Fodor's 58th edition

Europe

The complete guide, thoroughly up-to-date

Packed with details that will make your trip

What to see, what to skip

City strolls, countryside adventures

Smart lodging and dining options

Transportation tips, distances and directions

Key contacts, savvy travel tips

When to go, what to pack

Clear, accurate, easy-to-use maps

Fodor's Travel Publications • New York, Toronto, London, Sydney, Auckland
www.fodors.com

Fodor's Europe

EDITORS: Linda Cabasin, David Cashion, Sharron Wood

Editorial Contributors: Jennifer Abramsohn, Leslie Adler, Robert Andrews, Nuha Ansari, Beatrice Aranow, John Babb, Catherine Belonogoff, John Bigley, Carissa Bluestone, Kerry Brady Stewart, Jacqueline Brown, Ginanne Brownell, Mary Brunner, Philippe Candaele, Jeffrey Carson, Roland Chambers, Christine Cipriani, Peter Collis, Roderick Craig, Martha de la Cal, Bonnie Dodson, Charles Ferro, Robert Fisher, Aoife Fitzpatrick, Jane Foster, Ed Glinert, Katrin Gygax, Valerie Hamilton, Stewart Hennessey, Simon Hewitt, Geoff Hill, Lee Hogan, Alannah Hopkin, Anto Howard, Rosa Jackson, Gareth Jenkins, Raymond Johnston, Nicola Keegan, Shannon Kelly, Michael Kissane, Christina Knight, Carla Lionello, Mark Little, Joan Lofgren, Matthew Lombardi, Jennifer McDermott, Terence Mirabelli, Christopher Mooney, Ben Morse, Lauren Myers, Dan Navid, Heather O'Brian, Paris Permenter, Tim Perry, Ian Phillips, Marton Radkai, Tatiana Repkova, Patricia Rucidlo, Jürgen Scheunemann, George Semler, Ted Shoemaker, Edris Sitzer, Lewis Sitzer, AnneLise Sorensen, Jonette Stabbert, Melia Tatakis, Julie Tomasz, Susan Tuttle-Laube, Annie Ward, Alex Wijeratna, Devin Wilson, Kay Winzenried, Jeannie Wurz.

Editorial Production: Tom Holton

Maps: David Lindroth, *cartographer;* Rebecca Baer, Robert Blake, *map editors*

Design: Fabrizio La Rocca, *creative director;* Guido Caroti, *art director;* Jolie Novak, *senior picture editor;* Melanie Marin, *photo editor*

Cover Design: Pentagram

Production/Manufacturing: Robert B. Shields

Cover Photograph: Catherine Karnow

Copyright

58th Edition

ISBN 0-679-00862-4

ISSN 0362-0204

Special Sales

Fodor's Travel Publications are available at special discounts for bulk purchases for sales promotions or premiums. Special editions, including personalized covers, excerpts of existing guides, and corporate imprints, can be created in large quantities for special needs. For more information, contact your local bookseller or write to Special Markets, Fodor's Travel Publications, 280 Park Avenue, New York, NY 10017. Inquiries from Canada should be directed to your local Canadian bookseller or sent to Random House of Canada, Ltd., Marketing Department, 2775 Matheson Boulevard East, Mississauga, Ontario L4W 4P7. Inquiries from the United Kingdom should be sent to Fodor's Travel Publications, 20 Vauxhall Bridge Road, London SW1V 2SA, England.

PRINTED IN THE UNITED STATES OF AMERICA

10 9 8 7 6 5 4 3 2 1

CONTENTS

🌐 *Italic entries are maps.*

ON THE ROAD WITH FODOR'S

THE MORE YOU KNOW before you go, the better your trip will be. Europe's most fascinating small museum (or its most charming boutique or boisterous bistro) could be just around the corner from your hotel, but if you don't know it's there, it might as well be on the other side of the globe. That's where this book comes in. It's a great step toward making sure your next trip lives up to your expectations. As you plan, check out the Web as well. Guidebooks have been helping smart travelers find the special places for years; the Web is one more tool. Whatever reference you consult, be savvy about what you read, and always consider the source. Images and language can be massaged to make places appear better than they are. And one traveler's quaint is another's grimy. Here at Fodor's, and at our on-line arm, Fodors.com, our focus is on providing you with information that's not only useful but accurate and on target. Every day Fodor's editors put enormous effort into getting things right, beginning with the search for the right contributors—people who have objective judgment, broad travel experience, and the writing ability to put their insights into words. There's no substitute for advice from a like-minded friend who has just come back from where you're going, but our writers, having seen all corners of Europe, are the next best thing. They're the kind of people you'd poll for tips yourself if you knew them.

How to Use This Book

The section following this one, **New and Noteworthy,** cues you in on trends and happenings. Following that is Chapter 1, **Smart Travel Tips A to Z,** arranged alphabetically by topic. Under each listing you'll find tips and information that will help you accomplish what you need to in Europe. You'll also find addresses and telephone numbers of organizations and companies that offer destination-related services and detailed information and publications.

Chapters are in alphabetical order by country. Each covers the country's essential information A to Z, exploring, dining, lodging, nightlife and the arts, shopping, and side trips in cities and regions. Sites in major cities accompanied by maps are arranged alphabetically. Within regional sections, all restaurants and lodgings are grouped with the town. The Essentials list that ends all city or regional sections covers getting there and getting around. It also provides helpful contacts and resources.

Important Tip

Although all prices, opening times, and other details in this book are based on information supplied to us at press time, changes occur all the time in the travel world, and Fodor's cannot accept responsibility for facts that become outdated or for inadvertent errors or omissions. So **always confirm information when it matters,** especially if you're making a detour to visit a specific place.

Don't Forget to Write

Your experiences—positive and negative—matter to us. If we have missed or misstated something, we want to hear about it. We follow up on all suggestions. Contact the Europe editor at editors@fodors.com or c/o Fodor's, 280 Park Avenue, New York, New York 10017. And have a fabulous trip!

Karen Cure

Karen Cure
Editorial Director

NEW AND NOTEWORTHY

Austria

Recently opened in Vienna is the long-heralded **Museumsquartier,** a vast contemporary art and culture complex in what was once the Imperial Habsburg stables. It will display the world's largest collection of the works of Egon Schiele, as well as international art from 1900 to the present, plus a calendar of contemporary exhibitions. The Wiener Festwochen, Viennale Film Festival, and International Dance Festival will be held in the old winter training halls of the Spanish Riding School, which will also serve as performance venues for experimental music and theater events. Upcoming events in the **Vienna art world** include Italian travel landscapes by artists of the Austro-Hungarian Empire from around 1800 and an exhibit of sculptures from one of the most famous artists of the Baroque period, Franz Xaver Messerschmidt, both at the Belvedere Palace. The long-awaited reopening of the Albertina in autumn 2002 will kick off with an Edvard Munch exhibit. And Prince Liechtenstein plans to permanently display his own vast collection of art at the Liechtenstein Palace, which will open again as a museum sometime in 2002.

Baltic States

Popular weekend destinations for many Europeans, Estonia, Latvia, and Lithuania are relatively inexpensive, uncrowded, and provide the quality amenities found in most Western European tourist destinations. The states are spending more and more on **infrastructure improvements** and on maintaining their cities' old quarters, which are now looking as regal and splendid as they did when they were first built.

Belgium

The rich legacies of Belgium's Flemish and francophone cultures will be celebrated throughout 2002 as the **Royal Museums of Fine Arts** in Brussels continue to mark their bicentennial. A special exhibit opening at the end of the year will trace the museums' 200-year history, starting with the transfer of paintings from Paris and Versailles to Brussels in 1801. For two days in August, Brussels's famed Grand'Place will be transformed into a carpet of flowers as Belgium's prodigious production of begonias is used to create a floral tapestry in the cobbled square. In **Brugge,** the canal-laced medieval city often known as the Venice of the North, a host of special activities, including music, theater, film, and exhibitions will kick off in March under the city's rubric of the Cultural Capital of Europe. The nearby port city of Zeebrugge will host **Sail 2002,** a parade of sailing ships, for five days in August.

Bulgaria

The years 2000 and 2001 brought big changes to the city of **Sofia:** two major feature films were shot there, drawing international film crews and stars. Hope for a booming new film business, combined with an influx of money, has been a catalyst for the opening of new upscale hotels, the country's first top-notch multiplex theater, and the introduction of Western service standards in general.

Ploshtad Sveta Nedelya, Sofia's central plaza, has undergone massive reconstruction. Underneath the plaza, the brand-new metro station, decorated with archaeological finds unearthed during its construction, began to operate in 2000. To the west, the Central Market Hall (Tsentralna Hali) has been completed and unveiled as an enormous, bustling indoor bazaar. TSUM, formerly Sofia's biggest and drabbest department store, was reopened under new ownership as a sparkling, modern shopping mall.

The outstanding National History Museum, famous for its golden Thracian treasures, was relocated in 2000 from Vitosha Boulevard to a splendid new home in the former residence of deceased Communist leader Todor Zhivkov. The museum is now in palatial surroundings worthy of its awesome collection.

Cyprus

The attempt to **reunite** the Greek and Turkish sectors of Cyprus continues but so far has not been successful. The Cyprus Tourism Organization continues to support its **agritourism** project to encourage the renovation of traditional homes in villages as guest accommodations.

Czech Republic

Karlštejn castle, right outside Prague, underwent several months of renovation in 2001, right on the the heels of several decades of work done to fix up the Chapel of the Holy Rood in the massive main tower. In Prague, renovations are well underway on the Empire-style **U Hybernů exhibition hall,** the last building on touristy Na Příkopě to still be in need of a post-Communist-era facelift. Prague's **metro system** is not only adding new stations, but plans are underway to replace the Soviet-era metro cars with modern ones.

Denmark

The construction of the **Øresund bridge** between Copenhagen andMalmö, Sweden, was completed in June 2000, linking the two countries and creating what many hope will be a new binational metropolis. The bridge makes intercontinental and Scandinavian travel much simpler. The **Copenhagen Card,** allowing bus/train transportation around the region and admission to a number of sites, also offers discounts on many attractions in Malmö.

Finland

Festivals throughout Finland continue to attract top performers in jazz (Pori), big bands (Imatra), opera (Savonlinna), folk music (Kaustinen), and rock (Ruisrock in Turku). Popular festivals also celebrate theater (Tampere) and mixed arts (Helsinki). Finland's status as an Internet-savvy country is especially evident in the well-organized, accessible information available on the festivals. The Web site www.festivals.fi presents information on 62 festivals with a combined annual audience of more than 1.8 million visitors.

Lapland has become increasingly popular as a travel destination even in winter, as sports enthusiasts take advantage of the long ski season, from October to mid-May. A wide array of tourist facilities, snow safaris, and other special tours is available. **High-tech Finland** is taking advantage of the latest in Internet technology. For example, in 2000 the Cable Book Library in the center of Helsinki received the Bill and Melinda Gates Foundation award for its work in promoting access to information technology. It offers a wide range of services to its visitors, such as drop-in work stations and Web surfing stations. In addition, the Finnish Tourist Board has introduced a WAP-based (wireless application protocol) travel guide in English: wap.finlandtravelguide.com. While regular Web site information is still more convenient to use, watch for developments in such mobile phone–based Web pages. Another example of Finland's high-tech orientation is found in the Arktikum museum in Rovaniemi, which sells items from its gift shop on the Internet as "authentic Lappish Sami handicraft in e-commerce."

France

Jacques Chirac, mayor of Paris from 1977 until he became French president in 1995, suffered a blow to his 2002 reelection plans when his conservative RPR party was trounced by **Bertrand Delanoë** in the March 2001 mayoral election. Delanoë, an openly gay offical, became the first left-wing mayor of Paris for over a century after forging an alliance with ecologists that is sure to have repercussions on the Paris cityscape—more bike lanes, for starters.

A new "medieval" garden at the **Musée de Cluny** was planted in September 2000, containing 58 species of flora and fauna depicted in the museum's famous "Lady and the Unicorn" tapestries. Not so pretty were the city's wooded parks, the Bois de Boulogne and the Bois de Vincennes—still a desolate sight after losing thousands of trees in the hurricane that swept through Paris during Christmas 1999.

The elegant **Pont de Solférino footbridge,** linking the Tuileries Gardens to the Musée d'Orsay, finally opened late 2000 after treatment to its exotic wood, originally deemed "too slippery."

A striking aluminum and colored glass entrance canopy was raised over the entrance to **Palais-Royal Metro station,** near the Louvre, and a new RER station was opened at Bibliothéque, connecting with Metro Line 14, which has linked the giant new state library to Madeleine since 1999. Elsewhere, a new superfast **TGV track south of Lyon** was due to slash the 500-mile Paris–Marseille train run to just three hours as of June 2001, with brand new stations at Valence and Aix-en-Provence. Those who like their travel less frenetic should note the planned relaunch of the **Dieppe-Newhaven cross-Channel ferry,** after Dieppe Regional Council took the unprecedented step of buying up the Port of Newhaven on England's Sussex coast.

Germany

After years of debate, Berlin broke ground in 2001 for the national **Holocaust memorial,** which will consist of 2,600 concrete pillars. Also in Berlin, a collection finally arrived at the **Jewish Museum;** admirers previously toured the empty building simply for its remarkable architecture. Munich's long-awaited **Pinakothek der Moderne** opens its doors in spring 2002. The museum will house collections of modern art and industrial and graphic design, as well as architectural exhibits.

Great Britain

Post-millennium building frenzy has abated only slightly as museums and galleries strive to become more technological and visitor-friendly. Almost every museum, in fact, has been part of this whirlwind of activity, resulting in the glittering new Great Court of the British Museum; the latest technological gizmos at the staid British Library; the state-of-the-art Tate Modern; the multimillion-pound makeovers of the Sadler's Wells Theatre and the Royal Opera House; the new face of the National Portrait Gallery; and the scintillating space-age Earth Galleries at the Natural History Museum. Thanks to these attractions, swinging-again London now outranks its neighbors as Europe's most forward-looking spot.

Culturally, London is making a bid to catch up with its overseas rivals in terms of modern art, and the word here is that big is beautiful. Opened in May 2000, **Tate Modern** houses a huge number of artworks formerly hidden from public view due to lack of space in the old Millbank Gallery. Londoners on their way to Tate Modern on the South Bank, the Docklands developments, and ancient Greenwich with the regenerated "Greenwich Peninsula" have **new tube stations** on the ultramodern Jubilee Line, plus extra services on the time-honored mode of transport called Old Father Thames. Also on the south side of the Thames is the **British Airways London Eye,** where, since its opening in Februry 2000, the public has been lining up to see the unrivaled views of London and beyond from its see-through, podlike capsules.

The Queen's **Golden Jubilee year** (2002) will see much pomp and pageantry, and at Buckingham Palace there is extra celebration for the completion of the new entrance and expansion of the Queen's Gallery. The Royal Collection of old masterpieces will have twice the exhibition space, together with micro-gallery for perusing the collection on screen.

The **Bath Spa Project,** involving a new baths complex in the center of Bath, is due to open in late 2001.

Greece

With the **2004 Olympics** just around the corner, Greeks, who generally do things at the last minute, seem to have picked up the pace. The atmosphere is feverish with construction just about everywhere, but there's also a light shimmering on the horizon. Athens is finally on its way to becoming a more user-friendly city. Pedestrians seem to be winning back areas of the city from the motor car as more and more areas of downtown Athens are being declared off limits to traffic. Renovation projects have rescued many of the neoclassical buildings throughout Athens, and previously industrial and depressed areas adjacent to the center of town are now spilling over with theaters and charming restaurants. Even trees seem to have made a comeback. The projects are indeed numerous: construction has finally begun on an archaeological park that will link, in a charming promenade, the major historical sites in Athens. The ban has been lifted on construction in the Attica area and 28 new luxury hotels are under construction. The state beaches, now under the management of private businesses, are abuzz with water parks, sports amenities, and children's playgrounds; the Attica coastline is now one of the cleanest in the Mediterranean. Kilometers of the new Attica highway have been opened to the public, making the Eleftherios Venizelos Airport accessible. Super-fast, brand-new ferry-boats to distant islands have cut travel time to islands like Crete, Chios, and Rhodes in half.

Hungary

Grand old **Budapest** is seeing more and more development, from private restoration of crumbling buildings to city-funded projects, such as the increase in pedestrian-only zones and a new park on Erzsébet tér, in the center of downtown. Plans for a fourth metro line and a new national theater were stalled at press time, due to political tensions between state and city leaders, but Hungary's overall stability and continued attraction of foreign investment have fostered ongoing revitalization. Indeed, the theater and café culture seems no worse for politics. While many Hungarians can hardly afford to go out to eat, an emerging middle class has gradually instilled Budapest with a confidence unseen since the heady days of the Austro-Hungarian empire a century ago.

Slowly but surely Hungary continues to improve its **infrastructure,** helping it fill its increasingly important role as a link between Eastern and Western Europe. The airport in Budapest has seen major expansion in recent years, and major highways are undergoing significant upgrading and expansion. Last but not least, the once-antiquated telephone system has drastically improved in recent years—but travelers can still expect number changes and broken connections as progress continues.

Iceland

Iceland's **Keflavík International Airport** has expanded, allowing smoother handling of greater numbers of visitors. The budget air-charter company GO, which caters heavily to Web surfers, has given flagship carrier Icelandair healthy competition and made for some very attractive offers from both carriers. Domestic carrier Air Iceland has also been bolstered by a handsome government contract for maintaining domestic routes in case of the need for the medical airlifting of patients.

In the capital area, the major **public transportation companies** have merged so that tickets and routing are now controlled by single, coordinated management. Following the consolidation trend, a number of jeep, boating, and glacier tour operators now operate under one umbrella, Iceland Adventure.

As of press time, the area immediately surrounding the beautiful Snæfellsjökull of west Iceland is in the final stages of being approved as a **new national park.** Public opinion is also growing locally and abroad for a Highlands National Park, which would preserve Europe's largest remaining area of undeveloped wildlands and perhaps spare the land from the threat of submersion under reservoirs for generating hydroelectric power.

Ireland

Ireland's **economy** continues to **boom** and the extraordinary expansion of Dublin progresses without any sign of abating. With standards of living soaring and unemployment at an all-time low of around 5%, Ireland, and especially Dublin, is experiencing greater immigration than emigration. For the visitor this means a much more cosmopolitan city, where your waitress is as likely to be from Budapest as Blarney. New construction continues throughout the city, with the postmodern Four Seasons yet another addition to the high-end lodging sector. The spectacular new museum called the **Guinness Storehouse** promises to be one of Dublin's biggest attractions. At the top of the Storehouse is the **Gravity Bar,** with its 360-degree view over the whole city.

A major upgrading of Ireland's national routes continues unabated, yet as the **infrastructure** improves, traffic conditions seem to worsen. Cork, Galway, and Limerick are all seeing major increases in the number of cars, but it is in Dublin that congestion has begun to approach the level of that in other major European cities.

Cork's **Opera House** now has a new facade that unites the building to its recently extended neighbor, **Crawford Municipal Gallery,** creating a buzzy new artistic center. Patrick Street is now largely pedestrianized, contributing greatly to an improved and revitalized shopping district. In Sligo Town a long-overdue IR£3-million refurbishment of the Model Arts Centre, now known as the **Model and Niland Centre,** at last provides a fitting home for the magnificent collection of early-20th-century

Irish art and Yeats memorabilia, up to now housed in the town library.

In **Northern Ireland** the cease-fire by Republican and Loyalist militants has held for five years, and the Good Friday Agreement and Assembly elections of 1998 yielded the historic Northern Ireland Assembly, a fledgling, devolved government containing both Unionist and Republican ministers. Although continuing disagreements about the issue of disarmament have threatened to topple the Assembly and the agreement, it has survived, since neither most politicians nor the general public want to return to the turmoil of the past. In its short life, the agreement has already resulted in devolved government, an end to the south's constitutional claim to the north, a North-South Council to oversee coöperation on matters of mutual interest, and adherence to the principle that Northern Ireland will not leave the United Kingdom without the consent of a majority of the people of the province. Despite political discord, an air of social and economic rejuvenation predominates in Northern Ireland.

Italy

In 2001, **mad cow** (*mucca pazza*) disease had a dramatic effect on Italian eating habits. Although no one in Italy was infected, and only two cows were found to have been infected, Italians stopped eating beef en masse. As the EU banned veal and beef that came in contact with the bone and spinal marrow, restaurants were forced to grill alternative meats such as pork, but also buffalo and kangaroo imported from Australia. In Rome, the traditional offal and oxtail preparations are currently no longer available. In Pisa, work was completed to halt the ever-increasing tilt of the **Leaning Tower.** Plans are to reopen it to visitors in 2002.

Luxembourg

Luxembourgers enjoy a varied and active social life, but it is in the summer that the capital really comes alive with its **Summer in the City** festival. Beginning with an impressive fireworks display for the Grand Duke's Birthday and also the Duchy's National Day on June 22, the festival continues through the middle of September with street performers, concerts, and bands at the Place d'Armes. The final event of the festival is the **Schueberfouer,** a carnival complete with cotton candy and rides and a Ferris wheel offering a spectacular view of Luxembourg City and its remaining battlements.

The year 2001 saw the introduction of the **Muséeskaart,** valid for one, two, or three days for one adult or a family, which allows you entrance into the Casino Luxembourg, the Musée d'Histoire de la Ville de Luxembourg, the Musée National d'Histoire et d'Art, the Natur Musée, and Villa Vauban.

Malta

In early 2001 the Malta Tourism Authority reclassified all accommodation on the islands. In the process, the one-star hotel category disappeared; those that made the grade were classified as two star and those not up to scratch became "guest houses." The latter now are divided into two somewhat ambiguous categories, "standard" and "comfort."

Netherlands

The fifth world horticultural exhibition, **Floriade,** will take place in the Haarlemmermeer district close to Schiphol Airport from mid-April until mid-October 2002. This significant Dutch attraction is held once every ten years. Floriade 2002 is expected to draw more than three million international visitors. Every aspect of Dutch horticulture will be showcased, with more than 300 entries from at least 27 other countries also on display. One of the most dazzling spectacles is a valley of flowers, created with over a million bulbs.

Celebrating its 50th anniversary in 2002 is the **Efteling,** the Netherlands' most popular amusement park and one that has won major international awards. Located in Kaatsheuvel in North Brabant (the southern part of the country), it's one of the most magical places to take children. The Efteling will celebrate its anniversary with a new theater that seats 1,200 and an exciting show.

Amsterdam's renowned **Vondel Park** has undergone some changes since spring of 2001. There are many new landscaping features, including a small island with llamas, nesting islands for ducks and other aquatic birds, and the introduction of frogs and toads to the ponds. Whole areas of the park have been heavily planted with native flora, which should be well established by 2002.

Norway

Particular **annual events** that are worth attending are the National Day held every May 17, with celebrations in every village, town, and city throughout the country. In Oslo there is a three-hour-long and very festive Children's Parade. Most adults wear national costume and a sense of restrained national pride abounds. Other events include the Ski-jumping World Cup held at the Holmenkollen International Ski Jump in March. Meanwhile, the Oslo Horse Show is held in October and the Oslo Marathon in September.

Poland

Poland is seeing a **crisis in the historic Solidarity Party.** In 2000, the Solidarity presidential candidate came in third with an embarrassing 14 percent of the vote, losing to former Communist and current Social Democrat Aleksander Krasniewski, who first came to power by defeating Solidarityís patriarch Lech Walesa in 1995. Solidarity, which helped begin the domino like effect of bringing down communism in the eighties, no longer appeals to the majority of the population. The party, damaged by internal splits, will have to reorganize to survive.

Portugal

In Lisbon two ring-road systems and a **new north-south cross-city highway** linking the Ponte 25 de Abril with the northbound toll highway on the other side of town have gone a long way towards clearing traffic congestion in and around the city, but they are unforgiving if you take the wrong turn or miss your exit. A second road bridge across the Tagus, the 17-km (11-mi) **Ponte Vasco da Gama,** has made getting in and out of Lisbon a lot easier and a **new light suburban rail service** using the Ponte 25 de Abril crossing takes you in style and comfort across to the south bank. Radical restructuring and face-lifting has greatly improved passenger handling at Lisbon's international airport.

The left-in-place nucleus of Lisbon's World Exposition, EXPO'98, has become the leisure hub of an ambitious riverfront development site. Baptized **Parque das Nações** (Nations Park), the area includes concert halls, Europe's biggest oceanarium, restaurants, and Portugal's biggest bowling alley. As tourism grows in Lisbon, new hotels are springing up everywhere, mainly in the four- and five-star bracket. Redevelopment of the dockside area between the Cais do Sodré railway station and Alcântara has created a new and trendy nightlife center. Lisbon's **camping park** in the Monsanto woods reopened as a deluxe spot with vastly improved facilities.

Out along the coast at **Estoril,** landscaping and seawall renovation have extended and improved the breezy seaside promenade. The **Algarve** region is currently replacing its often-confusing road signs with clear, color-coded, easy to read markers.

Romania

The strict guidelines for its coveted **admission to NATO and the EU** have helped Romania to look realistically at what is necessary to rebuild the nation following its years under a dictatorship. With newly elected ex-Communist president Ion Iliescu, it is difficult to predict what direction the country will take. The government has agreed to discourage the country's long-standing policy of charging foreigners higher rates than Romanians. Visa regulations are constantly changing. Be sure to check before you travel.

Slovakia

Slovakia has been catching up fast with its neighbors the Czech Republic, Poland, and Hungary in their efforts to join the European Union. The country's westward orientation is reflected in both its infrastructure and people's mindset. The construction boom of supermarkets has been followed by an **explosion of dining facilities,** from fast-food joints and pizzerias to more upscale restaurants and cafés. Existing establishments have been forced to improve the quality of their services because of fiercer competition.

Skiing services in the High Tatras now pattern themselves after neighboring resorts in the Alps and include plenty of ski rentals, a free skibus from Štrbské Pleso, as well as, ski tows and cables. The **new golf facilities** of Veľká Lomnica in the High Tatras reflect the rising popularity of golf—a game considered exotic a decade ago in Slovakia.

The unique 120-year Slovak tradition of precisely marking hiking routes has been preserved by dozens of volunteers, and reliable tourist maps covering the whole country area can guide you throughout the 1,300 kilometers of marked trails. Another set of **recently developed maps** shows half of the 3,500 kilometers of **biking routes.**

Slovenia

Slovenia has a high standard of living compared to other Central and Eastern European countries, and it looks set to become one of the first, along with Hungary, to **enter the European Union.** Since gaining independence in 1991, low inflation, the stability of the Slovenian tolar, and international credibility have lead to increased prosperity, and the new generation of multilingual, highly educated Slovenes seem to have everything going for them.

Despite an image problem caused by the conflicts that have plagued its sister republics that once made up Yugoslavia, the tourist industry is thriving. Many hotels have been modernized, though care has been taken to conserve buildings of historic value. Dining out, if you don't mind the prices, is a joy, especially in the capital. Several museums have recently installed audiovisual presentations that transcend language barriers.

Spain

Starting at the end of 2000, Spain's **economy** began to slow down for the first time since 1994, though with revenues from such companies as Terra-Lycos, one of the largest Internet companies in the world, it definitely continues to hum.

Also in late 2000, UNESCO awarded Spain with five new **World Heritage Site** designations—in Tarragona, Lugo, Burgos, Valencia, and Vallde Boi—making Spain the world's leader with 36 sites (Italy is second with 33).

Sweden

Sweden continues to be one of the world's dominant players in the new **information-based economy.** Although many start-up companies (as well as established giants such as Ericsson) took their share of economic bumps and bruises in 2001, as a whole there remains an intense interest in the business possibilities of the Internet and wireless communications. During the last few years, Sweden has received substantial international press coverage for its innovative technological solutions, new management philosophies, and unique Web design. As a result, visitors will quickly notice many people with mobile phones (cell phone use is over 50 percent), lots of Internet cafés, and a widespread use of new technology. If there's an expensive new gadget on the market, chances are you'll see a stylish Stockholmer using it.

The **bridge** connecting Malmö and Copenhagen, which opened in the summer of 2000, continues to change the Öresund region in southern Sweden. The easy connection means greater economic exchange between Sweden and Denmark. What it means for tourists is a faster and easier way to bring a car across the water. Some boat and hydroplane service continues between the two cities.

Switzerland

Zurich's formerly industrial neighborhood, **Zurich West,** is undergoing extensive revitalization, with factories being converted into trendy restaurants, art galleries, and clubs. This area is quickly becoming a hotspot, with construction expected to continue into 2006.

Turkey

Named for Turkey's first female aviator, the Sabiha Gökçen International Airport in Kürtköy on the Asian side of the city became **Istanbul's second airport,** and welcomed its inaugural flight in January 2001. In November 2000 the European Union announced certain **reforms required** before Turkey could hope to become a member, including greater democratization and increased freedom of speech. But such reforms have been blocked by hard-line nationalists in Turkey's government causing the E.U. to say that, without the reforms, Turkish accession would be impossible until at least 2010. It seems that Turkey's century-old dream of becoming part of Europe is an increasingly distant prospect.

In 2000 the Turkish government redoubled its efforts to **reduce inflation,** which had had averaged a crippling 70%–80% per annum for more than a decade. By January 2001 it had succeeded in reducing annual inflation to 35.9%, compared with 68.9% one year earlier.

Europe

ICELAND
Reykjavík
NORWAY
Bergen
SCOTLAND
NORTHERN IRELAND
Edinburgh
North Sea
Belfast
IRELAND
Irish Sea
DENMARK
Dublin
UNITED KINGDOM
WALES
Hamburg
ENGLAND
NETHERLANDS
Cardiff
Amsterdam
The Hague
London
Rotterdam
English Channel
ATLANTIC OCEAN
Brussels
Bonn
BELGIUM
Frankfurt
Paris
LUXEMBOURG
FRANCE
Zürich
Bern
SWITZERLAND
Lyon
Milan
Monte Carlo
Nice
MONACO
Marseille
ANDORRA
PORTUGAL
Madrid
Florence
Lisbon
Barcelona
Corsica
SPAIN
Seville
Granada
Sardinia
Balearic Islands
Gibraltar
Mediterranean Sea
MOROCCO
ALGERIA
TUNISIA
0
400 miles
0
600 km

FINLAND
Gulf of Bothnia
Oslo
SWEDEN
Helsinki
Gulf of Finland
St. Petersburg
Tallinn
Stockholm
ESTONIA
Kattegat
Göteborg
Riga
LATVIA
Moscow
Copenhagen
LITHUANIA
Baltic Sea
Kaunas
RUSSIA
Vilnius
RUSSIA
Kaliningrad
Minsk
Berlin
POLAND
BELARUS
Warsaw
Kraków
Kiev
Prague
CZECH REPUBLIC
UKRAINE
SLOVAKIA
Vienna
Bratislava
Salzburg
MOLDOVA
Budapest
AUSTRIA
Chișinău
HUNGARY
SLOVENIA
Ljubljana
Zagreb
ROMANIA
CROATIA
Novi Sad
Bucharest
BOSNIA AND HERZEGOVINA
Belgrade
SERBIA
Black Sea
Adriatic Sea
Sarajevo
YUGOSLAVIA
BULGARIA
MONTENEGRO
KOSOVO
Rome
Priština
Sofia
Podgorica
Skopje
ITALY
MACEDONIA
Istanbul
Tiranë
ALBANIA
Ankara
Naples
TURKEY
GREECE
Aegean Sea
Ionian Sea
Athens
Sicily
CYPRUS
MALTA
Crete
Mediterranean Sea

World Time Zones

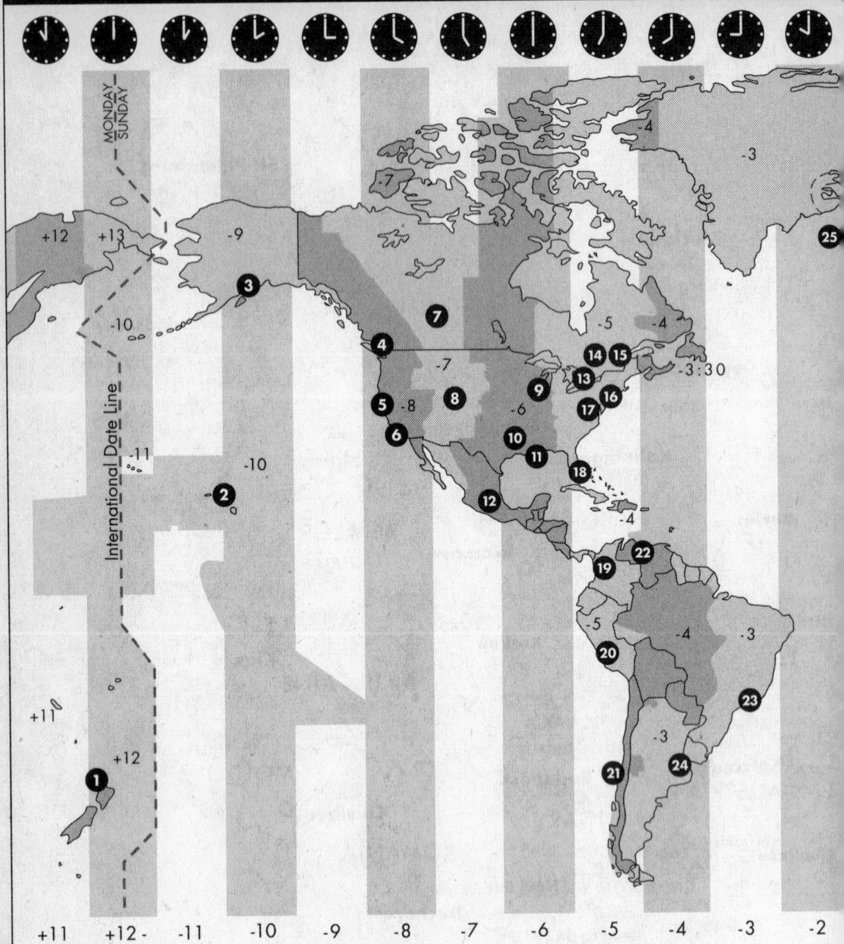

+11 +12 - -11 -10 -9 -8 -7 -6 -5 -4 -3 -2

Numbers below vertical bands relate each zone to Greenwich Mean Time (0 hrs). Local times frequently differ from these general indications, as indicated by light-face numbers on map.

Algiers, **29**
Anchorage, **3**
Athens, **41**
Auckland, **1**
Baghdad, **46**
Bangkok, **50**
Beijing, **54**
Berlin, **34**
Bogotá, **19**
Budapest, **37**
Buenos Aires, **24**
Caracas, **22**
Chicago, **9**
Copenhagen, **33**
Dallas, **10**
Delhi, **48**
Denver, **8**
Dublin, **26**
Edmonton, **7**
Hong Kong, **56**
Honolulu, **2**
Istanbul, **40**
Jakarta, **53**
Jerusalem, **42**
Johannesburg, **44**
Lima, **20**
Lisbon, **28**
London (Greenwich), **27**
Los Angeles, **6**
Madrid, **38**
Manila, **57**

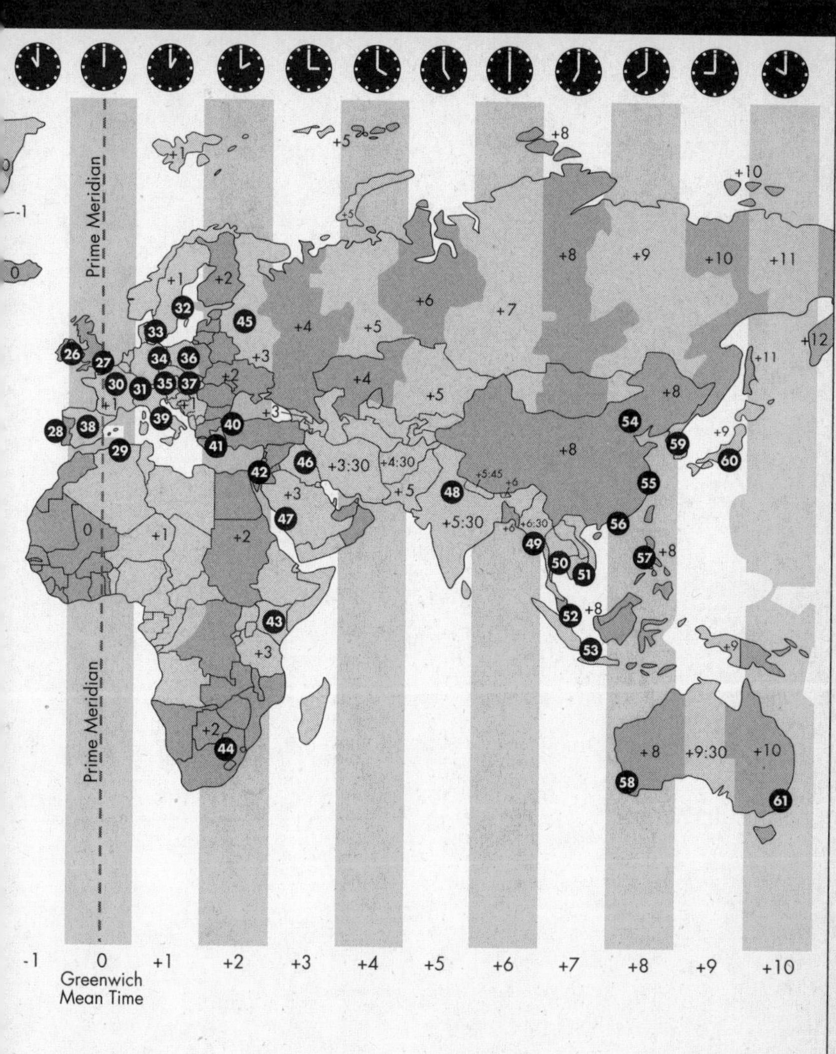

Mecca, **47**
Mexico City, **12**
Miami, **18**
Montréal, **15**
Moscow, **45**
Nairobi, **43**
New Orleans, **11**
New York City, **16**

Ottawa, **14**
Paris, **30**
Perth, **58**
Reykjavík, **25**
Rio de Janeiro, **23**
Rome, **39**
Saigon (Ho Chi Minh City), **51**

San Francisco, **5**
Santiago, **21**
Seoul, **59**
Shanghai, **55**
Singapore, **52**
Stockholm, **32**
Sydney, **61**
Tokyo, **60**

Toronto, **13**
Vancouver, **4**
Vienna, **35**
Warsaw, **36**
Washington, D.C., **17**
Yangon, **49**
Zürich, **31**

1 SMART TRAVEL TIPS A TO Z

AIR TRAVEL

Before booking, **compare different modes of transportation.** Many city pairs are so close together that flying hardly makes sense. For instance, it may take just half an hour to fly between London and Paris, but you must factor in time spent getting to and from the airports, plus check-in time. A 3-hour train ride from city center to city center seems a better alternative. It makes sense to **save air travel for longer distances**—say, between London and Rome, Paris and Vienna, Brussels and Stockholm—and do your local traveling from these hubs.

If you're flying so-called **national carriers,** full-fare tickets often remain the only kind available for one-way trips and restriction-free round-trips, and they are prohibitively expensive for most leisure travelers. On most European flights, your choice is between Business Class (which is what you get when paying full fare) and Economy (coach). Some flights are all Economy. First Class has ceased to exist in Europe. The most reasonable fares have long been nonrefundable and nontransferable round-trips (APEX fares), which require a Saturday night at the destination. But the near-monopoly that used to be enjoyed by these airlines is crumbling, and they have had to start offering less restrictive fares. Check before you fly.

Some national carriers reward transatlantic passengers with fixed-price flight coupons (priced at $100–$120) to destinations from their respective hubs and/or domestic or area air passes. These must be bought before leaving home. If you're young, **ask about youth stand-by fares,** which are available on a number of domestic and some international services.

Over the last few years, a substantial number of local airlines have been created to provide feeder services to major hubs and services between secondary city pairs. Do not, however, expect rock-bottom prices. **Seek advice from local branches of international travel agencies** like American Express or Carlson/Wagonlit.

Low-cost no-frills airlines base their fares on one-way travel, and a return ticket is simply twice the price. Advertised fares are always preceded by the word "from." To get the lowest fare, book two weeks ahead of time; it also helps to be flexible about your date of travel. In general, you have to book directly by calling the airline, credit card in hand. Some also accept reservations by fax. Reservation via Internet is available with companies such as the SABRE-powered Travelocity (www.travelocity.com) and Microsoft's Expedia (www.expedia.com). You can make secure payments via the Net and hunt the cheapest flight deals, as well as reserve hotels. You get a reservation number and pick up your boarding pass at the airport. Note that some flights use relatively distant secondary airports.

ARRIVALS

Passport control has become a perfunctory affair within most of the European Union (EU). The nine signatories to the Schengen Agreement (Austria, Belgium, France, Germany, Italy, Luxembourg, the Netherlands, Portugal, and Spain) have abolished passport controls for travelers between countries in that area, but individual countries can temporarily suspend it.

The most notable exception is Great Britain; when a number of flights from the U.S. arrive at Heathrow or Gatwick close together in the morning, **be prepared for a longish wait** (though rarely as long as Europeans have to wait at JFK in New York).

The Green Channel/Red Channel customs system in operation at most Western European airports and other borders is basically an honor system. If you have nothing to declare, walk through the Green Channel, where there are only spot luggage checks; if in doubt, go through the Red Channel. If you fly between two EU-member countries, go through the new **Blue Channel,** where there are no customs officers except the one who glances at baggage labels to make sure only people off EU flights get through. On average, you need to **count on at least half an hour from deplaning to getting out of the airport.**

BOOKING

When you book, **look for nonstop flights** and **remember that "direct" flights stop at least once.** Try to avoid connecting flights, which require a change of plane. For more booking tips and to check prices and make online flight reservations, log on to www.fodors.com.

CARRIERS

➤ U.S. AIRLINES: **American** (☎ 800/433–7300 in the U.S.; 0345/789–789 in the U.K., WEB www.aa.com). **Continental** (☎ 800/525–0280 in the U.S.; 0800/776–464 in the U.K., WEB www.continental.com). **Delta** (☎ 800/221–1212 in the U.S.; 0800/414–767 in the U.K., WEB www.delta.com). **Northwest** (☎ 800/225–2525 in the U.S.; c/o alliance partner KLM, call 0990/750–9000 in the U.K., WEB www.klm.com). **TWA** (☎ 800/221–2000 in the U.S.; 0845/733–3333 or 020/8814–0707 in the U.K., WEB www.twa.com). **United** (☎ 800/538–2929 in the U.S.; 0845/844–4777 in the U.K., WEB www.unitedairlines.com). **US Airways** (☎ 800/428–4322 in the U.S.; 0800/783–5556 in the U.K., WEB www.usairways.com).

➤ EUROPEAN AIRLINES: Austria: **Austrian Airlines** (☎ 800/843–0002 in the U.S.; 020/7434–7373 in the U.K., WEB www.aua.com). Belgium: **Sabena Belgian World Airlines** (☎ 800/955–2000 in the U.S.; 020/7494–2629 in the U.K., WEB www.sabena-usa.com). Bulgaria: **Balkan Bulgarian Airlines** (☎ 800/776–5706 in the U.S.; 020/7637–7637 in the U.K., WEB www.balkanairlines.bg). The Czech Republic and Slovakia: **Czech Airlines** (CSA, ☎ 212/765–6022 in the U.S.; 020/7255–1898 in the U.K., WEB www.csa.cz). Denmark: **Scandinavian Airlines** (SAS, ☎ 800/221–2350 in the U.S.; 0845/600–7767 in the U.K., WEB www.flysas.com). Finland: **Finnair** (☎ 800/950–5000 in the U.S.; 020/7408–1222 in the U.K., WEB www.finnair.com). France: **Air France** (☎ 800/237–2747 in the U.S.; 0845/084–5111 in the U.K., WEB www.airfrance.com). Germany: **LTU International Airways** (☎ 800/888–0200 in the U.S., www.ltu.com). **Lufthansa** (☎ 800/645–3880 in the U.S.; 0345/737–747 in the U.K., WEB www.lufthansa.com). Great Britain: **British Airways** (☎ 800/247–9297 in the U.S.; 0345/222–111 in the U.K., WEB www.british-airways.com). **Virgin Atlantic** (☎ 800/862–8621 in the U.S.; 0129/3747–747 in the U.K., WEB www.virgin-atlantic.com). Greece: **Olympic Airways** (☎ 800/223–1226 in the U.S.; 0870/606–0460 in the U.K., WEB www.oa-airways.com). Hungary: **Malév Hungarian Airlines** (☎ 212/757–6446; 800/223–6884 outside NY in the U.S., WEB www.baxter.net/malev). Iceland: **Icelandair** (☎ 800/223–5500 in the U.S.; 020/7874–1000 in the U.K., WEB www.icelandair.com). Ireland: **Aer Lingus** (☎ 888/474–7424 or 800/223–6537 in the U.S.; 01631/577–5700 in the U.K., WEB www.aerlingus.com). Italy: **Alitalia** (☎ 800/223–5730 in the U.S.; 020/8745–8200 in the U.K., WEB www.alitalia.it). Malta: **Air Malta** (☎ 800/756–2582 in the U.S.; 020/7292–4949 in the U.K., WEB www.airmalta.com). The Netherlands: **KLM Royal Dutch Airlines** (☎ 800/447–4747 in the U.S.; 0990/750–900 in the U.K., WEB www.klm.com). Norway: **SAS** (☎ 800/221–2350 in the U.S.; 0845/600–7767 in the U.K., WEB www.flysas.com). Poland: **LOT Polish Airlines** (☎ 800/223–0593 in the U.S.; 020/7580–5037 in the U.K., WEB www.lot.com). Portugal: **TAP Air Portugal** (☎ 800/221–7370 in the U.S.; 020/7630–0900 in the U.K., WEB www.tap.com). Romania: **Tarom Romanian Air Transport** (☎ 212/687–6013 in the U.S.; 020/7224–3693 in the U.K., WEB www.tarom.digero.net). Spain: **Iberia Airlines** (☎ 800/772–4642 in the U.S.; 020/7830–0011 in the U.K., WEB www.iberia.es). Sweden: **SAS** (☎ 800/221–2350 in the U.S.; 0845/600–7767 in the U.K., WEB www.flysas.com). Switzerland: **Swissair** (☎ 800/221–4750 in the U.S.; 020/7494–2629 in the U.K., WEB www.swissair.com). Turkey: **THY Turkish Airlines** (☎ 212/339–9650 in the U.S.; 0845/601–0956 in the U.K., WEB www.turkishairlines.com).

➤ FROM CANADA: **Air Canada** (☎ 888/247–2262, WEB www.aircanada.com). **Air Transat** (☎ 877/872–6728, WEB www.airtransat.com).

➤ FROM THE U.K.: **British Airways** (✉ 156 Regent St., London W1R

5TA, ☎ 0345/222–111, WEB www.britishairways.com). **British Midland** (☎ 0870/607–0555, WEB www.british-midland.com). **EasyJet** (☎ 0870/600–0000, WEB www.easyjet.com). **KLM U.K.** (☎ 0870/507–4074, WEB www.klm.com). **Ryanair** (☎ 0541/569–569, WEB www.ryanair.com). **Virgin Express** (☎ 0800/891–199, WEB www.virgin-express.com).

➤ FROM AUSTRALIA: **Qantas Airways** (☎ 13–12–11 in Australia; 020/7497–2571 in the U.K., WEB www.qantas.com).

➤ FROM IRELAND: **Aer Lingus** (☎ 01/705–3333 in Ireland; 01631/577–5700 in the U.K., WEB www.aerlingus.com).

➤ FROM NEW ZEALAND: **Air New Zealand** (☎ 09/3362–4242 or 0800/737–000 in New Zealand; 020/8741–2299 in the U.K., WEB www.airnewzealand.com).

➤ NO-FRILLS CARRIER RESERVATIONS WITHIN EUROPE: Belgium: **Virgin Express** (☎ 2/752–0505; 0800/891–199 in the U.K., WEB www.virgin-express.com) from Brussels to Milan, Rome, Nice, Madrid, Barcelona, Copenhagen, and London (Gatwick, Heathrow, Stansted); from Rome to Barcelona and Madrid; from London (Stansted) to Berlin and Shannon. Ireland: **Ryanair** (☎ 01/609–7800 in Ireland; 0541/569–569 in the U.K., FAX 0541/565–579 in the U.K., WEB www.ryanair.com) from Dublin to 12 U.K. destinations, to Paris (Beauvais) and Brussels (Charleroi); from London (Stansted, Luton, and Gatwick) to Dublin; from London (Stansted) to four other Irish destinations, five French destinations, four Scandinavian destinations, six Italian destinations, and Frankfurt. United Kingdom: **Buzz** (☎ 0870/240–7070, WEB www.buzzaway.com) from London (Stansted) to Bordeaux, Düsseldorf, Berlin, Frankfurt, Hamburg, Helsinki, Jerez (Spain), Lyon, Marseilles, Milan, Paris, and Vienna. **EasyJet** (☎ 0870/6000–000, WEB www.easyjet.com) from London (Luton) and Liverpool to Amsterdam, Barcelona, Belfast, Geneva, Madrid, Malaga, Nice; from London (Luton) to Athens, Palma de Mallorca, Zurich, and four Scottish destinations; from Geneva to Amsterdam, Barcelona, Liverpool, London (Luton, Gatwick, and Stansted), and Nice. **Go** (☎ 0845/605–4321, WEB www.go-fly.com) from London (Stansted) to Copenhagen, Edinburgh, Lyon, Munich, Prague, Zurich, ten Iberian destinations, and four Italian destinations.

CHECK-IN & BOARDING

Assuming that not everyone with a ticket will show up, airlines routinely overbook planes. When everyone does, airlines ask for volunteers to give up their seats. In return, these volunteers usually get a certificate for a free flight and are rebooked on the next flight out. If there are not enough volunteers, the airline must choose who will be denied boarding. The first to get bumped are passengers who checked in late and those flying on discounted tickets, so **get to the gate and check in as early as possible,** especially during peak periods.

Always **bring a government-issued photo I.D. to the airport;** even when it's not required, a passport is best.

CUTTING COSTS

The least expensive airfares to Europe must usually be purchased in advance and are non-refundable. It's smart to **call a number of airlines,** and when you are quoted a good price, **book it on the spot**—the same fare may not be available the next day. Always **check different routings** and look into using different airports. Travel agents, especially low-fare specialists (☞ Discounts & Deals, *below*), are helpful.

Consolidators are another good source. They buy tickets for scheduled international flights at reduced rates from the airlines, then sell them at prices that beat the best fare available directly from the airlines, usually without restrictions. Sometimes you can even get your money back if you need to return the ticket. Carefully read the fine print detailing penalties for changes and cancellations, and **confirm your consolidator reservation with the airline.**

When you **fly as a courier,** you trade your checked-luggage space for a ticket deeply subsidized by a courier service. There are restrictions on when you can book and how long you can stay.

Ask your airline about purchasing discount passes for intra-European flights before you leave the United States to save significantly on travel between European cities. If you're going to be covering a lot of ground, consider Europebyair.com, which sells intra-European flights to more than 150 cities for $99 per segment. They also offer unlimited flight passes good for 15 or 21 days.

➤ CONSOLIDATORS: **Cheap Tickets** (☎ 800/377–1000). **Discount Airline Ticket Service** (☎ 800/576–1600). **Unitravel** (☎ 800/325–2222). **Up & Away Travel** (☎ 212/889–2345). **World Travel Network** (☎ 800/409–6753).

➤ COURIERS: **Air Courier Association** (✉ 15000 W. 6th Ave., Suite 203, Golden, CO 80401, ☎ 800/282–1202, WEB www.aircourier.org). **International Association of Air Travel Couriers** (✉ 220 S. Dixie Hwy. #3, Box 1349, Lake Worth, FL, 33460, ☎ 561/582–8320, FAX 561/582–1581, WEB www.courier.org). **Now Voyager Travel** (✉ 74 Varick St., Suite 307, New York, NY 10013, ☎ 212/431–1616, FAX 212/219–1753 or 212/334–5243, WEB www.nowvoyagertravel.com).

➤ DISCOUNT PASSES: **Europebyair.com** (☎ 888/387–2479, WEB www.europebyair.com).

ENJOYING THE FLIGHT

For more legroom, **request an emergency-aisle seat.** Don't sit in the row in front of the emergency aisle or in front of a bulkhead, where seats may not recline. If you have dietary concerns, **ask for special meals when booking.** These can be vegetarian, low-cholesterol, or kosher, for example. On long flights, try to maintain a normal routine, to help fight jet lag. At night, **get some sleep.** By day, **eat light meals, drink water** (not alcohol), and **move around the cabin** to stretch your legs. For additional jet-lag tips consult *Fodor's FYI: Travel Fit & Healthy* (available at bookstores everywhere).

FLYING TIMES

Flights from New York to London take about 6½ hours, to Paris 7½ hours, to Frankfurt 7½ hours, and to Rome 8½ hours. From Sydney to London, flights take about 23 hours via Bangkok, to Paris 22¾ hours via Singapore, to Frankfurt 22 hours via Singapore, and to Rome 25 hours via Bangkok.

HOW TO COMPLAIN

If your baggage goes astray or your flight goes awry, complain right away. Most carriers require that you **file a claim immediately.**

➤ AIRLINE COMPLAINTS: U.S. Department of Transportation **Aviation Consumer Protection Division** (✉ C-75, Room 4107, Washington, DC 20590, ☎ 202/366–2220, WEB www.dot.gov/airconsumer). **Federal Aviation Administration Consumer Hotline** (☎ 800/322–7873).

RECONFIRMING

Depending on the airline or on whether your ticket was bought through a consolidator, you may have to reconfirm your flights a specified number of hours before departure. **Check with your travel agent or airline** when you buy your ticket.

AIRPORTS

See Essentials *in* city sections of country chapters.

DUTY-FREE SHOPPING

Duty-free shopping was eliminated for travelers between EU countries as of July 1, 1999. However, duty-free shopping still applies in non-EU countries, and tax-free shopping is available for tourists returning to non-EU countries from the EU. If you're looking for good deals associated with duty-free airport shopping, **check out liquor and beauty products,** although prices vary considerably. The amount of liquor you may buy is restricted, generally to two bottles.

Some airport concourses, notably in Amsterdam, Copenhagen, and Shannon, have practically been transformed into shopping malls, selling everything from electronics and chocolates to fashion and furs. These are tax-free rather than duty-free shops; if this is your last stop before leaving the EU, there's no VAT and you can **avoid the tax-refund rigmarole** (☞ Taxes, *below*).

BIKE TRAVEL

BIKES IN FLIGHT

Most airlines accommodate bikes as luggage, provided they are dismantled and boxed. Airlines sell bike boxes, which are often free at bike shops, for about $5 (it's at least $100 for bike bags). International travelers can sometimes substitute a bike for a piece of checked luggage at no charge; otherwise, the cost is about $100. Domestic and Canadian airlines charge $25–$50.

BOAT & FERRY TRAVEL

Ferry routes for passengers and vehicles link the countries surrounding the North Sea, the Irish Sea, and the Baltic Sea; Italy with Greece; and Spain, France, Italy, and Greece with their respective islands in the Mediterranean. Longer ferry routes—between, for instance, Britain and Spain or Scandinavia—can help you **reduce the amount of driving and often save time.** A number of modern ships offer improved comfort and entertainment ranging from one-armed bandits to gourmet dining.

FARES & SCHEDULES

See individual country chapters, or contact operators for specific information on fares and schedules.

➤ BOAT & FERRY INFORMATION: Ferry operators between the British Isles and the Continent include **Brittany Ferries** (✉ Millbay Docks, Plymouth PL1 3EW, ☎ 0870/900–9746, WEB www.brittanyferries.com) from Plymouth to Roscoff (Brittany) and Santander (Spain), from Poole to Cherbourg, and from Portsmouth to Caen and St. Malo; **DFDS Seaways** (✉ Scandinavia House, Parkeston Quay, Harwich, Essex CO12 4QG, ☎ 0990/333–000 or 0125/524–0240; 800/533–3755 in the U.S., WEB www.dfdsseaways.com), from Harwich to Esbjerg (Denmark), Hamburg, and Gothenburg and from Newcastle-upon-Tyne to IJmuiden, 20 mi west of Amsterdam and (summer season) to Gothenburg and Hamburg; **Fjord Line** (✉ International Ferry Terminal, Royal Quays, North Shields NE29 6EE, ☎ 0191/296–1313), from Newcastle to Bergen/Stavanger/Haugesund (Norway); **Hoverspeed** (✉ International Hoverport, Marine Parade, Dover, Kent CT17 9TG, ☎ 0870/240–8070 or 0990/240–241, WEB www.hoverspeed.com), Dover–Calais, Dover–Oostende, Folkestone–Boulogne, and Newhaven–Dieppe; **Irish Ferries** (✉ Reliance House, Water St., Liverpool L2 8TP, ☎ 0990/171–717, WEB www.irishferries.ie), Holyhead–Dublin and Pembroke–Rosslare; also Rosslare (Ireland; reservations 01/638–3333) to Cherbourg, and Roscoff; **P&O European Ferries** (✉ Peninsular House, Wharf Rd., Portsmouth, PO2 8TA, ☎ 0870/242–4999, WEB www.poef.com) sails Portsmouth to Cherbourg, Le Havre, and Bilbao (Spain), and Cairnyarn (Scotland)–Larne (Belfast); **P&O North Sea Ferries** (✉ King George Dock, Hedon Rd., Hull HU9 5QA, ☎ 0148/237–7177, WEB www.ponsf.com), from Hull to Rotterdam and Zeebrugge; **P&O Stena Line** (✉ Channel House, Channel View Rd., Dover, Kent CT17 9TJ, ☎ 0870/600–0600 or 0130/486–4003, WEB www.posl.com), Dover–Calais; **SeaFrance** (✉ Eastern Docks, Dover, Kent CT16 1JA, ☎ 0870/571–1711 or 0130/421–2696, WEB www.seafrance.co.uk), Dover–Calais; **Stena Line** (✉ Charter House, Park St., Ashford, Kent TN24 8EX, ☎ 0990/707–070 or 0123/364–7022, WEB www.stenaline.co.uk), Harwich–Hook of Holland, Holyhead–Dun Laoghaire (Dublin), Fishguard–Rosslare, and Stranraer (Scotland)–Belfast; and **Swansea Cork Ferries** (✉ Harbour Office, Kings Dock, Swansea SA1 1SF, ☎ 01792/456–116, WEB www.commerce.ie/cs/scf), Swansea–Cork (mid-Mar.–early Nov.).

BUS TRAVEL

International bus travel is rapidly expanding in Europe, thanks to changing EU rules and the Channel Tunnel, but it still has some way to go before it achieves the status of a natural choice, except in Britain and Sweden. In other northern European countries, bus services exist mostly to supplement railroads.

Within several southern European countries—including Portugal, Greece, parts of Spain, and Turkey—the bus has supplanted the train as the main means of public transportation, and is often quicker and more comfortable, with more frequent service, than the antiquated national rolling stock. Be prepared to discover that the bus is more expensive. Competition among lines is keen, so **ask about air-conditioning and reclining seats before you book.**

Eurolines comprises 30 motor-coach operators of international scheduled services, all no-smoking. They also transport passengers within each country. The 30-nation network serves more than 500 destinations with services ranging from twice weekly to five times daily. Eurolines has its own coach stations in Paris (✉ 28 av. du Général de Gaulle at Bagnelot; métro: Gallieni), Brussels (80 rue du Progrès, next to the Gare du Nord), and Amsterdam (adjacent to the Amstel Railway Station). In other cities, coaches depart from railway stations or municipal bus terminals.

From the U.K., Eurolines links London with 400 destinations on the European Continent and Ireland, from Stockholm to Rome, from Dublin to Bucharest. All are via Calais, using either ferry services or Le Shuttle/Eurotunnel under the English Channel. Buses leave from Victoria Coach Station (adjoining the railway station). Services link up with the National Express network covering the U.K.

National or regional tourist offices have information about bus services. For reservations on major lines before you go, **contact your travel agent at home.**

CUTTING COSTS

The **Busabout** service can take you to more than 70 cities in Europe with two options: the consecutive pass or the flexipass. If you're planning a whirlwind European tour on a small budget, two weeks of consecutive travel will run you $249; three weeks $359; and one month $479. For a more leisurely pace, the flexipass gives you ten nonconsecutive traveling days in a two-month period for $399 or up to twenty days of nonconsecutive travel in a three-month period for $719. There are also links to London ($45 supplement), Athens (a Greek Island Pass takes you to five islands for a $79 supplement), and Morocco.

There is an on-board guide who not only provides local information but, with notice, can book campsites, bungalows, budget hotels, or hostels.

The **Eurolines Pass** allows unlimited travel between 40 European cities on scheduled bus services. A 30-day summer pass costs $379 ($329 for those under 26 or over 60); a 60-day pass costs $449 ($409). Passes can be bought from Eurolines offices and travel agents in Europe and from the companies listed below.

➤ DISCOUNT PASSES: In the U.S.: Eurolines Passes can be purchased from **DER Travel Services** (✉ 9501 W. Devon Ave., Rosemont, IL 60018, ☎ 847/692–6300 in IL; 800/782–2424), and from most Hostelling International and all STA offices (☞ Students in Europe, *below*).

➤ BUS INFORMATION: **Busabout (UK) Ltd.** (✉ Victoria Bus Station, 258 Vauxhall Bridge Rd., London, SW1V 1BF, ☎ 020/7950–1661, FAX 020/7950–1661, WEB www.busabout.com). **Eurolines** (✉ 52 Grosvenor Gardens, London SW1 WOAU, ☎ 0990/143–219 or 020/7730–8235, WEB www.eurolines.com). **Eurolines (UK)** (✉ 4 Cardiff Rd., Luton LU1 1HX, ☎ 01582/404–511, FAX 01582/400–694). For brochures, timetables, and sales agents in the U.S. and Canada, contact the **Eurolines Pass Organization** (✉ Keizersgracht 317, 1016 EE Amsterdam, The Netherlands, ☎ 020/625–3010, FAX 020/420–6904).

CAMERAS & PHOTOGRAPHY

The *Kodak Guide to Shooting Great Travel Pictures* (available at bookstores everywhere) is loaded with tips.

➤ PHOTO HELP: **Kodak Information Center** (☎ 800/242–2424).

EQUIPMENT PRECAUTIONS

Don't pack film and equipment in checked luggage, where it is much more susceptible to damage. X-ray machines used to view checked luggage are becoming much more powerful and therefore are much more likely to ruin your film. Always **keep film and tape out of the sun.** Carry an extra supply of batteries, and **be prepared to turn on your camera or camcorder** to prove to security personnel that the device is real. Always **ask for hand inspection of film,** which becomes clouded after repeated exposure to airport X-ray machines, and **keep videotapes away from metal detectors.**

CAR RENTAL

The great attraction of renting is obviously that you become independent of public transport. Cost-wise, you should **consider renting a car only if you are with at least one other person;** single travelers pay a tremendous premium. Car rental costs vary from country to country; rates in Scandinavia and Eastern Europe are particularly high. If you're visiting a number of countries with varying rates, it makes sense to **rent a vehicle in the cheapest country.** For instance, if you plan to visit Normandy, the same company that rents you a car for a weekly rate of $246 in Paris will rent you one for $159 in Brussels, adding a few hours to your trip but at a 35% savings.

Picking up a car at an airport is convenient but often costs extra (up to 10%) as rental companies pass along the fees charged to them by airports.

Sample rates: London, $39 a day and $136 a week for an economy car with air-conditioning, a manual transmission, and unlimited mileage; Paris, $60 a day and $196 a week; Madrid, $37 a day and $132 a week; Rome, $49 a day and $167 a week; Frankfurt, $18 a day and $91 a week. These figures do not include tax on car rentals, which ranges from 15% to 21%.

➤ MAJOR AGENCIES: **Alamo** (☎ 800/522–9696; 020/8759–6200 in the U.K., WEB www.alamo.com). **Avis** (☎ 800/331–1084; 800/879–2847 in Canada; 02/9353–9000 in Australia; 09/525–1982 in New Zealand; 0870/606–0100 in the U.K., WEB www.avis.com). **Budget** (☎ 800/527–0700; 0870/156–5656 in the U.K., WEB www.budget.com). **Dollar** (☎ 800/800–6000; 0124/622–0111 in the U.K., where it's affiliated with Sixt; 02/9223–1444 in Australia, WEB www.dollar.com). **Hertz** (☎ 800/654–3001; 800/263–0600 in Canada; 020/8897–2072 in the U.K.; 02/9669–2444 in Australia; 09/256–8690 in New Zealand, WEB www.hertz.com). **National Car Rental** (☎ 800/227–7368; 020/8680–4800 in the U.K., WEB www.nationalcar.com).

CUTTING COSTS

To get the best deal, **book through a travel agent who will shop around.** If you think you'll need a car in Europe but are unsure about when or where, ask your travel agent to check out Kemwel's CarPass. This gives the benefit of pre-paid vouchers with the flexibility of last-minute bookings in Europe. Unused vouchers are refunded. Do **look into wholesalers,** companies that do not own fleets but rent in bulk from those that do and often offer better rates than traditional car-rental operations. Payment must be made before you leave home. Short-term leasing can save money if you need a rental for more than 17 days. Kemwel and Europe by Car are among the wholesalers offering such deals.

➤ WHOLESALERS: **Auto Europe** (☎ 207/842–2000 or 800/223–5555, FAX 207/842–2222, WEB www.autoeurope.com). **Europe by Car** (☎ 212/581–3040 or 800/223–1516, FAX 212/246–1458, WEB www.europebycar.com). **DER Travel Services** (✉ 9501 W. Devon Ave., Rosemont, IL 60018, ☎ 800/782–2424, FAX 800/282–7474 for information; 800/860–9944 for brochures, WEB www.dertravel.com). **Kemwel Holiday Autos** (☎ 800/678–0678, FAX 914/825–3160, WEB www.kemwel.com).

INSURANCE

When driving a rented car you are generally responsible for any damage to or loss of the vehicle. Before you rent, see what coverage your personal auto-insurance policy and credit cards provide.

Before you buy collision coverage, check your existing policies—you may already be covered. However, collision policies that car-rental companies sell for European rentals usually do not include stolen-vehicle coverage. Note that in Italy, all car-rental companies make you buy theft-protection policies.

REQUIREMENTS & RESTRICTIONS

Your own driver's license is acceptable virtually everywhere. An International Driver's Permit is a good idea, especially if your travel is likely to include Eastern Europe; it's available from the American or Canadian automobile association, and, in the United Kingdom, from the Automobile Association or Royal Automobile Club. These international permits are universally recognized; having one in your wallet may save you a problem with the local authorities.

SURCHARGES

Before you pick up a car in one city and leave it in another, **ask about drop-off charges or one-way service fees,** which can be substantial. Note, too, that some rental agencies charge extra if you return the car before the time specified in your contract. To avoid a hefty refueling fee, **fill the tank just before you turn in the car,** but be aware that gas stations near the rental outlet may overcharge.

CAR TRAVEL

Unless you're in a rush to get from A to B, you will find it rewarding to **avoid the freeways and use alternative routes.**

Motorway tolls can easily add $25 a day to your costs in driving through France, and there are toll roads throughout southern Europe, as well as charges for many tunnels. When crossing borders into Switzerland, you're charged 40 Swiss francs (about $30) for a *vignette* that entitles you to use Swiss freeways for a year. To get a handle on costs, **ask the national tourist office or car rental firm about tolls before you travel.**

If you are driving a rented car, **be sure to carry the necessary papers provided by the rental company.** For U.K. citizens, if the vehicle is your own, you will need proof of ownership, a certificate of roadworthiness (known as a Ministry of Transport, or MOT, road vehicle certificate), up-to-date vehicle registration or tax certificate, and a Green Card proof of insurance, available from your insurance company (fees vary depending on destination and length of stay).

Border controls have been abolished within the EU (except in the U.K., Ireland, Scandinavia, and Greece). The border posts are still standing, but drivers whiz through them without slowing down. Truck traffic is generally routed to separate checkpoints.

Drivers traveling between Great Britain and the Continent can now **consider using the Eurotunnel,** the train carrying cars, buses, motorbikes, and trucks, plus their passengers, through the Channel Tunnel between Folkestone and Calais in 35 minutes. The shuttle trains operate continuously—three to four trains per hour—and reservations are not needed, but to avoid queueing, tickets can be bought in advance from travel agents or by credit card from **Eurotunnel** (☎ 03/2100–6100 in France, 0990/353–535 in the U.K.). Prices vary according to length of stay on the Continent, as well as the season and time of travel. Prices given are for return fares, with the maximum rate applying in the peak July and August holiday period. A short break (less than 5 days) costs £139–£225, and a standard return costs £219–£325. Club Class gives you the right to priority queueing and entry to the Club Class lounge for a premium of 25%–35%. To calculate single fares simply divide by two. Note that you must make advance reservations to benefit from promotional fares and special offers. *See* The Channel Tunnel, *below.*

AUTO CLUBS

➤ In Australia: **Australian Automobile Association** (☎ 02/6247–7311).

➤ In Canada: **Canadian Automobile Association** (CAA, ☎ 613/820–1890 for membership).

➤ In New Zealand: **New Zealand Automobile Association** (☎ 09/377–4660).

➤ In the U.K.: **Automobile Association** (AA, ☎ 0990/500–600). **Royal Automobile Club** (RAC, ☎ 0990/722–722 for membership; 0345/121–345 for insurance).

➤ In the U.S.: **American Automobile Association** (☎ 800/564–6222).

EMERGENCY SERVICES

You must carry a reflecting red triangle (to be placed 30 meters behind your car in case of breakdown). A first-aid kit and fire extinguisher are strongly recommended.

GASOLINE

Be prepared: gasoline costs three to four times more than in the United States, due to heavy taxes. The better fuel economy of European cars offsets the higher price to some extent.

ROAD CONDITIONS

During peak vacation periods, main routes can be jammed with holiday traffic. In the United Kingdom, **try to avoid driving during any of the long bank-holiday (public holiday) weekends,** when motorways are invariably clogged. The tunnels carrying traffic between Italy and the countries to the north are often overburdened with truck traffic; cross the Alps on a weekend, if you can. In France, Greece, Spain, and Italy, huge numbers of people still take a fixed one-month vacation in August, so **avoid driving** during *le départ,* the first weekend in August, when vast numbers of drivers head south; or *le retour,* when they head back.

RULES OF THE ROAD

Establishing a speed limit for German motorways has proved a tougher nut than any government could crack. On the rest of the Continent, the limit is generally 120 kph (74 mph), but the cruising speed is mostly about 140 kph (about 87 mph). In the United Kingdom, the speed limit is 112 kph (70 mph), but there, too, passing at considerably higher speed is not uncommon. In suburban and urban zones, the speed limit is much lower. For safe driving, **stay in the slower lane unless you want to pass, and make way for faster cars wanting to pass you.**

In the United Kingdom, the Republic of Ireland, Malta, Cyprus, and Gibraltar, cars drive on the left. In other European countries, traffic is on the right. If you're coming off the Eurotunnel's shuttle, or ferries from Britain or Ireland to the Continent (or vice versa), beware the transition. *See* individual country chapters for national speed limits and rules of the road.

THE CHANNEL TUNNEL

Short of flying, the "Chunnel" is the fastest way to cross the English Channel: 35 minutes from Folkestone to Calais, 60 minutes from motorway to motorway, or 3 hours from London's Waterloo Station to Paris's Gare du Nord.

➤ Car Transport: **Le Shuttle** (☎ 0870/535–3535 in the U.K.).

➤ Passenger Service: In the U.K.: **Eurostar** (☎ 0870/518–6186), **InterCity Europe** (☎ 0870/584–8848 for credit-card bookings). In the U.S.: **BritRail Travel** (☎ 800/677–8585), **Rail Europe** (☎ 800/942–4866, WEB www.raileurope.com).

CHILDREN IN EUROPE

If you are renting a car, don't forget to **arrange for a car seat** when you reserve. Children under twelve may not travel in the front seat.

For general advice about traveling with children, consult *Fodor's FYI: Travel with Your Baby* (available in bookstores everywhere).

FLYING

If your children are two or older, **ask about children's airfares.** As a general rule, infants under two not occupying a seat fly at greatly reduced fares or even for free. When booking, **confirm carry-on allowances** if you're traveling with infants. In general, for babies charged 10% of the adult fare you are allowed one carry-on bag and a collapsible stroller; if the flight is full, the stroller may have to be checked or you may be limited to less.

Experts agree that it's a good idea to use safety seats aloft for children weighing less than 40 pounds. Airlines set their own policies: U.S. carriers usually require that the child be ticketed, even if he or she is young enough to ride free, since the seats must be strapped into regular seats. Do **check your airline's policy about using safety seats during takeoff and landing.** And since safety seats are not allowed everywhere in the plane, get your seat assignments early.

When reserving, **request children's meals or a freestanding bassinet** if you need them. But note that bulkhead seats, where you must sit to use the bassinet, may lack an overhead bin or storage space on the floor.

LODGING

Most hotels in Europe allow children under a certain age to stay in their parents' room at no extra charge, but others charge for them as extra adults; be sure to **find out the cutoff age for children's discounts.**

SIGHTS & ATTRACTIONS

Places that are especially appealing to children are indicated by a rubber-duckie icon (🐥) in the margin.

CONSUMER PROTECTION

Whenever shopping or buying travel services in Europe, **pay with a major credit card,** if possible, so you can cancel payment or get reimbursed if there's a problem. If you're doing business with a particular company for the first time, **contact your local Better Business Bureau and the attorney general's offices** in your state and (for U.S. businesses) the company's home state as well. Have any complaints been filed? Finally, if you're buying a package or tour, always **consider travel insurance** that includes default coverage (☞ Insurance, *below*).

➤ BBBs: **Council of Better Business Bureaus** (✉ 4200 Wilson Blvd., Suite 800, Arlington, VA 22203, ☎ 703/276–0100, FAX 703/525–8277, WEB www.bbb.org).

CRUISE TRAVEL

Europe is a major cruise center, with eight seas (Adriatic, Aegean, Baltic, Black, Ionian, Mediterranean, North, and Tyrrhenian) and the Atlantic Ocean. From the majesty of Norway's fjords to the ruins of ancient Greece, the region has more than one could possibly hope to see on one cruise vacation. **Select your ship as carefully as you choose your itinerary.** Cruises sail in Europe from April through November.

To learn how to plan, choose, and book a cruise-ship voyage, check out Cruise How-to's on www.fodors.com and consult *Fodor's FYI: Plan & Enjoy Your Cruise* (available in bookstores everywhere).

➤ CRUISE LINES: **Abercrombie & Kent** (✉ 1520 Kensington Rd., Suite 212, Oak Brook, IL 60523, ☎ 630/954–2944 or 800/323–7308). **Celebrity Cruises** (✉ 1050 Caribbean Way, Miami, FL 33132, ☎ 305/539–6000 or 800/437–3111). **Clipper Cruise Line** (✉ 7711 Bonhomme Ave., St. Louis, MO 63105, ☎ 314/727–2929 or 800/325–0010). **Crystal Cruises** (✉ 2049 Century Park E, Suite 1400, Los Angeles, CA 90067, ☎ 800/446–6620). **Cunard Line Limited** (6100 Blue Lagoon Dr., Suite 400, Miami, FL 33126, ☎ 800/929–9595). **Holland America Line** (✉ 300 Elliott Ave. W, Seattle, WA 98119, ☎ 800/426–0327). **Orient Lines** (✉ 1510 S.E. 17th St., Fort Lauderdale, FL 33316 ☎ 954/527–6660 or 800/333–7300). **Princess Cruises** (✉ 10100 Santa Monica Blvd., Los Angeles, CA 90067, ☎ 310/553–1770; 800/774–6237 for brochures). **Radisson Seven Seas Cruises** (✉ 600 Corporate Dr., Suite 410, Fort Lauderdale, FL 33334, ☎ 800/333–3333). **Royal Caribbean International** (✉ 1050 Caribbean Way, Miami, FL 33132, ☎ 305/539–6000; 800/255–4373 for brochures). **Royal Olympic Cruises** (✉ 805 Third Ave., 18th floor, New York, NY 10022, ☎ 212/397–6400; 800/872–6400; 800/368–3888 in Canada). **Silversea Cruises** (✉ 110 E. Broward Blvd., Fort Lauderdale, FL 33301, ☎ 954/522–4477 or 800/722–9955). **Special Expeditions** (✉ 720 Fifth Ave., New York, NY 10019, ☎ 212/765–7740 or 800/762–0003). **Windstar Cruises** (✉ 300 Elliott Ave. W, Seattle, WA 98119, ☎ 800/258–7245).

CUSTOMS & DUTIES

When shopping, **keep receipts** for all purchases. Upon reentering the country, **be ready to show customs officials what you've bought.** If you feel a duty is incorrect or object to the way your clearance was handled, note the inspector's badge number and ask to see a supervisor. If the problem isn't resolved, write to the appropriate authorities, beginning with the port director at your point of entry.

IN AUSTRALIA

Australian residents who are 18 or older may bring home $A400 worth of souvenirs and gifts (including jewelry), 250 cigarettes or 250 grams of tobacco, and 1,125 ml of alcohol (including wine, beer, and spirits). Residents under 18 may bring back $A200 worth of goods. Prohibited items include meat products. Seeds, plants, and fruits need to be declared upon arrival.

➤ INFORMATION: **Australian Customs Service** (Regional Director, ✉ Box 8, Sydney, NSW 2001, Australia, ☎ 02/9213–2000, FAX 02/9213–4000, WEB www.customs.gov.au).

IN CANADA

Canadian residents who have been out of Canada for at least seven days may bring home C$750 worth of goods duty-free. If you've been away fewer than seven days but more than 48 hours, the duty-free allowance drops to C$200; if your trip lasts 24–48 hours, the allowance is C$50. You may not pool allowances with family members. Goods claimed under the C$750 exemption may follow you by mail; those claimed under the lesser exemptions must accompany you. Alcohol and tobacco products may be included in the seven-day and 48-hour exemptions but not in the 24-hour exemption. If you meet the age requirements of the province or territory through which you reenter Canada, you may bring in, duty-free, 1.14 liters (40 imperial ounces) of wine or liquor *or* 24 12-ounce cans or bottles of beer or ale. If you are 19 or older you may bring in, duty-free, 200 cigarettes and 50 cigars. Check ahead of time with the Canada Customs Revenue Agency or the Department of Agriculture for policies regarding meat products, seeds, plants, and fruits.

You may send an unlimited number of gifts worth up to C$60 each duty-free to Canada. Label the package UNSOLICITED GIFT—VALUE UNDER $60. Alcohol and tobacco are excluded.

➤ INFORMATION: **Canada Customs Revenue Agency** (✉ 2265 St. Laurent Blvd. S, Ottawa, Ontario K1G 4K3, Canada, ☎ 204/983–3500 or 506/636–5064; 800/461–9999 in Canada, WEB www.ccra-adrc.gc.ca).

IN EUROPE

Since the EU's 1992 agreement on a unified European market, the same customs regulations apply to all 15 member states (Austria, Belgium, Denmark, Finland, France, Germany, Great Britain, Greece, Ireland, Italy, Luxembourg, the Netherlands, Portugal, Spain, and Sweden). If you arrive from another EU country, you do not have to pass through customs.

Duty-free allowances for visitors from outside the EU are the same whatever your nationality (but you have to be over 17): 200 cigarettes or 50 cigars or 100 cigarillos or 250 grams of pipe tobacco; 1 liter of spirits or 2 liters of fortified or sparkling wine or liqueurs; 2 liters of still table wine; 60 milliliters of perfume; 250 milliliters of toilet water (note: 1 U.S. quart equals 0.946 liters); plus $200 worth of other goods, including gifts and souvenirs. Unless otherwise noted in individual country chapters, there are no restrictions on the import or export of currency. These limits remained in force after June 30, 1999, when duty-free shopping for travel within the EU was abolished.

See individual country chapters on non-EU countries for information on their import limits.

IN NEW ZEALAND

Homeward-bound residents 17 or older may bring back $700 worth of souvenirs and gifts. Your duty-free allowance also includes 4.5 liters of wine or beer; one 1,125-ml bottle of spirits; and either 200 cigarettes, 250 grams of tobacco, 50 cigars, or a combination of the three up to 250 grams. Prohibited items include meat products, seeds, plants, and fruits.

➤ INFORMATION: **New Zealand Customs** (Custom House, ✉ 50 Anzac Ave., Box 29, Auckland, New Zealand, ☎ 09/300–5399, FAX 09/359–6730, WEB www.customs.govt.nz).

IN THE U.K.

If you are a U.K. resident and your journey was wholly within the European Union (EU), you won't have to pass through customs when you return to the United Kingdom. If you plan to bring back large quantities of alcohol or tobacco, check EU limits beforehand. From countries outside the European Union, you may bring home, duty-free, 200 cigarettes or 50 cigars; 1 liter of spirits or 2 liters of fortified or sparkling wine or liqueurs; 2 liters of still table wine; 60 ml of perfume; 250 ml of toilet water; plus £145 worth of other goods, including gifts and souvenirs. If returning from outside the EU, prohibited items include meat products, seeds, plants, and fruits.

➤ INFORMATION: **HM Customs and Excise** (✉ Dorset House, Stamford St., Bromley, Kent BR1 1XX, U.K., ☎ 020/7202–4227, WEB www.hmce.gov.uk).

IN THE U.S.

U.S. residents who have been out of the country for at least 48 hours (and who have not used the $400 allowance or any part of it in the past 30 days) may bring home $400 worth of foreign goods duty-free.

U.S. residents 21 and older may bring back 1 liter of alcohol duty-free. In addition, regardless of your age, you are allowed 200 cigarettes and 100 non-Cuban cigars. Antiques, which the U.S. Customs Service defines as objects more than 100 years old, enter duty-free, as do original works of art done entirely by hand, including paintings, drawings, and sculptures.

You may also mail or ship packages home duty-free: up to $200 worth of goods for personal use, with a limit of one parcel per addressee per day (except alcohol or tobacco products or perfume worth more than $5); label the package PERSONAL USE and attach a list of its contents and their retail value. Do not label the package UNSOLICITED GIFT or your duty-free exemption will drop to $100. Mailed items do not affect your duty-free allowance on your return.

➤ INFORMATION: **U.S. Customs Service** (✉ 1300 Pennsylvania Ave. NW, Room 6.3D, Washington, DC 20229, WEB www.customs.gov; inquiries ☎ 202/354–1000; complaints c/o 1300 Pennsylvania Ave. NW, Room 5.4D, Washington, DC 20229; registration of equipment c/o Office of Passenger Programs, ☎ 202/927–0530).

DINING

See discussions of dining in individual country chapters. The restaurants we list are the cream of the crop in each price category.

RESERVATIONS & DRESS

Reservations are always a good idea: we mention them only when they're essential or not accepted. We mention dress only when men are required to wear a jacket or a jacket and tie.

DISABILITIES & ACCESSIBILITY

Getting around in many European cities and towns can be difficult if you're using a wheelchair, as cobblestone-paved streets and sidewalks are common in older, historic districts. Generally, newer facilities (including museums, transportation, hotels) provide easier access for people with disabilities.

LODGING

Contact a support organization at home to see whether they have publications with lists of approved accommodation. The U.S.-based Society for the Advancement of Travel for the Handicapped (SATH) is dedicated to promoting access for travelers with disabilities. The British nonprofit Holiday Care Service produces an annual guide, *The Holiday Care Service Guide to Accessible Accommodation and Travel,* which lists more than 1,000 establishments inspected for access by Holiday Care in association with the National Tourist Boards. It has sections on accessible transportation, identifies accessible tourist attractions, and suggests sample itineraries.

➤ SUPPORT ORGANIZATIONS: **Holiday Care Service** (✉ 2nd floor, Imperial Bldgs., Victoria Rd., Horley, Surrey, RH6 7PZ, ☎ 0129/377–4535, FAX 0129/378–4647, WEB www.holidaycare.org.uk). **The Society for the Advancement of Travel for the Handicapped** (SATH; ✉ 347 Fifth Ave., Suite 610, New York, NY 10016, ☎ 212/447–7284, FAX 212/725–8253).

RESERVATIONS

When discussing accessibility with an operator or reservations agent, **ask hard questions.** Are there any stairs, inside *or* out? Are there grab bars next to the toilet *and* in the shower/tub? How wide is the doorway to the room? To the bathroom? For the most extensive facilities meeting the latest legal specifications, **opt for newer accommodations.**

➤ COMPLAINTS: **Aviation Consumer Protection Division** (☞ Air Travel, *above*) for airline-related problems. **Civil Rights Office** (✉ U.S. Department of Transportation, Departmental Office of Civil Rights, S-30, 400 7th St. SW, Room 10215, Washington, DC 20590, ☎ 202/366–4648, FAX 202/366–9371, WEB www.dot.gov/ost/docr/index.htm) for problems with surface transportation. **Disability Rights Section** (✉ U.S. Department of Justice, Civil Rights Division, Box 66738, Washington, DC 20035-6738, ☎ 202/514–0301 or 800/514–0301; 202/514–0383 TTY; 800/514–0383 TTY, FAX 202/307–1198, WEB www.usdoj.gov/crt/ada/adahom1.htm for general complaints.

TRAVEL AGENCIES

In the United States, the Americans with Disabilities Act requires that travel firms serve the needs of all travelers. Some agencies specialize in working with people with disabilities.

➤ TRAVELERS WITH MOBILITY PROBLEMS: **Access Adventures** (✉ 206 Chestnut Ridge Rd., Scottsville, NY 14624, ☎ 716/889–9096, dltravel@prodigy.net), run by a former physical-rehabilitation counselor. **CareVacations** (✉ No. 5, 5110–50 Ave., Leduc, Alberta T9E 6V4, Canada, ☎ 780/986–6404 or 877/478–7827, FAX 780/986–8332, WEB www.carevacations.com), for group tours and cruise vacations. **Flying Wheels Travel** (✉ 143 W. Bridge St., Box 382, Owatonna, MN 55060, ☎ 507/451–5005 or 800/535–6790, FAX 507/451–1685, WEB www.flyingwheelstravel.com).

➤ TRAVELERS WITH DEVELOPMENTAL DISABILITIES: **New Directions** (✉ 5276 Hollister Ave., Suite 207, Santa Barbara, CA 93111, ☎ 805/967–2841 or 888/967–2841, FAX 805/964–7344, WEB www.newdirectionstravel.com). **Sprout** (✉ 893 Amsterdam Ave., New York, NY 10025, ☎ 212/222–9575 or 888/222–9575, FAX 212/222–9768, WEB www.gosprout.org).

DISCOUNTS & DEALS

Be a smart shopper and **compare all your options** before making decisions. A plane ticket bought with a promotional coupon from travel clubs, coupon books, and direct-mail offers or on the Internet may not be cheaper than the least expensive fare from a discount ticket agency. And always keep in mind that what you get is just as important as what you save.

DISCOUNT RESERVATIONS

To save money, **look into discount reservations services** with toll-free numbers, which use their buying power to get a better price on hotels, airline tickets, even car rentals. When booking a room, always **call the hotel's local toll-free number** (if one is available) rather than the central reservations number—you'll often get a better price. Always ask about special packages or corporate rates.

When shopping for the best deal on hotels and car rentals, **look for guaranteed exchange rates,** which protect you against a falling dollar. With your rate locked in, you won't pay more, even if the price goes up in the local currency.

➤ AIRLINE TICKETS: ☎ **800/FLY–ASAP.**

➤ HOTEL ROOMS: **Hotel Reservations Network** (☎ 800/964–6835, WEB www.hoteldiscount.com). **International Marketing & Travel Concepts** (☎ 800/790–4682, WEB www.imtc-travel.com). **Players Express**

Vacations (☏ 800/458-6161, WEB www.playersexpress.com). **Steigenberger Reservation Service** (☏ 800/223-5652, WEB www.srs-worldhotels.com). **Travel Interlink** (☏ 800/888-5898, WEB www.travelinterlink.com). **Turbotrip.com** (☏ 800/473-7829, WEB www.turbotrip.com).

PACKAGE DEALS

Don't confuse packages and guided tours. When you buy a package, you travel on your own, just as though you had planned the trip yourself. Fly/drive packages, which combine airfare and car rental, are often a good deal. If you **buy a rail/drive pass,** you may save on train tickets and car rentals. All Eurail- and Europass holders get a discount on Eurostar fares through the Channel Tunnel. A German Rail Pass is also good for travel aboard some KD River Steamers and some Deutsche Touring/Europabus routes. Greek Flexipass options may include sightseeing, hotels, and plane tickets.

ELECTRICITY

To use electric-powered equipment purchased in the U.S. or Canada, **bring a converter and adapter.** The electrical current in Europe is 220 volts, 50 cycles alternating current (AC); wall outlets in most of Europe take plugs with two round prongs; Great Britain, Malta, and Cyprus use plugs with three oblong prongs and mains current is at 240 volts.

If your appliances are dual-voltage, you'll need only an adapter. Don't use 110-volt outlets marked FOR SHAVERS ONLY for high-wattage appliances such as blow-dryers. Most laptops operate equally well on 110 and 220 volts and so require only an adapter.

GAY & LESBIAN TRAVEL

Although big cities like Amsterdam, London, and Paris have a visible and happening gay scene (the newly elected mayor of Paris is openly gay), most of Europe has a view of homosexuality similar to that found away from big cities in the U.S.

➤ GAY- & LESBIAN-FRIENDLY TRAVEL AGENCIES: **Different Roads Travel** (✉ 8383 Wilshire Blvd., Suite 902, Beverly Hills, CA 90211, ☏ 323/651-5557 or 800/429-8747, FAX 323/651-3678, lgernert@tzell.com). **Kennedy Travel** (✉ 314 Jericho Turnpike, Floral Park, NY 11001, ☏ 516/352-4888 or 800/237-7433, FAX 516/354-8849, WEB www.kennedy-travel.com). **Now Voyager** (✉ 4406 18th St., San Francisco, CA 94114, ☏ 415/626-1169 or 800/255-6951, FAX 415/626-8626, WEB www.nowvoyager.com). **Skylink Travel and Tour** (✉ 1006 Mendocino Ave., Santa Rosa, CA 95401, ☏ 707/546-9888 or 800/225-5759, FAX 707/546-9891, WEB www.skylinktravel.com), serving lesbian travelers.

INSURANCE

The most useful travel-insurance plan is a comprehensive policy that includes coverage for trip cancellation and interruption, default, trip delay, and medical expenses (with a waiver for pre-existing conditions).

Without insurance you will lose all or most of your money if you cancel your trip, regardless of the reason. Default insurance covers you if your tour operator, airline, or cruise line goes out of business. Trip-delay covers expenses that arise because of bad weather or mechanical delays. Study the fine print when comparing policies.

If you're traveling internationally, a key component of travel insurance is coverage for medical bills incurred if you get sick on the road. Such expenses are not generally covered by Medicare or private policies. U.K. residents can buy a travel-insurance policy valid for most vacations taken during the year in which it's purchased (but check pre-existing-condition coverage). British and Australian citizens need extra medical coverage when traveling overseas.

Always **buy travel policies directly from the insurance company**; if you buy them from a cruise line, airline, or tour operator that goes out of business you probably will not be covered for the agency or operator's default, a major risk. Before making any purchase, **review your existing health and home-owner's policies** to find what they cover away from home.

➤ TRAVEL INSURERS: In the U.S.: **Access America** (✉ 6600 W. Broad St., Richmond, VA 23230, ☎ 800/284–8300, FAX 804/673–1491, WEB www.etravelprotection.com), **Travel Guard International** (✉ 1145 Clark St., Stevens Point, WI 54481, ☎ 715/345–0505 or 800/826–1300, FAX 800/955–8785, WEB www.noelgroup.com).

➤ INSURANCE INFORMATION: In the U.K.: **Association of British Insurers** (✉ 51–55 Gresham St., London EC2V 7HQ, U.K., ☎ 020/7600–3333, FAX 020/7696–8999, WEB www.abi.org.uk). In Canada: **RBC Travel Insurance** (✉ 6880 Financial Dr., Mississauga, Ontario L5N 7Y5, Canada, ☎ 905/791–8700, 800/668–4342 in Canada, FAX 905/816–2498, WEB www.royalbank.com). In Australia: **Insurance Council of Australia** (✉ Level 3, 56 Pitt St., Sydney NSW 2000, ☎ 02/9253–5100, FAX 02/9253–5111, WEB www.ica.com.au). In New Zealand: **Insurance Council of New Zealand** (✉ Box 474, Wellington, New Zealand, ☎ 04/472–5230, FAX 04/473–3011, WEB www.icnz.org.nz).

LANGUAGE

A phrase book and language-tape set can help get you started. *Fodor's French for Travelers, Fodor's German for Travelers, Fodor's Italian for Travelers,* and *Fodor's Spanish for Travelers* (available at bookstores everywhere) are excellent.

LODGING

For discussions of accommodations in Europe, *see* the Lodging sections in individual country chapters. The lodgings we list are the cream of the crop in each price category. When pricing accommodations, always ask what facilities are included and what costs extra.

APARTMENT & VILLA RENTALS

If you want a home base that's roomy enough for a family and comes with cooking facilities, **consider a furnished rental.** These can save you money, especially if you're traveling with a group. Home-exchange directories sometimes list rentals as well as exchanges.

➤ INTERNATIONAL AGENTS: **At Home Abroad** (✉ 405 E. 56th St., Suite 6H, New York, NY 10022, ☎ 212/421–9165, FAX 212/752–1591, WEB www.athomeabroadinc.com). **Drawbridge to Europe** (✉ 98 Granite St., Ashland, OR 97520, ☎ 541/482–7778 or 888/268–1148, FAX 541/482–7779, WEB www.drawbridgetoeurope.com). **Hideaways International** (✉ 767 Islington St., Portsmouth, NH 03801, ☎ 603/430–4433 or 800/843–4433, FAX 603/430–4444, WEB www.hideaways.com; membership $129). **Hometours International** (✉ Box 11503, Knoxville, TN 37939, ☎ 865/690–8484 or 800/367–4668, WEB thor.he.net/INSERT TILDEhometour/). **Interhome** (✉ 1990 N.E. 163rd St., Suite 110, N. Miami Beach, FL 33162, ☎ 305/940–2299 or 800/882–6864, FAX 305/940–2911, WEB www.interhome.com). **Vacation Home Rentals Worldwide** (✉ 235 Kensington Ave., Norwood, NJ 07648, ☎ 201/767–9393 or 800/633–3284, FAX 201/767–5510, WEB www.vhrww.com). **Villanet** (✉ 11556 1st Ave. NW, Seattle, WA 98177, ☎ 206/417–3444 or 800/964–1891, FAX 206/417–1832, WEB www.rentavilla.com). **Villas and Apartments Abroad** (✉ 1270 Avenue of the Americas, 15th floor, New York, NY 10020, ☎ 212/897–5045 or 800/433–3020, FAX 212/897–5039, WEB www.vaanyc.com). **Villas International** (✉ 950 Northgate Dr., Suite 206, San Rafael, CA 94903, ☎ 415/499–9490 or 800/221–2260, FAX 415/499–9491, WEB www.villasintl.com).

HOME EXCHANGES

If you would like to exchange your home for someone else's, **join a home-exchange organization,** which will send you its updated listings of available exchanges for a year and will include your own listing in at least one of them. It's up to you to make specific arrangements.

➤ EXCHANGE CLUBS: **HomeLink International** (✉ Box 47747, Tampa, FL 33647, ☎ 813/975–9825 or 800/638–3841, FAX 813/910–8144, WEB www.homelink.org; $98 per year). **Intervac U.S.** (✉ Box 590504, San Francisco, CA 94159, ☎ 800/756–

4663, FAX 415/435–7440, WEB www.intervacus.com; $93 yearly fee includes one catalogue and on-line access).

HOSTELS

No matter what your age, you can **save on lodging costs by staying at hostels.** In some 4,500 locations in more than 70 countries around the world, Hostelling International (HI), the umbrella group for a number of national youth-hostel associations, offers single-sex, dorm-style beds and, at many hostels, rooms for couples and family accommodations. Membership in any HI national hostel association, open to travelers of all ages, allows you to stay in HI-affiliated hostels at member rates; one-year membership is about $25 for adults (C$26.75 in Canada, £9.30 in the U.K., $30 in Australia, and $30 in New Zealand); hostels run about $10–$25 per night. Members have priority if the hostel is full; they're also eligible for discounts around the world, even on rail and bus travel in some countries.

➤ ORGANIZATIONS: **Hostelling International—American Youth Hostels** (✉ 733 15th St. NW, Suite 840, Washington, DC 20005, ☎ 202/783–6161, FAX 202/783–6171, WEB www.hiayh.org). **Hostelling International—Canada** (✉ 400–205 Catherine St., Ottawa, Ontario K2P 1C3, Canada, ☎ 613/237–7884, FAX 613/237–7868, WEB www.hostellingintl.ca). **Youth Hostel Association of England and Wales** (✉ Trevelyan House, 8 St. Stephen's Hill, St. Albans, Hertfordshire AL1 2DY, U.K., ☎ 0870/8708808, FAX 01727/844126, WEB www.yha.org.uk). **Australian Youth Hostel Association** (✉ 10 Mallett St., Camperdown, NSW 2050, Australia, ☎ 02/9565–1699, FAX 02/9565–1325, WEB www.yha.com.au). **Youth Hostels Association of New Zealand** (✉ Level 3, 193 Cashel St., Box 436, Christchurch, New Zealand, ☎ 03/379–9970, FAX 03/365–4476, WEB www.yha.org.nz).

HOTELS

All hotels listed have private bath unless otherwise noted.

RESERVING A ROOM

See individual country chapters for details on last-minute reservation services.

➤ TOLL-FREE NUMBERS: **Best Western** (☎ 800/528–1234, WEB www.bestwestern.com). **Choice** (☎ 800/221–2222, WEB www.hotelchoice.com).**Clarion** (☎ 800/252–7466, WEB www.hotelchoice.com). **Comfort** (☎ 800/228–5150, WEB www.comfortinn.com). **Forte** (☎ 800/225–5843, WEB www.forte-hotels.com). **Hilton** (☎ 800/445–8667, WEB www.hilton.com). **Holiday Inn** (☎ 800/465–4329, WEB www.basshotels.com). **Hyatt Hotels & Resorts** (☎ 800/233–1234, WEB www.hyatt.com). **Inter-Continental** (☎ 800/327–0200, WEB www.interconti.com). **Marriott** (☎ 800/228–9290, WEB www.marriott.com). **Le Meridien** (☎ 800/543–4300, WEB www.lemeridien-hotels.com). **Nikko Hotels International** (☎ 800/645–5687, WEB www.nikkohotels.com). **Quality Inn** (☎ 800/228–5151, WEB www.qualityinn.com). **Radisson** (☎ 800/333–3333, WEB www.radisson.com). **Ramada** (☎ 800/228–2828, WEB www.ramada.com). **Renaissance Hotels & Resorts** (☎ 800/468–3571, WEB www.renaissancehotels.com/). **Ritz-Carlton** (☎ 800/241–3333, WEB www.ritzcarlton.com). **Sheraton** (☎ 800/325–3535, WEB www.starwood.com). **Wyndham Hotels & Resorts** (☎ 800/822–4200, WEB www.wyndham.com).

MONEY MATTERS

Admission prices throughout this guide are included for attractions that charge more than $10 or the equivalent. Prices throughout this guide are given for adults. Substantially reduced fees are almost always available for children, students, and senior citizens. For information on taxes, *see* Taxes, *below*.

ATMS

ATMs are ubiquitous throughout Europe; you can draw local currency from an ATM in most airports as soon as you deplane.

CREDIT CARDS

Throughout this guide, the following abbreviations are used: **AE,** American Express; **DC,** Diners Club; **MC,** MasterCard; and **V,** Visa.

CURRENCY

On January 1, 2002, the new single European Union (EU) currency, the euro, will finally become the official currency of the eleven countries participating in the European Monetary Union: Austria, Belgium, Finland, France, Germany, Ireland, Italy, Luxembourg, the Netherlands, Portugal, and Spain. Denmark, Great Britain, Greece, and Sweden, although a part of the EU, are not yet part of the monetary union, and therefore will retain the use of their local currencies. At press time (summer 2001), just how graceful this long-awaited physical debut of the much touted euro will be was up for discussion. Those traveling at the beginning of 2002 take note: All banks, businesses, and money machines will be stocked in euros as of January 1, 2002, but there will be a short transition period where the local currencies of the eleven participating countries will co-exist with the euro. Which means that in France, you may buy your morning baguette with your remaining francs and receive euros in return.

Your best bet is to change your old European currency into euros the minute you arrive in Europe (or before you leave), and for once, it doesn't really matter where, because the rate between the monetary union members and the euro was irrevocably fixed in late 1999, thus eliminating any fluctuations in the market and any need for commission.

Although it might take Europeans a little getting used to, the euro will make life for the European traveler much, much easier. Gone are the days when a day trip to Belgium from France meant changing money into yet another currency and paying additional commissions. To make things even easier for travelers from the United States, the euro was created as a direct competitor with the U.S. dollar, which means that their values are quite similar. At press time (summer 2001), one euro was equal to US$.90. It is also equal to 1.37 Canadian dollars, 1.74 Australian dollars, 2.15 New Zealand dollars, and .62 pounds sterling.

In the euro system there are eight coins: 1 and 2 euros, plus 1, 2, 5, 10, 20, and 50 centimes, or cents, of the euro. All coins have one side that has the value of the euro on it and the other side with each country's unique national symbol. There are seven colorful notes: 5, 10, 20, 50, 100, 200, and 500 euros. Notes have the principal architectural styles from antiquity onwards on one side and the map and the flag of Europe on the other and are the same for all countries.

CURRENCY EXCHANGE

For the most favorable rates, **change money through banks.** Although ATM transaction fees may be higher abroad than at home, ATM rates are excellent because they are based on wholesale rates offered only by major banks. You won't do as well at exchange booths in airports or rail and bus stations, in hotels, in restaurants, or in stores. To avoid lines at airport exchange booths, **get a bit of local currency before you leave home.**

➤ EXCHANGE SERVICES: **International Currency Express** (☎ 888/278–6628 for orders, WEB www.foreignmoney.com). **Thomas Cook Currency Services** (☎ 800/287–7362 for telephone orders and retail locations, WEB www.us.thomascook.com).

TRAVELER'S CHECKS

Do you need traveler's checks? It depends on where you're headed. If you're going to rural areas and small towns, go with cash; traveler's checks are best used in cities. Lost or stolen checks can usually be replaced within 24 hours. To ensure a speedy refund, buy your own traveler's checks—don't let someone else pay for them: irregularities like this can cause delays. The person who bought the checks should make the call to request a refund.

PACKING

You should **pack more for the season than for any particular dress code.** In general, northern and central Europe have cold, snowy winters, and the Mediterranean countries have mild winters, though parts of southern Europe can be bitterly cold, too. In the Mediterranean resorts **bring a warm jacket for mornings and evenings,** even in summer. The mountains usually are warm on summer days, but the weather is unpredictable, and the nights are generally cool.

For European cities, **pack as you would for an American city:** formal outfits for first-class restaurants and nightclubs, casual clothes elsewhere. Jeans are perfectly acceptable for sightseeing and informal dining. Sturdy walking shoes are appropriate for the cobblestone streets and gravel paths that fill many of the parks and surround some of the historic buildings. For visits to churches, cathedrals, and mosques, **avoid shorts and revealing outfits.** In Italy, women cover their shoulders and arms (a shawl will do). Women, however, no longer need to cover their heads in Roman Catholic churches. In Greece many monasteries bar women wearing pants; long skirts are often provided at the entrance as a cover-up for both women wearing pants and men dressed in shorts. In Turkey, women must have a head covering; a long-sleeved shirt and a long skirt or slacks are required.

To discourage purse snatchers and pickpockets, **take a handbag with long straps** that you can sling across your body, bandolier-style, and with a zippered compartment for money.

If you stay in budget hotels, **take your own soap.**

In your carry-on luggage, **pack an extra pair of eyeglasses or contact lenses and enough of any medication** you take to last the entire trip. You may also ask your doctor to write a spare prescription using the drug's generic name, since brand names may vary from country to country. In luggage to be checked, **never pack prescription drugs or valuables.** To avoid customs delays, carry medications in their original packaging. And don't forget to carry with you the addresses of offices that handle refunds of lost traveler's checks. Check *Fodor's How to Pack* (available in bookstores everywhere) for more tips.

CHECKING LUGGAGE

How many carry-on bags you can bring with you is up to the airline. Most allow two, but not always, so make sure that everything you carry aboard will fit under your seat or in the overhead bin, and get to the gate early. Note that if you have a seat at the back of the plane, you'll probably board first, while the overhead bins are still empty.

If you are flying internationally, note that baggage allowances may be determined not by piece but by weight—generally 88 pounds (40 kilograms) in first class, 66 pounds (30 kilograms) in business class, and 44 pounds (20 kilograms) in economy.

Airline liability for baggage is limited to $1,250 per person on flights within the United States. On international flights it amounts to $9.07 per pound or $20 per kilogram for checked baggage (roughly $640 per 70-pound bag) and $400 per passenger for unchecked baggage. You can buy additional coverage at check-in for about $10 per $1,000 of coverage, but it excludes a rather extensive list of items, shown on your airline ticket.

Before departure, **itemize your bags' contents** and their worth, and label the bags with your name, address, and phone number. (If you use your home address, cover it so potential thieves can't see it readily.) Inside each bag, **pack a copy of your itinerary.** At check-in, **make sure that each bag is correctly tagged** with the destination airport's three-letter code. If your bags arrive damaged or fail to arrive at all, file a written report with the airline before leaving the airport.

PASSPORTS & VISAS

When traveling internationally, **carry your passport** even if you don't need one (it's always the best form of I.D.) and **make two photocopies of the data page** (one for someone at home and another for you, carried separately from your passport). If you lose your passport, promptly call the nearest embassy or consulate and the local police.

ENTERING EUROPE

Citizens of the United States, Canada, United Kingdom, Ireland, Australia, and New Zealand need passports for travel in Europe. Visas may also be required for visits to or through Turkey, Poland, Estonia, Latvia,

Romania, Hungary, and the Czech and Slovak Republics even for short stays or train trips, and in some cases must be obtained before you'll be allowed to enter. Check with the nearest consulate of the country you'll be visiting for visa requirements and any other applicable information.

PASSPORT OFFICES

The best time to apply for a passport or to renew is in fall and winter. Before any trip, check your passport's expiration date, and, if necessary, renew it as soon as possible.

➤ AUSTRALIAN CITIZENS: **Australian Passport Office** (☎ 131–232, WEB www.dfat.gov.au/passports).

➤ CANADIAN CITIZENS: **Passport Office** (☎ 819/994–3500; 800/567–6868 in Canada, WEB www.dfait-maeci.gc.ca/passport).

➤ NEW ZEALAND CITIZENS: **New Zealand Passport Office** (☎ 04/494–0700, WEB www.passports.govt.nz).

➤ U.K. CITIZENS: **London Passport Office** (☎ 0870/521–0410, WEB www.ukpa.gov.uk) for fees and documentation requirements and to request an emergency passport.

➤ U.S. CITIZENS: **National Passport Information Center** (☎ 900/225–5674; calls are 35¢ per minute for automated service, $1.05 per minute for operator service; WEB www.travel.state.gov/npicinfo.html).

SAFETY

Europe, and Great Britain in particular, has been plagued in recent years by what has now become an agricultural crisis. The first cases of bovine spongiform encephalopathy (BSE), commonly known as "mad cow disease," surfaced in Great Britain in the mid-1980s. BSE is a fatal degenerative disease contracted by cattle. When contaminated beef is eaten by humans, it can result in Creutzfeldt-Jakob Disease (CJD), an extremely rare brain-wasting illness fatal to humans.

Europe reacted swiftly to the threat, placing a ban on all beef exported from Great Britain for a short period and immediately banning all use of feed prepared with animal by-products. People are still wary, but at press time the risk of contracting the disease was considered extremely remote. The Centers for Disease Control and Prevention (www.cdc.gov) reported "The current risk for infection with the BSE agent among travelers to Europe is extremely small, if it exists at all." But, as always, stay informed.

At press time (summer 2001), Great Britain, and to a much lesser extent France and the Netherlands, was affected by yet another crisis, foot and mouth disease. Foot and mouth disease affects animals almost exclusively; human cases are extremely rare, and the United Kingdom Ministry of Agriculture, Fisheries, and Food considers it harmless to humans. Nevertheless, it has had a catastrophic effect on the British economy due to the fact that all animals suspected of being infected must be slaughtered immediately.

To limit the spread of foot and mouth disease, some hiking routes and coastal footpaths were closed, especially in north and southwestern England, and certain festivities were cancelled. Some rural tourist attractions were also closed due to the crisis, though at press time many had reopened. Also expect stringent border controls, with an enforced ban on carrying English dairy and farm products out of the territory, and you might have to disinfect your luggage and shoes before leaving the country. Again, read the press and stay informed. The Open Britain web site (www.openbritain.gov.uk) has all the latest information, so you can check before you go.

SENIOR-CITIZEN TRAVEL

Radisson SAS Hotels in Europe offer discounts of 25% or more to senior citizens, subject to availability. You need a confirmed reservation.

To qualify for age-related discounts, **mention your senior-citizen status up front** when booking hotel reservations (not when checking out) and before you're seated in restaurants (not when paying the bill). When renting a car, ask about promotional car-rental discounts, which can be cheaper than senior-citizen rates.

➤ EDUCATIONAL PROGRAMS: **Elderhostel** (✉ 11 Ave. de Lafayette, Boston,

MA 02111-1746, ☎ 877/426–8056, FAX 877/426–2166, WEB www.elderhostel.org). **Interhostel** (✉ University of New Hampshire, 6 Garrison Ave., Durham, NH 03824, ☎ 603/862–1147 or 800/733–9753, FAX 603/862–1113, WEB www.learn.unh.edu). **Folkways Institute** (✉ 14600 S.E. Aldridge Rd., Portland, OR 97236-6518, ☎ 503/658–6600 or 800/225–4666, FAX 503/658–8672, WEB www.folkwaystravel.com).

STUDENTS IN EUROPE

Students in Europe are entitled to a wide range of discounts on admission and transportation. An **International Student Identity Card,** issued by Council Travel (☞ I.D.s & Services, *below*), helps. The globally recognized ISIC card is issued by local student travel organizations that are members of the International Student Travel Confederation, best found by consulting their Web site (www.istc.org).

Many U.S. colleges and universities have study-abroad programs or can connect you with one, and numerous institutions of higher learning in Europe accept foreign students for a semester or year's study. Check with your college administration or contact the CIEE for contacts and brochures.

If you're between 18 and 26, the Ibis hotel chain will let you have a room for $50 or less, provided you show up after 9 PM and they have a room free. You'll be asked for your student I.D. Your chances are best on weekends. There are more than 400 Ibis hotels in Europe, most of them in France.

➤ I.D.s & Services: **Council Travel** (CIEE; ✉ 205 E. 42nd St., 15th floor, New York, NY 10017, ☎ 212/822–2700 or 888/268–6245, FAX 212/822–2699, WEB www.councilexchanges.org) for mail orders only, in the U.S. **Travel Cuts** (✉ 187 College St., Toronto, Ontario M5T 1P7, Canada, ☎ 416/979–2406 or 800/667–2887 in Canada, FAX 416/979–8167, WEB www.travelcuts.com).

TAXES

VALUE-ADDED TAX

Information about national tax-refund programs is given in the A to Z section at the beginning of each country chapter.

Global Refund is a V.A.T. refund service that makes getting your money back hassle-free. The service is available Europe-wide at 130,000 affiliated stores. In participating stores, **ask for the Global Refund refund form** (called a Shopping Cheque). Have it stamped like any customs form by customs officials when you leave the European Union (be ready to show customs officials what you've bought). Then take the form to one of the more than 700 Global Refund counters—conveniently located at every major airport and border crossing—and your money will be refunded on the spot in the form of cash, check, or a refund to your credit-card account (minus a small percentage for processing).

➤ V.A.T. Refunds: **Global Refund** (✉ 99 Main St., Suite 307, Nyack, NY 10960, ☎ 800/566–9828, FAX 845/348–1549, WEB www.globalrefund.com).

TELEPHONES

Telephone systems in Europe are in flux; expect new area codes and extra digits in numbers. Keep in mind that some countries now rely on phone cards; it's a good idea to buy one. Country codes appear in the A to Z section at the beginning of each country chapter. Cellular telephone companies unfortunately opted for different standards in the U.S. and Europe, so only the most sophisticated models with dual or triple band possibilities will function on both sides of the Atlantic. Functionality of both cell phones and pagers will also depend on the kind of subscription you have with your cell-phone company.

INTERNATIONAL CALLS

Consult individual country chapters for information.

LONG-DISTANCE SERVICES

AT&T, MCI, and Sprint access codes make calling long distance relatively convenient, but you may find the local access number blocked in many hotel rooms. First ask the hotel operator to connect you. If the hotel operator balks, ask for an international operator, or dial the international operator yourself. One way to improve your odds of getting connected to your long-distance carrier is to travel with more than one company's calling card (a hotel may block Sprint, for example, but not MCI). If all else fails, call from a pay phone.

TIME

Most of continental Europe ticks at Central European Time (CET), one hour ahead of Greenwich Mean Time (GMT), which prevails in Great Britain, Ireland, Iceland, Portugal, and Madeira. Eastern European countries including the Baltic States (Estonia, Latvia, and Lithuania), Romania, Bulgaria, Greece, and Turkey are two hours ahead of GMT. In most of mainland Europe clocks are turned back one hour during the night of the last Saturday/Sunday in March and put forward one hour on the last Saturday/Sunday night in October.

Europe uses the 24-hour (or "military") clock for everything from airplane departures to opening arias. After noon continue counting forward: 13:00 is 1 PM, 14:00 is 2 PM, etc.

TOURS & PACKAGES

Because everything is prearranged on a prepackaged tour or independent vacation, you spend less time planning—and often get it all at a good price.

BOOKING WITH AN AGENT

Travel agents are excellent resources. But it's a good idea to collect brochures from several agencies as some agents' suggestions may be influenced by relationships with tour and package firms that reward them for volume sales. If you have a special interest, **find an agent with expertise in that area**; ASTA (☞ Travel Agencies, *below*) has a database of specialists worldwide.

Make sure your travel agent knows the accommodations and other services of the place being recommended. Ask about the hotel's location, room size, beds, and whether it has a pool, room service, or programs for children, if you care about these. Has your agent been there in person or sent others whom you can contact? Do some homework on your own, too: local tourism boards can provide information about lesser-known and small-niche operators, some of which may sell only direct.

BUYER BEWARE

Each year consumers are stranded or lose their money when tour operators—even large ones with excellent reputations—go out of business. So **check out the operator.** Ask several travel agents about its reputation, and try to **book with a company that has a consumer-protection program.** (Look for information in the company's brochure.) In the United States, members of the National Tour Association and the United States Tour Operators Association are required to set aside funds to cover your payments and travel arrangements in the event that the company defaults. It's also a good idea to choose a company that participates in the American Society of Travel Agents' Tour Operator Program (TOP); ASTA will act as mediator in any disputes between you and your tour operator.

Remember that the more your package or tour includes the better you can predict the ultimate cost of your vacation. Make sure you know exactly what is covered, and **beware of hidden costs.** Are taxes, tips, and transfers included? Entertainment and excursions? These can add up.

➤ TOUR-OPERATOR RECOMMENDATIONS: **American Society of Travel Agents** (☞ Travel Agencies, *below*). **National Tour Association** (NTA; ✉ 546 E. Main St., Lexington, KY 40508, ☎ 859/226–4444 or 800/682–8886, WEB www.ntaonline.com). **United States Tour Operators Association** (USTOA; ✉ 342 Madison Ave., Suite 1522, New York, NY 10173, ☎ 212/599–6599 or 800/468–7862, FAX 212/599–6744, WEB www.ustoa.com).

TRAIN TRAVEL

Some national high-speed train systems have begun to link up to form the nucleus of a pan-European system. On a long journey, you still have to change trains a couple of times, for the national railways are jealously guarding their prerogatives. Deregulation, so far achieved only in Britain and the Netherlands, is vigorously pushed by the European Commission. French TGV (Trains à Grande Vitesse), which serve most major cities in France, have been extended to Geneva, Lausanne, Bern, Zürich, Turin, and Milan. They connect with the latest generation of Italy's tilting Pendolino trains, also called Eurostar Italia. Italy's service extends beyond the country's borders with a service from Turin to Lyon and, in a joint venture with the Swiss Railways, from Milan to Geneva and Zürich. Express Thalys trains operate from Brussels to Paris on high-speed tracks and from Brussels to Amsterdam and Cologne on conventional track. Germany's equally fast ICE trains connect Hamburg and points in between with Basel, and Mannheim with Munich.

High-speed trains travel at speeds of up to 190 mph on dedicated track and over 150 mph on old track, covering the distance from Paris to Marseille in just over 4 hours, Hamburg to Munich in less than 6. They have made both expensive sleeper compartments and budget *couchettes* (seats that convert into bunks) all but obsolete. Their other attraction is the comfort of a super-smooth ride. The flip side is the reservations requirement; rather than just hopping on the next train, you need to **reserve in advance or allow enough time to make a reservation at the station.**

The **Orient Express,** a glamorous recreation of a sumptuous past, takes two days to cover the distance from London to Venice, and if you want to know the price, you can't afford it. The Swiss Railways operate special services that allow you to enjoy superb scenery and railway buffs to admire the equally superb railroad technology. The **Panoramic Express** takes 3 hours to travel from Montreux via Gstaad to Interlaken; the **Glacier Express** (7½ hours) runs from Zermatt to St. Moritz and also offers en-route gourmet dining as befits these famous resorts; and the **Bernina Express,** the most spectacular, runs from Chur over the 7,400-ft Bernina Pass (where you can turn around; each leg takes 2½ hours), or you can continue to Tirano in Italy (4 hours, with connections to Lugano and Milan). Holders of a Swisspass can travel on all three, but reservations are needed. For additional information on rail services and special fares, contact the national tourist office of the country (☞ Visitor Information, *below*).

CLASSES

Virtually all European systems, including the high-speed ones, operate a two-class system. First class costs substantially more and is usually a luxury rather than a necessity. Some of the poorer European countries retain a third class, but avoid it unless you're an adventure-minded budget traveler.

CUTTING COSTS

To save money, **look into rail passes.** But be aware that if you don't plan to cover many miles you may come out ahead by buying individual tickets.

Before you invest in a discount pass, compare the cost against the point-to-point fares on your actual itinerary. (Rates given in this section are valid through December 2001, the latest available at press time.) EurailPasses provide unlimited first-class rail travel for the duration of the pass in 17 European countries: Austria, Belgium, Denmark, Finland, France, Germany, Greece, Hungary, the Irish Republic, Italy, Luxembourg, the Netherlands, Norway, Portugal, Spain, Sweden, and Switzerland (but not the United Kingdom). If you plan to rack up miles, get a standard pass. These are available for 15 days ($554, £390), 21 days ($718, £506), one month ($890, £627), two months ($1,260, £887), and three months ($1,558, £1,097). Note that you will have to pay a supplement for certain high-speed trains—half the fare on Eurostar.

In addition to standard EurailPasses, check out special rail-pass plans. Among these are the Eurail Youthpass (in second class for those under 26, from $388/£273 to $1,089/£767), the Eurail Saverpass (which gives a discount for 2 to 5 people traveling together; a minimum of two people; from $470/£332 to $1,324/£932 per person), and the Eurail Flexipass (which allows 10 or 15 travel days within a two-month period, $654/£461 and $862/£607, respectively). This is also available at a youth rate. If you're going to travel in just one part of Europe, look into a regional pass, such as the East Europe Pass.

If your plans call for only limited train travel, consider Europass, which costs less money than a EurailPass and is available in first class only for adults and second class only for travelers under 26. It has a number of conditions. It is valid only in France, Germany, Italy, Spain, and Switzerland, but "associated countries" can be added at an extra charge. These are Austria/Hungary, the Benelux area, Greece, and Portugal, to a maximum of 2 extensions. You also get from 5 to 15 travel days during a two-month time period. The other side of the coin is that a Europass costs a couple of hundred dollars less than the least expensive EurailPass. A Europass Adult ranges in price from $348/£254 to $728/£603, a Europass Youth from $233/£170 to $513/£431.

It used to be the rule that non-Europeans had to **purchase Eurail passes before leaving** for Europe. This remains the recommended option, but you can now buy a pass in person within six months of your arrival in Europe from Rail Europe (☞ Train Information, *below*) in London. Also remember that you need to **book seats ahead even if you are using a rail pass**; seat reservations are required on the cross-Channel Eurostar service and European high-speed trains, and are a good idea on other trains that may be crowded—particularly around Easter and at the beginning and end of European vacation periods. You will also need to purchase sleeper or couchette (sleeping berth) reservations separately.

European nationals and others who have resided in Europe for at least six months qualify for the **InterRail Pass.** It used to be exclusively for young people but can now also be purchased, at a premium, by older travelers. This entitles you to unlimited second-class travel within up to eight zones you have preselected. One zone for 22 days, for instance, costs £129 for travelers under 26 (£185 for over 26); all zones for one month, £229 (£319). InterRail Passes can be bought only in Europe at main railway stations, or in the United Kingdom from Rail Europe in London (☞ Train Information, *below*).

FROM THE U.K.

Sleek, high-speed Eurostar trains use the Channel Tunnel to link London (Waterloo) with Paris (Gare du Nord) in 3 hours and with Brussels (Gare du Midi) in 2 hours, 40 minutes. When the British build their high-speed rail link to London (St. Pancras), probably in 2003, another half hour will be shaved off travel time. There are a minimum of 14 daily services to Paris and 10 to Brussels.

Many of the trains stop at Ashford (Kent), and all at the Lille-Europe station in northern France, where you can change to French TGV trains to Brittany, southwest France, Lyon, the Alps, and the Riviera, eliminating the need to transfer between stations in Paris.

Passengers headed for Germany and the Netherlands can buy through tickets via Brussels to Cologne (5½ hours) and Amsterdam (5 hours, 45 minutes). Eurostar does not accept EurailPasses but allows discounts of 40%–50% to passholders. Check for special prices and deals before you book. Or, if money is no object, you can choose the Premium First Class (to Paris only), complete with limo delivery and pick-up at the stations, improved catering, and greater comfort.

Conventional boat trains from London are timed to dovetail with ferry departures at Channel ports. The ferries connect with onward trains at the main French, Belgian, Dutch and Irish ports. Be sure to ask when making your reservation which London railway station to use.

INDIVIDUAL COUNTRY PASSES

Single-country passes are issued by most national railways, and the majority are sold by Rail Europe

(☞ Train Information, *below*, and individual country chapters). Great Britain has a number of rail passes, including the Visitor's Travelcard for train and bus discounts and the BritRail Pass and the BritRail Flexi Pass for train discounts. These British passes must be purchased before you leave home from a BritRail agent (☞ Train Information, *below*).

FARES & SCHEDULES

A good rail timetable is indispensable if you're doing extensive rail traveling. The Thomas Cook Timetables are updated monthly. There's also an annual summer edition (limited to Britain, France, and the Benelux).

➤ TRAIN INFORMATION: **BritRail Travel International** (☎ 800/677–8585). **CIT Tours Corp.** (✉ 15 W. 44th St., 10th floor, New York, NY 10036, ☎ 800/248–7245 for rail; 800/248–8687 for tours and hotels, rail@cit-rail.com for rail; tour@cit-tours.com for tours and hotels). **DER Travel Services** (☞ Discount Passes, Eurolines, *in* Bus Travel, *above*). **Eurostar** (☎ 800/942–4866; 805/482–8210 in U.S.; 0990/186–186 in the U.K.; 0123/361–7575 to the U.K. from other countries, WEB www.eurostar.com). **Rail Europe** (in the U.S.: ✉ 226–230 Westchester Ave., White Plains, NY 10604, ☎ 800/942–4866, FAX 800/432–1329, info@raileurope.com, WEB www.raileurope.com; in Canada: ✉ 2087 Dundas E., Suite 105, Mississauga, Ontario L4X 1M2, ☎ 905/602–4195; in the U.K.: ✉ 179 Piccadilly, and Victoria Station, London W1V 8BA, ☎ 0990/848–848 in the U.K.; 020/7647–4900 to the U.K. from other countries). **Venice Simplon-Orient Express** (✉ Sea Containers House, 20 Upper Ground, London SE1 9PF, ☎ 800/524–2420 in the U.S.; 020/7805–5100 in the U.K.; 0870/161–5060 brochures, WEB www.orient-express.com).

TRAVEL AGENCIES

A good travel agent puts your needs first. Look for an agency that has been in business at least five years, emphasizes customer service, and has someone on staff who specializes in your destination. In addition, **make sure the agency belongs to a professional trade organization.** The American Society of Travel Agents (ASTA), with more than 26,000 members in some 170 countries, is the largest and most influential in the field. Operating under the motto "Without a travel agent, you're on your own," it maintains and enforces a strict code of ethics and will step in to help mediate any agent-client disputes if necessary. ASTA also maintains a Web site that includes a directory of agents. (If a travel agency is also acting as your tour operator, *see* Buyer Beware *in* Tours & Packages, *above.*)

➤ LOCAL AGENT REFERRALS: **American Society of Travel Agents** (ASTA; ✉ 1101 King St., Suite 200, Alexandria, VA 22314 ☎ 800/965–2782 24-hr hot line, FAX 703/739–7642, WEB www.astanet.com). **Association of British Travel Agents** (✉ 68–71 Newman St., London W1T 3AH, U.K., ☎ 020/7637–2444, FAX 020/7637–0713, WEB www.abtanet.com). **Association of Canadian Travel Agents** (✉ 130 Albert St., Suite 1705, Ottawa, Ontario K1P 5G4, Canada, ☎ 613/237–3657, FAX 613/237–7052, WEB www.acta.net). **Australian Federation of Travel Agents** (✉ Level 3, 309 Pitt St., Sydney NSW 2000, Australia, ☎ 02/9264–3299, FAX 02/9264–1085, WEB www.afta.com.au). **Travel Agents' Association of New Zealand** (✉ Level 5, Paxus House, 79 Boulcott St., Box 1888, Wellington 10033, New Zealand, ☎ 04/499–0104, FAX 04/499–0827, WEB www.taanz.org.nz).

VISITOR INFORMATION

For general information before you go, contact the national tourism offices.

➤ AUSTRIAN NATIONAL TOURIST OFFICE: **U.S.** (✉ Box 1142, Times Square Station, New York, NY 10108-1142, ☎ 212/944–6880, FAX 212/730–4568, WEB www.austria-tourism.at). **Canada** (✉ 2 Bloor St. E, Suite 3330, Toronto, Ontario M4W 1A8, ☎ 416/967–3381, FAX 416/967–4101). **U.K.** (✉ 14 Cork St., London, W1X 1PF, ☎ 020/7629–0461, FAX 020/7499–6038). **Australia and New Zealand** (✉ 36 Carrington St., 1st floor, Sydney, NSW 2000, ☎ 02/9299–3621, FAX 02/9299–3808). **Ireland** (✉ Merrion Hall, Strand Rd.,

Sandymount, Box 2506, Dublin 4, ☎ 01/283–0488, FAX 01/283–0531).

➤ Belgian National Tourist Office: **U.S.** (✉ 780 Third Ave., Suite 1501, New York, NY 10017, ☎ 212/758–8130, FAX 212/355–7675, WEB www.visitbelgium.com). **Canada** (✉ Box 760, Succursale NDG, Montréal, Québec H4A 3S2, ☎ 514/484–3594, FAX 514/489–8965). **U.K.** (✉ 31 Pepper St., London E14 9RW, ☎ 020/7458–2888, FAX 020/7458–2999).

➤ British Tourist Authority: **U.S.** (✉ 551 Fifth Ave., Suite 701, New York, NY 10176, ☎ 212/986–2200 or 800/462–2748, FAX 212/986–1188; 818/441–8265 24-hour fax information line, WEB www.visitbritain.com; walk-in service only: ✉ 625 N. Michigan Ave., Suite 1510, Chicago, IL 60611). **Canada** (✉ 5915 Airport Rd., Suite 120, Mississauga, Ontario L47V 1T1, ☎ 905/405–1840 or 888/847–4885, FAX 905/405–1835). **U.K.:** Britain Visitors Centre (✉ 1 Regent St., London SW1Y 4PQ, ☎ 0839/123–456; 0891/600–109 for 24-hour brochure line, costs 50p per minute; ✉ Thames Tower, Black's Rd., London, W6 9EL [no information by phone]). **Australia** (✉ Level 16, Gateway, 1 Macquarie Place, Sydney, NSW 2000, ☎ 02/9377–4400, FAX 02/9377–4499). **New Zealand** (✉ Dilworth Bldg., Suite 305, 3rd floor, Corner of Queen & Customs Sts., Auckland 1, ☎ 09/303–1446, FAX 09/377–6965). **Ireland** (✉ 18–19 College Green, Dublin 2, ☎ 01/670–8000, FAX 01/670–8244).

➤ Bulgaria: **U.S. and Canada** (Balkan Tourist USA, authorized agent, ✉ 20 E. 46th St., Suite 1003, New York, NY 10017, ☎ 212/338–6838 or 800/822–1106, FAX 212/822–5910). **U.K.** (Balkan Tourist UK, ✉ 111 Bartholomew Rd., London NW2 BJ, ☎ 020/7485–4584; Balkan Holidays, ✉ 19 Conduit St., London W1R 9TD, ☎ 020/7491–4499, FAX 020/7543–5577).

➤ Cyprus Tourist Office: **U.S. and Canada** (✉ 13 E. 40th St., New York, NY 10016, ☎ 212/683–5280, FAX 212/683–5282, WEB www.cyprustourism.org). **U.K.** (✉ 17 Hanover St., London W1R 0AA, ☎ 020/7569–8800, FAX 020/7499–4935); Turkish Republic of Northern Cyprus Tourist Office (✉ 29 Bedford Sq., London WC1B 3EG, ☎ 020/7631–1930, FAX 020/7631–1873).

➤ Czech Center: **U.S. and Canada** (✉ 1109 Madison Ave., New York, NY 10028, ☎ 212/288–0830, FAX 212/288–0971, WEB www.czechcenter.com). **Canada** (Czech Tourist Authority, ✉ c/o Czech Airlines, 401 Bay St., Suite 1510 Toronto, Ontario M5H 2Y4, ☎ 416/363–9928, FAX 416/363–0239). **U.K.** (✉ 95 Great Portland St., London W1N 5RA, ☎ 020/7291–9920, FAX 020/7436–1300; Czech and Slovak Tourist Centre, ✉ 16 Frognal Parade, Finchley Rd., London NW3 5HG, ☎ 020/7794–3263, FAX 020/7794–3265).

➤ Danish Tourist Board: **U.S. and Canada** (✉ 655 Third Ave., 18th floor, New York, NY 10017, ☎ 212/885–9700, FAX 212/885–9726, WEB www.dt.dk). **U.K.** (✉ 55 Sloane St., London SW1X 9SY, ☎ 020/7259–5959; 0900/160–0109 for 24-hour brochure line, costs 50p per minute, FAX 020/7259–5955).

➤ Estonian Tourist Office: **U.S.** (Consulate, ✉ 600 Third Avenue, 26th floor, New York, NY 10016, ☎ 212/883–0636, FAX 212/883–0648, WEB www.tourism.ee). **Canada** (Consulate, ✉ 958 Broadview Ave., Suite 202, Toronto, Ontario M4K 2R6, ☎ 416/461–0764, FAX 416/461–0353). **U.K.** (Embassy, ✉ 16 Hyde Park Gate, London, SW7 5DG, ☎ 020/7589–3428, FAX 020/7589–3430). **Australia** (Consulate, ✉ 86 Louisa Rd., Birchgrove, NSW 2041, ☎ 02/9810–7468, FAX 02/9818–1779).

➤ Finnish Tourist Board: **U.S. and Canada** (✉ 655 Third Ave., New York, NY 10017, ☎ 212/885–9700, FAX 212/885–9739, WEB www.mek.fi). **U.K.** (✉ 30–35 Pall Mall, London SW1Y 5LP, ☎ 020/7839–4048, FAX 020/7321–0696). **Australia** (✉ c/o Finnesse Communications, Level 4, 81 York St., Sydney, NSW 2000, ☎ 02/9290–1950, FAX 02/9290–1981).

➤ French Government Tourist Office: **U.S.** (☎ 900/990–0040 nationwide, 50¢ per minute; ✉ 444 Madison Ave., 16th floor, New York, NY 10022, FAX 212/838–7855, WEB www.francetourism.com; ✉ 676 N.

Michigan Ave., Chicago, IL 60611, FAX 312/337-6339; ✉ 9454 Wilshire Blvd., Suite 715, Beverly Hills, CA 90212, FAX 310/276-2835). **Canada** (✉ 1981 Ave. McGill College, Suite 490, Montréal, Québec H3A 2W9, ☎ 514/288-4264, FAX 514/845-4868). **U.K.** (✉ 178 Piccadilly, London W1V OAL, ☎ 0870/556-1434, 50p per minute, FAX 020/7493-6594). **Australia** (✉ 25 Bligh St., Sydney, NSW 2000, ☎ 02/9231-5244, FAX 02/9221-8682). **Ireland** (✉ 35 Lower Abbey St., Dublin 1, ☎ 01/703-4046, FAX 01/874-7324).

➤ GERMAN NATIONAL TOURIST OFFICE: **U.S.** (✉ 122 E. 42nd St., New York, NY 10168, ☎ 212/661-7200, FAX 212/661-7174, WEB www.deutschland-tourismus.de; ✉ 401 N. Michigan Ave., Suite 2525, Chicago, IL 60611, ☎ 312/644-0723, FAX 312/644-0724). **Canada** (✉ 175 Bloor St. E, Suite 604, Toronto, Ontario M4W 3R8, ☎ 416/968-1570, FAX 416/968-1986). **U.K.** (✉ Box 2695, London W1A 3TN, ☎ 020/7317-0908 or 0891/600-100 for brochures, 50p per minute, FAX 020/7495-6129). **Australia** (✉ Box A980, Sydney, NSW 1235, ☎ 02/9267-8148, FAX 02/9267-9035).

➤ GIBRALTAR INFORMATION BUREAU: **U.S. and Canada** (✉ 1156 15th St. NW, Suite 1100, Washington, DC 20005, ☎ 202/452-1108, FAX 202/452-1109, WEB www.gibraltar.gi). **U.K.** (Gibraltar Tourist Board, ✉ Arundel Great Court, 179 The Strand, London WC2R 1EH, ☎ 020/7836-0777, FAX 020/7240-6612).

➤ GREEK NATIONAL TOURIST ORGANIZATION: **U.S.** (✉ 645 Fifth Ave., New York, NY 10022, ☎ 212/421-5777, FAX 212/826-6940, WEB www.gnto.gr). **Canada** (✉ 1300 Bay St., Toronto, Ontario M5R 3K8, ☎ 416/968-2220, FAX 416/968-6533). **U.K.** (✉ 4 Conduit St., London W1R 0DJ, ☎ 020/7734-5997, FAX 020/7287-1369). **Australia** (✉ 51-57 Pitt St., Sydney, NSW 2000, ☎ 02/9241-1663, FAX 02/9235-2174).

➤ HUNGARIAN NATIONAL TOURIST OFFICE: **U.S. and Canada** (✉ 150 E. 58th St., 33rd floor, New York, NY 10155, ☎ 212/355-0240, FAX 212/207-4103, WEB www.hungarytourism.hu). **U.K.** (✉ Embassy of the Republic of Hungary, Commercial Section, 46 Eaton Pl., London SW1X 8AL, ☎ 020/7823-1032, FAX 020/7823-1459).

➤ ICELAND TOURIST BOARD: **U.S. and Canada: Scandinavia Tourism Inc.** (✉ 655 Third Ave., New York, NY 10017, ☎ 212/885-9700, FAX 212/885-9710, WEB www.goscandinavia.com). **U.K.** (✉ 172 Tottenham Court Rd., 3rd floor, London W1P 9LG, ☎ 020/8286-8008 for brochures; 020/7874-1000 for IcelandAir).

➤ IRISH TOURIST BOARD: **U.S.** (✉ 345 Park Ave., New York, NY 10154, ☎ 212/418-0800 or 800/223-6470, FAX 212/371-9052, WEB www.ireland.travel.ie). **Canada** (✉ 160 Bloor St. E, Suite 1150, Toronto, Ontario M4W 1B9, ☎ 416/487-3335, FAX 416/929-6783). **U.K.** (✉ Ireland House, 150 New Bond St., London W1Y 0AQ, ☎ 020/7493-3201, FAX 020/7493-9065). **Australia** (✉ 36 Carrington St., 5th floor, Sydney, NSW 2000, ☎ 02/9299-6177, FAX 02/9299-6323). **Ireland** (✉ Baggot Street Bridge, Dublin 2, ☎ 01/602-4000, FAX 01/605-7757).

➤ ITALIAN GOVERNMENT TRAVEL OFFICE (ENIT): **U.S.** (✉ 630 Fifth Ave., Suite 1565, New York, NY 10111, ☎ 212/245-4822, FAX 212/586-9249, WEB www.italiantourism.com; ✉ 500 N. Michigan Ave., Suite 2240, Chicago, IL 60611, ☎ 312/644-0996, FAX 312/644-3019; ✉ 12400 Wilshire Blvd., Suite 550, Los Angeles, CA 90025, ☎ 310/820-1898, FAX 310/820-6357). **Canada** (✉ 1 Pl. Ville Marie, Suite 1914, Montréal, Québec H3B 3M9, ☎ 514/866-7667, FAX 514/392-1429). **U.K.** (Italian State Tourist Board, ✉ 1 Princess St., London W1R 9AY, ☎ 020/7408-1254, FAX 020/7493-6695). **Australia** (✉ c/o Italian Chamber of Commerce Level 26, 44 Market St., Sydney, NSW 2000, ☎ 02/9262-1666, FAX 02/9262-1677).

➤ LITHUANIAN TOURIST BOARD: **U.S.** (Lithuanian Tourist Information Center, ✉ 40-24 235th St., Suite 100, Douglaston, NY 11363, ☎ 718/281-1623, FAX 718/423-3979, WEB www.tourism.lt). **Canada** (Embassy, 130 Albert St., Suite 204, Ottawa, Ontario K1P 5G4, ☎ 613/567–5458, FAX 613/567–5315). **U.K.** (Embassy, ✉ 84 Gloucester Pl., London W1H 3HN, ☎ 020/7486–6401, FAX 020/7468–6403).

➤ Luxembourg National Tourist Office: **U.S. and Canada** (✉ 17 Beekman Pl., New York, NY 10022, ☎ 212/935–8888, FAX 212/935–5896, WEB www.ont.lu). **U.K.** (✉ 122 Regent St., London W1R 5FE, ☎ 020/7434–2800, FAX 020/7734–1205).

➤ Malta National Tourist Office: **U.S. and Canada** (✉ 350 Fifth Ave., Suite 4412, New York, NY 10118, ☎ 212/695–9520, FAX 212/695–8229, WEB www.visitmalta.com). **U.K. and Ireland** (✉ 36–38 Piccadilly, London W1V 0PP, ☎ 020/7292–4900, FAX 020/7734–1880). **Australia** (✉ 403 George St., Sydney, NSW 2000, ☎ 02/9321–9154, FAX 02/9290–3641). **Ireland** (✉ 4 Inns Court, Winetavern St., Dublin 8, ☎ 01/405–8200, FAX 01/473–2962).

➤ Monaco Government Tourist Office and Convention Bureau: **U.S. and Canada** (✉ 565 Fifth Ave., New York, NY 10017, ☎ 212/286–3330, FAX 212/286–9890, WEB www.monaco-tourism.com). **U.K.** (✉ The Chambers, Chelsea Harbour, London SW10 0XF, ☎ 020/7352–9962 or 0500/006–114, FAX 020/7352–2103).

➤ Netherlands Board of Tourism: **U.S.** (✉ 225 N. Michigan Ave., Suite 1854, Chicago, IL 60601, ☎ 312/819–1500 or 888/464–6552, FAX 312/819–1740, WEB www.holland.com). **Canada** (✉ Box 1078, Toronto, Ontario M5C 2K5, ☎ 888/464–6552 in English; 888/729–7227 in French, FAX 416/363–1470). **U.K.** (✉ 18 Buckingham Gate, London SW1E 6LD, ☎ 020/7828–7900; 0906/871–7777 for 24-hour brochure line, costs 50p per minute, FAX 020/7828–7941).

➤ Norwegian Tourist Board: **U.S. and Canada** (✉ 655 Third Ave., Suite 1810, New York, NY 10017, ☎ 212/885–9700, FAX 212/885–9710, WEB www.goscandinavia.com). **U.K.** (✉ Charles House, 5 Lower Regent St., London SW1Y 4LR, ☎ 020/7839–6255, FAX 020/7839–6014).

➤ Polish National Tourist Office: **U.S. and Canada** (✉ 275 Madison Ave., Suite 1711, New York, NY 10016, ☎ 212/338–9412, FAX 212/338–9283, WEB www.polandtour.org). **U.K.** (✉ Remo House, 1st floor, 310–312 Regent St., London W1N 5AJ, ☎ 020/7580–8811, FAX 020/7580–8866).

➤ Portuguese National Tourist Office: **U.S.** (✉ 590 Fifth Ave., 4th floor, New York, NY 10036, ☎ 212/354–4403, FAX 212/764–6137, WEB www.portugal.org). **Canada** (✉ 60 Bloor St. W, Suite 1005, Toronto, Ontario M4W 3B8, ☎ 416/921–7376, FAX 416/921–1353). **Ireland** (✉ 54 Dawson St., Dublin 2, ☎ 01/670–9133, FAX 01/670–9141). **U.K.** (✉ 2nd floor, 22–25A Sackville St., London W1X 1DE, ☎ 020/7494–1441, or 0900/1600–370, 24-hour brochure line, costs 50p per minute, FAX 020/7494–1868).

➤ Romanian National Tourist Office: **U.S. and Canada** (✉ 14 E. 38th St., 12th floor, New York, NY 10016, ☎ 212/545–8484, FAX 212/251–0429). **U.K.** (✉ 83A Marylebone High St., London W1M 3DE, ☎ 020/7224–3692, FAX 020/7935–6435).

➤ Slovak Tourist Office: **U.S. and Canada** (Embassy, ✉ 2201 Wisconsin Ave., NW, Suite 250, Washington, DC 20007, ☎ 202/965–5160, FAX 202/965–5166, WEB www.sacr.sk). **U.K.** (Czech and Slovak Tourist Centre, ✉ 16 Frognal Parade, Finchley Rd., London NW3 5HG, ☎ 020/7794–3263, FAX 020/7794–3265).

➤ Slovenian Tourist Office: **U.S.** (✉ 345 E. 12th St., New York, NY 10003, ☎ 212/358–9686, FAX 212/358–9025, WEB www.slovenia-tourism.si). **U.K.** (✉ 2 Canfield Pl., London, NW6 3BT, ☎ 020/7371–3767, FAX 020/7371–3763).

➤ Tourist Office of Spain: **U.S.** (✉ 666 Fifth Ave., 35th floor, New York, NY 10103, ☎ 212/265–8822, FAX 212/265–8864, WEB www.ok-spain.org; ✉ 845 N. Michigan Ave., Suite 915 E, Chicago, IL 60611, ☎ 312/642–1992, FAX 312/642–9817; ✉ 8383 Wilshire Blvd., Suite 956, Los Angeles, CA 90211, ☎ 213/658–7188, FAX 213/658–1061; ✉ 1221

Brickell Ave., Suite 1850, Miami, FL 33131, ☎ 305/358–1992, FAX 305/358–8223). **Canada** (✉ 2 Bloor St. W, Suite 3402, Toronto, Ontario M4W 3E2, ☎ 416/961–3131, FAX 416/961–1992). **U.K.** (✉ 22–23 Manchester Sq., London W1M 5AP, ☎ 020/7486–8077 or 0891/669–920, 24-hour brochure line, costs 50p per minute, FAX 020/7486–8034).

➤ SWEDISH TRAVEL AND TOURISM COUNCIL: **U.S. and Canada** (✉ Box 4649, Grand Central Station, New York, NY 10163-4649, ☎ 212/885–9700, FAX 212/885–9764). **U.K.** (✉ 11 Montagu Pl., London W1H 2AL, ☎ 020/7870–5600; 0147/657–8811, 24-hour brochure line, FAX 020/7724–5872

➤ SWITZERLAND TOURISM: **U.S.** (✉ 608 Fifth Ave., New York, NY 10020, ☎ 212/757–5944, FAX 212/262–6116, WEB www.switzerlandtourism.ch; ✉ 222 N. Sepulveda Blvd., Suite 1570, El Segundo, CA 90245, ☎ 310/335–5980, FAX 310/335–5982; ✉ 501 Santa Monica Blvd., Suite 607, Los Angeles, CA 90401, ☎ 310/260–2421, FAX 310/260–2923). **Canada** (✉ 926 The East Mall, Etobicoke Toronto], Ontario M9B 6KI, ☎ 416/695–2090, FAX 416/695–2774). **U.K.** (✉ Swiss Centre, 1 New Coventry St., London W1V 8EE, ☎ 020/7734–1921, FAX 020/7851–1720). **Australia** (✉ Swissair Building, 33 Pitt St., Level 8, Sydney, NSW 2000, ☎ 02/9231–3744, FAX 02/9251–6531).

➤ TURKISH TOURIST OFFICE: **U.S.** (✉ 821 UN Plaza, New York, NY 10017, ☎ 212/687–2194, FAX 212/599–7568, WEB www.turkey.org; ✉ 1717 Massachusetts Ave. NW, Suite 306, Washington, DC 20036, ☎ 202/429–9844, FAX 202/429–5649). **Canada** (✉ 360 Albert St., Suite 801, Ottawa, Ontario K1R 7X7, ☎ 613/230–8654, FAX 613/230–3683). **U.K.** (✉ Egyptian House, 170–173 Piccadilly, London W1V 9DD, ☎ 020/7629–7771 or 0900/188–7755, 24-hour brochure line, costs 50p per minute, FAX 020/7491–0773).

➤ U.S. GOVERNMENT ADVISORIES: **U.S. Department of State** (✉ Overseas Citizens Services Office, Room 4811 N.S., 2201 C St. NW, Washington, DC 20520, ☎ 202/647–5225 for interactive hot line, WEB http://travel.state.gov/travel/html); enclose a self-addressed, stamped, business-size envelope.

WEB SITES

Do check out the World Wide Web when planning your trip. You'll find everything from weather forecasts to virtual tours of famous cities. Be sure to **visit Fodors.com** (www.fodors.com), a complete travel-planning site. You can research prices and book plane tickets, hotel rooms, rental cars, vacation packages, and more. In addition, you can post your pressing questions in the Travel Talk section and, in the site's Rants & Raves section, read comments about some of the restaurants and hotels in this book—and chime in yourself. Other planning tools include a currency converter and weather reports, and there are loads of links to travel resources.

Also check out the European Travel Commission's site, www.visiteurope.com.

WHEN TO GO

For information about travel seasons and for the average daily maximum and minimum temperatures of the major European cities, *see* the A to Z section *in* each country chapter.

➤ FORECASTS: **Weather Channel Connection** (☎ 900/932–8437), 95¢ per minute from a Touch-Tone phone.

2 ANDORRA

ANDORRA LA VELLA AND BEYOND

THE PRINCIPALITY OF ANDORRA has carved itself a niche in the world's imagination as a hiking, skiing, and trout-fishing paradise. This perception may cause some disappointment when you find yourself in a 20-mi traffic jam of bargain hunters on the one road through the country, but don't give up: if you avoid Spanish and French holidays, you will find that Andorra's upper reaches are still pristine.

In 1993, this 464-square-km (278-square-mi) tax haven, commercial oasis, winter-sports station, and mountain hideaway drafted a constitution and held elections, converting one of Europe's last pockets of feudalism into a modern democratic state and member of the United Nations. The bishop of Urgell and the president of France assumed symbolic roles as the co-heads of state of this unique Pyrenean country. Andorra originally fell through the cracks between France and Spain when Charlemagne founded the valley as an independent entity during his 8th-century battles with the Moors. In the 9th century, his heir, Charles the Bald, made the bishop of Urgell overlord of Andorra, a role contested by the French counts of Foix until a treaty providing for joint suzerainty was agreed upon in 1278. During the 16th century the French monarchy inherited these rights and eventually passed them on to the presidents of France.

This dual protection long allowed Andorra to thrive as a low-tax, duty-free haven. Europe's new semiborderless unity, however, has changed this special status, and Andorra is now in the process of developing an improved tourist industry and a more conventional economy. Andorra is administratively divided into seven parishes—Sant Julià de Lòria, Andorra la Vella, La Massana, Escaldes-Engordany, Encamp, Ordino, and Canillo—and each of these entities has its own tourist office.

Winter sports, mountain climbing and hiking, and the architectural and cultural heritage of its many Romanesque chapels, bridges, and medieval farms and town houses are Andorra's once and future stock in trade, although numbered bank accounts will surely not be disappearing anytime soon.

ANDORRA A TO Z

To research prices, get advice from other travelers, and book travel arrangements, visit www.fodors.com.

AIR TRAVEL

The nearest international airports are at Barcelona (210 km/130 mi) and in France, at Perpignan (128 km/79 mi) and Toulouse-Blagnac (196 km/122 mi).

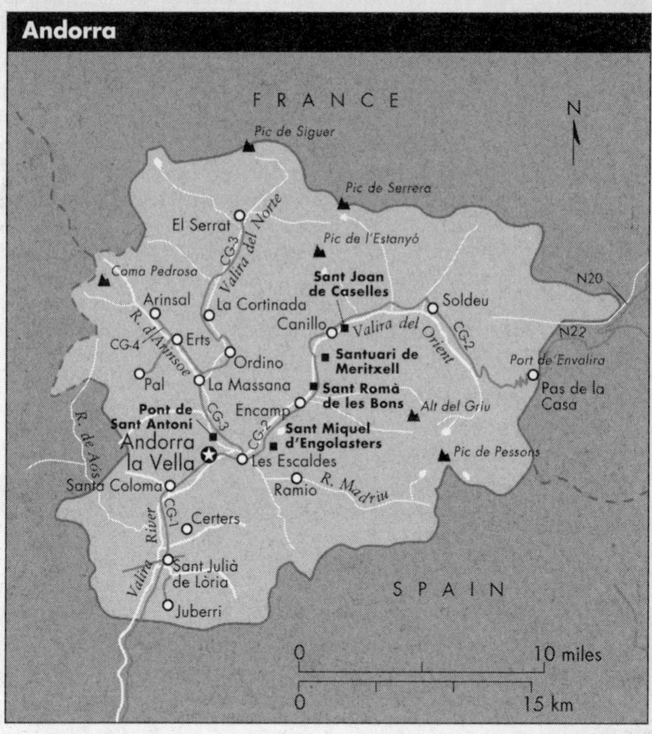

BUS TRAVEL

Barcelona is connected with Andorra la Vella by Eurolines buses, which leave Barcelona's El Prat airport's Terminal B (from in front of the Miró mural at the south end of the terminal) at 11 AM, 3 PM, and 8 PM. Buses to El Prat airport leave Andorra at 9:45, 2, and 7. Buses from Barcelona's Sants train station to Andorra leave at 6:15, 11:30, 3:30, and 8:30. Return buses to Sants station leave Andorra's Hotel Diplomatic at 9:15 AM, 1:30 PM, 6:30 PM, and 10:30 PM. In summer direct buses run from Perpignan and Toulouse to Andorra. The ride from Barcelona, Perpignan, or Toulouse to Andorra la Vella takes about three hours.

Minibuses connect Andorra's towns and villages, and fares are low; 150 ptas./€0.90 will take you 5 km (3 mi). Details on fares and services are available at hotels and from tourist offices.

BUSINESS HOURS

Banks are open weekdays 9–1 and 3–5, and Saturday 9–noon. They are closed Sunday. Andorra is predominantly Catholic; most chapels and churches are kept locked around the clock, the key being left at the closest house. Check with the local tourist office. Shops are open daily 9–8, though many are closed between 1 and 4.

CAR TRAVEL

The N-20 road from France into Spain via Andorra la Vella is curvy but good and handles the heaviest traffic. The spur north toward the ski resorts at La Massana and Ordino is also excellent. Once you leave the valley floor, the roads are narrow, winding, and best suited to four-wheel-drive vehicles, especially in snow. In winter, snow tires or chains are essential. Although the Puymorens Tunnel does not surface in Andorra, it does eliminate the switchbacks of the Puymorens mountain pass going through toward Spain from the northern entrance at L'Hospitalet, France. This pass is either dangerous or closed in bad weather.

The fastest, most direct route from Barcelona to Andorra la Vella (with about 4,500 ptas./€27.05 in tolls) runs through Terrassa, Manresa, the Tunel del Cadí, and the Cerdanya Valley via Bellver de Cerdanya and La Seu d'Urgell. Slightly longer but toll-free is the western approach to La Seu d'Urgell via N-11 to Igualada through Cervera and Oliana on C-1311. The eastern entrance into Andorra through Puigcerdà to Pas de la Casa is often a good way to avoid traffic. Andorra is 613 km (380 mi) from Madrid via Zaragoza, Lleida, and Seu d' Urgell, a six- to seven-hour drive. Barcelona to Andorra is 210 km (130 mi); Perpignan to Andorra is 128 (79 mi); Toulouse to Andorra is 196 km (122 mi).

CONSULATES

➤ CANADA: ✉ Nuñez de Balboa 35, Madrid, Spain, ☎ 91/225–9119.
➤ UNITED KINGDOM: ✉ Apartado de Correos 12111, Barcelona, Spain, ☎ 93/322–2151.
➤ UNITED STATES: ✉ Pg. Reina Elisenda 23, Barcelona, Spain, ☎ 93/280–2227.

CUSTOMS AND DUTIES

Crossing out of Andorra can be a problem. The French customs officers between Pas de la Casa and the Puymorens Tunnel sporadically stage mammoth roadblocks and may search anything. Spanish customs between Andorra la Vella and Seu d'Urgell can also be tricky. The established limits for all varieties of goods are specified in "Franquicias dels Viatgers," a leaflet distributed by the Andorra National Tourist Office in Barcelona or Andorra la Vella. No one seems to mind how often you pass through customs on a given day, however. So one way to score significant savings is to stay in a hotel on the Spanish side and make a half dozen trips through.

DINING

Andorra is developing a reputation for fine dining. There are good restaurants serving French, Spanish, or Catalan cuisine and plenty of spots where you can eat hearty Pyrenean fare at no great cost. Local dishes to look for include *escudella* (a hearty mountain stew); *trinchat* (mashed potatoes and cabbage with bacon); *estofat d'isard* (stewed mountain goat); *truite de carreroles* (omelet with wild mushrooms); *truite de ríu* (river trout); local cheeses, such as *formatge de tupí*; and *rostes amb mel* (ham baked with honey). Most restaurants offer both prix-fixe and à la carte menus.

Prices are for one main course at dinner.

CATEGORY	COST
$$$$	over 3,000 ptas. (€18)
$$$	2,000 ptas.–3,000 ptas. (€12–€18)
$$	1,000 ptas.–2,000 ptas. (€6–€12)
$	under 1,000 ptas. (€6)

MEALTIMES

Andorrans eat late: dinner doesn't usually get under way until 8 or 9, and lunch is a substantial meal served between 1:30 and 4.

RESERVATIONS AND DRESS

Casual dress is acceptable in all restaurants in Andorra, regardless of price category.

HOLIDAYS

January 1; March 14 (Constitution Day); Easter Monday; April 23 (St. George's Day); May 1 (Labor Day); Pentecost Monday (in May or June); June 24 (St. John's Day); September 8 (La Verge de Meritxell); November 1 (All Saints' Day); December 8 (Immaculate Conception); December 25; December 26 (St. Stephen's Feast).

LANGUAGE

Although less than half of the country's population of nearly 66,000 are native speakers of Catalan, this Provençal French-rooted Romance language is the principality's official language. Spanish, French, and English are also spoken by hotel and commercial personnel.

LODGING

The number of Andorran hotels continues to increase, and standards are rising. Decor is usually functional, but service is friendly and the facilities are excellent. Most hotels are open year-round. Reservations are necessary during July and August. Hotel rates often include at least two meals.

The following price ratings apply for two people in a double room.

CATEGORY	COST
$$$$	over 15,000 ptas. (€90)
$$$	10,000 ptas.–15,000 ptas. (€60–€90)
$$	7,500 ptas.–10,000 ptas. (€45–€60)
$	3,500 ptas.–7,500 ptas. (€21–€45)

MAIL AND SHIPPING

There are no postal codes in Andorra, but from Spain be sure to include "Principat d'Andorra" when you address your letter, to distinguish the country from the Spanish town of the same name.

➤ POST OFFICES: **Spanish post office** (✉ Carrer Joan Maragall 10). **French post office** (✉ 1 rue Père d'Urg).

POSTAL RATES

Postal service within the country is free.

MONEY MATTERS

Prices in Andorra are similar to those in neighboring France and Spain. The best bargains still available are products subject to state tax, such as tobacco, alcohol, perfume, and gasoline. Such staples as butter, cheese, and milk sold as surplus by member countries of the European Union (EU) are also cheaper in Andorra.

Here are some sample prices: soft drink, 175 ptas./€1.05; cup of coffee, 125–150 ptas./€0.75–€0.90; 1½-km (1-mi) taxi ride, 350 ptas./€2.10; ham sandwich, 500 ptas./€3.

CURRENCY

Until the introduction of the euro as the unified European currency, the Spanish peseta was the major Andorran currency, though French francs were equally acceptable. Prices are presently quoted in euros as well as in both national currencies. For exchange rates and coinage information, *see* Money Matters *in* the Spain and France chapters.

OUTDOORS AND SPORTS

Mountainous Andorra is a playground for hikers and backpackers. The mountains are high and the terrain is wild, so a degree of care and experience is advisable. There are three long-distance trails: the GR7, which runs from the French border near Pas de la Casa to Les Escaldes on the road from Andorra la Vella to Spain; the GR11, also called the Ordino Route, a high-mountain trail that stretches across the central range; and the GR P1, a potentially 5- to 10-day perimeter route running the crests around the Andorran border. There are 26 mountain refuges distributed throughout Andorra, so you can plan day treks and travel light. Some of the best hikes include the Estanys de Tristaina route from Ordino; the Vall de Madriu walk (6 hours each way) from Escaldes to Pas de la Casa's upper reaches; the hike to the Cirque de Pessons from Cortals above Encamp; the walk from Sant Julià de Lòria to the Canòlic sanctuary; and the Vall d'Incles walk up to the Estanys (tarns, or Pyrenean glacial ponds) de Juclar. Get details on treks and walks from local tourist offices.

PASSPORTS AND VISAS

Non-Europeans need a passport to cross the border; Europeans enter with only an identity card.

SHOPPING

Shopping has traditionally been one of Andorra's main attractions, but be careful: not all the goods displayed are at bargain prices. Good buys are such consumables as gasoline, perfume, butter, cheese, cigarettes, wine, whiskey, and gin. For cameras, tape recorders, and other imported items, compare prices and models carefully. Ask for the *precio último* (final price) and insist politely on *el descuento,* the 10% discount to which you are entitled as a visitor to Andorra.

The main shopping area is **Andorra la Vella.** There are also stores in all the new developments and in the towns close to the frontiers, namely Pas de la Casa and Sant Julià de Lòria. The **Punt de Trobada** center (✉ Ctra. d'Espanya, ☎ 843433), 2 km (1 mi) from the Spanish border, is bright, modern, and immense. **La Casa del Formatge** (✉ Av. Carlemany s/n, ☎ 821689) in Les Escaldes has more than 500 different kinds of cheeses from all over the world.

TELEPHONES

COUNTRY AND AREA CODES

The country code for Andorra is 376.

INTERNATIONAL CALLS

For assistance, call the local operator at 111. To call Andorra from Spain or France dial 00–376 and the six-digit local number. To dial long distance from Andorra dial 00, the country code of the country you are calling, and the local number.

LOCAL CALLS

For local directory assistance, dial 111. Andorra has no regional area codes. Most pay phones take phone cards issued by the telephone company, which may be purchased at *tabacs* (stores that sell tobacco and stamps).

TIPPING

Restaurant and café prices always include a 10%–15% service charge; it's customary to leave a similar amount in addition to the charge, but this is completely optional.

TRAIN TRAVEL

From Barcelona, take the train to Puigcerdà, then the bus to La Seu d'Urgell and Andorra la Vella; from Madrid, take the train to Lleida and then a bus to La Seu d'Urgell and Andorra la Vella. From Toulouse, take the train to Ax-les-Thermes and L'Hospitalet, where the bus to Pas de la Casa and Andorra la Vella meets the morning train. Alternatively, go on to Latour-de-Carol and take the bus from Puigcerdà to La Seu d'Urgell and Andorra la Vella.

WHEN TO GO

With reliable snowfall from December to early April, Andorra has excellent ski resorts at Soldeu, Arinsal, Pal, Pas de la Casa–Grau Roig, and Ordino–Arcalis and a cross-country center at La Rabassa. Winter brings a huge influx of skiing buffs, but consumers are eager to take advantage of Andorra's tax- and duty-free shopping all year long, making weekends and holidays a traffic nightmare any time of year. In early April, the first flush of spring flowers enlivens the slopes and valleys.

CLIMATE

Keep in mind that even in summer the nighttime temperatures can drop to freezing. The following are the average daily maximum and minimum temperatures for Andorra.

Jan.	43F	6C	**May**	62F	17C	**Sept.**	71F	22C
	30	1		43	6		49	10
Feb.	45F	7C	**June**	73F	23C	**Oct.**	60F	16C
	30	1		39	4		42	6
Mar.	54F	12C	**July**	79F	26C	**Nov.**	51F	10C
	35	2		54	12		35	2
Apr.	58F	14C	**Aug.**	76F	24C	**Dec.**	42F	6C
	39	4		53	12		31	1

EXPLORING ANDORRA

Exploring Andorra takes time. The roads are narrow and steep, the views compel frequent stops, and every village has its secret treasures. Do as much sightseeing on foot as time permits. Key sites to visit include Andorra la Vella's Casa de la Vall, Ordino's aristocratic Casa d'Areny Plandolit, Sispony's bourgeois Museu Casa Rull, and Encamp's Cal Cristo, a typical farmer's dwelling. Andorra's Romanesque patrimony, surprisingly abundant, features two bridges and 34 chapels. Natural treasures include Pyrenean ponds and peaks such as the 9,708-ft Pic de Coma Pedrosa.

Andorra la Vella

The capital's pivotal attraction, outside its shops and restaurants, is the **Casa de la Vall** (House of the Valley), overlooking the town's main square. Constructed in 1580, this massive and medieval bulk of stone is the seat of the Andorran government and the repository of notable Gothic frescoes, some of which were carefully moved here from village churches high in the Pyrenees. The kitchen is particularly interesting, with its collection of ancient copper pots and other culinary implements. ✉ *Carrer de la Vall s/n.* ⏲ *Mon.–Sat. 9–1 and 3–7, Sun. 10–2.*

$$–$$$ ✕ **Borda Estevet.** A borda with a very Pyrenean feel, this simple spot offers a selection of Spanish and Andorran dishes, beef cooked and served *à la llosa* (on hot slabs of slate), and three private dining rooms in addition to the main dining room. ✉ *Ctra. Comella 2,* ☎ *864026. AE, DC, MC, V. Closed Sun. in Aug.*

$$–$$$ ★ ✕ **Celler d'En Toni.** This small, rustic restaurant in the center of Andorra la Vella serves some of the best food in the principality, a blend of Mediterranean and Pyrenean cuisines. Known primarily as a restaurant, Celler d'En Toni also rents rooms, which are adequate but not luxurious. The quality of the restaurant more than compensates. ✉ *Verge del Pilar 4,* ☎ *821252,* FAX *821872. 17 rooms. Restaurant. AE, DC, MC, V.*

$$–$$$ ★ ✕ **Molí dels Fanals.** This quiet restaurant occupies an antique *borda* (a typical stone Andorran mountain refuge) with a fireplace and wooden paneling. The Catalan cuisine here uses consistently high-

quality ingredients. Try the *magret de canard* (breast of duck) with grapes and port. ✉ *Carrer Dr. Vilanova 9 (Borda Casadet),* ☎ *821381. AE, DC, MC, V. Closed Mon. and last 2 wks in Aug. No dinner Sun.*

$$–$$$ ✕ **Versailles.** A tiny and authentic French bistro with only 10 tables, Versailles is nearly always packed. The cuisine is primarily French with occasional Andorran specialties such as *escudella barrejada* (a thick vegetable and meat soup) or *civet de jabalí* (stewed wild boar). ✉ *Cap de Carrer 1,* ☎ *821331. AE, DC, MC, V.*

$$$$ **Andorra Park.** The Park is a grand building away from the city's congestion. The hotel bar is a popular watering hole for local society. Outside are a pretty garden, a pitching and putting green, and an ample terrace. The deluxe guest rooms have private balconies. ✉ *Carrer Les Canals 24,* ☎ *820979,* FAX *820983,* WEB *www.uha.ad. 40 rooms. Restaurant, pool. AE, DC, MC, V.*

$$$$ **Hotel Crowne Plaza.** The Crowne Plaza is the pinnacle of Andorra's lodging options, combining the finest service and most comprehensive comfort in the principality. The rooms (all suites) are spacious and flawlessly decorated in bright colors. ✉ *Carrer Prat de la Creu 88,* ☎ *874444,* FAX *874445,* WEB *www.uha.ad. 133 suites. Restaurant, pool, sauna, garden, parking (fee). AE, DC, MC, V.*

$$$$ **Hotel Ibis.** This hotel is part of the Accor chain, which includes the neighboring Novotel and the Mercure. The hotel restaurant, the Brasserie, is a bright and friendly spot with quick and convenient service and fare. The rooms, sleek and modern, are impeccable but characterless. ✉ *Av. Meritxell 58,* ☎ *820777,* FAX *828245,* WEB *www.ibishotel.com. 63 rooms. Restaurant. AE, DC, MC, V.*

$$$$ ★ **Hotel Mercure.** The large, modern Mercure is widely considered one of the capital's best hotels. The rooms are spacious and the furnishings smartly contemporary. The outdoor terrace is a pleasant spot to relax and watch the bustle below. ✉ *Carrer de la Roda,* ☎ *873602,* FAX *828552,* WEB *www.mercure.com. 150 rooms. Restaurant, pool. AE, DC, MC, V.*

$$$–$$$$ **Hotel Eden Roc.** Besides having all the comforts of larger hotels, the smaller Eden Roc offers an exceptional dining room, a terrace, and attentive personal service. ✉ *Av. Dr. Mitjavila 1,* ☎ *821000,* FAX *860319. 56 rooms. Restaurant. AE, V.*

Les Escaldes

The spa town, now virtually one with Andorra la Vella, is a 15-minute ★ walk from the Casa de la Vall. The Romanesque church of **Sant Miquel d'Engolasters** stands on a ridge northeast of the capital and can be reached on foot—allow a half day for the round-trip—or by automobile up a mountain road. The views are well worth the climb.

★ **Caldea** is an elaborate thermal spa complex barely 1 km (½ mi) from the center of Andorra la Vella, complete with steam rooms, Turkish baths, and snow patios. There are three restaurants, boutiques, an art gallery, and a cocktail bar open until 2 AM. Charges for the treatments vary; a five-day Andorra ski ticket will get you in for free. ✉ *Parc de la Mola 10, Les Escaldes,* ☎ *865777,* FAX *865656.*

$$$$ ★ ✕ **Roc Blanc.** Sleek, modern, and luxurious, with a wealth of facilities to pamper the body, from mud baths to acupuncture—that's what the Roc Blanc is all about. The rooms are large, there's a terrace, and the hotel's restaurants, La Brasserie, L'Entrecôte, and El Pi, serve Andorran and international specialties. ✉ *Plaça dels Co-Prínceps 5,* ☎ *871400,* FAX *860244,* WEB *www.rocblanc.com. 250 rooms. 3 restaurants, 2 pools. AE, DC, MC, V.*

Encamp

★ Just beyond Encamp, which is 6 km (4 mi) northeast of Andorra la Vella, is the 12th-century church of **Sant Romà de les Bons,** in a picturesque context of medieval buildings and mountain scenery.

★ **Cal Cristo** is another must-visit, a 19th-century farmer's dwelling that has been perfectly preserved down to the tiniest utensil. ✉ *Carrer dels Cavallers,* ☏ *831405.* ⏲ *Tues.–Sat. 9:30–1:30, 3–6:30, Sun. 10–2.*

The **funicamp telecabina** (cable car) carries hikers and sightseers from Encamp up to the Grau Roig ski resort. The telecabina connects hotels in the valley with the upper slopes and ski runs, alleviating the wicked winter traffic jams for which Andorra has become famous.

$ **Hotel La Mola.** This friendly spot, midway between the ski slopes and the bright lights of Andorra la Vella, is a comfortable choice that has all the basic facilities at half the price of some of the better-known Andorran hotels. ✉ *Av. Co-Princep Episcopal 62,* ☏ *831181,* FAX *833046. 48 rooms. Restaurant, pool. AE, DC, MC, V.*

Canillo

The **Santuari de Meritxell** is the home of the Virgin of Meritxell, the principality's patron saint. The original sanctuary was destroyed by fire in 1972; the new gray-stone building that replaced it looks remarkably like a factory, but the mountain setting is superb. ✉ *N-2, between Encamp and Canillo.* ⏲ *Wed.–Mon. 9–1 and 3–7.*

Just outside Canillo stands a **seven-armed Gothic cross** of stone (in fact, it has only six arms; one has been broken off). The Romanesque church of **Sant Joan de Caselles,** 2 km (1 mi) east of Canillo, is one of Andorra's treasures, with ancient walls of stone that has turned a lovely dappled gingerbread color over the centuries. The bell tower is stunning: three stories of weathered stone punctuated by rows of round-arch windows. Inside, a fine reredos (a wall or screen behind an altar), dating from 1525, depicts the life of St. John the Evangelist.

La Massana

★ **Pont de Sant Antoni** (St. Anthony Bridge), a Romanesque stone bridge spanning a narrow river, is just 3 km (2 mi) north of Andorra la Vella on the N-3 road toward La Massana. The rustic streets of the mountain town of La Massana are good for a picturesque stroll.

In Sispony the **Museu Casa Rull** offers a look at a typical wealthy burgher's house of the 17th century. ✉ *Carrer Major, Sispony,* ☏ *836919.* ⏲ *Tues.–Sat. 9:30–1:30, 3–6:30, Sun. 10–2.*

$$$–$$$$ ✕ **El Rusc.** A smallish flower-covered chalet 1 km (½ mi) from La Massana, El Rusc may be Andorra's top restaurant in both cost and quality. Chef Antoni Garrallá serves Basque cuisine and French and international specialties. Try the foie gras with onions or *besugo* (baked sea bream), a standard treat from the Basque country. ✉ *Ctra. de Arinsal,* ☏ *838200,* FAX *835180. Reservations essential. AE, DC, MC, V. Closed Mon. No dinner Sun.*

$$–$$$ ★ ✕ **La Borda de l'Avi.** This popular place specializes in lamb, goat, beef, quail, partridge, and trout cooked over coals. The three dining rooms can hold some 200 diners and, during the high season, often do. ✉ *Ctra. de Arinsal,* ☏ *835154. AE, DC, MC, V.*

Ordino

The tiny village of Ordino, 5 km (3 mi) northeast of La Massana, is known for its medieval church, **Sant Martíde la Cortinada.** Romanesque with Baroque altarpieces, the church also has 12th-century frescoes and unusual wooden furnishings.

Museu Casa d'Areny Plandolit is an aristocratic 18th-century manor house affording a rare glimpse into the life and luxuries of a noble Andorran family. ✉ *Carrer Major,* ☎ *836908.* ⏲ *Tues.–Sat. 9:30–1:30, 3–6:30, Sun. 10–2.*

$$$ 🏨 **Hotel Coma.** Surrounded by woods and meadows, this Swiss chalet-style hideaway just outside the village offers scenery, silence, and simple Andorran fare at affordable prices. ✉ *Ctra. General,* ☎ *835116,* FAX *837938. 48 rooms. Restaurant, pool. AE, DC, MC, V.*

La Cortinada

In this village is **Can Pal,** a fine example of medieval Andorran architecture. It is a privately owned manor house (strictly no admittance) with a dovecote attached. Note the turret perched high on the far side.

Santa Coloma

★ Santa Coloma's pre-Romanesque **Santa Coloma de les Bons** hermitage, the only Andorran church with a round tower, is the main attraction in this village 4 km (2½ mi) south of Andorra la Vella on CG-1. Parts of the church date from the 9th and 10th centuries. Twelfth-century Romanesque frescoes adorn the interior walls, while an 18th-century Baroque altarpiece presides.

$$–$$$$ ✕ **El Bon Racó.** Exactly what the name says it is—a good corner, nook, or retreat—it is a traditional borda in design. The place turns out fine Pyrenean home cooking at encouraging prices. Try to arrive early; it fills quickly, especially on weekends. ✉ *Av. Salou 86,* ☎ *822085. AE, DC, MC, V. Closed Sept. 8 and Dec. 25.*

Pas de la Casa

This conglomeration of high-rises and supermarkets is a sort of Andorran Smuggler's Notch, traditionally a place for French and Spanish shoppers to effect a quick sting while the kids are skiing and then retreat back to their respective countries. Known to be colder and snowier than any other point around, Pas de la Casa is a favorite ski resort, especially for visitors from the Cerdanya Valley in Spain.

$$$ 🏨 **Esqui d'Or.** At the very foot of the lift of what may be the snowiest ski resort in the Pyrenees (certainly in Andorra), this modern hotel is a handy resource if you can get a reservation for rooms overlooking the slopes. The menu evolves from buffet breakfast and lunch to serious cuisine at dinner. ✉ *Catalunya 9,* ☎ *855127,* FAX *855178,* WEB *www.andorra-welcome.com/catalan/hotel/encamp/hotel15.htm. 62 rooms. Restaurant. AE, DC, MC, V.*

Sant Julià de Lòria

Sant Julià de Lòria is the first parish you encounter coming into Andorra from Spain. It is the site of Andorra's only Nordic skiing facility. Around and above it are a number of unspoiled small villages. Fontaneda and its rustic Sant Miquel de Fontaneda chapel, in particular, are among Sant Julià de Lòria's finest sights.

$$–$$$ ★ 🏨 **Pol.** Gracefully modern surroundings and a friendly staff help make this hotel popular. A garden and terrace are part of the Pol's appeal, and its dance club is a busy nightspot. ✉ *Av. Verge de Canólich 52,* ☎ *841122,* FAX *841852,* WEB *www.uha.ad/Pol/Index.html. 80 rooms. Restaurant. AE, MC, V.*

ANDORRA ESSENTIALS

EMERGENCIES

➤ EMERGENCY SERVICES: Police (☎ 110). Mountain rescue (☎ 112). Ambulance (☎ 118). Medical and dental emergencies (☎ 116).

TOURS

Tours of Andorra la Vella and the surrounding countryside are offered by several firms; check with the tourist office for details or call Excursion Nadal or Sol i Neu Excursion.

➤ FEES AND SCHEDULES: **Excursion Nadal** (☎ 821138). **Sol i Neu Excursion** (☎ 823653).

TRAVEL AGENCY

➤ LOCAL AGENT REFERRALS: **Relax Travel Agency/American Express** (✉ Mossen Tremosa 12, Andorra la Vella, ☎ 822044, FAX 827055).

VISITOR INFORMATION

➤ TOURIST INFORMATION: **Andorra La Vella** (Sindicat d'Iniciativa/National Tourist Office; ✉ Carrer Dr. Vilanova, ☎ 820214, FAX 825823; Barcelona office, ✉ World Trade Center BCN, Moll de Barcelona, Ed. Nord, Planta Baixa 27, 08039, ☎ 93/508–8448 or 93/508–8449; city tourist office, ✉ Plaça de la Rotonda, ☎ 827117). **Canillo** (Unió Pro-Turisme, ✉ Caseta Pro-Turisme, ☎ FAX 851002). **Encamp** (Unió Pro-Foment i Turisme, ✉ Plaça Consell General, ☎ 831405, FAX 831878). **Escaldes-Engordany** (Unió Pro-Turisme, ✉ Plaça dels Co-Prínceps, ☎ 820963). **La Massana** (Unió Pro-Turisme, ✉ Plaça del Quart, ☎ 835693). **Ordino** (Oficina de Turisme, ✉ Cruïlla d'Ordino, ☎ 737080). **Pas de la Casa** (Unió Pro-Turisme, ✉ C. Bernat III, ☎ 855292). **Sant Julià de Lòria** (Unió Pro-Turisme, ✉ Plaça de la Germandat, ☎ 844345).

3 AUSTRIA

VIENNA, DANUBE VALLEY, SALZBURG, INNSBRUCK

AN OFT-TOLD STORY concerns an airline pilot whose prelanding announcement advised, "Ladies and gentlemen, we are on the final approach to Vienna Airport. Please make sure your seat belts are fastened, please refrain from smoking until you are inside the terminal, and please set your watches back 100 years."

Apocryphal or not, the pilot's observation suggests the allure of a country where visitors can sense something of what Europe was like before the pulse of the 20th century quickened to a beat that would have dizzied our great-grandparents. Today, the occasional gentleman will kiss a lady's hand just as in the days of the Habsburgs, and Lipizzan stallions still dance to Mozart minuets—in other words, Austria is a country that has not forgotten the elegance of its past.

Look beyond the postcard clichés of dancing white horses, the zither strains, and the singing of the Vienna Boys Choir, however, and you'll find a conservative-mannered yet modern country, one of Europe's richest, in which the juxtaposition of old and new often creates excitement—even controversy. Vienna has its sumptuous palaces, but it is also home to an assemblage of U.N. organizations housed in a wholly modern complex. Tucked away between storybook villages are giant industrial plants, one of which turns out millions of compact discs for Sony. The world's largest penicillin producer is hidden away in a Tirolean valley. And those countless glittering crystal objects you see in jewelry and gift stores around the world originate in a small village outside Innsbruck. By no means is the country frozen in a time warp: rather, it is the contrast between the old and the new that makes Austria such a fascinating place to visit.

So, too, does the fact that, poised as it is between East and West, Austria shares a culture with Europe but has deep roots as well in the lands that lie beyond to the east. It was Metternich who declared that "Asia begins at the Landstrasse," referring to Vienna's crucial role as the meeting place of East and West for 2,000 years, a role that new xenophobic political forces are trying to stem today: with the news in early 2000 that the anti-immigrant and extremist Freedom Party once spearheaded by Jörg Haider was to be admitted to the national cabinet, Austria's government was set on a collision course with members of the European Union who issued economic and political sanctions. The sanctions against Austria were lifted later in the year and Haider, as *Landeshauptmann* (governor) of the southern province of Carinthia, is no longer at the political forefront. Politics aside, Vienna's spectacular historical and artistic heritage—exemplified by the legacies of Beethoven, Freud, Klimt, and Mahler—remains to lure travelers. A fascinating

Austria (Österreich)

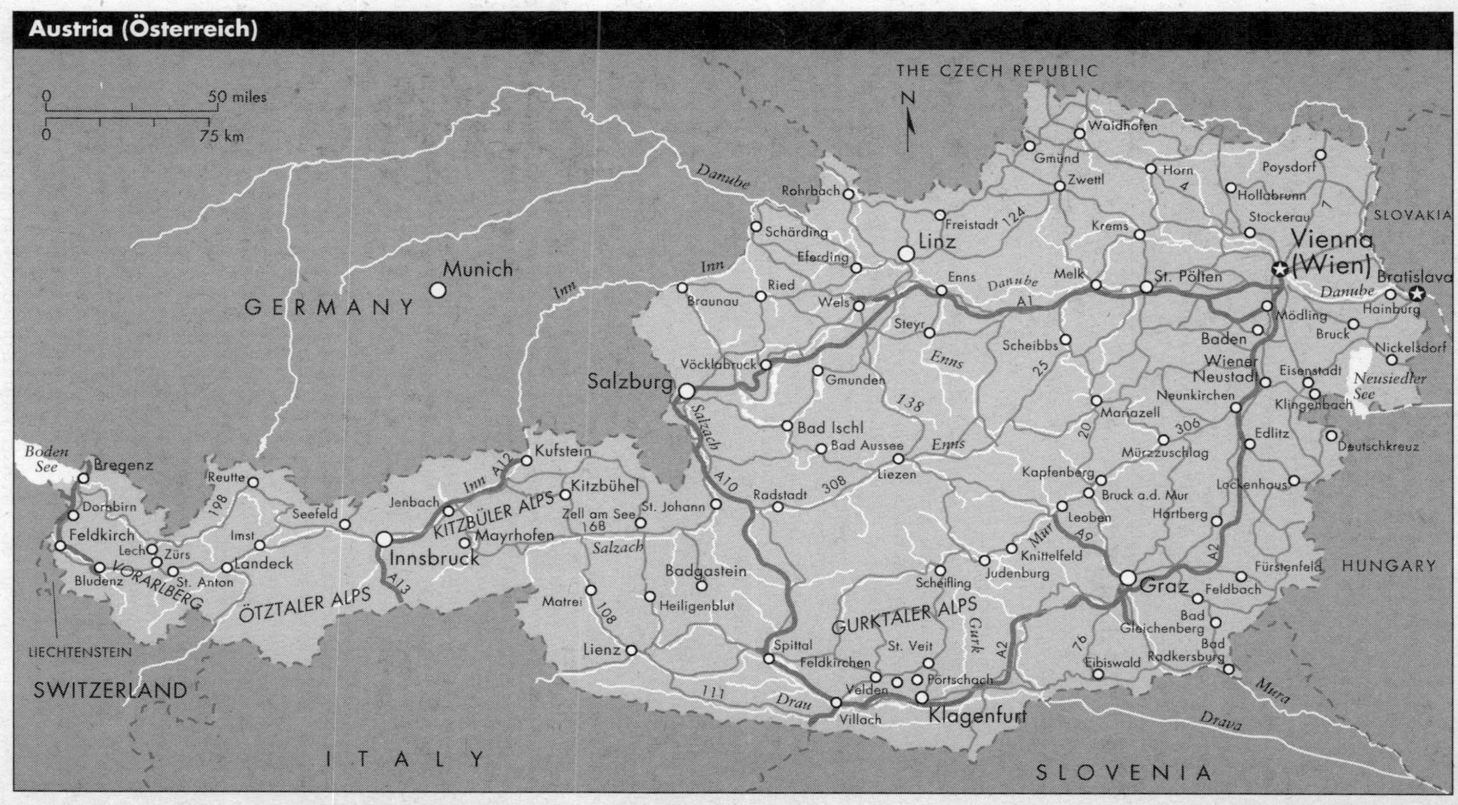

mélange of Apfelstrudel and psychoanalysis, Schubert and sausages, Vienna possesses a definite Old World charm that natives would be the last to underplay.

But as with most countries, the capital is only a small part of what Austria has to offer. A grand tour of the country reveals considerably more faces of Austria than the nine provinces would suggest: Salzburg—home every summer to one of the world's ritziest music festivals—is a departure point for the Salzkammergut lake country and the mountains of Land Salzburg; as the hub of the Alps, Innsbruck beckons skiers to explore the resorts of Lech, St. Anton, and Kitzbühel; finally, there's the scenic Wachau stretch of the Danube Valley.

AUSTRIA A TO Z

To research prices, get advice from other travelers, and book travel arrangements, visit www.fodors.com.

AIR TRAVEL

Austria's national airline, Austrian Airlines, flies to major worldwide destinations. Tyrolean Airlines offers service from Vienna to Graz, Linz, Innsbruck, Salzburg, and points outside Austria. Rheintalflug has service between Vienna and Altenrhein (Switzerland, near Bregenz), with bus connections to points in Voralberg. Be aware, though, that travel by air within the country is expensive.

➤ AIRLINES AND CONTACTS: **Austrian Airlines** (main office; ✉ Kärtner Ring 18, 1010 Vienna, ☎ 05/1789. Note that the 05 prefix must be dialed from anywhere in Austria). **Rheintalflug** (☎ 01/7007–36911). **Tyrolean Airlines** (☎ 01/70070).

BUS TRAVEL

Austria has an extensive national bus network run by the post office and railroads. Where trains don't go, buses do, and you'll find them (bright yellow for easy recognition) in the remotest regions. You can buy tickets onboard, and in the off-season there is no problem getting a seat, but on routes to favored ski areas during holiday periods reservations are essential. Bookings can be handled at the ticket office (there's one in most towns with bus service) or by travel agents. In most communities, bus routes begin and end at or near the railroad station, making transfers easy. Increasingly, coordination of bus service with railroads means that many of the discounts and special tickets available for trains apply to buses as well.

BUSINESS HOURS

BANKS AND OFFICES

Banks are open weekdays 8–noon or 12:30 and 1:30–3; until 5 on Thursday; closed Saturday. Hours vary from one city to another. Principal offices in cities stay open during lunch.

MUSEUMS AND SIGHTS

Museum opening days and times vary considerably from one city to another and depend on the season and other factors. Monday is often a closing day. Your hotel or the local tourist office will have current details.

SHOPS

Shops are open weekdays from 8 or 9 until 6, in shopping centers until 7:30, and Saturday until 5, although some may still close at noon or 1. Many smaller shops close for one or two hours at midday. Larger food markets are open weekdays from 7:30 to 7:30, Saturday to 5.

CAR TRAVEL

GASOLINE

Gas prices are among the most expensive in Europe, though eventually they will have to be lowered to conform with other EU countries. Currently it costs roughly AS14/€1.02 a liter for unleaded gasoline and AS12/€.87 a liter for diesel, and at nearly 4 liters to the gallon, the final tally can be quite hefty.

PARKING

Traffic congestion in major cities means that driving generally takes longer than taking public transportation. City planners' solutions have been to make driving as difficult as possible, with one-way streets and other tricks, and a car in town is far more of a burden than a pleasure. Daytime parking is very difficult. A *Parkschein,* available at most tobacconists and magazine stands, allows you to park for up to 90 minutes—they cost AS6/€.44 for 30 minutes, AS12/€.87 for 1 hour, and AS19/€1.39 for 90 minutes—although you can park for free on Saturday and Sunday (but not overnight). Display the paper on your dashboard. Parking in smaller towns and villages is much easier and not as restricted.

ROAD CONDITIONS

The Austrian highway network is excellent and roads are well maintained and well marked. Secondary roads may be narrow and winding, albeit very picturesque. The main routes (Autobahns), especially the A2 down to Carinthia and Italy, are packed during both Austrian and German school holidays.

RULES OF THE ROAD

Drive on the right. Seat belts are compulsory in front. Children under 12 must sit in the back, and smaller children must have a restraining seat. Speed limits are as posted; otherwise, 130 kph (80 mph) on expressways, 100 kph (62 mph) on other main roads, 50 kph (31 mph) in built-up areas. Some city areas have speed limits of 30 kph (19 mph). Be aware that speed is checked by radar, even in small towns, and fines are heavy. The right-of-way is for those coming from the right (especially in traffic circles) unless otherwise marked. All vehicles using the Autobahn (divided, mostly limited-access main highways, including the main highway from Vienna airport to the city) must display an Autobahn-Vignette toll sticker on the inside of the windshield. If you're renting a car in Austria it's already included, but if you're coming from another country you need to buy a 10-day sticker for AS105/€7.63. Two-month stickers cost AS300/€21.80. If you're caught without a sticker, the fine is a hefty AS3,000/€218.02. To apply for a Autobahn-Vignette, contact the ÖAMTC/Österreichischer Automobile-, Motorrad- und Touringclub.

➤ CONTACTS: **ÖAMTC/Österreichischer Automobile-, Motorrad- und Touringclub** (✉ Schubertring 3, A-1010, Vienna, ☎ 01/711997).

CUSTOMS AND DUTIES

Austria's duty-free allowances are as follows: 200 cigarettes or 50 cigars or 250 grams of tobacco; 2 liters of wine and 1 liter of spirits; 1 bottle of toilet water (about 250-milliliter size); and 50 milliliters of perfume for those age 17 and over arriving from non–European Union countries. Tourists also do not have to pay duty on personal articles brought into Austria temporarily for their own use.

DINING

Take your choice among full-fledged restaurants in every price category, plus sidewalk *Würstel* (sausage) stands, *Imbissstuben* (quick-lunch stops), cafés, *Heurigen* (wine taverns), self-service restaurants, and modest *Gasthäuser* (neighborhood establishments featuring local specialties). Most places post their menus outside. Shops (such as Eduscho) that sell coffee beans also offer coffee by the cup at prices considerably lower than those in cafés, though you can't sit down. Many Anker bakery shops also offer tasty *Schmankerl* (snacks) and coffee, and some offer a full breakfast. *Würstel* stands offer a tempting array of grilled sausages, including *Käsekrainer* (beef and melted cheese), served with a roll and mustard. A growing number of shops and snack bars offer pizza by the slice.

Prices are for one main course.

CATEGORY	MAJOR CITY	OTHER AREAS
$$$$	over AS325 (€23.61)	over AS225 (€16.3)
$$$	AS200–AS325 (€14.53–€23.61)	AS175–AS225 (€12.71–€16.35)
$$	AS125–AS200 (€9.08–€14.53)	AS125–AS175 (€9.08–€12.71)
$	Under AS125 (€9.08)	Under AS125 (€9.08)

MEALTIMES

A typical Austrian breakfast consists of rolls, cold cuts, cheese, and coffee. Lunch is usually the big meal of the day for Austrians unless they're dining out in the evening. *Jause* (coffee with cake) is taken in the late afternoon, and a light supper ends the day.

RESERVATIONS AND DRESS

A jacket and tie are generally advised for restaurants in the top two price categories. Otherwise casual dress is acceptable. When in doubt, it's best to dress up.

EMBASSIES

For consulates, *see* Vienna Essentials, *below.*

➤ CANADA: (✉ Laurenzerberg 2, 3rd floor of Hauptpost building complex, ☎ 01/531–38–3000).

➤ UNITED KINGDOM: (✉ Jauresg. 10, near Schloss Belvedere, ☎ 01/71613–5151).

➤ UNITED STATES: (✉ Boltzmanng. 16, ☎ 01/313–39).

HOLIDAYS

All banks and shops are closed on national holidays: January 1 (New Year's Day); January 6 (Epiphany); Easter Sunday and Monday; May 1 (May Day); Ascension Day; Pentecost Sunday and Monday; Corpus Christi; August 15 (Assumption); October 26 (National Day); November 1 (All Saints' Day); December 8 (Immaculate Conception); December 25–26. On the December 8 holiday, banks and offices are closed but most shops are open.

LANGUAGE

German is the official national language. In larger cities and most resort areas you will have no problem finding English speakers; hotel and restaurant employees, in particular, speak English reasonably well. Most younger Austrians speak at least passable English.

LODGING

All prices quoted here are for two people in a double room and include taxes. Although exact rates vary, a single room generally costs more than half the price of a comparable double. Breakfast at the roll-and-coffee level is often included in the room rate; full and sumptuous breakfast buffets, however, can involve a supplementary charge. Keep in mind that hotels outside Vienna may offer comprehensive rates that include breakfast *and* dinner; these are often excellent deals.

HOW TO USE THIS GUIDE

Great trips begin with great planning, and this guide makes planning easy. It's packed with everything you need—insider advice on hotels and restaurants, cool tools, practical tips, essential maps, and much more.

COOL TOOLS

Fodor's Choice Top picks are marked throughout with a star.

Great Itineraries These tours, planned by Fodor's experts, give you the skinny on what you can see and do in the time you have.

Smart Travel Tips A to Z This special section is packed with important contacts and advice on everything from how to get around to what to pack.

Good Walks You won't miss a thing if you follow the numbered bullets on our maps.

Need a Break? Looking for a quick bite to eat or a spot to rest? These sure bets are along the way.

Off the Beaten Path Some lesser-known sights are worth a detour. We've marked those you should make time for.

POST-IT® FLAGS

Dog-ear no more!

"Post-it" is a registered trademark of 3M.

Favorite restaurants • Essential maps • Frequently used numbers • Walking tours • Can't-miss sights • Smart Travel Tips • Web sites • Top shops • Hot [illegible]

nightclubs • Addresses • Smart contacts • Events • Off-the-beaten-path spots • Favorite restaurants • Essential maps • Frequently used numbers • Walking tours •

ICONS AND SYMBOLS

Watch for these symbols throughout:

★ Our special recommendations

✕ Restaurant

Lodging establishment

✕ Lodging establishment whose restaurant warrants a special trip

Good for kids

☞ Sends you to another section of the guide for more information

✉ Address

☎ Telephone number

FAX Fax number

WEB Web site

Admission price

Opening hours

$-$$$$ Lodging and dining price categories, keyed to strategically sited price charts. Check the index for locations.

①❶ Numbers in white and black circles on the maps, in the margins, and within tours correspond to one another.

ON THE WEB

Continue your planning with these useful tools found at **www.fodors.com**, the Web's best source for travel information.

"Rich with resources." —*New York Times*

"Navigation is a cinch." —*Forbes* "Best of the Web" list

"Put together by people bursting with know-how."
—*Sunday Times* (London)

Create a Miniguide Pinpoint hotels, restaurants, and attractions that have what you want at the price you want to pay.

Rants and Raves Find out what readers say about Fodor's picks—or write your own reviews of hotels and restaurants you've just visited.

Travel Talk Post your questions and get answers from fellow travelers, or share your own experiences.

On-Line Booking Find the best prices on airline tickets, rental cars, cruises, or vacations, and book them on the spot.

About our Books Learn about other Fodor's guides to your destination and many others.

Expert Advice and Trip Ideas From what to tip to how to take great photos, from the national parks to Nepal, Fodors.com has suggestions that'll make your trip a breeze. Log on and get informed and inspired.

Smart Resources Check the weather in your destination or convert your currency. Learn the local language or link to the latest event listings. Or consult hundreds of detailed maps—all in one place.

CATEGORY	MAJOR CITY	OTHER AREAS
$$$$	over AS4,000 (€290.70)	over AS2,700 (€196.22)
$$$	AS1,750–AS2,500 (€127.18–€181.69)	AS1,600–AS2,200 (€116.28–€159.88)
$$	AS1,000–AS1,750 (€72.67–€127.18)	AS1250–AS1,600 (€90.84–€116.28)
$	under AS1,000 (€72.67)	under AS900 (€65.41)

All prices are for two persons in a standard double room, including local taxes (usually 10%), service (15%), and breakfast (except in most $$$$ hotels).

CAMPING

Most campsites are well equipped, with water and toilet facilities. Some have hookups for RVs. Few campsites are open year-round. Summer or winter, make reservations well in advance to be sure of a site. In addition to campsites, mountain cabins are available on an overnight basis to Alpine hikers. For information, contact Österreichischer Alpenverein. Information on camping is available from the National Tourist Office.

➤ CONTACTS: **Österreichischer Alpenverein** (✉ Wilhelm-Greil-Str. 15, A-6020 Innsbruck, ☎ 0512/59547–34, FAX 0512/575528).

HOSTELS

Hosteling is well developed, although most locations are outside city centers. For information, contact Österreichischer Jugendherbergsverband (Austrian Hostel Association).

➤ HOSTEL ORGANIZATIONS: **Österreichischer Jugendherbergsverband** (✉ Schottenring 28, A-1010 Vienna, ☎ 01/533–5353, FAX 01/535–0861).

HOTELS

Austrian hotels and pensions are officially classified using from one to five stars. These grades broadly coincide with our own four-point rating system. No matter what the category, standards for service and cleanliness are high. All hotels in the upper three categories have either a bath or shower in the room; even the most inexpensive accommodations provide hot and cold water. Accommodations include castles and palaces, conventional hotels, *Gasthöfe* (country inns), and the more modest pensions. In summer, student dormitories offer a reasonably priced option to guests of all ages.

MAIL AND SHIPPING

American Express offices will hold mail at no charge for those carrying an American Express credit card or American Express traveler's checks.

➤ CONTACTS: **American Express** (✉ Kärntnerstr. 21–23, Vienna, ☎ 01/515–40–0; Mozartpl. 5–7, Salzburg, ☎ 0662/8080; Brixnerstr. 3, Innsbruck, ☎ 0512/582–4910).

POSTAL RATES

Airmail letters and postcards to the United States and Canada cost AS15/€1.09 minimum. Airmail letters and postcards to the United Kingdom cost AS7/€.51, and an aerogram costs AS13/€.94.

MONEY MATTERS

Austria has become expensive, but as inflation is relatively low, the currency has remained fairly stable. Vienna and Salzburg are the most expensive cities, along with fashionable resorts at Kitzbühel, Seefeld, Badgastein, Velden, Zell am See, Pörtschach, St. Anton, Zürs, and Lech. Many smaller towns near these resorts offer virtually identical facilities at half the price. Drinks in bars and clubs cost considerably more than in cafés or restaurants. Austrian prices include service and tax.

Sample prices include: cup of coffee in a café or restaurant, AS35/€2.54–AS58/€4.21; half a glass of draft beer, AS34/€2.47–AS48/€3.49; small glass of wine, AS28/€2.03–AS80/€5.81; Coca-Cola, AS28/2.03€; open sandwich, AS25/€1.82; theater ticket, AS200/€14.53–AS300/€21.80; concert ticket, AS250/€18.17–AS500/€36.34; opera ticket, AS600/€43.60 and up; 2-km (1.6-mi) taxi ride, AS60/€4.36.

CREDIT CARDS

Credit cards are not as widely used in Austria as they are in other European countries, and not all establishments that accept plastic take all cards. Some may require a minimum purchase if payment is to be made by card. Many restaurants take cash only. American Express has money machines in Vienna at its main office and at the airport. Many of the Bankomat money dispensers will also accept Visa cards if you have an encoded international PIN (Personal Identification Number).
➤ CONTACTS: **American Express** (main office; ✉ Kärntnerstr. 21–23).

CURRENCY

The unit of currency is the Austrian schilling (AS), divided into 100 groschen. There are AS20, AS50, AS100, AS500, AS1,000, and AS5,000 bills; AS1, AS5, AS10, and AS20 coins; and 10- and 50-groschen coins. At press time (summer 2001), the exchange rate was AS14.75 to the U.S. dollar, AS9.7 to the Canadian dollar, AS21.50 to the pound sterling, AS17.20 to the Irish punt, AS6.4 to the New Zealand dollar, AS8.4 to the Australian dollar, and AS1.95 to the South African rand. You may bring in any amount of either foreign currency or schillings and take out any amount with you.

The year 2002 spells the end of the schilling: January 1, 2002 sees the long-awaited introduction of coins and notes in the new European Union (EU) currency, the euro. Until March 2002, consumers will be able to make payments in both schillings and euros, though this could change. One euro is equivalent to 13.76 schillings, which is a fixed, irrevocable rate.

Exchange traveler's checks at a bank, a post office, or the American Express office to get the best rate. All charge a small commission; some smaller banks or "change" offices may give a poorer rate *and* charge a higher fee. All change offices at airports and at main train stations in major cities cash traveler's checks. In Vienna, bank-operated change offices with extended hours are found on Stephansplatz and at the main rail stations. Bank Austria machines on Stephansplatz, at Kärntnerstrasse 51 (to the right of the Opera), and at the Raiffeisenbank on Kohlmarkt (at Michaelerplatz) change bills from other currencies into schillings, but rates are poor and the commission hefty.

TAXES

VALUE-ADDED TAX (VAT)

A value-added tax (VAT) of 20% is charged on all sales and is automatically included in prices. If you purchase goods worth AS1,000/€72.67 or more and are not a citizen of an EU country, you can claim a refund of the tax either as you leave or after you've returned home. Ask the store clerk to fill out the necessary papers. Get them stamped at the airport or border crossing by customs officials (who may ask to see the goods). You can get an immediate refund of the VAT, less a service charge, at international airports or at main border crossings, or you can return the papers by mail to the shop(s). The VAT refund can be credited to your credit card account or remitted by check.

TELEPHONES

COUNTRY AND AREA CODES

The country code for Austria is 43. When dialing an Austrian number from abroad, drop the initial 0 from the local area code.

INTERNATIONAL CALLS

It costs considerably more to telephone *from* Austria than it does *to* Austria. Calls from post offices are least expensive. To avoid hotel charges, call overseas and ask to be called back; use an international credit card, available from AT&T and MCI. Use the AT&T access code to reach an operator. Another option for long-distance access is MCI WorldPhone. To make a collect call—you can't do this from pay phones—dial the operator and ask for an *R*-Gespräch (pronounced "air-ga-*shprayk*"). For international information dial 11812 for numbers in Germany, 11813 for numbers in other European countries, and 11814 for overseas numbers. Most operators speak English; if yours doesn't, you'll be passed along to one who does.

➤ ACCESS CODES: **AT&T** (☎ 0800-200-288). **MCI WorldPhone** (☎ 022/903–012).

LOCAL CALLS

Pay telephones take AS1, AS5, AS10, and AS20 coins. Emergency calls are free. Instructions are in English in most booths. The initial connection for a local call costs AS2. Insert AS1 or more to continue the connection when you hear the tone warning that your time is up. Phone cards, available at post offices, work in all phones marked WERTKARTENTELEFON. The cost of the call will be deducted from the card automatically. Phone numbers throughout Austria are currently being changed. A sharp tone indicates either no connection or that the number has been changed. Dial 11811 for numbers in Austria.

TIPPING

In restaurants, 10% service is included. Add anything from AS5/€.36 to AS50/€3.63, depending on the restaurant and the size of the bill, or about 5%. Leave the actual tip by telling the waiter the total amount you wish to pay—that is, the bill plus the tip—then remit the tip with the payment to the waiter (do not leave it on the table). Railroad porters and hotel porters or bellhops get AS10/€.73 per bag. Doormen get AS20/€1.45 for hailing a cab and assisting. Room service gets AS20/€1.45 for snacks and AS20/€1.45–AS40/€2.90 for full meals; in more expensive establishments, expect to tip on the higher side. Maids get no tip unless you stay a week or more, or unless a special service is rendered.

TRAIN TRAVEL

Austrian train service is excellent and efficient. The IC (InterCity) and EC (EuroCity) trains are the fastest, with a supplement of AS50/€3.63 included in the price of the ticket. If you are traveling outside the country, be sure to ask at the station whether an additional supplement is required. Some trains require it, and it costs more to buy it onboard. It's also a good idea to pay the extra AS48/€3.49 per ticket for a seat reservation, especially at peak holiday times, and year-round for travel to major destinations. If you're planning on doing a lot of traveling within Austria, it might be a good idea to purchase a *Vorteilskarte* which enables you to travel for half-price within Austria. It's good for one year and costs AS1,100/€79.94.

VISITOR INFORMATION

The Central Tourist Office is for phone inquiries and hotel assistance. For city tourist offices, *see* Visitor Information in the Essentials sections for Vienna, Salzburg, and Innsbruck, *below.*

➤ TOURIST INFORMATION: **Central Tourist Office** (national tourist office; ✉ Margaretenstr. 1, A-1040 Vienna, ☎ 01/211140, FAX 01/216–8492).

WHEN TO GO

Austria has two tourist seasons. The summer season technically starts around Easter, reaches its peak in July, and winds down in September. In summer, Vienna moves outdoors. May, June, September, and October are the most temperate months, and the most affordable. The winter cultural season starts in October and runs into June; winter sports get under way in December and last until the end of April, although you can ski in certain areas well into June and on some of the highest glaciers year-round. Some events—the Salzburg Festival is a prime example—occasion a substantial increase in hotel and other prices.

CLIMATE

Summer can be warm; winter, bitterly cold. The southern region is usually several degrees warmer in summer, several degrees colder in winter. Winters north of the Alps can be overcast and dreary, whereas the south basks in winter sunshine. The following are the average daily maximum and minimum temperatures for Vienna.

Jan.	34F	1C	**May**	67F	19C	**Sept.**	68F	20C
	25	– 4		50	10		53	11
Feb.	38F	3C	**June**	73F	23C	**Oct.**	56F	14C
	28	– 3		56	14		44	7
Mar.	47F	8C	**July**	76F	25C	**Nov.**	45F	7C
	30	– 1		60	15		37	3
Apr.	58F	15C	**Aug.**	75F	24C	**Dec.**	37F	3C
	43	6		59	15		30	– 1

VIENNA

Vienna has been characterized as an "old dowager of a town"—an Austro-Hungarian empress widowed in 1918 by the Great War. It's not just the aristocratic and courtly atmosphere, with monumental doorways and facades of former palaces at every turn. Nor is it just that Vienna (Wien in German) has a higher proportion of middle-aged and older citizens than any other city in Europe, with a concomitant air of stability, quiet, and respectability. Rather, it's these factors—combined with a love of music; a discreet weakness for rich food (especially cakes); an adherence to old-fashioned and formal forms of address; a high regard for the arts; and a gentle mourning for lost glories—that preserve the enchanting elegance of Old World dignity.

Exploring Vienna

Numbers in the margin correspond to points of interest on the Vienna map.

Most main sights are in the inner zone, the oldest part of the city, encircled by the Ring, once the course of the city walls and today a broad, tree-lined boulevard. Carry a ready supply of AS10 coins; many places of interest have coin-operated tape-recording machines that provide English commentaries. As you wander around, train yourself to look upward; some of the most memorable architectural delights are found on upper stories and along roof lines. Note that addresses throughout the chapter ending with "-strasse" or "-gasse" (both meaning "street") are abbreviated "str." or "g." respectively (Augustinerstrasse will be "Augustinerstr."; Dorotheergasse will be "Dorotheerg.").

The Heart of Vienna

1 **Albertina.** Some of the greatest Old Master drawings—including Dürer's *Praying Hands*—are housed in this unassuming building, home to the world's largest collection of drawings, sketches, engravings, and etchings. Other highlights include works by Rembrandt, Michelangelo, and Correggio. The building is undergoing restoration and is scheduled to reopen in September 2002. (⊠ *Augustinerstr. 1,* ☎ *01/581–3060–21.* ⏲ *Tues.–Sun. 10–5.*

3 **Augustinerkirche** (St. Augustine's Church). The interior of this 14th-century church has undergone restoration; while much of the earlier Baroque ornamentation was removed in the 1780s, the gilt organ decoration and main altar remain as visual sensations. This was the court church; the Habsburg rulers' hearts are preserved in a chamber here. On Sunday, the 11 AM mass is sung in Latin. ⊠ *Josefspl.*

23 **Figarohaus** (Mozart Memorial Rooms). A commemorative museum occupies the small apartment in the house on a narrow street just east of St. Stephen's Cathedral where Mozart lived from 1784 to 1787. It was here that the composer wrote *The Marriage of Figaro* (hence the nickname Figaro House) and, some claim, spent the happiest years of his life. Fascinating Mozart memorabilia are on view, unfortunately displayed in an inappropriately modern fashion. ⊠ *Domg. 5,* ☎ *01/513–6294.* ⏲ *Tues.–Sun. 9–6.*

25 **Freud Museum.** The original famous couch is gone (there's a replica), but the apartment in which Sigmund Freud developed modern psychiatry and treated his first patients is otherwise generally intact. Other rooms include a reference library. ⊠ *Bergg. 19,* ☎ *01/319–1596.* ⏲ *July–Sept., daily 9–6; Oct.–June, daily 9–4.*

18 **Haus der Musik** (House of Music). It would be easy to spend an entire day at this new, ultra high-tech museum housed on several floors of an early 19th-century palace near Schwarzenbergplatz. There are special rooms dedicated to each of the great Viennese composers—Haydn, Mozart, Beethoven, Strauss, and Mahler—complete with music samples and manuscripts. There are also dozens of interactive computer games. You can even record your own CD with a variety of everyday sounds. ⊠ *Seilerstätte 30,* ☎ *01/51648,* WEB *haus-der-musik-wien.at.* ⏲ *Daily 10–10. Restaurant, café. U-Bahn: U1, U2, U4 Karlsplatz, then Streetcar D to Schwarzenbergpl.*

32 **Heeresgeschichtliches Museum** (Museum of Military History). Designed by Theophil Hansen, this impressive neo-Gothic building houses war artifacts ranging from armor and Turkish tents confiscated from the Turks during the 16th-century siege of Vienna to fighter planes and tanks. Also on display is the bullet-riddled car that Archduke Franz Ferdinand and his wife were riding in when they were assassinated in Sarajevo in 1914. ⊠ *Arsenal 3, Bldg. 18,* ☎ *01/795–610.* ⏲ *Sat.–Thurs. 9–5. Tram 18/Ghegastr., near the Belvedere.*

★ 7 **Hofburg** (Imperial Palace). This centerpiece of Imperial Vienna is actually a vast complex comprising numerous buildings, courtyards, and other must-sees. Start with the magnificent domed entry—**Michaelertor** (St. Michael's Gate), the principal gateway to the Hofburg—and go through the courtyards to the vast, grassy Heldenplatz (Hero's Square), on the front. The palace complex, with sections dating from the 13th through 18th centuries, includes the **Augustinerkirche,** the **Nationalbibliothek**—its central room is one of the most spectacular Baroque showpieces anywhere—and the **Hofburgkapelle,** home to the Vienna Boys Choir. Here, too, are the famous **Spanische Reitschule**—where the Lipizzaners go through their paces—and three fascinating

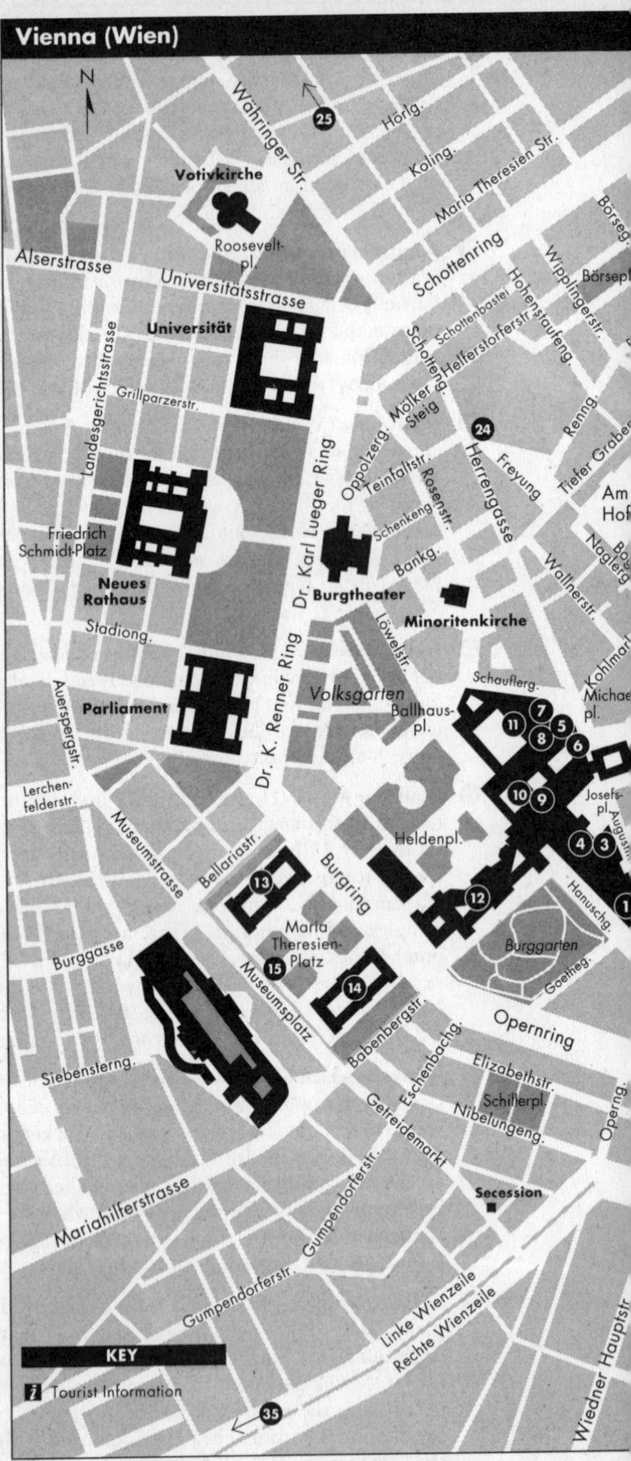
Vienna (Wien)
N
Währinger Str.
Hörlg.
Koling.
Maria Theresien Str.
Börseg.
Votivkirche
Roosevelt-pl.
Alserstrasse
Universitätsstrasse
Schottenring
Börsepl.
Wipplingerstr.
Hohenstaufeng.
Schottenbastei
Helferstorferstr.
Schotteng.
Mölker Steig
Universität
Landesgerichtsstrasse
Grillparzerstr.
Renng.
Tiefer Graben
Oppolzerg.
Teinfaltstr.
Rosenstr.
Herrengasse
Freyung
Am Hof
Naglerg.
Dr. Karl Lueger Ring
Schenkeng.
Bankg.
Friedrich Schmidt-Platz
Neues Rathaus
Burgtheater
Minoritenkirche
Wallnerstr.
Löwelstr.
Stadiong.
Kohlmarkt
Schauflerg.
Michaelerpl.
Volksgarten
Ballhaus-pl.
Auerspergstr.
Parliament
Dr. K. Renner Ring
Josefs-pl.
Augustinerstr.
Lerchenfelderstr.
Museumstrasse
Heldenpl.
Bellariastr.
Burgring
Hanuschg.
Maria Theresien-Platz
Burggarten
Burggasse
Museumsplatz
Goetheg.
Babenbergstr.
Opernring
Eschenbachg.
Elizabethstr.
Schillerpl.
Siebensterng.
Getreidemarkt
Nibelungeng.
Operng.
Secession
Gumpendorferstr.
Mariahilferstrasse
Linke Wienzeile
Rechte Wienzeile
Wiedner Hauptstr.
KEY
Tourist Information

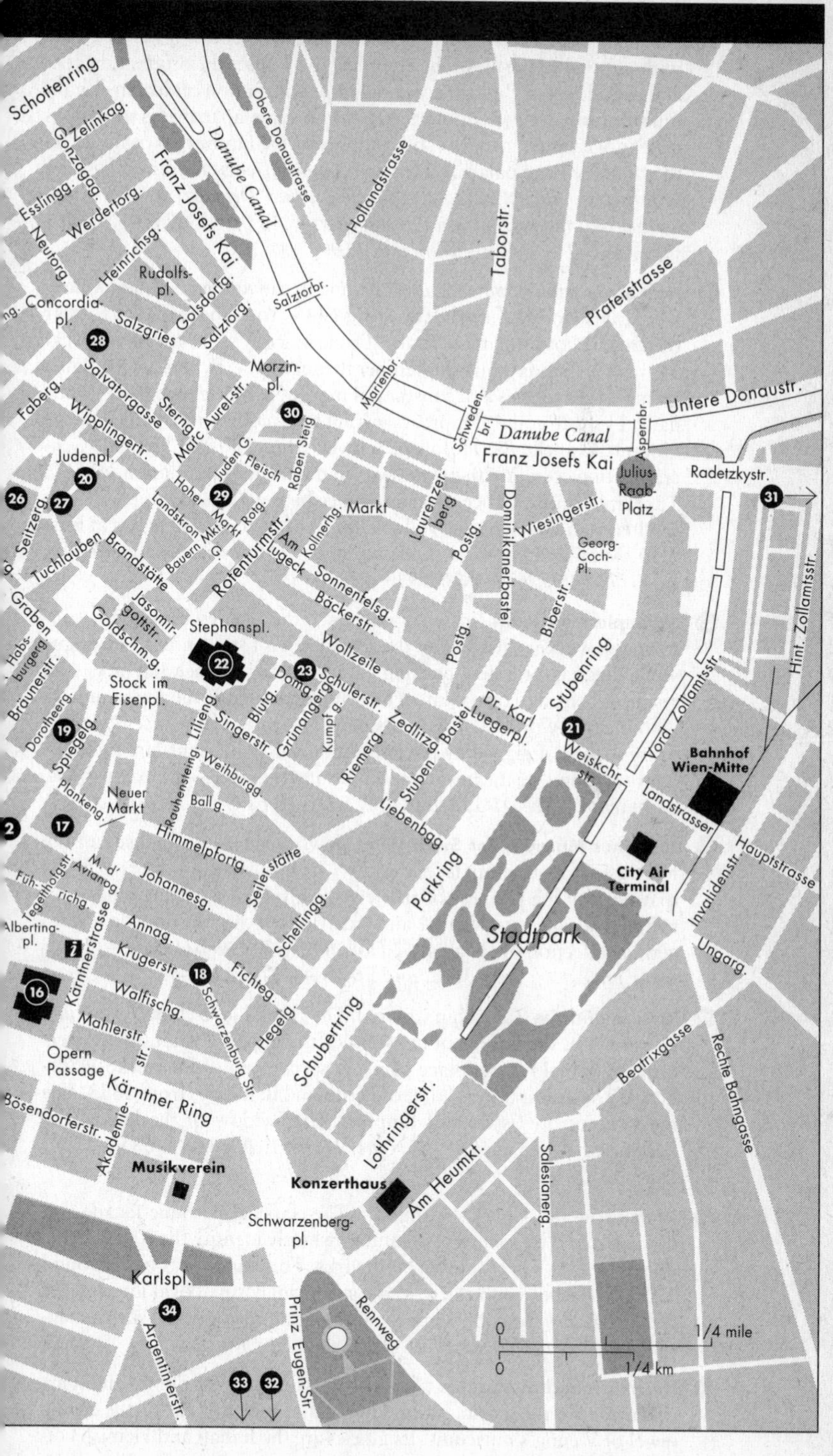
Schottenring
Zelinkag.
Gonzagag.
Esslingg.
Neutorg.
Werdertorg.
Franz Josefs Kai
Danube Canal
Obere Donaustrasse
Hollandstrasse
Taborstr.
Praterstrasse
Heinrichsg.
Rudolfs-pl.
Golsdorfg.
Salztorbr.
Concordia-pl.
Salzgries
Salztorg.
28
Morzin-pl.
Salvatorgasse
Faberg.
Wipplingerstr.
Sterng.
Marc Aurel-str.
30
Marienbr.
Schweden-br.
Danube Canal
Aspernbr.
Untere Donaustr.
Franz Josefs Kai
Julius-Raab-Platz
Radetzkystr.
31
Judenpl.
20
26
27
Juden G.
Fleisch Markt
Raben Steig
Hoher Markt
Landskron
Bauern Mkt.
Rotg.
29
Seitzerg.
Tuchlauben
Brandstätte
Rotenturmstr.
Am Lugeck
Kollnerhg.
Laurenzer-berg
Postg.
Dominikanerbastei
Wiesingerstr.
Georg-Coch-Pl.
Sonnenfelsg.
Bäckerstr.
Biberstr.
Hint. Zollamtsstr.
Graben
Jasomir-gottstr.
Goldschm.g.
Stephanspl.
22
Wollzeile
Postg.
Stubenring
Habs-burgerg.
Bräunerstr.
Stock im Eisenpl.
23
Domg.
Schulerstr.
Blutg.
Grünangerg.
Kumpf g.
Dr. Karl Luegerpl.
Vord. Zollamtsstr.
Dorotheerg.
19
Spiegelg.
Lilieng.
Singerstr.
Zedlitzg.
Stuben Bastei
Riemerg.
21
Weiskchr.-str.
Bahnhof Wien-Mitte
Planken g.
Neuer Markt
Weihburgg.
Rauhensteing.
Ball g.
Liebenbgg.
Landstrasser
2
17
Himmelpfortg.
Seilerstätte
Parkring
City Air Terminal
Hauptstrasse
Füh-richg.
Tegetthofgstr.
M. d'Avianog.
Johannesg.
Invalidenstr.
Albertina-pl.
Kärntnerstrasse
Annag.
Schellingg.
Stadtpark
Ungarg.
Krugerstr.
18
Fichteg.
16
Walfischg.
Schwarzenburg Str.
Mahlerstr.
Hegelg.
Schubertring
Beatrixgasse
Rechte Bahngasse
Opern Passage
Kärntner Ring
Bösendorferstr.
Akademie-str.
Lothringerstr.
Salesianerg.
Musikverein
Konzerthaus
Am Heumkt.
Schwarzenberg-pl.
Karlspl.
34
Argentinierstr.
Prinz Eugen-Str.
Rennweg
0
1/4 mile
0
1/4 km
33
32

museums: the **Silberkammer,** the **Schauräume in der Hofburg,** and the **Schatzkammer,** as well as the **Schmetterlinghaus** (Butterfly House), alive with unusual butterflies. The complex also houses the office of the federal presidency, a glittering chandelier-lit convention center, an elegant multipurpose hall (Redoutensaal), and private apartments as well as lesser government offices. The complex of the Hofburg is centered on the ☞ **Neue Burg** palace. ✉ *Hofburg: main streets circling complex—Opernring, Augustinerstr., Schauflerg., and Dr. Karl Renner-Ring, Schmetterlinghaus: entrance in Burggarten,* ☎ *01/533–7570.* ⏲ *Apr.–Oct., daily 10–5; Nov.–Mar., daily 10–4.*

10 **Hofburgkapelle** (Court Chapel). Home to the renowned Vienna Boys Choir, this Gothic chapel dates from 1449. You'll need tickets to hear the angelic boys sing mass (only 10 side balcony seats afford views) at 9:15 AM on Sunday, mid-September through June; tickets are available from travel agencies at a substantial markup, at the chapel itself (open daily 11:30–1 and 3–5), or by writing two months in advance to the Hofmusikkapelle (✉ Hofburg, Schweizerhof, A-1010 Vienna). General seating costs AS70; prime seats in the front of the church, AS380. The City Tourist Office can sometimes help with ticket applications. Limited standing room is available for free; get to the chapel by at least 8:30 AM on Sunday for a shot at a spot. ✉ *Hofburg, Schweizer Hof,* ☎ *01/533–9927–71,* FAX *01/533–9927–75.*

20 **Judenplatz Museum.** In what was once the old Jewish ghetto, construction workers discovered the remains of a 13th-century synagogue while digging for a new parking garage. Simon Wiesenthal (a Vienna resident) helped to turn it into a museum dedicated to the Austrian Jews who died in World War II. Outside is a concrete cube resembling library shelves, designed by Rachel Whiteread. Downstairs are three exhibition rooms on medieval Jewish life and the synagogue excavations. ✉ *Judenpl. 8,* ☎ *01/535–0431.* ⏲ *Sun.–Thurs. 10–6, Fri. 10–2.*

19 **Jüdisches Museum der Stadt Wien** (Jewish Museum). Housed in the former Eskeles town palace, the city's Jewish Museum offers exhibits that portray the richness of the Jewish culture and heritage that contributed so much to Vienna and Austria. On the top floor is a staggering collection of Judaica. ✉ *Dorotheerg. 11,* ☎ *01/535–0431,* WEB *www.jmw.at.* ⏲ *Sun.–Wed. and Fri. 10–6, Thurs. 10–8.*

17 **Kapuzinerkirche** (Capuchin Church). The ground-level church is nothing unusual, but the basement crypt holds the imperial vault, the **Kaisergruft,** the final resting place of many sarcophagi of long-dead Habsburgs. The oldest tomb is that of Ferdinand II; it dates from 1633. The most recent one is that of Empress Zita, widow of the last of the kaisers, who died in 1989. ✉ *Neuer Markt 1,* ☎ *01/512–6853–12.* ⏲ *Daily 9:30–4.*

★ 34 **Karlskirche** (St. Charles's Church). The classical Baroque facade and dome flanked by vast twin columns instantly identify the Karlskirche, one of the city's best-known landmarks. The church was built around 1715 by Fischer von Erlach. In the surprisingly small oval interior, the ceiling has airy frescoes, while the Baroque altar is adorned with a magnificent sunburstlike array of gilded shafts. ✉ *Karlspl.*

★ 14 **Kunsthistorisches Museum** (Art History Museum). One of the finest art collections in the world, housed in palatial splendor, this is the crown jewel of Vienna's museums. Its glories are the Italian and Flemish collections, assembled by the Habsburgs over many centuries. The group of paintings by Pieter Brueghel the Elder is the largest in existence. The large-scale works concentrated in the main galleries shouldn't distract you from the masterworks in the more intimate side wings. One level down is the remarkable Kunstkammer (Art Cabinet) displaying priceless objects created for the Habsburg emperors. These include curiosities made of gold, silver, and crystal (including Cellini's salt cellar). ✉ *Maria-Theresien-Pl.,* ☎ *01/525–240.* ⏲ *Tues.–Wed. and Fri.–Sun. 10–6, Thurs. 10–9.*

6 Lipizzaner Museum. To learn more about the extraordinary Lipizzan horses of the Spanish Riding School, visit the adjacent museum set in what used to be the imperial pharmacy. Exhibits document the history of the Lipizzaners through paintings, photographs, and videos giving an overview from the 16th century to the present. A visit to the nearby stables—part of the Spanish Riding School complex—allows you to see the horses up close through a window. ✉ *Reitschulg. 2,* ☎ *01/533–7811,* FAX *01/533–3853.* *Combination ticket with morning training session at the Spanish Riding School AS140/€10.17.* ⏲ *Daily 9–6.*

15 Museumsquartier (Museum Quarter). Scheduled to open in the summer of 2001, this vast culture center, which claims to be the largest of its kind in the world, will be housed in what was once the Imperial Court Stables. The 250-year-old Baroque complex is ideally situated near the Hofburg Palace in the heart of the city. Four museums are planned, the **Leopold Museum** (⏲ Wed.–Thurs., Sat.–Mon. 11–7, Fri. 11–9), to contain the Egon Schiele collection, the **Museum moderner Kunst Stiftung Ludwig** (⏲ Tues.–Wed., Fri.–Sun. 10–6, Thurs. 10–9), or modern art museum, the **Kunsthalle** (⏲ Fri.–Wed. 10–7, Thurs. 10–10), an art hall to be used for special exhibits, and a children's museum, the **ZOOM Kinder Museum** (⏲ Mon.–Fri. 8–5, Sat.–Sun. 10–5:30). The annual Wiener Festwochen (theater arts festival) and the International Tanzwochen (dance festival) will be held in the former winter riding hall. In addition to all this, there will be an architecture center for contemporary design, a theater where the annual Viennale Film Festival will be held, and shops, cafés, and art galleries. ✉ *Museumspl. 1–5,* ☎ *01/523–5881,* WEB *www.museumsquartier.at. U-Bahn: U2 Babenbergerstr./U2, U3 Volkstheater.*

21 Museum für angewandte Kunst (MAK) (Museum of Applied Arts). This fascinating museum contains a large collection of Austrian furniture, porcelain, art objects, and priceless Oriental carpets. The museum puts on changing exhibitions of contemporary art, with artists ranging from Chris Burden to Nam June Paik. The museum also houses the popular MAK Cafe. ✉ *Stubenring 5,* ☎ *01/711–36–0.* ⏲ *Tues.–Wed., Fri.–Sun. 10–6, Thurs. 10–9. U-bahn: U3 Stubentor.*

★ **4 Nationalbibliothek** (National Library). The focus here is on the stunning Baroque central hall—one of Europe's most magnificently decorated spaces. Look for the fascinating collection of globes on the third floor. ✉ *Josefspl. 1,* ☎ *01/534–100 library; 01/534–10–297 globe museum.* ⏲ *Library: hrs vary, generally May 7–Oct. 26, Mon.–Wed., Fri.–Sat. 10–4, Thurs. 10–7, Sun. 10–2; Oct. 27–May 6, Mon.–Sat. 10–2. Globe museum: Mon.–Wed. and Fri. 11–noon, Thurs. 2–3.*

13 Naturhistorisches Museum (Natural History Museum). The twin building opposite the art-filled Kunsthistorisches Museum houses ranks of assorted showcases filled with stuffed animals, but such special collections as butterflies are better presented. There are dinosaur skeletons, of course. Here also is the Venus of Willendorf, a 25,000-year-old statuette discovered in Lower Austria. ✉ *Maria-Theresien-Pl.,* ☎ *01/521–77–0.* ⏲ *Thurs.–Mon. 9–6:30, Wed. 9–9.*

12 Neue Burg (New Wing of the Imperial Palace). This 19th-century edifice—Hitler announced the annexation of Austria from its balcony in 1938—now houses a series of museums whose exhibits range from musical instruments (Beethoven's piano) to weapons (tons of armor) to the collections of the **Völkerkunde** (Ethnological) and **Ephesus** (Classical Antiquity) museums. ✉ *Heldenpl. 1,* ☎ *01/525–240.* ⏲ *Ethnological museum: Tues.–Sun. 10–6. Ephesus musuem: Wed.–Mon. 10–6.*

★ ❾ **Schatzkammer** (Imperial Treasury). An almost overpowering display includes the magnificent crown jewels, the imperial crowns, the treasure of the Order of the Golden Fleece, regal robes, and other secular and ecclesiastical treasures. The imperial crown of the Holy Roman Empire is more than 1,000 years old. ✉ *Hofburg, Schweizer Hof,* ☎ *01/533–7931.* ⏲ *Wed.–Mon. 10–6.*

❽ **Schauräume in der Hofburg** (Imperial Apartments). The long, repetitive suite of conventionally luxurious rooms has a poignant feel. The decoration (19th-century imitation of 18th-century rococo) tries to look regal but ends up looking merely official. Among the few signs of genuine life are Emperor Franz Josef's spartan, iron field bed, and Empress Elizabeth's wooden gymnastics equipment. Obsessed with her looks, she suffered from anorexia and was fanatically devoted to exercise. ✉ *Michaelerpl. 1; entrance under Michaelertor dome,* ☎ *01/533–7570.* ⏲ *Daily 9–4:30.*

★ ⓫ **Silberkammer** (Court Silver and Tableware Museum). See how royalty dined in this brilliant showcase of imperial table settings. Little wonder Marie-Antoinette—who, as a child of Maria Theresa, grew up in Schloss Schönbrunn—had a taste for extreme luxury. You can buy a combination ticket, which includes the imperial apartments around the corner. ✉ *Burghof inner court, Michaelertrakt,* ☎ *01/533–7570.* ⏲ *Daily 9–4:30.*

★ ❺ **Spanische Reitschule** (Spanish Riding School). Probably the most famous interior in Vienna, the riding arena of the Spanish Riding School—wedding-cake white and crystal-chandeliered—is where the beloved white Lipizzaner horses train and perform dressage when they are not stabled in stalls across the Reitschulgasse to the east side of the school. For performance schedules and tickets, write to the Spanische Reitschule (✉ Hofburg, A-1010 Vienna) *at least* three months in advance. The AmEx office sometimes has a few last-minute tickets, but expect a 22% service charge. You can watch the 10 AM–noon training sessions Tuesday–Friday during much of the performance season (tickets only at the door) but the full-scale rehearsal session on Saturday requires advance booking for tickets through travel agencies, as does, needless to say, the main dressage performance offered on Sunday. ✉ *Michaelerpl. 1, Hofburg,* ☎ *01/533–9031–0,* FAX *01/535–0186.* 🎫 *AS250/€18.17–AS900/€65.40, standing room AS200/€14.53, morning training sessions AS100/€7.27; classical dressage sessions with music AS250/€18.17, available only through travel agencies.* ⏲ *Tues.–Sun., Mar.–June and Sept.–mid-Dec.; closed tour wks.*

⓰ **Staatsoper** (State Opera House). Considered one of the best opera houses in the world, the Staatsoper is a focus of Viennese social life as well. Almost totally destroyed in the last days of World War II (only the walls and front foyers were saved), it was rebuilt in its present, simpler elegance and reopened in 1955. Tickets for seats can be expensive and scarce, but among the very best bargains in Vienna are the Staatsoper standing-room tickets, available for each performance at delightfully affordable prices—as low as AS50 (€3.70). Backstage tours are also available. ✉ *Opernring 2,* ☎ *01/514–4426–13.*

★ ㉒ **Stephansdom** (St. Stephen's Cathedral). The towering Gothic spires and gaudy 19th-century tile roof of the city's central landmark still dominate the skyline. The oldest parts of the structure are the 13th-century entrance, the soaring **Riesentor** (Great Entry), and the **Heidentürme** (Heathens' Towers). Inside, the church is mysteriously shadowy, filled with an array of monuments, tombs, sculptures, paintings, and pulpits. Despite numerous Baroque additions—and extensive wartime damage—the atmosphere seems authentically medieval. Climb the 343 steps of the south tower—der alte Steffl (Old Stephen) as the Viennese call it—for a stupendous view over the city. If you take a 30-minute tour of the crypt, you can see the copper jars in which the entrails of the Habsburgs are carefully preserved. ⊠ *Stephanspl.,* ☎ *01/515–520.* ⊙ *Guided tour Mon.–Sat. at 10:30 and 3, Sun. at 3; evening tour Jun.–Sept., Sat. at 7; catacombs tour Mon.–Sat. from 10–11:30 and 1:30–4:30 every half hr, Sun. from 1:30–4:30 every half hr. North Tower elevator to Pummerin bell Apr.–Jun. and Sept., daily 9–6; Jul.–Aug., daily 9–6:30; Nov.–Mar., daily 8:30–5.*

2 **Theater Museum.** Housed in the noted 18th-century Palais Lobkowitz—Beethoven was a regular visitor here—this museum covers the history of theater in Vienna and the rest of Austria. A children's museum in the basement—alas, open only by appointment—is reached, appropriately, by a slide. ⊠ *Lobkowitzpl. 2,* ☎ *01/512–8800–0.* ⊙ *Tues., Thurs.–Sun. 10–5, Wed. 10–8.*

Other Corners of Vienna

26 **Am Hof.** The name of this remarkable square translates simply as "at court." On the east side of Am Hof, most of the Baroque overlay both inside and out on the massive **Kirche am Hof** (also known as the Church of the Nine Choirs of Angels) dates from the 1600s. In style, the somewhat dreary interior is reminiscent of those of many Dutch churches. In the northeast corner of the square check out what is possibly the most ornate fire station in the world. You'll find an open-air antiques market in the square on Thursday and Friday in summer and frequent seasonal markets at other times. ⊠ *Bounded by Tiefer Graben on west, Naglerg. on south, and Seitzerg. on east.*

29 **Hoher Markt.** This ancient cobblestone square with its imposing central monument celebrating the betrothal of Mary and Joseph sits atop **Roman ruins** (⊠ Hoher Markt 3, ☎ 01/535–5606), remains of the 2nd-century Roman legion encampment. On the north side of Hoher Markt is the amusing **Anker-Uhr,** a clock that marks the hour with a parade of moving figures. The figures are identified on a plaque at the lower left of the clock. ⊠ *Judeng. and Fisch-hof Str.*

31 **Hundertwasserhaus** (Hundertwasser House). This structure is an eccentric modern masterpiece envisioned by the late Austrian avant-garde artist Friedensreich Hundertwasser—an astonishing apartment complex marked by turrets, towers, unusual windows, and uneven floors. The nearby **KunstHaus Wien** (Vienna House of Art; ⊠ Untere Weissgerberstr. 13, ☎ 01/712–0491) is an art museum designed by the artist; it offers a floor of his work plus changing exhibits of other modern art. ⊠ *Kegelg. and Löweng.* ⊙ *Daily 10–7.*

28 **Maria am Gestade** (St. Mary's on the Bank). When built around 1400, this was a church for fishermen from the nearby canal, hence the name. Note the arched stone doorway and the ornate carved-stone-latticework "folded hands" spire. ⊠ *Salvatorg. and Passauer Pl.*

30 **Ruprechtskirche** (St. Rupert's Church). Vienna's oldest church, dating from the 11th century, is usually closed but sometimes opens for local art shows and summer evening classical concerts. ⊠ *Ruprechtspl.*

★ 33 **Schloss Belvedere** (Belvedere Palace). On a rise overlooking the city, this Baroque-era palace is one of the showpieces of Vienna. It was commissioned by Prince Eugene of Savoy and built by Johann Lukas von Hildebrandt in 1721–22. The palace consists of two separate buildings, one at the foot of the hill and the other at the top. The Upper Belvedere houses a gallery of 19th- and 20th-century Viennese art, featuring works by Klimt (including his world-famous painting *The Kiss*), Schiele, Waldmüller, and Makart; the Lower Belvedere has a Baroque museum together with exhibits of Austrian art of the Middle Ages. Take Streetcar D toward the Südbahnhof to reach the Belvedere. ✉ *Prinz-Eugen-Str. 27,* ☎ *01/79557–100.* ⌚ *Tues.–Sun. 10–5.*

★ 35 **Schloss Schönbrunn** (Schönbrunn Palace). The Versailles of Vienna, this magnificent Baroque residence with grandly formal gardens was built for the Habsburgs between 1696 and 1713. The complex has been a summer residence for such personages as Maria Theresa and Napoléon. Kaiser Franz Josef I was born and died here. His "office" (kept as he left it in 1916) is a touching reminder of his spartan life. In contrast, other rooms are filled with truly spectacular imperial elegance. The ornate reception areas are still used for state occasions. A guided tour leading through more than 40 of the palace's 1,441 rooms is the best way to see inside the palace (the most dazzling salons start at No. 21). Ask to see the **Berglzimmer,** ornately decorated ground-floor rooms generally not included in tours. To get to the palace, take the U4 subway line from Karlsplatz in the city center to Schönbrunn. ✉ *Schönbrunner Schloss-Str.,* ☎ *01/81113–239.* *AS145/€10.54 with guided tour; AS120/€8.72 without tour (40 rooms).* ⌚ *Apr.–Oct., daily 8:30–5; Nov.–Mar., daily 8:30–4:30.*

On the grounds of the Schönbrunn Palace is the **Tiergarten** (zoo), Europe's oldest menagerie, established in 1752 to amuse and educate the court. It houses an extensive assortment of animals; the original Baroque enclosures now serve as viewing pavilions, with the animals housed in effective, modern settings. ☎ *01/877–9294–0.* ⌚ *Nov.–Jan., daily 9–4:30; Feb., daily 9–5; Mar. and Oct., daily 9–5:30; Apr., daily 9–6; May–Sept., daily 9–6:30.*

Pathways lead up through the formal gardens to the **Gloriette,** an 18th-century Baroque folly on the rise behind Schloss Schönbrunn built to afford superb views of the city. A café is inside. ⌚ *Daily 9–5.*

The **Wagenburg** (Imperial Coach Collection), near the entrance to the palace grounds, displays splendid examples of bygone conveyances, from ornate children's sleighs to the grand carriages built to carry the coffins of deceased emperors in state funerals. ☎ *01/877–3244.* ⌚ *Nov.–Mar., Tues.–Sun. 10–4; Apr.–Oct., daily 9–6.*

Wander the grounds to discover the **Schöner Brunnen** (Beautiful Fountain) for which the Schönbrunn Palace is named; the re-created but convincing massive **Römische Ruinen** (Roman Ruins); and the great glass **Palmenhaus** (Palm House), with its orchids and exotic plants. ✉ *Palm House: nearest entrance Hietzing,* ☎ *01/877–5087–406.* ⌚ *Nov.–Mar., daily 8:30–4:30; Apr. and Oct., daily 9:30–4:30 May–Sept., daily 9:30–5:30.*

24 **Schottenkirche, Museum im Schottenstift** (Scottish Church and Museum). Despite its name, the monks who founded this church around 1177 were actually Irish, not Scots. The present imposing building dates from the mid-1600s. In contrast to the plain exterior, the interior bubbles with cherubs and angels. The Benedictines have set up a small but worthwhile museum of mainly religious art, including a late-Gothic winged altarpiece removed from the church when the interior was given a Baroque overlay. The museum entrance is in the courtyard. ✉ *Freyung 6,* ☎ *01/534–98–600.* ⌚ *Thurs.–Sat. 10–5, Sun. noon–5.*

27 **Uhrenmuseum** (Clock Museum). Tucked away on several floors of a lovely Renaissance structure is an amazing collection of clocks and watches. Try to be here when the hundreds of clocks strike the noon hour. ✉ *Schulhof 2,* ☎ *01/533–2265.* ⌚ *Tues.–Sun. 9–4:30.*

Vienna Environs

Wienerwald (Vienna Woods). You can reach a small corner of the historic Vienna Woods by streetcar and bus: take a streetcar or the U-2 subway line to Schottentor/University and, from there, Streetcar 38 (Grinzing) to the end of the line. To get into the woods, change in Grinzing to Bus 38A. This will take you to the Kahlenberg, which provides a superb view out over the Danube and the city. You can take the bus or hike to the Leopoldsberg, the promontory over the Danube from which Turkish invading forces were repulsed during the 16th and 17th centuries. Grinzing itself is a village out of a picture book. Unfortunately, it is sometimes a tour-bus mecca. For less touristy wine villages, try Sievering (Bus 39A), Neustift am Walde (U-4, U-6 subway to Spittelau, then Bus 35A), or the suburb of Nussdorf (Streetcar D).

Dining

In the mid-1990s Vienna, once a culinary backwater, produced a new generation of chefs willing to slaughter sacred cows and create a *Neue Küche,* a new Vienna cuisine. This trend relies on lighter versions of the old standbys and clever combinations of such traditional ingredients as *Kürbiskernöl* (pumpkin-seed oil) and fruit sauces instead of butter and cream. Austria also claims the distinction of having more organic farms than any other country in Europe, so restaurants feature some of the healthiest, freshest foods around.

In a first-class restaurant you will pay as much as in most other Western European capitals. But you can still find good food at refreshingly low prices in the simpler restaurants, particularly at neighborhood Gasthäuser (rustic inns) in the suburbs. Remember if you eat your main meal at noon (as the Viennese do), you can take advantage of the luncheon specials available at most restaurants and in cafés. For details and price-category definitions, *see* Dining *in* Austria A to Z, *above.*

$$$–$$$$ ★ ✕ **Steirereck.** Generally conceded to be the most famous restaurant in Austria, Steirereck consistently ranks high on critics' lists. You can choose from three elegant settings: the intimate Kaminstüberl with its Renaissance-style fireplace and decorative columns; the sunny, plant-filled Winter Garden; or the light, spacious room filled with French Impressionist reproductions. Fish choices are plentiful and may include delicate smoked catfish or turbot in an avocado crust. Also good is the lamb with crepes and spinach cooked simply with garlic and olive oil. At the end of the meal, you can sample an outstanding selection of cheeses from the cheese cellar. ✉ *Rasumofskyg. 2, A-1030,* ☎ *01/713–3168. Reservations essential. Jacket and tie. AE, DC, MC, V. Closed Sat.–Sun.*

$$–$$$ ★ ✕ **Artner.** This modern, pleasantly lit spot has one of the most innovative menus in the city and is unique in showcasing superb wines and goat cheeses from its own 350-year-old winery and farm in the Carnuntum region east of Vienna. Signature dishes include free-range chicken with basil risotto, or pike perch in a zucchini crust, and home-made pasta topped with fresh basil and diced ruby-red tomatoes. Lamb and veal dishes have the same tempting nouvelle flair. ✉ *Florag. 6 (entrance on Neumanng.),* ☎ *01/503–5033. AE, DC, MC, V. No lunch weekends.*

$$–$$$ ✕ **Bauer.** As soon as you're seated in this pretty 17th-century house with its bay window and dusky-rose walls, you know you're in for a treat. A variety of freshly baked breads and a light herbed spread are brought to your table while you're perusing the seasonal menu, which might include the unusual but delicious light cream of chestnut soup with truffles, fillet of *Zander* (pike perch) in a sesame crust, or a big, tender steak with homemade potato chips. ✉ *Sonnenfelsg. 17,* ☎ *01/512–9871. Reservations essential. AE. Closed Sun.–Mon. No lunch.*

$$–$$$ ✕ **Palmenhaus.** Twenty-ft-high palm trees and exotic plants decorate this airy restaurant, in the old Hofburg Palace conservatory at the back of the Burggarten. There's a blackboard that lists daily fresh-fish specials, and several vegetarian dishes are also offered, such as pumpkin gnocchi. It's also worth a stop for coffee and a pastry. In fine weather, tables are set outside on the terrace overlooking the park. Service can be slow. ✉ *Burggarten (or through Goetheg. gate after 8 PM),* ☎ *01/533–1033. Reservations essential. DC, MC, V.*

$$–$$$ ★ ✕ **Vincent.** Across the Danube canal from Schwedenplatz on a quiet residential street, Vincent has several dining rooms. The offerings change every few days, and it's possible to order à la carte from the two set menus. You might start with baby shrimp and smoked salmon in a dill cream sauce, followed by little crispy pike perch with a salad of field greens. Main courses could include a big tender filet mignon or game hen with black truffles and polenta, all washed down with a superb Austrian sauvignon blanc from the Donauland. Serving until midnight, it's a perfect choice for dining after the opera or theater. ✉ *Grosse Pfarrg. 7,* ☎ *01/214–1516. Reservations essential. AE, D, MC, V. Closed Sun. No lunch.*

$–$$$ ★ ✕ **Frank's.** A cavernous cellar-like restaurant with aged brick walls, arches, and candlelight is not exactly what you'd expect to find inside the ultramodern central post office building. People come to Frank's for fun, and to choose from the vast selection of pizzas, burgers (both chicken and beef), salads, and pastas. There are also plenty of vegetarian and fresh-fish items. From October to April, Frank's offers a popular Sunday brunch, featuring, among other American-style staples, bagels and Bloody Marys. ✉ *Laurenzerberg 2/entrance Postpassage Schwedenpl.,* ☎ *01/533–7805. Reservations essential. D, MC, V. Closed Sun. May–Sept. No lunch Sat.*

$–$$$ ✕ **MAK Cafe.** In the Museum of Applied Arts, also known as MAK, this is one of the "scene" places in Vienna. The menu changes frequently and includes lots of vegetarian items. One staple is the delicious pierogi stuffed with either potatoes or minced beef. In summer sit outside in the shaded inner courtyard. ✉ *Stubenring 3–5,* ☎ *01/714–0121. No credit cards. Closed Mon.*

$–$$$ ✕ **Neu Wien.** As the name says, this is a taste of the new Vienna. The vaulted interior is enlivened by cheeky modern art. The eclectic menu changes frequently, but look for the herbed goat-cheese salad with basil oil dressing or veal with tagliatelle in a truffle sauce. ✉ *Bäckerstr. 5, near St. Stephen's,* ☎ *01/512–0999. Reservations essential. MC, V. Closed weekends in summer. No lunch.*

$–$$ ✕ **Brezl Gwölb.** Housed in a medieval pretzel factory between Am Hof and Judenplatz, this snug restaurant fills up fast at night. Try the scrumptious *Tyroler G'röstl,* home-fried potatoes with slivered ham and onions served in a blackened skillet. Best tables are downstairs in the authentic medieval cellar, which looks like a set from *Phantom of the Opera.* ✉ *Ledererhof 9,* ☎ *01/533–8811. AE, DC, MC, V.*

$–$$ ✕ **Figlmüller.** Known for its gargantuan Wiener schnitzel—so large it usually overflows the plate—Figlmüller is always packed with diners sharing benches and long tables. Food choices are limited, and everything is à la carte. Try to get a table in the "greenhouse" passageway area. ✉ *Wollzeile 5 (passageway from Stephansdom),* ☎ *01/512–6177. No credit cards. Closed Aug.*

$–$$ ★ ✕ **Hansen.** Housed downstairs in the Börse (Vienna Stock Exchange), this unique restaurant is also an exotic, upscale flower market. The decor is modern and elegant, with close-set tables covered in white linen. The menu highlights Mediterranan-inspired dishes such as scampi risotto or spaghettini with oven-dried tomatoes in a black-olive cream sauce. There are also Austrian dishes done with a fresh, light slant. Lunch is the main event here, though you can also come for breakfast or a pretheater dinner. ✉ *Wipplingerstr. 34,* ☏ *01/532–0542. Reservations essential. AE, DC, MC, V. Closed Sun. and after 8 PM.*

$–$$ ✕ **Lebenbauer.** Vienna's premier vegetarian restaurant even has a no-smoking room, rare in this part of Europe. Specialties include soy and fennel in a curry sauce with ginger, pineapple and wild rice, spinach tortelloni in a Gorgonzola sauce, or tender flying duck breast in a marsala sauce with roasted chestnuts and pumpkin polenta. ✉ *Teinfaltstr. 3, near Freyung,* ☏ *01/533–5556–0. AE, DC, MC, V. Closed Sat.–Sun. and first 2 wks in Aug.*

Lodging

Vienna's first district (A-1010) is the best base for visitors because it's so close to most of the major sights, restaurants, and shops. This accessibility translates, of course, into higher prices. Try bargaining for discounts at the larger international chain hotels during the off-season. For details and price-category definitions, *see* Lodging *in* Austria A to Z, *above.*

$$$$ 🏨 **Bristol.** Opposite the Staatsoper (State Opera House), the Bristol has one of the finest locations in the city. The accent here is on tradition, from the brocaded walls to the Biedermeier period furnishings in the public rooms and some of the bedrooms. The building dates from 1892, and during the 1945–55 occupation it was the U.S. military headquarters. ✉ *Kärntner Ring 1, A-1010,* ☏ *01/515–16–0,* FAX *01/515–16–550,* WEB *www.westin.com/bristol. 141 rooms. 2 restaurants, café. AE, DC, MC, V.*

$$$$ 🏨 **Imperial.** The hotel is as much a palace today as when it was formally opened in 1873 by Emperor Franz Josef. The emphasis is on Old Vienna elegance and privacy; the guest list is littered with famous names, from heads of state to Michael Jackson. The beautiful rooms are furnished in antique style, though only the first three floors are part of the original house and have high ceilings; subsequent floors were added in the late 1930s. Included in the room price is limousine transfer from the airport or train station. ✉ *Kärntner Ring 16, A-1010,* ☏ *01/501–10–0,* FAX *01/501–10–410,* WEB *www.luxurycollection.com/imperial. 128 rooms. Restaurant, café. AE, DC, MC, V.*

$$$$ ★ 🏨 **Palais Schwarzenberg.** Set against a vast formal park, the palace, built in the early 1700s, seems like a country estate (though just a few minutes' walk from the heart of the city). The public salons are grand and glorious, while each guest room is individual and luxuriously appointed, with original artworks adorning the walls. A renovated wing has ultramodern suites by Italian designer Paolo Piva. You don't have to be a guest here to come for a drink, coffee, or light lunch, served outside on the terrace in summer or beside a roaring fireplace in the main sitting room in winter. ✉ *Schwarzenbergpl. 9, A–1030,* ☏ *01/798–4515–0,* FAX *01/798–4714,* WEB *www.palais-schwarzenberg.com. 44 rooms. Restaurant, bar, pool. AE, DC, MC, V.*

$$$$ ★ 🏨 **Sacher.** The grand old Sacher dates from 1876, and it has retained its sense of history over the years while providing luxurious, modern-day comfort. The corridors are a veritable art gallery, and the exquisitely furnished bedrooms also contain original artwork. The location directly behind the Opera House could hardly be more central, and the ratio

of staff to guests is more than two to one. Meals in the Red Room or Anna Sacher Room are first-rate; the Café Sacher, of course, is legendary. ✉ *Philharmonikerstr. 4, A-1010, ☎ 01/514–56–0, FAX 01/514–57–810, WEB www.sacher.com. 108 rooms. Restaurant, bar. AE, DC, MC, V.*

$$$ ★ **Altstadt.** A real gem, this small hotel was once a patrician home. Rooms are large, with all the modern comforts, though they retain an antique feel. The English-style lounge has a fireplace and plump floral sofas. The breakfast room is bright. You're one streetcar stop or a pleasant walk from the main museums. ✉ *Kircheng. 41, A-1070, ☎ 01/526–3399–0, FAX 01/523–4901. 25 rooms. AE, DC, MC, V.*

$$$ **König von Ungarn.** This utterly charming hotel is tucked away in the shadow of St. Stephen's. Rooms are furnished with country antiques (some have Styrian wood-paneled walls) and come with walk-in closets and double sinks in the sparkling bathrooms. The two suites are two-storied. ✉ *Schulerstr. 10, A-1010, ☎ 01/515–84–0, FAX 01/515–848. 33 rooms. Restaurant. DC, MC, V.*

$$–$$$ **Austria.** Tucked away on a tiny cul-de-sac, this older house offers the ultimate in quiet only five minutes' walk from the heart of the city. The high-ceilinged rooms are pleasing in their combination of dark wood and lighter walls; the decor is mixed, with Oriental carpets on many floors. The nice courtyard terrace is a perfect place to sip coffee. ✉ *Wolfeng. 3/Fleischmarkt 20, A-1010, ☎ 01/515–23–0, FAX 01/515–23–506. 46 rooms, 40 with shower, 6 with bath. AE, DC, MC, V.*

$$–$$$ ★ **Regina.** This dignified old hotel sits regally on the edge of the Altstadt, commanding a view of Sigmund Freud Park. The high-ceilinged rooms are quiet, spacious, and attractively decorated, and most have charming sitting areas. Freud, who lived nearby, used to eat breakfast in the hotel's café every morning. Buffet breakfast is included. ✉ *Rooseveltpl. 15, A-1090, ☎ 01/404–460, FAX 01/408–8392, WEB www.kremslehner.hotels.or.at. 125 rooms. Restaurant. AE, DC, MC, V.*

$$ **Kärntnerhof.** Behind the "Schönbrunn yellow" facade of this elegant 100-year-old house, set on a quiet cul-de-sac, lies one of the friendliest small hotels in the city center. The dated lobby is cheered by a gorgeously restored Biedermeier elevator. Guest rooms are functionally decorated but clean and serviceable. Pets are welcome. ✉ *Grashofg. 4, A-1010, ☎ 01/512–1923–0, FAX 01/513–2228–33. 43 rooms, 35 with shower, 8 with bath. AE, DC, MC, V.*

$$ ★ **Museum.** Located in a beautiful Belle Époque mansion just a five-minute walk from the Art History and Natural History museums, this elegant pension offers large, comfortable rooms with TV. There is also a pretty, sunny sitting room with deep, stuffed sofas and wing-back chairs, perfect for curling up in with a good book. This is a popular place, so book ahead. ✉ *Museumstr. 3, A-1070, ☎ 01/523–44–260, FAX 01/523–44–2630. 15 rooms. AE, DC, MC, V.*

$$ **Zur Wiener Staatsoper.** A great deal of loving care has gone into this family-owned hotel near the State Opera, reputed to be one of the Viennese settings in John Irving's *The Hotel New Hampshire.* Rooms are small but have high ceilings and are charmingly decorated with pretty fabrics. ✉ *Krugerstr. 11, A-1010, ☎ 01/513–1274, FAX 01/513–1274–15. 22 rooms with shower. AE, MC, V.*

$ ★ **Pension Riedl.** Across the square from the Postsparkasse—the famous 19th-century postal savings bank designed by Otto Wagner—this small establishment offers pleasant rooms with cable TV. As an added touch, breakfast is delivered in your room. Friendly owner Maria Felser is happy to arrange concert tickets and tours. ✉ *Georg-Coch-Pl. 3/4/10 (near Julius-Raab Pl.), A-1010, ☎ 01/512–7919, FAX 01/512–7919–8. 7 rooms with bath, 1 with shower. DC, MC, V. Closed last wk in Jan. and first 2 wks in Feb.*

$ ☎ **Reimer.** The cheery, comfortable Reimer is in a prime location just off the Mariahilferstrasse. Rooms have high ceilings and large windows. Breakfast is included. ✉ *Kircheng. 18, A-1070,* ☏ *01/523-6162,* FAX *01/524-3782. 14 rooms, 8 with shower, 6 with bath. MC, V.*

Nightlife and the Arts

The Arts

MUSIC

Classical concerts are held in the **Konzerthaus** (✉ Lothringerstr. 20, ☏ 01/712-1211), featuring the Vienna Symphonic Orchestra, which also occasionally plays modern and jazz pieces. The **Musikverein** (✉ Bösendorferstr. 12, ☏ 01/505-8190-0) is the home of the acclaimed Vienna Philharmonic Orchestra. Tickets can be bought at their box offices or ordered by phone. Tickets to various musical events are sold through the **Vienna Ticket Service** (☏ 01/534-1775, FAX 01/534-1328 or 01/534-1726).

THEATER AND OPERA

Check the monthly program published by the city; posters also show opera and theater schedules. The **Staatsoper,** one of world's great opera houses, presents major stars in its almost-nightly original-language performances. The **Volksoper** offers operas, operettas, and musicals, also in original-language performances. Performances at the **Akadamietheater** and **Burgtheater** are in German. Tickets for the Staatsoper, the Volksoper, and the Burg and Akademie theaters are available at the **central ticket office** (✉ Bundestheaterkassen, Hanuschg. 3, ☏ 01/514-44-2959), open weekdays 8-6, weekends and holidays 9-noon, to the left rear of the Staatsoper. Tickets go on sale a month before performances. Unsold tickets can be obtained at the evening box office. Tickets can be ordered three weeks or more in advance in writing, by fax (FAX 01/514-44-2969), or a month in advance by phone (☏ 01/513-1513). Standing-room tickets for the Staatsoper are a great bargain.

Theater is offered in English at **Vienna's English Theater** (✉ Josefsg. 12, ☏ 01/402-1260-0). The **International Theater** (✉ Porzellang. 8, ☏ 01/319-6272) is also a popular choice for seeing plays in English.

Nightlife

The central district for nightlife in Vienna is nicknamed the **Bermuda-Dreieck** (Bermuda Triangle). Centered on Judengasse/Seitenstettengasse, next to St. Ruprecht's, a small Romanesque church, the area is jammed with everything from good bistros to jazz clubs.

CABARETS

Most cabarets are expensive and unmemorable. One leading option is **Casanova** (✉ Dorotheerg. 6, ☏ 01/512-9845), which emphasizes striptease. A popular cabaret-nightclub is **Moulin Rouge** (✉ Walfischg. 11, ☏ 01/512-2130), where there are floor shows and some striptease.

CAFÉS

A quintessential Viennese institution, the coffeehouse, or café, is club, pub, and bistro all rolled into one. To savor the atmosphere of the coffeehouses you must take your time: set aside an afternoon, a morning, or at least a couple of hours, and settle down in one of your choice. There is no need to worry about overstaying your welcome, even over a single small cup of Mokka—although in some of the more opulent coffeehouses this cup of coffee and a pastry can cost as much as a meal.

Alte Backstube (✉ Langeg. 34, ☏ 01/406-1101), in a gorgeous Baroque house—with a café in front and restaurant in back—was once a bakery and is now a museum as well. **Café Central** (✉ Herreng. 14, ☏ 01/

533–3763–26) is where Trotsky played chess; in the Palais Ferstel, it's one of Vienna's most beautiful cafés. **Cafe Landtmann** (✉ Dr. Karl Leuger Str. 4, ☎ 01/532–0621), next to the dignified Burgtheater, with front-row views of the Ringstrasse, was reputedly Freud's favorite café. A 200-year-old institution, **Demel** (✉ Kohlmarkt 14, ☎ 01/535–1717–0) is the grande dame of Viennese cafés. The elegant front rooms have more atmosphere than the airy modern atrium, while the first room is reserved for nonsmokers. Order the famous coffee and compare the Sacher torte with the one served up at the Sacher—for more than a hundred years there has been an ongoing feud over who owns the original recipe. **Gerstner** (✉ Kärntnerstr. 11–15, ☎ 01/512–496377) is in the heart of the bustling Kärntnerstrasse, and one of the more modern Viennese cafés. Popular here is the Bruegel torte, a marzipan and chocolate pastry. **Museum** (✉ Friedrichstr. 6, ☎ 01/586–5202), with its original interior by the architect Adolf Loos, draws a mixed crowd and has an ample supply of newspapers. The **Sacher** (✉ Philharmonikerstr. 4, ☎ 01/512–1487) is hardly a typical Vienna café; more a shrine to plush gilt and marzipan, it's both a must-see and a must-eat, despite the crowds of tourists here to order the world's ultimate chocolate cake.

DISCOS

Atrium (✉ Schwarzenbergpl. 10, A-1040, ☎ 01/505–3594) is open Monday through Saturday and draws a lively young crowd. **Eden Bar** (✉ Lilieng. 2, ☎ 01/512–7450) is the leading spot for the well-heeled, mature crowd with a live band offered most nights. **Havana** (✉ Mahlerstr. 11, ☎ 01/513–2075) is great for salsa dancing and draws the twentysomething crowd. The **U-4** (✉ Schönbrunnerstr. 222, ☎ 01/815–8307) ranks high among the young set who like their music loud.

NIGHTCLUBS

A former 1950s cinema just off the Kärntnerstrasse, **Kruger** (✉ Krugerstr. 5, ☎ 01/512–2455) now draws the crowds with its deep leather sofas and English gentleman's club atmosphere. **First Floor** (✉ corner of Seitenstetteng. and Rabensteig., ☎ 01/533–7866) is actually one floor up from ground level and garners the attractive thirtysomething crowd. An outdoor glass elevator whisks you up to the **Skybar** (✉ Kärntnerstr. 19, ☎ 01/513–1712–25) at the top of the Steffl department store, where dramatic views and piano music set the mood.

WINE TAVERNS

Some of the city's atmospheric *Heurige*, or wine taverns, date from as far back as the 12th century. Open at lunchtime as well as evenings, the **Augustinerkeller** (✉ Augustinerstr. 1, ☎ 01/533–1026), in the Albertina building, is a cheery wine tavern with live, schmaltzy music after 6 PM. The **Esterházykeller** (✉ Haarhof 1, ☎ 01/533–3482), in a particularly mazelike network of rooms, has good wines. The **Zwölf Apostelkeller** (✉ Sonnenfelsg. 3, ☎ 01/512–6777), near St. Stephen's, has rooms that are down, down, down underground.

Shopping

Boutiques

Famous names line the **Kohlmarkt** and **Graben** and their respective side streets, as well as the side streets off **Kärntnerstrasse.**

Folk Costumes

The main resource for exquisite Austrian *Trachten* (native dress) is **Loden-Plankl** (✉ Michaelerpl. 6, ☎ 01/533–8032).

Food and Flea Markets

The **Naschmarkt** (foodstuffs market; ✉ between Rechte and Linke Wienzeile) is a sensational open-air market offering specialties from around the world. The fascinating **Flohmarkt** (flea market; subway U-4 to Kettenbrückeng.), open Saturday 8–4, operates year-round beyond the Naschmarkt. An **Arts and Antiques Market** (✉ beside Danube Canal near Salztorbrücke) has a mixed selection, including some high-quality offerings. It's open May–September, Saturday 2–6 and Sunday 10–6. Check Am Hof square for antiques and collectibles on Thursday and Friday from late spring to early fall. Also look for the seasonal markets in Freyung Square.

Shopping Districts

Kärntnerstrasse is lined with luxury boutiques and large emporiums. The Viennese do much of their in-town shopping in the many department and specialty stores of **Mariahilferstrasse.**

Vienna Essentials

AIRPORTS AND TRANSFERS

All flights use Schwechat Airport, about 16 km (10 mi) southwest of Vienna.

➤ AIRPORT INFORMATION: **Schwechat Airport** (☎ 01/7007–0).

TRANSFERS

Buses leave the airport for the city air terminal, Wien-Mitte Landstrasse Hauptstrasse (✉ Am Stadtpark, ☎ 01/5800–33369), by the Hilton, on every half hour from 5 to 6:30 AM and every 20 minutes from 6:50 AM to 11:30 PM; after that, buses depart every hour until 5 AM. Buses also run every hour (Apr.–Sept., weekends every ½ hr) from the airport to the Westbahnhof (West Train Station) and the Südbahnhof (South Train Station). The one-way fare for all buses is AS70/€5.09. The S7 train (called the *Schnellbahn*) shuttles every half hour between the airport and the Landstrasse/Wien-Mitte (city center) and Wien-Nord (north Vienna) stations; the fare is AS34/€2.47 and it takes about 35 minutes. Follow the signs picturing a train to the basement of the airport. A taxi from the airport to downtown Vienna costs about AS400/€29.07–AS500/€36.34; agree on a price in advance. Cabs (legally) do not meter this drive, as airport fares are more or less fixed (legally again) at about double the meter fare. The cheapest cab service is C+K Airport Service, charging a set price of AS290/€21, though you should give another AS30/€2.18 as tip. C+K will also meet your plane at no extra charge if you let them know in advance.

➤ CONTACTS: **C+K Airport Service** (☎ 01/44444).

BIKE TRAVEL

Vienna has hundreds of miles of marked cycle routes, including reserved routes through the center of the city. Paved cycling routes parallel the Danube. For details, get the city brochure on cycling. Bicycles can be rented at a number of locations and can be taken on the Vienna subway (with the exception of the U-6 line) year-round all day Sunday and holidays from 9 to 3, after 6:30 on weekdays, and, from May through September, after 9 AM Saturday. You'll need a half-fare ticket for the bike.

BUS TRAVEL WITHIN VIENNA

Inner-city buses are numbered 1A through 3A and operate weekdays until about 7:40 PM, Saturday until 7 PM. Reduced fares are available for these routes (buy a *Kurzstreckenkarte*; it allows you four trips for AS38/€2.76) as well as designated shorter stretches (roughly two to four stops) on all other bus and streetcar lines. Streetcars and buses are numbered or lettered according to route, and they run until about midnight. Night buses marked *N* follow 22 special routes every half hour between 12:30 AM and 4:30 AM. Get a route plan from any of the public transport or VORVERKAUF offices. The fare is AS25/€1.82, payable on the bus unless you have a 24-hour, three-day, or eight-day ticket; then you need only pay an AS10/€.73 supplement. The central terminus is Schwedenplatz. Streetcars 1 and 2 run the circular route around the Ring clockwise and counterclockwise, respectively.

CAR TRAVEL

The main access routes are the expressways to the west and south (Westautobahn A1, Südautobahn A2). Routes leading to the downtown area are marked ZENTRUM.

Unless you know your way around the city, a car is more of a nuisance than a help. The center of the city is a pedestrian zone, and city on-street parking is a problem. Observe signs; tow-away is expensive. In winter, overnight parking is forbidden on city streets with streetcar lines. Overnight street parking in districts I, VI, VII, VIII, and IX is restricted to residents with stickers; check before you leave a car on the street, even for a brief period. However, you can park in the inner city for free on Saturday, Sunday, and holidays and at night from 7 PM until midnight, but check street signs first.

CONSULATES

➤ UNITED KINGDOM: (✉ Jauresg. 10, near Schloss Belvedere, ☎ 01/71613–5151).

➤ UNITED STATES: (✉ Gartenbaupromenade, Parkring 12A, in Marriott building, ☎ 01/313–39).

EMERGENCIES

If you need a doctor, ask your hotel, or in an emergency, phone your embassy or consulate. In each neighborhood, one pharmacy (*Apotheke*) in rotation is open all night and weekends; the address is posted on each area pharmacy.

➤ EMERGENCY SERVICES: **Ambulance** (☎ 144). **Police** (☎ 133).

ENGLISH-LANGUAGE MEDIA

➤ BOOKSTORES: **Big Ben Bookshop** (✉ Alserstr. 4, Courtyard 1, No. 17, ☎ 01/409–3567). **British Bookshop** (✉ Weihburgg. 24–26, ☎ 01/512–1945–0; ✉ Mariahilferstr. 4, ☎ 01/522–6730). **Shakespeare & Co.** (✉ Sterng. 2, ☎ 01/535–5053).

SUBWAY TRAVEL

Subway (U-bahn) lines—stations are marked with a huge blue "U"—are designated U-1, U-2, U-3, U-4, and U-6, and are clearly marked and color-coded. Trains run daily until about 12:30 AM. Additional services are provided by fast suburban trains, the S-bahn, indicated by a stylized blue "S" symbol. Both are tied into the general city fare system.

TAXIS

Cabs can be flagged on the street if the FREI (free) sign is lit. You can also dial ☎ 60160, 31300, or 40100 to request one. All rides around town are metered. The initial fare is AS35/€2.54, but expect to pay AS80/€5.81–AS100/€7.27 for an average city ride. There are additional charges for luggage, and a surcharge of AS16/€1.16 is added at night, on Sunday, and for telephone orders. Tip the driver AS5/€.36–AS8/€.58 by rounding up the fare.

TOURS

BUS TOURS

Tours will take you to cultural events and nightclubs, and there are daytime bus trips to the Danube Valley, Salzburg, and Budapest, among other spots. Check with the City Tourist Office or your hotel.

The following are city orientation tours. Prices are similar, but find out whether you will visit or just drive past Schönbrunn and Belvedere palaces and whether admission fees are included. Cityrama provides city tours with hotel pickup. Vienna Sightseeing Tours offers a short highlights tour or a lengthier one to the Vienna Woods, Mayerling, and other sights near Vienna. Tours start in front of or beside the Staatsoper on the Operngasse.

➤ FEES AND SCHEDULES: **Cityrama** (☎ 01/534–130). **Vienna Sightseeing Tours** (☎ 01/712–4683–0).

WALKING TOURS

Guided walking tours in English are available almost daily and include such topics as "Jewish Vienna." Check with the City Tourist Office or your hotel.

TRAIN TRAVEL

Vienna has four train stations. The Westbahnhof is for trains to and from Linz, Salzburg, and Innsbruck and to and from Germany, France, and Switzerland. The Südbahnhof is for trains to and from Graz, Klagenfurt, Villach, and Italy. The Franz-Josefs-Bahnhof, or Nordbahnhof, is for trains to and from Prague, Berlin, and Warsaw. Go to the Wien-Mitte/Landstrasse Hauptstrasse station for local trains to and from the north of the city. Budapest trains use both the Westbahnhof and Südbahnhof, and Bratislava trains both Wien-Mitte and the Südbahnhof, so check.

TRANSPORTATION AROUND VIENNA

Vienna addresses include a roman numeral that designates in which of the city's 23 districts the address is located. The first district (I, the inner city) is bounded by the Ringstrasse and the Danube Canal. The 2nd through 9th (II–IX) districts surround the inner city, starting with the 2nd district across the Danube Canal and running clockwise; the 10th through the 23rd (X–XXIII) districts form a second concentric ring of suburbs.

Vienna is fairly easy to explore on foot; much of the heart of the city—the area within the Ringstrasse—is a pedestrian zone. Public transportation is comfortable, convenient, and frequent, though not cheap. Tickets for buses, subways, and streetcars are available in subway stations and from dispensers on buses and streetcars. Tickets in multiples of five are sold at cigarette shops—look for the sign TABAK-TRAFIK—or at the window marked VORVERKAUF at such central stations as Karlsplatz or Stephansplatz. A block of five tickets costs AS95/€6.90, a single ticket AS19/€1.38, a 24-hour ticket AS60/€4.36, a three-day tourist ticket AS150/€10.90, and an eight-day ticket AS300/€21.80. Maps and information in English are available at the Stephansplatz, Karlsplatz, and Praterstern U-bahn stations.

The Vienna Card, available for AS210/€15.26 at tourist and transportation information offices and most hotels, gives you unlimited travel for 72 hours on city buses, streetcars, and the subway; reductions on selected museum entry fees; plus tips and discounts on various attractions and selected shopping throughout the city.

TRAVEL AGENCIES

➤ LOCAL AGENTS: **American Express** (✉ Kärntnerstr. 21–23, ☎ 01/515–40–0). **Ökista** (✉ Garnisong. 7, A-1090, ☎ 01/401–480). **Österreichisches Verkehrsbüro** (Austrian Travel Agency; ✉ Friedrichstr. 7, A-1010, ☎ 01/588–000, FAX 01/58800–280).

VISITOR INFORMATION

➤ TOURIST INFORMATION: **City Tourist Office** (✉ Am Albertinapl. 1, A-1010, ☎ 01/211–14–222).

THE DANUBE VALLEY

Austria contains some of the most beautiful stretches of the Danube (Donau), extending about 88 km (55 mi) west of Vienna. The river rolls through the celebrated Wachau, a gloriously scenic valley that offers magnificent countryside, some of Austria's best food and wine, and comfortable—in some cases elegant—accommodations. Above the river are the ruins of ancient castles. The abbeys at Melk and Göttweig, with their magnificent libraries, dominate their settings. Vineyards sweep down to the river, which is lined with fruit trees that burst into blossom every spring. People here live close to the land, and at certain times of year vintners open their homes to sell their own wines and produce. Roadside stands offer flowers, fruits, vegetables, and wines. This is also a region of legend: the Danube shares with the Rhine the story of the mythical Nibelungen, defenders of Siegfried, hero of German myth.

The most delightful way to approach the Wachau is by boat, but car and train routes are also scenically splendid. From Vienna you can follow the southern Danube bank, crossing at Melk and returning along the north bank. Vienna to Melk is about 112 km (70 mi), the return along the north bank about 109 km (68 mi).

Klosterneuburg

The massive **Stift Klosterneuburg** (abbey) dominating this market town was established in 1114; treasures in its museum include an enameled altar dating from 1181. The abbey is a major agricultural landowner in the region, and its extensive vineyards produce excellent wines. ✉ *Stiftspl. 1,* ☎ *02243/411–0,* WEB *www.stift-klosterneuburg.at.* ⏲ *1-hr. tour Mon.–Sat. at 9:30, 10:30, 1:30, 2:30, 3:30, 4:30, Sun. at 11, 2 (English language), 1:30, 2:30, 3:30, 4:30.*

Designed by Heinz Tesar, the new **Sammlung Essl** contemporary art museum, features the work of artists created after 1945. The permanent collection includes pieces by regional artists, such as Hermann Nietsch and Arnulf Rainer, and changing exhibits have celebrated contemporary notables like Nam June Paik. The emphasis here is on "new," and the museum also hosts special evening concerts highlighting the work of various modern composers. To get to the Sammlung Essl museum, take the U-4 to Heilegenstadt, then transfer to Bus 239 to Klosterneuberg. ✉ *An der Donau–Au 1,* ☎ *0800/232–800,* FAX *02243/370–5022.* ⏲ *Tues.–Sun. 10–5, Wed. 10–9.*

Göttweig

You will see **Stift Göttweig** high above the Danube Valley long before you reach it. This impressive 11th-century Benedictine abbey affords sensational panoramas of the Danube Valley; you can stroll the grounds and visit the chapel. ✉ *Rte. 303, on south bank of Danube, opposite Krems, Furth bei Göttweig,* ☎ *02732/85581–231.* ⏲ *Daily 10–5; tours (minimum 8 people) Easter–Oct., daily at 10, 11, 2, 3, and 4.*

$$$–$$$$ ★ ✕🏨 **Landhaus Bacher.** This is one of Austria's best restaurants, elegant but entirely lacking in pretension. The innovative style of Lisl Wagner-Bacher, the top female chef in the country, is constantly changing, but lamb and fish specialties are always present. Be sure to try the potato soup with truffles, served in a huge, hollowed-out potato, or the fresh cheese ravioli in an artichoke ragout. Try dining in the garden in summer. ✉ *Südtirolerpl. 208, Mautern,* ☎ *02732/82937–0. Reservations essential. DC, V. Closed Mon.–Tues. and Jan. 7–Feb.*

Melk

The **Benediktinerstift Melk** (Benedictine Abbey of Melk) is one of the most impressive in Europe, commandingly perched above the Danube.

Danube Valley

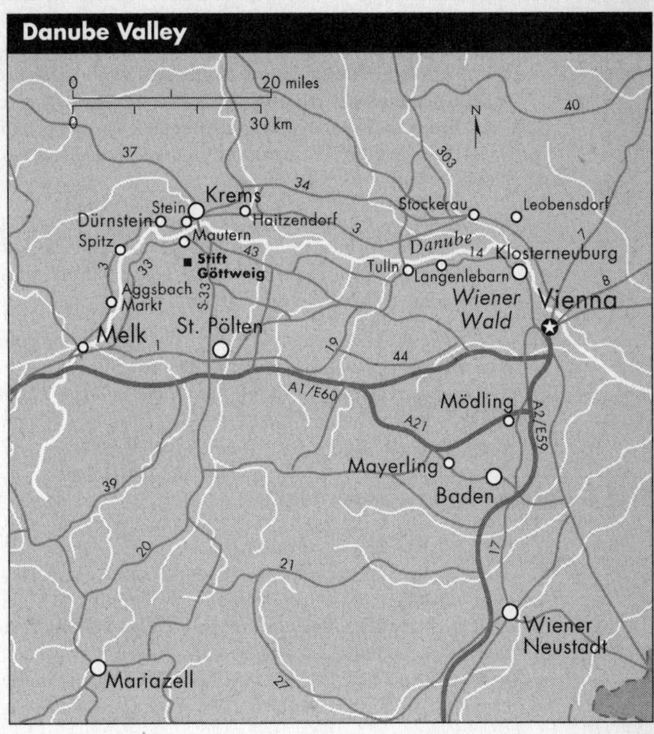

This is one of Austria's monumental, major sights, with its library rich in art as well as books; the ceiling frescoes are particularly memorable. ✉ *Abt Berthold Dietmayr-Str. 1,* ☎ *02752/555-232,* FAX *02752/555-249.* ⏲ *Apr. 15–Nov. 15, daily 9–6 (ticket office closes at 5); Nov. 16–Apr. 14, daily 9–5 (ticket office closes at 4).*

$$–$$$$ ★ **Stadt Melk.** Nestled below the golden abbey in the center of the village square, this elegant restaurant has been well known ever since the Duke and Duchess of Windsor dined here long ago. Though the decor is decidedly Biedermeier, the food is nouvelle Austrian, and may include duck in a honey glaze or chicken breast stuffed with leeks and accompanied by corn and potato croquettes. There are also 16 rather plain guest rooms upstairs if you feel like making a night of it. ✉ *Hauptpl. 1, A-3390,* ☎ *02752/52475,* FAX *02752/52475–19. AE, DC, MC, V.*

Dürnstein

Across the river from Melk, the romantic road hugs the Danube, heading north toward Dürnstein and Krems. The beautiful medieval town of Dürnstein is associated with Richard the Lion-hearted, who was imprisoned in its now-ruined castle for 13 months in 1192–93. The town is also known for its fine hotels, restaurants, and wines and for its gloriously Baroque Stiftskirche (church).

$$$$ ★ **Richard Löwenherz.** This former cloister, justifiably a Romantik hotel member, sits above the Danube. Room furnishings include antiques and every comfort. The restaurant is excellent, as are the house wines. ✉ *Dürnstein 8, A-3061,* ☎ *02711/222,* FAX *02711/222–18. 40 rooms. Restaurant, bar, pool. AE, DC, MC, V. Closed Nov.–Mar.*

Krems/Stein an der Donau

Remnants of the ancient city wall are prominent in this town more than 1,000 years old, with its Renaissance, Gothic, and Baroque monuments.

Krems and Stein sit at the center of Austria's foremost wine-growing region. You can explore the town center, the churches, and view the Danube from lookout points perched high above the town. **Weinkolleg Kloster Und** is a wine museum in a beautifully restored cloister in Und, tucked between Krems and Stein. ✉ *Undstr. 6,* ☎ *02732/73073–0.* 💶 *AS200/€14.53, including tasting.* ⏲ *Daily 11–7. Closed Dec. 23–mid-Mar.*

Stein, with its 16th-century houses, is virtually part of adjacent Krems. Look for the former **Imperial Toll House** and the 14th-century **Minoritenkirche,** a church that now serves as a museum with temporary exhibitions, just off the main street.

$$ 🏨 **Alte Post.** A 16th-century house with an arcade courtyard, the inn is conveniently positioned right in the center of Krems. In good weather the courtyard is used for dining. ✉ *Obere Landstr. 32, A–3500, Krems,* ☎ *02732/82276–0,* FAX *02732/84396. 24 rooms, 8 with bath. Restaurant. No credit cards. Closed Jan.–mid-Mar.*

The Danube Valley Essentials

BOAT AND FERRY TRAVEL

Travel upstream, with stops at Krems, Dürnstein, Melk, and points between. Return to Vienna by boat or by train from Melk (combination tickets available). Check in Vienna with DDSG Blue Danube Schiffahrt for ferry schedules.

➤ BOAT AND FERRY INFORMATION: **DDSG Blue Danube Schiffahrt** (✉ Friedrichstr. 7, Vienna, ☎ 01/588–800, FAX 01/588–80–440).

CAR TRAVEL

If you're pressed for time, take the Autobahn to St. Pölten, turn north onto Route S-33, and follow the signs to Melk. For a more scenic route, follow the south shore of the Danube via Klosterneuburg and Greifenstein, taking Routes 14, 19, 43, and 33. Cross the Danube at Melk, and then return to Vienna along the north bank of the river (Rte. 3).

TOURS

Vienna travel agencies offer tours of the Wachau ranging from one-day outings to longer excursions.

TRAIN TRAVEL

Depart from the Westbahnhof for Melk, and then take the bus along the north bank of the Danube to Dürnstein and Krems. Side bus trips can be made from Krems to Göttweig.

VISITOR INFORMATION

➤ TOURIST INFORMATION: **Lower Austria Tourist Office** (✉ Walfischg. 6, Vienna, ☎ 01/513–8022, FAX 01/513–8022–30). **Dürnstein** (✉ Parkpl. Ost, ☎ 02711/219). **Klosterneuburg** (✉ Niedermarkt 4, Postfach 6, ☎ 02243/32038). **Krems/Stein an der Donau** (✉ Undstr. 6, ☎ 02732/82676). **Melk** (✉ Babenbergerstr. 1, ☎ 02752/52307–410).

SALZBURG

Salzburg, best known as the birthplace of Wolfgang Amadeus Mozart, receives its greatest number of visitors every summer during its music festival, the world-famous Salzburger Festspiele. Dominated by a fortress on one side and the Kapuzinerberg, a small mountain, on the other, this Baroque city is best explored on foot, for many of its most interesting areas are pedestrian precincts. Besides the festival, the city has innumerable other attractions. Thanks to the powerful prince-archbishops of the Habsburg era, few other places offer an equivalent abundance of Baroque splendor. Many sites are identifiable from the film that made Salzburg a household name in the United States, *The Sound of Music.* No matter what season you visit, bring an umbrella: Salzburg is noted for sudden, brief downpours.

Exploring Salzburg

Numbers in the margin correspond to points of interest on the Salzburg map.

The Salzach River separates Salzburg's old and "new" towns; for the best perspective on the old, climb the Kapuzinerberg (follow pathways from Linzergasse or Steingasse). For another postcard view, look toward the fortress through the Mirabell gardens, behind Mirabell palace. The sweeping panorama from the fortress itself offers the reverse of both perspectives. Wander along Getreidegasse, with its quaint wrought-iron shop signs and the Mönchsberg standing sentinel at the far end. Don't neglect the warren of interconnecting side alleys: these shelter a number of fine shops and often open onto impressive inner courtyards that are guaranteed to be overflowing with flowers in summer.

14 **Alter Markt** (Old Market Square). In the heart of the Altstadt (Old City) is the Alter Markt, the old marketplace and center of secular life in past centuries. Salzburg's narrowest house is squeezed into the north side of the picturesque 17th-century square, filled in summer with flower stalls. Look into the former court pharmacy (Hof-Apotheke) for a touch of centuries past. ✉ *Judeng., Getreideg., Goldg.*

6 **Carolino Augusteum Museum** (Historical Museum). The city museum is devoted to art, archaeology, and fascinating musical instruments. ✉ *Museumspl. 1,* ☎ *0662/841134–0.* ⏲ *July–Sept., Tues.–Wed., Fri.–Sun. 10–6, Thurs. 9–8; Oct.–June, Tues.–Wed., Fri.–Sun. 9–5, Thurs. 9–8.*

★ 10 **Dom** (Cathedral). The cathedral-square setting is close to perfection, while the sheer mass of the cathedral itself gives a suggestion of the onetime power of the prince-archbishops who ruled the region. You enter through great bronze doors. A small museum shows off centuries of church treasures. ✉ *Dompl. 1,* ☎ *0662/840442.* ⏲ *May 20–Oct. 29, Mon.–Sat. 10–5, Sun. 1–6.*

★ 11 **Festung Hohensalzburg** (Salzburg Fortress). To reach the 12th-century fortress that dominates the city, walk up the narrow Festungsgasse at the back end of Kapitalplatz. From here, you can either follow the footpath up the hill or take a five-minute ride on the funicular, or Festungsbahn. On a sunny day you can hike up Festungsgasse, turning frequently to enjoy the changing panorama of the city below. The terrace restaurant overlooks a *stunning* panorama. A main attraction is **St. George's Chapel,** built in 1501. A year later, in 1502, the chapel acquired the 200-pipe barrel organ, which is played daily in summer at 7 AM, 11 AM, and 6 PM. ✉ *Mönchsberg 34,* ☎ *0662/842430–11.* ⏲ *Oct.–May., daily 8–6; June–Sept., daily 8–7; 50-min tour every ½ hr Nov.–Mar., daily 10–4:30; Apr.–June and Sept.–Oct., daily 9:30–5; July–Aug., daily 9–5:30.*

9 **Franziskanerkloster** (Franciscan Monastery). A tall, graceful spire marks this 13th-century church, whose modest Romanesque nave soars abruptly into a Gothic fan vault over the Baroque altar. Check for mass—frequently one of Mozart's—on Sunday at 9 AM. ✉ *Franziskanerg. 5,* ☎ *0662/843629–0.* ⏲ *Daily 6:30 AM–7:30 PM.*

2 **Friedhof St. Sebastian** (Cemetery of St. Sebastian). This secluded spot is the setting for the scene near the end of *The Sound of Music* when

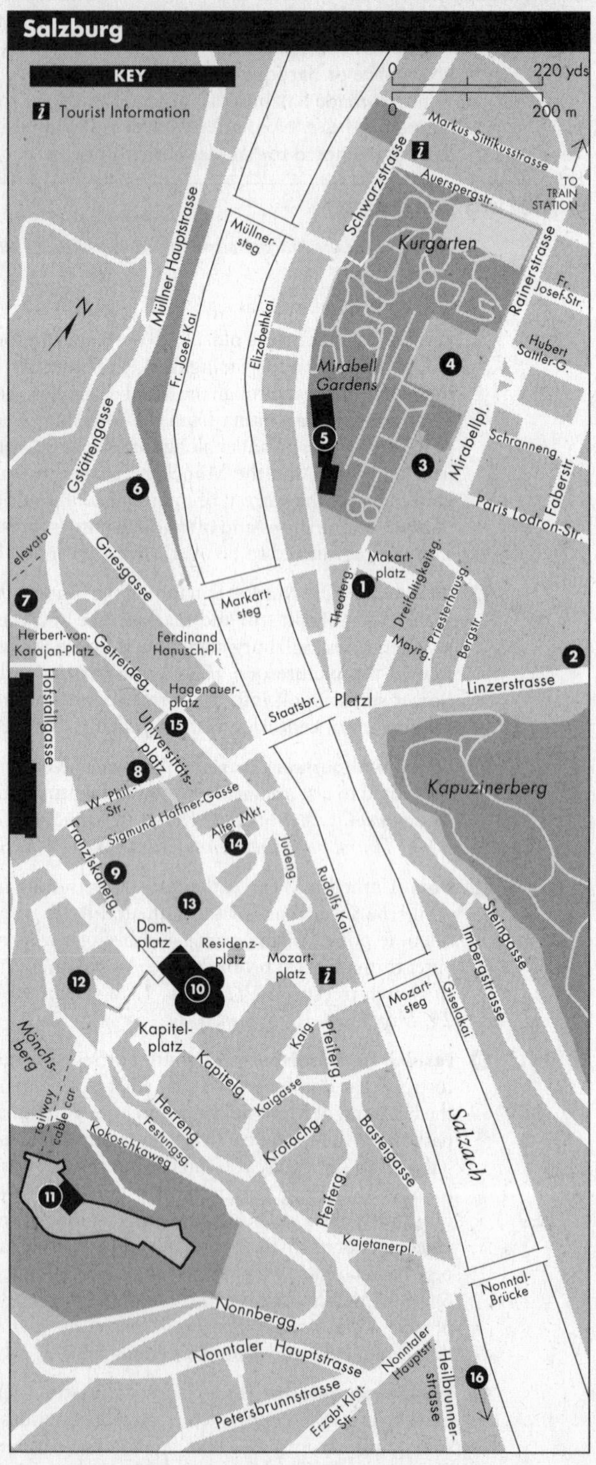

Salzburg
KEY
Tourist Information
0
220 yds
200 m
N
Markus Sittikusstrasse
TO TRAIN STATION
Auerspergstr.
Schwarzstrasse
Kurgarten
Rainerstrasse
Fr. Josef-Str.
Hubert Sattler-G.
Müllner Hauptstrasse
Müllnersteg
Fr. Josef Kai
Elisabethkai
Mirabell Gardens
Mirabellpl.
Schranneng.
Faberstr.
Paris Lodron-Str.
Gstättengasse
Griesgasse
elevator
Makartplatz
Dreifaltigkeitsg.
Priesterhausg.
Theaterg.
Markartsteg
Herbert-von-Karajan-Platz
Getreideg.
Ferdinand Hanusch-Pl.
Mayrg.
Bergstr.
Linzerstrasse
Hagenauerplatz
Staatsbr.
Platzl
Hofstallgasse
Universitätsplatz
Kapuzinerberg
W. Phil.-Str.
Sigmund Haffner-Gasse
Alter Mkt.
Judeng.
Rudolfs Kai
Franziskanerg.
Steingasse
Imbergstrasse
Domplatz
Residenzplatz
Mozartplatz
Mozartsteg
Giselakai
Mönchsberg
Kapitelplatz
Kaig.
Pfeiferg.
Kapitelg.
Kaigasse
railway
cable car
Herreng.
Kokoschkaweg
Festungsg.
Krotachg.
Basteigasse
Salzach
Pfeiferg.
Kajetanerpl.
Nonntal-Brücke
Nonnbergg.
Nonntaler Hauptstrasse
Nonntaler Hauptstr.
Heilbrunnerstrasse
Petersbrunnstrasse
Erzabt Klot-Str.

the von Trapps are nearly captured. The cemetery was commissioned in the late 16th century by Prince-Archbishop Wolf Dietrich and built in the arcaded style of an Italian *campo santo*. Wolf Dietrich's brightly tiled mausoleum is unusual for Austria. Also buried here are Mozart's widow, Constanze, and his father, Leopold (by the central path leading to the mausoleum). ✉ *Linzerg. 41.* ⏲ *Daily 7–7.*

★ 8 **Kollegienkirche** or Universitätskirche (University Church). Completed by Fischer von Erlach in 1707, this is one of the purest examples of Baroque architecture in Austria. Unencumbered by rococo decorations, the modified Greek-cross plan has a majestic dignity worthy of Palladio. ✉ *Universitätspl.,* ☎ *0662/841–327–72.* ⏲ *Apr.–Oct., Mon.–Sat. 9–7, Sun. 10–7; Nov.–Mar., Mon–Sat. 9–4, Sun. 10–4.*

1 **Mozart-Wohnhaus** (Mozart Residence). The house where the Mozart family lived for some years includes a small recital hall and the Mozart Audio and Film Museum. Purchasing combination tickets with Mozarts Geburtshaus is cheaper than buying tickets at each place individually. ✉ *Makartpl. 8,* ☎ *0662/874227–40.* ⏲ *Daily 10–6 (last tickets at 5:30 PM).*

5 **Mozarteum und Marionettentheater** (Mozart Center and Marionette Theater). This is the main research facility devoted to the work of Salzburg's most famous native son, Wolfgang Amadeus Mozart. Inside the complex are the **University Mozarteum** (☎ 0662/88908–0); the **International Mozarteum Foundation** (✉ Schwarzstr. 26, ☎ 0662/88940), whose courtyard contains the summerhouse (accessible only by special appointment) in which Mozart wrote *The Magic Flute*; and the **Marionettentheater,** home to the extraordinary Salzburg Marionette Theater. The south end of the Mozarteum complex on Makartplatz includes the **Landestheater** (Provincial Theater), where operas, operetta, ballet, and dramas are staged during winter months when the larger festival buildings are closed. ✉ *Marionettentheater, Schwarzstr. 24,* ☎ *0662/872406–0,* FAX *0662/882141.* *AS250/€18.17–AS500/€36.34.* ⏲ *Box office Mon.–Sat. 9–1 and 2 hrs before marionette performance; Salzburg season May–Sept., Dec. 25, Mozart Week (Jan.), Easter.*

★ 15 **Mozarts Geburtshaus** (Mozart's Birthplace). The house at the head of the tiny Hagenauerplatz in which the famed composer was born is now a museum packed with Mozart memorabilia. Purchasing combination tickets with the Mozart-Wohnhaus is cheaper than buying tickets at each place individually. ✉ *Getreideg. 9,* ☎ *0662/844313.* ⏲ *Daily 9–6 (last tickets at 5:30 PM).*

13 **Residenz** (Residence). The palatial complex on Residenzplatz includes the prince-archbishops' historic and sumptuous living quarters and ceremonial reception rooms. The **Residenzgalerie** has an outstanding collection of 16th- through 19th-century European art. Combination tickets can provide entry to both sites. ✉ *Residenzpl. 1,* ☎ *0662/8042–2690; 0662/840451 art collection.* ⏲ *Residence daily 10–5 (closed two wks before Easter). Tours by arrangement. Art collection daily 10–5 (closed Wed. Oct.–Mar.).*

3 **Salzburger Barockmuseum** (Salzburg Baroque Museum). A focal point of the celebrated Mirabell Gardens, the museum stands between Mirabellplatz and the Orangerie. The museum displays 17th- and 18th-century paintings and sketches, including works by the Neopolitan painter Luca Giordano and the Austrian Baroque painter Johann Michael Rottmayr, as well as a Bernini sculpture. You can wander through the Baroque gardens behind the city's main theater complex and discover a dramatic view of the Old City with the fortress in the background. ✉ *Orangeriegarten,* ☎ *0662/877432.* ⏲ *Daily 9–5 during Summer Festival; rest of year, Tues.–Sat. 9–noon, 2–5, Sun. 10–1.*

16 **Schloss Hellbrunn** (Hellbrunn Castle). Take Bus 55 from the city center to Hellbrun, 6 km (4 mi) south of Salzburg, to reach this popular attraction. The castle was built in the 17th century, and its rooms have some fine trompe-l'oeil decorations. To entertain Salzburg's great prince-archbishops, its gardens contain an ingenious system of **Wasserspiele**—hidden jets of water conceived by someone with an impish sense of humor: expect to get sprinkled by surprise. ✉ *Fürstenweg, 37, Hellweg,* ☎ *0662/820372.* ⏲ *Apr. and Oct., daily 9–4:30; May–Sept., daily 9–5:30. Evening tours in July–Aug., hourly 6–10* PM.

In the Hellbrunn park complex is the **Tiergarten** (zoo; ☎ 0662/820176, ⏲ Oct.–Feb., daily 8:30–4; Mar.–Apr., daily 8:30–4:30; May–mid-June, daily 8:30–6; mid-June–mid-Sept., Fri.–Sat. 8:30 AM–9 PM; Sept. 15–30, daily 8:30–5:30), outstanding for the way in which the animals are housed in natural surroundings. The **Monatsschlössl,** the historic hunting lodge, houses a small folklore museum.

4 **Schloss Mirabell** (Mirabell Palace and Gardens). Built by Prince-Archbishop Wolf Dietrich for his mistress, the elegant complex now houses the city's registrar; many couples come here to be married. The foyer and staircase, decorated with cherubs, are splendid examples of Baroque excess. The gardens are where the von Trapp children "Do-re-mi-ed" in *The Sound of Music.* ✉ *Mirabellpl., off Makartpl.,* ☎ *0662/848586.* ⏲ *Mon.–Tues., Fri. 9–1; Wed.–Thurs. 1–5.*

7 **Spielzeugmuseum** (Toy Museum). Once a hospital, the Bürgerspital now houses a toy and musical instruments museum within its Renaissance arcades. There's a combined ticket with the Carolino Augusteum Museum, cathedral excavations, and the Folklore Museum at Schloss Hellbrunn. Nearby on Herbert-von-Karajan-Platz is the 15th-century royal **Pferdeschwemme** (Horse Drinking Trough). ✉ *Bürgerspitalg. 2,* ☎ *0662/847560,* ⏲ *July–Sept., Tues.–Sun. 10–6; Oct.–June, Tues.–Sun. 9–5.*

12 **Stift St. Peter** (St. Peter's Abbey). Late-Baroque style marks this sumptuous edifice tucked beneath the mountain. Originally a Romanesque basilica, it preserves a front portal dating from 1245. Inside, the low-ceilinged aisles are painted in rococo candy-box style. The cemetery lends an added air of mystery to the monks' caves cut into the cliff. The catacombs attached to the church can be visited by guided tour. ✉ *St. Peter Bezirk, just off Kapitalpl.,* ☎ *0662/844578–0.* ⏲ *May–Sept., Tues.–Sun. 10:30–5; Oct.–Apr., Wed.–Thurs. 10:30–3:30, Fri.–Sun. 10:30–4.*

The Arts

Festivals

Information and tickets for the main **Salzburger Festspiele** (Salzburg Festival), held in late July and August, as well as the Easter Festival (early April) and the Pentecost Concerts (late May), can be obtained from Salzburger Festspiele (✉ Postfach 140, A-5010 Salzburg, FAX 0662/8045–760 Summer Festival; 0662/8045–790 Easter Festival, WEB www.salzburgfestival.com). Write or fax ahead, as it is difficult (but not impossible) to obtain tickets for festival performances once you are in Salzburg.

Opera, Music, and Art

Theater and opera are presented in the three auditoriums of the **Festspielhaus** (✉ Hofstallg. 1, ☎ 0662/8045–579 ticket office). Opera, operettas, ballet, and drama are offered at the **Landestheater** (✉ Schwarzstr. 22, ☎ 0662/871–512–21). Concerts are the specialty at the **Mozarteum** (✉ Schwarzstr. 26, ☎ 0662/873154). Chamber music has a grand venue at the **Schloss Mirabell** (✉ Mirabellpl., off Makartpl., ☎ 0662/848586 tickets). Special art exhibitions are often held in the **Rupertinum** (✉ Wiener-Philharmoniker-G. 9, ☎ 0662/8042–2336). An outstanding art venue is the **Galerie Welz** (✉ Sigmund-Haffner-G. 16, ☎ 0662/841771–0, FAX 0662/841771–20).

Dining

This is a tourist town, and popular restaurants are always crowded, so make reservations well ahead, particularly during festival times. Most restaurants are open daily during festival season. For details and price-category definitions, *see* Dining *in* Austria A to Z, *above.*

$$–$$$$ ✕ **Bei Bruno.** A short walk from Schloss Mirabell, this intimate restaurant in the luxurious Bristol hotel is a perfect choice for after-concert dining. The food is nouvelle Austrian, specializing in fresh fish, lightly prepared, and the menu changes frequently to showcase what's in season, such as the delicious *Kurbisrisotto* (pumpkin risotto) with black truffles, and garlic and rosemary game hen with lentils and polenta soufflé. ✉ *Makartpl. 4,* ☎ *0662/878417. AE, DC, MC, V, Closed Sun.*

$$–$$$$ ★ ✕ **Pfefferschiff.** The "Pepper Ship" is the top-ranked eatery in Salzburg, located 2–3 km (1–2 mi) northeast of the center in a pretty rectory adjacent to a pink-and-cream chapel. Klaus Fleischhaker, an award-winning chef, and his wife Petra make sure guests feel pampered in the country-chic atmosphere, which features polished wooden floors, antique hutches, and tables set with fine bone china. Look for scampi tempura with asparagus and arugula, lobster crepes, or *Seeteufel* (monkfish) in an olive crust with pesto polenta. For dessert try the sublime rhubarb tartelette with buttermilk ice cream. A taxi is the least stressful way of getting here, but if you have your own car, drive along the north edge of the Kapuzinerberg toward Hallwang and then Söllheim. ✉ *Söllheim 3, A-5300 Hallwang,* ☎ *0662/661242,* FAX *0662/661841. Reservations essential. AE.*

$$–$$$ ✕ **Zum Eulenspiegel.** Delicious food matches the unique setting in this house, which is hundreds of years old. Tables are set with white linen in wonderful nooks and crannies reached by odd staircases. It's right in the middle of the Old City, and the staff speaks English. Try the potato goulash with chunks of sausage and beef in a creamy paprika sauce, or the house specialty, fish stew Provençale. These are served at lunch, or all day in the bar downstairs. ✉ *Hagenauerpl. 2,* ☎ *0662/843180–0,* FAX *0662/843180–6. Reservations essential. AE, DC, MC, V. Closed Sun. except during festival, and Jan.–mid-Mar.*

$–$$$ ✕ **St. Peter Stiftskeller.** This is one of oldest restaurants in Europe. The courtyard, with its gray stone archways and vine-trellised walls, couldn't be more dramatic. The food, however, tends to be on the heavy side with an emphasis on pork, sauerkraut, and dumplings. Still, it's worth the experience. ✉ *St. Peter District I/4,* ☎ *0662/841–2680. MC, V.*

$–$$ ✕ **Bistro Bio Terra.** Located inside the Rupertinum Galerie, this casual vegetarian restaurant serves tasty dishes entirely free of animal products or preservatives. The chef takes Italian recipes and creates his own vegetarian versions. The blackboard menu changes daily, but look for bruschetta with a variety of toppings or tomato tagliatelle in a tomato cream sauce with sautéed vegetables. You could make an entire meal of the enticing antipasti bar. ✉ *Philharmonikerg. 9,* ☎ *06222/849414. No credit cards.* ⏲ *June–Aug. until 10 PM; Sept.–May until 5:30. Closed Mon. except during Summer Festival.*

$–$$ ★ ✕ **Ristorante Pizzeria al Sole.** Next to the Mönchsberg elevator, this Italian restaurant is owned by two friendly brothers who regularly travel over the border to Italy to bring back the freshest ingredients. The thin-crust pizzas are especially scrumptious, with a wide variety of toppings. Pasta dishes are numerous and delicious, such as spaghettini with tuna and black olives. Try the panna cotta with fresh strawberries for dessert. Sit upstairs in a pretty room lined with Venetian prints or in the more casual downstairs area. ✉ *Gstätteng. 15,* ☎ *0662/843284. AE, DC, MC, V.*

$–$$ ✕ **Zum Fidelen Affen.** The name means "At the Faithful Ape," which explains the ape motifs in this popular *Gasthaus,* dominated by a round copper-plated bar and stone pillars under a vaulted ceiling. Besides the beer on tap, the kitchen offers tasty Austrian dishes, such as Tyrolean cheese ravioli with a light topping of chopped, fresh tomatoes and basil or spinach spätzle in a ham and cheese gratiné. ✉ *Priesterhausg. 8,* ☎ *0662/877361. No credit cards. Closed Sun. No lunch.*

Lodging

Hotel reservations are always advisable and are imperative at festival times (both Easter and summer). Be aware that many hotels charge higher prices during festival times. For details and price-category definitions, *see* Lodging *in* Austria A to Z, *above.*

$$$$ **Goldener Hirsch.** The "Golden Stag" has the best location of all Salzburg's luxury hotels, right down the street from Mozart's Birthplace. Rooms in this nearly 600-year-old town house have a simple, rustic charm with bright rag rugs; the stag motif is everywhere, even on the lamp shades, which were hand-painted by an Austrian countess. ✉ *Getreideg. 37, A-5020,* ☎ *0662/8084–0,* FAX *0662/843–349,* WEB *www.goldenerhirsch.com. 70 rooms. Restaurant. AE, DC, MC, V.*

$$$$ ★ **Hotel Sacher Salzburg.** Clientele at this beautiful hotel on the banks of the Salzach River has ranged from the Beatles and the Rolling Stones to, more recently, Hillary and Chelsea Clinton. It's owned by the Gürtler family, who also own the Hotel Sacher in Vienna. Each room is different, but all are exquisitely decorated, with care and attention given to every possible whim or need, and the staff is warm and friendly. Room prices include a delicious buffet breakfast, complete with Sekt (Austrian sparkling wine). *Schwarzstr. 5–7, A-5020,* ☎ *0662/88977–0 or 0662/889–7714,* FAX *0662/88977–551,* WEB *www.sacher.com. 120 rooms. 4 restaurants. AE, DC, MC, V.*

$$$$ ★ **Schloss Mönchstein.** Its own magical universe, this palatial mountain retreat is surrounded by gardens and hiking trails, yet just minutes from the city center. Within the ancient, ivy-covered walls are luxurious rooms, some hung with tapestries and others featuring pretty views of the woods with Salzburg in the distance. Service is pleasant and discreet. Getting in and out of town calls for a car or taxi, unless you are willing to negotiate the many steps into town or the nearby Mönchsberg elevator, itself an eight-minute walk away. ✉ *Mönchsberg 26, A-5020,* ☎ *0662/848555–0,* FAX *0662/848559,* WEB *www.monchstein.at. 17 rooms. Restaurant, bar, café, tennis court. AE, DC, MC, V.*

$$–$$$ ★ **Wolf Dietrich.** Rooms in this small hotel are charmingly decorated, some with Laura Ashley fabrics, and have extra amenities, such as VCRs and sitting areas. Rooms in the back look out over the looming Gaisberg and the cemetery of St. Sebastian. ✉ *Wolf Dietrich-Str. 7, A-5020,* ☎ *0662/871275,* FAX *0662/882320,* WEB *www.salzburg-hotel.at. 30 rooms. Restaurant, pool. AE, DC, MC, V.*

$$ **Blaue Gans.** The "Blue Goose" has recently undergone a total overhaul, and the result couldn't be more appealing. Care has been taken to keep its Old World charm intact, and the ancient wood beams, winding corridors, and low archways add to the fun. Rooms are spacious and have contemporary furnishings, whitewashed walls with cheeky framed posters, and cheerful curtains. A few have skylights. Its location right on Getreidegasse makes this 500-year-old hotel a top choice, so reserve early. ✉ *Getreideg. 43, A-5020,* ☎ *0662/841317 or 0662/*

842–4910, FAX 0662/842–4919, WEB www.blauegans.at. 44 rooms. Restaurant. AE, DC, MC, V.

Shopping

Shopping centers on Griesgasse, Getreidegasse, and Alter Markt in the Old City and Platzl and Linzer Strasse on the other side of the river. Look for quality handicrafts at **Salzburger Heimatwerk** (✉ Residenzpl. 9, ☎ 0662/842–1100).

Salzburg Essentials

AIRPORTS AND TRANSFERS

All flights go via Salzburg Airport, 4 km (2½ mi) west of the city.

➤ AIRPORT INFORMATION: **Salzburg Airport** (☎ 0662/851211 or 0662/85–6364–11).

TRANSFERS

Buses leave for the Salzburg train station at Südtirolerplatz every 15 minutes during the day, every half hour at night until 10 PM. Journey time is about 20 minutes. Taxi fare runs about AS150/€10.90–AS170/€12.35.

BIKE TRAVEL

A bicycle is useful only if you want to tackle some of the outlying areas. Marked bicycle paths show the way.

BUS TRAVEL TO AND FROM SALZBURG

The central bus terminal is in front of the train station, the Salzburg Hauptbahnhof. The postal bus terminal is another bus line servicing Austria.

➤ BUS INFORMATION: **Central bus terminal** (✉ Südtirolerpl. 1, ☎ 0662/872150, FAX 0662/93000-5359, WEB www.oebb.at). **Postal bus terminal** (✉ Andreas-Hofer-Str. 9, ☎ 0662/4660–333, FAX 0662/4660–335, WEB www.vor.at).

BUS TRAVEL WITHIN SALZBURG

Bus and trolleybus service is frequent and reliable; route maps are available from the tourist office or your hotel. Save money by buying a daily pass for AS40/€2.91. A 24-hour pass is no longer available.

CAR TRAVEL

Salzburg has several Autobahn exits; study the map. Parking is available in the cavernous garages under the Mönchsberg, near the city center, and in other garages around the city; look for the large blue P signs.

Don't even think of traveling in Salzburg by car. The old part of the city is a pedestrian zone. Many other parts of the city have restricted parking (indicated by a blue pavement stripe), reserved either for residents with permits or for a restricted period. Get parking tickets from coin-operated dispensers on street corners; instructions are also in English.

CONSULATES

➤ UNITED KINGDOM: (✉ Alter Markt 4, ☎ 0662/848133).

➤ UNITED STATES: (✉ Alter Markt 1/3, ☎ 0662/848776, FAX 0662/849777).

EMERGENCIES

➤ EMERGENCY SERVICES: **Ambulance** (☎ 144). **Police** (☎ 133).

➤ PHARMACIES: Pharmacies (*Apotheken*) stay open nights and weekends on rotation; a sign is posted outside each pharmacy listing which are open.

ENGLISH-LANGUAGE MEDIA

BOOKS

American Discount concentrates on popular paperbacks and magazines. Most good bookstores have some books in English. Hintermayer sells discount paperbacks in English.

➤ BOOKSTORES: **American Discount** (✉ Waagpl. 6, ☎ 0662/845640). **Hintermayer** (✉ Goldg. 3, ☎ 0662/875–7541).

TAXIS

At festival time, taxis are too scarce to hail on the street, so order through your hotel porter or call the number below.

➤ TAXI COMPANIES: (☎ 0662/8111 or 0662/1715).

TOURS

BUS TOURS

There are guided bus tours of the city and its environs, but buses cannot enter much of the Altstadt (Old City).

➤ FEES AND SCHEDULES: **Bob's Special Tours** (✉ Rudolfskai 38, ☎ 0662/849511–0, FAX 0662/849512). **Panorama Tours** (✉ Schranneng. 2/2, ☎ 0662/883211–0). **Salzburg Sightseeing Tours** (✉ Mirabellpl. 2, ☎ 0662/881616).

SPECIAL-INTEREST TOURS

Many tour operators offer *Sound of Music* excursions through the city; those given by Bob's Special Tours are among the friendliest. All tour operators can organize chauffeur-driven tours for up to eight people and it's a good way to orient yourself. Your hotel will have details.

WALKING TOURS

The folder "Salzburg—The Art of Taking It All In at a Glance" describes a one-day self-guided walking tour and is available at the Salzburg City Tourist Office.

TRAIN TRAVEL

Salzburg's main train station is at Südtirolerplatz. For train information, call the number below. For seat reservations, go to the Österreichische Bundesbahnen Zugauskunft office inside the train station.

➤ TRAIN INFORMATION: **Train Information** (☎ 0662/1717).

TRANSPORTATION AROUND SALZBURG

Salzburg is compact and most distances are short. This is a city to explore on foot, but take an umbrella, as surprise showers are legendary. Consider purchasing the Salzburg Card, available at most hotels, travel agencies, and the city tourist office. *SalzburgKarten* are good for 24, 48, or 72 hours at AS230/€16.71, AS320/€23.25, and AS410/€29.80, respectively, and allow no-charge entry to most museums and sights, use of public transport, and special discount offers.

You can also take a *Fiaker* (horse-drawn cab); Fiakers on the Residenzplatz cost AS420/€30.52 (up to four people) for 20–25 minutes, AS820/€59.60 for 50 minutes.

TRAVEL AGENCIES

➤ LOCAL AGENTS: **American Express** (✉ Mozartpl. 5–7, ☎ 0662/8080–0, FAX 0662/8080–171). **Columbus** (✉ Münzg. 1, ☎ 0662/842755, FAX 0662/842755–5).

VISITOR INFORMATION

The Mozartplatz Information Office is open daily except Sunday. The Central Station Information Office is open daily. The Salzburg City Tourist Office is the main tourist office. It is open Mon.–Thurs. 8–4, Fri. 8–1:30, closed Sat.–Sun.

➤ TOURIST INFORMATION: **Central Station Information Office** (Hauptbahnhof/main train station; ✉ Bahnsteig 2A, ☎ 0662/88987–340). **Mozartplatz Information Office** (Stadtverkehrsbüro; ✉ Mozartpl. 5, ☎ 0662/88987–340). **Salzburg City Tourist Office** (✉ Auerspergstr. 7, ☎ 0662/88987–0, FAX 0662/88987–66).

INNSBRUCK

Ringed by mountains and sharing the valley with the Inn River, Innsbruck is compact and very easy to explore on foot. The medieval city—it received its municipal charter in 1239—owes much of its fame and charm to its unique location. To the north, the steep, sheer sides of the Alps rise like a shimmering blue-and-white wall from the edge of the city, an awe-inspiring backdrop for the mellow green domes and red roofs of the picturesque Baroque town.

Exploring Innsbruck

Numbers in the margin correspond to points of interest on the Innsbruck map.

Modern-day Innsbruck retains close associations with three historic figures: Emperor Maximilian I and Empress Maria Theresa (both responsible for much of the city's architecture), and Andreas Hofer, a Tyrolean patriot. You will find repeated references to these names as you tour the city and its historic core—the Altstadt.

8 **Annasäule** (St. Anne's Column). This memorial commemorates the withdrawal of Bavarian forces in the war of the Spanish Succession in 1703 on St. Anne's Day. From here you'll have a classic view of Innsbruck and the glorious mountains. ✉ *Maria-Theresien-Str.*

3 **Domkirche** (Cathedral). Built in 1722 and dedicated to St. James, the church has an interior with dramatic painted ceilings and a high-altar portrait of the Madonna by Lucas Cranach the Elder dating from about 1520. ✉ *Dompl. 6.* ⏲ *Sat.–Thurs. 6 AM–noon, Fri. 2–5.*

★ 1 **Goldenes Dachl** (The Golden Roof). The ancient mansion with its gold-roof (copper tiles gilded with 31 pounds of gold) balcony is the city's foremost landmark. The balcony was a reviewing stand. The building now houses a **Museum Maximilianeum** (Maximilian Museum), which focuses on the life and works of the Habsburg ruler between 1490 and 1519. A combined ticket also gives you entry to the Ferdinandeum and the Stadtturm, the 15th-century city tower across the street. ✉ *Herzog Friedrich-Str. 21,* ☎ *0512/581111.* ⏲ *Oct.–Apr., daily 10–12:30 and 2–5; May–Sept., daily 10–6.*

9 **Helblinghaus** (Helbling House). Dating from 1560, this Gothic town house in a 1730 makeover received a facade of ornate blue-and-white rococo decoration that remains one of Innsbruck's most beautiful sights. ✉ *Herzog Friedrich-Str.*

★ 2 **Hofburg** (Imperial Palace). Dating from 1460, the rococo palace has an ornate reception hall decorated with portraits of Maria Theresa's ancestors. ✉ *Rennweg 1,* ☎ *0512/587186.* ⏲ *Daily 9–5.*

★ 4 **Hofkirche** (Court Church). Maximilian's mausoleum is surrounded by 24 marble reliefs portraying his accomplishments, as well as 28 oversize bronze statues of his ancestors. Andreas Hofer is also buried here. Don't miss the heavily decorated altar of the 16th-century **Silberne Kapelle** (Silver Chapel). ✉ *Universitätsstr. 2,* ☎ *0512/584302.* ⏲ *Mon.–Sat. 9–5.*

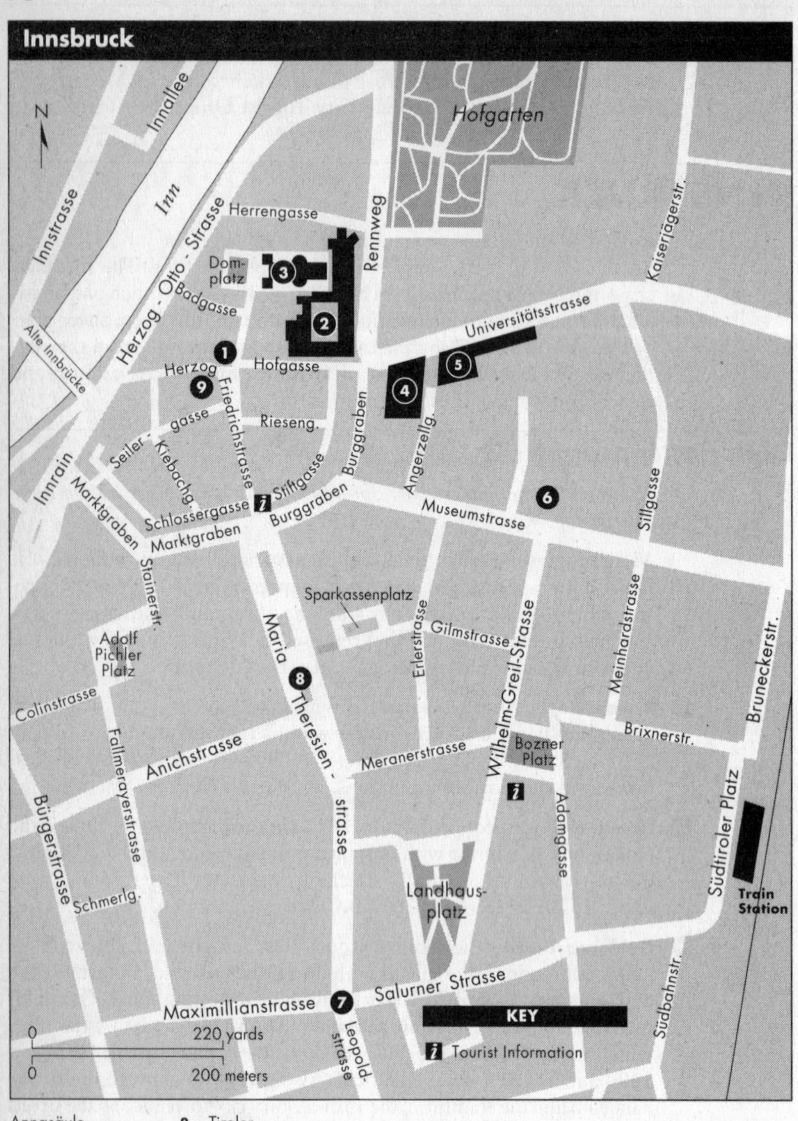

Annasäule 8
Domkirche 3
Goldenes Dachl 1
Helblinghaus 9
Hofburg 2
Hofkirche 4
Tiroler Landesmuseum Ferdinandeum 6
Tiroler Volkskunstmuseum . . . 5
Triumphpforte 7

6 **Tiroler Landesmuseum Ferdinandeum** (Tyrolean Provincial Museum). Austria's largest collection of Gothic art is here as well as paintings from the 19th and 20th centuries. ✉ *Museumstr. 15,* ☎ *0512/59489.* ⊙ *May–Sept., Sun.–Wed., Fri.–Sat. 10–5, Thurs. 10–5 and 7–9; Oct.–Apr., Tues.–Sat. 10–noon and 2–5, Sun. 10–1.*

5 **Tiroler Volkskunstmuseum** (Tyrolean Folk Art Museum). In the Hofkirche complex, this fascinating museum exhibits costumes and farmhouse rooms decorated in styles ranging from Gothic to rococo. There's a combined ticket with the Hofburg. ✉ *Universitätsstr. 2,* ☎ *0512/584302.* ⊙ *Mon.–Sat. 9–5, Sun. 9–noon.*

7 **Triumphpforte** (Triumphal Arch). In honor of the marriage of Leopold (son of Maria Theresa and Francis I, brother of Marie-Antoinette, and later Kaiser Leopold II) to Maria Ludovica of Tuscany, the arch was built in 1765. It expresses the joy of the marriage on one side and the sadness at the death of Francis I, who died suddenly during the wedding celebrations, on the other. ✉ *Maria-Theresien-Str.*

The Arts

Most hotels have a monthly calendar of events (in English). The City Tourist Office sells tickets to most events. The leading venue for operas, musicals, and concerts is the **Tiroler Landestheater** (✉ Rennweg 2, ☎ 0512/520744). Other major performances are held at the **Kongresshaus** (✉ Rennweg 3, ☎ 0512/5936–0).

Dining

Innsbruck gives you a chance to sample hearty Tyrolean cooking, such as *Tyroler G'röstl,* a tasty potato hash with onion and bacon, and *Schlutzkrapfen,* a local version of ravioli. Don't forget to check out some of the city's delightful coffeehouses. For details and price-category definitions, *see* Dining *in* Austria A to Z, *above.*

$$$$ ★ ✕ **Schwarzer Adler.** The leaded-glass windows and rustic Tirolean decor of this intimate, romantic restaurant in the Schwarzer Adler hotel provide the perfect backdrop for a memorable meal. Specialties include *Schweinfilet* (pork fillet) stuffed with spinach and mushrooms in a puff pastry, and grilled freshwater trout. ✉ *Kaiserjägerstr. 2,* ☎ *0512/587109,* FAX *0512/561697. Reservations essential. Jacket and tie. AE, DC, MC, V. Closed Sun. and mid-Jan.*

$$$–$$$$ ✕ **Ottoburg.** You can sit in a bay window in one of the upstairs rooms overlooking the Altstadt in this medieval gray-stone town house with charming red-and-white shutters. A best bet is the fresh salmon accompanied by a *Kartoffelpuffer,* a big crispy hash brown. ✉ *Herzog Friedrich-Str. 1A,* ☎ *0512/584338. AE, DC, MC, V.*

$$$–$$$$ ★ ✕ **Tiroler Stuben.** This restaurant has a broad seasonal menu, including lots of vegetarian choices. Try the *Schlutzkrapfen* (Tyrolean ravioli) or a simple, succulent roast chicken with potato salad. ✉ *Alpotel Tirol, Innrain 13 (Ursulinenhof),* ☎ *0512/577931. Reservations essential. AE, MC, V.*

$–$$$$ ✕ **Sweet Basil.** This popular restaurant in the heart of the Altstadt has small, intimate rooms with stone-vaulted ceilings and a candlelit underground bar. The eclectic menu offers everything from Caesar salads to steaks and chicken, as well as heaping bowls of pasta. ✉ *Herzog-Friedrich-Str. 31,* ☎ *0512/584996. AE, DC, MC, V.*

$–$$$ ★ ✕ **Sacher Café.** The famous Sacher Café of Vienna is now also in Innsbruck, in the prestigious setting of the Hofburg palace complex. Choose from a variety of delectable pastries to go along with the excellent coffee, and sit back and enjoy the elegant red-damask surroundings. Croissant sandwiches and full meals are also offered. ✉ *Rennweg 1, ☎ 0512/565–626, FAX 0512/565–6266. AE, DC, MC, V.*

$–$$ ✕ **Philippine.** The tempting food here is primarily vegetarian. You might start with polenta topped with Gorgonzola and ruby-red tomatoes and then go on to whole-wheat *Schlutzkrapfen* with browned butter or pumpkin risotto with pumpkin seeds, ginger, and Parmesan. Several fish dishes have recently been added, including salmon in cream sauce with spinach. The restaurant has a light, cheerful ambience, and tables are candlelit at night. ✉ *Corner of Müllerstr. and Tempelstr., ☎ 0512/589157. MC, V. Closed Sun. and holidays.*

$ ✕ **Theresien Bräu.** This multilevel brewhouse in the center of town is decorated to give the appearance of the inside of a ship. An assortment of seafaring gear is scattered throughout, such as fishnets, steamer trunks, and even rowboats. But the focus here is on beer, brewed right on the premises. Meals and snacks include zucchini ragout with polenta gratiné, or *Tafelspitz,* a boiled beef dish. People of any age can be found here, but be prepared for loud music. ✉ *Maria-Theresien-Str. 51–53, ☎ 0512/587580, FAX 0512/587580–5. AE, DC, MC, V.*

Lodging

Many travelers use Innsbruck hotels as home bases for excursions into the surrounding countryside—book far in advance for accommodations. Most hotels offer or can arrange transport to ski areas. For details and price-category definitions, *see* Lodging *in* Austria A to Z, *above.*

$$$$ **Goldener Adler.** Mozart, Goethe, and more recently John Glenn and the king and queen of Norway have stayed here. This traditional hotel, a 600-year-old house with stone walls, winding staircases, and a variety of nooks and crannies, has mostly spacious rooms, though a few readers have complained about closetlike rooms on the upper floors. The location is ideal, in the heart of the Old City. ✉ *Herzog Friedrich-Str. 6, A-6020, ☎ 0512/586334, FAX 0512/584409. 40 rooms. 2 restaurants. AE, DC, MC, V.*

$$$ **Alpotel Tirol.** Abundant space, comfort, and modern style are the keys in this hotel on the edge of the Altstadt. The staff is particularly helpful. Many rooms have balconies overlooking the quiet garden and mountains. The Tiroler Stuben restaurant is unusually good. ✉ *Innrain 13 (Ursulinenpassage), A-6020, ☎ 0512/577931, FAX 0512/577931–15. 75 rooms. Restaurant. AE, DC, MC, V.*

$$$ **Innsbruck.** This is one of the city's newest and finest hotels. From some of the modern rooms you'll get gorgeous views of the Old City, and, from those on the river side, of the Nordkette mountains directly behind. ✉ *Innrain 3, A-6020, ☎ 0512/59868–0, FAX 0512/572280. 111 rooms. Restaurant, indoor pool. AE, DC, MC, V.*

$$$ **Weisses Rössl.** The White Horse beckons visitors with bright orange geranium windowboxes and rustic charm, and you can't beat the location in the center of the Altstadt. Rooms are plain and modern. ✉ *Kiebachg. 8, A-6020, ☎ 0512/583–057, FAX 0512/58–30–575, WEB www.roessl.at. 13 rooms. Restaurant. MC, V.*

$$ ★ **Weisses Kreuz.** Occupying an honored position in the Altstadt, the White Cross is a lovely inn that dates from 1465. Mozart stayed here. ✉ *Herzog Friedrich-Str. 31, A-6020, ☎ 0512/59479, FAX 0512/59479–90. 39 rooms, 20 rooms with shower, 19 with bath. Restaurant. AE, V.*

$ **Innsbrücke.** The snug modern rooms at the front of this modest town house look across the river toward the Old City. You're five minutes from the center on foot, or from the railroad station by Bus A or K. ✉ *Innstr. 1, A-6020, ☎ 0512/28–1934, WEB www.innsbruck.nethotels.com/innbruecke. 30 rooms, 13 with bath. AE, DC, MC, V.*

Shopping

The main central shopping district is concentrated around the Old City, along Maria-Theresien-Strasse, Maximilianstrasse, Anichstrasse, Burggraben, Museumstrasse, and Wilhelm-Greil-Strasse and their side streets. A new shopping destination worthy of note in the Altstadt is **Kaiser Max,** a unique five-story "shopping center" with 20 stores featuring exclusive Tyrolean handcrafts, including the famous Giesswein clothing, jewelry, hand-blown glass, edibles, and much more. Portal is under the **Stadtturm**. For groups, handcraft demonstrations can be scheduled with a few days' notice by calling the Giesswein store at ☎ 0512/570669 (✉ Herzog-Freidrich-Str. 23). For local handicrafts, you can try **Tiroler Heimatwerk** (✉ Meraner Str. 2–4, ☎ 0512/582320).

Innsbruck Essentials

AIRPORTS AND TRANSFERS

The airport is 4 km (2½ mi) to the west of the city. For flight information, call the number below.

➤ AIRPORT INFORMATION: **Flight information** (☎ 0512/22525–304).

TRANSFERS

Buses (Line F) to the city center (Maria-Theresien-Str.) run every 20 minutes and take about 20 minutes. Get your ticket from the bus driver; it costs AS21/€1.53. Taxis should take no more than 10–15 minutes into town, and the fare is between AS120/€8.72 and AS150/€10.90.

BUS TRAVEL TO AND FROM INNSBRUCK

The Innsbruck terminal is to the right of the main train station. Routes extend from here throughout the Tirol.

➤ BUS INFORMATION: **Terminal** (✉ Südtiroler-Pl., ☎ 0512/585155).

BUS TRAVEL WITHIN INNSBRUCK

Service is frequent and efficient. Most bus and streetcar routes begin or end at Südtiroler-Platz, in front of the main train station. A bus is the most convenient way to reach the six major ski areas outside the city, and it is free when you use the special buses provided. From the Old City, the buses leave from in front of the Tiroler Landestheater, or from the corner of Innrain and Marktgraben, near the Inn River. Ask at your hotel for more information.

CAR TRAVEL

Within Innsbruck, a car is a burden except for getting out of town. Much of the downtown area is a pedestrian zone or paid-parking only; get parking vouchers at tobacco shops, coin-operated dispensers, or the City Tourist Office.

EMERGENCIES

Pharmacies (*Apotheken*) stay open nights and weekends on a rotation system. Signs outside each pharmacy, and notices in local newspapers, list which ones will be open.

➤ EMERGENCY SERVICES: **Ambulance** (☎ 144). **Police** (☎ 133).

TAXIS

Taking a taxi is not much faster than walking, particularly along the one-way streets and in the Altstadt. To order a radio cab, phone one of the numbers listed below.

➤ TAXI COMPANIES: **Radio Cab** (☎ 0512/1718, 0512/5311, or 0512/45500).

TOURS

BUS TOURS

Two-hour bus tours covering the city's highlights leave from the hotel information office at the railroad station (✉ Südtiroler-Pl.) daily at noon. In summer, additional buses are scheduled at 2, and there are shorter tours Monday through Saturday at 10:15, noon, 2, and 3:15. Individual private tours are available with advance reservation. Contact your hotel or the tourist office.

TRAIN TRAVEL

The city's main station is at Südtiroler-Platz, about a 15-minute walk from the Altstadt. Numbers for train information and ticket reservations are listed below.

➤ TRAIN INFORMATION: **Ticket reservations** (☎ 0512/1700). **Train information** (☎ 0512/1717).

TRAVEL AGENCIES

➤ LOCAL AGENTS: **American Express** (✉ Brixnerstr. 3, ☎ 0512/582491, FAX 0512/573385). **Österreichisches Verkehrsbüro** (✉ Brixnerstr. 2, ☎ 0512/520790, FAX 0512/520–7985).

VISITOR INFORMATION

Österreichischer Alpenverein has information on Alpine huts and mountaineering. Pick up a free *Club Innsbruck* card at your hotel for free use of ski buses and discount ski-lift passes. The *Innsbruck Card* (good for 24, 48, and 72 hours at AS260/€18.90, AS330/€23.98, and AS400/€29.07, respectively) gives you admission to all the museums and mountain cable cars, plus free bus and tram transportation.

➤ TOURIST INFORMATION: **Innsbruck Tourismus** (City Tourist Office; ✉ Burggraben 3, ☎ 0512/5356–30, FAX 0512/535643). **Österreichischer Alpenverein** (✉ Wilhelm-Greil-Str. 15, ☎ 0512/59547–19, FAX 0512/575528).

4 BALTIC STATES

ESTONIA, LATVIA, LITHUANIA

ESTONIA, LATVIA, LITHUANIA: these three small countries in northeastern Europe have weathered centuries of domination by Germans, Swedes, Russians, and Poles; fought countless battles to preserve at least their dignity; and won their independence twice in the 20th century. The three countries share terrain and history. Nevertheless, since breaking free of the Soviet Union in 1990 and 1991, the Baltics have been quietly reconstructing their individual national identities, societies, and economies, and each is resolute about its distinctness.

While building sustainable democracies out of the rubble of post-Soviet republics, Estonia, Latvia, and Lithuania have pursued very different alliances. Estonia, with linguistic and geographic affinities to Helsinki, looks every bit as Scandinavian and Western as its neighbor across the Gulf of Finland. Latvia, with a huge Russian population, still retains some of the chaos of its former eastern nemesis but has emerged as the most cosmopolitan country of the three. Lithuania was slower in embracing the West but since 1996 has made great strides, renewing contacts and relations with Poland in an effort to hitch itself to the EU and NATO's rising star.

Although there aren't many world-famous attractions in the Baltics, the region's obscurity may actually be the best thing about it. Another plus for the English speaker is that it is becoming increasingly easy to roam the three Baltic capitals of Tallinn, Rīga (Riga), and Vilnius without encountering language barriers. The landscape itself is also free of barriers; everywhere in the Baltics you'll find unspoiled forests and beaches, as well as people whose initial aloofness toward strangers often gives way to genuine friendliness.

Baltic States A to Z

For country-specific details about money, phones, and so on, *see* the appropriate sections, *below;* the following is general information on all three Baltic states.

To research prices, get advice from other travelers, and book travel arrangements, visit www.fodors.com.

BUSINESS HOURS

Banks are open weekdays 9–4, but some open as early as 8 and close as late as 7. Most are closed on Saturday, but some stay open 9–3. Museums are generally open Wednesday–Sunday 11–5. Some stay open until 6. Shops open between 10 and 11 and close between 5 and 7, with shorter hours on Saturday. Most shops are closed on Sunday.

Estonia, Latvia, Lithuania

CUSTOMS AND DUTIES

Duty-free allowances are 250 grams of tobacco, 1 liter of spirits, 1 liter of wine, and 10 liters of beer (3 liters of wine and 5 liters of beer in Lithuania).

Since the export of antiques and historic artifacts is strictly controlled, before you export an old item be sure to contact the Division of Export of Culture Objects in Estonia, the Ministry of Culture in Latvia, or the Committee of Cultural Heritage in Lithuania. Generally a 10%–20% duty is charged on goods more than 50 years old and native to the country; up to 100% duty is charged on goods more than 100 years old made in a foreign country but bought in the Baltics.

➤ INFORMATION: Estonia: **Division of Export of Culture Objects** (☎ 2/448–501). Latvia: **Ministry of Culture** (☎ 721–4100). Lithuania: **Committee of Cultural Heritage** (☎ 2/724–005).

DINING

Native dishes predominate: usually meat, potatoes, and root-vegetable salad. Nevertheless, the dining scene in the capitals has improved in recent years. Tallinn, Riga, and Vilnius all offer an array of authentic international cuisine. Riga has the most upscale restaurants, while Vilnius has the best international cuisine. In Tallinn international dining predominates, but diners may still find some good national cuisine.

Prices are for a main course at dinner.

CATEGORY	COST
$$$$	over $20
$$$	$15–$20
$$	$8–$15
$	under $8

RESERVATIONS AND DRESS

Casual dress is acceptable in all restaurants. Jeans and tennis shoes, however, are not appropriate for high-priced establishments.

EMBASSIES

➤ ESTONIA: **Australia** (✉ Kopli 25, Tallinn, ☎ 650–9308, FAX 667–8444). **Canada** (✉ Toom-kooli 13, Tallinn, ☎ 627–3311, FAX 627–3312). **United Kingdom** (✉ Wismari 6, Tallinn, ☎ 667–4700, FAX 667–4723). **United States** (✉ Kentmanni 20, Tallinn, ☎ 631–2021, FAX 660–5549).

➤ LATVIA: **Australia** (✉ Raiņa 3, Riga, ☎ 722–2383, FAX 722–2314). **Canada** (✉ Doma laukums 4, Riga, ☎ 722–6315, FAX 783–0140). **United Kingdom** (✉ Alunāna 5, Riga, ☎ 733–8126, FAX 733–8132). **United States** (✉ Raiņa 7, Riga, ☎ 721–0005, FAX 728–0047).

➤ LITHUANIA: **Australia** (✉ Totorių 15, Vilnius, ☎ 2/223–369, FAX 2/223–369). **Canada** (✉ Gedimino 64, Vilnius, ☎ 2/220–853, FAX 2/220–884). **United Kingdom** (✉ Antakalnio 2, Vilnius, ☎ 2/222–070, FAX 2/727–579). **United States** (✉ Akmenų 6, Vilnius, ☎ 2/223–031, FAX 2/312–819).

LODGING

Rooms in all hotels listed have private bath or shower unless otherwise noted. Most have individual heating and air-conditioning units.

Prices are for two people sharing a double room and include breakfast.

CATEGORY	COST*
$$$$	over $120
$$$	$80–$120
$$	$40–$80
$	under $40

PASSPORTS AND VISAS

Australian, British, Irish, New Zealand, and U.S. citizens can stay in Estonia visa-free for up to 90 days. Canadian citizens need a visa to enter Estonia. Australians, Canadians, and New Zealanders need visas for Latvia; a 90-day visa can be purchased from consulates outside Latvia, and 10-day visas can be purchased for 12Ls at the Riga airport. Australian, British, Canadian, Irish, New Zealand, and U.S. citizens can stay in Lithuania visa-free for up to 90 days. A 10-day visa can be issued at the Vilnius airport for 160Lt if your country of citizenship does not have a Lithuanian embassy or consulate or you are a citizen of an EU country.

VISITOR INFORMATION

➤ Tourist Information: **Estonia:** ⊠ Raekoja plats 10, Tallinn, ☎ 645–7777, FAX 645–7778, WEB www.tourism.tallinn.ee. **Latvia:** ⊠ Rātslaukums 6, Riga, ☎ 704–4377, FAX 720–7100, WEB www.latviatravel.com. **Lithuania:** ⊠ Pilies 42, Vilnius, ☎ FAX 2/620–762, WEB www.vilnius.lt; ⊠ Airport arrivals hall, Rodūnės kelias 2, Vilnius, ☎ 8–299/99–721).

WHEN TO GO

Midsummer sees an influx of tourists and an exodus by locals. For local color and temperate weather, visit in late spring or early autumn.

CLIMATE

The Baltic States' climate is temperate but tends to be cool and damp. The rainy season is in early summer. The snowy, cold winter season lasts from November through March. Summers, though warm, are generally wet and humid. August tends to see the smallest amount of rain in all three Baltic States. The average daily temperatures for Estonia, Latvia, and Lithuania, in that order, are as follows:

Jan.	26F	- 3C	**May**	46F	8C	**Sept.**	56F	13C
	28F	- 2C		52F	11C		55F	13C
	27F	- 3C		50F	10C		57F	14C
Feb.	24F	- 4C	**June**	63F	17C	**Oct.**	45F	7C
	32F	0C		57F	14C		45F	7C
	24F	4C		67F	20C		44F	6C
Mar.	32F	0C	**July**	65F	18C	**Nov.**	37F	3C
	34F	1C		60F	16C		36F	2C
	34F	1C		69F	20C		32F	0C
Apr.	43F	6C	**Aug.**	60F	15C	**Dec.**	30F	- 1C
	49F	9C		59F	15C		31F	- 1C
	48F	9C		62F	17C		30F	- 1C

ESTONIA

The country's history is sprinkled liberally with long stretches of foreign domination, beginning in 1219 with the Danes, followed without interruption by the Germans, Swedes, and Russians. Only after World War I, with Russia in revolutionary wreckage, was Estonia able to declare its independence. But shortly before World War II, in 1940, that independence was usurped by the Soviets, who—save for a brief three-year occupation by Hitler's Nazis—proceeded to suppress all forms of national Estonian pride for the next 50 years. Estonia finally regained independence in 1991. In the early 1990s Estonia's own Riigikogu (Parliament), not some other nation's puppet ruler, handed down from the Upper City reforms that forced Estonia to blaze its post-Soviet trail to the European Union. In 1997 the country got the nod from Brussels to join the EU in the future, an endorsement of Estonia's progress toward a sustainable market economy.

Estonia A to Z

AIR TRAVEL

There are no direct flights between Estonia and the United States. Estonian Air operates from Copenhagen, Frankfurt, Hamburg, Helsinki, London, Riga, Stockholm, Vienna, and Vilnius. American carriers partnered with Finnair, LOT, Lufthansa, and SAS have good connections. Copterline helicopters fly the 18-minute trip between Helsinki and Tallinn daily.

➤ AIRLINES AND CONTACTS: **Copterline helicopters** (☏ 645–1818).

BOAT AND FERRY TRAVEL

Passenger ships—including frequent ferries and hydrofoils—connect Tallinn with Helsinki and Stockholm. Boat service to and from Tallinn is minimal and dependent on weather from October to March.

BUS TRAVEL

Public transportation tickets purchased from nearly any kiosk cost 10EEK. Purchased from the driver, they are 15EEK. Express tickets cost 15EEK from a kiosk or 20EEK from the driver. A single type of ticket is valid on buses, trolleys, and streetcars. Punch your ticket in the machine mounted on a pole in the bus upon boarding or be fined up to 420EEK. Public transportation operates 6 AM–midnight. Intercity bus trips cost 70EEK–150EEK. For bus schedules call the bus station.

➤ BUS INFORMATION: **Bus station** (☏ 601–0386).

CAR RENTAL

Cars may be rented starting at 700EEK a day from Avis, Budget, Hertz, or National.

➤ MAJOR AGENCIES: **Avis** (☏ 605–8222). **Budget** (☏ 605–8600). **Hertz** (☏ 605–8923). **National** (☏ 605–8071).

CAR TRAVEL

An international or national driver's license bearing a photograph is acceptable in Estonia. Drive on the right. Most roads are not up to Western standards, but major thoroughfares tend to be in better condition than secondary roads, where potholes and unpaved ways are common. Gas costs 10EEK per liter.

EMERGENCIES

➤ CONTACTS: **Police** (☏ 110). **Ambulance/Fire** (☏ 112). **Tallinn Central Hospital** (☏ 620–7010). **Doctor: Sinu Arst Family Practice** (☏ 631–5440). **Dentist: Baltic Medical Partners** (☏ 601–0550). **Pharmacy: Rohupood** (☏ 668–4870).

HOLIDAYS

January 1; February 24 (Independence Day); Good Friday; Easter; May 1 (May Day); June 3 (Whitsuntide); June 23 (Victory Day); June 23, 24 (St. John's Day/Midsummer); August 20 (Day of Restoration and Independence); December 25, 26.

LANGUAGE

Estonian, which belongs to the Finno-Ugric family, is the official language. However, many people in cities speak English perfectly. Most Estonians will ignore attempts to communicate in Russian, though the 30% of the population that is ethnically Russian is happy to speak it.

MAIL AND SHIPPING

A 20-gram letter to the United States costs 7EEK, a postcard 6.70EEK. A 20-gram letter to Europe costs 5.50EEK, a postcard 5.20EEK. The main post office is open weekdays 8–8, Saturday 8–6. Stamps are sold at post offices only.

➤ POST OFFICE: **Main post office** (✉ Narva 1, Tallinn, ☎ 625–7300).

MONEY MATTERS

A cup of coffee or tea costs 20EEK; a glass of beer 35EEK; a main dish at a local, medium-priced restaurant 50EEK–60EEK. Admission to museums and galleries costs 10EEK–20EEK. If you're staying in Tallinn from one to three days, the best deal is the Tallinn Card, which can be purchased at the tourist office, all points of entry, and some hotels. It allows visitors free access to public transportation, free admission to museums, a free bus and walking tour, and discounts at shops and restaurants in Tallinn.

CURRENCY

The monetary unit in Estonia is the kroon, which is divided into 100 senti. There are notes of 1, 2, 5, 10, 25, 50, 100, and 500EEK and coins of 5, 10, 20, and 50 senti and 1EEK. At press time (summer 2001) the rate of exchange was 16.62EEK to the U.S. dollar, 11.09EEK to the Canadian dollar, 24.88EEK to the pound sterling, 19.87EEK to the Irish punt, 9.29EEK to the Australian dollar, 7.39EEK to the New Zealand dollar, and 2.19EEK to the South African rand. National banks, with branches in all major and most minor cities, change cash and traveler's checks at fair commissions; most also give advances on a Visa or MasterCard. Credit cards are widely accepted in Estonia.

TAXIS

Taxis are expensive around hotels and ferry, bus, and train stations, cheaper within the city center; it's best to telephone for one. Taxi fares generally start at 6EEK or 8EEK and increase by 4EEK or 6EEK per kilometer (½ mi) in the daytime, more at night or in bad weather. Drivers are bound by law to display an operating license and a meter. In-town journeys cost up to 50EEK.

➤ TAXI COMPANIES: **Esra** (☎ 642–5425). **Tulika** (☎ 612–0000).

TELEPHONES

COUNTRY AND AREA CODES

The country code for Estonia is 372. There is no city code for phone numbers in Tallinn, though there is for other areas.

INTERNATIONAL CALLS

➤ ACCESS CODE: **AT&T** (☎ 8–008001001).

LOCAL CALLS

Pay phones take phone cards worth 30EEK, 50EEK, or 100EEK. Buy cards at any kiosk.

➤ INFORMATION: **Telephone information** (☎ 626–1111).

TIPPING

At restaurants a 10% service charge is sometimes added and an 18% VAT is included in the price of dishes on the menu but may be listed separately on your bill. Tipping is not obligatory; for excellent service, add 10%.

TOURS

➤ FEES & SCHEDULES: **CDS Tours** (✉ Raekoja plats 17, ☎ 650–4150). **Reisiekspert** (✉ Roosikrantsi 17, ☎ 610–8600, FAX 631–3083).

Exploring Estonia

Tallinn

Tallinn's tiny Old Town, the most impressive in the region, has romantic towers, ankle-wrenching cobblestone streets, cozy nooks, city-wall cafés, and a dozen other attractions—all within 1 square km (.4 square mi). In the 1990s, Vanalinn (the lower Old Town)—historically the domain of traders, artisans, and ordinary citizens—sprouted glitzy neon signs in otherwise charming alleys and sights. The stately, sedate Toompea (Upper Town), a hillock that was the site of the original Estonian settlement, is on the burial mound of Kalev, the epic hero of Estonia. Toompea Castle, crowning the hill, is now the seat of the country's parliament and is not open to visitors.

The 19th-century Russian Orthodox **Aleksandr Nevski Khram** (Alexander Nevsky Cathedral), which houses the country's largest bell, is a symbol of the centuries of Russification this country has endured. ✉ *Lossi pl. 10, Toompea,* ☎ *644–3484.* ⏲ *Daily 8–7.*

Wander through the ages in the ancient stone galleries and narrow hallways of the **Dominiiklaste Kloostri Muuseum** (Dominican Monastery Museum), founded in 1246 and now displaying 15th- and 16th-century stone carvings. At 5 PM enjoy a half-hour Baroque music concert. ✉ *Vene 16, Vanalinn,* ☎ *644–4606.* ⏲ *Daily 11–7.*

The Lutheran **Toomkirik** (Dome Church), the oldest church in the country, was founded by the occupying Danes in the 13th century and rebuilt in 1686. ✉ *Toom-kooli 6, Toompea,* ☎ *644–4140.* ⏲ *Tues.–Sun. 9–5.*

The Baroque **Kadriorg Palace Foreign Art Museum,** built for Catherine I by her husband Peter the Great in 1721, merits a visit not just for its impressive and thorough exhibition of 16th- to 20th-century art, but also for the palace's architectural beauty and manicured gardens. Reopened in July 2000 after renovations, Kadriorg Palace offers a glimpse into a history from Russian imperial splendor to Soviet Socialist Realist art, with Estonian and European masterpieces along the way. ✉ *Weizenbergi 37, Tallinn,* ☎ *644–9340.* ⏲ *Tues.–Sun. 11–6.*

★ At the southern end of the Old Town looms the magnificent, six-story tower **Kiek-in-de-Kök** (Low German for "peep in the kitchen"), so called because during the 15th century one could peer into the kitchens of lower town houses from here. The tower houses a museum of contemporary art and ancient maps and weapons. ✉ *Komandandi 2, Vanalinn,* ☎ *644–6686.* ⏲ *Tues.–Fri. 10:30–5:30, weekends 11–4:30.*

The 15th-century **Niguliste kirik** (Church of St. Nicholas), part of the Estonian Art Museum, is famed for its fragment of a treasured frieze, Bernt Notke's (1440–1509) *Danse Macabre,* a haunting depiction of death. ✉ *Niguliste 3, Vanalinn,* ☎ *644–9911.* ⏲ *Wed.–Fri. 10–6, weekends 11:30–6.*

The stocky guardian of the northernmost point of the Old City, **Paks Margareeta** (Fat Margaret) is a 16th-century fortification named for a particularly hefty cannon it housed. Now it contains a Maritime Museum. ✉ *Pikk 70, Vanalinn,* ☎ *641–1412.* ⏲ *Wed.–Sun. 10–6.*

★ **Raekoja Plats** (Town Hall Square) has a long history of intrigue, executions, and salt (Tallinn's main export in the Middle Ages). Take a guided tour of the only surviving original Gothic **town hall** in northern Europe. Old Thomas, its weather vane, has been atop the town hall since 1530. Near the center of the square, an L-shape stone marks the site of a 17th-century execution, where a priest was beheaded for killing a waitress who had offered him a rock-hard omelet. Across the square stands the town **apothecary,** which dates from 1422. ✉ *Raekoja plats 11,* ☎ *644–2132.* ⏲ *Daily 9–5.*

Just a 15-minute drive from the center, the 207-acre **Rocca al Mare** (Open-air Ethnographic Museum) provides a breath of fresh air and an informative look into Estonia's past from farm architecture to World War II–era deportations. ✉ *Vabaõhumuuseumi 12, Tallinn,* ☎ *654–9117.* ⌚ *Daily 10–6.*

$$$$ ✕ **Gloria.** Though you may order à la carte here, the eclectic *menu dégustation* for about 780EEK is sure to surprise and satisfy. To maintain its tradition of decadence, Gloria offers a *tabacalera* (tobacco shop) and an extensive wine cellar. ✉ *Müürivahe 2,* ☎ *644–6950. Reservations essential. Jacket and tie. MC, V.*

$$$ ✕ **Le Bonaparte.** Enjoy traditional French food in a house dating from the 13th century and now restored to look as it did in the 17th century. The seasonal menu represents a solid collection of French favorites and benefits from the restaurant's on-premises patisserie and wine cellar. ✉ *Pikk 45,* ☎ *646–4444. MC, V.*

$$ ✕ **Olde Hansa.** In a 15th-century building in the Old Town, this restaurant re-creates a medieval atmosphere with waiters in period costume, candlelit tables, and historic Eastern European recipes for such dishes as nobleman's smoked filet mignon in mushroom sauce and wild boar with game sauce and forest berries. The honey beer is out of this world, and the old-fashioned food is always fresh and tasty. ✉ *Vanaturg 1,* ☎ *627–9020. MC, V.*

$$ ✕ **Vasilio.** Remind your tastebuds of their existence with a long meal at this authentic Greek restaurant. Though the menu is in Estonian, the eager-to-please waiters are happy to describe in detail each sumptuous item on the menu. ✉ *Vene 6,* ☎ *644–9591. MC, V.*

$ ✕ **Café Anglais.** With an excellent view of Old Town square, this second-floor café attracts a steady clientele with its nightly live jazz and refreshingly light menu of sandwiches, soups, and salads. ✉ *Raekoja plats 14,* ☎ *644–2160. No credit cards.*

$ ✕ **Creperie Chez Grigou.** A bit of Paris in Tallinn: the black-clad waitresses are friendly and the enticing crepes are filled with ham, cheese, mushrooms, zucchini, or even banana. Candlelight, excellent espresso drinks, and old-time jazz music greet a hip, laid-back clientele. ✉ *Müürivahe 23,* ☎ *631–4337. No credit cards.*

$$$$ 🏨 **Park Consul Schlössle.** In three medieval warehouses in the Old Town, Tallinn's most luxurious hotel has unparalleled service and historic charm. The sauna is free for guests. ✉ *Pühavaimu 13–15, EE10123,* ☎ *699–7700,* FAX *699–7777,* WEB *www.consul-hotels.com/pcschloessle. 23 rooms. Restaurant. DC, MC, V.*

$$$–$$$$ 🏨 **Olümpia.** This high-rise offers a variety of rooms. Amenities include a conference hall, a sauna overlooking the city, and a splendid breakfast buffet. Request a room with a view of the Old Town. ✉ *Liivalaia 33, EE0001,* ☎ *631–5555,* FAX *631–5675,* WEB *www.olympia.ee. 405 rooms. 2 restaurants, pool, sauna, exercise room. AE, DC, MC, V.*

$$ 🏨 **Express Hotel.** Just a few minutes' walk from the center of the Old Town, the Express Hotel is extremely democratic—all rooms here are identical and cost exactly the same price. For a no-frills, good value, this is a good choice. ✉ *Sadama 1, EE0001,* ☎ *667–8700,* FAX *667–8800,* WEB *www.olympia.ee. 166 rooms. Restaurant. AE, DC, MC, V.*

$$ 🏨 **Hotel Central.** The Central may have precious little of the personality of more expensive establishments, but as a standard, mid-range hotel it stands out with solid and efficient service. The luxury rooms are a better value than the economy rooms. ✉ *Narva 7c, EE0001,* ☎ *633–9800,* FAX *633–9900,* WEB *www.olympia.ee. 225 rooms. 2 restaurants. AE, DC, MC, V.*

$ 🏨 **Eeslitall.** Right in the middle of the Old Town, this budget hotel has sparely furnished rooms with common showers and toilets. Double rooms have a choice of one double bed or two singles. ✉ *Dunkri 4, EE0001,* ☎ *631–3755,* FAX *631–3210,* WEB *www.eeslitall.ee. 9 rooms. Restaurant. No credit cards.*

The Islands

Some 1,500 time machines float off the western coast of Estonia, embodying what the country was all about before World War II. The Soviets feared a mass exodus to the West, so these islands have largely been off-limits for the past 50 years. Only two islands, Saaremaa and Hiiumaa, are easily accessible, through port towns about 100 km (62 mi) south of Tallinn. **Kuressaare,** the capital of **Saaremaa,** is a town of only 16,000 but proudly lays claim to an almost wholly intact Gothic castle, complete with turrets and moat. Visiting the modest cliffs and beaches round out a trip to the island. **Hiiumaa,** and its center of **Kärdla,** is quieter still, with nothing more audacious than some windmills and a few birds to disturb this perfect retreat.

LATVIA

Latvia, and particularly Riga, is fiercely distinct from the other two Baltic States in a number of ways. German influence was stronger here than elsewhere, as the 14th-century Knights of the Sword used this as their base. When the Soviets forcibly incorporated Latvia into the Soviet Union in 1944, the effects of Russification were more devastating. Today 45% of Latvia is Russian-speaking; in Riga, Russians, Ukrainians, and Belorussians are the majority. This has created a palpable tension: Latvians are angered because their culture has been suppressed for 50 years. Russians are peeved that most of them have yet to be given citizenship here.

Latvia A to Z

AIR TRAVEL

Air Baltic operates from Budapest, Copenhagen, Frankfurt, Geneva, Helsinki, London, Stockholm, Tallinn, Vilnius, Warsaw, and Zürich. British Airways, Finnair, LOT, Lufthansa, SAS, and Swissair connect from the United States.

BOAT AND FERRY TRAVEL

Passenger ships connect Riga with Kiel (in Germany) and Stockholm.

BUS TRAVEL

Public transportation costs 20s and runs 5:30 AM–midnight. Some routes have 24-hour service. Buy bus tickets from the conductor on the bus. Tram and trolleybus tickets are sold at kiosks. Intercity bus trips cost less than 5Ls. For bus schedules call the 20s per minute toll number at the bus station.

➤ Bus Information: **Bus Station** (☎ 900–0009).

CAR RENTAL

Cars may be rented from 40Ls a day; lower rates are available for longer rental terms. Rental agencies include Avis, Baltijos Autolīzingas, and Hertz.

➤ Major Agencies: **Avis** (☎ 720–7353). **Hertz** (☎ 720–7980).

➤ Local Agencies: **Baltijos Autolīzingas** (☎ 733–4480).

CAR TRAVEL

An international or national driver's license bearing a photograph is acceptable in Latvia. Drive on the right. Roads are not up to Western standards. Gas costs 30s per liter.

EMERGENCIES

For medical attention in Riga, contact the English-speaking doctors at Ars. For a 24-hour pharmacy that delivers nonprescription drugs to your door, phone Rudens aptieka.

➤ CONTACTS: **Police** (☎ 02). **Ambulance** (☎ 03). **Doctor: Ars** (☎ 720–1001 or 720–1007). **Dentist: A+S Health Center** (☎ 728–9516). **Rudens aptieka** (☎ 724–4322).

HOLIDAYS

January 1; Good Friday; Easter; May 1 (Labor Day); June 23, 24 (St. John's Day/Midsummer); November 18 (Independence Day, 1918); December 24–26; December 31.

LANGUAGE

The country's official language is Latvian, which belongs to the Baltic branch of the Indo-European family of languages; the unofficial language is Russian. Most Latvians will answer you if addressed in Russian, but more and more speak perfect English.

MAIL AND SHIPPING

The main post office is open weekdays 7 AM–11 PM, weekends 8 AM–10 PM.

➤ POST OFFICE: **Main post office** (✉ Brīvības 19, Riga, ☎ 701–8738).

POSTAL RATES

A 20-gram letter to the United States costs 40s, a postcard 30s. To Europe a 20-gram letter costs 30s, a postcard 20s.

MONEY MATTERS

A cup of coffee or tea costs 40s; a glass of local beer 1Ls; a medium-priced local dish 3Ls–5Ls. Admission to museums and galleries costs around 1Ls.

CURRENCY

The monetary unit in Latvia is the lat (Ls), which is divided into 100 santīmi(s). There are notes of 5, 10, 20, 50, 100, and 500 lat, coins of 1 and 2 lat and 1, 2, 5, 10, 20, and 50 santīmi. At press time (summer 2001) the rate of exchange was 62s to the U.S. dollar, 41s to the Canadian dollar, 92s to the pound sterling, 74s to the Irish punt, 34s to the Australian dollar, 27s to the New Zealand dollar, and 8s to the South African rand. Banks change cash and traveler's checks at fair commissions; most also give advances on a Visa or MasterCard. Credit cards are widely accepted.

TAXIS

Taxis are expensive around Riga's hotels and ferry, bus, and train stations, cheaper within the city center; for best results, telephone for one. The official rate is 30s per kilometer (½ mi) in the daytime and 40s at night or in bad weather. Drivers must display an operating license and a meter. Stick to the state cabs with orange and black markings. Insist that the meter be turned on; if there is no meter, choose another taxi or decide on a price beforehand. Riga Taxi and Rīgas Taksometru Parks are by and large trustworthy taxi companies.

Shared taxis accommodate up to 10 people and are cheap and comfortable. They operate on virtually every bus and trolleybus line. Tariffs are 20s and 30s. Passengers may embark at any regular bus stop and disembark anywhere along the route.

➤ TAXI COMPANIES: **Riga Taxi** (☎ 800–1010). **Rîgas Taksometru Parks** (☎ 733–4041).

TELEPHONES

COUNTRY AND AREA CODES

The country code for Latvia is 371. Though there is no area code for numbers in Riga, there are for other regions of the country.

INTERNATIONAL CALLS

➤ ACCESS CODE: AT&T (☎ 700–7007).

LOCAL CALLS

Pay phones take phone cards worth 2, 3, or 5 Ls. Buy cards at any kiosk.
➤ INFORMATION: **Telephone information** (☎ 800–8080).

TIPPING

At restaurants a service charge of 10% is sometimes added and an 18% VAT is automatically included. Tipping is not obligatory, but for excellent service, add 10%.

TOURS

Latvia Tours offer tours of Riga on Monday, Wednesday, Saturday, and Sunday, with regional tours on other days.
➤ FEES & SCHEDULES: **Latvia Tours** (☎ 708–5057).

TRAIN TRAVEL

Electric trains are the preferable mode of transport for getting around Latvia. Tickets cost less than 5Ls. For train schedule information call Central Station.
➤ TRAIN INFORMATION: **Central Station** (☎ 583–2134).

Exploring Latvia

Riga

Riga has an upscale, big-city feel unmatched in the region. The capital is almost as large as Tallinn and Vilnius combined and is the business center of the area. Original, high-quality restaurants and hotels have given Riga something to brag about.

Although Riga's Old Town is its calling card, it is also the city of Art Nouveau. Long avenues of complex and sometimes whimsical interwar Jugendstil facades hint at Riga's grand past. Many were designed by Mikhail Eisenstein, the father of Soviet director Sergei. This style dominates the city center; you can see the finest examples at Alberta 2, 2a, 4, 6, 8, and 13; Elizabetes 10b; and Strēlnieku 4a.

The fiercely Gothic **Melngavlvju Nams** (Blackheads House) was built in 1344 as a hotel for wayfaring merchants (who wore black hats). Partially destroyed during World War II and leveled by the Soviets in 1948, the extravagant, ornate building was renovated and reopened in 2000 for Riga's 800th anniversary. The facade is a treasured example of Dutch Renaissance work. ✉ *Strēlnieku laukums,* ☎ *721–0269.* ⏲ *Tues.–Sun. 10–5.*

The **Brīvdabas muzejs** (Open-air Ethnographic Museum) is well worth the 9-km (5-mi) trek from downtown. At this countryside living museum farmsteads and villages have been crafted to look like those in 18th- and 19th-century Latvia, and costumed workers engage in traditional activities (beekeeping, smithing, and so on). ✉ *Brīvības 440,* ☎ *799–4515.* ⏲ *Daily 10–5.*

★ The central **Brīvības piemineklis** (Freedom Monument), a 1935 statue whose upheld stars represent Latvia's united peoples (the Kurzeme, Vidzeme, and Latgale), was the rallying point for many nationalist protests during the late 1980s and early 1990s. ✉ *Brīvības and Raiņa.*

In **Doma laukums** (Dome Square), the nerve center of the Old Town, the stately 1210 **Doma baznīca** (Dome Cathedral) dominates. Reconstructed over the years with Romanesque, Gothic, and Baroque bits, this place of worship is astounding for its architecture as much as for its size. The massive 6,768-pipe organ is among the largest in Europe, and it is played nearly every evening at 7 PM. Check at the cathedral for schedules and tickets. ✉ *Doma laukums,* ☎ *721–3213.* ⏲ *Tues. 11–6, Wed.–Fri. 1–6, Sat. 10–2.*

★ The **Okupācijas muzejs** (Latvian Occupation Museum) details the devastation of Latvia at the hands of the Nazis and Soviets during World War II as well as the Latvians' struggle for independence in September 1991. In front of the museum is a monument to the Latvian sharpshooters who protected Lenin during the 1917 revolution. ✉ *Strēlnieku laukums 1,* ☎ *721–2715.* ⏲ *Daily 11–5.*

★ At **Rīgas motormuzejs** (Motor Museum) the Western cars on display can impress, but the Soviet models—including Stalin's iron-plated limo and a Rolls-Royce totaled by Brezhnev himself—are the most fun. ✉ *Eizenšteina 6,* ☎ *709–7170.* ⏲ *Tues.–Sun. 10–6.*

Latvia's restored 18th-century **Nacionālā Opera Doms** (Opera House), where Richard Wagner once conducted, is worthy of a night out. ✉ *Box office, Teatra 10/12,* ☎ *722–5803.* ⏲ *Daily 10–7.*

Towering **Pētera baznīca** (St. Peter's Church), originally built in 1209, had a long history of annihilation and conflagration before being destroyed most recently in 1941. Rebuilt by the Soviets, it lacks authenticity but has a good observation deck on the 200-ft spire. ✉ *Skārņu 19.* ⏲ *Tues.–Sun. 10–7.*

The **TrīsBrāļi** (Three Brothers)—a trio of houses on Mazā Pils—show what the city looked like before the 20th century. The three oldest stone houses in the capital (No. 17 is the oldest, dating from the 15th century) span several styles, from the medieval to the Baroque. The middle house is the city's **architecture museum.** ✉ *Mazā Pils 17, 19, 21,* ☎ *722–0779.* ⏲ *Weekdays 9–5, Sat. noon–4.*

The **Valsts mākslas muzejs** (National Art Museum) has a gorgeous interior equipped with imposing marble staircases linking several large halls of 19th- and 20th-century Latvian paintings. ✉ *Kr. Valdemara 10a,* ☎ *732–5021.* ⏲ *Wed.–Mon. 11–5.*

$$$–$$$$ ✕ **Symposium.** One of Riga's premier dining establishments, Symposium serves outstanding Mediterranean cuisine, with an emphasis on seafood dishes, in a softly lit dining room to the strains of classical music. ✉ *Dzirnavu 84/1,* ☎ *724–2545. MC, V.*

$$$–$$$$ ✕ **Vincents.** Named for Van Gogh, this restaurant has a menu with a sensational collection of international delicacies. It attracts an international clientele from Mstislav Rostropovich and José Carreras to the princes and princesses of Europe. ✉ *Elizabetes 19,* ☎ *733–2634. MC, V.*

$$–$$$ ✕ **Charlestons.** This restaurant has achieved a level of informal class and hearty good taste from breakfast to dinner. The front café is perfect for a quiche or croissant and coffee, while the main dining room and summer terrace invite long, leisurely lunches and dinners. ✉ *Blaumaņa 38/40,* ☎ *777–0573. MC, V.*

$ ✕ **Paddy Whelan's.** Riga's unofficial expat hideout is a great place to find inexpensive pub grub and informal atmosphere. Visit the **Roisin Dubh** (Black Rose) upstairs for more expensive Irish dishes or a late-night pint. ✉ *Grēcinieku 4,* ☎ *733–2634. MC, V.*

$ ✕ **Staburags.** In an Art Nouveau building in downtown Riga, Staburags may be the capital's best place to sample Latvian national cuisine, with such dishes as roast leg of pork, sauerkraut, all manner of potato dishes, and smoked chicken. ✉ *Čaka 55,* ☎ *729–9787. No credit cards.*

$$$$ **Grand Palace Hotel.** Outstanding service, 19th-century decor, and a enviable location right in the heart of Riga make the Grand Palace truly a grand place in which to relax in luxury. ✉ *Pils 12, LV1050,* ☎ *704–4000,* FAX *704–4001,* WEB *www.consul-hotels.com/grandpalace. 56 rooms. 2 restaurants, sauna. DC, MC, V.*

$$$$ **Radisson SAS Daugava.** Popular with conference-goers and business travelers, this branch of the Radisson chain does not disappoint. Its position across the river from Old Town means an extra walk into town, but the unique vistas compensate. ✉ *Kugu 24, LV1050,* ☎ *706–1111,* FAX *706–1100,* WEB *www.radisson.com. 361 rooms. Restaurant, pool, sauna. AE, DC, MC, V.*

$$–$$$ **Konventa Sēta.** In a charming complex of buildings dating from the Middle Ages, this hotel has rooms with a clean, white Scandinavian aesthetic and medieval details. ✉ *Kalēju 9/11, LV1050,* ☎ *708–7501,* FAX *708–7515,* WEB *www.derome.lv. 140 rooms. Restaurant. AE, DC, MC, V.*

$$ **Raudi un Draugi.** This small hotel affords a great location for a low price; it's clean, efficiently run, and simple. Large rooms for families are available. ✉ *Mārstaļu 1/3, LV1050,* ☎ *722–0372,* FAX *724–2239. 47 rooms. MC, V.*

Jūrmala

The Latvian name of this string of four small towns means "seaside," and for a 20-km (12-mi) stretch that is exactly what you get. Once a sought-after vacation spot for Soviet elite, this area today is home to a variety of Russian and Latvian vacationers. The beach is clean and the Soviet-era main street has been renovated. Frequent electric trains (crowded in summer) make the 40-minute trip from Riga.

Gauja Nacionālais Parks

About one hour east of the capital, Gauja National Park, populated by friendly people and a helpful forestry staff, feels light-years away. Latvia's deepest river valley, at 280 ft, is little more than a dip, but the gently flowing Gauja and the 13th-century ruins of **Turaidas Pils** (Turaida Castle), built by the Knights of the Sword, near Sigulda provide amusement, ancient graffiti, and a bobsled track. ✉ *53 km (33 mi) east of Riga; Sigulda visitor center: Pils 4a,* ☎ *2/971–335.*

LITHUANIA

Lithuania has historically been the invader, not the invaded. In 1386, the country formed a union with Poland, and over the following 400 years the joint kingdom stretched from the Baltic to the Black Sea. Poland took the leading role until the late 18th century, but Lithuanians still remember their time as a European superpower. Russification ensued, followed by a short period of independence (during which Kaunas was the capital, as Vilnius was occupied by Poland). Hundreds of thousands of Lithuanians were deported by the Soviets in the 1940s and 1950s, but today's population is 80% Lithuanian, with only 10% Russian-speaking. However, the Jewish population—which had thrived here since the 1400s—was decimated during World War II.

Lithuania A to Z

AIR TRAVEL

No direct flights link Lithuania and the United States. Lithuanian Airlines operates from Amsterdam, Berlin, Copenhagen, Frankfurt, Helsinki, London, Paris, Stockholm, and Warsaw. Finnair, Lufthansa, and SAS offer good connections.

BUS TRAVEL

Public transportation costs 80c at kiosks and 75c from the driver. Buy tickets separately for buses and trolleybuses. Punch your ticket upon boarding or be fined 20Lt. Most public transportation operates 5:30 AM–midnight. Intercity bus trips cost between 8Lt and 40Lt. For bus schedules phone Televerslas or the bus station.

➤ BUS INFORMATION: **Televerslas** (☎ 2/231–414). **Bus station** (☎ 2/704–000).

CAR RENTAL

Cars may be rented from 250Lt a day from Avis, Baltijos Autolīzingas, or Hertz.

➤ MAJOR AGENCIES: **Avis** (☎ 2/306–820). **Hertz** (☎ 2/726–940).

➤ LOCAL AGENCIES: **Baltijos Autolīzingas** (☎ 2/319–632.

CAR TRAVEL

An international or national driver's license bearing a photo is acceptable in Lithuania. Drive on the right. Main roads tend to be in good condition—better than those in Latvia or Estonia. Secondary roads, however, are commonly unpaved and have potholes. Gas costs 2Lt per liter.

EMERGENCIES

➤ CONTACTS: **Police** (☎ 02). **Ambulance** (☎ 03). **Doctor: Baltic-American Clinic** (☎ 2/342–020). **Dentist: Dentamed** (☎ 2/227–582). **Pharmacy: Gedimino Vaistinė** (☎ 2/624–930).

HOLIDAYS

January 1; February 16 (Independence Day); March 11 (Restoration of Lithuania's Independence); Easter; July 6 (Day of Statehood); November 1 (All Saints' Day); December 25, 26.

LANGUAGE

Lithuanian is the official language; however, English, Russian, and, to a certain degree, Polish are spoken in Vilnius.

MAIL AND SHIPPING

The main post office is open weekdays 7–7, Saturday 9–4.

➤ POST OFFICE: **Main post office** (✉ Gedimino 7, ☎ 2/616–759).

POSTAL RATES

A 20-gram letter to the United States or Europe costs 1.70Lt, a postcard 1.20Lt.

MONEY MATTERS

A cup of coffee or tea costs 3Lt–5Lt; a glass of local beer 8Lt; a medium-priced dish at a local restaurant 12Lt–15Lt. Admission to museums and galleries costs about 4Lt.

CURRENCY

The monetary unit in Lithuania is the lita, which is divided into 100 centas. There are notes of 1, 2, 5, 10, 20, 50, 100, and 200 litas and coins of 1, 2, and 5 litas and 1, 2, 5, 10, 20, and 50 centas. At press time (summer 2001) the rate of exchange was 4Lt to the U.S. dollar, 2.68Lt to the Canadian dollar, 6Lt to the pound sterling, 4.81Lt to the Irish punt, 2.24Lt to the Australian dollar, 1.78Lt to the New Zealand dollar, and 53c to the South African rand. National banks, with branches in all major and most minor cities, change cash and traveler's checks at fair commissions; most also give advances on a Visa card. Credit cards are widely accepted.

TAXIS

Taxis in Vilnius can be expensive around hotels and the bus and train stations. It's best to telephone for one. Taxi fares generally start at 1.30Lt and increase by 1Lt to 1.30Lt per kilometer (½ mi) in the daytime, more at night or in bad weather. Drivers must display an operating license and a meter. In-town journeys cost up to 10Lt. Try Baltas Taxi and Vilniaus Taxi.

Shared taxis accommodate up to 10 people and are cheap and comfortable. They operate on virtually every bus and trolleybus line. Tariffs are 1Lt to 2Lt. Passengers may embark at any regular bus stop and disembark anywhere along the route.
➤ TAXI COMPANIES: **Baltas Taxi** (☎ 2/220–909). **Vilniaus Taxi** (☎ 2/228–888 or 2/229–403).

TELEPHONES

COUNTRY AND AREA CODES

The country code for Lithuania is 370. The area code in Vilnius is 2.

INTERNATIONAL CALLS

➤ ACCESS CODE: **AT&T** (☎ 8–196).

LOCAL CALLS

Pay phones accept cards worth 7Lt. Buy phone cards from any post office or Lietuvos Spauda kiosk.
➤ INFORMATION: **Telephone information** (☎ 2/757–009).

TIPPING

At restaurants a service charge of 7% is sometimes added and an 18% VAT is included in the price of dishes on the menu but may be listed separately on your bill. Add 10% if you've received excellent service.

TOURS

Vilnius City Tour runs walking tours of Vilnius and minibus tours of the region.
➤ FEES & SCHEDULES: **Vilnius City Tour** (☎ 2/611–800).

TRAIN TRAVEL

Domestic train trips cost between 8Lt and 40Lt. For schedules call the train station. Beware that certain trains running from Vilnius to Poland cross Belarus. Avoid these trains, as you need a Belorussian transit visa to cross a mere 48 km (30 mi) of Belarus along the way. Trains are slower and less comfortable than buses.
➤ TRAIN INFORMATION: **Train station** (☎ 2/630–086).

Exploring Lithuania

Vilnius

What Vilnius has is *soul.* Good jazz, friendly faces, and amazingly cheap restaurants are a way of life here. The Old Town is somewhat shabby around the edges—it is, after all, the biggest in Central and Eastern Europe—but those structures that have been renovated shine in Baroque glory, and some that haven't been renovated house a living pulse as homes for the city's artsy squatters.

Founded by Lithuanian Grand Duke Gediminas in the 14th century. Vilnius was an important center of Lithuanian, Polish, and Jewish culture until World War II. Now this former "Jerusalem of the East" is Lithuania's bustling capital—a national symbol to extradited Poles, a ghost town to the 150,000 Jews who once lived here, and home to 100,000 displaced Russians. It has museums, lush parks, a wealth of Baroque churches, and myriad courtyards, many with cafés.

★ Vilnius's main cathedral, **Arkikatedra Bazilika,** has been a national symbol for centuries; inside is the dazzling 17th-century Chapel of St. Kazimieras. Originally a temple to Perkūnas, one of Lithuania's many pagan gods, the building became a church in the 13th century, when Lithuania converted from paganism to Christianity; it was the last European country to do so. The cathedral was used for other purposes under Communism; the church reclaimed the cathedral in the 1980s. ✉ *Katedros 1,* ☎ *2/611–127.* ⏲ *Daily 2–6.*

★ The **Aušros Vartai** (Gates of Dawn) is the only one remaining of Vilnius's nine 16th-century gates. Beyond it to the right, a door leads to the **Chapel of Our Lady of Vilnius,** a room whose walls are covered with metal and silver hearts and that contains an icon of the Virgin Mary renowned for its healing powers. Many of the devout climb on their knees up the steps to this holy place, converted into a chapel in 1671 and remade in neoclassical style in 1829. ✉ *Aušros Vartų.*

Wind past the good-natured, beer-drinking youth of Kalnų Parkas and mount Castle Hill, topped by the 13th-century **Gedimino bokštas** (Gedimino Tower), once part of the city's fortifications. Inside the tower is the **Vilniaus Pilies Muziejus** (Vilnius Castle Museum; ✉ Arsenalo 5, ☎ 2/617–453; ⏲ daily 11–6), which has outstanding city views.

To the east you can see the **Trijų Kryžių Kalnas** (Hill of Three Crosses), which are said to commemorate seven Franciscan monks killed on the hill by pagans; four of them were thrown into the river below (hence only three crosses).

During the early 1900s Vilnius was Europe's major center of Yiddish education and literature. By the end of World War II, all but 600 of Vilnius's 100,000 Jews had been killed. Today the **Jewish quarter** contains almost no trace of the once-thriving culture. The single remaining **synagogue** (✉ Pylimo 39) survived only because the Nazis used it as a medical-supply warehouse. To learn about Vilnius's Jewish heritage, visit the **Valstybinis Žydų Muziejus** (State Jewish Museum). ✉ *Pylimo 4,* ☎ *2/613–003.* ⏲ *Mon.–Thurs. 10–5:30, Fri. 10–4.*

★ In the New Town, at the **Genocido Aukų Muziejus** (KGB Museum), plaques take you through a litany of horrors in the basement of the former KGB prison. Hundreds of Lithuanians were killed here, and hundreds of thousands more were deported to Siberia by the Soviet regime during the 1940s and '50s. ✉ *Aukų 2a,* ☎ *2/622–449.* ⏲ *Tues.–Sun. 10–4.*

The amazing Gothic facade of the 16th-century **Šv Onos Bažnyčia** (St. Anne's Church) was created using 33 different types of brick. It's said that when Napoléon passed through town, he wanted to take the church back to Paris "in the palm of his hand." ✉ *Maironio 8,* ☎ *2/611–236.* ⏲ *Weekdays 6:30–8:30 PM, weekends 9–7:30.*

The Baroque 17th-century **Šv Kazimiero bažnyčia** (St. Casimir's Church) is named for the city's patron saint, Prince Casimir Jagiellon. During Russia's reign a cupola replaced the familiar crown. Today the church is a popular spot for Sunday-afternoon organ recitals. ✉ *Didžioji 34,* ☎ *2/221–715.* ⏲ *Mon.–Sat. 4–6:30, Sun. 8–1:30.*

The **Šv Petro ir Povilo** (Church of Sts. Peter and Paul) has an astounding Baroque interior, with nearly 2,000 ornate, white-stucco figures and an extraordinary boat-shape glass chandelier. ✉ *Antakalnio 1,* ☎ *2/340–229.* ⏲ *Mon.–Sat. 8–4:30, Sun. 10–8.*

The best collection of Lithuanian fine art is at the **Vilniaus Paveikslų Galerija** (Vilnius Picture Gallery), which displays 16th- to 19th-century paintings, as well as a number of sculptures and some early pottery and folk art. The interior of what was a palace from the 17th through the 19th centuries has been handsomely restored. ✉ *Didžioji 4,* ☎ *2/224–258.* ⏲ *Tues.–Sat. noon–6, Sun. noon–5.*

Vilniaus Universiteto (Vilnius University), founded by the Jesuits in 1570, is a complex of 12 courtyards. Highlights include the **observatory,** with its 18th-century zodiac engravings (note that it is not open to the public), and the Gothic **Sts. Johns' Church** (☎ 2/611–795), begun in 1387. ✉ *Šv Jono 12.*

$$ ✕ **Freskos.** The dining room is furnished with antiques and props from the opera and theater. The Continental menu might offer pepper steak or grilled chicken breast salad. A salad bar, a dessert cart, and local beer are also available. ✉ *Didžioji 31,* ☎ *2/618–133. MC, V.*

$ ✕ **Prie Parlamento.** The apple crumble here enjoys legendary status among diners. The informal atmosphere, hearty English breakfasts, and innovative pub grub all make for a satisfying meal. Visit the cellar dance club Ministerija at night for drinks, pop music dancing, and a friendly crowd. ✉ *Gedimino 46,* ☎ *2/621–606. MC, V.*

$ ✕ **Ritos Sleptuvė.** Lithuanian-American Rita Dapkus, who gave up political life to start cooking, serves authentic Chicago-style pizza, great steaks, the best Tex-Mex in Lithuania, and Vilnius's best breakfast. ✉ *Goštauto 8,* ☎ *2/626–117. AE, MC, V.*

$ ✕ **Žaltvysklė.** Part of the Vilnius University complex of buildings, this Hungarian café has a Gothic interior. The inexpensive menu concentrates on Hungarian cuisine but also offers national dishes from Lithuania and Bulgaria. ✉ *Pilies 11,* ☎ *2/687–173. MC, V.*

$ ✕ **Žemaičių smuklė.** The huge and delicious portions of roasted meats, fresh vegetables, and cooked potatoes, the friendly service, and the cabin-like interior and medieval summer patio make this restaurant one of the best places to sample Lithuanian cuisine. ✉ *Vokiečių 24,* ☎ *2/616–573. MC, V.*

$$$$ 🏨 **Narutis.** This Old Town hotel has spacious, well-appointed rooms. The restored building dates from the 16th century and has an unbeatable location. ✉ *Pilies 24, 2001,* ☎ *2/222–894,* FAX *2/622–882. 30 rooms. 2 restaurants. AE, MC, V.*

$$$$ 🏨 **Radisson SAS Astorija Hotel Vilnius.** Radisson-quality rooms in this late-19th-century building have a touch of the antique thrown in. As the only international chain property in town, this hotel sets the standard for service in Vilnius. ✉ *Didžioji 35/2, 2001,* ☎ *2/220–110,* FAX *2/221–762,* WEB *www.radisson.com. 120 rooms. Restaurant. AE, DC, MC, V.*

$$$$ 🏨 **Stikliai.** Rooms at this inn dating from the 17th century are lavish and elegant, with a hint of British colonial meets Martha Stewart: comfortable, with lots of flower prints, antique baskets, and knickknacks. ✉ *Gaono 7, 2001,* ☎ *2/627–971,* FAX *2/223–870,* WEB *www.iti.lt/stikliai/. 29 rooms. 2 restaurants. AE, MC, V.*

$$$ 🏨 **Naujasis Vilnius.** Across the river from Old Town, the "New Vilnius" hotel offers colorful rooms with modern decor and a helpful, efficient staff. ✉ *Ukmergės 14, 2011,* ☎ *2/726–756,* FAX *2/723–161,* WEB *www.is.lt/LTF/Nvhome.htm. 102 rooms. Restaurant. AE, MC, V.*

$$ 🏨 **Lietuvos Telekomas Svečių Namai.** Run by Lithuanian Telecom and near Old Town, this small, modern hotel offers rooms with all the amenities and none of the personality of the more expensive hotels. ✉ *Vivulskio 13a, 2009,* ☎ *2/313–533,* FAX *2/652–782. 10 rooms. Restaurant. MC, V.*

$ 🏨 **JNN Hostel.** This hostel across the river from the Old Town has a youthful ambience but impeccably clean rooms. ✉ *Ukmergės 25, 2600,* ☎ *2/722–270,* FAX *2/725–651. 10 rooms. Restaurant, pool. MC, V.*

Neringa

Also known as the Courland Spit, this tiny 100-km-long (62-mi-long) strip of land 315 km (195 mi) west of Vilnius via ferry from Klaipeda ranks among Europe's most fascinating natural features. Although only half of the spit is Lithuanian—the other half belongs to the Russian exclave of Kaliningrad—there's plenty of space for playing on the beach. Of the two tiny villages, **Nida,** about 50 km (31 mi) down the two-lane road, is the more developed, with bigger dunes and a more popular beach. The sleepy town of **Juodkrantė,** 25 km (15 mi) out on the spit, feels less like a resort.

5 BELGIUM

BRUSSELS, ANTWERP, GHENT, BRUGGE

BELGIUM IS A CONNOISSEUR'S DELIGHT. The land of Brueghel and Van Eyck, Rubens and Van Dyck, and Ensor and Magritte is where their best work can still be seen. Belgian culture was and remains that of a bourgeois, mercantile society. Feudal lords may have built Belgium's many castles, and the clergy its splendid churches, but merchants and craftsmen are responsible for the guild houses and sculpture-adorned town halls of Brussels, Antwerp, Ghent, and Brugge.

This small country offers surprising variety, from the beaches and dunes of the North Sea coast and the tree-lined canals and big sky of the "platte (flat) land" to the rolling Brueghel country around Brussels and the sheer cliffs and dense woods of the Ardennes. The state of Belgium is one of Europe's youngest, but its territory has been fought over for centuries by invaders from all sides. Julius Caesar called the Belgae the bravest of the tribes that defied the Roman legions. Since then, the land we now call Belgium has been fought over and conquered by the Franks, the dukes of Burgundy, the Spanish, the Austrians, and the French. Finally, after the defeat of Napoléon in 1815, Belgium was forcibly amalgamated with Holland into the United Kingdom of the Netherlands.

With independence from their Dutch rulers in 1830, Belgium began forging a national identity. The independent state of Belgium was universally recognized in 1831 as a monarchy under its first king, Leopold I, and his heirs have continued to hold the throne to the present day. The current monarch, Albert II, was crowned in 1993.

The Belgians are inveterate individualists—witness the endless variations of Art Nouveau in the Belle Epoque town houses that line many a prosperous street. The art of living well has been cultivated since the days of the great Burgundian wedding feasts, when members of the ruling dynasty were joined with other royal houses. The country continues to claim an amazing number of eating places dedicated to haute cuisine. Whole families often celebrate a first communion, an engagement, or a birthday in an expensive restaurant.

Belgium packs nearly 6 million Dutch-speaking Flemings and just over 4 million French-speaking Walloons into a country the size of Vermont or Wales. The presence of two major language communities enriches its intellectual life but also creates constant political and social tension. The creation in the mid-1990s of three largely self-governing regions—Flanders, Wallonia, and the City of Brussels, which is bilingual and multicultural—has only emphasized these divisions.

Belgium's neutrality was violated during both world wars, when much of its architectural heritage was destroyed and great suffering was in-

Belgium (Belgique, België)

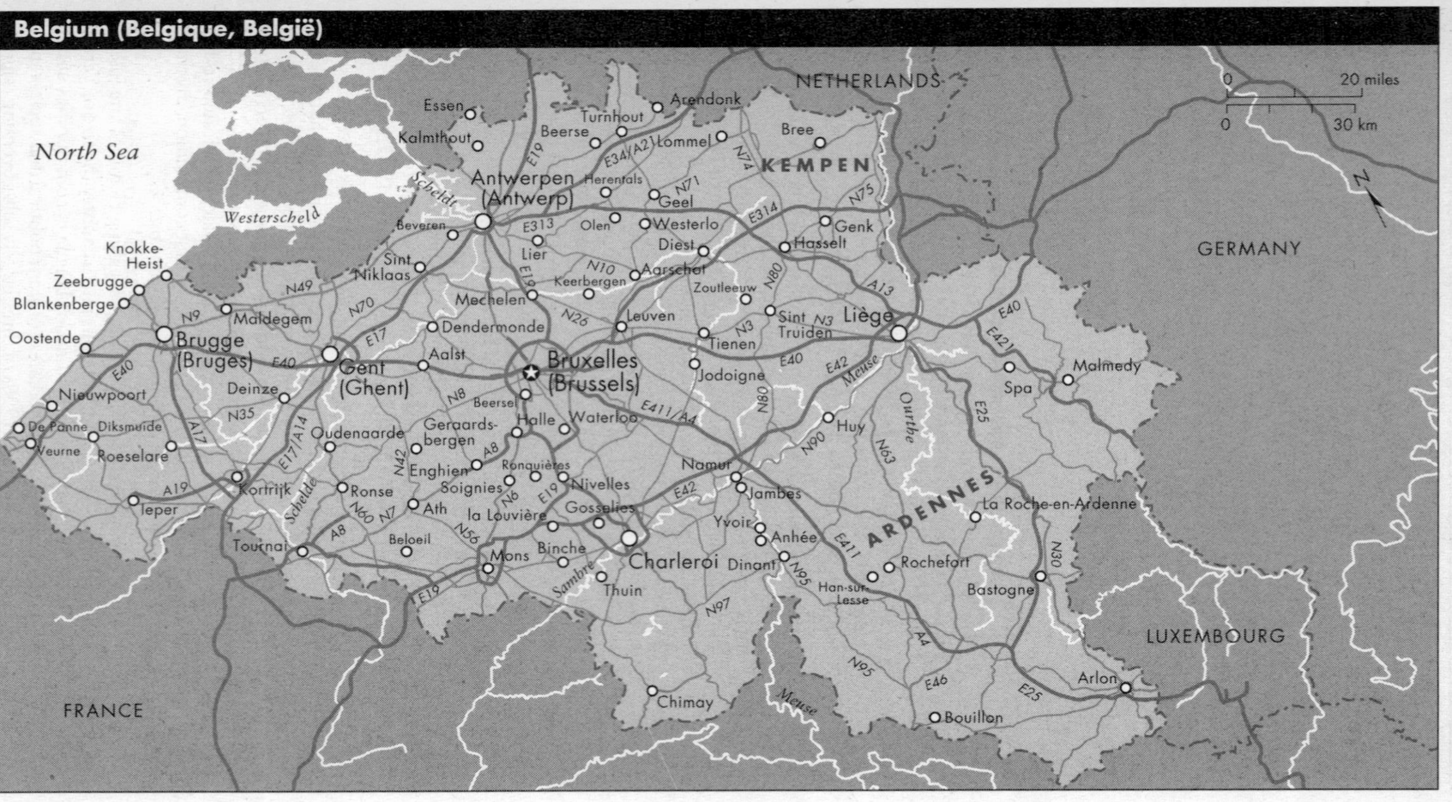

flicted by the occupying forces. This may be why Belgium staunchly supports the European Union (EU), which has guaranteed peace in Western Europe for the past 50 years. As the home of most of the EU institutions, Brussels has to some become a synonym for a faceless bureaucracy, but this is unfair to both the city and the so-called Eurocrats. For the Belgian government, maintaining the trust of the people without pandering to extremist linguistic-political divisions looks to be a tall order.

BELGIUM A TO Z

To research prices, get advice from other travelers, and book travel arrangements, visit www.fodors.com.

AIR TRAVEL

There are no domestic air services.

BIKE TRAVEL

You can rent a bicycle from Belgian National Railways at 35 stations throughout the country; train travelers get reduced rates. These bikes are serviceable, but not the state-of-the-art mountain bikes you can rent in specialized outlets. Bicycling is easy in the flat northern and coastal areas; in the hilly south and east it's more strenuous. There are bicycle lanes in many Flemish cities, where car use is being discouraged, but cycling in downtown Brussels can be downright dangerous.

BUS TRAVEL

Local city buses (STIB/MIVB) serve greater Brussels and the closer suburbs. Small towns and the outlying suburbs are served by independent transport companies De Lijn (within Flanders) and TEC (within Wallonia). Intercity bus services are rudimentary. Check at the tourist office or train station.

BUSINESS HOURS

Banks are usually open weekdays 9 AM–4 or 4:30 PM; some close for an hour at lunch. Currency exchange facilities (*bureaux de change* or *wisselkantoren*) are usually open evenings and weekends, but you'll get a better rate in banks during the week. For instant cash, ATMs are nearly everywhere (but not at railway stations) and accept major credit cards. Museums are generally open 10 AM–5 PM Tuesday through Sunday. Many museums will refuse to admit you after 4:15 PM or so. Large stores are open weekdays and Saturday from 9:30 or 10 AM to 6:30 or 7 PM and generally stay open an hour later on Friday. "Night" shops, for newspapers, tobacco, drinks, and limited grocery items, are open seven days a week from 6 PM until dawn.

CAR TRAVEL

On-street parking often requires you to display a ticket dispensed from not-always-obvious coin-operated machines generally in the middle of the block. Old-fashioned meters still line some streets. Parking garages provide another option, but few stay open past 10 PM. On no account park in front of a garage or a building bearing a towing sign: being towed is expensive and time-consuming.

Road signs are written in the language of the region, so you need to know that Antwerp is Antwerpen in Dutch and Anvers in French; likewise, Brugge is Bruges in French, and Brussels is Bruxelles in French and Brussel in Dutch; Ghent is Gent (Dutch) and Gand (French). Even more confusing, Liège and Luik are the same place, as are Louvain and Leuven, and Namur and Namen. Yet more difficult is Mons (French) and Bergen (Dutch), or Tournai (French) and Doornik (Dutch). On the

Brussels-Liège/Luik motorway, signs change language with alarming frequency as you crisscross the Wallonia-Flanders border. Finally, *Uitrit* is Dutch for exit.

ROAD CONDITIONS

Belgium has an excellent system of toll-free expressways, and the main roads are generally very good. Road numbers for main roads have the prefix *N* for national roads; highways and expressways are prefixed by *A* or *E*.

RULES OF THE ROAD

All motorists must hold a valid national or international driver's license. Drive on the right and pass on the left; passing on the right is forbidden. Seat belts are compulsory in both front and rear seats. Every car must have a triangle-shaped warning sign to be used in the event of a breakdown or accident. Unless otherwise posted, traffic on the right has right-of-way at intersections. Adhere strictly to this rule, as there are few stop or yield signs. Never, ever assume that someone with priority will stop if you don't. Pedestrians have priority on marked crossings, and vehicles in traffic circles have priority over those entering them—even if they're coming from the right. Buses have priority over cars, and trams have absolute priority; they will ring bells or sound horns if you're obstructing them, and they will hit you if they can't stop. Maximum speed limits are 120 kph (75 mph) on highways, 90 kph (55 mph) on major roads, and 50 kph (30 mph) in cities. Lower limits are frequently imposed. The maximum permitted blood alcohol level is 0.05%, a level you can reach with two glasses of beer or one glass of wine.

CUSTOMS AND DUTIES

For details on imports and duty-free limits for visitors from outside the EU, *see* Customs & Duties *in* Chapter 1.

DINING

Most Belgians take eating seriously and are discerning about fresh produce and innovative recipes. At the top end of the scale, *menus dégustation* (tasting menus) offer a chance to sample small portions of a large selection of the chef's finest dishes. Many brasseries and neighborhood restaurants have risen to the challenge of making eating out more affordable, and animated ambience amply compensates for a more limited cuisine.

Belgian specialties include *lapin à la kriek* (rabbit in cherry-flavored beer), *anguilles au vert* (eels in a green herb sauce), *waterzooi* (a creamy fish or chicken stew), and *moules/frites* (fresh steamed mussels served with french fries). Other local specialties are *chicons* (Belgian endive); marvelous white asparagus from Mechelen, at its best in April; and tiny, sweet shrimp fresh from the North Sea. For lunch, cold cuts, a *croque monsieur* (grilled ham-and-cheese sandwich), and *jambon d'Ardennes* (smoked Ardennes ham) are popular, as is the *tartine au fromage blanc* (an open-face sandwich of dark bread with soft white cheese, served with chopped radishes and spring onions).

Fixed-price menus are widely available and often represent considerable savings. Menus and prices are posted outside most restaurants, but it's a good idea to check availability before you sit down in tourist areas. Reservations are a must in finer establishments. Few restaurants have no-smoking sections, and many welcome dogs.

Prices are for one for main course at dinner and include a whopping 21% value-added tax. Belgian restaurants include a 16% service charge on all bills. Look for fixed-price menus or the daily special (*plat du jour* or *dagschotel*); if you sacrifice choice, you can eat well for less than BF700 in many good restaurants. Restaurant prices are roughly the same in Brussels and other cities.

CATEGORY	COST
$$$$	over BF1,200 (€30)
$$$	BF900–BF1,200 (€22–€30)
$$	BF500–BF900 (€12–€22)
$	under BF500 (€12)

MEALTIMES

Most hotels serve breakfast until 10 AM. Belgians usually eat lunch between 1 and 3 PM. The main meal of the day is dinner, which most Belgians eat between 7 and 10 PM; peak dining time used to be about 8 PM but is now creeping closer to 9 PM. Dining well after 10:30 PM is something of a challenge, although a few student hangouts near the main university campuses stay open late.

RESERVATIONS & DRESS

Jacket and tie are required only in the most exclusive establishments. Most Belgians favor casual wear; open-neck shirts, slacks, and jeans popular with all age groups. Women usually dress up more than men.

EMBASSIES

➤ AUSTRALIA: (✉ Rue Guimard 6, 1040 Brussels, ☎ 02/286–0500).
➤ CANADA: (✉ Av. de Tervuren 2, 1040 Brussels, ☎ 02/741–0611).
➤ IRELAND: (✉ Rue Froissart 81, 1040 Brussels, ☎ 02/230–5337).
➤ NEW ZEALAND: (✉ Sq. de Meeus 1, 7/F, 1000 Brussels, ☎ 02/512–1040).
➤ SOUTH AFRICA: (✉ Wetstraat 26, 1000 Brussels, ☎ 02/285–4400).
➤ UNITED KINGDOM: (✉ Rue d'Arlon 85, 1040 Brussels, ☎ 02/287–6211).
➤ UNITED STATES: (✉ Bd. du Régent 25-27, 1000 Brussels, ☎ 02/508–2111).

HOLIDAYS

January 1; Easter Monday; May 1 (Labor Day); June 1 (Ascension); Pentecost or Whit Monday(last Monday in May); July 21 (Belgian National Day); August 15 (Assumption); November 1 (All Saints' Day); November 11 (Armistice Day); December 25.

LANGUAGE

Language is a sensitive subject and exerts an unhealthy influence on politics at the national and regional levels. There are three official languages in Belgium: French, spoken primarily in the south of the country (Wallonia); Dutch, spoken in the north (Flanders); and German, spoken in a small area in the east near the German border. Brussels is bilingual, with both French and Dutch officially recognized, though the majority of residents are francophones. Many people speak English in Brussels and throughout Flanders; in Wallonia, English-speakers tend to be thin on the ground. Belgian French and Dutch both contain slight differences from the corresponding languages spoken in the neighboring countries to the south and north.

LODGING

As the self-proclaimed capital of Europe, Brussels attracts high-powered visitors, and many luxury hotels have been built to accommodate them. Over weekends and during July and August, business travelers are few and far between, so prices come down to BF5,000/€124 or less. New hotels catering to cost-conscious travelers have also been built, where doubles cost less than BF3,000/€76. Rates change considerably and without notice, so verify your rate when making a reservation.

Hotel prices, including sales tax and service charge, are usually posted in each room. All prices listed below are for two people in a standard double room, excluding a 16% service charge and a 14.9% room tax. The tax is slightly lower at suburban hotels.

CATEGORY	BRUSSELS	OTHER CITIES
$$$$	over BF9,000/€223	over BF7,500/€186
$$$	BF6,500–BF9,000 (€161–€223)	BF5,500–BF7,500 (€136–€186)
$$	BF3,500–BF6,500 (€87–€161)	BF2,500–BF5,500 (€62–€136)
$	under BF3,500 (€87)	under BF2,500 (€62)

B&BS

B&Bs are now an attractive option, thanks to self-regulation and higher standards. Contact local tourist offices.

CAMPING

Belgium is well supplied with camping and caravan (trailer) sites. For details contact the Royal Camping & Caravaning Club de Belgique. Both the Flemish and Walloon tourist offices publish guides to recommended campsites in their respective regions.

➤ ORGANIZATIONS: **Royal Camping & Caravaning Club de Belgique** (✉ Av. Villa 5, Brussels, ☎ 02/537–3681).

HOSTELS

For information about youth hostels in Brussels and Wallonia, contact Les Auberges de la Jeunesse. For Flanders, contact Vlaamse Jeugdherbergcentrale. The youth organization Connections makes travel arrangements for young people.

➤ ORGANIZATIONS: **Les Auberges de la Jeunesse** (✉ Rue de la Sablonnière 28, Brussels, ☎ 02/219–5676). **Connections** (✉ Rue du Midi 19–21, Brussels, ☎ 02/550–0100).**Vlaamse Jeugdherbergcentrale** (✉ Van Stralenstraat 40, 2060 Antwerp, ☎ 03/232–7218).

HOTELS

You can trust Belgian hotels, almost without exception, to be clean and of a high standard. The ritzier hotels in city centers tend to be like luxury hotels around the globe. Smaller, family-owned hotels are much more personal. Brugge is especially well supplied with romantic hideaways. BTR (Belgian Tourist Reservations) handles reservations free.

➤ ORGANIZATIONS: **BTR** (Belgian Tourist Reservations; ✉ Bd. Anspach 111, Brussels, ☎ 02/513–7484, FAX 02/513–9277).

MAIL AND SHIPPING

First-class (airmail) letters and postcards to the United States cost BF34, second-class (surface) BF23. Airmail letters and postcards to the United Kingdom cost BF21, second-class BF19. All international first-class mail must be marked with a blue A-PRIOR sticker (available in post offices). The central post office is open 24 hours a day, seven days a week.

➤ POST OFFICES: **Central post office** (✉ Av. Frosny 1, 1060 Brussels).

MONEY MATTERS

Costs in Brussels are roughly on a par with those in London and New York. All taxes and service charges (tips) are included in hotel and restaurant bills and taxi fares. Gasoline prices are steep, but highways are toll-free.

Cup of coffee in a café, BF50/€1.25–BF60/€1.50; a glass of draft beer, BF50/€1.25–BF70/€1.75; a glass of wine, about BF120/€2.97. A single bus/metro/tram ride BF50/€1.24; theater tickets from about BF500/€12.40.

CURRENCY

Belgium, as one of the euro zone currency countries, will introduce euro (€) notes and coins on January 1, 2002. The euro and the Belgian franc (BF) will circulate simultaneously through February 2002. Banks and ATMs will give all money in euros. Shops and restaurants are encouraged to give change in euros whenever possible. Prices are marked in both euros and Belgian francs. In Belgian francs there are bills of 100, 200, 500, 1,000, 2,000, and 10,000 francs and coins of 1, 5, 20, and 50 francs. At press time (summer 2001), the exchange rate was BF42.66 to the U.S. dollar, BF28.94 to the Canadian dollar, BF64.03 to the pound sterling, BF51.22 to the Irish punt, BF25.57 to the Australian dollar, BF20.20 to the New Zealand dollar, BF6.17 to the South African rand, and BF40.34 to the euro.

VALUE ADDED TAX (V.A.T.)

One option often suggested by diamond jewelers in Antwerp is that you pay the full amount by credit card. After you have had the invoice stamped by customs at your last port of call in the EU, you mail it back to the store of purchase, and the VAT amount will be credited to your credit card or bank account.

TELEPHONES

COUNTRY & AREA CODES

The country code for Belgium is 32. Under a new dialing procedure, all calls within the country must include the regional telephone code. When dialing Belgium from outside the country, drop the first zero in the regional code.

INTERNATIONAL CALLS

Buy a high-denomination telecard and make a direct call from a phone booth. For credit card and collect calls, dial AT&T, MCI Worldphone, or Sprint Global One.

➤ ACCESS CODES: **AT&T** (☎ 0800–10010), **MCI Worldphone** (☎ 0800–10012), **Sprint Global One** (☎ 0800–10014).

PUBLIC PHONES

Pay phones work mostly with telecards, available at post offices, supermarkets, neighborhood shops, railway stations, and many newsstands. Cards are sold in denominations of BF200, BF500, and BF1,000. An average local call costs BF20. Coin-operated phones (on the platforms of metro stations) take 5- and 20-franc coins. All telephone numbers must be preceded by their area code prefix, regardless of the location in Belgium from where the call is made.

TIPPING

A tip (*service compris* or *service inclusief*) is always included in restaurant and hotel bills and in taxi fares. Railway porters expect BF30/€0.75 per item on weekdays and BF40/€1.00 per item on weekends. For bellhops and doormen, BF100/€2.50 is adequate. Give movie ushers BF20/€0.50 per person in your party, whether or not they show you to your seat. If no fixed price is indicated, tip washroom attendants BF10/€0.25. And tip doormen at bars, nightclubs, or discos at least BF50/€1.25 if you're planning to go back.

TRAIN TRAVEL

Fast and frequent trains connect all main towns and cities. Reduced tariffs are available for daily and weekend return trips, for large families, groups, senior citizens, and young people under 26. Check with the train station to see what specials are currently on offer. A Benelux Tourrail Ticket allows unlimited travel throughout Belgium, Luxembourg, and the Netherlands for any five days over a one-month period. People under 26 can purchase a Go Pass, valid for 10 second-class, one-way trips within Belgium in a six-month period. Special weekend round-trip tickets are valid from Friday morning to Monday night: a 40% reduction is available on the first traveler's ticket and a 60% reduction on companions' tickets.

VISITOR INFORMATION

Each region has its own tourist office. The national Flemish office and the national French-speaking office are at the same address in Brussels and share a ground-floor Tourist Information Office.

➤ TOURIST INFORMATION: **National Flemish office** (☎ 02/504–0300). **Tourist Information Office** (✉ rue du Marché-aux-Herbes 63, ☎ 02/504–0390).

WHEN TO GO

The tourist season runs from early May to late September and peaks in July and August, when the weather is warmest. May and September offer the advantage of generally clear skies and smaller crowds, but be prepared for rain any time of the year.

CLIMATE

Temperatures range from around 65°F in May to an average of 73°F in July and August. In winter they drop to an average of about 40°F to 45°F. Snow is unusual except in the mountains of the Ardennes, where skiing is popular. On the coast and in the Ardennes, freezing fogs can reduce visibility to 5 yards and render road surfaces glassy.

The following are the average daily maximum and minimum temperatures for Brussels.

Jan.	40F	4C	**May**	65F	18C	**Sept.**	69F	21C
	30	– 1		46	8		51	11
Feb.	44F	7C	**June**	72F	22C	**Oct.**	60F	15C
	32	0		52	11		45	7
Mar.	51F	11C	**July**	73F	23C	**Nov.**	48F	9C
	36	25		4	12		38	3
Apr.	58F	14C	**Aug.**	72F	22C	**Dec.**	42F	6C
	41	5		54	12		32	0

BRUSSELS

Brussels has become synonymous with the European Union and the project to unite the continent, but while diplomats, politicians, lobbyists, and journalists have flocked to the city, it's far from becoming gray and faceless. Brussels's strength is its diversity. A bilingual city where French- and Dutch-speaking communities are too often divided, Brussels is home to all the cultures of Europe—east and west—as well as Americans, Canadians, Congolese, Rwandans, Vietnamese, Turks, and Moroccans. Art Nouveau flourished in Brussels as nowhere else, and its spirit lives on in gloriously individualistic town houses. Away from the winding alleys of the city center, parks and squares are plentiful, and the Bois de la Cambre, at the end of Avenue Louise, leads straight into a forest as large as the city itself.

Exploring Brussels

You need to give yourself at least two days to explore the many riches of Brussels, devoting one day to the lower town (whose cobblestones call for comfortable walking shoes) and the other to the great museums and uptown shopping streets.

Around the Grand'Place

The Grand'Place, whose gilded splendor makes it one of Europe's most impressive squares, serves as an anchor for an area where the ghosts of the past mingle with a lively contemporary scene. Narrow, cobbled streets radiate off the square, with a rich offering of cafés, restaurants, and souvenir shops.

Numbers in the margin correspond to points of interest on the Brussels map.

9 **Cathédrale des Sts-Michel-et-Gudule.** The names of the archangel and an obscure 7th-century local saint have been joined for the cathedral of Brussels. Begun in 1226, it combines architectural styles from the Romanesque to full-blown Gothic. The chief treasures are the stained-glass windows inspired by the drawings of Bernard Van Orley, an early 16th-century court painter. The ornately carved pulpit (1699) depicts Adam and Eve being expelled from the Garden of Eden. In the crypt are remnants of the original 11th-century Romanesque church. ✉ *Parvis Ste-Gudule,* ☎ *02/217–8345.* ⏲ *Daily 7:30–6.*

★ 7 **Centre Belge de la Bande Dessinée** (Belgian Comic Strip Center). This unique museum celebrates the comic strip, focusing on such famous Belgian graphic artists as Hergé, Tintin's creator; Morris, the progenitor of Lucky Luke; and many others. There are a library, a bookshop, and an airy brasserie. The display is housed in what used to be a draper's wholesale warehouse, designed in 1906 by Art Nouveau pioneer Victor Horta (1861–1947) and restored to its former glory in 1989. ✉ *Rue des Sables 20,* ☎ *02/219–1980,* WEB *www.fumetti.org/cbc/cbc.htm.* ⏲ *Tues.–Sun. 10–6.*

5 **Galeries St-Hubert.** The oldest covered shopping arcade in western Europe—and still one of its most elegant—was constructed in 1847 and is filled with shops, restaurants, cafés, and theaters. Diffused daylight penetrates the gallery from the glazed vaults high above, and neoclassical gods and heroes look down from their sculpted niches. Midway through, the gallery is traversed by **rue des Bouchers,** which forms the main restaurant area. Caveat: the more lavish the display of food outside, the poorer the cuisine inside. ✉ *Between rue du Marché-aux-Herbes and rue d'Arenberg.*

★ 1 **Grand'Place.** The ornate Baroque guild houses here, with their burnished facades, were completed in 1695, just three years after a French bombardment destroyed everything but the Town Hall. The houses are topped by gilded statues of saints and heroes, so vividly rendered that they seem to call out to each other. Thus the end result of Louis XIV's folly is Europe's most sumptuous market square and the heart of the city. On summer nights, music and colored light flood the entire square. Shops, restaurants, and taverns occupy most ground floors. The Maison des Brasseurs houses the **Brewery Museum** (✉ Grand'Place 10, ☎ 02/511–4987). The Grand'Place comes enchantingly alive during local festivals such as the Ommegang, a magnificent historical pageant re-creating Emperor Charles V's reception in the city (first Tues. and Thurs. in July). ✉ *Rue au Beurre, rue du Chair et du Pain, rue des Harengs, rue de la Colline, rue de l'Étuve, rue de la Tête d'Or.*

2 **Hôtel de Ville** (Town Hall). Dominating the Grand'Place, the Town Hall is around 300 years older than the guild houses that line the square. The slender central tower, combining boldness and light, is topped by a statue of the archangel Michael crushing the devil under his feet. The halls are embellished with some of the finest examples of local tapestries from the 16th, 17th, and 18th centuries. ✉ *Grand'Place,* ☎ *02/279–*

Brussels (Bruxelles, Brussel)

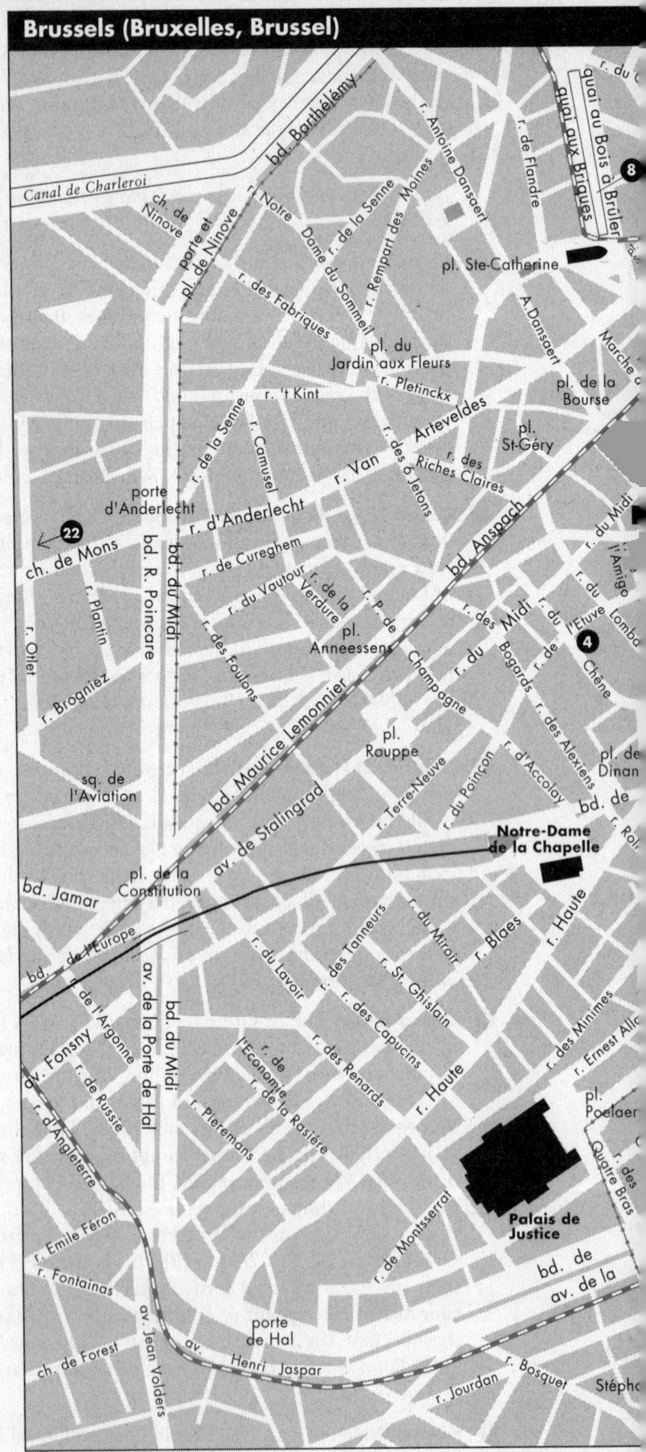

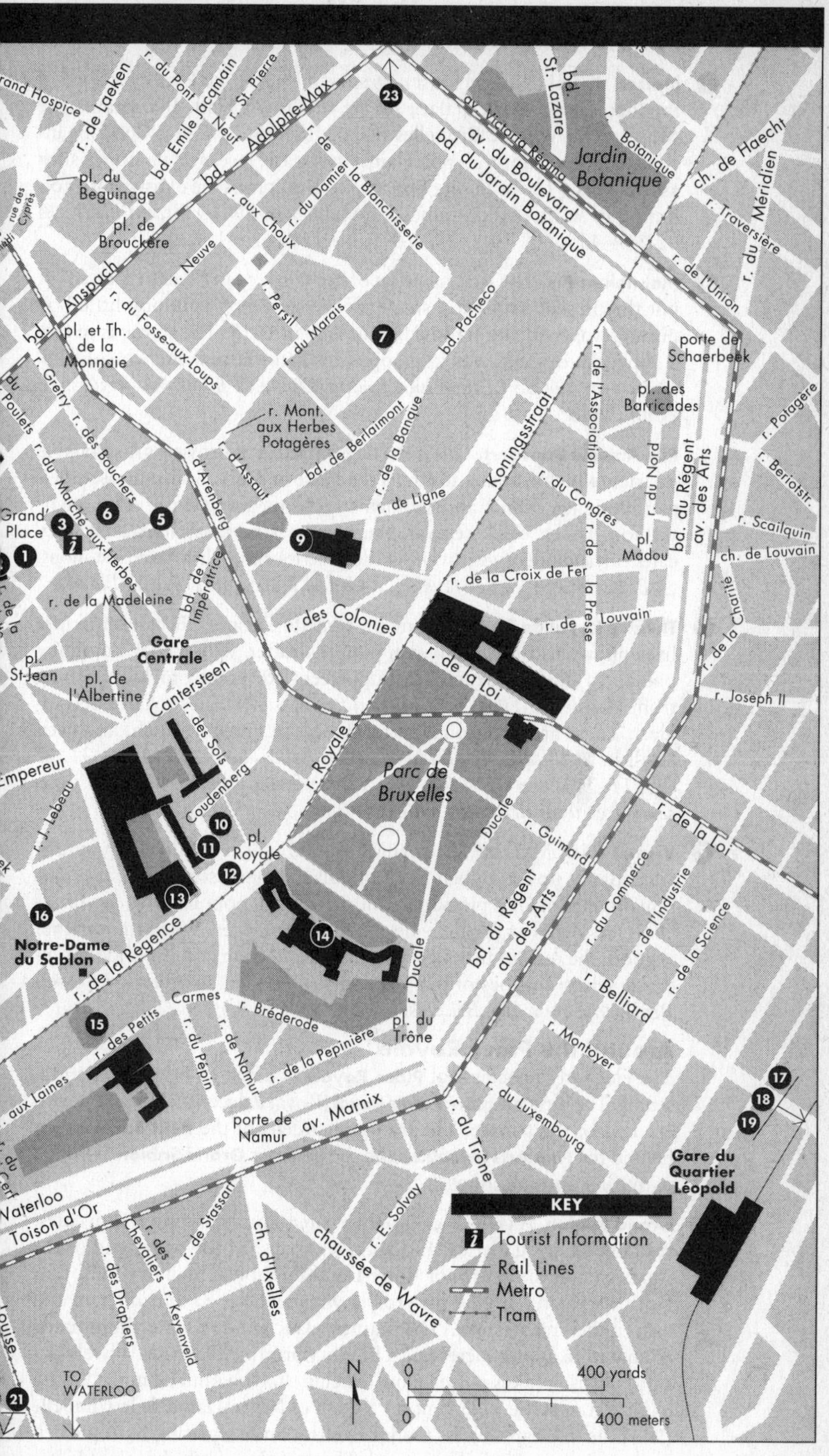

Jardin Botanique
Parc de Bruxelles
Gare Centrale
Notre-Dame du Sablon
Gare du Quartier Léopold
Grand' Place
pl. du Beguinage
pl. de Brouckère
pl. et Th. de la Monnaie
pl. St-Jean
pl. de l'Albertine
pl. Royale
pl. du Trône
pl. des Barricades
pl. Madou
porte de Schaerbeek
porte de Namur
bd. Adolphe-Max
bd. Anspach
bd. Emile Jacqmain
bd. du Jardin Botanique
bd. St. Lazare
bd. Pacheco
bd. de Berlaimont
bd. de l'Impératrice
bd. du Régent
av. des Arts
av. du Boulevard
av. Victoria Regina
av. Marnix
Koningsstraat
Cantersteen
ch. de Haecht
ch. de Louvain
ch. d'Ixelles
chaussée de Wavre
r. de Laeken
r. du Pont Neuf
r. St. Pierre
r. Neuve
r. aux Choux
r. du Damier
r. de la Blanchisserie
r. Persil
r. du Marais
r. du Fosse-aux-Loups
r. Mont. aux Herbes Potagères
r. d'Arenberg
r. d'Assaut
r. de la Banque
r. de Ligne
r. des Bouchers
r. du Marché-aux-Herbes
r. de la Madeleine
r. des Colonies
r. de la Loi
r. Royale
r. des Sols
Coudenberg
r. J. Lebeau
r. de la Régence
r. des Petits Carmes
r. Bréderode
r. de la Pepinière
r. du Pépin
r. de Namur
r. aux Laines
r. Ducale
r. Guimard
r. du Commerce
r. de l'Industrie
r. de la Science
r. Belliard
r. Montoyer
r. du Luxembourg
r. du Trône
r. E. Solvay
r. de Stassart
r. des Chevaliers
r. des Drapiers
r. Keyenveld
r. du Congres
r. de la Croix de Fer
r. de Louvain
r. de la Presse
r. de l'Association
r. du Nord
r. Botanique
r. Traversière
r. du Méridien
r. de l'Union
r. Potagère
r. Beriotstr.
r. Scailquin
r. de la Charité
r. Joseph II
r. Grétry
r. des Poulets
Waterloo
Toison d'Or
TO WATERLOO
KEY
Tourist Information
Rail Lines
Metro
Tram
N
0
400 yards
0
400 meters

2340. ⏲ *English-speaking tours Tues. 11:30 and 3:15, Wed. 3:15, Sun. 12:15. No individual visits.*

3 **Maison du Roi** (King's House). Despite the name, no king ever lived in this neo-Gothic–style palace facing the Town Hall. It contains the **Musée de la Ville de Bruxelles** (City Museum), whose collections include Gothic sculptures, porcelain, silverware, lace, and paintings such as Brueghel's *The Wedding Procession.* Don't miss the extravagant collection of some 600 costumes for Manneken-Pis. ✉ *Grand'Place,* ☎ *02/279–4350.* ⏲ *Tues.–Fri. 10–5, weekends 10–1.*

4 **Manneken-Pis.** The first mention of the "little man" dates from 1377, but the present version, a small bronze statue of a chubby little boy peeing, was made by Jérôme Duquesnoy in 1619. The statue is in fact a copy; the original was kidnapped by 18th-century French soldiers. ✉ *Corner rue de l'Étuve and rue du Chêne, 3 blocks southwest of Grand'Place.*

Rue Antoine Dansaert. This is the flagship street of Brussels's fashionable quarter, which extends south to the Place St-Géry. Boutiques sell Belgian-designed men's and women's fashions along with other high-fashion names. Slick restaurants, trendy bars, jazz clubs, and cozy cafés rub shoulders with avant-garde galleries and stylish furniture shops. ✉ *Between rue Van Artevelde at Grand'Place and Porte de Flandre.*

6 **Théâtre Royal de Toone** (Toone Marionette Theater). Brussels folklore lives on in this tiny, family-run puppet theater, with a cozy adjoining pub and a small museum. The puppeteers irreverently tackle anything from *Hamlet* to *The Three Musketeers* in the broadest of Brussels dialect. There are occasional performances in French, Dutch, and even English. ✉ *Impasse Schuddeveld 6 off Petite rue des Bouchers 21,* ☎ *02/511–7137 or 02/513–5486.* *Performances BF400/€10, museum free with ticket for show.* ⏲ *Tues.–Sat. 8:30* PM.

8 **Vismet** (Fish Market). The canals around which this lively quay district sprang up have been filled in, but the many seafood restaurants remain, making it a pleasantly animated area, popular with the Bruxellois (residents of Brussels) despite the high prices. When the weather is good, the restaurants all set up tables and chairs on the wide promenade where cargoes of fish were once unloaded. ✉ *Quai au Bois-à-Brûler and quai aux Briques.*

Around the Place Royale

The elegantly neoclassical **Place Royale** is home of Brussels' art museums. The rather austere **Palais Royal** (Royal Palace) anchors the northern end of the square. The tranquil gardens of the **Petit Sablon,** just behind the **Fine Arts Museum,** and the gracious **Grand Sablon** are lined with tony antique shops.

★ 16 **Grand Sablon.** A well-to-do, sophisticated square, it's alive with cafés, restaurants, art galleries, and antiques shops. At the upper end of the square stands the church of **Notre-Dame du Sablon,** built in flamboyant Gothic style in 1304 by the crossbowmen who used to train here and now under restoration. The stained-glass windows are illuminated from within at night, creating a kindly warmth. Weekends, a lively antiques market takes place below the church. Downhill from the Grand Sablon stands the 12th-century church of **Notre-Dame de la Chapelle** (✉ Pl. de la Chapelle). Its Gothic exterior and surprising Baroque belfry have been splendidly restored. This was the parish church of Pieter Brueghel the Elder (1520–69); he is buried here in a marble tomb.

13 **Musée d'Art Ancien** (Fine Arts Museum). The collection of Old Masters focuses on Flemish and Dutch paintings from the 15th to the 19th

century. In the Brueghel Room is one of the world's finest collections of Pieter the Elder's works, including *The Fall of Icarus;* the Rubens Room holds paintings by that master. The museum displays works by Hieronymus Bosch, Memling, Van Dyck, and many others. An underground passage links it with the adjacent Museum of Modern Art. ✉ *Rue de la Régence 3,* ☎ *02/508–3211,* WEB *www.fine-arts-museum.be.* ⏲ *Tues.–Sun. 10–5*

★ ⓫ **Musée d'Art Moderne** (Museum of Modern Art). Housed in an exciting feat of modern architecture, the museum descends eight floors into the ground around a central light well. Its strength lies in the quality of Belgian modern art: not only Magritte's luminous fantasies, Delvaux's nudes in surrealist settings, and James Ensor's hallucinatory carnival scenes but also the works of artists such as Léon Spilliaert, Constant Permeke, Leo Brusselmans, and Rik Wouters from the first half of the century; the post-war COBRA group, including Pierre Alechinsky and Henri Michaux; and on to contemporary works. ✉ *Pl. Royale 1–2,* ☎ *02/508–3211,* WEB *www.fine-arts-museum.be.* ⏲ *Tues.–Sun. 10–5.*

★ ❿ **Musée Instrumental** (Musical Instruments Museum). Seven thousand instruments, from the Bronze Age to today, make up this extraordinary collection. The saxophone family is well represented, as befits the country of its inventor, Adolphe Sax (1814–94). In the spring of 2000 the museum took up residence in the **Old England** building, a glass-and-steel Art Nouveau masterpiece designed by Paul Saintenoy (1862–1952) for the British-owned department store Old England in 1899. ✉ *Rue Montagne-de-la-Cour 2,* ☎ *02/545–0130,* WEB *www.mim.fgov.be.* 🎫 *BF150/€3.72.* ⏲ *Tues., Wed., Fri. 9:30–5, Thurs. 9:30–8, Weekends 10–5. Concerts Thurs. at 8.*

⓮ **Palais Royal** (Royal Palace). The palace facing the Royal Park was rebuilt in 1904 to suit the expansive tastes of Leopold II (1835–1909). The king's architect, Alphonse Balat, achieved his masterpiece with the monumental stairway and the Throne Hall. The Belgian royal family uses this address only on state occasions. When the Belgian flag is flying, you'll know that the king is in Brussels. ✉ *Pl. des Palais,* ☎ *02/551–2020.* ⏲ *July 22–early Sept., Tues.–Sun. 10–4.*

⓯ **Petit Sablon.** Statues of the counts of Egmont and Horne, who were executed by the Spanish in 1568, hold pride of place here. The tranquil square is surrounded by a magnificent wrought-iron fence, topped by 48 small statues representing Brussels's medieval guilds. ✉ *Rue de la Régence.*

⓬ **Place Royale.** This white, symmetrical square is neoclassical Vienna transposed to Brussels. From here you have a superb view over the lower town. The Coudenberg Palace once stood here. Underneath the square, excavations have revealed the *Aula Magna* (Great Hall), where the Flanders-born king of Spain and Holy Roman emperor Charles V (1500–58) was crowned and where he also announced his abdication two years before his death. The name of the palace lives on in the 18th-century church St-Jacques-sur-Coudenberg. In the center of the square stands the equestrian statue of Godefroid de Bouillon (1060–1100), leader of the First Crusade and ruler of Jerusalem. ✉ *Jct. rue de la Régence, rue Royale, rue de Namur, and rue Montagne-de-la-Cour.*

Elsewhere in Brussels

⓱ **Autoworld.** This mecca for vintage car aficionados comprises a collection of more than 400 vehicles, all in working order. The surprise star of the show is the Belgian-made Minerva, a luxury car from the early '30s. ✉ *Parc du Cinquantenaire 11,* ☎ *02/736–4165,* WEB *www.autoworld.be.* ⏲ *Daily: Apr.–Sept. 10–6; Oct.–Mar. 10–5.*

18 **European Union Institutions.** The various offices of the European Commission are centered on Rond Point Schuman (Metro: Schuman). The rounded glass summit of the **European Parliament** building (✉ Rue Wiertz 43) looms behind the Gare de Luxembourg. ✉ *Rond Point Schuman, rue de la Loi, rue Archimède, bd. Charlemagne, rue Wiertz.*

20 **Hôtel Hannon** (Hannon Mansion). The flowering of Art Nouveau produced this handsome, original town house designed by Jules Brunfaut (1852–1942) in 1903, now a gallery devoted to contemporary photography. In the interior, note the staircase with its romantic fresco, as well as the stained glass. ✉ *Av. de la Jonction 1,* ☎ *02/538–4220.* ⏲ *Aug. 16–July 14, Tues.–Sun. 1–6. Metro: Near Musée Horta; trams 91 and 92 from Place Louise.*

19 **Koninklijke Museum voor Midden-Afrika** (Africa Museum). King Leopold II (1835–1909) was sole owner of the Congo (later Zaire, and now the Republic of Congo)—a colonial adventure that brought great wealth to the exploiters and untold misery to the exploited. He built a museum outside Brussels to house some 250,000 objects emanating from his domain. The museum has since become a leading research center for African studies. ✉ *Leuvensesteenweg 13, Tervuren,* ☎ *02/769–5211,* WEB *www.africamuseum.be.* ⏲ *Tues.–Fri. 10–5, weekends 10–6. Tram 44 from Square Montgomery.*

★ 22 **Maison d'Erasme** (Erasmus House). In the middle of a nondescript neighborhood in Anderlecht, this remarkable redbrick 16th-century house was home to the great humanist Erasmus in 1521. Every detail is authentic, with period furniture, paintings by Holbein and Bosch, prints by Dürer, and first editions of Erasmus's works, including *In Praise of Folly.* ✉ *Rue du Chapître 31,* ☎ *02/521–1383.* ⏲ *Mon., Wed.–Thurs., and weekends 10–noon and 2–5. Metro: St-Guidon.*

23 **Mini-Europe.** At the foot of the landmark **Atomium**, this popular attraction in a 5-acre park is a collection of 300 models (on a 1:25 scale) of buildings from the 15 EU countries. ✉ *Brupark,* ☎ *02/478–0550.* *BF420.* ⏲ *Sept.–June, daily 9:30–5; July–Aug., daily 9:30–7, Fri. nights and weekends in July and August until 11. Metro: Heysel.*

Musée des Enfants (Children's Museum). Few kids don't fall in love with this educational center for 2- to 12-year-olds. They get to plunge their arms into sticky goo, dress up in eccentric costumes, walk through a hall of mirrors, and take photographs with an oversize camera. ✉ *Rue du Bourgmestre 15,* ☎ *02/640–0107.* ⏲ *Sept.–July, Wed. and weekends 2:30–5. Trams 93 and 94.*

★ 21 **Musée Horta** (Horta Museum). Victor Horta, the Belgian master of Art Nouveau, designed this building for himself and lived and worked here until 1919. From cellar to attic, every detail of the house displays the exuberant curves of the Art Nouveau style. Horta's aim was to put nature and light back into daily life, and here his floral motifs give a sense of opulence and spaciousness where in fact space is very limited. ✉ *Rue Américaine 25,* ☎ *02/543–0490.* ⏲ *Tues.–Sat. 2–5:30. Tram 91 or 92 from Pl. Louise.*

Dining

Brussels is one of the great dining cities in the world. Three thousand-odd restaurants are supplemented by a multitude of fast-food establishments and snack bars, and most cafés also offer *petite restauration* (light meals). Fixed-price menus, especially in top-dollar restaurants, sometimes cost only half of what you would pay dining à la carte, and the quality of your meal is likely to be just as good. There's less smoking than in the past, but no-smoking areas are rare. For price categories, *see* Dining *in* Belgium A to Z, *above.*

$$$$ ★ ✕ **Comme Chez Soi.** Master chef Pierre Wynants runs Brussels's most celebrated restaurant, and the array of toques and stars he has earned is well-deserved. One all-time favorite, fillet of sole with a white wine mousseline and shrimp, is always on the menu, but the perfectionist owner-chef is constantly creating new culinary masterpieces. This stunning Art Nouveau restaurant is small, so reserve well ahead; you may have to wait up to six weeks for a table. Don't be put off by the scruffy neighborhood. ✉ *Pl. Rouppe 23,* ☎ *02/512–2921. Reservations essential. Jacket and tie. AE, DC, MC, V. Closed Sun.–Mon., July, and Dec. 25–Jan. 1.*

$$$–$$$$ ★ ✕ **La Truffe Noire.** Luigi Ciciriello's "Black Truffle" is a spacious eatery with cuisine that draws on classic Italian and modern French cooking. Carpaccio, prepared at the table, comes with strips of truffle and Parmesan, while main courses include pigéon de Vendé with truffles and steamed John Dory with truffles and leeks. ✉ *Bd. de la Cambre 12,* ☎ *02/640–4422. Reservations essential. Jacket and tie. AE, DC, MC, V. Closed Sun., Mon., and last 3 weeks in Aug.*

$$–$$$$ ★ ✕ **Sea Grill.** Gigantic etched-glass murals convey the cool of the Arctic fjords that provide inspiration and ingredients for one of Belgium's best seafood restaurants. Chef Yves Mattagne's gift for applying meat preparations to fish is showcased in dishes like noisettes of tuna Rossini, while house classics include whole sea bass baked in salt and Brittany lobster pressed at your table. ✉ *Radisson SAS, rue du Fossé-aux-Loups 47,* ☎ *02/227–3120. Jacket and tie. AE, DC, MC, V. Closed Sun. and 4 wks in July–Aug. No lunch Sat.*

$$$ ★ ✕ **L'Ogenblik.** With green-shaded lamps over marble-topped tables, sawdust on the floor, and ample servings, l'Ogenblik is a true bistro. The long and imaginative menu changes frequently but generally includes mille-feuille with lobster and salmon, and saddle of lamb with spring vegetables. The kitchen stays open until after midnight, making it a favorite for artists and actors after the show. ✉ *Galerie des Princes 1,* ☎ *02/511–6151. AE, DC, MC, V. Closed Sun.*

$$–$$$ ✕ **Aux Armes de Bruxelles.** One of the few restaurants to escape the "tourist trap" label on this hectic street, Aux Armes has three rooms with a lively atmosphere: The most popular section overlooks the street theater outside, but locals prefer the cozy rotunda. It offers the classics of Belgian cooking—tomatoes stuffed with tiny shrimp, *waterzooi* (a creamy fish or chicken stew), and mussels steamed in white wine. ✉ *Rue des Bouchers 13,* ☎ *02/511–5598. AE, DC, MC, V. Closed Mon. and mid-June–mid-July.*

$–$$$ ★ ✕ **Les Salons de Wittamer.** The elegant upstairs rooms at Brussels's best-known patisserie house a stylish breakfast and lunch restaurant, where meals are topped off with the establishment's celebrated pastry or ice-cream concoctions. ✉ *Pl. du Grand Sablon 12–13,* ☎ *02/512–3742. AE, DC, MC, V. Closed Mon.*

$$ ✕ **Au Stekerlapatte.** In the shadow of the monstrous Palais de Justice, this bustling Marolles bistro is packed nightly with diners craving liberal portions of Belgian specialties. Try black pudding with caramelized apples, sauerkraut, beef fried with shallots, grilled pig's trotters, or spareribs. ✉ *Rue des Prêtres 4,* ☎ *02/512–8681. MC, V. Closed Sun. Closed Sun. and Mon. Jul.–Aug. No lunch.*

$$ ✕ **Au Vieux St-Martin.** Belgian specialties dominate the menu here, and portions are generous. The restaurant claims to have invented the now ubiquitous *filet américain* (the well-seasoned Belgian version of steak tartare). The walls are hung with bright contemporary paintings, and picture windows face the pleasant square. ✉ *Pl. du Grand Sablon 38,* ☎ *02/512–6476. AE, MC, V.*

$–$$ ✕ **Kasbah.** An Aladdin's den of stained-glass lamps and dark, sumptuous decor, this is one of the best of the capital's many North African restaurants. Steaming portions of couscous and *tajines* (Moroccan casseroles with fish or meat, usually involving fruit, vegetables, and spices) are served in this lively restaurant. ✉ *Rue Antoine Dansaert 20,* ☏ *02/502–4026. AE, MC, V.*

$–$$ ✕ **Léon.** Critics deride it as McMoules-frites, but this century-old eatery is enormously popular, with franchises across Belgium and even in Paris and Japan. The secret is heaping plates of steaming mussels, specialties such as *anguilles au vert* (eels in green sauce), free children's menus, and great fries. It's loud, brightly lit—and has a charm all its own. ✉ *Rue des Bouchers 18,* ☏ *02/511–1415. AE, DC, MC, V.*

$–$$ ★ ✕ **Taverne Falstaff.** This huge tavern with an Art Nouveau interior fills up for lunch and keeps going until the wee hours. The ever-changing crowd, from students to pensioners, consumes onion soup, filet mignon, salads, and other brasserie fare. On the heated terrace, a favorite meeting point for groups, the surliness of the waiters is legendary. ✉ *Rue Henri Maus 17–21,* ☏ *02/511–8987. AE, DC, MC, V.*

$ ✕ **Chez Patrick.** This old-timer next to the Grand'Place has been dishing up good, honest Belgian food for nearly 70 years, in an unpretentious, old-fashioned setting with waitresses in black and white and specials chalked up on the mirrors. Expect large, tasty portions of shrimp croquettes, salmon and endives cooked with beer, and chicken with *kriek* (cherry-flavored beer) and cherries. ✉ *Rue des Chapeliers 6,* ☏ *02/511–9815. AE, DC, MC, V. Closed Mon.*

$ ✕ **Le Pain Quotidien.** These bakeries–cum–snack bars have spread like wildfire all over Brussels (and even to New York and Boston in the U.S.) with the same formula: copious salads, hearty homemade soups, and delicious open sandwiches on farm-style bread, served at a communal table from 7:30 AM to 7 PM. ✉ *Rue des Sablons 11,* ☏ *02/513–5154;* ✉ *Rue Antoine Dansaert 16,* ☏ *02/502–2361; and other locations. Reservations not accepted. No credit cards.*

Lodging

The main hotel districts are around the Grand'Place, the Place de Brouckère, and in the avenue Louise shopping area. If you have a problem finding accommodations, go to the TIB tourist office in the Hôtel de Ville at the Grand'Place or telephone BTR (Belgian Tourist Reservations, ☏ 02/513–7484) for their free service. Weekend and summer discounts, often of 50% or more, are available in almost all hotels; be sure to check when you book. Most new hotels have set aside rooms or floors for nonsmokers and offer a limited number of rooms equipped for people with disabilities. For price categories, *see* Lodging *in* Belgium A to Z, *above.*

$$$$ ★ 🏨 **Amigo.** Although it was built in the 1950s, this family-owned hotel off the Grand'Place has the charm of an earlier age. Each room is individually decorated, often in silk, velvet, and brocades, and most have marble bathrooms. Some 60 rooms, omitted from the most recent refurbishment, are more modestly priced. Ask for a quiet room, away from the main tourist trail. ✉ *Rue de l'Amigo 1–3, 1000,* ☏ *02/547–4747,* FAX *02/513–5277,* WEB *www.rfhotels.com. 185 rooms, 7 suites. Restaurant. AE, DC, MC, V.*

$$$$ 🏨 **Brussels Hilton.** The 27-story Hilton was one of the capital's first high-rises, dating from the 1960s, and remains a distinctive landmark with great views of the inner town. Corner rooms are the most desirable; there are four floors of executive rooms and superb business facilities. The second-floor Maison du Boeuf restaurant is much appreciated by Brussels gourmets. The hotel is in the luxury avenue de la Toison d'Or and boulevard de Waterloo shopping area, overlooking the tiny Parc d'Egmont. ✉ *Bd. de Waterloo 38, 1000,* ☎ *02/504–1111,* FAX *02/504–2111. 430 rooms, 39 suites. 2 restaurants. AE, DC, MC, V.*

$$$$ **Conrad International.** Opened by the Hilton group in 1993, the Conrad combines the European grand hotel tradition with American tastes and amenities, and has become *the* place to stay for visiting dignitaries. Rooms are spacious, with three telephones, bathrobes, and in-room checkout. The Maison de Maître restaurant maintains the same high standard, and the large bar is pleasantly clublike. ✉ *Av. Louise 71, 1050,* ☎ *02/542–4242,* FAX *02/542–4200,* WEB *www.hilton.com. 269 rooms, 15 suites. 2 restaurants. AE, DC, MC, V.*

$$$$ **Manos Stéphanie.** This former town house, opened as a hotel in 1992, has a marble lobby, Louis XV furniture, and elegant rooms. Service is friendly, breakfast is included, and children under 12 stay free. ✉ *Chaussée de Charleroi 28, 1060,* ☎ *02/539–0250,* FAX *02/537–5729,* WEB *www.manoshotel.com. 55 rooms, 7 suites. Bar. AE, DC, MC, V.*

$$$$ ★ **Le Méridien.** Opened in 1995, Le Méridien is Brussels's newest luxury hotel, in a convenient area opposite the Gare Centrale. The marble and gilt-edged lobby recalls palatial Parisian hotels, and the restaurant sets out brightly colored Limoges china. Rooms, in dark blue or green, come with three telephones, large desks, and data ports. ✉ *Carrefour de l'Europe 3, 1000,* ☎ *02/548–4211,* FAX *02/548–4080,* WEB *www.meridien.be. 224 rooms, 12 suites. Restaurant. AE, DC, MC, V.*

$$$$ **Le Metropole.** Built in 1895, this restored Belle Epoque masterpiece is the last trace of elegance in what was once one of Brussels's most charming squares. The lobby has a high coffered ceiling, chandeliers, and Oriental rugs, while the staircase and original lift are as stunning as they were when Sarah Bernhardt stayed here. The theme extends to the restaurant and the café, which opens onto a heated terrace. Most guest rooms are in discreet pastel shades and Art Deco style. ✉ *Pl. de Brouckère 31, 1000,* ☎ *02/217–2300,* FAX *02/218–0220,* WEB *www.metropole.be. 400 rooms, 10 suites. 2 restaurants. AE, DC, MC, V.*

$$$$ **Radisson SAS.** This excellent 1990 hotel has guest rooms decorated with great panache in four different styles: Scandinavian, Asian, Italian, and Art Deco. A portion of the 12th-century city wall forms part of the atrium. Children under 17 stay free; check weekend rates. ✉ *Rue du Fossé-aux-Loups 47, 1000,* ☎ *02/219–2828,* FAX *02/219–6262. 263 rooms, 18 suites. 3 restaurants. AE, DC, MC, V.*

$$$ **Le Dixseptième.** In this stylish 17th-century hotel, originally the residence of the Spanish ambassador, each room is named for a Belgian artist. Suites are up a splendid Louis XV staircase, and the standard rooms surround an interior courtyard. Whitewashed walls, bare floors, exposed beams, and colorful textiles are the style here. Some rooms have kitchenettes; suites have working fireplaces and fax machines. ✉ *Rue de la Madeleine 25, 1000, 1000,* ☎ *02/539–0250,* FAX *02/502–6424. 24 rooms, 12 suites. AE, DC, MC, V.*

$$ **Orion.** This residential hotel accepts overnight guests; it's a good choice for families. The exterior is plain, but the location on the Vismet is plum. Rooms have pull-out twin beds; junior suites sleep four. All have kitchenettes. ✉ *Quai au Bois-à-Brûler 51, 1000,* ☎ *02/221–1411,* FAX *02/221–1599. 169 rooms. Breakfast room. AE, DC, MC, V.*

$ **Bed & Brussels.** This upscale B&B accommodations service arranges stays with 100 host families in Brussels or surrounding areas, most of them with room to spare after children have flown the coop. Many rooms come with private bath, and breakfast with the hosts is included. ✉ *Rue Gustave Biot 2,* ☎ *02/646–0737,* FAX *02/644–0114,* WEB *www.bnb-brussels.be. MC, V.*

$ 🏨 **Matignon.** Only the Belle Epoque facade of this family-run hotel opposite the stock exchange was preserved when it was converted into a hotel in 1993. The lobby is tiny to make room for the bustling café-brasserie. Rooms are small but have large beds (and large TVs), and the duplex suites are good value for families. It's noisy but very central. ✉ *Rue de la Bourse 10, 1000,* ☎ *02/511–0888,* FAX *02/513–6927. 26 rooms, 9 suites. Restaurant. AE, DC, MC, V.*

$ ★ 🏨 **Welcome Hotel.** Owners Michel and Sophie Smeesters expanded this charming establishment in 2000, but are committed to remaining the smallest hotel in Brussels. The rooms, with king- or queen-size beds, would be a credit to far more expensive establishments; it's essential to book well ahead. There's a charming breakfast room, and Michel is also chef at the excellent seafood restaurant around the corner, La Truite d'Argent. ✉ *Rue du Peuplier 5, 1000,* ☎ *02/219–9546,* FAX *02/217–1887,* WEB *www.hotelwelcome.com. 10 rooms, 3 apartments for stays of at least one month. Restaurant. AE, DC, MC, V.*

Nightlife and the Arts

The Arts

The best way to find out what's going on in Brussels—and throughout the country—is to buy a copy of the English-language weekly the *Bulletin.* It's published every Thursday.

FILM

Movies are mainly shown in their original language (indicated as v.o., or *version originale*). Complete listings appear in the *Bulletin.* For unusual movies or screen classics, visit the **Musée du Cinéma** (Film Museum; ✉ Rue Baron Horta 9, ☎ 02/507–8370), where three sound films and two silents with piano accompaniment are shown every evening. Unfortunately, those under 16 are not admitted.

MUSIC

Major symphony concerts and recitals are held at the **Palais des Beaux-Arts** (✉ Rue Ravenstein 23, ☎ 02/507–8200). Chamber music is best enjoyed at the intimate **Conservatoire Royal de Musique** (✉ Rue de la Régence 30, ☎ 02/511–0427). Free Sunday morning concerts take place at various churches, including the Cathédrale Sts-Michel-et-Gudule. You can also experience a Sunday morning concert at the **Église des Minimes** (✉ Rue des Minimes 62). **Ancienne Belgique** (✉ Bd. Anspach 110, ☎ 02/548–2424) hosts folk, rock, pop, funk, and jazz concerts.

OPERA AND DANCE

The national opera company, based at the handsome **Théâtre Royal de la Monnaie** (✉ Pl. de la Monnaie, ☎ 070/233939), stages productions of international quality. Touring dance and opera companies often perform at **Cirque Royal** (✉ Rue de l'Enseignement 81, ☎ 02/218–2015).

THEATER

The **Théâtre Royal du Parc** (✉ Rue de la Loi 3, ☎ 02/505–3030) stages productions of Molière and other French classics. Avant-garde theater is performed at **Théâtre Varia** (✉ Rrue du Sceptre 78, ☎ 02/640–8258). **Théâtre de Poche** (✉ Chemin du Gymnase 1a, in the Bois de la Cambre, ☎ 02/649–1727) presents unusual and modern productions.

Nightlife

BARS

There's a café on virtually every corner in Brussels, and all of them serve beer from morning to late at night. If you crave a young crowd, try **Au Soleil** (✉ Rue Marché au Charbon 86, ☎ 02/513–3430) in the fashionable place St-Gery–rue A. Dansaert part of town. The lively **Beurss-**

chouwburg-Café (✉ Rue Auguste Orts 22, ☎ 02/513–8290) attracts earnestly trendy young Flemish intellectuals. **Le Cirio** (✉ Rue de la Bourse 18, ☎ 02/512–1395) is a typical *bruin café* with 1900s-era advertisements and price lists on the mirror-lined walls. Another 1900-style café-bar with a lost-in-time atmosphere is **À La Mort Subite** (✉ Rue Montagne-aux-Herbes-Potagères 7, ☎ 02/513–1318). On the Grand'-Place, **Le Cerf** (✉ Grand'Place 20, ☎ 02/511–4791) is particularly pleasant, with atmosphere and furnishings out of the 17th century. Only a 10-minute stroll from the Grand'Place is **La Fleur en Papier Doré** (✉ Rue des Aléxiens 53, ☎ 02/511–1659), a quaint tavern with a surrealist decor that appeals to an artsy crowd. **Le Greenwich** (✉ Rue des Chartreux 7, ☎ 02/511–4167), a chess club–cum–café, is where Magritte used to play. **Rick's Café Américain** (✉ Av. Louise 344, ☎ 02/648–1451) is a favorite with the American and British expat community. Like most other western European cities, Brussels has a sizable number of "Irish" bars. **James Joyce** (✉ Rue Archimède 34, ☎ 02/230–9894) was the first in Brussels and is the most genuinely Gaelic.

DANCE CLUBS

In all the clubs the action starts at 10 or after. Electronica fans prefer **Fuse** (✉ Rue Blaes 208, ☎ 02/511–9789), a bunker-style techno haven with regular gay and lesbian nights. **Griffin's** (✉ Rue Duquesnoy 5, ☎ 02/505–5555), at the Royal Windsor Hotel, appeals to young adults and business travelers. **Le Mirano Continental** (✉ Chaussée de Louvain 38, ☎ 02/227–3970) remains the glitzy hangout of choice for the self-styled beautiful people.

JAZZ

Most of Brussels's dozen or so jazz haunts present live music only on certain nights; check before you go. **New York Café Jazz Club** (✉ Chaussée de Charleroi 5, ☎ 02/534–8509) is an American restaurant by day and a modern jazz hangout on Friday and Saturday evenings. **Sounds Jazz Club** (✉ Rue de la Tulipe 28, ☎ 02/512–9250), a big café, emphasizes jazz-rock, blues, and other modern trends. **Travers** (✉ Rue Traversière 11, ☎ 02/218–4086), a café–cum–jazz club, is a cramped but outstanding showcase for the country's leading players.

Shopping

Gift Ideas

Belgium is where the *praline*—rich chocolate filled with flavored creams, liqueur, or nuts—was invented. Try Corné Toison d'Or, Godiva, Neuhaus, or the lower-priced Leonidas, available at shops throughout the city. **Wittamer** (✉ Pl. du Grand Sablon 12, ☎ 02/512–3742) is an excellent patisserie with a sideline in superb chocolates. **Pierre Marcolini** (✉ Pl. du Grand Sablon 39, ☎ 02/514–1206) is the boy wonder of the chocolate world. Exclusive handmade pralines can be bought at **Mary** (✉ Rue Royale 73, ☎ 02/217–4500), official purveyor of chocolates to the Belgian court.

Only the Val-St-Lambert mark guarantees handblown, hand-carved Belgian lead crystal. Many stores sell crystal tableware and ornaments, including **Art & Selection** (✉ Rue du Marché-aux-Herbes 83, ☎ 02/511–8448) near the Grand'Place.

When shopping for lace, ask whether it is genuine handmade Belgian or machine-made in East Asia. **Maison F. Rubbrecht** (✉ Grand'Place 23, ☎ 02/512–0218) sells authentic Belgian lace. For a choice of old and modern lace, try **Manufacture Belge de Dentelles** (✉ Galerie de la Reine 6–8, ☎ 02/511–4477).

Markets

On Saturday (9–6) and Sunday (9–2), the upper end of the Place du Grand Sablon becomes an open-air **antiques and book market** with more than 100 stalls. The **Vieux Marché** (✉ Pl. du Jeu de Balle), open daily 7–2, is a flea market worth visiting for the authentic atmosphere of the working-class Marolles district. To make real finds, get here early.

Shopping Districts

The shops in the **Galeries St-Hubert** sell mostly luxury goods or gift items. The **rue Neuve** and the **City 2** mall are good for less expensive boutiques and department stores. Avant-garde clothes are sold in boutiques on **rue Antoine Dansaert,** near the stock exchange.

Uptown, **avenue Louise,** with the arcades Galerie Louise and Espace Louise, counts a large number of boutiques selling expensive clothes and accessories. The **boulevard de Waterloo** is home to the same fashion names as Bond Street and Rodeo Drive. The **Grand Sablon** has more charm; this is the center for antiques and art galleries.

Side Trip

Waterloo, where Napoléon was finally defeated by the British and Prussian armies on June 18, 1815, lies 19 km (12 mi) to the south of the city; take the TEC bus "W" or Bus 365a from Place Rouppe to the town of Waterloo. The Waterloo Tourist Office (✉ Chaussée de Bruxelles 149, ☎ 02/354–9910) is in the center of town.

The **Wellington Museum,** in the former inn where the general established his headquarters, displays maps and models of the battle and military memorabilia. ✉ *Chaussée de Bruxelles 147,* ☎ *02/354–7806.* ⏲ *Apr.–Sept., daily 9:30–6:30; Oct.–Mar., daily 10:30–5.*

Just 4½ km (3 mi) south of town, and accessible by TEC Bus 365a, is the battlefield. The **Visitors' Center** has an audiovisual reconstruction, and the Panorama next door illustrates memorable phases of the battle. You can also book guides to take you around the battlefield. ✉ *Rte. du Lion 252–254, Braine–l'Alleud,* ☎ *02/385–1912.* ⏲ *Apr.–Oct., daily 9:30–5:30; Nov.–Feb. daily 10:30–4; Mar., daily 10:30–5.* 🎫 *Guides BF1,500/€37 for 1 hr; BF3,000/€74 for 3 hrs.*

Overlooking the battlefield is the **Butte du Lion,** a pyramid-shaped mound with a 28-ton cast-iron lion standing at the top. The Lion Mound was erected in honor of the Prince of Orange, leader of the Dutch-Belgian troups, who was wounded on this spot. After climbing 226 steps, you will be rewarded with a great view of the site.

Brussels Essentials

AIRPORTS AND TRANSFERS

All international flights arrive at Brussels National Airport at Zaventem (sometimes called simply Zaventem), 15 km (9 mi) northeast of the city center.

➤ AIRPORT INFORMATION: Flight information (☎ 0900–70000).

TRANSFERS

Shuttle trains run between Brussels Airport and all three main railway stations in Brussels: South (Midi), Central (Central), and North (Nord). The Airport City Express runs four times per hour, from about 6 AM to midnight, seven days a week. The journey takes 18 minutes. A one-way ticket costs BF140/€3.50 (1st class) or BF90/€2.25 (2nd class). A taxi to the city center takes about a half hour and costs about BF1,000/€25.

BOAT AND FERRY TRAVEL

Hoverspeed operates a Hovercraft catamaran service between Dover and Calais, carrying cars and foot passengers. Travel time is 35 minutes. Hoverspeed also offers pedestrian-only "SeaCat" service between Dover and Oostende, with travel time just under two hours. Trains at either end connect with London and Brussels. P&O North Sea Ferries operates an overnight ferry service between Hull and Zeebrugge.

➤ BOAT & FERRY INFORMATION: **Hoverspeed** (☎ 44/870–5240241 in the U.K.). **P&O North Sea Ferries** (☎ 0990/980980 in the U.K.; 050/542222 in Europe).

BUS TRAVEL TO AND FROM BRUSSELS

Eurolines operates up to three daily express services from and to Amsterdam, Berlin, Frankfurt, Paris, and London. The Eurolines Coach Station in Brussels adjoins the Gare du Nord.

➤ BUS INFORMATION: **Eurolines** (✉ Pl. de Brouckère 50, ☎ 02/217–0025). **Eurolines Coach Station** (✉ Rue du Progrès 80, ☎ 02/203–0707).

METRO, TRAM, AND BUS TRAVEL WITHIN BRUSSELS

The Métro (subway), trams (streetcars), and buses are parts of a unified system. All are clean and efficient. A single ticket, valid for one hour's travel, costs BF50/€1.25. The best buy is a 10-trip ticket for BF340/€8.50 or a one-day card costing BF130/€3.25. Tickets are sold in metro stations and at newsstands. Single tickets can be purchased on the bus or tram.

CAR TRAVEL

If you use Le Shuttle under the English Channel or a ferry to Calais, note that the E40 (via Oostende and Brugge) connects with the French highway, cutting driving time from Calais to Brussels to under two hours.

EMERGENCIES

Every pharmacy displays a list of pharmacies on duty outside normal hours.

➤ DOCTORS & DENTISTS: **Doctor/Pharmacy**: Information about all-night and weekend services: ☎ 02/479–1818. **Dentist** (☎ 02/426–1026).

➤ EMERGENCY SERVICES: **Police** (☎ 101). **Ambulance and Fire Brigade** (☎ 100).

➤ HOT LINES: **Lost/Stolen Bank/Credit Cards** (☎ 070/344344). **24-Hour English-Speaking Info and Crisis Line** (☎ 02/648–4014).

ENGLISH-LANGUAGE MEDIA

➤ BOOKSTORES: **The Reading Room** (✉ Av. Georges Henri 503, ☎ 02/734–7917). **Sterling Books** (✉ Rue du Fossé-aux-Loups 38, ☎ 02/223–6223). **Waterstone's** (✉ Bd. Adolphe Max 71–75, ☎ 02/219–2708).

TOURS

BUS TOURS

Expertly guided half-day English-language coach tours are organized by ARAU, from March through November, including "Brussels 1900: Art Nouveau" (every Sat.) and "Brussels 1930: Art Deco" (every 3rd Sat.). Admission is BF600/€15. Tours begin in front of Hotel Métropole on Place de Brouckère. Chatterbus tours (early June–Sept.) include visits by minibus or on foot to the main sights. De Boeck Sightseeing Tours operates city tours with multilingual cassette commentary. They also conduct tours of Antwerp, the Ardennes, Brugge, Ghent, Ieper, and Waterloo.

➤ FEES & SCHEDULES: **ARAU** (✉ Bd. Adolphe Max 55, ☎ 02/219–3345 information and reservations). **Chatterbus** (✉ Rue des Thuyas 12, ☎ 02/673–1835). **De Boeck Sightseeing Tours** (✉ Rue de la Colline 8, Grand'Place, ☎ 02/513–7744).

PRIVATE GUIDES

Qualified guides are available for individual tours from the TIB. Three hours costs BF3,200/€79 for up to 20 people.

➤ Fees & Schedules: **TIB** (☎ 02/513–8940).

WALKING TOURS

Chatterbus organizes visits (early June–Sept.) on foot or by minibus to the main sights and a walking tour with a visit to a bistro. Walking tours organized by the tourist office depart from the Brussels Tourist Office (TIB) in the Town Hall, May–September, Monday–Saturday.

TAXIS

Cabs don't cruise for fares; call Taxis Verts to have one pick you up. Taxis here are among the most expensive in Europe. The tip is included in the fare.

➤ Taxi Companies: **Taxis Verts** (☎ 02/349–4949).

TRAIN TRAVEL

Ten Eurostar passenger trains a day link Brussels's Gare du Midi with London's Waterloo station via the Channel Tunnel in two hours, 40 minutes. A one-way trip costs BF9,750/€242 in business class and from BF5,000/€124 in economy; rail pass holders qualify for 50% discounts. Reservations are required. Check-in is 20 minutes before departure.

All rail services between Brussels and Paris are on Thalys high-speed trains (1 hr, 25 mins). A one-way trip costs BF3,750/€92 ("Confort 1"), BF2,150/€53 ("Confort 2"). Reservations are required.

➤ Train Information: **Eurostar** (☎ 0900–10366 information; 0900/10–177 telephone sales). **Thalys** (☎ 070/667788 information; 0900/10366 reservations).

TRAVEL AGENCIES

➤ Local Agent Referrals: **American Express** (✉ Houtweg 24, 1170 Brussels, ☎ 02/245–2250). **Carlson Wagonlit Travel** (✉ Bd. Clovis 53, 1040 Brussels, ☎ 02/287–8811).

VISITOR INFORMATION

At Tourist Information Brussels you can buy a Tourist Passport (BF300/€7)—a one-day public transport card and BF2,000/€50 worth of museum admissions and reductions.

➤ Tourist Information: **Tourist Information Brussels** (TIB; ✉ Hôtel de Ville, Grand'Place, ☎ 02/513–8940).

ANTWERP

Antwerp's Dutch name is Antwerpen, close enough to be confused with *handwerpen,* and thereby hangs a tale. The Roman soldier Silvius Brabo is said to have cut off and flung into the water the hand of the giant who exacted a toll from boatmen on the river. *Hand* is hand, and *werpen* means throwing. The tale explains the presence of severed hands on the city's coat of arms.

Great prosperity came to Antwerp in the 16th century, during the reign of Charles V. A hundred years later, Rubens and his contemporaries made the city an equally important center of the arts. Craftsmen began practicing diamond-cutting at about this time, and the city is still the world leader in the diamond trade, with an annual turnover of more than $20 billion. In spite of being 88 km (55 mi) up the River Scheldt, it is Europe's second-largest port after Rotterdam. Antwerp is the principal city of Flanders, and the Antwerpers, convinced they are a cut above most others, don't mind at all their Spanish-derived nickname: *Sinjoren* (señores).

Exploring Antwerp

Numbers in the margin correspond to points of interest on the Antwerp map.

The Old City—a short subway ride from the Central Station—is the heart of Antwerp and best explored on foot. Rubens and his contemporaries seem to be everywhere, in churches, art museums, and splendid Renaissance mansions. Antwerp is also known as the City of Madonnas. You'll see a statuette of Our Lady on many a street corner.

8 **Bourlaschouwburg** (Bourla Theater). Dating from the 1830s, this handsome neoclassical theater fell into neglect before being restored to gold-and-velvet glory in 1995. Sunday brunch in the opulent café is booked up weeks in advance. ⊠ *Komedieplaats 18,* ☎ *03/231–0750.*

12 **Centraal Station** (Central Station). This railway station is special. Leopold II (1835–1909), a monarch not given to understatement, had it built in 1905 as a neo-Baroque cathedral to the railway age, with splendid staircases and a magnificently vaulted ticket-office hall. ⊠ *Koningin Astridplein,* ☎ *03/233–3915.*

11 **Dierentuin** (Antwerp Zoo). The residents are housed in style in this huge, well-designed complex: giraffes and ostriches in an Egyptian temple, rhinoceroses in a Moorish villa, okapis around an Indian temple. Other attractions are a winter garden, a planetarium, an aquarium, and a good restaurant. ⊠ *Koningin Astridplein 26,* ☎ *03/202–4540.* *BF460.* ⊙ *Dec.–Jan., daily 9–4:30; Feb. and mid-Oct.–Nov., daily 9–4:45; 1st ½ Mar. and 1st ½ Oct., daily 9–5:15; mid-Mar.–June and Sept., daily 9–5:45; July–Aug., daily 9–6:15.*

1 **Grote Markt.** The heart of the Old City, a three-sided square, is dominated by a huge fountain topped by a statue of Silvius Brabo, the giant-killer. The Renaissance **Stadhuis** (City Hall) flanks one side of the square, and guild houses the other two. ⊠ *Jct. Suikerrui, Oude Koornmarkt, Handschoenmarkt, Kaasrui, Hofstraat, and Nosestraat.*

6 **Koninklijk Museum voor Schone Kunsten** (Royal Museum of Fine Arts). This huge museum south of the Old City contains more than 1,500 paintings by Old Masters, including magnificent works by Van Eyck, Memling, Rubens, Van Dyck, Jordaens, Hals, and Brueghel. The first floor has more modern paintings, including works by Magritte, Delvaux, and James Ensor. ⊠ *Leopold de Waelplaats 2,* ☎ *03/238–7809.* ⊙ *Tues.–Sun. 10–5.*

★ 7 **Museum Mayer van den Bergh.** A passionate 19th-century collector, Mayer van den Bergh amassed almost 4,000 works of art, the best of which are displayed in the small museum that bears his name. The masterpiece is Brueghel's great *Dulle Griet* (*Mad Meg*), an antiwar allegory. In 1894 Mayer van den Bergh bought the painting for a mere BF488. ⊠ *Lange Gasthuisstraat 19,* ☎ *03/232–4237.* ⊙ *Tues.–Sun. 10–5.*

★ 5 **Museum Plantin-Moretus.** Religious dissident, humanist, and printer extraordinaire Christophe Plantin (1514–89) founded a printing house that flourished for three centuries. Two typefaces designed here, Plantin and Garamond, are still in use. The presses continue to work. Among the treasures are portraits by Rubens as well as many first editions, engravings, and a copy of the Gutenberg Bible. The luxurious private apartments and editorial offices can also be visited. ⊠ *Vrijdagmarkt 22,* ☎ *03/221–1450.* ⊙ *Tues.–Sun. 10–5.*

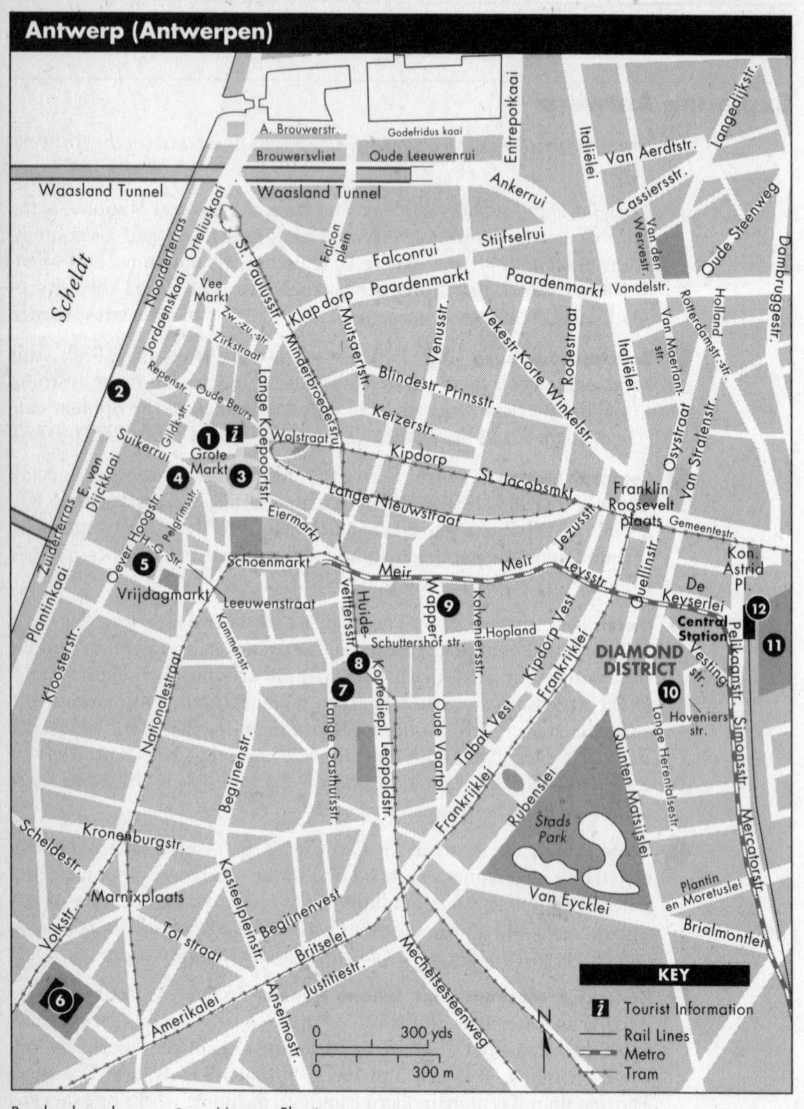

Bourlaschouwburg . . 8
Centraal Station . . . 12
Dierentuin 11
Grote Markt 1
Koninklijk Museum voor Schone Kunsten 6
Museum Mayer van den Bergh 7
Museum Plantin-Moretus 5
Onze-Lieve-Vrouwekathedraal . . . 3
Provinciaal Diamantmuseum . . . 10
Rubenshuis 9
Steen 2
Vlaeykensgang 4

★ 3 **Onze-Lieve-Vrouwekathedraal** (Cathedral of Our Lady). You'll see the white, 404-ft spire of Antwerp's Gothic masterpiece from far away. Starting in 1352, a succession of architects worked on it for more than 200 years, but the ensemble is completely coherent. The paintings and statuary it contained have repeatedly been plundered, most recently by the army of the French Revolution. The cathedral's remaining treasures include four Rubens altarpieces. His *Descent from the Cross* is flanked by panels showing Mary's visit to Elizabeth and the presentation of Jesus in the Temple; these are among the most delicate biblical scenes ever painted. ✉ *Handschoenmarkt,* ☎ *03/213–9940.* ⏲ *Weekdays 10–5, Sat. 10–3, Sun. 1–4.*

10 **Provinciaal Diamantmuseum** (Provincial Diamond Museum). This remarkable museum traces the long and often bloody history of the search for these precious stones. You are guided through the diamond production process, from extraction to the sparkling gem. There's also a 19th-century diamond workshop and a treasure room of jewelry. The museum is around the corner from the **diamond district** (✉ Hoveniersstraat). ✉ *Lange Herentalsestraat 31–33,* ☎ *03/202–4890.* ⏲ *Daily 10–5; cutting demonstrations Sat. afternoon.*

9 **Rubenshuis** (Rubens House). Rubens lived here from 1610 until his death in 1640. The mansion, a reconstruction based on his original designs, gives a vivid impression of the artist's life as wealthy court painter and diplomat. The mezzanine overlooks the studio where Rubens and his pupils worked. His widow promptly sold 300 paintings when he died, but a few Rubens originals do hang in the house. ✉ *Wapper 9,* ☎ *03/232–4747.* ⏲ *Tues.–Sun. 10–5.*

2 **Steen.** This 9th-century fortress is the oldest building in Antwerp. It was used as a prison for centuries, and the crucifix where condemned men said their final prayers is still in place. The Steen now houses the **National Scheepvaartmuseum** (National Maritime Museum). ✉ *Steenplein,* ☎ *03/232–0850.* ⏲ *Tues.–Sun. 10–4:45.*

4 **Vlaeykensgang.** Time has stood still in this cobblestone alley in the center of town, which captures the mood and style of the 16th century. There's no better place to linger on a Monday night, when the carillon concert rings out from the cathedral.

Dining

Dining in Antwerp's many fine restaurants has a distinctly French flavor, making full use of the excellent ingredients from the surrounding farmland. Naturally, seafood has pride of place on the dinner tables of this port city. For details and price-category definitions, *see* Dining *in* Belgium A to Z, *above.*

$$$–$$$$ ✕ **'t Fornuis.** In the heart of Old Antwerp, this old and cozy restaurant, decorated in traditional Flemish style, serves some of the best food in the city. The menu changes frequently, but truffled sweetbreads with wild truffle sauce is a house classic. ✉ *Reyndersstraat 24,* ☎ *03/233–6270. Reservations essential. AE, DC, MC, V. Closed weekends and 3 wks in Aug.*

$$$ ★ ✕ **De Matelote.** The gifted chef at this tiny restaurant in a narrow, Old City street concocts such inventive dishes as grilled asparagus with fresh morels and a poached egg, and langoustines in a light curry sauce. Some say it's also the best fish restaurant in town. ✉ *Haarstraat 9,* ☎ *03/231–3207. Reservations essential. AE, DC, MC, V. Closed Sun. and June. No lunch Mon. and Sat.*

$$–$$$ ★ ✕ **Neuze Neuze.** Five tiny houses cobbled together form a handsome, split-level restaurant with whitewashed walls, dark-brown beams, and a blazing fireplace. The inventive dishes include sautéed goose liver with caramelized pineapple and scallops with rhubarb preserve. ✉ *Wijngaardstraat 19,* ☎ *03/232–5783. AE, DC, MC, V. Closed Sun., 1st wk. in Jan., and 2 wks. in Aug. No lunch Sat.*

$$–$$$ ★ ✕ **Sir Anthony Van Dijck.** On Antwerp's most famous alley is a classy brasserie, with an interior courtyard and tables grouped around stone pillars under high, massive beams. The menu changes monthly, but expect such items as salad liègeoise with smoked salmon and caramelized onions, duck à l'orange, and tuna steak. There are two seatings a night. ✉ *Vlaeykensgang, Oude Koornmarkt 16,* ☎ *03/231–6170. Reservations essential. AE, DC, MC, V. Closed Sun., Aug., Christmas–New Year's, and Easter week.*

$$ ✕ **'t Hofke.** This restaurant is worth visiting for its location alone—it's in the Vlaeykensgang alley, where time seems to have stood still. The cozy dining room has the look and feel of a private home, and the menu includes a large selection of salads and omelets, as well as scampi in cream with cognac and calves' liver with Roquefort. ✉ *Oude Koornmarkt 16,* ☎ *03/233–8606. No credit cards.*

$–$$ ✕ **Cirque Belge.** Replicas of the Atomium and the Manneken Pis, portraits of famous Belgians, paintings of national products from beer to Rizla papers: here's Belgium's answer to Belgian-bashers, a knowingly kitsch extravaganza with well-executed, locally inspired cuisine and a huge range of beers. Try fish soup, rabbit in beer, or fried beef in shallots. ✉ *Groenplaats 33–34,* ☎ *03/232–9439. AE, MC, V.*

$–$$ ✕ **Hungry Henrietta.** Father and son run this stylish Antwerp institution next to the church where Rubens is buried. You can dine in the garden when the weather's good. Fillet of salmon with endive, quail salad, and leg of lamb are on the menu. ✉ *Lomardenvest 19,* ☎ *03/232–2928. AE, DC, MC, V. Closed Sun., Mon.*

$–$$ ✕ **Zuiderterras.** This stark glass-and-black-metal café and restaurant was designed by avant-garde architect bOb (his spelling) Van Reeth in 1993. Snack on one of the inventive salads or splurge on some great *waterzooi,* and enjoy the view of the river on one side or the cathedral and the Old Town on the other. ✉ *Ernest Van Dijckkaai 37,* ☎ *03/234–1275. AE, DC, MC, V.*

$ ✕ **Kiekekot.** Antwerp students satisfy their craving for spit-roasted chicken and french fries at this no-frills "chicken coop," which offers a juicy half chicken for about BF250/€6 nearly all night. ✉ *Grote Markt 35,* ☎ *03/232–1502. MC, V. Closed Tues.*

Lodging

The Antwerp City Tourist Office keeps track of the best hotel prices and can make reservations for you up to a week in advance. Write or fax for a reservation form. It also maintains a list of some 25 recommended bed-and-breakfast accommodations from BF1,200/€30 to BF2,000/€50. For details and price-category definitions, *see* Lodging *in* Belgium A to Z, *above.*

$$$$ ★ **De Witte Lelie.** Three step-gabled 16th-century houses have been combined to make the "White Lily" Antwerp's most exclusive hotel. Personal service is the watchword in the 10-room hotel, decorated mostly in white, with colorful carpets and modern art on the walls. Sumptuous breakfasts are served on a loggia opening up on the inner courtyard. ✉ *Keizerstraat 16–18, 2000,* ☎ *03/226–1966,* FAX *03/234–0019,* WEB *www.hotels-belgium.com. 4 rooms, 6 suites. AE, DC, MC, V.*

$$$$ 🏨 **Hilton Antwerp.** Incorporating the turn-of-the-20th-century Grand Bazaar building, the five stories of the Hilton, built in 1993, are architecturally compatible with the much older buildings on Groenplaats. Rooms have three telephones, safes, and desks. Afternoon tea is served in the marble-floored lobby. The restaurant, Het Vyfde Seizoen, will satisfy gourmets. ✉ *Groenplaats, 2000,* ☎ *03/204–1212,* FAX *03/204–1213,* WEB *www.hilton.com. 183 rooms, 18 suites. 2 restaurants. AE, DC, MC, V.*

$$$ 🏨 **Classic Hotel Villa Mozart.** This small, modern hotel in an old building in a pedestrian area could not be more central—next door to the cathedral. The rooms, equipped with business-class features, air-conditioning, and safes, are slightly cramped, but many overlook the cathedral. ✉ *Handschoenmarkt 3, 2000,* ☎ *03/231–3031,* FAX *03/231–5685,* WEB *www.bestwestern.be. 25 rooms. Restaurant, in-room safes. AE, DC, MC, V.*

$$$ ★ 🏨 **Firean.** An Art Deco gem built in 1929, Hotel Firean is family operated. There's a tiny bar–cum–breakfast room, where eggs are served in floral-print cozies. The location is not central, but a tram to the Old Town runs outside the door. ✉ *Karel Oomsstraat 6, 2018,* ☎ *03/237–0260,* FAX *03/238–1168,* WEB *www.hotels-belgium.com. 9 rooms, 6 in annex next door. AE, DC, MC, V.*

$$$ 🏨 **Hyllit.** The Hyllit (1995) stands on the corner of De Keyserlaan, Antwerp's prestige shopping street, with its entrance on Appelmansstraat, the gateway to the diamond district (reception on second floor). Rooms are decorated in muted colors and equipped with office-type desks. There's a roof-top buffet breakfast room and full room service. ✉ *De Keyserlei 28–30, 2018,* ☎ *03/202–6800,* FAX *03/202–6890,* WEB *www.hyllithotel.be. 24 rooms, 56 suites. Breakfast room. AE, DC, MC, V.*

$–$$ 🏨 **Pension Cammerpoorte.** The rooms (some with a view of the cathedral) are decorated in bright pastels and sad-clown art, and many can comfortably house a family of four. A buffet breakfast, included in the price, is served in the tidy brick-and-lace café. There's no elevator for the four floors. ✉ *Steenhouwersvest 55, 2000,* ☎ *03/231–2836,* FAX *03/226–2843. 16 rooms with shower. Café. AE, DC, MC, V.*

Shopping

In fashion, Antwerp has become a center second only to Milan, thanks to a group of designers who burst on the scene as the Antwerp Six. Inspired by their success, other young designers have achieved prominence; check out the boutiques in the De Wilde Zee district and along Huidevetterstraat and Schuttershofstraat. Ready-to-wear by Raf Simons and Martin Margiela can be found at **Louis** (✉ Lombardenstraat 2, ☎ 03/232–9872). **Dries Van Noten** (✉ Nationalestraat 16, ☎ 03/233–9437) has a beautiful boutique, Modepaleis, that's not to be confused with the drab Van Noten shop opposite.

If you plan to invest in diamonds, it makes sense to do so in the world's leading diamond center. If you're not an expert, your best bet is **Diamondland** (✉ Appelmansstraat 33a, ☎ 03/234–3612), in whose spectacular showrooms you can see both loose and mounted diamonds.

Antwerp Essentials

AIRPORTS AND TRANSFERS

Antwerp International Airport is 5½ km (3 mi) southeast of the city. There are several flights a day to and from London City Airport. Most passengers arrive via Brussels National Airport (Zaventem), which is linked with Antwerp by hourly bus service (50 mins one-way).

➤ Airport Information: **Antwerp International Airport** (☎ 03/285–6500 flight information).

TRANSFERS

Buses to Antwerp's Centraal Station leave every 20 minutes; travel time is about 15 minutes.

CAR TRAVEL

Expressways from Amsterdam, Eindhoven, Aachen, Liège, Brussels, and Ghent converge on Antwerp's inner-city ring expressway. It's a 10-lane racetrack, so be sure you're in the correct lane well before you exit.

TOURS

BOAT TOURS

Flandria operates 90-minute boat trips on the River Scheldt, departing from the Steenplein pontoon (next to the Steen) from Easter through September (BF260/€6.45), as well as boat tours of the enormous port (2½ hrs), which leave from Quay 13 near Londonstraat, May–October (BF450/€11.15).

➤ Fees & Schedules: **Flandria** (☎ 03/231–3100).

PRIVATE GUIDES

Qualified personal guides can be engaged through the City Tourist Office, which requires a couple of days' notice. The price for two hours is BF1,500/€37.

TRAM TOURS

Touristram operates 50-minute tram tours with cassette commentary in the Old City and old harbor area. Tickets (BF150/€3.70) are sold on the tram.

➤ Fees & Schedules: **Touristram** (✉ Groenplaats, ☎ 03/480–9388).

TRAIN TRAVEL

Frequent fast trains run between Antwerp (Centraal Station) and Brussels; the trip takes 35 minutes.

➤ Train Information: **Centraal Station** (☎ 03/204–2040).

TRAM TRAVEL

In the downtown area, the tram is the most convenient means of transportation. Some lines have gone underground (look for signs marked M); the most useful line runs between Centraal Station (Metro: Diamant) and the Groenplaats (for the Old City). A single ride costs BF40/€1, a 10-ride ticket BF290/€7, and a day pass BF110/€3. For detailed transportation maps, stop at the tourist office.

VISITOR INFORMATION

➤ Tourist Information: **Toerisme Stad Antwerpen** (Antwerp City Tourist Office; ✉ Grote Markt 15, ☎ 03/232–0103, FAX 03/231–1937).

GHENT

Ghent—spelled Gent in Dutch and known to French-speakers as Gand—is the home of one of the world's greatest works of art, Van Eyck's *Adoration of the Mystic Lamb*. The city center may come straight out of the Middle Ages, but this is a dynamic, modern town with a long-established rebellious streak. It was weavers from Ghent, joined by others from Brugge, who took up arms to defeat the French cavalry in 1302. Charles V (1500–58) was born here, but that did not prevent an uprising against Spanish rule from being cruelly crushed. Centuries later, a weaver saved Ghent from decline by stealing a newfangled spinning mule from England and starting Ghent's industrial revolution. Later, socialists battled here for workers' rights, and Ghent became the site of Belgium's first Flemish-speaking university. The militant tradition continues to this day: while the city commemorated Charles's 500th birthday in 2000, many academics and locals vehemently opposed the festivities.

Exploring Ghent

The best spot to start a walk around the center is Sint-Michielsbrug (St. Michael's Bridge), with its view of Ghent's three glorious medieval steeples. The closest is the severe early Gothic Sint-Niklaaskerk (St. Nicholas's Church); behind it is the Belfort (Belfry) from 1314. In the background rises the honey-colored tower of Sint-Baafskathedraal (St. Bavo's Cathedral) in Brabant Gothic. The classic walk around the Old City takes you up to the Gravensteen (Castle of the Counts) and then, on the opposite shore of the River Leie, to the Stadhuis (Town Hall) and the cathedral. Many historic buildings are lit up every night from May through October (and Friday and Saturday nights the rest of the year), making an evening walk a memorable experience.

Belfort (Belfry). Three hundred ft high, it symbolizes the power of the guilds during the 14th century. The spire was added for the world's fair of 1913, based on the original plans. A 52-bell carillon hangs on the fifth floor but can only be visited with a guide. ✉ *Sint-Baafsplein,* ☎ *09/269–3730.* ⏲ *Mid-Mar.–mid-Nov., daily 10–12:30 and 2–5:30; guided visits at 10 mins past hr, afternoons only, May–Sept.*

★ **Graslei.** This quay along the Leie River, between St. Michael's Bridge and Gras Bridge, is best seen from the Korenlei across the river. Once the center of Ghent's trade, it is lined with a row of Baroque guild houses and other buildings, among them the 12th-century **Koornstapelhuis** (Granary), used for 600 years.

Gravensteen. The ancient castle of the counts of Flanders hulks up like a battleship near the confluence of the Leie and Lieve Canal, the 700-year-old waterway that links the city with Brugge. First erected in 1180, the castle has been rebuilt a number of times, most recently in the 19th century. A gruesome display of torture instruments indicates how feudal power was maintained. The spinning mules that made Ghent a textile center were first installed here. ✉ *Sint-Veerleplein,* ☎ *09/225–9306.* ⏲ *Apr.–Sept., daily 9–6; Oct.–Mar., daily 9–5.*

Museum voor Schone Kunsten (Fine Arts Museum). Paintings and sculptures from the Middle Ages to the mid-20th century are displayed here. The collection includes two outstanding paintings by Hieronymus Bosch, *St. Jerome* and *The Bearing of the Cross,* and a fine selection of Belgian art from the late 19th and early 20th centuries. ✉ *Nicolaas de Liemaeckereplein 3,* ☎ *09/222–1703.* ⏲ *Tues.–Sun. 9:30–5.*

★ **Sint-Baafskathedraal** (St. Bavo's Cathedral). In the baptistry is the stupendous 24-panel *Adoration of the Mystic Lamb,* completed in 1432 by Jan Van Eyck (1389–1441), who is said to have invented the technique of painting with oil. To the medieval viewer, the painting was a theological summation of the relationship between God and the world. The cathedral has several other treasures, notably a Rubens masterpiece, *The Conversion of St. Bavo,* in which the artist painted himself as a convert in a red cloak. ✉ *Sint-Baafsplein,* ☎ *09/225–1626,* WEB *www.gent.be/gent/english/index.htm.* ⏲ *Cathedral Apr.–Oct., daily 8:30–6; Nov.–Mar., daily 8:30–5. Chapel Apr.–Oct., Mon.–Sat. 9:30–5, Sun. 1–5; Nov.–Mar., Mon.–Sat., 10:30–4, Sun. 2–5. No visits to cathedral or chapel during services.*

Stedelijk Museum voor Actuele Kunst (Municipal Museum for Contemporary Art). SMAK, as it is known, has made a significant impact on Belgium's contemporary art scene since opening in Ghent's City Park in 1999. Esteemed curator Jan Hoet has put together a collection that includes everything from Joseph Beuys to Francis Bacon. In a town filled with history, Hoet dares to be new. ✉ *Citadelpark,* ☎ *09/221–1703,* FAX *09/221–7109.* ⏲ *Tues.–Sun. 10–6.*

Stadhuis (Town Hall). You notice immediately that this 16th-century building reflects two distinct architectural styles, the result of crippling tax increases imposed by Charles V that forced a halt in construction. The older Gothic section, with its lacelike tracery, was begun early in the 16th century. The structure was finished at the end of the same century in a more sober Renaissance style. ✉ *Botermarkt,* ☎ *09/266–5222.* ⏲ *Guided visits only, May–Oct., Mon.–Thurs. at 3.*

Dining

Ghent's contribution to Belgian gastronomy is the creamy fish or chicken stew *waterzooi,* which most menus offer. For details and price-category definitions, *see* Dining *in* Belgium A to Z, *above.*

$$$–$$$$ ★ ✕ **Waterzooi.** This tiny restaurant stands on a square distinguished by 16th- and 17th-century buildings facing the Gravensteen. It serves such specialties as waterzooi (what else) and turbot with pepper sauce. ✉ *Sint-Veerleplein 2,* ☎ *09/225–0563. Reservations essential. Jacket and tie. AE, DC, MC, V. Closed Wed., Sun., and 3 wks in July–Aug.*

$$ ★ ✕ **'t Buikske Vol.** Patershol, formerly a district where textile workers lived, has become a charming residential area. Probably the best among its trendy eateries, the Buikske Vol presents such well-prepared dishes as grilled turbot, fillet of beef with onion confit, and sweetbreads with rabbit. ✉ *Kraanlei 17,* ☎ *09/225–1880. AE, DC, V. Closed Sun., Wed., Easter wk, and 1st ½ of Aug. No lunch Sat.*

$$ ✕ **Pakhuis.** An old warehouse has been converted into an enormously popular brasserie, with marble-top tables, parquet floors, and a huge oak bar. There's an oyster bar to supplement such basic brasserie fare as knuckle of ham with mustard and steak tartare. ✉ *Schuurkenstraat 4,* ☎ *09/223–5555. AE, DC, MC, V. Closed Sun. No lunch Sat.*

$–$$ ★ ✕ **Cassis.** In a tranquil setting combining beamed ceilings, light wood and wicker chairs, Cassis offers both traditional Belgian specialties and huge, inventive salads presented as artfully as a Flemish still life. ✉ *Vrijdagmarkt 5,* ☎ *09/223–8546. AE, MC, V.*

$ ✕ **Taverne Keizershof.** Touristy taverns are much the same all over Belgium, but this one is popular with locals—always a good sign. The daily plates are large portions of hearty Belgian food. ✉ *Vrijdagmarkt 47,* ☎ *09/223–4446. MC, V. Closed Mon.*

Lodging

A number of Ghent hotels catering to trade-show visitors stand near the Expo Center. There are not so many in the Old Town, but they do include one of the oldest hotels in Europe. For details and price-category definitions, *see* Lodging *in* Belgium A to Z, *above.*

$$$$ 🏨 **Sofitel.** The Ghent outpost of this classy and comfortable French hotel chain is a converted Art Nouveau building, decorated in warm brown and beige and excellently situated in the heart of the Old City. The bathrooms are palatial. ✉ *Hoogpoort 63, 9000,* ☎ *09/233–3331,* FAX *09/233–1102. 124 rooms, 3 suites. Restaurant. AE, DC, MC, V.*

$$ ★ **Erasmus.** From the flagstone and wood-beam library-lounge to the stone mantels in the bedrooms, every inch of this noble 16th-century house has been scrubbed, polished, and bedecked with period ornaments. Even the tiny garden has been carefully manicured. ✉ *Poel 25, 9000,* ☎ *09/224–2195,* FAX *09/233–4241. 11 rooms. AE, DC, MC, V. CP.*

$$ **Gravensteen.** This handsome 19th-century mansion, restored to its original Second Empire style, has a superb canal-front location, a few steps from the castle of the counts. Some rooms are small but tasteful; 10 more luxurious rooms overlook the canal. ✉ *Jan Breydelstraat 35, 9000,* ☎ *09/225–1150,* FAX *09/225–1850,* WEB *www.gravensteen.be. 49 rooms, 2 suites. AE, DC, MC, V.*

$$ **Sint-Jorishof.** Napoléon stayed here, and so did Mary of Burgundy and Emperor Charles V, for this hotel has been operating since 1228, making it one of the oldest in Europe. Much of its Gothic spirit has been preserved, especially in the reception area and the restaurant, which serves classic French fare. There are only four rooms in the main building; the rest are in two converted 18th-century houses across the street. ✉ *Botermarkt 2, 9000,* ☎ *09/224–2424,* FAX *09/224–2640,* WEB *http://hotels-belgium.com/gent/cour-st-georges.htm. 4 rooms in main building, 24 in annex. Restaurant. AE, DC, MC, V. CP.*

Ghent Essentials

CAR TRAVEL

Ghent is just off the six-lane E40 from Brussels, which continues to Brugge and the coast. Traffic can be bumper-to-bumper on summer weekends. It is generally lighter on the E17 from Antwerp. Finding your way in and out of the city center can be extremely tricky; advance preparation is a good idea.

TOURS

BOAT TOURS

Sightseeing boats depart from landing stages at Graslei, Easter–October, and Korenlei, from April–mid-November, for 35-minute trips. Admission is BF170/€4.20.

➤ FEES & SCHEDULES: **Sightseeing boats** (☎ 09/225–1505); Korenlei (☎ 09/223–8853).

PRIVATE GUIDES

Your Ghent experience can be much enhanced by a personal guide; call Gidsenbond van Gent (Association of Ghent Guides). The charge is BF1,700/€42 for the first two hours, BF850/€21 per additional hour.

➤ FEES & SCHEDULES: **Gidsenbond van Gent** (☎ 09/233–0772, FAX 09/233–0865).

TRAIN TRAVEL

Nonstop trains depart for Gent-Sint-Pieters every half hour from Gares du Midi, Central, and Nord in Brussels. Travel time to Ghent is 28 minutes.

➤ TRAIN INFORMATION: **Gares du Midi, Central, and Nord** (Brussels; ☎ 02/203–3640 OR 09/221–4444).

TRANSPORTATION AROUND GHENT

Most of the sights are within a 1-km (½-mi) radius of the Town Hall, and by far the best way to see them is on foot. You can rent bikes at the train station or in the center, and much of the city center is closed to cars.

VISITOR INFORMATION

➤ TOURIST INFORMATION: **Dienst voor Toerisme** (Tourist Office; ✉ Belfort, Botermarkt 17a, ☎ 09/266–5232).

BRUGGE

Brugge (or Bruges, as it is known to French- and most English-speakers) represents the flowering of commerce and culture in the Middle Ages. The city had the good fortune to be linked with the North Sea by a navigable waterway and became a leading member of the Hanseatic League during the 13th century. Splendid marriage feasts were celebrated here; that of Charles the Bold, Duke of Burgundy (1433–77), to Margaret of York in 1468 is commemorated in the annual Holy Blood Procession. Disaster struck when the link with the sea silted up in the 15th century, but this past misfortune is responsible for Brugge's present glory: little has changed over the last 500 years in this city of interlaced canals, making it a living museum in the best possible sense.

Exploring Brugge

Numbers in the margin correspond to points of interest on the Brugge (Bruges) map.

The center of Brugge is virtually reserved for pedestrians; you need to remember that cobbled streets call for good walking shoes. Brugge draws visitors in droves, but there's always a quiet corner away from the crowd. Try to do your exploring in the early evening or early morning when the day trippers are not around and the city is at its most magical.

❻ **Arentshuis.** The Brugge-born English artist Frank Brangwyn (1867–1956) was one of several British Romantics who lived in the city and influenced the reconstruction of many buildings in a pseudo-Gothic style. Many of his brooding paintings of Brugge are on view here. On the ground floor is the **Kantmuseum** (Lace Museum), containing outstanding examples of a craft long and lovingly practiced in Brugge. ⊠ *Dijver 16,* ☎ *050/448711.* ⊙ *Apr.–Sept., daily 9:30–5; Oct.–Mar., Wed.–Mon. 9:30–5.*

★ ❿ **Begijnhof** (Beguinage). The Begijnhof has been an oasis of peace for 750 years. The first Beguines were widows of fallen crusaders. They were not nuns but lived a devout life while serving the community. Although the last Beguines left the close of small, whitewashed houses in 1930, a Benedictine community has replaced them, and you may join them, discreetly, for vespers and masses in their small church. ⊠ *Off Wijngaardstraat,* ☎ *050/330011.* ⊙ *Masses and vespers held intermittently from dawn to dusk.*

❶ **Belfort** (Belfry). There's a panoramic view of the town from the top of the 270-ft-high (366 steps!) Belfort, which dominates the Markt, the city's ancient market square. The Belfort has a carillon notable even in Belgium, where they are a matter of civic pride. ⊠ *Markt 7.* ⊙ *Apr.–Sept., daily 9:30–5; Oct.–Mar., daily 9:30–12:30 and 1:30–5. Carillon concerts Oct.–mid-June, Wed. and weekends 2:15–3; mid-June–Sept., Mon., Wed., and Sat. 9 PM–10 PM, Sun. 2:15–3.*

★ ❷ **Burg.** This magical medieval square is the focal point of ancient Brugge. The **Stadhuis** (Town Hall), a jewel of Gothic architecture in white sandstone from the 14th century, has an ornate facade adorned with a multitude of statues. It is linked with the graceful Renaissance **Oude Griffie** (Old Recorder's House) by a bridge arching over the narrow Blinde Ezelstraat. ⊠ *Stadhuis: Burg 12.* ⊙ *Apr.–Sept., daily 9:30–5; Oct.–Mar., daily 9:30–12:30 and 2–5.*

★ ❺ **Groeninge Museum.** This small museum enjoys a worldwide reputation for its superb collection of Flemish Primitives and includes Van Eyck's *Virgin and Canon Van der Paele,* Memling's *Moreel Triptych,*

Brugge (Bruges)

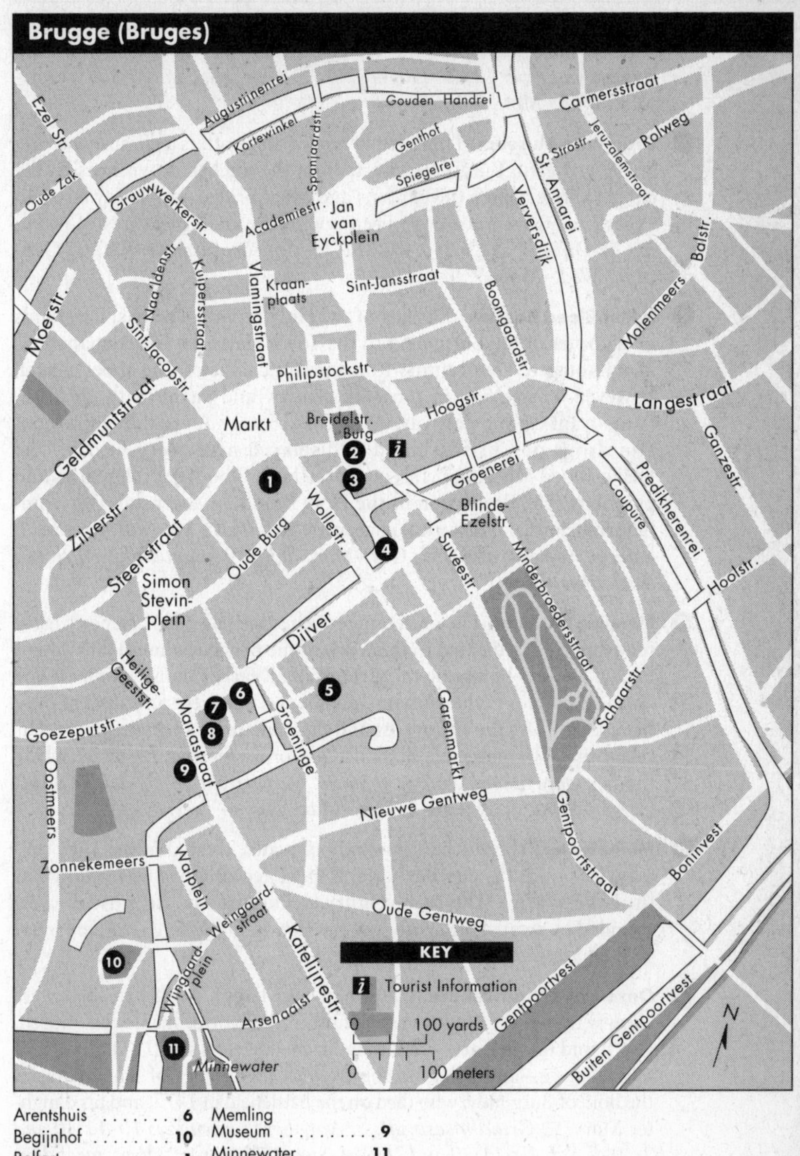

Arentshuis	6
Begijnhof	10
Belfort	1
Burg	2
Groeninge Museum	5
Gruuthuse Museum	7
Heilig-Bloed Basiliek	3
Memling Museum	9
Minnewater	11
Onze-Lieve-Vrouwekerk	8
Reien	4

arguably his most intensely spiritual work, Hieronymus Bosch's surrealistic *Last Judgment,* and Pieter Brueghel's *Preaching of John the Baptist.* ✉ *Dijver 12,* ☎ *050/448711.* ⏲ *Apr.–Sept., daily 9:30–5; Oct.–Mar., Wed.–Mon. 9:30–5.*

7 **Gruuthuse Museum.** This 15th-century palace offers a glimpse into life at the powerful Burgundy court, from the kitchen downstairs to the chapel above. Catch the gardens and canal bridge on a sunny day and experience what must have been one of the great pleasures of nobility. ✉ *Dijver 17,* ☎ *050/448711,* ⏲ *Apr.–Sept., daily 9:30–5; Oct–Mar., Wed.–Mon. 9:30–5.*

3 **Heilig-Bloed Basiliek** (Basilica of the Holy Blood). The basilica stands on a corner of the Burg, next to the Town Hall. The lower chapel has kept its austere 12th-century Romanesque character. The upper chapel, however, was rebuilt in the 15th century and again, with an ultra-flamboyant Gothic stairway, in the 19th century. A vial thought to contain drops of Christ's blood is displayed here every Friday. The **Heilig-Bloed Museum** (Museum of the Holy Blood) has reliquaries and paintings. The **Procession of the Holy Blood** on Ascension Day combines religious and historical pageantry. ✉ *Burg.* ⏲ *Museum Apr.–Sept., daily 9:30–noon and 2–6; Oct.–Mar., daily 10–noon and 2–4; closed Wed. afternoon.*

★ 9 **Memling Museum.** The museum, reopened in June 2001 after extensive renovation, is dedicated to the work of the Brugge painter Hans Memling (c. 1430–94), among the greatest of all early Flemish painters. The six masterpieces in the museum include the altarpiece *St. John the Baptist and St. John the Evangelist* and the miniatures adorning the St. Ursula shrine. The museum is housed in the former **Sint-Janshospitaal,** where the sick were nursed for 700 years. ✉ *Mariastraat 38,* ☎ *050/448711.* ⏲ *Apr.–Sept., daily 9:30–5; Oct.–Mar., Thurs.–Tues. 9:30–5.*

11 **Minnewater.** This enchanting body of water, created in the 13th century, was once the city harbor and more recently has been known as the Lake of Love. The 16th-century lockkeeper's house is usually surrounded by swans, the symbol of the city. ✉ *Off Wijngaardplein, next to Begijnhof.*

8 **Onze-Lieve-Vrouwekerk** (Church of Our Lady). At 381 ft, the severe spire is the tallest brick construction in the world. Inside the church, you'll find notable art—including Michelangelo's small *Madonna and Child* statue—and splendid tombs with the effigies of Duke Charles the Bold of Burgundy, who died on the battlefield in 1477, and his daughter Mary. ✉ *Gruuthusestraat.* ⏲ *Apr.–Sept., weekdays 10–11:30 and 2:30–5, Sat. 10–11:30 and 2:30–4, Sun. 2:30–5; Oct.–Mar., weekdays 10–11:30 and 2:30–4:30, Sat. 10–11:30 and 2:30–4:30, Sun. 2:30–4:30.*

★ 4 **Reien** (Canals). The canals of Brugge with their arching stone bridges can be explored both by boat and on foot along the quays. They give the city its special character. From **Steenhouwersdijk** you see the brick rear gables, which are all that remains of the old county hall. Next to the little **Huidenvettersplein,** with its 17th-century guild houses, is **Rozenhoedkaai;** from here the view of the heart of Brugge includes the pinnacles of the Town Hall, the basilica, and the belfry.

Dining

Along Brugge's quiet streets you'll find some of Belgium's finest dining. The Markt, however, is ringed with unremarkable restaurants catering to the tourist trade. For details and price-category definitions, *see* Dining *in* Belgium A to Z, *above.*

$$$$ ★ ✕ **De Karmeliet.** Owner-chef Geert Van Hecke, one of Belgium's best, works in this lovely 18th-century house. His inventive kitchen creates a festival of flavors: goose liver with truffled potatoes, roast langoustines with endive in an apple-and-curry juice, cod carpaccio with asparagus. ✉ *Langestraat 19,* ☎ *050/338259. Reservations essential. Jacket and tie. AE, DC, MC, V. Closed Mon. No dinner Sun.*

$$$ ✕ **'t Bourgoensche Cruyce.** In a romantic canal-side setting, this restaurant has salmon-and-copper decor that is reflected in the water. The cuisine is equally romantic: panfried langoustines with wild mushrooms, tournedos of salmon with bacon, turbot medallions with coriander and caramelized leeks (reservations essential; closed Tues., Wed., and 1st wk in July). The establishment has eight cozy guest rooms furnished in traditional Flemish style; four face the canal. ✉ *Wollestraat 41,* ☎ *050/337926,* FAX *050/341968. 8 rooms. Restaurant. AE, DC, MC, V. Closed mid-Nov.–mid-Dec.*

$$–$$$$ ✕ **Breidel-De Coninc.** Famed for fresh mussels and other seafood, this simple, but well-appointed, restaurant stands between the Markt and the Burg. While there are token offerings of eel and steak, the focus is on the basics—a huge crock heaped with shiny, blue-black shells. ✉ *Breidelstraat 24,* ☎ *050/339746. AE, MC, V. Closed Wed. and June.*

$ ✕ **Straffe Hendrik.** This daytime pub is attached to the brewery, dating from 1546, that produces the crystal-clear beer of the same name. It also serves quite acceptable pub grub, and you can tour the facilities. The square is among Brugge's most charming. ✉ *Walplein 26,* ☎ *050/332697. No credit cards.*

$ ✕ **Taverne Oud Handbogenhof.** Here's an authentic Flemish inn, with a big courtyard shaded by linden trees. It's much favored by locals, always a good sign. Specialties are spareribs with garlic sauce and salmon with scallops and shrimp in white sauce. ✉ *Baliestraat 6,* ☎ *050/331945. MC, V. Closed Mon., 1st wk in July, and Jan. No lunch Tues., Wed.*

Lodging

In proportion to its size, Brugge has a large number of hotels, many of them romantic, canal-side residences popular for second honeymoons. Prices are relatively high, but so are standards. Many hotels offer package deals. For details and price-category definitions, *see* Lodging *in* Belgium A to Z, *above*.

$$$ 🏨 **De Castillion.** This restaurant and hotel was the residence of 18th-century bishop Jean-Baptiste de Castillion. Drinks and coffee are served in a handsome Art Deco salon. Fillet of venison in a Pomerol stock and turbot and scampi on a bed of tagliatelle with a curry sauce are among the offerings (reservations essential; jacket and tie required; no dinner Sun., no lunch Mon.–Tues.). The rooms in the hotel side vary considerably in size and price. Their decor ranges from rustic to modern. ✉ *Heilige Geeststraat 1,* ☎ *050/343001,* FAX *050/339475,* WEB *www.youniware.be/castillion. 18 rooms, 2 suites. Restaurant. AE, DC, MC, V.*

$$$ ★ 🏨 **De Tuileriëen.** A 15th-century mansion with Venetian glass windows has been converted into a patrician hotel and decorated with discreet antique reproductions. Canal-side rooms have great views; courtyard rooms are quieter. ✉ *Dijver 7, 8000,* ☎ *050/343691,* FAX *050/340400,* WEB *www.hoteltuilerieen.com. 22 rooms, 23 suites. Pool. AE, DC, MC, V.*

$$$ 🏨 **Die Swaene.** This hotel has "romantic" written all over it: canal-side location, four-poster beds, candles, and marble nymphs in every nook and cranny: honeymoon heaven. The restaurant ($$$$; closed Wed., 3 wks in July, 3 wks in Jan.; no lunch Thurs.) is a serious contender as one of the best in this gourmet city: goose liver, sweetbreads, and grilled turbot are among its treats. ✉ *Steenhouwersdijk 1, 8000,*

☎ *050/342798,* FAX *050/336674,* WEB *www.dieswaene-hotel.com. 22 rooms, 2 suites. Restaurant, pool. AE, DC, MC, V.*

$$$ **Walburg.** One of Brugge's grandest 19th-century town houses, a few blocks from the Burg, was converted into a hotel in 1996. The rooms, decorated in different color schemes, with period Marie Antoinette furniture and marble bathrooms, are a generous 750 square ft—and the suite twice as large. ✉ *Boomgaardstraat 13, 8000,* ☎ *050/349414,* FAX *050/336884. 12 rooms, 1 suite. Restaurant, bar. AE, DC, MC, V.*

$$ ★ **Egmond.** Every room in this manorlike inn on Minnewater has a garden view, as well as parquet floors and the odd fireplace or dormer ceiling. The hotel is a pleasant retreat from the bustle of the center, 10 minutes away. The bathrooms are tiny. ✉ *Minnewater 15, 8000,* ☎ *050/341445,* FAX *050/342940,* WEB *www.egmond.be. 9 rooms. No credit cards.*

$ ★ **De Pauw.** At this family-run hotel, the warmly furnished rooms have names rather than numbers, and breakfast comes with six kinds of bread, cold cuts, and cheese. The two rooms that share a shower down the hall are a super value. ✉ *Sint-Gilliskerkhof 8, 8000,* ☎ *050/337118,* FAX *050/345140. 8 rooms, 6 with bath. MC, V.*

Brugge Essentials

CAR TRAVEL

Brugge is about an hour's drive from Brussels on the E40 motorway to the coast. Holiday weekend traffic is heavy. Unless you are driving to a hotel, leave your car at one of the parking lots or garages at the entrance to the Old City.

TOURS

CARRIAGE TOURS

The horse-drawn carriages that congregate in the Markt are an expensive way of seeing the sights. They are available March–November, daily 10–6; a 35-minute trip will cost BF1,000/€25. The carriages take up to five people.

BOAT TOURS

Boat trips along the city canals are run by several companies and depart from five separate landings. Boats ply the waters March–November, daily 10–6. They leave every 10–15 minutes, and a 30-minute trip costs BF190/€5.

BUS TOURS

Fifty-minute minibus tours of the city center leave every hour on the hour from the Markt in front of the post office.

TRAIN TRAVEL

Trains run twice an hour from Brussels (Gare du Midi, Central, or Nord) to Brugge. The station is south of the canal that circles the downtown area; it is a pleasant walk to the Minnewater, Begijnhof, and on to the city center. Travel time from Brussels is 53 minutes.

➤ TRAIN INFORMATION: **Belgian National Railways** (☎ 050/382382).

TRANSPORTATION AROUND BRUGGE

The center of Brugge is best explored on foot, as car and bus access is severely restricted. This makes for bicycle heaven; ask the tourist office for information on where to rent one.

VISITOR INFORMATION

➤ TOURIST INFORMATION: **Toerisme Brugge** (Brugge Tourist Office; ✉ Burg 11, ☎ 050/448686, FAX 050/448600). Contact them well in advance for tickets to the Holy Blood Procession.

6 BULGARIA

SOFIA, THE BLACK SEA COAST, INLAND BULGARIA

BULGARIA, WITH MOUNTAINS AND SEASIDES, modern cities and medieval villages, is an enigmatic land where rustic beauty coexists with decaying remnants of a Communist past. Lying in the eastern half of the Balkan Peninsula, Bulgaria was the closest ally of the former Soviet Union until the 1989 overthrow of Communist Party head Todor Zhivkov. Since then, Bulgaria, which is striving to become a member of the European Union, has struggled toward democracy and a free-market economy. Due to continued reform as well as Bulgaria's support during the Kosovo conflict, the country has become a serious contender among countries in line for membership to the EU.

Corruption, massive unemployment, and skyrocketing inflation resulting in a decreasing standard of living severely tested the patience of Bulgarians after 1989. In January 1997, as the lev plunged, Bulgarians took to the streets. Protests and strikes immobilized the country and forced the Socialist Party government to hold early elections. April 1997 elections gave the opposition coalition (UDF; Union of Democratic Forces) a plurality. Though the new government headed by Prime Minister Ivan Kostov has not yet pulled Bulgaria completely out of the economic crisis that's made it one of the poorest countries in Europe, there are definite improvements. Over the past four years, the lev has been pegged to the German mark and is finally stable, the Mafia is not nearly as prevalent or powerful, and the country is enjoying the most optimistic atmosphere in years. Food and goods are plentiful, though more affordable for the upper-crust and visitors making a Western salary.

One of the most important advances is the new law that as of June 2001 Bulgarians were granted the right to visa-free tourism throughout the European Union. While foreign travel still poses a formidable financial barrier for most, the repeal of the restriction cannot be underestimated, as for years Bulgarians have existed inside a jail formed by the country's border. Spirits are high, while costs are low. It is an excellent time to visit Bulgaria.

Endowed with long Black Sea beaches, the rugged interior Balkan Range, and fertile Danube plains, Bulgaria has much to offer year-round. The Black Sea coast, the country's eastern border, is particularly alluring, with secluded coves and fishing villages built amid Byzantine and Roman ruins, and wide, shallow beaches that have been developed into resorts. The terrain of the beautiful interior is ideal for hiking and skiing. In the more remote areas hides a tranquil world of forested ridges, spectacular valleys, and small villages where donkey-drawn carts are still the primary transport.

Bulgaria (Bŭlgariya)

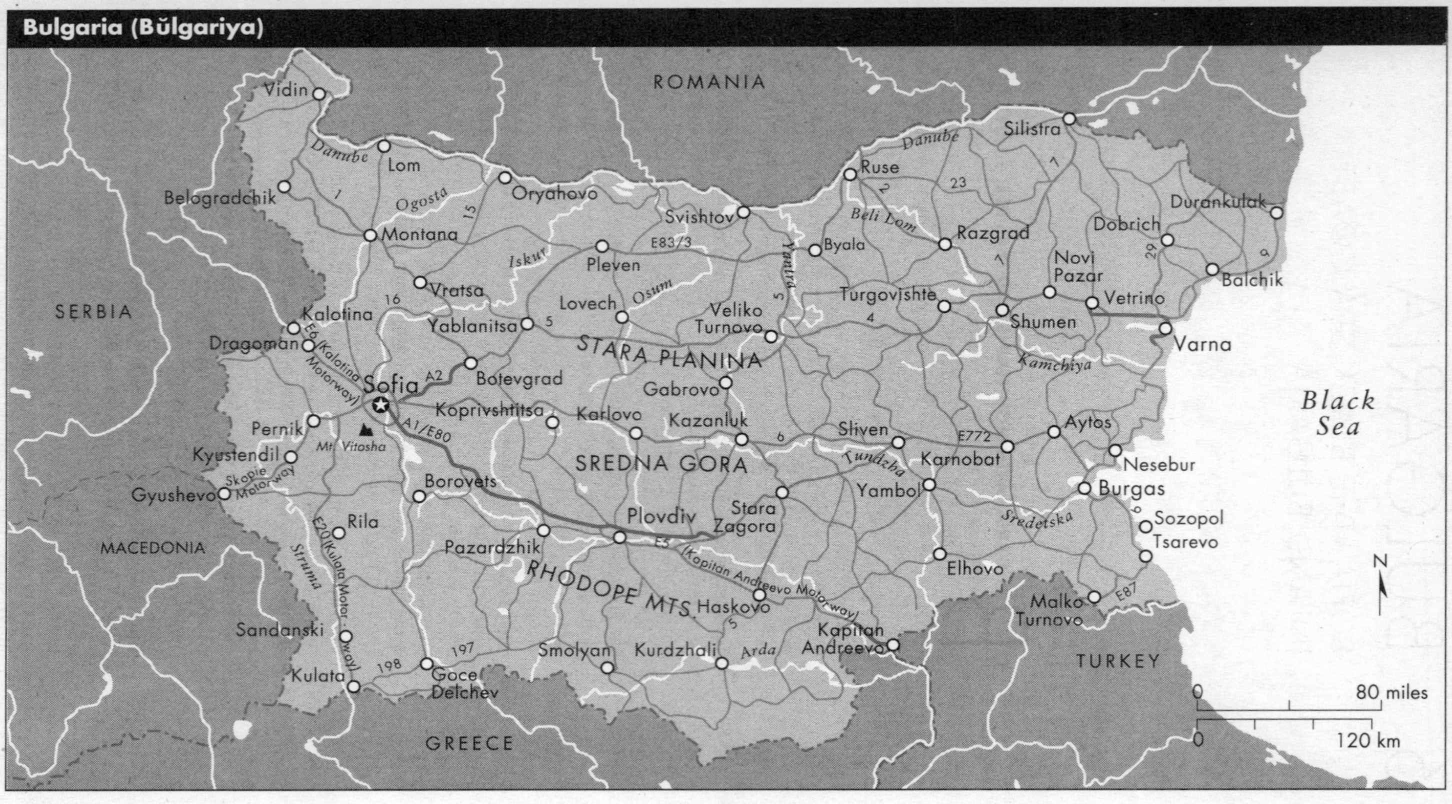

Founded in AD 681 by the Bulgars, a Turkic tribe from Central Asia, Bulgaria was already a crossroads. Archaeological finds in Varna, on the Black Sea coast, give proof of civilization from as early as 4600 BC. Part of the Byzantine Empire from 1018 to 1185, Bulgaria was occupied by the Turks from 1396 until 1878. Today, Bulgaria has Eastern-influenced architecture, Turkish fast food, Greek ruins, Soviet monuments, and European outdoor cafés. Five hundred years of Muslim occupation and nearly half a century of Communist rule did not wipe out Christianity. The country's 120 monasteries, with their icons and numerous frescoes, chronicle the development of Bulgarian cultural and national identity.

The capital, Sofia, sits picturesquely in a valley near Mt. Vitosha. Rich with history and culture, the city also has good hotels, a variety of restaurants, and a vibrant Mediterranean-style nightlife. Veliko Turnovo, just north of the Balkan Range in the center of the country and the capital from the 12th through 14th centuries during the Second Bulgarian Empire, still has medieval ramparts and vernacular architecture. Plovdiv, a university town southeast of Sofia, has a particularly picturesque Old Quarter as well as one of the world's best-preserved Roman amphitheaters. Varna, the site of one of Europe's first cultural settlements, is a summer beach playground and among the most important ports on the Black Sea.

BULGARIA A TO Z

To research prices, get advice from other travelers, and book travel arrangements, visit www.fodors.com.

AIR TRAVEL

Balkan Airlines is currently the only carrier within Bulgaria, and has regular services to Varna and Burgas, the biggest ports on the Black Sea. Since 1999, Balkan no longer has flights to the United States. For group travel or chartered flights within Bulgaria on Balkan, call to speak with an agent.

➤ AIRLINES AND CONTACTS: **Balkan Airlines** (✉ 12 pl. Narodno Subranie Sofia, ☎ 02/981–5170). **Group travel or chartered flights agent** (☎ 02/984–481).

BOAT AND FERRY TRAVEL

Modern luxury vessels cruise the Danube from Passau in Germany to Ruse. Hydrofoils link main communities along the Bulgarian stretches of the Danube and the Black Sea, and there are coastal excursions from some Black Sea resorts. A ferry from Vidin to Calafat links Bulgaria with Romania. Contact a travel agent for reservations.

BUS TRAVEL

An increasing number of private bus firms link all the major towns. Buses tend to be luxurious, air-conditioned, and faster than trains. Bus stations are generally close to the train station. Buy tickets a day or two in advance (but no more than a week). Within the cities a regular system of trams and trolley buses operates for a single fare of 25 stotinki. In Sofia booths at bus stops sell tickets; outside the city you can pay the driver. Group Travel is the chief bus service in the country.

➤ BUS INFORMATION: **Group Travel** (✉ ticket office, 106 bul. Vasil Levski in the First Bank Building, ☎ 02/320–122).

BUSINESS HOURS

Banks are open weekdays 9–5. Museums are usually open 9–5 but are often closed on Monday or Tuesday. Shops are open Monday–Saturday 9–7; some are open on Sunday. A few *denonoshni magazini* (day-and-night minimarkets) in the city center are open 24 hours.

CAR RENTAL

Renting cars in Bulgaria is no bargain—unlike almost everything else, the cost of renting a car from a major Western firm is higher here than in other European countries. Three international car-rental firms have offices in Sofia and other major towns: Hertz, Avis, which can be found at both the Sheraton Sofia Hotel and at the Sofia airport, and Europcar, which operates out of Sofia Airport as well. Two agencies rent cars with drivers: Balkantour and Balkantourist both arrange for chauffeurs, which are actually not much more expensive than renting the car alone.

➤ MAJOR AGENCIES: **Avis** (☒ Sheraton Sofia Hotel, 5 pl. St. Nedelya, ☎ 02/981–1082, ☒ Sofia Airport, ☎ 02/738–023). **Europcar** (☒ Sofia Airport, ☎ 02/981-0334). **Hertz** (☒ 47 bul. Vasil Levski (☎ 02/980–0461).

➤ LOCAL AGENCIES: **Balkantour,** (☒ 27 bul. Stamboliiski, ☎ 02/988–55–43). **Balkantourist** (☒ 1 bul. Vitosha, ☎ 02/87–51–92).

CAR TRAVEL

AUTO CLUBS

For motorist information contact the Bulgarian Automobile Touring Association.

➤ IN BULGARIA: **Bulgarian Automobile Touring Association** (SBA; ☒ 3 ul. Pozitano Sofia, ☎ 02/980–3308).

EMERGENCIES

In case of breakdown call the number below. SBA trucks carry essential spares. Fiat, Ford, Volkswagen, Peugeot, and Mercedes-Benz all have car-service operations in Bulgaria. Other important numbers for drivers are the road police and ambulance.

➤ CONTACTS: **Ambulance** (☎ 150). **Breakdowns** (☎ 146). **Road Police** (☎ 165).

GASOLINE

Stations are regularly spaced on main roads but may be few and far between. All are marked on Balkantourist's motoring map. A listing of 24-hour gas stations in Sofia can be found in the *Sofia City Guide,* an English-language brochure for sale at news kiosks and free at major hotels.

PARKING

Bulgaria's parking laws are liberal, and if there's not a place on the street, you can often park on the sidewalk. Just be sure you're not blocking a driveway or another car, and never park where there's a NO PARKING sign (a red circle with a line through it). If you are in doubt, check with the hotel, restaurant, or sight you are visiting.

ROAD CONDITIONS

Main roads are generally well engineered, although some routes are poor and narrow for the volume of traffic they have to carry. A large-scale expressway construction program has begun to link the main towns. Completed stretches run from Kalotina—on the Serbian border—to Sofia, and from Sofia to Plovdiv.

RULES OF THE ROAD

Drive on the right. The speed limit is 120 kph (70 mph) on highways, 50 or 60 kph (31 or 36 mph) in built-up areas, and 80 kph (50 mph) elsewhere. You must take out collision, or Casco, insurance to drive a rented car. You are required to carry a first-aid kit, fire extinguisher, and triangle-shaped breakdown sign in the vehicle. Front seat belts must be worn. The drunk-driving laws are strict—you are expected not to drive after you have had more than one drink. If you're pulled over, be prepared to pay on the spot a fine determined by the officer. In theory, you need an international drivers' license to drive in Bulgaria. In practice, for the time being, any foreign driver's license along with passport suffices.

CUSTOMS AND DUTIES

You may import duty-free into Bulgaria 250 grams of tobacco products, 1 liter of hard liquor, and 2 liters of wine. Declare items of greater value—computers, camcorders, and the like—so there will be no problems with Bulgarian customs officials on departure. Failure to declare items of value can result in a fine or even police detainment when you attempt to leave.

DINING

In Bulgaria you have a choice between predictable hotel dining, which often includes international cuisines, and more adventurous outings to restaurants or cafés, where the menu may be in Cyrillic. The best bets are the small, folk-style restaurants called *mehanas,* which serve regional specialties, often at shared tables.

Bulgarian national dishes are closely related to their Greek and Slav counterparts: basic Balkan cooking includes lamb and potatoes, pork sausages called *kebapche,* and a popular salad called *shopska salata,* made with feta-style sheep cheese, tomatoes, cucumbers, peppers, and onions. Bulgaria produces sumptuous fruits and vegetables. Try the rich, amber-color *bolgar* grapes and orange-red apricots. Bulgaria invented *kiselo mlyako* (yogurt), and there is excellent *tarator* (cold yogurt soup with sliced cucumber and garlic) in summer. *Banitsa* (butter, cheese, and phyllo dough pastry) is often eaten for breakfast. Syrupy baklava and chocolate or *palachinki* (nut- and honey-stuffed crepes) are favorite desserts.

Bulgarian wines are good, usually full-bodied, dry, and inexpensive. The national drink is *rakia*—either *slivova* (plum) or *grozdova* (grape) brandy—but other hard alcohol and beer are popular, too. Coffee is strong and is often drunk along with a cold beverage, such as cola or a lemon drink.

Prices are for one main course at dinner.

CATEGORY	COST
$$$$	over 18 leva
$$$	13 leva–18 leva
$$	6 leva–12 leva
$	under 6 leva

RESERVATIONS AND DRESS

In Sofia, formal dress (jacket and tie) is customary at $$$$ restaurants. Casual dress is appropriate elsewhere.

EMBASSIES

➤ United Kingdom: (✉ 38 bul. Levski, Sofia, ☎ 02/980–1220).
➤ United States: (✉ 1 ul. Suborna, Sofia, ☎ 02/980–5241).

HOLIDAYS

January 1; March 3 (Treaty of San Stefano Day); Orthodox Easter; May 1 (Labor Day); May 24 (Sts. Cyril and Methodius—creators of the Cyrillic alphabet—Commemoration Day); December 24–26 (Christmas); September 21–22 (Bulgarian Liberation Day.)

LANGUAGE

The official language, Bulgarian, is written in Cyrillic and is close to Old Church Slavonic, the root of all Slavic languages. English, though becoming popular with the young, is rarely understood outside major hotels and restaurants. It is essential to remember that in Bulgaria a nod of the head means "no" and a shake of the head means "yes."

LODGING

There is a wide choice of accommodations, ranging from the old, state-run hotels—most of them dating from the 1960s and '70s—to new, private hotels, apartment rentals, rooms in private homes, and campsites. While you'll find comfortable modern chain hotels in Sofia, lodging in the countryside still tends to suffer from temperamental wiring and erratic plumbing.

Prices are for two people in a double room. At the leading hotels you can pay in either U.S. dollars or leva; the less expensive hotels accept only leva. Foreign currency can be exchanged for leva at the reception desk in most hotels.

CATEGORY	SOFIA	OTHER AREAS
$$$$	over 300 leva	over 100 leva
$$$	150 leva–300 leva	70 leva–100 leva
$$	80 leva–150 leva	40 leva–70 leva
$	under 80 leva	under 40 leva

APARTMENT AND VILLA RENTALS

Rented accommodations are a growth industry, with planned modern complexes as well as picturesque cottages. Cooking facilities tend to be meager, and meal vouchers are included in the deal. An English-speaking manager is generally on hand. Such accommodations usually aren't offered in Sofia but can often be found on the Black Sea coast and in Plovdiv and Veliko Turnovo.

➤ LOCAL AGENTS: **Balkan Tour Sofia** (✉ 27 bul. Stamboliiski, ☎ 02/988–5543). **Balkan Tourist** (✉ 1 bul. Vitosha, ☎ 02/987–5192, WEB www.balkantourist.net).

HOTELS

Most of the formerly government-owned or -operated hotels in Sofia, Plovdiv, and the bigger Black Sea cities have been privatized. Some state-owned hotels in smaller towns are still in the process of privatization and may be closed for renovation. Outside Sofia call ahead to hotels to get the latest information. Most hotels have restaurants and bars; the large, modern ones have swimming pools, shops, and other facilities.

PRIVATE ACCOMMODATIONS

Staying in private homes, with arrangements made by private-room agencies, is becoming a popular alternative to hotels; it not only cuts costs but also means increased contact with Bulgarians. Booking offices are in most main tourist areas. In Sofia contact Balkantour Ltd. Balkan Tourist can also help with Sofia lodgings. Take your own towels, soap, and other necessities.

➤ LOCAL AGENTS: **Balkantour Ltd.** (✉ 27 bul. Stamboliiski, ☎ 02/988–5543 or 02/987–7233). **Balkan Tourist** (✉ 1 bul. Vitosha, ☎ 02/987–5192, WEB www.balkantourist.net).

MAIL AND SHIPPING

The postal code for Sofia is 1000. To receive mail in Bulgaria (an iffy proposition), you can have it sent to PISMO DO POISKVANE, CENTRAL POST OFFICE, followed by the name of the city where you want to pick it up. Mail is held for one week. Do not send anything valuable in the mail and don't be surprised if your mail doesn't arrive. A more expensive but surer option is to use the private courier DHL.

➤ MAJOR SERVICES: **DHL** (✉ 50 bul. Patriarch Evtimii, ☎ 916–133–60).

POSTAL RATES

Letters up to 10 grams to North America cost 80 stotinki; to the United Kingdom, 70 stotinki. Rates change constantly with inflation, so ask for the current price at the post office.

MONEY MATTERS

The favorable exchange rate makes prices seem extremely low by international standards. The greatest expense is lodging, but it is possible to cut costs by choosing the more moderate hotels or staying in a private room in a Bulgarian house or apartment. Taxi and public transport fares, museum and theater admissions, and meal prices in most restaurants are quite low.

Because of fluctuating exchange rates, the following price list can be used only as a rough guide. A trip on a tram, trolley, or bus, 40 stotinki; theater ticket, 2–8 leva; coffee in a moderate restaurant, 1 lev; bottle of wine in a moderate restaurant, 4–9 leva; museum admission, 1–3 leva.

CREDIT CARDS

The major international credit cards are accepted in larger stores and in the most expensive hotels and restaurants, but before you place an order, check to see whether or not you can use your card. Outside Sofia, and at any small restaurant or hotel, credit cards are almost always worthless. Bring cash. If you run into a problem, Western Union opened an office in Sofia in 2000, where you can send and receive money wires.

➤ CONTACTS: **Western Union** (✉ 70 bul. Vitosha, ☎ 953–4153).

CURRENCY

As of January 1, 2000, 1 lev was pegged to 1 DM, and Bulgarian bills of less then 1 lev are obsolete. Stotinki, which had been rendered worthless during the period of hyperinflation, are once again in use in the new currency system. As before, 100 stotinki equals 1 lev. There are bills of 1, 2, 5, 10, 20, and 50 leva, and coins of 1, 2, 5, 10, 20, and 50 stotinki. Although prices are sometimes quoted in dollars, all goods and services (except the most expensive hotels and international airline tickets) must be paid for in leva. You may import any amount of foreign currency, including traveler's checks, and exchange foreign currency at banks, hotels, airports, border posts, and the plentiful private exchange offices (which offer the best rates and take no commission). Bring new, clean U.S. bills, as counterfeiting is a recent phenomenon, and torn or marked currency will be turned away. It is possible to change traveler's checks at a few select locations, such as the airport and some major hotels, but commissions are exorbitant. In small towns traveler's checks are worthless. ATMs are plentiful only in Sofia, but found also in Plovdiv, Varna, and Burgas. As of summer 2001, the exchange rate was 2.28 leva to the U.S. dollar, 1.43 leva to the Canadian dollar, 3.25 leva to the pound sterling, 2.68 leva to the Irish punt, 141 leva to the Australian dollar, 99 stotinki to the New Zealand dollar, and 29 stotinki to the South African rand.

PASSPORTS AND VISAS

All visitors need a valid passport. Americans do not need visas when traveling as tourists for 30 days or less. Other tourists, traveling independently, should inquire about visa requirements at a Bulgarian embassy or consulate before entering the country. Many package tours are exempt from the visa requirement.

TELEPHONES

Prior to 2000, a 2-leva coin (now outdated) was used to make local phone calls. Now, you must pay 50 stotinki at the post office or a street kiosk for a *zheton*–a special coin that works in zheton pay phones. A better plan than purchasing a handful of zhetoni coins is to make calls from your hotel (for a surcharge) or from pay phones using one of the two types of card phones, *Betkom* and *Bulfon,* both of which can also be used for long-distance calls throughout Bulgaria and Europe. Phone cards can be purchased at post offices, hotels, and numerous street kiosks. Coin-operated phones are silver, Betkom phones are blue, and Bulfon phones are orange.

COUNTRY AND AREA CODES

For international calls to Bulgaria, the country code is 359. The access code for Sofia is 2 from outside Bulgaria and 02 from within.

INTERNATIONAL CALLS

Calls to the United States can be made from Bulfon or Betkom phones by using a local calling card to reach the international operator and then a long-distance calling card to reach the States. In Sofia direct-dial calls to the United States can also be made from the international phone office (½ block west of the main post office). You can also place a call using an AT&T USA Direct international operator.

➤ ACCESS CODES: **AT&T USA Direct** (☎ 00–800–0010).

TIPPING

Tips of 10% of the bill are appropriate for waiters and taxi drivers; hotel employees also receive tips ($1 or the equivalent for bellhops; 10%–20% for staff at expensive hotels, 10% in leva at smaller hotels).

TRAIN TRAVEL

In Sofia buy tickets in advance at the ticket office (in the underpass below the National Palace of Culture) to avoid long lines at the station. In other cities get your tickets at the station. It's best to take an *ekspresni* (express) or *burzi* (fast) train, as they are the fastest and most comfortable. *Putnicheski* (slow) trains are very old and painfully slow. Trains tend to be crowded; seat reservations are obligatory on expresses. *Purva clasa* (first class) is not much more expensive than second class and is worth it. From Sofia there are six main routes: to Varna or Burgas on the Black Sea coast; to Plovdiv and beyond to the Turkish border; to Dragoman and the Serbian border; to Kulata and the Greek border; and to Ruse on the Romanian border.

TRANSPORTATION AROUND BULGARIA

Bulgaria uses the following abbreviations in addresses: *ul.* (*ulitsa*) is street; *bul.* (*bulevard*) is boulevard; *pl.* (*ploshtad*) is square.

VISITOR INFORMATION

➤ TOURIST INFORMATION: **Balkan Tour Sofia** (✉ 27 bul. Stamboliiski, ☎ 02/988–5543). **Balkan Tourist** (✉ 1 bul. Vitosha, ☎ 02/987–5192, WEB www.balkantourist.net).

WHEN TO GO

The ski season lasts from mid-December through March; the Black Sea coast season runs from May through October, reaching its peak in July and August. Fruit trees blossom in April and May; in May and early June the blossoms are gathered in the Valley of Roses; in October the fall colors are at their best.

CLIMATE

Summers are warm; winters are crisp and cold. The coastal areas enjoy considerable sunshine. March and April are the wettest months inland.

Even when the temperature climbs, the Black Sea breezes and the cooler mountain air prevent the heat from being overwhelming.

The following are the average daily maximum and minimum temperatures for Sofia.

Month	F	C	Month	F	C	Month	F	C
Jan.	35F	2C	**May**	69F	21C	**Sept.**	70F	22C
	25	– 4		50	10		52	11
Feb.	39F	4C	**June**	76F	24C	**Oct.**	63F	17C
	27	– 3		56	14		46	8
Mar.	50F	10C	**July**	81F	27C	**Nov.**	48F	9C
	33	1		60	16		37	3
Apr.	60F	16C	**Aug.**	79F	26C	**Dec.**	38F	4C
	42	5		59	15		28	– 2

SOFIA

Bulgaria's bustling capital stands on the high Sofia Plain, ringed by mountain ranges: the Balkan Range to the north; the Lyulin Mountains to the west; part of the Sredna Gora Mountains to the southeast; and, to the southwest, Mt. Vitosha—the city's playground—which rises to more than 7,600 ft. In the 1870s Sofia was still part of the Ottoman Empire, and one mosque still remains today. Most of the city was planned after 1880, and following the destruction of World War II many of the main buildings were rebuilt in the Socialist style. The area has been inhabited for about 7,000 years, but driving in from the airport, your first impression may be of a city besieged by hasty development, dominated by an expanse of nightmarish Socialist-era block housing. Moving towards the center from the suburbs, however, the unpleasantness soon gives way to eclectic urban charm, spacious parks, open-air cafés, and broad streets filled with an incongruous mix of Western sports cars and old-fashioned farmers' wagons laden with firewood.

Exploring Sofia

Numbers in the margin correspond to points of interest on the Sofia map.

There are enough intriguing museums and musical performances to merit a lengthy stay, but you can see the main city sights in two days and enjoy the serenity of Mt. Vitosha on a third day.

5 **Banya Bashi Dzhamiya** (Banya Bashi Mosque). This distinctive building, consisting of a large dome and a lone minaret, a legacy from the centuries of Turkish rule, was built in the 16th century. Loudspeakers on the minaret call the city's Muslim minority to prayer every day. ✉ *Bul. Maria Luiza at ul. Triyaditsa.*

(child icon) 15 **Borisova Gradina** (Boris's Garden). Dilapidated benches, stray dogs, overflowing garbage dumpsters, an empty lake, a dry fountain, and neglected statues of Communist leaders mar this former haven. Nevertheless, it is huge, central, and important to the city's inhabitants. The wild woods surrounding it are good for a stroll. In summer, ice-cream vendors, children in rented battery-operated minicars, a first-class outdoor disco, and a surprisingly pristine public pool with water slides for children bring life to the park. ✉ *Bul. Bulgaria between bul. Tsar Osvoboditel and bul. Dragan Tsankov.*

★ 13 **Hram-pametnik Alexander Nevski** (Alexander Nevski Memorial Church). The neo-Byzantine structure with glittering onion domes

Sofia

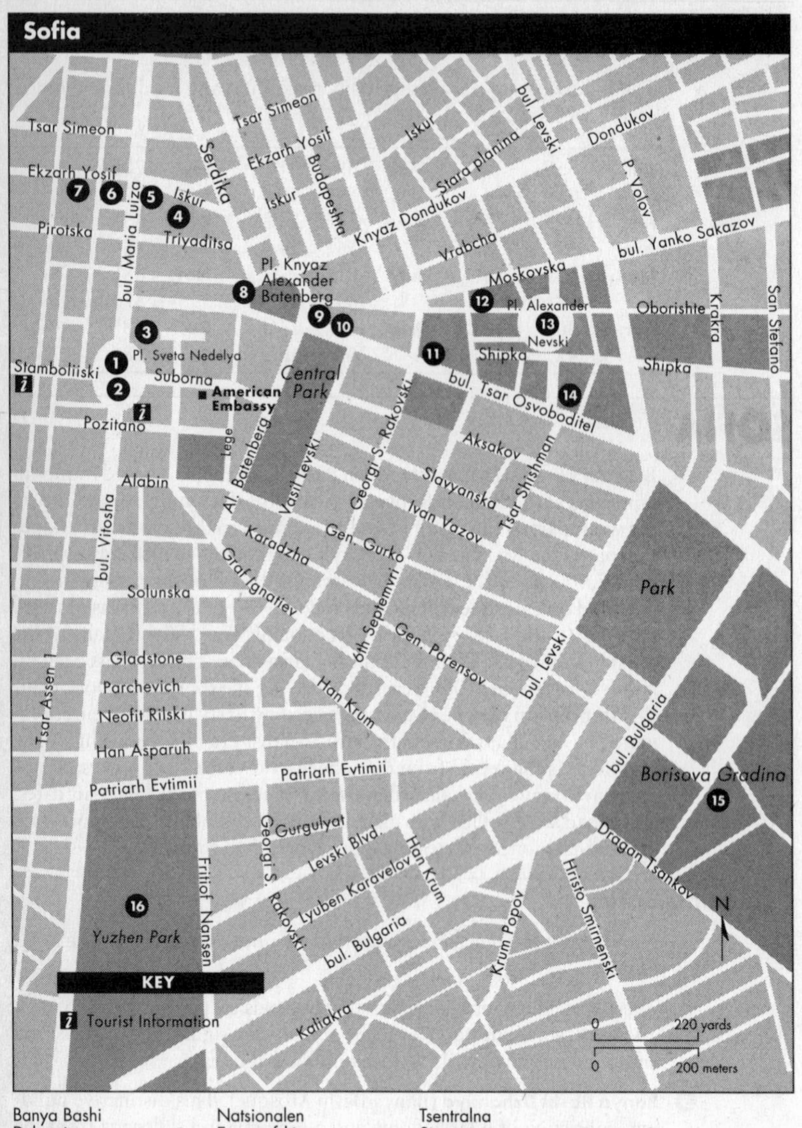

Banya Bashi Dzhamiya 5
Borisova Gradina 15
Hram-pametnik Alexander Nevski . . 13
Narodno Subranie 14
Natsionalen Dvorets na Kulturata 16
Natsionalen Etnografski Muzei 10
Natsionalna Hudozhestvena Galeria 9
Partiyniyat Dom 8
Ploshtad Sveta Nedelya 1
Rotonda Sveti Georgi 3
Tsentralna Sinagoga 7
Tsentralnata Banya 4
Tsentralni Hali 6
Tsurkva Sveta Nedelya 2
Tsurkva Sveta Sofia 12
Tsurkva Sveti Nikolai 11

dominates the city. It was built by the Bulgarian people at the beginning of the 20th century as a mark of gratitude to their Russian liberators. Inside are Venetian mosaics; magnificent frescoes; and space for a congregation of 5,000. Attend a service to hear the superb choir, and, above all, don't miss the fine collection of icons in the **Kripta Museo** (Crypt Museum). ✉ *Pl. Alexander Nevski,* ☎ *02/981–5775,* WEB *www.sofia.com/sightseeing/capital.htm.* ⏲ *Wed.–Mon. 10–5.*

14 **Narodno Subranie** (National Assembly). During the January 1997 uprising, CNN immortalized this squat building by repeatedly broadcasting clips of Bulgarian protesters smashing the windows and attempting to drag barricaded members of the Socialist parliament onto the plaza. Topped by the Bulgarian national flag, it is adorned with an inscription reading "Unity Makes Strength," referring to the unification of the country in 1885, a few years after the defeat of the Turks. In front of the building is a monument to the Russians, who helped in the battle against the Turks, surmounted by an equestrian statue of Russian Tsar Alexander II. ✉ *Bul. Tsar Osvoboditel at pl. Narodno Subranie.*

16 **Natsionalen Dvorets na Kulturata** (National Palace of Culture). The large modern building houses halls for conventions and cultural events, as well as the city's first top-notch cinema mulitplex, opened in 2001. Its multilevel underpass is equipped with a train-ticket office, shops, restaurants, discos, and a bowling alley. The park to the north draws crowds of rollerblading, skateboarding, and bike-riding teenagers. Younger children skitter around in rented battery-operated minicars. ✉ *Yuzhen Park, 1 pl. Bulgaria.*

10 **Natsionalen Etnografski Muzei** (National Ethnographic Museum). The former palace of the Bulgarian tsar currently houses displays of costumes, crafts, and tools illustrating life in the country's rural areas as late as the 19th century. ✉ *1 pl. Alexander Batenberg,* ☎ *02/987–4191.* ⏲ *Wed.–Sun. 10:30–noon and 1:30–5:30,* 🎫 *2.50 leva.*

★ **Natsionalen Istoricheski Muzei** (National History Museum). This extraordinary museum is even more of must-see, now that it's been relocated to the splendid and palatial mansion that was formerly the residence of deceased and controversial Communist leader Todor Zhivkov. The vast collections include priceless Thracian treasures, Roman mosaics, enameled jewelry from the First Bulgarian Kingdom (AD 600–AD 1018), and glowing religious art that survived the years of Ottoman oppression. The museum is now a ten-minute taxi ride from the center. City bus lines 2 and 69 pass the museum on their way out of town. ✉ *Residencia Boyana, The Ring Road Km 11,* ☎ *02/955–4280.* 🎫 *4.50 leva.* ⏲ *Weekdays 9:30–6:30.*

9 **Natsionalna Hudozhestvena Galeria** (National Art Gallery). In the west wing of the former tsar's palace is a collection of outstanding Bulgarian works, as well as a section devoted to foreign art. ✉ *1 pl. Alexander Batenberg,* ☎ *02/980–0093.* ⏲ *Tues.–Sun. 10:30–6,* 🎫 *3 leva, 9 leva for a guided tour.*

8 **Partiyniyat Dom** (The Party House). The former headquarters of the Bulgarian Communist Party is prominent on a vast square. The imposing Stalinist-style building now houses the administrative offices of the parliament. The pole on top of the building looks bare without the gigantic red star it once supported. ✉ *pl. Alexander Batenberg.*

1 **Ploshtad Sveta Nedelya** (St. Nedelya Square). From this large, bustling, and open square in the center of town, the shopping street bulevard Vitosha stretches south and bulevard Maria Luisa north. Vendors sell flowers, nuts, and toys; fortune-tellers use hamsters to predict your fu-

ture; and Gypsies congregate to perform. The square, with the brand-new metro operating underneath, is a good starting point for an exploration of the main sights. ✉ *Bordered by bul. Vitosha, bul. Maria Luiza, and bul. Stamboliiski.*

3 **Rotonda Sveti Georgi** (Rotunda of St. George). On the northeast side of St. Nedelya Square, in the courtyard of the Sheraton Sofia Balkan Hotel, stands this unusual artifact. Built in the 4th century as a Roman temple, it has served as both a mosque and a church. Recent restoration revealed gorgeous medieval frescoes, which were unveiled in the much-awaited public opening in 2000. ✉ *2 pl. St. Nedelya.*

7 **Tsentralna Sinagoga** (Central Synagogue). This spectacular structure topped with an enormous dome is surrounded by five smaller domes and six towers. Constructed in 1909, it has been renovated after decades of disuse and is in use as a synagogue again. ✉ *Ul. Ekzarh Yosif.* ⏲ *Daily 11–2 and 4–6.*

4 **Tsentralnata Banya** (The Central Baths). For years this former Ottoman mineral bathhouse was in ruins. Renovations, begun in 1997, have restored the outside of the splendid building, and the domes gleam once again. The amazing interior is still closed, but repairs are under way and, by the spring of 2002 it should open again as a public bathhouse. At the spring in the adjacent park, Sofians line up to fill plastic bottles with hot mineral water, thought to cure respiratory diseases and ensure longevity. ✉ *Bul. Maria Luiza at ul. Triyaditsa.*

6 **Tsentralni Hali** (Central Market Hall). Once one of the most beautiful buildings in Sofia, the hall served as the central market during Communist times. Allowed to fall into ruin, it was closed for renovations for years. During the summer of 2000 it was completed and reopened as a modern indoor bazaar that retains the bustling marketplace atmosphere of years past. ✉ *Bul. Maria Luiza at ul. Ekzarh Yosif.*

2 **Tsurkva Sveta Nedelya** (St. Nedelya Church). This 19th-century church, with its huge dome ringed by small windows, dominates the south side of St. Nedelya Square. It is the latest in a series of churches that have occupied the site since the Middle Ages. Behind it is bulevard Vitosha, a lively pedestrian street with stores and cafés. ✉ *Pl. St. Nedelya.*

12 **Tsurkva Sveta Sofia** (Church of St. Sofia). Dating from the 6th century, this simple brick edifice became in the mid-14th century the namesake for the city of Sofia. ✉ *North side of pl. Alexander Nevski.*

11 **Tsurkva Sveti Nikolai** (Church of St. Nicholas). This ornate Russian structure was erected between 1912 and 1914. ✉ *Bul. Tsar Osvoboditel at ul. Rakovski.*

Dining

Sofia teems with restaurants and cafés offering high-quality but inexpensive international cuisines. If you can tolerate cigarette smoke and crowded seating, the most authentic eating experience is in a mehana, or tavern, where the music is loud and diners relax for hours over rakia and salads.

$$–$$$$ ★ ✕ **Otvut Aleyata, Zad Shkafut** (Beyond the Alley, Behind the Cupboard). In a beautiful old house with a patio strung with flickering lights, this small, casually elegant restaurant serves such Bulgarian and Pan-European dishes as chicken stuffed with Roquefort, Russian salad, veal marsala, beef with béchamel sauce, and *yogurt-loo* (Turkish spiced sausage with pita bread and fresh yogurt). The staff speaks English, there are menus in English, and it is one of the few places that provide the kind of Western service that foreigners tend to expect—such as taking back a cold or undercooked dish. ✉ *31 ul. Budapeshta,* ☎ *02/83–5581. Reservations essential. No credit cards.*

$$–$$$$ ✕ **Restaurant Barbecue.** With a rooftop terrace for summer evenings, a cozy fireplace for winter feasts, and an indoor table-side barbecue used to grill high-quality meat and fish, this mehana is truly a fine Bulgarian restaurant. For starters, try the authentic *monastirski salata,* (monastery salad traditionally eaten by monks) a combination of white beans, vegetables and *pastarma* (dried Bulgaria sausage), or the mushrooms stuffed with pâté de fois gras and Roquefort. In addition to barbecued meat, fish, and chicken, they have lobster, crab, and a number of excellent veal and duck entrées. ✉ *38 ul. Tsar Assen II,* ☎ *02/462–803. Reservations recommended. No credit cards.*

$$–$$$$ ★ ✕ **Rotiserie Nationale.** The Rotiserie eclipses all other Sofia restaurants for high-caliber atmosphere and first-class cuisine. Expect to be greeted with a free cocktail and to be escorted into a cellar outfitted for medieval dining decadence. You can feast on duck in orange sauce, succulent roast lamb, pâté de foie gras, Caesar salads, and pears flambé as musicians stroll between the long banquet tables adorned with golden candelabras. Nowhere in the West can you experience such luxury, complete with carafes of excellent homemade wine, at the Rotiserie's price of less than $20 per person. You won't get past the host without reservations, a jacket, and dress shoes. ✉ *Ul. Hristo Belchev at ul. Neofit Rilski,* ☎ *02/980–1717. Reservations essential. V.*

$$–$$$$ ✕ **Stenata** (The Wall). Just behind the Roman Wall market, this elegant restaurant is dug out of a cellar of aged stone, giving it a romantic air of antiquity. Candles illuminate arched doorways and archaeological artifacts, and the menu is as sophisticated as the ambience. Wines from around the world compliment Continental fare such as salmon *le sud,* roast lamb, veal medallions with fettuccine, stuffed crab, or a salad of wild mushrooms and French cheese. Individual-size layered ice-cream cakes and a decadent assortment of flavored crèmes brûlées are for desert, and the proprietor is known for sending over surprises of complimentary after dinner aperitifs. This is a place for intimate celebrations. ✉ *10 ul. Nerazdelni,* ☎ *02/963–0313. V.*

$–$$$ ✕ **Club Stargaloto.** Neither the most expensive nor the most sophisticated restaurant in Sofia, this is one of the few high-quality and locally popular Bulgarian restaurants that offers a decent mixture of Western service and authentic Balkan ambience. There is often live folk music, as well as regional specialties such as *kebapche* (spicy Balkan pork sausage) and *meshana skara* (assorted barbecued meats), albeit in a Mafia-drenched, sometimes touristy atmosphere. ✉ *116 bul. Rakovski,* ☎ *02/980–7170. AE, MC, V.*

$–$$ ✕ **Baalbeck.** Local businesspeople like this Middle Eastern restaurant just off central Slaveikov Square. It's seedy in appearance, but it prepares fast lunches of delicious falafel, hummus, and tabouleh. Sit downstairs for a quick bite wrapped in pita bread to go, or dine upstairs if you want your *doner kebap* (a lamb, beef, or chicken skewer) on a plate. ✉ *6 ul. Vasil Levski. No credit cards.*

$–$$ ✕ **Dani's.** The perfect spot for a leisurely lunch, this friendly café ranks number one with foreigners living in Sofia. Sponge-painted arty walls surround the tiny dining area, where Sofia's hip gourmets drink wine and share enormous, eclectic salads, such as the green bean, potato, and tuna fish feast. Dani's bakes its bread fresh on the premises and each salad is served with an enormous loaf and herb butter. The soup of the day is always excellent, the perfect accompaniment to a grilled chicken, red pepper, and feta cheese sandwich. It's always packed, so be patient. In the summer, sit on the sidewalk terrace and enjoy a cappuccino, Israeli lemonata, or American apple pie. ✉ *18 ul. Angel Kunchev,* ☎ *02/987–4548. No credit cards.*

$–$$ ✕ **Ugo 2.** Ugo was the first 24-hour restaurant in Sofia. A pizzeria run by teenagers in the basement of a bulevard Vitosha block, it quickly became one of the trendiest and most beloved hangouts in Sofia. Brand-new in 2000, Ugo 2 is the upscale sister of the original Ugo, with romantic lighting, tasteful art, top-notch service, and—unbelievably—the same dirt-cheap, addictive menu, including tomato-and-feta-stuffed baked potatoes, smoked-chicken-and-hot-pepper pizza, spaghetti bolognese, and a choice of eight different enormous fresh salads. Wine and beer here are inexpensive and good. ✉ *68 ul. Neophit Rilski,* ☎ *02/987–2152. No credit cards.*

Lodging

Although inexpensive lodging can be found in Sofia, the standard Western chain hotels that cater to foreigners charge nearly Western rates. If you are looking for less expensive lodging, **Balkantourist** (✉ 1 bul. Vitosha, ☎ 02/987–5192) can help you find rooms in private homes at better prices. If you want, they can also book you in a state-owned hotel. You shouldn't have trouble finding a room, even if you arrive in town without a reservation.

$$$$ **Castle Hotel Hrankov.** This hotel at the foot of Mt. Vitosha is a cross between a beige-and-white mountain chalet and a castle with turrets and oversize doorways. Stars like Harvey Keitel, Mira Sorvino, and Jean Claude Van Damme have called it home while filming movies in the city. The hotel has windows facing the mountain, plush carpets, chandeliers, and a clean, bright ambience as well as the best fitness center in the city, with squash and tennis courts, an Olympic-size swimming pool, and ski facilities. ✉ *53 ul. Krusheva Gradina, Dragalevtsi 1415,* ☎ *02/91–909,* FAX *02/967–2985. 360 rooms. 4 restaurants, pool. AE, DC, MC, V.*

$$$$ ★ **Sheraton Sofia Hotel Balkan.** This first-class hotel has a central location that can't be matched. Rooms are basic (for the price) and businesslike with dark decor. Suites are more lavish, with brighter decor, bigger bathtubs, and views of the ploshtad Sveta Nedelya. A daytime café and nighttime bar called Capital, in the hotel's north wing, draws an upscale crowd for lunch, ice cream, coffee, and evening drinks. ✉ *5 pl. Sveta Nedelya, 1000,* ☎ *02/981–65–41,* FAX *02/980–64–64. 187 rooms. 3 restaurants. AE, DC, MC, V.*

$$$–$$$$ ★ **Hotel Kempinski Zografski–Sofia.** The towering, luxurious hotel is designed in Japanese minimalist style. Guest rooms are basic: big beds, TVs, large bathrooms with bathtubs, mini-refrigerators, and desks. The hotel also has a shopping arcade and the most expensive restaurant in the entire country, Sakura, Bulgaria's one and only spot for sushi. ✉ *100 bul. James Bourchier, 1407,* ☎ *02/62–518,* FAX *02/681–225. 454 rooms. 5 restaurants, pool. AE, DC, MC, V.*

$$$ **Gloria Palace.** Just south of the ploshtad Sveta Nedelya stands the brightly painted purple Gloria Palace. With marble floors, rich purple curtains, and gold accents, the lobby reflects the decor of the ornate guest rooms. Large beds, fluffy towels, two stellar suite apartments, and room service presented with flair show that this palace is striving to be fit for a king. ✉ *20 bul. Maria Luiza, 1000,* ☎ *02/980–7895,* FAX *02/980–7894. 28 rooms. 2 restaurants. AE, DC, MC, V.*

$$$ **Hotel Maria Luiza.** The closest thing Sofia has to a modern yet cozy bed-and-breakfast, this upscale, private hotel has comfortable, cheery rooms and a friendly staff. The hotel is a narrow six stories, in a renovated stretch of turn-of-the-20th-century buildings. Fruit baskets and chocolates greet guests in the rooms, windows face out toward the Banya

Bashi Mosque, and the bathrooms have big, glass Western-style showers. ✉ *29 bul. Maria Luiza, 1000,* ☎ *02/91–044,* FAX *02/980–3355. 21 rooms. Restaurant. AE, DC, MC, V.*

$$ 🏨 **Bulgaria.** Despite its central location, this small hotel is quiet and old-fashioned. Dark and decorated with antiques, it is private, somber, and serious. Guests are more likely to be Eastern European business travelers than Westerners or tourists on holiday. ✉ *4 bul. Tsar Osvoboditel, 1000,* ☎ *02/870–191,* FAX *02/88–41–77. 85 rooms. Restaurant. No credit cards.*

$ 🏨 **Hotel Rotasar.** Opened in 2000, this clean and cozy little hotel is an incredible value. Secure rooms are tight but modern and efficient with televisions, refrigerators, and comfy low-to-the-ground Bulgarian beds. All rooms have big bathrooms with sparkling fixtures and showers. The price includes the daily delivery of a delicious and varied Bulgarian breakfast in bed, with fruit, yogurt, eggs, pastries, and cheese. Just off the road leading to the airport. ✉ *Ul. Liditze and ul. Kosta Lulchev, 1000,* ☎ *02/971–4571,* FAX *02/971–4574. 22 rooms. AE, MC, V.*

Nightlife and the Arts

The Arts

For a list of cultural events in Sofia, pick up a copy of *Sofia City Info Guide* at the American Express office or at hotels. Newsstands in Sofia now carry the helpful *Sofia Echo,* an English-language newspaper that includes news and entertainment listings.

FILM

Most movie theaters show recent foreign films in their original languages with Bulgarian subtitles. **The NDK Multiplex** (✉ Yuzhen Park, in the NDK underpass, ☎ 957-2911) with six top-notch theaters and three cafés, opened to much fanfare in 2000. The classy **Mir Theater** (✉ 6 ul. Denkoglu, ☎ 02/986–1135) is one of the city's best. **The Levski** (✉ 30 ul. Yanko Sakugov, ☎ 02/46–7171) is another high-quality cinema.

GALLERIES

The city has a number of good art galleries. The **City Art Gallery** (✉ 1 ul. Gen. Gurko, ☎ 02/87–21–81) displays permanent exhibits of both 19th-century and modern Bulgarian paintings as well as changing exhibits showcasing contemporary artists. The art gallery of the **Sts. Cyril and Methodius International Foundation** (✉ pl. Alexander Nevski, ☎ 02/986–6530) has a collection of Indian, African, Japanese, and Western European paintings and sculptures. The art gallery of the **Union of Bulgarian Artists** (✉ 6 ul. Shipka, ☎ 02/43–351) exhibits contemporary Bulgarian art.

MUSIC

The standard of music in Bulgaria is high, whether it's performed in opera houses or symphony halls or at concerts of folk music, with its close harmonies and colorful stage displays. For ballet and opera tickets, go to the **Sofia National Opera House** (✉ 1 ul. Vrabcha, at 58 bul. Dondukov, ☎ 02/987–7011). Buy concert and symphony tickets at the **Bulgarian Concert Hall** (✉ 1 ul. Aksokov, ☎ 02/987–7656), where the Sofia Philharmonic Orchestra performs every Thursday night at 7:30.

Nightlife

BARS AND NIGHTCLUBS

The **Blaze Club** (✉ 36 ul. Slavianska, ☎ 02/988–1423) is where the young and hip go for dance music after the bars on ulitsa Shishman shut their doors. **J.J. Murphy & Co.** (✉ 6 ul. Karnigradska, ☎ 02/980–2870) is a dark, wood-paneled Irish pub (opened by an Irish couple in 1999 but passed to Bulgarian owners) frequented by Bulgarians as well as foreigners for its extensive selection of beers from around the world and tasty appetizers. The **Capital Diner** (✉ 5 pl. Sveta Nedelya, inside the Sheraton Hotel, ☎ 02/986–7963) is a new (2000) and extremely swanky bar for people-watching, drawing international films-stars on location, foreigners, local politicians, celebrities, models, and businesspeople for stiff drinks and a pricey menu that satisfies a discerning crowd. Looking for live music? Check out the rock and jazz lineup at **Swingin' Hall** (✉ 8 bul. Dragan Tsankov, ☎ 02/963–0696).

CASINOS

You can try your luck at the **International Casino Club Sheraton** (✉ 5 pl. St. Nedelya, ☎ 02/981–5747). **Princess Casino International** (✉ Novotel Europa, 131 bul. Maria Luiza, ☎ 02/931–0077) offers 8 roulette tables, 5 poker tables, 7 blackjack tables, and 200 slot machines.

DISCOS

Brand-new, with three floors of beautiful people and famous DJs from all over Europe, **Escape** (✉ 1 ul. Angel Kunchev, ☎ 988–5922) rivals the best techno and house music clubs in Western Europe and New York, and all for a mere 3 leva cover. For more casual all-night dancing action, try **Chervilo** (Lipsticks; ✉ 48 bul. Tsar Osvoboditel, ☎ 981–6633), where you get salsa lessons and sangria at the Wednesday Latino party. **Black Label Whiskey Bar** (✉ bul. Rakovski and bul. Tsar Osvoboditel, ☎ 02/981–6633) is located adjacent to Chervilo, a situation that makes bar-hopping easy. Drawing a classier, slightly older crowd for rhythm and blues as well as whiskey and cigars, this new club (opened in 2000) has less dancing and more iffy Mafia types. **Spartacus** (✉ bul. Vasil Levski and bul. Tsar Osvoboditel, in the underpass in front of Sofia University) is Sofia's first *mixed* club, attracting the city's avant garde, both gay and straight.

Shopping

Department Stores

Bonjour (✉ 2 pl. Slaveikov; ✉ 93 ul. Alabin; ✉ 97 bul. Levski, ☎ 962–5000) stocks everything from food and wine to sporting goods, gifts, and cosmetics. The drab Tsentralen Universalen Magazin, better known as **TSUM** (Central Department Store; ✉ 2 bul. Maria Luiza, ☎ 926–0600) and formerly Sofia's biggest department store, has received a face-lift for the new millennium. As of summer 2000, the entire building had been converted into a sparkling and bustling Western-style shopping mall with privately rented boutiques and cafés.

Gifts and Souvenirs

The **Galeria Natalie** (✉ ul. Gurko 38, ☎ 980–7603) carries an excellent assortment of national arts, including pottery, paintings and woven rugs. **Bulgarian Artists Magazin #10** (✉ 4 ul. Tsar Shishman, ☎ 980–6927) is the best of the many co-ops where Bulgarian artists display their wares; this particular shop features top-quality paintings, sculptures, hand-knitted clothes, hand-crafted jewelry, and blown glass. There is a good selection of arts and crafts at the shop of the **Union of Bulgarian Artists** (✉ 6 ul. Shipka). The outdoor **arts and crafts market** around Alexander Nevski Cathedral specializes in lace and linen at reasonable prices. For a large variety of **crafts and souvenirs,** visit the underpass between St. Nedelya Church and the Central Department Store.

In the year 2000, fashion shopping in Sofia suddenly became more adventurous when many outdated boutiques on bul. Vitosha and surrounding streets received much-needed face-lifts. Try the Bulgarian **DIKA,** with beautifully designed suits and sportswear for women (✉ 65 Vitosha, ☎ 981–8172). **Incognito** is great for fun, cutting edge Italian street-fashion (✉ 70 Patriarch Evtimii, ☎ 988–0499). You can find stunningly elegant Greek cocktail creations at **Raxevksy** (✉ 48 ul. Gurko, ☎ 980–9687). Looking for jewelry? Unique gold and silver creations abound at **Loisir Jewelers** (✉ 63 Vitosha, ☎ 988–0025). For men's fashions, **Hugo Boss** (✉ 1 ul. Legue) is a pricey alternative to Bulgarian designs.

For recordings of Bulgarian music, go to the underpass below the National Palace of Culture, where there are stalls selling music.

There are still some rare antiques deals in Sofia; ulitsa Rakovski is particularly full of antiques dealers. **Letostrui** (✉ 157 ul. Rakovski, ☎ 983–6332 or 988–0025) is a reputable (if expensive) place to start your search. For excellent regional wines and tobacco, **Bai Gencho** (✉ 24 bul. Yanko Sakazov) has one of the best selections.

Shopping Districts

Bulevard Vitosha is a lively street with many upscale shops. Moderately priced and stylish boutiques are on **ulitsa Graf Ignatiev.** The quintessential shopping excursion is to the outdoor **Zhenski Pazaar** (✉ ul. Stefan Stambolov, between ul. Tsar Simeon and bul. Slivnitsa), the women's market, so called for the endless stalls worked by women from neighboring villages who hawk everything from homemade brooms and lace to produce and used electronic equipment.

Side Trips

Both Boyana (8 km/5 mi southwest of Sofia) and Dragalevtsi (9 km/5½ mi south of Sofia) are pleasant day trips to the Mt. Vitosha vicinity and can be reached by Bus 64 from Sofia.

Boyana

The little medieval **Boyana Church** is well worth a visit, as is the small, elegant restaurant of the same name, next door. The church is closed for restoration, but a replica, complete with copies of the exquisite 13th-century frescoes, is open to visitors. ✉ *Ul. Belite Brezi.* ⏲ *Daily approx. noon–4.*

$–$$$ ✕ **Boyansko Hanche.** At the foot of Mt. Vitosha, this charming and authentic (but touristy) mehana offers Bulgarian specialties, folk music, and dance shows with audience participation nightly at 9 PM. In the summer they have an exciting Black Sea coast firewalking exhibition in the outdoor garden. Locals tout this mehana as the perfect spot for entertaining or holding a boisterous celebration. ✉ *Boyana district, 31 ul. Sevastokrator Kaloyan,* ☎ *02/563–016. No credit cards.*

Dragalevtsi

The **Dragalevtsi Monastery** stands in beech woods above the village. The complex is still used as a convent, but you can visit the 14th-century church with its outdoor frescoes. ✉ *3 km (2 mi) past Vodenicharski Mehani restaurant, Dragalevtsi.*

You can take chairlifts (beside Vodenicharski Mehani restaurant) from Dragalevtsi to the delightful resort complex of 👶 **Aleko.** In winter, it has bunny runs and sledding. In the summer, kids can run on the mountain and pick berries, hike, and look at the wildlife. From Aleko you can continue on foot for about an hour to the top of **Rezen Maluk,** the nearest peak. There are well-marked walking and ski trails.

$$–$$$ ✕ **Vodenicharski Mehani** (Miller's Tavern). Made up of three old mills linked together, this tavern stands at the foot of Mt. Vitosha. A folklore show and a menu of Bulgarian specialties provide an authentic atmosphere. Try the *gyuvech* (potatoes, tomatoes, peas, and onions baked in an earthenware dish). ✉ *Dragalevtsi district (Bus 64), at southern end of town next to chairlift,* ☎ *02/67–10–21 or 02/67–10–01. No credit cards.*

Sofia Essentials

AIRPORTS AND TRANSFERS

All international flights arrive at Sofia Airport.

➤ AIRPORT INFORMATION: **Sofia Airport** (☎ 02/79–80–35; 02/72–06–72 international flights; 02/72–24–14 domestic flights).

TRANSFERS

Bus 84 from Sofia University serves the airport. At the airport taxi stand fares to the center are fixed at $20 (or 42 leva). If you speak some Bulgarian and know where you're going, private taxis outside the terminal will get you there for less than half the official price. Agree on the fare before starting. The Tourist Service Travel Agency operates a $5 (or 9-leva) airport shuttle, with service *to* the airport *from* the city center only.

➤ CONTACTS: The **Tourist Service Travel Agency** (✉ 127 ul. Rakovski, ☎ 02/988–8108).

BUS TRAVEL WITHIN SOFIA

Buses, trolleys, and trams run fairly often. Buy a ticket from the ticket stand near the streetcar stop and punch it into the machine on board. (Watch how other people do it.)

CAR RENTAL

You can hire a car with a driver through Balkantourist, Balkantour Ltd., or your hotel. You can also rent a car at the airport or from one of the city's car-rental agencies.

CAR TRAVEL

From Greece, take E-20, passing through the checkpoint at Kulata; from Turkey, take E-5, passing through the checkpoint Kapitan–Andreevo. Border crossings to Romania are at Vidin on E-79 and at Ruse on E-97 and E-85.

EMERGENCIES

➤ DOCTORS AND DENTISTS: **Pirogov Emergency Hospital** (☎ 02/5–15–31).

➤ EMERGENCY SERVICES: **Police** (☎ 166). **Fire** (☎ 160). **Ambulance** (☎ 150).

➤ 24-HOUR PHARMACIES: **Apteka** (✉ 5 pl. St. Nedelya, ☎ 02/87–59–89).

TOURS

Guided tours of Sofia and environs are arranged by Balkantourist or Balkantour Ltd. or by major hotels. Among the possibilities are three- to four-hour tours of the principal city sights by car or minibus or a longer four- to five-hour tour that goes as far as Mt. Vitosha.

TAXIS

Hail Express Taxi, Sofia City Taxi, and Radio Taxicabs in the street or at a stand (avoid taxis parked in front of hotels as they target foreigners and charge higher prices). Always take a taxi with a phone number written on the side so you know you are traveling with a legitimate company. The rate should be 30–40 stotinki per km during the day, 40–50 at night. There is a minimal surcharge for taxis ordered by phone in Sofia. To tip, round out the fare by 5%–10%.

➤ TAXI COMPANIES: **Express Taxi** (☎ 91919), **Sofia City Taxi** (☎ 1263), **Radio Taxi** (☎ 1282); **English speaking dispatcher** (☎ 973–2121).

TRAIN TRAVEL

➤ TRAIN INFORMATION: **Tsentralna Gara** (Central Station; ✉ northern edge of city, ☎ 02/3–11–11 or 02/843–33–33). **Ticket offices** (✉ in underpass below National Palace of Culture, ☎ 02/658–402; ✉ 1 pl. Bulgaria, ☎ 02/59–01–36; Rila International Travel Agency, ✉ 5 ul. Gurko, ☎ 02/87–07–77).

TRANSPORTATION AROUND SOFIA

The main sights are concentrated in the center, so the best way to see the city is on foot.

TRAVEL AGENCIES

➤ LOCAL AGENT REFERRALS: **American Express** (✉ 1 ul. Vasil Levski, ☎ 02/981–42–01). **Carlson Wagonlit Travel** (✉ 10 ul. Lege, ☎ 02/980–81–26). **Jamadvice Travel & Tours** (✉ 10 ul. Assen Zlatarov, ☎ 02/944–1520).

VISITOR INFORMATION

➤ TOURIST INFORMATION: **Balkantourist** (✉ 1 bul. Vitosha, ☎ 02/987–5192, WEB www.balkantourist.com). **Balkantour Ltd.** (✉ 27 bul. Stamboliiski, ☎ 02/988–5543 or 02/987–7233).

THE BLACK SEA COAST

Bulgaria's most popular resort area attracts visitors from all over Europe. Its sunny, sandy beaches are backed by the easternmost slopes of the Balkan Range and, to the south, by the Strandzha Mountains. Although the tourist centers tend to be huge, state-built complexes with a somewhat lean feel, they have modern amenities. Slunchev Bryag (Sunny Beach), the largest of the resorts, with more than 100 hotels, has plenty of children's amusements and play areas but is closed November through April.

The historic port of Varna is a good center for exploration. A focal point of land and sea transportation for the region, it has museums, a variety of restaurants, and a lively nightlife in summer. The nearby fishing villages of Nesebâr and Sozopol to the south are more attractive and tranquil. Hotels tend to be scarce in these villages, but private lodgings are easily arranged through local accommodation agencies. Besides water sports, tennis and horseback riding are available.

Varna

Bulgaria's third-largest city is easily reached by rail (about 7½ hours by express) or road from Sofia. If you plan to drive, allow time to see the **Pobiti Kamuni** (Stone Forest), monumental petrified tree trunks just off the Sofia–Varna road between Devnya and Varna. The ancient city of Varna, named Odyssos by the Greeks, became a major Roman trading center and is now an important shipbuilding and industrial city. With its beaches and tourism, Varna has become cosmopolitan; it even holds an international Film Festival each August.

The **Archeologicheski Muzei** (Archaeological Museum) is one of the great—if lesser known—museums of Europe. The splendid collection includes the world's oldest gold treasures from the Varna necropolis of the 4th millennium BC, as well as Thracian, Greek, and Roman artifacts and richly painted icons. ✉ *41 bul. Maria Luiza, in park,* ☎ *052/23–70–57 or 052/212–41.* ⏲ *Tues.–Sat. 10–5.*

The pedestrian-only **ploshtad Nezavisimost** marks the center of town. To the east, **ulitsa Knyaz Boris I** is lined with shops, cafés, and restaurants. Take a look at the lavish murals in the monumental **Tsurkva Yspenie Bogorodichno** (Cathedral of the Assumption), built between 1880

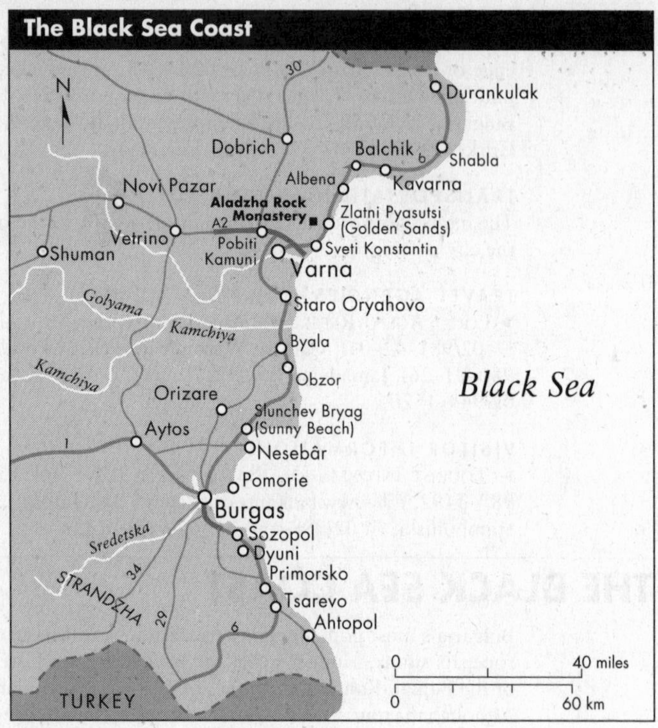

and 1886. ✉ *Pl. Mitropolit Simeon.* ⏲ *May–Sept., daily 10–6; Oct.–Apr., daily 10–1 and 4–5:30.*

In the extensive and luxuriant **Primorski Park** (Seaside Park) are restaurants, an open-air theater, and the **Copernicus Astronomy Complex** (☎ 052/244–109), open weekdays 8–noon and 2–5, near the main entrance. ✉ *Southern end of bul. Primorski.*

Wander through the remains of the **Rimski Termi** (Roman Baths), dating from the 2nd through the 3rd centuries. Signs in English detail the various steps of the bath ritual. ✉ *Ul. Han Krum just south of Tsurkva Sveta Bogoroditsa.*

The 1602 **Tsurkva Sveta Bogoroditsa** (Church of the Holy Virgin) is worth a look for its beautifully carved iconostasis. ✉ *Ul. Han Krum at ul. Knyaz Alexander Batenberg.*

Running north from the cathedral is **ulitsa Vladislav Varnenchik,** with shops, movie theaters, and eateries. In the city gardens stands the **Starata Chasovnikova Kula** (Old Clock Tower; ✉ pl. Nezavisimost), built in 1880 by the Varna Guild Association. The magnificent Baroque **Stoyan Buchvarov Dramatichen Teatur** (Stoyan Bucharov Drama Theater; ✉ Pl. Nezavisimost) presents local and national theater productions, as well as opera and symphonic concerts.

The restored **ulitsa Stari Druzhi** is lined with restaurants, taverns, and coffeehouses. The **Morski Muzei** (Marine Museum) has displays on the early days of navigation on the Black Sea and the Danube. ✉ *2 bul. Primorski,* ☎ *052/222–586.* ⏲ *Weekdays 8–4.*

$–$$ ✕ **Paraklisa.** Antiquated and charming, this garden dining spot has a friendly mehana atmosphere. The menu offers classic Bulgarian cuisine and a wide variety of rakias and wines. The *pulneni chushki* (peppers stuffed with cardamom-spiced pork and rice) are especially good, though the restaurant is best known for its delicious vegetarian dishes such as *tarator* (cold yogurt and cucumber soup) and *tikvichki sus kiselo mlyako* (panfried zucchini in buttery yogurt sauce). ✉ *47 bul. Primorski s/n opposite Marine Museum,* ☎ *052/223–495. No credit cards.*

$–$$ ✕ **Restaurant UCCA.** Garnering great praise for it's traditional domestic Bulgarian cuisine, this restaurant has developed a loyal following among Varna locals. From the full menu of Bulgarian "comfort food," one of the best dishes is the *gyevech* (a hearty stew of chicken, pork or beef, potatoes, and green beans in a tangy tomato sauce). ✉ *84, ul. Macedonia,* ☎ *052/602–898. No credit cards.*

$$$$ ★ **Grand Varna.** The Grand Varna is surrounded by a well-kept beachside forest and has 24-hour room service, minibars, decent fitness equipment, and marble bathrooms. It is one of the first Black Sea resorts to deliver the Western details lacking in some of even the highest-quality Eastern European hotels. Suites have fantastic views, and it's just a few minutes on foot to the beach. ✉ *8 km (5 mi) north of the Varna city center, dir. Sveti Konstantin (follow signs), 9006,* ☎ *052/361–904,* FAX *052/386–1920. 200 rooms, 32 suites. Restaurant. AE, DC, MC, V.*

Albena

The newest and most modern Black Sea resort has a long, wide beach and clean sea. Some of its 35 hotels have extensive hydrotherapy facilities. The contemporary conveniences of this present-day tourist village come with a smaller dose of local charm, inflated prices, and menus and street signs in German and Russian. This is a resort for people seeking amenities but not necessarily the true Bulgaria.

$–$$ ✕ **Bambuka.** This open-air restaurant serves mainly grilled, picnic-style Bulgarian seafood and salads, but the dinner menu includes earthenware pots of *kavarma* (meat and vegetable stew) and *gyuvech* (stewed chunks of vegetables and lamb). ✉ *Bul. Bryag, off E-87, Albena exit,* ☎ *05722/624–04. No credit cards.*

$$$$ **Albena Resort Dobrudzha.** The mineral-water health spa is the main attraction at this big, comfortable hotel. ✉ *Bul. Bryag, off E-87, Albena exit, 9620,* ☎ *05722/620–20,* FAX *05722/622–16,* WEB *www.albena.com. 275 rooms. 3 restaurants, 2 pools. AE, DC, MC, V.*

Slunchev Bryag

This enormous popular resort, known as **Sunny Beach** in English, offers safe beaches, gentle tides, and facilities for children. It has a variety of beachside restaurants, kiosks, and playgrounds. Rapid Socialist construction left behind huge, ugly hotels that line a gorgeous crescent-shape beach.

$$–$$$ ✕ **Hanska Shatra** (Tent Inn). In the hills above the sea, this combination restaurant and nightclub has been built to resemble the tents of the Hans (Bulgarian rulers) of old. It has entertainment well into the night. Take a taxi or have someone from your hotel draw a map. Like many Bulgarian beach resort restaurants, it is in the woods off poorly marked, unlit roads, but don't let that keep you from one of the most enjoyable evenings on the Black Sea. ✉ *Off E-87, 4¾ km (3 mi) west of Slunchev Bryag,* ☎ *0554/28–11. No credit cards.*

$$$ ★ **Globus.** Popular with tour groups and usually full, with a lively, holiday atmosphere, the hotel is among the best in the area. The rooms are brighter, cleaner, and more modern (with bigger, better-equipped bathroom facilities, such as enclosed showers) than those in many other hotels. ✉ *Slunchev Bryag 8240,* ☎ *0554/222–45. 140 rooms. Restaurant, pool. AE, DC, MC, V.*

$$ 🏨 **Chaika.** Among the bargain hotels (though rates double June–September), the Chaika is cozy, with a sea-facing location, just off the cleanest and prettiest stretch of beach. It is close to the best restaurants and cafés, on the way out of town toward the quaint neighboring village of Nesebâr. ✉ *Slunchev Bryag 8240,* ☎ *0554/223–08. 36 rooms, 4 suites. No credit cards.*

Nesebâr

★ Just 10 minutes by bus or car south of Sunny Beach is a painters' and poets' retreat. It would be hard to find a town that exudes a greater sense of age than this ancient settlement, founded by the Greeks 25 centuries ago on a rocky peninsula reached by a narrow causeway. Among its vine-covered houses are richly decorated medieval churches. Don't miss the frescoes and the dozens of small, private, cozy pubs.

$$–$$$ ✕ **Kapitanska Sreshta.** The ancient charm of this old fisherman's restaurant makes it one of the most photographed buildings in Nesebâr. Its authentic interior and top-quality seafood draw Bulgarian tourists, and the waiters in naval costumes provide friendly service to boisterous crowds. ✉ *Ul. Chaika,* ☎ *0554/34–29. No credit cards.*

Burgas

Bulgaria's second-largest port on the Black Sea has two main streets, ulitsa Aleksandrovska and bulevard Bogoridi, which intersect to form a quaint town center teeming with outdoor cafés, bars, shops, and excellent seafood restaurants. Burgas is famed for spectacular windsurfing as well. An especially pleasant walk is through the **Primorska Gradina** (Seaside Park), with its expansive beach and pedestrian alleyways winding through the adjacent gardens. There is little reason to visit this summer seaside city during the off-season, when the streets are empty and cafés closed.

$–$$$ ✕ **Cheren Peter.** This elegant and inexpensive hideaway is on the more sedate side of town. The cuisine is Bulgarian—everything from a big *ovcharska salata* (shepherd salad: tomatoes, cucumbers, mushrooms, peppers, feta cheese, and boiled eggs) to moussaka, grilled meats, and dessert crepes. ✉ *26 ul. Gurko,* ☎ *056/801–572. No credit cards.*

$$$ 🏨 **Bulgaria.** Rooms at this high-rise hotel in the center of town are modern but basic, with TVs, showers, and desks. Popular with tour groups and business travelers, it has its own nightclub and a restaurant set in a mock winter garden. ✉ *21 ul. Aleksandrovska, 8000,* ☎ *056/842–610. 200 rooms. Restaurant. DC, MC, V.*

Sozopol

★ Nestled in Byzantine ruins, the fishing port of Sozopol, with narrow, cobbled streets leading down to the harbor, was Apollonia, the oldest of the Greek colonies in Bulgaria. It is now a popular haunt for Bulgarian and, increasingly, foreign writers and artists, who find private accommodations in the rustic Black Sea–style houses, so picturesque with their rough stone foundations and unpainted wood slats on the upper stories. **Lotos** (✉ ul. Ropotamo, ☎ 05514/429) can arrange for rental of apartments and houses. Sozopol hosts the **Apollonia Arts Festival** each September, which draws musicians, playwrights, painters, dancers, and actors from all of Europe.

Black Sea Coast Essentials

TOURS

Excursions can be arranged from all resorts. There are bus excursions to Sofia from Albena and Slunchev Bryag; a one-day bus and boat trip along the Danube from neighboring resorts Zlatni Pyasutsi and Sveti Konstantin, as well as Albena; and a multiday bus tour of Bulgaria, including the Valley of Roses, departing from Zlatni Pyasutsi, Sveti Konstantin, and Albena. All tours are run by local tourist agencies. In Varna, Adonis 45 Travel Agency arranges individual tours.

➤ FEES AND SCHEDULES: **Adonis 45 Travel Agency** (✉ 51 ul. Slivnitsa, ☎ 052/603–051, FAX 052/658–215).

TRANSPORTATION AROUND THE BLACK SEA COAST

Buses make frequent runs up and down the coast. Cars and bicycles can be rented. A regular boat service travels the north-bound Varna–Sveti Konstantin (St. Konstantin)–Zlatni Pyasutsi (Golden Sands)–Albena–Balchik route.

VISITOR INFORMATION

➤ TOURIST INFORMATION: **Albena** (✉ bul. Bryag, off E-87, km 1.5, ☎ 05722/27–21). **Burgas** (✉ Hotel Primorets, 1 ul. Knyaz Batenberg, ☎ 056/841–147). **Nesebâr** (✉ 8 ul. Chaika, ☎ 0554/58–30). **Slunchev Bryag** (☎ 0554/23–25). **Varna** (✉ Varnenski Brjag, 3 ul. Moussala, ☎ 052/361–904 or 052/222–272).

INLAND BULGARIA

Inland Bulgaria, despite limited hotel facilities and sometimes complicated public transportation (modern Plovdiv withstanding), has its own distinctive flavor. Wooded and mountainous, the interior is dotted with attractive museum villages (entire settlements are listed for preservation because of their historic cultural value) and ancient towns. The foothills of the Balkan Range, Stara Planina (old mountains), lie parallel to the lower Sredna Gora Mountains, with the verdant Rozova Dolina (Valley of Roses) between them. In the Balkan Range is the ancient capital of Veliko Turnovo; south of the Sredna Gora stretches the fertile Thracian plain, home to Bulgaria's second-largest city, Plovdiv. Between Sofia and Plovdiv lies the enchanting old town of Koprivshtitsa. To the south, in the Rila Mountains, is Borovets, the first of the mountain resorts.

Koprivshtitsa

★ One of Bulgaria's showpiece villages, Koprivshtitsa is set in mountain pastures and pine forests, about 3,050 ft up in the Sredna Gora range. It is 105 km (65 mi) from Sofia, reached by a minor road south from the Sofia–Kazanluk expressway. During the 19th century, Koprivshtitsa became a prosperous trading center with close ties to Istanbul. The architecture of this period, called the National Revival or Bulgarian Renaissance style, is marked by carved woodwork on broad verandas and overhanging eaves, brilliant colors, and courtyards with studded wooden gates. For centuries artists, poets, and wealthy merchants have made their homes here, and many of the historic houses are now open as museums.

$–$$ ✕ **Byaloto Konche.** Uphill from the town square, this intimate, family-owned restaurant is decorated in the National Revival style and offers traditional Bulgarian dishes. ✉ *2 ul. Generilo,* ☎ *07184/22–50. No credit cards.*

$ 🏨 **Drelekova.** It's a unique experience to stay in this brightly painted, restored, and well-preserved period house from the Bulgarian Renaissance. It has only 12 private rooms, and is extremely popular, so reserve ahead. ✉ *2 ul. Petur Zhilkov, 2090,* ☎ *07184/2911 (in Sofia call 978–3511). 12 double rooms. No credit cards.*

$ 🏨 **Hotel Byaloto Konche.** This charming inn offers rustic rooms furnished in the traditional National Revival style, with woven rugs and low beds. One room has a fireplace. ✉ *2 ul. Generilo 2, 2090,* ☎ *07184/22–50. 6 rooms without bath. Restaurant. No credit cards.*

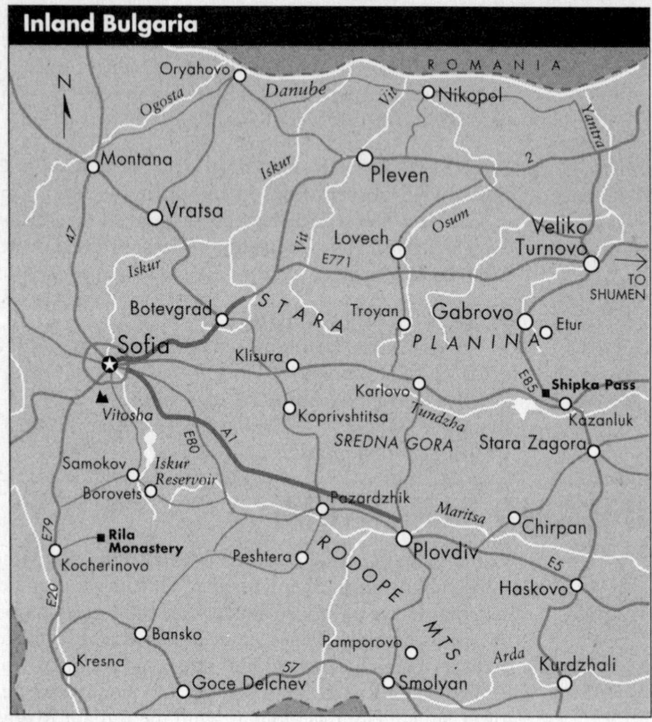

Troyan

Troyan is a tiny, sleepy, old place. A couple of miles from town stands the **Troyanski Monastir** (Troyan Monastery), built during the 1600s in the heart of the mountains. Its church was painstakingly remodeled during the 19th century, and its icons, wood carvings, and frescoes are classic examples of National Revival art. Here at the monastery, monks still brew the nation's most famous brand of rakia, Troyankso Slivova. ✉ *5 km (3 mi) east of Troyan.* ⏲ *Daily 8–6.*

Veliko Turnovo

This town of panoramic vistas, about 200 km (124 mi) northeast of Sofia, rises up against steep mountain slopes through which the Yantra River runs its jagged course. From the 12th through 14th centuries, Veliko Turnovo was the capital of the Second Bulgarian Kingdom. Damaged by repeated Ottoman attacks, and again by an earthquake in 1913, it has been reconstructed and is now a museum city of marvelous relics. Ideally, you should begin at a vantage point above the town in order to get an overview of its design and character.

In a large, National Revival–style house, the **Muzei Vuzrazhdaneto i Uchreditelnoto Subranie** (Museum of the National Revival and Constitutional Assembly) has three floors of exhibits. The first floor holds a collection of medieval icons and local craftwork; the second has photos and documents detailing the national liberation movement; the third houses the hall where the first Bulgarian parliament drafted the country's first constitution. ✉ *2 ul. Nicola Picolo,* ☎ *062/29–821.* ⏲ *Wed.–Sun. 8–noon and 1–5.*

Tsarevets, a hill on the east end of town, almost encircled by the Yantra River, is where the palace and patriarchate of the Second Bulgarian Kingdom stood. The area is under restoration, and steep paths and stairways provide opportunities to view the extensive ruins of the royal palace.

Thursday through Saturday in the summer, the hill is illuminated at 10 PM with a spectacular laser light show. Every day during the summer on the bridge leading to the castle ruins, surreal, life-size puppets enact scenes relating to the castle and Bulgarian history. The prominent feature on the south side of Tsarevets is **Balduinova Kula** (Baldwin's Tower), the 13th-century prison of Baldwin of Flanders, onetime Latin emperor of Constantinople. On the west side of the hill stands the 13th-century **Tsurkva na Chetirideset Muchenitsi** (Church of the Forty Martyrs), with its Turnovo-school frescoes and two inscribed columns, one dating from the 9th century. On the north side of Tsarevets, the **Tsurkva na Sveti Petur i Pavel** (Church of Sts. Peter and Paul) has vigorous murals both inside and out. Across the river to the west, reached by a bridge near the Forty Martyrs, the restored **Tsurkva na Sveti Dimitur** (Church of St. Dimitrius) was built on the spot where the Second Bulgarian Kingdom was proclaimed in 1185.

Near the center of town is **ulitsa Samovodene,** lined with restored crafts workshops—a fascinating place to linger and a good place to find souvenirs, Turkish candy, or a charming café.

$–$$ ✕ **Bolyarska Izba** (Bolyar's Hut). In the center of the busy district just north of the river, this unpretentious eatery is a favorite with locals, many of whom order the house *sarmi* (rose, cabbage or vine leaves stuffed with rice). ✉ *Ul. St. Stambolov,* ☎ *no phone. No credit cards.*

$$$$ 🏨 **Veliko Turnovo Interhotel.** Right in the middle of the most historic part of the town, this modern hotel (refurbished in 2000 when purchased by Interhotel) offers some of the best facilities in its class. Rooms are big and airy with all the amenities, such as TVs, phones, desks, and modern bathrooms. ✉ *2 ul. Emil Popov, 5000,* ☎ *062/633–975. 195 rooms. 2 restaurants, pool. AE, DC, MC, V.*

$$–$$$ 🏨 **Yantra.** The Yantra has some of the best views in town, looking across the river to Tsarevets. It also has a decent restaurant with a balcony that provides the best vantage point of the great vista. ✉ *1 pl. Velchova Zavera, 5000,* ☎ *062/620–931,* FAX *062/620–128. 60 rooms, 40 with shower. Restaurant. AE, DC, MC, V.*

Etur

This historic village sits on the banks of the Sivek, a small branch of the Yantra River, 9 km (6 mi) south of Gabrovo. The mill here is still powered by a stream, and local craftspeople continue to be trained in traditional skills.

Kazanluk

In this town at the eastern end of the Valley of Roses, you can trace the history of rose cultivation, Bulgaria's oldest industry. Each June the town hosts the Festival of Roses, which features folk dancing, art exhibits, and rose-picking demonstrations.

Plovdiv

★ Bustling with college students and new businesses, Bulgaria's second-largest city, Plovdiv, is one of the oldest settlements in Europe and now a major industrial, cultural, and intellectual center. Closed to cars to preserve the original cobblestone, the breathtaking, lantern-lit **Stariat Grad** (Old Town) lies on the hillier southern side of the Maritsa River.

Below the medieval gateway of Hisar Kapiya, the **Georgiadieva Kushta** (Georgiadi House) is a grandiose example of National Revival–style architecture; it also contains a small museum dedicated to the April 1876 uprising against the Turks. ✉ *1 ul. Starinna.* ⏲ *Wed.–Sun. 9:30–12:30 and 2–5.*

The old **Kapana District** (✉ northwest of pl. Stamboliiski) has narrow, winding streets lined with restored shops and cafés. The exquisite hilltop **Rimski amfiteatur** (Roman amphitheater), discovered and excavated in 1981, has been sensitively renovated. In summer the theater is used for dramatic and musical performances. ✉ *Ul. Tsar Ivailo.*

The **Natsionalen Archeologicheski Muzei** (National Archaeological Museum) holds a replica of the 4th-century BC Panagjuriste Gold Treasure and a wealth of ancient Thracian artifacts from Plovdiv and the surrounding region. ✉ *1 pl. Suedinenie,* ☎ *032/55–82–98.* ⏲ *Tues.–Sun. 9–12:30 and 2–5:30.*

The **Natsionalen Etnografski Muzei** (National Ethnographic Museum) in the former home of a Greek merchant, Arghir Kuyumdzhioglu, is an elegant example of the National Revival style, which made its first impact in Plovdiv. The museum is filled with artifacts from that fertile period. ✉ *2 ul. Chomakov,* ☎ *032/22–56–56.* ⏲ *Tues.–Sun. 9–noon and 2–5.*

The steep, narrow **ulitsa Strumna** is lined with workshops and boutiques, some reached through little courtyards. Beyond the railings and past the jewelry and leather vendors in the center of Stamboliiski Square stand the remains of a 2nd-century **Rimski stadion** (Roman stadium). ✉ *Ul. Saborna and ul. Knyaz Alexander I.*

$–$$$ ✕ **Puldin.** On a hill in the center of old town, this folk restaurant has a romantic subterranean dining room complete with a waterfall and live piano music. Order the excellent *pulneni chushki* (peppers stuffed with meat, spices, and rice), served with yogurt, for a taste of Bulgarian home cooking. ✉ *3 ul. Knyaz Tseretelev,* ☎ *032/631–720. AE, DC, MC, V.*

$–$$ ✕ **Alafrangite.** This charming mehana, in a restored 19th-century house with a vine-covered courtyard, is in the old part of town. One of the specialties is *kuopoolu* (vegetable puree of baked eggplant, peppers, and tomatoes). ✉ *17 ul. Nektariev,* ☎ *032/22–98–09 or 032/26–95–95. No credit cards.*

$–$$ ✕ **Restaurant Starata Kushta.** In a renovated 19th-century house in the old quarter, you'll find traditional fare such as *cirene po shopski* (hot feta cheese with herbs, tomatoes, and peppers in an earthenware pot). ✉ *19 ul. Nektariev,* ☎ *032/26–68–42. No credit cards.*

$$$$ 🏨 **Novotel Plovdiv.** This large, modern and well-equipped five star Novotel has all the conveniences expected of a western luxury hotel. ✉ *2 ul. Zlato Boyadzhiev, 4000,* ☎ *032/652–505,* FAX *032/551–979. 322 rooms. Restaurant, pool. AE, DC, MC, V.*

$$$ 🏨 **Maritsa.** Reopened in 2001 after a year of reconstruction, this glitzy high-quality hotel boasts a great combination of location (across from the fairgrounds) and service, at an affordable price. Though some of the new Las Vegas–style opulence is overdone, the rooms are freshly painted, modern, and business-efficient with desks. ✉ *42 bul. Tsar Boris Obedinitel, 4000,* ☎ *032/552–735. 212 rooms. Restaurant, café, gym. AE, DC, MC, V.*

Borovets

Slightly more than 4,300 ft up the northern slopes of the Rila Mountains, this is an excellent walking center and winter-sports resort. It is well equipped with hotels, folk-style taverns, and ski schools. The winding mountain road leads back to Sofia, 70 km (43 mi) from here, past Iskur Reservoir, the largest lake in the country.

Rila

★ **Rilski Monastir** (Rila Monastery), founded by Ivan of Rila in the 10th century, lies in a steep, forested valley past the village of Rila. The monastery has suffered so frequently from fire that most of it is now a grand National Revival reconstruction, although a rugged 14th-century tower has survived. The striking mountain retreat is home to flocks of storks. Part of the complex has been turned into a museum, and some of the monks' cells are now guest rooms. You can see 14 small chapels with frescoes from the 15th and 17th centuries, a lavishly carved altarpiece in the new Church of the Assumption, the sarcophagus of Ivan of Rila, icons, and ancient manuscripts.

Inland Bulgaria Essentials

TOURS

Organized tours set out from Sofia, each covering different points of interest. Check with your hotel information desk or with Balkantourist or Balkantour Ltd.

TRANSPORTATION AROUND INLAND BULGARIA

Rail and bus services cover all parts of inland Bulgaria, but the best bet is to rent a car. To hire a driver, check with Balkantourist or Balkantour Ltd.

VISITOR INFORMATION

➤ TOURIST INFORMATION: **Plovdiv** (Balkan VIP Tours, ✉ Hall 8, Fairground, ☎ 032/563–430). **Veliko Turnovo** (E.A.D. Yantra, ✉ 2 ul. Emil Popov, ☎ 062/620–065).

7 CYPRUS

THE REPUBLIC OF CYPRUS, NORTHERN CYPRUS

THE MEDITERRANEAN ISLAND of Cyprus was once a center for the cult of the Greek goddess Aphrodite. Wooded and mountainous, with a 648-km (403-mi) coastline, Cyprus lies just off the southern coast of Turkey. Fruits and fish are plentiful. The summers are hot and dry, the springs gentle. In winter, visitors can ski in the Troodos Mountains in morning and sunbathe on the beach in the afternoon.

Cyprus's strategic position in the eastern Mediterranean has made it subject to regular invasions by powerful empires. Greeks, Phoenicians, Assyrians, Egyptians, Persians, Romans, and Byzantines—all have ruled here. In 1191, Richard the Lion-Hearted, leader of the Third Crusade, took possession of Cyprus. A year later he sold Cyprus to the Knights Templar, who resold it to Guy de Lusignan, the deposed King of Jerusalem. Guy's descendants ruled the island until the late 15th century, when it was annexed by the Venetians. From the 16th through 19th centuries it was ruled by the Turks. It became a British colony in 1914.

Vestiges of the diverse cultures that have ruled here dot the island. Many fortifications built by the Crusaders and the Venetians still stand. The tomb of the prophet Muhammad's aunt (Hala Sultan Tekke), on the shore of the great salt lake, is one of Islam's most important shrines. A piece of the true cross is said to be kept in the monastery of Stavrovouni, and Paphos has the remains of a pillar to which St. Paul was allegedly tied when he was beaten for preaching Christianity.

The upheavals are not over. Following independence in 1960, the island became the focus of contention between Greeks and Turks. Currently some 84% of the population is Greek and 12% Turkish. Since 1974 Cyprus has been divided by a thin buffer zone—occupied by United Nations (UN) forces—between the Turkish Cypriot north and the Greek Cypriot south. The zone cuts right through the capital city of Nicosia. Talks aimed at uniting the communities into one bizonal federal state have been going on for years. Both communities have comfortable tourist facilities, but entry through the northern part, which is recognized only by Turkey, makes access to the south impossible.

THE REPUBLIC OF CYPRUS

The Republic of Cyprus A to Z

To research prices, get advice from other travelers, and book travel arrangements, visit www.fodors.com.

AIR TRAVEL

There are no direct flights between Cyprus and the United States. Cyprus Airways and British Airways fly direct from London to Larnaca and Paphos. Cyprus Airways also operates from many continental and Mediterranean cities. Other carriers include KLM from Amsterdam.

➤ AIRLINES AND CONTACTS: **British Airways** (☎ 2/761166). **Cyprus Airways** (☎ 2/663054, WEB www.cyprusairways.com). **KLM** (☎ 2/671616).

BOAT AND FERRY TRAVEL

Passenger ships connect Cyprus (Limassol and Larnaca) with various Greek, Italian, Egyptian, and Middle Eastern ports.

BUS TRAVEL

This is the cheapest form of transportation in urban areas; the fare is 40¢. Buses operate every half hour and cover an extensive network. In Nicosia, buses run until 7:30 PM (6:30 PM October–April). In tourist areas during the summer services are extended until midnight. Intercity bus fares range between C£2 and C£3. For information on the Nicosia–Limassol–Paphos route and the Limassol–Larnaca–Ayia Napa route, call the numbers listed below.

➤ BUS INFORMATION: **Limassol–Larnaca–Ayia Napa information** (☎ 04/654890). **Nicosia–Limassol–Paphos information** (☎ 02/463989).

BUSINESS HOURS

BANKS AND OFFICES

Banks are open September–June, weekdays 8:30–12:30 and Monday afternoons 3:15–4:45; July and August, weekdays 8:15–12:30. Some have special afternoon tourist services and will cash traveler's checks weekdays 3–6 October–April, 4–7 May–September, and Saturday 8:30–noon year-round.

MUSEUMS AND SIGHTS

Museum hours vary; it pays to check ahead. Generally, museums are closed for lunch and on Sunday. Most ancient monuments are open from dawn to dusk.

SHOPS

Shops open between 8 and 9 and close at 6 PM November–March, 7 PM April–May and mid-September–October, 7:30 PM June–mid-September. Between June and mid-September, they close for the afternoon summer break daily 1–4 and throughout the year at 2 on Wednesday and Saturday and all day Sunday. In tourist areas shops may stay open late and on Sunday in summer.

CAR RENTAL

Cars may be rented from C£17 per day, less off-season. Rental agencies are located in all major cities as well as at the Larnaca Airport. Visitors can use a valid International Driver's License or their national driver's license, provided it is valid for the class of vehicle they rent.

CAR TRAVEL

GASOLINE

Gas costs about 38¢ per liter.

ROAD CONDITIONS

Main roads between large towns are good. Minor roads can be unsurfaced, narrow, and winding.

RULES OF THE ROAD

Drive on the left. International traffic signs are used. The maximum speed limit is 100 kph (62 mph) on the motorways; in cities the speed limit is 50 kph (31 mph) unless otherwise posted. Use of front seat belts is compulsory. Children under the age of five are not permitted to sit in the front passenger seat.

CONSULATES, EMBASSIES, AND HIGH COMMISSIONS

➤ CANADA: **Consulate of Canada** (✉ 4 Annis Komninis, Nicosia, ☎ 02/766699, FAX 02/459096).

➤ UNITED KINGDOM: **U.K. British High Commission** (✉ Alexandrou Palli, Box 21978, Nicosia, ☎ 02/861100, FAX 02/777198).

➤ UNITED STATES: **United States Embassy** (✉ Gonia Metochiou and Ploutarchou, Egkomi, Nicosia, ☎ 02/776400, FAX 02/780944).

CUSTOMS AND DUTIES

Duty-free allowances are 250 grams of tobacco, 1 liter of spirits or 2 liters of wine, 0.6 liters of perfume, and up to C£100 in other goods. The export of antiques (items that are more than 100 years old) and historic artifacts is strictly forbidden unless a license is obtained from the Department of Antiquities in Nicosia.

➤ INFORMATION: **Department of Antiquities** (☎ 02/865864).

DINING

The top hotels offer a good variety of both local and international food at good prices; large buffets are especially popular. Meals in local restaurants or tavernas usually start with a variety of *mezes* (appetizers), followed by kabobs, dolmas, stews, fresh fish, and various lamb dishes. Meals end with fruit or honey pastries and Greek coffee. By law, all establishments must display a menu with government-approved prices, which include the 10% service charge and 8% value-added tax. Food is relatively cheap, and the quality is good.

Prices are for one main course at dinner.

CATEGORY	COST*
$$$	over C£7
$$	C£5–C£7
$	under C£5

RESERVATIONS AND DRESS

Casual dress is acceptable in most restaurants in Cyprus, regardless of price category, although those in major hotels may require more formal clothing.

EMERGENCIES

For information in English about pharmacies that are open late and on holidays, call an area pharmacy information number, listed below by city. Medical problems can be handled in Nicosia's Nicosia General Hospital.

➤ CONTACTS: **Ambulance, Police, and Fire Brigade** (☏ 199). **Nicosia General Hospital** (☏ 02/451111; 02/452760 for ambulance). **Pharmacies** (☏ 1412 in Nicosia; 1415 in Limassol; 1414 in Larnaca; 1416 in Paphos).

HOLIDAYS

January 1; January 6 (Epiphany); February 10 (Green Monday); March 25 (Greek Independence Day); Greek Orthodox Easter; April 1 (Greek Cypriot National Day); May 1 (Labor Day); Pentecost Monday; August 15 (Assumption); October 1 (Cyprus Independence Day); October 28 (Greek National Day); December 24–26.

LANGUAGE

Greek is the main language, but English is widely spoken in hotels, tavernas, and other tourist haunts. Off the beaten path, sign language may have to do.

The Republic of Cyprus government has carried out a controversial exercise to spell all place names as they are pronounced in Greek. Hence Nicosia becomes Lefkoşa, Larnaca is Larnaka, Limassol is Lemesos, and Paphos is Pafos. Internationally, the original names remain, and in Cyprus both spellings are currently in use.

LODGING

Prices are for two people sharing a double room and include breakfast.

CATEGORY	COST*
$$$$	over C£80
$$$	C£60–C£80
$$	C£40–C£60
$	under C£40

HOTELS

All hotels listed have private bath or shower, but check when making reservations. Most have at least partial air-conditioning. In resort areas many hotel apartments have kitchens.

MAIL AND SHIPPING

Post offices are open Monday, Tuesday, Thursday, and Friday 7:30–1:30 and 3–5, Wednesday 7:30–1:30, and Saturday 9–11 AM. Stamps are also sold at hotels, newsstands, and kiosks.

POSTAL RATES

A 20-gram letter to the United States costs 36¢, a postcard 31¢. To Europe a 20-gram letter costs 31¢, and a postcard 26¢.

MONEY MATTERS

A cup of coffee or tea in the Republic of Cyprus costs 60¢–C£1; a glass of beer 75¢–C£1; a kabob around C£1.25–C£1.75; a bottle of local wine C£1.75–C£4.50.

CURRENCY

The monetary unit in the Republic of Cyprus is the Cyprus pound (C£), which is divided into 100 cents. There are notes of C£1, C£5, C£10, and C£20 and coins of 1, 2, 5, 10, 20, and 50 Cyprus cents. At press time (summer 2001) the rate of exchange was C£0.64 to the U.S. dollar, C£0.41 to the Canadian dollar, C£0.92 to the pound sterling, C£0.74 to the Irish punt, C£0.33 to the Australian dollar, C£0.29 to the New Zealand dollar, and C£.08 to the South African rand.

PASSPORTS AND VISAS

No visas are necessary for holders of valid passports from the United States, Canada, the United Kingdom, or mainland European countries.

TAXIS

PRIVATE TAXIS

Private taxis operate 24 hours throughout the island. They are generally very cheap within towns but far more expensive than service taxis between towns. Telephone from your hotel or hail one in the street. Urban taxis have an initial charge of 65¢ and then 22¢ per kilometer (½ mi) in the daytime, more at night. Drivers are bound by law to run a meter. In-town journeys range from C£1.50 to about C£3.

SERVICE TAXIS

Shared taxis accommodate four to seven passengers and are a cheap, fast, and comfortable way to travel between the main towns: Nicosia, Limassol, Larnaca, and Paphos. Tariffs are C£1.65–C£4.25. Seats must be booked by phone, and passengers may embark/disembark anywhere within the town. The taxis run every half hour (Monday–Saturday 5:45 AM–6:30 PM). Sunday service is less frequent and must be booked one day ahead. On Sundays and public holidays, expect taxi service from 7 AM–5:30 PM from September through May, from 7 AM–6:30 PM from June through August. Contact Karydas, Kypros Taxi Office, or Acropolis Vasos.

➤ TAXI COMPANIES: **Karydas** (☎ 02/755353 in Nicosia; 05/362061 in Limassol; 06/233181 in Paphos). **Kypros Taxi Office** (☎ 02/751811 in Nicosia; 05/363979 in Limassol). **Acropolis Vasos** (☎ 02/760111 in Nicosia; 04/655555 in Larnaca).

TELEPHONES

COUNTRY AND AREA CODES

The country code for Cyprus is 357.

INTERNATIONAL CALLS

To reach an AT&T, MCI, or Sprint long-distance operator, dial one of the access numbers listed below. Public phones may require the deposit of a coin or use of a phone card when you call these numbers.

➤ ACCESS CODES: **AT&T** (☎ 080–90010). **MCI** (☎ 080–90000). **Sprint** (☎ 080–90001).

LOCAL CALLS

Pay phones take 2¢, 5¢, 10¢, and 20¢ coins, but most popular these days are those taking Telecards. These have values of C£3, C£5, or C£10 and can be purchased at post offices, banks, souvenir shops, and kiosks. For telephone information dial 192 in all towns.

TIPPING

A service charge of 10% and an 8% value-added tax (VAT) are included in all bills. If service has been especially good, add 5%.

TOURS

Licensed guides can be hired for half-day (starting at C£29) and full-day (starting at C£46) tours; a list of licensed guides is available from the Cyprus Tourism Organization. Try Cyprus Tourist Guides for half-day and full-day trips and expect to pay C£30–C£48. Night tours typically include dinner at a taverna, folk dancing, and bouzouki music. In seaside resorts hotels or travel agencies can arrange coastal cruises.
➤ FEES AND SCHEDULES: **Cyprus Tourist Guides** (✉ Box 24942, Nicosia 1355, ☎ 02/765755, FAX 02/766872, WEB www.cytourguides.com).

VISITOR INFORMATION

➤ TOURIST INFORMATION: **Nicosia** (national office, ✉ Aristokyprou 11, Laiki Geitonia, ☎ 02/674264, FAX 02/331644; local office, ✉ Laiki Yitonia, ☎ 02/444264). **Larnaka** (✉ Democratias Sq., ☎ 04/654322). **Larnaka International Airport** (✉ Democratias Sq., ☎ 04/634000). **Limassol** (✉ Spyros Araouzos St., ☎ 05/362756). **Paphos** (✉ Gladstone St., ☎ 06/232841).

WHEN TO GO

The tourist season runs throughout the year, but prices are lower November–March.

CLIMATE

Spring and fall are best, usually warm enough for swimming but not uncomfortably hot. The rainy season is in January and February, and it often snows in the Troodos Mountains from January through March. July and August are always very hot and dry. The following are the average daily maximum and minimum temperatures for Nicosia.

Jan.	59F	15C	**May**	85F	29C	**Sept.**	92F	33C
	42	5		58	14		65	18
Feb.	61F	16C	**June**	92F	33C	**Oct.**	83F	28C
	42	5		65	18		58	14
Mar.	66F	19C	**July**	98F	37C	**Nov.**	72F	22C
	44	7		70	21		51	10
Apr.	75F	24C	**Aug.**	98F	37C	**Dec.**	63F	17C
	50	10		69	21		45	7

Exploring the Republic of Cyprus

Nicosia

The capital is twice divided. Its picturesque Old City is contained within 16th-century Venetian fortifications that separate it from the wide, tree-lined streets, large hotels, and high-rises of the modern section. The second division is political and more noticeable. The so-called Green Line (set up by the UN) divides the island between the Republic of Cyprus and Turkish-occupied Northern Cyprus. It is possible to arrange a day trip from the Greek to the Turkish sector through the official checkpoint in Nicosia (Ledra Palace), though it is essential to return by 5 PM. If you are late, you will not be allowed to re-enter into the Republic of Cyprus. You will be forced to depart from Northern Cyprus. There are no official representatives of countries other than Turkey in the northern sector, so contact your consulate before crossing the line to confirm safety.

★ In the Greek sector **Laiki Yitonia,** at the southern edge of the Old City, is an area of winding alleys and traditional architecture that is being completely renovated. Among its important sites is the **Archbishopric,** which houses several museums. Tavernas, cafés, and crafts workshops line the shaded, cobbled streets. Just to the west lies Ledra Street, where modern shops alternate with yet more crafts shops. Head north to visit the tiny Greek Orthodox **Tripiotis** church (✉ Solonos 47–49), which dates from 1690 and is decorated with an ornately carved golden iconostasis and silver-covered icons.

The **Leventis Municipal Museum of Nicosia** traces the city's history from 3000 BC to the present, with exhibits on crafts and daily life. ✉ *17 Ippocratous St.,* ☎ *02/451475.* ⏲ *Tues.–Sun. 10–4:30.*

Housed in a wing of the archiepiscopal palace built in 1960 in neo-Byzantine style, the **Archbishop Makarios III Cultural Foundation** consists of the **Byzantine Art Museum,** with fine displays of icons spanning 1,000 years, and the **Greek War of Independence Gallery,** with a collection of maps, paintings, and mementos of 1821. ✉ *Archbishop Kyprianou Sq.,* ☎ *02/456781.* ⏲ *Weekdays 9–1, 2–5, Sat. 9–1.*

The **Museum of the National Struggle** has dramatic displays of the Cypriot campaigns against the British from 1955 to 1959. ✉ *Archbishop Kinyras 7,* ☎ *02/302465.* ⏲ *Weekdays 8–2 and 3–5:30.*

★ The **Cyprus Folk Art Museum,** housed in the 14th-century part of the archiepiscopal palace, has demonstrations of ancient weaving techniques and displays of ceramics and olive and wine presses. ✉ *Archbishop Kyprianou Sq.,* ☎ *02/463205.* ⏲ *Weekdays 9–1, 2–5, Sat. 10–1.*

Don't miss **Ayios Ioannis** (St. John's) Cathedral, built in 1662 within the courtyard of the archiepiscopal palace. Look for the 18th-century murals illustrating important moments in Cypriot religious history and including a depiction of the tomb of St. Barnabas. ✉ *Archbishop Kyprianou Sq.* ⏲ *Mon.–Sat. 8–noon and 2–4.*

The **Famagusta Gate,** now a cultural center, houses exhibitions, a lecture hall, and a theater. ✉ *Athina St.,* ☎ *02/430877.* ⏲ *Weekdays 10–1 and 4–7.*

★ Outside the city walls stands the **Cyprus Museum.** It has archaeological displays ranging from Neolithic to Roman times. This stop is essential to an understanding of the island's ancient sites. ✉ *Museum St.,* ☎ *02/302189.* ⏲ *Mon.–Sat. 9–5, Sun. 10–1.*

The neoclassical **Municipal Theater** (✉ Museum St., ☎ 02/463028) seats 1,200 people and stages events throughout the year, including Greek-language dramas and concerts. The lush **Municipal Gardens** (✉ opposite Cyprus Museum) are a well-maintained oasis of greenery in the city.

$$$ ✕ **Plaka Tavern.** One of the oldest eating establishments in the city, in the heart of Engomi, offers up to 30 different meze dishes, including such unusual items as snails and okra with tomatoes. ✉ *8 Stylianou Lena,* ☎ *02/446498. AE, DC, MC, V.*

$$$ ✕ **Trattoria Romantica.** The fare is Italian, and the atmosphere is distinctly friendly, with no shortage of advice available on any topic relating to Cyprus. There's a roaring fire in winter and service in the courtyard outside in summer. ✉ *13 Evagora Pallikaridi,* ☎ *02/376161. AE, DC, MC, V. Closed Sun.*

$$$$ ★ 🏨 **Cyprus Hilton.** The Hilton is among the island's best hotels, with extensive sports facilities, a skylit indoor pool, and dancing. An executive wing offers business facilities. ✉ *Archbishop Makarios Ave., Box 22023, 1516,* ☎ *02/377777,* FAX *02/377788,* WEB *www.hilton.com. 298 rooms, 17 suites. 2 restaurants, 2 pools. AE, DC, MC, V.*

$$$$ 🏨 **Holiday Inn.** In the Old City, near commercial and historic districts, this member of the chain opened in 1995. Its amenities include Japanese, international, and health-food restaurants and a rooftop pool with a garden. ✉ *70 Regina St., Box 21212, 1504,* ☎ *02/665131,* FAX *02/*

673337, WEB www.holidayinn.com. 140 rooms. 4 restaurants, 2 pools. AE, DC, MC, V.

$$$ **Cleopatra Hotel.** This hostelry offers a convenient location, cordial service, and well-prepared food served poolside. ✉ *8 Florina St., Box 21397, 1507,* ☎ *02/671000,* FAX *02/670618,* WEB *www.hotelworld.com. 90 rooms. Restaurant, pool. AE, DC, MC, V.*

Ayia Napa

Once a small fishing village, 30 km (19 mi) east of Larnaca, Ayia Napa is anchored by a 16th-century monastery and is renowned for its white-sand beaches and views of the brilliant sea. Today its many restaurants and hotels reflect the town's transformation into Cyprus's premier vacationland.

$$$ **Nissi Beach.** This modern, air-conditioned hotel is set in magnificent gardens overlooking a sandy beach 3 km (2 mi) outside town. Some accommodations are in bungalows, which do not have kitchens. Amenities include a dive shop, a health club, and more. ✉ *Nissi Ave., Box 30010, 5340,* ☎ *03/721021,* FAX *03/721623,* WEB *www.nissibeach.com. 270 rooms, 166 bungalows. Restaurant, pool. AE, DC, MC, V.*

$$ **Pernera Beach Sun Hotel.** This budget hotel has a view of the beach. All rooms are air-conditioned. ✉ *Pernera Beach, Box 33005, 5340,* ☎ *03/831011,* FAX *03/831020. 156 rooms. AE, DC, MC, V.*

Larnaca

The seaside resort with its own airport, 51 km (32 mi) southeast of Nicosia, has a flamboyant Whitsuntide celebration, Cataklysmos, as well as fine beaches, palm trees, and a modern harbor. In the marina district the **Larnaca Museum** displays treasures, including outstanding sculptures and Bronze Age seals. ✉ *Kimon and Kilkis Sts.,* ☎ *04/630169.* ⏲ *Mon.–Wed. and Fri. 9–2:30, Thurs. 9–2:30 and 3–5.*

Kition, the old Larnaca of biblical times, was one of the most important ancient city-kingdoms. Architectural remains of temples date from the 13th century BC. ✉ *Kyman St., north of Larnaca Museum.* ⏲ *Weekdays 9–2:30.*

The **Pierides Collection** is a private assemblage of more than 3,000 pieces distinguished by its Bronze Age terra-cotta figures. ✉ *Paul Zenon Kitieos St. 4, near Lord Byron St.,* ☎ *04/652495.* ⏲ *Mid-June–Sept., Mon.–Sat. 9–1 and 4–7; Oct.–mid-June, weekdays 9–1 and 3–6, Sat. 9–1.*

The 17th-century **Turkish fort** contains finds from Hala Sultan Tekke and Kition. ✉ *Within sight of marina on seafront.* ⏲ *June–Sept., daily 7:30–7; Oct.–May, Mon.–Wed. and Fri. 7:30–5, Thurs. 7:30–6.*

In the town center stands one of the island's more important churches, **Ayios Lazarus** (Church of Lazarus), resplendent with icons. It has a fascinating crypt containing Lazarus's sarcophagus. ✉ *Plateia Agiou Lazarou.* ⏲ *Sept.–Mar., Mon.–Sat. 8–12:30 and 2:30–5; Apr.–Aug., Mon.–Sat. 8–12:30 and 3:30–6:30.*

South of Larnaca on the airport road is the 6.5-square-km (2½-square-mi) **Salt Lake.** In winter it's a refuge for migrating birds. On the lake's ★ edge a mosque stands in an oasis of palm trees guarding the **Hala Sultan Tekke**—burial place of the prophet Muhammad's aunt, Umm Haram, and an important Muslim shrine. ✉ *Salt Lake.* ⏲ *June–Sept., daily 9–7:30; Oct.–May, daily 9–5.*

The 11th-century **Panayia Angeloktistos** church, 11 km (7 mi) south of Larnaca, has extraordinary Byzantine wall mosaics that date from the 6th and 7th centuries. ✉ *Rte. B4, Kiti.* ⏲ *Sept.–May, Mon.–Sat.*

8–noon, Sun. 8–noon and 2–4; June–Aug., Mon.–Sat. 8–noon and 2–5, Sun. 8–noon and 2–4.

On a mountain 40 km (25 mi) west of Larnaca stands the **Stavrovouni** (Mountain of the Cross) monastery. It was founded by St. Helena in AD 326; the present buildings date from the 19th century. The views from here are splendid. Ideally, you should visit the monastery in a spirit of pilgrimage rather than sightseeing, out of respect for the monks. Male visitors are allowed inside the monastery daily sunrise–sunset, except between noon and 3 (between noon and 1, Oct.–May).

$$ ✕ **Monte Carlo.** The outdoor seating at this spot along the road to the airport is on a balcony extending over the sea. Service is efficient, and the dining area is clean. Try the fish and meat mezes and casseroles. ✉ *28 Pigiale Pasa Ave.,* ☏ *04/653815. AE, DC, MC, V.*

$–$$ ✕ **Omiros.** This family-owned restaurant is best known for its fish meze, a true feast of 24 dishes fresh from the sea. Menu items also include red mullet, calamari, octopus, lamb chops, and pork kabobs. ✉ *Pigiale Pasa Ave., Stadem Court 3,* ☏ *04/653521. AE, DC, MC, V.*

$$$$ 🏨 **Golden Bay.** Comfort is paramount at this beach hotel east of the town center. All rooms have balconies and views of the sea. The extensive sports facilities make it an ideal spot. ✉ *Larnaca-Dhekelia Rd., Box 40741, 6306,* ☏ *04/645444,* FAX *04/645451,* WEB *www.lordos.com.cy. 194 rooms. 2 restaurants, 2 pools. AE, DC, MC, V.*

$$$ 🏨 **Sandy Beach Hotel.** Between Larnaca and Dhekelia, this beach hotel has a health club and tennis court. All rooms have twin beds and a partial sea view. ✉ *Larnaca–Dekeleia Rd., 8 km (5 mi) from Larnaca, Box 40857, 6307,* ☏ *04/646333,* FAX *04/646900,* WEB *www.sandybeachhotel.com. 195 rooms, 5 suites. 3 restaurants, 2 pools. AE, DC, MC, V.*

Phikardou

In this museum village south of Nicosia, many rural houses have remarkable woodwork; they also contain the household furnishings used a century ago. Official tour guides are available in the village. ✉ *Machairas Alicosia Rd. via Klirou; 1½ km (1 mi) east of Gourri,* ☏ *02/337715 in Nicosia.* ⏲ *Hrs vary.*

Limassol

A commercial port and wine-making center on the south coast, Limassol, 75 km (47 mi) from Nicosia, is a bustling, cosmopolitan town. Luxury hotels, apartments, and guest houses stretch along 12 km (7 mi) of seafront. The town's nightlife is the liveliest on the island. In the center, the elegant, modern shops of Makarios Avenue contrast with those of the old part of town, where local handicrafts prevail.

★ The 14th-century **Limassol Fort** was built on the site of a Byzantine fortification. Richard the Lion-Hearted and Berengaria of Navarre are said to have married here in 1191. The **Cyprus Medieval Museum** in the castle displays medieval armor and relics. ✉ *Near old port,* ☏ *05/330419.* ⏲ *Mon.–Sat. 9–5, Sun. 10–1.*

For a glimpse of Cypriot folklore, visit the **Folk Art Museum.** The collection includes national costumes and fine examples of weaving and other crafts. ✉ *Agiou Andreou 253,* ☏ *05/362303.* ⏲ *Oct.–May, Mon.–Wed. and Fri. 8:30–1:30 and 3–5:30, Thurs. 8:30–1:30; June–Sept., Mon.–Wed. and Fri. 8:30–1:30 and 4–6:30, Thurs. 8:30–1:30.*

At the annual **Limassol Wine Festival** in September, local wineries offer free samples and demonstrate traditional grape-pressing methods. There are open-air music and dance performances. The **KEO Winery,** just west of the town, welcomes visitors. ✉ *Roosevelt Ave., toward the new port,* ☏ *05/362053.* ⏲ *Tours weekdays at 10.*

★ **Kolossi Castle,** a Crusader fortress of the Knights of St. John, was constructed in the 13th century and rebuilt in the 15th. ✉ *Road to Paphos.* ⏲ *June–Sept., daily 7:30–5:30; Oct.–May, daily 7:30–5.*

Kourion (Curium), west of Limassol, has Greek and Roman ruins. In the **amphitheater,** classical and Shakespearean plays are sometimes staged. Next to the theater is the **Villa of Eustolios,** a summer house built by a wealthy Christian. A nearby **Roman stadium** has been partially rebuilt. The **Apollo Hylates** (Sanctuary of Apollo of the Woodlands), an impressive archaeological site, stands 3 km (2 mi) farther on. ✉ *Main Paphos Rd.* ⏲ *June–Sept., daily 7:30–5; Oct.–May, daily 8–4:45.*

$$$ ✕ **Scottis Steak House.** Just off the city's main thoroughfare, Makarios Avenue, this serves some of the best steaks available in Cyprus. ✉ *38 Souli St.,* ☎ *05/335173. AE, DC, MC, V.*

$$ ✕ **Porta.** A varied menu of international and Cypriot dishes, such as *foukoudha* barbecue (grilled strips of steak) and trout baked in prawn and mushroom sauce, is served in this restored warehouse. On many nights you'll be entertained by soft live music. ✉ *17 Yenethliou Mitella, Old Castle,* ☎ *05/360339. MC, V.*

$$$$ ★ **Four Seasons Hotel.** One of the premier hotels in Cyprus, this property is not part of the international chain but offers comparable elegance. The spacious rooms have marble baths; many also have balconies with sea views. Guest services include a spa, a dive shop, a children's club, tennis and squash courts, and a gym. ✉ *Old Limassol–Nicosia Rd., Box 57222, 3313,* ☎ *05/310222,* FAX *05/310887. 190 rooms, 18 suites. 3 restaurants, 3 pools. AE, DC, MC, V.*

$$$$ ★ **Le Meridien.** The striking lobby of this large, luxurious hotel is pink marble and glass. The amenities are first-class and include scuba diving, a kids' center, a health club, and a heated indoor pool. ✉ *Old Limassol–Nicosia Rd., Box 56560, 3308,* ☎ *05/862000,* FAX *05/634222,* WEB *www.lemeridien-cyprus.com. 232 rooms, 69 suites. 3 restaurants, 2 pools. AE, DC, MC, V.*

$ **Azur Beach.** This fine apartment hotel has a good sandy beach and helpful management. ✉ *Potamios Yermasoyias, Box 51318, 3504,* ☎ *05/322667,* FAX *05/321897. 24 1-bedroom apartments, 12 studios, 60 rooms. 2 restaurants. DC, MC, V.*

$ **Continental.** A great sea view adds to the appeal of this family hotel close to the castle. ✉ *137 Spyros Araouzos Ave., Box 50398, 3604,* ☎ *05/362530,* FAX *05/373030. 30 rooms. AE, V.*

Troodos Mountains

North of Limassol, these mountains, which rise to 6,500 ft, have shady cedar and pine forests and cool springs. Small, painted churches in the Troodos and Pitsilia Foothills are rich examples of a rare indigenous art form. **Asinou Church,** near the village of Nikitari, and **Agios Nikolaos tis Stegis** (St. Nicholas of the Roof), south of Kakopetria, are especially noteworthy. The **Tall Trees Trout Farm** is an oasis serving delicious meals of fresh fish. In winter, skiers take over the mountains; **Platres,** in the foothills of Mt. Olympus, is the principal resort. At the **Kykkos** monastery, founded in 1100, the prized icon of the Virgin is reputed to have been painted by St. Luke.

Petra tou Romiou

The legendary **birthplace of Aphrodite**—Greek goddess of love and beauty—is just off the main road between Limassol and Petra. Signs in Greek and English identify the offshore rock that is viewed from the shoreline.

Paphos

In the west of the island and 142 km (88 mi) southwest of Nicosia, Paphos combines superb sea swimming with archaeological sites and a rich history. The center is modern.

The **Paphos District Archaeological Museum** displays pottery, jewelry, and statuettes from Cyprus's Roman villas. ✉ *43 Grivas Dighenis Ave., Ktima,* ☎ *06/240215.* ⏲ *Weekdays 7:30–2:30, 3–5.*

★ There are notable 6th-century mosaics and icons in the **Byzantine Museum.** ✉ *7 Andreas Ioannou St.,* ☎ *06/231392.* ⏲ *Oct.–May, weekdays 9–12:30, 2–5, Sat. 9–12:30; June–Sept., weekdays 9–12:30, 4–7, Sat. 9–12:30.*

The charming **Ethnographical Museum** re-creates various rooms of typical old houses, including furnishings, fabrics, and kitchen and agricultural utensils. ✉ *1 Exo Vrysi,* ☎ *06/232010.* ⏲ *May–Sept., weekdays 9–1 and 2–5, Sat. 9–1, Sun. 10–1; Oct.–Apr., weekdays 9–1 and 2–5, Sat. 9–1, Sun. 10–1.*

Don't miss the elaborate **Roman mosaics** in the **Roman Villa of Theseus,** the **House of Dionysos,** and the **House of Aion.** The town bus stops nearby. ✉ *Kato Paphos (New Paphos), near harbor,* ☎ *06/240217.* ⏲ *June–Sept., daily 7:30–5; Oct.–May, daily 8–5.*

★ The **Tombs of the Kings,** an early necropolis, date from 300 BC. The coffin niches are empty, but a powerful sense of mystery remains. ✉ *Kato Paphos (New Paphos),* ☎ *06/240295.* ⏲ *Weekdays 7:30–5, weekends 9–5.*

$$ ✕ **Chez Alex Fish Tavern.** The well-established tavern serves only fresh fish (the catch of the day) and fish mezes. ✉ *7 Constantia St., Kato Paphos,* ☎ *06/234767. AE, DC, MC, V.*

$$$$ ★ **Azia Beach Hotel.** Ninety percent of the rooms at this expansive hotel perched up on rugged cliffs have a sea view. The resort offers tennis, squash, and a health center. ✉ *Akamas Ave., Box 62108, 8061,* ☎ *06/247800,* FAX *06/246883,* WEB *www.lemeridien-cyprus.com. 179 rooms, 4 suites. 3 restaurants, 2 pools. AE, DC, MC, V.*

$$$$ ★ **Coral Beach Hotel and Resort.** Just 10 minutes from the town of Paphos, this luxurious seaside hotel has Mediterranean-style rooms. Guest facilities include a complete spa, scuba diving, and an arts and crafts workshop. ✉ *Coral Bay, Box 624222, 8099,* ☎ *06/621711,* FAX *06/621742. 420 rooms. 5 restaurants, 2 pools. AE, DC, MC, V.*

$$$$ **Paphos Beach.** Surrounded by gardens, this hotel has a wealth of facilities. Water sports are a major draw here. Accommodations are either in the main hotel or in roomy bungalows on the grounds. ✉ *Posidonos St., Box 60136, 8125,* ☎ *06/233091,* FAX *06/242818. 224 rooms, 20 bungalows. 3 restaurants, pool. AE, DC, MC, V.*

$$$ **Amalthia Beach Hotel.** This hotel on the beach amid banana groves has a friendly, personal atmosphere. The impressive, open lobby overlooks the water, and the rooms have balconies with sea views. ✉ *8574 Kissonerga Rd., Box 60323, 8102,* ☎ *06/247777,* FAX *06/245963,* WEB *www.lemeridien-cyprus.com. 168 rooms. Restaurant, 2 pools. AE, DC, MC, V.*

$$ **Hilltop Gardens Hotel Apartments.** All apartments have a view of the sea, just 500 yards away. The decor is a pleasant mixture of traditional Cypriot village style, including wooden furniture, and modern touches. ✉ *Off Tombs of the Kings Rd., Box 60185, 8101,* ☎ *06/243111,* FAX *06/248229. 48 apartments. Pool. AE, DC, MC, V.*

Polis

Just past the town's fishing harbor of Latchi, and 48 km (30 mi) north of Paphos, are the **Baths of Aphrodite,** a natural pool where the goddess is said to have seduced her swains. The wild, undeveloped Akamas Peninsula is perfect for a hike.

$$$$ ★ **Anassa.** *Anassa* is the Greek word for "queen," and this upscale accommodation overlooks a stretch of coastline from an exclusive setting filled with Greek motifs and frescoes. Suites vary in size from studios to expansive accommodations. All rooms have a Mediterranean decor and include a private balcony or terrace. ✉ *Polis-Baths of Aphrodite Rd., Box 60136, 8125,* ☎ *06/322800 or 800/323–7500,* FAX *06/322900. 184 suites. 4 restaurants, 2 pools. AE, DC, MC, V.*

NORTHERN CYPRUS

There are two important things to bear in mind in Northern Cyprus. One is that public holidays follow those in Turkey, with additional public holidays on May 1 (Labor Day), July 20 (Peace and Freedom Day), and November 15 (Independence Day). The other is to note that, although English is widely spoken, Turkish, not Greek, is the predominant language and Turkish names designate the cities and towns: Nicosia is known as Lefkoşa, Kyrenia as Girne, and Famagusta as Gazimağusa. Visitors are also advised to obey the NO PHOTOGRAPHS signs wherever they appear.

Northern Cyprus A to Z

To research prices, get advice from other travelers, and book travel arrangements, visit www.fodors.com.

AIR TRAVEL

Cyprus Turkish Airlines, Istanbul Airlines, and Turkish Airlines run all flights via mainland Turkey, usually with a change of plane at Istanbul. There are also nonstop flights from Adana, Ankara, Antalya, and İzmir to Ercan Airport, 24 km (15 mi) from Lefkoşa. It is not possible to enter the Republic of Cyprus from Northern Cyprus unless you are returning from a day trip from Lefkoşa.

BOAT AND FERRY TRAVEL

Ferries run from Turkey: from Mersin to Gazimağusa and from Antalya and Tasucu to Girne.

BUS TRAVEL

Minibuses and the shared *dolmuş* (taxis) are the cheapest forms of transportation. Service is frequent on main routes. A minibus from Lefkoşa to Girne costs about $1.50 and to Gazimağusa about $1.80, with slightly lower fares if you get off before the final destination. The price of a seat in a dolmuş remains the same wherever you get off and, for the same trips, would cost approximately the same as a minibus at about $1.50 and $1.80, respectively.

BUSINESS HOURS

From May through September, most of the main tourist sites are open daily 8–7, but check before you visit.

CAR TRAVEL

See By Car *in* The Republic of Cyprus A to Z, *above.*

DINING

Prices are for one main course at dinner.

CATEGORY	COST*
$$$	over $17
$$	$10–$17
$	$5–$10

LODGING

Prices are for one night for two people sharing a double room and include breakfast.

CATEGORY	COST*
$$$$	Over $150
$$$	$100–$150
$$	$50–$100
$	Under $50

MONEY MATTERS

Prices for food and accommodations tend to be lower than those in the Republic of Cyprus. However, with the exception of Turkish wines and spirits, most foreign drinks are slightly more expensive. A cup of coffee costs around $1, a glass of beer about $1.50. Wine is around $3 per glass. A 35-km (22-mi) taxi ride costs about $25.

CURRENCY

The monetary unit in Northern Cyprus is the Turkish lira (TL). There are bills for 100,000; 250,000, 500,000, 1,000,000, 5,000,000, and 10,000,000 TL; and coins for 10,000, 25,000, 50,000 and 100,000 TL. The Turkish lira is subject to considerable inflation, so most of the prices in this section are quoted in U.S. dollars.

VISITOR INFORMATION

➤ TOURIST INFORMATION: **Department of Tourism Marketing** (✉ Selçuklu Caddesi, Lefkoşa; mailing address, Selçuklu Cad., Lefkoşa KKTC, Mersin 10, Turkey, ☎ 392/228–9629, FAX 392/228–9625). **Regional tourism offices** (☎ 392/366–2864 in Gazimağusa; 392/815–2145 in Girne; 392/228–9629 in Lefkoşa).

Exploring Northern Cyprus

Lefkoşa (Nicosia)

The Turkish half of the city is the capital of Northern Cyprus. A walk around the Old City, within the encircling walls, is rich with glimpses from the Byzantine, Lusignan, and Venetian past. In addition to Venetian fortifications, it contains the **Selimiye Mosque,** originally the 13th-century Cathedral of St. Sophia and a fine example of Gothic architecture to which a pair of minarets has been added. ✉ *Selimiye St.* ⏲ *Oct.–Apr., weekdays 8–1 and 2–5; May–Sept., Mon. 7:30–1 and 2–6, Tues.–Fri. 7:30–2.*

Near the Girne Gate is the **Mevlevi Tekke ve Etnografi Müzesi** (Mevlevi Shrine and Ethnographic Museum), the former home of the Mevlevi Dervishes, a Sufi order. The building now houses a museum of Turkish history and culture. ✉ *Girne St.* ⏲ *Oct.–Apr., weekdays 8–1 and 2–5; May–Sept., Mon. 7:30–1 and 2–6, Tues.–Fri. 7:30–2.*

$$ ★ ✕ **Cyprus Kitchen.** This restaurant offers some of the finest authentic Cypriot cuisine in Northern Cyprus, with a superb range of starters and grilled meats. The interior is crammed with mementoes of village life, from a plough and loom to handicrafts. ✉ *Atatürk Caddesi No. 39, Gönyeli,* ☎ *392/223–1694. MC, V. Reservations essential.*

Girne (Kyrenia)

Of the coastal resorts, Girne, with its yacht-filled harbor, is the most appealing. There are excellent beaches to the east and west of the town. **Girne Castle,** overlooking the harbor, is Venetian. It now houses the Batık Gemi Müzesi (Shipwreck Museum), whose prize possession is the remains of a ship that sank around 300 BC. ⏲ *May–Sept., daily 8–7; Oct.–Apr., daily 8–5.*

The fantastic ruins of the **St. Hilarion Kalesi** (Castle of St. Hilarion) stand on a hilltop 11 km (7 mi) southwest of Girne. It's a strenuous walk, so take a taxi (about $30 round-trip from Girne); the views are breathtaking. ⏲ *Daily 8–5.*

The romantic ruins of the former **Bella Pais Manastiri** (Abbey of Bellapais), built in the 12th century by the Lusignans, are just as impressive. They lie on a mountainside 6 km (4 mi) southeast of Girne, overlooking the coastal plain. ⏲ *Oct.–Apr., weekdays 8–1 and 2–5; May–Sept., Mon. 7:30–1 and 2–6, Tues.–Fri. 7:30–2.*

$–$$ ✕ **Niazi's.** Less picturesque than the restaurants ringing the harbor, this place serves much better food with excellent grilled foods, including *şeftali kebab* (meatballs), a Turkish Cypriot specialty, and homemade desserts. ✉ *Kordonboyu Caddesi,* ☎ *392/815–2160. MC, V.*

$$$ **Jasmine Court.** Next to its own beach in Girne, the luxurious hotel is a resort in its own right, with air-conditioned rooms, palm tree–shaded poolside terraces, sports facilities, a casino, and a disco. ✉ *Temmuz Cad. 20, Girne, Mersin 10, Turkey,* ☎ *392/815–1450,* FAX *392/815–1488,* WEB *www.lemeridien-cyprus.com. 143 rooms. Restaurant, pool. MC, V.*

$$ **Dome Hotel.** Despite the gleaming marble of the lobby and restaurant, this doyen of Girne's hotels still has a nostalgic air of faded 1960s grandeur. Rooms on the seaside may have a slightly battered decor but are superbly located almost literally over the water. ✉ *Kordonboyu Caddesi, Girne, Mersin 10, Turkey,* ☎ *392/815–2453,* FAX *392/815–2772. 170 rooms. Restaurant, pool. MC, V.*

Gazimağusa (Famagusta)

Gazimağusa, the chief port of Northern Cyprus, has massive and well-preserved Venetian walls and the late-13th-century Gothic Cathedral of St. Nicholas, now Lala Mustafa Pasha Mosque. The Old Town, within the walls, is the most intriguing district to explore.

Salamis, on the seashore north of Gazimağusa, is an ancient ruined city and perhaps the most dramatic archaeological site on the island. St. Barnabas and St. Paul arrived in Salamis and established a church near here. Most of the ruins date from the Roman Empire, including a well-preserved theater, an amphitheater, villas, and superb mosaic floors. After surviving earthquakes and pirate raids, the city was abandoned in the 7th century AD when the population moved to what is now Gazimağusa. Much of ancient city is overgrown with a tangle of bushes and dune grass, which only serve to enhance the site's serene, poignant beauty. ⏲ *Oct.–Apr., daily 8–5; May–Sept., daily 8–7.*

8 CZECH REPUBLIC

PRAGUE, SIDE TRIPS: BOHEMIA AND MORAVIA

FOR ALL ITS HISTORY, the Czech Republic is a very young nation. After a peaceful revolution overthrew a Communist regime that had been in power for 40 years, Czechoslovakia split in 1993 as its two constituent republics, Czech and Slovak, formed independent countries.

Formed from the ruins of the Austro-Hungarian Empire at the end of World War I, Czechoslovakia appeared to withstand the threat of divisive nationalism and brought stability to the potentially volatile region. During the difficult 1930s, the Czechoslovak republic stood as the model democracy in Central Europe. In the 1960s a courageous Slovak, Alexander Dubček, led the 1968 Prague Spring, an intense period of national renewal. Students and opponents of the Communist regime in both Prague and Bratislava toppled the ruling party in 1989.Czechoslovakia proved to be an artificial creation that masked important and long-standing cultural differences between two outwardly similar peoples. The old Czech lands of Bohemia and Moravia, whose territory makes up most of the Czech Republic, can look to a rich cultural history that goes back a millennium, and they played pivotal roles in the great religious and social conflicts of European history. Slovakia, by contrast, languished for centuries as an agrarian outpost of the Hungarian empire. Given the state of the Slovaks' national ego, independence was probably inevitable.

Since the 1989 revolution, Prague, the Czech capital, has become one of Europe's top destinations. Forget old impressions of neglect and melancholy; Prague exudes an atmosphere of enthusiasm and provides such conveniences as English-language newspapers, attentive service, loads of upscale shopping choices, and restaurateurs who will try to find you a seat even if you don't have a reservation. Musicians and writers find new inspiration in the city that once harbored Mozart and Kafka. Spectacular Gothic, Baroque, and Art Nouveau treasures stand in glorious counterpoint to drab remnants of socialist architecture.

Outside the capital you can discover everything from imperial spas to modern industrial cities. Don't pass up the lovely towns and castles of southern Bohemia: the Renaissance river town of Český Krumlov ranks among Central Europe's grandest sights.

CZECH REPUBLIC A TO Z

To research prices, get advice from other travelers, and book travel arrangements, visit www.fodors.com.

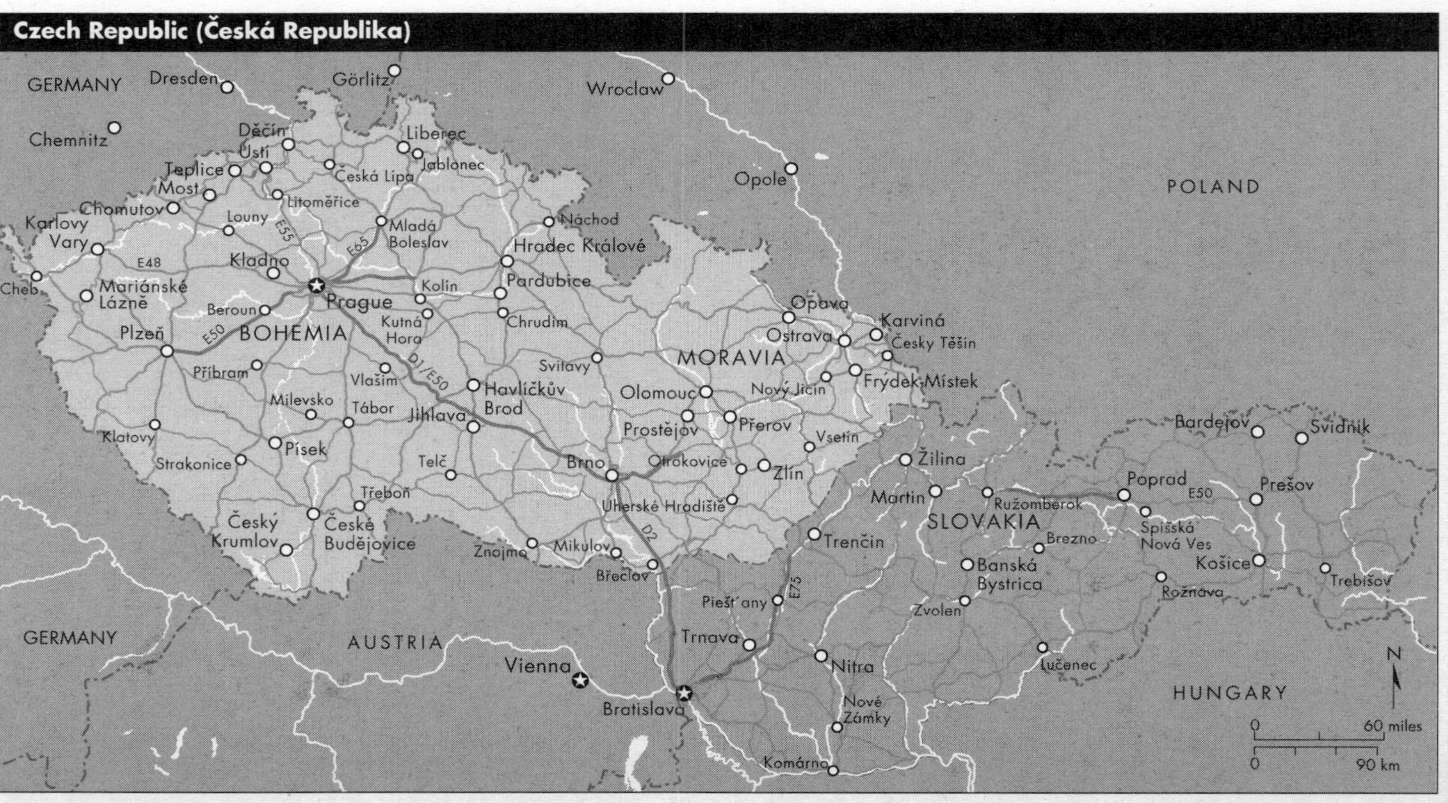
Czech Republic (Česká Republika)
GERMANY
Dresden
Görlitz
Wroclaw
Chemnitz
Děčín
Ústí
Liberec
Jablonec
Teplice
Most
Česká Lípa
Litoměřice
Chomutov
Karlovy Vary
Louny
E55
Mladá Boleslav
E65
Náchod
Hradec Králové
Opole
POLAND
E48
Kladno
Cheb
Mariánské Lázně
Prague
Kolín
Pardubice
Beroun
Kutná Hora
Chrudim
Plzeň
E50
BOHEMIA
Opava
Karviná
Ostrava
Český Těšín
MORAVIA
Příbram
Vlašim
D1/E50
Svitavy
Frýdek-Místek
Havlíčkův Brod
Olomouc
Nový Jičín
Milevsko
Tábor
Jihlava
Prostějov
Přerov
Bardejov
Svidník
Klatovy
Písek
Vsetín
Žilina
Strakonice
Telč
Brno
Otrokovice
Zlín
Poprad
Prešov
Třeboň
Uherské Hradiště
Martin
Ružomberok
SLOVAKIA
Český Krumlov
České Budějovice
D2
Trenčín
Brezno
Spišská Nová Ves
Znojmo
Mikulov
Břeclav
Banská Bystrica
Košice
Trebišov
Piešťany
E75
Zvolen
Rožňava
GERMANY
AUSTRIA
Trnava
Nitra
Lučenec
Vienna
Bratislava
HUNGARY
N
Nové Zámky
0
60 miles
0
90 km
Komárno

AIR TRAVEL

Good air service links Prague with several other towns, including Ostrava in Moravia and Bratislava and Poprad (for the High Tatras) in Slovakia. Prices are reasonable. Make reservations at Čedok offices or directly at ČSA (Czech Airlines).

➤ AIRLINES AND CONTACTS: **ČSA** (Czech Airlines; ☎ 02/2010–4115 or 02/2011–1111).

BUS TRAVEL

A reasonable bus network provides quicker service than trains at somewhat higher prices (low by Western standards). Buses are often full. Reserve your seat in advance, especially on long-distance routes.

BUSINESS HOURS

Banks are open weekdays 8–5. Museums are usually open Tuesday–Sunday 10–5. Shops are generally open weekdays 9–6; some close for lunch between noon and 2. Many larger ones are also open Saturday and Sunday.

CAR TRAVEL

EMERGENCIES

Emergency road service offers help for stranded motorists.

➤ CONTACTS: **Emergency road service** (☎ 123).

GASOLINE

At about 120 Kč ($3.25) a gallon, gasoline is expensive. Look for service stations along main roads on the outskirts of towns and cities.

ROAD CONDITIONS

Main roads are usually good, if sometimes narrow. An expressway links Plzeň, Prague, Brno, and Bratislava. If you plan to do much exploring, pick up an *Auto Atlas,* available in bookstores and souvenir shops.

RULES OF THE ROAD

Drive on the right. Speed limits are 50 kph (31 mph) in urban areas, 90 kph (55 mph) on open roads, and 130 kph (81 mph) on expressways. Seat belts are compulsory everywhere; drinking and driving is strictly prohibited. A permit sticker is required to drive on expressways and other four-lane highways. It costs 800 Kč per year, 200 Kč per month, or 100 Kč for 10 days. They are sold at border crossings, post offices, and some service stations. A law that took effect in 2001 gives pedestrians the right of way at intersections, although it is catching on slowly.

CUSTOMS AND DUTIES

You may import duty-free 200 cigarettes, 50 cigars, 1 liter of spirits, 2 liters of wine, and gifts with a total value of 1,000 Kč. Goods worth up to 3,000 Kč (approximately US$90) are not liable for duty upon arrival. Declare items of greater value (jewelry, computers, and so on) on arrival to avoid problems with customs officials on departure. You may only export antiques that are certified as not of historical value. Reputable dealers will advise. Play safe, and also save your receipts.

DINING

Dining options include restaurants; the *vinárna* (wine cellar), which covers anything from inexpensive wine bars to swank restaurants; the more down-to-earth *pivnice* or *hospody* (beer taverns); cafeterias; and coffee shops and snack bars. Make reservations at all but the humblest places during high season. Privatization has brought more culinary variety, especially in Prague. Be wary of food bought from street vendors, as sanitary conditions may not be ideal.

Prague ham makes a favorite first course. The most typical main dish is roast pork (or duck or goose) with sauerkraut. Also try the outstanding trout, carp, and other freshwater fish. Crepes, here called *palačinky,* are ubiquitous and may come with savory or sweet fillings. Dumplings in various forms, generally with a rich gravy, accompany many dishes. A typical Czech breakfast is cold cuts and spreadable cheese or jam with rolls, washed down with coffee.

Prices are reasonable, even in some of the more expensive restaurants.

Prices are for one main course at dinner.

CATEGORY	COST
$$$$	over 360 Kč
$$$	230 Kč–360 Kč
$$	120 Kč–230 Kč
$	under 120 Kč

MEALTIMES
Lunch is usually from 11:30 to 2 or 3; dinner from 6 to 9:30 or 10. At places open all day, it's easier to get a table during off-hours.

RESERVATIONS AND DRESS
A jacket and tie are recommended for $$$$ and $$$ restaurants. Informal dress is appropriate elsewhere.

EMBASSIES

➤ AUSTRALIA: The Honorary Consulate and Trade Commission of Australia (✉ Na Ořechovce 38, ☎ 02/2431–0071 or 02/2431–0743).
➤ CANADA: (✉ Mickiewiczova 6, Hradčany, ☎ 02/7210–1800).
➤ IRELAND: (✉ Tržiště 13, ☎ 02/5753–0061).
➤ NEW ZEALAND: (consulate; ✉ Dykova 19, ☎ 02/5753–0061).
➤ SOUTH AFRICA: (✉ Ruska 65, Vršovice, ☎ 02/6731–1114).
➤ UNITED KINGDOM: (✉ Thunovská 14, Malá Strana, ☎ 02/5753–0278).
➤ UNITED STATES: (✉ Tržiště 15, Malá Strana, ☎ 02/5753–0663, WEB www.usis.cz).

HOLIDAYS

January 1; Easter Sunday and Monday; May 1 (Labor Day); May 8 (Liberation Day); July 5 (Sts. Cyril and Methodius); July 6 (Jan Hus); October 28 (Czech National Day); November 17 (Uprising of Student for Freedom and Democracy); December 24–26.

LANGUAGE

Czech, which belongs to the Slavic family of languages along with Russian, Polish, and Slovak, uses the Latin alphabet like English but adds special diacritical marks to make certain sounds: č is written for the "ch" sound, for instance. Unlike words in many other languages, Czech words are spelled phonetically, and the emphasis is almost always on the first syllable. You'll find a growing number of English-speakers, especially among young people and in the tourist industry. German is generally understood throughout the country.

LODGING

Accommodations in the Czech Republic range from hotels, motels, private lodgings, and hostels to campsites. Renovated older properties have great character and style. There is a shortage of reasonably affordable hotel rooms during the peak season, so make reservations well in advance. Private room agencies offer a variety of lodgings. The standards of facilities and services in the less expensive categories hardly match those in the West, so don't be surprised by faulty plumbing or indifferent reception clerks. Unless otherwise noted, rooms include bath.

Prices are for double rooms, generally including breakfast. Prices at the lower end of the scale apply to low season. Expect a 15%–25%

rate increase at certain periods, such as Christmas, New Year's, Easter, or during festivals.

CATEGORY	PRAGUE	OTHER AREAS
$$$$	over 5,300 Kč	over 2,600 Kč
$$$	2,700 Kč–5,300 Kč	1,300 Kč–2,600 Kč
$$	1,400 Kč–2,700 Kč	650 Kč–1,300 Kč
$	under 1,400 Kč	under 650 Kč

CAMPING

Maps showing the locations of the many campgrounds around the country are available at bookstores and tourist offices. Several campgrounds in Prague operate year-round; the Prague Information Service (PIS) has a list.

HOSTELS

IYH members can book reservations at any of 25-odd hostels across the country, including three in Prague (350 Kč and up, including breakfast), at KMC. IYH cards are also sold here (250 Kč) and at CKM Youth Travel Service.

In Prague most hostels are open to everyone and generally operate year-round. One of these is Hostel Estec. Ask at accommodation agencies about hostels outside Prague. Rates start at 300 Kč per person at hostels not affiliated with IYH.

➤ ORGANIZATIONS: **CKM Youth Travel Service** (✉ Mánesova 77, Prague 1, ☎ 02/2272–1595). **Hostel Estec** (✉ Vaníčkova 5, 160 00 Prague 6, ☎ 02/5721–0410 or 02/527344, FAX 02/5721–5263. **KMC** (✉ Karolíny Světlé 30, 160 00 Prague 6, ☎ 02/2222–0081, WEB www.kmc.cz/English.htm).

HOTELS

Hotels are officially graded with from one to five stars, using the international classification system. Outside Prague and the spa resorts, few hotels carry more than three stars. Bills can be paid in koruny. (Check to see if your hotel insists on hard currency; some hotels refuse to accept credit cards.) Breakfast is often included in the room price.

PRIVATE LODGINGS

Many travel agencies in Prague offer accommodation in private homes. Such rooms are invariably cheaper and often more comfortable than hotel rooms, though you may have to sacrifice some privacy. The largest room-finding service is probably AVE in the main and Holešovice train stations and at the airport (all branches are open daily). Insist on a room in the city center, however, or you may find yourself in a dreary, far-off suburb. Another helpful agency is City of Prague Accommodation Service. Elsewhere, look along main roads for signs that read ROOM FREE (room available) or, in German, ZIMMER FREI or PRIVATZIMMER. Offices of the travel bureau Čedok and the Prague Information Service (PIS) can also help you find private accommodations.

➤ CONTACTS: **AVE** (☎ 02/2422–3463). **City of Prague Accommodation Service** (✉ Haštalská 7, ☎ 02/2481–3022).

MAIL AND SHIPPING

POSTAL RATES

First-class (airmail) letters to the United States and Canada cost 13 Kč up to 20 grams, postcards 9 Kč. First-class (airmail) letters to the United Kingdom cost 9 Kč up to 20 grams, postcards 7 Kč.

RECEIVING MAIL

If you don't know where you'll be staying, American Express mail service is a great convenience, available at no charge to anyone holding an American Express credit card or carrying American Express traveler's checks. You can also have mail held *poste restante* (general delivery) at post offices in major towns, but the letters should be marked *Pošta 1,* to designate the city's main post office. The poste restante window is at the main post office in Prague. You will be asked for identification when you collect your mail.

➤ POST OFFICES: **American Express** (✉ Václavské náměstí 56 [Wenceslas Square]). **Main Post Office** (✉ Jindřišská ul. 14, Prague).

MONEY MATTERS

Costs are highest in Prague and only slightly lower in the main Bohemian resorts and spas, though even in these places you can now find inexpensive accommodations in private homes. The least expensive area is southern Moravia. Note that many public venues in Prague and the Czech Republic continue the odious practice of adhering to a separate pricing system for Czechs and for foreigners. (Foreigners may be charged double or more on museum admission, for example.)

Cup of coffee, 30 Kč; beer (½ liter), 16 Kč–30 Kč; Coca-Cola, 20 Kč; ham sandwich, 30 Kč; 1½-km (1-mi) taxi ride, 50 Kč–70 Kč; museum and castle admission, 20 Kč–300 Kč.

CURRENCY

The unit of currency in the Czech Republic is the crown, or koruna (plural koruny), written as Kč, and divided into 100 haléřů (hellers). There are bills of 50, 100, 200, 500, 1,000, and 5,000 koruny and coins of 10, 20, and 50 hellers and 1, 2, 5, 10, 20, and 50 koruny. At press time (summer 2001), the rate of exchange was 36.75 Kč to the U.S. dollar, 24.53 Kč to the Canadian dollar, 55.19 Kč to the pound sterling, 44.48 Kč to the Irish punt, 21.01 Kč to the Australian dollar, 16.62 Kč to the New Zealand dollar, and 4.86 Kč to the South African rand. Banks and ATMs give the best rates. Banks and private exchange outlets, which litter Prague's tourist routes, charge either a set fee or a percentage of the transaction or both. It's wise to compare. The koruna is fully convertible and can be purchased outside the country and changed into other currencies, but you should keep your receipts and convert your koruny before you leave the country just to be sure.

PASSPORTS AND VISAS

ENTERING THE CZECH REPUBLIC

United States, Canadian, and British citizens need only a valid passport to visit the Czech Republic as tourists. United States citizens may stay for 30 days without a visa; British and Canadian citizens, six months. Australians need tourist visas to enter the Czech Republic; the visa is less expensive if obtained at a Czech embassy or consulate outside the Czech Republic; at the Czech Republic border, it costs 1,600 Kč.

TELEPHONES

To use a public phone, buy a phone card at a newsstand or tobacconist. Cards cost 175 Kč for 50 units or 320 Kč for 100 units. CzechMate cards worth 500 or 750 Kč of telephoning—ideal for long-distance calls—are also sold at post offices. To place a call, lift the receiver, insert the card, and dial.

COUNTRY AND AREA CODES

The Czech Republic's country code is 420.

INTERNATIONAL CALLS

Some special international pay-phone booths in central Prague will take 5 Kč coins or accept phone cards that allow automatic dialing. You will also find coin and card booths at the main post office (✉ Jindřišská 14, near Václavské náměstí [Wenceslas Square]); the entrance for telephone service is in this building but around the corner on Politických vězňů. The international dialing code is 00. Dial 0132 for international inquiries to the United States, Canada, or the United Kingdom. Calls can be placed using AT&T USA Direct, MCI, and Sprint international operators. International rates vary according to destination.

➤ ACCESS CODES: **AT&T USA Direct** (☎ 0042–000101). **MCI** (☎ 0042–000112). **Sprint** (☎ 0042–087187).

LOCAL CALLS

Local calls cost one unit.

TIPPING

A service charge is rarely added to restaurant bills. Give a tip for good service directly to the waiter when you pay your bill. As a rule of thumb, round up to the next multiple of 10 (i.e., if the bill comes to 83 Kč, give the waiter 90 Kč). Give 10% on big or group tabs. For taxis, consider 10% a reasonable tip. In the better hotels doormen should get 20 Kč for each bag they carry to the check-in desk; bellhops get up to 40 Kč each for taking them up to your rooms. In $$ or $ hotels plan to lug your own baggage.

TRAIN TRAVEL

The country has an extensive rail network. Fares are relatively low and trains are crowded. You have to pay a small supplement on EuroCity (EC) and InterCity (IC) trains. Most long-distance trains have dining cars; overnight trains between main centers have sleeping cars.

TRANSPORTATION AROUND THE CZECH REPUBLIC

Traveling in the Czech Republic is relatively simple once you know the basic street-sign words: *ulice* (street), abbreviated to *ul.* (note that common usage often drops ulice in a printed address), *náměstí* (square), abbreviated to *nám.*, and *třída* (avenue). In most cases blue signs on buildings mark the street address.

VISITOR INFORMATION

Many towns have an information office ("Infocentrum") or private tourist bureau, often in the main square. The ubiquitous Čedok, now a private travel agency, has offices in all larger towns.

➤ TOURIST INFORMATION: **Čedok** (main office; ✉ Na Příkopě 18, 111 35 Prague 1, ☎ 02/2419–7111).

WHEN TO GO

Organized sight-seeing tours run from April or May through October (year-round in Prague). Some monuments, especially castles, either close entirely or curtail their hours in winter. Hotel rates may decrease in the off-season except during festivals. May, the month of fruit blossoms, is the time of the Prague Spring International Music Festival. Huge crowds clog Prague sites in spring, summer, and early fall.

CLIMATE

The following are the average daily maximum and minimum temperatures for Prague.

Jan.	36F	2C	**May**	66F	19C	**Sept.**	68F	20C
	25	– 4		46	8		50	10
Feb.	37F	3C	**June**	72F	22C	**Oct.**	55F	13C
	27	– 3		52	11		41	5
Mar.	46F	8C	**July**	75F	24C	**Nov.**	46F	8C
	32	0		55	13		36	2
Apr.	58F	14C	**Aug.**	73F	23C	**Dec.**	37F	3C
	39	4		55	13		28	– 2

PRAGUE

Poets, philosophers, and the Czech-in-the-street have long sung the praises of Praha (Prague), also referred to as the Golden City of a Hundred Spires. Like Rome, Prague is built on seven hills, which slope gently or tilt precipitously down to the Vltava (Moldau) River. The riverside location, enhanced by a series of graceful bridges, makes a great setting for two of the city's most notable features: its extravagant, fairy-tale architecture and its memorable music. Mozart claimed that no one understood him better than the citizens of Prague, and he was only one of several great masters who lived or lingered here.

It was under Karel IV (Charles IV), in the 14th century, that Prague first became the seat of the Holy Roman Empire—virtually the capital of Western Europe—and acquired its distinctive Gothic imprint. The medieval inheritance is still here under the overlays of graceful Renaissance and exuberant Baroque. Prague escaped serious wartime damage, but it didn't escape neglect. During the 1990s, however, artisans and their workers have restored dozens of the city's historic buildings with care and sensitivity.

Exploring Prague

Numbers in the margin correspond to points of interest on the Prague map.

Shades of the five medieval towns that combined to form Prague linger in the divisions of its historic districts. On the flat eastern shore of the Vltava River are three areas arranged like nesting boxes: **Josefov** (the old Jewish Quarter) within **Staré Město** (Old Town) bordered by **Nové Město** (New Town). **Malá Strana** (Lesser Quarter) and **Hradčany** (Castle District) perch along the river's hillier west bank. Spanning the Vltava is **Karlův most** (Charles Bridge), which links the Old Town to the Lesser Quarter; everything within the historic center can be reached on foot in a half hour or less from here.

Nové Město and Staré Město (New Town and Old Town)

New Town is over 500 years old, and only new when compared to Old Town, which dates back to the 12th century. Both neighborhoods have a mix of Renaissance, Baroque, and modern architecture. Old Town has the slight advantage in historic sites, with its world famous Astronomical Clock Tower and Old Town Square. New Town, with its store-packed Wenceslas Square and multiple department stores, has the lead in shopping. Almost every street in this area has a building or monument worth checking out.

11 **Betlémská kaple** (Bethlehem Chapel). The martyr and national hero Jan Hus thundered his reform teachings from the chapel pulpit during the early 15th century. The structure was rebuilt in the 1950s, but the little door through which Hus came to the pulpit is original, as are some of the inscriptions on the wall. ⊠ *Betlémské nám.* ⊙ *Apr.–Sept., daily 9–6; Oct.–Mar., daily 9–5.*

3 **Celetná ulice.** Medieval kings took this street on their way to their coronation at Prague Castle. The **Royal Route** continues past the Gothic spires of the Týn Church in Old Town Square; it then crosses Charles Bridge and goes up to the castle. Along the route stands every variety of Romanesque, Gothic, Renaissance, and Baroque architecture.

10 **Clam-Gallas palác** (Clam-Gallas Palace). Squatting on a constricted site in the heart of the Old Town, this pompous Baroque palace was de-

Prague (Praha)

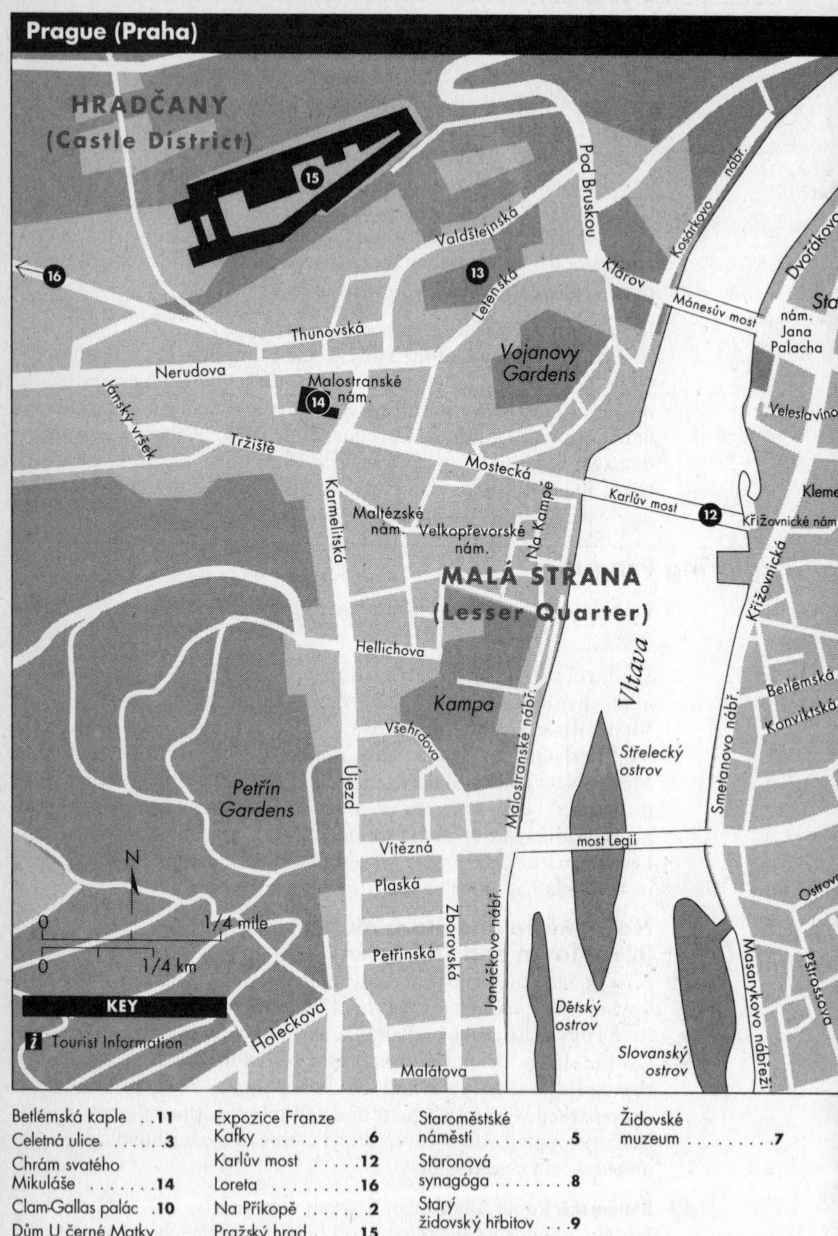

Betlémská kaple . . 11	Expozice Franze Kafky 6	Staroměstské náměstí 5	Židovské muzeum 7
Celetná ulice 3	Karlův most 12	Staronová synagóga 8	
Chrám svatého Mikuláše 14	Loreta 16	Starý židovský hřbitov . . . 9	
Clam-Gallas palác . 10	Na Příkopě 2	Václavské náměstí . . 1	
Dům U černé Matky Boží 4	Pražský hrad 15	Valdštejnská zahrada 13	

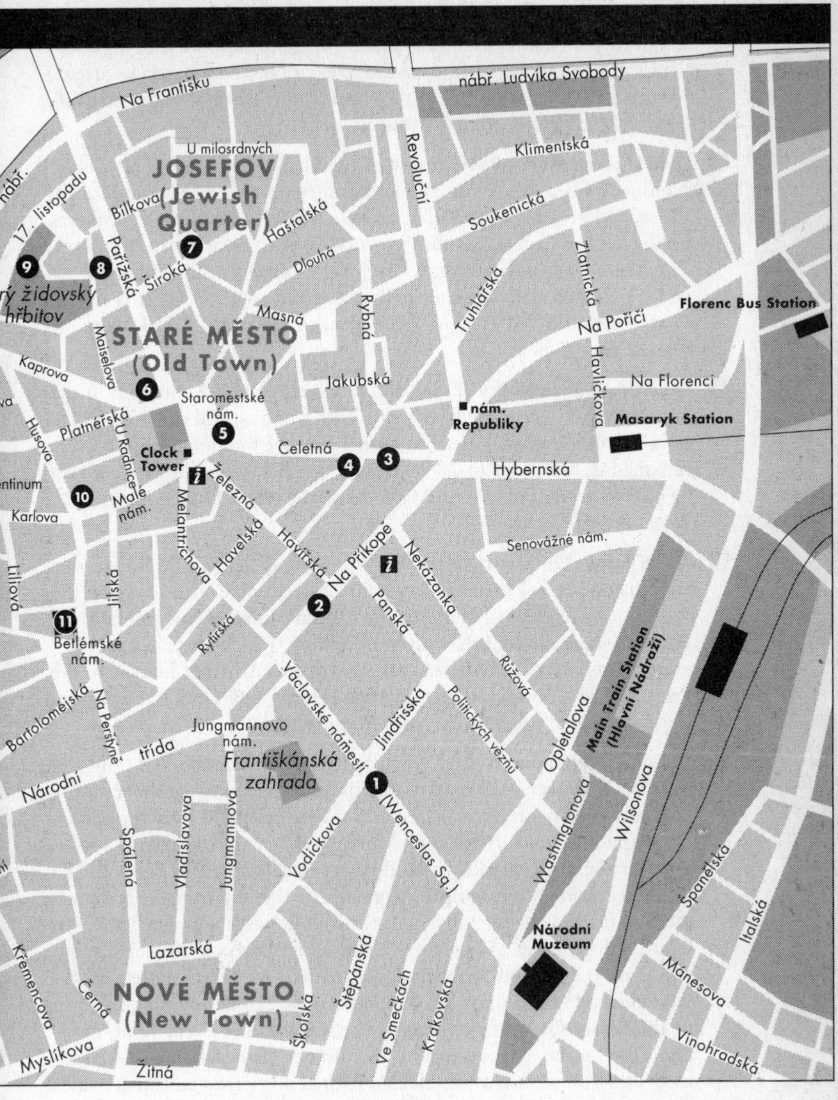
nábř. Ludvíka Svobody
Na Františku
U milosrdných
JOSEFOV (Jewish Quarter)
17. listopadu
Břílkova
Pařížská
Široká
Haštalská
Dlouhá
Masná
Revoluční
Klimentská
Soukenická
Truhlářská
Zlatnická
Rybná
starý židovský hřbitov
STARÉ MĚSTO (Old Town)
Maiselova
Kaprova
Jakubská
Staroměstské nám.
Na Poříčí
Havlíčkova
Na Florenci
Florenc Bus Station
Masaryk Station
nám. Republiky
Platnéřská
Husova
U Radnice
Clock Tower
Celetná
Hybernská
Karlova
Malé nám.
Melantrichova
Železná
Havelská
Havířská
Na Příkopě
Nekázanka
Senovážné nám.
Panská
Liliová
Jilská
Betlémské nám.
Rytířská
Václavské náměstí
Jindřišská
Politických vězňů
Růžová
Main Train Station (Hlavní Nádraží)
Bartolomějská
Na Perštýně
Jungmannovo nám.
třída
Národní
Františkánská zahrada
(Wenceslas Sq.)
Opletalova
Washingtonova
Wilsonova
Vodičkova
Spálená
Vladislavova
Jungmannova
Lazarská
Štěpánská
Ve Smečkách
Krakovská
Národní Muzeum
Španělská
Italská
Mánesova
Vinohradská
Křemencova
Černá
NOVÉ MĚSTO (New Town)
Školská
Myslíkova
Žitná

signed by the great Viennese architect J. B. Fischer von Erlach. All the sculptures, including the titans that struggle to support the two doorways, are the work of one of the great Bohemian Baroque artists, Matthias Braun. Peek inside at the superb staircase or attend an evening concert. ✉ *Husova 20,* WEB *www.ahmp.cz.*

❹ **Dům U černé Matky Boží** (House of the Black Madonna). This Cubist building adds a jolt to the architectural styles along Celetná ulice. In the second decade of the 20th century, several leading Czech architects boldly applied Cubism's radical reworking of visual space to structures. The Black Madonna, designed by Josef Gočár, is unflinchingly modern yet topped with an almost Baroque tile roof. ✉ *Celetná ul. (at Ovocný trh),* ☎ *2421–1732,* WEB *www.ecn.cz/cmvu/DCMB_a.htm.* ⌚ *Tues.–Sun. 10–6.*

❻ **Expozice Franze Kafky** (Franz Kafka's Birthplace). A museum in the house displays photos, editions of Kafka's books, and other memorabilia from the author's life. The corner that the building stands on was renamed in his honor in 2000. (Kafka's grave lies in the New Jewish Cemetery at the Želivského Metro stop.) ✉ *Nám. Franze Kafky 5.* ⌚ *Tues.–Fri. 10–6, Sat. 10–5.*

❷ **Na Příkopě.** Once part of the moat surrounding the Old Town, this street is now an elegant (in places) pedestrian mall. It leads from the bottom of Wenceslas Square to the **Obecní dům** (Municipal House), Prague's most lavish Art Nouveau building, which reopened in 1997 after a controversial two-year refurbishment. A bridge links it to the **Prašná brána** (Powder Tower), a 19th-century neo-Gothic restoration of the medieval original. ✉ *Nám. Republiky.*

★ ❺ **Staroměstské náměstí** (Old Town Square). The commercial center of the Old Town is now a remarkably harmonious hub—architecturally beautiful and relatively car-free and quiet. Looming over the center, the twin towers of **Kostel Panny Marie před Týnem** (Church of the Virgin Mary before Týn) look forbidding despite Disneyesque lighting. The large Secession-style **sculptural group** in the square's center commemorates the martyr Jan Hus, whose followers completed the Týn Church during the 15th century. The white Baroque **Kostel svatého Mikuláše** (Church of St. Nicholas) is tucked into the square's northwest angle. It was built by Kilian Ignatz Dientzenhofer, co-architect also of the Lesser Quarter's church of the same name. Every hour, mobs converge on the Astronomical Clock Tower of the **Staroměstská radnice** (Old Town Hall) as the clock's 15th-century mechanism activates a procession that includes the 12 Apostles. A skeleton figure of Death tolls the bell. ✉ *Pařížská, Dlouhá, Celetná, Železná, Melantrichova, and Kaprova.*

❽ **Staronová synagóga** (Old-New Synagogue). A small congregation still attends the little Gothic Old-New Synagogue, one of Europe's oldest surviving houses of Jewish prayer. Men are required to cover their heads upon entering; skull caps are sold for a small fee at the door. ✉ *Červená 3 at Pařížská.* ☎ *02/2481– 0099,* WEB *www.jewishmuseum.cz.* ⌚ *Sun.–Thurs. 9–5, Fri. 9–2.*

★ ❾ **Starý židovský hřbitov** (Old Jewish Cemetery). The crowded cemetery is part of **Josefov,** the former Jewish quarter, and is one of Europe's most unforgettable sights. Here, ancient tombstones lean into one another; below them, piled layer upon layer, are thousands of graves. Many gravestones—they date from the mid-14th to the late 18th centuries—are carved with symbols indicating the name, profession, and attributes of the deceased. If you visit the tomb of the 16th-century scholar Rabbi Löw, you may see scraps of paper covered with prayers or requests stuffed into the cracks. In legend, the rabbi protected Prague's Jews with the help of a *golem,* or artificial man; today he still receives appeals for assistance. ✉ *Entrance at Pinkas Synagogue, Široká 3.* ☏ *02/2481–0099,* WEB *www.jewishmuseum.cz.*

❶ **Václavské náměstí** (Wenceslas Square). In the Times Square of Prague hundreds of thousands voiced their disgust for the Communist regime in November 1989 at the outset of the "Velvet Revolution." The "square" is actually a broad boulevard that slopes down from the **Národní muzeum** (National Museum) and the equestrian **statue of St. Václav** (Wenceslas). ✉ *Between Wilsonova and jct. Na příkopě and 26 Října.*

❼ **Židovské muzeum** (Jewish Museum). The rich exhibits in Josefov's Pinkas Synagogue, Maisel Synagogue, Klaus Synagogue, Ceremonial Hall, and the newly renovated Spanish Synagogue, along with the Old Jewish Cemetery, make up the museum. Jews, forced to fulfill Adolf Hitler's plan to document the lives of the people he was trying to exterminate, gathered the collections. They include ceremonial objects, textiles, and displays covering the history of Bohemia's and Moravia's Jews. The interior of the Pinkas Synagogue is especially poignant, as it is painted with the names of 77,297 Jewish Czechs killed during World War II. Pinkas Synagogue also contains a permanent exhibition of drawings by children who were interned at the Terezín (Theresienstadt) concentration camp from 1942 to 1944. ✉ *Museum ticket offices: U starého hřbitova 3a and Široká 3.* ⏲ *Apr.–Oct., Sun.–Fri. 9–6; Nov.–Mar., Sun.–Fri. 9–4:30; closed Sat. and Jewish holidays. Old-New Synagogue closes 2–3 hrs early on Fri.*

Karlův Most and Malá Strana (Charles Bridge and the Lesser Quarter)

Many of the houses in the charmingly quaint Lesser Side have large signs above the door with symbols such as animals or religious figures. These date to the time before houses were numbered, when each house was referred to by name. Aristocrats built palaces here during the 17th century to be close to Prague Castle. Many of their private gardens have evolved into pleasant public parks with strutting peacocks. Some of the former palaces have become embassies, but increased security makes it hard to have more than a quick glance at the exterior.

⓮ **Chrám svatého Mikuláše** (Church of St. Nicholas). Designed by the late-17th-century Dientzenhofer architects, father and son, this is among the most beautiful examples of the Bohemian Baroque, an architectural style that flowered in Prague after the Counter-Reformation. On clear days you can enjoy great views from the tower. ✉ *Malostranské nám.* ⏲ *Sept.–May, daily 9–4; June–Aug., daily 9–6.*

★ ⓬ **Karlův most** (Charles Bridge). As you stand on this statue-lined stone bridge, unsurpassed in grace and setting, you see views of Prague that would be familiar to its 14th-century builder Peter Parler and to the artists who started adding the 30 sculptures in the 17th century. Today, nearly all the sculptures on the bridge are skillful copies of the originals, which have been taken indoors to be protected from the polluted air. The 12th on the left (starting from the Old Town side of the bridge) depicts St. Luitgarde (Matthias Braun sculpted the original, circa 1710). In the 14th on the left, a Turk guards suffering saints. (F. M. Brokoff sculpted the original, circa 1714.) The bridge itself is a gift to Prague from the Holy Roman emperor Charles IV. ✉ *Between Mostecká ul. on Malá Strana side and Karlova ul. on Old Town side.*

⓭ **Valdštejnská zahrada** (Wallenstein Gardens). This is one of the most elegant of the many sumptuous Lesser Quarter gardens. In the 1620s the Habsburgs' victorious commander, Czech nobleman Albrecht of Wallenstein, demolished a wide swath of existing structures in order to build his oversize palace with its charming walled garden. A covered outdoor stage of late-Renaissance style dominates the western end. ✉ *Entrance, Letenská 10.* ⏲ *May–Sept., daily 9–7.*

OFF THE BEATEN PATH

VILLA BERTRAMKA – While in Prague, Mozart liked to stay at the secluded estate of his friends the Dušeks. The house is now a small museum packed with Mozart memorabilia. From Karmelitská ulice in Malá Strana, take Tram 12 south to the Anděl Metro station; walk down Plzeňská ulice a few hundred yards, and take a left at Mozartova ulice. ✉ *Mozartova ul. 169, Smíchov,* ☎ *02/543893.* ⏲ *Daily 9:30–6.*

Pražský Hrad and Hradčany (Prague Castle and the Castle District)

No feature dominates the city more than Prague Castle, which, due to its hilltop location, can be seen from most of the city. The neighborhood in front of the castle once housed astronomers, alchemists, counts, and clergy hoping to obtain royal favors. Some of the palaces near the castle have become museums, others are used by government ministries. A large number of churches can be found here as well. Some offer tours, others can only be viewed after early-morning religious services.

16 **Loreta.** This Baroque church and shrine are named for the Italian town to which angels supposedly transported the Virgin Mary's house from Nazareth to save it from the infidel. The glory of its fabulous treasury is the monstrance *The Sun of Prague,* with its 6,222 diamonds. Arrive on the hour to hear the 27-bell carillon. ✉ *Loretánské nám. 7.* ⏲ *Tues.–Sun. 9–noon and 1–4:30.*

★ 15 **Pražský hrad** (Prague Castle). From its narrow hilltop, the monumental castle complex has witnessed the changing fortunes of the city for more than 1,000 years. The castle's physical and spiritual core, **Chrám svatého Víta** (St. Vitus Cathedral), took from 1344 to 1929 to build, so you can trace in its lines architectural styles from high Gothic to Art Nouveau. The eastern end, mostly the work of Peter Parler, builder of the Charles Bridge, is a triumph of Bohemian Gothic. "Good King" Wenceslas (in reality a mere prince, later canonized) has his own chapel in the south transept, dimly lit and decorated with fine medieval wall paintings. Note the fine 17th-century carved wooden panels on either side of the chancel. The left-hand panel shows a view of the castle and town in November 1620 as the defeated Czech Protestants flee into exile. The three easternmost chapels house tombs of Czech princes and kings of the 11th to the 13th centuries, although Charles IV and Rudolf II lie in the crypt, the former in a bizarre modern sarcophagus. On the southern facade of the cathedral, the 14th-century glass and quartz mosaic of the Last Judgment, long clouded over, has been restored to its original, brightly colored appearance.

Behind St. Vitus's, don't miss the miniature houses of **Zlatá ulička** (Golden Lane). Its name, and the apocryphal tale of how Holy Roman emperor Rudolf II used to lock up alchemists here until they transmuted lead into gold, may come from the gold-beaters who once lived here. Knightly tournaments often accompanied coronation ceremonies in the **Královský palác** (Royal Palace), next to the cathedral, hence the broad Riders' Staircase leading up to the grandiose Vladislavský sál (Vladislav Hall), with its splendid late-Gothic vaulting and Renaissance windows. Oldest of all the castle's buildings, though much restored, is the complex of **Bazilika svatého Jiří** (St. George's Basilica and Convent). The basilica's cool Romanesque lines hide behind a glowing salmon-color Baroque facade. The ex-convent houses a superb collection of Bohemian art from medieval religious sculptures to Baroque paintings. The castle **ramparts** afford glorious vistas of Prague's fabled hundred spires rising above the rooftops. ✉ *Approach via Nerudova, Staré zámecké schody, or Keplerova. Main castle ticket office in Second Courtyard,* ☎ *02/2437–3368,* WEB *www.hrad.cz/index_uk.html.* 🎫 *100 Kč; tickets valid 3 days; admits visitors to cathedral, Royal Palace, and St. George's Basilica (but not convent gallery), and Powder Tower.* ⏲ *Oct.–Mar., daily 9–4; Apr.–Sept., daily 9–5. Castle gardens Apr.–Oct., daily 9–5.*

Dining

Eating out is important to Prague residents; make reservations whenever possible. For details and price-category definitions, *see* Dining *in* Czech Republic A to Z, *above.*

$$$$ ✕ **Circle Line Brasserie.** Elegant yet decidedly unstuffy, this dining spot tucked into a restored Baroque palace in Malá Strana offers delicious nouvelle cuisine specialties. Appetizers and main courses may include hare terrine with sun-dried plums and apricots; roasted lamb sweetbreads with truffle sauce; and grilled veal ribs with mustard-seed sauce. A pianist plays unintrusively each evening; service is gracious and discreet. ✉ *Malostranské nám. 12, Malá Strana,* ☎ *02/5753–0021. Reservations essential. AE, DC, MC, V.*

$$$$ ✕ **Peklo.** This subterranean chamber beneath a former monastery was once a favorite drinking spot of the highly temperamental King Wenceslas IV. The old wine cellar has been replaced by a restaurant that serves meals such as fillet of devil's hoof and offers a good selection of Czech and French wines. The atmosphere is unbeatable and the service is attentive. ✉ *Strahovské nádvoří 1/132, Prague 1,* ☎ *02/2051–6652. AE, MC, V.*

$$$$ ✕ **U Zlaté Hrušky.** Careful restoration has returned this restaurant to its original 18th-century style. It specializes in Moravian wines, which are well matched with fillet steaks and goose liver. ✉ *Nový Svět 3, Hradčany,* ☎ *02/2051–5356. Reservations essential. AE, V.*

$$$$ ★ ✕ **Vinárna V Zátiší.** Impeccably gracious service and serene surroundings make an evening at the "Still Life" one of Prague's most memorable dining experiences. Continental cuisine is exquisitely prepared and presented—fish and game specialties are outstanding. The wine list is extensive, with special emphasis on French vintages. ✉ *Liliová 1, Staré Město,* ☎ *02/2222–1155. Reservations essential. AE, MC, V.*

$$$–$$$$ ★ ✕ **U Modré Kachničky.** The exuberant, eclectic decor is as attractive as the Czech and international dishes, which include steaks, duck, and game in autumn, and Bohemian trout and carp. ✉ *Nebovidská 6, Malá Strana,* ☎ *02/5732–0308. Dinner reservations essential. AE, V.*

$$$ ★ ✕ **Palffy palác.** The faded charm of an Old World palace makes this a lovely, romantic spot for a meal. Very good Continental cuisine is served with elegance that befits the surroundings. Try the potatoes au gratin or chicken stuffed with goat cheese. Surprisingly, brunches here are not worth the price. Dining is also possible on the terrace in summer. ✉ *Valdštejnská 14, Malá Strana,* ☎ *02/5731–2243. MC, V.*

$$$ ✕ **U Mecenáše.** This wine restaurant manages to be both medieval and elegant despite the presence of swords and battle axes. Try to get a table in the back room. The chef specializes in thick, juicy steaks served with a variety of sauces. ✉ *Malostranské nám. 10, Malá Strana,* ☎ *02/5753–1631. Reservations essential. AE, MC, V.*

$$ ✕ **Chez Marcel.** This authentic French bistro on a quiet, picturesque street offers a little taste of Paris in the center of Prague's Old Town. French owned and operated, Chez Marcel has an extensive menu suitable for lingering over a three-course meal (French cheeses, salads, pâtés, rabbit, and some of the best steaks in Prague) or just a quick espresso. ✉ *Haštalská 12, Staré Město,* ☎ *02/231–5676. No credit cards.*

$$ ✕ **Dynamo.** With a consistent clientele of beautiful people, this little green diner is one of the trendiest spots on what is fast becoming a veritable restaurant row. Dynamo's quirky menu offers tasty variations on Continental themes, such as liver and apples on toast, and succulent eggplant filled with grilled vegetables. ✉ *Pštrossova 221/29, Nové Město,* ☎ *02/294224. AE, MC, V.*

$$ ★ ✕ **Kavárna Slavia.** This legendary hangout for the best and brightest of the Czech arts world—from composer Bedřich Smetana and poet Jaroslav Seifert to then-dissident Václav Havel offers a spectacular view both inside and out. Its Art Deco decor is a perfect backdrop for people-watching, and the vistas (the river and Prague Castle or the National Theater) are a compelling reason to linger over an espresso. ✉ *Smetanovo nábřeží 1012/2, Nové Město,* ☎ *02/2422–0957. No credit cards.*

$$ ✕ **U Sedmi Švábů.** A medieval theme accents the truly old-fashioned Bohemian fare that includes millet pudding and mead. The less adventuresome can opt for the roast meat and poultry dishes. A special knight's feast requires 24 hours' advance notice. At the bottom of the stairs you can find a dungeon. ✉ *Janský vršek 14, Malá Strana, Prague 1,* ☎ *02/5753–1455.*

$–$$ ✕ **Novoměstský pivovar.** Always packed with out-of-towners and locals alike, this microbrewery-restaurant is a maze of rooms, some painted in mock-medieval style, others decorated with murals of Prague street scenes. Pork knee (*vepřové koleno*) is a favorite dish. The beer is the cloudy, fruity, fermented style exclusive to this venue. ✉ *Vodičkova 20, Prague 1,* ☎ *02/2223–2448. AE, MC, V.*

$ ✕ **Bohemia Bagel.** The casual, American-owned and child-friendly Bohemia Bagel serves a good assortment of fresh bagels from raisin-walnut to "supreme," with all kinds of spreads and toppings. The thick soups are among the best in Prague for the price, and the bottomless cups of coffee (from gourmet blends) are a further draw. ✉ *Újezd 16, Malá Strana,* ☎ *02/531002. No credit cards.*

$ ✕ **Česká hospoda v Krakovské.** Right off Wenceslas Square, this clean pub noted for its excellent traditional fare is the place to try Bohemian duck. Pair it with cold Krušovice beer. ✉ *Krakovská 20, Nové Město,* ☎ *02/2221–0204. No credit cards.*

$ ✕ **Country Life.** A godsend for Praguers and travelers, this health-food cafeteria offers a bounteous (and fresh) salad bar and daily rotating meat-free specials. The dining area has that rare Prague luxury for a low-end eating establishment: no blaring techno music. There's table service evenings after 6:30. It's off the courtyard connecting Melantrichova and Michalská streets. ✉ *Melantrichova 15, Staré Město,* ☎ *02/2421–3366. No credit cards. Closed Sat.*

$ ✕ **Pivovarský dům.** Beer made on the premises is the main attraction here. They make not only traditional Pilsner-style but also a rotating choice of coffee, cherry, or even eucalyptus beer. The menu offers well-made traditional pub fare such as *guláš* with dumplings. Peek at the vats behind the glass to see beer fermenting. ✉ *Lipová 20, Prague 2,* ☎ *02/9621–6666. No credit cards.*

$ ✕ **U Zlatého Tygra.** This crowded hangout is the last of a breed of authentic Czech pivnice. The smoke and stares preclude a long stay, but it's worth a visit for such pub staples as ham and cheese plates or roast pork. The service is surly, but the beer is good. ✉ *Husova 17, Staré Město,* ☎ *02/2422–9020. Reservations not accepted. No credit cards.*

Lodging

Many of Prague's older hotels have been renovated, and new establishments in old buildings ornament the Old Town and Lesser Quarter. Very few hotel rooms in the more desirable districts go for less than $100 per double room in high season; most less-expensive hotels are far from the center of Prague. Private rooms and pensions remain the best budget deal. For details and price-category definitions, *see* Lodging *in* Czech Republic A to Z, *above.*

$$$$ 🏨 **Diplomat.** Completed in 1990, the Diplomat fuses style with Western efficiency. A 10-minute taxi or subway ride from the Old Town, it's convenient to the airport. The hotel is modern and tasteful, with a huge, sunny lobby and comfortable rooms. ✉ *Evropská 15, 160 00 Prague 6,* ☎ *02/2439–4111,* FAX *02/2439–4215,* WEB *www.diplomat-hotel.cz. 369 rooms, 13 suites. 2 restaurants. AE, DC, MC, V.*

$$$$ ★ 🏨 **Dům U Červeného Lva.** In Malá Strana, a five-minute walk from Prague Castle's front gates, the Baroque House at the Red Lion is an intimate, immaculately kept hotel. The spare but comfortable guest rooms have parquet floors, 17th-century painted-beam ceilings, superb antiques, and all-white bathrooms with brass fixtures. The two top-floor rooms can double as a suite. There is no elevator, and stairs are steep. ✉ *Nerudova 41, 118 00 Prague 1,* ☎ *02/537–239 or 02/538–192,* FAX *02/538–193. 8 rooms. 2 restaurants. AE, DC, MC, V.*

$$$$ ★ 🏨 **Hoffmeister.** On a picturesque (if a bit busy) corner near the Malostranská Metro station, this is one of the most stylish small hotels in the city. Rooms have finely crafted wood built-ins and luxuriously appointed bathrooms. Museum-quality prints by the proprietor's father hang throughout the hotel. ✉ *Pod Bruskou 7, 118 00 Prague 1,* ☎ *02/5101–7111,* FAX *02/5101–7120,* WEB *www.hoffmeister.cz. 38 rooms. Restaurant. AE, DC, MC, V.*

$$$$ 🏨 **Kampa.** An early Baroque armory turned hotel, the Kampa is tucked away in a residential corner of the Lesser Quarter. The rooms are clean, if spare, but the bucolic setting one block from the river as well as a lovely park compensate for its relative remoteness. ✉ *Všehrdova 16, 118 00 Prague 1,* ☎ *02/5732–0508 or 02/732–0404,* FAX *02/5732–0262. 84 rooms. Restaurant. AE, DC, MC, V.*

$$$$ ★ 🏨 **Palace Praha.** The Art Nouveau–style Palace is Prague's most elegant and luxurious hotel, though it now faces competition from other luxury hotels. Rooms have high ceilings, marble baths with phones, and minibars with complimentary snacks and beverages. Its central location just off Wenceslas Square offers more convenience than local character. ✉ *Panská 12, 110 00 Prague 1,* ☎ *02/2409–3111,* FAX *02/2422–1240,* WEB *www.palacehotel.cz. 125 rooms. Restaurant. AE, DC, MC, V.*

$$$ 🏨 **Hotel U staré paní.** "The Old Lady" is a delightfully cozy hotel only a five-minute walk from Old Town Square, in a renovated building on one of Prague's most atmospheric Old Town lanes. Comfortable rooms are decorated in soft tones with simple Scandinavian-style furnishings. One of Prague's best jazz clubs has concerts nightly here in the basement. (Yes, it is soundproofed.) ✉ *Michalská 9, 110 00 Prague 1,* ☎ *02/267267, 02/264920, or 02/261655,* FAX *02/267–9841, 02/267267, or 02/264920. 18 rooms. Restaurant. AE, MC, V.*

$$$ 🏨 **Opera.** Once the lodging of choice for divas performing at the nearby State Theater, the Opera greatly declined under the Communists. The mid-'90s saw the grand fin-de-siècle facade rejuvenated with a perky pink-and-white paint job and the installation of bathrooms and TVs in all rooms. Comfy wing chairs add to the rooms, which are decorated in tan and white. ✉ *Těšnov 13, 110 00 Prague 1,* ☎ *02/231–*

5609, FAX 02/231–1477, WEB www.hotel-opera.cz. 64 rooms, plus 4 suites. Restaurant, bar. AE, DC, MC, V.

$$ **Balkán.** The hotel is a spiffy yellow building on an otherwise drab street not far from the Lesser Quarter. Rooms are small, simple, clean: white spreads and walls, tan paneling, lacy curtains. Request a room at the back, as the hotel is on a major street, one block from the tram stop. ✉ *Svornosti 28, 150 00 Prague 5,* ☎ FAX *02/5732–7180. 24 rooms. Breakfast not included. Restaurant. AE.*

$$ **Central.** Quite conveniently, this hotel lives up to its name, with a site near Celetná ulice and Náměstí Republiky. Rooms are sparely furnished, but all have baths. The Baroque glories of the Old Town are steps away. ✉ *Rybná 8, 110 00 Prague 1,* ☎ *02/2481–2041,* FAX *02/232–8404. 62 rooms, 4 suites. Restaurant, bar. AE, MC, V.*

$ **Pension Unitas.** Operated by the Christian charity Unitas in an Old Town convent, this well-run establishment has sparely furnished rooms, all of which are no-smoking. Note that an adjacent 3-star hotel, Cloister Inn, shares the same address and phone number. ✉ *Bartolomějská 9, 110 00 Prague 1,* ☎ *02/232–7700,* FAX *02/232–7709. 34 rooms without bath. Reserve well in advance, even for off-season. Restaurant. No credit cards.*

$ **Penzion Sprint.** Basic, clean, no-frills rooms, most of which have their own tiny bathrooms, make the Sprint a fine budget choice. The rustic-looking pension is on a quiet residential street in the outskirts of Prague about 20 minutes from the airport; tram 18 rumbles directly to Old Town. ✉ *Cukrovarnická 64, 160 00 Prague 6,* ☎ *02/312–3338,* FAX *02/3335–1837,* WEB *web.telecom.cz/penzionsprint. 21 rooms. AE, MC, V.*

Nightlife and the Arts

The Arts

Prague's cultural life is one of its top attractions—and its citizens like to dress up and participate; performances can be booked far ahead. Monthly programs of events are available at the PIS, Čedok, or hotels. The English-language newspaper *Prague Post* carries detailed entertainment listings. The main ticket agency for classical music is **Bohemia Ticket International** (✉ Na Příkopě 16, ☎ 02/2421–5031). **Ticketpro** (✉ Salvátorská 10, ☎ 02/2481–4020, FAX 02/2481–4021) sells tickets for most rock and jazz events, as well as theatrical performances and some tours. For major concerts, opera, and theater, it's much cheaper to buy tickets at the box office.

CONCERTS

Performances are held in many palaces and churches. Too often, programs lack originality (how many different ensembles can play the *Four Seasons* at once?), but the settings are lovely and the acoustics can be superb. Concerts at the **churches of St. Nicholas** in both the Old Town Square and the Lesser Quarter are especially enjoyable. At **St. James's Church** on Malá Štupartská (Old Town) cantatas are performed amid a flourish of Baroque statuary.

The excellent Czech Philharmonic plays in the intimate, lavish Dvořák Hall in the **Rudolfinum** (✉ Nám. Jana Palacha, ☎ 02/2489–3111). The lush home of the Prague Symphony, **Smetana Hall,** reopened in 1997 along with the rest of the Obecní dům building (✉ Nám. Republiky 5, ☎ 02/2200–2100 or 02/2200–2101).

OPERA AND BALLET

Opera is of an especially high standard in the Czech Republic. One of the main venues in the grand style of the 19th century is the beautifully restored **Národní divadlo** (National Theater: ✉ Národní třída 2,

☏ 02/2490–1448). The **Statni opera Praha** (State Opera of Prague: ✉ Wilsonova 4, ☏ 02/265353), formerly the Smetana Theater, is another historic site for opera lovers. The **Stavovské divadlo** (Estates Theater: ✉ Ovocný trh 1, ☏ 02/2421–5001) hosts opera, ballet, and theater performances by the National Theater ensembles. Mozart conducted the premiere of *Don Giovanni* here.

PUPPET SHOWS

This traditional form of Czech entertainment, generally adaptations of operas performed to recorded music, has been given new life at the **Národní divadlo marionet** (National Marionette Theater: ✉ Žatecká 1, ☏ 02/232–3429).

THEATER

A dozen or so professional companies play in Prague to packed houses. Nonverbal theater abounds as well, notably "black theater," a melding of live acting, mime, video, and stage trickery that, despite signs of fatigue, continues to draw crowds. The popular **Archa Theater** (✉ Na Poříčí 26, ☏ 02/232–8800) offers avant-garde and experimental theater, music, and dance and hosts world-class visiting ensembles, including the Royal Shakespeare Company. **Laterna Magika** (Magic Lantern; ✉ Národní třída 4, ☏ 02/2491–4129) is one of the more established producers of black-theater extravaganzas.

Nightlife

DISCOS AND CABARET

Discos catering to a young crowd blast sound onto lower Wenceslas Square. The newest dance music plays at the ever-popular **Radost FX** (✉ Bělehradská 120, Prague 2, ☏ 02/251210).

Four clubs in one can be found at the renovated spa building near the Charles Bridge **Karlový lázně** (✉ Novotného lávka), which has several live acts or DJs nightly and a café with Internet access in the daytime.

JAZZ AND ROCK CLUBS

Jazz clubs are a Prague institution, although foreign customers keep them in business. Excellent Czech groups play the tiny **AghaRTA** (✉ Krakovská 5, ☏ 02/2221–1275); arrive well before the 9 PM show time to get a seat with a sight line. Top jazz groups (and the odd world-music touring ensemble) play **Jazz Club U staré paní** (✉ Michalská 9, ☏ 02/264920) in Old Town. **Malostranská Beseda** (✉ Malostranské nám. 21, ☏ 02/5753–2092) is a funky hall for rock, jazz, and folk. At **Palác Akropolis** (✉ Kubelíkova 27, ☏ 02/2271–2287) you can hear world music, well-known folk, rock, and jazz acts, plus DJs. **Reduta** (✉ Národní třída 20, ☏ 02/2491–2246), the city's best-known jazz club for three decades, stars mostly local talent. Hip locals congregate at **Roxy** (✉ Dlouhá 33, ☏ 02/2481–0951) for everything from punk to funk to New Age tunes.

Shopping

Many of the main shops are in and around Old Town Square and Na Příkopě, as well as along Celetná ulice and Pařížská. On the Lesser Quarter side, Nerudova has the densest concentration of shops.

Department Stores

The biggest downtown department store is **Kotva** (✉ Nám. Republiky 8), which grows flashier and more expensive every year. **Bílá Labut'** (✉ Na Poříčí 23) is a good-value option. The basement supermarket at **Tesco** (✉ Národní třída 26) is the best and biggest in the center of the city.

Specialty Shops

Shops specializing in Bohemian crystal, porcelain, ceramics, and antiques abound in Old Town and Malá Strana and on Golden Lane at Prague Castle. Look for the name **Dílo** (✉ Staroměstské nám. 15, Old Town; ✉ U Lužického semináře 14, Malá Strana) for glass and ceramic sculptures, prints, and paintings by local artists. **Lidová Řemesla** (✉ Jilská 22, Old Town; ✉ Mostecká 17, Malá Strana) shops stock wooden toys, elegant blue-and-white textiles, and charming Christmas ornaments made from straw or pastry. **Moser** (✉ Na Příkopě 12, ☎ 02/2421–1293) is the source for glass and porcelain.

Side Trips

The castle and spa region of Bohemia and the history-drenched villages of Moravia make excellent (and convenient) excursions from Prague. Buses or trains link the capital with every corner of the Bohemian region; transportation to towns in Moravia takes longer (three hours or more from the capital) but is also dependable.

Bohemia's Spas and Castles

The Bohemian countryside is a restful world of gentle hills and thick woods. It is especially beautiful during fall foliage season or in May, when the fruit trees that line the roads are in blossom. Two of the most famous of the Czech Republic's scores of spas lie in such settings: Karlovy Vary (Karlsbad) and Mariánské Lázně (Marienbad). During the 19th and early 20th centuries, European royalty and aristocrats came to ease their overindulged bodies (or indulge them even more) at these spas.

South Bohemia, a country of lonely castles, green hills, and quiet fish ponds, is sprinkled with exquisite medieval towns, many of them undergoing much-needed rehabilitation. In such towns as Tábor, the Hussite reformist movement was born during the early 15th century, sparking a series of religious conflicts that engulfed all of Europe. Countering the Hussites from Český Krumlov was the powerful Rožmberk family, who scattered castles over the countryside and created lake-size "ponds" in which to breed highly prized carp, still the focus of a Czech Christmas dinner.

Praguers love to spend weekends in the **Berounka Valley,** where two magnificent castles rise up over the river.

Karlštejn, less than an hour from Prague off Route E50 (direction Beroun), is an admirable restoration of the 14th-century castle built by Charles IV. It was built to protect the crown jewels of the Holy Roman Empire. The castle itself underwent a few months of renovation in 2001. Decades of renovation work on the main tower's Chapel of the Holy Rood, with its walls covered with gold leaf and semi-precious stones, have also finally been completed. Reservations must be made in advance to see the chapel. ✉ *Karlštejn,* ☎ *0311/681617.* ⏲ *Nov.–Mar., Tues.–Sun. 9–3; Apr. and Oct., Tues.–Sun. 9–4; May–June and Sept., Tues.–Sun. 9–5; July–Aug., Tues.–Sun. 9–6.*

The main attractions of **Křivoklát** are its glorious woodlands, a favorite royal hunting ground in times past. The castle is about an hour from Prague. ✉ *Křivoklát,* ☎ *0313/558440.* ⏲ *Apr.–May and Sept.–Dec., Tues.–Sun. 9–4; June–Aug., Tues.–Sun. 9–6.*

★ About two hours from Prague by car on route E48, **Karlovy Vary,** or Karlsbad, was named for the Holy Roman emperor Charles IV. While he was in pursuit of a deer during a hunt, the animal supposedly led him to the main spring of Vřídlo. Over the years the spa attracted not only many of the crowned heads and much of the blue blood of Europe but

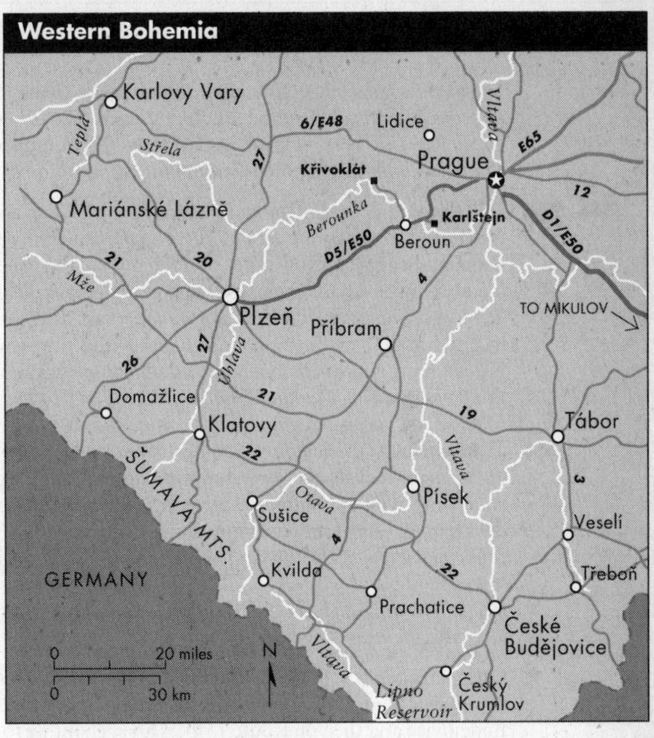

also leading musicians and writers. Its confident bourgeois architecture nestles in a deep, forested valley; the meandering Teplá River divides the town down the middle. The elegant, old spa part of town is lined with fanciful turn-of-the-20th-century buildings in soft colors. Four colonnades (free-standing covered pedestrian walkways), one of wrought iron, one of carved wood, one of stone, and one of steel and glass, allow leisurely strolling and sipping of mineral waters. The waters from the spa's 12 springs are uniformly foul-tasting: sip them while nibbling rich Karlovy Vary *oplatky* (wafers), and then resort to the "13th spring," Karlovy Vary's tangy herbal liqueur known as Becherovka.

$$$$ 🏨 **Dvořák.** Opened in 1991, this Austrian-built hotel in the center of town has imaginative decor, with whimsical white furniture, pale peach walls, and lacy curtains. The view from the front rooms looks out onto the Teplá River and rose gardens in season. The staff is cheerful and utterly professional. ✉ *Nová louka 11, 360 21,* ☎ *017/322–4145,* FAX *017/322–2814,* WEB *www.hotel-dvorak.cz. 76 rooms, 3 suites. Restaurant. AE, DC, MC, V.*

$$$–$$$$ ★ 🏨 **Grandhotel Pupp.** Founded in 1701, the Pupp still has a fine 18th-century hall, the Slavnostní sál. It's one of the oldest surviving hotels in Europe, with glittering names—past and present—in its guest register. For more elegance, request a room furnished in 19th-century period style; other rooms were redecorated in a functional way under communism. ✉ *Mírové nám. 2, 360 91,* ☎ *017/310–9111,* FAX *017/322–4032,* WEB *www.pupp.cz. 220 rooms. 2 restaurants. AE, DC, MC, V.*

$$–$$$ 🏨 **Thermal.** This unappealing 1970s gray high-rise is solidly anchored at one end of Karlovy Vary's colonnade. Its rooms are not special but the balconies of all front-facing rooms afford a magical view over the entire colonnade and the rolling hills of the town. The Thermal's heated outdoor pool, built into a hillside and open year-round, allows similar gorgeous vistas. ✉ *I. P. Pavlova 11, 360 00 Karlovy Vary,* ☎

017/321–1111, FAX *017/322–6992,* WEB *www.hotel.cz/thermal. 145 rooms. 2 restaurants, pool. AE, DC, MC, V.*

The sanatoriums and colonnades of **Mariánské Lázně** (Marienbad) are impressively arrayed around an oblong park. The town has one of the Czech Republic's best golf courses and hosts a PGA European Tour event. The resort is about three hours from Prague, on Route 21 off Route E50.

$$$–$$$$ **Palace.** Built during the spa's heyday in 1875, this elegant five-story building is in the resort center. Turrets sprout at the top of the bright white-and-canary-yellow hotel, and the myriad balconies have swirling metal railings. Chandeliers and gold-color plating glisten in the public rooms. The comfortable guest rooms are less ostentatious, decorated in peach tones, with simple light fixtures and fluted white furniture. No-smoking rooms are available, as are complete spa services on-site. ✉ *Hlavní třída 67, Mariánské Lázně, 353 01,* ☎ *0165/622222,* FAX *0165/624262. 40 rooms, 5 suites. Restaurant, spa. AE, DC, MC, V.*

$$$ **Bohemia.** At this lemon-yellow spa resort beautiful crystal chandeliers in the main hall set the stage for a comfortable and elegant stay. The rooms are well appointed in soothing pale tones. To be really decadent request one of the enormous suites overlooking the park. The staff can arrange spa treatments and horseback riding. Rates are significantly lower in fall and winter. ✉ *Hlavní třída 100, Mariánské Lázně, 353 01,* ☎ *0165/623251,* FAX *0165/622943. 62 rooms, 4 suites. Restaurant. AE, MC, V.*

★ Once the main seat of the Rožmberks, Bohemia's noblest family, **Český Krumlov,** about four hours south of Prague (on Route E55 to České Budějovice and then on Route 159), is an enchanting town with its imposing Renaissance **Hrad** (castle; ☎ 0337/711465, WEB www.ckrumlov.cz/uk/i_index.htm), complete with romantic elevated walkways; a round, pastel-hued tower; and an 18th-century theater that still hosts performances. The castle is open April and October, Tuesday–Sunday 9–4; May–August, Tuesday–Sunday 8–5; and September, Tuesday–Sunday 9–5. The Vltava River snakes through the town, which has steeply stacked steps on either bank linking various levels and twisting narrow lanes that converge on **Náměstí Svornosti,** the Old Town's main square. A number of notable Renaissance houses add an air of formality to this exquisite place. The **Mezinárodní kulturní centrum Egona Schieleho** (Egon Schiele Center) exhibits the work of the painter, a frequent visitor to the town, and other 20th-century artists. ✉ *Široká 70–72, Český Krumlov,* ☎ *0337/704–011.* *100 Kč.* ⏲ *Daily 10–6 (inquire locally about winter closures).*

$$$$ **Růže.** The stone exterior clearly shows its Renaissance monastery past, but the lobby is modern. Most of the (smallish) rooms were modernized in the '70s with violet as the color of choice; they have tiny Gothic windows. ✉ *Horní ul. 153, Český Krumlov, 381 01,* ☎ *0337/711141,* FAX *0337/711128. 71 rooms. Restaurant. AE, MC, V.*

$$ ★ **Na louži.** Wooden shutters on the street level set the old but cared-for atmosphere of this friendly pub-restaurant and the five immaculate small rooms upstairs, which are furnished with cozy country-style beds and wardrobes. ✉ *Kájovská 66, Český Krumlov, 381 01,* ☎ FAX *0337/711280,* WEB *www.ck.ipex.cz/hotlouze/en. 7 rooms. Restaurant. No credit cards.*

After Jan Hus's death at the stake in 1415, his proto-Protestant followers established an egalitarian commune on a fortified bluff above the Lužnice River. Jan Žižka, a one-eyed general, led the zealots of **Tábor** (1½ hrs from Prague on Route E55) and shaped them into Europe's most-feared army. The town itself became a weapon of defense: its twisting streets were designed to confuse the enemy. A labyrinth of tunnels and cellars below the town served as both living quarters and link with the outer defenses. The story is told in the **Husitské muzeum** (Hussite Museum). ✉ *Křivkova 31, Tábor.* ⏲ *Apr.–Nov., daily 8:30–4; Dec.–Mar. on request.*

Moravian Towns

Moravia, with its peaceful villages and small towns three to four hours southeast of Prague, is the easternmost of the historic Czech Lands, sharing a lightly populated border with Bohemia.

A former center of Jewish life and learning in the Habsburg Empire, **Mikulov** (about 4 hrs southeast of Prague on Route 620 off E55) now bears few traces of its scholarly past. Today the town is known for its wine making. During the grape harvest in October, head for the limestone hills surrounding the town—tradition dictates that a knock on the door of a private *sklípek* (wine cellar) will lead to a tasting session. The town's Baroque-and-Gothic **Zámek Mikulov** (château) contains a wine-making museum where you can see a 22,000-gallon wine cask from 1643. ☎ *0625/2255.* ⏲ *Apr.–Oct., Tues.–Sun. 9–4.*

$$$ **Rohatý Krokodýl.** This classic hotel ("The Horned Crocodile") is perfectly in keeping with the town's look in that it is a long, low white building on a street that dates back to the Renaissance. Furnishings are simple, modern, and immaculate. The restaurant is outstanding. ✉ *Husova 8, Mikulov, 692 01,* ☎ *0625/510692,* FAX *0625/522695,* WEB *www.rohatykrokodyl.cz. 14 rooms. Restaurant. AE, MC, V.*

Amid the farmlands and industrial centers of middle Moravia, **Olomouc,** three hours from Prague on Route 462 off E50, comes as an unexpected joy. The city retains its rambling Old Town, partially circled by high brick fortifications. The Renaissance town hall and the tall, impossibly ornate Trinity column compete for attention on **Horní náměstí,** the main square. At the eastern end of the Old Town are the neo-Gothic **Dóm svatého Václava** (Cathedral of St. Wenceslas; ✉ Václavskenám., Olomouc), one of the glories of Moravia, and a ruined 12th-century **palace** (✉ Dómská ul., Olomouc) with an exquisite row of Romanesque stone windows.

$$$ **Hotel U Dómu.** This cozy, well-cared-for establishment run by the Jiříček family is steps from the cathedral. Spacious rooms (all including kitchenettes and large bathrooms) are furnished with simple, Scandinavian-style furniture, pastel carpeting, and white walls; tasteful, original watercolors decorating the rooms are by local artists. Service is friendly and obliging. ✉ *Dómská 4, Olomouc, 772 00,* ☎ *068/522–0502,* FAX *068/522–0501. 6 rooms. Kitchenettes, bar, café. AE, MC, V.*

It is a surprise to come upon trim little **Telč,** with its neat, formal architecture, nestled in such bucolic countryside on Route 406 (E50 and 19). Only the Renaissance facades, each fronted by arcades and topped with rich gables, are visible, and although these are colorful, cute, and well maintained, often the buildings behind them are falling apart. The Renaissance theme carries over to the **Zámek Telč** (château), whose architecture and decoration form a rare pre-Baroque example of stylistic unity. ☎ *066/962821.* ⏲ *Apr.–Oct., Tues.–Sun. 9–4.*

Prague Essentials

AIRPORTS AND TRANSFERS

All international flights arrive at Prague's Ruzyně Airport, about 20 km (12 mi) from downtown.

➤ AIRPORT INFORMATION: **Ruzyně Airport,** ☎ 02/367760 or 02/2011–3314.

TRANSFERS

The private Cedaz minibus shuttle links the airport and Náměstí Republiky. Shuttles run every 30–60 minutes between 5:30 AM and 9 PM daily. The trip costs 90 Kč one-way and takes about 30 minutes. On regular Bus 119 the cost is 12 Kč, but you'll need to change to the subway at the Dejvická station to reach the center. By taxi, expect to pay 600 Kč to the center. Only one city-authorized firm, FIX, is permitted to pick up customers at the airport. (You may take any taxi *to* the airport, however.)

BUS TRAVEL TO AND FROM PRAGUE

The Czech bus network (ČSAD) operates from a station near Prague's main train station. Take Metro B or C to the Florenc stop.

➤ BUS INFORMATION: **ČSAD** (✉ Křižíkova 4, ☎ 02/121999).

BUS AND TRAM TRAVEL WITHIN PRAGUE

Trams are often more convenient than the Metro for short hops. Most bus lines connect outlying suburbs with the nearest Metro station. Trams 50–59 and buses numbered 500 and above run all night—at, however, intervals of up to an hour—after the Metro stops.

CAR TRAVEL

In the center of the city, meters with green stripes let you park up to six hours; an orange stripe indicates a two-hour limit. Blue-marked spaces are reserved for local residents. (Parking boots may be attached to offending vehicles.) There is an underground parking lot near Old Town Square.

➤ PARKING: **Underground parking lot** (✉ Alšovo nábřeží).

EMERGENCIES

Be prepared to pay in cash for medical treatment, whether you are insured or not. The Lékárna U Andělais 24-hour pharmacy is near the Anděl metro station, and the Lékárna Palackého 24-hour pharmacy is located downtown.

➤ EMERGENCY SERVICES: **Police** (☎ 158). **Ambulance** (☎ 155).

➤ HOSPITALS: **Foreigners' Department of Na Homolce Hospital** (☎ 02/5727–2146 and 02/5727–1111 weekdays; 02/5292–2403 and 02/807756 evenings and weekends). **American Medical Center** (☎ 02/807756; 02/807757; 02/807758 weekdays).

➤ 24-HOUR PHARMACIES: **Lékárna U Anděla** (✉ Štefánikova 6, Prague 1, ☎ 02/537039). **Lékárna Palackého** (✉ Palackého 5, Prague 1, ☎ 02/2494–6982).

ENGLISH-LANGUAGE MEDIA

The Knihkupectví U černé Matky Boží is good for hiking maps and atlases; go downstairs).

➤ BOOKSTORES: **Anagram Bookshop** (✉ Týn 4, Prague 1). **Big Ben Bookshop** (✉ Malá Štupartská 5, Prague 1). **Globe Bookstore and Coffeehouse** (✉ Pštrossova 6, Prague 1). **Knihkupectví U černé Matky Boží** (✉ Celetná ul. 34 at Ovocný trh, Prague 1. **U Knihomola** (✉ Mánesova 79, Prague 2).

SUBWAY TRAVEL

Prague's three modern Metro lines are easy to use and relatively safe. They provide the simplest and fastest means of transportation, and most new maps of Prague mark the routes. The Metro runs from 5 AM to midnight, seven days a week.

TAXIS

Regulations have set taxi rates at 25 Kč initial fee and 17 Kč per kilometer plus 4 Kč per minute waiting time. Drivers must also display a small license, although this has not stopped fare-related problems. It is still advisable to order a taxi in advance by telephone. Try AAA for quick, reliable service. Profitaxi is also fast and efficient. Some larger hotels have their own fleets, which are a little more expensive.

Note: Do not pick up cabs waiting at taxi stands in the tourist areas: many of these drivers have doctored their meters and have other tricks to rip you off.

➤ TAXI COMPANIES: **AAA** (☎ 02/14014). **Profitaxi** (☎ 02/14035).

TOURS

BUS TOURS

Čedok offers a daily three-hour tour of the city, starting at 10 AM from two offices. Martin-Tour offers a tour departing from Náměstí Republiky and three other Old Town points four times daily. PIS arranges guided tours at its Na Příkopě and Old Town Square locations.

Čedok's one-day tours out of Prague include excursions to the lovely medieval town of Kutná Hora, the unusual sandstone formations of the "Bohemian Paradise" region, famous spa towns and castles, wineries, and the Terezín ghetto.

➤ FEES & SCHEDULES: **Čedok** (✉ Na Příkopě 18; ✉ Pařížská 6, ☎ 02/2419–7111). **Martin-Tour** (☎ 02/7122–2227). **PIS** (☎ 02/2448–2569).

PRIVATE GUIDES

Contact Čedok or PIS to arrange a personal walking tour of the city. Prices start at around 400 Kč per hour.

SPECIAL-INTEREST TOURS

For cultural tours call Čedok. These include visits to the Jewish quarter, performances of folk troupes, Laterna Magika, opera, and concerts.

TRAIN TRAVEL

The main station is Hlavní Nádraží, not far from Wenceslas Square. Some international trains use Nádraží Holešovice, on the same Metro line (C) as the main station.

➤ TRAIN INFORMATION: **Hlavní Nádraží** (✉ Wilsonova ul.). **Nádraží Holešovice** (✉ Vrbenského ul.). **Domestic and international schedules** (for both stations; ☎ 02/2422–4200, 02/2461–4030, or 02/2461–4031).

TRANSPORTATION AROUND PRAGUE

Public transportation is a bargain. *Jízdenky* (tickets) can be bought at hotels, newsstands, and dispensing machines in Metro stations. Transport passes for unlimited use of the system for 1 day (70 Kč) up to 15 days (280 Kč) are sold at some newsstands and at the windows marked DP or JÍZDENKY in the main Metro stations. Be sure to validate your pass by signing it where indicated. A basic 12-Kč ticket allows one hour's travel, with unlimited transfers (90 minutes on weekends and between 8 PM and 5 AM weekdays) on the Metro, tram, and bus network within the city limits. Cheaper 8-Kč tickets are good for a tram or bus ride up to 15 minutes without transferring, or 30 minutes on the Metro including transfers between lines; on the Metro, though, you cannot travel more than four stops from your starting point. For the Metro punch the ticket in the station before getting onto the escalators; for buses and trams punch the ticket inside the vehicle. (Enter the tram or bus through any door and stick the tickets horizontally—and gently—into the little yellow machines, which should "stamp" them with the date and time; it's an acquired trick of hand-eye coordination; ask for help from another passenger if your machine is not cooperating, which is often the case.) If you fail to validate your ticket you may be fined 400 Kč by a ticket inspector.

Note: Prague has quite a pickpocketing racket, to which the police apparently turn a blind eye. Be very wary of raucous groups of people making a commotion as they get on and off trams and metros; generally they are working the passengers. Keep close watch on your belongings and purses on crowded streets and in crowded sites.

TRAVEL AGENCIES

➤ LOCAL AGENT REFERRALS: **American Express** (✉ Václavské nám. 56, ☎ 02/2280–0223; 02/2280–0222 lost/stolen credit cards, FAX 02/2221–1131). **Thomas Cook** (✉ Národní třída 28, ☎ 02/2110–5371).

VISITOR INFORMATION

The English-language weekly *Prague Post* lists current events and entertainment programs.

➤ TOURIST INFORMATION: **Čedok** (main office; ✉ Na Příkopě 18, near Wenceslas Sq., ☎ 02/2419–7111; other branches, ✉ Rytířská 16 and ✉ Pařížská 6). **Prague Information Service** (PIS; ✉ Na Příkopě 20 and Staroměstské nám. 22, ☎ 02/2448–2569).

➤ TOURIST BUREAUS OUTSIDE PRAGUE: **Český Krumlov** (Infocentrum; ✉ Nám. Svornosti 1, ☎ 0337/711183). **Karlovy Vary** (✉ Ul. Dr. Bechera 21–23, ☎ 017/22281). **Mariánské Lázně** (Infocentrum; ✉ Hlavní 47, ☎ 0165/622474 or 0165/5892). **Mikulov** (Regional Tourist Center; ✉ Nám. 32, ☎ FAX 0625/2855). **Olomouc** (✉ Horní nám., ☎ 068/551–3385). **Tábor** (✉ Žižkovo nám., ☎ 0361/252385). **Telč** (✉ Town hall; Nám. Zachariáše z Hradce 10, ☎ 066/962233).

9 DENMARK

COPENHAGEN, FYN AND THE CENTRAL ISLANDS, JYLLAND AND THE LAKES

EBULLIENCE AND A SENSE OF HUMOR have always been Danish trademarks. One might expect a country comprising more than 400 islands to develop an island mentality, but the Danes are famous for their friendliness. They even have a word—*hyggelig*—for the feeling of well-being that comes from their own brand of cozy hospitality.

The stereotype of melancholic Scandinavia simply doesn't hold here: either in the café-studded streets of the larger cities, where musicians and fruit vendors hawk their wares to passersby, or in the tiny coastal towns, where the fishing boats are as brightly painted as fire trucks. Even the country's indoor-outdoor museums, where history is brought to life in clusters of reconstructed buildings out in the open, indicate that Danes don't choose to keep experience behind glass.

This is a land of well-groomed agriculture, where every available acre is planted in orchards, forests, or crops. Nowhere are you far from water as you drive on and off the ferries and bridges linking the three regions of Jylland (Jutland), Fyn (Funen), and Sjælland (Zealand).

The surrounding sea has shaped Denmark's history. The Vikings, unparalleled seafarers, had seen much of the world by the 8th century. Today the Danes remain expert navigators, using their 7,314 km (4,544 mi) of coastline both for sport—there are regattas around Sjælland and Fyn—and for fishing and trading. Copenhagen is also proving itself as one of the most popular cruise ports in northern Europe.

Long one of the world's most liberal countries, Denmark has a highly developed social welfare system. Hefty taxes are the subject of grumbling and jokes, but Danes remain proud of their state-funded medical and educational systems.

The country that gave the world Isak Dinesen, Hans Christian Andersen, and Søren Kierkegaard has a long-standing commitment to culture and the arts. In what other nation does the royal couple translate the writings of Simone de Beauvoir or the queen design costumes for the ballet? The Royal Danish Ballet is world renowned, and even in the provinces there are numerous theater groups and opera houses.

Perhaps Denmark's greatest charm is its manageable size—about half that of Maine or 4½ times the size of Wales (43,070 square km/16,629 square mi). The combined ferry and train ride from Esbjerg, on the western coast of Jylland, to Copenhagen, on the eastern coast of Sjælland, takes just over three hours. From the capital you can make comfortable, unhurried expeditions by boat, car, bus, or train to explore one of the world's most civilized countries.

Denmark (Danmark)
North Sea
Skagerrak
TO GREENLAND
TO FAROE ISLANDS
Skagen
Hirtshals
Hjørring
Frederikshavn
Sæby
SWEDEN
Brønderslev
Hanstholm
Læsø
Aalborg
Limfjord
Thisted
Limfjord
Aalborg Bugt
Kattegat
Nykøbing
Hadsund
Lemvig
Skive
Struer
Viborg
Anholt
Holstebro
Jylland
Randers
Grenå
Ringkøbing
Herning
Silkeborg
Århus
Ebeltoft
Skanderborg
Horsens
Samsø
Tisvildeleje
Hornbæk
Helsingør
Grindsted
Nykøbing
Hillerød
Skjern
Billund
Vejle
Frederikssund
Humlebæk
Samsøbælt
Kalundborg
Holbæk
Copenhagen
Esbjerg
Holsted
Fredericia
Storebælt
Jyderup
Roskilde
Middelfart
Fanø
Kolding
Kerteminde
Sjælland
Amager
Odense
Slagelse
Ringsted
Køge
Køge Bugt
Ribe
Vojens
Assens
Fyn
Rømø
Nyborg
Korsør
Skærbæk
Haderslev
Lillebælt
Næstved
St. Heddinge
Fåborg
Åbenrå
Langeland
Karrebæksminde
Tønder
Svendborg
Als
Troense
Tranekær
Vordingborg
Sønderborg
Rudkøbing
Stege
Ærøskøbing
Marstal
Nakskov
Møn
Ærø
Nykøbing
Maribo
Falster
Rødby
TO BORNHOLM
Nysted
Lolland
Ostsee
SWEDEN
Baltic Sea
GERMANY
Bornholm
Rønne
N
0
50 miles
0
75 km

DENMARK A TO Z

To research prices, get advice from other travelers, and book travel arrangements, visit www.fodors.com.

BIKE TRAVEL

Some say the Danes have the greatest number of bikes per capita in the world. Indeed, with its flat landscape and uncrowded roads, Denmark is a cyclist's paradise. You can rent bikes at some train stations and many tourist offices, as well as from private firms. Contact the Dansk Cyklist Forbund (Danish Cyclists' Association) for additional information. The Danish Tourist Board publishes the pamphlet "Cycling Holiday in Denmark." In the warmer months, you'll also see Bycykler (City Bikes) parked at special bike stands placed at 200–300 meter intervals all around the center of town. Deposit DKr20 and pedal away. The bikes are often dented, but they do function. You'll get your deposit back when you return the bike.

➤ CONTACTS: **Dansk Cyklist Forbund** (✉ Rømersg. 7, DK 1362 Copenhagen, ☎ 33/32–31–21, WEB www.dcf.dk).

BOAT AND FERRY TRAVEL

There is frequent service to Germany, Poland, Sweden, Norway, and the Faroe Islands (in the Atlantic Ocean, north of Scotland), as well as to Britain. Domestic ferries provide service between Jylland, Fyn, and Sjælland and to the smaller islands, 100 of which are inhabited. Danish State Railways and several private shipping companies publish timetables in English; you should reserve on both domestic and overseas routes. Ask about off-season discounts.

BUS TRAVEL

Traveling by train or bus is easy, as Danish State Railways (DSB) and a few private companies cover the country with a dense network of train services, supplemented in remote areas by buses.

➤ BUS INFORMATION: **Danish State Railways** (☎ 70/13–14–15 information, WEB www.dsb.dk).

BUSINESS HOURS

BANKS AND OFFICES

Banks in Copenhagen are open weekdays 9:30–4 and Thursday until 6. Several bureaux de change, including those at Copenhagen's central station and airport, stay open until 10 PM. Outside Copenhagen, banking hours vary.

MUSEUMS AND SIGHTS

Museums are generally open 10–3 or 11–4 and closed Monday. In winter, opening hours are shorter, and some museums close for the season. Check the local papers or ask at tourist offices.

SHOPS

Small shops and boutiques are open weekdays 10–5:30; most stay open Friday until 7 or 8 and close on Saturday at 1 or 2. On the first and last Saturday of every month, most shops stay open until 4 or 5. Call to double-check weekend opening hours for specific stores to avoid disappointment.

CAR TRAVEL

EMERGENCIES

Members of organizations affiliated with Alliance International de Tourisme (AIT), including American AAA and British AA, can get technical and legal assistance from the Forenede Danske Motorkøretøjer (Danish Motoring Organization). All highways have emergency phones, and you can also phone your car-rental company for help. If you cannot drive your car to a garage for repairs, the rescue corps, Falck, can help anywhere, night or day.

➤ CONTACTS: **Falck** (☎ 44/92–22–22). **Forenede Danske Motorkøretøjer** (✉ Firskovvej 32, DK 2800 Lyngby, ☎ 45/27–07–07, WEB www.fdm.dk).

GASOLINE

Gas costs more than DKr8 a liter. Reality check: that's about US$5 a gallon.

PARKING

In areas with signs reading PARKERING/STANDSNING FORBUDT (no parking and no stopping) you are allowed a three-minute grace period to load and unload. In towns, automated parking-permit machines are used. Drop in coins, push the silver button, and a ticket marked with the expiration time will drop down. Display the ticket clearly on the dashboard. Parking for an hour costs DKr6–DKr20 in Copenhagen, DKr7 elsewhere. In some areas signs post parking regulations. All cars have a plastic dial on the inside of their windshields. Set the dial to the time you leave your car.

ROAD CONDITIONS

Roads here are good and largely traffic-free (except around Copenhagen); you can reach many islands by toll-free bridges. The Storebæltsbro connecting Sjæland and Fyn, and the Øresundsbro between Copenhagen and Malmö, Sweden take tolls.

RULES OF THE ROAD

To drive you will need a valid license, and if you're using your own car it must have a certificate of registration and national plates. A triangular hazard-warning sign is compulsory in every car and is provided with rentals. The driver and all passengers must wear seat belts. Headlights must always be on—even in the daytime. Motorcyclists must always wear helmets and use headlights. All drivers must pay attention to cyclists, who use the outer right lane and have the right-of-way.

Drive on the right and give way to traffic from the left. A red-and-white triangular yield sign, or a line of white triangles across the road, means you must yield to traffic on the road you are entering. Do not turn right on a red light. Speed limits are 50 kph (30 mph) in built-up areas; 100 kph (60 mph) on highways; and 80 kph (50 mph) on other roads. If you are towing a trailer, you must not exceed 70 kph (40 mph). Speeding, and drinking and driving, especially, are punished severely.

CUSTOMS AND DUTIES

For details on imports and duty-free limits, *see* Customs and Duties *in* Chapter 1.

DINING

Danes take their eating seriously, and traditional Danish food, however simple, is excellent, with an emphasis on fresh ingredients, few spices, and careful presentation. Fish and meat are both of top quality in this fishing and farming country, and both are staple ingredients of the famous *smørrebrød* (open-faced sandwiches). Some smørrebrød are huge meals in themselves: you may be faced with a dauntingly large (but nonetheless delicious) mound of fish or meat, slathered with condiments, all atop either *rugbrød* (rye bread) or *franskbrød* (French bread). Another specialty is *wienerbrød,* a confection far superior to anything billed as "Danish pastry" elsewhere.

All Scandinavian countries have versions of the cold table, but Danes claim that theirs, *det store kolde bord,* is the original and the best. It's a celebration meal; the setting of the long table is a work of art—often with lighted candles and silver platters—and the food itself is a minor miracle of design and decoration. In hotels and restaurants the cold table is served at lunch only, though you will find a more limited version at hotel breakfasts—a good bet for budget travelers, since you can eat as much as you like.

Denmark offers more than 50 varieties of beer, made by a dozen or so breweries; the best-known suds are Carlsberg and Tuborg, both made by the same company. If you like harder stuff, try *snaps,* the aquavit traditionally drunk with cold food, especially herring. A note about smoking: Danes, like many Europeans, regard smoking as an inalienable right. Militant insistence that they abstain will be regarded as either hysteria or comedy. A polite tone requesting they blow their smoke away from you may prove more effective.

Meal prices vary little between town and country. Prices are for one main course at dinner.

CATEGORY	COPENHAGEN	OTHER AREAS
$$$$	over DKr200	over DKr170
$$$	DKr120–DKr200	DKr120–DKr170
$$	DKr80–DKr120	DKr80–DKr120
$	under DKr80	under DKr80

MEALTIMES

The Danes start work early, which means they generally eat lunch at noon. Evening meals are also eaten early, so make sure you have dinner reservations for 9 at the latest. Bars and cafés stay open later, and most offer at least light fare.

RESERVATIONS AND DRESS

The Danes are fairly casual, and few restaurants require a jacket and tie. Even in the most chic establishments the tone is elegantly casual.

EMBASSIES

All embassies are in Copenhagen.

➤ CANADA: (✉ Kristen Bernikowsg. 1, 1105 KBH , ☎ 33/48–32–00).
➤ IRELAND: (✉ Østbanegade 21, 2100 KBH, Ø, ☎ 35/42–32–33).
➤ SOUTH AFRICA: (✉ Gammel Vartov Vej 8, DK-2900 Hellerup, ☎ 39/18–01–55).
➤ UNITED KINGDOM: (✉ Kastelsvej 40, 2100 KBH Ø, ☎ 35/44–52–00).
➤ UNITED STATES: (✉ Dag Hammarskjölds Allé 24, 2100 KBH Ø, ☎ 35/55–31–44).

HOLIDAYS

January 1; Easter (Thursday–Monday); Common Prayer (May); Ascension (40 days after Easter); June 5 (Constitution Day; shops close at noon); Whitsun/Pentecost (10 days after Ascension); December 24–26 (Christmas).

LANGUAGE

Danish is a difficult tongue for foreigners—except those from Norway and Sweden—to understand, let alone speak. Danes are good linguists, however, and almost everyone, except perhaps elderly people in rural areas, speaks English well in addition to a third language, usually French or German.

LODGING

Accommodations in Denmark range from the spare and comfortable to the resplendent. Even inexpensive hotels have invested in good materials and good, firm beds in simple designs. However, when you make reservations, pin down details so you get what you want. Many hotels are in century-old buildings; room sizes, even in top hotels, can vary enormously; the smallest have sloping ceilings and cubbyhole-size doubles. Also ask about noise caused by traffic or adjacent rooms. If you have preferences, ask for them specifically and get a confirmation in writing. Many Danes prefer a shower to a bath, so if you particularly want a tub, ask for it, but be prepared to pay more. Except in the case of rentals, breakfast and taxes are usually included in prices, though this seems to be changing. Check when making a reservation.

All prices are for a standard double room, excluding service charges and 14.9% room tax. The tax is slightly lower at suburban hotels.

CATEGORY	COPENHAGEN	OTHER AREAS
$$$$	over DKr1,700	over DKr1,400
$$$	DKr1,400–DKr1,700	DKr1,200–DKr1,400
$$	DKr900–DKr1,400	DKr900–DKr1,200
$	under DKr900	under DKr900

APARTMENT AND VILLA RENTALS

Many Danes rent out their summer homes—an ideal option if you want to see the countryside in a more relaxed way. A simple house with room for four costs from DKr1,000 per week to five times that much during the summer high season. Contact the Danish Tourist Board for details.

CAMPING

Denmark has more than 500 approved campsites, with a rating system of one, two, or three stars. To camp you need an International Camping Carnet or Danish Camping Pass (available at any campsite and valid for one year). For more details on camping and discounts for groups and families, contact Campingrådet.

➤ CONTACTS: **Campingrådet** (✉ Hesseløg. 16, DK 2100 Copenhagen Ø, ☎ 39/27–88–44, WEB www.campingraadet.dk).

FARM VACATIONS

This is perhaps the best way to see how the Danes live and work. You stay on a farm and share meals with the family; you can even help with the chores. The minimum stay is three nights; bed-and-breakfast is about DKr150, and half board (an overnight with breakfast and one hot meal) runs DKr245. Full board, an overnight with three meals, can be arranged. There is a 50% discount for children under 11. Contact Ferie på Landet (Holiday in the Country) for details.

➤ CONTACTS: **Ferie på Landet** (✉ Ceresvej 2, 8410 Ronde, ☎ 70/10–41–90, FAX 75/60–21–90, WEB www.bondegaardsferie.dk).

HOSTELS

The 101 youth hostels in Denmark are open to everyone regardless of age. If you have an International Youth Hostels Association card (obtainable before you leave home), the rate is roughly DKr100 for a single bed, DKr150–DKr300 for a private double room. Without the card, there's a surcharge of about DKr30 per person. For more information, contact Danhostel Danmarks Vandrehjem or American Youth Hostels.

➤ CONTACTS: **Danhostel Danmarks Vandrehjem** (✉ Vesterbrog. 39, DK 1620 Copenhagen V, ☎ 33/31–36–12, FAX 33/31–36–26, WEB www.danhostel.dk).

HOTELS

Luxury hotels in the city or countryside offer rooms of a high standard; in a manor-house hotel you may find yourself sleeping in a four-poster bed. Less expensive accommodations, however, are uniformly clean and comfortable.

INNS

A cheaper and charming alternative to hotels are the old stagecoach *kroer* (inns) scattered throughout Denmark. You can save money by contacting Kro Ferie (Inn Holiday) to invest in a book of Inn Checks, valid at 84 inns. Each check costs about DKr640 per couple and includes one overnight stay in a double room as well as breakfast. Family checks, for three (DKr720) and four (DKr800), are also available. Order a free catalog from Kro Ferie and choose carefully; the organization includes some chain hotels bereft of even a smidgen of inn-related charm. Some also tack a DKr150 surcharge on the price of a double.

➤ CONTACTS: **Kro Ferie** (✉ Vejlevej 16, DK 8700 Horsens, Jylland, ☎ 75/64–87–00, WEB www.dansk-kroferie.dk).

MAIL AND SHIPPING

If you do not know where you will be staying, your mail can be addressed to "poste restante" and sent to any post office. If no post office is specified, letters will be sent to the main post office in Copenhagen.

➤ CONTACTS: **Copenhagen Main Post Office** (✉ Tietgensg. 37, DK 1704).

POSTAL RATES

Surface and airmail letters, aerograms, and postcards to the United States and Canada cost DKr5.50 for 20 grams. Airmail letters and postcards to the United Kingdom and other EU countries cost DKr4.50. Stamps are sold at post offices and some shops.

MONEY MATTERS

Denmark's economy is stable, and inflation remains reasonably low. The standard and the cost of living are high, especially for such luxuries as alcohol and cigarettes. Prices are highest in Copenhagen; the least expensive areas are Fyn and Jylland.

Sample prices include: cup of coffee, DKr14–DKr25; bottle of beer, DKr20–DKr35; soda, DKr10–DKr15; ham sandwich, DKr22–DKr40; 1½-km (1-mi) taxi ride, DKr50.

CURRENCY

The monetary unit in Denmark is the krone (kr., DKr, or DKK), which is divided into 100 øre. At press time (summer 2001), the krone stood at DKr8.20 to the U.S. dollar, DKr5.27 to the Canadian dollar, DKr11.71 to the pound sterling, DKr9.46 to the Irish punt, DKr4.50 to the Australian dollar, DKr3.49 to the New Zealand dollar, and DKr1.05 to the South African rand. Most well-known credit cards are accepted in Denmark, though it would be wise to inquire about American Express and Diners Club beforehand. Traveler's checks can be cashed in banks and in many hotels, restaurants, and shops.

TAXES

VALUE-ADDED TAX (VAT)

Visitors from a non-EU country can save about 15% on purchases over DKr300 by obtaining a refund of the value-added tax (VAT) at the more than 1,500 shops displaying TAX FREE signs. If the shop sends your purchase directly to your home address, you pay only the sales price, exclusive of VAT. If you want to take the goods home yourself, pay the full price in the shop and get a VAT refund at the Danish duty-free shopping center at the Copenhagen Airport. There is a charge for these services. Get a copy of the *Tax-Free Shopping Guide* from the Danish Tourist Board.

TELEPHONES

COUNTRY AND AREA CODES

The country code for Denmark is 45.

DIRECTORY AND OPERATOR ASSISTANCE

To ask an operator, most of whom speak English, for local assistance, dial 118; for an international operator, dial 113.

INTERNATIONAL CALLS

Dial 00, then the country code, area code, and the desired number. You can reach AT&T, MCI, and Sprint by dialing one of the access codes below.

➤ ACCESS CODES: **AT&T** (☎ 800/10010). **MCI WorldCom** (☎ 800/10022). **Sprint** (☎ 800/10877).

LOCAL CALLS

Pay phones take DKr1, DKr2, DKr5, and DKr10 coins. You must use area codes even when dialing a local number. Calling cards, which are sold at Danish State Railways stations, post offices, and some kiosks, cost DKr30, DKr50, DKr75, or DKr150 and are increasingly necessary as pay phones that accept coins become a thing of the past.

TIPPING

Some restaurants, usually larger ones, add a service charge. Waiters do not expect a tip, but appreciate one. Rule of thumb: round up the bill if you got good food and service. Hotel porters should get around DKr5 per bag; you should also leave DKr1 or DKr2 for the use of a public toilet if there is an attendant.

TRAIN TRAVEL

Hourly intercity trains connect the main towns in Jylland and Fyn with Copenhagen and Sjælland, using high-speed diesels, called IC-3s, on the most important stretches. All these trains make the seven-minute tunnel crossing of the Store Bælt (Great Belt), the waterway separating Fyn and Sjælland. Seat reservations on intercity trains and IC-3s are optional, but you must have a reservation if you plan to cross the Great Belt. Buy tickets at stations for trains, buses, and connecting ferry crossings (buses allow you to buy tickets on board). For most cross-country trips, children between 4 and 11 accompanied by an adult travel free, though they must have a seat reservation (DKr15). Ask about discounts for senior citizens and groups.

FARES AND SCHEDULES

The ScanRail pass affords unlimited train travel throughout Denmark, Finland, Norway, and Sweden, as well as restricted ferry passage in and beyond Scandinavia. It is available for 5 days of travel within 15 days, 10 days within a month, or 21 days. Buy your tickets in the United States: they are available in Denmark, but they are more expensive. Various discounts are offered to holders of the pass by hotel chains and other organizations; ask DER, RailEurope, or your travel agent for details.

VISITOR INFORMATION

The main tourist information office is the Danish Tourist Board. Youth information is available in Copenhagen at Ungdoms Information.

➤ TOURIST INFORMATION: **Danish Tourist Board** (✉ Danmarks Turistråd; Bernstoffsg. 1, DK 1577 Copenhagen V, ☎ 70/22–24–42, WEB www.dt.dk; ✉ Tivoli grounds; plus Helsingør, Hillerød, Køge, Roskilde, Gilleleje, Hundersted, and Tisvildeleje). **Ungdoms Information** (✉ Rådhusstr. 13, ☎ 33/73–06–50).

WHEN TO GO

Most travelers visit Denmark during the warmest months, July and August, but there are advantages to going in May, June, or September, when sights are less crowded and many establishments offer off-season discounts. However, few places in Denmark are ever unpleasantly crowded, and when the Danes make their annual exodus to the beaches, the cities have even more breathing room. In the winter months days are short and dark, and important attractions, including Copenhagen's Tivoli Gardens, are closed. It's worth noting, however, that winter holidays are beautiful and especially cozy—even Tivoli reopens with its special Christmas market.

CLIMATE

The following are the average daily maximum and minimum temperatures for Copenhagen.

Jan.	36F	2C	**May**	61F	16C	**Sept.**	64F	18C
	28	- 2		46	8		51	11
Feb.	36F	2C	**June**	67F	19C	**Oct.**	54F	12C
	28	- 2		52	11		44	7
Mar.	41F	5C	**July**	71F	22C	**Nov.**	45F	7C
	31	- 1		57	14		38	3
Apr.	51F	11C	**Aug.**	70F	21C	**Dec.**	40F	4C
	38	3		56	14		34	1

COPENHAGEN

When you arrive in Copenhagen Airport on the isle of Amager, as you taxi into the city you are met with no startling skyline, no seething metropolis. Instead, elegant spires and central cobbled streets characterize Scandinavia's most populous capital and one of its oldest towns. It is not divided like most other cities into single-purpose districts; instead it is a rich, multilayered capital where people work, play, shop, and live throughout its central core. Surrounded by water, be it sea or canal, and connected by bridges and drawbridges, it has a maritime atmosphere that is indelible.

Exploring Copenhagen

Numbers in the margin correspond to points of interest on the Copenhagen map.

When Denmark ruled Norway and Sweden during the 15th century, Copenhagen was the capital of all three countries. Today it is still a lively northern capital, with about 1 million inhabitants. It's a city meant for walking, the first in Europe to recognize the value of pedestrian streets in fostering community spirit. As you stroll through the cobbled streets and squares, you'll find that Copenhagen combines the excitement and variety of big-city life with a small-town atmosphere. If there's such a thing as a cozy metropolis, this is it.

In Copenhagen you're never far from water, whether sea or canal. The original city itself is built upon two main islands, Slotsholmen and Christianshavn, connected by drawbridges. The ancient heart of the city is intersected by two heavily peopled walking streets—part of the five such streets known collectively as Strøget—and around them curls a maze of cobbled streets packed with tiny boutiques, cafés, and restaurants—all best explored on foot. In summer, when Copenhagen moves outside, the most engaging views of city life are from sidewalk cafés in the sunny squares. Walk down Nyhavn Canal, once the haunt of a salty crew of sailors, now gentrified and filled with chic restaurants.

16 **Amalienborg** (Amalia's Castle). During the fall and winter, when members of the royal family return to their principal residence as they have since 1784, the Royal Guard and band march through the city at noon

Amalienborg 16
Børsen 10
Botanisk Have 25
Carlsberg Bryggeri . .32
Christiansborg Slot . . .5
Den Lille Havfrue . . .20
Frihedsmuseet 18
Heligånds Kirken . . .31
Hirschsprungske Samling 27
Kastellet 19
Københavns Synagoge 22
Kongelig Teater 13
Kongelige Bibliotek . . .7
Kunstindus-trimuseet 17
Lurblæserne 2
Marmorkirken 15
Nationalmuseet 4
Nikolaj Kirken 12
Ny Carlsberg Glyptotek 30
Nyhavn 14
Rådhus Pladsen 1
Rosenborg Slot 24
Rundetårn 23
Statens Museum for Kunst 26
Strøget 3
Teatermuseum 8
Thorvaldsen Museum 6
Tivoli 29
Tøjhusmuseet 9
Tycho Brahe Planetarium 28
Vor Frelsers Kirken 11
Vor Frue Kirken 21

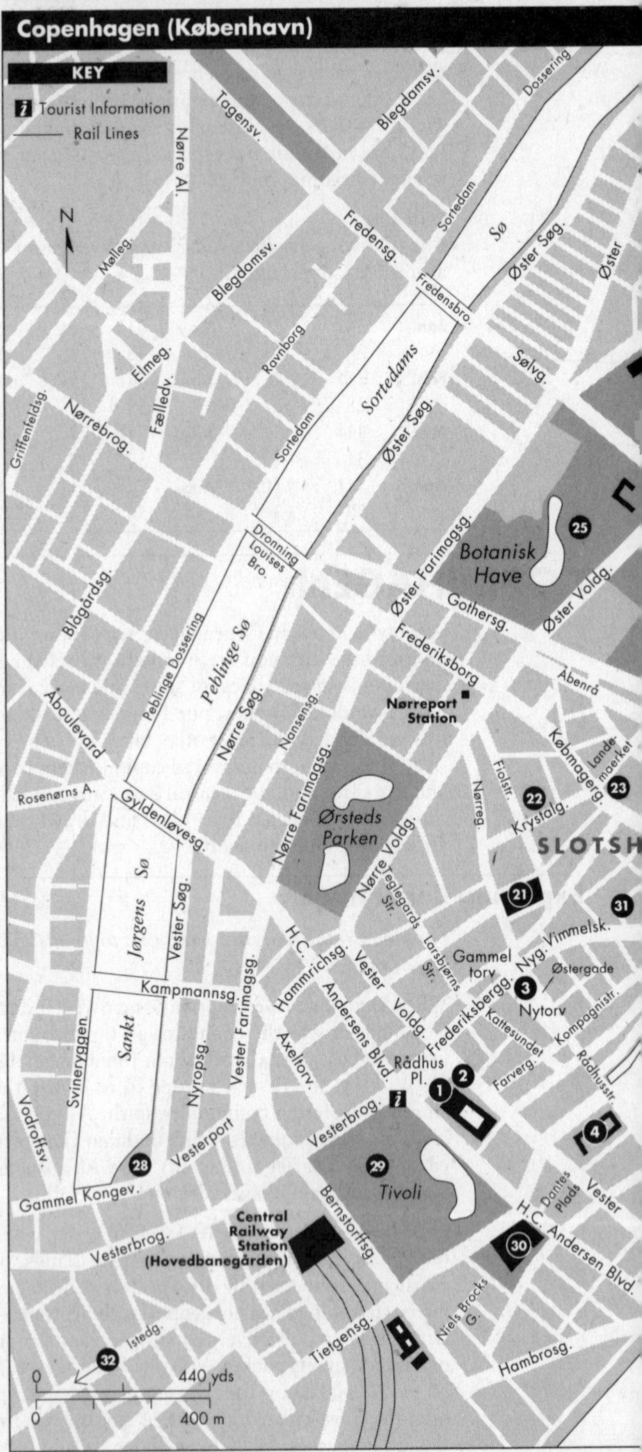

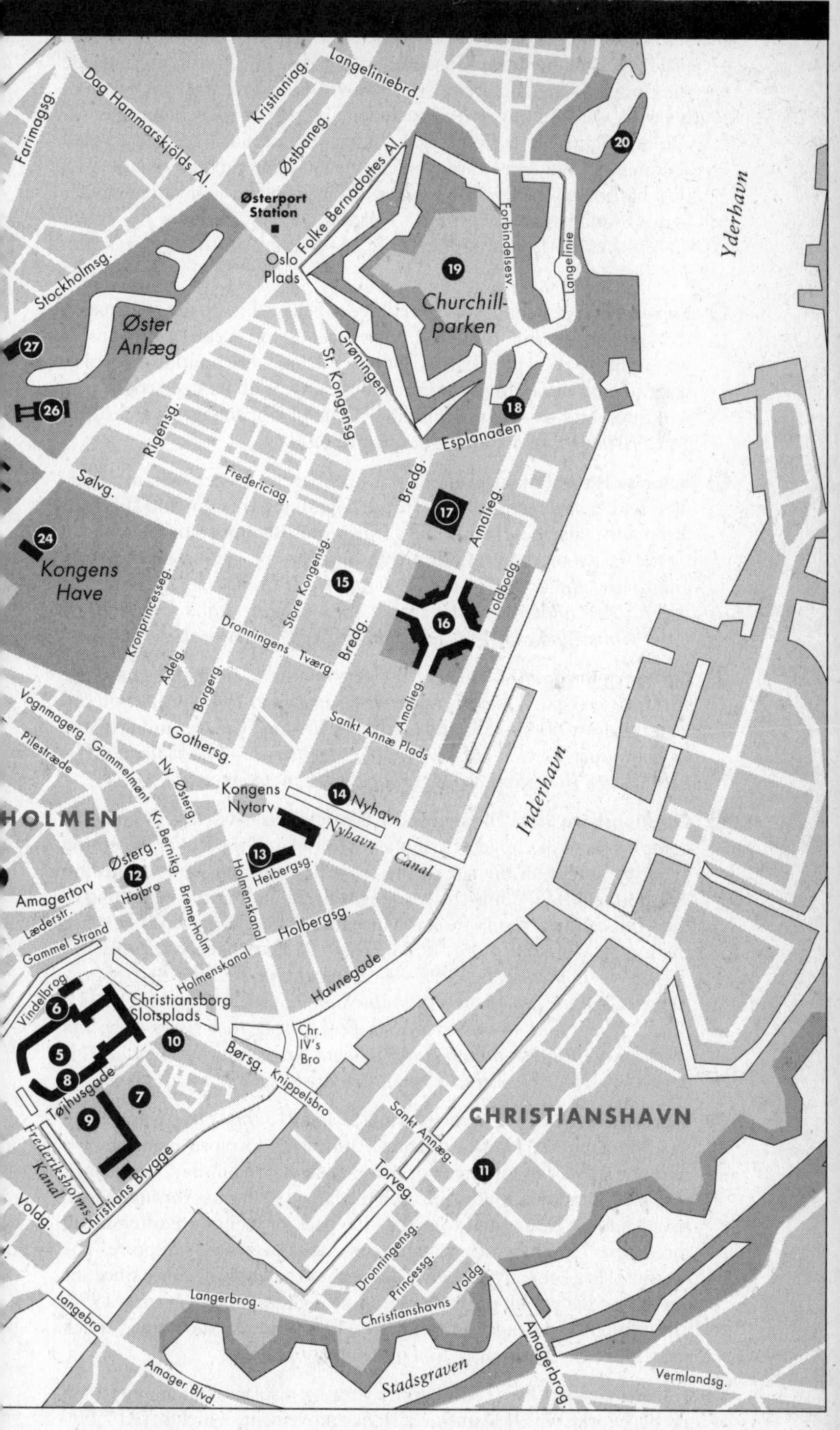

Langeliniebrd.
Dag Hammarskjölds Al.
Kristianiag.
Farimagsg.
Østbaneg.
Folke Bernadottes Al.
Østerport Station
Oslo Plads
Forbindelsesv.
Langelinie
Yderhavn
Stockholmsg.
Øster Anlæg
Churchill-parken
Grønningen
St. Kongensg.
Rigensg.
Esplanaden
Sølvg.
Fredericiag.
Bredg.
Amalieg.
Kongens Have
Kronprincesseg.
Store Kongensg.
Toldbodg.
Dronningens Tværg.
Adelg.
Borgerg.
Amalieg.
Vognmagerg.
Gammelmønt
Pilestræde
Gothersg.
Sankt Annæ Plads
Inderhavn
Ny Østerg.
Kongens Nytorv
Nyhavn
HOLMEN
Kr. Bernikg.
Nyhavn Canal
Østerg.
Heibergsg.
Amagertorv
Højbro
Bremerholm
Holmenskanal
Læderstr.
Holbergsg.
Gammel Strand
Holmenskanal
Havnegade
Vindelbrog
Christiansborg Slotsplads
Chr. IV's Bro
Børsg.
Knippelsbro
Tøjhusgade
Sankt Annæg.
CHRISTIANSHAVN
Frederiksholms Kanal
Christians Brygge
Torveg.
Voldg.
Dronningensg.
Princessg.
Langerbrog.
Christianshavns Voldg.
Langebro
Amagerbrog.
Stadsgraven
Amager Blvd.
Vermlandsg.

to change the palace guard. Amalienborg's other main attraction is the second division of the Royal Collection (the first is at Rosenborg), housed inside the **Amalienborg Museum.** Among the collection's offerings are the study of King Christian IX (1818–1906) and the drawing room of his wife, Queen Louise. Also included are a set of rococo banquet silver, highlighted by a bombastic Viking ship centerpiece, and a small costume exhibit. Afterward, you can view visiting yachts along the castle's harbor, as well as the modern sculptures and manicured flower beds of **Amalienhaven** (Amalia's Gardens). ✉ *Amalienborg Pl.,* ☎ *33/40–10–10.* ⏲ *May–late Oct., daily 11–4; late Oct.–Apr., Tues.–Sun. 11–4.*

10 **Børsen** (Stock Exchange). This edifice is believed to be the oldest such structure still in use, though it functions only on special occasions. It was built by the 16th-century monarch King Christian IV, a scholar, warrior, and the architect of much of the city. With its steep roofs, tiny windows, and gables, the building is one of Copenhagen's treasures. ✉ *Christiansborg Slotspl. Not open to public.*

25 **Botanisk Have** (Botanical Garden). Copenhagen's 25-acre botanical garden, with a spectacular Palm House containing tropical and subtropical plants, upstages the palatial gardens of **Rosenborg Slot** (Rosenborg Castle). Also on the grounds are an observatory, geological museum, and cactus and orchid house. ✉ *Gothersg. 128,* ☎ *35/32–22–40.* 🎫 *Free.* ⏲ *Grounds May–Aug., daily 8:30–6; Sept.–Apr., daily 8:30–4. Palm House daily 10–3. Cactus House Wed. and Sun. 1–3.*

32 **Carlsberg Bryggeri** (Carlsberg Brewery). Granite elephants guard the entrance to the first Carlsberg brewery, opened in 1847; inside you can visit the draft-horse stalls and **Carlsberg Visitors' Centre,** and taste the local product. ✉ *Gl. Carlsbergvej 11,* ☎ *33/27–13–14,* WEB *www.carlsberg.dk.* ⏲ *Tues.–Sun. 10–4; groups book in advance.*

★ 5 **Christiansborg Slot** (Christiansborg Castle). This massive gray complex contains the Folketinget (Parliament House) and the Royal Reception Chambers. It is on the site of the city's first fortress, built by Bishop Absalon in 1167. While the castle was being built at the beginning of the 20th century, the National Museum excavated the ruins beneath the site. ✉ *Christiansborg,* ☎ *33/92–64–92 Christiansborg ruins; 33/37–55–00 Folketinget; 33/92–64–92 reception chambers.* ⏲ *Christiansborg ruins: Jan.–Sept. 30, Mon.–Sun. 9:30–3:30; Oct. 1–Dec. 31, Tues., Thurs., Sat.–Sun. 9:30–3:30. Folketinget: tour times vary; call ahead. Reception chambers: June 5–Sept., daily; guided tours only, 11, 1, 3; Oct.–Dec. 31, Tues., Thurs., weekends, guided tours 11, 3.*

20 **Den Lille Havfrue** (The Little Mermaid). In 1913 this statue was erected to commemorate Hans Christian Andersen's lovelorn creation. It's now the subject of hundreds of travel posters. On Sunday, **Langelinie,** the spit of land you follow to reach the famed nymph, is thronged with promenading Danes and tourists—the pack of whom are often much more absorbing to watch than the somewhat overrated sculpture. The mermaid has been mysteriously decapitated a couple of times since she was set on her perch; the most recent incident took place in early 1998, and though her head was returned within a week, she gained much more publicity without it. ✉ *Langelinie promenade.*

18 **Frihedsmuseet** (Liberty Museum). Evocative displays commemorate the heroic World War II Danish resistance movement, which saved 7,000 Jews from the Nazis by hiding them and then smuggling them across to Sweden. ✉ *Churchillparken,* ☎ *33/13–77–14.* ⏲ *Tues.–Sat. 10–4, Sun. 10–5.*

31 **Heligånds Kirken** (Church of the Holy Ghost). This church on Strøget contains a marble font by the sculptor Bertel Thovaldsen (1770–1844) in its 18th-century choir. ✉ *Niels Hemmingsensg. 5, Amagertorv section of Strøget,* ☎ *33/12–95–55.* ⏲ *Weekdays 9–1, Sat. 10–noon.*

27 **Hirschsprungske Samling** (Hirschsprung Collection). This cozy museum displays works from Denmark's golden age of painting, the mid-19th-century school of Naturalism pioneered by C. W. Eckersberg, whose pictures contain a remarkable wealth of detail and technical skill combined with limpid, cool, luminescent color. Other prominent painters of the trend include Christian Købke and Julius Exner. The Hirschsprungske also has a collection of paintings by the late-19th-century artists of the Danish Skagen school, as well as interiors with furnishings from the artists' homes. ✉ *Stockholmsg. 20,* ☎ *35/42–03–36,* WEB *www.dhs.dk.* ⏲ *Thurs.–Mon. 11–4, Wed. 11–9.*

19 **Kastellet** (Citadel). Once surrounded by two rings of moats, this building was the city's main fortress during the 17th century, but, in a grim reversal during World War II, the Germans used it as one of their headquarters during their occupation of Denmark. The lovely green area around it, **Churchillparken,** cut throughout with walking paths, is a favorite among the Danes, who flock here on weekends. If you have time, walk past the spired **St. Alban's,** an Anglican church that stands at the park's entrance. ✉ *Churchillparken.* ⏲ *Grounds daily 6 AM–sunset.*

22 **Københavns Synagoge** (Copenhagen Synagogue). This synagogue was designed by the contemporary architect Gustav Friedrich Hetsch, who borrowed from the Doric and Egyptian styles in creating the arklike structure. ✉ *Krystalg. 12.* ⏲ *Daily services 4:15.*

13 **Kongelig Teater** (Royal Theater). The home of Danish opera and ballet as well as theater occupies the southeast side of Kongens Nytorv. The Danish Royal Ballet remains one of the world's great companies, with a repertoire ranging from classical to modern. On the western side of the square you'll see the stately facade of the **D'Angleterre,** the grandest of Copenhagen's hotels. ✉ *Tordenskjoldsg. 3,* ☎ *33/69–69–69,* WEB *www.kgl-teater.dk. Not open for tours.*

7 **Kongelige Bibliotek** (Royal Library). This library houses the country's largest collection of books, newspapers, and manuscripts. Look for early records of the Viking journeys to America and Greenland and the statue of the philosopher Søren Kierkegaard in the garden. A dark marble annex next door, known as the Black Diamond, has reading rooms, a ground-floor performance space, and a bookstore. ✉ *Søren Kierkegaards Pl. 1,* ☎ *33/47–47–47,* WEB *www.kb.dk.* ⏲ *Mon.–Sat. 10–7.*

17 **Kunstindustrimuseet** (Museum of Decorative Art). The highlights of this museum's collection are a large assortment of European and Asian handicrafts, as well as ceramics, silver, and tapestries. The quiet library full of design tomes and magazines doubles as a primer for Danish functionalism with its Le Klint paper lamp shades and wooden desks. ✉ *Bredg. 68,* ☎ *33/18–56–56,* WEB *www.kunstindustrimuseet.dk.* ⏲ *Special exhibits Tues.–Fri. 10–4, weekends noon–4; permanent exhibition Tues.–Fri. 1–4, weekends noon–4.*

2 **Lurblæserne** (Lur Blower Column). Topped by two Vikings blowing an ancient trumpet called a *lur,* this column erected in 1914 displays a good deal of artistic license—the lur dates from the Bronze Age, 1500 BC, whereas the Vikings lived a mere 1,000 years ago. The monument is a starting point for sightseeing tours of the city. ✉ *East side of Rådhus Pl.*

15 **Marmorkirken** (Marble Church). The ponderous Frederikskirke, commonly called the Marmorkirken, is a Baroque church that was begun in 1749 in high-priced Norwegian marble and stood unfinished (because of budget constraints) from 1770 to 1874. It was finally completed and consecrated in 1894. Perched around the exterior are 16 statues of various religious leaders from Moses to Luther, and below them stand sculptures of outstanding Danish ministers and bishops. ✉ *Frederiksgade 4,* ☎ *33/15–01–44.* ⏲ *Mon.–Tues. and Thurs.–Sat. 10–6, Sun. noon–5, with service at 10:30.*

4 **Nationalmuseet** (National Museum). This museum has extensive collections chronicling Danish cultural history to modern times and displays of Egyptian, Greek, and Roman antiquities. You can see Viking runic stones in the Danish cultural history section. The children's museum is an excellent place to ease kids into the joys of history; though the original relics are secured behind glass, there is plenty of stuff, including clothing and a school, to play in and with. ✉ *Ny Vesterg. 10,* ☎ *33/13–44–11,* WEB *www.natmus.dk.* ⏲ *Tues.–Sun. 10–5.*

12 **Nikolaj Kirken** (St. Nicholas Church). In Østergade, the easternmost of the streets that make up Strøget, you cannot miss the green spire of this building. The present structure was built in the 20th century; the previous one, dating from the 13th century, was destroyed by fire in 1728. Today the building is no longer a church but an art gallery and exhibition center. ✉ *Nikolaipl.,* ☎ *33/93–16–26.* ⏲ *Daily noon–5.*

★ 30 **Ny Carlsberg Glyptotek** (New Carlsberg Sculpture Museum). This elaborate neoclassical building houses one of Europe's greatest collections of Greek and Roman antiquities and sculpture. A modern wing houses an impressive pre-Impressionist collection including works from the Barbizon school; Impressionist paintings, with works by Monet, Sisley, and Pissarro; and a post-Impressionist section, with 50 Gauguin paintings plus 12 of his very rare sculptures. ✉ *Dantes Pl. 7,* ☎ *33/41–81–41,* WEB *www.glyptoteket.dk.* ⏲ *Tues.–Sun. 10–4.*

★ 14 **Nyhavn** (New Harbor). You can relax with a beer in one of the most gentrified parts of the city, a longtime haunt of sailors. Now restaurants and cafés outnumber tattoo shops. The name refers to both the street and the canal leading southeast out of Kongens Nytorv. The area still gets rowdy on long, hot summer nights, with Scandinavians reveling against the backdrop of a fleet of old-time sailing ships and well-preserved 18th-century buildings. Hans Christian Andersen lived at numbers 18 and 20. Nearer to the harbor are old shipping warehouses, including two—Nyhavn 71 and the Admiral—that have been converted into comfortable hotels. ✉ *East of Kongens Nytorv.*

★ 1 **Rådhus Pladsen** (City Hall Square). This hub of Copenhagen's commercial district is the best place to start a stroll. The Renaissance-style building dominating it is the **Rådhuset** (Town Hall), completed in 1905. A statue of Copenhagen's 12th-century founder, Bishop Absalon, sits atop the main entrance. Inside, you can see the first World Clock, an astrological timepiece invented and built by Jens Olsen and set in motion in 1955. You can take a guided tour partway up the 350-ft **tower** for a panoramic view. ✉ *Square in Strøget at eastern end of Vesterbrog. and western end of Frederiksbergg.,* ☎ *33/66–25–82.* ⏲ *Rådhus Mon.–Wed. and Fri. 9:30–3, Thurs. 9:30–4, Sat. 9:30–1. Tours in English weekdays at 3, Sat. at 10 and 11. Tower tours Oct.–May, Mon.–Sat. at noon; June–Sept., Mon.–Sat. at 10, noon, and 2. Call to confirm hrs.*

★ 24 **Rosenborg Slot** (Rosenborg Castle). This Renaissance palace—built by jack-of-all-trades Christian IV—houses the Crown Jewels, as well as a collection of costumes and royal memorabilia. Don't miss Christian IV's pearl-studded saddle. ✉ *Øster Voldg. 4A,* ☎ *33/15–32–86.* ⏲ *Nov.–Dec. 17 and Jan.–Apr., Tues.–Sun. 11–2; May–Sept., daily 10–4; Oct., daily 11–3.*

23 **Rundetårn** (Round Tower). It is said that Peter the Great of Russia drove a horse and carriage up the 600 ft of the inner staircase of this round tower, built as an observatory in 1642 by Christian IV. It's a formidable walk, but the view is worth it, and there is sometimes an astronomer available to answer questions. At the base of the tower is the university church, Trinitas; halfway up the tower you can take a break at the tower's art gallery. ✉ *Købmagerg. 52A,* ☎ *33/73–03–73.* ⏲ *Tower: Sept.–May, Mon.–Sat. 10–5, Sun. noon–5; June–Aug., Mon.–Sat. 10–8, Sun. noon–8. Observatory and telescope: mid-Oct.–mid-Mar., Tues.–Wed. 7–10 PM; June 20–Aug. 10, Sun. 1–4.*

26 **Statens Museum for Kunst** (National Art Gallery). The original 100-year-old building and a new, modern structure house works of Danish art from the golden age (early 19th century) to the present, as well as paintings by Rubens, Dürer, the Impressionists, and other European masters—but the space also includes a children's museum, an amphitheater, a documentation center and study room, a bookstore, and a restaurant. ✉ *Sølvg. 48–50,* ☎ *33/74–84–94,* WEB *www.smk.dk.* ⏲ *Tues., Thurs.–Sun. 10–5, Wed. 10–8.*

3 **Strøget.** Frederiksberggade is the first of the five pedestrian streets that make up Strøget, Copenhagen's shopping district and promenade area. Walk past the cafés and trendy boutiques to the double square of **Gammeltorv** and **Nytorv,** where, farther along, the street is paved with mosaic tiles. Outside the posh displays of the fur and porcelain shops the sidewalks have the festive aura of a street fair. **Kongens Nytorv** (King's New Market) is the square marking the end of Strøget.

8 **Teatermuseum** (Theater Museum). Built in 1767 in the Royal Court, this museum is devoted to exhibits on theater and ballet history. You can wander around the boxes, stage, and dressing rooms to see where it all happened. ✉ *Christiansborg Ridebane 18,* ☎ *33/11–51–76.* ⏲ *Wed. 2–4, weekends noon–4.*

★ 6 **Thorvaldsen Museum.** The 19th-century Danish sculptor Bertel Thorvaldsen, whose tomb stands in the center of the museum, was greatly influenced by the statues and reliefs of classical antiquity. In addition to his own works, the collection includes drawings and paintings by others that illustrate the influence of Italy on the artists of Denmark's golden age. ✉ *Porthusg. 2,* ☎ *33/32–15–32,* WEB *www.thorvaldsens-museum.dk.* ⏲ *Tues.–Sun. 10–5.*

★ 29 **Tivoli.** In the 1840s the Danish architect Georg Carstensen convinced King Christian VIII that an amusement park would be the perfect opiate for the masses, arguing that "when people amuse themselves, they forget politics." In the season from May through September, about 4 million people come through the gates. Tivoli is more sophisticated than a mere fun fair: it offers a pantomime theater and an open-air stage, elegant restaurants, and frequent classical, jazz, and rock concerts in addition to a museum chronicling its own history. On weekends there are elaborate fireworks displays. Try to see Tivoli at least once by night, when the trees are illuminated along with the Chinese Pagoda and the main fountain. In recent years Tivoli has also been opened a month before Christmas with a gift and decorations market and children's rides. Most of the restaurants are also open, but there are plenty of less expensive food stalls serving everything from Asian specialties to mulled wine. ✉ *Vesterbrog. 3,* ☎ *33/15–10–01,* WEB *www.tivoli.dk.* ⏲ *May–*

mid-Sept., and at Christmas time, daily 11 AM–midnight, Fri.–Sat. until 1 AM.

9 **Tøjhusmuseet** (Royal Armory). The Renaissance structure was built by King Christian IV. It houses impressive displays of uniforms, weapons, and armor in an arched hall 200 yards long. ✉ *Tøjhusg. 3,* ☎ *33/11–60–37,* WEB *www.thm.dk.* ⏲ *Tues.–Sun. noon–4.*

28 **Tycho Brahe Planetarium.** This modern, cylindrical building has astronomy exhibits and an Omnimax theater that takes visitors on a simulated journey up into space and down into the depths of the seas (reservations are advised for the theater). Because these films can be disorienting, planetarium officials do not recommend them for children under seven. ✉ *Gammel Kongevej 10,* ☎ *33/12–12–24,* WEB *www.tycho.dk.* 🎫 *Exhibition and theater DKr70.* ⏲ *Daily 10:30–9.*

11 **Vor Frelsers Kirken** (Our Savior's Church). Legend has it that the staircase encircling the fantastic green-and-gold spire of this 1696 Gothic structure was built curling the wrong way around, and that when its architect reached the top and saw what he had done, he jumped. ✉ *Skt. Annæg. 9,* ☎ *31/57–63–25.* ⏲ *Weekdays 9–1. Closed during services and special functions; call ahead.*

21 **Vor Frue Kirken** (Church of Our Lady). This has been Copenhagen's cathedral since 1924, but the site itself has been a place of worship since the 13th century, when Bishop Absalon built a chapel here. The spare, neoclassical facade is a 19th-century innovation repairing damage suffered during Nelson's bombing of the city in 1801. If the church is open, you can see Thorvaldsen's marble sculptures of Christ and the Apostles. Afterward, if you're on your way to the Nørreport train station, you'll pass the stoic, columned **Københavns Universitet** (Copenhagen University; ✉ Nørregade 10). It was built in the 19th century on the site of the medieval bishops' palace. ✉ *Pilestræde 67,* ☎ *33/14–41–28.* ⏲ *Weekdays 8:30–5.*

Dining

Food is one of the great pleasures in Copenhagen, a city with more than 2,000 restaurants. Traditional Danish fare spans all the price categories: you can order a light lunch of smørrebrød, snack from a store kolde bord, or dine on lobster and Limfjord oysters. You can also enjoy fast food Danish style, in the form of *pølser* (hot dogs) sold from trailers on the street. Team any of this with some pastry from a bakery (the shops displaying an upside-down gold pretzel), and you've got yourself a meal on the go. Many restaurants close for Christmas, roughly from December 24 through December 31. For details and price-category information, *see* Dining *in* Denmark A to Z, *above.*

$$$$ ★ ✕ **Kommandanten.** The 300-year-old building, once the apartment of the Commander of Copenhagen, houses Scandinavia's most celebrated restaurant. The ever-varying set-course menu follows what's freshest at the market, including sliced breast of guinea fowl with quail eggs or wild duck with confit. Expect adventurous French cooking of the highest caliber and service attuned to the lift of an eyebrow. If possible, book before your trip—this epicurean favorite seats only 50. ✉ *Ny Adelgade 7,* ☎ *33/12–09–90,* WEB *www.kommandanten.dk. AE, DC, MC, V. Closed Sun..*

$$$$ ★ ✕ **Kong Hans Kaelder.** In this hushed cloister with medieval vaulted ceilings you'll find one of the city's outstanding restaurants. The menu is classic French, with a focus on the creative use of local ingredients, including mushrooms brought by bicycle from nearby forests. You haven't tasted salmon like this before, prepped for 36 hours in the restau-

rant's own cold smoker. Save room for the outstanding selection of gourmet cheeses, many homemade. ✉ *Vingårdstr. 6,* ☎ *33/11–68–68,* WEB *www.konghans.dk. AE, DC, MC, V. Closed Sun.–Mon. June–mid-July and Aug.; mid–late July; and Easter wk. No lunch.*

$$$$ ✕ **Krogs.** Fish is to Denmark what wine is to France, and the reigning champion among Copenhagen seafood restaurants remains venerable Krogs, equal to the best in food and tops in local charm and history. Gilded mirrors, high ceilings, and 19th-century paintings are a study in old-fashioned opulence, as is a menu including grilled lobster with vanilla polenta, poached fish in Parmesan bouillon, and the locally famous bouillabaisse. ✉ *Gammel Strand 38,* ☎ *33/15–89–15,* WEB *www.krogs.dk. Reservations essential. AE, DC, MC, V. Closed Sun., and around Christmas, Easter.*

$$$ ★ ✕ **Els.** Said to be a favorite of the queen, Els is a piece of Danish history, largely unchanged since it first catered to the theater crowd in 1853. The flip side of the restaurant's proud past is an occasionally supercilious attitude toward foreigners, but a touch of stiffness seems in keeping with the 19th-century tiles, Renaissance-style painted muses, and antique samovar greeting you at the bar. Enjoy fine French cooking with a focus on fish, and wild game and fowl. ✉ *Store Strandstr. 3,* ☎ *33/14–13–41. Reservations essential. AE, DC, MC, V.*

$$$ ✕ **L'Alsace.** In the cobbled courtyard of Pistolstraede and hung with paintings by Danish surrealist Wilhelm Freddie, this restaurant is peaceful and quiet. The menu includes a hearty *choucroute* (sauerkraut) with sausage and pork, plus fruit tarts and cakes for dessert. ✉ *Ny Østerg. 9,* ☎ *33/14–57–43. AE, DC, MC, V. Closed Sun.*

$$$ ✕ **Le Sommelier.** Classic French country cooking is served here with a dazzling selection of wines by the glass. Enjoy the popular steamed mussels, homemade foie gras, or pigeon breast with mushrooms and glazed beets. Take a break from worrying about secondhand smoke and give in to the European ambience: patrons can select from 30 brands of cigarettes to go with any of 12 varieties of coffee. ✉ *Bredg. 63,* ☎ *33/11–45–15,* WEB *www.lesommelier.dk. AE, DC, MC, V. Closed between lunch and dinner sittings, approx. 4–6. Closed Christmas–New Year.*

$$$ ✕ **Schiøtt's.** The city's newest modern French hit, this cozy cellar restaurant offers superb creative fare in the Provençal style, including flavorful shoulder of lamb with peppers, eggplant, and olives. It offers an elegant experience at the price. The walk along the Christianhavn Canal adds to the pleasure on warm summer nights. ✉ *Overgaden neden vandet 17,* ☎ *32/54–54–08,* WEB *www.schoetts.dk. AE, DC, MC, V. Closed around Christmas and Easter.*

$$$ ✕ **Victor.** This French-style corner café has great people-watching and bistro fare. It's best during weekend lunches, when Danes gather for such specialties as rib roast, homemade pâté, smoked salmon, and cheese platters. Careful ordering here can get you an inexpensive meal. ✉ *Ny Østerg. 8,* ☎ *33/13–36–13,* WEB *www.cafevictor.dk. AE, DC, MC, V.*

$$ ✕ **El Meson.** Ceiling-hung pottery, knowledgeable waiters, and a top-notch menu make this Copenhagen's best Spanish restaurant. Choose carefully for a moderately priced meal, which might include beef spiced with spearmint, lamb with honey sauce, or paella for two. ✉ *Hauser Pl. 12,* ☎ *33/11–91–31. AE, DC, MC, V. Closed Sun. No lunch.*

$$ ✕ **Havfruen.** A full-size wooden mermaid swings decorously from the ceiling in this small, rustic fish restaurant in Nyhavn. Natives love the maritime-bistro ambience and the daily-evolving French and Danish menu. ✉ *Nyhavn 39,* ☎ *33/11–11–38. DC, MC, V. Closed Sun.*

$$ ★ ✕ **Ida Davidsen.** Five generations old (counting Ida's children, Oscar and Ida Maria), this world-renowned lunch spot has become synonymous with smørrebrød. Choose from these creative open-face sandwiches, piled high with such ingredients as pâté, bacon, and steak tartare, or even kangaroo, or opt for smoked duck served with a beet salad and potatoes. ✉ *St. Kongensg. 70,* ☎ *33/91–36–55. Reservations essential. AE, DC, MC, V. Closed weekends and July. No dinner.*

$$ ✕ **Olsen's.** Urban-modern in appearance, this popular spot prides itself on its *husmandskost*—old-fashioned Danish food, carefully prepared and served with gusto. For a truly local experience order the *flæskesteg* (roast pork) and enjoy the fat and rind, as Danes do. ✉ *St. Kongensg. 66,* ☎ *33/93–91–95,* WEB *www.olsen.dk. AE, DC, MC, V. May be closed for part of July.*

$ ✕ **Lai Hoo.** Denmark's Princess Alexandra, a native of Hong Kong, is a fan of this Chinese restaurant near the city's main square. The lunch specialty is an inspired variety of steamed dumplings (dim sum), and for dinner the best bet is the fixed menu—try the salt-baked prawns in pepper or the luscious lemon duck. ✉ *St. Kongensg. 18,* ☎ *33/93–93–19. DC, MC, V.*

$ ✕ **Quattro Fontane.** On a corner west of the lakes, one of Copenhagen's busiest Italian restaurants is a noisy, two-story affair packed tight with marble-top tables and a steady flow of young Danes. Chatty Italian waiters serve cheese or beef ravioli, cannelloni, linguine with clam sauce, and thick pizzas. Reservations are essential on weekends. ✉ *Guldbersg. 3,* ☎ *35/39–39–31. No credit cards.*

$ ★ ✕ **Riz Raz.** On a corner off Strøget, this Middle Eastern restaurant packs in young and old, families, and singles every night and on weekends. The very inexpensive all-you-can-eat buffet is heaped with healthy dishes, including lentils, falafel, bean salads, and occasionally pizza. Reservations are essential on weekends. ✉ *Kompagnistr. 20,* ☎ *33/15–05–75,* WEB *www.rizraz.dk. DC, MC, V.*

Lodging

Copenhagen is well served by a wide range of hotels, which are almost always clean, comfortable, and well run. Most but not all Danish hotels include a substantial breakfast in the room rate. Summertime reservations are a good idea, but if you should arrive without one, try the hotel booking service at the Danish Tourist Board. They can also give you a "same-day, last-minute price," which is about DKr400–DKr500 for a double hotel room. This service will also locate rooms in private homes, with rates starting at about DKr300 for a double. Try the **Ungdoms Information** lodging service (✉ Rådhusstr. 13, ☎ 33/73–06–50) for budget accommodations. For details and price-category definitions, *see* Lodging *in* Denmark A to Z, *above*.

$$$$ ★ **D'Angleterre.** The grande dame of Copenhagen hotels underwent major changes during the 20th century, but the hotel still retains its Old World, old-money aura. The rooms are done in pinks and blues, with overstuffed chairs and antique escritoires and armoires. Bathrooms sparkle with brass, mahogany, and marble. If you are a light sleeper, choose a back room; some guests complain of noise from the nearby bars, as well as early morning deliveries. ✉ *Kongens Nytorv 34, DK 1051 KBH K,* ☎ *33/12–00–95,* FAX *33/12–11–18,* WEB *www.remmen.dk/hda.htm. 110 rooms, 20 suites. 2 restaurants, pool. AE, DC, MC, V.*

$$$$ **Radisson SAS Scandinavia.** Near the airport, this is one of northern Europe's largest hotels and Copenhagen's token skyscraper. An immense lobby, with cool, recessed lighting and streamlined furniture, gives access to the city's first (and only) casino. Guest rooms are large and somewhat institutional but offer every modern convenience. Breakfast is not included in the rates. ✉ *Amager Blvd. 70, DK 2300 KBH S,* ☎ *33/96–50–00,* FAX *33/96–55–00,* WEB *www.radissonsas.com. 542 rooms, 52 suites. 4 restaurants, pool. AE, DC, MC, V.*

$$$ **Kong Frederik.** West of Rådhus Pladsen, near Strøget, this intimate hotel is a cozy version of its big sister, D'Angleterre. The sunny Queen's Garden restaurant serves a breakfast buffet (not included in the rate); rooms are elegant with Oriental vases, mauve carpets, and all modern amenities. ✉ *Vester Voldg. 25, DK 1552 KBH K,* ☎ *33/12–59–02,* FAX *33/93–59–01,* WEB *www.remmen.dk/hkf.htm. 110 rooms, 17 suites. Restaurant. AE, DC, MC, V.*

$$$ **Neptun.** The centrally sited Neptun has been in business for nearly 150 years and shows no signs of flagging. Guest rooms decorated with blond wood are favored by Americans. Though charming, this Best Western hotel can become very busy with tour groups. Moreover, because it is housed in a old building, room sizes vary greatly, and so does the noise from the street. Ask for details when booking a room. ✉ *Skt. Annæ Pl. 18, DK 1250 KBH K,* ☎ *33/13–89–00,* FAX *33/14–12–50. 123 rooms, 14 suites. Restaurant. AE, DC, MC, V.*

$$$ **Nyhavn 71.** In a 200-year-old warehouse overlooking the old ships of Nyhavn, this quiet hotel is a good choice for privacy-seekers. The maritime interiors have been preserved with their original plaster walls and exposed brick. Rooms are tiny but cozy, with warm woolen spreads, dark woods, soft leather furniture, and exposed timbers. ✉ *Nyhavn 71, DK 1051 KBH K,* ☎ *33/11–85–85,* FAX *33/93–15–85,* WEB *www.nyhavnhotel.dk. 84 rooms. Restaurant. AE, DC, MC, V.*

$$$ **The Phoenix.** This luxury hotel welcomes guests with crystal chandeliers and gilt touches everywhere. The staff switch languages as they register business and cruise guests. Suites and executive-class rooms have Biedermeier-style furniture and 18-karat-gold-plated bathroom fixtures, but the standard rooms are very small, at barely 9 by 15 ft. If you're a light sleeper, ask for a room above the second floor to avoid street noise. ✉ *Bredg. 37, DK 1260 KBH K,* ☎ *33/95–95–00,* FAX *33/33–98–33,* WEB *www.phoenix.dk. 208 rooms, 7 suites. Restaurant. AE, DC, MC, V.*

$$ **Ascot.** A charming old building downtown, this family-owned hotel has a classically columned entrance and an excellent breakfast buffet. Rooms have colorful geometric-pattern bedspreads and cozy bathrooms. A few have kitchenettes. Repeat guests often ask for their regular rooms. Be warned: in recent years, a nearby late-night disco has disturbed some guests. Be sure to ask for a room as far away from it as possible. The restaurant serves breakfast only. ✉ *Studiestr. 61, DK 1554 KBH K,* ☎ *33/12–60–00,* FAX *33/14–60–40. 161 rooms, 4 suites. Restaurant. AE, DC, MC, V.*

$$ **Copenhagen Admiral.** Overlooking old Copenhagen and Amalienborg, the monolithic Admiral, once a grain warehouse, now offers historic but airy accommodations. With massive stone walls broken by rows of tiny windows, it's one of the less expensive top hotels, though in recent years it's been upping both frills and prices. Guest rooms are spare, with jutting beams and modern prints. ✉ *Toldbodg. 24–28, DK 1253 KBH K,* ☎ *33/11–82–82,* FAX *33/32–55–42,* WEB *www.admiralhotel.dk. 365 rooms. Restaurant. AE, DC, MC, V.*

$ **Cab-Inn Scandinavia.** Winter business travelers and budget-minded summer backpackers and families alike flock to Copenhagen's answer to Japanese-style hotel minirooms. More cozy than futuristic, shiplike "berths" are brightly decorated, all with standard furnishings, including a small wall-hung desk with chair. Around the corner, at Danasvej 32, is a sister hotel, the Cab-Inn Copenhagen, with 86 rooms. ✉ *Vodroffsvej 55, DK 1900 FR C,* ☎ *35/36–11–11,* FAX *35/36–11–14,* WEB *www.cab-inn.dk. 201 rooms with shower. AE, DC, MC, V.*

$ **Missionhotellet Nebo.** This budget hotel is between the main train station and Istedgade's seediest porn shops. Nonetheless, it's a prim hotel, comfortable and well maintained by a friendly staff. The dorm-like guest rooms are furnished with industrial carpeting, polished pine furniture, and soft duvet covers. Baths, showers, and toilets are clustered at the center of each hallway, and the breakfast restaurant downstairs has a tiny courtyard. ✉ *Istedg. 6, DK 1650 KBH V,* ☎ *31/21–12–17,* FAX *31/23–47–74,* WEB *www.nebo.dk. 88 rooms, 40 with bath. AE, DC, MC, V.*

$ **Triton.** Despite seedy surroundings, this streamlined hotel attracts a cosmopolitan clientele thanks to a central location in Vesterbro. The large rooms, in blond wood and warm tones, have new bathrooms and state-of-the-art fixtures. The buffet breakfast included in the price is exceptionally generous, and the staff is friendly. There are also family rooms, each with a separate bedroom and fold-out couch. The restaurant serves breakfast only. ✉ *Helgolandsg. 7–11, DK 1653 KBH K,* ☎ *31/31–32–66,* FAX *31/31–69–70,* WEB *www.accorhotel.dk. 123 rooms. Restaurant. AE, DC, MC, V.*

Nightlife and the Arts

English-language *Copenhagen This Week* has good information on musical and theatrical happenings, as well as on special events and exhibitions. WEB www.aok.dk is an excellent website for learning about shopping, dining, accommodations, and entertainment, in fact everything about Copenhagen (which is what AOK stands for). It also features similar information about other Danish cities. Concert and festival information is available from the **Dansk Musik Information Center** (DMIC; ✉ Gråbrødretorv 16, ☎ 33/11–20–66, WEB www.mic.dk. Copenhagen's main theater and concert season runs from September through May, and tickets can be obtained either directly from theaters and concert halls or from ticket agencies; ask your hotel concierge for advice. **Billetnet** (☎ 70/15–65–65, WEB www.billetnet.dk), a box-office service available at all large post offices, has tickets for most major events. Keep in mind that same-day purchases at the box office at **Tivoli** (✉ Vesterbrogade 3, ☎ 33/15–10–12) are half price if you pick them up after noon.

The Arts

MUSIC

Tivoli Concert Hall (✉ Tietensg. 20, ☎ 33/15–10–12) offers more than 150 concerts each summer, presenting a host of Danish and foreign soloists, conductors, and orchestras.

THEATER

The **Royal Theater** (✉ Kongens Nytorv, ☎ 33/14–10–02, WEB www.kgl-teater.dk) regularly holds theater, ballet, and opera performances. For English-language theater, try to catch a performance of the professional **London Toast Theatre** (☎ 33/22–86–86, WEB www.londontoast.dk).

Nightlife

Many of the city's restaurants, cafés, bars, and clubs stay open after midnight, some as late as 5 AM. Copenhagen is famous for jazz, but you'll find nightspots catering to musical tastes ranging from bop to ballroom music. In the inner city most discos open at 11 PM, have a cover charge (about DKr40), and pile on steep drink prices. A few streets behind the railway station is Copenhagen's red-light district, where sex shops share space with grocers. Although the area is fairly well lighted and lively, women may feel uncomfortable here alone at night.

JAZZ

The upscale **Copenhagen Jazz House** (✉ Niels Hemmingsensg. 10, ☎ 33/15–26–00, WEB www.jazzhouse.dk) attracts European and some international talent to its chic, modern barlike ambience. **La Fontaine** (✉ Kompagnistr. 11, ☎ 33/11–60–98) is Copenhagen's quintessential jazz dive, with sagging curtains, impenetrable smoke, crusty lounge lizards, and the random barmaid nymph; for jazz lovers, the bordello mood and Scandinavian jazz talent make this a must. **Tivoli Jazzhouse Mantra** (✉ Vesterbrog. 3, ☎ 33/11–11–13), Tivoli's jazz club, lures some of the biggest names in the world.

NIGHTCLUBS AND DANCING

The young set gets down on the disco floor in the fashionable **Park Café** (✉ Østerbrog. 79, ☎ 35/26–63–42). Mellower folks come for brunch when the place transforms back to its Old World roots, or to check out the movie theater next door. **Rosie McGees** (✉ Vesterbrog. 2A, ☎ 33/32–19–23) is a very popular English-style pub with Mexican food and dancing. **Sabor Latino** (✉ Vester Voldg. 85, ☎ 33/11–97–66) is the U.N. of discos, with an international crowd dancing to salsa and other Latin beats. Among the most enduring clubs is **Woodstock** (✉ Vesterg. 12, ☎ 33/11–20–71), where a mixed audience grooves to 1960s classics.

Shopping

Strøget's pedestrian streets are synonymous with shopping.

Specialty Shops

Just off Østergade is **Pistolstræde,** a typical old courtyard filled with intriguing boutiques. Farther down the street toward the town-hall square is a compound that includes several important stores: **Georg Jensen** (✉ Amagertorv 4, ☎ 33/11–40–80), one of the world's finest silversmiths, gleams with a wide array of silver patterns and jewelry. Don't miss the **Georg Jensen Museum** (✉ Amagertorv 6, ☎ 33/14–02–29), which showcases glass and silver creations ranging from tiny, twisted-glass shot glasses to an $85,000 silver fish dish. **Royal Copenhagen Porcelain** (✉ Amagertorv 6, ☎ 33/13–71–81) carries both old and new china, plus porcelain patterns and figurines.

Bang & Olufsen (✉ Østerg. 3–5, ☎ 33/15–04–22) offers reasonable prices for radios, TVs, and stereo equipment in its own upscale shop. Along Strøget, at furrier **Birger Christensen** (✉ Østerg. 38, ☎ 33/11–55–55), you can peruse designer clothes and chic furs. **FONA** (✉ Østerg. 47, ☎ 33/15–90–55) carries stereo equipment, including the superior design and sound of Bang & Olufsen. **Illum** (✉ Østerg. 52, ☎ 33/14–40–02) is a department store that has a fine basement grocery and eating arcade. Don't confuse Illum with **Illums Bolighus** (✉ Amagertorv 10, ☎ 33/14–19–41), where designer furnishings, porcelain, quality clothing, and gifts are displayed in near-gallery surroundings. **Magasin** (✉ Kongens Nytorv 13, ☎ 33/11–44–33), one of the largest department stores in Scandinavia, offers all kinds of clothing and gifts, as well as an excellent grocery department.

Side Trips

Klampenborg

Just north of town, accessible by S-train or the coastal road Strandvejen, is the **Dyrehave** ("deer park"), a favorite escape for area city dwellers. What began as hunting grounds for Danish royalty is now a forest preserve of enormous beech and fir trees. Put on your walking shoes and admire the thatched cottages, the royal hunting lodge with its stone sphinxes and gods, and the roaming herds of imported deer. Tucked inside is Bakken, which claims to be the world's oldest amusement park; it's open April–August. ✉ *Dyrehavevej 62, 2930 Klampenborg,* ☎ *36/63–35–44.*

Helsingør

Shakespeare immortalized both the town and the castle when he chose Helsingør's **Kronborg Slot** (Kronborg Castle) as the setting for *Hamlet.* Completed in 1585, the present gabled and turreted structure is about 600 years younger than the fortress we imagine as the setting of Shakespeare's tragedy. Inside are a 200-ft-long dining hall, the luxurious chapel, and the royal chambers. The ramparts and 12-ft-thick walls are a reminder of the castle's role as a coastal bulwark—Sweden is only a couple of miles away. Helsingør town—about 47 km (29 mi) north of Copenhagen—has a number of picturesque streets with 16th-century houses. Frequent trains stop at Helsingør station, and then it's a 20-minute walk around the harbor to the castle. ✉ *Kronborg Slot,* ☎ *49/21–30–78.* ⏲ *Easter and May–Sept., daily 10:30–5; Oct. and Apr., Tues.–Sun. 11–4; Nov.–Mar., Tues.–Sun. 11–3.*

Humlebæk

The town, 35 km (22 mi) and a half-hour train ride from Copenhagen, is part of the "Danish Riviera" on the North Sjælland coast. Its chief landmark is **Louisiana,** a world-class modern art collection set in an elegant, rambling structure with views of the sound. A combined train fare (from Copenhagen) and admission (DKr103) is available from DSB. A 10-minute walk from the station, the museum is also accessible by the E4 highway and the more scenic Strandvejen, or coastal road. ✉ *Gammel Strandvej 13,* ☎ *49/19–07–19,* WEB *www.louisiana.dk.* ⏲ *Thurs.–Tues. 10–5, Wed. 10–10.*

Roskilde

For a look into the past, head 30 km (19 mi) west of Copenhagen to the bustling market town of Roskilde. The principal city of Denmarkduring Viking times, it remained one of the largest towns in northern Europe through the Middle Ages. Today the legacy of its 1,000-year history lives on in its spectacular cathedral. Built on the site of one of Denmark's first churches, the **Domkirke** (cathedral) has been the burial place of Danish royalty since the 15th century. The combined effect of their tombs is striking—from the magnificent shrine of Christian IV to the simple brick chapel of Frederik IX. ✉ *Domkirkepl.,* ☎ *46/35–27–00.* ⏲ *Subject to change; call ahead.*

★ A 10-minute walk south and through the park takes you to the water and the **Vikingeskibshallen** (Viking Ship Museum). Inside are five exquisitely reconstructed Viking ships discovered at the bottom of Roskilde Fjord in 1962. ✉ *Strandengen,* ☎ *46/30–02–00.* ⏲ *Apr.–Oct., daily 9–5; Nov.–Mar., daily 10–4.*

Copenhagen Essentials

AIRPORTS & TRANSFERS

The main airport for both international and domestic flights is Copenhagen Airport, 10 km (6 mi) southeast of town.

TRANSFERS

Trains from the airport's sleek new subterranean train station take less than 10 minutes to zip into Copenhagen's main station. Buy a ticket upstairs in the airport train station (DKr18); three trains an hour go into Copenhagen, while a fourth travels farther to Roskilde. Bus service to the city is frequent. The airport bus to the central station leaves every 15 minutes: the trip takes about 25 minutes, with a fare of about DKr50 (pay on the bus). Public buses cost about DKr18 and run as often but take longer. Bus 250S takes you to Rådhus Pladsen, the city-hall square. A taxi ride takes 15 minutes and costs about DKr150, though slightly more after 4 PM and weekends.

BIKE TRAVEL

More than half the 5 million Danes are said to ride bikes, which visitors use as well. Bike rental costs DKr50–DKr200 a day, though weekly rates are available, with a deposit of DKr300–DKr1,000. Contact Københavns Cykler or Østerport Cykler.

➤ BIKE RENTAL: **Københavns Cykler** (✉ Central Station, ☎ 33/33–86–13). **Østerport Cykler** (✉ Oslo Plads, ☎ 33/33–85–13).

BUS TRAVEL WITHIN COPENHAGEN

Buses and suburban trains operate on the same ticket system and divide Copenhagen and environs into three zones. Tickets are validated on the time system: on the basic ticket, which costs DKr11 for an hour, you can travel anywhere in the zone in which you started. You can buy a discount *klip kort* (clip card), equivalent to 10 basic tickets, for DKr85. Call the 24-hour information service for zone information. Buses and S-trains run from 5 AM (6 AM on Sunday) to 12:30 AM. A reduced network of buses drives through the night.

➤ BUS INFORMATION: **Information service** (☎ 36/45–45–45 buses; 70/13–14–15 S-trains; wait for the Danish message to end and an operator will answer).

CAR TRAVEL

Copenhagen is a city for walkers, not drivers. The charm of its pedestrian streets is paid for by a complicated one-way road system and difficult parking. Leave your car in the garage: attractions are relatively close together, and public transportation is excellent.

EMERGENCIES

If you use the dental emergency service listed below, expect to pay cash. Emergency doctor fees are also payable in cash only, and nighttime visits include a DKr350 surcharge.

➤ DOCTORS AND DENTISTS: **Dental Emergency Service** (✉ Tandlægevagten 14, Oslo Pl., near Østerport station, ☎ 35/38–02–51). **Doctor** (☎ 33/93–63–00 weekdays 8–4; 38/88–60–41 daily after 4 PM).

➤ EMERGENCY SERVICES: **Auto Rescue/Falck** (☎ 70/10–20–30). **Police, fire, ambulance** (☎ 112).

➤ 24-HOUR PHARMACIES: **Steno Apotek** (✉ Vesterbrog. 6C, ☎ 33/14–82–66). **Sønderbro Apotek** (✉ Amagerbrog. 158, Amager area, ☎ 32/58–01–40).

ENGLISH-LANGUAGE MEDIA

➤ BOOKSTORES: **Arnold Busck** (✉ Købmagerg. 49, ☎ 33/73–35–00). **Boghallen** (✉ Rådhus Pl. 37, ☎ 33/47–25–60).

TAXIS

The computer-metered Mercedeses and Volvos are not cheap. The base charge is DKr22, plus DKr10–DKr13 per kilometer (½ mi). A cab is available when it displays the green sign FRI (free); you can either hail a cab (though this can be difficult outside the center), pick one up at a taxi stand, or call the number listed below.

➤ TAXI COMPANIES: (☎ 35/35–35–35).

TOURS

BOAT TOURS

The Harbor and Canal Tour by boat leaves from Gammel Strand and the east side of Kongens Nytorv; it runs from April through mid-October, daily every half hour from 10 to 5.

BUS TOURS

Several bus tours, conducted by Copenhagen Excursions, leave from the Lur Blowers Column in Rådhus Pladsen, late March–September.

➤ FEES AND SCHEDULES: **Copenhagen Excursions** (☎ 32/54–06–06).

PRIVATE GUIDES

The Danish Tourist Board can recommend multilingual guides for individual needs; travel agents have details on hiring a limousine and guide.

SINGLE-DAY TOURS

The Danish Tourist Board has full details relating to excursions outside the city, including visits to castles (such as Hamlet's castle) and the Viking Ship Museum.

WALKING TOURS

The Danish Tourist Board supplies maps and brochures and can recommend a walking tour.

TRAIN TRAVEL

Copenhagen's clean and convenient central station, Hovedbanegården, is the hub of the country's train network. Intercity express trains leave hourly, on the hour, from 6 AM to 10 PM for principal towns in Fyn and Jylland. Find out more from DSB Information at the central station. You can make reservations at the central station as well as most other stations, and through travel agents.

➤ TRAIN INFORMATION: **DSB Information** (☎ 70/13–14–15). **Hovedbanegården** (✉ just south of Vesterbrog, ☎ 33/14–88–00).

TRANSPORTATION AROUND COPENHAGEN

The best bet for visitors is the Copenhagen Card, affording unlimited travel on buses and suburban trains (S-trains), admission to some 60 museums and sights around metropolitan Copenhagen and Malmö, Sweden, and a reduction on the ferry crossing to Sweden. Buy the card, which costs about DKr155 (24 hours), DKr255 (48 hours), or DKr320 (72 hours)—half price for children ages 5 to 11—at bus/train stations, tourist offices, and hotels or from travel agents.

TRAVEL AGENCIES

➤ LOCAL AGENTS: **Carlson Wagonlit Travel** (✉ Ved Vesterport 6, ☎ 33/63–78–78). **DSB Rejsebureau Terminus** (✉ Central Station, ☎ 33/14–11–26). **Spies** (✉ Nyropsg. 41, ☎ 70/10–42–00).

FYN AND THE CENTRAL ISLANDS

It was Hans Christian Andersen, the region's most famous native, who dubbed Fyn (Funen) the "Garden of Denmark." Part orchard, part farmland, Fyn is sandwiched between Sjælland and Jylland. With its tidy, rolling landscape, seaside towns, manor houses, and castles, it is one of Denmark's loveliest islands. Its capital—1,000-year-old Odense, in the north—is the birthplace of Hans Christian Andersen; his life and works are immortalized here in two museums. Fyn is also the site of two of Denmark's best-preserved castles: 12th-century Nyborg Slot, in the east, and 16th-century Egeskov Slot, near Svendborg, in the south. From Svendborg it's easy to hop on a ferry and visit some of the smaller islands, such as Tåsinge, Langeland, and Ærø, whose main town, Ærøskøbing, with its twisting streets and half-timber houses, seems caught in a time warp.

Fyn has a wide range of hotels and inns, many of which offer off-season (October through May) rates, as well as special weekend deals. The islands also have numerous campsites and youth hostels, all clean and attractively located. Some, like Odense's youth hostel, are set in old manor houses. Contact local tourist offices for information.

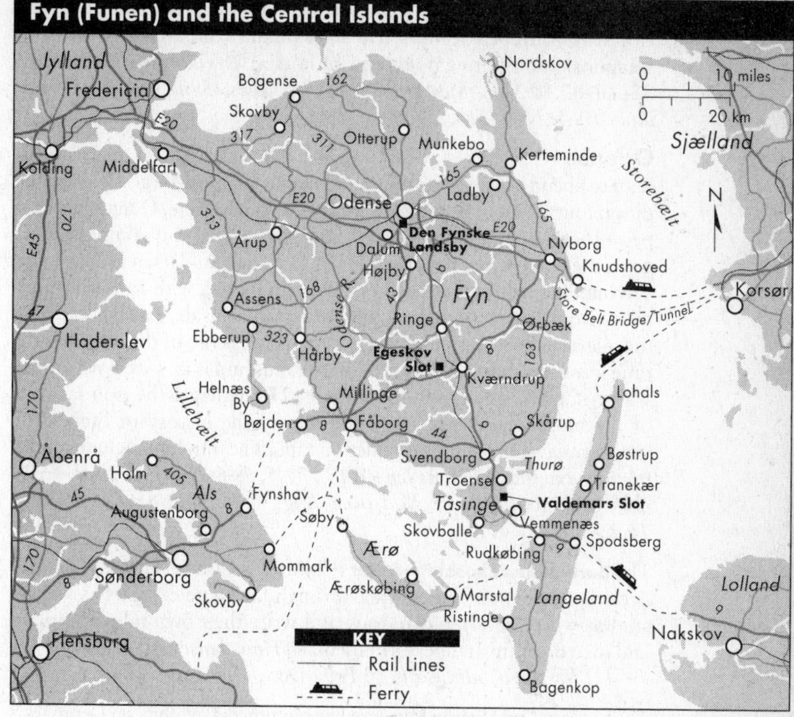

Nyborg

This 13th-century town was Denmark's capital during the Middle Ages, as well as an important stop on a major trading route between Sjælland and Jylland. From 1200 to 1413, Nyborg housed the Danehof, the early Danish parliament. Nyborg's major landmark is its 12th-century **Nyborg Slot** (Nyborg Castle). It was here that Erik Glipping granted the first Danish constitution, the Great Charter, in 1282. ✉ *Slotspl.,* ☎ *65/31–02–07,* WEB *www.museer-nyborg.dk.* ⏲ *Mar.–May and Sept.–mid-Oct., Tues.–Sun. 10–3; June–Aug., daily 10–4; schedule changes, check times; closed from Nov.–Mar..*

$$$$ 🏨 **Hesselet.** This modern hotel tucked into the Fyn landscape affords views of the Store Belt bridge and paths down to the sea. Inside it's a refined English-cum-Asian sanctuary with impeccable service. The guest rooms are furnished with cushy, modern furniture, and most have splendid views. ✉ *Christianslundsvej 119, DK 5800,* ☎ *65/31–30–29,* FAX *65/31–29–58,* WEB *www.hesselet.dk. 43 rooms, 3 suites. Restaurant, indoor pool. AE, DC, MC, V.*

Kerteminde

Coastal Kerteminde is Fyn's most important fishing village and a picturesque summer resort. Stroll down Langegade to see its half-timber houses.

$$$ ✕ **Rudolf Mathis.** You can enjoy delectable fish and seafood specialties and a splendid view of Kerteminde Harbor at this traditional Danish restaurant. ✉ *Dosseringen 13, 13 km (8 mi) northeast of Odense on Rte. 165,* ☎ *65/32–32–33. AE, DC, MC, V. Closed Dec. 18–Mar. 1; Sun.–Mon. in Mar.; Mon. in Apr.*

Ladby

If you're a Viking enthusiast, stop in the village of Ladby to see the **Ladbyskibet** (Ladby Ship), the 1,100-year-old underground remains of a Viking chieftain's burial, complete with his 72-ft-long ship. The warrior was equipped for his trip to Valhalla (the afterlife) with his weapons, four hunting dogs, and 11 horses. ✉ *Vikingevej 123,* ☎ *65/32–16–67.* ⏲ *Mar.–May and Sept.–Oct., Tues.–Sun 10–4; June–Aug., daily 10–5; Nov.–Feb., Wed.–Sun. 11–3.*

Odense

Plan to spend at least one night in Denmark's third-largest city. In addition to its museums and pleasant pedestrian streets, Odense is an especially charming provincial capital. If you can't take quaintness, don't go to the **H. C. Andersens Hus** (Hans Christian Andersen House). The surrounding district has been carefully preserved, with cobbled pedestrian streets and low houses with lace curtains. Inside, exhibits use photos, diaries, drawings, and letters to convey a sense of the man and the time in which he lived. Attached to the museum is an extensive library with Andersen's works in more than 127 languages (he is in fact one of the most widely published authors in the history of literature), where you can listen to fairy tales on tape. The museum includes child-friendly exhibits. ✉ *Hans Jensenstr. 37–45,* ☎ *66/13–13–72 ext. 4611,* WEB *www.odmus.dk.* ⏲ *Mid-June–Aug., daily 9–7; Sept.–mid-June, Tues.–Sun. 10–4.*

The **Børnekulturehuset Fyretøjet** (Children's Culture House, The Tinderbox) museum includes walk-through fairy-tale exhibits as well as studios where children can draw and write their own tales and plays and then dress up and perform them. ✉ *Hans Jensenstr. 21,* ☎ *66/14–44–11,* WEB *www.odmus.dk.* ⏲ *Feb.–Dec., Tues.–Sun. 10–4.*

The modern **Carl Nielsen Museum** has multimedia exhibits on Denmark's most famous composer (1865–1931) and his wife, the sculptor Anne Marie Carl Nielsen (1863–1945). ✉ *Claus Bergsg. 11,* ☎ *66/13–13–72, ext. 4671 or 66/14–88–14, ext. 4601,* WEB *www.odmus.dk.* ⏲ *Apr.–May and Sept.–Oct., Thurs.–Sun. noon–4; June–Aug., Tues.–Sun. noon–4; Nov.–Mar., Thurs.–Fri 4–8, weekends noon–4.*

Odense's **Møntergården** (Museum of Cultural and Urban History) fills four houses representing Danish architectural styles from the Renaissance to the 18th century, all grouped around a shady, cobbled courtyard. Inside are dioramas, an extensive coin collection, clothing, toys, and tableaux. ✉ *Overg. 48–50,* ☎ *66/13–13–72, ext. 4611,* WEB *www.odmus.dk.* ⏲ *Tues.–Sun. 10–4.*

★ **Brandts Passage,** off Vestergade, is a heavily boutiqued walking street. At the end of the passage, in what was once a textile factory, is a four-★ story art gallery, the **Brandts Klædefabrik,** incorporating the **Museet for Foto Kunst** (Museum for Photographic Art), **Danmarks Grafiske Museum** (Danish Graphics Museum), and **Kunst Hallen** (Art Hall), with temporary exhibits for video art. It's well worth the short walk to see Fyn's rendition of a New York SoHo loft. ✉ *37–43 Brandts Passage,* ☎ *66/13–78–97,* WEB *www.brandts.dk.* ⏲ *Tues.–Sun. 10–5.*

Don't neglect **Den Fynske Landsby** (Fyn Village); an enjoyable way to get here is to travel down the Odense River by boat. The open-air museum village is made up of 20 farm buildings, including workshops, a vicarage, a water mill, and a windmill. There's a theater, too, with summertime adaptations of Andersen's tales. ✉ *Sejerskovvej 20,* ☎ *66/13–13–72, ext. 4642,* WEB *www.odmus.dk.* ⏲ *Apr.–mid-June and mid-Aug.–Oct., Tues.–Sun. 10–5; mid-June–mid-Aug., daily 9:30–7; Nov.–Mar., Sun. 11–3.*

$$ ✕ **Le Provence.** A few minutes from the pedestrian street, this restaurant, with its cozy orange-and-yellow dining room, puts a Danish

twist on Provençal cuisine, with such specialties as truffle soup or frogs' legs served with an Armagnac sauce. ✉ *Pogstr. 31,* ☎ *66/12–12–96,* WEB *www.le-provence.dk. DC, MC, V.*

$ ✕ **Målet.** A lively crowd calls this sports club its neighborhood bar. Next to steaming plates of schnitzel served in a dozen ways, soccer is the delight of the house. ✉ *Jernbaneg. 17,* ☎ *66/17–82–41. Reservations not accepted. No credit cards.*

$$$ **Grand Hotel.** They don't make spacious, gracious places like this anymore. Dating from 1897, the Grand offers spruced-up fin-de-siècle elegance. The lobby decor is cool and green, with a sweeping staircase and a spectacular Pompeian-red dining room. Guest rooms are ample and comfortable. ✉ *Jernbaneg. 18, DK 5000,* ☎ *66/11–71–71,* FAX *66/14–11–71,* WEB *www.firsthotels.com. 138 rooms. Restaurant. AE, DC, MC, V.*

$$ **Hotel Ansgar.** This hotel maintains a cozy, modest, English-style ambience. The rooms—done in rather dark colors—have a mix of old and new furniture. ✉ *Østre Stationsvej 32, DK 5000,* ☎ *66/11–96–93,* FAX *66/11–96–75,* WEB *www.hotel.ansgar.dk. 64 rooms. Restaurant. AE, MC, V.*

$ **Hotel Ydes.** If you're a student or are budget-conscious and tired of barracks-type accommodations, this bright, colorful hotel is a good bet. The plain, white, hospital-style rooms are clean and comfortable. ✉ *Hans Tausensg. 11, DK 5000,* ☎ *66/12–11–31,* WEB *www.ydes.dk. 28 rooms, 27 with shower. Restaurant. AE, DC, MC, V.*

Fåborg

Four times a day, the lovely little 12th-century town of Fåborg echoes with the dulcet chiming of the Klokketårnet (Bell Tower) carillon, the largest in Fyn. Dating from 1725, the **Den Gamle Gård** (Old Merchant's House) presents the cultural history of Fyn. ✉ *Holkeg. 1,* ☎ *62/61–33–38.* ⏲ *Mid-May–Sept., daily 10:30–4:30, April 1–May 14 and Sept. 16–Oct 31, 11–3.*

The **Fåborg Museum for Fynsk Malerkunst** (Fyn Painting Museum) displays the compositions—dating mainly from 1880 to 1920—of Fyn painters, filled with the dusky light that so often illuminates Scandinavian painting. ✉ *Grønneg. 75,* ☎ *62/61–06–45,* WEB *www.faaborgmuseum.dk.* ⏲ *Apr.–May and Sept.–Oct., daily 10–4; June–Aug., daily 10–5; Nov.–Mar., Tues.–Sun. 11–3.*

$$$$ **Falsled Kro.** Once a smuggler's hideaway, this 500-year-old institution is one of Denmark's most elegant inns. A favorite among well-heeled Europeans, it has sumptuously appointed cottages with European antiques and stone fireplaces. The restaurant combines French and Danish cuisines, employing ingredients from its own garden and markets in faraway Lyon. ✉ *Assensvej 513, DK 5642 Millinge, 13 km (8 mi) northwest of Fåborg on Millinge-Assens Hwy.,* ☎ *62/68–11–11,* FAX *62/68–11–62,* WEB *www.falsledkro.dk. 14 rooms, 3 apartments. Restaurant. AE, DC, MC.*

$$$ **Steensgård Herregårdspension.** A long avenue of beeches leads to this 700-year-old moated manor house 7 km (4½ mi) northwest of Fåborg. Rooms are elegant, with antiques, four-poster beds, and yards of silk damask. The fine restaurant serves wild game from the manor's own preserve. ✉ *Steensgård 4, DK 5642 Millinge,* ☎ *62/61–94–90,* FAX *62/61–78–61,* WEB *www.herregaardspension.dk. 18 rooms. Restaurant. AE, DC, MC, V. Closed Jan.–Feb..*

Svendborg

★ The southernmost town in Fyn is the gateway to the country's southern islands. Just north of Svendborg is **Egeskov Slot** (Egeskov Castle), one of the best-preserved island castles in Europe. Egeskov means "oak forest," and an entire one was felled around 1540 to form the piles on which the rose-stone structure was erected. The park contains noteworthy Renaissance, Baroque, English, and peasant gardens and an antique-car museum. This is still a private home, but a few rooms, including the trophy-filled hunting room, are open to the public. ✉ *Egeskovg. 18, Kværndrup, 15 km/9 mi north of Svendborg,* ☎ *62/27–10–16,* WEB *www.egeskov.com.* *Castle and museum DKr115.* ⏲ *Castle May–June and Aug.–Sept., daily 10–5; July, daily 10–7. Museum May and Sept., daily 10–5; June and Aug., daily 9–6; July, daily 9–8.*

$ ✕ **Ærø.** A dim hodgepodge of ship parts and maritime doodads, this harborside restaurant is peopled by brusque waitresses and serious local trenchermen. The menu remains staunchly old-fashioned, focusing on *frikadeller* (fried meatballs), fried *rødspætte* (plaice) with hollandaise sauce, and dozens of smørrebrød options. ✉ *Brøg. 1 ved Ærøfærgen,* ☎ *62/21–07–60. DC, MC, V. Closed Sun.*

Ærø

Take the car ferry to **Søby** at the northern tip of Ærø island, the "Jewel of the Archipelago," where roads wend their way through fertile fields and past thatched farmhouses. South from Søby is the charming town of **Ærøskøbing,** on the island's north coast. Once you've spent an hour walking through its cobbled 17th- and 18th-century streets, you'll understand its great appeal.

$ **Ærøhus.** The half-timber building with a steep red roof looks like a rustic cottage on the outside and a great-aunt's house on the inside. Hanging pots and slanted walls highlight the public areas; pine furniture and cheerful curtains and duvets keep the guest rooms simple and bright. Apartments, all with kitchenettes, occupy an annex. The garden's eight cottages have small terraces. ✉ *Vesterg. 38, Ærøskøbing DK 5970 Ærøskøbing,* ☎ *62/52–10–03,* FAX *62/52–21–23,* WEB *www.aeroehus-hotel.dk. 30 rooms, 18 with bath; 8 cottages; 37 apartments. Restaurant. AE, DC, MC, V. Closed Dec. 24 and Jan..*

Troense

On the island of Tåsinge, pretty Troense is one of Denmark's best-preserved villages. Once the home port for countless sailing ships, both Viking and, later, commercial, the harbor today is stuffed with pleasure yachts. Dating from around 1640, **Valdemars Slot** (Valdemars Castle), now a sumptuously furnished home, is one of Denmark's oldest privately owned castles. Upstairs rooms are appointed to the smallest detail. Downstairs is the castle church, illuminated only by candlelight. There's a restaurant beneath the church. The sister café overlooks Lunkebugten, a bay with one of south Fyn's best stretches of beach. ✉ *Slotsalleen 100, Troense,* ☎ *62/22–61–06,* WEB *www.valdemarsslot.dk.* ⏲ *May and Sept.–Oct., daily 10–5; June–Aug., daily 10–6. Call to confirm opening hrs.*

$$$ ✕ **Restaurant Valdemars Slot.** Beneath the castle, this domed restaurant is all romance and prettiness, with pink carpet and candlelight. Fresh ingredients from France and Germany and game from the castle's preserve are the essentials for an ever-changing menu, which includes such specialties as venison with cream sauce and duck breast à l'orange. The less expensive café, Euel-Brockforff, serves traditional Danish food. ✉ *Slotsalleen 100, Troense,* ☎ *62/22–59–00,* WEB *www.valdemarsslot.dk. AE, MC, V. Closed Nov.–Mar. except to groups of 4 or more with several days' notice.*

Langeland

Tåsinge is connected with the island of Langeland by a causeway bridge. The largest island in the southern archipelago, Langeland is rich in relics of the past, including a castle, a thatched village, and a sculpture garden, and the beaches are worth scouting out.

Fyn and the Central Islands Essentials

TOURS

At the tourist board, pick up a copy of the free booklet "In the Footsteps of Hans Christian Andersen"; it describes a very enjoyable walking tour that you take at your own pace. From Medieval Odense to the Odense of Today Tour, offered July–August, Tuesday–Thursday at 11, also organized by the tourist board, takes you on a tour of the town through the ages.

A day trip to Odense leaves from Copenhagen's city-hall square at 9 AM every Sunday from mid-May to mid-September. Lasting about 11 hours, the trip includes stops at several picturesque villages and a lightning-speed visit to Egeskov Castle.

TRANSPORTATION AROUND FYN AND THE CENTRAL ISLANDS

The best starting point is Nyborg, on Fyn's east coast, just across the Great Belt from Korsør, on Sjælland. "The other Chunnel"—this one connecting Sjælland to Fyn—opened for rail traffic in 1997 and for cars in 1998. From Nyborg the easiest way to travel is by car, though public transportation is good. Distances on Fyn and its islands are short, but there is much to see and you can easily spend two or three days here, circling the islands from Nyborg or using Odense or Svendborg as a base from which to make excursions.

VISITOR INFORMATION

➤ TOURIST INFORMATION: **South Fyn Tourist Board** (✉ Centrumpl., Svendborg, ☎ 62/21–09–80). **Nyborg** (✉ Torvet 9, ☎ 65/31–02–80). **Odense** (✉ Rådhuset, ☎ 66/12–75–20, WEB www.odenseturist.dk).

JYLLAND AND THE LAKES

A region of carefully groomed pastures punctuated by stretches of rugged beauty, the peninsula of Jylland (Jutland) is the only part of Denmark that is naturally attached to the mainland of Europe; its southern boundary forms the frontier with Germany. Moors and sand dunes cover a tenth of the peninsula—the windswept landscapes of Isak Dinesen's short stories can be seen in the northwest—and the remaining land is devoted to agriculture and forestry. On the east side of the peninsula, facing Fyn, wooded fjords run inland for miles. Beyond rustic towns and stark countryside, Jylland possesses gracious castles, parklands, and the famed Legoland. Ribe, Denmark's oldest town, lies to the south; to the east is Århus, Denmark's second-largest city, with superb museums and a new concert hall. If you are in this region directly after touring Fyn, head northwest from Odense through Middlefart and then on to Vejle. By train, either from Odense or Copenhagen, the starting point is Kolding, to the south of Vejle.

Kolding

Don't miss the 13th-century **Koldinghus** castle, a royal residence during the Middle Ages. Rebuilt in the 15th century, it was destroyed by fire in the early 1800s. Modern efforts to restore the structure took nearly 20 years, but they culminated in the European Nostra Prize for restoration in 1993. Perched at the edge of the Kolding Fjord is the massive redbrick quadrangle centered on a courtyard. The castle floors are made of raw oak, and its walls are alternately spare and white or

Jutland (Jylland)

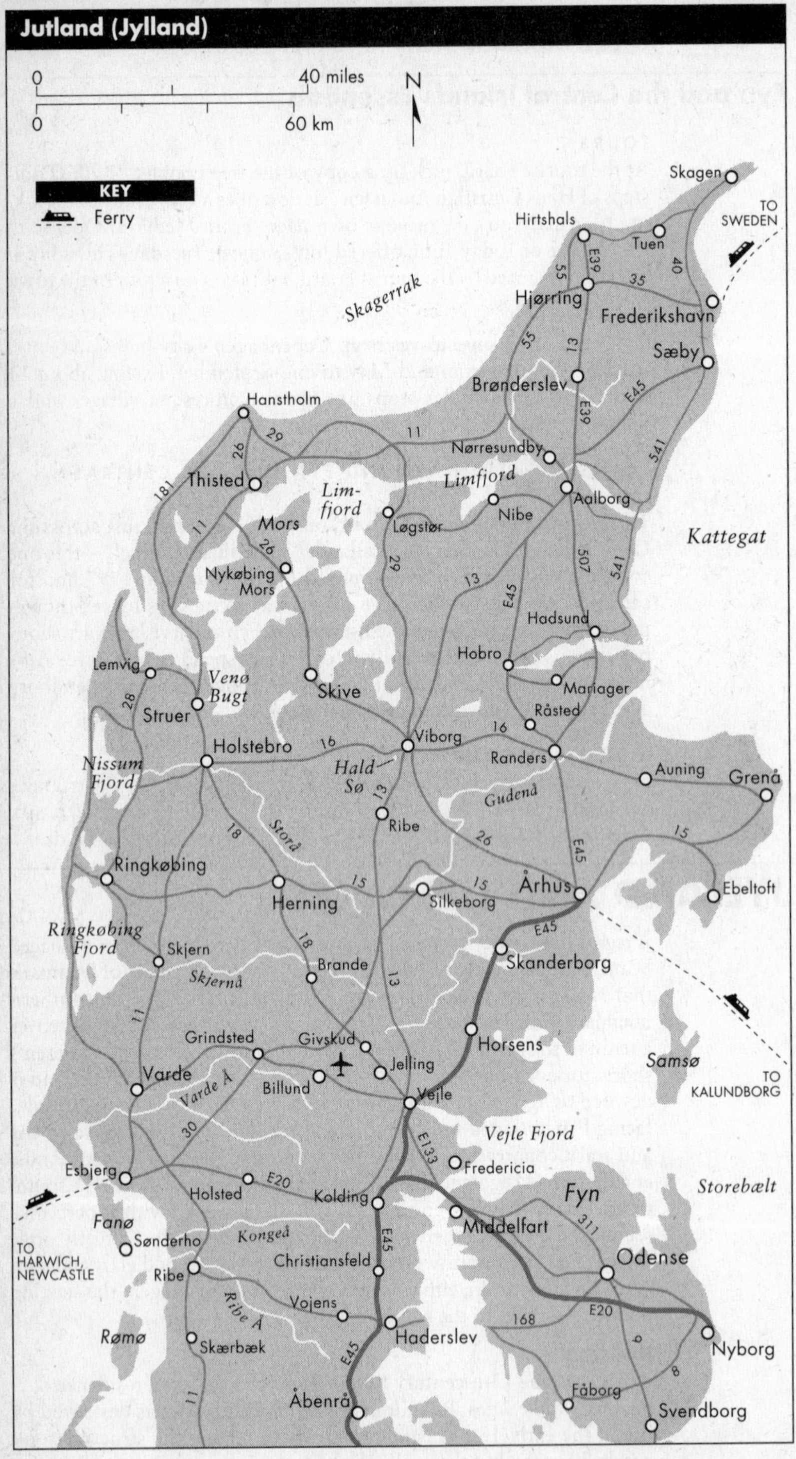

lined with iron plates. ✉ *Markdanerg.,* ☎ *75/50–15–00,* WEB *www.koldinghus.dk.* ⌚ *Daily 10–5.*

The **Geografiske Have** (Geographical Garden) has a rose garden with more than 120 varieties, as well as some 2,000 other plants from all parts of the world, arranged geographically. ✉ *Christian den IV Vej,* ☎ *75/50–38–80,* WEB *www.geografiskehave.dk.* ⌚ *May–Sept., daily 10–6.*

Vejle

Beautifully positioned on the fjord amid forest-clad hills, Vejle faces the strait that divides Jylland and Fyn. You can hear an old Dominican monastery clock chiming the hours; the clock survives, but the monastery itself was long ago torn down to make room for the town's imposing 19th-century city hall.

$$$$ **Munkebjerg.** Seven kilometers (4½ mi) southeast of town, surrounded by a thick beech forest and majestic views of the Vejle Fjord, this elegant hotel provides privacy. Overlooking the forest, rooms are furnished in blond pine and soft green; the lobby is rustic. Of the two top-notch restaurants, one specializes in French cuisine, the other in very Danish fare. Amenities include a heliport. ✉ *Munkebjergvej 125, DK 7100,* ☎ *76/42–85–00,* FAX *75/72–08–86,* WEB *www.munkebjerg.dk. 148 rooms. 2 restaurants, pool. AE, DC, MC, V.*

Jelling

Here are two 10th-century burial mounds, all that remains from the court of King Gorm the Old and his wife, Thyra. Between the mounds are the Jelling **Runestener** (runic stones), one of which, "Denmark's Certificate of Baptism," is decorated with the oldest known figure of Christ in Scandinavia. The stone was erected by Gorm's son, King Harald Bluetooth, who brought Christianity to the Danes in AD 960.

Silkeborg

The region between Silkeborg, on the banks of the Gudenå in Jylland's lake district, and Skanderborg to the east reveals some of Denmark's loveliest scenery. The best way to explore the area is by water; the Gudenå winds its way some 160 km (100 mi) through lakes and wooded hillsides down to the sea. You can take an excursion boat or, better still, a rare old coal-fired paddle steamer, the ***Hjejlen,*** which runs in summer and is based at Silkeborg. Ever since 1861 it has been paddling its way through narrow stretches of fjord where the treetops meet overhead to the foot of Denmark's highest hill, the Himmelbjerget, which rises all of 438 ft at Lake Julso. You can clamber up the narrow paths through the heather and trees to the top of the hill, where there is an 80-ft tower erected in 1875 in memory of King Frederik VII. ✉ *Havnen, Silkeborg,* ☎ *86/82–07–66 reservations.* 🎫 *Round-trip DKr90, DKr50 for children.* ⌚ *Departs Silkeborg Harbor June 29–Aug. 2 at 10 and 1:45.*

One of Silkeborg's chief attractions can be seen in the **Kulturhistoriske Museum** (Museum of Cultural History), which houses the 2,200-year-old Tollund Man, whose corpse was preserved naturally in a nearby bog. ✉ *Hovedgaardsvej 7,* ☎ *86/82–14–99,* WEB *silkeborgmuseum.dk.* ⌚ *Mid-Apr.–late Oct., daily 10–5; late Oct.–mid-Apr., Wed. and weekends noon–4.*

Århus

Denmark's second-largest city is at its liveliest during the 10-day **Århus Festival** in late August, which brings together everything from classical concerts to jazz and folk music, clowning, theater, exhibitions, beer tents, and sports. The town's cathedral, the 15th-century **Domkirke,** is Denmark's longest church; it contains a beautifully executed three-panel altarpiece. Whimsical sketches enliven the ceiling. ✉ *Bispetorv,* ☎ *86/12–38–45.* ⊙ *Jan.–Apr. and Oct.–Dec., Mon.–Sat. 10–3; May–Sept., Mon.–Sat. 9:30–4.*

Århus's 13th-century **Vor Frue Kirken** (Church of Our Lady), formerly attached to a Dominican abbey, has an eerie but interesting crypt church rediscovered in 1955 and dating from 1060, one of the oldest preserved stone churches in Scandinavia. The vaulted space contains a replica of an old Roman crucifix. ✉ *Frue Kirkepl.,* ☎ *86/12–12–43.* ⊙ *Sept.–Apr., weekdays 10–2, Sat. 10–noon; May–Aug., weekdays 10–4, Sat. 10–2.*

The town's open-air museum, the **Den Gamle By** (Old Town), is composed of 65 half-timber houses, a mill, and a millstream. The meticulously re-created period interiors range from the 15th to the early 20th century. ✉ *Viborgvej,* ☎ *86/12–31–88,* WEB *www.dengamleby.dk.* ⊙ *Jan., daily 11–3; Feb.–Mar., daily 11–4; Apr.–May and Sept.–Oct., daily 10–5; June–Aug., daily 9–6; Nov.–Dec., daily 10–4.*

★ In a 250-acre forest just south of Århus, the indoor-outdoor **Moesgård Forhistorisk Museum** (Prehistoric Museum) displays ethnography and archaeology, including the Grauballe Man, a well-preserved corpse from 2,000 years ago. Take the Prehistoric Trail through the forest, which leads past Stone and Bronze Age displays to some reconstructed houses from Viking times. ✉ *Ny Moesgård Allé 20, Højbjerg,* ☎ *89/42–11–00.* ⊙ *Jan.–mid-Mar. and Oct.–Dec., Tues.–Sun. 10–4; mid-Mar.–Sept., daily 10–5.*

$ ✕ **Bryggeriet Sct. Clemens.** At this popular brewpub, you can sit among copper kettles and quaff the local recipe, which is unfiltered and without additives, just like in the old days. Between the spareribs and Australian steaks, you won't go hungry either. ✉ *Kannikeg. 10–12,* ☎ *86/13–80–00. AE, MC, V.*

$$$ **Hotel Royal.** Open since 1838, Århus's grand hotel has hosted such greats as Arthur Rubinstein and Marian Anderson. Guests are welcomed into a stately lobby appointed with Chesterfield sofas, modern paintings, and a winding staircase leading to the accommodations above. The plush rooms vary in style and decor, but all have rich drapery, velour- and brocade-covered furniture, and marble bathrooms. ✉ *Store Torv 4, DK 8100,* ☎ *86/12–00–11,* FAX *86/76–04–04,* WEB *www.hotelroyal.dk. 102 rooms, 8 suites. Restaurant. AE, DC, MC, V.*

$ **Youth Hostel Pavilionen.** As in all Danish youth and family hostels, rooms here are clean, bright, and functional, and the secluded, wooded setting near the fjord is downright beautiful. Keep in mind that it does get noisy, with carousing business parties mixed in with budget-conscious backpackers. There's a kitchen for guests' use. The cafeteria serves breakfast only. ✉ *Marienlundsvej 10, DK 8240,* ☎ *86/16–72–98,* FAX *86/10–55–60. 30 rooms, 11 with shower; 4 communal showers and toilets. AE, MC, V. Closed mid-Dec.–mid-Jan.*

Aalborg

This city guards the narrowest point of the Limfjord, the great waterway of northern Jylland and the gateway between north and south. Here you'll find charming combinations of new and old, twisting lanes filled with medieval houses and, nearby, broad modern boulevards. Jomfru Ane Gade, a tiny cobbled street in the center of Aalborg, is lined with restaurants, inns, and sidewalk cafés. The magnificent five-story **Jens Bangs Stenhus** (Jens Bang's Stone House; ✉ Østerågade 9, ☎ 98/12–50–56), dating from 1624, has an atmospheric restaurant and an excellent wine cellar. The Baroque cathedral, **Budolfi Kirken** (Butolph

Church; ✉ Gammel Torv), is consecrated to English St. Butolph. The 15th-century **Helligaandsklosteret** (Monastery of the Holy Ghost; ✉ C. W. Obelspl., next to Budolfi Kirken), one of Denmark's best-preserved, is now a home for the elderly.

$$ ★ ✕ **Duus Vinkælder.** This amazing cellar is part alchemist's den, part neighborhood bar. Most people come for a drink before or after dinner, but you can also get a light bite. In summer the menu is chiefly smørrebrød, but during the winter you can order such specialties as pølser, frikadeller, *biksemad* (cubed potato, meat, and onion hash), and the restaurant's specialty, pâté. ✉ *Østerå 9,* ☏ *98/12–50–56. Reservations essential. No credit cards. Closed Sun.*

$$ ✕ **Spisehuset Kniv og Gaffel.** In a 400-year-old building parallel to Jomfru Ane Gade, the busy "Knife and Fork" is crammed with oak tables balancing on crazy slanting floors and lit by candles. Its year-round courtyard is a veritable greenhouse. Young waitresses negotiate the mayhem to deliver inch-thick steaks, the house specialty. ✉ *Maren Turisg. 10,* ☏ *98/16–69–72. DC, MC, V. Closed Sun.*

$$$$ 🏨 **Helnan Phønix.** In a sumptuous old mansion, this hotel is popular with international and business guests. Rooms are luxuriously furnished with plump chairs and polished dark-wood furniture; in some the original raw beams are still intact. The Brigarden restaurant serves excellent Danish cuisine. ✉ *Vesterbro 77, DK 9000,* ☏ *98/12–00–11,* FAX *98/16–31–66,* WEB *www.helnan-phonix-hotel.dk. 210 rooms, 2 suites. Restaurant. AE, DC, MC, V.*

Skagen

The picturesque streets and luminous light of the town have inspired both painters and writers. Michael and Anna Ancher, P.S. Krøyer, and other artists settled here and founded what has become known as the Skagen school of painting; you can see their work in the **Skagens Museum.** ✉ *Brøndumsvej 4,* ☏ *98/44–64–44,* WEB *www.skagensmuseum.dk.* ⏲ *Apr. and Oct., Tues.–Sun. 11–4; May and Sept., daily 10–5; June–Aug., daily 10–6; Nov.–Mar., Wed.–Fri. 1–4, Sat. 11–4, Sun. 11–3.*

$$ 🏨 **Brøndums Hotel.** A few minutes from the beach, this 150-year-old gabled inn is furnished with antiques and Skagen-school paintings. The 21 guest rooms in the main building, without TVs or phones, are old-fashioned, with wicker chairs, Oriental rugs, and pine and four-poster beds. Some are beginning to show their age, but 25 annex rooms are more modern. Reserve well in advance for the summer months. The hotel has a fine Danish-French restaurant with a lavish cold table. ✉ *Anchersvej 3, DK 9990,* ☏ *98/44–15–55,* FAX *98/45–15–20,* WEB *www.broendums-hotel.dk. 46 rooms, 13 with bath. Restaurant. AE, DC, MC, V.*

Viborg

Dating from the 8th century, the town started out as a trading post and a place of pagan sacrifice. Later it became a center of Christianity, with monasteries and its own bishop. The 1,000-year-old **Haervejen,** the old military road that starts near here, was once Denmark's most important connection with the outside world. Legend has it that during the 11th century, King Canute set out from Viborg to conquer England, which he subsequently ruled from 1016 to 1035. Built in 1130, Viborg's **Domkirke** (cathedral; ✉ Mogensg., ☏ 87/25–52–50) was once the largest granite church in the world. The crypt, restored and reopened in 1876, is all that remains of the original building. Its 20th-century biblical frescoes were painted by Danish artist Joakim Skovgaard.

Hald Sø

There's terrific walking country beside Hald Sø (Hald Lake) and on the nearby heather-clad Dollerup Bakker (Dollerup Hills). At a small kiosk near the lake that sells snacks and sweets you can pick up a map.

Herning

In this old moorland town, you'll find a remarkable circular building with an exterior frieze by Carl-Henning Pedersen (b. 1913); it houses the **Carl-Henning Pedersen and Else Afelt Museum.** Just next door is the Hernings Kunst Museum (Herning Art Museum; ☎ 97/12–10–33). The convex outer wall of the collar-shape building, a shirt factory until 1977, is lined with a 722-ft-long frieze. The two museums are set within a sculpture park. ✉ *Birk Centerpark 1–3,* ☎ *97/22–10–79.* ⏲ *Hours for both museums: Nov.–Apr., Tues.–Sun. noon–5; May–June, Sept.–Oct., Tues.–Sun. 10–5; July, daily 10–5.*

Ribe

The medieval center in Denmark's oldest town is preserved by the Danish National Trust. From May to mid-September, a night watchman walks around the town telling of its ancient history and singing traditional songs. Visitors can join him in the main square each night at 10.

$$$ **Hotel Dagmar.** In the middle of Ribe's quaint center, this cozy, half-timber hotel encapsulates the charm of the 16th century, with stained-glass windows, frescoes, sloping floors, and carved chairs. The lavish rooms are all appointed with antique canopy beds, fat armchairs, and chaise longues. The fine French restaurant serves such specialties as fillet of salmon in sorrel cream sauce and marinated *foie gras de canard* (duck liver). ✉ *Torvet 1, DK 6760,* ☎ *75/42–00–33,* FAX *75/42–36–52,* WEB *www.hoteldagmar.dk. 50 rooms. Restaurant. AE, DC, MC, V.*

Billund

★ **Legoland** is a park filled with scaled-down versions of cities, towns, and villages; working harbors and airports; a Statue of Liberty; a statue of Sitting Bull; a Mt. Rushmore; a safari park; even a Pirate Land—all constructed of millions of Lego bricks. There are also exhibits of toys from pre-Lego days, including Legoland's showpiece, Titania's Palace, a sumptuous dollhouse built in 1907 by Sir Neville Wilkinson for his daughter. The park also has the double-football-field-size Castleland extravaganza, where guests arrive through a serpentine dragon ride to enjoy rides and restaurants. Everything inside is made of 45 million Lego bricks, including the wizards and warlocks, dragons and knights that inhabit it. That is until you get to the theme restaurant, the Knight's Barbecue, where waiters in Middle Ages garb hustle skewered haunches of beef and typical fare of the period. ✉ *Legoland,* ☎ *75/33–13–33,* WEB *www.legoland.dk.* *DKr140–DKr150.* ⏲ *Mid-Apr.–Oct., daily 10–8.*

Jylland and the Lakes Essentials

CAR TRAVEL

Although there is good train and bus service between all the main cities, this region is best visited by car. The delightful nearby islands are suitable only if you have ample time, as many involve an overnight stay.

TOURS

Guided tours are scarce in these parts; stop by any tourist office for maps and suggestions for a walking tour. Århus also offers a "Round and About the City" tour, which leaves from the tourist board daily at 10 AM from mid-June to mid-August.

VISITOR INFORMATION

The Danish Tourist Board maintains a central Web site with links to all regional offices, listed below.

➤ TOURIST INFORMATION: **Aalborg** (✉ Østerå 8, Aalborg, ☎ 98/12–60–22). **Århus** (✉ Rådhuset, Århus, ☎ 89/40–67–00). **Billund** (✉ c/o Legoland A/S, Billund, ☎ 75/33–19–26). **Danish Tourist Board** (☎ 70/22–24–42, WEB www.dt.dk). **Herning** (✉ Torvet 1A, Herning, ☎ 96/27–22–22). **Kolding** (✉ Axeltorv 8, Kolding, ☎ 76/33–21–00). **Randers** (✉ Erhvervens Hus, Tørvebryggen 12, Randers, ☎ 86/42–44–77). **Ribe** (✉ Torvet 3–5, Ribe, ☎ 75/42–15–00). **Silkeborg** (✉ Åhavevej Haven, Godthåbsvej 4, Silkeborg, ☎ 86/82–19–11). **Vejle** (✉ Banegaardspl. 6, ☎ 75/82–19–55). **Viborg** (✉ Nytorv 9, Viborg, ☎ 86/61–16–66).

10 FINLAND

HELSINKI, THE SOUTH COAST, THE LAKELANDS, FINNISH LAPLAND

IF YOU LIKE MAJESTIC OPEN SPACES, fine architecture, and the Nordic quality of life, Finland is for you. It is a land of lakes—187,888 at the last count—and forests, whose people prize their natural surroundings while expanding the frontiers of modern design and high technology.

The music of Sibelius echoes the mood of this Nordic landscape. Both can swing from the somber nocturne of midwinter darkness to the tremolos of sunlight slanting through pine and bone-white birch, ending with the diminuendo of a sunset as it fades into the next day's dawn. Similarly, the Finnish people reflect the changing moods of their land and climate. Their affinity with nature has produced some of the world's greatest designers and architects. Many American cities have buildings designed by Alvar Aalto and the Saarinens, Eliel and his son Eero. Today Finland is also increasingly known for its high-tech achievements, especially by the mobile-phone giant Nokia.

While Internet connections in Finland are more numerous per capita than anywhere else in the world, the country's more than 5.1 million inhabitants continue to treasure their vast silent spaces. They won't always appreciate back-slapping familiarity—least of all in the sauna, widely regarded in the land that gave the traditional bath its name as a spiritual, as well as a cleansing, experience. Nevertheless, Finns are not unlikely to strike up impromptu conversations in pubs or provide generous help for a lost tourist.

Until 1917 Finland (in Finnish, Suomi) was under the domination of Sweden and Russia. After more than 600 years under the Swedish crown and 100 under the tsars, the country bears marks of the two cultures, such as a small but influential Swedish-speaking minority and a scattering of onion-dome Orthodox churches. The Finns themselves, neither Scandinavian nor Slavic, are descendants of the wandering Finno-Ugric peoples, who settled on the swampy shores of the Gulf of Finland before the Christian era. Finnish is one of the Finno-Ugric languages; it is related to Estonian and, distantly, to Hungarian.

There is a tough, resilient quality to the Finns. No other people fought the Soviets to a standstill as the Finns did in the Winter War of 1939–40. They are stubborn, self-sufficient, and patriotic, yet not aggressively nationalistic. Having overcome a severe recession and a daunting rate of unemployment during the early 1990s, Finland became assertive in international markets, proud of its technology leaders as well as its sports figures and increasingly aware of what it has to offer the rest of Europe. In 1995 Finland joined the European Union, aiming for greater economic and political security and strengthening its profile by pro-

Finland (Suomi)

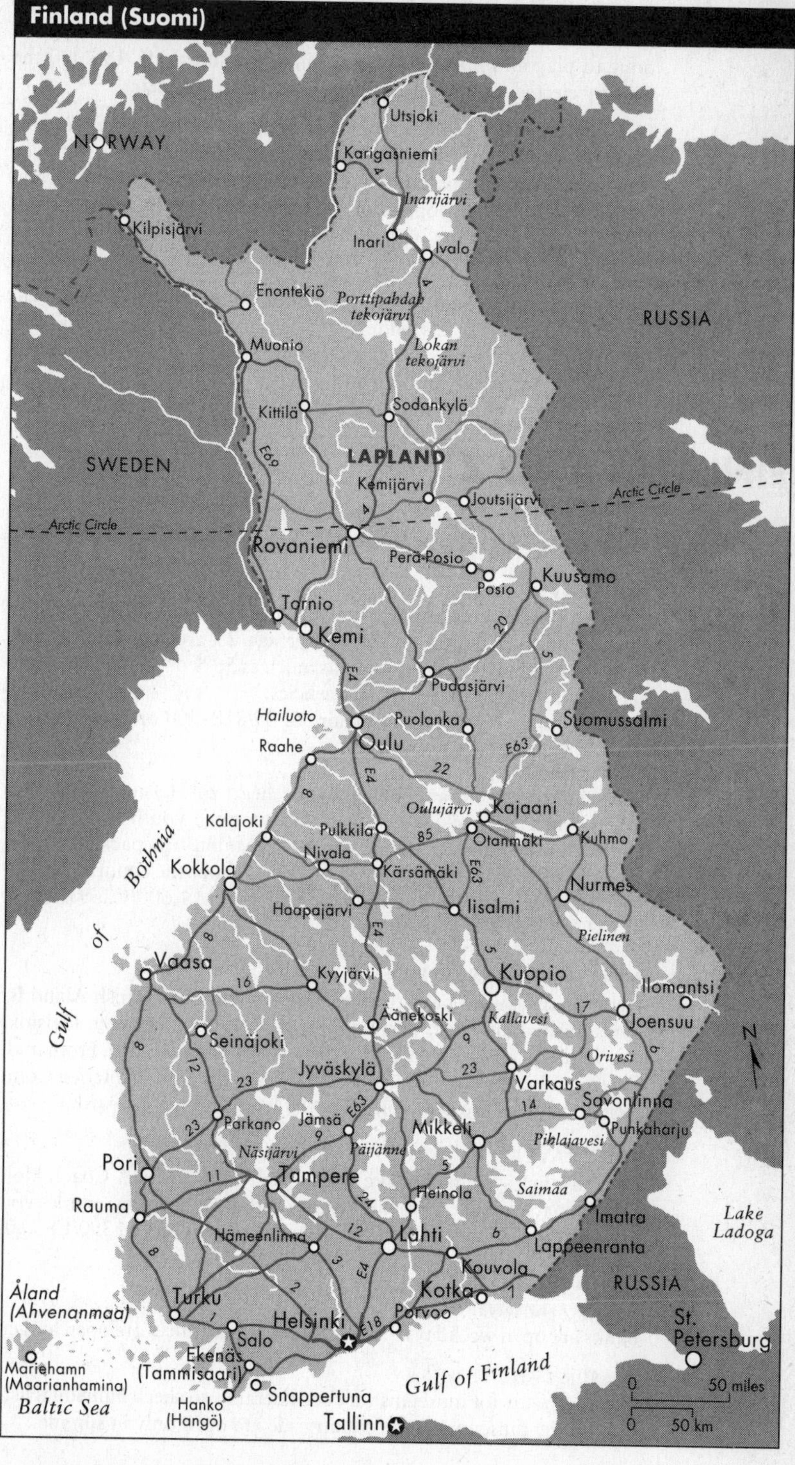

moting the union's "northern dimension." Finland was one of the first countries in the world to grant women the vote, and women continue to play an important role in Finnish political life. In 2000 the country elected its first female president, Tarja Halonen.

Finland's extensive public transport system offers an efficient and affordable way to cover beautiful expanses of lakeland and forest. The atmosphere in the capital, Helsinki, with its outdoor summer bars and cafés and multilingual population, is far more cosmopolitan than it was a decade ago. An influx of Russians and Estonians is also evidence of Finland's new, more open relationship with its eastern neighbors.

"The strength of a small nation lies in its culture," noted Johan Vilhelm Snellman, Finland's leading 19th-century statesman and philosopher. As though inspired by this thought, Finns—who are among the world's top readers—continue to nurture a rich cultural climate, as is illustrated by 900 museums and a slew of summer festivals.

FINLAND A TO Z

To research prices, get advice from other travelers, and book travel arrangements, visit www.fodors.com

AIR TRAVEL

Finnair operates an elaborate network of flights linking 25 towns in Finland. Finnair grants visitors under age 25 a discount on flights booked ahead, with reductions of as much as 50% or more. These tickets are available at major travel agencies.

➤ AIRLINES AND CONTACTS: **Finnair** (☏ 09/818–800 or 9800/3466).

BIKE TRAVEL

Well-marked cycle paths run into the heart of Helsinki and other towns and cities. Bikes can be rented at some youth hostels. The Finnish Youth Hostel Association offers round-trip packages from Helsinki to any of its hostel locations throughout the country, including bike rental and hostel accommodation, for FM 1,600/€269 (7 days) or FM 2,820/€474 (14 days).

BOAT AND FERRY TRAVEL

Helsinki and Turku have regular sea links with the Finnish Åland Islands in the Baltic Sea. Ferry and hydrofoil traffic between Helsinki and Tallinn is also convenient for one- to two-day side trips. From mid-June to mid-August you can cruise the lakes of the Finnish interior. Complete timetables are available from the Finnish Tourist Board.

BUS TRAVEL

Finland's bus system can take you virtually anywhere. A Coach Holiday Ticket, available from bus stations and travel agencies, entitles you to 1,000 km (625 mi) of bus travel within two weeks for FM 390/€65.60.

BUSINESS HOURS

BANKS AND OFFICES

Banks are open weekdays 9:15–4:15; exchange offices are open longer.

MUSEUMS AND SIGHTS

Opening hours for museums vary considerably, so check individual listings. Many museums in the countryside are open only in summer.

SHOPS

Shops are generally open weekdays 9–6, Saturday 9–2. Department stores and supermarkets stay open until 8 or 9 on weekdays and 5 or 6 on Saturday. Shops may also open on Sunday during June, July, and August and on four other Sundays in the year—usually in December for Christmas shopping. Shops in the tunnel complex beneath Helsinki's main railway station are open daily, including holidays, until 10 PM.

CAR TRAVEL

EMERGENCIES

The Automobile and Touring Club of Finland (Autoliitto) operates a 24-hour information service for club members and members of foreign auto clubs. Report accidents without delay to the insurance company listed on the rental-car documents or to the Finnish Motor Insurers' Centre (Liikennevakuutuskeskus), as well as to the police.

➤ CONTACTS: **The Automobile and Touring Club of Finland** (✉ Hämeentie 105 A, 00550 Helsinki, ☎ 09/7258–4400; 24-hour information service, 09/7747–6400, FAX 09/7258–4460). **Finnish Motor Insurers' Centre** (✉ Bulevardi 28, 00120 Helsinki, ☎ 09/680–401).

GASOLINE

Gasoline costs about FM 6.2/€1.05 per liter.

PARKING

Major cities offer multistory garages; most towns have on-street meters. In Helsinki there is no free on-street parking. In areas with no meters drivers must display a *pysäköintilippu* (parking voucher), for sale at R-kiosks and gas stations, on their dashboard.

ROAD CONDITIONS

Finland has an expanding network of efficient major roads, some of which are multilane. In the north, you can expect long stretches of dirt road, which become difficult to negotiate during the spring thaw. Away from the larger towns traffic is light, but take elk and reindeer warning signs seriously.

RULES OF THE ROAD

Speed limits (usually marked) are 50 kph (30 mph) in built-up areas and 80–100 kph (50–62 mph) in the country and on main roads, 120 kph (74 mph) in summer on some highways. Low-beam headlights must be used at all times outside city areas, seat belts are compulsory (for all seats), and you must carry a warning triangle in case of a breakdown.

CUSTOMS AND DUTIES

For details on imports and duty-free limits, *see* Customs and Duties *in* Chapter 1.

DINING

As in other parts of Scandinavia, the *seisovapöytä* (buffet table) is often a work of art as well as a feast. Some special Finnish dishes are *poronkäristys* (reindeer casserole); salmon, herring, and various freshwater fish; and *lihapullat* (meatballs with a creamy sauce). In the autumn, local mushrooms such as the *suppelovahvero* (a funnel-shaped chanterelle) are a nice complement to meat and game. For a delicious dessert, try *lakka* (cloudberries), which grow above the Arctic Circle and are frequently used in sauces for ice cream. Inexpensive lunches are served in *kahvila* (coffee shops) and *baari* (usually cafés, not bars).

Prix-fixe menus, which usually include two courses and coffee, are served in many establishments and are often a good deal. Also, restaurants that specialize in expensive dishes such as reindeer or pheasant may have less expensive, sometimes vegetarian, options on the menu. A service charge (*palvelupalkkio*) will be included in the check. If you want to leave an additional tip—though it really isn't necessary—round the figure off to the nearest FM 5 or FM 10. Heavy taxation is evident in wine and hard liquor prices in restaurants. Beer is a tasty and moderately priced alternative.

CATEGORY	COST
$$$$	over FM 150 (€25.25)
$$$	FM 100–FM 150 (€16.80–€25.25)
$$	FM 50–FM 100 (€8.40–€16.80)
$	under FM 50 (€8.40)

MEALTIMES

The Finns generally eat early at home, but restaurants run on a later schedule. Breakfast is usually from 7 to 10, lunch runs from 11 or noon to 1 or 2, and dinner from 7 to midnight.

RESERVATIONS AND DRESS

Except for the most elegant establishments, where a jacket and tie are preferred, casual attire is acceptable for restaurants in all price categories; jeans are not allowed in some more expensive dining rooms.

EMBASSIES

There are consular offices for Australia and New Zealand in Helsinki.

➤ CANADA: (✉ Pohjoisesplanadi 25B, 00101 Helsinki, ☎ 09/171–141).

➤ IRELAND: (✉ Erottajankatu 7A, 00131 Helsinki, ☎ 09/646–006).

➤ UNITED KINGDOM: (✉ Itäinen Puistotie 17, 00140 Helsinki, ☎ 09/228–65100).

➤ UNITED STATES: (✉ Itäinen Puistotie 14, 00140 Helsinki, ☎ 09/171–931).

EMERGENCIES

➤ CONTACTS: **National emergency number** (☎ 112). **Police** (☎ 10022).

HOLIDAYS

January 1; January 6 (Epiphany); Good Friday, Easter, and Easter Monday; May 1 (May Day); Ascension (in May); Pentecost/Whitsunday (mid-May to early June); June 23 (Midsummer); All Saints' Day (first Saturday in November); December 6 (Independence Day); December 25–26.

LANGUAGE

The official languages of Finland are Finnish and Swedish. Only about 6% of the total population speaks Swedish, but in some areas, such as the west coast and in pockets close to Helsinki, Swedish speakers form a local majority. English is widely spoken in Helsinki and by young Finns around the country. In Finnish Lapland the native Sámi (pronounced *Sah*-me) population speaks three different dialects of a language distantly related to Finnish. Note that the Finnish letters ä and ö and the Swedish å come at the end of the alphabet.

LODGING

Finland offers a full range of accommodations: hotels, motels, boardinghouses, bed-and-breakfasts, rental chalets and cottages, farmhouses, youth hostels, and campsites. Standards are generally high. Prices are for two people in a double room on a weekday and include breakfast and service charges. Weekend and summer rates tend to be significantly lower. Most rates are listed on hotel Web sites.

CATEGORY	HELSINKI	OTHER AREAS
$$$$	over FM 1200 (€204)	over FM 800 (€136)
$$$	FM 800–FM 1,200 (€136–€204)	FM 600–FM 800 (€102–€136)
$$	FM 500–FM 800 (€85–€136)	FM 500–FM 600 (€85–€102)
$	under FM 500 (€85)	under FM 500 (€85)

CAMPING

Finland has about 350 campsites, and about 200 of them belong to the Finnish Travel Association (Suomen Matkailuliitto) network. Lists are available from the Finnish Travel Association Camping Department and the Finnish Tourist Board.

➤ CONTACTS: **Finnish Travel Association Camping Department** (✉ Atomitie 5C, 00370 Helsinki, ☎ 09/622–6280, FAX 09/654–358).

FARMHOUSE AND COTTAGE RENTALS

Found mainly outside Helsinki, these provide the least expensive accommodations; local tourist offices have lists of available properties. Comfortable (not luxurious) accommodations cost approximately FM 1,500/€252–FM 5,000/€841 per week for a four-person rental. A central reservations agency is Lomarengas (Finnish Country Holidays).

➤ CONTACTS: **Lomarengas** (✉ Hämeentie 105D, 00550 Helsinki, ☎ 09/5766–3350, FAX 09/5766–3355, WEB www.lomarengas.fi).

HOSTELS

Hostels range from empty schools to small manor houses. The Finnish Tourist Board and the Finnish Youth Hostel Association can provide a list of hostels. There are no age restrictions, and prices range from FM 60/€10 to FM 180/€30 per bed and FM 80/€13.46–FM 305/€51.30 per person in single or double rooms, with a discount of FM 15/€2.52 for YHA members.

➤ CONTACTS: **Finnish Youth Hostel Association** (YHA; ✉ Yrjönkatu 38B, 00100 Helsinki, ☎ 09/565–7150, FAX 09/565–71510, WEB www.srmnet.org).

HOTELS

Most hotels in Finland are modern or recently renovated; a few occupy fine old manor houses. Rooms usually have a bath or shower, and virtually all hotels have saunas. Prices generally include breakfast and often a morning sauna and swim. The Finncheque voucher system offers good discounts mid-May through September. For additional information inquire at Suomen Hotellivaraukset Oy (Hotel Reservations in Finland, Ltd.).

➤ CONTACTS: **Suomen Hotellivaraukset Oy** (✉ Korkeavuorenkatu 47B, 00130 Helsinki, ☎ 09/686–0330; 0800/55155 toll-free in Finland, FAX 09/686–03310).

SUMMER HOTELS

Some university student housing is turned into "summer hotels" from June through August; they offer modern facilities at reasonable prices. The Finnish Youth Hostel Association publishes "Hostellit," which lists summer hotels as well as youth hostels. Free copies are available at the Finnish Tourist Board and the Finnish Youth Hostel Association.

RESERVING A ROOM

If you haven't reserved a room before arriving in Helsinki, you can make reservations through a travel agency or at the Hotel Booking Centre; the booking service is free by phone, fax, or e-mail; if the reservation is booked in person, the charge is FM 30/€5.05 per room or FM 20/€3.35 per hostel bed in Helsinki, FM 40/€6.73 for reservations outside Helsinki.

➤ CONTACTS: **Hotel Booking Centre** (✉ Rautatieasema [train station], west wing, ☎ 09/2288–1400, FAX 09/2288–1499, WEB www.helsinki-expert.fi/hotel).

MAIL AND SHIPPING

If you're uncertain about where you'll be staying, have mail sent to you marked "poste restante" and addressed to the post office in the appropriate town or Helsinki's main post office. American Express offers free mail service to cardholders.

➤ CONTACTS: **American Express** (✉ Clients' Mail, American Express, c/o Area Travel Agency, Mikonkatu 2D, 00100 Helsinki). **Main Post Office** (✉ Mannerheiminaukio 1A, 00100; poste restante Helsinki 10, Elielinaukio 2F).

POSTAL RATES

Airmail letters and postcards to destinations within Finland (up to 50 grams) and to all other countries (up to 20 grams) cost FM 3.60/€.61.

MONEY MATTERS

Prices are highest in Helsinki. The prices of many goods include an 18% sales tax; the tax on food is less.

Some sample prices include: cup of coffee, FM 7/€.76–FM 10/€1.08; glass of beer, starting from FM 15/€2.52; soft drink, FM 13/€2.19; ham sandwich, FM 15/€2.50–FM 20/€3.35; 2-km (1-mi) taxi ride, FM 35/€5.90–FM 50/€8.40 (depending on time of day).

CURRENCY

The unit of currency in Finland is the Finnish mark, divided into 100 penniä. There are bills of FM 20, 50, 100, 500, and 1,000 Finnish marks. Coins are 10 and 50 penniä and FM 1, FM 5, and FM 10. At press time (summer 2001), the exchange rate was FM 6.39 to the U.S. dollar, FM 4.13 to the Canadian dollar, FM 9.30 to the pound sterling, FM 7.55 to the Irish punt, FM 3.37 to the Australian dollar, FM 2.77 to the New Zealand dollar, and FM 0.83 to the South African rand. The euro is equivalent to FM 5.94, a fixed rate. January 1, 2002 sees the introduction of the new euro coins and notes. Finland will be switching currency to the euro in March 2002. Marks will cease to exist. Credit cards are widely accepted, even in many taxicabs. Traveler's checks can be cashed only in banks.

Prepaid electronic cash cards that process even the smallest cash transactions at public pay phones, vending machines, and fast-food outlets are very popular in Finland and can be purchased at kiosks.

TAXES

Non-EU residents who purchase goods worth more than FM 250/€42.05 in any shop marked TAX FREE FOR TOURISTS can get a 12%–16% refund (10% on food). Show your passport and the store will give you a check for the appropriate amount, which you can cash at your final point of departure from the EU.

TELEPHONES

Telephone numbers in Finland vary in length from four to eight digits. Business phone numbers may also have special prefix codes (020 or 010), which are country-wide but are charged at only local rates.

COUNTRY AND AREA CODES

The country code for Finland is 358.

INTERNATIONAL CALLS

You can dial Britain and the United States directly from anywhere in Finland. Calls to other countries can be made from telegraph offices, which are marked TELE or LENNÄTIN and are usually next to a post office. An operator will assign you a booth and collect payment at the end of the call. To dial numbers from outside Finland, omit the zero at the beginning of the city code. To make a direct international phone call from Finland, dial 999, 990, or 994, then the country code and phone number. You can reach long-distance operators, or get help from directory assistance, by dialing one of the numbers listed below.

➤ ACCESS CODES: **AT&T** (☎ 9800–10010). **Directory assistance abroad** (☎ 020–208). **MCI** (☎ 9800–10280). **Sprint** (☎ 9800–10284).

LOCAL CALLS

To avoid exorbitant hotel surcharges on calls, use public pay phones, and have some FM 1 and FM 5 coins ready. For information about telephone service, call Elisa Communications, Sonera, or, for help, call local directory assistance.

➤ CONTACTS: **Elisa Communications** (☎ 010/26000). **Sonera** (☎ 0204/01). **Local directory assistance** (☎ 118).

PHONE CARDS

Many pay phones accept only a phone card; the *Sonera Kortti, Elisa Kortti,* and other cards are available at post offices, R-kiosks, and some grocery stores. They come in increments of FM 30, FM 50, FM 100, and FM 150. Several local phone companies also offer cards, and some pay phones only accept certain cards.

TIPPING

You can give taxi drivers small coins. Train and airport porters have a fixed charge. It's not necessary to tip hotel doormen for carrying bags to the check-in counter, but give bellhops FM 5/€.85–FM 10/€1.70 for carrying bags to your room. A coat-check room fee of FM 5/€.85 is usually clearly posted; if not, give about FM 10/€1.70, depending on the number in your party.

TRAIN TRAVEL

Finland's comfortable and clean rail system extends to all main centers of the country. A Finnrail Pass gives unlimited first- or second-class travel within a set time; the 3-day pass costs FM 650/€109.30 (FM 980/€164.80 for first-class), the 5-day pass FM 870/€146.30 (FM 1,310/€220.35), and the 10-day pass FM 1,180/€198.45 (FM 1,700/€285.90). Children pay half-fare. In Finland the Finnrail Pass is available from VR Finnish Railways.

CUTTING COSTS

The ScanRail Pass allows unlimited train travel throughout Denmark, Finland, Norway, and Sweden and comes in various denominations: 5 days of travel within 15 days (FM 1,130/€190.05 second class, FM 1,523/€390.05 first class) or 21 days (FM 1,725/€290.10 second class, 2,319/€390.05 first class). Discounts or free connections on certain ferries and buses are included. Certain hotel chains and organizations also offer discounts to pass holders. In the United States call Rail Europe, or DER, which also offers a 21-day pass.

➤ TRAIN INFORMATION: **DER** (☎ 800/782–2424). **Norvista** (☎ 0171/409–7334). **Rail Europe** (☎ 800/438–7245). **VR Finnish Railways** (☎ 09/707–5700, FAX 09/707–4237).

VISITOR INFORMATION

Many festivals are scheduled throughout the country, especially in summer. For information contact Finland Festivals.

➤ TOURIST INFORMATION: **Finnish Tourist Board Tourist Information Office** (✉ Eteläesplanadi 4, 00100 Helsinki, ☎ 09/4176–9300, FAX 09/4176–9301, WEB www.mek.fi). **Finland Festivals** (✉ Uudenmaankatu 36D, 00120 Helsinki, ☎ 09/612–6760 or 09/6126–7611, FAX 09/6126–7610, WEB www.festivals.fi).

WHEN TO GO

Summer is marked by long hours of sunlight and cool nights. Though many establishments close or reduce hours off-season, the advantages to off-season travel are many: fewer mosquitoes, spectacular fall foliage, and cross-country skiing.

CLIMATE

You can expect warm days in Helsinki from mid-May and in Lapland from mid-June. Hot weather, with temperatures well into the 80s, is not uncommon in July and August. The midnight sun can be seen from May through July, depending on the region. Even in Helsinki, summer nights are brief and never really dark; in midwinter daylight lasts only a few hours.

The following are average daily maximum and minimum temperatures for Helsinki.

Jan.	30F	– 1C	**May**	64F	18C	**Sept.**	53F	11C
	26	– 3		48	9		39	4
Feb.	34F	1C	**June**	60F	16C	**Oct.**	46F	8C
	24	– 4		48	9		36	2
Mar.	36F	2C	**July**	68F	20C	**Nov.**	32F	0C
	26	– 3		55	13		26	– 3
Apr.	46F	8C	**Aug.**	64F	18C	**Dec.**	32F	0C
	32	0		53	12		24	– 4

HELSINKI

Built on the peninsulas and islands of the Baltic shoreline, Helsinki is a city of the sea. Streets curve around bays, bridges arch between islands, and ferries carry traffic to islands farther offshore. The smell of the sea hovers over the city, and there is a constant bustle in the harbors as the huge ships that ply the Baltic drop and lift anchor.

The city covers a total of 1,140 square km (433 square mi), including some 315 islands, with at least 30% of the metropolitan area reserved for parks and other open spaces. Most of Helsinki's sights, however, are crowded onto a single peninsula.

In the 16th century the Swedish king Gustav Vasa, at that time ruler of Finland as well, was determined to woo trade away from the Estonian city of Tallinn and the Hanseatic League. Helsinki was founded next to the rapids of the Vantaa River on June 12, 1550, by a group of Finns who had settled here upon the king's orders.

Over the next three centuries, Turku, on Finland's west coast, was the country's political and intellectual capital. Helsinki took center stage only when Sweden ceded Finland to Russia in 1809. Tsar Alexander I turned Finland into an autonomous grand duchy, proclaiming Helsinki its capital in 1812. Around the same time, much of Turku burned to the ground, and its university was forced to move to Helsinki. From then on Helsinki's position as Finland's first city was assured.

Just before the tsar's proclamation, a fire destroyed many of Helsinki's traditional wooden buildings, making it necessary to build a new city center. The German-born architect Carl Ludvig Engel was entrusted with the project, and thanks to him Helsinki has some of the purest neoclassical architecture in the world. Add to this foundation the stunning outlines of the Jugendstil (Art Nouveau) period of the early 20th century and more modern buildings designed by native Finnish architects, and you have a capital city as architecturally eye-catching as it is unlike those of the rest of Europe.

Exploring Helsinki

Numbers in the margin correspond to points of interest on the Helsinki map.

17 **Eduskuntatalo** (Parliament House). This imposing, colonnaded, red-granite structure was built between 1927 and 1931. The legislature has one of the world's highest ratios of women to men. ✉ *Mannerheimintie 30,* ☎ *09/432–2027,* WEB *www.eduskunta.fi.*

19 **Finlandiatalo** (Finlandia Hall). The lake Töölönlahti forms the backdrop of this important cultural venue. Architect Alvar Aalto designed this creative, marble and black-granite building to be functional: the tower and inclined roof enhance acoustics in the concert hall. ✉ *Karamzinkatu 4,* ☎ *09/402–4246,* WEB *www.finlandia.hel.fi.* ⏲ *Concerts usually Wed. and Thurs. nights.*

Kaivopuisto (Well Park). This elegant district was favored by Russian high society during the 19th century. Now it is a residential area for diplomats and a popular strolling ground. ✉ *Close to ferry terminals, between Puistokatu and Ehrenströmintie.*

Katajanokka. Nineteenth-century brick warehouses in this district have been converted into boutiques, galleries, crafts studios, and restaurants. ✉ *East of Kanavaranta and the Orthodox cathedral.*

3 **Katumuseo/Helsingin Kaupunginmuseo** (Street Museum/Helsinki City Museum). Walk down this block of Sofiankatu from the esplanade to Senate Square and step through various periods of Helsinki's history. The Helsinki City Museum, which displays art, furniture, illustrations, literature, and archives, including a model of Helsinki in the 1870s, a pharmacy, and home interiors from the 18th to the 20th centuries, is on the same street. ✉ *Sofiankatu 4,* ☎ *09/169–3933,* WEB *www.hel.fi/kaumuseo.* ⏲ *Weekdays 9–5, weekends 11–5.*

★ 1 **Kauppatori** (Market Square). The colorful, bustling market beside the South Harbor attracts customers for freshly cut flowers, fruit, and vegetables, as well as handicrafts from small country villages—all sold by vendors in bright orange tents. Closer to the dock are fresh fish from the waters of the Baltic. You can't miss the curvaceous ***Havis Amanda*** statue watching over the busy square. ✉ *Eteläranta and Pohjoisesplanadi.* ⏲ *Sept.–May, weekdays 6:30–2, Sat. 6:30–3; June–Aug., weekdays 6:30–2 and 3:30–8, Sat. 6:30–3, Sun. 9–4.*

2 **Kaupungintalo** (City Hall). This light-blue building on Pohjoisesplanadi (North Esplanade), the political center of Finland, is the home of city government offices. ✉ *Pohjoisesplanadi 1,* ☎ *09/169–3757.*

24 **Korkeasaari Eläintarha** (Helsinki Zoo). Here snow leopards and reindeer thrive in the cold Finnish climate and children can climb on outdoor play equipment. The ferry departs from the Market Square approximately every 30 minutes from May through September. Alternatively, you can catch the bus at Erottaja or Herttoniemi (weekends), or take the metro to the Kulosaari stop, cross under the tracks, and then follow the signs 20 minutes to the zoo. ✉ *Korkeasaari Island,* ☎ *09/169–5969,* WEB *www.hel.fi/zoo.* ⏲ *Mar.–Apr., daily 10–6; May–Sept., daily 10–8; Oct.–Feb., daily 10–4.*

15 ***Mannerheimin patsas*** (statue of Marshal Mannerheim). In front of the main post office, the bronze equestrian gazes down Mannerheimintie, named in his honor. No man in Finnish history is as revered as Baron Carl Gustaf Mannerheim, the military and political leader who guided Finland through the first half of the 20th century. ✉ *Mannerheimintie.*

Eduskuntatalo	17
Finlandiatalo	19
Gallen-Kallela Museum	23
Katumuseo/ Helsingin Kaupunginmuseo	3
Kauppatori	1
Kaupungintalo	2
Korkeasaari Eläintarha	24
Mannerheimin patsas	15
Nykytaiteenmuseo (Kiasma)	16
Presidentinlinna	6
Rautatieasema	13
Senaatintori	4
Seurasaaren Ulkomuseo	22
Stockmann's	11
Suomen Kansallismuseo	18
Suomen Kansallisooppera	20
Suomen Kansallisteatteri	14
Suomenlinna	9
Svenska Teatern	10
Temppeliaukion Kirkko	21
Tuomiokirkko	5
Uspenskin Katedraali	7
Valtion Taidemuseo	12
Vanha Kauppahalli	8

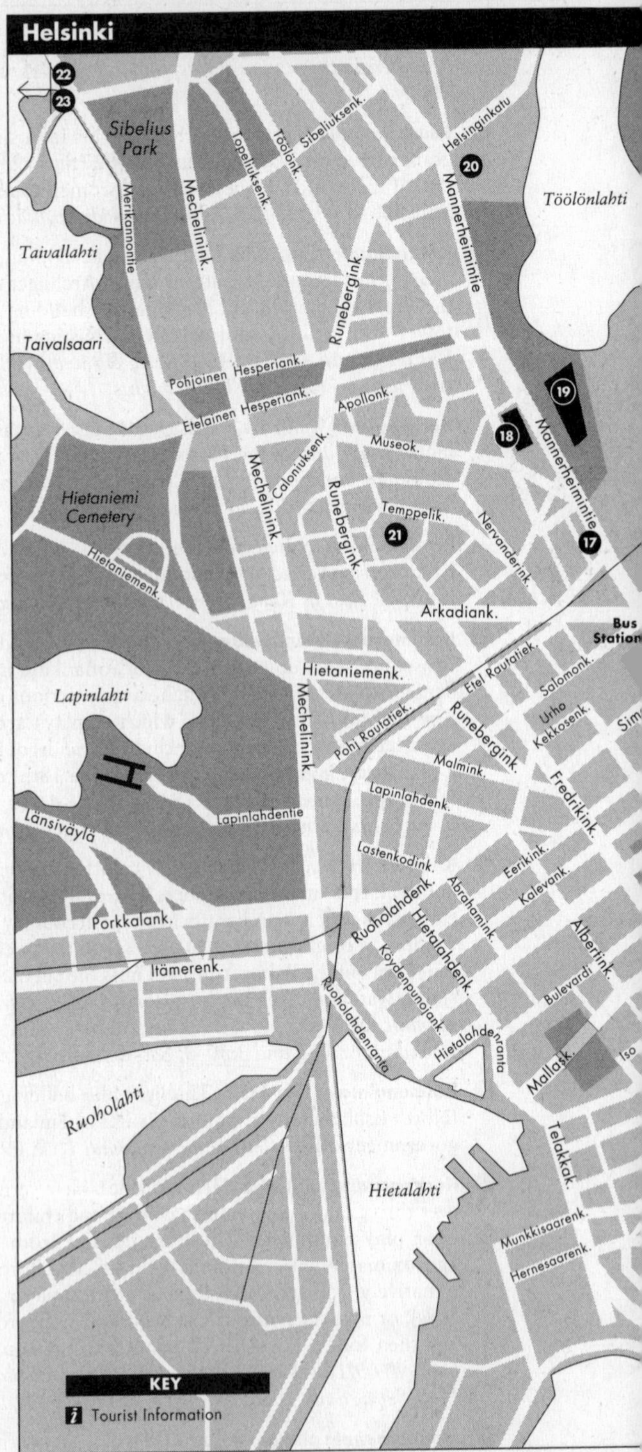

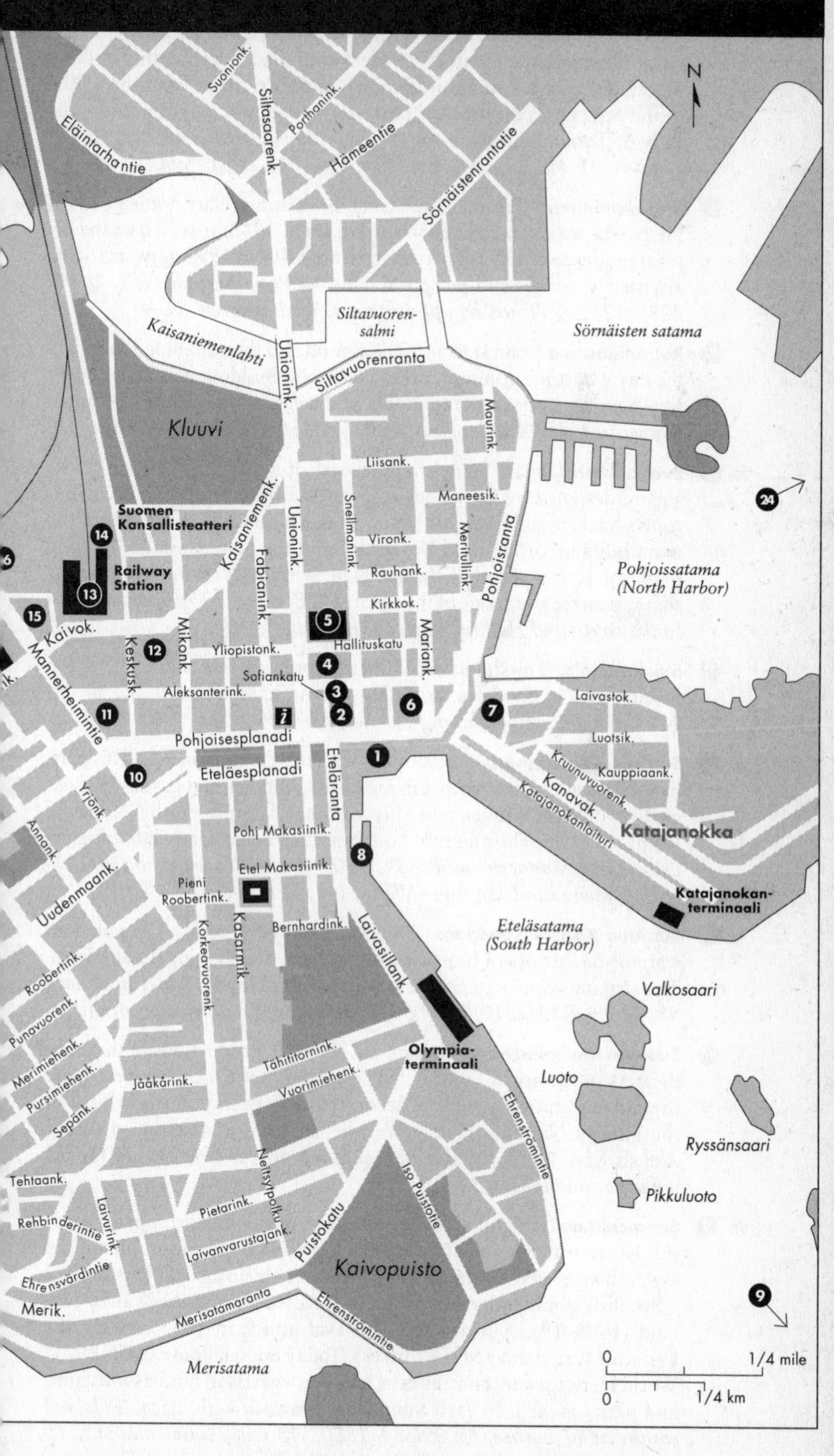

Suonionk.
Siltasaarenk.
Porthamink.
Eläintarhantie
Hämeentie
Sörnäistenrantatie
Siltavuorensalmi
Sörnäisten satama
Kaisaniemenlahti
Unionink.
Siltavuorenranta
Kluuvi
Maurink.
Liisank.
Maneesik.
Snellmanink.
Meritullink.
Pohjoisranta
Suomen Kansallisteatteri
Kaisaniemenk.
Fabianink.
Vironk.
Rauhank.
Railway Station
Kirkkok.
Pohjoissatama (North Harbor)
Kaivok.
Mannerheimintie
Keskusk.
Mikonk.
Yliopistonk.
Hallituskatu
Mariank.
Sofiankatu
Aleksanterink.
Laivastok.
Luotsik.
Pohjoisesplanadi
Eteläesplanadi
Eteläranta
Kruunuvuorenk.
Kauppiaank.
Kanavak.
Katajanokanlaituri
Katajanokka
Yrjönk.
Annank.
Pohj Makasiinik.
Etel Makasiinik.
Pieni Roobertink.
Uudenmaank.
Kasarmik.
Korkeavuorenk.
Bernhardink.
Laivasillank.
Katajanokanterminaali
Eteläsatama (South Harbor)
Roobertink.
Valkosaari
Punavuorenk.
Tähtitornink.
Olympiaterminaali
Merimiehenk.
Vuorimiehenk.
Luoto
Jääkärink.
Pursimiehenk.
Ehrenströmintie
Sepänk.
Ryssänsaari
Tehtaank.
Neitsytpolku
Iso Puistotie
Pikkuluoto
Pietarink.
Rehbinderintie
Laivurink.
Laivanvarustajank.
Puistokatu
Kaivopuisto
Ehrensvärdintie
Merik.
Merisatamaranta
Merisatama
0
1/4 mile
0
1/4 km
N

16 **Nykytaiteenmuseo (Kiasma)** (Museum of Contemporary Art). Praised for the boldness of its curved steel shell but condemned for its encroachment on the territory of the Mannerheim statue, this striking museum displays a wealth of Finnish and foreign art from the 1960s to the present. Look for the "butterfly" windows, and don't miss the view of Töölönlahti from the café. ✉ *Mannerheiminaukio 2.* ☎ *09/1733–6501,* WEB *www.kiasma.fi.* ⏲ *Tues. 9–5, Wed.–Sun. 10–10.*

6 **Presidentinlinna** (President's Palace). Built as a private home in 1818, the palace was converted for use by tsars in 1843. It served as the official residence of Finnish presidents from 1919 to 1993; now its rooms are used as offices and reception halls. ✉ *Pohjoisesplanadi 1,* ☎ *09/2288–1222.* ⏲ *Tours by appointment, Wed. and Sat. 11–4.*

13 **Rautatieasema** (train station). The station and the adjoining square are the city's bustling commuter hub. The solid building was designed by Eliel Saarinen, one of the founders of the early 20th-century National Romantic style. ✉ *Kaivokatu,* ☎ *09/7071; 09/707–5700 reservations.*

★ **4** **Senaatintori** (Senate Square). The heart of neoclassical Helsinki, the square designed by Carl Ludvig Engel is a harmonious blend of Europe's ancient architectural styles. In addition to **Tuomiokirkko,** the main building of Helsinki University and the State Council Building flank the square. **Kiseleff Bazaar Hall,** with cafés and gift and crafts shops, is on the south side of the square. ✉ *Bordered by Aleksanterinkatu to the south and Hallituskatu to the north.*

11 **Stockmann's.** This huge department store has the latest in Finnish fashion and is good for browsing. ✉ *Aleksanterinkatu 52,* ☎ *09/1211,* WEB *www.stockmann.fi.* ⏲ *Weekdays 9–9, Sat. 9–6.*

★ **18** **Suomen Kansallismuseo** (National Museum). Eliel Saarinen and his partners blend allusions to Finnish medieval churches and castles with elements of Art Nouveau in this vintage example of the National Romantic style. The museum houses archaeological, and ethnological exhibits. ✉ *Mannerheimintie 34,* ☎ *09/40501,* WEB *www.nba.fi/NATMUS/Kmeng.html.* ⏲ *Tues.–Wed. 11–8, Thurs.–Sun. 11–6.*

20 **Suomen Kansallisooppera** (Finnish National Opera). The splendid state-of-the-art opera house is set in a park overlooking Töölönlahti. The striking white exterior has clean, modern lines. ✉ *Helsinginkatu 58,* ☎ *09/4030–2210; 09/4030–2350 tours,* WEB *www.operafin.fi.*

14 **Suomen Kansallisteatteri** (National Theater). Productions in the three theaters inside are in Finnish. The elegant granite facade overlooking the railway station square is decorated with quirky reliefs typical of the Finnish National Romantic style. In front is a statue of writer Aleksis Kivi. ✉ *North side of Rautatientori,* ☎ *09/1733–1331,* WEB *www.nationaltheatre.fi.*

★ **9** **Suomenlinna** (Finland's Castle). Frequent ferries link Kauppatori with this island fortress, which was begun in 1748 by Finnish units of the Swedish army. Its six islands were Sweden's shield against Russia until a Swedish commander surrendered to Russia during the War of Finland (1808–19). A heavy British naval attack in 1855, during the Crimean War, damaged the fortress. Today Suomenlinna, a UNESCO World Heritage site, continues as a military garrison but has museums and parks as well. In early summer it is awash with lilacs. ✉ *Island southeast of harbor,* ☎ *09/684–1880,* WEB *www.suomenlinna.fi.* ⏲ *Tours June–Aug., daily at 10:30, 1, and 2:30.*

10 **Svenska Teatern** (Swedish Theater). All performances at this circular theater are in Swedish; many are musicals. ✉ *Pohjoisesplanadi 2,* ☎

09/6162–1411, WEB *www.svenskateatern.fi.* ⏲ *Box office daily noon–performance time.*

★ 21 **Temppeliaukion Kirkko** (Temple Square Church). In a labyrinth of streets west of the Opera, this strikingly modern church is carved out of rock and topped with a copper dome. ✉ *Lutherininkatu 3,* ☎ *09/494–698.* ⏲ *Weekdays 10–8, Sat. 10–6, Sun. noon–1:45 and 3:15–5:45. Closed Tues. 1–2 and during weddings, concerts, and services.*

5 **Tuomiokirkko** (Lutheran Cathedral). Completed in 1852, the domed cathedral dominates the Senaatintori and serves as a symbol of Helsinki. Organ concerts take place on Sundays at 8 PM June–August. ✉ *Yliopistonkatu 7,* ☎ *09/709–2455.* ⏲ *June–Aug., Mon.–Sat. 9–6, Sun. noon–4; Sept.–May, weekdays 10–5, Sat. 10–6, Sun. 10–4.*

★ 7 **Uspenskin Katedraali** (Uspenski Cathedral). The redbrick Orthodox cathedral, completed in 1868, looms over the east side of Kauppatori. ✉ *Kanavakatu 1,* ☎ *09/634–267.* ⏲ *Tues.–Fri. 9:30–4, Sat. 9:30–2, Sun. noon–3.*

12 **Valtion Taidemuseo** (Finnish National Gallery). The best traditional Finnish art is housed in this complex, which includes the **Ateneum,** one of three museums organized under the National Gallery umbrella. The museum displays Finnish art from the 18th century to the 1960s, as well as changing shows, and has an excellent bookshop and a café. ✉ *Kaivokatu 2–4,* ☎ *09/173–36401,* WEB *www.fng.fi.* ⏲ *Tues. and Fri. 9–6, Wed.–Thurs. 9–8, weekends 11–5.*

8 **Vanha Kauppahalli** (Old Market Hall). On the western shore of the South Harbor, near the huge ferry dock for boats from Sweden, Poland, and Estonia, the brick market hall is worth a visit for its amazing spreads of meat, fish, and other delights. ✉ *Eteläranta, along the South Harbor.* ⏲ *Mon.–Thurs. 8–5, Fri. 8–6, Sat. 8–3.*

Elsewhere in Helsinki

23 **Gallen-Kallela Museum.** Akseli Gallen-Kallela (1865–1931), one of Finland's greatest artists, lived in this studio-home, which now displays his heroic paintings and landscapes from the Golden Age of Finnish art. To get to the estate, take Tram 4 in front of the City Sokos department store on Mannerheimintie. From the Munkkiniemi stop transfer to Bus 33, or walk the 2 km (1 mi) through the woods. ✉ *Gallen-Kallelantie 27, Tarvaspää Espoo,* ☎ *09/541–3388.* ⏲ *Mid-May–Aug., daily 10–6; Sept.–mid-May, Tues.–Sat. 10–4, Sun. 10–5.*

22 **Seurasaaren Ulkomuseo** (Seurasaari Open-Air Museum). Evoking the Finnish countryside within the city, this museum showcases traditional rural architecture and lifestyles on a wooded island. A highlight is the ornate **Karunan Kirkko** (Karuna Church) from 1686. Seurasaari also has a restaurant and several beaches, including a secluded clothing-optional strand. ✉ *Seurasaari, island 5 km (3 mi) west of city center; Bus 24 from Swedish Theater,* ☎ *09/4050–9660 in summer; 09/4050–9327 in winter,* WEB *www.nba.fi/MUSEUMS/SEURAS/Seurseng.htm.* ⏲ *Museum June–Aug., Mon.–Tues. and Thurs.–Sun. 11–5, Wed. 11–7; May 15–31 and Sept. 1–15, weekdays 9–3, weekends 11–5; Sept. 16–Nov. 21, weekends 11–5.*

Dining

Although Russian restaurants are among the star attractions here, do seek out Finnish specialties—pheasant, reindeer, hare, and grouse—accompanied by wild berries and exotic mushrooms. Some expensive establishments close on Sundays or weekends. For details and price-category information, *see* Dining *in* Finland A to Z, *above*.

$$$$ ★ ✕ **Alexander Nevski.** In a city famed for fine Russian cuisine, Alexander Nevski has the best. Echoing the Russian-French style of 19th-century St. Petersburg, the decor is dominated by palm trees and shades of green. Sample the game specialties and blinis. ✉ *Pohjoisesplanadi 17,* ☎ *09/639–610. AE, DC, MC, V.*

$$$$ ✕ **Savoy.** With its airy, Alvar Aalto–designed dining room overlooking the Esplanade, the Savoy is a frequent choice for business lunches. Unusual combinations include whitefish baked with liver and cabbage and baked pheasant with white turnip, apple, and truffle. ✉ *Eteläesplanadi 14,* ☎ *09/684–4020. AE, DC, MC, V. Closed weekends.*

$$$–$$$$ ★ ✕ **Bellevue.** Established in 1917, Bellevue is one of Helsinki's oldest Russian restaurants, in both decor and cuisine. The fillet à la Novgorod (a traditional ox fillet prepared with carrots, barley, and sauerkraut) and chicken Kiev are the authentic articles here. ✉ *Rahapajankatu 3,* ☎ *09/179–560. AE, DC, MC, V. No lunch weekends.*

$$$–$$$$ ✕ **Havis Amanda.** Across the street from the *Havis Amanda* statue, this gracious restaurant, with its classic Scandinavian interior, is a seafood institution. The sophisticated menu offers local fish specialties with Continental accents. ✉ *Pohjoisesplanadi 17,* ☎ *09/666–882. AE, DC, MC, V. Closed Sun. Sept.–May.*

$$$–$$$$ ✕ **Sipuli.** In a brick warehouse dating from the late 19th century, Sipuli takes its name from the golden onion-shape cupolas that adorn the Orthodox Uspenski Cathedral nearby. The food is French in style with a Finnish flair; try the fennel soup with forest mushroom ravioli. ✉ *Kanavaranta 3,* ☎ *09/179–900. AE, DC, MC, V. Closed weekends, except dinner for groups.*

$$$ ✕ **Troikka.** The Troikka takes you back to tsarist times in decor, paintings, and music. Try the *pelmeny* (small meat dumplings served with sour cream). ✉ *Caloniuksenkatu 3,* ☎ *09/445–229. AE, DC, MC, V. Closed Sun., weekends in July.*

$$–$$$ ✕ **Töölönranta.** Combining contemporary Finnish architecture and a view of Töölö Bay, the light, international cuisine here highlights wok dishes. The patio catches the evening sun. ✉ *Helsinginkatu 56,* ☎ *09/454–2100. AE, DC, MC, V. Closed Sun. mid-Sept.–Apr.*

$$ ✕ **Kuu.** For the true character of Helsinki, try simple, friendly, and atmospheric Kuu ("Moon"), which has retained its local character since the 1960s. The menu is homey Finnish fare with monthly themes, such as elk. ✉ *Töölönkatu 27,* ☎ *09/2709–0973. AE, DC, MC, V.*

$$ ✕ **Maxill.** This café-bar hybrid is popular with the after-work crowd. The menu is light and trendy; try the salad with goat cheese croutons. ✉ *Korkeavuorenkatu 4,* ☎ *09/638–873. AE, DC, MC, V.*

$$ ✕ **Ravintola Perho.** This restaurant is associated with Helsinki's culinary school and emphasizes Finnish food; try the fish dishes and a beer from their own microbrewery. ✉ *Mechelininkatu 7,* ☎ *09/5807–8600. AE, DC, MC, V.*

$$ ✕ **Wellamo.** Unbeatable for cheerful intimacy and local character, the restaurant holds spontaneous piano recitals and often displays art on its walls. Fried Baltic herring and the house chocolate cake are highlights of the simple but hearty Finnish menu. ✉ *Vyökatu 9,* ☎ *09/663–139. AE, DC, MC, V. Closed Mon.*

$–$$ ★ ✕ **Kynsilaukka /Garlic.** This cozy yet sophisticated restaurant appeals to the senses with fresh, beautifully prepared food highlighting garlic. Stellar dishes include the garlic cream soup and bouillabaise; for dessert try the classic crepes with cloudberry sauce. A generous four-course lunch menu and the fact it's open on holidays help make it a local favorite. ✉ *Fredrikinkatu 22,* ☎ *09/651–939. AE, DC, MC, V.*

$ ✕ **Zucchini.** For a vegetarian lunch or just coffee and dessert, Zucchini is a cozy hideaway with quiet music, magazines, and a few sidewalk tables. Pizzas, soups, and salads are all tasty here. ✉ *Fabianinkatu 4,* ☎ *09/622–2907. DC, MC, V. No dinner.*

Lodging

Helsinki's hotels have a reputation for being extremely expensive, but this is true only of the very top stratum. Special summer and weekend offers are common. Generous breakfast buffets are nearly always included in the room price. Most hotels cater to business travelers, but standard rooms tend to be small. For details and price-category information, *see* Lodging *in* Finland A to Z, *above.*

$$$$ ★ **Hotel Kämp.** Opposite the Esplanade Park stands this splendid turn-of-the-20th-century cultural landmark, restored in 1999. Expect the ultimate in luxury, service, and decor. ✉ *Pohjoisesplanadi 29, 00100,* ☎ *09/576–1111,* FAX *09/576–1122,* WEB *www.luxurycollection.com. 179 rooms, including suites. 2 restaurants. AE, DC, MC, V.*

$$$$ ★ **Scandic Hotel Continental Helsinki.** The host of various diplomatic guests, this hotel has many amenities (fax machines, printers) in rooms. It's close to Finlandia Hall, the Finnish National Opera, National Museum, and the Museum of Contemporary Art; the restaurant, Olivo, serves Mediterranean dishes and has a separate wine bar. ✉ *Mannerheimintie 46, 00260,* ☎ *09/40551,* FAX *09/4055–3255,* WEB *www.scandic-hotels.com. 512 rooms. 2 restaurants, pool. AE, DC, MC, V.*

$$$$ **Scandic Hotel Marski.** Opposite Stockmann's department store, the Marski has suites that are the last word in modern luxury, and all rooms are soundproof, shutting out traffic noise. ✉ *Mannerheimintie 10, 00100,* ☎ *09/68061,* FAX *09/642–377,* WEB *www.scandic-hotels.com. 236 rooms, 6 suites. Restaurant. AE, DC, MC, V.*

$$$$ **Sokos Hotel Torni.** Be sure to take in the striking views of Helsinki from the Atelier Bar and from the higher floors of the original part of this hotel, built in 1903. Some old-section rooms on the courtyard have high ceilings with original carved-wood details and wooden writing desks. ✉ *Yrjönkatu 26, 00100,* ☎ *09/131–131,* FAX *09/131–1361,* WEB *www.sokoshotels.fi. 139 with shower, 15 with bath; 9 suites. 2 restaurants. AE, DC, MC, V. Closed Dec. 25.*

$$$$ ★ **Strand Inter-Continental.** This waterfront hotel has granite and marble in the lobby and modern designer bedrooms. There is a choice of cuisines—Pamir's elegant offerings of seafood, steak, and game, or the Atrium Plaza for lighter meals. ✉ *John Stenberginranta 4, 00530,* ☎ *09/3935–3255,* FAX *09/393–5255,* WEB *www.interconti.com. 200 rooms. 2 restaurants, pool. AE, DC, MC, V.*

$$$ **Cumulus Airport Hotel.** Proximity to the airport and a shuttle for the 3¼ km (2 mi) to town are the keys to this hotel. Rooms are small. ✉ *Robert Huberintie 4, 01510 Vantaa,* ☎ *09/4157–7100,* FAX *09/4157–7101,* WEB *www.cumulus.fi. 276 rooms. Restaurant, pool. AE, DC, MC, V.*

$$$ ★ **Cumulus Seurahuone.** This hotel across from the train station has rooms that range from sleek and modern to formal and classic with crystal chandeliers and brass bedsteads. The street-side rooms are not always quiet. ✉ *Kaivokatu 12, 00100,* ☎ *09/69141,* FAX *09/691–4010,* WEB *www.cumulus.fi. 118 rooms. Restaurant. AE, DC, MC, V.*

$$$ **Radisson SAS Hesperia Hotel Helsinki.** Built in 1972, the updated hotel remains Finnish with a modern flair. It's just a short stroll from the center of the city. ✉ *Mannerheimintie 50, 00260,* ☎ *09/43101,* FAX *09/431–0995,* WEB *www.radisson.com. 383 rooms. Restaurant, pool. AE, DC, MC, V.*

$$$ **Rivoli Jardin.** The high-class town house is tucked into the heart of Helsinki's shopping and business center. All rooms face the courtyard, which is free of traffic noise. ✉ *Kasarmikatu 40, 00130,* ☎ *09/177–880,* FAX *09/656–988,* WEB *www.rivoli.fi. 55 rooms. AE, DC, MC, V.*

$$$ **Scandic Hotel Grand Marina.** This renovated early 19th-century customs warehouse sits in the posh Katajanokka Island neighborhood. Friendly service and modern facilities have made the hotel a success. ✉ *Katajanokanlaituri 7, 00160,* ☎ *09/16661,* FAX *09/664–764,* WEB *www.scandic-hotels.com. 462 rooms. 2 restaurants. AE, DC, MC, V.*

$$$ **Scandic Hotel Kalastajatorppa Helsinki.** In the posh Munkkiniemi neighborhood, this hotel offers luxury in a quiet seaside setting. The best rooms are in the seaside annex, and all are large and airy. Rooms in the main building may be equipped with bath and terrace or with showers only. ✉ *Kalastajatorpantie 1, 00330,* ☎ *09/45811,* FAX *09/458–1668,* WEB *www.scandic-hotels.com. 235 rooms, 8 suites. 2 restaurants, 2 pools. AE, DC, MC, V.*

$$ **Arthur.** A property of the Helsinki YMCA, on a quiet, central street, Arthur is unpretentious and comfortable. ✉ *Vuorikatu 19, 00100,* ☎ *09/173–441,* FAX *09/626–880,* WEB *www.hotelarthur.fi/international/. 144 rooms. Restaurant. AE, DC, MC, V.*

$$ **Aurora.** About 2 km (1 mi) from the city center, just opposite the Linnanmäki amusement park, the hotel has reasonable prices, cozy rooms, and good facilities. ✉ *Helsinginkatu 50, 00530,* ☎ *09/770–100,* FAX *09/7701–0200. 70 rooms. Restaurant. AE, DC, MC, V.*

$$ **Hotel Helka.** Privately owned by the Finnish YWCA, this is a pleasant, affordable alternative to the higher-priced chain hotels in Helsinki. Situated in the heart of the city, the Helka is surprisingly quiet, thanks to double windows. Furnishings are in light wood and mixed pastels. The Aurinko restaurant has a sunny atmosphere and an open kitchen, where dishes with an international accent are prepared at reasonable prices; choose from a very good wine selection. ✉ *Pohjoinen Rautatiekatu 23A, 00100,* ☎ *09/613–580,* FAX *09/441–087,* WEB *www.helka.fi. 147 rooms, 3 suites. Restaurant. AE, DC, MC, V.*

$$ **Marttahotelli.** Run by a century-old women's association, the hotel has small but pleasant rooms. It is a 10-minute walk from the railway station. ✉ *Uudenmaankatu 24, 00120,* ☎ *09/618–7400,* FAX *09/618–7401,* WEB *www.marttahotelli.fi. 44 rooms, 1 suite. AE, DC, MC, V.*

$ **Academica.** This summer hotel is a standard student dormitory during the school year. Its simple rooms and the impressive array of exercise facilities make this an excellent value. ✉ *Hietaniemenkatu 14, 00100,* ☎ *09/1311–4334,* FAX *09/441–201,* WEB *www.hyy.fi/domus. 115 rooms. Pool. AE, DC, MC, V. Closed Sept.–May.*

Nightlife and the Arts

The Arts

For a list of events pick up *Helsinki This Week*, available in hotels and tourist offices. In summer the guide lists a telephone number for recorded program information in English. Published every two months, *Helsinki Happens* also lists events and provides more detailed cultural background. Tickets for small concerts at clubs and restaurants are available from **Lippupalvelu** (✉ Mannerheimintie 5 (Kaivopiha), ☎ 0600–10020 FM 20/€3.35 per call plus a local call charge; 0600–10495 FM 4.95/€.83 per minute plus a local call charge; 3589/6138–6246 from abroad). Call **Tiketti** (✉ Forum shopping center, Kukontori, ☎ 0600/11616 FM 3.95/€.66, plus a local call charge).

CONCERTS

Finlandiatalo (Finlandia Hall; ✉ Karamzininkatu 4, ☎ 09/402–4246) is the home of the Helsinki Philharmonic. **Savoy Theater** (✉

Kasarminkatu 46–48, ☎ 09/169–3703) presents ballet and world music. The **Sibelius Academy** (✉ Pohjois Rautatiekatu 9, ☎ 09/405–4662) hosts a broad range of classical music, including orchestral, choral, chamber music, and jazz, by guest artists and students. **Temppeliaukio Kirkko** (Temppeliaukion Church; ✉ Lutherinkatu 3, ☎ 09/494–698) is a favorite venue for choral and chamber music.

FESTIVALS

The **Helsinki Festival** (✉ Lasipalatsi, Mannerheimintie 22–24, 00100 Helsinki, ☎ 09/6126–5100, FAX 09/6126–5161), one of the largest in the Nordic region, presents music, dance, and poetry performances and art exhibits during two weeks in August and September.

THEATER

Summertime productions (in Finnish or Swedish) in such bucolic settings as Suomenlinna Island, Keskuspuisto Park, Mustikkamaa Island, and the Rowing Stadium (operettas) make enjoyable entertainment. Check *Helsinki This Week* for listings. Also try the splendid **Suomen Kansallisooppera** (Finnish National Opera; ✉ Helsinginkatu 58, ☎ 09/4030–2211).

Nightlife

BARS AND LOUNGES

Helsinki This Week lists all the pubs and clubs. **Cantina West** (✉ Kasarmikatu 23, ☎ 09/622–0900) is a Tex-Mex bar and restaurant with live music Thursday–Saturday. **Kaarle XII** (✉ Kasarmikatu 40, ☎ 09/612–9990) is in one of Helsinki's striking Jugendstil buildings: the young and beautiful are drawn here for dancing on weekends. Founded in 1867, **Kappeli** (✉ Eteläesplanadi 1, ☎ 09/179–242) brews its own beer. At **Storyville** (✉ Museokatu 8, ☎ 09/408–007), jazz musicians complement New Orleans–style cuisine.

Molly Malone's (✉ Kaisaniemenkatu 1C, ☎ 09/5766–7500) is a popular Irish pub. **Angleterre** (✉ Fredrikinkatu 47, ☎ 09/647–371) is a cozy English ale house run by an award-winning cellar master and frequented by the Helsinki professional crowd. The **William K** bars located around in the city center (✉ Annankatu 3, ☎ 09/680–2562; ✉ Mannerheimintie 72, ☎ 09/409–484; ✉ Fredrikinkatu 65, ☎ 09/693–1427; ✉ Fleminginkatu 6, ☎ 09/821–816) offer an excellent selection of European ales.

NIGHTCLUBS

Helsinki's largest and most famous club is the **Hesperia Nightclub** (✉ Radisson SAS Hotel Hesperia, Mannerheimintie 50, ☎ 09/43101). **Kaivohuone** (✉ Kaivopuisto/Well Park, ☎ 09/684–1530) is a summertime favorite in an attractive park setting.

Shopping

Department Stores

Stockmann's (☞ Exploring Helsinki, *above*).

Markets

In good weather you'll find a variety of goods at the **Hietalahti Flea Market** (✉ Hietalahti at west end of Bulevardi). **Kauppatori** (✉ Market Sq.), next to the South Harbor, is an absolute must year-round.

Shopping Districts

Helsinki's prime shopping districts run along **Pohjoisesplanadi** (North Esplanade) and **Aleksanterinkatu** in the city center. Along **Pohjoisesplanadi** and **Eteläesplanadi** (✉ bordering the gardens), you'll find Finland's design houses. Look for antiques shops in the **Kruununhaka** (✉ behind Senate Sq.) neighborhood.

Specialty Shops

Forum (✉ Mannerheimintie 20, ☎ 09/694–1498) is a modern, multistory shopping mall carrying clothing, gifts, books, and toys. The **Kiseleff Bazaar Hall** (✉ Aleksanterinkatu 22–28) has shops specializing in handicrafts, toys, knitwear, and children's items. You can shop until 10 PM in stores along the **Tunneli** (✉ underneath the train station).

Aarikka (✉ Pohjoisesplanadi 27, ☎ 09/652–277; Eteläesplanadi 8, ☎ 09/175–462) offers wooden jewelry, toys, and gifts. **Artek** (✉ Eteläesplanadi 18, ☎ 09/613–250) is known for its Alvar Aalto–designed furniture and ceramics. **Hackman Shop Arabia** (✉ Pohjoisesplanadi 25, ☎ 0204/393–501) sells Finland's Arabia china and Iittala glass. **Kalevala Koru** (✉ Unioninkatu 25, ☎ 09/171–520) specializes in jewelry based on ancient Finnish designs; most jewelers also sell a selection of the designs. **Marimekko** (✉ Pohjoisesplanadi 31, ☎ 09/177–944; ✉ Eteläesplanadi 14, ☎ 09/170–704) sells women's clothing, household items, and gifts made from its textiles. **Pentik** (✉ Pohjoisesplanadi 27, ☎ 09/625–558) has tasteful pottery and household goods.

Side Trip

Hvitträsk, a dramatic and romantic log villa designed by Eliel Saarinen and his partners Herman Gesellius and Armas Lindgren, was their shared home and studio in the early 20th century and is now a museum. Art exhibitions are also held here. This forested estate 30 km (19 mi) west of Helsinki has exhibits, a restaurant, a café, a shop, and a lakeside sauna with swimming. Bus 166 will take you from Helsinki's main bus station, or take the train to Luoma and follow the signs, about 2 km (1 mi), or to Masala and take a taxi. ✉ *Luoma, Kirkkonummi,* ☎ *09/4050–9630.* ⏲ *June–Aug., daily 10–7; Sept.–Oct. and Apr.–May, daily 11–6; Nov.–Mar., Tues.– Sun. 11–5.*

Helsinki Essentials

AIRPORTS AND TRANSFERS

All international flights arrive at Helsinki–Vantaa Airport.

➤ AIRPORT INFORMATION: **Helsinki–Vantaa Airport** (✉ Tuusulan Rte., ☎ 9600–8100 information).

TRANSFERS

Finnair buses make the trip between Helsinki–Vantaa Airport and the city center two–three times an hour, stopping behind the Inter-Continental Helsinki and at the Finnair Terminal next to the train station. The ride takes about 35 minutes and costs FM 25/€4.20. A local bus service (Bus 615) will also take you to the train station and costs FM 15/€2.50 for the 40-minute ride. Expect to pay between FM 100/€16.80 and FM 140/€23.55 for a taxi into the city center. The Airport Taxi minivan service drops you at your destination for FM 60/€10.10 per person, FM 80/€13.45 for two people.

BOAT AND FERRY TRAVEL

Ships arriving from Rostock, Germany, and Stockholm dock at Katajanokanlaituri. Finnjet-Silja makes the trip June 3–September 11; Viking Line makes the trip year-round. Silja Line ships from Stockholm, Sweden; it arrives at Olympialaituri.

In summer regular boat service links the South Harbor Kauppatori (Market Square) with the Suomenlinna and Korkeasaari, site of Helsinki Zoo. Schedules and prices are listed on signs at the harbor.

➤ BOAT AND FERRY INFORMATION: **Finnjet-Silja** (✉ Mannerheimintie 2, ☎ 09/18–041). **Katajanokanlaituri** (✉ east side of South Harbor).

Olympialaituri (✉ west side of South Harbor). **Silja Line** (✉ Mannerheimintie 2, ☎ 09/18–041). **Viking Line** (✉ Mannerheimintie 14, ☎ 09/12351).

BUS TRAVEL TO AND FROM HELSINKI

The main long-distance bus station is Linja-autoasema (bus station). Many local buses arrive and depart from Rautatientori (Railway Station Square). For information on long-distance transport, call Matka Huolto/Helsingin Linja-autoasema, which charges FM 6.34/€1.07 for the call in addition to local charges.

➤ BUS INFORMATION: **Matka Huolto/Helsingin Linja-autoasema** (✉ off Mannerheimintie, between Salomonkatu and Simonkatu, ☎ 0200–4010).

CONSULATES

➤ AUSTRALIA: (✉ Museokatu 25B, 00100, ☎ 09/447–223).

➤ NEW ZEALAND: **Honorary Consul General of New Zealand, c/o Kohdematkat** (✉ Hietalahdenranta 13, 00180, ☎ 09/615–615).

EMERGENCIES

➤ DOCTORS AND DENTISTS: **Dentist** (☎ 09/736–166). **Doctor** (☎ 10023).

➤ EMERGENCY SERVICES: **Ambulance** (☎ 112). **Police** (☎ 112 or 10022).

➤ 24-HOUR PHARMACIES: **Yliopiston Apteekki** (University Pharmacy; ✉ Mannerheimintie 96, ☎ 09/4178–0300).

ENGLISH-LANGUAGE MEDIA

➤ BOOKSTORES: **Akateeminen Kirjakauppa** (Academic Bookstore; ✉ Pohjoisesplanadi 39, ☎ 09/12141). **Suomalainen Kirjakauppa** (Finnish Bookstore; ✉ Aleksanterinkatu 23, ☎ 09/651–855).

SUBWAY TRAVEL

Helsinki's subway (Metro) line runs from Ruoholahti, west of the city center, to Mellunmäki and Vuosaari, in the eastern suburbs. It operates Monday–Saturday 5:33 AM–11:23 PM, Sunday 6:38 AM–11:23 PM.

TAXIS

Taxis are all marked TAKSI. Meters start at FM 30/€5.05, the fare rising on a per-kilometer basis. A listing of all taxi companies appears in the white pages; they charge from the point of dispatch. The main phone number for taxi dispatch is listed below.

➤ TAXI COMPANIES: **Taxi dispatch** (☎ 700–700).

TOURS

BOAT TOURS

J. L. Runeberg has all-day boat tours to the charming old wooden town of Porvoo, with departures at 10 AM several days a week May 19–September 2.

➤ FEES AND SCHEDULES: **J. L. Runeberg** (✉ departs from Kauppatori, ☎ 019/524–3331, WEB www.msjlruneberg.fi).

GUIDED TOURS

Guided tours are offered through Helsinki Expert. You can book one of their scheduled tours at the Helsinki City Tourist Office, or call them directly.

➤ FEES AND SCHEDULES: **Helsinki Expert** (✉ Lönnrotinkatu 7B, 00120 Helsinki, ☎ 09/2288–1600 for scheduled tours, 09/2288–1222 for individualized tours, WEB www.helsinkiexpert.fi).

TRAIN TRAVEL

Helsinki's main rail gateway is the Rautatieasema (train station).

➤ TRAIN INFORMATION: **Rautatieasema** (✉ city center, off Kaivokatu, ☎ 09/707–5700 information).

TRANSPORTATION AROUND HELSINKI

The center of Helsinki is compact and best explored on foot. If you want to use public transportation, your best buy is the Helsinki Kortti (Helsinki Card), which offers unlimited travel on city public transportation, free entry to many museums, a free sightseeing tour, and a variety of other discounts. It's available for one, two, or three days. You can buy it (for FM 135/€22.70, FM 175/€29.45, and FM 205/€34.50, respectively) at some hotels and travel agencies, Stockmann's department store, the Hotel Booking Centre, some R-kiosks in the city center, and the Helsinki City Tourist Office. The Helsinki City Transport tourist ticket entitles you to unlimited travel on all buses, trams, subways, and local trains in Helsinki. It is valid for one, three, or five days and costs FM 25/€4.20, FM 50/€8.40, or FM 75/€12.60. For timetable and ticket information for Helsinki's comprehensive and generally efficient public transport system, call the 24-hour line.

Tickets for buses, streetcars, local trains, and the subway may be purchased at subway stations, R-kiosks, and shops displaying the Helsinki city transport logo (two curving black arrows on a yellow background). Standard single tickets valid on all transport, and permitting transfers within the whole network for within an hour of the time stamped on the ticket, cost FM 10/€1.70 and can be bought on trams and buses. Single tickets bought beforehand, at the City Transport office in the railway station tunnel or at one of the many R-kiosk shops, for example, cost FM 8/€1.35. A 10-trip ticket sold at R-kiosks costs FM 75/€12.60. Most of Helsinki's major points of interest, from Kauppatori to the Opera House, are along the 3T tram line; the Helsinki City Tourist Office distributes a free pamphlet called "Helsinki Sightseeing: 3T."

➤ LOCAL AGENTS: **24-hour transportation information line** (☎ 0100–111).

TRAVEL AGENCIES

➤ LOCAL AGENTS: **American Express** (✉ Area Travel Agency, Mikonkatu 2D, 00100 Helsinki, ☎ 09/818–383). **Finland Travel Bureau** (Suomen Matkatoimisto; ✉ Kaivokatu 10A, PL 319, 00100 Helsinki, ☎ 09/18261).

VISITOR INFORMATION

➤ TOURIST INFORMATION: **Helsinki City Tourist Office** (✉ Pohjoisesplanadi 19, ☎ 09/169–3757, FAX 09/169–3839, WEB www.hel.fi). **The Finnish Tourist Board Tourist Information Office** (✉ Eteläesplanadi 4, ☎ 09/4176–9300, FAX 09/4176–9301, WEB www.mek.fi).

SOUTH COAST

A magical world of 30,000 islands stretches along Finland's coastline, forming a magnificent archipelago in the Gulf of Finland and the Baltic. On the coast, Turku, the former Finnish capital, was the main gateway through which cultural influences reached Finland over the centuries. Westward from Turku lies the rugged and fascinating Åland Islands group, an autonomous province of its own. Many of Finland's oldest towns, chartered by Swedish kings, lie in the southwest—hence the predominance of the Swedish language here. It is a region of flat, often mist-soaked rural farmland and villages of picturesque, traditional wooden houses.

Snappertuna

Snappertuna, 70 km (43 mi) west of Helsinki, is a farming town with a proud hilltop church, a charming homestead museum, and a castle set in a small dale. The handsome, restored ruin of **Raaseporin Linna** (Raseborg Castle) is believed to date from the 12th century. In summer, concerts, dramas, and old-time market fairs are staged here. Guided tours are arranged by the local tourist office (☎ 019/278–6540). ✉ *Keskuskatu 90,* ☎ *019/234–015.* ⏲ *May and Aug. 16–Aug. 31, daily 10–5; June–Aug. 15, daily 10–8; Sept., weekends 10–5.*

Ekenäs (Tammisaari)

Tammisaari, more commonly known by its Swedish name, Ekenäs, has a colorful Old Quarter, 18th- and 19th-century buildings, and a lively marina. In summer the sun glints off the water and marine traffic is at its peak. The **Tammisaaren Museo** (Tammisaari Museum) is the provincial museum of western Uusimaa and provides a taste of the region's culture and history. ✉ *Kustaa Vaasan katu 11,* ☎ *019/263–3161.* ⏲ *May 20–July, Tues.–Sun. 11–4; Aug.–May 19, Tues.–Thurs. 6–8 PM.*

$ **Ekenäs Stadshotell and Restaurant.** This modern, airy hotel is set amid fine lawns and gardens right in the heart of Ekenäs. Some rooms have private balconies, and all have wide windows and comfortable modern furnishings. ✉ *Pohjoinen Rantakatu 1, 10600 Tammisaari,* ☎ *019/241–3131,* FAX *019/246–1550,* WEB *www.ekenas.fi. 16 rooms, 2 suites. Restaurant, pool. AE, DC, MC, V.*

Hanko

In the coastal town of Hanko (Hangö), you'll find long stretches of beach—about 30 km (19 mi) in total—and some of the most fanciful private homes in Finland, their porches edged with gingerbread iron- and woodwork, and whimsical towers sprouting from their roofs. Hanko is also a popular sailing center.

Fortified in the 18th century, Hanko lost its defenses to the Russians in 1854, during the Crimean War. Later Hanko became a popular spa town for Russians, then the port from which more than 300,000 Finns emigrated to North America between 1880 and 1930.

Turku

Founded at the beginning of the 13th century, Turku is the nation's oldest city and was the original capital of Finland. The city has a long history as a commercial and intellectual center; the site of the first Finnish university, it now has two major universities, the Finnish University of Turku and the Swedish-speaking Åbo Akademi. With a population of more than 170,000, Turku is the fifth-largest city in Finland; its significant commercial harbor is active year-round and is a departure point for daily ferries to Stockholm and the beautiful Åland archipelago.

Known jointly as **Aboa Vetus/Ars Nova,** the Museum of Archaeology and History and the Museum of Contemporary Art exhibit excavated medieval archaeological remains along with the modern-art collection of the former Villa von Rettig Museum. Look for Picasso's *Swordsman* as well as works by Auguste Herbin (1882–1960) and Max Ernst (1891–1976). ✉ *Itäinen Rantakatu 4–6,* ☎ *02/250–0552,* WEB *www.aboavetusarsnova.fi.* ⏲ *May–Aug., daily 11–7; Sept.–Apr., Thurs.–Sun. 11–7.*

The **Luostarinmäen Kasityöläismuseo** (Luostarinmäki Handicrafts Museum) is a collection of wooden houses and buildings containing shops and workshops where traditional crafts are demonstrated and sold. ✉ *Vartiovuorenkatu 4,* ☎ *02/262–0350,* WEB *www.turku.fi/museo.* ⏲ *Mid-Apr.–mid-Sept., daily 10–6; mid-Sept.–mid-Apr., Tues.–Sun. 10–3.*

Where the Aura flows into the sea stands **Turun Linna** (Turku Castle), one of the city's most important historical monuments. The oldest part of the fortress was built at the end of the 13th century, and the newer part dates from the 16th century. The vaulted chambers evoke a sense of the domestic lives of the Swedish royals. A good gift shop and a pleasant café are on the castle grounds. ✉ *Linnankatu 80,* ☎ *02/262–0300,* WEB *www.turku.fi/museo/english/castle.htm.* ⏲ *Mid-Apr.–mid-Sept., daily 10–6; mid-Sept.–mid-Apr., Mon. 2–7, Tues.–Sun. 10–3.*

The **Turun Taidemuseo** (Turku Art Museum) holds some of Finland's most famous paintings, including works by Akseli Gallen-Kallela, and a broad selection of turn-of-the-20th-century Finnish art and contemporary works. Due to renovation, exhibits are temporarily being held on the Vartiovuorenmäki hill, in the Old Observatory (Vartiovuorenmäen Tähtitorni). ✉ *Vartiovuorenmäki,* ☎ *02/274–7570,* WEB *www.turuntaidemuseo.fi.* ⏲ *Old Observatory Apr.–Sept., Tues. and Fri.–Sat. 10–4, Wed.–Thurs. 10–7, Sun. 11–6; Oct.–Mar., Tues.–Wed. and Fri.–Sat. 10–4, Thurs. 10–7, Sun. 11–6.*

The 700-year-old **Turun Tuomiokirkko** (Turku Cathedral) remains the seat of the archbishop of Finland. Although it was partially gutted by fire in 1827, the cathedral has been completely restored and celebrated its 700th anniversary in 2000. The cathedral museum includes a collection of medieval church vestments, silver chalices, and wood sculptures. ✉ *Turun Tuomiokirkko,* ☎ *02/251–0651,* WEB *www.turunsrk.fi/english/church/kk-tuomi.htm.* ⏲ *Mid-Apr.–mid-Sept., daily 9–8; mid-Sept.–mid-Apr., daily 9–7.*

$$–$$$ ✕ **Calamare.** At this hotel restaurant, try the fried *kuha* (pike-perch) with beet terrine for a taste of local specialties. Calamare has impressive views of the Auajoki River and a Mediterranean atmosphere with Roman-style statues and palm trees. ✉ *Linnankatu 32,* ☎ *02/336–300. AE, DC, MC, V.*

$$–$$$ ✕ **Suomalainen Pohja.** Next to the Turku Art Museum, this Finnish restaurant has a splendid view of an adjacent park. Seafood, poultry, and game dishes are good here; try noisettes of reindeer. ✉ *Aurakatu 24,* ☎ *02/251–2000. AE, DC, MC, V. Closed weekends.*

$$$–$$$$ 🏨 **Park Hotel.** The castlelike Park Hotel in the heart of Turku is one of Finland's most unusual lodgings. Rooms have high ceilings and antique furniture. ✉ *Rauhankatu 1, 20100 Turku,* ☎ *02/273–2555,* FAX *02/251–9696. 21 rooms. Restaurant. AE, DC, MC, V.*

South Coast Essentials

AIR TRAVEL

Turku Airport is about 7 km (4½ mi) from the city center. Finnair flies to Helsinki, Mariehamn, and Stockholm.

BOAT AND FERRY TRAVEL

Passenger-car ferries depart daily from Turku's harbor for Stockholm and Åland. Contact Silja Line or Viking Line for details and timetables. Their services are similar, although Viking is known for being more budget-oriented.

➤ Boat and Ferry Information: **Silja Line** (☎ 09/18–041, FAX 09/180–4279, WEB www.silja.fi). **Viking Line** (☎ 09/12351, FAX 09/647–075, WEB www.vikingline.fi).

BUS TRAVEL

Regular daily bus services run between Helsinki and Turku. The trip takes about 2½ hours. Turku offers a 24-hour Tourist Ticket (FM 20) for unlimited public transport access; it can be purchased on buses.

CAR TRAVEL

The main route between Helsinki and Turku is fast and normally traffic-free. A parallel, more picturesque route to the south takes you at a leisurely pace through the smaller towns closer to the coast.

TOURS

Turku TouRing offers area tours.

➤ FEES AND SCHEDULES: **Turku TouRing/City Tourist Information Office** (✉ Aurakatu 4, 20100 Turku, ☎ 02/262–7444, FAX 02/262–7674, WEB www.turku.fi/turkutouring).

TRAIN TRAVEL

Turku is served by fast train services to Helsinki and Tampere several times a day. The Pendolino high-speed train also operates between Helsinki and Turku, cutting travel time to under two hours.

VISITOR INFORMATION

➤ TOURIST INFORMATION: **Hanko** (Tourist Information Office; ✉ Box 14, 5 Raatihuoneentori, 10901 Hanko, ☎ 019/220–3411, FAX 019/220–3261). **Turku** (Turku TouRing/City Tourist Information Office; ✉ Aurakatu 4, 20100 Turku, ☎ 02/262–7444, FAX 02/233–6488).

THE LAKELANDS

In southeastern and central Finland, the light has a softness that seems to brush the forests, lakes, and islands, changing the landscape throughout the day. For centuries this beautiful region was a much-contested buffer between the warring empires of Sweden and Russia. The Finns of the Lakelands prevailed by sheer *sisu* (guts), and now their descendants thrive amid the rough beauty of the terrain.

Savonlinna

The center of Savonlinna is a series of islands linked by bridges. An open-air market flourishes alongside the main quay. Savonlinna was once the hub of the passenger fleet serving Saimaa, the largest lake system in Europe. Now cruise boats dominate lake traffic.

★ First built in 1475 to protect Finland's eastern border, the castle **Olavinlinna** rises majestically out of the lake, retaining its medieval character. It is one of Scandinavia's best-preserved historic monuments and houses two museums, one that displays items from the castle and another with icons and other Russian Orthodox items both from Finland and Russia. The **Savonlinna Opera Festival** is held in the courtyard each July. Contact the Opera Ticket Office (✉ Olavinkatu 27, 57130 Savonlinna, ☎ 015/476–750, FAX 015/476–7540) well in advance for tickets. ✉ *10-min walk southeast from quay,* ☎ *015/531–164,* WEB *www.operafestival.fi.* ⏲ *June–mid-Aug., daily 10–5; mid-Aug.–May, daily 10–3.*

The **Savonlinnan maakunta museo** (Savonlinna Provincial Museum) is the home of the 19th-century steam schooners SS *Salama,* SS *Mikko,* and SS *Savonlinna.* ✉ *Riihisaari Island, near Olavinlinna,* ☎ *015/571–4712.* ⏲ *Sept.–June, Tues.–Sun. 11–5; July–mid–Aug., daily 11–6; boats mid-May–mid-Aug. during museum hrs.*

$$$ ✕ **Rauhalinna.** This romantic turn-of-the-20th-century timber villa was built by a general in the imperial Russian army. From town it's 16 km (10 mi) by road, 40 minutes by boat. Both food and atmosphere are Old Russian, touched by Finnish accents. Try the blini or game dishes. ✉ *Lehtiniemi,* ☎ *015/739–5432, 015/517–640 in summer. Reservations essential. AE, DC, MC, V. Closed Aug. 13–June 1.*

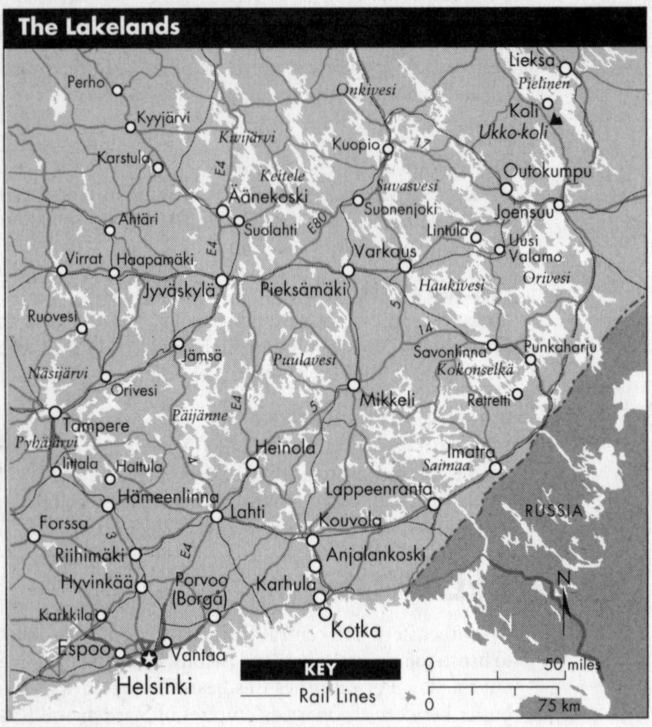

$$–$$$ ✕ **Majakka.** Centrally located, Majakka serves Finnish home cooking in a family atmosphere. Try the pepper steak in cream sauce. Reservations are essential during festival season. ✉ *Satamakatu 11,* ☎ *015/531–456. AE, DC, MC, V.*

$$ ✕ **Paviljonki.** An affiliate of the Savonlinna restaurant school, this convenient spot just 1 km (½ mi) west of the city serves classic Finnish dishes. ✉ *Rajalahdenkatu 4,* ☎ *015/574–9303. DC, MC, V.*

$$$–$$$$ 🏨 **Seurahuone.** In this hotel near the market and passenger harbor, rooms are small but modern. The restaurant moves into the open air in summer. ✉ *Kauppatori 4–6, 57130,* ☎ *015/5731,* FAX *015/273–918. 84 rooms. Restaurant. AE, DC, MC, V.*

$$$ 🏨 **Casino Spa.** The Casino Spa has a bucolic lakeside setting on an island linked by a pedestrian bridge to the center of town. Rooms are basic with brown cork floors and simple furnishings; all but one have a balcony. ✉ *Kylpylaitoksentie, Kasinosaari, 57130,* ☎ *015/73950,* FAX *015/272–524. 80 rooms. Restaurant, pool. AE, DC, MC, V.*

Punkaharju

This breathtaking ridge of pine-covered rocks predates the Ice Age. Sometimes narrowing to only 25 ft, it rises out of the water to separate the lakes on either side.

Take an excursion (by boat or bus) to **Taidekeskus Retretti** (Retretti Art Center), the largest privately owned art center in Scandinavia, to see changing exhibits, multimedia programs, and children's events. ✉ *Just south of Punkaharju,* ☎ *015/775–2200,* FAX *015/644–314.* 🎫 *FM 70/€11.80.* ⏲ *June and Aug., daily 10–5; July, daily 10–6.*

The nearby **Lusto–Suomen Metsämuseo ja Metsätietokeskus** (Lusto Finnish Forest Museum) has displays on every aspect of forestry, from the industrial to the artistic, and all sides of Finland's close relationship with its most abundant natural resource, including demonstrations and theme days. Make an appointment for a guided tour. ✉ *Lustontie 1, 58450, Punkaharju,* ☎ *015/345–100.* ⊙ *Jan.–Apr. and Oct.–Dec., Tues.–Sun. 10–5; May and Sept., daily 10–5; June–Aug., daily 10–7.*

$$$ **Punkaharju National Hotel.** Near the Retretti Art Center, this building was constructed as a gamekeeper's lodge for Tsar Nicholas I in 1845 but has since been enlarged and restored. Now it's a restful spot for a meal or an overnight visit. ✉ *Punkaharju 2, 58450,* ☎ *015/739–611,* FAX *015/441–784,* WEB *www.lomaliitto.fi. 24 rooms. Restaurant. AE, DC, MC, V.*

Kuopio

The 11½-hour boat trip from Savonlinna to Kuopio may be the best opportunity you'll get to appreciate the soul of the Finnish Lakelands. Meals are available on board. The boat arrives at Kuopio's passenger harbor, where you'll find a small evening market daily from 3 to 10.

★ Kuopio's tourist office is close to the **Tori** (marketplace), one of Finland's most colorful outdoor markets, which sells produce, flowers, handicrafts, and the Finnish market version of fast food: sausages and fried fish served with potatoes. ✉ *City center.* ⊙ *May–Sept., weekdays 7–5, Sat. 7–3; Oct.–Apr., weekdays 7–3, Sat. 7–2.*

The **Ortodoksinen Kirkkomuseo** (Orthodox Church Museum) has an unusual collection of religious art from the monasteries of Karelia (the eastern province of Finland, part of which is now in Russia). ✉ *Karjalankatu 1,* ☎ *017/287–2244.* ⊙ *May–June and Aug., Tues.–Sun. 10–4; July, Tues.–Sun. 11–5; Sept.–Apr., weekdays noon–3, weekends noon–5.*

Puijo Näkötorni (Puijo Tower), an observation and communications tower, is best visited at sunset, when the lakes shimmer with reflected light. It has two observation decks and a revolving restaurant on top, from which you can enjoy the views. ✉ *3 km (2 mi) northwest of Kuopio,* ☎ *017/209–560.* ⊙ *May–Aug., Mon.–Sat. 9–10, Sun. 1–8.*

Valamon Luostari (Valamo Monastery) in Heinävesi, between Varkaus and Joensuu, is a center for Orthodox religious and cultural life in Finland. Precious 18th-century icons and other sacred objects are housed in the main church and in the icon conservation center. On the grounds are a café-restaurant, hotel, and hostel accommodations. Guided tours are offered daily June through August, and at other times of year by appointment. ✉ *Uusi Valamo,* ☎ *017/570–111; 017/570–1504 hotel reservations,* FAX *017/570–1510.* ⊙ *Oct.–Feb., daily 8 AM–9 PM; Mar.–Sept., daily 7 AM–9 PM.*

$$ ✕ **Musta Lammas.** Finnish dishes are served in this former beer cellar. Specialties include steamed arctic char with warm Waldorf salad. ✉ *Satamakatu 4,* ☎ *017/581–0458. AE, DC, MC, V. Closed Sun.*

$$ ✕ **Sampo.** The specialty here is whitefish. The atmosphere is unpretentious and lively, and the location in the town center is convenient. ✉ *Kauppakatu 13,* ☎ *017/261–4677. AE, DC, MC, V.*

$$$ **Scandic Hotel Kuopio.** The best equipped of local hotels, the Scandic has all the advantages of a lakefront location while being close to the center of town. Rooms are spacious by European standards, with parquet floors. ✉ *Satamakatu 1, 70100,* ☎ *017/195–111,* FAX *017/195–170,* WEB *www.scandic-hotels.com. 134 rooms. Pool. AE, DC, MC, V.*

$$ **Hotel-Spa Rauhalahti.** Sports-oriented travelers and families flock to this high-energy setting. Close to the lakeshore and 5 km (3 mi) from the town center, Rauhalahti offers lively activities and conveniences for all ages and interests. ✉ *Katiskaniementie 8, 70700,* ☎ *017/473–111,* FAX *017/473–470,* WEB *www.rauhalahti.com. 106 rooms, 20 apartments, 26 hostel rooms. 3 restaurants. AE, DC, MC, V.*

Tampere

Cotton and textile manufacturers put Tampere on the map as a traditional center of industry, but the city is now known for its high-tech companies and large universities. The mobile-phone giant Nokia got its start in a small city of the same name nearby; don't be surprised to see many of the locals strolling down Tampere's compact main street, Hämeenkatu, with a *kännykä* ("little hand," or cell phone) in use. Tampere's 200,000 inhabitants also nurture an unusually sophisticated cultural environment, with the international festivals of short film (March) and theater (August) among the most popular offerings.

From about the year 1000, this part of Finland was a base from which traders and hunters set out on their expeditions to the north. It was not until 1779 that a Swedish king, Gustav III, founded Tampere. A Scotsman by the name of James Finlayson came to the city in 1882 and established a factory for spinning cotton. The firm of Finlayson is still one of the country's large industrial enterprises.

An isthmus, little more than 1 km (½ mi) wide at its narrowest point, separates the lakes Näsijärvi and Pyhäjärvi, and at one spot the waters of one rush through to the other down the Tammerkoski Rapids. Their natural beauty has been preserved despite the factories on either bank, and the distinctive public buildings of the city grouped around them add to the overall effect.

The **Amurin Työläismuseokortteli** (Amuri Museum of Workers' Housing) consists of more than 30 apartments in a collection of wooden houses, plus a sauna, a bakery, a haberdashery, and more from the 1880s to the 1970s. Its café has garden seating in summer. ✉ *Makasiininkatu 12,* ☎ *03/314–6690.* ⏲ *Mid-May–mid-Sept., Tues.–Sun. 10–6.*

On the east side of town the modern **Kalevan Kirkko** (Kaleva Church) is a soaring monument to light and space designed by Reima (1923–93) and Raili (b. 1926) Pietilä, the famous architect couple who also designed the Tampere city library. ✉ *Liisanpuisto 1.* ⏲ *May–Aug., daily 9–6; Sept.–Apr., daily 11–3.*

The **Lenin Museo** (Lenin Museum) occupies the hall where Lenin and Stalin first met; memorabilia and temporary exhibits document the life of Lenin and the Russian Revolution. ✉ *Hämeenpuisto 28, 3rd fl.,* ☎ *03/276–8100,* WEB *www.tampere.fi/culture/lenin/.* ⏲ *Weekdays 9–6, weekends 11–4.*

The **Museokeskus Vapriikki** (Museum Centre Vapriikki) is home to 700,000 pieces that illustrate the city's role in Finnish history. Housed in a former factory complex that dates from the 1880s, the permanent exhibit focuses on local history, while other displays cover archaeological finds and modern art. ✉ *Veturiaukio 4,* ☎ *03/3146–6966,* WEB *www.tampere.fi/vapri.* ⏲ *Tues., Thurs.–Sun. 10–6, Wed. 10–8.*

Among Reima Pietilä's many unusual structures in Tampere is the **Tampere pääkirjasto** (Tampere Central Library), nicknamed "metso" (wood grouse) for its unusual shape; it exhibits the Moomintroll books of Finnish author Tove Jansson. ✉ *Pirkankatu 2,* ☎ *03/314–614.* ⏲ *Sept.–May, weekdays 9:30–8, Sat. 9:30–3; June–Aug., weekdays 9:30–7, Sat. 9:30–3.*

The **Tuomiokirkko** (cathedral), built in 1907, displays some of the best-known masterpieces of Finnish mural art. ✉ *Tuomiokirkonkatu 3.* ⏲ *May–Aug., daily 9–6; Sept.–Apr., daily 11–3.*

The **Särkänniemi Peninsula** holds many attractions. **Särkänniemen Huvikeskus** (Särkäniemi Amusement Center) is a recreation complex made up of an amusement park, a children's zoo, a planetarium, and an aquarium with a separate "dolphinarium." Within Särkäniemi, the **Sara Hildénin Taidemuseo** (Sara Hildén Art Museum) is a striking example of Finnish architecture, displaying works by such modern artists as Chagall, Klee, Miró, and Picasso. ✉ *Särkänniemi,* ☏ *03/248–8111; 9800–4242 main complex information,* WEB *www.sarkanniemi.fi.* *Joint admission FM 150/€25.20.* ⏲ *Daily 11–6.*

Särkänniemi's 550-ft **Näsinneula Observation Tower,** the tallest in Finland, dominates the Tampere skyline. At the top are an observatory and a revolving restaurant. The contrast between the industrial maze of Tampere at your feet and the serenity of the lakes stretching out to meet the horizon is unforgettable. ✉ *Särkänniemi.* ☏ *03/248–8111 main complex information.* ⏲ *June–Aug., daily 11 AM–midnight; Sept.–May, Tues.–Sat. 10 AM–midnight, Sun.–Mon. 10–9.*

On the **"Poet's Way"** boat tour along Lake Näsijärvi, the boat passes through the agricultural parish of Ruovesi, where J. L. Runeberg, Finland's national poet, once lived. Many artists and writers spend their summers by the straits of Visuvesi. ✉ *Finnish Silverline and "Poet's Way," Laukontori 10A3,* ☏ *03/212–4804.* *Round-trip fare FM 340/€57.18; optional bus return.*

$$–$$$ ★ ✕ **Astor.** A choice of moderately priced brasserie fare and a more sophisticated menu is served in a cozy yet elegant atmosphere off the main square. ✉ *Aleksis Kivenkatu 26,* ☏ *03/260–5700. DC, MC, V.*

$$–$$$ ✕ **Laterna.** Located in a tsarist-era hotel and once the haunt of artists and writers, Laterna offers Russian fare with a Finnish twist. Enjoy a variety of live music in a charming main dining room and cozy side parlors. ✉ *Puutarhakatu 11,* ☏ *03/272–0241. AE, DC, MC, V.*

$$–$$$ ✕ **Tiiliholvi.** A romantic cellar in an Art Nouveau building with a colorful past, Tiiliholvi offers Finnish haute cuisine and the best wine selection in town. ✉ *Kauppakatu 10,* ☏ *03/272–0231. AE, DC, MC, V. Closed Sun.*

$$$ **Sokos Hotel Ilves.** Soaring above newly gentrified old warehouses near the city center, the hotel has some rooms with spectacular views of the city and Pyhäjärvi and Näsijärvi lakes. ✉ *Hatanpään valtatie 1, 33100,* ☏ *03/262–6262,* FAX *03/262–6263,* WEB *www.sokoshotels.fi. 336 rooms. 3 restaurants, pool. AE, DC, MC, V.*

$$ **Sokos Hotel Tammer.** A beautiful historic hotel overlooking a park, the Hotel Tammer has a grand dining room and modern rooms. ✉ *Satakunankatu 13, 33100,* ☏ *03/262–6265,* FAX *03/262–6266,* WEB *www.sokoshotels.fi. 83 rooms, 4 suites. Restaurant. AE, DC, V.*

$ **Iltatähti Apartment Hotel.** In the center of town, this hotel offers pleasant and unpretentious accommodation at budget rates. ✉ *Tuomiokirkonkatu 19, 33100,* ☏ *03/315–161,* FAX *03/3151–6262. 40 rooms. No credit cards.*

Iittala

The **Iittala Lasikeskus** (Iittala Glass Center) offers museum tours for groups and has a shop. Top designers produce the magnificent glass; the seconds are bargains you won't find elsewhere. ✉ *14500 Iittala,* ☏ *0204/396–230.* ⏲ *Museum May–Aug., daily 10–6; Sept.–Apr., daily 10–5. Shop May–Aug., daily 9–8; Sept.–Apr., daily 10–6.*

Hämeenlinna

Hämeenlinna's secondary school has educated many famous Finns, among them composer Jean Sibelius (1865–1957). The only surviving timber house in the town center is **Sibeliuksen syntymäkoti** (Sibelius's Birthplace), a modest dwelling built in 1834. One of the rooms houses the harmonium Sibelius played as a child. ✉ *Hallituskatu 11,* ☏ *03/621–2755.* ⏲ *May–Aug., daily 10–4; Sept.–Apr., daily noon–4.*

Hämeen Linna (Häme Castle) is Finland's oldest castle: Swedish crusaders began building it in the 13th century. At times a granary and a prison, the lakeshore castle is now restored and open to the public for tours and exhibitions; it sits 1 km (½ mi) north of Hämeenlinna's town center. ✉ *Kustaa III:n katu 6,* ☎ *03/675–6820.* ⏲ *May–Aug. 14, daily 10–6; Aug. 15–Apr., daily 10–4.*

The **Hämeenlinnan Taidemuseo** (Hämeenlinna Art Museum), housed in a 19th-century granary designed by Carl Ludvig Engelas and in a second granary in the same courtyard, exhibits Finnish art from the 19th and 20th centuries and foreign art from the 17th century; works evacuated from Vyborg in 1939 form the core of the collection. ✉ *Viipurintie 2,* ☎ *03/621–2669.* ⏲ *Tues.–Wed. and Fri.–Sun. noon–6, Thurs. noon–8.*

$$$ ★ **Rantasipi Aulanko.** One of Finland's top hotels, Rantasipi Aulanko sits on the lakeshore in a beautifully landscaped park 6½ km (4 mi) from town. All rooms have wall-to-wall carpeting and overlook the golf course, the park, or the lake. ✉ *Aulanko Puisto (Aulanko Park), 13210,* ☎ *03/658–801,* FAX *03/682–1922,* WEB *www.htk.fi/hml/conferen/venue9.htm. 245 rooms. Pool. AE, DC, MC, V.*

Hattula

The interior of medieval **Hattulan Kirkko** (Hattula Church), 8 km (5 mi) north of Hämeenlinna in Hattula, has vivid frescoes of biblical scenes dating from around 1510. ✉ *Hattula,* ☎ *03/672–3383 during open hrs; 03/631–1540 at other times.* ⏲ *May 15–Aug. 15, daily 11–5; other times by appointment.*

Riihimäki

The **Suomen Lasimuseo** (Finnish Glass Museum) in Riihimäki, 35 km (22 mi) south of Hämeenlinna, has an outstanding display on the history of glass from early Egyptian times to the present, artfully arranged in an old glass factory. ✉ *Tehtaankatu 23, Riihimäki,* ☎ *019/741–7494,* WEB *www.riihimaki.fi/lasimus.* ⏲ *May–Aug., daily 10–6; Sept.–Dec. and Feb.–Apr., Tues.–Sun. 10–6. Closed Jan..*

$$ ✕ **Lehmushovi.** In a manor house in a park near the Glass Museum, Lehmushovi offers Finnish and international cuisine. ✉ *Lehmustie 5,* ☎ *019/738–946. Reservations essential DC, MC, V.*

The Lakelands Essentials

AIR TRAVEL

Airports in the Lakelands are at Tampere, Mikkeli, Jyväskylä, Varkaus, Lappeenranta, Savonlinna, Kuopio, and Joensuu.

BUS TRAVEL

Buses are the best form of public transport into the region, with frequent connections to lake destinations from most major towns. The ride from Helsinki to Savonlinna takes six hours.

CAR TRAVEL

The region is vast, so the route you choose will depend on your destination. Consult Autoliitto (Automobile and Touring Club of Finland) or tourist boards for route advice.

TOURS

➤ FEES AND SCHEDULES: **Häme Tourist Service** (Raatihuoneenkatu 11, 13100 Hämeenlinna, ☎ 03/621–2388, FAX 03/621–2716).

TRAIN TRAVEL

Trains run from Helsinki to Lahti, Mikkeli, Imatra, Lappeenranta, Joensuu, and Jyväskylä.

TRANSPORTATION AROUND THE LAKELANDS

In Tampere you can buy a 24-hour Tourist Ticket from the city tourist office that allows unlimited travel on city transportation.

VISITOR INFORMATION

➤ TOURIST INFORMATION: **Hämeenlinna** (✉ Raatihuoneenkatu 11, 13100 Hämeenlinna, ☎ 03/621–2388). **Kuopio** (✉ Haapaniemenkatu 17, 70110 Kuopio, ☎ 017/182–584). **Savonlinna** (✉ Puistokatu 1, 57100 Savonlinna, ☎ 015/517–510). **Tampere** (✉ Verkatehtaankatu 2, Box 487, 33100 Tampere, ☎ **03/3146–6680**).

FINNISH LAPLAND

Lapland is a region of great silences, with endless forests and fells. Settlers in Finnish Lapland have walked gently and left the landscape almost unspoiled. The oldest traces of human habitation in Finland have been found in Lapland, where hoards of Danish, English, and even Arabian coins indicate active trading many centuries ago. Until the 1930s, Lapland was still largely unexploited, and any trip to the region was an expedition. Its isolation ended when the Arctic Highway was completed, connecting Rovaniemi with the Arctic Sea.

Only about 4,000 native Sámi live in Lapland; the remainder of the province's population of 203,000 is Finnish. Recent grassroots efforts to preserve Sámi language and traditions have been largely successful. Sámi craftspeople create beautiful objects and clothing out of the materials readily at hand: wood, bone, and reindeer pelts.

While winter in Lapland brings with it the fascinating northern lights and reindeer roundups, beautiful weather often complements summer's nightless days. In early fall nature's colors are spectacular.

Exploring Lapland

Rovaniemi

Rovaniemi is the Lapland administrative and communications hub. Nearly razed by the retreating German army in 1944, Rovaniemi is today a modern university town and business center strongly influenced by Alvar Aalto's architecture. One notable structure is the **Lappia-Talo** (Lappia House; ✉ Hallituskatu 11, ☎ 016/322–2944), an Aalto-designed concert and congress center.

★ You can get a good instant introduction to the region and its natural history at the **Arktikum** (Arctic Research Center), 1 km (½ mi) north of Lappia-Talo. It houses the Lapland Provincial Museum, with exhibits on Sámi culture. ✉ *Pohjoisranta 4,* ☎ *016/317–840,* WEB *www.arktikum.fi.* ⏲ *May–June 15, daily 10–6; June 16–Aug. 15, daily 9–7; Aug. 16–31, daily 10–6; Sept.–Apr., Tues.–Sun. 10–6.*

$$ ✕ **Fransmanni.** In the Sokos Hotel Vaakuna in downtown Rovaniemi, this restaurant specializes in international, Finnish, and Sámi dishes. ✉ *Koskikatu 4,* ☎ *016/332–211. AE, DC, MC, V.*

$$ ✕ **Ounasvaaran Pirtit.** This town favorite, a small restaurant decorated in traditional Lapp wooden style and focused on a welcoming open fireplace, serves traditional Finnish and Sámi fare. "Kotas," traditional Lappish huts, are available for group dining. ✉ *Antinmukka 4,* ☎ *016/369–056. Reservations essential. MC, V.*

$$$ 🏨 **Rantasipi Hotel Pohjanhovi.** With its pleasant location overlooking the Kemi River, this hotel is a favorite with travelers to the north. ✉ *Pohjanpuistikko 2, 96200,* ☎ *016/33711,* FAX *016/313–997,* WEB *www.randburg.com/fi/hotelran.html. 212 rooms, 4 suites. 2 restaurants, pool. AE, DC, MC, V.*

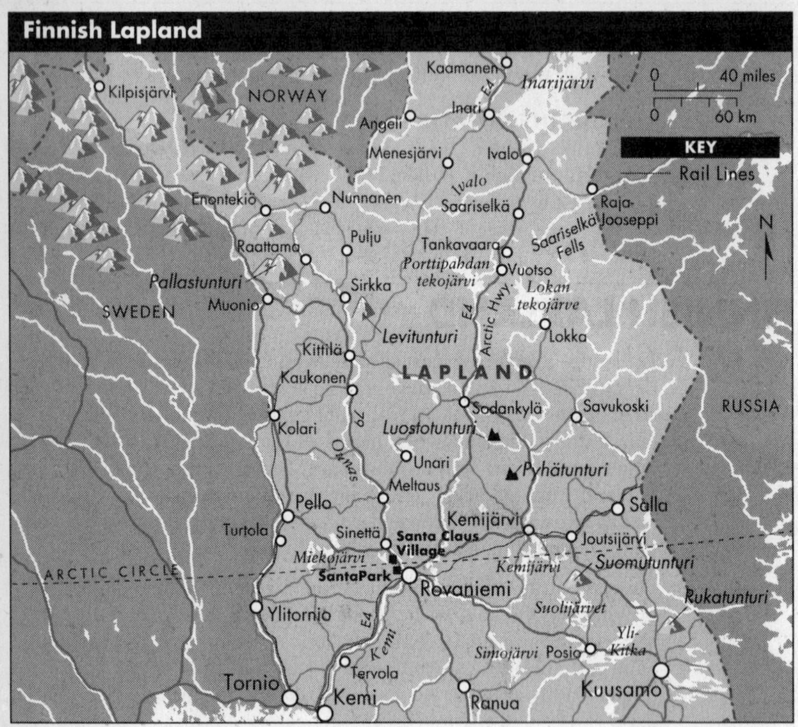

$$$ **Scandic Hotel Rovaniemi.** This modern hotel is in the heart of town. Some rooms have individual saunas or hot tubs. ✉ *Koskikatu 23, 96200,* ☎ *016/460–6000,* FAX *016/460–6666,* WEB *www.scandic-hotels.com. 167 rooms. 2 restaurants, bar. AE, DC, MC, V.*

$$$ ★ **Sky Hotel Rovaniemi.** The views of the town and the surrounding area are fantastic from this tranquil, full-service hotel perched on Ounasvaara Mountain, 3 km (2 mi) from town. Most rooms have saunas. ✉ *96400,* ☎ *016/335–3311,* FAX *016/318–789,* WEB *www.fintravel.com/rovaniemi/hotel/skyhotel/. 69 rooms. Restaurant. AE, DC, MC, V.*

$$$ **Sokos Hotel Vaakuna.** Opened in 1992, the Vaakuna has small rooms in pastel shades. The club here is a center of Rovaniemi nightlife. ✉ *Koskikatu 4, 96200,* ☎ *016/332–211,* FAX *016/332–2199,* WEB *www.sokoshotels.fi. 157 rooms, 2 suites. 2 restaurants. AE, DC, MC, V.*

$$ **Best Western Hotel Oppipoika.** Rooms here are spacious and comfortable. The restaurant offers a variety of Lapland specialties. ✉ *Korkalonkatu 33, 96200,* ☎ *016/338–8111,* FAX *016/346–969,* WEB *www.fintravel.com/rovaniemi/hotel/oppipoika/. 40 rooms. 2 restaurants, pool. AE, DC, MC, V.*

Arctic Circle

SantaPark, a Christmas theme park deep inside a rocky cavern, offers a Magic Sleigh Ride, a Puppet Circus, and a Christmas Carousel, among other attractions. Take the Santa Train from the park to **Santa Claus Village,** where you can shop for gifts and have your purchases shipped with a special Santa Claus Land stamp; stop along the way at the Reindeer Park to see Santa's sleigh team. ✉ *Arctic Circle, 96930,* ☎ *016/333–0000 park; 016/356–2157 village,* FAX *016/333–0020 park; 016/356–2096 village,* WEB *www.santapark.com.* *Park FM 120/€20.20.* *Park June 15–Aug. 19, daily 10–6; Nov. 23–Jan. 13, daily 10–6. Village June–Aug., daily 8–8; Sept.–May, daily 10–5.*

Tankavaara

Tankavaara is the most accessible and best developed of several gold-panning areas in Lapland. The **Kultamuseo** (Gold Museum) tells the centuries-old story of Lapland's hardy fortune seekers. In the summer months guides will show you how to wash gold dust and tiny nuggets from the dirt of an ice-cold stream. ✉ *Arctic Hwy. 4, Kultakylä,* ☎ *016/626–158,* WEB *www.urova.fi/home/kulta/emuseo.htm.* ⏲ *June–Aug. 15, daily 9–6; Aug. 16–Sept., daily 9–5; Oct.–May, daily 10–4.*

$$ ✕ **Wanha Waskoolimies.** Sámi specialties predominate at this attractive café-restaurant at the Gold Museum; try the gold prospector's reindeer steak. ✉ *Tankavaaran kultakylä,* ☎ *016/626–158. DC, V.*

Saariselkä

From here you can set off into the true wilderness; during the snowy months, it has some of the finest cross-country and downhill skiing in Finland. More than 2,500 square km (965 square mi) of this magnificent area have been set aside as **Urho Kekkosen kansallispuisto** (Urho Kekkonen National Park; ✉ Northern Lapland Tourism, Honkapolku 3, 99830 Saariselkä, ☎ 016/668–402, FAX 016/668–403).

$$$ 🏨 **Riekonlinna.** This is the most recent and best-equipped addition to the developing tourist complex on the fringes of the wilderness fells. Catering to sports enthusiasts, it offers a wide range of facilities, including a children's play room, ski maintenance, and storage room. ✉ *99830,* ☎ *016/679–4455,* FAX *016/679–4456,* WEB *www.riekkoparvi.fi. 124 rooms. AE, DC, MC, V.*

Ivalo

Just south of here, the highway passes the **Ivalojoki** (Ivalo River). Join a canoe trip down its swift waters to Lake Inari. The modern community of Ivalo is the main center for northern Lapland.

$ 🏨 **Hotel Ivalo.** Modern and fully equipped, the Hotel Ivalo is right on the river and about 1 km (½ mi) from the village center. One of its two restaurants serves Lapland specialties. ✉ *Ivalontie 34, 99800,* ☎ *016/688–111,* FAX *016/661–905,* WEB *www.saunalahti.fi/~hotivalo. 94 rooms. 2 restaurants, pool. AE, DC, MC, V.*

$ 🏨 **Kultahippu.** Here, next to the Ivalo River, you can patronize the "northernmost nightclub in Finland." The hotel has cozy rooms. ✉ *Petsamontie 1, 99800,* ☎ *016/661–825,* FAX *016/662–510,* WEB *www.kultahippuhotel.fi/. 30 rooms. Restaurant. AE, DC, MC, V.*

Inari

The huge island-studded expanses of Inarijärvi (Lake Inari), north of Ivalo, offer endless possibilities for wilderness exploration. Lakeside Inari, home of the Sámi Parliament, is a good base for summer boat excursions. Set in the oldest inhabited region of northern Lapland and named after the Lapp word for village or living space, the new **SIIDA Center** hosts a variety of exhibits on the Sámi people and the northern seasons. The center houses the **Saamelaismuseo** (Sámi Museum) and the **Ylä-Lapin luontokeskus** (Northern Lapland Nature Center). The Nature Center includes the **Metsähallitus** (Forest and Park Service; ☎ 0205/647–740, FAX 0205/647–750), which provides camping and fishing permits and advice on exploring the wilderness. A 17-acre open-air museum is open during the summer. ✉ *Hwy. 4 by Lake Inari,* ☎ *016/665–212,* FAX *016/665–156,* WEB *www.siida.fi.* ⏲ *June–Sept., daily 9–8; Oct.–May, Tues.–Sun. 10–5.*

$ 🏨 **Inarin Kultahovi.** This renovated old inn stands on the wooded bank of a swiftly flowing river. ✉ *99870,* ☎ *016/671–221,* FAX *016/*

671–250, WEB *www.saariselka.fi/kultahovi/. 29 rooms. Restaurant. DC, MC, V.*

Lapland Essentials

AIR TRAVEL

Finnair domestic flights link Oulu and Rovaniemi with Ivalo, Enontekiö, Kemi, and Sodankylä. Finnair also has daily flights directly from Helsinki to Kuusamo. The SAS-owned Air Botnia also serves Lapland's airports.

➤ AIRLINES AND CONTACTS: **Air Botnia** (☎ 09/6151–2900).

BUS TRAVEL

Buses leave five times daily from Rovaniemi to Inari (five hours) and Ivalo (four hours). Taxi stands are at most bus stations.

CAR TRAVEL

The Arctic Highway will take you north from Rovaniemi at the Arctic Circle to Inari, just below the 69th parallel.

TOURS

For information on tours in the area, contact Lapland Travel Limited.

➤ FEES AND SCHEDULES: **Lapland Travel Ltd.** (✉ Koskikatu 1, **Box 8156,** 96101 Rovaniemi, ☎ 016/332–3422, FAX 016/332–3411).

VISITOR INFORMATION

➤ TOURIST INFORMATION: **Inari and Saariselkä** (Northern Lapland Tourism; ✉ Honkapolku 3, 99800 Saariselkä, ☎ 016/668–402, FAX 016/668–403). **Rovaniemi** (✉ Koskikatu 1, Rovaniemi 96200, ☎ 016/346–270 or 016/322–2279, FAX 016/342–4650). **Sodankylä** (✉ Jäämerentie 3, 99600 Sodankylä, ☎ 016/618–168, FAX 016/613–478).

11 FRANCE

PARIS, THE ILE-DE-FRANCE, THE LOIRE VALLEY, NORMANDY, BURGUNDY AND LYON, PROVENCE, THE CÔTE D'AZUR

LIKE THE HIGH-SPEED TRAINS speeding toward the Channel Tunnel, France has been on the move. This is particularly evident in Paris: in the last two decades no other European capital has seen as much building at such a pharaonic pace. I. M. Pei's glass pyramid at the Louvre and the postmodern Grande Arche de la Défense are just two examples of the architecturally dramatic monuments that have shocked purists and set the city abuzz.

But France's attachment to its heritage also persists, as major restorations of the Champs-Élysées and the Tuileries Gardens in Paris have proved. The world's most magnificent châteaux—Vaux-le-Vicomte and Fontainebleau in the Ile-de-France, Chenonceau and Chambord in the Loire Valley—have remained testaments to France's illustrious nobility and are veritable histories of France in stone. The spires of Chartres and Claude Monet's gardens in Giverny have continued to demonstrate France's glorious artistic and architectural legacy. Everywhere you go, you'll see scenery cultivated and tempered by the hand of man. The land seems to have been molded and trimmed with a strange, unerring instinct for proportion, and this celebrated Gallic measure is visible everywhere. You will be conscious of it in Notre-Dame de Paris, Versailles, the Place de la Concorde, Rouen Cathedral; in hundreds of places where an unerring *sens du plastique,* or artistic sense, has managed to impart itself to stone, iron, paint, and glass in such a way that these monuments still have the power, centuries after they were created, to lift the human spirit.

The Loire Valley and the Ile-de-France are easily accessible from Paris. But to really experience France, you must travel farther afield. Go west to stolidly Norse Normandy, home of Camembert, Calvados (apple brandy), the D-day landings, and dramatic Mont-St-Michel overlooking the English Channel (*La Manche* to the French). Head southeast to Burgundy, famed for its wine, and explore the hills of Beaujolais, en route to Lyon, a city that competes with Paris—and Dijon—for the title of France's gastronomic capital. Then wend your way south along the towering Rhône Valley to Provence, for the warm colors and the sweet smell of lavender. After feasting your eyes on Provence's orange tile roofs, the ocher earth, and bright, luminous air—so memorably captured in the paintings of Paul Cézanne—continue on to the Côte d'Azur, for the stars, the sun, and the beaches along the bright blue waters of the Mediterranean.

The best way to get by in France is to try out a little French—a simple *"Bonjour"* (Good day) or a *"Parlez-vous anglais?"* (Do you speak English?) will go a long away. Do as the French do: you'll be surprised,

France

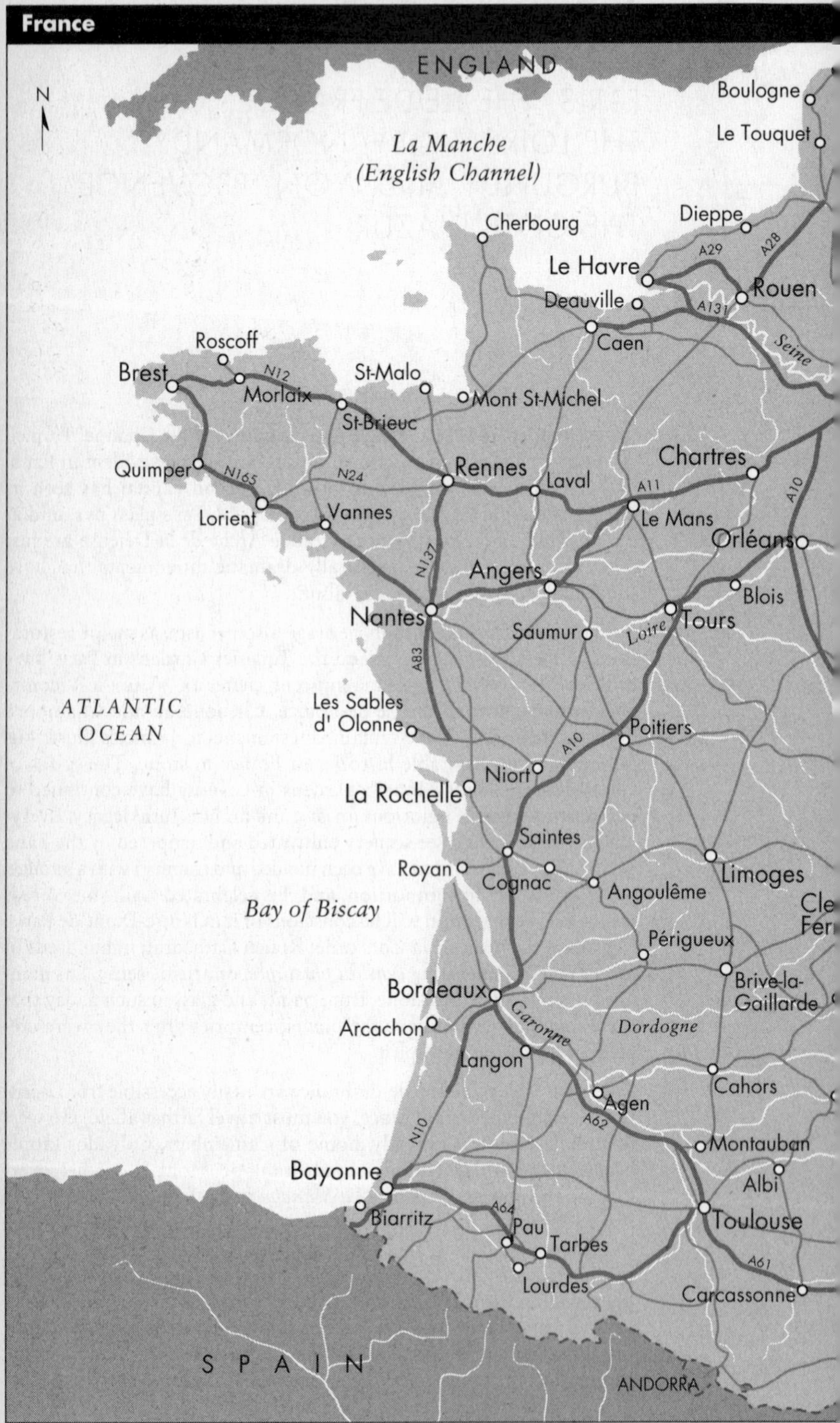
ENGLAND
N
La Manche
(English Channel)
Boulogne
Le Touquet
Dieppe
Cherbourg
A29
A28
Le Havre
Rouen
Deauville
A131
Caen
Seine
Roscoff
Brest
N12
Morlaix
St-Malo
Mont St-Michel
St-Brieuc
Rennes
Chartres
Quimper
N165
N24
Laval
A11
A10
Lorient
Vannes
Le Mans
Orléans
N137
Angers
Blois
Nantes
Tours
Saumur
Loire
A83
ATLANTIC
OCEAN
Les Sables
d' Olonne
Poitiers
A10
Niort
La Rochelle
Saintes
Limoges
Royan
Cognac
Angoulême
Bay of Biscay
Périgueux
Brive-la-
Gaillarde
Bordeaux
Garonne
Arcachon
Dordogne
Langon
Cahors
Agen
A62
N10
Montauban
Albi
Bayonne
Biarritz
A64
Toulouse
Pau
Tarbes
A61
Lourdes
Carcassonne
SPAIN
ANDORRA

Calais
BELGIUM
Lille
A26
Arras
Amiens
Cambrai
St. Quentin
A16
A1
Beauvais
Laon
Reims
A4
LUXEMBOURG
Corsica
Bastia
Calvi
Corte
Ajaccio
N198
Bonifacio
Metz
Paris
Châlons-en-Champagne
A5
A26
Nancy
Strasbourg
Fontainebleau
Troyes
A35
GERMANY
Sens
A31
Colmar
Auxerre
Mulhouse
Belfort
A6
A36
Dijon
Besançon
Bourges
Nevers
Beaune
Autun
A71
SWITZERLAND
Saône
Montluçon
Mâcon
Bourg-en-Bresse
Lyon
Rhône
A72
A43
Chambéry
ITALY
A49
Grenoble
Aurillac
Le Puy
A75
Rhône
Rodez
Montélimar
Gap
Millau
Sisteron
Avignon
A57
Nîmes
Monte Carlo
Nice
A9
Montpellier
Aix-en-Provence
A8
Cannes
Marseille
Narbonne
Toulon
A19
Perpignan
0
50 mi
0
75 km
Mediterranean Sea
Corsica

for instance, at how quickly a surly waiter will melt if you fight a smirk with a smirk. Take time out from your busy sightseeing schedule to match that French passion for the daily rituals. Linger over a coffee in the afternoon or a bottle of wine at dinner and your own experience will be all the more authentic and satisfying. By the end of your stay you will probably agree with the observation that "Everyone has two countries, his or her own and France."

FRANCE A TO Z

To research prices, get advice from other travelers, and book travel arrangements, visit www.fodors.com.

AIR TRAVEL

Flying time to Paris is 7½ hours from New York, 9 hours from Chicago, and 11 hours from Los Angeles. Some major airlines also fly into Nice. Domestic air travel in France is less expensive than it used to be, and there are more flights all over the country; major hubs in France include Lyon, Nice, Marseille, Bordeaux, and Toulouse. (Train service, however, may be faster when you consider time spent getting to and from the airport.)

CARRIERS

Most domestic flights from Paris leave from Orly on Air France; it flies all over the country. Air Liberté flies from Paris to the Côte d'Azur and the southwest region of France.

➤ AIRLINES AND CONTACTS: **Air France** (☎ 800/237–2747 in the U.S.; 08–02–80–28–02 in France). **Air Liberté** (☎ 08–03–80–58–05).

AIRPORTS

The major gateways to France are the airports outside Paris: Orly and Charles de Gaulle, often referred to as Roissy.

➤ AIRPORT INFORMATION: **Charles de Gaulle** (☎ 01–48–62–22–80). **Orly** (☎ 01–49–75–52–52).

BIKE TRAVEL

The French are great bicycling enthusiasts—witness the Tour de France—and there are many good bicycling routes in France. For 44 frs/€6.70 a day (55 frs/€8.40 for a 10-gear touring bike) you can rent a bike from one of 240 train stations; you need to show your passport and leave a deposit of 1,000 frs/€153 or a Visa or MasterCard. Bikes may be taken as accompanied luggage from any station in France; some trains in rural areas don't even charge for this. Tourist offices supply details on the more than 200 local shops that rent bikes, as well as mountain bikes (known as VTT, or *Vélos Touts Terrains*), or you can get the SNCF brochure "Guide du Train et du Vélo" from any station.

BOAT AND FERRY TRAVEL

Canal and river vacations are popular: you can either take an organized cruise or rent a boat and plan your own leisurely route. Contact a travel agent for details or ask for a "Tourisme Fluvial" brochure in any French tourist office.

BUS TRAVEL

Because of the excellent train service, long-distance buses are rare; they're found mainly where train service is scarce. Bus tours are organized by SNCF. Long-distance routes to many European cities are covered by Eurolines.

➤ BUS INFORMATION: **Eurolines** (✉ 28 av. Général-de-Gaulle, 93170 Bagnolet, ☎ 01–49–72–51–51, métro: Galliéni).

BUSINESS HOURS

BANKS AND OFFICES

Banks are open weekdays 9:30–5, with variations; most close for at least an hour at lunch.

MUSEUMS AND SIGHTS

Museums are closed one day a week (often Monday or Tuesday) and on national holidays. Usual hours are from 9 or 10 to 5 or 6. Many museums close for lunch (noon–2); on Sunday many are open afternoons only.

SHOPS

Shops in big towns are open from 9 or 9:30 to 7 or 8 without a lunch break; though it's still rare, an increasing number are now open on Sunday. Smaller shops often open earlier and close later but take a lengthy lunch break (12:30–3 or 4). This siesta-type schedule is more typical in the south of France. Corner grocery stores frequently stay open until around 10 PM.

CAR TRAVEL

EMERGENCIES

If your car breaks down on a highway, go to a roadside emergency telephone and call the breakdown service. If you have a breakdown anywhere else, find the nearest garage or contact the police (dial ☎ 17).

GASOLINE

Gas is expensive, especially on expressways and in rural areas. Don't let your tank get too low—you can go for many miles in the country without passing a gas station—and keep an eye on pump prices as you go. These vary enormously; from 6.50 to 7.80 frs (€1 to 1.2) per liter. The cheapest gas can be found at *hypermarchés* (superstores).

PARKING

Parking is a nightmare in Paris and often difficult in other large towns. Meters and ticket machines (pay and display) are common: make sure you have a supply of 1-, 2-, 5-, and 10-fr coins, or equivalent in euro coins (1 and 2 euros, plus 1, 2, 5, 10, 20, and 50 centimes, or cents, of the euro). Parking is free during August in most of Paris, but be sure to check the signs. In smaller towns parking may be permitted on one side of the street only—alternating every two weeks—so pay attention to signs.

ROAD CONDITIONS

France's roads are classified into five types, numbered and prefixed *A*, *N*, *D*, *C*, or *V*. Roads marked *A* (Autoroutes) are expressways. There are excellent links between Paris and most French cities but poor ones between the provinces (the principal exceptions being A26 from Calais to Reims, A62 between Bordeaux and Toulouse, and A9/A8 the length of the Mediterranean coast). It's often difficult to avoid Paris when crossing France—just try to steer clear of the rush hours (7–9:30 AM and 4:30–7:30 PM). A *péage* (toll) must be paid on most expressways: the rate varies but is roughly 1 fr/€.15 per 3 km (1½ mi). The *N* (Route Nationale) roads—which are sometimes divided highways—and *D* (Route Départementale) roads are usually wide and fast, and driving along them can be a real pleasure. Don't be daunted by the smaller C (Chemin Communal) and *V* (Chemin Vicinal) roads, either. The yellow regional Michelin maps—on sale throughout France—are invaluable.

RULES OF THE ROAD

You may use your own driver's license in France, but you must be able to prove you have third-party insurance. Drive on the right and yield to drivers coming from the right if there is no solid white line. Seat belts are obligatory for all passengers, and children under 12 may not travel in the front seat. Speed limits are 130 kph (80 mph) on expressways, 110 kph (70 mph) on divided highways, 90 kph (55 mph) on other roads, 50 kph (30 mph) in towns. French drivers break these limits and police dish out hefty on-the-spot fines with equal abandon.

CUSTOMS AND DUTIES

For details on imports and duty-free limits, *see* Customs and Duties *in* Chapter 1.

DINING

Eating in France is serious business, at least for two of the three meals each day. For a light meal try an informal café or brasserie (steak and french fries remains the classic) or a picnic (a baguette with ham, cheese, or pâté is a perfect combination). Reservations are advised at most restaurants, particularly in summer. French breakfasts are relatively modest—strong coffee, fruit juice if you insist, and croissants.

RATINGS

Prices are per person and are for a main course only; note that when prices are quoted for a restaurant which only offers prix fixe (set-price) complete dinners, it is given a price category that reflects this prix-fixe price. Tax (19.6%) and service are included in these prices, but not wine.

CATEGORY	PARIS AND THE CÔTE D'AZUR	OTHER AREAS
$$$$	over 250 frs (€38)	over 180 frs (€27.48)
$$$	150 frs–250 frs (€23–€38)	120 frs–180 frs (€18.32–€27.48)
$$	80 frs–150 frs (€12–€23)	70 frs–120 frs (€10.70–€18.32)
$	under 80 frs (€12)	under 70 frs (€10.70)

MEALTIMES

Dinner is the main meal and usually begins at 8. Lunch begins at noon in the countryside, and 12:30 or 1 (seldom later) in towns.

RESERVATIONS AND DRESS

Jacket and tie are recommended for $$$$ and $$$ restaurants and at some of the more stylish $$ restaurants as well. When in doubt, it's best to dress up. Otherwise casual dress is appropriate (though be aware that casual in Paris means stylish and no shorts or sneakers).

EMBASSIES

➤ AUSTRALIA: (✉ 4 rue Jean-Rey, 15e, ☎ 01–40–59–33–00, métro: Bir-Hakeim).

➤ CANADA: (✉ 35 av. Montaigne, 8e, ☎ 01–44–43–29–00, métro: Franklin-D.-Roosevelt).

➤ NEW ZEALAND: (✉ 7 ter rue Léonardo-da-Vinci, 16e, ☎ 01–45–00–24–11, métro: Victor-Hugo).

➤ UNITED KINGDOM: **United Kingdom** (✉ 35 rue du Faubourg–St-Honoré, 8e, ☎ 01–44–51–31–00, métro: Concorde).

➤ UNITED STATES: **United States** (✉ 2 av. Gabriel, 8e, ☎ 01–43–12–22–22, métro: Concorde).

HEALTH

FOOD AND DRINK

Tap water is perfectly safe, though not always very palatable (least of all in Paris). Mineral water is a good alternative; there's a vast choice of *eaus plates* (still) and *eaux gazeuses* (fizzy).

HOLIDAYS

January 1; Easter Monday (usually late March or early April); May 1 (Labor Day); May 8 (VE Day); Ascension (usually early May); Pentecost Monday (usually mid-May); July 14 (Bastille Day); August 15 (Assumption); November 1 (All Saints' Day); November 11 (Armistice); December 25.

LANGUAGE

The French study English for a minimum of four years at school and, although few are fluent, their English is probably better than the French of most Americans. English is widely understood in major tourist areas, and in most hotels there is likely to be at least one person who can converse with you. Even if your own French is rusty, try to master a few words: people will greatly appreciate your efforts.

LODGING

France has a wide range of accommodations, from rambling old village inns to stylishly converted châteaux to modern hotels. Prices must, by law, be posted in the hotel room and include taxes and service. Prices are usually listed by room, not per person, and don't usually include breakfast. In smaller rural hotels, you may be expected to have your evening meal at the hotel, too.

The quality of accommodations, particularly in older properties, can vary greatly from room to room; if you don't like the room you're given, ask to see another. When making reservations, state your preference for *une chambre à deux lits* (twin beds) or *une chambre à grand lit* (double bed) and for *douche* (shower) or *baignoire* (tub)—the latter always costs more.

It's always a good idea to make hotel reservations in Paris and other major tourist destinations as far in advance as possible, especially in late spring, summer, or fall. If you arrive without a reservation, tourist offices in major train stations and most towns may be able to find a hotel for you.

RATINGS

Prices are for standard double rooms and include tax (19.6%) and service charges.

CATEGORY	PARIS AND THE CÔTE D'AZUR	OTHER AREAS
$$$$	over 1,200 frs (€184)	over 800 frs (€123)
$$$	750 frs–1,200 frs (€115–€184)	500 frs–800 frs (€76.33–€123)
$$	450 frs–750 frs (€68.70–€115)	250 frs–500 frs (€38.16–€76.33)
$	under 450 frs (€68.70)	under 250 frs (€38.16)

APARTMENT AND VILLA RENTALS

Renting an apartment or a *gîte* (furnished house) for a week or month can be more convenient and save you money if you're traveling with a group or family. The French Government Tourist Offices in New York and London are good sources for information about rentals. Gîtes de France has a list of gîtes for rent: indicate the region that interests you or order the annual nationwide guide (140 frs/€21).

The following agencies list houses and apartments for rent: At Home Abroad; At Home in France; Orion; Paris Appartements Services; and Ville et Village.

➤ RENTAL LISTINGS: **At Home Abroad** (✉ 405 E. 56th St., Suite 6H, New York, NY 10022, ☎ 212/421–9165, FAX 212/752–1591). **At Home in France** (✉ Box 643, Ashland, OR 97520, ☎ 541/488–9467, FAX 541/488–9468). **Gîtes de France** (✉ 59 rue St-Lazare, 75009 Paris, ☎ 01–49–70–75–75, FAX 01–42–81–28–53). **Orion** (✉ 30 pl. d'Italie, 75013 Paris, ☎ 01–40–78–54–54; 800/546–4777; 212/688–9538 in the U.S., FAX 01–40–78–54–55; 212/688–9467 in the U.S.). **Paris Appartements Services** (✉ 69 rue d'Argout, 75002, ☎ 01–40–28–01–28, FAX 01–40–28–92–01). **Ville et Village** (✉ 2124 Kittredge St., Suite 200, Berkeley, CA 94704, ☎ 510/559–8080, FAX 510/559–8217).

BED-AND-BREAKFASTS

Known as *chambres d'hôte,* B&Bs are becoming increasingly popular in rural areas and can be a great bargain. Check local tourist offices for details, or contact Gîtes de France, a national organization listing B&Bs all over France.

➤ RESERVATION SERVICES: **Gîtes de France** (✉ 59 rue St-Lazare, 75009 Paris, ☎ 01–49–70–75–75).

CAMPING

A guide to France's campsites is published by the Fédération Française de Camping et de Caravaning.

➤ CONTACTS: **Fédération Française de Camping et de Caravaning** (✉ 78 rue de Rivoli, 75004 Paris, ☎ 01–42–72–84–08).

HOSTELS

Some of the hostels in France are quite nice and even have double rooms; age restrictions may apply. Contact the Fédération Unie des Auberges de Jeunesse for information.

➤ HOSTEL ORGANIZATIONS: **Fédération Unie des Auberges de Jeunesse** (✉ 27 rue Pajol, 75018 Paris, ☎ 01–44–89–87–27, FAX 01–44–89–87–10).

HOTELS

First-time travelers to France (or anywhere else in Europe, for that matter), take note: not only are hotel rooms here small by American standards, they are also rarely as well appointed. Unless you have booked into a top-tier address, do not expect to find a spacious room with all the latest conveniences. The hotels we have chosen can be relied upon to offer clean linens, conscientious service, and considerable charm. Rest assured that the bathrooms, though sometimes small, will be clean and comfortable, but don't be surprised to find the bed a bit saggy or the carpet in the hall a little threadbare.

MAIL AND SHIPPING

If you're uncertain where you'll be staying, have mail sent to American Express (if you're a card member) or Thomas Cook; mail labeled "poste restante" is also accepted at most French post offices.

POSTAL RATES

Letters and postcards to the United States and Canada cost 4.40 frs/€.67 for 20 grams. Letters to the United Kingdom cost 3 frs/€.46 for up to 20 grams, as do letters within France. Postcards cost 2.70 frs/€.41 within France and to EU countries. Stamps can be bought in post offices (La Poste) and cafés sporting a red TABAC sign outside.

MONEY MATTERS

There's no way around it: France is expensive. But many travel basics—hotels, restaurants, plane, and train tickets—can be made more affordable by planning ahead, taking advantage of prix-fixe menus, and staying in smaller, family-run places. Prices are highest in Paris and on the Côte d'Azur, though even in these areas you can find reasonable accommodations and food.

Prices vary greatly depending on the region, proximity to tourist sights, and—believe it or not—whether you're sitting down (and where—inside or on the terrace) or standing up in a café! Here are a few samples: cup of coffee, 6–12 frs/€.92–1.84; glass of beer, 10–25 frs/€1.53–

3.84; soft drink, 10–20 frs/€1.53–3; ham sandwich, 15–25 frs/€2.30–3.84; 1½-km (1-mi) taxi ride, 35 frs/€5.38.

CURRENCY

January 1, 2002, sees the French franc replaced by the new European Union (EU) currency, the euro, worth precisely 6.55957 francs. Coins and notes in French francs (subdivided into 100 centimes) will be gradually withdrawn from circulation over the first few months of 2002. International credit cards and traveler's checks are widely accepted throughout France, except in some rural areas.

In France, the long-awaited physical debut of the much touted euro will begin in a rather confusing manner; all banks, businesses, and money machines will be stocked in euros as of January 1, but French francs will *also* be valid until midnight February 17, a six-week period when you can still buy that newspaper with francs but receive your change in euros. Your best bet is to change your remaining francs into euros the minute you arrive in France, and for once it doesn't really matter where because the rate between the franc and the euro was irrevocably fixed in late 1999 (1 euro = 6.55957 frs), thus eliminating any fluctuations in the market and any need for commission. If anyone tries to charge you a commission when you are changing French francs into euros, stop the transaction immediately.

However, there is a big difference between exchanging old francs (set rate, with no commissions, and no worries) and exchanging dollars (competition, plus fluctuation and diverse commissions), or, in fact, any other non-European Union currencies, such as Japanese yen and British pounds. For these monies, which still fluctuate in value against the euro, you still need to follow the old guidelines, such as shopping around for the best exchange rates and checking the rates before leaving home. At press time (summer 2001), the U.S. dollar bought 7.1 francs, the Canadian dollar 4.7 francs, the pound sterling 10.4 francs, the Irish punt 8.3 francs, the Australian dollar 3.9 francs, the New Zealand dollar 3.1 francs, and the South African rand 0.9 francs. The U.S. dollar brought €1.11, the Canadian dollar €.71, the Irish punt €1.26, the Australian dollar €.57, the New Zealand dollar €.45, and the South American rand €.13.

SHOPPING

People don't usually bargain in shops where prices are clearly marked, but they do at outdoor markets and flea markets.

TAXES

All taxes must be included in posted prices in France. The initials TTC (*toutes taxes comprises,* which means taxes included) are sometimes included on price lists, but they are superfluous. Restaurant and hotel prices must *by law* include taxes and service charges: if they are tacked onto your bill as additional items, you should complain.

VALUE-ADDED TAX

A value-added tax of 19.6%, known in France as the TVA, is imposed on most consumer goods. Non–European Union residents age 15 and over can reclaim part of this tax. To qualify, your purchases in a single shop must total at least 2,000 frs/€307. The amount of the refund varies from shop to shop but usually hovers between 13% and 16%. The major department stores have simplified the refund process with special desks where the *bordereaux* (export sales invoices) are prepared.

TELEPHONES

French phone numbers have 10 digits. All phone numbers have a two-digit prefix determined by zone: Paris and the Ile-de-France, 01; the northwest, 02; the northeast, 03; the southeast, 04; and the southwest, 05.

COUNTRY AND AREA CODES

The country code for France is 33 and for Monaco 377. To call France from the United States, dial 011 (for all international calls), then dial 33 (the country code), and the number in France, minus any initial 0. To dial France from the United Kingdom, dial 00–33, then the number in France, minus any initial 0.

INTERNATIONAL CALLS

To call a foreign country from France, dial 00 and wait for the tone, then dial the country code, area code, and number. You can also contact your long distance carrier directly and charge your call to your calling card or make a collect call.

➤ ACCESS CODES: **AT&T** (☎ 08–00–99–00–11). **MCI** (☎ 08–00–99–00–19). **Sprint** (☎ 08–00–99–00–87).

LOCAL CALLS

To make calls within a region or to another region in France, simply dial the full, 10-digit number. A local call in France costs 60 centimes for the first minute and 22 centimes for every minute after that; cheaper rates apply between 7 PM and 8 AM and between noon Saturday and 8 AM Monday. Dial ☎ 12 for local operators.

PUBLIC PHONES

Telephone booths can almost always be found at post offices, cafés, and métro stations. Some French pay phones take 1-, 2-, and 5-fr coins (1-fr minimum), but most phones are now operated by *télécartes* (phone cards), sold in post offices, métro stations, and cafés with red TABAC signs by unit (cost: 48.60 frs/€7 for 50 units, 96.70 frs/€14.87 for 120 units).

TIPPING

The bill in a bar or restaurant includes service, but it's customary to leave some small change unless you're dissatisfied. The amount varies, from 30 centimes for a beer to 10–30 frs/€1.53–4.61 after a meal. Tip taxi drivers and hairdressers about 10%. Give ushers in theaters 1–2 frs/€.30. Cloakroom attendants will expect nothing if there is a sign saying POURBOIRE INTERDIT (tipping forbidden); otherwise give them 5 frs/€.76. Washroom attendants usually get 2 frs/€.30—a sum that is often posted. Bellhops should get 10 frs/€1.53 per item. If you stay in a moderately priced hotel for more than two or three days, it is customary to leave something for the chambermaid—perhaps 10 frs/€1.53 per day. Expect to tip 10 frs/€1.53 for room service—but nothing is expected if breakfast is routinely served in your room. Service station attendants get nothing for giving you gas or oil, and 5 or 10 frs/€.76–1.53 for checking tires. Train and airport porters get a fixed sum (6–10 frs/€.92–1.53) per bag. Museum guides should get 5–10 frs/€.76–1.53 after a guided tour. Tip tour guides (and bus drivers) 10 frs/€1.53 or more after an excursion.

TRAIN TRAVEL

SNCF, the French national railroad, is fast, punctual, comfortable, and comprehensive. The TGV (*Trains à Grande Vitesse*), with a top speed of 300 kph (190 mph), are the best domestic trains, heading southeast from Paris to Lyon, Marseille, the Côte d'Azur, and Switzerland; west to Nantes; southwest to Bordeaux; and north to Lille and Brussels. The new TGV Méditerranée line, which opened in 2001, connects Valence with Avignon, Aix, and Marseilles (with a branch line further to Nîmes), reducing the trip from Paris to Provence from five hours to two hours and 55 minutes. TGVs require a seat reservation (easily obtained at the ticket window or from an automatic machine).

You must punch your train ticket in one of the orange machines (*composteurs*) you'll encounter alongside platforms. Slide your ticket in face-up and wait for a "clunk" sound. (The small yellow tickets and automatic ticket barriers used for most suburban Paris trains are similar to those in the métro/RER.) The ticket collectors will present you with an on-the-spot fine of 100 frs/€15.38 if your ticket hasn't been validated before boarding.

On overnight trains you choose between *wagons-lits* (private sleeping cars), which are expensive, and *couchettes* (bunks), which sleep six to a compartment in second class and four to a compartment in first class (sheet and pillow provided) and are cheaper (90 frs/€13.80). Ordinary compartment seats do not pull together to enable you to lie down. In summer special night trains from Paris to Spain and the Côte d'Azur are geared for a younger market, with discos and bars.

FARES AND SCHEDULES

As an example, the cost of a second-class ticket for the Paris–Lyon route is normally 324 frs/€49.84 but climbs to 410 frs/€63 during the morning and evening rush hours. Seat reservations are reassuring but seldom necessary on other French trains, except at holiday times.

If France is your only destination in Europe, consider purchasing a France Rail Pass, which allows three days of unlimited train travel in a one-month period. Prices range from $180 to $210 for one or two adults in first or second class. Additional days may be added for extra fees in either class. Other options include the France Rail 'n Drive Pass (combining rail and rental car), France Rail 'n Fly Pass (rail travel and one air journey within France), and the France Fly, Rail 'n Drive Pass (a rail, air, and rental-car program all in one).

France is one of 17 countries in which you can use Eurailpasses, which provide unlimited first-class rail travel, in all of the participating countries, for the duration of the pass. Fees are $554 for 15 days, $890 for one month. If your plans call for only limited train travel, look into a Europass, which costs less money than a Eurailpass. The Inter-Rail pass (which can be bought in Europe) covers second-class rail travel, in up to 28 countries (sub-divided into 8 zones), and prices range from 1,798 frs/€274 for one zone for 3 weeks to 2,064 frs/€467 for all 8 zones for one month.

CUTTING COSTS

Various reduced-fare passes are available from major train stations in France and from SNCF travel agents. To find out information about these passes, log on to www.europeonrail.com. When traveling together, two people (who don't have to be a couple) can save money with the Découverte à Deux. Just say you're traveling together when you make a reservation or buy the tickets, and you will get a 25% discount during "périodes bleues" (blue periods; weekdays and not on or near any holidays—calendars are available at stations). Senior citizens (over 60) qualify for the *Carte Senior* (290 frs/€44.27 for four trips), and young people (under 26) qualify for the *Carte 12/25* (270 frs/€41.22). You can get 50% discounts in blue periods. The *Carte Enfant* + (350 frs/€53.43) enables children under 12 and up to four accompanying adults to travel at half- or quarter-price, depending on the travel period. Other discounts are available if you book 30 or 8 days before traveling (*Découverte J30* or *Découverte J8*). If you don't benefit from any of these reductions and plan on traveling at least 1,000 km (620 mi) round-trip (including several stops), look into purchasing a *Billet Séjour.* This ticket gives you a 25% reduction if you stay over a Sunday and travel only during blue periods.

➤ TRAIN INFORMATION: SNCF (✉ 88 rue St-Lazare, 75009 Paris, ☎ 08–36–35–35–35, WEB www.sncf.com).

VISITOR INFORMATION

➤ TOURIST INFORMATION: **France On-Call** (☎ 410/286–8310, ⏲ weekdays 9–7, WEB www.francetourism.com). **Chicago** (✉ 676 N. Michigan Ave., 60611). **London** (✉ 178 Piccadilly, W1V OAL, ☎ 171/6399–3500, FAX 171/6493–6594). **Los Angeles** (✉ 9454 Wilshire Blvd., Suite 715, Beverly Hills 90212). **Montréal** (✉ 1981 av. McGill College, Suite 490, Québec H3A 2W9). **New York City** (✉ 444 Madison Ave., 16th floor, 10022).

WHEN TO GO

June and September, free of midsummer crowds, are the best months to be in France. June has the advantage of long daylight hours; slightly cheaper prices and many warm days (often lasting well into October) make September attractive. The second half of July and all of August are spoiled by inflated prices and huge crowds on the beaches, and the heat can be stifling in southern France. Paris, though pleasantly deserted, can be stuffy in August, too. Anytime between March and November offers a good chance to soak up some sun on the Côte d'Azur. The weather in Paris and the Loire is unappealing before Easter (lots of rain and chilly temperatures). If you're dreaming of Paris in the springtime, May (not April) is your best bet.

CLIMATE

North of the Loire (including Paris), France has a northern European climate—coldish winters, pleasant if unpredictable summers, and frequent rain. Southern France has a Mediterranean climate: mild winters; long, hot summers; and sunshine much of the year. The more Continental climate of eastern and central France is a mixture of these two extremes: winters can be very cold and summers mighty hot. France's Atlantic coast has a temperate climate even south of the Loire, with the exception of the much warmer Biarritz. The following are the average daily maximum and minimum temperatures for Paris and Marseille.

PARIS

Jan.	43F	6C	**May**	68F	20C	**Sept.**	70F	21C
	34	1		49	10		53	12
Feb.	45F	7C	**June**	73F	23C	**Oct.**	60F	16C
	34	1		55	13		46	8
Mar.	54F	12C	**July**	76F	25C	**Nov.**	50 F	10C
	39	4		58	15		40	5
Apr.	60F	16C	**Aug.**	75F	24C	**Dec.**	44 F	7C
	43	6		58	15		36	2

MARSEILLE

Jan.	50F	10C	**May**	71F	22C	**Sept.**	77F	25C
	35	2		52	11		58	15
Feb.	53F	12C	**June**	79F	26C	**Oct.**	68F	20C
	36	2		58	14		51	10
Mar.	59F	15C	**July**	84F	29C	**Nov.**	58F	14C
	41	5		63	17		41	5
Apr.	64F	18C	**Aug.**	83F	28C	**Dec.**	52F	11C
	46	8		63	17		37	3

PARIS

If there's a problem with a trip to Paris, it's the embarrassment of riches that faces you. No matter which Paris you choose—-touristy Paris, historic Paris, fashion-conscious Paris, pretentious bourgeois Paris, thrifty Paris, the legendary bohemian arty Paris of undying attraction—one thing is certain: you will find your own Paris, one that is vivid, exciting, often unforgettable. Paris is a city of vast, noble perspectives and intimate, ramshackle streets, of formal *espaces vertes* (green open spaces) and quiet squares—and this combination of the pompous and the private is one of the secrets of its perennial pull.

For the first-timer, there will always be several "musts" at the top of the list, but a visit to Paris will never be quite as simple as a quick look at Notre-Dame, the Louvre, and the Eiffel Tower. Every *quartier,* or neighborhood, has its own treasures, and you should be ready to explore—a very pleasant prospect in this most elegant of cities.

Exploring Paris

Numbers in the margin correspond to points of interest on the Paris map.

As world capitals go, Paris is surprisingly compact. With the exceptions of the Bois de Boulogne and Montmartre, you can easily walk from one major sight to the next. The city is divided in two by the River Seine, with two islands (Ile de la Cité and Ile St-Louis) in the middle. The Left—or south—Bank has a more intimate, bohemian flavor than the haughtier Right Bank. The east–west axis from Châtelet to the Arc de Triomphe, via the rue de Rivoli and the Champs-Élysées, is the principal thoroughfare for sightseeing and shopping on the Right Bank.

The **Carte Musées–Monuments** pass, which allows you access to most Paris museums and monuments, can be obtained from museums or major métro stations (one-day pass, 80 frs/€12; three days, 160 frs/€24; five days, 240 frs/€36). Note, however, that this pass may only be useful to you if you plan to see *a lot* of museums in the allotted days.

The perfect introduction to Paris? Begin at the beginning—Notre-Dame and the little island of Ile de la Cité, where Paris was first settled more than 2,000 years ago. After visiting the nearby Gothic jewel of the Sainte-Chapelle, head over to the Louvre—home to the *Venus de Milo,* the *Winged Victory,* and the ironic, haunting smile of the *Mona Lisa*—then wander through the gardens of the Tuileries to the city's heart, Place de la Concorde. Take a boat along the Seine for a waterside rendezvous with the Eiffel Tower, and consider finishing off with dinner in Montmartre. Papa Hemingway was right: Paris is truly a moveable feast.

From Notre-Dame to the Latin Quarter

No matter how you first approach Paris—historically, geographically, emotionally—it is the river Seine that summons us, the Seine which harbors two islands, the Ile de la Cité and the Ile St-Louis, within the very center of Paris. Of them, it is the Ile de la Cité that forms the historic ground zero of the city. It was here that the earliest inhabitants of Paris, the Gaulish tribe of the Parisii, settled in about 250 BC). Here you'll find the great, brooding cathedral of Notre-Dame, the jewel-like Sainte-Chapelle, and the Conciergerie, last haunt of Queen Marie-Antoinette. To the east lies the smaller island of the Ile St-Louis—one of Paris's most romantic nooks—while across the river on the Left Bank of the Seine is the bohemian Quartier Latin, with its warren of steep sloping streets, populated largely by Sorbonne students and academics.

29 **Conciergerie.** Bringing a tear to the eyes of Ancien Régime devotées, this is the famous prison in which dukes and duchesses, lords and ladies, and, most famously, Queen Marie-Antoinette were imprisoned during the French Revolution before being bundled off for their date with the guillotine. You can still see the queen's cell and chapel and the superb vaulted 14th-century hall, the **Salles des Gens d'Armes** (Hall of the Men-at-Arms). The **Tour de l'Horloge** (Clock Tower) near the entrance on quai de l'Horloge has a clock that has been ticking off time since 1370. ✉ *1 quai de l'Horloge,* ☎ *01–53–73–78–50.* ⏲ *Apr.–Sept., daily 9:30–6:30; Oct.–Mar., daily 10–5. Métro: Cité.*

32 **Ile St-Louis.** Of the two islands in the Seine—the Ile de la Cité is located just to the west—it is the Ile St-Louis that best retains the loveliness of *le Paris traditionnel.* A tiny universe unto itself, shaded by trees, bordered by Seine-side quais, and overhung with ancient stone houses, the island has long been a coveted address for Parisians—Voltaire, Daumier, Cézanne, Baudelaire, Chagall, Helena Rubenstein, and the Rothschilds are just some of the lucky people who have called the St-Louis home. In summer, crowds line up for a scoop from Berthillon's ice-cream shop—savor your cone of *glace de Grande Marnier* by strolling along the isle's Seine-side streets. *Métro: Pont-Marie.*

★ 31 **Notre-Dame.** The cathedral of Notre-Dame remains Paris's historic and geographic heart, a place of worship for more than 2,000 years (the present building is the fourth on this site). Victor Hugo's Quasimodo sought sanctuary in its towers, kings and princes married before its great altar, and Napoléon crowned his empress here. The magnificent structure was begun in 1163, making it one of the earliest Gothic cathedrals, but wasn't finished until 1345. The interior is at its lightest and least crowded in the early morning. Window space is limited and filled with shimmering stained glass; the circular rose windows in the transept are particularly delicate. The 387-step climb up the towers is worth the effort for a perfect view of the gargoyles and Paris. ✉ *Pl. du Parvis.* ⏲ *Cathedral daily 8–7, treasury (religious and vestmental relics) weekdays 9:30–6:30. Métro: Cité.*

30 **Panthéon.** This Temple to the Famous started life as a church (1758–89). Since the Revolution, the crypt has harbored the remains of such national heroes as Voltaire, Rousseau, and Zola. The austere interior is ringed with Puvis de Chavannes's late-19th-century frescoes, relating the life of Geneviève, patron saint of Paris, and contains a swinging model of the giant pendulum used here by Léon Foucault in 1851 to prove the earth's rotation. ✉ *Pl. du Panthéon,* ☎ *01–44–32–18–00.* ⏲ *Daily 10–6:15. Métro: Cardinal-Lemoine.*

28 **Place Dauphine.** At the western tail end of the Ile de la Cité, this charming plaza was built by Henri IV. The triangular place is lined with some 17th-century houses which the writer André Maurois felt represented the very quintessence of Paris and France; take a seat on the park bench and see if you agree. *Métro: Cité.*

★ 30 **Sainte-Chapelle** (Holy Chapel). One of the most beauteous achievements of the Middle Ages and home to the most ancient stained-glass windows in Paris, this chapel was built by Louis IX in the 1240s to house the Crown of Thorns he had bought from Emperor Baldwin. A lower chapel leads to the dazzling upper chapel, whose walls—if you can call them that—are almost completely made of stained glass. Like an enormous magic lantern, the scenes illuminate more than a thousand figures from stories of the Bible. Try to attend a candlelit concert here. ✉ *4 bd. du Palais,* ☎ *01–53–73–78–51.* ⏲ *Apr.–Sept., daily 9:30–6:30; Oct.–Mar., daily 10–5. Métro: Cité.*

33 **Sorbonne.** Students at Paris's ancient university—one of the oldest in Europe—used to listen to lectures in Latin, which explains why the surrounding area is known as the Latin Quarter. You can visit the main courtyard and peek into the lecture halls if they're not in use. The Baroque chapel is open only during exhibitions. ✉ *Rue de la Sorbonne. Métro: Cluny–La Sorbonne.*

From the Louvre to the Arc de Triomphe

From the gleaming glass pyramid entrance of the Louvre, the world's greatest museum, you can see the Arc de Triomphe standing foursquare at the top of the city's most famous avenue, the Champs-Élysées. Between the Louvre and the Arc lies the city's spiritual heart—the elegant Place de la Concorde.

5 **Arc de Triomphe** (Triumphal Arch). This 164-ft arch was planned by Napoléon to celebrate his military successes. Yet when Empress Marie-Louise entered Paris in 1810, it was barely off the ground. Napoléon had been dead for 15 years when the Arc de Triomphe was finished in 1836. The arch looms over Place Charles-de-Gaulle, referred to by Parisians as **L'Étoile** (The Star), one of Europe's most chaotic traffic circles. Short of attempting a death-defying dash, your only way to get over to the Arc de Triomphe is to take the pedestrian underpass. France's Unknown Soldier is buried beneath the archway; the flame is rekindled every evening at 6:30. ✉ *Pl. Charles-de-Gaulle,* ☎ *01–55–37–73–77.* ⏲ *Easter–Oct., daily 9:30 AM–11 PM; Nov.–Easter, daily 10 AM–10:30 PM. Métro, RER: Charles-de-Gaulle–Étoile.*

6 **Champs-Élysées.** The cosmopolitan pulse of Paris beats strongest along this gracefully sloping, 2-km (1-mi) avenue, originally laid out in the 1660s by André Le Nôtre as parkland sweeping away from the Tuileries. There isn't much sign of that pastoral past these days, as you stroll by the cafés, restaurants, airline offices, car showrooms, movie theaters, and chic arcades that occupy its upper half. For a look at its more regal past, note the two 19th-century garden pavilion restaurants, Laurent and Ledoyen. *Métro: George-V, Franklin-D.-Roosevelt, Champs-Élysées–Clemenceau.*

7 **Grand Palais** (Grand Palace). This so-called palace built for the World Exhibition of 1900 is closed for renovation and is unlikely to reopen before at least 2003; but you can still visit the **Palais de la Découverte** (Palace of Discovery), with scientific and mechanical exhibits and a **planetarium.** ✉ *Av. Winston-Churchill,* ☎ *01–56–43–20–21.* ⏲ *Palais de la Découverte Tues.–Sat. 9:30–6, Sun. 10–7. Métro: Franklin-D.-Roosevelt.*

8 **Jardin des Tuileries** (Tuileries Gardens). Immortalized in many Impressionist masterpieces by Renoir, Pissarro, and Monet, these enormous formal gardens are lined with trees, ponds, and statues. At the far end of the Tuileries, leading toward the Louvre, is the **Arc du Carrousel,** a dainty triumphal arch erected more quickly (1806–08) than its big brother at the far end of the Champs-Élysées. *Métro: Concorde, Tuileries.*

★ 12 **Louvre.** Leonardo da Vinci's *Mona Lisa* and *Virgin and Saint Anne,* Van Eyck's *Madonna of Chancellor Rolin,* Giorgione's *Concert Champêtre,* and Delacroix's *Liberty Guiding the People* . . . you get the picture. Once a royal palace, now the world's largest and most famous museum, the Louvre has been given fresh purpose by over a decade of expansion, renovation, and reorganization, symbolized by I. M. Pei's daring glass pyramid that now serves as the entrance to both the museum and an underground shopping arcade, the **Carrousel du Louvre.** Many thousands of treasures are newly cleaned and lit, so plan on see-

Paris

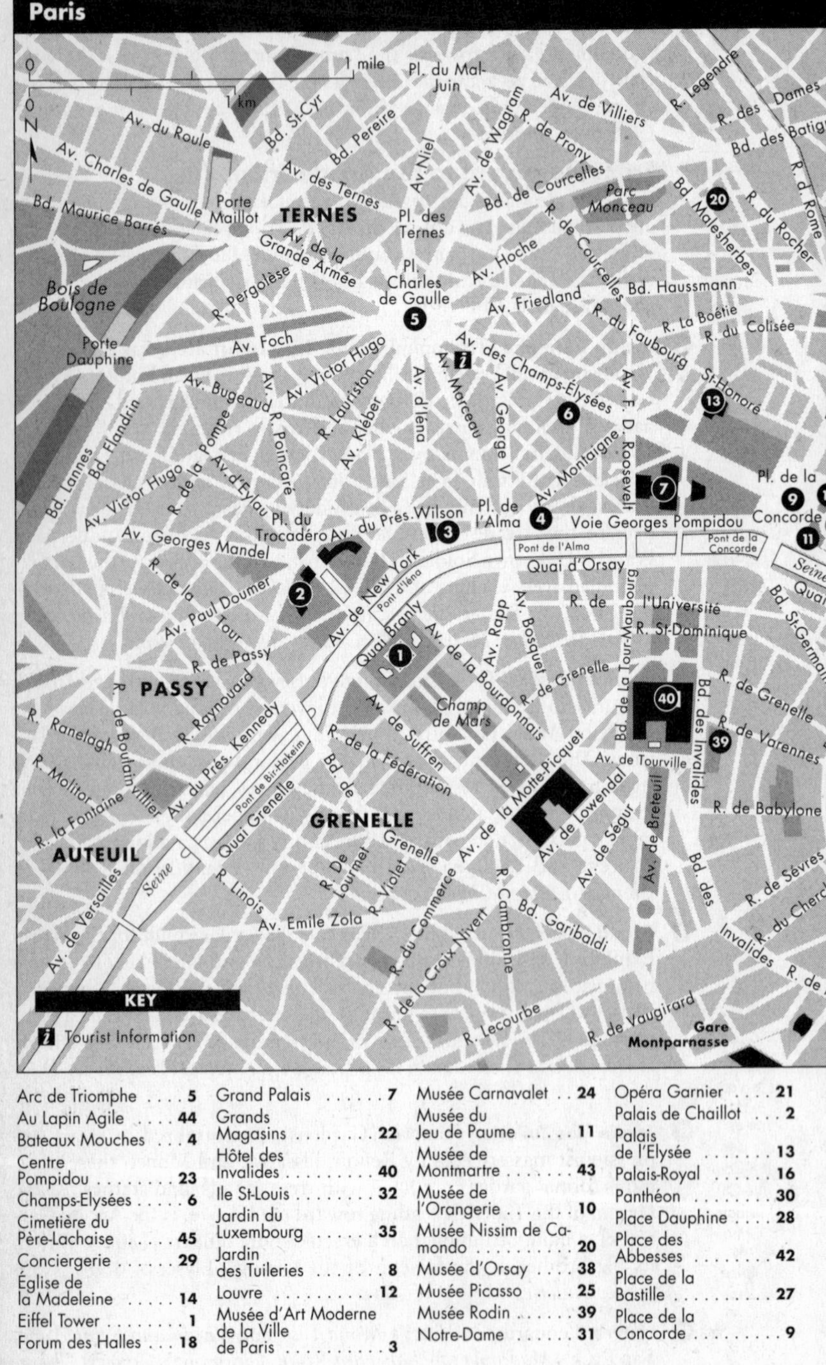

Arc de Triomphe 5
Au Lapin Agile 44
Bateaux Mouches . . . 4
Centre Pompidou 23
Champs-Elysées 6
Cimetière du Père-Lachaise 45
Conciergerie 29
Église de la Madeleine 14
Eiffel Tower 1
Forum des Halles . . . 18
Grand Palais 7
Grands Magasins 22
Hôtel des Invalides 40
Ile St-Louis 32
Jardin du Luxembourg 35
Jardin des Tuileries 8
Louvre 12
Musée d'Art Moderne de la Ville de Paris 3
Musée Carnavalet . . 24
Musée du Jeu de Paume 11
Musée de Montmartre 43
Musée de l'Orangerie 10
Musée Nissim de Camondo 20
Musée d'Orsay 38
Musée Picasso 25
Musée Rodin 39
Notre-Dame 31
Opéra Garnier 21
Palais de Chaillot . . . 2
Palais de l'Elysée 13
Palais-Royal 16
Panthéon 30
Place Dauphine 28
Place des Abbesses 42
Place de la Bastille 27
Place de la Concorde 9

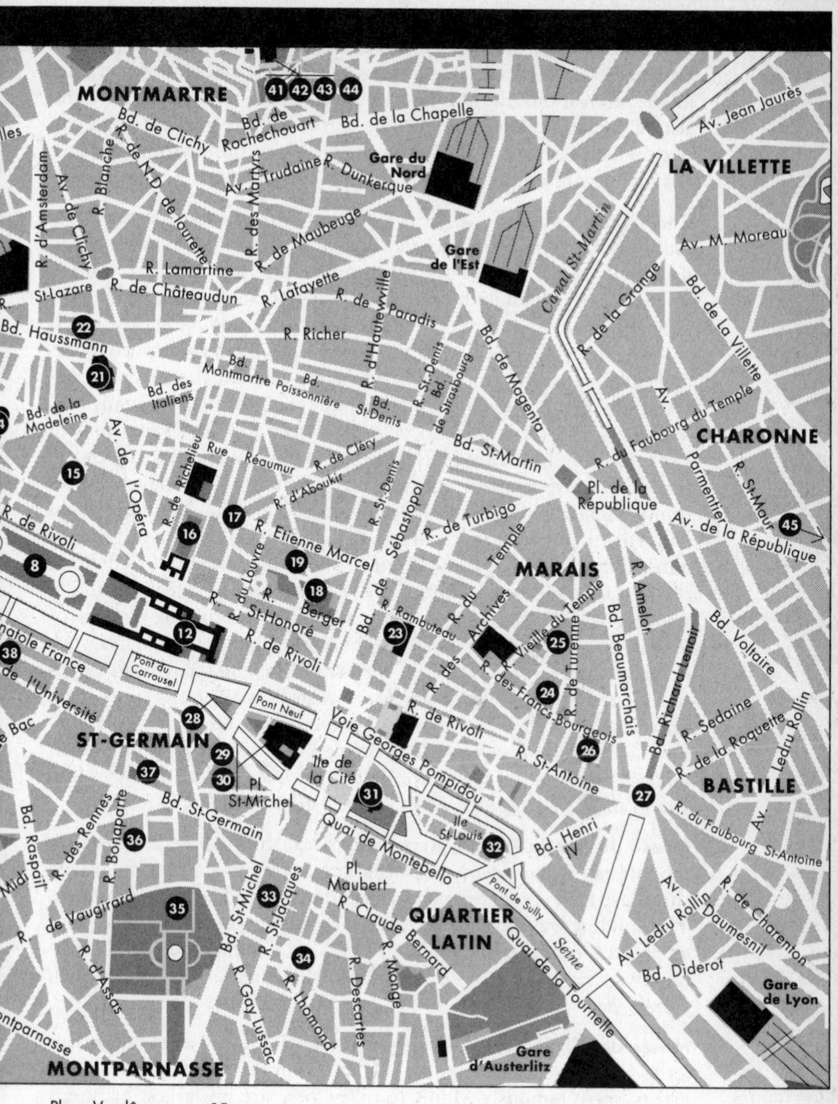

Place Vendôme	**15**
Place des Victoires	**17**
Place des Vosges	**26**
Sacré-Coeur	**41**
Sainte-Chapelle	**30**
St-Eustache	**19**
St-Germain-des-Prés	**37**
St-Sulpice	**36**
Sorbonne	**33**

ing it all—from the red-brocaded Napoléon III salons to the fabled Egyptian collection, from the 186-carat Regent Diamond to the rooms crowded with Botticellis, Caravaggios, Poussins, and Géricaults. After all the renovations, the Louvre is now a coherent, unified structure and search parties no longer need to be sent in to find you and bring you out. In fact, Pei's new Louvre has emerged less cramped and more rationally organized.

The main attraction for some is a portrait of the wife of a certain Florentine millionaire, Francesco da Gioconda, better known as Leonardo da Vinci's *Mona Lisa* (in French, *La Joconde*), painted in 1503. It's smaller than you might have imagined, kept behind glass, and invariably encircled by a mob of tourists intent on studying her (or she is studying them?). Turn your attention instead to some less-crowded rooms and galleries nearby, where Leonardo's fellow Italians are strongly represented: Fra Angelico, Giotto, Mantegna, Raphael, Titian, and Veronese. El Greco, Murillo, and Velázquez lead the Spanish; Van Eyck, Rembrandt, Frans Hals, Brueghel, Holbein, and Rubens underline the achievements of northern European art. The English collection is highlighted by works of Lawrence, Reynolds, Gainsborough, and Turner. French frontrunners include works by Poussin, Fragonard, Chardin, Boucher, and Watteau—together with David's *Oath of the Horatii*, Géricault's *Raft of the Medusa*, and Delacroix's *Liberty Guiding the People*. Famous statues include the soaring *Victory of Samothrace*—remember Audrey Hepburn's fine-boned take on this work in *Funny Face*?—the celebrated *Venus de Milo*, and the realistic Egyptian *Seated Scribe*. New rooms for ancient Persian, Arab, and Greek art opened in 1997. ✉ *Palais du Louvre (it's faster to enter through the Carrousel du Louvre mall on rue de Rivoli than through the pyramid),* ☎ *01–40–20–51–51 information,* WEB *www.louvre.com.* ⏲ *Mon. and Wed. 9 AM–9:45 PM, Thurs.–Sun. 9–6. Métro: Palais-Royal.*

11 **Musée du Jeu de Paume.** Renovations transformed this museum, at the entrance to the Tuileries Gardens, into an ultramodern, white-walled showcase for excellent temporary exhibits of bold contemporary art. The building was once the spot of *jeu de paume* games (literally, palm game—a forerunner of tennis). ✉ *1 pl. de la Concorde,* ☎ *01–42–60–69–69.* ⏲ *Tues. noon–9:30, Wed.–Fri. noon–7, weekends 10–7. Métro: Concorde.*

10 **Musée de l'Orangerie** (Orangery Museum). This museum in the Tuileries Gardens contains fine early 20th-century French works by many artists, most famously Monet (on view here are his largest paintings of *Water Lilies*); it should reopen in 2002 after renovation. ✉ *Pl. de la Concorde,* ☎ *01–42–97–48–16.* ⏲ *Wed.–Mon. 9:45–5:15. Métro: Concorde.*

9 **Place de la Concorde.** Flanked by elegant neoclassical buildings, this huge square is often choked with traffic and perhaps at its most scenic come nightfall, when its floridly beautiful fountains are illuminated. More than 1,000 people, including Louis XVI and Marie-Antoinette, were guillotined here in the early 1790s. The obelisk, a gift from the viceroy of Egypt, originally stood at Luxor and was erected here in 1833; the top was gilded in 1998. *Métro: Concorde.*

The Faubourg St-Honoré

Fashions change, but the Faubourg St-Honoré—the area just north of the Champs-Élysées and the Tuileries—firmly maintains its tradition of high style. As you progress from the President's Palace, past a wealth of art galleries and the Neoclassic Madeleine Church to the stately place Vendôme, you will see that all is luxury and refinement here. On the ritzy square, famous boutiques sit side by side with famous banks—after all, elegance and finance has never been an unusual combination. Leading names in modern fashion are found farther east on Place des Victoires. Sublimely Parisian is the Palais-Royal and its elegant gardens.

14 **Église de la Madeleine.** With its uncompromising array of columns, this church, known simply as La Madeleine, looks more like a Greek temple. Inside, the walls are richly decorated, with plenty of gold glinting through the murk. The church was designed in 1814 but not consecrated until 1842, after futile efforts to turn the site into a train station. ✉ *Pl. de la Madeleine.* ⏲ *Mon.–Sat. 7:30–7, Sun. 8–7. Métro: Madeleine.*

18 **Forum des Halles.** Since the city's much-lamented central glass-and-iron market halls were torn down during the late 1960s, the area has been transformed into a trendy—albeit slightly seedy—shopping complex, the Forum des Halles. A topiary garden basks in the shadow of the nearby **Bourse du Commerce** (Commercial Exchange) and bulky church of **St-Eustache.** *Métro: Les Halles; RER: Châtelet–Les Halles.*

13 **Palais de l'Élysée** (Élysée Palace). This "palace," known to the French simply as L'Élysée, where the French president lives, works, and receives official visitors, was originally constructed as a private mansion in 1718 and has housed presidents only since 1873. ✉ *55 rue du Faubourg St-Honoré. Not open to the public. Métro: Miromesnil.*

16 **Palais-Royal.** This erstwhile Royal Palace, built in the 1630s and now partly occupied by the Ministry of Culture, has a beautiful garden bordered by arcades and boutiques, and an adjacent courtyard with modern, candy-stripe columns by Daniel Buren. Once home to the Bourbon kings, it is still a coveted residential address (Colette was one resident) and is home to the famous Le Grand Véfour restaurant. ✉ *Pl. André-Malraux. Métro: Palais-Royal.*

15 **Place Vendôme.** Mansart's rhythmically proportioned example of 17th-century urban architecture is one of the world's most opulent squares. Top jewelers compete for attention with the limousines that draw up outside the Ritz hotel. The square's central pillar was made from the melted bronze of 1,200 cannons captured by Napoléon at the Battle of Austerlitz in 1805. That's Napoléon at the top, disguised as a Roman emperor. *Métro: Tuileries.*

17 **Place des Victoires.** This circular square, home to many of the city's top fashion boutiques, was laid out in 1685 by Jules-Hardouin Mansart in honor of the military victories (*victoires*) of Louis XIV. The Sun King gallops along on a bronze horse in the middle. *Métro: Sentier.*

19 **St-Eustache.** This colossal church, also known as the Cathedral of Les Halles, was erected between 1532 and 1637 and testifies to the stylistic transition between Gothic and classical architecture. ✉ *2 rue du Jour. Métro: Les Halles; RER: Châtelet–Les Halles.*

From the Eiffel Tower to Pont de l'Alma

The Eiffel Tower lords it over this southwest area of Paris. Across the way, in the Palais de Chaillot on Place du Trocadéro, are a number of museums. In this area, too, is where you get the Bateaux Mouches, the boats that ply the Seine on their tours of Paris by water.

4 **Bateaux Mouches.** These popular motorboats set off on their hour-long tours of Paris waters regularly (every half hour in summer). ✉ *Pl. de l'Alma,* ☎ *01–40–76–99–99,* WEB *www.bateaux-mouches.fr. Métro: Alma-Marceau.*

1 **Eiffel Tower** (Tour Eiffel). What is now the worldwide symbol of Paris nearly became 7,000 tons of scrap iron when its concession expired in

1909—now much loved, it was once widely derided by Parisians as too big and too modern. Only its potential use as a radio antenna saved the day. Architect Gustave Eiffel, whose skill as an engineer earned him renown as a builder of iron bridges, created his tower for the World Exhibition of 1889. Restoration in the 1980s didn't make the elevators any faster—long lines are inevitable unless you come in the evening (when every girder is lit in glorious detail, with a special eye-popping display that goes off on the hour)—but decent shops and two good restaurants were added. The view from 1,000 ft up will enable you to appreciate the city's layout and proportions. ✉ *Quai Branly,* ☎ *01–44–11–23–23,* WEB *www.tour-eiffel.fr.* ⏲ *July–Aug., daily 9 AM–midnight; Sept.–June, Sun.–Thurs. 9 AM–11 PM, Fri.–Sat. 9 AM–midnight. Métro: Bir-Hakeim; RER: Champ-de-Mars.*

3 **Musée d'Art Moderne de la Ville de Paris** (City of Paris Museum of Modern Art). Both temporary exhibits and a permanent collection of top-quality 20th-century art can be found at this modern art museum. It takes over, chronologically speaking, where the Musée d'Orsay leaves off. ✉ *11 av. du Président-Wilson,* ☎ *01–53–67–40–00.* ⏲ *Tues.–Sun. 10–5:30, Wed. 10–8:30. Métro: Iéna.*

2 **Palais de Chaillot** (Chaillot Palace). This honey-color, Art Deco culture center facing the Seine, perched atop tumbling gardens with sculpture and fountains, was built in the 1930s. It houses three museums: the **Musée de la Marine** (Maritime Museum), with a salty collection of seafaring paraphernalia; the **Musée de l'Homme** (Museum of Mankind), an anthropology museum with an array of prehistoric artifacts; and the **Musée des Monuments Français** (French Monuments Museum), whose painstaking replicas of statues and archways is under restoration after a fire (this museum is set to reopen—as the "Cité de l'Architecture"—by 2003). ✉ *Pl. du Trocadéro.* ⏲ *Wed.–Mon. 10–5. Métro: Trocadéro.*

The Grand Boulevards

The focal point of this walk is the uninterrupted avenue that runs in almost a straight line from St-Augustin, the city's grandest Second Empire church, to Place de la République, whose very name symbolizes the ultimate downfall of the imperial regime. The avenue's name changes six times along the way, which is why Parisians refer to it as the *Grands Boulevards.*

22 **Grands Magasins** (Department Stores). Paris's most venerable department stores can be found behind the Opéra: **Galeries Lafayette** has an elegant turn-of-the-20th-century glass dome, **Au Printemps** an excellent view from its rooftop cafeteria. ✉ *Bd. Haussmann. Métro: Havre-Caumartin.*

★ 20 **Musée Nissim de Camondo.** The French perfected the *art de vivre*—the art of living—in the 18th century in elegant, luxurious salons. In today's Paris, it's hard to experience that fabled age for yourself, so thank Dieu for this *hôtel particulier* (private mansion), magnificently furnished with beautiful furniture, *boiseries* (carved wood panels), and bibelots of the rococo and neoclassical periods. ✉ *63 rue de Monceau,* ☎ *01–53–89–06–40.* ⏲ *Wed.–Sun. 10–5. Métro: Villiers.*

★ 21 **Opéra Garnier.** Still the world's most glamorous theater, "home" to the infamous Phantom, and setting for some of Degas's most famous ballet paintings, the original Paris opera house was the flagship building of the Second Empire (1851–70). Architect Charles Garnier fused elements of neoclassical architecture—like the bas-reliefs on the newly cleaned facade—in an exaggerated combination imbued with as much subtlety as a Wagnerian cymbal crash. If you can't catch one of the ballet or opera performances, just visit the museum here, which allows you to walk through the Grand Foyer, whose staircase is so spectacular it makes even a count feel like a mouse, and to also view the lavishly upholstered auditorium, a monument of the super-opulent Napoléon III style, though now adorned with a ceiling painted by Marc Chagall in 1964. ✉ *Pl. de l'Opéra,* ☎ *01–40–01–22–63.* ⏲ *Daily 10–5. Métro: Opéra.*

The Marais and the Bastille

The Marais is one of the city's most historic, picturesque, and sought-after residential districts. The gracious architecture of the 17th and early 18th centuries sets the tone. Today, most of the Marais's *hôtels particuliers*—loosely, "mansions," onetime residences of aristocratic families—have been restored by rich, with-it couples, and many of the buildings are now museums. There are trendy boutiques and cafés among the kosher shops of the traditionally Jewish neighborhood around rue des Rosiers. On the eastern side of the neighborhood is Place de la Bastille, site of the infamous prison stormed on July 14, 1789, an event that came to symbolize the beginning of the French Revolution. The surrounding Bastille quarter is filled with galleries, shops, theaters, cafés, restaurants, and bars.

23 **Centre Pompidou** (Pompidou Center). The futuristic, funnel-top Pompidou Center was built in the mid-1970s and named in honor of former French president Georges Pompidou (1911–74). The center soon attracted more than 8 million visitors a year—five times more than intended—and was closed from 1997 to January 2000 for top-to-bottom renovation. The center is most famous for its **Musée National d'Art Moderne** (Modern Art Museum), covering 20th-century art from Fauvism and Cubism to postwar abstraction and video constructions. Other highlights include the new and chic Georges rooftop restaurant and the glass-tubed elevator that snakes up the side of the building. On the sloping piazza below is the **Atelier Brancusi** (Brancusi's Studio), four reconstituted rooms crammed with works by Romanian-born sculptor Constantin Brancusi. ✉ *Pl. Georges-Pompidou,* ☎ *01–44–78–12–33,* WEB *www.centrepompidou.fr.* ⏲ *Wed.–Mon. noon–10. Métro: Rambuteau.*

★ 24 **Musée Carnavalet.** Once the home of 17th-century Madame de Sévigné, this is now a museum devoted to the decorative arts and the history of Paris. Along with riveting objects of the French kings, there are also magnificent 17th- and 18th-century period salons on view, including recreations of Marcel Proust's cork-lined bedroom and the late 19th-century Fouquet jewelry shop. ✉ *23 rue de Sévigné,* ☎ *01–44–59–58–58.* ⏲ *Tues.–Sun. 10–5:40. Métro: St-Paul.*

25 **Musée Picasso** (Picasso Museum). The Hôtel Salé, an elegant mansion, is home to an extensive collection of little-known paintings, drawings, and engravings donated to the state by Picasso's heirs in lieu of death duties. Picasso, who loved to play the bohemian, actually loved the aristocratic lifestyle, so he would have been happy to have seen his paintings in this luxurious house. ✉ *5 rue de Thorigny,* ☎ *01–42–71–25–21.* ⏲ *Wed.–Mon. 9:30–5:30. Métro: St-Sébastien.*

27 **Place de la Bastille.** Nothing remains of the fortress stormed at the outbreak of the French Revolution; the soaring gilt-edge column, topped by the figure of Liberty, commemorates Parisians killed in the long-forgotten uprising of 1830. Also on the square is the modern, glass-fronted **Opéra de la Bastille** (Bastille Opera), opened in 1989 in commemoration of the Revolution's bicentennial. Rather more appealing is the **Viaduc des Arts** (Arts Viaduct), which leads off down avenue

Daumesnil: a disused railway viaduct converted into boutiques below and a planted walkway on top. *Métro: Bastille.*

★ 26 **Place des Vosges.** The oldest monumental square in Paris—and probably still its most nobly proportioned—the place des Vosges was laid out by Henri IV at the start of the 17th century. Originally known as place Royale, it has kept its Renaissance beauty nearly intact, although its buildings have been softened by time, their pale pink brick crumbling slightly in the harsh Parisian air and the darker stone facings pitted with age. In the far corner is the **Maison de Victor Hugo** (Victor Hugo Museum), containing souvenirs of the great poet's life and many of his surprisingly able paintings and ink drawings. ✉ *Maison de Victor Hugo: 6 pl. des Vosges,* ☎ *01–42–72–10–16.* ⏲ *Tues.–Sun. 10–5:45. Métro: St-Paul.*

From St-Germain to Les Invalides

This area of the Left Bank extends from the lively St-Germain neighborhood (named for the oldest church in Paris and still one of Paris's richest residential quarters) to the stately area around the Musée d'Orsay and Les Invalides. Other highlights are the city's most colorful park, the Jardin du Luxembourg; the Palais Bourbon, home to the National Assembly; and the Musée Rodin. South of St-Germain is Montparnasse, which had its cultural heyday in the first part of the 20th century, when it was *the* place for painters and poets to live.

★ 40 **Hôtel des Invalides.** Soaring above expansive if hardly manicured lawns, Les Invalides was founded by Louis XIV in 1674 to house wounded (*invalid*) war veterans. Les Invalides itself remains an outstanding Baroque ensemble, designed by Libéral Bruant and Jules Hardouin-Mansart. Its second church, the Église du Dôme, is graced by the city's most elegant dome and is home to **Napoléon's Tomb,** where you can breathe the fumes of hubris amidst all the marble columns and onyx trim. The adjacent **Musée de l'Armée** is a museum with a collection of arms, armor, and uniforms, while the **Musée des Plans-Reliefs** contains a fascinating collection of scale models of French towns dating from the 17th century. ✉ *Pl. des Invalides,* ☎ *01–44–42–37–72.* ⏲ *Apr.–Sept., daily 10–6; Oct.–Mar., daily 10–4:30. Métro: La Tour-Maubourg.*

35 **Jardin du Luxembourg** (Luxembourg Gardens). A favorite subject for 19th-century painters, Paris's most famous Left Bank park has tennis courts, flower beds, tree-lined alleys, and a large pond (with toy boats for rent alongside). The **Palais du Luxembourg** (Luxembourg Palace), built by Queen Maria de' Medici at the beginning of the 17th century in answer to Florence's Pitti Palace, houses the French Senate and is not open to the public. *Métro: Odéon; RER: Luxembourg.*

★ 38 **Musée d'Orsay** (Orsay Museum). This museum, in a spectacularly renovated former train station, is one of Paris's star attractions, thanks to its imaginatively housed collections of the arts (mainly French) spanning the period 1848–1914. The chief artistic attraction is its Impressionist collection, which includes some of the most celebrated paintings in the world, including Manet's *Déjeuner sur l'Herbe* (*Lunch on the Grass*) and Renoir's depiction of a famous dancehall called *Le Moulin de la Galette,* to name just two among hundreds. Other highlights include Art Nouveau furniture, a faithfully restored Belle Epoque restaurant, and a model of the Opéra quarter beneath a glass floor. The restaurant here is set in a dazzling 19th-century foyer. ✉ *1 rue de la Légion d'Honneur,* ☎ *01–40–49–48–14,* WEB *www.musee-orsay.fr.* ⏲ *Tues.–Wed., Fri.–Sat. 10–6, Thurs. 10–9:45, Sun. 9–6. Métro: Solférino; RER: Musée d'Orsay.*

★ 39 **Musée Rodin** (Rodin Museum). The Faubourg St-Germain, studded with private mansions owned by the aristocracy and the rich, remains for the most part behind closed gates but get a peek at this fabled neighborhood by visiting the 18th-century Hôtel Biron, onetime home of the sculptor Auguste Rodin (1840–1917) and today a gracious setting for his work. In back is a pretty garden with Rodin works and hundreds of rosebushes. ✉ *77 rue de Varenne,* ☎ *01–44–18–61–10.* ⏲ *Tues.–Sun. 9:30–5:45. Métro: Varenne.*

37 **St-Germain-des-Prés.** The oldest church in Paris was first built to shelter a relic of the true cross, brought back from Spain in AD 542. The chancel was enlarged and the church consecrated by Pope Alexander III in 1163 (the church tower dates from this period). ✉ *Pl. St-Germain-des-Prés.* ⏲ *Weekdays 8–7:30, weekends 8 AM–9 PM. Métro: St-Germain-des-Prés.*

36 **St-Sulpice.** Stand back and admire the impressive 18th-century facade of this enormous 17th-century church. The unequal, unfinished towers strike a quirky, fallible note at odds with the chillingly impersonal interior, embellished only by the masterly wall paintings by Delacroix—notably *Jacob and the Angel*—in the first chapel on the right. ✉ *Pl. St-Sulpice. Métro: St-Sulpice.*

Montmartre

On a dramatic rise above the city is Montmartre, site of the Sacré-Coeur Basilica (try to catch a sunset or sunrise over Paris from its terrace) and home to a once-thriving artistic community. Visiting Montmartre means negotiating a lot of steep streets and flights of steps. Some of the streets are now totally given over to the tourist trade, but if you wander and follow your nose, you can still find quiet corners that retain the poetry that once allured Toulouse-Lautrec and other great artists.

★ 44 **Au Lapin Agile.** One of the most picturesque spots in Paris, this legendary bar-cabaret (open nights only) is a miraculous survivor from the 19th century. Founded in 1860, its adorable maison-cottage was a favorite subject of painter Maurice Utrillo, and it soon became the home-away-from-home for Braque, Modigliani, Apollinaire, Vlaminck, and most famously, Picasso. ✉ *22 rue des Saules,* ☎ *01–46–06–85–87.* ⏲ *Tues.–Sun. 9 PM–2 AM. Métro: Lamarck-Caulaincourt.*

43 **Musée de Montmartre** (Montmartre Museum). In its turn-of-the-20th-century heyday, Montmartre's historical museum was home to an illustrious group of painters, writers, and assorted cabaret artists. ✉ *12 rue Cortot,* ☎ *01–46–06–61–11.* ⏲ *Tues.–Sun. 11–6. Métro: Lamarck-Caulaincourt.*

42 **Place des Abbesses.** This triangular square is typical of the picturesque, slightly countrified style that has made Montmartre famous. The entrance to the Abbesses métro station, a curving, sensuous mass of delicate iron, is one of Guimard's two original Art Nouveau entrance canopies left in Paris. The innovative brick and concrete Art Nouveau church of St-Jean de Montmartre overlooks the square. *Métro: Abbesses.*

41 **Sacré-Coeur.** If you start at Anvers métro station and head up rue de Steinkerque (full of budget clothing shops), you'll be greeted by the most familiar and spectacular view of the Sacré-Coeur, perched proudly atop the Butte Montmartre. The basilica was built in a bizarre, mock-Byzantine style between 1876 and 1910; although no favorite with aesthetes, it has become a major Paris landmark. It was constructed as an act of national penitence after the disastrous Franco-Prussian War of 1870—a Catholic show of strength at a time of bitter church-state conflict. ✉ *Pl. du Parvis-du-Sacré-Coeur. Métro: Anvers.*

45 **Cimetière du Père-Lachaise** (Father Lachaise Cemetery). This cemetery forms a veritable necropolis with cobbled avenues and tombs competing in pomposity and originality. Leading incumbents include Frédéric Chopin, Marcel Proust, Jim Morrison, Edith Piaf, and Gertrude Stein. Get a map at the entrance and track them down. ✉ *Entrances on rue des Rondeaux, bd. de Ménilmontant, and rue de la Réunion.* ⏲ *Apr.–Sept., daily 8–6; Oct.–Mar., daily 8–5. Métro: Père-Lachaise, Gambetta, Philippe-Auguste.*

Dining

Forget the Louvre, the Tour Eiffel, and the Bateaux Mouches—the real reason for a visit to Paris is to dine at its famous temples of gastronomy. Whether you get knee-deep in white truffles at Alain Ducasse or merely discover pistacchioed sausage (the poor man's caviar) at a classic corner bistro, you'll discover that food here is an obsession, an art, a subject of endless debate. And if the lobster soufflé is delicious, the historic ambience is often more so. Just request Empress Josephine's table at Le Grand Véfour and find out.

Right Bank

$$$$ ★ ✕ **Alain Ducasse.** Mega-star chef Alain Ducasse took over the restaurant of the Hotel Plaza-Athénée (beloved of yankee glitterati) in mid-2000. The rosy rococo salons have been updated with metallic organza over the chandeliers and, in a symbolic move, Ducasse has made time stand still by stopping the clock. Overlooking the prettiest courtyard in Paris, this makes for a setting as delicious as Ducasse's roast lamb garnished with "crumbs" of dried fruit or duckling roasted with fig leaves. However, the presentation *sur la table*—there are few sauce "paintings," orchid blossoms, or other visual adornments to garnish Ducasse's creations—could be enhanced (especially at these prices). ✉ *Hotel Plaza-Athénée, 27 av. Montaigne,* ☎ *01–53–67–66–65. Reservations essential. AE, DC, MC, V. Closed Sat. and Sun. No lunch Mon.–Wed.. Métro: Alma-Marceau.*

$$$$ ★ ✕ **Le Grand Véfour.** Originally built in 1784, set in the arcades of the Palais-Royal, this place is still a contender for the prize of Most Beautiful Restaurant in Paris, thanks to its 19th-century painted-glass and gilt setting. Everyone from Napoléon to Jean Cocteau has dined beneath the golden *boiseries* (wainscoting)—nearly every seat bears a plaque commemorating a famous patron and you can request to be seated at your idol's table. Chef Guy Martin pleases all with his foie gras–stuffed ravioli and truffled veal sweetbreads. Book way in advance. ✉ *17 rue Beaujolais, 1*[er]*,* ☎ *01–42–96–56–27. Reservations essential several wks in advance. Jacket and tie. AE, DC, MC, V. Closed Fri. dinner, weekends and Aug. Métro: Palais-Royal.*

$$$–$$$$ ★ ✕ **Les Ambassadeurs.** Looking as if Madame de Pompadour might stroll in the door any moment, Les Ambassadeurs offers a setting right out of Versailles—not surprisingly, since this 18th-century mansion was built by Louis XV. Honey-hued marble walls and gleaming chandeliers make a sumptuous setting for chef Dominique Bouche, who likes to mix luxe with more down-to-earth flavors: potato pancakes topped with smoked salmon, caviar-flecked scallops wrapped in bacon with tomato and basil, duck with rutabaga, turbot with cauliflower. It's also difficult to fault the view of place de la Concorde, the distinguished service, or the memorable wine list. ✉ *10 pl. de la Concorde,* ☎ *01–44–71–16–16. Reservations essential. Jacket and tie at dinner. AE, DC, MC, V. Métro: Concorde.*

$$$–$$$$ ★ ✕ **Taillevent.** Once the most traditional of all Paris luxury restaurants, this grande dame is suddenly the object of a certain uncharacteristic buzz, since new chef Michel Del Burgo arrived. He's jazzed up the clas-

sic menu with such creations as cod on white Paimpol beans in an emulsion of olive oil and meat juice garnished with red pepper. Decor has also been updated—the 19th-century salons are now accented with abstract paintings. The well-priced wine list is probably one of the top 10 in the world. ✉ *15 rue Lamennais,* ☎ *01–45–63–39–94. Reservations essential 3–4 wks in advance. Jacket and tie. AE, MC, V. Closed weekends and Aug. Métro: Charles-de-Gaulle–Étoile.*

$$–$$$ ✕ **Bofinger.** Settle in to one of the tables dressed in crisp white linens, under the gorgeous Art Nouveau glass cupola, and enjoy fine classic brasserie fare, such as oysters, grilled sole, or fillet of lamb. Note that the no-smoking section here is not only enforced but is also in the prettiest part of the restaurant. ✉ *5–7 rue de la Bastille,* ☎ *01–42–72–87–82. AE, DC, MC, V. Métro: Bastille.*

$$–$$$ ✕ **Chez Georges.** When you ask sophisticated bankers, aristocrats, and antiques dealers to name their favorite bistro, many choose Georges. The traditional bistro cooking is good—herring, sole, kidneys, steak, and *frîtes* (fries)—but the atmosphere is better. ✉ *1 rue du Mail, 2e,* ☎ *01–42–60–07–11. AE, DC, MC, V. Closed Sun. and Aug. Métro: Sentier.*

$$–$$$ ✕ **La Fermette Marbeuf.** Why have a blow-out at (sometimes disappointing) Maxim's when you can enjoy this magically beautiful Belle Epoque room, a favorite haunt of French TV and movie stars who adore the Art Nouveau mosaic and stained-glass mise-en-scène. The menu features solid, updated classic cuisine. ✉ *5 rue Marbeuf,* ☎ *01–53–23–08–00. AE, DC, MC, V. Métro: Franklin-D.-Roosevelt.*

$$–$$$ ★ ✕ **Macéo.** If you want to enjoy classic French food with a modern spin, then Macéo delivers in have-your-*gateau*-and-eat-it-too fashion. Contemporary lamps add a bold touch to the otherwise classic dining room, painted brick-red and cream. With its reasonably priced set menus (220 frs/€34 at lunch and 250 frs/€38 in the evening), this is an ideal spot for an elegant yet relaxed meal after a day at the Louvre and Palais Royal gardens. ✉ *15 rue des Petits-Champs,* ☎ *01–42–97–53–85. MC, V. Closed Sun. No lunch Sat. Métro: Palais-Royal.*

$$–$$$ ★ ✕ **Spoon, Food and Wine.** Star chef Alain Ducasse's blueprint of a bistro for the 21st century has a do-it-yourself fusion-food menu that allows you to mix and match dishes diversely American, Asian, and Italian in origin. Sign of the future? There are many salads and vegetable and grain dishes on the menu. Reservations are as coveted as Sharon Stone's Burberry shoes—call a month ahead—but you can drop in for a snack at the bar. Come late for the models and movie stars. ✉ *14 rue de Marignan,* ☎ *01–40–76–34–44. Reservations essential several wks in advance. AE, MC, V. Métro: Franklin-D.-Roosevelt.*

$$ ✕ **Café Runtz.** Next to the noted theater of Salle Favart, this friendly bistro has been given an overhaul by star decorator Jacques Garcia. Old brass gas lamps on each table and rich *boiseries* (woodwork) create a cozy and Flaubertian atmosphere. The fare is tasty, hearty, and, in the main, Alsatian. ✉ *16 rue Favart,* ☎ *01–42–96–69–86. AE, MC, V. Closed Sun. and Aug. No lunch Sat. Métro: Richelieu-Drouot.*

$$ ★ ✕ **La Grande Armée.** The Costes brothers' brasserie near the Arc de Triomphe has knockout decor designed by Jacques Garcia, whose super-opulent re-creations of historic salons have won the hearts of the super-rich everywhere. Here he's unleashed an exotic Napoléon-III bordello decor—think black lacquered tables, leopard upholstery, Bordeaux velvet—for a carefully tousled clientele picking at those dishes that chic Parisians like best these days. ✉ *3 av. de la Grande Armée,* ☎ *01–45–00–24–77. AE, DC, MC, V. Métro: Charles-de-Gaulle–Étoile.*

$$ ✕ **Le Poquelin.** The theaterlike scenery gives this welcoming little restaurant an atmosphere that's both elegant and relaxed. Owners Maggie and Michel Guillaumin proudly serve classic French cooking with

a twist, such as duck breast topped with foie gras. The popular, regularly changing "Menu Molière" is excellent value. ✉ *17 rue Molière, ☎ 01–42–96–22–19. AE, DC, MC, V. Closed Sun. No lunch Sat or Mon.. Métro: Palais-Royal.*

$$ ✕ **Le Repaire de Cartouche.** Near the Cirque d'Hiver in the Bastille, this split-level, 1950s-style bistro with dark-wood decor is the latest good-value sensation in Paris. Young chef Rodolphe Paquin is a creative and impeccably trained cook who does a stylish take on earthy French regional dishes. ✉ *99 rue Amelot, 11e, ☎ 01–47–00–25–86. Reservations essential. MC, V. Closed Sun., Mon. and Aug. Métro: Filles du Calvaire.*

$$ ★ ✕ **Le Safran.** Masterminded by passionate chef Caroll Sinclair, Le Safran almost exclusively offers food that is prepared with organic produce—red mullet stuffed with cèpe mushrooms and *gigot de sept heures* (leg of lamb cooked for seven hours) are two signature dishes. The little room is pretty, intimate, and painted in sunny saffron. ✉ *29 rue d'Argenteuil, ☎ 01–42–61–25–30. MC, V. Closed Sun. Métro: Tuileries, Pyramides.*

$ ✕ **Chartier.** This cavernous 1896 restaurant enjoys a huge following among budget-minded students, solitary bachelors, and tourists. You may find yourself sharing a table with strangers as you study the long, old-fashioned menu of such favorites as hard-boiled eggs with mayonnaise, steak tartare, and roast chicken with fries. ✉ *7 rue du Faubourg-Montmartre, ☎ 01–47–70–86–29. Reservations not accepted. AE, DC, MC, V. Métro: Montmartre.*

$ ✕ **Le Kitsch.** Fighting the good fight against ennui, this fun place is a favorite in the arty Bastille neighborhood. There's more than a touch of Pee-Wee's Playhouse here, thanks to the faux-stucco walls, plastic children's furniture, and naif paintings of cats. ✉ *10 rue Oberkampf, ☎ 01–40–21–94–14. No credit cards. Métro: Oberkampf.*

$ ✕ **Ladurée.** Pretty enough to bring a tear to Proust's eye, this ravishing *salon de thé* (tea salon) looks barely changed from 1862. The famous lemon and caramel macaroons, little tea sandwiches, and a slew of teas are on tap here. A new branch—one that also boasts a time-burnished ambience—is at 75 av. des Champs-Élysées. ✉ *16 rue Royale, ☎ 01–42–60–21–79. AE, MC, V. Métro: Madeleine.*

Left Bank

$$$ ✕ **59 Poincaré.** Famed chef Alain Ducasse's new luxe bistro (actually the old haunt of his main restaurant) was originally intended to be a variant of his Monaco restaurant Bar et Boeuf ("Sea Bass and Beef")—but, always the businessman, he quickly adapted to the "mad cow" scare with a menu featuring vegetables, lamb, lobster, and fruit. Downstairs is a sleek modern brasserie where you can drop in for a quick meal, while the upstairs Belle Epoque dining room is now adorned with photos of farmers, gadgets on the tables, and a hip soundtrack. ✉ *59 av. Raymond-Poincaré, ☎ 01–44–05–66–10. Reservations essential. AE, DC, MC, V. Closed Sun. and Mon. Métro: Victor-Hugo.*

$$$ ★ ✕ **Hélène Darroze.** Hélène Darroze has been crowned the newest female culinary star in Paris, thanks to the creative flair she has given the tried-and-true classics of southwestern French cooking, from the lands around Albi and Toulouse. You know it's not going to be *la même chanson,* or the same old thing, when you spot the resolutely contemporary Tse & Tse tableware and red-and-purple color scheme. The downside? High prices, dainty servings, and often unprofessional service, so you might opt for the downstairs bistro, which offers the same dishes but in even smaller, tapas-style portions. ✉ *4 rue d'Assas, ☎ 01–42–22–00–11. AE, DC, MC, V. Closed Sun. No lunch Sat. Métro: Sèvres-Babylone.*

$$–$$$ ✕ **Alcazar.** Englishman Sir Terence Conran's stunning, large new brasserie—a remake of a famed 19th-century spot—is one of the chicest spots in town. Young French chef Guillaume Lutard has created a regularly changing, appealingly innovative menu. Recently revamped to satisfy cool Parisians' evolving tastes, the menu now even features "so British" fish-and-chips. For 115 frs/€18 you can snack on a main dish with a glass of wine at the funky bar. ✉ *62 rue Mazarine,* ☎ *01–53–10–19–99. Reservations essential. AE, DC, MC, V. Métro: Odéon.*

$$ ✕ **Le Bouillon Racine.** Originally a *bouillon,* a Parisian soup restaurant popular at the turn of the 20th century, this two-story place is now a delightfully renovated Belle Epoque oasis with a good Franco-Belgian menu. ✉ *3 rue Racine, 6e,* ☎ *01–44–32–15–60. Reservations essential. AE, MC, V. Métro: Odéon.*

$$ ✕ **La Coupole.** This world-renowned, cavernous spot in Montparnasse practically defines the term brasserie. It might have lost its intellectual aura since restoration (the Art Deco murals look better than ever), but La Coupole has been popular since the days when Jean-Paul Sartre and Simone de Beauvoir were regulars and is still great fun. Expect the usual brasserie menu—including perhaps the largest shellfish platter in Paris—choucroute, and a wide range of over-the-top desserts. ✉ *102 bd. du Montparnasse,* ☎ *01–43–20–14–20. AE, DC, MC, V. Métro: Vavin.*

$$ ✕ **Thoumieux.** Delightfully Parisian, this place charms with red velour banquettes, yellow walls, and bustling waiters in white aprons. Budget prices for rillettes, duck confit, and cassoulet make Thoumieux—owned by the same family for three generations—popular. Don't come with gourmet expectations but for a solid, gently priced meal. ✉ *79 rue St-Dominique,* ☎ *01–47–05–49–75. AE, MC, V. Métro: Invalides.*

$–$$ ✕ **Bistro Mazarin.** Leave the tourists on boulevard St-Germain and join local gallery owners and students at this casual bistro for bags of atmosphere and sturdy, satisfying food made to order with fresh ingredients. Lentil salad, steak with Roquefort sauce or one of two daily fish specials, and a pitcher of the house wine make for a decent meal. In good weather, the terrace offers great people-watching potential. ✉ *42 rue Mazarine,* ☎ *01–43–29–99–01. AE, MC, V. Métro: Mabillon.*

$–$$ ✕ **Brasserie de l'Ile St-Louis.** In one of the most picturesque parts of the city, this brasserie serves good food on a great terrace. ✉ *55 quai de Bourbon,* ☎ *01–43–54–02–59. No credit cards. Métro: Pont Marie.*

$–$$ ★ ✕ **Les Pipos.** The tourist-trap restaurants along the romantic rue de la Montagne Ste-Genevieve are enough to make you despair—and then you stumble across this corner bistro, bursting with chatter and laughter. Slang for students of the famous Ecole Polytechnique nearby, Les Pipos is everything you could ask of a Latin Quarter bistro: the space is cramped, the food substantial (the cheese comes from the Lyon market), and conversation flows as freely as the wine. ✉ *2 rue de L'Ecole Polytechnique,* ☎ *01–43–54–11–40. No credit cards. Closed Sun. Métro: Maubert-Mutualité.*

Lodging

Right Bank

$$$$ ★ **Costes.** Baron de Rothschild hasn't invited you this time? No matter—just stay here at Jean-Louis and Gilbert Costes's sumptuous hotel and you won't know the difference. The darling of the fashion and media set, the place conjures up the palaces of Napoléon III, with stunning rooms swathed in rich garnet and bronze tones and luxurious fabrics. ✉ *239 rue St-Honoré, 75001,* ☎ *01–42–44–50–50,* FAX *01–42–44–50–01. 85 rooms. Restaurant, bar. AE, DC, MC, V. Métro: Tuileries.*

$$$$ ★ **Crillon.** You can't spend the night at Versailles but the next best thing may be the Crillon. Built by Louis XV and one of Paris's grandest 18th-century palaces, this famed hotel has welcomed royal guests from Marie-Antoinette (who took music lessons here) to Hollywood heavyweights. Most rooms are lavishly decorated with rococo and Directoire antiques, crystal and gilt wall sconces, and gold-leaf fittings. The sheer quantity of marble in the lobby and the luxurious Les Ambassadeurs restaurant is staggering, as is the location, right on place de la Concorde. ✉ *10 pl. de la Concorde, 75008,* ☎ *01–44–71–15–00; 800/888–4747 in the U.S,* FAX *01–44–71–15–02. 115 rooms, 45 suites. 2 restaurants, 2 bars. AE, DC, MC, V. Métro: Concorde.*

$$$$ ★ **Meurice.** One of the finest hotels in the world is now even finer, thanks to the multi-million-dollar face-lift given this treasure by the Sultan of Brunei. Few salons are as splendorous as the famous dining room here—all gilt boseries, pink roses, and Edwardian crystal—while guest rooms, furnished with Persian carpets, marble mantelpieces, and ormolu clocks, are now more soigné than ever. ✉ *228 rue de Rivoli, 75001,* ☎ *01–44–58–10–10,* FAX *01–44–58–10–15. 160 rooms, 36 suites. 2 restaurants, bar. AE, DC, MC, V. Métro: Tuileries, Concorde.*

$$$$ **Pavillon de la Reine.** This magnificent hotel, filled with Louis XIII–style fireplaces and antiques, is in a mansion reconstructed from original plans. Ask for a duplex with French windows overlooking the first of two flower-filled courtyards behind the historic Queen's Pavilion. ✉ *28 pl. des Vosges, 75003,* ☎ *01–40–29–19–19; 800/447–7462 in the U.S.,* FAX *01–40–29–19–20. 30 rooms, 25 suites. Bar, breakfast room, free parking. AE, DC, MC, V. Métro: Bastille, St-Paul.*

$$–$$$ **Louvre Forum.** This friendly hotel is a find: smack in the center of town, it has clean, comfortable, well-equipped rooms (with satellite TV) at extremely reasonable prices. ✉ *25 rue du Bouloi, 75001,* ☎ *01–42–36–54–19,* FAX *01–42–33–66–31. 27 rooms, 16 with shower. AE, DC, MC, V. Métro: Louvre.*

$$ **Axial Beaubourg.** A solid bet in the Marais, this hotel in a 16th-century building has beamed ceilings in the lobby and in the six first-floor rooms. Most guest rooms have pleasant if functional decor, and all have satellite TV. The Centre Pompidou and the Picasso Museum are five minutes away. ✉ *11 rue du Temple, 75004,* ☎ *01–42–72–72–22,* FAX *01–42–72–03–53. 39 rooms with bath. AE, DC, MC, V. Métro: Hôtel-de-Ville.*

$$ **Bretonnerie.** This small hotel is in a 17th-century *hôtel particulier* (town house) on a tiny street in the Marais. Rooms are Louis XIII style, complete with upholstered walls, but vary considerably in size from spacious to cramped. ✉ *22 rue Ste-Croix-de-la-Bretonnerie, 75004,* ☎ *01–48–87–77–63,* FAX *01–42–77–26–78. 27 rooms, 3 suites. MC, V. Métro: Hôtel-de-Ville.*

$$ ★ **Caron de Beaumarchais.** The theme of this intimate jewel is the work of Caron de Beaumarchais, who wrote *The Marriage of Figaro* in 1778. Rooms are faithfully decorated to reflect the taste of 18th-century French nobility. The second- and fifth-floor rooms with balconies are the largest; those on the sixth floor have views across Right Bank rooftops. ✉ *12 rue Vieille-du-Temple, 75004,* ☎ *01–42–72–34–12,* FAX *01–42–72–34–63. 19 rooms, 2 with shower. AE, DC, MC, V. Métro: Hôtel-de-Ville.*

$$ **Deux-Iles.** This converted 17th-century mansion on the picturesque Ile St-Louis has long won plaudits for charm and comfort. Flowers and plants are scattered throughout the stunning main hall and tapestries cover the exposed stone walls. The delightfully old-fashioned rooms, blessed with exposed beams, are small but airy and sunny. ✉ *59 rue St-Louis-en-l'Ile, 75004,* ☎ *01–43–26–13–35,* FAX *01–43–29–60–25. 17 rooms. AE, MC, V. Métro: Pont-Marie.*

$$ **Place des Vosges.** A loyal, eclectic clientele swears by this small, historic Marais hotel on a delightful street just off place des Vosges. The Louis XIII–style reception area and rooms with oak-beamed ceilings, rough-hewn stone, and a mix of rustic finds from secondhand shops evoke the old Marais. ✉ *12 rue de Birague, 75004,* ☎ *01–42–72–60–46,* FAX *01–42–72–02–64. 16 rooms with bath. AE, DC, MC, V. Métro: Bastille.*

$$ **St-Louis.** Louis XIII–style furniture and oil paintings set the tone in the public areas in this 17th-century town house on the romantic Ile St-Louis. Rooms are much simpler and more standard, but exposed beams and stone walls make them appealing. Breakfast is served in the atmospheric cellar. ✉ *75 rue St-Louis-en-l'Ile, 75004,* ☎ *01–46–34–04–80,* FAX *01–46–34–02–13. 21 rooms with bath. MC, V. Métro: Pont-Marie.*

$$ **Vieux Marais.** This pleasingly old-fashioned hotel with a turn-of-the-20th-century facade is on a quiet street in the heart of the Marais. Rooms are bright, impeccably clean, and equipped with satellite TV; try to get one overlooking the just-renovated courtyard. ✉ *8 rue du Plâtre, 75004,* ☎ *01–42–78–47–22,* FAX *01–42–78–34–32. 30 rooms with bath. MC, V. Métro: Hôtel-de-Ville.*

$ **Castex.** In a Revolution-era building in the Marais, this hotel is a bargain hunter's dream. Rooms are low on frills but squeaky clean, the owners are friendly, and the prices are rock-bottom, which ensures that the hotel is often booked months ahead by a largely young, American clientele. There's no elevator, and the only TV is on the ground floor. ✉ *5 rue Castex, 75004,* ☎ *01–42–72–31–52,* FAX *01–42–72–57–91. 27 rooms, 23 with shower. MC, V. Métro: Bastille.*

$ **Grand Hôtel Jeanne-d'Arc.** If you're on a budget, you're sure to get your money's worth at this hotel near place des Vosges in the Marais. Though rooms are on the spartan side, they are clean, well-maintained, and fairly spacious. The staff is welcoming and friendly. ✉ *3 rue de Jarente, 75004,* ☎ *01–48–87–62–11,* FAX *01–48–87–37–31. 36 rooms with bath. MC, V. Métro: St-Paul.*

Left Bank

$$$$ **Montalembert.** Whether appointed with traditional or contemporary furnishings, rooms at the Montalembert are all about simple lines and chic luxury. Ask about special packages if you're staying for more than three nights. ✉ *3 rue de Montalembert, 75007,* ☎ *01–45–49–68–68; 800/628–8929 in the U.S.,* FAX *01–45–49–69–49. 50 rooms, 6 suites. Restaurant, bar. AE, DC, MC, V. Métro: Rue du Bac.*

$$$$ ★ **Relais St-Germain.** The interior-designer owners of this hotel have exquisite taste and a superb respect for tradition and detail. Moreover, rooms are at least twice the size of those at other area hotels. Much of the furniture was selected with a knowledgeable eye from the city's *brocantes* (secondhand dealers). Breakfast is included. ✉ *9 carrefour de l'Odéon, 75006,* ☎ *01–43–29–12–05,* FAX *01–46–33–45–30. 21 rooms, 1 suite. AE, DC, MC, V. Métro: Odéon.*

$$$–$$$$ ★ **Hôtel d'Aubusson.** Set in an historic house and now one of the finest *petite hôtels de luxe* in the city, this place has original Aubusson tapestries, Versailles-style parquet floors, a chiseled stone fireplace, and restored antiques. Even the smallest rooms are a good size by Paris standards, and all are decked out in rich burgundies, greens, or blues. The 10 best rooms have canopied beds and ceiling beams. In summer, you can have your breakfast or predinner drink in the paved courtyard. ✉ *33 rue Dauphine, 75006,* ☎ *01–43–29–43–43,* FAX *01–43–29–12–62. 49 rooms with bath. AE, MC, V. Métro: Odéon.*

$$$ **Jardin du Luxembourg.** Blessed with a charming staff and a stylish look, this hotel is one of the most sought-after in the Latin Quarter. Rooms are a bit small (common for this neighborhood) but intelligently furnished to save space, and warmly decorated *à la provençale.* Ask for one with a balcony overlooking the street. ✉ *5 impasse Royer-Collard, 75005,* ☎ *01–40–46–08–88,* FAX *01–40–46–02–28. 27 rooms. AE, DC, MC, V. Métro: Luxembourg.*

$$–$$$ ★ **Le Tourville.** Here is a rare find: an intimate, upscale hotel at affordable prices. Each room has crisp, virgin-white damask upholstery set against pastel or ocher walls, a smattering of antiques, original artwork, and fabulous old mirrors. ✉ *16 av. de Tourville, 75007,* ☎ *01–47–05–62–62; 800/528–3549 in the U.S.,* FAX *01–47–05–43–90. 27 rooms, 3 junior suites. Bar. AE, DC, MC, V. Métro: École Militaire.*

$$ **Bonaparte.** The congeniality of the staff only makes a stay in this intimate place more of a treat. Old-fashioned upholsteries, 19th-century furnishings, and paintings create a quaint feel in the relatively spacious rooms. And the location in the heart of St-Germain is nothing short of fabulous. ✉ *61 rue Bonaparte, 75006,* ☎ *01–43–26–97–37,* FAX *01–46–33–57–67. 29 rooms with bath. MC, V. Métro: St-Germain-des-Prés.*

$$ **Hôtel de l'Université.** Staying at this hotel in a 17th-century town house between boulevard St-Germain and the Seine feels like going back in time. Guest rooms have English and French antiques and original fireplaces. Ask for one with a terrace on the fifth floor. ✉ *22 rue de l'Université, 75007,* ☎ *01–42–61–09–39,* FAX *01–42–60–40–84. 27 rooms with bath. AE, MC, V. Métro: Rue-du-Bac.*

$$ **Latour Maubourg.** In the residential heart of the 7e arrondissement, a stone's throw from Les Invalides, this hotel is homey and unpretentious. With just 10 rooms, the accent is on intimacy and personalized service. ✉ *150 rue de Grenelle, 75007,* ☎ *01–47–05–16–16,* FAX *01–47–05–16–14. 9 rooms, 1 suite. MC, V. Métro: La Tour–Maubourg.*

$–$$ **Aramis–St-Germain.** Get great value for your money at this hotel, which, surprisingly, is part of the Best Western chain. It is understated yet classically French. Rooms have damask bedspreads and sturdy cherry-wood armoires. ✉ *124 rue de Rennes, 75006,* ☎ *01–45–48–03–75; 800/528–1234 in the U.S.,* FAX *01–45–44–99–29. 42 rooms. Bar. AE, DC, MC, V. Métro: St-Placide.*

$ **Familia.** The hospitable Gaucheron family bends over backward for you. About half the rooms feature romantic sepia frescoes of celebrated Paris scenes; others have exquisite Louis XV–style furnishings or nice mahogany pieces. Book a month ahead for one with a walk-out balcony on the second or fifth floor. ✉ *11 rue des Écoles, 75005,* ☎ *01–43–54–55–27,* FAX *01–43–29–61–77. 30 rooms, 16 with shower. AE, MC, V. Métro: Cardinal-Lemoine.*

$ **Grandes Écoles.** This delightfully intimate hotel looks and feels like a country cottage dropped smack in the middle of the Latin Quarter. It is off the street and occupies three buildings on a beautiful, leafy garden, where breakfast is served in summer. Parquet floors, Louis-Philippe furnishings, lace bedspreads, and the absence of TV all add to the rustic ambience. ✉ *75 rue du Cardinal Lemoine, 75005,* ☎ *01–43–26–79–23,* FAX *01–43–25–28–15. 51 rooms with bath. MC, V. Métro: Cardinal-Lemoine.*

Nightlife and the Arts

For detailed entertainment listings, look for the weekly magazines *Pariscope, L'Officiel des Spectacles, Zurban,* and *Figaroscope.* The **Paris Tourist Office**'s 24-hour English-language hot line (☎ 08–36–68–31–12) and Web site (WEB www.paris-touristoffice.com/index_va.html) are also good sources of information about weekly events.

Tickets can be purchased at the place of performance (beware of scalpers: counterfeit tickets have been sold); otherwise, try your hotel or a travel agency such as **Opéra Théâtre** (✉ 7 rue de Clichy, 9e, ☎ 01–40–06–01–00, métro: Trinité). For most concerts, tickets can be bought at the music store **FNAC** (✉ 1–5 rue Pierre Lescot, Forum des Halles, 1er, ☎ 01–49–87–50–50, métro: Châtelet–Les Halles). **Virgin Megastore** (✉ 52 av. des Champs-Élysées, 8e, ☎ 08–03–02–30–24, métro: Franklin-D.-Roosevelt) has a particularly convenient ticket booth. Half-price tickets for same-day theater performances are available at the **Kiosques Théâtre** (✉ across from 15 Pl. de la Madeleine, métro: Madeleine), and in front of the Gare Montparnasse (✉ Pl. Raoul Dautry, 14e, métro: Montparnasse-Bienvenüe). Both are open Tuesday–Saturday 12:30–8, Sunday 12:30–4. Expect to pay a 16-fr/€2.44 commission per ticket and to wait in line.

The Arts

CLASSICAL MUSIC AND OPERA

Inexpensive organ or chamber music concerts take place in many churches throughout the city. Following are other venues for opera, orchestral concerts and recitals. **Cité de la Musique** (✉ in the Parc de La Villette, 221 av. Jean-Jaurès, 19e, ☎ 01–44–84–44–84, métro: Porte de Pantin) presents a varied program of classical, experimental, and world music concerts in a postmodern setting. **Opéra de la Bastille** (✉ Pl. de la Bastille, 12e, ☎ 08–36–69–78–68, WEB www.opera-de-paris.fr, métro: Bastille) is the main venue for opera; however, grand opera deserves a grand house (not the modern Bastille one), so you might plan your trip around dates when the troupe presents an opera at the spectacular and historic Opéra Garnier, about twice a year. The Orchestre de Paris and other leading international orchestras play regularly at the **Salle Pleyel** (✉ 252 rue du Faubourg-St-Honoré, 8e, ☎ 08–25–00–02–52, métro: Ternes). **Théâtre des Champs-Élysées** (✉ 15 av. Montaigne, 8e, ☎ 01–49–52–50–50, métro: Alma-Marceau) is worth seeing just for its elegantly restored, plush Art Deco decor.

DANCE

Opéra Garnier (✉ Pl. de l'Opéra, 9e, ☎ 08–36–69–78–68, WEB www.opera-de-paris.fr, métro: Opéra), the "old Opéra," now concentrates on dance: in addition to being the home of the well-reputed Paris Ballet, it also bills a number of major foreign troupes. The **Théâtre de la Ville** (✉ 2 pl. du Châtelet, 4e, métro: Châtelet; ✉ 31 rue des Abbesses, 18e, métro: Abbesses, ☎ 01–42–74–22–77 for both) is the place for contemporary dance.

FILM

Paris has hundreds of cinemas. Admission is generally 40 frs/€6–55 frs/€8.4, with reduced rates at some theaters on Monday. In principal tourist areas such as the Champs-Élysées and Les Halles, and on the boulevard des Italiens near the Opéra, theaters show English films marked *"version originale"* (v.o., i.e., not dubbed). Classics and independent films often play in Latin Quarter theaters. **Cinémathèque Française** (✉ 42 bd. de Bonne-Nouvelle, 10e, ☎ 01–56–26–01–01, métro: Bonne-Nouvelle; ✉ Palais de Chaillot, 7 av. Albert de Mun, ☎ 01–56–26–01–01, métro: Trocadéro) shows classic French and international films Wednesday–Sunday.

THEATER

There is no Parisian equivalent to Broadway or the West End, although a number of theaters line the Grands Boulevards between the Opéra and République. Shows are mostly in French. The **Comédie Française** (✉ Pl. Colette, 1er, ☎ 01–44–58–15–15, métro: Palais-Royal) performs distinguished classical drama by the likes of Racine, Molière, and Corneille. The **Théâtre de la Huchette** (✉ 23 rue de la Huchette, 5e, ☎ 01–43–26–38–99, métro: St-Michel) is a tiny venue where Ionesco's short plays make a deliberately ridiculous mess of the French language. The **Théâtre de l'Odéon** (✉ Pl. de l'Odéon, 6e, ☎ 01–44–41–36–36, métro Odéon) has made pan-European theater its primary focus.

Nightlife

BARS AND CLUBS

The hottest area at the moment is around Ménilmontant and Parmentier, and the nightlife is still hopping in and around the Bastille. The Left Bank tends to be more subdued. The Champs-Élysées is making a strong comeback, though the crowd remains predominantly foreign. Gay and lesbian bars are mostly concentrated in the Marais (especially around rue Ste-Croix-de-la-Bretonnerie) and include some of the most happening addresses in the city.

If you want to dance the night away, some of the best clubs are the following: **Les Bains** (✉ 7 rue du Bourg-l'Abbé, 3e, ☎ 01–48–87–01–80, métro: Étienne-Marcel) opened in 1978 and back in the disco era was often featured in French *Vogue*—believe it or not, this is still a hot ticket and difficult to get past the velvet rope. **Le Gibus** (✉ 18 rue du Faubourg du Temple, 11e, ☎ 01–47–00–78–88, métro: République) hosts big concerts in its theater, but its cellars are *the* place for trance, techno and jungle. **Queen** (✉ 102 av. des Champs-Élysées, 8e, ☎ 01–53–89–08–90, métro: George-V) is one of the most talked-about nightclubs in Paris: everyone lines up to get in. Monday is disco night.

Paris has many bars; following is a sampling: **Amnésia Café** (✉ 42 rue Vieille-du-Temple, 4e, ☎ 01–42–72–16–94, métro: St-Paul) attracts a young, professional gay and lesbian crowd. **Barramundi** (✉ 3 rue Taitbout, 9e, ☎ 01–47–70–21–21, métro: Richelieu-Drouot) is one of Paris's hubs of nouveau-riche chic; the lighting is dim, the copper bar long. **Buddha Bar** (✉ 8 rue Boissy d'Anglas, 8e, ☎ 01–53–05–90–00, métro: Concorde) offers one of the most glittery settings in Paris—a bar overlooks the main restaurant, with its towering gold-painted Buddha contemplating enough Dragon Empress chinoiserie for five MGM movies. **Café Charbon** (✉ 109 rue Oberkampf, 11e, ☎ 01–43–57–55–13, métro: St-Maur/Parmentier) is set in a beautifully restored 19th-century café. **Le Fumoir** (✉ 6 rue Amiral de Coligny, 1er, ☎ 01–42–92–00–24, métro: Louvre) is a fashionable spot for cocktails, with comfy leather sofas and a library. **Polo Room** (✉ 3 rue Lord Byron, 8e, ☎ 01–40–74–07–78, métro: George-V) is the very first Martini bar in Paris; there are polo photos on the walls, regular live jazz concerts, and DJs every Friday and Saturday night. **Wax** (✉ 15 rue Daval, 11e, ☎ 01–40–21–16–16, métro: Bastille) is worth a trip simply for its decor—orange and pink walls, multicolored squiggles on the columns, and moulded plastic banquettes by the window; this is one of the most happening places in the city musicwise, with DJs spinning techno and house every evening.

CABARETS

Paris's cabarets are household names, shunned by Parisians and beloved of foreign tourists, who flock to the shows. Prices range from 200 frs (simple admission plus one drink) to more than 800 frs (dinner plus show). **Crazy Horse** (✉ 12 av. George-V, 8e, ☎ 01–47–23–32–32, métro: Alma-Marceau) shows more bare skin than anyone else. **Lido** (✉ 116 bis av. des Champs-Élysées, 8e, ☎ 01–40–76–56–10, métro: George-V) shows are oceans of feathers and sequins. **Moulin Rouge** (✉ 82 bd. de Clichy, 18e, ☎ 01–53–09–82–82, métro: Blanche) has come a long way since the days of the cancan.

JAZZ CLUBS

Paris is one of the great jazz cities of the world. For nightly schedules consult the magazines *Jazz Hot, Jazzman,* or *Jazz Magazine.* Nothing gets going till 10 or 11 PM, and entry prices vary widely from about 40 frs to more than 100 frs. **New Morning** (✉ 7 rue des Petites-Écuries, 10e, ☎ 01–45–23–51–41, métro: Château-d'Eau) is a premier spot for serious fans of avant-garde jazz, folk, and world music. The greatest names in French and international jazz play at **Le Petit Journal** (✉ 71 bd. St-Michel, 5e, ☎ 01–43–26–28–59, RER: Luxembourg); it's closed Sunday. **Le Petit Opportun** (✉ 15 rue des Lavandières–Ste-Opportune, 1er, ☎ 01–42–36–01–36, métro: Châtelet), in a converted bistro, often has top-flight American soloists with French backup.

ROCK CLUBS

Lists of upcoming concerts are posted on boards in the FNAC stores. Following are the best places to catch big French and international stars: **L'Olympia** (✉ 28 bd. des Capucines, 9e, ☎ 01–47–42–25–49, métro: Opéra) once hosted legendary concerts by Jacques Brel and Edith Piaf, but the theater has since been completely rebuilt. **Palais Omnisports de Paris-Bercy** (✉ 8 bd. de Bercy, 12e, ☎ 08–25–03–00–31, métro: Bercy) is the largest venue in Paris and is where English and American pop stars perform. **L'Élysée Montmartre** (✉ 72 bd. Rochechouart, 18e, ☎ 01–55–07–06–00, métro: Anvers) dates from Gustave Eiffel, its builder, who, it is hoped, liked a good concert; emerging French and international rock groups appear here.

Shopping

Boutiques

Only Milan can compete with Paris for the title of Capital of European Chic. The top designer shops are found on **avenue Montaigne, rue du Faubourg-St-Honoré,** and **place des Victoires.** The area around **St-Germain-des-Prés** on the Left Bank is a mecca for small specialty shops and boutiques and has recently seen an influx of the elite names in haute couture. The top names in jewelry are grouped around the **place Vendôme,** and scores of trendy boutiques can be found around **Les Halles.** Between the pre-Revolution mansions and tiny kosher food stores that characterize the **Marais** are numerous gift shops and clothing stores. Search for bargains on the streets around the foot of Montmartre, or in the designer discount shops (Cacharel, Rykiel, Chevignon) along **rue d'Alésia** in Montparnasse.

Department Stores

Au Bon Marché (✉ 24 rue de Sèvres, 7e, métro: Sèvres-Babylone). **Au Printemps** (✉ 64 bd. Haussmann, 9e, métro: Havre-Caumartin). **Galeries Lafayette** (✉ 40 bd. Haussmann, 9e, métro: Chaussée-d'Antin). **La Samaritaine** (✉ 19 rue de la Monnaie, 1er, métro: Pont-Neuf). **Marks & Spencer** (✉ 35 bd. Haussmann, 9e, ☎ 01–47–42–42–91, métro: Havre-Caumartin, Auber, or Opéra).

Food and Flea Markets

Every *quartier* (neighborhood) has at least one open-air food market. Some of the best are on rue de Buci, rue Mouffetard, rue Montorgueuil, rue Mouffetard, and rue Lepic. Sunday morning till 1 PM is usually a good time to go; they are likely to be closed Monday.

The **Marché aux Puces de St-Ouen** (métro Porte de Clignancourt), just north of Paris, is one of Europe's largest flea markets; it's open Saturday–Monday. Best bargains are to be had early in the morning. Smaller flea markets also take place at **Porte de Vanves** and **Porte de Montreuil** (weekends only).

Gifts

Old prints are sold by ***bouquinistes*** (secondhand booksellers) in stalls along the banks of the Seine. **Les Caves Augé** (✉ 116 bd. Haussmann,

8e, métro: St-Augustin) is one of the best wine shops in Paris. **Fauchon** (✉ 30 pl. de la Madeleine, 8e, métro: Madeleine) is perhaps the world's most famous gourmet food shop. **Hédiard** (✉ 21 pl. de la Madeleine, 8e, métro: Madeleine) is a foodie mecca with a seductive array of comestibles. **Guerlain** (✉ 47 rue Bonaparte, 6e, métro: Mabillon) carries legendary French perfumes. The **Maison du Chocolat** (✉ 56 rue Pierre-Charron, 8e, ☎ 01–47–23–38–25, métro: Franklin-D.-Roosevelt; ✉ 8 bd. de la Madeleine, 9e, ☎ 01–47–42–86–52, métro: Madeleine; ✉ 225 rue du Faubourg St-Honoré, 8e, ☎ 01–42–27–39–44, métro: Ternes) is the place for chocolate. The **Musée des Arts Décoratifs** (✉ 107 rue de Rivoli, 1er, métro: Palais-Royal) has super chic home decorations.

Paris Essentials

AIRPORTS AND TRANSFERS

International flights arrive at either Charles de Gaulle Airport (known as Roissy to the French), 24 km (15 mi) northeast of Paris, or at Orly Airport, 16 km (10 mi) south of the city. Both airports have two terminals.

TRANSFERS

Both airports have train stations from which you can take the RER, the local commuter train, to Paris. The advantages of this are speed, price (49 frs/€7.50 to Paris from Roissy, 57 frs/€8.70 from Orly via the shuttle-train Orlyval with a change to the RER at Antony), and the RER's direct link with the métro system. The disadvantage is having to lug your bags around. Taxi fares between the airports and Paris are about 160 frs/€24.42 (Orly) and 230 frs/€35.11 (Roissy), with a 6-fr/€.92 surcharge per bag. The Paris Airports Service takes you by eight-passenger van to your destination in Paris from Roissy: 140 frs/€21.50 (one person) or 170 frs/€26 (two); Orly: 110 frs/€16.90 (one), 130 frs/€20 (two), less for groups. You need to book at least two days in advance (there are English-speaking clerks).

From Roissy, Air France Buses (open to all) leave every 15 minutes from 5:40 AM to 11 PM. The fare is 60 frs/€9.20 and the trip takes from 40 minutes to 1½ hours during rush hour. You arrive at the Arc de Triomphe or Porte Maillot, on the Right Bank by the Hôtel Concorde-Lafayette. From Orly, buses operated by Air France leave every 12 minutes from 6 AM to 11 PM and arrive at the Air France terminal near Les Invalides on the Left Bank. The fare is 45 frs/€6.90, and the trip takes between 30 and 60 minutes, depending on traffic. Alternatively, the Roissybus, operated by Paris Transport Authority (RATP), runs directly to and from rue Scribe, by the Opéra, every 15 minutes and costs 48 frs/€7.32. RATP also runs the Orlybus to and from Denfert-Rochereau and Orly every 15 minutes for 35 frs/€5.34; the trip takes around 35 minutes.

➤ TAXIS AND SHUTTLES: Paris Airports Service (☎ 01–49–62–78–78, FAX 01–49–62–78–79).

BUS TRAVEL TO AND FROM PARIS

See Bus Travel *in* Transportation *in* France A to Z, *above*.

BUS TRAVEL WITHIN PARIS

Most buses run from around 6 AM to 8:30 PM; some continue until midnight. Routes are posted on the sides of buses. *Noctambus* (night buses) operate from 1 AM to 6 AM between Châtelet and nearby suburbs. They can be stopped by hailing them at any point on their route. You can use your métro tickets on the buses, or you can buy a one-ride ticket on board. You need to show weekly/monthly/special tickets to the driver; if you have individual tickets, state your destination and be prepared to punch one or more tickets in the red and gray machines on board the bus.

CAR TRAVEL

Expressways converge on the capital from every direction: A1 from the north (225 km/140 mi to Lille); A13 from Normandy (225 km/140 mi to Caen); A4 from the east (500 km/310 mi to Strasbourg); A10 from the southwest (580 km/360 mi to Bordeaux); and A7 from the Alps and Côte d'Azur (465 km/290 mi to Lyon). Each connects with the *périphérique,* the beltway, around Paris. Exits are named by *porte* (gateway), not numbered. The "Périphe" can be fast—but gets very busy; try to avoid it between 7:30 and 10 AM and between 4:30 and 7:30 PM.

EMERGENCIES

Automatic phone booths can be found at various main crossroads for use in police emergencies (Police-Secours) or for medical help (Services Médicaux).

➤ DOCTORS AND DENTISTS: **Dentist** (☎ 01–43–37–51–00), open 24 hrs. **Doctor** (☎ 01–47–07–77–77).

➤ EMERGENCY SERVICES: **Ambulance** (☎ 15 for emergencies; 01–45–67–50–50). **Police** (☎ 17).

➤ HOSPITALS: **American Hospital** (✉ 63 bd. Victor-Hugo, Neuilly, ☎ 01–46–41–25–25). **British Hospital** (✉ 3 rue Barbès, Levallois-Perret, ☎ 01–47–58–13–12).

➤ 24-HOUR PHARMACIES: **Pharmacie Dérhy** (✉ 84 av. des Champs-Élysées, ☎ 01–45–62–02–41), open 24 hrs. **Pharmacie Première** (✉ 204 bd. de Sébastopol, 4e, ☎ 01–48–87–62–30), open until 2 AM.

ENGLISH-LANGUAGE MEDIA

Most newsstands in central Paris sell *Time, Newsweek,* and the *International Herald Tribune,* as well as the English dailies. Some English-language bookstores include the ones listed below.

➤ BOOKSTORES: **Brentano's** (✉ 37 av. de l'Opéra). **Galignani** (✉ 224 rue de Rivoli). **Shakespeare & Co.** (✉ 37 rue de la Bûcherie). **W. H. Smith** (✉ 248 rue de Rivoli).

MÉTRO TRAVEL

Fourteen métro lines crisscross Paris and the nearby suburbs, and you are seldom more than a five-minute walk from the nearest station. It's essential to know the name of the last station on the line you take, since this name appears on all signs within the system. A connection (you can make as many as you please on one ticket) is called a *correspondance.* At junction stations illuminated orange signs bearing the names of each line terminus appear over the corridors that lead to the various correspondances.

The métro connects at several points in Paris with RER trains that race across Paris from suburb to suburb: RER trains are a sort of supersonic métro and can be great time-savers. All métro tickets and passes are valid for RER and bus travel within Paris.

Some lines and stations in the seedier parts of Paris are a bit risky at night—in particular, Line 2 (Porte-Dauphine–Nation) and the northern section of Line 13 from St-Lazare to St-Denis/Asnières. The long, bleak corridors at Jaurès and Stalingrad are a haven for pickpockets and purse snatchers. But the Paris métro is relatively safe, as long as you don't walk around with your wallet in your back pocket or travel alone (especially women) late at night.

Paris Métro

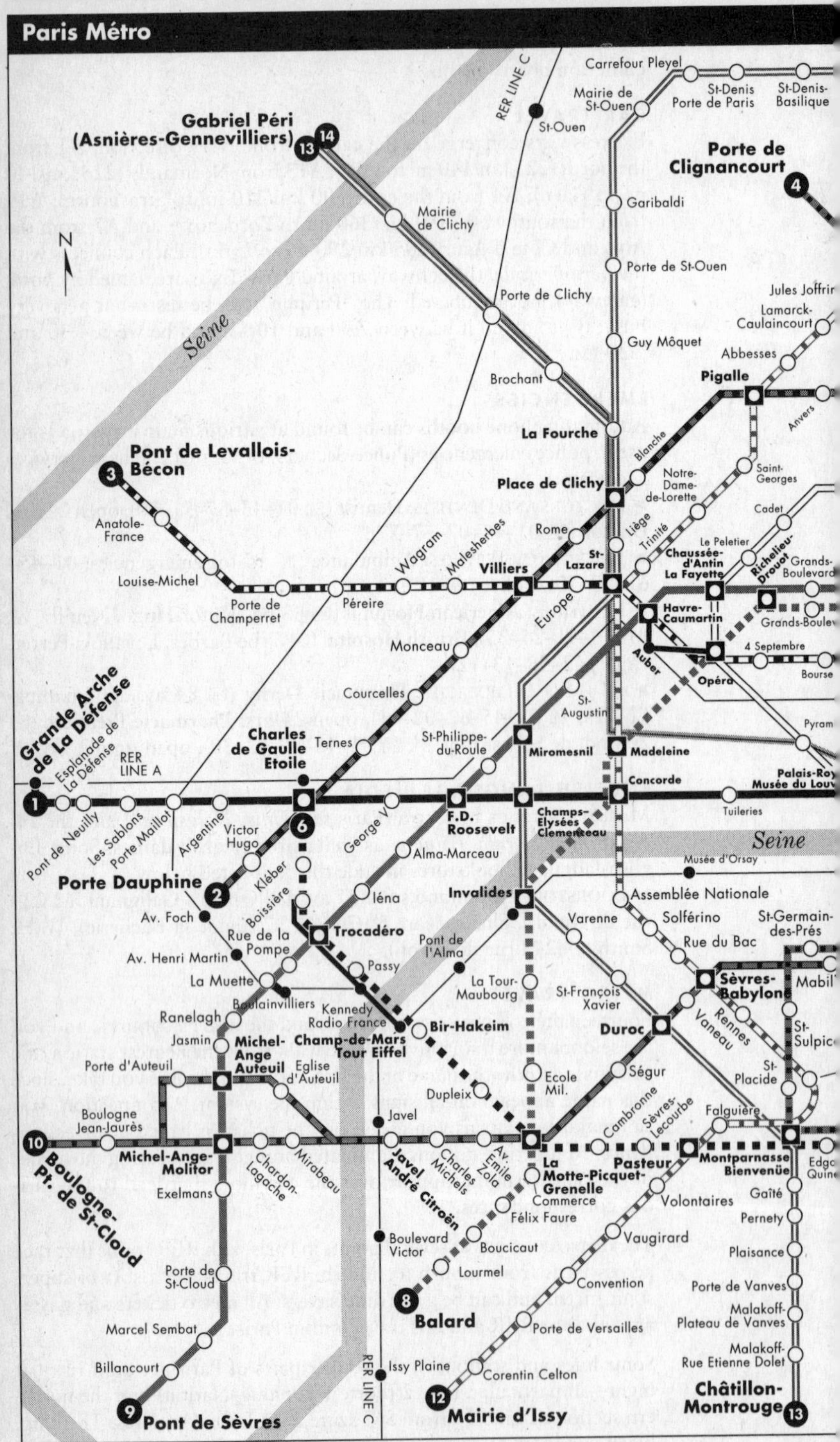

Gabriel Péri (Asnières-Gennevilliers)
Mairie de Clichy
Porte de Clichy
Brochant
Carrefour Pleyel
Mairie de St-Ouen
St-Ouen
St-Denis Porte de Paris
St-Denis-Basilique
Porte de Clignancourt
Garibaldi
Porte de St-Ouen
Guy Môquet
La Fourche
Jules Joffrin
Lamarck-Caulaincourt
Abbesses
Pigalle
Anvers
Blanche
Place de Clichy
Notre-Dame-de-Lorette
Saint-Georges
Cadet
Le Peletier
Rome
Liège
Trinité
St-Lazare
Villiers
Chaussée-d'Antin La Fayette
Richelieu-Drouot
Grands-Boulevards
Havre-Caumartin
Auber
Opéra
4 Septembre
Bourse
Europe
St-Augustin
Miromesnil
Madeleine
Concorde
Pyramides
Palais-Royal Musée du Louvre
Tuileries
Seine
RER LINE C
RER LINE A
Pont de Levallois-Bécon
Anatole-France
Louise-Michel
Porte de Champerret
Péreire
Wagram
Malesherbes
Monceau
Courcelles
Ternes
Charles de Gaulle Etoile
St-Philippe-du-Roule
F.D. Roosevelt
Champs-Elysées Clemenceau
Grande Arche de La Défense
Esplanade de La Défense
Pont de Neuilly
Les Sablons
Porte Maillot
Argentine
Victor Hugo
Porte Dauphine
George V
Alma-Marceau
Iéna
Kléber
Boissière
Av. Foch
Rue de la Pompe
Av. Henri Martin
Trocadéro
Passy
Pont de l'Alma
Invalides
Musée d'Orsay
Assemblée Nationale
Varenne
Solférino
Rue du Bac
St-Germain-des-Prés
La Muette
Boulainvilliers
Kennedy Radio France
Bir-Hakeim
Champ-de-Mars Tour Eiffel
La Tour-Maubourg
St-François Xavier
Sèvres-Babylone
Mabillon
Rennes
Vaneau
St-Sulpice
St-Placide
Duroc
Ranelagh
Jasmin
Michel-Ange Auteuil
Eglise d'Auteuil
Porte d'Auteuil
Ecole Mil.
Ségur
Dupleix
Cambronne
Sèvres-Lecourbe
Falguière
Javel
Boulogne Jean-Jaurès
Michel-Ange-Molitor
Chardon-Lagache
Mirabeau
Javel André Citroën
Charles Michels
Av. Emile Zola
La Motte-Picquet-Grenelle
Pasteur
Montparnasse Bienvenüe
Edgar Quinet
Boulogne-Pt. de St-Cloud
Exelmans
Commerce
Félix Faure
Volontaires
Gaîté
Pernety
Boulevard Victor
Boucicaut
Vaugirard
Plaisance
Lourmel
Convention
Porte de Vanves
Porte de St-Cloud
Balard
Porte de Versailles
Malakoff-Plateau de Vanves
Marcel Sembat
Malakoff-Rue Etienne Dolet
Billancourt
Issy Plaine
Corentin Celton
Châtillon-Montrouge
Pont de Sèvres
Mairie d'Issy
N

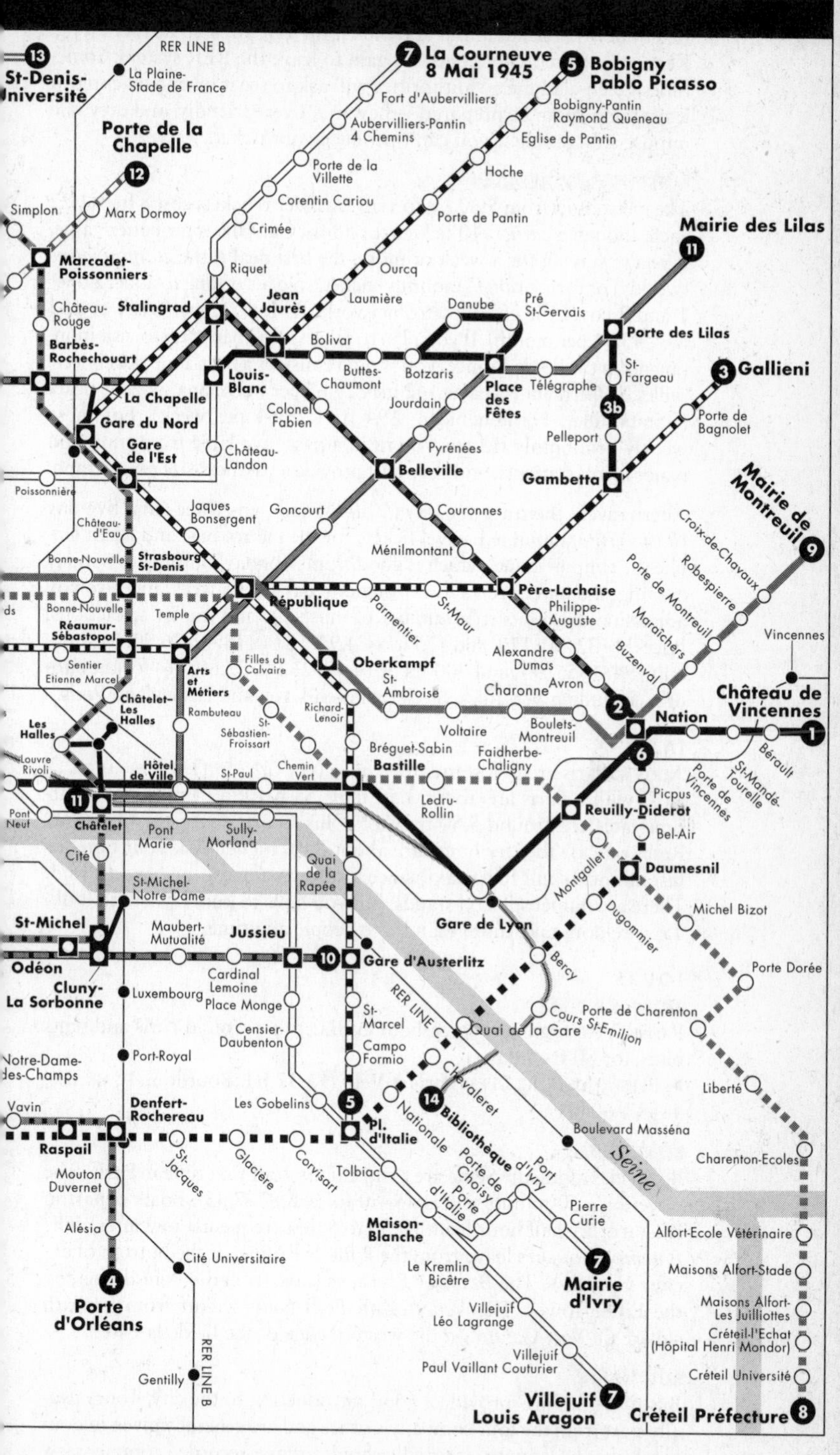

St-Denis-Université
La Plaine-Stade de France
RER LINE B
La Courneuve 8 Mai 1945
Bobigny Pablo Picasso
Fort d'Aubervilliers
Bobigny-Pantin Raymond Queneau
Aubervilliers-Pantin 4 Chemins
Eglise de Pantin
Porte de la Chapelle
Porte de la Villette
Hoche
Simplon
Marx Dormoy
Corentin Cariou
Porte de Pantin
Mairie des Lilas
Crimée
Marcadet-Poissonniers
Riquet
Ourcq
Laumière
Danube
Pré St-Gervais
Château-Rouge
Stalingrad
Jean Jaurès
Porte des Lilas
Bolivar
Barbès-Rochechouart
Louis-Blanc
Buttes-Chaumont
Botzaris
Place des Fêtes
Télégraphe
St-Fargeau
Gallieni
La Chapelle
Jourdain
Colonel Fabien
Porte de Bagnolet
Gare du Nord
Pelleport
Gare de l'Est
Château-Landon
Pyrénées
Belleville
Gambetta
Poissonnière
Mairie de Montreuil
Jaques Bonsergent
Goncourt
Couronnes
Château-d'Eau
Croix-de-Chavaux
Ménilmontant
Bonne-Nouvelle
Strasbourg St-Denis
Robespierre
République
Père-Lachaise
Porte de Montreuil
Bonne-Nouvelle
Temple
Parmentier
St-Maur
Philippe-Auguste
Maraîchers
Réaumur-Sébastopol
Vincennes
Alexandre Dumas
Buzenval
Sentier
Filles du Calvaire
Oberkampf
Etienne Marcel
Arts et Métiers
St-Ambroise
Avron
Charonne
Châtelet-Les Halles
Château de Vincennes
Rambuteau
Richard-Lenoir
Nation
Les Halles
Voltaire
St-Sébastien-Froissart
Boulets-Montreuil
Bréguet-Sabin
Faidherbe-Chaligny
Bérault
Louvre Rivoli
Hôtel de Ville
Chemin Vert
St-Mandé-Tourelle
St-Paul
Bastille
Porte de Vincennes
Picpus
Ledru-Rollin
Reuilly-Diderot
Pont Neuf
Châtelet
Pont Marie
Sully-Morland
Bel-Air
Cité
Quai de la Rapée
Montgallet
Daumesnil
St-Michel-Notre Dame
Dugommier
Michel Bizot
St-Michel
Maubert-Mutualité
Jussieu
Gare de Lyon
Odéon
Gare d'Austerlitz
Bercy
Porte Dorée
Cluny-La Sorbonne
Cardinal Lemoine
Luxembourg
Place Monge
RER LINE C
Porte de Charenton
Censier-Daubenton
St-Marcel
Cours St-Emilion
Quai de la Gare
Port-Royal
Campo Formio
Notre-Dame-des-Champs
Chevaleret
Liberté
Vavin
Les Gobelins
Bibliothèque
Denfert-Rochereau
Pl. d'Italie
Nationale
Boulevard Masséna
Raspail
St-Jacques
Glacière
Corvisart
Porte de Choisy
Port d'Ivry
Seine
Charenton-Ecoles
Mouton Duvernet
Tolbiac
Porte d'Italie
Pierre Curie
Alésia
Maison-Blanche
Alfort-Ecole Vétérinaire
Cité Universitaire
Le Kremlin Bicêtre
Maisons Alfort-Stade
Mairie d'Ivry
Porte d'Orléans
Villejuif Léo Lagrange
Maisons Alfort-Les Juilliottes
Créteil-l'Echat (Hôpital Henri Mondor)
RER LINE B
Villejuif Paul Vaillant Couturier
Créteil Université
Gentilly
Villejuif Louis Aragon
Créteil Préfecture

Access to métro and RER platforms is through an automatic ticket barrier. Slide your ticket in flat and pick it up as it pops up farther along. Keep your ticket; you'll need it again to leave the RER system. Sometimes green-clad métro authorities will ask to see it when you enter or leave the station: be prepared—they aren't very friendly, and they will impose a large fine if you can't produce your ticket.

FARES AND SCHEDULES

The métro runs from 5:30 AM to 1:15 AM. Métro tickets cost 8 frs/€1.22 each, though a *carnet* (10 tickets for 58 frs/€8.90) is a far better value. If you're staying for a week or more, the best deal is the *coupon jaune* (weekly) or *carte orange* (monthly) ticket, sold according to zone. Zones 1 and 2 cover the entire métro network (85 frs/€13 per week or 285 frs/€43.51 per month). If you plan to take a suburban train to visit monuments in the Ile-de-France, you should consider a four-zone ticket (Versailles, St-Germain-en-Laye; 142 frs/€21.67 per week) or a six-zone ticket (Rambouillet, Fontainebleau; 194 frs/€29.61 per week). For these weekly or monthly tickets, you need a pass (available from train and major métro stations), and you must provide a passport-size photograph.

Alternatively, there are one-day (*Mobilis*) and two-, three-, and five-day (*Paris Visite*) unlimited travel tickets for the métro, bus, and RER. Unlike the coupon jaune, which is good from Monday morning to Sunday evening, the latter are valid starting any day of the week and give you admission discounts to a number of museums and tourist attractions. Prices are 32, 90, 120, and 175 frs (€4.90, 13.80, 18.40, 26.90) for Paris only; 94, 175, 245, and 300 frs (€14.40, 26.90, 37.60, 46) for the suburbs, including Versailles, St-Germain-en-Laye, and Disneyland Paris.

TAXIS

Taxis in Paris aren't a standard vehicle type or color. Daytime rates (7 to 7) within Paris are about 3.50 frs/€.53 per km (½ mi), and nighttime rates are around 5.80 frs/€.89, plus a basic charge of 13 frs/€2. Rates outside the city limits are about 30% higher. Ask your hotel or restaurant to call for a taxi, since cruising cabs can be hard to find. There are numerous taxi stands, but you have to know where to look. Taxis seldom take more than three people at a time.

TOURS

BICYCLE TOURS

Paris à Vélo organizes three-hour cycling tours around Paris and rents bikes for 80 frs a day.

➤ FEES AND SCHEDULES: **Paris à Vélo** (✉ 37 bd. Bourdon, 4e, ☎ 01-48-87-60-01).

BOAT TOURS

Boat rides along the Seine are a must if it's your first time in Paris. The price for a 60-minute trip is 45–50 frs (€6.87–7.63). Boats depart in season every half hour from 10:30 to 5 (less frequently in winter). The *Bateaux Mouches* leave from the Pont de l'Alma, at the bottom of avenue George-V. The *Bateaux Parisiens* leave from the Pont d'Iéna, by the Eiffel Tower. The *Vedettes du Pont-Neuf* set off from beneath square du Vert-Galant on the western edge of the Ile de la Cité.

BUS TOURS

Bus tours of Paris provide a good introduction to the city. Tours usually start from the tour company's office and are generally given in double-decker buses with either a live guide or tape-recorded commentary. They last two to three hours and cost about 150 frs/€23. Tour operators also have a variety of theme tours (historic Paris, modern Paris, Paris by night) that last from 2½ hours to all day and cost up to 390 frs/€60, as well as excursions to Chartres, Versailles, Fontainebleau, the Loire Valley, and Mont-St-Michel (for a cost of 195–970 frs, or €30–149). Cityrama is one of the largest bus operators in Paris; it also runs minibus excursions that pick you up and drop you off at your hotel. Paris Vision is another large bus tour operator.

➤ FEES AND SCHEDULES: **Cityrama** (✉ 4 pl. des Pyramides, 1[er], ☎ 01–44–55–60–00). **Paris Vision** (✉ 214 rue de Rivoli, 1[er], ☎ 08–00–03–02–14).

PRIVATE GUIDES

Tours of Paris or the surrounding areas by limousine or minibus for up to seven passengers for a minimum of three hours can be organized. The cost starts at about 300 frs/€46 per hour. Contact Paris Major Limousines, Paris Bus, or Cityscope.

➤ CONTACTS: **Cityscope** (✉ 11 bis bd. Haussmann, 9e, ☎ 01–53–34–11–91). **Paris Bus** (✉ 22 rue de la Prévoyance, Vincennes, ☎ 01–43–65–55–55). **Paris Major Limousines** (✉ 14 rue Atlas, 19e, ☎ 01–44–52–50–00).

WALKING TOURS

Numerous special-interest tours concentrate on historical or architectural topics. Most are in French and cost between 40 and 60 frs (€6 and 9.2). Details are published in the weekly magazines *Pariscope* and *L'Officiel des Spectacles* under the heading "Conférences."

TRAIN TRAVEL

Paris has five international stations: Gare du Nord (for northern France, northern Europe, and England via Calais or the Channel Tunnel); Gare de l'Est (for Strasbourg, Luxembourg, Basel, and central Europe); Gare de Lyon (for Lyon, Marseille, the Côte d'Azur, Geneva, and Italy); Gare d'Austerlitz (for the southwest France and Spain); and Gare St-Lazare (for Normandy and England via Dieppe). The Gare Montparnasse serves western France (Nantes, Rennes, and Brittany) and is the terminal for the TGV Atlantic service from Paris to Tours, Poitiers, and Bordeaux. Call SNCF for information. You can reserve tickets at any Paris station regardless of the destination. Go to the Grandes Lignes counter for travel within France or to the Billets Internationaux desk if you're heading out of France.

➤ TRAIN INFORMATION: **SNCF** (☎ 08–36–35–35–35, WEB www.sncf.com).

TRANSPORTATION AROUND PARIS

Paris is relatively small as capital cities go, and most of its prize monuments and museums are within walking distance of one another. A river cruise is a pleasant way to get an overview. The most convenient form of public transportation is the métro; buses are a slower alternative, though they do allow you to see more of the city. Taxis are not that expensive but are not always so easy to find. Car travel within Paris is best avoided because finding parking is difficult and there is often a lot of traffic.

TRAVEL AGENCIES

➤ LOCAL AGENTS: **American Express** (✉ 11 rue Scribe, 9[e], ☎ 01–47–77–77–07). **Wagons-Lits** (✉ 32 rue du Quatre-Septembre, 2e, ☎ 01–42–66–15–80).

VISITOR INFORMATION

The Paris Tourist Office is open daily 9–8. It has branches at all mainline train stations except Gare St-Lazare.

➤ TOURIST INFORMATION: **Paris Tourist Office** (✉ 127 av. des Champs-Élysées, ☎ 01–49–52–53–54; 01–49–52–53–56 for recorded information in English, WEB www.paris-touristoffice.com).

ILE-DE-FRANCE

The region surrounding Paris is called Ile-de-France, although it isn't actually an *île* (island). But the area is figuratively isolated from the rest of France by three rivers—the Seine, the Oise, and the Marne—that weave meandering circles around its periphery. If you are visiting Paris—and France—for the first time, this is an excellent place to get a taste of French provincial life, with its palpably slower pace.

Parts of the area are fighting a losing battle against the encroaching capital, but you can still see the countryside that was the inspiration for the Impressionists and other 19th-century painters, as well as a wealth of architecture dating from the Middle Ages and Renaissance. The most famous sights are Chartres—one of the most beautiful French cathedrals—and Versailles, the monumental château of Louis XIV, the Sun King. Before the completion of Versailles, king and court resided in the delightful château of St-Germain-en-Laye, west of Paris—an easy day trip from the capital, as are the châteaux of Vaux-le-Vicomte and Fontainebleau, and Disneyland Paris.

The region can be covered in a series of loops: travel west from Paris to see Versailles, Rambouillet, and Chartres; east to Disneyland; and southeast to Fontainebleau and Vaux-le-Vicomte. Most of these sights are under 80 km (50 mi) away from Paris, including Disneyland, which is just 32 km (20 mi) east of the city via A4 (or take the RER-A train, stopping at Marne-la-Vallée-Chessy). Chartres and Giverny are a little farther away, but they're still easily manageable—and particularly enjoyable—side trips from the capital.

Versailles

Versailles is the location of one of the world's grandest palaces—and in fact, a grand town, since the château's opulence had to have a setting to match. Wide, tree-lined boulevards, bordered by massive 18th-century mansions, fan out from the palace; avenue de Paris, in the middle, is broader than the Champs-Élysées. From the imposing Place d'Armes, you enter the Cour d'Honneur, a sprawling cobbled forecourt. Right in the middle, the statue of Louis XIV, the Sun King, stands triumphant, surveying the town built to house those of the 20,000 noblemen, servants, and hangers-on who weren't quick enough to grab one of the 3,000 beds in the château.

★ The **Château de Versailles** took 50 years to complete. Hills were flattened, marshes drained, forests transplanted, and water from the Seine channeled from several miles away to supply the magnificent fountains. Visit the **Grands Appartements** (State Rooms), rooms that made up the royal quarters, and the famous **Galerie des Glaces** (Hall of Mirrors), where the controversial Treaty of Versailles, asserting Germany's responsibility for World War I, was signed in 1919. Both can be visited without a guide, but you can get an audio tour in English. It was hardly surprising that Louis XIV's successors rapidly felt out of sync with the bicep-flexing Baroque bombast of his great salons. Louis XV and Louis XVI preferred to cower in the **Petits Appartements** (Private Apartments), where the royal family and friends lived in relative intimacy; guided tours take you through these jewel-like rooms. Elsewhere are two showstoppers: the icily marble chapel and the magnificent opera house—one of the first oval rooms in France, built in the north wing for Louis XV in 1770.

After all this grandeur, the park outside is the ideal place to get your breath back. Although badly damaged by a hurricane at Christmas 1999, the château's vast **park** remains a masterpiece of formal landscaping by

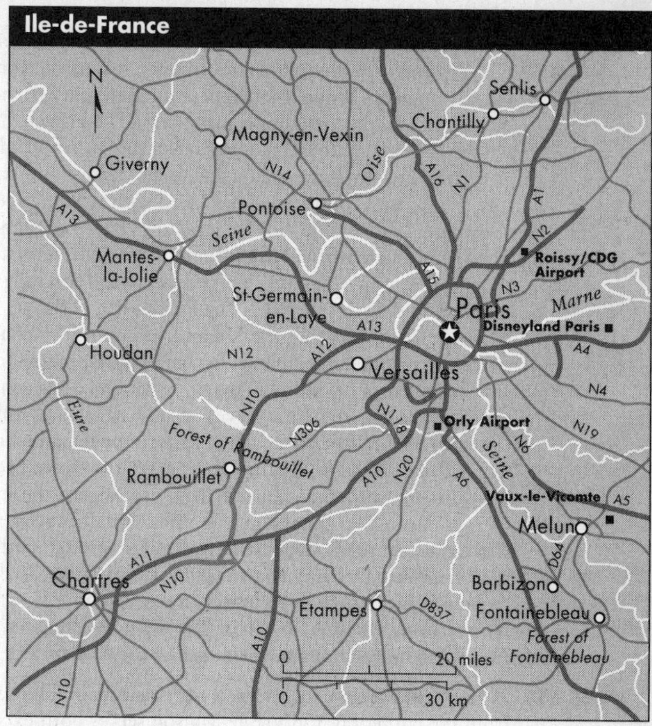

Andre Le Nôtre. At one end of the Petit Canal, which crosses the Grand Canal at right angles, is the **Grand Trianon,** a scaled-down pleasure palace built in the 1680s. The **Petit Trianon,** nearby, is a sumptuously furnished 18th-century mansion that is one of the landmarks of French Neoclassicism, commissioned by Louis XV; Marie-Antoinette would flee here to avoid the stuffy atmosphere of the court. Nearby, she built the **Hameau**—a tiny village, complete with dairy and water mill, where she led a make-believe life pretending to be a shepherdess with flocks of perfumed sheep. Its fairytale spell is still seductive—no wonder Toni (to use the queen's nickname) didn't see the Revolution coming. ☏ *01–30–84–76–18,* WEB *www.chateauversailles.fr.* ⏲ *Château Apr.–Sept., Tues.–Sun. 9–6:30; Oct.–Mar., Tues.–Sun. 9–5:30. Galerie des Glaces Tues.–Sun. 9:45–5. Opéra Tues.–Sun. 9:45–3:30. Tours of Petits Appartements and opera house every 15 mins Tues.–Sun. Park daily 7 AM–dusk. Grand Trianon and Petit Trianon Tues.–Sun. noon–5:30.*

$$$$ ★ ✕ **Les Trois Marches.** If your tour of Versailles has left you feeling a little hungry and more than a little regal, promenade over to the Trianon Palace hotel and this restaurant, long recognized as one of the best in Ile-de-France. Celebrated chef Gérard Vié's take on *cuisine bourgeoise* is one of the luxest, and most delectable, around. The restaurant has a fetching and huge terrace open in pleasant weather. ✉ *1 bd. de la Reine,* ☏ *01–39–50–13–21. Reservations essential. Jacket and tie. AE, DC, MC, V. Closed Aug.*

$$ ✕ **Quai No. 1.** Barometers, sails, and model boats fill this small, charming seafood restaurant. In summer you can enjoy your meal on the terrace. Home-smoked salmon and sauerkraut with fish are specialties; any dish on the two prix-fixe menus is a good value. ✉ *1 av. de St-Cloud,* ☏ *01–39–50–42–26. MC, V. Closed Mon. No dinner Sun.*

Chartres

As Versailles is the climax of French secular architecture, Chartres is the religious apogee—an extraordinary fusion of Romanesque and Gothic elements brought together at a moment when the flame of medieval faith burned brightest. Long before you reach Chartres, you'll see this famous cathedral towering over the plain and wheatfields. The attractive old town, steeped in religious history and dating from before the Roman conquest, is still laced with winding medieval streets; elsewhere, unfortunate modern structures have raised their ugly heads.

★ The Gothic **Cathédrale Notre-Dame** is the sixth Christian church on the site; despite a series of fires, it has remained basically the same since the 12th and 13th centuries. The **Portail Royal** (Royal Portal) on the main facade, presenting the life and triumph of the Savior, is one of the country's finest examples of Romanesque sculpture. Inside, the 12th- and 13th-century windows, many of which have been restored over the past decade, come alive even in dull weather, thanks to the deep Chartres blue of the stained glass: its formula remains a mystery to this day. All the descriptive prose and poetry that have been lavished on this supreme cathedral can only begin to suggest the strange sense of the numinous that the whole ensemble imparts even to nonbelievers. The cathedral tours (twice a day Monday through Saturday; the cost is 30 frs/€4.6) by local institution Malcolm Miller are legendary; you can reach him at the telephone number below. ✉ *Crypte: 16 cloître-Notre-Dame,* ☎ *02–37–21–56–33,* WEB *www.chartres.com.* ⏲ *Tours in English daily noon and 2:45; ask at the Maison des Clercs.*

$$–$$$ ✕ **La Vieille Maison.** In a refitted 14th-century building a stone's throw from the cathedral, the Vieille Maison serves both excellent nouvelle cuisine and traditional dishes. Try the regional "Menu Beauceron," for the homemade foie gras and duck dishes. ✉ *5 rue au Lait,* ☎ *02–37–34–10–67. AE, MC, V. Closed Mon. No dinner Sun.*

$$ ✕ **Buisson Ardent.** This attractive restaurant, in an old, oak-beamed building opposite the Vieille Maison, serves such dishes as chicken ravioli with leeks or rolled beef with spinach. ✉ *10 rue au Lait,* ☎ *02–37–34–04–66. AE, DC, MC, V. No dinner Sun.*

$$$ 🏨 **Grand Monarque.** The most popular rooms in this 18th-century coaching inn are in a separate turn-of-the-20th-century building overlooking a garden. The hotel also has an excellent restaurant with a good choice of prix-fixe menus for 170, 240, and 295 frs. ✉ *22 pl. des Épars, 28000,* ☎ *02–37–21–00–72,* FAX *02–37–36–34–18. 53 rooms. Restaurant. AE, DC, MC, V.*

Giverny

This small village is a place of pilgrimage for art lovers enticed by the
★ **Maison et Jardin Claude Monet** (Claude Monet's House and Garden). The house where Monet worked and lived for more than 40 years has been faithfully restored; the kitchen with its cool blue tiles and the buttercup-yellow dining room are particularly striking. However, the real pull is the colorful garden and especially the famous lily pond with its Japanese bridge, which was one of Monet's favorite subjects. ✉ *84 rue Claude-Monet,* ☎ *02–32–51–28–21,* WEB *www.giverny.org.* ⏲ *Apr.–Oct., Tues.–Sun. 10–6.*

After touring the many-acred "Monet" on view at the artist's home, you may wish to see some real paintings at the airy **Musée Américain** (American Museum), along the same road as Monet's House. It displays works by American Impressionists who were influenced by—and often studied with—Claude Monet. On site is a fine and expensive restaurant and a garden "quoting" some of Monet's plant compositions. ✉ *99 rue Claude-Monet,* ☎ *02–32–51–94–65.* ⏲ *Apr.–Oct., Tues.–Sun. 10–6.*

$$ ✕ **Les Jardins de Giverny.** This restaurant, with a tile-floor dining room overlooking a rose garden, is a few minutes' walk from Monet's house. Enjoy the 130-fr lunch menu or choose from a repertoire of inventive dishes such as foie gras spiked with Calvados or scallops with wild mushrooms. ✉ *1 rue Milieu,* ☏ *02–32–21–60–80. AE, MC, V. Closed Mon., Feb., and first half of Nov.*

Fontainebleau

During the early 16th century the flamboyant François I transformed the medieval hunting lodge of Fontainebleau into a magnificent Re-
★ naissance palace, the **Château de Fontainebleau.** His successor, Henri II, covered the palace with his initials, woven into the *D* for his mistress, Diane de Poítiers. When he died, his queen, Catherine de' Médicis, carried out further alterations, later continued under Louis XIV. However, it was Napoléon who made a Versailles, as it were, out of Fontainebleau by spending lavishly to restore the neglected property to its former glory. Before he was exiled to Elba, he bade farewell to his Old Guard in the courtyard now known as the **Cour des Adieux** (Court of Farewell), with its elegant horseshoe staircase. The **Grands Appartements** (State Rooms) are the main attractions of any visit to the château; these include the **Galerie François Ier** (Francis I Gallery) and a covered bridge (built 1528–30) looking out over the Cour de la Fontaine. The magnificent **Salle de Bal** (Ballroom) is nearly 100 ft long, with wood paneling, 16th-century frescoes and gilding, and, reputedly, the first coffered ceiling in France, its intricate pattern echoed by the splendid 19th-century parquet floor. If you're here on a weekday, you may also be able to join a guided tour (in French) of the **Petits Appartements** (Private Apartments), used by Napoléon and Joséphine, and the **Musée Napoléon** (Napoleonic Museum), which has some mementos, including the leader's imperial uniform. ✉ *Pl. du Général-de-Gaulle,* ☏ *01–60–71–50–70.* ⏲ *Wed.–Mon. 9:30–5. Call ahead for tour schedule.*

$$$$ ★ ✕🏨 **Aigle-Noir.** This may be Fontainebleau's costliest hotel, but you can't go wrong if you request one of the rooms overlooking either the garden or the château. Late-18th- or early 19th-century reproduction furniture evokes a Napoleonic mood. The restaurant, Le Beauharnais, serves subtle, imaginative cuisine; reservations are essential and jacket and tie are recommended. ✉ *27 pl. Napoléon-Bonaparte, 77300,* ☏ *01–60–74–60–00,* FAX *01–60–74–60–01. 56 rooms. Restaurant, pool. AE, DC, MC, V.*

$$ 🏨 **Londres.** The balconies of this small hotel overlook the palace and the Cour des Adieux; the 1830 facade is preserved by government order. Inside, the decor is dominated by Louis XV furniture. ✉ *1 pl. du Général-de-Gaulle, 77300,* ☏ *01–64–22–20–21,* FAX *01–60–72–39–16. 11 rooms. Restaurant, bar. AE, DC, MC, V. Closed mid-Dec.–early Jan., one week Aug.*

Vaux-le-Vicomte

★ The **Château de Vaux-le-Vicomte** is one of the greatest monuments of 17th-century France. Too grand for some: when owner Nicolas Fouquet, the royal finance minister, threw a housewarming party in 1661, Sun King Louis XIV threw a fit of jealousy, hurled Fouquet in the slammer on trumped-up fraud charges, and promptly began building Versailles to prove just who was boss—after signing up Fouquet's architectural supergroup (Louis Le Vau for design, André Le Nôtre in the gardens, and Charles Le Brun on all lead murals). From your point of view, though, Fouquet's *folie de grandeur* (delusions of grandeur) will probably be a treat. ☏ *01–64–14–41–90,* WEB *www.vaux-le-vicomte.com.* ⏲ *Mid-Mar.–Nov. 11, daily 10–6. Candlelight visits May–mid-Oct., Thur. and Sat. 8* PM*–midnight.*

Disneyland Paris

Get a dose of American pop culture in between visits to the Louvre and the Left Bank. Disneyland Paris is east of the capital, in Marne-la-Vallée, and easily accessible by RER from the city.

The theme park, less than 1½ km (½ mi) across, is ringed by a railroad with whistling steam engines. In the middle of the park is the soaring Sleeping Beauty Castle, surrounded by a plaza from which you can enter each of the "lands": **Frontierland, Adventureland, Fantasyland,** and **Discoveryland.** In addition, **Main Street U.S.A.** connects the castle to the entrance. Also included in the complex is **Disney Village,** an entertainment center with restaurants, a theater, dance clubs, shops, a post office, and a tourist office. ☎ *01–60–30–60–30,* WEB *www.disneylandparis.com.* *Apr.–Sept. and Christmas period: 225 frs/€34.35 (435 frs/€66.41 for 2-day Passport, 610 frs/€93.12 for 3-day Passport); Oct.–Mar., except Christmas period: 170 frs/€25.95 (330 frs/€50.38 for 2-day Passport, 460 frs/€70.7 for 3-day Passport); includes admission to all individual attractions within the park but not meals. AE, DC, MC, V.* ⏲ *Mid-June–mid-Sept., daily 9 AM–10 PM; mid-Sept.–mid-June, daily 10–8; Christmas period and spring school holidays, daily 9–8.*

$–$$ ✕ **Disneyland Restaurants.** The park is peppered with places to eat, ranging from snack bars and fast-food joints to full-service restaurants—all with a distinguishing theme. Eateries serve nonstop as long as the park is open. ☎ *01–60–45–65–40. Sit-down restaurants: AE, DC, MC, V ; no credit cards at counter-service restaurants.*

$$–$$$$ **Disneyland Hotels.** The resort has 5,000 rooms in six hotels, all a short distance from the park, ranging from the luxurious Disneyland Hotel to the not-so-rustic Camp Davy Crockett. Free transportation to the park is available at every hotel. To book a room, contact the Central Reservations Office. ✉ *Central Reservations Office, Box 100, 77777 Marne-la-Vallée cedex 4,* ☎ *01–60–30–60–30; 407/934–7639 in the U.S.,* FAX *01–49–30–71–00. All hotels have at least 1 restaurant and indoor swimming pool. AE, DC, MC, V.*

Ile-de-France Essentials

The region is reached only from Paris by car and by regular RER train service. But you might find it convenient to group some sights together: Versailles, Rambouillet, and Chartres are all on the Paris–Chartres train line; Fontainebleau and Vaux-le-Vicomte are within a few miles of each other.

CAR TRAVEL

The region is reached easily from Paris by car. A13 links Paris (from Porte d'Auteuil) to Versailles. You can get to Chartres on A10 from Paris (Porte d'Orléans). For Fontainebleau take A6 from Paris (Porte d'Orléans). Vaux-le-Vicomte is 6 km (4 mi) northeast of Melun via N36 and D215. The 32-km (20-mi) drive along A4 from Paris to Disneyland Paris takes about 30 minutes, longer in heavy traffic. Disneyland is 4 km (2½ mi) off A4; follow the signs for the park.

TOURS

Following are two private companies that organize regular half-day and full-day tours from Paris to Chartres, Fontainebleau, and Versailles with English-speaking guides. Tours are subject to cancellation, and reservations are suggested.

➤ FEES AND SCHEDULES: **Cityrama** (✉ 4 pl. des Pyramides, 1er, Paris, ☎ 01–44–55–60–00). **Paris Vision** (✉ 214 rue de Rivoli, 1er, Paris, ☎ 08–00–03–02–14).

TRAIN TRAVEL

Three lines connect Paris with Versailles; the trip takes about 30 minutes. RER-C5 to Versailles Rive Gauche station takes you closest to the château; trains from Paris (Gare Montparnasse) stop at Versailles Chantiers and continue to Chartres. Trains from Gare St-Lazare stop at La Défense en route to Versailles Rive Droite. Fontainebleau is served by 20 trains a day from Gare de Lyon; a bus leaves from the station (which is in neighboring Avon) for the château. The RER-A4 line goes to Disneyland Paris. Vaux-le-Vicomte is a 7-km (4-mi) taxi ride from the nearest station at Melun, served by regular trains from Paris and Fontainebleau. The taxi ride costs about 80 frs/€12.30–100 frs/€15.30.

➤ TRAIN INFORMATION: SNCF (☏ ☏ 08–36–35–35–35, WEB www.sncf.com).

VISITOR INFORMATION

➤ TOURIST INFORMATION: **Chartres** (✉ Pl. de la Cathédrale, ☏ 02–37–21–50–00). **Disneyland Paris** (✉ B.P. 100, 77777 Marne-la-Vallée cedex, ☏ 01–60–30–60–30). **Fontainebleau** (✉ 4 rue Royale, ☏ 01–60–74–99–99). **Versailles** (✉ 7 rue des Réservoirs, ☏ 01–39–50–36–22).

THE LOIRE VALLEY

The valley watered by the broad and shallow Loire and caught in a diaphanous web of subtly shifting light is one of the most beautiful areas of France. It was here in the 15th and 16th centuries that the kings of France chose to build their fabulous *châteaux d'agrément,* or pleasure castles, and these châteaux remain the chief attractions of a region rich in history. They often line the rocky banks of the Loire and its tributaries—the Rivers Cher, Indre, Vienne, and Loir (with no *e*), and in these stately houses, castles, and fairy-tale palaces, Renaissance elegance is often combined with fortresslike medieval mass. The Loire Valley was fought over by France and England during the Middle Ages until, inspired by Joan of Arc, the "Maid of Orléans" (scene of her most rousing military success), France finally managed to expel the English.

The Loire Valley's golden age came under François I (1515–47), France's flamboyant contemporary of England's Henry VIII. He hired Renaissance craftsmen from Italy and hobnobbed with the aging Leonardo da Vinci, his guest at Amboise. You can see his salamander emblem in many châteaux.

Most of the sights covered here are close to the Loire River along the 170-km (105-mi) stretch between Blois and Saumur. If you're coming from Paris, Châteaudun and Vendôme make attractive stops en route to Blois. Tours, 58 km (36 mi) west of Blois, is the region's major city. Saumur, Chinon, and Amboise are the other main historic towns.

Blois

With its forest of towers and tumbling alleyways, Blois is the most attractive of the major Loire towns. It is best known for its massive **Château de Blois,** a mixture of four different styles: Feudal (13th century), Gothic-Renaissance Transition (circa 1500), Renaissance (circa 1520), and Classical (circa 1635). ☏ *02–54–90–33–33.* ⏲ *Apr.–Aug., daily 9–6; Sept.–Mar., daily 9–noon and 2–5:30.*

$$ ✕ **Au Rendez-vous des Pêcheurs.** This restaurant near the Loire, below the château, serves chef Christophe Cosme's inventive desserts and seafish specialties. ✉ *27 rue du Foix,* ☏ *02–54–74–67–48. MC, V. Closed Aug. and Sun. No dinner Mon.*

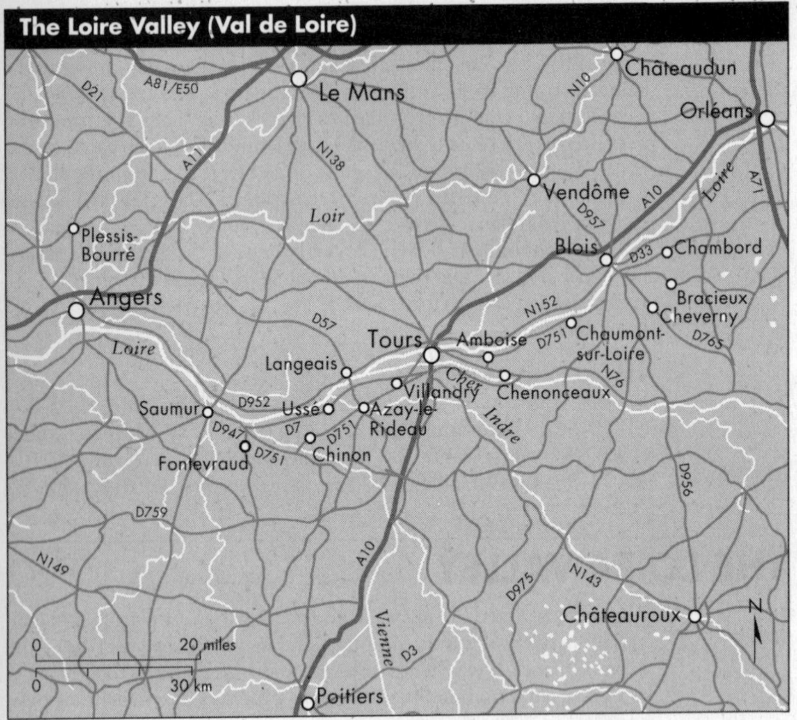

$$ ✕🏨 **Médicis.** Your best bet in Blois, this smart, friendly hotel 1 km (½ mi) from the château has comfortable rooms. Each is furnished differently, but all share the same joyous color scheme. Chef-owner Christian Garanger's cooking is innovative classical—*coquilles St-Jacques* (scallops) with a pear fondue, for instance. ✉ *2 allée François-I, 41000,* ☎ *02–54–43–94–04,* FAX *02–54–42–04–05. 11 rooms, 1 suite. Restaurant. AE, DC, MC, V. Closed Jan.*

Chambord

★ The largest of the Loire châteaux, the palatial **Château de Chambord** (begun in 1519), is in the heart of a vast forest. Another forest is on the roof: 365 chimneys and turrets, representing architectural self-indulgence at its least squeamish. Grandeur or a mere 440-room folly? Judge for yourself, but don't miss the superb spiral staircase—rumored to have been designed by Leonardo da Vinci—or the chance to saunter over the rooftop terrace. ☎ *02–54–50–40–28.* ⏲ *July–Aug., daily 9:30–6:45; Apr.–June and Sept.–Oct., daily 9:30–6:15; Nov.–Mar. 9–5:15.*

$$ ★ 🏨 **Grand St-Michel.** Considering its location across from the château, the St-Michel is reasonably priced. The best rooms are those with a splendid view of the château and the forest backdrop. ✉ *103 pl. St-Michel, 41250,* ☎ *02–54–20–31–31,* FAX *02–54–20–36–40. 38 rooms, 31 with bath or shower. Restaurant. MC, V. Closed mid-Nov.–mid-Dec.*

Amboise

This bustling town has two star attractions. The **Château d'Amboise,** dating from 1500, has splendid grounds, a rich interior, and fine views of the river from the battlements. But it wasn't always so peaceful: in 1560, more than 1,000 Protestant "conspirators" were hanged from these battlements during the Wars of Religion. ☎ *02–47–57–00–98.* ⏲ *July–Aug., daily 9–6:30; Sept.–June, daily 9–noon and 2–5:30.*

The **Clos-Lucé,** a 15th-century brick manor house, was the last home of Leonardo da Vinci, who was invited to stay by François I and died here in 1519. His engineering genius is illustrated by models based on his plans and sketches. ✉ *2 rue du Clos-Lucé,* ☎ *02–47–57–62–88.* ⏲ *Sept.–June, daily 9–6; July–Aug., daily 9–7.*

$–$$ ✕🏨 **Le Blason.** This delightful, small hotel is two blocks behind the château; Rooms 109 and 229 are especially nice. The pretty little restaurant has a seasonal menu that begins at 95 frs/€14.6 and might include roast lamb with garlic or medallions of pork. ✉ *11 pl. Richelieu, 37400,* ☎ *02–47–23–22–41,* FAX *02–47–57–56–18. 29 rooms. Restaurant. AE, DC, MC, V. Closed mid-Jan.–mid-Feb. No lunch Tues.*

Chenonceaux

The small village of Chenonceaux, on the Cher River, is best known as the site of the "most romantic" of all the Loire châteaux. The early 16th-★ century **Château de Chenonceau** (without the *x*) straddles the tranquil Cher like an unfinished bridge and was the magical abode for several of France's most famous ladies, including Diane de Poitiers—who received the chateau as a gift from King Henri II, only to have to give it back to his wife, Catherine de Médicis, on his death—and Madame Dupin, the latter so beloved by the townspeople that they spared her home from destruction during the worst days of the French Revolution. Thankfully—since this is truly the most beautiful château in France (at least from the outside), surrounded by elegant gardens and plane trees and mirrored in the river; its symmetrical style is basically Italianate in design since Catherine had Philibert de l'Orme design the signature gallery hall that spans the width of the river. Inside are fine paintings, colossal fireplaces, and richly worked ceilings, restored by the owners, the Menier family of sugar fame and fortune. A museum with wax figures depicting scenes from the château's history is in an outbuilding. Be sure to enjoy the gardens and walk along the embankment to see the Loir flowing under Chenonceau's arcades; boats are available for hire for a ride along the riverbanks. ☎ *02–47–23–90–07.* ⏲ *Mid-Nov.–Jan. 9–4:30, Feb.–mid-Mar. and mid-Sept.–mid-Nov., daily 9–5:30; mid-Mar.–mid-Sept. 9–7.*

$$–$$$ ✕🏨 **Bon Laboureur & Château.** Since 1882, four generations of the Jeudi family have run this elegant inn. Rooms in the old house are comfortably traditional; those in the former stables are larger and more modern; the biggest are in the converted manor house across the street. Dine on such excellent dishes as *poêlée de St-Jacques* (sautéed scallops) with fresh wild mushrooms. ✉ *6 rue du Dr-Bretonneau, 37150,* ☎ *02–47–23–90–02,* FAX *02–47–23–82–01. 37 rooms. Restaurant, pool. AE, DC, MC, V. Closed Jan. and mid-Nov.–mid-Dec.*

$$ ★ ✕🏨 **Roseraie.** What the Roseraie may lack in style, compared to its illustrious neighbor the Bon Laboureur, it makes up for with the joyful welcome of its English-speaking hosts, Laurent and Sophie Fiorito. Rooms are simple but spacious and quiet—especially those overlooking the garden—and copious meals are served in the rustic dining-room. ✉ *7 rue du Dr-Bretonneau, 37150,* ☎ *02–47–23–90–09,* FAX *02–47–23–91–59. 15 rooms. Restaurant, pool. AE, DC, MC, V. Closed mid-Nov.–mid-Feb.*

Tours

The largest city along the Loire, with 250,000 inhabitants, Tours was extensively damaged in World War II. But the timber-framed houses in the medieval center of Tours, the attractive old quarter around Place Plumereau, were tastefully restored.

★ The **Cathédrale St-Gatien** (1239–1484) numbers among France's most impressive churches. The influence of local Renaissance sculptors and craftsmen is evident on the ornate facade. The stained glass in the choir is particularly delicate; some of it dates from 1320. ✉ *Rue Lavoisier.*

$$$$ ★ ✕🏨 **Jean Bardet.** Bardet, one of France's top 20 chefs, showcases produce from his own rare herb and exotic vegetable garden in his kitchen. Signature dishes include baby eel in red wine or oysters poached in Muscadet on a puree of watercress. Reservations are essential, and the restaurant doesn't serve lunch Monday or, November through March, dinner Sunday and Monday. Rooms and suites at this stately mansion, though luxurious, are on the exorbitant side. For real style, hire Bardet's Rolls-Royce Silver Shadow II to take you on a tour of the Loire. ✉ *Château de Belmont, 57 rue Groison, 37100,* ☎ *02–47–41–41–11,* FAX *02–47–51–68–72. 16 rooms, 5 suites. Restaurant, pool. AE, DC, MC, V.*

$$$ ★ 🏨 **Univers.** The Univers is the best hotel in central Tours. Murals in the lobby depict some of the famous people who have stayed here since it opened in 1846: Winston Churchill, Sarah Bernhardt, Maurice Chevalier, Rudyard Kipling, Ernest Hemingway, Edith Piaf, and the Duke of Windsor. Rooms in this old hotel are all slightly different and all cleverly designed; wood paneling and soft colors give them warmth; most look onto the garden. ✉ *5 bd. Heurteloup, 37000,* ☎ *02–47–05–37–12,* FAX *02–47–61–51–80. 77 rooms, 8 suites. Restaurant. AE, DC, MC, V.*

Villandry

★ The **Château de Villandry,** near the Cher River, is known for its painstakingly relaid 16th-century **gardens,** which are now the finest example extant of French Renaissance garden design in France. Green-thumbers flock here to gaze at the long avenues of 1,500 manicured lime trees and the gigantic terraces planted with rare species of flowers and vegetables. The château interior was restored in the mid-19th century. Note the painted and gilded ceiling from Toledo and the collection of Spanish pictures. ☎ *02–47–50–02–09.* ⏲ *June–Sept., château daily 9–6, gardens daily 9–8; Oct.–May, château daily 9:30–12:30 and 2–5:30, gardens daily 9 AM–dusk.*

Azay-le-Rideau

One of the region's prettiest châteaux is the early 16th-century **Château d'Azay-le-Rideau.** Its high roof and fairy-tale corner turrets are reflected in the Indre River, which surrounds the château like a lake. This graceful ensemble compensates for the château's spartan interior, as does the charm of the surrounding village. ☎ *02–47–45–42–04.* ⏲ *July–Aug., daily 9:30–7; Apr.–June and Sept., daily 9:30–6; Oct.–Mar., daily 9:30–noon and 2–5.*

Ussé

The **Château d'Ussé**—actually in the village of Rigny-Ussé—claims to be the setting of the French fairy tale *Sleeping Beauty.* Its bristling turrets, terraces, and forest backcloth are undeniably romantic. Be sure to visit the dainty Renaissance chapel in the park. ☎ *02–47–95–54–05.* ⏲ *June–Aug., daily 9–6:30; Apr.–May and Sept., daily 9–noon and 2–6:45; mid-Feb.–Mar. and Oct.–mid-Nov., daily 9–noon and 2–6.*

Chinon

Chinon is an ancient town nestled by the Vienne River, with a rock-of-ages castle patrolling the horizon. The town is a warren of narrow, cobbled streets (some are pedestrian-only) lined with half-timber medieval houses. Since both the village and the château are on steep, cobbled slopes, it's a good idea to wear comfortable walking shoes. The 12th-century **Château de Chinon,** with walls 400 yards long, is mainly in ruins, though there's a small museum in the **Logis Royal** (Royal Chambers). The **Tour de l'Horloge** (Clock Tower), whose bell has sounded the hours since 1399, contains the **Musée Jeanne d'Arc** (Joan of Arc Museum). ☎ *02–47–93–13–45.* ⏲ *Nov.–mid-Mar., daily 9–12:30 and 2–5:30; mid-Mar.–June and Sept., daily 9–6; July–Aug., daily 9–7; Oct., daily 9–5.*

The **Musée du Vin** (Wine Museum), in a vaulted cellar beneath one of Chinon's fine medieval streets, has a fascinating presentation about vine growing and wine and barrel making. ✉ *12 rue Voltaire*

$$$ ✕🏨 **Château de Marçay.** In this 15th-century château, 6 km (4 mi) south of Chinon via D49 and D116, David Grandjeu prepares excellent cuisine—carpaccio of duck, and tournedos of salmon in a Chinon wine sauce. Rooms are furnished with antiques; beams and gables add warmth. Those on the ground floor in the west wing have private patios; the ones in the pavilion near the château, though pleasantly furnished, have less charm. ✉ *Route du Château, 37500 Marçay,* ☎ *02–47–93–03–47,* FAX *02–47–93–45–33. 34 rooms. Restaurant, pool, tennis court. AE, DC, MC, V. Closed Feb.–mid-Mar.*

$$ 🏨 **France.** Just off the main square is this hotel in the town's oldest buildings. Built in the 16th century, it was home to many notables until the Revolution when it became a hotel. Rooms are all comfortable, but ask for one of the more refurbished ones with a view of the castle. The ground-floor restaurant (closed Tuesday and no lunch Wednesday) serves Italian cuisine. ✉ *47 pl. du Général-de-Gaulle, 37500,* ☎ *02–47–93–33–91,* FAX *02–47–98–37–03. 27 rooms. Restaurant. AE, DC, MC, V. Closed 2nd ½ Nov.*

Saumur

The prosperous town of Saumur is famous for its riding school, wines, and castle. The **Château de Saumur**—a white 14th-century castle—towers above the river. It is home to two outstanding museums: the **Musée des Arts Décoratifs** (Decorative Arts Museum), featuring porcelain and enamels, and the **Musée du Cheval** (Horse Museum), with saddles, stirrups, skeletons, and Stubbs engravings. ☎ *02–41–40–24–40.* ⏲ *July–Sept., daily 9–6:30; Oct. and Apr.–June, daily 9–11:30 and 2–6; Nov.–Mar., Wed.–Mon. 9:30–noon and 2–5:30.*

$$–$$$ ✕🏨 **Anne d'Anjou.** Close to the center of town, this hotel facing the river has a view of the château (floodlit at night) perched above. Inside the 18th-century building, the simple rooms are filled with both old furniture and contemporary decor; Room 102 has wood-panel paintings and Empire furnishings. The outstanding restaurant, Les Ménestrels, serves imaginative regional cuisine. ✉ *32 quai Mayaud, 49400,* ☎ *02–41–67–30–30,* FAX *02–41–67–51–00. 45 rooms, 2 suites. Restaurant. AE, DC, MC, V.*

The Loire Valley Essentials

CAR TRAVEL

The easiest way to visit the Loire châteaux is by car; N152 hugs the riverbank and offers excellent sightseeing possibilities.

TOURS

Bus tours of the main châteaux leave daily in summer from Tours, Blois, and Saumur: Ask at the relevant tourist offices for latest times and prices. Most châteaux insist that you follow one of their tours of their interiors; try to get a booklet in English before joining the tour, as most are in French.

TRAIN TRAVEL

Trains run along the Loire Valley every two hours, supplemented by local bus services. A peaceful way to explore the region is to rent a bicycle at one of the SNCF train stations.

➤ TRAIN INFORMATION: SNCF (☎ ☎ 08–36–35–35–35, WEB www.sncf.com).

VISITOR INFORMATION

➤ TOURIST INFORMATION: **Blois** (✉ 3 av. du Dr-Jean-Laigret, ☎ 02–54–90–41–41). **Saumur** (✉ pl. de la Bilange, ☎ 02–41–40–20–60). **Tours** (✉ 78 rue Bernard-Palissy, ☎ 02–47–70–37–37).

NORMANDY

Jutting out into the Channel, Normandy has had more connections with the English-speaking world, from the invasions of William the Conqueror to those of troops during World War II, than any other part of France. Come here not only to see historic monuments but to explore the countryside, rich with apple orchards, lush meadows, and sandy beaches.

The historic cities of Rouen and Caen, capitals of Upper and Lower Normandy, respectively, are full of churches and museums. The Seine Valley is lined with abbeys and castles from all periods; along the coast are remnants of the D-Day landings. Normandy also has one of France's most enduring tourist attractions: Mont-St-Michel, a remarkable Gothic abbey perched on a rocky mount off the Cotentin peninsula. Étretat and Fécamp on the Alabaster Coast and Deauville, Trouville, and Honfleur on the Côte Fleurie (Flower Coast) are among Normandy's many seaside resorts. Normandy is also recognized as one of France's finest gastronomic regions for its excellent cheeses, cider, Calvados, and wide range of seafood dishes. The A13 expressway linking Paris to Rouen and Caen, becoming the fast N13 highway as its spears on to Bayeux and Cherbourg, is the backbone of Normandy. The new A84 expressway from Caen to Avranches (near Mont St-Michel) was completed in 2001.

Rouen

Numbers in the margin correspond to points of interest on the Rouen map.

Although blitzed during World War II, Rouen retains much medieval charm. The square where Joan of Arc was burned at the stake in 1431 has been transformed beyond recognition, but the adjacent rue du Gros-Horloge, with its giant Renaissance clock built in 1527, fires the
1 imagination. You may be familiar with the facade of Rouen's **Cathédrale Notre-Dame** from Claude Monet's famous series of paintings. The simple Romanesque **Tour St-Romain** on the left dates from 1145 and the more intricate **Tour de Beurre** (Butter Tower) on the right was built in the 15th century in a Flamboyant Gothic style. The cast-iron steeple, the tallest in France, was added in the 19th century. In the courtyard to the left is the **Portal des Libraires** (Booksellers' Portal), illustrating scenes from the Last Judgment; the dead are rising from their coffins while God begins to separate the good from the bad with terrifying detail. The cathedral caught fire twice during the war; Hitler ordered his troops to rescue it the first time, and the Rouennais saved it from Allied bombs the second time. Inside, note the 160-ft tower above the crossing on its four massive pillars, and the richly carved staircase in the north transept. ✉ *Pl. de la Cathédrale.* ⏲ *Mon.–Sat. 8–7, Sun. 8–6.*

The name of the pedestrian rue du Gros-Horloge, Rouen's most pop-
2 ular street, comes from the **Gros-Horloge** itself, a giant Renaissance clock; in 1527 the Rouennais had a splendid arch built especially for it. A 15th-century belfry gives you the chance to study the iron mechanism. ✉ *Rue du Gros-Horloge.* ⏲ *Wed.–Mon. 10–1 and 2–6.*

Normandy (Normandie)

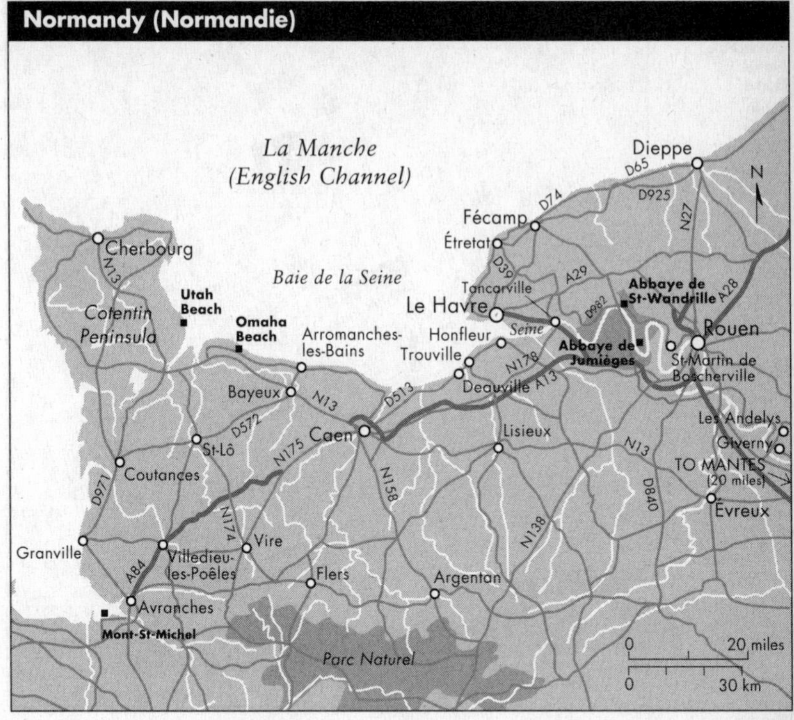

3 The Renaissance **Palais de Justice** (Law Courts), the most impressive civic building in Rouen, dates from the early 16th century. The facade bristles with a forest of turrets, pinnacles, gables, and buttresses. ✉ *34–36 rue des Juifs.*

4 Exactly what the shape of the modern **Église Jeanne d'Arc** (Joan of Arc Church) is supposed to represent is unclear; the flames of St. Joan's funeral pyre? A fish? An overturned boat? Built in 1979, in the old market square on the site of Joan of Arc's execution, this modern church showcases some pleasantly incongruous 16th-century stained glass, rescued from a church bombed in 1944. Outside, the exact spot where St. Joan was burnt alive is marked by a concrete and metal cross. ✉ *Pl. du Vieux-Marché.* ⏲ *Daily 10–12:15 and 2–6, except Fri. and Sun. morning.*

5 **Abbaye St-Ouen,** an airy, beautifully proportioned 14th-century abbey-church, has splendid medieval stained glass and one of France's most sonorous 19th-century organs. ✉ *Pl. du Général-de-Gaulle,* ☎ *02–32–08–13–90.* ⏲ *Mid-Mar.–Oct., Wed.–Mon. 8–noon and 2–6; Nov.–mid-Dec. and mid-Jan.–mid-Mar., Wed., Sat., and Sun. 10–12:30 and 2–6.*

6 The **Musée des Beaux-Arts** (Fine Arts Museum) specializes in 17th- and 19th-century French painting, with an emphasis on works by local artists and a collection of macabre paintings by Rouen-born painter Théodore Géricault. ✉ *26 bis rue Jean-Lecanuet,* ☎ *02–35–71–28–40.* ⏲ *Wed.–Mon. 10–6.*

7 At the **Musée de la Céramique** (Ceramics Museum), you can see examples of local earthenware; Rouen used to be a renowned faience-making center, reaching its heyday in the early 18th century. ✉ *Rue Faucon,* ☎ *02–35–07–31–74.* ⏲ *Wed.–Mon. 10–1 and 2–6.*

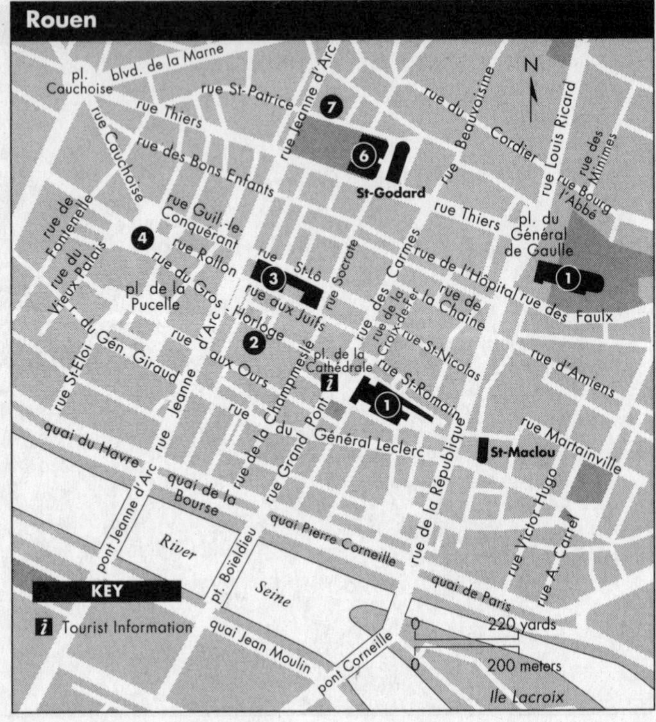

$$–$$$ ✕ **La Couronne.** Built in 1345, La Couronne is supposedly the oldest inn in France. Amid the oak beams, leather upholstery, and woodwork is a sculpture collection. The traditional cuisine features homemade foie gras and the famous "canard rouennais" (duck with blood sauce). Don't forget to try the famous *Normand Soufflé au Grand Marnier* for dessert. ✉ *31 Pl. du Vieux-Marché,* ☎ *02–35–71–40–90. Reservations essential. AE, DC, MC, V.*

$$ ✕🏨 **Le Vieux Carré.** This lovely little hotel with its tree-lined courtyard is situated in the heart of old Rouen. Rooms are small, practical, and comfortable—simply furnished with a taste for the exotic. Request one of the rooms on the third floor for a good view of the cathedral. ✉ *34, rue Ganterie, 76000,* ☎ *02–35–71–67–70,* FAX *02–35–71–19–17. 14 rooms. AE, V, MC, D.*

$$ 🏨 **Cathédrale.** This appealing hotel is in a medieval building on a narrow pedestrian street behind the cathedral (you can sleep soundly: the cathedral bells don't boom out the hour at night). Rooms are petite but neat and comfortable. ✉ *12 rue St-Romain, 76000,* ☎ *02–35–71–57–95,* FAX *02–35–70–15–54. 24 rooms. MC, V.*

Étretat

Claude Monet painted in Étretat as well as in Rouen and Giverny, immortalizing the site's rough cliff formations long before the advent of postcards. The white **Falaises d'Étretat** (Étretat Cliffs) are just as famous in France as Dover's are in England. Two immense archways—walls of stone hollowed out by the sea—lead to neighboring beaches at low tide. For a view over the bay and the **Aiguille** (Needle), which is an enormous rock towering in the middle, take the little path up the **Falaise d'Aval** (Aval Cliff).

$ ✕ **Roches Blanches.** Just off the beach, this family-owned restaurant is a concrete, post–World War II eyesore. But the views and the superbly fresh seafood are another story. ✉ *Rue de l'Abbé-Cochet,* ☎ *02–35–27–07–34. Reservations essential. MC, V. Closed Tues.–Thurs. (Wed. only July–early Sept.), Jan., and Oct.*

$–$$ ✕🏨 **Hôtel La Résidence.** This gorgeous hotel, set in a 16th-century house, is located in the heart of Étretat just 2 km (1 mi) from the sea. The cheapest rooms are just that, with both the bathroom and the shower located in the hallway, while the most expensive have both an in-room bathroom and a Jacuzzi. The brasserie-type restaurant located on the ground floor, Le Salamandre, showcases an organic, farm-raised cuisine. ✉ *4 blvd. René-Coty, 76790,* ☎ *02–35–27–02–87,* FAX *02–35–27–17–07. 15 rooms. Restaurant. AE, MC, V.*

$$$ 🏨 **Donjon.** This charming ivy-covered château, in a park overlooking the town, has lovely views of the bay. Rooms are individually furnished, spacious, and comfortable. For a spectacular view, request the Oriental suite, the Horizon, or the Majorie rooms. Reliable French cuisine is served with flair in the cozy, romantic restaurant. Rooms are reserved on a half-board basis on weekends. ✉ *Chemin de St-Clair, 76790,* ☎ *02–35–27–08–23,* FAX *02–35–29–92–24. 11 rooms. Restaurant, pool. AE, DC, MC, V.*

Honfleur

Toward the end of the last century, pretty Honfleur, once an important port for maritime expeditions, became a favorite spot for vacationers and painters, including the Impressionists. In summer or on weekends, be prepared for lines at restaurants and cafés. Its lively cobbled streets, harbors full of colorful yachts, and the **Église Ste-Catherine**—a 15th-century wooden church—make it the most picturesque town on the Normandy coast.

$$–$$$ ✕ **L'Assiette Gourmande.** When chef Gérard Bonnefoy comes into the dining room at Honfleur's unsung top restaurant, he decides what you would enjoy after a few minutes of conversation. Maybe you'll be lucky enough to have the superb coquilles St-Jacques grilled with sautéed asparagus in a raspberry vinaigrette and orange sauce. ✉ *2 quai des Passagers,* ☎ *02–31–89–24–88. AE, DC, MC, V. Closed Mon. except July–Aug.*

$$–$$$$ 🏨 **Hôtel l'Ecrin.** Dating from the days of Napoléon III, this elegant manor may be located in the center of town but it is a quiet and calm delight. The charming Madame Blais welcomes guests to her highly stylized living room that has gold just about everywhere gold can go. Each guest room has its own style. Request a room in the main house, as the views from the annex overlook the parking lot. ✉ *19 rue Eugène-Boudin, 14602,* ☎ *02–31–14–43–45,* FAX *02–31–89–24–41. 26 rooms. MC, V.*

Trouville–Deauville

Although separated only by the little Touques River, the popular resort towns of Trouville and Deauville are vastly different in mood. Deauville is the fancier of the two, with its palaces, casino, horse racing, and film festival. Some would say all the style is artificial: the town was built from scratch in the 1860s and is invaded each weekend by wealthy Parisians (thereby earning it the title of Paris's honorary 21st arrondisement). Neighboring Trouville retains an active fishing fleet and working population and is less damaging to the wallet. Its beach is arguably larger and more scenic, tucked in beneath a corniche. High season is kicked off in July and culminates with the American Film Festival the first week in September. If you are planning a visit at this time, reserve in advance and request written confirmation.

$$$$ ✕🏨 **Normandy.** The fashionable and monied from Paris have been attracted to this hotel, with its traditional Norman facade and underground passage to the casino, since it opened in 1912. Request a room with a sea view. The gourmet restaurant serves a wide array of fish dishes and meat with creamy Normandy sauces. Ask your concierge about the special prices guests here have at the luxurious thalassotherapy center. ✉ *38 rue Jean-Mermoz, 14800 Deauville,* ☎ *02–31–98–66–22; 800/223–5652 for U.S. reservations,* FAX *02–31–98–66–23. 291 rooms. AE, DC, MC, V.*

$–$$ 🏨 **Carmen.** This straightforward, unpretentious little hotel is around the corner from the casino and a block from the sea. Rooms range from plain and inexpensive to comfortable and moderate. The owners, the Bude family, are on hand to give advice. ✉ *24 rue Carnot, 14360 Trouville,* ☎ *02–31–88–35–43,* FAX *02–31–88–08–03. 18 rooms. Restaurant. AE, DC, MC, V. Closed Jan.–mid-Feb. and 10 days in Oct.*

Bayeux

Bayeux, a few miles inland from the D-Day beaches, was the first French town freed by the Allies in June 1944. It's known primarily as the home ★ of **Bayeux Tapestry** (La Tapisserie de la Reine Mathilde, or Queen Mathilda's Tapestry), which tells the epic story of William's conquest of England in 1066. You can rent headphones in English with scene-by-scene commentary. ✉ *13 bis rue de Nesmond,* ☎ *02–31–51–25–55.* ⊙ *May–Aug., daily 9–7; mid-Sept.–Apr., daily 9:30–12:30 and 2–6.*

Dominating the heart of Bayeux is the **Cathédrale Notre-Dame** (✉ rue de Bienvenu), a harmonious mixture of Norman (Romanesque) and Gothic architecture. Note the portal on the south side of the transept, depicting the assassination of English archbishop Thomas à Becket in Canterbury Cathedral in 1170.

The **Musée de la Bataille de Normandie** (Battle of Normandy Museum), overlooking the British Military Cemetery, traces the Allied advance against the Nazis in June and July of 1944. ✉ *Bd. Général-Fabian-Ware,* ☎ *02–31–92–93–41.* ⊙ *May–mid-Sept., daily 9:30–6:30; mid-Sept.–Apr., daily 10–noon and 2–6.*

$$ ✕ **Les Quatre Saisons.** This restaurant, in the Grand Hôtel du Luxembourg, is one of the best in town. The classical repertoire of Normandy dishes ranges from chicken roasted with cider to veal in a sauce scented with calvados. ✉ *25 rue des Bouchers,* ☎ *02–31–92–00–04. AE, DC, MC, V.*

$$$$ ✕🏨 **Chenevière.** In a late-19th-century grand manor in parkland between Bayeux and the coast, this elegant hotel has rooms with modern furnishings, floor-to-ceiling windows, and flowered bedspreads that add a splash of color. The restaurant serves classic Norman cuisine. ✉ *Les Escures, 14520 Commes (9 km/5½ mi north of Bayeux via D6),* ☎ *02–31–51–25–25,* FAX *02–31–51–25–20. 19 rooms. Restaurant. AE, MC, V.*

$$ 🏨 **Churchill.** This friendly, family-run inn in an old town house is within walking distance of Bayeux's major attractions. Rooms vary in shape and size; furnishings are modest and functional. ✉ *14 rue St-Jean, 14400,* ☎ *02–31–21–31–80,* FAX *02–31–21–41–66. 31 rooms. AE, DC, MC, V. Closed Dec.–Mar.*

Arromanches-les-Bains

Not much remains to mark the furious fighting waged hereabouts in World War II. In the bay off Arromanches, however, some elements of the floating harbor are still visible: the best view can be had from the terraced platform on D65 above the town. A few hundred yards out to sea you can see numerous vestiges of **Mulberry B**, an artificial concrete harbor built for the landings. (American troops landed farther up the coast on Omaha Beach, where Mulberry A was destroyed by a storm soon after.)

The **Musée du Débarquement** (Normandy Landings Museum) on the seafront shows the D-Day landing plan and a film (in English) about the operation. ✉ *Pl. du 6-Juin,* ☎ *02–31–22–34–31.* ⏲ *May–Sept., daily 9–7; Oct.–Dec. and Feb.–Apr., daily 9:30–12:30 and 1:30–5.*

$$ **Hôtel Victoria.** A well-maintained, charming stone manor, completed with chandeliered main salon, the Victoria is located just 2 km (1 mi) from the sea. Request a room either on the second floor of the main house or one of the cozy, reasonably priced smaller rooms in the attic. ✉ *Tracy-Sur-Mer, 14117,* ☎ *02–31–22–35–37,* FAX *02–31–22–93–38. 14 rooms. V. Closed Oct.–Mar.*

Mont-St-Michel

★ Fabled Mont-St-Michel, an offshore rock crowned by the spire of a medieval abbey, is perhaps the most spectacular site in France—and certainly the most-visited outside Paris. The best views can be had on the road from Avranches, to the east. The mount's fame comes not just from its location—until the causeway (to be replaced in 2002 by a bridge to allow the tide to circulate) was built, it was cut off from the mainland at high tide—but also from the dramatic nature of its construction during the 8th century, when tons of granite were brought from the nearby Chausey Islands and hauled up the 265-ft peak. It has been a pilgrimage site ever since. The first small chapel to St. Michael, erected by the bishop of Avranches in 709, was centuries later replaced by a large church and buildings, in which for nearly 800 years Benedictine monks peacefully prayed, studied, and worked. **La Merveille** (The Wonder) is the name given to the cluster of Gothic buildings on top. What looks like a fortress is in fact a series of architectural layers that trace the evolution of French architecture from Romanesque to late Gothic. Napoléon ultimately turned it into a prison, and then romantic connoisseurs had the settlement restored to full medieval glory. You can join a guided tour (in English).

To view the wonders of Mont-St-Michel is not a simple matter. Entering the tiny island by three massive stone gates, you must climb its long single street, the Grand-Rue, which is at first a steep ramp and later becomes a stairway. By the time you have passed the ramparts and reached the celebrated *escalier de dentelle* (lace staircase) to the gallery of the abbey church, you have climbed no fewer than 900 steps. For most of the year Mont-St-Michel—officially a small village with a permanent population of fewer than 100—is surrounded by sandy beach. The best time to see it is during the high tides of spring and fall, when the sea comes pounding in—dangerously fast—and encircles the mount. Try to enjoy an overnight stay, so you can truly appreciate the peace and solitary grandeur of the mount without the daytime crowds. ☎ *02–33–60–14–14.* ⏲ *May–Sept., daily 9:30–11:30 and 1:30–6; Oct.–Apr., Wed.–Mon. 9:30–4:30.*

$$$ ✕ **Terrasses Poulard.** In this overpriced collection of town houses, each room is named after a famous Norman personality and styled accordingly. Several have breathtaking views of the bay; others look out onto a little garden. The restaurant, famous for its light, fluffy omelettes, is crowded with tourists and lined with posters and photographs recalling illustrious past visitors. ✉ *Grande-Rue, 50116,* ☎ *02–33–60–14–09,* FAX *02–33–60–37–31. 29 rooms. Restaurant. AE, DC, MC, V.*

$$ **La Roche Torin.** This small, ivy-clad manor house, 9 km (6 mi) east of Mont-St-Michel, is an appealing alternative to the high-priced hotels on the mount. Rooms are pleasantly old-fashioned. ✉ *34 rte. de la*

Roche-Torin, 50220 Courtils, ☎ *02–33–70–96–55,* FAX *02–33–48–35–20. 13 rooms, 1 suite. Restaurant. MC, V. Closed mid-Nov.–mid-Mar.*

Normandy Essentials

BUS TRAVEL

For towns not covered by trains, there is a bus network; CNA covers Upper Normandy from Rouen to Le Havre; Auto-Cars Gris runs buses from Fécamp to Le Havre and Étretat; Bus Verts covers the coast from Honfleur to Caen and Bayeux and the D-Day sites.

➤ BUS INFORMATION: **CNA** (☎ ☎ 02–35–52–92–29). **Auto-Cars Gris** (☎ ☎ 02–35–28–19–88). **Bus Verts** (✉ ☎ 02–31–44–77–44).

CAR TRAVEL

Normandy is best visited by car.

TOURS

The following companies run daily bus excursions from Paris to Mont-St-Michel for approximately 980 frs/€149.60, with a guided tour in English, meals, and admission included. This is not for the faint of heart, as buses depart Paris at 7:15 AM and return late, at 10:30 PM.

➤ FEES AND SCHEDULES: **Cityrama** (✉ 4 pl. des Pyramides, 75001 Paris, ☎ 01–44–55–61–00). **Paris Vision** (✉ 214 rue de Rivoli, 75001 Paris, ☎ 08–00–03–02–14).

TRAIN TRAVEL

Though trains leave regularly from Paris to Rouen, Caen, and Bayeux, limited connections make cross-country traveling difficult and time-consuming. Visiting many of the historic monuments and towns—such as Honfleur and Mont-St-Michel, which have no train station—means using buses, which run infrequently.

➤ TRAIN INFORMATION: **SNCF** (☎ ☎ 08–36–35–35–35, WEB www.sncf.com).

VISITOR INFORMATION

➤ TOURIST INFORMATION: **Les Andelys** (✉ rue Philippe-Auguste, ☎ 02–32–54–41–93). **Bayeux** (✉ 3 rue St-Jean, ☎ 02–31–51–28–28). **Deauville** (✉ rue Victor-Hugo, ☎ 02–31–14–40–00). **Étretat** (✉ pl. Maurice-Guillard, ☎ 02–35–27–05–21). **Honfleur** (✉ 9 rue de la Ville, ☎ 02–31–89–23–30). **Mont-St-Michel** (✉ Corps de Garde des Bourgeois, ☎ 02–33–60–14–30). **Rouen** (✉ 25 pl. de la Cathédrale, ☎ 02–32–08–32–40).

BURGUNDY AND LYON

For a region whose powerful, late-medieval dukes held sway over the largest tract of Western Europe and whose current image is closely allied to its expensive wine, Burgundy is a place of surprisingly rustic, quiet charm. Its leading religious monument is the Romanesque basilica in Vézelay, once an important pilgrimage center and today a tiny village hidden in rolling hills. The heart of Burgundy is the dark, brooding Morvan Forest. Dijon, the region's only city, retains something of its medieval opulence, but its present reputation is essentially gastronomic. Top restaurants abound. The vineyards leading down toward Beaune are among the world's most distinguished and picturesque. The vines continue to flourish as you head south along the Saône Valley, through the Mâconnais and Beaujolais, toward Lyon, one of France's most appealing cities.

Burgundy is best visited by car. Its meandering country roads invite leisurely exploration. There are few big towns, and traveling around

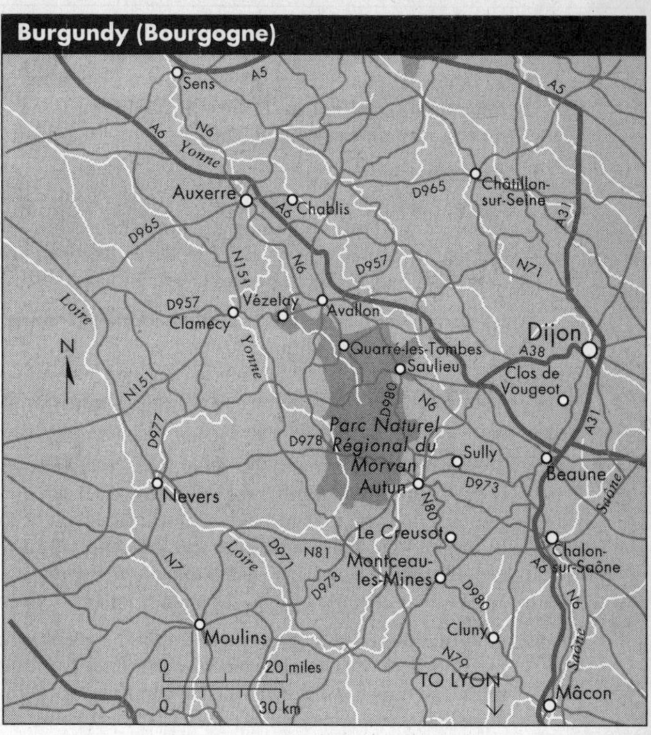

by train is unrewarding, especially as the infrequent cross-country trains steam along at the speed of a legendary Burgundy snail. However, the TGV (high-speed trains) zip out of Paris to Dijon (75 minutes), Mâcon (100 minutes), and Lyon (2 hours). It makes sense for Sens to be your first stop on the way down to Burgundy, as it is just 120 km (75 mi) southeast of Paris on N6—a fast, pretty road that hugs the Yonne Valley south of Fontainebleau. Take A6, if you are in a hurry. Zigzag across N6 and A6, taking the smaller roads that lead off them. A6, which turns into A7, is the highway to the Mediterranean and will take you close to Auxerre, Dijon, Beaune, Mâcon, and Lyon, then down the Rhône valley to Provence.

Sens

Sens is home to France's senior archbishop and is dominated by the 12th-century **Cathédrale St-Étienne.** This is one of the oldest cathedrals in France and has a foursquare facade topped by towers and an incongruous little Renaissance campanile. The vast, harmonious interior contains outstanding stained glass of various periods.

The roof of the 13th-century **Palais Synodal** (Synodal Palace), alongside Sens's cathedral, is notable for its diamond tile motif—misleadingly (and incongruously) added in the mid-19th century by medieval monument restorer Viollet-le-Duc. Annexed to the Palais Synodal is an ensemble of Renaissance buildings. Inside is a museum with archaeological finds from the Gallo-Roman period. The cathedral treasury, on the museum's second floor, is one of the richest in France. ☎ *03–86–64–46–27.* ⏲ *June–Sept., daily 10–noon and 2–6; Oct.–May, Wed. and weekends 10–noon and 2–6, Mon. and Thurs.–Fri. 2–6.*

$$ ★ ✕🏨 **Hôtel de Paris et de la Poste.** Owned for the last several decades by the Godard family, the modernized Paris & Poste, which began life as a post house in the 1700s, is a convenient and pleasant stopping

point. Rooms are clean and well equipped. But it is the traditional restaurant, padded green leather armchairs in the lounge, and little curved wooden bar that give this place its comfy charm. ✉ *97 rue de la République, 89100,* ☎ *03–86–65–17–43,* FAX *03–86–64–48–45. 25 rooms. Restaurant. AE, DC, MC, V.*

Auxerre

Auxerre is the jewel of Burgundy's Yonne region—a beautifully laid-out town with three imposing and elegant churches climbing the large hill that is its perch over the Yonne River. Its steep, undulating streets are full of half-timbered houses in every imaginable style and shape.

Its main feature is the muscular **Cathédrale St-Étienne,** rising majestically from the squat houses around it. It was built between the 13th and 16th centuries and has a powerful north tower similar to that at Clamecy. ✉ *Pl. St-Étienne,* ☎ *03–86–52–31–68.* ⏲ *Easter–Nov., Mon.–Sat. 9–noon and 2–6, Sun. 2–6.*

The earliest aboveground section of the former **Abbaye de St-Germain** is the 12th-century Romanesque bell tower. But the extensive underground crypt was inaugurated by Charles the Bald in 859 and contains its original Carolingian frescoes and Ionic capitals. ✉ *Pl. St-Germain,* ☎ *03–86–51–09–74.* ⏲ *Guided tours of the crypt Oct.–Apr., daily at 10, 11, and 2–5; May–Sept., daily every half hr between 10 and 5:30.*

$$ ✕ **Jardin Gourmand.** As its name implies, this restaurant has a pretty garden where you can eat in summer. The interior of this former manor house is equally congenial. Terrine of pheasant breast is a specialty: hope that the starter of snails with barley and chanterelles and the *gêlée de raisin de chablis* (chablis grape gelatin) dessert are available. ✉ *56 bd. Vauban,* ☎ *03–86–51–53–52. AE, MC, V. Closed Mon.*

$$$ ★ 🏨 **Château de Ribourdin.** Retired farmer Claude Brodard began building his *chambres d'hôtes* (B&B) in an old stable six years ago, and the result is cozy, comfortable, and reasonably priced. Château de la Borde, named for a small manor nearby, is the smallest, sunniest, and most intimate room. ✉ *89240 Chevannes (8 km/5 mi southwest of Auxerre on D1),* ☎ *03–86–41–23–16,* FAX *03–86–41–23–16. 5 rooms. No credit cards.*

Chablis

Famous for its dry white wine, Chablis makes an attractive excursion 16 km (10 mi) to the east of Auxerre, along D965. Beware of village tourist shops selling local wines at unpalatable prices. The surrounding vineyards are dramatic: their steeply banked hills stand in contrast to the region's characteristic gentle slopes.

$$–$$$ ★ ✕🏨 **Hostellerie des Clos.** The moderately priced, simple yet comfortable rooms at this inn have floral curtains and wicker tables with chairs. Most of all, come here for chef Michel Vignaud's fine cooking; it's the best in the region. (The restaurant is closed Wednesday.) ✉ *18 rue Jules-Rathier, 89800,* ☎ *03–86–42–10–63,* FAX *03–86–42–17–11. 26 rooms. Restaurant. AE, MC, V. Closed late Dec.–mid-Jan.*

Vézelay

Burgundy's leading religious monument is the Romanesque basilica in Vézelay, once an important pilgrimage center and today a tiny village hidden in rolling hills. The **Basilique Ste-Madeleine** is perched on a rocky crag, with commanding views of the surrounding countryside. It rose to fame during the 11th century as the resting place of the relics of St. Mary Magdalene and became a departure point for the great pilgrimages to Santiago de Compostela in northwest Spain. The church was rescued from decay by the 19th-century Gothic Revival architect Viollet-le-Duc and counts as one of the foremost Romanesque buildings in existence. ✉ *Pl. de la Basilique,* ☎ *03–86–33–39–50.* ⏲ *Daily 8–8, except during offices Mon.–Sat. 12:30–1:15 and 6–7, Sun. 11–12:15.*

$$$$ ✕🏨 **L'Espérance.** In St-Père-sous-Vézelay, a neighboring village, enjoy chef Marc Meneau's subtle and original cuisine at one of France's premier restaurants (closed Tuesday, Wednesday lunch, and February; reservations and jacket and tie are required). A second restaurant, Le Pré des Marguerites, serves simpler, more traditional, less expensive fare. Rooms in the main house are pretty but rather small; the others, in nearby buildings, are slightly larger. ✉ *89450 St-Père-sous-Vézelay,* ☎ *03–86–33–39–10,* FAX *03–86–33–26–15. 44 rooms. Restaurant. AE, DC, MC, V. Closed Feb.*

Dijon

Dijon is both the capital of Burgundy and of gastronomy. Testimony ★ to Dijon's bygone splendor is the **Palais des Ducs** (Ducal Palace), now one of France's leading art museums. The tombs of Philip the Bold and John the Fearless head a rich collection of medieval objects and Renaissance furniture. ✉ *Cour de Bar du Palais des États,* ☎ *03–80–74–52–70.* ⏲ *Wed.–Mon. 10–6.*

With its spindlelike towers, delicate arches gracing its facade, and 13th-century stained glass, the church of **Notre-Dame** (✉ rue de la Préfecture) is one of the city's highlights. Among the city's oldest churches, the **Cathédrale St-Bénigne** (✉ pl. St-Bénigne) is comparatively austere; its chief glory is the 11th-century crypt—a forest of pillars surmounted by a rotunda. The relatively new church of **St-Michel** (✉ pl. St-Michel) is notable for its chunky Renaissance facade. Don't miss the exuberant 15th-century gateway at the **Chartreuse de Champmol** (✉ just off av. Albert 1er beyond the train station)—all that remains of a former ★ charterhouse. Next to the Chartreuse de Champmol is the **Puits de Moïse,** the so-called Well of Moses, with six large, realistic statues of saints that are among the most celebrated creations of the late Middle Ages. It was designed by Flemish master Claus Sluter, who also created the tombs of the dukes of Burgundy.

A leisurely trip south of Dijon in the direction of Beaune takes you through some of the world's most famous **vineyards.** Route D122 wends its way past such properties as Gevrey-Chambertin and Chambolle-Musigny, then joins N74 at Chambolle-Musigny.

$$$–$$$$ ✕ **Billoux.** Jean-Pierre Billoux's three-year-old restaurant in the center of Dijon is one of the best-kept secrets of Burgundy. The house specialties are inventive, the welcome always convivial, and the wine list reads like a who's who of the regions best—but not necessarily best-known—winemakers. ✉ *13 pl. de la Libération,* ☎ *03–80–38–05–05. Reservations essential. AE, DC, MC, V. Closed Sun. night and Mon.*

$ ✕ **Bistrot des Halles.** Of the many restaurants in the area, this one is the best value. Well-prepared dishes range from escargots to beef bourguignon with braised endives. Dine either at the sidewalk tables or inside, where mirrors and polished wood dominate. ✉ *8 rue Bannelier,* ☎ *03–80–49–94–15. MC, V. No dinner Sun.*

$$–$$$ ✕🏨 **Chapeau Rouge.** A player piano in the bar and elegant staircase give this hotel a charm that the rooms, though clean and well appointed, lack. The restaurant is renowned as a haven of classic regional cuisine. ✉ *5 rue Michelet, 21000,* ☎ *03–80–30–28–10,* FAX *03–80–30–33–89. 30 rooms. Restaurant, bar. Reservations essential AE, DC, MC, V.*

$$$–$$$$ 🏨 **Hôtel Sofitel Dijon–La Cloche.** The best hotel in Dijon, in use since the 19th century, La Cloche is a successful cross between luxury chain and grand hotel. Try to get a room overlooking the tranquil back garden, also the backdrop for the greenhouse restaurant La Rotonde. ✉

14 pl. Darcy, 21000, ☎ 03–80–30–12–32, FAX 03–80–30–04–15. 53 rooms, 15 suites. 2 restaurants, bar. AE, DC, MC, V.

Clos de Vougeot

Visit Clos de Vougeot to see its *grange viticole* (wine-making barn), surrounded by its famous vineyard. Begun by Cistercian monks during the 12th century and completed during the Renaissance, the **Château du Clos de Vougeot** is famous as the seat of Burgundy's elite company of wine lovers, the Confrérie des Chevaliers du Tastevin. They gather here in November at the start of an annual three-day festival, Les Trois Glorieuses. ☎ *03–80–62–86–09.* ⏲ *Apr.–Sept., daily 9–6:30; Oct.–Mar., weekdays and Sun. 9–11:30 and 2–5:30, Sat. 9–5.*

Beaune

★ Despite the hordes of tourists, Beaune remains one of the most attractive French provincial towns. The **Hospices de Beaune** (or Hôtel Dieu), founded in 1443 as a hospital, owns some of the region's finest vineyards. Its history is retraced in a museum that also has Rogier van der Weyden's Flemish masterpiece *The Last Judgment.* ✉ *Hospices de Beaune,* ☎ *03–80–24–45–00.* ⏲ *Apr.–mid-Nov., daily 9–6:30; mid-Nov.–Mar., daily 9–11:30 and 2–5:30.*

Tapestries relating the life of the Virgin hang in Beaune's 12th-century main church, the **Collégiale Notre-Dame** (✉ off av. de la République). In the candlelit cellars of the **Marché aux Vins** (Wine Market) you can, for the price of admission, taste as many of the regional wines as you wish. ✉ *Rue Nicolas Rolin,* ☎ *03–80–25–08–20.* ⏲ *Daily 9:30–noon and 2–6.*

$$ ✕ **L'Écusson.** Don't be put off by its unprepossessing exterior. This is a comfortable, friendly, thick-carpeted restaurant with good-value prix-fixe menus. Showcased is chef Jean-Pierre Senelet's surefooted culinary mastery in such dishes as boar terrine with dried apricot and juniper berries. ✉ *Pl. Malmédy,* ☎ *03–80–24–03–82. Reservations essential. AE, DC, MC, V. Closed Feb., early July, and Sun. No dinner Wed.*

$–$$ ★ ✕ **Le Gourmandin.** Chef Alain Billard and host Isabelle Crotet serve regional fare at their intimate bistro—pork shank and shoulder stewed with beans and cabbage, called *potée Bourguignonne,* is a delicious staple—and a good range of wines from small vineyards. ✉ *8 pl. Carnot,* ☎ *03–80–24–07–88. MC, V. Nov.–Feb., closed Tues., no lunch Wed.; Mar.–Oct., closed Tues., no dinner Mon.; Jan.–Feb. variable.*

$$ 🏨 **Hôtel de la Cloche.** In the heart of town, this welcoming hotel in a 15th-century residence has neat rooms decorated with care. The best have full baths; the smaller, delightful attic rooms have shower only. ✉ *40–42 rue Faubourg-Madeleine, 21200,* ☎ *03–80–24–66–33,* FAX *03–80–24–04–24. 22 rooms. Restaurant. AE, MC, V. Closed late Dec.–mid-Jan.*

Cluny

Famous for its medieval abbey, which represented the finest flowering of the Romanesque style, Cluny was once the center of a vast Christian empire. Founded in the 10th century, the **Ancienne Abbaye** (Old Abbey) was the biggest church in Europe until the 16th century, when St. Peter's was built in Rome. Now in ruins, it still gives an idea of its original grandeur. The **Clocher de l'Eau-Bénite,** a majestic bell tower, crowns the only remaining part of the abbey church, the south transept. The 13th-century **farinier** (flour mill) has a fine oak and chestnut roof and a collection of Romanesque capitals from the vanished choir. The **Musée Ochier,** in the abbatial palace, contains Europe's foremost Romanesque lapidary museum. Vestiges of both the abbey and the village constructed around it are conserved here, as well as part of the *bibliothèque des moines* (monks' library). ☎ *03–85–59–12–79.* ⏲ *Abbey and museum Nov.–mid-Feb., daily 10–noon and 2–4; mid-Feb.–Mar., daily 10–noon and 2–5; Apr.–June, daily 9:30–noon and 2–6; July–Aug., daily 9–7; Sept., daily 9–6; Oct., daily 9:30–noon and 2–5.*

$$$ ✕ **Bourgogne.** The old-fashioned hotel building, dating from 1817, stands where other parts of the abbey used to be. It has a small garden and an atmospheric restaurant serving comfort cuisine, such as *volaille de Bresse au Noilly et morilles* (Bresse chicken with Noilly Prat and morilles). (Lunch is not served on Tuesday and Wednesday.) ✉ *Pl. de l'Abbaye, 71250,* ☎ *03–85–59–00–58,* FAX *03–85–59–03–73. 15 rooms. Restaurant. AE, DC, MC, V. Closed mid-Nov.–early Mar.*

Lyon

Numbers in the margin correspond to points of interest on the Lyon map.

Lyon, one of France's "second" cities, is easily accessible by car or train. Much of the city has an enchanting air of untroubled prosperity, and the dining choices are plentiful. It's easy to walk its pedestrian streets and explore its sights. If you have a few days, you can visit Vieux Lyon (Old Lyon) on the western bank of the Saône River; the old Roman district of Fourvière above it; and La Presqu'île between the Saône and the Rhône, which is the main downtown area, with shops, restaurants, bars, and theaters. For 90 frs you can purchase a three-day museum pass, the "Clés de Lyon."

It's easy to get around the city on the subway. A single ticket costs 8 frs/€1.22, a 10-ticket book 68 frs/€10.40. A day pass for bus and métro is 24 frs/€3.66 (available from bus drivers and machines in the métro).

1 The cliff-top silhouette of the **Basilique de Notre-Dame-de-Fourvière** is the city's most striking symbol: the 19th-century basilica is a mishmash of styles with an interior that's pure overkill. Climb the observatory heights for the view, instead, and then go to the nearby Roman remains. ✉ *Pl. de Fourvière.* ⏲ *Basilica daily 8–noon and 2–6. Observatory Easter–Oct., daily 10–noon and 2–6; Nov.–Easter, weekends 2–6.*

2 Two ruined, semicircular **Théâtres Romains** (Roman Theaters) are tucked into the hillside, just down from the summit of Fourvière. The **Grand Théâtre**, the oldest Roman theater in France, was built in 15 BC. The smaller **Odéon** was designed for music and poetry performances. ✉ *Colline Fourfière.* ⏲ *Daily 9 AM–dusk.*

3 At the **Musée de la Civilisation Gallo-Romaine** (Gallo-Roman Civilization Museum), statues, mosaics, vases, coins, and tombstones from Lyon's Roman precursors are on display. ✉ *17 rue Clébert,* ☎ *04–72–38–81–90.* ⏲ *Wed.–Sun. 9:30–noon and 2–6.*

4 Housed in the city's largest ensemble of Renaissance buildings, the **Musée Historique de Lyon** (Lyon Historical Museum) has a collection of medieval sculpture, furniture, pottery, paintings, and engravings. ✉ *1 pl. du Petit-Collège,* ☎ *04–78–42–03–61.* ⏲ *Wed.–Mon. 10:45–6.*

5 The best museum in Lyon is the **Musée des Beaux-Arts** (Fine Arts Museum). It houses sculpture, classical relics, and an extensive collection of Old Masters and Impressionists. ✉ *20 pl. des Terreaux,* ☎ *04–72–10–17–40.* ⏲ *Wed.–Sun. 10:30–6.*

6 The barrel-vaulted **Opéra de Lyon,** a reincarnation of a moribund 1831 building, was built in the early 1990s. It incorporates a columned exterior, soaring glass vaulting, neoclassical public spaces, and the latest backstage magic. ✉ *Pl. de la Comédie,* ☎ *04–72–00–45–00; 04–72–00–45–45 tickets.*

Basilique de Notre-Dame-de-Fourvière 1
Musée de la Civilisation Gallo-Romaine 3
Musée des Arts Décoratifs . . . 7
Musée des Beaux-Arts . . . 5
Musée Historique de Lyon 4
Musée Historique des Tissus . . . 8
Opéra de Lyon 6
Théâtres Romains 2

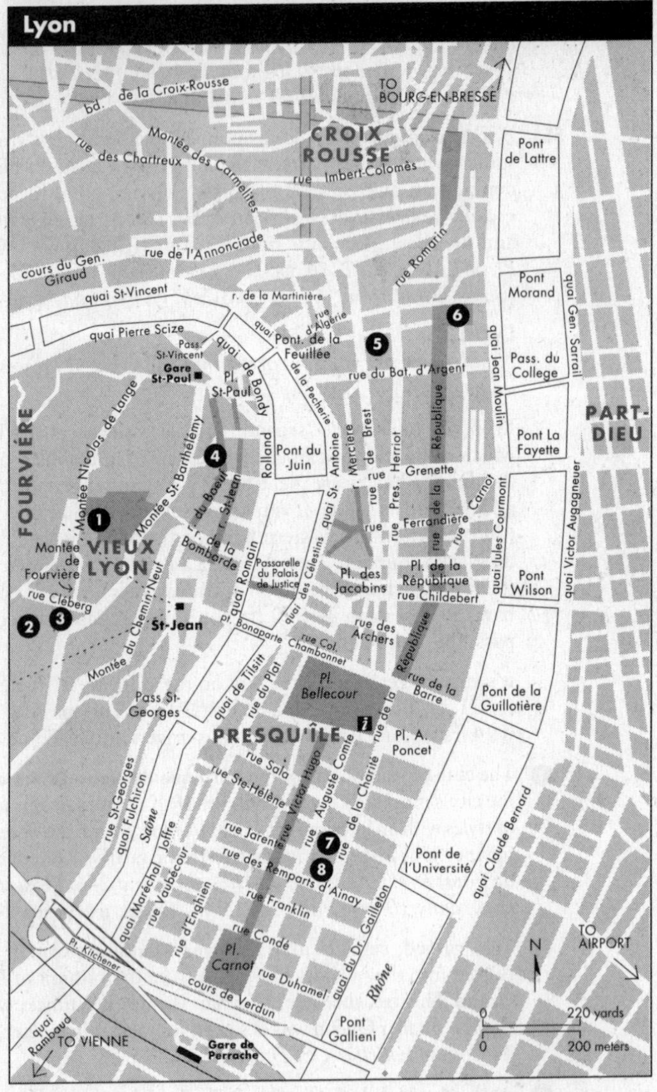

★ ❼ In an 18th-century mansion, the **Musée des Arts Décoratifs** (Decorative Arts Museum) has fine collections of silverware, furniture, objets d'art, porcelain, and tapestries. ✉ *34 rue de la Charité,* ☎ *04–78–38–42–00.* ⏲ *Tues.–Sun. 10–5:30.*

❽ On display at the **Musée Historique des Tissus** (Textile History Museum) is a fascinating exhibit of intricate carpets, tapestries, and silks (silk- and clothmaking made Lyon famous). ✉ *34 rue de la Charité,* ☎ *04–78–38–42–00.* ⏲ *Tues.–Sun. 10–5:30.*

$$$$ ★ ✕ **Léon de Lyon.** Chef Jean-Paul Lacombe's innovative uses of the region's butter, cream, and foie gras put this restaurant, in an old house, at the forefront of the city's gastronomic scene. ✉ *1 rue Pléney,* ☎ *04–72–10–11–12. Reservations essential. Jacket required. AE, MC, V. Closed Sun.–Mon. and early–late Aug.*

$$ ★ ✕ **Les Muses.** High up under the glass vault of the Opéra de Lyon is this small restaurant run by Philippe Chavent. The nouvelle cuisine is

excellent, especially the salmon in butter sauce with watercress mousse. The best value at dinner is the 159-fr menu. ✉ *Opéra de Lyon,* ☎ *04–72–00–45–58. Reservations essential. AE, MC, V.*

$ ✕ **Brunet.** Tables are crammed together in this tiny *bouchon* (tavern) with past menus inscribed on mirrors and a few photographs. The food is good, traditional Lyonnais fare. ✉ *23 rue Claudia,* ☎ *04–78–37–44–31. MC, V. Closed Sun.–Mon. and Aug.*

$$$$ ★ **La Cour des Loges.** Young Lyonnais architects teamed with Italian designers to transform four Renaissance mansions into one of Lyon's most stylish hotels. Rooms range from fairly small to comfortably large and are either classic or contemporary in design. ✉ *6 rue du Boeuf, 69005,* ☎ *04–72–77–44–44,* FAX *04–72–40–93–61. 63 rooms. Restaurant, bar. AE, DC, MC, V.*

$$–$$$ **Grand Hôtel des Beaux-Arts.** Half of the rooms at this hotel are "inspired worlds" where an artist has developed a theme through his paintings. Some rooms are traditionally furnished. ✉ *Rue du Président Édouard-Herriot, pl. des Jacobins, 69002,* ☎ *04–78–38–09–50,* FAX *04–78–42–19–19. 75 rooms. AE, DC, MC, V.*

$ **Bed et Breakfast à Lyon.** This nonprofit agency can house you for one night or several. The agency is open weekdays 9:30 AM–8 PM. ✉ *3 bis rue de la Garenne, 69005,* ☎ *04–72–16–95–01,* FAX *04–78–59–58–62. No credit cards.*

Burgundy and Lyon Essentials

AIR TRAVEL

AIRPORTS

The international airport for the region is in Satolas, 26 km (16 mi) east of Lyon. Air France and other major airlines have connecting services from Paris.

➤ AIRPORT INFORMATION: **Satolas** (☎ 04–72–22–72–21 flight information).

BUS TRAVEL

Plenty of private bus companies cover the region.

CAR TRAVEL

Larger towns can be reached by train, but to see smaller towns you need a car. A6 is the main route through the region (Lyon is 463 km/287 mi south of Paris). N6 is a slower, prettier option.

TOURS

Write to the Comité Régional de Tourisme (Regional Committee of Tourism) for information on regional tours using Dijon as a base, including wine tastings and visits to the famous religious sites. Contact the Comité Régional du Tourisme Rhône-Alpes (Regional Committee of Tourism for Rhône-Alpes) for information on Lyon (and the Alps).

➤ FEES AND SCHEDULES: **Comité Régional de Tourisme** (✉ B.P. 1602, 21035 Dijon). **Comité Régional du Tourisme Rhône-Alpes** (✉ 78 rte. de Paris, 69260 Charbonnières-les-Bains, ☎ 04–72–59–21–59).

TRAIN TRAVEL

The TGV to Lyon leaves from Paris (Gare de Lyon) hourly and arrives in just two hours. Six TGVs also go daily between Charles de Gaulle airport and Lyon. From Lyon there is frequent train service to other points. In addition, buses leave Lyon for smaller towns in the region. Dijon has two local train routes: one linking Sens, Joigny, Montbard, Dijon, Beaune, Chalon, Tournus, and Mâcon; and the other connecting Auxerre, Avallon, Clamecy, and Nevers.

➤ TRAIN INFORMATION: **SNCF** (☎ 08–36–35–35–35, WEB www.sncf.com).

VISITOR INFORMATION

➤ TOURIST INFORMATION: **Auxerre** (✉ 1 quai de la République, ☎ 03–86–52–06–19, WEB www.burgundy-tourism.com). **Beaune** (✉ rue de l'Hôtel-Dieu, ☎ 03–80–26–21–30, WEB www.beaune-burgundy.com). **Dijon** (✉ 29 pl. Darcy, ☎ 03–80–44–11–44, WEB www.ot-dijon.fr). **Lyon** (✉ pl. Bellecour, ☎ 04–72–77–69–69; ✉ av. Adolphe Max, near cathedral, ☎ 04–72–77–69–69; ✉ Perrache train station). **Sens** (✉ pl. Jean-Jaurès, ☎ 03–86–65–19–49).

PROVENCE

As you approach Provence there is a magical moment when the north is finally left behind: cypresses and red-tile roofs appear; you hear the jingling of cicadas and catch the scent of wild thyme and lavender—and all of this is against a backdrop of harsh, brightly lit landscapes that inspired the paintings of Paul Cézanne and Vincent van Gogh. Roman remains litter the ground in well-preserved profusion. The amphitheaters in Nîmes and Arles (both are still used for spectacles that include bullfighting), the aqueduct at Pont du Gard, and the mausoleum in St-Rémy-de-Provence are considered the best of their kind in existence.

A number of towns have grown up along the Rhône Valley owing to its historical importance as a communications artery. The biggest is bustling Marseille, but Avignon and Arles have more picturesque charm. North of Marseille lies Aix-en-Provence, with an old-time elegance that reflects its former role as regional capital. Extending the traditional boundaries of Provence westward, historic Nîmes has been included. The Côte d'Azur is also part of this region but has an identity of its own.

Avignon

A warren of medieval alleys nestling behind a protective ring of stocky towers, Avignon is where seven exiled popes camped between 1309 and 1377 after fleeing from the corruption of Rome. The dominant ★ building within the town walls is the colossal **Palais des Papes** (Papal Palace). It's really two buildings: the severe **Palais Vieux** (Old Palace), built between 1334 and 1342 by Pope Benedict XII, a member of the Cistercian order, which frowned on frivolity; and the more decorative **Palais Nouveau** (New Palace), built in the following decade by the arty, lavish Pope Clement VI. Magnificent frescoes relieve the austere stone, stripped during the Revolution. ✉ *Pl. du Palais-des-Papes,* ☎ *04–90–27–50–00.* ⊙ *Apr.–July and Oct., daily 9–7; Aug.–Sept., daily 8–7; Nov.–Mar., daily 9:30–5:45.*

The 12th-century **cathédrale** near the Palais des Papes contains the Gothic tomb of Pope John XII. Beyond the cathedral is the **Rocher des Doms** (Bluff of the Doms), a large park from which there are fine views of the town and the river.

The medieval **Petit Palais** (Small Palace) was once home to cardinals and archbishops. Nowadays it contains an outstanding collection of Old Masters. ✉ *21 pl. du Palais,* ☎ *04–90–86–44–58.* ⊙ *Sept.–June, Wed.–Mon. 9:30–noon and 2–6; July–Aug., Wed.–Mon. 10:30–6.*

The 12th-century **Pont St-Bénezet** (St. Bénezet Bridge)—the "pont d'Avignon" of nursery-song fame—is an easy walk from the Petit Palais if you want a demi-inspection of the bridge (only half of it remains). Pick up a cassette tour at the Palais des Papes. ✉ *Port du Rocher,* ☎ *04–90–27–50–00.* ⊙ *Apr.–July and Oct., daily 9–7; Aug.–Sept., daily 8–8; Nov.–Mar., daily 9:30–5:45.*

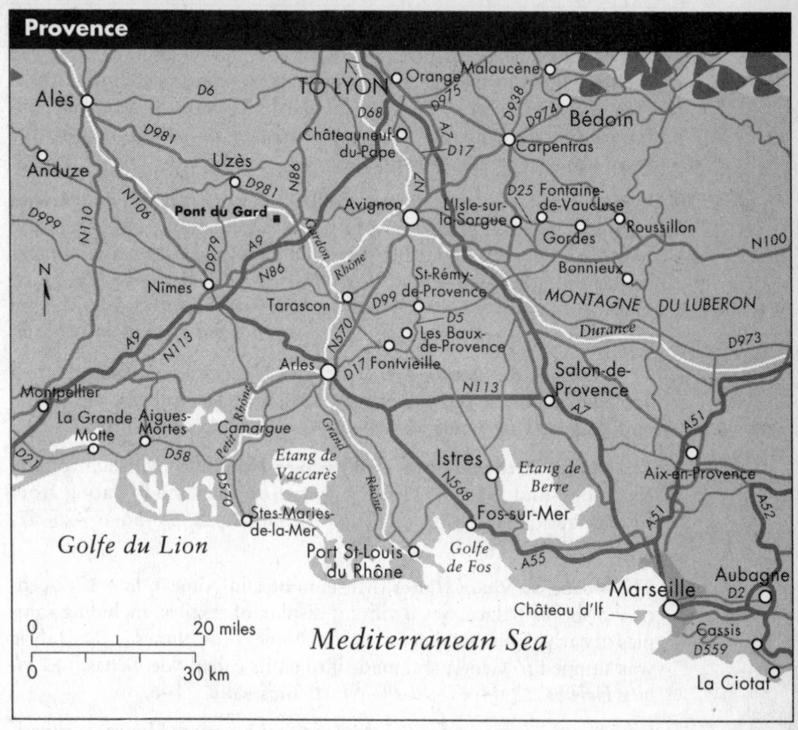

The **Musée Calvet,** an 18th-century Palladian-style manor, contains an extensive collection of mainly French paintings from the 16th century on. ✉ *65 rue Joseph-Vernet,* ☎ *04–90–86–33–84.* ⏲ *Wed.–Mon. 10–noon and 2–6.*

$$ ★ ✕ **La Cuisine de Reine.** Glassed into a white-stone cloister, this chic bistro offers a commedia dell'arte decor and a young, laid-back waitstaff. The blackboard lists eclectic dishes: duck in rosemary honey, and rosy herbed lamb chops. On Saturday, join the cashmere-and-loafer set for the 120-fr brunch buffet. ✉ *83 rue Joseph-Vernet,* ☎ *04–90–85–99–04. AE, DC, MC, V. Closed Sun.*

$$$$ ★ ✕🏨 **Hôtel de la Mirande.** Rich with exquisite reproduction fabrics and beeswaxed antiques, this design-mag dream of a hotel is just below the Papal Palace. Its enclosed garden is a breakfast and dinner oasis, and its central lounge is a skylit and jazz-warmed haven. Rooms are both gorgeous and comfy. ✉ *Pl. de la Mirande, 84000,* ☎ *04–90–85–93–93,* FAX *04–90–86–26–85. 19 rooms, 1 suite. Restaurant, bar. AE, DC, MC, V.*

$$ 🏨 **Hôtel du Blauvac.** Just off rue de la République and place de l'Horloge, this 17th-century nobleman's home has been divided into guest rooms. Many have exposed stonework, aged-oak detailing, and tall windows that look, alas, onto backstreet walls. Pretty fabrics and a warm, familial welcome more than compensate, however. ✉ *11 rue de la Bancasse, 84000,* ☎ *04–90–86–34–11,* FAX *04–90–86–27–41. 16 rooms. Breakfast room. AE, DC, MC, V.*

Pont du Gard

Twenty minutes west of Avignon looms the well-preserved Pont du Gard, a huge, three-tier aqueduct erected 2,000 years ago as part of a 48-km (30-mi) canal supplying water to Roman Nîmes. Its setting, spanning a rocky gorge 150 ft above the Gardon River, is nothing less than spectacular.

Nîmes

Though it's a feisty rat-race of a town today, few cities have preserved such visible links with their Roman past as Nîmes, which lies 20 km (12½ mi) southwest of the Pont du Gard (via N86). A three-day, 60-fr "passport," available from the tourist office, admits you to the town's museums and monuments.

★ In the heart of downtown Nîmes, the flawlessly preserved Roman **Arènes** (Arena) has a seating capacity of 21,000. An inflatable roof covers it in winter for concerts and exhibitions; bullfights and tennis tournaments are held in it in summer. ✉ *Bd. Victor-Hugo,* ☎ *04–66–67–29–11.* ⏲ *May–Sept., daily 9–6:30; Oct.–Apr., daily 9–noon and 2–5:30. Closed during concerts and férias (festivals), mid-Feb, end of May, end of Sept.*

At the **Musée des Beaux-Arts** (Fine Arts Museum), you can admire a vast Roman mosaic and works by Poussin, Brueghel, Rubens, and Rodin. ✉ *Rue de la Cité-Foulc,* ☎ *04–66–67–38–21.* ⏲ *Tues.–Sun. 11–6.*

The **Musée Archéologique et d'Histoire Naturelle** (Museum of Archaeology and Natural History) is rich in local finds dating from Roman antiquity. ✉ *Bd. de l'Amiral-Courbet,* ☎ *04–66–67–25–57.* ⏲ *Tues.–Sun. 11–6.*

The **Musée du Vieux Nîmes** (Museum of Old Nîmes), in a 17th-century bishop's palace, has a vibrant display of textiles, including samples of early denim, which came from Nîmes ("de Nîmes"). The fabric was shipped to Genoa and made into pants called "de Gênes." ✉ *Pl. aux Herbes,* ☎ *04–66–36–00–64.* ⏲ *Tues.–Sun. 11–6.*

Smack in the town center, the **Maison Carrée** (Square House), a superb Roman temple dating from the 1st century AD, is now a gallery for tiny exhibitions. So classically delightful are the lines of this temple that Thomas Jefferson had it copied for Virginia's state capitol. ✉ *Bd. Victor-Hugo.* ⏲ *May–Oct., daily 9–7; Nov.–Apr., daily 9–noon and 2–6.*

$ ★ ✕ **Chez Jacotte.** Duck into an Old Town back alley and into this cross-vaulted grotto that embodies Nîmes's Spanish-bohemian flair. Watch for blackboard specials such as scrambled eggs with truffles and asparagus. ✉ *15 rue Fresque (Impasse),* ☎ *04–66–21–64–59. MC, V. Closed Sun.–Mon. No lunch Sat.*

$$ **La Baume.** In the heart of scruffy Old Nîmes, this noble 17th-century *hôtel particulier* (mansion) has been reincarnated as a stylish hotel. The stenciled beam ceilings, cross vaults, and archways counterbalance hot ocher tones, swagged raw cotton, leather, and halogen lights. ✉ *21 rue Nationale, 30000,* ☎ *04–66–76–28–42,* FAX *04–66–76–28–45. 33 rooms. AE, DC, MC, V.*

Arles

Charming little Arles was once considered the "Rome of the North"—thanks to the many structures built here by the ancient Romans—and it was later home to both Gauguin and van Gogh. For 55 frs/€8.39 you can purchase a joint ticket to all the monuments and museums.

The town's most notable sight is the 26,000-capacity **Arènes** (Arena), built in the 1st century AD for circuses and gladiator combats. ✉ *Rond-Point des Arènes,* ☎ *04–90–49–36–74.* ⏲ *Apr.–Sept. daily 9–7; Oct.–Mar. daily 10–4:30.*

Close by are the scanty remains of Arles's **Théâtre Antique** (Roman Theater); the bits of marble columns scattered around the grassy enclosure hint poignantly at the theater's onetime grandeur. ✉ *Rue du Cloître,* ☎ *04–90–49–36–74.* ⏲ *Apr.–Sept., daily 9–7; Oct.–Mar., daily 10–4:30.*

The **Museon Arlaten,** housed in a 16th-century mansion, displays costumes and headdresses, puppets, and waxworks. They were all lovingly assembled by the great 19th-century Provençal poet Frédéric Mistral. ✉ *29 rue de la République,* ☎ *04–90–93–58–11.* ⏲ *Apr.–Sept., daily 9:30–12:30; Oct.–Mar., daily 10–12:30 and 2–5:30.*

★ Classed as a world treasure by UNESCO because of its magnificent portal sculpture, the extraordinary Romanesque **Église St-Trophime** (✉ pl. de la République) dates from the 11th century.

★ Tucked discreetly behind St-Trophime is a peaceful haven, the **Cloître St-Trophime** (St. Trophime Cloister). A Romanesque treasure worthy of the church, it is one of the loveliest cloisters in Provence. ☎ *04–90–49–36–74.* ⏲ *Apr.–Sept., daily 9–7; Oct.–Mar., daily 10–4:30.*

The fountains of the **Jardin d'Hiver** (Winter Garden) figure in several of van Gogh's paintings. Firebrand Dutchman Vincent van Gogh produced much of his best work—and chopped off the lobe of his ear—in Arles during a frenzied 15-month spell (1888–90) just before his suicide at 37. Markers throughout Arles note settings he painted. ✉ *East end of bd. des Luces.*

Alongside the Rhône and a little to the west of downtown is the modern, high-concept **Musée de l'Arles Antique** (Museum of Arles Antiquities), displaying historical artifacts excavated in the region of Arles. ✉ *Presque'île du Cirque Romain, south side of town (across N113), by the Rhône,* ☎ *04–90–18–88–88.* ⏲ *Mar.–Oct., daily 9–7; Nov.–Feb., daily 10–5.*

$ ✕ **L'Affenage.** A smorgasbord of Provençal hors d'oeuvres draws loyal locals to this former fire-horse shed. They come here for heaping plates of fried eggplant, tapenade, chickpeas in cumin, and lamb chops grilled in the great stone fireplace. ✉ *4 rue Molière,* ☎ *04–90–96–07–67. AE, MC, V. Closed Sun. and 3 wks in Aug. No dinner Wed.*

$$$$ ★ 🏨 **Nord-Pinus.** J. Peterman would feel right at home in this quintessentially Mediterranean hotel on place du Forum; Hemingway did. Travel relics, kilims, oil jars, wrought iron, and colorful ceramics create a richly atmospheric stage set. ✉ *Pl. du Forum, 13200,* ☎ *04–90–93–44–44,* FAX *04–90–93–34–00,* WEB *www.nord-pinus.com. 25 rooms. Brasserie, bar. AE, DC, MC, V.*

$$$ 🏨 **Arlatan.** Once home to the counts of Arlatan, this 15th-century stone house stands on the site of a 4th-century basilica, and a glass floor reveals the excavated vestiges under the lobby. Rows of rooms—each decorated with a chic, light hand—horseshoe around a lovely fountain courtyard. Seven new garden rooms have modern decor, and a pool is in the works. ✉ *26 rue du Sauvage, 13200,* ☎ *04–90–93–56–66,* FAX *04–90–49–68–45,* WEB *www.hotel-arlatan.fr/caht1.htm. 37 rooms, 7 suites. AE, DC, MC, V.*

$ ★ 🏨 **Le Clo'tre.** Built as a private home for the head of the Cloisters, this grand old medieval building has luckily fallen into the hands of a friendly couple devoted to making the most of its historic details. ✉ *16 rue du Cloitre, 13200,* ☎ *04–90–96–29–50,* FAX *04–90–96–02–88. 30 rooms. AE, MC, V.*

St-Rémy-de-Provence

Something felicitous has happened in this market town—a steady infusion of style, of art, of imagination—all brought by people with a respect for local traditions and a love of Provençal ways. Here more than anywhere you can meditate quietly on antiquity, browse through redolent markets with basket in hand, peer down the very row of plane trees you remember from a Van Gogh, and also enjoy urbane galleries, cosmopolitan shops, and specialty food boutiques.

Founded in the 6th century BC, St-Rémy-de-Provence was known as Glanum to the Greeks and Romans. Its Roman **Mausolée** (Mausoleum) was erected around 20 BC to the memory of Caius and Lucius Caesar, grandsons of the emperor Augustus. The **Arc Triomphal** (Triumphal Arch) is a few decades younger but has suffered more heavily than the mausoleum. All who crossed the Alps entered Roman Glanum through this gate, decorated with reliefs of battle scenes depicting Caesar's defeat and the capture of the Gauls. Excavations of **Glanum** began in 1921, and much of the Greek and Roman towns has now been unearthed. The remains are less spectacular than the arch and mausoleum, but are still fascinating. ✉ *Off D5, toward Les Baux,* ☎ *04–90–92–64–04.* ⏲ *Apr.–Sept., daily 9–7; Oct.–Mar., daily 9–noon and 2–5.*

You can examine many of the finds from Glanum—statues, pottery, and jewelry—at the **Musée Archéologique** (Archaeology Museum) in the center of St-Rémy. ✉ *Hôtel de Sade, rue Parage,* ☎ *04–90–92–64–04.* ⏲ *Feb.–Mar. and Oct., Tues.–Sun. 10–noon and 2–5; Apr.–Sept., Tues.–Sun. 10–noon and 2–6; Nov.–Dec., Wed. and weekends 10–noon and 2–5.*

$–$$ ★ ✕ **Le Bistrot des Alpilles.** This landmark institution still draws a loyal international set for classic regional specialties discreetly and unpretentiously served: *brandade gratiné* (salt-cod pestled and browned), leg of lamb, and fresh fruit tarts. ✉ *15 bd. Mirabeau,* ☎ *04–90–92–09–17. AE, MC, V. Closed late Jan.–early Feb.*

$$$$ ✕🏨 **Domaine de Valmouraine.** In this genteel inn on a broad park, overstuffed English-country decor mixes cozily with cool Provençal stone and timber. The restaurant features fresh game, seafood, local oils, and truffles. English owner Judith McHugo makes clients feel like weekend guests in a manor house. ✉ *Petite rte. des Baux (D27), 13210,* ☎ *04–90–92–44–62,* FAX *04–90–92–37–32. 14 rooms. Restaurant, pool. AE, DC, MC, V.*

$$ ★ ✕🏨 **Château de Roussan.** In a majestic landmark park, this extraordinary 18th-century château is being valiantly preserved by managers without a rich owner to back them. Glorious period furnishings are buttressed with bric-a-brac, and the bathrooms have an afterthought air. There are more cats and dogs than staff—but lovers of atmosphere will blossom in this three-dimensional costume-drama. ✉ *Petite rte. de Tarascon, 13210,* ☎ *04–90–92–11–63,* FAX *04–90–92–50–59. 22 rooms. Restaurant. AE, DC, MC, V.*

Gordes

Gordes was once an unknown, unspoiled hilltop village; it has now become a famous, unspoiled hilltop village surrounded by luxury vacation homes, modern hotels, restaurants, and B&Bs. No matter: the ancient stone village still rises above the valley in painterly hues of honey gold. The only way to see the interior of the **château** is to view its ghastly collection of photo paintings by pop artist Pol Mara, who lived in Gordes. ☎ *04–90–72–02–75.* ⏲ *Wed.–Mon. 10–noon and 2–6.*

$$$ 🏨 **Domaine de l'Enclos.** This cluster of stone cottages overlooking the arid hills offers privacy and autonomy as well as a warm welcome. Antique tiles and fresh faux-patinas keep it looking fashionably old. The atmosphere is surprisingly warm and familial for an inn of this sophistication. ✉ *Rte. de Sénanque, 84220,* ☎ *04–90–72–71–00,* FAX *04–90–72–03–03. 7 rooms, 6 apartments. Restaurant, pool. AE, MC, V.*

Aix-en-Provence

★ Few towns are as well preserved as the traditional capital of Provence: elegant Aix-en-Provence, birthplace of the Impressionist Paul Cézanne (1839–1906) and the novelist Émile Zola (1840–1902). The celebrated, graceful, lively avenue **cours Mirabeau** is the town's nerve center. It divides Old Aix in half, with narrow medieval streets to the north and 18th-century mansions to the south.

The sumptuous Hôtel Boyer d'Éguilles, erected in 1675, is worth a visit for its fine woodwork and murals, but is best known as the **Muséum d'Histoire Naturelle** (Natural History Museum). The highlight is the rare collection of dinosaur eggs. ✉ *6 rue Espariat,* ☎ *04–42–26–23–67.* ⏲ *Sept.–May, daily 10–noon and 1–5; June–Aug., daily 10–6.*

The evocative architectural mishmash that is **Cathédrale St-Sauveur** (✉ rue Gaston-de-Saporta) houses the remarkable 15th-century *Tryptique du Buisson Ardent* (Burning Bush Triptych) by Nicolas Froment, now open to viewing only on Tuesday afternoons.

The Archbishop's Palace, next to the cathedral, is now home to the **Musée des Tapisseries** (Tapestry Museum). Its highlight is a magnificent series of 17 tapestries made in Beauvais that date, like the palace itself, from the 17th and 18th centuries. ✉ *28 pl. des Martyrs de la Résistance,* ☎ *04–42–23–09–91.* ⏲ *Wed.–Mon. 10–noon and 2–5:45.*

The **Musée du Vieil Aix** (Museum of Old Aix), in a 17th-century mansion, displays an eclectic assortment of local treasures, from faience to *santons* (terra-cotta figurines). ✉ *17 rue Gaston-de-Saporta,* ☎ *04–42–21–43–55.* ⏲ *Apr.–Oct., Tues.–Sun. 10–noon and 2–6:30; Nov.–Mar., Tues.–Sun. 10–noon and 2–5.*

At the **Musée-Atelier de Paul Cézanne** (Cézanne's Studio) no major pictures are on display, but his studio remains as he left it at the time of his death in 1906, top coat, bowler hat, ginger jar, and all. ✉ *9 av. Paul-Cézanne,* ☎ *04–42–21–06–53.* ⏲ *Daily 10–noon and 2–6.*

A precious few of Cézanne's oils and watercolors can be found at the **Musée Granet.** ✉ *13 rue Cardinale,* ☎ *04–42–38–14–70.* ⏲ *Wed.–Mon. 10–noon and 2–6.*

$$$ ★ ✕ **Le Clos de la Violette.** Aix's best restaurant lies north of town in a residential district near the Cézanne atelier. Chef Jean-Marc Banzo uses only fresh, local ingredients in his nouvelle and traditional recipes. The weekday lunch menu is more moderately priced. ✉ *10 av. de la Violette,* ☎ *04–42–23–30–71. AE, MC, V. Closed Sun. No lunch Mon.*

$$ ✕ **Brasserie Les Deux Garcons.** There's standard brasserie fare here—stick to the shellfish or the smoked-duck salad—but eating isn't what you come here for. It's the linen-decked sidewalk tables facing onto the cours Mirabeau, and the white-swathed waiters snaking between the chairs that creates the laid-back allure here. ✉ *53 cours Mirabeau,* ☎ *04–42–26–00–51. MC, V.*

$$–$$$ 🏨 **Nègre-Coste.** This elegant 18th-century town house has luxurious Old World decor downstairs, and a long-overdue redecoration has left rooms upstairs with fresh tiled bathrooms and a new Provençal look. And where else can you lean over the cours Mirabeau with your morning café-crème in hand? ✉ *33 cours Mirabeau, 13100,* ☎ *04–42–27–74–22,* FAX *04–42–26–80–93. 37 rooms. AE, DC, MC, V.*

$–$$ ★ 🏨 **Quatre Dauphins.** In a noble hôtel particulier in the quiet Mazarin quarter, this modest but impeccable lodging has pretty, comfortable little rooms spruced up with Provençal decor. ✉ *55 rue Roux Alphéran, 13100,* ☎ *04–42–38–16–39,* FAX *04–42–38–60–19. 13 rooms. MC, V.*

Marseille

Much maligned, Marseille is often given wide berth by travelers. Their loss—the city is an eyepopper: its cubist jumbles of blinding-white stone rise up over a picture-book seaport crowned by larger-than-life neo-Byzantine churches (immortalized by Hollywood in the 1962 Leslie Caron film *Fanny*), while the labyrinthine Old Town is painted in broad strokes of saffron and robin's-egg blue. Feisty and fond of broad gestures, Marseille is a dynamic city, as cosmopolitan now as when the Phocaeans first founded it.

The picturesque **Vieux Port** (Old Harbor) is the heart of Marseille; avenue Canebière leads to the water's edge. A short way down the quay on the right (as you look out to sea) is the elegant 17th-century **Hôtel de Ville** (Town Hall). The Maison Diamantée, behind the Town Hall, is a 16th-century mansion housing the **Musée du Vieux Marseille** (Old Marseille Museum), displaying local costumes, pictures, and figurines. ✉ *2 rue de la Prison,* ☎ *04–91–13–89–00.* ⏲ *Call for hrs.*

Against the backdrop of industrial docks, the various domes of Marseille's pompous, striped neo-Byzantine **Cathédrale de la Major** (✉ Esplanade de la Tourette) look utterly incongruous. Too bad Napoléon III chopped down part of the original Romanesque treasury next door to make room; this, thank heaven, is now being restored and rebuilt.

The grid of narrow, tumbledown streets leading off rue du Panier is called simply Le Panier (The Basket). Apart from the ambience, Le Panier is worth visiting for the elegantly restored 17th-century hospice now known as the **Centre de la Vieille Charité** (Center of the Old Charity). It now houses a top-drawer archaeology museum. ✉ *2 rue de la Charité,* ☎ *04–91–14–58–80.* ⏲ *May–Sept., Tues.–Sun. 11–6; Oct.–Apr., Tues.–Sun. 10–5.*

The church of **Notre-Dame de la Garde,** with its great gilded statue of the Virgin, stands sentinel high over the old port below. Naif ex-votos displayed inside are the main draw. Hike to the top or take Bus 60 from cours Jean-Ballard. ✉ *Pl. du Colonel-Edon,* ☎ *04–91–13–40–80.* ⏲ *May–Sept., daily 7 AM–8 PM; Oct.–Apr., daily 7–7.*

Take time to drive the scenic 5-km (3-mi) coast road (corniche du Président-J.-F.-Kennedy) and stop at the magical **Vallon des Auffes,** a tiny castaway fishing port typical of greater Marseille. From the corniche du Président-J.-F.-Kennedy there are breathtaking views across the sea toward the rocky **Îles de Frioul,** which can be visited by ferries that leave from Vieux Port frequently throughout the day. On one, the **Chateau d'If** was the very real prison to the fictional Count of Monte Cristo.

$ ✕ **Étienne.** This tiny Le Panier hole-in-the-wall has more than just a good fresh-anchovy pizza from the wood-burning oven. There is also fried squid, a slab of rare-grilled beef, and the quintessential *pieds et paquets,* Marseille's earthy classic of sheep's feet and stuffed tripe. ✉ *43 rue de la Lorette,* ☎ *no phone. No credit cards.*

$$$ ★ **Mercure Beauvau Vieux Port.** Real antiques, burnished wood, a touch of brass, and deep carpet underfoot give this intimate urban hotel genuine Old World charm—and you can't beat the views from port-side balconies. ✉ *4 rue Beauvau, 13001,* ☎ *04–91–54–91–00; 800/637–2873 for U.S. reservations,* FAX *04–91–54–15–76. 71 rooms. Bar. AE, DC, MC, V.*

Provence Essentials

BUS TRAVEL

All the major centers—Avignon, Arles, Nimes, Aix-en-Provence—are connected by bus lines; some of these routes venture out to neighboring villages.

CAR TRAVEL

Provence's key attractions are not far apart. Traveling by car is the most rewarding way to get around, especially if you want to go to the smaller villages and explore the landscape. Speedy highways descend from Lyon and split at Orange to go to Nîmes and Montpellier or Aix-en-Provence and Marseille en route to the Côte d'Azur.

TOURS

The tourist offices in many towns, including Nîmes, Avignon, Aix-en-Provence, and Marseille, give walking tours.

TRAIN TRAVEL

If you're limited to public transportation, Avignon makes the best base for both train and bus connections. Avignon is where the TGV from Paris and Lyon splits for either the run down to Marseille or to Montpellier. From Marseille, trains run along the coast to Nice and Monaco.

➤ TRAIN INFORMATION: **SNCF** (☎ 08–36–35–35–35, WEB www.sncf.com).

VISITOR INFORMATION

➤ TOURIST INFORMATION: **Aix-en-Provence** (✉ 2 pl. du Général-de-Gaulle, ☎ 04–42–16–11–61). **Arles** (✉ esplanade Charles-de-Gaulle, ☎ 04–90–18–41–21). **Avignon** (✉ 41 cours Jean-Jaurès, ☎ 04–90–82–65–11). **Marseille** (✉ 4 La Canebière, ☎ 04–91–13–89–00). **Nîmes** (✉ 6 rue Auguste, ☎ 04–66–67–29–11). **St-Rémy-de-Provence** (✉ pl. Jean Jaurés, ☎ 04–90–92–05–22).

THE CÔTE D'AZUR

Few places in the world have the same pull on the imagination as France's fabled Côte d'Azur, the Mediterranean coastline stretching from St-Tropez in the west to Menton on the Italian border. Cooled by the Mediterranean in the summer and warmed by it in winter, the climate is almost always pleasant. Avoid the area in July and August, however, unless you love crowds.

The Côte d'Azur's coastal resorts may live exclusively for the tourist trade and have often been ruined by high-rises, but the hinterlands remain relatively untarnished. The little villages perched high on the hills behind medieval ramparts seem to belong to another century. One of them, St-Paul-de-Vence, is the home of the Maeght Foundation, one of the world's leading museums of modern art. Artists have played a considerable role in popular conceptions of the Côte d'Azur, and their presence is reflected in the number of art museums: the Musée Picasso in Antibes, the Musée Renoir and the Musée d'Art Moderne Méditerranée in Cagnes-sur-Mer, the Musée Jean Cocteau in Menton, and entire museums devoted to Chagall and Matisse in Nice.

Although the tiny principality of Monaco, which lies between Nice and Menton, is a sovereign state, with its own army and police force, its language, food, and way of life are French—but with a strong Italian accent.

The distance between St-Tropez and the border with Italy is only 120 km (75 mi), so most places are, in fact, within a day's journey. For the drama of mountains and sea, take one of the famous Corniche roads, which traverse the coastline at various heights over the Mediterranean from Nice to the Italian frontier.

St-Tropez

St-Tropez was just another pretty fishing village until it was "discovered" in the 1950s by the "beautiful people," a fast set of film stars, starlets, and others who scorned bourgeois values while enjoying bourgeois bank balances. Today, its summer population swells from 6,000 to 60,000, and the top hotels and nightclubs are jammed. In winter

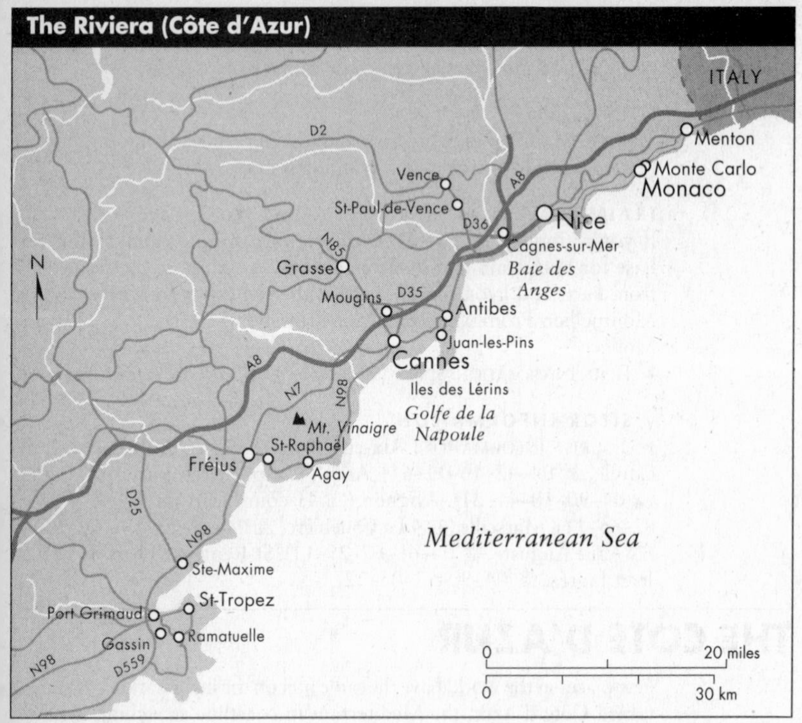

it's hard to find a restaurant open. The best times to visit, therefore, are early summer or fall. May and June are perhaps the best months, when the town lets its hair down during two local festivals.

The **Vieux Port** (Old Harbor) is the liveliest part of town, with plenty of outdoor cafés for good people-watching. Between the old and new harbors, in a cleverly converted chapel, is the **Musée de l'Annonciade** (Annunciation Museum), housing paintings by artists drawn to St-Tropez between 1890 and 1940, including Signac, Matisse, Derain, and Van Dongen. ✉ *Quai de l'Épi,* ☎ *04–94–97–04–01.* ⏲ *June–Sept., Wed.–Mon. 10–noon and 3–7; Oct.–May, Wed.–Mon. 10–noon and 2–6.*

Across place de l'Hôtel de Ville is the **Vieille Ville** (Old Town), where twisting streets, designed to break the impact of the terrible mistral (the cold, dry, northerly wind common to this region), open onto tiny ★ squares and fountains. The long climb up to the **Citadelle** rewards you with a splendid view across the gulf to Ste-Maxime, a quieter if heavily built-up and less posh family resort with a decent beach and reasonably priced hotels.

Easily visited from St-Tropez is the old Provençal town of **Ramatuelle** on a rocky spur 440 ft above the sea. Six kilometers (4 mi) north of Ramatuelle is the hilltop village of **Gassin,** a lovely place to escape the heat of the shoreline.

$$–$$$ ✕🏨 **La Résidence de la Pinède.** This balustraded white villa and its broad annex sprawl elegantly along a private waterfront (pay extra for a seaside room). The fair-sized rooms and sunny colors add to the charms of this resort. The restaurant features the skills of chef Herve Quesnel: truffle ravioli, sautéed prawns on basil-perfumed scrambled eggs, and fresh fig tarts. ✉ *Plage de la Bouillabaisse, 83991,* ☎ *04–94–55–*

91–00, FAX *04–94–97–73–64. 39 rooms, 4 suites. Restaurant, pool. AE, DC, MC, V. Closed mid-Oct.–Mar.*

Cannes

In 1834 a chance event was to change the town of Cannes forever. Lord Brougham, Britain's lord chancellor, was en route to Nice when an outbreak of cholera forced the authorities to freeze all travel. Trapped in Cannes, he fell in love with the place and built himself a house to use as an annual refuge from the British winter. The English aristocracy, czars, kings, and princes soon caught on, and Cannes became a community for the international elite. Grand palace hotels were built to cater to them, and Cannes came to symbolize dignified luxury. Today, Cannes is also synonymous with the International Film Festival.

Stroll along seafront **La Croisette,** an elegant promenade. Along the promenade are cafés, boutiques, and luxury hotels. Almost all beaches are private, but that doesn't mean you can't use them, only that you must pay for the privilege. Behind the promenade is the town and, beyond, the hills with the villas of the very rich. Only a few steps inland is the ★ Old Town, known as **Le Suquet,** with its steep, cobbled streets and its 12th-century watchtower.

$ ★ ✕ **Bouchon d'Objectif.** Popular and unpretentious, this tiny bistro serves inexpensive Provençale fare prepared with a sophisticated twist. An ever-changing display of photography adds a hip touch to the simple ocher-and-aqua setting. ✉ *10 rue Constantine,* ☎ *04–93–99–21–76. AE, MC, V. Closed Mon.*

$$$ **Majestic.** Of the luxury hotels lining La Croisette, this one has an air of aristocratic discretion (though prices are mega-deluxe). Rooms are spacious and traditional, though refreshingly pastel. ✉ *14 La Croisette, 06400,* ☎ *04–92–98–77–00,* FAX *04–93–38–97–90. 304 rooms. Restaurant, pool. AE, DC, MC, V. Closed mid-Nov.–Dec.*

$$ ★ **Molière.** Plush, intimate, and low-key, this low-price hotel has small rooms in cool shades of peach and indigo. Nearly all overlook a vast enclosed front garden. ✉ *5 rue Molière, 06400,* ☎ *04–93–38–16–16,* FAX *04–93–68–29–57. 42 rooms. AE, MC, V. Closed mid-Nov.–late Dec.*

$ **Albert Ier.** In a quiet residential area above the Forville market, this neo–Art Deco mansion is in a tiny enclosed garden. It's a 10-minute walk downhill to La Croisette and the beach. ✉ *68 av. de Grasse, 06400,* ☎ *04–93–39–24–04,* FAX *04–93–38–83–75. 11 rooms. MC, V.*

Antibes

On the east side of Cannes and Napoule Bay nestle Antibes and Juan-les-Pins, two villages that flow into one another with no perceptible boundary on either side of the peninsula, the Cap d'Antibes. Antibes, an older village, dates from the 4th century BC, when it was a Greek trading port. Every morning except Monday, the market on the Cours Masséna comes alive with exotic spices, hand-packed regional products, and colorful produce.

The Grimaldis, the family that rules Monaco, built the **Château Grimaldi** in the 12th century on the remains of a Roman camp. Today, the château's main attraction is the Musée Picasso (Picasso Museum), a bounty of the great artist's paintings, ceramics, and lithographs inspired by the sea and Greek mythology. ✉ *Pl. du Château,* ☎ *04–93–90–54–20.* ⏲ *June–Sept., Tues.–Sun. 10–6; Oct.–May, Tues.–Sun. 10–noon and 2–6.*

$$ ★ ✕ **Le Brûlot.** In this busy bistro, one street back from the market, chef Christian Blancheri hoists anything from suckling pigs to apple pies in and out of his roaring wood oven. ✉ *3 rue Frédéric-Isnard,* ☎ *04–93–34–17–76. MC, V. Closed Sun., last 2 wks of Aug., last wk Dec.–1st wk Jan. No lunch Sun.–Wed.*

$$$$ ★ **Belles Rives.** The home-away-from-home for F. Scott Fitzgerald and his wife Zelda (chums of the Murphys), this lovingly restored charmer proves that what's old is new again: this hotel's Neoclassic Moderne chic draws France's stylish young set. The terrace restaurant over the water is magical. ✉ *Bd. E.-Baudoin, 06160 Juan-les-Pins, Cap d'Antibes,* ☎ *04–93–61–02–73,* FAX *04–93–67–43–51. 42 rooms. Restaurant, bar, air-conditioning. AE, MC, V. Closed late-Oct.–mid-Apr.*

$$ **Le Mimosa.** The fabulous setting, in a hilltop garden studded with tall palms, mimosa, and tropical greenery, makes up for the hike down to the beach. Rooms are small and modestly decorated in Victorian florals, but ask for a balcony: many look over the garden and sizable pool. ✉ *Rue Pauline, Antibes 06160,* ☎ *04–93–61–04–16,* FAX *04–92–93–06–46. 34 rooms. Pool. MC, V. Closed Oct.–Apr.*

St-Paul-de-Vence

18 km (11 mi) north of Nice, 4 km (2 mi) south of Vence.

The most commercially developed of Provence's hilltop villages and second only to Mont-St-Michel for its influx of tourists, St-Paul is nonetheless a magical place when the crowds thin. Artists—Chagall, Bonnard, and Miró—were drawn to its light, its pure air, its wraparound views, and its honey-color stone walls. Film stars loved its lazy yet genteel ways, lingering on the garden-bower terrace of the famous inn of the Colombe d'Or, and challenging the locals to a game of pétanque under the shade of the plane trees.

★ Many people come to St-Paul just to visit the **Fondation Maeght,** founded in 1964 by art dealer Aimé Maeght. It's not just a small modern art museum but an extraordinary marriage of the arc-and-plane architecture of José Sert; the looming sculptures of Miró, Moore, and Giacometti; and a humbling hilltop setting of pines, vines, and flowing planes of water. ☎ *04–93–32–81–63.* ⏲ *July–Sept., daily 10–7; Oct.–June, daily 10–12:30 and 2:30–6.*

★ On the outskirts of Vence, toward St-Jeannet, the **Chapelle du Rosaire** (Chapel of the Rosary) was decorated with beguiling simplicity and clarity by Matisse between 1947 and 1951. "Despite its imperfections I think it is my masterpiece . . . the result of a lifetime devoted to the search for truth," wrote Matisse, who designed it when he was in his eighties and nearly blind. ✉ *Av. Henri-Matisse,* ☎ *04–93–58–03–26.* ⏲ *Tues. and Thurs. 10–11:30 and 2–5:30.*

$$$–$$$$ ✕ **Colombe d'Or.** This idyllic old auberge was the heart and soul of St-Paul's artistic revival, and the cream of 20th-century France lounged together under its fig trees—Picasso and Chagall, Maeterlinck and Kipling, Marcel Pagnol (*Manon des Sources*) and Jacques Prévert (*Les Enfants du Paradis*). Yves Montand and Simone Signoret met and married here, and current film stars make appearances from time to time. They do so more in homage to the inn's resonant history and *pastorale* atmosphere than for its food. ✉ *Pl. Général-de-Gaulle, 06570,* ☎ *04–93–32–80–02. AE, DC, MC, V. Closed mid-Nov.–late Dec.*

$$$$ ✕ **St-Paul.** Right in the center of the labyrinth of stone alleys, with views over the ancient ramparts, this luxurious inn (a Relais & Châteaux property) fills a noble 15th-century house with Provençal furniture, quarried stone, and lush fabrics. The restaurant, serving sophisticated regional specialties, is a cut above as well. (Off-season, the restaurant is closed Wednesday, and lunch is not served Thursday.) ✉ *86 rue Grande, 06570,* ☎ *04–93–32–65–25,* FAX *04–93–32–52–94. 18 rooms. Restaurant, bar, air-conditioning. AE, DC, MC, V. Closed early Jan.–mid-Feb.*

Nice

Numbers in the margin correspond to points of interest on the Nice map.

With a population of 350,000 and its own university, Nice is the undisputed capital of the Côte d'Azur. Founded by the Greeks as Nikaia, it has lived through several civilizations and was attached to France only in 1860. It consequently has a profusion of Greek, Italian, British, and French styles and a raffish, seductive charm. It also has a labyrinthine Old Town, an opera house, museums, and flourishing markets—all strung along an open stretch of pebble beach.

1 **Place Masséna** is a fine square built in 1815 to celebrate a local hero: one of Napoléon's most successful generals. Stroll through the Jardin
2 Albert to get to the **Promenade des Anglais** (English Promenade), built by the English community here in 1824. Nowadays dense traffic detracts from the peaceful setting, but it's a pleasant strand between town and sea with fine views of the Baie des Anges (Bay of Angels).

3 In the **Palais Masséna** (Masséna Palace) is a museum of city history with eclectic treasures ranging from Garibaldi's death sheet to Empress Josephine's tiara. ✉ *65 rue de France,* ☎ *04–93–88–11–34.* ⏲ *Call for hrs; renovations pending for a 2001 reopening.*

4 The **Musée des Beaux-Arts Jules-Chéret** (Jules Chéret Fine Arts Museum) was built in 1878 as a palatial mansion for a Russian princess. The rich collection has paintings by Sisley, Bonnard, and Vuillard; sculptures by Rodin; and ceramics by Picasso. ✉ *33 av. des Baumettes,* ☎ *04–92–15–28–28.* ⏲ *May–Sept., Tues.–Sun. 10–noon and 2–6; Oct.–Apr., Tues.–Sun. 10–noon and 2–5.*

The Cours Saleya flower market and the narrow streets in Vieux Nice (Old Nice) are the prettiest parts of town: while you're market-brows-
5 ★ ing, stop in to see the 18th-century **Chapelle de la Miséricorde** (Chapel of the Misericord), renowned for its ornate Baroque interior and sculpted decoration. At the northern end of the Old Town is the vast Italian-style
6 **Place Garibaldi**—all yellow-ocher buildings and formal fountains. The
7 imposing **Musée d'Art Modern** (Modern Art Museum), off Place Garibaldi, has an outstanding collection of French and international abstract and figurative art from the late 1950s onward. ✉ *Promenade des Arts,* ☎ *04–93–62–61–62.* ⏲ *Wed.–Mon. 11–6, Fri. 11–10.*

8 The **Musée National Message Biblique Chagall** (Marc Chagall Museum of Biblical Themes) has a superb, life-affirming collection of Chagall's (1887–1985) late works, including the 17 huge canvases of *The Message of the Bible,* which took 13 years to complete. ✉ *Av. du Dr-Ménard,* ☎ *04–93–53–87–20.* ⏲ *July–Sept., Wed.–Mon. 10–6; Oct.–June, Wed.–Mon. 10–5.*

9 A 17th-century Italian villa amid Roman remains contains the **Musée Matisse** (Matisse Museum), with paintings and bronzes by Henri Matisse (1869–1954), who lived nearly 40 years in Nice. ✉ *164 av. des Arènes-de-Cimiez,* ☎ *04–93–81–08–08.* ⏲ *Apr.–Sept., Wed.–Mon. 10–6; Oct.–Mar., Wed.–Mon. 10–5.*

10 Next door to the Matisse Museum, the **Musée Archéologique** (Archaeology Museum) displays finds from the Roman city that once flourished here. ☎ *04–93–81–59–57.* ⏲ *Apr.–Sept., Tues.–Sun. 10–noon and 2–6; Oct.–Mar., 10–1 and 2–5.*

$$ ★ ✕ **La Mérenda.** The back-to-bistro boom climaxed here when superstar chef Dominique Le Stanc took over this tiny, unpretentious landmark of Provençale cuisine. Now he and his wife work in the miniature open kitchen creating the ultimate versions of stuffed sardines, pistou,

Nice

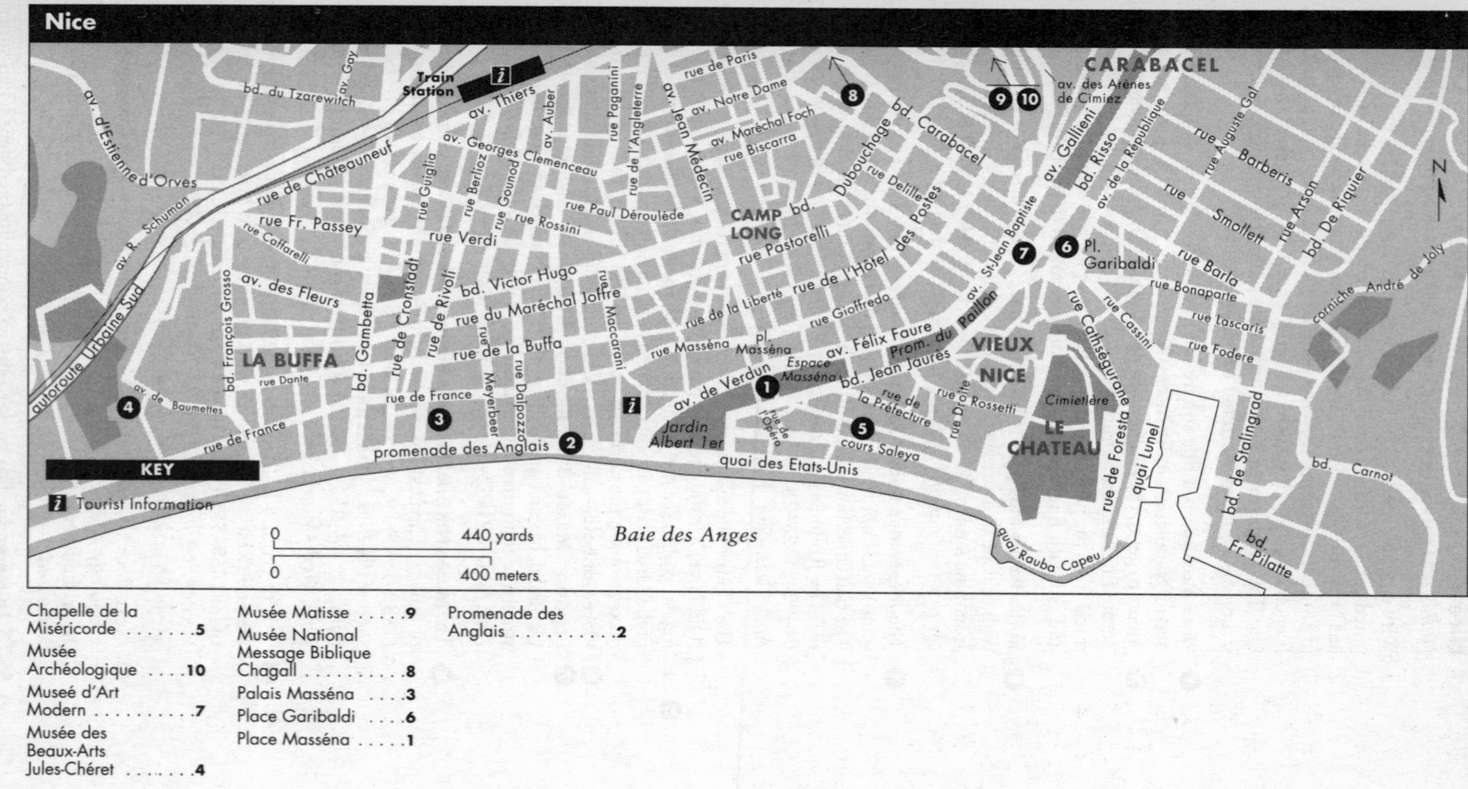

Chapelle de la Miséricorde 5
Musée Archéologique 10
Museé d'Art Modern 7
Musée des Beaux-Arts Jules-Chéret 4
Musée Matisse 9
Musée National Message Biblique Chagall 8
Palais Masséna 3
Place Garibaldi 6
Place Masséna 1
Promenade des Anglais 2

and slow-simmered *daubes* (beef stews). Stop by in person to reserve entry to the inner sanctum. ✉ *4 rue de la Terrasse,* ☎ *no phone. No credit cards. Closed weekends, last wk in July, and 1st 2 wks in Aug.*

$$ ★ **Windsor.** This is a memorably eccentric hotel with a vision: most of its white-on-white rooms either have frescoes of mythic themes or are works of artists' whimsy. But the real draw of this otherworldly place is its astonishing city-center garden. ✉ *11 rue Dalpozzo, 06000,* ☎ *04–93–88–59–35,* FAX *04–93–88–94–57. 57 rooms. Restaurant, bar, pool. AE, DC, MC, V.*

Monaco

Sixteen kilometers (10 mi) along the coast east of Nice lies tiny Monaco—tax-free haven for retired tennis stars, lucky billionaires, and one of the gaudiest royal families in Europe. As it is completely overbuilt with modern structures, it requires a fine eye to ferret out Monaco's legendary elegance of yesteryear. Though there is no frontier, it is a different country; when dialing numbers from outside Monaco, including France, you must prefix the call with "377."

For more than a century Monaco's livelihood was centered beneath the copper roof of its splendid **casino.** The oldest section dates from 1878 and was conceived by Charles Garnier, architect of the Paris opera house. ✉ *Pl. du Casino,* ☎ *92–16–21–21. Persons under 21 not admitted.* *European rooms 50 frs/€7.63; English Club and Monte-Carlo Sporting Club rooms 100 frs/€15; access to slot machines free.* ⏲ *Daily noon–4 AM.*

Monaco Town, the principality's Old Quarter, has many vaulted passageways and exudes an almost tangible medieval feel. The magnificent **Palais du Prince** (Prince's Palace), a grandiose Italianate structure with a Moorish tower, was largely rebuilt in the 19th century. The Grimaldi dynasty has lived and ruled here since 1297. The spectacle of the **Changing of the Guard** occurs each morning at 11:55; inside, guided tours take you through the state apartments (June-October only). In a wing of the palace with separate access, the **Palace Archives** and **Musée Napoléon** (Napoleonic Museum) remain open throughout the year. ✉ *Pl. du Palais,* ☎ *93–25–18–31.* ⏲ *Palais du Prince June–Oct., daily 9:30–6:30; Musée Napoléon and Palace Archives Tues.–Sun. 9:30–6:30.*

Monaco's **cathédrale** (✉ 4 rue Colonel Bellando de Castro) is a late-19th-century neo-Romanesque confection in which Philadelphia-born Princess Grace lies entombed in splendor along with other past members of the Grimaldi dynasty.

At the **Musée Océanographique** (Oceanography Museum), also an internationally renowned research institute founded by Prince Albert and run for years by underwater explorer Jacques Cousteau (1910–97), the aquarium is the undisputed highlight. ✉ *Av. St-Martin,* ☎ *93–15–36–00.* ⏲ *July–Aug., daily 9–8; Sept. and Apr.–June, daily 9–7; Oct.–Mar., daily 9:30–7; Nov.–Feb., daily 10–6.*

The Moneghetti area is the setting for the **Jardin Exotique** (Exotic Plants Garden), where 600 varieties of cacti and succulents cling to a vertiginous rock face overlooking the city and coast. Your ticket to the Jardin Exotique also allows you to explore the caves next door and to visit the adjacent **Musée d'Anthropologie Préhistorique** (Museum of Prehistoric Anthropology). ✉ *Bd. du Jardin Exotique,* ☎ *93–15–29–80.* ⏲ *Mid-May–mid-Sept., daily 9–7; mid-Sept.–mid-May, daily 9–6.*

$$$$ ★ ✕ **Louis XV.** Swimming in gilt and boiseries, the decor here is sumptuously splendid—even so, it never manages to upstage superstar chef Alain Ducasse and his beautifully conceived "country cooking," where

ravioli with foie gras and truffles slum happily alongside salt cod and tripe. It's horribly expensive, but probably worth it. ✉ *Hôtel de Paris, pl. du Casino,* ☎ *92–16–30–01. Reservations essential. AE, DC, MC, V. Closed Tues.–Wed. (except dinner July–Aug.) and late Nov.–late Dec.*

$$–$$$ ✕ **Castelroc.** With its pine-shaded terrace across from the entrance to the Prince's Palace, this is one of the more popular lunch spots in town. Monaco specialties, such as stockfish, *anchoïade* (anchovy paste), and *petits farcis* (stuffed vegetables) alternate with seafood, stylishly prepared. ✉ *Pl. du Palais,* ☎ *93–30–36–68. AE, MC, V. Closed Sat. and late Nov.–mid-Jan.*

$$$$ **Hôtel de Paris.** At this famed establishment, elegance, expense, luxury, dignity, and Old World charm are the watchwords. Built in 1864, it still exudes the gold-plated splendor of an era when kings and grand dukes were pampered here. Tunnels lead to the more discreet sister hotel, the Hermitage. ✉ *Pl. du Casino, 98000,* ☎ *92–16–30–00,* FAX *92–16–38–50,* WEB *www.montecarloresort.com/en/en.html/hot_index.html. 245 rooms. 4 restaurants, 2 pools. AE, DC, MC, V.*

$$ **Alexandra.** The friendly proprietress, Madame Larouquie, makes you feel right at home in this central, comfortable spot. Who cares if the color schemes clash and decor is spare, when the baths are big and newly redone? ✉ *35 bd. Princesse-Charlotte, 98000,* ☎ *93–50–63–13,* FAX *92–16–06–48. 56 rooms. AE, DC, MC, V.*

The Côte d'Azur Essentials

AIRPORTS

More than 30 airlines serve the International Aéroport Nice-Côte d'Azur. Air France flights leave for Paris more than 15 times a day.

BUS TRAVEL

Taking local buses (marked GARE ROUTIÈRE) or a guided tour is necessary to visit Grasse, Vence, and other inland areas if you're traveling by public transportation. The main routes between towns are serviced by SAP and Phoceens-Cars bus companies.

CAR TRAVEL

A8 is the only way to get around the Côte d'Azur quickly (keep lots of change handy for tolls). A car is best for exploring the hill towns perched behind the Côte d'Azur.

TOURS

SNCF runs many organized tours (contact the Nice Tourist Office) to areas otherwise hard to reach. Boats operate from Nice to Marseille; from St-Tropez to the charming Hyères Islands; and from Antibes, Cannes, and Juan-les-Pins to the Lérins Islands.

TRAIN TRAVEL

A train line follows the coast from Marseille to the Italian border, providing excellent access to the seaside resort towns.

➤ TRAIN INFORMATION: **SNCF** (☎ ☎ 08–36–35–35–35, WEB www.sncf.com).

VISITOR INFORMATION

➤ TOURIST INFORMATION: **Antibes** (✉ 11 pl. Général-de-Gaulle, ☎ 04–92–90–53–00). **Cannes** (✉ Palais des Festivals La Croisette, 04–93–39–24–53). **Juan-les-Pins** (✉ 51 bd. Charles-Guillaumont, ☎ 04–92–90–53–05). **Monaco** (✉ 2a bd. des Moulins, ☎ 377/92–16–61–66). **Nice** (✉ av. Thiers, ☎ 04–92–14–48–00; ✉ 5 av. Gustave-V, ☎ 04–93–87–60–60). **St-Tropez** (✉ quai Jean-Jaurès, ☎ 04–94–97–45–21).

12 GERMANY

MUNICH, THE BLACK FOREST, FRANKFURT, THE RHINE, HAMBURG, BERLIN, SAXONY AND THURINGIA

NO MATTER WHAT PART of Germany you visit, within its reconstructed cities and ancient towns are the thick layers of history: Roman relics keep company with medieval castles, Baroque palaces with rococo chapels, and half-timbered inns with communist-era apartment blocks.

The country of oompah, cuckoo clocks, and Mercedes-Benz also gave the world Gutenberg, Luther, Bach, Beethoven, Goethe, and Marx. Germans are industrious and heavily philosophical, and they take their leisure time just as seriously. The great outdoors has always been an important escape. Crystal-clear Alpine lakes are only a short train ride from boisterous Munich. The Black Forest offers spas and hiking trails. Sprawling Berlin is filled with its own lakes and green parklands. The German trains that link these various regions are fast, clean, and punctual, and a drive on a speed limit–free autobahn will give you an idea of just how fast those BMWs and Mercedeses are built to go.

Every town and village, and many a city neighborhood, manages at least one *Fest* a year, when the beer barrels are rolled out and sausages are thrown on the grill. The seasons have their own festivities: Fasching (carnival) heralds the end of winter, beer gardens open up with the first warm rays of sunshine; fall is celebrated with the Munich Oktoberfest; and Advent brings colorful pre-Christmas markets.

Berlin rolls off the tongue of cosmopolitan travelers in the same breath as Paris and London, as the ever-buzzing capital city offers much in terms of arts, architecture, and nightlife. Though the east and west halves of the city are now seamless, the chance to witness a European city still becoming itself is a rare one.

GERMANY A TO Z

To research prices, get advice from other travelers, and book travel arrangements, visit www.fodors.com

AIR TRAVEL

Germany's national airline, Lufthansa, serves all major cities. LTU International Airways serves Düsseldorf, Frankfurt, Hannover, and Munich. A British Airways subsidiary, Deutsche BA, competes with Lufthansa on many domestic routes, serving Berlin, Hamburg, Munich, Düsseldorf, Köln, and Bonn with substantially lower fares.

➤ AIRLINES AND CONTACTS: **Deutsche BA** (☎ 089/9759–1500, WEB www.deutsche-ba.de). **Lufthansa** (☎ 0180/380–3803 in Germany, WEB www.lufthansa.com). **LTU International Airways** (☎ 800/888–0200 in the U.S.; 0211/941808 in Germany, WEB www.ltu.de).

Germany (Deutschland)

THE CZECH REPUBLIC
AUSTRIA
SWITZERLAND
FRANCE
BELGIUM
LUX.
Dresden
Köln
Aachen
Bonn
Siegen
Marburg
Alsfeld
Erfurt
Weimar
Eisenach
Gera
Chemnitz
Zwickau
Saalfeld
Suhl
Meiningen
Plauen
Hof
Münchberg
Coburg
Giessen
Fulda
Koblenz
Rhine
Wiesbaden
Mainz
Frankfurt-am-Main
Bingen
Mosel
Trier
Darmstadt
Main
Würzburg
Bamberg
Bayreuth
Nürnberg
Fürth
Rothenburg-o-d-Tauber
Mannheim
Ludwigshafen
Heidelberg
Saarbrücken
Speyer
Heilbronn
Karlsruhe
Stuttgart
Regensburg
Straubing
Deggendorf
Passau
Danube
Baden-Baden
Tübingen
Offenburg
Ulm
Neu-Ulm
Augsburg
Isar
Munich
Inn
Biberach
Memmingen
Freiburg
Tuttlingen
Ravensburg
Wangen
Rheinfelden
Konstanz
Bodensee
Garmisch-Partenkirchen
Bad Reichenhall
Berchtesgaden
E45
3
E31
E35
7
E40
4
E441
72
E44
9
E42
5
81
E51
6
E50
E56
E41
8
E52
A7
18

BIKE TRAVEL

Bicycles can be rented at more than 160 train stations throughout Germany, mainly from April through October, though some are offered year-round. The cost is DM 6/€3–DM 25/€12.50 per day. You may have to leave cash or your passport as a deposit. You must return the bike to the station at which you rented it. Special types, such as mountain bikes at Alpine stations and children's bikes are also available. Bikes are allowed on all trains except the InterCity Express. With other express trains you must make advance reservations and pay DM 16/€8. On non-express trains the charge is DM 6/€3 and no reservation is required. The railroad has a nationwide bicycle hotline.

➤ BIKE RENTALS: **Bicycle hotline** (☎ 0180/319–4194).

BOAT AND FERRY TRAVEL

The Köln-based Viking KD operates overnight cabin trips on the Rhine, Mosel, Saar, Neckar, Danube, Elbe, and Main rivers. Köln-Düsseldorfer Deutsche Rheinschiffahrt runs day trips on the Rhine and Mosel; its U.S. representative is JFO Cruise Service Corp. Services on the Danube (Donau) between Degendorf, Germany, and Vienna are operated by Donauschiffahrt Wurm & Köck. In summer, car ferries and passenger ships cross the Bodensee (Lake Constance) on Germany's south border.

➤ BOAT AND FERRY INFORMATION: **Donauschiffahrt Wurm & Köck** (✉ Höllg. 26, D-94032 Passau, ☎ 0851/929–292, FAX 0851/35518, WEB www.donauschiffahrt.de). **Köln-Düsseldorfer Deutsche Rheinschiffahrt** (✉ Frankenwerft 35, D-50667 Köln, ☎ 0221/208–8318 or 800/346–6525 in the U.S., FAX 0221/208–8345, WEB www.rivercruises.com). **Viking KD** (✉ Hohestr. 68–82, D-50667 Köln, ☎ 0221/2586–0 or 877/668–4546 in the U.S., FAX 0221/2586–208, WEB www.vikingrivercruises.com).

BUS TRAVEL

Long-distance bus services in Germany are part of the Europe-wide Europabus network. Services are neither as frequent nor as comprehensive as those on the rail system. All Europabus services have a bilingual attendant and offer small luxuries that you won't find on the more basic, though still comfortable, regular services. Travel agents and Deutsche Touring offices can provide details and take reservations.

➤ BUS INFORMATION: **Deutsche Touring** (DTG; ✉ Am Römerhof 17, D-60486 Frankfurt/Main, ☎ 069/790–3261, FAX 069/790–3156, WEB www.touring-germany.com).

BUSINESS HOURS

Banks are usually weekdays from 8:30 or 9 to 3 or 4 (5 or 6 on Thursday). Some close from 12:30 to 1:30. Branches at airports and main train stations open as early as 6:30 AM and close as late as 10:30 PM. Museums are generally open Tuesday through Sunday 10–5. Some close for an hour or more at lunch. Many stay open until 8 or 9 on Wednesday or Thursday. Larger stores open weekdays 9:30–8, Saturday 9:30–4. Smaller shops close around 6:30 PM.

CAR TRAVEL

EMERGENCIES

In the event of a breakdown, ADAC, a major automobile organization, gives free help and advice to tourists, though you have to pay for spare parts, plus labor and mileage for a tow truck. Autobahns have regularly spaced telephones; look for call boxes on minor roads.

➤ CONTACTS: **ADAC** (✉ Am Westpark 8, D-81373 Munich, ☎ 089/76760, FAX 089/76762801, WEB www.adac.de). **Emergency number** (☎ 01802/222–222, or from a cell phone, 222–222).

GASOLINE

Unleaded gas and diesel are generally available all over Germany, and leaded fuel is being phased out. The price of a liter of gas may range from DM 2/€1 to DM 2.50/€1.50, depending on the grade.

PARKING

Daytime parking in cities is very difficult and parking restrictions are not always clearly marked. Better to use a parking garage or lot than risk having your car towed. In German garages you must pay immediately on returning to retrieve your car, not when driving out. Put the ticket you got on arrival into the machine and pay the amount displayed. Retrieve the ticket, go to your car, and upon exiting, insert the ticket in a slot to get the barrier raised. Parking-meter spaces are free at night.

ROAD CONDITIONS

The autobahn system in Germany is of the highest standard. These roads are marked either *A* (on blue signs), meaning intra-German highways, or *E* (on green signs), meaning they form part of the Europe-wide *Europastrasse* network. All autobahns are toll free. Local roads are called *Bundesstrassen* and are marked by their number on a yellow sign.

RULES OF THE ROAD

Officially, there's no speed limit on autobahns, although signs recommend that motorists stay below 130 kph (80 mph). Blue signs on autobahns recommend the minimum speed on that stretch. Germans are fast drivers, and autobahn speeds of more than 160 kph (100 mph) are common. Unless you're driving at that speed, stay in the right-hand lane on autobahns, and use the left-hand lanes only for passing. There are speed limits on other roads—100 kph (60 mph) on Bundesstrassen, 80 kph (50 mph) on country roads, between 30 kph (18 mph) and 60 kph (36 mph) in built-up urban areas. Fines for exceeding the speed limit can be heavy. Penalties for driving under the influence of alcohol are even more severe, so make sure to keep within the legal limit—equivalent to the consumption of two small beers or a glass of wine.

CUSTOMS AND DUTIES

For details on imports and duty-free limits, *see* Customs and Duties *in* Chapter 1.

DINING

The range of dining experiences in Germany is vast: everything from high-priced contemporary cuisine to street-vendor *Würste* (sausages). Countrywide, seek out *Gaststätten, Gasthäuser,* or *Gasthöfe*—local inns—for traditional and regional specialties. Beer gardens in Bavaria, *Apfelwein* (alcoholic apple cider) taverns in Frankfurt, and *Kneipen* (pubs) in Berlin nearly always offer the best value and local atmosphere. Just about every town will have a *Ratskeller,* a cellar restaurant in the town hall, where exposed beams, sturdy tables, and immense portions are the rule. Be aware that salt is used liberally in many dishes.

Every part of the country has its local brew. Say "*Helles*" or "*Export*" if you want light beer; "*Dunkles*" if you want dark beer. Bavaria's *Weissbier* is a sour but refreshing beer brewed from wheat. Germany is also a major producer of wine (mostly white). All wines are graded in one of three basic categories: *Tafelwein* (table wine); *Qualitätswein* (fine wine); and *Qualitätswein mit Prädikat* (top-quality wine).

Prices are for one main course at dinner.

CATEGORY	COST
$$$$	over DM 50 (€26)
$$$	DM 40–DM 50 (€21–€26)
$$	DM 30–DM 40 (€16–€21)
$	under DM 30 (€16)

MEALTIMES

Breakfast, served from 6:30 to 10, often consists of cold meats, cheeses, rolls, and fruit. Many city hotels offer Sunday brunch. Lunch is served from around 11:30 to around 2; dinner is generally from 6 until 9:30, or earlier in some quiet country areas. Big-city hotels and popular restaurants serve later. Lunch tends to be the main meal—try the *Tageskarte*, or suggested menu, for maximum nourishment at minimum outlay.

RESERVATIONS AND DRESS

Jacket and tie are advised for restaurants in the $$$ and $$$$ categories. In Germany, even casual attire is dressier than in the United States and Britain. Think "business casual."

EMBASSIES

Consulate offices are in Frankfurt, Hamburg, and Munich.

➤ AUSTRALIA: ✉ Friedrichstr. 200, Berlin, ☎ 030/880–0880.

➤ CANADA: ✉ International Trade Center, Friedrichstr. 95, Berlin, ☎ 030/261–1161.

➤ IRELAND: ✉ Friedrichstr. 200, Berlin, ☎ 030/220–720.

➤ NEW ZEALAND: ✉ Friedrichstr. 60, Berlin, ☎ 030/260–210.

➤ SOUTH AFRICA: ✉ Friedrichstr. 60, Berlin, ☎ 030/220–730.

➤ UNITED KINGDOM: ✉ Wilhelmstr. 70–71, Berlin, ☎ 030/204–570.

➤ UNITED STATES: ✉ Neustädtische Kirchstr. 4–5, Berlin, ☎ 030/85030.

HOLIDAYS

January 1; January 6 (Epiphany—Bavaria, Baden-Württemberg, and Saxony-Anhalt only); Good Friday; Easter Monday; May 1 (Worker's Day); Ascension, Pentecost Monday, in May; May 30 (Corpus Christi—south Germany only); August 15 (Assumption Day—Bavaria and Saarland only); October 3 (German Unity Day); November 1 (All Saints' Day–Baden Württemberg, Bavaria, North Rhine Westphalia, Rheinland-Pfalz and Saarland only); December 24–26.

LANGUAGE

Among Germany's many dialects, probably the most difficult to comprehend is Bavaria's. Virtually everyone can also speak *Hochdeutsch*, the German equivalent of Oxford English. Many people under age 40 speak some English.

LODGING

The standard of German hotels, from luxury properties (of which the country has more than its fair share) to the humblest pension, is excellent. You can expect courteous service; clean and comfortable rooms; and, in rural areas especially, considerable Old German atmosphere.

The country has numerous *Gasthöfe* or *Gasthäuser* (country inns); pensions or *Fremdenheime* (guest houses); and, at the lowest end of the scale, *Zimmer*, meaning rooms, normally in private houses. Look for the sign ZIMMER FREI (rooms free) or ZU VERMIETEN (for rent). A red sign reading BESETZT means there are no vacancies.

Major hotels in cities often have lower rates on weekends or when business is quiet. If you're lucky, you can find reductions of up to 60%.

Likewise, rooms reserved after 10 PM will often carry a discount. Tourist offices can provide lists of hotels offering *Pauschalangebote* (low-price inclusive weekly packages). Many winter resorts lower their rates for the periods immediately before and after the Christmas and New Year's high season.

The following chart is for hotels throughout Germany. In Berlin and Hamburg, price categories are about DM 50/€25 higher than those for other major cities. Breakfast is usually, but not always, included in the room rate.

CATEGORY	COST
$$$$	over DM 350 (€180)
$$$	DM 250–DM 350 (€128–€180)
$$	DM 150–DM 250 (€77–€128)
$	under DM 150 (€77)

*Prices are for standard double rooms and include tax.

APARTMENT AND VILLA RENTALS

Apartments and houses have reasonable rates, with reductions for longer stays. Rates for short- or medium-term stays usually include charges for gas and electricity. Local and regional tourist offices have lists of apartments in their areas.

CAMPING

Some 5,500 campsites in Germany are listed, along with many other European sites, by the German Camping Club. Sites tend to be crowded in summer, so make reservations a day or two ahead. Prices at ordinary campsites range from DM 20/€10 to DM 50/€26 per night for two adults, a car, and a tent or trailer. Some higher-priced facilities come replete with pool, sports facilities, and entertainment programs.

➤ CONTACTS: **German Camping Club** (DCC; ✉ Mandlstr. 28, D-80802 Munich, ☎ 089/380–1420, FAX 089/334737, WEB www.camping-club.de).

CASTLE HOTELS

The prices at *Schloss*, or castle, hotels are mostly moderate; some of the simpler establishments, however, may lack a little in the way of comfort, and furnishings can be basic. On the whole they're delightful, with antiques, imposing interiors, and out-of-the-way locations.

➤ CONTACTS: **Euro-Connection** (✉ 7500 212th St. SW, Suite 103, Edmonds, WA 98026, ☎ 800/645–3876). **European Castle Hotels & Restaurants** (✉ Postfach 1111, D-67142 Deidesheim an der Weinstrasse, ☎ 06326/700–030, FAX 06326/700–022, WEB www.european-castle-hotels.com).

HOSTELS

Germany's more than 600 *Jugendherberge* (youth hostels) are among the most efficient and up-to-date in Europe. Many are in castles. There's an age limit of 27 in Bavaria; elsewhere, there are no restrictions, though those under 20 take preference if space is limited. You must be a member of a national hosteling association or Hostelling International (HI) in order to stay at a hostel. Rates range from $10 to $20 per night. The DJH Service GmbH provides a complete list of German hostels for DM 14.80/€7.50 and has information on regional offices around the country. Hostels must be reserved well in advance for midsummer, especially in eastern Germany. Bookings for hostels can be made only by calling hostels directly.

➤ HOSTEL ORGANIZATIONS: **DJH Service GmbH** (✉ Postfach 1462, D-32704 Detmold, ☎ 05231/74010, FAX 05231/7401–49, WEB www.djh.de).

HOTELS

Lists of hotels are available from the Deutsche Hotel- und Gaststättenverband and from all regional and local tourist offices. Tourist offices will also make reservations for you—they usually charge a nominal fee—but may have difficulty doing so after 4 PM in peak season and on weekends. There is also an excellent, nationwide reservations service, Tourismus Service, which is open weekdays 9–6 and Saturday 9–1. In cities, trade fairs fill hotels year-round, so book well in advance.

Ringhotels are individually owned and managed hotels in the medium price range. Many are in the countryside or in pretty villages. Package deals of two to three days are available. Among the most delightful places to stay and eat in Germany are the aptly named Romantik Hotels and Restaurants. All are in historic buildings and are personally run by the owners. The emphasis generally is on solid comfort, good food, and style.

Smaller hotels do not provide much in terms of bathroom amenities. You may even have to request a washcloth.
➤ HOTEL INFORMATION: **Deutscher Hotel- und Gaststättenverband** (DEHOGA ✉ Am Weidendamm 1, D-10117 Berlin, ☎ 030/726–2520, FAX 030/726–25242, WEB www.dehoga.de). **Ringhotels** (✉ Belfortstr. 6–8, D-81667 Munich, ☎ 089/458–7030, FAX 089/458–70331, WEB www.ringhotels24.de). **Romantik Hotels and Restaurants** (✉ Horsteiner Str. 34, D-63791 Karlstein am Main, ☎ 06188–95020, FAX 06188–6007, WEB www.romantikhotels.com). **Tourismus Service GmbH** (✉ Yorckstr. 23, D-79110 Freiburg im Breisgau, ☎ 0761/885810, FAX 0761/8858129, WEB www.tourismus-service.com).

FARM VACATIONS

Almost every regional tourist office has listings of farms, by area, offering bed-and-breakfast, apartments, or whole farmhouses to rent. The German Agricultural Association produces an annual catalog of more than 2,000 farm lodgings, all of them inspected and graded. The brochure costs DM 19.50/€10, whether in bookstores or postpaid.
➤ CONTACTS: **German Agricultural Association** (DLG; ✉ Eschborner Landstr. 122, D-60489 Frankfurt am Main, ☎ 069/247–880, FAX 069/247–88–110, WEB www.landtourismus.de).

MAIL AND SHIPPING

You can arrange to have mail sent to you in care of any German post office; have the envelope marked "Postlagernd." This service is free. Alternatively, if you have an American Express card or travelers checks, or have booked a vacation with American Express you can have mail sent to any American Express office in Germany; there's no charge.

POSTAL RATES

Airmail letters to the United States and Canada cost DM 3/€1.50; postcards cost DM 2/€1. Airmail letters to the United Kingdom cost DM 1.10/€.55; postcards cost DM 1/€.50.

MONEY MATTERS

The most expensive cities are Berlin, Frankfurt, Hamburg, and Munich. Costs are somewhat lower in eastern Germany, but businesses that cater specifically to visitors are increasingly charging western German rates. Some sample prices include: cup of coffee, DM 3.50/€1.80; mug of beer in a beer hall, DM 6/€3; soft drink, DM 3.50/€1.80; ham sandwich, DM 5.50/€2.80; 3-km (2-mi) taxi ride, DM 12/€6.

CREDIT CARDS

All major U.S. credit cards are accepted in Germany. German ATMs accept four-digit PIN numbers.

➤ REPORTING LOST CARDS: **American Express:** ☏ 01805/840–840. **Diners Club:** ☏ 05921/861–234. **MasterCard:** ☏ 0800/819–1040. **Visa:** ☏ 08008/149–100.

CURRENCY

The year 2001 marked the final switch from the Deutsche Mark (DM) to the common European euro (€). Both D-marks and euros can theoretically be used until July 1, 2002, though the transition is likely to be all but complete in March 2002. You may get your change in euros even if you pay in marks during the transition period. The mark is divided into 100 pfennige. There are bills of 5 (rare), 10, 20, 50, 100, 200, 500, and 1,000 marks and coins of 1, 2, 5, 10, and 50 pfennige and 1, 2, and 5 marks. At press time, the mark stood at DM 2.24 to the U.S. dollar, DM 1.39 to the Canadian dollar, DM 3.11 to the pound sterling, DM 2.48 to the Irish punt, DM 1.16 to the Australian dollar, DM.92 to the New Zealand dollar, and DM.27 to the South African rand. The euro is equivalent to DM 1.95, a fixed rate.

TAXES

German goods carry a 16% value-added tax (VAT). Multiply the cost of an item by 13.8% to determine how much of the cost is VAT. When making a purchase, ask for a Global Refund Cheque or an *Ausfuhr-Abnehmerbescheinigung* form.

TELEPHONES

COUNTRY AND AREA CODES

Germany's country code is 49. When calling Germany from outside the country, drop the initial 0 in the regional code.

INTERNATIONAL CALLS

Calls can be made from just about any telephone booth, most of which are card operated. If you expect to do a lot of calling, international or local, purchase a telephone card. Collect calls can be made by dialing 0180/2001033 (this is also the number to call if you have problems dialing out). You can make international calls from post offices, too, even those in small country towns. Calls to the United States, day or night, cost 48 pf per minute, no matter the length of the call. Pay the clerk at the end of your call, adding a DM 2/€1 service fee.

➤ ACCESS CODES: **AT&T** (☏ 0800–888012). **MCI WorldCom** (☏ 0130–0012). **Sprint** (☏ 0800-888013).

LOCAL CALLS

Card phones have largely replaced coin-operated ones. Cards cost DM 12/€6 or DM 50/€25 (the latter good for DM 60/€30 worth of calls) and are sold at post offices, newsstands, and exchange places. If you need an operator, dial 0180/2001033. Calls made from a public phone cost 20 pfennigs a minute and are much cheaper than those made through a hotel.

TIPPING

Overtipping is as frowned upon as not tipping at all. In restaurants service is included (under the heading *Bedienung,* at the bottom of the check), and it is customary to round out the check to the next mark or two, a practice also commonplace in cafés, beer halls, and bars. For taxi drivers, also round out to the next mark or two. Railway and airport porters (if you can find any) have their own scale of charges, but round out the requested amount to the next mark. Hotel porters get DM 1/€50 per bag. Doormen are tipped the same amount for small services, such as calling a cab. Room service should be rewarded with at least DM 2/€1 every time you use it. Maids should get about DM 2/€1 per day. Double all these figures at luxury hotels. Service-station attendants get 50 pf/€25 or DM 1/€50 for checking oil and tires or cleaning windshields.

TRAIN TRAVEL

The Deutsche Bahn is a very efficient rail service. Journeys between the centers of many cities—Munich–Frankfurt, for example—can be completed faster by rail than by plane. The Frankfurt–Hamburg InterCity Express train takes 3 hours, 35 minutes one-way. InterCity Night and CityNightLine trains are "rolling hotels" with dining cars and shower and lavatory in each sleeping compartment, and overnight D-class trains also have sleepers. Seat reservations (highly advisable on the high-speed InterCity, EuroCity, and InterCity Express trains) cost DM 7/€3.50. City and large town stations have lockers.

CUTTING COSTS

A EurailPass is good over the entire German rail network. There is also a German Rail Pass, not available to Germans, for travel over the entire German rail network for 4 to 10 days within a single month. It can be purchased for first- or second-class travel. A Twin Pass does the same for two people traveling together and is even cheaper per person. A Youth Pass, sold to those ages 12–25, is for second-class travel only. These passes are also good for travel on tour routes, such as the ones along the Romantic and Castle roads served by Deutsche Touring and Rhine and Mosel river day trips. Passes are sold by travel agents and DER Travel in the United States and by Deutsche Bahn in Germany.

The *Schönes Wochenend Ticket* (Happy Weekend Ticket) provides unlimited weekend travel for up to five persons on local trains only for as little as DM 8/€4 per person. The *Guten Abend Ticket* (Good Evening Ticket) provides great savings between 7 PM and 2 AM on all trains except sleepers.

➤ TRAIN INFORMATION: **DER Travel Services** (☞ Travel Agents, *below*). **Deutsche Bahn** (DB) (German Railway; ☎ 01805/996–633, WEB www.bahn.de).

TRAVEL AGENTS

A very large travel agency, Deutsches Reisebüro (DER) has 353 offices, in just about every section of every German city (check the telephone book). All offer a full range of travel services, from tours and hotel bookings to car rentals, rail, and plane tickets. The tours it organizes are also sold by travel agents.

➤ DER ABROAD: **DER Travel Services** (✉ 9501 W. Devon Ave., Rosemont, IL 60018, ☎ 800/782–2424, FAX 800/860–9944 for a brochure, 888/337–8687 fax on demand service, WEB www.dertravel.com).

VISITOR INFORMATION

See Chapter 1 for the GNTB's office abroad.

➤ TOURIST INFORMATION: **German National Tourist Board** (GNTB; ✉ Beethovenstr. 69, D-60325 Frankfurt/Main, ☎ 069/974–640, FAX 069/751–903, WEB www.visits-to-germany.com).

➤ WINE INFORMATION: **Deutsches Wein Institut** (✉ Gutenbergplatz 3–5, 55116 Mainz, ☎ 06131/282–933, WEB www.deutschewein.de). **German Wine Information Bureau** (✉ 245 5th Ave., #2204, New York, NY 10016, ☎ 212/896–3336, WEB www.germanwineusa.org).

WHEN TO GO

The main tourist season runs from May through late October, when the weather is best and hundreds of folk festivals take place. The Rhine area has wine harvest events galore in early fall; an events calendar from the German Wine Information Bureau can help you time your visit. Winter-sports season in the Bavarian Alps runs from Christmas through mid-March.

CLIMATE

Germany's climate is generally temperate. Summers are usually sunny and warm, though the north half of Germany seems to have more than its share of overcast and wet days. Winters vary from mild and damp to very cold and bright. In Alpine regions spring often comes late, with snow flurries well into April. Only in southern Bavaria (Bayern) will you find strikingly variable weather, which is caused by the *Föhn,* a warm Alpine wind that brings sudden barometric changes and gives rise to clear but oppressive conditions in summer and causes snow to disappear overnight in winter. The following are the average daily maximum and minimum temperatures for Munich.

Jan.	35F	1C	**May**	64F	18C	**Sept.**	67F	20C
	23	– 5		45	7		48	9
Feb.	38F	3C	**June**	70F	21C	**Oct.**	56F	13C
	23	– 5		51	11		40	4
Mar.	48F	9C	**July**	74F	23C	**Nov.**	44F	7C
	30	– 1		55	13		33	0
Apr.	56F	14C	**Aug.**	73F	23C	**Dec.**	36F	2C
	38	3		54	12		26	– 3

MUNICH

Munich (München in German) is sometimes referred to as the nation's "secret capital." Flamboyant and easygoing, the city of beer and Baroque is starkly different from the sometimes stiffly Prussian-influenced Berlin; the gritty and industrial Hamburg; or the hardheaded, commercially driven Frankfurt. Munich is known for its good-natured and relaxed charm—Gemütlichkeit, they call it. The Bavarian city is a crazy mix of high culture (visit its world-class opera house and art galleries) and wild abandon (witness the vulgar frivolity of Oktoberfest or the very un-German high-jinks of *Fasching,* the Bavarian version of Carnival). The 19th-century King Ludwig I of Bavaria brought much international prestige to his home city after declaring: "I want to make Munich a town that does such credit to Germany that nobody knows Germany unless he has seen Munich." He kept his promise with an architectural and artistic renaissance—before abdicating in the wake of a wild romance with an Irish-born courtesan, Lola Montez.

Exploring Munich

Numbers in the margin correspond to points of interest on the Munich map.

Munich's Old Town has been rebuilt so often that it no longer has that homogeneous look found in other German cities. Still, its attractions lie fairly close to one another.

★ 19 **Alte Pinakothek** (Old Picture Gallery). This major art gallery contains celebrated Old Master paintings, including works by Dürer, Rembrandt, Rubens, and Murillo. Built by Leo von Klenze at the beginning of the 19th century to house King Ludwig I's collections, the massive

Munich (München)

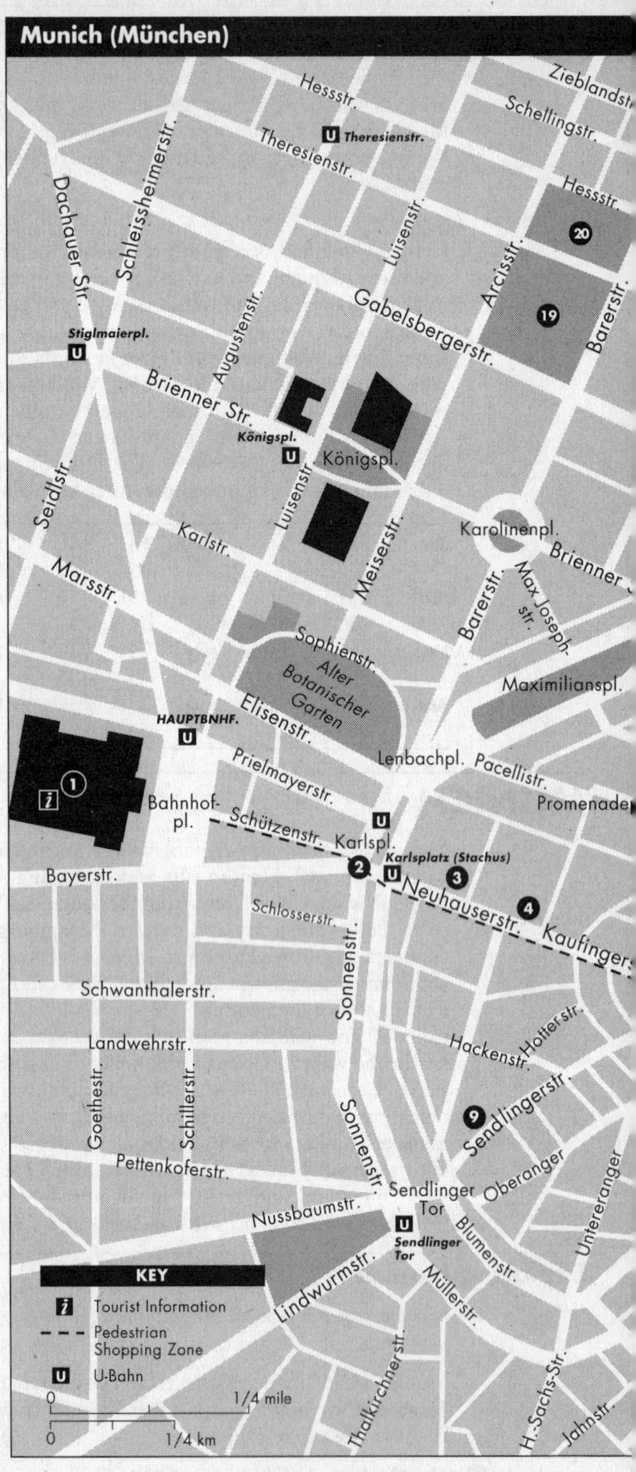

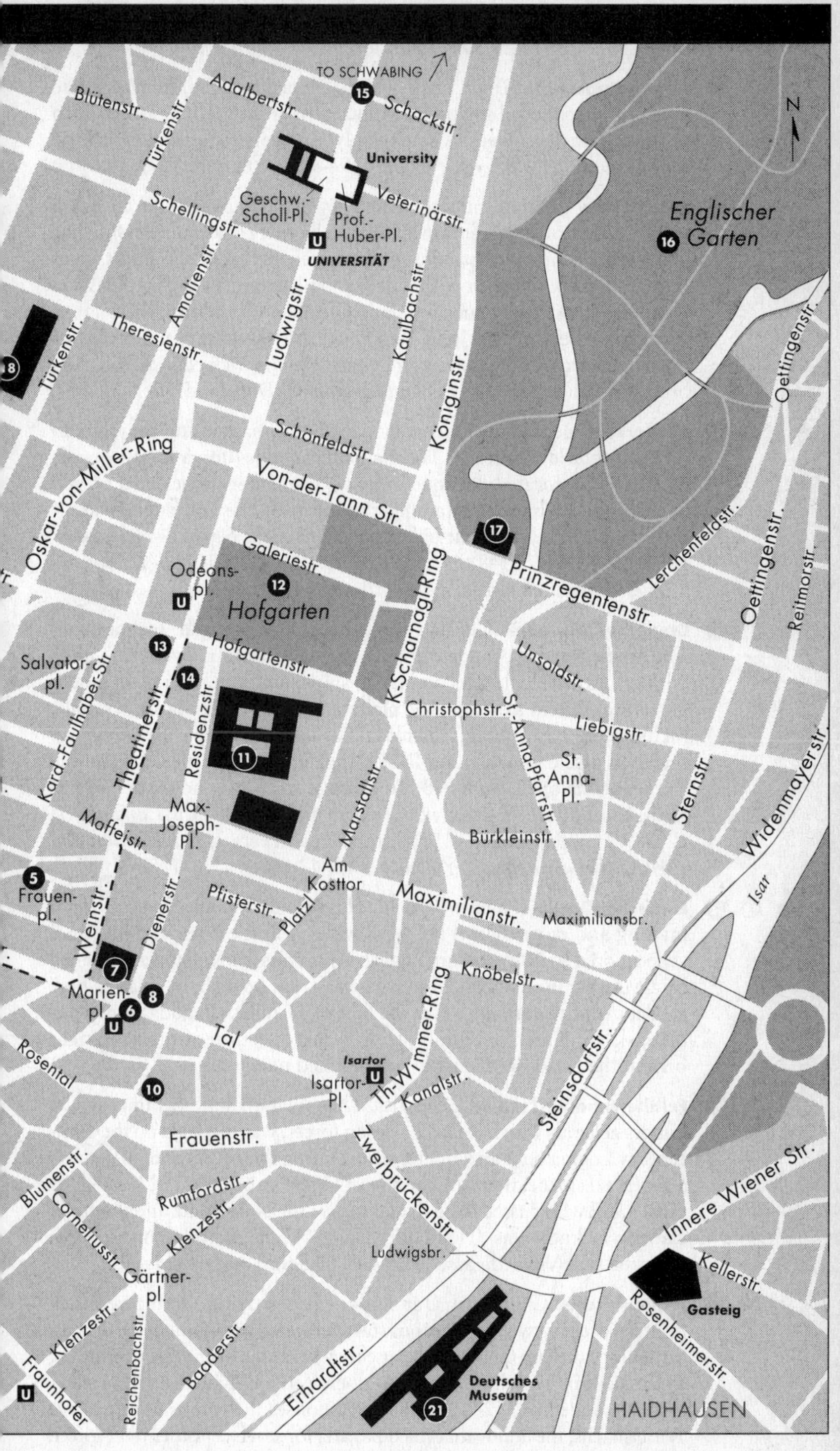

TO SCHWABING
Blütenstr.
Adalbertstr.
Schackstr.
Türkenstr.
University
Veterinärstr.
Schellingstr.
Geschw.-Scholl-Pl.
Prof.-Huber-Pl.
UNIVERSITÄT
Englischer Garten
Amalienstr.
Kaulbachstr.
Theresienstr.
Ludwigstr.
Türkenstr.
Oettingenstr.
Königinstr.
Schönfeldstr.
Oskar-von-Miller-Ring
Von-der-Tann Str.
Galeriestr.
Odeons-pl.
Hofgarten
K.-Scharnagl-Ring
Prinzregentenstr.
Lerchenfeldstr.
Oettingenstr.
Reitmorstr.
Hofgartenstr.
Unsoldstr.
Salvator-pl.
Kard.-Faulhaber-Str.
Theatinerstr.
Residenzstr.
Christophstr.
Liebigstr.
St.-Anna-Pfarrstr.
St. Anna-Pl.
Sternstr.
Widenmayerstr.
Marstallstr.
Max-Joseph-Pl.
Maffeistr.
Bürkleinstr.
Frauen-pl.
Am Kosttor
Pfisterstr.
Platzl
Maximilianstr.
Maximiliansbr.
Isar
Weinstr.
Dienerstr.
Knöbelstr.
Marien-pl.
Tal
Rosental
Isartor
Isartor-Pl.
Th.-Wimmer-Ring
Kanalstr.
Steinsdorfstr.
Frauenstr.
Zweibrückenstr.
Blumenstr.
Corneliusstr.
Rumfordstr.
Klenzestr.
Innere Wiener Str.
Ludwigsbr.
Kellerstr.
Gärtner-pl.
Gasteig
Klenzestr.
Reichenbachstr.
Baaderstr.
Rosenheimerstr.
Erhardtstr.
Fraunhofer
Deutsches Museum
HAIDHAUSEN

brick edifice is itself an architectural treasure. ✉ *Barerstr. 27,* ☎ *089/2380–5216.* ⊙ *Tues.–Sun. 10–5, until 10 PM Thur.*

8 **Altes Rathaus** (Old Town Hall). The 1474 medieval building has a fine assembly room used for official functions, although it is rarely open to the public. Its tower is a satisfyingly atmospheric setting for a little toy museum. ✉ *Marienpl.,* ☎ *089/294–001.* ⊙ *Daily 10–5:30.*

★ 9 **Asamkirche** (Asam Church). Munich's most unusual church has a suitably extraordinary entrance, framed by raw rock foundations. The insignificant church door, crammed between its craggy shoulders, gives little idea of the splendor within. It was built around 1730 by the Asam brothers—Cosmas Damian and Egid Quirin—next door to their home. They dedicated it to St. John Nepomuk, a 14th-century monk. Inside is a riot of decoration: gilding, frescoes, statuary, rich rosy marble, and billowing stucco clouds. ✉ *Sendlingerstr.* ⊙ *Daily 9–5:30.*

3 **Bürgersaal.** Behind the modest facade of this unassuming church is an unusual split-level interior. The main Oberkirche (upper level) consists of a richly decorated Baroque oratory. The Unterkirche (lower level) is a cryptlike chapel containing the tomb of the courageous Jesuit priest Rupert Mayer, an outspoken opponent of the Nazis. ✉ *Neuhauserstr. 14,* ☎ *089/223–884.* ⊙ *Oberkirche Mon.–Sat. 11–1, Sun. 9–12:30; Unterkirche Mon.–Sat. 6:30 AM–7 PM, Sun. 7–7.*

★ 21 **Deutsches Museum** (German Museum of Science and Technology). The six floors and 30 departments of this enormous museum—filled with aircraft, vehicles, locomotives, ships, and machinery—is an engineering student's dream. The planetarium has up to six shows daily, including a Laser Magic display. Nature and adventure films are screened at the wraparound IMAX theater. The Internet Café on the third floor is open daily 9–3. To arrange for a two-hour tour in English, call 089/2179–252 two weeks in advance. ✉ *Museumsinsel 1,* ☎ *089/21790; 089/211–25180 to reserve tickets at planetarium and IMAX,* WEB *www.fdt.de.* ⊙ *Daily 9 AM–11 PM.*

★ 16 **Englischer Garten** (English Garden). This seemingly endless park (5 km/3 mi long and more than ½ km/¼ mi wide) is in the open and informal style favored by 18th-century English aristocrats (though it was designed by a Massachusetts-born Torey). You can rent boats here, relax in beer gardens (the most famous is at the foot of a Chinese Pagoda), ride your bike, ski in winter, or simply stroll. A large section of the park right behind the **Haus der Kunst** is a designated nudist area.

14 **Feldherrnhalle** (Hall of Generals). This open-air hall of fame, which honors generals who have led Bavarian forces, was modeled on the 14th-century Loggia dei Lanzi in Florence. During the 1930s and '40s it was a key Nazi shrine, marking the site of Hitler's abortive 1923 rising, or putsch. All who passed the hall had to give the Nazi salute and the street came to be known as "Heil Hitler-Gasse." To avoid the salute, people took the tiny Viscardigasse behind it. ✉ *South end of Odeonspl.*

★ 5 **Frauenkirche** (Church of Our Lady). This soaring Gothic redbrick masterpiece has two incongruous towers topped by onion-shape domes, symbols of the city (perhaps because they resemble brimming beer mugs, cynics claim). The church was built between 1474 and 1494; the towers were added in 1524–25. The crypt houses the tombs of numerous Wittelsbachs, the family that ruled Bavaria for seven centuries until forced to abdicate in 1918. For a view of the city, you can take an elevator to a tower's observation platform. ✉ *Frauenpl.,* ☎ *089/290–0820.* ⊙ *Tower elevator Apr.–Oct., Mon.–Sat. 10–5.*

❶ **Hauptbahnhof** (Main Train Station). The city tourist office is here, with maps and helpful information. ✉ *Bahnhofpl.,* ☎ *089/2333–0256.*

⓱ **Haus der Kunst** (House of Art). The grandiose portico of this vast art gallery identifies the building as one of Munich's few remaining Nazi-era monuments, opened officially in 1938 by Hitler himself. Excellent art and photography exhibitions are often accompanied by theatrical and musical "happenings." ✉ *Prinzregentenstr. 1,* ☎ *089/211–270.* ⏲ *Tues.–Wed. and Fri.–weekends 10–5, Thurs. 10–8.*

⓬ **Hofgarten** (Royal Garden). The formal garden was once part of the royal palace grounds. It is bordered on two sides by arcades designed in the 19th century by the royal architect Leo von Klenze. ✉ *Hofgartenstr., north of Residenz.*

❷ **Karlsplatz** (Charles Square). Known locally as the Stachus, this busy intersection has one of Munich's most popular fountains, a circle of water jets that cool city shoppers and office workers on hot summer days.

★ ❻ **Marienplatz** (Square of Our Lady). Surrounded by shops, restaurants, and cafés, this square is named for the 1638 gilt statue of the Virgin Mary that has been watching over it for nearly four centuries.

❹ **Michaelskirche** (St. Michael's Church). One of the most magnificent Renaissance churches in Germany, this spacious and handsome structure is decorated throughout in plain white stucco. It was built during the late 16th century for the Jesuits and was closely modeled on Il Gesù, the Jesuit church in Rome. More than 40 members of the Wittelsbach royal family, including King Ludwig II, are buried in the crypt. ✉ *Neuhauserstr. 6,* ☎ *089/551–99257.* ⏲ *Crypt weekdays 10–1 and 2–4:30, Sat. 10–3. Guided tours Wed. at 2.*

⓴ **Neue Pinakothek** (New Picture Gallery). The art gallery that Ludwig I built to house his "modern" collections was destroyed during World War II and replaced by this exhibition hall in 1981. It's a superb, skylit setting for one of the finest collections of 19th-century European paintings and sculpture in the world. ✉ *Barerstr. 29,* ☎ *089/2380–5195.* 🎟 *Free Sun.* ⏲ *Tues.–Sun. 10–5, until 8 Thurs.*

❼ **Neues Rathaus** (New City Hall). Munich's present city hall was built between 1867 and 1908 in the fussy, turreted, neo-Gothic style so beloved by King Ludwig II. At 11, noon, and 9 daily (also June–September at 5), the central tower's *Glockenspiel,* or chiming clock, swings into action with two tiers of dancing and jousting figures. An elevator serves an observation point near the top of one of the towers. ✉ *Marienpl.,* ☎ *089/2331.* ⏲ *Tower Mon.–Thurs. 9–4, Fri. 9–1.*

⓲ **Pinakothek der Moderne** (Modern Art Gallery). This long-awaited museum might finally open in the spring of 2002. Five art and architectural collections will reside in the striking glass-and-concrete complex: galleries of modern art, industrial and graphic design, the Bavarian State collection of graphic art, and the Technical University's architectural museum. ✉ *Türkenstr. at Gabelsbergerstr., and Luisenstr. at Theresienstr.,* ☎ *089/238–05118.*

⓫ **Residenz** (Royal Palace). This mighty palace, whose history goes back to the 14th century, was the home of the Wittelsbach dukes for more than three centuries. Its several major attractions include the rooms of the palace itself, the glittering **Schatzkammer** (treasury; ⏲ Tues.–Sun. 10–4:30), and the small rococo **Cuvilliés Theater.** ✉ *Residenzmuseum Max-Joseph-Pl. 3, enter at Residenzstr. 1,* ☎ *089/290–671* ⏲ *Tues.–Sun. 10–4.*

★ **Schloss Nymphenburg** (Nymphenburg Palace). The summer palace of the Wittelsbachs stands magnificently in its own park in the western suburb of Nymphenburg. The oldest parts date from 1664, but the bulk of the work undertaken during the reign of Max Emmanuel between 1680 and 1730. The interiors are exceptional, especially the **Steinerner Saal,** a rococo masterpiece in green and gold extending over two floors and richly decorated with stucco and grandiose frescoes. Summer chamber-music concerts take place here. Portraits of the many women who caught the eye of Ludwig I adorn the **Schönheits Galerie** (Gallery of Beauties). The rococo **Amalienburg** (Hunting Lodge) on the grounds was built by François Cuvilliés, architect of the theater in Munich's Residenz. The palace also contains the **Marstallmuseum** (Museum of Royal Carriages); a sleigh that belonged to Ludwig II is included among the opulently decorated vehicles. On the floor above, the **Nymphenburger Porzellan** (Nymphenburg Porcelain Gallery) exhibits porcelain produced here between 1747 and the 1920s. The **Museum Mensch und Natur** (Museum of Man and Nature) is in the north wing. Take Tram 17 or Bus 41 from the city center to the Schloss Nymphenburg stop. ☎ *089/179–080.* ⏲ *Apr.–Sept., Tues.–Sun. 9–12:30 and 1:30–5; Oct.–Mar., Tues.–Sun. 10–12:30 and 1:30–4. Amalienburg and gardens daily.*

15 **Siegestor** (Victory Arch). Modeled on the Arch of Constantine in Rome, the arch was built to honor the achievements of the Bavarian army during the Wars of Liberation (1813–15) against Napoleon. The writing on the gable facing the inner city reads: "Dedicated to victory, destroyed by war, admonishing peace." ✉ *Start of Leopoldstr.*

13 **Theatinerkirche** (Theatine Church). This church was built for the Theatine monks in the mid-17th century, though its striking yellow-stucco facade, with twin eye-catching domes, was added only in the following century. The superb interior stucco work is being renovated and can only be glimpsed through drop cloths and scaffolding until 2003. The gaping space before the Feldherrnhalle and Theatinerkirche is often used for outdoor stage events. ✉ *Theatinerstr. 22.*

★ 10 **Viktualienmarkt** (Food Market). The city's open-air market has a wide range of produce—German and international goods, Bavarian beer, and French wines—and benches to eat at. ✉ *Southeast of Marienpl. via Tal or Rindermarkt.* ⏲ *Mon.–Sat. 7–6:30.*

Side Trips

KZ-Gedenkstätte Dachau (Dachau Concentration Camp Memorial Site). Although the 1,200-year-old town of Dachau attracted hordes of painters and artists from the mid-19th century until World War I, it is now best known as the site of Germany's first concentration camp. Opening in 1933, the camp held more than 206,000 political dissidents, Jews, homosexuals, clergy, and other "enemies" of the Nazis; more than 32,000 prisoners died here. Photographs, contemporary documents, the few remaining cell blocks, and the grim crematorium create a somber picture of the camp. The town of Dachau is a 20-minute ride from Marienplatz on the S-2 suburban railway line. To get to the concentration camp site take Bus 724 or 726 from the train station or town center. Both stop near the entrance. ✉ *Alte Römerstr. 75,* ☎ *08131/71007.* *Free.* ⏲ *Tues.–Sun. 9–5. Guided English tour June–Aug., Tues.–Sun. 12:30; Sept.–May., weekends 12:30.*

★ **Schloss Neuschwanstein** (Neuschwanstein Castle). The "fairy-tale" king, Ludwig II, had a deep love of theater and his last castle soars from its mountainside like a stage creation (it was conceived by a set designer—no wonder Walt Disney used it as the model for his own Disneyland castle). The king spent less than six months in the country residence before his death, and the interior was never finished. The Byzantine-style throne room is without a throne; Ludwig died before one could be installed. Probably more important to Ludwig were the murals depicting characters from Wagner's operas. Chamber concerts are held in September in the gaily decorated minstrels' hall (for details call the Verkehrsamt, Schwangau, ☎ 08362/81980).

More than 1 million people pass through Neuschwanstein and Hohenschwangau, the nearby castle in which he was born, every year. With a deposit or credit card number you can book your timed-entrance tickets in advance through **Verwaltung Hohenschwangau** (✉ Alpseestr. 12, D-87645 Hohenschwangau, ☎ 08362/930–830, FAX 0832/930–8320). There is a DM 3/€1.5 processing fee per ticket. You can cancel or change entrance times up to two hours before the confirmed entrance time. The castle lies 105 km (65 mi) southwest of Munich, and road signs to the castle read KONIGSCHLÖSSER. After parking in the village, you can take a horse-drawn carriage to the castle, or a bus to the outlook called Aussichtspunkt Jugend; from there it's only a 10-minute walk. The uphill walk from the village takes 25 minutes. ✉ *Hohenschwangau.* ⏲ *Guided tours Apr.–Sept., daily 8:30–5:30; Oct.–Mar., daily 10–4.*

Dining

Munich claims some of the most noted restaurants in Germany. For local cuisine, Munich's wood-paneled, flagstone beer restaurants and halls serve food sturdy enough for the large servings of beer.

$$$$ ✕ **Am Marstall.** Book a window table and nod to the promenaders a nose away on Maximilianstrasse. The cuisine has won the restaurant a Michelin star with its accent on the best of France and Germany—succulent lamb raised on salt-soaked pastures of coastal Brittany, for instance, or venison from the hunting grounds of Lower Bavaria. ✉ *Maximilianstr. 16,* ☎ *089/2916–5511. Reservations essential. Jacket and tie. AE, MC, V. Closed Mon.*

$$$$ ★ ✕ **Tantris.** Chef Hans Haas's creative cuisine has kept Tantris among the top five dining establishments in Munich. Specialties include shellfish and creamed potato soup and roasted wood pigeon with scented rice. The minimalist look includes bare concrete and garish orange-and-yellow decor. ✉ *Johann-Fichte-Str. 7,* ☎ *089/361–9590. Reservations essential. Jacket and tie. AE, DC, MC, V. Closed Sun.*

$–$$$$ ★ ✕ **Hackerhaus.** This upscale beer restaurant on one of Munich's ritziest streets is full of bric-a-brac and mementos that hark back to its origins as a medieval brewery. Since 1570, beer has been brewed or served here at the birthplace of one of the city's largest breweries—Hacker-Pschorr. Duck into one of the cozy rooms and choose a hearty soup; then try a plate of *Käsespätzle* (egg noodles with melted cheese). ✉ *Sendlingerstr. 14,* ☎ *089/260–5026. AE, DC, MC, V.*

$–$$ ★ ✕ **Dukatz.** The high-ceilinged and light-filled *Literaturhaus* (House of Literature) hums with talk of publishing contracts and literary gossip. The excellent cuisine combines traditional German with a light Gallic touch: lamb's tripe melting in a rich champagne sauce, for instance. Some of the readable artwork is by New York artist Jennifer Holtzer, such as the statement at the bottom of your coffee cup saying, "More eroticism, gentlemen!" ✉ *Salvatorpl. 1,* ☎ *089/291–9600. Reservations essential. No credit cards. No dinner Sun.*

$–$$ ✕ **Hundskugel.** Munich's oldest tavern, dating from 1440, is also one of the city's tiniest and snuggest, so don't expect privacy. You'll share a bench-table with the regulars and dine on traditional Bavarian fare—the *Spanferkel* (roast suckling pig) is particularly good. On fine days, an equally tiny beer garden beckons. ✉ *Hotterstr. 18,* ☎ *089/264–272. No credit cards. Closed Sun.*

$ ✕ **Augustiner Keller.** This 19th-century establishment is the flagship beer restaurant of one of Munich's oldest breweries, Augustiner. The decor of the two baronial hall–like rooms emphasizes wood—from the refurbished parquet floors to the barrels from which the beer is drawn. Bavarian specialties such as *Tellerfleisch*—cold roast beef with lashings of horseradish, served on a big wooden board—fill the daily menu. ✉ *Arnulfstr. 52,* ☎ *089/594–393. AE, DC, MC, V.*

$ ✕ **Cohen's.** Cohen's revives the old Jewish Central-European tradition of serving healthy cooking with hospitality and good cheer. Enjoy a few hearty latkes or a standard gefilte fish doused with excellent Golan wine from Israel. The kitchen is open from 12:30 until about 10:30. ✉ *Theresienstr.31,* ☎ *089/280–9545. AE, MC, V.*

$ ✕ **Dürnbräu.** A fountain plays outside this picturesque old Bavarian inn. Inside, it's crowded and noisy. Expect to share a table (the 21-ft table in the middle of the place is a favorite); your fellow diners will range from businesspeople to students. The food is resolutely traditional. Try the cream of spinach soup and the boiled beef. ✉ *Dürnbräug. 2,* ☎ *089/222–195. AE, DC, MC, V.*

$ ✕ **Gasthaus Isarthor.** The wooden tables here host a social mix of actors, government officials, apprentice craftspersons, journalists, and retirees. Besides pork roasts, roast beef with onions, boiled beef, and the like, the house specialty is the Augustiner beer from a wooden barrel, tapped once a day at around 6 PM. When the barrel is empty, that's it for the day. ✉ *Kanalstr. 2,* ☎ *089/227–753. MC.*

$ ✕ **Hofbräuhaus.** Crowds of singing, shouting, swaying beer drinkers fill the cavernous, smoky, stone vaults of the Hofbräuhaus. If you're not here solely to drink, try the Bavarian food in the more subdued upstairs restaurant, where the service is not so brusque. It's between Marienplatz and Maximilianstrasse. ✉ *Platzl 9,* ☎ *089/221–676. Reservations not accepted. MC, V.*

$ ✕ **Prinz Myshkin.** This gourmet vegetarian restaurant mixes Italian and Asian influences. You have the choice of antipasti, homemade gnocchi, tofu and stir-fried dishes, and excellent wines. If your hunger is only moderate, you can get half portions. The airy room has a majestically vaulted ceiling. ✉ *Hackenstr. 2,* ☎ *089/265–596. MC, V.*

Lodging

Munich's hotels are often full year-round. If you plan to visit during the *Mode Wochen* (fashion weeks) in March and September or during Oktoberfest at the end of September, make reservations at least several months in advance. Munich's tourist offices will handle only written or drop-in requests for reservations assistance. Write or fax the **Fremdenverkehrsamt** (✉ Sendlingerstr. 1, D-80313 Munich, FAX 089/233–0300, WEB www.munich-tourist.de). Tourist offices at the Hauptbahnhof or at the Rathaus (City Hall) on Marienplatz help find rooms. Rates are often but not always lower in suburban hotels—and taking the 15-minute U-bahn or S-bahn ride into town is easy.

$$$$ **Bayerischer Hof.** Germany's most respected family-owned hotel, the Bayerischer Hof began its rich history by hosting Ludwig I's guests. Public rooms are grandly laid out with antiques, paintings, marble, and painted wood. Laura Ashley–decorated rooms face the city center. Rooms facing the interior courtyard are the least expensive and begin at DM 495/€254. ✉ *Promenadepl. 2–6, D-80333,* ☎ *089/21200,* FAX *089/212–0906,* WEB *www.bayerischerhof.de. 396 rooms. 3 restaurants, pool. AE, DC, MC, V.*

$$$$ ★ **Kempinski Hotel Vier Jahreszeiten.** Close to the heart of the city, the Vier Jahreszeiten—Four Seasons—has been playing host to the world's wealthy and titled for more than a century. Elegance and luxury set the tone; many rooms have handsome antique pieces. ✉ *Maximilianstr. 17, D-80539,* ☎ *089/21250; 516/794–2670 reservations in U.S.,* FAX *089/2125–2000,* WEB *www.kempinski-vierjahreszeiten.de. 268 rooms, 38 suites. 2 restaurants, pool. AE, DC, MC, V.*

$$$–$$$$ ★ **Admiral.** The small, privately owned Admiral enjoys a quiet side-street location and its own garden, close to the Isar River and Deutsches Museum. Many of the simply furnished and warmly decorated bedrooms have a balcony overlooking the garden. Bowls of fresh fruit are part of the friendly welcome awaiting guests. The breakfast buffet is a dream, complete with homemade jams, in-season strawberries, and Italian and French delicacies. ✉ *Kohlstr. 9, D-80469,* ☎ *089/216–350,* FAX *089/293–674,* WEB *www.hotel-admiral.de. 33 rooms. Bar, parking (fee). AE, DC, MC, V.*

$$$–$$$$ **Eden Hotel Wolff.** Chandeliers and dark-wood paneling in the public rooms underline the old-fashioned elegance of this downtown favorite (it's across from the train station and the airport bus terminal). The rooms are comfortable, and most are spacious. Dine on excellent Bavarian specialties in the intimate Zirbelstube restaurant. ✉ *Arnulfstr. 4, D-80335,* ☎ *089/551–150,* FAX *089/5511–5555,* WEB *www.ehw.de. 209 rooms, 7 suites. Restaurant. AE, DC, MC, V.*

$$$–$$$$ **Torbräu.** In the shadow of one of Munich's ancient city gates, this snug hotel offers comfortable rooms decorated in plush and ornate Italian style. The location is excellent, as it's midway between the Marienplatz and the Deutsches Museum (and around the corner from the Hofbräuhaus). ✉ *Tal 41, D-80331,* ☎ *089/242–340,* FAX *089/242–34235,* WEB *www.torbraeu.de. 83 rooms, 3 suites. Restaurant, pool. AE, MC, V.*

$$$ **Biederstein.** The hotel is a rather uninspired block of a building, but it fits into its old Schwabing surroundings. At the rim of the Englischer Garten, the Biederstein has many advantages: peace and quiet, for one, excellent service, and comfortable, well-appointed rooms that were carefully renovated. ✉ *Keferstr. 18, D-80335,* ☎ *089/389–9970,* FAX *089/389–997389. 34 rooms, 7 suites. Bar. AE, DC, MC, V.*

$$–$$$ **Adria.** This modern, comfortable hotel is in the middle of Munich's museum quarter. Rooms are large and tastefully decorated, with old prints on the pale pink walls, Oriental rugs on the floors, and flowers beside the large double beds. A spectacular breakfast buffet (including a glass of sparkling wine) is included in the rate. ✉ *Liebigstr. 8a, D-80538,* ☎ *089/293–081,* FAX *089/227–015. 46 rooms. AE, MC, V.*

$$–$$$ **Advokat.** Owner Kevin Voigt designed much of the furniture of his exquisite hotel and had it made by Italian craftsmen. The Italian touch is everywhere, from the sleek, minimalist lines of the bedroom furniture and fittings to the choice prints and modern Florentine mirrors on the walls. If you value modern taste over plush luxury, this is the hotel for you. ✉ *Baaderstr. 1, D-80469,* ☎ *089/216–310,* FAX *089/216–3190,* WEB *www.hotel-advokat.de. 50 rooms. AE, DC, MC, V.*

$ **Hotel-Pension am Siegestor.** An ancient, wood-paneled elevator carries you in style to the fourth-floor reception area of this charming little hotel between Schwabing's main boulevard and the university quarter. Rooms on the fifth floor, tucked up under the eaves, are particularly cozy. None has a private bath, but each floor has its own bathroom. ✉ *Akademiestr. 5, D-80799,* ☎ *089/399–550 or 089/399–551,* FAX *089/343–050. 20 rooms with shared bath. No credit cards.*

$ **Hotel-Pension Beck.** American and British guests receive a particularly warm welcome from the Anglophile owner of the rambling, friendly Beck. Rooms are furnished in pinewood. The pension is near museums and the Englischer Garten. ✉ *Thierschstr. 36, D-80538,* ☎ *089/220–708 or 089/225–768,* FAX *089/220–925,* WEB *www.bst-online.de/pension.beck. 44 rooms, 7 with shower. MC, V.*

Nightlife and the Arts

The Arts

The **Gasteig Kulturzentrum** (✉ Rosenheimerstr. 5, ☎ 089/480–980) is the massive glass-and-brick complex on the hill above the eastern end of the Ludwigsbrücke. It's home to the Munich Philharmonic Orchestra, the main city library, and a variety of theaters, galleries, and cafés. Details of concerts and theater performances are available from the "Vorschau" or "Monatsprogramm" booklets obtainable at most hotel reception desks. Some hotels will make ticket reservations; otherwise book tickets at the two kiosks on the concourse below Marienplatz, or use one of the **ticket agencies** in the city center: Max Hieber Konzertkasse (✉ Liebfrauenstr. 1, ☎ 089/290–08014) or the Residenz Bücherstube (✉ Residenzstr. 1, ☎ 089/220–868 concert tickets only).

CONCERTS

Munich's **Philharmonic Orchestra** performs in one of Germany's finest concert halls, the Philharmonie at the Gasteig Kulturzentrum. Tickets are sold at the box office. The Bavarian Radio Orchestra also performs Sunday concerts at the Gasteig. In summer, concerts are held at Schloss Nymphenburg and in the open-air interior courtyard of the Residenz.

OPERA

Munich's Bavarian State Opera company is world famous, and tickets for major productions in its permanent home, the **Nationaltheater** (✉ Maximilianstr. 11, ☎ 089/2185–1920), are often difficult to come by. Try at the evening box office, which opens on the south side of the theater one hour before performances. Book far in advance through the tourist office for the annual opera festival held in July and August.

THEATER

More than 20 companies perform throughout the city. Compact opera productions and plays are often performed at the **Altes Residenztheater/Cuvilliés-Theater** (✉ Max-Joseph-Pl.; entrance on Residenzstr., ☎ 089/2185–1920. Regular English-language productions of the American Drama Group Europe are staged in the **Amerikahaus** (✉ Karolinenplatz 3, ☎ 089/552–5370).

Nightlife

BARS, CABARET, NIGHTCLUBS

Munich's media types have turned the **Alter Simpl** (✉ Turkenstr. 57, ☎ 089/272–3083) into an unofficial press club. The **Havana** (✉ Herrnstr. 3, ☎ 089/291–884) does its best to look like a run-down Cuban dive, drawing a chic clientele. **O'Reilly's Irish Cellar Pub** (✉ Maximilianstr. 29, ☎ 089/293–311) pours genuine Irish Guinness. Great Caribbean cocktails and a powerful Irish-German Black and Tan (Guinness and strong German beer) are served at the English nautical–style **Pusser's New York Bar** (✉ Falkenturmstr. 9, ☎ 089/220–500). In the Lehel district, **Scalar** (✉ Seitzstr. 12, ☎ 089/215–79–636) is designed to the last corner in modern, sleek style and draws a fairly mixed crowd of designer people. The bar **Schumann's** (✉ Maximilianstr. 36, ☎ 089/229–060) has a shabby New York look, but the clientele is Munich chic.

DANCE CLUBS

Clubs abound in the side streets off Freilitzschstrasse, surrounding Münchener Freiheit in Schwabing. Munich's spectacular dance club center, the **Kunstpark Ost** (✉ Grafingerstr. 6, ☎ 089/490–02928, S-bahn, bus, and tram stops are at Ostbahnhof), is in a former pasta factory with 13 "entertainment areas," including several clubs and music bars. At **Maximilian's** (✉ Maximilianspl. 16, ☎ 089/223–252), the stylish crowd packs a throbbing cellar into the early hours. The **Nachtcafe** (✉ Maximilianspl. 5, ☎ 089/595–900) is open all night on weekends. **P 1** (✉ Haus der Kunst, Prinzregentenstr. 1, ☎ 089/294–252) is the queen of them all, with a series of tiny dance floors and a great sound system. P 1 is allegedly the trendiest club in town, but good luck making it past the bouncer. Tops of the lot (quite literally) is the **Skyline** (✉ Münchner Freiheit, ☎ 089/333–131), at the top of the Hertie department store building.

JAZZ CLUBS

The popular and tiny **Mr. B's** (✉ Herzog-Heinrich-Str. 38, ☎ 089/534–901) is run by New Yorker Alex Best, who also mixes great cocktails. Munich's longest-established jazz haunt, the **Schwabinger Podium** (✉ Wagnerstr. 1, ☎ 089/399–482), has taken to offering rock music as well as traditional jazz; it's packed nightly. The **Unterfahrt** (✉ Kirchenstr. 96, ☎ 089/448–2794), in Munich's latest "quartier Latin," Haidhausen, has traditional and mainstream jazz.

Shopping

Munich has an immense central shopping area, 2 km (1 mi) of pedestrian streets stretching from the train station to Marienplatz and north to Odeonsplatz. The two main streets here are Neuhauserstrasse and Kaufingerstrasse. For upscale shopping, Maximilianstrasse, Residenzstrasse, and Theatinerstrasse are unbeatable and contain a fine array of classy and tempting stores. Schwabing, north of the university, has shops on Schellingstrasse and Hohenzollernstrasse.

Antiques

Blumenstrasse, Türkenstrasse, and Westenriederstrasse have antiques shops of every description, while those that line Prannerstrasse, behind the classy Bayerischer Hof Hotel, concentrate on treasures that usually end up in museums. The open-air Auer Dult fairs sell antiques; they're held on Mariahilfplatz at the end of April, July, and October.

Department Stores

Most of the major department stores are along Maffeistrasse, Kaufingerstrasse, and Neuhauserstrasse. **Hertie** (✉ Bahnhofpl. 7, ☎ 089/55120) is the largest and, some claim, the best department store in the city; it has a stylish delicatessen, a champagne bar, and a bistro. **Kaufhof** has two central Munich stores (✉ Karlspl. 22–24, opposite Hertie, ☎ 089/51250; ✉ corner Marienpl., ☎ 089/231–851); both offer a wide rang[e] of goods in the middle price range. Upscale **Karstadt** (✉ Neuhause[r]str. 18, ☎ 089/290–230) has an abundance of Bavarian arts and craf[ts].

Gift Ideas

Many shops specialize in beer-related souvenirs, but **Ludwig Mory** [...] Marienpl. 8, ☎ 089/224–542) is about the best. Munich is als[o] home of the famous **Porzellan Manufaktur Nymphenburg** (Nym[phen]burg Porcelain Factory; ✉ Odeonspl. and Briennerstr., ☎ 08[9/...] 428; ✉ Nördliche Schlossrondell 8, in front of Schloss Nym[phen]burg, ☎ 089/1791–9710).

Munich Essentials

AIRPORTS AND TRANSFERS

Munich's Franz Josef Strauss (FJS) Airport, named for a f[...] premier, is 28 km (17 mi) northeast of the city center.

➤ AIRPORT INFORMATION: Flughafen München (☎ 089/9[...]

TRANSFERS

The S-8 and S-1 suburban train lines link FJS Airport with the main train station (Hauptbahnhof). Trains leave every 10 minutes, and the trip takes around 40 minutes. Several intermediate stops are made, including the Ostbahnhof (convenient for lodgings east of the Isar River) and such city-center stations as Marienplatz. A one-way ticket costs DM 15.20/€7.60, or DM 12.80/€6.40 if you purchase a multiple-use "strip" ticket. A family of up to five (two adults and three children under 15) can make the trip for DM 28/€14 with a Tageskarte ticket.

Bus service is slower and more expensive (DM 16/€8) than the S-bahn link, unless you are doing a round trip to and from Munich, in which case it costs 26 DM/€13. A taxi costs between DM 90 DM/€45 and DM 110 DM/€55. If you are driving from the airport into the city, follow the MÜNCHEN autobahn signs to A92 and A9. Once on the A92, watch carefully for the signs to Munich; many motorists miss the sign and end up headed toward Stuttgart.

BUS TRAVEL TO AND FROM MUNICH

Munich has no central bus station. Long-distance buses arrive at and depart from the north side of the train station on Arnulfstrasse.

CAR RENTAL

All Hauptbahnhof (train station) offices are in the mezzanine-level gallery above the Deutsche Bahn information and ticket center. Airport offices are in the central area, Zentralbereich.

➤ MAJOR AGENCIES: **Avis** (✉ Airport, ☎ 089/975–97600; ✉ Hauptbahnhof, ☎ 089/550–2251; ✉ Nymphenburgerstr. 61, ☎ 089/1260–0020; ✉ Balanstr. 74, ☎ 089/403–091). **Europcar** (✉ Airport, ☎ 089/973–5020; ✉ Hauptbahnhof, ☎ 089/550–1341; ✉ Hirtenstr. 14, ☎ 089/557–145). **Hertz** (✉ Airport, ☎ 089/978–860; ✉ Hauptbahnhof, ☎ 089/550–2256; ✉ Nymphenburgerstr. 81, ☎ 089/129–5001). **Sixt** (✉ Airport, ☎ 089/526–2525; ✉ Hauptbahnhof, ☎ 089/550–2447; ✉ Seitzstr. 9, ☎ 089/223–333).

CAR TRAVEL

From the north (Nürnberg, Frankfurt), leave the autobahn at the Schwabing exit and follow the STADTMITTE signs. The autobahn from Stuttgart and the west ends at Obermenzing; again, follow the STADTMITTE signs. The autobahns from Salzburg and the east, from Garmisch and the south, and from Lindau and the southwest all join up with the city beltway, the Mittlerer Ring. The city center is well posted. Once in Munich it's best to get around on foot and by public transportation.

CONSULATES

➤ CANADA: ✉ Tal 29, ☎ 089/219–9570.

➤ IRELAND: ✉ Mauerkircherstr. 1a, ☎ 089/985–723.

➤ UNITED KINGDOM: ✉ Bürkleinstr. 10, ☎ 089/211–090.

➤ UNITED STATES: ✉ Königinstr. 5, ☎ 089/28880.

MERGENCIES

DOCTORS AND DENTISTS: **Dentist** (☎ 089/723–3093).

MERGENCY SERVICES: **Ambulance, Fire Department, and Paramedid** (☎ 112). **Police** (☎ 110).

RMACIES: **Europa-Apotheke** (✉ Schützenstr. 12, near Haupt- ☎ 089/595–423). **Internationale Ludwigs-Apotheke** (✉ str. 11, ☎ 089/260–3021).

ENGLISH-LANGUAGE MEDIA

➤ BOOKSTORES: **Anglia English Bookshop** (✉ Schellingstr. 3, ☎ 089/283–642). **Hugendubel** (✉ Marienpl. 22, ☎ 089/23890; ✉ Karlspl. 3, ☎ 089/552–2530).

TAXIS

Munich's cream-color taxis are numerous. Hail them in the street or call ☎ 089/21610 (there's an extra charge of DM 2/€1 if you call). Rates start at DM 5/€2.50. Expect to pay DM 14–DM 16/€7–€8 for a short trip within the city. There is a DM 1/€.50 charge for each piece of luggage.

TOURS

BIKE TOURS

City Hopper Touren offers daily escorted bike tours March–October. Bookings must be made in advance, and starting times are negotiable. Radius Touristik has bicycle tours from May through the beginning of October at 10:15 and 2; the cost, including bike rental, is DM 15/€7.50. Mike's Bike Tours is run by a young American who hires German students to take visitors on a two- to three-hour spin through Munich. The tours start daily at the Old Town Hall, the Altes Rathaus, at 11:20 and 3:50. They cost DM 28/€14, including bike rental.

➤ FEES AND SCHEDULES: **City Hopper Touren** (☎ 089/272–1131). **Mike's Bike Tours** (☎ 089/651–4275). **Radius Touristik** (✉ Arnulfstr. 3, opposite Platforms 30–36 in the Hauptbahnhof, ☎ 089/596–113).

BUS TOURS

City bus tours are operated by Panorama Tours. The blue buses operate year-round, departing daily from in front of the Hertie department store on Bahnhofplatz. The one-hour tour of Munich highlights costs DM 19/€9.50. A 2½-hour city tour departs daily at 10 AM and includes brief visits to the Alte Pinakothek, the Peterskirche, and Marienplatz for the glockenspiel. An afternoon tour, also 2½ hours and starting at 2:30 PM, includes a tour of Schloss Nymphenburg. The cost of each tour is DM 33/€16.50. Another 2½-hour tour, departing Saturday, Sunday, and Monday at 10 AM, includes a visit to the Bavaria film studios. The cost is DM 39/€19.50. A four-hour tour, starting daily at 10 AM and 2:30 PM includes a visit to the Olympic stadium. The cost is DM 49/€24.50. Panorama Tours also runs trips to attractions outside the city, including the "Royal Castles Tour" (Schlösserfahrt) of "Mad" King Ludwig's dream palaces. The cost is DM 78/€40.

➤ FEES AND SCHEDULES: **Panorama Tours** (✉ Arnulfstr. 8, ☎ 089/5502–8995; for the "Royal Castles Tour," call 098/5490–7560).

WALKING TOURS

Two-hour tours of the old city center are given daily in summer (March–October) and on Friday and Saturday in winter (November–February). Tours organized by the visitor center start at 10:30 and 1 in the center of Marienplatz. The cost is DM 16/€8. Munich Walks conducts tours of the old city and sites related to the Third Reich era. The cost is DM 15/€7.50. Tours depart daily at 11 from the Hauptbahnhof, outside the EurAide office by Track 11.

➤ FEES AND SCHEDULES: **Munich Walks** (☎ 0177/227–5901).

TRAIN TRAVEL

All long-distance services arrive at and depart from the main train station, the Hauptbahnhof. Trains to and from destinations in the Bavarian Alps usually use the adjoining Starnbergerbahnhof. For tickets and information go to the station or to the ABR travel agency on Bahnhofplatz.

TRANSPORTATION AROUND MUNICH

Downtown Munich is only about 1½ km (1 mi) square, so it can easily be explored on foot. Other areas—Schwabing, Nymphenburg, the Olympiapark—are best reached on the efficient and comprehensive public transportation network, which includes buses, streetcars, U-bahn (subways), and S-bahn (suburban trains). Tickets are good for the entire network, and you can break your trip as many times as you like using just one ticket, provided you travel in one direction within a given period of time. If you plan to make only a few trips, buy *Streifenkarten* (strip tickets)—blue for adults, red for children. A 10-strip ticket costs DM 16/€8. All tickets must be validated when you begin your trip; punch them in the automatic machines at station entrances and on all buses and streetcars.

The best buy is the *Tageskarte* (all-day ticket): up to two adults and three children can use this ticket for unlimited journeys between 9 AM and the end of the day's service (about 2 AM). It costs DM 12.50/€6.40 for the inner zone, which covers central Munich. A Tageskarte for the entire system, extending to the Starnbergersee and Ammersee, costs DM 26/€13.30. Holders of a Eurail Pass, a Youth Pass, an InterRail Card, or a DB Tourist Card travel free on all S-bahn trains.

The tourist office's "Welcome Card" includes unlimited U-bahn, tram, and bus travel within city limits and reduced entry to museums, art galleries, palaces, and other attractions. It costs DM 12/€6 for one day and DM 30/€15 for three days. A three-day card for two people costs DM 44/€22. The Partner-Tageskarte ticket provides unlimited travel for up to five people (maximum of two adults, plus three children under 15). It is valid weekdays from 9 AM to 6 AM the following day and at any time on weekends. The costs are DM 14/€7 for an inner-zone ticket and DM 28/€14 for the entire network. A three-day card is also available, costing DM 22/€11 for a single and 35 DM/€17.50 in the partner version.

TRAVEL AGENCIES

➤ LOCAL AGENTS: **DER** (✉ Bahnhofpl. 2, ☎ 089/5514–0100). **American Express** (✉ Promenadepl. 6, ☎ 089/290–900).

VISITOR INFORMATION

➤ TOURIST INFORMATION: **Info-Service** (✉ at Rathaus, Marienpl., ☎ 089/2332–8242; ✉ Bahnhofpl. 2, ☎ 089/233–0300, WEB www.munich-tourist.de).

THE BLACK FOREST

A little over a century ago the Black Forest (Schwarzwald) was one of the wildest stretches of countryside in Europe. But then the deep hot springs first enjoyed by the Romans were rediscovered, and small, forgotten villages became wealthy spas. The friendly and hospitable region is still extensively forested, though bouts with acid rain and a fierce windstorm in 1999 have wreaked considerable havoc. The area also offers large, open valleys and stretches of verdant farmland. The Black Forest is the southernmost German wine region and the custodian of some of the country's best traditional foods. Black Forest pine cone–smoked ham and Black Forest cake—kirsch-soaked layers of chocolate cake with sour cherry and whipped cream filling—are among the most famous. The region retains its vibrant clock-making tradition—the origin of a lucrative precision mechanics industry—and woodcarving is still a viable occupation here. Well-marked trails invite hikers in spring and fall and cross-country skiers in winter.

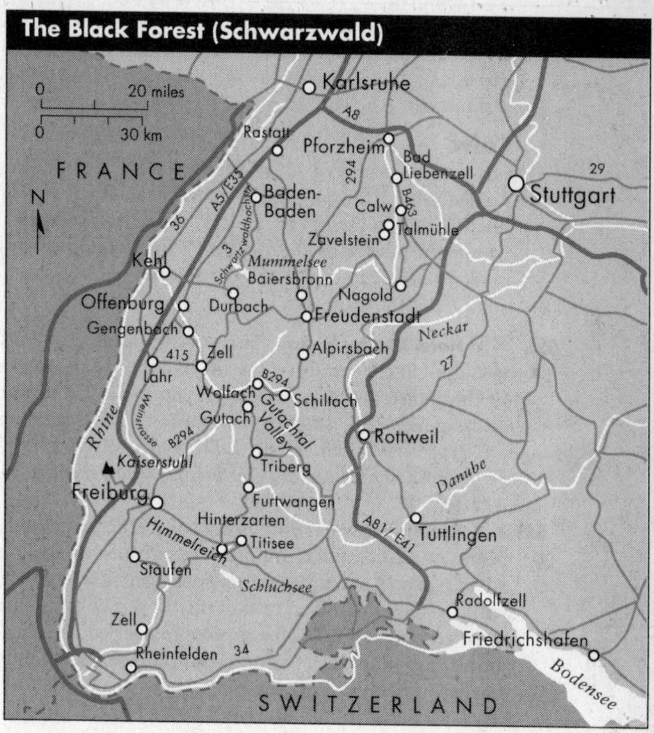

The Black Forest (Schwarzwald)

You can tour the region by all means of transportation, taking in parts of the Black Forest High Road, Low Road, Spa Road, Wine Road, and Clock Road. Crossing all the regions of the Black Forest, these roads start in the north in Pforzheim and go as far south as Staufen (approximately 200 km/125 mi) before descending into the Rhine Valley and returning north along the Rhine River to Baden-Baden (approximately 90 km/56 mi).

Pforzheim

This ancient Roman city, almost completely destroyed by World War II bombing, does not retain any Old World charm, but close by is lovely countryside for exploring. Worth visiting is the **Schmuckmuseum** (Jewelry Museum) in the Reuchlinhaus, which has a magnificent collection of centuries of jewelry dating back to 3000 BC. ✉ *Jahnstr. 42,* ☎ *07231/392–126.* ⏲ *Tues.–Sun. 10–5.*

Bad Liebenzell

The first stop on B–463 is one of the Black Forest's oldest spas, with the remains of 15th-century installations. A special site, too, is the actual fortress of Liebenzell, with a well-preserved 13th-century tower of red sandstone. It is a favorite destination for outings, and has a restaurant. The rest of the fortress is home to a seminar house. In Bad Liebenzell itself, you can take the waters at the **Paracelsusbad Lido Complex** (Paracelsus Swimming Pool Center) on the Nagold riverbank. ☎ *07052/408–250.* 🎫 *DM 30/€15 for 3 hrs in bath; DM 24/€12.30 for 3½ hrs in sauna.* ⏲ *Bath: Apr.–Oct., Mon.–Sat. 8 AM–9 PM, Sun. 8–8; Nov.–Mar., Mon.–Thurs. and Sat. 8:30 AM–9 PM, Sun. and Fri. 8:30–8. Sauna: year-round, Mon.–Thurs. 1–10, Fri. 1–11, Sat. 9 AM–11 PM, Sun. 9–8. Women only in the sauna Thurs.*

$$$ ✕🏨 **Kronen Hotel.** A large modern wing updates this comfortable hotel. The kitchen, which services the hotel's three restaurants, prides itself on its healthful cuisine with lots of fresh vegetables and herbs, whole-grain products, and fruit. ✉ *Badweg 7, D-75378,* ☎ *07052/4090,* FAX *07052/409–420,* WEB *www.kronenhotel.de. 43 rooms. 3 restaurants. AE, DC, V.*

Calw

Lovely half-timbered Calw (pronounced "calve") lies south of Bad Liebenzell. It's famous native son is Nobel Prize–winning novelist and poet Hermann Hesse (1877–1962). The **Hermann Hesse Museum** recounts the author of *Steppenwolf*'s life in photographs, manuscripts, books, and documents (English translation). ✉ *Marktpl. 30,* ☎ *07051/7522.* ⏲ *Tues.–Sun. 11–5.*

$$$ ★ ✕🏨 **Hotel Kloster Hirsau.** This country-house hotel just outside Calw in Calw-Hirsau stands on the site of a 900-year-old monastery, whose Gothic cloisters are still largely intact. In the restaurant, such regional dishes as *Schneckensuppe* (snail soup) and pork fillet in mushroom sauce are served. ✉ *Wildbaderstr. 2, D-75365,* ☎ *07051/96740,* FAX *07051/51795,* WEB *www.hotel/kloster/hirsau.de. 43 rooms. Restaurant, pool. AE, MC, V.*

$$ ✕🏨 **Ratsstube.** Most of the original features, including 16th-century beams and brickwork, are preserved at this historic house in the center of Calw. Rooms aren't spacious, but they are brightly decorated with pastel colors. The restaurant ($) serves such sturdy, traditional German fare as *Zwiebelrostbraten* (pan-fried beefsteak with onions), or the finer wild duck in orange sauce. A salad buffet will take care of smaller appetites, and lunchtime always has a special dish at special rates. ✉ *Marktpl. 12, D-75365,* ☎ *07051/92050,* FAX *07051/70826. 13 rooms. Restaurant. AE, MC, V.*

Nagold

The town of Nagold lies at the confluence of two gently flowing rivers, the Nagold and the Waldach. The elliptical street plan harks back to the town's founding over 750 years ago; half-timbered buildings, the Romanesque Remigius church, and the modest, hilltop remains of a medieval castle are other reminders of its long history.

$–$$ ✕ **Adler.** This 17th-century half-timbered inn has the kind of ambience lesser establishments can't imitate with false beams. The menu emphasizes traditional Swabian dishes. Veal in mushroom sauce and venison (in season) are reliable favorites. Rooms here cost about DM 156/€80. ✉ *Badstr. 1,* ☎ *07452/869–000,* FAX *07452/869–00200. AE. Closed Mon.*

Freudenstadt

This small town lies south of Nagold in the middle of lush farmland. Flattened by the French two weeks before the end of World War II, it was painstakingly restored. Arcaded shops surround the market square, which is as large as several football fields. The 17th-century **Protestant parish church**'s L shape was designed with two naves but a single pulpit. The idea was that the sexes could not see each other during services but would keep their eyes on the preacher. There are several sculptures of angels along the edge of the ceiling.

$$ ✕ **Ratskeller.** If it's cold outside, ask for a place near the *Kachelofen,* a large, traditional tile stove. Swabian dishes usually on the menu are Zwiebelrostbraten, served with sauerkraut, and pork fillet with mushroom gravy. In season, there's venison, and a specialty is the homemade trout roulade with crab sauce. ✉ *Marktpl. 8,* ☎ *07441/2693. V. Closed Wed.*

$$$ ✕ **Warteck.** Flowers spill over, even in the nooks and crannies between the leaded-pane windows, and continue in the color scheme of the rest of the house. The menu strikes a delicious balance between local and extraregional cuisine. Choices include succulent lamb in wild herbs, or *Leipziger Allerlei*, a vegetable stew with river crabs. In season the *Spargel* (asparagus) is dressed in an aromatic hazelnut vinaigrette. ✉ *Stuttgarter Str. 14, D-72250,* ☎ *07441/91920. DC, MC, V. Closed Tues.*

$$$ ★ ✕🏨 **Schwarzwaldhotel Birkenhof.** A woodland setting and a wide range of sports facilities are principal attractions of this motel-like hostelry above town. Its two restaurants offer sturdy Black Forest fare. ✉ *Wildbaderstr. 95, D-72250,* ☎ *07441/8920,* FAX *07441/4763. 62 rooms. 2 restaurants, pool, sauna, solarium, squash, bowling alley. AE, DC, MC, V.*

$$ ✕🏨 **Bären.** The Montigels have owned the sturdy old Gasthof Bären since 1878. Rooms are modern but contain such homey touches as farmhouse-style bedsteads and cupboards. The beamed restaurant (closed Monday and Friday) is a favorite with the locals. Its menu includes Swabian dishes (roasts in heavy sauces, fried *Maultaschen*, those giant raviolis), and lighter fare. The trout is caught locally. ✉ *Langestr. 33, D-72250,* ☎ *07441/2729,* FAX *07441/2887. 33 rooms. Restaurant, parking Restaurant is closed for lunch except on Sun. V.*

Baiersbronn

This mountain resort (7 km/4 mi northwest of Freudenstadt), in the midst of the northern Black Forest, is blessed with two of Germany's leading hotel-restaurants—both for hospitality and cuisine. Skiing, golfing, and horseback riding are among the area's activities.

$$$$ ★ ✕🏨 **Bareiss.** This luxury modern resort hotel is almost too big for the little town of Mitteltal near Baiersbronn. Inside, it has rooms with dark-wood furniture and tapestry-papered walls and others with a light and airy Laura Ashley decor. Its elegant Restaurant Bareiss ($$$–$$$$; closed Monday and Tuesday) serves imaginative nouvelle cuisine and carefully selected wines (30 brands of champagne alone). There are two other restaurants to suit your fancy as well. The hotel and its spa are among the best-equipped in the Black Forest. Suites have their own saunas, solariums, and whirlpool baths. ✉ *Gärtenbühlweg 14, D-07442 Mitteltal/Baiersbronn,* ☎ *07442/470,* FAX *07442/47320,* WEB *www.relaischateaux.fr/bareiss. 53 rooms, 37 apartments, 10 suites. 3 restaurants, 6 pools. AE, DC, MC, V.*

$$–$$$ ★ ✕🏨 **Traube Tonbach.** The award-winning mountain hotel has three outstanding restaurants—the Schwarzwaldstube, serving classic French cuisine (closed Monday and Tuesday); the Köhlerstube, offering international fare; and the Bauernstube, renowned for its Swabian dishes. The hotel is in an idyllic setting, each room enjoying sweeping views. Guests are nearly outnumbered by a small army of extremely helpful and friendly staff. ✉ *Tonbachstr. 237, D-72270,* ☎ *07442/4920,* FAX *07442/492–692,* WEB *www.traube-tonbach.de. 108 rooms, 55 apartments, 12 suites. 3 restaurants, 3 pools. AE, DC, MC, V.*

$–$$ ✕🏨 **Hotel Lamm.** The half-timber exterior of this 200-year-old building presents a clear picture of the traditional Black Forest hotel within. Rooms are furnished with heavy oak fittings and some fine antiques. In its beamed restaurant ($) you can order fish taken from the hotel's trout pools. ✉ *Ellbacherstr. 4, D-072270 Mitteltal/Baiersbronn,* ☎ *07442/4980,* FAX *07442/49878,* WEB *www.lamm-mitteltal.de. 48 rooms. Restaurant, pool. AE, DC, MC, V.*

Wolfach

South of Freudenstadt on B–294, Wolfach has a glass factory, the ★ **Dorotheen-Glashütte,** that is one of the last of its kind—glass is blown by centuries-old techniques. You can watch the teams making vases or blowing and etching drinking glasses. The large sales room has all kinds of objects that make excellent souvenirs, as well as a Christmas display. ✉ *Glashüttenweg 4,* ☎ *07834/751.* ⏲ *Daily. 9–4:30; shop open until 5.30; closed Sun. and holidays Jan. 1–Apr. 30.*

Gutach

The town lies south of Wolfach in Gutachtal, a valley famous for its traditional costumes. If you're here on holidays (and some Sundays), you'll see the married women sporting black pom-poms on their hats to denote their matronly status (red pom-poms are for the unmarried). Gutach is best known for the **Vogtsbauernhof,** an outdoor museum consisting of old Black Forest buildings. ☎ *7831/93560.* ⏲ *Late Mar.–early Nov., daily 8:30–6.*

Triberg

This town is the site of Germany's highest **★waterfalls,** plunging nearly 509 ft. The area around the falls is also renowned for pom-pom hats, straw-covered farmhouses, cuckoo clocks, and mountain railways. It is the starting place for walks through forests and valleys following the route of the cuckoo-clock traders. The ride on the **Schwarzwaldbahn** (Black Forest Railway) Offenburg–Villingen line, which passes through Triberg, is one of Germany's most scenic.

The **Schwarzwaldmuseum** (Black Forest Museum) has exhibits related to Black Forest culture. The oldest clock dates from 1640; its simple wooden mechanism is said to have been carved with a bread knife. Barrel organs and fairground organs from Berlin are newcomers to the collection. ✉ *Wallfahrtstr. 4,* ☎ *07722/4434.* ⏲ *May–Oct., daily 9–6, Nov. 1–14 and Dec. 16–Apr., daily 10–5; Nov. 15–Dec. 15, weekends 10–5.*

$ ★ ✕🏨 **Hotel-Restaurant-Pfaff.** This old post-and-beam restaurant, with its blue *Kachelofen* (tiled stove) attracts people of all stripes for a luxurious yet affordable meal of regional specialties. The Pfaff has been in family ownership since 1882. It stands right at the gateway to the famous cascade of Triberg. ✉ *Hauptstr. 85, D-78098 Triberg,* ☎ *07722/4479,* FAX *07722/7879,* WEB *www.hotel-pfaff.com. 23 rooms. Restaurant. AE, D, MC, V.*

$$$–$$$$ ★ ✕🏨 **Romantik Parkhotel Wehrle.** This enchanting building in the center of town has been welcoming guests since 1707. Its vine-covered facade dominates the marketplace. The comfortable rooms are individually furnished, often in Biedermeier style. The service is impeccable, and there is a special menu ($$$–$$$$) for the restaurant's outstanding trout. ✉ *Gartenstr. 24, D-78098,* ☎ *07722/86020,* FAX *07722/860–290,* WEB *www.romantikhotels.com/Triberg. 50 rooms, 1 apartment, 1 suite. 2 restaurants, 1 pool. AE, DC, MC, V.*

Furtwangen

Clock enthusiasts visit Furtwangen for its **Uhren Museum** (Clock Museum), the largest of its kind in Germany. It charts the development of Black Forest clocks, especially the cuckoo clock. The collection includes a cabinet timepiece weighing more than a ton, making various sounds (such as a rooster's crow in the morning), and with little mechanical plays performed automatically at various times in the Christian calendar. ✉ *Robert-Gerwig-Pl. 11,* ☎ *07723/920–117.* ⏲ *Apr.–Oct., daily 9–6; Nov.–Mar., daily 10–5.*

Titisee

The 2½-km-long (1½-mi-long) lake, set in a mighty forest, is the star attraction of the lakeland region. It becomes invariably crowded in summer with boats and windsurfers, and there are endless souvenir shops.

$$ ✕🏨 **Romantik Hotel Adler Post.** In the Neustadt district of Titisee, about 5 km (3 mi) from the lake, the solid, old building has been in the Ketterer family for more than 140 years. The guest rooms are comfortably and traditionally furnished. The hotel's restaurant ($) is noted for its regional cuisine. ✉ *Hauptstr. 16, D-79822 Titisee–Neustadt,* ☎ *07651/5066,* FAX *07651/3729,* WEB *www.romantikhotels.com/Titisee-Neustadt. 30 rooms. Restaurant, pool. AE, DC, MC, V. Closed mid-Mar.–early Apr..*

Hinterzarten

This lovely 800-year-old town is the most popular resort for cross-country skiing and hiking in the southern Black Forest. Some buildings date from the 12th century, among them **St. Oswalds Kirche** (St. Oswald's Church), built in 1146. Hinterzarten's oldest inn, **Weisses Rossle,** has operated since 1347.

$$$$ ✕🏨 **Park Hotel Adler.** This hotel, established in 1446, stands on grounds that are ringed by the Black Forest. Marie-Antoinette once ate here. In its Grill Restaurant ($), Continental cuisine is served. You can order regional dishes in the rustic Alte Ecke. All rooms are sumptuously appointed. ✉ *Adlerpl. 3, D-79856,* ☎ *07652/1270,* FAX *07652/127–717,* WEB *www.parkhotel.de. 46 rooms, 32 suites. 2 restaurants, pool. AE, DC, MC, V.*

Schluchsee

The largest of the Black Forest lakes, mountain-enclosed Schluchsee is a diverse resort, attracting swimmers, windsurfers, fishers, and, in winter, skiers, skaters, and tobogganers. At 4,900 ft, the neighboring Feldberg is the region's highest mountain and offers the best downhill skiing, and many attractive walks may be made in the environs.

Freiburg

Perched on the western slopes of the Black Forest, this is one of the region's largest and loveliest cities; it was founded as a free market town in the 12th century. Towering over Freiburg's rebuilt medieval streets ★ is its most famous landmark, the **Münster** (Cathedral). The church, which took three centuries to build—from 1200 to 1513—has one of the finest spires in the world. ✉ *Münsterpl.,* ☎ *0761/31099.* ⏲ *Münster tours Mon. and Fri. 2:30, Wed.–Thurs. and weekends 10:30.*

The Old Town is traffic-free, and every day but Sunday the square in front of the cathedral, **Münsterplatz,** teems with the town market, where you can buy everything from herbs to hot sausage. The 16th-century red Kaufhaus, with its statue-decorated facade, overlooks it.

$–$$ ✕ **Kühler Krug.** Wild game and goose-liver terrine are among the specialties at this restaurant, which has even given its name to a distinctive saddle-of-venison dish. There's also a range of freshwater fish available. ✉ *Torpl. 1,* ☎ *0761/29103. MC, V. Closed Wed.*

$–$$ ✕ **Oberkirchs Weinstuben.** Next to the Renaissance Kaufhaus, this wine cellar is a bastion of tradition and local Gemütlichkeit. Approximately 20 Baden wines are served by the glass, from white Gutedel to red Spätburgunder. The proprietor personally bags some of the game that ends up in the kitchen. Fresh trout is another specialty. ✉ *Münsterpl. 22,* ☎ *0761/202–6868. AE, MC, V. Closed Sun. and Jan. 10–Feb. 2.*

$ ✕ **Karchers Weinstube.** This Weinstube is full of locals and is just like the ones described in romantic novels—with old, shoe-scrubbed floor, well-worn tables, wood furnishings and paneling, a large and diverse wine list, excellent and basic dishes served with *Rösti* (fried potatoes) or *Schupfnudel* (oblong potato-based dumplings) and—in season—*Feldsalat* (lamb's lettuce). ✉ *Eisenbahnstr. 29,* ☎ *0761/202–870. No credit cards.*

$ ✕ **Freiburger Salatstuben.** Vegetarian food is prepared in creative ways—try the homemade whole-wheat noodles with cauliflower in a pepper cream sauce—and served cafeteria style. It gets crowded with university students at peak hours. ✉ *Am Martinstor-Löwenstr. 1,* ☎ *0761/35155. No credit cards. Closed Sun. No dinner Fri. and Sat.*

$$$$ ★ ✕🏨 **Colombi.** Freiburg's most luxurious hotel also has the city's finest and most original kitchen. You can order hearty Black Forest fare in a rustic room with hand-fashioned country chairs or imaginatively prepared dishes in an elegant dining room. The two reconstructed 18th-century farmhouse guest cottages are stunningly furnished and decorated with antiques. ✉ *Am Colombi Park/Rotteckring 16, D-79098,* ☎ *0761/21060,* FAX *0761/31410,* WEB *www.colombi.de. 80 rooms, 12 suites. Restaurant. AE, DC, MC, V.*

$$$ ★ ✕🏨 **Zum Roten Bären.** A showpiece of the Ring group, this inn, which dates from 1311, has very comfortable lodging and excellent dining in a cozy warren of restaurants and taverns. The two basement floors of cellars date from the 12th century and are well stocked with fine wines. ✉ *Oberlinden 12, D-79098,* ☎ *0761/387–870,* FAX *0761/36916,* WEB *www.roterlbaeren.de. 25 rooms, 3 suites. 3 restaurants. AE, DC, MC, V.*

$$–$$$ ✕🏨 **Victoria.** Owners Astrid and Bertram Späth have gone to great lengths to make their unique and excellent hostelry eco-friendly: hardwood floors are wet-vacuumed to prevent dust, beds have special mattresses and covers, eco-friendly cleaning products are used, and the electricity is supplied by renewable resources. The result was the InternationaL Hotel & Restaurant Association's Environmental Award 2000. Each night, a mixed crowd fills the Café Colonial Hemingway. ✉ *Eisenbahnstr. 54, D-79098,* ☎ *0761/207340,* FAX *0761/20734–444. 63. Restaurant, bar, free parking, free travel on local transit with DM 50/€25 deposit. AE, DC, MC, V.*

$$ 🏨 **Rappen Hotel.** The Rappen is in the center of Old Town overlooking the marketplace and the cathedral (and overhearing the bustle of the former and the bells of the latter). The rooms have a bright, fresh color scheme. The comfortable restaurant offers more than 200 regional wines. ✉ *Am Münsterpl. 13, D-79098,* ☎ *0761/31353,* FAX *0761/382–252. 25 rooms, 13 with bath. Restaurant. AE, DC, MC, V.*

Staufen

This small town, some 20 km (12 mi) south of Freiburg, claims the inquisitive Dr. Faustus as one of its early burghers. Faustus, who reputedly made a pact with the Devil, was the subject of Goethe's 1808 drama, *Faust.* Faustus allegedly lived in room 5 at the inn **Gasthaus zum Löwen** (✉ Hauptstr. 47) and died there of "a broken neck."

En Route From Staufen turn northward toward Baden-Baden along the **Weinstrasse** (Wine Road) skirting the French border to your left, through vineyards that produce the prized Baden wine. All the vineyards offer tastings, so don't hesitate to drop in and try one or two.

Leave the Weinstrasse at the town of Lahr and head inland, on B–415, through the narrow Schuttertal valley to Zell, and from there to the **Schwarzwaldhochstrasse** (Black Forest High Road). This is the land of fable and superstition, and if you're here during the misty days of autumn, stop off at the mystery-shrouded lake called the **Mummelsee.**

Baden-Baden

★ Fashionable Baden-Baden, idyllically set in a wooded valley of the northern Black Forest, sits atop the extensive underground hot springs that gave the city its name (*Baden* means "baths"). The Romans first exploited the springs, which were rediscovered a couple of centuries ago.

By the end of the 19th century, there was scarcely a crowned head of Europe who had not dipped into the healing waters.

One of the grand buildings of Baden-Baden's Belle Epoque is the pillared 1820s **Kurhaus** (Spa), part of the complex that includes a manicured park, a theater, shops, hotels, restaurants, and Germany's oldest casino, which opened its doors in 1838. Visitors are required to sign a declaration that they enter with sufficient funds to settle subsequent debts. Passports are necessary as proof of identity and jacket and tie are required. Guided tours are offered. ✉ *Kaiserallee 1,* ☎ *07221/210–60.* ⏲ *Tours Apr.–Sept., daily 9:30–11:30, Oct.–Mar., daily 10–11:30 AM).*

At Baden-Baden's famous Roman baths, the **Friedrichsbad,** you take the waters just as the Romans did nearly 2,000 years ago—nude. The Caracalla-Therme are an alternative for those uncomfortable with the idea of mixed nude bathing. The remains of the Roman baths that lie beneath the Friedrichsbad can be visited from April through October. ✉ *Römerpl. 1,* ☎ *07221/275–920.* 🎟 *3 hrs, DM 28/€14.35 (DM 48/€24.60 with massage).* ⏲ *Mon.–Sat. 9 AM–10 PM, Sun. noon–8. Children under 18 not admitted.*

The **Caracalla-Therme** (Caracalla Baths) are a huge, modern complex with five indoor pools, two outdoor pools, numerous whirlpools, a solarium, and a "sauna landscape"—you look out through windows at the countryside while you bake. ✉ *Römerpl. 11,* ☎ *07221/275–940.* 🎟 *2 hrs, DM 18/€9.20; 3 hrs, DM 24/€12.30.* ⏲ *Daily 8 AM–10 PM.*

$$$–$$$$ ✕ **Le Jardin de France.** This clean, crisp little French restaurant, whose owners are Alsatian, emphasizes elegant dining in simple surroundings. The duck may be cooked with raisins, figs, nuts, and a gingerbread cookie, or the crayfish with chanterelles. ✉ *Rotenbachtalstr. 10,* ☎ *07221/300–7860. AE, DC, MC, V Closed Mon.–Tues.*

$ ✕ **Weinstube Zum Engel.** The Frölich family has been in charge of the Angel (in the suburb of Neuweier) for four generations. It is an ideal place for traditional German food such as sauerbraten or Wiener schnitzel. The selection of wines, served by the glass, does supreme justice to the fine local vintages. ✉ *Mauerbergstr. 62,* ☎ *07223/57243. No credit cards. Closed Mon.–Tues., and 2 wks in Mar.*

$$$–$$$$ ★ ✕🏨 **Romantik Hotel Der Kleine Prinz.** Each room of this beautifully modernized 19th-century mansion is decorated in a different style, from romantic art nouveau to city chic. Chef Berthold Krieger combines flair with unmistakable German thoroughness, elevating the restaurant ($$$–$$$$) to a leading position in demanding Baden-Baden. ✉ *Lichtentalerstr. 36, D-76530,* ☎ *07221/3464,* FAX *07221/38264,* WEB *www.derkleineprinz.de. 23 rooms, 17 suites. Restaurant. AE, DC, MC, V.*

$$$$ 🏨 **Brenner's Park Hotel & Spa.** This stately, palatial hotel set in a private park had its beginnings 129 years ago. All rooms are luxuriously furnished and appointed. The spa provides further pampering. ✉ *Schillerstr. 6, D-76530,* ☎ *07221/9000,* FAX *07221/38772,* WEB *www.brenners-park.de. 68 rooms, 32 suites. 2 restaurants, pool. AE, DC, MC.*

$$ 🏨 **Merkur.** The Merkur has large and comfortable rooms. Quality is self-evident, and guests return again and again. A pretty breakfast room greets you in the morning, where a solid breakfast is provided. Ask for the special arrangements for longer stays. ✉ *Merkurstr. 8,,* ☎ *07221/3030,* FAX *07221/303–333,* WEB *www.hotel-merkur.com. 36 rooms. Restaurant. AE, D, MC, V.*

$ 🏨 **Hotel am Markt.** The Bogner family has run the place for more than three decades—a relatively short length of time for this 250-plus-year-old building. It's friendly, popular, and right in the center of town. ✉ *Marktpl. 17–18, D-76530,* ☎ *07221/22747,* FAX *07221/391–887. 28 rooms, 14 with bath. Restaurant. AE, DC, MC, V.*

The Black Forest Essentials

AIR TRAVEL

The nearest airports are in Stuttgart; Strasbourg, in the neighboring French Alsace; and the Swiss border city of Basel, just 64 km (40 mi) from Freiburg.

BUS TRAVEL

The bus system works closely with the German railways to reach every corner of the Black Forest. At train stations you will find either a bus station right near the entrance or signs directing you to the central bus stations (ZOB). For more information on bus travel, contact the Regionalbusverkehr Südwest.

➤ FARES AND SCHEDULES: **Regionalbusverkehr Südwest** (Regional Bus Lines, ☎ 0721/84060 in Karlsruhe).

CAR TRAVEL

The Rhine Valley autobahn, the A5, runs the entire length of the Black Forest and connects at Karlsruhe with the rest of the German expressway network. Well-paved, single-lane highways traverse the region.

TOURS

Freiburg Kultur offers bus tours of the Black Forest, beginning from Freiburg. Prices start at DM 49/€24.50. The group also leads in-depth tours of Freiburg itself (DM 10/€5).

➤ FEES AND SCHEDULES: **Freiburg Kultur** (✉ Rotteckring 14 Freiburg, ☎ 0761/290–7447WEB www.freiburg-kultour.com).

TRAIN TRAVEL

A main north–south train line follows the Rhine Valley, carrying EuroCity and InterCity trains that call at hourly intervals at Freiburg and Baden-Baden, connecting them directly with Frankfurt and many other German cities. Local lines connect most Black Forest towns, and two local east–west services, the Black Forest Railway and the Höllental Railway, are spectacular scenic runs.

VISITOR INFORMATION

Tourismus Marketing provides information on all areas of the Black Forest. Other local tourist information centers are listed by town below.

➤ TOURIST INFORMATION: **Baden-Baden** (✉ Solmsstr. 1, D-76530, ☎ 07221/275–2001, WEB www.baden-baden.de). **Freiburg** (✉ Rotteckring 14, D-79098, ☎ 0761/388-1880). **Freudenstadt** (✉ Promenadenpl. 1, D-72250, ☎ 07441/8640, WEB www.freudenstadt.de). **Pforzheim** (✉ Marktpl. 1, D-75175, ☎ 07231/19433, WEB www.pforzheim.de). **Schluchsee** (✉ Kurverwaltung, Fischbacherstr. 7, D-79859, ☎ 07656/7732, WEB www.schluchsee.de). **Tourismus Marketing** (regional tourist authority; ✉ Bertoldstr. 45, D-79098 Freiburg, ☎ 0761/296–2260).

FRANKFURT

Originally a Roman settlement, Frankfurt later served as one of Charlemagne's two capitals (the other being Aachen). Still later, the electors of the Holy Roman Empire met here to choose and crown the emperor. It is also the birthplace of the poet and dramatist Johann Wolfgang von Goethe (1749–1832). Virtually flattened by bombs during World War II, Frankfurt now bristles with skyscrapers, the visible signs of the city's role as Germany's financial capital. Five of the largest banks in Germany are headquartered here.

Exploring Frankfurt

Numbers in the margin correspond to points of interest on the Frankfurt map.

The neighborhood around the Hauptbahnhof (main train station), site of many major hotels, is mostly devoted to business, but be careful of the seedy red-light district nearby. The Old Town has some restored medieval buildings. On the south bank of the Main River, the old quarter of Sachsenhausen has been sensitively preserved and is full of taverns and museums. The neighborhood is the home of the famous *Apfelwein* (apple wine or cider) taverns, with long tables, backless benches, schmaltzy murals on the walls, and sing-alongs.

15 **Alte Oper** (Old Opera House). Built between 1873 and 1880, Frankfurt's Old Opera House was beautifully reconstructed after World War II. The building today serves as multipurpose performance hall. Tickets to events can range from DM 20/€10 to nearly DM 300/€150. Even if you don't go to a performance, it's worth having a look at the ponderous and ornate lobby. ⊠ *Opernpl.,* ☎ *069/134–0400,* WEB *www.alte-oper-frankfurt.de.*

13 **Börse** (Stock Exchange). The Börse was founded by Frankfurt merchants in 1558 to establish some order in their often chaotic dealings, but the present building dates from the 1870s. This center for Germany's stock and money market also has a visitor's gallery. ⊠ *Börsenpl.,* ☎ *069/21010,* WEB *www.deutsche-boerse.com.* ⏲ *Visitor's gallery weekdays 10:30–1:30.*

14 **Fressgasse** (Pig-Out Alley). The proper name of one of the city's liveliest thoroughfares is Grosse Bockenheimer Strasse, but Frankfurters have given it this sobriquet because of the amazing choice of delicatessens, wine merchants, cafés, and restaurants. ⊠ *Opernpl. to Hauptwache.*

★ 12 **Goethehaus und Goethemuseum** (Goethe House and Museum). The birthplace of Germany's most famous poet is furnished with many original pieces that belonged to his family. Although the original house was destroyed by Allied bombing, it has been carefully rebuilt and restored in every detail. The adjoining museum contains manuscripts in Goethe's own hand, works of art that inspired him (he was an amateur painter), and works associated with his literary contemporaries. ⊠ *Grosser Hirschgraben 23–25,* ☎ *069/138–800,* WEB *www.goethehaus-frankfurt.de.* ⏲ *Apr.–Sept., weekdays 9–6, weekends 10–4; Oct.–Mar., weekdays 9–4, weekends 10–4.*

1 **Hauptwache.** This square serves as the hub of the city's transportation network. The attractive Baroque building with a steeply sloping roof is the actual Hauptwache (main guard), a municipal guardhouse built in 1729. Today it houses a café and a tourist information office. ⊠ *Zeil and Grosse Eschenheimer Str.*

11 **Jüdisches Museum** (Jewish Museum). In the former Rothschild Palace, this museum tells the story of Frankfurt's Jewish quarter, which prior to the Holocaust was the second-largest Jewish community in Germany. The archives include 5,000 books and a large photograph collection. ⊠ *Untermainkai 14–15,* ☎ *069/212–3500,* WEB *www.juedischesmuseum.de.* ⏲ *Tues. and Thurs.–Sun. 10–5, Wed. 10–8.*

8 **Kaiserdom** (Imperial Cathedral). Because the Holy Roman emperors were chosen and crowned here from the 16th to 18th century, the Church of St. Bartholomew is commonly known as the Kaiserdom, even though it isn't the seat of a bishop. It was built largely between the 13th and 15th centuries, and most of its original treasures survived the bombs

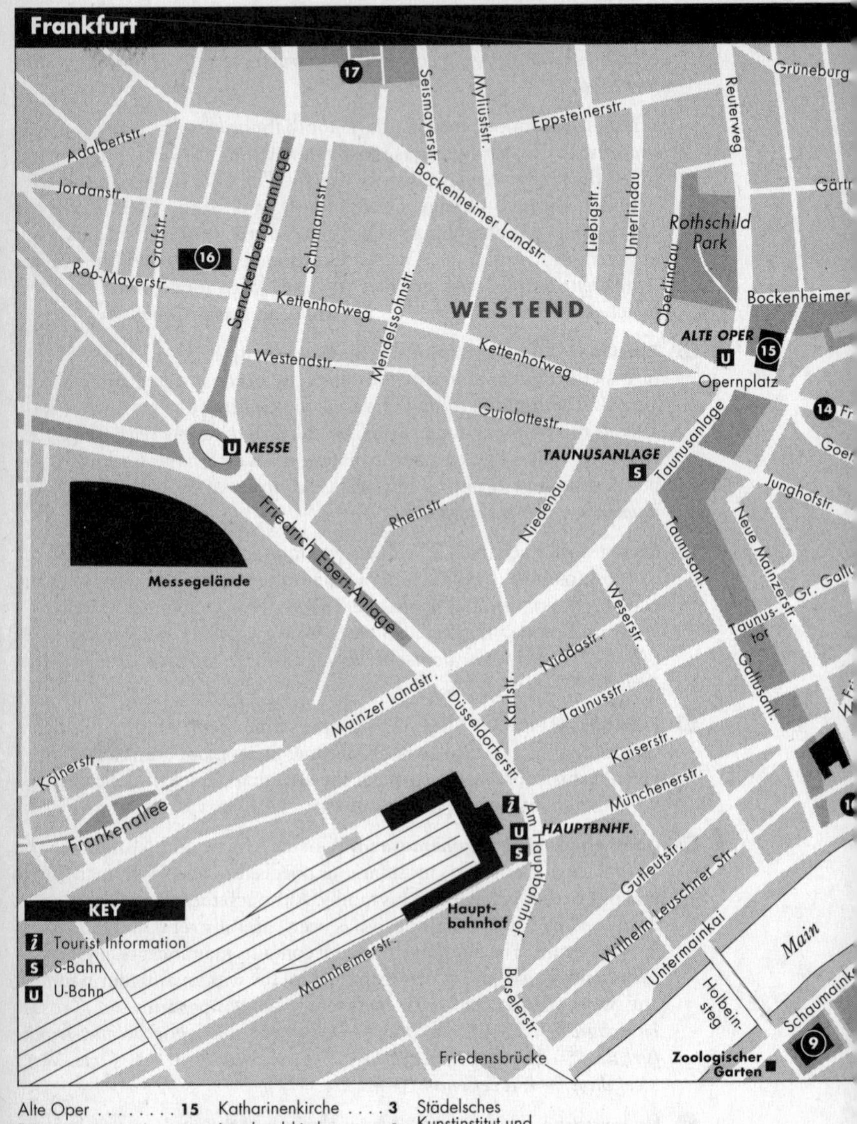

Alte Oper 15
Börse 13
Fressgasse 14
Goethehaus und Goethemuseum 12
Hauptwache 1
Jüdisches Museum 11
Kaiserdom 8

Katharinenkirche 3
Leonhardskirche 4
Naturkundemuseum Senckenberg 16
Nikolaikirche 7
Palmengarten 17
Römer 6
Römerberg Square 5

Städelsches Kunstinstitut und Städtische Galerie 10
Städtische Galerie Liebieghaus 9
Zeil 2

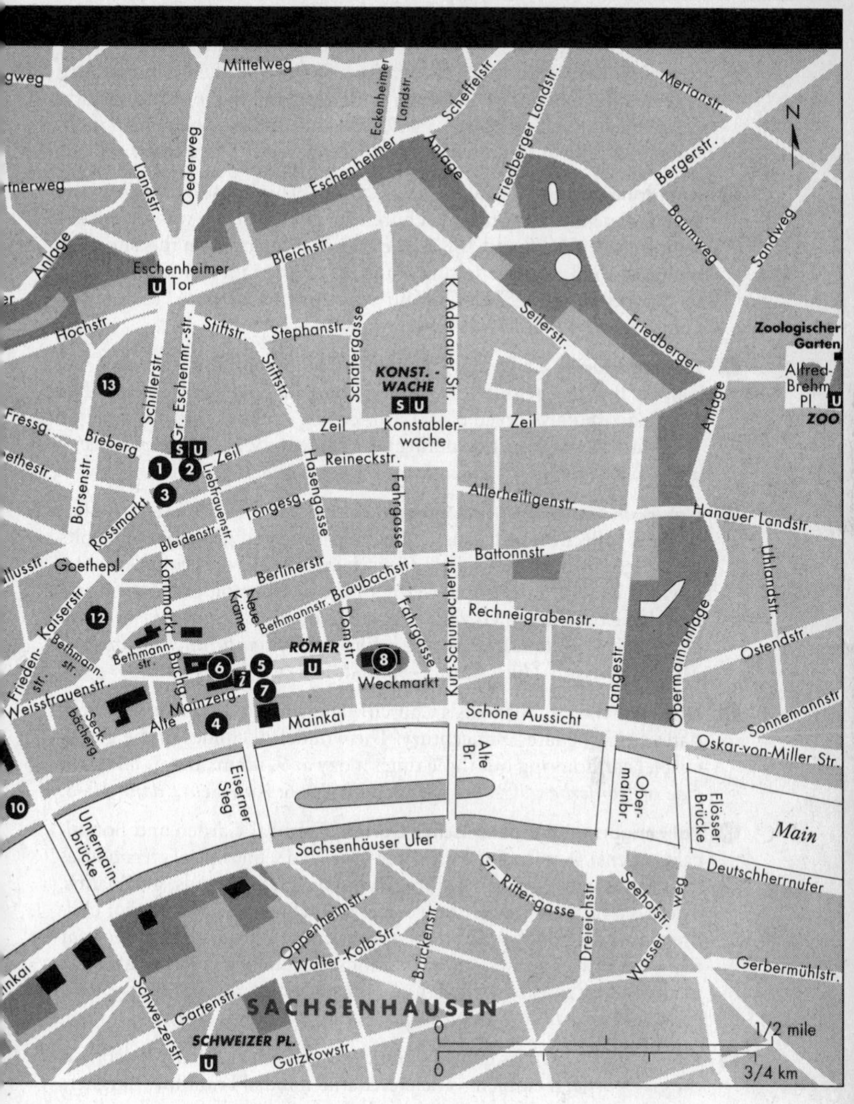
Mittelweg
Eckenheimer Landstr.
Scheffelstr.
Merianstr.
Friedberger Landstr.
Oederweg
Landstr.
Eschenheimer Anlage
Anlage
Bergerstr.
Baumweg
Sandweg
Bleichstr.
Eschenheimer Tor
Hochstr.
Stiftstr.
Stephanstr.
Schäfergasse
K. Adenauer Str.
Seilerstr.
Friedberger Anlage
Zoologischer Garten
Alfred-Brehm Pl.
ZOO
KONST.-WACHE
Konstablerwache
Zeil
Schillerstr.
Gr. Eschenmr.-str.
Fressg.
Bieberg
Reineckstr.
Hasengasse
Fahrgasse
Allerheiligenstr.
Hanauer Landstr.
Börsenstr.
Rossmarkt
Liebfrauenstr.
Töngesg.
Bleidenstr.
Goethepl.
Battonnstr.
Uhlandstr.
Kornmarkt
Berlinerstr.
Braubachstr.
Kurt-Schumacherstr.
Neue Kräme
Bethmannstr.
Domstr.
Recheigrabenstr.
Langestr.
Obermainanlage
Kaiserstr.
Frieden-str.
Weissfrauenstr.
Buchg.
RÖMER
Weckmarkt
Ostendstr.
Alte Mainzerg.
Seckbächerg.
Mainkai
Schöne Aussicht
Sonnemannstr.
Oskar-von-Miller Str.
Eiserner Steg
Alte Br.
Obermainbr.
Flösser Brücke
Main
Untermainbrücke
Sachsenhäuser Ufer
Deutschherrnufer
Gr. Ritter-gasse
Seehofstr.
Wasserweg
Oppenheimstr.
Walter-Kolb-Str.
Brückenstr.
Dreieichstr.
Gerbermühlstr.
Schweizerstr.
Gartenstr.
SACHSENHAUSEN
SCHWEIZER PL.
Gutzkowstr.
1/2 mile
3/4 km

of World War II. The tall, red-sandstone tower (almost 300 ft high) was added between 1415 and 1514. The view from the top is an exciting panorama. In 1953 excavations in front of the main entrance revealed the remains of a Roman settlement and the foundations of a Carolingian imperial palace. ✉ *Dompl. 1.* ⏲ *Mon.–Thur. and Sat. 9–noon and 2:30–6, Fri. and Sun. 2:30–6 (closes at 5 in winter).*

3 **Katharinenkirche** (St. Catherine's Church). This house of worship, the first independent Protestant church in Gothic style, was originally built between 1678 and 1681. The church it replaced on this site, dating from 1343, was the setting of the first Protestant sermon preached in Frankfurt, in 1522. Goethe was confirmed here. ✉ *An der Hauptwache.* ⏲ *Weekdays 2–6.*

4 **Leonhardskirche** (St. Leonard's Church). This beautifully preserved 13th-century building with five naves has some fine old stained glass. The hanging, ornately carved piece of the ceiling vault was already a major Frankfurt tourist attraction during the 17th century. ✉ *Am Leonhardstor and Untermainkai.* ⏲ *Tues.–Sun. 10–noon and 3–6.*

16 **Naturkundemuseum Senckenberg** (Natural History Museum). An important collection of fossils, animals, plants, and geological exhibits is upstaged by the famous diplodocus dinosaur—the only complete specimen of its kind in Europe. Many of the exhibits on prehistoric animals have been designed with children in mind. ✉ *Senckenberganlage 25,* ☎ *069/75420,* WEB *www.senckenberg.uni-frankfurt.de/sme.htm.* ⏲ *Mon.–Tues. and Thurs.–Fri. 9–5, Wed. 9–8, weekends 9–6.*

7 **Nikolaikirche** (St. Nicholas's Church). This small red-sandstone church dates from the late 13th century. The wonderful chimes of the glockenspiel carillon ring out three times a day at 9, noon, and 5. ✉ *South side of Römerberg.* ⏲ *Oct.–Mar., daily 10–6; Apr.–Sept., daily 10–8.*

17 **Palmengarten und Botanischer Garten** (Tropical Garden and Botanical Gardens). A splendid cluster of tropical and semitropical greenhouses contains a wide variety of flora, including cacti, orchids, and palms. There is a little lake where you can rent rowboats, a play area for children, a wading pool, and a miniature railway. During most of the year there are flower shows and exhibitions; in summer, concerts are held in an outdoor music pavilion. ✉ *Siesmayerstr. 63,* ☎ *069/2123–3939.* ⏲ *Mar.–Oct., daily 9–6; Nov.–Jan., daily 9–4; Feb., daily 9–5.*

6 **Römer** (City Hall). Its gabled Gothic facade with an ornate balcony is the city's official emblem. The mercantile-minded Frankfurt burghers used the complex of three patrician buildings not only for political and ceremonial purposes but also for trade fairs and other commercial ventures. Banquets to celebrate the coronations of the Holy Roman emperors were mounted starting in 1562 in the **Kaisersaal** (Imperial Hall). Impressive, full-length 19th-century portraits of the 52 emperors of the Holy Roman Empire line the walls of the banquet hall. ✉ *West side of Römerberg,* ☎ *069/2123–4814.* ⏲ *Kaisersaal daily 10–1 and 2–5. Closed during official functions.*

5 **Römerberg.** This square north of the Main River, lovingly restored after wartime bomb damage, is the historical focal point of the city. The **Römer** and the **Nikolaikirche** are found here. The fine 16th-century **Fountain of Justitia** (Justice) stands in the center of the square. At the coronation of Emperor Matthias in 1612, wine flowed from the fountain instead of water. ✉ *Between Braubachstr. and the Main River.*

★ 10 **Städelsches Kunstinstitut und Städtische Galerie** (Städel Art Institute and Municipal Gallery). One of Germany's important art collections has paintings by Dürer, Vermeer, Rembrandt, Rubens, Monet, Renoir, and other great masters. The section on German Expressionism is particularly strong, with works by Frankfurt artist Max Beckmann. ✉ *Schaumainkai 63,* ☎ *069/605–0980.* ⏲ *Tues. and Thurs.–Sun. 10–5, Wed. 10–8.*

❾ **Städtische Galerie Liebieghaus** (Liebieg Municipal Museum of Sculpture). The sculpture collection here spans from antiquity to the Middle Ages, from the Renaissance to the Baroque era, and is considered one of the most important in Europe. Some pieces are exhibited in the lovely gardens surrounding the house. ✉ *Schaumainkai 71,* ☎ *069/2123–8617.* ⏲ *Tues. and Thurs.–Sun. 10–5, Wed. 10–8.*

❷ **Zeil.** The heart of Frankfurt's shopping district is this ritzy pedestrian thoroughfare. The major department stores lie between the Hauptwache and Konstablerwache train stations. ✉ *East of Hauptwache.*

Dining

Many of the fancier restaurants in Frankfurt serve bargain lunch menus, and you should make reservations in advance for any meal. At Sachsenhausen *Apfelwein* (apple-wine) taverns, just find space at one of the long tables. Foods traditionally served with apple wine include *Rippchen* (cured pork chop on a mound of sauerkraut), boiled potatoes and boiled eggs with Frankfurt's traditional green sauce, and *Handkäs mit Musik* (soft cheese, onions, vinegar, and oil on bread).

$$$$ ★ ✕ **Erno's Bistro.** This tiny, unpretentious place in a quiet Westend neighborhood is one of the best restaurants in Frankfurt. The French bistro's specialty, fish, is often flown in daily from France. When its clientele, the well-heeled elite of the business community, are unlikely to be in town, Erno's closes its doors. The three-course midday menu for DM 49/€24.50 is a steal. ✉ *Liebigstr. 15,* ☎ *069/721–997. Reservations essential. AE, DC, MC, V. Closed weekends and July–early Aug.*

$$$–$$$$ ★ ✕ **Gargantua.** One of Frankfurt's most creative chefs, Klaus Trebes, who doubles as a food columnist, serves up new versions of German classics and French-accented dishes in a Westend dining room. His menu features such dishes as artichoke risotto with goose liver, lentil salad with stewed beef, and grilled dorade served on pureed white beans and pesto. One corner of the restaurant is reserved for those who only want to sample the outstanding wine list. ✉ *Liebigstr. 47,* ☎ *069/720–718. AE, DC, MC, V. Closed Sun. No lunch Sat.*

$–$$ ✕ **Altes Zollhaus.** Very good versions of traditional German specialties are served in this beautiful, 200-year-old half-timber house on the edge of town. Try a game dish. In summer you can eat in the beautiful garden. To get here, take bus 30 from Konstablerwache to Heiligenstock, or drive out on Bundestrasse 521 in the direction of Bad Vilbel. ✉ *Friedberger Landstr. 531,* ☎ *069/472–707. AE, DC, MC, V. Closed Mon. No lunch, except Sun.*

$–$$ ✕ **Kangaroo's.** The main dining room of this very popular, Australia-theme restaurant is glass-roofed and lush with greenery. The decor includes highway signs warning of kangaroos ahead. The adventurous can try the "Australia Platter" with kangaroo, crocodile, and emu meat (but Aussies, too, eat beef, chicken, and salads). ✉ *Rahmhofstr. 2–4,* ☎ *069/131–0339. AE, DC, MC, V.*

$ ✕ **Café Laumer.** The ambience of an old-time Viennese café, with a subdued decor and rear garden, is well preserved here. It owes its literary tradition to Theodor Adorno, a philosopher and sociologist of the "Frankfurt School," who drank his daily coffee here. It's open for breakfast, lunch, and afternoon coffee and closes at 7 PM. ✉ *Bockenheimer Landstr. 67,* ☎ *069/727912. DC, MC, V. No dinner.*

$ ✕ **Edelweiss.** Homesick Austrians enjoy their native cuisine at this rustic restaurant with a terrace. Dishes include the genuine Wiener schnitzel, and Kaiser Franz Josef's favorite, *Tafelspitze,* made of boiled beef with a chive sauce. Then there's the roast chicken with a salad made of "earth apples" (potatoes) and the beloved *Kaiserschmarrn*: egg pancakes with raisins, apples, cinnamon, and jam. ✉ *Schweizer Str. 96,* ☎ *069/619696. AE, DC, MC, V.*

$ ✕ **Sand.** The emphasis at this Lebanese restaurant is on lamb, and there is a wide selection of hors d'oeuvres, with spiced vegetables, lamb sausages, sheep cheese, and yogurt. It also, unaccountably, has a bar where you can get skillfully made American cocktails, a rarity even in Frankfurt. Most of the tables are in a pleasant courtyard to the rear, which is covered in inclement weather with a sliding translucent roof. A blind pianist helps with the mood Fridays and Saturdays. ✉ *Kaiserstr. 25,* ☎ *069/2424–9440. AE, DC, MC, V. Closed Sun. No lunch Sat.*

$ ★ ✕ **Wäldches.** This is Frankfurt's busiest brewpub, in a countrified location nevertheless handy to a rapid-transit station, and a favorite stop for bikers and hikers. By noon on pleasant summer Sundays, the big beer garden can be standing room only. The home-brewed light and dark beers go nicely with the largely German cuisine. If you like the beer, you can take some of it with you in an old-fashioned bottle. ✉ *Am Ginnheimer Wäldchen 8,* ☎ *069/520522. No credit cards.*

$ ✕ **Zum Wagner.** The kitchen produces the same hearty German dishes as other apple-wine taverns, only better. Try the *Tafelspitz mit Frankfurter grüner Sosse* (stewed beef with a sauce of green herbs) or come on Friday for fresh fish. Beer and wine are served as well as cider. This Sachsenhausen classic succeeds in being touristy and traditional all at once. ✉ *Schweizer Str. 71,* ☎ *069/612–565. No credit cards.*

Lodging

Businesspeople descend on Frankfurt year-round, so most hotels in the city are expensive (many offer significant reductions on weekends) and frequently book up well in advance. The majority of the larger hotels are around the main train station, a 15- to 20-minute walk from the Old Town.

$$$$ **Hessischer Hof.** This is the choice of many businesspeople, not just because it's near the fairgrounds but for the air of class that pervades its handsome interior (the exterior is nondescript). Many of the public-room furnishings are antiques owned by the family of the princes of Hesse. Guest rooms are done in either a British or Biedermeier style. Jimmy's is one of the cult bars in town. ✉ *Friedrich-Ebert-Anlage 40, 60325.* ☎ *069/7540–0,* FAX *069/7540–2924,* WEB *www.hessischer-hof.de. 100 rooms, 17 suites. Restaurant, bar. AE, DC, MC, V.*

$$$–$$$$ ★ **Gravenbruch Kempinski.** At a parkland site in leafy Neu Isenburg (a 15-minute drive south of Frankfurt), this sophisticated hotel maintains the atmosphere of the 16th-century manor around which it was built. Some of the luxuriously appointed rooms and suites are arranged as duplex penthouse apartments. Ask for a room overlooking the lake. ✉ *An der Bundestr. 459, D-63243 Neu-Isenburg,* ☎ *06102/5050,* FAX *06102/505–900,* WEB *www.kempinski-frankfurt.com. 255 rooms, 28 suites. 2 restaurants, bar, pool. AE, DC, MC, V.*

$$$–$$$$ ★ **Steigenberger Hotel Frankfurter Hof.** The Victorian Frankfurter Hof is one of the city's oldest hotels. The atmosphere throughout is one of old-fashioned, formal elegance, with burnished woods, fresh flowers, and thick-carpeted hush. Kaiser Wilhelm once slept here. Although it fronts a courtyard, you must enter it through a modest side entrance. ✉ *Am Kaiserpl., D-60311,* ☎ *069/21502,* FAX *069/215–900,* WEB

www.frankfurter-hof.steigenberger.com. 332 rooms, 10 suites. 2 restaurants. AE, DC, MC, V.

$$$ ★ **Art Hotel Robert Mayer.** In a turn-of-the-20th-century villa, each room has been decorated by a different Frankfurt artist, with furniture designs by the likes of Rietveld and Frank Lloyd Wright. The room designed by Therese Traube contrasts abstract newspaper collage with a replica Louis XIV armchair. Breakfast is included in the price of the room. ✉ *Robert-Mayer-Str. 44, D-60486,* ☎ *069/9709–100,* FAX *069/9709–1010,* WEB *www.art-hotel-robert-mayer.de. 11 rooms, 1 suite. AE, DC, MC, V.*

$–$$$ ★ **Maingau.** You'll find this pleasant hotel-restaurant in the middle of the lively Sachsenhausen quarter. Rooms are modest but spotless, comfortable, and equipped with TVs; the room rate includes a substantial breakfast buffet. Though the hotel is inexpensive, the restaurant, Maingau-Stuben, is anything but! ✉ *Schifferstr. 38–40, D-60594,* ☎ *069/609–140,* FAX *069/620–790. 100 rooms. Restaurant. AE, MC.*

$$ ★ **Hotel Nizza.** This beautiful Victorian building is furnished with selected antiques, and the proprietor added a modern touch in three bathrooms with her own artistic murals. The name of the hotel reflects the lush Mediterranean flora of its roof garden, where you can have breakfast in good weather with views of rooftops and the skyline. ✉ *Elbestr. 10, 60329,* ☎ *069/242538–0,* FAX *069/242538–30. 24 rooms, 18 with bath. Breakfast room. MC, V.*

$ **Hotel-Schiff *Peter Schlott*.** The hotel ship is moored on the Main River in the suburb of Höchst, a 15-minute train or tram ride from the city center. Guest cabins are on the small side, but the river views more than compensate. ✉ *Mainberg, D-65929,* ☎ *069/3004–643,* FAX *069/307–671,* WEB *www.hotel-schiff-schlott.de/. 19 rooms, 10 with shower. Restaurant. AE, MC, V.*

$ **Waldhotel Hensels Felsenkeller.** It's a long walk from public transportation, but it's clean, very inexpensive, and in a beautiful setting right on the edge of the city forest. Rooms are basic; the less expensive ones have shared showers. The nearest stop is Buchrainstrasse on tram lines 15 and 16. ✉ *Buchrainstr. 95, D-60599,* ☎ *069/652–086,* FAX *069/658–379. 16 rooms, 7 with bath. Restaurant. MC, V.*

Nightlife and the Arts

Frankfurt was a real pioneer in the German jazz scene, and also, of late, has done much for the development of techno music. In the fall the German Jazz Festival takes place in conjunction with the Music Fair. Sachsenhausen (Frankfurt's "Left Bank") is a good place to start for bars, clubs, and Apfelwein taverns. The increasingly hip Nordend has an almost equal number of bars and clubs but fewer tourists.

The Arts

Other than at the performance venue, tickets can be purchased from the tourist office at Römerberg 27 and from box offices like **Frankfurt Ticket GmbH** (✉ Hauptwache Passage, ☎ 069/134–0400). The most glamorous venue for classical or pop music concerts is the **Alte Oper** (Old Opera House; ✉ Opernpl., ☎ 069/134–0400). Tickets to performances can range from DM 20/€10 to nearly DM 300/€154. The world-renowned **Frankfurt Ballet** (Städtische Bühnen; ✉ Untermainanlage 11, ☎ 069/2123–7999) is under the very modern direction of American William Forsythe.

Nightlife

BARS AND DANCE CLUBS

There's live music most nights at the cellar Irish pub **An Sibin** (✉ Wallstr. 9, ☎ 069/603–2159), along with Guinness right out of the keg and some good pub grub. It's closed Sunday. The tiny, cozy **Balalaika** (✉ Dreikönigstr. 30, ☏ 069/612–226), in Sachsenhausen, provides intimacy and live music without charging the fancy prices you'd expect at such a place. The Eurotower's **Living XXL** (✉ Kaiserstr. 29, ☏ 069/242–9370) is a huge bar-restaurant. On Friday and Saturday a "subdued" disco is geared to the preferences of the banking community, but the club also hosts regular gay entertainment.

JAZZ CLUBS

The oldest jazz cellar in Germany, **Der Frankfurter Jazzkeller** (✉ Kleine Bockenheimer Str. 18a, ☏ 069/288–537) was founded by legendary trumpeter Carlo Bohländer. Its hot, modern jazz is often free (but the cover can also run around DM 25/€13). You might hear 1940s or '50s jazz, blues, funk, rock, or punk at **Dreikönigskeller** (✉ Färberstr. 71, ☏ 069/629–273). It's patronized mostly by students, as well as a sprinkling of older, hip people, all smoking as voraciously as the musicians. **Sinkkasten** (✉ Brönnerstr. 5–9, ☏ 069/280–385), a Frankfurt institution, is a class act for jazz, rock, pop, and African music.

Frankfurt Essentials

AIRPORTS AND TRANSFERS

Frankfurt Airport, the busiest and biggest airport in mainland Europe, is about 10 km (6 mi) southwest of the city. The airport railroad station is served by 84 long-distance InterCity trains a day. The airport also doubles as a shopping mall whose stores are not subject to Germany's strict closing laws.

➤ AIRPORT INFORMATION: **Flughafen Frankfurt Main** (☏ 069/6903–0511).

TRANSFERS

Getting into Frankfurt from the airport is easy. The S-8 (S-bahn) runs from the airport to downtown, stopping at the Hauptbahnhof (main train station) and then at the central Hauptwache square. Trains run at least every 15 minutes and the ride takes about as long; the one-way fare is DM 6.10/€3.10. InterCity and InterCity Express (ICE) trains to and from most major German cities also stop at the airport. Taxis from the airport downtown take about 20 minutes (double that in rush hour); the fare averages DM 35/€18. If you're driving, take the B-43 main road, following signs for STADTMITTE (Downtown).

BUS TRAVEL TO AND FROM FRANKFURT

Long-distance buses connect Frankfurt with more than 200 other European cities. Buses leave from the south side of the Hauptbahnhof. Tickets and information are available from Deutsche Touring.

CAR RENTAL

➤ MAJOR AGENCIES: **Avis** (✉ Schmidtstr. 39, ☏ 069/730–111). **Europcar** (✉ Kennedyallee 280, ☏ 069/6772–0291). **Hertz** (✉ Hanauer Landstr. 117, ☏ 069/449–090).

CAR TRAVEL

Frankfurt is the junction of many major autobahns. The most important are the A-3, running south from Köln and then on to Würzburg, Nürnberg, and Munich; and the A-5, running south from Giessen and then on to Mannheim, Heidelberg, Karlsruhe, and the Swiss-German border at Basel. A complex series of beltways surrounds the city. If you're driving to Frankfurt on the A-5 from either north or south, exit at Nordwestkreuz and follow A-66 to the Nordend district, just north of downtown. Driving south on A-3, exit onto A-66 and follow the signs to Frankfurt-Höchst and then the Nordwestkreuz. Driving west on

A-3, exit at the Offenbacher Kreuz onto A-661 and follow the signs for Frankfurt-Stadtmitte (City Center).

CONSULATES

➤ Australia: ✉ Grüneburgweg 58–62, ☎ 069/905–580.
➤ United Kingdom: ✉ Bockenheimer Landstr. 42, ☎ 069/170–0020.
➤ United States: ✉ Siesmayerstr. 21, ☎ 069/75350.

EMERGENCIES

Listings, in German, of pharmacies and pet doctors are available after hours through the hotline ☎ 069/011500.
➤ Doctors and Dentists: **Dental Emergencies** (☎ 069/660–7271).
➤ Emergency Services: **Fire** (☎ 112). **Medical Emergencies** (☎ 069/19292). **Police** (☎ 110).
➤ 24-hour Pharmacies: ☎ 069/011500.

ENGLISH-LANGUAGE MEDIA

The American Forces Network's radio signal is full of American news, sports, and music. Its AM broadcast (primarily talk) is at 873; the FM signal (primarily music) is at 98.7.
➤ Bookstores: **British Bookshop** (✉ Börsenstr. 17, ☎ 069/280–492).

MAIL

Note that the official address for Frankfurt includes "Main" after the city name in any variety of ways—Frankfurt/Main, Frankfurt am Main, Frankfurt/M, to cite a few.

TAXIS

Cabs are not always easy to hail from the sidewalk; some stop, while others will pick up only from the city's numerous taxi stands or outside hotels or the train station. Fares start at DM 3.80/€1.90 (DM 5/€2.50 in the wee hours) and increase by a per-kilometer (½ mi) charge of DM 2.80/€1.40 for the first three, DM 2.50/€1.30 thereafter. Count on paying DM 13/€6.70 for a short city ride.
➤ Taxi Companies: ☎ 069/250–001 or 069/230–033.

TOURS

BUS AND TROLLEY TOURS

Bus tours run by the tourist office and Gray Line take in all the main sights. The city transit authority runs a brightly painted old-time streetcar—the *Ebbelwoi Express* (Cider Express)—on weekend and holiday afternoons. Departures are from the Bornheim-Mitte U- and S-bahn station and the fare is DM 6/€3. Deutsche Touring will take you outside Frankfurt to Rothenburg, Heidelberg, and the Black Forest.
➤ Fees and Schedules: **City Transit Authority** (☎ 069/2132–2425). **Deutsche Touring** (✉ Am Römerhof 17, ☎ 069/790–350). **Gray Line** (☎ 069/230–492, WEB www.lts.de). **Main tourist office** (✉ Römerberg 27, ☎ 069/212–38708, WEB www.tcf.frankfurt-main.de).

BOAT TOURS

Pleasure boats of the Primus Line cruise the Main and Rhine rivers from Frankfurt, sailing as far as the Loreley and back in a day.
➤ Fees and Schedules: **Frankfurter Personenschiffahrt** (✉ Mainkai 36, ☎ 069/281–884, WEB www.aschaffenburg.personenschiffe.de).

TRAIN TRAVEL

EuroCity and InterCity trains connect Frankfurt with all other German cities and many major European ones. The InterCity Express (ICE) line links Frankfurt with Hamburg, Munich, and several major German cities. All long-distance trains arrive at and depart from the Hauptbahnhof.

TRANSPORTATION AROUND FRANKFURT

Frankfurt's efficient, well-integrated public transportation system consists of the U-bahn (subway), S-bahn (suburban railway), Strassenbahn (streetcars), and buses. During rush hours the subway is sometimes the fastest way to get around. Fares for the entire system are uniform but based on a complicated zone system. Tickets may be purchased from automatic vending machines accepting coins and notes at most stations and stops. Bus drivers sell tickets only at stops without a vending machine. Weekly and monthly tickets are available at central ticket offices and newsstands. For further information or assistance call ☏ 069/27307–0. The Frankfurt tourist office sells a Frankfurt Card (DM 12/€6 for one day, DM 19/€9.50 for two days) entitling you to unlimited travel within Frankfurt, a trip to the airport, and reduced, usually half-price, admission to 15 museums.

TRAVEL AGENCIES

➤ LOCAL AGENTS: **American Express** (✉ Kaiserstr. 10, ☏ 069/210–5111).

VISITOR INFORMATION

➤ FRANKFURT TOURIST OFFICE: ✉ Römerberg 27, ☏ 069/2123–8800; main train station; ✉ Am Hauptbahnhof, Main Hall, ☏ 069/2123–8849;mailing address, ✉ Tourismus und Congress GmbH, Kaiserstr. 56, D-60329, WEB www.frankfurt.de.

THE RHINE

For the Romans, who established forts and colonies along its western bank, the Rhine was the frontier between civilization and the barbaric German tribes. Roman artifacts are exhibited in museums throughout the region. In the Middle Ages the river's importance as a trade artery made it the focus of conflict between princes, nobles, and archbishops. Many of the picturesque castles that crown its banks were the homes of robber barons who held up or exacted tolls on passing ships.

For poets and composers, the Rhine—or *Vater Rhein* (Father Rhine), as the Germans call it—has been a source of inspiration. According to legend, the Loreley, a treacherous, craggy rock, was home to a beautiful and bewitching maiden who lured sailors to a watery grave. The Rhine does not belong to Germany alone, but the German span of it has the most spectacular scenery—especially the 190-km (120-mi) stretch between Mainz and Köln (Cologne) known as the Middle Rhine. This is a land of steep and thickly wooded hills, vineyards, tiny villages hugging the banks, and a succession of brooding castles.

Köln

The largest German city on the Rhine is Köln (Cologne), first settled by the Romans in 38 BC. Charlemagne restored the city's fortunes in the 9th century, appointing its first archbishop and ensuring its ecclesiastical prominence for centuries.

By the Middle Ages Köln was the largest city north of the Alps, and as a member of the powerful Hanseatic League it was more important commercially than either London or Paris. Ninety percent of the city was destroyed in World War II, and the rush to rebuild it shows in some of the blocky, uninspired architecture. Whatever the city's aesthetic drawbacks, the Altstadt (Old Town), within the line of the medieval city walls, has great charm, and at night it throbs with life. Towering over the Old Town is the ★**Kölner Dom** (Cologne Cathedral), an extraordinary Gothic edifice dedicated to St. Peter and the Virgin. At 515 ft high, the two western towers of the cathedral were by far the tallest structures in the world when they were finished. The length of the build-

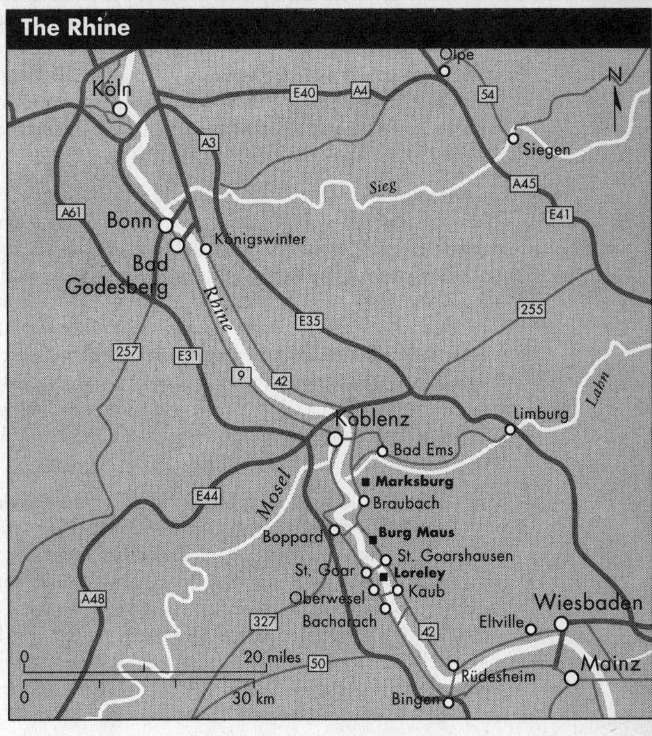

ing is 469 ft; the width of the nave is 148 ft; and the highest part of the interior is 139 ft. The cathedral was built to house what were believed to be the relics of the Magi, the three kings or wise men who paid homage to the infant Jesus. Today the relics are kept just behind the altar, in the same enormous gold-and-silver reliquary in which they were originally displayed. In the last chapel on the left as you face the altar is the Gero Cross, a monumental oak crucifix dating from 971 and impressive for its simple grace. The *Adoration of the Kings* (1440), a triptych by Stephan Lochner, Köln's most famous medieval painter, is to the right. More treasures can be seen in the **Dom Schatzkammer** (Cathedral Treasury), including the silver shrine of Archbishop Engelbert, who was stabbed to death in 1225. ✉ *Dompl.*, ☎ *0221/925–84730*, WEB *www.koelner-dom.de.* ⏲ *Treasury Apr.–Oct., Mon.–Sat. 9–5, Sun. 1–4; Nov.–Mar., Mon.–Sat. 9–4, Sun. 1–4.*

★ The **Museum Ludwig** is dedicated to art from the beginning of the 20th century to the present day. Its pop art collection includes Andy Warhol, Jasper Johns, Robert Rauschenberg, Claes Oldenburg, and Roy Lichtenstein. The **Agfa Foto-Historama** (Agfa Photography Museum) here has one of the world's largest collections of historic photographs. ✉ *Bischofsgartenstr. 1*, ☎ *0221/2212–2379*, WEB *www.museenkoeln.de.* ⏲ *Tues. 10–8, Wed.–Fri. 10–6, weekends 11–6..*

★ Paintings span the years 1300 to 1900 at the **Wallraf-Richartz-Museum.** The Master of the Saint Veronica and Stefan Lochner are represented by two luminous works, *The Last Judgment* and *The Madonna in the Rose Bower.* Large canvases by Rubens, who spent his youth in Köln, hang prominently, as do outstanding works by Rembrandt, Van Dyck, Frans Hals, Tiepolo, Canaletto, and Boucher. ✉ *Martinstr. 39*, ☎ *0221/2212–2393*, WEB *www.museenkoeln.de.* 🎫 *DM 10/€5.* ⏲ *Tues. 10–8, Wed.–Fri. 10–6, weekends 11–6.*

★ Opposite the Dom is the **Römisch-Germanisches Museum** (Roman-German Museum), built from 1970 to 1974 around the Dionysus mosaic that was unearthed during the construction of an air-raid shelter in 1941. The huge mosaic, more than 300 ft square, once covered the dining-room floor of a wealthy Roman trader's villa. ✉ *Roncallipl. 4,* ☎ *0221/221–24438.* ⊙ *Tues.–Sun. 10–5.*

The **Altes Rathaus** (Old Town Hall) will reopen to visitors in mid-2002. This is the oldest town hall in Germany; there was a seat of local government here in Roman times, and directly below the current Rathaus are the remains of the Roman city governor's headquarters, the Praetorium. Standing on pedestals at one end of the town hall are figures of prophets, made in the early 15th century. Ranging along the south wall are nine additional statues, the *Nine Good Heroes,* carved in 1360. Charlemagne and King Arthur are among them. Beneath a small glass pyramid by the south corner of the Rathaus is the **Mikwe,** a 12th-century ritual bath from the medieval Jewish quarter. ✉ *Alter Markt.* ⊙ *Mon.–Thurs. 7:30–4:45, Fri. 7:30–2.*

Köln's colorful old section near the river, the **Martinsviertel** (St. Martin's Quarter; ✉ between Lintg. and Gürzenichstr.), is an attractive combination of reconstructed, high-gabled medieval buildings; winding alleys; and tastefully designed modern apartments and business quarters. Head here at night—the place comes alive at sunset. During the day you can visit its churches. **Gross St. Martin** (Great St. Martin) is Martinsviertel's parish church. It's the most outstanding of Köln's 12 Romanesque churches. ✉ *Lintg.,* ☎ *0221/164–25650.* ⊙ *Weekdays 10:15–6, Sat. 10–12:30 and 1:30–6, Sun. 2–4.*

At the edge of Martinsviertel, within a 12th-century cathedral, the **Schnütgen Museum** is a treasure house of medieval art from the Rhine region. Don't miss the crucifix from the St. George Church or the original stained-glass windows and carved figures from the Kölner Dom. Many of the exhibits—intricately carved ivory book covers, rock-crystal reliquaries, illuminated manuscripts—require intense concentration to be appreciated. ✉ *Cäcilienstr. 29,* ☎ *0221/221–23620.* ⊙ *Tues.–Fri. 10–5, every first Wed. until 8, weekends 11–5.*

The exquisite, Romanesque **St. Gereon's** church stands on the site of an old Roman burial ground, six blocks west of the train station. An enormous dome rests on walls that were once clad in gold mosaics. Roman masonry still forms part of the structure, which is believed to have been built over the grave of its namesake, the 4th-century martyr and patron saint of Köln. ✉ *Gereonsdriesch 2–4,* ☎ *0221/134–922.* ⊙ *Mon.–Sat. 9–12:30, 1:30–6, Sun. 1:30–6.*

$$$ ✕ **Bizim.** This is one of the best Turkish restaurants in Germany. Forget shish kebab and prepare yourself for scampi with tarragon sauce, eggplant-coated lamb fillets with a garlic yogurt sauce, or quail grilled on a rosemary spit and served in its own juices. The four-course lunch menu (DM 55/€28) is highly recommended. ✉ *Weideng. 47–49,* ☎ *0221/131581. Reservations essential. AE, D, MC, V. Closed Sun.–Mon.*

$$$ ★ ✕ **Le Moissonnier.** Part of the charm of this restaurant—among the best in the city—is its lack of pretension. In contrast to the gray neighborhood, the turn-of-the-20th-century bistro decor radiates warmth from its mirrors, Tiffany-style lamps, and painted flowers. Chef Eric Menchon's cuisine is French at its base, but he intertwines global influences, serving dishes such as scampi with caraway seeds wrapped in potatoes with a white-bean sauce and oyster hash, or a bouillabaisse with thick turbot and calamari and ginger balls. ✉ *Krefelder Str. 25,* ☎ *0221/729479,* FAX *0221/7325461. Reservations essential. No credit cards. Closed Sun.–Mon.*

$–$$$ ✕ **Früh am Dom.** For real down-home German food, few places compare with this former brewery. Bold frescoes on the vaulted ceilings establish the mood, and such dishes as *hämmchen* (pork shank) provide an authentically Teutonic experience. ✉ *Am Hof 12–14,* ☎ *0221/258–0396. No credit cards.*

$$$$ ★ ✕🏨 **Excelsior Hotel Ernst.** The Empire-style lobby in sumptuous royal blue, bright yellow, and gold is striking, and a similar, boldly conceived grandeur extends to all the public rooms in this 1863 hotel. Old Master paintings (including a Van Dyck) are everywhere; you'll be served breakfast in a room hung with Gobelin tapestries. Guest rooms are intimate in scale, with spectacular marble bathrooms and ultramodern fixtures. The lacquered wood–paneled restaurant serves classic French cuisine imaginatively prepared. ✉ *Trankg. 1–5, D-50667,* ☎ *0221/2701,* FAX *0221/135–150. 140 rooms. Restaurant. AE, DC, MC, V.*

$$$$ ★ 🏨 **Hotel im Wasserturm.** What used to be Europe's tallest water tower is now an 11-story luxury hotel-in-the-round. The neoclassic look of the brick exterior was retained by order of Cologne conservationists. The ultramodern interior was the work of the French designer Andrée Putman. The 11th-floor restaurant has a view of the city. ✉ *Kayg. 2, D-50676,* ☎ *0221/20080,* FAX *0221/200–8888,* WEB *www.hotel-im-wasserturm.de. 54 rooms, 34 suites. Restaurant, bar. AE, DC, MC, V.*

$$ 🏨 **Chelsea.** This hotel has a strong following among artists and art dealers, and decor is a cross between Rietveld, Philippe Starck, and a half-dozen others. The bathrooms and bathtubs are luxuriously roomy and there is no end of mirrors. Breakfast is served until noon. It's just 20 minutes away from the city center on foot, 10 by subway or tram. ✉ *Jülicherstr. 1, D-50674,* ☎ *0221/234755,* FAX *0221/239137. 30 rooms. Restaurant. AE, DC, V.*

$$ 🏨 **Das Kleine Stapelhäuschen.** One of the few houses along the riverbank to have survived World War II bombings, this is among the very oldest buildings in Köln. You can't beat the location, overlooking the river and right by Gross St. Martin; rooms make up in quaintness for what they lack in luxury. ✉ *Fischmarkt 1–3, D-50667,* ☎ *0221/257–7862,* FAX *0221/257–4232. 31 rooms. AE, MC, V.*

Bonn

The staid city of Bonn, former capital of West Germany, lies 28 km (17 mi) south of Köln. Compared to that in other cities, life in Bonn's streets, old markets, pedestrian malls, parks, and handsome Südstadt residential area is unhurried. The town center is a car-free zone; an inner-ring road circles it with parking garages on the perimeter. A convenient parking lot is just across from the railway station and within 50 yards of the tourist office.

Bonn's late-Romanesque, 900-year-old **Münster** (Cathedral) has a massive octagonal main tower, a soaring spire, and an ornate rococo pulpit. It saw the coronations of two Holy Roman emperors (in 1314 and 1346). ✉ *Münsterpl.,* ☎ *0228/633–344.* ⏲ *Daily 7–7.*

★ The **Beethovenhaus** (Beethoven Museum) displays scores, a grand piano, and ear trumpets in the house where the composer was born. ✉ *Bonng. 20,* ☎ *0228/981–7525.* ⏲ *Apr.–Oct., Mon.–Sat. 10–6, Sun. 11–4; Nov.–Mar., Mon.–Sat. 10–5, Sun. 11–4.*

The **Kunst- und Austellungshalle der Bundesrepublik Deutschland** (Art and Exhibition Hall of the German Federal Republic) is one of the Rhineland's most important venues for exhibitions about culture and science. ✉ *Friedrich-Ebert-Allee 2,* ☎ *0228/9171200.* ⏲ *Tues.–Wed. 10–9, Thurs.–Fri. and Sun. 10–7, Sat. 9–9.*

The town of Königswinter (12 km/7 mi northeast of Bonn) has one of the most-visited castle sites on the Rhine, **Drachenfels.** Its ruins crown the highest hill in the Siebengebirge (Seven Hills). The castle was built in the 12th century by the archbishop of Köln.

$ ✕ **Em Höttche.** Travelers have been dining at this rustic tavern since the late 14th century; today it offers one of the best-value lunches in town. The food is hearty, and the portions are large. ✉ *Markt 4,* ☎ *0228/690–009. Reservations not accepted. No credit cards. Closed last 2 wks in Dec.*

$ ✕ **Haus Daufenbach.** Behind the stark white exterior, the mood is rustic, with simple wooden furniture and antlers on the walls. Specialties include *Spanferkel* (suckling pig) and a range of imaginative salads. Wines come from the restaurant's own vineyards. ✉ *Brüderg. 6,* ☎ *0228/969–4600. No credit cards.*

$$$ **Domicil.** A group of buildings around a courtyard has been stylishly converted into a hotel of great charm and comfort. The rooms are decorated in styles from fin-de-siècle romantic to Italian modern. ✉ *Thomas-Mann-Str. 24–26, D-53115,* ☎ *0228/729–090,* FAX *0228/691–207. 42 rooms. Restaurant. AE, DC, MC, V. Closed Dec. 25–Jan. 1.*

$$ **Sternhotel.** For good value and a central location in the Old Town, the family-run "Star" is tops. Rooms are small, but all are pleasantly furnished. Snacks are available at the café. ✉ *Markt 8, D-53111,* ☎ *0228/72670,* FAX *0228/726–7125. 80 rooms. Café. AE, DC, MC, V.*

Koblenz

This city began as a Roman camp more than 2,000 years ago and flourished thanks to its strategic location at the sharp conflux of the Rhine and Mosel rivers known as the **Deutsches Eck** (German Corner). A huge equestrian statue of Kaiser Wilhelm I, the Kaiser-Wilhelm-Denkmal, marks the spot. The historical sights of the **Altstadt** (Old Town) stand side by side with boutiques, pubs, and cafés near the squares Am Plan and Florinsmarkt. For a taste of contemporary Germany, visit the **Löhr Center,** a large shopping mall on the edge of the Altstadt.

Within a lovely 16th-century building near the Mosel promenade, the artworks of the **Mittelrhein Museum** span millennia. ✉ *Florinsmarkt 15,* ☎ *0261/129–2520.* ⏲ *Tues.–Sat. 10:30–5, Sun. 11–6.*

The 13th-century Deutschherrenhaus near the Rhine promenade is home to the **Museum Ludwig** and its fine collection of modern art. ✉ *Danziger Freiheit 1,* ☎ *0261/304–040.* ⏲ *Tues.–Sat., 10:30–5, Sun. 11–6.*

A stone's throw from the Museum Ludwig is **St. Kastor Kirche** (St. Castor's Church), stunning for its combination of Romanesque and Gothic elements. It was here that Louis the Pious negotiated plans for the Treaty of Verdun in 842. ✉ *Kastorhof.* ⏲ *Daily 9–6.*

Across the river from Koblenz, on the Rhine's east bank, towers the city's most spectacular castle, **Festung Ehrenbreitstein.** The fortifications of this vast structure date from the 1100s, although the bulk of it was built during the 16th and 17th centuries. To reach the fortress take the *Sesselbahn* (cable car, DM 12.50/€6.40 with castle visit). ☎ *0261/974–2444.* ⏲ *Castle daily 9:30–5. Cable car Apr., May, Oct., daily 10–4:50; June–Aug., daily 9–5:50; Sept., daily 10–5:50.*

$–$$ ★ ✕ **Café Balthazar.** The multistory atrium of a historic house (once a furniture store) has been turned into a very classy, yet comfortable, meeting place for all ages. Amidst fabulous Art Nouveau decor, complete with huge palm trees, you can have any one of your "three meals a day," coffee and cake, or simply snacks and drinks. Weekends, the lower level is a disco. The huge terrace is on Görres Square. ✉ *Firmungstr. 2, Am Görrespl.,* ☎ *0261/100–5833. MC, V.*

$$–$$$ **Hotel Mercure.** This high-rise on the Rhine is next to the city's conference and events center, the Rhein-Mosel-Halle, and a short walk to all major sights. Rooms are modern and well appointed; some have fabulous views. ✉ *Julius-Wegeler-Str. 6, D-56068,* ☎ *0261/1360,* FAX *0261/136–1199. 167 rooms, 1 suite. 2 restaurants. AE, DC, MC, V.*

$–$$ **Contel Hotel An Der Mosel.** The Hundertwasser-inspired, Art Nouveau look of this hotel is unique. Behind the colorful facade there are pleasant, modern rooms (some with waterbeds). You can dine on a terrace surrounded by artificial pools and eclectic "works of art." ✉ *Pastor-Klein-Str. 11, D-56073,* ☎ *0261/40650,* FAX *0261/406–5188. 185 rooms, 7 apartments. Restaurant. AE, DC, MC, V.*

Rhine Gorge

Between Koblenz and Rüdesheim, the Rhine flows through the 65-km (40-mi) Rhine Gorge. The Rhine lives up to its legends and lore here and flows past the greatest concentration of Rhine castles, which cling to the steep, terraced slopes. The river loops at Rüdesheim and passes by the world-renowned vineyards of the Rheingau en route to Mainz.

★ **Marksburg** castle, south of Koblenz, is on the east bank of the river, 500 ft above the town of Braubach. Built in the 12th century to protect silver and lead mines in the area, it is the only land-based castle in the entire Middle Rhine Valley never to have been destroyed. Within its massive walls are a collection of weapons and manuscripts, a medieval botanical garden, and a restaurant. ☎ *02627/206,* WEB *www.marksburg.de.* ⏲ *Easter–Oct., daily 10–5; Nov.–Easter, daily 11–4. Closed last wk Dec..*

The Rhine makes its largest loop just before passing the quiet old town of **Boppard,** once a bustling city of the Holy Roman Empire. Now its Roman and medieval past come to life at the site of its 4th-century fort and in a museum within the 14th-century electors' castle. Notable churches include the **Karmeliterkirche** (Carmelite Church), with two Baroque altars, and the Romanesque church of **St. Severus.** From Boppard there is a wonderful view across the Rhine to the ruined castles of **Liebenstein** and **Sterrenberg.**

$$–$$$ ✕ **Best Western Hotel Bellevue.** This imposing turn-of-the-20th-century building has an elegant white-and-yellow facade and faces directly onto the river. Afternoon tea, dinner, and Sunday lunch are accompanied by piano music. Try the hearty *Reblaus-Teller* of pork medallions in a grape sauce. Another restaurant ($–$$) offers sumptuous buffets. ✉ *Rheinallee 41–42, D-56154 Boppard,* ☎ *06742/1020,* FAX *06742/102–602,* WEB *www.bellevue.bestwestern.de. 92 rooms. 2 restaurants, bar, pool. AE, DC, MC, V.*

$$–$$$ ★ ✕ **Zum weissen Schwanen.** Just south of Marksburg castle you'll find a warm welcome at this historic, half-timber inn and mill. Next to a 13th-century town gateway, it is a thoroughly charming place to overnight or enjoy well-prepared regional specialties, contemporary German cuisine, and an excellent selection of wines. Rooms have period furniture ranging from Biedermeier to Belle Epoque. ✉ *Brunnenstr. 4, D-56338 Braubach,* ☎ *02627/559 or 9820,* FAX *02627/8802,* WEB *www.rhein-lahn-info.de/zum-weissen-schwanen. 16 rooms, 2 suites. Restaurant. AE, DC, MC, V. Restaurant closes for 3 wks in summer, and Wed. No lunch except Sun..*

St. Goar

South of Boppard, this little town is crowded against the steep gorge cliff and shadowed by the imposing ruin of **Burg Rheinfels** (Rhine Cliff Castle), built in the mid-13th century. A battle with the French destroyed it in 1797. Inside is an exquisite model of the complete fortress. ☎ *06741/383.* ⏲ *Apr.–Oct., daily 9–6; Nov.–Mar., weekends 10–5.*

Just across from the town of St. Goar is **St. Goarshausen** (an hourly ferry service runs between them), which lies at the foot of two 14th-century castles whose names, **Katz** (Cat) and **Maus** (Mouse), reflect one of the many power plays on the Rhine. Katz is not open to the public, but Maus has a terrace café and falconry demonstrations.

The **Loreley rock** is only a couple of miles from St. Goarshausen; follow the road marked with LORELEY-FELSEN signs. Here the Rhine takes a sharp turn around a rocky, shrub-covered headland. This is the narrowest and shallowest part of the Middle Rhine, full of treacherous currents. According to legend the maiden Lore sat on the rock here, combing her golden hair and singing a song so irresistible that passing sailors forgot the navigational hazards and were swept to their deaths.

$$$ ★ ✕🏨 **Schloss-Hotel & Villa Rheinfels.** High above St. Goar and directly opposite Burg Rheinfels, this hotel offers modern comfort and expansive views from the restaurant terrace. The main restaurant, Auf Scharfeneck ($$–$$$), serves regional specialties, and evenings the Burgschänke offers rustic fare in the cellar. The *Wispertal Forelle* (trout from the nearby Wisper Valley) is highly recommended. ✉ *Schlossberg 47, D-56329 St. Goar,* ☎ *06741/8020,* FAX *06741/802–802,* WEB *www.schlosshotel-rheinfels.de. 54 rooms. 2 restaurants, pool. AE, DC, MC, V.*

$–$$$ ★ ✕🏨 **Hotel Landsknecht.** The Nickenig family makes everyone feel at home in their riverside restaurant and hotel north of St. Goar. In the Vinothek you can sample Joachim Lorenz's prize-winning Bopparder Hamm wines. These go well with the restaurant's hearty local dishes, such as *Rheinische Kartoffelsuppe* (Rhenish potato soup). Friday evenings in summer there is a BBQ on the splendid Rhine terrace. Rooms are individually furnished and quite comfortable; some offer a Rhine view (Nos. 4, 5, and 8 are especially nice). ✉ *Rhinugerstr. (B–9), D-56329 St. Goar-Fellen,* ☎ *06741/2001,* FAX *06741/7499,* WEB *www.hotel-landsknecht.de. 14 rooms. Restaurant. AE, DC, MC, V. Closed mid-Dec.–Feb.*

Oberwesel

Sixteen of the original 21 medieval towers and much of the town wall still stand in Oberwesel, south of St. Goar on the west bank of the Rhine. The **Liebfrauenkirche** (Church of our Lady) is known as the "red church" for its exterior, and has one of Germany's oldest altars (1331).

$ ✕ **Historische Weinwirtschaft.** Tables in the flower-laden garden in front of this stone house are at a premium in the summer, yet seats in the nooks and crannies indoors are just as inviting. Ask Iris Marx, the ebullient proprietor, to translate the menu (it's in local dialect) of regional dishes. The wine list features 32 wines by the glass. ✉ *Liebfrauenstr. 17,* ☎ *06744/8186. AE, MC, V. Closed Tues. and Jan. No lunch except Sun. May–Sept.*

$$$$ ★ ✕🏨 **Burghotel Auf Schönburg.** Above the Rhine and the town of Oberwesel stands this 12th-century castle turned hotel. Antique furnishings and historical rooms (library, chapel, prison tower) add to the ambience. The wooden-beamed restaurant (closed Monday) serves such satisfying dishes as lentil soup with mushroom ravioli or rack of lamb in an herb crust. ✉ *D-55430 Oberwesel,* ☎ *06744/93930,* FAX *06744/1613,* WEB *www.hotel-schoenburg.com. 20 rooms. Restaurant. DC, MC, V. Closed Jan.–Mar.*

Kaub

Opposite this medieval village, south of the Loreley on the east side of the river, is one of the most-photographed sites of the Middle Rhine region. Like a small sailing ship bristling with sharp-pointed towers, the **Pfalzgrafenstein** castle sits on a tiny island in the middle of the Rhine. Never destroyed, the Pfalz provides a good look at sparse medieval living quarters. A boat from Kaub goes to the island. ⌚ *Easter–Sept. 9–1, 2–6; Oct.–Easter 9–1, 2–5. Closed Dec. and Mon. in winter.*

$ ★ ✕🏨 **Zum Turm.** Next to a medieval *Turm* (tower) near the Rhine, this little inn offers spacious, modern guest rooms on the floors above its cozy restaurant (dinner only; closed Tuesday) and terrace. Fish, game, and produce come from either local farms or from the market halls of Paris. The daily set menus (3–6 courses) are always excellent options. ✉ *Zollstr. 50, D-56349 Kaub,* ☎ *06774/92200,* FAX *06774/922–011,* WEB *www.rhein-hotel-turm.com. 6 rooms. Restaurant. DC, MC, V. Closed 2 wks in Feb. and 2 wks. in Nov..*

Bacharach

This well-preserved medieval village, complete with remains of its 14th-century walls, has been one of the Middle Rhine's most picturesque wine towns for centuries.

$–$$$ ★ ✕ **Weinhaus Altes Haus.** This medieval house is a favorite setting for films and photos. The cheerful proprietor uses the freshest ingredients possible and buys her meat and game from local butchers and hunters. *Rieslingrahmsuppe* (Riesling cream soup), *Reibekuchen* (potato pancakes), and the hearty *Hunsrücker Teller* (boiled beef with horseradish sauce) are favorites. She offers a good selection of wines from the family's own vineyards. ✉ *Oberstr. 61,* ☎ *06743/1209. AE, MC, V. Closed Wed. and mid-Dec.–Easter.*

$ ✕ **Gutsausschank Zum Grünen Baum.** Fritz Bastian runs this cozy tavern in a house dating from 1579. He is the sole owner of the vineyard Insel Heyles'en Werth on the island opposite Bacharach. The "wine carousel" is a great way to sample a full range of flavors and styles (15 wines), at best under the tutelage of the congenial host. Snacks are served, including delicious homemade, air-dried *Schinken* (ham). ✉ *Oberstr. 63,* ☎ *06743/1208. No credit cards. Closed Thur. and Feb.*

Rüdesheim

Tourism and wine are the heart and soul of Rüdesheim, and best epitomized by the **Drosselgasse** (Thrush Alley). The narrow, pub-lined lane is abuzz with merrymaking from noon to well past midnight every day from Easter through October. Rüdesheim is a gateway to the Rhine Gorge region so be sure to secure lodging well in advance.

High above Rüdesheim and visible for miles stands "Germania," a colossal female statue crowning the **Niederwald-Denkmal** (Niederwald Monument). It commemorates the rebirth of the German Empire after the Franco-Prussian War (1870–71). You can reach the monument on foot, by car (via Grabenstrasse), or by *Seilbahn* (cable car). There is also a *Sessellift* (chairlift) to and from Assmannshausen, a red wine enclave, on the west side of the hill. ✉ *Oberstr. 37,* ☎ *06722/2402.* ⌚ *Mid-Mar.–Oct., daily 9:30–4 (June–Sept. until 6:30).*

$–$$ ✕ **Rüdesheimer Schloss.** In a former tithe house built in 1729, this wine tavern specializes in Hessian cuisine and Rheingauer Riesling and Spätburgunder wines from the Breuer family's estate and other nearby wineries. The selection of older vintages is remarkable. Start with the delectable *Sauerkrautsuppe* (sauerkraut soup). Benedictine-style *Schloss Ente* (duck with dates and figs), *Ochsenbrust* (boiled breast of beef) and *Woihinkel* (chicken in Riesling sauce) are all excellent. ✉ *Drosselg.,* ☎ *06722/90500. AE, DC, MC, V. Closed Jan.–Mar.*

$$$ ★ ✕🏨 **Hotel Krone Assmannshausen.** This elegant, antiques-filled hotel and restaurant ($$$$) in Assmannshausen offers first-class service. Classic cuisine prepared by chef Willi Mittler and wines from the fam-

ily's own vineyards, as well as an overall superb collection of wines, make for very memorable meals indoors or on the terrace overlooking the Rhine. ✉ *Rheinuferstr. 10, D-65385 Rüdesheim–Assmannshausen,* ☎ *06722/4030,* FAX *06722/3049,* WEB *www.ila-chateau.com. 46 rooms, 12 suites. Restaurant, pool. AE, DC, MC, V.*

$$–$$$ ★ **Breuer's Rüdesheimer Schloss.** Hosts Susanne and Heinrich Breuer have beautifully integrated modern designer decor into the historic walls of this stylish hotel. The Constantinescu suite (No. 20) and the Rhine suite (No. 14), with its large terrace, are especially popular; most rooms offer a vineyard view. Cellar or vineyard tours and wine tastings can be arranged. ✉ *Steing. 10, D-65385,* ☎ *06722/90500,* FAX *06722/47960,* WEB *www.ruedesheimer-schloss.com. 18 rooms, 3 suites. Restaurant. AE, DC, MC, V. Closed late Dec.–early Jan..*

Eltville

Eltville is the geographic heart of the Rheingau, 14 km (9 mi) west of Wiesbaden and 16 km (10 mi) north of Mainz. Its half-timber buildings crowd narrow streets that date from Roman times. Today the town is well known for the production of *Sekt,* sparkling German wine (Champagne by any other name, though the French ensured it could not legally be called that by including a stipulation in the Treaty of Versailles in 1919). About 3 km (2 mi) from Eltville, near the village of ★ Kiedrich, lies **Kloster Eberbach** (Eberbach Abbey) in a secluded valley. The former Cistercian monastery has Romanesque and Gothic buildings that look untouched by time. Its viticultural tradition spans nearly nine centuries. You can sample wines year-round in the wine shop or restaurants on the grounds. ✉ *Stiftung Kloster Eberbach, northwest of Eltville via Kiedrich,* ☎ *06723/91780,* WEB *www.klostereberbach.de.* ⏲ *Apr.–Oct. daily 10–6; Nov.–Mar. weekdays 10–4, weekends 11–4.*

Mainz

This bustling modern city of nearly 200,000 lies on the west bank of the Rhine, at the mouth of the Main River. Once the seat of powerful ★ archbishops, the city still has as its focal point the **Dom,** one of the finest Romanesque cathedrals in Germany, dating mostly from the late 11th through 13th centuries, with an imposing Baroque spire added in the 18th century. ✉ *Domstr. 3,* ☎ *06131/253–412.* ⏲ *Apr.–Oct., weekdays 9–6:30; Nov.–Mar., weekdays 9–5. Year-round, Sat. 9–4, Sun. 12:45–2:45 and 4–5 (winter) or 6:30 (summer).*

★ The **Gutenberg Museum** honors the printing pioneer Johannes Gutenberg, who invented movable type around 1450 in Mainz. The museum houses a replica workshop that demonstrates his work and one of the Bibles he printed. ✉ *Liebfrauenpl. 5,* ☎ *06131/122–640,* WEB *www.gutenberg-museum.de.* ⏲ *Tues.–Sat. 9–5, Sun. 11–3.*

The collection of the **Römisch-Germanisches Museum** (Roman-Germanic Museum) in the Kurfürstliches Schloss (Elector's Palace) chronicles cultural developments in the area up to the early Middle Ages. ✉ *Ernst-Ludwig-Pl. on Grosse Bleiche,* ☎ *06131/91240.* ⏲ *Tues.–Sun. 10–6.*

★ The **Landesmuseum** (Museum of the State of Rheinland-Pfalz), housed in the former electors' stables, has exhibits that range from the Stone Age to the 20th century. Roman masonry, paintings by Dutch masters, and artworks from the Baroque to Art Nouveau periods are among the highlights. ✉ *Grosse Bleiche 49–51,* ☎ *06131/28570.* ⏲ *Tues. 10–8, Wed.–Sun. 10–5.*

The Gothic church of **St. Stephan** stands on a hilltop near Schillerplatz. Six vivid blue stained-glass windows by painter Marc Chagall (1887–1995) grace its choir. ✉ *Kleine Weissg. 12, via Gaustr.,* ☎ *06131/231–*

640. ⏲ Feb.–Nov., Mon.–Sat. 10–noon and 2–5; Dec.–Jan., Mon.–Sat. 10–noon and 2–4:30, afternoon only on Sun.

$–$$ ✕ **Heilig Geist.** Beneath the vaulted ceilings of this upbeat café-bistro-bar you can enjoy elaborate salads, creative fish and meat dishes, and *Croustarte,* an upscale version of pizza. ✉ *Mailandsg. 11,* ☎ *06131/ 225–757. No credit cards.*

$$$$ ★ ✕🏨 **Hilton International.** A terrific location by the Rhine and high standards of service and comfort make the Hilton an ideal choice. The buffets in the Römische Weinstube are excellent, as is the fare in the Brasserie. ✉ *Rheinstr. 68, D-55116,* ☎ *06131/2450,* FAX *06131/245–589. 433 rooms. 2 restaurants, casino. AE, DC, MC, V.*

$–$$ 🏨 **Hotel Weinhaus Rebstock.** This is a friendly inn in a 15th-century house in the heart of the Old Town. Ask for a room with a private bath and cathedral view. The Hertie department store's garage provides the closest parking. ✉ *Heiliggrabg. 6, near Bischofspl., D-55116,* ☎ *06131/230–317,* FAX *06131/230–318. 11 rooms. No credit cards.*

The Rhine Essentials

BOAT AND FERRY TRAVEL

Köln-Düsseldorfer Deutsche Rheinschiffahrt has daily cruises between Köln and Frankfurt from Easter through October. Many smaller, family-operated boat companies offer daytime trips and often, nighttime dinner-dance cruises. Check with local tourist offices for details.

➤ BOAT AND FERRY INFORMATION: **Hebel-Line** (☎ 06742/2420).

CAR TRAVEL

Frankfurt is 126 km (78 mi) from Koblenz, 175 km (109 mi) from Bonn, and 190 km (118 mi) from Köln (the A-3 links Frankfurt with Köln and passes near Koblenz and Bonn). The most spectacular stretch of the Rhineland is between Mainz and Koblenz, which takes in the Rhine Gorge. Highways hug the river on each bank (B-42 on the north/eastern side, and B-9 on the south/western side), and car ferries crisscross the Rhine at many points.

TOURS

Both day and overnight cruises visit towns along the Rhine. The local shipping company, Personenschiffahrt Merkelbach, has river tours. Rhein und Moselschiffahrt Gerhard Colée-Hölzenbein organizes tours of the Mosel and Rhine rivers. The tourist offices in Mainz and Köln offer English-language walking tours.

➤ FEES AND SCHEDULES: **Personenschiffahrt Merkelbach** (☎ 0261/ 76810). **Rhein und Moselschiffahrt Gerhard Colée-Hölzenbein** (☎ 0261/37744, FAX 0261/16640).

TRAIN TRAVEL

One of the best ways to visit the Rhineland in very limited time is to take the scenic, two-hour train journey from Mainz north to Köln along the western bank of the river.

VISITOR INFORMATION

The Rhineland regional tourist office, Rheinland-Pfalz-Information, provides general information on the region. The (partially) bilingual events calendar, *Veranstaltungskalender Rheinland-Pfalz Feste,* gives a comprehensive overview of wine, regional, and folk festivals, as well as cultural events. The German Wine Information Bureau has brochures on area vineyards and harvest festivals.

➤ TOURIST INFORMATION: **Bacharach** (Tourist-Information; ✉ Oberstr. 45, D-55422, ☎ 06743/919–303, FAX 06743/919–304, WEB www.rhein-nahe-touristik.de). **Bonn** (Bonn Information; ✉ Windeckstr. 2

am Münsterpl., D-53111, ☎ 0228/775–000, WEB www.bonn.de). **Boppard** (Tourist-Information; ✉ Marktpl., D-56154, ☎ 06742/3888, FAX 06742/81402, WEB www.boppard.de). **Koblenz** (Tourist-Information; ✉ Bahnhofsplatz 7, D-56068, ☎ 0261/31304, FAX 0261/100–4388, WEB www.koblenz.de). **Köln** (Köln Tourismus Office; ✉ Unter Fettenhenen 19, D-50667, ☎ 0221/221–23345, WEB www.koeln.de). **Mainz** (Touristik-Zentrale; ✉ Brückenturm am Rathaus, D-55116, ☎ 06131/286–210 WEB www.info–mainz.de). **Rheinland-Pfalz-Information** (✉ Löhrstr. 103–105, D-56068 Koblenz, ☎ 0261/915–200, FAX 0261/915–2040, WEB www.rlp-info.de). **Rüdesheim** (Tourist-Information; ✉ Geisenheimer Str. 22, D-65385, ☎ 06722/19433, FAX 06722/3485, WEB www.ruedesheim.de).

HAMBURG

Water—in the form of the Alster Lakes and the Elbe River—is Hamburg's defining feature. The city-state's official title, the Free and Hanseatic City of Hamburg, reflects its kingpin status in the medieval Hanseatic League, a union that dominated trade on the North and the Baltic seas. The city is still a major port, with 33 docks and 500 berths for oceangoing vessels. The seafaring life has created the city's most distinct attractions, from the fish market to the red-light district.

Exploring Hamburg

Numbers in the margin correspond to points of interest on the Hamburg map.

Within the remaining traces of its old city walls, downtown Hamburg combines the seamiest, steamiest streets of dockland Europe with sleek avenues of shops. The city is easy to explore on foot.

❷ **Alter Botanischer Garten** (Old Botanical Gardens). This green and open park in Wallringpark specializes in rare and exotic plants. Tropical and subtropical species grow under glass in hothouses, and specialty gardens—including herbal and medicinal—cluster around an old moat. ✉ *Stephanspl.*, ☎ *no phone.* ⏲ *Daily 8–6.*

★ ❼ **Erotic Art Museum.** Sexually provocative art from 1520 to the present is showcased here with great taste and decorum. Photography exhibits take place in a building on Bernhard-Nocht-Strasse. ✉ *Nobistor 10a at Reeperbahn and Bernhard-Nocht-Str. 69*, ☎ *040/3174–757*, WEB *www.erotic-art-museum.hamburg.de. Minimum age 16.* ⏲ *Sun.–Thurs. 10 AM–midnight, Fri.–Sat. 10 AM–1 AM. U-bahn: St. Pauli.*

★ ❺ **Fischmarkt** (Fish Market). Freshly caught fish are only part of a compendium of wares on sale at the popular Fischmarkt in Altona. In fact you can find almost anything—from live parrots and palm trees to armloads of flowers and bananas, valuable antiques to fourth-hand junk. ✉ *Between Grosse Elbestr. and St. Pauli Landungsbrücken.* ⏲ *Apr.–Sept., Sun. 5 AM–10 AM; Oct.–Mar., Sun. 7 AM–10 AM.*

❶ **Hauptbahnhof** (Main Train Station). The cast-iron-and-glass station is a breathtaking example of imperial German pride. It was opened in 1906 and is the largest structure of its kind in Europe. The enormous 394-ft-long structure is accentuated by a 460-ft-wide glazed roof that is supported only by pillars at each end. ✉ *Steintorpl.*

⓫ **Jungfernstieg.** Classy jewelers and chic clothing boutiques line this wide promenade looking out over the Alster Lakes.

❿ **Krameramtswohnungen** (Shopkeepers' Guild Houses). The shopkeepers' guild built this tightly packed group of courtyard houses between 1620 and 1626 for members' widows. The house marked "C" is open to the public. Tour buses stop here, and some of the houses have been converted to shops. ✉ *Historic House "C," Krayenkamp 10,* ☎ *040/3750–1988.* ⏲ *Tues.–Sun. 10–5. U-bahn: Rödingsmarkt.*

★ ⓮ **Kunsthalle** (Art Gallery). This prestigious exhibition hall's paintings include works by practically all the great northern European masters from the 14th through the 20th century. The 1996 postmodern cube contains a modern art collection, with works by Andy Warhol, Joseph Beuys, Georg Baselitz, and David Hockney. ✉ *Glockengiesserwall 1,* ☎ *040/42854–2612,* WEB *www.hamburger-kunsthalle.de.* ⏲ *Tues.–Wed., Fri.–Sun. 10–6, Thurs. 10–9.*

❻ **Landungsbrücken** (Landing Bridges). Harbor cruises depart from these main terminals. ✉ *Near St. Pauli and Hafenstr.*

❽ **Museum für Hamburgische Geschichte** (Museum of Hamburg History). The museum's vast collection of artifacts charts the history of Hamburg from its origins in the 9th century to the present. ✉ *Holstenwall 24,* ☎ *040/42841–2380.* ⏲ *Tues.–Sun. 10–6, Mon. 1–5.*

❸ **Planten un Blomen.** This park has beautifully groomed plant, flower, and water gardens. The Japanese Garden is Europe's largest. ✉ *Stephanspl.,* ⏲ *Mar.–Oct., daily 9–4:45; Nov.–Feb., daily 9–3:45.*

★ ⓭ **Rathaus** (Town Hall). This pompous neo-Gothic building has 647 rooms, 6 more than Buckingham Palace. Only the state rooms are open to visitors. ✉ *Rathausmarkt,* ☎ *040/428–310,* WEB *www.hamburg.de.* ⏲ *English-language tours Mon.–Thur. hourly 10:15–3:15, Fri.–Sun. hourly 10:15–1:15.*

⓬ **Rathausmarkt** (Town Hall Square). The large square, with its surrounding arcades, was laid out after Hamburg's Great Fire of 1842. The architects drew on St. Mark's in Venice for inspiration. ✉ *Bordered by Johannesstr., Alter Wall, Adolphsbrücke, and Adolphspl.*

❹ **Reeperbahn.** The red-light Reeperbahn is the major thoroughfare of the St. Pauli district. It offers a broad menu of entertainment besides striptease and sex shows. Beyond this strip, St. Pauli is dominated by its riverfront, which gives it a maritime, though run-down, appeal.

⓯ **Speicherstadt** (Warehouse District). These harbor warehouses, with a rich overlay of gables and turrets, store and process every conceivable commodity, from coffee and spices to raw silks. You can't enter the buildings, but the nonstop activity will give you a good sense of a port at work. ✉ *St. Annenufer 2, Block R,* ☎ *040/321–191,* WEB *www.speicherstadtmuseum.de.* ⏲ *Tues.–Sun. 10–5. U-bahn: Messberg.*

★ ❾ **St. Michaeliskirche** (St. Michael's Church). The finest baroque church in northern Germany, St. Michael's has a distinctive 433-ft brick-and-iron tower bearing the largest tower clock in Germany, 26 ft in diameter. Just above the clock is the viewing platform, which affords a magnificent panorama. ✉ *St. Michaeliskirche,* ☎ *040/376–780,* WEB *www.st-michaelis.de.* ⏲ *Apr.–Sept., Mon.–Sat. 9–6, Sun. 11:30–5:30; Oct.–Mar., Mon.–Sat. 10–5, Sun. 11–5:30.*

Dining

A flotilla of boats brings a wide variety of fish to Hamburg's harbor. One of the most celebrated of the robust local specialties is *Aalsuppe* (eel soup), a tangy concoction resembling bouillabaisse. *Räucheraal* (smoked eel) is also worth sampling. The sailors' favorite is *Labskaus,* a stew made from pickled meat, potatoes, and sometimes herring; it is usually garnished with a fried egg, sour pickles, and beets.

Hamburg

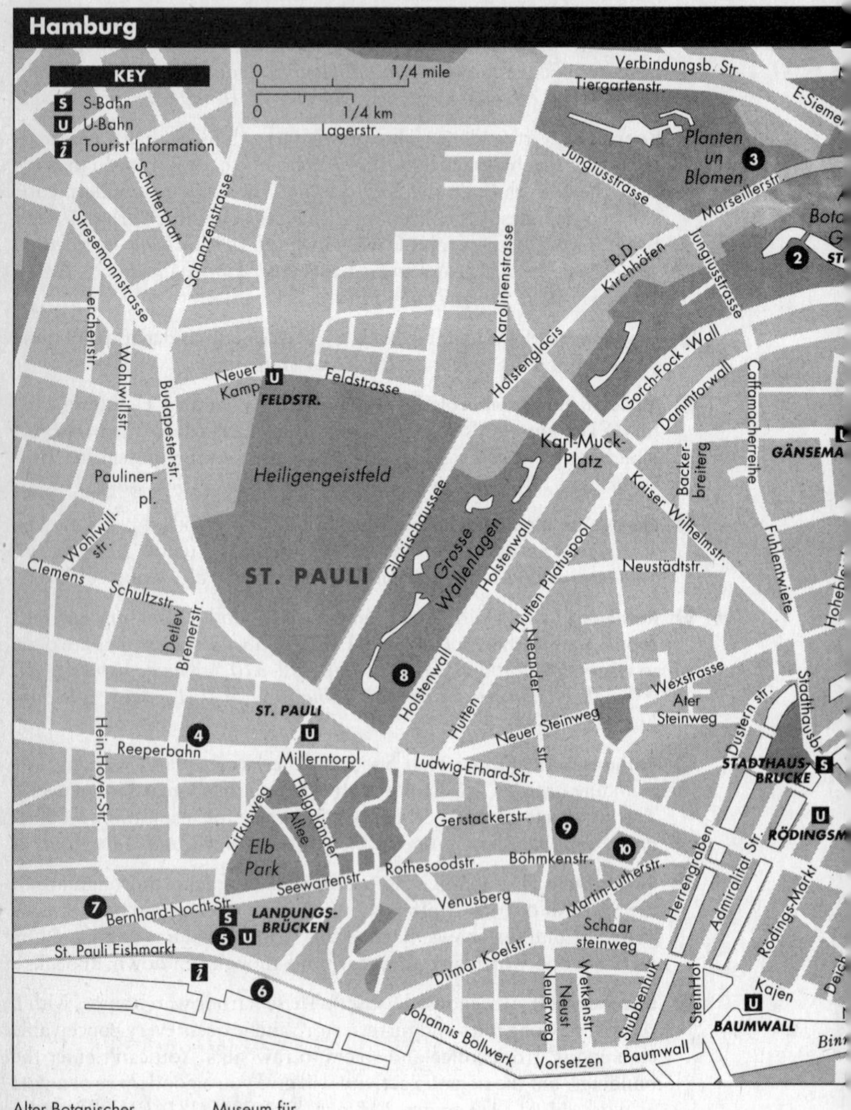
KEY
S-Bahn
U-Bahn
Tourist Information
0 1/4 mile
0 1/4 km
Verbindungsb. Str.
Tiergartenstr.
E-Siemens
Lagerstr.
Planten un Blomen
Jungiusstrasse
Marseillerstr.
Schulterblatt
Schanzenstrasse
Stresemannstrasse
Lerchenstr.
Wohlwillstr.
Karolinenstrasse
B.D. Kirchhöfen
Holstenglacis
Gorch-Fock-Wall
Dammtorwall
Caffamacherreihe
Neuer Kamp
FELDSTR.
Feldstrasse
Budapesterstr.
Karl-Muck-Platz
GÄNSEMA
Backerbreiterg
Paulinenpl.
Heiligengeistfeld
Kaiser Wilhelmstr.
Fuhlentwiete
Wohlwillstr.
Clemens
Schultzstr.
ST. PAULI
Glacischaussee
Grosse Wallenlagen
Holstenwall
Pilatuspool
Neustädtstr.
Detlev Bremerstr.
Hutten
Neander str.
Wexstrasse
Ater Steinweg
Stadthausbr
Hein-Hoyer-Str.
Reeperbahn
ST. PAULI
Millerntorpl.
Neuer Steinweg
Ludwig-Erhard-Str.
Dustern str.
STADTHAUS-BRUCKE
Zirkusweg
Helgoländer Allee
Elb Park
Gerstackerstr.
RÖDINGSM
Seewartenstr.
Rothesoodstr.
Böhmkenstr.
Herrengraben
Admiralitat Str.
Bernhard-Nocht-Str.
LANDUNGS-BRÜCKEN
Venusberg
Martin-Lutherstr.
Schaar steinweg
Rödings-Markt
St. Pauli Fishmarkt
Ditmar Koelstr.
Neuerweg
Neust
Wetkenstr.
Stubbenhuk
SteinHof
Kajen
Johannis Bollwerk
Vorsetzen
Baumwall
BAUMWALL

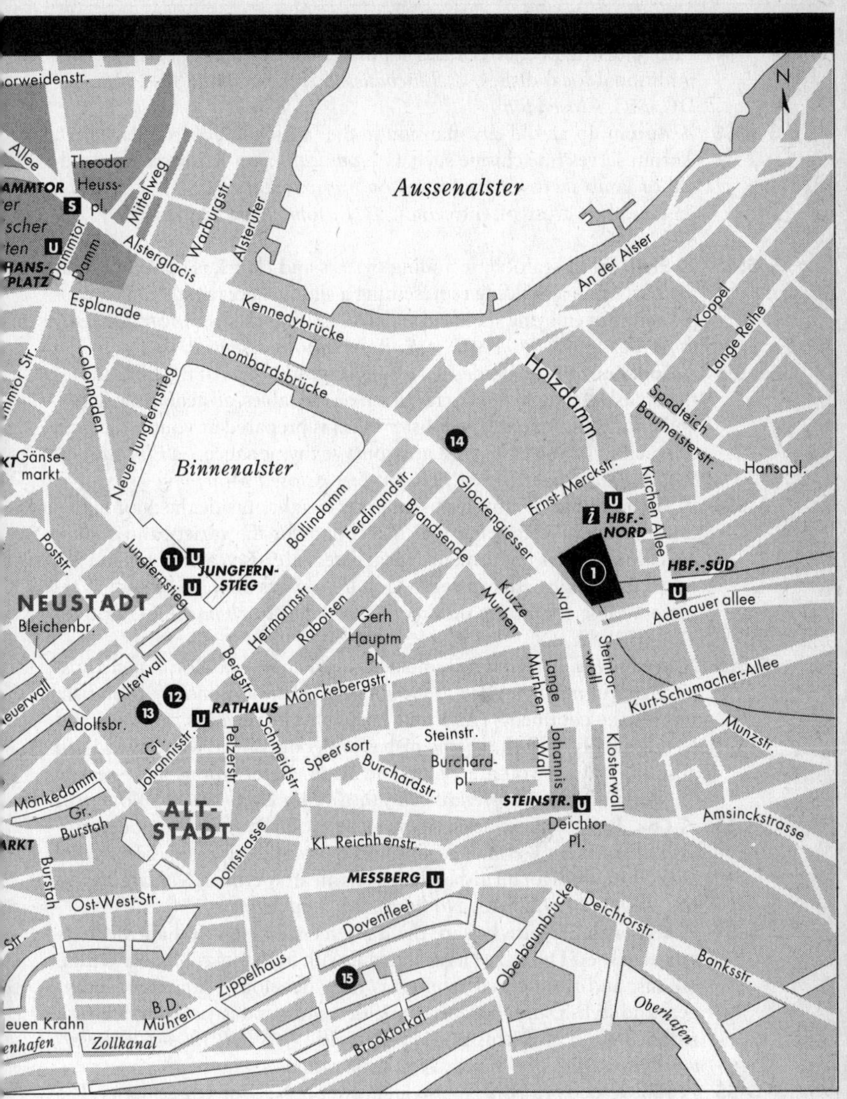
Aussenalster
Binnenalster
NEUSTADT
ALT-
STADT
Theodor
Heuss-
pl.
Alsterglacis
Esplanade
Kennedybrücke
Lombardsbrücke
Holzdamm
An der Alster
Koppel
Lange Reihe
Spadteich
Baumeisterstr.
Hansapl.
Ernst-Merckstr.
HBF.-
NORD
HBF.-SÜD
Kirchen Allee
Adenauer allee
Glockengiesser
wall
Steintor-
wall
Kurt-Schumacher-Allee
Munzstr.
Brandsende
Ferdinandstr.
Ballindamm
Neuer Jungfernstieg
Colonnaden
Jungfernstieg
JUNGFERN-
STIEG
Hermannstr.
Raboisen
Gerh
Hauptm
Pl.
Kurze
Murhen
Lange
Murhen
Johannis
Wall
Mönckebergstr.
RATHAUS
Bergstr.
Schmeidstr
Pelzerstr.
Gr.
Johannisstr.
Alterwall
Adolfsbr.
Bleichenbr.
Poststr.
Gänse-
markt
Speer sort
Steinstr.
Burchardstr.
Burchard-
pl.
Klosterwall
STEINSTR.
Deichtor
Pl.
Amsinckstrasse
Mönkedamm
Gr.
Burstah
Burstah
Domstrasse
Kl. Reichhenstr.
MESSBERG
Ost-West-Str.
Dovenfleet
Zippelhaus
Oberbaumbrücke
Deichtorstr.
Banksstr.
Oberhafen
Brooktorkai
B.D.
Mühren
Zollkanal
Alsterufer
Warburgstr.
Mittelweg
Dammtor
Damm
Alle
Allee
N

$$$–$$$$ ★ ✕ **Landhaus Scherrer.** A popular, country house–style restaurant in the Altona district, Scherrer fuses sophisticated nouvelle specialties with traditional local dishes. ✉ *Elbchaussee 130,* ☎ *040/880–1325. AE, DC, MC. Closed Sun.*

$–$$$$ ★ ✕ **Aurum.** In an old city mansion in the fashionable Karolinenviertel, Aurum serves fine cuisine such as *Lammcaree mit Rosmarinjus,* (saddle of lamb in rosemary sauce) or *Merrettichkruste vom Entrecote,* (horseradish crust of entrecote). ✉ *Karolinenstr. 32,* ☎ *040/4318–8432. MC.*

$–$$$$ ★ ✕ **Rive.** Fresh seafood, including oysters and clams, is served right at the harbor, in a building representing a ship, where mostly media people hang out enjoying spectacular views. ✉ *Van der Smissen Str. 1, Kreuzfahrt-Center,* ☎ *040/3805–919. Reservations essential. AE.*

$$–$$$ ✕ **Landhaus Dill.** A fin-de-siècle building with views of the Elbe houses this stylish restaurant, with crisp linen on the tables, glistening tile floors, and exquisite entrées. The lobster salad is prepared at your table, and the rack of lamb comes with an aromatic thyme sauce. ✉ *Elbchaussee 94,* ☎ *040/390–5077. AE, DC, MC, V. Closed Mon.*

$–$$$ ✕ **Fischerhaus.** Hamburg's fish market is right outside the door of this traditional old restaurant, which accounts for the variety and quality of seafood dishes on its menu. Meat eaters are also catered to, and the soups (especially fish) are legendary. It's always busy, so be sure to reserve a table and arrive on time. ✉ *St. Pauli Fischmarkt 14,* ☎ *040/314–053. AE, DC, MC, V.*

$–$$$ ★ ✕ **Weite Welt.** In an old fish smokehouse, owner Niko Bornhofen's hospitality will make you feel right at home. His food, mostly fresh fish, crosses the continents (Asia and Europe). The menu is inventive and changes daily, and the theme dishes are good value. Weite Welt is an absolute must if you are visiting St. Pauli. Reservations are essential on weekends. ✉ *Grosse Freiheit 70,* ☎ *040/3191–214. V. No lunch.*

$$ ★ ✕ **Cox.** Reliable Cox never goes out of style. The food, a modern fusion of southern German cuisine and Austrian recipes, uses fresh and healthy produce for all dishes. It attracts an artsy crowd. ✉ *Lange Reihe 68,* ☎ *040/249422. AE. No lunch Sun. and Mon.*

$–$$ ✕ **Eisenstein.** A sure bet are the daily menus or the Italian-Mediterranean dishes. The Pizza Helsinki (made with fresh tomatoes, sour cream, onions, and fresh cured salmon) is truly delicious. The crowd is upbeat and stylish, and the setting, a 19th-century industrial complex with redbrick walls, is very rustic. ✉ *Friedensallee 9,* ☎ *040/3904–606. Reservations essential for dinner. No credit cards.*

$–$$ ✕ **Nil.** Nestled in an old '50s-style shoe shop, Nil spans three floors. The kitchen turns out seafood and modern German fare such as *Zicklein mit Bohnen- und Topinamburgemüse* (baked kid, served with beans and Jerusalem artichokes). ✉ *Neuer Pferdemarkt 5,* ☎ *040/4397–823. Reservations essential for dinner. No credit cards. Closed Mon.–Tues.*

$ ★ ✕ **Genno's.** Owners Mathias Barth and Eugen Albrecht make you feel at home with warm service and tasty dishes. The cuisine is made up anything the two owners like to eat themselves, for example, *Putenleber in Apfel-Balsamicosauce und Kartoffelpüree,* (liver in apple-balsamico sauce and mashed potatoes). The restaurant has only 16 seats, so on weekends especially a reservation is essential. ✉ *Hammer Steindamm 123,* ☎ *040/202567. No credit cards. Dinner only. Closed Sun.*

Lodging

Hotels are often full, and rates are high, although special weekend reductions are common. The tourist office can help you with reservations; try the **HAM-Hotline** (☎ 040/3005–1300, WEB www.hamburg-tourism.de) to secure a room.

$$$$ ★ **Dorint am Alten Wall.** The rooms of this sleek hotel are furnished with timeless design furniture, huge beds (by German standards, that is) and even bigger marble bathrooms. The central location by the main shopping district and the hotel's bistro run by Le Canard–chef Josef Viehauser make this hotel a great choice. ✉ *Alter Wall 38–46, D-20457,* ☎ *040/369–500,* FAX *040/369–501,* WEB *www.dorint.de. 224 rooms, 18 suites. Restaurant. AE, DC, MC, V.*

$$$$ ★ **Kempinski Hotel Atlantic Hamburg.** The sumptuous Atlantic has been a focal point of Hamburg's social scene since it opened in 1909. Rooms, whether traditionally furnished or more modern, exude an understated luxury, and suites are just short of palatial; the service is swift and hushed. ✉ *An der Alster 72–79, D-20099,* ☎ *040/28880,* FAX *040/24729,* WEB *www.kempinski.atlantic.de. 241 rooms, 13 suites. 2 restaurants. AE, DC, MC, V.*

$$$$ ★ **Park Hyatt Hamburg.** This ultramodern hotel is hidden behind the historic walls of the Levanethaus, an old warehouse, close to the downtown area. Guest rooms have bright and stylish furnishings; the pool and fitness area is breathtaking. If you are bored with the Old World atmosphere of other first-class hotels, this is the place to stay. ✉ *Bugenhagenstr. 8–10, D-20095,* ☎ *040/3332–1234,* FAX *040/3332–1235,* WEB *www.hamburg.hyatt.com. 251 rooms, 31 apartments. 2 restaurants, pool. AE, DC, MC, V.*

$$–$$$$ ★ **Gastwerk Hotel Hamburg.** In a century-old, redbrick gas plant, the new Gastwerk is the most stylish accommodation in town. The simple but incredibly chic furnishings reflect industrial design, but the materials are still natural. ✉ *Daimlerstr. 67, D-22761,* ☎ *040/890–620,* FAX *040/890–6220,* WEB *www.gastwerk-hotel.de. 90 rooms, 10 suites. Restaurant. AE, MC, V.*

$$$ ★ **Hotel Prem.** Most guests are regulars who have their favorite rooms; no two rooms are alike. The Adenauer Suite (named for the chancellor who stayed here), for example, is traditionally furnished, including an antique chaise longue and a period writing desk in a small alcove with a lake view. ✉ *An der Alster 9, D-20099,* ☎ *040/2483–4040,* FAX *040/2803–851,* WEB *www.hotel-prem.de. 51 rooms, 3 suites. Restaurant, bar. AE, DC, MC, V.*

$$ **Hotel Hafen Hamburg and Hotel Residenz Hafen Hamburg.** In a complex just across the famous St. Pauli Landungbrücken, both hotels are good value. The older Hotel Hafen Hamburg, with its smaller but nicely renovated rooms, offers a great view of the harbor, while the ultramodern Hotel Residenz Hafen annex has more comfort. A very good deal are the Residenz's double rooms, which come at the price of a single room. ✉ *Seewartenstr. 7–9, D-20459,* ☎ *040/3111–3600,* FAX *040/3111–3755,* WEB *www.hotel-hamburg.de. 230 rooms, 10 suites, and 125 rooms. 2 restaurants. AE, DC, MC, V.*

$$ ★ **Hotel Village.** Until 1991, the small and charming Hotel Village was a typical brothel near the main train station. The decor of the 14 rooms—glossy red-and-black carpets and wallpaper—is a nod to the hotel's past. The service is extremely friendly and casual. ✉ *Steindamm 4, D-20099,* ☎ *040/246–137,* FAX *040/4503–0030. 14 rooms. AE, MC, V.*

$$ **Kronprinz.** For its down-market location (on a busy street opposite the train station) and its moderate price, the Kronprinz is a surprisingly attractive hotel. Rooms are individually styled, modern but homey; ask for N. 45, with its mahogany and red-plush decor. ✉ *Kirchenallee 46, D-20099,* ☎ *040/271–407,* FAX *040/280–1097. 73 rooms. Restaurant. AE, DC, MC, V.*

$$ ★ **Wedina.** Rooms at this small hotel are neat, compact, and completely renovated. When making a reservation, ask for a room in the stylish 100-year-old-plus "Yellow House," which is rustic Italian in style and

has an elegant parquet floor. ✉ *Gurlittstr. 23, D-20099,* ☎ *040/243–011,* FAX *040/280–3894. 27 rooms. Bar. AE, DC, MC, V.*

$ **Hotel Monopol.** The family-owned Hotel Monopol offers a safe and clean stay in the heart of Europe's most bizarre red-light district. The small rooms are not up-to-date, but the service is warm. This hotel is as local as it can get. ✉ *Reeperbahn 48, D-20359,* ☎ *040/311–770,* FAX *040/3117–7151. 82 rooms. Restaurant, bar. AE, DC, MC, V.*

Nightlife and the Arts

From about 10 PM on, the Reeperbahn springs to life, and *everything* is for sale. Among the Reeperbahn's even rougher side streets, the most notorious is the Grosse Freiheit, which means "Great Freedom." The area is not just a red-light district, however. Side streets have a mixture of yuppie bars, restaurants, and theaters that are somewhat more refined than the seamen's bars and sex shops. Hans-Albers-Platz is a center of this revival. The **Grosse Freiheit Nr. 7** (✉ Grosse Freiheit 7, ☎ 040/311–151) used to be a sailors' hangout and now serves as a pub and venue for live music. The bar **La Paloma** (✉ Gerhardstr. 2, ☎ 040/314–512) is stylish. Variety shows pack the house at **Theater Schmidt** (✉ Spielbudenpl. 27–28, ☎ 040/3177–8899).

For higher culture, head to the **Hamburgische Staatsoper** (✉ Grosse Theaterstr. 35, ☎ 040/356–868. It's the leading northern German venue for opera and ballet. The Hamburg Ballet is directed by American John Neumeier. Both the Hamburg Philharmonic and the Hamburg Symphony Orchestra appear at the **Musikhalle** (✉ Johannes-Brahms-Pl., ☎ 040/346–920).

Hamburg Essentials

AIRPORTS AND TRANSFERS

Fuhlsbüttel, Hamburg's international airport, is 11 km (7 mi) northwest of the city.

➤ AIRPORT INFORMATION: **Fuhlsbüttel** (☎ 040/50750. WEB www.ham-airport.de).

TRANSFERS

An Airport-City-Bus runs nonstop between the airport and Hamburg's Hauptbahnhof at 20-minute intervals between 5:40 AM and 10:30 PM. Tickets are DM 8/€4.10 per person. The Airport-Express (Bus 110) runs every 10 minutes between the airport and the Ohlsdorf U- and S-bahn stations, a 17-minute ride from the main train station. The fare is DM 6.90/€3.45.

BUS TRAVEL TO AND FROM HAMBURG

Hamburg's bus station, the Zentral-Omnibus-Bahnhof, is right behind the Hauptbahnhof (main train station).

➤ BUS INFORMATION: **Zentral-Omnibus-Bahnhof** (ZOB; ☎ 040/247–575).

CAR RENTAL

➤ MAJOR AGENCIES: **Avis** (✉ Airport, ☎ 040/5075–2314; ✉ Drehbahn 15–25, ☎ 040/341–651; ✉ Herderstr. 52, ☎ 040/220–1188). **Hertz** (✉ Airport, ☎ 040/5935–1367; ✉ Kirchenallee 34–36, opposite the Hauptbahnhof, ☎ 040/2801–201). **Sixt** (✉ Airport, ☎ 040/593–9480; ✉ Spaldingstr. 110, ☎ 040/232–393).

CAR TRAVEL

Hamburg is easier to handle by car than are many other German cities and is relatively uncongested with traffic. Incoming autobahns connect with Hamburg's three beltways, which then take you smoothly to the downtown area. Follow the signs for STADTZENTRUM (downtown).

CONSULATES

➤ IRELAND: ✉ Feldbrunnenstr. 43, ☎ 040/4418–6213.
➤ NEW ZEALAND: ✉ Heimhuder Str. 56, ☎ 040/442–5550.
➤ UNITED KINGDOM: ✉ Harvestehuder Weg 8a, ☎ 040/448–0320.
➤ UNITED STATES: ✉ Alsterufer 28, ☎ 040/411–710.

EMERGENCIES

➤ DOCTORS AND DENTISTS: **Dentist** (☎ 040/11500).
➤ EMERGENCY SERVICES: **Ambulance and Fire Department** (☎ 112). **Medical Emergencies** (☎ 040/228–022). **Police** (☎ 110).

ENGLISH-LANGUAGE MEDIA

➤ BOOKSTORES: **Frensche International** (✉ Spitalerstr. 26c, ☎ 040/327–585).

TAXIS

Taxi meters start at DM 4/€2.05, and the fare is DM 2.30/€1.17 (DM 2.50/€1.28 at night and on weekends) per kilometer (½ mi), plus 50 pfennigs/€0.25 for each piece of luggage.
➤ TAXI COMPANIES: ☎ 040/441–011, 040/686–868, or 040/611–061.

TOURS

BUS TOURS

Bus tours of the city, with a guide who rapidly describes sights in both German and English, leave from Kirchenallee (in front of the Hauptbahnhof) at regular intervals. A bus tour lasting 1¾ hours sets off daily and costs DM 35/€17.90. For DM 45/€23, one of the bus tours can be combined with two one-hour boat trips on the Alster Lake and the Elbe River.
➤ FEES AND SCHEDULES: **AG Hamburg Rundfahrt** (☎ 040/641–3731).

BOAT TOURS

HADAG tours of the harbor leave every half hour in summer, less frequently during the winter, from Landungsbrücken (Piers) 1, 2, 3, and 7. The one-hour tour costs DM 15/€7.50. A special harbor tour with an English-speaking guide leaves Pier 1 at 11:15 daily from March through November (same price). Bordparty-Service cold buffet dinner cruises (DM 69/€36) include as much beer as you dare to drink. Cruises depart on Saturdays at 8 PM, from between Piers 6 and 9. Fifty-minute cruises of the Alster lakes leave from the Jungfernstieg.
➤ FEES AND SCHEDULES: **Alster Touristik** (☎ 040/357–4240). **Bordparty-Service** (✉ Landungsbrücken, Pier 9, ☎ 040/313–687). **HADAG** (☎ 040/311–7070, 040/313–130, 040/313–959, 040/3178–2231 for English-language tour).

TRAIN TRAVEL

Hamburg is a terminus for main-line service to northern Germany. All trains to German and international destinations stop at the Hauptbahnhof and regional trains also stop at Hamburg-Altona.
➤ TRAIN INFORMATION: **Hamburg-Altona** (✉ Scheel-Plessen-Str. 17, ☎ 040/19419). **Hauptbahnhof** (✉ Adenauerallee 78, ☎ 040/19419).

TRANSPORTATION AROUND HAMBURG

The comprehensive city and suburban transportation system includes the U-bahn (subway) network, which connects with the S-bahn (suburban train lines), and an exemplary bus service. Tickets cover travel by all three, as well as by harbor ferry. The one- and three-day Hamburg CARD allows free travel on all public transportation within the city, free admission to state museums, and discounts of approximately 30% on most bus, train, and boat tours. For information about this card inquire at tourist offices. For information on the public-transportation system, contact the Hamburg Passenger Transport Board.

➤ CONTACTS: **Hamburg Passenger Transport Board** (HVV; ✉ Steinstr. 1, ☎ 040/19449. WEB www.hvv.de).

TRAVEL AGENCIES

➤ LOCAL AGENTS: **Hapag-Lloyd** (✉ Verkehrspavillon Jungfernstieg, ☎ 040/328–560). **Reiseland American Express** (✉ Ballindamm 39, ☎ 040/309–080).

VISITOR INFORMATION

➤ HAMBURG TOURIST OFFICES: **Hauptbahnhof** (Main Train Station; ✉ Steintorpl., at Kirchenallee main exit, ☎ 040/3005–1200). **St. Pauli Landungsbrücken** (Boat Landings; ✉ between Piers 4 and 5, ☎ 040/300–51200, WEB www.hamburg-tourism.de).

BERLIN

Germany's capital has evolved into a cosmopolitan metropolis. A royal residence during the 15th century, Berlin came into its own under the rule of King Friedrich II (1712–86)—Frederick the Great—whose liberal reforms and artistic patronage led the city's development into a major cultural capital. In the 20th century Hitler and his supporters destroyed Berlin's reputation for tolerance and plunged it headlong into the war that led to its wholesale destruction, and to its eventual division by the infamous Wall. Erected in 1961, the Wall was finally breached in the "Peaceful Revolution" of 1989. Berlin is again on the cutting edge, drawing curious and adventuresome visitors.

Exploring Berlin

Unlike most other large German cities, Berlin is a young and partly planned capital, with streets organized in a unusually clear manner. Yet Berlin is laid out on an epic scale—so allow plenty of time to get around.

Western Berlin

The western districts include Charlottenburg, Tiergarten, Kreuzberg, and Schöneberg, and the entire area is best known for the constant commerce on Kurfürstendamm. The boulevard of shops, art galleries, restaurants, and bars stretches 3 km (2 mi) through the downtown.

Numbers in the margin correspond to points of interest on the Western Berlin map.

★ 14 **Ägyptisches Museum** (Egyptian Museum). This small but outstanding museum is home to the portrait bust of Nefertiti known around the world. The 3,300-year-old queen is the centerpiece of a fascinating collection of Egyptian antiquities that includes some of the finest-preserved mummies outside Cairo. ✉ *Schlosstr. 70,* ☎ *030/3435–7311 or 030/3090–5555,* WEB *www.smb.spk-berlin.de.* ⏲ *Tues.–Sun. 10–6.*

17 **Bildungs- und Gedenkstätte Haus der Wannsee-Konferenz** (Educational and Memorial Site House of the Wannsee Conference). This elegant Berlin villa hosted the fateful Wannsee-Konferenz held on January 20, 1942, when Nazi leaders planned the systematic deportation and genocide of Europe's Jewish population. This conference and its results are illustrated in an exhibition. From the U-Bahn Wannsee station take Bus 114. ✉ *Am Grossen Wannsee 56–58,* ☎ *030/805–0010,* WEB *www.ghwk.de.* ⏲ *Mon.–Sun. 10–6.*

★ 7 **Brandenburger Tor** (Brandenburg Gate). Berlin's premier landmark was built in 1788 to celebrate the triumphant Prussian armies. The gate was cut off by the Wall, and it became a focal point of celebrations marking the reunification of Berlin and of all Germany. The square behind the gate, **Pariser Platz** (Paris Square), has regained its prewar design. Just a few hundred yards to the south of the gate, Germany's national **Holocaust Mahnmal** (Holocaust Memorial) is being built. ✉ *Unter den Linden at Pariser Pl.,* WEB *www.brandenburger-tor.de.*

18 **Dahlemer Museen** (Dahlem Museums). This unique complex of four museums includes the **Ethnologisches Museum** (Ethnographic Museum), famous for its artifacts from Africa, Asia, the South Seas, and the Americas. The other museums present early European cultures, ancient Indian culture, and East Asian art. ✉ *Lansstr. 8, subway line U-2 to Dahlem-Dorf,* ☎ *030/8301–438,* WEB *www.smb.spk-berlin.de.* ⏲ *Tues.–Fri. 10–6, weekends 11–6.*

16 **Grunewald** (Green Forest). Together with its Wannsee lakes, this splendid forest is the most popular retreat for Berliners, who come out in force, swimming, sailing their boats, tramping through the woods, and riding horseback. In winter a downhill ski run and ski jump operate on the modest slopes of Teufelsberg hill. Excursion steamers ply the Wannsee, the Havel River, and the Müggelsee. ✉ *Southwest of downtown western Berlin.*

★ 11 **Haus am Checkpoint Charlie.** The museum reviews events leading up to the Wall's construction and displays actual tools and equipment, records, and photographs documenting methods used by East Germans to cross over to the West. ✉ *Friedrichstr. 43–45,* ☎ *030/253–7250,* WEB *www.mauer-museum.com.* ⏲ *Daily 9 AM–10 PM.*

12 **Jüdisches Museum** (Jewish Museum). This jagged structure designed by architect Daniel Libeskind has received much acclaim. The history and culture of Germany's Jewish communities are the theme of the exhibits. ✉ *Lindenstr. 9–14,* ☎ *030/2599–3300,* WEB *www.jmberlin.de.*

★ 3 **Kaiser-Wilhelm-Gedächtniskirche** (Kaiser Wilhelm Memorial Church). This landmark, which once symbolized West Berlin, is a dramatic reminder of the futile destructiveness of war. The shell of the tower is all that remains of the 19th-century church. Adjoining the tower are a new church and bell tower. ✉ *Breitscheidpl.,* ☎ *030/218–5023,* WEB *www.gedaechtniskirche.com.* ⏲ *Old Tower Mon.–Sat. 10–4, Memorial Church daily 9–7.*

★ 9 **Kulturforum** (Cultural Forum). With its unique ensemble of museums, galleries, and libraries, the complex is a cultural jewel. It's also home to the Berlin Philharmonic orchestra. ✉ *Matthäikirchstr. 1,* ☎ *030/2548–8132, 030/2548–8232 or 030/2548–8301,* WEB *www.berlin-philharmonic.com.* ⏲ *Box office weekdays 3:30–6, weekends 11–2.*

The **Kunstgewerbemuseum** (Museum of Decorative Arts) displays arts and crafts of Europe from the Middle Ages to the present. ✉ *Matthäikirchpl. 10,* ☎ *030/266–2902.* ⏲ *Tues.–Fri. 10–6, weekends 11–6.*

The **Gemäldegalerie** (Painting Gallery) reunites formerly separated collections from eastern and western Berlin. One of Europe's finest art galleries, it has an extensive selection of European paintings from the 13th through 18th centuries, among them works by Dürer, Cranach the Elder, and Holbein, as well as of the Italian masters—Botticelli, Titian, Giotto, Lippi, and Raphael. ✉ *Matthäikirchpl. 8,* ☎ *030/2660; 030/2090–5555 for all state museums in Berlin,* WEB *www.smb.spk-berlin.de.* ⏲ *Tues.–Wed. 10–6, Thurs. 10–10, Fri.–Sun. 10–6.*

The **Neue Nationalgalerie** (New National Gallery), designed by Mies van der Rohe, exhibits artwork from the 19th and 20th centuries. ✉

Western Berlin

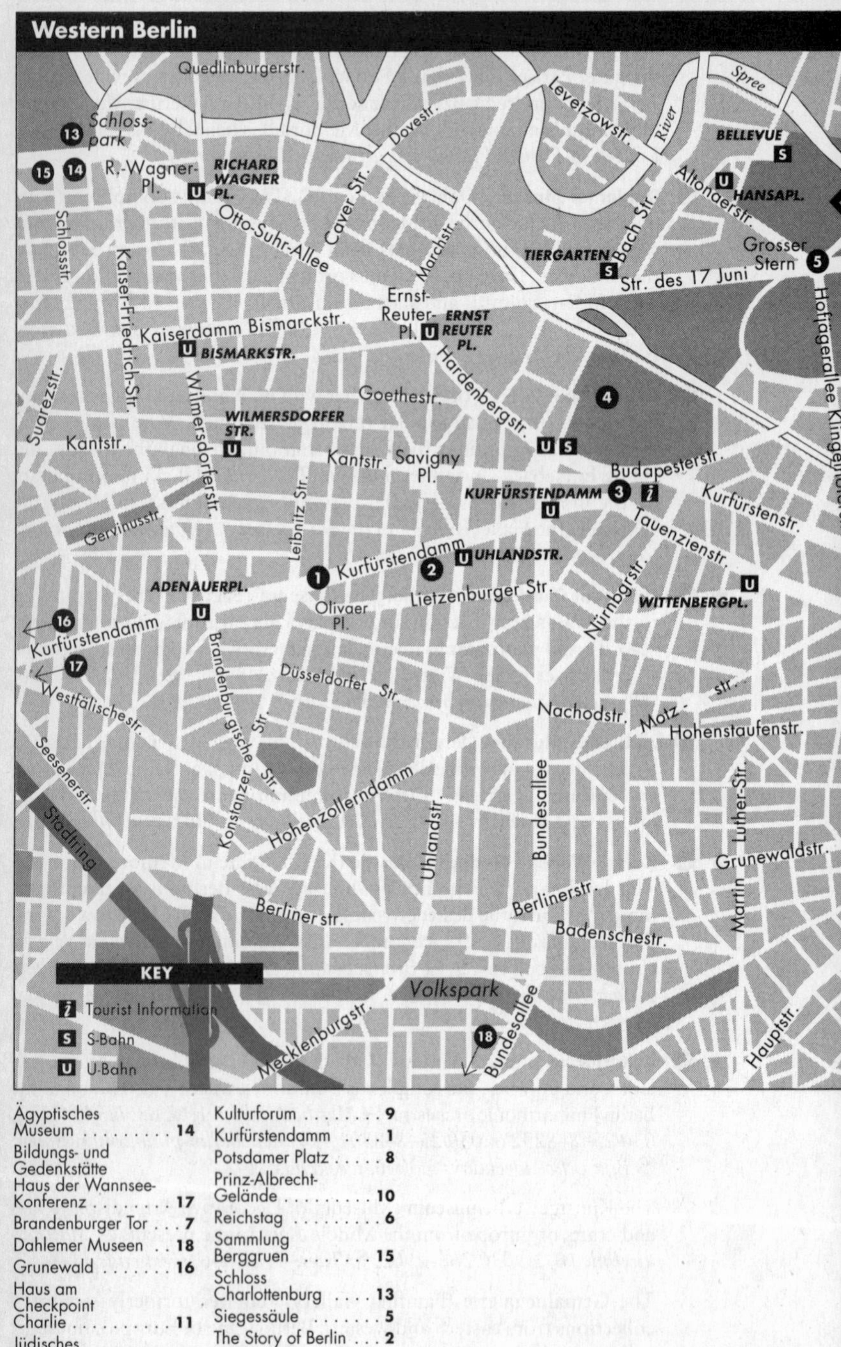

Ägyptisches Museum **14**
Bildungs- und Gedenkstätte Haus der Wannsee-Konferenz **17**
Brandenburger Tor . . . **7**
Dahlemer Museen . . **18**
Grunewald **16**
Haus am Checkpoint Charlie **11**
Jüdisches Museum **12**
Kaiser-Wilhelm-Gedächtniskirche . . . **3**
Kulturforum **9**
Kurfürstendamm **1**
Potsdamer Platz **8**
Prinz-Albrecht-Gelände **10**
Reichstag **6**
Sammlung Berggruen **15**
Schloss Charlottenburg **13**
Siegessäule **5**
The Story of Berlin . . . **2**
Zoologischer Garten **4**

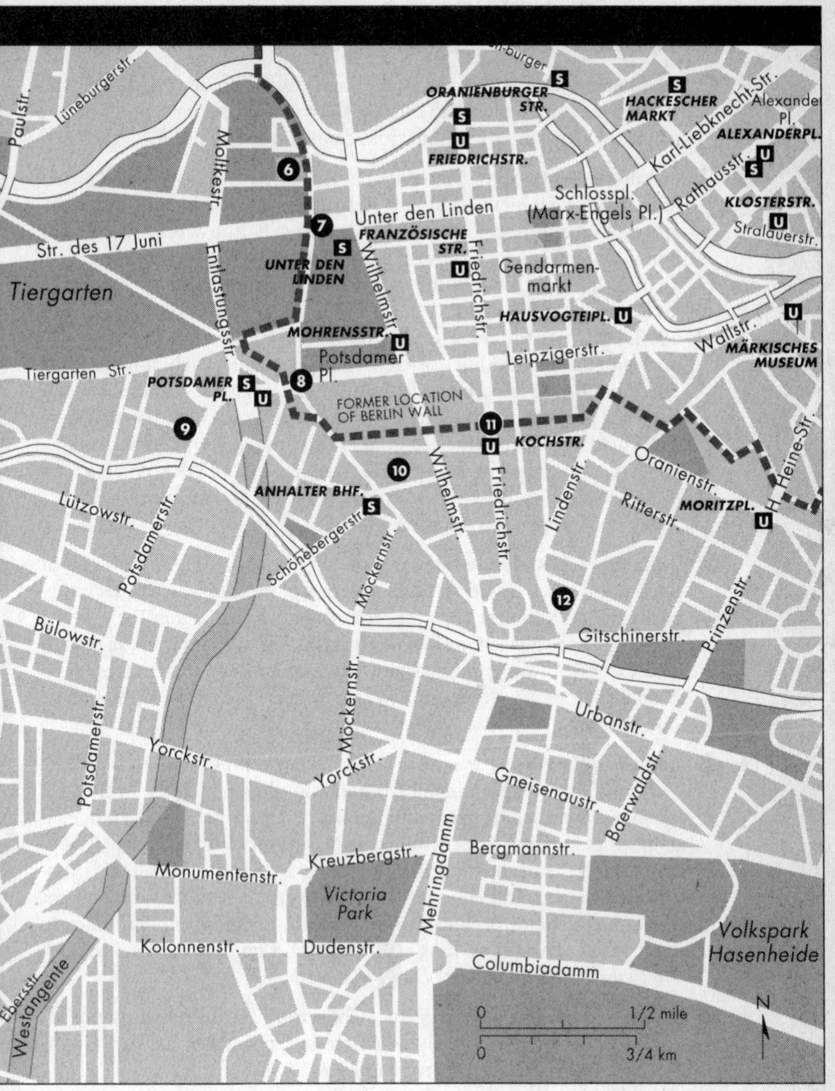

ORANIENBURGER STR.
HACKESCHER MARKT
Alexanderpl.
ALEXANDERPL.
Karl-Liebknecht-Str.
FRIEDRICHSTR.
Rathausstr.
KLOSTERSTR.
Stralauerstr.
Schlosspl. (Marx-Engels Pl.)
Unter den Linden
FRANZÖSISCHE STR.
UNTER DEN LINDEN
Gendarmenmarkt
HAUSVOGTEIPL.
MÄRKISCHES MUSEUM
Wallstr.
Leipzigerstr.
MOHRENSSTR.
Potsdamer Pl.
POTSDAMER PL.
FORMER LOCATION OF BERLIN WALL
KOCHSTR.
Oranienstr.
Ritterstr.
MORITZPL.
H. Heine-Str.
Lindenstr.
ANHALTER BHF.
Paulstr.
Lüneburgerstr.
Moltkestr.
Entlastungsstr.
Str. des 17 Juni
Tiergarten
Tiergarten Str.
Wilhelmstr.
Friedrichstr.
Lützowstr.
Potsdamerstr.
Schöneberger Str.
Möckernstr.
Bülowstr.
Gitschinerstr.
Prinzenstr.
Urbanstr.
Yorckstr.
Gneisenaustr.
Baerwaldstr.
Bergmannstr.
Kreuzbergstr.
Mehringdamm
Monumentenstr.
Victoria Park
Kolonnenstr.
Dudenstr.
Columbiadamm
Volkspark Hasenheide
Eberstr.
Westangente
0 1/2 mile
0 3/4 km
N
6
7
8
9
10
11
12

Potsdamer Str. 50, ☎ *030/266–2662,* WEB *www.smb.spk-berlin.de.* ⏲ *Tues.–Fri. 9–6, weekends 10–6.*

★ ❼ **Kurfürstendamm.** Ku'damm, as Berliners call the boulevard, throbs with activity day and night. The **Europa Center,** a shopping center, and the square in front of it are a buzzing, central meeting point.

★ ❽ **Potsdamer Platz.** Sony, Mercedes Benz, Asea Brown Boveri, and others have built their new company headquarters at this entirely reconstructed square, once Europe's busiest plaza before World War II. The **Sony Center** is an architectural marvel designed by German-American architect Helmut Jahn. Within it, the **Filmmuseum Berlin** (✉ Potsdamer Str. 2, ☎ 030/300–9030. ⏲ Tues., Wed., Fri., weekends 10–6, Thurs. 10–8. WEB www.filmmuseum-berlin.de) presents the history of moviemaking and memorabilia of German movie stars, including Marlene Dietrich. Also in the center is the Kaisersaal ("Emperor's Hall"), a café from the prewar Grand Hotel Esplanade that was located on this spot. The **Potsdamer Platz Arkaden** houses 140 upscale shops, a musical theater, a variety stage, cafés, a movie complex, a 3D-IMAX cinema, and even a casino. ✉ *Arkaden Alte Potsdamer Str. 7,* ☎ *Arkaden 030/2559–2766.* ⏲ *Arkaden weekdays 9:30–8, Sat. 9:30–4.*

❿ **Prinz-Albrecht-Gelände** (Prince Albrecht Grounds). The buildings that once stood here housed the headquarters of the Gestapo, the secret security police, and other Nazi security organizations. After the war, the buildings were leveled; in 1987, what was left of them was excavated. The exhibit "Topography of Terrors" documents their history and Nazi atrocities. ✉ *Niederkirchnerstr. 8,* ☎ *030/2545–090,* WEB *www.topographie.de.* ⏲ *Oct.–Apr., daily 10–6; May.–Sept., daily 10–8.*

★ ❻ **Reichstag** (German Parliament). The monumental building served as Germany's seat of parliament from its completion in 1894 until 1933, when it was gutted by fire under suspicious circumstances. Remodeled under the direction of British architect Sir Norman Foster, the Reichstag is once again hosting the Deutscher Bundestag, Germany's federal parliament. You can view the chambers on a short tour, and get a stunning view of Berlin from underneath the glass cupola. Lines to enter the Reichstag are long. ✉ *Platz der Republik 1,* ☎ *030/2270,* WEB *www.bundestag.de.* ⏲ *Daily 8 AM–10 PM.*

★ ⓯ **Sammlung Berggruen** (Berggruen Collection). This small museum focuses on modern art, with work from such artists as Van Gogh, Cézanne, Picasso, Giacometti, and Klee. ✉ *Schlosstr. 1,* ☎ *030/3269–580,* WEB *www.smb.spk-berlin.de.* ⏲ *Tues.–Fri. 10–6, weekends 11–6.*

★ ⓭ **Schloss Charlottenburg.** Built at the end of the 17th century by King Frederick I for his wife, Queen Sophie Charlotte, this grand palace and its magnificent gardens were progressively enlarged for later royal residents and now include museums. ✉ *Luisenpl., U-7 subway line to Richard-Wagner-Pl. station; from station walk east along Otto-Suhr-Allee,* ☎ *030/3209–1275,* WEB *www.smb.spk-berlin.de.* ⏲ *Tues.–Fri. 9–5, weekends 10–5.*

❺ **Siegessäule** (Victory Column). The memorial, erected in 1873, commemorates four Prussian military campaigns. It stands at the center of the 630-acre **Tiergarten** (Animal Park), the former hunting grounds of the Great Elector. After climbing 285 steps to its 213-ft summit, you'll be rewarded with a fine view of Berlin. ✉ *Am Grossen Stern,* ☎ *030/391–2961.* ⏲ *Nov.–Mar., daily 9:30–5:30; Apr.–Oct., weekdays 9:30–7, weekends 9:30–6:30.*

❷ **The Story of Berlin.** An effective mixture of history museum, theme park, and movie theater covers 800 years of Berlin's history. An old nuclear

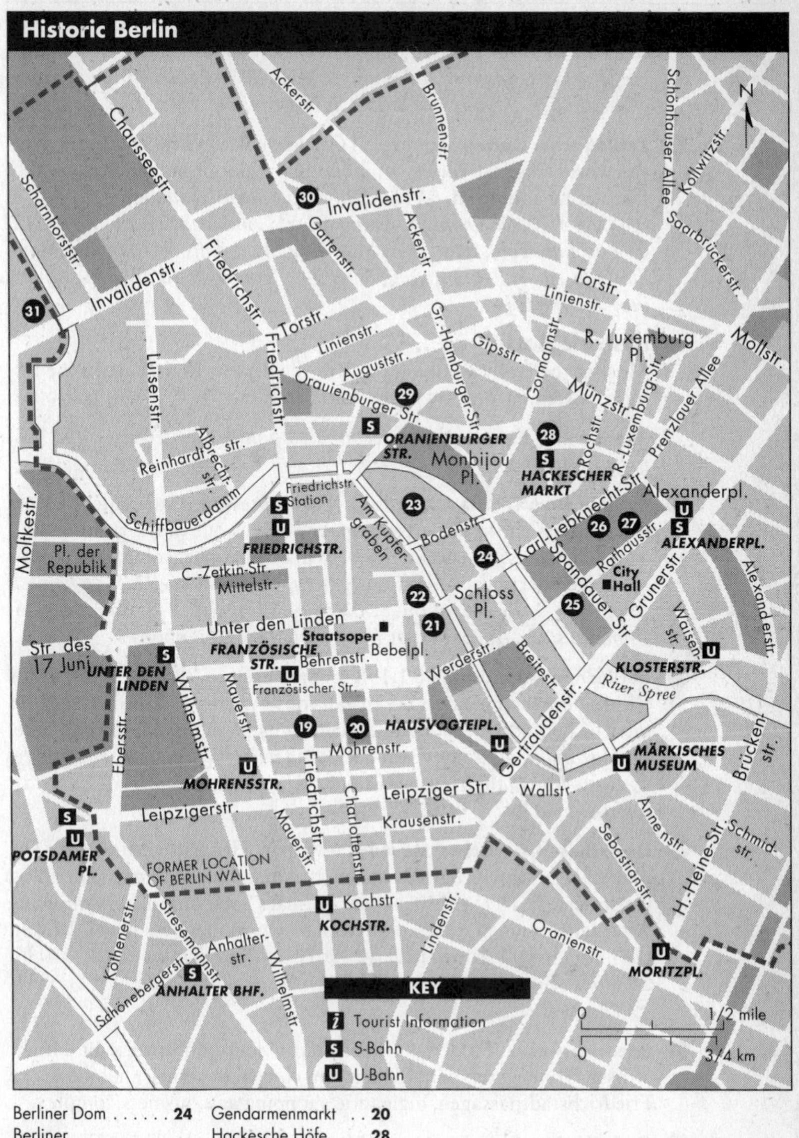

Berliner Dom 24
Berliner Fernsehturm 27
Deutsches Historisches Museum 22
Friedrichstrasse 19
Gedenkstätte Berliner Mauer 30
Gendarmenmarkt . . 20
Hackesche Höfe . . . 28
Hamburger Bahnhof 31
Kronprinzenpalais . . 21
Museumsinsel 23
Neue Synagoge . . . 29
Nikolaiviertel 25
St. Marienkirche . . . 26

shelter is part of the four-story structure. Many original objects are pieced together in an interactive design in the 26 rooms. ✉ *Ku'damm Karree, Kurfürstendamm 207–208,* ☎ *030/8872–0100,* WEB *www.story-of-berlin.de.* ⏲ *Daily 10–8 (last admission: 6).*

★ 4 **Zoologischer Garten** (Zoological Gardens). Berlin's enchanting zoo has the world's largest variety of individual types of fauna, along with a fascinating aquarium. ✉ *Hardenbergpl. 8 and Budapester Str. 34,* ☎ *030/254–010,* WEB *www.zoo-berlin.de.* 🎫 *Combined ticket DM 24/€12.* ⏲ *Zoo Jan.–Feb., daily 9–5; Mar.–late Mar., daily 9–5:30; late Mar.–late Sept., daily 9–6:30; Oct., daily 9–6; Nov.–Dec., daily, 9–5. Aquarium daily 9–6.*

Historic Berlin

Most of the really stunning parts of the prewar capital are in the historic eastern part of town, the Mitte district.

Numbers in the margin correspond to points of interest on the Historic Berlin map.

24 **Berliner Dom** (Berlin Cathedral). The impressive 19th-century cathedral with its enormous green copper dome is one of the great ecclesiastical buildings in Germany. More than 80 sarcophagi of Prussian royals are in the catacombs. ✉ *Am Lustgarten,* ☎ *030/2026–9119.* ⏲ *Church Mon.–Sat. 9–7, Sun. noon–8. Balcony Mon.–Sat. 9–7, Sun. noon–5. Imperial staircase and crypt Mon.–Sat. 9–8, Sun. noon–7.*

27 **Berliner Fernsehturm.** At 1,198 ft high, eastern Berlin's TV tower is 710 ft *taller* than western Berlin's. Its observation deck affords the best view of Berlin; the city's highest café, which revolves, is also up here. ✉ *Alexanderpl.,* ☎ *030/242–3333,* WEB *www.berlinerfernsehturm.de.* ⏲ *Nov.–Apr., daily 10 AM–midnight; May–Oct., daily 9 AM–1 AM (last admission at 11:30 PM).*

22 **Deutsches Historisches Museum** (German Historical Museum). The onetime Prussian Zeughaus (arsenal), a magnificent Baroque building constructed in 1695–1730, houses Germany's national history museum. After renovation and the addition of a new, modern wing by I. M. Pei, the museum will reopen in early 2002. ✉ *Unter den Linden 2.* ☎ *030/203–040,* WEB *www.dhm.de.* 🎫 *English-speaking guide DM 60/€31.* ⏲ *Thurs.–Tues. 10–6.*

★ 19 **Friedrichstrasse** (Frederick Street). Head south on historic Friedrichstrasse from Unter den Linden for chic new shops, including the **Friedrichstadtpassagen,** a gigantic shopping and business complex.

★ 30 **Gedenkstätte Berliner Mauer** (Memorial Site Berlin Wall). This is the only nearly original piece of the Berlin Wall left standing. The open-air museum shows a 230-ft-long piece of the whole Wall system, which consisted of two walls and a control path patrolled by border guards. ✉ *Bernauer Str. 111,* ☎ *030/4641–030.* ⏲ *Wed.–Sun. 10–5.*

20 **Gendarmenmarkt.** This historic square has the beautiful **Schauspielhaus**—built in 1818 and now one of the city's main concert halls—and twin cathedrals. The **Deutscher Dom** (German cathedral ☎ 030/2273–0431, ⏲ Sept.–May, Tues.–Sun. 10–6; June–Aug. Tues–Sun. 10–7) presents an official exhibit on German history. The **Französischer Dom** (French cathedral; ☎ 030/229–1760, ⏲ Tues.–Sat. noon–5, Sun. 11–5) houses a museum displaying the history of Huguenot immigrants in Berlin.

★ 28 **Hackesche Höfe** (Hackesche Warehouses). Built in 1905–07, the restored Hackesche Höfe are the finest example of Art Deco industrial architecture in Berlin. Its several bars and theaters are a center of nightlife. ✉ *Rosenthaler Str. 40–41,* WEB *www.hackeschehoefe.de.*

★ 31 **Hamburger Bahnhof** (Hamburg Train Station). A remodeled, early 19th-century train station and its huge and spectacular new wing—a stunning interplay of glass, steel, color, and sunlight—display an outstanding collection of contemporary art. German artists Joseph Beuys and Anselm Kiefer have works here, as do Andy Warhol, Cy Twombly, Robert Rauschenberg, and Robert Morris. ✉ *Invalidenstr. 50–51,* ☎ *030/3978–340,* WEB *www.smb.spk-berlin.de.* ⏲ *Tues., Wed., Fr. 10–6, Thurs. 10–10, weekends 11–6.*

21 **Kronprinzenpalais** (Crown Prince's Palace). This magnificent Baroque-style building was constructed in 1732 for Crown Prince Friedrich (who later became Frederick the Great). ✉ *Unter den Linden 3.*

★ 23 **Museumsinsel** (Museum Island). This unique complex contains four world-class museums. The **Nationalgalerie** (National Gallery; ✉ Bodestr.) has 19th- and 20th-century paintings and sculptures, mostly by German artists. The **Altes Museum** (Old Museum; entrance on ✉ Lustgarten) collections include Roman and Greek sculptures and other antique exhibits as well as German postwar art and works by the Old Masters. The **Pergamonmuseum** (Pergamon Museum; ✉ Am Kupfergraben), one of Europe's greatest museums, takes its name from its principal exhibit, the Pergamon Altar, a monumental Greek sculpture dating from 180 BC that occupies an entire city block. The museums are free the first Sunday of the month. Due to the continuing reconstruction of the Museumsinsel, the Bodemuseum will be closed in 2002. ✉ *Museumsinsel (right from Unter den Linden along Spree Canal via Am Zeughaus and Am Kupfergraben),* ☎ *030/2090–5577 or 030/2090–5560 all museums,* WEB *www.smb.spk-berlin.de.* ⏲ *All museums Tues.–Sun. 10–6.*

29 **Neue Synagoge** (New Synagogue). Completed in 1866, in Middle Eastern style, this was one of Germany's most beautiful synagogues until it was seriously damaged on Kristallnacht, November 9, 1938, when synagogues and Jewish stores across Germany were vandalized, looted, and burned. Today the outside is perfectly restored, and the interior is connected to the **Centrum Judaicum** (Jewish Center), an institution of culture and learning. ✉ *Oranienburger Str. 28/30,* ☎ *030/2840–1316,* WEB *www.cjudaiucum.de.* ⏲ *Sun.–Thurs. 10–6, Fri. 10–2.*

25 **Nikolaiviertel** (Nikolai Quarter). Berlin's oldest historic quarter is filled with shops, cafés, and restaurants. Nikolaikirchplatz has Berlin's oldest building, the **Nikolaikirche** (St. Nicholas's Church), dating from 1230. ✉ *Nikolaikirchpl.,* ☎ *030/240–020.* ⏲ *Tues.–Sun. 10–6.*

26 **St. Marienkirche** (Church of St. Mary). This medieval church, one of the finest in Berlin, is worth a visit for its late-Gothic fresco *Der Totentanz* (*Dance of Death*). The cross on top of the church tower was an everlasting annoyance to communist rulers, as its golden metal was always mirrored in the windows of the Fernsehturm TV tower, the pride of socialist construction genius. ✉ *Karl-Liebknecht-Str. 8,* ☎ *030/242–4467.* ⏲ *Mon.–Thurs. 10–4, weekends noon–4. Free tours Mon.–Tues. at 1, Sun. at noon.*

Dining

Typical Berliner meals include *Eisbein mit Sauerkraut* (knuckle of pork with sauerkraut), *Spanferkel* (suckling pig), *Berliner Schüsselsülze* (potted meat in aspic), and *Currywurst* (chubby and very spicy frankfurters sold at wurst stands).

$$$$ ★ ✕ **First Floor.** Chef Matthias Buchholz's traditional German fare earned him a Michelin star. The menu changes according to the season and

his moods, but most of the dishes are new interpretations of German dishes such as *Müritzlammrücken in Olivenkruste mit Bohnenmelange* (Müritz lamb back in olive crust, served with green beans). ✉ *Hotel Palace, Budapester Str. 42,* ☎ *030/2502–1020. Reservations essential. AE, DC, MC, V. No lunch Sat.*

$$$$ ★ ✕ **VAU.** VAU's excellent German fish and game dishes offer daring combinations such as *Ente mit gezupftem Rotkohl, Quitten und Maronen* (duck with selected red cabbage, quinces, and sweet chestnuts). The VAU's cool interior is all style and modern art. ✉ *Jägerstr. 54/55,* ☎ *030/202–9730. Reservations essential. AE, DC, MC, V. Closed Sun.*

$$$ ★ ✕ **Borchardt.** At this fashionable meeting place, columns, red plush benches, and an Art Nouveau mosaic create the impression of a 1920s salon. Entrées lean to French preparations. ✉ *Französische Str. 47,* ☎ *030/2038–7110. Reservations essential. AE, V.*

$$–$$$ ✕ **Paris Bar.** This Charlottenburg restaurant attracts a polyglot clientele of film stars, artists, and executives. The cuisine is creative but medium-quality French. ✉ *Kantstr. 152,* ☎ *030/313–8052. AE.*

$–$$ ✕ **Hackescher Hof.** The restaurant is without question one of the most "in" places in town and a great place to experience the upswing in the old East. The food is a mixture of contemporary international cuisine and beefy German cooking—there is also a special dinner menu with more refined dishes. ✉ *Rosenthaler Str. 40/41,* ☎ *030/2835–293. Reservations essential. AE, MC, V.*

$–$$ ✕ **Reinhard's.** Berliners of all stripes meet here in the Nikolai Quarter to enjoy the carefully prepared entrées and to sample spirits from the amply stocked bar. *Adlon* (honey-glazed breast of duck) is one of the house specialties. Reinhard's has a smaller, more elegant restaurant on the Ku'damm. ✉ *Poststr. 28,* ☎ *030/242–5295;* ✉ *Kurfürstendamm 190,* ☎ *030/881–1621. Reservations essential on weekends. AE, DC, MC, V.*

$–$$$ ★ ✕ **Schwarzenraben.** At its white-clothed tables, the rich and beautiful of the new metropolis gather to enjoy their success. The cooking lets you discover new Italian recipes such as Milanese veal hocks. ✉ *Neue Schönhauser Str. 13,* ☎ *030/2839–1698. Reservations essential. AE, DC, MC, V.*

$ ★ ✕ **Café Oren.** This popular Jewish vegetarian eatery is next to the Neue Synagoge. The restaurant buzzes with loud chatter all evening, and the atmosphere and service are friendly. The small backyard is a wonderful spot to enjoy a cool summer evening or a warm autumn afternoon. ✉ *Oranienburger Str. 28,* ☎ *030/282–8228. AE, V.*

$ ★ ✕ **Grossbeerenkeller.** The cellar restaurant, with its massive, dark-oak furniture and decorative antlers, is one of the most original dining spots in town. Owner and bartender Ingeborg Zinn-Baier presents such dishes as *Sülze vom Schweinekopf mit Bratkartoffeln und Remoulade* (diced pork with home fries and herb sauce). ✉ *Grossbeerenstr. 90,* ☎ *030/2513–064. No credit cards. Closed Sun.*

$ ✕ **Zur Letzten Instanz.** Established in 1621, Berlin's oldest restaurant combines the charming atmosphere of Old World Berlin with a limited (but tasty) choice of dishes. The emphasis here is on beer, both in the recipes and in the mug. Service can be erratic, though engagingly friendly. ✉ *Waisenstr. 14–16,* ☎ *030/242–5528. AE, DC, MC, V.*

Lodging

Make reservations well in advance. Prices for rooms can fluctuate wildly based on season and day of the week.

$$$$ **Bristol Hotel Kempinski.** This grand hotel in the heart of the city has the best of Berlin's shopping on its doorstep. All rooms and suites are luxuriously decorated and equipped, with marble bathrooms, cable TV,

and English-style furnishings. Kids under 12 stay free if they share their parents' room. ✉ *Kurfürstendamm 27, D-10719,* ☎ *030/884–340,* FAX *030/883–6075,* WEB *www.kempinski-bristol.de. 301 rooms, 52 suites. 2 restaurants, bar, pool. AE, DC, MC, V.*

$$$$ ★ **Four Seasons Hotel Berlin.** Smooth and up-to-date services such as portable phones complement turn-of-the-20th-century luxury here. Thick red carpets, heavy crystal chandeliers, and a romantic restaurant with an open fireplace make for a sophisticated and serene atmosphere. ✉ *Charlottenstr. 49, D-10117,* ☎ *030/20338,* FAX *030/2033–6119,* WEB *www.fourseasons.com. 162 rooms, 42 suites. Restaurant. AE, DC, MC, V.*

$$$$ ★ **Grand Hyatt Berlin.** Within reborn Potsdamer Platz, the Grand Hyatt provides large guest rooms with dark cherry-wood furniture, marble bathrooms, and Bauhaus artist photographs. A special attraction of the first-class hotel is the top-floor gym and swimming pool, which has a great view of Berlin's skyline. ✉ *Marlene-Dietrich-Pl. 2, D-10785,* ☎ *030/2553–1234,* FAX *030/2553–1235,* WEB *berlin.hyatt.com. 327 rooms, 16 suites. Restaurant, bar, pool. AE, DC, MC, V.*

$$$$ ★ **Hotel Adlon Berlin.** This elegant hotel next to Pariser Platz has managed to live up to its almost mythical predecessor, the old Hotel Adlon, which, until its destruction during World War II, was considered Europe's premier resort. The new Adlon has impeccable service. The city's priciest guest rooms are furnished in '20s style with dark-wood trimmings and bathrooms in black granite and bright marble. ✉ *Unter den Linden 77, D-10117,* ☎ *030/22610,* FAX *030/2261–2222,* WEB *www.hotel-adlon.de. 335 rooms, 51 suites. 3 restaurants, pool. AE, DC, MC, V.*

$$$$ ★ **Hotel Palace.** This is probably the most individualized luxury hotel in town and the only one in the heart of western downtown. Each room has its own design, mostly in dark blues or reds and fitting woods. The spacious business and corner suites are a good deal. ✉ *Europa-Center, Budapester Str. 26, D-10789,* ☎ *030/25020,* FAX *030/2502–1161,* WEB *www.palace.de. 239 rooms, 43 suites. 3 restaurants, 2 bars. AE, DC, MC, V.*

$$$–$$$$ **Heinrich-Heine City-Suites.** This new apartment hotel close to the historic Nikolai Quarter offers junior suites, which are among the best deals in town. All rooms have a full kitchen as well a mini-office. The hotel's extra services include a newspaper and fresh German rolls every morning. ✉ *Heinrich-Heine-Pl. 11, D-10179,* ☎ *030/278–040,* FAX *030/2780–4780. 38 apartments. AE, DC, MC, V.*

$$–$$$ **Hotel Astoria.** This is one of the most traditional, privately owned and run hotels in Berlin and it shows: rooms, service, and the restaurant all have a personal touch. Rooms are spacious, though the 1980s furniture is outdated. The location is good for exploring Kurfürstendamm, yet it's on a quiet street. ✉ *Fasanenstr. 2, D-10623,* ☎ *030/3124–067,* FAX *030/3125–027,* WEB *www.hotelastoria.de. 31 rooms, 1 suite. AE, DC, MC, V.*

$–$$ **Charlottenburger Hof.** A creative flair and a convenient location across from the Charlottenburg S-bahn station make this low-key hotel a great value for no-fuss travelers. The variety of rooms can suit friends, couples, or families. Kurfürstendamm is a 10-minute walk, taxis are easy to catch at the S-bahn station, and the bus to and from Tegel airport stops a block away. ✉ *Stuttgarter Pl. 14, D-10627,* ☎ *030/32–90–70,* FAX *030/323–3723,* WEB *www.charlottenburger-hof.de. 46 rooms with bath or shower. AE, MC, V.*

$$ ★ **Hotel-Pension Dittberner.** The Dittberner, close to Olivaer Platz and Kurfürstendamm, is a family-run hotel in a turn-of-the-20th-century house. Some of the furniture is worn, but the warm atmosphere and

the breakfast buffet more than make up for it. ✉ *Wielandstr. 26, D-10707,* ☏ *030/8846–950,* FAX *030/8854–046. 22 rooms. No credit cards.*

$$–$$$ ★ **Riehmers Hofgarten.** Surrounded by the bars and restaurants of the colorful Kreuzberg district, this hotel has fast connections to the center of town. The 19th-century building's high-ceiling rooms are stylishly furnished. ✉ *Yorckstr. 83, D-10965,* ☏ *030/7809–8800,* FAX *030/7809–8808,* WEB *www.hotel-riehmers-hofgarten.de. 20 rooms. Restaurant. AE, MC, V.*

$–$$ **Hotel am Scheunenviertel.** This simply furnished but well-kept small hotel offers personal service, a wonderful breakfast buffet, and three restaurants (Mexican, Russian, and German) next door. If you want to indulge in Berlin's hip nightlife, you'll be near the cultural and entertainment hot spots. ✉ *Oranienburger Str. 38, D-10117,* ☏ *030/282–2125,* FAX *030/282–1115. 18 rooms with shower. AE, DC, MC, V.*

Nightlife and the Arts

The Arts

The quality of opera and classical concerts in Berlin is high. One of the centrally located ticket agencies in the western downtown area is **Hekticket office** (✉ Zoo Palast movie theater, Karl–Liebknecht–Str. 12, ☏ 030/2431–2431). Details about what's going on in Berlin can be found in *Berlin–the magazine*, an English-language monthly magazine published by Berlin's Tourism Board; *Berlin Programm*, a monthly guide to arts, museums, and theaters; and the magazines *prinz, tip,* and *zitty,* which appear every two weeks and provide full arts listings.

CONCERTS

The Berlin Philharmonic, one of the world's leading orchestras, performs in the **Philharmonie** (✉ Matthäikirchstr. 1, ☏ 030/2548–8132 or 030/2548–8301). The **Konzerthaus Berlin** (✉ Gendarmenmarkt, ☏ 030/2030–92101) is an historic concert venue.

OPERA AND BALLET

The **Deutsche Oper** (German Opera House; ✉ Bismarckstr. 35, ☏ 030/343–8401), by the U-bahn stop of the same name, is home to both opera and ballet. The grand **Staatsoper Unter den Linden** (German State Opera; ✉ Unter den Linden 7, ☏ 030/2035–4555) is Berlin's main opera house. **Komische Oper** (Comic Opera House; ✉ Behrenstr. 55–57, ☏ 030/4799–7400) presents opera and dance performances.

VARIETY SHOWS

Variety shows thrive in Berlin. Intimate and intellectually entertaining is the **Bar jeder Vernuft** (✉ Schaperstr. 24, ☏ 030/8831–582). Hilarious shows that even non-German speakers can appreciate are at the **Chamäleon Varieté** (✉ Rosenthaler Str. 40/41, ☏ 030/2827–118). The world's largest circus is at the **Friedrichstadtpalast** (✉ Friedrichstr. 107, ☏ 030/2326–2326). The small but classy **Wintergarten** (✉ Potsdamer Str. 96, ☏ 030/2308–8230 or 030/2500–8888) pays romantic homage to the '20s. The **Grüner Salon** (✉ Freie Volksbühne, Rosa-Luxemburg-Pl., ☏ 030/2859–8936) is one of Berlin's hip venues for live music, cabaret, and dancing. The programs change almost daily.

Nightlife

With more than 6,000 *Kneipen* (pubs), bars, and clubs, nightlife in Berlin is no halfhearted affair. The centers of this nocturnal scene are around Savignyplatz in Charlottenburg; Nollendorfplatz and its side streets in Schöneberg; Oranienstrasse and Wienerstrasse in Kreuzberg; Kollwitzplatz in the Prenzlauer Berg district; and Oranienburger Strasse, Rosenthaler Platz, and Hackesche Höfe in Mitte.

BARS AND DANCE CLUBS

A young gay and lesbian crowd frequents the casual, hip **Anderes Ufer** (✉ Hauptstr. 157, ☎ 030/784–1578). It has a mellow atmosphere and 1950s and '60s music. A Berlin classic, **Bar am Lützowplatz** (✉ Am Lützowpl. 7, ☎ 030/262–6807) has the longest bar counter in town. Women sip American cocktails while flirting with the handsome bartenders. High-tech **Blu** (✉ Marlene-Dietrich-Pl. 4, ☎ 030/8261–882), high above the Potsdamer Platz, offers soul and funk music on three floors. The crowd is mixed—teenagers from East Berlin dance next to young managers. The view of the Berlin skyline is magnificent. A clubby gay and hetero crowd mingles within the red-velvet walls of rowdy **Kumpelnest 3000** (✉ Lützowstr. 23, ☎ 030/261–6918). The historic **Leydicke** (✉ Mansteinstr. 4, ☎ 030/216–2973) is a must for out-of-towners. The proprietors operate their own distillery and have a superb selection of sweet wines and liqueurs.

JAZZ CLUBS

Call the tourist office for details on the annual fall international Jazz Fest. Jazz groups from around the world appear throughout the year at the **A-Trane** (✉ Pestalozzistr. 105, ☎ 030/3132–550). The older and more traditional **Quasimodo** (✉ Kantstr. 12a, ☎ 030/312–8086) mostly hosts well-known Jazzrock or, at times, country bands.

Shopping

The liveliest and most famous shopping area in western Berlin is the Kurfürstendamm and its side streets, especially between Breitscheidplatz and Olivaer Platz. Running east from Breitscheidplatz is Tauentzienstrasse. The Potsdamer Platz Arkaden is the shopping mall on Potsdamer Platz. Eastern Berlin's best shops are along Friedrichstrasse.

Antiques

On weekends from 10 to 5, the colorful and lively antiques and handicrafts fair on **Strasse des 17. Juni** swings into action. Not far from **Wittenbergplatz,** several streets are strong on antiques, including Eisenacher Strasse, Fuggerstrasse, Keithstrasse, Kalckreuthstrasse, Motzstrasse, and Nollendorfstrasse.

Department Stores

Galeries Lafayette (✉ Französische Str. 23, ☎ 030/209–480), off Friedrichstrasse, carries almost exclusively French products, including designer clothes, perfume, and produce. The small but most luxurious **Department Store Quartier 206** (✉ Friedrichstr. 71, ☎ 030/2094–6240) offers primarily French designer clothes, perfumes, and home accessories. One of Berlin's classiest department stores is the **Kaufhaus des Westens** (KaDeWe; ✉ Tauentzienstr. 21, ☎ 030/21210); the food department occupies the whole sixth floor. The main department store in eastern Berlin, **Galleria Kaufhof** (✉ Alexanderpl. 9, ☎ 030/247–430), is at the north end of Alexanderplatz. **Wertheim** (✉ Kurfürstendamm 181, ☎ 030/883–8152) has a large selection of fine wares. **Stilwerk** (✉ Kantstr. 17, ☎ 030/315–150) is an upscale mall with 48 shops and restaurants all catering to design and style.

Gift Ideas

Fine porcelain is still produced at the **Königliche Porzellan Manufaktur** (Royal Prussian Porcelain Factory, or KPM). This delicate, handmade, hand-painted china is sold at KPM's store (✉ Kurfürstendamm 27, ☎ 030/8867–210) and the factory salesroom (✉ Wegelystr. 1, ☎ 030/390–090), where seconds are sold at reduced prices. The **Gipsformerei der Staatlichen Museen Preussicher Kulturbesitz** (Plaster Sculpture of the Prussian Cultural Foundation State Museums; ✉ Sophie-Charlotten-Str. 17, ☎ 030/3267–690) sells plaster casts of the Egyptian queen Nefertiti and other museum treasures.

Berlin Essentials

AIRPORTS AND TRANSFERS

Tegel airport is 7 km (4 mi) from downtown. Tempelhof, even closer to downtown, is used for commuter plane traffic. Schönefeld airport is about 24 km (15 mi) from downtown; it is used primarily for charter flights to Asia and southern and eastern Europe. You can reach all three airports by calling the central service phone number.

➤ AIRPORT INFORMATION: **Central Service** (☎ 0180/500–0186, WEB www.berlin-airport.de).

TRANSFERS

Buses 109 and X09 run every 10 minutes between Tegel airport and downtown. The journey takes 30 minutes; the fare is DM 4/€2 and covers all public transportation throughout Berlin. A taxi costs about DM 25/€13. If you're driving from the airport, follow signs for the STADTAUTOBAHN (City Freeway). Tempelhof is right on the U-6 subway line, in the center of the city. A shuttle bus leaves Schönefeld airport every 10–15 minutes for the nearby S-bahn station. S-bahn trains leave every 10 minutes for the Friedrichstrasse and Zoologischer Garten stations. The trip takes about 30 minutes; the fare is DM 4/€2. Taxi fare to your hotel is about DM 40/€20.50–DM 55/€28, and the trip takes about 40 minutes.

BUS TRAVEL TO AND FROM BERLIN

Berlin is linked by bus to 170 European cities. You can reserve seats at the central bus terminal or through DER or other travel agencies.

➤ BUS INFORMATION: **Central bus terminal** (✉ junction Masurenallee 4–6 and Messedamm, ☎ 030/301–8028).

CAR RENTAL

➤ MAJOR AGENCIES: **Avis** (✉ Schönefeld Airport, ☎ 030/6091–5710; ✉ Tegel Airport, ☎ 030/4101–3148; ✉ Budapester Str. 43, at Europa Center, ☎ 030/230–9370; ✉ Holzmarktstr. 15–18, ☎ 030/240–7940, WEB www.avis.de). **Europcar** (✉ Schönefeld Airport, ☎ 030/634–9160; ✉ Tegel Airport, ☎ 030/417–8520; ✉ Kurfürstenstr. 101–104, ☎ 030/235–0640, WEB www.europcar). **Hertz** (✉ Schönefeld Airport, ☎ 030/6091–5730; ✉ Tegel Airport, ☎ 030/4170–4674; ✉ Tempelhof Airport, ☎ 030/6981–9892; ✉ Budapester Str. 39, ☎ 030/261–1053, WEB www.hertz.de). **Sixt** (✉ Schönefeld Airport, ☎ 030/6091–5690; ✉ Tegel Airport, ☎ 030/4101–2886; ✉ Tempelhof Airport, ☎ 030/6951–3816; ✉ Nürnberger Str. 65, ☎ 030/212–9880; ✉ Leipziger Str. 104, ☎ 030/243–9050, WEB www.sixt.de).

CAR TRAVEL

The eight roads linking the western part of Germany with Berlin have been incorporated into the country-wide autobahn network, but be prepared for traffic jams, particularly on weekends. Follow signs for BERLIN–ZENTRUM to reach downtown.

EMBASSIES

See Germany A to Z.

EMERGENCIES

Pharmacies in Berlin offer late-night service on a rotating basis. Every pharmacy displays a notice indicating the location of the nearest shop with evening hours.

➤ DOCTORS AND DENTISTS: **Dentist emergency assistance** (☎ 030/8900–4333).

➤ EMERGENCY SERVICES: **Ambulance** (☎ 030/112). **Emergency poison assistance** (☎ 030/19240). **Police** (☎ 030/110).

➤ HOSPITALS: **Charite** (✉ Schumannstr. 20–21, Mitte, ☎ 030/28020).

➤ HOT LINES: **International Emergency Hotline** (☎ 030/3100–3222 or 030/3100–3243). **American Hotline** (☎ 0177/814–1510).

➤ 24-HOUR PHARMACIES: **Apotheken-Notdienst** (Emergency pharmaceutical assistance; ☎ 01189).

ENGLISH-LANGUAGE MEDIA

➤ BOOKSTORES: **Buchhandlung Kiepert** (✉ Hardenbergstr. 4–5, ☎ 030/311–880). **Dussmann Kulturkaufhaus** (✉ Friedrichstr. 90, ☎ 030/20250). **Hugendubel** (✉ Tauentzienstr. 13, ☎ 030/214060).

TAXIS

The base rate is DM 4/€2, after which prices vary according to a complex tariff system. If your ride will be short, ask in advance for the special Kurzstreckentarif, which is DM 5/€2.60 for rides of less than 2 km (1 mi) or five minutes. Figure on paying around DM 15 for a ride the length of Kurfürstendamm. Hail cabs in the street or at taxi stands, or order one by calling one of the numbers below. U-bahn employees will call a taxi for passengers after 8 PM.

➤ TAXI COMPANIES: ☎ 030/210–101, 030/210–202, 030/443–322, or 030/261–026.

TOURS

BUS TOURS

Bus tours of Berlin are more or less identical, covering Berlin's major sights, as well as day trips to Potsdam. The Berlin tour costs DM 25/€12.80 to DM 47/€24; Potsdam and Sanssouci Palace tour costs DM 65/€33.

➤ FEES AND SCHEDULES: **Berliner Bären Stadtrundfahrt** (BBS; ✉ Seeburgerstr. 19b, ☎ 030/3519–5270). **Berolina Stadtrundfahrten** (✉ Kurfürstendamm 220, corner Meinekestr. 3, ☎ 030/8856–8030, WEB www.berolina-berlin.com). **Bus Verkehr Berlin** (BVB; ✉ Kurfürstendamm 229, ☎ 030/885–9880, WEB www.bvb.net). **Severin & Kühn** (✉ Kurfürstendamm 216, ☎ 030/8804–190).

BOAT TOURS

Tours of downtown Berlin's canals take in sights such as the Charlottenburg Palace and Museum Island. Tours depart from several bridges and piers, such as Hansabrücke in Tiergarten, Kottbusser Bridge in Kreuzberg, Potsdamer Brücke, and Haus der Kulturen der Welt in Tiergarten. Tickets start at DM 8/€4 (one way). For details contact the tourist office.

WALKING TOURS

A walking tour is one of the best ways to familiarize yourself with Berlin's history and sights, and several companies offer native English speakers and thematic tours from which to choose.

➤ FEES AND SCHEDULES: **Berlin Walks** (☎ 030/301–9194, WEB www.berlinwalks.com). **Brewer's Best of Berlin** (☎ 030/2839–1433). **Insider Tours** (☎ 030/692–3149, WEB www.insidertour.de).

TRAIN TRAVEL

Most trains to and from Berlin pass through Bahnhof Zoo. Trains to the north and east usually stop at Lichtenburg station.

TRANSPORTATION AROUND BERLIN

The city has an excellent public transportation system: a combination of U-bahn and S-bahn lines, buses, and streetcars. For DM 4.20/€2.10, you can buy a ticket that covers travel on the entire downtown system (fare zones A and B) for two hours. Buy a *Kurzstreckentarif* for a short trip; it allows you to ride six bus stops or three U-bahn or S-bahn stops for DM 2.50/€1.30. The Day Card, for DM 12/€6.10, is valid until 3 AM of the day of validation.

The BerlinWelcomeCard is the best deal. At DM 32/€16.50 for three days, it entitles one adult and up to three children to unlimited travel as well as free or reduced-fare sightseeing trips and admission to museums, theaters, and other events. If you're caught without a validated ticket, the fine is DM 60/€31. Tickets are available from vending machines at U-bahn and S-bahn stations or from bus drivers. For information call the Berliner Verkehrsbetriebe or go to the information office on Hardenbergplatz, directly in front of the Bahnhof Zoo train station.
➤ CONTACTS: **Berliner Verkehrsbetriebe** (BVG; Berlin Public Transportation; ☎ 030/2561 or 030/19449, WEB www.bvg.de).

TRAVEL AGENCIES

➤ LOCAL AGENTS: **Euroaide** (✉ Hardenbergpl., inside the Zoologischer Garten train station, ☎ 030/2974–9241). **Reiseland American Express Reisebüro** (✉ Wittenbergpl., Bayreuther Str. 37, ☎ 030/2147–6293; ✉ Friedrichstr. 172, ☎ 030/2015–5721).

VISITOR INFORMATION

➤ TOURIST INFORMATION: **Berlin Tourismus Marketing GmbH** (main tourist office: ✉ Europa Center; ✉ Brandenburger Tor; ✉ Tegel Airport; by mail: ✉ Berlin Tourismus Marketing, ✉ Am Karlsbad 11, D-10785 Berlin). **Berlin-Hotline** (☎ 030/250–025 or 0190/754–040, [€1.20 per minute], FAX 030/2500–2424. WEB www.berlin.de).

SAXONY AND THURINGIA

Saxony and Thuringia—the states' names alone conjure up images of kingdoms and forest legends, of cultural riches and booming industrial enterprises. Since German reunification, the world's admiration has returned to Saxony's museum-rich capital, Dresden; Leipzig's musical and literary traditions; and Meissen's porcelain works. Largely rural Thuringia was always a popular East German holiday destination. The German Enlightenment movement was spearheaded in Weimar, as was the short-lived German democracy, the Weimar Republic.

Dresden

Saxony's capital city sits majestically on the banks of the Elbe River. Although it suffered appalling damage during World War II, it has been lovingly rebuilt. Italianate influences abound, most pronounced in the glorious rococo and Baroque buildings.

The magnificent **Semperoper** (Semper Opera House) was built in 1838–41 by architect Gottfried Semper. Wagner's *The Flying Dutchman* and *Tannhäuser* (conducted by the composer) and nine operas by Richard Strauss premiered here. Tickets to performances are often hard to get; try booking through your travel agent before you go or ask at your hotel. As a last resort, line up at the evening box office, the Abendkasse, left of the main entrance, about half an hour before the performance. ✉ *Theaterpl.,* ☎ *0351/491–1496 tours; 0351/49110 or 0351/491–11730 tickets,* WEB *www.semperoper.de.* ⏲ *Tour hrs vary but run daily 10–3, most often 2–3.*

Saxony and Thuringia

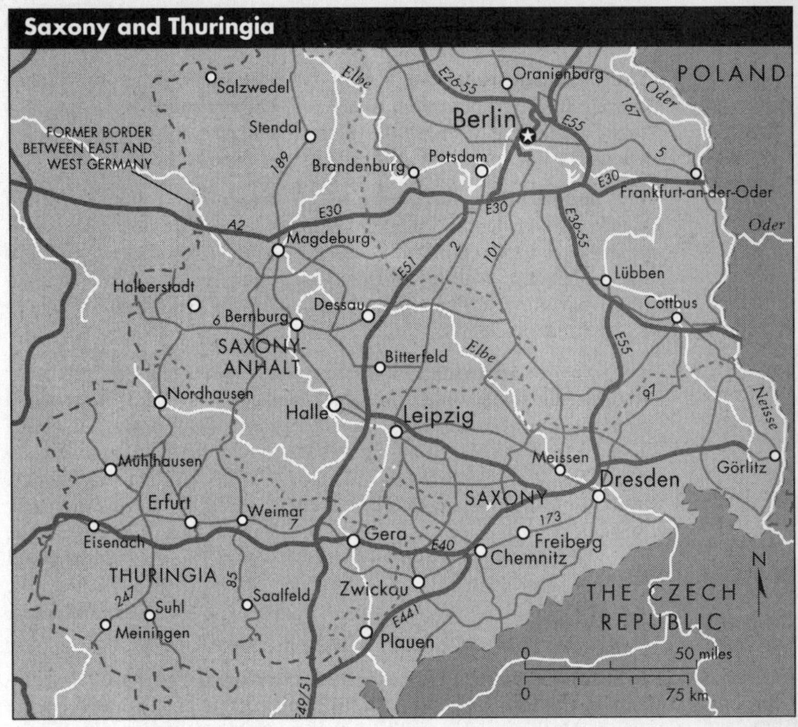

★ The largely 18th-century **Zwinger** palace complex is among the greatest examples of Baroque architecture in Europe. Completely enclosing a central courtyard of lawns and pools, six linked pavilions are adorned with a riot of sandstone garlands, nymphs, and other ornamentation and sculpture, created under the direction of Matthäus Daniel Pöppelmann. The complex is home to the world-renowned **Sempergalerie** (Semper Gallery), whose Gemäldegalerie Alte Meister (Gallery of Old Masters) contains works by Dürer, Holbein the Younger, Rembrandt, Vermeer, Raphael, Correggio, and Canaletto. The **Porzellansammlung** (Porcelain Museum) is famous for its Meissen pieces, but will be closed until mid-2002. ✉ *Theaterpl., follow Sophienstr.,* ☎ *0351/491–4619,* WEB *www.staatl-kunstsammlungen-dresden.de.* ⏲ *Sempergalerie Tues.–Sun. 10–6.*

Despite its name, the **Neumarkt** (New Market) serves as the historic heart of old Dresden. The mighty Baroque **Frauenkirche** (Church of Our Lady), once Germany's greatest Protestant church, is being slowly reconstructed on the square. Off the Neumarkt, on Augustusstrasse, is the 16th-century **Johanneum**, once the royal stables. It's outer wall features a prime example of Meissen porcelain art: a 335-ft-long mural of Saxon rulers (from 1123 to 1904) in procession. ✉ *Bordered by Schlosstr., Landhausstr., Tzschirnerpl., and Brühlsche G.*

Dresden's leading art museum, the **Albertinum,** is housed in a massive, imperial-style building. The **Gemäldegalerie Neue Meister** (New Masters Gallery) displays outstanding 19th- and 20th-century European works. The **Grünes Gewölbe** (Green Vault; entered from Georg-Treu-Platz), named after the collection's original home in the palace of August the Strong, showcases unique objets d'art fashioned from gold, silver, ivory, amber, and other precious and semiprecious materials. Next door, the **Skulpturensammlung** (Sculpture Collection) includes ancient Egyptian and classical objects and Italian Mannerist works.

✉ *Am Neumarkt at Brühlsche Terrasse,* ☎ *0351/4914–619,* WEB *www. staatl-kunstsammlungen-dresden.de.* ⏲ *Fri.–Wed. 10–6.*

The **Katholische Hofkirche** (Catholic Court Church) is Saxony's largest church. In the crypt are the tombs of 49 Saxon rulers and a precious vessel containing the heart of August the Strong. ✉ *Schlosspl.,* ☎ *No phone.* ⏲ *Weekdays 9–5, Sat. 10–5, Sun. noon–4:30.*

The **Sächsische Porzellanmanufaktur Dresden** (Saxonian Porcelain Company Dresden), 9 km (5½ mi) southwest of Dresden in Freital, is where Dresden's renowned porcelain is made. Exquisite examples of the porcelain are sold in all Dresden department stores, and the Freital showroom sells items as well. ✉ *Bachstr. 16, Freital,* ☎ *0351/647–1310.* ⏲ *Mon.–Sat. 9–5.*

The romantic **Schloss Pillnitz** (Pillnitz palace) was a summer retreat for King August the Strong. The palace, built in 1720–22, is surrounded by a landscaped garden and two smaller palaces, the Wasserpalais (closed Tuesday) and the Bergpalais (closed Monday). Both buildings were designed in Germany's late Baroque faux–Chinese pagoda style. Today, they house the **Kunstgewerbemuseum**, which showcases not only Baroque furniture and craft, but also modern design. To get here, take Tram 10 from the central train central towards Striesen, exit there and continue with Tram 12 (to Schillerplatz), change there again and take bus 83 to Pillnitz. ✉ *Kleinzschachwitz,* ☎ *0351/2613–201,* WEB *www. staatl-kunstsammlungen.de.* ⏲ *May–Nov., daily 10–6.*

$–$$ ✕ **Ristorante Bellotto im Italienischen Dörfchen.** This Baroque structure on the Elbe was built to house Italian craftsmen working on the nearby Hofkirche. Now it's a restaurant and café, with a shady beer garden and fine river views. The Italian influence is still in evidence—in the decor and on the menu, where pasta dishes are heavily favored. ✉ *Theaterpl. 3,* ☎ *0351/498–1681. AE, DC, MC, V.*

$ ★ ✕ **Sophienkeller.** One of the jolliest and most original restaurants in eastern Germany, the Sophienkeller offers truly Saxon dishes and strong beer, making it one of the city's most popular restaurants. ✉ *Taschenberg 3,* ☎ *0351/497–260. AE, MC, V.*

$$$$ ★ 🏨 **Kempinski Hotel Taschenbergpalais Dresden.** The rebuilt historic Taschenberg Palace—the work of architect Matthäus Daniel Pöppelmann—provides expensive pampering in the romantic heart of old Dresden. ✉ *Am Taschenberg 3, D-01067,* ☎ *0351/49120,* FAX *0351/491–2812,* WEB *www.kempinski-dresden.de/. 188 rooms, 25 suites. 2 restaurants, pool. AE, DC, MC, V.*

$$$–$$$$ ★ 🏨 **artotel Dresden.** Inside the artotel are more than 600 works by Dresden-born painter and sculptor A. R. Penck, as well as designs by Italian interior architect Denis Santachiara. The hotel's heavily styled rooms and service have genuine first-class appeal at considerably lower prices. ✉ *Astra-Allee 33, D-01067,* ☎ *0351/49220,* FAX *0351/492–2777,* WEB *www.artotel.de. 158 rooms, 16 suites. 3 restaurants, pool. AE, DC, MC, V.*

$$$ 🏨 **Westin Bellevue Dresden.** Across the river from the Zwinger palace, the opera, and the main museums, this modern hotel cleverly incorporates an old restored mansion. Guest rooms have elegant, Old World charm. The service is outstanding. ✉ *Grosse-Meissner-Str. 15, D-01097,* ☎ *0351/8050,* FAX *0351/8051–609,* WEB *www.westin-bellevue.com. 323 rooms, 16 suites. 3 restaurants, pool. AE, DC, MC, V.*

$$–$$$ 🏨 **Hotel am Terrassenufer.** Dresden's court painter Canaletto Belotto (1720–80) painted the very vistas you can see from this 12-story hotel on the Elbe River terrace. Rooms have bright, cherry-wood-veneer furniture and fresh pastel color schemes; all have views of the river and the Old Town. ✉ *Am Terrassenufer 12, D-01067,* ☎ *0351/440–9500,*

FAX 0351/440–9600, WEB *www.hotel-terrassenufer.de. 190 rooms, 6 suites. Restaurant. AE, DC, MC, V.*

$ **Hotel Schloss Röhrsdorf.** Surrounded by rolling parkland, this country palace is just a short drive from Dresden. Rooms have mostly modern furnishings but some original antique touches. The vaulted restaurant is of equally high standard. The hotel has stables, and the terrain is ideal for riding. ✉ *Hauptstr. 3, D-01809 Röhrsdorf,* ☎ *0351/285–770,* FAX *0351/2857–7263. 21 rooms, 1 suite. Restaurant, bar. AE, MC, V.*

Meissen

This romantic city on the Elbe River, 25 km (16 mi) northwest of Dresden, is known the world over for its porcelain, bearing the crossed blue swords trademark. The first European porcelain was made in this area, and in 1710 the royal porcelain workshop was established.

The **Staatliche Porzellan-Manufaktur Meissen** (Meissen's state porcelain works) outgrew its castle workshop in the mid-19th century and is now on the outskirts of town. In one of the buildings are a **Schauwerkstatt** (demonstration workshop) and a **Schauhalle** (museum), whose Meissen collection rivals that of the Porcelain Museum in Dresden. ✉ *Talstr. 9,* ☎ *03521/468–700,* WEB *www.meissener-porzellan.de.* ⏲ *Museum, Nov.–May, daily 9–5; May–Oct., daily 9–6.*

Leipzig

With a population of about 560,000, Leipzig is the second-largest city (after Berlin) in eastern Germany. Since the Middle Ages, it has been an important market town and a center for printing, publishing, and the fur business. Its year-round industrial fairs maintain Leipzig's position as a commercial center. Yet it is music and literature that most people associate with Leipzig; Johann Sebastian Bach (1685–1750) was the organist and choir director at St. Thomas's Church, and the composer Richard Wagner was born in Leipzig in 1813. One of the greatest battles of the Napoleonic Wars, and one that led to the ultimate defeat of the French general—the Battle of the Nations—was fought here in 1813.

The unique **Hauptbahnhof** (central train station), with its 26 platforms, majestic staircase, great arched ceiling, and more than 150 shops, is Europe's largest train station. ✉ *Willy-Brandt-Pl.,* ☎ *0341/19419.*

Leipzig's showpiece is its large **Markt** (market square). On one side of it is the Renaissance **Altes Rathaus** (Old City Hall), which houses the **Stadtgeschichtliches Museum** (City History Museum). Small streets leading off the Markt attest to Leipzig's rich trading past. Tucked in among them are glass-roofed shopping arcades. ✉ *Markt 1,* ☎ *0341/965–130.* ⏲ *City Hall and museum Tues. 2–8, Wed.–Sun. 10–6.*

Mädlerpassage (Mädler Mall) is the best shopping arcade, where references to Goethe's *Faust* lurk in every marble corner. Goethe set a scene in the Auerbachs Keller restaurant here. ✉ *Grimmaischestr.*

★ Johann Sebastian Bach worked for 27 years at **Thomaskirche** (St. Thomas's Church), composing most of his cantatas for the church's boys' choir, whose tradition continues today. ✉ *Thomaskirchhof (just off Grimmaischestr.),* ☎ *0341/9602–855,* WEB *www.thomaskirche.org.* ⏲ *Daily 9–6.*

★ **Nikolaikirche** (St. Nicholas's Church) is more impressive inside than out; it has an ornate 16th-century pulpit and an unusual diamond-pattern ceiling supported by classical pillars crowned with palm-tree-like flourishes. Demonstrations at the church in 1989 are credited with helping to bring down the Communist regime. ✉ *Nikolaikirchhof,* ☎ *0341/960–5270,* WEB *www.nikolaikirche.de.* ⏲ *Daily 10–6.*

★ The city's most outstanding museum, the **Museum der Bildenden Künste** (Museum of Fine Arts), is of international stature, especially strong in German and Dutch Old Masters. ✉ *Grimmaischestr. 1–7,* ☎ *0341/216–9914.* ⏲ *Tues. and Thurs.–Sun. 10–6, Wed. 1–9:30.*

The **Opernhaus** (Opera House; ✉ Augustuspl. 12, ☎ 0341/126–1261) is a center of the city's music life. The **Neues Gewandhaus** (✉ Augustuspl. 8, ☎ 0341/127–0280) is home to a first-class orchestra.

$$ ✕ **Kaiser Maximilian.** Leipzig's best Mediterranean restaurant serves inventive Italian and French dishes in an elegant yet modern setting, dominated by a cool design with high and undecorated walls and black leather seats. ✉ *Neumarkt 9–19,* ☎ *0341/9986–900. Reservations essential AE, MC, V.*

$–$$ ★ ✕ **Auerbachs Keller.** Established in 1530, this restaurant was made famous by Goethe's *Faust* and became an indispensable part of Leipzig life. Saxon dishes, often with Faustian names, head the menu. ✉ *Mädlerpassage, Grimmaischestr. 2–4,* ☎ *0341/216–100. Reservations essential. AE, MC, V.*

$–$$ ★ ✕ **Barthels Hof.** The beamed and paneled *Gasthaus* restaurant is a local favorite and serves hearty Saxon food with an international touch. The breakfast buffet is impressive, too. ✉ *Hainstr. 1,* ☎ *0341/141–310. AE, DC, MC, V.*

$ ✕ **Paulaner Hutter Culinaria Restaurant.** Munich's Paulaner brewery has transformed a historic corner of Leipzig into a vast complex combining a restaurant, banquet hall, café, and beer garden. There's something for everyone here, from intimate dining to noisy, Bavarian-style tavern-table conviviality. ✉ *Klosterg. 3–5,* ☎ *0341/211–3115. AE, DC, MC, V.*

$$$$ ★ 🏨 **Hotel Fürstenhof Leipzig.** One of the country's most luxurious hotels is in the Löhr-Haus, a revered old mansion. The spacious rooms are decorated with cherry-wood designer furniture. The fitness and swimming pool facilities are among the best in eastern Germany. ✉ *Tröndlinring 8, D-04105,* ☎ *0341/1400,* FAX *0341/1403–700,* WEB *www.arabellasheraton.com. 84 rooms, 8 suites. Restaurant, pool. AE, DC, MC, V.*

$$$–$$$$ 🏨 **Hotel Inter-Continental Leipzig.** The imposing high-rise "Interconti" offers outstanding service, but the place lacks atmosphere, despite a Japanese restaurant and garden. Rooms have every extravagance, including bathrooms with marble floors and walls. ✉ *Gerberstr. 15, D-04105,* ☎ *0341/9880,* FAX *0341/988–1229,* WEB *www.interconti.com. 426 rooms, 21 suites. 3 restaurants, pool. AE, DC, MC, V.*

$$–$$$$ 🏨 **Renaissance Leipzig Hotel.** In a city of trade fairs, this large hotel in the heart of old Leipzig attracts business travelers for its hushed atmosphere and its large, elegant rooms. The hotel's restaurant, Four Seasons, serves light Asian cuisine. ✉ *Grosser Brockhaus 3, D-04103,* ☎ *0341/12920,* FAX *0341/1292–800,* WEB *RenaissanceHotels.com. 295 rooms, 61 suites. Restaurant, pool. AE, DC, MC, V.*

Weimar

Sitting prettily on the Ilm River between the Ettersberg and Vogtland hills, Weimar has a place in German political and cultural history all out of proportion to its size (population 63,000). It is here that Goethe and the poet and dramatist Friedrich von Schiller were neighbors, Carl Maria von Weber (1786–1826) wrote some of his best music, and Liszt presented the first performance of Wagner's *Lohengrin.* Walter Gropius founded his Bauhaus design school in Weimar in 1919, and in 1919–

20 the German National Assembly drew up the constitution of the Weimar Republic.

A statue of Goethe and Schiller stand in **Theaterplatz,** in front of the National Theater. ★ The **Goethe-Nationalmuseum** (Goethe National Museum) showcases Weimar during the lifetime of Goethe, Herder, Schiller, and the like. It also integrates the **Goethehaus** (Goethe House), Goethe's home for 47 of his 57 years in Weimar. The museum is testimony not only to the great man's literary might but also to his interest in the sciences, particularly medicine, and his administrative skills (and frustrations) as Weimar's exchequer. ✉ *Frauenplan 1, 2 blocks south of Theaterpl.,* ☎ *03643/545–320,* WEB *www.weimar-klassik.de.* ⏲ *Jan.–Mar., Tues.–Sun. 9–4; Apr.–mid-May, Tues.–Sun. 9–6; mid-May–Aug., Tues.–Sun. 9–7; Sept.–Oct., Tues.–Sun. 9–6; Nov.–Dec., Tues.–Sun. 9–4.*

On a tree-shaded square around the corner from Goethe's house is the green-shuttered **Schillerhaus,** in which Friedrich Schiller and his family spent an all-too-brief but happy three years (the poet died here in 1805). His study, dominated by the desk at which he probably completed *Wilhelm Tell,* is tucked up underneath the mansard roof. ✉ *Schillerstr. 17,* ☎ *03643/545–350,* WEB *www.weimar-klassik.de.* ⏲ *Jan.–Mar., Tues.–Sun. 9–4; Mar.–mid-May, Tues.–Sun. 9–6; mid-May–Aug., Tues.–Sun. 9–7; Sept.–Oct., Tues.–Sun. 9–6; Oct.–Dec., Tues.–Sun., 9–4.*

Weimar's 16th-century castle, the **Stadtschloss** (City Palace), has a restored classical staircase, festival hall, and falcon gallery. The castle's impressive art collection includes paintings by Cranach the Elder and early 20th-century works by such artists as Böcklin, Liebermann, and Beckmann. ✉ *Burgpl. 4, around corner from market square,* ☎ *03643/5460,* WEB *www.kunstsammlungen-weimar.de.* ⏲ *Apr.–late Oct., Tues.–Sun. 10–6; late Oct.–Mar., Tues.–Sun. 10–4:30.*

Goethe's beloved **Gartenhaus,** a country cottage, is set amid parkland on the banks of the river Ilm. He wrote much poetry and began his masterly *Iphigenie auf Taurus* here. You can soak up the rural atmosphere along the river footpaths. ✉ *Goethepark,* ☎ *03642/545–375.* ⏲ *Jan.–Mar., Tues.–Sun. 9–4; Apr.–mid-May, Tues.–Sun. 9–6; mid-May–Aug., Tues.–Sun. 9–7; Sept.–Oct., Tues.–Sun. 9–6; Nov.–Dec., Tues.–Sun. 9–4.*

North of Weimar, in the Ettersberg Hills, is a blighted patch of land that contrasts cruelly with the verdant countryside that so inspired ★ Goethe: **Buchenwald,** where between 1937 and 1945 some 65,000 men, women, and children from 35 countries died from disease, starvation, or gruesome medical experiments. There are three small exhibition areas. ✉ *Buchenwald Str.; take public Bus No. 6 from Goethepl.,* ☎ *03643/4300,* WEB *www.buchenwald.de.* ⏲ *May–Sept., Tues.–Sun. 9:45–6; Oct.–Apr., Tues.–Sun. 8:45–5.*

$ ✕ **Hotel Thüringen.** The hotel's velvet drapes and chandeliers, makes the restaurant seem expensive, but the menu of regional dishes, such as Thüringer roast beef, is remarkably moderately priced. ✉ *Brennerstr. 42,* ☎ *03643/903–675. AE, DC, MC, V.*

$ ✕ **Scharfe Ecke.** Thuringia's traditional *Knödeln* (dumplings) are best here. But be patient; they're made to order and take at least 20 minutes to prepare. The Knödeln come with just about every dish, from roast pork to venison stew. The ideal accompaniment is beer. ✉ *Eisfeld 2,* ☎ *03643/202–430. No credit cards. Closed Mon.*

$$$ ★ 🏨 **Hotel Elephant.** The Elephant, dating from 1696, is famous for its charm—even through the communist years. Goethe, Schiller, and Liszt are some of the illustrious names in the hotel register. Book well in ad-

vance. ✉ *Markt 19, D-99423,* ☎ *03643/8020,* FAX *03643/802–610,* WEB *www.weimar.de/hotel-elephant. 97 rooms, 5 suites. 2 restaurants. AE, DC, MC, V.*

$$$ 🏨 **Hilton Weimar.** Weimar's most modern hotel combines lavishness and smooth-running service. The riverside Belvedere Park that Goethe helped plan is just across the road. Weimar's center is a hike in the other direction, but buses are frequent. ✉ *Belvederer Allee 25, D-99425,* ☎ *03643/7220,* FAX *03643/722–741,* WEB *www.hilton.com. 294 rooms, 6 suites. 2 restaurants, pool. AE, DC, MC, V.*

$$ 🏨 **Amalienhof VCH Hotel.** Book far ahead to secure a room here. The friendly little hotel dates from 1825 and is near Weimar's attractions. Double rooms have first-rate antique reproductions; public rooms have the real thing. ✉ *Amalienstr. 2, D-99423,* ☎ *03643/5490,* FAX *03643/549–110,* WEB *www.vch.de. 22 rooms, 9 apartments. AE, MC, V.*

Saxony and Thuringia Essentials

BOAT AND FERRY TRAVEL

The Sächsische Dampfschiffahrt (Saxonian Steamer Company) of inland boats, including paddle side-wheelers, plies the River Elbe, starting in Dresden (at the Terassenufer) or at the beautiful forested border town of Bad Schandau and proceeding on into the Czech Republic.

➤ BOAT AND FERRY INFORMATION: **Sächsische Dampfschiffahrt** (✉ Hertha-Lindner-Str. 10, D-01067 Dresden, ☎ 0351/866–090 or 0351/4906–114, WEB www.saechsische-dampfschiffahrt.de).

CAR TRAVEL

The autobahn and secondary roads crisscross Saxony and Thuringia. Resurfacing of some of the Communist-built highways has resulted in the lifting of the previous strictly enforced 100-kph (62-mph) speed limits on autobahns. Gas stations can be scarce.

TAXIS

Taxis in Dresden are inexpensive. Leipzig has plenty of cabs because of the trade fairs. Weimar's chief attractions are close to one another, but you may want to take a taxi from the main train station, which is somewhat removed from the city center.

TOURS

BUS TOURS

Contact the tourist offices in Leipzig and Dresden about the cities' English-language bus tours.

TRAIN TOURS

Deutsche Bahn's small-gauge line penetrates deep into the Saxony countryside and the Fichtelgebirge mountains.

WALKING TOURS

Walking tours are either regularly scheduled, or can be arranged, by city tourist offices.

TRAIN TRAVEL

InterCity, EuroCity, and InterCity Express trains connect Dresden, Meissen, Leipzig, and Weimar with Berlin and other major German cities, with InterRegio services completing the express network; older and slower D- and E-class trains connect smaller towns.

TRANSPORTATION AROUND SAXONY AND THURINGIA

Most areas are accessible by bus, but service is infrequent and connects chiefly with rail lines. In Dresden, Meissen, Leipzig, and Weimar, public buses and streetcars are cheap and efficient. Leipzig has an S-bahn (suburban rail) system. Tickets must be obtained in advance, at various prices according to the number of rides in a block. Get S-bahn tickets at the main railway station.

TRAVEL AGENCY

➤ LOCAL AGENT REFERRALS: **Reiseland American Express** (✉ Ludwigsburger Str. 9, D-04209 Leipzig, ☎ 0341/426–840; ✉ Willy-Brandt-Platz 5, D-04109 Leipzig, ☎ 0341/961–7373; ✉ Dohnaer Str. 246, D-01239 Dresden, ☎ 0351/2881–109, WEB www.americanexpress.de).

VISITOR INFORMATION

Most of the region's larger cities offer special tourist (exploring) cards such as the Dresdencard, Hallecard, Leipzigcard, or Weimarcard, which include discounts at museums, concerts, hotels, and restaurants or special sightseeing packages for up to three days.

➤ TOURIST INFORMATION: **Dresden** (Tourist-Information; ✉ Prager Str. 10, D-01069, ☎ 0351/491–920, WEB www.dresden.de). **Leipzig** (Leipzig Tourist Service e.V.; ✉ Sachsenpl. 1, D-06108, ☎ 0341/104–260, WEB www.leipzig.de). **Meissen** (Tourist-Information; ✉ An der Frauenkirche 3, D-01662, ☎ 03521/41940, WEB www.meiland.de/meissen). **Weimar** (Tourist-Information; ✉ Markt 10, D-99421, ☎ 03643/24000, WEB www.weimar.de).

13 GREAT BRITAIN

LONDON, WINDSOR TO BATH, CAMBRIDGE, YORK, THE LAKE DISTRICT, EDINBURGH

WHEN YOU VISIT LONDON, chances are you'll glimpse St. Paul's Cathedral riding high and white over the rooftops of the city skyline, just as it does in Canaletto's 18th-century views of the Thames. The great cathedral glows honey-gold, breathtakingly floodlit by night, its details and proportions testimony to the genius of architect Christopher Wren. Then, on second glance, you'll note that St. Paul's is being nudged by modern, glittering skyscrapers, with glass-and-steel tower blocks marching two abreast the length of London Wall. The juxtaposition should give you pause: clearly, when you come to see the sights of Britain, you ought not to miss the greatest sight of all, which is the unconquered, nearly 2,000-year-long continuity of English society.

From Baroque-era cathedrals to the latest postmodern structures, from prehistoric Stonehenge to Regency Bath, from one-pub Cotswold villages to London's Mod Brit restaurants, Great Britain is a spectacular tribute to the strength—and flexibility—of tradition. Here you'll find soaring medieval cathedrals; grand country mansions of the aristocracy filled with paintings, furniture, and tapestries, set in elegantly landscaped grounds; and grim fortified castles, whose gray-stone walls held fast against all challengers. But there is more to Britain than a historical theme park aspect: many of the pleasures of exploration derive from the ever-changing variety of its countryside. A day's drive from York, for example, will take you through stretches of wild, heather-covered moorland, ablaze with color in the fall; or past the steep, sheep-dotted mountainsides of the Dales, in which isolated hamlets are scattered.

Wandering off the beaten track will also allow you to discover Britain's many distinctive rural towns and villages, which move at a notably slower pace than do the metropolitan centers. A medieval parish church, a high street of 18th-century buildings accented by occasional survivors from earlier centuries, and perhaps a grandiose Victorian town hall, all still in use today, help to convey a sense of a living past. This continuity of past into present can be generously experienced in such a celebrated place as Stratford-upon-Avon. It's even more evident in the little town of Chipping Campden, set in the rolling Cotswold Hills, or Bury St. Edmunds, in the gentle Suffolk countryside east of Cambridge. In such places the visitor's understanding is often aided by small museums devoted to local history, full of intriguing artifacts and information on trade, traditions, and social life. These towns are likely places to look for specialty goods, including knitwear, pottery, and glass, the result of a 1990s renaissance in craftsmanship.

In contrast is the dazzling—at times hectic—pace of life in London. Today, Britain's swinging-again capital is much in the news, and the city's sizzling art, dining, style, and fashion scenes have done much to transform London's stodgy and traditional image. Thanks to such figures as artist Damien Hirst, designer-provocateur Alexander McQueen, and, of course, Tony Blair, the young(ish) prime minister, London continues to make headlines around the world. London has become Europe's most future-active capital with a slew of goodies, including the gigantic Tate Modern art gallery and the British Museum with its sparkling new glass-roofed Great Court, which have set the city alight.

Finally, it is important to remember that Great Britain consists of three nations—England, Scotland, and Wales—and that 648 km (402 mi) north of London lies the capital city of Edinburgh, whose streets and monuments bear witness to the often turbulent and momentous history of the Scottish people.

GREAT BRITAIN A TO Z

To research prices, get advice from other travelers, and book travel arrangements, visit www.fodors.com.

AIR TRAVEL

Britain offers an extensive network of internal air routes, run by about six different airlines. Hourly shuttle services operate every day between London and Glasgow, Edinburgh, Belfast, and Manchester. Seats are available on a no-reservations basis, and you can generally check in about a half hour before flight departure time.

BIKE TRAVEL

Most towns—including London—offer bike-rental facilities. Any bike shop or tourist information center should be able to direct you to the nearest rental firm. Rental fees can be as little as £5 per day, plus a fairly large deposit, though this can often be put on your credit card. If you're planning a tour and would like information on rental shops and special holidays for cyclists, contact a British Tourist Authority office in the United States before you leave home. In Britain contact the Cyclists' Touring Club.

➤ ORGANIZATIONS: **Cyclists' Touring Club** (✉ Cotterell House, 69 Meadrow, Godalming, Surrey GU7 3HS, ☎ 01483/417217).

BOAT AND FERRY TRAVEL

Britain offers more than 2,430 km (1,507 mi) of navigable inland waterways—rivers, lakes, canals, locks, and loughs—for leisure travel. Particular regions, such as the Norfolk Broads in East Anglia, the Severn Valley in the West Country, and the lochs and canals of Scotland are especially inviting. Although there are no regularly scheduled waterborne services, hundreds of yachts, canal boats, and motor cruises are available throughout the year. The Inland Waterways Association is a popular source for maps and guidebooks. British Waterways can assist with maps and information. For boat-rental operators along Britain's several hundred miles of historic canals and waterways, contact the Association of Pleasure Craft Operators.

➤ BOAT AND FERRY INFORMATION: **Association of Pleasure Craft Operators** (✉ 35A High St., Newport, Shropshire TF10 7AT, ☎ 01952/813572). **British Waterways** (✉ Customer Services, Willow Grange, Church Rd., Watford WD1 3QA, ☎ 01923/201120, WEB www.britishwaterways.co.uk). **Inland Waterways Association** (✉ Box 114, Rickmansworth, Hertfordshire WD3 1ZY, ☎ 01923/711114).

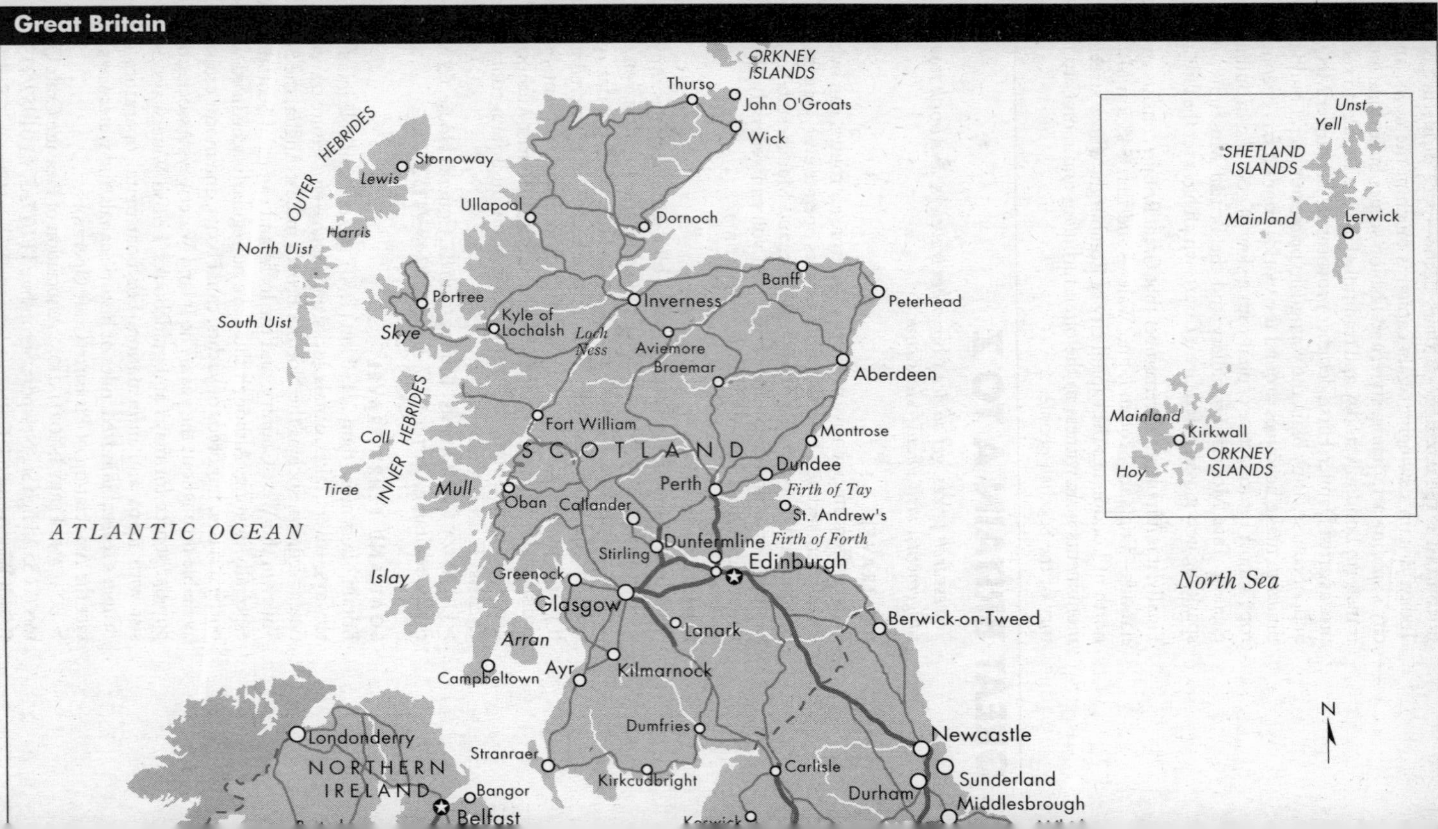
ORKNEY ISLANDS
Thurso
John O'Groats
Wick
OUTER HEBRIDES
Stornoway
Lewis
Ullapool
Dornoch
Harris
North Uist
Banff
Portree
Inverness
Peterhead
Kyle of Lochalsh
Loch Ness
South Uist
Skye
Aviemore
Braemar
Aberdeen
Fort William
Montrose
Coll
INNER HEBRIDES
SCOTLAND
Dundee
Perth
Firth of Tay
Tiree
Mull
Oban
Callander
St. Andrew's
ATLANTIC OCEAN
Dunfermline
Firth of Forth
Stirling
Edinburgh
Islay
Greenock
Glasgow
Lanark
Berwick-on-Tweed
Arran
Ayr
Kilmarnock
Campbeltown
Dumfries
Londonderry
Newcastle
Stranraer
Carlisle
NORTHERN IRELAND
Kirkcudbright
Sunderland
Durham
Bangor
Middlesbrough
Belfast
Unst
Yell
SHETLAND ISLANDS
Mainland
Lerwick
Mainland
Kirkwall
ORKNEY ISLANDS
Hoy
North Sea
N

Armagh
Isle of Man
Kendal
Scarborough
Lancaster
York
Blackpool
Bradford
Leeds
Kingston-upon-Hull
Irish Sea
Bolton
Manchester
Grimsby
Liverpool
Birkenhead
Doncaster
REPUBLIC OF IRELAND
Dublin
Holyhead
Sheffield
Llandudno
Skegness
Lincoln
Boston
The Wash
ENGLAND
Stoke-on-Trent
Nottingham
Cromer
Derby
Norwich
Great Yarmouth
Shrewsbury
Stamford
Peterborough
Leicester
Wolverhampton
Lowestoft
Aberystwyth
Birmingham
Coventry
Cambridge
Bury St. Edmunds
WALES
Stratford
Northampton
Ipswich
St. George's Channel
Fishguard
Banbury
Harwich
Gloucester
Colchester
Oxford
LONDON
Swansea
Newport
Swindon
Windsor
Pembroke
Bristol
Cardiff
Reading
Canterbury
Bath
Maidstone
Bristol Channel
Dover
Folkestone
Barnstaple
Taunton
Salisbury
Winchester
Reigate
Tunbridge Wells
Strait of Dover
Yeovil
Southampton
Brighton
0
50 miles
100 miles
0
50 km
100 km
150 km
Bude
Dorchester
Exeter
Bournemouth
Isle of Wight
Portsmouth
Bodmin
Torquay
Plymouth
English Channel
Penzance
Scilly Isles
Land's End
Falmouth
FRANCE

BUS TRAVEL

Bus prices are invariably half those of train tickets, and the network is just as extensive. There is one important semantic difference to keep in mind when discussing bus travel in Britain. Buses (either double- or single-decker) are generally part of the local transportation system in towns and cities and make frequent stops. Coaches, on the other hand, are comparable to American Greyhound buses and are used only for long-distance travel.

National Express offers the largest number of routes of any coach operator in Britain. It also offers a variety of discount tickets, including the Discount Coachcard and the Tourist Trail Pass for overseas visitors. The Discount Coachcard (£8) provides a 20%–30% reduction on journeys made within a year and is available only to students and those under 25 years or over 50. The Tourist Trail Pass offers discounted rates for several ranges of days' travel. Passes can be bought in London's Victoria Coach Station or at any of 1,200 National Express agents nationwide. Information about all coach services, from timetables to ticket purchase by credit card, can be obtained from the National Express Information Office at Victoria Coach Station, and, for information on coach services in Scotland, from Scottish Citylink.

➤ BUS INFORMATION: **National Express Information Office** (✉ Victoria Coach Station, Buckingham Palace Rd., SW1 9TP, ☎ 0870/580–8080). **Scottish Citylink** (✉ St. Andrew Sq., Edinburgh, Scotland, ☎ 0870/550–5050).

BUSINESS HOURS

Banks are open weekdays 9:30–4:30. Some have extended hours on Thursday evening, and a few are open on Saturday morning. Museum hours vary considerably from one part of the country to another. In large cities most are open Tuesday–Saturday 10–5; many are also open on Sunday afternoon. The majority close one day a week. Be sure to double-check the opening times of historic houses, especially if the visit involves a special trip; most stately houses in the countryside are closed November–March. Shops are open Monday–Saturday 9–5:30, and many are open Sunday. Outside the main centers most shops close at 1 PM once a week, often Wednesday or Thursday. In small villages many also close for lunch. In large cities—especially London—department stores stay open for late-night shopping (usually until 7:30 or 8) one day midweek.

CAR TRAVEL

Parking in London and in other large cities can be a nightmare. On-street meters are hard to find and can be very expensive. Cheaper pay-and-display lots (the driver inserts money into a machine to receive a sticker for the car with the amount of time allowed for parking) are common in smaller towns and suburban areas. But wherever you are, in town or city, beware of yellow or red lines. A single yellow line denotes no parking during the daytime. Double yellow lines or red lines indicate a more extensive prohibition on stopping. The exact times are indicated on signs, usually attached to lampposts. Illegal parking can result in having your vehicle removed or its wheel clamped, which can lead to a great deal of inconvenience as well as a hefty fine. In central London, where there is a good bus and underground service and taxis are plentiful, the use of a car is not recommended. If you must drive, an indispensable insider's reference book is the *London Parking Guide* (£4.99, Two Heads Publishing), available at good bookstores.

EMERGENCIES

The main automobile help groups are similar to the A.A.A. in the States. The Automobile Association runs a 24-hour breakdown service, as does the Royal Automobile Club. Most motorways have emergency phones along the route that connect the caller to the nearest police station. If you are driving extensively through Britain, membership in the AA can be useful for many reasons; you can also sign up through car-rental agents. If you are a member of the A.A.A. check your membership details, as you may be entitled to roadside assistance in Great Britain via a reciprocal agreement.

➤ CONTACTS: **Automobile Association** (AA; ☎ 0870/550–0600; 0990/500600 membership). **Royal Automobile Club** (☎ 0870/572–2722).

GASOLINE

In Britain gas (called petrol) pumps measure in liters. (There are 5 American gallons to 4 British gallons—for that amount, you will get about 20 liters.) At press time the price of gasoline was about 85p per liter, for lead-free. The price generally rises in spring and autumn with government tax increases, and you'll find the cheapest prices at the supermarket pumps. Unleaded gasoline is predominant, denoted by green stickers on fuel pumps and pumplines. Premium and Super Premium are the two varieties, and most cars run on regular premium.

ROAD CONDITIONS

Britain has superhighways (called motorways) running almost the length of the country, with links connecting them in the South, West, Midlands, and North. Motorways, given the prefix *M* on maps and road signs and shown in blue, have two or three lanes in each direction and are designed for high-speed rather than scenic travel. The other primary roads are A roads. Shown on maps as red and green lines, they connect town to town. Some bypass town centers and have fast stretches of divided (two-lane dual carriageway) highway. These are shown as thicker, black-edged lines on maps. Most other routes, yellow B roads, are the roads once designed for horses and carriages. Although they—and the even narrower, winding, white unclassified village roads—will allow you to see much more of the real Britain, your journey could end up taking twice the time. In remote country areas, road travel can be slow, especially in an icy winter. Good maps are available from the AA (Automobile Association) and the RAC (Royal Automobile Club); for in-depth exploring try the Ordnance Survey 1:50,000-series maps. These show every road, track, and footpath in the country. You might also consult the very useful Ordnance Survey *Motoring Atlas,* available at many bookstores.

RULES OF THE ROAD

You can use either a U.S. driver's license or an International Driver's License in Britain. Drive on the left-hand side of the road and pay close attention to the varying—and abruptly changing—speed limits. Seat belts are obligatory for front-seat passengers (and back-seat ones when the cars are fitted with them). In general, speed limits are 30 mph in the center of cities and built-up areas; 40 mph in suburban areas; 70 mph on motorways, divided highways, and dual carriageways; and 60 mph on all other roads.

CUSTOMS AND DUTIES

For details on imports and duty-free limits, *see* Customs and Duties *in* Chapter 1.

DINING

British food used to be put down for its lack of imagination and its mediocrity. Today, numerous chefs have taken such giant steps that London is now one of the world's greatest cities for dining out. Across Britain, the problem may be not so much bad food as expensive food. The best of traditional British cooking, deeper into the country, uses top-quality, fresh, local ingredients: wild salmon; spring lamb; distinctive handmade cheeses; myriad, almost forgotten, fruit varieties; and countless types of seasonal vegetables. Nearly all restaurant menus include vegetarian dishes, and interesting ethnic cuisines, especially Asian, can be found in the main street of even the smaller towns and villages.

Prices are for a main course at dinner.

CATEGORY	COST
$$$$	over £22
$$$	£16–£22
$$	£9–£15
$	under £9

MEALTIMES

These vary somewhat, depending on the region of the country you are visiting. But in general breakfast is served between 7:30 and 9 and lunch between noon and 2 (in the North the latter meal is called dinner). Tea—a famous British tradition and often a meal in itself—is generally served between 4 and 5:30. Dinner or supper is served between 7:30 and 9:30, sometimes earlier, but rarely later outside the metropolitan areas. High tea, at about 6, replaces dinner in some areas—especially in Scotland—and in large cities, pre- and after-theater suppers are often available. Note that many upscale restaurants close for 10 days during Easter and/or Christmas and for several weeks in July, August, or September. Call ahead.

RESERVATIONS AND DRESS

Jacket and tie are suggested for the more formal restaurants in the top price categories, but, in general, casual chic or informal dress is acceptable in most establishments.

EMBASSIES

➤ CANADIAN HIGH COMMISSION: (✉ McDonald House, 1 Grosvenor Sq., London W1X 0AB, ☎ 020/7258–6600).

➤ UNITED STATES: (✉ 24 Grosvenor Sq., London W1A 1AE, ☎ 020/7499–9000).

HOLIDAYS

Parliament isn't the only institution to decide which days are national holidays: some holidays are actually subject to royal proclamation. England and Wales: New Year's Day; Good Friday and Easter Monday; May Day (first Monday in May); Spring Bank Holiday (last Monday in May); August Bank Holiday (last Monday in August); Christmas Day and Boxing Day (day after Christmas). A national holiday is also to be announced for the Queen's Golden Jubilee celebrations.

LODGING

Britain offers a wide variety of accommodations, ranging from enormous, top-quality, top-price hotels to simple, intimate farmhouses and guest houses. Note that many smaller establishments close for 10 days during Christmas and sometimes for several weeks in July or August. Call ahead.

Prices are for two people in a double room and include all taxes.

CATEGORY	LONDON	OTHER AREAS
$$$$	over £230	over £150
$$$	£160–£230	£100–£150
$$	£100–£160	£60–£100
$	under £100	under £60

B&B'S

In Britain these are small, simple establishments, not the upscale option Americans know by this name. They offer modest, inexpensive accommodations, usually in a family home. Few rooms have private bathrooms, and most B&Bs offer no meals other than breakfast. Guest houses are a slightly larger, somewhat more luxurious, version. Both provide the visitor with an excellent glimpse of everyday British life.

CAMPING

Britain offers an abundance of campsites. Some are large and well equipped; others are merely small farmers' fields, offering primitive facilities. For information contact the British Tourist Authority in the United States or the Camping and Caravanning Club.

➤ ORGANIZATIONS: **Camping and Caravanning Club** (✉ Greenfields House, Westwood Way, Coventry CV4 8JH, ☎ 01203/694995).

FARMHOUSES

Farmhouses rarely offer professional hotel standards, but they have a special appeal: the rustic, rural experience. Prices are generally very reasonable. A car is vital for a successful farmhouse stay. The Farm Holiday Bureau, a network of farming and country people who offer B&B accommodations, is a good source for regional tourist board inspected and approved properties. These properties are listed in the *Stay on a Farm* guide, produced by the bureau.

➤ ORGANIZATIONS: **Farm Holiday Bureau** (✉ National Agricultural Centre, Stoneleigh Park, Kenilworth, Warwickshire CV8 2LZ, ☎ 01203/696909).

HISTORIC BUILDINGS

To spend your vacation in a Gothic temple, an old lighthouse on an isolated island, or maybe in an apartment at Hampton Court Palace, contact one of the half dozen organizations in Great Britain that have specially adapted, modernized historic buildings to rent. A leading organization that rents such buildings is the Landmark Trust; these properties do not have TVs. The National Trust, Portmeirion Cottages, and the upscale Rural Retreats also rent historic buildings.

➤ ORGANIZATIONS: **Landmark Trust** (✉ Shottesbrooke, Maidenhead, Berkshire SL6 3SW, ☎ 01628/825925, WEB www.landmarktrust.co.uk). **National Trust** (✉ Box 536, Melksham, Wiltshire SN12 8SX, ☎ 01225/791199). **Portmeirion Cottages** (✉ Hotel Portmeirion, Gwynedd, Wales LL48 6ET, ☎ 01766/770228). **Rural Retreats** (✉ Retreat House, Station Rd., Blockley, Moreton-in-Marsh GL56 9DZ, Gloucestershire, ☎ 01386/701177).

HOLIDAY COTTAGES

Furnished apartments, houses, cottages, and trailers are available for weekly rental in all areas of the country. These vary from quaint, cleverly converted farmhouses to brand-new buildings set in scenic surroundings. The British Tourist Authority booklet "Self Catering Holiday

Homes" is available from the BTA office in New York. Lists of rental properties are available free of charge from local Tourist Information Centres in Britain. Discounts of up to 50% apply during the off-season (October through March).

HOSTELS

The more than 350 youth hostels throughout England, Wales, and Scotland range from very basic to very good. Many are in remote and beautiful areas; others are on the outskirts of large cities. Despite the name, there is no age restriction. The accommodations are inexpensive and generally reliable and usually include cooking facilities. For additional information contact the YHA Headquarters.

➤ ORGANIZATIONS: **YHA Headquarters** (✉ Trevelyan House, 8 St. Stephen's Hill, St. Albans, Hertfordshire AL1 2DY, ☎ 01727/855215).

HOTELS

British hotels vary greatly, and there is no reliable official system of classification. Most have rooms with private bathrooms, although there are still many hotels—usually older ones—that offer some rooms with only sinks; in this case, showers and bathtubs (and toilets) are usually just down the hall. Many also have "good" and "bad" wings. Be sure to check the room before you take it. Generally, British hotel prices include breakfast, but beware: many offer only a Continental breakfast—often little more than tea and toast. A hotel that includes a traditional British breakfast in its rates is usually a good bet. Hotel prices in London can be significantly higher than in the rest of the country, and sometimes the quality does not reflect the extra cost. Tourist information centers all over the country will reserve rooms for you, usually for a small fee. A great many hotels offer special weekend and off-season bargain packages.

UNIVERSITY HOUSING

In larger cities and in some towns, certain universities offer their residence halls to paying vacationers. The facilities available are usually compact sleeping units, and they can be rented on a nightly basis. For information contact the British Universities Accommodation Consortium.

➤ ORGANIZATIONS: **British Universities Accommodation Consortium** (✉ Box 1498, University Park, Nottingham NG7 2RD, ☎ 01159/504571).

MAIL AND SHIPPING

POSTAL RATES

Airmail letters to the United States and Canada cost 45p for 10 grams; postcards, 40p; aerograms, 40p. Letters and postcards to Europe weighing up to 20 grams cost 36p. Letters within the United Kingdom: first-class, 27p; second-class and postcards, 19p.

RECEIVING MAIL

If you're uncertain where you'll be staying, you can arrange to have your mail sent to American Express. The service is free to cardholders and AmEx traveler's check holders; all others pay a small fee. You can also collect letters at London's Main Post Office. Ask to have the mail addressed as the recipient's name appears on his or her passport, to "poste restante" or "to be called for" and mailed to the Main Post Office. For collection, hours are weekdays 8 AM–8 PM, Saturday 9 AM–8 PM. You'll need your passport or other official form of identification. This service can be arranged at post offices throughout Britain.

➤ POST OFFICES: **American Express** (✉ 6 Haymarket, London SW1Y 4BS). **Main Post Office** (✉ Trafalgar Square, 24–28 William IV Street, London WC2N 4DL).

MONEY MATTERS

In general, transportation in Britain is expensive in comparison to other countries. You should take advantage of the many reductions and special fares available on trains, buses, and subways. Always ask about these when buying your ticket.

London now ranks with Tokyo as one of the world's most expensive hotel capitals. Finding budget accommodations—especially during July and August—can be difficult; you should try to book well ahead if you are visiting during these months. Dining out at top-of-the-line restaurants can be prohibitively expensive, but there are new chains of French-Italian–style café-brasseries, along with a large number of pubs and ethnic restaurants that offer excellent food at reasonable prices.

The gulf between prices in the capital and outside is wide. Be prepared to pay a value-added tax (VAT) of 17½% on almost everything you buy; in nearly all cases it is included in the advertised price.

Costs: in London, cup of coffee, £1–£2; pint of beer, £1.80–£2.20; glass of wine, £2–£4; soda, 80p–£1.50; 2-km (1-mi) taxi ride, £3; ham sandwich, £1.75–£3.50.

CURRENCY

The British unit of currency is the pound sterling (£), divided into 100 pence (p). Bills are issued in denominations of £5, £10, £20, and £50. Coins are £2, £1, 50p, 20p, 10p, 5p, 2p, and 1p. Scottish banks issue Scottish currency, of which all coins and notes—with the exception of the £1 notes—are accepted in England. At press time (summer 2001) the pound stood at £.68 to the U.S. dollar, £.44 to the Canadian dollar, £.81 to the Irish punt, £.35 to the Australian dollar, £.29 to the New Zealand dollar, and £.09 to the South African rand.

Traveler's checks are widely accepted in Britain, and many banks, hotels, and shops offer currency-exchange facilities. You will have to pay a £2 commission fee wherever you change them; banks offer the best rates, yet even these fees vary. If you are changing currency, you will have to pay (on top of commission) based on the amount you are changing. In London and other big cities, *bureaux de change* abound, but it definitely pays to shop around: they charge a flat fee and it's often a great deal more than that at other establishments, such as banks. American Express foreign exchange desks do not charge a commission fee on AmEx traveler's checks. Credit cards are universally accepted, and the most commonly used are MasterCard and Visa.

SALES TAX

Foreign visitors from outside Europe can avoid Britain's 17½% value-added tax (VAT) by taking advantage of the following two methods. By the Direct Export method, the shopkeeper arranges the export of the goods and does not charge VAT at the point of sale. This means that the purchases are sent on to your home separately. If you prefer to take your purchase with you, try the Retail Export scheme, run by most large stores: the special Form 407 (provided only by the retailer) is attached to your invoice. You must present the goods, form, and invoice to the customs officer at the last port of departure from the EU. Allow plenty of time to do this at the airport, as there are often long lines. The form is then returned to the store and the refund forwarded to you, minus a small service charge. For inquiries call the local Customs & Excise office listed in the telephone directory.

TELEPHONES

COUNTRY AND AREA CODES

The United Kingdom's country code is 44. When dialing a number in Britain from abroad, drop the initial 0 from the local area code.

DIRECTORY AND OPERATOR ASSISTANCE

For information anywhere in Britain, dial ☎ 192. For the operator, dial ☎ 100. For assistance with international calls, dial ☎ 155.

INTERNATIONAL CALLS

The cheapest way to make an overseas call is to dial it yourself. But be sure to have plenty of coins or phone cards close at hand (newsagents sell budget-rate international phone cards, such as First National and America First, which can be used from any phone by dialing an access number, then a personal identification number). After you have inserted the coins or card, dial 00 (the international code), then the country code—1 for the United States—followed by the area code and local number. You call also make calls through AT&T, MCI, Worldphone, or Sprint Global One long-distance operators. To make a collect or other operator-assisted call, dial ☎ 155.

➤ ACCESS CODES: **AT&T** (☎ 0800/0130011). **MCI, Worldphone** (☎ 0800/890222). **Sprint Global One** (☎ 0800/890877 or 0500/890877).

LOCAL CALLS

Public telephones are plentiful in British cities, especially London. British Telecom is gradually replacing the distinctive red phone booths with generic glass and steel cubicles, but the traditional boxes still remain in the countryside. The workings of coin-operated telephones vary, but there are usually instructions in each unit. Most take 10p, 20p, 50p, and £1 coins. A phone card is also available; it comes in denominations of 10, 20, 50, and 100 units and can be bought in a number of retail outlets. Card phones, which are clearly marked with a special green insignia, will not accept coins. You can often use your credit card, although this is a more expensive option.

A local call before 6 PM costs 15p for three minutes; this doubles to 30p for the same from a pay phone. A daytime call to the United States will cost 24p a minute on a regular phone (weekends are cheaper), 80p on a pay phone. Each large city or region in Britain has its own numerical prefix, which is used only when you are dialing from outside the city. In provincial areas the dialing codes for nearby towns are often posted in the booth.

AREA CODES

Some area codes and local numbers in the U.K. changed in 2000. There is one area code for London—020—followed by a prefix, either 7 (for inner London) or 8 (for outer London), before the 7-digit phone number. So, for example, for a phone call to inner London, you would dial 020/7242–4444; for outer London, 020/8242–4444.

TIPPING

Some restaurants and most hotels add a service charge of 10%–15% to the bill. If this has been done, you're under no obligation to tip further. If no service charge is indicated, add 10%–15% to your total bill, unless you are unhappy with the service given. Taxi drivers should also get 10%–15%, although it's not obligatory. You are not expected to tip theater or cinema ushers, elevator operators, or bartenders in pubs. Hairdressers and barbers should receive 10%–15%.

TRAIN TRAVEL

The old single national operator British Rail (BR) has been broken up into individual private operators. Dogged by poor performance, old rolling stock, and a major rail crash in 2000, tracks and services throughout the country are working on a major investment and overhaul programme to bring the service up to safety and speed levels which used to be the bywords for excellence in previous days. For information on train travel, contact National Rail Enquiries.

The country's rail network links London with every major city in the country, and to France and Belgium via the Channel tunnel. The most modern high-speed trains travel up to 140 mph and offer comfortable, air-conditioned cars, both first and second class, with restaurant or buffet facilities. Local train services are not as reliable, particularly around such congested city centers as London. In general, seat reservations are not necessary except during peak vacation periods and on popular medium- and long-distance routes. Charges for reserving a standard-class seat start from £1, although reservation charges are complimentary when booking by phone.

FARES AND SCHEDULES

Rail fares are high when compared with those in other countries. However, the network does offer a wide, and often bewildering, range of ticket discounts. Information and tickets can be obtained from information offices in each station, Rail Travel Centres within the larger train stations, and by phone to National Rail Enquiries.

If you are planning to travel only short distances, be sure to buy inexpensive same-day return tickets ("cheap day returns"). These cost only slightly more than ordinary one-way ("single"), standard-class tickets but can be used *only* after 9:30 AM and on weekends. Other special offers are regional Rover tickets, giving unlimited travel within local areas, and Saver returns, allowing greatly reduced round-trip travel during off-peak periods.

➤ TRAIN INFORMATION: **National Rail Enquiries** (☎ 0845/548–4950).

VISITOR INFORMATION

For National Tourist Board addresses and phone numbers, *see* Visitor Information *in* Chapter 1. For regional and city tourist boards, *see* Visitor Information *in* the Essentials section for the region, *below.*

WHEN TO GO

Many walking paths and sights closed by the February 2001 outbreak of foot-and-mouth disease (which affects animals) were reopening by summer 2001, but check with the British Tourist Authority or www.openbritain.gov.uk for current information.

CLIMATE

On the whole, Britain's winters are rarely bitter, except in the north and Scotland. Wherever you are, and whatever the season, be prepared for sudden changes. Take an umbrella and raincoat wherever you go, particularly in Scotland, where the temperatures can be somewhat cooler.

The following are the average daily maximum and minimum temperatures for London.

Jan.	43F	6C	**May**	62F	17C	**Sept.**	65F	19C
	36	2		47	8		52	11
Feb.	44F	7C	**June**	69F	20C	**Oct.**	58F	14C
	36	2		53	12		46	8
Mar.	50F	10C	**July**	71F	22C	**Nov.**	50F	10C
	38	3		56	13		42	6
Apr.	56F	13C	**Aug.**	71F	22C	**Dec.**	45F	7C
	42	6		56	13		38	3

London

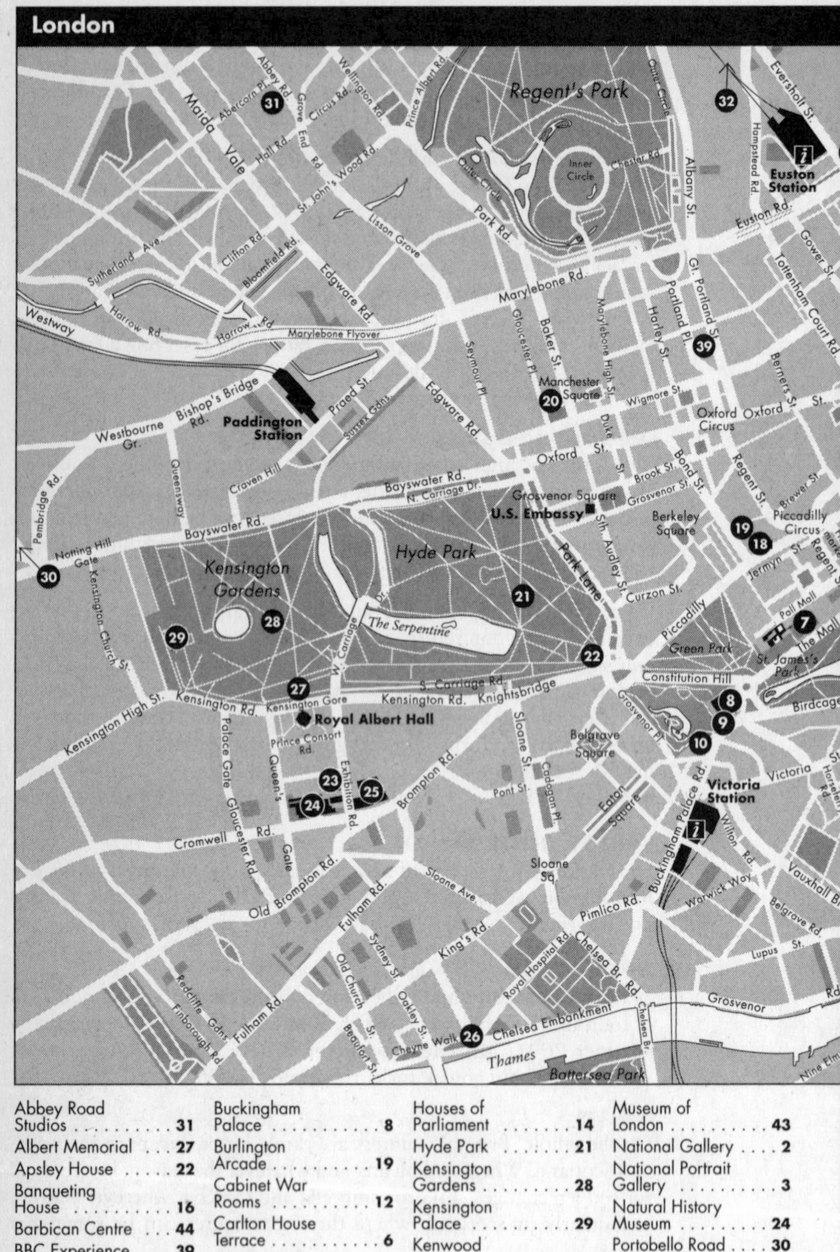

- Abbey Road Studios . . . 31
- Albert Memorial . . . 27
- Apsley House . . . 22
- Banqueting House . . . 16
- Barbican Centre . . . 44
- BBC Experience . . . 39
- British Library . . . 33
- British Museum . . . 40
- Buckingham Palace . . . 8
- Burlington Arcade . . . 19
- Cabinet War Rooms . . . 12
- Carlton House Terrace . . . 6
- Cheyne Walk . . . 26
- Covent Garden . . . 34
- Horse Guards Parade . . . 17
- Houses of Parliament . . . 14
- Hyde Park . . . 21
- Kensington Gardens . . . 28
- Kensington Palace . . . 29
- Kenwood House . . . 32
- The Mall . . . 5
- Museum of London . . . 43
- National Gallery . . . 2
- National Portrait Gallery . . . 3
- Natural History Museum . . . 24
- Portobello Road . . . 30
- Queen's Gallery . . . 9

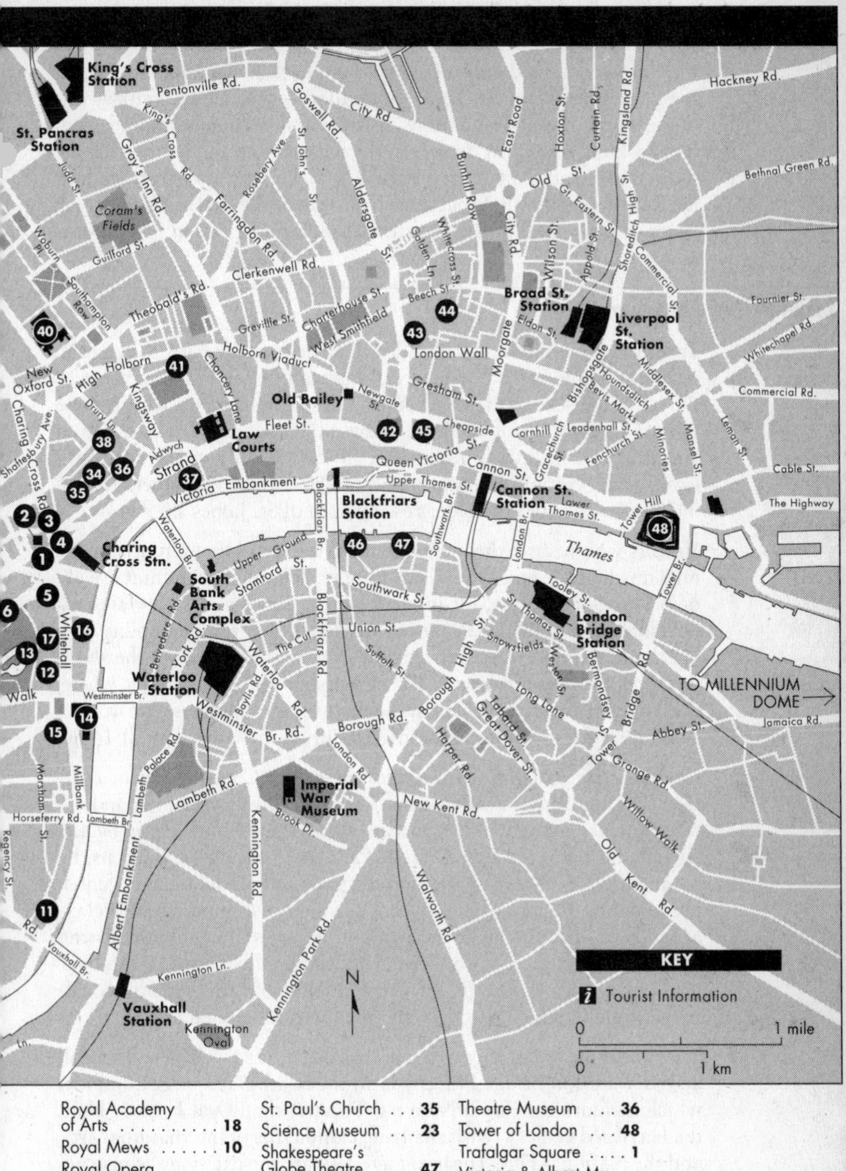

Royal Academy of Arts **18**
Royal Mews **10**
Royal Opera House **38**
St. James's Palace . . . **7**
St. Martin-in-the-Fields **4**
St. Mary-le-Bow **45**
St. Paul's Cathedral **42**
St. Paul's Church . . . **35**
Science Museum . . . **23**
Shakespeare's Globe Theatre **47**
Sir John Soane's Museum **41**
Somerset House **37**
Tate Britain **11**
Tate Modern **46**
Ten Downing Street **13**
Theatre Museum . . . **36**
Tower of London . . . **48**
Trafalgar Square **1**
Victoria & Albert Museum **25**
Wallace Collection **20**
Westminster Abbey **15**

LONDON

If London contained only its famous landmarks—Buckingham Palace, Big Ben, Parliament, the Tower of London—it would still rank as one of the world's great destinations. A city that loves to be explored, London beckons with great museums, royal pageantry, and houses that are steeped in history. Marvel at the Duke of Wellington's house, track Jack the Ripper's shadow in Whitechapel, then get Beatle-ized at Abbey Road. From the East End to the West End, you'll find London is a dickens of a place.

Exploring London

Traditionally London has been divided between the City, to the east, where its banking and commercial interests lie, and Westminster, to the west, the seat of the royal court and of government. It is in these two areas that you will find most of the grand buildings that have played a central role in British history: the Tower of London and St. Paul's Cathedral, Westminster Abbey and the Houses of Parliament, Buckingham Palace, and the older royal palace of St. James's.

Visitors who restrict their sightseeing to the well-known tourist areas miss much of the best the city has to offer. Within a few minutes' walk of Buckingham Palace, for instance, lie St. James's and Mayfair, two neighboring quarters of elegant town houses built for the nobility during the 17th and early 18th centuries and now notable for the shopping opportunities they house. The same lesson applies to the City, where, tucked away in quiet corners, stand many of the churches Christopher Wren built to replace those destroyed during the Great Fire of 1666.

Other parts of London worth exploring include Covent Garden, a former fruit and flower market converted into a lively shopping and entertainment center where you can wander for hours enjoying the friendly bustle of the streets. Hyde Park and Kensington Gardens, by contrast, offer a great swath of green parkland across the city center, preserved by past kings and queens for their own hunting and relaxation. A walk across Hyde Park will bring you to the museum district of South Kensington, with three major national collections: the Natural History Museum, the Science Museum, and the Victoria & Albert Museum, which specializes in the fine and applied arts.

The south side of the River Thames has its treats as well. A short stroll across Waterloo Bridge brings you to the South Bank Arts Complex, which includes the Royal National Theatre, the Royal Festival Hall, the Hayward Gallery (with changing exhibitions of international art), and the National Film Theatre. Here also are the exciting reconstruction of Shakespeare's Globe theater and its sister museum, and the new home, at Bankside Power Station, of the Tate Gallery of Modern Art—and now called simply Tate Modern. The London Eye observation wheel gives the most stunning views—to the west are the Houses of Parliament and Big Ben; to the east the dome of St. Paul's looks smaller on London's changing modern architectural skyline. The Millennium Bridge leaps across the Thames like a so-called steel "blaze of light" joining Tate Modern to St. Paul's in the city. London, although not simple of layout, is a rewarding walking city, and this remains the best way to get to know its nooks and crannies. The infamous weather may not be on your side, but there's plenty of indoor entertainment to keep you amused if you forget the umbrella.

Westminster

Numbers in the margin correspond to points of interest on the London map.

Westminster is the royal backyard—the traditional center of the royal court and of government. Here, within 1 km (½ mi) or so of one another, are nearly all of London's most celebrated buildings, and there is a strong feeling of history all around you. Generations of kings and queens have lived here since the end of the 11th century—including the current monarch.

16 **Banqueting House.** On the right side of the grand processional avenue known as Whitehall—site of many important government offices—stands this famous monument of the English Renaissance period. Designed by Inigo Jones in 1625 for court entertainments, it is the only part of Whitehall Palace, the monarch's principal residence during the 16th and 17th centuries, that did not burn down in 1698. It has a magnificent ceiling by Rubens, and outside is an inscription that marks the window through which King Charles I stepped to his execution. ✉ *Whitehall, SW1,* ☎ *020/7930–4179,* WEB *www.hrp.org.uk.* 🎟 *£3.60, includes free audio guide.* ⏲ *Mon.–Sat. 10–5 (closed on short notice for banquets, so call first). Tube: Westminster, Embankment, Charing Cross.*

8 **Buckingham Palace.** Supreme among the symbols of London, indeed of Britain generally, and of the royal family, Buckingham Palace tops many must-see lists—although the building itself is no masterpiece and has housed the monarch only since Victoria moved here from Kensington Palace at her accession in 1837. Located at the end of the Mall, the palace is the London home of the queen and the administrative hub of the entire royal family. When the queen is in residence (normally on weekdays except in January, August, September, and part of June), the royal standard flies over the east front. Inside are dozens of ornate 19th-century-style state rooms used on formal occasions. The private apartments of Queen Elizabeth and Prince Philip are in the north wing. Parts of Buckingham Palace are open to the public during August and September; during the entire year, the former chapel, bombed during World War II and rebuilt in 1961, is the site of the **Queen's Gallery,** which shows treasures from the vast royal art collections. The ceremony of the **Changing of the Guard** takes place in front of the palace at 11:30 daily, April–July, and on alternate days during the rest of the year. Arrive early, as people are invariably stacked several deep along the railings, whatever the weather. ✉ *Buckingham Palace Rd., SW1,* ☎ *020/7839–1377; 020/7799–2331 24-hr information; 020/7321–2233 credit-card reservations (50p booking charge),* WEB *www.royal.gov.uk.* 🎟 *£11.* ⏲ *Early Aug.–early Oct. (confirm dates, which are subject to queen's mandate), daily 9:30–4:15. Tube: St. James's Park, Victoria.*

12 **Cabinet War Rooms.** It was from this small maze of 17 bomb-proof underground rooms—in back of the hulking Foreign Office—that Britain's World War II fortunes were directed. During air raids the Cabinet met here—the Cabinet Room is still arranged as if a meeting were about to convene. Among the rooms are the Prime Minister's Room, from which Winston Churchill made many of his inspiring wartime broadcasts, and the Transatlantic Telephone Room, from which he spoke directly to President Roosevelt in the White House. ✉ *Clive Steps, King Charles St., SW1,* ☎ *020/7930–6961,* WEB *www.iwm.org.uk.* 🎟 *£4.80.* ⏲ *Apr.–Sept., daily 9:30–5:15; Oct.–Mar., daily 10–5:15. Tube: Westminster.*

6 **Carlton House Terrace.** This Regency-era showpiece on the Mall was built in 1827–32 by John Nash in imposing white stucco and with massive Corinthian columns. It is home to the Institute of Contemporary

Arts. ✉ *The Mall, W1,* ☎ *020/7930–3647,* WEB *www.ica.org.uk.* ⏲ *Daily noon–9:30, later for some events. Tube: Charing Cross.*

17 **Horse Guards Parade.** The former tiltyard of Whitehall Palace is the site of the annual ceremony of Trooping the Colour, when the queen takes the salute in the great military parade that marks her official birthday on the second Saturday in June (her real one is on April 21). Demand for tickets is great, and tickets are available for the ceremony, as well as the queenless rehearsals on the preceding two Saturdays (for information, call ☎ 020/7414–2479). There is also a daily guard-changing ceremony outside the guard house, on Whitehall, at 11 AM (10 on Sunday)—one of London's best photo-ops. ✉ *Whitehall, opposite Downing St., SW1. Tube: Westminster.*

14 **Houses of Parliament.** The Houses of Parliament are among the city's most famous and photogenic sights. The Clock Tower keeps watch on Parliament Square, in which stand statues of everyone from Richard the Lionhearted to Abraham Lincoln, and, across the way, Westminster Abbey. Also known as the **Palace of Westminster,** this was the site of the monarch's main residence from the 11th century until 1512; the court then moved to the newly built Whitehall Palace. The only parts of the original building to have survived are the **Jewel Tower,** which was built in 1365 as a treasure-house for Edward III, and **Westminster Hall,** which has a fine hammer-beam roof. The rest of the structure was destroyed in a disastrous fire in 1834 and was rebuilt in the newly popular mock-medieval Gothic style. The architect, Augustus Pugin, designed the entire place, right down to the Gothic umbrella stands. This newer part of the palace contains the debating chambers and committee rooms of the two Houses of Parliament—the Commons (whose members are elected) and the Lords (whose members are appointed or inherit their seats). There are no tours of the palace, but the public is admitted to the Public Gallery of each House; expect to wait in line for several hours (the line for the Lords is generally much shorter than that for the Commons). The most famous features of the palace are its towers. At the south end is the 336-ft **Victoria Tower.** At the other end is **St. Stephen's Tower,** or the Clock Tower, better known, but inaccurately so, as **Big Ben;** that name properly belongs to the 13-ton bell in the tower on which the hours are struck. Big Ben himself was probably Sir Benjamin Hall, commissioner of works when the bell was installed in the 1850s. A light shines from the top of the tower during a night sitting of Parliament. Be sure to have your name placed in advance on the waiting list for the twice-weekly tours of the private residence of the Lord Chancellor within the Palace of Westminster. You can also apply in advance for the special "line of route" tour—open only to overseas visitors—by writing to the **Parliamentary Education Unit** (✉ House of Commons Information Office, House of Commons, London, SW1A 2TT) at least a month in advance of your visit. ✉ *St. Stephen's Entrance, St. Margaret St., SW1,* ☎ *020/7219–3000; 020/7219–4272 Commons information; 020/7219–3107 Lords information; 020/7219–2184 Lord Chancellor's Residence.* ⏲ *Commons Nov.–June, Mon.–Thurs. 2:30–10, Fri. 9:30–3 (although not every Fri.); Lords Nov.–June, Mon.–Thurs. 2:30–10; Lord Chancellor's Residence Tues. and Thurs. Closed Easter wk and 3 wks at Christmas. Tube: Westminster. Jewel Tower, Abingdon St.,* ☎ *020/7222–2219.* ⏲ *Apr.–Sept., daily 10–6; Oct., daily 10–5; Nov.–Mar., daily 10–4.* WEB *www.parliament.uk*

5 **The Mall.** The splendid and imperial **Admiralty Arch** guards the entrance to The Mall, the noted ceremonial way that leads alongside **St. James's Park** to Buckingham Palace. The Mall takes its name from a game called *palle maille,* a version of croquet that James I imported from France

and Charles II popularized during the late 1600s. The park was developed by successive monarchs, most recently by George IV in the 1820s, having originally been used for hunting by Henry VIII. Join office workers relaxing with a lunchtime sandwich, or stroll here on a summer's evening when the illuminated fountains play and Westminster Abbey and the Houses of Parliament are floodlit. Toward Buckingham Palace, along the Mall, you'll pass the foot of the imposing **Carlton House Terrace.** *The Mall, Cockspur St., Trafalgar Sq., SW1. Tube: Charing Cross.*

★ ❷ **National Gallery.** Generally ranked right after the Louvre, the National Gallery is one of the world's greatest museums. Occupying the long neoclassical building on the north side of Trafalgar Square, it contains works by virtually every famous artist and school from the 14th through the 19th centuries. Its galleries overflow with masterpieces, including Jan van Eyck's *Arnolfini Marriage,* Leonardo da Vinci's *Burlington Virgin and Child,* Velásquez's *The Toilet of Venus* (known as "The Rokeby Venus"), and Constable's *Hay Wain.* The collection is especially strong on Flemish and Dutch masters, Rubens and Rembrandt among them, and on Italian Renaissance works. The museum's Brasserie is an excellent spot for lunch. ✉ *Trafalgar Sq., WC2,* ☎ *020/7747–2885,* WEB *www.nationalgallery.org.uk.* ⏲ *Daily 10–6, Wed. until 9 (special exhibition in Sainsbury Wing, Wed. until 10); 1-hr free guided tour of whole gallery starts at Sainsbury Wing daily at 11:30 and 2:30; and 6.30 Wed. Tube: Charing Cross, Leicester Sq.*

❸ **National Portrait Gallery.** This fascinating collection contains portraits of well-known (and not-so-well-known) Britons, including monarchs, statesmen, and writers. It provides a separate research center for the study of British portraiture, a bookstore, a café, and a top-floor restaurant with viewing area across to the river. Don't miss the Victorian and early 20th-century galleries. ✉ *2 St. Martin's Pl., at foot of Charing Cross Rd., WC2,* ☎ *020/7312–2463 recorded information,* WEB *www.npg.org.uk.* ⏲ *Mon.–Wed., Sat.–Sun. 10–6, Thurs.–Fri. 10–9. Tube: Charing Cross, Leicester Sq.*

❾ **Queen's Gallery.** This former chapel at the south side of Buckingham Palace is due to re-open in February 2002, to coincide with the queen's Golden Jubilee, after a complete renovation, expansion, and technological update. A Standing Gallery displays a selection of paintings, and the Graphic Art Gallery exhibits drawings and watercolors, while the original main gallery shows changing exhibitions including fine furniture, porcelain and decorative arts. In the micro gallery you can view other works in Her Majesty's vast art collection, not on display but on screen. ✉ *Buckingham Palace Rd., SW1,* ☎ *020/7799–2331,* WEB *www.royal.gov.uk.* ⏲ *Opening hours and prices not available at press time. Tube: St. James's Park, Victoria.*

❿ **Royal Mews.** Unmissable children's entertainment, this museum is the home of Her Majesty's Coronation Coach. Some of the queen's horses are stabled here and the elaborately gilded state coaches are on view. ✉ *Buckingham Palace Rd.,* ☎ *020/7799–2331,* WEB *www.royal.gov.uk.* 🎫 *£4.60.* ⏲ *Aug. 2–Sept., Mon.–Thurs. 10:30–4:30; Oct.–Aug. 1, Mon.–Thurs. noon–4. Tube: St. James's Park, Victoria.*

❹ **St. Martin-in-the-Fields.** Soaring above Trafalgar Square, this landmark church may seem familiar to many Americans because James Gibbs's classical-temple-with-spire design became a pattern for churches in early Colonial America. Built in about 1730, the distinctive neoclassical church is the site for regular lunchtime music recitals (tickets for free lunchtime concerts and evening concerts are available from the Box Office in the crypt). The crypt is a hive of lively activity, with a café, bookshop, plus the **London Brass-Rubbing Centre,** where you can make your own souvenir knight, lady, or monarch from replica tomb brasses for about £5. ✉ *Trafalgar Sq., WC2,* ☎ *020/7930–0089; 020/7839–8362 credit-card bookings for evening concerts,* WEB *www.stmartin-in-the-fields.org.* ⏲ *Church daily 8–8; crypt Mon.–Sat. 10–8, Sun. noon–6. Tube: Charing Cross, Leicester Sq..*

11 **Tate Britain.** By the river to the north of Chelsea, on traffic-laden Millbank, the Tate—now renamed Tate Britain, after the opening of the new Tate Modern south of the river, is the most important collection of modern British art. "Modern" is slightly misleading, as the gallery's collection consists of British art from 1545 to the present, including works by Thomas Gainsborough, Sir Joshua Reynolds, and George Stubbs from the 18th century; and by John Constable, William Blake, and the Pre-Raphaelite painters from the 19th century (don't miss Sir John Everett Millais's unforgettable *Ophelia*). Also on display is one of the highlights of the Tate's collections, the incredible Turner Bequest, consisting of the personal collection of England's greatest romantic painter, J. M. W. Turner. ✉ *Millbank, SW1,* ☎ *020/7887–8000; 020/7887–8008 recorded information,* WEB *www.tate.org.uk.* ⏲ *Daily 10–5:50. Tube: Pimlico.*

13 **Ten Downing Street.** As you walk along Whitehall, past government offices, you'll note, on the north side of the street, the entrance to Downing Street, a row of unassuming 18th-century houses. The prime minister's official office is at No. 10, with a private apartment on the top floor (although Tony Blair and his family don't use this as their main address). The chancellor of the exchequer, the finance minister, occupies No. 11. The street is gated off from the main thoroughfare. Nearby, in the middle of Whitehall, is the **Cenotaph,** a stone national memorial to the dead of both world wars. At 11 AM on the Sunday closest to the 11th day of the 11th month, the queen and other dignitaries lay flowers in tribute here. ✉ *Whitehall, SW1. Tube: Westminster.*

1 **Trafalgar Square.** This is the center of London, by dint of a plaque on the corner of the Strand and Charing Cross Road from which distances on U.K. signposts are measured. It is the home of the **National Gallery** and of one of London's most distinctive landmarks, **Nelson's Column,** a tribute to one of England's favorite heroes, Admiral Lord Horatio Nelson, who routed the French at the Battle of Trafalgar in 1805. Constantly alive with Londoners and tourists alike, roaring traffic, and pigeons, it remains London's "living room"—great events, such as New Year's, royal weddings, elections, and sporting triumphs, will always see the crowds gathering in the city's most famous square. ✉ *Trafalgar Sq., SW1. Tube: Charing Cross.*

★ 15 **Westminster Abbey.** The most ancient and important of London's great churches, it is here that Britain's monarchs are crowned. Most of the abbey dates from the 13th and 14th centuries. The main nave is packed with atmosphere and memories, as it has witnessed many splendid coronation ceremonies, royal weddings, and funerals. It is also packed with crowds—so many, in fact, that there is an admission fee to the main nave (always free, of course, for participants in religious services). **Henry VII's Chapel,** an exquisite example of the heavily decorated late-Gothic style, was not built until the early 1600s, and the twin towers over the west entrance are an 18th-century addition. There is much to see inside, including the tomb of the Unknown Warrior, a nameless World War I soldier buried, in memory of the war's victims, in earth brought with his corpse from France; and the famous Poets' Corner, where England's great writers—Milton, Chaucer, Shakespeare, et al.—are memorialized and some are actually buried. Behind the high altar are the royal tombs, including those of Queen Elizabeth I; Mary, Queen of Scots; and Henry V. In the Chapel of Edward the Confessor stands the Coronation Chair.

It is all too easy to forget, swamped by the crowds trying to see the abbey's sights, that this is a place of worship. Early morning is a good moment to catch something of the building's atmosphere. Better still, take time to attend a service. Photography is not permitted. ✉ *Broad Sanctuary, SW1,* ☎ *020/7222–5152.* *£5; Undercroft, Pyx Chamber, Chapter House, and Treasury £2.50 (£1 if you bought ticket to abbey).* ⏲ *Mon.–Sat. 9–3:45 (last admission Sat. 1:45). Undercroft, Pyx Chamber treasury, and Chapter House, Apr.–Oct., daily 10:30–5:30; Nov.–Mar., daily 10:30–4. Abbey closed weekdays and Sun. to visitors during services.*

St. James's and Mayfair

These are two of London's most exclusive neighborhoods, where the homes are fashionable and the shopping is world class. You can start by walking west from Piccadilly Circus along Piccadilly, a busy street lined with some very English shops (including Hatchards, the booksellers; Swaine, Adeney Brigg, the equestrian outfitters; and Fortnum & Mason, the department store that supplies the queen's groceries).

22 **Apsley House.** Once known, quite simply, as No. 1, London, this was long celebrated as the best address in town. Built by Robert Adam in the 1770s, this was where the Duke of Wellington lived from the 1820s until his death in 1852. It has been kept as the Iron Duke liked it, his uniforms and weapons, his porcelain and plate, and his extensive art collection displayed in opulent 19th-century rooms. Unmissable, in every sense, is the gigantic Canova statue of a nude (but fig-leafed) Napoléon Bonaparte, Wellington's archenemy. ✉ *149 Piccadilly, SW1,* ☎ *020/7499–5676,* WEB *www.vam.ac.uk.* *£4.50; includes free sound guides.* ⏲ *Tues.–Sun. 11–4:30. Tube: Hyde Park Corner.*

39 **BBC Experience.** To celebrate its 75th anniversary, the BBC opened the doors of its own in-house museum in 1997. Included are an audiovisual show, an interactive section, and, of course, a massive gift shop. Admission is on a prebooked and timed system. ✉ *Broadcasting House, Portland Pl., W1,* ☎ *0870/603–0304,* WEB *www.bbc.co.uk.* *£7.50.* ⏲ *Daily 9:30–5:30. Tube: Oxford Circus.*

19 **Burlington Arcade.** This perfectly picturesque covered walkway dates from 1819. Here, shops sell cashmere sweaters, silk scarves, handmade chocolates, and leather-bound books. If not the choice shopping spot it once was, it still makes a great photo-op, particularly if you can snap the uniformed beadle (he ensures that no one runs, whistles, or sings here) on duty. ✉ *Off Piccadilly, W1. Tube: Piccadilly Circus.*

18 **Royal Academy of Arts.** On the north side of Piccadilly, the grand marble pile of **Burlington House** contains the offices of many learned societies and the headquarters of the Royal Academy. The RA, as it is generally known, stages major visiting art exhibitions. Once most famous for its Summer Exhibition (May–August)—a chaotic hodgepodge of works by living and mostly conservative British artists—the RA has now adopted an impressive schedule of temporary art exhibitions that ranks among the most prestigious and cutting-edge in the country. ✉ *Burlington House, Piccadilly, W1,* ☎ *020/7300–8000; 020/7300–5760 recorded information,* WEB *www.royalacademy.org.uk.* ⏲ *Sat.–Thurs. 10–6, Fri. 10–8:30. Tube: Piccadilly Circus, Green Park.*

7 **St. James's Palace.** This historic royal palace is the current residence of the Prince of Wales. Although the earliest parts of the lovely brick

building date from the 1530s, it had a relatively short career as the center of royal affairs—from the destruction of Whitehall Palace in 1698 until 1837, when Victoria became queen and moved the royal household down the road to Buckingham Palace. Today, the palace is closed to the public, but your viewfinder will love the picturesque exterior and regimental guard on duty. ✉ *Friary Court, Pall Mall, SW1. Tube: Green Park.*

20 **Wallace Collection.** A palatial town-house museum, the Wallace is important, exciting, undervisited—and free. As at the Frick Collection in New York, the setting here, Hertford House, is part of the show—built for the Duke of Manchester and now stuffed with armor, exquisite furniture, and great paintings, including Bouchers, Watteaus, Fragonard's *The Swing,* and Frans Hals's *Laughing Cavalier.* The modernized basement floor is used for educational activities, and has a Watercolour Gallery. The museum courtyard provides yet more exhibition space and an upscale restaurant. ✉ *Hertford House, Manchester Sq., W1,* ☏ *020/7935–0687,* WEB *www.the-wallace-collection.org.uk.* ⏲ *Mon.–Sat. 10–5, Sun. noon–5. Tube: Bond Street.*

Hyde Park, Kensington, and Beyond

When in need of elbow room, Londoners head for Hyde Park and Kensington Gardens. Viewed by natives as their own private backyards, they form an open swath across central London, and in and around them are some of London's most noted museums and monuments.

27 **Albert Memorial.** Magnificently restored in 1998 to its original gilded glory, this florid monument of the 19th century commemorates Queen Victoria's much-loved husband, Prince Albert, who died in 1861 at the age of 42. The monument, itself the epitome of high Victorian pomp and circumstance, commemorates the many socially uplifting projects of the prince, among them the Great Exhibition of 1851, whose catalog he is holding. The memorial is directly opposite the Royal Albert Hall. ✉ *Kensington Gore. Tube: Knightsbridge.*

26 **Cheyne Walk.** The most beautiful spot in Chelsea—one of London's most arty (and expensive) residential districts—this Thamesside street is adorned with Queen Anne houses and legendary addresses. Author George Eliot died at No. 4 in 1880; Pre-Raphaelite artist Dante Gabriel Rossetti lived at No. 16. Two other resident artists were James McNeill Whistler and J. M. W. Turner.

21 **Hyde Park.** Along with the smaller St. James's and Green parks to the east, Hyde Park started as Henry VIII's hunting grounds. Nowadays, it remains a tranquil oasis from urban London—-tranquil, that is, except for Sunday morning, when soapbox orators take over **Speakers' Corner,** near the northeast corner of the park (feel free to get up and holler if you fancy spreading your message to the masses). Not far away, along the south side of the park, is **Rotten Row,** which was Henry VIII's royal path to the hunt—*la route du roi*—hence the name. It's still used by the Household Cavalry, the queen's guard. You can see them leave on horseback, in full regalia, at around 10:30 or await their exhausted return at about noon.✉ *Bounded by the Ring, Bayswater Rd., Park La., and Knightsbridge,* ☏ *020/7298–2100,* WEB *www.royalparks.co.uk.* ⏲ *Daily 5–midnight. Tube: Hyde Park Corner, Lancaster Gate, Marble Arch, Knightsbridge.*

28 **Kensington Gardens.** More formal than neighboring Hyde Park, Kensington Gardens was first laid out as palace grounds and adjoins Kensington Palace. George Frampton's 1912 **Peter Pan,** a bronze of the boy who lived on an island in the Serpentine and never grew up, overlooks the Long Water. His creator, J. M. Barrie, lived at 100 Bayswater

Road, not 500 yards from here. At the **Round Pond,** you can feed the swans. Nearby is boating and swimming in the **Serpentine,** an S-shape lake. Refreshments can be had at the lakeside tearooms. The **Serpentine Gallery** (☎ 020/7402–6075) holds noteworthy exhibitions of modern art. ⊠ *Bounded by the Broad Walk, Bayswater Rd., the Ring, and Kensington Rd.,* WEB *www.royalparks.co.uk* ⊙ *Daily dawn–dusk. Tube: Lancaster Gate or Queensway.*

(29) **Kensington Palace.** This has been a royal home since the late 17th century. From the outside it looks less like a palace than a country house, which it was until William III bought it in 1689. Queen Victoria spent a less-than-happy childhood at Kensington Palace and Princess Diana a less-than-happy marriage. Called the "royal ghetto," the palace is home to many Windsors (they live in a distant section cordoned off from the public). Kensington Palace's state apartments have been restored to how they appeared in Princess Victoria's day. Drop in on the Orangery here for a very elegant cup of tea. ⊠ *The Broad Walk, Kensington Gardens, W8,* ☎ *020/7937–9561,* WEB *www.hrg.org.uk.* *£9.50, including admission to the Dress Collection.* ⊙ *Daily 10–5. Tube: High Street Kensington.*

(24) **Natural History Museum.** Housed in an ornate late-Victorian building with striking modern additions, this museum features displays on such topics as human biology and evolution. ⊠ *Cromwell Rd., SW7,* ☎ *020/7942–5000,* WEB *www.nhm.ac.uk.* ⊙ *Mon.–Sat. 10–5:50, Sun. 11–5:50. Tube: South Kensington.*

(30) **Portobello Road.** North of Kensington Gardens is the lively **Notting Hill** district, full of stylish restaurants and cafés where some of London's trend-setters gather. The best-known attraction in this area is Portobello Road, where a lively antiques and bric-a-brac market is held each Saturday (arrive at 6 AM for the best finds); the southern end is focused on antiques, the northern end on food, flowers, and secondhand clothes. The street is also full of regular antiques shops that are open most weekdays.

(23) **Science Museum.** The leading national collection of science and technology, this museum has extensive hands-on exhibits on outer space, astronomy, and hundreds of other subjects. The dramatic Wellcome Wing, a £45 million modern addition to the museum, is devoted to contemporary science, medicine, and technology. It also includes a 450-seat IMAX cinema. ⊠ *Exhibition Rd., SW7,* ☎ *020/7942–4000,* WEB *www.sciencemuseum.org.uk.* ⊙ *Daily 10–6. Tube: South Kensington.*

★ (25) **Victoria & Albert Museum.** The V&A, as it is commonly known, originated during the 19th century as a museum of the decorative arts and has extensive collections of costumes, paintings, jewelry, and crafts from every part of the globe. Don't miss the sculpture court, the vintage couture collections, and the great Raphael Room. The provocative architectural addition of *The Spiral* is scheduled to open in 2005, but for now visitors will have to content themselves with the impressive British Galleries chronicling the last 400 years of British history, design, and life. ⊠ *Cromwell Rd., SW7,* ☎ *020/7942–2000,* WEB *www.vam.ac.uk.* ⊙ *Daily 10–5:45, Wed. Late View Wed. 6:30–9:30, last Fri. of the month 6–10. Tube: South Kensington.*

Covent Garden

The Covent Garden district—which lies just to the east of Soho—has gone from a down-at-the-heels area to one of the busiest, most raffishly enjoyable parts of the city. Continental-style open-air cafés create a very un-English atmosphere, with vintage fashion boutiques, art galleries, and street buskers attracting crowds.

34 **Covent Garden.** You could easily spend several hours exploring the block of streets north of the Strand known as Covent Garden. The heart of the area is a former wholesale fruit and vegetable market—made famous as one of Eliza Doolittle's haunts in *My Fair Lady*—established in 1656. The **Piazza,** the Victorian Market Building, is now a vibrant shopping center, with numerous boutiques, crafts shops, and cafés. On the south side of the market building is the **Jubilee market,** with crafts and clothing stalls. The section is anchored by **St. Paul's Church** and the **Royal Opera House.** For interesting specialty shops, head north of the Market Building. Shops on **Long Acre** sell maps, art books and materials, and clothing; shops on **Neal Street** sell clothes, pottery, jewelry, tea, housewares, and goods from East Asia. ✉ *Bounded by the Strand, Charing Cross Rd., Long Acre, and Drury La., WC2. Tube: Charing Cross, Covent Garden, Leicester Sq.*

38 **Royal Opera House.** This is the fabled home of the Royal Ballet and Britain's finest opera company. The glass-and-steel Floral Hall is the most wonderful feature, and visitors can wander in during the day and enjoy the Piazza concourse and the Amphitheatre Bar, which gives a splendid panorama across the city, or listen to a free lunchtime chamber concert. ✉ *Bow St., WC2,* ☎ *020/7240–1200 or 020/7304–4000,* WEB *www.royaloperahouse.org. Tube: Covent Garden.*

35 **St. Paul's Church.** A landmark of the Covent Garden market area, this 1633 church, designed by Inigo Jones, is known as the Actors' Church. Inside are numerous memorials to theater people. Look for the open-air entertainers performing under the church's portico. ✉ *Bedford St., WC2. Tube: Covent Garden.*

37 **Somerset House.** A royal palace once stood on the site, but was replaced in the 18th century with a classic structure by William Chambers. For the first time in over one hundred years, it is open to visitors who can view the 18th-century chambers, including the Seamen's Waiting Hall, the Nelson Stair, and Navy Commissioners' Barge. Lighting up the vaults is London's latest museum of intricate works of silver, gold snuff boxes and Italian mosaics, **The Gilbert Collection. The Hermitage Rooms** also house objects with foreign origins; they are the new permanent home for some of the treasures from Russia's eponymous premier museum. The Courtauld Institute of Art occupies the north building of Somerset House. Here, London's finest Impressionist and Postimpressionist collection spans from Bonnard to Van Gogh (Manet's *Bar at the Folies-Bergère* is the star), with bonus post-Renaissance works. Arts events are held in the Italianate courtyard between the Courtauld and the rest of Somerset House. Cafés and a river terrace complete the clutch of cultural delights that visitors can reach directly by walkway from Waterloo Bridge. ✉ *The Strand, WC2* ☎ *020/7845–4600, 020/7240–4080 Gilbert Collection, 020/7845–4630 Hermitage,* WEB *www.somerset-house.org.uk.* ⏲ *Courtauld Mon.–Sat. 10–6, Sun. noon–6 (last admission 5:15).* 🎫 *Somerset House, free; Gilbert Collection £4 (combined ticket to Gilbert and Courtauld Institute of Art £7, free admission to both Mon. 10–2); Hermitage Rooms £6.* ⏲ *Mon.–Sat. 10–6, Sun. noon–6 (last admission 5:15).*

36 **Theatre Museum.** A comprehensive collection of material on the history of the English theater, this museum traces the history not merely of the classic drama but also of opera, music hall, pantomime, and musical comedy. A highlight is the re-creation of a dressing room filled with memorabilia of former stars. ✉ *Russell St., WC2,* ☎ *020/7836–7891,* WEB *www.theatremuseum.org.* 🎫 *£4.50.* ⏲ *Tues.–Sun. 10–6. Tube: Covent Garden.*

Bloomsbury

Bloomsbury is a semiresidential district to the north of Covent Garden that contains some spacious and elegant 17th- and 18th-century squares. It could be called the intellectual center of London, as both the British Museum and the University of London are here. The area also gave its name to the Bloomsbury Group, a clique of writers and painters who thrived here in the early 20th century.

33 **British Library.** Since it opened in 1759, the British Library had always been housed in the British Museum on Gordon Square—but space ran out long ago, necessitating this grand new edifice, a few blocks north of the British Museum. The library's treasures: the Magna Carta, Gutenberg Bible, Jane Austen's writings, Shakespeare's First Folio, and music manuscripts by Handel are on view to the general public in the John Ritblat Gallery. The library's Piazza hosts a series of free concerts. ✉ *96 Euston Rd., NW1,* ☎ *020/7412–7332,* WEB *www.bl.uk.* ⌚ *Mon. and Wed.–Fri. 9:30–6, Tues. 9:30–8, Sat. 9:30–5, Sun. 11–5. Tube: Euston, King's Cross.*

★ 40 **British Museum.** The focal point in this fabled collection of antiquities is the unmissable techno-classical Great Court, where beneath a vast glass roof lies the museum's inner courtyard. The space also gives room for new galleries, an I.T. center for viewing the collection on screen, cafés, and shops. But back to the stuff of the museum—the priceless collection of treasures, including Egyptian, Greek, and Roman antiquities; Renaissance jewelry; pottery; coins; glass; and drawings from virtually every European school since the 15th century. Some of the highlights are the **Elgin Marbles,** sculptures that formerly decorated the Parthenon in Athens; the **Rosetta Stone,** which helped archaeologists to interpret Egyptian hieroglyphs; and the Chase Manhattan Gallery of **North America,** which has one of the largest collections of native culture outside the American Continent. The revered gold and blue Reading Room is open to the public and has banks of computers. It's best to pick one section that particularly interests you—to try to see everything would be an overwhelming and exhausting task. ✉ *Great Russell St., WC1,* ☎ *020/7636–1555,* WEB *www.thebritishmuseum.ac.uk.* ⌚ *Mon.–Sat. 10–5, Sun. noon–6. Tube: Tottenham Court Rd., Holborn, Russell Sq..*

★ 41 **Sir John Soane's Museum.** On the border of London's legal district, this museum, stuffed with antique busts and myriad decorative delights, is an eccentric, smile-inducing 19th-century collection of art and artifacts in the former home of the architect of the Bank of England. ✉ *13 Lincoln's Inn Fields, WC2,* ☎ *020/7405–2107,* WEB *www.soane.org.* ⌚ *Tues.–Sat. 10–5, also 6–9 PM 1st Tues. of every month. Tube: Holborn.*

The City and South Bank

The City, the commercial center of London, was once the site of the great Roman city of Londinium. Since those days, the City has been rebuilt innumerable times, and today, ancient and modern jostle each other elbow to elbow. Several of London's most famous attractions are here, along with the adjacent area across the Thames commonly called the South Bank. Here, Shakespeare's Globe Theatre, the new Tate Museum of Modern Art, and the British Airways London Eye—the world's largest Ferris-type wheel—are drawing both natives and visitors in droves.

44 **Barbican Centre.** A vast arts center built by the City of London, the Barbican takes its name from the watchtower that stood here during the Middle Ages. It contains a concert hall (where the London Symphony Orchestra is based), two theaters, an art gallery, a cinema, and several restaurants. The theaters are the London home of the **Royal**

Shakespeare Company. ☎ *020/7638–8891; 020/7628–3351 RSC backstage tour,* WEB *www.barbican.org.uk.* ⏲ *Barbican Centre Mon.–Sat. 9 AM–11 PM, Sun. noon–11; gallery Mon.–Sat. 10–7:30, Sun. noon–7:30; conservatory weekends noon–5:30 when not in use for private function (call first). Tube: Moorgate, Barbican.*

43 **Museum of London.** At **London Wall,** so called because it follows the line of the wall that surrounded the Roman settlement, the Museum of London enables you to come to grips with a great deal of the city's history. Oliver Cromwell's death mask, Queen Victoria's crinolined gowns, Selfridge's Art Deco elevators, and the Lord Mayor's Coach are just some of the goodies here. ✉ *London Wall, EC2,* ☎ *020/7600–0807.* 🎫 *£5 (free 4:30–5:50; tickets are good for one year).* ⏲ *Mon.–Sat. 10–5:50, Sun. noon–5:50. Tube: Barbican.*

45 **St. Mary-le-Bow.** This church, a landmark of the Cheapside district, was rebuilt by Christopher Wren after the Great Fire; it was built again after being bombed during World War II. It is said that to be a true Cockney, you must be born within the sound of Bow bells. This was the marketplace of medieval London (the word *ceap* is Old English for "to barter"), as the street names hereabouts indicate: Milk Street, Ironmonger Lane, and so on. Despite rebuilding, many of the streets still run on the medieval pattern. ✉ *Cheapside, EC2.* ⏲ *Mon.–Thurs. 6:30–5:45, Fri. 6:30–4, weekends special services only. Tube: Mansion House.*

★ 42 **St. Paul's Cathedral.** London's symbolic heart, St. Paul's is Sir Christopher Wren's masterpiece. Its dome—the world's third largest—can be seen from many an angle in other parts of the city. The cathedral was completed in 1710 following the Great Fire. Wren was the architect who was also responsible for designing 50 City parish churches to replace those lost in that disaster. Fittingly, he is buried in the crypt under a simple Latin epitaph, composed by his son, which translates as: "Reader, if you seek his monument, look around you." The cathedral has been the site of many famous state occasions, including the funeral of Winston Churchill in 1965 and the ill-fated marriage of the Prince and Princess of Wales in 1981. In the ambulatory (the area behind the high altar) is the American Chapel, a memorial to the 28,000 U.S. servicemen and -women stationed in Britain during World War II who lost their lives while on active service. The greatest architectural glory of the cathedral is the dome. This consists of three distinct elements: an outer, timber-frame dome covered with lead; an interior dome built of brick and decorated with frescoes of the life of St. Paul by the 18th-century artist Sir James Thornhill; and, in between, a brick cone that supports and strengthens both. There is a good view of the church from the **Whispering Gallery,** high up in the inner dome. The gallery is so called because of its remarkable acoustics, whereby words spoken on one side can be clearly heard on the other, 107 ft away. Above this gallery are two others, both external, from which there are fine views over the City and beyond. ✉ *St. Paul's Churchyard, Paternoster Sq., Ludgate Hill, EC4,* ☎ *020/7236–4128,* WEB *www.stpauls.co.uk.* 🎫 *Cathedral, crypt, ambulatory, and gallery £5.* ⏲ *Cathedral Mon.–Sat. 8:30–4; ambulatory, crypt, and galleries Mon.–Sat. 9:30–4:15. Tube: St. Paul's.*

★ 47 **Shakespeare's Globe Theatre.** This spectacular theater is a replica of Shakespeare's open-roof Globe Playhouse (built in 1599, incinerated in 1613), where most of the playwright's great plays premiered. It stands 200 yards from the original, overlooking the Thames. It was built with the use of authentic Elizabethan materials, down to the first thatch roof in London since the Great Fire. Plays are presented in natural light (and sometimes rain), to 1,000 people on wooden benches in the "bays," plus 500 "groundlings," standing on a carpet of filbert shells and clinker, just as they did nearly four centuries ago. The main theater season runs from June through September, but throughout the year you can tour the Globe through admission to the **New Shakespeare's Globe Exhibition,** which opened in September 1999 and is the largest ever to focus on the Bard. In addition, productions are now scheduled throughout the year in a second, indoor theater, built to a design by the 17th-century architect Inigo Jones. Call for performance schedule. ✉ *New Globe Walk, Bankside (South Bank),* ☎ *020/7902–1500,* WEB *www.shakespeares-globe.org.* ⏲ *Daily 10–5.*

46 **Tate Modern.** Opposite St. Paul's Cathedral on the Thames in South Bank, this is the new branch of the museum formerly known as the Tate Gallery of Modern British Art, now boldly renamed the Tate Britain. The £100 million state-of-the-art transformation of the former Bankside Power Station by Swiss architects Herzog and de Meuron opened in May 2000 and firmly establishes this gallery as one of the great world-class modern art museums, continuing the picture—where the National Gallery finishes—from the 19th century on. ✉ *25 Summer St., SE1,* ☎ *020/7887–8000,* WEB *www.tate.org.uk.* ⏲ *Sun.–Thurs. 10–6, Fri.–Sat 10–10. Tube: Blackfriars or Southwark.*

★ 48 **Tower of London.** A guaranteed spine-chiller, this is one of London's most famous sights and one of its most crowded, too. Come as early in the day as possible and head for the Crown Jewels so you can see them before the crowds arrive. The tower served the monarchs of medieval England as both fortress and palace. Every British sovereign from William the Conqueror in the 11th century to Henry VIII in the 16th lived here, and it remains a royal palace, in name at least. The **White Tower** is the oldest and also the most conspicuous building in the entire complex. Inside, the **Royal Armouries,** England's national collection of arms and armor, occupy the ground floor. On the first floor, the **Chapel of St. John** is one of the few unaltered parts of the tower, and its simple, original architectural features makes it one of the most distinctive church interiors of its time in England.

The group of buildings which make up the old **Medieval Palace** is best entered by Water Lane, beside **Traitors' Gate**. There are three towers to explore: **St. Thomas's Tower,** which contains the monarch's rooms and lobby with waterside entrance (now known as Traitors' Gate); the Wakefield Tower; and Lanthorn Tower, both of which have more royal accommodations joined by a walkway along the battlements. In the furnished rooms of the **Wakefield Tower,** costumed actors describe daily life in the Medieval Palace and its evolution over the centuries. Henry VI is alleged to have been murdered in the Wakefield Tower in 1471, during England's medieval civil war, the Wars of the Roses. Among other buildings worth seeing is the **Bloody Tower.** The little princes in the tower—the uncrowned boy-king Edward V and his brother Richard, duke of York, supposedly murdered on the orders of the duke of Gloucester, later crowned Richard III—certainly lived in the Bloody Tower and may well have died here, too. It was a rare honor to be beheaded in private inside the tower on the Scaffold Site of Tower Green; most people were executed outside, on **Tower Hill,** where the crowds could get a much better view. The church of **St. Peter ad Vincula** has the burial places of the unfortunate queens and bishops who upset the Tudor monarchy and can be seen as part of a Yeoman's Tour.

The **Crown Jewels,** a breathtaking collection of regalia, precious stones, gold, and silver, used for the coronation of the present sovereign, are housed in the **Jewel House, Waterloo Barracks.** An exhibition illustrating their history precedes the gems themselves. The Royal Scepter contains the largest cut diamond in the world. The Imperial State Crown, made for the 1838 coronation of Queen Victoria, contains some 3,000 precious stones, largely diamonds and pearls. The jewels used to be housed in the **Martin Tower** (in less secure circumstances, when a daring Thomas Blood made an attempt to steal them in 1671), where an exhibit—Crowns and Diamonds—shows the making of the royal regalia and displays some state crowns made for earlier kings and queens. Look for the ravens—Hardey, George, Mumin, Cedric, Odin, Thor (who talks), and Gwylem—near the Wakefield Tower. Their presence at the Tower is traditional, and it is said that if they leave, the Tower will fall and England will lose her greatness. ✉ *Tower Hill, EC3N,* ☎ *020/7709–0765; 020/7680–9004 recorded information,* WEB *www.hrp.org.uk.* 🎫 *£11.* ⏲ *Mar.–Oct., Mon.–Sat. 9–5, Sun. 10–5; Nov.–Feb., Tues.–Sat. 9–4, Sun.–Mon. 10–4 (Tower closes 1 hr after last admission and all internal buildings close 30 mins after last admission, but to see all the attractions, allow at least 3 hrs). Yeoman Warder guides conduct tours daily from Middle Tower; no charge. Subject to weather and availability of guides, tours are conducted about every 30 mins until 3:30 in summer, 2:30 in winter.*

Hampstead

Hampstead is a quaint village within the city, where many famous poets and writers have lived. Today it is a fashionable residential area, with a main shopping street and some rows of elegant 18th-century houses. The heath is one of London's largest and most attractive open spaces.

31 **Abbey Road Studios.** Here, outside the legendary Abbey Road Studios (the facility is closed to the public), is the most famous zebra crossing in the world. Immortalized on the cover of the Beatles' *Abbey Road* album of 1969, this pedestrian crosswalk is a spot beloved to countless Beatlemaniacs and baby boomers, many of whom venture here to leave their signature on the white stucco fence that fronts the adjacent studio facility. Abbey Road is not in Hampstead but in adjacent St. John's Wood, an elegant residential suburb a 10-minute ride on the tube from central London. ✉ *3 Abbey Rd., NW8,* WEB *www.abbeyroad.co.uk. Tube: St. John's Wood.*

32 **Kenwood House.** On the north side of the heath is Kenwood House, built in the 17th century and remodeled by Robert Adam at the end of the 18th century. The house contains a collection of superb paintings by Rembrandt, Turner, Reynolds, Van Dyck, and Gainsborough—and *The Guitar Player,* probably the most beautiful Vermeer in England. Unfortunately, only one grand Adam interior remains. The house's lovely landscaped grounds provide the setting for symphony concerts in summer. ✉ *Hampstead La., NW3,* ☎ *020/8348–1286.* ⏲ *Easter–Aug., Sat.–Mon., Tues., and Thurs. 10–6, Wed. and Fri. 10:30–6; Dec.–Easter, Sat.–Mon., Tues., and Thurs. 10–4, Wed. and Fri. 10:30–5; Sept.–Nov. Sat.–Mon., Tues., and Thurs. 10–4, Wed. and Fri. 10:30–4. Tube: Golder's Green, then Bus 210.*

Greenwich

Home to a number of historical and maritime attractions, Greenwich—situated on the Thames some 8 km (5 mi) east of central London—is an ideal destination for a day out. You can get to Greenwich by Underground, by riverboat from Westminster and Tower Bridge piers, and by Thames Line's high-speed river buses.

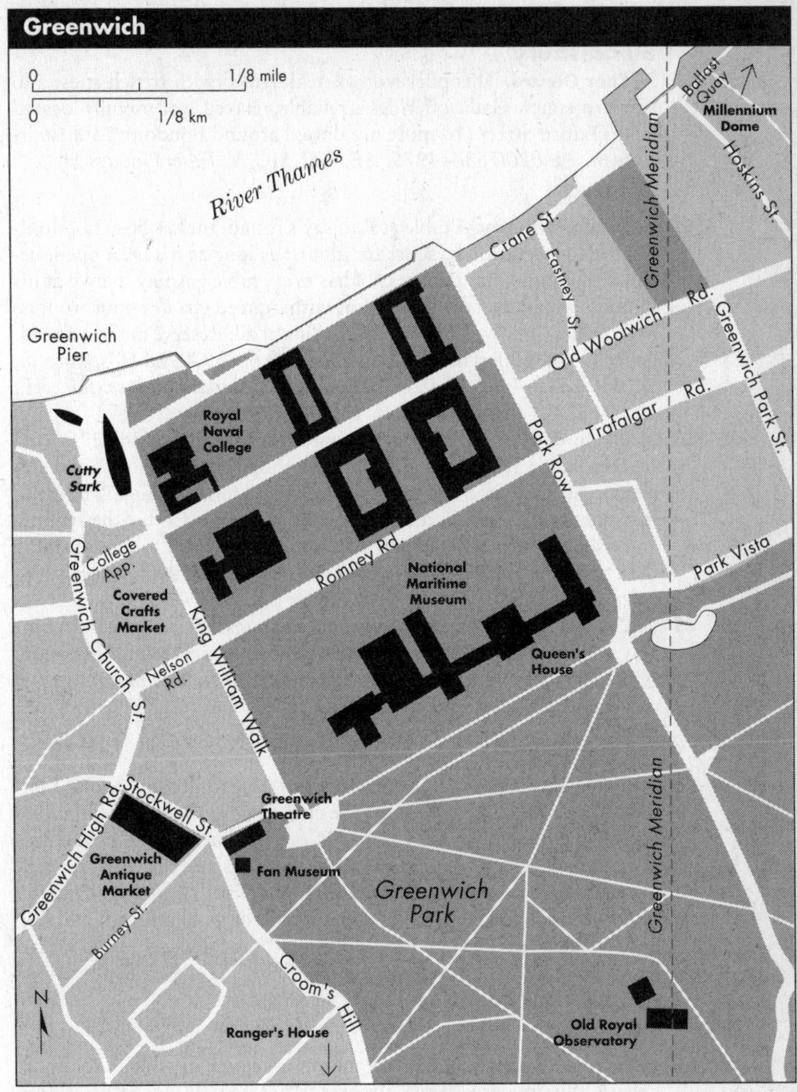

Cutty Sark. Now in dry dock is the glorious 19th-century clipper ship *Cutty Sark.* ✉ *King William Walk, SE10,* ☎ *020/8858–3445,* WEB *www.cuttysark.org.uk.* ⏲ *Daily 10–5. DLR: Cutty Sark.*

National Maritime Museum. A treasure house of paintings, maps, models, and, best of all, ships from all ages, this is a fascinating museum. Don't miss the ornate royal barges.✉ *Romney Rd., SE10,* ☎ *020/8858–4422.* ⏲ *Mon.–Sat. 10–6, Sun. noon–6. DLR: Greenwich.*

Old Royal Observatory. Stand astride both hemispheres in the courtyard of the Old Royal Observatory, where the prime meridian—0° longitude—is set. The observatory is at the top of the hill, behind the National Maritime Museum and Royal Naval College, in the attractive **Greenwich Park,** which was originally a royal hunting ground. Founded in 1675, the observatory has original telescopes and other astronomical instruments on display. ✉ *Greenwich Park, SE10,* ☎ *020/8858–4422,* WEB *www.rog.nmm.ac.uk.* ⏲ *Daily 10–5. DLR: Greenwich.*

Dining

Bloomsbury

$$–$$$ ✕ **Chez Gérard.** This purveyor of steak-*frîtes* (with french fries) and similarly simple Gallic offerings is reliable, relaxed, and usefully located near Oxford Street (10 more are dotted around London). ✉ *8 Charlotte St.,* ☎ *020/7636–4975. AE, DC, MC, V. Tube: Goodge St.*

Chelsea

$$$$ ★ ✕ **Gordon Ramsay.** A table at Ramsay's restaurant has been London's toughest reservation to score for almost as long as it's been open, because the soccer star turned chef has every table gasping in awe at his famous cappuccino of white beans with sautéed *girolles* (mushrooms) and truffles, followed by—well, anything at all. Reserve months ahead; go for lunch (£30) if money is an object. ✉ *68–69 Royal Hospital Rd.,* ☎ *020/7352–4441 or 020/7352–3334. Reservations essential. AE, DC, MC, V. Closed weekends. Tube: Sloane Sq.*

$$–$$$ ✕ **Bluebird.** Here's Sir Terence Conran's great "gastrodome"—food market, brasserie, fruit stand, butcher shop, kitchen shop, and café-restaurant, all housed in a snappy King's Road former garage. The menu has more than a nod in the Asia-Pacific direction. Go for the synergy and visual excitement—Conran's chefs share a tendency to promise more than they deliver. ✉ *350 King's Rd.,* ☎ *020/7559–1000. Reservations essential. AE, DC, MC, V. Tube: Sloane Sq.*

$$ ✕ **Chutney Mary.** London's stalwart Indian restaurant provides a fantasy version of the British Raj, with colonial cocktails and authentic re-creations of comforting, rich dishes, such as *dum ka murgh* (baked chicken with poppy seed, green chilies, and onion). ✉ *535 King's Rd.,* ☎ *020/7351–3113. Reservations essential. AE, DC, MC, V. Tube: Fulham Broadway.*

$$ ✕ **Zaika.** Zaika has zoomed in from nowhere to become one of London's finest Indian restaurants. The chef/patron, Vineet Bhatia, mixes age-old flavors with modern sensibilities and is pushing the boundaries of Indian cuisine. The restaurant is dark (muds and browns), refined, and subtle. You can't top the signature starter of *dhungar machli tikka*—tandoor home-smoked salmon with drips of mustard and dill. Sign off with cheeky chocolate samosas—"chocomosas"—and Indian ice cream. ✉ *257–259 Fulham Rd.,* ☎ *020/7351–7823. Reservations essential. AE, MC, V. Tube: South Kensington.*

The City

$$ ✕ **St. John.** Resembling a stark monks' refectory crossed with an art gallery, this modern British innovator has equally uncompromising menus. Some loathe bone marrow and parsley salad, huge servings of braised pheasant with "black cabbage," or organ meats any which way, with English puddings and Malmsey wine to follow, but newspaper journalists and swank architects really love it. ✉ *26 St. John St.,* ☎ *020/7251–0848. Reservations essential. AE, DC, MC, V. Closed Sun. Tube: Farringdon.*

Covent Garden

$$$ ✕ **Asia de Cuba.** One of the trendiest restaurants, in *the* trendy hotel, in the trendiest city in the world, allegedly. Ian Schrager's Philippe Starck–designed hotel brings Cool Britannia to its apogee. AdeC, the lead restaurant at St. Martins Lane Hotel, feels like a dreamscape. The food is fusion, and you're supposed to share. The Thai beef salad with Asian greens and roasted coconut is delicious, as is the lobster Mai Tai with rum and red curry. Schrager is right: hotels (and their restaurants) are the new disco. ✉ *St. Martins Lane Hotel, 45 St. Martin's La.,* ☎ *020/7300–5588. AE, DC, MC, V. Tube: Leicester Sq.*

$$$ ★ ✕ **Rules.** This is probably the city's most beautiful restaurant—daffodil-yellow walls, Victorian oil paintings, and hundreds of framed engravings make up the history-rich setting—and certainly one of the oldest (it has been here since 1798). Rules is traditional from soup to nuts or, rather, from venison and Dover sole to trifle and Stilton. There's the odd nod to newer cuisines, but the clientele of expense accounters and tourists who want to feast where Dickens and Lillie Langtry once did remains. ✉ *35 Maiden La.,* ☎ *020/7836–5314. AE, DC, MC, V. Tube: Covent Garden.*

$$–$$$ ★ ✕ **The Ivy.** The epitome of style without pretentiousness, this restaurant beguiles everybody, including media, literary, and theatrical movers and shakers. The menu's got it all—fish-and-chips, sausage-and-mash, squid-ink risotto, sticky toffee pudding—and all are good. ✉ *1 West St.,* ☎ *020/7836–4751. Reservations essential. AE, DC, MC, V. Tube: Covent Garden.*

$–$$ ★ ✕ **Joe Allen.** Long hours (thespians flock here after the curtains fall in Theatreland) and a welcoming, brick-walled interior mean New York Joe's London branch is still swinging after more than two decades. The Modern American menu helps, with barbecued ribs with black-eyed peas, London's only available corn muffins, and roast monkfish with sun-dried-tomato salsa usually on tap. ✉ *13 Exeter St.,* ☎ *020/7836–0651. Reservations essential. AE, MC, V. Tube: Covent Garden.*

$ ✕ **busabe eathai.** You can't do better than this in Soho for £11. It's designed as a superior Thai canteen: diners sit at communal tables, but somehow it's still seductive. All around are deep bronzes, rattans, wooden benches, hardwood tables, low lights and watercolor paper lampshades. Good things include stir-fry chicken butternut squash, green chicken curry with pea aubergine, and seafood vermicelli. ✉ *106–110 Wardour St.,* ☎ *020/7255–8686. Reservations not accepted. AE, MC, V. Tube: Leicester Sq*

Kensington

$$–$$$ ★ ✕ **Bibendum.** Upstairs in the renovated 1911 Michelin Building, this Art Deco dining extravaganza continues to entice with a menu as Gallic and gorgeous as ever. From the scallops in citrus sauce to the herring in sour cream, all the dishes are unpretentious but admirably done. The separate Oyster Bar, downstairs, is another way to go. ✉ *81 Fulham Rd.,* ☎ *020/7581–5817. Reservations essential. AE, DC, MC, V. Tube: South Kensington.*

$$–$$$ ★ ✕ **La Poule au Pot.** One of London's most romantic restaurants, La Poule au Pot is superb for proposals (or assignations). Gallic and rustic, this is a corner of France in darkest Belgravia. The "Chelsea Set" love it; Americans do, too. It is candlelit at night—you could be in a rambling French country house. The country cooking is good (not spectacular). The *poule au pot* (stewed chicken) with uncut vegetables is strong and hearty. The service comes with *bonhomie.* ✉ *231 Ebury St.,* ☎ *020/7730–7763. Reservations essential. AE, DC, MC, V. Tube: Sloane Sq.*

Knightsbridge

$$$$ ★ ✕ **La Tante Claire.** One of London's best restaurants has successfully upped its pots and pans from Chelsea and moved to the Berkeley Hotel. Chef Pierre Koffmann still holds the reins over the kitchen, so you can expect his haute-cuisine fireworks, such as his signature dish of pigs' feet stuffed with mousse of white meat with sweetbreads and wild mushrooms. The set lunch menu (£28) is a genuine bargain. Lunch reservations must be made three or four days in advance, dinner reservations three to four weeks in advance. ✉ *Berkeley Hotel, Wilton Pl.,* ☎ *020/7823–2003. Reservations essential. Jacket and tie. AE, DC, MC, V. Closed Sun. No lunch Sat. Tube: Knightsbridge.*

$$$$ ★ ✕ **Zafferano.** Princess Margaret, Eric Clapton, Joan Collins (she asked that the lights be turned down), and any number of stylish folk have flocked to this Belgravia place, London's best exponent of *cucina nuova*. The fireworks are in the kitchen, not in the brick-wall-and-saffron-hue decor: pheasant with rosemary and black truffle, venison medallions with mash and roast cod, lentils and parsley sauce. The desserts are also *delizioso,* especially the Sardinian pecorino pastries served with undersweetened vanilla ice cream. The menus are prix fixe. Be sure to book early. ✉ *15 Lowndes St.,* ☎ *020/7235–5800. Reservations essential. AE, DC, MC, V. Tube: Knightsbridge.*

$$$ ✕ **Isola.** Isola guns to be the coolest restaurant in London, so don't be surprised to see Joseph Fiennes mooching in a corner. It is grown-up osteria fare cooked by a Frenchman, Bruno Loubet. Upstairs is banquette-and-booth power dining; downstairs is more glam—diners sit at leather "compromise sofas" amid chrome, mirrors, and molecular lighting. Head for the *zuppa di fagiano e farro* (pheasant soup with cabbage and farro) and the *faraona al forno* (wood-roasted guinea fowl with liver and mascarpone). ✉ *145 Knightbridge,* ☎ *020/7838–1044. Reservations essential. AE, DC, MC, V. Tube: Knightsbridge.*

$–$$ ✕ **The Enterprise.** One of the new luxury breed of gastro-pubs, this is perhaps the chicest of the lot—near Harrods and Brompton Cross, it's filled with decorative types. The menu isn't overly pretty—seared tuna and char-grilled asparagus, timbale of aubergine, salmon with artichoke hearts—but the ambience certainly is. ✉ *35 Walton St.,* ☎ *020/7584–3148. AE, MC, V. Tube: South Kensington.*

Mayfair

$$$$ ★ ✕ **Oak Room.** Marco Pierre White used to enjoy Jagger-like fame from his TV appearances and gossip column reports of his eruptions of fury. Sadly, things are duller, now that he has hung up his pans for good and concentrates on expanding his empire. However, his charges are superbly trained here at his most spectacular setting yet—all Belle Epoque soaring ceilings and gilded bits, and palms and paintings. Menus are prix fixe. ✉ *Le Meridien, 21 Piccadilly,* ☎ *020/7437–0202. Reservations essential. AE, DC, MC, V. Tube: Piccadilly Circus.*

$$$–$$$$ ✕ **Nobu.** Nobuyaki Matsuhisa already has New York, Tokyo, Malabu, and Los Angeles, and now he's taken London, with the same formula of new-style sashimi with a Peruvian influence (such as salmon, ever so slightly seared in sesame-seed oil), plus the famous *omakase* (chef's choice) meals. Nobu is in the Metropolitan, one of London's hippest hotels, with staff, attitude, clientele, and prices to match. Ubon (backwards for Nobu) has opened in Canary Wharf. ✉ *Metropolitan hotel, 19 Old Park La.,* ☎ *020/7447–4747. Reservations essential. AE, DC, MC, V. No lunch weekends. Tube: Hyde Park.*

$$ ✕ **Momo.** Momo is one of the hottest tickets in town. Algerian-born Mourad Mazouz—Momo to his friends—has stormed beau London with his casbah-like, Moroccan-inspired North African restaurant. Going Momo is a real experience. The seats are low and placed close together, and there's often live music. Downstairs is the souk-like members-only Kemia Bar, and next door is Mô—a Moroccan tearoom, open to all. The lamb merguez is recommended. ✉ *25 Heddon St.,* ☎ *020/7434–4040. Reservations essential. AE, DC, MC, V. Tube: Piccadilly Circus.*

Notting Hill

$$–$$$ ✕ **The Cow.** Tucked away in the backwaters of trendy Portobello-land, this is the nicest of a trio of foodie pubs that feed the neighborhood arty hipsters and media stars. The Cow is the child of Tom Conran, son of Sir Terence (who appears to own half of London's restaurants). It pretends to be a pub in County Derry, serving oysters, crab salad, and other

seafood with the beer and heartier food in the cozy restaurant upstairs. ✉ *89 Westbourne Park Rd.,* ☎ *020/7221–5400. Reservations essential (restaurant). AE, MC, V. Tube: Westbourne Park.*

$$–$$$ ✕ **Kensington Place.** Trendy and loud, this ever-popular place features enormous plate-glass windows through which to be seen and plenty of fashionable food—grilled foie gras with sweet-corn pancake and baked tamarillo with vanilla ice cream are perennials—but it's the fun buzz that draws the crowds. ✉ *201 Kensington Church St.,* ☎ *020/7727–3184. DC, MC, V. Tube: Notting Hill Gate.*

$$ ★ ✕ **192.** A noisy wine bar/restaurant just off Portobello Road, this is as much a social hangout for the local media mafia as a restaurant, especially on weekends, when you'll feel like you've gate-crashed a party—if you manage to get a table, that is. The appetizer list is best—many people order two of these instead of an entrée. Try the pastas, the seasonal salad (perhaps romanesco, broccoli, anchovy, and gremolata), the fish (cod, clams, chorizo, and saffron broth), or whatever sounds unusual. ✉ *192 Kensington Park Rd.,* ☎ *020/7229–0482. Reservations essential. AE, DC, MC, V. Tube: Notting Hill Gate.*

$ ✕ **Tootsies.** A useful burger joint characterized by loudish rock and vintage advertisements on the walls, Tootsies serves some of London's better burgers, as well as chili, chicken, BLTs, taco salad, apple pie, fudge cake, and ice cream. There are seven other branches. ✉ *120 Holland Park Ave.,* ☎ *020/7229–8567. Reservations not accepted. AE, MC, V. Tube: Holland Park.*

St. James's

$$–$$$ ★ ✕ **Le Caprice.** Fabulously dark and glamorous, with black walls and stark white tablecloths, Le Caprice is a perennial that does nothing wrong, from its efficient, nonpartisan (famous folk eat here often) service to its Pan-European menu (salmon fish cake with sorrel sauce; confit of goose with prunes). ✉ *Arlington House, Arlington St.,* ☎ *020/7629–2239. Reservations essential. AE, DC, MC, V. Tube: Green Park.*

Soho

$$$–$$$$ ✕ **Spoon +.** This is London's current top groovy destination. Set in Ian Schrager's Sanderson hotel and designed in that Salvador Dali way by Philippe Starck, the Frenchman Alain Ducasse's first London foray has become the place to see and be seen. The menu is a complicated DIY system where the diner has to pick 'n' mix the ingredients. Ask for help, or go for the chef-decides "Sexy Spoon" option (£95 a head, with wine.) The adjacent 80-ft Long Bar is definitely the London bar to be. ✉ *Sanderson Hotel, 50 Berners St.,* ☎ *020/7300–1444. Reservations essential. AE, DC, MC, V. Tube: Oxford Circus.*

$$–$$$ ✕ **Titanic.** Marco Pierre White, the noted chef who opened this—the splashiest in the tide of trend-driven dining spots—claims it was not inspired by the blockbuster film. But like the movie, this place has pulled in the crowds, plus a clientele of the young, loud, and fashionable. Decor is Art Deco ocean liner; dinner is fun and casual, ranging from fish-and-chips to squid-ink risotto to sticky toffee pudding and prices are lower than you'd expect for this corner of town. ✉ *81 Brewer St.,* ☎ *020/7437–1912. Reservations essential. AE, DC, MC, V. Tube: Piccadilly Circus.*

South Bank

$$–$$$ ★ ✕ **OXO Tower Brasserie and Restaurant.** London finally has a room with a view, and *such* a view. On the eighth floor of the beautifully revived OXO Tower Wharf building, near the South Bank Centre, this elegant space has Euro food with this year's trendy ingredients (acorn-fed black pig charcuterie with tomato and pear chutney is one example). The ceiling slats turn and change from white to midnight blue,

but who notices, with the London Eye and St. Paul's dazzling you across the water? ✉ *Barge House St., Southbank,* ☎ *020/7803–3888. AE, DC, MC, V. Tube: Waterloo.*

Lodging

Note that although British hotels have traditionally included breakfast in their nightly tariff, many of London's most expensive establishments charge extra for breakfast.

Bayswater

$$ ★ **Commodore.** This peaceful hotel of three converted Victorian town houses has some amazing (especially for the price) rooms—as superior to the regular ones (which usually go to package tour groups) as Harrods is to Kmart. Twenty are miniduplexes, with sleeping gallery. One (No. 11) is a real duplex, entered through a secret mirrored door, with a thick-carpeted, *very* quiet bedroom upstairs and its toilet below. ✉ *50 Lancaster Gate, W2 3NA,* ☎ *020/7402–5291,* FAX *020/7262–1088,* WEB *www.commodore-hotel.com. 90 rooms. AE, MC, V. Tube: Lancaster Gate.*

$$ **London Elizabeth.** Steps from Hyde Park and the Lancaster Gate tube, this family-owned gem has one of the prettiest hotel facades in London. The charm continues inside—foyer and lounge are crammed with coffee tables and chintz drapery, lace antimacassars, and little chandeliers. The Anglo-Irish staff is friendly and helpful. ✉ *Lancaster Terr., W2 3PF,* ☎ *020/7402–6641,* FAX *020/7224–8900,* WEB *www.londonelizabethhotel.co.uk. 55 rooms. Restaurant. AE, DC, MC, V. Tube: Lancaster Gate.*

$ **Columbia.** The public rooms in these five joined Victorians are as big as museum halls, painted in icy hues of powder blue and buttermilk, or paneled in dark wood. At one end of the day they contain the hippest band in town drinking pints; at the other, there are sightseers sipping coffee. Rooms are clean, high-ceilinged, and sometimes very large—it's just a shame that teak veneer and avocado bathroom suites haven't made it back into the style bible yet. ✉ *95–99 Lancaster Gate, W2 3NS,* ☎ *020/7402–0021,* FAX *020/7706–4691,* WEB *www.columbiahotel.co.uk. 103 rooms. Restaurant. AE, MC, V. Tube: Lancaster Gate.*

Bloomsbury

$ **Morgan.** This family-run hotel in an 18th-century terrace house has rooms that are small but comfortably furnished and look friendly and cheerful. The tiny paneled breakfast room is straight out of a dollhouse. The back rooms overlook the British Museum. ✉ *24 Bloomsbury St., WC1B 3QJ,* ☎ *020/7636–3735,* FAX *020/7636–3045. 15 rooms with shower, 5 apartments. MC, V. Tube: Russell Sq.*

$ **Ridgemount.** The kindly owners, Mr. and Mrs. Rees, make you feel at home in this tiny hotel by the British Museum. There's a homey, cluttered feel in the public areas, and some bedrooms overlook a leafy garden. ✉ *65 Gower St., WC1E 6HJ,* ☎ *020/7636–1141. 34 rooms, 9 with bath. MC, V. Tube: Goodge St.*

Chelsea, Kensington, and Holland Park

$$$$ ★ **Blakes.** Patronized by musicians and film stars, this hotel is one of the most exotic in town. Its Victorian exterior contrasts with the 1980s ultrachic interior, an arty mix of Biedermeier and bamboo, four-poster beds, and chinoiserie, all dramatically lit in film noir style. The bedrooms have individual designs ranging from swaths of black moiré silk to blood-red and lily-white in the 007 suite. ✉ *33 Roland Gardens, SW7 3PF,* ☎ *020/7370–6701,* FAX *020/7373–0442. 52 rooms. Restaurant. AE, DC, MC, V. Tube: South Kensington.*

$$$$ ★ **Halcyon.** Discretion and decadent decor make this expensive, enormous, wedding-cake Edwardian desperately desirable. The Blue Room has moons and stars, the Egyptian Suite is canopied like a bedouin tent, and on and on. All guest rooms are different but large, with the high ceilings and big windows of the Holland Park vernacular. ✉ *81 Holland Park, W11 3RZ,* ☎ *020/7727–7288,* FAX *020/7229–8516,* WEB *www.halcyon-hotel.co.uk. 42 rooms. Restaurant. AE, DC, MC, V. Tube: Holland Park.*

$$$ ★ **The Gore.** Every wall of every room in this friendly and quiet hotel near the Albert Hall is smothered in prints and etchings, and antiques pepper the rooms. Some are spectacular follies—such as Tudor-style Room 101, with its minstrel gallery and four-poster. The crowd here is elegant and arty. ✉ *189 Queen's Gate, SW7 5EX,* ☎ *020/7584–6601,* FAX *020/7589–8127,* WEB *www.gorehotel.com. 54 rooms. Restaurant. AE, DC, MC, V. Tube: Gloucester Rd..*

$$$ **Portobello.** A faithful core of chic visitors returns again and again to this eccentric hotel in a Victorian terrace near the Portobello Road antiques market. Some rooms are tiny, but the ambience of '60s swinging London, the ecclesiastical antiques, and the peaceful vista of the gardens in back make up for it. ✉ *22 Stanley Gardens, W11 2NG,* ☎ *020/7727–2777,* FAX *020/7792–9641. 22 rooms. Restaurant. AE, DC, MC, V. Closed 10 days at Christmas. Tube: Notting Hill.*

$ **Abbey House.** Standards are high and the rooms unusually spacious in this hotel in a fine residential block near Kensington Palace and Gardens. ✉ *11 Vicarage Gate, W8,* ☎ *020/7727–2594. 16 rooms with shared bath. No credit cards. Tube: High Street Kensington.*

$ **The Vicarage.** This has long been a favorite for the budget-minded. Family-owned, set on a leaf-shaded street just off Kensington Church Street, the Vicarage is set in a large, white Victorian house. Bedrooms are traditional and comfortable, with solid English furniture. Definitely a charmer—but it is beginning to fray around the edges. ✉ *10 Vicarage Gate, W8 4AG,* ☎ *020/7229–4030,* WEB *www.londonvicaragehotel.com. 19 rooms. No credit cards. Tube: High Street Kensington.*

Knightsbridge, Belgravia, and Victoria

$$$$ **The Lanesborough.** Brocades and Regency stripes, moiré silks and fleurs-de-lis, antiques, oils, and reproductions in gilded splendor—everything undulates with richness in this upscale conversion of the old St. George's Hospital at Hyde Park Corner. To register you just sign the book, then retire to your room to find a personal butler, business cards with your in-room fax and phone numbers, VCR and CD player, umbrella, robe, huge flacons of unguents for bath time, and a drinks tray. ✉ *1 Lanesborough Pl., SW1X 7TA,* ☎ *020/7259–5599,* FAX *020/7259–5606,* WEB *www.lanesborough.com. 95 rooms. 2 restaurants. AE, DC, MC, V. Tube: Hyde Park Corner.*

$$$$ **The Rubens.** The Rubens hotel claims to treat its guests like royalty—after all, you're only a stone's throw from the real thing, with Buckingham Palace just across the road. And if this is how Her Majesty lives, then we've all got reason to be jealous. With well-appointed rooms and a location that could not be more truly central, this elegant hotel provides the sort of deep comfort needed to soothe away a hard day's sightseeing. ✉ *39 Buckingham Palace Rd., SW1W 0PS,* ☎ *020/7834–6600,* FAX *020/7233–6037,* WEB *www.redcarnationhotels.com. 180 rooms. Restaurant. AE, DC, MC, V. Tube: Victoria.*

$$$–$$$$ **Basil Street.** Family-run for some 80 years, this is a gracious Edwardian hotel on a quiet street. The rooms are filled with antiques, as are the various lounges, hushed like libraries with polished wooden floors and Oriental rugs. It sounds swanky, but Basil Street is more like home. ✉ *Basil St., SW3 1AH,* ☎ *020/7581–3311,* FAX *020/7581–3693,* WEB

www.thebasil.com. 80 rooms. Restaurant. AE, DC, MC, V. Tube: Knightsbridge.

$$$–$$$$ ★ **The Pelham.** Magnificent 18th-century pine paneling in the drawing room, glazed chintz and antique lace, four-posters in some rooms, fireplaces in others—all make this hotel feel more like an elegant home. It's near the big museums, and 24-hour room service and business services are available. ✉ *15 Cromwell Pl., SW7 2LA,* ☎ *020/7589–8288,* FAX *020/7584–8444,* WEB *www.firmdale.com. 50 rooms. Restaurant. AE, MC, V. Tube: South Kensington.*

$ **London County Hall Travel Inn Capital.** Don't get too excited—this neighbor of the luxurious new Marriott in the County Hall complex lacks the fabled river view (it's at the back of the grand former seat of local government, on the south side of the Thames). Still, you get an incredible value, with the standard facilities of the cookie-cutter rooms of this chain: TV, tea/coffeemaker, en suite bath-shower, and foldout beds that let you accommodate two children at no extra charge. You're looking at £50 a night for a family of four, in the shadow of Big Ben. *That's* a bargain. ✉ *Belvedere Rd., SE1 7PB,* ☎ *020/7902–1600,* FAX *020/7902–1619,* WEB *www.travelinn.co.uk. 312 rooms. Restaurant. AE, MC, V. Tube: Westminster.*

West End

$$$$ **Brown's.** Close to Bond Street, Brown's is like a country house in the middle of town, with wood paneling, grandfather clocks, and large fireplaces. Founded in 1837 by Lord Byron's "gentleman's gentleman," James Brown, it has attracted Anglophilic Americans ever since. Both Theodore and Franklin Delano Roosevelt stayed here. ✉ *34 Albemarle St., W1X 4BT,* ☎ *020/7493–6020,* FAX *020/7493–9381,* WEB *www.brownshotel.com. 118 rooms. Restaurant. AE, DC, MC, V. Tube: Green Park.*

$$$$ ★ **Claridge's.** This hotel has one of the world's classiest guest lists. The liveried staff is friendly, and the rooms are luxurious. The hotel was founded in 1812, but the present decor is either 1930s Art Deco or country-house style. Have a drink or afternoon tea in the Foyer and hear the Hungarian mini-orchestra. The rooms are spacious, the sweeping staircase grand. The hotel includes a fitness center and meeting rooms. Pause for breath. It's worth a visit if you are the sort that hankers after personal butler service, and you don't mind paying for it. ✉ *Brook St., W1A 2JQ,* ☎ *020/7629–8860 or 800/223–6800,* FAX *020/7499–2210,* WEB *www.savoy-group.co.uk. 200 rooms. Restaurant. AE, DC, MC, V. Tube: Bond St..*

$$$$ ★ **Covent Garden Hotel.** Clearly London's most relentlessly chic, extrastylish hotel, this former 1880s-vintage hospital is in the midst of the artsy Covent Garden district and is now the London home-away-from-home for a mélange of off-duty celebrities, actors, and style mavens. Theatrically baronial, the public rooms will keep even the most picky atmosphere-hunter happy. ✉ *10 Monmouth St., WC2H 9HB,* ☎ *020/7806–1000,* FAX *020/7806–1100,* WEB *www.firmdale.com. 46 rooms, 4 suites. Restaurant. AE, MC, V. Tube: Covent Garden.*

$$$$ **Dukes.** This small Edwardian hotel in a cul-de-sac in St. James's is perennially popular, an oasis of peace and elegant comfort in the heart of London. The top-floor suites are real finds for their views, antiques, and homey comfort. ✉ *35 St. James's Pl., SW1A 1NY,* ☎ *020/7491–4840,* FAX *020/7493–1264,* WEB *www.dukeshotel.co.uk. 80 rooms. Restaurant. AE, DC, MC, V. Tube: Green Park.*

$$$$ ★ **Savoy.** This grand, historic, late-Victorian hotel has been the byword for luxury for just over a century. Hemingway loved its American Bar, and Elizabeth Taylor spent her first honeymoon here. Spacious bedrooms have antiques and cream plasterwork, and the best ones over-

look the Thames. More than a hint of dazzling 1920s style remains. ✉ *Strand, WC2R 0EU,* ☎ *020/7836–4343,* FAX *020/7240–6040,* WEB *www.savoy-group.co.uk. 224 rooms. 3 restaurants, indoor pool. AE, DC, MC, V. Tube: Aldwych.*

$$$ **Hazlitt's.** Still Soho's only hotel, this, the last home of William Hazlitt, the essayist (1778–1830), is crammed with prints on every wall, Victorian claw-foot baths, assorted antiques, plants, and bits of art. There's no elevator, the sitting room is minuscule, floors can be creaky and bedrooms tiny, but Hazlitt's legion of devotees doesn't mind. And who needs room service when you stay on Restaurant Row? ✉ *6 Frith St., W1V 5TZ,* ☎ *020/7434–1771,* FAX *020/7439–1524,* WEB *www.gorehotel.com. 23 rooms. AE, DC, MC, V. Tube: Piccadilly.*

$$ **Bryanston Court.** Three 18th-century houses have been converted into a traditional English family-run hotel with open fires and comfortable armchairs. The bedrooms are contemporary. ✉ *56–60 Great Cumberland Pl., W1H 7FD,* ☎ *020/7262–3141,* FAX *020/7262–7248,* WEB *www.bryanstonhotel.com. 56 rooms. AE, DC, MC, V. Tube: Marble Arch.*

$$ **The Fielding.** Tucked away in a quiet alley, steps from the Royal Opera House, this cozy place is so adored by its regulars that you must book ahead. It's shabby-homey in decor and attitude—there's no elevator, only one room has a bathtub (most have showers), and there's no room service or restaurant, but it's cute and handy for the theater. ✉ *4 Broad Ct., Bow St., WC2B 5QZ,* ☎ *020/7836–8305,* FAX *020/7497–0064. 24 rooms. AE, DC, MC, V. Tube: Covent Garden.*

Nightlife and the Arts

The Arts

The most comprehensive list of events in the London arts scene can be found in *Time Out,* a weekly magazine available at most newsstands and bookstores. The city's evening paper, the *Evening Standard,* carries listings, as do the major Sunday papers, the daily *Independent* and *Guardian,* and, on Friday, the *Times.*

BALLET

The Royal Opera House is the traditional home of the world-famous **Royal Ballet.** As well as favorites like *The Nutcracker,* there are revivals of such productions as *Coppélia* which was originally presented by Dame Ninette de Valois, the founder of the company. Prices start at £2 (for ballet matinees). Bookings should be made well in advance. The **English National Ballet** and visiting companies perform at the Coliseum (☎ 020/7632–8300). In addition, the City Ballet of London performs at the **Peacock Theatre** (☎ 020/7863–8222). **Sadler's Wells Theatre** (☎ 020/7863–8000) hosts regional ballet and international modern dance troupes. Prices are reasonable. A popular venue for modern and experimental dance is **The Place** (☎ 020/7380–1268).

CONCERTS

Ticket prices for symphony orchestra concerts are still relatively moderate—between £5 and £35, although you can expect to pay more to hear big-name artists on tour. If you can't book in advance, arrive half an hour before the performance for a chance at returns.

The London Symphony Orchestra is in residence at the **Barbican Arts Centre** (☎ 020/7638–8891), although other top symphony and chamber orchestras also perform here. The **South Bank Centre** (☎ 020/7960–4242), which includes the Royal Festival Hall and the Queen Elizabeth Hall, is another major venue for choral, symphonic, and chamber concerts. For less expensive concert going, try the **Royal Albert Hall** (☎ 020/7589–8212) during the summer Promenade season; special tickets for standing room are available at the hall on the night of performance. Note, too, that the concerts are jumbo-screen broadcast in Hyde Park, but even a seat on the grass here requires a paid ticket. The **Wigmore Hall** (☎ 020/7935–2141) is a small auditorium, ideal for recitals. Inexpensive lunchtime concerts take place all over the city in smaller halls and churches, often featuring string quartets, vocalists, jazz ensembles, and gospel choirs. **St. John's, Smith Square** (☎ 020/7222–1061), a converted Queen Anne church, has a popular schedule of concerts. It has a handy cafeteria in the crypt.

FILM

Most West End cinemas are in the area around Leicester Square and Piccadilly Circus. Tickets average £8.50. Matinees and Monday evenings are cheaper, and some theaters offer student discounts. Cinema clubs screen a wide range of films: classics, Continental, underground, rare, or underestimated masterpieces. A temporary membership fee is usually about £1. One of the best cinema clubs is the **National Film Theatre** (☎ 020/7928–3232), part of the South Bank Centre.

OPERA

The **Royal Opera** presides over the main venue for opera in London, the fabled Royal Opera House (✉ Covent Garden, WC2E 9DD, ☎ 020/7304–4000), which ranks with the Metropolitan Opera House in New York in every way except, surprisingly, expense. Ballet matinees can cost as little as £2, although prices escalate to £150 for a top-price opera. Conditions of purchase vary—call for information.

The **Coliseum** (☎ 020/7632–8300) is the home of the English National Opera Company (ENO), whose productions are staged in English and are often innovative and exciting. Prices are lower than for the Royal Opera, ranging from £5 to £55. The ENO sells same-day seats for as low as £2.50.

THEATER

London's theater life can more or less be divided into three categories: the government-subsidized national companies; the commercial, or "West End," theaters; and the fringe. The **Royal National Theatre Company** (NT) shares the laurels as the top national repertory troupe with the Royal Shakespeare Company. In similar fashion to the latter troupe, the NT presents a variety of plays by writers of all nationalities, ranging from the classics of Shakespeare to specially commissioned modern works. The NT is based at the South Bank Centre (☎ 020/7452–3000 box office). The **Royal Shakespeare Company** (RSC) is based at the Barbican Centre (☎ 020/7638–8891 or 01789/403–403 box office). The RSC has terminated their summer season in London, although their winter season remains. In summer you can see the company's productions as it tours different theaters around the country. For general inquiries, phone the central box office in Stratford-Upon-Avon (☎ 020/7638–8891 or 01789/403–403). If you're visiting London in the summer, you can make up for the absence of the RSC by booking tickets at the spectacular new reconstruction of the famed Elizabethan-era **Shakespeare's Globe Theatre** (☎ 020/7401–9919 box office) on the South Bank, which offers open-air, late-afternoon performances from June through September.

The **West End theaters** stage musicals, comedies, whodunits, and revivals of lighter plays of the 19th and 20th centuries, often starring TV celebrities. Occasionally there are more serious productions, including successful productions transferred from the subsidized theaters, such as RSC's *Les Liaisons Dangereuses* and *Les Misérables*. The two dozen or so established **fringe theaters,** scattered around central London and the immediate outskirts, frequently present some of London's most intriguing productions, if you're prepared to overlook occasional rough staging and uncomfortable seating.

Most theaters have an evening performance at 7:30 or 8 Monday–Saturday, and a matinee twice a week (Wednesday or Thursday, and Saturday). Expect to pay from £10 for a seat in the upper balcony and at least £25 for a good seat in the stalls (orchestra) or dress circle (mezzanine)—more for musicals. Tickets may be booked in person at the theater box office, over the phone by credit card, or through ticket agents, such as **Ticketmaster** (☎ 020/7344–0055). The **SOLT Kiosk** in Leicester Square sells half-price tickets on the day of performance for about 25 theaters; there is a small service charge. It's open Monday–Saturday 2–6:30, Sunday noon–3. Beware of scalpers!

Nightlife

London's nightspots are legion; here are some of the best known. For up-to-the-minute listings, buy *Time Out* magazine.

CABARET

The best comedy in town can be found in the big, bright **Comedy Store** (✉ Haymarket House, Oxendon St., near Piccadilly Circus, ☎ 020/7344–0234).

JAZZ CLUBS

Pizza Express (✉ 10 Dean St., W1, ☎ 020/7437–9595 or 020/7439–8722) is the capital's best-loved chain of pizza houses, but it is also one of London's principal jazz venues, with music every night except Monday in the basement restaurant. Eight other branches also have live music; check the listings for details. **Ronnie Scott's** (✉ 47 Frith St., W1, ☎ 020/7439–0747) is the legendary Soho jazz club where international performers regularly take the stage.

NIGHTCLUBS

Café de Paris (✉ 3–4 Coventry St., W1V 7FL, ☎ 020/7734–7700) opened in 1914 and is one of London's most glamour-puss settings, once the haunt of royals and stars such as Noël Coward, Marlene Dietrich, Fred Astaire, and Frank Sinatra. **Hanover Grand** (✉ 6 Hanover Sq., W1, ☎ 020/7499–7977) is a swank and opulent big West End club that attracts TV stars and others in the entertainment business for funky U.S. garage on Fridays and glam disco on Saturdays. The lines outside get long, so dress up to impress the bouncers. **Ministry of Sound** (✉ 103 Gaunt St. SE1, ☎ 020/7378–6528) is more of an industry than a club, with its own record label, line of apparel, and, of course, DJs. Inside, there are chill-out rooms, dance floors, promotional Sony Playstations, Absolut shot bars—all the club kid's favorite things. If you are one, and you only have time for one night out, make it here. Kitschy **Stringfellows** (✉ 16–19 Upper St. Martin's La., WC2, ☎ 020/7240–5534) has an art deco upstairs restaurant, mirrored walls, and a dazzling light show in the downstairs dance floor.

ROCK

The **Forum** (✉ 9–17 Highgate Rd., Kentish Town, ☎ 020/7344–0044), a little out of the way, is a premier venue for medium-to-big acts. **100 Club** (✉ 100 Oxford St., W1, ☎ 020/7636–0933) is a basement dive that's always been there for R&B, rock, jazz, and beer. The **Shepherds Bush Empire** (✉ Shepherds Bush Green, W12, ☎ 020/7771–2000) is a major venue for largish acts in West London. The **Borderline** (✉ Otange Yard, off Manette St., W1V, ☎ 020/7734–2095) is a central subterranean room with fake southwestern decor that puts on a surprisingly good array of Americana, blues and indie rock.

Shopping

Shopping is one of London's great pleasures. Different areas retain their traditional specialties, and it's fun to seek out the small crafts, antiques, and gift stores, designer-clothing resale outlets, and national department-store chains.

Shopping Districts

Centering on the King's Road, **Chelsea** was once synonymous with ultrafashion; it still harbors some designer boutiques, plus antiques and home furnishings stores. A something-for-everyone neighborhood, **Covent Garden** has numerous clothing chain stores, stalls selling crafts, and shops selling gifts of every type—bikes, kites, herbs, beads, hats, you name it. **Kensington**'s main drag, Kensington High Street, is a smaller, classier version of Oxford Street, with Barkers department store, and a branch of Marks & Spencer at the eastern end. Try Kensington Church Street for expensive antiques, plus a little fashion. Venture out to the W11 and W2 neighborhoods around the Holland Park–Westbourne Grove end of **Notting Hill,** and you'll find specialty shops for clothes, accessories, and home living, with must-have status, plus lots of fashionable bistros for sustenance. Kensington's neighbor, **Knightsbridge** has Harrods, of course, but also Harvey Nichols, the chicest clothes shop in London, and many expensive designers' boutiques along Sloane Street, Walton Street, and Beauchamp Place. Adjacent Belgravia is also a burgeoning area for posh designer stores.

Bond Street, Old and New, is the elegant lure in **Mayfair,** with the *hautest* of haute couture and jewelry outposts, plus fine art. South Molton Street offers high-price, high-style fashion—especially at Browns—and the tailors of Savile Row are of worldwide repute. Crowded and a bit past its prime, **Oxford Street** is lined with tawdry discount shops. However, Selfridges, John Lewis, and Marks & Spencer are wonderful department stores, and there are interesting boutiques secreted off Oxford Street, just north of the Bond Street tube stop, in little St. Christopher's Place and Gees Court. Check out the cobbled streets in West Soho, behind Liberty in Regent Street, for handcrafted jewelry, designer gear, and stylish cafés. Perpendicular to Oxford Street lies **Regent Street**—famous for its curving path—with possibly London's most pleasant department store, Liberty's, as well as Hamley's, the capital's toy mecca. Shops around once-famous **Carnaby Street** stock designer youth paraphernalia and at least 57 varieties of T-shirts. The fabled English gentleman buys much of his gear at stores in **St. James's**: handmade hats, shirts, and shoes; silver shaving kits; and hip flasks. Here is also the world's best cheese shop, Paxton & Whitfield. Don't expect any bargains in this neighborhood.

Street Markets

Street markets are one aspect of London life not to be missed. Here are some of the more interesting markets:

Bermondsey. Arrive as early as possible for the best treasure. ✉ *Tower Bridge Rd., SE1.* ⏲ *Fri. 4 AM–1 PM. Tube to London Bridge or Bus 15 or 25 to Aldgate and then Bus 42 over Tower Bridge to Bermondsey Sq.*

Camden Lock. The youth center of the world, apparently, it's good for cheap clothes and boots. The canalside antiques, crafts, and junk markets are also picturesque and very crowded. ✉ *Chalk Farm Rd., NW1.* ⏲ *Shops Tues.–Sun. 9:30–5:30, stalls weekends 8–6. Tube or Bus 24 or 29 to Camden Town.*

Camden Passage. The rows of little antiques stalls are a good hunting ground for silverware and jewelry. Stalls open Wednesday and Saturday, but there is also a books and prints market on Thursday. Surrounding shops are open the rest of the week. ✉ *Islington, off Upper St., N1.* ⏲ *Wed. and Sat. 8:30–3. Tube or Bus 19 or 38 to Angel.*

Petticoat Lane. Look for budget-priced leather goods, gaudy knitwear, and fashions, plus cameras, videos, stereos, antiques, books, and bric-a-brac. ✉ *Middlesex St., E1.* ⏲ *Sun. 9–2. Tube: Liverpool St., Aldgate, Aldgate East.*

Portobello Market. Saturday is the best day for antiques, though this neighborhood is London's melting pot, becoming more vibrant every year. Find fabulous small shops, the city's trendiest restaurants, and a Friday and Saturday flea market at the far end at Ladbroke Grove. ✉ *Portobello Rd., W11.* ⏲ *Fri. 5 AM–3 PM, Sat. 6 AM–5 PM. Tube or Bus 52 to Notting Hill Gate or Ladbroke Grove, or Bus 15 to Kensington Park Rd.*

London Essentials

AIR TRAVEL TO AND FROM LONDON

International flights to London arrive at either Heathrow Airport, 24 km (15 mi) west of London, or Gatwick Airport, 43 km (27 mi) south of the capital. Most flights from the United States go to Heathrow. although Gatwick has grown from a European airport into one that serves 21 scheduled U.S. destinations. A third airport, Stansted, is to the east of the city. It handles mainly European and domestic traffic, although there is a scheduled service from New York.

British Airways is the national flag carrier and offers mostly nonstop flights from 18 U.S. cities to Heathrow and Gatwick airports. Other major carriers serving Heathrow and Gatwick airports in Great Britain include American Airlines and Virgin Atlantic, which serve Heathrow and Gatwick; Continental, Delta, Northwest, and TWA, which serve Gatwick; and United, which serves Heathrow.

➤ AIRLINES AND CONTACTS: **American Airlines** (☎ 800/433–7300; 020/8572–5555 in London). **British Airways** (☎ 800/AIRWAYS; 0845/7222–1111 in London). **Continental** (☎ 800/231–0856; 0800/776464 in London). **Delta** (☎ 800/241–4141; 0800/414767 in London). **Northwest Airlines** (☎ 800/447–4747; 0870/507–4074 in London). **TWA** (☎ 800/892–4141; 0345/333333 in London). **United** (☎ 800/241–6522; 0845/844–4777 in London). **Virgin Atlantic** (☎ 800/862–8621; 01293/747747 serves London).

AIRPORT TRANSFERS

Airport Travel Line gives information and takes advance bookings on transfers to town and between airports, including National Express as listed below. The Heathrow Express train links the airport with Paddington Station in only 15 minutes. It costs £12, and service departs every 15 minutes from 5:10 AM to 11:40 PM. The Piccadilly Line serves Heathrow (all terminals) with a direct Underground (subway) link, costing £3.50. Airbus A2 costs £7 and leaves every 30 minutes 6 AM–9:30 PM to Euston and King's Cross stations among other stops, but the trip can be lengthy, as there are around 14 other stops en route. National Express Jetlink 777 coaches leave every 30 minutes to Victoria Coach Station direct and are the same price, from 5:40 AM–9:30 PM. Cars and taxis drive into London from Heathrow, often through heavy traffic, and cost £30–£40. Add a tip of 10%–15% to the basic fare.

From Gatwick the quickest way to London is the nonstop rail Gatwick Express, costing £10.20 one-way and taking 30 minutes to reach Victoria Station. Trains run every 15 minutes 5:20 AM–midnight, then hourly 1:35 AM–5:20 AM. The hourly bus service by National Express Jetlink 777 takes about 90 minutes, hourly, 4:15 AM–9:15 PM, and costs £7 one-way. Stops include Marble Arch, Hyde Park Corner, Baker Street, Finchley Road, and Hendon Central, but there are sometimes delays. From Gatwick taxi fare is at least £50, plus tip; traffic can be very heavy.

➤ INFORMATION: **Airport Travel Line** (☎ 0870/574–7777). **Heathrow Express** (☎ 0845/600–1515). **Airbus A2** (☎ 0870/574–7777). **National Express** (☎ 0870/580–8080).

BUS TRAVEL TO AND FROM LONDON

The National Express coach service has routes to more than 1,200 major towns and cities in the United Kingdom. It's considerably cheaper than the train, although the trips usually take longer. National Express offers two types of service: ordinary service makes frequent stops for refreshment breaks (although all coaches have toilet and washroom facilities and reclining seats); Rapide and Flightlink services have stewardess and refreshment facilities on board. Day returns are available on both, but booking is advised on the Rapide service.

➤ BUS INFORMATION: **National Express** (✉ Victoria Coach Station, Buckingham Palace Rd., SW1, ☎ 0870/580–8080).

BUS TRAVEL WITHIN LONDON

London's bus system consists of bright red double- and single-deckers, plus other buses of various colors. Destinations are displayed on the front and back, with the bus number on the front, back, and side. Not all buses run the full length of their route at all times. Some buses are still operated with a conductor whom you pay after finding a seat, but these days you will more often find one-person buses, in which you pay the driver upon boarding.

Buses stop only at clearly indicated stops. Main stops—at which the bus should stop automatically—have a plain white background with a red LT symbol on it. There are also request stops with red signs, a white symbol, and the word REQUEST added; at these you must hail the bus to make it stop. Smoking is not allowed on any bus. Although you can see much of the town from a bus, *don't* take one if you want to get anywhere in a hurry; traffic often slows travel to a crawl, and during peak times you may find yourself waiting at least 20 minutes for a bus and not being able to get on it once it arrives. If you intend to go by bus, ask at a Travel Information Centre for a free bus map.

All journeys within the central zone are £1, and all others outside are 70p. Travel from the outer to the central zone costs £1. Travelcards are good for tube, bus, and British Rail trains in the Greater London zones. There are also a number of bus passes available for daily, weekly, and monthly use, and prices vary according to zones. A photograph is required for monthly bus passes.

CAR TRAVEL

The best advice is to avoid driving in London because of the ancient street patterns and the chronic parking restrictions. One-way streets also add to the confusion.

EMERGENCIES

Bliss Chemist is the only pharmacy in the center of London which is open round the clock. The leading chain drugstore, Boots at Piccadilly Circus, is open until 8 PM seven days, while Boots at 151 Oxford Street is open until 8 PM Thursdays. (Note: a prescription can only be filled if issued by a British registered doctor.)

➤ EMERGENCY SERVICES: **Police, fire brigade, or ambulance** (☎ 999).

➤ 24-HOUR PHARMACIES: **Bliss Chemist** (✉ 5 Marble Arch, W1, ☎ 020/7723–6116). **Boots** (✉ 44 Piccadilly Circus, W1, ☎ 020/7734–6126, or (✉ 151 Oxford St., W1, ☎ 020/7409–2857).

TAXIS

London's black taxis are famous for their comfort and for the ability of their drivers to remember the city's mazelike streets. Hotels and main tourist areas have ranks (stands) where you wait your turn to take one of the taxis that drive up. You can also hail a taxi if the flag is up or the yellow FOR HIRE sign is lighted. Fares start at £1.40 and increase by units of 20p per 281 yards or 55.5 seconds until the fare exceeds £8.60. After that, it's 20p for each 188 yards or 37 seconds. Surcharges are a tricky extra, which range from 40p for additional passengers or bulky luggage to 60p for evenings 8 PM–midnight, and until 6 AM on weekends and public holidays—at Christmas it zooms to £2 and there's 40p extra for each additional passenger. Fares are occasionally raised from year to year. Tip taxi drivers 10%–15% of the tab.

TOURS

BOAT TOURS

In summer, narrow boats and barges cruise London's two canals, the Grand Union and Regent's Canal; most vessels operate on the latter, which runs between Little Venice in the west (the nearest tube is Warwick Ave. on the Bakerloo Line) and Camden Lock (about 200 yards north of Camden Town tube station). Canal Cruises offers three or four cruises daily March–October on the *Jenny Wren* and all year on the cruising restaurant *My Fair Lady.* Jason's Trip operates one-way and round-trip narrow-boat cruises on this route. Trips last 1½ hours. The London Waterbus Company operates this route year-round with a stop at London Zoo: trips run daily April–October and weekends only November–March.

All year boats cruise up and down the Thames, offering a different view of the London skyline. In summer (April–October) boats run more frequently than in winter—call to check schedules and routes. Following is a selection of the main routes. For trips down river from Charing Cross to Greenwich Pier and historic Greenwich, call Catamaran Cruisers, or Westminster Passenger Boat Services which runs the same route from Westminster Pier. Thames Cruises goes to Greenwich and onwards to the Thames Barrier. Westminster Passenger Service Upriver runs through summer to Kew and Hampton Court from Westminster Pier. A Sail and Rail ticket combines the modern wonders of Canary Wharf and Docklands development with the history of the riverside by boat. Tickets are available year-round from Westminster Pier or Tower Gateway. Most of the launches have a public-address system and provide a running commentary on passing points of interest. Depending upon the destination, river trips may last from one to four hours.

➤ FEES AND SCHEDULES: **Canal Cruises** (☎ 020/7485–4433). **Catamaran Cruisers** (☎ 020/7839–3572). **Jason's Trip** (☎ 020/7286–3428). **London River Services** (☎ 020/7941–2400). **London Waterbus Company** (☎ 020/7482–2660). **Sail and Rail** (☎ 020/7363–9700). **Thames Cruises** (☎ 020/7930–3373). **Westminster Passenger Boat Services** (☎ 020/7930–4097). **Westminster Passenger Service Upriver** (☎ 020/7930–2062).

BUS TOURS

There is a choice of companies, each providing daily tours, departing (8:30–9 AM) from central points, such as Haymarket (check with the individual company). You may board or alight at any of the numerous stops to view the sights, and re-board on the next bus. Tickets are bought from the driver, good for all day, and prices vary according to the type of tour, although around £12 is the benchmark. The specialist in hop on–hop off tours is London Pride with friendly, informative staff on easily recognizable double-decker buses. The Original London Sightseeing Tour also offers frequent daily tours, departing from 8:30 AM from Baker Street (Madame Tussaud's), Marble Arch (Speakers' Corner), Piccadilly (Haymarket), or Victoria (Victoria Street) around every 12 minutes (less often out of peak summer season). The Big Bus Company runs a similar operation with a Red and Blue tour. The Red is a two-hour tour with 18 stops, and the Blue, one hour with 13. Both start from Marble Arch, Speakers' Corner. Evan Evans offers good bus tours which also visit major sights just outside the city. Another reputable agency that operates bus tours is Frames Rickards.

➤ FEES AND SCHEDULES: **The Big Bus Company** (☎ 020/8944–7810). **Evan Evans** (☎ 020/8332–2222). **Frames Rickards** (☎ 020/7837–3111). **London Pride** (☎ 020/7520–2050). **Original London Sightseeing Tour** (☎ 020/8877–1722).

EXCURSIONS

London Transport, Evan Evans, and Frames Rickards all offer day excursions (some combine bus and boat) to places of interest within easy reach of London, such as Windsor, Hampton Court, Oxford, Stratford-upon-Avon, and Bath. Prices vary and may include lunch and admission prices or admission only. Alternatively, make your own way, cheaply, to many of England's attractions on Green Line Coaches.

➤ FEES AND SCHEDULES: **Green Line Coaches** (☎ 020/8668–7261 or 0870/574–7777).

WALKING TOURS

One of the best ways to get to know London is on foot, and there are many guided and themed walking tours from which to choose. Two of the London-on-foot sightseeing experts are the Original London Walks and, for a more historical accent, Historical Walks, but your best bet is to peruse the variety of leaflets at a London Tourist Information Centre. The duration of the walks varies (usually one–three hours), and you can generally find one to suit even the most specific of interests.

If you'd rather explore on your own, then the City of London Corporation has laid out a Heritage Walk that leads through Bank, Leadenhall, and Monument; follow the trail by the directional stars set into the sidewalks. A map of this walk can be found in *A Visitor's Guide to the City of London,* available from the City Information Centre across from St. Paul's Cathedral. The Silver Jubilee Walkway covers 16 km (10 mi) and is marked by a series of silver crowns set into the sidewalks; Parliament Square makes a good starting point. For the Golden Jubilee year of 2002, there are some new sidewalk plaques and diversions along the way. The Thames Path is a National Trail that has been revamped along the modernized Docklands and south bank city route, and covers some 291 km (180 mi) from the river's source in Gloucestershire to the Thames Barrier; for information, call London Docklands Visitor Centre. Several guides offering further walks are available in bookshops. One of the most fascinating is *Secret London,* by Andrew Duncan (New Holland).

➤ FEES AND SCHEDULES: **Original London Walks** (☎ 020/7624–3978). **Historical Walks** (☎ 020/8668–4019). **London Docklands Visitor Centre** (☎ 020/7512–1111). **London Walking Forum** (WEB www.londonwalking.com).

TRAIN TRAVEL

London is served by no fewer than 15 main-line train stations, so be absolutely certain of the station for your departure or arrival. All have Underground stops either in the train station or within a few minutes' walk from it, and most are served by several bus routes. The principal routes that connect London to other major towns and cities are on an InterCity network. Seats can be reserved by phone only with a credit card. You can, of course, apply in person to any British Rail Travel Centre or directly to the station from which you depart.

Charing Cross Station serves southeast England, including Canterbury, Margate, Dover/Folkestone, and ferry ports. Euston/St. Pancras serves East Anglia, Essex, the Northeast, the Northwest, and North Wales, including Coventry, Stratford-upon-Avon, Birmingham, Manchester, Liverpool, Windermere, Glasgow, and Inverness, northwest Scotland. King's Cross serves the east Midlands; the Northeast, including York, Leeds, and Newcastle; and north and east Scotland, including Edinburgh and Aberdeen. Liverpool Street serves Essex and East Anglia. Paddington serves the south Midlands, west and south Wales, and the west country, including Oxford. Victoria serves southern England, including Gatwick Airport, Brighton, Dover/Folkestone and ferry ports, and the south coast. Waterloo serves the southwestern United Kingdom, including Salisbury, Portsmouth, Southampton, and Isle of Wight. Waterloo International is for the Eurostar to Europe.

If you're combining a trip to Great Britain with stops on the Continent, you can either drive your car onto a *Le Shuttle* train through the Channel Tunnel (35 minutes from Folkestone to Calais) or book a seat on the Eurostar high-speed train service to Paris or Brussels).

FARES AND SCHEDULES

Fare structures are slowly changing as the formerly nationalized British Rail is now run by various independent operators. Generally speaking, it is less expensive to buy a return (round-trip) ticket, especially for day trips not far from London, and you should always inquire at the information office about discount fares. You can hear a recorded summary of timetable and fare information to many destinations by calling the appropriate "dial and listen" numbers listed under Rail in the telephone book. The telephone information number listed below gets you through to any of the stations.

➤ TRAIN INFORMATION: (☎ 0845/748–4950).

TRAVEL AGENCIES

➤ LOCAL AGENT REFERRALS: **American Express** (✉ 6 Haymarket, WC2, ☎ 020/7930–4411; 89 Mount St., W1, ☎ 020/7499–4436). **Thomas Cook** (✉ 1 Marble Arch, W1, ☎ 020/7530–7100; 184 Kensington High St., W8, ☎ 020/7707–2300; and other branches).

UNDERGROUND TRAVEL

Known as "the tube," London's extensive Underground system is by far the most widely used form of city transportation. Trains run both beneath and aboveground out into the suburbs, and all stations are clearly marked with the London Underground circular symbol. (A SUBWAY sign refers to an under-the-street crossing.) Trains are all one class; smoking is *not* allowed on board or in the stations.

There are 10 basic lines—all named. The Central, District, Northern, Metropolitan, and Piccadilly lines all have branches, usually taking you to the outlying sections of the city, so be sure to note which branch is needed for your particular destination. Electronic platform signs tell you the final stop and route of the next train, and some signs indicate how many minutes you'll have to wait for the train to arrive. Begun in the Victorian era, the Underground is still being expanded and improved. The supermodern Jubilee line extension sweeps from Green Park to south of the river, with connections to Canary Wharf and the Docklands, and east to Stratford. The zippy Docklands Light Railway

(DLR) runs through the Docklands with a new extension to the *Cutty Sark* and maritime Greenwich.

From Monday through Saturday, trains begin running just after 5 AM; the last services leave central London between midnight and 12:30 AM. On Sunday, trains start two hours later and finish about an hour earlier. The frequency of trains depends on the route and the time of day, but normally you should not have to wait more than 10 minutes. A pocket map of the entire tube network is available free from most Underground ticket counters.

FARES AND SCHEDULES

For both buses and tube fares, London is divided into six concentric zones; the fare goes up the farther afield you travel. Ask at Underground ticket counters for the LT booklet "Fares and Tickets," which gives all details. You must buy a ticket before you travel. Many types of travel cards can be bought from Pass Agents that display the sign: tobacconists, confectioners, newsagents, and mainline overground rail stations.

For one trip between any two stations, you can buy an ordinary single (one-way ticket) for travel anytime on the day of issue; if you're coming back on the same route the same day, then an ordinary return (round-trip ticket) costs twice the single fare. Singles vary in price from £1.40 to £3.40 for a six-zone journey—not a good option for the sightseer who wants to make several journeys. A Carnet (£10) is a convenient book of 10 single tickets to use in central zone 1 only. Note that these prices are subject to increases.

Travelcards allow unrestricted travel on the tube, most buses, and British Rail trains in the Greater London zones and are valid weekdays after 9:30 AM, weekends, and all public holidays. They cannot be used on airbuses, night buses, or for certain special services. There are different options available: a One Day Travelcard costs £3.80–£4.50; Weekend Travelcards, for the two days of the weekend and on any two consecutive days during public holidays, run £5.70–£6.70. Family Travelcards are one-day tickets for one or two adults with one to four children and cost £3–£3.60 with one child; extra children cost 60p each. Adults do not have to be related to the children or even to each other.

Visitor's Travelcards are the best bet for visitors, but they must be bought before leaving home (they're available in both the United States and Canada). They are valid for periods of three, four, or seven days ($25, $32, $49, respectively) and can be used on the tube and virtually all buses and British Rail services in London.

➤ UNDERGROUND INFORMATION: (☎ 020/7222–1234, 24 hours). Travelers with disabilities should call for the free leaflet "Access to the Underground" (☎ 020/7918–3312).

VISITOR INFORMATION

Visitorcall is the London Tourist Board's 24-hour phone service—a premium-rate (60p per minute) recorded information line, with different numbers for theater, events, museums, sports, transportation around town, and so on. Call to access the list of options, or see the separate categories in the telephone directory.

➤ TOURIST INFORMATION: **London Tourist Information Centre** (✉ Victoria Station Forecourt). **Britain Visitor Centre** (✉ 1 Regent St., Piccadilly Circus, SW1Y 4NX; ⏲ Weekdays 9–6:30, weekends 10–4, WEB www.visitbritain.com). **London Tourist Board** (☎ 09068/663344 Visitorcall, WEB www.londontown.com)

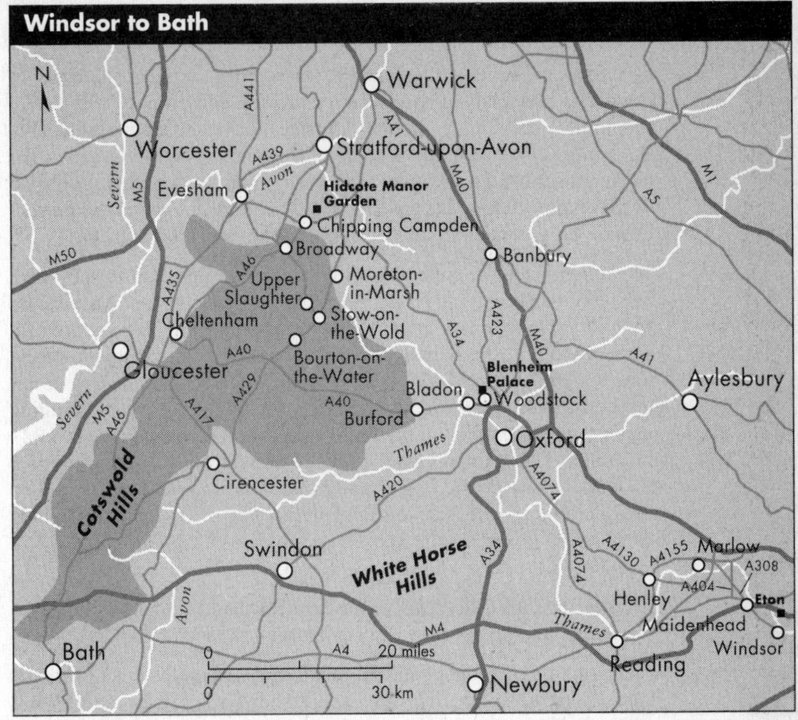

WINDSOR TO BATH

If you follow the Thames, England's second-longest river, along its course, you embark on a journey through historic towns, verdant countryside, and some of the loftiest homes ever erected. West of London, Windsor has housed the royal family since William the Conqueror. Many of England's traditions have been born on or nearby the Thames: horse-racing at Ascot; the Henley Royal Regatta; Oxford University; and even William Shakespeare. Blenheim Palace and Warwick Castle are emblems of grandeur in their own right, while Bath's 18th-century streets recall an age more elegant than our own.

Windsor

★ **Windsor Castle,** 34 km (21 mi) west of London, has housed the royal family since the 11th century. In the 14th century Edward III revamped the old castle, building the Norman gateway, the great round tower, and new apartments. Almost every monarch since then has added new buildings or improved existing ones; over the centuries the medieval fortification has been transformed into the lavish royal palace you see today.

In the queen's state apartments, the **Grand Reception Room,** the **Green and Crimson Drawing Rooms,** and the **State and Octagonal Dining Rooms** have been restored to their former glory after the fire of 1992. The ceiling of St. George's Hall, where the queen gives state banquets, has a green oak roof, and the largest hammerbeam roof to have been built during the 20th century looms magnificently over the 600-year-old hall. The private chapel of the royal family has also been redesigned, with a stained-glass window commemorating the fire of 1992 and the restoration work that subsequently took place. All restored rooms, except the private chapel, are open to the public. Be aware that the State Apartments are sometimes closed when the queen is in residence; call ahead to check.

St. George's Chapel, more than 230 ft long with two tiers of great windows and hundreds of gargoyles, buttresses, and pinnacles, is one of the noblest buildings in England. Inside, above the choir stalls, hang the banners, swords, and helmets of the Knights of the Order of the Garter, the most senior Order of Chivalry. The many monarchs buried in the chapel include Henry VIII and George VI, father of the present queen. (St. George's Chapel is closed to the public on Sunday.)

The magnificent art collection at Windsor contains paintings by such masters as Rubens, Van Dyck, and Holbein; drawings by Leonardo da Vinci; and Gobelin tapestries. There are splendid views across to Windsor Great Park, the remains of a former royal hunting forest. Make time to view **Queen Mary's Doll's House,** a charming miniature country house with every detail complete, including electricity, running water, and real books on the library shelves. It was designed in 1921 by architect Sir Edwin Lutyens for the present queen's grandmother. ✉ *Windsor Castle,* ☎ *01753/868286.* 🎫 *£10.50, £22 family ticket; Doll's House £1 extra (included in family ticket) or separately (including entry to the precincts).* ⏲ *Mar.–Oct., Mon.–Sat. 10–5:30, Sun. 8:30–6:30 (last admission at 4); Nov.–Feb., daily 10–4 (last entrance at 3).*

After seeing the castle, stroll around the town and enjoy the shops; antiques are sold on cobbled Church Lane and Queen Charlotte Street.

An attraction to delight children (of all ages) is **Legoland,** set in woodland 3¼ km (2 mi) outside Windsor. Hands-on activities indoors and out include building, driving, and boating. For more information ask at the Windsor tourist office. ✉ *B3202, Bracknell/Ascot Rd.,* ☎ *0990/040404.* 🎫 *£17.* ⏲ *Mar.–June and Sept.–Jan., daily 10–6; July–Aug., daily 10–8.*

$$ ✕ **Ye Harte and Garter.** Opposite Windsor Castle, in the hotel of the same name, this restaurant has a reasonably priced carvery offering a range of meats alongside the full à la carte menu. There is also a snack bar for sandwiches and light meals. ✉ *High St.,* ☎ *01753/863426. AE, DC, MC, V.*

Henley

Henley has been famous since 1839 for the rowing regatta it holds each year around the first Sunday in July. The social side of the regatta is as entertaining as the races themselves; elderly oarsmen wear brightly colored blazers and boater hats, and women flaunt their smartest summer suits. The town is worth exploring for its small but good selection of specialty shops. The Red Lion Hotel near the 200-year-old bridge has been visited by kings, dukes, and writers. **St. Mary's Church** has a 16th-century "checkerboard" tower made of alternate squares of flint and stone. The **Chantry House,** a 1420 merchant's house later converted into a school for impoverished boys, is an unspoiled example of the rare overhanging timber-frame design. ✉ *Hart St.,* ☎ *01491/577062.* ⏲ *For church services or by appointment.*

Oxford

Numbers in the margin correspond to points of interest on the Oxford map.

Oxford is more than a university town. It has been one of the two forerunners of English erudition since the 13th century, and is pristinely preserved. Tiny alleys, grimacing gargoyles, honey-color stone, and the ubiquitous "dreaming" spires make for an unforgettable experience. Oxford University comprises 40 independent colleges, and many of the magnificent chapels and dining halls are open to visitors—times and (in some cases) entry charges are displayed at the entrance lodges. Some colleges are open only in the afternoons during university semesters, when the undergraduates are in residence; access is often restricted to the chapels, dining rooms (called halls), and libraries. All are closed during exams, usually from mid-April to late June, when the May Balls are held. The best way to gain access is to join a walking tour led by an official Blue Badge guide. These two-hour tours leave up to five times daily from the Tourist Information Centre.

One of the most delightful walks through Oxford is along the **banks of the River Cherwell,** either through the University Parks area or through Magdalen College to Addison's Walk. Along the way you can watch the undergraduates idly punting a summer's afternoon away. Better still, rent one of these narrow flat-bottom boats yourself—but be warned: navigating is more difficult than it looks!

7 **Ashmolean Museum.** The Ashmolean is Britain's oldest public museum, holding noted collections of Egyptian, Greek, and Roman artifacts; Michelangelo drawings; and European silverware. ✉ *Beaumont St.,* ☎ *01865/278000,* WEB *www.ashmol.ox.ac.uk.* ⏲ *Tues.–Sat. 10–5, Sun. 2–5.*

4 **Balliol College.** The doors between the inner and outer quadrangles of Balliol still bear the scorch marks from the flames that burned Archbishop Cranmer and Bishops Latimer and Ridley at the stake in 1555 for their Protestant beliefs. ✉ *Broad St.,* WEB *www.balliol.ox.ac.uk* ⏲ *Daily 2–5.*

10 **Bodleian Library.** Begun in 1602 and one of the oldest libraries in the world, part of the Bodleian is housed in the spectacular Radcliffe Camera and contains an unrivaled collection of manuscripts. Limited sections of the Bodleian can be visited on a **tour.** Otherwise, the general public can visit only the Divinity School, a superbly vaulted room with changing exhibitions of manuscripts and rare books. ✉ *Broad St.,* ☎ *01865/277165; 01865/277188 (tour).* ⏲ *Tours mid-Mar.–Oct., weekdays at 10:30, 11:30, 2, and 3; Nov.–mid-Mar., weekdays at 2 and 3; occasional Sat. morning tours.*

3 **Christ Church College.** Built in 1546, Christ Church is the site of Oxford's largest quadrangle, "Tom Quad," named after the huge bell (6¼ tons) that hangs in the gate tower. Its 800-year-old chapel in one corner has been Oxford's cathedral since the time of Henry VIII. The college's medieval dining hall contains portraits of many famous alumni, including John Wesley, William Penn, and 13 of Britain's prime ministers. Lewis Carroll was a teacher of mathematics here for many years. ✉ *St. Aldate's,* WEB *www.chch.ox.ac.uk.* ⏲ *Mon.–Sat. 9:30–4:30, Sun. 2–4:30.*

Christ Church Picture Gallery. In Canterbury Quadrangle, this connoisseur's delight exhibits paintings by Tintoretto, Veronese, and Van Dyck. ✉ *Oriel Square,* ☎ *01865/276172.* ⏲ *Mon.–Sat. 10:30–1 and 2–4:30, Sun. 2–4:30 (until 5:30 in summer).*

Magdalen Bridge. At the foot of this famous Oxford landmark you can rent a punt (a shallow-bottomed boat that is poled slowly up the river) for £10 an hour. You may wish, like many an Oxford student, to spend a summer afternoon punting—while dangling your champagne bottle in the water to keep it cool. ✉ *High St.*

1 **Magdalen College.** Founded in 1458, with an impressive main quadrangle and a supremely monastic air, Magdalen is one of the most impressive of Oxford's colleges; scenic highlights include the Deer Park

Oxford

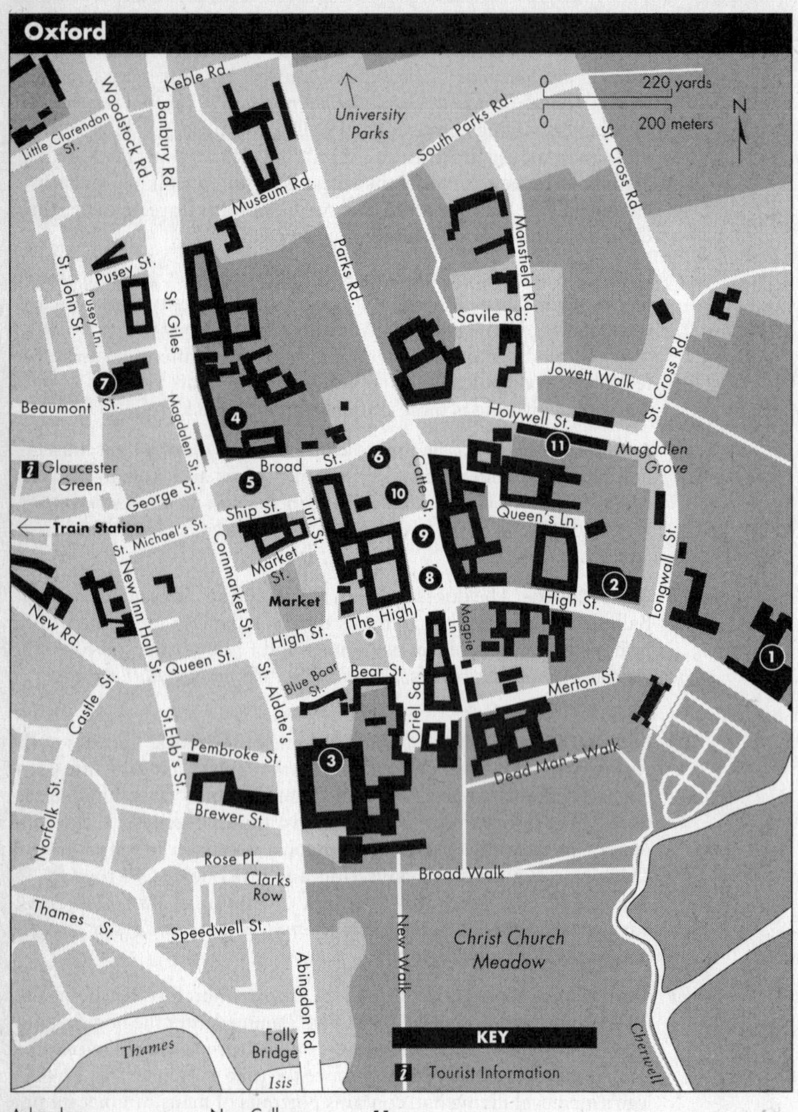

Ashmolean Museum 7
Balliol College 4
Bodleian Library . . . 10
Christ Church College 3
Magdalen College 1
New College 11
Oxford Story 5
Radcliffe Camera . . . 9
St. Edmund Hall 2
Sheldonian Theatre 6
University Church . . . 8

and Addison's Walk—the grounds which Cardinal Wolsey, Oscar Wilde, and Dudley Moore once called home. ⏲ *Daily 2–6.* WEB *www.magd.ox.ac.uk*

⓫ **New College.** Founded in 1379, it has extensive gardens, partly enclosed by the medieval city wall, and a notorious row of gargoyles. Famous alumni include Hugh Grant and Richard Mason, who published his international best-seller *The Drowning People*) only months after first "coming up" to Oxford. ✉ *Holywell St.,* WEB *www.new.ox.ac.uk.*

❺ The **Oxford Story.** This multimedia presentation explores the university's 800-year history. ✉ *Broad St.,* ☎ *01865/790055.* 🎫 *£5.70.* ⏲ *Daily with seasonal variations.*

❾ **Radcliffe Camera.** Behind University Church, this striking English Baroque structure is adorned with marble urns, massive columns, and one of the largest domes in Britain. It is not open to the public.

❷ **St. Edmund Hall.** On Queen's Lane, St. Edmund (or "Teddy") Hall has one of the smallest and most picturesque quadrangles, with an old well in the center. ⏲ *Daily 1 PM–dusk.*

❻ **Sheldonian Theatre.** Architect Christopher Wren designed this to look like a semicircular Roman amphitheater, complete with front gate topped by gigantic busts of the ancient emperors. ✉ *Broad St.,* ☎ *01865/277299.* ⏲ *Mar.–mid-Nov., Mon.–Sat. 10–12:30 and 2–4:30; mid-Nov.–Feb., Mon.–Sat. 10–12:30 and 2–4. Closed 10 days at Christmas and Easter, also for student events.*

❽ **University Church.** The 14th-century tower of this central church (officially known as St. Mary the Virgin) provides a splendid panoramic view of the city's famous skyline. The Convocation House, accessible from Radcliffe Square, serves generous portions—cafeteria style—under the room in which OxFam was founded. ☎ *01865/243806.* ⏲ *Tower Easter Mon.–Sept., daily 9:15–7; Oct.–Easter, daily 9:15–5.*

$$$$ ★ ✕ **Le Petit Blanc.** The more hip cousin to Le Manoir aux Quat'Saisons in Great Milton, this is the finest place to eat in all of Oxford and certainly sophisticated by any connoisseur's standards. The menu never ceases to produce edibly innovative and visually stunning exemplars of nouvelle cuisine. The 10-minute walk north of the city center and the dent you might put on your credit card are worth it. ✉ *71–72 Walton St.,* ☎ *01865/510999,* WEB *www.manoir.co.uk. AE, DC, MC, V.*

$$–$$$ ✕ **Gee's.** This brasserie in a conservatory, formerly a florist's shop, is just north of the town center. The menu offers French and English dishes, including a good fish selection, and the place is popular with both town and gown. ✉ *61 Banbury Rd.,* ☎ *01865/553540. AE, MC, V.*

$–$$ ✕ **Café Joe's.** For some of the best eggs Benedict in the valley, cross the Magdalene Bridge out of town, take the center fork, and pass its take-out sibling, Espresso Joe, on the left. Here, students "living out" sip lattés and read the broadsheets in comfortable style. ✉ *21 Cowley Road,* ☎ *01865/201120. MC, V.*

$$$$ ✕🏨 **Old Bank Hotel.** This hotel opened its doors in 1999 and has earned a reputation for bringing some style to the city. From the sleek lobby, set subtly back from the High Street, to the subdued designer decor, the former Barclay's Bank has a cosmopolitan air—disrupted only by the occasional lapse in service. Oxford's most central hotel, with a restaurant that has become a favorite of many, it has more than one asset to bank your money on. ✉ *92–94 High St., OX1 4BN,* ☎ *01865/799599,* FAX *01865/799598,* WEB *www.oxford-hotels-restaurants.co.uk. 43 rooms. Restaurant, bar, lounge. AE, DC, MC, V.*

$$$$ ★ **Old Parsonage.** Well respected since it opened in 1660, this gabled country-house hotel is a dignified and romantic escape from the surrounding the city center. Dark-wood panelling in the lobby and tasteful chintz patterns in the rooms are far from trendy, but expeditious room service and memorable gourmet meals by an open fire keep people coming back. ✉ *1 Banbury Rd., OX2 6NN,* ☎ *01865/310210,* FAX *01865/311262,* WEB *www.s-h-systems.co.uk. 30 rooms. Restaurant. AE, DC, MC, V.*

$$$–$$$$ **The Randolph.** Oxford's landmark hotel has undergone extensive restoration of its beautiful Victorian Gothic interior (unfortunately, this has not extended to some of the very squeaky floorboards, an annoyance at night). It's across from the Ashmolean Museum. ✉ *Beaumont St., OX1 2LN,* ☎ *01865/247481,* FAX *01865/791678. 104 rooms, 4 suites. Restaurant. AE, DC, MC, V.*

Woodstock

★ Home to dukes of Marlborough, Vanderbilts, and Churchills, **Blenheim Palace,** about 13 km (8 mi) north of Oxford on A44 (Woodstock Road), is not the most spectacular house in England just because of its history. The sheer Baroque grandeur—its vast pile of towers, colonnades, and porticoes—leaves no visitor impassive. Blenheim was built in neoclassical style in the early 18th century by architect Sir John Vanbrugh; it stands in 2,500 acres of beautiful gardens created later in the 18th century by the English landscape gardener "Capability" Brown. Soldier and statesman John Churchill, first duke of Marlborough, built the house on land given to him by Queen Anne as a reward for his defeat of the French at the Battle of Blenheim in 1704. The house is filled with fine paintings—don't miss the grand John Singer Sargent portrait of the ninth duke and his wife, Consuelo Vanderbilt—tapestries, and furniture. Winston Churchill, a descendant of Marlborough, was born in the palace; some of his paintings are on display, and there is an exhibition devoted to his life. A cafeteria is on the grounds, as are a famous topiary maze, butterfly house, and other amusements. ✉ *Woodstock,* ☎ *01993/811091,* WEB *www.blenheimpalace.com.* ⏲ *Mid-Mar.–Oct., daily 10:30–4:45; grounds year-round daily 9–4:45.*

Sir Winston Churchill (1874–1965) is buried in the nearby village of **Bladon.** His grave in the small tree-lined churchyard is all the more touching for its simplicity.

Just outside the back gates of Blenheim Palace is the village of **Woodstock.** Extraordinarily civilized, it's filled with beautiful shops, some elegant 18th-century buildings, and historic hotels, such as the Bear (☎ 08704/008202), the Feathers (☎ 01993/812291), and the Blenheim Guest House and Tea Rooms (☎ 01993/813814), the last set just outside the imperial back gates of the palace. Stay here instead of in Oxford and take the 15-minute bus ride back and forth to the college town.

Stratford-upon-Avon

Numbers in the margin correspond to points of interest on the Stratford-upon-Avon map.

A34 runs northwest from Oxford and Blenheim across the Cotswold Hills to Stratford-upon-Avon, the hometown of William Shakespeare. Even without its most famous son, Stratford would be worth visiting. The town's timbered buildings bear witness to its prosperity during the 16th century, when it was a thriving craft and trading center. Attractive buildings from the 18th century add to the town's historic feel.

The main places of Shakespearean interest are run by the **Shakespeare Birthplace Trust** (☎ 01789/204016). They all have similar opening

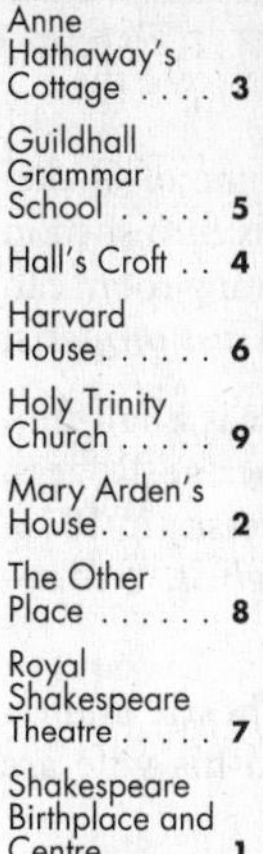

Stratford-upon-Avon

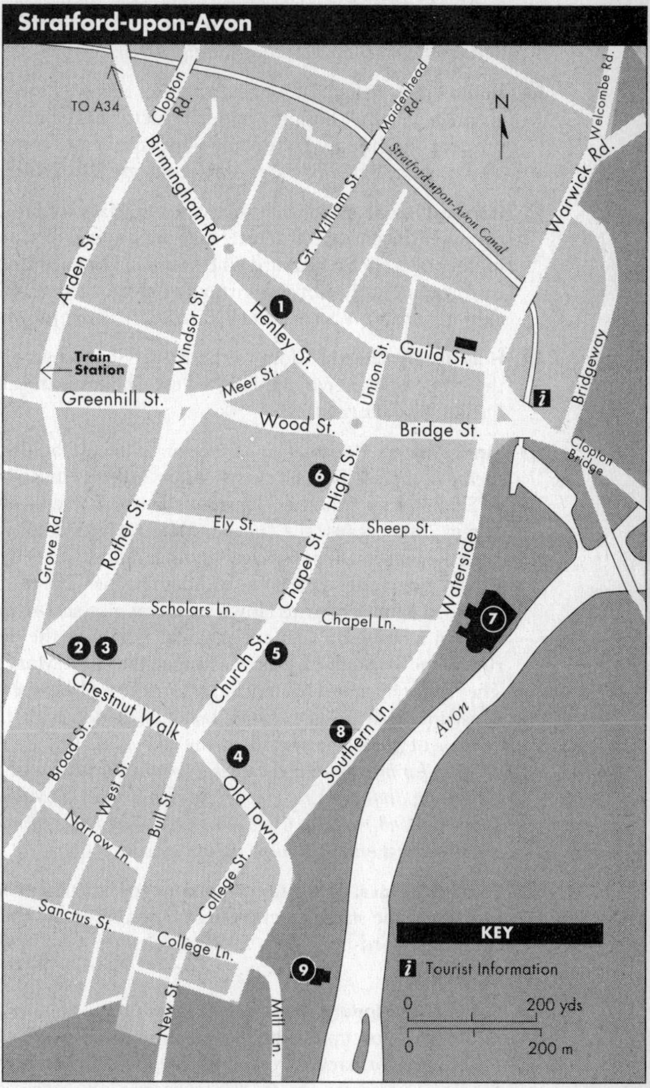

times, and you can get a combination ticket for them all—£12—or pay separate entry fees if you want to visit only one or two. ⏲ *Shakespeare's Birthplace and Anne Hathaway's Cottage: mid-Mar.–mid-Oct., Mon.–Sat. 9–5, Sun. 9:30–5; mid-Oct.–mid-Mar., Mon.–Sat. 9:30–4, Sun. 10–4. Nash's House, Hall's Croft, and Mary Arden's House: mid-Mar.–mid-Oct., Mon.–Sat. 9:30–5, Sun. 10–5; mid-Oct.–mid-Mar., Mon.–Sat. 10–4, Sun. 10:30–4 (last entry for all sights 30 mins before closing). www.stratford-upon-avon.co.uk and* WEB *www.shakespeare.org.uk*

★ ❸ **Anne Hathaway's Cottage.** Set in Shottery on the edge of the town, this is the early home of the playwright's wife. This thatched house is one of the most picturesque sights in Britain. ✉ *Cottage La., Shottery,* ☎ *01789/292100. A Shakespeare Birthplace Trust property.*

❺ **Guildhall Grammar School.** Along the main thoroughfare of Church Street are almshouses built by the Guild of the Holy Cross in the early 15th century. Farther along is the town school, which Shakespeare probably attended as a boy and which is still used to educate the young of

Stratford. ✉ *Church St., near Chapel La.,* ☎ *01789/293351.* ⏲ *Easter and summer school vacations, daily 10–6.*

❹ **Hall's Croft.** A fine Tudor town house, this was the home of Shakespeare's daughter Susanna and her doctor husband; it is furnished in the decor of the day. The doctor's dispensary and consulting room can also be seen. ✉ *Old Town. A Shakespeare Birthplace Trust property.*

❻ **Harvard House.** Next to the Garrick Inn, Harvard House is a half-timbered 16th-century structure that was home to Catherine Rogers, mother of the John Harvard who founded Harvard University in 1636. Unfortunately, the house is virtually unfurnished. ✉ *High St.* ⏲ *May–Sept. Contact the Shakespeare Birthplace Trust for hrs.*

❾ **Holy Trinity Church.** Close to the Royal Shakespeare Theatre and on the bank of the Avon, this is where Shakespeare and his wife are buried. ✉ *Trinity St.*

❷ **Mary Arden's House.** The hamlet of Wilmcote holds the fifth Shakespeare Birthplace Trust property—Mary Arden's House—the family home of Shakespeare's mother. This bucolic site attracted a flurry of attention in 2000 because the Tudor farmhouse considered for years to have been the home of Shakespeare's mother (and so named) was discovered to have been instead the home of Adam Palmer. The farmhouse has been renamed Palmer's Farm. However, it was also shown that Mary Arden lived in a house on Glebe Farm, which adjoins the farmhouse and is run by the Trust; this has now assumed the name Mary Arden's House. The Tudor farmhouse and farm form the **Shakespeare Countryside Museum,** with crafts exhibits, falconry demonstrations, a café, and a garden of trees mentioned in the plays. ✉ *Off A3400,* ☎ *01789/293455 for information on special events,* WEB *www.shakespeare.org.uk.* 🎫 *£5.50; Shakespeare Trust joint ticket £12.* ⏲ *Mid-Mar.–mid-Oct., Mon.–Sat. 9:30–5, Sun. 10–5; mid-Oct.–mid-Mar., Mon.–Sat. 10–4, Sun. 10:30–4; last entry 30 mins before closing.*

❽ **The Other Place.** This auditorium for experimental productions stands just down the street from the Royal Shakespeare Theatre. ✉ *Waterside, Stratford-upon-Avon, Warwickshire CV37 6BB,* ☎ *01789/295623.*

❼ **Royal Shakespeare Theatre.** The most famous Shakespearean theater in the world occupies a perfect position on the bank of the Avon—try to see a performance if you can. The company (always referred to as the RSC) performs several Shakespeare plays each season, as well as scripts by a wide variety of other playwrights, between March and January. For a fascinating insight into how the theater operates, join one of the backstage tours, led twice daily (four times on Sunday). Beside the main theater is the smaller **Swan.** Modeled on an Elizabethan theater, the Swan stages productions in the round. It also provides entry to the RSC collection of paintings, props, and memorabilia; visit it either on one of the backstage tours or on your own. It's best to book well in advance for RSC productions, but a few tickets for the day of performance are always available, and it is also worth asking if there are any returns. ✉ *The Royal Shakespeare Theatre, Stratford-upon-Avon, Warwickshire CV37 6BB,* ☎ *01789/296655; 01789/403403 box office; 01789/412602 tours,* WEB *www.rsc.org.uk.*

★ ❶ **Shakespeare Birthplace and Centre.** This holy shrine for Shakespeare lovers also contains a small museum with costumes used in the BBC's versions of the plays and an exhibition of the playwright's life and work. ✉ *Henley St. A Shakespeare Birthplace Trust property.*

$$$ ✕ **Box Tree Restaurant.** In the Royal Shakespeare Theatre, this elegant restaurant overlooks the river and is a favored spot for pre- and post-theater dining. Specialties include roast rack of lamb and grilled Scotch beef fillet. There is a prix-fixe menu. ✉ *Waterside,* ☎ *01789/293226. AE, MC, V. Closed when theater is closed.*

$$–$$$ ✕ **The Opposition.** Near the Royal Shakespeare Theatre, the Opposition caters to the pre- and post-theater dining crowd (as do all sensible restaurants in Stratford). It is extremely popular with the locals, so book in advance. The American and Continental dishes change each month—if you're lucky there will be Cajun chicken. ✉ *13 Sheep St.,* ☎ *01789/269980. Reservations essential. MC, V.*

$ ✕ **The Slug and Lettuce.** Don't let the name put you off—this pine-paneled pub serves excellent meals. Favorites are chicken breast baked in avocado and garlic, and poached cushion of salmon. ✉ *38 Guild St.,* ☎ *01789/299700. Reservations essential. AE, MC, V.*

$$$$ **Shakespeare Hotel.** For a touch of typical Stratford, stay at this timbered Elizabethan town house in the heart of the town, close to the theater and to most of the attractions. It has been luxuriously modernized while still retaining its Elizabethan character. ✉ *Chapel St., CV37 6ER,* ☎ *08704/008182,* FAX *01789/415411,* WEB *www.stratford-upon-avon.co.uk/shakespeare.htm. 74 rooms. AE, DC, MC, V.*

$$$ **Falcon County Hotel.** Licensed as an alehouse since 1640, it still has a friendly inn atmosphere. The heavily beamed rooms in the older part are small and quaint; those in the modern extension are in standard international style. ✉ *Chapel St., CV37 6HA,* ☎ *01789/279953,* FAX *01789/414260. 84 rooms. Restaurant. AE, DC, MC, V.*

$$ **Caterham House.** Built in 1830, this elegantly furnished building is within an easy walk of the theater. You may spot an actor or two among the guests. ✉ *58 Rother St., CV37 6LT,* ☎ *01789/267309,* FAX *01789/414836. 10 rooms. MC, V.*

Warwick

Warwick, some 13 km (8 mi) north of Stratford along A46, is an unusual mixture of Georgian redbrick and Elizabethan half-timber buildings, although some unattractive postwar developments have spoiled ★ the town center. **Warwick Castle** is one of the finest medieval structures of its kind in England, towering on a precipice above the River Avon. Most of the present buildings date from the 14th century. The interior contains magnificent collections of armor, paintings, and furniture, and a waxworks display by Madame Tussaud's. Outside, peacocks strut in the 60 acres of landscaped riverside gardens. A restored Victorian boathouse has a flora-and-fauna exhibition and a nature walk. ✉ *Castle Hill,* ☎ *01926/495421.* ⏲ *Easter–Oct., daily 10–6; Nov.–Easter, daily 10–5 (last entry 30 mins before closing).*

The Cotswolds

Near the spires and shires of Shakespeare Country is a region that conjures up "olde Englande" at its most blissfully rural: the Cotswolds. If you've come in search of picture-postcard English countryside, with soft rolling hills and mellow stone-built villages, this is your destination. From Stratford take an easy detour via A3400 and B4632 into this region, which is marked by high, bare hills patterned by patches of ancient forest and stone walls that protect the sheep that have grazed here from the earliest times.

The gateway to the Cotswolds is **Cheltenham,** once rivaling Bath for Georgian elegance. Although much of it is marred by modern developments, there are still some fine examples of the Regency style in its graceful secluded villas, lush gardens, and leafy crescents and squares. If you visit this historic health resort in the spring or summer—take either M4 and M5 north from Bath, or M5 south from Birmingham, turning east on A40—be sure to explore elegant Landsdowne Terrace, Pittville Spa, Sherborne Walk, and Montpellier Walk. Cheltenham may look in part like a Gilbert & Sullivan stage set but it is also home to the progressive **Cheltenham Festival of Literature,** held in October.

From Cheltenham, take B4632 to reach the Cotswolds proper. Two ★ kilometers (1 mi) southeast of Winchcombe is **Sudeley Castle,** the home and burial place of Catherine Parr (1512–48), Henry VIII's last wife. Restored by the Dent-Brocklehurst family, the Tudor-age mansion is surrounded by the most beautiful rose gardens in England, where Shakespeare performances are given in the summer. ✉ *Winchcombe,* ☎ *01242/604357,* WEB *www.stratford.co.uk.* ⏲ *Castle: Apr.–late-Oct., daily 11–5; gardens, grounds, plant center, and shop: early Mar.–late-Oct., daily 10:30–5:30.*

The tiny village of Stanway is landmarked by **Stanway House,** which dates from the Jacobean era and is familiar to many, thanks to its starring role in many TV dramas, including *The Buccaneers.* J. M. Barrie, author of *Peter Pan,* often rented this house in summer, and his thatched-roof cricket pavilion adorns the grounds. ✉ *Stanway,* ☎ *01386/584469.* ⏲ *Aug.–Sept., Tues. and Thurs. 2–5 (other times by appt. only for groups of at least 20).*

In the storybook hamlet of Snowshill lies the perfect Cotswold house, ★ **Snowshill Manor,** a 17th-century house overflowing with the amazing collections of bric-a-brac formed by Charles Paget Wade. ✉ *Snowshill,* ☎ *01386/852410.* ⏲ *Apr.–Oct., Wed.–Sun. noon–5; also Mon. in July and Aug. (grounds open May–Sept., Wed.–Sun. 11–5:30); last admission 30 mins before closing.*

Broadway is the Cotswold town to end all Cotswold towns. William Morris first discovered this village in the late 19th century, and lovers of rural England have journeyed there ever since to enjoy its many picturesque houses, tea parlors, and antiques shops.

The Cotswolds in a microcosm is the idyllic town of **Chipping Campden,** announced from afar by the soaring steeple of **St. James.** Look for the group of almshouses built in 1624 on High Street and raised above street level and for the gabled **Market Hall,** built three years later by Sir Baptiste Hycks for the sale of local produce. The historic **Silk Mill** has been renovated for crafts shops.

★ Six kilometers (4 mi) outside Chipping Campden is **Hidcote Manor Garden,** a 20th-century garden created around a Cotswold manor house (not open to the public). The lovely garden—which some connoisseurs consider the finest in Britain—consists of a series of open-air rooms divided by walls and hedges, each in a different style. Nearby is the fairy-tale hamlet of Hidcote Bartrim. ✉ *Hidcote Bartrim,* ☎ *01386/438333,* WEB *www.ntrustsevern.org.uk.* ⏲ *Apr.–Sept., Mon., Wed., Thurs., and weekends 10:30–6:30, also Tues. 10:30–6:30 in June–July, Oct. 10:30–5:30; last admission 1 hr before closing.*

Stow-on-the-Wold is the highest, as well as the largest, town in the Cotswolds. Built around a wide square, Stow's imposing golden-stone houses have been discreetly converted into a good number of quality antiques stores.

Bourton-on-the-Water is the most classic of the Cotswold "water" villages. The River Windrush runs through town, crossed by low stone bridges. Follow the stream and its ducks to the old mill, now home to the **Cotswold Motor Museum and Toy Collection,** to enjoy exhibits of vintage cars and re-created stores. ✉ *Sherborne St.,* ☎ *01451/821255.* ⏲ *Mar.–Oct., daily 10–6.*

$$$$ ★ **Lygon Arms.** Mullioned windows, a gorgeous 17th-century stone facade, baronial fireplaces, and rooms that once sheltered Charles I and Oliver Cromwell make this one of the most luxurious hotels of the Cotswolds. On the main street of Broadway, the inn also has 3 acres of private gardens. ✉ *High St., Broadway WR12 7DU,* ☎ *01386/ 852255,* FAX *01386/858611,* WEB *savoy-group.co.uk. 65 rooms. Restaurant, indoor pool. AE, DC, MC, V.*

$$$$ **Queen's Hotel.** Overlooking Imperial Gardens from the center of Cheltenham's Promenade, this classic Regency building has welcomed visitors since 1838. Decor is very British, though there's a taste of France, too: one of the hotel's two restaurants is Le Petit Blanc, open to nonresidents and a great place to sample French provincial cooking. ✉ *The Promenade, Cheltenham GL50 1NN,* ☎ *0870/4008107; 01242/ 266800 (restaurant),* FAX *01242/224145,* WEB *www.forte-hotels.com. 79 rooms. 2 restaurants. AE, DC, MC, V.*

$$ **Coombe House.** This neat guest house has comfortable bedrooms, an attractive garden, and ample parking. ✉ *Rissington Rd., Bourton-on-the-Water GL54 2DT,* ☎ *01451/821966,* FAX *01451/810477,* WEB *www.coombehousecotswolds.co.uk. 6 rooms. DC, MC, V. Closed Nov.–Mar..*

Bath

Numbers in the margin correspond to points of interest on the Bath map.

Bath lies at the southern end of the Cotswolds (at the end of A46), some 113 km (70 mi) from Stratford. A perfect 18th-century city, perhaps the best-preserved in all Britain, it is a compact place, easy to explore on foot; the museums, elegant shops, and terraces of magnificent town houses are all close to one another. Bath's golden age came about when the city became England's fashionable center for taking the waters. The architect John Wood created a harmonious vision from the mellow local stone, building beautifully executed terraces and crescents throughout the city. After promenading through the town, stop at either the Pump Room for morning coffee or afternoon tea in grand surroundings (perhaps listening to the music of a string quartet), or Sally Lunn's, where the famous Sally Lunn bun is still baked.

2 **Abbey.** Next to the Pump Room is the town abbey, built in the 15th century. There are superb fan-vaulted ceilings in the nave and a multimedia show about the abbey's history in the adjacent Heritage Vaults. ✉ *Abbey Churchyard.* ⏲ *Abbey Apr.–Sept., Mon.–Sat. 9–6; Oct.–Mar., Mon.–Sat. 9–4:30; Heritage Vaults Mon.–Sat. 10–4.*

5 **Assembly Rooms.** Near the Circus, these Assembly Rooms are frequently mentioned by Jane Austen in her novels of early 19th-century life. Set in a neoclassical mansion, the salons now house a Museum of Costume that displays dress styles from Beau Nash's day to the present. ✉ *Bennett St.,* ☎ *01225/477789.* ⏲ *Daily 10–5.*

★ 3 **The Circus.** To the north of Sawclose, you can admire some of the finest Georgian architecture at Queen Square and Gay Street, but the heart of Georgian Bath is the perfectly proportioned Circus, begun in 1754. Three Georgian terraces, with a frieze running round them, outline the round garden in the center.

8 **Holburne Museum.** Housed in an elegant 18th-century building, this museum contains a superb collection of 17th- and 18th-century fine art, silverware, and decorative arts. ✉ *Great Pulteney St.,* ☎ *01225/ 466669,* WEB *www.bath.ac.uk/holburne.* ⏲ *Mid-Feb.–mid-Dec., Tues.–Sat. 10–5, Sun. 2:30–5:30.*

Abbey 2
Assembly Rooms 5
The Circus . . . 3
Holburne Museum and Crafts Study Centre 8
No. 1 Royal Crescent 4
Pulteney Bridge 7
Roman Baths Museum 1
Theatre Royal 6

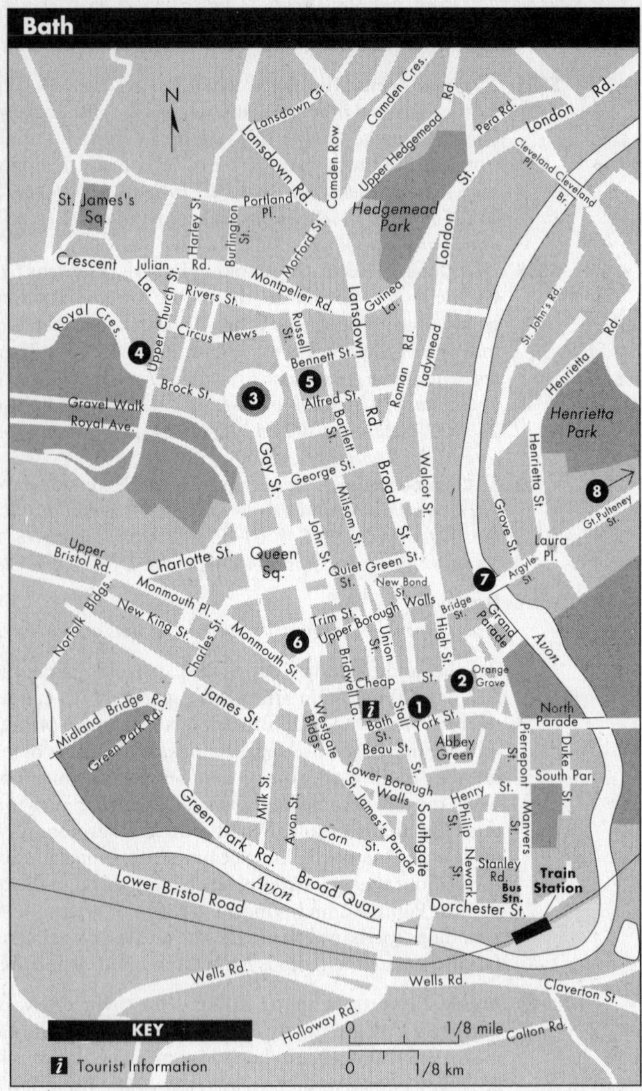

★ ❹ **No. 1 Royal Crescent.** On Bath's most graceful crescent, this house is furnished as it might have been when Beau Nash, the master of ceremonies and arbiter of 18th-century Bath society, lived in the city. The rooms allow a delightful peek into the gracious lifestyles of the Age of Enlightenment. ☏ *01225/428126,* WEB *www.bath-preservation-trust.org.uk.* ⌚ *Mid-Feb.–Oct., Tues.–Sun. 10:30–5; Nov., Tues.–Sun. 10:30–4.*

❼ **Pulteney Bridge.** One of the most charming and picturesque sights in Bath is this 18th-century span, whose design was based on the Ponte Vecchio of Florence. Lined with little shops, the bridge is the only work of Robert Adam in the city. The graceful Avon flows beneath, with ornamental gardens to one side.

★ ❶ **Roman Baths Museum.** The Romans were the first to take the waters at Bath, and they built a temple in honor of their goddess Minerva and a sophisticated series of baths to make full use of the curative hot springs. To this day, these springs gush from the earth at a constant temperature of 115.7°F (46.5°C). Underneath the 18th-century Pump Room, you can see the excavated remains of almost the entire baths complex. ✉ *Abbey Churchyard,* ☎ *01225/477785.* ⏲ *Apr.–July and Sept., daily 9–6; Aug., daily 9–6 and 8–10; Oct.–Mar., daily 9:30–5.*

6 **Theatre Royal.** This theater opened in 1805 and was restored in 1982. Next door the former home of Beau Nash—the dictator of fashion for mid-18th-century society in Bath—and his mistress Juliana Popjoy is now a restaurant called Popjoy's.

$$$ ✕ **Popjoy's Restaurant.** Beau Nash entertained the best of 18th-century society here, and Popjoy's retains its air of elegance. Diners can choose between dining on the ground floor or upstairs in a lovely Georgian drawing room. ✉ *Sawclose,* ☎ *01225/460494. Reservations essential. AE, DC, MC, V. Closed Sun.*

$$$ ✕ **Pump Room.** In addition to the famous morning coffee, lunches, and afternoon tea served here, often to music by a string trio. The adjoining Terrace Restaurant has views over Bath and is also open for evening meals (prix fixe) during the Bath Festival and in August and December. Reservations are a must for evening. ✉ *Abbey Churchyard,* ☎ *01225/444477. AE, MC, V. No dinner Sept.–Nov. or Jan.–July.*

$$ ✕ **Number Five.** This candlelit bistro off Pulteney Bridge has a relaxed ambience and offers tasty homemade soups or more elaborate dishes such as roast quail on wild rice and char-grilled loin of lamb. ✉ *5 Argyle St.,* ☎ *01225/444499. AE, DC, MC, V. Closed Sun. No lunch Mon.*

$$$$ ★ ✕🏨 **Queensberry Hotel.** In a quiet residential street near the Circus, this intimate, elegant hotel is in three 1772 town houses built by the architect John Wood for the Marquis of Queensberry. Renovations have preserved the Regency touches, and below stairs the Olive Tree restaurant serves English and Mediterranean dishes. ✉ *Russell St., BA1 2QF,* ☎ *01225/447928,* FAX *01225/446065,* WEB *www.bathqueensberry.com. 29 rooms. Restaurant. MC, V. Closed Dec. 24–30.*

$$$$ ★ 🏨 **Royal Crescent.** The ultimate in luxury living, in a gracious, lavishly converted building, the hotel stands on one of England's most famous terraces. Each bedroom has been individually designed to recapture the elegance of Bath's heyday. The hotel's formal Pimpernel's restaurant wins consistent praise. ✉ *16 Royal Crescent, BA1 2LS,* ☎ *01225/823333,* FAX *01225/339401,* WEB *www.royalcrescent.co.uk. 25 rooms, 19 suites. Restaurant. AE, DC, MC, V.*

$$–$$$ 🏨 **Paradise House.** It's a steep uphill climb from the center of Bath, but you'll be rewarded by a wonderful prospect of the city from the upper stories of this Georgian guest house. It features open fires in winter and a lush, secluded garden for the spring and summer. ✉ *88 Holloway, BA2 4PX,* ☎ *01225/317723,* FAX *01225/482005,* WEB *www.paradise-house.co.uk. 11 rooms. AE, DC, MC, V. Closed last wk. in Dec.*

Windsor to Bath Essentials

BUS TRAVEL

Regular long-distance services leave from Victoria Coach Station. National Express has runs on the route. Oxford Bus Company serves the region. The Green Line bus leaves from Eccleston Bridge, behind London's Victoria train station, *not* from the Coach Station itself. Make sure you catch the fast direct service, which takes 45 minutes and runs hourly; the stopping services take up to 1¼ hours.

➤ BUS INFORMATION: **Green Line** (☎ 020/8668–7261). **National Express** (☎ 0870/580–8080). **Oxford Bus Company** (☎ 01865/785400, WEB www.oxfordbus.co.uk).

CAR TRAVEL

M4 and M40 are the main highways out of London serving Oxford, the Cotswolds, and Bath. Once you're clear of London, take to the country roads and explore tiny villages and the best of the English countryside.

TOURS

Evan Evans operates daily one-day tours to Oxford, Stratford, and the Cotswolds. Frames Rickards runs full-day sightseeing tours to Windsor, Stratford-upon-Avon, Oxford, and Bath. Golden Tours runs four-day trips to Oxford, Stratford, and the Cotswolds from London. Guide Friday offers excellent open-top bus tours of Windsor, Oxford, the Cotswolds, and Shakespeare Country.

➤ FEES AND SCHEDULES: **Evan Evans** (☎ 020/7950–1777). **Frames Rickards** (☎ 020/7837–3111). **Golden Tours** (☎ 020/7233–7030). **Guide Friday** (☎ 01865/790522 Windsor and Oxford; 01789/294466 Stratford; 01225/444102 Bath, WEB www.guidefriday.com).

TRAIN TRAVEL

Windsor is easy to reach by train from London, either from Waterloo direct to Windsor and Eton Riverside (50 minutes), or from Paddington to Windsor Central, changing at Reading (45 minutes); there are two trains per hour on each route. Regular fast trains run from Paddington to Oxford and Bath, and less frequent and slower services requiring at least one change, to Stratford. An alternative route to Stratford is from London's Euston Station to Coventry, from which there are hourly bus connections on the Stratford Blue line.

➤ TRAIN INFORMATION: **National Rail Enquiries** (☎ 08457/484950, WEB www.nationalrail.co.uk). **Stratford Blue line** (☎ 01788/535555).

VISITOR INFORMATION

➤ TOURIST INFORMATION: **Bath** (✉ Abbey Chambers, Abbey Churchyard, Bath, ☎ 01225/477101, WEB www.visitbath.co.uk). **Oxford** (✉ The Old School, Gloucester Green, ☎ 01865/726871, WEB www.oxford.gov.uk). **Stow-on-the-Wold** (✉ Hollis House, The Square, ☎ 01451/831082). **Stratford** (✉ Bridgefoot, next to Clopton Bridge, ☎ 01789/293127, WEB www.stratford-upon-avon.co.uk). **Warwick** (✉ The Court House, Jury St., ☎ 01926/492212). **Windsor** (✉ 24 High St., ☎ 01753/743900, WEB www.windsor.gov.uk).

CAMBRIDGE

Cambridge, home of England's second-oldest university, is an ideal place to explore. There have been students here since the late 13th century, and virtually every generation after that has produced fine buildings, often by the most distinguished architects of its day. The result is a compact gallery of the best of English architecture. There is also good shopping in the city, and you can enjoy relaxing riverside walks. Cambridge is 87 km (54 mi) north of London, 66 km (41 mi) northwest of Colchester, and 102 km (63 mi) southwest of Norwich.

Exploring Cambridge

Numbers in the margin correspond to points of interest on the Cambridge map.

The university is in the very heart of Cambridge. It consists of a number of colleges, each of which is a separate institution with its own distinct character. Undergraduates join an individual college and are taught by dons, who are known as "fellows." Each college is built around a series of courts, or quadrangles; because students and fellows live in

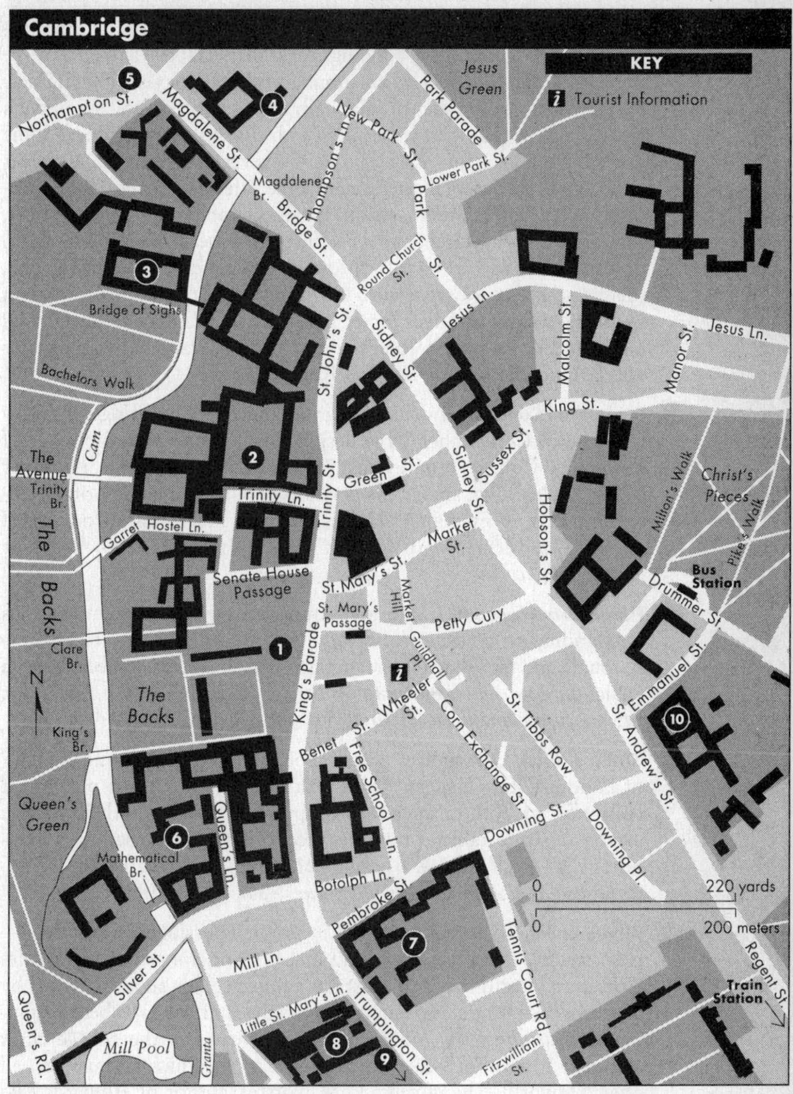

Emmanuel College 10
Fitzwilliam Museum 9
Kettle's Yard 5
King's College 1
Magdalene College 4
Pembroke College . . . 7
Peterhouse College 8
Queen's College 6
St. John's College . . . 3
Trinity College 2

these quadrangles, access is sometimes restricted. Visitors are not normally allowed into college buildings other than chapels, halls, and some libraries; some colleges levy an admission charge for certain buildings. Public visiting hours vary dramatically from college to college, and it's best to call ahead or to check first with the city tourist office. Some general guidelines for visiting hours, however, can be noted. Colleges close to visitors during the main exam time, late May to mid-June. Term-time (when classes are in session) means October through December, January through March, and April through June, while summer term, or vacations, run from July through September. If you have time, there's no better way to absorb Cambridge's unique atmosphere than by hiring a punt at Silver Street Bridge or at Magdalene Bridge and navigating down past St. John's or upstream to Grantchester, the pretty village made famous by the poet Rupert Brooke.

⑩ **Emmanuel College.** Evident throughout much of Cambridge, the master hand of Christopher Wren designed the chapel and colonnade of Emmanuel College, founded in 1584. The college was an early center of Puritan learning; among the portraits of famous members of the college hanging in Emmanuel Hall is one of John Harvard, founder of Harvard University. ✉ *St. Andrew's St.,* ☎ *01223/334200,* WEB *www.emma.cam.ac.uk.*

⑨ **Fitzwilliam Museum.** Cambridge's most renowned museum contains outstanding art collections (including paintings by Constable, Gainsborough, and the French Impressionists) and antiquities (especially from ancient Egypt). ✉ *Trumpington St.,* ☎ *01223/332900,* WEB *www.fitzmuseum.cam.ac.uk.* ⊙ *Tues.–Sat. 10–5, Sun. 2:15–5.*

⑤ **Kettle's Yard.** Originally a private house owned by a former curator of London's Tate Gallery, Kettle's Yard is home to a fine permanent collection of 20th-century art, sculpture, furniture, and decorative arts. A separate gallery provides space for a regular program of exhibitions. ✉ *Castle St.,* ☎ *01223/352124,* WEB *www.kettlesyard.co.uk.* ⊙ *House Tues.–Sun. 2–4; gallery Tues.–Sat. 11:30–5, Sun. 2–5:30.*

★ ① **King's College.** The high point of King's—and possibly of Cambridge—is its chapel, started by Henry VI in 1446 and a masterpiece of late-Gothic architecture, with a great fan-vaulted ceiling supported only by a tracery of soaring side columns. Behind the altar hangs Rubens's painting *Adoration of the Magi.* Every Christmas Eve the college choir sings the Festival of Nine Lessons and Carols, which is broadcast all over the world. The novelist E. M. Forster, author of *Howards End* and *A Passage to India,* studied at King's, as did the war poet Rupert Brooke. King's runs down to the **"Backs,"** the tree-shaded grounds on the banks of the River Cam, which is the background of many of the colleges. ✉ *King's Parade,* ☎ *01223/331447,* WEB *www.kings.cam.ac.uk.* ⊙ *Chapel term-time, Mon. 9:30–4:30, Tues.–Fri. 9:30–3:30, Sat. 9:30–3:15, Sun. 1:15–2:15; summer, Mon.–Sat. 9:30–4:30, Sun. 1:15–2:15 and 5–5:30.*

④ **Magdalene College.** Across Magdalene (pronounced *maud*-lin) Bridge, a cast-iron 1820 structure, is Magdalene College, distinguished by pretty redbrick courts. It was a hostel for Benedictine monks for more than 100 years before the college was founded in 1542. The college's **Pepys Library** contains the books and desk of the 17th-century diarist Samuel Pepys. Admission to the library is free and it's open April–September, Monday–Saturday 11:30–12:30 and 2:30–5:30; October–March, Monday–Saturday 2:30–3:30. ✉ *Magdalene St.,* ☎ *01223/332100,* WEB *www.magd.cam.ac.uk.*

7 **Pembroke College.** The first court of Pembroke College (1347) has some buildings dating from the 14th century. On the south side, Christopher Wren's chapel—his first major commission, completed in 1665—looks like a distinctly modern intrusion. You can walk through the college, around a delightful garden, and past the fellows' bowling green. ✉ *Trumpington St.,* ☎ *01223/338100.*

8 **Peterhouse College.** Cambridge's oldest college was founded in 1281 by the Bishop of Ely. Parts of the dining hall date from 1290; the chapel, in late-Gothic style, dates from 1632. On the river side of the buildings is a large and tranquil deer park. ✉ *Trumpington St.,* ☎ *01223/338200,* WEB *www.pet.cam.ac.uk.*

6 **Queen's College.** One of the most eye-catching colleges, Queen's (1446) is named after the respective consorts of Henry VI and Edward IV. The college's Mathematical Bridge (best seen from the Silver Street road bridge) is an arched wooden structure that was originally held together by gravity; when it was taken apart to see how Isaac Newton did it, no one could reconstruct it without using nails. The present bridge, dating from 1902, is securely bolted. ✉ *Queen's La.,* ☎ *01223/335511,* WEB *www.quns.cam.ac.uk.* ⏲ *Daily 1:45–4:30.*

3 **St. John's College.** St. John's is Cambridge's second-largest college, founded in 1511 by Henry VII's mother, Lady Margaret Beaufort. The famous copy of the Bridge of Sighs in Venice is here, reaching across the Cam to the mock-Gothic New Court (1825). ✉ *St. John's St.,* ☎ *01223/338600,* WEB *www.joh.cam.ac.uk.* ⏲ *Weekdays 10–5:30, weekends 9:30–5:30.*

2 **Trinity College.** This is the largest college, with almost 700 undergraduates, established by Henry VIII in 1546. It has a handsome 17th-century Great Court, around which are sited the chapel, hall, gates, and a magnificent library by Christopher Wren—colonnaded and seemingly constructed as much of light as of stone. In the massive gatehouse is Great Tom, a large clock that strikes each hour and that figured in the race around the quadrangle at the heart of the movie *Chariots of Fire.* Prince Charles was an undergraduate here in the late 1960s. ✉ *St. John's St.,* ☎ *01223/338400,* WEB *www.trin.cam.ac.uk.* ⏲ *College daily 10–6; library weekdays noon–2, Sat. term time 10:30–12:30.*

$$–$$$ ★ ✕ **Midsummer House.** A classy restaurant set beside the River Cam, Midsummer House is lovely in summer. There's a comfortable conservatory. Set-price menus for lunch and dinner offer a selection of robust yet sophisticated European and Mediterranean dishes. Choices might include tender lamb or the best from the fish market adorned with inventively presented vegetables. ✉ *Midsummer Common,* ☎ *01223/369299. Reservations essential. AE, DC, MC, V. Closed Mon. No lunch Sat., no dinner Sun.*

$–$$ ✕ **Brown's.** This huge, airy French-American–style brasserie-diner was converted from the outpatient department of the old Addenbrooke's Hospital opposite the Fitzwilliam Museum. Large fans still keep things cool in the pale yellow dining room. The wide-ranging menu runs from toasted tuna sandwiches, steak-mushroom-and-Guinness pie, hamburgers, and salads to venison or gigot of lamb; check the daily specials, too—there's usually fresh fish and pasta. ✉ *23 Trumpington St.,* ☎ *01223/461655. AE, MC, V.*

$$$$ ★ **Garden Moat House Hotel.** Set among the colleges, this luxurious modern hotel makes the most of its peaceful riverside location—it even rents out its own punts. Its gardens, lounge, cocktail bar, and conservatories all have river views, as do most of the smart guest rooms—if you want one, ask when you make your reservation. A leisure center

incorporates an indoor pool, a gym, a sauna, and a steam room. ✉ *Granta Pl., Mill La., CB2 1RT,* ☎ *01223/259988,* FAX *01223/316605. 118 rooms. Restaurant, pool. AE, DC, MC, V.*

$$$ **Arundel House.** This hotel occupies a converted terrace of Victorian houses overlooking the river Cam and Jesus Green, while a pleasing conservatory and patio-garden out back offers a calm hideaway. The bedrooms are comfortably furnished with locally made mahogany furniture; Continental breakfast is included in the room rate, and a full breakfast is available for an extra charge. ✉ *53 Chesterton Rd., CB4 3AN,* ☎ *01223/367701,* FAX *01223/367721. 105 rooms. Restaurant. AE, DC, MC, V.*

Cambridge Essentials

BUS TRAVEL TO AND FROM CAMBRIDGE

There are 14 buses daily from Victoria Coach Station that take just under two hours.

➤ Bus Information: (☎ 0990/808080).

CAR TRAVEL

M11 is the main highway from London to Cambridge. The main car-rental companies have offices in Cambridge.

TOURS

BUS TOURS

Guide Friday, in Cambridge, operates a city open-top bus tour every 15 minutes throughout the day (October–May, half-hourly); tickets (£7.50) can be bought from the driver, the office at Cambridge train station, or the Cambridge Tourist Information Center. You can join the tours at the station or at any of the specially marked bus stops throughout the city.

➤ Fees and Schedules: **Guide Friday** (☎ 01223/362444).

WALKING TOURS

The Cambridge Tourist Information Centre offers two-hour guided walking tours of the city and the colleges daily; tickets (£5.75) are available up to 24 hours in advance. Various theme tours are also offered, including combined walking-punting tours and 1½-hour evening pub tours. Booking is essential—the tours are very popular.

TRAIN TRAVEL

Half-hourly trains from London's Liverpool Street Station and King's Cross Station run to Cambridge. Because of problems with the British rail network, average journey times now vary from 1½ to 2 hours, depending on the day of week or time of day.

➤ Train Information: (☎ 0345/484950).

VISITOR INFORMATION

➤ Tourist Information: **Cambridge Tourist Information Centre** (✉ Wheeler St., off King's Parade, CB2 3QB, ☎ 01223/322640, FAX 01223/463385).

YORK

Once England's second city in terms of population and importance, ancient York has survived the ravages of time, war, and industrialization to remain one of northern Europe's few preserved walled cities, although in terms of physical size it is considerably smaller than northern England's main cities. King George VI, father of the present Queen, remarked that the history of York is the history of England. Even in a brief visit to the city, you can see evidence of life from every era since the Ro-

Castle Museum **3**
Jorvik Viking Center **2**
Merchant Adventurers' Hall **6**
National Railway Museum **7**
Shambles . . . **4**
Stonegate . . . **5**
York Minster **1**

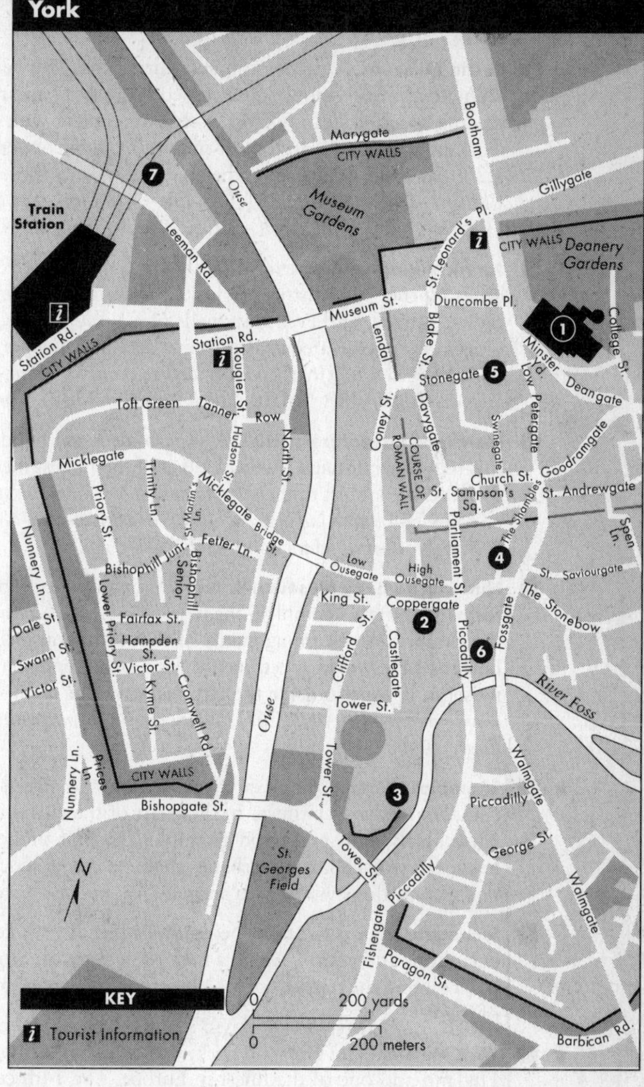

mans, not only in museums but also in the very streets and houses. York—41 km (25 mi) northeast of Leeds, 133 km (82 mi) south of Newcastle—is set in a fertile plain, dotted with ancient abbeys and grand aristocratic mansions, that leads westward to the hidden valleys and jagged, windswept tops of the Yorkshire Dales and northward to the brooding mass of the North York Moors. This is a land quite different from the south of England—it's emptier, and less aggressively materialistic.

Exploring York

Numbers in the margin correspond to points of interest on the York map.

You can get a first, memorable overview of the city by taking a stroll along the **city walls.** Originally they were earth ramparts erected by York's Viking kings to repel raiders; the present stone structure dates from the 14th century. A narrow paved walk runs along the top (originally 5 km/3 mi in circumference), passing over York's distinctive fortified gates, or "bars," and providing delightful views across rooftops and gardens.

★ ❸ **Castle Museum.** A debtor's prison during the 18th century, this museum now offers a number of detailed exhibitions and re-creations, including a cobblestone Victorian street complete with crafts shops; a working water mill; and, most important, the Coppergate Helmet, a 1,200-year-old Anglo-Saxon helmet, one of only three ever found. ✉ *Clifford St.,* ☎ *01904/653611.* ⏲ *Apr.–Oct., Mon.–Sat. 9:30–5:30, Sun. 10–5:30; Nov.–Mar., Mon.–Sat. 9:30–4:30, Sun. 10–4.*

❷ **Jorvik Viking Centre.** On this authentic Viking site, you can take another journey into history—whisked back in little "time cars" to the sights, sounds, and even the smells of a Viking street, which archaeologists have re-created in astonishing detail. ✉ *Coppergate,* ☎ *01904/653211,* WEB *www.jorvik-viking-centre.co.uk.* ⏲ *Apr.–Oct., daily 9–7; Nov.–Mar., daily 9–5:30 (last admission 2 hrs before closing).*

❻ **Merchant Adventurers' Hall.** A superb medieval building (1357–68), this hall was built and owned by one of the richest medieval guilds; it contains the largest timber-frame hall in York. ✉ *Fossgate,* ☎ *01904/654818,* WEB *www.kidsnet.co.uk.* ⏲ *Mid-Mar.–mid-Nov., daily 8:30–5; mid-Nov.–mid-Mar., Mon.–Sat. 8:30–3:30.*

❼ **National Railway Museum.** Britain's national collection of locomotives forms part of this complex, the world's largest train museum. Among the exhibits are gleaming giants of the steam era, including *Mallard,* holder of the world speed record for a steam engine (126 mph). The museum lies just outside the city walls, by the train station. ✉ *Leeman Rd.,* ☎ *01904/621261,* WEB *www.tourist-information-uk.com.* ⏲ *Daily 10–6.*

★ ❹ **Shambles.** Within York's city walls the narrow streets still follow the complex medieval pattern. In the heart of the city is the Shambles, a particularly well preserved example; the half-timbered shops and houses have such large overhangs that you can practically reach from one second-floor window to another.

❺ **Stonegate.** This is a narrow pedestrian street of 18th-century (and earlier) shops and courts. Along a narrow passage off Stonegate, at 52A, you will find the remains of a 12th-century Norman stone house—one of the very few surviving in England.

★ ❶ **York Minster.** The glory of York, this is the largest Gothic church in England and one of the finest in Europe. The 14th-century nave has soaring columns and intricate tracery, the choir screen portrays whimsical images of the kings of England, and the mighty rose window—just one of 128 stained-glass windows in the Minster—commemorates the marriage of Henry VII and Elizabeth of York. Visit the exquisite 13th-century **Chapter House** and the Roman and Saxon remains in the **Undercroft Museum and Treasury.** The 275 steps of the **Central Tower** lead to an unrivaled view of the city and the countryside beyond. The **Crypt** contains some of the cathedral's oldest and most valuable treasures, among them the Romanesque 12th-century statue of a heavy-footed Virgin Mary. ✉ *Duncombe Pl.,* ☎ *01904/624426 for York Minster Undercroft Museum and Treasury, Chapter House, Crypt, and Central Tower,* WEB *www.yorkminster.org.* ⏲ *Minster Apr.–Oct., daily 7 AM–8:30 PM; Nov.–Mar., daily 7–6. Undercroft, Chapter House, Crypt, and Central Tower Apr.–Oct., Mon.–Sat. 10–5:30, Sun. 1–5:30; Nov.–Mar., Mon.–Sat. 10–4:30, Sun. 1–4:30.*

$$–$$$ ✕ **19 Grape Lane.** The narrow, slightly cramped restaurant is housed
★ in a typically leaning timbered York building in the heart of town. It

serves modern English food from a blackboard of such specials as grilled wild boar sausages, and the substantial puddings are always a treat. ✉ *19 Grape La.,* ☎ *01904/636366. MC, V. Closed Sun., 1 wk at Christmas, 2 wks in Feb., 2 wks in Sept.*

$–$$ ✕ **Varsity.** At lunchtime in this airy brasserie you can feast on a set three-course menu of simple French food, one of the city's best bargains. At dinner prices increase, but not outrageously so, and the dishes become more elaborate: choose from warming seasonal soups, confit of duck, or that old brasserie standby, *moules marinières* (mussels). ✉ *2 Lendal,* ☎ *01904/655222. MC, V.*

$$$ **Dean Court.** This large Victorian house once provided accommodation for the clergy of York Minster, which looms just across the road. Refurbished to a high quality, it now has comfortably furnished rooms with plump sofas, TVs, and fine views overlooking the Minster. The restaurant serves good English cuisine, including a hearty Yorkshire breakfast. ✉ *Duncombe Pl., YO1 2EF,* ☎ *01904/625082,* FAX *01904/620305. 40 rooms. Restaurant. AE, DC, MC, V.*

$$–$$$ **Savages.** Despite its name, this small hotel on a leafy road near the town center is eminently refined, with a reputation for attentive service. Once a Victorian home, it has a stylish and comfortable interior, and there's a bar in which to relax. ✉ *15 St. Peter's Grove, Clifton, YO3 6AQ,* ☎ *01904/610818,* FAX *01904/627729. 21 rooms. Restaurant. AE, DC, MC, V.*

$ **Abbey Guest House.** This pretty, no-smoking, terraced guest house—formerly an artisan's house—is a 10-minute walk from the train station and town center. Although small, it's very clean and friendly, with a peaceful garden right on the river and ducks pottering about outside. Picnic lunches and evening meals can be arranged on request. ✉ *14 Earlsborough Terr., Marygate, YO3 7BQ,* ☎ *01904/627782. 7 rooms, 2 with bath. AE, MC, V.*

Side Trips: Fountains Abbey and Castle Howard

★ Thirty-two kilometers (21 mi) northwest of York, along B6265, you'll find that the majestic ruins of **Fountains Abbey,** with its own high tower and soaring 13th-century arches, make a striking picture on the banks of the River Skell. Founded in 1132, the abbey still possesses many of its original buildings, and the National Trust operates informative free guided tours around them; tours run April–October only, usually at 1:30, 2:30, and 3:30. The extensive ruins are set beside an 18th-century water garden and deer park, **Studley Royal,** combining lakes, ponds, and even a diverted river, while waterfalls splash around classical temples, statues, and a grotto. ✉ *Off B6265,* ☎ *01765/608888; 01765/601005 weekends,* WEB *www.fountainsabbey.org.uk.* ⏲ *Nov.–Jan., Sat.–Thurs. 10–5 (or dusk); Feb.–Mar. and Oct., daily 10–5 (or dusk); Apr.–Sept., daily 10–7.*

Newby Hall—reached along pleasant country roads 5 km (3 mi) east of Fountains Abbey—has some restored interiors by the 18th-century master architect Robert Adam and some equally celebrated gardens with a collection of rare roses. ✉ *Skelton-on-Ure,* ☎ *01423/322583,* WEB *www.newbyhall.co.uk.* ⏲ *Easter–Oct., Tues.–Sun. grounds 11–5, house noon–5.*

★ Twenty-four km (15 mi) northeast of York is **Castle Howard,** one of the grandest and most opulent stately homes in Britain. Its magnificent silhouette is punctuated by stone chimneys and a graceful central dome. Many people know it best as Brideshead, the home of the Flyte family in Evelyn Waugh's tale of aristocratic woe, *Brideshead Revisited*; this was where much of the TV series was filmed. The audacity and confidence of the great Baroque house are startling, proclaiming the wealth and importance of the Howards and the utter self-assurance of its architect, Sir John Vanbrugh. Castle Howard took 60 years to build (1699–1759) and it was worth every year. A magnificent central hallway dwarfs all visitors, and there is no shortage of grandeur elsewhere: vast family portraits, delicate marble fireplaces, immense tapestries, and a great many marble busts. Outside, the stately theme continues in one of the most stunning neoclassical landscapes in England. ✉ *Coneysthorpe,* ☎ *01653/648333,* WEB *www.castlehoward.co.uk.* *House and gardens £7.* ⏲ *House mid-Mar.–Oct., daily 11–4:30; grounds daily 10–5.*

York Essentials

BUS TRAVEL TO AND FROM YORK

National Express buses to York leave from London's Victoria Coach Station. Average travel time is 4½ hours to York.

➤ BUS INFORMATION: **National Express** (☎ 0990/808080).

CAR TRAVEL

Take the A1, the historic main route from London to the north, which branches east onto the A64 near Tadcaster for the final 19 km (12 mi) to York. Alternatively, take the M1, then the M18, and finally the A1. The drive from London takes a minimum of four hours.

TOURS

BUS TOURS

Guide Friday runs frequent city tours of York that allow you to get on and off the bus as you please (£7.50, £5.50 if booked in advance). It also conducts tours of the surrounding countryside, including Fountains Abbey and Castle Howard. Yorktour also offers tours to Castle Howard.

➤ FEES AND SCHEDULES: **Guide Friday** (✉ De Grey Rooms, Exhibition Sq., ☎ 01904/640896). **Yorktour** (☎ 01904/641737).

WALKING TOURS

The York Association of Voluntary Guides arranges short walking tours around the city each morning at 10:15, with additional tours at 2:15 PM April–October, and one at 7 PM July–August.

➤ FEES AND SCHEDULES: **York Association of Voluntary Guides** (✉ De Grey Rooms, Exhibition Sq., ☎ 01904/640780).

TRAIN TRAVEL

Great North-Eastern Railways serves York from London King's Cross. Journeys on the fastest trains take two-and-a-half hours.

➤ TRAIN INFORMATION: **Great North-Eastern Railways** (☎ 0345/484950).

VISITOR INFORMATION

➤ TOURIST INFORMATION: (✉ De Grey Rooms, Exhibition Sq., North Yorkshire, YO1 2HB, ☎ 01904/621756; ✉ York railway station, ☎ 01904/621756; ✉ 20 George Hudson St., ☎ 01904/554488).

THE LAKE DISTRICT

Poets Wordsworth and Coleridge can probably be held responsible for the development of the Lake District as a tourist destination. They, and other English men of letters, found it an inspiring setting for their work—and fashion, and thousands of visitors, have followed. The district, created in the 1970s as a national park from parts of the old counties of Cumberland, Westmorland, and Lancashire, combines so much that

The Lake District

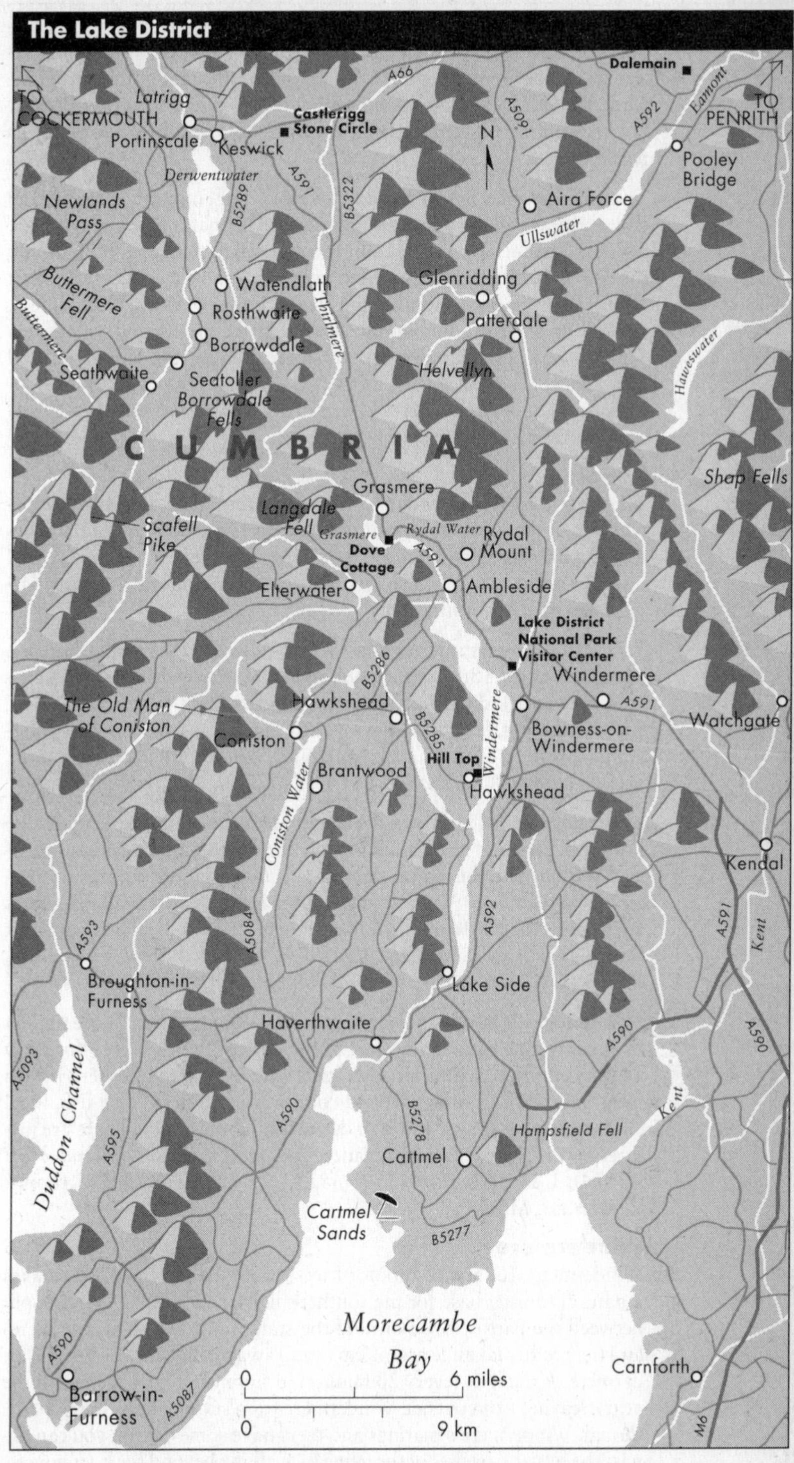
TO COCKERMOUTH
Latrigg
Portinscale
Keswick
Castlerigg Stone Circle
A66
Dalemain
A5091
A592
Eamont
TO PENRITH
Pooley Bridge
N
Derwentwater
A591
B5322
B5289
Newlands Pass
Aira Force
Ullswater
Buttermere Fell
Buttermere
Watendlath
Rosthwaite
Borrowdale
Thirlmere
Glenridding
Patterdale
Haweswater
Seathwaite
Seatoller
Borrowdale Fells
Helvellyn
CUMBRIA
Shap Fells
Grasmere
Langdale Fell
Grasmere
Rydal Water
Dove Cottage
Rydal Mount
Scafell Pike
Elterwater
Ambleside
Lake District National Park Visitor Center
Windermere
B5286
The Old Man of Coniston
Hawkshead
Coniston
B5285
Windermere
A591
Watchgate
Bowness-on-Windermere
Hill Top
Brantwood
Hawkshead
Coniston Water
Kendal
A592
A5084
A593
A591
Kent
Broughton-in-Furness
Lake Side
Haverthwaite
A590
A590
A5093
Duddon Channel
A590
B5278
Kent
Hampsfield Fell
A595
Cartmel
Cartmel Sands
B5277
Morecambe Bay
A590
0
6 miles
0
9 km
Carnforth
Barrow-in-Furness
A5087
M6

is magnificent in mountain, lake, and dale that entrancing vistas open out at each corner of the road. In addition to Wordsworth and Coleridge, other literary figures who made their homes in the region include De Quincey, Ruskin, Arnold, and the children's writer Beatrix Potter. Walking is perhaps the best way to discover the delights of this peaceful area.

The Lake District lies in the northwest of England, the entire region contained within the county of Cumbria. The major gateway from the south is Kendal; from the north, the gateway is Penrith—both are on the M6 motorway. The southern lakes and valleys contain the most popular destinations, notably the largest body of water, Windermere, as well as such quintessential Lake District towns and villages as Kendal, Bowness, Ambleside, Grasmere, Elterwater, Coniston, and Hawkshead. Among the northern lakes, south of Keswick and Cockermouth, you have the best chance to get away from the crowds and soak up the Lake District experience.

Kendal

The ancient town of Kendal—113 km (70 mi) north of Manchester—was one of the most important textile centers in northern England before the Industrial Revolution. Away from the busy main road, you'll discover narrow, winding streets and charming courtyards, many dating from medieval times.

Take a stroll along the River Kent, where—close to the Parish Church—you can visit the 18th-century **Abbott Hall.** Here the **Museum of Lakeland Life and Industry** offers interesting exhibits on blacksmithing, wheelwrighting, farming, weaving, printing, local architecture, and regional customs. ✉ *Kirkland,* ☎ *01539/722464,* WEB *www.abbothall.org.uk.* ⏲ *Apr.–Oct., daily 10:30–5; Nov.–Mar., daily 10:30–4.*

At the northern end of town the **Kendal Museum** details splendidly the flora and fauna of the Lake District. It also contains displays on Alfred Wainwright, the region's most avid chronicler of countryside matters, who died in 1991. His multivolume Lake District walking guides are famous the world over; you'll see them in every local book and gift shop. ✉ *Station Rd.,* ☎ *01539/721374,* WEB *www.kendalmuseum.org.* ⏲ *Apr.–Oct., daily 10:30–5; Nov.–Mar., daily 10:30–4.*

$ ✕🏨 **The Punch Bowl Inn.** Hidden along a country road in the hamlet of Crosthwaite, 8 km (5 mi) west of Kendal, the Punch Bowl—formerly a 16th-century coaching inn—delights with its inspired Modern British food (reservations essential) and comfortable rooms. Fresh fish, local lamb, warming soups, and rich desserts all hit the spot. There are just three rooms; book well in advance. ✉ *Crosthwaite, near Kendal (off A5074), LA8 8HR,* ☎ *015395/68237,* FAX *015395/68875. 3 rooms. Restaurant. MC, V.*

Windermere

★ Windermere, 16 km (10 mi) northwest of Kendal on the A591, makes a natural touring base for the southern half of the Lake District—split between the part of town around the station (known as Windermere) and the prettier lakeside area ½ km (¼ mi) away, called Bowness-on-Windermere. A minibus (every 20 minutes in summer, hourly the rest of the year), leaving from outside Windermere train station, links the two. Although Windermere's marinas and piers have some charm, you can bypass the busier stretches of shoreline by walking beyond the boat houses, which offer a fine view across the lake. A **ferry** crosses the water at this point to reach Far Sawrey and the road to Hawkshead; the crossing takes just a few minutes. ⏲ *Ferries run every 20 mins Mon.–Sat. 6:50 AM–9:50 PM, Sun. 9:10 AM–9:50 PM; Oct.–Easter until 8:50 PM.*

$$ ✕ **Porthole Eating House.** In an intimate 18th-century house in the center of Bowness, the small restaurant has a largely Italian menu with homemade pasta and excellent meat and fish dishes. In winter a large open fire adds to the ambience. ✉ *3 Ash St., Bowness-on-Windermere, ☎ 015394/42793. AE, DC, MC, V. Closed Tues. and mid-Dec.–late Feb. No lunch Sat.*
★

$$$$ **Miller Howe.** This small, white Edwardian country-house hotel is beautifully situated, with views across Windermere to the Langdale Pikes. The bedrooms have exceptional individual style—fresh and dried flowers are everywhere. The outstanding restaurant (reservations essential; jacket and tie) is renowned for its experimental, almost theatrical take on British cuisine—every night is a new performance. Menus change with the season. The room rate includes breakfast and dinner. ✉ *Rayrigg Rd., Bowness-on-Windermere LA23 1EY, ☎ 015394/42536, FAX 015394/45664, WEB www.millerhowe.com. 13 rooms. Restaurant. AE, DC, MC, V. Closed Jan.*
★

$ **Brendan Chase.** This well-maintained lodging is in the heart of Windermere's B&B-land, not far from the train station but about 2 km (1 mi) or so from the lake—though some rooms have distant water views. A full breakfast (English or vegetarian) sets you up for the day. ✉ *1–3 College Rd., Windermere LA23 1BU, ☎ 015394/45638. 8 rooms, 3 with bath. No credit cards.*

Brockhole

Five kilometers (3 mi) northwest of Windermere on the A591, a magnificent lakeside mansion houses the **Lake District National Park Visitor Centre,** which offers a fine range of exhibitions about the Lake District, including useful interpretative displays about the local ecology, flora, and fauna. The gardens are at their best in the spring, when floods of daffodils cover the lawns and the azaleas burst into bloom. ✉ *Ambleside Rd., ☎ 015394/46601. ⌚ Easter–late Oct., daily 10–5.*

Ambleside

The small town of Ambleside sits at the head of Lake Windermere—6½ km (4 mi) north of Brockhole, along the A591—making it a popular center for Lake District excursions. The town suffers terribly from tourist overcrowding in high season; Wednesday is particularly busy, when the local market takes place. However, it's easy enough to escape the crowds. Follow A593 west out of Ambleside and take the turning for the nearby village of **Elterwater,** a good stop for hikers. The B5343 continues west from here to **Langdale Fell,** where you can take one of several excellent walks: there are information boards at the various parking places.

$$ ✕ **Glass House.** This exciting conversion of an old watermill switches from a café by day to a thoroughly modern restaurant by night—with Mediterranean flavors, panfried fish, and char-grilled meats forming the mainstay of the menu. ✉ *Rydal Rd., ☎ 015394/32137. Reservations essential for dinner. MC, V.*

$ **Britannia Inn.** The Britannia is a friendly inn in the heart of splendid walking country, with quaint little rooms and hearty homemade English food served in the bar. The four guest rooms across the road in the Maple Tree Corner annex are a few pounds cheaper, but you'll have to walk over to the inn for breakfast. ✉ *Elterwater, on B5343, 6 km (4 mi) west of Ambleside, LA22 9HP, ☎ 015394/37210, FAX 015394/37311. 13 rooms, 9 with shower. Restaurant. MC, V.*
★

$ **3 Cambridge Villas.** Ambleside abounds in inexpensive B&Bs, but you'd be hard pressed to find a more welcoming spot than this—a lofty Victorian house right in the center, with hosts who know a thing or two about local walks. ✉ *Church St., LA22 9DL, ☎ 015394/32307. 8 rooms, 4 with shower. No credit cards. Closed Dec.–Jan.*

Rydal Mount

If there's one poet associated with the Lake District, it is William Wordsworth, who made his home at Rydal Mount, 2 km (1 mi) northwest of Ambleside, from 1813 until his death 37 years later. Wordsworth and his family moved to these grand surroundings when he was nearing the height of his career, and his descendants still live here, surrounded by his furniture, portraits, and the 4½-acre garden laid out by the poet himself. ✉ *Rydal, Ambleside,* ☎ *015394/33002.* ⏲ *Mar.–Oct., daily 9:30–5; Nov.–Feb., Wed.–Mon. 10–4. Closed 3 wks in Jan.*

Grasmere

The heart of Wordsworth country, Grasmere is one of the most typical of Lake District villages, sited on a tiny, wood-fringed lake 2 km (1 mi) north of Dove Cottage, 6½ km (4 mi) northwest of Ambleside, and made up of crooked lanes lined with charming slate-built cottages. Wordsworth lived on the town's outskirts for almost 50 years—at Rydal Mount and Dove Cottage—and he, his wife Mary, his sister Dorothy, and his daughter Dora are buried in Grasmere churchyard.

★ **Dove Cottage** is the leading literary shrine of the Lake District. Located 2½ km (1½ mi) northwest of Rydal Mount, this was Wordsworth's home from 1799 until 1808, and the tiny house still contains many personal belongings. Dove Cottage is also headquarters of the Centre for British Romanticism, which documents the literary contributions made by Wordsworth and his sister, Dorothy, Samuel Taylor Coleridge, Thomas De Quincey, and Robert Southey. ✉ *The Wordsworth Trust, Dove Cottage, Grasmere LA22 9SH,* ☎ *015394/35544,* WEB *www.wordsworth.org.uk.* ⏲ *Mid-Feb.–mid-Jan., daily 9:30–5.*

$$ ✕ **The Swan.** The handsome, flower-decked, 300-year-old Swan, a former coaching inn on the main road just outside Grasmere, keeps a fire in the lounge grate, an oak-beam restaurant serving Lake District specialties, and elegant guest rooms that combine space with fine views. ✉ *Grasmere, on the A591, LA22 9RF,* ☎ *015394/35551,* FAX *015394/35741. 36 rooms. Restaurant. AE, DC, MC, V.*

$ **Banerigg House.** You don't have to spend a fortune to find appealing lakeside lodgings in Grasmere. This turn-of-the-20th-century family house, 1½ km (¾ mi) south of the village, offers well-appointed, no-smoking rooms, most with lake views. ✉ *Lake Rd., LA22 9PW,* ☎ *015394/35204. 7 rooms, 5 with bath. No credit cards.*

Coniston

Formerly a copper-mining village, Coniston is now a small lake resort and boating center at the foot of the **Old Man of Coniston** (2,635 ft), 13 km (8 mi) south of Grasmere. Tracks lead up from the village past an old mine to the peak, which you can reach in about two hours, though many experienced hikers include the peak in an enervating seven-hour circular walk from the village.

★ Just outside Coniston is **Brantwood,** the home of Victorian artist, critic, and social reformer John Ruskin (1819–1900). Here, in the rambling white 18th-century house, you'll find a collection of Ruskin's own paintings, drawings, and books. The extensive grounds were laid out by Ruskin himself. It's an easy drive to Brantwood from Coniston, but it's much more agreeable to travel here by ferry across the lake. Services are available from the Coniston Launch (Easter–October, hourly departures; fewer sailings in winter) and the steam yacht *Gondola* (April–October, four–five trips daily), both departing from Coniston Pier. ✉ *Brantwood,* ☎ *015394/41396,* WEB *www.airtime.co.uk.* ⏲ *Mid-Mar.–mid-Nov., daily 11–5:30; mid-Nov.–mid-Mar., Wed.–Sun. 11–4.*

Hawkshead

Just outside the attractive village of Hawkshead, **Hill Top** was the home of author and illustrator Beatrix Potter, most famous for her *Peter Rabbit* stories. Now run by the National Trust, the tiny house is a popular—and often crowded—spot; admission is strictly controlled. Try to avoid visiting on summer weekends and during school vacations. The house is 3 km (2 mi) south of Hawkshead on the B5285, though you can also approach via the car ferry from Bowness-on-Windermere. ✉ *Near Sawrey, Ambleside,* ☎ *015394/36269.* ⏲ *Apr.–Oct., Sat.–Wed. 11–5.*

Ullswater

Hemmed in by towering hills, Ullswater, 10 km (6 mi) southwest of Penrith along A592, is the region's second-largest lake, in a spectacular setting. Some of the finest views are from A592 as it hugs the lake's western shore, through Glenridding and Patterdale at the southern end. Here, you're at the foot of Helvellyn (3,118 ft), which lies to the west. Arduous footpaths run from the road between Glenridding and Patterdale and pass by Red Tarn, at 2,356 ft the highest Lake District tarn.

Aira Force, 8 km (5 mi) north of Patterdale, just off the A592, is a spectacular series of waterfalls pounding through a wooded ravine to feed into Ullswater. From the parking lot (parking fee charged), it's a 20-minute walk to the falls—bring sturdy shoes in wet weather. Just above Aira Force in the woods of Gowbarrow Park, William Wordsworth and his sister, Dorothy, were walking on April 15, 1802. Dorothy remarked that she had never seen "daffodils so beautiful." Wordsworth was inspired by his sister's words to write one of the best-known lyric poems in English, "I Wandered Lonely as a Cloud."

Keswick

The great Lakeland mountains of Skiddaw and Blencathra brood over the gray slate houses of Keswick (pronounced *Kezz*-ick), 22 km (14 mi) west of Ullswater, on the scenic shores of Derwentwater Lake. Many of the best hiking routes radiate from here, so it is more of a touring base than a tourist destination. People stroll the congested, narrow streets in boots and corduroy hiking trousers, and there are plenty of mountaineering shops in addition to hotels, guest houses, pubs, and restaurants.

★ To understand why **Derwentwater** is considered one of England's finest lakes, take a short walk from the town center to the lake shore, and follow the Friar's Crag path—about 15 minutes' level walk from the center of Keswick. This pine-tree-fringed peninsula is a favorite vantage point, with its view over the lake, the surrounding ring of mountains, and many tiny wooded islands. Ahead you will see the crags that line the **Jaws of Borrowdale** and overhang a dramatic mountain ravine. Between late March and November, cruises set off every hour in each direction from a wooden dock at the lake shore.

$$$–$$$$ ★ ✕🏨 **Keswick Country House Hotel.** Built to serve railroad travelers in the 19th century, the Keswick has all the grandeur and style of that age, although it has been modernized. The room rate includes dinner, as well as breakfast, though you can opt for a stay without dinner if you wish. ✉ *Station Rd., CA12 4NQ,* ☎ *017687/72020,* FAX *017687/71300. 74 rooms. Restaurant. AE, DC, MC, V.*

$–$$ ✕🏨 **Highfield Hotel.** Overlooking the lawns of Hope Park, a few minutes' walk from lake or town, this family-run hotel preserves such features as its idiosyncratic turret rooms and even a former attached chapel, now used as a four-poster bedroom. Dinner serves up Lake District delights. ✉ *The Heads, CA12 5ER,* ☎ *017687/72508. 19 rooms. Restaurant. MC, V. Closed mid-Nov.–Jan.*

Cockermouth

This attractive little town, 22 km (14 mi) northwest of Seatoller, at the confluence of the Derwent and Cocker rivers, is slightly larger than Keswick and has a maze of narrow streets that's a delight to wander. It was the birthplace of William Wordsworth and his sister, Dorothy, whose childhood home, **Wordsworth House,** is a typical 18th-century north-country gentleman's home, now owned by the National Trust. ✉ *Main St.,* ☎ *01900/824805.* ⏲ *Apr.–Oct., weekdays 11–5; July–Aug., Mon.–Sat. 11–5.*

Lake District Essentials

BOAT AND FERRY TRAVEL

Windermere Lake Cruises employs its handsome fleet of modern launches and vintage cruisers—the largest ships on the lake—in regular service between Ambleside, Bowness, Brockhole, and Lakeside. A Freedom of the Lake ticket (£9.50) gives unlimited travel on any of the ferries for 24 hours.

➤ BOAT AND FERRY INFORMATION: **Windermere Lake Cruises** (☎ 015394/43360).

BUS TRAVEL

National Express serves the region from London's Victoria Coach Station. Average travel time to Kendal is just over 7 hours; to Windermere, 7½ hours; and to Keswick, 8¼ hours. Stagecoach Cumberland operates year-round throughout the Lake District, with reduced service on weekends and bank holidays. A One-day Explorer Ticket (£5.50) is valid on all routes.

➤ BUS INFORMATION: **National Express** (☎ 0990/808080). **Stagecoach Cumberland** (☎ 01946/63222).

CAR TRAVEL

Take M1 north from London to M6, leaving at exit 36 and joining A590/A591 west (around the Kendal bypass to Windermere) or at exit 40, joining A66 directly to Keswick and the northern lakes. Travel time to Kendal is about four hours, to Keswick five–six hours. Car-rental companies are few and far between in the Lakes; rent in London or York before your trip.

Roads within the region are generally good, although many of the minor routes and mountain passes can be steep and narrow. Warning signs are normally posted if snow has made a road impassable. In July and August and during public holiday weekends, expect heavy traffic.

OUTDOORS AND SPORTS

Every hamlet, village, and town provides scores of walking opportunities; stores throughout the region stock equipment, books, and maps. Always check on weather conditions before setting out, as mist or rain can roll in without warning. For short, local walks consult the tourist information centers, which can provide maps, guides, and advice. The other main source of information is the Lake District National Park Visitor Center.

TOURS

From Easter through October, the National Park Authority at Brockhole, near Windermere, arranges half-day or full-day walks introducing you to the history and natural beauties of the Lake District. Mountain Goat Holidays provides half- and full-day minibus sightseeing tours with skilled local guides.

➤ INFORMATION: **Mountain Goat Holidays** (☎ 015394/45161). **National Park Authority** (☎ 015394/46601).

TRAIN TRAVEL

InterCity West Coast serves the region from London's Euston Station. Take an InterCity train bound for Carlisle, Edinburgh, or Glasgow, and change at Oxenholme for the branch line service to Kendal and Windermere. Average travel time to Windermere (including the change) is 4½ hours. The Lakeside & Haverthwaite Railway Co. runs vintage steam trains in summer (and at Christmas) between Lakeside and Haverthwaite along Lake Windermere's southern tip.

➤ TRAIN INFORMATION: **InterCity West Coast** (☎ 0345/484950). **Lakeside & Haverthwaite Railway Co.** (☎ 015395/31594).

VISITOR INFORMATION

➤ TOURIST INFORMATION: **Ambleside** (✉ Central Buildings, Market Cross, ☎ 015394/32582). **Cumbria Tourist Board** (✉ Ashleigh, Holly Rd., Windermere, Cumbria LA23 2AQ, ☎ 015394/44444). **Grasmere** (✉ Red Bank Rd., ☎ 015394/35245). **Kendal** (✉ Town Hall, Highgate, ☎ 01539/725758). **Keswick** (✉ Moot Hall, Market Sq., ☎ 017687/72645). **Windermere** (✉ The Gateway Centre, Victoria St., ☎ 015394/46499).

EDINBURGH

Scotland and England *are* different—and let no Englishman tell you otherwise. Although the two nations have been united in a single kingdom since 1603, Scotland retains its own marked political and social character, with separate legal and educational systems quite distinct from those of England. Indeed, since July 1999 there has been once again a Scottish Parliament, which at present sits in the Assembly Hall on the Mound. In late 2003, the Parliament will move to its permanent home in a building designed by Barcelona architect Enric Miralles, on a site adjacent to the Palace of Holyroodhouse.

Exploring Edinburgh

Numbers in the margin correspond to points of interest on the Edinburgh map.

The key to understanding Edinburgh is to make the distinction between the Old and New Towns. Until the 18th century the city was confined to the rocky crag on which its castle stands, straggling between the fortress at one end and the royal residence, the Palace of Holyroodhouse, at the other. In the 18th century, during a time of expansion known as the Scottish Enlightenment, the city fathers fostered the construction of another Edinburgh, one a little to the north. In 1767 the competition to design the New Town was won by a young and unknown architect, James Craig. His plan was for a grid of three east–west streets, balanced at each end by a grand square. The plan still survives, despite commercial pressures. Princes, George, and Queen streets are the main thoroughfares, with St. Andrew Square at one end and Charlotte Square at the other. The mostly residential New Town, with elegant squares, classical facades, wide streets, and harmonious proportions, remains largely intact and lived in today.

12 **Arthur's Seat.** The open grounds of Holyrood Park enclose Arthur's Seat, Edinburgh's distinctive, originally volcanic minimountain, with steep slopes and miniature crags. ✉ *Holyrood Park.*

★ 16 **Calton Hill.** Steps and a road lead up to splendid views north across the Firth (estuary) of Forth to the Lomond Hills of Fife and south to the Pentland Hills. Among the various monuments on Calton Hill are a partial reproduction of Athens's **Parthenon,** begun in 1824 but left

Edinburgh

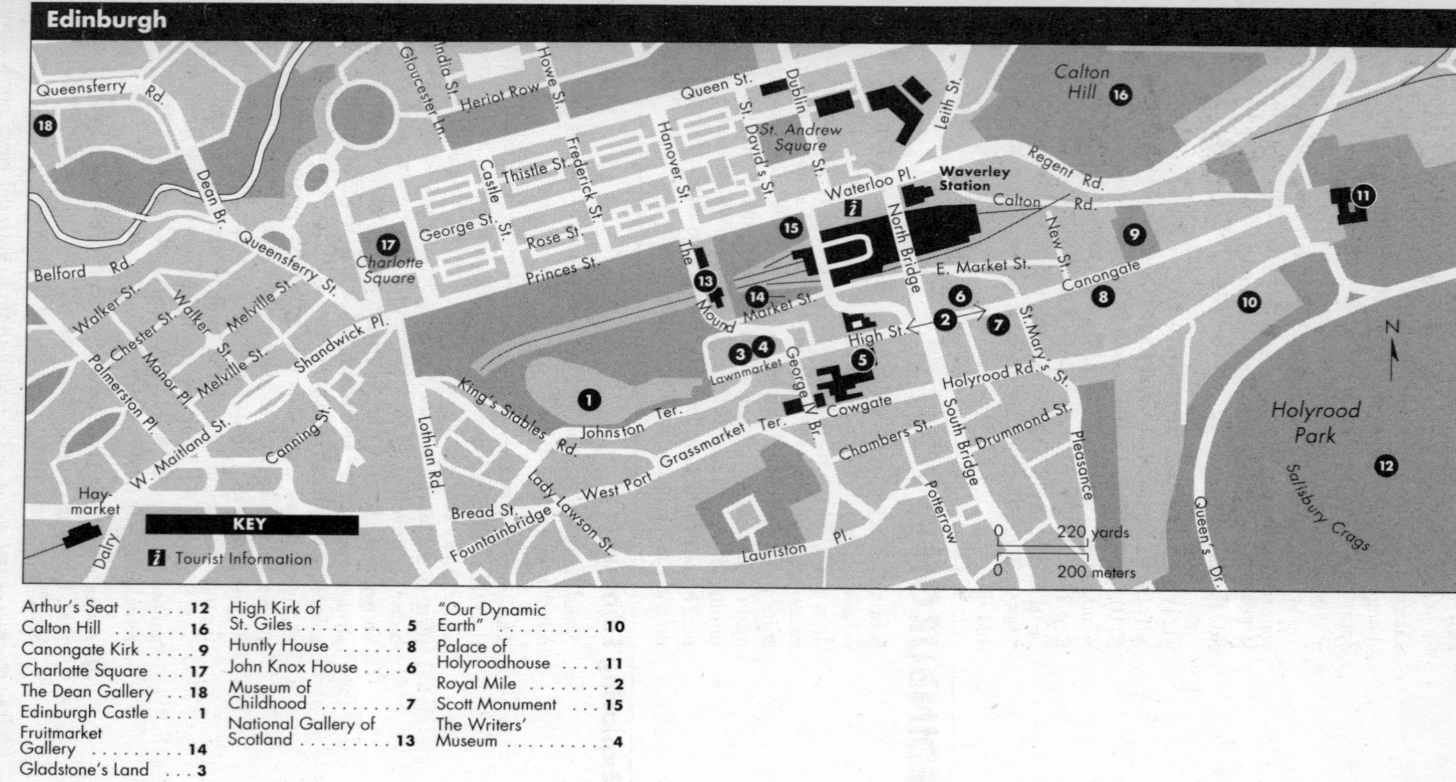

Arthur's Seat 12
Calton Hill 16
Canongate Kirk 9
Charlotte Square . . . 17
The Dean Gallery . . 18
Edinburgh Castle 1
Fruitmarket Gallery 14
Gladstone's Land . . . 3
High Kirk of St. Giles 5
Huntly House 8
John Knox House 6
Museum of Childhood 7
National Gallery of Scotland 13
"Our Dynamic Earth" 10
Palace of Holyroodhouse 11
Royal Mile 2
Scott Monument . . . 15
The Writers' Museum 4

incomplete because the money ran out; the **Nelson Monument;** and the **Royal Observatory.** ✉ *North side of Regent Rd.,* WEB *www.ebs.hw.ac.uk/EDC/guide/calton.html.*

9 Canongate Kirk. In the graveyard of this church, built in 1688, are buried some notable Scots, including the economist Adam Smith and the poet Robert Fergusson. ✉ *Canongate.*

17 Charlotte Square. The centerpiece of the New Town opens out at the western end of George Street. The palatial facade of the north side was designed by the great Scottish neoclassical architect Robert Adam.

18 The Dean Gallery. Directly opposite **The Scottish National Gallery of Modern Art,** the Dean Gallery is dedicated to displaying the whole of 20th-century art. The building itself is a treasure, converted from a neoclassical building, circa 1833, into an exciting contemporary space. ✉ *Belford Road.,* ☎ *0131/624–6200,* WEB *www.natgalscot.ac.uk* ⏲ *Mon–Sat. 10–5. Sun 12–5.* 🎫 *Free.*

★ **1 Edinburgh Castle.** The brooding symbol of Scotland's capital and the nation's martial past, the castle dominates the city center. Its attractions include the city's oldest building—the 11th-century **St. Margaret's Chapel;** the **Crown Room,** where the Regalia of Scotland are displayed; **Old Parliament Hall;** and **Queen Mary's Apartments,** where Mary, Queen of Scots, gave birth to the future King James VI of Scotland (who later became James I of England). In addition, military features include the **Scottish National War Memorial** and the **Scottish United Services Museum.** The **Castle Esplanade,** the wide parade ground at the entrance to the castle, hosts the annual Edinburgh Military Tattoo—a grand military display staged during a citywide festival every summer. ✉ *Castlehill,* ☎ *0131/225–9846,* WEB *www.ebs.hw.ac.uk/EDC/guide/edincas.html.* ⏲ *Apr.–Sept., daily 9:30–5:15; Oct.–Mar., daily 9:30–4:15.*

14 Fruitmarket Gallery. Adjacent to Waverly Station is this lively contemporary space that always has something cool and thoughtful going on. If you need a moment to gather your thoughts, take a latté and reflect through the sheet glass that there's another much larger gallery directly across the road, **The City Art Centre,** just waiting to be discovered. ✉ *45 Market Street.,* ☎ *0131/225–2383,* WEB *www.fruitmarket.co.uk.* ⏲ *Mon.–Sat. 11–6, Sun. 12–5.* 🎫 *Free.*

The elegant **Georgian House** in Charlotte Square is furnished to show the domestic arrangements of a prosperous late-18th-century Edinburgh family. ✉ *7 Charlotte Sq.,* ☎ *0131/225–2160.* ⏲ *Mar.–Oct., Mon.–Sat. 10–5, Sun. 2–5; Nov.–Dec., Mon.–Sat. 11–4, Sun. 2–4 (last admission at 3:30).*

3 Gladstone's Land. This six-story property cared for by the National Trust for Scotland dates from 1620. It has an arcaded front and first-floor entrance typical of the period and is furnished in the style of a merchant's house of the time; there are magnificent painted ceilings. ✉ *477B Lawnmarket,* ☎ *0131/226–5856.* ⏲ *Easter–Oct., Mon.–Sat. 10–5, Sun. 2–5 (last entrance at 4:30).*

5 High Kirk of St. Giles. Often called St. Giles's Cathedral, this historic structure dates from the 12th century; the impressive choir was built during the 15th century. ✉ *High St.,* ☎ *0131/225–9442.* ⏲ *Mon.–Sat. 9–5 (7 in summer), Sun. 1–5 and for services.*

8 Huntly House. Built in 1570, this museum presents Edinburgh history and social life. ✉ *142 Canongate,* ☎ *0131/529–4143.* ⏲ *Mon.–Sat. 10–5, Sun. during festival 2–5.*

6 **John Knox House.** Its traditional connections with Scotland's celebrated religious reformer are tenuous, but this 16th-century dwelling gives a flavor of life in the Old Town during Knox's time. ✉ *45 High St.,* ☎ *0131/556–2647.* ⊙ *Mon.–Sat. 10–5 (last admission at 4:30) during festival 10–6:30.*

7 **Museum of Childhood.** Even adults may well enjoy this celebration of toys. The museum was the first in the world to be devoted solely to the history of childhood. ✉ *42 High St.,* ☎ *0131/529–4142,* FAX *0131/558–3103.* ⊙ *Mon.–Sat. 10–5, Sun. during festival 2–5.*

★ 13 **National Gallery of Scotland.** Works by Old Masters and the French Impressionists and a good collection of Scottish paintings make this one of Britain's best national galleries. It is small enough to be taken in easily on one visit. There may be a charge for special exhibitions. The Dean Gallery houses the 20th-century art collection of the National Gallery of Scotland. (✉ *The Mound,* ☎ *0131/624–6200.* ⊙ *Mon.–Sat. 10–5, Sun. 12–5. Print Room weekdays 10–12:30 and 2–4:30, by arrangement.*

10 **Our Dynamic Earth.** Directly opposite the home of the Scottish Parliament building, this attraction is a testament to the successful integration of state-of-the-art technology in entertainment and learning. From the big bang to the unknown future you will travel through every environment on earth and encounter creatures you never even knew existed. ✉ *Holyrood Road,* ☎ *0131/550–7800,* WEB *www.dynamicearth.co.uk.* ⊙ *Easter–Oct., daily 10–6; Nov.–Easter, Wed.–Sun. 10–5 (last entry 1¼ hrs before closing).*

★ 11 **Palace of Holyroodhouse.** Still the Royal Family's official residence in Scotland, the palace was built as a guest house for the Abbey of Holyrood, founded in 1128 by Scottish king David I. It was extensively remodeled by Charles II in 1671. The state apartments, with their collections of tapestries and paintings, can be visited. ✉ *East end of Canongate,* ☎ *0131/556–7371; 0131/556–1096 recorded information,* WEB *lynn.efr.hw.ac.uk/EDC/guide/holyrood.html.* ⊙ *Apr.–Oct., daily 9:30–5:15; Nov.–Mar., daily 9:30–3:45. Closed during royal and state visits.*

2 **Royal Mile.** The backbone of the Old Town, the Royal Mile starts immediately below the Castle Esplanade. It consists of a number of streets running into one another—Castlehill, Lawnmarket, High Street, and Canongate—leading downhill to the Palace of Holyroodhouse. The many original Old Town "closes," narrow alleyways enclosed by high tenement buildings, reward exploration with a real sense of the former life of the city. ✉ *Between Edinburgh Castle and the Palace of Holyroodhouse.*

The Royal Yacht *Britannia*. At last an opportunity to see how the other half lives. This excursion is pure voyeurism at its best. A no port-hole-barred tour of the most famous ship in the world; from the Queen's former sitting room to the engine room. ✉ *Britannia Ocean Drive, Leith. Guide Friday and Lothian Buses both offer a bus service from Waverly Bridge, just off Princes St..* ☎ *0131/555–5566.* ⊙ *Year-round (times vary).*

15 **Scott Monument.** This unmistakable 200-ft-high Gothic spire was built in the 1840s to commemorate Sir Walter Scott (1771–1832), the celebrated novelist of Scots history. ✉ *Princes St.,* ☎ *0131/529–4068.* ⊙ *Mon.–Sat. 9–4, Sun. 10–4; Summer Mon.–Sat. 9–8, Sun. 10–6.*

4 **The Writers' Museum.** Housed in Lady Stair's House, a town dwelling dating from 1622, this museum recalls Scotland's literary heritage with exhibits on Sir Walter Scott, Robert Louis Stevenson, and Robert Burns. A superb complement for any visit to The Writer's Museum is

the McEwan's Edinburgh Literary Pub Tour ✉ *Lady Stair's Close, Lawnmarket,* ☎ *0131/529–4901.* ⏲ *Mon.–Sat. 10–5, Sun. during festival 2–5.*

Dining

Edinburgh's restaurants make the most of Scotland's excellent game, fish, shellfish, beef, and lamb.

$$$$ ★ ✕ **La Pompadour.** The decor in this hotel-restaurant, with its subtle plasterwork and rich murals, is inspired by the France of Louis XV. A sophisticated French menu is accented with Scottish delicacies. ✉ *Caledonian Hilton Hotel, Princes St.,* ☎ *0131/459–9988. Reservations essential. AE, DC, MC, V. No lunch weekends.*

$$$$ ✕ **Witchery by the Castle.** This spooky haunt comes complete with a lugubrious, cavernous interior set with flickering candles, broomsticks, and cabalistic insignia. However, there's nothing spooky about the excellent Scottish-accented French food. ✉ *352 Castlehill, Royal Mile,* ☎ *0131/225–5613. Reservations essential. AE, DC, MC, V.*

$$$ ★ ✕ **Martin Wishart.** Nestling modestly on the shore of the Water of Leith, this intimate, contemporary-styled restaurant is slightly out of town but worth every penny on the taxi fare. A rising star of the international culinary scene, it will woo you with an impeccable menu of French-influenced and beautifully presented food. ✉ *54 The Shore, Leith, EH2 1DJ,* ☎ *0131/553–3557. Reservations essential. MC, V.*

$$$ ✕ **A Room in the Town.** Though slightly off the beaten track, this cheerful bistro is in one of the most picturesque parts of the New Town. Dishes come with sauces that have a sweet edge to suit the Celtic taste, but the large variety on the menu would whet any palate. Amusing pseudo-classical murals festoon the walls, pop music plays gently, and the service is informal but excellent. Pick something from the lively wine list or bring your own bottle. It can sometimes get a bit smoky. ✉ *16 Howe St., EH3,* ☎ *0131/225–8204. DC, MC, V.*

$$ ✕ **The Dome.** The splendid interior of this former bank, with its painted plasterwork and central dome, provides an elegant backdrop for relaxed dining. Or you might opt for a drink at the central bar, a favored spot for sophisticates to wind down after work. The toasted BLT sandwiches are almost big enough for two, but if you're ravenous, the eclectic menu offers many other options. ✉ *14 George St., EH2 2PF,* ☎ *0131/624–8624. AE, DC, MC, V.*

$$ ✕ **Howie's.** Howie's is a simple neighborhood bistro. The steaks are tender Aberdeen beef, the Loch Fyne herring are sweet-cured to Howie's own recipe, and the clientele is lively. ✉ *29 Waterloo Place,* ☎ *0131/556–5766. MC, V. No lunch Mon.;* ✉ *63 Dalry Rd.,* ☎ *0131/313–3334. MC, V. No lunch Mon.;*

$$ ✕ **Petit Paris.** Serving classic French farmhouse cuisine, Petit Paris is appropriately situated in the area of the Old Town where the agricultural market was once held. Offerings on the menu might include cassoulet, Toulouse sausage, *boudin* (black pudding sausage), or quail, as well as more standard fare such as steak. ✉ *38 Grassmarket,* ☎ *0131/226–2442. MC, V.*

$ ✕ **Beehive Inn.** One of the oldest pubs in the city, the Beehive snuggles in the Grassmarket, under the majestic shadow of the castle. The upstairs Rafters restaurant lies hidden in an attractive and spacious attic room, crammed with weird and wonderful junk. Open only for dinner, it features mostly steaks and fish: try the charcoal-grilled Scottish salmon. ✉ *18/20 Grassmarket,* ☎ *0131/225–7171. AE, DC, MC, V. No lunch.*

Lodging

Many of Edinburgh's accommodations are very central, with New Town B&B establishments being especially convenient.

$$$$ **Caledonian Hilton Hotel.** "The Caley" echoes the days of the traditional great railway hotel, though the neighboring station has long since been demolished. The imposing Victorian decor has been lovingly preserved and embellished. There are also three excellent restaurants: **La Pompadour; Chisholms,** offering a less pricey Scottish menu; and **Henry J. Bean's,** a U.S.–style diner. ✉ *Princes St., EH1 2AB,* ☎ *0131/459–9988,* FAX *0131/225–6632. 246 rooms. 3 restaurants. AE, DC, MC, V.*

$$$$ ★ **Channings.** Five Edwardian terraced houses make up this elegant hotel in an upscale neighborhood minutes from Princes Street. Restrained colors, antiques, quiet rooms, and great views toward Fife (from the north-facing rooms) set the tone. The restaurant offers excellent value, especially at lunchtime; try the hot-smoked salmon with coriander and saffron risotto. ✉ *12–16 S. Learmonth Gardens, EH4 1EZ,* ☎ *0131/315–2226,* FAX *0131/332–9631. 48 rooms. Restaurant. AE, DC, MC, V.*

$$ ★ **17 Abercromby Place.** An exceptional standard is set at this Georgian terraced B&B in the center of the New Town. There are stunning views from the top-floor rooms. The host and the hostess both enjoy meeting guests and are very helpful, and—unusual for this part of town—there is off-street car parking. ✉ *17 Abercrombie Pl., EH3 6LB,* ☎ *0131/557–8036,* FAX *0131/558–3453. 10 rooms. MC, V.*

$$ ★ **Stuart House.** This B&B is within 15 minutes' walk of the city center, in a Victorian terraced house with some fine plasterwork. The decor suits the structure: bold colors, floral fabrics, and generously curtained windows combine with antique and traditional-style furniture and chandeliers to create an opulent ambience. Smoking is not permitted. ✉ *12 E. Claremont St., EH7 4JP,* ☎ *0131/557–9030,* FAX *0131/557–0563,* WEB *www.stuart-house-hotel.co.uk. 7 rooms. AE, DC, MC, V.*

The Arts

The *List,* available from newsagents throughout the city, as well as the *Day by Day List* and *Events 2000,* available from the Information Centre, carry the most up-to-date details about cultural events. The *Scotsman,* an Edinburgh daily, also carries reviews in its arts pages on Monday and Wednesday, and daily during the festival.

EDINBURGH FESTIVAL

The **Edinburgh International Festival,** a celebration of music, dance, and drama staged each summer (August 11–31 in 2002), draws international artists of the highest caliber. The **Festival Fringe** (information: ✉ 180 High St., ☎ 0131/226–5257; 0131/226–5259 during festival only, FAX 0131/220–4205, WEB www.eif.co.uk), the unruly child of the official festival, spills out of halls and theaters all over town, offering visitors a cornucopia of theatrical and musical events—some so weird they defy description. At the official festival you'll see top-flight performances by established artists, while at a Fringe event you might catch a new star or a new art form or a controversial new play. Advance information, programs, and ticket sales for the festival are available from the **Edinburgh International Festival Office** (✉ Castlehill, EH1 1ND, ☎ 0131/473–2001, FAX 0131/473–2003).

OTHER FESTIVALS

The **Edinburgh Military Tattoo** (information: Edinburgh Military Tattoo Office, ✉ 32 Market St., EH1 1QB, ☎ 0131/225–1188, FAX 0131/225–8627) may not be art, but it is certainly entertainment. This celebration of martial music and skills (in 2002, held August 2–24) is set on the Castle Esplanade. Dress warmly for late-evening shows. Even if it rains, the show most definitely goes on!

Edinburgh Essentials

AIR TRAVEL TO AND FROM EDINBURGH

British Airways operates a shuttle service from London's Heathrow Airport to Edinburgh; reservations are not necessary. Flying time from London is 1 hour, 15 minutes. British Midland also flies from Heathrow. KLM UK flies from Stansted to Edinburgh. EasyJet offers bargain fares from London Luton to Edinburgh. Transatlantic flights direct to Scotland use Glasgow Airport, with regular rail connections to Glasgow city center and on to Edinburgh.

➤ AIRLINES AND CONTACTS: **British Airways** (☎ 0345/222111). **British Midland** (☎ 0345/554–554). **EasyJet** (☎ 0990/29–29–29). **KLM UK** (☎ 0870/5074074).

BUS TRAVEL TO AND FROM EDINBURGH

Regular service is operated by National Express between Victoria Coach Station, London, and St. Andrew Square bus station, Edinburgh, twice a day. The journey takes approximately eight hours.

➤ BUS INFORMATION: **National Express** (☎ 0990/808080, FAX 0141/332–8055).

BUS TRAVEL WITHIN EDINBURGH

Lothian BUSES is the main provider within Edinburgh. A Day Saver Ticket (£2.20), allowing unlimited one-day travel on the city's buses, can be purchased in advance.

➤ BUS INFORMATION: **Lothian BUSES** (✉ 27 Hanover St., ☎ 0131/555–6363; ✉ Waverley Bridge, ☎ 0131/554–4494).

CAR TRAVEL

London and Edinburgh are 656 km (407 mi) apart; allow a comfortable nine hours for the drive. The two principal routes to the Scottish border are A1 (mostly a small but divided road) or the eight-lane M1, then M6. From there, the choice is between the four-lane highway A74, which can be unpleasantly busy, followed by A701 or A702, or the slower but much more scenic A7 through Hawick. All the main car-rental agencies have offices in Edinburgh.

Driving in Edinburgh has its quirks and pitfalls, but competent drivers should not be intimidated. Metered parking in the center city is scarce and expensive, and the local traffic wardens are alert. Illegally parked cars are routinely wheel-clamped and towed away, and getting your car back will be expensive. After 6 PM the parking situation improves considerably, and you may manage to find a space quite near your hotel, even downtown. If you park on a yellow line or in a resident's parking bay, be prepared to move your car by 8 AM the following morning, when the rush hour gets under way.

CONSULATES

➤ UNITED STATES: (✉ 3 Regent Terr., ☎ 0131/556–8315).

EMERGENCIES

➤ EMERGENCY SERVICES: **Police, ambulance, fire** (☎ 999).

➤ 24-HOUR PHARMACIES: **Boots** (✉ 48 Shandwick Pl., west end of Princes St., ☎ 0131/225–6757).

TOURS

BUS TOURS

Lothian BUSES operates tours in and around the city.

THE MCEWAN'S EDINBURGH LITERARY PUB TOUR

This exceptional tour has gradually moved from a niche to mainstream cultural necessity. A dramatic duologue performed by professional actors takes you on a memorable journey through 300 years of Scottish literary history, fact and fiction. From The Old Town—to The New, the action is well paced across four charming pubs of literary merit and gives new meaning to the term "pub scrawl". All tours leave from The Beehive Inn and, by arrangement, can combine supper packages.
➤ FEES AND SCHEDULES: ✉ 97B West Bow, Suite 2, EH1 2JP, ☎ 0131/225–6665, 0131/225–6667.

TAXIS

Taxi stands can be found throughout the downtown area, most conveniently at the west end of Princes Street, South St. David Street, and North St. Andrew Street (the latter two just off St. Andrew Sq.), Waverley Market, Waterloo Place, and Lauriston Place. You can also hail any taxi displaying an illuminated FOR HIRE sign.

TRAIN TRAVEL

Regular trains run from London's King's Cross Station to Edinburgh Waverley; the fastest journey time is just over 4 hours.
➤ TRAIN INFORMATION: **King's Cross Station** (☎ 0345/484950).

VISITOR INFORMATION

➤ TOURIST INFORMATION: **Edinburgh and Scotland Information Centre** (✉ 3 Princes St. (adjacent to Waverley Station), ☎ 0131/473–3800, FAX 0131/473–3881).

14 GREECE

ATHENS, THE NORTHERN PELOPONNESE, MAINLAND GREECE, CORFU, THE AEGEAN ISLANDS

IT CAN BE DISORIENTING for a visitor conditioned by textbooks, college Greek, and Keats' Grecian urn to arrive in Athens and find the natives roaring around in sports cars and talking about the latest nouvelle restaurant. Shouldn't they look like the truncated statues in the British Museum and have brows habitually crowned with wild olive? Incongruous as it may seem, most Greeks have two arms and two legs attached to the torso in the normal places. The torso itself is not swathed in mother's best percale bedsheet. As the lucky traveler soon learns, although their countryside may be bleached and stony, the Greeks themselves provide the vibrant color that has long since vanished from classical monuments once saturated with pigment, blue, gold, and vermilion, under the eye-searing Aegean sun.

The land itself is a stunning presence, dotted with cypress groves, vineyards, and olive trees; carved into gentle bays or dramatic coves bordered with startling white sand; or articulated into rolling hills and rugged mountain ranges that plunge into the sea. In Greece, indeed, you cannot travel far across the land without encountering the sea, or far across the sea without encountering one of its roughly 2,000 islands. Approximately equal in size to New York State, or roughly the size of England, Greece has 15,019 km (9,312 mi) of coastline, more than any other country of its size. The sea is everywhere, not on three sides only but at every turn, reaching into the shoreline like a probing hand. This natural beauty and the sharp, clear light of sun and sea, combined with plentiful archaeological treasures, make Greece one of the world's most inviting and rewarding countries to visit.

Western poetry, music, architecture, politics, medicine, law—all had their birth centuries ago in Greece. Among the mountains of mainland Greece are Mt. Olympus, whose cloud-capped peak was the fabled home of the Greek gods, and Mt. Parnassus, favorite haunt of the sun god, Apollo, and the nine Muses. Romantic and beautiful remains of the ancient past—the Acropolis and the Parthenon, the temples of Delphi, the Tombs of the Kings in Mycenae—and later Byzantine churches, Crusader castles and fortresses, and Ottoman minarets dot the country.

Of the many hundreds of islands and islets scattered across the Aegean Sea, in the east, and the Ionian Sea, in the west, fewer than 250 are still inhabited. This world of the farmer, fisherman, and seafarer has largely been replaced by the world of the tourist. More than 10 million vacationers visit Greece each year, almost doubling the entire native population. Once-idyllic beaches have become overcrowded and noisy, and fishing harbors have become flotilla-sailing centers. But

Greece (Ellada)

Black Sea
TURKEY
Kastanies
Istanbul
Komotini
Didymotiho
Xanthi
THRACE
E90
Avdira
Makri
Alexandroupoli
Sea of Marmara
Thassos
Samothrace
Troy
Limnos
Lesvos
Mytilini
Plomari
TURKEY
Aegean Sea
Hios
Hios
Mesta
Pirgi
Izmir (Smyrna)
Ephesus
Andros
Andros
Samos
Samos
Pythagorio
Ikaria
Agios Kirykos
Tinos
Tinos
Ermoupoli
Syros
Mykonos
Delos
Patmos
Paros
Naxos
Leros
Bodrum (Halicarnassus)
Kos
Kos
CYCLADES
Amorgos
Ios
Astypalea
Nissyros
Symi
Rhodes
Oia
Fira
Santorini
Anafi
DODECANESE
Tilos
Kameiros
Halki
Lindos
Rhodes
Sea of Crete
Karpathos
Kassos
Heraklion
Mallia
Knossos
Siteia
Agios Nikolaos
Phaestos
Ierapetra

traditional Greece survives: pubs and bars stand next door to *ouzeri* (informal eateries that serve appetizers and ouzo), *kafeneia* (Greek coffeehouses) are as popular as discos, and pizza and hamburger joints must compete with tavernas.

Although mass tourism has transformed the main centers, it is still possible to strike out and discover your own place among the smaller islands and the miles of beautiful mainland coastline. Except for an occasional scarcity of accommodations, especially in high summer, this is the ideal way to see traditional Greece. If you explore this fascinating country with open eyes, you'll enjoy it in all its forms: its slumbering cafés and buzzing tavernas; its elaborate religious rituals; its stark, bright beauty; and the generosity and curiosity of its people.

GREECE A TO Z

To research prices, get advice from other travelers, and book travel arrangements, visit www.fodors.com.

AIR TRAVEL

CARRIERS

Air Greece flies from Athens to Rhodes, Mytilini, Corfu, Kavala, and Heraklion and Hania in Crete. Cronus Airlines flies regularly from Athens to Thessaloniki, as well as to Heraklion and Hania. Olympic Airways has service between Athens and most large cities and islands in Greece.
➤ AIRLINES AND CONTACTS: **Air Greece** (✉ Fillelinon 22, Syntagma, Athens, ☎ 01/324–4457 reservations). **Cronus Airlines** (✉ Othonos 10, Syntagma, Athens, ☎ 01/994–4444 reservations). **Olympic Airways** (✉ Fillelinon 15, near Syntagma, Athens, ☎ 01/966–6666 reservations; 01/936–3363 through 01/936–3366 for flight arrival and departure information).

AIRPORTS

Ellinikon Airport, Athens's main airport, where most international flights land, lies about 10 km (6 mi) from the city center. For information on Olympic Airways flights, call the West Terminal information line; for other carriers, call the East Terminal. Some airlines also use the New Charter Terminal (Terminal B), just before the East Terminal on the former U.S. military base; the terminal operates May through October.
➤ AIRPORT INFORMATION: **Ellinikon Airport** (✉ Vas. Georgiou B' 1, ☎ 01/936–3363 through 3366 West Terminal; 01/969–4466 arrivals and departures East Terminal; 01/969–4531 passenger paging for East Terminal; 01/997–2686 or 01/997–2581 New Charter Terminal).

BIKE AND MOPED TRAVEL

Dune buggies, bicycles, mopeds, and motorcycles can be rented on the islands. Use extreme caution. Helmets, technically compulsory for motorcyclists, are not usually available, and injuries are common.

BOAT AND FERRY TRAVEL

Frequent car ferries and hydrofoils leave from Piraeus, the port of Athens, for the central and southern Aegean islands and Crete. Boats to such nearby islands as Evia, Andros, Mykonos, and Tinos also leave from Rafina, east of Athens. Ships to the Ionian islands usually sail from Patras and Igoumenitsa. Buy your tickets two or three days in advance, especially if you are traveling in summer or taking a car. Reserve your return journey or continuation soon after you arrive. Timetables change frequently, and boats may be delayed by weather conditions, so your plans should be flexible.

BUS TRAVEL

Travel with the regional KTEL bus network is inexpensive, usually comfortable, and relatively fast. Bus timetables are available from EOT offices. In summer and on holiday weekends, make reservations or buy tickets a few days before your planned trip. Board early, as passengers often have a loose attitude about assigned seating; if smoking bothers you, get a seat away from the driver, who is exempt from the no-smoking regulations.

BUSINESS HOURS

BANKS AND OFFICES

Office and shopping hours vary from season to season. Check with your hotel for up-to-the-minute information on opening and closing times. Banks are open weekdays 8–2, except Friday, when they close at 1:30; they are closed weekends and public holidays. In Athens one branch of the National Bank of Greece has extended hours for foreign exchange only, open Monday–Thursday 3:30–6:30, Friday 3–6:30, Saturday 9–3, Sunday 9–1. Even smaller towns have at least one bank with an ATM.

➤ CONTACTS: **National Bank of Greece** (✉ Karageorgi Servias 2, Syntagma, ☎ 01/334–0011).

MUSEUMS AND SIGHTS

Museums and archaeological sites are open 8:30–3 off-season, or winter (November–mid-April). Depending on available personnel, sites usually stay open longer mid-April–October, sometimes as late as 7 PM in July and August. Many museums are closed one day a week, usually Monday. Archaeological sites and museums are closed January 1, March 25, Good Friday morning until noon, Easter Sunday, May 1, and December 25–26; for the reduced visiting hours on other holidays, check the handout from EOT.

SHOPS

Shops may stay open from 9 AM to 9 PM in summer, though most stores close Monday, Wednesday, and Saturday afternoons around 3 or 4 PM. On Tuesday, Thursday, and Friday, many shops close between about 3 and 5 PM. In winter (October–mid-April) hours are slightly reduced, though this changes every year. Supermarkets are open weekdays until about 8:30 PM, with reduced hours on Saturday. In tourist areas such as Athens's Plaka, souvenir shops stay open late.

CAR TRAVEL

EMERGENCIES

The Automobile and Touring Club of Greece (ELPA) assists tourists with breakdowns free of charge if they belong to AAA or to ELPA (35,500 dr./€102.95 per year, good for discounts on emergency service throughout Europe); otherwise, there is a charge. ELPA also provides tourist information to drivers.

➤ CONTACTS: **Automobile and Touring Club of Greece** (✉ Messoghion 395, 15343 Agia Paraskevi, ☎ 01/606–8800; 104 throughout Greece for emergency; 174 for tourist information, FAX 01/606–8981).

GASOLINE

At press time, gas cost about 260 dr./€0.77–280 dr./€0.83 a liter. Gas pumps and service stations are everywhere, and lead-free gas is widely available. In rural areas and on the islands many stations are closed evenings.

PARKING

In Greece's half-dozen large cities, downtown street parking and lots are extremely hard to find. It's often cheaper to leave your car at the hotel and take a cab or bus. Elsewhere, parking is easy.

ROAD CONDITIONS

Greece has one of the highest ratios in Europe of collisions to the number of cars on the road. The National Road can be nightmarish with its inadequate signposting, remarked lanes, and constant repair work; tolls range from 250 dr./€0.73 to 900 dr./€2.65, depending on the distance traveled. You also need nerves of steel to drive in the cities, but many country roads, though narrow, are free of traffic.

RULES OF THE ROAD

Non-EU citizens must have an international driver's license. Driving is on the right, and although seat belts are compulsory, don't expect this or any other driving rule to be obeyed. The speed limit is 120 kph (74 mph) on the National Road (follow the temporary speed signs where it's under repair), 90 kph (54 mph) outside built-up areas, and 50 kph (31 mph) in town.

CUSTOMS AND DUTIES

For details on imports and duty-free limits, *see* Customs and Duties *in* Chapter 1.

IN GREECE

You may bring in only one each of such expensive portable items as camcorders and computers. You should register these with Greek customs upon arrival, to avoid any problems when taking them out of the country again. Foreign banknotes amounting to more than $2,500 must be declared for re-export, although there are no restrictions on traveler's checks; foreign visitors may export no more than 100,000 drachma in Greek currency.

DINING

The principal elements of Greek cuisine are fish; grilled and roasted meats, especially lamb; and fresh vegetables, such as eggplant, tomatoes, and beans, inventively combined with lots of olive oil and seasoned with lemon juice, garlic, onion, and oregano. Let your senses guide you—visit the kitchen and point to what looks appetizing; try the regional specialties and barrel wine whenever possible. Your best bet is to choose the tavernas and slightly more upscale *estiatoria* (restaurants) that are frequented by most Greeks. Both serve oven-baked dishes and stove-top stews called *magirefta,* prepared in advance and often served at room temperature. If you're in a fish taverna, ask to see the daily catch to check for freshness, choose your fish, and have it weighed before it's cooked; prices are by the kilo. Another alternative is an ouzeri or *mezedopolion,* where you order plates of appetizers, called *mezedes,* instead of an entrée. Recently, several upscale restaurants have begun serving what could be dubbed "nouvelle Mediterranean," with local ingredients unusually combined and imaginatively presented. Traditional fast food in Greece consists of the *gyro* (pronounced "*yee*-ro"), slices of grilled meat with tomato and onions in pita bread; souvlakia (shish kebab); toasted sandwiches called *tost,* which you fill from an array of ingredients ranging from red peppers to fried bacon to smoked eggplant dip; and pastries known as *pites,* stuffed with spinach, cheese, or meat—but hamburgers and pizzas are also found everywhere.

Prices are for one main course.

CATEGORY	ATHENS/MAIN ISLAND TOWNS	OTHER AREAS
$$$$	over 16,000 dr. (€47.06)	over 15,000 dr. (€44.12)
$$$	10,000dr.–16,000 dr. (€29.42–€47.06)	9,000 dr.–15,000 dr. (€26.47–€44.12)
$$	5,500 dr.–10,000 dr. (€16.18–€29.42)	5,000 dr.–9,000 dr. (€14.71–€26.47)
$	under 5,500 dr. (€16.18)	under 5,000 dr. (€14.71)

MEALTIMES

Lunch in Greek restaurants is served from 12:30 until 3. Dinner begins at about 9 and is served until 12:30 in Athens and until midnight outside Athens.

RESERVATIONS AND DRESS

Throughout the Greek islands you can dress informally for dinner, even at expensive restaurants; in Athens, jackets are appropriate at the top-price restaurants.

EMBASSIES

New Zealand maintains a consular office in Athens (☞ Athens Essentials, *below*).

➤ AUSTRALIA: (✉ D. Soutsou 37, Athens, ☎ 01/645–0404).

➤ CANADA: (✉ Gennadiou 4, Athens, ☎ 01/727–3400).

➤ IRELAND: (✉ Vas. Konstantinou 7, Athens, ☎ 01/723–2771).

➤ UNITED KINGDOM: (✉ Ploutarchou 1, Athens, ☎ 01/723–6211 through 6219; 01/727–2600).

➤ UNITED STATES: (✉ Vasilissis Sofias 91, Athens, ☎ 01/721–2951 through 2959).

HOLIDAYS

January 1; January 6 (Epiphany); February 26 (Clean Monday and first day of Lent); March 25 (Independence Day); Good Friday; Greek Easter Sunday; Greek Easter Monday; May 1 (Labor Day); June 3 (Pentecost); August 15 (Assumption); October 28 (Ochi Day); December 25–26.

LANGUAGE

English is widely spoken in hotels and elsewhere, especially by young people, and even in out-of-the-way places someone is always happy to lend a helping word. In this guide names are given in the Roman alphabet according to the Greek pronunciation.

LODGING

Greece offers a range of lodgings from spartan campgrounds to family-run pensions to luxurious resorts complete with a pseudo-village (bakery, church, café) on the premises. If you plan to visit during Easter week (Catholic or Orthodox) or from mid-June through August, reserve well in advance. In August on the islands, even the most basic rooms are hard to find, as that's when most Greeks take their monthlong vacation. Off-season, you usually can negotiate room rates.

Prices quoted are for a double room in high season, including taxes but not breakfast unless so indicated.

CATEGORY	COST
$$$$	over 55,000 dr. (€161.77)
$$$	35,000 dr.–55,000 dr. (€102.95–€161.77)
$$	19,000 dr.–35,000 dr. (€55.89–€102.95)
$	under 19,000 dr. (€55.89)

APARTMENT AND VILLA RENTALS

Most areas have pensions—usually clean, bright, and recently built—and self-catering apartments. On islands, owners wait for tourists at the harbor, and signs in English throughout villages indicate rooms available. You can also query the tourist police or the municipal tourist information office. Accommodations are harder to find in smaller resort towns during the winter and beginning of spring. Check the rooms first, for quality and location. Also, make sure you feel comfortable with the owners if they live on the premises.

CAMPING

There are numerous privately owned campgrounds, with amenities ranging from basic to elaborate (those operated by the tourist organization are cushier than most). Contact the Greek Camping Association or the Greek National Tourist Organization (EOT) for more information.

➤ CONTACTS: **Greek Camping Association** (✉ Solonos 102, 10680 Athens, ☎ FAX 01/362–1560).

HOSTELS

Hostels operate in major tourist areas but often close from season to season, so contact the Greek Youth Hostel Organization. The YWCA puts up overnight female guests.

➤ HOSTEL ORGANIZATIONS: **Greek Youth Hostel Organization** (✉ Damareos 75, 11633 Athens, ☎ 01/751–9530, FAX 01/751–0616). **YWCA** (✉ Amerikis 11, 10672 Athens, ☎ 01/362–4291 through 4293, FAX 01/362–2400).

HOTELS

Greek hotels are classified by the government as De Luxe (L) and A–E. Within each category quality varies greatly, but prices usually don't. Still, you may come across an A-class hotel that charges less than a B-class, depending on facilities. In this guide, hotels are classified according to price. All $$$$ and $$$ hotels are assumed to have air-conditioning, and unless indicated, all hotel rooms have private baths.

Prices quoted by hotels usually include service, local taxes, and VAT; many include breakfast. Often you can negotiate the price, sometimes by eliminating breakfast. The official price should be posted on the back of the door or inside a closet. Booking a room through a local travel agency may reduce the price substantially. You can contact a hotel directly or write one month in advance for reservations to the Hellenic Chamber of Hotels. The chamber also has a desk inside the National Bank of Greece to help visitors find rooms; it's open weekdays 8:30–2, Saturday 9–1. During high season, larger resort hotels may insist that guests take half board.

➤ CONTACTS: **Hellenic Chamber of Hotels** (✉ Stadiou 24, 10564 Athens, ☎ 01/331–0022 through 01/331–0026, FAX 01/322–5449, WEB users.otenet.gr/~grhotels/english.html; ✉ National Bank of Greece, Karageorgi Servias 2, 10564 Athens, ☎ 01/323–7193).

TRADITIONAL SETTLEMENTS

State organized, these establishments house guests in buildings representative of the local architecture. Many settlements are described in a free brochure from EOT, as well as in the English-language *Traditional Inns in Greece: Alternative Forms of Tourism* (published by Vertical Advertising-Publishing), available in foreign-language bookstores.

MAIL AND SHIPPING

Letters are sometimes lost in the mail; it's best to send important items registered. Most post offices are open weekdays 8–2. In Athens the main offices stay open late (weekdays 7:30 AM–8 PM, Saturday 7:30–2, Sunday 9–2). You can have your mail addressed to "poste restante" and sent to any post office in Greece, where you can pick it up once you show your passport. Or have it mailed to American Express offices. The service is free for holders of American Express cards or traveler's checks. Other AmEx offices are in Thessaloniki, Patras, Corfu, Rhodes, Santorini, Mykonos, Skiathos, and Heraklion in Crete.

➤ CONTACTS: **American Express** (✉ Ermou 2 Athens 10563). **Athens Post Offices** (✉ Aiolou 100, 10200; Syntagma Square at Mitropoleos).

POSTAL RATES

Airmail letters and postcards for delivery within Europe cost 170 dr./€.5 for 20 grams and 270 dr./€.75 for 50 grams, for outside Europe 200 dr./€.59 for 20 grams and 300 dr./€.89 for 50 grams. All parcels must be inspected; bring them open and with wrapping materials to the nearest post office. In Athens parcels that weigh more than 2 kilograms (4½ pounds) must be brought to Mitropoleos 60 or to the Spiromiliou arcade off Voukourestiou Street.

MONEY MATTERS

Fluctuations in currency make it impossible to do accurate budgeting in advance; watch the exchange rates. On the whole, Greece offers good value compared with many other European countries. A modest hotel in a small town will charge only slightly lower rates than a modest hotel in Athens, with the same amenities. The same is true of restaurants. Some sample prices include: cup of coffee, 800 dr./€2.36–1,100 dr./€3.24; bottle of beer, 700 dr./€2.06–900 dr./€2.65; soft drink, 500 dr./€1.48; grilled cheese sandwich, 850 dr./€2.5; 2-km (1-mi) taxi ride, around 500 dr./€1.48. Admission to most museums and archaeological sites is free on Sunday from November through March.

CURRENCY

The Greek monetary unit is the drachma (dr.). Banknotes are in denominations of 100, 200, 500, 1,000, 5,000, and 10,000 dr.; coins, 5, 10, 20, 50, 100, and 500. At press time (summer 2001), there were 355 dr. to the U.S. dollar, 240 dr. to the Canadian dollar, 532 dr. to the pound sterling, 426 dr. to the Irish punt, 212 dr. to the Australian dollar, 168 dr. to the New Zealand dollar, and 51.39 dr. to the South African rand. Daily exchange rates are prominently displayed in banks. Greece is one of 12 nations adopting the euro, the single European Union currency. Coins and bills will be issued in January 2002, and in a few months the drachma will cease to exist. One euro is equivalent to 340 dr.

SHOPPING

Prices in large stores are fixed. Bargaining may take place in small, owner-managed souvenir and handicrafts shops and in antiques shops. In flea markets bargaining is expected. You are required to have an export permit (not normally given if the piece is of any value) for antiques and Byzantine icons, but replicas can be bought fairly cheaply, although even these require a certificate stating they are copies.

TAXES

VALUE-ADDED TAX (VAT)

Prices quoted in shops include the value-added tax (VAT). If you are a citizen from a non-EU country, you may get a VAT refund on products worth 40,000 dr./€117.64 or more (including VAT) bought in Greece from licensed stores, which usually display the Tax-Free Shopping sticker. Ask the shop to complete a refund form called a Tax-Free Check, which Greek customs will stamp after viewing the item to make sure you are exporting it. Send the refund form back to the shop for repayment by check or credit card.

TELEPHONES

COUNTRY AND AREA CODES

The country code for Greece is 30. When dialing Greece from outside the country, drop the first zero in the regional telephone code.

DIRECTORY AND OPERATOR ASSISTANCE

For directory information, dial 131; many of the operators speak English. Many places are listed under the owner's name, not the official name, so you must know the name of the establishment's owner, even if it is a taverna or shop. For operator-assisted calls and international directory information in English, dial 161.

INTERNATIONAL CALLS

You can buy phone cards with 100 units (2,500 dr./€7.35), 500 units (5,000dr./€14.71), and 1,000 units (10,000 dr./€29.42) for use at card phones. Kiosks frequently have metered phones for long-distance calls, but their location is often on a bustling street corner. For more privacy, go to the local OTE (Hellenic Telecommunications Organization) office. There is a three-minute minimum charge for operator-assisted station-to-station and person-to-person connections. Numbers for major companies with long-distance operator assistance are listed below.

➤ ACCESS CODES: **AT&T** (☎ 00/800–1311). **Worldphone (MCI)** (☎ 00/800–1211). **Sprint** (☎ 00/800–1411).

LOCAL CALLS

Many kiosks have pay telephones for local calls only. You pay the kiosk owner 20 dr./€.06 per call after you've finished, unless it was a lengthy call, in which case you pay for the number of units you racked up. It's easier to buy a phone card from an OTE office, kiosks, or convenience shops and use it at card phones. The price drops about 50% for long-distance calls daily 10 PM–8 AM; for local calls, Sundays 10 PM–8 AM.

TIPPING

By law a service charge is figured into the price of a meal, but unless the waiter was rude or inept, it is customary to leave an additional 8%–10%. During the Christmas and Greek Easter holiday periods, restaurants add an obligatory 18% holiday bonus to your bill for the waiters. Tip porters 200 dr./€.58 per bag; in better hotels maids get about 200 dr./€.58 per day. For taxi drivers Greeks usually round off the fare to the nearest 100 dr./€.29. Hairdressers receive 10%. In legitimate theaters tip ushers 200 dr./€.58; at the cinema give 100 dr./€.29 if you take a program. On cruises, cabin and dining-room stewards get about 600 dr./€1.77 per day; guides receive about the same.

TRAIN TRAVEL

The main railway line runs north from Athens, dividing into three lines at Thessaloniki. The main line continues to Skopje and Belgrade, a second line goes east to the Turkish border and Istanbul, and a third line heads northeast to Sofia, Bucharest, and Budapest. The Peloponnese in the south is served by a narrow-gauge line dividing at Corinth into the Tripolis–Kalamata section and the Patras–Kalamata section. Call the number listed below for general information and timetables daily 7 AM–9 PM.

FARES AND SCHEDULES

➤ TRAIN INFORMATION: **Train Information** (☎ 01/529–7777 for general information; 145 for recorded departure timetable of trains [in Greek] within Greece; 147 for a Greek recording of departure times for trains to Europe).

VISITOR INFORMATION

In Greek addresses, the word "street" is not used; the abbreviation for the word *Platia* (square) is Pl. In city addresses, the name of the district follows the name of the street.

Tourist police, at most popular tourist sites, can answer questions in English about transportation, steer you to an open pharmacy or doctor, and locate phone numbers of hotels, rooms, and restaurants. There are Greek National Tourist Organization (EOT) offices throughout the country. Often more helpful are municipal tourism offices.

WHEN TO GO

May, June, September, and October are the most temperate and least-crowded months to visit Greece. The heat can be unpleasant in late June through August, especially in Athens, although the situation is somewhat alleviated when millions leave the city in August, taking their overheated cars with them. On the islands a brisk northwesterly wind, the *meltemi,* can make life more comfortable. The winter months tend to be cold virtually everywhere but with many sunny days.

CLIMATE

The following are the average daily maximum and minimum temperatures for Athens.

Jan.	55F	13C	**May**	77F	25C	**Sept.**	84F	29C
	44	6		61	16		67	19
Feb.	57F	14C	**June**	86F	30C	**Oct.**	75F	24C
	44	6		68	20		60	16
Mar.	60F	16C	**July**	92F	33C	**Nov.**	66F	19C
	46	8		73	23		53	12
Apr.	68F	20C	**Aug.**	92F	33C	**Dec.**	58F	15C
	52	11		73	23		47	8

ATHENS

Athens is the point to which all roads lead in Greece and from which many tours take off if for no reason other than that the greatest sight of "the glory that was Greece" is here: the Parthenon and other legendary buildings of the Acropolis. But this perpetual shrine of Western civilization, set high on a rocky bluff, dominates and overlooks a 21st-century boomtown. In 1834, when it became the capital of modern Greece, Athens had a population of fewer than 10,000. Now it houses more than a third of the entire Greek population—around 4.4 million. Needless to say, romantic travelers, nurtured on the truth and beauty of Keats's Grecian urn, are surprised to find that most of Athens has succumbed to that red tubular glare that owes only its name, neon, meaning new, to the Greeks. A modern concrete city has engulfed the old village and sprawls for 388 square km (244 square mi), covering all the surrounding plain from the sea to the encircling mountains. The city has an air-pollution problem, caused mainly by traffic fumes; in an attempt to lessen the congestion, private cars are forbidden in central Athens on alternate workdays. Still, Athens's vibrancy makes it one of the most exciting cities in Europe, and the sprawling cement has failed to overwhelm the astonishing reminders of the fabled ancient metropolis.

Although Athens covers a huge area, the major landmarks of the ancient Greek, Roman, and Byzantine periods are close to the modern city center. You can stroll from the Acropolis to the other sites, taking time to browse in shops and relax in cafés and tavernas along the way.

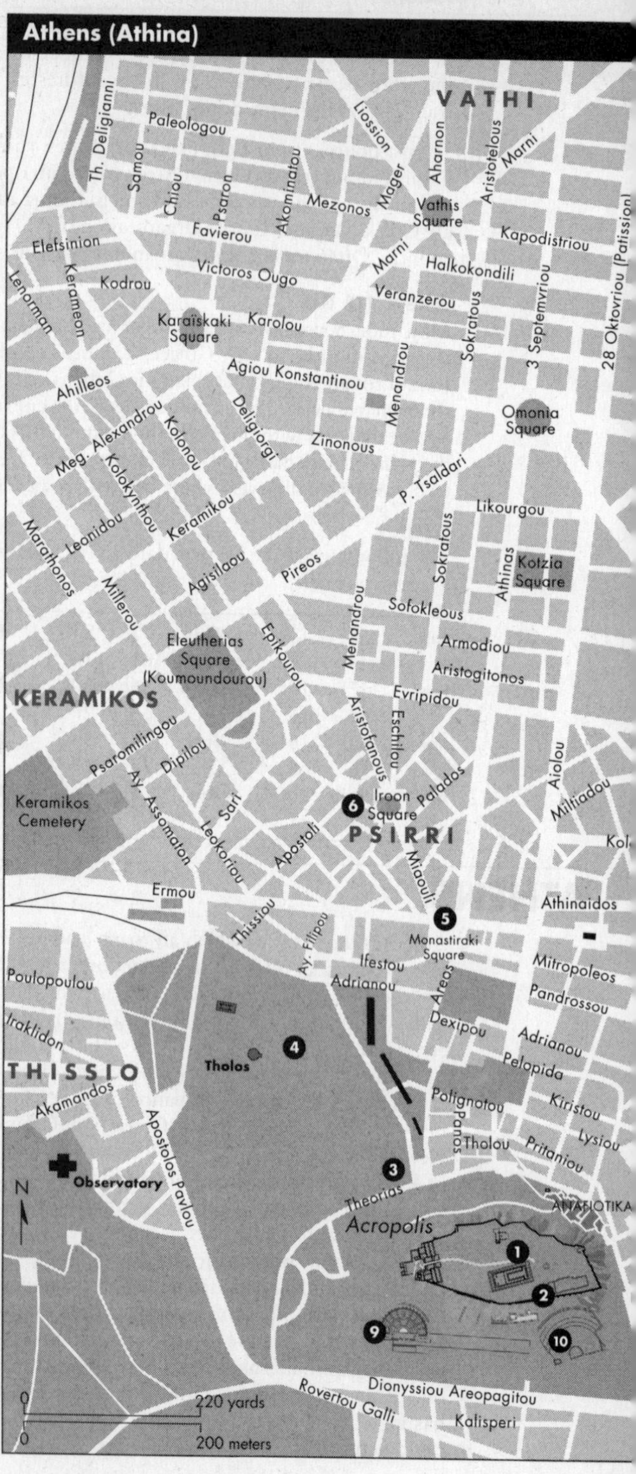
Athens (Athina)
VATHI
Th. Deligianni
Paleologou
Samou
Chiou
Psaron
Akominatou
Liossion
Mager
Aharnon
Aristotelous
Marni
Mezonos
Vathis Square
Favierou
Kapodistriou
Elefsinion
Victoros Ougo
Halkokondili
28 Oktovriou (Patission)
Kerameon
Kodrou
Veranzerou
Lenorman
Karaïskaki Square
Karolou
Sokratous
3 Septemvriou
Menandrou
Agiou Konstantinou
Ahilleos
Omonia Square
Deligiorgi
Meg. Alexandrou
Kolonou
Zinonous
Kolokynthou
P. Tsaldari
Likourgou
Keramikou
Marathonos
Leonidou
Athinas
Kotzia Square
Agisilaou
Pireos
Millerou
Sofokleous
Eleutherias Square (Koumoundourou)
Epikourou
Armodiou
Aristogitonos
KERAMIKOS
Evripidou
Aristofanous
Eschilou
Psaromilingou
Dipilou
Ay. Assomaton
Aiolou
Keramikos Cemetery
Sari
Iroon Square
Palados
Miltiadou
Leokoriou
Apostoli
PSIRRI
Miaouli
Ermou
Thissiou
Athinaidos
Ay. Filipou
Monastiraki Square
Ifestou
Mitropoleos
Poulopoulou
Adrianou
Areos
Pandrossou
Dexipou
Iraklidon
Adrianou
Pelopida
THISSIO
Tholos
Polignotou
Kiristou
Akamandos
Panos
Tholou
Lysiou
Pritaniou
Apostolos Pavlou
Observatory
N
Theorias
ANAFIOTIKA
Acropolis
Dionyssiou Areopagitou
Rovertou Galli
Kalisperi
0
220 yards
0
200 meters

Strefi
NEAPOLIS
Tossitsa
Boumboulinas
Zaimi
Notara
Stournara
Solomou
Kapodistriou
Kaningos Square
Kaningos
Themistokleous
Em. Benaki
Zoodohou Pigis
Harilaou Trikoupi
Arachovis
Dervenion
Eressou
Methonis
Kallidromiou
Smolenski
Issavron
Tsimiski
Voulgaroktonou
Komninon
Vatatzi
Velissariou
Laskareos
Jossif Damaskinou
Kosma Melodou
Doxapatri
Sarantapichou
Asklepiou
N. Ouranou
Dafnomili
Mavromichali
Ippokratous
Navarinou
Didotou
Akademias
Panepistimiou (Venizelou)
Stadiou
Aristidou
Municipal Cultural Center
Skoufa
Massalias
Solonos
Sina
Omirou
Chersonos
Sindesmou
Fokilidou
Anagnostopoulou
Tsakalof
Lykavitou
LIKAVITOS
Agios Giorgos
Marasli
Aristippou
Kleomenous
Loukianou
Spefsipou
Korai
Dragatsaniou
Klafthmonos Sq.
Paparigopoulou
Ch. Lada
Amerikis
Dimokritou
Voukourestiou
Pindarou
KOLONAKI
Patriarhou Ioakim
Ploutarchou
Alopekis
Karneadou
Ypsilantou
Irodotou
Schliemann's Mansion
Kanari
Merlin
Kolonaki Square
Koumbari
okotroni
Praxitelous
Karageorgi Servias
Perikleos
Vas. Georgiou A
Vasilissis Sofias
Ermou
Voulis
Syntagma Square
Parliament
Mourouzi
Rigilis
Likiou
Herod Atticus
Pendeli
Mitropoleos
Filellinon
Nikis
Vasilissis Amalias
Apollonos
National Gardens
Vasileos Georgiou B'
Nikodimou
PLAKA
Souri
Kidathineon
Scholiou
Adrianou
Tripodon
Thespidos
Zappion
Vasileos Konstantinou
Pafsaniou
Arianou
Eratosthenous
Agras
Epimenidou
Lysikratous
Goura
Pitakou
Vironos
Vasilissis Olgas
Arditos Hill
Plastira Square
19
18
16
17
15
14
13
12
11
8
7

The Acropolis and Filopappou, two craggy hills sitting side by side; the ancient and Roman agoras (marketplaces); and Kerameikos, the first cemetery, form the core of ancient and Roman Athens.

Exploring Athens

Numbers in the margin correspond to points of interest on the Athens map.

The central district of modern Athens is small, stretching from the Acropolis to Mt. Lycabettus, with its small white church on top. The layout is simple: three parallel streets (Stadiou, Panepistimiou, and Akademias) link two main squares (Syntagma and Omonia). Try to wander off this beaten tourist track: seeing the Athenian butchers in the central market near Monastiraki sleeping on their cold marble slabs during the heat of the afternoon siesta may give you more of a feel for the city than looking at hundreds of fallen pillars. In summer, closing times often depend on the site's available personnel, but throughout the year, arrive at least 45 minutes before the official closing time to ensure that you can buy a ticket. Flash photography is forbidden in museums. The Ministry of Culture's website (www.culture.gr) provides a good description of museums and archaeological sites, although the hours are often out-of-date.

7 **Agios Eleftherios** (St. Eleftherios). What's fascinating about the city's former cathedral is that the walls of this 12th-century Byzantine church incorporate reliefs—fanciful figures and zodiac signs—from buildings that date back to the classical period. The church is also known as Little Mitropolis and Panagia Gorgoepikoos (Virgin Who Answers Prayers Quickly), based on its 13th-century icon, said to perform miracles. ✉ *Pl. Mitropolis,* ☎ *No phone.* ⏲ *Hrs depend on services, but usually open daily 8–1.*

★ 1 **Akropolis** (Acropolis). Even in its bleached and silent state, the Parthenon—the great Panathenic temple that crowns the Acropolis, the tablelike hill that represented the "upper city" of ancient Athens—has the power to stir the heart as few other ancient relics can. Seeing it bathed in the sunlight of the south, or sublimely swathed in moonglow, one marvels at the continuing vitality of this monument of ageless intellect. Well, not completely ageless. The Athenians built this complex during the 5th century BC to honor the goddess Athena, patron of the city. The first ruins you'll see are the **Propylaia,** the monumental gateway that led worshipers from the temporal world into the spiritual world of the sanctuary; now only the columns of Pentelic marble and a fragment of stone ceiling remain. Above, to the right, stands the graceful **Naos Athenas Nikis** or **Apterou Nikis** (Wingless Victory). The temple was mistakenly called the latter because common tradition often confused Athena with the winged goddess Nike. The elegant and architecturally complex **Erechtheion,** most sacred of the shrines of the Acropolis and later turned into a harem by the Turks, has emerged from repair work with dull, heavy copies of the caryatids (draped maidens) supporting the roof. The **Acropolis Museum** houses five of the six originals, their faces much damaged by acid rain. The sixth is in the British Museum in London.

The **Parthenonas** (Parthenon) dominates the Acropolis and indeed the Athens skyline. Designed by Ictinus, with Phidias as master sculptor, it was completed in 438 BC and is the most architecturally sophisticated temple of that period. Even with hordes of tourists wandering around the ruins, it still inspires wonder. The architectural decorations were originally painted vivid red and blue, and the roof was of marble tiles, but time and neglect have given the marble pillars their golden-white shine, and the beauty of the building is all the more stark and striking. The British Museum houses the largest remaining part of the original 532-ft frieze (the Elgin Marbles), but Greece has long been campaigning for its return. The building has 17 fluted columns along each side and eight at the ends; these were cleverly made to lean slightly inward and to bulge, counterbalancing the natural optical distortion. The Parthenon was made into a brothel by the Romans, a church by the Christians, and a mosque by the Turks. The Turks also stored gunpowder in the Propylaia. When this was hit by a Venetian bombardment in 1687, 28 columns of the Parthenon were blown out and a fire raged for two days, leaving the temple in its present condition. Piece by piece, the entire Parthenon complex is now undergoing conservation, as part of an ambitious 20-year rescue plan launched with international support in 1983 by Greek architects. ✉ *Top of Dionyssiou Areopagitou,* ☎ *01/321–4172 or 01/321–0219.* ⏲ *May–Oct., daily 8–6:30; Nov.–Apr., daily 8:30–2:30.*

❹ **Archaia Agora** (Ancient Agora). Now a sprawling confusion of stones, slabs, and foundations, this was the civic center and focal point of community life in ancient Athens, where Socrates met with his students while merchants haggled over the price of olive oil. It is dominated by the best-preserved Doric temple in Greece, the **Hephaisteion,** built during the 5th century BC. Nearby, the Stoa Attalou (Stoa of Attalos II), reconstructed in the mid-1950s by the American School of Classical Studies in Athens, houses the **Museo tis Agoras** (Museum of Agora Excavations). The museum offers a glimpse of everyday life in ancient Athens, its objects ranging from a child's terra-cotta chamber pot to the shards (*ostraka,* from which the word "ostracism" is derived) used in secret ballots to recommend banishment of Themistocles and other powerful citizens. ✉ *Three entrances: from Monastiraki, on Adrianou; from Thission, on Apostolos Pavlou; from Acropolis, on descent along Ag. Apostoli,* ☎ *01/321–0185.* ⏲ *Tues.–Sun. 8:30–3.*

❸ **Areios Pagos** (Areopagus). From this rocky outcrop, ancient Athens's supreme court, you can view the Propylaia, the Agora, and the modern city. Legend claims it was here that Orestes was tried for the murder of his mother, and much later St. Paul delivered his Sermon to the Unknown God, so moving that a senator named Dionysius was converted and became the first bishop of Athens. ✉ *Opposite Acropolis entrance.* ⏲ *Always open.*

★ ⓳ **Ethniko Archaiologiko Museo** (National Archaeological Museum). Among the collection of antiquities are the sensational archaeological finds of Heinrich Schliemann in 1874 at Mycenae; 16th-century BC frescoes from the Akrotiri ruins on Santorini; and the 6½-ft-tall bronze sculpture *Poseidon,* an original work of circa 470 BC that was found in the sea off Cape Artemision. ✉ *28 Oktovriou (Patission) 44, 10-min walk north of Pl. Omonia,* ☎ *01/821–7717.* ⏲ *May–Oct., Mon. 12:30–7, Tues.–Fri. 8–7; Nov.–Apr., Mon. 10:30–5, Tues.–Sun. 8:30–3.*

★ ⓯ **Goulandri Museo Kikladikis ke Ellinikis Archaias Technis** (Goulandris Museum of Cycladic and Greek Ancient Art). The collection spans 5,000 years, with nearly 100 exhibits of the Cycladic civilization (3000–2000 BC), including many of the marble figurines that so fascinated such artists as Picasso and Modigliani. ✉ *Neofitou Douka 4 or Irodotou 1,* ☎ *01/722–8321 through 8323,* WEB *www.cycladic-m.gr.* ⏲ *Mon. and Wed.–Fri. 10–4, Sat. 10–3.*

❾ **Irodion** (Odeon of Herod Atticus). This hauntingly beautiful 2nd-century AD theater was built Greek-style into the hillside but with typical

Roman archways in its three-story stage building and barrel-vaulted entrances. Now restored, it hosts Athens Festival performances. ✉ *Dionyssiou Areopagitou across from Propylaia,* ☎ *01/323–2771.* ⏲ *Open only to audiences during performances.*

★ ⓰ **Likavitos** (Mt. Lycabettus). Athens's highest hill borders Kolonaki, a residential quarter worth a visit if you enjoy window-shopping and people-watching. A steep funicular climbs to the summit, crowned by whitewashed Agios Giorgios chapel. The view from the top—pollution permitting—is the finest in Athens. ✉ *Base: 15-min walk northeast of Syntagma; funicular every 10 min from Ploutarchou 1 at Aristippou (take minibus 060 from Kanaris St. or Pl. Kolonaki, except Sun.),* ☎ *01/722–7065.* ⏲ *Nov.–Apr., daily 9:15 AM–11:45 PM; May–Oct., daily 9:15 AM–12:45 AM. Closed Nov.*

❺ **Monastiraki.** The old Turkish bazaar area takes its name from Panayia Pantanassa Church, commonly called Monastiraki (Little Monastery); it once flourished as a convent, perhaps dating from the 10th century. Near the church stands the Tzistarakis Mosque (1759), exemplifying the East-West paradox that characterizes Athens. But the district's real draw is the Sunday flea market, centered on tiny Abyssinia Square and running along Ifestou and Kynetou streets where Greeks bargain with wildly gesturing hands and dramatic facial expressions. Everything's for sale, from gramophone needles to old matchboxes, from nose rings to lacquered eggs and cool white linens. ✉ *South of junction Ermou and Athinas Sts.*

★ ❷ **Museo Akropoleos** (Acropolis Museum). Tucked into one corner of the Acropolis, this institution contains superb sculptures, including the caryatids and a collection of colored *korai* (statues of women dedicated to Athena, patron of the ancient city). ✉ *Southeastern corner of Acropolis,* ☎ *01/323–6665.* ⏲ *Mid-Apr.–Oct., Mon. 11–6, Tues.–Sun. 8–6; Nov.–mid-Apr., Mon. 10:30–2:30, Tues.–Sun. 8:30–3.*

⓭ **Panathinaiko Stadio** (Panathenaic Stadium). A reconstruction of the ancient Roman stadium in Athens, this gleaming-white marble structure was built for the first modern Olympic Games in 1896 and seats 80,000 spectators. ✉ *Near junction Vas. Konstantinou and Vas. Olgas,* ☎ *no phone.* ⏲ *Daily 9–2.*

⓫ **Pili tou Adrianou** (Hadrian's Arch). Built in AD 131–32 by Emperor Hadrian to show where classical Athens ended and his new city, Hadriaopolis, began, the Roman archway with Corinthian pilasters bears an inscription on the side facing the Acropolis that reads, THIS IS ATHENS, THE ANCIENT CITY OF THESEUS. But the side facing the Temple of Olympian Zeus proclaims, THIS IS THE CITY OF HADRIAN AND NOT OF THESEUS. ✉ *Junction Vas. Amalias and Dionyssiou Areopagitou.*

★ ❽ **Plaka.** Stretching east from the Agora, this is almost all that's left of 19th-century Athens, a lovely quarter with winding walkways, neoclassical houses, and such sights as the **Museo Ellinikis Laikis Technis** (Greek Folk Art Museum; ✉ Kidathineon 17, ☎ 01/322–9031, ⏲ Tues.–Sun. 10–2), with a collection dating from 1650, and the Roman Agora's **Aerides** (Tower of the Winds; ✉ Pelopidas and Aiolou, ☎ 01/324–5220, ⏲ Tues.–Sun. 8:30–3), a 1st-century BC water clock. Just down the street from the Tower of the Winds in a neoclassical mansion is the delightful **Museo Ellinikon Laikon Musikon Organon** (Museum of Greek Popular Musical Instruments; ✉ Diogenous 1–3, ☎ 01/325–0198, ⏲ Tues., Thurs.–Sun. 10–2, Wed. noon–6), which gives a crash course in the development of Greek music, with three floors of instruments and headphones so visitors can appreciate recorded sounds made by such unusual organs as goatskin bagpipes and the Cretan lyra. Admission is free. The **Mnimeio Lysikratous** (Monument of Lysikrates; ✉ Herefondos and Lysikratous Sts.) is one of the few surviving tripods on which stood the award given to the producer of the best play in the Dionysia festival. Above Plaka, at the northeastern base of the Acropolis, is **Anafiotika,** the closest thing you'll find to a village in Athens. Take time to wander among its whitewashed, bougainvillea-framed houses and tiny churches.

6 **Psirri.** During the day, little in this former industrial district indicates that at night this rapidly changing quarter becomes a whirl of theaters, clubs, and restaurants, dotted with dramatically lit churches and lively squares. Whether you want to dance on tabletops to live Greek music, sing along with a soulful accordion player, salsa in a Cuban club, or just watch the hoi polloi go by as you snack on trendy or traditional mezedes, this is the place. ✉ *Off Ermou St., centered on Iroon and Ag. Anargiron Squares.*

12 **Stiles Olymbiou Dios or Olymbion** (Temple of Olympian Zeus). Begun during the 6th century BC, this temple was larger than all other temples in Greece when it was finally completed 700 years later. It was destroyed during the invasion of the Goths in the 4th century; only a few towering, sun-browned columns remain. ✉ *Vas. Olgas 1,* ☎ *01/922–6330.* ⏲ *Tues.–Sun. 8:30–3.*

17 **Syntagma** (Constitution Square). At the top of the square stands the **Vouli** (Parliament), formerly the royal palace, completed in 1838 for the new monarchy. From the Parliament you can watch the changing of the Evzone honor guard at the **Mnimeio Agnostou Stratiotou** (Tomb of the Unknown Soldier), with its text from Pericles's famous funeral oration and a bas-relief of a dying soldier modeled after a sculpture on the Temple of Aphaia in Aegina. The most elaborate ceremony takes place on Sunday, when the sturdy young guards don their *foustanellas* (kilts) with 400 pleats, one for each year of the Ottoman occupation. The procession usually arrives in front of Parliament at 11:15 AM. Pop into the gleaming **Stathmo Syntagma** (Syntagma Metro station: ✉ at upper end of Syntagma Square) to take a look at artifacts from the subway excavations artfully displayed and a vast cross-section of the earth behind glass with the finds in chronological layers, from a skeleton in its ancient grave to traces of the 4th century BC road to Mesogeia, to a Turkish cistern. The Metro station is open daily 5 AM until midnight. On the square's southern side sits the lush **Ethnikos Kipos** (National Garden), its dense foliage, gazebos, and trellised walkways offering a quick escape from the center's bustle. For young visitors, there are two playgrounds, a miniature zoo, duck pond, and refreshments at the stone cottage café. ✉ *Corner of Vas. Sofias and Vas. Amalias.*

10 **Theatro Dionyssou** (Theater of Dionysus). In this theater dating from about 330 BC, the ancient dramas and comedies were performed in conjunction with bacchanalian feasts. The throne in the center was reserved for the priest of Dionysus: it is adorned with regal lions' paws, and the back is carved with reliefs of satyrs and griffins. ✉ *Dionyssiou Areopagitou opposite Mitsaion,* ☎ *01/322–4625.* ⏲ *May–Oct., daily 8–6; Nov.–Apr., daily 8:30–2:30.*

18 **Vivliothiki, Panepistimio, Akademia** (Old University complex). These three dramatic buildings belong to the University of Athens, designed by the Hansen brothers in the period after independence and built of white Pentelic marble, with tall columns and decorative friezes. In the center is the Panepistimio, the Senate House of the university; on the right is the Akademia, or Academy, flanked by statues of Athena and Apollo; and on the left is the Vivliothiki, or National Library. ✉

Panepistimiou between Ippokratous and Sina, ☎ *01/361–4413 Vivliothiki; 01/361–4301 Panepistimio; 01/360–0207 or 01/360–0209 Akademia.* ⏲ *Vivliothiki Sept.–July, Mon.–Thurs. 9–8, Fri.–Sat 9–2. Other buildings weekdays 9–2.*

14 **Vizantino Museo** (Byzantine Museum). Housed in an 1848 mansion built by an eccentric French aristocrat, the museum has a unique collection of icons, re-creations of Greek churches throughout the centuries, and a very beautiful 14th-century Byzantine embroidery of the body of Christ, in gold, silver, yellow, and green. Sculptural fragments provide an excellent introduction to Byzantine architecture. ✉ *Vas. Sofias 22,* ☎ *01/721–1027.* ⏲ *Tues.–Sun. 8:30–3.*

Dining

Search for places with at least a half dozen tables occupied by Athenians—they're discerning customers. For details and price-category information, *see* Dining *in* Greece A to Z, *above.*

$$$$ ✕ **Vardis.** A meal at this French restaurant is worth the ride to the northern suburb of Kifissia. The chef is committed to the classics and to quality ingredients—he brings in sweetwater crayfish from Orhomenos and tracks down rare large shrimp from Thassos island. The clientele may be a little sedate, but the food dazzles. Especially good are the superb crayfish linguine, caramelized lamb cutlets with morel and porcini mushrooms, and salt-crusted duck filled with foie gras and served with a fragrant sherry sauce. The splendid desserts include a soufflé of Grand Marnier and forest berries, crème brûlée, and pear with dark chocolate and espresso sauce. ✉ *Diligianni 66, in Pentelikon Hotel, Kefalari, Kifissia,* ☎ *01/623–0650 through 0656. Reservations essential. AE, DC, MC, V. Closed Sun. and Aug. No lunch.*

$$$–$$$$ ★ ✕ **Aristera-Dexia.** Chef Chrisanthos Karalomengos enjoyed such a stellar reputation from his last hit restaurant (the now-defunct Vitrina) that his latest creation was an instant success. His forte is fusion—exciting, artful combinations such as pheasant sausage with parsnips in Madeira sauce; a tower of *haloumi* (Cypriot cheese) and feta croquettes in a melon-mirin-chili sauce; sardine tempura with black sesame and a vinaigrette with port and dried figs; or the Greek version of sushi, raw squid on a puree of eggplant with anchovies and trout roe. Though located in a less than desirable neighborhood, the restaurant is strikingly designed, with two large partitions dividing the large room (hence, the name "Left-Right") and a glass runway offering a peek at the cellar below, which houses one of the most extensive wine collections in the city. Diners exit through an art gallery. ✉ *Andronikou 3, Rouf,* ☎ *01/342–2380. Reservations essential. AE, MC, V. Closed Sun. No lunch.*

$$$–$$$$ ★ ✕ **To Varoulko.** Chef Lefteris Lazarou is constantly trying to outdo himself, with magnificent results. You can sample such appetizers as crab salad studded with mango and grapes, with bits of leek to cut the sweetness; fresh mullet roe from Messolonghi laced with honey and accompanied by cinnamony cauliflower puree; or carpaccio made from *petrobarbouno* (a kind of rockfish). Although the restaurant is most famous for monkfish, it offers a mind-boggling array of other seafood dishes: red mullet marinated in lemon and swirled with fuchsia-colored beet creme; cockles steamed in Limnos sweet wine; and lobster with wild rice, celery, and champagne sauce. ✉ *Deligeorgi 14, Piraeus,* ☎ *01/411–2043 or 01/422–1283. Reservations essential. AE, DC, MC, V. Closed Sun. and Aug. No lunch.*

$$$ ✕ **Boschetto.** The restaurant pampers diners with its park setting, expert maître d', and creative nouvelle Italian food. The specialty here is fresh pasta, such as the shrimp cannelloni, green gnocchi with Gorgonzola sauce, or ravioli with duck livers and truffle zabaglione. Entrées may include sea bass with a potato crust, succulent rooster in Riesling, and grilled wild buffalo steak with a sauce of coffee, fig and Mavrodaphne wine. End your meal with the crema cotta followed by the finest espresso in Athens. The tables tend to be close together; reserve near the window or in the courtyard during the summer. ✉ *Alsos Evangelismos, Hilton area,* ☎ *01/721–0893 or 01/722–7324. Reservations essential. AE, V. Closed Sun. and 2 wks in Aug. No lunch Oct.–Apr.*

$$$ ✕ **Spondi.** This vaulted stone–interior restaurant used to suggest a medieval wine cellar, but now, after redecoration, the ambience is as cool and contemporary as the cuisine. Savor the artichoke terrine with duck confit or black ravioli with honeyed leek and shrimp. Interesting entrées may include a perfectly grilled John Dory with a spirited orange and mustard sauce; lamb tail so tender it falls from the bone, with couscous, raisins and cumin; and chicken with foie gras, truffles, and asparagus in porcini sauce. In good weather, you can sit in the bougainvillea-draped courtyard. ✉ *Pirronos 5, Pangrati,* ☎ *01/756–4021 or 01/752–0658. Reservations essential. AE, DC, MC, V. No lunch.*

$$–$$$ ✕ **Azul.** The space may be a bit cramped, but the food is heavenly. Start with mushrooms stuffed with nuts and *anthotiro* cheese (soft, mild, low-fat white cheese made from goat's and sheep's milk), or salmon and trout in pastry with champagne sauce. The spaghetti *à la nona* (godmother's) with chamomile, Gorgonzola, and bacon is an unparalleled combination. Other memorable dishes are beef fillet with raisins and cedar needles, and chicken prepared with lemon leaves. In summer, Azul sets up tables outside. ✉ *Haritos 43, Kolonaki,* ☎ *01/725–3817. Reservations essential. AE, DC, MC, V. Closed last 2 wks in Aug. and Sun. Oct.–Apr. No lunch.*

$$–$$$ ✕ **Kollias.** Friendly owner Tassos Kollias creates his own dishes, ranging from the humble to the aristocratic: fried whole squid in its ink; sea urchin salad; cuttlefish stew with broccoli and cream; lobster with lemon, balsamic vinegar, and a shot of honey. He's known for bringing in the best-quality catch, whether mullet from Messolonghi or oysters culled by Kalymnos sponge divers, and his prices are usually 25% lower than most fish tavernas. A fitting end to the meal: fresh *loukoumades* (sweet fritters) or *bougatsa* (custard in phyllo). Ask for directions when you call—even locals get lost trying to find this obscure street in the working-class quarter of Piraeus. ✉ *Stratigou Plastira 3, near junction of Dramas and Kalokairinou, Tabouria,* ☎ *01/461–9150 or 01/462–9620. Reservations essential weekends. AE, DC, MC, V. Closed Aug. No lunch Mon.–Sat., no dinner Sun.*

$$–$$$ ✕ **Kouzina-Cine Psirri.** Once a dilapidated wood factory, this chic dining space features lots of stone, golden wood, and a partial glass floor that reveals the wine cellar. The best place to be is the roof terrace with its view of the illuminated Acropolis and the nearby observatory. The talented chef comes up with creative Greek cuisine. Try the appetizer of crab with smoked eggplant puree and fennel root or fish soup accompanied by grilled skate; then move on to such entrées as boar with watermelon chutney, or grilled rooster breast with kumquats. ✉ *Sarri 40, Psirri,* ☎ *01/321–5534 or 01/321–2476. Reservations essential. MC, V. Closed Mon.*

$$ ✕ **Margaro.** Near Piraeus, next to the Naval Academy, this popular, no-nonsense fish taverna serves just four items, along with excellent barrel wine: fried crayfish, fried red mullet, fried *marida* (a small white fish), and huge Greek salads. Tables on the terrace offer a view of the busy port. If it's crowded, you may be asked to go into the kitchen and prepare your own salad! Try to arrive between 6 and 8 PM, before Greeks eat dinner; reservations are not accepted. ✉ *Hatzikyriakou 126, Piraeus,* ☎ *01/451–4226. No credit cards. Closed 15 days at Greek Easter. No dinner Sun.*

$$ ✕ **Stous 7 Anemous.** The decor is a bit of postmodern pastiche, but the playful food with intense flavors is impressive here. For appetizers sample the fried Dodoni feta wrapped in sesame-enhanced crust and served with marinated tomatoes and walnut sauce, or the tortillas filled with octopus. Main dishes might include lamb ribs with a refreshing kiwi chutney spiked with mint; moist pork fillet with a dense coffee-black currant sauce; and grilled tuna with tomato, thyme, and chamomile. End your meal with the almond pastry (*amigdaloto*) with tsipouro. ✉ *Astiggos 17 (from Ermou 121), Monastiraki,* ☎ *01/324–0386. Reservations essential. AE, DC, MC, V. Closed Aug.*

$$ ✕ **Tade Efi Anna.** Near the end of the Ermou pedestrian zone, this stylish restaurant serves Greek regional cuisine with a modern touch. Try perhaps the best *pita Kaisarias* in Athens (the spicy, cured meat called *pastourmas* with tomato and Kasseri cheese in a crisp phyllo) or *melitzanes amigdalou* (thinly sliced eggplant layered with tomatoes and cheese with a thick topping of crushed almonds). The rabbit is cooked with cinnamony prunes and fresh spinach, and the chicken fillet is first wrapped around Gruyère, then baked in a crust of pistachios. ✉ *Ermou 72, Monastiraki,* ☎ *01/321–3652. V. Closed Mon. and June–Aug.*

$$ ★ ✕ **Vlassis.** Relying on recipes from Thrace, Roumeli, Thessaly, and the islands, the chefs whip up Greek home cooking in generous portions. Musts are the peppery cheese dip called *tirokafteri,* pastitsio (made here with bits of lamb liver), *lahanodolmades* (cabbage rolls), goat with oil and oregano, and octopus *stifado* (stew), tender and sweet with lots of onions. ✉ *Paster 8, Platia Mavili (near American embassy),* ☎ *01/646–3060. Reservations essential. No credit cards. Closed Aug.–mid-Sept. No dinner Sun.*

$ ✕ **Karavitis.** A neighborhood favorite, this taverna near the Olympic Stadium has warm-weather garden seating and a winter dining room decorated with huge wine casks. Classic Greek cuisine is well prepared here, including pungent *tzatziki* (yogurt-garlic dip), *bekri meze* (lamb chunks in a spicy red sauce), and *stamnaki* (beef baked in a clay pot). ✉ *Arktinou 35 and Pausaniou 4, Pangrati,* ☎ *01/721–5155. No credit cards. Closed around Aug. 15 for a week. No lunch.*

$ ★ ✕ **O Platanos.** Set in a picturesque courtyard, this is one of Plaka's oldest yet least touristy tavernas. The waiters are fast but far from ingratiating, and the place is packed with Greeks. Don't miss the oven-baked potatoes, roast lamb, green beans in savory olive oil, and exceptionally cheap but delicious barrel retsina. ✉ *Diogenous 4, Plaka,* ☎ *01/322–0666. No credit cards. Closed Sun.*

$ ✕ **Sigalas-Bairaktaris.** Run by the same family for more than a century, this is one of the best places to eat in Monastiraki. After admiring the painted wine barrels and black-and-white stills of Greek film stars, go to the window case to view the day's *magirefta*—beef *kokkinisto* (stew with red sauce), spicy meat patties seasoned with clove—or sample the gyro platter. Appetizers include tiny cheese pies with sesame seeds, tender mountain greens, and fried zucchini with a garlicky dip. ✉ *Pl. Monastiraki 2, Monastiraki,* ☎ *01/321–3036. AE, MC, V.*

Lodging

It's always advisable to reserve a room. Hotels are clustered around the center of town and along the seacoast toward the airport. Modern hotels are more likely to be air-conditioned and to have double-glazed windows; the center of Athens can be so noisy that it's hard to sleep. For details and price-category definitions, *see* Lodging *in* Greece A to Z, *above.*

$$$$ ★ 🏨 **Andromeda Athens Hotel.** On a quiet street near the U.S. embassy and the city's concert hall, this small, luxury hotel prides itself on its business clientele, but the meticulous service and sumptuous decor (Persian carpets, Italian pastels, designer furniture) will be enjoyed by all. For those who need to be plugged in, all rooms have an ISDN digital connection. The restaurant has excellent Polynesian and Chinese cuisine. The hotel also operates a property across the street with security system and 12 executive suites (one- and two-room apartments), which include fully equipped kitchenettes. ✉ *Timoleondos Vassou 22, Pl. Mavili, 11521,* ☎ *01/641–5000,* FAX *01/646–6361,* WEB *www.slh.com. 30 rooms, 5 suites, 4 penthouses. Restaurant. AE, DC, MC, V.*

$$$$ 🏨 **Athens Hilton.** A 200-year-old olive tree with a Turkish cannonball in its branches adds an earthy touch to the marble lobby. About a 20-minute walk from Syntagma, this is still ranked in the top tier of Athens hotels after nearly 30 years; a shuttle takes guests downtown during the day. The rooms, in muted colors, all have balconies and double-glazed windows, as well as fine views of either the Acropolis or Mt. Ymittos. The Galaxy bar has an outdoor terrace overlooking an enchanting Athens panorama. ✉ *Vas. Sofias 46, 11528,* ☎ *01/728–1000 or 01/728–1100 reservations,* FAX *01/728–1111; 01/725–1919 reservations,* WEB *www.hilton.com. 454 rooms, 19 suites. 4 restaurants, pool, wading pool. AE, DC, MC, V.*

$$$$ ★ 🏨 **Divani Apollon Palace.** For those who love the sea or need a break from city bustle, this grand modern hotel is the perfect solution. Towering above the posh, residential area of Kavouri, the seaside resort offers a casual ambience but sophisticated service and sparkling facilities. Take a few laps in the indoor pool, spend a hour on the tennis court, dip into the Aegean across the street (lined with a shady stretch of lawn and a few seafood tavernas), arrange to play a round of golf at the Glyfada links 3 km (2 mi) away, or take the hotel shuttle to Glyfada for some serious shopping (the van continues on to downtown Athens). The airy white-and-yellow rooms all have balconies with sea view, satellite-pay TV, and direct-dial phones with voice mail. The suites even have fireplaces. Best, though, are the hotel's large, gleaming public spaces, the outdoor pool with hydromassage, and the comfy Pelagos Bar with its leather sofas. The hotel is 3 km (2 mi) from the airport's international terminal, and limo service is available. ✉ *Ag. Nikolaou 10 and Iliou, Vouliagmeni, 16671,* ☎ *01/891–1100,* FAX *01/965–8010,* WEB *www.divaniapollon.gr. 286 rooms, 7 suites. 2 restaurants, 2 pools, 1 wading pool. AE, DC, MC, V.*

$$$$ 🏨 **Grande Bretagne.** Built in 1842, the G. B. is an Athens landmark, and its guest list testifies to its colorful history, with such visitors as Edith Piaf, Jackie Kennedy, royalty, and rock stars. A face-lift in 1992 restored the hotel: the lobby has Oriental rugs, tapestries, and ornate chandeliers, and the coveted Syntagma rooms have large balconies and Acropolis views. There are also "smart" rooms, with desk, printer, fax, photocopier, and a direct telephone line with voice mail, and the third floor is no-smoking. ✉ *Vas. Georgiou A' 1, Pl. Syntagma, 10564,* ☎ *01/333–0000; 01/331–5555 through 5559 reservations,* FAX *01/322–8034; 01/322–2261; 01/333–0910 reservations,* WEB *www.hotel-grandebretagne-ath.gr. 364 rooms, 23 suites. Restaurant. AE, DC, MC, V.*

$$$$ 🏨 **N. J. V. Athens Plaza.** At an exclusive Syntagma Square address, the fresh, spacious rooms, in gray and burgundy, come equipped with minibar, direct-dial phones with voice mail, satellite and pay TV, and large marble bathrooms with phone extensions. The few rooms in the back are quieter, but even those on the front are quiet, due to double glazing and air-conditioning. Non-smoking rooms are available. The suites on the eighth and ninth floors have sitting areas, breathtaking Acropolis views, and interiors decked out with designer fabrics and furnishings. ✉ *Vas. Georgiou A' 2, Pl. Syntagma, 10564,* ☎ *01/335–2400,* FAX *01/323–5856. 182 rooms, 15 suites. Restaurant. AE, DC, MC, V.*

$$$–$$$$ **Kefalari Suites.** In a turn-of-the-20th-century building among the neoclassical mansions and tree-lined boulevards of the suburb of Kifissia, the hotel offers imaginative themed suites (i.e., Malmaison, Jaipur) at prices lower than those of downtown deluxe hotels. The suites include kitchenettes with utensils, refrigerators, satellite TV, queen-size beds, modem connection, and verandas or balconies; guests share the sundeck, which has a whirlpool tub. Continental deluxe breakfast (cheese, cold cuts, cereal, yogurt, cake) is included in the room rate. ✉ *Pentelis 1 and Kolokotroni, Kefalari, Kifissia, 14562,* ☎ *01/623–3333,* FAX *01/623–3330,* WEB *www.kefalarisuites.gr. 13 suites. AE, DC, MC, V.*

$$$ **Electra Palace.** At the Plaka's edge, this hotel has cozy rooms in warm hues with TV and plenty of storage space, for comparatively low prices in this category. Rooms from the fifth floor up are smaller but have larger balconies and Acropolis views. The renovated roof garden has a bar, a pool and whirlpool tub, barbecue in summer, and stunning Acropolis views. One of the city's best buffet breakfasts (sausage, pancakes, home fries) is included in the price. ✉ *Nikodimou 18, Plaka, 10557,* ☎ *01/337–0000,* FAX *01/324–1875. 106 rooms, 5 suites. Restaurant, pool. AE, DC, MC, V.*

$$ **Acropolis View Hotel.** Major sights are just a stone's throw away from this hotel tucked into a quiet neighborhood below the Acropolis. About half of the agreeable rooms with balconies have Parthenon views. There is a roof garden, staff members in the homey lobby are efficient, and buffet breakfast is included in the price. ✉ *Webster 10, Acropolis, 11742,* ☎ *01/921–7303, 01/921–7304, or 01/921–7305,* FAX *01/923–0705,* WEB *www.acropolisview.gr. 32 rooms. Air-conditioning. DC, MC, V.*

$$ **Athens Cypria Hotel.** A cool oasis in the city center, this hotel is a few minutes from Syntagma Square, offering a reasonably priced alternative for those who want convenience and comfort. Enter the vaguely Art Deco lobby from the quiet street to find simple and clean air-conditioned guest rooms, done in shades of blue and furnished with satellite TV and standard amenities. Some of the upper floors open out onto a balcony; those on the sixth floor have Acropolis views. American buffet breakfast is included in the price. ✉ *Diomias 5, Syntagma, 10557,* ☎ *01/323–8034 through 8038,* FAX *01/324–8792. 71 rooms. Bar, air-conditioning. AE, V.*

$$ **Hotel Achilleas.** This modern, family-owned hotel is just a few minutes from Syntagma but priced at the low end of its category. It has plain but spacious rooms with TV, direct-dial phones, mini-bar, safe, and air-conditioning. At press time, the hotel was undergoing a major renovation to qualify for a higher government rating, so expect changes for the better. Breakfast is served in an interior courtyard filled with jungly plants and marble-topped blue tables. ✉ *Lekka 21, Syntagma, 10562,* ☎ *01/322–5826, 01/322–8531, or 01/323–3197,* FAX *01/322–2412,* WEB *www.tourhotel.gr/achilleas/. 36 rooms. Air-conditioning. AE, DC, MC, V.*

$$ **Plaka Hotel.** Close to the ancient sights and the Monastiraki Square Metro, this hotel has a roof garden overlooking the Plaka district's rooftops to the Parthenon. Double-glazed windows cut down the noise; the highest floors are the quietest. All rooms have TV and are simply furnished; those in back from the fifth floor up have the best Acropolis views. ✉ *Kapnikareas 7 and Mitropoleos, Plaka, 10556,* ☎ *01/322–2096 through 2098,* FAX *01/322–2412,* WEB *www.plakahotel.gr. 67 rooms. Air-conditioning. AE, DC, MC, V.*

$–$$ **Acropolis House.** Ensconced in a 19th-century Plaka residence, this pension is frequented by artists and academics who appreciate its large rooms, original frescoes, and genteel owners. All rooms have private bathrooms, though about 10 have their bath immediately outside in the hallway. Most rooms have air-conditioning, and a full breakfast is included in the price. ✉ *Kodrou 6–8, Plaka, 10558,* ☎ *01/322–2344 or 01/322–6241,* FAX *01/324–4143. 20 rooms. V.*

$–$$ **Adams Hotel.** Favored by young people for its clean rooms and good value, this quiet hotel sits across from Ayia Aikaterini church in Plaka. Most of the rooms have balconies and many, including all on the top floor, enjoy splendid views of the Acropolis. The four rooms that don't have air-conditioning are cooled by ceiling fans. Four cheaper rooms have their private bath outside the room. ✉ *Herefondos 6 at Thalou, Plaka, 10558,* ☎ *01/322–5381 or 01/324–6582,* FAX *01/323–8553,* WEB *www.greektravel.com/adams. 14 rooms. Air-conditioning. MC, V.*

$ **Art Gallery Pension.** On a side street not far from the Acropolis, this friendly, handsome house has an old-fashioned look, with family paintings on the muted white walls, comfortable beds, hardwood floors, and ceiling fans. Many rooms have balconies with views of Filopappou or the Acropolis. ✉ *Erecthiou 5, Koukaki, 11742,* ☎ *01/923–8376 or 01/923–1933,* FAX *01/923–3025. 21 rooms, 2 suites. No credit cards. Closed Nov.–Feb..*

$ **Attalos Hotel.** Gentlemanly owner Kostas Zissis's personality is reflected in the friendly, helpful atmosphere of this central hotel, just a few minutes from the trendy Psirri district. It has a rooftop garden, and 12 rooms have fine views of the Acropolis or Lycabettus; 37 rooms include balconies. All have direct-dial phone and TV. Try to get a room in the back, where there's less street noise, though it's also reduced by double-glazed windows. ✉ *Athinas 29, Monastiraki, 10554,* ☎ *01/321–2801 through 2803,* FAX *01/324–3124,* WEB *www.attalos.gr. 80 rooms. Air-conditioning. AE, V.*

Nightlife and the Arts

The English-language newspapers *Athens News* and *Kathemerini,* inserted in the *International Herald Tribune,* list current performances, gallery openings, and films. The free magazine *Now in Athens,* distributed at various hotels and EOT, offers extensive information on culture and entertainment in the capital.

The Arts

The **Athens Festival** (box office; ✉ arcade at Stadiou 4, ☎ 01/322–1459) runs from late June through September with concerts, opera, ballet, folk dancing, and drama. Performances are in various locations, including the theater of Herod Atticus (Irodion; ☎ 01/323–2771 box office) below the Acropolis and Mt. Lycabettus (☎ 01/722–7233 or 01/722–7209). Tickets range in price from 4,000 dr./€11.77 to 20,000 dr./€58.83 and are available a few days before the performance.

The **Krystalleia Festival** stages local and international musical and dance groups from June through July and September in the stately Plakendias mansion (✉ 16 km/10 mi northeast of Athens on Mt. Pendeli). The concurrent **Pendelis Festival** (end July and Sept.) focuses on classical music, often importing international orchestras to take advantage of the acoustics of the mansion. For information on the festivals, contact EOT. Tickets run from 2,000 dr./€5.89 to 5,000 dr./€14.71 and are usually sold at major record stores in downtown Athens.

Though rather corny, the **sound-and-light shows** (✉ Pnyx theater box office off Dionyssiou Areopagitou opposite Acropolis, ☎ 01/922–6210 or 01/928–2907), held April–October nightly at 9, display the

Acropolis with dramatic lighting and a brief narrated history. The box office opens at 8:20 PM, admission is 1,500 dr./€4.42 and performances are in English.

CONCERTS AND OPERAS

Greek and world-class international orchestras perform September through June at the **Megaron Athens Concert Hall** (✉ Vas. Sofias and Kokkali, ☎ 01/728–2333, FAX 01/728–2300; downtown box office, Arcade at Stadiou 4, ☎ 01/322–1459). Information and tickets are available weekdays 10–6 and Saturday 10–4. Prices range from 1,500 dr./€4.42 to 22,000 dr./€64.71; there is a substantial discount for students and those 8–18. Inexpensive and often free classical concerts are held November through May at the **Philippos Nakas Conservatory** (✉ Ippokratous 41, ☎ 01/363–4000, FAX 01/360–2827). Tickets cost 2,000 dr./€5.89 to 3,000 dr./€8.83

DANCE

The lively **Dora Stratou Troupe** (✉ Theater, Filopappou Hill, ☎ 01/921–4650; 01/324–4395 troupe's offices, FAX 01/324–6921, WEB users.hol.gr/~grdance) performs Greek and Cypriot folk dances in authentic costumes. Tickets cost 4,000 dr./€11.77. Performances are from the end of May to the end of September, Tuesday–Sunday at 10:15 PM and Wednesday and Sunday at 8:15.

FILM

Almost all Athens cinemas now show foreign films; for listings, consult the *Athens News* and the *Kathemerini* insert in the *International Herald-Tribune*. Tickets run about 2,000 dr./€5.89–2,300 dr./€6.77 In summer, films are also shown in open-air cinemas called *therina*.

Nightlife

Athens has an active nightlife; most bars and clubs stay open at least until 3 AM. Drinks are rather steep (about 1,800 dr./€5.29–2,500 dr./€7.35) but generous. Often there is a surcharge on weekends at the most popular clubs, which also have bouncers. Few clubs take credit cards for drinks. In summer many downtown dance clubs move to the seaside. Ask your hotel for recommendations and check ahead for summer closings. For a uniquely Greek evening, visit a club featuring *rembetika* music, a type of blues, or the popular *bouzoukia* (clubs with live bouzouki music). In the larger bouzouki venues, there is usually a per-person minimum or an overpriced, second-rate prix-fixe menu; a bottle of whiskey costs about 42,000 dr./€123.53.

BARS

Balthazar (✉ Tsoha 27, Ambelokipi, ☎ 01/644–1215 or 01/645–2278), in a neoclassical house, has a lush garden courtyard and subdued music. **Banana Moon** (✉ Vas. Olgas 1, Zappio, ☎ 01/321–5414) offers both a lively bar with a glamorous crowd and quieter tables set among the trees of the National Gardens; in winter the bar moves across the street. With low-key music and a romantic park setting, **Parko** (✉ Eleftherias Park, Ilisia, ☎ 01/722–3784) is another summer favorite. Cinema stars, romancing couples, girlfriends, the local Lotto vendor—all show up at **En Delfois** (✉ Skoufa 75 on Delfon pedestrian zone, Kolonaki, ☎ 01/360–8269) for its see-and-be-seen atmosphere in a friendly setting with good snacks, eclectic music played at conversational level, and generous drinks. **Folie** (✉ Eslin 4, Ambelokipi, ☎ 01/646–9852) has a congenial crowd of all ages dancing to reggae, Latin, funk, and ethnic music. Of the bars for the under-40 crowd, mainstream **Privilege** (✉ Pireos 130 and Alkioneos, Gazi, ☎ 01/347–7388) is especially popular, though tough to get into. **Plus Soda** (✉ Ermou 161, Thissio,

☎ 01/345–6187), the dance temple of Athens, is very popular and sometimes hard to gain entrance to. Both Privilege and Plus Soda usually move to the seaside in summer. Glitzy **Wild Rose** (✉ Panepistimiou 10, Syntagma, ☎ 01/364–2160) is an Athens classic, with predominantly house music and some rock. You'll find an artsy, happy crowd enjoying the playlist that runs from cabaret to ethnic to freestyle at the bar-restaurant **Multi-Culti** (✉ Ag. Theklas 8, Psirri, ☎ 01/324–4643).

BOUZOUKIA

Apollon Palace (✉ Syngrou 259, Nea Smyrni, ☎ 01/942–7580 through 7583) is the most popular place with Athenians who want to hear Greece's singing stars, such as Antonis Remos and Stelios Dionyssiou. It's closed Monday–Tuesday. Decadence reigns at the slightly more casual **Iera Odos** (✉ Iera Odos 18–20, Kerameikos, ☎ 01/342–8272 through 8275) as diners dance the seductive *tsifteteli* to big names like Notis Sfakianakis. It's closed Sunday–Monday.

LIVE ROCK, JAZZ, BLUES

The laid-back **House of Art** (✉ Santouri 4 and Sarri, Psirri, ☎ 01/321–7678) hosts small groups. The premier venue for international jazz and blues bands is the sophisticated **Half Note Jazz Club** (✉ Trivonianou 17, Mets, ☎ 01/921–3310 or 01/923–2460). Lively **Hi-Hat Cafe** (✉ Dragoumi 28 and Krousovou 1, Hilton, ☎ 01/721–8171) also hosts international artists. Most big names in popular music perform at the informal **Rodon** (✉ Marni 24, Platia Vathis, ☎ 01/524–7427); in summer, they usually appear at the outdoor Lycabettus amphitheater. Summer also heralds the three-day **Rockwave Festival** in mid-July, usually held somewhere on the Athens coast (Ticket House box office; ✉ Panepistimiou 42 in arcade, ☎ 01/360–8366 or check with downtown record stores). Past acts have included Patti Smith and Prodigy.

REMBETIKA CLUBS

Rembetika, the blues sung by refugees from Asia Minor who came to Greece in the 1920s, still enthralls Greeks. At **Stathmos** (✉ Mavromateon 22, Pedion Areos, ☎ 01/883–2393 or 01/822–0883), the band usually starts off slowly but by 1 AM is wailing to a packed dance floor. At **Mnissikleous** (✉ Mnissikleous 22 and Lyceiou, Plaka, ☎ 01/322–5558 or 01/322–5337), the authentic music of popular *rembetis* Bobis Goles draws audience participation.

Shopping

Antiques

Pandrossou Street in Monastiraki is especially rich in shops selling small antiques and icons. Keep in mind that fakes are common and that you must have government permission to export objects from the Classic, Hellenistic, Roman, or Byzantine periods. For serious antiques collecting, including carved dowry chests, head to **Martinos** (✉ Pandrossou 50, ☎ 01/321–2414). **Motakis** (✉ Pl. Abyssinia 3 in basement, ☎ 01/321–9005) sells antiques and other beautiful old objects. At **Nasiotis** (✉ Ifestou 24, ☎ 01/321–2369) you may uncover interesting finds in a basement stacked with engravings, old magazines, and books, including first editions.

Flea Markets

The **Sunday-morning flea market** (✉ Pandrossou and Ifestou Sts.) sells everything from secondhand guitars to Russian caviar. However little your treasured find costs, you should haggle. On weekdays in **Ifestou,** where coppersmiths have their shops, you can pick up copper wine jugs, candlesticks, and cookware for next to nothing.

Gift Ideas

Better tourist shops sell copies of traditional Greek jewelry; silver filigree; Skyrian pottery; onyx ashtrays and dishes; woven bags; attractive rugs, including flokatis; worry beads in amber or silver; and blue-and-white amulets to ward off the *mati* (evil eye). Reasonably priced natural sponges from Kalymnos also make good gifts. **Goutis** (✉ Dimokritou 40, Kolonaki, ☎ 01/361–3557) has an eclectic assortment of costumes, embroidery, and old, handcrafted silver items. **Ilias Kokkonis** (✉ Stoa Arsakeiou 8, Omonia, enter from Panepistimiou or Stadiou, ☎ 01/322–1189 or 01/322–6355) stocks any flag you've hankered after—large or small, from any country. **Mati** (✉ Voukourestiou 20, Syntagma, ☎ 01/362–6238) has finely designed amulets to battle the evil eye, as well as a collection of monastery lamps and candlesticks. **Mazarakis** (✉ Voulis 31–33, Syntagma, ☎ 01/323–9428) offers a large selection of flokatis and will ship.

Greeks spend hours heatedly playing *tavli*, or backgammon. To take home a set of your own, look for the hole-in-the-wall, no-name shop affectionately called **Baba** (✉ Ifestou 30, Monastiraki, ☎ 01/321–9994), which sells boards and pieces in all sizes and designs. For an inexpensive gift pick up some freshly ground Greek coffee and the special coffee pot called *briki* at **Miseyiannis** (✉ Levendis 7, Kolonaki, ☎ 01/721–0136).

Handicrafts

The **Kentro Ellinikis Paradosis** (Center of Hellenic Tradition; ✉ Mitropoleos 59, Monastiraki, ☎ 01/321–3023) is an outlet for quality handicrafts. The **Organismos Ethnikos Pronoias** (National Welfare Organization; ✉ Ipatias 6, and Apollonos, Plaka, ☎ 01/321–8272) displays work by Greek craftspeople—stunning handwoven carpets, flat-weave kilims, hand-embroidered tablecloths, and flokatis.

At **Amorgos** (✉ Kodrou 3, Plaka, ☎ 01/324–3836) the owners make wooden furniture using motifs from regional Greek designs. They also sell needlework, handwoven fabrics, hanging ceiling lamps, shadow puppets, and other decorative accessories. The Greek cooperative **EOMMEX** (✉ Mitropoleos 9, Syntagma, ☎ 01/323–0408) operates a showroom with folk and designer rugs made by more than 30 weavers around the country.

Jewelry

Prices for gold and silver are much lower in Greece than in many Western countries, and jewelry is of high quality. Many shops in Plaka carry original-design pieces available at a good price if you bargain hard enough. Great values in gold, often designed by the owners, can be purchased at **Byzantino** (✉ Adrianou 120, Plaka, ☎ 01/324–6605). For more expensive items, the Voukourestiou pedestrian mall off Syntagma Square has a number of the city's leading jewelry shops. The baubles at **J. Vourakis & Fils** (✉ Voukourestiou 8, ☎ 01/331–1087) are both unique modern designs and older, collector's items. **Xanthopoulos** (✉ Voukourestiou 4, ☎ 01/322–6856) carries diamond necklaces, magnificently large gems, and the finest pearls; you can also order custom-made jewelry.

Some of the most original work in gold can be had at **Fanourakis** (✉ Patriarchou Ioakeim 23, Kolonaki, ☎ 01/721–1762; ✉ Evangelistrias 2, Mitropoleos, ☎ 01/324–6642; ✉ Panagitsas 6, Kifissia, ☎ 01/623–2334), where contemporary Athenian artists use gold almost like a fabric—creasing, scoring, and fluting it. **LALAoUNIS** (✉ Panepistimiou 6, Syntagma, ☎ 01/361–1371) showcases pieces by Ilias Lalaounis, who takes his ideas from nature, biology, and ancient Greek pieces.

The **Benaki Museum gift shop** (✉ Koumbari 1, at Vas. Sofias, Kolonaki, ☎ 01/362–7367) has finely rendered copies of classical jewelry. The **Goulandris Cycladic Museum** (✉ Neofitou Douka 4, Kolonaki, ☎ 01/724–9706) carries modern versions of ancient jewelry designs.

Music

CDs of Greek music are much cheaper before they've been exported. One of the biggest selections, along with knowledgeable English-speaking staff, is at the **Virgin Megastore** (✉ Stadiou 7–9, Syntagma, ☎ 01/331–4788 through 4796), where you can listen before you purchase.

Side Trips

Mikrolimano

The pretty, crescent-shape harbor of Mikrolimano is famous for its many seafood restaurants. Although it has become increasingly touristy, its delightful atmosphere remains intact, and the harbor is crowded with elegant yachts. Terraces of lovely houses are tucked up against the hillsides. Take the Metro from Monastiraki Square to the Neo Faliron station; it's only 10 minutes' walk from there.

Moni Kaisarini

★ Outside central Athens, on the slopes of Mt. Ymittos (ancient Mt. Hymettus), stands Moni Kaisariani (Kaisariani Monastery), one of the city's most evocative Byzantine remains. The well-restored 11th-century monastery, built on the site of a sanctuary of Aphrodite, has some beautiful frescoes dating from the 17th century. Nearby are a basilica and a picnic site with a superb panorama of the Acropolis and Piraeus. Take a taxi or Bus 224 (in front of the Byzantine museum) to the end of the line; then walk 35 minutes along the paved road that climbs Mt. Ymittos. ✉ *Ethnikis Antistaseos,* ☎ *01/723–6619.* ⏲ *Monastery Tues.–Sun. 8:30–3; grounds daily sunrise–sunset.*

Athens Essentials

AIRPORTS AND TRANSFERS

Ellinikon Airport lies about 10 km (6 mi) from the city center.

➤ AIRPORT INFORMATION: **Ellinikon Airport** (✉ Vas. Georgiou B' 1, ☎ 01/936–3363 through 3366 West Terminal; 01/969–4466 arrivals and departures; 01/969–4531 passenger paging for East Terminal; 01/997–2581 New Charter Terminal).

TRANSFERS

An express bus service connects the East, West, and New Charter terminals; Syntagma Square; Omonia Square; and Piraeus. The express bus (No. E93) runs between the three terminals every 40 minutes around the clock. Between the terminals and Athens, the express bus (No. E91) runs around the clock, about every 30 minutes. You can catch the bus on Syntagma Square between Ermou and Mitropoleos streets or off Omonia Square on Stadiou and Aiolou. From the airport terminals to Piraeus (Pl. Karaiskaki), the express bus (No. E19) leaves about every hour, from 5 AM to midnight. The fare is 250 dr./€.74, 500 dr./€1.48 from 11:30 PM until 5:30 AM (for schedules check with EOT). You can also take the regular city line (No. B2) from Syntagma Square to the West Terminal (for Olympic Airways flights) from about 4:30 AM to 11:50 PM every 15 minutes for most of the day; fare is 120 dr./€.36. It's easier to take taxis: about 2,500 dr./€7.36 to Piraeus; 1,500 dr./€4.42 between terminals; 2,700 dr./€7.95 to the center, more if there is traffic. The price goes up by about two-thirds between midnight and 5 AM.

BOAT AND FERRY TRAVEL

Most ships from the Greek islands dock at Piraeus (port authority), 10 km (6 mi) from the center. EOT distributes boat schedules updated every Wednesday; you can also call a daily Greek recording by dialing 143 for departure times. From the main harbor you can take the nearby Metro right into Omonia Square (150 dr./€.45) or Syntagma Square (change at Omonia, take the line going to Ethniki Aminas, 250 dr./€.74) The trip takes 25–30 minutes. A taxi takes longer because of traffic and costs around 2,500 dr./€7.36. As the driver may wait until he fills the taxi with several passengers headed in the same direction, it's faster to walk to the main street and hail a cab there. If you arrive by hydrofoil in the smaller port of Zea Marina, take Bus 905 or Trolley 20 to the Piraeus Metro. At Rafina port, which serves some of the closer Cyclades and Evia, taxis are hard to find. KTEL buses, which are located slightly uphill from port, leave every 30 minutes from about 5:30 AM until 9:30 PM and cost 500 dr./€1.48.

➤ BOAT AND FERRY INFORMATION: **KTEL** (☎ 01/821–0872). **Piraeus** (☎ 01/451–1311 through 1319). **Rafina Port** (☎ 0294/22–300).

BUS TRAVEL TO AND FROM ATHENS

Greek buses serving parts of northern Greece, including Thessaloniki, and the Peloponnese (Corinth, Olympia, Nauplion, Epidavros, Mycenae) arrive at Terminal A. Those traveling from Evia, most of Thrace, and central Greece, including Delphi, pull in to Terminal B; you must call each region's ticket counter for information. EOT provides a phone list. From Terminal A, take Bus 051 to Omonia Square; from Terminal B, take Bus 24 downtown. To get to the stations, catch Bus 051 at Zinonos and Menandrou off Omonia Square for Terminal A and Bus 024 on Amalias Avenue in front of the National Gardens for Terminal B. International buses drop their passengers off on the street, usually in the Omonia or Syntagma Square area or at Stathmos Peloponnisos.

Most buses to the east Attica coast, including those for Sounion (1,250 dr./€3.67 for inland route and 1,300 dr./€3.83 on coastal road) and Marathon (800 dr./€2.36), leave from the KTEL terminal, which is on the corner Mavromateon and Alexandras near Pedion Areos park.

➤ BUS INFORMATION: **KTEL terminal** (✉ Platia Aigyptiou, ☎ 01/821–3203 for information on bus to Sounion; 01/821–0872 for information on bus to Marathon). **Terminal A** (✉ Kifissou 100, ☎ 01/512–4910). **Terminal B** (✉ Liossion 260, ☎ 01/831–7096 Delphi; 01/831–7173 Livadia [Ossios Loukas via Distomo]; 01/831–1431 Trikala [Meteora])).

BUS TRAVEL WITHIN ATHENS

EOT can provide bus information, as can the Organization for Public Transportation. The office itself is open to visitors weekdays 7:30–3. The fare on buses and trolleys is 120 dr./€.36; monthly passes are sold at the beginning of each month for 5,000 dr./€14.71 (bus and trolley). Purchase tickets at curbside kiosks or from booths at terminals. Validate your ticket in the orange machines when you board to avoid a fine. Buses run from the center to all suburbs and nearby beaches from 5 AM until about midnight. For suburbs north of Kifissia, change at Kifissia's main square, Platia Platanou.

➤ BUS INFORMATION: **Organization for Public Transportation** (✉ Metsovou 15, ☎ 185, 7:30–3 and 7 PM–9 PM).

CAR TRAVEL

You enter Athens by the Ethniki Odos (or National Road, as the main highways going north and south are known) and then follow signs for the center. Leaving Athens, routes to the National Road are marked with signs in English; they usually name Lamia for the north and Corinth or Patras for the southwest.

CONSULATES

➤ New Zealand: (✉ Kifissias 268, Halandri, ☎ 01/687–4700 or 01/687–4701).

EMERGENCIES

You can call an ambulance in the event of an emergency, but taxis are often faster. Most hotels will call a doctor or dentist for you; you can also contact your embassy for referrals to both. Not all hospitals are open nightly; ask your hotel to check for you, or dial 106 for a Greek listing. The *Athens News* often lists available emergency hospitals, as do most Greek newspapers. Many pharmacies in the center have someone who speaks English, or try Thomas. For late-night pharmacies, call the information line, or check the *Athens News*. For auto accidents, call the city police.

➤ Emergency Services: **Ambulance** (☎ 166). **City Police** (☎ 100). **Coast Guard** (☎ 108). **Fire** (☎ 199). **Tourist police** (✉ Dimitrakopoulou 77, Koukaki, ☎ 171).

➤ 24-hour Pharmacies: **Late-night Pharmacy Information Line** (☎ 107; information in Greek).

ENGLISH-LANGUAGE MEDIA

➤ Bookstores: **Booknest** (✉ Folia tou Bibliou, Panepistimiou 25–29, ☎ 01/322–9560). **Compendium** (✉ Nikis 28, upstairs, ☎ 01/322–1248). **Eleftheroudakis** (✉ Nikis 4, near Syntagma, ☎ 01/322–9388; ✉ Panepistimiou 17, ☎ 01/331–4180). **Pantelides** (✉ Amerikis 11, ☎ 01/362–3673).

SUBWAY TRAVEL

Line 1 runs from Piraeus to Omonia Square and then on to Kifissia, with downtown stops at Thission, Monastiraki, Omonia, and Platia Victorias (near the National Archaeological Museum). Line 2 runs from Sepolia to Syntagma, with a stop at the train stations (Stathmos Larissis) and, as far as Dafne, including a stop for the Acropolis. Line 3 runs from Syntagma to the Greek armed forces' "Pentagon" (Ethnikis Aminas) and includes a stop at Athens's concert hall and the American embassy (Megaron). The fare is 150 dr./€.45 if you stay only on Line 1; otherwise, it's 250 dr./€.74.

TAXIS

Although you can find an empty taxi, it's often faster to call out your destination to one carrying passengers; if the taxi is going in that direction, the driver will pick you up. Most drivers speak basic English. The meter starts at 200 dr./€.59, and even if you join other passengers, you must add this amount to your final charge. The minimum fare is 500 dr./€1.48. The basic charge is 71 dr./€.21 per kilometer (⅔ mi); this increases to 130 dr./€.39 between midnight and 5 AM or if you go outside city limits. There are surcharges for holidays (120 dr./€.36), trips to and from the airport (300 dr./€.89), and rides to, but not from the port, train stations, and bus terminals (150 dr./€.45). There is also a 50 dr./€.14 charge for each suitcase over 10 kilograms (22 pounds), but drivers expect 100 dr./€.29 for each bag they place in the trunk anyway. Waiting time is 2,300 dr./€6.77 per hour. Make sure drivers turn on the meter and use the high tariff ("Tarifa 2") only after midnight; if you encounter trouble, threaten to go to the police. Radio taxis charge an additional 400 dr./€1.18 for the pickup or 600 dr./€1.77 for a later appointment. Some fairly reliable services are Athina 1, Hellas, Kosmos, and Parthenon.

➤ TAXI COMPANIES: **Athina 1** (☎ 01/921–7942). **Hellas** (☎ 01/645–7000 or 01/801–4000). **Kosmos** (☎ 1300). **Parthenon** (☎ 01/532–3300).

TOURS

BUS TOURS

All tour operators offer a four-hour morning bus tour of Athens, including a guided tour of the Acropolis and its museum (10,500 dr./€32.35). Make reservations at your hotel or at a travel agency; many are situated around Filellinon and Nikis streets off Syntagma Square.

PRIVATE GUIDES

All the major tourist agencies can provide English-speaking guides for personally organized tours, or call the Union of Official Guides. Hire only those licensed by the EOT; a four-hour tour including the Acropolis and its museum costs about 28,000 dr./€82.36.

➤ CONTACTS: **Union of Official Guides** (✉ Apollonas 9A, ☎ 01/322–9705, FAX 01/323–9200).

SINGLE- AND MULTIPLE-DAY TOURS

A one-day tour to Delphi costs 21,500 dr./€63.30 with lunch included, 19,000 dr./€55.89 without lunch; a two-day tour to Mycenae, Nauplion, and Epidauros costs 34,000 dr./€100, including half board in first-class hotels; and a full-day cruise from Piraeus, visiting the islands of Aegina, Poros, and Hydra, costs 20,500 dr./€60.20, including buffet lunch on the ship.

SPECIAL-INTEREST TOURS

For folk dancing take a four-hour evening tour (April–October; 10,000 dr./€29.42) that begins with a sound-and-light show of the Acropolis and goes on to a performance of Greek folk dances in the open-air theater nearby. Another tour offers a dinner show at a taverna in the Plaka area for around 14,000 dr./€41.18. For efficient service, go first to CHAT Tours. For organized adventure travel, contact Trekking Hellas or F-Zein.

TRAIN TRAVEL

Athens has two railway stations, side by side, not far from Omonia Square off Diliyianni street. International trains and those coming from north of Athens use Stathmos Larissis. Take Trolley 1 from the terminal to Omonia Square or the Metro to Omonia and Syntagma squares. Trains from the Peloponnese use the marvelously ornate Stathmos Peloponnisos. To Omonia and Syntagma squares take Bus 057 or the Metro. As the phones are almost always busy, it's easier to get departure times from the main information phone service and call about seat availability or buy tickets at a railway office downtown, open Monday–Saturday 8–2.

➤ TRAIN INFORMATION: **Railway offices** (✉ Sina 6, ☎ 01/529–8910; Filellinon 17, ☎ 01/323–6747; ✉ Karolou 1, ☎ 01/529–7006 through 7007). **Stathmos Larissis** (☎ 01/529–8837). **Stathmos Peloponnisos** (☎ 01/529–8735).

TRANSPORTATION AROUND ATHENS

Many of the sights and most of the hotels, cafés, and restaurants are within a fairly small central area. It's easy to walk everywhere, though sidewalks are often obstructed by parked cars. You can buy a monthly pass covering the metro, buses, and trolleys for 10,000 dr./€29.42 at the beginning of each month. Validate your ticket by stamping it in the orange machines at the entrance to the platforms, or you will be fined.

TRAVEL AGENCIES

➤ LOCAL AGENTS: **American Express** (✉ Ermou 2, ☎ 01/324–4975 through 4975, FAX 01/322–7893). **CHAT Tours** (✉ 4 Stadiou, ☎ 01/

322–2886, FAX 01/323–5270). **Condor Travel** (✉ Stadiou 43, ☎ 01/321–2453 or 01/321–6986, FAX 01/321–4296). **F-Zein** (✉ Syngrou 132, 5th floor, ☎ 01/921–6285, FAX 01/922–9995). **Key Tours** (✉ Kallirois 4, ☎ 01/923–3166, FAX 01/923–2008). **Travel Plan** (✉ Christou Lada 9, ☎ 01/323–8801 through 8804, FAX 01/322–2152). **Trekking Hellas** (✉ Fillelinon 7, 3rd floor, ☎ 01/331–0323 through 0326, FAX 01/323–4548).

VISITOR INFORMATION

➤ TOURIST INFORMATION: EOT (✉ Amerikis 2, near Syntagma, ☎ 01/331–0565 or 01/331–0692; ✉ Ellinikon Airport, East Terminal [arrivals], ☎ 01/961–2722 or 01/969–4500; ✉ Piraeus, EOT Building, 1st floor, Zea Marina, ☎ 01/452–2591 or 01/452–2586).

THE NORTHERN PELOPONNESE

Suspended from the mainland of Greece like a large leaf, the ancient land of Pelops offers beautiful scenery—rocky coasts, sandy beaches, mountains—and a fascinating variety of ruins: temples, theaters, mosques, churches, palaces, and medieval castles built by crusaders. Legend and history meet a few miles south of the isthmus of Corinth, in Mycenae, where Agamemnon, Elektra, and Orestes played out their grim family tragedy. This city dominated the entire area from the 18th through the 12th centuries BC and may even have conquered Minoan Crete. After German archaeologist Heinrich Schliemann's excavations in 1874 uncovered gold-filled graves and a royal palace, Mycenae became a world-famous archaeological site.

Exploring the Northern Peloponnese

From Athens, head west across the Corinth Canal (84 km/52 mi) to ancient Corinth (detour off the National Road; otherwise you'll whiz by the canal on the new bridge before you know it). Head south to Mycenae (4 km/2½ mi off the road at Fichtion), and then turn off at Argos via Tiryns for Nauplion (63 km/39 mi from Corinth). The ancient theater of Epidauros is another 26 km (16 mi) east. From Epidauros you can return to Athens, joining the National Road at Corinth, or backtrack to Argos, where the road continues through the rugged mountains of Arcadia to ancient Olympia (191 km/118 mi from Argos). North of Olympia (122 km/76 mi) lies Patras, from where you can return to Athens on the National Road, an exceptionally beautiful drive along the coast. If you want to go on to Delphi, cross the gulf at Rion-Antirion en route.

Corinth

★ When you cross the **Gefira Isthmou** or Isthmos (Corinth Canal), you will have entered the Peloponnese. The ancients once winched their ships across a paved slipway nearby, then talked for centuries about carving a canal through the limestone. The modern throughway was completed in 1893; you can watch the ships go by from the narrow bridge, 197 ft above the water.

At the site of **Archaia Korinthos** (Ancient Corinth) lie remains of the Doric **Naos Apollonos** (Temple of Apollo), built during the 6th century BC and one of the few buildings that still stood when Julius Caesar decided to restore Corinth. A **museum** contains finds from the excavations. ✉ *9 km (6 mi) west of Corinth,* ☎ *0741/31–207; 0741/31–480 (24 hrs).* ⏲ *May–Oct., daily 8–7; Nov.–Apr., daily 8–6.*

Looming over ancient Corinth, the limestone **Acrocorinthos** (Acrocorinth) was one of the best naturally fortified citadels in Europe,

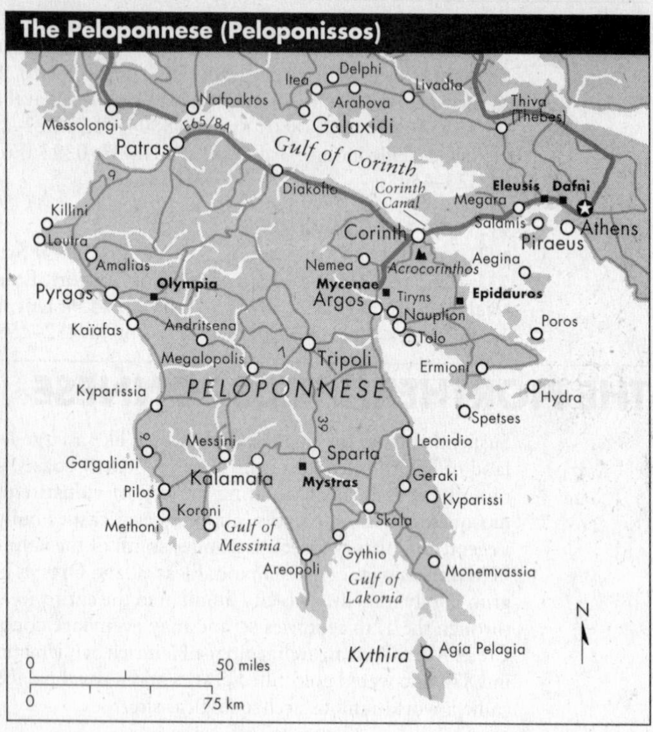

where citizens retreated in times of invasions and earthquakes. Various excavations indicate the many additions made by Romans, Franks, Venetians, and Turks. Take a taxi from ancient Corinth (about 1,500 dr./€4.42) or follow the signs by car. ✉ *Take road outside the ticket office in ancient Corinth, where taxis often wait for visitors, 3½ km (2¼ mi) up to tourist pavilion, then walk 10 mins to Acrocorinth gate,* ☎ *0741/31–266.* ⏲ *May–Oct., daily 8–7; Nov.–Apr., daily 8–5.*

Mycenae

★ Ancient Mykines (Mycenae) was the fabulous stronghold of the Achaean kings of the 13th century BC. Destroyed in 468 BC, it was forgotten until 1874, when Heinrich Schliemann, who had discovered the ruins of ancient Troy, uncovered the remains of this fortress city. Mycenae was the seat of the doomed House of Atreus—of King Agamemnon and his wife, Clytemnestra (sister of Helen of Troy), and of their ill-fated children, Orestes and Elektra. When Schliemann uncovered six shaft graves (so named because the kings were buried standing up) of the royal circle, he was certain that one was the tomb of Agamemnon. The gold masks and diadems, daggers, jewelry, and other treasures found in the graves are now in the National Archaeological Museum in Athens. The new local **museum** is dedicated to archaeological studies. You'll also see the monumental **Pili ton Leonton (Lion Gate)**, dating from 1250 BC; the **castle ruins** crowning the bleak hill; and the astounding beehive tomb **Thisavros tou Atrea** (Treasury of Atreus), built into the hillside outside the massive fortification walls, all remnants of the first great civilization in continental Europe. ☎ *0751/76–585; 0751/76–801 through 803.* ⏲ *May–Oct., daily 8–7; Nov.–Apr., daily 8–5.*

Argos

One of the oldest continuously inhabited towns in Greece and prominent during the 8th century BC, Argos has a grand central square and an **archaeological museum,** which displays neolithic pottery, Roman objects, and finds from the Mycenaean tombs. ✉ *Platia Argos at Vas. Olgas and Kallergi 1,* ☎ *0751/68–819.* ⏲ *Tues.–Sun. 8:30–3.*

$ ✕ **I Spilia.** This countryside taverna is known for its specialty, *bogana* (baby lamb slow-cooked in a wood-burning oven that is sealed airtight with mud, giving the meat a wonderful smoky flavor). Call ahead to make sure the chef saves you some. He makes more than 30 local specialties, including wild artichoke salad, spit-roasted goat, and *tirolagana* (a fried bread made with feta, green onions, dill, and special sheep's milk). ✉ *Tripoleos 165, 3 km (2 mi) from Argos on old national road to Tripolis,* ☎ *0751/62–300 or 0751/67–154. No credit cards. No lunch Mon.–Sat.*

Tiryns

Homer described Tirintha (Tiryns) as "the wall-girt city" for its ramparts, built of gigantic limestone blocks (the largest weighs 15 tons), which ancients thought could be handled only by giants. The remains, including the walls, date mostly from the 13th century BC, when Tiryns was one of the most important Mycenaean cities. ✉ *On Argos-Nauplion road, 4 km (2½ mi) before Nauplion,* ☎ *0752/22–657.* ⏲ *May–Oct., daily 8–7; Nov.–Apr., daily 8:30–3.*

Nauplion

A favorite weekend getaway for Athenians, Nauplion is a picturesque town on the Gulf of Argos, dominated by brooding Venetian fortifications. Modern Greece's first king lived for a year or two within the ★ walls of the high fortress, **Palamidi,** when Nauplion was the capital of Greece. His courtiers had to climb 999 steps to reach him; you can still climb the long staircase (steps begin near the Cultural Center and the courts) or drive up to the fortress. Guards on this large site generally stop letting visitors in one hour before closing time, and they usher out all visitors 15 minutes before the gates close. ✉ *Above town,* ☎ *0752/28–036.* ⏲ *May–Oct., daily 8–7; Nov.–Apr., daily 8:30–2:45.*

Wander for at least a few hours through the narrow streets and shady squares of the **Palia Poli** (Old Town), lined with a mix of Venetian, Turkish, Frankish, and Byzantine buildings. The Venetian naval arsenal on the main town square houses an **archaeological museum** with Mycenaean finds, including a 7th-century BC Gorgon mask from Tiryns. ✉ *East side of Pl. Constitution,* ☎ *0752/27–502.* ⏲ *Tues.–Sun. 8:30–3.*

$$ ✕ **Savouras.** The best-known seafood taverna in town, Savouras continues to maintain its high standards of freshness and simple but successful presentations of such specialties as grilled cod, as well as more expensive catch—red mullet, pandora, dorado. ✉ *Bouboulinas 79,* ☎ *0752/27–704. AE, MC, V.*

$ ✕ **Karamanlis.** A favorite with former Greek president Karamanlis, this taverna near the courthouse is crowded at lunch with civil servants who come for its tasty magirefta. The fish soup makes a good appetizer, as do the melt-in-your-mouth *gigantes yiachni* (giant beans with fresh tomato), followed by savory *yiouvetsi* (lamb or beef baked with orzo-shaped noodles). ✉ *Bouboulinas 1,* ☎ *0752/27–668. No credit cards. Closed Greek Easter.*

$ ✕ **Omorfo Tavernaki.** Snug and inviting, this mezedopolion serves up such appetizers as *tiroboukies* (cheese "bites") and croquettes made from wild greens, as well as some unusual dishes, such as Constantinople souvlaki, marinated in yogurt and garlic. ✉ *Vas. Olgas and Kotsonopoulou 1,* ☎ *0752/25–944. Reservations essential weekends. No credit cards. No lunch Mon.–Sat. Sept.–May.*

$$$$ ★ **Candia House.** This beautifully decorated hotel 17 km (10½ mi) south of Nauplion on sandy Candia Beach weds good taste with comfort. Fresh flowers, antiques, paintings by Greek artists, and handcrafted mirrors are just some of the special touches. Other facilities include a saltwater pool, a playroom with board games, and a gym. The "bio-breakfast" included in the price offers fresh vegetable dishes, salads, and homemade bread. ✉ *Candia-Irion, 21100,* ☎ *0752/94–060 through 063; 01/347–1503 off-season,* FAX *0752/94–480; 01/347–4732 off-season,* WEB *www.candiahouse.gr. 10 suites. Restaurant, pool, beach. AE, DC, MC, V. Closed Nov.–Mar. except holidays.*

$$$ **Amalia.** The Amalia occupies a fine neoclassical building in large gardens 3 km (2 mi) outside town, on the sea and close to the beach, on the way to ancient Tiryns. The public rooms are spacious and comfortable, and service is attentive. A buffet breakfast is included. ✉ *National Rd. to Argos outside Nauplion, 21100,* ☎ *0752/24–401; 01/323–7301 through 7309 reservations,* FAX *0752/24–400; 01/323–8792 reservations,* WEB *www.greekhotel.com/amalia. 175 rooms, 1 suite. Restaurant, pool. AE, DC, MC, V.*

$$ ★ **O Nausimedon.** Near the entrance of the Old Town, this lovely hotel is in a refurbished 19th-century residence. Most of its high-ceilinged rooms have antiques accompanied by such modern amenities as air-conditioning and TV. The quiet house sits across from the city park and has a large garden with palms. Full breakfast with homemade sweets is included. ✉ *Sidiras Merarhias 9, 21100,* ☎ *0752/25–060,* FAX *0752/26–913. 10 rooms, 3 bungalows. Air-conditioning. AE, V.*

$ **Byron.** This gracious hotel in the Old Town is in a rose-and-blue 18th-century house. Rooms include period furnishings, TV, and air-conditioning. The owners have added another building (buttercup-yellow with green shutters), with four spacious rooms, mostly decorated island-style, also with TV and air-conditioning. Guests eat breakfast on a pretty terrace atop the old Turkish bath, overlooking the town and the gulf. ✉ *Platonos 2, Platia Agios Spiridonos, 21100,* ☎ *0752/22–351,* ☎ FAX *0752/26–338,* WEB *www.otenet.gr/byronhotel. 18 rooms. Air-conditioning. AE, MC, V.*

Epidauros

★ Epidauros was the sanctuary of Asklepios, the Greek god of healing. You can visit the foundations of the temples and ancient hospital, as well as the **museum.** The site you must not miss is the ancient **open-air theater,** which seats 14,000. In summer, during the Festival of Ancient Drama, plays are staged here, but it merits a visit at any time of year. The acoustics are so good that you can sit in the top row and hear a whisper on stage. ☎ *0753/22–009.* ⏲ *Theater: May–Oct., daily 8–7; Nov.–Apr., daily 8–6. Museum: May–Oct., Tues.–Sun. 8–7, Mon. noon–7; Nov.–Apr., Tues.–Sun. 8–6, Mon. noon–6.*

Olympia

Just east of the modern village of Olympia, a few miles from the sea, ★ lies **Archaia Olympia** (Ancient Olympia), where the Olympic Games were first held in 776 BC. A huge assembly hall was built here to hold the 10,000 representatives of the Arcadian League. The games continued to be celebrated every four years until AD 393, when the Roman emperor Theodosius I, a Christian, banned these "pagan rites." Women were excluded from watching the games under penalty of death; women's games were held a few weeks earlier. Archaeologists still uncover statues and votive offerings among the pine trees surrounding the **stadium,** the imposing ruins of the **Naos Dios** (Temple of Zeus), and the **Heraion** (Temple of Hera) within the sacred precinct. The **museum,** which lies a few hundred yards north of the sanctuary, includes pedimental sculptures from the Zeus temple and the 4th-century BC head of the Hera cult statue and a well-preserved Hermes sculpted by Praxiteles, both from the Heraion. ☎ *0624/22–517 stadium and site; 0624/22–742 museum.* ⏲ *Site: May–Oct., weekdays 8–7, weekends 8:30–3; Nov.–Apr., weekdays 8–5, weekends 8:30–3. Museum: May–Oct., Mon. 12:30–7, Tues.–Fri. 8–7, weekends 8:30–3; Nov.–Apr., Mon. 10:30–5, Tues.–Fri. 8–5, weekends 8:30–3.*

$$ ✕ **O Kladeos.** Named for the river it borders, this *koutouki* (a tiny eatery) is big with locals. Sit near the fireplace in winter, in the shade of the plane tree in summer. The food is simple but classic Greek: codfish with garlic dip, fried squid, lamb in oil-oregano sauce, *saganaki* (pan-fried cheese), and charcoal-grilled dorado and shrimp. ✉ *Ancient Olympia beside river,* ☎ *0624/23–322. No credit cards. Closed Oct.–Apr. No lunch.*

$$ ★ ✕ **Taverna Ambrosia.** Family matriarch Kyria Sofia cooks up excellent magirefta such as *papoutsakia* (sliced eggplant topped with minced meat), rabbit in lemon, *briam* (like ratatouille), baked tomatoes and peppers stuffed with rice, and the specialty, lamb stewed in lemon sauce. ✉ *Near train station, behind archaeological museum, Oikismou Kambo,* ☎ *0624/23–414. AE, MC, V.*

$$ ✕ **Thraka.** This family-run taverna has a large variety of home-cooked food including *lahanodolmades* (cabbage leaves stuffed with minced meat) and beef stifado made with vinegar and garlic. The two kinds of baklava are from the family's pastry shop. ✉ *Vasiliou Bakopanou and Praxitelis Kondili,* ☎ *0624/22–575; 0624/22–475 off-season. AE, DC, MC, V. Closed Nov.–Mar. (meals by special arrangement).*

$ ✕ **Bacchus.** If you're at the ancient site and want to break for lunch, follow signs to the nearby village of Miraka, recently renamed Archaia (ancient) Pissa. You can try such hearty dishes as rooster with handmade noodles called *hilopites* (order one day before), charcoal-broiled chicken, lamb or goat in oregano sauce, and spit-roasted meats on weekends. ✉ *Archaia Pissa, 3 km (2 mi) outside Olympia, turn off on Tripolis Rd.,* ☎ *0624/22–498. V. No lunch Nov.–Jan.*

$$ 🏨 **Hotel Europa.** Run by the gracious Spiliopoulos family, this Best Western hilltop hotel overlooks the mountains of Arcadia, Alfios Valley, and the distant sea. All rooms have air-conditioning and marble bathrooms; most face the pool, where a grill operates in summer. Buffet breakfast is included. ✉ *Off road to ancient Olympia, at Oikismou Drouva, 27065,* ☎ *0624/22–650, 0624/22–700, or 0624/22–750,* FAX *0624/23–166,* WEB *www.bestwestern.com. 82 rooms. Restaurant, air-conditioning, pool. AE, DC, MC, V.*

$$ 🏨 **Olympic Village.** Surrounded by vineyards, the hotel has simple rooms with views of the surrounding vineyards, modern baths, wooden furniture, and comfortable public spaces. The restaurant serves excellent Greek food such as *arnaki fricassee* (lamb with spinach and rice) and *giouvetsi* (beef cooked in a clay pot with vegetables). ✉ *Pyrgos-Olympia road (about 300 yards from site), 27065,* ☎ *0624/22–211,* FAX *0624/22–812. 51 rooms. Restaurant, air-conditioning, pool. AE, MC, V. Closed Nov.–Feb.*

$ 🏨 **Pelops.** The Australian owner has taken a standard '60s Greek hotel, across from the main church, and decorated each room differently, with knickknacks, chintz, and lace curtains, producing an old-fashioned feel. The quiet rooms have orthopedic mattresses, anti-allergic pillows, and telephones; most have balconies. The vine-shaded bar is open in summer. The substantial breakfast (only 1,500 dr./4.42) includes cereals, stewed fruit, fresh milk, french toast, eggs, homemade cake and jams, and steaming hot coffee and herbal tea. ✉ *Varela 2, 27065,* ☎ *0624/22–543 or 0624/22–792,* FAX *0624/22–213. 25 rooms. Restaurant. MC, V. Closed Nov.–Feb.*

Patras

Patras, the third-largest city in Greece and its main western port, is the business hub of the Peloponnese. The city's prettiest features are its arcaded streets and its squares surrounded by neoclassical buildings. The Byzantine **Kastro** (fortress), built on the site of the ancient acropolis, affords a fine view along the coast. **Agiou Andrea** (Cathedral of St. Andrew; ✉ west side of harbor at end of Agiou Andreou, ☎ 061/330–644), open daily 7:30 AM–8 PM, reputedly the largest in Greece and built on the site of the crucifixion of St. Andrew, is also worth exploring. Its treasure is the saint's silver-mounted skull, returned to Patras in 1964 after 500 years in St. Peter's Cathedral, Rome.

Eight km (5 mi) outside Patras is the **Achaia Clauss Winery,** founded in the mid-1800s by Baron von Klauss. You can take a tour and sample the area's mavrodafni wine, a dessert wine named for the Baron's love, who died prematurely. Take Bus 7 from downtown, get off at the Kato Filagio stop, and walk 766 yards, or take a taxi (about 1,300 dr./€3.83). ✉ *Achaia,* ☎ *061/325–051.* ⏲ *May–Oct., daily 10–7; Nov.–Apr., daily 9–5.*

$$ ★ ✕ **Ditis.** When the diver-owner closes up shop in summer to indulge his love of the sea, locals mourn. The humble decor of his fish taverna belies the masterful seafood dishes he prepares: delectable *kakavia* (Greek fish stew); crayfish with pepperoncini; squid that's stuffed with shrimp, cheese, peppers, and onion, then foil-wrapped and buried in the charcoal; and anchovies cooked with carrot, dill, and fennel. The fresh local fish includes sargus, pandora, swordfish, and gildhead, depending on the season. ✉ *Norman and Gambetta 44,* ☎ *061/432–554. No credit cards. Closed Sun. and July–Sept.*

$ ✕ **Lavyrinthos (Taverna tou Antipa).** This classic taverna with wine barrels, old lamp fixtures, and a cozy loft serves such traditional Greek dishes as rabbit in lemon and pungent homemade potato salad. After your meal be sure to try a shot of *detoura,* a local liqueur similar to cognac and flavored with cinnamon and clove. ✉ *Poukevil 44 near Platia Vas. Olgas,* ☎ *061/226–436. No credit cards. Closed Sun.*

$$$$ ★ **Porto Rio Hotel and Casino.** Play a set of tennis or a round of beach volleyball, go for an afternoon dip, then head for the casino at this 35-acre beachside hotel complex across from a small medieval fort at Rion, about 8 km (5 mi) from Patras. Most rooms have outstanding views. Buffet breakfast is included. ✉ *Rio-Patroon National Rd., 26500,* ☎ *061/992–212,* FAX *061/992–115,* WEB *www.portorio-casino.gr. 235 rooms, 13 suites, 48 bungalows. 2 restaurants (1 in summer), bar, 2 pools. AE, DC, MC, V.*

$$$$ ★ **Primarolia Art Hotel.** Pinch yourself or you'll think you're dreaming when you walk into this small luxury hotel, which seems a veritable museum devoted to the history of modern design. Every space has been lovingly arranged, with decor that mingles disparate elements—a blue Egg chair by Arne Jacobsen; Ingo Maurer lighting; Fornasetti café tables; a Le Corbusier conference table—into a glorious visual feast that's warm, inviting, and chic. Six of the rooms have a sea view, while some have balconies. All have showers with hydromassage, satellite TV, video telephones, and a minibar stocked with beluga caviar and oysters, if you should so desire. ✉ *Othonos-Amalias 33 near the train station, 26223,* ☎ *061/240–740,* FAX *061/623–559,* WEB *www.arthotel.gr. 14 rooms. Restaurant, bar. AE, DC, MC, V.*

$$ **Rannia.** The Rannia stands on Queen Olga Square, the loveliest plaza in Patras. It's just two blocks from the waterfront and within walking distance of the bus and train stations. The clean, quiet rooms all have balconies; many have air-conditioning. ✉ *Riga Fereou 53, Platia Vas.*

Olgas, 26500, ☎ *061/220–114,* ☎ FAX *061/220–537. 30 rooms. Air-conditioning.*

Nightlife and the Arts

In late June, the new **Festival Naupflion** stages classical music concerts in Palamidi fortress and the former Turkish mosque; for information, contact the Nauplion tourist police. The **Festival of Ancient Drama** in the ancient theater at Epidauros takes place from mid-July to mid-September; the smaller Micro Theatro (Little Theater) nearby simultaneously hosts concerts and dance performances. Tickets for the drama festival can be bought before performances (☎ 0753/22–026 box office; 0753/22–006; 0753/22–008 festival offices) or in advance from the festival box office in Athens (✉ Stadiou 4, ☎ 01/322–1459). For information on the Micro Theatro program, call the ancient Epidauros town hall (☎ 0753/41–250) or the Megaron concert hall in Athens (☎ 01/728–2333). A venue modeled on an ancient theater but with state-of-the-art lighting and sound near the Olympia sanctuary hosts the summer **Festival Olympias,** an eclectic mix of performances ranging from Paco Pena to the White Oak Dance Project. Ticket booths are located throughout the region, or call the Olympia tourist police or the local town hall (☎ 0624/22–250). Patras also stages a **summer arts festival** July through August. Check with the Patras International Festival office (✉ Koryllon 2, Old Municipal Hospital, Old Town, ☎ 061/279–008) for details. A few weeks before Greek Orthodox Lent, Patras holds **Carnival** celebrations, including Sunday's Grand Parade, with floats and entrants competing for the best costume. Buy tickets for Grand Parade seats at the kiosk in Vas. Georgiou Square or at the Carnival office in the Municipal Cultural Center (✉ Koryllon 2, Old Municipal Hospital, Old Town, ☎ 061/279–008 or 061/226–063).

Northern Peloponnese Essentials

BOAT AND FERRY TRAVEL

In summer, hydrofoils leave Zea Marina in Athens for Nauplion; it's a good idea to reserve a seat.

➤ BOAT AND FERRY INFORMATION: **Hydrofoils** (☎ 01/418–7000).

BUS TRAVEL

The regional bus associations (KTEL) run frequent service from Athens to Nauplion (where you change for Mycenae), Epidauros, Corinth, Patras, and Olympia.

CAR TRAVEL

The roads are fairly good, and driving can be the most enjoyable (if not economical) way to see the area, once you get off the National Road.

TOURS

Available tours include one-day (21,500 dr./€64.71 with lunch, 18,500 dr./€55.89 without lunch) or two-day (34,000 dr./€100) trips to Mycenae, Nauplion, and Epidauros; four-day trips to those sites, as well as Olympia and Delphi (107,000 dr./€314.71); and a five-day excursion to all major sites in the Peloponnese, as well as Delphi and Meteora (144,000 dr./€423.53).

➤ FEES & SCHEDULES: **CHAT Tours** (✉ Stadiou 4, Athens, ☎ 01/322–2886, FAX 01/323–5270). **Key Tours** (✉ Kallirois 4, Athens, ☎ 01/923–3166, FAX 01/923–2008).

TRAIN TRAVEL

You can take a train from Athens to Corinth, where the route splits, heading either south to Argos and Nauplion, or west along the coast to Patras, and then south to Pyrgos and the branch line to Olympia. There is a substantial discount on round-trip tickets.

VISITOR INFORMATION

➤ TOURIST INFORMATION: **Nauplion** (Tourist information: ✉ 25th Martiou across from OTE, ☎ 0752/24–444; tourist police: ✉ P. Koundourioti 14 in police station, ☎ 0752/28–131). **Olympia** (Municipal tourist information office: ✉ Kondili 75, ☎ 0624/23–100; tourist police: ✉ Spiliopoulou 5, ☎ 0624/22–550 or 0624/22–100). **Patras** (EOT: ✉ Filopimenos 26, ☎ 061/620–353; tourist police: ✉ Norman and Iroon Politechniou [harbor welcome station], ☎ 061/451–833 or 061/451–893; Olympic Airlines: ✉ Aratou 17–19, Platia Vas. Olgas, ☎ 061/222–901 through 903; Automobile and Touring Club of Greece: ✉ Patroon Athinon 18, ☎ 061/425–411, ☎ FAX 061/426–416).

MAINLAND GREECE

The dramatic rocky heights of mainland Greece provide an appropriate setting for humanity's attempt to approach divinity. The ancient Greeks placed their gods on snowcapped Mt. Olympus and chose the precipitous slopes of Parnassus, "the navel of the universe," as the site for Delphi, their most important religious center. Many centuries later, pious Christians built a great monastery (Hosios Loukas) in a remote mountain valley. Others settled on the rocky peninsula of Athos, the Holy Mountain. Later, devout men established themselves precariously on top of strange, towerlike rocks and, to be closer to God, built such monasteries as those at Meteora, which remain among the most spectacular sights in Greece.

Exploring Mainland Greece

En route to Delphi from Athens via the National Road, take the turnoff for the ancient city of Thiva (Thebes), 90 km (56 mi) northwest of Athens. After detouring to the monastery of Hosios Loukas (turn off at Distomo village, 20 km/12 mi from Livadia), continue to Delphi. The road climbs a spur of Mt. Parnassus, past Arahova, known for its lively après-ski scene and handmade rugs of brightly colored wools; it also offers a better range of dining and lodging options than Delphi, if you're staying in the area. From Arahova it's a short, spectacular drive through the Pleistos gorge to the ancient site (179 km/111 mi northwest of Athens). After Delphi the road descends in sharp bends to lackluster Lamia (another 82 km/51 mi), then heads northwest to Kalambaka and Meteora (139 km/86 mi from Lamia).

Thiva

Thiva (Thebes), of which little remains, was the birthplace of legendary Oedipus, who unwittingly fulfilled the prophecy of the Delphic Oracle by slaying his father and marrying his mother.

Hosios Loukas

★ Nestled in a serene upland valley is **Moni Osiou Louka** (Monastery of Hosios Loukas), a fine example of Byzantine architecture and decoration. Built during the 11th century to replace the earlier shrine of a local saint, it has some of the world's finest Byzantine mosaics. ☎ *0267/22–797.* ⏲ *May–mid-Sept., daily 8–2 and 4–7; mid-Sept.–mid-Nov., and Mar.–Apr., daily 8–6; mid-Nov.–Feb., daily 8–5.*

Delphi

★ At the edge of Delphi loom the Phaedriades, twin cliffs split by the Castalian spring. It was here that pilgrims to the Delphic Oracle came for purification. To the ancient Greeks Delphi was the center of the uni-

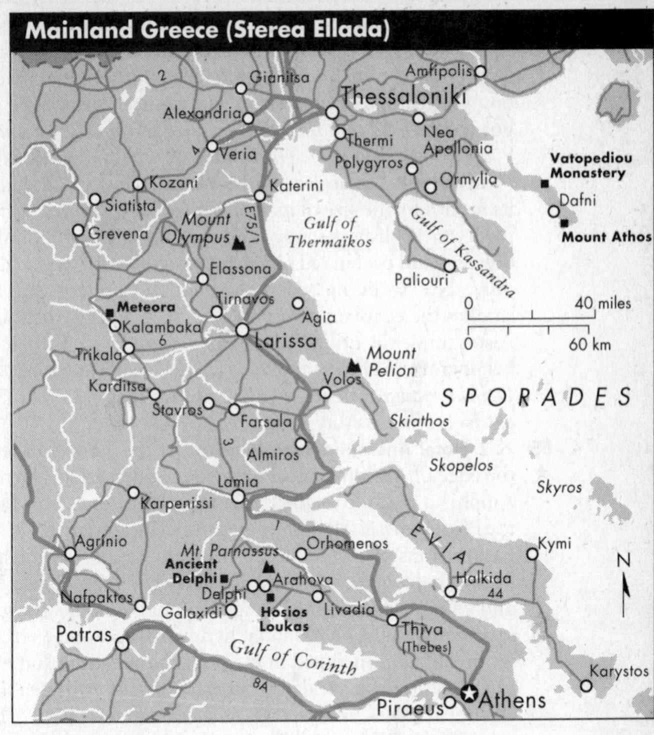

Mainland Greece (Sterea Ellada)

verse, because two eagles released by the gods at opposite ends of the earth met here. For hundreds of years the worship of Apollo and the pronouncements of the oracle made Delphi the most important religious center of ancient Greece. When first excavated in 1892, most of the ruins were found to date from the 5th through the 3rd centuries BC. As you walk up the **Iera Odos** (Sacred Way) to the **Naos Apollonos** (Temple of Apollo), the **theater,** and the **stadium,** you'll see Mt. Parnassus above; silver-green olive trees below; and, in the distance, the blue Gulf of Itea. East of the main site, about 500 ft down the road, is the area with the temple of **Athena Pronaia,** from which many of the museum's best sculptures came; the **gymnasium**; and the **Tholos,** the rotunda. If you come here in the early morning or evening, avoiding the busloads of tourists, you will feel the power and beauty of the place. ☏ *0265/82–312.* ⏲ *May–Oct., weekdays 8–7, weekends 8:30–3; Nov.–Apr., daily 8:30–3.*

Don't miss the bronze charioteer (early 5th century BC) in the **Delphi Museum.** Other works of art here include a statue of Antinoüs, Emperor Hadrian's lover; fragments of a 6th-century BC silver-plated bull, the largest example of an ancient statue in precious metal; and the stone *omphalos,* representing the navel of the earth. ☏ *0265/82–312.* ⏲ *May–Oct., weekdays 8–7, weekends 8:30–3; Nov.–Apr., daily 8:30–3.*

$ ✕ **Karaouli.** This warm, low-key taverna serves delicious regional cuisine along with barrel wine from Distomo: the lightest cabbage rolls, spicy local sausage and spit-roasted meats (*kontosouvli*), baked red peppers stuffed with four cheeses, roasted *formaella* (a local sheep's milk cheese), and *tiganopsomo* (cheese bread). For dessert: a large portion of creamy sheep's yogurt topped with quince preserves. ✉ *Arahova–Delphi road at entrance to Delphi,* ☏ *0267/31–001. No credit cards. Closed mid-June–mid-Sept.*

$ ✕ **Taverna Karathanasis.** The tiny kitchen at this taverna, open since 1930, turns out suitably vintage classics ranging from boiled goat (winter only) to *pita tou pappou* (grandfather's pie) made with mountain greens, and lamb stewed with spinach or cooked in an air-tight pot (gastra). ✉ *Arahova–Delphon road on central square, Arahova, 9 km (6 mi) east of ancient Delphi,* ☎ *0267/31–360. No credit cards.*

$ ✕ **Taverna P. Dasargiris (Barba Yiannis).** In a town that once counted its wealth by the size of its flocks, the oldest taverna is fittingly known for its meat dishes—baby lamb ribs, *kontosouvli,* lamb stewed with oregano and beef in red sauce, both served with the local noodles, *hilopites.* Not to be missed is the chunky eggplant dip; the cook first smokes the eggplant over charcoal, then adds garlic, oil, and vinegar. Also sample the grilled beef patties stuffed with formaella, Gouda, or kefalograviera cheese; and the dark red local wine, *brusco.* ✉ *Arahova–Delfon road across from OTE, Arahova,* ☎ *0267/31–291. No credit cards. No lunch May–Oct.*

$$ ★ ✕🏨 **Hotel Anemolia Best Western.** At this homey hotel on a bluff at the edge of Arahova, most of the large guest rooms have a view of the Amphissa plain from their balconies; some days you can see as far as the Peloponnese. All of the comfortable rooms have TV and some have bathtubs instead of showers; the eight newest rooms have fireplaces but no balconies; half feature a loft. The lobby has a large fireplace and country antiques. The indoor pool overlooks the greenery; other facilities include a bar, sauna, hydromassage, and exercise room. Buffet breakfast is included in the price. Note that in summer, the hotel's low season, the price drops substantially. ✉ *Arahova–Delphon road, Arahova 32004,* ☎ *0267/31–640 through 641; 0267/31–643 through 644,* FAX *0267/31–642,* WEB *www.bestwestern.com. 63 rooms. Restaurant, pool. AE, DC, MC, V.*

$$ 🏨 **Apollo.** Owned and operated by a husband-and-wife team, this hotel is lovely. The *saloni* (living room) with fireplace has traditional wall hangings and old prints among its carefully selected furnishings. The cheerful rooms have light-wood furniture set off by blue quilts and striped curtains, with pretty bathroom tiles and TVs. Many have wood balconies with black-iron railings, and a full breakfast is included. ✉ *Vas. Pavlou and Friderikis 59B, Delphi 33054,* ☎ *0265/82–580 or 0265/82–244,* FAX *0265/82–455. 21 rooms. Air-conditioning. MC, V. Closed weekdays Nov.–Mar.*

$$ 🏨 **Hotel Acropole-Delphi.** This friendly, family-run hotel has a garden and a spectacular view—dramatic mountainside and a sea of olive groves. The rooms are furnished with carved Skyrian pieces, traditional linens, and paintings. All rooms have TV and direct-dial phones. Buffet breakfast is included. ✉ *Filellinon 13, 33054,* ☎ *0265/82–675,* FAX *0265/83–171. 42 rooms. Air-conditioning. AE, DC, MC, V.*

$$ 🏨 **Villa Filoxenia-Apollo.** Rustic, charming, and lovingly decorated, this hotel has such amenities as electronic keys and air-conditioning and a lounge with fireplace and game area. Rooms include TVs and most have balconies and a view. Full breakfast is included. ✉ *Vas. Pavlou and Friderikis 15, Delphi 33054,* ☎ *0265/83–114,* FAX *0265/82–455. 14 rooms. Air-conditioning. MC, V. Closed weekdays Nov.–Mar.*

Meteora

Kalambaka serves as the base for visits to the monasteries of Meteora, which sit atop gigantic pinnacles that tower almost 1,000 ft above the plain. Monks and supplies once reached the top on ladders or in baskets; now steps are cut into the rocks, and some of the monasteries can easily be reached by car. Of the original 24 monasteries, only 6 can now be visited. Appropriate dress for women requires skirts to the knee (not shorts), and men should wear long pants. The fortresslike

Varlaam monastery (☎ 0432/22–277) is easy to reach and has beautiful Byzantine frescoes. It is open May through October, 9 to 2 and 3:20 to 5 (closed Friday); from November through April it is open 10 to 3 (closed Thursday and Friday). For an idea of what living in these monasteries was like 300 years ago, climb the steep rock steps to the **Megalo Meteoron** (☎ 0432/22–278). It is open May through October, 9 to 1 and 3 to 6 (closed Tuesday); from November through April it is open 9 to 1 and 3 to 5 (closed Tuesday and Wednesday). Allow time for the trek up if it's nearing midday or evening closing time.

In Kalambaka stop at the **Koimisis tis Theotokou** (Dormition of the Virgin), built in the first half of the 12th century by Emperor Manuel Comnenos, though some historians believe it was founded during the 7th century on the site of a temple of Apollo (classical drums from columns and other fragments are incorporated into the walls). The church also has vivid 16th-century frescoes. ✉ *North end of town; follow signs from Platia Riga Fereou,* ☎ *0432/24–962.* ⏲ *May–Oct., daily 7–1 and 3–7; Nov.–Apr., daily 7–10 and 3:30–6:30.*

$$ ★ ✕ **Restaurant Meteora.** A local favorite since 1925, this family restaurant on the upper square relies on the cooking of matriarch Ketty Gertzou, who prepares such dishes as *soutzoukakia* (spicy minced meat patties), lamb fricassee, stifado, *ladera* (vegetables cooked in olive oil), and chicken in wine with green peppers and garlic. ✉ *Ekonomou 4, on Platia Dimarchiou,* ☎ *0432/22–316. No credit cards. Closed Nov.–Mar. No dinner.*

$–$$ ✕ **Ziogas.** Master-griller Grigoris chooses only the freshest local meats and barbecues them to perfection over burning wood—try the pork chops, the lamb ribs, or the succulent *kokkoretsi* (spit-roasted meat roll made of lamb entrails). ✉ *On Patriarchou Dimitriou (road from Kalambaka to Meteora), Kastraki,* ☎ *0432/22–286. No credit cards. No lunch Mon.–Sat. No dinner Sun.*

$ ✕ **To Lakario.** At this *tsipouradiko,* mezedes are served with carafes of tsipouro, a liqueur similar to raki. The day's plates may include leek pie, charcoal-grilled potatoes, codfish with garlic dip, *piperonati* (baked eggplant, peppers, and cheese), onion-potato croquettes, and pork sautéed in wine, *tigania.* Seafood is also available: mussels in red sauce, grilled cuttlefish, marinated octopus. ✉ *28 Oktovriou 38,* ☎ *0432/24–871. No credit cards. Closed first 2 wks in Aug.*

$$$ ★ 🏨 **Amalia.** The area's best hotel is about 4 km (2½ mi) outside Kalambaka. The low-lying complex has spacious, handsomely decorated public rooms with touches such as Byzantine-style frescoes, as well as a garden. The rooms are done in soothing colors and have large beds, art prints, and wooden balconies. Buffet breakfast is included. ✉ *Trikalon 14, 42200,* ☎ *0432/72–216; 0432/72–217; 01/323–7301 reservations,* FAX *0432/72–457; 01/323–8792 reservations,* WEB *www.greekhotel.com/amalia. 171 rooms, 2 suites. Restaurant, pool. AE, DC, MC, V.*

$$ 🏨 **Hotel Antoniadis.** This reliable hotel in Kalambaka has pastel rooms with carpeting and TVs. Many rooms have a view of the Meteora monasteries. During the sweltering summers the hotel opens its rooftop pool. ✉ *Trikalon 148, 42200,* ☎ *0432/24–387 or 0432/23–419,* FAX *0432/24–319. 69 rooms. Restaurant, air-conditioning, pool. V.*

$ ★ 🏨 **Kastraki.** Step out on the balcony and bid good morning to the massive rocks that seem to loom over this great little hotel in a village on the road from Kalambaka to Meteora. All rooms have air-conditioning, balcony, and TV. Those who want to fortify themselves before trekking to the monasteries can have the optional buffet breakfast (2,500 dr./€7.37), which includes yogurt and homemade cake and fruit compotes. ✉ *Patriarchou Dimitriou A', 42200 Kastraki,* ☎ *0432/75–336,* ☎ FAX *0432/75–335. 28 rooms. V.*

Mainland Greece Essentials

TOURS

Call travel agencies in Athens for tours of mainland Greece, such as a two-day trip to the Meteora monasteries (39,900 dr./€117.65), a three-day trip to Delphi and Meteora (79,900 dr./€235.29), or a six-day excursion to northern Greece, including Delphi, Meteora, Thessaloniki, and its outlying archaeological sites (210,000 dr./€617.65).

TRANSPORTATION AROUND MAINLAND GREECE

Although it's easiest to visit the region by car, there is very good train and bus service between the main towns, and between each town and Athens.

VISITOR INFORMATION

➤ TOURIST INFORMATION: **Delphi** (Municipal tourist office: ✉ Vas. Pavlou and Friderikis 12, ☎ 0265/82–900; tourist police: ✉ Aggelos Sikelianou 3, ☎ 0265/82–222). **Meteora** (Tourist information office: ✉ Kondili 38, ☎ 0432/75–306; tourist police: ✉ Pindou and Ioanninon, Kalambaka, ☎ 0432/75–100).

CORFU

Temperate, multihued Corfu—of emerald mountains; turquoise waters lapping rocky coves; ocher and pink buildings; shimmering silver olive leaves; scarlet roses, bougainvillea, jacaranda, and lavender wisteria spread over cottages—could have inspired Impressionism. The island—which lies strategically in the northern Ionian Sea at the entrance to the Adriatic, opposite northwestern Greece and Albania—has a colorful history reflecting the commingling of Corinthians, Romans, Goths, Normans, Venetians, French, Russians, and British. Today, more than a million visitors a year—most from England and many from Europe—enjoy, and in summer, crowd its evocative capital city, isolated beaches, stylish restaurants, and resorts. The island combines neoclassical villas and eco-sensitive resorts, horse-drawn carriages and Jaguars—simplicity and sophistication—in an alluring mix. Its desirability, however, makes it expensive. The island of Corfu is small enough to cover completely in a few days. Roads vary from gently winding to spiraling, but they're generally well marked, and all lead to Corfu town, which recalls a stage set for a Verdi opera.

Along the east coast mid-island, **Corfu** town occupies the central prong of a three-pronged peninsula. On the southern prong is Paleopolis (Old Town) and on the northern is the Old Fort (now the backdrop for summer sound-and-light shows), walled in the 8th century. The remains of the medieval Venetian town here are scanty. If you arrive from Igoumenitsa or Patras, on mainland Greece, your ferry will dock at the **Old Port** on the north side of town, west of the **New Fortress** (1577–78) (on promontory northwest of the old fortress and medieval town), built by the Venetians and expanded by the French and the British to protect the town from a possible Turkish invasion. You can now wander through the maze of tunnels, moats, and fortifications.

The **Esplanade** (✉ between Old Fortress and Old Town), the huge, open parade ground on the land side of the canal, is central to the life of the town and is one of the most beautiful *spianadas* (esplanades) in Greece. It is bordered on the west by a street lined with seven- and eight-story Venetian and English Georgian houses, and arcades, called the **Liston** (modeled, by the French under Napoléon, on the Parisian rue de Rivoli). Cafés spill out into the passing scene, and Corfiot celebrations, games, and trysts occur in the sun and shadows.

The oldest cultural institution in modern Greece, the **Corfu Reading Society,** contains archives (dating back several centuries) of the Ionian islands. In the early 19th century, Corfu was the literary center of Greece. One of the island's loveliest buildings, it has an exterior staircase leading up to a loggia. ✉ *Kapodistriou.* ⏲ *Sat.–Wed. 9–1, Thurs.–Fri. 9–1 and 5–8.*

The **Garrison Church of St. George** (1830) in the Old Fortress has a Doric portico. In summer there's folk dancing, and in August sound-and-light shows relate the fortress's history. The views from here, east to the Albanian coast and west over the town, are splendid. ✉ *In middle of Old Fortress.* ⏲ *Daily 8–7.*

$$$ ✕ **Aegli.** This 35-year-old restaurant on the Liston serves more than 100 different dishes, both local and international. The tables in front overlook the nonstop parade on the promenade. ✉ *Liston,* ☏ *0661/31949. AE, DC, MC, V. Closed Dec.–Feb.*

$$$ ✕ **The Venetian Well.** On the most charming little square in the Old Town, built around a 17th-century well, this romantic restaurant seems too evocative and perfect to be true. The dining rooms in the handsome Venetian building are painted the classic Greek blue. Creative entrées might include duck with kumquats or wild boar. ✉ *Pl. Kremasti,* ☏ *0661/44761. AE, DC, MC, V.*

$ ✕ **O Yiannis.** One of the nicest in Corfu, this restaurant is unpretentious and full of locals. It's also cheap: you'll be hard-pressed to tally up 5,000 dr./€14.71 on the great barrel wine and wonderful food. Check out the ancient photos of Corfu's old-timers. ✉ *Sophia Kremona and Iassonos-Sossipatrou 30, Anemomilos,* ☏ *0661/31066. Reservations not accepted. No credit cards.*

$$$$ 🏨 **Corfu Palace.** Overlooking the bay, 100 yards from the center of town, this elegant hotel is one of the most beautiful in all of Greece. Tasteful and comfortable best describe its Old World grandeur. The spacious rooms, furnished in various styles (Louis XIV and Empire), have satellite TV and wide balconies with splendid views. The hotel also has two of Corfu's most luxurious restaurants. ✉ *Democratias 2, 49100,* ☏ *0661/39485,* FAX *0661/31749,* WEB *www.corfupalace.com. 110 rooms. 2 restaurants, 2 bars, 2 pools. AE, DC, MC, V.*

$$$ 🏨 **Cavalieri Hotel.** In this 17th-century, eight-story mansion, once Count Flamburiari's, on the arcade of the Liston, get a room on the fourth or fifth floor with a number ending in 2, 3, or 4 for a breathtaking view of the Old Fort. The recently renovated building is swank yet graceful and chock-full of history. Have a drink at the usually empty but delightful English-style wood-paneled bar. Best of all is the roof garden, which offers light meals and the most remarkable view in town. ✉ *4 Kapodistriou, 49100,* ☏ *0661/39041,* FAX *0661/39336,* WEB *www.cavalierihotel.com. 50 rooms. Restaurant. AE, DC, MC, V.*

$ 🏨 **Hotel Konstantinoupoulis.** A hotel for more than 200 years, this can be most ambitiously called traditional. But rooms are reasonably clean and acceptable if you're on a budget. It's opposite the dock for car ferries to the islands, with a great view of the old port. ✉ *Zavitsianou 11, Old Port, 49100,* ☏ *0661/39826. 44 rooms with shared baths. No credit cards.*

Kanoni

Outside Corfu town, at Kanoni, the site of the ancient capital, you may behold the most famous view on Corfu. A French cannon once stood in this hilly landscape, which is now built up and often noisy because of the nearby airport. From Kanoni, against the backdrop of the green slopes of Mount Ayia Deka, is the serene view of two tiny islets: One, **Moni Viahernes,** is reached by causeway. The other islet, **Pontikonisi** (Mouse Island), has a **white convent** and, beyond, tall cypresses guarding the **13th-century chapel.** You can take a little launch or pedal boat to visit it—or even swim there.

Elsewhere in the environs outside Corfu town are two fabled palaces and gardens open to visitors: **Mon Repos,** built by Robert Adam in 1831, used by English Lord High Commissioners and birthplace of England's Prince Philip, and, in the village of Gastouri, **Achilleion,** the Greek retreat of Empress Elisabeth of Austria.

Corfu Essentials

BOAT AND FERRY TRAVEL

Passenger ships stop at Corfu twice a week, April to October. Minoan Lines runs the ship service. Ferries from Igoumenitsa on the mainland leave every hour in summer and every two hours off-season, landing in Corfu town (two hours) and in Lefkimmi, at the southern tip of Corfu (45 minutes).

➤ BOAT AND FERRY INFORMATION: **Minoan Lines** (✉ Akti Poseidonos 28, Piraeus, ☎ 01/419–9900, FAX 01/413–5000).

BUS TRAVEL

KTEL Corfu buses leave Athens three or four times a day. Bus travel on Corfu is inexpensive, and the bus network covers the island. The Spilia bus company's terminal is at the New Port. Buses also run from the San Rocco bus company's depot.

➤ BUS INFORMATION: **KTEL Corfu** (☎ 0661/39985 or 0661/30627; 01/512–9443 for Athens branch). **San Rocco** (✉ Pl. San Rocco, ☎ 0661/31595). **Spilia** (✉ Avramiou, ☎ 0661/30627).

CAR TRAVEL

By car, the best route from Athens is the National Road via Corinth to the Rio/Antirio ferry, then to Igoumenitsa (472 km/274 mi), where you take the ferry to Corfu. Call the Touring Club of Greece for information.

➤ CONTACTS: **Touring Club of Greece** (☎ 104).

TOURS

Many agencies run half-day tours of Old Corfu town, and tour buses go daily to all the sights on the island. Tickets and information are available at travel agencies all over town.

VISITOR INFORMATION

➤ TOURIST INFORMATION: **Greek National Tourist Organization** (GNTO or EOT: ✉ Kapodistriou 1, ☎ 0661/37520, 0661/37638, or 0661/37639, FAX 0661/30298). **Tourist Police** (✉ Kapodistriou 1, ☎ 0661/30265).

THE AEGEAN ISLANDS

The islands of the Aegean have colorful legends of their own—the Minotaur in Crete; the lost continent of Atlantis, which some believe was Santorini; and the Colossus of Rhodes, to name a few. Mykonos has windmills, dazzling whitewashed buildings, hundreds of tiny red-domed churches on golden hillsides, and small fishing harbors. Visitors to Santorini sail into a vast volcanic crater and anchor below the island's forbidding cliffs. Crete, with its jagged mountain peaks, olive orchards, and vineyards, contains the remains of the Minoan civilization. In

The Aegean Islands (Ta Nissia tou Aegaiov)

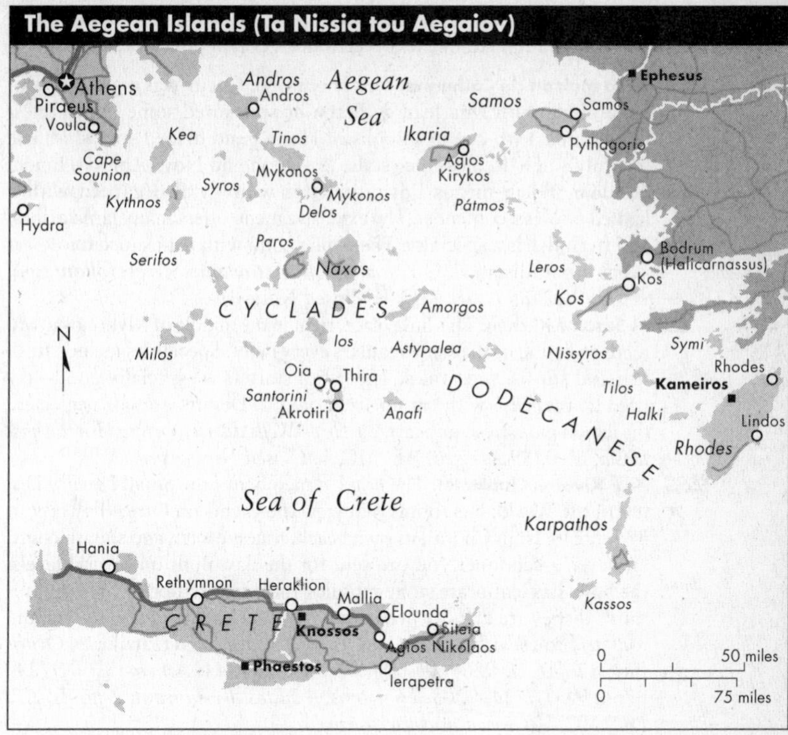

Rhodes a bustling modern town surrounds a walled medieval city and a castle; volcanic ash has preserved a 1500 BC village in Santorini.

Mykonos

Mykonos's chief village, also called Mykonos, is the Cyclades' best-preserved; it is a maze of narrow, flagstone streets lined with two-story whitewashed houses, many with flower-filled balconies, outdoor stairways, and blue or red doors and shutters. Every morning women scrub the sidewalks and streets in front of their homes, undaunted by passing donkeys. During the 1960s the bohemian jet set discovered Mykonos, and many old houses are now shops, restaurants, bars, or discos; the nightlife, both gay and straight, is notorious. The rich arrive by yacht, the middle class by plane, the backpackers and Athenians by boat. It is *the* holiday destination for the young, lively, and liberated.

If you stay more than a day, pay a quick visit to the **archaeological museum** to get a sense of the island's history; the most significant local find is a 7th-century BC *pithos* (storage jar) showing the Greeks emerging from the Trojan Horse. ✉ *East end of port,* ☎ *0289/22–325.* ⏲ *Tues.–Sun. 8:30–3.*

From the museum stroll down to the esplanade, where islanders promenade in the evening, or meander through the town, whose confusing ★ layout evolved to foil pirates. In a picturesque neighborhood called **Venetia** (Little Venice) at the southwest end of the port, a few of the old houses have been turned into stylish bars, and wooden balconies hang over the water. In the distance, lined up like toy soldiers on the high hill, are the **Mykonos windmills**; until 40 years ago, wind power was used to grind the island's grain.

Mykoniots claim that 365 churches and chapels dot their landscape, one for each day of the year. The most beautiful, **Paraportiani** (Our

Lady of the Postern Gate; ✉ Anargon), is really three churches imaginatively combined, like a confectioner's dream gone mad.

$$$$ ✕ **La Maison de Catherine.** This is onnister, Coeur was a great art patron (along with Duc Jean de Berry, he sponsored some of the finest illuminated 15th-century Books of Hours) and helped spread a taste for Italy's new Renaissance style. ✉ –noon and Nov.–Apr. No lunch.

$$$ ✕ **Edem.** Edem means Eden, and this white-walled garden with a lighted pool is a contender. The extensive menu offers many lamb dishes, and fresh fish is a specialty. The panna cotta with fruit sauce for desert keeps it paradisial. ✉ *On an alley off Matoyianni Street; follow sign,* ☎ *0289/22–855. AE, MC, V. Closed Nov.–Apr.*

$$ ✕ **Sesame Kitchen.** This little place, right in the middle of Mykonos town, tends to be full of the same regulars every night. Specialties include fresh fish and stir-fry vegetables. The list of starters is especially good—try fried goat cheese with caramelized onions. Deserts are not neglected; the lemon pie is fresh and tart. ✉ *Three Wells district, below Hotel Anastassia,* ☎ *0289/24–710. AE, MC, V. Closed Nov.–Apr.*

$$$$ ★ ✕ **Kivotos ClubHotel.** The hotel, a member of the Small Luxury Hotels of the World, has rooms that view the yachts on Ornos bay (about 3½ km/2 mi from Chora), its own beach, fitness center, and squash court, and even a schooner you can rent for the day. Built on several levels, the hotel has elaborate stone mosaics and much sculpture. The restaurant's dishes are artfully presented—the chicken stuffed with feta and tomato comes with a spoon each of fava, lentils, and tzatziki. ✉ *Ornos Bay, 84600,* ☎ *0289/24–094,* FAX *0289/22–844; Athens:* ☎ *01/724–6766,* FAX *01/724–9203. 26 rooms, 4 suites. Restaurant, 2 pools. AE, DC, MC, V. Closed mid-Oct.–Apr.*

$$$$ ★ **Cavo Tagoo.** This medley of white cubical suites perched above a small beach has been much praised for its architecture. The hotel is about 10 minutes' walk from the port; all rooms have balconies or terraces with superb sea views. Its poolside restaurant serves excellent haute Mediterranean cuisine. ✉ *Road to Ayios Stefanos, 84600 Mykonos, 400 yards from town,* ☎ *0289/23–692,* FAX *0289/24–923; Athens:* ☎ *01/643–0233,* FAX *01/644–5237. 68 rooms, 5 suites. Restaurant, seawater pool. DC, MC, V. Closed Nov.–mid-Apr.*

$$$ **Ilio Maris.** The spacious lobby of this attractive hotel has painted beams, a stone floor, and whitewashed walls. But the place isn't just pretty, it's practical—you're just five minutes from town on foot, and if you're driving you'll probably find a parking spot right out front. ✉ *Despotiko area 84600,* ☎ *0289/23–755,* FAX *0289/24–309. 28 rooms. AE, MC, V.*

$ **Myconian Inn.** This unpretentious, pleasant hotel, whose balconies overlook the port, is both convenient and peaceful. Many younger tourists who want to be far away from the disco beat stay here. Breakfast is included. ✉ *Petasos, 84600 Mykonos,* ☎ *0289/22–663 or 0289/23–420,* FAX *0289/27–269. 15 rooms. Air-conditioning. No credit cards. Closed Nov.–Mar.*

Delos

★ Thirty minutes by caïque from Mykonos, little dry Delos was the islands' ancient religious center, sacred to Apollo and Artemis. Its **Exedra ton Leonton** (Terrace of the Lions), a weathered row of nine Naxian marble sculptures from the 7th century BC (relocated in early 2000 to the museum), overlooks the dried-up sacred lake. Another highlight is a group of houses of the Hellenistic and Roman periods, with their fine floor mosaics *in situ.* Museum, theater, houses—the site is endlessly rich and needs exploring time. Tuesday through Sunday, **boats** leave Mykonos from 8:30 to 9:30 and return from 12:30 to 1:30, depending on winds (☎ 0289/22–259).

Santorini

★ The best way to approach Santorini, or Thira, is to sail into its spectacular bay, once the vast crater of the volcano, and dock beneath its black-and-red cliffs, which rise up to 1,000 ft above the sea. Passenger ferries dock at the grungy new port, Athinios, where visitors are met by buses, taxis, and hotel touts. The houses and churches of the main town, **Fira,** cling inside the rim in dazzling white contrast to the somber cliffs. The ride to Fira takes about a half hour, and from there you can make connections to **Oia,** or Ia, the serene town at the northern tip. Though crowded in summer, tiny Oia, pictured on dozens of advertisements for Greece, is famous for its marine sunset. Be sure to try the local wines—a number of wineries offer tours and tastings (Antinopoulos is a good bet). The volcanic soil produces a unique range of flavors, from light and dry to rich and aromatic.

The island's volcano erupted violently around 1500 BC, destroying its Minoan civilization. At **Akrotiri,** on the south end of Santorini, the remains of a Minoan city buried by volcanic ash are being excavated. The site, once a prosperous town some think is the legendary Atlantis, is remarkably well preserved. Its charming frescoes are in Athens, but the island wants them back. There are plans to temporarily close the site for further excavation, so check ahead before visiting. ☎ *0286/81–366.* ⏲ *Tues.–Sun. 8:30–3.*

At **Archaia Thira** (Ancient Thera), a clifftop site on the east coast of the island, a town founded before the 9th century BC has a theater, agora, houses, fortifications, and temples. Though only foundations remain, it is very romantic; you can easily imagine its famed dances performed by naked youths. ⏲ *Tues.–Sun. 8:30–3.*

Museum of Prehistoric Thera. This modern, spacious, handsome museum contains artifacts from Akrotiri and other excavation sites. You'll find frescoes, vases, tools, figurines—all beautifully displayed. Look for ancient Thera's symbol, the swallow. ✉ *Fira,* ☎ *0286/23–217* ⏲ *Tues.–Sun. 8:30–3.*

$$$$ ✕ **1800.** A group of new restaurants has sprung up in rapidly developing Oia, but this elegant old favorite, in an atmospheric captain's mansion, remains at the very top. Veal with tomato sauce and eggplant, zucchini pie with cheese and onions—everything is good. ✉ *Main pedestrian lane, Oia,* ☎ *0286/71–485. AE, DC, MC, V. Closed mid-Nov.–mid-Apr.*

$$$ ✕ **Selene.** At this longtime favorite overlooking the bay, the creative cooking develops traditional Santorini fare into Mediterranean elegance. The fava balls with tomato caper sauce and *brodedo* (fish, squid, octopus, prawns, and other shellfish in a clay pot) are both based on local recipes. ✉ *Fira,* ☎ *0286/22–249. MC, V. Closed Nov.–Mar.*

$$ ★ ✕ **Camille Stefani.** On the seaside walkway of black Kamari beach, below ancient Thira, is one of the island's best restaurants. It serves seafood and Greek and Continental cuisine. Begin with the *lahano dolmades* (stuffed cabbage), a plate of fava, and moist tomato croquettes, and continue with one of the 16 versions of beef, pork, or chicken fillet. Try a glass of the mellow Santorini Lava red wine. Locals eat here. ✉ *Beach road, Kamari,* ☎ *0286/31–716. AE, DC, MC, V. Closed Dec.–mid-Feb.*

$ ★ ✕ **Nikolas.** This simple, congenial, and vintage taverna is one of the few places in town that stays open in winter. Arrive early, as the cook runs out of food around midnight. The menu on the chalkboard offers barrel wine and a delicious choice of classic Greek dishes, including stifado, stuffed cabbage rolls, and mountain greens. ✉ *Erithrou Stavrou, Fira,* ☎ *0286/24–550. No credit cards.*

$$$$ ★ **Aigialos Traditional Houses.** These former cave houses have been redesigned, each differently, with traditional elegance, privacy, and comfort. Balconies overlook the bay, flowers decorate the rooms, and all the amenities are discretely present. The restaurant is good, too. ✉ *Follow signs from Hypapantis walkway, 84700 Fira,* ☎ *0286/25–191 through 195,* FAX *0286/22–856. 16 houses. AE, MC, V. Closed Nov.–mid-Apr.*

$$$$ **Perivolas Traditional Houses.** Built into the cliffside at the outskirts of beautiful Oia, these authentic cave houses, some of them 200 and 300 years old, have been restored and individually decorated in Cycladic style. They overlook the sea and offer comfortable accommodations complete with kitchenettes and terraces. Check out the pool, which seems to hang over the cliff. ✉ *84702 Oia,* ☎ *0286/71–308,* FAX *0286/71–309. 14 houses. Pool. No credit cards. Closed Nov.–Mar.*

$$$ **Atlantis Villas.** If you don't mind stairs, descend to this beautiful hotel on Oia's cliffside, 600 ft above the sea, which offers separate apartments of varied configuration with splendid sunset sea views, comfort, quiet, and amenities. ✉ *Down from main walkway, 84702 Oia,* ☎ *0286/71–214,* FAX *0286/71–312. 19 houses. Pool. AE, DC, MC, V. Closed mid-Oct.–mid-Apr.*

$–$$ **Delfini II.** Near Fira's center, this hotel has rooms decorated with old handcrafted objects and ceramics. Rooms include refrigerators; apartments have kitchens and private balconies. Guests make use of the terrace with a sea view, an umbrella pergola, and sun beds. ✉ *Between cathedral and Ayios Minas church, 84700 Fira,* ☎ *0286/22–780 or 0286/24–340,* FAX *0286/22–780; 0286/22–371 off-season. 4 rooms, 3 apartments. No credit cards. Closed Nov.–Mar.*

Rhodes

The large island of Rhodes, 11 km (7 mi) off the coast of Turkey, is the chief island of the Dodecanese. The northern end is one of Greece's major vacation centers. The island is large and not always beautiful, but it has fine beaches, ancient ruins, and an excellent climate. It makes a good base for visiting other islands of the Dodecanese, with their mixture of Aegean and Turkish architecture.

The town of **Rhodes** has an attractive harbor with fortifications; the gigantic bronze statue of the Colossus of Rhodes, incorrectly rumored to have straddled the entrance, was one of the wonders of the ancient world. The walled **Old City** is full of crooked, cobbled streets and echoes of antiquity. It's also full of the trappings of tourism, mainly evident in pubs and bars that cater to the large European market. The Old City was built by crusaders—the Knights of St. John—on the site of an ancient city. The knights ruled the island from 1309 until they were defeated by the Turks in 1522.

★ On the Street of the Knights stands the Knights' Hospital. Behind it the **archaeological museum** has ancient pottery and sculpture, including two voluptuous statues of Aphrodite. ✉ *Platia Mouseiou (Museum Square), reached by wide staircase from Hospital,* ☎ *0241/31–048.* ⊙ *May–Oct., Tues.–Fri. 8 AM–9 PM, weekends 8:30–3; Nov.–Apr., Tues.–Fri. 8:30–3.*

The medieval **Palati ton Ippoton** (Palace of the Knights), destroyed in 1856 by a gunpowder explosion, was restored by the Italians as a summer retreat for Mussolini. It is now a museum. Note its splendid Hellenistic and Roman floor mosaics. ✉ *Ippoton,* ☎ *0241/23–359.* ⊙ *May–Oct., Tues.–Fri. 8–7, weekends 8:30–3; Nov.–Apr., Tues.–Fri. 8:30–2:40, weekends 8:30–3.*

★ The **walls** of Rhodes's Old City are among the greatest medieval monuments in the Mediterranean. For 200 years the knights strengthened them, making them up to 40 ft thick in places and curving the surfaces to deflect cannonballs. You can take a walk on about half of the 4-km (2½-mi) road along the top of the fortifications. The tour begins from the courtyard of the Palace of the Knights at the end of Ippoton Street. ✉ *Old Town,* ☎ *0241/23–359.* ⏲ *Tours Tues. and Sat. at 2:45 (arrive at least 15 mins early).*

★ The enchanting village of **Lindos** ornaments the eastern coast. You can climb the winding path and steep stairs to the ruins of the ancient acropolis, **Akropoli tis Archaias Lindou.** The sight of its beautiful colonnade—part of the sanctuary to Athena Lindaia—with the sea far below is unforgettable. Look for little St. Paul's Harbor, beneath the cliffs of the acropolis; seen from above, it appears to be a lake, as rocks obscure its entrance. ✉ *Above town,* ☎ *0241/75–674.* ⏲ *May–Oct., Tues.–Sun. 8–6; Nov.–Apr., Tues.–Sun. 8:30–2:40.*

$$$$ ★ ✕ **Alexis.** The owners spare no effort to present the very best seafood—whether fresh lobster; mussels from nearby Simi steamed with onion, fennel, and white wine; or such specialties as sea urchin, limpets, and sea snail. ✉ *Sokratous 18, Old Town,* ☎ *0241/29–347. Reservations essential. AE, MC, V. No lunch June–Aug.*

$$$$ ✕ **Ta Kioupia.** Antique farm implements hang on the walls at this Rhodes landmark, and tables are elegantly set with linens, fine china, and crystal. Food arrives on large platters, and for a fixed price you select what pleases your eye: carrot bread, pine-nut salad, oven-baked meatballs with leeks, *tiropites* (four-cheese pie), and rooster kebab. ✉ *Tris, about 7 km (4¼ mi) from Rhodes town,* ☎ *0241/91–824. Reservations essential. AE, V. Closed Jan. No lunch.*

$$ ✕ **Dinoris.** In a cavernous hall built in 1530 as a stable for the knights, this establishment has long specialized in fish. For mezes try the variety platter of *psarokeftedakia* (fish balls made from a secret recipe), mussels, shrimp, and lobster. ✉ *Platia Mouseiou 14A, Old Town,* ☎ *0241/25–824. Reservations essential Mar.–Sept. AE, MC, V.*

$$ ★ ✕ **Palia Istoria.** Ensconced in an old house with genteel murals, this mezedopolion is a visual treat. Entrées include pork tenderloin in wine, fresh salmon in champagne sauce, and shrimp ouzo with orange juice. A taxi ride here from the center costs about 700 dr. ✉ *Mitropoleos 108, Ayios Dimitrios,* ☎ *0241/32–421. Reservations essential. MC, V. Closed mid-Dec.–mid-Jan. No lunch.*

$ ✕ **Taverna Nisiros.** Once the home of an Aga, this simple taverna dishes up traditional Greek fare in the large courtyard or in the cozy interior decorated with sheep bells and kilims. Sample the strong barrel wine or a fiery souma (or raki). ✉ *Ayiou Fanouriou 45–47, Old Town,* ☎ *0241/31–471. AE, MC, V.*

$$$$ ★ 🏨 **Grecotel Rhodos Imperial.** The buildings zigzag down the hillside like stacked red, blue, and yellow boxes. Linked by a pedestrian tunnel to the beach, the resort is just 4 km (2½ mi) from Rhodes town. Guests can play tennis, jet ski and windsurf, rent a mountain bike, or just amble along in pedal boats. The crisp, modern rooms all have balconies, about two-thirds of them with sea views. ✉ *Ialyssou Ave., Box 316, 85100 Ixia,* ☎ *0241/75–000,* FAX *0241/76–690; Athens:* ☎ *01/725–0920,* FAX *01/725–7671. 402 rooms, 42 suites. 3 restaurants, 3 pools. AE, DC, MC, V. Closed Nov.–mid-Mar.*

$$$ 🏨 **S. Nikolis' Hotel.** This small hotel within the Old Town is away from the most crowded tourist area. The rooms, in several 14th-century buildings, are outfitted with dark, rustic furniture; TV; air-conditioning (except in the apartments, which have fans); and refrigerators. They look out toward the spacious courtyard or the old city walls. De-

pending on the suite, different "honeymoon" features include a whirlpool tub, king- or queen-size beds, bathtub, loft, and balconies. A roof terrace lets guests enjoy a view over the town with the buffet breakfast. ✉ *Ippodamou 61, 85100 Rhodes,* ☎ *0241/34–561,* FAX *0241/32–034. 10 rooms, 4 suites, 4 apartments. Restaurant. AE, DC, MC, V.*

$$ **Spartalis Hotel.** Convenient if you have to catch a boat from the harbor, this is in Rhodes's New Town. Many rooms in the simple but lively hotel have balconies overlooking the bay, and there is a terrace for breakfast. The rooms on the street are noisy. ✉ *Plastira 2, 85100 Rhodes,* ☎ *0241/24–371,* FAX *0241/20–406. 79 rooms. AE, DC, MC, V. Closed Nov.–Mar.*

Crete

Greece's largest island, lying in the south Aegean, was the center of Europe's earliest civilization, the Minoan, which flourished from about 2000 BC to 1200 BC. Crete was struck a mortal blow in about 1450 BC by an unknown cataclysm, perhaps political.

★ The most important Minoan objects are in the **archaeological museum** in Heraklion, Crete's largest (and least attractive) city. The museum's treasures include the frescoes and ceramics from Knossos and Agia Triada depicting Minoan life, the snake goddesses, and the Phaestos disc, with Europe's first writing. ✉ *Xanthoudidou 1, Platia Eleftherias,* ☎ *081/226–092.* ⏲ *May–Oct., Mon. 12:30–7, Tues.–Sun. 8–7; Nov.–Apr., Mon. 12:30–5, Tues.–Sun. 8–5.*

Not far from Heraklion is the partly reconstructed, sublimely evoca-
★ tive palace of **Knossos.** From 2000 BC to 1400 BC it was the chief site of Europe's first civilization. Note the simple throne room, with its tiny gypsum throne, pipes for running water, and splendid decorations. Its complexity and rituals probably suggested the myth of the Minotaur: the monstrous man-bull, offspring of Queen Pasiphae and a white bull, was confined by King Minos to the labyrinth. ☎ *081/231–940.* ⏲ *May–Oct., daily 8–7; Nov.–Apr., daily 8–5.*

In addition to archaeological treasures, Crete has beautiful snow-capped mountain scenery and many beach resorts along the north coast. **Mallia,** in addition to another extensive palace ruin, has good sandy beaches. Two other highly developed beach resorts, Ayios Nikolaos and the nearby Elounda, lie farther east.

Western Crete, with soaring mountains, deep gorges, and rolling olive orchards, is much less visited. The region is rich in Byzantine churches, Venetian monasteries, and interesting mountain villages. The town of
★ **Rethymnon** is dominated at its western end by the **Fortezza,** one of the largest and best-preserved Venetian castles in Greece. In the town's old section, you'll come across carved-stone Renaissance doorways belonging to vanished mansions; fountains; wooden Turkish houses; and one of the few surviving minarets in Greece. It belongs to the **Neratzes mosque,** and you can climb its 120 steps for a panoramic view. The carefully restored Venetian **loggia** is the clubhouse of the local nobility. The small Venetian **harbor,** with its 13th-century lighthouse, comes to life in summer, with restaurant tables cluttering the quayside.

★ **Hania** is one of the most attractive towns in Greece. Work your way through the covered market, then through the maze of narrow streets to the waterfront. Walk along the inner harbor, past the Venetian arsenals and around to the old lighthouse, for a magnificent view of the town with the White Mountains looming beyond. Behind the outer harbor, Theotokopoulou and Zambeliou streets lead you into the alleys where almost all the houses are Venetian or Turkish, and to the **archaeological museum.** The finds come from all over western Crete: the painted Minoan clay coffins and elegant Late Minoan pottery indicate the region's Bronze Age wealth. ✉ *Halidon 24,* ☎ *0821/90–334.* ⏲ *May–Oct., Tues.–Sun. 8:30–7; Nov.–Apr., Tues.–Sun. 8:30–3.*

In summer, boat service operates along the southwest coast, stopping at **Paleochora,** the area's main resort. **Elafonissi** islet has white-sand beaches and black rocks set in a turquoise sea (to get there you wade across a narrow channel). A good road on the west coast from Elafonissi north accesses beaches that are rarely crowded even in summer, ★ including **Falasarna,** near Crete's northwest tip.

$$ ★ ✕ **Vaonakis.** The lively owner is known for his *leventia* (big-hearted manliness) and his taverna's fine cooking: memorable Cretan mezedes, such as handmade dolmades with tomato and carrot; fried *galantera,* made with the intestines of milk-fed lamb; and pepper croquettes with white cheese, fried eggplants, and baby squash. Leave room for the *mizithrokaltsouna* (pastries filled with sweet local ricotta and served hot with honey). ✉ *Pigianos Kambos, Rethymnon, near El Greco Hotel,* ☎ *0831/72–252. No credit cards. No lunch weekdays Oct.–Mar.*

$$ ✕ **Vassilis.** Watch the boats bobbing along the jetty at this congenial taverna. Don't miss the daily fish soup and such Cretan dishes as *koukouvayia* (a local roll soaked in wine, tomato, oil, and herbs). The owners also make their own rosé. ✉ *Nearchou 10, old harbor, Rethymnon,* ☎ *0831/22–967. V.*

$–$$ ✕ **Samaria.** The taverna has a loyal clientele that yearns for Greek food the way their grandmothers used to make it: *stamnas* (meat, usually beef, oven-cooked with carrots and potatoes in individual ceramic bowls), soutzoukakia, stuffed tomatoes, and creamy pastitsio (try a quarter kilo), ideal with the barrel retsina. The taverna stays open until very late. ✉ *El. Venizelou 39–40, Rethymnon,* ☎ *0831/24–681. V.*

$$ ✕🏨 **Doma.** This converted 19th-century mansion 3 km (2 mi) from the center of Hania has the welcoming atmosphere of a private home: the sitting room has a fireplace and armchairs with embroidered scarlet bolsters. The dining room, where the owner serves dinner on request (lamb cooked with white wine and Cretan mountain herbs, for example), has a memorable view across the bay to the old town. Many rooms have air-conditioning; ask for one overlooking the garden to reduce street noise. There is even an elevator. ✉ *El. Venizelou 124, 73100 Hania,* ☎ *0821/51–772,* FAX *0821/41–578. 28 rooms. Dining room. MC, V. Closed Nov.–Mar.*

$$$$ ★ 🏨 **Elounda Beach.** This is one of Greece's most renowned seaside resorts, 9 km (6 mi) north of Ayios Nikolaos. The complex, set in beautiful grounds—the pool is cleverly landscaped among carob trees—includes a miniature Greek village, complete with kafenion and church, minigolf, two beaches, and a disco. Many of the suites—bliss!—have their own swimming pool. ✉ *Elounda, 72053,* ☎ *0841/41–412,* FAX *0841/41–373; Athens:* ☎ *01/360–7120,* FAX *01/360–3392. 120 rooms, 43 bungalows, 37 suites. 4 restaurants, pool. AE, DC, MC, V. Closed Nov.–Mar..* WEB *www.eloundabeach.gr*

$$ ★ 🏨 **Casa Delfino.** This tranquil hotel in the heart of Hania's Old Town was once part of a Venetian Renaissance palace; you can still see the original stonework throughout the building and the beautiful pebble mosaic in the atrium. Set around a courtyard, the rooms are decorated in cool pastel colors. Four apartments, available at a higher price, are decorated with 17th-century objects and may have such features as a private terrace, sea view, or hydromassage. ✉ *Theofanous 9, Palea Poli, 73100 Hania,* ☎ *0821/93–098 or 0821/87–400,* FAX *0821/96–500. 16 rooms. Air-conditioning. AE, DC, MC, V.*

$$ ★ 🏨 **Nostos.** Dating from the 1400s, this building seems to have housed all the peoples who passed through Hania: the renovated Venetian

palazzo contains remains of an Ottoman bath and living quarters; it was also the site of the town's first Orthodox church. The roof garden is resplendent with honeysuckle, bougainvillea, and grapes. Antique kitchenware adorns the breakfast room. All rooms have balconies and fans; two have sea views. ✉ *Zambeliou 46, Palio Limani, 73131 Hania,* ☎ *0821/94–740,* FAX *0821/54–502. 12 studios. MC, V.*

Aegean Islands Essentials

AIR TRAVEL

There is frequent air service from Athens to each island, but in summer and on holidays it's vital to book well in advance.

BOAT AND FERRY TRAVEL

The simplest way to visit the Aegean Islands is by cruise ship. These usually stop at the four most popular islands—Mykonos, Rhodes, Crete, and Santorini. Car and passenger ferries sail to these destinations from Piraeus. Boats for Mykonos also leave from Rafina, 32 km (20 mi) north of Athens. En route from Piraeus you pass one of the great sights of Greece: the Temple of Poseidon looming on a hilltop at Cape Sounion.

TOURS

AEGEAN CRUISES

From April through October many cruises go to the islands from Piraeus. Try Golden Sun Cruises or Royal Olympic Cruises. Most cruise agencies also have downtown Athens representatives.

➤ Fees and Schedules: **Golden Sun Cruises** (✉ Akti Miaouli 71, Piraeus, ☎ 01/428–7894, FAX 01/428–7898). **Royal Olympic Cruises** (✉ Akti Miaouli 87, Piraeus, ☎ 01/429–0700 reservations, FAX 01/429–0638).

VISITOR INFORMATION

➤ Tourist Information: **Crete** (EOT: ✉ Kriari 40, Megaron Pantheon building, Hania, ☎ 0821/92–943, ☎ FAX 0821/92–624; ✉ Xanthoudidou 1, Heraklion, ☎ 081/244–462, 081/228–225, or 081/228–203; ✉ El. Venizelou beach road, Rethymnon, ☎ 0831/29–148; tourist police: ✉ Karaiskaki 60, Hania, ☎ 0821/73–333; ✉ Dikaiosinis 10, Heraklion, ☎ 081/283–190 or 081/289–614; ✉ El. Venizelou beach road next to EOT, Rethymnon, ☎ 0831/28–156; ELPA: ✉ G. Papandreou 46–50, Heraklion, ☎ 081/289–440). **Mykonos** (Hotel Reservations office: ✉ Port, next to tourist police, ☎ 0289/24–540); Association of Rental Rooms and Apartments: ✉ Port, next to tourist police, ☎ 0289/24–860; tourist police: ✉ Port, ☎ 0289/22–482). **Rhodes** (EOT: ✉ Archbishop Makarios and Papagou, Rhodes town, ☎ 0241/23–655; municipal tourism office: ✉ Platia, Rimini, ☎ 0241/35–945; tourist police: ✉ Archbishop Makarios and Papagou, entrance on Karpathou, Rhodes town, ☎ 0241/27–423. **Santorini** tourist police: ✉ next to KTEL bus station, ☎ 0286/22–649).

15 HUNGARY

BUDAPEST, THE DANUBE BEND, LAKE BALATON

HUNGARY SITS, proudly but precariously, at the crossroads of Central Europe, having retained its own identity despite countless invasions and foreign occupation by great powers of the East and West. Its industrious, resilient people have a history of brave but doomed uprisings: against the Turks in the 17th century, the Habsburgs in 1848, and the Soviet Union in 1956. Each upheaval has resulted in a period of readjustment, a return to politics as the art of the possible.

The 1960s and '70s saw matters improve politically and materially for most Hungarians. Communist party leader János Kádár remained relatively popular at home and abroad, allowing Hungary to improve trade and relations with the West. The bubble began to burst during the 1980s, however, when the economy stagnated and inflation escalated. The peaceful transition to democracy began when young reformers in the party shunted aside the aging Mr. Kádár in 1988 and began speaking openly about multiparty democracy, a market economy, and cutting ties with Moscow. Events quickly gathered pace, and by spring 1990, as the Iron Curtain disappeared, Hungarians went to the polls in the first free elections in 40 years. A center-right government took office, sweeping away the Communists and their renamed successor party, the Socialists, who finished fourth. Eleven years later, the nation entered the new millennium guided by an entirely new generation, the center-right FIDESZ party led by Prime Minister Viktor Orbán, only 35 years old when he was elected in 1998.

In bald mathematical terms, the total area of Hungary (Magyarország) is less than that of Pennsylvania. Two rivers cross the country: the Duna (Danube) flows from the west through Budapest on its way to the southern frontier, the smaller Tisza from the northeast across the Great Plain (Nagyalföld). Western Hungary is dominated by the largest lake in Central Europe, Lake Balaton. Although overdevelopment is advancing, the northern lakeshore is still dotted with Baroque villages and Old World spas, and the surrounding hills are covered with vineyards. In eastern Hungary, the Nagyalföld is steeped in the romantic culture of the Magyars (the Hungarians' name for themselves), with its spicy food, strong wine, and proud *csikós* (horsemen).

However, it is Budapest, a city of more than 2.5 million people, that draws travelers from all over the world. Bisected by the Danube, the city has a split personality; villas and government buildings cluster in the hills of Buda to the west, whereas an imposing array of hotels, restaurants, and shopping areas crowds the flatlands of Pest.

Hungary (Magyarország)

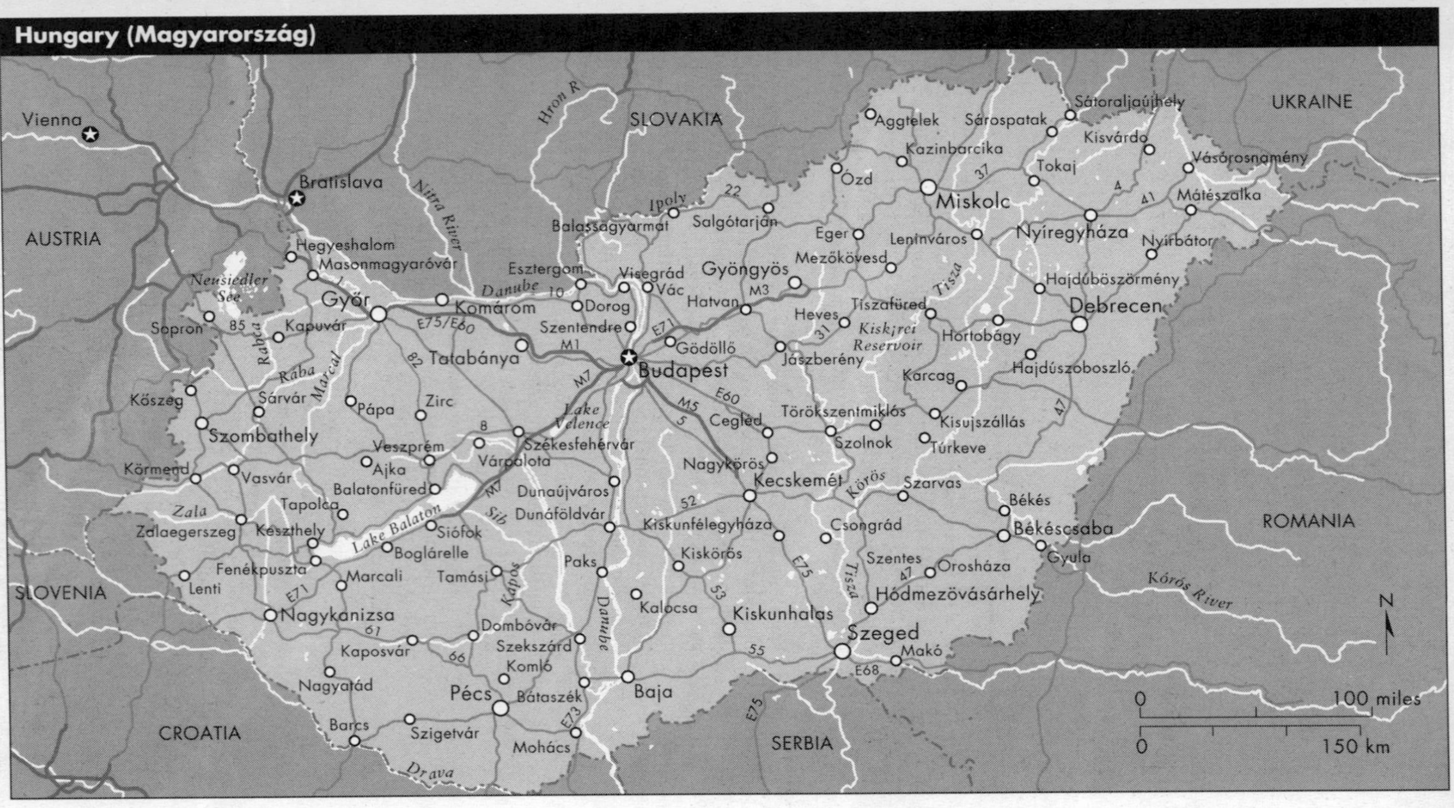

Hungarians, known for their hospitality, enjoy talking with foreigners. Hungarians of all ages share a deep love of music, and wherever you go you will hear it, whether it's opera performed at Budapest's opera house or simply Gypsy violinists serenading you at dinner.

HUNGARY A TO Z

To research prices, get advice from other travelers, and book travel arrangements, visit www.fodors.com.

BIKE TRAVEL

A land of rolling hills and flat plains, Hungary lends itself to bicycling. For brochures and general information on bicycling conditions and suggested routes, try Tourinform or contact the Magyar Kerékpáros Túrázók Szövetsége (Bicycle Touring Association of Hungary).

➤ Bike Information: **Magyar Kerékpáros Túrázók Szövetsége** (✉ V, Bajcsy-Zsilinszky út 31, 2nd floor, apt. 3, Budapest, ☎ 1/332–7177).

BOAT AND FERRY TRAVEL

Boat travel is possible in many parts of Hungary. Budapest, of course, straddles a major international waterway—the Danube. Vienna is six hours away by hydrofoil, and many Hungarian resorts are accessible by either hydrofoil or boat. For information about excursions or pleasure cruises, contact MAHART Tours.

➤ Boat and Ferry Information: **MAHART Tours** (✉ V, Belgrád rakpart, Budapest, ☎ 1/318–1704 or 1/318–1586).

BUS TRAVEL

Long-distance buses link Budapest with many main cities in Eastern and Western Europe. Services to the eastern part of the country leave from Népstadion station. Buses to the west and south leave from the main Volán bus station in the inner city, but the station will be relocated to a less central location in 2002 to accommodate the total restructuring planned for Erzsébet tér. Buses are inexpensive and tend to be crowded, so reserve your seat.

➤ Bus Information: **Népstadion station** (✉ IX, Hungária körút 46–48, Budapest, ☎ 1/252–4496). **Volán bus station** (✉ V, Erzsébet tér, Budapest, ☎ 1/318–2122).

BUSINESS HOURS

BANKS & OFFICES

Banks are generally open weekdays 8–2 or 3, often with a one-hour lunch break around noon; most close at 1 on Friday.

MUSEUMS & SIGHTS

Museums are generally open 10–6 Tuesday–Sunday; many stop selling admission 30 minutes before closing. Note that some museums change their opening and closing times by an hour or so at the beginning and end of peak seasons based on visitor traffic; it's prudent to double-check hours. Many have free admission one day a week.

SHOPS

Department stores are open weekdays 10–5 or 6, Saturday until 1. Grocery stores are generally open weekdays 7–6 or 7, Saturday until 1; "nonstops" or *éjjeli-nappali* (24-hour convenience stores) are (theoretically) open 24 hours.

CAR TRAVEL

To drive in Hungary, U.S. and Canadian visitors are supposed to have an International Driver's License—although their domestic licenses are usually accepted—and U.K. visitors may use their own domestic licenses.

EMERGENCIES

The Magyar Autó Klub (Hungarian Automobile Club) runs a 24-hour "Yellow Angels" breakdown service.

➤ CONTACTS: **Magyar Autó Klub** (✉ XIV, Francia út 38/B, Budapest, ☎ 1/345–1744).

GASOLINE

Gas stations are plentiful in and around major cities, and major chains have opened modern full-service stations on highways in the provinces. A liter of *ólommentes benzin* (unleaded gasoline) costs about 250 Ft. and is usually available at all stations, as is diesel.

ROAD CONDITIONS

There are three classes of roads: highways or "motorways" (designated by the letter "M" and a single digit), secondary roads (designated by a two-digit number), and minor roads (designated by a three-digit number). Highways and secondary roads are generally well maintained. Minor roads vary; tractors and horse-drawn carts may slow you down in rural areas. Tolls on major highways help fund the upgrading of many of the country's motorways.

RULES OF THE ROAD

Drive on the right. Unless otherwise noted, the speed limit in developed areas is 50 kph (30 mph), on main roads 80–100 kph (50–62 mph), and on highways 120 kph (75 mph). Speed limit signs are scarce compared to those in the United States. Seat belts are compulsory, as is the use of headlights (except in developed areas), and drinking alcohol is prohibited—there is a zero tolerance policy, and the penalties are severe.

CUSTOMS AND DUTIES

Objects for personal use may be imported freely. If you are over 16, you may also bring in 250 cigarettes or 50 cigars or 250 grams of tobacco, plus 2 liters of wine, 1 liter of spirits, 5 liters of beer, and 0.25 liters of perfume. A customs charge is made on gifts valued in Hungary at more than 27,000 Ft.

Keep receipts of any purchases from Konsumtourist, Intertourist, or Képcsarnok Vállalat. A special permit is needed for works of art, antiques, or objects of museum value. You are entitled to a VAT refund on new goods (i.e., not works of art, antiques, or objects of museum value) valued at more than 50,000 Ft.

For further customs information, inquire at the Hungarian Customs Office. If you can't speak Hungarian, ask the English-speaking staff at Tourinform for help.

➤ INFORMATION: **Hungarian Customs Office** (✉ IX, Mester u. 7, Budapest, ☎ 1/456–9500 or 1/470–4121).

DINING

Although prices are steadily increasing, plenty of good, affordable restaurants offer a variety of Hungarian dishes. Meats, rich sauces, and creamy desserts predominate, but you can also find vegetarian dishes and salads, even out of season. Don't miss a chance to sample some of Hungary's excellent wines. Egri Bikavér, or "bull's blood," Hungary's best-known red wine, goes well with almost any meal. A regular restaurant is likely to be called either a *vendéglő* or an *étterem*. You also have the option of eating in a *büfé* (snack counter), an *eszpresszó* (café), or a *söröző* (pub). Be sure to visit a *cukrászda* (pastry shop). Keep in mind that typical Hungarian breakfasts consist of cold cuts and bread; if the start of your day requires specially prepared omelets or blueberry muffins, be sure to inquire about your hotel's breakfast offerings ahead of time.

One caveat: many restaurants have a fine-print policy of charging for each slice of bread consumed from the bread basket. General overcharging is not unheard of, either. Authorities in Budapest, however, have been cracking down on establishments reported for overcharging. Don't order from menus without prices, and don't accept dining or drinking invitations from women hired to lure people into shady situations.

Prices are per person for a main course at dinner. Prices in Budapest tend to be a good 30% higher than elsewhere in Hungary.

CATEGORY	COST
$$$$	over 3,500 Ft.
$$$	2,500 Ft.–3,500 Ft.
$$	1,500 Ft.–2,500 Ft.
$	under 1,500 Ft.

MEALTIMES

Hungarians eat dinner early—you risk offhand service and cold food after 9 PM. Lunch, the main meal for many, is served from noon to 2. Some restaurants are introducing simple breakfast menus catering to Western travelers and expats.

RESERVATIONS AND DRESS

At most moderately priced and inexpensive restaurants, casual but neat dress is acceptable. Only in the most expensive Budapest establishments are a jacket and tie sometimes required.

EMBASSIES

➤ AUSTRALIA: (✉ XII, Királyhágó tér 8–9, Budapest 1126, ☎ 1/457–9777).

➤ CANADA: (✉ Mailing address: XII, Budakeszi út 32, Budapest 1121; ✉ Street address: XII, Zugligeti út 51–53, Budapest 1121, ☎ 1/275–1200).

➤ UNITED KINGDOM: (✉ V, Harmincad u. 6, Budapest 1051, ☎ 1/266–2888).

➤ UNITED STATES: (✉ V, Szabadság tér 12, Budapest 1054, ☎ 1/475–4400).

HOLIDAYS

January 1; March 15 (Anniversary of 1848 Revolution); Easter and Easter Monday; May 1 (Labor Day); Pentecost; August 20 (St. Stephen's and Constitution Day); October 23 (1956 Revolution Day); December 24–26.

LANGUAGE

Hungarian (Magyar) tends to look and sound intimidating to English-speakers. Generally, older people speak some German, and many younger people speak at least rudimentary English, which has become the most popular language to learn. It's a safe bet that anyone in the tourist trade will speak at least one of the two languages.

LODGING

Lodging ranges from sophisticated hotels to guest houses, private rooms, and campsites.

The following price categories are for a double room with bath, including VAT but not breakfast, during the peak season; rates are markedly lower off-season and in the countryside, sometimes under $20 for two. For single rooms with bath, count on about 80% of the double-room rate. As most large hotels require payment in hard currency, rates are given in dollars below.

During the peak season (June–August), full board may be compulsory at some of the Lake Balaton hotels, although this is increasingly rare. During the off-season (in Budapest, September–March; at Lake Balaton and the Danube Bend, May and September), rates can be considerably lower than those given above and are frequently negotiable.

CATEGORY	BUDAPEST	BALATON AND DANUBE BEND
$$$$	over $200	over $70
$$$	$140–$200	$50–$70
$$	$80–$140	$30–$50
$	under $80	under $30

APARTMENT AND VILLA RENTALS

Apartments in Budapest and cottages at Lake Balaton, available for short- and long-term rental, can be the most economical lodging for families. Contact tourist offices in Hungary and abroad for rates and reservations. A Budapest apartment or a luxury cottage for two on Lake Balaton may cost anywhere from $40 to $60 a day. You can make bookings in Budapest at the Tribus Hotel Service, which is open 24 hours a day. Although some enterprising locals stand outside tourist offices and at train stations offering tourists their apartments for lower than official rates, the risk of being taken for a ride far outweighs the savings. The IBUSZ Accommodation Centre has extensive rental listings. On the Buda side, a good rental agency is Cooptourist. Amadeus Apartments oversees five apartments that cost roughly $45 a night (two-night minimum), including airport transport.

➤ LOCAL AGENTS: **Amadeus Apartments** (✉ VIII, Üllői út 197, Budapest, ☎ 30/942–2893, FAX 1/302–8268). **Cooptourist** (✉ XI, Bartók Béla út 4, Budapest, ☎ 1/466–5349). **IBUSZ Accommodation Centre** (✉ V, Ferenciek tere 10, Budapest, ☎ 1/485–2767 or 1/485–2769, FAX 1/337–1205). **Tribus Hotel Service** (✉ V, Apáczai Csere János u. 1, Budapest, ☎ 1/266–8042 or 1/318–5776, FAX 1/266–8159, WEB www.tribus.hu).

CAMPING

Most of the some 300 campsites in Hungary are open from May through September. An average rate is about $12 a day per site in Budapest and the Balaton region, slightly less elsewhere. Children under 14 often get a 50% reduction. Camping is permitted only in designated areas. For information contact travel agencies or Tourinform, where you can pick up a detailed map locating campsites around the country.

GUEST HOUSES AND PRIVATE LODGINGS

Also called *panziók* (pensions), small guest houses lying just outside the heart of the city or town provide simple accommodations well suited to people on a budget. These usually include a private bathroom, and many also offer breakfast. A room for two in Budapest with breakfast and private bath will cost around the equivalent of $50–$70 per night in peak season, less at other times. Arrangements can be made through local tourist offices or travel agents abroad.

In the provinces, rooms that you are offered directly are likely to be clean and in a relatively good neighborhood. Look for a placard reading either SZOBA KIADÓ or—in German—ZIMMER FREI (room for rent). The rate per night for a double room in Budapest or at Lake Balaton is $20–$30 (which usually includes the use of a bathroom but not breakfast). Reservations can also be made by any tourist office.

HOSTELS

Most hostels in Budapest are in university dorms and open only when school is not in session (typically July and August). Hostels have no age limits or membership requirements, and they offer a 10% discount to HI (Hostelling International) cardholders. Most have no curfews and offer 24-hour reception service. The Hungarian Youth Hostel Federation in Budapest publishes an informative, annual directory of hostels throughout the country and provides information. Budapest's main hostel agency, Mellow Mood Kft./Travellers' Youth Hostels, operates year-round hostels. Be sure to book in advance in summer. Hostels are uncommon outside Budapest, but some towns open their university dorms to travelers during July and August; inquire at the local tourist office. The atmosphere and price at these dorms is about the same as at a hostel.

➤ HOSTEL ORGANIZATIONS: **Hungarian Youth Hostel Federation** (✉ VII, Almássy téri Szabadidő központ, Almássy tér 6, 4th floor, Budapest, ☎ FAX 1/352–1572, ext. 203 and 204). **Mellow Mood Kft./Travellers' Youth Hostels** (✉ Dózsa György út 152, Budapest H-1134 Budapest, ☎ 1/340–8585 or 1/329–8644, ☎ FAX 1/320–8425, WEB www.travellers-hostels.com).

HOTELS

Don't expect a bargain on your hotel room in Budapest: high-season rates at established hotels rival those of most Western capitals. There are few expensive hotels outside Budapest, but the moderately priced hotels are generally comfortable and well run. Unless otherwise noted, breakfast is not included.

MAIL AND SHIPPING

Two post offices in Budapest offer extended hours. Keleti is open daily 7 AM–9 PM. Nyugati is open Mon.–Sat. 7 AM–9 PM, Sun. 8 AM–10 PM. Each is near one of Budapest's main train stations.

General delivery service is available through any post office in Budapest, including the main downtown branch (✉ Magyar Posta 4. sz., H-1052 Budapest, Városház utca 18); the envelope should have your name written on it, as well as "posta maradó" (poste restante) in large letters. The roman-numeral prefix listed in a Budapest street address refers to one of the city's 22 districts. Postal addresses include a zip code but not the roman numeral.

➤ POST OFFICES: **Keleti** (Eastern; ✉ VIII, Baross tér 11c, Budapest, ☎ 1/312–1200). **Nyugati** (Western; ✉ VI, Teréz körút 51, Budapest, ☎ 1/322–1099).

POSTAL RATES

Postage for an airmail letter to the United States costs about 150 Ft.; an airmail letter to the United Kingdom and elsewhere in Western Europe costs about 140 Ft. Airmail postcards to the United States cost about 106 Ft. and to the United Kingdom and elsewhere in Western Europe, about 96 Ft.

MONEY MATTERS

The forint was significantly devalued over the past few years and continues its decline, but inflation has dramatically decreased to around 9% from an annual rate of more than 25%. Although you receive more forints for your dollar, prices have risen to keep up with inflation. Nevertheless, even with inflation and the 25% value-added tax (VAT) in the service industry, enjoyable vacations with all the trimmings remain less expensive than in nearby Western European cities such as Vienna.

Sample prices include: cup of espresso, 200 Ft.; bottle of beer at a bar or restaurant, 300 Ft.–400 Ft.; soft drinks, 200 Ft.; 2-km (1-mi) taxi ride, 600 Ft.; museum admission 300 Ft.–600 Ft.

ATMS

Hundreds of ATMs have appeared throughout the capital and in other major towns. Some accept Plus network bank cards and Visa credit cards, others Cirrus and MasterCard. You can withdraw forints only (automatically converted at the bank's official exchange rate) directly from your account; most levy a 1% or $3 service charge. Many cash-exchange machines, into which you feed paper currency for forints, have also sprung up.

CURRENCY

The unit of currency is the forint (Ft.). There are bills of 200, 500, 1,000, 2,000, 5,000, 10,000, and 20,000 forints and coins of 1, 2, 5, 10, 20, 50, and 100 forints. At press time (summer 2001), the exchange rate was 274 Ft. to the U.S. dollar, 186 Ft. to the Canadian dollar, 411 Ft. to the pound sterling, 329 Ft. to the Irish punt, 165 Ft. to the Australian dollar, 130 Ft. to the New Zealand dollar, and 39 Ft. to the South African rand.

There is still a black market in hard currency, but changing money on the street is risky and illegal, and the bank rate almost always comes close. Stick with banks and official exchange offices.

TRAVELER'S CHECKS

Eurocheque holders can cash personal checks in all banks and in most hotels. Many banks now also cash American Express and Visa traveler's checks. American Express has a full-service office in Budapest, and a smaller branch on Castle Hill—in the Sisi Restaurant, closed January–mid-March—offers only currency exchange. Hungary's first Citibank offers full services to account holders, including a 24-hour ATM.

➤ CONTACTS: **American Express** (✉ V, Deák Ferenc u. 10, Budapest, ☎ 1/235–4330 travel service; 1/235–4349 cardmember services, FAX 1/235–4303; ✉ In Sisi Restaurant, ☎ 1/224–0118). **Citibank** (✉ V, Vörösmarty tér 4, Budapest).

PASSPORTS AND VISAS

U.S., British, and Canadian citizens must carry a valid passport.

TAXES

VALUE-ADDED TAX (V.A.T.)

You are entitled to a VAT (ÁFA, in Hungarian) refund on new goods (i.e., not works of art, antiques, or objects of museum value) valued at more than 50,000 Ft. (VAT inclusive). Cash refunds are given only in forints. If you made your purchases by credit card, you can file for a credit to your card or to your bank account (again in forints), but this process is slow at best. If you intend to apply for the credit, make sure you get customs to stamp the original purchase invoice before you leave the country. For more information, pick up a tax refund brochure from any tourist office or hotel, or contact a tax refund agency. Intel Trade Rt. assists both individuals and foreign companies. Global Refund Magyarország Rt. is exclusively for individuals.

➤ V.A.T. REFUNDS: **Global Refund Magyarország Rt.** (✉ II, Bég u. 3–5, Budapest, ☎ 1/212–4906). **Intel Trade Rt.** (✉ I, Csalogány u. 6-10, Budapest, ☎ 1/356–9800).

TELEPHONES

COUNTRY AND AREA CODES

The country code for Hungary is 36.

DIRECTORY AND OPERATOR ASSISTANCE

For operator-assisted calls within Hungary, dial ☎ 191. Dial 198 for directory assistance throughout the country. Operators are unlikely to speak English. A safer bet is to consult *The Phone Book,* an English-language yellow pages–style telephone directory that also has cultural and tourist information; it's free in most major hotels, at many restaurants, and at English-language bookstores.

INTERNATIONAL CALLS

Direct calls to foreign countries can be made from Budapest and all major provincial towns by dialing 00 and waiting for the international dialing tone; on pay phones the initial charge is 60 Ft. Operator-assisted international calls can be made by dialing 190. To reach a long-distance operator, call AT&T, MCI, or Sprint.

➤ ACCESS CODES: **AT&T** (☎ 06–800–01111). **MCI** (☎ 06–800–01411). **Sprint** (☎ 06–800–01877).

LOCAL CALLS

The cost of a three-minute local call is 20 Ft. Pay phones use 10, 20, 50, and 100 Ft. coins. Most towns in Hungary can be dialed direct—dial 06 and wait for the buzzing tone, then dial the local number. It is unnecessary to use the city code, 1, when dialing within Budapest.

While Hungary's telephone system continues to be modernized, phone numbers are subject to change—usually without forewarning and sometimes several times. A recording in Hungarian and English may provide the new number. If you're having trouble getting through, ask your concierge to check the number.

PUBLIC PHONES

Gray card-operated telephones are common in Budapest and the Balaton region. The cards—available at post offices, newsstands, and kiosks—come in units of 60 (800 Ft.) and 90 (1,800 Ft.) calls.

TIPPING

Four decades of socialism didn't alter the Hungarian habit of tipping. Hairdressers and taxi drivers expect 10%–15% tips, while porters should get a dollar or two or a few hundred forints. Cloakroom attendants receive 100 Ft.–200 Ft., as do gas pump attendants if they wash your windows or check your tires. Unless otherwise noted, gratuities are not automatically included in restaurant bills; when the waiter arrives with the bill, you should immediately add a 10%–15% tip to the amount and pay the waiter, as it is not customary to leave a tip on the table. If a Gypsy band plays exclusively for your table, you can leave 200 Ft. in the plate provided.

TRAIN TRAVEL

Travel by train from Budapest to other large cities or to Lake Balaton is cheap and efficient. Remember to take a *gyorsvonat* (express train) and not a *személyvonat* (local), which can be extremely slow. A *helyjegy* (seat reservation), which costs about 370 Ft., is advisable for all Inter-City trains, which provide rapid, express service among Hungary's major cities.

Only Hungarian citizens are entitled to student discounts; non-Hungarian senior citizens (men over 60, women over 55), however, are eligible for a 20% discount. For more information about rail travel contact the MÁV Passenger Service.

FARES AND SCHEDULES

➤ TRAIN INFORMATION

MÁV Passenger Service (✉ VI, Andrássy út 35, Budapest, ☎ 1/461–5500 international information; 1/461–5400 domestic information).

VISITOR INFORMATION

➤ TOURIST INFORMATION: **Tourinform** (✉ Vörösmarty tér, at Vigadó u., H-1052 Budapest, ☎ 1/438–8080; 06/80–660–044 automated telephone service, ⊙ open 24 hours; ✉ Sütő u. 2, H-1052 Budapest, ☎ 1/317–9800, ⊙ open daily 8–8. www.hungarytourism.hu; WEB www.tourinform.hu).

WHEN TO GO

Many of Hungary's major fairs and festivals take place in the spring and fall. During July and August, Budapest can be hot and the resorts at Lake Balaton crowded, so spring (May) and the end of summer (September) are the ideal times to visit.

CLIMATE

The following are average daily maximum and minimum temperatures for Budapest.

Jan.	34F	1C	**May**	72F	22C	**Sept.**	73F	23C
	25	– 4		52	11		54	12
Feb.	39F	4C	**June**	79F	26C	**Oct.**	61F	16C
	28	– 2		59	15		45	7
Mar.	50F	10C	**July**	82F	28C	**Nov.**	46F	8C
	36	2		61	16		37	3
Apr.	63F	17C	**Aug.**	81F	27C	**Dec.**	39F	4C
	45	7		61	16		30	– 1

BUDAPEST

Budapest, lying on both banks of the Danube, unites the hills of Buda and the wide boulevards of Pest. It was the site of a Roman outpost in the 1st century, and the modern city was not created until 1873, when the towns of Óbuda, Pest, and Buda were joined. The resulting capital is the cultural, political, intellectual, and commercial heart of the nation; for the 20% of the nation's population who live here, anywhere else is just "the country."

Much of the charm of a visit to Budapest consists of unexpected glimpses into shadowy courtyards and long vistas down sunlit cobbled streets. Although some 30,000 buildings were destroyed during World War II and in 1956, the past lingers on in the often crumbling architectural details of the antique structures that remain and in the memories and lifestyles of Budapest's citizens.

Exploring Budapest

The principal sights of the city fall roughly into three areas, each of which can be comfortably covered on foot. The Budapest hills are best explored using public transportation. Many street names have been changed since 1989 to purge all reminders of the Communist regime—you can sometimes still see the old name, negated with a victorious red *x*, next to the new. The 22 districts of Budapest are referred to in addresses with Roman numerals, starting with I for the Várhegy (Castle Hill) district; V, VI, and VII indicate the main downtown areas.

Várhegy

Numbers in the margin correspond to points of interest on the Budapest map.

Most of Buda's main sights are on Várhegy (Castle Hill), a long, narrow plateau laced with cobblestone streets, clustered with beautifully preserved Baroque, Gothic, and Renaissance houses and crowned by the stately Royal Palace. Painstaking reconstruction work has been in progress here since the area was nearly leveled during World War II.

❺ **Hadtörténeti Múzeum** (Museum of Military History). The collection here includes uniforms and regalia, many belonging to the Hungarian generals who took part in the abortive uprising against Austrian rule in 1848. Other exhibits trace the military history of Hungary from the original Magyar conquest in the 9th century up to the middle of the 20th century. English-language tours can be arranged in advance. ✉ *I, Tóth Árpád sétány 40,* ☎ *1/356–9522,* WEB *www.militaria.hu.* ⏲ *Apr.–Sept., Tues.–Sun. 10–6; Oct.–Mar., Tues.–Sun. 10–4.*

★ ❸ **Halászbástya** (Fishermen's Bastion). This wondrous porch overlooking Pest and the Danube was built at the turn of the 20th century as a lookout tower to protect what was once a thriving fishing settlement. Its neo-Romanesque columns and arches frame views over the city and the river. ✉ *I, behind Mátyás templom.*

★ ❶ **Királyi Palota** (Royal Palace, also known as Buda Castle). The Nazis made their final stand here and left it a blackened wasteland. Under the rubble archaeologists discovered the medieval foundations of the palace of King Matthias Corvinus, who, in the 15th century, presided over one of the most splendid courts in Europe. The rebuilt palace is now a vast museum complex and cultural center. ✉ *I, south of Szent György tér.*

In the castle's northern wing, the **Ludwig Múzeum** (Ludwig Museum) houses a collection of more than 200 pieces of Hungarian and contemporary world art, including works by Picasso and Lichtenstein. ✉ *I, Buda Castle (Wing A), Dísz tér 17,* ☎ *1/375–7533.* ⏲ *Tues.–Sun. 10–6.*

The central section of the palace houses the **Magyar Nemzeti Galéria** (Hungarian National Gallery), which exhibits a wide range of Hungarian fine art. Names to look for are Munkácsy, a 19th-century Romantic painter, and Csontváry, an early Surrealist admired by Picasso. Tours for up to five people with an English-speaking guide can be booked in advance. ✉ *I, Buda Castle (Wing C), Dísz tér 17,* ☎ *1/375–7533; 1/224–3700, ext. 423 for tours.* ⏲ *Mid-Mar.–Nov., Tues.–Sun. 10–6; Dec.–mid-Mar., Tues.–Sun. 10–4.*

The **Budapesti Történeti Múzeum** (Budapest History Museum), the southern block of the palace, displays a permanent exhibit of the city's history from Buda's liberation from the Turks in 1686 through the 1970s. The 19th- and 20th-century photos and videos of the castle, the Chain Bridge, and other Budapest monuments can provide a helpful orientation to the city. Down in the cellars are the original medieval vaults of the palace, a palace chapel, and more royal relics. ✉ *I, Buda Castle (Wing E), Szt. György tér 2,* ☎ *1/375–7533,* WEB *www.btm.hu.* ⏲ *Mar.–mid-May and mid-Sept.–Oct., Wed.–Mon. 10–6; mid-May–mid-Sept., daily 10–6; Nov.–Feb., Wed.–Mon. 10–4.*

★ ❷ **Mátyás templom** (Matthias Church). This venerable church with its distinctive roof of colored, diamond-pattern tiles and skeletal Gothic spire dates from the 13th century. Built as a mosque by the Turks, it was destroyed and reconstructed during the 19th century, only to be bombed during World War II. Only the south porch survives from the original structure. The Habsburg emperors were crowned kings of Hungary here. High mass is held every Sunday at 10 AM with an orchestra and choir, and organ concerts are often held in the summer on Friday at 8 PM. Visitors are asked to remain at the back of the church during services (it's least intrusive to come after 9:30 AM weekdays and between 1 PM and 5 PM Sunday and holidays). ✉ *I, Szentháromság tér 2,* ☎ *1/355–5657.* ⏲ *Church daily 7 AM–8 PM, treasury daily 9:30–5:30.*

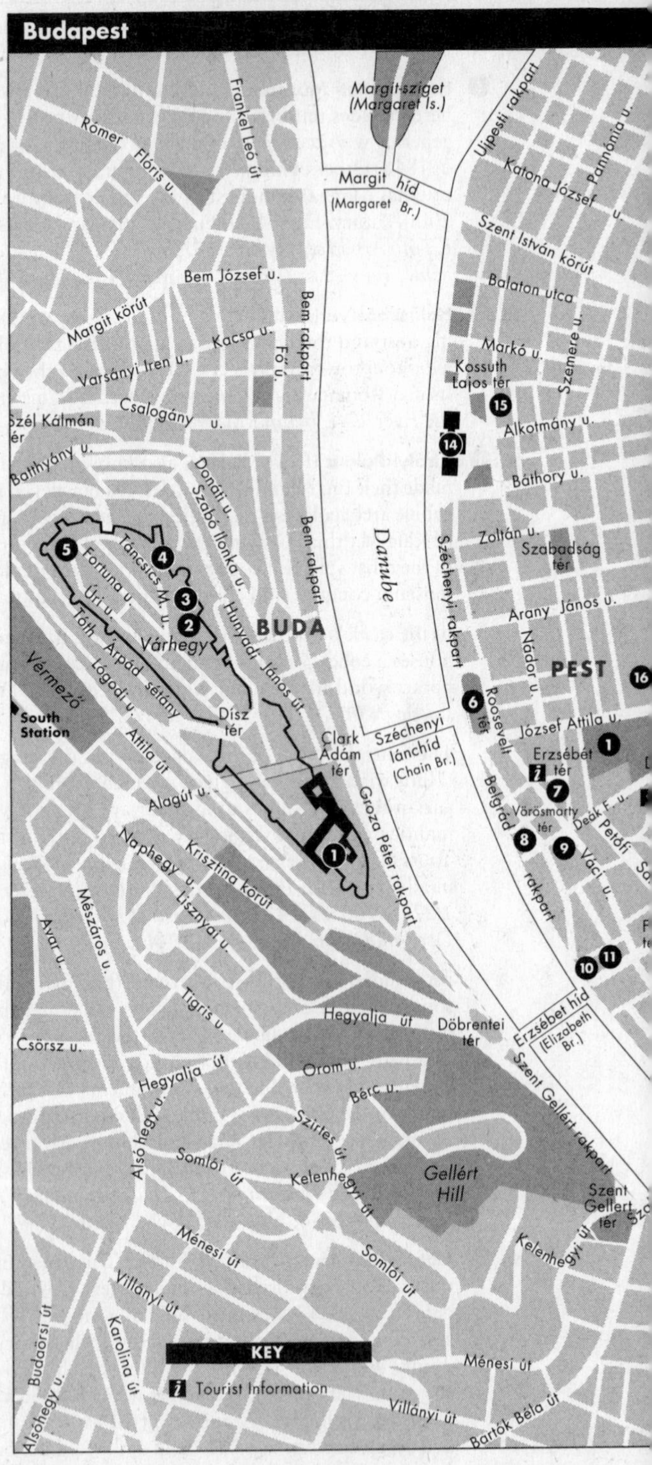
Budapest
Margit-sziget (Margaret Is.)
Margit híd (Margaret Br.)
Frankel Leó út
Római
Flóris u.
Újpesti rakpart
Pannónia u.
Katona József u.
Szent István körút
Balaton utca
Bem József u.
Bem rakpart
Margit körút
Kacsa u.
Fő u.
Markó u.
Szemere u.
Varsányi Iren u.
Kossuth Lajos tér
Csalogány u.
Alkotmány u.
Széll Kálmán tér
Batthyány u.
Báthory u.
Donáti u.
Szabó Ilonka u.
Danube
Zoltán u.
Szabadság tér
Táncsics M. u.
Fortuna u.
Úri u.
Tóth Árpád sétány
Hunyadi János út
Széchenyi rakpart
Arany János u.
Nádor u.
BUDA
PEST
Várhegy
Vérmező
South Station
Lógodi u.
Attila út
Dísz tér
Clark Ádám tér
Széchenyi lánchíd (Chain Br.)
Roosevelt tér
József Attila u.
Erzsébet tér
Alagút u.
Vörösmarty tér
Deák F. u.
Belgrád rakpart
Petőfi
Váci u.
Naphegy u.
Krisztina körút
Groza Péter rakpart
Lisznyai u.
Mészáros u.
Avar u.
Tigris u.
Hegyalja út
Döbrentei tér
Erzsébet híd (Elizabeth Br.)
Csörsz u.
Orom u.
Szent Gellért rakpart
Bérc u.
Alsó hegy u.
Szirtes út
Somlói út
Kelenhegyi út
Gellért Hill
Szent Gellért tér
Ménesi út
Villányi út
Budaörsi út
Karolina út
Alsóhegy u.
KEY
Tourist Information
Bartók Béla út

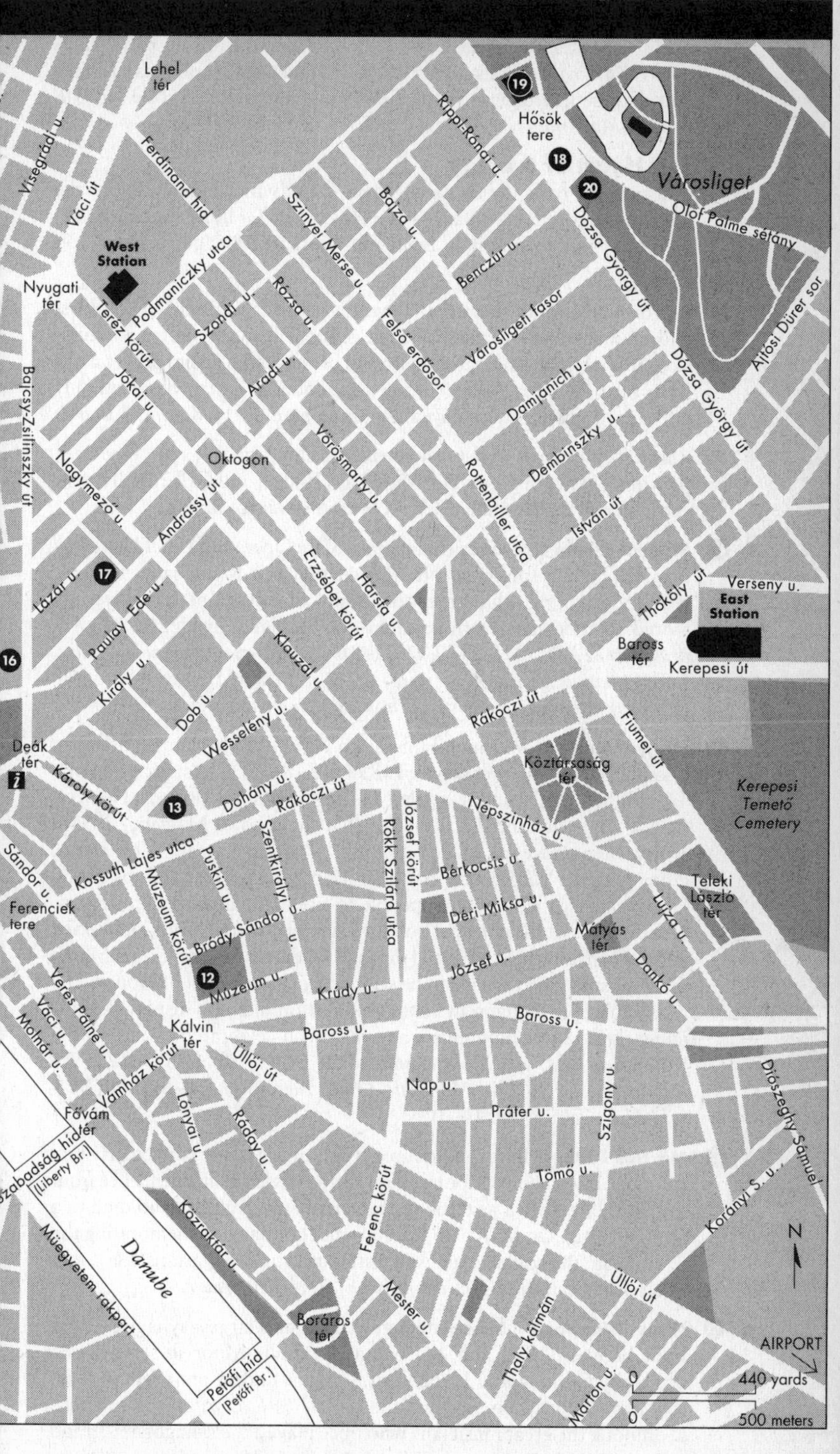

Lehel tér
Visegrádi u.
Váci út
Ferdinand híd
West Station
Nyugati tér
Teréz körút
Podmaniczky utca
Szondi u.
Rózsa u.
Szinyei Merse u.
Bajza u.
Rippl-Rónai u.
Hősök tere
Városliget
Olof Palme sétány
Benczúr u.
Felső erdősor
Városligeti fasor
Dózsa György út
Ajtósi Dürer sor
Jókai u.
Aradi u.
Damjanich u.
Bajcsy-Zsilinszky út
Nagymező u.
Oktogon
Andrássy út
Vörösmarty u.
Rottenbiller utca
Dembinszky u.
István út
Lázár u.
Paulay Ede u.
Erzsébet körút
Hársfa u.
Thököly út
Verseny u.
East Station
Baross tér
Kerepesi út
Király u.
Klauzál u.
Dob u.
Wesselény u.
Rákóczi út
Fiumei út
Deák tér
Károly körút
Dohány u.
Köztársaság tér
Kerepesi Temető Cemetery
Népszínház u.
József körút
Rökk Szilárd utca
Szentkirályi u.
Puskin u.
Kossuth Lajos utca
Múzeum körút
Sándor u.
Ferenciek tere
Bérkocsis u.
Déri Miksa u.
Teleki László tér
Luiza u.
Mátyás tér
Bródy Sándor u.
Múzeum u.
Krúdy u.
József u.
Dankó u.
Kálvin tér
Baross u.
Veres Pálné u.
Váci u.
Molnár u.
Vámház körút
Üllői út
Lónyai u.
Ráday u.
Nap u.
Práter u.
Szigony u.
Diószeghy Sámuel
Fővám tér
Szabadság híd (Liberty Br.)
Tömő u.
Műegyetem rakpart
Danube
Közraktár u.
Ferenc körút
Korányi S. u.
Mester u.
Bokáros tér
Thaly Kálmán
Márton u.
Petőfi híd (Petőfi Br.)
AIRPORT
0 440 yards
0 500 meters
N

❹ **Zenetörténeti Múzeum** (Museum of Music History). The handsome, 18th-century gray-stone palace that once belonged to the noble Erdődy family hosts intimate recitals of classical music and displays rare manuscripts and antique instruments. ✉ *I, Táncsics Mihály u. 7,* ☎ *1/214–6770.* ⏲ *Mid-Mar.–mid-Nov., Tues.–Fri. 10–5, Sat.–Sun. 10–6.*

The Heart of the City

Pest fans out from the Belváros (Inner City), which is bounded by the Kiskörút (Little Ring Road). The Nagykörút (Grand Ring Road) describes a wider semicircle from the Margaret Bridge to the Petőfi Bridge.

⓫ **Belvárosi plébánia templom** (Inner-City Parish Church). The oldest church in Pest dates from the 12th century. It incorporates a succession of Western architectural styles and preserves a Muslim prayer niche from the time when the Turks ruled the country. Liszt, who lived only a few yards away, often played the organ here. ✉ *V, Március 15 tér 2.*

★ **Korzó.** This elegant promenade runs south along the Pest side of the river, providing views of Castle Hill, the Chain Bridge, and Gellért Hill on the other side of the Danube. ✉ *V, from Eötvös tér to Március 15 tér.*

★ ⓱ **Magyar Állami Operaház** (Hungarian State Opera House). Flanked by a pair of marble sphinxes, this 19th-century neo-Renaissance treasure was the crowning achievement of architect Miklós Ybl. It has been restored to its original ornate glory—particularly inside. ✉ *VI, Andrássy út 22,* ☎ *1/331–2550; 1/332–8197 for tours,* WEB *www.opera.hu. Foreign-language tours (45 mins) daily at 3 PM and 4 PM; meet at the Sphinx statue in front of opera house on right-hand side.*

⓬ **Magyar Nemzeti Múzeum** (Hungarian National Museum). The stern, classical edifice was built between 1837 and 1847. On its steps, on March 15, 1848, Petőfi Sándor recited his revolutionary poem, "Nemzeti Dal" ("National Song"), declaring "By the God of Magyar, / Do we swear, / Do we swear, chains no longer / Will we wear." This poem, along with the "12 Points," a formal list of political demands by young Hungarians, called upon the people to rise up against the Habsburgs. Celebrations of the national holiday—long banned by the Communist regime—are now held here (and throughout the city) every year on March 15. A host of royal relics can be seen in the domed Hall of Honor. The museum's epic Hungarian history exhibition includes displays chronicling the end of Communism and the much-celebrated exodus of the Russian troops. ✉ *IX, Múzeum körút 14–16,* ☎ *1/338–2122,* WEB *www.hnm.hu.* ⏲ *Mid-Mar.–mid-Oct., Tues.–Sun. 10–6; mid-Oct.–mid-Mar., Tues.–Sun. 10–5.*

❿ **Március 15 tér** (March 15 Square). This square is not particularly picturesque, but it commemorates the 1848 struggle for independence from the Habsburgs with a statue of the poet Petőfi Sándor, who died in a later uprising. On March 15, the national holiday commemorating the revolution, the square is packed with patriotic Hungarians. ✉ *V, end of Apácai Csere János u. just north of Erzsébet Bridge.*

★ ⓭ **Nagy Zsinagóga** (Great Synagogue). Europe's largest synagogue was built between 1844 and 1859 in a Byzantine-Moorish style. Desecrated by German and Hungarian Nazis, it underwent years of massive restorations, completed in the fall of 1996. Liszt and Saint-Saëns are among the great musicians who once played the synagogue's grand organ. ✉ *VII, Dohány u. 2–8,* ☎ *1/342–1335.* ⏲ *Mid-Mar.–Nov., Mon.–Thurs. 10–5, Fri. 10–3, Sun. 10–1. Closed Jewish holidays.*

★ ⓯ **Néprajzi Múzeum** (Museum of Ethnography). Elegant both inside and out, this museum has impressive, exhaustive exhibits—captioned in English—of folk costumes and traditions. ✉ *V, Kossuth Lajos tér 12,* ☎ *1/332–6340,* WEB *www.neprajz.hu.* ⏲ *Mar.–Oct., Tues.–Sun. 10–6; Nov.–Feb., Tues.–Sun. 10–5.*

14 **Országház** (Parliament). The riverfront's most striking landmark is the imposing neo-Gothic Parliament, now minus the red star on top, designed by Imre Steindl. Although it is still a workplace for the nation's legislators, the interior can now be seen during regular guided tours that show off the gilded cathedral ceilings, frescoed walls, intricate glass windows, and majestic stairways (of which there are some 20 km in the building!). The highlight is the nation's Holy Crown, made for Hungary's first king, St. Stephen, 1,000 years ago. The crown, Hungary's national symbol, was relocated from the National Museum and now rests on a velvet pillow flanked by two sword-wielding uniformed guards under Parliament's soaring central cupola. One-hour tours in English are held daily at 10 and 2. Purchase tickets at Gate X, to the right of the main entrance steps. You are advised to arrive at least a half-hour early. ✉ *V, Kossuth Lajos tér,* ☎ *1/441–4904 or 1/441–4415,* WEB *www.mkogy.hu.* ⏲ *Weekdays 8–6, Sat. 8–4, Sun. 8–2.*

6 **Roosevelt tér** (Roosevelt Square). On this picturesque square opening onto the Danube you'll find the 19th-century neoclassical **Magyar Tudományos Akadémia** (Hungarian Academy of Sciences) and the 1907 **Gresham Palota** (Gresham Palace), a crumbling tribute to the age of Art Nouveau currently undergoing massive renovations and eventually to become a Four Seasons hotel. ✉ *V, at Pest end of Széchenyi lánchíd (Chain Bridge).*

★ **Széchenyi lánchíd** (Chain Bridge). The most beautiful of the Danube's eight bridges, the Széchenyi lánchíd was built twice: once in the 19th century and again after it was destroyed by the Nazis. ✉ *Spanning the Danube between I, Clark Ádám tér, and V, Roosevelt tér.*

16 **Szent István Bazilika** (St. Stephen's Basilica). Dark and massive, the 19th-century basilica is one of the landmarks of Pest. It was planned early in the 19th century as a neoclassical building, but by the time it was completed more than 50 years later, it was decidedly neo-Renaissance. The mummified right hand of St. Stephen, Hungary's first king and patron saint, is preserved in the Szent Jobb Chapel; the guard will illuminate it for you for a minimal charge. A climb up to the cupola (or a lift on the elevator) affords a sweeping city view. Restorations are under way, with a target completion date of 2005, so some part of the structure is likely to be under scaffolding when you visit. ✉ *V, Szt. István tér,* ☎ *1/317–2859.* ⏲ *Church Mon.–Sat. 7–7, Sun 1–7. Szt. Jobb Chapel Apr.–Sept., Mon.–Sat. 9–5; Oct.–Mar., Mon.–Sat. 10–4. Cupola mid-Apr.–Oct., daily 10–5.*

9 **Váci utca** (Váci Street). Lined with expensive boutiques and dozens of souvenir shops, this pedestrian-only thoroughfare is Budapest's most upscale shopping street and one of its most kitschy tourist areas. Váci utca stretches south of Kossuth Lajos utca, making the total length extend from Vörösmarty tér to the Szabadság Bridge. ✉ *V, south from Vörösmarty tér.*

8 **Vigadó tér** (Vigadó Square). This square, opening onto a grand Danube view, is named for the **Vigadó concert hall**. The hall was built in an eclectic mix of Byzantine, Moorish, and Romanesque styles; the facade even draws upon the ceremonial knots from the uniforms of the Hungarian hussars. Liszt, Brahms, and Bartók all performed here. Completely destroyed during World War II, it has been faithfully rebuilt. ✉ *V, off the Korzó, between Vigadó u. and Deák Ferenc u.*

7 **Vörösmarty tér** (Vörösmarty Square). In this handsome square in the heart of the Inner City, street musicians and sidewalk cafés combine to make one of the liveliest, albeit sometimes too touristy, atmospheres in Budapest. It's a great spot to sit and relax—but prepare to be approached by caricature artists and money changers. ✉ *V, at northern end of Váci u.*

Hösök Tere and Városliget

Heroes' Square is the gateway to Városliget (City Park): a square km (almost ½ square mi) of recreation, entertainment, nature, and culture.

18 **Hösök tere** (Heroes' Square). Budapest's grandest boulevard, Andrássy út, ends at this sweeping piazza flanked by the Szépművészeti Múzeum and the Műcsarnok. In the center stands the 120-ft bronze **Millennium Emlékmű** (Millennium Monument), begun in 1896 to commemorate the 1,000th anniversary of the Magyar Conquest. Statues of Árpád and six other founders of the Magyar nation occupy the base of the monument, while Hungary's greatest rulers and princes stand between the columns on either side. ✉ *VI, Andrássy út at Dózsa György út.*

20 **Műcsarnok** (Palace of Exhibitions). This striking 1895 structure on Heroes' Square schedules exhibitions of contemporary Hungarian and international art and a rich series of films, plays, and concerts. ✉ *XIV, Dózsa György út 37,* ☎ *1/343–7401,* WEB *www.mucsarnok.hu.* ⏲ *Tues.–Sun. 10–6.*

19 **Szépművészeti Múzeum** (Fine Arts Museum). An entire section of this Heroes' Square museum is devoted to Egyptian, Greek, and Roman artifacts, including many rare Greco-Roman ceramics. The institution's collection of Spanish paintings is among the best of its kind outside Spain. Some wings are undergoing long-term renovation and may be closed when you visit. ✉ *XIV, Dózsa György út 41,* ☎ *1/343–9759,* WEB *www.szepmuveszeti.hu.* ⏲ *Tues.–Sun. 10–5:30.*

★ **Városliget** (City Park). Just behind Heroes' Square, this park harbors Budapest's zoo, the state circus, an amusement park, and the outdoor swimming pool of the Széchenyi mineral baths. Inside is **Vajdahunyad Vár** (Vajdahunyad Castle), an art historian's Disneyland, created for the millennial celebration in 1896 and incorporating architectural elements typical of various periods of Hungary's history all in one complex. ✉ *XIV, between Dózsa György út and Hungária körút, and Vágány u. and Ajtósi Dürer sor.*

Elsewhere in the City

Aquincum. The reconstructed remains of the capital of the Roman province of Pannonia, dating from the 1st century AD, lie in northern Budapest's Óbuda district. A varied selection of artifacts and mosaics has been unearthed, giving a tantalizing inkling of what life was like on the northern fringes of the Roman empire. The on-site **Aquincum Museum** displays the dig's most notable finds. ✉ *III, Szentendrei út 139,* ☎ *1/250–1650.* ⏲ *Mid-Apr.–late Apr. and Oct., Tues.–Sun. 10–5; May–Sept., Tues.–Sun. 10–6. Grounds open at 9.*

Jánoshegy (János Hill). A *libegő* (chairlift) will take you to the summit, the highest point in Budapest, where you can climb a lookout tower for the best view of the city. ✉ *Take Bus 158 from Moszkva tér to last stop, Zugligeti út,* ☎ *1/200–9993 or 1/394–3764.* ⏲ *Mid-May–mid-Sept., daily 9–5; mid-Sept.–mid-May (depending on weather), daily 9:30–4. Closed alternate Mon.*

Szobor Park (Statue Park). For a look at Budapest's too-recent Iron Curtain past, make the 30-minute drive out to this open-air exhibit cleverly nicknamed "Tons of Socialism." Forty-two Communist statues and memorials that once dominated the city have been exiled here since the political changes in 1989. You can wander among mammoth figures of Lenin and Marx while listening to songs from the Hungarian and Russian workers' movement blaring from loudspeakers. To get here by public transport, take the yellow Volánbus from stall 6 at Kosztolányi Dezső tér. ✉ *XXII, Balatoni út, corner of Szabadkai út,* ☎ FAX *1/227–7446,* WEB *www.szoborpark.hu.* ⏲ *Daily 10–dusk.*

Dining

Private restaurateurs are breathing excitement into the Budapest dining scene. You can choose from Chinese, Mexican, Italian, French, Indian, or various other cuisines—there are even vegetarian restaurants. Or you can stick to solid, traditional Hungarian fare. Be sure to check out the less expensive spots favored by locals. If you get a craving for sushi or tortellini, consult the restaurant listings in the *Budapest Sun, Where Budapest* magazine, and *Budapest in Your Pocket.* For details and price-category definitions, *see* Dining *in* Hungary A to Z, *above.*

$$$$ ★ ✕ **Gundel.** George Lang, Hungary's best-known restaurateur, showcases his country's cuisine at this turn-of-the-20th-century palazzo in City Park. Dark-wood paneling, rich navy-blue and pink fabrics, and tables set with Zsolnay porcelain make the oversize dining room plush and handsome. Violinist György Lakatos, of the Lakatos Gypsy musician dynasty, strolls from table to table playing folk music. Waiters in black tie serve traditional favorites such as tender beef tournedos topped with goose liver and forest mushroom sauce or excellent fish specialties. ✉ *XIV, Állatkerti út 2,* ☎ *1/321–3550. Reservations essential. AE, DC, MC, V. Closed daily 4–6:30.*

$$$$ ✕ **Vadrózsa.** This restaurant in a romantic old villa in Buda's exclusive Rózsadomb district is elegant to the last detail—even the service is white glove—and the garden is delightful in summer. Kitchen fortes include venison and a variety of grilled fish; the house specialty is grilled goose liver. ✉ *II, Pentelei Molnár u. 15,* ☎ *1/326–5817. Reservations essential. AE, DC, MC, V. Closed daily 3–7.*

$$$–$$$$ ✕ **Múzeum.** Named for its location just steps from the National Museum, this elegant salon with mirrors, mosaics, and swift waiters serves authentic Hungarian cuisine with a lighter touch. The salads are fresh, the Hungarian wines excellent, and the chef dares to be creative. ✉ *VIII, Múzeum körút 12,* ☎ *1/267–0375. DC, MC, V. Closed Sun.*

$$–$$$$ ✕ **Kacsa.** Hungarian and international dishes with a focus on duck are done with a light touch, with quiet chamber music in the background, in this small, celebrated restaurant just a few steps from the river. Try the crisp wild duck stuffed with plums. ✉ *II, Fő u. 75,* ☎ *1/201–9992. Reservations essential. AE, DC, MC, V. Closed daily 3–6. No lunch weekends.*

$$–$$$ ★ ✕ **Lou Lou.** Since it opened in 1995, this convivial bistro tucked onto a side street near the Danube has been the hottest restaurant in Budapest. Framed prints, low lighting, and candles conjure a tasteful, elegantly romantic atmosphere. Blending local and Continental cuisines, the menu includes excellent rack of lamb and succulent fresh salmon with lemongrass. ✉ *V, Vigyázó Ferenc u. 4,* ☎ *1/312–4505. Reservations essential. AE. Closed daily 3–6:30 and Sun. No lunch Sat.*

$$–$$$ ✕ **Művészinas.** This bustling, bistrolike restaurant in the heart of Pest has a romantic, old-world ambience. Dozens of Hungarian specialties fill the long menu, from sirloin "Budapest style" (smothered in a goose liver, mushrooms, and sweet-pepper ragout) to spinach-stuffed turkey breast in fragrant garlic sauce. Crepes with a seasonal fruit sauce are a sublime dessert. ✉ *VI, Bajcsy-Zsilinszky út 9,* ☎ *1/268–1439. Reservations essential. AE, MC, V.*

$$ ✕ **Bagolyvár.** George Lang opened this restaurant next door to his gastronomic palace, Gundel, in 1993. The immaculate dining room with soaring beamed ceilings has a familial yet professional atmosphere, and the kitchen produces first-rate daily menus of home-style Hungarian specialties. Soups are particularly good. Musicians entertain with cimbalom (gypsy dulcimer) music nightly from 7 PM. In warm weather there is outdoor dining on a roomy back patio. ✉ *VI, Állatkerti körút 2,* ☎ *1/343–0217. AE, DC, MC, V.*

$$ ✕ **Kisbuda Gyöngye.** This Budapest favorite, hidden away on a small street in Óbuda, is filled with mixed antique furniture, and its walls are covered with a patchwork of antique carved wooden cupboard doors. Try the fresh trout smothered in cream sauce with mushrooms and capers. ✉ *III, Kenyeres u. 34,* ☎ *1/368–6402 or 1/368–9246. Reservations essential. AE, DC, MC, V. Closed Sun.*

$–$$ ★ ✕ **Café Kör.** Vaulted ceilings, low lighting, and wood floors with Oriental-style rugs render a warm and classy atmosphere. Service is excellent. The kitchen has won tremendous popularity for its lighter touch on Hungarian and Continental meat dishes and ample salads. The Kör appetizer platter, generously piled with pâtés, Brie, vegetables, goose liver, salmon, and more, is perfect for sharing. Avoid the tables by the bathroom doors and immediately at the entrance. ✉ *V, Sas u. 17,* ☎ *1/311–0053. Reservations essential. No credit cards. Closed Sun.*

$–$$ ★ ✕ **Náncsi Néni.** "Aunt Nancy's" out-of-the-way restaurant is irresistibly cozy. The dining room feels like a country kitchen: chains of paprikas and garlic dangle from the low wooden ceiling, and shelves along the walls are crammed with jars of home-pickled vegetables. On the Hungarian menu (large portions!), turkey dishes are given a creative flair, such as breast fillets stuffed with apples, peaches, mushrooms, cheese, and sour cream. Special touches include an outdoor garden in summer and free champagne for all couples in love. Reservations are recommended. ✉ *II, Ördögárok út 80,* ☎ *1/397–2742. MC, V.*

$ ✕ **Tüköry Söröző.** At this traditional Hungarian spot, carnivores can sample the beefsteak tartare, topped with a raw egg; many say it's the best in town. ✉ *V, Hold u. 15,* ☎ *1/269–5027. AE, MC, V. Closed weekends.*

Lodging

Some 30 million tourists come to Hungary every year, and the boom has encouraged hotel building; several major new luxury properties are currently under construction in Budapest's best locales. If you arrive in Budapest without a reservation, go to the 24-hour Tribus Hotel Service or to one of the tourist offices at any of the train stations or at the airport. For details and price-category definitions, *see* Lodging *in* Hungary A to Z, *above*.

$$$$ ★ **Budapest Hilton.** Built in 1977 around a 13th-century monastery adjacent to the Matthias Church, this perfectly integrated architectural wonder overlooks the Danube from the best site on Castle Hill. Every ample room has a remarkable view. Service is of the highest caliber. ✉ *I, Hess András tér 1–3, H-1014,* ☎ *1/488–6600; 800/445–8667 in U.S. and Canada,* FAX *1/488–6688,* WEB *www.danubiusgroup.com/hilton. 295 rooms, 27 suites. 3 restaurants, air-conditioning. AE, DC, MC, V.*

$$$$ ★ **Hotel Inter-Continental Budapest.** Formerly the Forum Hotel, this boxy, modern riverside hotel consistently wins applause for its superior business facilities, friendly service, and gorgeous views across the Danube to Castle Hill. Sixty percent of the rooms face the river (and are slightly more expensive than those that don't). The hotel café, Bécsi

Kávéház, is locally renowned for its pastries—and the fitness facilities are similarly excellent. ✉ *V, Apáczai Csere János u. 12–14, H-1368,* ☎ *1/327–6333 or 800/327–0200 (in the U.S.),* FAX *1/327–6357,* WEB *www.interconti.com. 382 rooms, 16 suites. 2 restaurants, air-conditioning, pool. AE, DC, MC, V.*

$$$$ ★ **Kempinski Hotel Corvinus Budapest.** Afternoon chamber music sets the tone at this sleek luxury hotel. Rooms are spacious, with elegant contemporary decor accented by geometric blond-and-black Swedish inlaid woods. The large, sparkling bathrooms are the best in Budapest. ✉ *V, Erzsébet tér 7–8, H-1051,* ☎ *1/429–3777; 800/426–3135 in the U.S. and Canada,* FAX *1/429–4777,* WEB *www.kempinski-budapest.com. 340 rooms, 29 suites. 4 restaurants, air-conditioning, pool. AE, DC, MC, V.*

$$$$ ★ **Le Meridien Budapest.** From Persian carpets and heavy silk draperies in the hushed lobby to polished walnut surfaces and twinkling chandeliers in the guest rooms, refined Old World elegance is everywhere. In a 1913 historic landmark building in the heart of downtown Pest, this five-star hotel is well situated for business as well as sightseeing. Breakfast and afternoon high tea are served under the lobby's soaring stained-glass cupola. ✉ *V, Erzsébet tér 9–10, H-1051,* ☎ *1/429–5500; 800/225–5843 in the U.S. and Canada,* FAX *1/429–5555,* WEB *www.lemeridien-hotels.com. 192 rooms, 26 suites. Restaurant, air-conditioning, pool. AE, DC, MC, V.*

$$$ **art'otel.** A short walk up the Danube from the Chain Bridge, this hip new boutique hotel is the first of its kind in Budapest. Like its sibling properties in Berlin and Dresden, the hotel-cum-gallery is completely dedicated to the work of a single artist—in this case, American Donald Sultan. From the carpets to the paintings, the teacups to the bathrobes, the entire hotel is decorated with Sultan's designs. Interconnecting a new building and four 18th-century Baroque houses on the Buda riverfront, the art'otel adroitly blends old and new. Sleek contemporary furniture contrasts elegantly with restored original moldings and doorframes in the older buildings' rooms. Rates include breakfast. ✉ *I, Bem rakpart 16–19, H-1011,* ☎ *1/487–9487,* FAX *1/487–9488,* WEB *www.parkplazaww.com. 156 rooms, 9 suites. Restaurant, air-conditioning. AE, DC, MC, V.*

$$$ **Budapest Marriott.** At this sophisticated yet friendly hotel near downtown Pest, every detail sparkles, including the marble floors and dark-wood paneling in the lobby. Stunning vistas open from every guest room, the ballroom, and even the outstanding fitness room. Most rooms have a balcony. ✉ *V, Apáczai Csere János u. 4, H-1052,* ☎ *1/266–7000; 800/228–9290 in U.S. and Canada,* FAX *1/266–5000,* WEB *www.marriotthotels.com/BUDHU. 351 rooms, 11 suites. 3 restaurants, air-conditioning. AE, DC, MC, V.*

$$$ **Danubius Grand Hotel.** Set on a car-free island in the Danube and connected to a bubbling thermal spa (free for guests), the Danubius (formerly Ramada) Grand feels removed from the city but is still only a short taxi or bus ride away. This venerable hotel, built in 1873, has been completely modernized, yet retains its period look, with high ceilings and Old World furnishings. Room prices include breakfast. ✉ *XIII, Margit-sziget, H-1138,* ☎ *1/452–6200; 1/452–6251 reservations,* FAX *1/452–6262,* WEB *www.danubiusgroup.com/grand. 154 rooms, 10 suites. Restaurant, pool. AE, DC, MC, V.*

$$$ **Danubius Hotel Gellért.** Built in 1918 in the Jugendstil (Art Nouveau style), this grand old lady with its double-deck rotunda sits regally at the foot of Gellért Hill. One of Hungary's most prized spa hotels, it also houses ornate thermal baths—free to guests. Rooms range from palatial suites to tiny spaces and have either early 20th-century furnishings or newer, more basic contemporary decor. Rooms that face the building's inner core are drastically less expensive but cramped and

viewless. The Gellért has begun an ambitious overhaul, adding air-conditioning and refurnishing all rooms in the mood of the building's original style. Inquire about completed rooms when you reserve. Breakfast is included in the room rates. ✉ *XI, Gellért tér 1, H-1111,* ☎ *1/385–2200,* FAX *1/466–6631,* WEB *www.danubiusgroup.com/gellert. 220 rooms, 13 suites. Restaurant, 2 pools. AE, DC, MC, V.*

$$ **Astoria.** Revolutionaries and intellectuals once gathered in the marble-and-gilt Art Deco lobby here. Rooms are Empire-style and renovations have not obscured their charm. In fact, the addition of soundproofing was essential, as the Astoria stands at a busy downtown intersection. Breakfast is included. ✉ *V, Kossuth Lajos u. 19–21, H-1053,* ☎ *1/317–3411,* FAX *1/318–6798,* WEB *www.danubiusgroup.com/astoria. 124 rooms, 5 suites. Restaurant. AE, DC, MC, V.*

$$ **Carlton Budapest.** Tucked into an alleyway at the foot of Castle Hill, this spotless, modern hotel (formerly the Alba Hotel) is a short walk via the Chain Bridge from business and shopping districts. Rooms are snug and quiet, with white and pale-gray contemporary decor and quintessentially Budapestian views over rooftops and chimneys. A buffet breakfast is included in the room price. ✉ *I, Apor Péter u. 3, H-1011,* ☎ *1/224–0999,* FAX *1/224–0990. 50 rooms with bath, 45 with shower. Air-conditioning. AE, DC, MC, V.*

$$ ★ **Victoria.** The stately Parliament building is visible from every room of this intimate establishment right on the Danube. The absence of conventioneers is a plus, and the location—an easy walk from Castle Hill and downtown Pest—couldn't be better. Room rates include breakfast. ✉ *I, Bem rakpart 11, H-1011,* ☎ *1/457–8080,* FAX *1/457–8088,* WEB *www.victoria.hu. 27 rooms, 1 suite. AE, DC, MC, V.*

$ ★ **Kulturinnov.** One wing of a magnificent 1902 neo-Baroque castle now houses basic budget accommodations. Rooms come with two or three beds and are clean and peaceful; breakfast is included in the rates. The neighborhood—one of Budapest's most famous squares in the luxurious castle district—is magical. ✉ *I, Szentháromság tér 6, H-1014,* ☎ *1/355–0122,* FAX *1/375–1886. 16 rooms. AE, DC, MC, V.*

$ **Molnár Panzió.** Fresh air, peace, and quiet reign at this immaculate guest house high above Buda on Széchenyi Hill. Rooms in the octagonal main house are polyhedral, clean, and bright; most have distant views of Castle Hill and Gellért Hill, and some have balconies. Twelve rooms in a building next door are more private and have superior bathrooms. Service is friendly and professional, and the restaurant is first rate. A Finnish sauna and garden setting add to the pension's appeal. ✉ *XII, Fodor u. 143, H-1124,* ☎ *1/395–1873 or 1/395–1874,* ☎ FAX *1/395–1872,* WEB *www.hotel-molnar.hu. 23 rooms. Restaurant. AE, DC, MC, V.*

Nightlife and the Arts

The Arts

The English-language *Budapest Sun* lists some of the week's entertainment and cultural events. *Where Budapest,* free in most hotels, is a slightly richer source. Hotels and tourist offices distribute the monthly *Programme,* which contains details of all cultural events in the city. Buy tickets at venue box offices, your hotel desk, many tourist offices, or ticket agencies. For music in Budapest, try the **National Philharmonic Ticket Office** (✉ V, Mérleg u. 10, ☎ 1/318–0281). For various cultural events in Budapest, contact the **Vigadó Ticket Office** (✉ V, Vörösmarty tér 1, ☎ 1/327–4322).

Arts festivals begin to fill the calendar in early spring. The season's first and biggest, the **Budapest Spring Festival** (early to mid-March), showcases Hungary's best opera, music, theater, fine arts, and dance, as well as visiting foreign artists. The weeklong **BudaFest** opera and ballet festival (mid-August) takes place at the Opera House. Information and tickets are available from ticket agencies.

CONCERTS AND MUSICALS

Several excellent orchestras, such as the Budapest Festival Orchestra, are based in Budapest. Concerts frequently include works by Hungarian composers Bartók, Kodály, and Liszt. **Liszt Ferenc Zeneakadémia** (Franz Liszt Academy of Music; ✉ VI, Liszt Ferenc tér 8, ☎ 1/342–0179 or 1/341–4788) is Budapest's premier classical concert venue; orchestra and chamber music performances take place in its splendid main hall. Classical concerts are also held at the **Pesti Vigadó** (Pest Concert Hall; ✉ V, Vigadó tér 2, ☎ 1/327–4322). The **Régi Zeneakadémia** (Old Academy of Music; ✉ VI, Vörösmarty u. 35, ☎ 1/322–9804) is a smaller venue for chamber music. The 1896 **Vígszínház** (Comedy Theater; ✉ XIII, Pannónia út 1, ☎ 1/329–2340) presents mostly musicals. Operettas and Hungarian renditions of popular Broadway musicals are staged at the **Operett Színház** (Operetta Theater; ✉ VI, Nagymező u. 19, ☎ 1/269–3870).

OPERA AND DANCE

Budapest has two opera houses, one of which is the gorgeous neo-Renaissance **Magyar Állami Operaház** (Hungarian State Opera House; ✉ VI, Andrássy út 22, ☎ 1/353–0170), also the city's main venue for classical ballet. There's also the plainer **Erkel Színház** (Erkel Theater; ✉ VIII, Köztársaság tér, ☎ 1/333–0540).

The young **Trafó Kortárs Művészetek Háza** (Trafo House of Contemporary Arts; ✉ IX, Liliom u. 41, ☎ 1/456–2044) has become the hub of Budapest's modern and avant-garde dance and music productions. From May through September, displays of Hungarian folk dancing take place at the **Folklór Centrum** (Folklore Center; ✉ XI, Fehérvári út 47, ☎ 1/203–3868). The Hungarian State Folk Ensemble performs regularly at the **Budai Vigadó** (✉ I, Corvin tér 8, ☎ 1/225–1012). There are regular participatory folk-dance evenings—with instructions for beginners—at district cultural centers; consult the entertainment listings of *Where Budapest* and *Programme* for schedules and locations, or check with a hotel concierge.

Nightlife

Budapest is a lively city by night. Establishments stay open well past midnight, and Western European–style bars and British-style pubs have sprung up all over the city. For quiet conversation, hotel bars are a good choice, but beware of the inflated prices. Expect to pay cash for your night on the town. The city also has its share of seedy go-go clubs and "cabarets," some of which have been shut down for scandalously excessive billing and physical intimidation and assault. Avoid places where women lingering nearby "invite" you in, and never order without first seeing the price.

BARS

The most popular of Budapest's Irish pubs and a favorite expat watering hole is **Becketts** (✉ V, Bajcsy-Zsilinszky út 72, ☎ 1/311–1035, ⏲ Mon.–Fri. 5 PM–1 or 2 AM, Sat.–Sun. noon–1 or 2 AM), where Guinness flows amid polished-wood and brass decor. A hip, low-key crowd mingles at the stylish **Café Incognito** (✉ VI, Liszt Ferenc tér 3, ☎ 1/342–1471, ⏲ Mon.–Fri. 10 AM–midnight, Sat.–Sun. noon–midnight), with low lighting and funky music kept at a conversation-friendly volume by savvy DJs. **Café Pierrot** (✉ I, Fortuna u. 14, ☎ 1/375–6971) is an elegant café and piano bar on a small street on Castle Hill. The stylish, new **Vörös és Fehér** (VI, Andrássy út 41, ☎ 1/413–1545) wine bar, opened by the Budapest Wine Society, is the perfect place to taste Hungary's exceptional (and inexpensive) wines by the glass.

CASINOS

Most casinos are open daily from 2 PM until 4 or 5 AM and offer gambling in hard currency—usually dollars—only. You must be 18 to enter a casino in Hungary. The popular **Las Vegas Casino** (✉ V, Roosevelt tér 2, ☎ 1/317–6022) is centrally located in the Atrium Hyatt Hotel. In an 1879 building designed by the architect Miklós Ybl, who also designed the Hungarian State Opera House, the **Várkert Casino** (✉ I, Miklós Ybl tér 9, ☎ 1/202–4244) is the most attractive in the city.

JAZZ AND DANCE CLUBS

Established Hungarian headliners and young up-and-comers perform nightly at the **Jazz Garden** (✉ V, Veres Pálné u. 44/a, ☎ 1/266–7364). Shows start at 8:30 PM; there is a 500-Ft. cover charge.

With wrought-iron and maroon-velvet decor, the stylish but unpretentious **Fél 10 Jazz Club** (✉ VIII, Baross u. 30, ☎ 06/60–318–467) has a dance floor and two bars on three open levels. A welcoming, gay-friendly crowd flocks to late-night hot spot **Café Capella** (✉ V, Belgrád rakpart 23, ☎ 1/318–6231) for glittery drag shows (held nightly) and DJ'd club music. It's open Sun.–Thurs. 9 PM to 4 AM, and Fri.–Sat. until 5 AM. There's a 500-Ft. drink minimum every night, plus a cover charge (500 Ft. Wed.–Thurs. and Sun., 1,000 Ft. Fri.–Sat.; Mon.–Tues. no cover).

Shopping

You'll find plenty of expensive boutiques, folk art and souvenir shops, and classical record shops on or around **Váci utca,** Budapest's pedestrian-only promenade. Browsing among some of the smaller, less touristy, more typically Hungarian shops in Pest—on the **Kiskörút** (Small Ring Boulevard) and **Nagykörút** (Great Ring Boulevard)—may prove more interesting and less pricey. Artsy boutiques are springing up in the section of district V south of Ferenciek tere toward the Danube and around Kálvin tér. **Falk Miksa utca,** north of Parliament, is home to some of the city's best antiques stores. You'll also encounter Transylvanian women dressed in colorful folk costume standing on busy sidewalks selling their own handmade embroideries and ceramics at rock-bottom prices. Look for them at **Moszkva tér, Jászai Mari tér,** outside the **Kossuth tér Metro,** and around **Váci utca.**

For a Hungarian take on a most American concept, you can visit one of the many mega-malls springing up around the city. **Mammut** (✉ II, Lövőház u. 2–6, ☎ 1/345–8020) is in central Buda. It's open Monday–Saturday 10 AM–9 PM, Sunday 10–6. The **West End** (✉ Váci út 1–3, ☎ 1/238–7777), behind Nyugati train station in downtown Pest, comes complete with a waterfall and a T.G.I. Friday's restaurant. Hours are Sunday–Thursday 8 AM–1 AM, Friday–Saturday 8 AM–2 AM.

A good place for special gifts, **Holló Műhely** (✉ V, Vitkovics Mihály u. 12, ☎ 1/317–8103) sells the work of László Holló, a master wood craftsman who has resurrected traditional motifs and styles of earlier centuries. There are lovely hope chests, chairs, jewelry boxes, candlesticks, and more, all hand-carved and hand-painted with cheery folk motifs—a predominance of birds and flowers in reds, blues, and greens.

Stores specializing in Hungary's excellent wines have become a trend in Budapest. Among the best of them is the store run by the **Budapest Bortársaság** (Budapest Wine Society; ✉ I, Batthyány u. 59, ☎ 1/212–0262). The cellar shop, at the base of Castle Hill, always has an excellent selection of Hungary's finest wines, chosen by the wine society's discerning staff, who will happily help you with your purchases. Tastings are held Saturday afternoons from 2 to 5.

Markets

The magnificent, cavernous, three-story **Vásárcsarnok** (Central Market Hall; ✉ IX, Vámház körút 1–3) teems with shoppers browsing among stalls packed with salamis, red paprika chains, and other enticements. Upstairs you can buy folk embroideries and souvenirs.

A good way to find bargains (and adventure) is to make an early morning trip out to **Ecseri Piac** (✉ IX, Nagykőrösi út; take Bus 54 from Boráros tér), a vast, colorful, chaotic flea market on the outskirts of Budapest. Try to go Saturday morning, when the most vendors are out. Foreigners are a favorite target for overcharging, so be tough when bargaining.

Budapest Essentials

AIR TRAVEL TO AND FROM BUDAPEST

The only nonstop service between Budapest and the United States is aboard Malév.

➤ AIRLINES AND CONTACTS: **Malév** (☏ 06/40–212–121 toll free; 1/235–3804 sales and information).

AIRPORTS AND TRANSFERS

Hungary's international airport, Ferihegy is about 22 km (14 mi) southeast of the city. All Malév flights operate from Terminal 2a; other airlines use the new Terminal 2b. For same-day flight information call the airport authority, where automated information is available in English.

Minibuses marked LRI CENTRUM-AIRPORT-CENTRUM leave every half hour from 5:30 AM to 9:30 PM for Erzsébet tér (in front of the Kempinski Hotel) in downtown Budapest. The trip takes 30–40 minutes and costs around 900 Ft. The modern minivans of the reliable LRI Airport Shuttle take you to any destination in Budapest, door to door, for around 2,000 Ft., even less than the least expensive taxi—and most employees speak English. At the airport buy tickets at the LRI counter in the arrivals hall near baggage claim; for your return trip call ahead for a pick-up. There are also approved Airport Taxi stands outside both terminals, with fixed rates based on which district you are going to. The cost to the central districts is about 4,800 Ft. Going to the airport, the cost is 3,000 Ft. from Pest, 3,500 Ft. from Buda; call one day ahead to arrange for a pick-up.

➤ AIRPORT INFORMATION: **Airport Taxi** (☏ 1/341–0000). **Ferihegy** (☏ 1/296–9696; airport authority ☏ 1/296–7155). **LRI Airport Shuttle** (☏ 1/296–8555 or 1/296–6283).

BIKE TRAVEL

On Margaret Island in Budapest, Bringóvár rents four-wheeled pedaled contraptions called *Bringóhintós,* as well as traditional two-wheelers; mountain bikes cost about 850 Ft. per hour, 2,500 Ft. for 24 hours. One-speeders cost less. For more information about renting in Budapest, contact Tourism Office of Budapest.

➤ BIKE RENTALS: **Bringóvár** (✉ Hajós Alfréd sétány 1, across from the Thermal Hotel, ☏ 1/329–2746). **Tourism Office of Budapest** (✉ VI, Liszt Ferenc tér 11, ☏ 1/322–4098 or 1/342–9390).

BUS TRAVEL TO AND FROM BUDAPEST

Most buses to Budapest from the western region of Hungary and from Vienna arrive at Erzsébet tér station downtown. The station is likely to be relocated some time in 2002; check with Tourinform for details.

➤ BUS INFORMATION: **Erzsébet tér station** (✉ V, Erzsébet tér, ☏ 1/317–2966).

CAR TRAVEL

The main routes into Budapest are the M1 from Vienna (via Győr), the M5 from Kecskemét, the M3 from near Gyöngyös, and the M7 from the Balaton region.

EMERGENCIES

➤ DOCTORS AND DENTISTS: **R-Klinika** (☎ 1/325–9999 private English-speaking).
➤ EMERGENCY SERVICES: **Ambulance** (☎ 104; 1/200–0100 private English-speaking). **Police** (☎ 107).
➤ 24-HOUR PHARMACIES: **Gyógyszertár** (☎ 1/311–4439 in Pest; 1/355–4691 in Buda).

ENGLISH-LANGUAGE MEDIA

➤ BOOKSTORES: **Bestsellers** (✉ V, Október 6 u. 11, ☎ 1/312–1295). **Central European University Academic Bookshop** (✉ V, Nádor u. 9, ☎ 1/327–3096).

TAXIS

Taxis are plentiful and are a good value, but be careful to avoid the also plentiful rogue cabbies. The city of Budapest recently established a tariff ceiling for taxi drivers. For a hassle-free ride, avoid unmarked "freelance" taxis; stick with those affiliated with an established company. Rather than hailing a taxi in the street, your safest bet is to order one by phone; a car will arrive in about 5 to 10 minutes. The average initial charge for taxis ordered by phone is 250 Ft., to which is added about 200 Ft. per kilometer (½ mi) plus 50 Ft. per minute of waiting time. The best rates are offered by Citytaxi and Főtaxi.
➤ TAXI COMPANIES: **Citytaxi** (☎ 1/211–1111; English spoken). **Főtaxi** (☎ 1/222–2222).

TOURS

IBUSZ Travel, Cityrama, and Budapest Tourist organize a number of unusual tours, including horseback riding, bicycling, and angling, as well as visits to the National Gallery. These companies provide personal guides on request. Also check at your hotel's reception desk. The Chosen Tours offers an excellent three-hour combination bus and walking tour (about $17, hotel pick-up and drop-off included), Budapest Through Jewish Eyes, highlighting the sights and cultural life of the city's Jewish community.
➤ FEES AND SCHEDULES: **Chosen Tours** (☎ FAX 1/355–2202).

BOAT TOURS

From April through October, boats leave from the quay at Vigadó tér on 1½-hour cruises between the railroad bridges north and south of the Árpád and Petőfi bridges, respectively. The trip, organized by MAHART Tours, runs only on weekends and holidays until late April, then once or twice a day, depending on the season; the trip costs around 900 Ft.
➤ FEES AND SCHEDULES: **MAHART Tours** (☎ 1/318–1704).

BUS TOURS

Cityrama offers a three-hour city bus tour (about 6,000 Ft. per person). Year-round, IBUSZ Travel sponsors three-hour bus tours of the city that cost about 6,000 Ft; starting from Erzsébet tér, they take in parts of both Buda and Pest. Specify whether you prefer live or recorded commentary.
➤ FEES AND SCHEDULES: **Cityrama** (✉ V, Báthori u. 22, ☎ 1/302–4382 or 1/331–0043).

SINGLE-DAY TOURS

Excursions farther afield include daylong trips to the Puszta (Great Plain), the Danube Bend, the Eger wine region, and Lake Balaton. IBUSZ Travel offers trips to the Buda Hills and stays in many of Hungary's historic castles and mansions.

TRAIN TRAVEL

Call the MÁV Passenger Service for train information. Call one of the three main train stations in Budapest for information during off-hours (8 PM–6 AM): Déli, Keleti, and Nyugati. Trains for Vienna usually depart from Keleti station, those for Lake Balaton from Déli.

➤ TRAIN INFORMATION: **Déli** (Southern; ✉ XII, Alkotás u., ☎ 1/375–6293). **Keleti** (Eastern; ✉ VII, Rákóczi út, ☎ 1/313–6835). **Nyugati** (Western; ✉ V, Nyugati tér, ☎ 1/349–0115).

TRANSPORTATION AROUND BUDAPEST

Budapest is best explored on foot. The maps provided by tourist offices are not very detailed, so arm yourself with one from any of the bookshops in Váci utca or from a stationery shop or newsstand.

Roman-numeral prefixes in Budapest street addresses refer to one of the city's 22 districts. Full postal addresses do not cite a Roman numeral, as the district is indicated by the zip code. Getting around is easier if you learn a few basic terms: *utca* (abbreviated *u.*) and *út,* which mean "street" and "road" or "avenue," respectively; *tér* or *tere* (square); and *körút* (ring road).

The Budapest Transportation Authority (BKV) runs the public transportation system—the Metro (subway) with three lines, buses, streetcars, and trolleybuses—and it's cheap, efficient, and simple to use. Most of it closes down around 11:30 PM, but certain trams and buses run on a limited schedule all night. A *napijegy* (day ticket) costs about 800 Ft. (a *turista-jegy,* or three-day tourist ticket, costs around 1,600 Ft.) and allows unlimited travel on all services within the city limits. Metro stations or newsstands sell single-ride tickets for about 100 Ft. You can travel on all trams, buses, and on the subway with this ticket, but you can't change lines or direction.

Bus, streetcar, and trolleybus tickets must be canceled on board—watch how other passengers do it. Metro tickets are canceled at station entrances. Plainclothes agents wearing red armbands spot check frequently, often targeting tourists, and you can be fined 1,500 Ft. if you don't have a canceled ticket.

TRAVEL AGENCIES

➤ LOCAL AGENTS: **American Express** (✉ V, Déak Ferenc u. 10, ☎ 1/235–4330). **Getz International** (✉ V, Falk Miksa u. 5, ☎ 1/312–0649 or 1/269–3728). **Vista Travel Center** (✉ VI, Andrássy út 1, ☎ 1/269–6032 air tickets; 1/328–4030 train, bus, boat tickets and youth, student travel, WEB www.vista.hu/english/).

VISITOR INFORMATION

Vista Visitor Center/Café has created a uniquely welcoming environment for visitors seeking information about Budapest and Hungary. You can linger over lunch in the popular café, browse through brochures, and get information about (and make bookings for) tours, events, accommodations, and more from the young, English-speaking staff. Computer terminals are rented by the hour for Internet surfing and E-mailing; storage lockers are also available, as are international telephone stations with good rates.

The monthly *Where Budapest* magazine and the *Budapest in Your Pocket* guide are good sources. The English-language weekly the *Budapest Sun* covers news, business, and culture.

The Tourism Office of Budapest has developed the Budapest Card, which entitles holders to unlimited travel on public transportation; free admission to many museums and sights; and discounts on various purchases, entertainment events, tours, meals, and services from participating businesses. The cost is 3,400 Ft. for two days, 4,000 Ft. for three days; one card is valid for an adult plus a child under 14. Budapest Cards are sold at main metro ticket windows, tourist information offices, and hotels.

➤ TOURIST INFORMATION: **IBUSZ Travel** (main branch, ✉ V, Ferenciek tere 10, ☎ 1/485–2762, 06/20–944–9091, or 1/317–7767 tours and programs; one central branch, ✉ V, Vörösmarty tér 6, ☎ 1/317–0532). **Tourinform** (✉ Vörösmarty tér, at Vigadó u., H-1052 Budapest, ☎ 1/438–8080; 06/80–660–044 automated telephone service, ⏲ 24 hours; ✉ Sütő u. 2, H-1052 Budapest, ☎ 1/317–9800, ⏲ daily 8–8, www.hungarytourism.hu; WEB www.tourinform.hu). **Tourism Office of Budapest** (✉ VI, Liszt Ferenc tér 11, ☎ 1/322–4098 or 1/342–9390, FAX 1/342–2541; ✉ VII, Király u. 93, ☎ 1/352–1433; ✉ XIII, Nyugati pályaudvar, ☎ 1/302–8580; ✉ I, Tárnok u. 9–11, ☎ 1/488–0453). **Tribus Hotel Service** (✉ V, Apáczai Csere János u. 1, ☎ 1/318–5776 or 1/266–8042). **Vista Visitor Center/Café** (✉ VI, Paulay Ede u. 7, ☎ 1/267–8603).

THE DANUBE BEND

About 40 km (25 mi) north of Budapest, the Danube abandons its eastward course and turns abruptly south toward the capital, cutting through the Börzsöny and Visegrád hills. In this area, the Danube Bend, are the Baroque town of Szentendre, the hilltop castle ruins and town of Visegrád, and the cathedral town of Esztergom.

Here, in the heartland, are traces of the country's history—the remains of the Roman empire's frontiers, the battlefields of the Middle Ages, and relics of the Hungarian Renaissance. Just 40 minutes or 21 km (13 mi) north of Budapest is Szentendre, a popular day trip. To visit the entire area, two days, with a night in Visegrád or Esztergom, would be a better way to savor its charms.

Szentendre

The lively, flourishing artists' colony of Szentendre was first settled by Serbs and Greeks fleeing the advancing Turks in the 14th and 17th centuries. The narrow cobbled streets are lined with cheerfully painted houses, many now containing art galleries. Unfortunately, tacky souvenir shops have appeared, and in summer, the streets swarm with tourists. Part of the town's artistic reputation can be traced to the ceramic artist Margit Kovács, whose pottery blended Hungarian folk-art traditions with motifs from modern art. ★ The **Kovács Margit Múzeum** (Margit Kovács Museum), in a small, 18th-century merchant's house, is devoted to her work. ✉ *Vastag György u. 1,* ☎ *26/310–244,* WEB *www.pmmi.hu.* ⏲ *Mid-Mar.–Oct., daily 10–6; Nov.–mid-Mar., Tues.–Sun. 9–5. Last tickets sold 30 mins before closing.*

The **Szabadtéri Néprajzi Múzeum** (Open-Air Ethnography Museum) re-creates Hungarian peasant life and folk architecture of the 19th century. Crafts demonstrations are held in summer. ✉ *Sztaravodai út,* ☎ *26/312–304.* ⏲ *Apr.–Oct., Tues.–Sun. 9–5.*

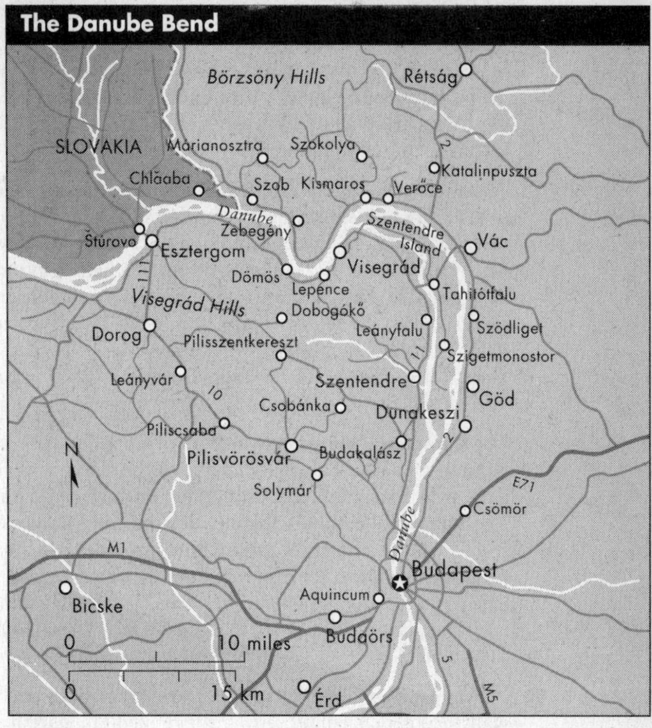

$$ ✕ **Rab Ráby.** This popular restaurant, decorated with wood beams and myriad eclectic antiques, is a great place for fish soup and fresh grilled trout. Reservations are essential in summer. ✉ *Péter Pál u. 1,* ☎ *26/310–819. AE, DC, MC, V.*

$ 🏨 **Bükkös Panzió.** Impeccably clean, this stylishly modernized old house is on a small canal just a few minutes' walk from the town center. The narrow staircase and small rooms give it a homey feel. Rates include breakfast. ✉ *Bükkös part 16, H-2000,* ☎ *26/312–021,* ☎ FAX *26/310–782,* WEB *www.hotels.hu/bukkos. 16 rooms. Restaurant. MC, V.*

Visegrád

This hilly village presided over by a mountaintop fortress was the seat of the kings of Hungary during the 14th century. The ruins of the palace of King Matthias on the main street have been excavated and reconstructed; there are jousting tournaments on the grounds of the fortress in June and a medieval festival in July. A winding road leads up to the haunting late-medieval fortress, **Fellegvár** (Citadel), from which you have a fine view of the Danube Bend. ☎ *26/398–101.* ⏲ *Mid-Mar.–Oct., daily 10–6; Nov.–mid-Mar., weekends 10–3 in good weather.*

$$$ ★ 🏨 **Silvanus.** Set high up on Fekete hill, this hotel is renowned for its spectacular views and offers hiking trails through the forest. Rooms are bright and clean. A buffet breakfast is included in the rates. ✉ *Feketehegy, H-2025,* ☎ *26/398–311 or 26/597–511,* FAX *26/597–516,* WEB *www.danubiusgroup.com/beta. 94 rooms, 8 suites. Restaurant, air-conditioning, indoor pool. AE, DC, MC, V.*

$ 🏨 **Hotel Honti.** This intimate, alpine-style pension, named for its owner, József Honti, is in a quiet neighborhood close to the Danube ferry. A stream running between the two houses amplifies the country atmosphere. ✉ *Fő u. 66, H-2025,* ☎ *26/398–120,* FAX *26/397–274,* WEB *www.hotels.hu/honti. 30 rooms, 2 suites. No credit cards.*

Esztergom

This primarily Baroque town stands on the site of a Roman fortress. St. Stephen, the first Christian king of Hungary, was crowned here in the year 1000. The kings are long gone, but Esztergom is still the home of the archbishop of Esztergom, the cardinal primate, head of the Catholic church in Hungary.

Thousands of pilgrims visit the imposing **Bazilika** (basilica), the largest in Hungary, which stands on Vár-domb (Castle Hill) overlooking the town. It was here that anti-Communist Cardinal József Mindszenty was finally reburied in 1991, ending an era of religious intolerance and persecution. The cathedral's treasury houses a valuable collection of ecclesiastical art. ✉ *Szt. István tér,* ☎ *33/411–895.* ⏲ *Basilica Mar.–Oct., daily 7–6; Nov.–Feb., daily 7–4. Treasury Mar.–Oct., daily 9–4:30; Nov.–Dec., Tues.–Sun. 11–3:30. Treasury closed Good Fri. and Holy Sat., and Jan.–Feb.*

The **Keresztény Múzeum** (Museum of Christian Art) is in the Prímási Palota (Primate's Palace). It is one of the finest art galleries in Hungary, with a large collection of early Hungarian and Italian paintings. The Italian collection, coupled with the early Renaissance paintings from Flanders and the Lower Rhine, provides insights into the transition of European sensibilities from medieval Gothic to the humanistic Renaissance. ✉ *Mindszenty tér 2,* ☎ *33/413–880.* ⏲ *Mid-Mar.–mid-Oct., Tues.–Sun. 10–6; mid-Oct.–Dec., Tues.–Sun. 10–5. Closed Jan.–mid-Mar.*

$$ ✕ **Prímáspince.** This restaurant's vaulted ceilings and exposed brick walls make a charming setting for refined Hungarian and Continental fare. The veal paprikas with homemade cheese curd and dill dumplings is a good, hearty bet. ✉ *Szt. István tér 4,* ☎ *33/313–495. AE, DC, MC, V. No dinner Jan.–Mar.*

$$ **Ria Panzió.** In this small, friendly guest house near the cathedral, most rooms face a garden courtyard. Rates include breakfast. ✉ *Batthyány u. 11–13, H-2500,* ☎ *33/313–115,* FAX *33/401–429. 15 rooms. AE, MC, V.*

$ **Alabárdos Panzió.** Downhill from the Basilica, this cozy, remodeled house provides an excellent view of Castle Hill. Rooms (doubles and quads) are small but less cramped than at other pensions. Breakfast is included in the rates. ✉ *Bajcsy-Zsilinszky u. 49, H-2500,* ☎ FAX *33/312–640. 21 rooms. No credit cards.*

The Danube Bend Essentials

BOAT AND FERRY TRAVEL

The best way to get around on the Danube is by boat or hydrofoil. The three main centers—Szentendre, Esztergom, and Visegrád—all have connections with one another and with Budapest. Contact MAHART Tours for schedules.

➤ BOAT AND FERRY INFORMATION: **MAHART Tours** (☎ 1/318–1704).

BUS TOURS

IBUSZ Travel organizes daylong bus trips from Budapest along the Danube stopping in Esztergom, Visegrád, and Szentendre. Cityrama runs full-day bus tours to Visegrád, Esztergom, and Szentendre, returning to Budapest by boat, from May through September, Wednesday–Sunday. Both tours include lunch and admission fees.

➤ FEES AND SCHEDULES: **Cityrama** (☎ 1/302–4382). **IBUSZ Travel** (☎ 1/485–2762, 1/485–2763, or 1/317–7767).

BUS TRAVEL

Regular bus service connects Szentendre, Esztergom, and Visegrád with one another and with Budapest.

TRAIN TRAVEL

Szentendre is most easily reached by HÉV commuter rail, departing from the Batthyány tér Metro in Budapest; the trip takes about 40 minutes and costs around 270 Ft.

VISITOR INFORMATION

➤ TOURIST INFORMATION: **Budapest** (Tourinform; ✉ Vörösmarty tér, at Vigadó u., H-1052 Budapest, ☎ 1/438–8080; 06/80–660–044 automated telephone service; ✉ Sütő u. 2, H-1052 Budapest, ☎ 1/317–9800). **Esztergom** (Grantours; ✉ Széchenyi tér 25, ☎ FAX 33/413–756). **Szentendre** (Tourinform; ✉ Dumsta J. u. 22, ☎ 26/317–965).

LAKE BALATON

Lake Balaton, the largest lake in Central Europe, stretches 80 km (50 mi) across western Hungary. It is within easy reach of Budapest. Sometimes known as the nation's playground, it helps to make up for Hungary's much-lamented lack of coastline. On its hilly northern shore, ideal for growing grapes, is Balatonfüred, the country's oldest spa town.

The national park on the Tihany Peninsula is just to the south, and regular boat service links Tihany and Balatonfüred with Siófok on the southern shore. This shore is flatter and more crowded with resorts, cottages, and high-rise hotels once used as Communist trade-union retreats. The south shore's waters are shallower than those of the north: you can walk out for nearly 2 km (1 mi) before they deepen.

The region grows more crowded every year (July and August are the busiest times), but a few steps along any side road will still lead you to a serene landscape of vineyards and old stone houses. A circular tour taking in Veszprém, Balatonfüred, and Tihany could be managed in a day, but two days, with a night in Tihany or Balatonfüred, would be more relaxed and allow for a detour to Herend and its porcelain factory.

Veszprém

Hilly Veszprém, though not on the lake itself, is the center of cultural ★ life in the Balaton region. **Veszprémi Várhegy** (Castle Hill), a charming hilltop district of well-preserved buildings, is the most attractive part of town. **Hősök Kapuja** (Heroes' Gate), at the entrance to the district, houses a small exhibit on Hungary's history. Just past the gate and down a little alley to the left is the **Tűztorony** (Fire Tower); note that the lower level is medieval while the upper stories are Baroque. There is a good view of the town and surrounding area from the castle balcony. The tower is open May–October, daily 10–6.

Vár utca, the only street in the castle area, leads to a small square in front of the **Püspök Palota** (Bishop's Palace) and the cathedral; outdoor concerts are held here in summer. Vár utca continues past the square up to a terrace erected on the north staircase of the castle. Stand beside the modern statues of St. Stephen and his queen, Gizella, for a far-reaching view of the old quarter of town.

$ ✕ **Skorpio.** This city-center eatery might look like an Alpine hut, but the excellent Hungarian and Continental menu offers grilled meats and tasty, creamy sauces. ✉ *Virág Benedek út 1,* ☎ *88/420–319. No credit cards.*

$ ✕ **Szürkebarát Borozó.** The plain off-white walls of the Gray Monk Tavern may be less than inspiring, but the hearty Hungarian fare at this cellar restaurant in the city center more than compensates. For an unusual (but very Hungarian) appetizer, try the paprika-spiced *velős pirítós* (marrow on toast; missing from the English menu and sometimes unavailable); or for a main course, gnaw away at "Ms. Baker's Pork Hoofs." ✉ *Szabadság tér 12,* ☎ *88/327–684. No credit cards.*

Herend

Herend is the home of some of Hungary's most renowned hand-painted porcelain. The **Herendi Porcelángyár** (Herend Porcelain Factory), founded in 1839, displays many rare pieces in its museum. An exhibit about the process of making porcelain is housed across the street. ✉ *Kossuth Lajos u. 144,* ☎ *88/261–144.* ⏲ *Apr.–Sept., daily 10–6; Oct.–Mar., Tues.–Sun. 10–4. Call ahead to confirm hours.*

Balatonfüred

Balatonfüred first grew famous as a spa catering to people suffering from heart disease, but thanks to its good beaches and proximity to Budapest, it's now the most popular resort on the lake. The town also lies in one of Hungary's finest wine-producing regions. In the main square, strong-smelling medicinal waters bubble up under a colonnaded pavilion. Down at the shore, the Tagore sétány (Tagore Promenade) is a wonderful place to stroll and watch the swans glide by.

$$ ✕ **Baricska Csárda.** From its perch atop a hill at the southwestern end of town, this rambling, reed-thatched inn overlooks vineyards toward the river. The hearty fare includes roasted trout and *fogas* (a freshwater fish of the Balaton region) as well as desserts crammed with sweet poppy-seed filling. In summer, colorful Gypsy wedding shows are held nightly. ✉ *Baricska dülő, off Rte. 71 (Széchenyi út) behind the Shell station,* ☎ *87/343–105. AE, V. Closed mid-Nov.–mid-Mar.*

$$ ✕ **Tölgyfa Csárda.** A prime hilltop location gives this tavern breathtaking views over the steeples and rooftops of Balatonfüred and the Tihany peninsula. The menu and decor are the equals of a first-class Budapest restaurant, and there's live Gypsy music in the evening. ✉ *Meleghegy hill (at end of Csárda u.),* ☎ *87/343–036. No credit cards. Closed late Oct.–mid-Apr.*

$$$$ 🏨 **Annabella.** The cool, spacious guest quarters in this Miami-style high-rise are especially pleasant in summer. Overlooking the Tagore Promenade and Lake Balaton, it has access to excellent water-sports facilities. All rooms have balconies; for the best vistas, request a room on a high floor with a view of the Tihany peninsula. Room rates include breakfast. Five suites have air-conditioning. ✉ *Deák Ferenc u. 25, H-8230,* ☎ *87/342–222,* FAX *87/483–029,* WEB *www.danubiusgroup.com. 383* *rooms, 5 suites. 3 restaurants, 2 pools. AE, DC, MC, V. Closed mid-Oct.–mid-Apr..*

$$ 🏨 **Park.** Hidden on a side street in town but close to the lakeshore, this family-run spot is noticeably calmer than Füred's bustling main hotels. Rooms are large and bright, with high ceilings and tall windows. However, the decor is uninspired, Eastern Bloc style, with low, narrow beds and plain upholstery. Suites have large, breezy balconies but small bathrooms. Breakfast is included in the room rates. ✉ *Jókai u. 24, H-8230,* ☎ FAX *87/343–203,* WEB *www.balaton.hu/parkhotel. 38 rooms, 3 suites. Restaurant. No credit cards.*

Tihany

★ A short trip by boat or car takes you from Balatonfüred to the **Tihanyi fél-sziget** (Tihany Peninsula), a national park rich in rare flora and fauna. As you walk from the ferry port, follow green markers to the Oroszkút (springs) or red ones to the top of Csúcs-hegy, where there is a great view of the lake.

★ The village of Tihany, with its **Bencés Apátság** (Benedictine Abbey), is on the lake's northern shore. The abbey building houses a **museum** with exhibits related to the Balaton area. Also worth a look are the pink angels floating on the ceiling of the abbey church. Organ concerts are held weekend nights in July and the first half of August. ✉ *Első András tér 1,* ☎ *87/448–405 abbey; 87/448–650 museum,* WEB *www.osb.hu/tihany.* ⏲ *May–Sept., Mon.–Sat. 9–6, Sun. 11–6; Nov.–Mar., Mon.–Sat. 10–3:30, Sun. 11–3:30; Apr. and Oct., Mon.–Sat. 10–4:30, Sun. 11–4:30; open holidays year-round from 11 (after mass).*

$$ ✕ **Pál Csárda.** Two thatched cottages house this simple restaurant, where cold fruit soup and fish stew are the specialties. You can eat in the garden, which is decorated with gourds and strands of peppers. ✉ *Visszhang u. 19,* ☎ *87/448–605. Reservations not accepted. AE, MC, V. Closed Oct.–Mar.*

$ ✕ **Halásztanya.** The location on a twisting, narrow street and evening Gypsy music contribute to the popularity of this restaurant, which specializes in fish. ✉ *Visszhang u. 11,* ☎ *87/448–771. Reservations not accepted. AE, MC, V. Closed Nov.–Easter.*

$$$ ★ 🏨 **Kastély.** Lush, landscaped gardens surround this stately neo-Baroque mansion on the water's edge. Inside, it's all understated elegance; rooms have soaring ceilings and beautiful views. Next door, a newer, less attractive building houses the Kastély's sister, the Park Hotel, which has less expensive but ugly rooms. Breakfast is included in the rates. ✉ *Fürdőtelepi út 1, H-8237,* ☎ *87/448–611,* FAX *87/448–409,* WEB *www.hotelfured.hu. 25 rooms, 1 suite. Restaurant. AE, DC, MC, V. Closed mid-Oct.–mid-Apr..*

$$ 🏨 **Kolostor.** Cozy, wood-paneled rooms are built into an attic above a popular restaurant and brewery in the heart of Tihany village. Rates include breakfast. ✉ *Kossuth u. 14, H-8237,* ☎ FAX *87/448–009. 5 rooms. Restaurant. MC, V. Closed Nov.–Mar.*

Lake Balaton Essentials

CAR TRAVEL

Highway 71 runs along the northern shore; M7 covers the southern.

TOURS

IBUSZ Travel has several tours to Balaton from Budapest; inquire at the main office in Budapest. Other tours more easily organized from hotels in the Balaton area include boat trips to vineyards and folk music evenings.

TRAIN TRAVEL

Trains from Budapest serve all the resorts on the northern shore; a separate line links the resorts of the southern shore.

TRANSPORTATION AROUND LAKE BALATON

Buses connect most resorts, and regular ferries link the major ones. On summer weekends traffic can be heavy, and driving around the lake can take quite a while; because of the crowds, you should also book bus and train tickets in advance. In winter, schedules are curtailed, so check ahead.

VISITOR INFORMATION

➤ Tourist Information: **Budapest** (Tourinform, ✉ Vörösmarty tér, at Vigadó u., H-1052 Budapest, ☎ 1/438–8080; 06/80–660–044 automated telephone service; ✉ Sütő u. 2, H-1052 Budapest, ☎ 1/317–9800). **Balatonfüred** (Balatontourist, ✉ Tagore sétány 1, ☎ 87/343–471 or 87/342–822; Tourinform, ✉ Petőfi S. u. 8, ☎ 87/342–237). **Tihany** (Tourinform, ✉ Kossuth L. u. 20, ☎ 87/448–804; Tihany Tourist, ✉ Kossuth L. u. 11, ☎ 87/448–481). **Veszprém** (Tourinform, ✉ Rákóczi u. 3, ☎ 88/404–548).

16 ICELAND

REYKJAVÍK AND THE COUNTRYSIDE

DON'T BE FOOLED BY ITS NAME. Iceland is anything but icy, with only 11% of the country covered by glaciers. Considering the country's high latitude, summers in Iceland are relatively warm, and the winter climate is milder than New York's. Indeed, during summer, with its lava and lushness, Iceland bears an uncanny resemblance to Hawaii, with coastal farms nestled in pastoral lowlands where livestock graze beside pristine streams.

Iceland's chilly name can be blamed on Hrafna-Flóki, a 9th-century settler who failed to store up enough fodder to see his livestock through the winter. Leaving in a huff, he passed a fjord filled with pack ice and cursed the country with a name that has stuck ever since.

The second-largest island in Europe, Iceland lies in the middle of the North Atlantic, where the warm Gulf Stream from the south meets cold currents from the north, creating a choice breeding ground for fish, which provide the nation with 70% of its export revenue. Iceland itself emerged from the bed of the Atlantic Ocean as a result of volcanic activity, which is ongoing. Every five years, on average, this fire beneath the earth breaks out in an eruption, sometimes even below glaciers. Fiery forces also heat the hot springs and geysers that bubble and spout in many parts of the country. Other geothermal water keeps public swimming pools comfortable and heats most homes and buildings, helping to keep the air smog-free.

Except for fish and agricultural products, most consumer goods are imported to Iceland, contributing to a high cost of living. Economic stability and reforms in recent years, however, have been bringing prices down to competitive levels with those of the rest of Scandinavia and not so different from those of Europe in general.

The first permanent settlers came from Norway in 874, though a handful of Irish monks likely arrived a century earlier. In 1262, Iceland came under foreign rule by Norway and later Denmark, and did not regain full independence until 1944. Today, 60% of the country's 275,000 people live in the capital area of Reykjavík.

ICELAND A TO Z

To research prices, get advice from other travelers, and book travel arrangements, visit www.fodors.com

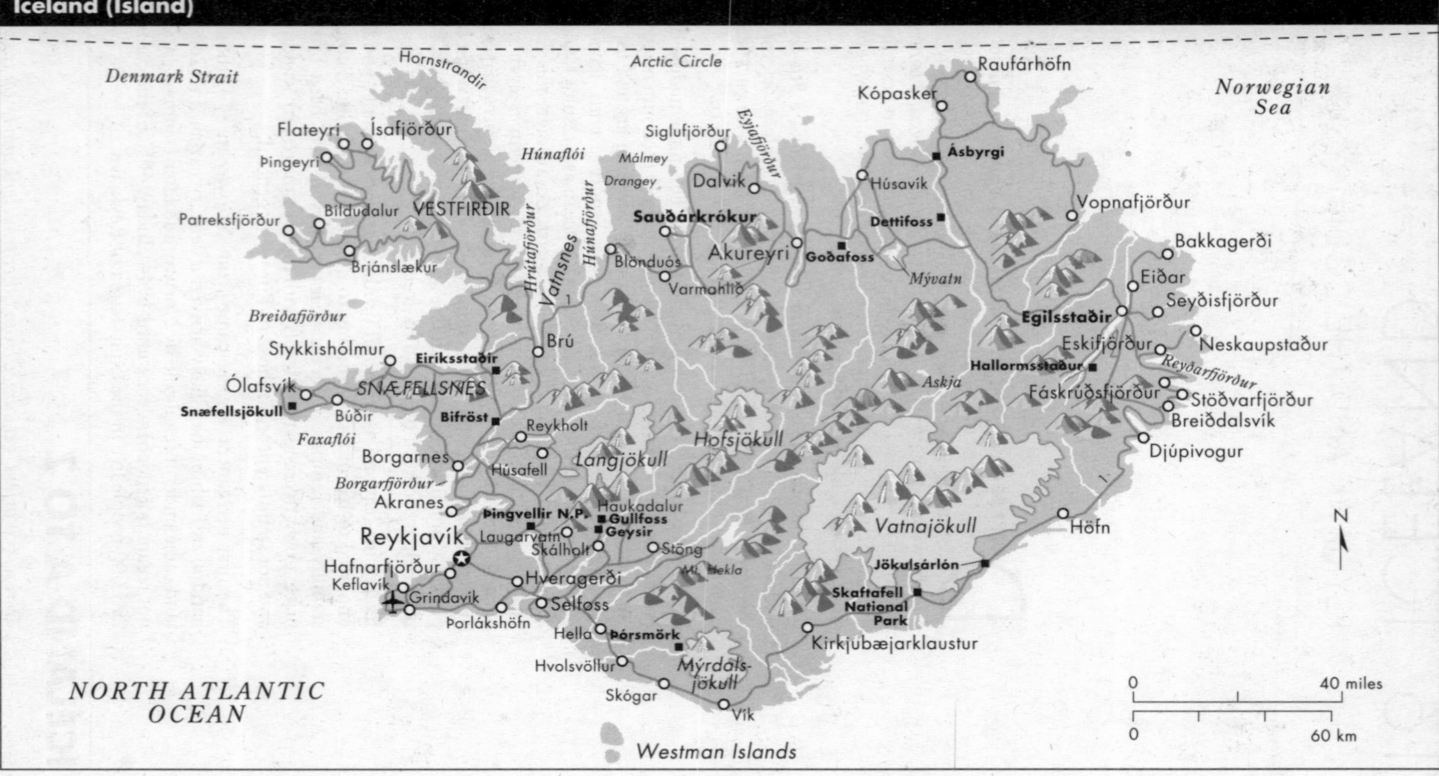
Iceland (Ísland)
Denmark Strait
Hornstrandir
Arctic Circle
Norwegian Sea
Raufárhöfn
Kópasker
Ásbyrgi
Húsavík
Dettifoss
Vopnafjörður
Bakkagerði
Eiðar
Seyðisfjörður
Egilsstaðir
Neskaupstaður
Eskifjörður
Reyðarfjörður
Hallormsstaður
Fáskrúðsfjörður
Stöðvarfjörður
Breiðdalsvík
Djúpivogur
Höfn
Askja
Mývatn
Goðafoss
Akureyri
Eyjafjörður
Siglufjörður
Dalvík
Málmey
Drangey
Sauðárkrókur
Blönduós
Varmahlíð
Húnaflói
Húnafjörður
Hrútafjörður
Vatnsnes
Flateyri
Ísafjörður
Þingeyri
Bíldudalur
VESTFIRÐIR
Patreksfjörður
Brjánslækur
Breiðafjörður
Stykkishólmur
Eiríksstaðir
Brú
Ólafsvík
SNÆFELLSNES
Snæfellsjökull
Búðir
Bifröst
Reykholt
Faxaflói
Borgarnes
Húsafell
Langjökull
Hofsjökull
Borgarfjörður
Akranes
Haukadalur
Þingvellir N.P.
Gullfoss
Geysir
Vatnajökull
Reykjavík
Laugarvatn
Skálholt
Stöng
Hafnarfjörður
Mt. Hekla
Jökulsárlón
Keflavík
Hveragerði
Grindavík
Selfoss
Skaftafell National Park
Þorlákshöfn
Hella
Þórsmörk
Kirkjubæjarklaustur
Hvolsvöllur
Mýrdalsjökull
Skógar
Vík
NORTH ATLANTIC OCEAN
Westman Islands
N
0
40 miles
0
60 km

AIR TRAVEL

Daily flights go to most of the larger towns. Although plane travel is expensive, special family fares, package tours, and vacation tickets are available. The airport departure fee is IKr1,805.

BOAT AND FERRY TRAVEL

The car-and-passenger ferry *Baldur,* operated by Sæferðir, links the West Fjords with the village of Stykkishólmur on the Snæfellsnes Peninsula. The ferry *Herjólfur* travels to the Westman Islands from Þorlákshöfn on the south coast. Smyril Line calls during summer at the east coast town of Seyðisfjörður, sailing from Norway, Denmark, Scotland's Shetland Islands, and the Faroe Islands. For information, contact Smyril Line or Norræna Ferðaskrifstofan. Information on boat trips linking several coastal spots with Ísafjörður on the West Fjords can be obtained from Vesturferðir.

➤ BOAT AND FERRY INFORMATION: ***Baldur*** (☎ 438–1450 at Stykkishólmur or ☎ 456–2020 at Brjánslækur, WEB www.saeferdir.is). **Herjólfur** (✉ Básaskersbryggja, IS-900 Westman Islands, ☎ 481–2800, FAX 481–2991). **Norræna Ferðaskrifstofan** (✉ Laugavegur 3, IS-101 Reykjavík, ☎ 562–6362, FAX 552–9450). **Smyril Line** (✉ Passenger Dept., Box 370, FR–110 Thorshavn, Faroe Islands, ☎ 298–315–900, FAX 298–315–707, WEB www.smyril-line.fo). **Vesturferðir** (☎ 456–5111, FAX 456–5185, WEB www.vesturferdir.is).

BUS TRAVEL

An extensive network of buses serves most parts of Iceland, though some routes operate only in summer. Many cross-country buses have bike racks. The Air Bus Rover package, allows travelers to fly one-way and return by coach. The bus network is coordinated at Bifreiðastöð Íslands; its terminal is on the northern rim of Reykjavík Airport.

➤ BUS INFORMATION: **Bifreiðastöð Íslands** (BSÍ; ✉ Vatnsmýrarvegur 10, Reykjavík, ☎ 552–2300, FAX 552–9973, WEB www.BSI.is).

BUSINESS HOURS

Banks are open weekdays 9:15–4. Some branches are also open Thursday 5–6. Museums are usually open 1–4:30, but some open as early as 10 and others stay open until 7. Some may be closed Monday. Shops are open weekdays 9–6 and Saturday 10–4, shopping malls daily 10–8, and grocery stores longer, including Sunday afternoon.

CAR TRAVEL

An international driver's license is required. Car-rental agencies are located at most airports and in many towns, but better deals can often be had in packages from your local travel agency.

EMERGENCIES

Rural service stations and garages are few and far between, but the main roads are patrolled, and fellow motorists are helpful. The general emergency number is available 24 hours throughout Iceland.

➤ CONTACTS: **Emergencies** (☎ 112).

GASOLINE

Gasoline prices are high, IKr93–IKr98 per liter depending on octane rating. Service stations are spaced no more than half a day's drive apart. Service stations in the Reykjavík area are open Monday–Saturday 7:30 AM–8 PM; hours outside the city vary.

ROAD CONDITIONS

Most of the Ring Road, which encircles the island, is two-lane asphalt. Other roads can be bumpy, often along gravel, dirt, or lava track—but the scenery is worth it. Be alert for loose livestock. Use extra caution when approaching single-lane bridges or on blind hills (*blindhæð*). A four-wheel-drive vehicle is vital for remote roads such as those in the highlands, which may be impassable until July. If you drive over the highlands, it is best to travel in convoy, especially when crossing unbridged rivers. For information on road conditions and the availability of gasoline off the beaten track, call Vegagerð Ríkisins (Public Roads Administration).

➤ CONTACTS: **Vegagerð Ríkisins** (☎ 563–1500 or 800–6316 for 24-hr summer road status in English, WEB www.vegag.is).

RULES OF THE ROAD

Traffic outside Reykjavík is generally light, but roads have only one lane going in each direction. Speed limits are 90 kph (55 mph) in rural areas on the Ring Road, 70 kph (42 mph) on secondary open roads, and 30–50 kph (20–30 mph) in urban areas. Drivers are required by law to use headlights at all times. Seat belts are required for all occupants.

CUSTOMS AND DUTIES

Tourists may bring in 6 liters of beer or 1 liter of wine containing up to 21% alcohol, 1 liter of liquor with up to 47% alcohol, and 200 cigarettes.

DINING

Restaurants are small and diverse. You can expect superb seafood, beef, and lamb, and the fresh fish is not to be missed—surely some of the best you'll ever have. In addition to a growing array of award-winning cheeses, dairy products include the unique *skýr* (pronounced "skeer"), a thick, creamy, protein-rich dairy product, which is available plain or with various fruits. Besides native cuisine, ethnic eateries range from Asian, Mexican, and Indian to French and Italian. Pizzas, hamburgers, and the tasty national version of the hot dog, with crisped onion bits, are widely available.

Prices are for a main course at dinner and include taxes and service charges.

CATEGORY	COST
$$$$	over IKr 3,000
$$$	IKr 2,000–IKr 3,000
$$	IKr 1,200–IKr 2,000
$	under IKr 1,200

MEALTIMES

Dinner, served between 6 and 9, is the main meal. A light lunch is usually served between noon and 2. Most restaurants are open from midmorning until midnight.

RESERVATIONS AND DRESS

Neat, casual dress is acceptable in all but the most expensive restaurants, where jacket and tie are recommended.

EMBASSIES

There is a Canadian consular office in Reykjavík (☞ Reykjavík Essentials, *below*).

➤ UNITED KINGDOM: (✉ Laufásvegur 31, Reykjavík IS-108, ☎ 550–5100).

➤ UNITED STATES: (✉ Laufásvegur 21, Reykjavík IS-101, ☎ 562–9100).

HOLIDAYS

January 1; Good Friday; Easter Monday; First Day of Summer (celebrated in late April—a vestige of the very optimistic Old Norse calendar); May 1 (Labor Day); Ascension (in May); Pentecost (in late May or early June); Seamen's Day (the first or second Sunday in June); June 17 (Independence Day); Public Holiday (first Monday in August); December 24 (from noon)–26; December 31 (half-day off).

LANGUAGE

The language is Icelandic, a highly inflected North Germanic tongue that is little changed from that originally spoken by the island's Norse settlers. In fact, an official committee invents new words for modern usage to keep Icelandic pure. You'll encounter three unique letters in Icelandic: the "thorn," þ, is pronounced as a forced "th" as in "throw"; the "eth," ð, is a soft "th" as in "breath" and never starts a proper noun; the Scandinavian ligature æ is pronounced as a long "i" as in "bike." Otherwise, the "j" is pronounced as a "y." But not to worry: English proficiency is widespread, particularly among the young.

LODGING

Hotels are clean, quiet, and friendly. Reykjavík and most villages also have guest houses and private accommodations. Outside Reykjavík you'll also find some hostels and other accommodations where private baths may not be available. If you tour Iceland on your own, get a list of hotels and guest houses in the various regions from the Tourist Information Center.

Prices are for two people sharing a double room at high season.

CATEGORY	REYKJAVÍK	OTHER AREAS
$$$$	over IKr 20,000	over IKr 15,000
$$$	IKr 15,000–IKr 20,000	IKr 10,000–IKr 15,000
$$	IKr 10,000–IKr 15,000	IKr 5,000–IKr 10,000
$	under IKr 10,000	under IKr 5,000

FARM ACCOMMODATIONS

Staying at farms is an excellent way to become acquainted with Iceland: some 120 participating farms are listed with Icelandic Farm Holidays. Many offer fishing, touring with a guide, and horseback riding.
➤ CONTACTS: **Icelandic Farm Holidays** (✉ Síðumúli 13, IS-108 Reykjavík, ☎ 570–2700, FAX 570–2799, WEB www.farmholidays.is).

HOSTELS

Information on the 30 hostels around the country can be obtained from the Icelandic Youth Hostel Association.
➤ HOSTEL ORGANIZATIONS: **Icelandic Youth Hostel Association** (✉ Sundlaugavegur 34, IS-105 Reykjavík, ☎ 553–8110, FAX 588–9201, WEB www.hostel.is).

HOTELS

A Sleep-As-You-Please voucher is available from Samvinn Travel, entitling holders to stay at a selection of hotels and guest houses all over Iceland; it costs IKr10,000 for seven nights.
➤ CONTACTS: **Samvinn Travel** (✉ Sætún 1, Box 910, IS-105 Reykjavík, ☎ 569–1070, WEB www.samvinn.is).

HUTS

Outside Reykjavík, the Icelandic Touring Association operates a number of spartan huts for mountaineers and hikers in remote areas.
➤ CONTACTS

Icelandic Touring Association (✉ Mörkin 6, IS-108 Reykjavík, ☎ 568–2533, FAX 568–2535).

MAIL AND SHIPPING

You can have your mail sent to the post office in any town or village in Iceland. In Reykjavík, have mail sent to the downtown post office.

Post Offices: DOWNTOWN POST OFFICE (✉ R/O PÓSTHÚSSTRÆTI, IS-101 REYKJAVÍK).

POSTAL RATES

Airmail letters cost IKr75 to the United States and IKr50 to Europe.

MONEY MATTERS

Like many islands, Iceland is on the expensive side. Hotels and restaurants cost about 20% more in Reykjavík than elsewhere in the country. Interestingly, though, prestige goods, such as Armani clothes, Rolex watches, and top labels in perfumes and jewelry, are often good buys for travelers, once the value-added tax is refunded.

Some sample prices include: cup of coffee or tea (with refills) or soft drink, IKr150; bottle of beer, IKr300; sandwich or snack, IKr350; 3-km (2-mi) taxi ride, IKr650.

CURRENCY

The Icelandic monetary unit is the króna (plural krónur), which is abbreviated kr locally and IKr or ISK internationally. Coins are the IKr1, 5, 10, 50, and 100. Krónur bills are in denominations of 500, 1,000, 2,000, and 5,000. At press time (summer 2001), the rate of exchange was IKr87 to the U.S. dollar, IKr57 to the Canadian dollar, IKr125 to the pound sterling, IKr100 to the Irish punt, IKr46 to the Australian dollar, IKr37 to the New Zealand dollar, and IKr11 to the South African rand.

CURRENCY EXCHANGE

Most major foreign currency is easily exchanged for krónur at Icelandic banks, but Icelandic money is virtually unavailable abroad. Almost all businesses accept major credit cards, even for small amounts. Currency exchange is also provided by the Change Group, open May–September, daily 8:30–8, and October–April, daily 8:30–6.

➤ EXCHANGE SERVICES: **Change Group** (✉ Bankastræti 2, Reykjavík, ☎ 552–3735).

TAXES

VALUE-ADDED TAX (V.A.T.)

A 24.5% *virðisaukaskattur* (value-added tax, or VAT), abbreviated VSK, applies to most goods and services. It's usually included in the price tag, tacitly making up 19.68% of the total; if not, that fact must be stated. Foreign visitors can claim a partial refund on the VAT, or 15% of the purchase price, provided they bought at least IKr5,000 worth of goods at one time. Souvenir stores issue "tax-free checks" that simplify collecting the VAT rebates as you depart Iceland, at the international airport terminal or ferry building. To qualify, keep your purchases (except woolens) in tax-free packages, and show them to customs officers along with a passport and the tax-free check.

TELEPHONES

Iceland's phone system is entirely digital and is part of the Nordic Mobile Telephone (NMT) system and the GSM global cellular phone network. Coverage for phones with NMT capability includes all but the remotest areas of Iceland, whereas the GSM system, which once reached mostly coastal areas, is expanding by leaps and bounds and may match the NMT range by press time. Cellular phones are ubiquitous. When calling Icelandic numbers whose prefix is 800, the charge is the same, regardless of where you're calling from within the country. A novel result of Iceland's small size and intimate society is that the country's phone books are organized by first names rather than last.

COUNTRY AND AREA CODES

The country code for Iceland is 354. All the country's local numbers are seven digits, with the first three giving a rough idea of location in lieu of area codes. Except for the country's 800 numbers, distance determines the cost of the call. Non-800 numbers starting with 8 often indicate cellular phones.

INTERNATIONAL CALLS

For assistance with overseas calls dial 115; for direct international calls dial 00. You can reach AT&T, World Phone, and Sprint Global One by dialing their access codes.

➤ ACCESS CODES: **AT&T** (☎ 800–9001). **Sprint Global One** (☎ 800–9003). **World Phone** (☎ 800–9002).

LOCAL CALLS

Pay phones usually take IKr10 and IKr50 coins and are found in hotels, some shops, and post offices; outdoor telephone booths are sparse. Phone cards costing IKr500 are sold at post offices, hotels, and some stores. For operator assistance with local calls dial 119, for information 118, for collect calls 115.

TIPPING

Tipping is not customary in Iceland.

VISITOR INFORMATION

➤ TOURIST INFORMATION: **Icelandic Tourist Board** (✉ Gimli, Lækjargata 3, IS-101 Reykjavík, ☎ 535–5500, FAX 535–5501, WEB www.goiceland.org/). **Tourist Information Center** (✉ Bankastræti 2, IS-101 Reykjavík, ☎ 562–3045, FAX 562–3057, WEB www.icetourist.is).

WHEN TO GO

Although it is a great year-round destination, Iceland is easiest to visit from May to mid-November. From June through July, the sun barely sets, and it never gets dark. In December the sun shines for only three hours a day, but on clear, cold nights anytime from September through March you may see the northern lights dancing among the stars.

CLIMATE

Weather in Iceland is unpredictable: in June, July, and August, sunny days alternate with spells of rain showers and chilling winds, or even snow in the highlands. Winter temperatures fluctuate wildly around freezing, often getting as high as 50°F (10°C) or as low as –14°F (–10°C). In general, the climate in the north is stable and continental, in the south fickle and maritime.

Below are average daily maximum and minimum temperatures for Reykjavík.

Jan.	35F	2C	**May**	50F	10C	**Sept.**	52F	11C
	28	– 2		39	4		43	6
Feb.	37F	3C	**June**	54F	12C	**Oct.**	45F	7C
	28	– 2		34	7		38	3
Mar.	39F	4C	**July**	57F	14C	**Nov.**	39F	4C
	30	– 1		48	9		32	0
Apr.	43F	6C	**Aug.**	56F	14C	**Dec.**	36F	2C
	33	1		47	8		29	– 2

REYKJAVÍK

Reykjavík has a small, generally safe city center, clean air, and plenty of open spaces. Icelanders' diet of fresh local seafood may give a clue to their longevity, contentment, and attractiveness as a people. For a city of 110,000, Reykjavík offers an astonishingly wide range of artistic events—the main cultural season is winter, but plenty goes on in summer as well. In June of even-numbered years, Reykjavík hosts a two-week arts festival with a strong international flavor. Most nightlife is in or near the city center; it's liveliest on weekends. If weather is good, this can make for a carnival-like atmosphere, with hundreds or even thousands spilling into Lækjartorg Square when pubs begin closing in the wee hours.

Exploring Reykjavík

Numbers in the margin correspond to points of interest on the Reykjavík map.

Old Midtown, the capital's original core, is the city's highlight, with classic buildings, a park, museums, shops, galleries, and a plethora of cafés. Between World War II and the mid-1960s, a middle belt of residential neighborhoods, such as Vesturbær, was established. Extending from the once separate community of Seltjarnarnes, well west of Old Midtown, to the salmon-populated Elliðaá River in the east, these areas have small, inviting parks. Besides lovely flower beds and large trees (by Icelandic standards), homes present the Icelandic flair for wildly colored rooftops. Since the late 1960s, suburbs such as the sprawling Breiðholt have sprung up outside town. These austere areas offer few attractions, other than showing how a lot of the modern population lives. Old Midtown can be browsed on foot; elsewhere, the city's bus system is an efficient, inexpensive option.

A practical option for visitors is purchase of a Reykjavík Tourist Card at the Tourist Information Center. The card permits unlimited bus use and admission to any of the capital area's seven pools and many museums—a bargain whether you buy it for one (IKr900), two (IKr1,200), or three days (IKr1,500).

18 **Árbæjarsafn** (Open-Air Folk Museum). This authentic "village" of relocated 18th- and 19th-century houses, 20 minutes southeast of downtown, is well worth the trip. ✉ *Árbær, Bus 10 from Hlemmur bus station,* ☎ *577–1111.* ⏲ *June–Aug., Tues.–Sun. 10–6.*

14 **Arnarhóll.** A statue of the Viking **Ingólfur Arnarson,** whose family first settled Iceland in 874, dominates this hill, which overlooks the bay. To the north is the ultramodern, glossy-black **Seðlabanki** (Central Bank). Behind Ingólfur is the copper-green **High Courts** building nestled beside the **National Theater** and old **Library,** dating from the early 20th century. ✉ *Arnarhóll.*

17 **Ásmundarsafn** (Ásmundur Sveinsson Sculpture Museum). Some originals by this sculptor (1896–1982), depicting ordinary working people, myths, and folktale episodes, are exhibited in the museum's gallery and studio as well as in the surrounding garden and chosen spots in Reykjavík. ✉ *Sigtún, 5-min ride from Hlemmur Station on Bus 5,* ☎ *553–2155.* ⏲ *June–Sept., daily 10–4; Oct.–May, daily 1–4.*

★ 2 **Austurvöllur** (East Field). This green square in Old Midtown is truly the heart of Reykjavík. The 19th-century **Alþingishús** (Parliament House), one of the oldest stone buildings in Iceland, faces the square and houses meetings of the world's oldest operating parliament, which dates from 930. A statue of Jón Sigurðsson (1811–79), the nationalist who led Iceland toward independence, stands in the square's center. ✉ *Bounded by Kirkjustræti and Pósthússtræti.*

Reykjavík

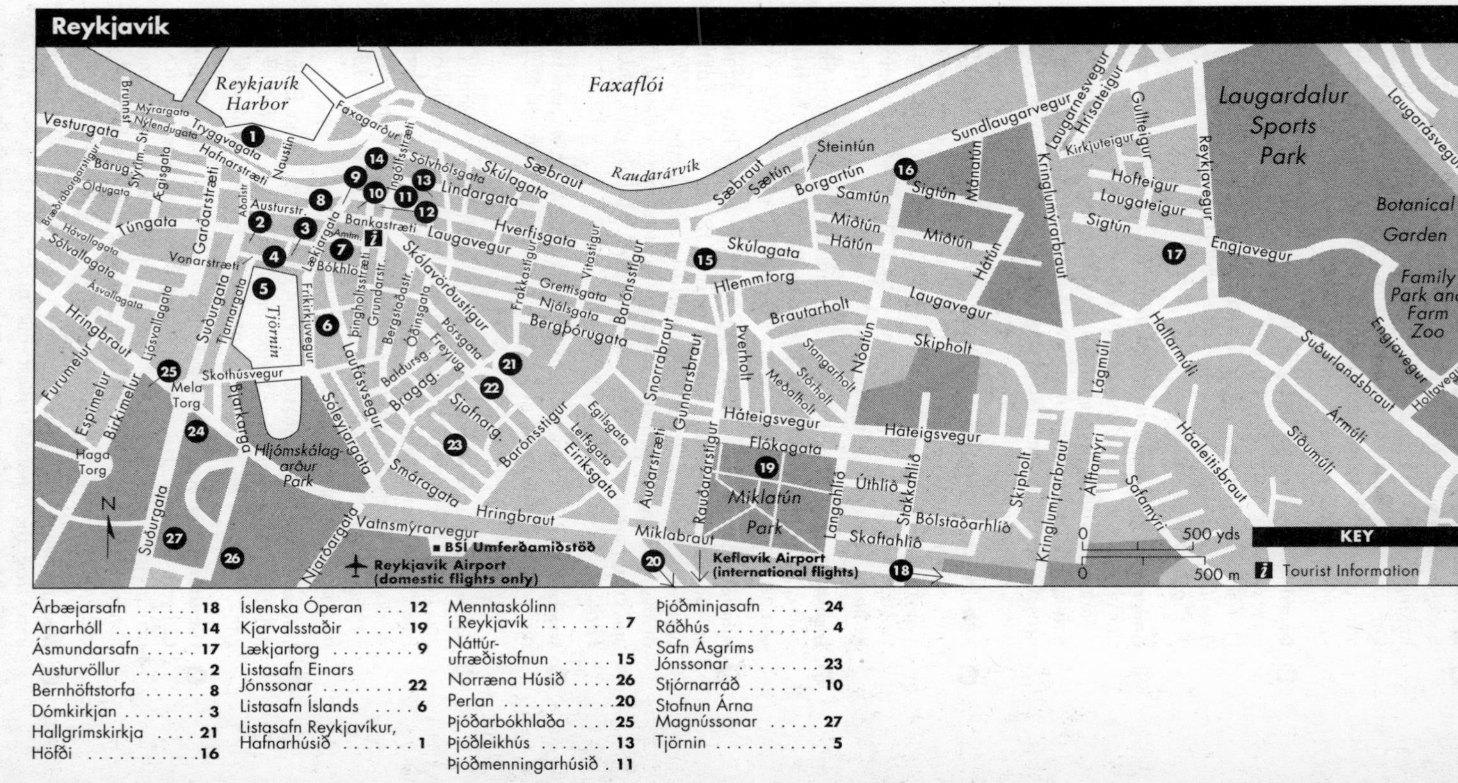

- Árbæjarsafn 18
- Arnarhóll 14
- Ásmundarsafn 17
- Austurvöllur 2
- Bernhöftstorfa 8
- Dómkirkjan 3
- Hallgrímskirkja 21
- Höfði 16
- Íslenska Óperan . . . 12
- Kjarvalsstaðir 19
- Lækjartorg 9
- Listasafn Einars Jónssonar 22
- Listasafn Íslands 6
- Listasafn Reykjavíkur, Hafnarhúsið 1
- Menntaskólinn í Reykjavík 7
- Náttúrufræðistofnun 15
- Norræna Húsið 26
- Perlan 20
- Þjóðarbókhlaða 25
- Þjóðleikhús 13
- Þjóðmenningarhúsið . 11
- Þjóðminjasafn 24
- Ráðhús 4
- Safn Ásgríms Jónssonar 23
- Stjórnarráð 10
- Stofnun Árna Magnússonar 27
- Tjörnin 5

8 **Bernhöftstorfa.** Picturesque, two-story, mid-19th-century wooden houses typify this small hill, which rises from Lækjargata, the main street linking the peaceful park by Tjörnin Lake with the busy city center. One corner of the lake is fed by warm water that does not freeze, creating a destination for birds year-round. ✉ *Just east of Lækjargata and just south of Bankastræti.*

3 **Dómkirkjan** (Lutheran Cathedral). This 18th-century stone church, with a treasured baptismal font carved by sculptor Bertel Thorvaldsen (1768/70–1844), stands by Kirkjustræti, or Church Street. ✉ *Austurvöllur,* ☎ *551–2113.* ⏲ *Mon.–Tues. and Thurs.–Fri. 9–5, Wed. 10–5. Closed during services.*

21 **Hallgrímskirkja** (Hallgrímur's Church). Forty years in the making, this church was finally completed in the 1980s. Its 210-ft gray concrete tower, visible from almost anywhere in the city, is open to the public, allowing a panoramic view of the city and its expansive suburbs. ✉ *Top of Skólavörðustígur,* ☎ *551–0745.* ⏲ *May–Sept., daily 9–6; Oct.–Apr., daily 10–6.*

16 **Höfði.** Mikhail Gorbachev and Ronald Reagan met here for the Reykjavík Summit of 1986. Rumored to be haunted, the house now serves as a venue for city functions. It is decorated with some of the city's art and opens to the public in summer, on the first Sunday of each month. ✉ *Near junction of Borgartún and Nóatún.*

12 **Íslenska Óperan** (Icelandic Opera). Reminiscent of old-fashioned movie houses, this building was, in fact, Iceland's first cinema. The resident company performs here in winter. ✉ *Ingólfsstræti,* ☎ *551–1475.*

19 **Kjarvalsstaðir** (Reykjavík Municipal Art Museum). This municipal art museum, named for Jóhannes Kjarval (1885–1972), the nation's best-known painter, displays the artist's lava landscapes and images of mystical beings. It also shows works by contemporary Icelandic artists and great masters, as well as visiting exhibits. ✉ *Flókagata, Miklatún Park,* ☎ *552–6131.* ⏲ *Daily 10–6.*

9 **Lækjartorg** (Brook Square). A focal point of Old Midtown, this square opens onto **Austurstræti**, a semipedestrian shopping street. ✉ *Junction of Bankastræti and Lækjargata.*

22 **Listasafn Einars Jónssonar** (National Gallery of Einar Jónsson). Cubic and fortresslike, this building was once the home and studio of Iceland's leading early 20th-century sculptor (1874–1954). His monumental works explore mystical subjects. The sculpture garden is always open. ✉ *Njarðargata,* ☎ *551–3797.* ⏲ *June–mid-Sept., Tues.–Sun. 1:30–4; mid-Sept.–Nov. and Feb.–May, weekends 1:30–4.*

6 **Listasafn Íslands** (National Gallery). A collection of Icelandic art fills the stately white building overlooking Tjörnin Lake. ✉ *Fríkirkjuvegur 7,* ☎ *562–1000,* WEB *www.natgall.is.* ⏲ *Tues.–Sun. noon–6.*

1 **Listasafn Reykjavíkur, Hafnarhúsið** (Harbor House, Reykjavík Municipal Gallery). The huge gallery was converted as part of the capital's participation as a Cultural City of Europe 2000. Among the holdings are hundreds of works by the expatriate Icelandic pop artist Erró. ✉ *Tryggvagötu 17,* ☎ *511–5155.* ⏲ *Wed. and Fri. 11–6, Thurs. 11–7.*

7 **Menntaskólinn í Reykjavík** (Reykjavík Grammar School). Many graduates from the country's oldest educational institution, established in 1846, have gone on to dominate political and social life in Iceland. ✉ *Corner of Amtmannsstígur and Lækjargata.*

15 **Náttúrufræðistofnun** (Museum of Natural History). One of the last great auks is on display here, along with other exhibits that focus on Icelandic natural history. ✉ *Hlemmtorg, Hverfisgata 116,* ☎ *562–9822,* WEB *www.ni.is.* ⊙ *Tues., Thurs., and weekends 1:30–4.*

26 **Norræna Húsið** (Nordic House). Designed by Finnish architect Alvar Aalto, this blue-and-white cultural center hosts exhibitions, lectures, and concerts; it has a library and a coffee shop. ✉ *Sæmundargata,* ☎ *551–7030,* WEB *www.nordice.is.* ⊙ *Exhibitions daily 2–7, coffee shop daily 9–5.*

20 **Perlan** (The Pearl). The gleaming glass dome perches like a space station on a hill atop six huge hot-water tanks that provide hot water for much of the capital area. Paths in the wooded slopes and the warm effluent water at the shoreline draw many locals for sport and relaxation. Two man-made geysers—one inside, erupting frequently, and Strókur on the south slope, spouting without pumps on the same pressure and release system as in natural geysers—complement the site. Also inside you'll find a balcony with splendid views, a coffee shop, an ice-cream bar, and a fine restaurant. ✉ *Öskjuhlíð Hill,* ☎ *562–0200.* ⊙ *Daily 11:30–10.*

25 **Þjóðarbókhlaða** (National and University Library). Clad in red aluminum, this 1994 edifice is hard to miss. It houses a substantial collection. ✉ *Corner of Birkimelur and Hringbraut,* ☎ *563–5600,* WEB *www.bok.hi.is.* ⊙ *Weekdays 9–7, Sat. 10–5.*

13 **Þjóðleikhús** (National Theater). The interior of this structure reflects the basalt lava columns that are typical in Icelandic geology. It is a venue for the biennial Reykjavík Arts Festival and, from fall to spring, diverse cultural events and drama. ✉ *Hverfisgata 19,* ☎ *551–1200.*

11 **Þjóðmenningarhúsið** (National Culture House). Crests on the facade of this impressive classic building, once the National Library, name prominent Icelandic literary figures. Lavishly renovated, it now houses diverse changing cultural exhibits. ✉ *Hverfisgata 15,* ☎ *545–1400,* FAX *562–3427,* WEB *www.kultur.is/vefurinn/kulturhus.htm.* ⊙ *Daily 11–5.*

24 **Þjóðminjasafn** (National Museum). On display are Viking artifacts, national costumes, weavings, carvings, and silver. ✉ *Suðurgata 141,* ☎ *530–2200.* ⊙ *Mid-May–mid-Sept., Tues.–Sun. 11–5; late Sept.–early May, Tues., Thurs., and weekends noon–5.*

4 **Ráðhús** (Reykjavík City Hall). Inside are a tourist information desk, a large-scale relief map of Iceland, and a coffee shop. Modern architecture and nature meet here—not only with Tjörnin Lake to the south, but with water seeping over moss on the building's north wall. ✉ *Vonarstræti and Tjarnargata,* ☎ *563–2000.* ⊙ *Weekdays 8:20–4:15; coffee shop, weekdays 11–6, weekends noon–6.*

23 **Safn Ásgríms Jónssonar** (Ásgrímur Jónsson Collection). Works by this well-regarded post-Impressionist painter (1876–1958) are displayed in his house, left otherwise untouched since his death. ✉ *Bergstaðastræti 74,* ☎ *551–3644.* ⊙ *June–Aug., Tues.–Sun. 1:30–4; Sept.–Nov. and Feb.–May, weekends 1:30–4.*

10 **Stjórnarráð** (Government House). Once a jail, this white, 18th-century building now houses the offices of Iceland's prime minister. ✉ *Lækjartorg, on seaward side of Bankastræti.*

27 **Stofnun Árna Magnússonar** (Árni Magnússon Manuscript Institute). Named for Árni Magnússon (1663–1730), who was instrumental in preserving priceless manuscripts, this facility houses what is arguably Iceland's greatest cultural treasure. Ancient volumes, some made of calf-

skin or vellum and illuminated, contain many of the sagas and much of the mythical poetry that established medieval Icelandic literature as some of the greatest in the world. ✉ *Suðurgata, University of Iceland,* ☎ *525–4010.* ⏲ *Mid-June–Sept., Mon.-Sat. 2–6.*

❺ **Tjörnin.** This natural, shallow lake is haven to a variety of birds, from majestic swans to elegant Arctic terns. In colder winters, skaters venture out onto it. At the south end of the lake, **Hljómskálagarður Park** is a fine spot to relax. ✉ *Bounded by Tjarnargata/Bjarkargata on west and Fríkirkjuvegur/Sóleyjargata on east.*

Dining

Most Reykjavík restaurants offer excellent seafood and lamb dishes. Winter menus often include game, such as goose, ptarmigan, or reindeer. Lavish winter holiday buffets offer innumerable varieties of seafood, meats, and desserts. Evening reservations are necessary on weekends in the better restaurants. Some offer discounts at lunch, or daily specials or tourist menus that may beat some entrée prices. For details and price-category definitions, *see* Dining *in* Iceland A to Z, *above.*

$$$$ ✕ **Gallery at Hótel Holt.** The walls of this distinguished hotel dining room are covered with Icelandic art from the owner's private collection. You can indulge in such mouthwatering seafood as gravlax and grilled halibut, and there's a fabulous wine list to match. ✉ *Hotél Holt, Bergstaðastræti 37,* ☎ *552–5700. AE, DC, MC, V.*

$$$$ ★ ✕ **Perlan.** In this rather formal revolving restaurant under "The Pearl" dome, you may pay a bit more for the food—including Icelandic fish and lamb dishes—but the splendid view, especially at sunset, justifies the expense. ✉ *Öskjuhlíð,* ☎ *562–0200. AE, DC, MC, V. No lunch.*

$$$–$$$$ ✕ **Hjá Sigga Hall á Oðinsvé.** Iceland's own TV celebrity chef reigns at this intimate hotel restaurant creating delicious and innovative offerings of fish, lamb, and, in season, game. ✉ *Oðinstorg,* ☎ *552–5090. AE, DC, MC, V.*

$$$ ✕ **Við Tjörnina.** The imaginative seafood here, including marinated cod cheeks and, in season, *tindabikkja* (starry ray), is served on the second floor of a typical early 20th-century house clad in corrugated iron. Lunch specials are an enticing value. ✉ *Templarasund 3,* ☎ *551–8666,* FAX *561–8666,* WEB *www.islandia.is/~vidtjornina/. AE, MC, V.*

$$ ✕ **Potturinn og pannan.** This cozy restaurant on the edge of the downtown area boasts a varied menu of seafood, lamb, beef, pork, and chicken, as well as an ever-popular salad bar. ✉ *Brautarholt 22,* ☎ *551–1690. MC, V.*

$$ ✕ **Þrír Frakkar hjá Úlfari.** Housed in an unassuming building in an older part of town, this restaurant features truly traditional Icelandic food emphasizing the sea's bounty, including the novelty whale-meat sushi. The bright annex overlooks a tiny, tree-filled park. ✉ *Baldursgata 14,* ☎ *552–3939. MC, V.*

$ ✕ **Hús málarans.** The name means "The Painter's House," and that's what this building was called until the 1970s, when the old paint shop closed. Now it's a thriving café with menu items showing influence from Mexico to Japan. On Thursdays, live jazz upstairs adds even more flavor. ✉ *Bankastræti 7a,* ☎ *562–3232. MC, V.*

Lodging

Hotels run the gamut from elegant to simple, classic to modern. For details and price-category definitions, *see* Lodging *in* Iceland A to Z, *above.*

$$$$ 🏨 **Radisson SAS Saga Hótel.** All rooms above the fourth floor have spectacular views. Hillary Clinton and her entourage stayed here during an official visit, occupying nearly 200 rooms. Like her, you can enjoy a full range of services, nearby museums, shops, and restaurants. ✉ *Hagatorg, IS-107, ☎ 525–9900, FAX 525–9909. 216 rooms, 9 suites. 2 restaurants. AE, DC, MC, V.*

$$$–$$$$ **Hótel Borg.** Elegant Art Deco rooms retain their original style but are equipped with CD players and coffeemakers. Expansion into upper floors has created unique rooms, including a luxurious tower suite. ✉ *Pósthússtræti 11, IS-101, ☎ 551–1440, FAX 551–1420, WEB www.hotelborg.is. 50 rooms, 3 suites. Restaurant. AE, DC, MC, V.*

$$$–$$$$ **Hótel Holt.** One of Reykjavík's finest hotels, the Holt has superb service and the exquisite Gallery Restaurant. Rooms are on the small side but, like the aptly named restaurant, are warmed by works of leading Icelandic artists and snuggled in a peaceful residential neighborhood. ✉ *Bergstaðastræti 37, IS-101, ☎ 552–5700, FAX 562–3025, WEB www.holt.is. 42 rooms, 12 suites. Restaurant. AE, DC, MC, V.*

$$$ **Hótel Esja, Icelandair Hotel.** With its in-house Planet Pulse health facility, this hotel pampers its guests with spa therapies and a wide variety of exercise options, including personal trainers. Rooms in the box layer-cake building of blue panels and glass are appealingly decorated in neutral colors; those facing north have a view of the hotel's namesake mountain. At press time, plans for a major expansion were going on the drawing board, but the hotel should remain open with service uncompromised. ✉ *Suðurlandsbraut 2, IS-108, ☎ 505–0950, FAX 505–0955, WEB www.icehotel.is/esja. 160 rooms, 12 suites. Restaurant. AE, DC, MC, V.*

$$$ **Hótel Reykjavík.** This hotel's unimposing facade incorporates a vertical wedge of windows to channel light inward; rooms have smart, Nordic-style furnishings. A hidden wing has now added more than two dozen rooms to this conveniently located hotel. ✉ *Rauðarárstígur 37, IS-105, ☎ 562–6250, FAX 562–6350, WEB www.hotelreykjavik.is. 79 rooms, 8 suites. 2 restaurants. AE, DC, MC, V.*

$$ **FossHótel Lind.** Though indulging in few frills, the Lind offers clean, comfortable rooms. It's near the Hlemmur bus station and a 15-minute walk from downtown. ✉ *Rauðarárstígur 18, IS-105, ☎ 562–3350, FAX 562–3351, WEB www.fosshotel.is. 56 rooms. Restaurant. DC, MC, V.*

$$ **Hotel Leifur Eiríksson.** Across from Reykjavík's biggest church, this hotel is convenient to countless boutiques, galleries, and city attractions. ✉ *Skólavörðustígur 45, IS-101, ☎ 562–0800, FAX 562–0804. 29 rooms. Restaurant. MC, V.*

$–$$ **Tower Guesthouse.** Stylishly decorated apartment units are convenient to the shopping street Laugavegur, but quietly tucked a block away. Have breakfast or unwind on the balconies, one of which has a Jacuzzi open to all guests. ✉ *Gretisgata 6, IS-101, ☎ 562–3350, FAX 552–5581, WEB www.towerguesthouse.homestead.com. 3 apartments. Full kitchen with each unit. MC, V.*

$ **Hotel Garður.** A student dormitory convenient to the National Museum and downtown, it is open as a hotel only from June through August. The rooms are basic but modern. ✉ *Hringbraut, IS-107, ☎ 551–5656. 44 rooms with shared bath. AE, DC, MC, V. Book through City Hotel, ☎ 511–1155, FAX 552–9040. WEB www.cityhotel.is*

Shopping

The main shopping street starts at Lækjartorg, heads east up the hill as Bankastræti, and continues on to become Laugavegur where the street Skólavörðustígur angles down from the facade of Hallgrímskirkja. Skólavörðustígur has been reborn as a center for distinctive custom jewelry, Icelandic-designed fashions, arts, crafts, and leatherwork.

At the **Handknitting Association of Iceland** (✉ Skólavörðustígur 9, ☎ 552–1890) you can buy high-quality hand knits through a cooperative. The **Kringlan Mall** (✉ junction of Miklabraut and Kringlumýrarbraut) offers indoor shelter for shopping when the cold winds blow outside. **Rammagerðin** (✉ Hafnarstræti 19, ☎ 551–7910) stocks a wide range of Icelandic clothes and souvenirs. For other bargains, try the weekend flea market, **Kolaprotið** (✉ harborside in the Customs House on Geirsgata) between 11 and 5.

Reykjavík Essentials

AIRPORTS AND TRANSFERS

Flights from the United States and Europe arrive at Keflavík Airport, 50 km (31 mi) south of Reykjavík. Reykjavík Airport is the central hub of domestic air travel in Iceland.

➤ AIRPORT INFORMATION: **Keflavík Airport** (☎ 505–0500). **Reykjavík Airport** (☎ 569–4100).

TRANSFERS

Flybus automatically connects with all flights to and from Keflavík. The trip into town takes 45 minutes. Terminals are at Hótel Loftleiðir and Hótel Esja, with requested stops in Garðabær and Hafnarfjörður. Taxis are also available.

➤ TAXIS AND SHUTTLES: **Flybus** (☎ 562–1011).

BUS TRAVEL TO AND FROM REYKJAVÍK

Central Reykjavík is served by two bus stations: Lækjartorg and Hlemmur. These punctuate the popular shopping street, Laugavegur, near its west end and midpoint.

BUS TRAVEL WITHIN REYKJAVÍK

Buses run from 7 AM to around midnight, some slightly later on weekends. The flat fare for Reykjavík and suburbs is IKr150 for adults. Exact change may be required. Strips of tickets are available from bus drivers and at stations. If you need to change buses, ask for a *skiptimiði* (free transfer ticket, pronounced "*skiff*-ti-mi-thi").

CONSULATES

➤ CANADA: (✉ Suðurlandsbraut 10, IS-101, ☎ 568–0820).

EMERGENCIES

Many pharmacies are open at night and on weekends. Lyf & heilsa apotek has two relatively convenient locations, listed below. More information may also be obtained by calling the pharmacy information line, also listed below.

➤ DOCTORS AND DENTISTS: **Dentist** (☎ 575–0505 for recorded information). **Doctor** (☎ 544–4114).

➤ EMERGENCY SERVICES: **Police, ambulance, fire** (☎ 112).

➤ LATE-NIGHT PHARMACIES: **Lyf & heilsa apotek** (✉ Austerver, Háaleitisbraut 68, ☎ 581–2101; ✉ Domus Medica, Egilsgötu 3, ☎ 563–1020). **Pharmacy information line** (☎ 551–8888).

ENGLISH-LANGUAGE MEDIA

➤ BOOKSTORES: **Bókabúð Steinars** (✉ Bergstaðastræti 7, ☎ 551–2030). **Eymundsson-Penninn** (✉ Austurstræti 18, ☎ 511–1130 or 511–1140). **Mál og menning** (✉ Laugavegur 18, ☎ 552–4240).

TAXIS

Rates start at about IKr400; few in-town taxi rides exceed IKr900.

➤ TAXI COMPANIES: **BSR** (☎ 561–0000 or 561–1720). **Bæjarleiðir** (☎ 553–3500). **Hreyfill** (☎ 588–5522).

TOURS

SINGLE- AND MULTIPLE-DAY TOURS

Most longer tours operate between June and September and cost from IKr25,000 to IKr150,000 per person, including accommodations and three meals a day. On some tours you'll stay in hotels, on others in tents. Such tours typically last from 3 to 19 days. One-day tours from Reykjavík include above all the classic circle to Gullfoss Waterfall, the hot-spring area at Geysir, and the founding site of Parliament at Þingvellir. Tours can be booked through bus companies, airlines, and travel agencies. For information on reliable tour operators, contact the Icelandic Tourist Board.

TRAVEL AGENCIES

➤ LOCAL AGENTS: **Guðmundur Jónasson Travel** (✉ Borgartún 34, IS-105, ☎ 511–1515, FAX 511–1511, WEB www.gjtravel.is). **Samvinn Travel** (✉ Sætún 1, Box 910, IS-105, ☎ 569–1070, FAX 552–7796, WEB www.samvinn.is). **Úrval–Útsýn Travel** (✉ Lágmúli 4, IS-108, ☎ 585–4000 or 800–6300, FAX 585–4065, WEB www.urvalutsyn.is).

THE COUNTRYSIDE

Incredible natural contrasts appear throughout Iceland's beautiful countryside. Magnificent, diverse fjords impart a scenic wrinkle to all coasts except the south, which is marked by spacious plains, foothills, and bizarre black sands crowned by pristine white glaciers. The interior highlands, a challenge to reach, are raw wonderlands of panorama and solitude. You are never far from cool waterfalls, steamy hot-springs, or snowcapped summits.

The amount of countryside you can cover depends on time. And there's plenty of that during the summer midnight sun. Trips from Reykjavík can easily be expanded to several rewarding days in the neighboring southern or western regions. To circle the country via the Ring Road (Road 1), allow at least a week, so you have time to explore spectacular attractions along the way. There can be up to 170 km (105 mi) between towns and gas stations.

The South

You reach the rich piedmont and coastal farmlands of the south by descending the plateau east of Reykjavík along the Ring Road. Look off-shore toward the southeast on your way down, and you may see Vestmannaeyjar (the Westman Islands) in the distance. Once down, you'll quickly come upon the village of Hveragerði, noted for greenhouses and health retreats. Larger Selfoss is 15 minutes away and straddles the Ölfusá River. Much farther east you reach tiny Skógar, and you'll have lots of time to practice pronouncing it before you reach Kirkjubæjarklaustur (hint: *keer*-kyew-*bye*-yar-kler-ster). Next you'll reach the stunning **Skaftafell National Park.** But should you see a 50-year-old yellow jeep en route, show some tolerance, since the driver is nearing 90 (that's years, not mph) and is one of two bachelor brothers whose huge farmstead is at the awesome bluffs of Lómagnúpur. The region is anchored at Höfn (harbor) í Hornafjörður. This whole area, laced by major glacial rivers and some of the country's best-known waterfalls, like majestic Gullfoss and pure-white Skógafoss, is charged with geothermal springs, such as Geysir, namesake for spouting springs the world over.

Crowning the countryside are noteworthy peaks. Mt. Hekla, once said to be where lost souls were banished, is alive and well, last erupting (as of press time) in early 2000. The volcanic network under Europe's largest glacier, Vatnajökull, is also active. Resulting meltwater from a 1996 eruption pushed forward huge boulders and expanded the vast black sands of Skeiðarársandur, which cover a sizable part of the central south coast. Skiers, snowmobilers, and ice climbers find thrills at Vatnajökull, the world's largest temperate glacier. Don't miss the unique geology, flora, and fauna of Skaftafell National Park, with Hvannadalshnjúkur, Iceland's highest peak, just beyond its borders.

Hveragerði

Hveragerði, about 40 km (25 mi) east of Reykjavík, has hot springs and fruit and vegetable greenhouses. An unabashed tourist stop is the greenhouse **Eden,** where homegrown bananas have astonished visitors for years.

$$$–$$$$ **Hótel Örk.** Few hotels match the extras here, which include tennis courts, a pool, golf, and a sauna. Meals in the ground-floor restaurant are reasonable. Staff can book "spa cure" retreat packages at the nearby health clinic. *Breiðamörk 1, IS-810, 483–4700, FAX 483–4775, WEB www.keyhotel.is. 85 rooms. Restaurant, pool. DC, MC, V.*

$ **Ból Youth Hostel & Ljósbrá Guesthouse.** Rooms in the hostel have up to five beds and share kitchen facilities. The guest house has five doubles with bath. Staff are a trove of information. *Hveramörk 14, IS-810, 483–4198 hostel, FAX 483–4088, 483–4588 guesthouse, FAX 483–4088. 20 beds. MC, V. Closed mid-Sept.–mid-May.*

Selfoss

Selfoss, on the turbulent Ölfusá River, is the south's largest community. With many diverse services, it is home to the nation's largest dairy plant.

$$$ **Hótel Selfoss.** On the glacial riverbanks, this hotel is a perfect base for visits to inland sites or the coast. The restaurant is the town's best eatery. A new wing is planned for mid-2002. *Eyravegur 2, IS-800, 482–2500, FAX 482–2524, WEB www.ka.is. 20 rooms. Restaurant. AE, MC, V.*

Skógar

Skógar, 120 km (75 mi) east of Selfoss, is near one of the country's most picturesque waterfalls, **Skógafoss.** What you see from the bottom is the final drop in a series of cascades and rapids that reward the hiker. The town also boasts one of the country's best rural museums, **Byggðarsafniði Skógar** (just east of Hótel Edda Skógar), whose curator is a walking encyclopedia and has been commended for his efforts with the Falcon Medal of Honor, the nation's highest distinction.

$$ **Hótel Edda Skógar.** Close to the Skógafoss waterfall, and near a dramatic glacial backdrop, this airy summer hotel has views of the sea and lush green slopes. *Skógar IS-861, 487–8870, FAX 487–8858. 34 rooms without bath. Restaurant. AE, MC, V. Closed Sept.–May.*

Kirkjubæjarklaustur

Aptly named Kirkjubæjarklaustur (or "church farm cloister") was the site of a medieval convent. When the volcano Laki erupted in 1783, producing the greatest amount of lava from a single eruption in recorded history, its deposits reshaped the landscape. A tiny chapel commemorates the pastor whose prayers are said to have stopped the lava before it reached these habitations. Two lovely nearby waterfalls and a first-rate August chamber-music festival are among local attractions. At the foot of Systrafoss waterfalls, beneath the town bluffs, visit **Kirkjubæjarstofa** (Kirkjubæjar Center; Klausturvegur 2, IS–880, 487–4645) for exhibits on regional nature and culture.

$$$–$$$$ **Hotel Kirkjubæjarklaustur, Icelandair Hotel.** This excellent facility is open year-round. For liquid and solid refreshment, head to the bar and restaurant in the spacious newer building. ✉ *Klausturvegur 6, IS-880,* ☎ *487–4799,* FAX *487–4614,* WEB *www.icehotel.is. 73 rooms, 57 with shower. Restaurant, pool (summers). MC, V.*

Skaftafell National Park

★ Near the foot of Skaftafellsjökull Glacier, you can hike from lowland sands into lush foothills, and on to hidden glacial canyons and stunning mountaintops. If you're lucky, you will glimpse Iceland's highest summit, Hvannadalshnjúkur Peak, rising 6,950 ft just outside the park borders. About 32 km (20 mi) east of the park is the adventure world of **Jökulsárlón,** where you can tour the glacial lagoon's eerie ice floes by boat.

$$ **Hótel Skaftafell.** Near Skaftafell National Park, this hotel has an unmatched setting. Rooms come in three varieties: contemporary with private bath, spartan without bath, and, last, without bed linens for which you provide a sleeping bag. The latter two share bathrooms, but kitchen facilities are a plus. ✉ *Freysnes, Öræfi, IS-785,* ☎ *478–1945,* FAX *478–1946,* WEB *www.hotelskaftafell.is. 53 rooms, 43 with bath. Restaurant. AE, MC, V.*

$ **Skaftafell National Park Campground and Service Center.** This spacious campground has excellent facilities. ✉ *Skaftafell National Park, Rte. 998 off Ring Road 1,* ☎ *478–1627. MC, V. Closed Sept.–June.*

Höfn

Höfn, the major port community of the southeast, offers fine views of Europe's largest glacier, **Vatnajökull,** and the adjacent mountains.

$ ✕ **Kaffi Hornið.** Despite its name, which means Coffee Corner, this is more than just a coffee spot. Buffets, a salad bar, and piping-hot soups make this log-cabin eatery popular with locals and travelers alike. ✉ *Hafnarbraut 42,* ☎ *478–2600. MC, V.*

$$$ **FossHótel Vatnajökull.** This hotel with spectacular views of the glacier has a nationwide reputation for quality accommodations and excellent cooking. ✉ *Lindarbakki, Hornafjörður, IS-780,* ☎ *478–2555,* FAX *478–2444,* WEB *www.fosshotel.is. 26 rooms. Restaurant. MC, V. Closed Sept. 16–Jan. 1.*

$$$ **Hótel Höfn.** With splendid views of both mountains and sea, this hotel also has impeccable rooms. There's an emphasis on dining, whether in the upper-level restaurant, where sumptuous buffets and reindeer steak may be found, or in the ground-level bistro, where you can have lobster 101 ways (almost). ✉ *Hornafjörður, IS-780,* ☎ *478–1240,* FAX *478–1996,* WEB *www.icehotel.is. 36, 32 with bath. Restaurant. MC, V.*

Westman Islands

This cluster of islets off Iceland's south coast again became the focus of world attention when Keiko, the Orca whale that starred in the movie *Free Willy,* was brought to **Heimaey,** the largest of the Westman Islands. In a roomy sea pen he has thrived from the day he arrived. If all goes according to plan, by the time this book comes out he may be roving ambassador for Heimaey.

Heimaey has one of Iceland's best natural-history museums, the **Fiska- og náttúrugripasafn** (Fish and Nature Research Center); its reliable work was pivotal in returning Keiko to the Icelandic waters from which he was taken in the 1970s. ✉ *Heiðarvegur 12,* ☎ *481–1997.* ⊙ *May–Aug., daily 11–5; Sept.–Apr., weekends 3–5.*

On the first weekend of August, thronging islanders celebrate the 1874 grant of Icelandic sovereignty with a **festival** on Heimaey. The population and hundreds of visiting revelers move into a tent city in Herjólfsdalur (Herjólfur's Valley), a 10-minute stroll west of town, for a raucous extended weekend of bonfires, fireworks, dance, and song.

The nearby **Surtsey,** which erupted onto the scene as a new island in 1963, is preserved for ecological research and is closed to the public.

The East

Bustling fishing towns and villages dot Iceland's east coast. As names such as Stöðvarfjörður, Fáskrúðsfjörður, and Reyðarfjörður testify, each village has its own fjord. Farming thrives in the valleys, which enjoy almost continental summers.

Djúpivogur

Some of the oldest buildings in Djúpivogur, a trading post since the 1500s, date from the Danish monopoly that ended in 1855. One, **Langabúð** (✉ second house inland from the pier, ☎ 478–8220), besides being a local museum and coffee shop, pays tribute to the late master woodcarver and sculptor Ríkarður Jónsson, whose ornate Rococo mirror frame, done to complete his apprenticeship, would fit handsomely in any Tuscan palace. Nearby, pyramidal Mt. Búlandstindur, legendary as a force of mystical power, rises to 6,130 ft.

$$ **Hótel Framtíð.** A large dining room, where fish is the forte, and an annex, all in square-hewn Finnish timber, give this friendly harborside hotel a country look. ✉ *Vogaland 4, IS-765,* ☎ *478–8887,* FAX *478–8187,* WEB *www.isholf.is/framtid. 18 rooms. Restaurant. AE, MC, V.*

$ **Berunes Youth Hostel.** This hostel offers lodging for 25 people in two-, three-, and four-person rooms. There are two separate cottages for five and seven people. Reserve in advance fall–spring. ✉ *Beruneshreppur, IS-765,* ☎ FAX *478–8988. 30 beds. MC, V.*

Breiðdalsvík

Commerce in this tiny village of a few hundred souls dates from 1883. The hamlet offers stores, a hotel, and boats.

$$ **Hótel Bláfell.** The hotel has a cozy, rustic interior and a homey, award-winning restaurant. ✉ *Sólvellir 14, IS-760,* ☎ *475–6770,* FAX *475–6668,* WEB *www.centrum.is/~blafell. 23 rooms, 17 with bath. Restaurant. MC, V.*

Seyðisfjörður

Although it's hard to believe now, the quaint village of Seyðisfjörður was one of Iceland's major trading ports in the 1800s, when tall sailing ships plied the crowded fjord. Beautiful wooden houses and buildings in Norwegian style attest to its affluent past. Nowadays in summer, the ferry *Norröna* cruises regularly into harbor from Europe. Summer Wednesday-evening concerts and exhibitions abound; for information contact the tourist office.

$$ **Hótel Seyðisfjörður.** In a classic Norse-style wooden house, this hotel overlooking the dramatic fjord puts out a varied buffet on summer Wednesdays, accompanied by live music. Rooms are tidy and cozy but not lavish. ✉ *Austurvegur 3, IS-710,* ☎ *472–1460,* FAX *472–1570. 8 rooms. Restaurant. AE, MC, V.*

Egilsstaðir

Egilsstaðir, commercial hub of the eastern sector, has an airport equipped for international flights. The town straddles the Ring Road and lies on the eastern shore of Lake Lögurinn, reputed home of a wormlike serpent that guards a treasure chest. Named ***Lagarflótsormurinn*** like the monster, a pleasure ship now plies the glacially murky waters, scanning for supernatural spouts of steam. ✉ *Main River Bridge, ☎ 896–6452, FAX 471–2414.*

The **Bright Nights in June** festival offers opera and classical music, while contrasting tastes are served by an international jazz festival of long standing. For information on the music, as well as nearby attractions, contact the Marketing Office of East Iceland (✉ Campground, IS-700 Egilsstaðir, ☎ 471–2000, FAX 472–1751). The nation's largest forest, **Hallormsstaðarskógur,** is 25 km (15 mi) south of Egilsstaðir. Native birch and planted aspen, larch, and spruce have grown tall here. The woods are ideal for walkers and horseback riders. Cross the valley bridge from the forest to visit **Skriðuklaustur** (☎ 471–2990), an unusual stone-covered mansion built by the writer Gunnar Gunnarsson, and donated by him to the state for an agricultural research station and visiting artist's residence.

$$ **Hótel Hérað, Icelandair Hotel.** Offering views of the nearby meadows and glacial lake, this modern hotel is convenient to Egilsstaðir's shops and the town pool. ✉ *Miðvangur 5–7 IS-700, ☎ 471–1500, FAX 471–1501. 36 rooms. Restaurant. AE, D, MC, V.*

$$ **Hótel Svartiskógur.** This pleasant countryside haven has plain but inviting rooms behind a stream, well away from traffic. Breakfast and previously ordered meals are available. ✉ *Svartiskógur IS-701, northwest of Egilsstaðir, 23 km (14½ mi) on Ring Road 1, turn 8 km (5 mi) north on Road 917 to Vopnafjörður, ☎ 471–1030, FAX 471–1016. 11 rooms. MC, V Closed Oct.–Apr., except by arrangement for groups.*

The North

The north coast is deeply gouged by fjords, from Vopnafjörður in the east to Hrútafjörður (Rams' Fjord) in the west. In fact, Eyjafjörður, the country's longest, dips far inward to Akureyri, the "Capital of the North." In the region's midsection, large, well-established farms, some dating from Viking times, have thrived in fertile valleys, whose rivers attract salmon fishers.

Húsavík

★ Húsavík is a charming port with a uniquely painted timber church. Handy to nearby winter sports, it is also a base for summer hiking. Whale watchers have had amazing success (99%) on tours aboard restored oak boats. The new **Hvalamiðstöð á Húsavík** (Húsavík Whale Center) has exhibits on Iceland's history as a whaling nation and on the biology of these behemoths. ✉ *Sólbrekka 21, ☎ 464–2520. ⏲ May–Aug., daily 9–9; Sept.–Apr., upon request.*

★ The true jewel of this area is **Mývatn,** a lake surrounded by fascinating "false" and eruptive craters, as well as varied, abundant birdlife. More duck species nest here than at any other lake on earth, and the harlequin duck and Barrow's goldeneye exist nowhere else in Europe. Bring head nets if you visit in summer, because the lake is rightly named for midges.

In the region around Mývatn, shrub lands, lava barrens, and black sands are traversed by rivers with impressive waterfalls. At **Goðafoss** (Waterfall of the Gods), the leader of the pagan Norse faith at Parliament in the year 1000 tossed his religious icons into the waterfall to signal his acceptance of Christianity. Thundering **Dettifoss** on Jökulsá (Glacier River), southeast of Húsavík via the Tjörnes Peninsula, is Europe's most powerful waterfall, and its lengthy canyon is a national park. Also protected is the nearby hollow of **Ásbyrgi,** which, according to legend, is a giant hoofprint left by Sleipnir, the eight-legged horse of the ancient Norse god Óðinn.

$$$ **Hótel Húsavík.** Two new eateries and plenty of help in booking area day tours make this recently renovated hotel an attractive option. ✉ *Ketilsbraut 22, IS-640,* ☎ *464–1220,* FAX *464–2161,* WEB *www.hotel-husavik.is. 44 rooms. Café, bar. AE, D, MC, V.*

$$$ **Hótel Reynihlíð.** This well-situated, comfortable hotel provides an information service and restaurant for hungry travelers. The on-site eatery, Gamli Bærinn, is a friendly café by day, congenial pub by night. ✉ *Mývatn, IS-660 Reykjahlíð,* ☎ *464–4170,* FAX *464–4371,* WEB *www.reynihlid.is. 41 rooms. Restaurant. AE, DC, MC, V.*

$$$ **LykilHótel Skútustaðir.** The area's newest hotel has a delightful dining area with stunning views of the lake and landscape. ✉ *Skútustaðir, IS-660,* ☎ *464–4455,* FAX *551–6031,* WEB *www.keyhotel.is. 32 rooms. Restaurant. MC, V. Closed Sept. 16–May 14.*

$$ **Hótel Reykjahlíð.** This peaceful hotel is on the shore of Lake Mývatn, and bird-watchers can spot many of the lake's species right from their windows. Rooms have baths and all essentials, but nature supplies the luxury here. ✉ *Mývatn, IS-660 Reykjahlíð,* ☎ *464–4142,* FAX *464–4336,* WEB *www.reykjahlid.is. 7 rooms. Restaurant. MC, V.*

Akureyri

Akureyri's natural surroundings are unrivaled. Several 18th- and 19th-century wooden houses give the city a sense of history, as well as architectural variety. **Lystigarðurinn** (Arctic Botanic Gardens) has more than 400 species of flora native to Iceland and neighboring Greenland. ✉ *Eyrarlandsvegur.* ⏲ *Daily 8 AM–11 PM.*

With the northernmost 18-hole golf course in the world, Akureyri hosts the **Arctic Open Golf Tournament** during the unending days of midsummer. For details, contact local tourist information.

$$$$ **Hótel KEA.** Centrally located at the end of a pedestrian shopping lane, this first-class hotel has an excellent ground-level restaurant, Rósagarðurinn, serving haute cuisine. Room furnishings are elegant mahogany. ✉ *Hafnarstræti 87-89, IS-602,* ☎ *460–2000,* FAX *460–2060,* WEB *www.hotelkea.is. 73 rooms. Restaurant. AE, DC, MC, V.*

$$$ **LykilHótel (Key Hotel) Norðurland.** Rooms here are pleasantly decorated with Danish furnishings. The sitting room has an impressive view. ✉ *Geislagata 7, IS-600,* ☎ *462–2600,* FAX *462–7962,* WEB *www.keyhotel.is. 34 rooms. Restaurant. MC, V.*

$$ **Hótel Edda.** This summer hotel in a school dormitory is known for quality service and good meals. ✉ *Menntaskólinn v/Hrafngilstræti, IS-600,* ☎ *461–1434,* FAX *461–1423,* WEB *www.edda.is. 79 rooms, 14 with bath. Restaurant. MC, V. Closed Sept.–June 17.*

$ **Hostelling in Akureyri.** Accommodations run from bunks for those with sleeping bags, to separate, completely equipped cottages that sleep six comfortably. Kitchen facilities are available. ✉ *Stórholt 1, IS-600,* ☎ *462–3657 or 894–4299,* FAX *461–2549,* WEB *www.hostel.is. 17 rooms without bath. Hostel only closed Dec. 16–Jan. 9. MC, V.*

Sauðárkrókur

In summer, boat trips from the coastal town of Sauðárkrókur to Drangey and Málmey islands offer striking views of the fjord and bird cliffs.

$$$ **FossHótel Áning.** Views from the tidy, austere rooms of this summer hotel are of either the nearby mountains or the fjord. Hiking, golfing, horseback riding, boat touring, and river rafting can be arranged from here. ✉ *Sæmundarhlíð, IS-550,* ☎ *453–6717 or 562–4000,* FAX *453–6087,* WEB *www.fosshotel.is. 65 rooms. Restaurant. MC, V.*

The West

At Iceland's dragon head—the rugged fjords at Europe's western tip—seabirds vastly outnumber people. Due south is the long arm of Snæfellsnes Peninsula, with the awe-inspiring Snæfellsjökull volcano. South of that peninsula lies Borgarfjörður, where wide farmlands steeped in the history of the Viking sagas still fire the imagination of visitors.

Ísafjörður

The uncrowned capital of the West Fjords and one of the most important fishing towns in Iceland hosts a renowned Easter week ski meet. With its quaint buildings and lively cultural activities, the town is a convenient jumping-off point for tours to Hornstrandir, the splendidly peaceful, desolate coast north of the 66th parallel that is inhabited by millions of seabirds.

$$$ **Hótel Ísafjörður.** A stone's throw from the sea, this hotel is great for families. The modern structure is decorated in Scandinavian style, and the restaurant offers haute cuisine, with delicious emphasis on fresh seafood. ✉ *Silfurtorg 2, IS-400,* ☎ *456–4111,* FAX *456–4767. 32 rooms. Restaurant. AE, MC, V.*

Stykkishólmur

Stykkishólmur is an active small port community, with a beautifully sheltered harbor. Classic timber houses, many lovingly restored, and some dating from as early as 1828, reveal its distinguished past, when many of the now-abandoned islets of Breiðafjörður were settled.

$ ✕ **Narfeyrarstofa.** This charming, tiny eatery in an old timber building serves homemade quiches, coffee, light entrées, and desserts daily until midnight in summer. In winter it's purely a coffee and dessert spot, but impromptu live music can spring up almost anytime. ✉ *Aðalgata 3,* ☎ *438–1119. MC, V.*

$$$ **FossHótel Stykkishólmur.** The town's largest hotel has views of the harbor and neighboring mountains. The restaurant features lamb, seafood, and, in season, puffin and other seabirds. ✉ *Borgarbraut 6, IS-340,* ☎ *430–2100,* FAX *430–2101,* WEB *www.fosshotel.is. 33 rooms. Restaurant. MC, V.*

Snæfellsjökull

Literally the high point on Snæfellsnes Peninsula is Snæfellsjökull, the entrance in Jules Verne's novel *Journey to the Center of the Earth*. This stupendous, glacier-covered, conical summit, according to local legend, possesses supernatural energies and is home to hidden folk.

Ólafsvík

Commerce has been carried on in this village, under the north shoulder of Snæfellsjökull, since 1687. From here you can hike to the top of the glacier or arrange snowmobile tours.

$$$ **Höfði Guest House.** This family-style harborside hotel has a charming restaurant that serves fresh local fare such as trout and halibut. ✉ *Ólafsbraut 20, IS-355,* ☎ *436–1650,* FAX *436–1651. 18 rooms with bath. Restaurant. AE, MC, V.*

The Countryside Essentials

TOURS

Aptly named Iceland Adventure can arrange a wide variety of exciting tours, be it glacier jeep safaris, skiing, snowmobiling, or river-rafting. ➤ FEES AND SCHEDULES: **Iceland Adventure** (☎ 577–5500, FAX 577–5511, WEB www.atours.is).

TOURS IN THE SOUTH

Boat tours can be arranged on arrival at the Jökulsárlón glacial lagoon. Jórvik Aviation offers spectacular sightseeing flights around and to Skaftafell National Park or can be chartered to anywhere in the country. Öræfaferðir, a father-son outfit, puts together tours ranging from ice climbing to hiking Iceland's highest mountain, to seal- and birdwatching. Toppferðir has four-wheel-drive glacier tours leaving from Hotel Vatnajökull. Westman Islands Travel offers informative, reasonably priced sightseeing by boat and bus in the Westman Islands.

➤ FEES AND SCHEDULES: **Jökulsárlón** (☎ 478–1065 or 852–0631). **Jórvik Aviation** (✉ Box 5308, Reykjavík, ☎ 562–5101, FAX 562–5201, WEB www.jorvik.is). **Öræfaferðir** (✉ Hofsnes-Öræfi, IS-785 Fagurhólsmýri, ☎ 478–1682, WEB www.simnet.is/coast-mountains/). **Toppferðir** (✉ Lindarbakki, Höfn in Hornafjörður, ☎ 478–2666). **Westman Islands Travel** (✉ Herjólfsgata 4, IS-900, ☎ 481–2922).

TOURS IN THE NORTH

In Húsavík, Norðursigling–North Sailing offers whale-watching aboard classic oak ships.

➤ FEES AND SCHEDULES: **Norðursigling–North Sailing** (✉ Box 122, IS-640 Húsavík, ☎ 464–2350).

TOURS IN THE WEST

Eyjaferðir runs boat tours. Snowmobile trips to the top of Snæfellsjökull are arranged for groups at Snjófell. West Tours runs adventure trips to isolated parts of the West Fjords.

➤ FEES AND SCHEDULES: **Eyjaferðir** (✉ Egilshús, Stykkishólmur, ☎ 438–1450). **Snjófell** (✉ Arnarstapi, ☎ 435–6783). **West Tours** (✉ Box 37, Ísafjörður, ☎ 456–5111).

VISITOR INFORMATION

➤ TOURIST INFORMATION: **Akureyri** (✉ Hafnarstræti 82, ☎ 462–7733). **Egilsstaðir** (✉ Campsite, ☎ 471–2320, WEB www.east.is). **Höfn** (✉ Campsite, Hafnarbraut, ☎ 478–1500). **Húsavík** (✉ Safnarhús/Museum, ☎ 464–1173). **Ísafjörður** (✉ Hafnarstræti 6, ☎ 456–5121). **Kirkjubæjarklaustur** (✉ Klausturvegur 10, ☎ 487–4620). **Mývatn** (✉ Eldá Travel, Mývatnssveit, ☎ 464–4220, WEB www.elda.is); contact Reykjahlíðarskóli School (☎ 464–4390) June–August. **Ólafsvík** (✉ Pakkhúsið, ☎ 436–1543). **Selfoss Tryggvaskáli** (✉ next to Ölfusá River bridge, ☎ 482–1704). **Seyðisfjörður** (✉ Vesturvegur 8, ☎ 472–1551, WEB www.sfk.is).

17 IRELAND

DUBLIN, DUBLIN TO CORK, CORK TO GALWAY, GALWAY TO DONEGAL, NORTHERN IRELAND

FOR A SMALL ISLAND COUNTRY isolated on the westernmost extreme of the continent, Ireland has nevertheless managed to strut its way around the European stage. Economically it has traditionally been a mere understudy to the major European powers (especially Great Britain); politically its influence is minimal; and yet everyone knows of the Irish, and they all cast a slightly envious eye at this mysterious island of romance.

Never more so than now. The booming economy has heralded a level of prosperity and development never before enjoyed, particularly in the capital city of Dublin. One-third of the country's very young population lives in the city, which is as much a college town as a center of government. Galleries, art-house cinemas, elegant shops, coffeehouses, and a stunning variety of restaurants are springing up on almost every street. Along with a welcome influx of immigrants from all corners of the globe, these factors are transforming the provincial capital that once suffocated Joyce into a city almost as cosmopolitan as the Paris to which he fled.

The pace of life outside Dublin is more relaxed. Indeed, the farther you travel from the metropolis, the more you'll be inclined to linger. Apart from such sporting attractions as championship golf, horse racing, angling, and the native games of hurling and Gaelic football, the thing to do in Ireland is to stop, take a deep breath of some of the best air in the western world, and look around.

The lakes of Killarney—a chain of azure lakes surrounded by wild, boulder-strewn mountains—are justifiably among the country's most famous attractions. The Ring of Kerry is a gift from the gods to touring motorists, an out-and-back daylong adventure through lush green mountain and valley, and on down to the sea. By contrast, the lunar landscape of County Clare's eerie limestone desert, the Burren, must be explored on foot if you're to enjoy its rare alpine and Mediterranean flowers. Likewise, if you want to stand on the summit of the Cliffs of Moher to watch the Atlantic breakers bite into the ancient rocks 710 ft below, you'll have to get out of your car—even in the rain, and it often rains in Clare. If you love history, there are plenty of delightful castles and great stately houses peppering the banks of the old River Shannon, the spine of the nation. Throughout the country, prehistoric and early Christian ruins and remains hint at the awesome age of civilization on this ancient island. Alternatively, you could just visit a bookstore and pick up anything by the great writers of Ireland; let James Joyce, William Butler Yeats, John Millington Synge, or Seamus Heaney be your travel guide as you seek out the places made famous in their works.

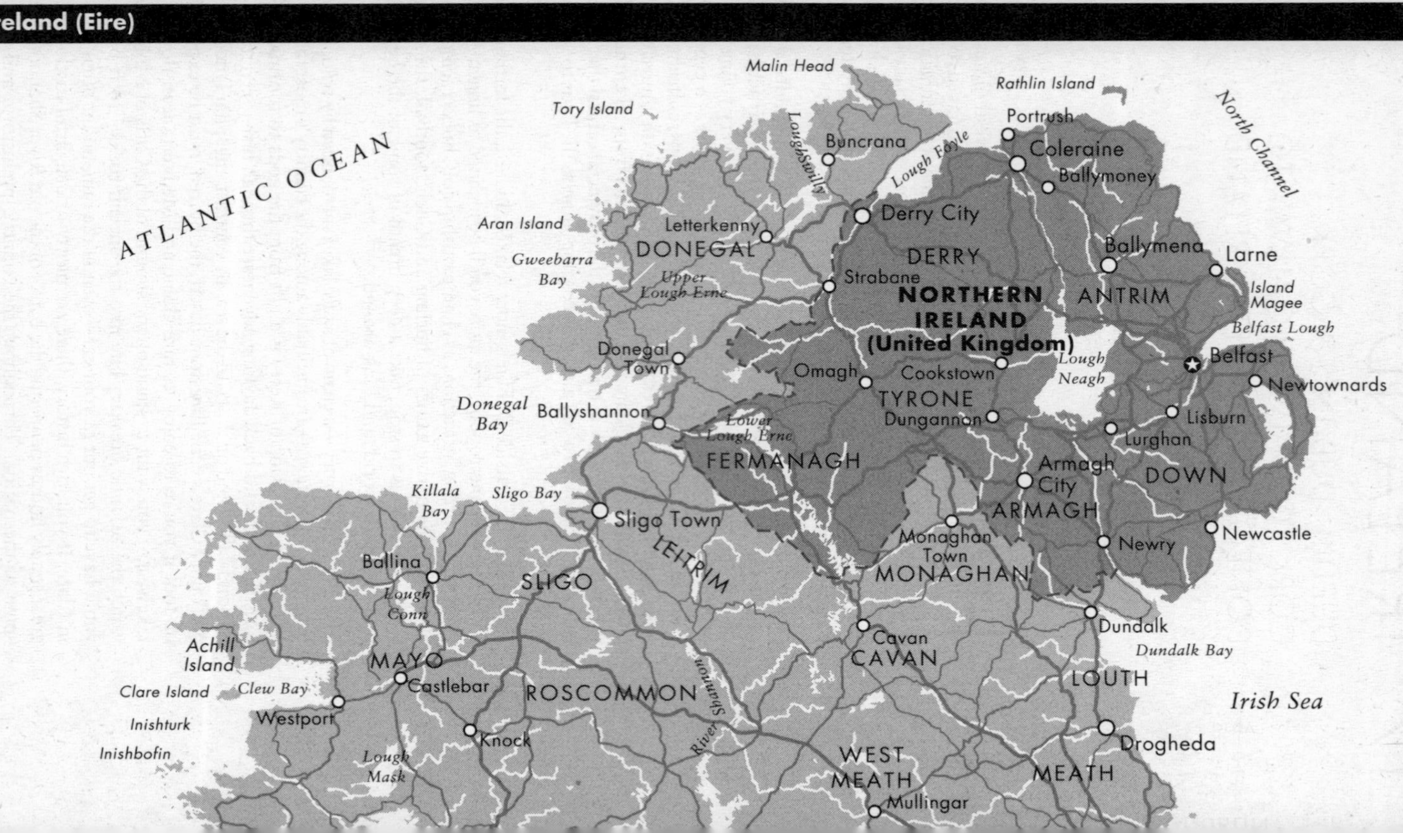
Malin Head
Rathlin Island
North Channel
Tory Island
Portrush
Coleraine
Ballymoney
Buncrana
Lough Swilly
Lough Foyle
ATLANTIC OCEAN
Aran Island
Letterkenny
DONEGAL
Derry City
DERRY
Ballymena
Larne
Island Magee
Gweebarra Bay
Upper Lough Erne
Strabane
NORTHERN IRELAND (United Kingdom)
ANTRIM
Belfast Lough
Belfast
Newtownards
Donegal Town
Omagh
Cookstown
Lough Neagh
TYRONE
Dungannon
Lisburn
Donegal Bay
Ballyshannon
Lower Lough Erne
Lurghan
FERMANAGH
Armagh City
DOWN
ARMAGH
Killala Bay
Sligo Bay
Sligo Town
LEITRIM
Monaghan Town
MONAGHAN
Newry
Newcastle
Ballina
Lough Conn
SLIGO
Dundalk
Dundalk Bay
Cavan
CAVAN
Achill Island
MAYO
Castlebar
ROSCOMMON
River Shannon
LOUTH
Irish Sea
Clare Island
Clew Bay
Westport
Inishturk
Knock
Drogheda
Inishbofin
Lough Mask
WEST MEATH
MEATH
Mullingar

REPUBLIC OF IRELAND
GALWAY
Lough Corrib
Galway City
Ballinasloe
Athlone
DUBLIN
Dublin
Dun Laoghaire
Bray
Naas
OFFALY
KILDARE
Galway Bay
Aran Islands
Birr
Portlaoise
LAOISE
Athy
Wicklow Town
WICKLOW
CLARE
Ennis
Roscrea
Nenagh
Arklow
CARLOW
KILKENNY
Kilrush
Limerick City
Thurles
Gorey
TIPPERARY
Kilkenny Town
LIMERICK
Cashel
Mouth of the Shannon
Listowel
Newcastle West
Tipperary
WEXFORD
Clonmel
Carrick-on-Suir
Wexford Town
Tralee
Dingle Peninsula
WATERFORD
Waterford City
Mallow
Fermoy
Killarney
Dingle Bay
Dungarvan
Blasket Islands
KERRY
CORK
Cork City
Iveragh Peninsula
Youghal
Midleton
Cobh
St. George's Channel
Bandon
Skellig Rocks
Kenmare Bay
Bantry Bay
Clonakilty
Skibbereen
Mizen Head
N
0
40 miles
0
60 km

IRELAND A TO Z

To research prices, get advice from other travelers, and book travel arrangements, visit www.fodors.com.

ADDRESSES

We have tried to provide full addresses for hotels, restaurants, and sights, though many of Ireland's villages and towns are so tiny they barely have street names, much less house numbers. If in doubt, ask for directions.

AIR TRAVEL

Distances are not great in Ireland, so airplanes play only a small role in internal travel. There are daily flights from Dublin to Belfast, Derry, Shannon, Cork, Waterford, Kerry, Knock, and Galway; all flights take about 30 minutes. There is frequent service to the Aran Islands, off Galway Bay, from Connemara Airport, Galway; the flight takes about six minutes.

BIKE TRAVEL

Biking can be a great way to get around Ireland. For information about renting bikes, contact Bord Fáilte. Rates average IR£8/€10.15 per day or IR£40/€50.80 per week. You must pay a IR£30/€38.10 deposit. Be sure to make reservations, especially in July and August. If you rent a bike in the Republic, you may *not* take it into Northern Ireland; nor may you take a bike rented in Northern Ireland into the Republic.

BOAT AND FERRY TRAVEL

Exploring Ireland's lakes, rivers, and canals is a delightful, offbeat way to get to know the country. Motor cruisers can be chartered on the Shannon, the longest river in the British Isles. Bord Fáilte has details of the wide choice of trips and operators available. For drifting through the historic Midlands on the Grand Canal and River Barrow, contact Celtic Canal Cruisers.

➤ BOAT AND FERRY INFORMATION: **Celtic Canal Cruisers** (✉ 24th Lock, Tullamore, Co. Offaly, ☎ 0506/21861).

BUS TRAVEL

Bus Éireann (Irish Bus) runs bus service in the Republic. The 15-day Rambler ticket gives unlimited travel by bus in the Republic and is an excellent value at IR£105/€133.30 (IR£145/€184.10 for all of Ireland). It can be purchased from any city bus terminal and is valid for travel on any 15 days in a 30-day period. The provincial bus system operated by Bus Éireann is widespread—more so than the train system—although service can be infrequent in remote areas. In Northern Ireland, all buses are operated by the state-owned Ulsterbus.

➤ BUS INFORMATION: **Bus Éireann** (☎ 01/836–6111).

BUSINESS HOURS

Banks are open weekdays 10–4 and until 5 on Thursday. In small towns they may close for lunch from 12:30 to 1:30. Museums are usually closed on Mondays but open Tuesday–Saturday 10–5, and Sunday 2–5. Always make a point of checking, however, as hours can change unexpectedly. Shops are open Monday–Saturday 9–5:30, closing earlier on Wednesday, Thursday, or Saturday, depending on the locality. Most shops, however, remain open until 9 PM on Thursday.

CAR TRAVEL

PARKING

Parking in towns (especially Dublin) can be difficult. Signs with the letter P indicate parking lots, but if there's a stroke through the P, keep away or you'll collect a stiff fine, normally around IR£15/€19.05. After 6 PM, restrictions are lifted. Give lot attendants about 50p/€.65 when you leave.

ROAD CONDITIONS

Ireland is one country in which a car is more or less essential to really get around. Despite improvements in public transportation, both the train and bus networks are limited, and many of the most intriguing regions are accessible only by car. Distances in Ireland seem short, but roads are narrow and often twisting and hilly, and side attractions are numerous, so you should aim for a daily mileage of no more than 240 km (149 mi). You'll find that driving past an ever-changing and often dramatic series of unspoiled landscapes is very much part of the fun. Outside the cities, the traffic is normally light, though you can easily find yourself crawling down country lanes behind an ancient tractor or a flock of sheep.

All principal roads are designated by the letter *N*, meaning National Primary Road. Thus, the main highway north from Dublin is N1, the main highway northwest is N2, and so on. Divided highways, or motorways—designated by blue signs and the letter *M*—take the place of some N roads. They are the fastest way to get from one point to another, but use caution, as they can end as abruptly as they begin. Road signs are usually in both Irish and English; in isolated parts of the northwest and Connemara, most are in Irish only, so make sure you have a good road map. A sensible rule to follow at unmarked intersections is to keep going straight if there's no sign directing you to do otherwise. Distances on the green signposts are in kilometers; white signposts give distances in miles.

RULES OF THE ROAD

Driving is on the left. There is a general speed limit of 96 kph (60 mph) on most roads; in towns, the limit is 48 kph (30 mph). In some areas, the limit is 64 kph (40 mph); this is always clearly posted. At traffic circles (roundabouts), which are the main form of interchange, traffic from the right takes priority. Seat belts must be worn by the driver and front-seat passengers. Children under 12 must ride in the back. The drunk-driving laws are strict, limiting the driver to less than one pint of beer.

CUSTOMS AND DUTIES

For details on imports and duty-free limits, *see* Customs and Duties *in* Chapter 1.

DINING

Ireland is in the throes of a food revolution. Many of today's Irish chefs are young and have traveled widely and absorbed the best influences of Europe, North America, and the Pacific Rim. The result is a pan-European cuisine that has moved beyond the age-old roast-beef-and-Yorkshire-pudding habit of the old Anglo-Irish country houses. In its place an innovative, indigenous style is emerging, marrying simple treatments of traditional courses—nettle soup, oysters, wild salmon—with more exotic dishes featuring unusual combinations of the best local, often organic, ingredients.

Despite the new sophistication, there are many examples of traditional cooking, particularly in pubs serving lunches of Irish stew, boiled bacon and cabbage, or steamed mussels. Pubs are one of the pillars of Irish society, worth visiting as much for conversation and music as for a good drink. The national drink, Guinness, is a pitch-black, malted stout, one of the great beers of the world.

Hotel dining rooms vary in quality, but the best country-house hotels offer some of the finest dining in Europe, and most of these welcome guests, whether you're staying overnight or not.

Prices are per person for a dinner main course. Sales tax is included in the price. Many places add a 10%–15% service charge—if not, a 10% tip is fine. For the Northern Ireland dining price chart, *see* Northern Ireland Essentials.

CATEGORY	COST
$$$$	over IR£23 (€29)
$$$	IR£17–IR£23 (€21–€29)
$$	IR£10–IR£16 (€13–€20)
$	under IR£10 (€13)

MEALTIMES

Always check breakfast times in advance. It's usually 7–10, but some hotels serve from 7 to 11. Most offer a full Irish breakfast, with cereal followed by bacon, eggs, sausage, and, sometimes, black-and-white pudding. Lunch, from noon to 2 (or even 3), is a leisurely affair. Some hotels serve afternoon tea and scones. Most people go out for dinner after 8; if you want to eat earlier, watch for early-bird menus, typically served from 6:30 to 7:30.

RESERVATIONS AND DRESS

People dress up for dinner at the top restaurants, but a jacket is ordinarily sufficient. Ties are rarely essential. Nice casual wear is usually acceptable.

EMBASSIES

For information on consulates in Northern Ireland, *see* Northern Ireland Essentials, *below.*

➤ AUSTRALIA: (✉ Fitzwilton House, Fitzwilton Terr., Dublin 2, ☎ 01/676–1517).
➤ CANADA: (✉ 65 St. Stephen's Green, Dublin 2, ☎ 01/478–1988).
➤ SOUTH AFRICA: (✉ Alexandra House, 2nd floor, Earlsfort Terrace, Dublin 2, ☎ 01/661–5553).
➤ UNITED KINGDOM: (✉ 31 Merrion Rd., Dublin 2, ☎ 01/205–3700).
➤ UNITED STATES: (✉ 42 Elgin Rd., Ballsbridge, Dublin 4, ☎ 01/668–8777).

HOLIDAYS

January 1; St. Patrick's Day; Good Friday; Easter Monday; May 6 (May Holiday); Whitmonday; August 5 (August Holiday); October 28 (October Holiday); and December 25–26 (Christmas and St. Stephen's Day).

LANGUAGE

Officially, Irish (Gaelic) is the first language of the Republic, but the everyday language of the vast majority of Irish people is English. Except for isolated parts of the northwest and Connemara, where many signs are not translated, most signs in the country are written in English, with an Irish translation. There is one important exception to this rule, with which you should familiarize yourself: FIR (pronounced "fear") and MNÁ (pronounced "muh-*naw*") translate, respectively, into "men" and "women." The Gaeltacht (pronounced "*gale*-tocked")—areas in which Irish *is* the everyday language of most people—comprises only 6% of the land, and all its inhabitants are, in any case, bilingual.

LODGING

Accommodations in Ireland range from deluxe castles and stately homes to thatched cottages and farmhouses to humble bed-and-breakfasts. Standards everywhere are high, and they—along with prices—

continue to rise. The days of considering Ireland your basic bargain destination are long gone. Pressure on hotel space reaches a peak between June and September, but it's a good idea to make reservations in advance at any time of the year, particularly at the more expensive spots. Accommodations are more economical in winter, although some—particularly in the west and the northwest—are closed from October through March.

Prices are for two people in a double room, based on high-season (June–mid-September) rates, including value-added tax (VAT) and service charges. For the Northern Ireland lodging price chart, *see* Northern Ireland Essentials.

CATEGORY	COST
$$$$	over IR£180 (€229)
$$$	IR£140–IR£180 (€178–€229)
$$	IR£100–IR£140 (€127–€178)
$	under IR£100 (€127)

BED-AND-BREAKFASTS

Bed-and-breakfast means just that. The bed can vary from a four-poster in the wing of a castle to a feather bed in a whitewashed farmhouse or the spare bedroom of a modern home. Rates are generally around IR£25/€32 per person, though these can vary significantly. Although many larger B&Bs have rooms with bath or shower, in some you'll have to use the bathroom in the hall.

CAMPING

Ireland has a variety of beautifully sited campgrounds and trailer parks, but be prepared for wet weather. All are listed in *Caravan and Camping in Ireland,* available from Bord Fáilte.

GUEST HOUSES

Some smaller hotels are graded as guest houses. To qualify, they must have at least five bedrooms, but in major cities they often have many more. A few may have restaurants; those that do not will often provide evening meals by arrangement. Otherwise these rooms can be as comfortable as those of a regular hotel, and in major cities they offer very good value for the money, compared with the $ hotels.

HOTELS

In general, hotels charge per person. In most cases (but not all, especially in more expensive places), the price includes a full breakfast. Value-added tax (VAT) is included, but some hotels—again, usually the more expensive ones—add a 10%–15% service charge. This should be mentioned in their price list. If it's not, a tip of between 10% and 15% is customary—if you think the service is worth it. In $$ and $ hotels, be sure to specify whether you want a private bath or shower; the latter is cheaper. Off-season (October–May) prices are reduced by as much as 25%.

RESERVING A ROOM

Rooms can be reserved directly from the United States and elsewhere; ask your travel agent for details. Local tourist board offices can also make reservations, as can Bord Fáilte's (the Irish Tourist Board, pronounced "Board *Fall*-cha") Central Credit Card Reservations Service. Bord Fáilte has an official grading system and publishes a detailed price list of all approved accommodations, including hotels, guest houses, farmhouses, B&Bs, and hostels. No hotel may exceed this price without special authorization from Bord Fáilte; prices must also be displayed in every room. Don't hesitate to complain either to the manager or to Bord Fáilte, or both, if prices exceed this maximum.

➤ TOLL-FREE NUMBERS: **Bord Fáilte Central Credit Card Reservations Service** (✉ Suffolk St., Dublin 2, ☎ 1800/668–668 in Ireland; 800/398–4376 in the U.S., FAX 01/605–7787).

MAIL AND SHIPPING

A general delivery service is operated free of charge from Dublin's General Post Office.

➤ POST OFFICES: **General Post Office** (✉ O'Connell St., Dublin 1, ☎ 01/705–7000).

POSTAL RATES

Airmail rates to the United States, Canada, and the Commonwealth are 45p for letters and postcards. Letters and postcards to Britain and continental Europe cost 32p.

MONEY MATTERS

Dublin is expensive—an unfortunate state of affairs that manifests itself most obviously in hotel rates and restaurant menus. You can generally keep costs lower if you visit Ireland on a package tour. Alternatively, consider staying in a guest house or a B&B; they provide an economical and atmospheric option. The rest of the country—with the exception of the better-known hotels and restaurants—is less expensive than Dublin. That the Irish themselves complain bitterly about the high cost of living is partly attributable to the rate of value-added tax (VAT)—a stinging 21% on "luxury" goods and 12½% on hotel accommodations. For instance, while a double room in a moderately priced Dublin hotel will cost about IR£90/€114, with breakfast, the current rate for a country B&B is around IR£25/€32 per person. Modest, small-town hotels generally charge around IR£40/€50 per person.

Sample prices include: cup of coffee, IR£1/€1.30; pint of beer, IR£2.30/€3; Coca-Cola, 95p/€1.20; a sandwich, IR£1.80/€2.30; 2-km (1-mi) taxi ride, IR£4/€5.10.

CURRENCY

The unit of currency in Ireland is the pound, or punt (pronounced "poont"), written as IR£ to avoid confusion with the pound sterling (£). The currency is divided into the same denominations as in Britain, with IR£1 divided into 100 pence (written *p*). The North uses British currency; Irish punts, or pounds, are not accepted. Although the Irish pound is the only legal tender in the Republic, U.S. dollars and British currency are often accepted in large hotels and shops licensed as bureaux de change. Banks give the best rate of exchange. There is likely to be some variance in the rates of exchange between Ireland and the United Kingdom (which includes Northern Ireland). Change U.K. pounds at a bank when you get to Ireland (pound coins not accepted); change Irish pounds before you leave. Ireland is a member of the European Monetary Union (EMU) and since January 1, 1999, all prices have been quoted in pounds and euros. January 2002 is to see the introduction of the euro coins and notes and the gradual withdrawal of the local currency. The rate of exchange at press time (summer 2001) was 82p/€1.05 to the U.S. dollar, 55p/€.71 to the Canadian dollar, IR£1.25/€1.60 to the pound sterling, 47p/€.60 to the Australian dollar, 39p/€.50 to the New Zealand dollar, and 12p/€.15 to the South African rand.

TAXES

VALUE-ADDED TAX (VAT)

Visitors from outside Europe can take advantage of the "cash-back" system on value-added tax (VAT) in two ways. The first is by having your invoice receipt stamped by customs on departure and mailing it back to the store for VAT refund. You must, however, verify at the time of purchase that the store operates by this system. The second and more popular option is to use one of the private cash-back companies, which charge a commission.

TELEPHONES

COUNTRY AND AREA CODES

The country code for the Republic of Ireland is 353; for Northern Ireland it's 44.

INTERNATIONAL CALLS

In the Republic and Northern Ireland, calls to the United States and Canada can be made by dialing 001 followed by the area code. For calls to the United Kingdom, dial 0044 followed by the number, dropping the beginning zero. For long-distance operators, call one of the service providers below.

➤ ACCESS CODES: **AT&T** (☎ 800/550–000). **MCI** (☎ 800/551–001). **Sprint** (☎ 800/552–001).

LOCAL CALLS

Pay phones can be found in all post offices and most hotels and bars, as well as in street booths. Local calls cost 20p/€.25 for three minutes, calls within Ireland cost about 80p/€1.00 for three minutes, and calls to Britain cost about IR£2/€2.50 for three minutes. Telephone cards are available at post offices and most newsagents. Prices range from IR£2/€2.50 for 10 units to IR£8/€10.15 for 50 units. Card booths are as common as coin booths. Rates go down by about a third after 6 PM and all day Saturday and Sunday. Northern Ireland is part of the United Kingdom telephone system; a local call costs 10p/€.15.

TIPPING

Some hotels and restaurants will add a service charge of about 12% to your bill, so tipping isn't necessary unless you've received particularly good service. But if there is no service charge, you might want to add a minimum of about 10% to the total. You don't tip in pubs, but if there is waiter service in a bar or hotel lounge, leave about 50p. Tip taxi drivers about 10% of the fare if the taxi has been using its meter. For longer journeys, where the fare is agreed upon in advance, a tip will not be expected unless some kind of commentary (solicited or not) has been provided. In luxury hotels porters and bellhops will expect IR£1/€1.30; elsewhere, 50p/€.65 is adequate. Hairdressers normally expect a tip of about IR£1/€1.30.

TRAIN TRAVEL

The Irish Republic's train services are generally reliable, reasonably priced, and comfortable, though trains in Ireland travel more slowly than in other places in Europe. Iarnód Eíreann (Irish Rail) and Bus Éireann are independent components of the state-owned public transportation company Coras Iompair Eíreann (CIE). All the principal towns are easily reached from Dublin, though services between provincial cities are roundabout. To reach Cork City from Wexford, for example, you have to go via Limerick Junction. It is often quicker, though perhaps less comfortable, to take a bus. Most mainline trains have two classes: standard and superstandard. Round-trip tickets are usually cheapest.

CUTTING COSTS

Eurailpasses are not valid in Northern Ireland. The Irish Explorer Rail & Bus Pass, for use on Ireland's railroads, bus system, or both, covers all the state-run and federal railways and bus lines throughout the Republic of Ireland. It does not apply to the North or to transportation within the cities. The Emerald Isle Card offers unlimited bus and train travel anywhere in Ireland and Northern Ireland, valid within cities as well. In Northern Ireland, Rail Runabout tickets entitle you to seven days' unlimited travel on scheduled rail services April–October. Even if you have a rail pass, be sure to book seats ahead of time.

➤ Train Information: **Iarnód Eíreann** (☎ 01/836–6222).

VISITOR INFORMATION

For information on travel in the Irish Republic, contact the headquarters of the Irish Tourist Board.

➤ Tourist Information: **Irish Tourist Board (Bord Fáilte)** (✉ Baggot St. Bridge, Dublin 2, ☎ 1850/230–330, FAX 01/602–4100).

WHEN TO GO

June to mid-September is Ireland's high season, but the country's attractions are not as dependent on the weather as those in most other northern European countries, and the scenery is just as attractive in the off-peak times of fall and spring.

CLIMATE

In all seasons you can expect rain, although the sun is often out moments after a squall passes. Winters are mild though wet; summers can be warm and sunny, but there's always the risk of a sudden shower. No one ever went to Ireland for a suntan. The following are the average daily maximum and minimum temperatures for Dublin.

Jan.	46F	8C	**May**	60F	15C	**Sept.**	63F	17C
	34	1		43	6		48	9
Feb.	47F	8C	**June**	65F	18C	**Oct.**	57F	14C
	35	2		48	9		43	6
Mar.	51F	11C	**July**	67F	19C	**Nov.**	51F	11C
	37	3		52	11		39	4
Apr.	55F	13C	**Aug.**	67F	19C	**Dec.**	47F	8C
	39	4		51	11		37	3

DUBLIN

Europe's most intimate capital has become a boomtown—the soul of the Republic of Ireland is in the throes of what may be the nation's most dramatic period of transformation since the Georgian era. Dublin is riding the back of its "Celtic Tiger" economy, and massive construction cranes are hovering over both shiny new hotels and old Georgian houses. Irish culture is hot: in recent years, Patriot Michael Collins became a Hollywood box-office star, Frank McCourt's *Angela's Ashes* conquered best-seller lists in the United States and was made into a movie, and *Riverdance* became a worldwide old-Irish mass jig. Because of these and other attractions, travelers are coming to Dublin in ever-greater numbers, so don't be surprised if you stop to consult your map in Temple Bar—the city's most happening neighborhood—and are swept away by the ceaseless flow of bustling crowds. Dublin has become a colossally entertaining, engaging city—all the more astonishing considering its gentle size. The quiet pubs and little empty backstreets might be harder to find now that Dublin has been "discovered," but a bit of effort and research can still unearth the old "Dear Dirty Dumpling," a city that Joyce was so fond of.

Exploring Dublin

Numbers in the margin correspond to points of interest on the Dublin map.

Originally a Viking settlement, Dublin sits on the banks of the River Liffey, which divides the city north and south. The liveliest round-the-clock spots, including Temple Bar and Grafton Street, are on the south side, although a variety of construction projects on the north side are helping to reinvigorate these areas. The majority of the city's most notable buildings date from the 18th century—the Georgian era—and, although many of its finer Georgian buildings disappeared in the redevelopment of the '70s, enough remain to recall the elegant Dublin of centuries past. Dublin is small as capital cities go, with a compact downtown area, and the best way to soak in the full flavor of the city is on foot. Literary Dublin can still be recaptured by following the footsteps of Leopold Bloom's progress, as described in James Joyce's *Ulysses.* Trinity College, alma mater of Oliver Goldsmith, Jonathan Swift, and Samuel Beckett, among others, is a green, Georgian oasis, alive with students.

South of the Liffey

South of the Liffey are graceful squares and fashionable terraces from Dublin's elegant heyday, and, interspersed with some of the city's leading sights, this area is perfect for an introductory city tour. You might begin at O'Connell Bridge—as Dublin has no central focal point, most natives regard it as the city's Piccadilly Circus or Times Square—then head south down Westmoreland Street to Parliament House. Continue on to Trinity College—the Book of Kells, Ireland's greatest artistic treasure, is on view here—then eastward to Merrion Square and the National Gallery; south to St. Stephen's Green and Fitzwilliam Square; west to Dublin's two beautiful cathedrals, Christ Church and St. Patrick's; and end with dinner in a Temple Bar restaurant overlooking the Liffey.

2 **Bank of Ireland.** With a grand facade of marble columns, the Bank of Ireland is one of Dublin's most striking buildings. Across the street from the front entrance to Trinity College, the Georgian structure was once the home of the Irish Parliament. Built in 1729, it was bought by the Bank of Ireland in 1803. Hurricane-shape rosettes adorn the coffered ceiling in the pastel-hued, colonnaded, clerestoried main banking hall, once the Court of Requests, where citizens' petitions were heard. Just down the hall is the original House of Lords, with tapestries, an oak-panel nave, and a 1,233-piece Waterford glass chandelier; ask a guard to show you in. Visitors are welcome during normal banking hours; a brief guided tour is given every Tuesday at 10:30, 11:30, and 1:45. ✉ *2 College Green,* ☏ *01/677–6801.* ⏲ *Mon.–Wed. and Fri. 10–4, Thurs. 10–5.*

17 **Christ Church Cathedral.** You'd never know from the outside that the first Christianized Danish king built a wooden church at this site in 1038; thanks to the extensive 19th-century renovation of its stonework and trim, the cathedral looks more Victorian than Anglo-Norman. Stone construction was begun in 1172 by Strongbow, a Norman baron and conqueror of Dublin for the English crown. The vast, sturdy **crypt,** with its 12th- and 13th-century vaults, is Dublin's oldest surviving structure and the building's most notable feature. At 6 PM on Wednesdays and Thursdays you can enjoy a choral evensong. ✉ *Christ Church Pl. and Winetavern St.,* ☏ *01/677–8099.* ⏲ *Daily 9:45–5.*

16 **City Hall.** Facing the Liffey from the top of Parliament Street, this grand Georgian municipal building (1769–79), once the Royal Exchange, was designed by Thomas Cooley. It has a central rotunda encircled by 12 columns, a fine mosaic floor, and 12 frescoes depicting Dublin legends and ancient Irish historical scenes. The building is now home to an exhibition tracing the evolution of Ireland's 1,000-year-old capital.

Abbey Theatre 21
Bank of Ireland 2
Ceol 30
Christ Church Cathedral 17
City Hall 16
Custom House 20
Dublin Castle 15
Dublin Civic Museum 4
Dublin Writers Museum 26
Four Courts 28
Geneaological Office 6
General Post Office 22
Grafton Street 3
Guinness Brewery and Storehouse 34
Ha'penny Bridge . . . 23
Hugh Lane Municipal Gallery of Modern Art 27
Kilmainham Gaol 33
Leinster House 9
Marsh's Library 13
Merrion Square 11
National Gallery of Ireland 10
National Library 7
National Museum . . . 8
O'Connell Bridge 19
Old Jameson Distillery 29
Parnell Square 25
Phoenix Park 31
Rotunda Hospital . . . 24
Royal Hospital Kilmainham 32
Royal Irish Academy 5
St. Patrick's Cathedral 14
St. Stephen's Green 12
Temple Bar 18
Trinity College 1

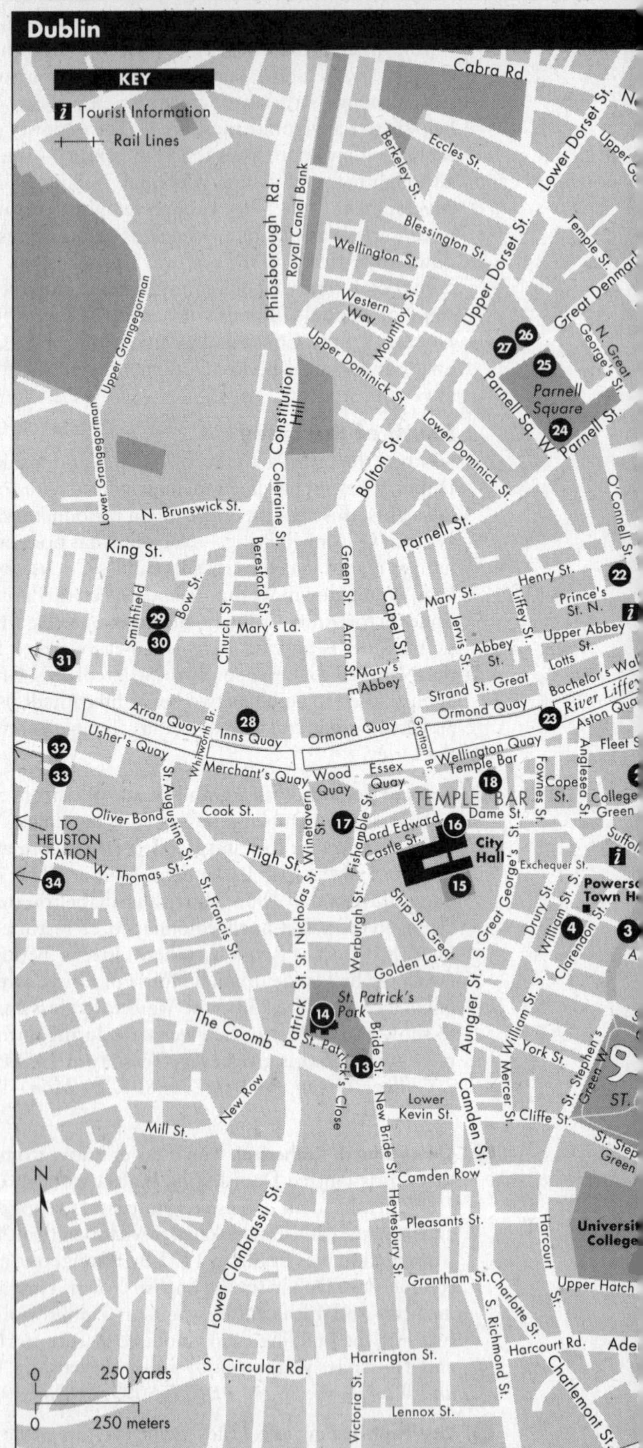

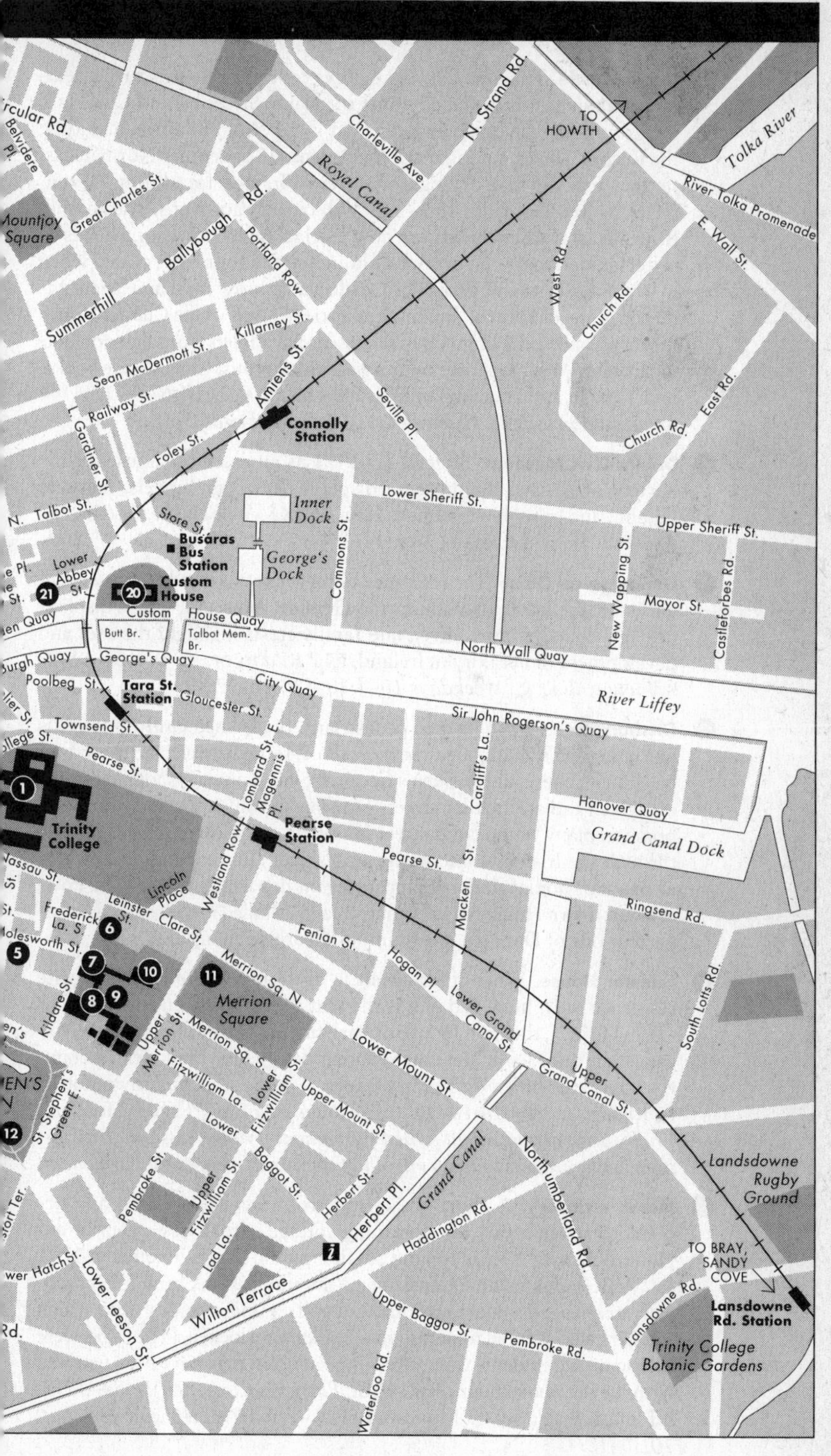

Connolly Station
Busáras Bus Station
Custom House
Tara St. Station
Pearse Station
Trinity College
Merrion Square
Mountjoy Square
River Liffey
Royal Canal
Grand Canal
Grand Canal Dock
Inner Dock
George's Dock
Tolka River
TO HOWTH
TO BRAY, SANDY COVE
Landsdowne Rugby Ground
Lansdowne Rd. Station
Trinity College Botanic Gardens
North Wall Quay
Sir John Rogerson's Quay
Custom House Quay
City Quay
George's Quay
Hanover Quay
Amiens St.
N. Strand Rd.
Pearse St.
Lower Mount St.
Northumberland Rd.
Haddington Rd.
Wilton Terrace
Pembroke Rd.
Ringsend Rd.

✉ *Dame Street,* ☎ *01/672–2204,* WEB *www.dublincorp.ie.* ⏲ *Mon.–Sat. 10–5:15, Sun. 2–5.*

15 **Dublin Castle.** The film *Michael Collins* captures this structure's near-indomitable status in the city. Just off Dame Street behind City Hall, the grounds of the castle encompass a number of buildings, including the **Record Tower,** a remnant of the original 13th-century Norman castle that was the seat of English power in Ireland for almost 7½ centuries, as well as various 18th- and 19th-century additions. The lavishly furnished **state apartments** are now used to entertain visiting heads of state. Guided tours run every half hour, but the rooms are closed when in official use, so call first. The **Castle Vaults** now hold an elegant little patisserie and bistro. The castle is also the home of the **Chester Beatty Library.** Among the library's exhibits are clay tablets from Babylon dating from 2700 BC, Japanese color wood-block prints, Chinese jade books, and Turkish and Persian paintings. ✉ *Castle St.,* ☎ *01/677–7129,* WEB *www.dublincastle.ie.* ⏲ *Weekdays 10–5, weekends 2–5.*

4 **Dublin Civic Museum.** Built in 1765–71 as an assembly house for the Society of Artists, the museum displays drawings, models, maps of Dublin, and other civic memorabilia. ✉ *58 S. William St.,* ☎ *01/679–4260.* ⏲ *Tues.–Sat. 10–6, Sun. 11–2.*

6 **Genealogical Office.** The reference library here is a good place to begin ancestor tracing. It also houses the **Heraldic Museum,** where displays of flags, coins, stamps, silver, and family crests highlight the uses and development of heraldry in Ireland. ✉ *2 Kildare St.,* ☎ *01/661–8811,* WEB *www.nli.ie.* ⏲ *Weekdays 10–4:30, Sat. 10–12:30.*

★ 3 **Grafton Street.** Open only to pedestrians, brick-lined Grafton Street is one of Dublin's vital spines: the most direct route between the front door of Trinity College and Stephen's Green; the city's premier shopping street, off which radiate smaller streets housing stylish shops and pubs; and home to many of the city's street musicians and flower sellers. Browse through the Irish and international designer clothing and housewares at **Brown Thomas,** Ireland's most elegant department store. The **Powerscourt Town House** is a shopping arcade installed in the covered courtyard of one of Dublin's most famous Georgian mansions.

9 **Leinster House.** When it was built in 1745 it was the largest private residence in Dublin. Today it is the seat of Dáil Eireann (pronounced "Dawl Erin"), the Irish House of Parliament. The building has two facades: the one facing Merrion Square is designed in the style of a country house; the other, on Kildare Street, is in the style of a town house. ✉ *Kildare St.,* ☎ *01/618–3000,* WEB *www.irlgov.ie.* ⏲ *Tours Mon. and Fri. by prior arrangement (when Parliament is not in session). Dáil visitors' gallery access with an introduction from a member of Parliament.*

13 **Marsh's Library.** A short walk west from Stephen's Green and accessed through a tiny but charming cottage garden lies a gem of old Dublin: the city's—and Ireland's—first public library, opened in 1701 to "All Graduates and Gentlemen." Its interior has been left practically unchanged since it was built—it still contains "cages" into which scholars who wanted to peruse rare books were locked. (The cages were to discourage students who, often impecunious, may have been tempted to make the books their own.) ✉ *St. Patrick's Close,* ☎ *01/454–3511,* WEB *www.kst.dit.ie.* ⏲ *Mon. and Wed.–Fri. 10–12:45 and 2–5, Sat. 10:30–12:45.*

★ 11 **Merrion Square.** Created between 1762 and 1764, this tranquil Georgian square is lined on three sides by some of Dublin's best-preserved Georgian town houses. Even when the flower gardens are not in bloom, the vibrant green grounds, dotted with sculpture and threaded with meandering paths, are worth a walk. **No. 1,** at the northwest corner, was the home of Sir William and Sperenza Wilde, Oscar's parents. ✉ *East end of Nassau St.* ⏲ *Daily sunrise–sunset.*

★ ⑩ **National Gallery of Ireland.** On the west side of Merrion Square, this 1854 building contains the country's finest collection of Old Masters—treasures include Vermeer's *Woman Writing a Letter* (twice stolen from Sir Alfred Beit and now safe at last), Gainsborough's *Cottage Girl,* and Caravaggio's *The Arrest of Christ.* The gallery's restaurant is one of the city's best spots for an inexpensive, top-rate lunch. Free guided tours are available on Saturday at 3 PM and on Sunday at 2:15, 3, and 4. ✉ *Merrion Sq. W,* ☎ *01/661–5133,* WEB *www.nationalgallery.ie.* ⏲ *Mon.–Wed. and Fri.–Sat. 10–5:30, Thurs. 10–8:30, Sun. 2–5.*

⑦ **National Library.** The collections here include first editions of every major Irish writer. Temporary exhibits are held in the entrance hall, off the colonnaded rotunda. The main reading room, opened in 1890, has a dramatic dome ceiling. ✉ *Kildare St.,* ☎ *01/661–8811,* WEB *www.nli.ie.* ⏲ *Mon.–Wed. 10–9, Thurs.–Fri. 10–5, Sat. 10–1.*

⑧ **National Museum.** On the other side of Leinster House from the National Library, the museum is most famous for its spectacular collection of Irish artifacts from 7000 BC to the present, including the Tara Brooch, the Ardagh Chalice, the Cross of Cong, and a fabled hoard of Celtic gold jewelry. Upstairs, Viking Age Ireland is a permanent exhibit on the Norsemen, featuring a full-size Viking skeleton, swords, leather works recovered in Dublin and surrounding areas, and a replica of a small Viking boat. ✉ *Kildare St.,* ☎ *01/660–1117,* WEB *www.museum.ie.* ⏲ *Tues.–Sat. 10–5, Sun. 2–5.*

⑲ **O'Connell Bridge.** Strange but true: the main bridge spanning the Liffey is wider than it is long. The north side of the bridge is dominated by an elaborate memorial to Daniel O'Connell, "The Liberator," erected as a tribute to the great 19th-century orator's achievement in securing Catholic Emancipation in 1829. Today **O'Connell Street,** one of the widest in Europe, is less a street to loiter in than to pass through on your way to elsewhere. **Henry Street,** to the left just beyond the General Post Office, is, like a downscale Grafton Street, a busy pedestrian thoroughfare where you'll find throngs of Dubliners out doing their shopping. A few steps down Henry Street off to the right is the colorful **Moore Street Market,** where street vendors recall their most famous ancestor, Molly Malone, by singing their wares—mainly flowers and fruit—in the traditional Dublin style.

⑤ **Royal Irish Academy.** The country's leading learned society houses important manuscripts in its 18th-century library. Just below the academy is the **Mansion House,** the official residence of the Lord Mayor of Dublin. Its Round Room, the site of the first assembly of Dáil Eireann in January 1919, is now used mainly for exhibitions. ✉ *19 Dawson St.,* ☎ *01/676–2570,* WEB *www.ria.ie.* ⏲ *Weekdays 9:30–5.*

⑭ **St. Patrick's Cathedral.** Legend has it that St. Patrick baptized many converts at a well on the site of the cathedral in the 5th century. The building dates from 1190 and is mainly early English Gothic in style. At 305 ft, it is the longest church in the country. In the 17th century Oliver Cromwell, dour ruler of England and no friend of the Irish, had his troops stable their horses in the cathedral. It wasn't until the 19th century that restoration work to repair the damage was begun. St. Patrick's is the national cathedral of the Anglican Church in Ireland and has had many illustrious deans. The most famous was Jonathan Swift, author of *Gulliver's Travels,* who held office from 1713 to

1745. Swift's tomb is in the south aisle. Memorials to many other celebrated figures from Ireland's past line the walls. "Living Stones" is the cathedral's permanent exhibition celebrating Saint Patrick's place in the life of the city. Matins (9:45 AM) and evensong (5:35 PM) are still sung on most days, a real treat for the music lover. ✉ *Patrick St.,* ☎ *01/453–9472,* WEB *www.stpatrickscathedral.ie.* ⏲ *May and Sept.–Oct., weekdays 9–6, Sat. 9–5, Sun. 10–11 and 12:30–3; June–Aug., weekdays 9–6, Sat. 9–4, Sun. 9:30–3 and 4:15–5:15; Nov.–Apr., weekdays 9–6, Sat. 9–4, Sun. 10–11 and 12:45–3.*

⓬ **St. Stephen's Green.** Dubliners call it simply Stephen's Green; green it is—strikingly so, year-round (you can even spot a palm tree or two). Among the park's many statues are a memorial to Yeats and another to Joyce by Henry Moore. The north side is dominated by the magnificent **Shelbourne Méridien Hotel**. A drink in one of its two bars, or afternoon tea in the elegant Lord Mayor's Room is the most financially painless way to soak in the old-fashioned luxury.

★ ⓲ **Temple Bar.** Dublin's hippest neighborhood—bordered by Dame Street to the south, the Liffey to the north, Fishamble Street to the west, and Westmoreland Street to the east—is the city's version of the Latin Quarter, the playing ground of "young Dublin." Representative of the improved fortunes of the area, with its narrow, winding pedestrian-only cobblestone streets, is the **Clarence** (✉ 6–8 Wellington Quay, ☎ 01/670–9000), a favorite old Dublin hotel now owned by Bono and the Edge of U2. The area is chock-full of small hip stores, art galleries, and inexpensive restaurants and pubs. The **Irish Film Centre** (✉ 6 Eustace St., ☎ 01/679–5744) is emblematic of the area's vibrant mix of high and alternative culture.

★ ❶ **Trinity College.** Ireland's oldest and most famous college is the heart of college-town Dublin. Trinity College, Dublin (officially titled Dublin University but familiarly known as Trinity), was founded by Elizabeth I in 1592 and offered a free education to Catholics—providing they accepted the Protestant faith. As a legacy of this condition, until 1966 Catholics who wished to study at Trinity had to obtain a dispensation from their bishop or face excommunication. Today more than 70% of Trinity's students are Catholics, an indication of how far away those days seem now.

The pedimented, neoclassical Georgian facade, built between 1755 and 1759, consists of a magnificent portico with Corinthian columns. The design is repeated on the interior, so the view from outside the gates and from the quadrangle inside is the same. On the quad's lawn are statues of two of the university's illustrious alumni—statesman Edmund Burke and poet Oliver Goldsmith. Other famous students include the philosopher George Berkeley (who gave his name to the northern California city), Jonathan Swift, Thomas Moore, Oscar Wilde, John Millington Synge, Bram Stoker, Edward Carson, and Samuel Beckett. The 18th-century building on the left, just inside the entrance, is the **chapel.** There's an identical building opposite, the **Examination Hall.** The oldest buildings are the library in the far right-hand corner, completed in 1712, and a 1690 row of redbrick buildings known as the **Rubrics,** which contains student apartments.

Ireland's largest collection of books and manuscripts is housed in **Trinity College Library,** entered through the library shop. Its principal treasure is the Book of Kells, generally considered the most striking manuscript ever produced in the Anglo-Saxon world. Only a few pages from the 682-page, 9th-century gospel are displayed at a time, but an informative exhibit has reproductions of many of them. At peak hours you may have to wait in line to enter the library; it's less busy early in the day. Don't miss the grand and glorious Long Room, an impressive 213 ft long and 42 ft wide, which houses 200,000 volumes in its 21 alcoves. ☎ *01/677–2941,* WEB *www.bookofkells.ie.* ⏲ *Mon.–Sat. 9:30–4:45, Sun. noon–4:30.*

In the Thomas Davis Theatre in the Arts Building, **"Dublin Experience"** is an audiovisual presentation devoted to the history of the city over the last 1,000 years. ☎ *01/677–2941.* ⏲ *Late-May–Oct., daily 10–5; shows every hr on the hr.*

North of the Liffey

The Northside city center is a mix of densely thronged shopping streets and slightly run-down sections of once-genteel homes, which are now being bought up and renovated. There are some classic sights in the area, including gorgeous Georgian monuments—the Custom House, the General Post Office, Parnell Square, and the Hugh Lane Gallery—and two landmarks of literary Dublin, the Dublin Writers Museum and the James Joyce Cultural Center, hub of Bloomsday celebrations. A good way to begin is by heading up O'Connell Street to Parnell Square and the heart of James Joyce Country.

21 **Abbey Theatre.** Ireland's national theater was founded by W. B. Yeats and Lady Gregory in 1904. Works by Yeats, Synge, O'Casey, Kavanagh, and Friel have premiered here. The original building was destroyed in a fire in 1951; the present, rather austere theater was built in 1966. It has some noteworthy portraits and mementos in the foyer. Seats are usually available for about IR£12/€15.25; all tickets are IR£8/€10.15 for Monday performances. ✉ *Lower Abbey St.,* ☎ *01/878–7222,* WEB *www.abbeytheatre.ie.*

20 **Custom House.** Extending 375 ft on the north side of the Liffey, this is the city's most spectacular Georgian building (1781–91), the work of James Gandon, an English architect. The central portico is linked by arcades to the pavilions at each end. A statue of Commerce tops the graceful copper dome; additional allegorical statues adorn the main facade. Republicans set the building on fire in 1921, but it was completely restored; it now houses government offices and a visitor center tracing the building's history and significance, and the life of Gandon. ✉ *Custom House Quay,* ☎ *01/876–7660.* ⏲ *Mid-Mar.–Oct, weekdays 10–5:30, weekends 2–5:30; Nov–mid-Mar., Wed.–Fri. 10–5, Sun. 2–5:30.*

★ 26 **Dublin Writers Museum.** Two restored 18th-century town houses on the north side of Parnell Square, an area rich in literary associations, lodge one of Dublin's finest cultural sights. Rare manuscripts, diaries, posters, letters, limited and first editions, photographs, and other mementos commemorate the lives and works of the nation's greatest writers, including Joyce, Shaw, Wilde, Yeats, and Beckett. The bookshop and café make this an ideal place to spend a rainy afternoon. ✉ *18–19 Parnell Sq. N,* ☎ *01/872–2077,* WEB *www.visitdublin.com.* ⏲ *June–Aug., Mon.–Sat. 10–6, Sun. 11–5; Sept.–May, Mon.–Sat. 10–5, Sun. 11–5.*

22 **General Post Office.** The GPO (1818), still a working post office, is one of the great civic buildings of Dublin's Georgian era, but its fame derives from the role it played during the Easter Rising. Here, on Easter Monday, 1916, the Republican forces stormed the building and issued the Proclamation of the Irish Republic. After a week of shelling, the GPO lay in ruins; 13 rebels were ultimately executed. Most of the original building was destroyed; only the facade—you can still see the scars of bullets on its pillars—remained. ✉ *O'Connell St.,* ☎ *01/872–8888,* WEB *www.anpost.ie.* ⏲ *Mon.–Sat. 8–8, Sun. 10:30–6:30.*

23 **Ha'penny Bridge.** This heavily trafficked footbridge crosses the Liffey at a prime spot: Temple Bar is on the south side, and the bridge provides the fastest route to the thriving Mary and Henry Street shopping areas to the north. Until early in this century, a half-penny toll was charged to cross it. Yeats was one among many Dubliners who found this too high a price to pay—more a matter of principle than of finance—and so made the detour via O'Connell Bridge.

★ 27 **Hugh Lane Municipal Gallery of Modern Art.** The imposing Palladian facade of this town house, once the home of the Earl of Charlemont, dominates the north side of Parnell Square. Sir Hugh Lane, a nephew of Lady Gregory (Yeats's patron), collected Impressionist paintings and 19th-century Irish and Anglo-Irish works. Among them are canvases by Jack Yeats (W. B.'s brother) and Paul Henry. The late Francis Bacon's partner donated the entire contents of the artist's studio to the Hugh Lane Gallery, where it has been reconstructed. ✉ *Parnell Sq.,* ☎ *01/874–1903,* WEB *www.hughlane.ie.* ⏲ *Tues.–Thurs. 9:30–6, Fri.–Sat. 9:30–5, Sun. 11–5.*

25 **Parnell Square.** This is the Northside's most notable Georgian square and one of Dublin's oldest. Because fashionable hostesses liked passersby to be able to peer into the first-floor reception rooms of the elegant brick-face town houses and admire the distinguished guests, their windows are much larger than the others.

24 **Rotunda Hospital.** Founded in 1745 as the first maternity hospital in Ireland or Britain, the Rotunda is now most worth a visit for its **chapel,** with elaborate plasterwork, appropriately honoring motherhood. The Gate Theatre, housed in an extension, attracts large crowds with its fine repertoire of classic Irish and European drama. ✉ *Parnell St.,* ☎ *01/873–0700.*

Dublin West

If you're not an enthusiastic walker, hop a bus or find a cab to take you to these sights in westernmost Dublin.

★ 30 **Ceol.** "Ceol" is the Irish word for music, and this museum tells the ancient story of Celtic music in a thoroughly modern fashion. Computerized exhibits allow you to customize your learning, and touch screens give access to recordings of the masters of the genre plus hundreds of film clips of them performing. The Stories Room contains a priceless oral history of musicians and storytellers from the early part of the 20th century. A children's area includes an ingenious game of musical twister, allowing kids to play along with a tune using parts of their body to play the notes. *Smithfield Village,* ☎ *01/817–3820,* WEB *www.ceol.ie.* ⏲ *Mon.–Sat. 10–6, Sun. 12–6.*

28 **Four Courts.** Today the seat of the High Court of Justice of Ireland, the Four Courts are James Gandon's second Dublin masterpiece, built between 1786 and 1802. The courts were destroyed during the Troubles of the 1920s and restored by 1932. Its distinctive copper-covered dome atop a colonnaded rotunda makes this one of Dublin's most recognizable buildings. You are allowed to listen in on court proceedings, which can often be interesting, educational, even scandalous. ✉ *Inns Quay,* ☎ *01/872–5555,* WEB *www.courts.ie.* ⏲ *Daily 10:30–1 and 2:15–4.*

★ 34 **Guinness Brewery and Storehouse.** Founded by Arthur Guinness in 1759, Ireland's all-dominating brewery is on a 60-acre spread west of Christ Church Cathedral; it is the most popular tourist destination in town. The brewery itself is closed to the public, but the Storehouse is a spectacular tourist attraction with a high-tech exhibition about the brewing process of the "dark stuff." Located in a cast-iron and brick warehouse, it covers six floors built around a huge central glass atrium. But without doubt the star attraction is the top floor **Gravity Bar,** with it's 360°, floor-to-ceiling glass walls and a stunning view over the city. ✉ *St. James's Gate,* ☎ *01/408–4800,* WEB *www.guinness.com.* ⏲ *April–Sept., Mon.–Sat. 9:30–7, Sun. 11–5; Oct.–Mar., daily 9:30–5.*

33 **Kilmainham Gaol.** This grim, forbidding structure was where leaders of the 1916 Easter Rising, including Pádrig Pearse and James Connolly, were held before being executed. A guided tour and a 30-minute audiovisual presentation relate a graphic account of Ireland's political history over the past 200 years from a Nationalist viewpoint. ✉ *Inchicore Rd.,* ☎ *01/453–5984,* WEB *www.heritageireland.ie.* ⏲ *Apr.–Sept., daily 9:30–5; Oct.–Mar., weekdays 9:30–4, Sun. 10–5.*

29 **Old Jameson Distillery.** The birthplace of one of Ireland's best whiskeys has been fully restored and offers a fascinating insight into the making of *uisce batha,* or "holy water," as whiskey is known in Irish. There is a 40-minute guided tour of the old distillery, a 20-minute audiovisual tour, and a complimentary tasting. ✉ *Bow St.,* ☎ *01/807–2355,* WEB *www.irish-whiskey-trail.com.* ⏲ *Daily 9:30–5:30; tours every ½ hr.*

★ 31 **Phoenix Park.** Europe's largest public park encompasses 1,752 acres of verdant lawns, woods, lakes, playing fields, a zoo, a flower garden, and two residences—those of the president of Ireland and the ambassador for the United States. A 210-ft-tall obelisk, built in 1817, commemorates the Duke of Wellington's defeat of Napoléon. It is a runner's paradise, but Sunday is the best time to visit, when all kinds of games are likely to be in progress.

★ 32 **Royal Hospital Kilmainham.** A short ride by taxi or bus from the city center, this structure is regarded as the most important 17th-century building in Ireland. Completed in 1684 as a hospice for soldiers, it survived into the 1920s as a hospital. The ceiling of the Baroque chapel is extraordinary. It now houses the **Irish Museum of Modern Art,** which displays works by such non-Irish greats as Picasso and Miró but concentrates on the work of Irish artists. ✉ *Kilmainham La.,* ☎ *01/612–9900,* WEB *www.modernart.ie.* ⏲ *Tues.–Sat. 10–5:30, Sun. noon–5:30; Royal Hospital tours every ½ hr; museum tours Wed. and Fri. at 2:30, Sat. at 11:30.*

Dining

Beyond the restaurants recommended here, the area between Grafton Street and South Great George's Street has many to offer, as does Temple Bar, just across Dame Street. It's also worth checking out suburban villages like Ranelagh, Blackrock, and Sandycove for good local restaurants.

$$$$ ✕ **The Commons Restaurant.** This restaurant is in a large, elegant room with French windows in the basement of Newman House, where James Joyce was a student in the original premises of University College Dublin. The seasonal menu encompasses a light treatment of classic themes. ✉ *85–86 St. Stephen's Green,* ☎ *01/478–0530. AE, DC, MC, V. Closed weekends.*

$$$$ ✕ **Le Coq Hardi.** John Howard has been running one of the best restaurants in Dublin in this Georgian house for many years. One of his signature dishes—a little old-fashioned, perhaps, but still popular—is Coq Hardi chicken stuffed with potatoes and mushrooms, wrapped in bacon before going into the oven, and finished off with a dash of Irish whiskey. ✉ *35 Pembroke Rd., Ballsbridge,* ☎ *01/668–9070. Reservations essential. AE, DC, MC, V. Closed Sun.*

$$$$ ★ ✕ **Patrick Guilbaud.** Everything is French here, including the eponymous owner, his chef, and the maître d'. Guillaume Le Brun's cooking is a fluent expression of modern French cuisine—not particularly flamboyant, but coolly professional. ✉ *Hotel Merrion, Merrion St.,* ☎ *01/676–4192. AE, DC, MC, V. Closed Sun.–Mon. and late Dec.–mid-Jan.*

$$$$ ★ ✕ **Thornton's.** Owner Kevin Thornton is one of the finest chefs in Ireland, and a visit to his town-house restaurant on the north bank of the Grand Canal is a must for serious foodies. The space is elegantly understated, the service is formal, and the French cuisine is exquisite, if expensive. ✉ *1 Portobello Rd.,* ☎ *01/454–9067. Reservations essential. AE, DC, MC, V. Closed Sun.–Mon. No lunch Sat.–Thurs.*

$$$ ✕ **Chapter One.** In the vaulted, stone-walled basement of the Dublin Writers Museum, this is one of the most notable restaurants in Northside Dublin. Dishes include pressed duck and black pudding terrine with a pear chutney, and grilled black sole with ravioli stuffed with salmon mousse. ✉ *18–19 Parnell Sq.,* ☎ *01/873–2266. AE, DC, MC, V. Closed Sun.–Mon. No lunch Sat.*

$$$ ✕ **Cooke's Café.** Johnny Cooke has turned this central, Californian-Mediterranean-style bistro into a cool spot. It's busy and service can be slow; the outdoor seating on nice summer days is a consolation. ✉ *14 S. William St.,* ☎ *01/679–0536. AE, DC, MC, V.*

$$–$$$ ✕ **Brownes Brasserie.** In this elegant restaurant, huge mirrors reflect the light from crystal chandeliers, glowing on jewel-colored walls and upholstery. The food is rich and heartwarming, with such classics as Irish smoked salmon and confit of duck with lentils. ✉ *22 St. Stephen's Green,* ☎ *01/638–3939. AE, DC, MC, V. No lunch Sat.*

$$–$$$ ✕ **Bruno's.** At this French–Mediterranean bistro on one of the busiest corners in Temple Bar, enjoy simple but stylish dishes ranging from starters of fresh crab claws with chilies, lemongrass, and tomato concassé to main dishes of char-grilled chicken with raisins, dried prunes, Moroccan semolina, and walnut dressing. ✉ *30 Essex St. E,* ☎ *01/670–6767. AE, DC, MC, V. Closed Sun.*

$$–$$$ ★ ✕ **La Stampa.** One of the most dramatic dining rooms in Dublin, La Stampa has huge gilt mirrors and elaborate candelabra that are gloriously over the top. The menu changes frequently to reflect an eclectic, international style. For a main course you may get rack of organic lamb with braised beans, tomatoes, and rosemary jus, or roast scallops with artichoke mash and a tomato vinaigrette. ✉ *35 Dawson St.,* ☎ *01/677–8611. AE, DC, MC, V. No lunch.*

$$ ✕ **Caviston's.** The Cavistons have been dispensing recipes for years from their fish counter and delicatessen in Sandycove, just south of the ferry port of Dun Laoghaire, 30 minutes by taxi or DART train south of Dublin. The fish restaurant next door is a lively and intimate spot for lunch, but you should book in advance. ✉ *59 Glasthule Rd., Dun Laoghaire,* ☎ *01/280–9120. MC, V. Closed Sun.–Mon. and late Dec.–early Jan. No dinner.*

$$ ✕ **Eden.** This popular brasserie-style restaurant overlooking one of Temple Bar's main squares turns out good contemporary cuisine, such as vegetarian buckwheat pancake filled with garlic, spinach, and cheddar, and duck leg confit with lentils. Try to go when there are open-air movies in the square. ✉ *Meeting House Sq.,* ☎ *01/670–5372. Reservations essential. AE, MC, V.*

$$ ✕ **The Lord Edward.** Creaking floorboards and an old fireplace give the impression of being in someone's drawing room at this restaurant, one of the oldest in the city. Start with classic fish dishes such as prawn cocktail or smoked salmon, followed by fresh and simply cooked Dover sole, salmon, or lobster. ✉ *23 Christ Church Pl.,* ☎ *01/454–2420. AE, DC, MC, V. No lunch Sat. Closed Sun.*

$ ✕ **Milano.** In a well-designed dining room with lots of brio, choose from a tempting array of inventive, thin-crust pizzas. ✉ *38 Dawson St.,* ☎ *01/670–7744; 18 Essex St. E, Temple Bar;* ☎ *01/670–3384. AE, DC, MC, V.*

Pub Food

Most pubs serve food at lunchtime, some throughout the day. Food ranges from hearty soups and stews to chicken curries, smoked salmon salads, and sandwiches. Expect to pay IR£4/€5.10–IR£6/€7.60 for a main course. Larger pubs tend to take credit cards.

✕ **Davy Byrne's.** James Joyce immortalized Davy Byrne's in *Ulysses.* Nowadays it's more akin to a cocktail bar than a Dublin pub, but it's good for fresh and smoked salmon, salads, and a hot daily special. ✉ *21 Duke St.,* ☎ *01/671–1298.*

✕ **Old Stand.** Conveniently close to Grafton Street, the Old Stand serves grilled food, including steaks. ✉ *37 Exchequer St.,* ☎ *01/677–7220.*

✕ **Porterhouse.** Ireland's first brewpub has an open kitchen and a dazzling range of beers—from pale ales to dark stouts. ✉ *16–18 Parliament St.,* ☎ *01/679–8847.*

✕ **Stag's Head.** The Stag's Head is a favorite of Trinity students and businesspeople, who come for one of the best pub lunches in the city. ✉ *1 Dame Ct.,* ☎ *01/679–3701.*

✕ **Zanzibar.** This is a spectacular and cavernous bar that looks as though it might be more at home in downtown Marakesh. While away an afternoon on one of its wicker chairs. ✉ *34–35 Lower Ormond Quay,* ☎ *01/878–7212.*

Cafés

Though Dublin has nowhere near as many cafés as pubs, it's easier than ever to find a good cup of coffee at most hours of the day or night.

✕ **Bewley's Coffee House.** The granddaddy of the capital's cafés, Bewley's has been supplying Dubliners with coffee and buns for more than a century. ✉ *78 Grafton St.; 12 Westmoreland St.; all* ☎ *01/677–6761.*

✕ **Kaffe Moka.** One of Dublin's hottest haunts for the caffeine-addicted, this spot has three hyperstylish floors and a central location in the heart of the city center. ✉ *39 S. William St.,* ☎ *01/679–8475.*

✕ **Thomas Read's.** By day it's a café, by night a pub. Its large windows overlooking a busy corner in Temple Bar make it a great spot for people-watching. ✉ *1 Parliament St.,* ☎ *01/671–7283.*

Lodging

On the lodging front Dublin is in the midst of a major hotel boom. For value stay in a guest house or a B&B; both tend to be in suburban areas—generally a 10-minute bus ride from the center of the city. **Bord Fáilte** can usually help find you a place to stay if you don't have reservations.

$$$$ 🏨 **Conrad Dublin International.** A subsidiary of Hilton Hotels, the Conrad is aimed at the international business executive. The seven-story redbrick and smoked-glass building is just off Stephen's Green. The spacious rooms are done in light brown and pastel greens. Alfie Byrne's, the main bar, attempts to re-create a traditional Irish pub atmosphere. ✉ *Earlsfort Terr., Dublin 2,* ☎ *01/676–5555,* FAX *01/676–5424,* WEB *www.conrad-international.ie. 182 rooms, 9 suites. 2 restaurants, bar. AE, DC, MC, V.*

$$$$ 🏨 **Jurys and the Towers.** These adjacent seven-story hotels, a short cab ride from the center of town, are popular with businesspeople and vacationers. Both have more atmosphere than most comparable modern hotels, though the Towers has an edge over Jurys, its older, larger, less expensive companion. ✉ *Pemroke Rd., Ballsbridge, Dublin 4,* ☎ *01/660–5000,* FAX *01/660–5540,* WEB *www.jurys.com.. Jurys: 288 rooms, 5 suites; the Towers: 100 rooms, 5 suites. 3 restaurants, pool. AE, DC, MC, V.*

$$$$ ★ **Merrion.** Four exactingly restored Georgian town houses make up part of this luxurious hotel. The stately rooms have been richly appointed in classic Georgian style down to the last detail. Leading Dublin restaurateur Patrick Guilbaud's eponymous restaurant is here. ✉ *Upper Merrion St., Dublin 2,* ☎ *01/603–0600,* FAX *01/603–0700,* WEB *www.merrionhotel.com. 127 rooms, 18 suites. 2 restaurants, 2 bars. AE, DC, MC, V.*

$$$$ ★ **Shelbourne Méridien Hotel.** Old-fashioned luxury prevails at this magnificent showplace, which has presided over Stephen's Green since 1824. Each room has its own fine, carefully selected furnishings. Those in front overlook the green; rooms in the back are quieter. The restaurant, 27 The Green, is one of the most elegant rooms in Dublin; Lord Mayor's Room, off the lobby, serves a lovely afternoon tea. ✉ *27 Stephen's Green, Dublin 2,* ☎ *01/663–4500; 800/543–4300 in the U.S.,* FAX *01/661–6006,* WEB *www.shelbourne.ie. 194 rooms, 9 suites. 2 restaurants, 2 bars. AE, DC, MC, V.*

$$$$ **Westbury.** This comfortable, modern hotel is right off the city's shopping mecca, Grafton Street. The spacious main lobby, where you can have afternoon tea, is furnished with antiques and large sofas. Rooms are rather utilitarian; the suites, which combine European decor with Japanese prints and screens, are more inviting. The flowery Russell Room serves formal lunches and dinners. ✉ *Grafton St., Dublin 2,* ☎ *01/679–1122,* FAX *01/679–7078,* WEB *www.jurys.com. 203 rooms, 8 suites. 2 restaurants, bar. AE, DC, MC, V.*

$$$–$$$$ **Chief O'Neill's.** Next door to the traditional music museum Ceol, this modern hotel has a huge lobby-bar area looking out onto a cobbled courtyard. Smallish, high-tech rooms all have chrome fixtures and minimalist furnishings. Top-floor suites have delightful rooftop gardens with views of the city on both sides of the Liffey. ✉ *Smithfield Village, Dublin 7,* ☎ *01/817–3838,* FAX *01/817–3839,* WEB *www.chiefoneills.com. 69 rooms, 4 suites. Restaurant, bar. AE, DC, MC, V.*

$$$–$$$$ **Hibernian.** An early 20th-century Edwardian nurses' home was converted into this hotel, retaining the distinctive red-and-amber brick facade. Every room is a different shape, though all are done in light pastels with deep-pile carpets. Public rooms are slightly small but are attractive in cheerful chintz and stripes. ✉ *Eastmoreland Pl., off Upper Baggot St., Dublin 4,* ☎ *01/668–7666,* FAX *01/660–2655,* WEB *hibernianhotel.com. 40 rooms. Restaurant, bar. AE, DC, MC, V.*

$$–$$$ **Central Hotel.** Established in 1887, this grand, old-style redbrick hotel is in the heart of the city. Rooms are small but have high ceilings and tasteful furnishings. The Library Bar on the second floor is one of the best spots in the city for a quiet pint. ✉ *1–5 Exchequer St., Dublin 2,* ☎ *01/679–7302,* FAX *01/679–7303,* WEB *www.centralhotel.ie. 67 rooms, 3 suites. Restaurant, 2 bars. AE, DC, MC, V.*

$$ ★ **Number 31.** Two strikingly renovated Georgian mews are connected via a small garden to the grand town house they once served; together they form a marvelous guest house a short walk from Stephen's Green. Owners Deirdre and Noel Comer offer gracious hospitality and made-to-order breakfasts. ✉ *31 Leeson Close, Dublin 2,* ☎ *01/676–5011,* FAX *01/676–2929,* WEB *www.number31.ie. 18 rooms. AE, MC, V.*

$$ **Paramount.** On the corner of Parliament Street and Essex Gate at the heart of Temple Bar, this medium-size hotel has kept its classy Victorian facade. The bedrooms are all dark woods and subtle colors, very 1930s; you just know if Bogart and Bacall ever come to Dublin they'll

have to stay here. If your fond of a tipple try the hotel's art-deco Turks Head Bar and Chop House. ✉ *Parliament Street and Essex Gate, Dublin 2,* ☎ *01/417–9900,* FAX *01/417–9904,* WEB *www.paramounthotel.ie. 70 rooms. Restaurant, bar. AE, DC, MC, V.*

$–$$ **Mount Herbert Hotel.** Close to the luxury hotels in the tree-lined inner suburb of Ballsbridge, a 10-minute DART ride from Dublin's center, the Loughran family's sprawling accommodation is popular with budget-minded visitors. Rooms are small, but all have 10-channel TVs and hair dryers. There's no bar on the premises, but there are plenty to choose from nearby. ✉ *7 Herbert Rd., Ballsbridge, Dublin 4,* ☎ *01/668–4321,* FAX *01/660–7077,* WEB *www.mountherberthotel.ie. 200 rooms. Restaurant. AE, DC, MC, V.*

$ ★ **Ariel Guest House.** Dublin's leading guest house is in a tree-lined suburb, a 10-minute walk from Stephen's Green, and close to a DART stop. Rooms in the main house are lovingly filled with antiques; those at the back of the house are more spartan; all are immaculate. Owner Michael O'Brien is a helpful and gracious host. ✉ *52 Lansdowne Rd., Dublin 4,* ☎ *01/668–5512,* FAX *01/668–5845,* WEB *www.ariel-house.com. 40 rooms. Breakfast room, wine bar. MC, V.*

$ **Avalon House.** Many young, independent travelers rate this cleverly restored, Victorian redbrick building the most appealing of Dublin's hostels. A 2-minute walk from Grafton Street and 5–10 minutes from some of the city's best music venues, it has a mix of dormitories, rooms without bath, and rooms with bath. The Avalon Café serves food until 10 PM, but is open as a common room after hours. ✉ *55 Aungier St., Dublin 2,* ☎ *01/475–0001,* FAX *01/475–0303,* WEB *www.avalon-house.ie. 312 beds. Bar, café. AE, MC, V.*

$ **Jurys Christchurch Inn.** Expect few frills at this functional budget hotel (part of an otherwise upscale hotel chain), where there's a fixed room rate for up to three adults or two adults and two children. The biggest plus: the pleasant location, facing Christ Church Cathedral and within walking distance of most city-center attractions. Rooms are in pastel colors. The bar serves a pub lunch, and the restaurant, breakfast and dinner. ✉ *Christchurch Pl., Dublin 8,* ☎ *01/454–0000,* FAX *01/454–0012,* WEB *www.jurys.com. 182 rooms. Restaurant, bar. AE, DC, MC, V.*

Nightlife and the Arts

The weekly magazines *In Dublin* and the *Big Issue* (at newsstands) contain comprehensive details of upcoming events, including ticket availability. *The Event Guide* also lists events and is free at many pubs and cafés. In peak season, consult the free Bord Fáilte leaflet "Events of the Week."

Cabarets

The following all have cabaret shows, with dancing, music, and traditional Irish song; they are open only in peak season (roughly May–October; call to confirm): **Abbey Tavern** (✉ Howth, Co. Dublin, ☎ 01/839–0307). **Clontarf Castle** (✉ Castle Ave., Clontarf, ☎ 01/833–2321). **Doyle Burlington Hotel** (✉ Upper Leeson St., ☎ 01/660–5222). **Jurys Hotel** (✉ Pembroke Rd., Ballsbridge, ☎ 01/660–5000).

Classical Music

The **National Concert Hall** (✉ Earlsfort Terr., ☎ 01/475–1666), just off Stephen's Green, is home to the National Symphony Orchestra of Ireland and is Dublin's main theater for classical music of all kinds. **St. Stephen's Church** (✉ Merrion Sq., ☎ 01/288–0663) has a regular program of choral and orchestral events.

Nightclubs

The **Kitchen** (✉ Essex St., ☎ 01/677–6635) is part-owned by U2 and attracts a young, vibrant clientele. The **POD** (✉ Harcourt St., ☎ 01/478–0166) is the city's hippest spot for twenty-somethings. **Rí Ra** (✉ Dame Court, ☎ 01/677–4835) means "uproar" in Irish, and on most nights the place does go a little wild; it's one of the best spots for no-frills, fun dancing in Dublin.

Pubs

Check advertisements in evening papers for folk, ballad, Irish traditional, or jazz music performances. The pubs listed below generally have some form of musical entertainment. The **Brazen Head** (✉ 20 Lower Bridge St., ☎ 01/677–9549)—Dublin's oldest pub, dating from 1688—has music every night. **Chief O'Neill's** (✉ Smithfield Village, ☎ 01/817–3838) has an open, airy bar-café. The **Cobblestone** (✉ N. King St., ☎ 01/872–1799) is a glorious house of ale in the best Dublin tradition. **Doheny & Nesbitt's** (✉ 5 Lower Baggot St., ☎ 01/676–2945) is frequented by local businesspeople, politicians, and legal eagles. In the **Horseshoe Bar** (✉ Shelbourne Méridien Hotel, St. Stephen's Green, ☎ 01/676–6471) you can eavesdrop on Dublin's social elite. **Kehoe's** (✉ 9 S. Anne St., ☎ 01/677–8312) is popular with students, artists, and writers. Locals and tourists bask in the theatrical atmosphere of **Neary's** (✉ 1 Chatham St., ☎ 01/676–2807). **O'Donoghue's** (✉ 15 Merrion Row, ☎ 01/661–4303) features some form of musical entertainment on most nights. The **Palace Bar** (✉ 21 Fleet St., ☎ 01/677–9290) is a journalists' haunt.

Theaters

Ireland has a rich theatrical tradition. The **Abbey Theatre** (✉ Marlborough St., ☎ 01/878–7222) is the home of Ireland's national theater company, its name forever associated with J. M. Synge, W. B. Yeats, and Sean O'Casey. The **Peacock Theatre** is the Abbey's more experimental small stage. The **Gaiety Theatre** (✉ S. King St., ☎ 01/677–1717) features musical comedy, opera, drama, and revues. The **Gate Theatre** (✉ Cavendish Row, Parnell Sq., ☎ 01/874–4045) is an intimate spot for modern drama and plays by Irish writers. The **Olympia Theatre** (✉ Dame St., ☎ 01/677–7744) has comedy, vaudeville, and ballet performances. The **Project Arts Centre** (✉ 39 E. Essex St., ☎ 01/679–6622) is an established fringe theater.

Shopping

The rest of the country is well supplied with crafts shops, but Dublin is the place to seek out more specialized items—antiques, haute couture, designer ceramics, books and prints, silverware and jewelry, and designer hand-knit items.

Shopping Centers and Department Stores

The shops north of the river—many of them chain stores and lackluster department stores—tend to be less expensive and less design-conscious. The one exception is the **Jervis Shopping Center** (✉ Jervis St. at Mary St., ☎ 01/878–1323), a major shopping center with chain stores as well as smaller boutiques. **Arnotts** (✉ Henry St., ☎ 01/805–0400) is Dublin's largest department store and carries a good range of cut crystal. **Brown Thomas** (✉ Grafton St., ☎ 01/605–6666) is Dublin's most elegant department store. **St. Stephen's Green Center** (✉ St. Stephen's Green, ☎ 01/478–0888) contains 70 stores in a vast Moorish-style glass-roof building.

Shopping Districts

Grafton Street is the most sophisticated shopping area in Dublin's city center. **Francis Street** and **Dawson Street** are the places to browse for antiques. **Nassau Street** and **Dawson Street** are for books; the smaller side streets are good for jewelry, art galleries, and old prints. The pedestrianized **Temple Bar** area, with its young, offbeat ambience, has a number of small art galleries, specialty shops (music and books), and inexpensive, trendy clothing shops. The area is further enlivened by buskers (street musicians) and street artists.

Bookstores

Fred Hanna's (✉ 29 Nassau St., ☎ 01/677–1255) sells old and new books, with a good choice of books on travel and Ireland. **Hodges Figgis** (✉ 56–58 Dawson St., ☎ 01/677–4754) is Dublin's leading independent, with a café on the first floor. **Waterstone's** (✉ 7 Dawson St., ☎ 01/679–1415) is the Dublin branch of the renowned British chain. **Hughes & Hughes** (✉ St. Stephen's Green Centre, ☎ 01/478–3060) has strong travel and Irish-interest sections. There is also a store at Dublin Airport.

Gift Items

Blarney Woollen Mills (✉ Nassau St., ☎ 01/671–0068) has a good selection of tweed, linen, and woolen sweaters. **Dublin Woolen Mills** (✉ Metal Bridge Corner, 41 Lower Ormond Quay, ☎ 01/677–5014), at Ha'penny Bridge, sells hand-knit and other woolen sweaters at competitive prices. **Kevin & Howlin** (✉ Nassau St., ☎ 01/677–0257) carries tweeds for men. **Kilkenny Shop** (✉ Nassau St., ☎ 01/677–7066) is good for contemporary Irish-made ceramics, pottery, and silver jewelry. **McDowell** (✉ 3 Upper O'Connell St., ☎ 01/874–4961), in business for more than 100 years, is a popular jewelry shop. **Tierneys** (✉ St. Stephen's Green Centre, ☎ 01/478–2873) carries a good selection of crystal, china, claddagh rings, pendants, and brooches.

Outdoor Markets

Moore Street (✉ Henry St.), a large mall behind the Ilac Center, is open from Monday to Saturday 9–6; stalls lining both sides of the street sell fruits and vegetables. A variety of bric-a-brac is sold at the **Liberty Market** on the north end of Meath Street, open on Friday and Saturday 10–6, Sunday noon–5:30. The indoor **Mother Redcap's Market,** opposite Christ Church, is open Friday, Saturday, and Sunday 10–5; come here for antiques and other finds.

Side Trips

The **Hill of Tara,** 33 km (21 mi) northwest of Dublin, was the religious and cultural capital of Ireland in ancient times. Its importance waned with the arrival of Christianity in the 5th century, and today its crest is, appropriately enough, crowned with a statue of the man who brought Christianity to Ireland—St. Patrick.

It was in the 8th-century abbey in **Kells,** 64 km (40 mi) north of Dublin, that the Book of Kells was completed; a facsimile can be seen in St. Columba's Church. Among the remains of the abbey are a well-preserved round tower and a rare example of a stone-roof church dating from the 9th century.

Dublin Essentials

AIRPORTS AND TRANSFERS

All flights arrive at Dublin Airport, 10 km (6 mi) north of town.

➤ Airport Information: (☎ 01/814–1111).

TRANSFERS

Express buses leave every 20 minutes from outside the Arrivals door for the central bus station in downtown Dublin. The ride takes about

30 minutes, depending on the traffic, and the fare is IR£3/€3.80. If you have time, take a regular bus for IR£1.15/€1.45. A taxi ride into town will cost from IR£12/€15.25 to IR£14/€17.80, depending on the location of your hotel; be sure to ask in advance if the cab has no meter.

BOAT AND FERRY TRAVEL

Irish Ferries has a regular car and passenger service directly into Dublin port from Holyhead in Wales. Stena Sealink docks in Dublin port (3½-hour service to Holyhead) and in Dun Laoghaire (High Speed Service, known as "HSS," which takes 99 minutes). Prices and departure times vary according to season, so call to confirm. In summer, reservations are strongly recommended. Dozens of taxis wait to take you into town from both ports, or you can take DART or a bus to the city center.

➤ BOAT AND FERRY INFORMATION: **Irish Ferries** (✉ Merrion Row, ☎ 01/661–0511). **Stena Sealink** (✉ Ferryport, Dun Laoghaire, ☎ 01/204–7777).

BUS TRAVEL TO AND FROM DUBLIN

The central bus station is Busaras; some buses also terminate near O'Connell Bridge. Bus Éireann provides express and provincial service.

➤ BUS INFORMATION: **Busaras** (✉ Store St. near the Custom House). **Bus Éireann** (☎ 01/836–6111).

BUS TRAVEL WITHIN DUBLIN

Dublin Bus provides city service, including transport to and from the airport. Most city buses originate in or pass through the area of O'Connell Street and O'Connell Bridge. If the destination board indicates AN LÁR, that means that the bus is going to the city center. Timetables (IR£2.50/€3.20) are available from Dublin Bus; the minimum fare is 55p/€.70.

➤ BUS INFORMATION: **Dublin Bus** (✉ 59 Upper O'Connell St., ☎ 01/873–4222).

CAR TRAVEL

The main access route from the north is N1; from the west, N4; from the south and southwest, N7; from the east coast, N11. All routes have clearly marked signs indicating the center of the city: AN LÁR. The M50 motorway encircles the city from Dublin Airport in the north to Tallaght in the south.

The number of cars in Ireland has grown exponentially in the last few years, and nowhere has their impact been felt more than in Dublin, where the city's complicated one-way streets are often congested. Avoid driving a car in the city except to get you into and out of it, and be sure to ask your hotel or guest house for clear directions when you leave.

EMERGENCIES

➤ DOCTORS AND DENTISTS: **Dentist: Dublin Dental Hospital** (☎ 01/662–0766). **Doctor: Eastern Help Board** (☎ 01/679–0700).

➤ EMERGENCY SERVICES: **Ambulance** (☎ 999). **Police** (☎ 999).

➤ PHARMACIES: **Hamilton Long** (☎ 01/874–8456).

TAXIS

Official licensed taxis, metered and designated by roof signs, do not cruise; they can be found beside the central bus station, at train stations, at O'Connell Bridge, Stephen's Green, College Green, and near major hotels. The initial charge is IR£1.80/€2.30, with an additional charge of about IR£1.60/€2.05 per 2 km (1 mi) thereafter (make sure the meter is on). Hackney cabs, which also operate in the city, have neither roof signs nor meters and will sometimes respond to hotels' requests for a cab. Negotiate the fare before your journey begins.

TOURS

BUS TOURS

Bus Éireann runs day trips to all the major sights around the capital. Gray Line Tours organizes bus tours of Dublin and its major sights; they also have daylong tours into the surrounding countryside and longer tours elsewhere (the price for excursion tours includes accommodations, breakfast, and admission). Dublin Bus runs a continuous guided open-top bus tour (IR£5/€6.35) that allows you to hop on and off the bus as often as you wish and visit some 15 sights along its route.

➤ FEES AND SCHEDULES: **Bus Éireann** (☎ 01/836–6111). **Dublin Bus** (☎ 01/873–0000). **Gray Line Tours** (☎ 01/670–8822).

SPECIAL INTEREST TOURS

Elegant Ireland arranges tours for groups interested in architecture and the fine arts; these include visits with the owners of some of Ireland's stately homes and castles.

➤ FEES AND SCHEDULES: **Elegant Ireland** (☎ 01/475–1665).

WALKING TOURS

The tourist office has leaflets giving information on a selection of walking tours, including "Literary Dublin," "Georgian Dublin," and "Pub Tours." Bord Fáilte has a "Tourist Trail" walk, which takes in the main sites of central Dublin and can be completed in about three hours, and a "Rock 'n Stroll" tour, which covers the city's major pop and rock music sites.

TRAIN TRAVEL

Irish Rail provides train service throughout the country. Dublin has three main stations. Connolly Station is the departure point for Belfast, the east coast, and the west. Heuston Station is the departure point for the south and southwest. Pearse Station is for Bray and connections via Dun Laoghaire to the Liverpool-Holyhead ferries.

An electric train commuter service, DART, serves the suburbs out to Howth, on the north side of the city, and to Bray, County Wicklow, on the south side. Fares are about the same as for buses. Street-direction signs to DART stations read STAISIUN/STATION.

➤ TRAIN INFORMATION: **Connolly Station** (✉ at Amiens St.). **Heuston Station** (✉ at Kingsbridge). **Irish Rail** (✉ 35 Lower Abbey St., ☎ 01/836–6222 information). **Pearse Station** (✉ on Westland Row).

TRAVEL AGENCIES

➤ LOCAL AGENTS: **American Express** (✉ 116 Grafton St., ☎ 01/677–2874). **Thomas Cook** (✉ 118 Grafton St., ☎ 01/677–1721).

VISITOR INFORMATION

In addition to the visitor information offices in the entrance hall of the headquarters of Bord Fáilte, Dublin Tourism has visitor information at the airport (Arrivals level), open daily 8 AM–10 PM; and at the Ferryport, Dun Laoghaire, open daily 10 AM–9 PM.

DUBLIN TO CORK

One good way to see the country is to drive southwest from Dublin to Cork, the Republic's second-largest city. On the way, you'll see the lush green fields of Ireland's famous stud farms and imposing Cashel, where Ireland built its reputation as the "Land of Saints and Scholars" while most of Europe was slipping into the Dark Ages.

Naas

The road to Naas (pronounced "*nace*") passes through the area known as the Pale—that part of Ireland in which English law was formally

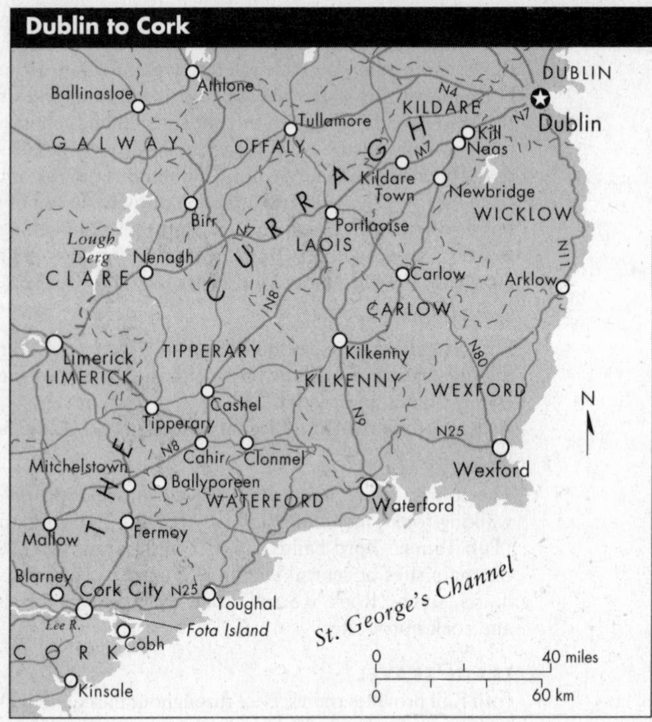

acknowledged up to Elizabethan times. The aesthetically mundane seat of County Kildare and a thriving market town in the heartland of Irish Thoroughbred country, Naas is full of pubs filled with jockeys discussing the merits of their stables. Naas has its own small racecourse, but **Punchestown Racecourse** (3 km/2 mi from Naas) has a wonderful setting amid rolling plains and is famous for its steeplechases.

The Curragh

The Curragh, 8 km (5 mi) southwest of Naas, just beyond the end of the bypass M7 and bisected by the main N7 road, is the biggest area of common land in Ireland, containing about 31 square km (12 square mi) and devoted mainly to grazing. It's also Ireland's major racing center, home to the **Curragh Racecourse** (☎ 045/441205), where the Irish Derby and other international horse races are run. In addition, the Irish army trains here, at the **Curragh Main Barracks.**

Kildare Town

The thriving economy of Kildare, 5 km (3 mi) from the Curragh on M7, is based on horse breeding. The town is also where St. Brigid founded a religious settlement in the 5th century; **St. Brigid's Cathedral** (✉ off Market Sq.) is a restoration of a 13th-century building.

If you're a longtime horse aficionado, or are just curious, the **National Stud Farm,** a main center of Ireland's racing industry, is well worth a visit. Also on the grounds, the National Stud Horse Museum recounts the history of the horse in Ireland. ✉ *South of Kildare Town about 2½ km (1½ mi), clearly signposted to left of market square,* ☎ *045/521617,* WEB *www.irish-national-stud.ie.* ⏲ *Mid-Feb.–mid-Nov., daily 9:30–6.*

★ The elegant **Japanese Gardens,** adjacent to the National Stud Farm, were laid out between 1906 and 1910 and are considered among the finest in Europe. ✉ *South of Kildare Town about 2½ km (1½ mi), clearly* *signposted to left of market square,* ☎ *045/521617,* WEB *www.irish-national-stud.ie.* ⏲ *Mid-Feb.–mid-Nov., daily 9:30–6.*

Cashel

Cashel is a market town on the busy Cork–Dublin road, which, in spite of the incessant heavy traffic running through it, retains some interesting Victorian shopfronts on its Main Street. The town has a lengthy history as a center of royal and religious power.

★ The awe-inspired, oft-mist-shrouded **Rock of Cashel** is one of Ireland's most-visited sites. The rock itself, which is a short walk from the north of the town, rises as a giant, circular mound 200 ft above the surrounding plain; it is crowned by a tall cluster of gray monastic remains. The kings of Munster held it as their seat for about seven centuries, and it was here that St. Patrick reputedly plucked a shamrock from the ground, using it as a symbol to explain the mystery of the Trinity, giving Ireland, in the process, its universally recognized symbol. ☎ *062/61437,* WEB *www.heritageireland.ie.* ⏲ *Mid-Mar.–mid-June, daily 9:30–5:30; mid-June–mid-Sept., daily 9–7:30; mid-Sept.–mid-Mar., daily 9:30–4:30.*

$$$ ✕ **Chez Hans.** Enjoy fresh local produce cooked with a French accent in this converted chapel at the foot of the famous rock. ✉ *Rockside,* ☎ *062/61177. MC, V. Closed Sun.–Mon. and first 3 wks in Jan. No lunch.*

$$$$ ✕🏨 **Cashel Palace.** Although in the town center, this magnificently restored 18th-century bishop's palace has great views of the Rock of Cashel from its back rooms. Inexpensive light meals are served all day in its bistro-style cellar restaurant. ✉ *Main St., Co. Tipperary,* ☎ *062/62707,* FAX *062/61521,* WEB *www.cashel-palace.ie. 23 rooms. 2 restaurants, bar. AE, DC, MC, V.*

Cahir

Cahir (pronounced "care") is a popular stopping place to break the Dublin–Cork journey. **Cahir Castle,** the town's main attraction, is a massive limestone structure dating from 1164 and built on rock in the middle of the river. There are guided tours and an audiovisual display in the lodge. ☎ *052/41011,* WEB *www.heritageireland.ie.* ⏲ *Apr.–mid-June and late Sept.–mid-Oct., daily 10–5:30; late June–mid-Sept., daily 9–7:30; late Oct.–Mar., daily 10–1 and 2–4:30.*

$ 🏨 **Kilcoran Lodge Hotel.** This handsome, sprawling, former 19th-century hunting lodge sits amid beautiful countryside 6 km (4 mi) outside Cahir on the main Cork–Dublin (N8) road. Rooms facing the front have the best views of the beautiful, heather-covered slopes; all have Victorian-style furnishings and comfortable beds. ✉ *Cahir, Co. Tipperary,* ☎ *052/41288,* FAX *052/41994,* WEB *www.tipp.ie. 23 rooms. Restaurant, bar. AE, DC, MC, V.*

Cork City

The road enters Cork City along the banks of the River Lee. In the center of Cork, the Lee divides in two, giving the city a profusion of picturesque quays and bridges. The name Cork derives from the Irish *corcaigh* (pronounced "corky"), meaning a marshy place. The city received its first charter in 1185 and grew rapidly during the 17th and 18th centuries with the expansion of its butter trade. It is the major metropolis of the south, and with a population of about 175,000, the second-largest city in Ireland. The main business and shopping center of Cork lies on the island created by the two diverging channels of the Lee, and most places of interest are within walking distance of the center. **Patrick Street** is the focal point; here you'll find the city's major department stores, **Roches** and **Brown Thomas.** If you look up above the plate-glass shop facades, you'll see examples of the bowfront Georgian windows that are emblematic of old Cork.

The famous bell tower of **St. Anne's Church,** the 120-ft Shandon Steeple, is on a hill across the river to the north of Cork's main shopping area. Shaped like a pepper pot, it houses the bells immortalized in the song "The Bells of Shandon." You can climb the tower and ring the bells over Cork. ✉ *Church St.* ⏲ *May–Oct., Mon.–Sat. 9:30–5; Nov.–Apr., Mon.–Sat. 10–3:30.*

The liveliest place in town to shop is the pedestrian-only **Paul Street** area, parallel to the northwest side of Patrick Street. Housed in the 1724 building that was once the city's Custom House, the **Crawford Municipal Art Gallery** at the top of Paul Street has an excellent collection of 18th- and 19th-century views of Cork and adventurous exhibits by modern artists. ✉ *Emmet Pl.,* ☎ *021/427–3377.* ⏲ *Weekdays 9–5, Sat. 9–1.*

$$$ ✕ **The Ivory Tower.** Seamus O'Connell, the young chef-owner of this restaurant off Patrick Street, concocts such adventurous dishes as blackened shark with banana ketchup, or wild duck with vanilla, sherry and jalapeños. The bare boards and stick-back chairs are offset by original works of art. ✉ *35 Princes St.,* ☎ *021/427–4665. MC, V. Closed Sun.–Mon.*

$ ★ ✕ **Isaac's.** In an old warehouse, this popular spot has modern art on the walls and Mediterranean-influenced food. Excellent local produce is used in such starters as warm potato salad with smoked bacon and black pudding. ✉ *48 MacCurtain St.,* ☎ *021/450–3805. MC, V.*

$$$ ✕🏨 **Jurys.** Beside the River Lee, a five-minute walk from the city center, this modern, two-story structure of smoked glass and steel is a popular local meeting place. The Glandore Restaurant serves an à la carte menu with the emphasis on fresh local produce. Rooms are spacious, with the best ones overlooking the internal patio garden and pool. ✉ *Western Rd., Co. Cork,* ☎ *021/427–6622,* FAX *021/427–4477,* WEB *www.jurys.com. 185 rooms. 2 restaurants. AE, DC, MC, V.*

$$$$ 🏨 **Hayfield Manor.** This fine luxury hotel is built to resemble a classic Georgian country house. It's beside the university campus, five minutes' drive from the city center. ✉ *Perrott Ave., off College Rd., Co. Cork,* ☎ *021/431–5600,* FAX *021/431–6839,* WEB *www.hayfieldmanor.ie. 53 rooms. Restaurant, bar. AE, DC, MC, V.*

$$ 🏨 **Hotel Isaac's.** This stylish city-center hotel has bright and cheerful rooms, with polished wood floors and rustic pine furniture. ✉ *48 MacCurtain St., Co. Cork,* ☎ *021/450–0011,* FAX *021/450–6355,* WEB *www.isaacs.ie. 36 rooms with bath. Restaurant. AE, MC, V.*

Cobh and Fota Island

If you're from the United States and have Irish roots, chances are your ancestors were among the thousands who sailed from the port of Cork. Cobh (pronounced "cove"), as it is known nowadays, is an attractive, hilly town, dominated by its 19th-century cathedral. From Cork, follow the signposts for Waterford on N25 along the northern bank of the River Lee. Alternatively, a suburban rail service leaves from Cork's **Kent Station** (☎ 021/450–6766 schedule) with stops in Cobh and Fota ★ Island. In the old Cobh railway station, the **Queenstown Project** recreates the experience of the emigrants who left the town between 1750 and the mid-20th century. It also tells the stories of the great transatlantic liners, including the *Titanic,* whose last port of call was Cobh, and the *Lusitania,* which was sunk by a German submarine off this coast on May 7, 1915. ☎ *021/481–3591,* WEB *www.cobhheritage.com.* ⏲ *Feb.–Nov., daily 10–6.*

Part of the **Fota Demesne,** a large estate on Fota Island, consists of a magnificent arboretum. Also on the estate is the 238-square-km (70-acre) Fota Wildlife Park, an important breeding center for cheetahs and wallabies. ☎ *021/481–2678,* WEB *www.fotawildlife.ie.* ⏲ *Mid-Mar.–Sept., daily 10–6.*

$$$$ ★ ✕🏨 **Ballymaloe House.** One of Ireland's best-known and most-admired country houses, Ballymaloe is the home of the Allen family, who welcome guests with gracious aplomb. Each guest room is an elegant variation on country-house style. Myrtle, the doyenne of Irish cooking, presides over the outstanding dining room. ✉ *29 km (18 mi) east of Cobh, Shanagarry, Midleton,* ☎ *021/465–2531,* FAX *021/465–2021,* WEB *www.ballymaloe.ie. 32 rooms. Restaurant, pool. AE, DC, MC, V.*

Blarney

Just north of Blarney is **Blarney Castle**—or what remains of it: the ruined central keep is all that's left of this mid-15th-century stronghold. The walls of the castle contain the famed **Blarney Stone,** in a wall below the castle's battlements; kissing the stone, it is said, endows you with the fabled "gift of gab." To kiss the stone, you must lie down on the battlements and lean your head way back. Nobody knows how the tradition originated, but Elizabeth I is credited with giving the word "blarney" to the language when, commenting on the unfulfilled promises of Cormac MacCarthy, Lord Blarney of the time, she remarked, "This is all Blarney; what he says he never means." ☎ *021/438–5252,* WEB *www.blarneycastle.ie.* ⏲ *Mon.–Sat. 9 AM–sundown, Sun. 9–5:30.*

Dublin to Cork Essentials

AIRPORTS

Cork Airport, 5 km (3 mi) south of Cork City on the Kinsale road, is used primarily for flights to and from the United Kingdom. Regular 30-minute internal flights are scheduled between Shannon and Dublin, Shannon and Cork, and Cork and Dublin.

➤ AIRPORT INFORMATION: **Cork Airport** (☎ 021/431–3131).

BIKE TRAVEL

➤ BIKE RENTALS: **Rothar Cycle Tours** (✉ 2 Bandon Rd., Cork City, ☎ 021/431–3133).

BUS TRAVEL

Bus Éireann operates Expressway services from Dublin to Cork City.

➤ BUS INFORMATION: **Bus Éireann** (☎ 01/836–6111, Dublin; 061/313333, Limerick; 021/450–8188, Cork; or 066/23566, Tralee). **Cork City Main Bus Terminal** (✉ Parnell Pl., ☎ 021/450–8188).

CAR TRAVEL

From Dublin, pick up N8 in Portlaoise for Cork City (257 km/160 mi); the journey time is about 3½ hours. A car is the ideal way to explore this area. Roads are generally narrow, two-lane motorways. All the main car-rental firms have desks at Cork Airport. Be sure to get a map of Cork City's complicated one-way street system.

TOURS

Arrangements Unlimited can arrange special-interest tours of the region for small or large groups. Bus Éireann operates a number of city tours and regional excursions from Parnell Place in Cork City.

➤ FEES AND SCHEDULES: **Arrangements Unlimited** (✉ 1 Woolhara Park, Douglas, Cork City, Co. Cork, ☎ 021/429–3873, FAX 021/429–2488). **Bus Éireann** (☎ 021/450–6066, WEB www.buseireann.ie).

TRAIN TRAVEL

The terminal in Cork City is Kent Station. There are direct service from Dublin and Tralee and a suburban line to Cobh.

➤ TRAIN INFORMATION: **Kent Station** (☎ 021/450–6766 information).

VISITOR INFORMATION

➤ TOURIST INFORMATION: **Cahir** (✉ Castle St., Co. Tipperary, ☎ 052/41453); open April–September. **Cashel** (✉ Town Hall, Co. Tipperary, ☎ 062/61333, FAX 062/61789); open April–September. **Cork City** (✉ Grand Parade, Cork City, ☎ 021/427–3251, FAX 021/427–3504); open year-round.

CORK TO GALWAY

The trip from Cork north to Galway is about 300 km (186 mi) and includes stops in Killarney and Limerick. The Shannon region around Limerick is littered with castles, both ruined and restored. Along the way, the Cork–Killarney road passes through the west Cork Gaeltacht—a predominantly Irish-speaking region—and begins its climb into the Derrynasaggart Mountains.

Killarney and Environs

Killarney itself is an undistinguished market town, well developed to handle the crowds that gather here in peak season. They come to drink in the famous scenery, located out of town toward the lakes that lie in a valley running south between the mountains. Much of Killarney's ★ lake district is within **Killarney National Park.** At the heart of the park is the 10,000-acre **Muckross Estate,** which is open daily, daylight hours. Cars are not allowed in the estate, so if you don't want to walk, rent a bicycle in town or take a trip in a jaunting car—a small two-wheel horse-drawn cart whose operators can be found at the gates to the estate and in Killarney. At the center of the estate is **Muckross House,** a 19th-century manor that contains the Kerry Country Life Experience. On the adjoining grounds is an Old World farm. ☎ *064/31440,* WEB *www.heritageireland.ie.* ⏲ *Sept.–June, daily 9–5:30; July–Aug., daily 9–7. Closed 1 wk at Christmas.*

To get an idea of the splendor of the lakes and streams—and of the massive glacial sandstone and limestone rocks and lush vegetation ★ that characterize the Killarney district—take a daylong tour of the **Gap of Dunloe,** as well as **the Upper Lake, Long Range, Middle and Lower lakes,** and **Ross Castle.** The central section, the Gap of Dunloe, is not suitable for cars, but horses and jaunting cars are available at **Kate Kearney's Cottage,** which marks the entrance to the gap.

$$$ ✕ **Gaby's Seafood.** Tile floors, pine booths, and red gingham tablecloths are the hallmarks of the cheerful, informal decor of this Killarney restaurant. Fresh seafood simply prepared is the specialty. ✉ *17 High St.,* ☎ *064/32519. AE, DC, MC, V. No breakfast or lunch. Closed Sun.*

$$ ✕ **Dingles.** The warm welcome supplied by Gerry Cunningham at his rustic restaurant in Killarney's center will make you feel like a local. His wife, Marie, creates such tasty dishes as baked crab and prawn au gratin or roast rack of Kerry lamb. ✉ *40 New St.,* ☎ *064/31079. AE, DC, MC, V. Closed Nov.–Mar. No lunch.*

$$$$ ★ ✕🏨 **Aghadoe Heights.** Its location on a bluff translates into unforgettable lake views—especially from the aerie of the famous hotel restaurant, Frederick's. The luxurious interior is a pleasant combination of the antique and the modern. ✉ *Aghadoe Heights, 4 km (2½ mi) outside Killarney on the Tralee side, signposted off the N22, Co. Kerry,* ☎ *064/31766,* FAX *064/31345,* WEB *www.aghadoeheights.com. 77 rooms, 3 suites. Restaurant, bar. AE, DC, MC, V.*

$$ 🏨 **Arbutus.** A good budget hotel in the town center, Arbutus has been in the same family since it was built more than 60 years ago. Ask for a room in the newer, second-story section. Its quiet bar draws a local

Cork to Galway

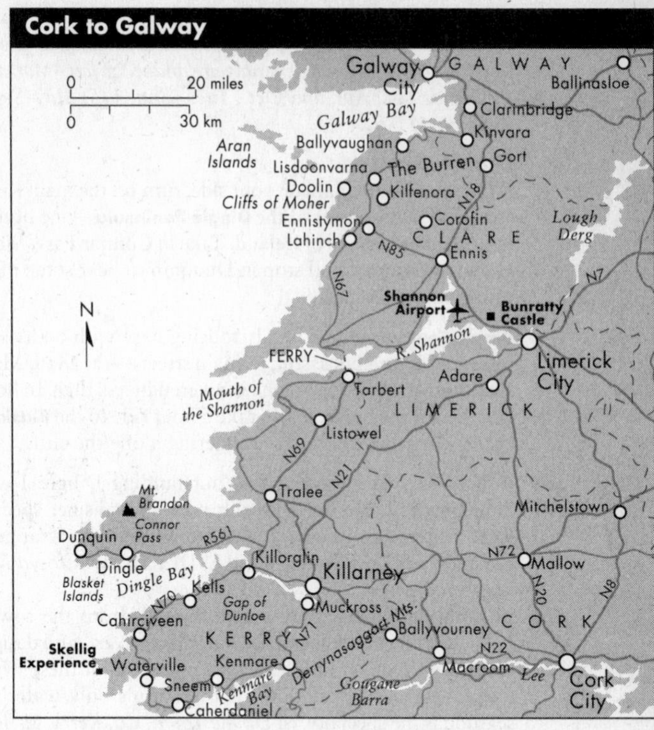

crowd. ✉ *College St., Killarney, Co. Kerry,* ☎ *064/31037,* FAX *064/34033. 44 rooms. Restaurant, bar. AE, DC, MC, V.*

Ring of Kerry

Running along the perimeter of the Iveragh Peninsula, the dramatic Ring of Kerry is probably the single most popular tourist route in Ireland. Stunning mountain and coastal views are around almost every turn. The only drawback: on a sunny day, it seems like half the tourists in Ireland are there. It's a daylong drive (176 km/109 mi round-trip) from Killarney; leave by N71 (the Kenmare road).

Kenmare

Kenmare is a small, mainly 19th-century market town at the head of Kenmare Bay. Across the water, as you drive out along the Iveragh Peninsula, are views of the gray-blue mountain ranges of the Beara Peninsula.

$$$$ ★ ✕🏨 **Park Hotel.** Spacious rooms with late-Victorian antiques and Italian marble–tile bathrooms distinguish this fine country-house hotel. Local ingredients and seafood star on the restaurant's sophisticated Irish-Continental menu (a jacket and tie are required). ✉ *Kenmare, Co. Kerry,* ☎ *064/41200,* FAX *064/41402,* WEB *www.parkenmare.com. 50 rooms. Restaurant, bar. AE, DC, MC, V. Closed Jan.–mid-Apr..*

Sneem

Sneem, on the estuary of the River Ardsheelaun, is one of the prettiest villages in Ireland. Look for "the pyramids" (as they are known locally), 12-ft-tall, traditional stone structures that look old but were completed in 1990 by Kerry-born artist James Scanlon.

Caherdaniel

The **Derrynane House** was once the home of the 19th-century politician and patriot Daniel O'Connell, "The Liberator." The south and east wings of the house are open to visitors and still contain much of the original furniture and other items associated with O'Connell. ☎ *066/947–5113,* WEB *www.heritageireland.ie.* ⊙ *Jan.–Mar. and Nov.–Dec., weekends 1–5; Apr. and Oct., Tues.–Sun. 1–5; May–Sept., Mon.–Sat. 9–6, Sun. 11–7.*

Dingle Area

If time and weather are on your side, turn off the main Killorglin–Tralee road and make a tour of the **Dingle Peninsula**—one of the wildest and least-spoiled regions of Ireland. Take in **Connor Pass, Mount Brandon, Gallarus Oratory,** and stop in **Dunquin** to hear some of Ireland's best traditional musicians.

Dingle Town itself is a handy touring base with crafts shops, seafood restaurants, and pubs; still, its main streets—the Mall, Main and Strand streets, and the Wood—can be covered in less than an hour. For an adventure off the beaten path, take a boat ride to the **Blasket Islands** and spend a few blissful hours wandering along the cliffs. ★

$$$ ★ ✕ **Beginish.** The food at this outstanding Dingle Town restaurant imaginatively interprets French nouvelle cuisine; specialties include local lobster and roast loin of lamb with phyllo-wrapped kidneys. ✉ *Green St.,* ☎ *066/915–1588. AE, DC, MC, V. Closed Mon. and mid-Nov.–mid-Mar.*

$$$ ✕🏨 **Dingle Skellig.** A five-minute walk from the town center, this hotel-restaurant is a showcase of Irish craft, art, and design. More than half the spacious rooms have sea views (ask for these when reserving). The Coastguard Restaurant is the town's only water's-edge eatery; seafood is the specialty. ✉ *Dingle Town, Co. Kerry,* ☎ *066/915–0200,* FAX *066/915–1501,* WEB *www.dingleskellig.com. 116 rooms. Restaurant, indoor pool. AE, DC, MC, V. Closed last wk in Dec.–Jan..*

$ 🏨 **Greenmount House.** This impeccably kept, modern B&B a short walk from the town center is renowned for its imaginative breakfasts. ✉ *Gortanora, Dingle Town, Co. Kerry,* ☎ *066/915–1414,* FAX *066/915–1974,* WEB *www.greenmounthouse.com. 12 rooms. MC, V.*

Tralee

County Kerry's capital and its largest town, Tralee has neither ruins nor quaint architecture, yet it makes a go at attracting visitors. Tralee has long been associated with its annual festival, during which, every September, a young woman of Irish descent is chosen to be the "Rose of Tralee." The **Kerry County Museum,** Tralee's major cultural attraction, traces the history of Kerry's people from 5000 BC to the present. ✉ *Ashe Memorial Hall, Denny St.,* ☎ *066/712–7777,* WEB *www.kc-museum.com.* ⊙ *Sept.–July, Mon.–Sat. 10–6; Aug., Mon.–Sat. 10–8.*

Adare

Adare is one of Ireland's most picture-perfect towns. A bit of England in the Old Sod, it has storybook thatch-roof cottages and Tudor-style churches. Visit the **Adare Heritage Centre** for a look back at the town's picturesque history. A seasonal tourist office is open here May through October. ✉ *Main St.,* ☎ *061/396666.* ⊙ *May–Sept., daily 9–6; Oct.–Apr., daily 10–5.*

$$$ 🏨 **Dunraven Arms.** Although Adare Manor, a Tudor-Gothic castle just across the road, is swankier, you get a warmer welcome at this old coaching inn. It's a handy first stop when arriving at Shannon Airport, about 40 km (25 mi) northwest. Guest rooms, decorated with antiques, are comfortable. ✉ *Adare, Co. Limerick,* ☎ *061/396633,* FAX *061/396541,* WEB *www.dunravenhotel.com. 76 rooms. Restaurant, bar, indoor pool. AE, DC, MC, V.*

Limerick City

Limerick is an industrial port and the third-largest city in the Republic (population 75,000). The area around the cathedral and the castle is the old part of the city, dominated by mid-18th-century buildings with fine Georgian proportions. Economic investment is helping to spiff up its former image as an unattractive city marked by high unemployment and a high crime rate. Frank McCourt's 1996 memoir *Angela's Ashes*—set in Limerick, where McCourt grew up desperately poor—has also helped to pique interest in the city.

In the Old Customs House on the banks of the Shannon in the city center, the **Hunt Museum** has the finest collection of Celtic and medieval treasures outside the National Museum in Dublin. ✉ *Rutland St.,* ☎ *061/312833,* WEB *www.ul.ie/~hunt.* ⏲ *May–Sept., Mon.–Sat. 10–5, Sun. 2–5; Oct.–Apr., Tues.–Sat. 10–5, Sun. 2–5.*

Built by the Normans in the early 1200s, **King John's Castle** still bears traces on its north side of the 1691 bombardment. Climb the drum towers for a good view of the town and the Shannon. Inside, exhibitions illustrate the history of Limerick. ✉ *Castle St.,* ☎ *061/411201,* WEB *www.shannonheritage.com.* ⏲ *Apr.–Sept., daily 9:30–5; Oct.–Mar., weekends 9:30–5.*

★ **Bunratty Castle** is one of three castles in the area that has nightly medieval banquets. The castle, once the stronghold of the princes of Thomond, is the most complete and—despite its Ye Olde World banquets—authentic medieval castle in Ireland, restored in such a way as to give an idea of life during the 15th and 16th centuries. The **Folk Park** on its grounds has farm buildings and crafts shops typical of the 19th century. *18 km (10 mi) west of Limerick City on N18,* ☎ *061/361511,* WEB *www.shannonheritage.com.* ⏲ *Daily 9:30–dusk (last entry 1 hr before closing).*

$$$$ ★ **Castletroy Park.** High standards of comfort are the rule at this well-designed modern hotel on the outskirts of town. ✉ *Dublin Rd., Co. Limerick,* ☎ *061/335566,* FAX *061/331117,* WEB *www.castletroy-park.ie. 107 rooms. 2 restaurants, indoor pool. AE, DC, MC, V.*

$$ **Greenhills.** This suburban, modern low rise is convenient for Shannon Airport and also makes a good touring base. The friendly owner-manager welcomes families. ✉ *Ennis Rd., Co. Limerick,* ☎ *061/453033,* FAX *061/453307. 55 rooms. Restaurant, indoor pool. AE, DC, MC, V.*

Ennis

Ennis, 37 km (23 mi) northwest of Limerick, and the principal town of County Clare, is a pleasant if unremarkable market town that's often bustling. It has always fostered traditional music, especially fiddle playing, and step dancing; at the end of May, it's the gathering place for the **Fleadh Nua** (pronounced "fla-nooa"), a festival of Irish music.

$$ ✕ **West County.** This lively modern hostelry is a popular stopping point on the Limerick–Galway road and is a five-minute walk from Ennis's historic town center. It caters to both vacationers and business travelers. Boru's Porterhouse serves traditional Irish fare including local steak and seafood. ✉ *Clare Rd., Ennis, Co. Clare,* ☎ *065/682–8421,* FAX *065/682–8801,* WEB *www.lynchotels.com. 152 rooms. 2 restaurants, 3 indoor pools. AE, DC, MC, V.*

Corofin

If you're searching for your Irish roots, Corofin's **Clare Heritage Center** has a genealogical service and information about doing research yourself. It also has displays on the history of the West of Ireland in the 19th century. ☎ *065/683–7955.* ⏲ *Apr.–Oct., daily 10–6; Nov.–Mar. (genealogy service only), weekdays 9–5; museum by appointment.*

Lisdoonvarna

Lisdoonvarna is a small spa town with several sulfurous and iron-bearing springs with radioactive properties. Its buildings reflect a mishmash of mock-architectural styles, which, depending on your taste, is either lovably kitschy or unappealingly tacky. The town has developed something of a reputation over the years as a matchmaking center, with bachelor farmers and single women converging here each year in late September for a Bachelors' Festival.

$$ ✕🏨 **Sheedy's Restaurant and Country Inn.** Originally a 17th-century farmhouse, this small, friendly, family-run hotel is only a short walk from both the town center and spa wells. Rooms are spotlessly clean and well cared for. Creative French-Irish cuisine is served at the moderately priced restaurant, and there is an informal Seafood Bar beside the lobby. ✉ *Co. Clare,* ☎ *065/707–4026,* FAX *065/707–4555,* WEB *www.sheedyscountryhouse.com. 11 rooms. Restaurant, bar. AE, DC, MC, V. Closed Oct.–Mar..*

$ 🏨 **Ballinalacken Castle.** It's not a castle but a converted Victorian shooting lodge on 100 acres of wildflower meadows, commanding a breathtaking view of the Atlantic. Rooms are modest but full of character. ✉ *Co. Clare,* ☎ *065/707–4025,* FAX *065/707–4025,* WEB *www.ballinalackencastle.ie. 12 rooms. Restaurant. AE, DC, MC, V. Closed early Oct.–Easter.*

The Burren

In the northwest corner of County Clare, the Burren (from the Irish word for "stony rock") is a strange, rocky limestone district—and a superb nature reserve, with a profusion of wildflowers that are at their best in late May. Huge colonies of birds—puffins, kittiwakes, shags, guillemots, and razorbills—nest along its coast. The **Burren Display Center** explains the extraordinary geology and wildlife of the area in a simple audiovisual display. ✉ *Kilfenora,* ☎ *065/708–8030,* WEB *homepage.eircom.net/~burrencentre.* ⏲ *Mid-Mar.–May and Sept.–Oct., daily 10–5; June–Aug., daily 10–6.*

The Cliffs of Moher

★ One of Ireland's most breathtaking natural sites, the majestic Cliffs of Moher rise vertically out of the sea in a wall that stretches over an 8-km (5-mi) swath and as high as 710 ft. **O'Brien's Tower** is a defiant, broody sentinel built at their highest point. The **visitor center,** at the base of the cliffs, beside the parking lot, has a tearoom and is a good refuge from passing rain squalls. It's open mid-February–April, daily 10–5; May–June and September, daily 10–6; July–August, daily 9:30–6:30. On a clear day the Aran Islands are visible from the cliffs, and in summer there are regular day trips to them from **Doolin,** a tiny village that claims three of the best pubs in Ireland for traditional music.

Ballyvaughan

A pretty waterside village with views of Galway Bay and the Aran Islands, Ballyvaughan makes a good base for exploring the Burren. At nearby **Aillwee Cave,** you can take a guided tour into the underworld of the Burren, where 3,415 ft of cave, formed millions of years ago, can be explored. ☎ *065/707–7036,* WEB *www.aillweecave.ie.* ⏲ *Early Mar.–June and Sept.–early Nov., daily 10–6 (last tour at 5:30); July–Aug., daily 10–7 (last tour at 6:30).*

$$ 🏨 **Hyland's Hotel.** Travelers have been looked after for 250 years at this comfortable, family-run coaching inn. The cheerful, unpreten-

tious restaurant specializes in local seafood and lamb. ✉ *Co. Clare,* ☎ *065/707–7037,* FAX *065/707–7131. 31 rooms. Restaurant. AE, MC, V. Closed Jan.*

Kinvara

The picture-perfect village of Kinvara is worth a visit, thanks to its gorgeous bay-side locale, great walking and sea angling, and numerous pubs. The town is best known for its early August sailing event, **Cruinniú na mBád** (Festival of the Gathering of the Boats). On a rock north of Kinvara Bay, the 16th-century **Dunguaire Castle** stands commanding the approaches from Galway Bay. ✉ *Co. Galway,* ☎ *091/637108,* WEB *www.shannonheritage.com.* ⏲ *May–Sept., daily 9:30–5; banquets at 5:30 and 8:30.*

Clarinbridge

Clarinbridge hosts Galway's annual **Oyster Festival,** which is held in September and features the superlative products of the village's oyster beds.

$ ✕ **Moran's of the Weir.** This waterside traditional thatched cottage is one of Ireland's simplest yet most famous seafood eateries. The specialty here is oysters, but crab, prawns, mussels, and smoked salmon are also served. ✉ *The Weir, Kilcolgan,* ☎ *091/796113. AE, MC, V.*

Cork to Galway Essentials

AIRPORTS

The most convenient international airport is Shannon, 25 km (16 mi) east of Ennis. Galway Airport, at Carnmore, near Galway City, is used mainly for internal flights.

➤ AIRPORT INFORMATION: **Galway Airport** (☎ 091/752874). **Shannon Airport** (☎ 061/471444).

BUS TRAVEL

Bus Éireann operates Expressway services from Dublin to Limerick City and Tralee and from Dublin, Cork City, and Limerick City to Ennis and Galway City. Information is also available at local tourist offices.

➤ BUS INFORMATION: **Bus Éireann** (☎ 01/836–6111, 061/313–333, 021/450–8188, or 066/712–3566).

CAR RENTAL

To rent a car at Shannon Airport call Avis or Budget; both agencies have offices in Killarney, as well.

➤ LOCAL AGENTS: **Avis** (✉ Killarney, ☎ 064/36655; ✉ Shannon Airport, ☎ 061/471094). **Budget** (✉ Killarney, ☎ 064/34341; ✉ Shannon Airport, ☎ 061/471361).

CAR TRAVEL

Though it's possible to explore the region by local and intercity bus services, you will need plenty of time; a car makes getting around much easier.

TOURS

Bus Éireann organizes day tours by bus from the Killarney and Tralee train stations; check with the tourist office or rail station for details. Destination Killarney arranges tours of Killarney and the Gap of Dunloe. Shannon Castle Tours has "Irish Nights" in Bunratty Folk Park or takes you to a medieval banquet at Bunratty Castle.

➤ FEES AND SCHEDULES: **Destination Killarney** (☎ 064/32638). **Shannon Castle Tours** (☎ 061/360788).

TRAIN TRAVEL

Trains run from Cork to Tralee, via Killarney, and from Cork to Limerick City. Trains for Galway City leave from Dublin's Heuston Station.

VISITOR INFORMATION

All visitor information offices are open weekdays 9–6 and Saturday 9–1.

➤ TOURIST INFORMATION: **Ennis** (✉ Arthur's Row, Town Centre, Co. Clare, ☎ 065/682–8366). **Killarney** (✉ Aras Fáilte, Beech Rd., ☎ 064/31633, FAX 064/34506). **Limerick City** (✉ Arthur's Quay, ☎ 061/317522, FAX 061/317939). **Shannon Airport** (☎ 061/471664). **Tralee** (✉ Ashe Memorial Hall, ☎ 066/7121288).

GALWAY TO DONEGAL

The trip from Galway to Donegal takes you through the rugged landscape of Connemara to the fabled Yeats country in the northwest and then skirts the borders of Northern Ireland. Although it passes through some of the wildest, loneliest, and most dramatic parts of Ireland, it takes in Galway City, which today has become a hip mini-Dublin.

Galway City

As almost any Galwegian will tell you, theirs is the fastest-growing city in all of Ireland. Nonetheless, its heart is a warren of compact streets. The city's medieval heritage is everywhere apparent, particularly in and around its main pedestrian-oriented street—the name of which changes from Williamsgate to William to Shop to High to Quay. For many Irish people, Galway is a favorite weekend getaway—it's in a beautiful spot, on the north shore of Galway Bay, where the River Corrib flows from Lough Corrib out into the sea. It's also a university town: University College Galway (or UCG as it's locally known) is a center for Gaelic culture. The town, too, has long attracted writers, artists, and musicians, who keep the traditional music pubs lively year-round—the de facto centers of culture.

On the west bank of the Corrib estuary, just outside of the town walls, is **Claddagh,** said to be the oldest fishing village in Ireland. **Salthill Promenade** is the place "to sit and watch the moon rise over Claddagh, and see the sun go down on Galway Bay"—in the words of the city's most famous song.

$$$ ✕ **Kirwan's Lane Creative Cuisine.** This restaurant serves a fashionable and sophisticated menu in striking minimalist surroundings. Rack of lamb comes with sweet-potato mash, while fresh local cod fillet is accompanied by spring onion risotto. ✉ *Kirwan's La.,* ☎ *091/568266. AE, DC, MC, V. Closed Sun.*

$–$$$$ ✕ **McDonagh's Seafood Bar.** An old Galway institution in the heart of the pedestrianized town center, this is part fish-and-chips bar, part serious seafood restaurant; try the famous Galway oysters here. ✉ 22 *Quay St.,* ☎ *091/565001. DC, MC, V.*

$$ ✕ **Malt House.** This cheerful pub-restaurant tucked away in an alley off High Street in the center of Old Galway has long been popular for good food—steaks, rack of lamb, prawns panfried in garlic butter—served in pleasantly informal surroundings. ✉ *Olde Malte Mall, High St.,* ☎ *091/567866. AE, DC, MC, V. Closed Sun. Oct.–Apr.*

$$$$ 🏨 **Galway Great Southern.** Expect to rub elbows with many native Irish visiting Galway at this grand, old-fashioned hotel presiding over Eyre Square. Rooms have high ceilings and Georgian-style furniture. A pianist often graces the spacious lobby, which, like the two bars, is a popular gathering spot. ✉ *Eyre Sq., Co. Galway,* ☎ *091/564041,*

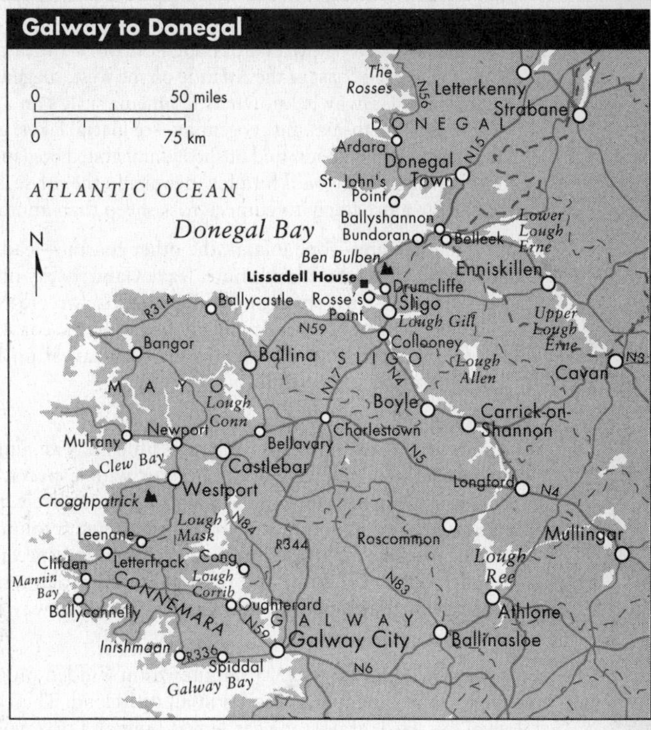

FAX *091/566704,* WEB *www.gsh.ie. 115 rooms. Restaurant, 2 bars, indoor pool. AE, DC, MC, V.*

$$$ **Ardilaun House.** This lovely 19th-century house is in a quiet, tree-lined suburb, midway between the city center and the Salthill promenade. For views of the bay, book an even-numbered room on the top floor; other rooms, which are just as pleasant, overlook the flower garden. ✉ *Taylor's Hill, Co. Galway,* ☎ *091/521433,* FAX *091/521–546,* WEB *www.ardilaunhousehotel.ie. 81 rooms, 7 suites. Restaurant, 2 bars, indoor pool. AE, DC, MC, V.*

$$ **Jurys Galway Inn.** At the foot of Galway's busy main Quay Street, this modern, four-story hotel offers good-quality budget accommodations. Each room is big enough for three adults or two adults and two children. ✉ *Quay St., Co. Galway,* ☎ *091/566444,* FAX *091/568415,* WEB *www.jurys.com. 128 rooms. Restaurant, bar. AE, DC, MC, V.*

The Aran Islands

Jutting from a belligerent ocean, the Aran Islands—Inishmore, Inishmaan, and Inisheer—are remote western outposts of the ancient province of Connaught. The islands have been populated for thousands of years, and the Irish-speaking inhabitants have adhered to the traditions of their ancestors. The best time to visit the islands is May and early June while the unusual, Burren-like flora is at its best and before the bulk of the visitors arrives.

★ **Rossaveal,** a port on the coast road beyond Spiddal, is the handiest port for a trip to the Aran Islands, 48 km (30 mi) off the coast. **Inis Meáin (Inishmaan),** the middle island, is the most unspoiled of the three; it's here that the traditional Aran lifestyle is most evident. Boats depart for Inishmaan from Rossaveal and less frequently from Galway. You can also fly daily from the **Connemara Airport** (☎ 091/593–034). WEB www.aran-islands.com

Connemara

Bordered by the long expanse of Lough Corrib on the east and the deeply indented, jagged coast of the Atlantic on the west, rugged, desolate western County Galway is known as Connemara. It's an area of spectacular, almost myth-making geography—of glacial lakes; gorgeous, silent mountains; lonely roads; and hushed, uninhabited boglands. In the midst of this wilderness, you'll find few people. In the off-season, especially, you're far more likely to come across sheep than another car.

Two main routes—one inland, the other coastal—lead through Connemara. To take the inland route, leave Galway City on the well-signposted outer-ring road and follow signs for N59—Moycullen, Oughterard, and Clifden. If you choose to go the coastal route, you'll travel due west from Galway City to Rossaveal on R336 through Salthill, Barna, and Spiddle.

Clifden

The principal town of Connemara, Clifden has an almost alpine setting, nestling on the edge of the Atlantic with a spectacular mountain backdrop. A good selection of small restaurants, lively bars with music most nights in the summer, some very pleasant accommodations, and excellent walks make the town a popular base, especially in July and August. A short (2-km/1-mi) walk along the beach road through the grounds of the ruined **Clifden Castle** is the best way to explore the seashore.

Kylemore Abbey, about 15 minutes from Clifden on N59, is one of the most photographed castles in all of Ireland. The vast Gothic Revival, turreted, gray-stone castle was built as a private home between 1861 and 1868. Today it's the home of Benedictine nuns. Three reception rooms and the main hall are open to the public, as are a crafts center and simple cafeteria. ✉ *Kylemore,* ☎ *095/41146,* WEB *www.kylemoreabbey.com.* ⏲ *Crafts shop mid-Mar.–Nov., daily 10–6; cafeteria Easter–Nov., daily 9:30–6; grounds Easter–Nov., daily 9 AM–dusk; exhibition and gardens Easter–Nov., daily 9–5:30.*

$$ ✕▣ **Erriseask House.** This rambling, modern house, on the rocky shore of Mannin Bay, is a stylish, comfortable accommodation. Owner-chef Stefan Matz has won many awards for his fine cooking; freshly turf-smoked fillet of beef is a house specialty. ✉ *Ballyconneely, Co. Galway,* ☎ *095/23553,* FAX *095/23639,* WEB *www.erriseask.connemara-ireland.com. 8 rooms, 5 suites. Restaurant. AE, DC, MC, V. Closed Nov.–Apr..*

Letterfrack

The 5,000-acre **Connemara National Park** lies just southeast of the village of Letterfrack (14 km/9 mi north of Clifden on N59). The park's **visitor center** covers the area's history and ecology. You can also get details on the many excellent walks and beaches in the area. ☎ *095/41054,* WEB *www.heritageireland.ie.* ⏲ *Park daily. Visitor center Apr.–May and Sept., daily 10–5:30; June, daily 10–6:30; July–Aug., daily 9:30–6:30.*

$$$ ★ ✕▣ **Renvyle House.** The extraordinary setting—a lake is at the front door and the Atlantic Ocean is at the back—distinguishes this country house. The elegant rooms all have breathtaking views. The cheerful, softly lit restaurant's table d'hôte menu emphasizes fresh local fish and lamb. ✉ *Renvyle, Co. Galway,* ☎ *095/43511,* FAX *095/43515,* WEB *www.renvyle.com. 65 rooms. Restaurant, pool. AE, DC, MC, V. Closed Jan.–Feb.*

Westport

Westport is a quiet, mainly 18th-century town overlooking Clew Bay—a wide expanse of water studded with nearly 400 islands. The distinctive silhouette of **Croagh Patrick,** a 2,540-ft mountain, dominates the town. Today some 25,000 pilgrims climb it on the last Sunday in July in honor of St. Patrick, who is believed to have spent 40 days fasting on its summit in AD 441. Whether he did or not, the climb is an exhilarating experience and can be completed in about three hours; it should be attempted only in good weather, however.

$$ ✕ **Quay Cottage.** On the harbor front, a short distance from the town center, this tiny cottage decorated with a nautical theme is both an informal wine bar and a seafood restaurant. ✉ *The Harbour,* ☎ *098/26412. AE, MC, V. Closed Jan. No lunch.*

$$ 🏨 **Delphi Lodge.** In the heart of spectacular mountains-and-lakes scenery, this sporting lodge is heavily stocked with fishing paraphernalia. The owner, Peter Mantle, is a valuable storehouse of information and stories. Guests dine together. ✉ *6 km (4 mi) off N59, northwest of Leenane, Co. Mayo,* ☎ *095/42211,* FAX *095/42296,* WEB *http://ireland.iol.ie/~delfish. 12 rooms. Restaurant, bar. MC, V. Closed mid-Dec.–mid-Jan..*

$$ 🏨 **Olde Railway Hotel.** This Victorian hotel on the town center's tree-lined mall offers both character and comfort. ✉ *The Mall, Co. Mayo,* ☎ *098/25605,* FAX *098/25090,* WEB *www.anu.ie/railwayhotel. 14 rooms. Restaurant. AE, DC, MC, V. Closed mid-Jan.–mid-Feb..*

Sligo Area

County Sligo is noted for its seaside resorts, the famous golf course at Rosses Point (just outside Sligo Town), and its links with Ireland's most famous 20th-century poet, W. B. Yeats. **Sligo Town** is the best place to begin a tour of Yeats Country. In the throes of an economic boom, Sligo retains all the charm of smaller, sleepier villages, yet by day it's as lively and crowded as Galway City. The **Model and Niland Centre** houses collections of works by the poet's brother, Jack B. Yeats, and a fine collection of early 20th-century Irish art, as well as memorabilia of Yeats the poet. The latter's grave is in Drumcliff, beneath the slopes of Ben Bulben, just north of town. ✉ *The Mall,* ☎ *071/41405.* ⏲ *Daily 10–5 and during performances.*

★ From Sligo Town, you can take a boat or drive up to **Lough Gill** and see the Lake Isle of Innisfree and other places immortalized in Yeats's poetry. Fourteen kilometers (9 mi) northwest of Sligo Town is **Lissadell House,** a substantial mansion dating from 1830 that features prominently in Yeats's writings. It was the home of Constance Gore-Booth, later Countess Markeviecz, who took part in the 1916 uprising. ☎ *071/63150,* WEB *www.ireland-northwest.travel.ie.* ⏲ *June–mid-Sept., Mon.–Sat. 10:30–12:30 and 2–4:30.*

$ ✕ **Bistro Bianconi.** The decor is all white: blond wood and white-tile floors. But the food is a colorful array of gourmet pizzas, baked in the wood-burning oven with toppings both traditional and innovative. ✉ *44 O'Connell St., Sligo Town,* ☎ *071/41744. AE, MC, V. No lunch.*

$$$ ✕🏨 **Markree Castle.** A pastoral, 1,000-acre estate is home to this 17th-century, family-owned hotel in a castle. Public rooms share a comfortable informality; guest rooms are idiosyncratic. The kitchen offers up an excellent table d'hôte menu, and on Sunday a traditional lunch attracts a sizable, family-oriented crowd. ✉ *Off N4, south of Sligo Town, Collooney, Co. Sligo,* ☎ *071/67800; 800/223–6510 in the U.S.,* FAX *071/67840,* WEB *www.markreecastle.ie. 30 rooms. Restaurant. AE, DC, MC, V.*

Donegal Town

Donegal is the gateway to the magnificent Northwest, with its rugged coastline and dramatic highlands. The town is centered on the triangular Diamond, where three roads converge (N56 to the west, and N15 to the south and the northeast) and the mouth of the River Eske pours gently into Donegal Bay. Near the north corner of the Diamond is **Donegal Castle,** built by clan leader Hugh O'Donnell in the 1470s. Ruins of the **Franciscan abbey,** founded in 1474 by Hugh O'Donnell, are a five-minute walk south of town at a spectacular site perched above the Eske.

$ ✕ **Blueberry Tea Room.** This pleasant restaurant and café is just across the street from Donegal Castle. ✉ *Castle St.,* ☎ *073/22933. V. Closed Sun. mid-Sept.–May.*

$$$$ ★ ✕🏨 **St. Ernan's House.** On its own wooded tidal island in Donegal Bay, five minutes south of town, St. Ernan's is one of the most spectacularly situated country houses in all of Ireland. Guest rooms are simple but elegant, with antiques and views of the bay. Dinner in the intimate dining room is prepared in Irish country-house style. ✉ *St. Ernan's Island, Co. Donegal,* ☎ *073/21065,* FAX *073/22098,* WEB *www.sainternans.com. 12 rooms. Dining room. MC, V. Closed Nov.–Easter.*

$$ ✕🏨 **Castle Murray House Hotel.** The original house has been extended and modernized to take full advantage of the exceptional panoramic views of the bay and distant mountains. The restaurant serves superb French cuisine. ✉ *21 km (13 mi) west of Donegal Town, St. John's Point, Dunkineely, Co. Donegal,* ☎ *073/37022,* FAX *073/37330. 10 rooms. Restaurant. MC, V. Closed mid-Jan.–mid-Feb. and Mon.–Tues. Oct.–mid-Jan. and mid-Feb.–Easter.*

Galway to Donegal Essentials

BIKE TRAVEL

Bikes can be rented from Celtic Cycles, Gary's Cycles, or John Mannion.

➤ Bike Rentals: **Celtic Cycles** (✉ Victoria Pl., Galway City, ☎ 091/566–606). **Gary's Cycles** (✉ Quay St., Sligo, ☎ 071/45418). **John Mannion** (✉ Railway View, Clifden, ☎ 095/21160).

BUS TRAVEL

Bus Éireann travels all over the region. McGeehan Coaches services County Donegal locally.

➤ Bus Information: **Bus Éireann** (☎ 01/836–6111). **McGeehan Coaches** (☎ 075/46150).

CAR RENTAL

➤ Local Agents: **Avis** (☎ 091/568886). **Budget** (☎ 091/564570 or 091/566376). **Murray's** (☎ 091/562222).

TAXIS

Taxis do not operate on meters; agree on the fare beforehand.

TOURS

CIE Tours International operates day tours of Connemara out of Galway City and bus tours into the Donegal highlands from Sligo train station; details are available from local tourist offices. Bus Éireann and Gray Line organize tours of the Boyne Valley and County Meath out of Dublin.

➤ Fees and Schedules: **Gray Line** (☎ 01/661–9666).

TRAIN TRAVEL

Trains to Galway, Westport, and Sligo operate from Dublin's Heuston or Connolly (Sligo) station. There is no train service north of Sligo.

VISITOR INFORMATION

All offices are open weekdays 9–6 and Saturday 9–1.

➤ TOURIST INFORMATION: **Galway City** (✉ off Eyre Sq., ☎ 091/563081, FAX 091/565201). **Sligo Town** (✉ Temple St., ☎ 071/61201, FAX 071/60360, WEB www.irealnd-northwest.travel.ie). **Westport** (✉ The Mall, ☎ 098/25711, FAX 098/26709).

NORTHERN IRELAND

Northern Ireland, a province ruled by the United Kingdom, boasts some of the most unspoiled scenery you could hope to find—the granite Mountains of Mourne; the Giant's Causeway, made of extraordinary volcanic rock; more than 320 km (200 mi) of coastline with long, unspoiled beaches and hidden coves; and rivers and island-strewn lakes that provide fabled fishing grounds, among them the largest freshwater lake in Europe, Lough Neagh. Northern Ireland also holds a great legacy in its celebrated descendants. Nearly one in six of the more than 4½ million Irish who made the fateful journey across the Atlantic to seek their fortune in the New World was from Ulster, and of this group (and from their family stock) more than a few left their mark in the United States: Davy Crockett, President Andrew Jackson, President Woodrow Wilson, General Stonewall Jackson, financier Thomas Mellon, merchant Paul Getty, writers Edgar Allan Poe and Mark Twain, and astronaut Neil Armstrong.

Belfast is the capital of Northern Ireland. A great Victorian success story, the city was once an industrial boomtown whose prosperity was built on trade—especially linen and shipbuilding (this is where the *Titanic* was built). You'll find some of the warmest, wryest people in all of Ireland here, a fair amount of construction, and, most of all, a palpable will to move beyond the infamous Troubles that plagued the city, and all of Northern Ireland, for almost three decades. With an ongoing, albeit uncertain, peace agreement in Northern Ireland since 1997, Nationalists and Unionists have been working together for the betterment of the province.

Belfast is fairly compact; its center is made up of roughly three contiguous areas that are easy to navigate on foot, though from the south end to the north it's about an hour's leisurely walk. At Belfast's southern end, the **Queen's University area** is easily the most appealing part of the city. This is where you'll find the university, the Botanic Gardens, fine 19th-century buildings, and many good pubs, restaurants, and B&Bs. Between University Street and Shaftesbury Square is the **Golden Mile,** with hotels, major civic and office buildings, and some restaurants, cafés, and stores. City Hall marks the northern boundary of the Golden Mile and the southern end of the (theoretically) pedestrian-only **central district,** which extends from Donegall Square north almost to St. Anne's Cathedral; this is the old heart of Belfast and has the highest concentration of retail outlets that Belfast has to offer. Behind St. Anne's is the **Cathedral Quarter,** a maze of cobbled streets that the city plans to transform over the next few years.

$$$ ★ ✕ **Deane's.** Celebrated Chef Michael Deane serves up delicious contemporary cuisine at his two-story restaurant—a brasserie downstairs and formal restaurant upstairs—in the center of Belfast. Deane's tastes are eclectic, though he has worked in Bangkok, and Thai influences particularly shine in his subtle way with spices. Squab is a Deane specialty, and the ravioli of lobster is a standout. ✉ *34–40 Howard St.,* ☎ *028/9033–1134 restaurant, 028/9056–0000 brasserie. AE, MC, V. Restaurant closed Sun.–Tue, brasserie closed Sun.–Mon.*

$$–$$$ ★ ✕ **Aldens.** East Belfast was a gastronomic wilderness until this modernist restaurant opened with chef Cath Gradwell at the helm, producing a seafood-rich menu at some of the most reasonable prices in town. The set dinner menus from Monday to Thursday are U.K.£14.95 for three courses. The mood is relaxed, the staff friendly and the wine list one of the best around. Try the pan-fried scallops with sticky rice to start, and roast fillet of brill with red wine sauce for a main course. Reservations are recommended. ✉ *229 Upper Newtownards Road, Belfast,* ☏ *028/9065–0079. AE, DC, MC, V. No lunch weekends, no dinner Sun.*

$$ ✕ **Cayenne.** Celebrity TV chefs Paul and Jeanne Rankin run this Golden Mile spot. Cayenne serves up fusion cuisine with an Asian twist; main dishes range from char-grilled rib eye, served with red onion and mushroom *bruschetta* (a type of Italian garlic bread), to wok-smoked salmon with Bombay potatoes and fresh coriander. Open until 11:15 PM, this is an excellent choice for a late meal after taking in an opera or concert. ✉ *Shaftesbury Sq. at end of Great Victoria St.,* ☏ *028/9033–1532. AE, DC, MC, V. Closed Sun. No lunch Sat.*

$$$$ **The McCausland Hotel.** Clean, simple lines and an aura of sumptuous minimalism are the hallmarks of this pair of 1867 grain warehouses, which have been turned into a luxury hotel. Each comfortable, contemporary guest room is well equipped, with a VCR and mini hi-fi. ✉ *34–38 Victoria St., Belfast, Co. Antrim BT1 3GH,* ☏ *028/9022–0200,* FAX *028/9022–0220,* WEB *www.slh.com. 60 rooms. 2 restaurants, bar. AE, DC, MC, V. Closed late Dec..*

$$ ★ **Ash-Rowan Guest House.** This outstanding B&B in a spacious Victorian home has guest rooms decorated in tasteful, individual styles; each has a private bath and TV. It was the marital home of Thomas Andrews, the designer of the ill-fated *Titanic.* ✉ *12 Windsor Ave., BT9 6EE,* ☏ *028/9066–1758,* FAX *028/9066–3227. 8 rooms with bath. MC, V. Closed Christmas week.*

$$ **Madison's.** A few minutes' walk from the university, this hotel is done in a modish Barcelona-inspired take on Art Nouveau. Rooms, in cool yellows and rich blues, are sparely furnished but comfortable. ✉ *59 Botanic Ave., BT7 1JL,* ☏ *028/9050–9800,* FAX *028/9050–9808,* WEB *www.mooneyhotelgroup.com. 35 rooms with bath. Restaurant, bar. AE, MC, V.*

Northern Ireland Essentials

AIRPORTS

Belfast International Airport at Aldergove is the North's principal air arrival point, 30½ km (19 mi) from Belfast. Belfast City Airport is the second airport, 6½ km (4 mi) from the city; it receives flights only from the United Kingdom.

➤ AIRPORT INFORMATION: **Belfast City Airport** (☏ 028/9045–7745). **Belfast International Airport at Aldergove** (☏ 028/9448–4848).

BUS TRAVEL

Ulsterbus runs a direct service between Dublin and Belfast. Questions regarding Ulsterbus, or any other bus service in Northern Ireland, can be dealt with by the central call center of Translink. The Republic's Bus Éireann also runs direct services between Dublin and Belfast.

➤ BUS INFORMATION: **Bus Éireann** (☏ 01/836–6111 in Dublin). **Translink** (☏ 028/9033–3000).

CAR RENTALS

All the major car-rental agencies have branches at Belfast International Airport; some also have branches at Belfast City Airport. If you're planning to take a rental car across the border into the Republic, inform the company and check its insurance procedures.

CAR TRAVEL

Many roads from the Republic into Northern Ireland were once closed for security reasons, but all are now open, leaving you with a score of legitimate crossing points to choose from. Army checkpoints at all approved frontier posts are rare, and few customs formalities are observed. The fast N1/A1 road connects Belfast to Dublin (160 km/100 mi) with an average driving time of just over two hours.

CONSULATES

➤ CANADA: (✉ 378 Stranmillis Rd., Belfast BT9 5EU, ☎ 028/9066–0212).

➤ NEW ZEALAND: (✉ New Balance House, 118A Lisburn Rd., Glenavy, Co. Antrim BT29 4NY, ☎ 028/9264–8098).

➤ UNITED STATES: (✉ Queen's House, 14 Queen St., Belfast BT1 6EQ, ☎ 028/9032–8239).

DINING

Prices are per person for a dinner main course. Sales tax is included in the price. Many places add a 10%–15% service charge—if not, a 10% tip is fine.

CATEGORY	COST
$$$$	over U.K.£18
$$$	U.K.£13–U.K.£18
$$	U.K.£7–U.K.£12
$	under U.K.£7

EMERGENCIES

➤ EMERGENCY SERVICES: **Ambulance, police, fire, and coast guard** (☎ 999 toll-free in all of Northern Ireland). **Belfast's main police station** (✉ 6–10 N. Queen St., ☎ 028/9065–0222).

LODGING

Prices are for two people in a double room, based on high season (June–mid-September) rates, including value-added tax (VAT) and service charges.

CATEGORY	COST
$$$$	over U.K.£120
$$$	U.K.£90–U.K.£120
$$	U.K.£60–U.K.£90
$	under U.K.£60

TOURS

Citybus runs two Belfast city tours. Ulsterbus operates half-day or full-day trips (June–September) from Belfast to surrounding areas. Historical Pub Tours of Belfast offers walking tours of the city's pubs on Thursdays at 7 PM and Saturdays at 5 PM.

➤ FEES AND SCHEDULES: **Citybus** (☎ 028/9024–6485). **Historical Pub Tours of Belfast** (☎ 028/9068–1278). **Ulsterbus** (☎ 028/9033–3000).

TRAIN TRAVEL

The Dublin–Belfast Express train, run jointly by Northern Ireland Railways and Iarnród Éireann (Irish Rail), travels between the two cities in about two hours. Six trains (check timetables, as some trains are much slower) run daily in both directions (three on Sunday) between Dublin and Belfast's misnamed Central Station. A free shuttle bus service from Belfast Central Station will drop you off at City Hall or Ulsterbus's city-center Europa Buscentre. You can change trains at Central Station for the city-center Great Victoria Street Station, which is adjacent both to the Europa Buscentre and the Europa Hotel.

➤ TRAIN INFORMATION: **Central Station** (✉ E. Bridge St., ☎ 028/9089–9411). **Europa Buscentre** (☎ 028/9033–3000). **Great Victoria Street Station** (✉ Great Victoria St., ☎ 028/9043–4424). **Northern Ireland Railways** (☎ 028/9089–9411). **Iarnród Éireann** (☎ 01/855–4477).

VISITOR INFORMATION

Northern Ireland Tourist Board Information Centre can provide contact information for local branches throughout Northern Ireland.

➤ TOURIST INFORMATION: **Northern Ireland Tourist Board Information Centre** (✉ 35 Donegall Place, BT1 5AU, ☎ 028/9023–1221 or 028/9024–6609, FAX 028/9023–9936 or 028/9031–2424, WEB www.discovernorthernireland.com).

18 ITALY

ROME, FLORENCE, TUSCANY, MILAN, VENICE, CAMPANIA

WHERE ELSE IN EUROPE can you find the blend of great art, delicious food and wine, and sheer verve that awaits you in Italy? This Mediterranean country has made a profound contribution to Western civilization, producing some of the world's greatest thinkers, writers, politicians, saints, and artists. Impressive traces of their lives and works can still be seen in Italy's great buildings and lovely countryside.

The whole of Italy is one vast attraction, but the triangle of its most-visited cities—Rome (Roma), Florence (Firenze), and Venice (Venezia)—represents the great variety found here. In Rome and Florence, especially, you can feel the uninterrupted flow of the ages, from the classical era of the ancient Romans to the bustle and throb of contemporary life being lived in centuries-old settings. Venice, by contrast, seems suspended in time, the same today as it was when it held sway over the eastern Mediterranean and the East. Each of these cities reveals a different aspect of the Italian character: the Baroque exuberance of Rome, Florence's serene stylishness, and the dreamy sensuality of Venice.

Trying to soak in Italy's rich artistic heritage poses a challenge. The country's many museums and churches draw hordes of visitors, all wanting to see the same thing at the same time. From May through September, the Sistine Chapel, Michelangelo's *David,* Piazza San Marco, and other key sights are more often than not swamped by mobs of tourists. Try to see the highlights at off-peak times. If they are open during lunch, this is often a good time. Seeing some attractions—such as the scrubbed facades of Rome's glorious Baroque churches—entails no opening hours and no lines at all.

Making the most of your time in Italy doesn't mean rushing through it. To gain a rich appreciation for Italy, don't try to see everything all at once. Practice the Italian-perfected *il dolce far niente*—the sweet art of idleness—which might mean skipping a museum to sit at a table in a pretty café, enjoying the sunshine and a cappuccino. Art—and life—is to be enjoyed, and the Italians can show you how.

ITALY A TO Z

To research prices, get advice from other travelers, and book travel arrangements, visit www.fodors.com.

AIR TRAVEL

Alitalia and some privately owned companies, such as Meridiana and Air One, in addition to other European airlines, provide service through-

Italy (Italia)
AUSTRIA
HUNGARY
SWITZERLAND
SLOVENIA
CROATIA
BOSNIA AND HERZEGOVINA
MONTENEGRO (YUGOSLAVIA)
FRANCE
MONACO
Adriatic Sea
Ligurian Sea
Golfo di Venezia
Corsica
Elba
ALPI
TRENTINO-ALTO ADIGE
FRIULI-VENEZIA GIULIA
VENETO
LOMBARDY
VALLE D'AOSTA
PIEDMONT
LIGURIA
EMILIA-ROMAGNA
TUSCANY
UMBRIA
THE MARCHES
THE DOLOMITES
Cortina d'Ampezzo
Bolzano
Trento
Belluno
Udine
Trieste
Treviso
Venice
Padua
Vicenza
Verona
Brescia
Bergamo
Lago di Garda
Lago di Como
Lago Maggiore
Como
Lugano
Milan
Pavia
Novara
Aosta
Mt. Blanc
Turin
Asti
Po
Adige
Genoa
San Remo
Rapallo
La Spezia
Parma
Mantua
Modena
Ferrara
Bologna
Ravenna
Rimini
SAN MARINO
Ancona
Macerata
Pescara
Florence
Pistoia
Lucca
Pisa
Livorno
Arno
Siena
Arezzo
Perugia
Assisi
Terni
Orvieto
Viterbo
Tiber
Grosseto
Civitavecchia
N

Rome
Tivoli
Termoli
MOLISE
Gargano Peninsula
Isernia
Cassino
Foggia
Anzio
Gaeta
CAMPANIA
APULIA
Bari
Naples
Vesuvius
Potenza
Brindisi
Lecce
Salerno
Capri
Paestum
BASILICATA
Taranto
Golfo di Taranto
SARDINIA
Olbia
Sassari
Cagliari
Tyrrhenian Sea
Cosenza
Crotone
Catanzaro
CALABRIA
Aeolian Islands
Messina
Reggio
Ionian Sea
Palermo
SICILY
Etna
Catania
Agrigento
Siracusa
Mediterranean Sea
ALGERIA
TUNISIA
Tunis
0
100 miles
0
150 km

out Italy. Most of them offer several types of discount fares; inquire at travel agencies or at Alitalia agencies in major cities.

BOAT & FERRY TRAVEL

Ferries connect the mainland with all the major islands. Car ferries operate to Sicily, Sardinia, Elba, Ponza, Capri (though taking a car here is not advised), and Ischia, among others. Lake ferries connect the towns on the shores of the Italian lakes: Como, Maggiore, Garda, and Iseo.

BUS TRAVEL

Regional bus companies provide service throughout Italy. Route information and timetables are usually available at tourist information offices and travel agencies, or at bus company ticket offices. One of the interregional companies providing long-distance service is SITA.

➤ BUS INFORMATION: **SITA** (☎ 800/373760 toll-free).

BUSINESS HOURS

Banks are open weekdays 8:30–1:30 and 2:45–3:45. Churches are usually open from early morning to noon or 12:30, when they close for about two hours or more, opening again in the afternoon until about 7 PM. National museums (*musei statali*) are usually open from 9 AM until 2 and are often closed on Monday, but there are many exceptions, especially at major museums. Non-national museums have entirely different hours, which may vary according to season. Most major archaeological sites are open every day from early morning to dusk, except some holidays. At all museums and sites, ticket offices close an hour or so before official closing time. Always check with the local tourist office for current hours and holiday closings. Shops are open, with individual variations, from 9 to 1 and from 3:30 or 4 to 7:30 or 8. They are open Monday–Saturday but close for a half day during the week; for example, in Rome most shops are closed on Monday morning, although food shops close on Thursday afternoon in fall–spring. All shops, including food shops, close Saturday afternoon in July and August, though a 1995 ordinance allows greater freedom. Some tourist-oriented shops and department stores—in downtown Rome, Florence, and Venice—are open all day, every day.

CAR TRAVEL

The extensive autostrada network (toll superhighways) connecting all major towns is complemented by equally well maintained but toll-free *superstrade* (express highways), *strade statali* (main roads), and *strade provinciali* (secondary roads). The Autostrada del Sole (A1) crosses the country from north to south, connecting Milan to Naples. From Salerno, the A3 brings you farther south to Reggio Calabria. The A4 from west to east connects Turin to Trieste.

All highways are clearly signposted and numbered. The ticket issued on entering an autostrada must be returned on leaving, along with the toll. On some shorter autostrade, mainly connections, the toll is payable on entering. Have small bills and change handy for tolls; shortchanging is a risk, so always count your change before leaving the toll booth. If you will be using autostrade extensively, buy a Viacard—an automated toll card—for 50,000 lire/€26, 100,000 lire/€52, or 150,000 lire/€77.50 at autostrada locations and some banks. Some automated booths also take an array of credit cards.

Parking is greatly restricted in the center of most cities. Parking in a Zona Disco is for limited periods. City garages cost up to 30,000 lire/€15.50 per day. Check with your hotel to determine the best place to park.

EMERGENCIES

Dial 116 for towing and repairs. Dial 113 for an ambulance and highway police.

GASOLINE

Gas costs about 2,050 lire/€1.05 per liter. Except on the autostrade, most gas stations are closed Sunday; they also close from 12:30 PM to 3:30 PM and at 7 PM for the night. Most gas stations do not accept credit cards. Self-service pumps, which usually accept only 10,000 lire notes, can be found in most cities and towns.

RULES OF THE ROAD

Driving is on the right. The speed limit on an autostrada is 130 kph (81 mph). It is 110 kph (70 mph) on state and provincial roads, unless otherwise marked. Other regulations are largely as in the United States except that the police have the power to levy severe on-the-spot fines. Italians drive fast and impatiently; don't be surprised when, on a winding two-lane highway, drivers zip into the ongoing-traffic lane to pass you if you are going too slowly. Call the Automobil Club Italiano (ACI, daily 8AM-8PM) for information in English about rules of the road, road conditions, car insurance, and travel tips.

➤ CONTACTS: **Automobil Club Italiano** (☏ 06/49982389).

CUSTOMS AND DUTIES

For details on imports and duty-free limits in Italy, *see* Customs and Duties *in* Chapter 1.

DINING

Generally speaking, a *ristorante* pays more attention to decor and service than does a *trattoria,* which is simpler and often family run. An *osteria* used to be a simple tavern, though now the term may be used to designate a chic and expensive eatery. A *tavola calda* offers hot dishes and snacks, with seating. A *rosticceria* offers the same to take out.

The menu is always posted in the window or just inside the door of an eating establishment. Note whether there are charges for *coperto* (cover) and *servizio* (service), which will increase your check amount. The coperto charge has been abolished in many eating places. Many restaurants offer a *menù turistico,* usually a complete meal, limited to a few entrées, at a reasonable price (including taxes and service, usually with beverages extra). Tap water is safe in large cities and almost everywhere else unless noted *non potabile.* Bottled mineral water is available everywhere, *gassata* (with bubbles) or *non gassata* (without bubbles). If you prefer tap water, ask for *acqua semplice.* Note that many restaurants close from Christmas through the first week in January and for a good part of August.

Prices are per person for a dinner main course, excluding tax or tip.

CATEGORY	ROME, FLORENCE, VENICE, MILAN	OTHER AREAS
$$$$	over 45,000 lire (€23)	over 35,000 lire (€18)
$$$	35,000 lire–45,000 lire (€18–€23)	25,000 lire–35,000 lire (€13–€18)
$$	25,000 lire–35,000 lire (€13–€18)	15,000 lire–25,000 lire (€8–€13)
$	under 25,000 lire (€13)	under 15,000 lire (€8)

MEALTIMES

Lunch is served in Rome from 1 to 3, dinner from 8 to 10:30 and sometimes later. Service begins and ends a half hour earlier in Florence and Venice and later in the south.

RESERVATIONS AND DRESS

Except for restaurants in the $$$$ and occasionally in the $$$ categories, where jacket and tie are advisable, neat, casual attire is acceptable.

HOLIDAYS

January 1; January 6 (Epiphany); Easter Sunday and Monday; April 25 (Liberation Day); May 1 (May Day); August 15 (Assumption, known as Ferragosto); November 1 (All Saints' Day); December 8 (Immaculate Conception); December 25–26.

The feast days of patron saints are observed locally. Many businesses and shops may be closed in Florence, Genoa, and Turin on June 24 (St. John the Baptist); in Rome on June 29 (Sts. Peter and Paul); in Palermo on July 15 (Santa Rosalia); in Naples on September 19 (San Gennaro); in Bologna on October 4 (San Petronio); in Trieste on November 3 (San Giusto); and in Milan on December 7 (St. Ambrose). Venice's feast of St. Mark is April 25, the same as Liberation Day, and the city also celebrates November 21 (Madonna della Salute).

LANGUAGE

Italy is accustomed to English-speaking tourists, and in major cities you will find that many people speak at least a little English. In smaller hotels and restaurants and on public transportation, knowing a few phrases of Italian comes in handy.

LODGING

Italy, especially Rome, Florence, and Venice, offers a good choice of accommodations, though rooms tend to be small. Room rates are on a par with those of most European capitals, although porters, room service, and in-house laundering are disappearing in all but the most elegant hotels. Taxes and service are included in the room rate. Although breakfast is usually quoted in the room rate, it's actually an extra charge that you can decline. Make your preference clear when booking or checking in. Air-conditioning also may be an extra charge. Specify if you care about having either a bathtub or shower, as not all rooms have both. In $$ and $ places showers may be the drain-in-the-floor type guaranteed to flood the bathroom. In older hotels room quality may be uneven; if you don't like the room you're given, ask for another. This applies to noise, too; some front rooms are bigger and have views but get street noise. Train stations in major cities have hotel-reservation service booths.

The following price categories are determined by the cost of two people in a double room.

CATEGORY	ROME, FLORENCE, VENICE, MILAN	OTHER AREAS
$$$$	over 500,000 lire (€258)	over 300,000 lire (€155)
$$$	350,000 lire–500,000 lire (€180–€258)	200,000 lire–300,000 lire (€103–€155)
$$	200,000 lire–350,000 lire (€103–€180)	100,000 lire–200,000 lire (€52–€103)
$	under 200,000 lire (€103)	under 100,000 lire (€52)

RENTALS AND AGRITOURISM

Short or long rental stays in town apartments or in rural villas or farms are a good option for families traveling with children and others who value independence and want a taste of living Italian-style. Agritourism, or the practice of staying on a working farm, usually for a week or more, is growing in popularity in rural areas throughout Italy, especially in Tuscany and Umbria. Agritourism accommodations range in style from rustic simplicity to country chic, and prices vary accordingly. Contact local APT tourist offices or visit the multilingual Web site, www.agriturist.it. You can also buy *Agriturism,* available in major bookstores; it's in Italian but has pictures and international symbols describing facilities.

CAMPING

Italy has a wide selection of campgrounds, and the Italians themselves have taken to camping, which means that beach or mountain sites will be crammed in July and August. A *carnet* (permit) is required in most campgrounds; get one from your local association before leaving home. You can buy a campsite directory such as the detailed multilingual guide published by the Touring Club Italiano or the more evocative *Guida ai Campeggi in Italia* (published by Demetra in Italian only but with international symbols), with color pictures of the most popular resorts. Alternatively, you can obtain *Campeggiare in Italia,* the free directory of campsites published by the Federazione Italiana del Campeggio by mail from the organization.

➤ CONTACTS: **Federazione Italiana del Campeggio** (✉ Casella Postale 23, 50041 Calenzano, Florence, ☎ 055/882391, FAX 055/8825918).

HOTELS

Italian hotels are classified by regional tourist boards from five-star (deluxe) to one-star (modest hotels and small inns). The established price of the room appears on a rate card on the back of the door of your room or inside the closet door, though you may be able to get a lower rate by asking. Any variations above the posted rate should be cause for complaint and should be reported to the manager and the police. Standards in one-star hotels are very uneven. At best, rooms are usually spotlessly clean but basic, with showers and toilets down the hall.

Low-season rates do not officially apply in Rome, Florence, and Milan, but you can usually bargain for discounted rates in Rome and Milan in summer and during weekends (when business travelers are few) and in Florence in winter. Ask for *"la tariffa scontata."* You can save on hotel accommodations in Venice and in such resorts as Sorrento and Capri during their low seasons—the winter (with the exception of Christmas holidays and Carnival in Venice), early spring, and late-autumn months.

MAIL & SHIPPING

The Italian mail system is notoriously erratic and can be excruciatingly slow. Allow up to 15 days for mail to and from the United States and Canada and about a week to and from the United Kingdom and within Italy. Posta Prioritaria (stationery and small packages up to 2 kg) and the more expensive Postacelere (up to 20 kg) are special-delivery services from the post office that guarantee delivery within 24 hours in Italy and three to five days abroad.

Correspondence can be addressed to you in care of the Italian post office. Letters should be addressed to your name, "c/o Ufficio Postale Centrale," followed by "Fermo Posta" on the next line, and the name of the city (preceded by its postal code) on the next. You can collect it at the central post office by showing your passport or photo-bearing ID and paying a small fee. American Express also has a general-delivery service. There's no charge for cardholders, holders of American Express Traveler's checks, or anyone who booked a vacation with American Express.

POSTAL RATES

Airmail letters and postcards to the United States and Canada cost 1,300 lire/€.65 for the first 20 grams; for heavier stationery you should go to the post office. Always stick a blue airmail tag (available at post offices) on your mail, or write "airmail" in big, clear characters to the side of the address. Postcards and letters (for the first 20 grams) to any EU country, including Italy, cost 800 lire/€.40. You can purchase stamps at post offices and tobacconists. Lightweight stationery sent as Posta Prioritaria to the United States and Canada costs 1,500 lire/€.75 (for the first 20 grams, double that for parcels up to 100 grams); to EU countries, including Italy, it costs 1,200 lire/€.60. As regular stamps are not valid for this service, make sure you buy the special golden Posta Prioritaria stamps. Postacelere rates to the United States and Canada range between 46,000 lire/€23.75 (30,000 lire/€15.50 to the United Kingdom and Europe) for parcels up to 500 grams (a little over a pound) and 358,000 lire/€184.90 (148,000 lire/€76.45 to the United Kingdom and Europe) for packages weighing 20 kilos. Contact Informazioni Poste Italiane for information in Italian about rates and local post offices' opening hours.

➤ CONTACTS: **Informazioni Poste Italiane** (☎ 160 [600 lire/€.30 per call]; 800/009966 [toll-free for information about Postacelere]).

MONEY MATTERS

Venice, Milan, Florence, and Rome are the more expensive Italian cities to visit. Taxes are usually included in hotel bills; there is a 20% tax on car rentals, usually included in the rates. A cup of espresso enjoyed while standing at a bar costs from 1,000 lire/€0.50 to 1,500 lire/€0.75, the same cup served at a table, triple that. At a bar, beer costs from 4,000 lire/€2.05 to 6,000 lire/€3.10, a soft drink about 3,000 lire/€1.55. A *tramezzino* (small sandwich) costs about 2,500 lire/€1.30, a more substantial one about 3,500 lire/€1.80–5,000 lire/€2.60. You will pay about 15,000 lire/€7.75 for a short taxi ride. Admission to a major museum is about 12,000 lire/€6.20.

CREDIT CARDS

Credit cards are generally accepted in shops and hotels but may not always be welcome in restaurants. When you wish to leave a tip beyond the 15% service charge that is usually included with your bill, leave it in cash rather than adding it to the credit card slip.

CURRENCY

The unit of currency in Italy is the lira (plural, lire). There are bills of 1,000, 2,000, 5,000, 10,000, 50,000, 100,000, and 500,000 lire (impossible to change, except in banks); coins are worth 50, 100, 200, 500, and 1,000 lire. In 1999 the new single currency of the European Union, the euro was introduced as a banking currency. Euros coins and notes will be issued in January 2002, and in a few months lire will be withdrawn from circulation. At press time (summer 2001) the exchange rate was 2,171 lire/€1.12 to the U.S. dollar, 1,376 lire/€.71 to the Canadian dollar, 3,108 lire/€1.60 to the pound sterling, 2,458 lire/€1.27 to the Irish punt, 1,054 lire/€.54 to the Australian dollar, 876 lire/€.45 to the New Zealand dollar, and 267 lire/€.14 to the South African rand.

When your purchases run into hundreds of thousands of lire, beware of being shortchanged, a dodge that is practiced at ticket windows, toll booths, and cashiers' desks, as well as in shops and even in banks. *Always count your change before you leave the counter.* Always carry some smaller-denomination bills for sundry purchases.

SALES TAX

Foreign tourists who have spent more than 300,000 lire/€155 (before tax) in one store can obtain a refund of Italy's value-added tax (IVA). At the time of purchase, with passport or ID in hand, ask the store for an invoice describing the article or articles and the total lire amount. If your destination when you leave Italy is a non-EU country, you must have the invoice stamped at customs upon departure from Italy; if your destination is another EU country, you must obtain the customs stamp upon departure from that country. Once back home—and within 90 days of the date of purchase—you must send the stamped invoice back to the store, which should forward the IVA rebate directly to you. If the store participates in the Europe Tax-Free Shopping System (those that do display a sign to the effect), things are simpler. Note that, to calculate the price without IVA, you don't subtract 20% from the price on the label, which already includes IVA. Instead, you need to subtract roughly 16.5%. Transaction fees which go to the companies providing the tax-free service are 3%–4%, so in this case you should expect to get only about 13% of the purchase price back.

TELEPHONES

COUNTRY AND AREA CODES

The country code for Italy is 39. Do not drop the 0 in the regional code when calling Italy.

INTERNATIONAL CALLS

To place an international call, insert a phone card, dial 00, then the country code, area code, and phone number. The cheaper and easier option, however, is to use your AT&T, MCI, or Sprint calling card. To make collect calls, dial the AT&T USADirect number below. For information and operators in Europe and the Mediterranean area, dial 15; for intercontinental service, dial 170.

➤ ACCESS CODES: **AT&T USADirect** (☎ 172–1011). **MCI Call USA** (☎ 172–1022). **Sprint Express** (☎ 172–1877).

LOCAL CALLS

For all local calls, you must dial the regional area codes, even in cities. Most local calls cost 200 lire/€.10 for two minutes. Pay phones take either 100-, 200-, or 500-lire coins or *schede telefoniche* (phone cards), purchased in bars, tobacconists, and post offices in either 5,000-10,000-, or 15,000-lire denominations. The phone card called Time Europa (50,000 lire/€25.80) is a good-value card for calling Europe and the United States, at only 540 lire/€.30 per minute. For directory information in Italy, dial 12.

SAFETY

Always be on guard against pickpockets and purse snatchers in the main tourist cities, particularly in crowded buses and trains in Rome, Milan, and Naples, and on board the vaporetti in Venice; in Naples, it's advisable to carry your bags on the side facing away from the street, as purse snatchers here more often than not ride scooters. Especially in Rome and Florence, watch out for bands of gypsy children, expert at lifting wallets. Keep the children at a distance, and don't be shy about shouting at them to stay away. Small cities and towns are usually safe.

TIPPING

Tipping practices vary depending on where you are. Italians tip smaller amounts in small cities and towns, often not at all in cafés and taxis north of Rome. The following guidelines apply in major cities.

In restaurants a 15% service charge is usually added to the total; it's customary to give the waiter an additional 5%–10%, depending on the service and on the quality of the meal. Charges for service are included in all hotel bills, but smaller tips to staff members are appreciated. In general, in a $$ hotel, chambermaids should be given about 1,500 lire/€.75 per day, or about 8,000 lire–10,000 lire (€4.15–€5.15) a week; bellhops should get 1,000 lire–2,000 lire (€.50–€1). Tip a minimum of 1,000 lire/€.50 for room service and valet service. Tip breakfast waiters 500 lire/€.25 per day per table (at end of stay). These amounts should be increased by 40% in $$$ hotels, doubled in $$$$ hotels. Give the concierge about 15% of the bill for services. Tip doormen about 500 lire/€.25 for calling a cab.

Taxi drivers are happy with 5%–10%, although Italians rarely tip them. Porters at railroad stations and airports charge a fixed rate per suitcase; tip an additional 500 lire/€.25 per person, more if the porter is very helpful. Tip service-station attendants 1,000 lire/€.50 if they are especially helpful. Tip guides about 2,000 lire/€1 per person for a half-day tour, more if they are very good.

TRAIN TRAVEL

The fastest trains on the FS (Ferrovie dello Stato), the state-owned railroad, are the Eurostar trains, for which you pay a supplement and for which seat reservations are required in both first and second class and are included in the cost of the ticket. Also fast are Intercity (IC) and Eurocity (EC) trains, for which you pay a supplement in both classes and for which reservations may be required. Trains designated *interregionale* are slower, making more stops. *Regionale* trains are locals, serving a single region. Throughout Italy, call FS for train information in Italian. If you plan on a lot of train traveling, the complete FS train schedule, sold at news stalls, is a good investment; the multilingual Web site has the complete FS train schedule.

You can buy tickets and make seat reservations at travel agencies displaying the FS symbol up to two months in advance, thereby avoiding long lines at station ticket windows. All tickets must be date-stamped in the small yellow or red machines near the tracks before you board. Once stamped, tickets are valid for six hours on distances of less than 200 km (124 mi) or for 24 hours on distances of 200 km or more. If you wish to stop along the way and your final destination is more than 200 km away, you can stamp the ticket a second time before it expires to extend its validity to a maximum of 48 hours from the time it was first stamped. You can get on and off at will for the duration of the ticket's validity. If you don't stamp your ticket in the machine, you must actively seek out a conductor to validate the ticket on the train, paying an extra 10,000 lire/€5.15 for the service. If you merely wait in your seat for him to collect your ticket, unless the train is overcrowded, you risk a heavier fine. You will pay a hefty surcharge if you purchase your ticket on board the train. Tickets for destinations within a 200-km (124-mi) range can be purchased at any *tabacchi* (tobacconist) inside the station. There is a refreshment service on most long-distance trains. Trains are very crowded at holiday times; always reserve. Traveling by night is inexpensive, but never leave your belongings unattended and make sure the door of your compartment is locked.

➤ TRAIN INFORMATION: FS (☎ 8488/880880, WEB www.fs-on-line.com).

VISITOR INFORMATION

Information is available at regional and local agencies, either the Azienda di Promozione Turistica (APT) or the Ente Provinciale per il Turismo (EPT), as well as municipal tourist offices and others known as Informazione e Accoglienza Turistica (IAT) or Pro Loco in small towns.

WHEN TO GO

The best months for sightseeing are April–June, September, and October, which are usually pleasant and not too hot.

CLIMATE

In general the northern half of the peninsula and the entire Adriatic Coast, with the exception of Apulia, are rainier than the rest of Italy. In Venice, fog and high tides are likely to be part of the landscape between November and February. The hottest months are July and August, when brief afternoon thunderstorms are common in inland areas. Winters are relatively mild in most places on the tourist circuit, but there are always some rainy spells. The following are average daily maximum and minimum temperatures for Rome and Milan.

ROME

Jan.	52F	11C	**May**	74F	23C	**Sept.**	79F	26C
	40	5		56	13		62	17
Feb.	55F	13C	**June**	82F	28C	**Oct.**	71F	22C
	42	6		63	17		55	13
Mar.	59F	15C	**July**	87F	30C	**Nov.**	61F	16C
	45	7		67	20		49	9
Apr.	66F	19C	**Aug.**	86F	30C	**Dec.**	55F	13C
	50	10		67	20		44	6

MILAN

Jan.	40F	5C	**May**	74F	23C	**Sept.**	75F	24C
	32	0		57	14		61	16
Feb.	46F	8C	**June**	80F	27C	**Oct.**	63F	17C
	35	2		63	17		52	11
Mar.	56F	13C	**July**	84F	29C	**Nov.**	51F	10C
	43	6		67	20		43	6
Apr.	65F	18C	**Aug.**	82F	28C	**Dec.**	43F	6C
	49	9		66	16		35	2

ROME

For 2,500 years, emperors, popes, and the citizens of the ages have left their mark on Rome, and the result is like nothing so much as a hustling, bustling open-air museum. Most of the city's major sights are in the *centro storico* (historic center), which lies between the long, straight Via del Corso and the Tiber River, and the adjacent area of *Roma antica* (ancient Rome), site of the Roman Forum and Colosseum. The best way to discover the city is to wander, taking time to notice the layers of history that make Rome unique. On your way between monuments and museums you'll walk into the past: medieval Rome, which covered the horn of land that pushes the Tiber toward the Vatican and extended across the river into Trastevere, and Renaissance Rome, which was erected upon medieval foundations and extended as far as the Vatican, with beautiful villas created in what were then the outskirts of the city.

Exploring Rome

Numbers in the margin correspond to points of interest on the Rome map.

The layout of the centro storico is irregular, but several landmarks serve as orientation points to identify the areas that most visitors come to see: the Colosseum, Pantheon, Piazza Navona, St. Peter's Basilica, the Spanish Steps, and the Baths of Caracalla. You'll need a good map to find

Arco di Costantino . . . 8
Campidoglio 2
Campo dei Fiori 34
Castel Sant'Angelo 21
Chiesa del Gesù 27
Colosseo 6
Domus Aurea 7
Fontana delle Tartarughe 26
Fontana di Trevi 16
Foro Romano 5
Galleria Borghese . . . 20
Galleria Doria Pamphili 28
Giardini Vaticani . . . 24
Isola Tiberina 36
Keats-Shelley Memorial House 15
Musei Capitolini 3
Musei Vaticani 25
Museo Etrusco di Villa Giulia 12
Palazzo Altemps 31
Palazzo Barberini . . . 18
Palazzo Farnese 35
Pantheon 30
Piazza Barberini 17
Piazza del Popolo . . . 10
Piazza di Spagna . . . 13
Piazza Navona 33
Piazza San Pietro . . . 22
Piazza Venezia 1
San Luigi dei Francesi 32
Santa Maria d'Aracoeli 4
Santa Maria della Concezione 19
Santa Maria del Popolo 11
Santa Maria sopra Minerva 29
Scalinata di Trinitá dei Monti 14
St. Peter's Basilica . . . 23
Terme di Caracalla . . . 9

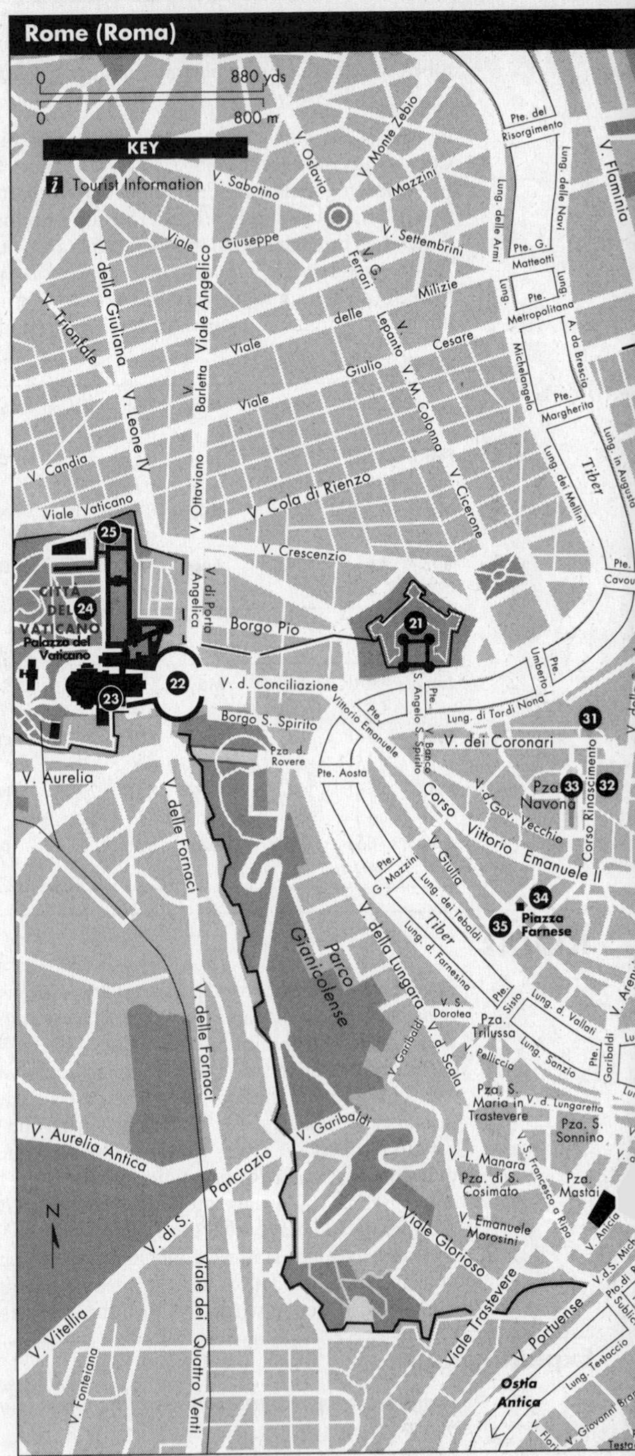

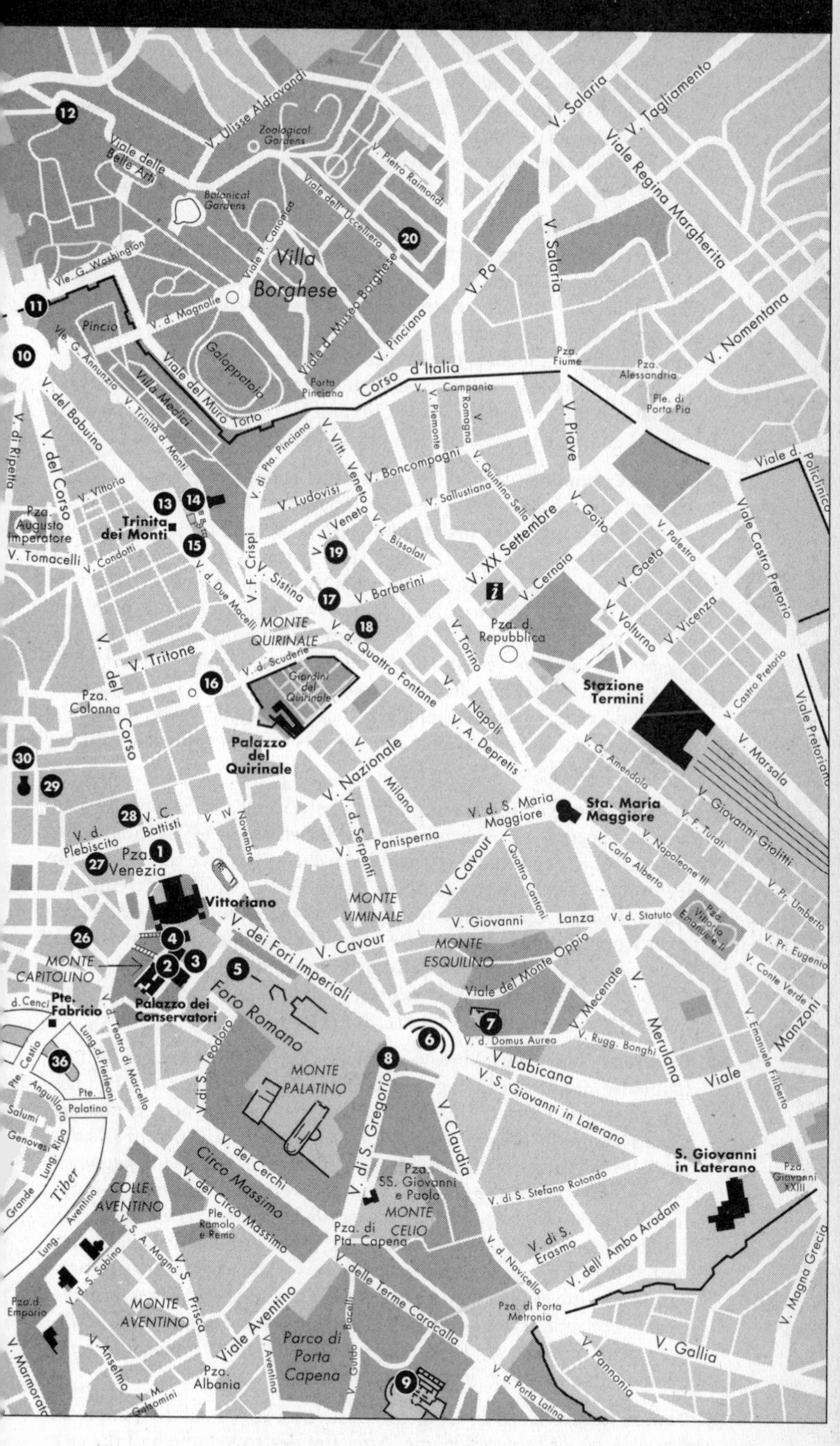

Villa Borghese
Zoological Gardens
Botanical Gardens
Pincio
Galoppatoio
Villa Medici
Trinita dei Monti
Pza. Augusto Imperatore
MONTE QUIRINALE
Giardini del Quirinale
Palazzo del Quirinale
Pza. Colonna
Pza. Venezia
Vittoriano
MONTE CAPITOLINO
Palazzo dei Conservatori
Pte. Fabricio
Foro Romano
MONTE PALATINO
Circo Massimo
COLLE AVENTINO
MONTE AVENTINO
Tiber
MONTE VIMINALE
MONTE ESQUILINO
Pza. d. Repubblica
Stazione Termini
Sta. Maria Maggiore
Pza. Vittorio Emanuele II
S. Giovanni in Laterano
Pza. Giovanni XXIII
MONTE CELIO
Pza. SS. Giovanni e Paolo
Pza. di Pta. Capena
Parco di Porta Capena
Pza. di Porta Metronia
Pza. Albania
Pza. Fiume
Pza. Alessandria
Ple. di Porta Pia
Porta Pinciana
Corso d'Italia
V. Salaria
Viale Regina Margherita
V. Nomentana
V. XX Settembre
V. Nazionale
V. Cavour
V. dei Fori Imperiali
V. Labicana
V. S. Giovanni in Laterano
Viale Aventino
V. d. Porta Latina
V. Gallia

your way around; newsstands offer a wide choice. Energetic sightseers will walk a lot, a much more pleasant way to see the city since traffic is barred from the center of town during the day; others might choose to take taxis, buses, or the Metro. If you are in Rome during a hot spell, do as the Romans do: start out early in the morning, have a light lunch and a long siesta during the hottest hours, then resume sightseeing in the late afternoon and end your evening with a leisurely meal outdoors, refreshed by cold Frascati wine and the *ponentino*, the cool evening breeze.

Ancient Rome

The geographic center of the city is at Piazza Venezia, site of the late-19th-century monument to the first king of a united Italy, Vittorio Emanuele. The most evocative ruins of the ancient city extend from the Campidoglio across the Foro Romano to the Colosseo and the Terme di Caracalla and include the Palatino and Circo Massimo. This is one of the world's most striking and significant concentrations of historic remains; stand at the back of the Campidoglio overlooking the Roman Forum and take in 2½ thousand years of history at a glance.

❽ **Arco di Costantino** (Arch of Constantine). The best preserved of Rome's triumphal arches, this 4th-century monument commemorates Constantine's victory over Maxentius at the Milvian Bridge. Just before this battle in AD 312, Constantine had a vision of a cross in the heavens and heard the words: "In this sign thou shalt conquer." The victory led not only to the construction of this majestic marble arch but also to a turning point in the history of Christianity: soon afterward a grateful—and converted—Constantine decreed that it was a lawful religion and should be tolerated throughout the empire. His newfound faith didn't seem to cure his imperial sticky fingers, however; the arch's decorations were pilfered from monuments to earlier emperors. ✉ *Piazza del Colosseo.*

❷ **Campidoglio** (Capitoline Hill). The majestic ramp and beautifully proportioned piazza are the handiwork of Michelangelo (1475–1564), who also designed the facades of the three palaces that face this square on Capitoline Hill. Palazzo Senatorio, at the center, is still the ceremonial seat of Rome's City Hall; it was built over the Tabularium, where ancient Rome's state archives were kept. The statue at the center of the square is a copy of an ancient Roman bronze of Marcus Aurelius (AD 120–180). The Capitoline Museums, the two palaces flanking the Senatorio, house the original. ✉ *Piazza del Campidoglio.*

★ ❻ **Colosseo** (Colosseum). Massive and majestic, this ruin is ancient Rome's hallmark monument, inaugurated in AD 80 with a program of games and shows that lasted 100 days. Before the imperial box, gladiators would salute the emperor and cry, "*Ave, imperator, morituri te salutant*" ("Hail, emperor, men soon to die salute thee"); it is said that when one day they heard the emperor Claudius respond, "Or maybe not," they became so offended that they called a strike. The Colosseum could hold more than 50,000 spectators; it was faced with marble, decorated with stuccos, and had an ingenious system of awnings to provide shade. It was built in just eight years. The Colosseum takes its name from a colossal, 118-ft statue of Nero that once stood nearby. ✉ *Piazza del Colosseo,* ☎ *06/7004261,* WEB *www.archeorm.arti.beniculturali.it.* ⏲ *Daily 9–2 hrs before sunset.*

❼ **Domus Aurea.** Nero's "Golden House" is a spectacular example of the excesses of Imperial Rome. After fire destroyed much of the city in AD 64, Nero took advantage of the resultant open space to construct a palace so large that contemporary accounts complained his house was bigger than the rest of the city. One wing of the building was given over to public functions, while the other served as the emperor's private residence. More than 150 rooms have been excavated, revealing a subterranean trove of ancient Roman architecture and some well-preserved Roman paintings decorating the walls. ✉ *Via della Domus Aurea,* ☎ *06/6990110 information; 06/39967700 reservations,* WEB *www.archeorm.arti.beniculturali.it.* ⏲ *Wed.–Mon. 9–7:45. Closed Tues..*

❺ **Foro Romano** (Roman Forum). Rome's foundations as a world capital and crossroads of culture are to be found here—literally. Excavations have shown that this site was in use as a burial ground as far back as the 10th century BC, hundreds of years before Rome's legendary founding by Romulus. But the Forum gained importance (and the name in use today) during Roman and Imperial times, when this marshy hollow was the political, commercial, and social center of Rome, and by extension, of the ancient world. The majestic ruins of temples and palaces visible today are fragments of the massive complex of markets, civic buildings, and houses of worship that dominated the city in its heyday. Wander down the **Via Sacra,** which runs the length of the Roman Forum, and take in the timeless view; then climb the **Colle Palatino** (Palatine Hill), where the emperors had their palaces and where 16th-century cardinals strolled in elaborate Italian gardens. From the *belvedere* (overlook) you have a good view of the **Circo Massimo** (Circus Maximus). Audio guides are available at the bookshop-ticket office at the Via dei Fori Imperiali entrance. ✉ *Entrances at Via dei Fori Imperiali and Piazza del Colosseo,* ☎ *06/6990110 or 06/39967700,* WEB *www.archeorm.arti.beniculturali.it.* ⏲ *Mon.–Sat. 9–2 hrs before sunset; Sun. and holidays 9–2.*

❸ **Musei Capitolini** (Capitoline Museums). The **Museo Capitolino** and **Palazzo dei Conservatori,** the palaces flanking Palazzo Senatorio on the Campidoglio, form a single museum holding some fine classical sculptures, including the gilded bronze equestrian statue of Marcus Aurelius that once stood on the pedestal in the piazza, as well as the *Dying Gaul,* the *Capitoline Venus,* and a series of portrait busts of ancient philosophers and emperors. In the courtyard of Palazzo dei Conservatori on the right of the piazza are mammoth fragments of a colossal statue of the emperor Constantine (circa 280–336). Inside are splendidly frescoed salons still used for municipal ceremonies, as well as sculptures and paintings. Don't miss the superb Baroque painting collection in the Pinacoteca, which holds masterpieces by Caravaggio and Rubens, among other stars. ✉ *Piazza del Campidoglio, off Piazza Venezia,* ☎ *06/39967800,* WEB *www.comune.roma.it.* ⏲ *Tues.–Sun. 9:30–7:30, Sat. open until 11 PM.*

❶ **Piazza Venezia.** Considered the geographical heart of the city, the square is dominated by the enormous marble monument (1911) honoring the first king of unified Italy, Vittorio Emanuele II (1820–78). Climb to the top of the "Vittoriano" for a stunning panorama over Rome. The piazza takes its name from the smaller but more historically important Palazzo Venezia, once Mussolini's headquarters. His most famous speeches were delivered from its balcony to the roaring crowds below. ✉ *Square at intersection of Via del Corso, Via del Plebiscito, and Via del Fori Imperiali.* ⏲ *Tues.–Sun. 10:30–1 hr before sunset.*

❹ **Santa Maria d'Aracoeli.** The 13th-century church on the Campidoglio can be reached by a long flight of steep stairs or, more easily, by way of the stairs on the far side of the Museo Capitolino. Stop in to see the medieval pavement, the Renaissance gilded ceiling that commemorates the victory of Lepanto, and the Pinturicchio (1454–1513) frescoes. ✉

Piazza Aracoeli, ☎ *06/6798155.* ⏲ *Oct.–May, daily 7–noon and 4–6; June–Sept., daily 7–noon and 4–6:30.*

9 **Terme di Caracalla** (Baths of Caracalla). The scale of the towering ruins of ancient Rome's most beautiful and luxurious public baths hint at their past splendor. Inaugurated by Caracalla in AD 217, the baths were used until the 6th century. An ancient version of a swank athletic club, the baths were open to all, though men and women used them separately; citizens could bathe, socialize, and exercise in huge pools and richly decorated halls and libraries. ✉ *Via delle Terme di Caracalla 52,* ☎ *06/39967700,* WEB *www.archeorm.arti.beniculturali.it.* ⏲ *Oct.–Mar., Mon. 9–1, Tues.–Sun. 9–3:30; Apr.–Sept., Mon. 9–1, Tues.–Sun. 9–6.*

Piazzas and Fountains

The lush park of Villa Borghese is dotted with pines and fountains and neoclassical "ruins." It is a happy conjunction of the pleasure gardens and palaces of Renaissance prelates on the site of ancient Roman villas. It also holds the world-class museums of the Galleria Borghese and Villa Giulia, both with histories of their own. The Pincio, the ancient Pincian Hill, is a belvedere over the city and a vantage point over elegantly planned Piazza del Popolo, below. Crossing the piazza are dedicated shoppers heading for Via del Corso's emporia and the boutiques of Via Condotti, towards the bustle of the Piazza di Spagna. The scene around the Fontana di Trevi is equally crowded, forcing the wishful to toss their coins into the fountain from center field.

★ 16 **Fontana di Trevi** (Trevi Fountain). A spectacular fantasy of mythical sea creatures and cascades of splashing water, this fountain is one of Rome's Baroque greats. The fountain as you see it was completed in the mid-1700s, but there had been a drinking fountain on the site for centuries. Pope Urban VIII (1568–1644) almost sparked a revolt when he slapped a tax on wine to cover the expenses of having the fountain repaired. Legend has it that a coin tossed into the fountain ensures a return trip to Rome. ✉ *Piazza di Trevi.*

20 **Galleria Borghese.** At the southeast corner of Villa Borghese, a park studded with pines and classical statuary, is this gallery created by Cardinal Scipione Borghese in the early 17th century as a showcase for his fabulous collection of ancient sculpture and Baroque painting. Highlights of the collection are the seductive reclining statue of Pauline Borghese by Canova (1757–1822) and some extraordinary works by Bernini (1598–1680), including the virtuoso *Apollo and Daphne.* The painting collection is no less impressive, with works by Caravaggio (1573–1610), Raphael (1483–1520), and Titian (circa 1488–1576), but the palace's restored magnificence is such that it would be a must-see even if it were empty. ✉ *Piazza Scipione Borghese, in Villa Borghese,* ☎ *06/8548577 for information; 06/32810 for reservations (press 2 for English),* WEB *www.galleriaborghese.it.* ⏲ *Winter, Tues.–Sun. 9–7; summer Tues.–Fri. 9–9, Sat. 9–midnight, Sun. 9–8 reservations required.*

15 **Keats-Shelley Memorial House.** To the right of the Spanish Steps is the house where Keats (1795–1821) died; the building is now a museum dedicated to English Romanticism and Keats and Shelley memorabilia. It also houses a library of works by Romantic authors. ✉ *Piazza di Spagna 26, next to the Spanish Steps,* ☎ *06/6784235,* WEB *www.Keats-Shelley-House.org.* ⏲ *Mon.–Fri. 9–1 and 3–6, Sat. 11–2 and 3–6.*

12 **Museo Etrusco di Villa Giulia** (Etruscan Museum of Villa Giulia). Pope Julius III (1487–1555) built this gracious Renaissance villa as a summer retreat. It's been turned into a fine museum dedicated to the Etruscans, central Italy's pre-Roman inhabitants. The collection, a well-explained cross-section of Etruscan statuary and sculpture, provides an introduc-

tion to this complex and ancient culture that is an interesting counterpoint to the city's usual emphasis on Imperial and Papal Rome. ✉ *Piazzale di Villa Giulia 9,* ☎ *06/3226571.* ⏲ *Tues.–Sat. 9–7, Sun. 9–2.*

18 **Palazzo Barberini** (Barberini Palace). Rome's most splendid 17th-century palace houses the **Galleria Nazionale di Arte Antica.** Its gems include Raphael's *La Fornarina* and many other fine paintings, some lavishly frescoed ceilings, and a suite of rooms decorated in 1782 on the occasion of the marriage of a Barberini heiress. ✉ *Via Barberini 18,* ☎ *06/4824184,* WEB *www.galleriaborghese.it.* ⏲ *Tues.–Sat. 9–7:30, Sun. 9–1.*

17 **Piazza Barberini.** This busy crossroads is marked by two Bernini fountains: the saucy **Fontana del Tritone** (Triton Fountain) in the middle of the square and the **Fontana delle Api** (Fountain of the Bees) at the corner of Via Veneto. Decorated with the heraldic Barberini bees, this latter shell-shaped fountain bears an inscription that was immediately seen as an unlucky omen by the superstitious Romans: it proclaimed that the fountain had been erected in the 22nd year of the reign of Pope Urban VIII, who commissioned it, whereas in fact the 21st anniversary of his election was still some weeks away. The incorrect numeral was hurriedly erased, but to no avail: Urban died eight days before the beginning of his 22nd year as pontiff. ✉ *Square at intersection of Via del Tritone, Via Vittorio Veneto, and Via Barberini.*

10 **Piazza del Popolo.** Designed by neoclassical architect Giuseppe Valadier in the early 1800s, this circular square is one of the largest and airiest in Rome. It's a pleasant spot for an afternoon stroll. The 3,000-year-old obelisk in the middle of the square, brought to Rome from Egypt by the emperor Augustus, once stood in the Circus Maximus. ✉ *Southern end of Via Flaminia and northern end of Via del Corso.*

13 **Piazza di Spagna.** The square is the heart of Rome's chic shopping district and a popular rendezvous spot, especially for the young people who throng the **Spanish Steps** on evenings and weekend afternoons. In the center of the elongated square, at the foot of the Spanish Steps, is the **Fontana della Barcaccia** (Old Boat Fountain) by Pietro Bernini (Gian Lorenzo's father). ✉ *Southern end of Via del Babuino and northern end of Via Due Macelli.*

19 **Santa Maria della Concezione.** In the crypt under the main Capuchin church, skeletons and scattered bones of some 4,000 dead Capuchin monks are arranged in odd decorative designs, intended as a macabre reminder of the impermanence of earthly life. ✉ *Via Veneto 27,* ☎ *06/4871185.* ⏲ *Fri.–Wed. 9–noon and 3–6.*

11 **Santa Maria del Popolo.** This medieval church rebuilt by Gian Lorenzo Bernini in Baroque style is rich in art; the pièces de résistance are two stunning Caravaggios in the chapel to the left of the main altar. ✉ *Piazza del Popolo,* ☎ *06/3610836.* ⏲ *Mon.–Sat. 7–7, Sun. 8–2 and 4:30–7:30.*

★ 14 **Scalinata di Trinitá dei Monti** (Spanish Steps). The 200-year-old stairway got its nickname from the nearby Spanish Embassy to the Holy See (the Vatican), though it was built with French funds in 1723, as the approach to the French church of **Trinità dei Monti** at the top of the steps. Rome's classic picture-postcard view is even more lovely when the steps are banked with blooming azaleas, from mid-April to mid-May. ✉ *Piazza di Spagna and Piazza Trinità dei Monti.*

Castel Sant'Angelo and the Vatican

Given that the Vatican is home to many of Rome's (and the world's) greatest art treasures, as well as being the spiritual home of a billion

Catholics, this area of the city is full of tourists and pilgrims almost year-round. Between the Vatican and the once-moated bulk of Castel Sant'Angelo, the pope's covered passageway flanks an enclave of workers and craftspeople, the old Borgo neighborhood, whose workaday charm is beginning to succumb to gentrification.

21 **Castel Sant'Angelo** (Sant'Angelo Castle). Transformed into a formidable fortress, this castle was originally built as the tomb of Emperor Hadrian (AD 76–138) in the 2nd century AD. In its early days it looked much like the Augusteo (Tomb of Augustus), which still stands in more or less its original form across the river. Hadrian's Tomb was incorporated into the city's walls and served as a military stronghold during the barbarian invasions. According to legend it got its present name in the 6th century, when Pope Gregory the Great, passing by in a religious procession, saw an angel with a sword appear above the ramparts to signal the end of the plague that was raging. Enlarged and fortified, the castle became a refuge for the popes, who fled to it along the Passetto, an arcaded passageway that links it with the Vatican.

Inside the castle are ancient corridors, medieval cells, and Renaissance salons, a museum of antique weapons, courtyards piled with stone cannonballs, and terraces with great views of the city. The highest terrace of all, under the bronze statue of the legendary angel, is the one from which Puccini's heroine Tosca threw herself to her death. **Ponte Sant'Angelo,** the ancient bridge spanning the Tiber in front of the castle, is decorated with lovely Baroque angels designed by Bernini. ✉ *Lungotevere Castello 50,* ☎ *06/6819111,* WEB *www.vatican.va.* ⏲ *Tues.–Sun. 9–8 (ticket office 9–7); longer hrs in summer.*

24 **Giardini Vaticani** (Vatican Gardens). The attractively landscaped gardens can be seen in a two-hour tour that shows you a few historical monuments, fountains, and the lovely 16th-century house of Pius IV (1499–1565), designed by Pirro Ligorio (1500–83), as well as the Vatican's mosaic school. Vistas from within the gardens give you a different perspective on the basilica itself. Reserve two or three days in advance. ✉ *Tickets: Piazza San Pietro,* ☎ *06/69884466.* 🎫 *20,000 lire/€10.35.* ⏲ *Tours Apr.–Oct., Mon.–Tues. and Thurs.–Sat. at 10; Nov.–Mar., Sat. at 10, weekdays by request for groups.*

★ 25 **Musei Vaticani** (Vatican Museums). One of the world's greatest collections of Western art, the holdings of the Vatican Museum are an embarrassment of riches that include Ancient Egyptian sarcophagi, Greek and Roman statuary, paintings by Giotto, Leonardo, and Raphael, and Michelangelo's magnificent frescoes in the Sistine Chapel. The nearly 8 km (5 mi) of displays are said to represent only a small part of the Vatican's holdings. The museums are almost unavoidably overwhelming, but four color-coded itineraries marked at the entrance and throughout the galleries help you make sense of it all. The shortest takes about 90 minutes, the longest more than four hours, depending on your rate of progress. All routes include the famed **Cappella Sistina** (Sistine Chapel). In 1508 Pope Julius II (1443–1513) commissioned Michelangelo to paint the more than 10,000 square ft of the chapel's ceiling. For four years Michelangelo dedicated himself to painting in the fresco technique, over wet plaster, and the result is one of the Renaissance's masterworks. Cleaning has removed centuries of soot and revealed the original and surprisingly brilliant colors of the ceiling and the *Last Judgment.* The chapel is almost always unpleasantly crowded—try to avoid the tour groups by going early or late. This is one instance in which a pair of binoculars and an illustrated or audio guide will contribute greatly to understanding and appreciating the work.

A complete list of the great works on display would go on for pages; don't-miss highlights, however, certainly include the Egyptian collection, the Roman mosaics and wall paintings, and the great classical- and Hellenistic-style statuary in the Belvedere Courtyard, including the *Laocoön*, the *Belvedere Torso* (which inspired Michelangelo), and the *Apollo Belvedere*. The **Stanze di Raffaello** (Raphael Rooms) are decorated with masterful frescoes, and there are more of Raphael's works in the **Pinacoteca** (Picture Gallery). Bored children may perk up in the whimsical **Sala degli Animali**, a seemingly forgotten room full of animal statuary. ✉ *Viale Vaticano*, ☎ *06/69884947*, WEB *www.vatican.va*. ⏲ *Easter wk and mid-Mar.–Oct., weekdays 8:45–3:45, Sat. 8:45–12:45; Nov.–mid-Mar. (except Easter), Mon.–Sat. 8:45–12:45; last Sun. of every month 8:45–12:45. Closed religious holidays (Jan. 1 and 6, Feb. 11, Mar. 19, Easter Sun. and Mon., May 1, Ascension Thurs., Corpus Christi, June 29, Aug. 15 and 16, Nov. 1, Dec. 8, Dec. 25 and 26) and Sun., excepting last Sun. of month. Note: Ushers at the entrance of St. Peter's Basilica and the Vatican Museums will not allow entry to persons with inappropriate clothing (no bare knees, shoulders, or low-cut shirts).*

22 **Piazza San Pietro** (St. Peter's Square). Gian Lorenzo Bernini designed this vast, circular piazza in the 17th century with an eye to the dramatic contrast between the dark, narrow medieval streets of the area and the wide open space of the piazza, presided over by the magnificence of St. Peter's Basilica. Unfortunately for art history, Mussolini had his own ideas about dramatic effect, which led him to raze much of the medieval neighborhood around the square to create Via della Conciliazione, the broad avenue that leads to the square today. Other aspects of Bernini's vision of architectural harmony remain, however: look for the stone disks in the pavement halfway between the fountains and the obelisk. From these points the colonnades seem to be formed of a single row of columns all the way around. The square was designed to accommodate crowds, and it has held up to 400,000 people at one time. At noon on Sunday when he is in Rome, the pope appears at his third-floor study window in the **Palazzo Vaticano**, to the right of the basilica, to bless the crowd in the square, and in warm months he blesses visitors from a podium on the basilica steps on Wednesday mornings. ✉ *End of Via Conciliazione*.

Since the Lateran Treaty of 1929, Vatican City has been an independent and sovereign state, which covers about 108 acres and is surrounded by thick, high walls. Its gates are watched over by the Swiss Guards, who still wear the colorful dress uniforms based on a Michelangelo design. Sovereign of this little state is the Pope of the Roman Catholic Church. For many visitors a **papal audience** is the highlight of a trip to Rome. Mass audiences take place on Wednesday morning in the square or in a modern audience hall (capacity 7,000) off the left-hand colonnade. Tickets are necessary. For audience tickets write or fax well in advance indicating the date you prefer, language you speak, and hotel in which you will stay. Or, apply for tickets in person on the Monday or Tuesday before the Wednesday audience. ✉ *Tickets: Prefettura della Casa Pontificia, 00120 Vatican City*, ☎ *06/69883273*, FAX *06/69885863*. ⏲ *Mon.–Tues. 9–1*.

★ 23 **St. Peter's Basilica** (Basilica di San Pietro). In all of its staggering grandeur and magnificence, St. Peter's Basilica is best appreciated as the lustrous background for ecclesiastical ceremonies thronged with the faithful. The original basilica was built in the early 4th century AD by the emperor Constantine, above an earlier shrine that supposedly marked the burial place of St. Peter. After more than 1,000 years, the decrepit old basilica had to be torn down. The task of building a new, much larger one took almost 200 years and employed the genius of many of the Renaissance's greatest architects, including Alberti (1404–72), Bramante (1444–1514), Raphael, Peruzzi (1481–1536), Antonio Sangallo the Younger (1483–1546), and Michelangelo, who died before the dome he had planned could be completed. The structure was finally finished in 1626.

The most famous work of art inside is Michelangelo's *Pietà* (1498), in the first chapel on the right as you enter the basilica. Michelangelo carved four statues of the Pietà, or Mary cradling her dead son; this one is the earliest and best known, two others are in Florence, and the fourth, the *Rondanini Pietà,* is in Milan. At the end of the central aisle is the bronze statue of St. Peter, its foot worn by centuries of reverent kisses. The bronze throne above the altar in the apse was created by Bernini to contain a simple wood-and-ivory chair believed to have once belonged to St. Peter. Bernini's baldachin over the papal altar was made with bronze stripped from the dome of the Pantheon at the order of Pope Urban VIII, one of the powerful Roman Barberini family. His practice of plundering ancient monuments for material with which to carry out his grandiose decorating schemes inspired the famous quip "*Quod non fecerunt barbari, fecerunt Barberini*" ("What the barbarians didn't do, the Barberinis did").

As you stroll up and down the aisles and transepts, notice the fine mosaic copies of famous paintings above the altars, the monumental tombs and statues, and the fine stuccowork. Stop at the **Museo Storico** (Historical Museum), which contains some priceless liturgical objects. ⏲ *Apr.–Sept., daily 9–6; Oct.–Mar., daily 9–5.*

The entrance to the so-called **Grotte Vaticane** (Vatican Grottoes), crypts containing chapels and the tombs of various popes, is in one of the huge piers under the dome, next to the central altar. It's best to leave this visit for last, as the crypt's only exit takes you outside the church. It occupies the area of the original basilica, over the necropolis, the ancient burial ground where evidence of what may be St. Peter's burial place has been found. ⏲ *Apr.–Sept., daily 7–6; Oct.–Mar., daily 7–5.*

To see the **roof and dome** of the basilica, take the elevator or climb the stairs in the courtyard near the exit from the Vatican Grottoes. From the roof you can climb a short interior staircase to the base of the dome for an overhead view of the basilica's interior. Then, and only if you are in good shape, you should attempt the very long, strenuous, and claustrophobic climb up the narrow stairs to the balcony of the lantern atop the dome, where you can look down on the Giardini Vaticani (Vatican Gardens) and out across all of Rome. ✉ *Entrance in courtyard to the left as you leave the basilica.* ⏲ *Apr.–Sept., daily 8–6; Oct.–Mar., daily 8–5.*

Free 60-minute tours of St. Peter's Basilica are offered in English daily (Monday–Saturday usually starting about 10 AM and 3 PM, Sunday at 2:30 PM) by volunteer guides. They start at the information desk under the basilica portico. At the Ufficio Scavi you can book special tours of the necropolis. Note that entry to St. Peter's, the Musei Vaticani, and the Gardens is barred to those wearing shorts, miniskirts, sleeveless T-shirts, and otherwise revealing clothing. Women can cover bare shoulders and upper arms with scarves; men should wear full-length pants or jeans. ✉ *Piazza San Pietro,* ☎ *06/69884466.* ⏲ *Apr.–Sept., daily 7–7; Oct.–Mar., daily 7–6. Closed during ceremonies in the piazza. Necropolis (left beyond Arco delle Campane entrance to Vatican):* ☎ *06/69885318. Apply a few days in advance to Ufficio Scavi, or try in morning for the same day. Office Mon.–Sat. 9–5.* WEB *www.vatican.va.*

Old Rome

The land between the Corso and the Tiber bend is packed with churches, patrician palaces, Baroque piazzas, and picturesque courtyards, with Piazza Navona as a magnificent central point. In between are narrow streets and intriguing little shops, interspersed with eating places and cafés that are a focus of Rome's easygoing, itinerant nightlife.

★ 34 **Campo dei Fiori** (Field of Flowers). This wide square is the site of Rome's best-loved morning market, a crowded and colorful circus of fruits, flowers, and fish, raucously peddled daily 9–2. If you'd rather watch than participate in the genial chaos, sit at one of the pleasant cafés that line the square. The hooded bronze figure brooding over the piazza is philosopher Giordano Bruno (1548–1600), who was burned at the stake here for heresy in 1600. ✉ *Piazza Campo dei Fiori.*

27 **Chiesa del Gesù.** This huge 16th-century church is a paragon of the Baroque style and the tangible symbol of the power of the Jesuits, who were a major force in the Counter-Reformation in Europe. Its interior gleams with gold and precious marbles, and it has a fantastically painted ceiling that flows down over the pillars, merging with painted stucco figures to complete the three-dimensional illusion. ✉ *Piazza del Gesù,* ☎ *06/697001.* ⏲ *Daily 7–noon and 4–7.*

26 **Fontana delle Tartarughe** (Turtle Fountain). The winsome turtles that are this 16th-century fountain's hallmark are thought to have been added around 1658 by Bernini as a low-budget way to bring the Renaissance fountain into the Baroque. Visit it on a stroll through Rome's former Jewish Ghetto, an atmospheric old neighborhood with medieval inscriptions and friezes on the old buildings on Via Portico d'Ottavia, and the remains of the Teatro di Marcello (Theater of Marcello), a theater built by Julius Caesar to hold 20,000 spectators. ✉ *Piazza Mattei.*

28 **Galleria Doria Pamphili.** You can visit this rambling palazzo, still the residence of a princely family, to view the gallery housing the family's art collection and also some of the magnificently furnished private apartments. ✉ *Piazza del Collegio Romano 2,* ☎ *06/6797323,* WEB *www.doriapamphilj.it.* ⏲ *Fri.–Wed. 10–5; private-apartments tours 10:30, 11, 11:30, noon. Closed May 1, Aug. 15, Nov. 1.*

36 **Isola Tiberina.** Built in 62 BC, Rome's oldest bridge, the **Ponte Fabricio,** links the Ghetto neighborhood on the Tiber's left bank to this little island, home to a hospital and the church of San Bartolomeo. The island has been dedicated to healing ever since a temple to Aesculapius was erected here in 291 BC. **Ponte Cestio** links the island with the Trastevere neighborhood on the right bank.

OFF THE BEATEN PATH

Ostia Antica (Ancient Ostia) – The well-preserved Roman port city of Ostia Antica, near the sea, is now a vast archaeological park just outside Rome, a lovely day trip into the ancient past. Wander through ancient markets and ruined houses, or bring a picnic and enjoy the sea breeze. There's regular train service from the Ostiense Station (Piramide Metro Bstop). ✉ *Via dei Romagnoli, Ostia Antica, not far from Fiumicino Airport,* ☎ *06/56358099,* WEB *www.itnw.roma.it/ostia/scavi.* ⏲ *Excavations: Tues.–Sun. 9 AM–1 hr before sunset. Museum: Tues.–Sun. 9–1:30.*

---

31 **Palazzo Altemps.** A 15th-century patrician dwelling, the palace is a showcase for the sculpture collection of the **Museo Nazionale Romano** (National Museum of Rome). Informative labels in English make it easy to appreciate such famous sculptures as the intricate carved reliefs on the *Ludovisi Sarcophagus* and the *Galata,* representing the heroic death of

a barbarian warrior. ✉ *Piazza Sant'Apollinare 46,* ☎ *06/6833566,* WEB *www.archeorm.arti.beniculturali.it.* ⏲ *Tues.–Sun. 9–7:45.*

35 **Palazzo Farnese.** Now the French Embassy, one of the most beautiful of Rome's many Renaissance palaces dominates Piazza Farnese, where Egyptian marble basins from the Terme di Caracalla have been transformed into fountains. Note the unique brickwork patterns on the palace's facade. ✉ *Piazza Farnese.*

★ 30 **Pantheon.** Lauded for millennia for its architectural harmony, the Pantheon is no less impressive in the 21st century. Built in 27 BC by Augustus's general Agrippa and totally rebuilt by Hadrian in the 2nd century AD, this unique temple (consecrated as a church in the Middle Ages) is a must-see. Notice the equal proportions of the height of the dome and the circular interior—unlike most angular buildings, the Pantheon is designed after a globe. The oculus, or opening in the ceiling, is meant to symbolize the all-seeing eye of heaven; in practice, it illuminates the building and lightens the heavy stone ceiling. In earlier times the dome was covered in bronze, later pilfered to construct the baldachin over the altar in St. Peter's. ✉ *Piazza della Rotonda,* ☎ *06/68300230.* ⏲ *Mon.–Sat. 9–6:30, Sun. 9–1.*

★ 33 **Piazza Navona.** This elongated 17th-century piazza traces the oval form of the underlying Circus of Diocletian. At the center, Bernini's lively **Fontana dei Quattro Fiumi** (Four Rivers Fountain) is a showpiece. The four statues represent rivers in the four corners of the world: the Nile, with its face covered in allusion to its then-unknown source; the Ganges; the Danube; and the River Plata, with its hand raised. You may hear the legend that this was Bernini's mischievous dig at Borromini's design of the facade of the church of **Sant'Agnese in Agone,** from which the statue seems to be shrinking in horror. In point of fact, the fountain was created in 1651; work on the church's facade began a year or two later. ✉ *North of Corso Vittorio Emanuele and west of Corso Rinascimento.*

32 **San Luigi dei Francesi.** The clergy of San Luigi considered Caravaggio's roistering and unruly lifestyle scandalous enough, but his realistic treatment of sacred subjects—seen in three paintings here—was just too much for them. They rejected his first version of the altarpiece and weren't particularly happy with the other two works either. Thanks to the intercession of Caravaggio's patron, an influential cardinal, they were persuaded to keep them—a lucky thing, since they are now recognized to be among the artist's finest paintings. Have a few 500-lire coins handy for the light machine. ✉ *Piazza San Luigi dei Francesi,* ☎ *06/688271.* ⏲ *Fri.–Wed. 7:30–12:30 and 3:30–7, Thurs. 7:30–12:30.*

29 **Santa Maria sopra Minerva.** Rome's only major Gothic church takes its name from the temple of Minerva over which it was built. Inside are some beautiful frescoes by Filippino Lippi (circa 1457–1504); outside in the square is a charming elephant by Bernini carrying an obelisk on its back. ✉ *Piazza della Minerva,* ☎ *06/6791217.* ⏲ *Daily 7–noon and 4–7.*

Dining

Rome has no shortage of restaurants, and what the city lacks in variety of fare is made up for by overall quality. Don't make the mistake of assuming that expensive restaurants serve better or more authentic food; in Rome, you may pay top dollar for nothing more than a flourish of linen and silver. Some of Rome's prime restaurants are worth the expense, but you'll often do better at a more unassuming trattoria or osteria. Romans eat out a lot, and there's a wide variety of Italian fast food that caters to workers on lunch breaks. These places serve anything from a fruit salad and fresh spinach to lasagna and deep-fried cod fillets. Unfortunately, non-Italian cuisines haven't really caught on in Rome, although there are a few excellent Eritrean and Ethiopian places near Termini and some less appealing Chinese restaurants throughout the center. That old Roman standby, the paper-thin, crispy wood-oven pizza, is a low-budget favorite among locals and travelers alike, as is its to-go cousin, the heartier *pizza al taglio*. During August and over Christmas many restaurants close for vacation.

$$$$ ✕ **La Rosetta.** The city's most elegant seafood restaurant, La Rosetta is still the place to go in Rome for artful presentations of first-rate fish. The space is elegant in its simplicity, with warm woods, fresh flowers, and a stunning display of fish at the entrance. Particularly good are the *vongole veraci* (sautéed clams), *tonnarelli ai frutti di mare* (poached fish on artichokes or potatoes), and sea bass with black truffles. Homemade desserts are worth saving room for. ✉ *Via della Rosetta 9,* ☎ *06/6861002. Dinner reservations essential. AE, DC, MC, V.* ⊙ *Closed Sun. and 2–3 weeks in Aug. No lunch Thurs. and Fri.*

$$$ ★ ✕ **Sangallo.** Small and intimate, this is an old-fashioned restaurant where the owner buys the fish himself, and where dinner is meant to last all night. The traditional menu leans heavily toward the gourmet, with dishes like oysters *tartare,* snapper with *foie gras,* Texas steaks and a fixed-price menu based on truffles. There are few tables in the tiny dining room, so make sure to book ahead. ✉ *Vicolo della Vaccarella 11/a,* ☎ *06/6865549. AE, DC, MC, V. Closed Sun., 1 wk in Jan., and 2 wks in Aug. No lunch Mon.*

$$–$$$ ✕ **Checchino dal 1887.** Carved out of a hillside made of potsherds from Roman times, Checchino serves the most traditional Roman cuisine—carefully prepared and served without fanfare—in a clean, sober environment. You can try the variety of meats that make up the soul of Roman cooking, including *trippa* (tripe) and *coratella* (sweetbreads). There's also plenty to choose from for those uninterested in innards. ✉ *Via di Monte Testaccio 30,* ☎ *06/5746318. AE, DC, MC, V. Closed Mon., Aug., and during Christmas. No dinner Sun.*

$$–$$$ ★ ✕ **Dal Bolognese.** This classic restaurant is a trendy choice for a leisurely lunch between sightseeing and shopping. An array of contemporary paintings decorates the dining room, but the real attraction is the lovely piazza—prime people-watching real estate. As the name of the restaurant promises, the cooking here adheres to the hearty tradition of Bologna, with delicious homemade *tortellini in brodo* (tortellini in broth), fresh pastas in creamy sauces, and *bollito misto* (steaming trays of boiled meats). ✉ *Piazza del Popolo 1,* ☎ *06/3611426. AE, DC, MC, V. Closed Mon. and Aug.*

$$–$$$ ✕ **Papà Baccus.** Italo Cipriani, owner of Rome's best Tuscan restaurant, takes his meat as seriously as any Tuscan, using real Chianina beef for the house special, *bistecca alla fiorentina* (grilled, thick bone-in steak). If you're avoiding beef, you can sample such dishes as Tuscan bean soup, and the sweet and delicate prosciutto from Pratomagno. The welcome here is warm, the service excellent, and the decor has the feel of an upscale trattoria. ✉ *Via Toscana 36,* ☎ *06/42742808. AE, DC, MC, V. Closed Sun., Aug., and during Christmas. No lunch Sat.*

$$ ✕ **Colline Emiliane.** Behind an opaque glass facade not far from Piazza Barberini lies this quiet, family-run restaurant reputed to serve the city's best classic Emilian cuisine: light homemade pastas, *tortelli di zucca* (pumpkin-filled ravioli), and meats ranging from *giambonetto di vitello* (roast veal) to *cotoletta alla bolognese* (fried veal cutlet with cheese and prosciutto). ✉ *Via degli Avignonesi 22,* ☎ *06/4818564. Reservations essential. MC, V. Closed Fri. and Aug.*

$$ ✕ **Il Simposio di Costantini.** At the classiest wine bar in town—done out in wrought-iron vines, wood paneling, and velvet—choose from about 30 wines in *degustazione* (available by the glass) or order a bottle from a list of more than 1,000 Italian and foreign labels sold in the shop next door. Food is appropriately fancy: marinated and smoked fish, designer salads, fine cured meats, terrines and pâtés, and stellar cheeses. ✉ *Piazza Cavour 16, near the Vatican,* ☎ *06/3211502. AE, DC, MC, V. Closed Sun. and Aug. No lunch Sat.*

$$ ★ ✕ **Myosotis.** The menu here rides a delicate line between tradition and innovation, focusing more on the freshness and quality of the ingredients than on elaborate presentation. Fresh pasta gets special attention on the extensive menu: it's rolled out by hand to order for the *stracci alla delizia di mare* (pasta with seafood). The wine list is ample, and the prices are honest. ✉ *Vicolo della Vaccarella 3/5,* ☎ *06/6865554. AE, DC, MC, V. Closed Sun. and 2 wks in Aug.*

$–$$ ✕ **Dal Toscano.** The hallmarks of this great family-run Tuscan trattoria near the Vatican are friendly and speedy service, an open wood-fired grill, and such classic dishes as *ribollita* (a dense bread and vegetable soup) and the prized bistecca alla fiorentina. Wash it all down with a strong Chianti. All desserts are homemade and delicious. ✉ *Via Germanico 58,* ☎ *06/39725717. AE, DC, MC, V. Closed Mon., Aug., and 2 wks in Dec.*

$ ✕ **Alfredo e Ada.** There's no place like home, and you'll feel like you're back there from the moment you squeeze into a table at this hole in the wall just across the river from Castel Sant'Angelo. There's no menu, just plate after plate of whatever Ada thinks you should try, from hearty, classic pastas to *involtini di vitello* (savory veal rolls with tomato) and homemade sausage. Sit back and enjoy—it's all good. ✉ *Via dei Banchi Nuovi 14,* ☎ *06/6878842. No credit cards. Closed weekends.*

$ ✕ **Da Gino.** Trastevere's most elegant pizzeria serves all the classics but with a style that sets it apart from its more rough-and-tumble neighbors. Delectably thin wood-oven pizza shares menu space with treats like *fritto di moscardini* (fried baby squid); the wine list shows a sommelier's touch. Outdoor tables on a bustling pedestrian street are refreshing in summer. ✉ *Via della Lungaretta 85,* ☎ *06/5803403. AE, MC, V. Closed Wed. Lunch Sun. only.*

$ ✕ **Perilli.** A bastion of authentic Roman cooking and trattoria charm since 1911 (the decor has changed very little), this is the place to go to try rigatoni *con pajata* (with veal's intestines)—if you're into that sort of thing. Otherwise the carbonara and *all'amatriciana* (spicy tomato sauce with pancetta) are classics. The house wine is a golden nectar from the Castelli Romani. ✉ *Via Marmorata 39,* ☎ *06/5742415. AE, DC, MC, V. Closed Wed.*

Lodging

Hotels listed are within walking distance of at least some sights and handy to public transportation. Those in the $$ and $ categories do not have restaurants but serve Continental breakfast. Rooms facing the street may get traffic noise throughout the night, and few hotels in the lower price categories have double-glazed windows. Ask for a quiet room—or bring earplugs. Always make reservations, even if only a few days in advance. Always inquire about discounts. Should you find yourself in the city without reservations, however, contact **HR** (✉ Termini Station; Aeroporto Fiumicino, ☎ 06/6991000), a hotel reservation service, or **EPT** (✉ Via Parigi 5, ☎ 06/48899253, FAX 06/4819316; ✉ near Piazza della Repubblica; ✉ Aeroporto Fiumicino, ☎ 06/65956074; ✉ Stazione Termini, ☎ 06/4871270). The Rome municipal tourist information booths will also help you find a room.

$$$$ **Dei Borgognoni.** This quietly chic hotel near Piazza Colonna is as central as you could want, yet the winding byway stage set gives you a sense of being off the beaten track. The centuries-old building provides spacious lounges, a glassed-in garden, and rooms well arranged to create an illusion of space, though they are actually compact. The hotel has a garage (fee), a rarity in such a central location. ✉ *Via del Bufalo 126, 00187,* ☎ *06/69941505,* FAX *06/69941501,* WEB *www.borgognoni.it. 51 rooms. AE, DC, MC, V.*

$$$$ ★ **Eden.** The historic Eden, a haunt of Hemingway, Ingrid Bergman, and Fellini, merits superlatives for dashing elegance and stunning vistas of Rome from the rooftop restaurant and bar (also from some of the most expensive rooms). Precious but discreet antique furnishings, fine linen sheets, and marble baths whisper understated opulence. ✉ *Via Ludovisi 49, 00187,* ☎ *06/478121,* FAX *06/4821584,* WEB *www.hoteleden.it. 101 rooms, 12 suites. Restaurant. AE, DC, MC, V.*

$$$$ **Hassler.** You can expect a cordial atmosphere and superb service at this hotel at the top of the Spanish Steps. The public rooms have an extravagant, somewhat dated decor, especially the clubby winter bar, garden bar, and the glass-roofed lounge, with gold marble walls and hand-painted tile floors. Elegant bedrooms are decorated in a variety of classic styles (the best feature is the frescoed walls). ✉ *Piazza Trinità dei Monti 6, 00187,* ☎ *06/699340,* FAX *06/6789991,* WEB *www.hotelhasslerroma.com. 85 rooms, 15 suites. Restaurant. AE, DC, MC, V.*

$$$ ★ **Britannia.** A quiet locale off Via Nazionale is only one of the attractions of this small, special hotel, where you will be coddled with luxury touches such as English-language dailies and local weather reports delivered to your room each morning. The well-furnished rooms (two with a rooftop terrace), frescoed halls, and lounge (where a rich breakfast buffet is served) attest the management really cares about superior service and value. ✉ *Via Napoli 64, 00184,* ☎ *06/4883153,* FAX *06/4882343,* WEB *www.italyhotel.com. 32 rooms, 1 suite. AE, DC, MC, V.*

$$$ ★ **Farnese.** An early 20th-century mansion, the Farnese is in a quiet but central residential district. Art Deco–style furniture is mixed with enchanting fresco decorations amid its compact rooms, plenty of lounge space, and a roof garden. ✉ *Via Alessandro Farnese 30, 00193,* ☎ *06/3212553,* FAX *06/3215129,* WEB *www.travel.it. 24 rooms. AE, DC, MC, V.*

$$$ **La Residenza.** A converted town house near Via Veneto, this hotel offers good value and first-class comfort at reasonable rates. Public areas are spacious and guest rooms are comfortable and have large closets and TVs. The hotel's clientele is mainly from the United States. Rates include a generous buffet breakfast. ✉ *Via Emilia 22, 00187,* ☎ *06/4880789,* FAX *06/485721,* WEB *www.venere.it. 21 rooms, 6 suites. V.*

$$–$$$ **Scalinata di Spagna.** An old-fashioned pensione loved by generations of romantics, this tiny hotel is booked solid for months ahead. Its location at the top of the Spanish Steps, inconspicuous little entrance, quaint hodgepodge of old furniture, and view from the terrace where you breakfast make it seem like your own special, exclusive inn. ✉ *Piazza Trinità dei Monti 17, 00187,* ☎ *06/6793006,* FAX *06/69940598. 15 rooms. MC, V.*

$$ **Amalia.** Handy to St. Peter's, the Vatican, and the Cola di Rienzo shopping district, this small hotel is owned and operated by the Consoli family—Amalia and her brothers. On several floors of a 19th-century building, it has large rooms with functional furnishings, TVs, minibars, pictures of angels on the walls, and gleaming marble bathrooms (hair dryers included). The Ottaviano stop of Metro A is a block away. ✉ *Via Germanico 66, 00192,* ☎ *06/39723356,* FAX *06/39723365,* WEB *www.hotelamalia.com. 30 rooms, 23 with bath. AE, MC, V.*

$ ★ **Margutta.** This small hotel near the Spanish Steps and Piazza del Popolo has an unassuming lobby but bright, attractive bedrooms with wrought-iron bedsteads and modern baths. ✉ *Via Laurina 34, 00187,* ☎ *06/3223674,* FAX *06/3200395. 24 rooms. AE, DC, MC, V.*

$ **Romae.** Near Termini Station, this mid-size hotel has clean, spacious rooms with light-wood furniture and small but bright bathrooms. The congenial, helpful management offers special winter rates and welcomes families. Low rates that include breakfast and free Internet access make this a good deal. ✉ *Via Palestro 49, 00185,* ☎ *06/4463554,* FAX *06/4463914,* WEB *www.hotelromae.com. 38 rooms. AE, MC, V.*

Nightlife and the Arts

You will find information on scheduled events and shows at EPT and municipal tourist offices or booths. The biweekly booklet *Un Ospite a Roma,* free from concierges at some hotels, is another source of information, as is *Wanted in Rome,* published on Wednesday, available at newsstands. There are listings in English in the back of the weekly *Roma C'è* booklet, with handy bus information for each listing; it is published on Thursday and sold at newsstands. If you want to go to the opera, the ballet, or a concert, it's best to ask your concierge to get tickets for you. They are sold at box offices only, just a few days before performances.

The Arts

CONCERTS

The main concert hall is the **Accademia di Santa Cecilia** (✉ Via della Conciliazione 4, ☎ 06/68801044). Concerts are held year-round; look for posters or for schedules in the publications mentioned above.

FILM

There are two original-language movie theaters in Rome, **Pasquino** (✉ Piazza Sant'Egidio, near Piazza Santa Maria in Trastevere, ☎ 06/5803622) and **Quirinetta** (✉ Via Minghetti 4, off Via del Corso near Piazza Venezia, ☎ 06/6790012). Programs are listed in Rome's daily newspapers, as well as the *Italy Daily* supplement to the *International Herald Tribune.* Several other movie theaters show films in English on certain days of the week; the listings in *Roma C'è* are reliable.

OPERA

The opera season runs from November or December through May, and performances are staged in the **Teatro dell'Opera** (✉ Piazza Beniamino Gigli, ☎ 06/48160255 or 06/481601). From May through August, the spectacular performances are held in the open air at one end of the Stadio Olimpico, Rome's soccer stadium. Smaller opera companies put up their own low-budget, high-quality productions in various venues. Look for posters advertising performances.

Nightlife

Rome's "in" nightspots change frequently, and many fade into oblivion after a brief moment of glory. The best places to find an up-to-date list are the weekly entertainment guide "Trovaroma," published each Thursday in the Italian daily *La Repubblica,* and *Roma C'è,* the weekly guide sold at newsstands.

BARS

More and more American-style bars are lining Rome's streets these days. Try Trastevere or the area west of Piazza Navona for a bit of bar-hopping. One of the grandest places for a drink in well-dressed company is **Le Bar** (✉ Via Vittorio Emanuele Orlando 3, ☎ 06/47091) of Le Grand Hotel. **Jazz Cafè** (✉ Via Zanardelli 12, ☎ 06/6861990), near Piazza Navona, is an upscale watering hole with good live music downstairs. **Flann O'Brien** (✉ Via Napoli 29, ☎ 06/4880418), one of a plethora of pubs that now monopolize the bar scene in Rome, has the feel of a good Irish pub. **Trinity College** (✉ Via del Collegio Romano 6, near Piazza Venezia, ☎ 06/6786472) has two floors of Irish pub trappings, with happy chatter and background music until 3 AM.

DISCOS AND NIGHTCLUBS

Testaccio's three-floor **Saint** (✉ Via Galvani 46, ☎ 06/5747945) has two discos designated "Paradiso" and "Inferno" (Heaven and Hell). You might spot an American celeb at **Gilda** (✉ Via Mario de' Fiori 97, ☎ 06/6784838), with a disco, piano bar, and live music. It's closed Monday and jackets are required. Just as exclusive is **Bella Blu** (✉ Via Luciani 21, ☎ 06/3230490), a club in Parioli that caters to Rome's thirtysomething elite.

MUSIC CLUBS

For the best live music, including jazz, blues, rhythm and blues, African, and rock, go to **Big Mama** (✉ Vicolo San Francesco a Ripa 18, ☎ 06/5812551). A membership card required for entry will set you back 20,000 lire/€10.35. Live performances of jazz, soul, and funk by leading musicians draw celebrities to **Alexanderplatz** (✉ Via Ostia 9, in the Vatican area, ☎ 06/39742171). The music starts about 10 PM, and you can have supper while you wait.

Shopping

Via Condotti, directly across from the Spanish Steps, and the streets running parallel to Via Condotti, as well as its cross streets, form the most elegant and expensive shopping area for clothes and accessories in Rome—head here first for top Italian and European designer shops. Lower-price fashions are on display at shops on **Via Frattina** and **Via del Corso.** Romans in the know do much of their shopping along **Via Cola di Rienzo** and **Via Nazionale.** For prints, browse among the stalls at **Piazza Fontanella Borghese** or stop in at the shops in the Pantheon area. For minor antiques **Via dei Coronari** and other streets in the Piazza Navona area are good. High-end antiques dealers are situated in **Via del Babuino** and its environs. The open-air markets near **Campo dei Fiori** and in other neighborhoods throughout the city provide an eyeful of local color.

Rome Essentials

AIRPORTS & TRANSFERS

Rome's principal airport is Aeroporto Leonardo da Vinci, usually known as Fiumicino. The smaller Ciampino, on the edge of Rome, is used as an alternative by international and domestic lines, especially for charter flights.

➤ AIRPORT INFORMATION: **Aeroporto Leonardo da Vinci** (✉ 29 km/18 mi southeast of Rome, ☎ 06/65953640 flight information). **Ciampino** (☎ 06/794941 flight information; WEB www.adr.it).

TRANSFERS

To get to downtown Rome from Fiumicino you have a choice of two trains. Ask at the airport (at EPT or train information counters) which one takes you closest to your hotel. The nonstop Airport–Termini express takes you directly to Track 22 at Termini Station, Rome's main train terminal, well served by taxis and the hub of Metro (subway) and bus lines. The ride to Termini takes 30 minutes; departures are hourly, beginning at 7:50 AM, with the final departure at 10:05 PM. Tickets cost 13,000 lire/€6.70. The other airport train (FM1) runs to Tiburtina station in Rome and beyond to Monterotondo, a suburban town to the east.

The main stops in Rome are at the Trastevere, Ostiense, and Tiburtina stations. At each of these you can find taxis and bus and/or Metro connections to various parts of Rome. This train runs from 6:35 AM to 12:15 AM, with departures every 20 minutes. The ride to Tiburtina takes 40 minutes. Tickets cost 8,000 lire/€4.15. For either train, buy your ticket at an automated vending machine (you need Italian currency) or the ticket office just before the train platforms. There are ticket counters at some stations (Termini Track 22, Trastevere, Tiburtina). Remember to date-stamp your ticket in one of the yellow machines near the track.

A taxi to or from Fiumicino costs 70,000 lire/€36.15–80,000 lire/€41.30, including extra charges for baggage and off-hours. At a booth inside the terminal you can hire a four- or five-passenger car with driver for a little more. If you decide to take a taxi, use only the yellow or the newer white cabs, in line at the official stand outside the terminal; make sure the meter is running. Gypsy cab drivers solicit your business as you come out of customs; they're not reliable, and their rates may be higher. Ciampino is connected with the Anagnina station of the Metro A by bus (runs every half hour). A taxi between Ciampino and downtown Rome costs about 35,000 lire/€18.

BIKE & MOPED TRAVEL

Pedaling through Villa Borghese, along the Tiber, and through the city center when traffic is light is a pleasant way to see the sights, but remember: Rome is hilly. Rental concessions are at the Piazza di Spagna and Piazza del Popolo Metro stops, and at Piazza San Silvestro and Largo Argentina. You will also find rentals at Viale della Pineta and Viale del Bambino on the Pincio, inside Villa Borghese. Collalti, just off Campo de' Fiori, leases and repairs bikes. St. Peter's Motor Rent rents bikes and mopeds. You can also rent a moped or scooter and mandatory helmet at Scoot-a-Long.

➤ BIKE AND MOPED RENTALS: **Collalti** (✉ Via del Pellegrino 82, ☎ 06/68801084). **Scoot-a-Long** (✉ Via Cavour 302, ☎ 06/6780206). **St. Peter's Motor Rent** (✉ Via di Porta Castello 43, near St. Peter's, ☎ 06/6875714).

BUS TRAVEL WITHIN ROME

Orange ATAC city buses (and a few streetcar lines) run from about 6 AM to midnight, with night buses (indicated N) on some lines. Bus lines 117 and 119, with compact electric vehicles, make a circuit of limited but scenic routes in downtown Rome. They can save you from a lot of walking, and you can get on and off as you please. The orange-and-blue J-Line buses are a handy alternative way to get across town; route information and tickets (1,900 lire/€1) are available at newsstands and tobacconists.

➤ BUS INFORMATION: **ATAC** (☎ 800/431784).

CAR TRAVEL

If you come by car, put it in a parking space (and note that parking in central Rome is generally either metered or prohibited) or a garage, and use public transportation. If you must park in a metered (blue-outlined) space, buy credits at the blue machines near parking areas, scratch off the time you've paid for, and display them on your dashboard. If you plan to drive into or out of the city, take time to study your route, especially on the GRA (Grande Raccordo Anulare, a beltway that encircles Rome and funnels traffic into the city, not always successfully). The main access routes to Rome from the north are the A1 autostrada from Florence and Milan and the Aurelia highway (SS 1) from Genoa. The principal route to or from points south, such as Naples, is the A2 autostrada.

EMBASSIES

➤ CANADA: (✉ Via Zara 30, ☎ 06/445981).
➤ UNITED KINGDOM: (✉ Via XX [pronounced "Venti"] Settembre 80a, ☎ 06/48903708).
➤ UNITED STATES: (✉ Via Veneto 121, ☎ 06/46741).

EMERGENCIES

Pharmacies are open 8:30–1 and 4–8. Some stay open all night, and all open Sunday on a rotation system; a listing of the neighborhood pharmacies open all night is posted at each pharmacy. The number below gives an automated list of three open pharmacies closest to the telephone from which you call. When calling for ambulance service, say *Pronto Soccorso* ("emergency room") and be prepared to give your address.
➤ EMERGENCY SERVICES: **Ambulance** (☎ 1188 or 06/5510). **Police** (☎ 113).
➤ HOSPITALS: **Salvator Mundi Hospital** (☎ 06/588961, WEB www.smih.pcn.net). **Rome American Hospital** (☎ 06/22551, WEB www.rah.it).
➤ 24-HOUR PHARMACIES: (☎ 1100).

ENGLISH-LANGUAGE MEDIA

➤ BOOKSTORES: **Anglo-American Bookstore** (✉ Via della Vite 102, ☎ 06/6795222, WEB www.aab.it). **Corner Bookstore** (✉ Via del Moro 48, Trastevere, ☎ 06/5836942). **Economy Book and Video Center** (✉ Via Torino 136, ☎ 06/4746877, WEB www.booksitaly.com). **Feltrinelli International** (✉ Via Emanuele Orlando 84, ☎ 06/4827878). **Open Door Bookshop** (Secondhand books, ✉ Via Lungaretta 25, ☎ 06/5896478).

METRO TRAVEL

The Metro (subway) is a fast and easy way to get around, but it doesn't serve many of the areas you'll probably want to visit, particularly Old Rome. It opens at 5:30 AM, and the last train leaves each terminal at 11:30 PM. Metro A runs from the eastern part of the city to Termini station and past Piazza di Spagna and Piazzale Flaminio to Ottaviano-S. Pietro, near St. Peter's and the Vatican museums. Metro B serves Termini, the Colosseum, and Tiburtina station (where the FM1 Fiumicino Airport train stops).

TAXIS

Taxis wait at stands and, for a small extra charge, can also be called by telephone. They're very difficult to hail, but you can try to flag down taxis whose roof lights are illuminated. The meter starts at 4,500 lire/€2.65; there are extra charges for night service (5,000 lire/€2.50 extra from 10 PM to 7 AM) and on Sunday and holidays, as well as for each piece of baggage. Use the yellow or the newer white cabs only, and be very sure to check the meter. To call a cab, dial one of the numbers listed below; the operator will give you a medallion number and arrival time.
➤ TAXI COMPANIES: (☎ 06/3570, 06/5551, 06/4994, or 06/88177).

TOURS

Most operators offer half-day excursions to Tivoli to see the Villa d'Este's fountains and gardens; Appian Line and CIT run half-day tours to Tivoli that also include Hadrian's Villa and its impressive ancient ruins. Operators also offer all-day excursions to Assisi, to Pompeii and/or Capri, and to Florence. For do-it-yourself excursions to Ostia Antica and other destinations, pick up information at the APT information offices. American Express, Appian Line, ATAC, and CIT all offer orientation tours of Rome.

➤ Fees and Schedules: **American Express** (✉ Piazza di Spagna 38, ☎ 06/67641). **Appian Line** (✉ P. Esquilino 6, ☎ 06/487861, WEB www.appianline.it). **ATAC** (✉ Information booth, Termini Station). **CIT** (✉ Piazza della Repubblica 65, ☎ 06/4620311, WEB www.citonline.it).

WALKING TOURS

Enjoy Rome offers a variety of walking and bicycling tours in English, including a nighttime tour of Old Rome. Scala Reale also has English-language tours. For more information contact city tourist offices.

➤ Fees and Schedules: **Enjoy Rome** (✉ Via Varese 39, ☎ 06/4451843, WEB www.enjoyrome.com). **Scala Reale** (✉ Via dell'Olmata 30, 00184 Rome, ☎ 06/4745673; 800/732–2863 ext. 4052 in the U.S., WEB www.scalareale.org).

TRAIN TRAVEL

Termini Station is Rome's main train terminal, although the Tiburtina, Ostiense, and Trastevere stations serve some long-distance trains, many commuter trains, and the FM1 line to Fiumicino Airport. For train information call the toll-free number below, or try the English-speaking personnel at the information office in Termini, or at any travel agency. Tickets and seats can be reserved and purchased at travel agencies bearing the FS (Ferrovie dello Stato) emblem. Tickets are sold up to two months in advance. Short-distance tickets are also sold at tobacconists and ticket machines in the stations.

➤ Train Information: (☎ 848/888088).

TRANSPORTATION AROUND ROME

Rome's integrated Metrebus transportation system includes buses and trams (ATAC), Metro and suburban trains and buses (COTRAL), and some other suburban trains (FS) run by the state railways. A ticket valid for 75 minutes on any combination of buses and trams and one admission to the Metro costs 1,500 lire/€.75 (time-stamp your ticket when boarding the first vehicle; you're supposed to stamp it again if you board another vehicle just before the ticket runs out, but few do). Tickets are sold at tobacconists, newsstands, some coffee bars, automated ticket machines in Metro stations, some bus stops, and at ATAC and COTRAL ticket booths. A BIG tourist ticket, valid for one day on all public transport, costs 6,000 lire/€3.10. A weekly ticket (Settimanale, also known as CIS) costs 24,000 lire/€12.40 and can be purchased only at ATAC and Metro booths.

TRAVEL AGENCIES

➤ Local Agents: **American Express** (✉ Piazza di Spagna 38, ☎ 06/67641). **CIT** (☞ *above*). **CTS** (youth and budget travel, discount fares; ✉ Via Genova 16, ☎ 06/4620431, WEB www.cts.it).

VISITOR INFORMATION

➤ Tourist Information: **APT** (Rome Provincial Tourist Agency, main office; ✉ Via Parigi 5, 00185, ☎ 06/48899253; Termini Station, ☎ 06/4871270; Fiumicino Airport, ☎ 06/65956074). **City tourist information booths** (✉ Largo Goldoni, corner of Via Condotti; Via del Corso in the Spanish Steps area; Via dei Fori Imperiali, opposite the entrance to the Roman Forum; Via Nazionale, at Palazzo delle Esposizioni; Piazza Cinque Lune, off the north end of Piazza Navona; Piazza Sonnino, in Trastevere; WEB www.romaturismo.it).

FLORENCE

The birthplace of the Renaissance and one of Europe's preeminent treasures, Florence draws visitors from all over the world. Lining the narrow streets of the historic center are 15th-century palazzi whose plain and sober facades often give way to delightful courtyards. The classical dignity of the High Renaissance and the exuberant invention of the Baroque are mostly absent in Florentine buildings; here, the typical exterior gives nothing away of the treasures contained within.

Exploring Florence

Numbers in the margin correspond to points of interest on the Florence map.

Founded by Julius Caesar, Florence was built in the familiar grid pattern common to all Roman colonies. Except for the major monuments, which are appropriately imposing, the buildings are low and unpretentious and the streets are narrow. At times Florence can be a nightmare of mass tourism. Plan, if you can, to visit the city in late fall, early spring, or even in winter to avoid the crowds. A special museum ticket valid for three days on the Michelangelo Trail includes the Galleria dell'Accademia, Cappelle Medicee, and the Museo del Bargello; it costs 25,000 lire/€12.90.

Piazza del Duomo and Piazza della Signoria

The area between Piazza del Duomo and Piazza della Signoria comprises the core of the centro storico. Piazza del Duomo has been the center of Florence's religious life for centuries; work began on the Duomo in 1296, and the structure that sprang from the site is testament to religious fervor and a wealthy populace. Via Calzaiouli links this piazza to Piazza della Signoria, the center of Florentine government since the end of the 13th century. The piazza is lined with Renaissance sculpture (some originals, some copies). The Galleria degli Uffizi, next to Palazzo Vecchio, houses one of the most important collections of Renaissance painting in the world.

★ 3 **Battistero** (Baptistery). In front of the Duomo is the octagonal baptistery, one of the city's oldest (modern excavations suggest its foundations date from the 4th to 5th and the 8th to 9th centuries) and most beloved buildings. The interior dome mosaics are famous but cannot outshine the building's renowned gilded bronze east doors (facing the Duomo), the work of Lorenzo Ghiberti (1378–1455). The ones you see at the Baptistery, however, are copies; the originals are preserved in the Museo dell'Opera del Duomo. ⊠ *Piazza del Duomo,* ☎ *055/2302885,* WEB *www.operaduomo.firenze.it.* ⊙ *Mon.–Sat. 12:30–6:30, Sun. 8:30–1:30.*

2 **Campanile** (Bell tower). This early 14th-century bell tower, designed by Giotto (1266–1337), is richly decorated with colored marble and sculpture reproductions; the originals are in the Museo dell'Opera del Duomo. The 414-step climb to the top is less strenuous than that to the cupola on the Duomo. ⊠ *Piazza del Duomo,* ☎ *055/2302885,* WEB *www.operaduomo.firenze.it.* ⊙ *Apr.–Oct., daily 9–7:30; Nov.–Mar., daily 9–6:50.*

★ 1 **Duomo.** The Cattedrale di Santa Maria del Fiore is dominated by a cupola representing a landmark in the history of architecture. Work began on the cathedral itself in 1296 under the supervision of master sculptor and architect Arnolfo di Cambio, and its construction took 140 years to complete. Gothic architecture predominates; the facade was added in the 1870s but is based on Tuscan Gothic models. Inside, the church is cool and austere, a fine example of the architecture of the period. Take a good look at the frescoes of equestrian figures on the left wall of the nave: the one on the right is by Paolo Uccello (1397–1475), the one on the left by Andrea del Castagno (circa 1419–57). The dome frescoes by Vasari

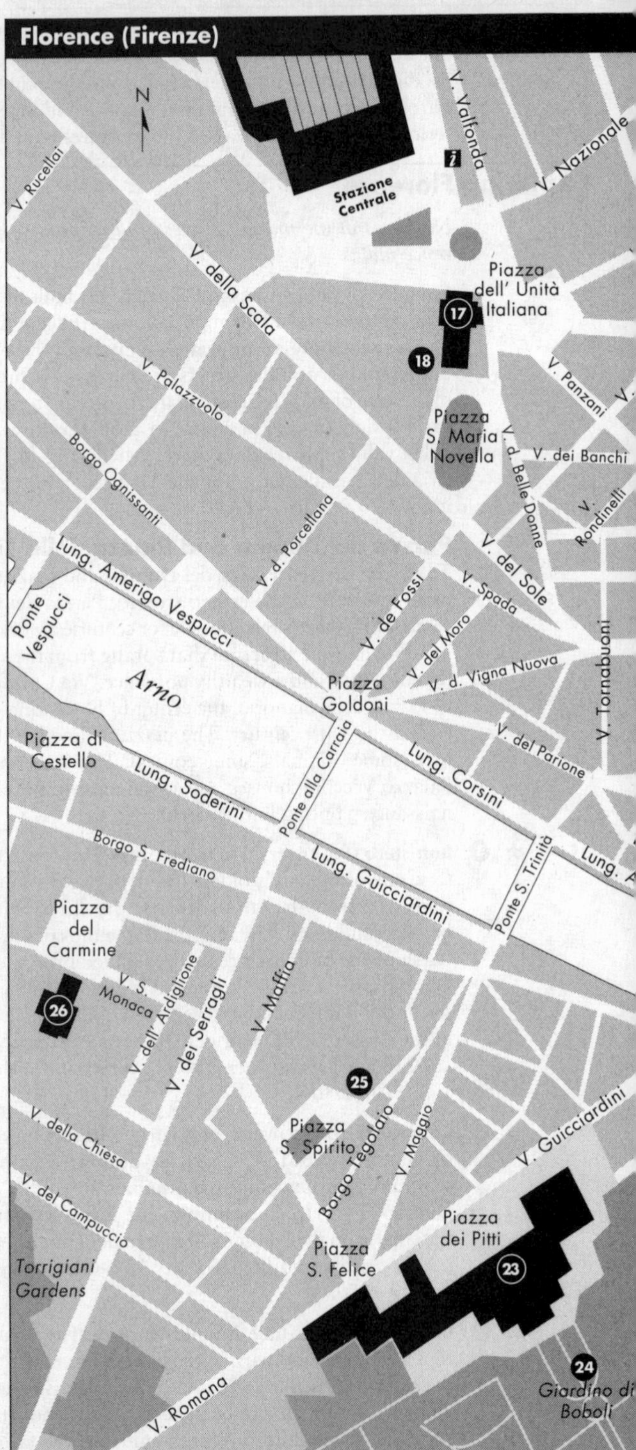

Florence (Firenze)
N
V. Rucellai
Stazione Centrale
V. Valfonda
V. Nazionale
V. della Scala
Piazza dell' Unità Italiana
17
18
V. Panzani
V. Palazzuolo
Piazza S. Maria Novella
V. d. Belle Donne
V. dei Banchi
V. Rondinelli
Borgo Ognissanti
V. d. Porcellana
V. del Sole
V. Spada
V. de Fossi
Lung. Amerigo Vespucci
Ponte Vespucci
V. del Moro
V. d. Vigna Nuova
V. Tornabuoni
Arno
Piazza Goldoni
V. del Parione
Piazza di Cestello
Lung. Soderini
Ponte alla Carraia
Lung. Corsini
Borgo S. Frediano
Lung. Guicciardini
Ponte S. Trinità
Piazza del Carmine
V. S. Monaca
26
V. dell' Ardiglione
V. dei Serragli
V. Maffia
25
V. della Chiesa
Piazza S. Spirito
Borgo Tegolaio
V. Maggio
V. Guicciardini
V. del Campuccio
Piazza dei Pitti
Torrigiani Gardens
Piazza S. Felice
23
24
Giardino di Boboli
V. Romana

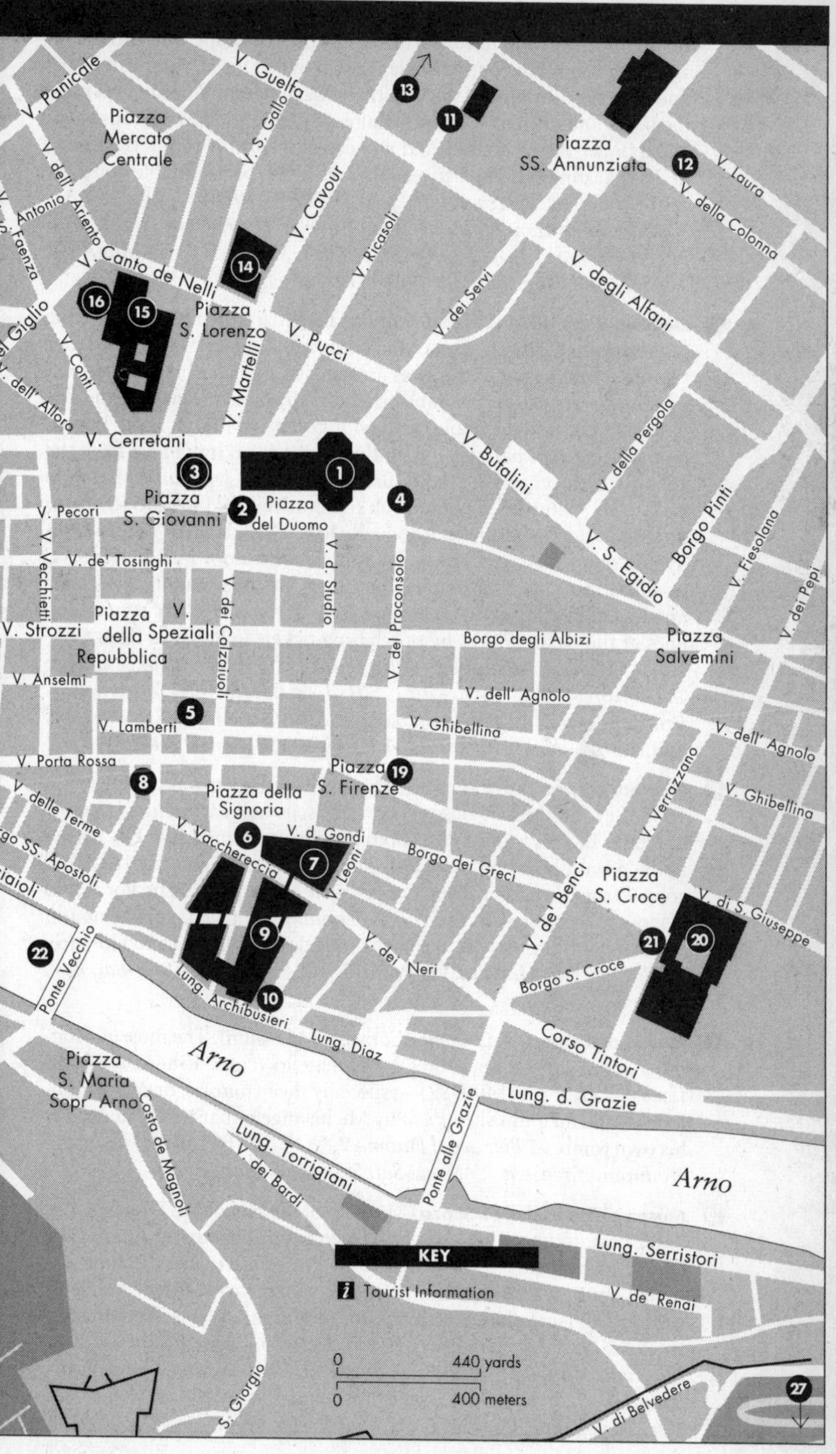
V. Panicale
Piazza Mercato Centrale
V. Guelfa
V. S. Gallo
V. Cavour
V. Ricasoli
Piazza SS. Annunziata
V. Laura
V. della Colonna
V. degli Alfani
V. dei Servi
V. dell' Ariento
V. S. Antonio
V. Faenza
V. Canto de Nelli
Piazza S. Lorenzo
V. del Giglio
V. Conti
V. dell' Alloro
V. Martelli
V. Pucci
V. Bufalini
V. della Pergola
V. Cerretani
Piazza S. Giovanni
Piazza del Duomo
V. Pecori
V. de' Tosinghi
V. Vecchietti
V. d. Studio
V. del Proconsolo
V. S. Egidio
Borgo Pinti
V. Fiesolana
V. dei Pepi
V. Strozzi
Piazza della Repubblica
V. Speziali
V. dei Calzaiuoli
Borgo degli Albizi
Piazza Salvemini
V. Anselmi
V. dell' Agnolo
V. Lamberti
V. Ghibellina
V. Porta Rossa
Piazza S. Firenze
V. Verrazzano
V. delle Terme
Piazza della Signoria
V. d. Gondi
Borgo SS. Apostoli
V. Vacchereccia
V. Leoni
Borgo dei Greci
V. de' Benci
Piazza S. Croce
V. di S. Giuseppe
V. dei Neri
Ponte Vecchio
Borgo S. Croce
Lung. Archibusieri
Lung. Diaz
Corso Tintori
Arno
Piazza S. Maria Sopr' Arno
Costa de Magnoli
Lung. Torrigiani
V. dei Bardi
Ponte alle Grazie
Lung. d. Grazie
Arno
Lung. Serristori
KEY
Tourist Information
V. de' Renai
0 440 yards
0 400 meters
S. Giorgio
V. di Belvedere

take second place to the dome itself, Brunelleschi's (1377–1446) greatest architectural and technical achievement. The dome was also the inspiration behind the one Michelangelo designed for St. Peter's in Rome and even for the dome of the Capitol in Washington. You can visit early medieval and ancient Roman remains of previous constructions excavated under the cathedral. And you can climb to the top of the dome, 463 exhausting steps up between the two layers of the double dome for a fine view. ✉ *Piazza del Duomo,* ☎ *055/2302885,* WEB *www.operaduomo.firenze.it.* ⊙ *Mon.–Wed., Fri.–Sat. 10–5, Thurs. and 1st Sat. of every month 10–3:20, other Sat. 8:30–5, Sun. 1–5. Crypt Mon.–Sat. 10–5. Dome Mon.–Sat. 8:30–6:20 (1st Sat. of month 8:30–3:20).*

★ 9 **Galleria degli Uffizi** (Uffizi Gallery). The Uffizi was built to house the administrative offices of the Medici, onetime rulers of the city. Later their fabulous art collection was arranged in a gallery on the top floor, which was opened to the public in the 17th century—making this the world's first modern public gallery. It comprises Italy's most important collection of paintings, with the emphasis on Italian art from the 13th to 16th centuries. Make sure you see the *Ognissanti Madonna* by Giotto (1266–1337), and look for Botticelli's (1445–1510) *Birth of Venus* and *Primavera* in Rooms X–XIV, Michelangelo's *Holy Family* in Room XXV, and works by Raphael next door in Room XXVI. In addition to its art treasures, the gallery offers a magnificent close-up view of the Palazzo Vecchio tower from the coffee bar. Avoid long lines at the ticket booths by purchasing tickets in advance from Consorzio ITA. ✉ *Piazzale degli Uffizi 6,* ☎ *055/23885. Advance tickets:* ✉ *Consorzio ITA, Piazza Pitti 1, 50121,* ☎ *055/294883,* WEB *www.uffizi.firenze.it.* 🎫 *12,000 lire/€6.20.* ⊙ *Apr.–Oct., Tues.–Sat. 8:30–10, Sun. 8:30–6; Nov.–Mar., Tues.–Sat. 8:30–6:50, Sun. 8:30–7.*

8 **Mercato Nuovo** (New Market). This open-air loggia was completed in 1551. Beyond the slew of souvenir stands, its main attraction is a copy of Pietro Tacca's bronze *Porcellino* (though it means *Little Pig,* it's actually a wild boar) on the south side, dating from around 1612 and copied from an earlier Roman work now in the Uffizi. The Porcellino is Florence's equivalent of the Trevi Fountain: put a coin in his mouth, and if it lands properly, it means that one day you'll return to Florence. ✉ *Via Por San Maria at Via Porta Rossa.* ⊙ *Market Tues.–Sat. 8–7, Mon. 1–7.*

★ 4 **Museo dell'Opera del Duomo** (Cathedral Museum). The museum contains some superb sculptures by Donatello (circa 1386–1466) and Luca della Robbia (1400–82)—especially their *cantorie,* or singers' galleries—and an unfinished *Pietà* by Michelangelo that was intended for his own tomb. ✉ *Piazza del Duomo 9,* ☎ *055/2302885,* WEB *www.operaduomo.firenze.it.* ⊙ *Mon.–Sat. 9:30–6:30, Sun. 8–2.*

10 **Museo di Storia della Scienza** (Museum of the History of Science). You don't have to know a lot about science to appreciate the antique scientific instruments presented here in informative, eye-catching exhibits. From astrolabes and armillary spheres to some of Galileo's own instruments, the collection is one of Florence's lesser-known treasures. ✉ *Piazza dei Giudici 1,* ☎ *055/2398876,* WEB *www.imss.fi.it.* ⊙ *Museum: Mon.–Sat. 9:30–6:30, Sun. 8–2. Planetarium: Mon., Wed.–Sat. 9:30–5, Tues. 9:30–1; open 10–1 2nd Sun. of the month; closed Dec. 25–26, Jan. 1 and 6, Easter and Easter Mon.*

5 **Orsanmichele** (Garden of St. Michael). For centuries this was an odd combination of first-floor church and second-floor granary. Today it serves as a museum, and the statues in the niches on the exterior (many of which are now copies) constitute an anthology of the work of em-

inent Renaissance sculptors, including Donatello, Ghiberti, and Verrocchio (1435–88). The tabernacle inside is an extraordinary piece by Andrea Orcagna (1308–68). Many of the original statues can be seen in the Museo di Orsanmichele contained within. ✉ *Via dei Calzaiuoli; museum entrance at via Arte della Lana,* ☎ *055/284944.* ⏲ *Guided visits Mon.–Fri. at 9, 10, and 11; non-guided opening hrs Sat.–Sun. 9–1 and 4–6. Closed 1st and last Mon. of month.*

❼ **Palazzo Vecchio** (Old Palace). Also called Palazzo della Signoria, this massive, fortresslike city hall was begun in 1299 and was taken over, along with the rest of Florence, by the Medici. Inside, the impressive, frescoed salons and the *studiolo* (little study) of Francesco I are the main attractions. ✉ *Piazza della Signoria,* ☎ *055/2768465.* ⏲ *Mon.–Wed., Fri.–Sat. 9–7, Thurs., Sun. 9–2.*

❻ **Piazza della Signoria.** This is the heart of Florence and the city's largest square. In the pavement in the center of the square a plaque marks the spot where Savonarola, the reformist Dominican friar who urged Florentines to burn their pictures, books, musical instruments, and other worldly objects, was hanged and then burned at the stake as a heretic in 1498. The square, the Fontana di Nettuno (Neptune Fountain) by Ammanati (1511–92), and the surrounding cafés are popular gathering places for Florentines and for tourists who come to admire the Palazzo della Signoria, the copy of Michelangelo's *David* standing in front of it, and the sculptures in the 14th-century Loggia dei Lanzi.

San Marco, San Lorenzo, Santa Maria Novella, Santa Croce

San Marco is the old neighborhood of the Medici, and their imprint is still very much in evidence today. Visual reminders of their power can be seen in the Cappelle Medicee and in San Lorenzo, which was the church that the Medici viewed as their very own. This area is teeming with churches filled with great works of art, and two must-see museums. The Accademia is home to Michelangelo's David, arguably the most famous sculpture in the world, and the Bargello boasts a collection of Renaissance sculpture that is unparalleled.

★ ⓰ **Cappelle Medicee** (Medici Chapels). These extraordinary chapels, part of the church of San Lorenzo complex, contain the tombs of practically every member of the Medici family, which guided Florence's destiny from the 15th century to 1737. Cosimo I (1519–74), a Medici whose acumen made him the richest man in Europe, is buried in the crypt beneath the **Cappella dei Principi** (Chapel of the Princes), and Donatello's tomb is next to that of his patron, Cosimo il Vecchio (1389–1464). Upstairs is a dazzling array of colored marble panels. Michelangelo's **Sagrestia Nuova** (New Sacristy) tombs of Giuliano and Lorenzo de' Medici are adorned with the justly famed sculptures of *Dawn* and *Dusk, Night* and *Day.* ✉ *Piazza di Madonna degli Aldobrandini,* ☎ *Reservations: 055/294 883,* WEB *www.sanlorenzo.com.* 💳 *11,000 lire/€5.70* ⏲ *Daily 8:15–5; closed 1st, 3rd, and 5th Mon. and 2nd and 4th Sun. of month.*

★ ⓫ **Galleria dell'Accademia** (Accademia Gallery). Michelangelo's *David* is a tour de force of artistic conception and technical ability, for he was using a piece of stone that had already been worked on by a lesser sculptor. Take time to see the forceful *Slaves,* also by Michelangelo; their rough-hewn, unfinished surfaces contrast dramatically with the highly polished, meticulously carved *David.* Michelangelo left the *Slaves* "unfinished," it is often claimed, to accentuate the figures' struggle to escape the bondage of stone. Actually, he simply abandoned them because his patron changed his mind about the tomb monument for which they were planned. Try to be first in line at opening time or go shortly before closing time so you can get the full impact without having to fight your way through the crowds. ✉ *Via Ricasoli 60,* ☎ *Reservations: 055/ 294 883; Galleria: 055/2388609,* WEB *www.mega.it.* 💳 *15,000 lire/€7.75* ⏲ *Apr.–Oct., Tues.–Sat. 8:30–10, Sun. 8:30–6; Nov.–Mar., Tues.–Sat. 8:30–6:50, Sun. 8:30–7.*

12 **Museo Archeologico** (Archaeological Museum). Fine Etruscan and Roman antiquities and a pretty garden are the draw here. ✉ *Via della Colonna 38,* ☎ *055/23575,* WEB *www.mega.it.* ⏲ *Mon. 2–7, Tues., Thurs. 8:30–7, Wed., Fri.–Sun. 8:30–2.*

21 **Museo dell'Opera di Santa Croce e Cappella dei Pazzi** (Museum of Santa Croce and Pazzi Chapel). From the cloister of the convent adjacent to Santa Croce you can visit the small museum and see what remains of the Cimbaue crucifix that was irreparably damaged by a flood in 1966, when water rose to 16 ft in parts of the church. The **Cappella dei Pazzi** in the cloister is an architectural gem by Brunelleschi. The interior is a lesson in spatial equilibrium and harmony. ✉ *Piazza Santa Croce,* ☎ *055/244619.* ⏲ *Mar.–Oct., Thurs.–Tues. 10–7; Nov.–Feb., Thurs.–Tues. 10–6.*

13 **Museo di San Marco.** A former Dominican convent houses this museum, which contains many works by Fra Angelico (1400–55). Within the same walls where the unfortunate Savonarola, the reformist friar, later contemplated the sins of the Florentines, Fra Angelico went humbly about his work, decorating many of the otherwise austere cells and corridors with brilliantly colored frescoes on religious subjects. Look for his masterpiece, the *Annunciation.* Together with many of his paintings arranged on the ground floor, just off the little cloister, they form a fascinating collection. ✉ *Piazza San Marco 1,* ☎ *055/2388608.* ⏲ *Mon.–Fri. 8:30–1:50, Sat. 8:30–6:50, Sun. 8:30–7. Closed 2nd and 4th Mon. of month.*

18 **Museo di Santa Maria Novella.** Adjacent to the church, this museum is worth a visit for its serene atmosphere and the faded Paolo Uccello frescoes from Genesis, as well as the **Cappellone degli Spagnoli** (Spanish Chapel), with frescoes by Andrea di Buonaiuto. ✉ *Piazza Santa Maria Novella 19,* ☎ *055/282187.* ⏲ *Wed.–Mon. 9–2.*

★ 19 **Museo Nazionale del Bargello.** This grim, fortresslike palace served in medieval times as a residence of Florence's chief magistrate and later as a prison. It is now a treasure trove of Italian Renaissance sculpture. In this historic setting you can see masterpieces by Donatello, Verrocchio, Michelangelo, and other major sculptors amid an eclectic array of arms and ceramics. For Renaissance enthusiasts this museum is on a par with the Uffizi. ✉ *Via del Proconsolo 4,* ☎ *055/2388606,* WEB *www.arca.net/db/musei/bargello.htm.* ⏲ *Daily 8:30–1:50. Closed 2nd and 4th Mon. of month and 1st, 3rd, and 5th Sun. of month.*

14 **Palazzo Medici-Riccardi.** Few tourists know about Benozzo Gozzoli's (1420–97) glorious frescoes in the tiny second-floor chapel of this palace, built in 1444 for Cosimo de' Medici (Il Vecchio, 1389–1464). Glimmering with gold, they represent the journey of the Magi as a spectacular cavalcade with cameo portraits of various Medici and the artist himself. ✉ *Via Cavour 1,* ☎ *055/2760340.* ⏲ *Thurs.–Tues. 9–7.*

15 **San Lorenzo.** The facade of this church was never finished, but the Brunelleschi interior is elegantly austere. Stand in the middle of the nave at the entrance, on the line that stretches to the high altar, and you'll see what Brunelleschi achieved with the grid of inlaid marble in the pavement. Every architectural element in the church is placed to create a dramatic effect of single-point perspective. The **Sagrestia Vecchia**

(Old Sacristy), decorated with stuccoes by Donatello, is attributed to Brunelleschi. ✉ *Piazza San Lorenzo,* ☎ *055/216634.* ⏲ *Church: Mon.–Sat. 7–12 and 3:30–5:30, Sun. 3:30–5. Old Sacristy: Mon.–Sat. 8–noon and 3:30–5:30, Sun. 3:30–5:30. Closed Dec. and Jan.*

★ 20 **Santa Croce.** The mighty church of Santa Croce was begun in 1294 and has become a pantheon for Florentine greats; monumental tombs of Michelangelo, Galileo (1564–1642), Machiavelli (1469–1527), and other Renaissance luminaries line the walls. Inside are two chapels frescoed by Giotto and another painted by Taddeo Gaddi (1300–66), as well as an *Annunciation* and crucifix by Donatello. But it is the scale of this grandiose church that proclaims the power and ambition of medieval Florence. ✉ *Piazza Santa Croce 16,* ☎ *055/244619.* ⏲ *Nov.–Mar., Mon.–Sat. 9:30–12:15 and 3–5:30, Sun. 3–5:30; Apr.–Oct., Mon.–Sat. 9:30–5:30 and Sun. 3–5:30.*

17 **Santa Maria Novella.** A Tuscan interpretation of the Gothic style, this handsome church should be seen from the opposite end of Piazza Santa Maria Novella for the best view of its facade. Inside are some famous paintings, especially Masaccio's (1401–28) *Trinity,* a Giotto crucifix in the sacristy, and Ghirlandaio's frescoes in the **Capella Maggiore** (Main Chapel). ✉ *Piazza Santa Maria Novella,* ☎ *055/210113.* ⏲ *Mon.–Sat. 7–noon and 3–6, Sun. 3–5.*

The Oltrarno

The Oltrarno, which means "beyond the Arno," is on the south side of the Arno. It's a neighborhood filled with artisans' workshops, and in that respect, it has changed little since the Renaissance. The gargantuan Palazzo Pitti stands as a sweeping reminder of the power of the Medici family, and there some lovely Renaissance churches, terrific restaurants, and first-rate shoe stores—all reason enough to cross over and explore.

24 **Giardini Boboli** (Boboli Gardens). The main entrance to this garden on a landscaped hillside is in the right wing of Palazzo Pitti. The garden was laid out in 1549 for Cosimo I's wife, Eleanora da Toledo, who made the Palazzo her home, and was further developed by later Medici dukes. ✉ *Enter through Palazzo Pitti,* ☎ *055/2651816.* ⏲ *Apr.–Oct., daily 8:15–5:30; Nov.–Mar., daily 8:15–4:30. Closed 1st and last Mon. of each month.*

23 **Palazzo Pitti.** This enormous palace is a 16th-century extravaganza the Medici acquired from the Pitti family after the latter had gone deeply into debt to build the central portion. The Medici enlarged the building, extending its facade along the immense piazza. Solid and severe, it looks like a Roman aqueduct turned into a palace. The palace houses several museums: the **Museo degli Argenti** (Silver Museum) displays the fabulous Medici collection of objects in silver and gold; another has the collections of the **Galleria d'Arte Moderna** (Gallery of Modern Art). The most famous museum, though, is the **Galleria Palatina** (Palatine Gallery), with an extraordinary collection of paintings, many hung frame-to-frame in a clear case of artistic overkill. Some are high up in dark corners, so try to go on a bright day. ✉ *Piazza Pitti,* ☎ *055/210323,* WEB *www.thais.it.* ⏲ *Museo degli Argenti Nov.–Mar., daily 8:30–1:50. Closed 2nd and 4th Sun. and 1st, 3rd, and 5th Mon. of month. Galleria Palatina Nov.–Mar., Tues.–Sat. 8:30–6:50, Sun. 8:30–8; Apr.–Oct., Tues.–Sat. 8:30 AM–10 PM, Sun. 8:30–7.*

★ 22 **Ponte Vecchio** (Old Bridge). Florence's oldest bridge appears to be just another street lined with goldsmiths' shops until you get to the middle and catch a glimpse of the Arno below. Spared during World War II by the retreating Germans (who blew up every other bridge in the city), it also survived the 1966 flood. It leads into the **Oltrarno,** where the atmosphere of working-class Florence is preserved amid fascinating artisans' workshops. ✉ *East of Ponte Santa Trinita and west of Ponte alle Grazie.*

27 **San Miniato al Monte.** One of Florence's oldest churches, this charming green-and-white marble Romanesque edifice is full of artistic riches, among them the gorgeous Renaissance chapel where a Portuguese cardinal was laid to rest in 1459 under a ceiling by Luca della Robbia. ✉ *Viale Michelangelo, or take stairs from Piazzale Michelangelo,* ☏ *055/2342731.* ⏲ *Mon.–Sat. 8–12:30 and 2–6, Sun. 8–6.*

26 **Santa Maria del Carmine.** The church is of little architectural interest but of immense significance in the history of Renaissance art. It contains the celebrated frescoes painted by Masaccio in the **Cappella Brancacci.** The chapel was a classroom for such artistic giants as Botticelli, Leonardo da Vinci (1452–1519), Michelangelo, and Raphael, since they all came to study Masaccio's realistic use of light and perspective and his creation of space and depth. ✉ *Piazza del Carmine,* ☏ *055/2382195.* ⏲ *Mon., Wed.–Sat. 10–5, Sun. 1–5.*

25 **Santo Spirito.** Its plain, unfinished facade is less than impressive, but this church is important because it is one of Brunelleschi's finest architectural creations. It contains some superb paintings, including a *Madonna* by Filippo Lippi. Santo Spirito is the hub of a colorful, trendy neighborhood of artisans and intellectuals. An outdoor market enlivens the square every morning except Sunday; in the afternoon, pigeons, pet owners, and pensioners take over. ✉ *Piazza Santo Spirito,* ☏ *055/210030.* ⏲ *Church: Thurs.–Tues. 9–noon and 4–6, Wed. 9–12. Cenacolo: Tues.–Sun. 10–2.*

Dining

Mealtimes in Florence are from 12:30 to 2:30 and 7:30 to 9 or later. Reservations are always advisable; to find a table at inexpensive places, get there early.

$$$$ ★ ✕ **Cibrèo.** The food at this classic Florentine trattoria is fantastic, from the first bite of seamless, creamy *crostini di fegatini* (savory Tuscan chicken liver spread on grilled bread) to the last bite of one of the melt-in-your-mouth-good desserts. If you thought you'd never try tripe, let alone like it, this is the place to lay any doubts to rest: the cold tripe salad with parsley and garlic is an epiphany. ✉ *Via dei Macci 118/r,* ☏ *055/2341100. Reservations essential. AE, DC, MC, V. Closed Sun.–Mon., July 25–Sept. 5, and Dec. 31–Jan. 7.*

$$$$ ✕ **Enoteca Pinchiorri.** A sumptuous Renaissance palace with high, frescoed ceilings and bouquets in silver vases provides the setting for this restaurant, one of the most expensive in Italy. Some consider it one of the best, and others consider it an expensive, non-Italian ripoff. Prices are high and portions are small. A variety of fish, game, and meat dishes are always on the menu, along with pasta combinations such as the *ignudi*—ricotta and cheese dumplings with a lobster and coxcomb fricassee. ✉ *Via Ghibellina 87,* ☏ *055/242777. Reservations essential. AE, MC, V. Closed Sun. and Aug. No lunch Mon.*

$$$ ✕ **Alle Murate.** This sophisticated restaurant features creative versions of classic Tuscan dishes. The main dining room has a rich, uncluttered look, with warm wood floors and paneling and soft lights. In a smaller adjacent room called the *vineria* (wine bar or bistro), you get the same splendid service and substantially reduced prices. Be warned that there's no middle ground with the wine list—only a smattering of inexpensive offerings before it soars to exalted heights. ✉ *Via Ghibellina 52/r,* ☏ *055/240618. AE, DC, MC, V. Closed Mon. No lunch.*

$$$ ★ ✕ **Beccofino.** Written on the menu is "*esercizi di cucina italiana*" (Italian cooking exercises), which is a disarmingly modest way to alert the diner that something wonderfully different is going on here. The interior has a pale-wood serpentine bar separating the ochre-walled wine bar from the green-walled restaurant. Chef Francesco Berardinelli has paid some dues in the United States, and it shows in the inventiveness of his food, which ends up tasting wholly and wonderfully Italian. The wine bar offers a shorter and less expensive menu; in the summer, you can enjoy this food on an outdoor terrace facing the Arno. ✉ *Piazza degli Scarlatti 1/r (Lungarno Guicciardini),* ☎ *055/290076. Reservations essential. MC, V. Closed Mon. Nov.–Mar.*

$$–$$$ ★ ✕ **La Giostra.** La Giostra, which means "carousel" in Italian, is owned and run by Prince Dimitri Kunz d'Asburgo Lorena. It has a clubby feel, with white walls and tablecloths and dim lighting accented with a few tiny blue lights twinkling on the ceiling. Try the unusually good pastas, maybe the *carbonara di tartufo,* decadently rich spaghetti with eggs and white truffles. Leave room for dessert: this might be the only show in town with a sublime tiramisu and a wonderfully gooey Sacher torte. ✉ *Borgo Pinti 12/r,* ☎ *055/241341. AE, DC, MC, V.*

$$ ✕ **Pallottino.** With its tile floor, photograph-filled walls, and wooden tables, Pallottino is the quintessential Tuscan trattoria, with such hearty, heartwarming classics as *pappa al pomodoro* (tomato and bread soup) and *peposo alla toscana* (beef stew laced with black pepper). The lunch special—*primo and secondo* (first and second courses)—could be, at 10,000 lire/€5, the best bargain in town. ✉ *Via Isola delle Stinche 1/r,* ☎ *055/289573. AE, DC, MC, V (no credit cards at lunch). Closed Mon. and Aug. 1–20.*

$–$$ ✕ **Baldovino.** This lively, brightly hued spot down the street from the church of Santa Croce is the brainchild of David and Catherine Gardner, expat Scots. From its humble beginnings as a pizzeria, it has evolved into something more. Happily, pizza is still on the menu, but now it shares billing with sophisticated primi and secondi. The menu changes monthly and offers such treats as *filetto di manzo alla Bernaise* (filet mignon with a light Béarnaise sauce). ✉ *Via San Giuseppe 22/r,* ☎ *055/241773. MC, V. Closed Mon. Nov.–Mar.*

$–$$ ✕ **Il Latini.** This may be the noisiest, most crowded trattoria in Florence. It's also a fun place to go precisely because it is so lively. Four big rooms are lined with bottles of wine and prints, and somehow they manage to feel cozy—perhaps because there are always a lot of happy Florentines tucking into their *salsicce e fagioli* (sausage and beans) or, in season, *agnello fritto* (fried lamb). Portions are big—you'll think you won't be able to eat it all, but you will. Reservations are advised. ✉ *Via dei Palchetti 6/r,* ☎ *055/210916. AE, DC, MC, V. Closed Mon. and 15 days over Christmas.*

$ ✕ **La Casalinga.** "Casalinga" means housewife, and this place has all the charm of a 1950s kitchen with Tuscan comfort food to match. There's not much interior decor beyond mediocre paintings cluttering the semi-paneled walls. Tables are set close together and the place is usually jammed, and with good reason. The menu is long, portions are plentiful, and service is prompt and friendly. If you eat ribollita anywhere in Florence, eat it here—the setting couldn't be more authentic. ✉ *Via Michelozzi 9/r,* ☎ *055/218624. AE, DC, MC, V. Closed Sun., 1 wk at Christmas, 3 wks in Aug. No lunch in July.*

Lodging

Hotel rooms are at a premium in Florence for most of the year. Reserve well in advance. If you arrive without a reservation, the **Consorzio ITA** office in the train station (✉ Stazione Centrale di Santa Maria

Novella), open 8:20 AM–9 PM, can help you, but there may be a long line (take a number and wait). Now that much traffic is banned in the centro storico, many central hotel rooms are quieter. Local traffic and motorcycles can still be bothersome, however, so check the decibel level before you settle in. From November through March, ask for special low winter rates.

$$$$ ★ **Brunelleschi.** Architects united a Byzantine tower, a medieval church, and a later building in a stunning structure in the very heart of the centro storico to make this unique hotel. Medieval stone walls and brick arches contrast pleasantly with the plush, contemporary decor. The comfortable, soundproof rooms are done in coordinated patterns and soft colors. ✉ *Piazza Sant'Elisabetta 3/r (off Via dei Calzaiuoli), 50122,* ☎ *055/27370,* FAX *055/219653,* WEB *www.hotelbrunelleschi.it. 96 rooms, 7 junior suites. Restaurant, bar. AE, DC, MC, V.*

$$$$ ★ **Excelsior.** Florentine hotels do not get much more exquisite or expensive than this. Rooms are decorated in Empire style but still feel up-to-date. High ceilings, dramatic views of the Arno, patterned rugs, and tasteful prints lend the rooms a sense of extravagant well-being. Public rooms have stained glass and acres of Oriental carpets strewn over marble floors. The opulence of 19th-century Florentine antiques is set off by charming old prints of the city and long mirrors. ✉ *Piazza Ognissanti 3, 50123,* ☎ *055/264201,* FAX *055/210278,* WEB *www.luxurycollection.com. 168 rooms. Restaurant. AE, DC, MC, V.*

$$$$ **Grand.** This Florentine classic provides all the luxuries. Rooms are decorated in either Renaissance or Empire style; the former have deep, richly hued damask brocades and canopied beds, the latter a lovely profusion of crisp prints and patterned fabric offsetting white walls. The overall effect is sumptuous, as is the view of either the Arno or a small courtyard lined with potted orange trees. Avoid the piano bar, which is high-priced karaoke. ✉ *Piazza Ognissanti 1, 50123,* ☎ *055/288781,* FAX *055/217400,* WEB *www.luxurycollection.com. 107 rooms. Restaurant, bar. AE, DC, MC, V.*

$$$$ **Hotel Savoy.** From the outside, it looks very much like the turn-of-the-19th-century building that it is. But step inside where sleek minimalism prevails at this hotel in the heart of the centro storico. Sitting rooms have a funky edge with their cream-colored walls dotted with contemporary prints and photographs. Many of the rooms, decorated in muted colors, with clean lines and soaring ceilings, overlook Piazza Repubblica and have views of the Duomo's cupola. ✉ *Piazza della Repubblica 7, 50123,* ☎ *055/27351,* FAX *055/2735888,* WEB *www.rfhotels.com. 98 rooms, 9 suites. Restaurant, bar. AE, DC, MC, V.*

$$$$ **Lungarno.** Rooms and suites in this hotel across the Arno from the Palazzo Vecchio and the Duomo have private terraces jutting out over the river. The chic decor approximates a breezily elegant home, with lots of crisp white fabrics trimmed in blue. Four suites in a 13th-century tower preserve exposed stone walls and old archways. More than 100 paintings and drawings—from Picassos to Cocteaus—hang in hallways and bedrooms. ✉ *Borgo San Jacopo 14, 50125,* ☎ *055/27261,* FAX *055/268437,* WEB *www.lungarnohotels.com. 60 rooms, 11 suites. Restaurant, bar. AE, DC, MC, V.*

$$$ ★ **Hermitage.** This place is centrally located and, given the price, a great bargain. All rooms are hung with lively wallpaper; some have views of the Palazzo Vecchio and others of the Arno. The rooftop terrace, where you can breakfast or enjoy a cocktail, is decked with flowers. The lobby feels like a friendly living room, with warm yellow walls. ✉ *Vicolo Marzio 1 (Piazza del Pesce, Ponte Vecchio), 50122,* ☎ *055/287216,* FAX *055/212208,* WEB *www.hermitagehotel.com. 27 rooms, 1 suite. MC, V.*

$$$ ★ Loggiato dei Serviti. Occupying a 16th-century former monastery, this attractively spare Renaissance building was originally a refuge for traveling priests. Vaulted ceilings, tasteful furnishings (some antique), canopied beds, and rich fabrics give you the feel of Old Florence while you enjoy modern creature comforts. ✉ *Piazza Santissima Annunziata 3, 50122,* ☎ *055/289592,* FAX *055/289595,* WEB *www.venere.it. 29 rooms. AE, DC, MC, V.*

$$$ ★ Monna Lisa. Housed in a 15th-century palazzo, parts of which date from the 13th century, this hotel retains some of its original wood coffered ceilings from the 1500s, as well as its original marble staircase. The rooms are on the small side, but they are tastefully decorated. The public rooms retain a 19th-century aura. ✉ *Borgo Pinti 27, 50121,* ☎ *055/2479751,* FAX *055/2479755,* WEB *www.monnalisa.it. 30 rooms. Bar. AE, DC, MC, V.*

$$$ Porta Faenza. A hospitable Italian-Canadian couple owns and manages this conveniently positioned hotel near the station. Spacious rooms in Florentine style and sparkling bathrooms that, though compact, have such amenities as hair dryers make this a good value. The staff is helpful and attentive to your needs. ✉ *Via Faenza 77, 50123,* ☎ *055/284119,* FAX *055/210101,* WEB *www.hotelportafaenza.it. 25 rooms. AE, DC, MC, V.*

$$ Alessandra. The location, a block from the Ponte Vecchio, and clean, ample rooms make this a good choice for basic accommodations at reasonable rates. The English-speaking staff makes sure guests are happy. ✉ *Borgo Santi Apostoli 17, 50123,* ☎ *055/283438,* FAX *055/210619,* WEB *www.hotelalessandra.com. 25 rooms, 9 without bath. AE, MC, V. Closed Dec. 10–26.*

$$ Hotel Ritz. Set amid a row of buildings facing the Arno, this family-managed hotel makes you feel as if you are a guest in a pretty, 19th-century Florentine home with 21st-century amenities. Most rooms have lovely views of either the Arno or the domed, red-roofed "skyline" of Florence. ✉ *Lungarno Zecca Vecchia 24, 50122,* ☎ *055/2340650,* FAX *055/240863,* WEB *www.florenceitaly.net. 30 rooms. AE, DC, MC, V.*

$$ ★ Morandi alla Crocetta. This charming and distinguished residence near Piazza Santissima Annunziata was once a monastery, and access is up a flight of stairs. It is furnished in the classic style of a Florentine home, and guests feel like privileged friends of the family. Small and exceptional, it is also a good value and must be booked well in advance. ✉ *Via Laura 50, 50121,* ☎ *055/2344747,* FAX *055/2480954,* WEB *www.hotelmorandi.it. 9 rooms. AE, DC, MC, V.*

$$ Pendini. The atmosphere of an old-fashioned Florentine pensione is intact here; bedrooms have floral wallpaper, pastel carpeting, and modern baths. Public rooms have a Belle Epoque look, with some antiques. It's central, and off-season rates here are a real bargain. ✉ *Via Strozzi 2, 50123,* ☎ *055/211170,* FAX *055/281807,* WEB *www.florenceitaly.net. 42 rooms. AE, DC, MC, V.*

$$ Villa Azalee. A five-minute walk from the train station and a short distance from the Fortezza da Basso (site of the Pitti fashion shows), this 19th-century villa deftly recalls its previous incarnation as a private residence. Some rooms have private terraces, many have views of the hotel's flower-filled garden. ✉ *Viale Fratelli Rosselli 44, 50123,* ☎ *055/214242,* FAX *055/268264,* WEB *www.villaazalee.it. 25 rooms. AE, DC, MC, V.*

$ ★ Bellettini. This small, central hotel occupies two floors of an old but well-kept building near San Lorenzo, in an area with many inexpensive restaurants. Rooms are ample, with Venetian or Tuscan decor, and bathrooms are modern. The management is friendly and helpful. ✉ *Via dei Conti 7, 50123,* ☎ *055/213561,* FAX *055/283551,* WEB *www.firenze.net. 27 rooms, 4 without bath. AE, DC, MC, V.*

$ ☎ **Nuova Italia.** Near the main train station and within walking distance of the sights, this homey hotel in a dignified palazzo is run by a genial English-speaking family. Rooms are clean and simply furnished, and the triple-glazed windows ensure restful nights. ✉ *Via Faenza 26, 50123,* ☎ *055/268430,* FAX *055/210941. 20 rooms. AE, MC, V.*

Nightlife and the Arts

The Arts

FILM

You can find movie listings in *La Nazione,* the daily Florence newspaper. English-language films are shown Tuesday–Sunday evenings at the **Cinema Astro** (✉ Piazza San Simone, near Santa Croce). Every Monday, first-run English language films are shown at the **Odeon** (✉ Piazza Strozzi). The **Goldoni** (✉ Via dei Serragli) offers first-run English-language films every Wednesday.

MUSIC

Most major musical events are staged at the **Teatro Comunale** (✉ Corso Italia 16, ☎ 055/2779236). The box office (closed Sunday and Monday) is open from 9 to 1 and a half hour before performances. It's best to order your tickets by mail, however, as they're difficult to come by at the last minute. Amici della Musica (Friends of Music) puts on a series of concerts at the **Teatro della Pergola** (box office; ✉ Via della Pergola 10a/r, ☎ 055/2479651). For information contact the **Amici della Musica** (✉ Via Alamanni 39, ☎ 055/2479651) directly.

Nightlife

BARS

Rex (✉ Via Fiesolana 23–25/r, Santa Croce, ☎ 055/2480331) has a trendy atmosphere and an arty clientele. The oh-so-cool vibe at **La Dolce Vita** (✉ Piazza del Carmine 6/r, ☎ 055/284595) attracts Florentines and occasionally the visiting American movie star.

NIGHTCLUBS

Central Park (✉ Via del Fosso Macinante 2, ☎ 055/353505) is a great spot if you want to put on your dancing shoes. **Maracaná** (✉ Via Faenza 4, ☎ 055/210298) serves as a restaurant and pizzeria featuring Brazilian specialties; at 11 PM, it transforms itself into a cabaret floor show and then into a disco until 4 AM. Remember to book a table if you want to eat. Young up-to-the-minute Florentines drink and dance 'til the wee hours at **Maramao** (✉ Via dei Macci 79/r, ☎ 055/244341), which opens at 11 PM and doesn't really get going until much before 2. **Space Electronic** (✉ Via Palazzuolo 37, ☎ 055/293082) has two floors, with karaoke upstairs and an enormous disco downstairs. **Yab** (✉ Via Sassetti 5/r, ☎ 055/215160) is one of the largest clubs, with a young clientele. Popular especially on Tuesday and Thursday nights, it packs in locals and foreigners.

Shopping

Markets

Don't miss the indoor, two-story **Mercato Centrale** (✉ Piazza del Mercato Centrale), near San Lorenzo, open in the morning Monday–Saturday. The **Mercato di San Lorenzo** (✉ Piazza San Lorenzo and Via dell'Ariento) is a fine place to browse for buys in leather goods and souvenirs; it's open Tuesday–Saturday 8–7 (June–September, Sunday 8–7).

Shopping Districts

Via Tornabuoni is the high-end shopping street. **Via della Vigna Nuova** is just as fashionable. Goldsmiths and jewelry shops can be found on and around the **Ponte Vecchio** and in the **Santa Croce** area, where there is also a high concentration of leather shops and inconspicuous shops selling gold and silver jewelry at prices much lower than those of the elegant jewelers near Ponte Vecchio. The convent of **Santa Croce** (✉ Via San Giuseppe 5/r; ✉ Piazza Santa Croce 16) houses a leather-working school and showroom. Antiques dealers can be found in and around the center but are concentrated on **Via Maggio** in the Oltrarno area. **Borgo Ognissanti** also has shops selling period decorative objects.

Florence Essentials

ADDRESSES

It is easy to find your way around in Florence: major sights can be explored on foot, as they are packed into a relatively small area. Wear comfortable shoes. The system of street addresses is unusual, with commercial addresses (those with an *r* in them, meaning *rosso,* or red) and residential addresses numbered separately (32/r might be next to or a block away from plain 32).

AIRPORTS AND TRANSFERS

The airport that handles most arrivals is Aeroporto Galileo Galilei, more commonly known as Aeroporto Pisa-Galilei. Some domestic and European flights use Florence's Aeroporto Vespucci.

➤ AIRPORT INFORMATION: **Aeroporto Galileo Galilei** (✉ Pisa, ☎ 050/500707, WEB www.pisa-aeroport.com). **Aeroporto Vespucci** (✉ Peretola, ☎ 055/373498, WEB www.safnet.it).

TRANSFERS

Pisa-Galilei Airport offers direct train service to the Stazione Centrale di Santa Maria Novella. There are hourly departures throughout the day, and the trip takes about 60 minutes. When departing, you can buy train tickets for the airport and check in for all flights leaving from Aeroporto Pisa-Galilei at the Florence Air Terminal at Track 5 of Santa Maria Novella. Aeroporto Vespucci is connected to downtown Florence by SITA bus.

BIKE AND MOPED TRAVEL

➤ BIKE AND MOPED RENTALS: **Alinari** (✉ Via Guelfa 85/r, ☎ 055/280500).

BUS TRAVEL TO AND FROM FLORENCE

For excursions outside Florence, to Siena, for instance, you take SITA near the Stazione Centrale di Santa Maria Novella. The CAP bus terminal is also near the train station.

➤ BUS INFORMATION: **CAP** (✉ Via Nazionale 13). **SITA** (bus terminal, ✉ Via Santa Caterina da Siena 17).

BUS TRAVEL WITHIN FLORENCE

Bus maps and timetables are available for a small fee at the Azienda Transporti Autolinee Fiorentine city bus information booths. The same maps may be free at visitor information offices. ATAF city buses run from about 5:15 AM to 1 AM. Buy tickets before you board the bus; they are sold at many tobacco shops and newsstands. The cost is 1,500 lire/€.75 for a ticket good for one hour, 2,500 lire/€1.30 for two hours, and 5,800 lire/€3 for four one-hour tickets, called a *multiplo.* A 24-hour tourist ticket (*turistico*) costs 6,000 lire/€3.10.

➤ BUS INFORMATION: **Azienda Transporti Autolinee Fiorentine** (ATAF; ✉ near Stazione Centrale di Santa Maria Novella; Piazza del Duomo 57/r).

CAR TRAVEL

The north–south access route to Florence is the Autostrada del Sole (A1) from Milan or Rome. The Florence–Mare autostrada (A11) links Florence with the Tyrrhenian coast, Pisa, and the A12 coastal autostrada. Parking in Florence is severely restricted.

CONSULATES

➤ UNITED KINGDOM: (✉ Lungarno Corsini 2, ☎ 055/284133).
➤ UNITED STATES: (✉ Lungarno Vespucci 38, ☎ 055/2398276).

EMERGENCIES

Pharmacies are open Sunday and holidays by rotation. Signs posted outside pharmacies list those open all night and on weekends. The pharmacy at Santa Maria Novella train station is always open.
➤ DOCTORS AND DENTISTS: **Tourist Medical Service** (✉ Via Lorenzo il Magnifico 59, ☎ 055/475411).
➤ EMERGENCY SERVICES: **Ambulance** (☎ 118). **Police** (☎ 113).

ENGLISH-LANGUAGE MEDIA

➤ BOOKSTORES: **BM Bookshop** (✉ Borgo Ognissanti 4/r, ☎ 055/294575). **Paperback Exchange** (✉ Via Fiesolana 31/r, ☎ 055/2478154). **Seeber** (✉ Via Tornabuoni 70/r, ☎ 055/215697).

TAXIS

Taxis wait at stands throughout the centro storico; you can also telephone them. Hailing them from the street is not done here. Use only authorized cabs, which are white with a yellow stripe or rectangle on the door. The meter starts at 4,500 lire/€2.30, with extra charges for nights, holidays, or radio dispatch.
➤ TAXI COMPANIES: (☎ 055/4798 or 055/4390).

TOURS

BUS TOURS

A bus consortium (through hotels and travel agents) offers tours in air-conditioned buses covering the important sights in Florence with a trip to Fiesole. The cost is about 48,000 lire/€24.80 for a three-hour tour, including entrance fees, and bookings can be made through travel agents.

Operators offer a half-day excursion to Pisa, usually in the afternoon, costing about 48,000 lire/€24.80, and a full-day excursion to Siena and San Gimignano, costing about 68,000 lire/€35. Pick up a timetable at ATAF information offices near the train station, at SITA. Also enquire at the APT tourist office.

SPECIAL INTEREST TOURS

Inquire at travel agents or at Turismo Verde for visits and stays at farm estates. The APT tourist office has information on garden tours in and around Florence.
➤ FEES AND SCHEDULES: **Turismo Verde** (✉ Via Verdi 5, ☎ 055/2344925).

TRAIN TRAVEL

The main station is Stazione Centrale di Santa Maria Novella. Florence is on the main north–south route between Rome, Bologna, Milan, and Venice. High-speed Eurostar trains reach Rome in less than two hours and Milan in less than three.
➤ TRAIN INFORMATION: **Stazione Centrale di Santa Maria Novella** (☎ 8488/88088 toll-free).

TRAVEL AGENCIES

➤ LOCAL AGENTS: **American Express** (✉ Via Dante Alighieri 22/r, ☎ 055/50981). **CIT Italia** (✉ Piazza Stazione 51/r, ☎ 055/284145). **Micos Travel Box** (✉ Via dell'Oriuolo 50–52/r, ☎ 055/2340228).

VISITOR INFORMATION

➤ TOURIST INFORMATION: **Azienda Promozione Turistica** (APT; ✉ Via Cavour 1/r, 50100, ☎ 055/290832).

TUSCANY

Tuscany is a blend of rugged hills, fertile valleys, and long stretches of sandy beaches that curve along the west coast of central Italy and fringe the pine-forested coastal plain of the Maremma. The gentle, cypress-studded green hills may seem familiar: Leonardo da Vinci and Raphael often painted them in the backgrounds of their masterpieces. Cities and towns here were the cradle of the Renaissance, which during the 15th century flourished most notably in nearby Florence. Come to Tuscany to enjoy its unchanged and gracious atmosphere of good living, and, above all, its unparalleled artistic treasures, many still in their original tiny old churches and patrician palaces.

Prato

Since the Middle Ages, Prato, 21 km (13 mi) northwest of Florence, has been Italy's major wool-producing center, and it remains one of the world's largest manufacturers of cloth. Ignore the drab industrial outskirts and devote some time to the fine old buildings in the centro storico, crammed with artwork commissioned by Prato's wealthy merchants during the Renaissance. Though in ruins, the formidable **Castello** (Castle) built for Frederick II Hohenstaufen, adjacent to Santa Maria delle Carceri, is an impressive sight, the only castle of its type to be seen outside southern Italy. ✉ *Piazza Santa Maria delle Carceri,* ☎ *0574/38207.* ⏲ *Nov.– Feb., Mon., Wed.–Fri. 10–4, Sat.–Sun. 10–5; Mar.–Oct., Mon. and Wed.–Sun. 10–1.*

The **Duomo,** reconstructed beginning in 1211, was decorated with paintings and sculptures by some of the most illustrious figures of Tuscan art. Among them was Fra Filippo Lippi, who executed scenes from the life of St. Stephen on the left wall and scenes from the life of John the Baptist on the right in the **Cappella Maggiore** (Main Chapel). ✉ *Piazza del Duomo,* ☎ *0574/26234.* ⏲ *Nov.–Apr., daily 7–12:30 and 3:30–7; May–Oct., daily 7–12:30 and 4–7:30.*

In the former bishop's palace, now the **Museo dell'Opera del Duomo** (Cathedral Museum), you can see reliefs by Donatello that were originally meant for the Pulpit of the Holy Girdle (Mary's belt, supposedly given to the apostle Thomas as evidence of her assumption into heaven; the relic is kept in a chapel of the cathedral). ✉ *Piazza del Duomo 49,* ☎ *0574/29339.* *10,000 lire/€5.15.* ⏲ *Mon., Wed.–Sat. 9:30–12:30 and 3–6:30, Sun. 9:30–12:30.*

The church of **Santa Maria delle Carceri** was built by Giuliano Sangallo in the 1490s and is a landmark of Renaissance architecture. ✉ *Piazza Santa Maria delle Carceri, off Via Cairoli and southeast of the cathedral,* ☎ *0574/27933.* ⏲ *Daily 7–noon and 4–7.*

$$$ ★ ✕ **Osvaldo Baroncelli.** This restaurant has been in the Baroncelli family for more than 50 years, and in that time they've perfected their menu. You'll be tempted to eat all of the perfectly fried olives that arrive warm, but save room for what's to come. The pastas are house made—the *tortelli di fagiano in salsa di scalogno con pancetta* (pheasant-stuffed tortelli with a shallot-infused bacon sauce) is wonderful. Reservations are advised. ✉ *Via Fra Bartolomeo 13,* ☎ *0574/23810. AE, MC, DC, V. Closed Sun. and 3 wks in Aug. No lunch Sat.*

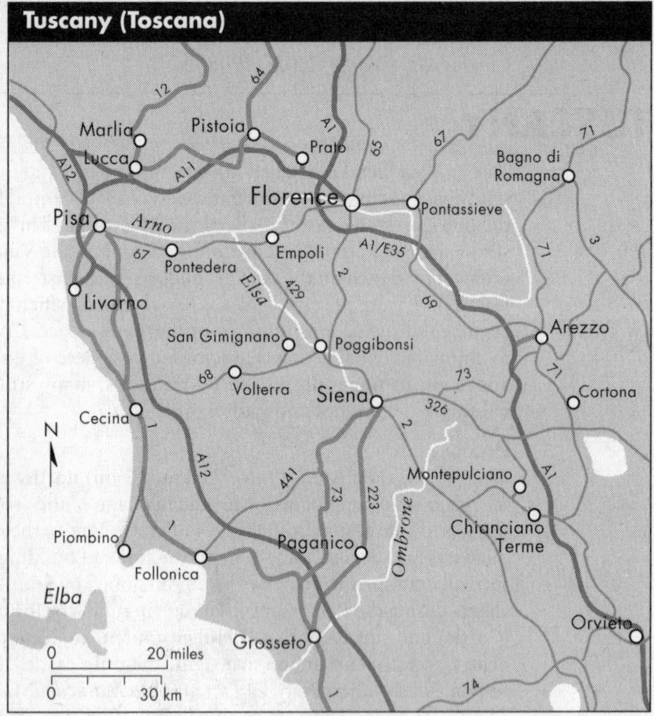

Pistoia

A floricultural capital of Europe, Pistoia—about 18 km (11 mi) northwest of Prato—is surrounded by greenhouses and plant nurseries. Flowers aside, Pistoia's main sights are all in the historic center, which has superb examples of Romanesque architecture. The Romanesque **Duomo** is flanked by a bell tower begun in the 12th century and faces the unusual Gothic baptistery. Inside the cathedral in a side chapel dedicated to St. James, the patron saint of Pistoia, is a massive **silver altar** that alone makes the stop in Pistoia worthwhile. Begun in 1287, this incredible piece of workmanship took nearly 200 years to complete. ✉ *Piazza del Duomo,* ☎ *0573/25095.* ⏲ *Church daily 8:30–12:30 and 3:30–7. Altar Mon.–Sat. 10–12 and 4–5:45, Sun. 11:20–12 and 4–5:30.*

North of the cathedral, the **Spedale del Ceppo** (Hospital of the Tree Trunk), founded in the 13th century, gets its name from the hollow trunk in which offerings were placed. On the facade is a superb frieze begun by Giovanni della Robbia (1469–1529) and completed by the workshop of Santi and Benedetto Buglioni between 1526 and 1528. ✉ *Piazza dell'Ospedale, Via delle Pappe.*

An architectural gem revealed in green-and-white marble, the medieval church of **San Giovanni Fuorcivitas** contains a *Visitation* by Luca della Robbia (1400–82), a painting attributed to Taddeo Gaddi, and a font that may have been executed by Fra Guglielmo, a Dominican friar, around 1270. ✉ *Via Cavour,* ⏲ *Daily 8–noon and 5–6:30.*

Though it is not as grand as the silver altar in the cathedral, many consider Pistoia's greatest art treasure to be Giovanni Pisano's powerfully sculpted pulpit, executed between 1298 and 1301 in the church of **Sant'-Andrea.** ✉ *Via Sant'Andrea,* ☎ *0573/21912.* ⏲ *Nov.–Mar., daily 8–12:30 and 3:30–5; Apr.–Oct., daily 8–12:30 and 3:30–7.*

$–$$ ★ ✕ **S. Jacopo.** This charming restaurant near the Duomo has white walls, tiled floors, and a gracious host in Bruno Lottini, a native Pistoian fluent in English. Tasteful prints and photographs on the walls play off nicely with the rustic blue linens that dress the tables. The menu has mostly regional favorites, such as the *maccheroni S. Jacopo,* wide ribbons of house-made pasta with a duck *ragù* (sauce), but they can turn out perfectly grilled squid as well. Save room for dessert, especially the apple strudel. ✉ *Via Crispi 15,* ☎ *0573/27786. AE, DC, MC, V. Closed Mon. No lunch Tues.*

Lucca

Any tour of Tuscany should include Lucca, with its handful of marvelously elaborate Romanesque churches and late-19th-century and early 20th-century Liberty facades along the Fillungo, its main shopping thoroughfare. Few cars are allowed in the historic center, making the city a pleasure to explore. For that very reason it's an excellent alternative to, or side trip from, Pisa, just 22 km (14 mi) away. First enjoy the views of Lucca and countryside from the parklike 16th-century ramparts. Then visit the churches that look suspiciously like oversized marble wedding cakes. Fanciful colonnettes decorate the facade of the 11th-century **Duomo**; inside is the 15th-century tomb of Ilaria del Carretto by Jacopo della Quercia (1374–1438). ✉ *Piazza San Martino,* ☎ *0583/490530.* ⌚ *Duomo Mon.–Fri. 7–6, Sat. 9:30–6:45, Sun. 9–9:50, 11:30–11:50, and 1–5. Tomb Mon.–Fri. 9:30–5:15, Sat. 9:30–6:45, Sun. 9–9:50, 11:30–11:50, and 1–5.*

Piazza del Anfiteatro Romano preserves the oval form of the Roman amphitheater over which it was built; there is a bustling outdoor market here on weekdays. The church of **San Frediano** is graced with an austere facade ornamented by 13th-century mosaic decoration. Inside, check out the exquisite reliefs by Jacopo della Quercia in the last chapel on the left and the bizarre mummy of St. Zita, patron saint of domestic servants. ✉ *Piazza San Frediano.* ⌚ *Mon.–Sat. 8:30–noon and 3–5, Sun. 10:30–5.*

One of the most fanciful facades in central Italy can be seen on the front of the church of **San Michele in Foro,** adorned with a marriage of arches and columns crowned by a statue of St. Michael. The church is an exceptional example of the Pisan Romanesque style and the decorative flair peculiar to Lucca. ✉ *Piazza San Michele.* ⌚ *Daily 7:40–noon and 3–6.*

The **Villa Reale** (Royal Villa), at Marlia, 8 km (5 mi) west of Lucca, was once the home of Napoléon's sister and has been restored by the Counts Pecci-Blunt. It is celebrated for its spectacular gardens, originally laid out in the 16th century and redone in the middle of the 17th century. Gardening buffs adore the legendary **Teatro di Verdura,** a theater carved out of hedges and topiaries; a music festival is usually held here during July and August. ✉ *Via Villa Reale, Marlia,* ☎ *0583/30108,* WEB *www.comunedicapannori.it.* ⌚ *Mar.–Nov., tours at 10, 11, 12, 3, 4, 5, and 6; Dec.–Feb., open by appointment only.*

$$ ★ ✕ **bucadisanantonio.** This restaurant has been around since 1782, and it's easy to see why. The white-walled interior hung with copper pots, expertly prepared food, and an able staff make dining here a real treat. The menu offers something for everyone—from the simple but blissful *tortelli lucchesi al sugo* (meat-stuffed pasta with a tomato and meat sauce) to such daring dishes as roast *capretto* (kid) with herbs. ✉ *Via della Cervia 3,* ☎ *0583/55881. AE, DC, MC, V. Closed Mon. and two weeks in Jan., two weeks in July. No dinner Sun.*

$–$$ ✕ **Osteria del Neni.** Tucked into a side street just a block away from San Michele, this delightful little place offers up tasty treats in a cozy atmosphere: the walls are a warm orange and it's dotted with wooden tables. All the pasta is made in-house, and if you're lucky enough to find *ravioli, spinaci e anatra in salsa di noci* (ravioli stuffed with duck and spinach and sauced with a dreamily creamy but light walnut sauce), by all means order it. The menu changes regularly; in the summer, the splendid food can be enjoyed al fresco. ✉ *Via Pescheria 3,* ☎ *0583/492 681. Reservations essential. MC, V. Closed Mon.*

$$$$ ★ **Locanda l'Elisa.** Surrounded by rosemary, lavender, and azaleas, this hotel preserves the intimacy of a well-furnished home: it's decorated in Empire style with 19th-century furniture, prints, and fabrics. The attached restaurant features Luccan specialties and elevates them to new heights. ✉ *Via Nuova per Pisa 1952, 55050,* ☎ *0583/379737,* FAX *0583/379019,* WEB *www.tuscany.net. 2 rooms, 8 suites. Restaurant, pool. AE, DC, MC, V. Closed Nov. 21– Dec. 21.*

$ **Piccolo Hotel Puccini.** Just a few steps away from the busy square and church of San Michele, this little hotel is quiet and calm. ✉ *Via di Poggio, 9, 55100,* ☎ *0583/55421,* FAX *0583/55421,* WEB *www.hotelpuccini.com. 14 rooms. AE, DC, MC, V.*

Pisa

If you cut through the kitschy atmosphere around the Leaning Tower, Pisa has much to offer. Its cathedral-baptistery-tower complex in Piazza dei Miracoli is among the most dramatic in Italy, and Piazza dei Cavalieri is a superb example of a Renaissance piazza. Pisa's treasures are more subtle than Florence's, to which it is inevitably compared. Pisa usually emerges the loser, and it shouldn't. Though it sustained heavy damage during World War II, many of its beautiful Romanesque structures are still preserved.

The **Battistero** (Baptistery) in front of the cathedral is known for its graceful form and for the pulpit carved by Giovanni Pisano's father, Nicola (1220–78). The Baptistery was begun in 1153 but not completed until around 1400. Ask one of the ticket takers if he'll sing for you inside the Baptistery. The acoustics are remarkable; a tip of 5,000 lire/€2.50 is appropriate. ✉ *Piazza dei Miracoli,* WEB *www.duomo.pisa.it.* ⏲ *June 22–Sept. 21, daily 8–7:40; Sept. 22–Dec. 21, Mar. 22–June 21, daily 9–5:40; Dec. 22–Mar. 21, daily 9–4:40.*

The **Camposanto** (Cemetery) is said to be filled with earth brought back from the Holy Land by Crusaders. Important frescoes, notably the *Drunkenness of Noah* by Renaissance artist Benozzo Gozzoli and a 14th-century *Triumph of Death,* are within. ✉ *Piazza dei Miracoli,* WEB *www.duomo.pisa.it.* ⏲ *June 22–Sept. 21, daily 8–7:40; Sept. 22–Dec. 21, Mar. 22–June 21, daily 9–5:40; Dec. 22–Mar. 21, daily 9–4:40.*

★ Pisa's **Duomo** is elegantly simple, its facade decorated with geometric and animal shapes. The cavernous interior is supported by 68 columns, and the pulpit is a prime example of Giovanni Pisano's work and one of the major monuments of the Italian Gothic style. The lamp suspended across from the pulpit is known as Galileo's Lamp; it's said to have inspired his theories on pendular motion. ✉ *Piazza del Duomo,* WEB *www.duomo.pisa.it.* ⏲ *Jun. 22–Sept. 21, daily 8–7:40; Sept. 22–Dec. 21, Mar. 22–June 21, daily 9–5:40; Dec. 22–Mar. 21, daily 9–4:40.*

$$ ✕ **Beny.** Apricot walls dotted with etchings of Pisa provide a warm atmosphere in this small, single-room restaurant specializing in fish. Flavorful, fresh dishes such as the *sformato di verdura* (a flan with Jerusalem artichokes) embellished with sweet gamberoni (a member of the shrimp family) dot the menu. ✉ *Piazza Gambacorti 22,* ☎ *050/*

25067. AE, DC, MC, V. Closed Sun. and no lunch Sat. Closed two weeks in Aug. and one week in Jan.

$-$$ ✕ **Osteria dei Cavalieri.** This charming osteria, a few steps from Piazza dei Cavalieri, is reason enough to come to Pisa. On offer are exquisitely grilled fish dishes, vegetarian dishes, and *tagliata,* thin slivers of rare beef. Finish your meal with a lemon sorbet bathed in Prosecco, and walk away feeling that you've eaten like a king at plebeian prices. ✉ *Via San Frediano 16,* ☎ *055/580858. AE, DC, MC, V. Closed Sun. and July 25–Aug. 25. No lunch Sat.*

Siena

One of Italy's best-preserved medieval towns, Siena is rich in both works of art and expensive antiques shops. Built on three hills, it is not an easy town to explore, for everything you'll want to see is either up or down a steep hill or stairway and many hotels are outside the old walls. But it is worth every ounce of effort. Siena was a center of learning and art during the Middle Ages, and almost all its public buildings and churches have enough artistic or historical merit to be worth visiting. You can buy a combined ticket for admission to the Biblioteca Piccolomini, Museo dell'Opera del Duomo, and the Battistero.

One of the finest Gothic cathedrals in Italy, Siena's **Duomo** is unique in displaying a mixture of religious and civic ornamentation on both its interior and exterior. The lovely inlaid marble floors and Nicola Pisano's (circa 1220–1284) pulpit, carved between 1266 and 1268, are highlights. The animated frescoes of papal history in the **Biblioteca Piccolomini** (Piccolomini Library) were painted by Pinturicchio. ✉ *Piazza del Duomo,* ☎ *0577/283048,* WEB *www.operaduomo.it.* ⏲ *Duomo Nov.–mid-Mar., daily 7:30–1 and 2:30–5; mid-Mar.–Oct., daily 9–7:30. Biblioteca Piccolomini Nov.–mid-Mar., daily 10–1 and 2:30–5; mid-Mar.–Oct., daily 9–7:30.*

The **Museo dell'Opera Metropolitana** (Cathedral Museum) contains some fine works of art, notably a celebrated *Maestà* by Duccio di Buoninsegna. ✉ *Piazza del Duomo,* ☎ *0577/283048,* WEB *www.operaduomo.it.* ⏲ *Nov.–mid-Mar., daily 9–1:30; mid-Mar.–Sept., daily 9–7:30; Oct., daily 9–6.*

★ The 13th-century **Palazzo Pubblico** (City Hall) dominates Piazza del Campo and houses the **Museo Civico** (Civic Museum), where there are noteworthy frescoes. ✉ *Piazza del Campo,* ☎ *0577/292226,* WEB *www.comune.siena.it.* ⏲ *Nov.–Jan., daily 10–4; Mar.–June and Oct., daily 10–7; July–Sept., daily 10 AM–11 PM.*

★ Fan-shaped, sloping **Piazza del Campo** is Siena's main center of activity, with 11 streets leading into it. Farsighted planning has preserved it as a medieval showpiece. This is the venue for the famous **Palio,** a breakneck, 90-second horse race that takes place twice each year, on July 2 and August 16. The **Torre del Mangia** (Bell Tower) of the Palazzo Pubblico offers a wonderful view (you'll have to climb 503 steps to reach it, however). ✉ *Piazza del Campo.* ⏲ *Daily 10–1 hr before sunset.*

$$$$ ✕ **Antica Trattoria Botteganova.** Just outside the city walls, north toward Chianti, the Botteganova is arguably the best restaurant in Siena. The interior, with high vaulting, is relaxed yet classy, and the service is first rate. Clean flavors, balanced combinations, and inviting presentations are the trademarks here. The menu changes every two months to reflect the season's bounty; three different tasting menus are also on offer. ✉ *Strada di Montevarchi, SS408, 2 km (1 mi) north of Siena,* ☎ *0577/284230. AE, DC, MC, V. Closed Mon.*

$ ★ ✕ **Enoteca I Terzi.** Near the Campo and the main shopping streets, this *enoteca* (wine bar), the ground floor of a 12th-century tower, is hard to beat for a good glass of wine from a lengthy and well-thought-out list. Owner Michele Incarnato offers not only a *degustazione* (tasting) menu where he pairs different wines with various dishes but also daily pasta dishes such as a sumptuous lasagna with smoked provolone. ✉ *Via dei Termini 7,* ☎ *0577/44329. AE, DC, MC, V. Closed Sun.*

$$$$ ★ **Certosa di Maggiano.** A 14th-century Carthusian monastery less than 2 km (1 mi) southeast of Siena has been converted into a luxe oasis furnished in impeccable style. The bedrooms have every comfort, and the atmosphere is that of an aristocratic family villa. In warm weather breakfast is served on the patio. Half-pension is required during high season, which increases the cost of the stay. ✉ *Strada di Certosa 82, 53100,* ☎ *0577/288180,* FAX *0577/288189,* WEB *www.certosadimaggiano.it. 18 rooms. Restaurant, pool. AE, MC, V.*

$$$ ★ **Palazzo Ravizza.** There might not be a more romantic and pretty place in the center of Siena than this quietly charming pensione just outside Porta San Marco and a short 10-minute walk to the Duomo. Rooms have high ceilings, antique furniture, big windows, and bathrooms decorated with handpainted tiles. The restaurant offers up tasty Tuscan classics, which can be eaten outdoors when it's warm. ✉ *Pian dei Mantellini, 34, 53100,* ☎ *0577/280462,* FAX *0577/221597,* WEB *www.palazzoravizza.it. 30 rooms, 4 suites. Restaurant. AE, DC, MC, V.*

$$$ **Park.** Just outside the walls of the old city, this is a handsome and sprawling 15th-century villa on its own well-equipped grounds, with a nine-hole golf course. The furnishings in the public areas strike an elegant balance between antique charm and patrician comfort. Guest rooms have bold, dark fabrics and modern appointments. ✉ *Via di Marciano 18, 53100,* ☎ *0577/44803,* FAX *0577/49020,* WEB *www.parkhotelsiena.it. 69 rooms. Restaurant, pool. AE, DC, MC, V.*

$$ **Antica Torre.** A cordial young couple runs this hotel in a restored centuries-old tower a 10-minute walk from Piazza del Campo. Rooms are smallish and are furnished sparingly but tastefully. Beam ceilings throughout and original brick vaults here and there are reminders of the tower's venerable history. ✉ *Via Fieravecchia 7, 53100,* ☎ FAX *0577/222255. 8 rooms. AE, DC, MC, V.*

San Gimignano

San Gimignano of the Beautiful Towers—to use its original name—is perhaps the most delightful of the Tuscan medieval hill towns, 31 km (20 mi) northwest of Siena. There were once more than 70 tall towers here, symbols of power for the wealthy families of the Middle Ages. Fifteen still stand, giving the town its unique skyline. The main street leads directly from the city gates to Piazza della Cisterna, with a quaint wellhead, and Piazza del Duomo.

The walls of the **Collegiata** (church), and those in the **Cappella della Santa Fina** (Chapel of St. Fina), are decorated with radiant frescoes by Domenico Ghirlandaio. In the pretty courtyard on the right as you descend the church stairs, there's a shop selling Tuscan and Deruta ceramics, which you'll also find in other shops along the Via San Giovanni. ✉ *Piazza del Duomo,* ☎ *0577/940316.* ⏲ *Apr.–Oct., weekdays 9:30–7:30, Sat. 9:30–5, Sun. 1–5; Nov.–Jan. 20, Mon.–Sat. 9:30–5, Sun. 1–5. Closed Jan. 21–Feb. 28.*

$$$ ✕ **Bel Soggiorno.** Bel Soggiorno is attached to a small hotel. It has fine views, refectory tables set with linen and candles, and leather-covered chairs. The menu, which changes frequently, offers such treats as *sorpresa in crosta* (spicy rabbit stew in a bread crust). ✉ *Via San Giovanni 91,* ☎ *0577/940375. AE, DC, MC, V. Closed Wed. and Jan. 6–Feb. 28*

$$ ✕ **La Mangiatoia.** Prices in this rustic trattoria off Via San Matteo are more moderate than at places with a view. The kitchen turns out simple country cooking. ✉ *Via Mainardi 5,* ☎ *0577/941528. No credit cards. Closed Tues., 3 wks in Nov., and 1 wk in Jan.*

$$ 🏨 **Pescille.** This rambling stone farmhouse, about 3 km (2 mi) outside San Gimignano, with a good view of the town, has been restored as a hotel and furnished in attractive, chic rustic style. ✉ *Località Pescille, 53037,* ☎ *0577/940186,* FAX *0577/940186. 50 rooms. Pool. AE, DC, MC, V. Closed Nov.–Mar.*

Arezzo

To appreciate Arezzo you have to delve into the town's centro storico, ignoring the industrialized suburbs. The city is one of Italy's three major gold jewelry production centers. In the old, upper town are an array of medieval and Renaissance buildings and a piazza that is a compendium of several eras. Tuscan art treasures abound in Arezzo, including frescoes by Piero della Francesca (1420–92), stained glass, and ancient Etruscan pottery. The old part of Arezzo was home to the poet Petrarch (1304–74), the artist Vasari (1511–74), and the satirical author Pietro Aretino (1492–1556).

The fine Gothic **Duomo** is decorated with richly colored 16th-century stained-glass windows and a fresco of a tender Magdalene by Piero della Francesca. ✉ *Piazza del Duomo,* ☎ *0575/23991.* ⏲ *Daily 7–12:30 and 3–6:30.*

Piazza Grande is an attractive, sloping square where an extensive open-air fair of antiques and old bric-a-brac is held the first weekend of every month. The shops around the piazza also specialize in antiques, with prices lower than those you will encounter in Florence. The colonnaded apse and bell tower of the Romanesque church of **Santa Maria della Pieve** grace one end of this pleasant piazza. ✉ *Corso Italia,* ☎ *0575/377678.* ⏲ *Daily 8–1 and 3–7.*

Next to what's left of an ancient Roman amphitheater and near the train station is the **Museo Archeologico** (Archaeological Museum), with a rich collection of Etruscan art, artifacts, and pottery. ✉ *Via Margaritone 10,* ☎ *0575/20882.* ⏲ *Daily 8:30–7.*

★ In the church of **San Francesco** are famous frescoes by Piero della Francesca, depicting *The Legend of the True Cross* on three walls of the choir. They were painted between 1452 and 1466 and are a stunning display of his skill and genius. ✉ *Via Cavour,* ☎ *0575/900404,* WEB *www.pierodellafrancesca.it.* ⏲ *Nov.–Mar., Mon.–Fri., 9–5:30, Sat. 9–5, Sun. 1–5; Apr.–Oct., Mon.–Fri. 9–7, Sat. 9–6:15, Sun. 1–6:15. Admission limited to 25 people at a time every 30 min. Reservations required.*

$$ ★ ✕ **Buca di San Francesco.** Travelers and passing celebrities come to this rustic and historic cellar restaurant for the 13th-century cantina atmosphere, but locals love it for the food, especially ribollita and *sformato di verdure* (vegetable flan). ✉ *Piazza San Francesco 1,* ☎ *0575/23271. AE, DC, MC, V. Closed Tues. and 2 wks in July. No dinner Mon.*

$$ ✕ **L'Agania.** The main draw to this central osteria is not its plain wood paneling and cheap furniture, but its good, inexpensive dishes such as *cinghiale* (wild boar), both as a second course and in a savory sauce with pasta. Also try the *griffi* (veal cheek in a tasty sauce with tomatoes and spices). ✉ *Via Mazzini 10,* ☎ *0575/295381. AE, DC, MC, V. Closed Mon. and 2nd wk in June.*

$$ 🏨 **Continental.** This hotel has fairly spacious rooms decorated in white and bright yellow, spic-and-span bathrooms, and the advantage of a central location within walking distance of all major sights. ✉ *Piazza*

Guido Monaco 7, 52100, ☎ 0575/20251, FAX 0575/350485, WEB www.hotelcontinental.com. 74 rooms. AE, DC, MC, V.

Cortona

Cortona, about 30 km (19 mi) south of Arezzo, has a peculiarly Tuscan brand of charm. This well-preserved, unspoiled medieval hill town is known for its excellent small museum and a number of fine antiques shops, as well as for its colony of foreign residents. The approach to Cortona from the east passes the Renaissance church of **Santa Maria del Calcinaio.** The heart of Cortona is formed by **Piazza della Repubblica** and the adjacent **Piazza Signorelli.**

The **Museo Diocesano** (Diocesan Museum) houses an impressive number of large and splendid paintings by native son Luca Signorelli (circa 1450–1523), as well as a beautiful *Annunciation* by Fra Angelico. ✉ *Piazza del Duomo 1, ☎ 0575/62830. ⏲ Apr.–Sept., Tues.–Sun. 9:30–1 and 3:30–7; Oct., Tues.–Sun. 10–1 and 3:30–6; Nov.–Mar., Tues.–Sun. 10–1 and 3–5.*

Picturesque **Palazzo Pretorio** (Praetorian Palace) houses a museum with a representative collection of Etruscan bronzes. Climb its centuries-old stone staircase to the **Museo dell'Accademia Etrusca** (Gallery of Etruscan Art). ✉ *Piazza Signorelli 9, ☎ 0575/630415. ⏲ Apr.–Sept., Tues.–Sun. 10–7; Oct.–Mar., Tues.–Sun. 10–5.*

$$ ✕ **Osteria del Teatro.** Just up the street from Teatro Signorelli, this small osteria is lined with photographs from theatrical productions spanning several decades. The food is deliciously simple—try the *filetto in crema di tartufo* (beef in a creamy tartufo sauce). ✉ *Via Maffei 5, ☎ 0575/630556. AE, DC, MC, V. Closed Wed. and 2 wks in Nov.*

Tuscany Essentials

BUS TRAVEL

Buses are a good alternative to driving; the region is crisscrossed by bus lines, which in some cases offer more frequent local service than trains, especially from Florence to Prato, a half-hour trip, and from Florence to Siena, which can take from 1¼ (by express bus) to 2 hours.

CAR TRAVEL

The best way to see the region is by car, taking detours to hill towns and abbeys. Roads throughout Tuscany are in good condition, though often narrow. The A1 autostrada links Florence with Arezzo and Chiusi (where you turn off for Montepulciano). A toll-free superstrada links Florence with Siena. For Chianti wine country scenery, take the S222 south of Florence through the undulating hills between Strada in Chianti and Greve in Chianti.

TOURS

American Express operates one-day excursions to Siena and San Gimignano out of Florence. CIT Italia operates regional tours, too.

➤ FEES AND SCHEDULES: **American Express** (✉ Via Dante Alighieri 22/r, ☎ 055/50981). **CIT Italia** (✉ Piazza Stazione 51/r, ☎ 055/284145).

TRAIN TRAVEL

The main train network connects Florence with Arezzo and Prato. Another main line runs to Pisa, and a secondary line goes from Prato to the coast via Lucca. Trains also connect Siena with Pisa, a two-hour ride.

➤ TRAIN INFORMATION: (☎ 8848/88088 toll-free).

VISITOR INFORMATION

➤ TOURIST INFORMATION: **Arezzo** (✉ Piazza della Repubblica 22, ☎ 0575/377678). **Cortona** (✉ Via Nazionale 42, ☎ 0575/630352). **Lucca** (✉ Piazzale Verdi, ☎ 0583/442944). **Pisa** (✉ Via Cammao 2, ☎ 050/560464). **Pistoia** (✉ Palazzo dei Vescovi, ☎ 0573/21622). **Prato** (✉ Piazza delle Carceri 15, ☎ 0574/24112, WEB www.prato.turismo.toscana.it). **San Gimignano** (✉ Piazza del Duomo, ☎ 0577/940008, WEB www.sangimignano.it).

MILAN

Milan, capital of all that is new in Italy, has a history spanning at least 2,500 years. Its fortunes, both as a great commercial trading center and as the object of regular conquest and occupation, are readily explained by its strategic position at the center of the Lombard Plain.

Exploring Milan

Numbers in the margin correspond to points of interest on the Milan map.

Virtually every invader in European history—Gaul, Roman, Goth, Longobard, and Frank—as well as a long series of rulers from France, Spain, and Austria, has taken a turn at ruling the city and the region. So if you are wondering why so little seems to have survived from Milan's antiquity, the answer is simple—war. Thanks to the great family dynasties of the Visconti and the Sforza, however, there are still great Gothic and Renaissance treasures to be seen, including Leonardo's unforgettable *Last Supper.* And thanks to new lords and ladies—like Armani and Prada—the city now dazzles as the design and fashion center of the world. Old and new come together at Milan's La Scala—Europe's most important opera house—where audiences continue to set sail for passion on the high C's.

7 **Basilica di Sant'Ambrogio** (Basilica of St. Ambrose). Noted for its medieval architecture, the church was consecrated by St. Ambrose in AD 387 and is the model for all Lombard Romanesque churches. Ancient pieces inside include a remarkable 9th-century altar in precious metals and enamels and some 5th-century mosaics. ✉ *Piazza Sant'Ambrogio,* ☎ *02/86450895.* ⏲ *Basilica Mon.–Sat., 7–12, 2:30–7, Sun. 3–8. Museum Mon., Wed.–Fri 10–12 and 3–5, Sat.–Sun. 3–5.*

5 **Castello Sforzesco.** Surrounded by a moat, this building is a somewhat sinister 19th-century reconstruction of the imposing 15th-century fortress built by the Sforzas, who succeeded the Viscontis as lords of Milan. It now houses collections of sculptures, antiques, and ceramics, including Michelangelo's *Rondanini Pietà,* his last work, left unfinished at his death. ✉ *Piazza Castello,* ☎ *02/62083284.* ⏲ *Tues.–Sun., 9–5:30.*

★ 1 **Duomo.** The massive Duomo, a mountain of marble fretted with statues, spires, and flying buttresses, sits—in all its Gothic drama—in the heart of Milan. The **Madonnina,** a gleaming gilt statue on the highest spire, is a city landmark. Take the elevator or walk up 158 steps to the roof for a view of the Lombard Plain and the Alps beyond. Dating from the 4th century, the **Baptistery** ruin is beneath the piazza; enter through the Duomo. ✉ *Piazza del Duomo,* ☎ *02/86463456.* ⏲ *Baptistery daily 9:30–5:15. Church daily 6:45–6:45.*

★ 2 **Galleria Vittorio Emanuele.** In this spectacularly extravagant late-19th-century, glass-top equivalent of the shopping mall, Milanese and visitors stroll, window shop, and sip pricey cappuccinos at trendy cafés.

Milan (Milano)

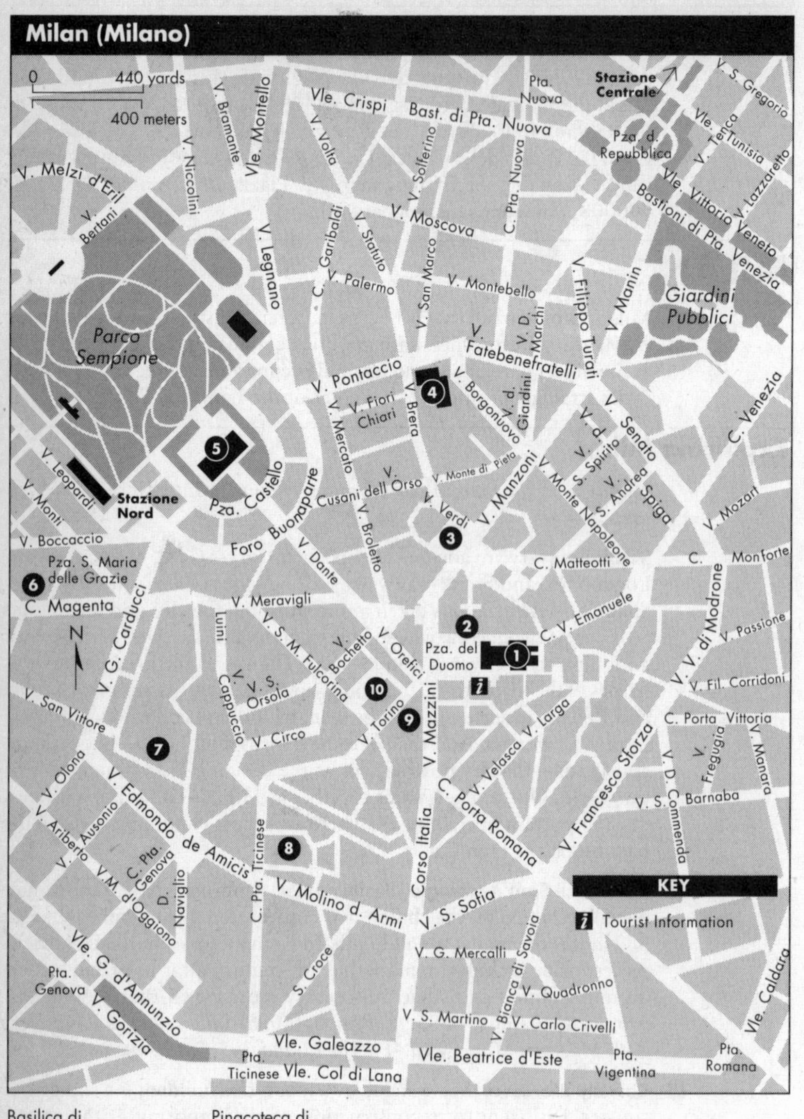

Basilica di Sant'Ambrogio 7
Castello Sforzesco 5
Duomo 1
Galleria Vittorio Emanuele 2
Pinacoteca Ambrosiana 10
Pinacoteca di Brera 4
San Lorenzo Maggiore 8
San Satiro 9
Santa Maria delle Grazie 6
Teatro alla Scala . . . 3

✉ *Piazza del Duomo, beyond the northern tip of cathedral's facade.* ⏲ *Daily 9:30–1 and 3:30–7.*

❿ **Pinacoteca Ambrosiana.** This museum, founded in the 17th century by Cardinal Federico Borromeo, is one of the city's treasures. Here you can contemplate works of art like Caravaggio's simple—yet revolutionary in the history of art—*Basket of Fruit* and Raphael's awesome preparatory drawing for *The School of Athens* in the Vatican, as well as paintings by Leonardo, Botticelli, Luini, Titian, and Brueghel, among others. The adjacent library, the Biblioteca Ambrosiana, also sometimes hosts exhibits and is considered to be the oldest Italian public library. ✉ *Piazza Pio XI, 2,* ☎ *02/80692225.* ⏲ *Museum Tues.–Sun. 10–5:30, library weekdays 9:30–5.*

★ ❹ **Pinacoteca di Brera** (Brera Painting Gallery). One of Italy's great fine art collections includes works by Mantegna (1431–1506), Raphael, and Titian. Most are of a religious nature, confiscated during the 19th century when many religious orders were suppressed and their churches closed. ✉ *Via Brera 28,* ☎ *02/722631.* *12,000 lire/€6.20.* ⏲ *Tues.–Sat. 9–5, Sun. 9–7.*

❽ **San Lorenzo Maggiore** (St. Lorenzo the Elder). Sixteen ancient Roman columns line the front of this sanctuary; 4th-century mosaics survive in the **Cappella di San Aquilino** (Chapel of St. Aquilinus). ✉ *Corso di Porta Ticinese.* ⏲ *Daily 7:30–6:45, mosaics can be viewed 9:30–6:30.*

❾ **San Satiro** (St. Satyr). This church is an architectural gem in which Bramante's perfect command of proportion and perspective, characteristic of the Renaissance, tricks the eye through a famous optical illusion and makes a small interior seem extraordinarily spacious and airy. ✉ *Via Torino.* ⏲ *Weekdays 7:30–11:30 and 3:30–6:30, weekends 9–noon and 3:30–7.*

★ ❻ **Santa Maria delle Grazie** (Madonna of Grace). Although portions of this church were designed by Bramante, it plays second fiddle to the **Cenacolo Vinciano,** the former rectory next door, where, over a three-year period, Leonardo da Vinci painted his megafamous *Last Supper.* The fresco has suffered more than its share of disasters, beginning with the experiments of the artist, who used untested pigments that soon began to deteriorate. Nevertheless, after a restoration, *The Last Supper* has regained a measure of clarity and luminosity. Reservations can be made Monday–Friday 9–6 and Saturday 9–2, and visitors are strongly advised to make them. ✉ *Piazza Santa Maria delle Grazie 2,* ☎ *02/89421146.* ⏲ *Tues.–Sun. 8–7.*

❸ **Teatro alla Scala.** In this world-famous institution, Verdi established his reputation and Maria Callas sang her way into opera lore. Its rich history is displayed in the attached **Museo Teatrale alla Scala** (Theatrical Museum at La Scala). The theater is scheduled to close for renovations in January 2002, after the events to mark the centenary of Verdi's death, although there are likely to be delays in the transfer to the Arcimboldi Theatre on the outskirts of Milan. ✉ *Piazza della Scala,* ☎ *02/8053418.* ⏲ *Mon.–Sat. 9–12, 2–5; May–Oct., also open these hours Sun. Theater viewing occasionally not possible during rehearsals and museum is expected to be temporarily shut down when opera house is transferred.*

Dining

Lombardy is home to some of Italy's freshest waters, and in the south some of the best pastureland, so you can be sure restaurants have choice selections of meats and fish. All are paired nicely with the crisp wines of the region.

$$$$ ★ ✕ **Savini.** The Savini is a Milanese institution, with red carpets and cut-glass chandeliers characteristic of its late-19th-century roots. The Milanese *risotto al salto* (rice cooked as a pancake, tossed in the pan) is excellent here, as are the *cotoletta di vitello* (breaded veal cutlets) and osso buco. ✉ *Galleria Vittorio Emanuele,* ☎ *02/72003433. AE, DC, MC, V. Closed Sun., Jan. 1–6 and 20 days in Aug.*

$$$–$$$$ ★ ✕ **Boeucc.** Milan's oldest restaurant, opened in 1696, is located on a square not far from La Scala. The interior is opulent, with fluted columns and chandeliers, and there's a garden for warm-weather dining. The Milanese specialties include *penne al branzino e zucchine* (penne with sea bass and zucchini sauce) and *gelato di castagne con zabaglione caldo* (chestnut ice cream with hot zabaglione). ✉ *Piazza Belgioioso 2,* ☎ *02/76020224. Reservations essential. AE. Closed Sat., Easter, Aug., and Dec. 24–Jan. 2. No lunch Sun.*

$$$ ✕ **Joia.** At this haute-cuisine restaurant near Piazza della Repubblica, delicious vegetarian dishes are artistically prepared by chef Pietro Leemann. A fish menu is also available, and the menu changes every three months. A no-smoking dining room is available. ✉ *Via Panfilo Castaldi 18,* ☎ *02/29522124. AE, DC, MC, V. Closed weekends, Aug., and Dec. 24–Jan. 8.*

$$–$$$ ✕ **Antica Trattoria della Pesa.** The late-19th-century decor and atmosphere, dark-wood paneling, and old-fashioned lamps still look much as they must have when this eatery opened 100 years ago. This is authentic Old Milan, and the menu is right in line, with risotto, minestrone, and osso buco. ✉ *Viale Pasubio 10,* ☎ *02/6555741,* FAX *02/29006859. AE, DC, MC, V. Closed Sun., Aug., and Dec. 24–Jan. 6.*

$–$$ ✕ **Al Rifiugio Pugliese.** Just outside the center of town, this restaurant is a lively, fun place to sample Pugliese specialties. ✉ *Via Costanza 2, at via Boni 16,* ☎ *02/48000917. AE, DC, MC, V. Closed 25 days in Aug., 10 days at Christmas.*

$–$$ ✕ **La Bruschetta.** This tiny, busy, first-class pizzeria near the Duomo also features specialties from Tuscany and other parts of Italy. Try the spaghetti *alle cozze e vongole* (with mussels and clams) or the grilled and skewered meats. ✉ *Piazza Beccaria 12,* ☎ *02/8692494. AE, V. Closed Mon., 3 wks in Aug., and 10 days at Christmas.*

$–$$ ✕ **Trattoria Milanese.** Between the Duomo and the Basilica of Sant'Ambrogio, this small, popular trattoria has been run by the same family in the same location since 1933. It's invariably crowded, especially at dinner, when the regulars love to linger. Food is classic regional in approach; good choices include risotto and *cotoletta alla Milanese* (veal Milanese style). ✉ *Via Santa Marta 11,* ☎ *02/8645199. DC, MC, V. Closed Tues., Aug., and Dec. 24–Jan. 6.*

Lodging

If Rome is the administrative and political capital of Italy, Milan is the bustling business heart. As such, hotels are plentiful, with efficient service and, for those hotels in the $$ and up categories, excellent standards. Stay as close to the city center as possible and always book well in advance.

$$$$ 🏨 **Four Seasons.** The elegant restoration of a 15th-century monastery in the middle of Milan's exclusive shopping district has produced a precious gem—with the highest rates in the city. The hotel blends European class with American comfort. Individually furnished rooms have opulent marble bathrooms; most rooms face the quiet courtyard. Il Teatro serves dinner only. ✉ *Via Gesù 8, 20121,* ☎ *02/77088,* FAX *02/77085000,* WEB *www.fourseasons.com. 118 rooms. 2 restaurants, bar. AE, DC, MC, V.*

$$$$ ★ **Grand Hotel Duomo.** Just 20 yards from the cathedral, this hotel's first- through third-floor rooms all overlook the church's Gothic gargoyles and pinnacles. The rooms are spacious and furnished in a snappy, contemporary style. ✉ *Via San Raffaele 1, 20121,* ☎ *02/8833,* FAX *02/86460454 or 02/86462027,* WEB *www.grandhotel-duomo.com. 153 rooms. Restaurant, bar. AE, DC, MC, V.*

$$$$ ★ **Palace.** This truly elegant hotel is one of the finest the city has to offer, with a personalized, attentive service to match and elegantly outfitted and upholstered guest rooms. ✉ *Piazza della Repubblica 20, 20124,* ☎ *02/6336,* FAX *02/654485,* WEB *www.westin.com. 244 rooms. Restaurant, bar. AE, DC, MC, V.*

$$$ **Hotel Spadari Al Duomo.** This charming, intimate four-star hotel near the Duomo and the Pinacoteca Ambroseum museum also houses its own private collection of art. Junior suites on the seventh floor have views of the cathedral. ✉ *Via Spadari 11, 20123,* ☎ *02/72002371,* FAX *02/861184,* WEB *www.spadarihotel.com. 39 rooms. Bar. AE, DC, MC, V. Closed Dec. 24–26 and Aug. 15–16.*

$$ **Ariston.** This hotel, near Milan's Duomo, was built according to bio-architectural principles, using natural materials and treating air with ionizers to improve air quality. Free Internet access is available in the lobby. Bicycles are available for guests to use in summer. ✉ *Largo Carrobbio 2, 20123,* ☎ *02/72000556,* FAX *02/72000914. 46 rooms. Bar. AE, DC, MC, V. Closed Aug.*

$$ **Canada.** This friendly, small hotel close to Piazza Duomo offers modern comfort at a reasonable price. ✉ *Via Santa Sofia 16, 20121,* ☎ *02/58304844,* FAX *02/58300282,* WEB *www.canadahotel.it. 35 rooms. Bar. AE, DC, MC, V.*

$$ **London.** Close to the Duomo, the London has clean, good-sized, simply furnished rooms and a friendly English-speaking staff. ✉ *Via Rovello 3, 20121,* ☎ *02/72020166,* FAX *02/8057037,* WEB *www.travel.europe.it. 29 rooms. Bar. MC, V. Closed Aug. and Dec. 24–Jan. 6.*

$ **Antica Locanda Leonardo** This small hotel is convenient to sites such as *The Last Supper* and the city center. There is a peaceful inner courtyard, and the staff is happy to provide information about getting tickets to the opera house, soccer games, and other Milan events. ✉ *Corso Magenta 78, 20123,* ☎ *02/463317,* FAX *02/48019012.,* WEB *www.leoluc.com. 20 rooms. Restaurant, bar. AE, DC, MC, V.Dec. 27–Jan. 1, 3 wks in Aug..*

$ **San Francisco.** In a residential area between the central station and the university, this medium-sized hotel is handy to subway and bus lines. It also has the advantages of a friendly management, rooms that are bright and clean, and a charming garden. ✉ *Viale Lombardia 55, 20131,* ☎ *02/2361009,* FAX *02/26680377,* WEB *www.hotel-sanfrancisco.it. 31 rooms. AE, DC, MC, V.*

Nightlife and the Arts

The Arts

Milan's famed **Teatro alla Scala** (✉ Piazza della Scala, Ufficio Biglietteria, Via Filodrammatici 2, ☎ 02/72003744) presents some of the world's most impressive operatic productions. The opera season begins December 7 (St. Ambrose Day) and runs through July. Opera is interspersed with a handful of ballets and a series of concerts by the theater's own musicians and other top names from around the world. Programs are available at principal travel agencies and tourist information offices in Italy and abroad.

Tickets are usually hard to come by, but your hotel may be able to help obtain them. For information on schedules, ticket availability, and ticket sales, the **Infotel Scala Service** (✉ Teatro alla Scala, Ufficio Biglietteria, Via Filodrammatici 2, ☎ 02/72003744, FAX 02/8607787) operates (with English-speaking staff) at the ticket office and is open daily noon–6 and until 8 in the evening when there are performances. Otherwise, you can check ticket availability and purchase tickets by credit card, on the 24-hour automated phone reservation system (☎ 02/860775) or on the opera house's Web site (WEB www.teatroallascala.org). Both services charge a 20% advance booking fee. You may also be able to book at CIT or other travel agencies (no more than 10 days before performance) for a 15% advance booking charge.

Nightlife

Head off to the Navigli or Brera district to have a drink or take advantage of one of the many happy hours that run from around 6:30 to 9:30. **La Banque** (✉ Via Bassano Porrone 6, ☎ 02/86996565), near Piazza La Scala, is an exclusive and expensive bar, disco, and restaurant popular for anything from an aperitivo to a night out on the town. **El Brellin** (✉ Vicolo Lavandai, at Alzaia Naviglio Grande, ☎ 02/58101351) is one of many bars in the Navigli district; it's closed Sunday evening but offers one of Milan's increasingly popular brunches on Sunday afternoon. **Magazzini Generali** (✉ Via Pietrasanta 14, ☎ 02/55211313), in an old warehouse, is a fun, futuristic place to dance and to hear concerts. It's closed on Sunday. For a quieter evening, the cinema **Mexico** (✉ Via Savona, 57, ☎ 02/48951802), although a bit out of the way, frequently shows films in English. **Nordest Caffe** (✉ Via P. Borsieri 35, ☎ 02/69001910) is an elegant bar featuring jazz concerts Wednesday and Thursday nights and classical music on Friday. It's closed on Saturday. Check out **Orient Express** (✉ Via Fiori Chiari 8, ☎ 02/8056227) in the Brera quarter for a bite to eat and live music. **Le Scimmie** (✉ Via Ascanio Sforza 49, ☎ 02/89402874) delivers cool jazz in a relaxed atmosphere.

Shopping

Milan is one of the most renowned fashion centers in the world, so it comes as no surprise that most shops sell clothing—designer names with designer price tags. Milan's most elegant shopping streets are **Via Monte Napoleone, Via Manzoni, Via della Spiga,** and **Via Sant'Andrea.** Head for **Corso Buenos Aires,** near the central train station, if the chic goods in other areas are a shock to your purse.

Milan Essentials

AIR TRAVEL TO AND FROM MILAN

As Lombardy's capital and the most important financial and commercial center in northern Italy, Milan is well connected with Rome and Florence by fast and frequent rail and air service. Flights in and out of Milan during winter months are often prone to delay due to heavy fog.

AIRPORTS AND TRANSFERS

Aeroporto Milano Linate handles mainly domestic and a limited number of European flights. Aeroporto Malpensa services intercontinental flights, as well as many European and domestic flights.

➤ AIRPORT INFORMATION: **Aeroporto Malpensa** (✉ 50 km/30 mi northwest of the city, ☎ 02/74852200). **Aeroporto Milano Linate** (✉ 11 km/7 mi east of Milan, ☎ 02/74852200). **Air traffic information** (☎ 02/74851).

TRANSFERS

The *Malpensa Express* train connects Malpensa airport with the Cadorna train station for 15,000 lire/€7.75 one-way or 20,000 lire/€10.35 for a 40-minute round-trip ride in the same day. Trains running to Cadorna from Malpensa leave every 30 minutes 7:45 AM–9:45 PM. Malpensa Express trains leave Cadorna for the airport every half hour 6:50 AM–8:20 PM. The agency also runs buses on the same route outside of these hours. In addition, buses connect both airports with Milan, stopping at the central station. Fare from Linate is 5,000 lire/€2.60 on the special airport bus or 1,500 lire/€0.75 on municipal Bus 73 (to Piazza San Babila); from Malpensa, it costs 13,000 lire/€6.70. A taxi from Linate to the center of Milan costs about 30,000 lire/€15.50 from Malpensa, about 130,000 lire/€67.15. Buses connecting airports leave Malpensa and Linate twice a day in each direction and cost 18,000 lire/€9.30.

➤ TRANSFER INFORMATION: ***Malpensa Express*** (☎ 02/27763).

CAR TRAVEL

From Rome and Florence take the A1 autostrada. From Venice take the A4. Parking is banned throughout Milan center, so park on the outskirts and use public transportation.

CONSULATES

➤ CANADA: (✉ Via Pisani 19, ☎ 02/67581).

➤ UNITED KINGDOM: (✉ Via San Paolo 7, ☎ 02/723001).

➤ UNITED STATES: (✉ Via Principe Amedeo 2, ☎ 02/290351).

EMERGENCIES

➤ DOCTORS AND DENTISTS: **Hospital and Doctor** (☎ 113).

➤ EMERGENCY SERVICES: **Ambulance** (☎ 118). **Carabinieri** (military police; ☎ 112). **Police** (☎ 113).

SUBWAY TRAVEL

Milan's subway network, the Metropolitana, is modern, fast, and easy to use. Signs marked MM indicate Metropolitana stations. There are, at present, three lines. The ATM has an information office. Tickets are sold at newsstands at every stop, and in ticket machines, some of which require exact change only. The fare is 1,500 lire/€.75, and the subway runs from 6:20 AM to midnight. Buses follow the subway routes aboveground for about an hour after the subway closes.

➤ SUBWAY INFORMATION: **ATM information office** (✉ mezzanine of the Duomo Metro station, ☎ 800/016857).

TAXIS

Use yellow cabs only. They wait at stands or can be called in advance.

➤ TAXI INFORMATION: **Yellow cabs** (☎ 02/5353).

TOURS

Three-hour morning sightseeing tours depart Tuesday–Sunday from Piazzetta Reale, next to the Duomo, at 9:30; they cost about 60,000 lire/€31 and are run by Autostradale Viaggi. Tickets can be purchased from the APT offices or aboard the bus. In addition, go to APT offices for information on three-hour walking tours of the city, held Monday mornings at 10. Guided tours to city museums (many of which do not have their own guides) and other Milan and nearby artistic and architectural attractions are also organized by the APT.

TRAIN TRAVEL

The main train station is Milano Centrale. Several smaller stations handle commuter trains. Rapid Intercity trains connect Rome and Milan daily, stopping in Florence and/or Bologna; a nonstop Intercity leaves Rome or Milan morning and evening, and the trip takes about four hours. Information on train hours can be found on the FS Web site.

➤ TRAIN INFORMATION: **FS Information** (WEB www.fs-on-line.it.). **Milano Centrale** (✉ Piazzale Duca d'Aosta, ☎ 848/888088).

TRANSPORTATION AROUND MILAN

Buy tickets for buses and streetcars at newsstands, tobacco shops, and bars. The fare is 1,500 lire/€.75. One ticket is valid for 75 minutes on all surface lines and one subway trip. Daily tickets valid for 24 hours on all public transportation lines are sold at the Duomo Metro station ATM (city transport authority) information office and at Milano Centrale Metro station. Twenty-four-hour tickets cost 5,000 lire/€2.60 48-hour tickets 9,000 lire/€4.65.

TRAVEL AGENCIES

➤ LOCAL AGENTS: **American Express Travel Agency** (✉ Via Brera 3, ☎ 02/72003693). **Compagnia Italiana Turismo** (CIT; ✉ Galleria Vittorio Emanuele, ☎ 02/863701).

VISITOR INFORMATION

➤ TOURIST INFORMATION: **APT Offices** (✉ Stazione Centrale, ☎ 02/72524370; ✉ Palazzo del Turismo, Via Marconi 1, ☎ 02/72524300).

VENICE

It was called La Serenissima Repubblica, a name suggesting the monstrous power and majesty of the city that was for centuries the unrivaled mistress of trade between Europe and the Far East, and the staunch bulwark of Christendom against the tides of Turkish expansion. Venice is a labyrinth of narrow streets and waterways, opening now and again onto an airy square or broad canal. Many of its magnificent palazzi are slowly crumbling; but far from making it a down-at-the-heels slum, somehow in Venice the shabby, derelict effect is magically transformed into one of beauty and charm. The place is romantic, especially at night when the lights from the vaporetti and the stars overhead pick out the gargoyles and arches of the centuries-old facades. Though the power and glory of its days as a wealthy city-republic are gone, the art and exotic aura remain.

Exploring Venice

Numbers in the margin correspond to points of interest on the Venice map.

To enjoy the city you will have to come to terms with the crowds of day-trippers, who take over the center around San Marco from May through September and during Carnival. Venice is cooler and more welcoming in early spring and late fall. Romantics like it in the winter, when prices are much lower, the streets are often deserted, and the sea mists impart a haunting melancholy to the *campi* (squares) and canals. Piazza San Marco is the pulse of Venice, but after joining with the crowds to visit the Basilica di San Marco and the Doge's Palace, strike out on your own and just follow where your feet take you—you won't be disappointed.

Piazza San Marco and the San Polo Neighborhood

Piazza San Marco alone would be worth a trip to Venice: an estimated 35,000 visitors a day come here to admire the sights that made Venice world famous well before the days of mass tourism; no wonder that the streets north and west of the square are clustered with fashion boutiques and expensive shops. The less crowded (and more affordable) San Polo district, with its lively alleys, is fun to explore on foot.

★ 3 **Basilica di San Marco** (St. Mark's Basilica). Half Christian church, half Middle Eastern mosque, this building was conceived during the 11th century to hold the relics of St. Mark the Evangelist, the city's patron saint. Inside are more than 43,055 square ft of golden mosaics, lending an extraordinarily exotic aura. Be sure to see the **Pala d'Oro,** a dazzling gilded silver screen encrusted with 1,927 precious gems and 255 enameled panels. The richly decorated facade is surmounted by copies of four famous gilded bronze horses; the originals are in the **museum** (☎ 041/5225205) upstairs. ✉ *Piazza San Marco,* ☎ *041/5225205.* ⏲ *Basilica Nov.–Apr., Mon.–Sat. 9:45–4:30, Sun. 1–4:30; May–Oct., Mon.–Sat. 9:45–5:30, Sun. 1–5:30 (last entry 30 mins before closing); tours June–Aug., Mon.–Sat.*

★ ❺ **Campanile di San Marco.** Venice's famous brick bell tower (325 ft tall, plus the angel) stood here for 1,000 years before it collapsed without warning one morning in 1912. It was swiftly rebuilt according to the old plan. In the 15th century, clerics found guilty of immoral behavior were suspended in wooden cages from the tower, sometimes forced to subsist on bread and water for as long as a year, other times left to starve. The stunning view from the tower on a clear day includes the Lido, the lagoon, and the mainland as far as the Alps, but, strangely enough, none of the myriad canals that snake through the city. ✉ *Piazza San Marco,* ☎ *041/5224064.* ⏲ *June–Sept., daily 9:30–9:30; Oct.–May, daily 9:30–sunset (last entry 30 mins before closing). Closed 2 wks in Jan.*

❷ **Museo Correr.** Exhibits here range from the absurdly high-soled shoes worn by 16th-century Venetian ladies (who walked with the aid of a servant on either side) to fine Venetian paintings and 11 rooms illustrating the period from the Napoleonic and Austrian occupation through the unification of Italy. Map buffs should not miss the huge, exceptionally detailed *Grande Pianta Prospettica* by Jacopo de' Barberi (circa 1440–1515), which faithfully portrays every inch of 16th-century Venice. The Quadreria (Picture Gallery) on the second floor features Gothic works by the *madoneri,* a group of Greek-Venetian artists who specialized in the painting of glittering gold Madonnas. ✉ *Piazza San Marco, Ala Napoleonica,* ☎ *041/5225625.* ⏲ *Apr.–Oct., daily 9–7; Nov.–Mar., daily 9–5 (last entry 1 hr before closing).*

★ ❹ **Palazzo Ducale** (Doge's Palace). During Venice's heyday, this was the epicenter of its great empire. More than just a palace, it was a combination White House, Senate, Supreme Court, torture chamber, and prison. The building's facade is a Gothic-Renaissance fantasia of pink-and-white marble. It is filled with frescoes, paintings, and a few examples of statuary by some of the Renaissance's greatest artists. Don't miss the famous view from the balcony, overlooking the piazza, St. Mark's Basin, and the church of San Giorgio Maggiore across the lagoon. ✉ *Piazzetta di San Marco,* ☎ *041/5224951.* 🎫 *24,000 lire/€12.40* ⏲ *Apr.–Oct., daily 9–7; Nov.–Mar., daily 9–5 (last entry 1½ hrs before closing). English tours daily 10:30; reservations essential.*

★ ❶ **Piazza San Marco.** In the most famous square in Venice—the only one called a *piazza*; the rest are called *campi* (fields)—pedestrian traffic jams clog the surrounding byways and even pigeons have to fight for space. The short side of the square opposite the Basilica of San Marco is known as the **Ala Napoleonica,** a wing built by order of Napoléon, enclosing it to form what he called "the most beautiful drawing room in all of Europe."

❻ **Santa Maria Gloriosa dei Frari.** This soaring Gothic brick church known simply as I Frari contains a number of the most important pictures in Venice. Paradoxically, as the principal church of the Franciscans it is austere in design, suitably reflecting the order's vows of poverty. Chief among the works is the magnificent Titian altarpiece,

Venice (Venezia)

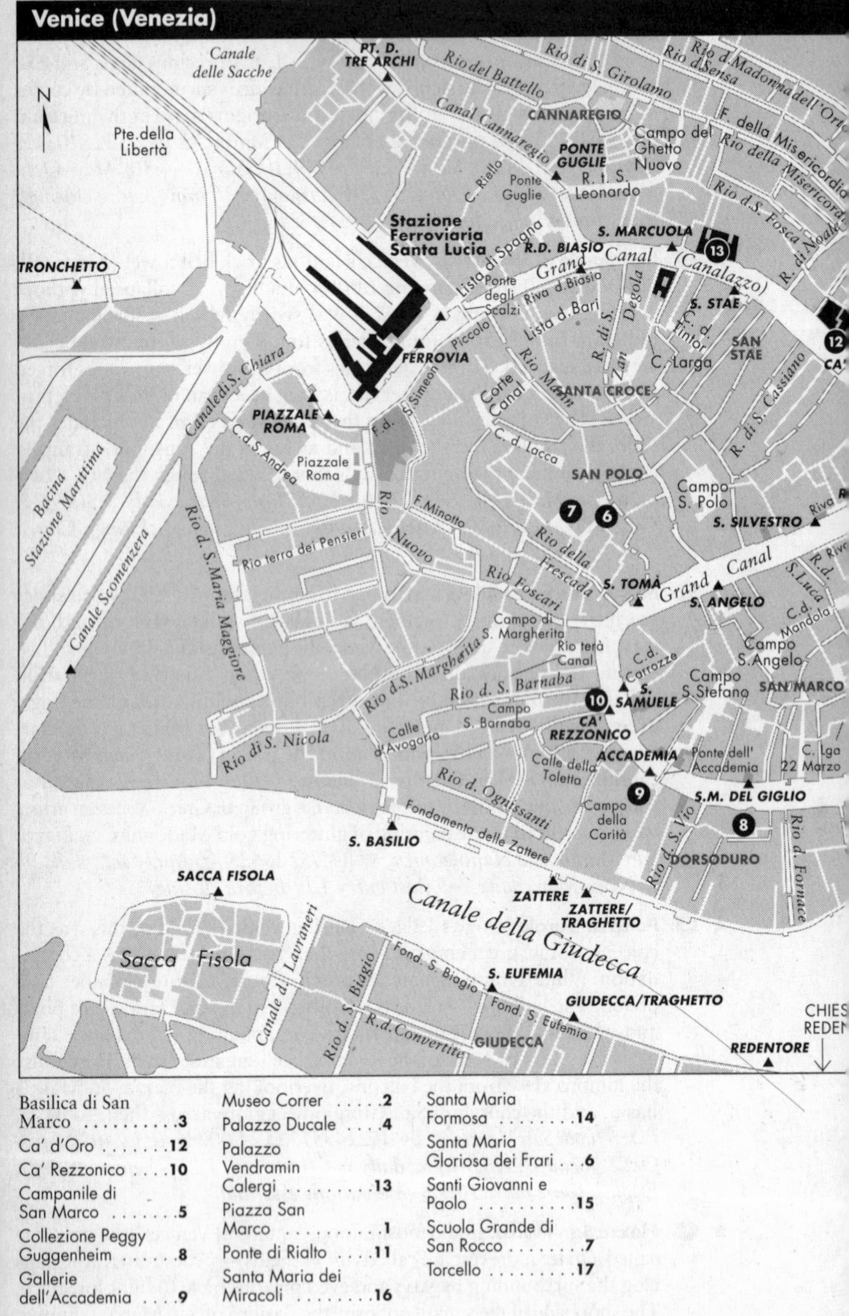

Basilica di San Marco 3
Ca' d'Oro 12
Ca' Rezzonico 10
Campanile di San Marco 5
Collezione Peggy Guggenheim 8
Gallerie dell'Accademia 9
Museo Correr 2
Palazzo Ducale 4
Palazzo Vendramin Calergi 13
Piazza San Marco 1
Ponte di Rialto 11
Santa Maria dei Miracoli 16
Santa Maria Formosa 14
Santa Maria Gloriosa dei Frari . . .6
Santi Giovanni e Paolo 15
Scuola Grande di San Rocco 7
Torcello 17

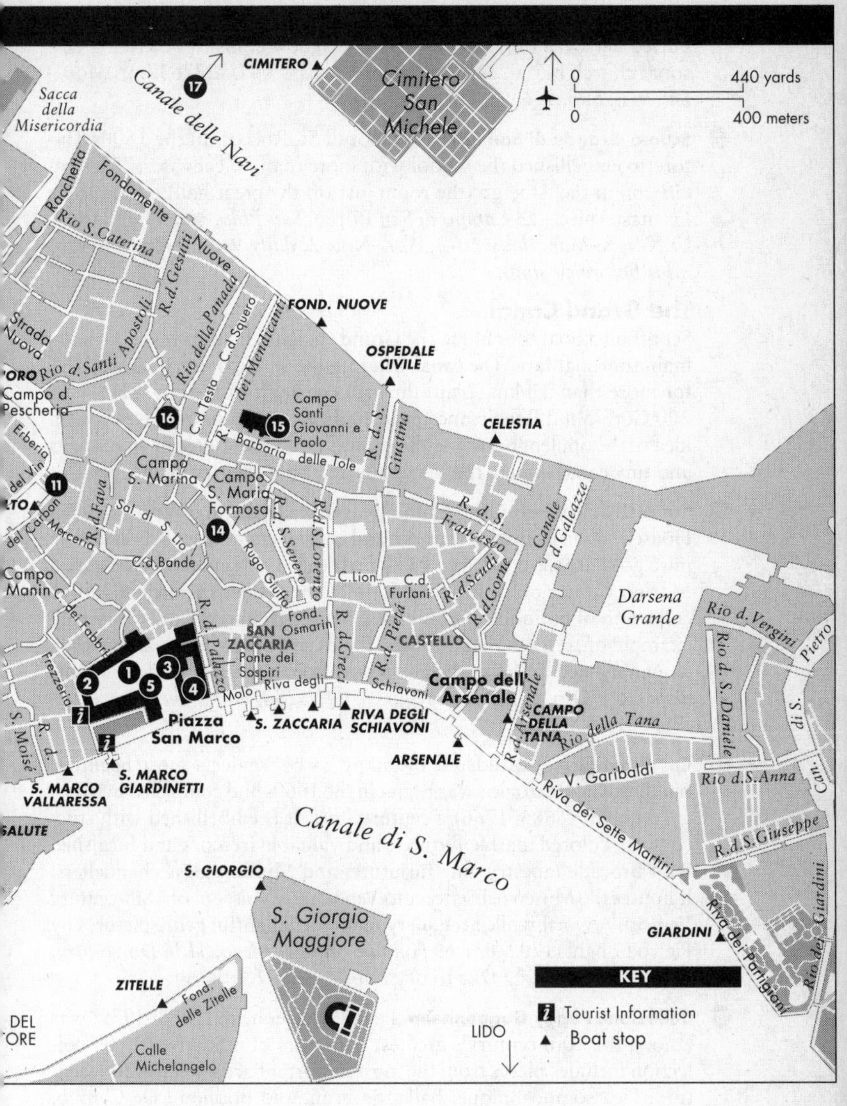

CIMITERO
Cimitero San Michele
Sacca della Misericordia
Canale delle Navi
0
440 yards
0
400 meters
Fondamente Nuove
C. Racchetta
Rio S. Caterina
R.d. Gesuiti
Rio della Panada
C.d.Squero
dei Mendicanti
Strada Nuova
Rio d. Santi Apostoli
FOND. NUOVE
OSPEDALE CIVILE
Campo d. Pescheria
Erberia
del Vin
C.d.Testo
Campo Santi Giovanni e Paolo
R. Barbaria delle Tole
R. d. S. Giustina
CELESTIA
Campo S. Marina
Campo S. Maria Formosa
del Carbon
Mercerie
R.d.Fava
Sol. di S. Lio
R.d. S.Severo
R.d.S.Lorenzo
R. d. S. Francesco
Canale d.Galeazze
C.d.Bande
Ruga Giuffa
C.Lion
C.d. Furlani
R.d.Scudi
R.d.Gorne
Darsena Grande
Campo Manin
C. dei Fabbri
R. d. Palazzo
Fond. Osmarin
R. d.Greci
R.d. Pietà
CASTELLO
Rio d.Vergini
S. Pietro
SAN ZACCARIA
Ponte dei Sospiri
Frezzeria
Molo
Riva degli Schiavoni
Campo dell' Arsenale
Rio d. S. Daniele
Piazza San Marco
S. ZACCARIA
RIVA DEGLI SCHIAVONI
R.d. Arsenale
CAMPO DELLA TANA
Rio della Tana
S. Moisè
R. d.
ARSENALE
V. Garibaldi
Rio d.S.Anna
Can.
S. MARCO GIARDINETTI
S. MARCO VALLARESSA
Riva dei Sette Martiri
SALUTE
Canale di S. Marco
R.d.S.Giuseppe
S. GIORGIO
S. Giorgio Maggiore
Riva dei Partigiani
GIARDINI
Rio dei Giardini
ZITELLE
Fond. delle Zitelle
Calle Michelangelo
LIDO
KEY
Tourist Information
Boat stop

the immense *Assumption of the Virgin,* over the main altar. Titian is buried here, the only one of 70,000 plague victims to be given a personal church burial. ✉ *Campo dei Frari,* ☎ *041/5222637.* ⏲ *Mon.–Sat. 9–6, Sun. 1–6.*

7 **Scuola Grande di San Rocco** (School of St. Rocco). In the 1500s Tintoretto embellished the school with more than 50 canvases. The *Crucifixion* in the Albergo (the room just off the great hall) is held to be his masterpiece. ✉ *Campo di San Rocco, San Polo,* ☎ *041/5234864.* ⏲ *Nov. 3–Mar., daily 10–4; Apr.–Nov. 2, daily 9–5:30 (last entry 30 mins before closing).*

The Grand Canal

Set off on a boat tour along the Grand Canal, which serves as Venice's main thoroughfare. The canal winds in the shape of a backwards "S" for more than 3½ km (2 mi) through the heart of the city, past some 200 Gothic and Renaissance palaces. The vaporetto tour gives you an idea of the opulent beauty of the palaces and a peek into the side streets and tiny canals where the Venetians go about their daily business.

★ 12 **Ca' d'Oro.** This exquisite Gothic palace was once literally a "Golden House," when its marble traceries and ornaments were embellished with pure gold. It was created in 1434 by the rich and enamored patrician Marino Contarini for his wife. It holds the **Galleria Franchetti**, a fine collection of antiquities, sculptures, paintings, and the only surviving example of frescoes that adorned the exterior of a Venetian building (commissioned by those who could not afford a marble facade). ✉ *Calle della Ca' d'Oro, 3933 Cannaregio,* ☎ *041/5238790.* ⏲ *Tue.–Sun. 8:15–7:15, Mon. 8:15–2.*

★ 10 **Ca' Rezzonico.** Considered by many to be Venice's most beautiful building, Ca' Rezzonico was begun in the 1660s and completed by Giorgio Massari (1686–1766) a century later. It is embellished with stuccowork, colored marble fixtures, and valuable frescoes and furnished with brocade tapestry, fine furniture, and Murano glass chandeliers. It houses the Museo del Settecento Veneziano (Museum of 18th-century Venice). A worthwhile art gallery includes delightful genre pictures by Pietro Longhi (1702–85). ✉ *Fondamenta Pedrocco, 3136 Dorsoduro,* ☎ *041/2410100.* ⏲ *Due to open in June 2001.*

8 **Collezione Peggy Guggenheim.** Peggy Guggenheim (1898–1979) was among the 20th century's greatest collectors of modern art. Her collection includes pieces from the most important artists of the 20th century: Picasso and Braque; Balla, Severini, and Boccioni; De Chirico; Kandinsky; Magritte; and Rothko, Motherwell, Pollock, and Bacon. ✉ *Palazzo Venier dei Leoni, entrance on Calle San Cristoforo, 701 Dorsoduro,* ☎ *041/5206288.* ⏲ *Wed.–Mon. 10–6.*

★ 9 **Gallerie dell'Accademia** (Accademia Gallery). Unquestionably the largest collection of Venetian art in the world, the Accademie Galleries include oils by Giovanni Bellini (1430–1516), Giorgione (1477–1511), Titian, and Tintoretto (1518–94) and superb later works by Veronese (1528–88) and Tiepolo (1696–1770). ✉ *Campo della Carità, Accademia, Dorsoduro,* ☎ *041/5222247.* ⏲ *Tues.–Sat. 8:15–7:15, Mon. 8:15–2.*

13 **Palazzo Vendramin Calergi.** This Renaissance gem dates from the 1480s. The German composer Wagner died in a room here in 1883 following the success of his *Parsifal.* Today the palace houses Venice's casino. ✉ *2040 Cannaregio, San Marcuola vaporetto stop.* ⏲ *Casino daily 11 AM–2:30 AM.* ☎ *041/5297111.*

★ 11 **Ponte di Rialto** (Rialto Bridge). The first permanent stone bridge across the Grand Canal, the Rialto was built in the late 1500s after a competition that attracted the best architects of the period, including Michelangelo, Palladio, and Sansovino. The job went to Antonio da Ponte, whose plan focused on structure rather than elaborate decoration and kept costs down at a time when the Republic's coffers were low due to continual wars against the Turks and the opening of oceanic trade routes. A single arcade, more than 91 ft in length, supports two rows of shops, with windows that open onto the often crowded central passage. The side paths offer a prime look at one of the city's most captured views: the Grand Canal full of gondolas and boats in the background. Make a point of seeing the adjacent Rialto food market and the fish market beyond it (Tuesday–Saturday mornings; fish market closed Monday). Ruga San Giovanni and Ruga del Ravano, beside the market, will bring you face to face with scores of shops. Start from the Salizzada San Giovanni side of the bridge.

North of San Marco

Fold the map away and it's easy to get lost in the picturesque neighborhoods north of San Marco: here low-key shops, bakeries, and tiny watering holes have not been replaced by tourist-oriented places and humble houses are festooned with laundry hung from lines stretched across the dark-green canals.

16 **Santa Maria dei Miracoli.** Perfectly proportioned and sheathed in marble, the late-15th-century church embodies the classical serenity of the early Renaissance. The interior is decorated with marble reliefs by the church's architect, Pietro Lombardo, and his son Tullio. ✉ *Campo Santa Maria Nova,* ☎ *041/5235293.* ⏲ *Mon.–Sat. 10–5, Sun. 1–5.*

14 **Santa Maria Formosa.** This graceful white marble church, built by Mauro Coducci in 1492, was grafted onto 11th-century foundations. Inside is a hodgepodge of Renaissance and Baroque styles. A small vegetable market bustles in the square weekday mornings. ✉ *Campo Santa Maria Formosa,* ☎ *041/5234645.* ⏲ *Mon.–Sat. 10–5, Sun. 1–5.*

15 **Santi Giovanni e Paolo.** This massive Dominican church is the twin (and rival) of the Franciscan Santa Maria Gloriosa dei Frari and contains a wealth of artwork. Twenty-five doges are buried here. Outside in the campo stands Verrocchio's magnificent equestrian monument of **Bartolomeo Colleoni** (1400–75), who fought for the Venetian cause during the mid-1400s. ✉ *Campo Santi Giovanni e Paolo,* ☎ *041/5237510.* ⏲ *Mon.–Sat. 8–12:30 and 3:30–6, Sun. 3:30–6.*

Venetian Lagoon

A vaporetto excursion to the main islands of the lagoon makes for a perfect escape from the busy streets of Venice. Start with Murano, famous for its glass furnaces; then continue to Burano, where fishermen painted their toy-like houses with the brightest colors possible to make them visible even in the thickest of the lagoon's fog; the further-flung Torcello has a dream-like atmosphere of its own, which makes it one of the most romantic places in the region.

17 **Torcello.** This is where the first Venetians landed in their flight from the barbarians 1,500 years ago. Even after many settlers left to found the city of Venice on the island of Rivo Alto (Rialto), Torcello continued to grow and prosper until its main source of income, wool manufacturing, was priced out of the marketplace. It's hard to believe now, looking at this almost deserted island, that in the 16th century it had 20,000 inhabitants and 10 churches.

The island's cathedral, **Santa Maria Assunta,** dates from the 11th century. The ornate Byzantine mosaics are testimony to the importance and wealth of an island that could attract the best artists and craftsmen of its day. The vast mosaic on the inside of the facade depicts the *Last Judgment* as artists of the 11th and 12th centuries imagined it: figures writhe in vividly depicted contortions of pain. Facing it, as if in mitigation, is the calm mosaic figure of the Madonna, alone in a field of gold above the staunch array of Apostles. ✉ *Torcello,* ☎ *041/730084.* ⏲ *June–Sept., daily 10:30–6; Oct.–May, daily 10–4.*

Dining

Venetians love seafood, and it figures prominently on most restaurant menus, sometimes to the exclusion of meat dishes. Fish is generally expensive, and you should remember when ordering that the price given on menus for fish as a main course is often per 100 grams, not the total cost of what you are served, which could be two or three times that amount. However, *sarde in saor* (fried sardines marinated with onions, vinegar, pine nuts and raisins) is a tasty traditional dish that can cost as little as a pizza. City specialties also include *pasta e fagioli* (pasta and bean soup), risotto, and the delicious *fegato alla veneziana* (liver with onions) served with grilled polenta.

$$$–$$$$ ✕ **Da Arturo.** The tiny Da Arturo is a refreshing change from the numerous seafood restaurants of which Venetians are so fond. The cordial proprietor prefers, instead, to offer varied and delicious seasonal vegetable and salad dishes, or tasty, generous meat courses such as *braciola alla veneziana* (pork chop schnitzel with vinegar). ✉ *Calle degli Assassini, 3656 San Marco,* ☎ *041/5286974. Reservations essential. No credit cards. Closed Sun., 10 days after Carnival, and Aug.*

$$$–$$$$ ★ ✕ **Osteria Da Fiore.** Long a favorite with Venetians, Da Fiore has been discovered by tourists, so reservations are imperative. It's known for its excellent seafood dinners, which might include such specialties as *pasticcio di pesce* (fish pie) and *seppioline* (little cuttlefish). Not easy to find, it's just off Campo San Polo. ✉ *Calle dello Scaleter, 2202/A San Polo,* ☎ *041/721308. Reservations essential. AE, DC, MC, V. Closed Sun.–Mon., Aug. 10–early Sept., and Dec. 25–Jan. 15.*

$$$ ✕ **Fiaschetteria Toscana.** Once the storehouse of a 19th-century wine merchant from Tuscany, this popular restaurant has long been a favorite of Venetians and visitors. Courteous, cheerful waiters serve such specialties as *rombo* (turbot) with capers, an exceptionally good *pasta alla buranella* (pasta with shrimp, au gratin), and zabaglione. ✉ *Campo San Giovanni Crisostomo, 5719 Cannaregio,* ☎ *041/5285281. AE, DC, MC, V. Closed Mon. lunch, Tues. and 4 wks in July–Aug.*

$$–$$$ ★ ✕ **Al Covo.** This small osteria changes its menu according to the day's bounty—mostly local seafood caught just hours before. Cesare Benelli and his American wife, Diane, insist on only the freshest ingredients and claim to not use butter or animal fats. Try the *zuppa di pesce* (fish broth) followed by the fish of the day either grilled, baked, or steamed. The flexible tasting menu at lunch is a good deal. ✉ *Campiello della Pescaria, 3968 Castello,* ☎ *041/5223812. No credit cards. Closed Wed. and Thurs., 2 wks in Aug., and 1 month between Dec. and Jan.*

$$ ★ ✕ **Alle Testiere.** A strong local following can make it tough to get one of the five tables at this tiny trattoria near Campo Santa Maria Formosa. Chef Bruno Gavagnin's dishes stand out for lightness and balance. Try the *gnocchetti con moscardini* (little gnocchi with tender baby octopus), or the baked turbot with radicchio di Treviso. A short but well-assembled wine list allows for some interesting combinations. Save room for a slice of homemade pear tart. ✉ *Calle del Mondo Novo, 5081 Castello,* ☎ *041/5227220. Reservations essential. MC, V. Closed Sun., 3 wks in Aug., and 3 wks in Dec.–Jan.*

$$ ✕ **Vini da Gigio.** An attractive, family-run establishment, this trattoria is on the quayside of a canal, just off the Strada Nuova. The service is affable and the food tasty, with homemade pasta, fish, and meat dishes and good draft wine. The barroom is pleasant and casual for lunch. ✉ *Fondamenta de la Chiesa, 3628A Cannaregio,* ☎ *041/5285140. AE, DC, MC, V. Closed Mon., 3 wks between Jan. and Feb., 1 wk in June, and 3 wks between Aug. and Sept.*

$ ★ ✕ **Ae Oche.** But for the clientele, there's not much Venetian about this saloon-like pizzeria with rows of imported stouts on the shelves and a no-smoking room. Eighty pizza combinations include the popular Campagnola, lavishly sprinkled with a mix of tomato, mozzarella, mushroom, Brie, and *speck* (smoked prosciutto), but purists should stick to the *margherita* with tomato, mozzarella, and basil. A selection of 16 salads plus a few pasta dishes make the Oche an ideal stop for a light meal between sights. ✉ *Calle delle Oche, 1552/a–b Santa Croce,* ☎ *041/5241161. AE, DC, MC, V. Closed Mon., Nov.–Dec.*

$ ✕ **L'Incontro.** This trattoria between San Barnaba and Campo Santa Margherita has a faithful clientele drawn by good food (excellent meat, but no fish) at reasonable prices. Menu choices include freshly made Sardinian pastas, juicy steaks, wild duck, boar, and (with advance notice) roast suckling pig. ✉ *Rio Terrá Canal, 3062A Dorsoduro,* ☎ *041/5222404. AE, D, MC, V. Closed Mon., Jan., and 2 wks in Aug. No lunch Tues.*

Lodging

Space in the time-worn but renovated palaces-cum-hotels is at a premium in this city, and even in the best hotel, rooms can be small and offer little natural light. Preservation restrictions on buildings often preclude the installation of such things as elevators and air-conditioning. On the other hand, Venice's luxury hotels can offer rooms of fabulous opulence and elegance, and even in the more modest hotels you can find comfortable rooms of great charm and character, sometimes with stunning views. Venice attracts visitors year-round, although the winter months, with the exception of Carnival time, are generally much quieter, and most hotels offer lower rates during this period. It is always worth booking in advance, but if you haven't, AVA (Venetian Hoteliers Association) booths will help you find a room after your arrival in the city.

$$$$ 🏨 **Danieli.** Parts of this rather large hotel are built around a 15th-century palazzo bathed in sumptuous Venetian colors. The downside is that the Danieli also has several modern annexes that some find bland and impersonal, and the lower-price rooms can be exceedingly drab. Still, celebrities and English-speaking patrons crowd its sumptuous four-story-high lobby, chic salons, and dining terrace with a fantastic view of St. Mark's Basin. ✉ *Riva degli Schiavoni, 4196 Castello, 30122,* ☎ *041/5226480,* FAX *041/5200208,* WEB *www.luxurycollection.com. 219 rooms, 11 suites. Restaurant. AE, DC, MC, V.*

$$$$ ★ 🏨 **Gritti Palace.** This haven of pampering luxury is like an aristocratic private home, with fresh flowers, fine antiques, lavish appointments, and Old World service. The dining terrace overlooking the Grand Canal is best in the evening when boat traffic dies down. ✉ *Campo Santa Maria del Giglio, 2467 San Marco, 30124,* ☎ *041/794611,* FAX *041/5200942,* WEB *www.luxurycollection.com. 87 rooms, 6 suites. Restaurant. AE, DC, MC, V.*

$$$–$$$$ ★ 🏨 **Metropole.** Guests can step from their water taxi or gondola into the lobby of this small, very well-run hotel, rich in precious antiques and just five minutes from Piazza San Marco. Many rooms have a view of the lagoon and others overlook the garden at the back. ✉ *Riva degli Schiavoni, 4149 Castello, 30122,* ☎ *041/5205044,* FAX *041/5223679,* WEB *www.hotelmetropole.com. 67 rooms, 7 suites. Restaurant. AE, DC, MC, V.*

$$$ **Londra Palace.** Fine views of the lagoon and the church of San Giorgio offer a soothing alternative to the concoction of plush carpets and costly tapestries that fill the over-the-top interiors of the Londra Palace, one of the grand hotels of Venice. Handsome Biedermeier tables, couches, and writing desks stand out against the numerous marble columns planted all around to support such heavy luxury. Rooms overlooking the Riva cost 10% more than the smaller, top-floor rooms with mansard ceilings. ✉ *Riva degli Schiavoni, 4171 Castello, 30122,* ☎ *041/5200533,* FAX *041/5225032,* WEB *www.hotelondra.it. 36 rooms, 17 suites. Restaurant. AE, DC, MC, V.*

$$ ★ **Accademia.** Hidden within the heart of Venice, this miniature Palladian villa—complete with canal-side garden—is one of the city's most enchanting hotels. It has plenty of atmosphere, with a touch of romance. Many rooms overlook the gardens. ✉ *Fondamenta Bollani, 1058 Dorsoduro, 30123,* ☎ *041/5210188,* FAX *041/5239152,* WEB *www.pensioneaccademia.it. 27 rooms, 25 with bath. AE, DC, MC, V.*

$$ **Ala.** The Ala is between San Marco and Santo Stefano, a few steps from the Santa Maria del Giglio vaporetto stop. Some rooms are large with coffered ceilings and old-style furnishings; smaller ones have more modern decor and orthopedic beds. Breakfast is served in a beautiful room overlooking a small canal. ✉ *2494 San Marco, 30124,* ☎ *041/5208333,* FAX *041/5206390,* WEB *www.hotelala.it. 85 rooms. AE, DC, MC, V.*

$$ ★ **La Calcina.** The Calcina sits in an enviable position along the sunny Zattere with views across the wide Giudecca Canal. You can sunbathe on the *altana* (wooden-roof terrace), or enjoy an afternoon tea in one of the reading corners of the shadowy, intimate hall with flickering candlelight and soft classical music. A stone staircase leads to the rooms upstairs (no elevator), with shiny wooden floors, Art Deco furnishings, and firm beds; some suffer from a lack of storage space. The annex nearby offers lower-priced rooms without a view. ✉ *780 Dorsoduro, 30123,* ☎ *041/5206466,* FAX *041/5227045,* WEB *www.veniceinfo.it. 42 rooms. AE, DC, MC, V.*

$$ **Wildner.** Rooms in this pleasant family-run, unpretentious pensione are spread over four floors (no elevator), half with a view of San Giorgio; the others (cooler and quieter in summer) overlook Campo San Zaccaria. ✉ *Riva degli Schiavoni, 4161 Castello, 30122,* ☎ *041/5227463,* FAX *041/5265615,* WEB *www.veneziahotels.com. 16 rooms. AE, DC, MC, V.*

$–$$ **Paganelli.** The lagoon views here so impressed Henry James that he wrote the Paganelli up in the preface to his *Portrait of a Lady.* This charming, small hotel on the waterfront has an annex on the quiet square of Campo San Zaccaria and is tastefully decorated in Venetian style. ✉ *Riva degli Schiavoni, 4687 Castello, 30122,* ☎ *041/5224324,* FAX *041/5239267,* WEB *www.gpnet.it. 22 rooms, 19 with bath. AE, MC, V.*

$ **Bucintoro.** Whistler once stayed here, and today the Bucintoro is still favored by artists, drawn by the lagoon views from every room. Slightly off the tourist track, this friendly, family-run hotel has clean and simple rooms. The price is unbeatable for such spectacular vistas. ✉ *Riva San Biagio, 2135 Castello, 30122,* ☎ *041/5223240,* FAX *041/5235224. 28 rooms, 25 with bath. Restaurant. No credit cards. Closed mid-Dec.–early Feb.*

$ ★ **Dalla Mora.** Tucked into the end of a quiet calle beyond the main flow of traffic, this hotel occupies two simple, well-maintained houses, both with a view. The cheerful, tiny entry hall leads upstairs to a delightful terrace. Rooms are spacious, with basic wooden furniture and tile floors. The annex across the calle has rooms without private bathrooms and others with only showers and sinks. Excellent quality for the price makes this a particularly good place to stay. ✉ *Off Salizzada*

San Pantalon, 42 Santa Croce, 30123, ☎ 041/710703, FAX 041/723006. 14 rooms, 6 with bath. AE, DC, MC, V.

Nightlife and the Arts

For a detailed listing of what's going on, pick up the monthly *Venezia News* from a newsstand. It has plenty of information in English about concerts, opera, ballet, theater, exhibitions, movies, sports, sightseeing, and a useful "Servizi" section with late-night pharmacies, operating hours for the busiest vaporetto and bus lines, and a listing of the main trains and flights from Venice.

The Arts

Venice is a stop for major traveling exhibits, from Maya art to contemporary art retrospectives. In odd years, usually from late June to early November, the **Biennale dell'Arte** exhibition draws the work of hundreds of contemporary international artists and holds events throughout the season, including the yearly Mostra Internazionale del Cinema (International Film Festival), which begins at the end of August.

CONCERTS

Although there are occasional jazz and Italian pop concerts in clubs around town, the vast majority of music played in Venice is classical. Vivaldi (Venice's most famous composer) is usually on the playbill; the churches of the Pietà, San Stae, Santo Stefano, and San Bartolomeo are frequent venues. For information on these often impromptu events, ask at the APT office and look for posters on walls and in restaurants and shops. **Kele e Teo Agency** (✉ Ponte dei Bareteri, 4930 San Marco, ☎ 041/5208722, FAX 041/5208913) and **Nalesso** (✉ Calle dello Spezier off Campo Santo Stefano, 2765 San Marco, ☎ 041/5203329) handle tickets for several musical events.

OPERA

The Teatro La Fenice is one of Italy's oldest opera houses, a pilgrimage site for all opera lovers and the scene of many memorable operatic premieres, including, in 1853, the dismal first-night flop of Verdi's *La Traviata.* The great opera house was badly damaged by fire in January 1996, and the meticulous restoration work—helped in large part by donations from opera lovers around the world—is expected to continue for several years. Until the Fenice reopens, opera, symphony, and ballet performances are held year-round at the **Palafenice** (✉ Cassa di Risparmio bank, Campo San Luca, ☎ 041/5210161; 041/786511 ticket information, WEB www.teatrolafenice.it), near the Tronchetto parking area.

Nightlife

For dancing, try the tiny **Disco Club Piccolo Mondo** (✉ 1056/A Dorsoduro, ☎ 041/5200371), near the Accademia Gallery. The large **Casanova** (✉ Lista di Spagna, 158/a Cannaregio, ☎ 041/2750199) is a restaurant-cabaret-disco with big projection screens, metallic walls, and red leather couches. **Fiddler's Elbow** (✉ Strada Nuova, 3847 Cannaregio, ☎ 041/5239930) offers all the typical trappings of an Irish pub: gab, grub, and frothy Guinness. The **Martini Scala Club** (✉ Calle del Cafetier, 1077 San Marco, ☎ 041/5224121) is an elegant piano bar with a restaurant. Tunes start at 10 PM and go until the wee hours.

Shopping

At **Gilberto Penzo** (✉ Calle Seconda dei Saoneri, 2681 San Polo, ☎ 041/719372) you'll find small-scale models of gondolas and their graceful oar locks known as *forcole.* **Norelene** (✉ Calle della Chiesa, 727 Dorsoduro, near the Guggenheim, ☎ 041/5237605) has hand-painted fabrics that make wonderful wall hangings or elegant jackets and chic scarves. **Venetia Studium** (✉ Calle Larga XXII Marzo, 2430 San Marco, ☎ 041/5229281) is famous for Fortuny-inspired lamps and elegant scarves.

Glass

There's a lot of cheap, low-quality Venetian glass for sale around town; if you want something better, try **l'Isola** (✉ Campo San Moisè, 1468 San Marco, ☎ 041/5231973), where Carlo Moretti's contemporary designs are on display. **Domus** (✉ Fondamenta dei Vetrai, Murano, ☎ 041/739215), on Murano, has a good selection of glass objects.

Shopping Districts

Le Mercerie, the **Frezzeria,** and **Calle dei Fabbri** are some of Venice's busiest shopping streets and lead off of Piazza San Marco.

Venice Essentials

AIRPORTS & TRANSFERS

➤ AIRPORT INFORMATION: **Aeroporto Marco Polo** (✉ 10 km/6 mi northeast of Venice on the mainland, ☎ 041/2609260 flight information).

TRANSFERS

The most direct way between the airport and downtown is by the Alilaguna launch, with regularly scheduled service until midnight; it takes about an hour to get to the landing (just off Piazza San Marco), stopping at the Lido on the way, and the fare is 17,000 lire/€8.80 per person, including bags. Blue ATVO buses make the 25-minute trip in to Piazzale Roma, where the road to Venice terminates; the cost is 5,000 lire/€2.60. From Piazzale Roma visitors will most likely have to take a vaporetto to their hotel. Water taxis (slick high-power motorboats called *motoscafi*) should cost about 140,000 lire/€72.30. Land taxis are available, running the same route as the buses; the cost is about 55,000 lire/€28.40.

➤ INFORMATION: **Alilaguna** (☎ 041/5235775). **Land Taxis** (☎ 041/5237774). **Water Taxis** (☎ 041/5235775).

BOAT & FERRY TRAVEL

BY GONDOLA

If you mustn't leave Venice without treating yourself to a gondola ride, take it in the quiet of the evening, when the churning traffic on the canals has died down, the palace windows are illuminated, and the only sounds are the muted splashes of the gondolier's oar. Make sure he understands that you want to see the *rii,* or smaller canals, as well as the Grand Canal. There's supposed to be a fixed minimum rate of about 120,000 lire/€61.95 for 50 minutes and a nighttime supplement of 30,000 lire/€15.50. Set the terms with your gondolier *before* stepping into his boat.

BY TRAGHETTO

Few tourists know about the two-man gondolas that ferry people across the Grand Canal at various fixed points. It's the cheapest and shortest gondola ride in Venice, and it can save a lot of walking. The fare is 700 lire/€0.35, which you hand to one of the gondoliers when you get on. Look for TRAGHETTO signs.

BY VAPORETTO

ACTV water buses run the length of the Grand Canal and circle the city. There are several lines, some of which connect Venice with the major and minor islands in the lagoon. The fare is 6,000 lire/€3.10

on all lines. A 24-hour tourist ticket costs 18,000 lire/€9.30, a three-day ticket 35,000 lire/€18.10, and a seven-day ticket 60,000 lire/€31; these are especially worthwhile if you are planning to visit the islands. Free timetables are available at the ticket office at Piazzale Roma. Timetables are posted at every landing stage, but there is not always a ticket booth operating. After 9 PM, tickets are available on the boats, but you must immediately inform the controller that you need a ticket. For this reason it may be useful to buy a *blocchetto* (book of tickets) in advance. Landing stages are clearly marked with name and line number, but check before boarding, particularly with the 52 and 82, to make sure the boat is going in your direction.

Line 1 is the Grand Canal local, calling at every stop, and continuing via San Marco to the Lido. (The trip takes about 45 minutes from the station to San Marco.) Other major lines are 41 and 42 (between San Zaccaria and Murano), 51 and 52 (between the railway station and the Lido), 61 and 62 (between the Lido and Murano), and 82 (a loop beginning and ending at San Zaccaria), all of which make stops at key locations along the way. At night, there is only line N, with boats every 30 minutes making stops at the Lido, San Zaccaria, Rialto, Piazzale Roma, Giudecca, and Zattere.

BY WATER TAXI

Motoscafi, or taxis, are excessively expensive, and the fare system is as complex as Venice's layout. A minimum fare of about 50,000 lire/€25.82 gets you nowhere, and you'll pay three times as much to get from one end of the Grand Canal to the other. *Always agree on the fare before starting out.* It's probably worth considering taking a water taxi only if you are traveling in a small group. Contact the Cooperativa San Marco.

➤ BOAT AND FERRY INFORMATION: **ACTV** (Daily 7:30 AM–8 PM, ☎ 041/5287886, WEB www.actv.it). **Cooperativa San Marco** (☎ 041/5222303).

CAR TRAVEL

PARKING

If you bring a car to Venice, you will have to pay for a garage or parking space during your stay. Do not be waylaid by illegal con artists often wearing fake uniforms who may try to flag you down and offer to arrange parking and hotels. Continue on until you reach the automated ticket machines.

Parking at Autorimessa Comunale costs 36,000 lire/€18.60 for 24 hours. The private Garage San Marco costs 35,000 lire/€18.10 for 12 hours and 48,000 lire/€24.80 for 24 hours. To reach the privately run Tronchetto parking area, follow the signs to turn right before Piazzale Roma. Parking costs 30,000 lire/€15.50 for 24 hours. Do not leave valuables in the car. There is a left-luggage office, open daily 8–8, next to the Pullman Bar on the ground floor of the municipal garage at Piazzale Roma. The AVA has arranged a discount of about 20% per day for hotel guests who use the Garage San Marco or Tronchetto parking facility. Ask for a voucher when you check into your hotel. Present the voucher when you pay the parking fee. A vaporetto (No. 82) runs from Tronchetto to Piazzale Roma and Piazza San Marco (also to the Lido in summer). In thick fog or when tides are extreme, a bus runs instead to Piazzale Roma, where you can pick up a vaporetto.

➤ CONTACTS: **Autorimessa Comunale** (✉ Piazzale Roma, end of S11 road, ☎ 041/2727301). **Garage San Marco** (✉ Piazzale Roma 467/f, end of S11 road, ☎ 041/5232213). **Tronchetto** (☎ 041/5207555).

CONSULATES

➤ UNITED KINGDOM: (✉ Campo della Carità, 1051 Dorsoduro, ☎ 041/5227207).

EMERGENCIES

Pharmacies are open weekdays 9–12:30 and 3:45–7:30, Saturday 9–12:45; a notice telling where to get late-night and Sunday service is posted outside every pharmacy.

➤ DOCTORS AND DENTISTS: **Doctor** (emergency room, Venice's hospital, ☎ 041/5230000).

➤ EMERGENCY SERVICES: **Ambulance** (☎ 118). **Carabinieri** (military police; ☎ 112). **General emergencies** (☎ 113).

TOURS

SINGLE-DAY TOURS

The Cooperativa San Marco organizes tours of the islands of Murano, Burano, and Torcello departing April–September, daily at 9:30 and 2:30, and October–March 1, daily at 2 PM, from the landing stage in front of Giardini Reali near Piazza San Marco. Tours last about 3½ hours and cost about 30,000 lire/€15.50. They do tend to be annoyingly commercial, however, and emphasize glass factory showrooms where you are pressured to buy, often at higher than standard prices.

American Express books a day trip to Padova by boat along the Brenta River, with stops at three Palladian villas. The tours run three days a week from March to October; the cost is about 120,000 lire/€61.95 per person; bookings need to be made the day before. Alternatively, the Palladio Villa Tour (by mini-bus, max. 8 people), besides a visit to the Palladian villas, includes a walking tour of Vicenza (190,000 lire/€98.15 per person). Other full-day excursions which can be booked at American Express focus on the hills of the Veneto, with stops in the towns of Marostica, Bassano del Grappa, Asolo, at Villa Barbaro at Maser, and at a vineyard along the Strada del Prosecco for a Prosecco wine tasting (175,000 lire/€90.38), and on the Dolomite mountains, with stops at the lake of Misurina and in Cortina d'Ampezzo (180,000 lire/€92.95 per person includes packet lunch). For these last three tours it is essential to make reservations a couple of weeks in advance.

➤ FEES AND SCHEDULES: **American Express** (✉ Salizzada San Moisè, 1471 San Marco, ☎ 041/5200844, FAX 041/5229937). **Cooperativa San Marco** (✉ just off Piazza San Marco, ☎ 041/2406736 or 041/5235775).

PRIVATE GUIDES

American Express can provide guides for walking or gondola tours of Venice, or cars with driver and guide for excursions on the mainland. Pick up a list of licensed guides and their rates from the main IAT office or directly contact the Guides' Association.

➤ CONTACTS: **Guides' Association** (✉ 750 San Marco, near San Zulian, ☎ 041/5209038, FAX 041/5210762). **IAT** (✉ San Marco 71/F, near the Museo Correr).

WALKING TOURS

American Express and other operators offer two-hour walking tours of the San Marco area, taking in the basilica and the Doge's Palace. The cost is about 45,000 lire/€23.25, including admission. From April 25 through November 15, American Express offers an afternoon walking tour that ends with a short gondola ride (about 50,000 lire/€25.80). Some tour operators offer group gondola rides with a serenade. The cost is about 50,000 lire/€25.80. From June through August, free guided tours of the Basilica di San Marco are offered by the Procuratoria; information is available at a desk in the atrium of the church (no tours on Sun.).

TRAIN TRAVEL

Make sure your train goes all the way to the Stazione Ferroviaria Santa Lucia. Some trains leave passengers at the Stazione Ferroviaria

Venezia-Mestre. All trains traveling to and from Santa Lucia stop at Mestre, so to get from Mestre to Santa Lucia, or vice versa (a 10-minute trip), take the first available train, remembering there is a *supplemento* (extra charge) for traveling on Intercity, Eurocity, and Eurostar trains and that if you board one of these trains without having paid in advance for this part of the trip, you are subject to a hefty fine. Since most tourists arrive in Venice by train, tourist services are conveniently located at Santa Lucia, including an APT information booth and baggage depot. Directly outside the train station are the main vaporetto landing stages; from here, vaporetti can transport you to your hotel's neighborhood. Be prepared with advance directions from the hotel and a good map.

➤ TRAIN INFORMATION: **APT** (☎ 041/5298727). **Stazione Ferroviaria Santa Lucia** (✉ Venice's northwest corner, ☎ 8488/88088 toll-free). **Stazione Ferroviaria Venezia-Mestre** (✉ on the mainland, ☎ 8488/880880 toll-free).

TRANSPORTATION AROUND VENICE

First-time visitors find that getting around Venice presents some unusual problems: the complexity of its layout (the city is made up of more than 100 islands, all linked by bridges); the bewildering unfamiliarity of waterborne transportation; the apparently illogical house numbering system and duplication of street names in its six districts; and the necessity of walking whether you enjoy it or not. This is the only way to reach many parts of Venice, so wear comfortable shoes and count on getting lost more than once. It's essential to have a good map showing all street names and water-bus routes; buy one at any newsstand.

TRAVEL AGENCIES

➤ LOCAL AGENTS: **American Express** (✉ Salizzada San Moisè, 1471 San Marco, ☎ 041/5200844, FAX 041/5229937). **Albatravel** (✉ Calle dei Fabbri 4538, San Marco, ☎ 041/5210123, FAX 041/5200781).

VISITOR INFORMATION

The Venetian Hoteliers Association (AVA) will make free same-day reservations for those who come in person to their booths at the Piazzale Roma (open daily 9 AM–10 PM), at the Santa Lucia train station (open daily 8 AM–9 PM), and at the Marco Polo airport (open daily 9 AM–10 PM); a deposit, which will be deducted from your hotel bill, is required to hold the room. Alternatively, Venezia Sì's offers free reservations over the phone (Mon.–Sat. 9 AM–7 PM).

➤ TOURIST INFORMATION: **AVA** (☎ 041/5228004; ✉ Piazzale Roma, ☎ 041/5231397; ✉ inside the Santa Lucia train station, ☎ 041/715288; ✉ Marco Polo airport, ☎ 041/5415133). **IAT Information booths** (✉ Santa Lucia train station, ☎ 041/5298727; ✉ 71/f San Marco, near the Museo Correr; Lido in summer, ✉ Gran Viale S. Maria Elisabetta 6A, ☎ 041/5265721, FAX 041/5298720, Tourist information over phone ☎ 041/5298711; weekdays 8:30–5). **Venezia Sì's** (☎ 800/843006; 0039/0415222264 outside Italy; FAX 0039/0415221242).

CAMPANIA

Campania, the region composed of Naples, the Amalfi coast, and the surrounding sun-drenched area, is where most people's preconceived ideas of Italy become a reality. You'll find beaches, good food that relies heavily on tomatoes and mozzarella, acres of classical ruins, and gorgeous scenery. The exuberance of the locals doesn't leave much room for efficient organization, however, and you may have to revise your concept of time; here minutes dilate into hours at the drop of a hat.

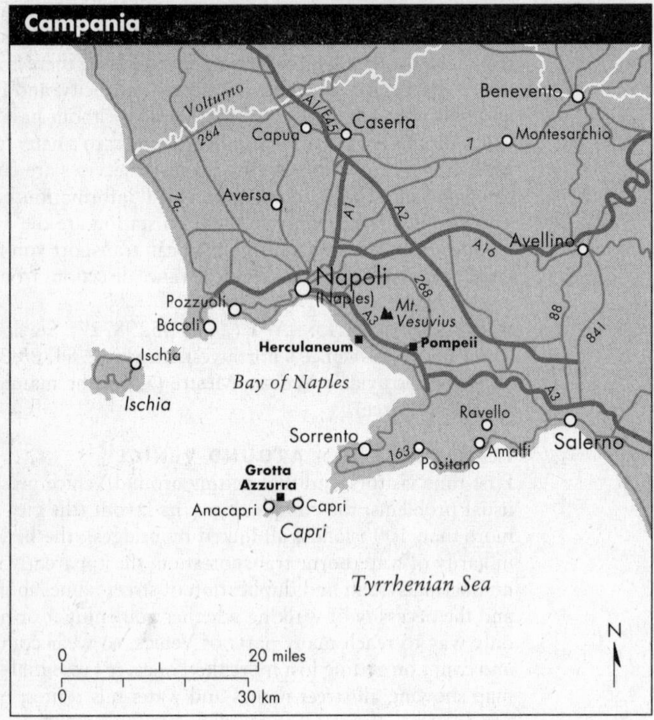

Once a city that rivaled Paris as a brilliant and refined cultural capital, Napoli (Naples) is afflicted by acute urban decay and chronic delinquency. You need patience, stamina, and a degree of caution to visit Naples on your own, but it's worth it for those who have a sense of adventure and the capacity to discern the enormous riches the city has accumulated in its 2,000-year history.

If you want the fun without the hassle, skip Naples and head for Sorrento, Capri, and the Amalfi coast, legendary haunts of the sirens who tried to lure Odysseus off course. Sorrento is touristy but has some fine old hotels and beautiful views; it's a good base for a leisurely excursion to Pompeii. Capri is a pint-size paradise, though sometimes too crowded for comfort, and the Amalfi coast offers enchanting towns and spectacular scenery.

Naples

Founded by the Greeks, Naples became a playground of the Romans and was ruled thereafter by a succession of foreign dynasties, all of which left traces of their cultures in the city and its environs. The most splendid of these rulers were the Bourbons, who were responsible for much of what you will want to see in Naples. Among the greatest relics of Bourbon powers in Naples is the 17th-century **Palazzo Reale** (Royal Palace), still furnished in the lavish Baroque style that suited them so well. ✉ *Piazza del Plebiscito,* ☎ *081/7944021.* ⏲ *Thurs.–Tues. 9–8.*

On the heights of the Vomero hill, the bastions of **Castel Sant'Elmo** (✉ Largo San Martino), open Tuesday–Sunday 9–7, occupy an evocative position with distant views over Naples and its bay. You can reach it by the **Montesanto funicular,** near Piazza Dante.

Also known as the Maschio Angioino, the massive stone **Castel Nuovo** (New Castle) was built by the city's Aragon rulers in the 13th century;

inside, the city's Museo Civico (Civic Museum) comprises mainly local artwork from the 15th to the 19th centuries, and there are also regular exhibitions. ✉ *Castel Nuovo, Piazza Municipio,* ☎ *081/7952003.* ⏲ *Castle Mon.–Sat. 9–7, courtyard only Sun. 9–1.*

The **Certosa di San Martino,** a Carthusian monastery restored in the 17th century, contains an eclectic collection of Neapolitan landscape paintings, royal carriages, and *presepi* (Christmas crèches). Check out the view from the balcony off Room 25. The museum lies on the Vomero Hill, near the Castel Sant'Elmo. ✉ *Museo Nazionale di San Martino,* ☎ *081/5781769.* ⏲ *Tues.–Fri. 8:30–7:30, weekends 9–7:30.*

★ The **Museo Archeologico Nazionale** (National Archaeological Museum) is generally dusty and unkempt, but it holds one of the world's great collections of antiquities. Greek and Roman sculptures, vividly colored mosaics, countless objects from Pompeii and Herculaneum, and an equestrian statue of the Roman emperor Nerva are all worth seeing. ✉ *Piazza Museo,* ☎ *081/440166.* ⏲ *Wed.–Mon. 9–7.*

★ The **Museo di Capodimonte** is housed in an 18th-century palace built by Bourbon king Charles III and surrounded by a vast park that affords sweeping views of the bay. The picture gallery is devoted to work from the 13th to 18th centuries, including many familiar works by Dutch and Spanish masters, as well as by the great Italians. Other rooms contain an extensive collection of porcelain and majolica from the various royal residences, some produced in the Bourbons' own factory right here on the grounds. ✉ *Parco di Capodimonte,* ☎ *081/7499111.* ⏲ *Tues.–Sun. 8:30–7:30.*

Santa Chiara was built during the early 1300s in Provençal Gothic style. A favorite Neapolitan song celebrates the quiet beauty of its cloister, decorated in delicate floral tiles. ✉ *Piazza Gesù Nuovo,* ☎ *081/5526209.* ⏲ *Apr.–Sept., daily 8:30–noon and 4–7; Oct.–Mar., daily 8:30–noon and 4–6.*

Via Toledo, also known as Via Roma, is great for strolling and watching the antics of the Neapolitans, whose daily lives are fraught with theatrical gestures and fiery speeches. They all seem to be actors in their own human comedy. The church **Gesù Nuovo,** with oddly faceted stone facade and elaborate Baroque interior, is off Via Toledo. ✉ *Piazza Gesù Nuovo,* ☎ *081/5518613.* ⏲ *Mon.–Sat. 6:30–12:45 and 4:15–7:30, Sun. 6:30–1:30.*

$$$ ✕ **La Sacrestia.** This lovely restaurant above Mergellina has a fine view from the delightful summer terrace. Traditional Neapolitan specialties of the day might be baked or steamed sea bass and linguine *in salsa di scorfano* (with scorpion-fish sauce). ✉ *Via Orazio 116,* ☎ *081/7611051. AE, DC, MC, V. Closed Sun. in July–Aug. and 2 wks in mid-Aug. No lunch Mon., no dinner Sun.*

$$ ✕ **Ciro a Santa Brigida.** Tables at this no-frills restaurant are arranged on two levels, and the decor is classic trattoria. This is the place to try traditional Neapolitan *sartù di riso* (a rich rice dish with meat and peas) and *melanzane alla parmigiana* or *polpette alla Ciro* (meatballs). There's pizza, too. ✉ *Via Santa Brigida 71, off Via Toledo,* ☎ *081/5524072. AE, DC, MC, V. Closed Sun. and 2 wks in Aug.*

$$$$ 🏨 **Excelsior.** On the shore drive, the Excelsior has splendid views of the bay from its front rooms. Spacious bedrooms are furnished in informal floral prints or more formal Empire style; all have a comfortable, traditional air. The salons are formal, with chandeliers and wall paintings, and the Terrazza restaurant enjoys stupendous views. ✉ *Via Partenope 48, 80121,* ☎ *081/7640111,* FAX *081/7649743,* WEB *www.excelsior.it. 136 rooms. Restaurant. AE, DC, MC, V.*

$$ 🏨 **Rex.** On the first two floors of an Art Nouveau building, the hotel, in a fairly quiet spot near the Santa Lucia waterfront, reveals a haphazard collection of 1950s modern, fake period pieces, and some folk art. ✉ *Via Palepoli 12, 80132,* ☎ *081/7649389,* FAX *081/7649227. 38 rooms. AE, DC, MC, V.*

$$ 🏨 **Splendid.** This is a light, airy, modern hotel in the Posillipo district, with inspiring views over the Phlegrean fields and across to Ischia and Capri. It offers excellent value, is fully equipped and comfortable, and has a classic style. ✉ *Via Manzoni 96, 80123,* ☎ *081/645462,* FAX *081/7146431. 45 rooms. Restaurant. AE, DC, MC, V.*

Herculaneum

★ Hercules is reputed to have founded Herculaneum (Ercolano), just 10 km (6 mi) southeast of Naples. The elite Roman resort was devastated by the same volcanic eruption that buried Pompeii in AD 79. Excavations have revealed that many died on the shore while attempting to escape, when a slow-moving mud slide embalmed the entire town by covering it with a 36-ft-deep blanket of volcanic ash and ooze. Though devastating for Herculaneum's residents, it preserved the site in pristine condition for nearly two millennia. ✉ *Corso Ercolano,* ☎ *081/7390963,* WEB *www.pompeiisites.org.* ⏲ *Apr.–Oct., daily 8:30–7:30 (ticket office closes at 6); Nov.–Mar., daily 8:30–5 (ticket office closes at 3:30).*

Pompeii

An estimated 2,000 of Pompeii's residents perished on that fateful August day. The ancient city of Pompeii was much larger than Herculaneum, and excavations have progressed to a much greater extent, though the remains are not as well preserved, due to some 18th-century scavenging for museum-quality artwork, most of which is displayed in Naples's Museo Archeologico Nazionale. This prosperous Roman city had an extensive forum, lavish baths and temples, and patrician villas richly decorated with frescoes. It's worth buying a detailed guide of the site to gain an understanding of the ruins and their importance.

★ Be sure to see the **Villa dei Misteri** (Villa of the Mysteries), with 1,900-year-old frescoes that retain rich detail and color depth. Have small change handy to tip the guards at the more important houses so they will unlock the gates for you. ✉ *Pompeii Scavi,* ☎ *081/8610744,* WEB *www.pompeiisites.org.* ⏲ *Apr.–Oct., daily 8:30–7:30 (ticket office closes at 6); Nov.–Mar., daily 8:30–5 (ticket office closes at 3:30).*

Sorrento

In the not-too-distant past, small Sorrento was a genteel resort for the fashionable elite. Now the town, 28 km (17 mi) southwest of Pompeii, has spread out along the crest of its fabled cliffs. The once-secret haunts of the few tourists who came for the magnificent coastline have been long discovered, and they are now ravaged by package tours. But nothing can dim the delights of the marvelous climate and view of the Bay of Naples. For the best views go to the **Villa Comunale,** near the old church of San Francesco (in itself worth a visit), planted with flowering vines. **Museo Correale,** in an attractive 18th-century villa, retains a collection of decorative arts and paintings of the Neapolitan school. ✉ *Via Correale,* ☎ *081/8781846.* ⏲ *Wed.–Mon. 9–2.*

$$$–$$$$ ✕ **Antica Trattoria.** Garden dining at this homey, hospitable spot is a joy in summer. Classic *pennette al profumo di bosco* (mini-penne with a creamy mushroom and ham sauce), fish, and *gamberetti freschi all'Antica Trattoria* (shrimp in a tomato sauce) are among the house specialties. ✉ *Via Giuliani 33,* ☎ *081/8071082. AE, DC, MC, V. Closed Mon. and 4 wks in Jan.–Feb.*

$$–$$$ ✕ **Parrucchiano.** One of the town's best and oldest, Parrucchiano features greenhouse-type dining rooms dripping with vines and dotted with

plants. Among the antipasti, try the *panzerotti* (pastry crust filled with mozzarella and tomato) and, for a main course, the *scaloppe alla sorrentina* (cutlets with mozzarella and tomato). ✉ *Corso Italia 71,* ☎ *081/8781321. MC, V. Closed Wed. in Nov.–Mar.*

$$ ✕ **Trattoria da Emilia.** You can sit outside here, right on the Marina Grande, and watch the life of the port go by. This simple, rustic restaurant with wooden tables has been run by Donna Emilia and her offspring since 1947 and provides typical Sorrento home cooking and a family atmosphere. Fried seafood is the specialty. ✉ *Via Marina Grande 62,* ☎ *081/8072720. No credit cards. Oct.–Mar. closed Tues. and evening [i.e., open all day all week in summer].*

$$$$ **Excelsior Vittoria.** In the heart of Sorrento, this hotel right on the cliff has Art Nouveau furnishings, some of which are grand, although faded. Tenor Enrico Caruso's bedroom is preserved as a relic; guest bedrooms are spacious and elegant in a late-19th-century style. ✉ *Piazza Tasso 34, 80067,* ☎ *081/8071044,* FAX *081/8771206,* WEB *www.exvitt.it. 109 rooms. Restaurant, pool. AE, DC, MC, V.*

$$$–$$$$ **Bellevue Syrene.** This exclusive hotel is set in a cliff-top garden close to the center of Sorrento. It retains its solid, old-fashioned comforts and sumptuous charm, with Victorian nooks and alcoves, antique paintings, and exuberant frescoes. ✉ *Piazza della Vittoria 5, 80067,* ☎ *081/8781024,* FAX *081/8783963,* WEB *www.sorrentopalace.it. 76 rooms. Restaurant. AE, DC, MC, V.*

$ **Mignon Meublé.** A good find for this price category and central location, it offers simple, stylish accommodation in a friendly atmosphere. Rooms are spacious and homey, and breakfast is brought to you. It's always in demand, so book well in advance. ✉ *Via Sersale 9, 80067,* ☎ *081/8073824,* FAX *081/5329001. 23 rooms. AE, DC, MC, V.*

$ **Settimo Cielo.** This is an excellent choice if you want to stay on the seafront without breaking your budget. The beach is steps away. Rooms are simple, modern, and all sea-facing. ✉ *Via Capo 27, 80060,* ☎ *081/8781012,* FAX *081/8073290. 20 rooms. Restaurant, pool. AE, DC, MC, V. Closed Nov.–mid-Mar.*

Capri

No matter how many day-trippers crowd onto the island, no matter how touristy certain sections have become, Capri remains one of Italy's loveliest places. Incoming visitors disembark at Marina Grande, from where you can take some time out for an excursion to the **Grotta Azzurra** (Blue Grotto). Be warned that this is one of the country's all-time great rip-offs: motorboat, rowboat, and grotto admissions are charged separately, and if there's a line of boats waiting, you'll have little time to enjoy the grotto's marvelous colors. At Marina Grande you can also take a boat excursion around the island. A cog railway or bus service takes you up to the deliberately commercial and self-consciously picturesque **Capri Town,** where you can stroll through the Piazzetta, a choice place from which to watch the action and window-shop in expensive boutiques. The **Giardini di Augusto** (Gardens of Augustus; ✉ Via Matteotti) has gorgeous views. To get away from the crowds, hike to ★**Villa Jovis,** one of the many villas that Roman emperor Tiberius built on the island. The walk takes about 45 minutes, with pretty views all the way and a final spectacular vista of the entire Bay of Naples and part of the Gulf of Salerno. ✉ *Villa Jovis, Via Tiberio,* ☎ *081/8370381.* ⏲ *Daily 9–1 hr before sunset.*

You can take the bus or a jaunty open taxi to Anacapri and look for the little church of **San Michele,** where a magnificent, hand-painted majolica tile floor shows you an 18th-century vision of the Garden of Eden. ✉ *Off Via Orlandi.* ⏲ *Easter–Oct., daily 9–7; Nov.–Easter, daily 9:30–5.*

Villa San Michele is the charming former home of Swedish scientist-author Axel Munthe. ✉ *Via Axel Munthe,* ☎ *081/837401.* ⏲ *May–Sept., daily 9–6; Nov.–Feb., daily 10:30–3:30; Mar., daily 9:30–4:30; Apr. and Oct., daily 9:30–5.*

$$$–$$$$ ★ ✕ **La Capannina.** Only a few steps away from Capri's social center, the Piazzetta, La Capannina has a delightful vine-hung courtyard for summer dining and a reputation as one of the island's best eating places. Antipasto features fried ravioli and eggplant stuffed with ricotta, and house specialties include chicken, scaloppine, and a refreshing, homemade lemon liqueur called *limoncello.* ✉ *Via Botteghe 12 bis and 14,* ☎ *081/8370732. AE, DC, MC, V. Closed mid-Nov.–mid-Mar. (except a week at New Year), and Wed. in Mar. and Oct.–mid-Nov.*

$$–$$$ ✕ **Al Grottino.** This small, family-run restaurant, with a handy location near the Piazzetta, displays autographed photographs of celebrity customers. House specialties are gnocchi with tomato sauce and mozzarella and *linguine ai gamberetti* (linguine with shrimp sauce). ✉ *Via Longano 27,* ☎ *081/8370584. AE, MC, V. Closed Tues. and Nov. 3–Mar. 20.*

$$–$$$ ✕ **La Pigna.** Ensconced in a glassed-in veranda and offering outdoor dining in a garden shaded by lemon trees, the Pigna is one of Capri's favorite restaurants. The specialties are a house-produced wine, *farfalle impazzite* (bow-tie pasta with seafood and tomato), and *aragosta alla luna caprese* (lobster with mozzarella, tomato, and basil). ✉ *Via Lo Palazzo 30, Capri Town,* ☎ *081/8370280. Reservations essential. AE, DC, MC, V.*

$$$–$$$$ ★ ✕🏨 **Villa Brunella.** The restaurant of this family-run hotel is on the lane leading to Punta Tragara and the Faraglioni. From that level you descend to the rooms and the pool on lower levels. Furnishings are tastefully casual and comfortable, the views serendipitous. ✉ *Via Tragara 24, 87003,* ☎ *081/8370122,* FAX *081/8370430,* WEB *www.caprionline.com. 20 rooms. Restaurant, pool. AE, DC, MC, V. Closed Nov.–Mar..*

$$$$ 🏨 **Quisisana.** One of Italy's poshest hotels is right in the center of the town of Capri. The rooms are spacious, and many have arcaded balconies with views of the sea; the decor is traditional or contemporary, with some antique accents. From the small terrace at the entrance you can watch all Capri go by, but the enclosed garden and pool in the back are perfect for getting away from it all. The bar and restaurant are casual but very elegant. ✉ *Via Camerelle 2, 80073,* ☎ *081/8370788,* FAX *081/8376080,* WEB *www.quisi.com. 149 rooms. Restaurant, bar. pool. AE, DC, MC, V. Closed Nov.–mid-Mar..*

$–$$ 🏨 **Villa Sarah.** Just a 10-minute walk from the Piazzetta, the Sarah is a whitewashed Mediterranean villa with a garden, and bright, simply furnished rooms. ✉ *Via Tiberio 3/A, 87003,* ☎ *081/8377817,* FAX *081/8377215,* WEB *www.villasarah.it. 20 rooms. Bar. AE, DC, MC, V. Closed Nov.–Mar..*

Positano

★ Positano's jumble of pastel houses topped by whitewashed cupolas clings to the mountainside above the sea. The town—the prettiest along this stretch of coast—attracts a sophisticated group of visitors and summer residents who find that its relaxed and friendly atmosphere more than compensates for the sheer effort of moving about this exhaustingly vertical town, most of whose streets are stairways. This former fishing village has now opted for the more regular and lucrative rewards of tourism and fashion. Practically every other shop is a boutique displaying locally made casual wear. The beach is the town's focal point, with a little promenade and a multitude of café-restaurants.

$$$ ✕ **'O Capurale.** Of all the popular restaurants on the beach promenade, 'O Capurale has the best food and lowest prices. Tables are set under vines on a breezy sidewalk in the summer, upstairs and indoors in winter. *Spaghetti con melanzane* (spaghetti with eggplant) and crepes *al formaggio* (with cheese) are tasty. ✉ *Via Regina Giovanna 12,* ☎ *089/875374. AE, DC, MC, V. Closed Nov.–mid-Feb.*

$$$$ 🏨 **Le Sirenuse.** The most fashionable hotel in Positano, in an 18th-century villa, has been in the same family for eight generations. The hotel is set into the hillside overlooking Positano's harbor. Most of the bedrooms face the sea. Because of the hotel's location, the dining room is like a long, closed-in terrace overlooking the village of Positano. The cuisine ranges from acceptable to excellent. ✉ *Via Cristoforo Colombo 30, 84017,* ☎ *089/875066,* FAX *081/811798,* WEB *www.sirenuse.it. 60 rooms. Restaurant. AE, DC, MC, V.*

$$$$ 🏨 **San Pietro.** Perched on the side of a cliff, this opulent hotel is eclectic and airy, with unusual antiques and, everywhere, hanging bougainvillea. The guest rooms are tastefully appointed, but the stupendous window views steal the show. The light, open dining room is verdant with plants. An elevator takes guests to the hotel's small beach area. ✉ *Via Laurito 2, 84017,* ☎ *089/875455,* FAX *089/811449,* WEB *www.ilsanpietro.it. 60 rooms. Restaurant. AE, DC, MC, V. Closed Nov.–Mar..*

$$$–$$$$ 🏨 **Palazzo Murat.** The location is perfect, in the heart of town, near the beachside promenade and set within a walled garden. The old wing is a historic palazzo, with tall windows and wrought-iron balconies; the newer wing is a whitewashed Mediterranean building with arches and terraces. You can relax in antiques-strewn lounges or on the charming vine-draped patio. ✉ *Via dei Mulini 23, 84017,* ☎ *089/875177,* FAX *089/811419,* WEB *www.palazzomurat.it. 31 rooms. Restaurant. AE, DC, MC, V. Closed Jan.–mid-Mar..*

$$ ★ 🏨 **La Fenice.** This tiny and unpretentious hotel beckons with bougainvillea-laden vistas, castaway cottages, and a turquoise pool, all perched over a private beach. Guest rooms—accented with coved ceilings, whitewashed walls, and native folk art—are simple havens of tranquillity (book the best, those closest to the sea, only if you can handle *very* steep walkways). Situated on the peaceful outskirts of town, this is, happily, open year-round. ✉ *Via G. Marconi 4, 84017,* ☎ *089/875513,* FAX *089/811309. 15 rooms. Pool. No credit cards.*

Amalfi

The coastal drive down to the resort town of Amalfi provides some of Italy's most dramatic and beautiful scenery. Amalfi itself is a charming maze of covered alleys and narrow byways straggling up the steep mountainside. The piazza just below the cathedral forms the town's heart—a colorful assortment of pottery stalls, cafés, and postcard shops grouped around a venerable old fountain. The exterior of the **cathedral** is its most impressive feature. The **cloisters,** with whitewashed arches and palms, are worth a glance, and the small **museum** in the adjoining crypt could inspire you to climb up all those stairs. ☎ *089/871059.* ⏲ *Duomo, cloister and museum: Apr.–June and Oct., daily 9–7; July–Sept., daily 9–9; Nov.–Mar., daily 10–12:30 and 2:30–5:30.*

$$$–$$$$ ✕ **La Caravella.** Tucked away under some arches lining the coast road, the Caravella has a pleasant interior decorated with paintings of old Amalfi. It's small and intimate, and proprietor Franco describes the cuisine as "*sfiziosa*" (taste tempting). Specialties include *linguine alla colatura di alici* (linguine with anchovies) based on a medieval recipe and *calamari ripieni* (stuffed squid). ✉ *Via M. Camera 12,* ☎ *089/871029. AE, MC, V. Closed Tues. and Nov.*

$$$$ ★ 🏨 **Santa Caterina.** A large mansion perched above terraced and flowered hillsides on the coast road just outside Amalfi proper, the Santa

Caterina is one of the best hotels on the entire coast. The rooms are tastefully decorated, and most have small terraces or balconies with great views. There are lounges and terraces for relaxing, and an elevator whisks guests down to the seaside saltwater pool, bar, and swimming area. Amid lemon and orange groves are two romantic villa annexes. ✉ *Strada Amalfitana 9, 84011,* ☎ *089/871012,* FAX *089/871351,* WEB *www.hotelsantacaterina.it. 66 rooms. Restaurant, pool. AE, DC, MC, V.*

Ravello

★ Ravello is on a high mountain bluff overlooking the sea 8 km (5 mi) north of Amalfi. The road up to it is a series of switchbacks, and the village itself clings precariously on the mountain spur. The village flourished during the 13th century and then fell into a tranquillity that has remained unchanged for the past six centuries. The town center is Piazza del Duomo, with its **cathedral,** founded in 1087. Note the fine bronze 12th-century doors and, inside, two pulpits richly decorated with mosaics: one depicts the story of Jonah and the whale; the other, more splendid mosaic is carved with fantastic beasts and rests on a pride of lions. Composer Richard Wagner once stayed in Ravello, and today there is a Wagner festival every summer on the garden terrace of the 11th-century **Villa Rufolo.** There is a Moorish cloister with interlacing pointed arches, beautiful gardens, an 11th-century tower, and a belvedere with a fine view of the coast. ✉ *Piazza Vescovado,* ☎ *089/857657.* ⏲ *Daily 9–sunset.*

At the entrance to the **Villa Cimbrone** complex is a small cloister that looks medieval but was actually built in 1917, with two bas-reliefs: one representing nine Norman warriors, the other illustrating the seven deadly sins. Then, the long avenue leads through peaceful gardens scattered with grottoes, small temples, and statues to a belvedere and terrace where, on a clear day, the view stretches out over the Mediterranean Sea. ✉ *Via Santa Chiara 26,* ☎ *089/857459.* ⏲ *Daily 9–sunset.*

$$$$ **Hotel Palumbo.** Of all the hotels on the Amalfi coast, the Hotel Palumbo is the most genteel—and one of the most costly. Occupying a 12th-century patrician palace furnished with antiques and provided with modern comforts, this hotel has an elegant, warm atmosphere. You won't quickly forget the lovely garden terraces, breathtaking views, and sumptuous upstairs dining room. Some bedrooms are small, but they are full of character. The rooms facing the sea are the choice ones—and the more expensive (those in the modern annex are considerably cheaper). You are required to take half- or full-board lodging except in winter when the restaurant is closed. ✉ *Via San Giovanni del Toro 16, 84010,* ☎ *089/857244,* FAX *089/858133,* WEB *www.hotel-palumbo.it. 20 rooms. Restaurant. AE, DC, MC, V.*

Campania Essentials

AIR TRAVEL

There are several daily flights between Rome and Naples's Aeroporto Capodichino, 8 km (5 mi) north of downtown Naples. From May through September there's direct helicopter service between Capodichino and Capri or Ischia.

➤ INFORMATION: **Aeroporto Capodichino** (☎ 081/7896259). **Aerotaxi** (☎ 081/5841481).

BOAT AND FERRY TRAVEL

Most boats and hydrofoils for the islands and the Sorrento peninsula leave from the Molo Beverello Pier, near Naples's Piazza Municipio;

there's also a hydrofoil station at Mergellina Pier. Passenger and car ferry service is frequent. Note that you cannot take cars onto Capri.

➤ HYDROFOILS: **Alilauro** (☎ 081/5522838). **Caremar** (☎ 081/5513882). **Navigazione Libera del Golfo** (NLG, ☎ 081/5527209). **SNAV** (☎ 081/7612348).

➤ PASSENGER AND CAR FERRIES: **Caremar** (☞ *above*). **Navigazione Libera del Golfo** (☞ *above*).

BUS TRAVEL

➤ BUS INFORMATION: **SITA** (☎ 081/5522176).

CAR TRAVEL

The Naples–Pompeii–Salerno toll road has exits at Herculaneum and Pompeii and connects with the tortuous coastal road to Sorrento and the Amalfi coast at the Castellammare exit. Parking within Naples is not recommended: window smashing and robbery are not uncommon.

TOURS

One-, two-, or three-day guided tours of the area depart from Rome. From Naples you can choose from a wide range of half-day and all-day tours on the mainland and to the islands.

➤ FEES AND SCHEDULES: **American Express** (✉ Rome, ☎ 06/67641). **Appian Line** (✉ Rome, ☎ 06/487861). **Carrani** (✉ Rome, ☎ 06/4880510 or 06/4742501). **Milleviaggi** (✉ Riviera di Chiaia 252, Naples, ☎ 081/7642064). **Tourcar** (✉ Piazza Matteotti 1, Naples, ☎ 081/5520429).

TRAIN TRAVEL

Many trains run between Rome and Naples from the Stazione Centrale every day; Intercity trains make the journey in less than two hours. There are several stations in Naples, and a network of suburban trains connects the city with diverse points of interest in Campania, most usefully the Circumvesuviana line, which runs to Herculaneum (Ercolano), Pompeii, and Sorrento. Naples has a Metropolitana (subway); though it's old and trains are infrequent, it beats the traffic. The fare is 1,500 lire/€0.80.

➤ TRAIN INFORMATION: **Circumvesuviana line** (☎ 081/7722444). **Stazione Centrale** (✉ Piazza Garibaldi, Naples, ☎ 1478/88088 information).

VISITOR INFORMATION

➤ TOURIST INFORMATION: **Capri** (✉ Marina Grande pier, ☎ 081/8370634; ✉ Piazza Umberto I, Capri Town, ☎ 081/8370686, WEB www.capritourism.com). **Naples** (EPT; ✉ Piazza dei Martiri 58, ☎ 081/405311, WEB www.ept.napoli.it; ✉ Stazione Centrale, ☎ 081/268779; ✉ Stazione Mergellina, ☎ 081/7612102; ✉ Aeroporto Capodichino, ☎ 081/7805761; Azienda Autonoma di Soggiorno, Cura e Turismo, AASCT; ✉ Piazza del Gesù, ☎ 081/5523328). **Sorrento** (✉ Via De Maio 35, ☎ 081/8074033, WEB www.sorrentotourism.com).

19 LUXEMBOURG

WHEN YOU TRY TO LOCATE LUXEMBOURG ON A MAP, look for "Lux," at the heart of Western Europe. Even abbreviated, the name runs over—west into Belgium, east into Germany, south into France—as the country's influence has done for centuries. The Grand Duchy of Luxembourg is a Rhode Island–size land that contains variety and contrasts out of all proportion to its size.

Luxembourg has a wild and beautiful highland country studded with castles rich in history. It has legendary vineyards producing great wines and a lovely farmland called Le Bon Pays. And, of course, it has its capital, with an ancient fortress towering above the south-central plain. Seen through early morning mists, Luxembourg City revives the magic of Camelot. Yet it is actually the nerve center of a 1,000-year-old seat of government and a bustling and important element of the European Union (EU).

One of the smallest countries in the United Nations, Luxembourg comprises only 2,586 square km (998 square mi). It is dwarfed by its neighbors, yet from its history of invasion, occupation, and siege, you might think the land was made of solid gold. Starting in AD 963, when Charlemagne's descendant Sigefroid started to build his castle atop the promontory of the Bock, the duchy encased itself in layer upon layer of fortifications until by the mid-19th century its very impregnability was considered a threat. The Castle of Luxembourg was ultimately dismantled in the name of peace, and the country's neutrality was "guaranteed" by the 1867 Treaty of London. But the Grand Duchy was to be invaded twice again, in 1914 and 1940. Its experiences during World War II convinced Luxembourg of the necessity to cooperate with all its neighbors to avoid conflicts. The entire country now flaunts new wealth, new political muscle, and the highest per capita income in Europe. Luxembourg bristles with international banks—enough to rival Switzerland—and just outside the Old City, a new colony has been populated by *fonctionnaires* of the EU.

There is an old saying that describes the life of the Luxembourgers—or Luxembourgeois, if you prefer the more elegant French appellation: "One Luxembourger, a rose garden; two Luxembourgers, a kaffeeklatsch; three Luxembourgers, a band." This is a country of parades and processions, good cheer, and a hearty capacity for beer and Moselle wine. In its traditions, values, and politics, Luxembourg remains more conservative than its neighbors. This may occasionally seem stifling to the younger generation of Luxembourgeois, but to the majority of their elders these attitudes express the age-old national motto, *Mir wëlle bleiwe wat mir sin.* ("We want to remain what we are.")

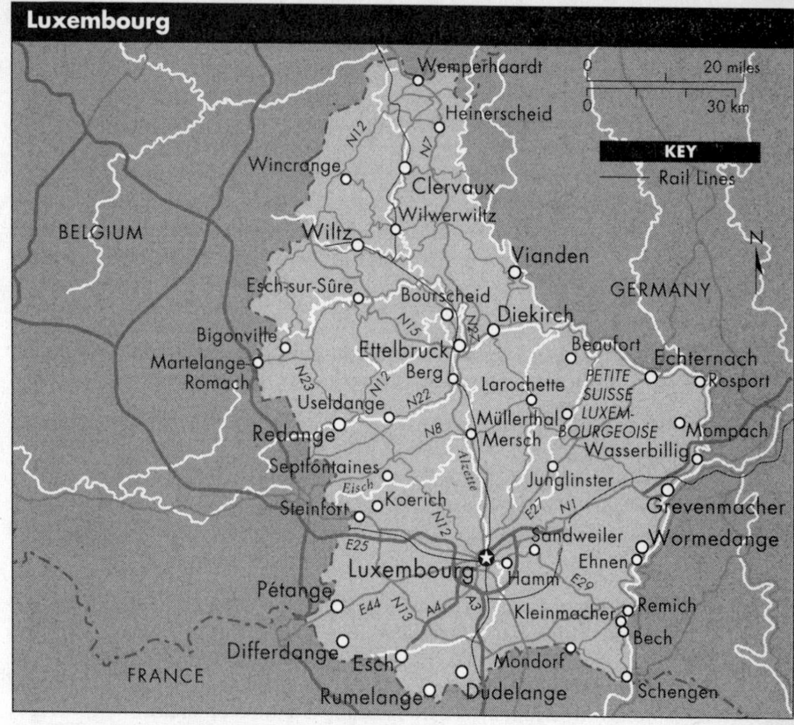

LUXEMBOURG A TO Z

BUSINESS HOURS

BANKS AND OFFICES

Banks are generally open weekdays 8:30–4, though some close for lunch (noon–2). In Luxembourg City, an automated exchange machine on rue de la Reine accepts banknotes of most foreign currencies. There is also a currency exchange booth at the airport that is open daily.

MUSEUMS AND SIGHTS

Museums' opening hours vary, so check individual listings. Most are closed Monday, and in the countryside some also close for lunch (noon–2).

SHOPS

Shops and department stores are generally open Monday 2–6 and Tuesday–Saturday 9–6. Some close for lunch (noon–2). A few small family businesses are open Sunday 8–noon.

CUSTOMS AND DUTIES

For information on customs regulations, *see* Customs and Duties *in* Chapter 1.

DINING

Restaurants in Luxembourg combine Gallic quality with Teutonic quantity. The best deals are at lunch, when you can find a plat du jour or *menu* (two or three courses included in the price) at bargain rates. Pizzerias, found everywhere, offer an inexpensive alternative. Service (10%) and sales tax (3%) are included in quoted prices.

Prices are for one main course at dinner.

CATEGORY	COST
$$$$	over Flux 1,300 (€32)
$$$	Flux 1,000–Flux 1,300 (€25–€32)
$$	Flux 700–Flux 1,000 (€17–€25)
$	under Flux 700 (€17)

MEALTIMES

Most hotels serve breakfast until 10. Luxembourgers shut down their computers at noon to rush home for a two-hour lunch. Dinner is eaten a bit earlier than in neighboring countries, generally between 7 and 10.

RESERVATIONS AND DRESS

Stylish, casual dress is expected in most restaurants; when in doubt, err on the side of formality. In expensive French restaurants, jacket and tie is a given.

EMBASSIES

➤ IRELAND: (✉ 28 Rte. D' Arlon, ☎ 450610).

➤ UNITED KINGDOM: (✉ Bd. F. D. Roosevelt 14, ☎ 229864).

➤ UNITED STATES: (✉ Bd. Emmanuel Servais 22, ☎ 460123).

HOLIDAYS

January 1; Carnival (mid-February to early March); Easter Monday; May 1 (May Day); Ascension (mid- to late May); Pentecost Monday; June 23 (National Day); August 15 (Assumption); November 1 (All Saints' Day); December 25–26. When a holiday falls on a Sunday, the following Monday is automatically a national holiday.

LANGUAGE

Native Luxembourgers speak three languages fluently: Luxembourgian (a Germanic language salted with French), German, and French. Many also speak English.

LODGING

Price categories are for a double room. Service (10%) and sales tax (3%) are included in posted rates. Check for special rates when making reservations.

CATEGORY	COST
$$$$	over Flux 9,000 (€223)
$$$	Flux 6,000–Flux 9,000 (€149–€223)
$$	Flux 3,000–Flux 6,000 (€74–€149)
$	under Flux 3,000 (€74)

CAMPING

The Grand Duchy is probably the best-organized country in Europe when it comes to camping. It offers some 120 sites, all with full amenities. Listings are published annually by the National Tourist Office.

HOSTELS

Inexpensive youth hostels are plentiful; many are housed in historic buildings. For information, contact Centrale des Auberges Luxembourgeoises.

➤ HOSTEL ORGANIZATIONS: **Centrale des Auberges Luxembourgeoises** (✉ 18 Place d'Armes, Box 374, L-2013 Luxembourg Ville, ☎ 225588).

HOTELS

Most hotels in Luxembourg City are relatively modern and range from the international style to smaller, family-run establishments. Many hotels offer reduced rates on weekends.

MAIL AND SHIPPING

Mail can be sent in care of BBL Travel American Express. This service is free for holders of American Express credit cards or traveler's checks.
➤ CONTACTS: **BBL Travel American Express** (✉ 3 rue Jean Piret, L-2350 Luxembourg Ville).

POSTAL RATES

Airmail postcards and letters to North America weighing less than 20 grams cost Flux 25/€.62. Letters and postcards to the United Kingdom cost Flux 18/€.45.

MONEY MATTERS

Luxembourg has a high standard and cost of living. Prices in the countryside are slightly lower than in Luxembourg City. Sample prices include: cup of coffee, Flux 55/€1.35–Flux 80/€2; glass of beer, Flux 55/€1.35–Flux 70/€1.75; movie admission, Flux 250/€6.20–Flux 300/€7.45; 5-km (3-mi) taxi ride, Flux 800/€20.

CURRENCY

In Luxembourg, the unit of currency is the franc (abbreviated "Flux"). Luxembourg issues its own currency in bills of 100, 1,000, and 5,000 francs and coins of 1, 5, 20, and 50 francs.

Luxembourg francs (and Belgian francs, which have the same value) will be accepted until February 28, 2002, after which only euros will be accepted. Euro banknotes and coins will be available beginning January 1, 2002. The euro is equal to Flux 40.34. At press time (summer 2001), the exchange rate was Flux 45.65 to the U.S. dollar, Flux 28.92 to the Canadian dollar, Flux 64.87 to the pound sterling, Flux 51.22 to the Irish punt, Flux 22.05 to the Australian dollar, Flux 18.29 to the New Zealand dollar, and Flux 5.62 to the South African rand.

TAXES

VALUE-ADDED TAX (VAT)

Purchases of goods for export may qualify for a value-added tax (called TVA, or *taxe value ajouté*) refund of 15%.

TELEPHONES

COUNTRY AND AREA CODES

The country code for Luxembourg is 352. Note that there are no area codes within the Grand Duchy.

DIRECTORY AND OPERATOR ASSISTANCE

To place operator-assisted calls, dial 0010.

INTERNATIONAL CALLS

The cheapest way to make an international call is to dial direct from a public phone. To reach an AT&T, MCI, or Sprint long-distance operator, dial one of the access codes below.
➤ ACCESS CODES: **AT&T** (☎ 0800–0111). **MCI** (☎ 0800–0112). **Sprint** (☎ 0800–0115).

LOCAL CALLS

You can find public phones on the street and in city post offices. A local call costs a minimum of Flux 5/€.12 from a public phone (slightly more from restaurants and gas stations). Post offices sell phone cards, called Telekaarten, in denominations from Flux 250/€6.20 to Flux 750/€18.60, which can be used in nearly all the country's phone booths. Many public phone booths no longer accept coins.

TIPPING

In hotels and restaurants, taxes and service charges are included in the bill. If you wish to tip further, round off the total to the nearest Flux

100. Bellhops and doormen appreciate a tip of Flux 50/€1.25 to Flux 100/€2.50. Porters at the railway station charge Flux 50/€1.25 per bag, to a maximum of Flux 150/€4. Taxi drivers expect a tip; add about 15% to the amount on the meter.

VISITOR INFORMATION

➤ Tourist Information: **Office National du Tourisme** (National Tourist Office; main branch, ✉ Gare Centrale, ☎ 481199; head office, ✉ B.P. 1001, L-1010 Luxembourg Ville, ☎ 428282–1, FAX 428282–38, WEB www.ont.lu; ✉ airport branch, ☎ 4282–8221).

WHEN TO GO

The main tourist season in Luxembourg is from early May through October, with spring and fall the most rewarding seasons to travel.

CLIMATE

In general, temperatures in Luxembourg are moderate. Be sure to pack rain gear. In the hilly north there is frequently snow in winter. The following are the average daily maximum and minimum temperatures for Luxembourg.

Jan.	37F	3C	**May**	65F	18C	**Sept.**	66F	19C
	29	– 1		46	8		50	10
Feb.	40F	4C	**June**	70F	21C	**Oct.**	56F	13C
	31	– 1		52	11		43	6
Mar.	49F	10C	**July**	73F	23C	**Nov.**	44F	7C
	35	1		55	13		37	3
Apr.	57F	14C	**Aug.**	71F	22C	**Dec.**	39F	4C
	40	4		54	12		32	0

LUXEMBOURG CITY

As you arrive in the capital of Luxembourg from the airport and cross the vast span of the Grande Duchesse Charlotte Bridge, you are greeted by an awe-inspiring panorama of medieval stonework fortifications fronted by massive gates. Then, after a left turn into boulevard Royal, you're back in the 20th century of BMW and Mercedes cars and glittering glass-and-concrete office buildings. A block away, in the Old City, the sedate pace of a provincial picture-book town delightfully returns.

Exploring Luxembourg City

Numbers in the margin correspond to points of interest on the Luxembourg City map.

The military fortifications and the Old Town, with its cobbled streets and inviting public squares, make for terrific exploring. In 1994 the United Nations Educational, Scientific, and Cultural Organization (UNESCO) declared these areas part of the world's cultural heritage.

★ 13 **Bock.** This stony promontory is Luxembourg's raison d'être. Jutting dramatically above the valley, the Bock once supported the castle built by the first duke of Luxembourg in AD 963. Taking in vertiginous views of the valley, you'll see the **Plateau du Rham** across the way, on the right and, before it, the massive towers of Duke Wenceslas's fortifications, which were built in 1390. The blocklike *casernes* (barracks) were added during the 17th century by the French. From the Bock you can gain access to 18th-century military tunnels. At the entrance, the **Crypte Archéologique du Bock** (Archaeological Crypt) offers a brief audiovisual history of Luxembourg from the 10th to 15th centuries. ✉ *Montée de Clausen,* ☎ *226753.* ⏲ *Mar.–Oct., daily 10–5.*

Luxembourg City (Luxembourg Ville)

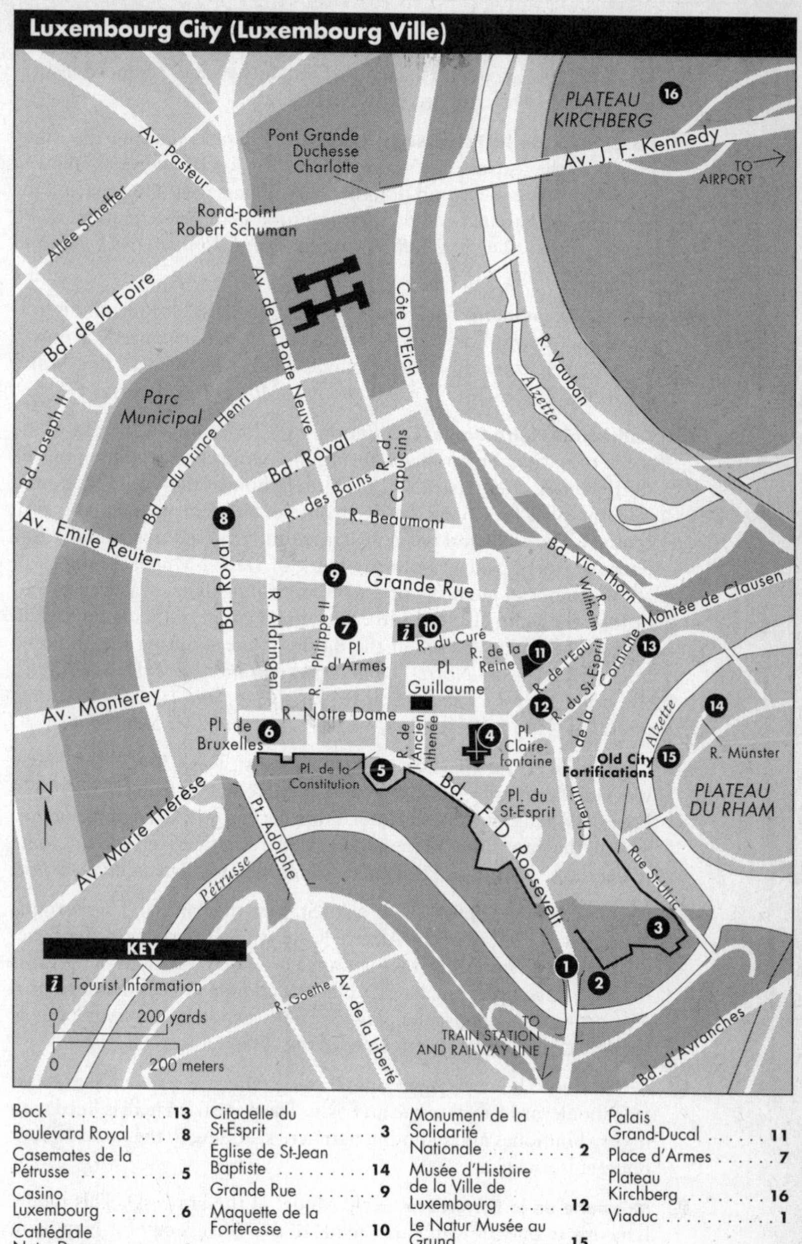

Bock **13**	Citadelle du St-Esprit **3**	Monument de la Solidarité Nationale **2**	Palais Grand-Ducal **11**
Boulevard Royal **8**	Église de St-Jean Baptiste **14**	Musée d'Histoire de la Ville de Luxembourg **12**	Place d'Armes **7**
Casemates de la Pétrusse **5**	Grande Rue **9**	Le Natur Musée au Grund **15**	Plateau Kirchberg **16**
Casino Luxembourg **6**	Maquette de la Forteresse **10**		Viaduc **1**
Cathédrale Notre-Dame **4**			

8 **Boulevard Royal.** Luxembourg's mini–Wall Street, once the site of the fortress's main moat, curves around the west and north sides of the Old City. It is lined with as many of the duchy's 220 financial institutions as could be crowded into five blocks.

5 **Casemates de la Pétrusse** (Pétrusse Casemates). During the many phases of the fortress-city's construction, the rock itself was hollowed out to form a honeycomb of underground passages. Those facing the Pétrusse Valley date from the 17th-century Spanish occupation. ✉ *Pl. de la Constitution,* ☎ *222809.* ⏲ *Easter and Whitsun weekends and July–Sept., daily 11–4.*

6 **Casino Luxembourg.** Far from being a gaming establishment, this gracious hall, where Franz Liszt played his last public concert, is now a gallery where contemporary art exhibitions are mounted. ✉ *Rue Notre-Dame 41,* ☎ *225045.* ⏲ *Wed. and Fri.–Mon. 11–6, Thurs. 11–8.*

4 **Cathédrale Notre-Dame.** Luxembourg's 17th-century cathedral is the scene of national pilgrimage during the two weeks beginning on the third Sunday after Easter. The pilgrimage honors the Virgin Mary and celebrates her for saving the city from the bubonic plague in the 14th century. The cathedral has an extravagantly carved portal and a fine Baroque organ gallery, both the work of Daniel Muller. In the crypt are the tombs of members of the present ruling dynasty as well as that of John the Blind (1296–1346), the gallant count of Luxembourg and king of Bohemia who fell at the Battle of Crécy during the Hundred Years' War. ✉ *Rue Notre-Dame (crypt entrance bd. F. D. Roosevelt).* ⏲ *Crypt Easter–Oct., weekdays 10–5, Sat. 8–6, Sun. 10–6; Nov.–Easter, weekdays 10–11:30 and 2–5, Sat. 8–11:30 and 2–5, Sun. 10–5.*

3 **Citadelle du St-Esprit** (Citadel of the Holy Spirit). This 17th-century citadel was built during a French occupation by Maréchal Vauban (1633–1707), Louis XIV's chief military engineer. From the "prow," take in a panoramic view of the three spires of the cathedral, the Alzette River, and the white tower of the European Parliament secretariat. ✉ *Plateau du St-Esprit.*

14 **Église de St-Jean Baptiste** (Church of St. John the Baptist). This Baroque church on the shore of the Alzette River was formerly part of a Benedictine abbey. Among its treasures are a cycle of the stations of the cross made of Limoges enamel and a Black Madonna once thought to provide protection against the plague. The riverside passageway outside the church has a wonderful view of the cliffs. ✉ *Rue Münster.*

9 **Grand Rue.** The city's main upscale shopping street runs west to east from boulevard Royal to rue du Fossé. The pedestrian mall is lined with luxury boutiques and tempting patisseries, adding to the Luxembourg bourgeois touch.

10 **Maquette de la Forteresse** (Scale Model of the Fortress). This model is a copy of one (now in Paris) made of the fortress-city for Napoléon in 1804, when the fortified complex was in its glory. ✉ *Rathskeller, rue du Curé,* ☎ *222809.* ⏲ *May–Sept., daily 10–5.*

2 **Monument de la Solidarité Nationale** (Monument to National Unity). Luxembourg was the only occupied country during World War II to stage a general strike against its occupiers. Hitler annexed the Grand Duchy and drafted its young men into the German army. This moving memorial honors Luxembourg's World War II casualties. Within the stark walls is a small, stained-glass chapel housing a symbolic tombstone. ✉ *Kanounenhiwel, Plateau du St-Esprit.*

★ 12 **Musée d'Histoire de la Ville de Luxembourg** (Luxembourg City Historical Museum). This interactive museum explores the city's history over 1,000 years. Visitors are provided with electronic cards to use the many touch-sensitive screens in their language of choice. A marriage of ancient buildings and contemporary technology, the museum invites visitors to descend in time and space in a panoramic elevator the size of an exhibition hall. ✉ *Rue du St-Esprit 14,* ☎ *229050–1 information line.* ⏲ *Tues.–Wed. and Fri.–Sun. 10–6, Thurs. 10–8.*

★ 15 **Le Natur Musée au Grund** (Museum of Natural History). Opened in 1996, the museum was formerly a women's prison. The building, dating from 1308, now houses collections and displays that explain the environment, past and present. The museum stands on the bank of the Alzette River in the heart of the **Grund** neighborhood; to get here in comfort, take the elevator from the Plateau du St-Esprit. ✉ *Rue Münster 23,* ☎ *462233–1 information,* WEB *www.mnhn.lu.* ⏲ *Mid-Sept.–May, Tues.–Fri. 2–6, Sat. 10–6; June–mid-Sept., Tues.–Sun. 10–6.*

11 **Palais Grand-Ducal** (Palace of the Grand Dukes). This restored palace is the city residence of the grand ducal family. Parts date from the 16th century, notably the section that once served as the town hall; a distinct Spanish-Moorish influence is obvious in the elaborate facade. Tickets for guided tours (often sold out) are available only at the City Tourist Office. ✉ *Rue du Marché-aux-Herbes.* ⏲ *Guided tours only; mid-July–mid-Aug., in English, weekdays 1–4, Sat. 10.*

7 **Place d'Armes.** Lined with symmetrical plane trees and strung with colored lights, this is the city's liveliest and most welcoming square. A bandstand (concerts are often held here on summer evenings), sidewalk cafés, fast-food joints, and a twice-monthly flea market constantly lure natives and tourists alike. From its southeast corner, a passage leads to the more dignified **Place Guillaume,** with the Hôtel de Ville (Town Hall); there's a farmers' market Wednesday and Saturday mornings. Next, as you continue southeast, comes the elegant, sloping **Place Clairefontaine,** adorned with a graceful statue of the much-loved Grande Duchesse Charlotte, who ruled from 1919 to 1964.

16 **Plateau Kirchberg.** Several European Union institutions, some major banks, the country's new Auchan shopping center, and the 10-screen Utopolis cinema complex lie in this district. ✉ *Across Grande Duchesse Charlotte Bridge (Bus 18 [direction Domaine du Kiem] from bd. Royal loops around area).*

1 **Viaduc.** The 19th-century bridge is also known as the *Passerelle* (footbridge), although it carries vehicular traffic from the railway station. A good starting point for exploring Luxembourg City, it spans the valley of the Pétrusse (now more a brook than a river), which has become a beautiful park. ✉ *From av. de la Gare to Plateau du St-Esprit.*

Dining

Today, leading chefs are taking traditional Luxembourg specialties—*jambon d'Ardennes* (raw-smoked ham served cold with pickled onions), *treipen* (blood pudding), and *écrevisses* (crayfish)—and giving them all a newer-than-now nouvelle spin. In the process, Luxembourg City is becoming a true capital *gastronomique.* Note that many upscale places offer a reasonably priced menu at lunch. For more details and price-category definitions, *see* Dining *in* Luxembourg A to Z, *above.*

$$$$ ★ ✕ **Clairefontaine.** The tastefully discreet luxury of this dining spot on the city's most attractive square draws government ministers, visiting dignitaries, and well-heeled gourmands. Chef-owner Tony Tintinger's inspirations include foie gras specialties, innovative fish dishes (soufflé of langoustines perfumed with anise), and such game offerings as

tournedos of doe with wild mushrooms. ✉ *Pl. de Clairefontaine 9,* ☎ *462211. Reservations essential. Jacket and tie. AE, DC, MC, V. Closed 2 wks in Aug., first wk in Nov., and Sun. No lunch Sat.*

$$$ ★ ✕ **Jan Schneidewind.** The chef-owner of this bandbox bistro serves excellent stuffed North Sea crab, panfried garlic-scented monkfish, and other seafood specialties. In August, this is virtually the only top-rank restaurant in town that stays open. ✉ *Rue du Curé 20,* ☎ *222618. AE, DC, MC, V. Closed Mon. and 2 wks in Sept. No lunch weekends.*

$$$ ✕ **La Lorraine.** Outstanding seafood is the specialty of this restaurant strategically situated on the Place d'Armes. A retail shop around the corner shows off the freshness of its wares. Baked skate (in hazelnut butter with capers) and puff pastry with sole and morels are good bets. ✉ *Pl. d'Armes 7,* ☎ *474620. AE, DC, MC, V. Closed Sun. and Aug.*

$$$ ✕ **Le Bouquet Garni.** A short walk from the Palais Grand-Ducal, this charming French restaurant in a wonderfully restored building is one of the city's best dining experiences. Chefs Lysiane and Thierry Duhr serve original dishes such as lobster ravioli in a frothy cappuccino bisque. ✉ *Rue de l'Eau 32,* ☎ *262006. AE, DC, MC, V. Closed Dec. 24–Jan. 4. Closed Sun. and lunch Sat.*

$$ ✕ **Chiggeri.** In the heart of the Old Town, Chiggeri offers both bistro and fine dining and is famous for its ever-changing wine list that features almost to 2,000 different wines. ✉ *Rue du Nord 15,* ☎ *229936,* WEB *www.chiggeri.lu. AE, DC, MC, V.*

$–$$ ★ ✕ **Ristorante Roma.** Luxembourg's first Italian restaurant, the Roma has been serving classic Italian food in an unpretentious, inviting atmosphere since the 1950s. Local favorites include the paper-thin carpaccio and fresh pasta. ✉ *Rue Louvigny 5,* ☎ *223692. AE, MC, V. Closed Mon. No dinner Sun.*

$ ★ ✕ **Ems.** Everybody in Luxembourg vies for one of the vinyl booths in this unpretentious but lively establishment. Its vast portions of mussels in a rich wine-and-garlic broth are best accompanied by french fries and a bottle of sharp, cold, and inexpensive Auxerrois or Rivaner. Ems is open until 1 AM. Reservations are essential on weekends. ✉ *Pl. de la Gare 30,* ☎ *487799. AE, DC, MC, V. No lunch Sat.*

$ ✕ **Mousel's Cantine.** Right next to the great Mousel brewery, this fresh, comfortable café serves heaping platters of local specialties—braised and grilled ham, sausage, broad beans, and fried potatoes—accompanied by crockery steins of creamy *Gezwickelte Béier* (unfiltered beer). ✉ *Montée de Clausen 46,* ☎ *470198. MC, V. Closed Sun. and 3 wks in Aug.*

$ ✕ **Oberweis.** Luxembourg's most famous patisserie also serves light lunches. You select your meal at the counter (quiche lorraine, spinach pie, and the like), and it is served at your table. ✉ *Grand Rue 19–20,* ☎ *470703,* WEB *www.oberweis.lu. AE, DC, MC, V. Closed Sun..*

Lodging

Hotels in the city center are more convenient to exploring than those clustered around the train station. There are also large, modern hotels near the airport and on the Plateau Kirchberg. For details and price-category definitions, *see* Lodging *in* Luxembourg A to Z, *above.*

$$$$ ★ **Le Royal.** In the city center, within steps of parks, shopping, and the Old Town, Le Royal is the best choice for luxury. It's solid, modern, and sleek, with pleasant lobbies on each floor and a health club. A wing has an exotic winter garden and a deluxe restaurant. ✉ *Bd. Royal 12, L-2449,* ☎ *2416161,* FAX *225948,* WEB *www.hotelroyal.lu. 190 rooms, 20 suites. 2 restaurants, indoor pool. AE, DC, MC, V.*

$$$ **Cravat.** This charming Luxembourg relic straddles the valley and the Old Town in the best location in the city. Corridors have a dated

air, but guest rooms are fresh and welcoming in a variety of tastefully retro styles. The Art Deco coffee shop has been updated but still draws fur-hatted ladies to tea. You can dine in their brasserie La Taverne, or have cocktails in the bar Le Trianon. Opened in April 2001, the restaurant Le Normandy offers upscale French cuisine. ✉ *Bd. F. D. Roosevelt 29, L-2450,* ☎ *221975,* FAX *226711,* WEB *www.hotelcravat.lu. 60 rooms. 2 restaurants, bar. AE, DC, MC, V.*

$$$ **Parc Belair.** This privately owned, family-run hotel a few blocks from the city center stands on the edge of the Parc de Merl. Rooms are a warm beige; those on the park are the quietest. The complex includes a separate restaurant with an outdoor café. A substantial buffet breakfast is included. The restaurant serves dinner only. ✉ *Av. du X Septembre 109, L-2551,* ☎ *442323,* FAX *444484,* WEB *www.hpb.lu. 52 rooms, 19 suites. Restaurant. AE, DC, MC, V.*

$$ **Ibis.** The hotel is across the street from the airport, with direct access to the motorway. You can walk from the airport or call the hotel to send its free shuttle. Not strong on personality, it does provide honest value for the money. Family rooms sleeping up to four are available. The forest begins just behind the hotel. ✉ *Rte. de Trèves, L-2632 Findel,* ☎ *438801,* FAX *438802,* WEB *http://webplaza.pt.lu/public/ibishote. 120 rooms. Restaurant. AE, DC, MC, V.*

$$ **Italia.** This is a find: a former private apartment house converted into hotel rooms, some with plaster detailing and vintage cabinetry. Rooms are solid and freshly furnished, all with tile bathrooms. The restaurant downstairs is one of the city's better Italian eateries. ✉ *Rue d'Anvers 15–17, L-1130,* ☎ *486626,* FAX *480807. 20 rooms. Restaurant. AE, DC, MC, V.*

$$ ★ **La Cascade.** A turn-of-the-20th-century villa has been converted into a hotel of considerable charm and elegance. There's a good French restaurant and a lovely terrace overlooking the Alzette River. A bus stops outside to take you to the city center, just over 2 km (1 mi) away. ✉ *Rue de Pulvermuhl 2, L-2356,* ☎ *428736,* FAX *424788. 9 rooms. Restaurant. AE, DC, MC, V.*

$$ **Sieweburen.** At the northwestern end of the city is this attractively rustic hotel, opened in 1991. There are a playground in front and woods in the back. The brasserie-style tavern, older than the rest of the property, is hugely popular, especially when its terrace is open. ✉ *Rue des Septfontaines 36, L-2534,* ☎ *442356,* FAX *442353. 14 rooms. Restaurant. MC, V. Closed 3 wks late Dec.–early Jan.*

$ **Carlton.** In this vast 1918 hotel near the train station you'll find roomy, quiet quarters. The beveled glass and the oak parquet and terrazzo floors are original—but so are the toilets, all down the hall. Each room has antique beds, floral-print comforters, and a sink; wooden floors, despite creaks, are spotless. ✉ *Rue de Strasbourg 9, L-2561,* ☎ *299660,* FAX *299664. 50 rooms without bath, 8 with shower. No credit cards.*

Shopping

Luxembourg City's principal shopping areas comprise the **Grand Rue** and its side streets, the recently revamped **Gare** (train station) area, and the **Auchan** shopping center on Kirchberg. Jewelry and designer fashions are particularly well represented. Luxembourg chocolates, called *knippercher,* are popular purchases at the best pastry shops. Luxembourg's most famous product is porcelain from **Villeroy & Boch** (✉ Rue du Fossé 2, ☎ 463343). Feast your eyes on their tableware, crystal, and cutlery at the glitzy main store; then buy—at a 20% discount—at the excellent second-quality factory outlet to the northwest of the city center (✉ Rue Rollingergrund 330, ☎ 468211).

Side Trips

The northern highlands that compose the celebrated Ardennes plateau were the hunting ground of emperors and dukes and have been fought over from time immemorial to World War II. Castles punctuate its hills and dominate the valleys; rocky rivers and streams pour off its slopes. In contrast, the Petite Suisse, to the northeast of the capital, presents a more smiling face. It's a hilly area of leafy woods, rushing brooks, and old farms, ideal for rustic picnicking and great hiking. An easy hour's drive from Luxembourg City will take you to any of the towns except Clervaux, which is a bit farther.

Echternach

Echternach's cobbled market square is a mix of Gothic arcades and medieval town houses. The River Sûre here forms the border with Germany, and large numbers of tourists cross over on weekends. Some 15,000 pilgrims participate every year in a dancing procession on the Tuesday after Pentecost, ending at the **Basilique St-Willibrord,** whose crypt, open daily 9:30–6:30, contains the tomb of the great English missionary St. Willibrord (658–739).

Painstakingly detailed reproductions of the illuminated manuscripts of the Echternach School are displayed in the **Musée de l'Abbaye** (Abbey Museum). ✉ *Parvis de la Basilique 11,* ☎ *727472.* ⏲ *Apr.–June and Sept.–Oct., daily 10–noon and 2–6; July–Aug., daily 10–6.*

Diekirch

In the Ardennes, Diekirch has a lovely little Romanesque church, **Église St-Laurent** (St. Lawrence's Church), with Merovingian tombs, and (south of town) the Devil's Altar, a Celtic dolmen. The **Musée National d'Histoire Militaire** (National Military History Museum) mainly commemorates the Battle of the Bulge, the last German counteroffensive, which began just before Christmas 1944. ✉ *Bamertal 10,* ☎ *808908.* ⏲ *Apr.–Oct., daily 10–6; Nov.–Mar., daily 2–6.*

Vianden

★ The medieval **Château de Vianden** is the most romantic sight in the Grand Duchy. Rearing up on a hill above the tiny village, and replete with conical spires and massive bulwarks, it vividly recalls Luxembourg's feudal past. ✉ *Grande Rue,* ☎ *849291.* ⏲ *Apr.–Sept., daily 10–6; Mar. and Oct., daily 10–5; Nov.–Feb., daily 10–4.*

Clervaux

Surrounded by deep-cleft hills, the town is noted for the 12th-century **Château de Clervaux,** which has become the permanent home for Luxembourg-born Edward Steichen's "Family of Man," arguably the greatest photographic exhibit ever assembled. Franklin Delano Roosevelt's ancestor Philip de Lannoi, set forth from this castle in 1621 to seek his fortune in America. ✉ *Grande Rue,* ☎ *522–4241.* ⏲ *Mar.–Dec., Tues.–Sun. 10–6.*

Bourscheid

★ The romantic ruins of the **Château de Bourscheid** loom 500 ft above the River Sûre, commanding three valleys. Restorations have made the ruin's rambling towers and walls more accessible. ✉ *Bourscheid Moulin-Plage,* ☎ *990570.* ⏲ *Apr., daily 11–5; May–June and Sept., daily 10–6; July–Aug., daily 10–7; Oct., daily 11–4; Nov.–Mar., weekends 11–4.*

Moselle

On the eastern border with Germany, this wide river turns into Luxembourg's seaside during the summer, with promenading and jet-skiing. The banks of the river are covered with vineyards where the Luxembourg Moselle wine and sparkling wine (*crement*) are grown. Famous for sparkling wines, the **Bernard Massard** cellars are open for tours and tastings. ✉ *8 rue Pont, Grevenmacher,* ☎ *7505451.* ⏲ *Daily 9:30–6.*

The valley can be best appreciated from aboard the ***MS Princess Marie-Astrid,*** which cruises along the Moselle. ✉ *Rte. du Vin 10, Grevenmacher,* ☎ *758275.*

Luxembourg City Essentials

AIRPORTS AND TRANSFERS

All international flights arrive at Luxembourg's Findel Airport, 6 km (4 mi) northeast of the city.

➤ AIRPORT INFORMATION: **Findel Airport** (☎ 47/982315).

TRANSFERS

Bus 9 links the airport, the city center, and the main bus depot, next to the train station. Tickets cost Flux 40/€1. A taxi costs Flux 700/€17.35–Flux 800/€19.85.

BIKE TRAVEL

Bicycling is an excellent way to see the city and outlying areas. Bikes can be rented in Luxembourg City at Vélo en Ville from April through October.

➤ BIKE RENTALS: **Vélo en Ville** (✉ Bisserwee 8, ☎ 4796–2383).

BUS TRAVEL WITHIN LUXEMBOURG CITY

Luxembourg City has highly efficient bus service. Information can be found at Aldringen Center, an underground station off boulevard Royal. A 10-ride ticket costs Flux 320/€7.95.

CAR TRAVEL

PARKING

On-street parking in Luxembourg City is difficult. If you're in Luxembourg for a day, use one of the underground parking lots or park at the Parking Glacis next to the Municipal Theater, five minutes' walk from the city center. If you arrive from the west, use the free Parking Stade (opposite the Stadium) on Route d'Arlon and take the shuttle bus (Flux 40/€1) to town. If you arrive from France, look for the park-and-ride facility Sud (south); from Germany, look for Kirchberg-FIL. You need local currency for the bus ride.

EMERGENCIES

Pharmacies in Luxembourg stay open nights on a rotation system; see signs listing late-night facilities outside each pharmacy.

➤ EMERGENCY SERVICES: **Ambulance, Doctor, Dentist** (☎ 112). **Police** (☎ 113).

ENGLISH-LANGUAGE MEDIA

For books and magazines in English, try Magasin Anglais. The English-language paper *Luxembourg News,* published on Thursdays, is available from newsagents in the city.

➤ BOOKSTORES: **Magasin Anglais** (✉ Allée Scheffer 13, ☎ 224925).

TAXIS

Taxi stands are near the Gare Centrale and the main post office; it is almost impossible to hail one in the street.

➤ TAXI COMPANIES: **Taxi dispatch** (☎ 480058 or 482233).

TOURS

BUS TOURS

Sales-Lentz runs 2¼-hour city bus tours, April–mid-November, from the war memorial on Place de la Constitution and from the bus station, as well as a 4¾-hour tour to Château de Vianden on weekends May–September.

➤ FEES AND SCHEDULES: **Sales-Lentz** (☎ 461818–1).

TRAIN TOURS

Pétrusse Express guided mini-train tours of the Old Town and the Pétrusse Valley run from the Place de la Constitution April–October.

➤ FEES AND SCHEDULES: **Pétrusse Express** (☎ 461617).

WALKING TOURS

A guided walking tour called "City Promenade," held November–Easter, Monday, Wednesday, and weekends at 2, leaves from Place d'Armes. The "Wenzel Walk" allows visitors to experience 1,000 years of history in 100 minutes. The walk starts at the Bock promontory and leads over medieval bridges and past ancient ruins. The Luxembourg City Tourist Office can provide a guide. The walk is offered Easter Saturday–October 31, daily at 3 PM. In addition to the Wenzel Walk, a guided city promenade takes place daily Easter Saturday–October 31 at 2:30 PM. For those who prefer exploring the city alone, tapes explaining the city's history and development can be rented from the Luxembourg City Tourist Office throughout the year.

➤ FEES AND SCHEDULES: **"City Promenade"** (☎ 222809).

TRAIN TRAVEL

Luxembourg is served by frequent direct trains from Paris (four hours) and Brussels (three hours). From Amsterdam (six hours), the journey is via Brussels. There are connections from most German cities via Koblenz. Outside Luxembourg City, three major train routes extend to the north, south, and east. All services are from the Gare Centrale.

➤ TRAIN INFORMATION: **Gare Centrale** (☎ 4990–4990).

TRAVEL AGENCIES

➤ LOCAL AGENTS: **BBL Travel American Express** (✉ 3 rue Jean Piret, ☎ 4924041). **Carlson/Wagonlit** (✉ Grande Rue 105, ☎ 460315). **Connections** (including youth travel; ✉ Grande Rue 70, ☎ 229933).

VISITOR INFORMATION

The "Luxembourg Card" provides admission to 31 major attractions in the capital and countryside and use of public transport throughout the Grand Duchy. It costs Flux 350/€8.70 for one day, Flux 600/€14.85 for two days, and Flux 850/€21 for three days; family cards are twice the price. Cards can be bought in hotels and tourist offices.

➤ TOURIST INFORMATION: **Luxembourg City Tourist Office** (✉ Pl. d'Armes, ☎ 222809). **Beaufort** (✉ Rue de l'Église 9, ☎ 836081). **Bourscheid** (✉ Château, ☎ 990564). **Clervaux** (✉ Château, ☎ 920072). **Diekirch** (✉ Esplanade 1, ☎ 803023). **Echternach** (✉ Porte St-Willibrord, Basilique, ☎ 720230). **Vianden** (✉ Maison Victor Hugo, rue de la Gare 37, ☎ 834257).

20 MALTA

VALLETTA, AROUND THE ISLANDS

HULKING MEGALITHIC TEMPLES, ornate Baroque churches, narrow Old World streets, and hilltop citadels are Malta's human legacy. Dizzying limestone cliffs, sparkling Mediterranean seas, and charming rural landscapes make up its natural beauty. Its three main islands—Malta, Gozo, and Comino—offer history, water sports, spectacular coastal views, and culinary delights.

In its 7,000 years of human habitation, Malta has been overrun by every major Mediterranean power: Phoenicians, Carthaginians, Romans, Byzantines, and Arabs; Normans, Swabians, Angevins, Aragonese, and the Knights of the Order of St. John of Jerusalem; the French, the British, and now tourists. The Germans and Italians tried to take it in World War II—their air raids were devastating—but could not.

The islands' history with the Knights of the Order of St. John has given them their lasting character. Charles V of Spain, more than 400 years before the Axis powers' assault, granted Malta to the Knights after the Ottoman Turks chased the military order of hospitalers out of Rhodes. Charles leased Malta to the order for one falcon a year, giving birth to the myth of the Maltese falcon. In 1565, when the forces of Süleyman the Magnificent laid siege to the islands, it was the Knights' turn, with the faithful backing of the Maltese, to send the Turks packing.

The handsome limestone buildings and fortifications that the wealthy Knights left behind are all around the islands. Malta has plenty of modern development, too—all the more reason to stick to the historic sights on Malta and head to quieter Gozo to relax and to enjoy the sea. You'll need at least four days to see Malta and Gozo; allow two or more for taking in Malta's splendid past, and then make your way to Gozo for a few days of the quiet life.

MALTA A TO Z

To research prices, get advice from other travelers, and book travel arrangements, visit www.fodors.com.

AIR TRAVEL

Malta Air Charter, a helicopter company, makes the 10-minute flight from Malta to Gozo several times daily.

➤ AIRLINES AND CONTACTS: **Malta Air Charter** (☎ 557905 or 662211).

BOAT AND FERRY TRAVEL

Daily car and passenger ferries run year-round from Ċirkewwa (northwest Malta) to Mġarr Harbor on Gozo. One service leaves weekdays from Pietà (near Valletta) for Gozo. Commuter ferry service links

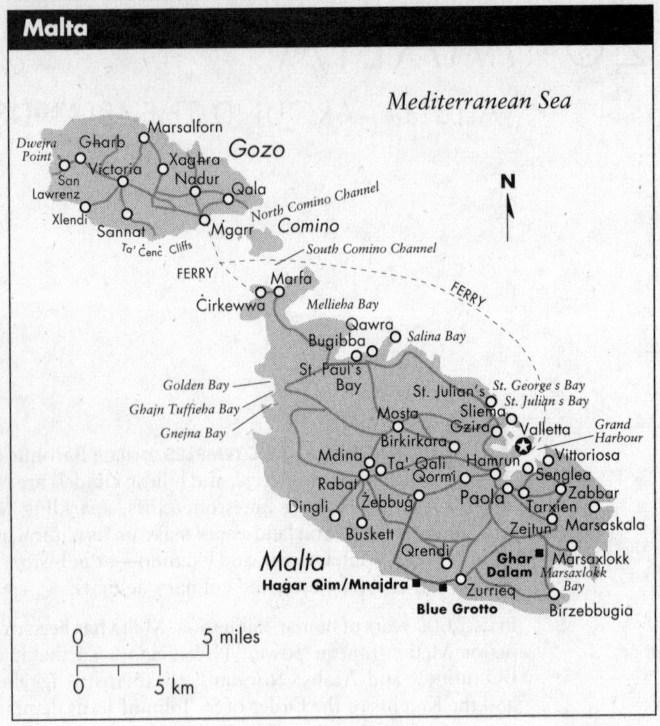

Sliema to Valletta. An express catamaran service operates irregularly from Pietà.

➤ BOAT AND FERRY INFORMATION: **Ferry information** (☎ 243964 in Malta; 556114, 556743 in Gozo).

BUS TRAVEL

Most routes across the island start at Valletta Terminal. Local fares on Malta's orange-colored fleet of new and retro buses are remarkably cheap: 15¢ for most trips, 18¢ for longer rides. With the help of the tourism bureau's map of the islands, on which bus routes are marked, and the Public Transportation Association's schedule listing the stops for each bus number (plus a little bit of luck and lots of patience), you can get almost anywhere on the island.

➤ BUS INFORMATION: **Public Transportation Association** (☎ 250007/9). **Valletta Terminal** (✉ Triton Fountain Sq., just outside main City Gate, ☎ 225916).

BUSINESS HOURS

BANKS AND OFFICES

Banks are generally open weekdays 8:30–2 and 4–7 and Saturday 8:30–12:45; from June through September they're open Friday until 3:30. The currency-exchange booths at the airport are open 24 hours, and there are ATMs throughout the islands.

MUSEUMS AND SIGHTS

Museums in both Malta and Gozo run by the Museums Department (☎ 230711) are open October–mid-June, Monday–Saturday 8:15–5, Sunday 8:15–4:15; mid-June–September, daily 7:45–2. They are closed on public holidays. Other museums' hours may vary slightly, so check locally.

SHOPS

Shops are open Monday–Saturday 9–1 and 4–7.

CAR TRAVEL

RULES OF THE ROAD

British driver's licenses are acceptable; Americans must have international licenses. Driving is on the left and, in spite of the relatively well signposted routes, challenging. Speed limits are 40 kph (25 mph) in towns, 65 kph (40 mph) elsewhere.

CUSTOMS AND DUTIES

You may bring into Malta, duty-free, 200 cigarettes or 50 cigars, one bottle of liquor, one bottle of wine, and one bottle of perfume. Up to Lm 1,000 in Maltese currency may be imported.

DINING

Traditional Maltese cuisine is Italian in origin, but "international" food is on most restaurant menus as well. Locally caught fish is a specialty. The national dish is *fenek* (rabbit); *braġjoli* (beef olives) and *lampuki* (dorado) pie are runners-up. Pastry coats fish, vegetables, cheese, and pasta dishes. Soups, *minestra* (minestrone), and *aljotta* (fish) especially, are common, and are delicious with daily baked crusty Maltese bread. Capers, the buds of the *caperis specicum* shrub that is native to the islands, are widely used. Native wine is abundant and inexpensive; look for medium-dry whites. Cisk lager is a local favorite, and try Hop Leaf pale ale for something with a bit more bite. Kinnie, a terrific non-alcoholic thirst quencher, is made from a "secret recipe" that includes bitter oranges.

Prices are for one main course at dinner.

CATEGORY	COST
$$$$	over Lm 5.50
$$$	Lm 4.50–Lm 5.50
$$	Lm 3.50–Lm 4.50
$	under Lm 3.50

RESERVATIONS AND DRESS

A jacket and tie are appropriate in higher-price restaurants. Otherwise, casual dress is acceptable.

EMBASSIES AND HIGH COMMISSIONS

➤ AUSTRALIA: **Australian High Commission** (✉ Villa Fiorentina, Ta' Xbiex Terrace, Ta' Xbiex, ☎ 338201).

➤ UNITED KINGDOM: **British High Commission** (✉ 7 St. Anne St., Floriana, ☎ 233134).

➤ UNITED STATES: (✉ St. Anne St., Development Office, 2nd floor, Floriana, ☎ 235960).

HOLIDAYS

January 1; February 10 (St. Paul's Shipwreck); March 19 (St. Joseph's Day); March 31 (Freedom Day); Good Friday; May 1 (Worker's Day); June 7 (Commemoration of First Maltese Nationalist Protest); June 29 (Sts. Peter and Paul); August 15 (Assumption, or Santa Marija); September 8 (Our Lady of Victories); September 21 (Independence Day); December 8 (Immaculate Conception); December 13 (Republic Day); December 25.

LANGUAGE

English and Maltese, a language of Arabic origin written in Roman script, are the official languages. Maltese pronunciations are as follows: *ċ* = ch (as in Ċirkewwa); *ġ* = j (Haġar); *ħ* = a barely perceptible h (Ħal

Saflieni); *j* = y (Dwejra); *M*= im (Mdina); *x* = sh (Marsaxlokk); *ż* = ts (Żebbuġ); and the plain *g* and *q* are silent, as in Għarb ("arb") and Haġar Qim ("*ha*-jar eem").

LODGING

Aside from the larger resort hotels in Buġibba, most quality accommodations in Malta can be found in the St. George's Bay and St. Julian's areas. In a bid to improve the standards of inexpensive lodgings, the tourism board launched a reclassification program at the end of 2000 to weed out substandard hotels. Several run-down properties have been closed; what's left are hotels that offer value for money and provide a set standard of service. On Gozo there are upscale hotels at Mgarr, Sannat, and San Lawrenz, but the best bet is to rent a farmhouse or villa. The limestone houses can be anywhere from 300 years to one month old; newer ones tend to be on the edges of towns. Insist on clear photographs and details in writing before sending a deposit.

Prices are for two people sharing a double room.

CATEGORY	COST
$$$$	over Lm 50
$$$	Lm 25–Lm 50
$$	Lm 12–Lm 24
$	under Lm 12

HOUSE RENTALS

In Victoria, Gozo's capital, Paradise Travel and Property Services, Ltd. has 15 farmhouses to rent for Lm 12–Lm 50. Be specific with your request: number of guests, old or new farmhouse, necessity of pool (usually unheated), telephone service, size of town, and so on. Linen and weekly maid service is provided. Paradise can also arrange car rentals. ➤ LOCAL AGENTS: **Paradise Travel and Property Services, Ltd.** (✉ 38 St. Sabina Sq., VCT 102, ☎ 562025, FAX 562026).

MAIL AND SHIPPING

POSTAL RATES

Airmail letters to the United States and Canada cost 22¢; postcards cost 22¢. Airmail letters and postcards to the United Kingdom cost 16¢.

MONEY MATTERS

Malta was once among the least expensive holiday destinations in Europe, but with the rapid development of tourism, prices have inevitably risen. Some sample prices, in Maltese currency, include: cup of coffee, 35¢; bottle of beer, 35¢; soft drink, 30¢; sandwich, 90¢; individual pizza, Lm 1.70.

CURRENCY

The unit of currency is the Maltese lira (Lm), also sometimes referred to as the pound; it's divided into 100 cents. There are Lm 2, 5, 10, and 20 bills. The 1¢ coin is bronze, and other coins—2¢, 5¢, 10¢, 25¢, 50¢, and Lm 1—are silver. At press time (summer 2001) the exchange rate was Lm 0.44 to the U.S. dollar, Lm 0.28 to the Canadian dollar, Lm 0.64 to the pound sterling, Lm 0.51 to the Irish punt, Lm 0.25 to the Australian dollar, Lm 0.23 to the New Zealand dollar, and Lm 0.06 to the South African rand.

TELEPHONES

COUNTRY AND AREA CODES

The country code for Malta is 356.

INTERNATIONAL CALLS

➤ ACCESS CODES: **Overseas operator** (☎ 194). **International dialing access code** (☎ 00). **AT&T Long-Distance** (☎ 0800–890110).

LOCAL CALLS

To reach an operator in Malta, dial 190. Public phones are mostly operated by phone cards, which may be purchased at many shops for Lm 2, Lm 3, Lm 5, and Lm 10.

TIPPING

A tip of 10% is expected when a service charge is not included.

TOURS

Sightseeing tours are arranged by local travel agents and most hotels. There are half-day, full-day, and "Malta by Night" bus tours; rates vary. Contact tourist offices for details. Malta Air Charter runs helicopter tours of the islands. Beware of cheap tours: officially licensed guides should wear an identification tag.

➤ FEES AND SCHEDULES: **Malta Air Charter** (☎ 559341/2 in Malta; 662211 in Gozo).

VISITOR INFORMATION

➤ TOURIST INFORMATION: **Malta Tourism Authority** (✉ 280 Republic St., Valletta CMR 02, ☎ 224444/5).

WHEN TO GO

Late April into June and late September through October have pleasantly warm weather, and the sea is delightful. Mid-June to early September can be too hot for comfort; November through March tends to be cool and occasionally rainy.

CLIMATE

The following are the average daily maximum and minimum temperatures for Valletta.

Jan.	58F	14C	**May**	71F	22C	**Sept.**	81F	27C
	50	10		61	16		7	22
Feb.	59F	15C	**June**	79F	26C	**Oct.**	75F	24C
	51	11		67	19		66	19
Mar.	61F	16C	**July**	84F	29C	**Nov.**	67F	20C
	52	11		72	22		60	16
Apr.	65F	18C	**Aug.**	85F	29C	**Dec.**	61F	16C
	56	13		73	23		54	12

VALLETTA

Malta's capital, the minicity of Valletta, has ornate palaces and museums protected by massive fortifications of honey-color limestone. Houses along the narrow streets have overhanging wooden balconies for people-watching from indoors. Generations ago they gave housebound women a window on the world of the street.

Exploring Valletta

The main entrance to town is through the City Gate (where all bus routes end), which leads onto Triq Repubblika (Republic Street), the spine of the grid-pattern city and the main shopping street. Triq Mercante (Merchant Street) parallels Repubblika to the east and is also good for strolling. From these two streets, cross streets descend toward the water; some are stepped. Valletta's compactness makes it ideal to explore on foot. Before setting out along Republic Street, stop at the tourist information office (just inside the city gate) for maps and brochures.

Barrakka ta' Fuq (Upper Barrakka Gardens). Where knights once honed their fencing skills under a covered loggia (now open to the sky), a troupe of cats and some greenery occupy this lofty lookout over the Grand Harbor and the Three Cities across the water. ⊠ *Castile Sq.* ⏲ *Daily dawn–dusk.*

★ **Casa Rocca Piccola.** The exquisitely cultured current owners, Nicolas and Frances de Piro d'Amico Inguanez, host tours of the last of the patrician houses still occupied. The treasures inside chart the history of the house, from a portable Baroque chapel for baptisms to a painting of "Miss Electricity," commissioned to mark the local contribution of an ambitious ancestor. New exhibits include a costume gallery and an underground bomb shelter, used by Valletta residents during the war. ⊠ *74 Triq Repubblika,* ☎ *231796,* WEB *tourist.vol.net.mt/casarocca.* ⏲ *Guided tours Mon.–Sat. 10, 11, noon, 1.*

Fort St. Elmo. Built in 1552 by the Knights to defend the harbor, it was completely destroyed during the siege of 1565 and rebuilt by succeeding military leaders. Today part of the fort houses the **War Museum** (☎ 222430), with its collection of military objects related to World War II, including the George Cross, a medal awarded to the people of Malta for bravery in 1942 by British King George VI. Also on display are an Italian E-Boat and one of the three Gloster Gladiator biplanes that defended the island. ⊠ *St. Elmo Pl., Valletta,* ☎ *226400.*

★ **Grand Masters' Palace.** The palace houses the president's office, and Malta's parliament meets here. Completed in 1574, the palace has a unique collection of Gobelin tapestries; the main hall is decorated with frescoes depicting the history of the Knights and the Great Siege. On view are works by Ribera, Van Loo, and Batoni. At the back of the building is the **Armoury of the Knights,** with exhibits of arms and armor through the ages. ⊠ *Palace Sq., Triq Repubblika,* ☎ *221221.*

★ **Great Siege of Malta and the Knights of St. John.** A walk-through presentation traces the order's history from its founding in 1099 in the Holy Land and its journeys from Jerusalem to Cyprus, Rhodes, and Malta. Also depicted are epic scenes from the Great Siege of 1565, the naval Battle of Lepanto, and the order's eviction from Malta by the French. ⊠ *Cafe Premier Complex, Treasury St.,* ☎ *247300,* WEB *www.cities.com.mt/great-siege.* ⏲ *Daily 9–4.*

Manoel Theater. If you are here in opera season, don't miss a show at the third-oldest theater in Europe, which had its opening night on January 9, 1732. Intimate and splendidly decorated, it was designed after Palermo's theater at the time. ⊠ *Old Theater St.,* ☎ *222618.* ⏲ *Guided tours weekdays 10:30 and 11:30, Sat. 11:30.*

★ **National Museum of Archaeology.** Housed in the Auberge de Provence (the hostel of the Knights from Provence), the museum has an excellent collection of finds from Malta's many prehistoric sites—Tarxien, Haġar Qim, and the Hypogeum at Paola. ⊠ *Triq Repubblika,* ☎ *233821.*

Sacra Infermeria (Hospital of the Knights). This gracious building near the seawall has been converted into the Mediterranean Conference Center. For an introduction to the island, see the *Malta Experience,* a multimedia presentation on the history of Malta that is given here daily on the hour. ⊠ *Mediterranean St.,* ☎ *243776.* ⏲ *Weekdays 9:30–4.*

★ **St. John's co-Cathedral.** Functional in design but lavishly decorated, the Order of St. John's own church (1578) is Malta's most important treasure. The Knights' colored-marble tombstones on the floor are gorgeous. Each of the side chapels was decorated by a national hostel of the Knights. Many of the paintings and the decoration scheme are by the island's beloved 17th-century painter Mattia Preti (b. 1613). The cathedral **museum** has illuminated manuscripts and a rich collection of Flemish tapestries. ✉ *Pjazza San Gwann.* ⏲ *Weekdays 9:30–12:30 and 1:30–4:30, Sat. 9:30–12:30.*

★ **St. Paul's Shipwreck Church.** The importance of St. Paul to the Maltese explains the work lavished on this Baroque marvel—its raised central vault, oval dome, and marble columns. The *os brachii* (arm bone) relic of the saint is housed in a chapel on the right, a splendid gated chapel is on the left, and a baptismal font stands by the entrance. ✉ *Triq San Pawl.*

Dining

$$$$ ✕ **The Carriage.** It feels like a prohibition-era secret when you ride the private elevator to the top floor, where you seem to be joining a stylish international party. Window tables have splendid views. Warm servers bring you ambitious fare that sometimes disappoints. ✉ *22/5 Valletta Buildings, South St.,* ☏ *247828. Reservations essential. Jacket and tie. AE, DC, MC, V. Closed Sun.–Mon. No dinner Tues.–Wed. No lunch Sat.*

$$$$ ✕ **Giannini.** Atop the quiet west end of Valletta's mighty bastions, this is among the city's most reserved and elegant restaurants. Leading politicians and the fashionable set dine here on haute Maltese-Italian cuisine. There is a lounge downstairs; the restaurant is on the fifth floor. ✉ *23 Windmill St.,* ☏ *237121. Reservations essential. AE, DC, MC, V. No dinner Sun.–Thurs., no lunch weekends.*

$$ ✕ **Lantern.** Two brothers run this friendly spot. The interior of the 18th-century town house on Valletta's western heights is spare but chummy, and the traditional Maltese food is flavorful. ✉ *20 Sappers St.,* ☏ *237521. V. Closed Sun.*

$$ ✕ **Trattoria Palazz.** In a limestone cellar beneath the city's public library, which the Knights of Malta built more than 270 years ago, this tiny, romantic hideaway cooks up tasty Maltese-Italian dishes. Specials are your best bet here. ✉ *43 Old Theater St.,* ☏ *226611. Reservations essential. AE, DC, MC, V. Closed Sun.*

$ ★ ✕ **Caffe Cordina.** On the ground floor of the original treasury of the Knights is Valletta's oldest café. Since 1837, this ornate, vaulted confectionery has produced hot, savory breakfast pastries and *qaghaq ta' l-ghasel* (honey rings). ✉ *244–45 Triq Repubblika,* ☏ *234385. AE, DC, MC, V.*

Lodging

$$$$ **Le Meridien Phoenicia.** The grande dame of Malta is just outside Valletta's City Gate and across from the busy bus terminus. Nonetheless, you can enjoy attractive lounges, a stunning dining room, and well-appointed guest rooms (standard rooms can be small). Service is inconsistent—from professional to haughty and surly. ✉ *The Mall, Floriana VLT 16,* ☏ *225241,* FAX *235254,* WEB *www.lemeridienphoenicia.com. 136 rooms. 2 restaurants, pool. AE, DC, MC, V.*

$$ **Castille.** In a 16th-century former palazzo, this tired-looking hotel with sagging mattresses and not-so-nice bathrooms is nevertheless the best bet for inexpensive accommodations in Valletta. Rooms are spacious, with good windows, and the staff is friendly. Book at least three months ahead. ✉ *348 St. Paul St., VLT 07,* ☏ *243677 or 243678,* FAX *243677. 39 rooms. Restaurant, café. AE, DC, MC, V.*

$$ ☎ **Osborne.** In budget-hotel-starved Valletta, the Osborne provides a foothold within the city walls. The spacious lounge downstairs and the rooftop sundeck are filled with adventuresome European travelers, but the rooms are smokey, dark, and worn. ✉ *50 South St., VLT 11,* ☎ *243656,* FAX *247293. 60 rooms. Restaurant. AE, DC, V.*

Shopping

Valletta's main shopping street, **Triq Repubblika,** is lined with touristy shops—pick up postcards and film here, and then venture onto side streets for a look at everyday Maltese wares. The **Government Craft Center** (✉ Pjazza San Gwann) has traditional handmade goods. At the **open-air market** (Triq Mercante), with some haggling you may snap up a good bargain.

Valletta Essentials

AIRPORTS AND TRANSFERS

Air Malta operates regular flights from most major European cities to Malta International Airport, 6 km (4 mi) south of Valletta. TWA and Air Malta penned a code-sharing agreement in February 2000, making travel from the United States to the islands easier, but not faster.

➤ AIRPORT INFORMATION: **Malta International Airport** (☎ 249600).

TRANSFERS

Local Bus 8 (15¢) passes through Luqa village on its way to Valletta, with a stop at the airport every 15 minutes. Taxis are also available, and fares (Lm 3–Lm 13) are paid at the taxi booth in the arrivals hall before the trip.

BOAT AND FERRY TRAVEL

Grimaldi Ferries operates a weekly car and passenger ferry between Malta and Salerno in southern Italy. Virtu Ferries runs car and passenger catamarans most days of the week between Malta, Catania, and Pozzallo on Sicily. Summer and winter schedules vary.

➤ BOAT AND FERRY INFORMATION: **Grimaldi Ferries** (☎ 226873, FAX 226876). **Virtu Ferries** (☎ 318854, FAX 314533).

BUS TRAVEL WITHIN VALLETTA

Although Bus 98 (15¢) circles the perimeter of the city every hour from the terminus by the City Gate, it is quicker to walk around Valletta. Buses do not run on streets within the city.

EMERGENCIES

➤ EMERGENCY SERVICES: **Ambulance** (☎ 196). **Fire** (☎ 199). **Police** (☎ 191).

➤ HOSPITALS: **Hospital** (✉ Gwardamangia, ☎ 241251).

TAXIS

Metered taxis are plentiful and extravagantly expensive. If you use one, be sure the meter is switched on when your trip starts, or bargain first.

TOURS

One-hour boat tours of Valletta's Grand Harbour leave regularly from Sliema jetty. Buy tickets at most travel agencies or on the boat. Licensed guides can be hired through local travel agencies.

TRAVEL AGENCIES

Local agencies have desks at most major hotels.

➤ LOCAL AGENTS: **American Express** (representative; ✉ Airways House, High St., Sliema, ☎ 344336). **Thomas Cook** (✉ Il-Pjazzetta, Tower Rd., Sliema, ☎ 322747 or 322748).

VISITOR INFORMATION

➤ TOURIST INFORMATION: **Valletta** (✉ 1 City Gate Arcade, ☎ 237747). **Malta International Airport** (☎ 69999603).

AROUND MALTA

The conurbation around Valletta varies in character. The Three Cities area has its Old World charms, while the urban sprawl of Sliema and St. Julian's is becoming increasingly commercialized with new hotels and expanding shopping areas. Malta's southern and eastern areas have prehistoric sites, as well as the stunning cliffs and waters around the Blue Grotto. The ancient and silent walled city of Mdina rises out of the center of the island. On the way to the ferry on the northwest end, parallel rift valleys alternate fertile terrain with barren, exposed hills and sandy or rocky coastline. Alas, the towns in this direction, such as Buġibba and Qawra, have largely been done in by interchangeable international resorts with no real Maltese character.

The Three Cities

East across the Grand Harbor from Valletta, the three cities of **Vittoriosa, Senglea,** and **Cospicua** are where the Knights of the Order of St. John first settled—and where crucial fighting took place in the Great Siege of the Turks in 1565. Vittoriosa, also called Birgu, is named for the victory over the Turks. The 5 km (3 mi) of great walls around the cities are the Cottonera Lines, built in the 1670s.

In **Vittoriosa/Birgu** in early October, hundreds of actors stage a Grand Master's crossing of the harbor, and monastery doors on Triq San Lawrenz open to the public for the **Birgu Festa.** On the narrow streets north of the main square you can loop from the Triq La Vallette to the Triq Majjistral on the right. Triq It-Tramuntana takes you past Baroque doorways, the Knights' Auberge d'Angleterre (Inn of England), and a Saracen-style house that is thought to date from the 1200s.

Below Birgu's main square, the **Church of St. Lawrenz** is the city's finest church, with the 17th-century painter Mattia Preti's *Martyrdom of San Lawrenz.* ✉ *Triq San Lawrenz, Birgu.*

The displays in Birgu's **Inquisitor's Palace** reveal less-discussed aspects of less-tolerant times in Malta. ✉ *Triq Il-Mina Il-Kbira, Birgu.*

At the tip of Senglea, **Gardjola Garden,** once a guard post, has great views and a turret carved with a vigilant eye and ear.

Sliema and St. Julian's

Sliema's shoreline, an almost-flashy commercial strip, is Malta's best spot for designer clothes shopping. St. Julian's Bay has a number of excellent restaurants and waterfront cafés. Heavily trafficked Paceville, just beyond St. Julian's, is where Malta's club-goers party at night. The town of Ta' Xbiex is equipped for yachts.

$$$$ ✕ **Barracuda.** Perched precariously on columns and commanding a superb view of St. Julian's Bay, this old house holds one of Malta's most delightful and efficiently run restaurants. Seafood is the drawing card here—choose from a variety caught the same day served with such sauces as cucumber and mint or tomatoes, black olives, and capers. ✉ *194–5 Main St., St. Julian's,* ☎ FAX *331817. AE, DC, MC, V.*

$$$$ ✕ **San Giuliano.** The large, second-story dining room overlooking Spinola Bay in St. Julian's permits some of the swankiest and slowest dining in Malta. The Italian chef prepares a delicious array of antipasti and knows that truly fresh fish caught the same day needs little fuss-ing. ✉ *Spinola Bay, St. Julian's,* ☎ *332000. Reservations essential. AE, DC, MC, V. No lunch Mon.*

$$$ ✕ **Peppino's.** This is the place to go if you want to be seen. The ground floor is a wine bar that also serves light meals. There's a good full-blown restaurant on the first floor. ✉ *St. George's Rd., St. Julian's,* ☎ *373200. AE, DC, MC, V.*

$$ ✕ **Ta' Kolina.** The only point of culinary interest on Sliema's waterfront, this untrendy spot serves traditional Maltese dishes—such as *timpana* (baked pasta covered with pastry), fresh cheese salad, bragjoli, and octopus. ✉ *151 Tower Rd., Sliema,* ☎ *335106. AE, DC, MC, V. No lunch.*

Paola and Tarxien

★ The **Ħal Saflieni Hypogeum,** a massive labyrinth of underground chambers, was used for burials more than 4,000 years ago. Many chambers are decorated with red ocher or fine carvings. ✉ *On road to Santa Lucija,* ☎ *233821.* ⏲ *By appointment.*

The three interconnecting **Tarxien Temples** have curious carvings, oracular chambers, and altars, all dating from about 2800 BC. Nearby are remains of an earlier temple from about 4000 BC. ✉ *Behind Paola's Church of Christ the King.*

Marsaxlokk

At the fishing and resort town Marsaxlokk on the southeast coast you can see the *luzzu,* Malta's multicolored, traditional fishing boat. Its vertical prow has Phoenician ancestry.

$$ ✕ **Ix-Xlukkajr.** Seafood is the draw at this harborside restaurant. Octopus marinated in garlic sauce is a wonderful cold starter. Try the whole-fish specials and, for dessert, homemade prickly-pear and kiwi ice creams. ✉ *Village Sq.,* ☎ *612109. MC, V. Closed Wed.*

Għar Dalam

The semifossilized remains of long-extinct species of dwarf elephants and hippopotamuses that roamed the island some 125,000 years ago were found in a **cave** here. The fossils are now on display in the small museum.

Ghajn Tuffieha Bay

This sandy beach on the northwestern side of Malta is wonderful for an afternoon by the sea. The sometimes bumpy bus (Route 47) ride takes you through the rolling countryside, which is patchworked with ancient stone walls and occasional fields of root crops.

Zurrieq

On the way to Zurrieq from Valletta you will pass limestone quarries, where orchards are planted, protected from the wind, after the limestone is exhausted. On the far side of town, **Wied-iz-Zurrieq** (Zurrieq Valley) runs along the road to a lookout over the towering walls of the Blue Grotto's bay. Across the water, tiny **Filfla,** flat-topped from British air-force target practice, is the smallest of the Maltese islands.

★ The turnoff for the **Blue Grotto** is 1 km (½ mi) beyond the lookout. A steep road takes you to the rocky inlet where noisy boats (Lm 2.50) leave for the grottoes (there are many) and the stained-glass-blue waters that splash their walls. Bring a bathing suit in case the water is calm enough for swimming. ✉ *Coast Rd.*

★ The 4,800-year-old **Haġar Qim** ("*ha*-jar eem") gives a clear picture of the massive scale of Malta's ancient limestone temples. The altars are well preserved, but the decoration (some of which is a reproduction)
★ is pitted. From the temple of **Mnajdra** ("mna-ee-dra"), on the edge of

a hill by the sea, views are superb. The temple is encircled by hard coralline limestone walls and has the typical, cloverlike trefoil plan. ✉ *Coast Rd.*

Dingli

With a car, you can drive south from Mdina to Dingli for a tour of the countryside, a look at the cliffs, and a tree fix at **Buskett Forest.** The forest surrounds **Verdala Castle,** which the Knights built as a hunting lodge in the 16th century. Now the president of Malta uses it to host distinguished visitors. It is not open to the public. ✉ *Buskett Rd.*

Mdina

★ In Malta's ancient, walled capital—the longtime stronghold of Malta's nobility—traffic is limited to residents' cars, and the noise of the world outside doesn't penetrate the thick, golden walls. The quiet streets are lined with sometimes block-long, still-occupied noble palaces.

★ The serene, Baroque **Mdina Cathedral** (dedicated to St. Peter and St. Paul) contains Mattia Preti's 17th-century painting *The Shipwreck of St. Paul.* In the cathedral museum are Dürer woodcuts and illuminated manuscripts. ✉ *Archbishop Sq.,* ☎ *454679.* ⏲ *Mon.–Sat. 9–1 and 1:30–4.*

Rabat

The town's name means "suburb"—of Mdina, in this case. The beautiful **St. Paul's Church** (✉ Parish Sq.) stands above a grotto where St. Paul reputedly took refuge after his shipwreck on Malta.

Catacombs run under much of Rabat. Up Triq Santa Agatha from Parish Square, the **Catacombs of St. Paul** are clean of bones but full of carved-out burial troughs. Don't forget the way out when you set off to explore. **St. Agatha's Crypt and Catacombs,** farther up the street, were beautifully frescoed between 1200 and 1480, then defaced by Turks in 1551. ✉ *St. Agatha St.*

Mosta

The **Rotunda** (Church of St. Mary) has the third-largest unsupported dome in Europe, after St. Peter's in Rome and Hagia Sophia in Istanbul. A German bomb fell through the roof during World War II—without detonating. ✉ *Rotunda Sq. (Buses 49 and 53).* ⏲ *Daily 9–noon and 3–6.*

GOZO AND COMINO

Gozo is a place to relax. Spend a morning in the walled, hilltop Cittadella; stroll around Victoria's narrow limestone-walled streets; look inside splendid local churches; and then head down for a swim at Ramla Bay or a boat ride from the Inland Sea at Dwejra ("dway-ra"). You can take great walks along the cliffs of Ta' Ċenċ ("ta chench") and San Lawrenz/Dwejra or hike past the centuries-old salt pans west of Marsalforn at Qbajjar.

Gozo has some superb restaurants, and local bakeries turn out tasty, crusty round loaves. The island's traditional craft is lace making, practiced by a diminishing number of older women who still make time for the intricacy of this labor of love. Like their Maltese counterparts, Gozitan men love to hunt, and native and migratory birds are either caged or shot. Most of the waist-high stone structures that dot Gozo's fields are blinds, and on autumn hunting-season mornings you'll hear the sporadic pop of rifles. The island has become increasingly popular for diving, especially at Xlendi Bay. The ferry docks at Mġarr Harbour, but this part of Gozo is unrepresentative. Go elsewhere.

Xagħra

The parish **Church of Our Lady of Victories** has two clock towers. One clock has the correct time, while the other is deliberately wrong to fool the devil. In the cliffs to the west is reputedly **Calypso's Cave,** of Homer's *Odyssey* fame, viewable only from a platform a good distance away.

★ Imagine domes rising from the heavy stone walls of eastern Xagħra's 5,800-year-old **Ġgantija Temples,** and you will get a sense of their original power. Each bears the classic five-apse plan that is the signature of Maltese megalithic temples. ✉ *Xagħra plateau.*

$$ ★ ✕ **Oleander.** Mario Attard prepares sophisticated local food at this village-square restaurant. The fresh tomato soup and pasta with anchovies, tomatoes, and black olives are spectacular. ✉ *10 Victory Sq.,* ☎ *557230. AE, MC, V. Closed Mon.*

$ ★ ✕ **Gester Restaurant.** This old-time luncheonette is run by sisters Gemma and Ester, who serve delicious, homey Gozitan food. Try peppered local sheep's milk cheese, rabbit in rich tomato sauce, lasagna, and the meadlike local "wine." ✉ *8th September Ave.,* ☎ *556621. No credit cards. Closed Sun. No dinner.*

$$$ 🏨 **Cornucopia.** This sprawling complex of hotel rooms, bungalows, and farmhouses lies on the western flank of town. Valley-view rooms (24 and 47 are the best), bungalows, and farmhouses are spacious and pleasant. Avoid all others. ✉ *10 Gnien Imrik St., Xagħra XRA 102,* ☎ *556486 or 553866,* FAX *552910. 45 rooms, 2 suites, 11 bungalows, 2 farmhouses, 2 apartments. Restaurant, 3 pools. AE, DC, MC, V.*

Nadur

Gozo's second-largest town has a substantial parish church with a colored Italian marble interior and French stained-glass windows.

★ Baker Joe at **Mekren's Bakery** (✉ Triq Tal-Ħanaq, 50 yards down the road to Ramla after first intersection in Nadur) makes some of Gozo's best bread—for 11¢ a loaf—and occasionally whips up sweet pastry or pizza.

Outside Nadur are two small beaches that were once considered secret. Anything but that now, tiny **San Blas Bay** to the north is accessed by a *very* steep descent on foot past citrus groves. **Ħondoq Bay,** to the east through the town of Qala, faces Comino. The beach isn't gorgeous, but the swims to rocky inlets are delightful.

Ramla Bay

The ocher-color sands at Ramla Bay cover Gozo's largest and most popular beach, which is ideal for swimming.

$ ✕ **Il-Werqa.** When the sunshine and the sea are no longer enough at this popular beach, take a few steps over to the fish shack with the cactus sign for its "special fish dinner," in which only today's catch is served. ✉ *Ramla Bay,* ☎ *559723. No credit cards. Closed mid-Nov.–Easter.*

Victoria

Gozo's capital is a charming old city with warrens of narrow streets, a hilltop Cittadella, and two main squares—Pjazza Independenza beneath the Cittadella and Pjazza San Franġisk. The splendid Baroque **St. George's Basilica** (✉ down Triq San Ġużepp from Pjazza Indepenża) has the most beautiful interior on Gozo. The original city here is the walled, hilltop **Cittadella.** It has steep, winding streets and great views from its ramparts. The **cathedral**'s dome fell in a 1693 earthquake; it is now simulated by a trompe l'oeil painting. A museum displays the cathedral's ceremonial silver. The intriguing **Folklore Museum** (✉ Triq Milite Bernardo) occupies three medieval houses. The **Archaeological Museum** (✉ Triq il-Katidral) exhibits objects from various ancient periods.

The street to the left of the cathedral leads to the **Cittadella Boutique** (✉ 4 Fosse St., ☎ 555953), a one-stop shop for high-quality local lacework and nicely packaged food items. It also serves light lunches of tomatoes, cheese, bread, and wine. It's closed Sunday.

$$$ ✕ **Brookie's.** In a stone farmhouse under the western walls of the Cittadella, Brookie's prepares some of the island's priciest and richest fare (cream is a favorite ingredient). A popular bar is on site, as well as a terrace and patio for drinks. Service can be erratic. ✉ *½ Triq Wied Sara,* ☎ *559524. AE, DC, MC, V. Closed Mon.*

Sannat

Sannat is a quiet village due south of Victoria and home to lace makers who work along the streets and a Baroque church. Beyond town, park your car along the dirt road and continue north and west for the spectacular Ta' Ċenċ cliffs and wildflowers in the fields around them.

$$$$ **Hotel Ta' Ċenċ.** Near the windy southern cliffs of Gozo, the understated hotel has an exclusivity unique for Malta. In spite of poorly lit rooms, the hotel is a quiet, memorable place to relax for a few days. There is private swimming at a rocky inlet a 10-minute drive away. ✉ *Ta' Ċenċ, near Sannat, VCT 112,* ☎ *556819 or 556830,* FAX *558199. 64 rooms, 19 suites. Restaurant, 2 pools. AE, DC, MC, V.*

Xlendi

The miniature, fjordlike Xlendi (that's "shlendi") is home to fishermen and an abundance of vacation apartments that have spoiled this splendid place. The promenade along the water is lined with cafés, and on Sunday families traditionally parade here in their finest.

Ghajn il-Kbira (The Great Fountain; ✉ Fontana, between Victoria and Xlendi Bay) was built in the 15th century to provide fresh spring water and laundry facilities for nearby Gozitans. Today, though it is still used for its original intent, you're just as likely to see a car being washed.

Malta's history, geography, and clear blue sea provide excellent opportunities for underwater exploration. Contact **St. Andrew's Divers Cove Ltd.** (✉ Shore St., Mġarr Harbour, ☎ 556441, FAX 561548, WEB www.digigate.net/standrews).

$$$ ★ **St. Patrick's Hotel.** This well-maintained mid-size hotel stands steps away from the bay. Harbor-view rooms are the best; avoid claustrophobic courtyard rooms. ✉ *Xlendi, VCT 115,* ☎ *562951 or 562952,* FAX *556598. 45 rooms, 4 penthouse rooms. Restaurant. AE, MC, V.*

Marsalforn and Qbajjar

On a bay north of Victoria, this former fishing village is a tourist factory out of character with the rest of the island. On the coast west of Marsalforn, past Qbajjar ("by-*jar*"), is a stretch of salt pans dating from the time of the Knights. June through September, troughs cut into the limestone flats are filled with seawater, left to evaporate, then scraped for the salt left behind. The coarse crystals are excellent for cooking. In season you can buy salt along the road here from the gatherers.

$$$$ ✕ **Auberge Ta' Frenċ.** In an atmospheric limestone farmhouse, this restaurant has Gozo's most refined service and classic cuisine. Seafood dishes are best here. ✉ *Marsalforn Rd.,* ☎ *553888. Reservations essential. AE, DC, MC, V. Closed Tues. and weekdays Jan.–Feb.*

Għarb

This far-west island village is one of the prettiest on Gozo. Its central square has a particularly handsome church. Visit the privately owned, 28-room **Għarb Folklore Museum** (✉ 99 Pjazza il-Knisja, ☎ 561929), which is worth a half-hour or so.

$$–$$$ ★ ✕ **Jeffrey's.** Chef-owner Jeffrey's interpretations of Gozitan classics in this romantic find are superb: a delicate brine-free fish soup, succulent braciola, and rabbit in a white wine and garlic sauce. Jeffrey harvests produce from his own farm and herbs from outside the kitchen. Reservations are essential; otherwise you will be unceremoniously shown to the door. ✉ *10 Triq L-Għarb,* ☎ *561006. Reservations essential. AE, MC, V. Closed Sun. and Nov.–Easter. No lunch.*

San Lawrenz and Dwejra

The **cliffs of San Lawrenz and Dwejra** ("dway-ra") are spectacular—especially at sunset. From Għarb, follow signs for the hamlet of San Lawrenz. Park where the road turns to dirt at the town's end and follow the road for a kilometer (½ mi) or so.

★ A must on Gozo is a ride (Lm 5 per boat) from the tiny **Inland Sea** through a natural tunnel under the cliffs out to the sea. Have the boatman loop around Dwejra Point to see the **Azure Window and Fungus Rock,** a huge limestone arch with unusual rock formations extending from the cliffs.

$$$$ ★ **San Lawrenz Leisure Resort.** This new hotel is built around the largest pool on the islands and has the best-equipped spa on Gozo. ✉ *Triq il-Rokon, San Lawrenz GRB104,* ☎ *558639,* FAX *562977,* WEB *www.sanlawrenz.com. 106 suites. Restaurant, 2 pools. AE, DC, MC, V.*

Comino

The 3-square-km (1-square-mi) island is populated by a handful of people year-round. Day-trippers walk the dirt paths and swim in the beautiful but overcrowded Blue Lagoon.

$$$$ **Comino Hotel.** Functionally modern, the Comino is the only hotel on the island. In spite of its private beach, abundant water sports, and a spirited new manager, the hotel needs to update rooms, public spaces, and furnishings. Day use of facilities is also available. ✉ *Comino,* ☎ *529821,* FAX *529826,* WEB *www.cominohotels.com. 95 rooms, 2 suites, 45 bungalows. Restaurant, 2 pools. AE, DC, MC, V. Closed mid-Nov.–late Mar..*

Gozo and Comino Essentials

BOAT AND FERRY TRAVEL

Hourly ferries leave from Ċirkewwa on Malta for Mġarr Harbour on Gozo. Passenger fares are Lm 1.75; car fares are Lm 5.75. Less frequent ferries go to Comino from Ċirkewwa and from Mġarr Harbor for Lm 2.

BUS TRAVEL

A bus service connects Victoria with the major towns in Gozo. A bus from the harbor to Victoria runs according to the ferry schedule.

➤ BUS INFORMATION: **Bus service** (☎ 562040).

CAR RENTAL

Ask about four-wheel-drive vehicles if you want to venture to Gozo's more remote sites—some of the island's roads are extremely bumpy and rutted.

➤ CONTACTS: **Mġarr Rent a Car** (✉ Mġarr Harbor, ☎ 556081 or 556098). **Mario's Taxi and Rent a Car** (✉ Victoria, ☎ 557242, FAX 551827).

EMERGENCIES

➤ EMERGENCY SERVICES: **Ambulance** (☎ 196). **Fire** (☎ 199). **Hospital** (☎ 561600). **Police** (☎ 191).

TOURS

Xlendi Pleasure Cruises' 40-ft *Gozo Princess* circles Gozo and Comino, stopping at scenic spots. The Lm 10.50 fare includes buffet meals, and you can swim from the boat.

➤ FEES AND SCHEDULES: **Xlendi Pleasure Cruises** (✉ Xlendi, ☎ 559967, FAX 555667).

VISITOR INFORMATION

➤ TOURIST INFORMATION: **Mġarr Harbour** (✉ ☎ 553343). **Victoria** (✉ Palm St., ☎ 561419).

21 THE NETHERLANDS

AMSTERDAM; HISTORIC HOLLAND; THE HAGUE, DELFT, AND ROTTERDAM

THE BUCOLIC IMAGES of windmills and wooden shoes that brought tourism here in the decades after World War II have little to do with the Netherlands today. Sure, tulips grow in abundance in the bulb district of Noord- and Zuid-Holland provinces, but today's Netherlands is no backwater operation: this tiny nation has an economic strength and cultural wealth that far surpass its size and population.

Sophisticated, modern Netherlands has more art treasures per square mile than just about any other country on earth, as well as a large number of ingenious, energetic citizens with a remarkable commitment to quality, style, and innovation. The 33,393 square km (16,033 square mi) of the Netherlands are just about half the area of the state of Maine or half the area of Scotland, and its population of nearly 16 million is slightly smaller than that of the state of Texas or twice the population of London. Formerly home to the most successful seafaring merchants, the country is still one of the world's most important distribution and transport hubs, and its banks have invested this wealth around the world. The country encourages internal accomplishments as well, particularly of a cultural nature. In the country, within a 120-km (75-mi) radius, are 10 major art museums and several smaller ones that together contain the world's richest and most comprehensive collection of Western art masterpieces from the 15th to 20th centuries. In the same small area are a half-dozen performance halls offering music, dance, and internationally known performing arts festivals.

The marriage of economic power and cultural wealth is nothing new to the Dutch; during the 17th century, for example, money raised through their colonial outposts overseas was used to buy or commission portraits and paintings by young artists such as Rembrandt, Hals, Vermeer, and Van Ruysdael. But it was not only the arts that were encouraged: the Netherlands was home to the philosophers Descartes, Spinoza, and Comenius; the jurist Grotius; the naturalist Van Leeuwenhoek, inventor of the microscope; and others like them who flourished in the country's enlightened tolerance. The Netherlands continues to subsidize its artists and performers, supporting an educational system in which creativity in every field is respected and nourished.

The Netherlands is the delta of Europe, located where the great Rhine and Maas rivers and their tributaries empty into the North Sea. Near the coast, it is a land of flat fields and interconnecting canals; in the center it is surprisingly wooded, and in the far south are rolling hills. About half of the Netherlands is below sea level.

Amsterdam is the focal point of the country's culture, as well as of a 60-km (37½-mi) circle of cities, known as the Randstad (agglomera-

The Netherlands (Nederland)

tion of cities), that includes the Hague (the Dutch seat of government and the world center of international justice), Rotterdam (the industrial center of the Netherlands and the world's largest port), and the historic cites of Haarlem, Leiden, Delft, and Utrecht.

The northern and eastern provinces are rural and quiet; the southern provinces that hug the Belgian border are lightly industrialized and sophisticated. The great rivers that cut through the heart of the country provide both geographical and sociological borders. The area "above the great rivers," as the Dutch phrase it, is peopled by tough-minded and practical Calvinists; to the south are more ebullient Catholics. A tradition of tolerance pervades this densely populated land; aware that they cannot survive alone, the Dutch are bound by common traits of ingenuity, personal honesty, and a bold sense of humor.

THE NETHERLANDS A TO Z

To research prices, get advice from other travelers, and book travel arrangements, visit www.fodors.com.

AIR TRAVEL

KLM Royal Dutch Airlines, under the banner of CityHopper, operates several domestic services connecting major cities. In this small country, however, you'd probably travel just as fast by car or train.

BIKE TRAVEL

The Netherlands is a cyclist-friendly country with specially designated cycle paths, signs, and picnic areas. Bikes can be rented at train stations in most cities and towns, and Dutch trains are cycle-friendly, too, with entryways designed to accommodate bicycles. You will need an extra ticket for the bike, however. There are some restrictions on carrying bicycles on trains, so check first. Advice on rentals and routes is available from offices of the Netherlands Board of Tourism in North America or in the Netherlands, or from local tourist offices.

BUS TRAVEL

The Netherlands has an excellent bus network between and within towns. Bus excursions can be booked on the spot and at local tourist offices. In major cities, the best buy is a *strippenkaart* ticket (Fl. 12.50/€6), which can be used for all bus, tram, and metro services. Each card has 15 strips, which are canceled either by the driver as you enter the bus or by the stamping machine at each door of the tram. More than one person can travel on a strippenkaart. You can buy it at train stations, post offices, some tourist offices, in Amsterdam at the public transport (GVB) ticket office in the plaza in front of the central railway station, and at many newsagents. A *dagkaart,* a travel-anywhere ticket (Fl. 11/€5, one day; Fl. 17.50/€8, two days; Fl. 22.50/€10, three days), covers all urban bus and streetcar routes. The Amsterdam Transport Pass gives you unlimited use of all forms of public transport, including the canal bus, for a day (Fl. 31.50/€14). National public transport information is available from the number listed below, at a cost of 75¢ per minute.

➤ BUS INFORMATION: **National public transport information** (☎ 0900/9292).

BUSINESS HOURS

BANKS AND OFFICES

Banks are open weekdays 9–5. Some banks are closed Monday mornings. GWK Border Exchange Offices at major railway stations are generally open Monday–Saturday 8–8, Sunday 10–4. GWK offices at border checkpoints and Schiphol Airport are open 24 hours.

MUSEUMS AND SIGHTS

Museums in Amsterdam are open daily. Elsewhere they close on Monday, but there are exceptions, so check with local tourist offices. In rural areas, some museums close or operate shorter hours in winter. Usual hours are 10–5.

SHOPS

Shops are open weekdays and Saturday 8:30 or 9–5:30 or 6, but outside the cities some close for lunch. Department stores and most shops do not open on Monday until 1 PM. In major cities there is usually late-night shopping until 9 PM on Thursday or Friday. Sunday opening, from noon to 5, varies from city to city.

CAR TRAVEL

EMERGENCIES

Experienced, uniformed mechanics of the *Wegenwacht* patrol the highways in yellow cars 24 hours a day. Operated by the Royal Dutch Touring Club (ANWB), they will help if you have car trouble. On major roads, ANWB also maintains phone boxes from which you can call for assistance. Otherwise call the number listed below. To use these services, you may be asked to take temporary membership in ANWB.

➤ CONTACTS: **ANWB** (☎ 0800/0888).

GASOLINE

Gas (*benzine* in Dutch) costs around Fl. 2.50/€1 per liter for regular, Fl. 2.60/€1.25 for super unleaded, and Fl. 1.75/€.75 for diesel.

PARKING

Parking in the larger towns is difficult and expensive, with illegally parked cars quickly towed away or subject to a wheel clamp. Fines for recovery or release from a clamp can top Fl. 300/€136. Consider parking on the outskirts and using the efficient public transportation. Watch for blue P&R (Park and Ride) signs on ring roads and approach roads to major towns.

ROAD CONDITIONS

The Netherlands has one of the best road systems in Europe. Multi-lane expressways (toll-free) link major cities, but the smaller roads and country lanes provide more picturesque routes. In towns, many streets are narrow, and you'll have to contend with complex one-way systems and cycle lanes. Be particularly vigilant for cyclists; they're ubiquitous, and they assume you'll give them the right of way. Information about weather and road conditions—in Dutch—can be obtained by calling the number below (75¢ per minute).

➤ CONTACTS: **Weather and road condition information** (☎ 0900/9622).

RULES OF THE ROAD

In the Netherlands your own driver's license is acceptable. Driving is on the right. The speed limit on expressways is 100 kph (62 mph) or 120 kph (75 mph); on city streets and in residential areas it is 50 kph (30 mph) or less, according to the signs. Note that slow traffic from the right has priority in urban areas and local roads. On traffic circles, drivers in the circle have priority. Front-seat riders are required to wear a seat belt, all other passengers are required to use available seat belts, and it is advisable to have children ride in the back seat. Drinking and driving is never advisable.

CUSTOMS AND DUTIES

For details on imports and duty-free limits, *see* Customs and Duties *in* Chapter 1.

DINING

The Dutch enjoy a wide variety of cuisines from traditional Dutch to Indonesian—the influence of the former Dutch colony. Breakfast includes several varieties of bread, butter, jam, ham, cheese, chocolate, boiled eggs, juice, and steaming coffee or tea. Lunch tends to be a *broodje* (sandwich) from the great selection of delicatessens. Dutch specialties for meals later in the day include *erwtensoep* (rich, thick pea soup with pieces of tangy sausage or pigs' knuckles) and *stamppot* (mashed potatoes and greens with *worst* [sausage]); both are usually served only in winter. *Haring* (herring) is particularly popular, especially the "new herring" caught between May and September and served raw, with a garnish of onions and pickles. At Indonesian restaurants, the chief item is *rijsttafel* (rice table), a meal made up of rice and 20 or more small meat, seafood, or vegetable dishes, many of which are hot and spicy. Eating places range from snack bars, fast-food outlets, and modest local cafés to haute cuisine restaurants of international repute. Of special note are the *bruin cafés* (brown cafés), characterful, traditional pubs that normally serve snack-type meals. They are so named because of the rich wooden furnishings and—some say—the centuries-old pipe-tobacco stains on the ceilings. The indigenous Dutch liquor is potent and warming *jenever* (gin), both "old" (matured) and "young."

Prices are for one main course at dinner.

CATEGORY	AMSTERDAM/MAIN CITIES	OTHER AREAS
$$$$	over Fl. 100 (€45)	over Fl. 85 (€39)
$$$	Fl. 70–Fl. 100 (€32–€45)	Fl. 55–Fl. 85 (€25–€39)
$$	Fl. 40–Fl. 70 (€18–€32)	Fl. 35–Fl. 55 (€16–€25)
$	under Fl. 40 (€18)	under Fl. 35 (€16)

MEALTIMES

Lunchtime is between 12:30 and 1. The Dutch eat dinner at around 6 or 7 PM, especially in the country and smaller cities, so many restaurants accept final orders at 9 PM and close at about 10. In larger cities dining hours vary, and some restaurants stay open until midnight.

RESERVATIONS AND DRESS

Jacket and tie are advised for restaurants in the $$$$ and $$$ categories. The tolerant Dutch accept casual outfits in most eateries.

EMBASSIES

All embassies are located in the Hague.

- ➤ AUSTRALIA: (✉ Carnegielaan 4, ☎ 070/3108200).
- ➤ CANADA: (✉ Sophialaan 7, ☎ 070/3123456).
- ➤ IRELAND: (✉ Dr. Kuyperstraat 9, ☎ 070/3630993).
- ➤ NEW ZEALAND: (✉ Carnegielaan 10, ☎ 070/3469324).
- ➤ SOUTH AFRICA: (✉ Wassenaarseweg 40, ☎ 070/3924501).
- ➤ UNITED KINGDOM: (✉ Lange Voorhout 10, ☎ 070/4270427).
- ➤ UNITED STATES: (✉ Lange Voorhout 102, ☎ 070/3109209).

HOLIDAYS

January 1 (New Year's Day); Easter; April 30 (Queen's Day); May 9 (Ascension); May 19–20 (Pentecost/Whitsunday and Whitmonday); December 25–26 Christmas.

LANGUAGE

Dutch is a difficult language for foreigners, but the Dutch are fine linguists, so almost everyone speaks at least some English, especially in larger cities and tourist centers.

LODGING

The Netherlands has a wide range of accommodations, from the luxurious, Dutch-owned international Golden Tulip hotel chain to traditional, small-town hotels and family-run guest houses. For adventurous travelers, the provinces abound with modest hostels, campgrounds, and rural bungalows.

Prices are for two persons sharing a double room.

CATEGORY	AMSTERDAM/MAIN CITIES	OTHER AREAS
$$$$	over Fl. 500 (€227)	over Fl. 350 (€159)
$$$	Fl. 300–Fl. 500 (€136–€227)	Fl. 200–Fl. 350 (€91–€159)
$$	Fl. 200–Fl. 300 (€91–€136)	Fl. 150–Fl. 200 (€68–€91)
$	under Fl. 200 (€91)	under Fl. 150 (€68)

B&BS

VVV provides lists of B&B and "pension" accommodations, which can be much cheaper than hotel accommodations, while introducing you to Dutch domestic life in the flesh. Bed & Breakfast Holland also provides B&B addresses in cities and rural areas around the country.

➤ RESERVATION SERVICES: **Bed & Breakfast Holland** (✉ Theophile de Bockstraat 3, 1058 TV, Amsterdam, ☎ 020/6157527, FAX 020/6691573).

HOTELS

Dutch hotels are generally clean, if not spotless, no matter how modest their facilities, and service is courteous and efficient. There are many moderate and inexpensive hotels, most of which are relatively small. In the provinces, the range of accommodations is more limited, but there are friendly, inexpensive family-run hotels that are usually centrally located. Some have good—if modest—dining facilities. Hotels generally quote room prices for double occupancy, and rates often include breakfast, service charges, and VAT. The prime tourist season in the Netherlands runs from April through October and peaks during school vacation periods (Easter, July, and August), when hotels may impose a 20% surcharge.

To book hotels in advance, you can use the free Netherlands Reservation Center. For a small fee, tourist offices can usually make reservations at short notice. Bookings must be made in person, however.

➤ CONTACTS: **Netherlands Reservation Center** (☎ 070/4195500, WEB www.hotelres.nl).

MAIL AND SHIPPING

If you're uncertain where you'll be staying, have mail sent to "poste restante, Hoofd Postkantoor" in major cities along your route (making sure that your name and initials are clear and correctly spelled), or to American Express offices, where a small fee is charged on collection to non–American Express customers.

POSTAL RATES

Airmail letters to the United States cost Fl. 1.60/€.75 for the first 20 grams; postcards cost Fl. 1.10/€.50; aerograms cost Fl. 1.30/€.60. Airmail letters to the United Kingdom cost Fl. 1.10/€.50 for the first 20 grams; postcards cost Fl. 1.10/€.50; aerograms cost Fl. 1.30/€.60.

MONEY MATTERS

The Netherlands is prosperous, with a high standard of living, so overall costs are similar to those in other northern European countries. Prices for hotels and services in major cities are 10%–20% higher than those in rural areas. Amsterdam and the Hague are the most expensive. Hotel and restaurant service charges and the 6% value-added tax (VAT) are usually included in the prices quoted. Some sample prices include: half bottle of wine, Fl. 25/€11; glass of beer, Fl. 3.50/€1.50; cup of coffee, Fl. 4/€2; ham and cheese sandwich, Fl. 5/€2.25; 2-km (1-mi) taxi ride, Fl. 14/€6.

CURRENCY

The unit of currency in the Netherlands is the guilder, written as NLG (for Netherlands guilder), Fl., or simply F. (from the centuries-old term for the coinage, florin). Each guilder is divided into 100 cents. Bills are in denominations of 10, 25, 50, 100, 250, and 1,000 guilders. Denominations over Fl. 100 are rarely seen, and many shops refuse to change them. Coins are 1, 2.5, and 5 guilders and 5, 10, and 25 cents. Don't confuse the 1- and 2.5-guilder coins and the 5-guilder and 5-cent coins. The Netherlands is one of 12 nations adopting the euro, the European Union currency. Coins and bills will be issued in January 2002, and in a few months guilders will cease to exist.

At press time (summer 2001), the exchange rate for the guilder was Fl. 2.30 to the U.S. dollar, Fl. 1.60 to the Canadian dollar, Fl. 3.60 to the pound sterling, Fl. 2.80 to the Irish punt, Fl. 1.30 to the Australian dollar, Fl. 1.10 to the New Zealand dollar, and Fl. 0.30 to the South African rand. The euro is equivalent to Fl. 2.20, a fixed rate.

TAXES

VALUE-ADDED TAX (VAT)

Purchases of goods in one store on one day amounting to Fl. 300/€136 or more qualify for a value-added tax, called BTW, refund of 19%, less a service charge. After the refund check has been validated by customs at the airport, you can submit it when you leave the Netherlands or exit the European Union, or by mail, and the refund will be credited to your credit card within 30 days. This arrangement is only valid if you export the goods within 30 days and submit the refund check within three months. Ask the salesperson for a VAT refund form.

TELEPHONES

COUNTRY AND AREA CODES

The country code for the Netherlands is 31. When dialing a number in the Netherlands from outside the country, drop the initial 0 from the local area code.

INTERNATIONAL CALLS

Direct-dial international calls can be made from any phone booth. To reach an AT&T, MCI (called WorldPhone in the Netherlands), or Sprint operator, dial one of the access codes below.

➤ ACCESS CODES: **AT&T** (☎ 0800/022–9111). **MCI** (☎ 0800/022–9122). **Sprint** (☎ 0800/022–9119).

LOCAL CALLS

All towns and cities have area codes that are used only when you are calling from outside the area. All public phone booths require phone cards, which may be purchased from post offices, railway stations, and newsagents for Fl. 10/€4.50, Fl. 25/€11, or Fl. 50/€23. Pay phones in bars and restaurants take 25¢ or Fl. 1 coins, but rates are often hiked. Dial 0800/0101 for an English-speaking operator.

TIPPING

Hotels and restaurants almost always include 10%–15% service and 6% VAT in their charges. Give a doorman Fl. 3 for calling a cab. Bellhops in first-class hotels should be tipped Fl. 2/€.90 for each bag they carry. Hat-check attendants expect at least Fl. 1/€.50, and washroom attendants get 50¢/€.25. Taxis in almost every town have a tip included in the meter charge, but round the fare to the next guilder nevertheless.

TRAIN TRAVEL

Fast, frequent, comfortable trains operate throughout the country. All trains have first- and second-class cars, and many intercity trains have buffet or dining-car services. Sometimes one train contains two separate sections that divide during the trip, so be sure you are in the correct car for your destination.

At major railway stations, look for blue columns marked REISWIJZER ("Route Finder"). For Fl. 1.25, paid with a telephone card, you can get a printout in English with door-to-door travel information that includes stops and connections on trains, buses, and trams. A booklet, "Exploring Holland by Train," is available at train stations.

CUTTING COSTS

To get the best value out of rail travel, purchase a pass. The Benelux Tourrail can be bought abroad, but the other passes are available only in the Netherlands. A Holland Rail Pass ticket allows unlimited travel throughout the Netherlands for 3 or 5 days within any 30-day period. Other options are a Dagkaart (one-day, travel-anywhere train ticket) or an OV-Dagkaart (one-day, travel-anywhere ticket for the train, bus, tram, and metro). From July through August, you can purchase a Zomertoer (summer tour) ticket for three days' travel within a 10-day period. You need your passport when you purchase these tickets. Ask about these fares at railway information bureaus or local tourist offices. An informative booklet, "Exploring Holland by Train," is available at train stations.

VISITOR INFORMATION

The VVV (acronym for the Vereniging voor Vreemdelingenverkeer, or national tourist offices) has branches in smaller towns; the information line below costs Fl. 1.05/€.50 per minute.

The *Museumjaarkaart,* which can be purchased from most museums and all VVV tourist offices, provides a year's free or discounted admission to almost 450 museums throughout the country. It costs Fl. 70/€32, Fl. 30/€14 if you're under 25. A photo and passport are required for purchase. Nearly all museums participate.

➤ TOURIST INFORMATION: **Netherlands Board of Tourism** (✉ Box 458, 2260 MG Leidschendam, Holland, ☎ 070/3705705, FAX 070/3201654). **VVV** (☎ 0900/4004040 telephone inquiries).

WHEN TO GO

Dutch bulb fields bloom from late March to the end of May. June is the ideal time to catch the warm weather and miss the crowds, but every region of the Netherlands has its season. Delft is luminous after a winter storm, and fall in the Utrecht countryside can be as dramatic as it is in New England.

CLIMATE

Summers are generally warm, but beware of sudden showers and blustery coastal winds. Winters are chilly and wet but are not without clear days. If the canals freeze over, then they immediately fill with keen skaters, the learners pushing along chairs. After a cloudburst, notice the watery quality of light that inspired Vermeer and other great Dutch painters. The following are the average daily maximum and minimum temperatures for Amsterdam.

Jan.	40F	4C	**May**	61F	16C	**Sept.**	65F	18C
	34	1		50	10		56	13
Feb.	41F	5C	**June**	65F	18C	**Oct.**	56F	13C
	34	1		56	13		49	9
Mar.	47F	8C	**July**	70F	21C	**Nov.**	47F	8C
	38	3		59	15		41	5
Apr.	52F	11C	**Aug.**	68F	20C	**Dec.**	41F	5C
	43	6		59	15		36	2

AMSTERDAM

Amsterdam is a gem of a city for the visitor. Small and densely packed with fine buildings, many dating from the 17th century or earlier, it is easily explored on foot or by bike.

Exploring Amsterdam

The old heart of the city consists of canals, with narrow streets radiating out like the spokes of a wheel. The hub of this wheel and the most convenient point to begin sightseeing is Centraal Station (Central Station). Across the street, in the same building as the Old Dutch Coffee House, is a tourist information office. The Rokin, once an open canal, is the main route from Central Station via the Dam to the Muntplein. Amsterdam's key points of interest can be covered within two or three days, including visits to one or two of the important museums and galleries. The city center is divided into districts that are easily covered on foot.

Around the Dam

Numbers in the margin correspond to points of interest on the Amsterdam map.

★ 14 **Anne Frankhuis** (Anne Frank House). Immortalized by the poignant diary kept by the young Jewish girl from 1942 to 1944, when she and her family hid here from the German occupying forces, this canal-side house also has an educational exhibition and documents about the Holocaust and civil liberty. ✉ *Prinsengracht 263,* ☎ *020/5567100,* WEB *www.annefrank.nl.* ⏲ *Apr.–Aug., daily 9–9 (except for May 4, 9–7); Sept.–Mar., daily 9–7 (except Christmas Day and New Year's Day, noon–7). Closed Yom Kippur.*

10 **Beurs van Berlage** (Berlage's Stock Exchange). This impressive building, completed in 1903, was designed by Hendrik Petrus Berlage (1856–1934), whose principles were to guide modernism. The sculpture and rich decoration of the plain brick interior are among modernism's embryonic masterpieces. It now houses two concert halls, a large exhibition space, and its own museum, which also offers the chance to climb the 138-ft-high tower for its superb views. ✉ *Beursplein 1,* ☎ *020/5304141.* ⏲ *Museum Tues.–Sun. 10–5.*

1 **Centraal Station** (Central Station). The flamboyant redbrick and stone portal was designed by P. J. H. Cuijpers (1827–1921) and built in 1884–89. Compare it with Cuijpers's other significant contribution to Amsterdam's architectural heritage—the Rijksmuseum. ✉ *Stationsplein.*

11 **Dam** (Dam Square). This is the broadest square in the old section of the town. Fishermen used to come here to sell their catch. Today it is a busy crossroads, circled with shops and bisected by traffic; it is also a popular spot for outdoor performers. At one side of the square stands a simple monument to Dutch victims of World War II. Eleven urns contain soil from the 11 provinces of the Netherlands, while a

12th contains soil from the former Dutch East Indies, now Indonesia. ✉ *Junction of Rokin, Damrak, Moses en Aaronstraat, and Paleisstraat.*

6 **De Waag** (The Weighhouse). Dating from 1488, when it was built as a city gate, this turreted, redbrick monument dominates the Nieuwmarkt (New Market) in the oldest part of Amsterdam. It became a weighhouse and was once the headquarters for ancient professional guilds. The magnificently restored **Theatrum Anatomicum,** up the winding stairs, was added in 1691 and set the scene for Rembrandt's painting the *Anatomy Lesson of Dr. Tulp*. The upper floors are now home to the media lab of the Society for Old and New Media, which hosts occasional conferences and exhibitions. Downstairs is a grand café and restaurant. ✉ *Nieuwmarkt 4,* ☎ *020/5579898,* WEB *www.waag.org.*

13 **Het Koninklijk Paleis te Amsterdam** (Royal Palace in Amsterdam). The vast, well-proportioned classical structure dominating the Dam was completed in 1655. It is built on 13,659 pilings sunk into the marshy soil. The great pediment sculptures are an allegorical representation of Amsterdam surrounded by Neptune and mythological sea creatures. Filled with opulent 18th- and early 19th-century furnishings, it is the official royal residence but is used only on high state occasions. ✉ *Dam,* ☎ *020/6248698.* ⏲ *Tues.–Thurs. 1–4; daily 12:30–5 in summer. Occasionally closed for state events.*

9 **Museum Amstelkring.** The facade carries the inscription "*Ons Lieve Heer Op Solder*" ("Our Lord in the Attic"). In 1578 Amsterdam embraced Protestantism and outlawed the church of Rome. The municipal authorities were so tolerant that secret Catholic chapels were allowed to exist; at one time there were 62 in Amsterdam alone. One such chapel was established in the attics of these three neighboring canalside houses, built around 1661, and services were held in the attics regularly until 1888, the year the St. Nicolaaskerk was consecrated for Catholic worship. Of interest are the Baroque altar with its revolving tabernacle, the swinging pulpit that can be stowed out of sight, and the upstairs gallery with its displays of religious artifacts. ✉ *Oudezijds Voorburgwal 40,* ☎ *020/6246604.* ⏲ *Mon.–Sat. 10–5, Sun. 1–5.*

5 **Nederlands Scheepvaartmuseum** (Netherlands Maritime Museum). This former naval warehouse maintains a collection of restored vessels and a replica of a three-masted trading ship from 1749. The museum explains the history of Dutch shipping, from dugout canoes right through to modern container ships, with maps, paintings, and models. ✉ *Kattenburgerplein 1,* ☎ *020/5232222.* ⏲ *Tues.–Sun. 10–5, only open Mon. on school holidays.*

3 **NEMO Science & Technology Center.** This interactive museum, formerly called newMetropolis, was designed by Renzo Piano, architect of the Centre Pompidou in Paris. Hands-on exhibits range from elementary physics to the latest technological gadgets. The rooftop terrace offers a panoramic view across the city. ✉ *Oosterdok 2, Prins Hendrikkade,* ☎ *0900/9191100 costs 75¢ per min,* WEB *www.e-NEMO.nl.* ⏲ *Tues.–Sun. 10–5.*

12 **Nieuwe Kerk** (New Church). This huge Gothic structure was gradually expanded until 1540, when it reached its present size. Gutted by fire in 1645, it was reconstructed in an imposing Renaissance style, as interpreted by strict Calvinists. The superb oak pulpit, the 14th-century nave, the stained-glass windows, and the great organ (1645) are all shown to great effect on national holidays, when the church is bedecked with flowers. As befits the Netherlands' national church, it is the site of all coronations, most recently that of Queen Beatrix in 1980. In democratic Dutch spirit, the church is also used as a meeting

Amsterdam Historisch Museum 16
Anne Frankhuis 14
Beurs van Berlage 10
Begijnhof 17
Bloemenmarkt 21
Centraal Station 1
Concertgebouw 32
Dam 11
De Waag 6
Engelse Kerk 17
Gouden Bocht 19
Het Koninklijk Paleis te Amsterdam 13
Jodenbreestraat 23
Joods Historisch Museum 27
Jordaan 35
Leidseplein 34
Muiderstraat 25
Munttoren 20
Museum Amstelkring 9
Museum het Rembrandthuis 24
Museum Willet-Holthuysen . . .22
Muziektheater/ Stadhuis 28
Nederlands Scheepvaartmuseum . .5
NEMO Science & Technology Center . . .3
Nieuwe Kerk 12
Oude Kerk 8
Portugese Israelitische Synagoge 26
Rijksmuseum 29
Rosse Buurt 7
Scheepvaartshuis 4
Schreierstoren 2
Spui 18
Stedelijk Museum . . .31
Van Gogh Museum 30
Vondelpark 33
Westerkerk 15

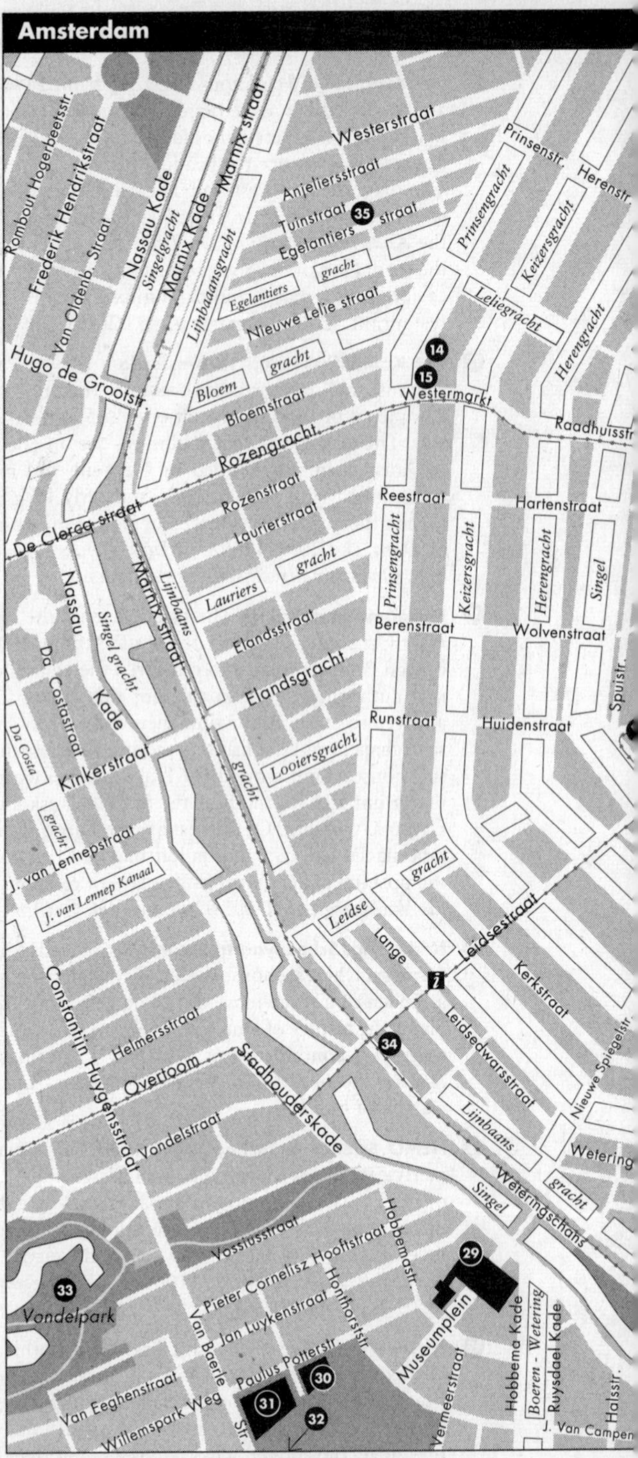

Amsterdam

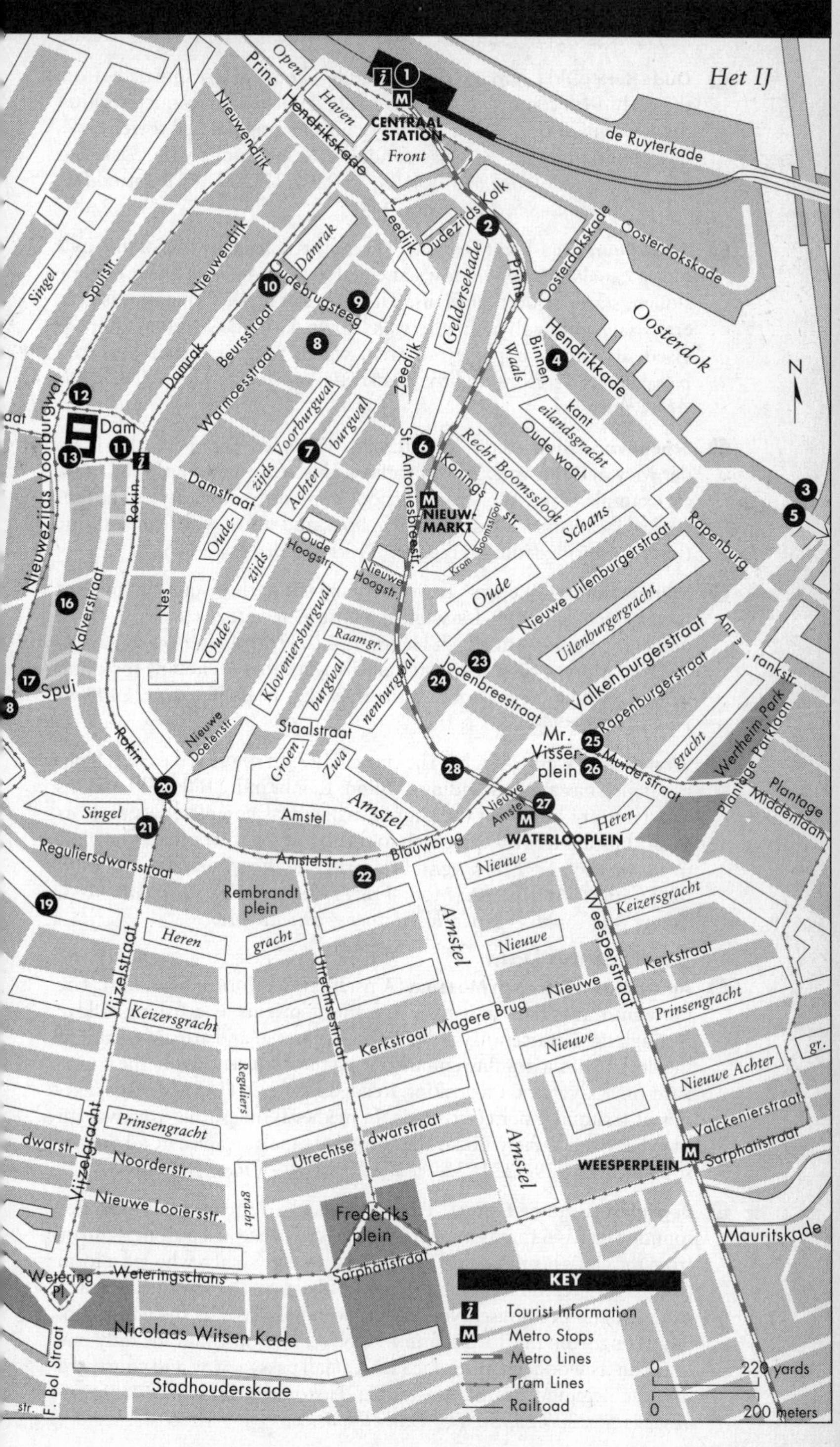

Het IJ
Open Haven
Prins Hendrikskade
CENTRAAL STATION
Front
de Ruyterkade
Nieuwendijk
Singel
Spuistr.
Damrak
Zeedijk
Oudezijds Kolk
Geldersekade
Oosterdokskade
Oosterdok
Prins Hendrikkade
Binnen Waals
eilandsgracht
kant
Oude waal
Oudebrugsteeg
Beursstraat
Warmoesstraat
Oudezijds Voorburgwal
Oudezijds Achterburgwal
Dam
Nieuwezijds Voorburgwal
Rokin
Damstraat
St. Antoniesbreestr.
NIEUWMARKT
Recht Boomssloot
Konings str.
Krom Boomssloot
Schans
Oude
Nieuwe Uilenburgerstraat
Uilenburgergracht
Rapenburg
Oude Hoogstr.
Nieuwe Hoogstr.
Kloveniersburgwal
Raamgr.
Groenburgwal
Zwanenburgwal
Nes
Kalverstraat
Spui
Jodenbreestraat
Valkenburgerstraat
Rapenburgerstraat
Mr. Visserplein
Muiderstraat
Wertheim Park
Plantage Parklaan
Plantage Middenlaan
Nieuwe Doelenstr.
Staalstraat
Amstel
Singel
Reguliersdwarsstraat
Amstelstr.
Blauwbrug
Nieuwe Amstel
WATERLOOPLEIN
Herengracht
Nieuwe Herengracht
Rembrandt plein
Keizersgracht
Nieuwe Keizersgracht
Weesperstraat
Kerkstraat
Nieuwe Kerkstraat
Magere Brug
Utrechtsestraat
Vijzelstraat
Reguliersgracht
Prinsengracht
Nieuwe Prinsengracht
Nieuwe Achtergracht
Valckenierstraat
Utrechtse dwarsstraat
dwarstr.
Noorderstr.
Nieuwe Looiersstr.
Vijzelgracht
WEESPERPLEIN
Sarphatistraat
Frederiksplein
Mauritskade
Wetering Pl.
Weteringschans
Nicolaas Witsen Kade
Stadhouderskade
F. Bol Straat
KEY
Tourist Information
Metro Stops
Metro Lines
Tram Lines
Railroad
0 220 yards
0 200 meters

place, has a lively café, and hosts temporary exhibitions and concerts. ✉ *Dam,* ☎ *020/6386909.* ⏲ *Daily 10–6; Thurs. until 10.*

8 **Oude Kerk** (Old Church). The city's oldest house of worship dates from the early 14th century, but it was badly damaged by iconoclasts after the Reformation. The church still retains its original bell tower and a few remarkable stained-glass windows. Rembrandt's wife, Saskia, is buried here. ✉ *Oudekerksplein 23,* ☎ *020/6258284,* WEB *www.oudekerk.nl.* ⏲ *Mon.–Sat. 11–5, Sun. 1–5.*

7 **Rosse Buurt** (Red-Light District). This area is defined by two of the city's oldest canals. In the windows at canal level, women in sheer lingerie slouch, stare, or do their nails. The area can be shocking, but is generally safe, although midnight walks down dark side streets are not advised. If you do explore the area, watch for purse snatchers and pickpockets. ✉ *Bordered by Oudezijds Voorburgwal and Oudezijds Achterburgwal.*

4 **Scheepvaartshuis** (Shipping Offices). Designed (1911–16) by J. M. der Mey and the Van Gendt brothers, this office building is the earliest example of the Amsterdam School's unique building style. The fantastical facade is richly decorated in brick and stone, with lead and zinc roofing pouring from on high. ✉ *Prins Hendrikkade 108–119.*

2 **Schreierstoren** (Weepers' Tower). Facing the harbor stands a lookout tower, erected in 1480, for women whose men were out at sea. A tablet marks the point from which Henrik (a.k.a. Henry) Hudson set sail on the *Half Moon* on April 4, 1609, on a voyage that eventually took him to what is now New York and the river that bears his name. ✉ *Prins Hendrikkade 94–95.*

15 **Westerkerk** (West Church). The church's 279-ft tower is the city's highest; it also has an outstanding carillon. Rembrandt (1606–69) and his son Titus are buried in the church, which was completed as early as 1631. In summer you can climb to the top of the tower for a fine view over the city. ✉ *Prinsengracht (corner of Westermarkt),* ☎ *020/6247766.* ⏲ *April–Sept., Mon.–Fri. 11–3; July–Aug., also Sat. 11–3. Tower June–Sept., 11–3. Closed during private services.*

South of the Dam

16 **Amsterdam Historisch Museum** (Amsterdam Historical Museum). The museum traces the city's history from its origins as a fishing village through the 17th-century golden age of material and artistic wealth to the decline of the trading empire during the 18th century. In the courtyard off Kalverstraat a striking Renaissance gate (1581) guards a series of tranquil inner courtyards. In medieval times, this area was an island devoted to piety. Today the bordering canals are filled in. ✉ *Kalverstraat 92,* ☎ *020/5231822.* ⏲ *Weekdays 10–5, weekends 11–5.*

★ 17 **Begijnhof** (Beguine Court). This is an enclosed square of almshouses founded in 1346 that is a surprising oasis of peace just a stone's throw from the city's hectic center. The Beguines were women who led a form of convent life, often taking the vow of chastity. The last Beguine died in 1974, and her house, No. 26, has been preserved as she left it. No. 34, dating from the 15th century, is the oldest house and the only one to retain its wooden Gothic facade. A small passageway and courtyard link the Begijnhof to the Amsterdam Historisch Museum. ✉ *Begijnhof 29,* ☎ *020/6233565.* ⏲ *Daily 9–dusk.*

21 **Bloemenmarkt** (Flower Market). Here floating stalls carry a bright array of freshly cut flowers and foliage, as well as an enviable variety of bulbs and plants. ✉ *Along Singel Canal, from Muntplein to Koningsplein.* ⏲ *Mon.–Sat. (occasionally Sun.) 8:30–6.*

17 **Engelse Kerk** (English Church). This church was given to Amsterdam's English and Scottish Presbyterians early in the 17th century. On the church wall and in the chancel are tributes to the Pilgrim Fathers, who sailed from Delftshaven (in Rotterdam) to the New World in 1620. Opposite the church is another of the city's secret Catholic chapels, whose exterior looks as though it were two adjoining houses, built in 1671. ✉ *Begijnhof.*

★ 19 **Gouden Bocht** (Golden Bend). The Herengracht (Gentlemen's Canal) is the city's most prestigious canal. The stretch of the canal from Leidsestraat to Vijzelstraat is named for the sumptuous patrician houses that line it. Seventeenth-century merchants moved here from the Amstel River to escape the byproducts of their wealth: noisy warehouses, unpleasant brewery smells, and the risk of fire in the sugar refineries. The houses display the full range of Amsterdam architectural detailing, from gables in a variety of shapes to elaborate Louis XIV–style cornices and frescoed ceilings. They are best seen from the east side of the canal. ✉ *Herengracht, Leidsestraat to Vijzelstraat.*

20 **Munttoren** (Mint Tower). Built in 1620 at this busy crossroads, the graceful tower that was later added to this former royal mint has a clock and bells that still seem to mirror the golden age. There are frequent carillon recitals. ✉ *Muntplein.*

22 **Museum Willet-Holthuysen.** Built in 1690, the elegant residence was bequeathed to the city of Amsterdam on condition that it be retained as a museum. It provides a peek into the lives of the city's well-heeled merchants. ✉ *Herengracht 605,* ☎ *020/5231870.* ⏲ *Weekdays 10–5, weekends 11–5.*

18 **Spui** (Sluice). In the heart of the university area, the lively square was a center for revolutionary student rallies in 1968. Now you'll find bookstores and bars, including cozy brown cafés. ✉ *Junction of Nieuwezijds Voorburgwal, Spuistraat, and Singel Canal.*

Jewish Amsterdam

The original settlers in the Jodenbuurt (old Jewish Amsterdam) were wealthy Sephardic Jews from Spain and Portugal, later followed by poorer Ashkenazic refugees from Germany and Poland. At the beginning of the 20th century this was a thriving community of Jewish diamond polishers, dyers, and merchants.

23 **Jodenbreestraat.** During World War II this street marked the southwestern border of the *Joodse wijk* (Jewish neighborhood), then a Nazi-controlled ghetto surrounded by barbed wire. The character of the area was largely destroyed in the name of progress in the guise of highway construction in 1965 and, more recently, by construction of both the Metro and the Muziektheater/Stadhuis complex. However, you can still find a flavor of times past by wandering around the quaint and peaceful canals and streets between the Rechtboomsloot and the Oude Schans.

27 **Joods Historisch Museum** (Jewish Historical Museum). This complex of four synagogues, the oldest dating from 1671, opened in 1987 as a unique museum. The succession of synagogues was gradually constructed to accommodate Amsterdam's growing community of Jews, many of whom had fled from oppression and prejudice elsewhere. Before the war, there were about 120,000 Jews here, but only 20,000 of them survived the Nazis and the war. Founded by American and Dutch Jews, the museum displays religious treasures in a clear cultural and historical context. Because the synagogues lost most of their treasures in the war, their architecture and history are more compelling than the ex-

hibits. ✉ *Jonas Daniël Meijerplein 2–4,* ☎ *020/6269945,* WEB *www.jhm.nl.* ⏲ *Daily 11–5. Closed Yom Kippur.*

25 **Muiderstraat.** This pedestrian area east of Waterlooplein retains much of the neighborhood's historic atmosphere. Notice the gateways decorated with pelicans, symbolizing great love; according to legend, the pelican will feed her starving young with her own blood. ✉ *Muiderstraat/Waterlooplein.*

★ 24 **Museum het Rembrandthuis** (Rembrandt's House). From 1639 to 1658, Rembrandt lived at Jodenbreestraat 4. For more than 20 years he used the ground floor as living quarters; the sunny upper floor was his studio. The museum has a superb collection of his etchings as well as work by his contemporaries. The modern new wing next door houses a multimedia auditorium, two new exhibition spaces, and a shop. ✉ *Jodenbreestraat 4–6,* ☎ *020/5200400,* WEB *www.rembrandthuis.nl.* ⏲ *Mon.–Sat. 10–5, Sun. 1–5. Closed Jan. 1.*

28 **Muziektheater/Stadhuis** (Music Theater/Town Hall complex). Amsterdammers come to the Town Hall section of the building by day to obtain driver's licenses, pick up welfare payments, and get married. They return by night to the rounded, marble-clad facade overlooking the Amstel River to see opera and ballet performed by the Netherlands' national companies. You can wander into the Town Hall for a look at some interesting sculptures and other displays. A guided tour of the Muziektheater takes you around the dressing rooms, dance studios, backstage, and even to the wig department. ✉ *Amstel 3,* ☎ *020/5518054.* ⏲ *Guided tours Wed. and Sat. at 3.*

★ 26 **Portugese Israelitische Synagoge** (Portuguese Israelite Synagogue). As one of Amsterdam's five neighboring synagogues, this was part of the largest Jewish religious complex in Europe. The beautiful, austere interior of the 17th-century building is still intact, even if the building itself is marooned on a traffic island. ✉ *Mr. Visserplein 3,* ☎ *020/6245351,* WEB *www.esnoga.com.* ⏲ *Apr.–Oct., Sun.–Fri. 10–4; Nov.–Mar., Sun.–Thurs. 10–4, Fri. 10–3. Closed Jewish holidays.*

The Museum Quarter

32 **Concertgebouw** (Concert Hall). The sounds of the country's foremost orchestra resonate in this imposing, classical building. The smaller of the two auditoriums is used for chamber music and solo recitals. The main hall hosts world-class concerts. ✉ *Concertgebouwplein 2–6,* ☎ *020/6718345.*

34 **Leidseplein.** This square is the pulsing heart of the city's nightlife. In summer you can enjoy the entertainment of street performers on the many café terraces. ✉ *Junction of Leidsestraat, Marnixstraat, and Weteringschans.*

★ 29 **Rijksmuseum** (State Museum). The museum, the most important of the Dutch museums, was founded in 1808, but the current, rather lavish building dates from 1885 and was designed by the architect of Central Station, P. J. H. Cuijpers. As well as Italian, Flemish, and Spanish paintings, there are also vast collections of furniture, textiles, ceramics, sculpture, and prints. The museum's fame, however, rests on its unrivaled collection of Dutch 16th- and 17th-century masters. Of Rembrandt's masterpieces, the *Night Watch,* concealed during World War II in a cave in Maastricht, was misnamed because of its dull layers of varnish; in reality it depicts the Civil Guard in daylight. Also worth searching out are Frans Hals's family portraits, Jan Steen's drunken scenes, Van Ruysdael's romantic but menacing landscapes, and Vermeer's glimpses of everyday life bathed in his limpid light. The Zuid

Vleugel (South Wing) houses a freshly displayed treasure trove of Eastern art. ✉ *Stadhouderskade 42,* ☎ *020/6747047,* WEB *www.rijksmuseum.nl.* ⏲ *Daily 10–5.*

31 **Stedelijk Museum** (Museum of Modern Art). The museum has a stimulating collection of modern art and ever-changing displays of the works of contemporary artists. Before viewing the paintings of Cézanne, Chagall, Kandinsky, and Mondrian, check the list of temporary exhibitions in Room 1. ✉ *Paulus Potterstraat 13,* ☎ *020/5732911,* WEB *www.stedelijk.nl.* ⏲ *Daily 11–5.*

★ 30 **Van Gogh Museum.** This museum contains the world's largest collection of the artist's works—200 paintings and nearly 500 drawings—as well as works by some 50 of his contemporaries. The main building was designed by Gerrit Rietvelt (1888–1964) and completed in 1972. It was renovated in 1999, and a new wing, designed by Japanese architect Kisho Kurokawa, was added to exhibit van Gogh's prints and accommodate temporary exhibitions, which focus on art from the late 19th and early 20th centuries. ✉ *Paulus Potterstraat 7,* ☎ *020/5705252,* WEB *www.vangoghmuseum.nl.* ⏲ *Daily 10–5:30.*

33 **Vondelpark.** Amsterdam's central park is an elongated rectangle of paths, lakes, and pleasant, shady greenery. A monument honors the 17th-century epic poet Joost van den Vondel, after whom the park is named. There are special children's areas with paddling pools and sandboxes. From June through August, the park hosts free outdoor concerts and plays Wednesday–Sunday. ✉ *Stadhouderskade.* ☎ *020/523–779,* WEB *www.openluchttheater.nl.*

The Jordaan

35 **Jordaan.** In this old part of Amsterdam the canals and side streets are named for trees, flowers, and plants. When it was the French quarter of the city, the area was known as *le jardin* (the garden), a name that over the years has become Jordaan. The best time to explore the district is on a Sunday morning or in the evening. The Jordaan has attracted many artists and is something of a bohemian quarter, where run-down buildings are being converted into restaurants, antiques shops, boutiques, and galleries. ✉ *Bordered by Prinsengracht, Lijnbaansgracht, Brouwersgracht, and Raadhuisstraat.*

Dining

Health-conscious Amsterdammers prefer set menus and early dinners. For traditionalists the NEDERLANDS DIS soup tureen sign is a promise of regional recipes and seasonal ingredients. For details and price-category definitions, *see* Dining *in* The Netherlands A to Z, *above.*

$$–$$$ ★ ✕ **La Rive.** The French cuisine, with an awe-inspiring "truffle menu" of dishes prepared with exotic (and expensive) ingredients, can be tailored to meet your every whim. Epicureans should inquire about the "chef's table": with a group of six you can sit at a table alongside the open kitchen and watch chefs prepare and describe each of your courses. At this world-class restaurant, you can also enjoy the city's most elegant view of the river Amstel, and, unusual for this country, a no-smoking section. ✉ *Amstel Inter-Continental Hotel, Professor Tulpplein 1,* ☎ *020/6226060. Jacket and tie. AE, DC, MC, V.*

$$–$$$ ✕ **Oesterbar.** The "Oyster Bar" specializes in seafood, grilled, baked, or fried. The upstairs dining room is more formal than the downstairs bistro, but prices don't vary. The sole is prepared in four different ways, or you can try the local specialties such as halibut and eel; oysters are a stimulating, if pricey, appetizer. ✉ *Leidseplein 10,* ☎ *020/6232988. AE, DC, MC, V.*

$$–$$$ ★ ✕ **'t Swarte Schaep.** The "Black Sheep" is named after a proverbial 17th-century sheep that roamed the area. With its creaking boards and array of copper pots, the interior is reminiscent of a ship's cabin. Classic Dutch dishes include scallops wrapped in bacon for starters and fillet of beef with hazelnuts as a filling main course. ✉ *Korte Leidsedwarsstraat 24,* ☎ *020/6223021. Reservations essential. Jacket and tie. AE, DC, MC, V.*

$–$$$ ★ ✕ **Excelsior.** The restaurant at the Hôtel de l'Europe offers a varied menu of French cuisine based on local ingredients. There are no fewer than 15 splendid set menus. Service is discreet and impeccable, and the view over the Amstel River, to the Muntplein on one side and the Muziektheater on the other, is the best in Amsterdam. ✉ *Hôtel de l'Europe, Nieuwe Doelenstraat 2–8,* ☎ *020/5311705. Reservations essential. Jacket and tie. AE, DC, MC, V. No lunch Sat.*

$$ ★ ✕ **De Silveren Spiegel.** In an alarmingly crooked 17th-century house, you can have an outstanding meal while you enjoy the personal attention of the owner at one of just a small cluster of tables. Local ingredients such as Texel lamb and wild rabbit are cooked with subtlety and flair. ✉ *Kattengat 4–6,* ☎ *020/6246589. AE, MC, V. Closed Sun.*

$–$$ ✕ **D' Theeboom.** Just behind the Dam, the ground floor of this historic canal-side warehouse has been converted into a stylish, formal restaurant offering a bargain lunchtime formula. The seasonal menu might include a delicious parcel of vegetables flavored with a selection of mushrooms, followed by carefully prepared red mullet with a saffron sauce. ✉ *Singel 210,* ☎ *020/6238420. AE, DC, MC, V. No lunch weekends.*

$–$$ ✕ **De Knijp.** Traditional Dutch food and French bistro fare are served here in a traditional Dutch environment. The mezzanine level is especially cozy. Alongside tamer dishes, there are seasonal game specialties including wild boar, ham with red cabbage, and fillet of hare. After-midnight dinner draws concert goers and performers from the neighboring Concertgebouw. ✉ *Van Baerlestraat 134,* ☎ *020/6714248. Reservations not accepted. AE, DC, MC, V.*

$–$$ ✕ **De Tropen.**The emphasis on the tropics is reflected in the decor, food, and background music in this small, intimate restaurant. Owner/chef Jacob Preyde is somewhat of a sensation on the Amsterdam scene with his innovative Carribean/Chinese fusion dishes. Pumpkin soup with saffron or parrotfish prepared with exotic herbs and spices are just some of the choices you may find on the ever-changing menu. His homemade cardamom ice cream is a favorite. ✉ *Palmgracht 39,* ☎ *020/4215528. MC, V. Closed Mon.–Tues. No lunch.*

$–$$ ✕ **Dynasty.** Surrounded by luxurious Oriental furniture and murals, you can savor dishes from Thailand, Malaysia, and China. Main-course delicacies include mixed seafood in banana leaves and succulent duck and lobster on a bed of watercress. In one of the city's most active nightlife areas, it can get very busy, but service is always impeccable. ✉ *Reguliersdwarsstraat 30,* ☎ *020/6268400. AE, DC, MC, V. Closed Tues. No lunch.*

$–$$ ✕ **Giulia's Ristorante.** Finely prepared meals from all the regions of Italy include many seafood dishes. Leave room for the ultimate chocolate dessert. The refined neoclassical interior is divided into several rooms. ✉ *Hobbemakade 63,* ☎ *020/6711263. AE, DC, MC, V. No lunch.*

$–$$ ✕ **In de Waag.** The lofty, beamed interior below the Theatrum Anatomicum has been converted into a grand café and restaurant. The reading table harbors computer terminals for Internet enthusiasts. Dinnertime brings a seasonal selection of hearty cuisine to be savored by candlelight. ✉ *Nieuwmarkt 4,* ☎ *020/4227772. AE, MC, DC, V.*

$–$$ ★ ✕ **L'Indochine.** This is one of the city's first ventures into Vietnamese food, and the chef's skillful preparation of the freshest ingredients, some specially imported, has been an immediate success. Sample the healthy, mint-flavored spring rolls or the meatier seared prawn and beef skewers to start, followed by lightly fried fish with vegetables in a subtly spiced sauce. ✉ *Beulingstraat 9,* ☎ *020/6275755. Reservations essential. AE, MC, V. Closed Mon. No lunch.*

$–$$ ✕ **Land van Walem.** Elegant breakfast and brunch options are served at this popular, all-day grand café on chic *ciabatta* (a crispy, white Italian bread), while at dinnertime the chefs prepare up-to-the-minute fusion cooking—and ask a higher price tag to go with it. ✉ *Keizersgracht 449,* ☎ *020/6253544. AE, MC, V.*

$–$$ ★ ✕ **Lonny's.** Lonny Gerungan's family have been cooks on Bali for generations—even preparing banquets for visiting Dutch royals. His plush restaurant in Amsterdam, draped in silky fabrics, serves the finest authentic Indonesian cuisine. Even the simplest rijsttafel is a feast of more than 15 delicately spiced dishes. ✉ *Rozengracht 46–48,* ☎ *020/6238950. Reservations essential. AE, DC, MC, V.*

$–$$ ✕ **Rose's Cantina.** A perennial favorite of the sparkling set, this place offers spicy Tex-Mex food, lethal cocktails, and a high noise level. Weekend reservations are essential. ✉ *Reguliersdwarsstraat 38,* ☎ *020/6259797. AE, DC, MC, V.*

$ ✕ **Het Gasthuys.** In this bustling restaurant you'll be served handsome portions of traditional Dutch home cooking—choice cuts of meat with excellent fries and piles of mixed salad. Sit at the bar or take a table high up in the rafters at the back. In summer the enchanting terrace on the canal side opens. ✉ *Grimburgwal 7,* ☎ *020/6248230. No credit cards.*

$ ✕ **Kantjil en de Tijger.** This lively Indonesian restaurant is a favorite with the locals and close to the bars on the Spui. The menu is based on three different rijsttafel, with a profusion of meat and vegetable dishes varying in flavor from coconut-milk sweet to peppery hot. ✉ *Spuistraat 291/293,* ☎ *020/6200994. AE, DC, MC, V. No lunch.*

$ ✕ **Song Kwae.** The traditional offerings in Amsterdam's Chinatown, based around the Nieuwmarkt and Zeedijk, have now been complemented by a surge of Thai restaurants, and this buzzing joint offers speedy service and quality food for a budget price. Alongside the traditional red and green Thai curries and the stir-fry options, there are specialties such as green papaya salad with crab. ✉ *Kloveniersburgwal 14,* ☎ *020/6242568. AE, DC, MC, V.*

$ ★ ✕ **Toscanini.** This cavernous, noisy Italian restaurant has superb cuisine and an enthusiastic regular clientele. Try a selection of antipasti followed by fresh pasta or the simple fish and meat dishes. ✉ *Lindengracht 75,* ☎ *020/6232813. Reservations essential. AE, DC, MC, V. No lunch.*

Lodging

Accommodations are tight from Easter to summer, so early booking is advised. For details and price-category definitions, *see* Lodging *in* The Netherlands A to Z, *above*.

$$$$ ★ 🏨 **Amstel Inter-Continental.** Amsterdam's grande dame opened in 1867 and was spectacularly renovated in 1992. The spacious rooms have Oriental rugs, brocade upholstery, Delft lamps, and a color scheme inspired by the warm, earthy tones of Makkum pottery. The Amstel is frequented by many of the nation's top businesspeople and sometimes hosts members of the royal family. ✉ *Professor Tulpplein 1, 1018 GX,* ☎ *020/6226060,* FAX *020/6225808,* WEB *www.interconti.com. 55 rooms, 25 suites. Restaurant, indoor pool. AE, DC, MC, V.*

$$$$ 🏨 **Blake's.** British designer Anouska Hempel opened her luxury hotel in 1999 and it became an immediate "in" spot. The beautifully appointed interior has an oriental influence and the entire hotel and courtyard offer serenity in a bustling city. The restaurant is one of Amsterdam's best ($$), with a Thai/French fusion kitchen. ✉ *Keijzersgracht 384, 1016 GB,* ☎ *020/5302010,* FAX *020/5302030,* WEB *www.blakes.site.nl. 15 rooms, 10 suites. Restaurant. AE, DC, MC, V.*

$$$$ ★ **Grand Amsterdam.** In 1991 Amsterdam's former city hall was converted into a luxury hotel. Parts of this elegant building date from the 16th century, but most of it belongs to the early 20th, when the country's best artists and architects were commissioned to create a building the city could be proud of. Features include a mural by Karel Appel, Jugendstil stained-glass windows, Gobelin tapestries, and palatially luxurious reception areas and rooms. The kitchen of the brasserie-style restaurant, Café Roux, is supervised by the incomparable Albert Roux. ✉ *Oudezijds Voorburgwal 197, 1012 EX,* ☎ *020/5553111,* FAX *020/5553222,* WEB *www.thegrand.nl. 160 rooms, 6 suites, 16 apartments. Restaurant, indoor pool. AE, DC, MC, V.*

$$$$ ★ **Hôtel de l'Europe.** Behind the stately facade of this building dating from the end of the 19th century is a full complement of modern facilities, as befits a hotel often ranked among the world's best. Large, bright rooms overlooking the Amstel are done in pastel colors; others have warm, rich colors and antiques. Apart from its world-renowned Excelsior restaurant, the hotel houses a sophisticated leisure complex. ✉ *Nieuwe Doelenstraat 2–8, 1012 CP,* ☎ *020/5311777,* FAX *020/5311778,* WEB *www.leurope.nl. 80 rooms, 20 suites. Restaurant, indoor pool. AE, DC, MC, V.*

$$$$ ★ **Pulitzer.** The Pulitzer is one of Europe's most ambitious hotel restorations, using the shells of a block of 24 17th- and 18th-century merchants' houses. Inside, the refined atmosphere is sustained by the modern art gallery and the lovingly restored brickwork, oak beams, and split-level rooms: no two are alike, and many rooms have antique furnishings to match the period architectural features. ✉ *Prinsengracht 315–331, 1016 GZ,* ☎ *020/5235235,* FAX *020/6276753,* WEB *www.starwood.com. 224 rooms, 3 suites, 4 apartments. Restaurant. AE, DC, MC, V.*

$$$ **Ambassade.** With its beautiful canal-side location, its Louis XV–style decoration, and its Oriental rugs, the Ambassade seems more like a stately home than a hotel. Service is attentive and room prices include breakfast in an elegant room overlooking the canal. For other meals, the neighborhood has a good choice of restaurants. ✉ *Herengracht 341, 1016 AZ,* ☎ *020/5550222,* FAX *020/5550277,* WEB *www.ambassade-hotel.nl. 52 rooms, 7 suites, 1 apartment. AE, DC, MC, V.*

$$$ **Canal House Hotel.** The new Irish owners of this canal-side hotel have maintained the same standards as the American owners who retired in 1999. They created a real sense of sleeping in the 17th century, opting for antiques rather than TVs as furnishings. Spacious rooms overlook the canal or the atmospheric garden. A hearty Dutch breakfast served in the breakfast room is included in the price. Children under age 14 are not permitted. ✉ *Keizersgracht 148, 1015 CX,* ☎ *020/6225182,* FAX *020/6241317,* WEB *www.canalhouse.nl. 26 rooms. AE, DC, MC, V.*

$$–$$$ **Golden Tulip Grand Hotel Krasnapolsky.** The fine Old World hotel is enhanced by the Winter Garden restaurant ($$), which dates from 1818. The large-scale expansion into neighboring buildings in the '90s has provided space for extensive conference and business facilities and an amazing selection of restaurants. The cosmopolitan atmosphere carries through all the well-equipped rooms, with decor ranging from Victorian to Art Deco. ✉ *Dam 9, 1012 JS,* ☎ *020/5549111,* FAX *020/6228607,* WEB *www.krasnapolsky.nl. 432 rooms, 1 suite, 36 apartments. 7 restaurants. AE, DC, MC, V.*

$$–$$$ **Hotel Seven Bridges.** Named for the view from its front steps, this small canal-house hotel has rooms decorated with individual flair. Oriental rugs warm wooden floors, and there are comfy antique armchairs and marble washstands. The Rembrandtsplein is nearby. For a stunning view, request a canal-side room, but make sure to reserve months in advance. One of the pleasures here is breakfast in bed. There are four attic rooms full of character that have shared bath facilities. ✉ *Reguliersgracht 31, 1017 LK,* ☎ *020/6231329. 10 rooms, 6 with shower or bath. AE, MC, V.*

$$ 🏨 **Atlas Hotel.** Known for its friendly atmosphere, this small hotel is in Amsterdam's most prestigious neighborhood, just a block from the Vondelpark. The moderate-size rooms are decorated in a comfortable, modern style. The main museums are within easy walking distance. ✉ *Van Eeghenstraat 64, 1071 GK,* ☎ *020/6766336,* FAX *020/6717633. 23 rooms. Restaurant. AE, DC, MC, V.*

$$ 🏨 **Hotel de Filosoof.** On a quiet street near Vondelpark, the hotel attracts artists, thinkers, and people looking for something a little unusual. Each room is decorated in a different philosophical or cultural motif—such as an Aristotle room and a Goethe room adorned with texts from *Faust.* A large Dutch breakfast is included in the price. ✉ *Anna van den Vondelstraat 6, 1054 GZ,* ☎ *020/6833013,* FAX *020/6853750,* WEB *www.xs4all.nl/~filosoof. 30 rooms. AE, MC, V.*

$–$$ ★ 🏨 **Agora.** The cheerful bustle of the nearby Singel flower market is reflected in this small hotel in an 18th-century house. Rooms are light and spacious, and some are decorated with vintage furniture; the best overlook the canal or the university. The Agora has a considerate staff, and the neighborhood is relaxed. Book well in advance. ✉ *Singel 462, 1017 AW,* ☎ *020/6272200,* FAX *020/6272202,* WEB *www.hotelagora.nl. 15 rooms, 13 with bath or shower. AE, DC, MC, V.*

$–$$ 🏨 **Hotel Washington.** On a peaceful street, the hotel is just a few blocks from the museum quarter and the Concertgebouw. Many of the world's top musicians find it the ideal place to reside when performing in Amsterdam. Period furniture and attentive service lend this small establishment a homey feel. All except the cheaper upper-floor rooms have bath or shower and toilet. ✉ *Frans van Mierisstraat 10, 1071 RS,* ☎ *020/6796754,* FAX *020/6734435. 24 rooms, 19 with bath or shower. AE, DC, MC, V.*

$ 🏨 **Amstel Botel.** The floating hotel moored near Central Station is an appropriate place to stay in watery Amsterdam. The rooms are small and basic, but the large windows offer fine views across the water to the city. Make sure you don't get a room on the land side of the vessel, or you'll end up staring at a postal sorting office. ✉ *Oosterdokskade 2, 1011 AE,* ☎ *020/6264247,* FAX *020/6391952,* WEB *www.amstelbotel.com. 174 rooms. AE, DC, MC, V.*

Nightlife and the Arts

The Arts

The arts flourish in cosmopolitan Amsterdam. The best source of information about performances is the monthly English-language *What's On in Amsterdam,* published by the VVV tourist office, where you can also secure tickets for the more popular events. *De Uitkrant* is available in Dutch and covers practically every event. You can also find the latest information and make personal or phone bookings for a small charge at the **Amsterdam Uitburo** (✉ Stadsschouwburg, Leidseplein 26, ☎ 0900/0191, 75¢ per minute, 9–9 daily).

CLASSICAL MUSIC

The **Concertgebouw** (✉ Concertgebouwplein 2–6, ☎ 020/6718345) is the home of one of Europe's finest orchestras. A smaller hall in the same building hosts chamber music, recitals, and even jam sessions. While ticket prices for international orchestras are high, most concerts are good value, and Wednesday lunchtime concerts at 12:30 are free.

FILM

The greatest concentration of movie theaters is around Leidseplein and near Muntplein. Most foreign films are subtitled rather than dubbed. Conveniently located close to Leidseplein, **City 1–7** (✉ Kleine Gartmanplantsoen 13–25, ☎ 0900/1458, 50¢ per min. for recorded info) has seven screens. **Pathe de Munt** (✉ Vijselstraat 15, ☎ 0900/1458, 50¢ per min for recorded info) is the largest multiplex cinema in Amsterdam, with thirteen screens.

OPERA AND BALLET

The Dutch national ballet and opera companies perform in the **Muziektheater** (✉ Waterlooplein, ☎ 020/6255455). Guest companies from other countries perform here during the Holland Festival in June. The country's smaller regional dance and opera companies usually include performances at the **Stadsschouwburg** (City Municipal Theater; ✉ Leidseplein 26, ☎ 020/6242311) in their schedules.

THEATER

Boom Chicago (✉ Leidseplein Theater, Leidseplein 12, ☎ 020/5307306, WEB www.boomchicago.nl) offers improvised comedy with a local touch. For experimental theater, contemporary dance, and colorful cabaret in Dutch, catch the shows at **Felix Meritis** (✉ Keizersgracht 324, ☎ 020/6231311).

Nightlife

Amsterdam has a wide variety of dance clubs, bars, and exotic shows. The more respectable—and expensive—after-dark activities are in and around Leidseplein and Rembrandtsplein; fleshier productions are on Oudezijds Achterburgwal and Thorbeckeplein. Most bars are open Sunday to Thursday to 1 AM and later on weekends, while clubs stay open until 5 AM or later. On weeknights very few clubs charge admission, though the livelier ones sometimes ask for a "club membership" fee of Fl. 20 or more. Watch out around the red-light district, where street-touts will offer tempting specials for louche clubs with floor shows—the experience may turn out to cost more than you bargained for.

CAFÉS AND BARS

Amsterdam, and particularly the Jordaan, is renowned for its brown cafés. There are also grand cafés, with spacious interiors, snappy table service, and well-stocked reading tables. Two other variants of Amsterdam's buzzing bar scene are the *proeflokalen* (tasting houses) and *brouwerijen* (breweries). The Dutch have a relaxed tolerance of the dreaded weed, to be encountered in "coffee shops" with the green leaves of the marijuana plant showing in the window.

Among more fashionable cafés is **Caffe Esprit** (✉ Spui 10, ☎ 020/6221967), serving delicious burgers and fine lunches; it is often used as a venue for radio and television interviews. The beamed interior of **De Admiraal Proeflokaal en Spijhuis** (✉ Herengracht 319, ☎ 020/6254334) is an intimate setting in which to enjoy the award-winning jenevers. **De Gijs** (✉ Lindegracht 249, ☎ 020/6380740) is an atmospheric brown café. **De Jaren** (✉ Nieuwe Doelenstraat 20, ☎ 020/6255771), a spacious grand café with a canal-side terrace, attracts young businesspeople, arts and media workers, and other trendy types. If Continental lagers no longer tickle your fancy, then the selection of home-brewed beers at **Maximiliaan Amsterdams Brouwhuis** (✉ Kloveniersburgwal 6, ☎ 020/6266280) is well worth sampling. At the **Rooie Nelis** (✉ Laurierstraat 101, ☎ 020/6244167), you can spend a rainy afternoon chatting with friendly strangers over homemade meatballs and a beer or apple tart and coffee. **Tweede Kamer** (✉ Heisteeg 6, just off the Spui, ☎ 020/4222236), named after the Dutch parliament's lower house, offers chess and backgammon in a convivial, civilized atmosphere permeated with the smoke of hemp.

CASINO

Holland Casino (✉ Max Euweplein 62, ☎ 020/6201006), just off Leidseplein, has blackjack, roulette, and slot machines in elegant, canalside surrounds. You'll need your passport to get in, and although you don't have to wear a tie, sneakers will not get you past the door; the minimum age is 18.

DANCE CLUBS

Dance clubs tend to fill up after midnight. The cavernous **Escape** (✉ Rembrandtsplein 11–15, ☎ 020/6221111) has taken on a much hipper mantle. The **iT** (✉ Amstelstraat 24, ☎ 020/6250111) is gay on Saturday. It's primarily straight on Thursday, Friday, and Sunday—but could never be accused of being straitlaced. **Seymour Likely Lounge** (✉ Nieuwezijds Voorburgwal 161, ☎ 020/4205663), has a lively, trendy crowd hopping to the latest music.

GAY AND LESBIAN NIGHTLIFE

Amsterdam has a vibrant gay and lesbian community. **Spijker** (✉ Kerkstraat 4, ☎ 020/6205919) is a popular late-night bar with a sociable pool table and pinball machine. The **Web** (✉ St. Jacobsstraat 6, ☎ 020/6236758) draws a leather/jeans crowd to its darker environs. **Cockring** (✉ Warmoestraat 96, ☎ 020/6239604) is a late-night dance bar that features special shows. **Café Rouge** (✉ Amstel 60, ☎ 020/4209881) is home to traditional Dutch oompapa music and frivolity. The **Amstel Taverne** (✉ Amstel 54, ☎ 020/6234254) is the oldest existing gay bar in Amsterdam and is an early-evening venue. The trendy set prevails at bars along the Reguliersdwarsstraat. A very mixed blend of different nationalities and ages meets early in the evening at **April** (✉ Reguliersdwarsstraat 37, ☎ 020/6259572). **Havana** (✉ Reguliersdwarsstraat 17, ☎ 020/6206788) sports a relaxed dance club on the first floor. The lesbian community meets at the **Saarein** (✉ Elandsstraat 119, ☎ 020/6234901), a traditional bar in the Jordaan. The younger set jives at **Vive La Vie** (✉ Amstelstraat 7, ☎ 020/6240114). There's a popular Saturday night women-only disco in the COC.

The **Gay & Lesbian Switchboard** (☎ 020/6236565) has friendly operators who provide up-to-the-minute information on events in the city, as well as general advice for gay or lesbian visitors. The **COC** (✉ Rozenstraat 14, ☎ 020/6263087), the Dutch lesbian and gay political organization, operates a coffee shop and weekend discos.

JAZZ CLUBS

The **Bimhuis** (✉ Oude Schans 73–77, ☎ 020/6233373) offers the best jazz and improvised music in town. The adjoining BIM café has a magical view across the Oude Schans canal.

ROCK CLUBS

Melkweg (✉ Lijnbaansgracht 234, ☎ 020/6241777) is a major rock and pop venue with its large auditorium; it also has a gallery, theater, cinema, and café. The **Paradiso** (✉ Weteringschans 6, ☎ 020/6264521), converted from a church, is a vibrant venue for rock, New Age, and even contemporary classical music.

Shopping

Department Stores

De Bijenkorf (✉ Dam 1), the city's number one department store, is excellent for contemporary fashions and furnishings. **Maison Bon-**

neterie (✉ Rokin 140; ✉ Beethovenstraat 32) is gracious, genteel, and understated. The well-stocked departments of **Vroom & Dreesmann** (✉ Kalverstraat 201) carry all manner of goods.

Gift Ideas

DIAMONDS

Since the 17th century, "Amsterdam cut" has been synonymous with perfection in the quality of diamonds. At the diamond-cutting houses, the craftsmen explain how a diamond's value depends on the four *c*'s—carat, cut, clarity, and color—before encouraging you to buy. There is a cluster of diamond houses on the Rokin. **Amsterdam Diamond Centre** (✉ Rokin 1–5, ☎ 020/6245787) is the largest institution on the Rokin. You can take a free guided diamond factory tour at **Gassan Diamonds** (✉ Nieuwe Uilenburgerstraat 173–175, ☎ 020/6225333).

PORCELAIN

The Dutch have been producing Delft, Makkum, and other fine porcelain for centuries. **Focke & Meltzer** (✉ Gelderlandplein 149, ☎ 020/644429) stores have been selling it since 1823. Pieces range from affordable, hand-painted, modern tiles to expensive Delft blue-and-white pitchers.

Markets

The **Bloemenmarkt** (flower market) on the Singel canal near the Muntplein is world-famous for its bulbs, many certificated for export, and cut flowers. Amsterdam's lively **Waterlooplein flea market,** open Monday–Saturday 9–5, next to the Muziektheater, is the ideal spot to rummage for secondhand clothes, inexpensive antiques, and other curiosities. In summer, you'll find etchings, drawings, and watercolors at the Sunday **art markets** on Thorbeckeplein and the Spui. There are as many English-language books as Dutch ones for browsing at the **book market** on the Spui, every Friday 10–4. A small but choice **stamp market,** open Wednesday and Saturday 1–4, is held on the Nieuwezijds Voorburgwal. **Kunst & Antiekmarkt De Looier** (De Looier Art & Antiques Market; ✉ Elandsgracht 109, ☎ 020/6249038) is a bustling, warrenlike indoor market, with myriad stalls selling everything from expensive antiques and art to kitschy bric-a-brac; it's open daily 11–5.

Shopping Districts

Leidsestraat, Kalverstraat, Utrechtsestraat, and Nieuwendijk, Amsterdam's chief shopping districts, have largely been turned into **pedestrian-only areas,** but watch out for trams and bikes nevertheless. The imposing **Kalvertoren** shopping mall (✉ Kalverstraat near Munt) has a rooftop restaurant with magnificent views of the city. **Magna Plaza** shopping center (✉ Nieuwezijds Voorburgwal 182), built inside the glorious turn-of-the-last-century post office behind the Royal Palace at the Dam, is *the* place for A-to-Z shopping in a huge variety of stores. The **Spiegelkwartier** (✉ Nieuwe Spiegelstraat and Spiegelgracht), just a stone's throw from the Rijksmuseum, is Amsterdam's antiques center, with galleries for wealthy collectors as well as old curiosity shops. **P. C. Hooftstraat,** and also Van Baerlestraat and Beethovenstraat, are the homes of haute couture and other fine goods. **Rokin** is hectic with traffic and houses a cluster of boutiques and renowned antiques shops selling 18th- and 19th-century furniture, antique jewelry, Art Deco lamps, and statuettes. The **Jordaan** to the west of the main ring of old canals, and the quaint streets crisscrossing these canals, is a treasure trove of trendy small boutiques and unusual crafts shops. **Schiphol Airport** tax-free shopping center is often lauded as the world's best.

Amsterdam Essentials

AIRPORTS AND TRANSFERS

Most international flights arrive at Amsterdam's Schiphol Airport. Immigration and customs formalities on arrival are relaxed, with no forms to be completed.

TRANSFERS

The best link is the direct rail line to the central train station, where you can get a taxi or tram to your hotel. The train runs every 10 to 15 minutes throughout the day and takes about a half hour. Make sure you buy a ticket before boarding, or ruthless conductors will impose a fine. Second-class single fare is Fl. 6.25/€3. Taxis from the airport to central hotels cost about Fl. 60/€27.

BIKE TRAVEL

Rental bikes are widely available for around Fl. 12.50/€6 per day with a Fl. 50/€23–Fl. 200/€91 deposit and proof of identity. Several rental companies are close to the central train station; ask at tourist offices for details. Lock your bike whenever you park it, preferably to something immovable. Also, check with the rental company to see what your liability is under their insurance terms. Take-a-Bike is under the main railway station, and you can get cheaper rates if you buy a *huurfietskaart* in combination with a train ticket. MacBike has various rental points around the center.

➤ BIKE RENTALS: **MacBike** (✉ Mr. Visserplein 2, ☎ 020/6200985; ✉ Marnixstraat 220, ☎ 020/6266964). **Take-a-Bike** (✉ Stationsplein 12, ☎ 020/6248391).

BOAT AND FERRY TRAVEL

The Canalbus (Fl. 19.50/€9 for a hop-on, hop-off day card) travels between the central train station and the Rijksmuseum. The Museum Boat (Fl. 22) stops near major museums.

BUS TRAVEL WITHIN AMSTERDAM

See ☞ Transportation Around Amsterdam, *below.*

CAR TRAVEL

The city's concentric ring of canals, one-way systems, hordes of cyclists, and lack of parking facilities make driving here unappealing. It's best to put your car in one of the parking lots on the edge of the old center and abandon it for the rest of your stay.

CONSULATES

➤ UNITED KINGDOM: (✉ Koningslaan 44, ☎ 020/6764343).
➤ UNITED STATES: (✉ Museumplein 19, ☎ 020/5755309).

EMERGENCIES

The Central Medical Service supplies names and opening hours of pharmacists and dentists, as well as doctors, outside normal surgery hours.

➤ DOCTORS AND DENTISTS: **Central Medical Service** (☎ 020/5923434).
➤ EMERGENCY SERVICES: **Police, Ambulance, Fire, and Rescue** (☎ 112).

ENGLISH-LANGUAGE MEDIA

➤ BOOKSTORES: **American Book Center** (✉ Kalverstraat 185, ☎ 020/6255537). **Athenaeum Boekhandel** (✉ Spui 14, ☎ 020/6226248). **English Bookshop** (✉ Lauriergracht 71, ☎ 020/6264230). **Waterstone's** (✉ Kalverstraat 152, ☎ 020/6383821).

TAXIS

Taxis are expensive: a 5-km (3-mi) ride costs around Fl. 26/€12. Taxis are not usually hailed on the street but are picked up at stands near stations and other key points, where you will see a yellow column. You can order a taxi by dialing Taxi Centrale (50¢ per minute). Taxi Direkt (22¢ per minute) is a taxi service supplying Amsterdam. Water taxis are more expensive than land taxis: standard-size water taxis—for up to eight people—cost Fl. 150/€68 for a half hour, and Fl. 100/€45 per 15 minutes thereafter. They offer a large range of catering services and are a popular way to enjoy the city or celebrate special occasions.

➤ TAXI COMPANIES: **Taxi Centrale** (☎ 0900/6777777). **Taxi Direkt** (☎ 0900–0724). **Water taxis** (☎ 020/5301090).

TOURS

BICYCLE TOURS

From April through October, guided bike tours are an excellent way to discover Amsterdam. There are also supervised tours to the idyllic countryside and quaint villages just north of the city. The three-hour city tour costs Fl. 32.50/€15, and the 6½-hour countryside tour costs Fl. 45/€20, arranged by Yellow Bike Guided Tours.

➤ FEES AND SCHEDULES: **Yellow Bike Guided Tours** (✉ Nieuwezijds Kolk 29, ☎ 020/6206940).

BOAT TOURS

The most enjoyable way to get to know Amsterdam is on a boat trip along the canals. Departures are frequent from points opposite Central Station, along the Damrak, and along the Rokin and Stadhouderskade (near the Rijksmuseum). For a tour lasting about an hour, the cost is around Fl. 15/€7, but the student guides expect a small tip for their multilingual commentary. A candlelight dinner cruise costs upward of Fl. 47.50/€21. Trips can be booked through the tourist office.

At Canal-Bike, a pedal boat for four costs Fl. 42/€19 per hour. The Museum Boat combines a scenic view of the city with seven stops near 20 museums. Tickets, good for the day and including discounted entry to museums, are Fl. 27.50/€12.

➤ FEES AND SCHEDULES: **Canal-Bike** (✉ corner of Leidsestraat and Keizersgracht; Leidsekade; Stadhouderskade opposite Rijksmuseum; Prinsengracht opposite Westerkerk; ☎ 020/6239886). **Museum Boat** (✉ Stationsplein 8, ☎ 020/5301090).

BUS TOURS

Guided bus tours provide an excellent introduction to Amsterdam. A bus-and-boat tour includes the inevitable trip to a diamond factory. Costing Fl. 25/€11–Fl. 35/€16, the comprehensive, 2½-hour tour can be booked through Key Tours or through Lindbergh.

➤ FEES & SCHEDULES: **Key Tours** (✉ Dam 19, ☎ 020/6235051). **Lindbergh** (✉ Damrak 26, ☎ 020/6222766).

WALKING TOURS

Amsterdam is a compact city of narrow streets and canals, ideal for exploring on foot. The tourist office issues seven excellent guides in English that detail walking tours around the center.

TRAIN TRAVEL

The city has excellent rail connections with the rest of Europe. Central Station is in the center of town.

➤ TRAIN INFORMATION: **Central Station** (✉ Stationsplein, ☎ 0900/9296 international service information, 50¢ per minute, and sometimes involving a long wait).

TRANSPORTATION AROUND AMSTERDAM

A zonal fare system is used for the public transportation system, which includes metro, tram, and bus. Tickets (starting at Fl. 3) are available from automated dispensers on the Metro or from the drivers on trams and buses; or buy a money-saving strippenkaart. Even simpler is the dagkaart, which covers all city routes for Fl. 11/€5. These discount tickets can be obtained from the main GVB ticket office (open weekdays 7–7 and weekends 8–7), in front of Central Station, and from many newsstands, along with route maps of the public transportation system. The Circle Tram 20 goes both ways around a loop that passes close to most of the main sights and offers a hop-on, hop-off ticket for one to three days.

TRAVEL AGENCIES

➤ LOCAL AGENTS: **American Express** (✉ Damrak 66, ☎ 020/5048787). **Holland International** (✉ Damrak 90, ☎ 020/5550808). **Key Tours** (✉ Dam 19, ☎ 020/6235051).

VISITOR INFORMATION

VVV Amsterdam Tourist Office has offices at Schiphol Airport, at Stationsplein 10, in front of Central Station in the Old Dutch Coffee House, as well as one in the station itself. The information number, listed below, costs Fl. 1.05 per minute, and the electronic queue has a long wait.
➤ TOURIST INFORMATION: **VVV Amsterdam Tourist Office** (✉ Schiphol Airport; ✉ Stationsplein 10, in front of Central Station in the Old Dutch Coffee House; ✉ Spoor 2 [Platform 2] inside the station, ☎ 0900/4004040).

HISTORIC HOLLAND

Between the historic towns, you'll see some of the Netherlands' windmill-dotted landscape and pass through centers of tulip-growing and cheese production. Apeldoorn is 90 km (56 mi) east of Amsterdam along highway A1, where the national park and royal palace are day trips in themselves. Amersfoort is an optional stop-off on the way. Arnhem is 15 km (9 mi) south of Apeldoorn on the A90, for trips to the open-air museum with children during summer months. The historically important centers of Utrecht, Gouda, and Leiden form an arc from the Groene Hart (Green Heart) of Holland toward the coast. Utrecht is 40 km (25 mi) southeast of Amsterdam on the A2. West of Utrecht, 36 km (22 mi) along the A12, you'll come to Gouda. Heading north on N11, you'll come to the ancient city of Leiden. The bulb fields of Lisse are halfway between Haarlem and Leiden, taking the N208 or the H206 coastal route. Haarlem, with its major museums, is 20 km (12 mi) directly west of Amsterdam on the A5.

Amersfoort

Although Amersfoort, east of Amsterdam on the way to Apeldoorn, is now a major industrial town, it has managed to retain much of its medieval character and charm. It was the birthplace of painter Piet Mondrian (1872–1944). A double ring of canals surrounds the town's old center. **Hovik** canal was once the harbor and loading quay. The **Koppelport** (✉ Kleine Spui), an imposing water gate across the Eem, dates from 1400. Turreted **Kamperbinnenpoort** (✉ Langstraat) is a land gate surviving from the 15th century. The graceful 335-ft-high **Onze Lieve Vrouwetoren** (Tower of Our Lady; ✉ Breestraat), on a Gothic church, has musical chimes that ring every Friday between 10 and 11 AM.

Museum Flehite, with its unusual medieval collections, gives insight into the history of the town. In the associated **St. Pieters-en-Bloklands**

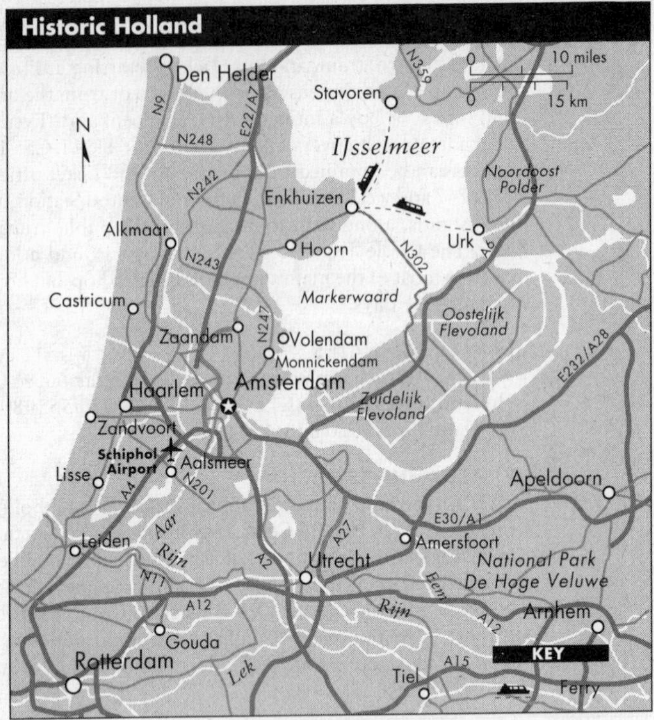

Gasthuis, a hospice founded in 1390, are a chapel and a medieval room. ✉ *Westsingel 50,* ☎ *033/4619987.* ⏲ *Tues.–Fri. 11–5, weekends 1–5.*

The **Culinair Museum Marienhof** (Culinary Museum), a convent during the 16th century, traces the history of eating and drinking, from prehistoric peoples, via the Roman period, through to the present day, sometimes accompanied by tasty demonstrations. ✉ *Kleine Haag 2,* ☎ *033/4631025.* ⏲ *Tues.–Fri. 11–5, weekends 1–5.*

Apeldoorn

★ The main attraction at Apeldoorn is the **Rijksmuseum Paleis Het Loo** (Het Loo Palace National Museum). Built during the late 17th century for William III, this former royal palace was the summer residence for the House of Orange from 1684 to 1972. It has been beautifully restored to illustrate the domestic surroundings enjoyed by the monarchs for more than three centuries. Royal memorabilia, silver, and ceramics are displayed, and there is a collection of old royal cars and carriages in the stables. ✉ *Koninklijkpark 1,* ☎ *055/5772400.* ⏲ *Tues.–Sun. 10–5.*

★ The **Nationale Park De Hoge Veluwe** (Hoge Veluwe National Park) is an area of moorlands, dense woods, and open meadows lying in the triangle formed by Arnhem, Apeldoorn, and Ede. Access for cars is restricted and there is a small fee, but you can park at one of the three main entrances and borrow a free bike. ✉ *5 km (3 mi) south of Apeldoorn on N304,* ☎ *0318/591627.* ⏲ *Nov.–Mar., daily 9–5:30; Apr., daily 8–8; May and Aug., daily 8 AM–9 PM; June–July, daily 8 AM–10 PM; Sept., daily 9–8; Oct., daily 9–7. Bezoekerscentrum and Museonder, daily 10–5.*

★ The **Kröller-Müller Museum** lies in the woods in the middle of the Hoge Veluwe National Park. The museum displays one of the finest collections of modern art in the world. It possesses 278 works by Vincent van Gogh, as well as paintings, drawings, and sculptures by Seurat, Redon, Braque, Picasso, and Mondrian. The building, too, is part of the experience; it seems to bring the museum's wooded setting right into the galleries with you. ✉ *Houtkampweg 6, Otterlo, in Nationale Park De Hoge Veluwe, 5 km (3 mi) from Apeldoorn on N304,* ☎ *0318/591241,* WEB *www.kmm.nl.* ⏲ *Tues.–Sun. 10–5, sculpture garden Tues.–Sun. 10–4:30.*

$$ ✕ **De Echoput.** Near Rijksmuseum Paleis Het Loo, this delightful restaurant is a member of the Alliance Gastronomique Néerlandaise, a guarantee of an excellent, classic French meal. Game from the surrounding forest is a specialty. An attractive terrace overlooks fountains and greenery for summer dining. ✉ *Amersfoortseweg 86,* ☎ *055/5191248. Reservations essential. AE, DC, MC, V. Closed Mon. No lunch Sat.*

$$$$ **Bilderberg Hotel de Keizerskroon.** In style and amenities it is a business hotel; in comfort and cordiality, a traveler's hotel; and in setting—at the edge of the town on a quiet street leading toward the woods—a weekend getaway. Three suites have an open hearth and a hot tub. ✉ *Koningstraat 7, 7315 HR, Apeldoorn,* ☎ *055/5217744,* FAX *055/5214737,* WEB *www.bilderberg.nl/keizerskroon. 91 rooms, 6 suites. Restaurant, indoor pool. AE, DC, MC, V.*

Arnhem

If you have children in tow, consider a visit to the **Nederlands Openlucht Museum** (Open-Air Museum) in Arnhem. In a 44-acre park, the curators have brought together more than 80 original buildings and furnishings from all over the Netherlands to establish a comprehensive display of Dutch rural architectural styles and to depict traditional ways of living since 1650. There are farmhouses and barns, workshops, and windmills—animals, too. Opened in 2000, an indoor exhibition space and panoramic theater accommodates visitors when the weather is inclement. ✉ *Schelmseweg 89,* ☎ *026/3576111.* *Fl. 23.25/€11.* ⏲ *Apr.–Oct., daily 10–5.*

Utrecht

The city of Utrecht was formerly the academic and religious center of the Netherlands. The gabled houses of Nieuwegracht, the canals with their sluice gates, the 13th-century wharves and storage cellars of Oudegracht, and an abundance of Gothic churches are just some of the city's key attractions. Utrecht hosts a number of internationally respected festivals, especially the annual Holland Festival of Early Music in the last week of August. If you arrive by rail, you pass through the enormous and ugly Vredenburg shopping center on the way to the beautiful, tree-lined Old Town.

The main cathedral square is a good point for orientation. The **Domkerk** is a late-Gothic cathedral with a series of fine stained-glass windows. The **Domtoren** (cathedral tower) opposite was connected to the cathedral until a hurricane destroyed part of the nave in 1674. It's open April–October, weekdays 10–5, weekends noon–5; November–March, weekends noon–5. The bell tower is the country's tallest, and its 465 steep steps lead to a magnificent view. A guide is essential in the tower's labyrinth of steps and passageways. ✉ *Domplein,* ☎ *030/2310403.* ⏲ *Tours on the hr: May–Sept., weekdays 10–5, Sat. 10–3:30, Sun. 2–4; Oct.–Apr., weekdays 11–4, Sat. 11–3:30, Sun. 2–4.*

★ The **Rijksmuseum van Speelklok tot Pierement** (National Museum of Mechanical Musical Instruments) is devoted to music machines—from music boxes to street organs and even musical chairs. During the tour, music students play some of the instruments. ✉ *Buurkerkhof 10,* ☎ *030/2312789.* ⏲ *Tues.–Sat. 10–5, Sun. 12–5.*

The **Museum Catharijneconvent** (Catherine's Convent Museum) contains the country's largest display of medieval art in addition to its collection of holy relics and vestments. ✉ *Nieuwegracht 63,* ☎ *030/2313835.* ⏲ *Tues.–Fri. 10–5, weekends 11–5.*

The **Centraal Museum** underwent a radical renovation that was completed in early 2000, bringing it into the 21st century with a bang that has not been received with unanimous awe. It houses a rich collection of contemporary art, especially applied arts, and exhibits about the city. There is a Viking ship (discovered in 1930), also a 17th-century dollhouse with period furniture, porcelain, and miniature Old Master paintings. A wing across the street is dedicated to the work of architect and designer Gerrit Rietveld (1888–1964). ✉ *Agnietenstraat 1,* ☎ *030/2362362.* ⏲ *Tues.–Sun. 11–5.*

An important part of the Centraal Museum's collection is the **Rietveld-Schröderhuis** (Rietveld-Schröder House), a 15-minute walk away in Utrecht's eastern suburbs. In 1924, architect Gerrit Rietveld (1888–1964), working with Truus Schröeder, designed what is considered to be the architectural pinnacle of de Stijl (The Style). The use of primary colors (red, yellow, blue) and black and white, as well as the definition of interior space, is unique and innovative even today. ✉ *Prins Hendriklaan 50a,* ☎ *030/2362362.* ⏲ *Tues.–Sun. 11–5.*

$–$$ ✕ **Polman's Huis.** A comfortable, classic café welcomes you to this restaurant; beyond, the spacious dining room has an incredibly high, cherub-decked ceiling. Attentive service accompanies well-prepared international cuisine, influenced by Asian as well as European palates. Vegetables are either steamed to perfection or given an exotic twist. ✉ *Keistraat 2,* ☎ *030/2313368. Reservations essential. MC, V.*

$ ✕ **De Soepterrine.** This snug restaurant offers 10 varieties of steaming homemade soups, including Dutch specialties such as thick erwtensoep. Each bowl comes with crusty bread and herb butter. Quiches and generous salads fill up extra corners. ✉ *Zakkendragerssteeg 40,* ☎ *030/2317005. Reservations not accepted. AE, DC, MC, V.*

$$ 🏨 **Malie Hotel.** The Malie is in a 19th-century row house on a quiet, leafy street a 15-minute walk from the old center. Rooms are vividly decorated though simply furnished. The breakfast room overlooks a garden and terrace. ✉ *Maliestraat 2, 3581 SL,* ☎ *030/2316424,* FAX *030/2340661,* WEB *www.maliehotel.nl. 45 rooms. AE, DC, MC, V.*

Gouda

Just a short walk from the railway station, the **Stadhuis** (City Hall) stands in fairy-tale Gothic majesty in the middle of the market square. The facade dates from 1450. Quirky mechanical figures in a mechanical clock to the right of the main entrance stir into action every hour, depicting Floris V granting Gouda its city rights in 1272. A special event held on the second Tuesday in December each year is Kaarsjesavond (Candle Night), when the city is illuminated by thousands of candles, an important local product, and enlivened with culinary and musical festivities. Gouda is perhaps most famous for its cheese. Brightly colored farm wagons arrive loaded with cheeses for the morning **Kaasmarkt** (Cheese Market; open June–Aug., Thurs. 10–12:30).

In the Baroque **Waag** (weigh house) to the side of the marketplace, the Kaasexposeum (cheese exhibition) explains the history of cheese and dairy products. ✉ *Markt 35–36,* ☎ *0182/529996.* ⏲ *Apr.–Oct., Mon.–Sat. 10–5, Sun. noon–5.*

Sint Janskerk (Church of St. John) has the longest nave in the country, primarily built during the 16th century. There are 64 glorious stained-glass windows depicting biblical and historical scenes, which you can examine through a telescope. The oldest windows date from 1555 and survived the bombardments of World War II in bomb-proof bunkers. The modern window in memory of the Holocaust is extremely moving. ✉ *Achter de Kerk 16,* ☎ *0182/512684.* ⏲ *Mar.–Oct., Mon.–Sat. 9–5; Nov.–Feb., Mon.–Sat. 10–4.*

The **Stedelijk Museum Het Catharina Gasthuis** (Catharina Hospice Municipal Museum) is a former poorhouse and hospital. Housed in a complex of historic buildings, exhibits include period furniture, galleries of paintings and prints, a former chapel with religious art, and a medieval torture chamber. ✉ *Oosthaven 10/Achter de Kerk 14,* ☎ *0182/588440.* ⏲ *Mon.–Sat. 10–5, Sun. noon–5.*

Leiden

Leiden is renowned for its spirit of religious and intellectual tolerance and for its university and royal connections. The university was founded by William the Silent as a reward to Leiden for its victory over the Spanish in the 1573–74 siege. During the war the dikes were opened and the countryside flooded so that the rescuing navy could sail right up to the city walls. The unusual **De Burcht** (The Keep; ✉ Burgsteeg 14), a man-made mound that formed part of the city's early fortifications, affords a spectacular view of the city.

The Pilgrim Fathers stayed in Leiden before they set out for Delftshaven on the first stage of their arduous voyage to the New World. Documents relating to their stay are kept in the library of the **Stedelijk Museum De Lakenhal.** The Public Reading Room of the **Stadsarchief** (City Record Office) has facsimiles of documents and other material of historical interest. ✉ *Dolhuissteeg 7,* ☎ *071/5120191 or 071/5165355.* ⏲ *Weekdays 9:30–5, Sat. 9–12:15.*

The **Leiden American Pilgrim Museum** displays a historic furniture collection in a 16th-century house, along with copies of documents relating to the Pilgrim Fathers. The American curator offers guided tours of the city's Pilgrim sights. ✉ *Beschuitsteeg 9,* ☎ *071/5122413.* ⏲ *Wed.–Sat. 1–5.*

Founded in 1590, the **Hortus Botanicus** (Botanical Garden) is among the oldest in the world. The highlights are ancient trees, a faithful reconstruction of a 16th-century garden, an herb garden, a Japanese garden, and an orangery. ✉ *Rapenburg 73,* ☎ *071/5277249.* ⏲ *Mar.–Oct., daily 10–6; Nov.–Feb., Sun.–Fri. 10–4.*

★ **Naturalis** (National Museum of Natural History) boasts superb collections of minerals, fossils, insects, and stuffed birds and animals in a spacious modern accommodation. The collections have been growing since Leiden University scientists started the museum in 1820, and now you will have the natural wonders of the world explained with the help of the latest technology. ✉ *Darwinweg,* ☎ *071/5687600,* WEB *www.naturalis.nl.* ⏲ *Tues.–Sun. 10–6; during school holidays, daily 10–6.*

Stedelijk Museum De Lakenhal (Cloth Hall Municipal Museum), a textile and antiques museum and art gallery, occupies a classical building constructed in 1639 for cloth merchants. Pride of place in the collection goes to the Dutch 16th- and 17th-century paintings, with works by Steen, Dou, Rembrandt, and, above all, Lucas van Leyden's *Last Judgment* (1526)—the first great Renaissance painting executed in what is now the Netherlands. Other rooms are devoted to furniture and to the history of Leiden's medieval guilds. ✉ *Oude Singel 28–32,* ☎ *071/5165360,* WEB *www.lakenhal.nl.* ⏲ *Tues.–Fri. 10–5, weekends and holidays noon–5.*

Molenmuseum de Valk (Windmill Museum) is housed in a windmill built in 1747, which was worked by 10 generations of millers until 1964. The seven floors contain the original machinery, an old forge, and living quarters. ✉ *2e Binnenvestgracht 1,* ☎ *071/5165353.* ⏲ *Tues.–Sat. 10–5, Sun. 1–5.*

St. Pieterskerk (St. Peter's Church) is associated closely with the Pilgrim Fathers, who worshiped here, and with their spiritual leader, John Robinson, who is buried here. ✉ *Pieterskerkhof 1a,* ☎ *071/5124319.* ⏲ *Daily 1:30–6.*

A narrow street by the **Persijnhofje** alms house (✉ Kloksteeg 21), dating from 1683, leads to the tree-lined **Rapenburg** canal, crossed by triple-arch bridges and bordered by stately 18th-century houses.

The **Rijksmuseum van Oudheden** (National Museum of Antiquities) is the country's leading archaeological museum. The prize exhibit is the entire 1st-century Temple of Taffeh, donated by the Egyptian government. ✉ *Rapenburg 28,* ☎ *071/5163163,* WEB *www.rmo.nl.* ⏲ *Tues.–Fri. 10–5, weekends and holidays noon–5.*

$ ✕ **Annie's Verjaardag.** A vaulted cellar full of students and a canal-side terrace make Annie's attractive in all weather. The selection of salads and baguettes is usually accompanied by a daily special, such as mussels or jugged hare. ✉ *Hoogstraat 1a,* ☎ *071/5125737. Reservations not accepted. MC.*

$ ✕ **Stadscafé Restaurant van der Werff.** From the Art Nouveau interior you can see the De Valk windmill framed across the water. The restaurant serves café fare throughout the day, and on Sunday afternoons the place swings to live jazz. In the evening there is an appetizing and adventurous dinner menu based on French cuisine. ✉ *Steenstraat 2,* ☎ *071/5130335. AE, DC, MC, V.*

$$–$$$ **Nieuw Minerva.** This family-run hotel is a conversion of six 16th-century buildings. The original part is decorated in Old Dutch style. The newer part is better equipped but has slightly less character. Many rooms overlook a quiet tributary of the Rhine. The restaurant serves an excellent three-course tourist menu with vegetarian, meat, and fish selections. ✉ *Boommarkt 23, 2311 EA,* ☎ *071/5126358,* FAX *071/5142674,* WEB *www.nieuwminerva.nl. 38 rooms, 1 suite. Restaurant. AE, DC, MC, V.*

$–$$ **Hotel De Doelen.** The spartan decor of this small hotel is in keeping with its origins as a 17th-century patrician's house, but the rooms are comfortable and modern. ✉ *Rapenburg 2, 2311 EV,* ☎ *071/5120527,* FAX *071/5128453,* WEB *www.dedoelen.com. 16 rooms. AE, DC, MC, V.*

Lisse

The **Keukenhof,** a 70-acre park and greenhouse complex, is planted each year to create a special exhibition of springtime flowering bulbs in 79 acres of landscaped gardens situated between Amsterdam, Leiden, and Haarlem. The world's largest flower show draws huge crowds to its woodland walks, greenhouse pavilions, and regimental lines of tulips, hyacinths, and daffodils. A new initiative is the Zomerhof (Summer Garden), with summer bulbs and tuberous plants such as lilies, anemones, begonias, and canna, as well as perennials. ✉ *Lisse, N208,* ☎ *0252/465555.* ⏲ *Late Mar.–late May, daily 8–7:30; early Aug.–mid-Sept., daily 9–6.*

Aalsmeer

Flowers are big business to the Dutch, and the Netherlands has the world's largest complex of flower auction houses. The biggest of these facilities (it also is the largest in the world) is the **Bloemenveiling** (flower auction) in Aalsmeer, close to Schiphol International Airport and Amsterdam.

In a building the size of three football fields, three auction rooms function simultaneously. Get there early; it's all over by 10 AM. ✉ *Legmeerdijk 313,* ☎ *0297/334567.* ⏲ *Weekdays 7:30–11 AM.*

Haarlem

With buildings notable for their secret inner courtyards and pointed gables, Haarlem resembles a 17th-century canvas by Frans Hals, the city's greatest painter. The area around the **Grote Markt** (market square) provides an architectural stroll through the 17th and 18th centuries.

The **Vleeshal** (meat market), near the Stadhuis (City Hall), dates from the early 1600s and has an especially fine gabled front. It now serves as an additional exhibition space for the Frans Hals Museum. ✉ *Grote Markt 16.* ⏲ *Mon.–Sat. 11–5, Sun. and holidays noon–5.*

The **Grote Kerk** (cathedral) is also known as the St. Bavo, to whom it is dedicated. Built between 1400 and 1550, it houses one of the world's finest organs, which has 5,000 pipes and was played by both Mozart and Handel. An annual organ festival is held here in July. ✉ *Grote Markt,* ☎ *023/5330877.* ⏲ *Apr.–Aug., Mon.–Sat. 10–4; Sept.–Mar., Mon.–Sat. 10–3:30.*

★ The **Teylers Museum** claims to be the oldest museum in the country. It was founded by a wealthy merchant in 1778 as a museum of science and the arts and has old showcases filled with mineral specimens as well as an intriguing collection of historic scientific instruments. It also has a fine collection of the Hague school of painting as well as drawings and sketches by Michelangelo, Raphael, and other non-Dutch masters. As the canvases in this building are shown in natural light, try to visit on a sunny day. ✉ *Spaarne 16,* ☎ *023/5319010,* WEB *www.teylersmuseum.nl.* ⏲ *Tues.–Sat. 10–5, Sun. and holidays noon–5.*

★ The **Frans Hals Museum,** in what was a 17th-century hospice, contains a marvelous collection of works by Hals (1585–1666); his paintings of the guilds of Haarlem are particularly noteworthy. The museum also has works of the artist's 17th-century contemporaries and an extensive contemporary collection, including paintings by the CoBrA school, including Corneille, Constant, and Appel. ✉ *Groot Heiligland 62,* ☎ *023/5115775,* WEB *www.franshalsmuseum.nl.* ⏲ *Mon.–Sat. 11–5, Sun. and holidays noon–5.*

$ ✕ **Café Restaurant Brinkman.** This elegant, classic grand café overlooks the magnificent Grote Kerk. You can while away the afternoon over a single coffee or choose from a wide menu of casseroles and grills with salad. ✉ *Grote Markt 9–13,* ☎ *023/5323111. AE, DC, MC, V.*

$$$ 🏨 **Golden Tulip Lion d'Or.** Just five minutes from the old city center and conveniently near the railway station, this comfortable but unprepossessing hotel offers a full range of luxuries. ✉ *Kruisweg 34–36, 2011 LC,* ☎ *023/5321750,* FAX *023/5329543,* WEB *www.goldentulip.nl. 32 rooms, 2 suites. Restaurant. AE, DC, MC, V.*

Historic Holland Essentials

CAR TRAVEL

The most convenient way to explore the countryside is by rented car from Amsterdam. All the towns listed above can also be reached by bus or train. Check with the tourist office in Amsterdam for help in planning your trip, or inquire at Central Station.

TOURS

The towns of Historic Holland are covered, in various combinations, by organized bus tours out of Amsterdam. Brochures for tour operators are available from the VVV Amsterdam Tourist Offices. The VVV office in Utrecht organizes several excursions, including a boat trip along the canals and a sightseeing flight over the city. There are also day trips to country estates, castles, and gardens.

VISITOR INFORMATION

In towns such as Apeldoorn and Gouda, which have few good hotels, B&B accommodations can be booked through the VVV.

➤ TOURIST INFORMATION: **Amersfoort** (VVV; ✉ Stationsplein 9–11, ☏ 0900/1122364, Fl. 1 per minute). **Apeldoorn** (VVV; ✉ Stationstraat 72, ☏ 0900/1681636, 80¢ per minute). **Arnhem** (VVV; ✉ Stationsplein 45, ☏ 0900/2024075, Fl. 1 per minute). **Gouda** (VVV; ✉ Markt 27, ☏ 0182/513666). **Haarlem** (VVV; ✉ Stationsplein 1, ☏ 0900/6161600, Fl. 1 per minute). **Leiden** (VVV; ✉ Stationsweg 2d, ☏ 0900/2222333, Fl. 1 per minute). **Lisse** (VVV; ✉ Grachtweg 53, ☏ 0252/414262). **Utrecht** (VVV; ✉ Vredenburg 90, ☏ 0900/4141414, 50¢ per minute).

THE HAGUE, DELFT, AND ROTTERDAM

The royal, diplomatic, and governmental seat of Den Haag, or 's-Gravenhage (the Hague), is the Netherlands' most dignified and spacious city. Its close neighbor is the leading North Sea beach resort of Scheveningen. Also nearby are Delft, a historic city with many canals and ancient buildings, and the energetic and thoroughly modern international port city of Rotterdam.

These cities are all linked by excellent train service. The Hague and Delft, only 14 km (9 mi) from each other, are both about 60 km (37 mi) southwest of Amsterdam and can be reached within an hour by fast, frequent trains. Rotterdam is a quarter of an hour farther.

By road the Hague is 50 km (31 mi) southwest of Amsterdam using the A4, then the A44. Delft is 60 km (37 mi) southwest of Amsterdam on the A4, then the A13, via the Hague. The A13 is also the trunk road to Rotterdam, 13 km (8 mi) farther south. Rotterdam is just 73 km (45 mi) south of Amsterdam.

The Hague

During the 17th century, when Dutch maritime power was at its zenith, the Hague was known as "the Whispering Gallery of Europe" because it was thought to be the secret manipulator of European politics. The Hague remains a powerful world diplomatic and juridical capital, as well as the seat of government for the Netherlands.

★ The gracious **Binnenhof** (Inner Court) complex is the site where William II built a castle when he adopted the Hague, then surrounded by forest, as the base for his hunting activities in 1250. It is now surrounded by early classical buildings that serve as offices for politicians working in the neighboring Parliament buildings. At the center is the imposing late-13th-century **Ridderzaal** (Knights' Hall). Inside are vast beams spanning a width of 59 ft, flags, and stained-glass windows. The city's heart is the **Hofvijver** (court pond), which was originally a protective moat and is now a reflecting pond filled with water lilies. Tours of the government buildings, new and old, in English are conducted by **Stichting Bezoekerscentrum Binnenhof** (Binnenhof Visitors Center), just to the right of the Ridderzaal. ✉ *Binnenhof 8a,* ☏ *070/3646144 tour reservations.* ⏲ *Mon.–Sat. 10–3:45; tours by appointment only.*

★ The **Mauritshuis** (Maurits' House), a small, perfectly proportioned neoclassical palace on the far side of the Binnenhof, dates from 1644. This former royal residence is one of the finest small art museums in the world. It contains a feast of art from the 17th century, including six works by

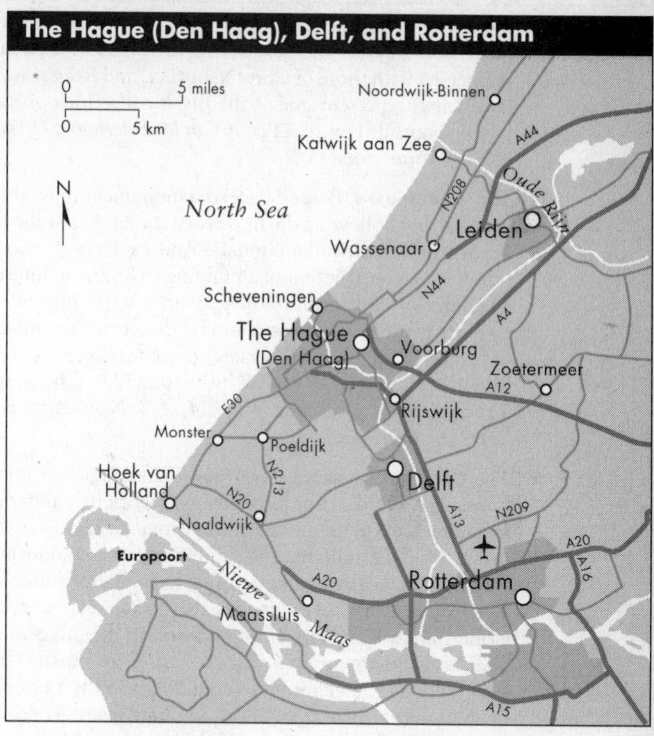

Rembrandt van Rijn (1606–69); of these the most powerful is the *Anatomy Lesson of Dr. Tulp,* a theatrical work depicting a dissection of the lower arm. Also here are the celebrated *Girl Wearing a Turban* and the glistening *View of Delft* by Jan Vermeer (1632–75), famous for his brilliant ability to capture the fall of light. ✉ *Korte Vijverberg 8,* ☎ *070/3023456,* WEB *www.mauritshuis.nl.* ⏲ *Tues.–Sat. 10–5, Sun. 11–5.*

Lange Voorhout is a large L-shape boulevard close to the Mauritshuis and Parliament buildings. During the 19th century, horse-drawn trams clattered along its cobbles and deposited dignitaries outside the various palaces, which are now primarily inhabited by embassies. The **Hoge Raad** (Supreme Court; ✉ Lange Voorhout 34) once belonged to William I, the first king of the Netherlands. With its redbrick stepped gable, the **Rode Kruis** (Dutch Red Cross) headquarters, in a former servants' house at No. 6, seems out of place on this stately avenue.

The **Museum Het Paleis** (Palace Museum; ✉ Lange Voorhout 74, ☎ 070/3624061), a former royal residence, is a dependence of **Gemeentemuseum Den Haag**, where temporary exhibitions are held in the state rooms.

The **Kloosterkerk** (Cloister Church; ✉ Lange Voorhout 4, corner Parkstraat), built in 1400, is the Hague's oldest church. In spring the adjoining square is covered with yellow and purple crocuses; on Thursday in summer it is the setting for a colorful antiques market.

Panorama Mesdag is a 400-ft painting-in-the-round that shows the nearby seaside town of Scheveningen as it looked in 1880. Hendrik Mesdag (1831–1915), a marine painter, used the muted colors of the Hague school in his calming seascape, as well as special perspective techniques. ✉ *Zeestraat 65,* ☎ *070/3644544,* WEB *www.mesdag.nl.* ⏲ *Mon.–Sat. 10–5, Sun. noon–5.*

Museum Mesdag (Mesdag Museum), the painter's former home, contains works by H. W. Mesdag and members of the Hague school interspersed with those of Corot, Courbet, and Rousseau. These delicate landscapes represent one of the finest collections of Barbizon School painting outside France. ✉ *Laan van Meerdervoort 7f,* ☎ *070/3621434.* ⏲ *Tues.–Sun. noon–5.*

The **Vredespaleis** (Peace Palace) is a monument to world peace through negotiation. Following the first peace conference at the Hague in 1899, the Scottish-American millionaire Andrew Carnegie donated $1.5 million for the construction of a building to house an international court. The interior and furniture display an eclectic mix of works donated by participating nations from around the world. The **International Court of Justice,** which rules on disputes between countries, has its headquarters here. ✉ *Carnegieplein 2,* ☎ *070/3022323,* WEB *www.icj-cij.org.* ⏲ *Tours May–Oct., weekdays 10, 11, 2, 3; Nov.–Apr., weekdays 11, 2, 3; reservations required.*

★ The **Gemeentemuseum Den Haag** (The Hague Municipal Museum) houses the world's largest collection of work by painter Piet Mondrian, including his last, unfinished work, *Broadway Boogie Woogie,* acquired in 1998 for $20 million. The exhibition traces Mondrian's stylistic development from figurative painting to refined, minimalist abstraction. The Hague School of painters is also amply represented, as well as the CoBrA artist Karel Appel. In addition to magnificent arts-and-crafts collections, there are two vast collections of musical instruments. H. P. Berlage's 1935 yellow-brick building itself is a fascinating example of the International Style. ✉ *Stadhouderslaan 41,* ☎ *070/3381111,* WEB *www.gemeentemuseum.nl.* ⏲ *Tues.–Sun. 11–5.*

Madurodam, between the Hague and Scheveningen, is a miniature Netherlands where the country's important buildings are duplicated at a scale of 1:25. No detail has been forgotten, from the lighthouse and 4½-km (3-mi) train track to the hand-carved furniture in the gabled houses. ✉ *George Maduroplein 1, the Hague,* ☎ *070/3553900,* WEB *www.madurodam.nl.* 🎫 *Fl. 22.* ⏲ *Sept.–mid-Mar., daily 9–6; mid-Mar.–June, daily 9–8; July–Aug., daily 9* AM*–10* PM*.*

$–$$$ ★ ✕ **Bistro-mer.** A notch above most other seafood restaurants in the Hague, Bistro-mer has a menu that ranges from the North Sea to the Mediterranean. Start with a selection of the three types of oyster they always have on ice. Portions are generous, and the food is cooked to perfection. There's a wood-paneled dining room for snug winter meals and an attractive glassed-in terrace for the summer. ✉ *Javastraat 9,* ☎ *070/3607389. AE, DC, MC, V. Closed Mon. No lunch weekends.*

$–$$ ✕ **Borobudur.** Tucked away in a little alley close to the Hague's concert hall and dance theater, this restaurant's attentive staff serves Indonesian dishes as well as a royal selection of festive rijsttafel, which offers myriad small tastes of the Orient. ✉ *Bagijnenstraat 23–25,* ☎ *070/3659691. AE, DC, MC, V. Closed Sun.–Mon. No lunch.*

$–$$ ✕ **Da Roberto.** Popular with politicians and the Hague's business elite, Roberto's is a quiet and classically chic restaurant where all the adventure goes into the cuisine. Italian standards and some ambitious variations are treated to elegant nouvelle cuisine presentation. ✉ *Noordeinde 196,* ☎ *070/3464977. AE, DC, MC, V. Closed Sun. No lunch Sat.*

$–$$ ✕ **Le Haricot Vert.** What was built in 1638 as a staff house for the nearby palace is nowadays an intimate, candlelit restaurant in the city center. Succulent meats swimming in sauce appear on large white plates with a colorful tangle of vegetables. Leave room for one of the sinfully laden dessert platters. ✉ *Molenstraat 9a–11,* ☎ *070/3652278. AE, DC, MC, V. No lunch Sun.–Wed.*

$$–$$$$ **Hotel Des Indes.** At the end of one of the Hague's most prestigious squares, the Des Indes is grace and gentility supreme. The once-private mansion was built for grand balls and entertainments; the rooms are arranged around the glamorous, marble-walled foyer. For more than 100 years it has hosted ambassadors and kings, dancers and spies. Rooms are spacious and classically styled; one suite offers a spectacular view across the city toward the coast. The historic restaurant ($$$), frequented by diplomats, serves French-style haute cuisine. ✉ *Lange Voorhout 54–56, 2514 EG,* ☎ *070/3612345,* FAX *070/3451721,* WEB *www.inter-conti.com. 70 rooms, 6 suites. Restaurant. AE, DC, MC, V.*

$–$$ **Hotel Corona.** Overlooking a charming square in the center of the city, this hotel has rooms decorated in a restful scheme of white, cream, and dove-gray. Mouthwatering dishes from its excellent Restaurant Marc Smeets include lamb with forest mushrooms and wild duck with sage and thyme. The lunch menu includes sandwiches and light meals. ✉ *Buitenhof 39–42, 2513 AH,* ☎ *070/3637930,* FAX *070/3615785. 26 rooms. Restaurant. AE, DC, MC, V.*

$ **Hotel Sebel.** This hotel is in a largely residential district between the city center and the Vredespaleis (Peace Palace). The rooms are invitingly spacious and light and have marble bathrooms. ✉ *Zoutmanstraat 40, 2518 GR,* ☎ *070/3608010,* FAX *070/3455855. 27 rooms. AE, DC, MC, V.*

Scheveningen

Scheveningen is adjacent to the Hague on the North Sea coast, with the **Scheveningse Bosjes** (Scheveningen Woods) separating it from the capital. A fishing village since the 14th century, Scheveningen became a popular beach resort in the 19th century. The beach itself, protected from tidal erosion by stone jetties, slopes gently into the sea in front of a high promenade that protects the boulevard and everything behind it from winter storms. During the summer, cafés and restaurants line the sandy beach, but you can escape to quieter environs by walking north of the pier along miles of untouched beach.

The **Pier,** completed in 1962, stretches 1,220 ft into the sea. The four circular buildings at its end contain a sun terrace and restaurant, an observation tower, an amusement center with a children's play area, and an underwater panorama. ✉ *Northern end of Boulevard.*

Sea Life Scheveningen on the beachfront is an ingeniously designed aquarium complex with a transparent underwater tunnel. You walk through it as if you were on the sea floor, with sharks, rays, eels, and octopuses swimming inches above your head. ✉ *Strandweg 13,* ☎ *070/3542100,* WEB *www.sealife.nl.* ⏲ *Sept.–June, daily 10–6; July–Aug., daily 10–8.*

$$$$ **Steigenberger Kurhaus Hotel.** At the turn of the last century this imposing spa hotel stood alone at the center of the beach as a fashionable resort. Rooms have tasteful, modern furnishings. The ballroom is still the hotel's focal point, with an extravagantly decorated ceiling, under which you can enjoy a superb buffet lunch at weekends. The **Vitalizee** spa (☎ 070/4166500), alongside the hotel's panoramic sea-view terrace, provides a refreshing and invigorating pampering no matter what the season and is open to residents and nonresidents alike. You can enjoy the suite of saunas and steam rooms, with optional massage, restorative therapies, and beauty treatments. ✉ *Gevers Deynootplein 30, 2586 CK,* ☎ *070/4162636,* FAX *070/4162646,* WEB *www.kurhaus.nl. 245 rooms, 10 suites. 2 restaurants. AE, DC, MC, V.*

Delft

Probably no town in the Netherlands is more intimate, more attractive, or more traditional than this minimetropolis, whose famous blue-and-white earthenware is popular throughout the world. Compact and easy to explore despite its web of canals, Delft is best discovered on foot—although canal-boat excursions are available April through October and horse-drawn trams leave from the marketplace. Every canal and street is lined with attractive Gothic and Renaissance houses.

In the marketplace, the only lively spot in this tranquil town, stands the **Nieuwe Kerk** (New Church), built in the 14th century, with its tall Gothic spire and a 48-bell carillon. The crypt has been the final resting place for all members of the Dutch royal family since the mid-16th century. ✉ *Markt,* ☎ *015/2123025.* ⏲ *Tower Mar.–Oct., Mon.–Sat. 9–6; Nov.–Feb., Mon.–Sat. 11–4.*

The **Stedelijk Museum Het Prinsenhof** (Prinsenhof Municipal Museum) was formerly the Convent of St. Agatha, founded in 1400; William of Orange was murdered here in 1584. The chapel dates from 1471; its interior is remarkable for the wooden statues under the vaulting ribs. Today the Prinsenhof's collection includes 16th- and 17th-century paintings by Delft masters, local silverware, and Delft ceramics. The **Volkenkundig Museum Nusantara** (Nusantara Ethnographic Museum), part of the same complex, has a collection of objects from the former Netherlands colonies in Indonesia. ✉ *St. Agathaplein 1,* ☎ *015/2602358.* ⏲ *Tues.–Sat. 10–5, Sun. 1–5.*

The **Oude Kerk** (Old Church), a vast Gothic monument from the 13th century, overlooks the Oude Delft canal, the city's oldest waterway. The beautiful tower, surmounted by a brick spire, lists somewhat alarmingly. ✉ *Heilige Geest Kerkhof,* ☎ *015/2123015.* ⏲ *Apr.–Nov., Mon.–Sat. 10–5.*

The timbered rooms of the **Lambert van Meerten Museum** have been filled with an extensive collection of old Dutch and foreign tiles and Delft pottery since the museum was founded in the home of this successful 19th-century industrialist in 1908. ✉ *Oude Delft 199,* ☎ *015/2602358.* ⏲ *Tues.–Sat. 10–5, Sun. 1–5.*

When decorated porcelain brought to the Netherlands from China on East India Company ships during the 17th century became so popular that Dutch potters felt their livelihood threatened, they set about creating pottery to rival the Chinese product. This resulted in Delftware. Only two manufacturers still make hand-painted Delftware, and at both workshops you can still see the craftspeople at work: **De Delftse Pauw** (✉ Delftweg 133, ☎ 015/2124920) and **Koninklijke Porceleyne Fles** (Royal Delft; ✉ Rotterdamsweg 196, ☎ 015/2512030).

$$ ✕ **L'Orage.** This canal-side restaurant serves delicious fish steeped in tantalizing sauces. The work of chef-owner Jannie Munk is influenced by French cuisine, but she bases many of her dishes on recipes from her native Denmark. Main courses might include grilled bass served on a bed of risotto and sun-dried tomatoes. ✉ *Oude Delft 111b,* ☎ *015/2123629. Reservations essential. AE, DC, MC, V. Closed Mon. No lunch.*

$–$$ ✕ **Spijshuis De Dis.** Seafood is a house specialty at this favorite neighborhood spot, where a friendly staff serves typically Dutch cuisine. The mussels with garlic sauce are delicious, and you can try such delicacies as roast quail. Lunch is served only to groups of 20 or more and it is essential to make reservations. ✉ *Beestenmarkt 36,* ☎ *015/2131782. AE, MC, V. Closed Wed.*

$$ 🏨 **Hotel De Ark.** This bright, airy hotel in the center of old Delft comprises three 17th-century canal houses joined so nearly every room has a view of either the canal or the garden in back. Rooms are clean and modern. ✉ *Koornmarkt 59–65, 2611 EC,* ☎ *015/2157999,* FAX *015/2144997,* WEB *www.deark.nl. 16 rooms, 9 apartments. AE, DC, MC, V.*

$–$$ ★ **Hotel de Plataan.** Converted in 1994 from a rather grand old post office building, the hotel was decorated by a local artist in 1950s-style cream and Bordeaux red. Most rooms have a kitchen nook. The classic Grand Café Quercus serves drinks and snacks. ✉ *Doelenplein 10–11, 2611 BP,* ☎ *015/2126046,* FAX *015/2157327,* WEB *www.hoteldeplataan.nl. 21 rooms, 3 suites. AE, DC, MC, V.*

$–$$ **Hotel Leeuwenbrug.** On one of the prettiest canals in Delft, this traditional Dutch family-style hotel is in a former patrician mansion and an annex. The mansion is simpler, with smaller rooms; the annex is more contemporary and businesslike. You can breakfast overlooking the canal; rooms on the top floor of the annex overlook the city. ✉ *Koornmarkt 16, 2611 EE,* ☎ *015/2147741,* FAX *015/2159759,* WEB *www.leeuwenbrug.nl. 38 rooms. AE, MC, V.*

Rotterdam

Rotterdam is one of the few thoroughly modern cities in the Netherlands and the site of the world's largest and busiest port. Art lovers know the city for its extensive and outstanding collection of art; philosophers recall it as the city of Erasmus. Representative of the city's adventuresome modern architecture is the **Erasmusbrug** (Erasmus Bridge), an extraordinary, single-span pylon bridge over the Maas River, nicknamed "the Swan." This forms the main link with the **Kop van Zuid,** Rotterdam's phenomenal ongoing redevelopment project in former docklands on the south bank.

In the city center a most intriguing series of cube-shape apartments balance on a tall stem. One of these precarious-looking houses, the **Kijk-Kubus** (literally, "viewing cube"), just east of the center, is open to the public. ✉ *Overblaak 70,* ☎ *010/4142285.* ⏲ *Mar.–Dec., daily 11–5; Jan.–Feb., Fri.–Sun. 11–5.*

The biggest surprise in Rotterdam is the remarkable 48-km-long (30-mi-long) **Europoort** (Europort; ✉ Willemsplein), which handles more than 300 million tons of cargo every year and more ships than any other port in the world. It is the delta for three of Europe's most important rivers (the Rhine, the Waal, and the Maas). You can get to the piers by tram or Metro (blue line to the Leuvehaven station) from the train station. The 1¼-hour harbor tour illuminates Rotterdam's vital role in world trade.

You can also survey the harbor from the vantage point of the **Euromast** observation tower. Get there via the RET Metro red line to Dijkszicht. ✉ *Parkhaven 20,* ☎ *010/4364811,* WEB *www.euromast.nl.* ⏲ *Daily 10–5.*

The inner harbor's hodgepodge of cranes, barges, steamships, and old shipbuilding machinery looks like a maritime junkyard and is a work in progress: volunteers are restoring the vessels and machinery. The open-air museum of shipbuilding, shipping, and communications is part of the **Maritiem Museum Prins Hendrik** (Prince Henry Maritime Museum), housed in a large gray building at the head of the quay. Moored in the inner harbor adjacent to the museum is the historic 19th-century Royal Dutch Navy warship *De Buffel.* Within the museum are exhibits devoted to the history and activity of the great port outside. ✉ *Leuvehaven 1,* ☎ *010/4132680,* WEB *www.mmph.nl/splash.htm.* ⏲ *Sept.–June, Tues.–Sat. 10–5, Sun. 11–5; July–Aug., Mon.–Sat. 10–5, Sun. 11–5.*

The **Museumpark,** an easy stroll along the canal from Eendrachtsplein Metro station, is a welcome contrast to the industrial might of the Europoort and the Netherlands' maritime history. Three of Rotterdam's ★ art institutions are sited around these landscaped gardens. The **Boijmans Van Beuningen Museum** has a section that includes the work of Brueghel, Bosch, and Rembrandt, as well as a renowned print gallery with works by artists such as Dürer and Cézanne. Dalí and Magritte mix with the Impressionists in the Modern Arts collection. ✉ *Museumpark 18–20,* ☏ *010/4419400,* WEB *boijmans.kennisnet.nl.* ⏲ *Tues.–Sat. 10–5, Sun. 11–5.*

The **Nederlands Architectuurinstituut** (Netherlands Institute of Architecture), designed by Jo Coenen, hosts innovative exhibitions and lectures in the field of architecture, town and country planning, and interior design from the 1800s to the present. ✉ *Museumpark 25,* ☏ *010/4401200,* WEB *www.nai.nl.* ⏲ *Tues. 10–9, Wed.–Sat. 10–5, Sun. 11–5.*

The **Kunsthal** (Art Hall) in Museumpark mounts all manner of major temporary exhibitions—from prehistoric bones to Picasso retrospectives to avant-garde rows of compact cars. ✉ *Westzeedijk 341,* ☏ *010/4400300,* WEB *www.kunsthal.nl.* ⏲ *Tues.–Sat. 10–5, Sun. 11–5.*

Delfshaven—spelled Delftshaven when the Pilgrims set sail from here—is the last remaining nook of old Rotterdam. Rows of gabled buildings and a windmill line the waterfront. Today Delfshaven is an up-and-coming area of trendy galleries, cafés, and restaurants. ✉ *Voorhaven. From Delfshaven Metro station, double back along Schiedamseweg, then turn right down Aelbrechtskolk.*

$$–$$$ ✕ **Parkheuvel.** This award-winning two-star restaurant, run by chef-owner Cees Helder, is said to be popular among the harbor barons, who can oversee their dockside territory from the bay windows of this tastefully modern, semicircular building. Luxuries such as truffle are added to the freshest ingredients, with the day's menu dictated by the availability of the best produce at that morning's markets. ✉ *Heuvellaan 21,* ☏ *010/4360530. AE, DC, MC, V. Closed Sun. No lunch Sat.*

$–$$$ ✕ **Parkzicht.** Beside a lake in the city's Maas Park, this airy 19th-century building has the sunniest terrace in town. Take time for a lazy lunch or high tea in the casual brasserie, join the trendy for a cocktail at the marble bar, or revel in a full dinner from the cosmopolitan menu in the upstairs restaurant. Influences run from Sumatra to Norway, and there is an oyster bar, as well as a selection of caviars to whet your appetite. ✉ *Kievitslaan 25,* ☏ *010/4368888. AE, DC, MC, V.*

$–$$ ✕ **Loos.** This stylish café is in one of the city's few remaining old neighborhoods. The fare is adventurous French-influenced Dutch, with such dishes as braised calf's tail with truffle sauces or sea bass stir-fried with vegetables. ✉ *Westplein 1,* ☏ *010/4117723. AE, MC, V. No lunch weekends.*

$$$–$$$$ 🏨 **Bilderberg Parkhotel.** Located on one of Rotterdam's main axes, within walking distance of all neighborhoods, this hotel was built as a town house in the late 19th century. In the early 1990s it was modernized, and a colossal steel-faced tower was constructed. The Empress serves fine French cuisine in the classical surroundings of the old wing of the hotel. ✉ *Westersingel 70, 3015 LB,* ☏ *010/4363611,* FAX *010/4364212,* WEB *www.bilderberg.nl/parkhotel. 187 rooms, 2 suites. Restaurant. AE, DC, MC, V.*

$$$ 🏨 **Golden Tulip Rotterdam.** Close to the river and at the heart of the shopping district, this hotel is a surprisingly beautiful Art Deco building in the midst of post-war architecture. The Takura serves Japanese fare, while more traditional meals are available in the brasserie. ✉ *Coolsingel/Aert van Nesstraat 4, 3012 CA,* ☎ *010/2067800,* FAX *010/4117423. 215 rooms. 2 restaurants. AE, DC, MC, V.*

$$$ **Hotel Inntel Rotterdam.** A location right on the riverside, with a view of the landmark Erasmus bridge, is ideal to get a feel for this world port. Le Papillon has great views of the harbor and serves traditional French cuisine. ✉ *Leuvehaven 80, 3011 EA,* ☎ *010/4134139,* FAX *010/4133222,* WEB *www.hotelinntel.com. 149 rooms. Restaurant, indoor pool, gym. AE, DC, MC, V.*

$–$$$ **Hotel New York.** The twin towers of the Hotel New York have been a feature of Rotterdam's skyline for almost a century. In the days of transatlantic liners, it was the head office of the Holland-America Line. Some rooms retain the original walnut paneling and restored Art Nouveau carpets, while others are modern in design. Downstairs, the huge café-restaurant serves everything from English afternoon tea to a choice of five different types of oyster. ✉ *Koninginnenhoofd 1, 3072 AD,* ☎ *010/4390500,* FAX *010/4842701. 72 rooms, 1 penthouse apartment. Restaurant. AE, DC, MC, V.*

$ **Grand Hotel Central.** For the traveler on a budget, this basic hotel is a reasonable bet and ideally located for shops, restaurants, and museums. Rooms in this late-19th-century building are spacious and airy with simple modern furniture. Breakfast is served in the large dining room. ✉ *Kruiskade 12, 3012 EH,* ☎ *010/4140744,* FAX *010/4125325. 64 rooms. AE, MC, V.*

The Hague, Delft, and Rotterdam Essentials

EMERGENCIES

The Doctors Telephone supplies names and opening hours of pharmacists and dentists, as well as doctors, outside normal surgery hours. Calls cost Fl. 1.05 per minute.

➤ EMERGENCY SERVICES: **Ambulance, Police, Fire, and Rescue** (☎ 112). **Doctors Telephone** (☎ 0900/8600 in the Hague; 010/4201100 in Rotterdam; 020/5923434 in Amsterdam).

TOURS

BOAT TOURS

In Scheveningen there are fishing-boat tours around the Dutch coast; Sportsviscentrum Trip 30 offers circle tours and seasonal fishing expeditions. In Delft, the tourist office organizes boat tours along the unspoiled canal system. Spido Rondvaarten, the main boat company, lets you cruise the port of Rotterdam on a basic tour of 1¼ hours (year-round), or choose one that lasts as long as nine hours (midsummer only). They also operate 2½-hour summer evening music-and-dinner cruises of the inner harbor. The pier can be reached by taking the RET Metro blue line toward Spijkenisse to the Leuvehaven station and walking to the end of the boulevard.

➤ FEES AND SCHEDULES: **Spido Rondvaarten** (✉ Willemsplein, ☎ 010/4135400). **Sportsviscentrum Trip 30** (☎ 070/3541122).

BUS TOURS

Sightseeing tours of the Hague can be arranged by or through the main VVV tourist office next to the train station. The two-hour Royal Tour by bus departs from this office at 1 PM Tuesday–Saturday from May to August, also on Sundays in July and August, and takes passengers past Queen Beatrix's residences. From April through September, daily two-hour bus tours of Rotterdam are conducted by the VVV Rotterdam Tourist Office, departing from the office at 1:30 PM.

WALKING TOURS

Scheveningen is for walkers. The Scheveningen VVV office has information about coastal strolls. Delft is best seen on foot. The VVV Delft Tourist Office organizes tours.

TRANSPORTATION AROUND THE HAGUE, DELFT, AND ROTTERDAM

The heart of the Hague and Delft are compact enough to be explored on foot. Scheveningen is reached from the Hague's center by bus or tram; public transportation is more convenient than driving because of severe parking problems at the resort. The RET Metro is an easy-to-use option for getting around Rotterdam; the two main branches (north–south and east–west) cross in the heart of the business district.

VISITOR INFORMATION

➤ TOURIST INFORMATION: **Delft** (VVV; ✉ Markt 83–85, ☏ 0900/3353888, Fl. 1 per minute). **The Hague** (VVV; ✉ Babylon Center, Koningin Julianaplein 30, next to Den Haag CS train station, ☏ 0900/3403505, 75¢ per minute). **Rotterdam** (VVV; ✉ Coolsingel 67, ☏ 0900/4034065, 50¢ per minute). **Scheveningen** (VVV; ✉ Gevers Deynootweg 1134, ☏ 0900/3403505, 75¢ per minute).

22 NORWAY

OSLO; THE COAST ROAD TO STAVANGER; THROUGH TELEMARK TO BERGEN; ABOVE BERGEN: THE FAR NORTH

ON NORWAY'S DRAMATIC WEST COAST, deep fjords knife into steep mountain ranges. Inland, cross-country ski trails follow frozen streams, and downhill trails slice through forests that are carpeted with wildflowers and berries in summer. In older villages, wooden houses spill down toward docks where Viking ships were once moored. Small fishing boats, pleasure craft, and large industrial oil tankers dot the maritime horizon.

Inhabited since 1700 BC, Norway is today a peaceful nation, but from the 8th to the 10th century AD the Vikings marauded as far afield as Seville and the Isle of Man and engaged in vicious infighting at home. This fierce spirit remained alive, despite Norway's subsequent centuries of subjugation by the Danes and Swedes. Independence came early in the 20th century but was tested during World War II, when the Germans occupied the country. Norwegian Resistance fighters rose to the challenge, eventually sabotaging Nazi efforts to develop atomic weapons.

The foundations for modern Norwegian culture were laid in the 19th century, during the period of union with Sweden, which lasted until 1905. Oslo blossomed at this time, and Norway produced its three greatest men of arts and letters: composer Edvard Grieg (1843–1907), playwright Henrik Ibsen (1828–1906), and painter Edvard Munch (1863–1944). Other notable Norwegians of this period were the polar explorers Roald Amundsen and Fridtjof Nansen.

The fjords, however, are Norway's true claim to fame. They were formed during an ice age a million years ago, when the ice cap created enormous pressure by burrowing deep into existing mountain-bound riverbeds. There was less pressure along the coast, so the entrances to most fjords are shallow, about 500 ft, while inland depths reach as much as 4,000 ft. Although Norway's entire coastline is notched with fjords, the most breathtaking sights are on the west coast between Stavanger and Trondheim, and the northern Helgeland coastline to the Lofoten Islands. From the sheltered villages deep in fjord country to the wildest windswept plateaus in Finnmark, Norway's natural beauty captivates both visitors and residents, transforming many into serious outdoor enthusiasts.

NORWAY A TO Z

To research prices, get advice from other travelers, and book travel arrangements, visit www.fodors.com.

AIR TRAVEL

Fares are high, so be sure to ask about the special rates available year-round within Norway. For longer distances, flying can be cheaper than renting a car. Inquire about Visit Norway and Visit Scandinavia passes, which provide relatively cheap domestic-flight coupons.

CARRIERS

Contact the following Norwegian airlines for more information: SAS, Braathens SAFE AS, and Widerøe.

➤ AIRLINES AND CONTACTS: **Braathens SAFE AS** (✉ Oslo Central Station, ☎ 81001200). **SAS** (✉ Oslo Central Station; beginning of Karl Johans Gt., ☎ 81003300). **Widerøe** (✉ Volls vei 6, Box 131, 1324 Lysaker, ☎ 67596600).

BOAT AND FERRY TRAVEL

Norway's long, fjord-indented coastline is served by an intricate network of ferries and passenger ships. A wide choice of services is available, from simple hops across fjords (saving many kilometers of traveling) and excursions among the thousands of islands to luxury cruises and long journeys up the coast. Most ferries carry cars. Reservations are required on journeys of more than one day but are not needed for simple fjord crossings. Fares and exact departure times depend on the season and the availability of ships. Contact Nortra (Norwegian Travel Association) or the Norway Information Centre for details (☞ Visitor Information, *below*).

One of the world's great sea voyages is aboard one of the mail-and-passenger Hurtigruta ships that run up the Norwegian coast from Bergen to Kirkenes, well above the Arctic Circle. Contact Tromsø Coastal Steamer Company.

➤ BOAT AND FERRY INFORMATION: **Tromsø Coastal Steamer Company** (main office; ✉ Tromsø, ☎ 77648200 or 81030000).

BUS TRAVEL

The Norwegian bus network makes up for some limitations of the country's train system, and several routes are particularly scenic. For example, the Nord-Norge Buss Service (North Norway Bus Service) goes from Fauske (on the train line to Bodø) to Sortland; from Sortland the Tromsø–innland rutebil (Tromsø–inland coach) goes right up to Kirkenes on the Russian–Norwegian border. Buses leave the Oslo area from Bussterminalen (Bus Terminal), close to the Oslo Sentralstasjon (Central Station). For general information about bus routes and schedules throughout the country, you can also call Norway Bussekspress.

➤ BUS INFORMATION: **Bussterminalen** (✉ Galleriet Oslo, Schweigaardsgt. 10, ☎ 23002449). **Nord-Norge Buss Service** (✉ 8400 Sortland, ☎ 76111111). **Norway Bussekspress** (☎ 82054300). **Tromsø–innland rutebil** (☎ 77852100).

BUSINESS HOURS

Banks are open weekdays 8:30–3:30; from June to August, hours are 8:15–3. Museums are usually open Tuesday–Sunday 10–3 or 4. Shops are usually open weekdays from 9 or 10 until 6 (Thursday until 7 or 8) and Saturday 9–3 or 4. Shopping malls are often open until 8 on weeknights.

Norway (Norge)

0
200 miles
0
300 km
North Cape
Vardø
Vadsø
Hammerfest
Kirkenes
ATLANTIC
OCEAN
Alta
Masi
Tromsø
Kantokeino
FINLAND
Harstad
Bardu
Norwegian
Sea
Narvik
Svolvoer
Lofoten
Vestfjorden
Bodø
Fauske
Saltdal
Arctic Circle
Mo i Rana
Umbukta
Sandnessjøen
Mosjøen
Brønnøysund
E6
SWEDEN
Gulf of Bothnia
Vikna
Namsos
Steinkjer
Trondheim
Meråker
Støren
Kristiansund N.
Molde
70
Oppdal
Ålesund
Røros
Tynset
E69
Dombås
Otta
Nordfjord
Koppang
Florø
Jostedalsbreen
Rena
Lillehammer
Sognefjorden
Lake Mjøsa
Hamar
Voss
E68
Eidsvoll
Bergen
Hardangerfjorden
7
Hønefoss
40
Oslo
11
Kongsberg
Sarpsborg
Baltic Sea
Haugesund
Drammen
Fredrikstad
Larvik
Oslofjord
Skien
Sandefjord
Stavanger
39
Evje
Arendal
Egersund
Skagerrak
Kattegat
Grimstad
Mandal
Kristiansand S.

CAR TRAVEL

EMERGENCIES

Norges Automobil Forbund (NAF), the Norwegian Automobile Association, patrols main roads and has emergency telephones on mountain roads. For NAF 24-hour service, dial the number listed below.

➤ CONTACTS: **Norges Automobil Forbund** (✉ Storgt. 2, 0155 Oslo, ☎ 81000606, 81000505, or 22341400, WEB www.naf.no).

GASOLINE

Gas costs NKr 8–NKr 9 per liter and diesel costs NKr 7–NKr 8 per liter. Gas stations are not hard to find in remote areas.

PARKING

Street parking in cities and towns is clearly marked. There are also municipal parking lots. You cannot park on main roads or on bends. Check the leaflet "Parking in Oslo," available free from the tourist office, at toll stations, and at the City Hall; or ask at your hotel.

ROAD CONDITIONS

Away from the major routes, roads are narrow and winding, so don't expect to average more than 50–70 kph (30–40 mph), especially in fjord country. Even the best roads suffer from frost, and mountain passes may be closed in winter. Snow tires (preferably studded) are advised in winter in most areas.

RULES OF THE ROAD

Driving is on the right. The speed limit is 90 kph (55 mph) on highways, 80 kph (50 mph) on main roads, 50 kph (30 mph) in towns, and 30–40 kph (18–25 mph) in residential areas. The use of headlights at all times is mandatory. For assistance contact Norges Automobil Forbund (☞ *above*). Remember to yield to the vehicle approaching from the right. Passing areas on narrow roads are marked with a white *M* (for *møteplass*) on a blue background.

CUSTOMS AND DUTIES

Residents of non-European countries who are over 18 may import duty-free into Norway 400 cigarettes or 500 grams of other tobacco products. Residents of European countries who are over 18 may import 200 cigarettes or 250 grams of other tobacco goods. Anyone can bring in souvenirs, gifts, perfume, and eau de cologne to a value of NKr 5,000 after being out of the country for more than 24 hours. Within 24 hours, you may bring in goods duty free valued up to NKr 2,000. Anyone over 20 may bring in 1 liter of liquor, 1 liter of wine, and 2 liters of beer or 2 liters of wine and 2 liters of beer. Travelers who are at least 18 years old may bring in 2 liters of wine and 2 liters of beer.

DINING

The Norwegian diet emphasizes protein and carbohydrates. Breakfast is usually a large buffet of smoked fish, cheeses, sausage, cold meats, and whole-grain breads accompanied by tea, coffee, or milk. Lunch is simple, usually *smørbrød* (open-face sandwiches). Restaurant and hotel dinners are usually three-course meals, often starting with soup and ending with fresh fruit and berries. Meals are generally expensive, so take hotel breakfast when it's offered. Spirits are not served on Sunday, although beer and wine are available in most establishments. Alcohol is very expensive and, except in restaurants, is sold only during strictly regulated hours at state-owned *vinmonopol* stores. Note that laws relating to drinking and driving are very strict.

Prices are for one main course at dinner.

CATEGORY	COST
$$$$	over NKr 250
$$$	NKr 150–NKr 250
$$	NKr 100–NKr 150
$	under NKr 100

MEALTIMES

Lunch is from noon to 3 at restaurants featuring a *koldtbord*—a Scandinavian buffet, primarily for special occasions and visitors, but locals generally eat lunch anywhere between 11:30 and 1. Dinner has traditionally been early, but in hotels and major restaurants it is now more often from 6 to 11.

RESERVATIONS AND DRESS

Unless otherwise indicated, jacket and tie or high-fashion casual wear is recommended for restaurants in the $$$$ and $$$ price categories; during the summer, neat casual dress is acceptable in most places.

EMBASSIES

Australia, Ireland, New Zealand, and South Africa have consular offices in Oslo (☞ Oslo Essentials, *below*).

➤ CANADA: (✉ Wergelandsvn. 7, 0244 Oslo, ☎ 22995300).

➤ UNITED KINGDOM: (✉ Thos. Heftyesgt. 8, 0244 Oslo, ☎ 23132700).

➤ UNITED STATES: (✉ Drammensvn. 18, 0244 Oslo, ☎ 22448550).

HOLIDAYS

January 1; Palm Sunday; Good Friday; Easter Sunday and Monday; May 1 (Labor Day); May 17 (Constitution Day); Ascension (mid-May to early June); Pentecost Sunday and Monday (late May to early June); December 25–26.

LANGUAGE

There are two official forms of the Norwegian language—*bokmål* and *nynorsk*—along with many dialects. As is typical of Scandinavian languages, Norwegian's additional vowels—æ, ø, and å—come at the end of the alphabet in the phone book.

English is the main foreign language taught in schools, and movies, music, and TV reinforce its popularity. It is widely spoken by people in larger cities and most commercial establishments.

LODGING

Prices are summer/weekend rates for two people in a double room with bath and include breakfast, service, and taxes. Overnight rates during the week can be NKr 200–NKr 300 extra.

CATEGORY	MAJOR CITIES	OTHER AREAS
$$$$	over NKr 1,300	over NKr 1,000
$$$	NKr 1,000–NKr 1,300	NKr 850–NKr 1,000
$$	NKr 800–NKr 1,000	NKr 650–NKr 850
$	under NKr 800	under NKr 650

CABIN AND HOME RENTALS

Norwegians escape to *hytter* (mountain cabins) whenever they have the chance. Stay in one for a week or two and you'll see why—magnificent scenery, pure air, edible wild berries, and a chance to hike, fish, or cross-country ski. For information on renting cabins, farms, or private homes, write to Den Norske Hytteformidling A.S., or get the brochure "Norsk Hytteferie" from tourist offices. An unusual alternative is to rent a *rorbu* (fisherman's dwelling) in the northerly Lofoten Islands. Contact Destination Lofoten.

➤ CONTACTS: **Den Norske Hytteformidling A.S.** (✉ Box 309, Sentrum, 0103 Oslo, ☎ 22356270, WEB www.hytte.com). **Destination Lofoten** (✉ Box 210, 8301 Svolvær, ☎ 76073000).

CAMPING

There are 1,160 registered campsites in the country, many in spectacular surroundings. Prices vary according to the facilities provided: a family with a car and tent can expect to pay about NKr 80–NKr 150 per night. Some campsites have log cabins available from between NKr 20 and NKr 600 per night. *Camping Norway* is available from tourist offices and the Norges Automobil Forbund.

➤ CONTACTS: **Norges Automobil Forbund** (NAF; ✉ Storgt. 2, 0105 Oslo, ☎ 22341400, WEB www.naf.no).

HOSTELS

Norway has about 100 hostels; some are schools or farms in winter.

➤ HOSTEL ORGANIZATIONS: **Norske Vandrerhjem** (NoVa; ✉ Dronningensgt. 26, 0154 Oslo, ☎ 23139300, WEB www.vandrerhjem.no).

HOTELS

Accommodations in Norway are usually spotless, and smaller establishments are often family-run. Service is attentive and considerate, right down to blackout curtains to block out the midnight sun. The Fjord Pass, which costs about NKr 85 (around $10), is valid for discounts at 250 establishments. Hotels in larger towns have special summer rates from late June to early August, and some chains have their own discount offers—see Norway's annual accommodation guide at tourist offices. Discounts in smaller hotels are offered to guests staying several days; meals are then included in the rate.

➤ CONTACTS: **Fjord Pass** (✉ Fjord Tours, Box 1752, 5024 Bergen, ☎ 55551630, WEB www.fjordpass.no).

MAIL AND SHIPPING

Opening times for post offices vary throughout the country, but in general they are weekdays 9–5 and Saturday 10–2. Post offices cash traveler's checks, exchange foreign currency, and provide postal services. All mailing addresses in Norway include a four-digit zip code. The Oslo Hoved Post Kontor (Oslo Main Post Office) is open weekdays 8–7, Saturday 10–3.

If you're uncertain about where you'll be staying, have your mail marked "poste restante" and sent to the town where you plan to pick it up. Your last name should be underlined. American Express offices will also hold mail (nonmembers pay a small fee on collection).

➤ POST OFFICE: **Oslo Hoved Post Kontor** (✉ Dronningensgt. 15).

POSTAL RATES

Letters and postcards to the United States cost NKr 7 for the first 20 grams. The rate within Europe is NKr 6 for the first 20 grams.

MONEY MATTERS

Norway has a high standard—and cost—of living, but there are ways to save money by taking advantage of special offers for accommodations and travel during the tourist season and on weekends.

Some sample prices include: cup of coffee, NKr 12–NKr 25; ½ liter of beer, NKr 35–NKr 55; soft drink, NKr 15–NKr 35; ham sandwich, NKr 30–NKr 50.

CURRENCY

The unit of currency in Norway is the krone, written as Kr. on price tags but officially NOK (bank designation), NKr, or kr. The krone is divided into 100 øre. Bills of NKr 50, 100, 200, 500, and 1,000 are in general use. Coins are in denominations of 50 øre and 1, 5, 10, and 20 kroner. Credit cards are accepted in most hotels, stores, restaurants, and many gas stations and garages, but generally not in smaller shops and inns in rural areas. The exchange rate at press time (summer 2001) was NKr 9.09 to the U.S. dollar, NKr 5.82 to the Canadian dollar, NKr 13.10 to the pound sterling, NKr 10.28 to the Irish punt, NKr 4.65 to the Australian dollar, NKr 3.73 to the New Zealand dollar, and NKr 1.13 to the South African rand.

SHOPPING

Prices of handmade articles are government controlled, and selection is widest in Oslo, so that's the best place to do your shopping: pewter, silver, glass, sheepskin, leather, painted-wood decorations, kitchenware, knitwear, and wall hangings all make special souvenirs.

TAXES

VALUE-ADDED TAX (VAT)

Much of the 23% Norwegian value-added tax (VAT) will be refunded to visitors who spend more than NKr 308 in any single store. Ask for a special tax-free check and show your passport to confirm that you are not a resident. All purchases must be sealed and presented together with the tax-free check at the tax-free counter at foreign ferry ports and at airports and border posts. The VAT will be refunded, minus a service charge. You can get general information about the tax-free system by calling the number below.

➤ VAT REFUNDS: **Tax-Free Information** (☎ 67156010).

TELEPHONES

COUNTRY AND AREA CODES

The international country code for Norway is 47.

DIRECTORY AND OPERATOR ASSISTANCE

For local information, dial 180. For international information, dial 181. For international collect calls, dial 115.

INTERNATIONAL CALLS

Cheap rates for international calls apply only after 10 PM. International calls can be made from any pay phone. For calls to North America, dial 00–1, then the area code and number. When dialing the United Kingdom, omit the initial zero of the area code. To reach an AT&T or MCI WorldCom operator, dial one of the access codes below.

➤ ACCESS CODES: **AT&T** (☎ 80019011). **MCI WorldCom** (☎ 80019912).

LOCAL CALLS

Domestic rates are reduced 5 PM–8 AM weekdays and all day on weekends. Area codes are not used in Norway. The cost of calls within the country varies according to distance: in Oslo, the cost goes up according to the amount of time used after the three-minute flat fee. The Oslo phone book has dialing information in English.

PUBLIC PHONES

Avoid using room phones in hotels. In public booths you can find card phones or coin phones. Be sure to read the instructions; some phones require the coins to be deposited before dialing, some after. You can buy telephone cards at Narvesen kiosks or at the post office. The largest coins generally accepted are NKr 10, although some new phones take NKr 20 coins. Most older phones take only NKr 1 or NKr 5 coins. The minimum deposit is NKr 2 or NKr 3, depending on the phone.

TIPPING

A 10%–12% service charge is added to most bills at hotels and restaurants. If you have had exceptional service, give an additional 5%–10% tip. Round off a taxi fare to the next higher unit, or a little more if the driver has been particularly helpful with luggage. If the porter helps with your luggage, give NKr 15–NKr 20. Tip with kroner only.

TRAIN TRAVEL

Trains are punctual and comfortable, and most routes are scenic. Lines fan out from Oslo and leave the coastline (except in the south) to buses and ferries. Reservations are required on all *ekspresstog* (express trains) and night trains. The Oslo–Bergen route is especially beautiful, and the Oslo–Trondheim–Bodø route takes you within the Arctic Circle. Do not miss the side trips from Myrdal to Flåm from the Oslo–Bergen line and Dombås to Åndalsnes from the Oslo–Trondheim line. NSB trains leave Oslo from Oslo Central Station.

FARES AND SCHEDULES

Two types of ScanRail passes, good in Norway, Sweden, Denmark, and Finland, are available, offering unlimited travel on a given number of travel days within a specified period (on 5 days out of 15 or 21 days out of 21). These are available in Norway through NSB, the Norwegian State Railways. A Norway Rail Pass, also available from NSB, offers a choice of one or two weeks unlimited rail travel or three travel days within a month within Norway. Reduced fares during off-peak times ("green" routes) are also available if booked in advance.

➤ TRAIN INFORMATION: **NSB** (Norwegian State Railways; ✉ Prinsensgt. 7–9, 0048 Oslo, ☎ 23150000 or 81500888, FAX 23150401, WEB www.nsb.no). **Oslo Central Station** (✉ Jernbanetorget, beginning of Karl Johans Gt.).

VISITOR INFORMATION

➤ TOURIST INFORMATION: **Nortra** (Norwegian Travel Association; ✉ Drammensvn. 40, Postboks 2893, Solli, 0230 Oslo, ☎ 22925200). **Norway Information Centre** (✉ Vestbanen, Brynjulf Bullspl. 1, 0250 Oslo, ☎ 23117880, WEB www.visitnorway.com; Oslo Central Station, east of Strandgt.). **Trafikanten** (✉ Oslo Central Station, east of Strandgt., ☎ 22177030; 177 for Oslo public transportation).

WHEN TO GO

Norway is an important winter sports center. January, February, and early March are good skiing months. Avoid late April, when sleet, rain, and repeated thaws may ruin the good skiing snow and leave roads—and spirits—in bad shape. The country virtually closes down for the five-day Easter holiday, when Norwegians make their annual migration to the mountains. In May the days are long and sunny, cultural life is still going strong, and *Syttende mai* (Constitution Day, May 17), with all its festivities, is worth a trip in itself. Norwegians tend to take their vacations in July and the first part of August. Summers are generally mild. With the midnight sun, even in the "southern" city of Oslo, night seems more like twilight around midnight, and dawn comes by 2 AM. The weather can be fickle, and rain gear and sturdy waterproof shoes are recommended even in summer.

CLIMATE

The following are the average daily maximum and minimum temperatures for Oslo.

Jan.	28F	– 2C	**May**	61F	16C	**Sept.**	60F	16C
	19	– 7		43	6		46	8
Feb.	30F	– 1C	**June**	68F	20C	**Oct.**	48F	9C
	19	– 7		50	10		38	3
Mar.	39F	4C	**July**	72F	22C	**Nov.**	38F	3C
	25	– 4		55	13		31	– 1
Apr.	50F	10C	**Aug.**	70F	21C	**Dec.**	32F	0C
	34	1		54	12		25	– 4

OSLO

Although it is one of the world's largest capital cities in area, Oslo has only about 500,000 inhabitants. In recent years the city has become more lively: shops are open later, and plentiful pubs, cafés, and restaurants are crowded at all hours, especially later in the week. The city celebrated its 1,000th anniversary in 2000.

Exploring Oslo

Numbers in the margin correspond to points of interest on the Oslo map.

The downtown area is compact, but the city limits include forests, fjords, and mountains, giving Oslo a pristine airiness that complements its urban dignity. Explore downtown on foot, and then venture beyond via bus, streetcar, or train.

★ 10 **Aker Brygge** (Aker Wharf). The quayside shopping and cultural center, with a theater, cinemas, and galleries among the stores and restaurants, is a great place to linger late into summer nights. It's in the central harbor—the heart of Oslo and head of the fjord. ✉ *Off Dokkvn.*, WEB *www.akerbrygge.no*

9 **Akershus Slott og Festning** (Akershus Castle and Fortress). This fortified harbor-front castle was built in 1299 and restored in 1527 by Christian IV of Denmark (Denmark then ruled Norway) after it was damaged by fire. Christian laid out the present city of Oslo (naming it Christiania, after himself) around his new residence; Oslo's street plan still follows his design. Some rooms are open for guided tours, and the grounds form a park. Also on the grounds are the **Forsvarsmuséet** (Defense Museum) and **Hjemmefrontmuseum** (Resistance Museum). Both give you a feel for the Norwegian fighting spirit throughout history and especially during the German occupation, when the Nazis set up headquarters on this site and had a number of patriots executed here. ✉ *Festningspl.*, ☎ *23093553 castle; 23093769 Forsvarsmuséet; 23093138 Hjemmefrontmuseum.* ⏲ *Castle May–mid-Sept., Mon.–Sat. 10–4, Sun. 12:30–4; Sept. and Apr., Sun. 12:30–4; guided tours May–Sept., Mon.–Sat. 11, 1, and 3, Sun. 1 and 3. Forsvarsmuséet June–Aug., weekdays 10–6, weekends 11–4; Sept.–May, weekdays 10–3, weekends 11–4. Hjemmefrontmuseum mid-Apr.–mid-June, weekdays 10–4, weekends 11–4; mid-June–Sept., weekdays 10–5, weekends 11–5; Oct.–mid-Apr., weekdays 10–3, weekends 11–4.*

7 **Astrup Fearnley Muséet.** This private museum collection was founded by a leading Oslo shipping family and displays postwar and contemporary works of art and sculptures by Norwegian and international artists, including pieces by the celebrated British artist Damien Hirst. Special exhibitions and guided tours are held regularly throughout the year. ✉ *Grev Wedels Pl. 9*, ☎ *22936060 or 22936015*, WEB *www.afmoma.no.* ⏲ *Tues.–Wed. and Fri. 11–5, weekends noon–5.*

Oslo

KEY

Tourist Information

Aker Brygge **10**
Akershus Slott og Festning **9**
Astrup Fearnley Muséet **7**
Ekebergsletta Parken **19**
Fram-Muséet **16**
Historisk Museum . . . **2**
Holmenkollbakken **21**
Kon-Tiki Muséet **15**
Munch-Muséet **17**
Muséet for Samtidskunst **8**
Nasjonalgalleriet . . . **3**
Nationaltheatret **4**
Norsk Folkemuseum **13**
Oslo Domkirke **6**
Oslo Ladegård **18**
Oslo Rådhus **12**
Slottet **1**
Stenersenmuséet . . . **11**
Stortinget **5**
Vigelandsparken . . **20**
Vikingskiphuset . . . **14**

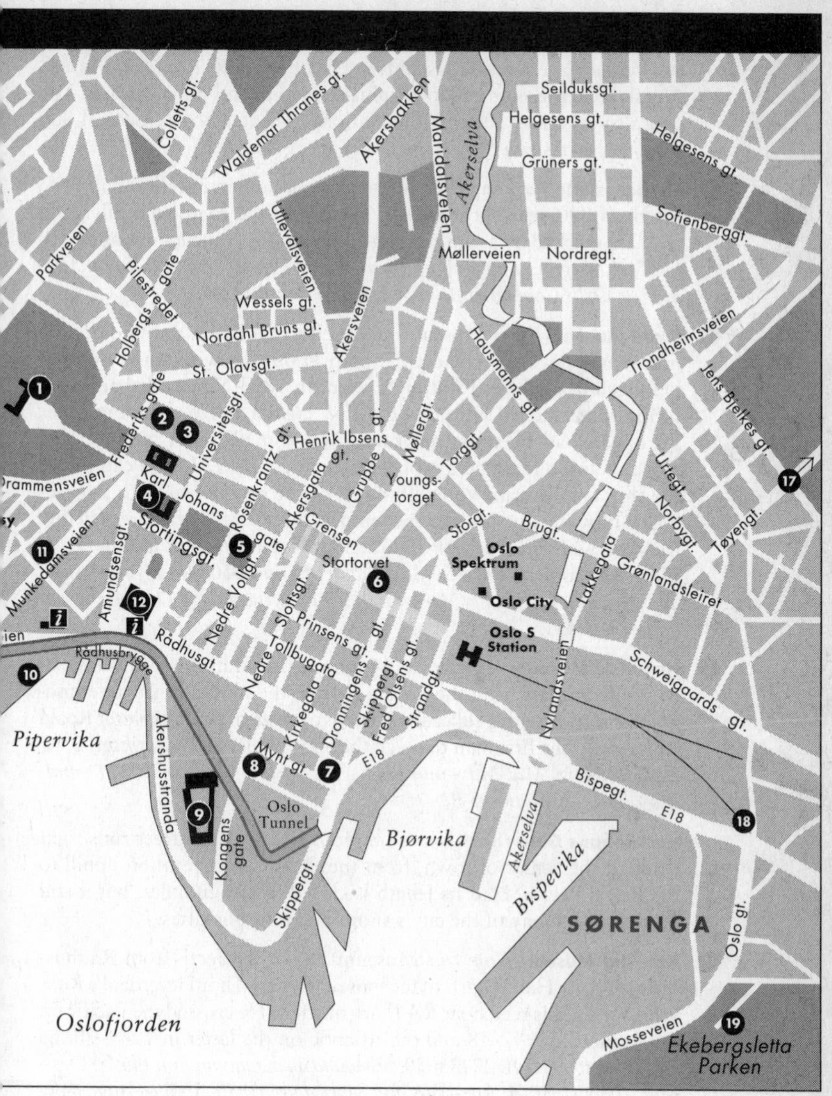

Seilduksgt.
Helgesens gt.
Grüners gt.
Helgesens gt.
Sofienberggt.
Akerselva
Maridalsveien
Akersbakken
Waldemar Thranes gt.
Colletts gt.
Parkveien
Pilestredet
Holbergs gate
Ullevålsveien
Møllerveien
Nordregt.
Wessels gt.
Nordahl Bruns gt.
St. Olavsgt.
Akersveien
Hausmanns gt.
Trondheimsveien
Jens Bjelkes gt.
Frederiks gate
Universitetsgt.
Henrik Ibsens gt.
Rosenkrantz' gt.
Akersgata
Grubbe gt.
Møllergt.
Torggt.
Youngs-torget
Urtegt.
Norbygt.
Tøyengt.
Drammensveien
Karl Johans gate
Stortingsgt.
Grensen
Storgt.
Brugt.
Oslo Spektrum
Lakkegata
Grønlandsleiret
Munkedamsveien
Amundsensgt.
Nedre Vollgt.
Stortorvet
Oslo City
Oslo S Station
Slottsgt.
Prinsens gt.
Rådhusgt.
Rådhusbrygge
Nedre Tollbugata
Kirkegata
Dronningens gt.
Skippergt.
Fred Olsens gt.
Strandgt.
Nylandsveien
Schweigaards gt.
Pipervika
Akershusstranda
Mynt gt.
E18
Bispegt.
Oslo Tunnel
Kongens gate
Bjørvika
Akerselva
Bispevika
Skippergt.
SØRENGA
Oslo gt.
Oslofjorden
Mosseveien
Ekebergsletta Parken

Bygdøy. In summer, ferries make the seven-minute run from Rådhusbryggen (City Hall Wharf) across the fjord to the Bygdøy peninsula, where there are several museums (☞ *Fram*-Muséet, *Kon-Tiki* Muséet, Norsk Folkemuseum, Vikingskiphuset, *below*) and some beaches. You can also take Bus 30 from the National Theater or the Central Station. ⏲ *Ferries run May–Sept., daily every ½ hr 8:15–5:45.*

19 **Ekebergsletta Parken.** The oldest traces of human habitation in Oslo are the 5,000-year-old stone carvings across the road from this park; they are marked by a sign reading FORTIDSMINNE (ancient monument). ✉ *Karlsborgvn.; take Trikk (Tram) 18 or 19 east from National Theater or Oslo Central Station to Sjømannsskolen stop.*

16 ***Fram*-Muséet** (*Fram* Museum). Housed in a triangular building, the museum is devoted to the polar ship *Fram,* the wooden vessel that belonged to explorer Fridtjof Nansen. In 1893 Nansen led an expedition that reached latitude 86°14′N, farther north than any other European had been at that time. Active in Russian famine-relief work, Nansen received a Nobel Peace Prize in 1922. You can board the ship and imagine yourself in one of the tiny berths with a force-9 gale blowing outside and the temperature dozens of degrees below freezing. ✉ *Bygdøynes,* ☎ *23282950,* WEB *www.fram.museum.no.* ⏲ *Mar.–Apr., daily 11–3:45; May and Sept., daily 10–4:45; June–Aug., daily 9–6:45; Oct., daily 10–4:45; Nov.–Feb., weekdays 11–2:45, weekends 11–3:45.*

2 **Historisk Museum** (Historical Museum). In addition to displays of daily life and art from the Viking period, the museum has an ethnographic section with a collection related to the great polar explorer Roald Amundsen, the first man to reach the South Pole. ✉ *Frederiksgt. 2,* ☎ *22859964.* ⏲ *Mid-May–mid-Sept., Tues.–Sun. 11–3; mid-Sept.–mid-May, Tues.–Sun. noon–3.*

Karl Johans Gate (Karl Johan's Street). Oslo's main street runs right through the center of town, from the Oslo Central Station uphill to the Royal Palace. Half its length is closed to automobiles, but it still bustles with many of the city's shops and outdoor cafés.

★ 15 ***Kon-Tiki* Muséet** (*Kon-Tiki* Museum). Take the ferry from Rådhusbryggen (City Hall Wharf) to the museum where Thor Heyerdahl's *Kon-Tiki* raft and his reed boat *RA II* are on view. He crossed the Pacific on the former in 1947–48 and the Atlantic on the latter in 1969–70. ✉ *Bygdøynesvn. 36,* ☎ *22438050,* WEB *www.media.uio.no/kon-tiki.* ⏲ *Oct.–Mar., daily 10:30–4; Apr.–May and Sept., daily 10:30–5; June–Aug., daily 9:30–5:45.*

★ 17 **Munch-Muséet** (Munch Museum). In 1940, four years before his death, Edvard Munch bequeathed much of his work to the city; the museum opened in 1963, the centennial of his birth. Although only a fraction of its 22,000 items—books, paintings, drawings, prints, sculptures, and letters—are on display, you can still get a sense of the tortured Expressionism that was to have such an effect on European painting. ✉ *Tøyengt. 53; Bus 29 from Rådhuset or T-bane from Nationaltheatret to Tøyen in northeast Oslo,* ☎ *23241400,* WEB *www.museumnett.no/munchmuseet.* ⏲ *June–mid-Sept., daily 10–6; mid-Sept.–May, Tues.–Wed. and Fri.–Sat. 10–4, Thurs. and Sun. 10–6.*

8 **Muséet for Samtidskunst** (Museum of Contemporary Art). Housed in the Norwegian Art Nouveau former Bank of Norway building, the museum displays Norwegian and international contemporary art. You will also find a library, a cafeteria, and a bookshop. ✉ *Bankpl. 4,* ☎ *22862210,* WEB *www.museumsnett.no/mfs.* ⏲ *Tues.–Wed. and Fri. 10–*

5, Thurs. 10–8, Sat. 11–4, Sun. 11–5. Guided tours weekends at 2. Special children's tours 1st Sun. of month at 2.

❸ **Nasjonalgalleriet** (National Gallery). Norway's largest public gallery has a small but high-quality selection of paintings by European artists, and there's an impressive collection of works by Scandinavian Impressionists. Here you can see Edvard Munch's most famous painting, *The Scream.* ✉ *Universitetsgt. 13,* ☎ *22200404,* WEB *www.museumsnett.no/nasjonalgalleriet.* ⏲ *Mon., Wed., and Fri., 10–6, Thurs. 10–8, weekends 10–4.*

❹ **Nationaltheatret** (National Theater). Statues of Bjørnstjerne Bjørnson, the nationalist poet who wrote Norway's anthem, and Henrik Ibsen, who wrote the plays *Peer Gynt, A Doll's House,* and *Hedda Gabler,* watch over Nationaltheatret. Ibsen worried that his works, packed with allegory, myth, and sociological and emotional angst, might not have appeal outside Norway. As it happened, they changed the face of modern theater around the world. ✉ *Stortingsgt. 15,* ☎ *22412710,* WEB *www.nationaltheatret.no.*

★ ⓭ **Norsk Folkemuseum** (Norwegian Folk Museum). Take the ferry from Rådhusbryggen (City Hall Wharf) and walk up a well-marked road to see centuries-old farmhouses that have been collected from all over the country and reassembled here. A whole section of 19th-century Oslo was moved here, as was a 12th-century wooden stave church. ✉ *Museumsvn. 10,* ☎ *22123666,* WEB *www.norskefolke.museum.no.* ⏲ *Oct.–Apr., daily 11–4; May–Sept., daily 10–6.*

❻ **Oslo Domkirke** (Oslo Cathedral). Consecrated in 1697 and subsequently much renovated, this rather austere cathedral is modest compared to those of other European capitals, but the interior is rich with treasures, such as the Baroque carved-wood altarpiece and pulpit. The ceiling frescoes by Hugo Lous Mohr were done after World War II. Look for arcades, small restaurants, and street musicians behind the cathedral. ✉ *Stortorvet 1.* ⏲ *Weekdays 10–4.*

⓲ **Oslo Ladegård** (The Manor). Now owned by the city council, this museum has scale models of Old Oslo on the site of the 13th-century Bispegård (Bishop's Palace). ✉ *St. Hallvards Pl., Oslogt. 13,* ☎ *22194468.* ⏲ *May–Sept., guided tours Wed. at 6 and Sun. at 3, and on request; book in advance.*

★ ⓬ **Oslo Rådhus** (City Hall). Designed by architects Arnstein Arneberg and Magnus Poulsson, the impressive redbrick City Hall opened officially on May 15, 1950. The courtyard friezes portraying scenes from Norwegian folklore literally pale in comparison to the marble-floored inside halls, where murals and frescoes bursting with color depict daily life, historical events, and Resistance activities in Norway. The elegant main hall has been the venue for the Nobel Peace Prize Ceremony since 1991. ✉ *Rådhuspl.,* ☎ *22861600.* ⏲ *May–Aug., Mon.–Sat. 9–5, Sun. noon–5; Sept.–Apr., Mon.–Sat. 9–3:30, Sun. noon–5. Tours weekdays at 10, noon, and 2.*

★ ❶ **Slottet** (Royal Palace). This neoclassical structure, completed in 1848, is as sober, sturdy, and unpretentious as the Norwegian character. The surrounding park is open to the public, though the palace is not. The changing of the guard takes place daily at 1:30. When the king is in residence—signaled by a red flag—the Royal Guard strikes up the band. ✉ *Drammensvn. 1,* ☎ *22048700.*

⓫ **Stenersenmuséet** (Stenersen Museum). The museum shows a representative collection of Norwegian art from 1850 to 1970, featuring works by Amaldus Nielsen, Ludvig O. Ravensberg, and Rolf E. Stenersen. In addition, the museum hosts special exhibitions, generally in photography and Nordic modern art. ✉ *Munkedamsv. 15,* ☎ *23493600.* ⏲ *Tues. and Thurs. 11–7, Wed. and Fri.–Sun. 11–5.*

5 **Stortinget** (Parliament). Built in 1866 by Swedish architect Emil Langelot, this bow-front, yellow-brick building is open to visitors by request when Parliament is not in session. A guide will take you around the frescoed interior and into the debating chamber. ✉ *Karl Johans Gt. 22,* ☎ *22313050.* ⏲ *Guided tours July–Aug.; public gallery, weekdays when parliament is in session.*

★ 20 **Vigelandsparken** (Vigeland's Park, also known as Frogner Park). Don't leave Olso without pondering Gustav Vigeland's sculptures—192 of them, with a total of 650 figures—in this park in northwest Oslo. Two works in particular continue to spark metaphysical ruminations: *Wheel of Life,* a circle in stone depicting the stages of human life, and *The Monolith,* nearly 50 ft high and covered with more than 100 linked human forms. The nearby Vigeland Museum, open-air restaurants, tennis courts, and swimming pools provide additional diversions. ✉ *Kirkevn. and Middelthunsgt.; Trikk 12 or 15 or T-bane train 1, 2, 3, 4, or 5 to Majorstuen.*

★ 14 **Vikingskiphuset** (Viking Ship Museum). Three remarkably intact 9th-century ships last used by Vikings on the shores of the Oslofjord as royal burial chambers are the treasures of this cathedral-like museum. Also on display are riches that accompanied the royal bodies on their last voyage. The ornate craftsmanship evident in the ships and jewelry dispels any notion that the Vikings were skilled only in looting and pillaging. ✉ *Huk Av. 35,* ☎ *22438379,* WEB *www.uio.no/vikingskiphuset.* ⏲ *Nov.–Mar., daily 11–3; Apr. and Oct., daily 11–4; May–Aug., daily 9–6; Sept., daily 11–5.*

Elsewhere in Oslo

21 **Holmenkollbakken** (Holmenkollen Ski Museum and Ski Jump). A structure towering 203 ft above the ground, Holmenkollen's ski jump is among the world's highest and the site of an international contest each year in March. Carved into the rock at its base is the Ski Museum. The scenic half-hour subway ride from downtown Oslo to the jump sweeps up behind the city to the ski-jump complex, which stands 1,322 ft above sea level. ✉ *Kongevn. 5, Holmenkollen; Frognerseter/Holmenkollen T-bane train from Nationaltheatret, to Holmenkollen; walk uphill to the jump,* ☎ *22923264,* WEB *www.skiforeningen.no.* ⏲ *Oct.–Apr., daily 10–4; May and Sept., daily 10–5; June–Aug., daily 9–8.*

Dining

Oslo's chefs are gaining recognition worldwide. Norwegian cuisine, based on products from the country's waters and farmland, is now firmly ingrained in the culinary melting pot. Menus change daily, weekly, or seasonally in many Oslo restaurants. For details and price-category information *see* Dining *in* Norway A to Z, *above.*

$$$$ ★ ✕ **Annen Etage.** Dine in splendid surroundings in this restaurant on the first floor of the Hotel Continental. Savor Norwegian gastronomy with a distinctive French accent—perfect for a special occasion. ✉ *Stortingsgt. 24–26,* ☎ *22824070. Reservations essential. AE, DC, MC, V.*

$$$$ ★ ✕ **Bagatelle.** This was the first restaurant with a Norwegian chef serving Norwegian food to receive international recognition. Choose the seven-course menu for the full range of chef Hellstrøm's talents. The chairs are comfortable, service is impeccable, and Norwegian contemporary art adorns the walls. The fish soup is a highlight. ✉ *Bygdøy allé 3,* ☎ *22121440. AE, DC, MC, V. Closed Sun. No lunch.*

$$$$ ★ ✕ **De Fem Stuer.** Chef Frank Halvorsen prepares food that is even better than the view from this restaurant near the Holmenkollen ski jump. Modern versions of Norwegian classics focus on fish and game. ✉ *Holmenkollen Park Hotel, Kongevn. 26,* ☎ *22922734. AE, DC, MC, V.*

$$$–$$$$ ✕ **Babette's Gjestehus.** This intimate restaurant has an international menu with a French accent. ✉ *Rådhuspassasjen,* ☎ *22416464. Reservations essential. AE, DC, MC, V. Closed Sun. No lunch.*

$$$–$$$$ ✕ **Restaurant Blom.** See and be seen at this upscale eatery frequented by Oslo's artistic community. Blom is for the distinguished palate, famous for Swiss-born chef Walter Kieliger's salmon and reindeer dishes. A well-stocked wine cellar. ✉ *Karl Johansgt. 41B,* ☎ *23139500. Reservations essential. AE, DC, MC, V.*

$$$ ★ ✕ **Theatercafeen.** One of the last Viennese-style cafés in northern Europe, this is a favorite with the literary and entertainment crowd. The pastry chef here also makes desserts for Norway's royal family. ✉ *Hotel Continental, Stortingsgt. 24–26,* ☎ *22824050. AE, DC, MC, V.*

$$–$$$ ✕ **Det Gamle Raadhus.** The "Old City Hall," Oslo's oldest restaurant, is in a building that dates from 1641. Specialties include seafood casserole. ✉ *Nedre Slottsgt. 1,* ☎ *22420107. AE, DC, MC, V. Closed Sun.*

$$ ★ ✕ **Dinner.** Its name does not identify the restaurant as specializing in Szechuan-style cuisine, but this is the best place for Chinese food, both hot and not so pungent. The mango pudding dessert is wonderful. ✉ *Stortingsgt. 22,* ☎ *22426890. AE, DC, MC, V. No lunch.*

$$ ✕ **Frognerseteren.** This restaurant specializing in fish and reindeer overlooks the city from just above the Holmenkollen ski jump. There is outdoor seating on the restaurant terrace, but the same view can be enjoyed from the glass-fronted upstairs rooms if it is too chilly to sit outside. ✉ *Holmenkollenvn. 200,* ☎ *22924040. DC, MC, V.*

$ ✕ **Kaffistova.** This unpretentious budget restaurant has a long history of high-quality homemade food. The meatballs are a real treat after an energetic morning walk. ✉ *Rosenkrantzgt. 8,* ☎ *23214210. AE, DC, MC, V.*

$ ✕ **Vegeta.** Take advantage of the all-you-can-eat specials at this down-to-earth spot. The restaurant is next to the Nationaltheatret bus station. ✉ *Munkedamsvn. 3B,* ☎ *22834020. Reservations not accepted. AE, DC, V.*

Lodging

Lodging in the capital is expensive. Prices for downtown accommodations are high, even for B&Bs, although just about all hotels have weekend, holiday, and summer rates (25%–50% reductions). Taxes and service charges, unless otherwise noted, are included. Breakfast is usually included also, but be sure to ask before booking your room. If you arrive and need a hotel the same day, ask about last-minute prices, which are generally discounted. The helpful accommodations bureau of the **Norway Information Centre** (☞ Visitor Information *in* Oslo Essentials, *below*) in the Oslo Central Station can help you find a room; apply in person and pay a fee of NKr 20. For details and price-category information, *see* Lodging *in* Norway A to Z, *above.*

$$$$ ★ 🏨 **Grand Hotel.** It's hard to beat the Grand's site on Oslo's main street, opposite Parliament. The hotel has comforts and history to match its name. Palmen, just off the lobby, is where Oslo matrons sip afternoon tea. ✉ *Karl Johans Gt. 31, 0159,* ☎ *23212000,* FAX *23212100,* WEB *www.rica.no. 287 rooms, 50 suites. 3 restaurants, pool. AE, DC, MC, V.*

$$$$ ★ 🏨 **Holmenkollen Park Rica.** The imposing building in the old romantic folkloric style stands near the ski jump in Holmenkollen. The rooms are bright, and most have balconies with excellent views of the city and

the fjord. ✉ *Kongevn. 26, 0390,* ☎ *22922000,* FAX *22146192,* WEB *www.rica.no. 221 rooms. 2 restaurants, pool. AE, DC, MC, V.*

$$$$ ★ **Hotel Continental.** The Brockmann family, owners of the hotel since 1900, have succeeded in combining the rich elegance of the 20th century with modern, comfortable living. Antique furniture and shiny white porcelain fixtures add a distinctive touch to the impeccably decorated rooms. The property stands in the heart of Oslo, between the Royal Palace and the City Hall. ✉ *Stortingsgt. 24–26, 0161,* ☎ *22824000,* FAX *22429689,* WEB *www.hotel-continental.no. 140 rooms, 19 suites. 3 restaurants. AE, DC, MC, V.*

$$$$ **Radisson SAS Scandinavia Hotel.** The SAS, across from the Royal Palace, is a comfortable business hotel with impeccable service, including an airport bus that stops right outside. ✉ *Holbergs Gt. 30, 0166,* ☎ *23293000,* FAX *23293001,* WEB *www.radisson.no. 488 rooms, 3 suites. 2 restaurants, pool. AE, DC, MC, V.*

$$$ **Best Western Hotel Bondeheimen.** Established to provide "down-home" accommodations for farmers on business in the big city, this may be Oslo's most Norwegian hotel. The rooms are simple and comfortable. ✉ *Rosenkrantz' Gt. 8, 0159,* ☎ *23214100,* FAX *23214101. 81 rooms. Restaurant. AE, DC, MC, V.* WEB *nettvik.no/handelskleiva/bestwestern*

$$$ **Radisson SAS Park Royal Hotel.** This clean, efficient hotel sits in Fornebu park by the shores of the Oslo fjord, 15 minutes from Oslo's center. ✉ *Fornebuparken, Box 1324, 1324 Lysaker,* ☎ *67823000,* FAX *67823001. 254 rooms, 14 suites. Restaurant. AE, DC, MC, V.* WEB *nettvik.no/handelskleiva/bestwestern*

$$ ★ **Best Western Ambassadeur Hotel.** On a quaint residential street, this hotel has individually designed rooms and personalized service. ✉ *Camilla Colletts vei 15, 0266,* ☎ *23272300,* FAX *22444791. 33 rooms, 8 suites. Pool. AE, DC, MC, V.* WEB *nettvik.no/handelskleiva/bestwestern*

$$ **Gabelshus Hotel.** Only five minutes from the center of town on an attractive side street in Frogner, Gabelshus has the feel of a large country house. The rooms are spacious and airy. ✉ *Gabels Gt. 16, 0272,* ☎ *23276500,* FAX *23276560. 43 rooms. Restaurant. AE, DC, MC, V.*

$$ **Golden Tulip Rainbow Hotel Stefan.** The service is cheerful and accommodating in this hotel in the center of town. Be sure to sample traditional Norwegian dishes at Oslo's best buffet lunch, served in the restaurant on the top floor. ✉ *Rosenkrantz' Gt. 1, 0159,* ☎ *23315500,* FAX *23315555,* WEB *www.rainbow-hotels.no. 139 rooms. Restaurant. AE, DC, MC, V.*

$$ **Tulip Inn Rainbow Cecil Hotel.** Known for its copious breakfast table, this hotel is right in the heart of town near the Parliament building. ✉ *Stortingsgt. 8, 0130,* ☎ *23314800,* FAX *23314850,* WEB *www.rainbow-hotels.no. 112 rooms. AE, DC, MC, V.*

$ **Rainbow Gyldenløve.** Rooms decorated in neutral tones are provided at a reasonable price. The hotel is on one of Oslo's busiest shopping streets. ✉ *Bogstadvn. 20, 0355,* ☎ *22601090,* FAX *22603390,* WEB *www.rainbow-hotels.no. 168 rooms. AE, DC, MC, V.*

$ **Tulip Inn Rainbow Hotel Munch.** This B&B-style hotel near the National Gallery has large, spartan rooms. ✉ *Munchsgt. 5, 0165,* ☎ *23219600,* FAX *23219601,* WEB *www.goldentulip.com. 180 rooms. AE, DC, MC, V.*

Nightlife and the Arts

The Arts

Considering the city's small population, Oslo has a surprisingly rich arts scene. Check the English-language monthly *What's On in Oslo,* available at the Norway Information Centre (☞ Visitor Information *in* Oslo Essentials, *below*).

FILM

All films are screened in the original language with Norwegian subtitles. Oslo has one of Europe's best cinema collections, with 30 screens. Call ☎ 82030000 for schedules for most of the city's theaters. For alternative and classic films, try **Cinemateket** (✉ Dronningensgt. 16, ☎ 22474505), the city's only independent cinema.

MUSIC

Oslo's modern **Konserthuset** (✉ Munkedamsvn. 14, ☎ 23113100) is the home of the Oslo Philharmonic. A smaller hall in the same building has folk dancing, held Monday and Thursday at 9 PM in July and August. At **Den Norske Opera** (The Norwegian Opera House; ✉ Storgt. 23, ☎ 23315000), performances usually start at 7:30; it's closed in July and August. **Herr Nilsen** (✉ C J Hambros pl. 5, ☎ 22335405) is an atmospheric bar with some of the best jazz acts in Norway. **Oslo Spektrum** (✉ Sonja Henies pl. 2, ☎ 22052900) is a large indoor show and concert venue. **Rockefeller/John Dee** (✉ Torggt. 16, ☎ 22203232) has concerts featuring well-known pop and rock acts.

THEATER

Winter is *the* cultural season, when the **Nationaltheatret** (National Theater; ☞ Exploring Oslo, *above*) presents modern plays (all in Norwegian), classics, and a good sampling of Ibsen. The modern theater complex **Det Norske Teatret** (The Norwegian Theater; ✉ Kristian IV's Gt. 8, ☎ 22424344), has musicals and plays (all in Norwegian).

Nightlife

NIGHTCLUBS AND BARS

Barock-Restauranthuset (✉ Universitetsgt. 26, ☎ 22424420), complete with elegant chandeliers and blaring techno pop, is where Oslo's young and beautiful people choose to dance. You'll find a friendly and lively older crowd at **Bristol Night Spot** (✉ Kristian IVs Gt. 7, ☎ 22826030), with music and dancing to match the youngsters elsewhere. **Baronen og Baronessen** (✉ Stortingsgt. 10, ☎ 22420470), a combination discotheque, piano bar, and restaurant, is one of the few places serving food until 4 AM. Students frequent the informal and intimate **Ett Glass** (✉ Karl Johansgt. 23, ☎ 22334079) café. Media people and students hang out at **Galleriet** (✉ Kristian IV's Gt. 12, ☎ 22422936), a three-story disco with live music sessions on the third floor. **Karl Johans Gate,** Olso's main downtown thoroughfare, is a lively and drunken place into the wee hours, with a good selection of music cafés and clubs, as well as more conventional nightspots, from which to choose. Dress codes apply at **Lipp** (✉ Olav V's Gt. 2, ☎ 22824060), a popular upscale predinner drinks bar (for people over 24); Lipp's restaurant serves international cuisine. **Smuget** (✉ Rosenkrantz' Gt. 22, ☎ 22425262) is a combination discotheque and bar with live rock and blues bands most nights of the week.

Shopping

Many of the larger stores are in the pedestrian-only areas between Stortinget and the cathedral. Shops stay open until 5 or 6 on weekdays, 7 or 8 on Thursdays, and 2 or 3 on Saturdays. Stores have extended hours the first Saturday of the month, known as "Super Saturday." One of Oslo's newest shopping areas, **Aker Brygge** (✉ Waterfront), a complex of booths, offices, and sidewalk cafés, is especially lively in summer and spring. The **Basarhallene** (✉ at back of the cathedral) is an art and handicrafts boutique center just around the corner from the many outdoor vendors and shops that line the pedestrian part of Karl Johans Gate. Check out the many shops and galleries on **Bogstadveien/Hegdehaugsveien** (✉ runs from Majorstua to Parkvn.).

Department Stores and Malls

Byporten (✉ Jernbanetorget 6, ☎ 23362160), open weekdays 10–9 and Saturday 10–6, is a modern complex with a number of eateries and 75 shops, including a well-stocked delicatessen and upscale housewares stores. **Glasmagasinet** (✉ Stortorvet 9, ☎ 22908900), open weekdays 10–7 and Saturday 10–6, has a large assortment of wares in 50 different stores, including souvenirs, glassware, and silver and pewter jewelry. Oslo's largest shopping mall, **Oslo City** (✉ opposite Central Station, ☎ 22938050), open weekdays 9–9 and Saturday 9–7, has more than 100 stores and businesses, including a bank, a travel agency, and a grocery store on the lower level. **Paléet** (✉ Karl Johans Gt., ☎ 22417086), open weekdays 10–8 and Saturday 10–5, is an elegant indoor shopping center with 45 shops and 12 restaurants. **Steen & Strøm** (✉ Kongengsgt. 23, ☎ 22100250), open weekdays 10–7 and Saturday 10–6, is an exclusive department store with six floors and 58 different shops plus a cafeteria.

Flea Markets

Every Saturday during spring, summer, and fall, there is a flea market at **Vestkanttorget** (✉ 2 blocks east of Frogner Park, junction of Professor Dahls Gt. and Eckerbergs Gt.). Check the papers for local *loppemarkeder* (flea markets) in schools and outdoor squares around town.

Side Trips

Høvikodden

Just outside Oslo is the **Henie-Onstad Kunstsenter** (Henie-Onstad Art Center), which displays an impressive collection of works by Léger, Munch, Picasso, Bonnard, and Matisse. The center was a gift from the Norwegian skater Sonja Henie and her husband, shipowner Niels Onstad. ✉ *About 12 km (7 mi) southwest of Oslo on E18,* ☎ *67804880,* WEB *www.hok.no.* ⏲ *Tues.–Thurs. 10–9, Fri.–Mon. 11–6.*

Vinterbro

Tusenfryd is Norway's largest amusement park, with more than 50 attractions, including carousels, a roller coaster, games, an outdoor stage, shops, and restaurants. Don't miss **Vikingelandet** (Viking Land), which re-creates life during the time of the Vikings, with trading centers, boat building, a blacksmith, jewelry making, and farm animals. One of the "Vikings" will also help you try your talent as an archer, or you can join "Leif Eriksson" on an expedition in the depths of a mountain cave. ✉ *1433 Vinterbro; about 20 km (12 mi) southeast of Oslo on E18,* ☎ *64976497.* ⏲ *Tusenfryd May–early June and mid-Aug.–mid-Sept., weekends 10:30–7; early June–mid-Aug., daily 10:30–7. Vikingelandet 2 wks in mid-June, weekdays 10:30–3, weekends 1–7; last wk in June–mid-Aug., daily 1–7.*

Lillehammer

At the top of the long finger of Lake Mjøsa, Lillehammer is reached by train from the Central Station in about two hours. A paddle steamer, D/S *Skibladner,* travels the length of the lake (six hours each way) in summer, making several stops. At the site of the 1994 Winter Olympics, Lillehammer's Olympic bobsled track, **Hunderfossen** (✉ about 5 km/3 mi north of town), is open for runs; you can book at the **Lillehammer Tourist Office** (✉ Lilletorget, ☎ 61259299 or 81548170). Lillehammer is also home of **Maihaugen,** one of the largest open-air museums in northern Europe. More than 100 old buildings have been relocated here, along with workshop interiors, antique tools, and the like. ✉ *Mai-*

haugvn. 1, ☎ 61288900, WEB www.maihaugen.museum.no. ⏲ Mid-May–May 31, daily 10–5; June–mid-Aug., daily 9–6; mid-Aug.–Sept., daily 10–5.

Oslo Essentials

AIRPORTS AND TRANSFERS

Gardermoen Airport, 37 km (23 mi) north of Oslo, is Oslo's main airport.

➤ AIRPORT INFORMATION: **Gardermoen Airport** (☎ flight information 81550250, WEB www.osl.no).

TRANSFERS

Taxis between downtown and Gardermoen cost between NKr 700 and NKr 800. Flybussen (airport bus) takes about 40 minutes from Galleri Oslo shopping center, stopping at Jernbanetorget (Oslo Central Station); the fare is NKr 55. The high-speed Airport Express Train carries passengers from Central Station to Gardermoen in 20 minutes; a one-way fare is NKr 120.

➤ TAXIS AND SHUTTLES: **Flybussen** (☎ 82054301).

CONSULATES

➤ AUSTRALIA: (✉ Jernbanetorget 2, 0106 Oslo, ☎ 22479170).

➤ IRELAND: (✉ Lilleakervn. 2C, 0283 Oslo, ☎ 22122000).

➤ NEW ZEALAND: (✉ Billingstadsletta 19 B, 1396 Billingstad, ☎ 66775330).

➤ SOUTH AFRICA: (✉ Drammensvn. 88C, 0271 Oslo, ☎ 22273220).

EMERGENCIES

➤ DOCTORS AND DENTISTS: **Dentist** (☎ 22176566).

➤ EMERGENCY SERVICES: **Ambulance** (☎ 113). **Fire** (☎ 110). **Police** (☎ 112).

➤ HOSPITALS: **Oslo Legevakt Emergency Clinic** (☎ 22118080).

➤ 24-HOUR PHARMACIES: **Jernbanetorgets Apotek** (☎ 22412482).

ENGLISH-LANGUAGE MEDIA

➤ BOOKSTORES: **Erik Qvist** (✉ Drammensvn. 16, ☎ 22542600). **Tanum Libris** (✉ Karl Johans Gt. 37–41, ☎ 22411100).

TAXIS

Taxis can be hailed on the street when the roof light is on, found at taxi stands, or ordered by phone, though during peak hours you may have to wait.

➤ TAXI COMPANIES: **Taxi** (☎ 22388090).

TOURS

CITY TOURS

Båtservice Sightseeing has a bus tour, five cruises, and one combination tour. HMK Sightseeing offers several bus tours in and around Oslo. Starting at noon and continuing at 45-minute intervals until 10 PM, the Oslo Train, which looks like a chain of dune buggies, leaves Aker Brygge for a 30-minute ride around the town center. Ask at the Norway Information Centre (☞ Visitor Information, *below*).

➤ FEES AND SCHEDULES: **Båtservice Sightseeing** (✉ Rådhusbryggen 3, ☎ 22200715). **HMK Sightseeing** (✉ Hegdehaugsvn. 4, ☎ 22208206).

PRIVATE GUIDES

The Norway Information Centre (☞ Visitor Information, *below*) can provide an authorized city guide for your own private tour. OsloTaxi also gives private tours.

➤ FEES AND SCHEDULES: **OsloTaxi** (✉ Trondheimsvn. 100, ☎ 22388070).

SPECIAL-INTEREST TOURS

The Norway Information Centre (☞ Visitor Information, *below*) can arrange four- to eight-hour motor safaris through the forests surrounding Oslo. In winter you can ride an old-fashioned sleigh or a horse through Hallingdal, northwest of the Oslo, with Vangen Skistue.

➤ FEES AND SCHEDULES: **Vangen Skistue** (✉ Laila and Jon Hamre, Fjell, 1404 Siggerud, ☎ 64865481).

TRAIN TRAVEL

Trains on international or domestic long-distance and express routes arrive at Oslo's Central Station. Suburban trains depart from the Central Station, Stortinget, and the Nationaltheatret stations.

➤ TRAIN INFORMATION: **Central Station** (✉ east of Strandgt.).

TRANSPORTATION AROUND OSLO

If you're using public transportation only occasionally, you can get tickets (NKr 20) at bus and subway (T-bane) stops. For NKr 50, the Dags Kort (One-day Card) gives 24 hours' unlimited travel on all public transportation, including the summer ferries to Bygdøy, Hovedøya, Langøya, and Gressholmen. The Flexikort gives you eight rides on the subway, bus, or trikk (the name given to Oslo's extensive tram network) for NKr 125, including transfers. For information on public transportation, call Trafikanten.

➤ CONTACTS: **Trafikanten** (✉ Oslo Central Station, ☎ 22177030 or 177).

TRAVEL AGENCIES

➤ LOCAL AGENTS: **Bennett** (✉ Linstowsgt. 6, ☎ 22597800). **Berg-Hansen Reisebyrå** (✉ Kongensgt. 6, ☎ 81550290). **Winge** (American Express; ✉ Karl Johans Gt. 33/35, ☎ 22004500).

VISITOR INFORMATION

Oslo Kortet (the Oslo Card)—valid for one, two, or three days—entitles you to free entrance to museums, public swimming pools, and the racetrack; unlimited travel on the Oslo transport system and Norwegian Railways commuter trains within the city limits; free parking on municipal streets and in some lots; and discounts at various stores, cinemas, and sports centers. You can get the card at Oslo's tourist information offices and hotels. A one-day card costs NKr 180; two-day, NKr 290; three-day, NKr 410. A one-day family card costs NKr 410.

➤ TOURIST INFORMATION: **Nortra** (Norwegian Travel Association; ✉ Drammensvn. 40, Postboks 2893, Sentrum, 0230 Oslo, ☎ 22925200). **Norway Information Centre** (✉ Vestbanen, Brynjulf Bullspl. 1, 0250 Oslo, ☎ 23117880; Oslo Central Station, WEB www.visitnorway.com).

THE COAST ROAD TO STAVANGER

Route E18 parallels the coast of Sørlandet, or Southern Norway, south of Oslo toward the busy port of Kristiansand. Beyond the city, the coast curves west and north to Stavanger. After Flekkefjord, follow the coast road (Route 44) past the fishing port of Egersund to Ogna, and then on to Stavanger. Sørlandet's whaling business has given way to canneries, lumber, paper production, and petrochemicals. Yet the beauty of this 608-km (380-mi) route remains, and you'll find seaside towns, rocky headlands, and stretches of forest. Travel between towns takes less than an hour in most cases. South of Stavanger is flat and stony Jæren, the largest expanse of level terrain in this mountainous country. The mild climate and the absence of good harbors caused the people here to turn to agriculture, and the miles of stone walls are a testament to their labor. It is also possible to reach Stavanger on an inland route through Telemark.

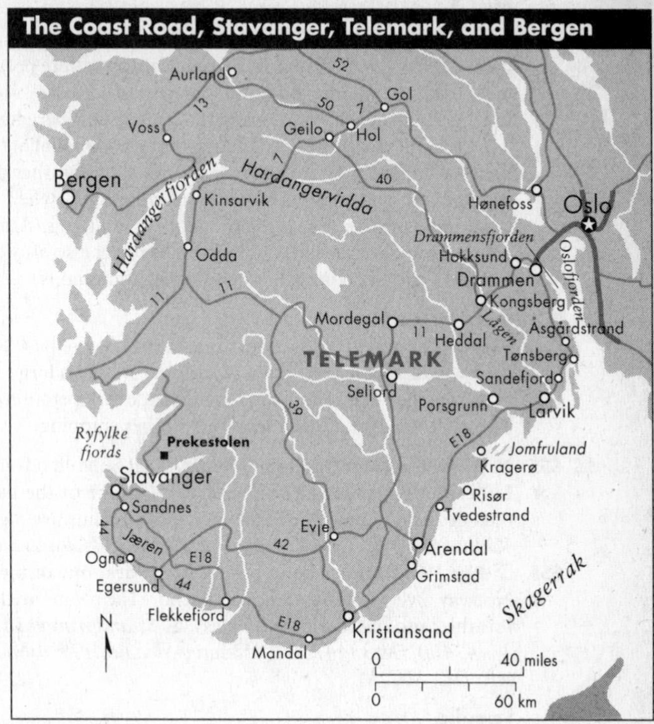

Drammen

Drammen lies on the bank of the wide Drammen River, 45 km (28 mi) long and popular for its salmon and trout fishing. The river was the city's main street during the centuries when the production of wood products (paper and cellulose) was the chief industry in Drammen. From May 10 through August you can join a five-hour guided tour aboard the 114-year-old sailing ship ***Christiane*** (☎ 95887560 tours), which sails south from Drammen to the attractive little village of Holmsbu. Holmsbu has a restaurant overlooking the small harbor and a number of attractive arts-and-crafts shops.

The center of Drammen has a great variety of shops and restaurants. **Bragernes Torg** is home to a sizable farmer's market. This large square is lined by several buildings dating from just after 1866, when a huge fire devastated the entire district. **Drammens Teatret,** also built after the great fire, has an impressive collection of ceiling paintings and crystal chandeliers. Designed by Emil Langlet, it was completed in 1870 and is a working theater and conference venue.

$$ ✕ **Spiraltoppen Café.** You'll find excellent views and food here atop Bragernes Hill. ✉ *Bragernesåsen,* ☎ *32263761. Reservations not accepted. AE, DC, MC, V.*

$$ 🏨 **Rica Park Hotel.** This comfortable and central hotel close to the station has been recently modernized. ✉ *Gamle Kirkepl. 3, 3019,* ☎ *32263600,* FAX *32263777,* WEB *www.rica.no. 96 rooms, 2 suites. 2 restaurants. AE, DC, MC, V.*

Åsgårdstrand

Edvard Munch painted many of his best works in Åsgårdstrand, where he spent seven summers in a small yellow frame house. **Munchs lille hus** is open to visitors June–August. ✉ *Munchsgt.,* ☎ *33031708.*

Tønsberg

Tønsberg was founded in 871; it is the site of the Oseberg Viking ship, discovered in 1903. Shipping, commerce, and culture prospered in Tønsberg from the Viking Age until the rise of Oslo as Norway's capital during the 14th century. During the 1700s, Tønsberg had a resurgence as a thriving whaling port. Today, on steep **Slottsfjellet** (Castle Hill; ✉ next to Tønsberg train station), the ruins of **Tønsberghus**, an extensive fortress and abbey, evoke the Middle Ages, when Tønsberg was the administrative center for the Norwegian kings. A model of Tønsberghus stands in the lookout tower. The tower also affords a panoramic view of Oslo fjord and the surrounding mountains.

Sandefjord

Attractive Sandefjord is a port that served as the base for the Norwegian whaling fleet until after World War II, when large-scale competition from the Soviet Union and Japan made the operation uneconomical. The port remains a busy depot for timber shipping.

$$–$$$ ★ ✕ **Ludl's Gourmet Odd Ivar Solvold.** Chef Solvold has taken over chef Ludl's duties preparing fish specialties in one of the best restaurants outside Oslo. The eight- and five-course menus are a great value. ✉ *Rådhusgt. 7,* ☎ *33462741. AE, DC, MC, V. Closed Sun.*

$$$ ★ **Rica Park Hotel.** The imposing Rica Park, one of the best hotels in Norway, overlooks Sandefjord's harbor. The rooms are large and comfortable, and the service is flawless. ✉ *Strandpromenaden 9, 3200,* ☎ *33447400,* FAX *33447500,* WEB *www.rica.no. 179 rooms. Restaurant. AE, DC, MC, V.*

Larvik

Larvik is the terminus for ferries to Frederikshavn, Denmark. It once looked to whaling for its livelihood but now concentrates on lumbering and ferrying.

The **Larvik Sjøfarts Museum** (Maritime Museum), in the former customs house, chronicles Larvik's seafaring history. ✉ *Kirkestredet 5,* ☎ *33130404.* ⏲ *Mid-May–June, mid-Aug.–Sept., Sun. noon–5; July–mid-Aug., daily noon–5.*

$$ **Quality Grand Hotel Farris.** Spotless rooms and attentive service are what you'll find at this large hotel overlooking the fjord. Sample the local fish soup and smoked meat platters in the hotel's restaurant. ✉ *Storgt. 38–40, 3256,* ☎ *33187800,* FAX *33187045,* WEB *www.choice.no. 88 rooms. Restaurant. AE, DC, MC, V.*

Risør

The coastal village of Risør is a sailing center; its picturesque harbor is lined with white-painted 19th-century patrician houses. If you're here in August, don't miss the town's wooden sailboat festival.

Arendal

Between 1850 and 1886, Arendal was one of the most important seafaring towns in Scandinavia. You can still discern a bit of that era in the tidy cottages and grandiose captains' houses within shouting distance of the docks. Explore Arendal's **Tyholmen Quarter,** the oldest part of the town, for a glimpse into this 19th-century world.

Arendals Rådhus (Arendal's City Hall) was created by the Danish architect Peder Krog Bonsach Jessen and constructed between 1812 and 1815. Built as a private home for one of Arendal's wealthy ship owners, it was converted to City Hall in 1844. Arendal hosts a popular speedboat race every summer.

$$ ✕ **Madam Reiersen.** Good, traditional rustic fare is served at this informal waterfront restaurant. Reservations are essential on summer weekends, when there is a great atmosphere and live music. ✉ *Nedre Tyholmsvn. 3,* ☎ *37021900. AE, DC, MC, V.*

$$$$ **Clarion Tyholmen Hotel.** This hotel is in the heart of the Old Town, which is filled with brightly painted houses. The views of the fjord are splendid. ✉ *Teaterpl. 2, 4801,* ☎ *37026800,* FAX *37026801,* WEB *www.choice.no. 60 rooms. 2 restaurants. AE, DC, MC, V.*

Kristiansand

The largest town in Sørlandet, Kristiansand has important air, sea, road, and rail links. It was laid out in the 17th century in a grid pattern, with the imposing **Christiansholm Festning** (fort) guarding the eastern harbor approach.

The open-air **Vest-Agder Fylkesmuseum** (County Museum) has 30 old buildings and farms rebuilt in the local style of the 18th and 19th centuries. ✉ *Kongsgård (Rte. E18, east of Kristiansand),* ☎ *38090228,* WEB *www.museumsnett.no/vafymuseum.* ⊙ *June–late Aug., Mon.–Sat. 10–6, Sun. noon–6; late Aug.–May, Sun. noon–5.*

Kristiansand Cannon Museum has the last remaining 38-cm caliber cannon in the world. The huge cannon installations were built by the Germans during World War II. ✉ *South of town, off E39,* ☎ *38085090.* ⊙ *May–mid-June and Sept.–Oct., Thurs.–Sun. 11–6; mid-June–Aug., daily 11–6.*

Children love the **Kristiansand Dyrepark** (Kristiansand Zoo), with five separate parks, including a water park, a forested park, an entertainment park, and a zoo. There's also **Kardemomme By** (Cardamom Town), a replicated storybook village. ✉ *4609 Kardemomme By,* ☎ *38049700.* *NKr 185.* ⊙ *Jan.–late June, daily 10–4; late June–Aug., daily 10–6; Sept.–Dec., daily 10–3.*

$$ ✕ **Sjøhuset.** Succulent seafood platters are the specialty of this antiques-filled restaurant housed in a converted salt factory. ✉ *Østre Strandgt. 12a,* ☎ *38026260. Reservations not accepted. AE, DC, MC, V.*

$$$ **Rica Travel Hotel.** Only a stone's throw from the Town Hall and cathedral, this hotel is also close to the harbor beach. Breakfast and evening buffet are included Monday–Thursday. ✉ *Dronningens Gt. 66, 4602,* ☎ *38021500,* FAX *38020119,* WEB *www.rica.no. 47 rooms. Restaurant. AE, DC, MC, V.*

Mandal

Norway's southernmost town is famous for its beach, salmon, and 18th- and 19th-century houses. Seafood lovers flock here for the shellfish festival held on the second weekend in August.

Flekkefjord

The road climbs and weaves its way through steep, wooded hills before descending to the fishing port of Flekkefjord, with its charming **Hollenderbyen,** or Dutch Quarter.

Ogna

Ogna is known for the stretch of unspoiled sandy beach that has inspired so many Norwegian artists, among them Kitty Kjelland.

Stavanger

Stavanger is a former trading town that became a focus (some environmentalists say victim) of the oil boom. It is now the fourth-largest city in Norway. Drilling platforms and oil tankers take the place of fishing boats in the harbor. In sharp contrast to the new high-rise complexes, there is an old quarter with cobbled lanes and clapboard houses at odd angles. The town is believed to date from the 8th century.

Stavanger's Anglo-Norman **Domkirke** (cathedral), next to the central market, was established in 1125 by the English bishop of Winchester. Norway and England had strong trading and ecclesiastical links throughout the Middle Ages. ✉ *City center, next to pond, Breiavatnet.*

Ledaal is a fine patrician mansion where the royal family resides when visiting Stavanger. The house reopened in 2001 after extensive restoration. ✉ *Eiganesvn. 45,* ☎ *51520618,* WEB *www.stavanger.museum.no.* ⊙ *Mid-June–mid-Aug., daily 11–4; mid-Aug.–mid-June, Sun. 11–4.*

Breidablikk manor house, designed by the architect Henrik Nissen, was built by a Norwegian shipping magnate between 1881 and 1882. An outstanding example of Norwegian "Swiss-style" chalet architecture, the property has been perfectly preserved inside and out. The rich interiors, complete with antiques, give an idea of how a well-to-do family would have lived in the late 19th century. ✉ *Eiganesvn. 40A,* ☎ *51526035,* WEB *www.stavanger.museum.no.* ⊙ *Mid-June–mid-Aug., daily 11–4; mid-Aug.–mid-June, Sun. 11–4.*

Ullandhaug is a reconstructed Early Iron Age farmstead, with authentic rough-hewn log dwellings erected around the excavated postholes of the original buildings. There are also demonstrations of Iron Age crafts using original tools. ✉ *Grannesvn., Ullandhaug,* ☎ *51846061,* WEB *www.stavanger.museum.no.* ⊙ *Mid-June–Aug., daily 11–4; early May–mid-June and Sept., Sun. noon–4.*

The **Norsk Hermetikkmuseum** (Canning Museum) in the heart of Old Stavanger is a reconstructed sardine factory that was in use between 1890 and 1920. ✉ *Øvre Strandgt. 88A,* ☎ *51534989,* WEB *www.stavanger.museum.no.* ⊙ *Mid-June–mid-Aug., daily 11–4; mid-Aug.–mid-June, Sun. 11–4; closed Dec.*

The **Utvanndrings Sentre** (Norwegian Emigration Center) specializes in genealogy and family research, helping to bridge the gap between Norway and the families of emigrants. ✉ *Nedre Strandgt. 31,* ☎ *51538860,* FAX *51538863.* ⊙ *Weekdays 9–3.*

The **Ryfylke fjords** north and east of Stavanger form the southern end of the fjord country. The city is a good base for exploring this region, with the "white fleet" of low-slung sea buses making daily excursions into even the most distant fjords of Ryfylke. Great for a heart-stopping view is Prekestolen (Pulpit Rock), a huge cube of rock with a vertical drop of 2,000 ft. You can join a tour to get here or you can do it on your own from mid-June to late August by taking the ferry from Fiskepiren across Hildefjorden to Tau, riding a bus to the Pulpit Rock Lodge, and walking 1½ to 2 hours to the rock.

$$$ **Comfort Hotel Grand.** On the edge of the town center, this hotel's rooms are comfortable and bright, done in white and pastels. In summer the rates drop significantly. ✉ *Klubbgt. 3, 4012,* ☎ *51895800,* FAX *51895710,* WEB *www.choice.no. 90 rooms. AE, DC, MC, V.*

$$–$$$ **Skagen Brygge Hotell.** Almost all the rooms are different in these three rehabilitated old sea houses, from modern to old-fashioned with exposed beams and brick-and-wood walls. The hotel can make reservations for you at any of 14 restaurants in the area and put the tab on your bill. ✉ *Skagenkaien 30, 4006,* ☎ *51850000,* FAX *51850001,* WEB *www.skagenbrygghotell.no. 106 rooms. AE, DC, MC, V.*

The Coast Road to Stavanger Essentials

BUS TRAVEL

Local buses cover the entire route, but they take much longer than the train. For details on fares and schedules, check with the tourist offices listed below or the Norway Information Centre in Oslo (☞ Visitor Information *in* Oslo Essentials, *above*).

CAR TRAVEL

Driving gives you the chance to stop at coastal villages that are either not served by trains or have only sporadic service. The route is simple: E18 as far as Flekkefjord, then Route 44 to Stavanger.

TOURS

In summer a daily boat excursion sets out from Oslo southwest to the coastal resorts of Kragerø; the long, thin island of Jomfruland; and Risør. You return the same day, and refreshments are served on board. Contact the Norway Information Centre (☞ Visitor Information *in* Oslo Essentials, *above*).

TRAIN TRAVEL

The Sørland line leaves from Oslo Central Station and goes all the way to Stavanger via Kristiansand. It has five departures daily to Kristiansand; three continue to Stavanger. The Oslo–Drammen stretch is an engineering feat that includes Norway's longest tunnel, an 11-km (7-mi) bore through sheer rock.

VISITOR INFORMATION

➤ TOURIST INFORMATION: **Arendal** (✉ Friholmsgt. 1, ☎ 37005544). **Drammen** (✉ Rådhuset, ☎ 32806210). **Flekkefjord** (✉ Main St., ☎ 38322131). **Kristiansand** (✉ Dronningensgt. 2, ☎ 38121314). **Larvik** (✉ Storgt. 48, ☎ 33139100). **Mandal** (✉ Bryggetgt., ☎ 38260820). **Risør** (✉ Strandgaten, ☎ 37152270). **Stavanger** (✉ Rosenkildehuset, Rosenkildetorget 1, ☎ 51859200). **Tønsberg** (✉ Nedre Langgt. 36B, ☎ 33310220).

THROUGH TELEMARK TO BERGEN

Bergen is Norway's second-largest city. To get here from Oslo, drive west through Telemark, a region marked by steep valleys, pine forests, lakes, and fast-flowing rivers full of trout. Morgedal, the cradle of skiing, is here. At the Haukeligrend crossroads, Route 11 really begins to climb, and you'll see why the Norwegians are so proud of keeping this route open all year. Hardangervidda, a wild mountain area and national park, was the stronghold of Norway's Resistance fighters during World War II. Farther west is the beautiful Hardangerfjord. Few places on earth match western Norway—the fabled land of the fjords—for spectacular scenic beauty.

Fjord transportation is good, as crossing fjords is a necessary as well as scenic way to travel in Norway. Hardangerfjorden, Sognefjord, and Nordfjord are three of the deepest and most popular.

One way to enjoy Telemark is to take a boat trip on the **Telemark Canal,** a heritage watercourse that cuts 105 km (65 mi) through the county from the coast to the foothills of the Hardanger highlands. The canal has 18 lock systems and is lined with pathways for cyclists. The lakes and views toward the mountains are breathtaking. Contact **Telemark Reiser** (✉ Box 3133, Handelstorget, 3707 Skien, ☎ 35900030, FAX 35900021) for more information.

Kongsberg

Kongsberg, founded in 1624 next to the fast-flowing Lågen River as a silver-mining town, is one of the gateways to Telemark. Forests give way to rocky peaks and desolate spaces farther into the plateau. Although there is no more mining, the old mines at Saggrenda are open for guided tours; contact the tourist office (☞ Visitor Information *in* Through Telemark to Bergen Essentials, *below*). In the town center is an 18th-century rococo church, which reflects the town's former source of wealth: silver. The **Norsk Bergverksmuseum** (Norwegian Mining Museum) includes the **Sølvverkets Samlinger** (Silver Mines Collection), the **Kongsberg Skimuseum** (Ski Museum), and **Den Kongelige Mynts Museum** (Royal Mint Museum). ✉ *Hyttegt. 3,* ☎ *32723200,* WEB *www.bvm.museum.no.* ⏲ *Mid-May–June, daily 10–4; July–mid-Aug., daily 10–5; mid-Aug.–Sept., daily noon–4; Oct.–mid-May, Sun. noon–4. Otherwise by appointment.*

$$ ✕ **Gamle Kongsberg Kro.** Hearty Norwegian dishes with a French accent are served at this café near Nybrofossen (the Nybro waterfall). ✉ *Thornesvn. 4,* ☎ *32731633. DC, MC, V.*

Heddal

★ Heddal is the first stop in Telemark. Here you'll find the **Heddal Stavkirke** (Heddal Church), Norway's largest stave church, built in 1147. Stave churches are built with wooden planks staked vertically into the ground or base and usually have some carved ornamentation on the doors and around the aisle. These churches date from the medieval period and are found almost exclusively in southern Norway. ☎ *35020400,* WEB *www.kirker.net/heddal.* ⏲ *Mid-May–mid-June and mid-Aug.–mid-Sept., daily 10–5; mid-June–mid-Aug., daily 9–7.*

Seljord

The attractive village of Seljord, on a lake of the same name, has ornamented wooden houses and a medieval church. The countryside by the lake is richer than that on the Telemark plateau; meadows and pastureland run down to the lakefront. Before you descend toward Seljord, you'll see the Lifjell area's highest peak, **Røydalsnuten** (4,235 ft), on the left.

Kinsarvik

The attractive village of Kinsarvik is on the Sørfjord. For the best view of the junction of the Sørfjord and the mighty Hardangerfjord, take the ferry to Utne. On the dramatic 30-minute ferry crossing, you will come to understand why this area was such a rich source of inspiration for Romantic composer Edvard Grieg.

$$$$ ★ 🏨 **Utne Hotel.** The white frame house dates from 1722, making this hotel one of the oldest in Norway. The wood-paneled, hand-painted dining room is decorated with copper pans, old china, and paintings. ✉ *5797 Utne,* ☎ *53666983,* FAX *53666950. 22 rooms with bath or shower. Restaurant. AE, DC, MC, V.*

$$$ 🏨 **Best Western Kinsarvik Fjord Hotel.** This handsome family-run hotel near the busy ferry port offers good views of Hardangerfjord and the glacier. The rooms are bright and spacious. ✉ *5780 Kinsarvik,* ☎ *53663100,* FAX *53667433, www.nettvik.no/handelskleiva/bestwestern. 70 rooms. Restaurant. AE, DC, MC, V.* WEB

Bergen

★ The road descends tortuously into Bergen, the capital of the fjords and Norway's second-largest city (population 219,000). The town was founded in 1070, and even before oil brought an influx of foreigners to Stavanger, Bergen was the most international Norwegian city, having been an important trading and military center when Oslo was still an obscure village. A member of the medieval Hanseatic League, it offered an ice-free harbor and convenient trading location on the west coast. Natives of Bergen still think of Oslo as a dour provincial town.

Despite numerous fires in its past, much of medieval Bergen has survived. Seven surrounding mountains set off the weathered wooden houses, cobbled streets, and Hanseatic-era warehouses of **Bryggen** (the harbor area).

The best way to get a feel for Bergen's medieval trading heyday is to visit the **Hanseatisk Museum.** One of the oldest and best-preserved of Bergen's wooden buildings, it is furnished in 16th-century style. ✉ *Finnegårdsgt. 1,* ☎ *55314189.* ⏲ *June–Aug., daily 9–5; Sept.–May, daily 11–2.*

The **Bergen Aquarium** overlooks the approach to the port of Bergen. Seals and penguins cavort in large pools, and the aquarium has one of Europe's most impressive collections of fish and marine invertebrates. There is also a spectacular video-in-the-round film on Norway's coastal flora and fauna. ✉ *Nordnesbakken 4,* ☎ *55557171.* ⏲ *May–Sept., daily 9–8; Oct.–Apr., daily 10–6.*

From behind Bryggen you can walk through the meandering back streets to the popular **Fløybanen** (Fløyen Funicular), which climbs a steep 1,070 ft to the top of Fløyen, one of the seven mountains guarding the city. ✉ *Øvregt.* ⏲ *May–Sept., weekdays every ½ hr 7:30 AM–11 PM, Sat. 8 AM–midnight, Sun. 9 AM–midnight.*

★ **Damsgaard Manor** is in the suburb of Laksevaag, 10 minutes by bus outside Bergen. Once the most splendid in the area, the house has been restored with gardens replanted as they might have been 200 years ago. ☎ *55325108,* FAX *55940870.* ⏲ *Late May–Aug., Tues.–Sun. 10–5; Sept.–late May, tours by appointment. Guided tours available*

$$$$ ✕ **Lucullus.** This French-inspired seafood restaurant is, appropriately enough, in the Neptun Hotel. It has an excellent wine cellar, with special emphasis on white wines to go with the fish. ✉ *Walckendorffsgt. 8,* ☎ *55901000,* FAX *55306800. AE, DC, MC, V. Closed Sun.*

$$$–$$$$ ★ ✕ **Fiskekrogen.** This cozy seafood restaurant, rustic-appearing but still upmarket, is housed in one of the old wooden buildings on Bryggen. Specialities include five varieties of lobster. ✉ *Torget 2,* ☎ *55559660,* FAX *55559662. AE, DC, MC, V.*

$$–$$$ ★ ✕ **Munkestuen Café.** This tiny mom-and-pop place is a hometown legend. Try the monkfish with hollandaise sauce or the fillet of roe deer with morels. Reserve a table early; they can be booked up to four weeks in advance. ✉ *Klostergt. 12,* ☎ *55902149. Reservations essential. AE, DC, MC, V. Closed weekends and 3 wks in July. No lunch.*

$$$$ 🏨 **Augustin Hotel.** This small but excellent hotel in the center of town has been restored to its original late–Art Nouveau character, complete with period furniture in the lobby. ✉ *C. Sundtsgt. 22–24, 5004,* ☎ *55304000,* FAX *55304010,* WEB *www.augustin.no. 82 rooms. Restaurant. AE, DC, MC, V.*

$$–$$$$ 🏨 **Radisson SAS Royal Hotel.** This hotel on the harbor is near a section of old, well-preserved warehouses and buildings. Ravaged by nine fires since 1170, the warehouses have been rebuilt each time in the same style. ✉ *Bryggen, 5003,* ☎ *55543000,* FAX *55324808,* WEB *www.radisson.no. 273 rooms. 2 restaurants. AE, DC, MC, V.*

$$–$$$ ★ 🏨 **Clarion Hotel Admiral.** Centrally located with fantastic views over the harbor, this hotel occupies a converted turn-of-the-20th-century warehouse. The elegant rooms are themed throughout with Jugenstil Art Nouveau features. Great service and excellent value. ✉ *C. Sundsgt. 9, 5804 Bergen,* ☎ *55236400,* FAX *55236464. 210 rooms. Restaurant, bar. AE, DC, MC, V.*

$–$$ **Tulip Inn Rainbow Hotel Bryggen Orion.** Facing the harbor in the center of town, the hotel is surrounded by Bergen's most famous sights. The rooms are decorated in warm, sunny colors. ✉ *Bradbenken 3, 5835,* ☎ *55318080,* FAX *55329414,* WEB *www.rainbow-hotels.no. 229 rooms. Restaurant. AE, DC, MC, V.*

Through Telemark to Bergen Essentials

AIR TRAVEL

Flesland Airport is 20 km (12 mi) south of Bergen.

BUS TRAVEL

Buses in the region rarely run more than twice a day; schedules are available at tourist offices or Nor-Way Bussekspress. All buses serving the Bergen region depart from Bergen's central bus station.

➤ Bus Information: **Central bus station** (✉ Strømgaten 8, ☎ 177). **Nor-Way Bussekspress** (✉ Bussterminalen, Galleri Oslo, ☎ 23002400; 81544444 within Norway).

CAR TRAVEL

E18 stretches from Oslo to Drammen and Route 11 from Drammen to Haukeli. From Haukeli to Kinsarvik you take Route 13. After the ferry crossing, Kinsarvik–Utne–Kvandal, follow Route 7 to Bergen.

TOURS

Bergen is the gateway to the fjords, and excursions cover most towns in the western part of the region as well as the fjords farther north. Contact the tourist information offices (☞ Visitor Information, *below*) for details of these constantly changing tours.

TRAIN TRAVEL

For Bergen, the Bergensbanen has five departures daily, plus an additional one on Sunday, in both directions on the Oslo–Bergen route. The only train service in the southern part of Telemark is the Oslo–Stavanger line (via Kristiansand).

VISITOR INFORMATION

➤ Tourist Information: **Bergen** (✉ Vaagsallmeningen 1, ☎ 55321480). **Kinsarvik** (✉ Public Library bldg., ☎ 53663112) is open mid-June–mid-August. **Kongsberg** (✉ Storgt. 35, ☎ 32735000).

ABOVE BERGEN: THE FAR NORTH

The fjords continue northward from Bergen all the way to Kirkenes, on Norway's border with the Republic of Russia. In the north you can hike, climb, fish, bird-watch (seabirds), see Samiland—the land of the Sami ("Lapps")—and experience the unending days of the midnight sun in June and July. The Lofoten Islands present the grand face of the "Lofoten Wall"—a rocky massif surrounded by the sea and broken into six pieces. Svolvær, the most populated island, has a thriving summer artists' colony. It's also known for Lofotfisket, a winter cod-fishing event. Cheaper accommodations are the rule in the north, whether you stay in hotels, cabins, campsites, guest houses, or *rorbuer*—fishermen's huts next to the sea with modern facilities.

Ålesund

★ Ålesund's pride is its unique, internationally recognized collection of Art Nouveau buildings constructed between 1904 and 1907 after the Great Fire. Romantic and colorful, these buildings line the narrow streets of the old town. Also attractive is **Brosundet** (the old harbor). This area on the west coast of Norway was one of the first places exposed after the Ice Age. Excavations in the Skjonghelleren cave on the nearby island of Valderøy have given evidence of Stone Age settlements that lived off plentiful fishing. Even today, much of the town's income derives from the fishing industry. *Klipfisk* (split, dried cod), which is exported worldwide, is the main ingredient for *bacalao,* a popular local dish whose name derives from the Portuguese for salted cod, and whose preparation was learned from Portuguese fishermen.

Atlantic Sea Park, 3 km (2 mi) west of Ålesund, has the largest aquarium in Scandinavia and is open all year. ☎ *70107060,* WEB *www.atlanterhavsparken.no.* ⏲ *Mid-June–mid-Aug., weekdays and Sun. 10–7, Sat. 10–5; mid-Aug.–mid-June, Mon.–Sat. 11-4, Sun. noon–5.*

$$ ✕ **Fjellstua.** This mountaintop restaurant has tremendous views over the surrounding peaks, islands, and fjords. The main dining room serves the widest variety of dishes and homemade desserts. ✉ *Fjellstua,* ☎ *70126582. AE, DC, MC, V. Closed mid-Dec.–early Feb.*

$$ ✕ **Sjøbua.** On an old wharf at Brunholmen, Sjøbua offers an excellent selection of the fresh-caught fare. You can even pick your own dinner from a saltwater aquarium. ✉ *Brunholmgt. 1,* ☎ *70127100. AE, DC, MC, V.*

$$$ 🏨 **Comfort Home Hotel Bryggen.** This dockside warehouse converted into a hotel has splendid views. ✉ *Apotekergt. 1–3, 6004,* ☎ *70126400,* FAX *70121180,* WEB *www.choice.no. 85 rooms. AE, DC, MC, V.*

$$$ 🏨 **Quality Scandinavie Hotel.** The impressive building dates from 1905. The rooms are decorated in blue, peach, and green, with reproduction Biedermeier furniture. ✉ *Løvenvoldgt. 8, 6002,* ☎ *70123131,* FAX *70132370,* WEB *www.choice.no. 65 rooms. 2 restaurants. AE, DC, MC, V.*

Trondheim

Trondheim sits at the southern end of Norway's widest fjord, Trondheimsfjord. This water-bound city, the third largest in the country, is where Norwegian rulers are traditionally crowned. It has a historic fish market worth seeing, as well as Scandinavia's two largest wooden buildings. One is a student dormitory and the other is the rococo **Stiftsgården,** built between 1774 and 1778, which became a royal palace in 1906. It is one of the highlights of Norwegian architecture, but the architect is unknown.

Construction of Scandinavia's largest medieval building, **Nidaros Domkirke** (Nidaros Cathedral), first started in 1070, but it suffered numerous fires and was not completed until 1969. The cathedral has been attracting pilgrims since the 11th century, following the miraculous preservation of the body of then-king Olaf Haraldsson, who died in 1030. He was worshipped as a saint soon after his death, and he is the patron saint of Norway. ✉ *Kongsgårdsgt. 2,* ☎ *73525333,* WEB *www.nidarosdomen.no.* ⏲ *Late June–late Aug., weekdays 9–6, Sat. 9–2, Sun. 1–4; late Aug.–mid-Sept. and May–late June, weekdays 9–3, Sat. 9–2, Sun. 1–4; mid-Sept.–Apr., weekdays noon–2:30, Sat. 11:30–2, Sun. 1–3.*

★ **Erkebispegården** (Archbishop's Palace) is adjacent to the cathedral and well worth exploration. The palace was the focal point of Norwegian Christendom in the 12th century, when clerical decisions made here applied not only in Norway but extended to the Faeroe Islands, the Shetland Islands, the Isle of Man, and Greenland. After the 16th century the palace declined in importance and began a new phase as a military garrison. Now this impressive stone building houses permanent sculpture and archaeology galleries, as well as changing exhibitions. ⏲ *Late June–late Aug., weekdays 10–5, Sat. 10–3, Sun. noon–5; late Aug.–late June, weekdays and Sat. 11–3, Sun. noon–4.*

$$$–$$$$ ★ ✕ **Bryggen.** A feast of traditional specialties is served at this popular restaurant near the Gamle Bybro (Old Town Bridge). There's also a cheaper brasserie, a lively pub, and a private dining room. ✉ *Øvre Bakklandet 66,* ☎ *73874242. AE, DC, MC, V.*

$$$ ✕ **Dickens.** In a 17th-century building in the Bryggen section of town, this charming restaurant is decorated in traditional Norwegian style. The menu includes national dishes as well as a variety of international specialties. ✉ *Kjøpmannsgt. 63,* ☎ *73515750. AE, DC, MC, V.*

$$ ★ ✕ **Tavern på Sverresborg.** Outside the city, at the open-air Folk Museum, this restaurant serves regional specialties. ✉ *Sverresborg,* ☎ *73520932. AE, DC, MC, V.*

$$$ **Brittania Hotel.** Rich in tradition and dating from the 19th century, this centrally located classic hotel boasts a splendid Moorish-style reception room, a piano bar, and a nightclub. ✉ *Dronningensgt. 5,* ☎ *73800800,* FAX *73800801. 240 rooms. Restaurant. AE, DC, MC, V.*

$$ ★ **Comfort Home Hotel Bakeriet.** The hotel is housed in a building that opened as a bakery in 1897. Few rooms look alike, but all are large and stylish in their simplicity, with natural-wood furniture and beige-and-red textiles. A light evening meal is included in the room rate. ✉ *Brattørgt. 2, 7010,* ☎ *73525200,* FAX *73502330,* WEB *www.choice.no. 109 rooms. AE, DC, MC, V.*

$–$$ **Hotel Ambassadeur.** Take in the dramatic view of fjord and coastline from the roof terrace of this hotel, about 300 ft from the market square. Breakfast and a light evening meal (weekdays only) are included. ✉ *Elvegt. 18, 7013,* ☎ *73527050,* FAX *73527052. 34 rooms. AE, DC, MC, V.*

Bodø

The last stop on the European rail system, Bodø is the first major town above the Polar Circle and, with its 40,000 inhabitants, the second-largest city in northern Norway. Bodø's modern airport has frequent flights daily serving most of the country. *Hurtigruten* (the Coastal Express ship) calls in twice a day, and a ferry will take you from Bodø straight to the Lofoten Islands. For boat excursions to coastal bird colonies on **Værøya,** Bodø is also the best base. The city was bombed by the Germans in 1940, but postwar reconstruction gave rise to the bustling modern city center, replete with lively shopping streets, a marina, and good restaurants and accommodations. A war memorial stands outside the stunning, contemporary **Bodø Domkirke** (Bodø Cathedral), its spire separated from the main building; inside are rich modern tapestries.

Norsk Luftfartssenter (Norwegian Aviation Museum) is divided into military and civilian sections. Among the attractions are an American U-2 spy plane, a Junkers JU 52, a Catalina antisubmarine aircraft, and the Mosquito Bomber. Try the flight simulator. ✉ *Olav V's Gt.,* ☎ *75508550.* ⏲ *Mid-June–mid-Aug., weekdays and Sun. 10–7, Sat. 10–5; mid-Aug.–mid-June, weekdays 10–4, weekends 11–5.*

Saltstraumen, the world's strongest tidal current, has inspired tales of ships' being sucked down in its maelstrom (whirlpool). It is one of nature's wonders as well as a paradise for anglers. A new visitor center opened here in 1996. ✉ *33 km (20 mi) south of Bodø,* ☎ *75560655.*

Kjærringøy Gamle Handelssted (Kjærringøy Old Trading Post) is 40 km (25 mi) north of Bodø. It has one of Norway's most important collections of buildings preserved from the 19th century, capturing part of the history of north Norwegian coastal life and culture. Norwegian author Knut Hamsun developed a special relationship to Kjerringøy, which became the setting for some of his best literary descriptions. For more information contact **Destination Bodø AS** (✉ Box 514, Sjøgt. 21, 8001 Bodø, ☎ 75526000).

$$$ **Radisson SAS Hotel Bodø.** This grand hotel pulses with life and has enough amenities—like bowling and live music—to keep you solidly entertained. The rooms are well supplied, and the service is impeccable. ✉ *Storgt. 2, 8006,* ☎ *75524100,* FAX *75527493,* WEB *www.radisson.no. 190 rooms. 2 restaurants. AE, DC, MC, V.*

$$ **Quality Hotel Diplomat.** Located centrally near the harbor, this comfortable hotel has a sauna, a solarium, and a gymnasium. ✉ *Sjøgt. 23A, 8006,* ☎ *75527000,* FAX *75547089,* WEB *www.choice.no. 113 rooms. 2 restaurants. AE, DC, MC, V.*

$ **Norrøna Hotell.** This B&B is comfortable, with a good view of the sea. ✉ *Storgt. 4B, 8006,* ☎ *75525550,* FAX *75523388,* WEB *www.norrona-hotell.bedre.no. 99 rooms. Restaurant. AE, DC, MC, V.*

Lofoten Islands

★ The Lofoten Islands archipelago is a 190-km (118-mi) chain of mountaintops rising from the bottom of the sea north of Bodø. In summer the local farms, fjords, and fishing villages become a tourist magnet. Between January and March, thousands of fishermen from all over the country head for Lofoten to the annual Lofoten Fishery, the world's largest annual cod-fishing event. **Svolvær,** the main town and administrative center for the villages on Lofoten Islands, is connected with the other islands by express boat and ferry, and by coastal steamer and air to Bodø. It has a thriving summer art colony. **Lofotr** (Viking Museum of Borg; ✉ 8360 Bøstad, ☎ 76084900), 67 km (42 mi) south of Svolvær on Route E10, has a reconstruction of a Viking chieftain's homestead. The year 900 is re-created inside, with a flickering fireplace and oil lamps. You may also bump into the chieftain himself; he tells many stories of raids and expeditions. The midnight sun is visible in Lofoten from May 27 to July 17. The best places to view it are Unstad and Eggum on **Vestvågøy** and Gimsøy and Laukvik on **Vågan.** It is also worth taking a fishing boat trip to see the impressive **Refsvikhula Cave.**

Narvik

Narvik is a rebuilt city, an ice-free seaport, and a major iron ore shipping center. An excellent railway connects it to the mines across the Swedish border. **Krigsminnemuséet** (War Memorial Museum) has gripping displays on wartime intrigue and suffering. ✉ *Kongensgt. near the main square,* ☎ *76944426.* ⏲ *Mar.–mid-June and mid-Aug.–Sept., daily 11–3; mid-June–mid-Aug., Mon.–Sat. 10–10, Sun. 10–4; tours arranged by appointment Oct.–Feb.*

$$ **Inter Nor Grand Royal Hotel.** An eager-to-please staff serves you at this handsome hotel near the train station. There are many possibilities for skiing and fishing nearby, as well as whale safaris. ✉ *Kongensgt. 64, 8500,* ☎ *76941500,* FAX *76977007. 107 rooms. 2 restaurants. AE, DC, MC, V.*

Harstad

Northeast of Lofoten on Hinnøya, Norway's largest island, is Harstad, where the population of 23,000 swells to 42,000 during the annual June cultural festival and the July deep-sea fishing festival.

Tromsø

Farther north on the mainland is Tromsø, self-dubbed "the Paris of the North" for its nightlife inspired by the midnight sun. Looming over the remote arctic university town are 6,100-ft peaks with permanent snowcaps. Tromsø trails off into the islands: half the 50,000 inhabitants of the town live offshore. Be sure to see the spectacular **Ishavskatedral** (Arctic Cathedral), with its eastern wall made entirely of stained glass. Coated in aluminum, the **Tromsø bridge** has triangular peaks that make a bizarre mirror for the midnight sun.

Part of Tromsø University, **Tromsø Museum** concentrates on science, the Sami, and northern church art. ✉ *Lars Thøringsvei 10, Folkeparken (take Bus 28),* ☎ *77645000.* ⏲ *June–Aug., daily 9–8; Sept.–May, Mon.–Tues. and Thurs.–Fri. 8:30–3:30, Wed. and Sat. noon–3, Sun. 11–4.*

$$$$ **Radisson SAS Hotel Tromsø.** Rooms in this central hotel have great views over the shoreline. ✉ *Sjøgt. 7, 9001,* ☎ *77600000,* FAX *77685474,* WEB *www.radisson.no. 195 rooms. 3 restaurants. AE, DC, MC, V.*

$$ **Comfort Saga Hotel.** On a pretty town square, this hotel has quiet and comfortable, if basic, rooms. Its restaurant serves affordable, hearty meals. ✉ *Richard Withs Pl. 2, 9008,* ☎ *77681180,* FAX *77682380,* WEB *www.choice.no. 66 rooms, 3 suites. Restaurant. AE, DC, MC, V.*

Hammerfest

With 10,000 inhabitants, Hammerfest is the world's northernmost town. Founded in 1789, it is an elegant, festive-looking port. In the late 19th century fire consumed it, and years later, defeated German troops destroyed the town as they retreated. Modern Hammerfest is the natural starting point for exploring Finnmark.

Discover **Sami culture** and try traditional Sami food on a trip to a *mikkelgammen* (Sami turf hut) just outside town through Hammerfest Turist AS (☎ 78412185). The city is also home to **Isbjørn Klubben** (Royal and Ancient Polar Bear Society), which has taxidermic displays of polar bears and other Arctic animals. ✉ *Town Hall ground floor,* ☎ *78413100,* WEB *www.hammerfest-turist.no/polarbear/.* ⏲ *June–Aug., weekdays 7–7; Sept.–May, daily 11:30–1:30.*

Far North Essentials

BOAT AND FERRY TRAVEL

One of the best ways to travel in northern Norway is aboard a *Hurtigruta* (contact Tromsø coastal steamer company for information), which starts out in Bergen and turns around 2,000 nautical km (1,250 mi) farther north at Kirkenes. Many steamers run this route, so you can stay in port for any length of time and pick up the next one coming through. Major tourist offices have schedules, and reservations are essential as far as a year in advance (☞ Visitor Information, *below*).

➤ BOAT AND FERRY INFORMATION: **Tromsø coastal steamer company** (☎ 77648200).

CAR TRAVEL

E6 and its feeder roads are the only routes available north of Trondheim, where the country narrows dramatically.

TRAIN TRAVEL

A major train route runs from Oslo to Trondheim, then to Bodø. From Bodø tours go to the Lofoten Islands by ferry. To reach the Nordkapp (North Cape), the northernmost mainland point in Europe, you must continue your trip by bus from Fauske. With a Scanrailpass you get a 50% discount on buses. From Narvik a train to Sweden departs twice a day. In summer a day trip through wild and beautiful scenery takes you to the Swedish border. Schedule and fare information is available from the tourist office at Narvik (☞ *below*).

VISITOR INFORMATION

➤ TOURIST INFORMATION: **Ålesund** (✉ Rådhuset, ☎ 70157600). **Bodø** (✉ Sjøgt. 21, ☎ 75548000). **Hammerfest** (✉ 9600, ☎ 78412185). **Harstad** (✉ Torvet 8, ☎ 77063235). **Lofoten Islands** (✉ 8300 Svolvær, ☎ 76073000). **Narvik** (✉ Kongensgt. 66, ☎ 76946033). **Tromsø** (✉ Storgt. 61, ☎ 77610000). **Trondheim** (✉ Munkegt. 19, ☎ 73929394).

23 POLAND

WARSAW, KRAKÓW AND ENVIRONS, GDAŃSK AND THE NORTH

POLES ARE FOND OF QUOTING, with a wry grimace, the old Chinese curse, "May you live in interesting times." The times were certainly interesting in 1990s Poland, the home of the Solidarity political-labor-social movement that sent shock waves through the Soviet Bloc in 1980, and the first Eastern European state to shake off Communist rule. But as the grimace implies, being on the firing line of history—something that the Poles are well used to—can be uncomfortable. Poles in the new millennium are looking forward to membership in the European Union (EU) to gain the stability that eluded Poland in the 20th century.

You will be constantly reminded in Poland that the return to free-market capitalism after more than 45 years of state socialism is an experiment on an unprecedented scale that has brought hardships for millions but also benefits for a growing percentage of the population. With 39 million inhabitants living in a territory of 312,677 square km (119,755 square mi), Poland in the 1990s was suspended between the Old World and the New, and the images can be confusing. Bright, new, privately owned shops with smiling assistants carry on business in shabby buildings that have not been renovated for decades. Billboards advertise goods that most Poles cannot afford. Many key public services have deteriorated as local authorities make valiant attempts to satisfy an increasingly demanding electorate with woefully insufficient funds. In 1999, the government introduced sweeping reform programs in the fields of education, health care, and social security.

The official trappings of the Communist state were quickly dismantled after the Solidarity victory in the 1989 elections. But Communism never sat easily with the Poles. It represented yet another stage in their age-old struggle to retain their identity in the face of pressure from large and powerful neighbors to the west and east. Since its foundation as a unified state on the great north European plain in the 10th century, Poland has stood at the heart of Europe, precisely at the halfway point on a line drawn from the Atlantic coast of Spain to the Ural Mountains. This has never been an enviable position. During the Middle Ages Poland fought against German advance; in the golden age of Polish history during the 16th and 17th centuries—of which you will be reminded by splendid Renaissance buildings in many parts of the country—Poland pushed eastward against her Slavic neighbors, taking Kiev and dreaming of a kingdom that stretched from the Baltic to the Black Sea. By the end of the 18th century Poland's territories were divided among the Austrian, Prussian, and Russian empires.

In the 20th century Poland fell victim to peculiarly vicious forms of dictatorship—from both the right and the left: the brutal Nazi occupation and imposition of Soviet rule. Poland's ancient cities—Kraków, Warsaw, Gdańsk—tell much of the tale of European history and culture. Its countryside offers unrivaled opportunities to escape from the present. Paradoxically, Communism—which after 1956 dropped attempts to collectivize agriculture and left the Polish farmer on his small, uneconomical plot—has left rural Poland in something of a time warp. Despite pollution, cornflowers still bloom, storks perch atop untidy nests by cottage chimneys, and horsepower still frequently comes in the four-legged variety. While the Poles have a certain wary reserve, they will win you over with their strong individualism—expressed through their well-developed sense of humor and their capacity for conviviality.

It's likely to take several generations before the physical and psychological traces of 45 years of Soviet rule fade, and at least 20 years until Poland "catches up" with the poorest EU member in terms of standard of living. Nevertheless, Poland became a NATO member in 1997. Poland, whose economy has seen a steady growth rate of five percent during the year 2000, is one of two other central European countries fast-tracked for European Union membership, possibly joining as early as 2004.

POLAND A TO Z

To research prices, get advice from other travelers, and book travel arrangements, visit www.fodors.com.

AIR TRAVEL

LOT, Poland's national airline, operates daily flights linking eight main cities: Warsaw, Kraków, Gdańsk, Wrocław, Szczecin, Poznań, Katowice, and Rzeszów. Fares begin at about $80 round-trip from Warsaw. Tickets and information are available from LOT or any travel agent. Be sure to book well in advance, especially for the summer season.

BUS TRAVEL

PKS is the national bus company. Polski Express is private and much nicer. Both offer long-distance service to most cities. Express buses, on which you can reserve seats, are somewhat more expensive than trains but often—except in the case of a few major intercity routes—get to their destinations more quickly. For really out-of-the-way destinations, the bus is often the only means of transportation. Bus stations are usually quite near railway stations. Tickets and information are best obtained from any travel agency, hotel, or the bus station itself.

➤ Bus Information: **PKS** (☎ 022/823–63–94) is the national bus company. **Polski Express** (☎ 022/620–03–30).

BUSINESS HOURS

Banks are open weekdays 8 or 9–3 or 6. Museum hours vary greatly but are generally Tuesday–Sunday 10–5. Among shops, food shops are open weekdays 7–7, Saturday 7–1 or 2; many are now open on Sunday, and there are a few all-night stores in most central shopping districts. Other stores are open weekdays 11–7 and Saturday 9–1 or 2.

CAR TRAVEL

EMERGENCIES

Poland's Motoring Association (PZMot) offers breakdown, repair, and towing services to members of various international insurance organizations; check with Orbis before you leave home. Carry a spare-parts kit. For emergency road help call ☎ 981.

GASOLINE

The price of gas is about zł 2.9 for a liter of high-octane fuel. Filling stations are located every 30 km (19 mi) or so and are usually open 6 AM–10 PM. More and more bright, clean, full-service 24-hour stations are opening each year, and they're often accompanied by fast-food restaurants or grocery stores.

ROAD CONDITIONS

Despite the extensive road network, a major increase in traffic in the 1990s and the lack of divided highways have made driving in Poland extremely dangerous. Minor roads tend to be narrow and encumbered with horse-drawn carts, bicycles, and pedestrians. If you're in a hurry, stick to roads marked E (express roads that in theory lead to a Polish border) or A (domestic express roads).

RULES OF THE ROAD

Driving is on the right. The speed limit on highways is 110 kph (68 mph) and on roads in built-up areas, 60 kph (37 mph). A built-up area is marked by a white rectangular sign with the name of the town on it. A new law was introduced in 1999 making it illegal to use cellular phones while driving.

CUSTOMS AND DUTIES

Persons over 18 may bring in duty-free: personal belongings, including musical instruments, one computer, one radio, one camera with 24 rolls of film, up to 250 cigarettes, 50 cigars, 1 liter of spirits, 2 liters of vodka, 2 liters of wine, and 5 liters of beer. Additional goods with a collective value of $75 may be brought into the country. The foreign currency limit is $5,200, and it must be declared on arrival.

➤ INFORMATION: **Customs information** (Warsaw: ☎ 022/650–28–73).

DINING

Polish food and drink are basically Slavic with Baltic overtones. The emphasis is on soups and meat (especially pork), as well as freshwater fish. Cream is a staple, and pastries are rich and often delectable. The most popular soup is *barszcz* (known to many Americans as borscht), a clear beet soup often served with such Polish favorites as sausage, cabbage, potatoes, sour cream, coarse rye bread, and beer. Other typical dishes are pierogi, which may be stuffed with savory or sweet fillings; *gołąbki* (cabbage leaves stuffed with minced meat); *bigos* (sauerkraut with meat and mushrooms); and *flaki* (a tripe soup). Polish beer is excellent; vodka is a specialty and is often downed before, during, and after meals.

Zajazdy (roadside inns) and *bar mleczny* (milk bars), which are often less expensive than regular restaurants, serve more traditional food. As elsewhere in Central Europe, cafés are a way of life in Poland and often serve delicious homemade pastries and ice cream.

Prices are for one main course at dinner.

CATEGORY	WARSAW/KRAKÓW	OTHER AREAS
$$$$	over zł 50	over zł 35
$$$	zł 35–zł 50	zł 20–zł 35
$$	zł 15–zł 35	zł 10–zł 20
$	under zł 15	under zł 10

MEALTIMES

Poles eat their main meal at around 2 PM, with a light supper at about 8 PM. Restaurants—especially in major cities—open around noon for lunch and serve dinner between 7 and 10 PM. Although many restaurants in the provinces close around 10 PM, more cosmopolitan establishments stay open until 11 PM or later. Most hotel restaurants serve the evening meal until 10:30.

RESERVATIONS AND DRESS

In Warsaw and Kraków jacket and tie is customary at $$$ and $$$$ restaurants. Casual dress is appropriate elsewhere.

EMBASSIES

All embassies are located in Warsaw. The United Kingdom has a consulate in Warsaw, and the United States maintains one in Kraków.

➤ AUSTRALIA: (✉ Ul. Nowogrodzka 11, ☎ 022/521–34–34, WEB www.ausembwa.it.com.pl).

➤ CANADA: (✉ Ul. Jerozolimskie 123, ☎ 022/584–31–00).

➤ UNITED KINGDOM: (✉ Al. Róż 1, ☎ 022/628–10–01, WEB www.britishembassy.pl).

➤ UNITED STATES: (✉ Al. Ujazdowskie 29–31, ☎ 022/628–30–41).

HEALTH

Tap water in major cities is unsafe to drink, so ask for bottled mineral water. Beware of meat dishes served in cheap snack bars.

HOLIDAYS

January 1; Easter Monday; May 1 (Labor Day); May 3 (Constitution Day); June 22 (Corpus Christi); August 15 (Assumption); November 1 (All Saints' Day); November 11 (Independence Day; rebirth of the Polish state in 1918); December 25, 26.

LANGUAGE

Polish is a Slavic language that uses the Roman alphabet but has several additional characters and diacritical marks. Because it has a high incidence of consonant clusters, most English speakers find it a difficult language to decipher, much less pronounce. Many older Poles speak German; the younger generation usually knows some English. In larger cities English is increasingly common, especially in hotels, but you may have difficulty in the countryside.

LODGING

Acceptable lodging can be found even in remote corners of the country. For luxurious, world-class accommodations you'll have to wait several more years before being satisfied with offerings outside Warsaw.

The following prices are a rate for two people in a double room with bath or shower and breakfast. These prices are in U.S. dollars; many hotels in Poland quote prices in American dollars or German marks because of the fluctuations in Polish currency.

CATEGORY	COST
$$$$	over $200
$$$	$100–$200
$$	$50–$100
$	under $50

APARTMENT AND VILLA RENTALS

Rooms can be arranged either in advance through a travel agent or on the spot at the local tourist information office. Villas, lodges, rooms, or houses are available. Daily rates vary from about $8 for a room to more than $150 for a villa.

HOTELS

The government rates hotel accommodations from one to five stars. A tourism law that took effect in July 1998 sets standards for each rating where none previously existed. Note that even the best hotels in Poland do not have a five-star rating—usually because they don't want to pay the 22% value-added tax that accompanies the honor.

Orbis hotels, owned by the state tourist office and currently undergoing privatization, have almost all been accorded three or four stars and guarantee a reasonable standard of cleanliness and service (although they tend to lack character). Most of them range in price from $$ to $$$$; the chain includes a number of foreign-built luxury hotels. In recent years Orbis hotels have faced competition from a growing number of privately owned lodgings, often part of international chains and mostly in the top price range. Discounts on various ranges of hotels and castles throughout the country are offered at www.hotelspoland.com.

Municipal hotels and Dom Turysty hotels are run by local authorities or the Polish Tourist Association. They are often rather old and can have limited bath and shower facilities. Standards are improving as many undergo renovations; prices are in the $$ category.

ROADSIDE INNS

Many roadside inns are quite attractive, offering inexpensive food and guest rooms at moderate rates.

MAIL AND SHIPPING

POSTAL RATES

Airmail letters abroad cost about zł 1.60 (depending on weight); postcards, zł 1.10. Post offices are open weekdays 8–8. At least one post office is open 24 hours in every major city. In Warsaw the 24-hour post office is at ulica Świętokrzyska 31.

MONEY MATTERS

Inflation in Poland is high by Western standards, although the rate has fallen to about 10% annually. Prices are highest in the big cities, especially Warsaw.

A cup of coffee, zł 3–zł 7; a bottle of beer, zł 4–zł 8; a soft drink, zł 2–zł 5; a ham sandwich, zł 4–zł 6; a 2-km (1-mi) taxi ride, zł 5.20.

CREDIT CARDS

Major credit cards are accepted in all major hotels, in the better restaurants and nightclubs, and for other tourist services. In small cafés and shops, especially in the provinces, credit cards are not accepted.

CURRENCY

The monetary unit in Poland is the złoty (zł), which is divided into 100 groszy (gr). There are notes of 10, 20, 50, 100, and 200 złotys, and coins in values of 1, 2, and 5 złotys and 1, 2, 5, 10, 20, and 50 groszys. At press time (summer 2001), the exchange rate was zł 4.38 to the U.S. dollar, zł 2.98 to the Canadian dollar, zł 6.57 to the pound sterling, zł 5.26 to the Irish punt, zł 2.64 to the Australian dollar, zł 2.08 to the New Zealand dollar, and zł 0.63 to the South African rand.

The złoty is exchangeable at a free-market rate in banks and at *kantory* (private exchange bureaus), which sometimes offer slightly better rates than banks do and are usually open until 8 PM. There are also cash machines throughout the country that accept most major credit cards as long as you have a personal identification number. (Bankomat currently has more than 500 machines in Poland.)

PASSPORTS AND VISAS

ENTERING POLAND

Citizens of the United States and the United Kingdom do not need visas for entry to Poland; Canadian citizens and citizens of other countries must apply to the Polish Consulate General in any country. (Canadians must pay the equivalent of C$89 and more for multiple-entry visas.) Visitors from Canada and other countries who are required to have visas must complete one application form and provide two photographs; allow one to two weeks for processing. Visas for Canadians are issued for 180 days but can be extended in Poland through the local province police headquarters.

TELEPHONES

COUNTRY AND AREA CODES

The international country code for Poland is 48. When dialing a number in Poland from outside the country, drop the initial 0 from the local area code.

DIRECTORY AND OPERATOR ASSISTANCE

For local directory information, dial 913; for Poland-wide directory information and dialing codes, dial 912; for international information and codes, dial 908.

INTERNATIONAL CALLS

Post offices and first-class hotels have booths at which you can use your calling card or pay after completing your call. If you need to place a call on a calling card, various international operators can be reached from Poland.

➤ ACCESS CODES: AT&T USA Direct (☎ 0–0800/111–1111). **MCI** (☎ 0–0800/111–2122). **Sprint Global One** (☎ 0–0800/111–3115).

LOCAL CALLS

Most public phones in Poland now take phone cards, and not coins. The cards can be used for either local or long-distance calls. The cards, which cost zł 6.41, zł 12.81, or zł 25.62 depending on how much time you are purchasing, are sold at kiosks, post offices, and hotels. When making a long-distance call, first dial 0, wait for the dial tone, then dial the rest of the number.

TIPPING

At restaurants, if service is not included, waiters get a standard 10% of the bill. On smaller bills, round upward to the nearest zł or two. Hotel porters and doormen get about zł 2 per bag.

TRAIN TRAVEL

Poland's PKP railway network is extensive and relatively inexpensive. Most trains have first- and second-class accommodations, but Western visitors usually prefer to travel first-class. You should arrive at the station well before departure time. The fastest trains are intercity and express trains, which require reservations. Orbis and other travel agents furnish information, reservations, and tickets. If you're traveling on overnight trains, reserve a berth in a first- or second-class car. Long-distance trains carry buffets.

FARES AND SCHEDULES

Polish trains run at three speeds—*ekspresowy* (express), *pośpieszny* (fast), and *osobowy* (slow)—and fares vary accordingly. You pay more for intercity and express, and round-trip tickets are priced at precisely double the one-way fare.

VISITOR INFORMATION

There is no national tourist office in Poland. State-run tourist offices are listed in individual cities' Essentials sections.

WHEN TO GO

The main tourist season runs from May through September. The best times for sightseeing are late spring and early fall. Major cultural events usually take place in the cities during the fall.

CLIMATE

The early spring is often wet and windy. Below are the average daily maximum and minimum temperatures for Warsaw.

Jan.	32F	0C	**May**	67F	20C	**Sept.**	66F	19C
	22	– 6		48	9		49	10
Feb.	32F	0C	**June**	73F	23C	**Oct.**	55F	13C
	21	– 6		54	12		41	5
Mar.	42F	6C	**July**	75F	24C	**Nov.**	42F	6C
	28	– 2		58	16		33	1
Apr.	53F	12C	**Aug.**	73F	23C	**Dec.**	35F	2C
	37	3		56	14		28	– 3

WARSAW

At the end of World War II Warsaw lay in ruins, a victim of systematic Nazi destruction. Only one-third of its prewar population survived the German occupation. The experience is visible everywhere in the memorial plaques describing mass executions of civilians and in the bullet holes still on the facades of some buildings. Surrounding the old districts is the modern Warsaw, built since the war in utilitarian Socialist and later styles, giving it a certain "Soviet" feel.

Exploring Warsaw

Numbers in the margin correspond to points of interest on the Warsaw map.

The sights of Warsaw are all relatively close to one another, making most attractions accessible on foot. A walking tour of the old historic district takes about two hours. A walk along the former Royal Route—the Trakt Królewski—which stretches south from Castle Square down Krakowskie Przedmieście, through Nowy Świat, and on along Aleje Ujazdowskie, considered by many locals to be Warsaw's finest street, is also worthwhile. Lined with magnificent buildings and embassies, it has something of a French flavor. The Muranów district is the site of Jewish Warsaw.

Stare Miasto (Old Town) and Nowego Miasto (New Town)

Both Old and New Town lay in rubble after the war; Varsovians painstakingly rebuilt these districts, reconstructing them after consulting old prints and paintings. The remarkable result is an area whose buildings are painted in warm pastel colors. If you did not know their tragic histories, you would think these buildings dated back hundreds of years.

7 **Barbakan** (Barbican). This pinnacled redbrick gate is a fine example of a 16th-century defensive fortification. From here you can see the partially restored wall that was built to enclose the Old Town and enjoy a splendid view of the Vistula River, with the district of Praga on its east bank. ✉ *Ul. Freta.*

3 **Bazylika Świętego Jana** (Cathedral of St. John). Dating from the 14th century, this is the oldest church in Warsaw. Several Polish kings were crowned here. ✉ *Ul. Świętojańska 8.*

10 **Kościół Najświętszej Marii Panny** (St. Mary's Church). This is the oldest church in the New Town, built as a parish church for the district by the princes of Mazovia in the early 15th century. St. Mary's has been destroyed and rebuilt many times throughout its history. The Gothic bell tower dates from the early 16th century. ✉ *Ul. Przyrynek 2.*

6 **Muzeum Historyczne Warszawy** (Historical Museum of Warsaw). This excellent museum detailing the history of the city has a 20-minute movie, *Warsaw Remembers,* describing the history of Warsaw and mostly made up of old footage. It is shown in English every day at noon. ✉ *Rynek Starego Miasta 28,* ☎ *022/635–16–25.* ⏲ *Tues. and Thurs. 11–6, Wed., Fri., Sat. 10–3:30, Sun. 10:30–4:30.*

5 **Muzeum Literatury Adama Mickiewicza** (Adam Mickiewicz Museum of Literature). This museum has manuscripts, mementoes, and portraits of Polish writers. ✉ *Rynek Starego Miasto 20,* ☎ *022/831–40–61.* ⏲ *Mon.–Tues. and Fri. 10–3, Wed.–Thurs. and Sat. 11–6, Sun. 11–5.*

8 **Muzeum Marii Skłodowskiej-Curie** (Marie Curie Museum). This beige-and-rose-color stone house was the birthplace of the Nobel Prize win-

ner for physics (1903)—for the discovery of radium and polonium (named after Poland)—and chemistry (1911). ✉ *Ul. Freta 16,* ☎ *022/831–80–92.* ⏲ *Tues.–Sat. 10–4, Sun. 10–2.*

1 **Plac Zamkowy** (Castle Square). Here a slender column supports the **statue of Zygmunt (Sigismund) III Wasa,** king of Poland and Sweden, who moved the country's capital from Kraków to Warsaw in the early 17th century. The city's oldest monument, it was the first to be rebuilt after World War II. ✉ *Junction ul. Miodowa and Krakowskie Przedmieście.*

9 **Rynek Nowego Miasta** (New Town Square). The center of the New Town is slightly more irregular and relaxed than its Old Town counterpart. The town was founded at the turn of the 15th century. Rebuilt after World War II in 18th-century style, the **Nowe Miasto** district has a spacious feeling to it. ✉ *Off ul. Freta.*

★ 4 **Rynek Starego Miasta** (Old Town Market Square). In summer the square is full of open-air cafés and tubs of flowering plants; artists display their talents for tourists year-round. At night the brightly lighted Rynek is the place to go for good food and atmosphere. The streets of the **Stare Miasto** have colorful medieval houses, cobblestone alleys, uneven roofs, and wrought-iron grillwork. A statue of a mermaid, the symbol of Warsaw, is in the middle of the square. ✉ *Junction ul. Piedarska and ul. Świętojańska.*

★ 2 **Zamek Królewski** (Royal Castle). The princes of Mazovia first built a residence here in the 14th century; its present Renaissance form dates from the reign of King Sigismund III, who needed a magnificent palace for his new capital. Reconstructed later than the Old Town, in the 1970s, the castle now gleams as it did in its earliest years, with gilt, marble, and wall paintings; it houses impressive art collections—including views of Warsaw by Canaletto's nephew Bernardo Bellotto (known in Poland as "Canaletto"), which were used to help rebuild the city after the war. ✉ *Pl. Zamkowy 4,* ☎ *022/657–21–70.* ⏲ *Daily 10–4; tours available in English.*

Trakt Królewski (The Royal Route)

All towns with kings had their Royal Routes; the one in Warsaw stretched south from Castle Square down Krakowskie Przedmieście, through Nowy Świat, and on along Aleje Ujazdowskie to Łazienki Park. Some of Warsaw's finest churches and palaces are along this route.

22 **Former headquarters of the Polish Communist Party.** This large, solid, gray building, erected in the Socialist-Realist architectural style, now houses banks and, until 2000, the Warsaw Stock Exchange, now located off of Ul. Prusa. ✉ *Corner Al. Jerozolimskie and Nowy Świat.*

17 **Galeria Zachęta** (Zachęta Gallery). Built during the last years of the 19th century by the Society for the Encouragement of the Fine Arts, the gallery was the site of the assassination of the first president of the post–World War I Polish Republic, Gabriel Narutowicz, by a right-wing fanatic in 1922. It has no permanent collection but organizes thought-provoking special exhibitions—primarily modern art and photography—in lofty, well-lit halls. It also has an excellent bookshop. ✉ *Pl. Małachowskiego 3,* ☎ *022/827–69–09.* ⏲ *Tues.–Sun. 10–6.*

26 **Gestapo Headquarters.** Now the Ministry of National Education, the building also houses a small museum that recalls the horrors that took place behind its peaceful facade. ✉ *Al. Szucha 25,* ☎ *022/629–49–19.* ⏲ *Wed. 9–5, Thurs. and Sat. 9–4, Fri. 10–5, Sun. 10–4.*

15 **Grób Nieznanego Żołnierza** (Tomb of the Unknown Soldier). The only surviving fragment of an early 18th-century Saxon palace, which

Warsaw (Warszawa)

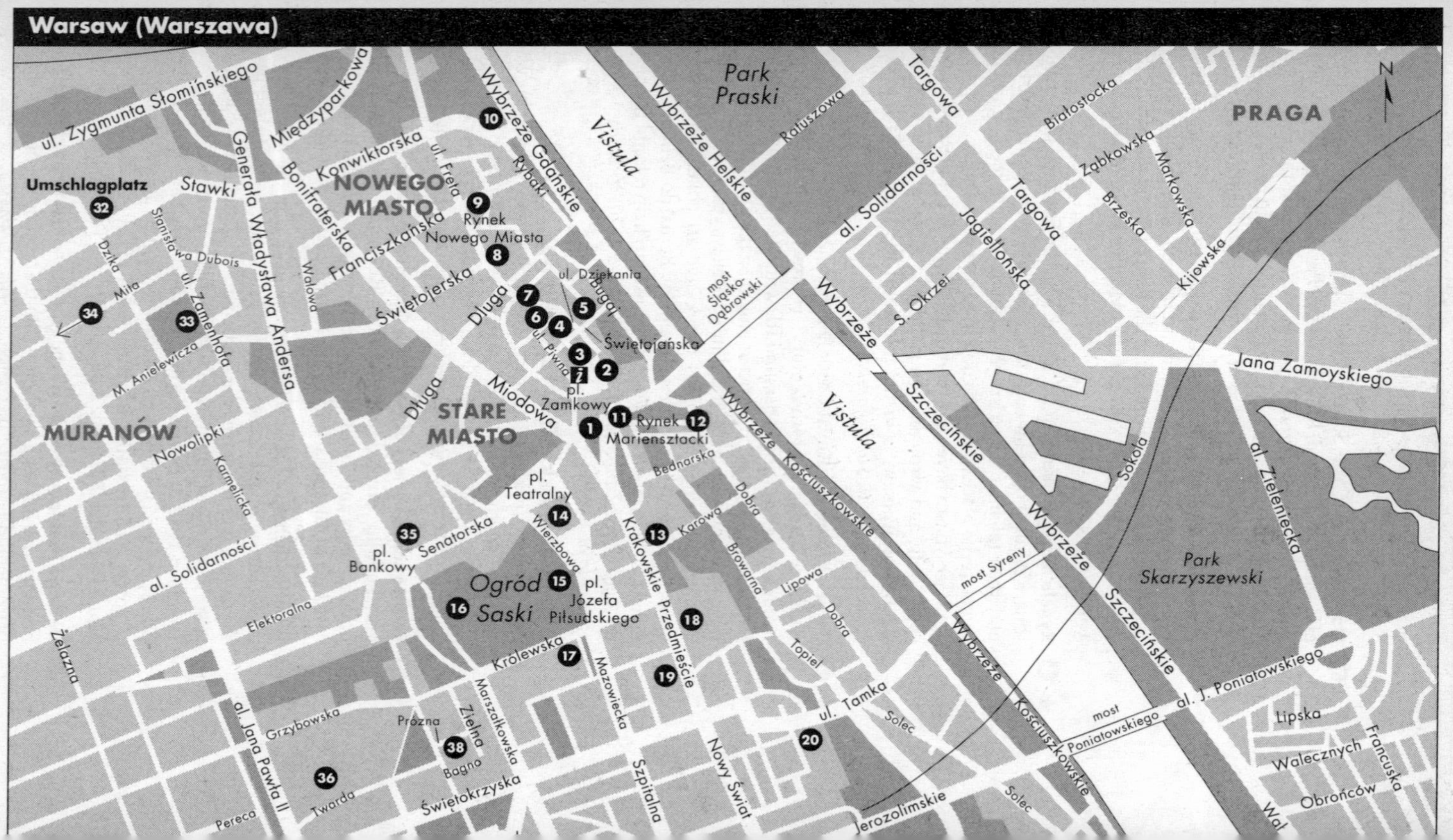

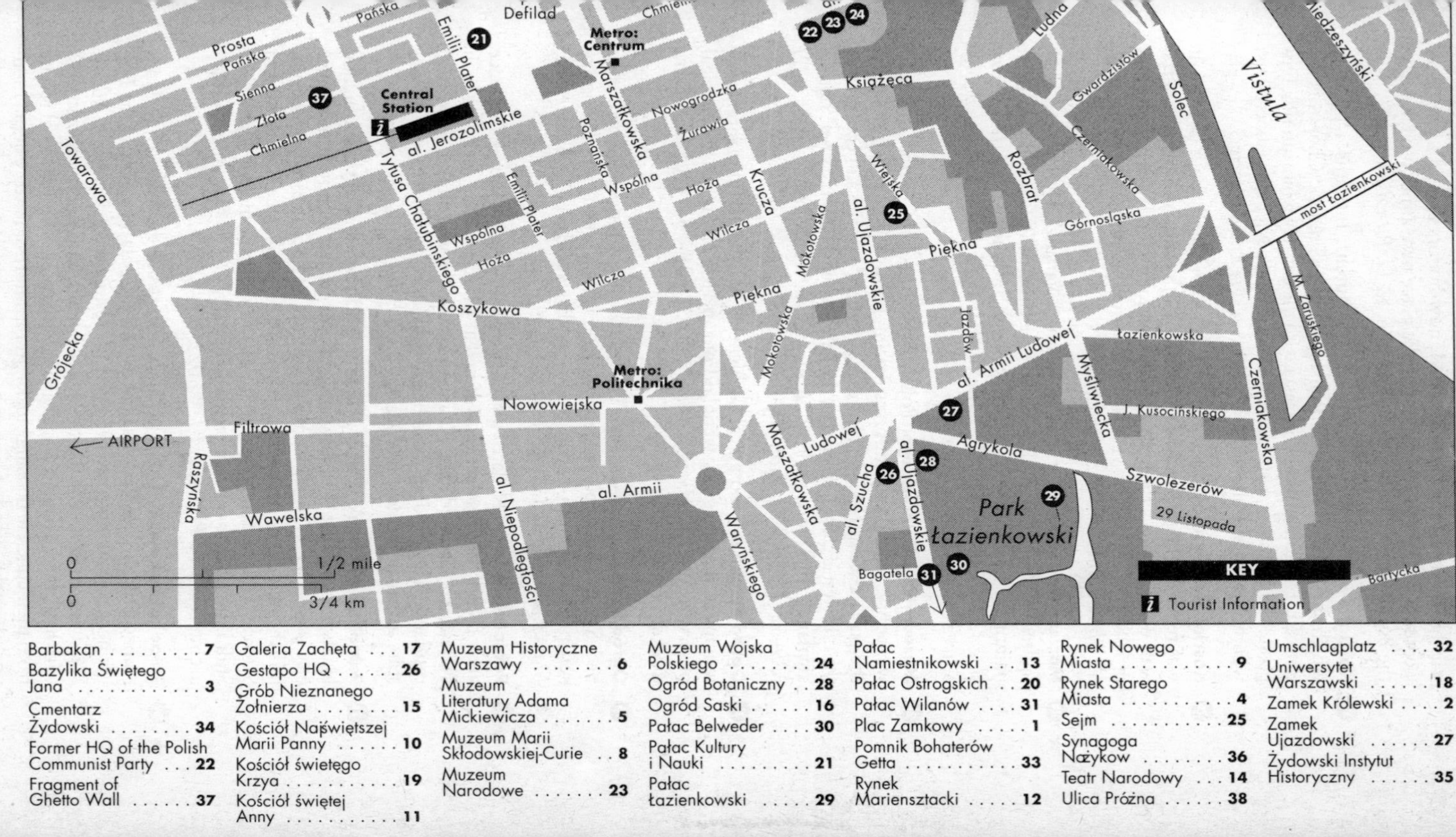

Barbakan 7
Bazylika Świętego Jana 3
Cmentarz Żydowski 34
Former HQ of the Polish Communist Party . . . 22
Fragment of Ghetto Wall 37
Galeria Zachęta . . . 17
Gestapo HQ 26
Grób Nieznanego Żołnierza 15
Kościół Najświętszej Marii Panny 10
Kościół świętego Krzya 19
Kościół świętej Anny 11
Muzeum Historyczne Warszawy 6
Muzeum Literatury Adama Mickiewicza 5
Muzeum Marii Skłodowskiej-Curie . . 8
Muzeum Narodowe 23
Muzeum Wojska Polskiego 24
Ogród Botaniczny . . 28
Ogród Saski 16
Pałac Belweder 30
Pałac Kultury i Nauki 21
Pałac Łazienkowski 29
Pałac Namiestnikowski . . . 13
Pałac Ostrogskich . . 20
Pałac Wilanów 31
Plac Zamkowy 1
Pomnik Bohaterów Getta 33
Rynek Mariensztacki 12
Rynek Nowego Miasta 9
Rynek Starego Miasta 4
Sejm 25
Synagoga Nożyków 36
Teatr Narodowy . . . 14
Ulica Próżna 38
Umschlagplatz 32
Uniwersytet Warszawski 18
Zamek Królewski 2
Zamek Ujazdowski 27
Żydowski Instytut Historyczny 35

was blown up by the Nazis in 1944, now honors Poland's war dead. Ceremonial changes of the guard take place here at noon on Sunday; the Polish army still uses the goose step. ✉ *Pl. Piłsudskiego.*

19 **Kościoł świętego Krzya** (Holy Cross Church). Inside is a pillar in which the heart of the great Polish composer Frédéric Chopin is entombed. The golden altar contrasts with the entirely white interior. Opposite the church is a statue of the astronomer Nicolaus Copernicus, who was born in Poland. ✉ *Ul. Krakowskie Przedmieście 3.*

11 **Kościół świętej Anny** (St. Anne's Church). Originally built in 1454, it was rebuilt in High Baroque style in the 17th century. A plaque on the wall outside marks the spot where Pope John Paul II celebrated mass in 1980, during his first visit to Poland after his election to the papacy. ✉ *Ul. Krakowskie Przedmieście 68.*

★ 23 **Muzeum Narodowe** (National Museum of Warsaw). The spacious, skylighted museum has an impressive collection of Polish and European paintings, Gothic icons, and works from antiquity. ✉ *Al. Jerozolimskie 3,* ☎ *022/629–30–93.* ⏲ *Tues.–Wed. and Fri. 10–4, Thurs. noon–5, weekends 10–5.*

24 **Muzeum Wojska Polskiego** (Polish Army Museum). With exhibits of weaponry, armor, and uniforms tracing Polish military history across the past 10 centuries, it captures the romance of the subject. Even if the museum is closed, stroll past the gates to see the military helicopters, airplanes, and tanks parked outside. ✉ *Al. Jerozolimskie 3,* ☎ *022/629–52–71.* ⏲ *Wed.–Sun. 10–4.*

28 **Ogród Botaniczny** (Botanical Gardens). These beautiful plantings belonging to the university were laid out in 1818. Note the neoclassical **observatory.** ✉ *Al. Ujazdowskie 4,* ☎ *022/628–75–14.* ⏲ *May–Oct., weekdays 9–8, weekends 10–7.*

16 **Ogród Saski** (Saxon Gardens). The palace park was designed by French and Saxon landscape gardeners; the gardens contain 18th-century sculptures, a man-made pond, and a sundial. ✉ *Corner ul. Marszałkowska and ul. Królewska.*

30 **Pałac Belweder** (Belvedere Palace). This 18th-century former residence and office of the president was vacated in 1995 by former president Lech Wałesa, who declared Pałac Namiestnikowski the new official presidential residence. The building could become a museum or lodging for official state guests in the next few years. ✉ *Ul. Belwederska 2.*

21 **Pałac Kultury i Nauki** (Palace of Culture and Science). With ironic humor, locals tell you that the best vantage point from which to admire their city is atop the 37-story Palace of Culture and Science. Why? Because it is the only point from which you can't see the Palace of Culture and Science. This wedding-cake-style skyscraper was a personal gift from Stalin. It is Warsaw's best example of early 1950s "Socialist Gothic" architecture. ✉ *Pl. Defilad 1,* ☎ *022/656–68–54.* ⏲ *Daily 9–6.*

★ 29 **Pałac Łazienkowski** (Łazienki Palace). Set inside the wonderfully landscaped French-style **Park Łazienkowski,** the palace, a gem of the Polish neoclassical style, was the private residence of Stanisław August Poniatowski (1732–98), the last king of Poland. It overlooks a lake stocked with huge carp. To many Varsovians, this park provides the ideal respite from their concrete housing blocks. At the impressionistic Chopin monument nearby, wonderful open-air concerts take place on summer Sundays. ✉ *Ul. Agrykola 1,* ☎ *022/621–62–41.* ⏲ *Tues.–Sun. 9:30–3.*

13 **Pałac Namiestnikowski** (Namiestnikowski Palace). Built during the 17th century by the Radziwiłł family (into which Jacqueline Kennedy's sis-

ter, Lee, later married), this palace at one time functioned as the administrative office of the tsarist occupiers. In 1955 the Warsaw Pact was signed here, and now the palace serves as the official residence of Poland's president. In the forecourt is an equestrian statue of Prince Józef Poniatowski, a nephew of the last king of Poland, and one of Napoléon's marshals. It is closed to the public and heavily guarded. ✉ *Krakowskie Przedmieście 46–48.*

20 **Pałac Ostrogskich** (Ostrogski Palace). Headquarters of the Chopin Society, the 17th-century mansion towers impressively above the street. The best approach is along the steps from ulica Tamka. In the 19th century the Warsaw Conservatory was housed here (Paderewski was one of its students); now used for Chopin concerts, it has a small museum with mementoes of the composer. ✉ *Ul. Okólnik 1,* ☎ *022/827–54–71.* ⏲ *Mon.–Wed. and Fri.–Sat. 10–2, Thurs. noon–6.*

★ 31 **Pałac Wilanów** (Wilanow Palace). Built by King Jan Sobieski, who in 1683 stopped the Ottoman advance on Europe at the Battle of Vienna, the palace later passed into the hands of Stanisław Kostka Potocki. Potocki amassed a major art collection and was responsible for the layout of the palace gardens. He opened Poland's first public museum here in 1805. The palace still houses much of the original furniture; there's also a striking display of 16th- to 18th-century Polish portraits on the first floor. Outside, to the left of the main entrance, is a romantic park with pagodas, summerhouses, and bridges overlooking a lake. There's also a **gallery** of contemporary Polish art on the grounds, and the stables to the right of the entrance house a **poster museum.** ✉ *Ul. Wiertnicza 1, 10 km (6 mi) from town center,* ☎ *022/842–81–01.* ⏲ *Museum Wed.–Mon. 9:30–2:30, park Wed.–Mon. until dusk.*

12 **Rynek Mariensztacki** (Mariensztat Square). At the bottom and to the left of a steeply sloping, cobbled street lies a quiet, leafy 18th-century square that is worth a detour. ✉ *Ul. Bednarska.*

25 **Sejm.** The Polish Houses of Parliament, with their round, white debating chamber, were built in the 1920s, after the rebirth of an independent Polish state. The building is not open to the public. ✉ *Ul. Wiejska 4–6.*

14 **Teatr Narodowy** (Opera House and National Theater). This columned theater was built in the 1820s and reconstructed after World War II. It has a grand dome that is adorned inside with abstract constellation art. The **Museum Teatralne** (Museum of Theatre; ☎ 022/826–52–13), on the first floor, is open Friday–Wednesday 10–2. ✉ *Pl. Teatralny,* ☎ *022/629-02–08.*

18 **Uniwersytet Warszawski** (University of Warsaw). Established in 1816, the university has been a center for independent political thinking; most student protests have started here. Near the university, in the small garden opposite ulica Bednarska, stands a monument to the great Polish poet Adam Mickiewicz. It was here that Warsaw University students gathered in March 1968, after a performance of Mickiewicz's until-then banned play, *Forefathers' Eve,* and set in motion the events that led to the toppling of Poland's longtime Communist leader Władysław Gomułka. ✉ *Krakowskie Przedmieście 26–28,* ☎ *022/620–03–81.*

27 **Zamek Ujazdowski** (Ujazdów Castle). Reconstructed in the 1980s, this is now the home of the **Centrum Sztuki Współczesnej** (Center for Contemporary Art), which hosts a variety of exhibitions by Polish, European, and North American artists. At the back, a terrace overlooks formal gardens laid out down to the Vistula. ✉ *Al. Ujazdowskie 6,* ☎ *022/628–12–71.* ⏲ *Tues.–Thurs. and weekends 11–5, Fri. 11–9.*

The Muranów District

The Muranów district is the historic heart of the old prewar Warsaw Jewish district and ghetto under the Nazi regime. In April 1943 the Jewish resistance began the Warsaw Ghetto uprising, which was suppressed by the Nazis with unbelievable ferocity; the Muranów district was flattened. Today there are only bleak gray apartment blocks here.

34 **Cmentarz Żydowski** (Jewish Cemetery). This active cemetery is an island of continuity amid destruction. It survived the war and, although badly neglected during the postwar period, is gradually being restored. Fine 19th-century headstones testify to the Jewish community's important role in Polish history and culture. ✉ *Ul. Okopowa 49–51.*

37 **Fragment of Ghetto Wall.** In the courtyard of this building, through the archway on the right, stands a 9½-ft-tall fragment of the ghetto wall that existed for one year from November 1940. ✉ *Ul. Złota 60.*

33 **Pomnik Bohaterów Getta** (Heroes of the Warsaw Ghetto). The simple monument to the heroes of the Warsaw Ghetto is a slab of dark granite with a bronze bas-relief. A monument—inscribed in Hebrew and Polish—also marks the site of the house at ulica Miła 18 in which the command bunker of the uprising was concealed. ✉ *Ul. Zamenhofa, between ul. Anielewicza and ul. Lewartowskiego.*

36 **Synagoga Nożykow** (Nozyk Synagogue). Founded in 1900 by Zelman and Ryfka Nożyk, the synagogue survived the war and is now the only active synagogue in Warsaw. ✉ *Ul. Twarda 6.*

38 **Ulica Próżna** (Prózna Street). This is the only thoroughfare in Jewish Warsaw where tenement buildings have been preserved on both sides of the street. The Lauder Foundation plans to restore the street to its original state. No. 9 belonged to Zelman Nożyk.

32 **Umschlagplatz.** From this rail terminus, hundreds of thousands of the ghetto's inhabitants were shipped in cattle cars to the extermination camp of Treblinka, about 100 km (60 mi) northeast of Warsaw. The school building to the right of the square was used to detain those who had to wait overnight for transport, and the beginning of the rail tracks survives on the right. At the entrance to the square is a **symbolic gateway**, erected in 1988 as a memorial on the 45th anniversary of the uprising. The first names of deportees are inscribed on the walls. ✉ *Corner ul. Stawki and ul. Dzika.*

35 **Żydowski Instytut Historyczny** (Jewish Historical Institute). Some 3 million Polish Jews were put to death by the Nazis during World War II, ending the enormous Jewish contribution to Polish culture, tradition, and achievement. The institute houses a genealogy project that acts as a clearinghouse of information on archival sources and on the history of towns and villages in which Polish Jews lived. The institute also houses a **museum** with photographs and displays of artifacts recalling a lost world. The nearby Sony building stands on the site of Warsaw's largest synagogue, which was blown up by the Nazis in May 1943 as a finale to the liquidation of the Jewish ghetto. ✉ *Ul. Tłomackie 3/5,* ☎ *022/827–92–21.* ⏲ *Mon.–Fri. 8–4, Thurs. 11–6.*

Dining

Interesting and ethnically diverse restaurants have sprung up over the city in the past few years, yet some of the most atmospheric dining rooms are still to be found on and around the Rynek Starego Miasta (Old Town Square). Reservations for dinner can be made by telephone (by your hotel receptionist if you don't speak Polish); in the case of expensive and fashionable restaurants, this is essential.

$$$$ ✕ **Belvedere.** Housed in the elegant, romantic 19th-century orangery in Łazienki Park, the restaurant has tables set among palms and waterfalls. The overpriced menu offers such traditional dishes as sliced breast of duck with a fruit sauce or, for a French touch, veal medallions in French pastry. ✉ *Łazienki Królewskie, entrance from ul. Parkowa,* ☎ *022/841–48–06. Reservations essential. AE, DC, MC, V.*

$$$ ✕ **Fukier.** This romantic restaurant with an opulent interior specializes in Polish cuisine with a European twist. Recognized as being one of the best restaurants in Poland, the beautifully restored townhouse has an original 15th century wine cellar. (✉ *Rynek Starego Miasta 27,* ☎ *022/831–58–08. AE, DC, MC, V.*

$$$ ★ ✕ **Karczma Gessler.** Three restaurants in one—the brick cellar, bathed in candlelight, serves traditional Polish recipes while music students often entertain. The ground floor houses a café and the first floor specializes in European cuisine. ✉ *Rynek Starego Miasta 21,* ☎ *022/831–44–27. Reservations essential. AE, DC, MC, V.*

$$ ✕ **Café Ejlat.** This Warsaw institution is owned by the Polish-Israeli Friendship Society and has a menu rich in Jewish specialties, including a halvah dessert, and contemporary Polish dishes. ✉ *Al. Ujazdowskie 47,* ☎ *022/628–54–72. AE, DC, MC, V.*

$$ ✕ **Pod Samsonem.** This simple, prewar Jewish-style (nonkosher) restaurant serves terrific traditional Polish food, but don't expect service with a smile. Order the borscht with dumplings. ✉ *Ul. Freta 3/5,* ☎ *022/831–17–88. AE, DC, MC, V.*

$$ ✕ **Qchnia Artystyczna.** This artsy place at the back of the Ujazdowski Castle is not for the stodgy. The service is getting better, and the mainly vegetarian menu is creative and filling. Sample the *naleśniki* (crepes stuffed with sweet cheese or fruit). In summer, outdoor tables overlook the park. ✉ *Ujazdowski Castle, al. Ujazdowskie 6,* ☎ *022/625–76–27. AE, DC, MC, V.*

$$ ★ ✕ **Restauracja Polska.** Decorated with antiques, floral prints, and fruits, the restaurant is a treat for the senses. The specialty here is nouvelle Polish cuisine, and the service is excellent. The royal carp with sour cream sauce is an update of the country's classic Christmas dish. ✉ *Ul. Nowy Świat 21,* ☎ *022/826–38–77. AE, DC, MC, V.*

$ ✕ **Czytelnik.** Intellectuals and politicians from the Parliament next door hang out at this cafeteria-style restaurant-café with homemade, upscale milk-bar cuisine: classic Polish soups, such as tomato and mushroom, and cutlets of various meats, from veal to pork to chicken. ✉ *Ul. Wiejska 12a,* ☎ *022/628–14–41. No credit cards. No dinner.*

$ ✕ **Miedzy Nami.** For the tragically hip, this restaurant has a boisterous lunch crowd. However, if you can stand the pretensions, they serve delicious salads and surprisingly good quesadillas. The specials can be hit or miss. There is no sign, so look for the white awnings. ✉ *Ul. Bracka 20,* ☎ *022/827–94–41. No credit cards.*

Lodging

Orbis hotels are reliable, offering standardized, functional rooms. Most show signs of wear, but bathrooms are usually up to Western European standards. Private accommodations are cheap and hospitable. Information and reservations are available through the Center for Tourist Information. **Syrena** (✉ Ul. Krucza 17, ☎ 022/628–75–40) arranges for rooms in private homes. Some hotels have lower prices during the winter months.

$$$$ ★ **Bristol.** This is Warsaw's most exclusive and luxurious hotel, where heads of state and celebrities stay when visiting the city. It was built in 1901 and once partially owned by Ignacy Paderewski, the pianist who was Poland's prime minister in 1919–20. The decidedly Polish Sunday brunch includes a caviar bar. ✉ *Krakowskie Przedmieście 42–44, 00–325,* ☎ *022/625–25–25,* FAX *022/625–25–77. 163 rooms, 43 suites. 2 restaurants, pool. AE, DC, MC, V.*

$$$$ **Marriott.** This Marriott's 40 stories (20 make up the hotel; the rest are office and retail shopping space) make it one of the tallest buildings in Warsaw. Its Italian restaurant, Parmizzano's, is among the best of its kind in the city. Cafe Vienna, on the mezzanine level, is a popular meeting place. ✉ *Al. Jerozolimskie 65–79, 00–697,* ☎ *022/630–63–06,* FAX *022/830–03–11,* WEB *www.marriotthotels.com/WAWPL. 487 rooms, 34 suites. 5 restaurants, pool. AE, DC, MC, V.*

$$$$ ★ **Sheraton.** Finished in 1996, this hotel stands near the Parliament and Embassy Row. The tastefully decorated rooms overlook a beautiful square. Service is impeccable, and there are small but excellent exercise facilities in the basement. ✉ *Ul. Prusa 2, 00–493,* ☎ *022/657–61–00,* FAX *022/657–62–00,* WEB *www.sheraton.com. 331 rooms, 21 suites. 2 restaurants, 2 lounges. AE, DC, MC, V.*

$$$$ **Victoria Inter-Continental.** The main advantage of this large 1970s hotel is its convenient location near the Old Town. It has the full range of Inter-Continental facilities. Ask for a room facing Victory Square. ✉ *Ul. Królewska 11, 00–065,* ☎ *022/657–80–11,* FAX *022/657–80–57,* WEB *www.orbis.pl/hot vic.html. 365 rooms. 3 restaurants, pool. AE, DC, MC, V.*

$$$ **Hotel Europejski.** This late-19th-century hotel has views overlooking the Royal Route. Rooms are spacious, and the location is so good that you may not mind the slightly shabby furnishings. ✉ *Krakowskie Przedmieście 13, 00–065,* ☎ *022/826–50–51,* FAX *022/826–11–11,* WEB *www.orbis.pl. 224 rooms, 13 suites. Restaurant. AE, DC, MC, V.*

$$ **Dom Chłopa.** This renovated 1950s hotel has bright, pine-furnished rooms with gleaming bathrooms. It is a five-minute walk from the primary shopping streets and the National Philharmonic. If you don't mind the noisy clientele of the nightclub on the ground floor, it's good value. ✉ *Pl. Powstańców Warszawy 2, 00–030,* ☎ *022/625–15–45,* FAX *022/625–21–40. 211 rooms. Restaurant. AE, DC, MC, V.*

$$ **MDM.** The rooms are slightly dreary, with brown bedspreads, but the place is clean and the bathrooms are up to Western standards. For a downtown hotel, you can't beat the price. The central location can be noisy, so request a room on one of the higher floors. ✉ *Pl. Konstytucji 1, 00–647,* ☎ *022/621–62–11,* FAX *022/621–41–73. 105 rooms, 5 suites. 2 restaurants. AE, DC, MC, V.*

Nightlife and the Arts

The Arts

The monthly *Warsaw Insider,* available at most major hotels, is the best English-language source (www.warsawinsider.com). If you read Polish, *Gazeta Wyborcza* and the monthly *IKS* (*Informator Kulturalny Stolicy*) or *City Magazine* have extensive listings. Cultural information is available by phone (☎ 022/629–84–89). Most operators speak only Polish, but you may get lucky and find one who speaks English. Tickets can be ordered at your hotel, at the theater, or through the ticket office of **Zasp** (✉ Al. Jerozolimskie 25, ☎ 022/621–93–83).

CONCERTS

The **National Philharmonic** (✉ Ul. Sienkiewicza 10, ☎ 022/826–72–81) is Poland's best concert hall. The **Royal Castle** (✉ Pl. Zamkowy 4, ☎ 022/657–21–70) has regular concerts in its stunning Great Assembly Hall. In summer free Chopin concerts are held at the Chopin monument in **Łazienki Park** on Sunday.

OPERA

Teatr Wielki (✉ Pl. Teatralny 1, ☎ 022/826–32–88) hosts the Grand Theater of Opera and Ballet. Its stage is one of Europe's largest. The beautiful, intimate **Warsaw Chamber Opera** (✉ Al. Solidarności 76b, ☎ 022/625–7510) theater is not to be missed.

THEATERS

There are still 17 major theaters in Warsaw, despite large cuts in state funding, attesting to Poles' love of this art form. The **Globe Theatre Group** (☎ 022/620–44–29) has a varied contemporary English-language repertory. **Teatr Narodowy** (✉ Pl. Teatralny 1, ☎ 022/826–32–88) is the oldest in Poland (it opened in 1765). **Żydowski Theater** (✉ Pl. Grzybowski 12/16, ☎ 022/620–70–25), Warsaw's Jewish Theater, stages performances in Yiddish.

Nightlife

BARS

Harenda (✉ Krakowskie Przedmieście 4/6, ☎ 022/826–29–00), with an outdoor terrace in summer, is open until 3 AM; jazz is played almost every night in the cellar bar. **Soma** (✉ Ul. Foksal 19, ☎ 022/828–21–33) is a bright, spacious bar/restaurant with comfy couches reminiscent of trendy spots found in London or New York. The Irish-owned **Morgan's** (✉ Ul. Okólnik 1, ☎ 022/826–81–38), below the Pałac Ostrogskich, stays open until the wee hours.

CAFÉS

Waršaw's *kawiarnia* (cafés), which move outdoors in summer, are busy meeting places, serving coffee and pastries in Central European style. **Café Blikle** (✉ Nowy Świat 35, ☎ 022/826–66–19) is a traditional, fashionable hangout on Warsaw's main shopping street; try the *pączki* (Polish doughnuts). **E. Wedel** (✉ Ul. Szpitalna 8, ☎ no phone), a venerable Warsaw institution, is best known for its thick, incredibly rich hot chocolate. **Cafe Barma** (✉ Ul. Marszalkowska 8, ☎ 022/629–65–36) serves great food and coffee—but they won't let you use your cell phone. The large glass facade of the **Modulor Café** (✉ Pl. Trzech Krzyży 8, ☎ 022/627–26–04) makes this the place to see and be seen. It serves good coffees and salads. **Nowe Miasto** (✉ Nowego Miasta 13/15, ☎ 022/831–43–79), a vegetarian café-cum-restaurant, is on the restored, quiet New Town Square. The large, bustling **Nowy Świat** (✉ Nowy Świat 63, ☎ 022/826–58–03) is good for people-watching and has a selection of foreign-language newspapers. The tiny, four-table café **Pożegnanie z Afrika** ("Out of Africa"; ✉ Ul. Freta 4/6, ☎ no phone) has aromatic coffees from all over the world but a limited selection of pastries. If you're craving a Starbuck's-style experience, then **TriBeCa Coffee** (✉ Ul. Bracka 22, ☎ no phone) is your place.

DANCE CLUBS

Barbados (✉ Ul. Wierzbowa 9, ☎ 022/827–71–61) draws corporate types to its small dance floor. The cavernous **Ground Zero** (✉ Ul. Wspólna 62, ☎ 022/625–43–80), a former bomb shelter, caters to crowds of varying ages; it has its own eatery, the Warsaw Tortilla Factory. **Labirynt** (✉ Ul. Smolna 12, ☎ 022/826–2220) plays mainstream pop and dance for an upscale crowd and has a two-lane bowling alley. The elegant **Piekarnia** (✉ Ul. Młocińa 11, ☎ 022/636–49–79) is where local and international DJs come to play. **Scena 2000** (✉ Ul. Armii Ludowej 3/5, ☎ 022/622–60–07) attracts aspiring Polish actors and models. **Tango** (✉ Ul. Smolna 15, ☎ 022/622–19–19) is an upmarket disco and cabaret.

JAZZ CLUBS

Hotel Bristol's plush **Column Bar** (✉ Ul. Krakowskie Przedmieście 42/44, ☎ 022/625–25–25) has live jazz on Friday nights. The cozy **Kaw-**

iarnia Literacka (✉ Krakowskie Przedmieście 87/89, ☎ 022/828–89–95), overlooking Castle Square, has classic jazz on Sunday evenings.

Shopping

Nowy Świat, Krakowskie Przedmieście, and ulica Chmielna are lined with boutiques selling good-quality leather goods, silver and amber jewelry, clothing, and trinkets. For the best selection of Polish wood carvings, including animals and nativity scenes, go to **Arex** (✉ Ul. Chopina 5A, ☎ 022/629–66–24). Try the **Cepelia** stores (✉ Pl. Konstytucji 5, ☎ 022/621–26–18; ✉ Rynek Starego Miasta 10, ☎ 022/831–18–05) for handicrafts such as glass, enamelware, amber, and hand-woven wool rugs. **Desa** (✉ Ul. Marszałkowska 34, ☎ 022/621–66–15) specializes in antiques (objects from before 1945 cannot be legally exported). **Galeria Plakatu** (✉ Rynek Starego Miasta 23, ☎ 022/831–93–06) has an excellent selection of Polish posters, many of which celebrate National Theater performances.

Warsaw Essentials

AIR TRAVEL TO AND FROM WARSAW

International flights arrive at Warsaw's Okęcie Airport just southwest of the city. Terminal 1 serves international flights; Terminal 2, next door, serves domestic flights.

➤ AIRPORT INFORMATION: **Okęcie Airport** (✉ Port Lotniczy, ☎ 022/650–42–20).

AIRPORTS AND TRANSFERS

The airport–city bus (about every 20 minutes from Platform 4; costs zł 5.60) and public Bus 175 (every 15 minutes; costs zł 2) run past almost all major downtown hotels. The trip takes about 25 minutes.

Avoid at all costs taxi drivers who approach you inside and those parked outside the arrivals hall. Your best bet is to go upstairs to the departure drop-off and hail a taxi (if the driver cannot take you, ask him to call one) or call ☎ 919 for a radio taxi (fare about zł 25). Some of the hotels will also pick you up (fare about zł 35).

BUS TRAVEL TO AND FROM WARSAW

Warsaw's central bus terminal is at Aleje Jerozolimskie 144.

BUS AND TRAM TRAVEL WITHIN WARSAW

Though often crowded, trams and buses are the cheapest way of getting around. They (including express buses) cost zł 2. Night buses run between 11:15 PM and 4:45 AM and require three tickets. Tickets may be bought in advance from Ruch newsstands or from bus drivers for zł 2.20. You must cancel your own ticket in a machine on the tram or bus when you get on; watch how others do it. Beware of very professional pickpockets.

CAR TRAVEL

Seven main access routes lead to the center of Warsaw. Highways E30 and E77 are the main arteries from the West. The city introduced paid street parking in 1999 for zł 1.40 per hour.

CONSULATES

➤ UNITED KINGDOM: (✉ Ul. Emilii Plater 28, ☎ 022/625–30–99).

EMERGENCIES

Call the number listed below for an ambulance and doctor, or call your embassy or the American Medical Center. Pharmacies in Warsaw stay open late on a rotational system. Signs listing the nearest open facility are posted outside every pharmacy. There is also a 24-hour pharmacy upstairs in the Central Train Station.

➤ EMERGENCY SERVICES: **Police** (☎ 997). **Ambulance and Doctor** (☎ 999). **American Medical Center** (AMC; ☎ 0602/243–024. ⏲ 24 hours).

➤ 24-HOUR PHARMACIES: Central Train Station (✉ Al. Jerozolimskie 54, ☎ 022/825–69–84).

ENGLISH-LANGUAGE MEDIA

➤ BOOKSTORES: **American Bookstore** (✉ Ul. Koszykowa 55, ☎ 022/660–56–37). **Bookland** (✉ Al. Jerozolimskie 64, ☎ 022/625–41–46). **Empik** (✉ Ul. Nowy Swiat 15/17, ☎ 022/625–67–94; ✉ Ul. Marszałkowska 116/122, ☎ 022/551–44–42).

SUBWAY TRAVEL

Warsaw's subway opened in spring 1995. The single line runs 17½ km (11 mi) from the southern suburbs to the city center (Kabaty to Centrum—by the Palace of Culture and Science), with an extension to ulica Świętokrzyska expected to open in 2001. It is clean and fast and costs the same as the tram and bus. Starting in 2001, tickets are now electronically cancelled once you enter the turnstiles. Trains run every five minutes during rush hours, every 15 minutes during off-peak hours.

TAXIS

Taxis are still relatively cheap—about zł 3.60 for the first kilometer (½ mi) and zł 1.60 for each additional kilometer—and are readily available at taxi stands. Beware of any that just have a TAXI sign on the top of the car with no company name—they do not have meters and may rip you off. Most major hotels have their own monogrammed fleets, but expect to pay more than you would for the efficient radio taxi service (☎ 919, English spoken), which is also considerably cheaper than taxis at stands.

TOURS

BUS TOURS

Bus tours of the city depart in the morning and afternoon from major hotels. Mazurkas Travel offers an excellent selection of tours around the city. Orbis also has half-day excursions into the surrounding countryside. Our Roots conducts four-hour tours of Jewish Warsaw.

BUGGY TOURS

Horse-drawn carriages can be rented at a negotiated price at the Old Town Market Square or Castle Square. Prices vary, but the average rate is zł 60 for a ride around the entire Old Town area.

➤ FEES AND SCHEDULES: **Mazurkas Travel** (✉ Ul. Długa 8/14, ☎ 022/635–66–33). **Orbis** (☞ Travel Agencies, *below*). **Our Roots** (☞ Travel Agencies, *below*).

TRAIN TRAVEL

Trains to and from Western Europe arrive at Dworzec Centralny in the center of town. For tickets contact a travel agent or your hotel or go to the train station.

➤ TRAIN INFORMATION: **Dworzec Centralny** (Central Station; ✉ Al. Jerozolimskie 54; ☎ 022/620–03–61 local train information; 022/620–45–12 international train information).

TRAVEL AGENCIES

➤ LOCAL AGENT REFERRALS: **American Express** (✉ Ul. Sienna 39, ☎ 022/581–51–00; ✉ Marriott Hotel, Al. Jerozolimskie 65/79, ☎ 022/630–69–52; for lost or stolen cards, call 022/625–40–30 6 AM–2 AM). **Carlson Wagonlit Travel** (✉ Ul. Nowy Świat 64, ☎ 022/826–04–31). **Orbis**

Hotels (✉ Ul. Bracka 16, ☎ 022/826–02–71. **Orbis Travel Office** ✉ Ul. Marszałkowska 142, ☎ 022/827–80–31). **Our Roots–Jewish Information and Tourist Bureau** (✉ Ul. Twarda 6, ☎ 022/620–05–56).

VISITOR INFORMATION

➤ TOURIST INFORMATION: **Center for Tourist Information** (✉ Pl. Zamkowy 1, ☎ 022/635–18–81). **Warsaw Tourist and Cultural Information** (✉ Central Train Station, Al. Jerozolimskie 54, ☎ 022/524–51–84).

KRAKÓW

Kraków, once the capital of Poland (before losing the honor to Warsaw in 1611) and seat of the country's oldest university, is one of the few Polish cities that escaped devastation during World War II. Today Kraków's fine ramparts, towers, facades, and churches, illustrating seven centuries of Polish architecture, have earned its Old Town a listing by UNESCO as one of the 12 great historic cities of the world.

The city's location—about 270 km (167 mi) south of Warsaw—makes it a good base for hiking and skiing trips in the mountains of southern Poland. Within exploring range from Kraków are the Polish shrine to the Virgin Mary at Częstochowa, and a grim reminder of man's capacity for inhumanity at Auschwitz (Oświęcim).

Exploring Kraków

Numbers in the margin correspond to points of interest on the Kraków map.

It seems a miracle that the marvelous old city of Kraków escaped World War II virtually undamaged. The city has three basic districts for touring: the Old Town, the Jewish quarter, and the Wawel. Each area can be seen in a half day or so, but more time can easily be spent.

1 **Barbakan** (The Barbican). This imposing, round, redbrick 15th-century fortress was part of the old city defense system. It stands in Planty Park, which, circling the Old Town, replaces the old walls, which were torn down in the mid-19th century. ✉ *Ul. Basztowa.*

2 **Brama Floriańska** (St. Florian's Gate). The surviving fragment of the city wall opposite the Barbakan, where students and amateur artists like to hang their paintings for sale in the summer, contains the Renaissance-period Municipal Arsenal. ✉ *Ul. Pijarska.*

9 **Collegium Maius** (Greater College). The pride of the oldest building of the world-renowned **Jagiellonian University,** founded in 1364, is the Italian-style arcaded courtyard. A **museum** (☎ 012/422–05–49; ⏲ weekdays 11–2:30, Sat. 11–1:30, call ahead for tours in English) contains the Copernicus globe, the first on which the American continents were shown, as well as astronomy instruments from the time of Kraków's most famous graduate. ✉ *Ul. Jagiellońska 15.* ⏲ *Courtyard Mon.–Sat. 8–6.*

5 **Kościół Mariacki** (Church of the Virgin Mary). Every hour, four short bugle calls drift down from the spire of this church. The notes are a centuries-old tradition that honors a trumpeter whose throat was pierced by an enemy arrow as he was warning his fellow citizens of an impending Tartar attack. Inside the church is a 15th-century wooden altarpiece—the world's largest—carved by Veit Stoss. The saints' faces are reputedly those of local burghers. ✉ *Rynek Główny.*

11 **Kościół na Skałce** (Church on the Rock). This Pauline church is the center of the cult of St. Stanisław, an 11th-century bishop and martyr.

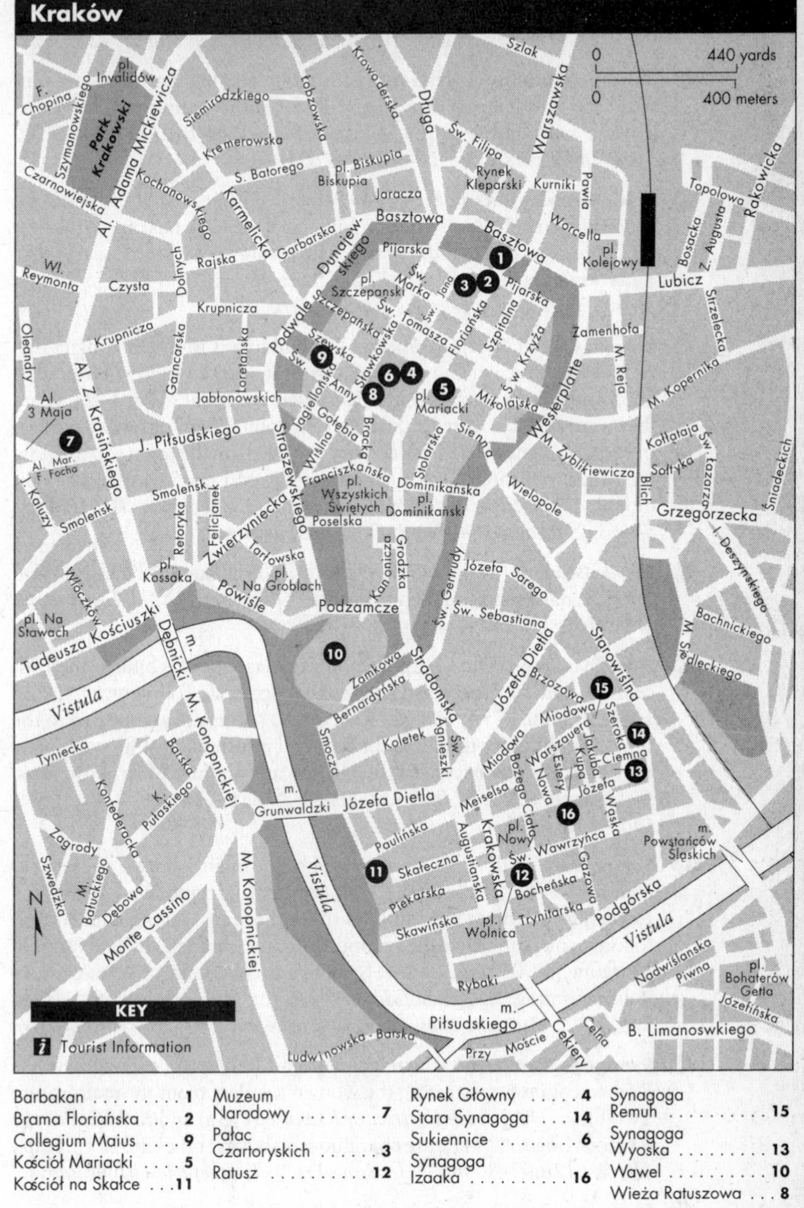

Barbakan 1
Brama Floriańska . . . 2
Collegium Maius 9
Kościół Mariacki 5
Kościół na Skałce . . . 11
Muzeum Narodowy 7
Pałac Czartoryskich 3
Ratusz 12
Rynek Główny 4
Stara Synagoga . . . 14
Sukiennice 6
Synagoga Izaaka 16
Synagoga Remuh 15
Synagoga Wyoska 13
Wawel 10
Wieża Ratuszowa . . . 8

Starting in the 19th century, it became the last resting place for well-known Polish writers and artists. ✉ *Ul. Skałeczna and ul. Paulińska.*

7 **Muzeum Narodowy** (National Museum). The highlights of this museum are Polish Art Nouveau and 20th-century paintings, as well as historic arms and uniforms. ✉ *Al. 3 Maja 1,* ☎ *012/634–33–77.* ⏲ *Tues. and Thurs.–Sun. 10–3:30, Wed. 10–6.*

★ 3 **Pałac Czartoryskich** (Czartoryski Palace). This branch of the National Museum, partially housed in the **Municipal Arsenal,** has one of the best art collections in Poland. Among its treasures is Leonardo da Vinci's *Lady with an Ermine.* ✉ *Ul. Św. Jana 19,* ☎ *012/422–55–66.* ⏲ *Tues.–Thurs. and weekends 10–3:30, Fri. 10–6.*

12 **Ratusz** (City Hall of Kazimierz). The building is in the Kazimierz district of Kraków, which was once a town in its own right, chartered in 1335 and named for its founder, Kazimierz the Great. After 1495, when they were expelled from Kraków by King John Albert, this was the home of Kraków's Jews. The 15th-century town hall on the town square, now the **Muzeum Etnograficzne** (Ethnographic Museum), displays a well-mounted collection of regional folk art. ✉ *Pl. Wolnica,* ☎ *012/430–55–63.* ⏲ *Mon. 10–6, Wed.–Fri. 10–3, weekends 10–2.*

4 **Rynek Główny** (Main Market Square). This is one of the largest and finest Renaissance squares in Europe. ✉ *Center of Old Town at ul. Floriańska and Św. Anny.*

14 **Stara Synagoga** (Old Synagogue). This synagogue was built in the 15th century and reconstructed in Renaissance style following a fire in 1557. Here, in 1794, Tadeusz Kościuszko successfully appealed to the Jewish community to join in the national insurrection. The synagogue now houses the **Museum of the History and Culture of Kraków Jews.** ✉ *Ul. Szeroka 24,* ☎ *012/422–20–81.* ⏲ *Sat.–Thurs. 9–3, Fri. 11–6. Closed 1st weekend of month.*

6 **Sukiennice** (Cloth Hall). In the center of the main square stands a covered market hall built in the 14th century but remodeled during the Renaissance. The ground floor is still in business, selling trinkets and folk-art souvenirs. On the second floor, in a branch of the **National Museum** (☎ 012/422–11–66), there's a collection of 19th-century Polish painting. ✉ *Rynek Główny.* ⏲ *Ground floor Mon.–Sat. 10–6, Sun. 10–5; Museum Tues.–Wed. and Fri.–Sun. 10–3:30, Thurs. 10–6.*

16 **Synagoga Izaaka** (Isaac Synagogue). This Renaissance synagogue has Roman columns separating the women's gallery from the main room. Two films, *The Jewish District of Kraków* (1936) and *Removal to the Kraków Ghetto* (1941), are continuously shown at the site. ✉ *Ul. Kupa 18,* ☎ *012/602–300–277.* ⏲ *Sun.–Fri. 9–7, except Jewish holidays.*

15 **Synagoga Remuh** (Remuh Synagogue). This tiny 16th-century synagogue is still used for worship. The cemetery, used by the Jewish community from 1533 to 1799, is the only well-preserved Renaissance Jewish burial ground in Europe. The so-called **New Cemetery** (✉ Ul. Miodowa), which contains many old headstones, was established in the 19th century. ✉ *Ul. Szeroka 40.* ⏲ *Sun.–Fri. 9–4, except Jewish holidays.*

13 **Synagoga Wysoka** (High Synagogue). This late-16th-century synagogue has a prayer room on the second floor. ✉ *Ul. Józefa 38,* ⏲ *Sat.–Thurs. 9–3:30, Fri. 9–6, closed Sun. and Jewish holidays.*

★ 10 **Wawel.** This impressive castle complex of Gothic and Renaissance buildings stands on fortifications that date from the 8th century. Inside the castle is a **museum** with an exotic collection of Asian tents captured from the Turks at the Battle of Vienna in 1683, as well as rare 16th-century

Flemish tapestries. **Katedra Wawelska** (Wawel Cathedral) is where, until the 18th century, Polish kings were crowned and buried. Until 1978 the cathedral was the principal church of Archbishop Karol Wojtyła, later Pope John Paul II. ✉ *Ul. Grodzka,* ☎ *012/422–51–55,* WEB *www.cyf-kr.edu.pl/wawel/emenu.htm.* ⏲ *Tues.–Sat. 9:30–3, Sun. 10–3.*

8 **Wieża Ratuszowa** (Town Hall Tower). Across from the Cloth Hall is all that remains of the 16th-century town hall. A climb up the winding staircase give you a good view of the town square from the two observation levels. Art exhibitions are held here in summer. ✉ *Rynek Główny.*

Dining

For details and price-category definitions, *see* Dining and Lodging *in* Poland A to Z, *above.*

$$$ ✕ **Chimera.** The vaulted ceilings and simple furnishings here are in sharp contrast to the creative cuisine, which adds a Continental flair to Polish game dishes. Try the roast venison in juniper sauce or the goose à la Dijon. The bar in the cellar hosts blues and folk music. ✉ *Ul. Świętej Anny 3,* ☎ *012/423–21–78. AE, DC, MC, V.*

$$$ ✕ **Hawelka.** Established in 1876 as a breakfast house by the merchant Antoni Hawelka, this Kraków institution specializes in Polish cuisine. The restaurant on the ground floor is casual and cheaper than the one upstairs, officially called Tetmajerowska. ✉ *Rynek Główny 34,* ☎ *012/422–47–53. AE, DC, MC, V.*

$$$ ★ ✕ **Pod Aniołami.** In summer the restaurant is in a courtyard; in winter it moves into a cozy cellar. The country-style kitchen turns out homemade bread and hearty entrées. The chef will roast an entire pig for a group. ✉ *Ul. Grodzka 35,* ☎ *012/421–39–99. No credit cards.*

$$$ ✕ **Wierzynek.** It was in a restaurant on this site, after a historic meeting in 1364, that the king of Poland wined and dined the Holy Roman Emperor Charles IV, five kings, and a score of princes. The current establishment serves traditional Polish specialties and excels in soups and game. ✉ *Rynek Główny 15,* ☎ *012/422–10–35. AE, DC, MC, V.*

$$ ✕ **Chłopskie Jadło.** This is the place for authentic Polish cuisine. The interior is a maze of rooms, each decked out like a Polish farmhouse with benches and chunky wooden picnic tables. The soups are outstanding. Try the *żurek* (sour cream soup). ✉ *Ul. Agnieszki 1,* ☎ *012/421–85–20. AE, DC, MC, V.*

$$ ✕ **Jama Michalikowa.** Kraków's most famous café serves good coffee and excellent, homemade ice cream. The decor pays homage to the site's cabaret days. ✉ *Ul. Floriańska 45,* ☎ *012/422–15–61. No credit cards.*

$$ ✕ **Kabaret Loch Camelot.** This little café is on a small street right off the main square. If you can get a table and a waiter's attention, it's a good place to get a glass of wine and soak up the lively atmosphere. It's also open in the morning for coffee. ✉ *Ul. Tomasza 17,* ☎ *022/421–01–23. No credit cards.*

Lodging

Hotel rooms are in short supply in Kraków, especially during the summer season, when it is absolutely essential to book well in advance. Rooms facing the street in the Old Town are often noisy at night. For details and price-category definitions, *see* Lodging *in* Poland A to Z, *above.*

$$$ 🏨 **Cracovia.** Large and Orbis-run, this five-story 1960s hotel is one of the few likely to have space during the busy summer months. The rooms are small and standardized but comfortable. Unfortunately, the hotel overlooks a traffic-laden square, but it also faces the National Museum.

✉ *Al. Marszałka F. Focha 1, 30–111,* ☎ *012/422–86–66,* FAX *012/421–95–86,* WEB *www.orbis.pl. 427 rooms. Restaurant. AE, DC, MC, V.*

$$$ **Forum.** This charmless hotel stands on the south bank of the Vistula, with a fine view of Wawel Castle. It's a bit far from the Old Town but has exercise facilities and a large selection of shops. There's also underground parking. ✉ *Ul. Marii Konopnickiej 28, 30–302,* ☎ *012/261–92–12,* FAX *012/269–00–80,* WEB *www.orbis.pl. 277 rooms. Restaurant, pool. AE, DC, MC, V.*

$$$ **Francuski.** This small, turn-of-the-20th-century hotel stands on a quiet street just inside the Old Town's ramparts. The atmosphere is intimate and the service friendly. Rooms are small but elegant in a homey, Eastern European way. The restaurant is tranquil and plush. ✉ *Ul. Pijarska 13, 31–015,* ☎ *012/422–51–22,* FAX *012/422–52–70,* WEB *www.orbis.pl. 42 rooms. Restaurant. AE, DC, MC, V.*

$$$ ★ **Grand.** An air of Regency elegance predominates at this late-19th-century hotel in the Old Town, although some Art Nouveau stained-glass windows have been preserved on the first floor. Rooms have reproduction period furniture and modern bathrooms and facilities. ✉ *Ul. Sławkowska 5–7, 31–014,* ☎ *012/421–72–55,* FAX *012/421–83–60. 56 rooms. Restaurant. AE, DC, MC, V.*

$$ **Continental.** This high-rise Orbis hotel is bland but comfortable. Its location, on the far side of Kraków Common, is a short taxi ride from the Old Town. Athletic facilities, such as horseback riding stables, are nearby. ✉ *Ul. Armii Krajowej 11, 30–150,* ☎ *012/637–50–44,* FAX *012/637–59–38,* WEB *www.orbis.pl. 305 rooms. Restaurant, pool. AE, DC, MC, V.*

$$ **Pollera.** This 150-year-old hotel is a bit on the shabby side but is a good value because of its location. The bathrooms were modernized in 1998, and the bedrooms received a face-lift in 1999. ✉ *Ul. Szpitalna 30, 31–024,* ☎ *012/422–10–44,* FAX *012/422–13–89. 42 rooms. Restaurant. AE, DC, MC, V.*

$$ **Saski.** Quaint and unpretentious, the Saski seems less hotel than it does early 1900s residence. Some of the spacious rooms were redecorated in 1997 and 1998. The small, dark restaurant is mainly frequented for breakfast. ✉ *Ul. Sławkowska 3, 31–014,* ☎ *012/421–42–22,* FAX *012/421–48–30. 63 rooms. Restaurant. AE, DC, MC, V.*

Side Trips

Oświęcim (Auschwitz)

Fifty kilometers (30 mi) west of Kraków is Oświęcim, better known by its German name, Auschwitz. Here 4 million victims, mostly Jews, were executed by the Nazis in the Auschwitz and Birkenau concentration camps. **Auschwitz** is now a museum, with restored crematoria and barracks housing dramatic displays of Nazi atrocities. The buildings at **Birkenau**, a 15-minute walk away, have been left just as they were found in 1945 by the Soviet Army. Oświęcim itself is an industrial town with good connections from Kraków; buses and trains leave Kraków periodically, and signs in Oświęcim direct visitors to the former camp. ✉ *Ul. Więźniów Oświęcimia 20,* ☎ *033/843–21–33.* ⏲ *Auschwitz Nov.–Mar., daily 8–4; Apr. and Oct., daily 8–5; May and Sept., daily 8–6; June–Aug., daily 8–7. Birkenau daily sunrise–sunset.*

Chevra Lomdei Mishnayot Synagogue / Auschwitz Jewish Center. This renovated early 20th-century synagogue is the only site of Jewish worship left standing in Oświęcim. Nazis destroyed the other 11, sparing this one to become a munitions depot. Next door is the Auschwitz Jewish Center, which has permanent exhibits on pre-war Polish Jewish life and a room devoted to genealogy research. ✉ *Plac Ks. Jana Skarbka 3–5,* ☎ *033/844–70–02,* WEB *www.ajcf.org.* ⏲ *Nov.–Feb., Sun.–Fri. 8:30–2; Mar.–Oct., Sun.–Fri. 8:30–5.*

Wieliczka

About 8 km (5 mi) southeast of Kraków is the oldest salt mine in Europe, in operation since the 13th century. The mine is on the UNESCO World Cultural Heritage list and is famous for its magnificent underground chapel hewn from crystal rock, the **Chapel of the Blessed Kinga** (Queen Kinga was a 14th-century Polish queen, later beatified). ✉ *Ul. Daniłowicza 10,* ☎ *012/278–73–34.* ⏲ *Daily 8–4.*

Częstochowa

Nearly 120 km (70 mi) from Kraków and reachable by regular trains and buses, Częstochowa is the home of the holiest shrine in a country that is some 95% Catholic. Inside the 14th-century **Pauline Monastery** on Jasna Góra (Light Hill) is the *Black Madonna,* a painting of Our Lady of Częstochowa attributed by legend to St. Luke. Here an invading Swedish army met heroic resistance from the Poles in 1655.

$ **Polonia.** The humble but charming Polonia makes a good base for exploring the monastery, and as most of the guests are pilgrims, the atmosphere is a mixture of piety and good fun. ✉ *Ul. Piłsudskiego 9, 42–200,* ☎ *034/324–23–88,* FAX *034/365–11–05. 62 rooms. Restaurant. AE, DC, MC, V.*

Wadowice

About 40 km (25 mi) southwest of Kraków is the little town of Wadowice, birthplace of Pope John Paul II. You can visit the **Muzeum Wadowice** (Wadowice Museum), in the house where he grew up. ✉ *Ul. Kościelna 7,* ☎ *033/823–26–62.* ⏲ *Tues.–Sun. 9–noon and 2–5.*

Kraków Essentials

AIR TRAVEL TO AND FROM KRAKÓW

Kraków can be reached by plane with direct flights from many major European cities and most Polish cities.

➤ AIRPORT INFORMATION: ☎ (012/411–67–00).

BUS TRAVEL TO AND FROM KRAKÓW

The bus station is across the street from the train station.

CAR TRAVEL

By car Kraków can be reached on major highways—E7 direct from Warsaw and E40 from Częstochowa.

CONSULATE

➤ UNITED STATES: (✉ Ul. Stolarska 9, ☎ 012/429–66–55, FAX 012/421–82–92).

TOURS

Bus or walking tours of Kraków and its environs are provided by Orbis and other travel agencies. Jardan Tours specializes in "Schindler's List" tours. Horse-drawn carriages can be rented at the main market square for a negotiated price.

TRAIN TRAVEL

Trains link Kraków with most major destinations in Poland; the station, Kraków Główny, is in the city center near the Old Town.

➤ TRAIN INFORMATION: Kraków Główny (✉ Pl. Kolejowy 1, ☎ 012/422–22–48 international information).

TRAVEL AGENCIES

➤ LOCAL AGENT REFERRALS: Jardan Tours (✉ Ul. Szeroka 2, ☎ 012/421–71–66). Orbis (✉ Rynek Glówny 41, ☎ 012/422–40–35; ✉ Al. Marszałka F. Focha 1, ☎ 012/421–98–80).

VISITOR INFORMATION

➤ TOURIST INFORMATION: **Częstochowa** (Częstochowa Informacja Turystyczna, ✉ Al. Najświętszej Marii Panny 64, ☎ 034/324–13–60). **Kraków** (✉ Jewish Cultural Center, Ul. Rabina Mieselsa 17, ☎ 012/423–55–95; ✉ Kraków 2000 Cultural Information Center, Ul. Świętej Jana 2, ☎ 012/421–77–87; ✉ Waweltur, Ul. Pawia 8, ☎ 012/422–67–65).

GDAŃSK AND THE NORTH

In contrast to Kraków and the south, Poland north of Warsaw is a land of castles, dense forests and lakes, and fishing villages and beaches. If you don't have a car, consider going straight to Gdańsk and making excursions from there.

Exploring Gdańsk and the North

By car from Warsaw, follow routes E77 and E62 through Płock. Continue through Włocławek to Toruń, where you can stay overnight. The route leading north from Toruń to Gdańsk passes through some of the oldest towns in Poland. Along the way are many medieval castles, manor houses, and churches that testify to the wealth and strategic importance of the area. Two short detours are a must: one is to Kwidzyń, to see the original 14th-century castle and cathedral complex, which is open to the public. The other is to Malbork.

For a different route back to Warsaw, follow highway E77 southeast along the edge of Poland's scenic lake district. The area is rich in natural and historic attractions. A side trip 42 km (26 mi) east of Ostróda takes you to the medieval town of Olsztyn. Another diversion, 17 km (10½ mi) west of Olsztynek, is the site of the Battle of Grunwald.

Gdańsk

Gdańsk, once the Free City of Danzig, contains one of Poland's beautifully restored Old Towns, displaying a rich heritage of Gothic, Renaissance, and Mannerist architecture. In 1997 Gdańsk celebrated its 1,000th anniversary. This is where the first shots of World War II were fired and where the first free trade union in the Soviet bloc, Solidarity, was born after strikes in August 1980. The city's Old Town has a wonderful collection of historic town houses and narrow streets. Splendid **ulica Długa** (best for shopping) and Długi Targ (Long Market) are great starting points for walks into other districts. The evocative **Pomnik Solidarnosci** (Solidarity Monument)—erected in honor of workers killed by the regime during strikes in 1970—stands outside the former Lenin shipyards. The nearby town of **Sopot** is Poland's most charming prewar seaside resort.

$$$$ ★ ✕ **Tawerna.** For traditional Polish and Germanic dishes such as pork cutlets and seafood, try this well-established restaurant overlooking the river. It's touristy, but the food is delicious. ✉ *Ul. Powroźnicza 19–20, off Długi Targ,* ☎ *058/301–41–14. AE, DC, MC, V.*

$$$$ ★ ✕ **Villa Hestia.** Built in 1894, the Sopot villa that houses this elegant restaurant is an architectural and artistic treasure. Still, the atmosphere is comfortable and the service is superb. The French-accented menu, based on Polish specialties, changes with every season. ✉ *Ul. Władysława IV 3/5,* ☎ *058/551–21–00. AE, DC, MC, V.*

$$$ ✕ **Euro.** Paisley prints and dark wood give this restaurant a tasteful look, matched by its classic menu. The pork chop stuffed with plums is a regional dish. ✉ *Ul. Długa 79/80,* ☎ *058/305–23–83. AE, DC, MC, V.*

$$$ ✕ **Pod Łososiem.** The name of this restaurant refers to salmon, which, if available on the day you visit, is highly recommended. Other fish and wild fowl such as duck and pheasant are good choices, too. The

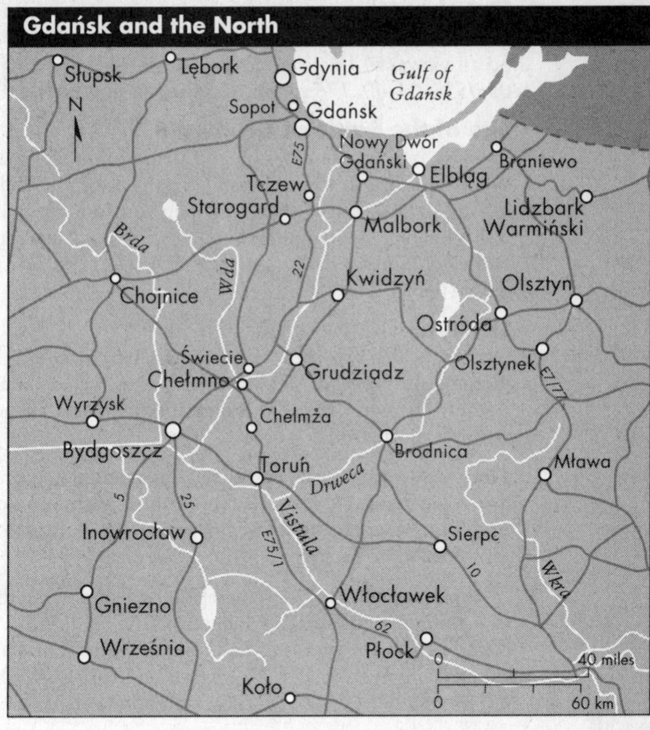

decor is overdone, but the service is pleasant. ✉ *Ul. Szeroka 54,* ☎ *058/301–76–52. AE, DC, MC, V.*

$$$ ✕ **Retman.** This restaurant, with ornate furniture and stained-glass windows, takes you back to the 18th century. The food specializes in Old-Gdańsk–style cuisine and speciality fish dishes. ✉ *Ul. Stagiewna 1,* ☎ *058/301–92–48. AE, DC, MC, V.*

$$$ 🏨 **Hanza.** Opened in 1998, this luxury hotel overlooks the picturesque harbor in Gdańsk. Its ultramodern decor is softened by warm colors and recessed lighting. The increasingly popular restaurant specializes in Continental cuisine. ✉ *Ul. Tokarska 6, 80–888,* ☎ *058/305–34–27,* FAX *058/305–33–86. 60 rooms. Restaurant. AE, DC, MC, V.*

$$$ 🏨 **Hewelius.** This 18-story hotel is within walking distance of the Old Town and is also close to the train and bus stations. The spacious, blandly furnished rooms have most modern conveniences. ✉ *Ul. Heweliusza 22, 80–861,* ☎ *058/321–00–00,* FAX *058/301–19–22,* WEB *www.orbis.pl/hot_hev.html. 281 rooms. Restaurant. AE, DC, MC, V.*

$$$ 🏨 **Holiday Inn Gdańsk.** The rooms on the front side of this hotel, which opened in 1999, overlook the central train station, and the property is just a few minutes' walk from the Old Town. The City Forum shopping center and T.G.I. Friday's, where breakfast is served, are connected to the property. ✉ *Podwale Grodzkie 9, 80–895,* ☎ *058/300–60–00,* FAX *058/300–60–03,* WEB *www.holiday-inn.com/gdanskpoland. 143 rooms, 19 suites. Restaurant. AE, DC, MC, V.*

$$ 🏨 **Grand.** With its magnificent location on the Bay of Gdańsk in the charming German-era seaside resort of Sopot, this prewar hotel is well worth the short commute. The rooms could have been restored more authentically, but the view from the restaurant is great. ✉ *Ul. Powstańców Warszawy 12/14, 81–718 Sopot,* ☎ *058/551–00–41,* FAX *058/551–61–24,* WEB *www.orbis.pl/hot_gras.html. 112 rooms. Restaurant. AE, DC, MC, V.*

$$ ☎ **Marina.** This modern high-rise hotel is a short taxi ride from the center of Sopot. The hotel is on the beach, and upper floors have ocean views. ✉ *Ul. Jelitkowska 20, 80–342,* ☎ *058/553–20–79,* FAX *058/553–04–60. 176 rooms. Restaurant, pool. AE, DC, MC, V.*

Site of the Battle of Grunwald

In 1410, in what was possibly the greatest battle of the Middle Ages, Władysław Jagiełło and his Polish-Lithuanian army annihilated the Grand Master of the Teutonic Order, Ulrich von Jungingen, and thousands of his knights. A small museum on the site explains the course of the battle. ✉ *17 km (11 mi) west of Olsztynek off Rte. 537.* ⏲ *May–Sept., daily 10–6.*

Olsztyn

Olsztyn, which was badly damaged during World War II, is more of a jumping-off point for the Mazurian Lakes region than a place of interest in its own right. The **Rynek** (marketplace) in the Old Town is worth a short stroll.

The town's 14th-century **castle** contains a **museum,** open Tuesday–Sunday 10–4, dedicated to local culture, and **Copernicus's quarters** on the first floor, where he lived for three years. ✉ *Ul. Zamkowa 1,* ☎ *089/527–95–96.* ⏲ *Tues.–Sun. 9–3.*

$ ☎ **Orbis Novotel.** This 1970s hotel is typical of the kind found in Poland. It is the most comfortable lodging in the area, set in beautiful surroundings on the shores of Lake Ukiel. Water sports and horseback-riding facilities are nearby. ✉ *Ul. Sielska 4A, 10–802,* ☎ *089/527–40–81,* FAX *089/527–54–03. 97 rooms. Restaurant. AE, DC, MC, V.*

Olsztynek

This otherwise drab town contains the **Muzeum Budownictwa Ludowego** (Museum of Folk Buildings), a collection of timber buildings, including a thatched church. The area's Lithuanian influence is evident, particularly in the museum's colorful mill. ✉ *Ul. Sportowa 21,* ☎ *089/519–21–64.* ⏲ *Mid-Apr.–Aug., daily 9–3; Sept., Tues.–Sun. 9–3.*

Malbork

★ This huge, redbrick, turreted castle was one of the most powerful strongholds in medieval Europe. From 1308 to 1457 it was the residence of the Grand Masters of the Teutonic Order. The Teutonic Knights were a thorn in Poland's side until their defeat at the Battle of Grunwald in 1410. Inside Malbork Castle is a museum with beautiful examples of amber—including lumps as large as melons and pieces containing perfect specimens of prehistoric insects. ✉ *Rte. 50, 58 km (36 mi) southeast of Gdańsk,* ☎ *055/272–33–64,* WEB *www.malbork.pl.* ⏲ *Museum Oct.–Apr., Tues.–Sun. 9–3; May–Sept., Tues.–Sun. 9–5. Grounds Oct.–Apr., daily 9–3; May–Sept., daily 9–6.*

Płock

Once you get through Płock's industrial area, you will find a lovely medieval city that was, for a short time, the capital of Poland. The 12th-century **Katedra** (cathedral), where two Polish kings are buried, has a **Muzeum Diecezjalne** (Diocesan Museum) that displays a collection of religious art as well as local folk pieces. ☎ *024/262–26–23.* ⏲ *Tues.–Fri. 9–3, weekends 9–4.*

In the remains of the dramatic 14th-century **Teutonic castle** is the **Muzeum Mazowieckie** (Mazovian Museum), with one of the best Art Nouveau collections in Poland. ☎ *024/262–44–91.* ⏲ *Apr.–Sept., Wed.–Sat. 10–3, Sun. 11–4; Oct.–Mar., Wed.–Sat. 10–1, Sun. 11–2.*

Toruń

Toruń, birthplace of Nicolaus Copernicus, is a medieval city that grew wealthy because of its location on the north–south trading route along the Vistula. In 1998 Toruń was placed on the UNESCO World Cultural Heritage List. Its **Old Town** district is a remarkably successful blend of Gothic buildings—churches, the town hall, and burghers' residences—and Renaissance and Baroque patrician houses. The town hall tower (1274) is the oldest in Poland.

$$$ ✕ **Petite Fleur.** In a cozy, redbrick cellar, this restaurant serves Polish and French specialties with care. ✉ *Ul. Piekary 25,* ☎ *056/663–44–00. No credit cards.*

$$ ✕ **Ost Gromada.** Excellent meat dishes and soups are served in a restored 17th-century interior. The restaurant, which is part of a small hotel, is only one block from Toruń's Old Town Square. ✉ *Ul. Żeglarska 10/14,* ☎ *056/622–60–60. AE, DC, MC, V.*

$$$ **Helios.** This friendly, medium-size Orbis hotel in the city center is within convenient walking distance from the Old Town. Request a room with a renovated bathroom—it's worth the higher rate. ✉ *Ul. Kraszewskiego 3, 87–100,* ☎ *056/619–65–50,* FAX *056/655–54–29,* WEB *www.orbis.pl/hot_hel.html. 108 rooms. Restaurant. AE, DC, MC, V.*

$$ **Kosmos.** A functional 1960s hotel, Kosmos had a face-lift in 1998. It's near the Vistula River, in the city center. ✉ *Ul. Popiełuszko 2, 87–100,* ☎ *056/622–89–00,* FAX *056/622–13–41,* WEB *www.orbis.pl/hot kos.html. 58 rooms. Restaurant. AE, DC, MC, V.*

Gdańsk and the North Essentials

GETTING AROUND

Gdańsk is a major transportation hub, with an international airport just outside town (and good bus connections to downtown) and major road and rail connections with the rest of the country.

TOURS

Orbis and other travel agencies arrange group and individual package tours of Toruń, Gdańsk, Poznań, and the surrounding areas.

VISITOR INFORMATION

➤ TOURIST INFORMATION: **Gdańsk** (Orbis, ✉ Ul. Heweliusza 22, ☎ 058/301–21–32). **Olsztyn** (Orbis, ✉ Ul. Dąbrowszczaków 1, ☎ 089/527–46–74). **Płock** (✉ Ul. Toomska 4, ☎ 024/262–94–97). **Toruń** (✉ Rynek Staromejski 1, ☎ 056/622–37–46; ✉ Orbis, Ul. Mostowa 7, ☎ 056/655–48–63).

24 PORTUGAL

LISBON; THE ESTORIL COAST, SINTRA, AND QUELUZ; THE ALGARVE

CLINGING TO THE WESTERN CUSP of the continent, insulated from Spain's arid plains and burning sun, Portugal is one of Europe's great surprises. It is a land of fine food and wine, spectacularly sited castles, medieval hilltop villages, and excellent beaches, but Portugal is also a land of miscellany and of delightful distinctions.

The landscape unfolds in astonishing variety from a mountainous, green interior to a sweeping coastline—Celtic and Moorish influences are evident in the land, its people, and their tongue. Given Portugal's long Atlantic coastline, it isn't surprising that most of its tumultuous history has revolved around the sea. From the charting of the Azores archipelago in 1427 to the discovery of Japan in 1542, Portuguese explorers unlocked the major sea routes to southern Africa, India, eastern Asia, and the Americas. The great era of exploration, known as the *descobrimentos,* reached its height during the 15th century under the influence of Prince Henry the Navigator. But the glories of the Portuguese empire were relatively short-lived, and the next several centuries saw dynastic instability, extravagant spending by feckless monarchs, natural disasters, and foreign invasion. Order was finally imposed in the 20th century by the drastic solution of a right-wing dictatorship. The regime lasted more than forty years, until a bloodless coup established democracy in 1974 and the process of modernization began.

Today Portugal is a stable country, its people keen to share in the prosperity offered by developments within the European Union (EU). This stability, born so shortly after revolution, demonstrates the inherent strength of the Portuguese psyche. Political confidence couldn't have been maintained without improvements in the economy, and there have been great strides forward since 1974—the highway system, in particular, has been completely overhauled as EU money has been used to modernize the country's infrastructure.

Lisbon, Portugal's centuries-old capital, is an engaging mixture of modernity and mellow age, where graceful old buildings hold their own with modern high-rises. The city's coastal and wooded environs give it an added dimension. Following its 1994 stint as the European City of Culture, Lisbon moved firmly into the international limelight by hosting Expo '98, the last great World Exposition of the 20th century. A startling regeneration program has improved the city center, its transportation, and public buildings. At the former Expo site—reclaimed shore northeast of the city's center—now the Parque das Nações (Park of the Nations), are riverside restaurants, exhibitions, concerts, a cable-car ride, and the stupendous Lisbon Oceanarium, the Expo's erstwhile centerpiece.

Portugal

0 50 miles
0 50 km
N
Minho
Valença
Viana do Castelo
Lima
N101
Serra do Gerês
N103
Bragança
Chaves
Barcelos
Braga
Póvoa de Varzim
Guimarães
Tâmega
A4/IP4
Mirandela
Vila do Conde
A3/IP1
Amarante
Vila Real
N102/IP2
Sabor
Mogadouro
Oporto
Penafiel
Douro
Duoro
Lamego
Espinho
Oliveira dos Azeméis
Moimenta da Beira
ATLANTIC OCEAN
S. Pedro do Sul
Albergaria-a-Velha
Vouga
Aveiro
Viseu
Pinhel
IP5
Sta. Comba Dão
Mealhada
Mira
Cantanhede
Mondego
Guarda
Coimbra
Serra da Estrêla
Covilhã
Figueira da Foz
A1/IP1/E1
Arganil
Fundão
Zêzere
Penamacor
N109
Pombal
N110
Serra da Gardunha
N233
Leiria
Batalha
Ourém
Proença-a-Nova
Castelo Branco
Nazaré
Tomar
IP2
Alcobaça
Fátima
Sra. do Aire
IP6
Abrantes
Nisa
Caldas da Rainha
Torres Novas
Tagus
N118
SPAIN
Obidos
Aveiras de Cima
Portalegre
Torres Vedras
Santarém
Ponte de Sor
Mafra
Tejo
Vila Franca de Xira
N8
Sorraia
Avis
Sintra
Lisbon
N10
A6
Badajoz
Estremoz
Elvas
Cascais
Estoril
Arraiolos
Montemor-o-Novo
A6/IP1
Sra. de Ossa
Seixal
A2/IP1
Vila Viçosa
Guadiana
Setúbal
Sado
A2
Évora
Reguengos
Cabo Espichel
Alcácer do Sal
N2
IP2
TO THE AZORES
IP1/E1
Ferreira do Alentejo
Moura
Beja
Sines
Santiago do Cacem
Vilaverde de Ficalho
Cabo de Sines
N122
Serpa
Castro Verde
Chança
Odemira
Ourique
Mértola
Mira
Guadiana
TO MADEIRA ISLAND
N120
Almodovar
Monchique
ALGARVE
Portimão
EN125
IP1
S. Brás de Alportel
Vila do Bispo
Lagos
Albufeira
Tavira
Vila Real de S. António
Cabo de S. Vicente
Sagres
Faro
Olhão

The sun-swept beaches of the Algarve in the country's south are some of Europe's most popular vacation areas. Off the beaten track, you can catch glimpses of a traditional life and culture, shaped by memories of empire and tempered by the experience of revolution.

PORTUGAL A TO Z

To research prices, get advice from other travelers, and book travel arrangements, visit www.fodors.com.

AIR TRAVEL

CARRIERS

TAP Air Portugal flies to Oporto and Faro, as well as to Madeira and the Azore Islands. Portugália has flights from Lisbon to Oporto and Faro. SATA-Air Açores flies from Lisbon to the Azores and takes care of inter-island traffic in the Azores archipelago.

➤ AIRLINES AND CONTACTS: **Portugália** (☎ 21/842–5500). **SATA-Air Açores** (☎ 21/843–7700). **TAP Air Portugal** (✉ Edifício Estação do Oriente, Av. Berlim, 1800 Lisbon, ☎ 80/820–5700).

BUS TRAVEL

Lisbon's main bus terminals are at the Oriente train station and the Arco do Cego. Major companies like Renex operate routes from the Lisbon stations to all parts of the country. The journey to Oporto, for example, takes three hours; it's about four hours to the Algarve. Try to buy tickets a day in advance. For information on particular routes, contact the main tourist office in Lisbon; for tickets, visit the terminals themselves or any travel agency.

➤ BUS INFORMATION: **Arco do Cego** (✉ Av. Duque de Ávila 12). **Oriente** (✉ Parque das Nações). **Renex** (☎ 21/888–2829).

BUSINESS HOURS

Banks are open weekdays 8:30–3. Lisbon has currency-exchange machines (around the Praçado Comércio and Praça dos Restauradores), as do other cities. Museums are generally open Tuesday to Sunday 10–6, often with last admittance at 5:30. Some are closed Tuesday morning; a few close for lunch. Most palaces close on Tuesday. Shops are open weekdays 9–1 and 3–7, Saturday 9–1. Shopping malls in Lisbon and other cities remain open until 10 PM or midnight and are often open on Sunday.

CAR TRAVEL

EMERGENCY SERVICES

All large garages in and around towns have breakdown services, and there are orange emergency (SOS) phones along turnpikes and highways. The national automobile organization, Automóvel Clube de Portugal, provides reciprocal membership with the American Automobile Association (AAA) and some European automobile associations.

➤ CONTACTS: **Automóvel Clube de Portugal** (✉ Rua Rosa Araújo 24/26, 1200-195 Lisbon, ☎ 21/318–0100).

GASOLINE

Gas prices are among the highest in Europe: around 183$00/€.90 per liter for unleaded 95 octane and 191$00/€.95 for unleaded 98 octane. Diesel is 130$00/€.65 per liter. Many gas stations are self-service, and credit cards are widely accepted.

PARKING

Parking lots and underground garages abound in major cities, but those in Lisbon and Oporto are pricey. It's often difficult to find a parking space near city-center hotels, though increasingly common parking meters are improving the situation.

ROAD CONDITIONS

Turnpikes and major highways that link Lisbon with Cascais, the Algarve, Oporto, and other main cities are in good shape. Minor roads are often winding with unpredictable surfaces. Local driving may be faster and less forgiving than you're used to; visitors, especially on unfamiliar Algarve roads, can cause problems: drive carefully.

In recent years, the principal east–west Algarve highway, EN 125, was widened and resurfaced, and construction of the IP1 Algarve highway (Via Infante D. Henrique) from the Spanish border to Albufeira has eliminated many horrendous bottlenecks. The IP5 in the north shortens the drive from Aveiro to the Spanish border, near Guarda, but it should be driven with great care. The IP4 connects Oporto through Vila Real to once-remote Bragança, and the A3 turnpike north from Oporto is a fast highway link between Lisbon and the northern frontier with Spain.

The A2–A6 turnpike system south from Lisbon reaches the Spanish frontier at Badajoz, linking up with the highway to Madrid, and, ultimately, with the entire European turnpike system. The southbound A2 reaches Grándola en route to the Algarve, and at press time (summer 2001), was scheduled to arrive at Castro Verde in 2001. There's good, fast access to Setúbal and to Évora and other Alentejo towns, though rush-hour traffic on the 25 de Abril bridge across the Tagus can be frustrating. An alternative is to take the 17-km (11-mi) Vasco da Gama bridge across the Tagus estuary to Montijo and then link up with southbound and eastbound roads.

RULES OF THE ROAD

Driving is on the right. At the junction of two roads of equal size, traffic coming from the right has priority. Vehicles in a traffic circle have priority over those entering it from any point. The use of seat belts is obligatory, and you must carry a reflective red warning triangle sign in your car for use in a breakdown. Horns should not be used in cities. The speed limit on turnpikes is 120 kph (74 mph); on other roads it is 90 kph (56 mph) and, in urban areas, 50 kph–60 kph (30 mph–36 mph).

CUSTOMS AND DUTIES

For details on imports and duty-free limits for visitors from outside the EU, *see* Customs and Duties *in* Chapter 1.

DINING

Traditional Portuguese cooking is undeniably on the heavy side. But culinary styles are changing fast. In Lisbon and the Algarve, for example, young chefs are adding lighter, adventurous touches to old favorites. Some tradition remains intact, though. Seafood is still a staple—*sardinhas assadas* (fresh-grilled sardines) are a summer delicacy, *caldeirada* is a piquant seafood stew, and *bacalhau* (dried salt cod) appears on all menus in a number of mouthwatering guises. Fresh lobster, crab, shrimp, tuna, sole, and squid are widely available. In the Algarve, *cataplana* is a must—a delectable mixture of clams, ham, tomatoes, onions, garlic, and herbs. Meat lovers wax rhapsodic over char-grilled *frango* (chicken), usually served with hot *piri-piri* (chili) sauce; northern-style *leitão da bairrada* (roast suckling pig); and the tasty *porco alentejana* (pork with clams), a southern specialty found throughout the country. Desserts—in particular the ubiquitous *doces de ovos* (egg-and-sugar confections) and *pudim flan* (egg custard)—are often too eggy and sweet for non-Portuguese tastes, but fresh fruit is usually on the menu. Water is safe, but you may prefer bottled water: *sem gas* for still, *com gas* for fizzy.

Much of the renowned cooking in Portugal, and certainly the best value for your money, is found in moderately priced restaurants, officially categorized as 2° (2nd class). The classification of a restaurant has more to do with space and facilities than with the food. Lower priced *tascas* (taverns, or bistros) and small, sometimes family-run restaurants are where discerning Lisboners go for a good meal. *Cervejarias* (pub–restaurants) and *marisqueiras* specialize in seafood. The food is usually good in these places, but however proletarian the trappings, seafood is always pricey. Shellfish (*mariscos*) is expensive and is often sold by weight in restaurants. This means that if you indulge in lobster, crab, prawns, and the like without watching the scales in an otherwise modestly priced eatery, you can end up paying more than you would for a non-*marisco* meal in a $$$$ place. At all restaurants be wary of appetizers you didn't order. You'll be charged extra even for eating one olive, and some of the appetizers can be quite expensive.

Prices are for a main course at dinner. Taxes and service are usually included in the bill, but a tip of 5%–10% is always appreciated.

CATEGORY	COST
$$$$	over 4,500$00 (€22.45)
$$$	3,500$00–4,500$00 (€17.45–€22.45)
$$	2,500$00–3,500$00 (€12.50–€17.45)
$	under 2,500$00 (€12.50)

MEALTIMES

Most hotels serve breakfast until 10. Lunch usually begins around 1 PM; dinner is served at about 8 PM.

RESERVATIONS AND DRESS

Neatness suffices for all but the most formal occasions; jacket and tie are advised for city restaurants in the $$$$ category; otherwise, casual dress is fine.

EMBASSIES

➤ CANADA: (✉ Av. da Liberdade 196–200, Lisbon, ☎ 21/316–4600).
➤ UNITED KINGDOM: (✉ Rua São Bernado 33, Lisbon, ☎ 21/392–4000).
➤ UNITED STATES: (✉ Av. Forças Armadas, Lisbon, ☎ 21/727–3300).

HOLIDAYS

January 1; Good Friday; Easter Sunday; April 25 (Anniversary of the Revolution); May 1 (Labor Day); Corpus Christi; June 10 (National Day); August 15 (Assumption); October 5 (Day of the Republic); November 1 (All Saints' Day); December 1 (Independence Day); December 8 (Immaculate Conception); December 25.

LANGUAGE

For English speakers, Portuguese is difficult to pronounce and understand (most people speak quickly and elliptically). If you have a fair knowledge of a Latin language, you may be able to read a little Portuguese, but be aware that, with some cognates, appearances can be deceptive—it's best to double-check terms in a dictionary. In large cities and major resorts many people speak English and, occasionally, French. Spanish is always understood.

LODGING

Portugal has some of the lowest rates in Europe. The government grades hotels with one to five stars. Non-hotel options include small family-owned *pensões* (pensions), rooms in country manor houses, villas, holiday apartments, campsites, and luxury *pousadas* (tourist hotels) in historic buildings. Rates depend on location and time of year. In the Algarve in winter, particularly January through March, room prices drop by as much as 40%. Book ahead in summer and at Easter and Christmas.

Tourist offices can help with reservations and provide free lists of the local hostelries. In Lisbon the airport and the downtown tourist information center have hotel reservation desks. If you arrive at a resort in summer without a reservation, you may be offered an inexpensive *quarto* (room) near a rail or bus station; always see the room before agreeing to take it.

Prices quoted are for two people in a double room based on high-season rates, including tax and service.

CATEGORY	COST
$$$$	over 50,000$00 (€249.40)
$$$	30,000$00–50,000$00 (€149.65–€249.40)
$$	10,000$00–30,000$00 (€49.90–€149.65)
$	under 10,000$00 (€49.90)

CAMPING

There are more than 150 campsites throughout the country, with a large concentration in the Algarve. Most are owned and run by local municipal governments. The main private operating chain is Orbitur; most local tourist offices can direct you to specific sites. For additional information contact Federação Portuguesa do Campismo (Portuguese Camping Federation).

➤ CONTACTS: **Federação Portuguesa do Campismo** (✉ Av. Col. Ed. Galhardo 24, 1199-007 Lisbon, ☎ 21/812–6900). **Orbitur** (✉ Rua Diogo do Couto 1–8, 1149-042 Lisbon, ☎ 21/811–7000).

COUNTRY AND MANOR HOUSES

Splendid country homes, manor houses, and historic buildings are available through programs in which private homeowners offer a room, breakfast, and sometimes dinner (on request). Properties are inspected and approved by the government and then advertised by private agencies. The Portuguese National Tourist Office in your home country can provide more information in advance of your trip; in Portugal, tourist offices can advise about the best local possibilities.

HOTELS AND POUSADAS

In addition to regular hotels, many towns have smaller inns called *estalagems* or *albergarias,* which usually provide breakfast only.

The 45 state-owned pousadas—in castles, old monasteries, or newer buildings on sites with particularly fine views—are luxury properties, but rates in low season can make them a good value. Contact Enatur Pousadas de Portugal or the national tourist organization in your home country.

➤ CONTACTS: **Enatur Pousadas de Portugal** (✉ Av. Santa Joana Princesa 10, 1749-090 Lisbon, ☎ 21/844–2001, FAX 21/844–2085, WEB www.pousadas.pt).

PENSIONS

The mainstay of budget accommodation in Portugal is the *pensão,* or pension, rated up to four stars and sometimes including meals in the price. Do some research—not all pensão rooms come with private baths or showers, and air-conditioning is standard only in higher-category accommodations. A *residencial* (between a pensão and a hotel), found in most towns, is similar; breakfast is usually included.

MAIL AND SHIPPING

The post office in the Praça dos Restauradores in Lisbon is open daily 8 AM–10 PM, and there's a 24-hour post office at the airport. Main post offices in towns are open weekdays 8:30–6; offices in rural areas close for lunch and at 6 PM weekdays and are closed weekends.

You can have mail sent care of American Express. Elsewhere in the country, post offices in major towns have "held mail" services (you simply have letters sent to you labeled "poste restante" at a particular post office address).

➤ MAJOR SERVICES: **American Express** (✉ Top Tours, Av. Duque de Loulé 108, 1050-093 Lisbon, ☎ 21/315–5885, FAX 21/315–5827).

MONEY MATTERS

The most expensive areas are Lisbon, the Algarve, and the tourist resorts along the Tagus estuary; the least expensive are country towns. The price of most items includes the European Union sales, or value-added, tax. Called VAT, or IVA in Portugal, of either 5% (for basic foodstuffs, medicines, and accommodation), 12% (restaurant bills), or 17% (other goods and services, including car rentals).

Some sample prices are: cup of coffee, 100$00/€.50–200$00/€1; bottle of beer, 150$00/€.75; soft drink, 125$00/€.60–175$00/€.90; 2-km (1-mi) taxi ride, 450$00/€2.25; city bus ride, 160$00/€.80; museum admission, 450$00/€2.25–600$00/€3.

CURRENCY

The unit of currency in Portugal is the escudo, which is divided into 100 centavos. Escudos come in bills of 500$00, 1,000$00, 2,000$00, 5,000$00, and 10,000$00. (In Portugal the dollar sign stands between the escudo and the centavo.) Owing to the complications of dealing with millions of escudos, 1,000$00 is always called a *conto*, so 10,000$00 is referred to as 10 contos. Coins come in denominations of 1$00, 5$00, 10$00, 20$00, 50$00, 100$00, and 200$00.

At press time (summer 2001), the exchange rate was 216 escudos to the U.S. dollar, 141 escudos to the Canadian dollar, 313 escudos to the pound sterling, 254 escudos to the Irish punt, 114 escudos to the Australian dollar, 93 escudos to the New Zealand dollar, 28 escudos to the South African rand, and 200 escudos to the euro. You can change money in hotels, but banks and *postos de cambio* (exchange offices) give better rates.

As Portugal is a member of the European Monetary Union (EMU), all prices have been quoted in escudos and euros since the start of 1999. Euro coins and notes are to be introduced January 1, 2002, from which point all non-cash transactions (such as credit-card purchases) are to be conducted in euros. The escudo will be gradually withdrawn until complete removal February 28, 2002.

SHOPPING

Bargaining is not the practice in city stores or shops, though it is sometimes possible in flea markets and antiques shops. The Centro de Turismo Artesanato ships goods abroad. By air to the United States, parcels take about three weeks; by sea, two months.

➤ CONTACTS: **Centro de Turismo Artesanato** (✉ Rua Castilho 61, 1200 Lisbon, ☎ 21/386–0879).

TAXES

SALES TAX

For non-EU residents, the IVA paid on individual items over 11,700$00/€58.35 can be reclaimed if you buy them in a tax-free associated shop. Ask for a special Tax-Free Shopping Cheque at the shop and get it stamped by airport customs, and the money can be refunded at the tax-free desk at the Lisbon airport.

TELEPHONES

Late in 1999 all telephone numbers in Portugal were reformatted. The old area codes dropped their introductory 0 in favor of the digit 2 and were incorporated into individual numbers. It is now necessary to dial the area code of the number you want to reach, beginning with a 2, whether your call is local or long distance. For instance, anyone calling a Lisbon number, either from within the Lisbon area or from outside of it, now dials 21 plus the individual number. In the case of the Algarve, depending on whether you're in the Tavira, Portimão, or Faro region, it would be 281, 282, or 289, plus the individual number. All phone numbers now have nine digits. The country code for Portugal is 351.

INTERNATIONAL CALLS

You can make international and collect calls from most public phones as well as from main post offices, which almost always have a supply of phone cabins (you're assigned a booth, and you pay at the end of the call). In larger towns you may be able to charge calls over 500$00/€2.50 to your MasterCard or Visa. Some phone booths accept international calls. For the operator, dial 171 for all international calls. For information, dial 177; for collect calls, 172. Access numbers to reach American long-distance operators are listed below.

➤ ACCESS CODES: **AT&T** (☎ 800/800–128). **MCI** (☎ 800/800–123). **Sprint** (☎ 800/800–187.

LOCAL CALLS

Older-style pay phones take 10$00, 20$00, and 50$00 coins; the newer models (with instructions in English) take 100$00 and 200$00 coins as well; 10$00 is the minimum payment for short local calls. Portugal Telecom card phones accept plastic phone cards of 50 or 120 units; you can buy these cards at post and phone offices, tobacco shops, and newsstands. As of March 1, 2002, coin-operated phones will accept only euro coins.

TIPPING

Service is included in bills at hotels and most restaurants. At hotels give the porter who takes your bags 200$00/€1 and leave the maid 200$00/€1 a day. If you dine regularly in the hotel, give your waiter 500$00/€2.50 to 1,000$00/€5 at the end of your stay; if you order wine with every meal, give the wine waiter somewhat less. Otherwise, tip 5%–10% on restaurant bills, except at inexpensive places, where you may just leave the difference in change. Taxi drivers get 10%; cinema and theater ushers who seat you, 50$00/€.25; train and airport porters, 100$00/€.50 per bag; hairdressers, around 10%.

TRAIN TRAVEL

Portugal has an extensive rail system. Trains are clean and leave on time, but there are few express runs except the one between Lisbon and Oporto, which takes just over three hours for the 338-km (210-mi) journey, and the one between Lisbon and the Algarve (four hours to Faro, five hours to Lagos). Try to buy tickets and reserve seats (at stations or through travel agents) two or three days in advance. Advance reservations are essential on Lisbon–Oporto and Lisbon–Algarve express trains. Trains to Madrid, Paris, and other parts of Europe depart from the Santa Apolonia Station in Lisbon and Coimbra (Paris only).

Special tourist passes are available through travel agents or at main train stations, valid for periods of 7, 14, or 21 days for first- and second-class travel on any domestic train service; mileage is unlimited. At press time (summer 2001), the cost was 18,500$00/€92.30 for 7 days, 31,000$00/€154.65 for 14 days, and 43,300$00/€216 for 21 days.

VISITOR INFORMATION

➤ TOURIST INFORMATION: **Green Line** (☎ 800/296–296 tourist help line within Portugal).

WHEN TO GO

The tourist season runs from spring through autumn, but some parts of the country, especially the Algarve, are balmy even in winter. Hotel prices are greatly reduced between November and February, except in Lisbon, where business visitors keep rates uniformly high throughout the year.

CLIMATE

Portugal's climate is temperate year-round. Even in August, the hottest month, the Algarve and the Alentejo are the only regions where the midday heat may be uncomfortable, but there you can go to the beaches to swim. What rain there is falls from November through June; December and January can be chilly at times, even on the Algarve, and very wet to the north, but there's no snow except in the mountains of the Serra da Estrela in the northeast. The almond blossoms and vivid wildflowers that cover the countryside start to bloom early in February.

The following are the average daily maximum and minimum temperatures for Lisbon.

Jan.	57F	14C	**May**	71F	21C	**Sept.**	79F	26C
	46	8		55	13		62	17
Feb.	59F	15C	**June**	77F	25C	**Oct.**	72F	22C
	47	8		60	15		58	14
Mar.	63F	17C	**July**	81F	27C	**Nov.**	63F	17C
	50	10		63	17		52	11
Apr.	67F	20C	**Aug.**	82F	28C	**Dec.**	58F	15C
	53	12		63	17		47	9

LISBON

Spread out over a string of hills on the north bank of the Tagus River estuary, Portugal's capital presents unending treats for the eye. Its wide boulevards are bordered by black-and-white mosaic sidewalks made of small cobblestones called *calçada*. Modern, pastel-color apartment blocks vie for attention with some of Europe's finest Art Nouveau structures. Tiled facades glint in the sun. Winding, hilly streets provide scores of vantage points with spectacular views of the river and the city.

With a population of around a million, Lisbon is a small capital by European standards. Its center stretches north from the spacious Praça do Comércio, one of the largest riverside squares in Europe, to the Rossío, a smaller square lined with shops and sidewalk cafés. This district, known as the Baixa (Lower Town), is one of the earliest examples of town planning on a large scale. The grid of parallel streets between the two squares was built after an earthquake and tidal wave destroyed much of the city in 1755. The Alfama, the old Moorish quarter that survived the earthquake, lies just east of the Baixa, and the Bairro Alto—an 18th-century quarter of restaurants, bars, and clubs—just to the west; Belém, an historic riverside district with restaurants, museums, palaces, and famed tourist sights like the Mosteiro dos Jerónimos, lies another 5 km (3 mi) to the west. Northeast of the center, the riverside Parque das Nações has the Lisbon Oceanarium—Europe's largest aquarium.

Lisbon (Lisboa)

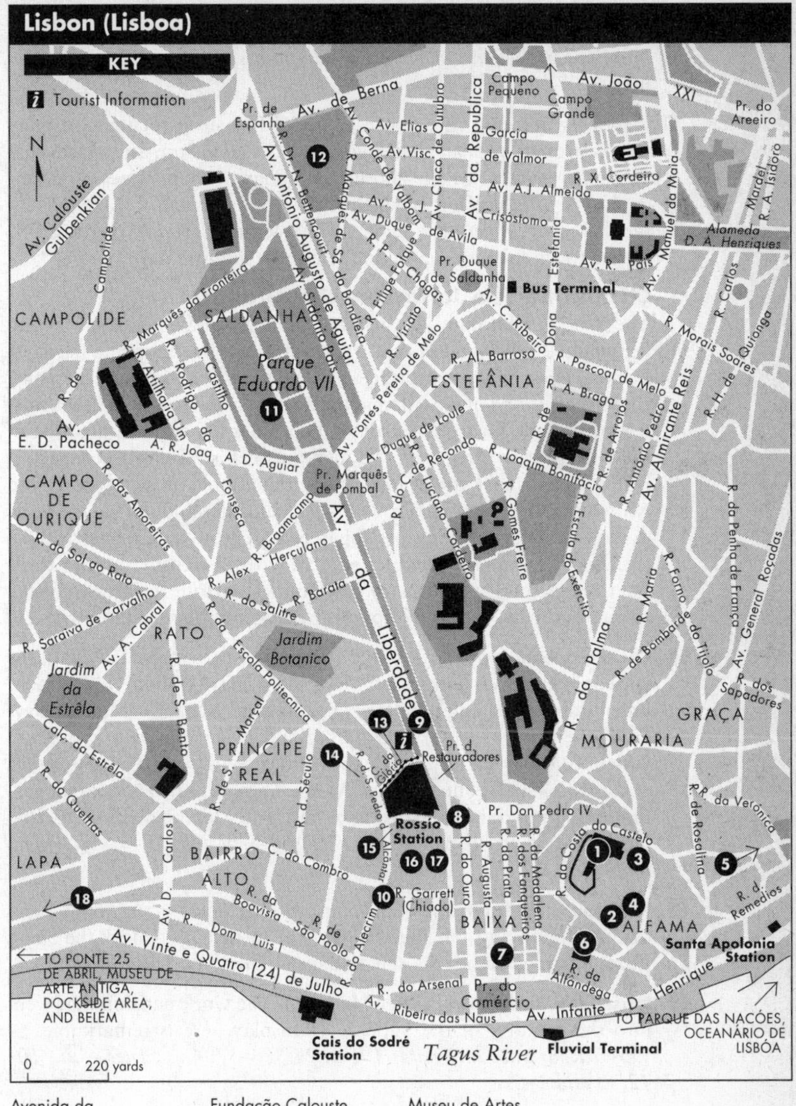

Avenida da Liberdade 9	Fundação Calouste Gulbenkian 12	Museu de Artes Decorativas 4
Baixa 7	Igreja de São Roque 15	Museu Nacional de Arte Antiga 18
Castelo de São Jorge 1	Igreja do Carmo . . . 16	Museu Nacional do Azulejo 5
Chiado 10	Instituto do Vinho do Porto 14	Parque Eduardo VII 11
Elevador da Glória 13	Miradouro de Santa Luzia 2	Rossío 8
Elevador de Santa Justa 17	Museu da Marioneta 3	Sé 6

Exploring Lisbon

Numbers in the margin correspond to points of interest on the Lisbon map.

Lisbon is not easy to explore on foot. The steep inclines of many streets present a tough challenge to the casual visitor, and places that appear to be close to one another on a map are sometimes on different levels. But the effort is worthwhile—judicious use of trams, the funicular railway, and the majestic city-center *elevador* (vertical lift) makes tours enjoyable even on the hottest summer day.

Castelo de São Jorge and the Alfama

The Moors, who imposed their rule on most of the southern Iberian Peninsula during the 8th century, left a subtle but enduring mark on Lisbon. Their most visible traces are in the medina-like pattern of narrow streets found in the Alfama, the quarter of narrow alleys that clusters around St. George's Castle and occupies the approximate site of the old Moorish settlement. Though the area is relatively compact, it is notoriously easy to get lost among the jumble of little streets and whitewashed houses with flower-laden balconies and red tile roofs. Its down-to-earth charm is most apparent in June, during the festivals of the Santos Populares (Popular Saints), when the entire quarter turns out to eat, drink, and be merry. The best way to tour the area is to take a taxi, Tram 28, or Bus 37 up to the castle and then walk down.

★ ❶ **Castelo de São Jorge** (St. George's Castle). Only vestiges remain of the ancient Roman, Visigothic, and Moorish origins of Lisbon's oldest monument, destroyed and rebuilt time and again over the centuries. Nevertheless, this is Lisbon's birthplace and it is a pleasant spot from which to survey the city. Inside the main gate are well-tended grounds and terraces with panoramic city views. There are entrances to the castle from Largo do Chão da Feira or Largo do Menino de Deus. ⊠ *Rua da Costa do Castelo,* ☎ *no phone.* ⏲ *Apr.–Sept., daily 9–9; Oct.–Mar., daily 9–7.*

❷ **Miradouro de Santa Luzia.** Stop at this overlook for sweeping views of the Alfama and the Tagus River. The terrace garden by the Santa Luzia Church catches the sun all day. ⊠ *Largo da Santa Luzia.*

❸ **Museu da Marioneta** (Puppet Museum). The workmanship that went into the creation of the puppets on display here is remarkable. ⊠ *Largo Rodrigues de Freitas 19,* ☎ *21/886–5794.* ⏲ *Tues.–Sun. 10–12:30 and 2–6.*

❹ **Museu de Artes Decorativas** (Museum of Decorative Arts). In a splendid 18th-century mansion with period furnishings, the museum has temporary exhibits of its art and furniture. It also conducts workshops that teach threatened handicrafts—bookbinding, carving, and cabinetmaking. ⊠ *Largo das Portas do Sol 2,* ☎ *21/881–4600.* ⏲ *Tues.–Sun. 10–5.*

❺ **Museu Nacional do Azulejo** (National Tile Museum). In the cloisters of the 16th-century Madre de Deus convent, this museum has a major and extremely lovely collection of 15th- to 20th-century tiles that trace the development of the art in Portugal from its introduction into Iberia by the Moors. The convent church has an ornate 18th-century interior with a splendid rococo altarpiece. ⊠ *Rua da Madre de Deus 4,* ☎ *21/814–7747.* ⏲ *Tues. 2–6, Wed.–Sun. 10–6 (last admission 5:30).*

★ ❻ **Sé** (Cathedral). Founded in 1150 to commemorate the defeat of the Moors three years earlier, the Sé has an austere Romanesque interior and a beautiful 13th-century cloister. The treasure-filled sacristy contains the relics of St. Vincent. ⊠ *Largo da Sé,* ☎ *21/886–6752.* ⏲ *Cathedral daily 9–noon and 2–6, sacristy daily 10–1 and 2–6.*

The Baixa and the Modern City

The Baixa, Lisbon's main shopping and banking district, opens on its northwestern end into the Praça dos Restauradores, the beginning of modern Lisbon, with Avenida da Liberdade running northwest to the green expanses of the Parque Eduardo VII.

9 **Avenida da Liberdade.** A stroll along the city's main avenue from the Praça dos Restauradores to the Parque Eduardo VII takes about 30 minutes, though you may want to stop at an open-air café in the esplanade that runs down the center of the tree-lined avenue. ⊠ *Between Praça dos Restauradores and Parque Eduardo VII.*

7 **Baixa** (Lower Town). The Baixa once housed trades and crafts now reflected in the street names: Rua dos Sapateiros (Cobblers' Street), Rua da Prata (Silversmiths' Street), and Rua do Ouro (Goldsmiths' Street). Scattered throughout are shoe shops, glittering jewelry stores, and a host of cafés and delicatessens that sell wines, cheeses, and pastries. ⊠ *Between the river and Rossío.*

10 **Chiado.** This chic district is home to some of the city's most fashionable shops. Rua Garrett, in particular, the Chiado's principal street, is lined with old department stores and a series of comfortable, turn-of-the-20th-century, wood-paneled coffee shops. Chiado's most famous coffee shop is the **Brasileira** (⊠ Rua Garrett 120, ☎ 21/346–9541), closed Sunday, which has a life-size statue of one of Portugal's great poets, Fernando Pessoa, seated at one of the sidewalk tables. ⊠ *Western side of Baixa.*

★ 12 **Fundação Calouste Gulbenkian** (Calouste Gulbenkian Foundation). One of Europe's finest collections of art and artifacts, collected by Armenian oil magnate Calouste Gulbenkian (1869–1955), is housed at this museum. The collection includes masterpieces by Rubens, Rembrandt, Gainsborough, and Rodin; Persian carpets; Chinese porcelain; ancient Egyptian art; Greek and Roman coins; and a room of Lalique jewelry. Two performance halls host concerts and and ballet productions. ⊠ *Av. de Berna 45,* ☎ *21/782–3000,* WEB *www.gulbenkian.pt.* ⏲ *Tues. 2–6, Wed.–Sun. 10–6.*

11 **Parque Eduardo VII** (Edward VII Park). The city's main park was named in honor of King Edward VII of England, who visited Lisbon in 1903. Rare flowers, trees, and shrubs thrive in the greenhouses. ⊠ *North end of Av. de Liberdade.* ⏲ *Apr.–Sept., daily 9–6; Oct.–Mar., daily 9–5.*

8 **Rossío.** Lisbon's main square since the Middle Ages is officially known as Praça Dom Pedro IV (whom the central statue commemorates), but is almost always referred to as *Rossío,* which loosely translates as Common Square. Renowned sidewalk cafés line the east and west sides of the square. ⊠ *Praça Dom Pedro IV.*

Bairro Alto and Lapa

Lisbon's Bairro Alto (Upper Town) is largely made up of 18th- and 19th-century buildings crowding narrow streets that house an exciting mixture of restaurants, theaters, nightclubs, fado houses, bars, and antiques shops. You can access the district by funicular railway and by street elevator.

13 **Elevador da Glória.** One of the finest approaches to the Bairro Alto is via the funicular railway in the northwest corner of Praça dos Restauradores. The ascent takes about two minutes; you are let out at the

São Pedro de Alcântara miradouro, facing the castle and the Alfama. ✉ *Calçada da Glória,* ☎ *21/363–2044.* ⏲ *Daily 7 AM–midnight.*

17 **Elevador de Santa Justa.** The elevator—enclosed in a Gothic-style tower created by Raul Mesnier, a Portuguese protégé of Gustave Eiffel—connects the Bairro Alto with Rua da Santa Justa in the Baixa. ✉ *Largo do Carmo,* ☎ *21/363–2044.* ⏲ *Daily 7 AM–midnight.*

15 **Igreja de São Roque.** The plain exterior of the Church of St. Roque belies its rich interior. Its flamboyant 18th-century **Capela de São João Baptista** (Chapel of St. John the Baptist) is adorned with rare stones and mosaics that resemble oil paintings. The **Museu de Arte Sacra** (Museum of Sacred Art) displays 16th- to 18th-century paintings. ✉ *Largo Trinidade Coelho,* ☎ *21/346–0361.* ⏲ *Church daily 8:30–5, museum Tues.–Sun. 10–1 and 2–5.*

16 **Igreja do Carmo** (Carmelite Church). The sacristy and nave of this church, the only sections to survive the 1755 earthquake, house the quirky **Museu Arqueológico** (Archaeological Museum), filled with everything from Roman coins to medieval sarcophagi. ✉ *Largo do Carmo,* ☎ *21/346–0473.* ⏲ *Apr.–Sept., daily 10–6; Oct.–Mar., daily 10–1 and 2–5.*

14 **Instituto do Vinho do Porto** (Port Wine Institute). Inside the cozy, club-like lounge you can sample the different types and vintages of Portugal's most famous beverage from the institute's formidably stocked cellars. ✉ *Rua de São Pedro de Alcântara 45,* ☎ *21/347–5707.* ⏲ *Mon.–Sat. 10–10.*

18 **Museu Nacional de Arte Antiga** (National Museum of Art). A beautiful collection of Portuguese art, mainly 15th–19th century, is exhibited at this 1884 museum in a 17th-century palace in the Lapa district, midway between the Baixa and Belém. Highlights are the *St. Vincent Altarpiece* (1467–70) by Nuno Gonçalves, Dürer's *St. Jerome,* and the Japanese lacquered *namban* screens depicting the arrival of the Portuguese in Japan in the 16th century. ✉ *Rua das Janelas Verdes,* ☎ *21/396–4151.* ⏲ *Tues. 2–6, Wed.–Sun. 10–6.*

Belém

Numbers in the margin correspond to points of interest on the Belém map.

For the best examples of the uniquely Portuguese, late-Gothic architecture known as Manueline, head for Belém, on the riverside at the southwestern edge of Lisbon. If you're traveling in a group of three or four, taxis are the cheapest way to get here; otherwise take the train from Cais do Sodré to Belém station or Tram 15 from the Praça do Comércio for a more colorful, if bumpier, journey.

21 **Monumento dos Descobrimentos** (Monument to the Discoveries). Erected in 1960, the tall, white, angular slab at the water's edge—a modern tribute to the seafaring explorers—overlooks what was the departure point for many a voyage. Take the elevator to the top for river views. ✉ *Av. de Brasília,* ☎ *21/301–6268.* ⏲ *Tues.–Sun. 9:30–7.*

★ 19 **Mosteiro dos Jerónimos** (Jerónimos Monastery). Conceived by King Manuel I at the beginning of the 16th century to commemorate the discoveries of Vasco da Gama, construction on the monastery began in 1502 and was financed by treasures brought back from the Portuguese "discoveries" in Africa, Asia, and South America. ✉ *Praça do Império,* ☎ *21/362–0034.* ⏲ *June–Sept., Tues.–Sun. 10–6:30; Oct.–May, Tues.–Sun. 10–1 and 2:30–5.*

20 **Museu de Marinha** (Maritime Museum). Portugal's long seafaring tradition is reflected in this huge collection of exhibits ranging from early

Monumento dos Descobrimentos . . . 21
Mosteiro dos Jerónimos . . . 19
Museu de Marinha 20
Museu Nacional dos Coches 23
Palácio da Ajuda . . . 24
Torre de Belém 22

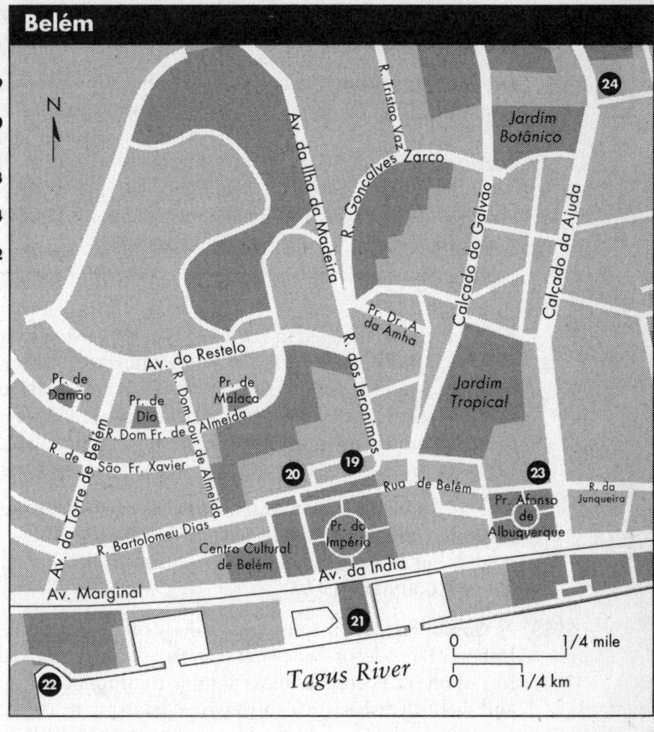

maps, model ships, and navigational instruments to fishing boats and royal barges. ✉ *Praça do Império (west end Jerónimos Monastery),* ☎ *21/362–0010.* ⏲ *Tues.–Sun. 10–6.*

23 **Museu Nacional dos Coches** (National Coach Museum). One of the largest collections of coaches in the world is on display at this former riding school. The most elaborate exhibits are three golden Baroque coaches made in Rome for King John V in 1716. ✉ *Praça Afonso de Albuquerque,* ☎ *21/361–0850.* ⏲ *Tues.–Sun. 10–6 (last admittance 5:30).*

24 **Palácio da Ajuda** (Ajuda Palace). Once a royal residence, this building now contains a collection of 18th- and 19th-century paintings, furniture, and tapestries. Guided tours are available on request. ✉ *Calçada da Ajuda,* ☎ *21/363–7095.* ⏲ *Thurs.–Tues. 10–5.*

★ 22 **Torre de Belém** (Belém Tower). With ornate balconies and domed turrets, this is one of the finest Manueline structures in the country—besides being a masterpiece of early 16th-century military architecture. Built on a basalt outcrop more than 200 m (656 ft) out in the water, the tower originally guarded the river approach to Lisbon. Land-reclamation works carried out over the centuries have brought the river bank up to its doorstep. ✉ *Av. da India,* ☎ *21/301–6892.* ⏲ *June–Sept., Tues.–Sun. 10–6:30; Oct.–May, Tues.–Sun. 10–1 and 2:30–5.*

Parque das Nacões

An ambitious urban renewal project 5 km (3 mi) northeast of the city center is revitalizing a stretch of riverfront by building on the infrastructure left from Expo '98. The leisure-oriented part of the development, Parque das Nacões, has Europe's biggest oceanarium, acres of landscaped park land, restaurants, a 10,000-seat indoor stadium, a marina, and a scenic cable-car ride. The area is easy to reach on the subway to Oriente, or, if you're driving from the south or east, on the

16-km (9-mi) Ponte Vasco da Gama (Vasco da Gama Bridge), which spans the Tagus.

Oceanário de Lisboa (Lisbon Oceanarium). This glass-and-stone structure, rising from the river and reached by footbridge, is the largest aquarium in Europe, with 15,000 fish, plants, seabirds, and mammals. It is the first aquarium to incorporate selected world ocean habitats (North Atlantic, Pacific, Antarctic, and Indian Ocean) within one complex. ✉ *Doca dos Olivais, Esplanada Dom Carlos I,* ☎ *21/891–7002.* ⏲ *Daily 10–7.*

Dining

Lifestyles have changed in Portugal over the past decade or so, and so has the Lisbon dining scene. Firmly established restaurants are holding their ground, but the pressure is on from a wave of newcomers, many of them attuned to lighter modern tastes. Foreign cuisine is ever more prominent—Chinese, Mexican, Italian, Brazilian, Russian, and Japanese restaurants are proliferating, and many of them are superb.

Restaurants in the low to middle price range often provide an *ementa turistica* (tourist menu), usually at lunchtime. These meals vary in quality but generally include three courses, a drink, and coffee, all for about 4,000$00/€19.95.

$$$$ ✕ **Gambrinus.** An inconspicuous door off a busy pedestrian street in Lisbon's Baixa leads somewhat surprisingly into the wood-paneled comfort of one of Portugal's most notable traditional restaurants. The fish and shellfish dishes are highly favored, along with a select wine list that is strong on long-established Portuguese labels. ✉ *Rua das Portas de S. Antão 23–25,* ☎ *21/346–8974 or 21/342–1466. AE, DC, MC, V.*

$$$–$$$$ ✕ **Casa da Comida.** The refined décor, complete with indoor garden, complements perfectly the polished service and quality cuisine at this longstanding feature on Lisbon's gourmet restaurant circuit. ✉ *Travessa das Amoreiras 1,* ☎ *21/388–5376. Reservations essential. AE, DC, MC, V.*

$$$–$$$$ ★ ✕ **Tavares.** Lisbon's oldest restaurant, and once a favorite of visiting millionaires, Tavares remains notable though its heyday is over. Handsome Edwardian furnishings fill the interior, and the menu is heavy with temptations like *perdiz na púcara* (partridge casserole in red wine), and *filetinhos de robalo com lagosta ao champagne* (fillets of rock bass braised with lobster in a champagne sauce). The wine list is top quality, but a bit unadventurous. ✉ *Rua Misericórdia 37,* ☎ *21/342–1112. Reservations essential. AE, DC, MC, V. Closed Sat. No lunch Sun.*

$$–$$$ ✕ **Bica do Sapato.** Installed like many of its new-wave brethren in a converted dockside warehouse, this airy restaurant, a favorite with TV stars and other trendy celebrities, serves food that is perfectly in sync with its contemporary lines: light and imaginative variations on traditional basics. ✉ *Av. Infante Dom Henrique, Armazém B, Cais da Bica a Santa Apolónia,* ☎ *21/881 0320. AE, DC, MC, V. No dinner Sun. and Mon..*

$$–$$$ ★ ✕ **Pap' Açorda.** Art and media types scramble for the closely packed tables in this former bakery at the heart of the Bairro Alto. Portuguese classics are skillfully and imaginatively adapted to modern tastes. The *açorda,* a bread-based seafood dish, is legendary among Bairro Alto gourmets. ✉ *Rua da Atalaia 57,* ☎ *21/346–4811. Reservations essential. AE, DC, MC, V.*

$–$$$ ★ ✕ **Bota Alta.** Lines form outside the door by 8 PM at this small tavern, one of the Bairro Alto's oldest and most popular restaurants. The menu is strong on traditional Portuguese dishes, among them a famed *almeijoas à Bulhão Pato* (clams steamed in a garlic and coriander sauce) and *carne de porco à alentejana* (pork sautéed with clams in white wine with garlic), which is one of the best in Lisbon. ✉ *Travessa da Queimada 37,* ☎ *21/342–7959. MC, V. Closed Sun. No lunch Sat.*

$–$$$ ✕ **A Travessa.** Hidden away in a lane in the old Madragoa quarter, this inviting bistro is on every Lisbon gourmet's phone list. Fresh fish dishes are popular and, as one of the owners is Belgian, Saturday nights are dedicated to mussels. Reservations are recommended Saturdays. ✉ *Travessa das Inglesinhas 28,* ☎ *21/390–2034. AE, DC, MC, V. Closed Sun. No lunch Sat.*

$–$$$ ✕ **XL.** Inventive cooking, inviting ambience, and late hours have made this restaurant a favorite dinner venue with the television and theater crowd, journalists, artists, and other midnight-oil burners fond of good fare. ✉ *Calçada da Estrela 57,* ☎ *21/395–6118. Reservations essential. AE, DC, MC, V. No lunch. Closed Sun.*

$ ✕ **1° de Maio**. Based on recipes from Portugal's rural heartland, the dishes at this former tavern in Bairro Alto are the work of Sr. and Sra. Santos, a husband and wife team of culinary genius. The wine list puts fancier restaurants to shame, and Sr. Santos is on hand with expert guidance. ✉ *Rua da Atalaia 8,* ☎ *21/342–6840. AE, MC, V. Closed Sun. No dinner Sat.*

$ ✕ **Sinal Vermelho.** This Bairro Alto restaurant updates the traditional Lisbon *adega* (a small wine tavern serving simple meals). Consider starting with a plate of clams drenched in oil and garlic, followed by any of the fresh fish dishes, which are rarely disappointing. Weekend reservations are essential. ✉ *Rua das Gáveas 89,* ☎ *21/346–1252. AE, MC, V. Closed Sun.*

Lodging

Accommodations in Lisbon range from major international chain hotels to small family-run establishments. For peak season reserve well in advance.

$$$$ ★ 🏨 **Lapa Palace.** In a unique Old Lisbon quarter where regal homes neighbor humble abodes with laundry-draped balconies, sits this converted 19th-century mansion. The luxurious guest rooms, suites, and public rooms run the gamut from neoclassical opulence to English country-house charm. ✉ *Rua Pau de Bandeira 4, 1249-021,* ☎ *21/394–9494,* FAX *21/395–0666,* WEB *www.orient-expresshotels.com. 109 rooms. Restaurant, bar, pool. AE, DC, MC, V.*

$$$$ ★ 🏨 **Ritz Four Seasons.** One of the finest hotels in Europe, the Ritz is renowned for excellent service. The large, handsomely decorated guest rooms have terraces, and the public rooms are ornate, with tapestries, antique reproductions, and fine paintings. ✉ *Rua Rodrigo da Fonseca 88, 1070-243,* ☎ *21/383–2020,* FAX *21/383–1783,* WEB *www.fourseasons.com. 284 rooms. Restaurant, bar. AE, DC, MC, V.*

$$$ ★ 🏨 **As Janelas Verdes.** This late-18th-century mansion has marvelously restored, individually furnished rooms. You can eat breakfast in an ivy-covered patio garden. Reservations are vital at this hotel; it's as popular as it is small. ✉ *Rua das Janelas Verdes 47, 1200-690,* ☎ *21/396–8143,* FAX *21/396–8144. 17 rooms. AE, DC, MC, V.*

$$$ 🏨 **Tivoli.** Facing Lisbon's main avenue, this comfortable, well-run establishment has a large public area furnished with inviting armchairs and sofas. The guest rooms are all pleasant, but those in the rear are quieter. ✉ *Av. da Liberdade 185, 1269-050,* ☎ *21/319–8900,* FAX *21/319–8950. 327 rooms. Restaurant, pool. AE, DC, MC, V.*

$$–$$$ 🏨 **Apartamentos Orion Eden.** This nine-floor *apart'hotel* in one of Lisbon's main downtown squares offers fully furnished and equipped apartments for one to four people. The rooms are bright and modern, and the building itself is a 1930s architectural landmark. ✉ *Praça dos Restau-*

radores 24, 1250-187, ☎ 21/321–6600, FAX 21/321–6666, WEB www. citadines.com. 134 rooms. Pool. AE, DC, MC, V.

$$–$$$ **Lisboa Plaza.** The staff at this family-owned hotel behind Avenida da Liberdade is friendly and helpful. The rooms are comfortable and pleasant and the bathrooms well-stocked. The room rate includes a generous buffet breakfast that aims to prepare you for tackling Lisbon's hilly streets. ✉ *Travessa do Salitre 5, 1269-066, ☎ 21/321–8218, FAX 21/343–0980. 106 rooms. Restaurant. AE, DC, MC, V.*

$$–$$$ ★ **York House.** This atmospheric residential hotel, built as a convent in the 17th century, is in a shady garden at the top of a long flight of steps. It has a good restaurant, and full or half board is available. Book well in advance: the place is small and has a loyal following. ✉ *Rua das Janelas Verdes 32, 1200-691, ☎ 21/396–2435, FAX 21/397–2793. 34 rooms. Restaurant. AE, DC, MC, V.*

$$ **Casa de São Mamede.** One of the first private houses to be built in Lisbon after the 18th-century earthquake, São Mamede has been handsomely restored and transformed into a relaxed guest house. Only breakfast is served; you're a 10-minute walk from the Bairro Alto. ✉ *Rua da Escola Politécnica 159, 1250-100, ☎ 21/396–3166, FAX 21/395–1896. 28 rooms. MC, V.*

$$ **Ibis Lisboa Saldanha.** Frills are not on the menu in this practical modern hotel, but in terms of comfort, service, and location, the value could hardly be bettered. The rooms are small, but adequately equipped. The buffet breakfast is extra. ✉ *Av. Casal Ribeiro 23, 1000-90, ☎ 21/319–1690, FAX 21/319–1699. 116 rooms. Restaurant. AE, DC, MC, V.*

$ **Aljubarrota.** An effusive welcome awaits you in this fourth-floor pensão (no elevator) in the Baixa. Rooms are small with linoleum floors, but neat and clean—antique tiles add character. Tiny balconies in some rooms have neck-craning views over the rooftops to the Castelo de São Jorge. The minimum stay is three nights. ✉ *Rua da Assunção 53, 1100-042, ☎ 21/346–0112. 12 rooms. MC, V.*

Nightlife and the Arts

Lisbon has a lively arts and nightlife scene. The weekend editions of the *Diario de Notícias* and *Publico* newspapers have listings of music, theater, film, and other entertainment. The free English/Spanish-language entertainment and culture guide *Follow Me,* published fortnightly, highlights major events in the city and is available at most hotel and tourism desks and at all ASK ME counters.

The Arts

Opera productions are presented infrequently at the **Teatro Nacional de São Carlos** (✉ Rua Serpa Pinto 9, ☎ 21/346–5914). The **Fundação Calouste Gulbenkian** (✉ Av. Berna 45, ☎ 21/793–5131) is the capital's main sponsor of and venue for music, ballet, and the visual arts. It presents the Great World Orchestras Cycle each year and the Early Music and Baroque Festival each spring. The **Centro Cultural de Belém** (✉ Praça do Império, ☎ 21/361–2400) hosts a full range of major concerts and exhibitions. Free recitals take place regularly at the Igreja do Carmo and Igreja de São Roque in the Bairro Alto, and at the Sé. Theater classics are performed in Portuguese at the **Teatro Nacional de D. Maria II** (✉ Praça Dom Pedro IV, ☎ 21/347–2246).

Most films in Lisbon appear in their original language with Portuguese subtitles. The best movie houses are on Avenida da Liberdade, and in big shopping centers such as **Amoreiras** (✉ Av. Eng. Duarte Pacheco, ☎ 21/383–1275), **Colombo** (✉ Av. Col. Militar, Benfica, ☎ 21/711–3200), and **Vasco da Gama** (✉ Av. D. João II, Lote 10502, in the Parque das Nações, across from Oriente Station, ☎ 21/893–0600).

Nightlife

DANCE CLUBS AND BARS

Once the undisputed center of Lisbon nightlife, the Bairro Alto has lost many of its young late-night habitues to the trendy bars and discos that have mushroomed along the city's waterfront. But the Old Quarter's narrow streets are still a fascinating warren of smoky bohemian bars, restaurants, and fado houses. The **Pavilhão Chines** (✉ Rua Dom Pedro V 89, ☎ 21/342–4729) bar is a good jumping-off place for an incursion into the quarter. Not far off, **Trumps** (✉ Rua Imprensa Nacional 104b, ☎ 21/397–1059) is the city's biggest gay dance club.

Along the waterfront between Santa Apolónia and the Ponte 25 de Abril, and encompassing the Avenida 24 de Julho, converted warehouses have become fashionable nightspots. **Salsa Latina** (✉ Gare Maritima de Alcântara, AlcâSul, ☎ 21/395–0550) is the place to go for the Latin American beat. Dancing, some nights to live music, begins at around 10:30. **Kapital** (✉ Av. 24 de Julho 68, ☎ 21/395–5963) is a nightlife classic, and still packs them in. The dance floor is dark and crowded, and the techno/rock music is deafening, but you can escape to a slightly quieter bar floor upstairs. **Lux** (✉ Av. Infante D. Henrique, Armazem, A, Cais da Pedra a Sta. Apolónia, ☎ 21/882–0890) is the trendy waterfront place for rubbing shoulders with celebrities. A bit upriver, the Parque das Nações has its own late-night scene, with popular bars, restaurants, and discos hugging the handsomely landscaped estuary waterfront.

MUSIC CLUBS

Fado is Portugal's equivalent of the blues. The songs, accompanied by the plaintive strains of the Portuguese guitar, are usually melancholy laments for lost lovers or unrequited love. The so-called *adegas típicas, restaurantes típicas,* and *casas de fado,* where people usually go to hear fado, belie the rustic wine cellar images their names suggest. They are mostly comfortable, mid- to upper-price range places where you can dine or have drinks while you listen. The entertainment usually starts around 10 PM, and reservations are advised. The **Adega do Machado** (✉ Rua do Norte 91, ☎ 21/342–8713) is a reliable fado spot in the Bairro Alto. In the Alfama, **Parreirinha d'Alfama** (✉ Beco do Espírito Santo 1, ☎ 21/886–8209) is one of the best fado houses, but you'll have to keep quiet—the regulars take their fado *very* seriously.

Shopping

Flea Markets

Feira da Ladra (Thieves' Market) takes place Tuesday morning and all day Saturday in the Largo de Santa Clara behind the Church of São Vicente, near the Alfama district. Every Sunday the **Feira de Domingo** (Sunday Market) is held in the Parque das Nações, near the waterfront on Rua da Pimenta. Though easy to spot, it is not always in the same place on the street. Call the Parque das Nações information office for the exact location (☎ 21/891–9333).

Gift Ideas

HANDICRAFTS

For embroidered goods and baskets from the Azores, try **Casa Regional da Ilha Verde** (✉ Rua Paiva de Andrade 4, Chiado). **Casa Ribeiro da Silva** (✉ Travessa Fiéis de Deus 69, Bairro Alto) is the place for handcrafted pottery. **Fábrica Sant'Ana** (✉ Rua do Alecrim 95, Bairro Alto) sells hand-painted ceramics and tiles. Fine porcelain can be found at **Vista Alegre** (✉ Largo do Chiado 18 and Rua Ivens 52, Bairro Alto). **Viúva Lamego** (✉ Largo do Intendente and Calçada do Sacramento 29) has a large selection of tiles and pottery.

JEWELRY AND ANTIQUES

Most antiques shops are along the Rua Escola Politénica, Rua Dom Pedro IV, Rua da Misericórdia, and Rua do Alecrim. **Antonio da Silva** (✉ Praça Luis de Camões 40), at the top of the Chiado, specializes in antique silver and jewelry. Look for Portuguese gold and silver filigree work at **Sarmento** (✉ Rua Aurea 251), in the Baixa.

LEATHER GOODS

Shoe stores abound in Lisbon, and some make shoes to order. You can buy leather gloves at a variety of specialty shops on Rua do Carmo and Rua Aurea. Fine leather handbags and luggage are sold at **Casa da Siberia** (✉ Rua Augusta 254, Baixa). Visit **Ulisses** (✉ Rua do Carmo 87, Chiado) for a fine selection of gloves.

Shopping Districts

The **Chiado** quarter is one of Lisbon's best shopping districts, with some of the city's oldest and most prestigious shops and an upscale shopping center with a large FNAC bookstore. The **Baixa,** from Restauradores square down to the River Tagus, is a popular shopping area. Designer boutiques and trees line the **Avenida da Liberdade.,** north of the Baixa. On Avenida Engenheiro Duarte Pacheco, west of Parque Eduardo VII, the blue-and-pink towers of the **Amoreiras Shopping Center** dominate the Lisbon skyline. **Colombo,** in the suburb of Benfica and reached directly by metro (Col. Militar–Luz), is the largest shopping mall on the Iberian Peninsula. The big **Vasco da Gama** mall in Parque das Naçóes is airy and attractive.

Lisbon Essentials

AIR TRAVEL TO AND FROM LISBON

For details, *see* Air Travel *in* Portugal A to Z, *above.*

AIRPORTS AND TRANSFERS

Lisbon's Portela Airport is on the northern edge of the city, about 7 km (4 ½ mi) from the city center.

➤ AIRPORT INFORMATION: **Portela Airport** (☎ 21/841–3700).

AIRPORT TRANSFERS

The Aerobus Hotel Shuttle runs every 20 minutes, 7 AM–9 PM, from outside the airport into the city center; tickets, available from the driver, are 460$00/€2.30 or 1,100$00/€5.50 and provide one or three days' travel, respectively, on all Lisbon buses and trams. The bus can drop you off at one of a list of hotels along its route. If you arrive on a TAP or TAP-booked flight, the bus is free: just present your boarding pass. Taxis into Lisbon run from about 1,200$00/€6 to 1,500$00/€7.50 and to Estoril or Sintra about 6,000$00/€29.95. For each piece of luggage in the trunk, add another 300$00/€1.50. No trains or subways link the airport and the city, but you can rent a car at the airport.

BOAT AND FERRY TRAVEL

Ferries cross the Tagus River from the Fluvial Terminal, adjacent to Praça do Comércio, to the suburb of Cacilhas and to the towns of Seixal, Montijo, and Barreiros. The six-minute crossing (daily 7 AM–9:30 PM) to Cacilhas is 110$00/€.55 one-way. Car-carrying ferries also run to Cacilhas from the quay at Cais do Sodré (10 minutes, 110$00/€.55 person, 250$00/€1.25 car) and from Belém to Porto Brandão (15 minutes, 110$00/€.55 person, 350$00/€1.75 car). These river trips are worth it simply for the fine views of the city. For details about two-hour cruises on the Tagus River, available April through October, contact Transtejo.

➤ BOAT AND FERRY INFORMATION: **Transtejo** (☎ 21/887–5058).

BUS TRAVEL TO AND FROM LISBON

Lisbon has two main bus terminals: Arco do Cego and Estação Oriente. The major national and international companies operate out of these two stations. Neither has a central information number; you have to call the individual bus companies. Rede Expressos is one of the companies at Arco do Cego. Renex operates out of Estação Oriente.

➤ BUS INFORMATION: **Arco do Cego** (✉ Av. Duque de Ávila, 12). **Estação Oriente** (✉ Parque das Nações, east of Sta. Apolonia Station). **Rede Expressos** (☎ 21/354–5439). **Renex** (☎ 21/888–2829).

BUS TRAVEL WITHIN LISBON

Buses and trams operate 6:30 AM–midnight. Take Tram 28 for an inexpensive tour of the city; buses to Costa da Caparica and Setúbal cross the Tagus bridge. In summer, old-fashioned trams run on tours through the city (3,000$00/€14.95 per person), departing from Praça do Comércio; call the public transportation company, Carris, for information.

➤ BUS INFORMATION: **Carris** (☎ 21/358–2334).

CAR RENTAL

➤ MAJOR AGENCIES: **Avis** (☎ 800/201002; 21/843–5550 airport). **Budget** (☎ 21/994–0443; 21/847–8803 airport). **Europcar International** (☎ 21/940–7790; 21/840–1176). **Hertz** (☎ 800/238238; 21/843–8660 airport).

CAR TRAVEL

Avoid driving around Lisbon yourself. Most central streets are choked with traffic during the day and parking spaces are always hotly contested; taxi drivers are skilled at navigating the one-way street system.

EMERGENCIES

Pharmacies are open weekdays 9–1, 3–7, and Saturday 9–1. A notice on the door indicates the nearest one open on weekends or after hours; a similar list appears in Lisbon's daily newspapers.

➤ EMERGENCY SERVICES: **Ambulance** (☎ 21/942–1111). **Police** (☎ 21/346–6141). **SOS Emergencies** (☎ 112).

➤ HOSPITALS: **British Hospital** (✉ Rua Saraiva de Carvalho 49, ☎ 21/395–5067).

SUBWAY TRAVEL

The Metro, short for Metropolitano, operates 6:30 AM–1 AM. Individual tickets are 100$00/€.50; a 10-ticket strip, a *caderneta,* is 850$00/€4.25. Unlimited-use daily tickets cost 270$00/€1.35. Watch out for pickpockets during rush hour.

➤ SUBWAY INFORMATION: **Metropolitano** (☎ 21/355–8457, WEB www.metrolisboa.pt).

TAXIS

Lisbon taxis are cream-color. When the TAXI sign on the roof is lit, the taxi is for hire. When only a green light is showing, the taxi is in use. Many city squares have taxi stands, or you can flag one down (on streets where stopping is allowed). Taxis are metered and take up to four passengers. Rates start at about 300$00/€1.50 and don't rise much higher than 1,200$00/€6. There's no per-person fee, but there is an extra charge for luggage.

TOURS

A half-day tour of Lisbon costs about 6,000$00/€29.95; a full-day trip north to Obidos, Nazaré, and Fatima runs about 15,000$00/€74.80 (including lunch), as does a full day east along the "Roman Route" to Évora and Monsaraz. Tour-company conglomerate Citirama has details about all the possible excursions. You can reserve through Citirama or any travel agent or hotel.

➤ FEES AND SCHEDULES: **Citirama** (✉ Av. Praia da Vitória 12-b, ☎ 21/355–8569 or 21/355–8564).

PRIVATE GUIDES

Contact the main Lisbon Tourist Office or the Syndicate of Guide Interpreters. The front desk at your hotel may also have a list of bilingual guides. Beware of unauthorized guides who try to "guide" you to a particular shop or restaurant.

➤ CONTACTS: **Syndicate of Guide Interpreters** (✉ Rua do Telhal 4, ☎ 21/346–7170).

TRAIN TRAVEL

International trains from Paris and Madrid arrive at the spectacular Estação Oriente, which has bus, subway, and taxi connections to all parts of the city. They continue on to the older terminal, just east of the city center. To get from Santa Apolonia to the central Praça dos Restauradores by public transport, take Bus 9, 39, 46, or 90.

➤ TRAIN INFORMATION: **Santa Apolonia** (☎ 21/888–4025).

TRANSPORTATION AROUND LISBON

Lisbon is hilly, and the sidewalks are paved with cobblestones, so walking can be tiring, even with comfortable shoes. But buses, trams, and the Metro system connect all parts of the city. A pass for unlimited rides on buses or trams is 500$00/€2.50 for one day (*bilhete um dia*), 1,075$00/€5.35 for three days (*bilhete tres dias*); the four-day (1,760$00/€8.80) or seven-day (2,490$00/€12.40) *Passe Turistico* (Tourist Pass), which you can buy at the Cais do Sodré Station train station, Restauradores metro station, and other terminals, is valid on the Metro as well as the Santa Justa elevator and Gloria and Bica funiculars. Otherwise, you pay a flat fee of 165$00/€.80 to the driver every time you ride a bus, tram, the Santa Justa elevator, or the funiculars. Buy your ticket in advance from a kiosk to get a 165$00/€.80 ticket that is valid for two separate journeys.

With the Lisboa Card (2,100$00/€10.50 for 24 hrs, 3,500$00/€17.45 for 48 hrs, or 4,500$00/€22.45 for 72 hrs) you get unlimited public transport and entrance to many of the city's museums. The best places to buy the card are the Turismo Lisboa desk in the arrivals area at the airport, the Turismo Lisboa desk at the Santa Apolónia railway station, the main National Tourist Office, and the Lisboa Welcome Center.

TRAVEL AGENCIES

➤ LOCAL AGENTS: **Viagens Abreu** (✉ Av. da Liberdade 158–160, ☎ 21/323–0200). **Marcus & Harting** (✉ Rossío 45–50, ☎ 21/346–9271). **Top Tours** (✉ Av. Duque de Loulé 108, ☎ 21/315–5877).

VISITOR INFORMATION

The two main sources of tourist information in Lisbon are the National Tourist Office and the Lisboa Welcome Center.

Additionally, the city has a number of ASK ME information desks, offering information specifically about Lisbon. There are three at the airport, one in the tourism office in Restauradores Square, one in the Santa Apolonia railway station, one in St. George's Castle, one on Rua Augusta, a main pedestrian thoroughfare in the Baixa, one in the Jerónimos Monastery, and one in the Lisboa Welcome Center.

➤ TOURIST INFORMATION: **Lisboa Welcome Center** (✉ Rua do Arsenal 15, ☎ 21/031–2815). **National Tourist Office** (main office: ✉ Palácio Foz, Praça dos Restauradores, at Baixa/Lower Town end of Av. da

Liberdade, ☎ 21/346–3643; airport office: ✉ Portela Airport, ☎ 21/849–3689).

THE ESTORIL COAST, SINTRA, AND QUELUZ

Extending 32 km (20 mi) west of Lisbon is a river and seaboard stretch of coastline known as the Costa do Estoril—the Estoril Coast, whose string of beaches has long served as a summer playground for Lisboners and tourists. The food here is some of the region's best, and sporting possibilities abound: golf courses, horseback riding, fishing, tennis, swimming, mountain climbing, hang gliding, and 4x4 excursions. Beaches vary in quality and cleanliness, though more and more display the blue flag of the Council of Europe, which sets high standards for unpolluted water and sand. The waters off Cascais and Estoril are calm. To the north, around Guincho's rocky promontory and along the Praia de Maças coast, the Atlantic is often windswept and rough—good for surfing and windsurfing.

To the north of Cascais and Estoril lie the mountains of Sintra and to the northeast, the historic 18th-century Queluz Palace. The villas and luxury *quintas* (country properties) of the wealthy, set back from the modern coastal development, still populate the Sintra hills and secluded parts of Estoril and Cascais.

Estoril

Despite latter-day development, the more secluded parts of Estoril, 26 km (16 mi) west of Lisbon, are still filled with grand homes and gardens. Many of the mansions date from the 19th century, when the town was a favorite escape for the European aristocracy. Estoril's blue-blooded air has dissolved somewhat, but it's still a cosmopolitan place of considerable charm. The best and longest local beach is in adjoining Monte Estoril.

The biggest casino in Europe, **Casino Estoril,** with gaming rooms, restaurants, floor show, and bars, is not just the hub of Estoril's nightlife; it also houses one of Portugal's major art galleries and hosts cultural events from craft shows to ballet performances. Admission to the casino complex and the 1,200 slot machines is free, but entrance to the gaming rooms is 1,000$00/€5 for a one-day ticket and 1,500$00/€7.50 for a week pass. The cost of dinner and the floor show begins at around 10,000$00/€49.90. ✉ *Parque do Estoril,* ☎ *21/466–7700.* ⏲ *Casino and restaurant 3 PM–3 AM, floor show nightly at 11.*

$–$$$$ ✕ **Estoril Mandarim.** This luxury Chinese restaurant aims to position itself among Europe's finest. Top Canton chef U Peng Kuan oversees the elaborate menu of Cantonese seafood, poultry, beef, and vegetarian dishes. Especially notable is the top-quality Chinese wine list. ✉ *Casino Estoril, Parque do Estoril,* ☎ *21/466–7270. AE, DC, MC, V. Closed Tues.*

$–$$$ ✕ **Restaurante Costa do Estoril.** One of the best deals in the area, this restaurant specializes in charcoal-grilled fish and has a terrace for warm-weather dining. Free fado performances take place Friday night 9:30–midnight. ✉ *Av. Amaral,* ☎ *21/468–1817. AE, MC, V. Closed Mon.*

$$$ ★ ✕🏨 **Hotel Palácio.** During World War II, exiled European aristocrats came here to wait out the war in grand style. Rooms are lavish, and those on the first, third, and fifth floors have balconies. Monumental columns, tiled floors, and chandeliers grace the common areas. The elegant Four Seasons restaurant ($$–$$$$) serves buffets around the garden pool in summer and seeks perfection with the freshest of

The Estoril Coast, Sintra, and Queluz

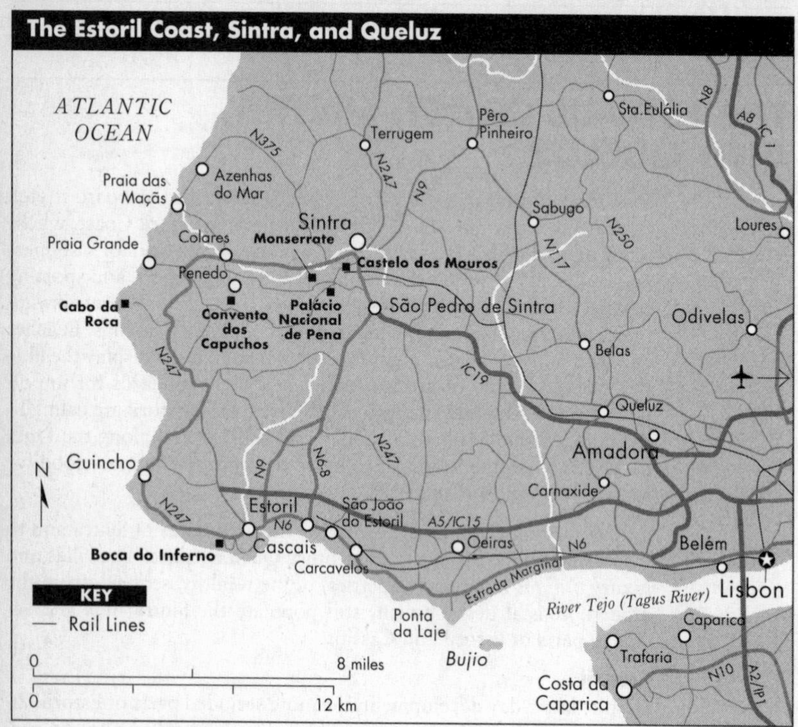

foods—the menu changes with the season. ✉ *Rua do Parque, 2769-504,* ☎ *21/468–0400,* FAX *21/468–4867. 162 rooms. Restaurant, pool. AE, DC, MC, V.*

Cascais

★ A former fishing village, Cascais (3¼ km/2 mi west of Estoril)—with three small, sandy bays—is now a heavily developed resort. Its small-town character is retained however, around the harbor and in the streets and squares off Largo 5 Outubro, which have lace shops, cafés, and restaurants galore.

The most-visited local attraction is the **Boca do Inferno** (Mouth of Hell), just 2 km (1¼ mi) west of Cascais, where the sea pounds into an impressive natural grotto. ✉ *Estrada da Boca do Inferno.*

The **Igreja de Nossa Senhora da Assunção** (Church of Our Lady of the Assumption) has paintings by the 17th-century Portuguese artist Josefa de Óbidos. ✉ *Largo da Assunção,* ☎ *no phone.* ⏲ *Daily 9–1 and 5–8.*

In an elegant 19th-century town house, the **Museu Conde de Castro Guimarães** (Museum of the Counts of Guimarães) displays 18th- and 19th-century paintings, ceramics, furniture, and locally excavated artifacts. The gem of the collection is an illumination of Lisbon in a 16th-century manuscript. The museum is on the grounds of the **Parque do Marechal Carmona** (Marechal Carmona Park), open daily 9–6, which has a shallow lake, a café, and a small zoo. ✉ *Estrada da Boca do Inferno,* ☎ *21/482–5407.* ⏲ *Tues.–Sun. 11–12:30 and 2–5.*

$$–$$$$ ✕ **Beira Mar.** Tucked behind the fish market, the Beira Mar serves traditional Portuguese seafood dishes. Watch the scales when choosing shellfish—it's often sold by weight and can be pricey. The atmosphere is comfortable and unpretentious. ✉ *Rua das Flores 6,* ☎ *21/483–0152. AE, DC, MC, V. Closed Tues.*

$$$–$$$$ ★ ✕🏨 **Hotel Albatroz.** The most luxurious of Cascais's hotels, this charming old house sits atop a rocky outcrop that was converted from an aristocrat's summer residence. The restaurant ($$–$$$$) offers superior sea views and specializes in fish dishes, like grilled sole or baked cod stuffed with ham. ✉ *Rua Frederico Arouca 100, 2750-353,* ☎ *21/483–2821,* FAX *21/484–4827,* WEB *www.albatrozhotel.pt. 42 rooms. Restaurant, pool. AE, DC, MC, V.*

$$$ 🏨 **Estoril Sol.** This luxurious high-rise hotel overlooking the Bay of Cascais may not beautify the coastline, but it offers modern comforts, including a health club and a large seawater pool. Nearly all of the spacious guest rooms have sweeping ocean views. ✉ *Parque Palmela, 2754-504 Cascais,* ☎ *21/483–9000,* FAX *21/483–2280,* WEB *www.hotelestorilsol.pt. 310. Restaurant, bar, pool. AE, DC, MC, V.*

$$ 🏨 **Baía.** In the center of town, this hotel looks directly out onto the old harbour and the little crescent of sand known as the fishermen's beach. The rooms are small, but well equipped and attractive, and some have balconies with views over the harbor. ✉ *Av. dos Combatentes da Gran Guerra, 2754-509,* ☎ *21/483–1033,* FAX *21/483–1095. 113 rooms. Restaurant, bar, pool. AE, DC, MC, V.*

Guincho

A superb wide beach overlooked by several seafood restaurants rests at Guincho, 11 km (7 mi) northwest of Cascais. Waves from the Atlantic pound onto the sand here even on the calmest of days, providing perfect conditions for windsurfing. But beware: the undertow at Guincho beach is notoriously dangerous, and even strong swimmers should take heed.

$$–$$$$ ✕🏨 **Fortaleza do Guincho.** Along one of the most beautiful stretches of Portugal's Atlantic coast sits this exquisite hotel, a former fort. The rooms are small but luxurious, and decorated in a mixture of period styles; the views they afford of the rocky shoreline are spectacular. The spacious and elegant restaurant ($$$–$$$$) is the hub of the establishment. The cooking is nouveau-ish French, coordinated by Strasbourg chef and restaurateur Antoine Westermann. ✉ *Estrada do Guincho, 2750-642,* ☎ *21/487–0491,* FAX *21/487–0431,* WEB *www.guinchotel.pt. 29 rooms. Restaurant. AE, DC, MC, V.*

Sintra

★ One of Portugal's oldest towns, Sintra—30 km (19 mi) northwest of Lisbon, and 13 km (8 mi) north of Estoril—was the summer residence of early Portuguese kings and aristocrats. By the 18th and 19th centuries its charms became widely known, as English travelers, poets, and writers—including an enthusiastic Lord Byron—were drawn by the region's beauty. On the second or fourth Sunday of the month, the Feira de São Pedro, known as the Sintra Fair by local English-speakers, takes place in the nearby village of São Pedro de Sintra, 2 km (1¼ mi) to the southeast.

The 8th-century **Castelo dos Mouros** (Moorish Castle) defied invaders until it was conquered by Dom Afonso Henriques, Portugal's first king, in 1147. Follow the steep, partially cobbled road up to the ruins or rent a horse-drawn carriage in Sintra. From the castle's serrated walls, you can see why its Moorish architects chose the site: the views falling away on all sides are breathtaking. ✉ *Estrada da Pena,* ☎ *no phone.* ⏲ *June–Sept., daily 10–7; Oct.–May, daily 9–5.*

★ At the center of the Old Town stands the 14th-century **Palácio Nacional de Sintra** (Sintra Palace). This twin-chimney building, a combination of Moorish and Gothic architectural styles, was once the summer residence of the House of Avis, Portugal's royal family. Today it's a museum exhibiting fine examples of Moorish-Arabic *azulejos* (tiles). ✉ *Largo Rainha D. Amelia,* ☎ *21/910–6840.* ⊙ *Thurs.–Tues. 10–5:30 (last admittance 5).*

★ The **Palácio Nacional de Pena** (Pena Palace), an extravaganza built by the king consort Ferdinand of Saxe-Coburg in 1840, is a cauldron of clashing styles, from Arabian to Manueline, and was home to the last kings of Portugal. The surrounding park is filled with trees and flowers brought from every corner of the Portuguese empire by Dom Fernando, consort to Dona Maria II, in the 1840s. It's a long but pleasant climb from Sintra to the palace—about 4 km (2½ mi). There's hourly bus service from the Sintra train station and town center. ✉ *Estrada da Pena,* (☎ *21/910–5340.* ⊙ *June–Sept., Tues.–Sun. 10–6:30 (last admittance 6); Oct.–May, Tues.–Sun. 10–5 (last admittance 4:30).*

Sintra Museu de Arte Moderna (Sintra Museum of Modern Art). The Berardo collection of modern European and American art, one of the finest private assemblages of modern painting and sculpture in Europe, is displayed here. ✉ *Av. Heliodoro Salgado,* ☎ *21/924–8170.* 🎫 *600$00/€3.* ⊙ *Tues.–Sun. 10–6.*

Quinta da Regaleira. Masonic symbolism and the mystical ideas of the Knights Templar are represented at this romantic palace built by a cocoa millionaire at the turn of the 20th century. Its turrets, gargoyles, and mysterious Well of Initiation would surely have delighted Charles Adams. ✉ *Estrada de Monserrate,* ☎ *21/910–6650,* WEB *www.regaleira.pt.* 🎫 *2,000$00/€10.* ⊙ *Visits must be booked in advance by phone.*

$–$$ ✕ **Tacho Real.** Truly old-fashioned Portuguese cooking is the attraction here. The *bacalhau no forno* (oven-baked salted cod) is outstanding. Wooden arches reveal that the building was once a stable. ✉ *Rua da Ferraria 4,* ☎ *21/923–5277. AE, DC, MC, V. Closed Wed.*

$ ✕ **Alcobaça.** Excellent fish dishes, including an *arroz de polvo* (octopus with rice) of local renown, are what habitués go for at this central and reasonably priced restaurant. ✉ *Rua das Padarias 7–11,* ☎ *21/923–1651. MC, V.*

$$$–$$$$ ★ 🏨 **Palácio de Seteais.** Formerly a palatial residence, this luxurious hotel 1 km (½ mi) from Sintra was built by the Dutch consul in Portugal in the 18th century. Its stately rooms are decorated with delicate wall and ceiling frescoes. ✉ *Rua Barbosa do Bocage 8, 2710-517,* ☎ *21/923–3200,* FAX *21/923–4277. 30 rooms. Restaurant, pool. AE, DC, MC, V.*

$$$ 🏨 **Lawrence's.** This small luxury establishment bills itself as the oldest hotel on the Iberian Peninsula, and it is probably right. Lord Byron stayed here in 1809, and many other famous people were guests in their time. The hotel re-opened in 1999 after total restoration. ✉ *Rua Consiglieri Pedroso 38–40, 2710-550,* ☎ *21/910–5500,* FAX *21/910–5505,* WEB *www.portugalvirtual.pt/lawrences. 16 rooms. Restaurant. AE, DC, MC, V.*

$$ ★ 🏨 **Quinta das Sequóias.** Down a side road and surrounded by gardens, this lovely manor house is just over 1 km (½ mi) from Sintra. It's a good touring base, and after a day of sightseeing you can unwind in the whirlpool tub or sauna. Dinner must be ordered in advance. Reservations are essential. ✉ *Apartado 4, 2711-901,* ☎ FAX *21/923–0342. 6 rooms. Pool. AE, DC, MC, V.*

$$ 🏨 **Tivoli Sintra.** From its perch in the center of Sintra, the Tivoli has views over the nearby valleys. The smart rooms provide space and comfort in equal measure. ✉ *Praça da República, 2710-616,* ☎ *21/923–3505,* FAX *21/923–1572,* WEB *www.tivoli.pt. 75 rooms. Restaurant. AE, DC, MC, V.*

Queluz

The town of Queluz, 15 km (9 mi) east of Sintra and 15 km (9 mi) northwest of Lisbon, is accessible by train directly from Lisbon or by way of the IC19/N249 road, which runs between Lisbon and Sintra.

★ Once you turn off the main road, it's hard to miss the magnificent **Palácio Nacional de Queluz** (Queluz Palace). Inspired in part by Versailles, the salmon-pink rococo palace begun by Dom Pedro III in 1747 was completed 40 years later. The landscaping and waterways are the work of the French designer Jean-Baptiste Robillon. The palace is now used for formal banquets and music festivals and houses visiting heads of state. A display of the elegant formal horsemanship known as haute ècole dressage, an art for which Portuguese riders are famed, is held in the gardens every Wednesday. ✉ *Rte. IC19,* ☎ *21/435–0039.* ⏲ *Wed.–Mon. 10–5 (last admittance 4:30).*

$$–$$$ ★ ✕🏨 **Pousada de Dona Maria I.** Marble hallways lined with prints of Old Portugal give way to high-ceiling rooms with 18th-century reproduction furniture in these former servants' quarters beneath the clock tower opposite the Queluz Palace. Across the street is the Cozinha Velha restaurant ($$–$$$$), set in an 18th-century palace kitchen and renowned for its faithful renderings of traditional Portuguese dishes. ✉ *Rte. IC19, 2745-191,* ☎ *21/435–6158,* FAX *21/435–6189,* WEB *www.pousadas.pt. 26 rooms. Restaurant. AE, DC, MC, V.*

The Estoril Coast, Sintra, and Queluz Essentials

BUS TRAVEL TO AND FROM THE ESTORIL COAST, SINTRA, AND QUELUZ

The best way to reach Cascais, Estoril, and Sintra is by train from Lisbon, but there are some useful bus connections between towns. The bus terminal outside the train station at Cascais has summer service to Guincho (15-minute trip) and Sintra (40 minutes). From the bus terminal outside the Sintra train station, there's year-round service to Cascais and Estoril (1 hour), and to the Moorish Castle and Pena Palace.

➤ BUS INFORMATION: **Terminal Rodoviário de Cascais** (☎ 21/483–6357).

CAR TRAVEL

The area is served by three main roads: the often congested four-lane coastal highway (the N6 Avenida Marginal), the IC19/N249 to Sintra, and the A5 expressway, which links Lisbon with Cascais.

TOURS

Most travel agents and guided-tour operators can reserve you a place on a guided tour, or you can contact the reception desk of your hotel. Half-day trips to Queluz, Sintra, or Estoril, or a tour of the area's royal palaces, cost around 8,000$00/€39.90; nine-hour tours of Mafra, Sintra, and Cascais cost 13,000$00/€64.85, including lunch.

TRAIN TRAVEL

A commuter train leaves every 15 to 30 minutes (5:30 AM–2:30 AM) from Cais do Sodré Station in Lisbon for the trip to Estoril and on to Cascais, two stops farther. A one-way ticket to both destinations is 210$00/€1.05. Trains from Lisbon's Rossío station run every 15 minutes to Queluz (20 minutes, 170$00/€.85), and on to Sintra, (40 minutes from Queluz, 170$00/€.85). The fare from Lisbon to Sintra is 210$00/€1.05. For current information about train services, call ☎ 21/888–4025.

VISITOR INFORMATION

➤ TOURIST INFORMATION: **Cascais** (✉ Rua Visconde da Luz 14, ☎ 21/486–8204). **Estoril** (✉ Arcadas do Parque, ☎ 21/466–3813). **Sintra** (✉ Praça da República 3, ☎ 21/923–1157; 21/924–1700; 21/924–1623 train station).

THE ALGARVE

The Algarve, Portugal's southernmost region, encompasses 240 km (150 mi) of sun-drenched coastline. Vacationers head here for clean, sandy beaches, top-quality sports facilities, fine hotels, championship golf courses, Mediterranean-type weather, and colorful local markets and cafés. Heavily developed since the 1960s, apartment complexes, hotels, and restaurants crowd every bay and cliff top in certain areas. Still, some fishing villages and secluded beaches remain untouched. The drive to Albufeira from Lisbon takes about three hours; allow another hour to reach either Faro or Lagos. (Regional authorities have been working to improve directional signs along roads, but sign posting remains inadequate.)

Monte Gordo

Pine woods and orchards break up the flat landscape around Monte Gordo, a town near the Spanish border 4 km (2½ mi) west of Vila Real de Santo António. Brightly colored houses dot the streets, which are laid out in an 18th-century grid pattern similar to that of the Baixa district in Lisbon. There's a long stretch of beach here, but beaches to the west, such as Praia Verde and Manta Rota, are equally attractive. You should have little trouble finding a spot on the sand, perhaps for a lunch of grilled sardines at one of the numerous beach-side bistros.

$ ✕ **Mota.** The Mota is a lively, unpretentious seafood restaurant with a covered terrace right on the ocean. ✉ *On beach at Monte Gordo,* ☎ *28/151–2340. AE, DC, MC, V.*

$–$$ 🏨 **Alcazar.** Unusual architecture and interior design mark this engaging hotel. The sinuous arches and low molded ceilings suggest the inside of a cave or an Arab tent. ✉ *Rua de Ceuta 9, 8900-149,* ☎ *28/151–0140,* FAX *28/151–0149. 95 rooms. Restaurant, pool. AE, DC, MC, V.*

Tavira

A tuna fishing port at the mouth of the River Gilão, 20 km (12 mi) west of Monte Gordo, Tavira has cobbled streets, a seven-arch Roman bridge, old Moorish defense walls crowning the central hill, and several churches of artistic and historical interest—not the least of which is **Santa Maria do Castelo** (St. Mary of the Castle), where the sons of King João I were knighted in the early 15th century for their part in taking the North African city of Ceuta from the Moors. Ferries to sand beaches on nearby **Ilha da Tavira** (Tavira Island), are available from the jetty at Quatro Águas (✉ 2 km [1 mi] east of town center)—it runs May–mid-October (150$00/€.75 roundtrip). Boats leave every 10 minutes or so July through August, and less frequently in other months, depending on demand. Another ferry runs May through mid-October from a quay in the center of town between the Roman Bridge and the market. The boats leave every 30 minutes (200$00/€1 roundtrip).

Olhão

Founded in the 18th century, this fishing port 22 km (14 mi) west of Tavira is notable for North African–style cube-shaped whitewashed buildings and for some of the best food markets in the Algarve (near the harbor). Ferries to the islands of **Armona** and **Culatra,** both of which have excellent beaches, are available from the jetty east of the town gardens. Schedules are available at the tourist office.

The Algarve

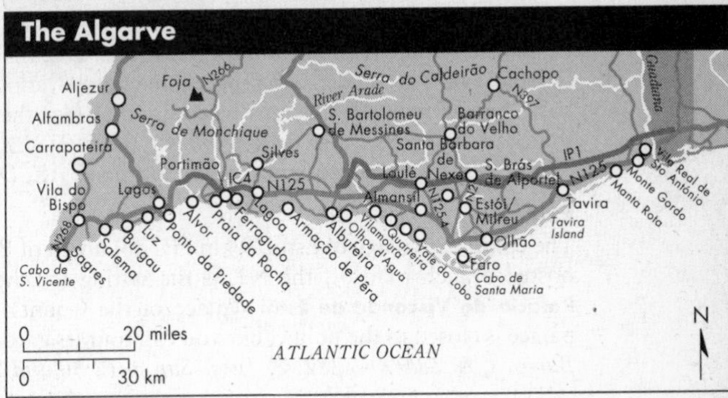

Faro

Founded by the Moors, Faro—provincial capital of the Algarve—was taken by Afonso III in 1249, ending the Arab domination of Portugal. A modern center 9 km (6 mi) west of Olhão, it is full of restaurants with international cuisines.

★ The best of the sights in Faro is surely the **Capela dos Ossos** (Chapel of the Bones) in the **Igreja do Carmo** (Carmelite Church), decorated with human bones taken from the monks' cemetery. ✉ *Largo do Carmo,* ☏ *no phone.* ⌚ *Weekdays 10–1 and 2:30–5, Sat. 10–1.*

★ In the older district, called the **Cidade Velha,** you can see remnants of medieval walls and gates. One of the gates, the **Arco da Vila,** with a white marble statue of St. Thomas Aquinas at the top, leads to the grand Largo da Sé (Cathedral Square). Surrounded by orange trees in the Largo da Sé is the restored **Gothic Sé.** (☏ 28/980–6632), open weekdays 10–5, and Saturdays 10–5 if there are no weddings.

At the **Museu Etnológico** (Ethnological Museum), lace-making, embroidery, and fishing displays show just how much the Algarve has changed over the years. ✉ *Rua do Pé da Cruz,* ☏ *no phone.* ⌚ *Weekdays 10–6.*

The Old Town's **Museu Municipal** (Municipal Museum), in a former convent, has a section devoted to the Roman remains found at the nearby archaeological site of Milreu. ✉ *Largo D. Afonso III,* ☏ *28/982–2042.* ⌚ *Weekdays 9:30–12:30 and 2–5.*

A large sand beach on Faro Island, the **Praia de Faro,** is connected by road (Bus 16 from the harbor gardens). Or you can take the ferry from the jetty below the old town to the beach at Farol on Culatra Island.

$$–$$$$ ✕ **Camané.** Carlos Manuel Martins and his wife, Graça, have made this Faro restaurant facing the lagoon a seafood Mecca. Algarve desserts, like the *tarte de amêndoa* (almond tart), an open pastry with a rich almond-and-egg filling, are especially good. Reservations are recommended for dinner. ✉ *Ilha de Faro (east side),* ☏ *28/981–7539. AE, DC, MC, V. Closed Mon.*

$ ✕ **Taska.** Mere mention of this small, cozy, family-run restaurant makes mouths water; the wide selection of seafood and market-fresh produce draw diners from far beyond the boundaries of Faro. ✉ *Rua do Alportel 38,* ☏ *28/982–4739. No credit cards.*

$$$ ★ 🏨 **Hotel Apartamento La Reserve.** High-class apartments, like duplexes with verandas and sea views, are available at this intimate luxury hotel in the hills of Santa Barbara, 10 km (6 mi) inland from Faro, complete with a tennis court and a surrounding six-acre park. The restaurant serves elegant Continental cuisine with a French accent. ✉ *Santa*

Bárbara de Nexe, 8000-712 Faro, ☎ 28/999–9494, FAX 28/999–9402. 12 studios, 8 duplexes. Restaurant, pool. AE, DC, MC, V.

$$ **Hotel Eva.** This modern, well-appointed hotel overlooking the yacht basin has rooms with spacious balconies that face the sea. There's a shuttle to the beach. ✉ *Av. da República 1, 8000-078,* ☎ *28/980–3354,* FAX *28/980–2304. 150 rooms. Restaurant, pool. AE, DC, MC, V.*

Estói

The charming village of Estói, 9 km (5½ mi) north of Faro, on a sign-posted branch road off the N2, is the setting for the 18th-century **Palácio do Visconde de Estói** (Palace of the Counts of Estói). The palace is closed to the public, but you can tour its gardens. ✉ *Rua da Barroca,* ☎ *28/999–7282.* ⊙ *Tues.–Sat. 9–12:30 and 2–5:30.*

Extensive Roman ruins at **Milreu** include a temple and mosaic fragments adorning some 3rd-century baths. ✉ *About 1 km (½ mi) north of Estói on N2-6,* ☎ *28/999–7823.* ⊙ *Tues.–Sun. 9:30–12:30 and 2–5.*

Loulé

Once a Moorish stronghold, the market town of Loulé, in the hills 17 km (10 mi) northwest of Faro, along the N125–4, is now best known for its crafts and the decorative white chimneys of its houses. You can usually see coppersmiths and leather workers toiling in their workshops along the narrow streets.

You can visit the partially restored ruins of the medieval Saracen **Castelo de Loulé,** which houses the town's archaeological and historical museum, the Museu Arqueológical de Loulé. ✉ *Rua D. Paio Peres Correia.* ⊙ *Weekdays 9–5:30, Sat. 10–5:30.*

The 13th-century parish church, **Igreja de São Clemente,** decorated with handsome tiles and wood carvings, contains an unusual wrought-iron pulpit. ✉ *Largo da Matriz.* ⊙ *At discretion of priest.*

Almancil

One of the best reasons to visit this nondescript town 10 km (6 mi) northwest of Faro is the 18th-century Baroque chapel of **São Lourenço** (St. Lawrence; ✉ N125, ☎ 28/939–5475)—filled with blue-and-white tile panels and intricate gilt work. The cottages beside it have been transformed into a lovely art gallery. The chapel, 3 km (2 mi) east of Almancil proper, is open Monday through Saturday 10–1 and 2–5.

Two major resorts are found in the area, south of Almancil. The **Vale de Lobo** resort sits in exclusive isolation on a beach about 2 km (1 mi) southwest of Almancil. The grand **Quinta do Lago** resort, famed for its golf, tennis, horseback riding, and water-sports facilities, is south-east of Almancil.

$$$$ **Hotel Quinta do Lago.** Green hills, pine woods, and golf courses surround this secluded and luxurious hotel on the rim of the Ria Formosa Natural Park, the wetland nature reserve that extends along the coast almost to the Spanish border. Most rooms have balconies with views over the Ria Formosa lagoon to the Island of Tavira. ✉ *Quinta do Lago, 8135-024,* ☎ *28/935-0350,* FAX *28/939-6393,* WEB *www.quinta-dolagohotel.com. 141. Restaurant, pool. AE, DC, MC, V.*

$$$–$$$$ **Le Meridien Dona Filipa.** On extensive, beautifully landscaped grounds near the beach, this lavish hotel has first-rate service, tennis courts, and discounts for nearby golf courses. ✉ *Vale de Lobo, 8135-901,* ☎ *28/935–7200,* FAX *28/935–7201,* WEB *www.lemeridien-hotels.com. 147 rooms. Restaurant, pool. AE, DC, MC, V.*

$$–$$$$ ✕ **Gigi.** You have to walk 400 m (¼ mi) across a wooden footbridge that begins near the Hotel Quinta do Lago entrance at the end of Rua André Jordão to reach this famed beachside restaurant, but seafood lovers

from around the world make the effort. Preparation is simple but masterly. Accompanying salads are skillfully constructed to harmonize with the food, and so is the wine list. ✉ *Praia da Quinta do Lago,* ☎ *96/404–5078. Reservations essential. AE, DC, MC, V. Closed Oct.–Feb.*

Vilamoura

A highly developed resort 10 km (6¼ mi) west of Almancil, Vilamoura is replete with luxury hotels, a casino, a large yacht marina, several golf courses, a major tennis center, and one of Europe's largest shooting centers. The beach is splendid, and there's more sand just 4 km (2½ mi) to the east at the neighboring market town of Quarteira, a quiet fishing village turned bustling high-rise resort.

$$–$$$$ **Hotel Vilamoura Marinotel.** Overlooking the Vilamoura marina, this hotel is one of the flagships of the Algarve's fleet of luxury hotels. The rooms are spacious and handsome; gardens lead down to the beach. ✉ *Vilamoura Resort, Apartado 676, 8125-410 Quarteira,* ☎ *28/938–9988,* FAX *28/938–9869,* WEB *www.nexus-pt.com/marinotel. 193 rooms, 16 suites. 3 restaurants, 2 pools. AE, DC, MC, V.*

$$–$$$ **Hotel Dom Pedro Golf.** In the heart of Vilamoura, the Dom Pedro is close to the casino and the beach. Each room is attractively furnished and has its own balcony; you can take advantage of golf privileges, tennis courts, and the health club. ✉ *Rua do Oceano Atlântico, 8125-410 Quarteira,* ☎ *28/930–0700,* FAX *28/930–0701. 263 rooms. Restaurant, pool. AE, DC, MC, V.*

Albufeira

Like many Algarve towns, Albufeira, 10 km (6 ¼ mi) west of Vilamoura, was a sleepy fishing village that mushroomed into a large and popular resort. But with its steep, narrow streets and hundreds of whitewashed houses clutching the slopes, Albufeira retains a distinctly Moorish flavor. The town has a lively fish market (open daily), caves and grottoes along its coast, and an active nightlife.

$–$$$$ ✕ **La Cigale.** Nine kilometers (5½ mi) east of Albufeira proper, overlooking its own little beach, this restaurant—one of the best—offers both French and Portuguese cuisine. ✉ *Olhos d'Agua 8200-591 Albufeira,* ☎ *28/950–1637. AE, DC, MC, V. Closed Dec.–Feb.*

$$–$$$ ✕ **Cabaz da Praia.** From its cliff-side terrace, this long-established restaurant has a spectacular view of the main beach. There's fine French–Portuguese cooking here—fish soup, imaginative fish plates, and chicken with seafood. ✉ *Praça Miguel Bombarda 7,* ☎ *28/951–2137. AE, MC, V. Closed Dec. No lunch Sat.*

$$ ✕ **A Ruina.** A rustic restaurant on the beach, built on several levels, this is the place for good views and charcoal-grilled seafood. ✉ *Cais Herculano, Praia dos Pescadores,* ☎ *28/951–2094. AE, DC, MC, V.*

$$$–$$$$ ★ **Sheraton Algarve.** On a spectacular cliff-top site by the sea 8 km (5 mi) east of town, this hotel blends Moorish courtyards, fountains, and terraces, and fine Portuguese tiles and furnishings. The hotel has a sauna, a nine-hole golf course, tennis courts, and access by an exterior elevator to the beach. A buffet breakfast is included. ✉ *Praia da Falésia, Apartado 644, 8200-909,* ☎ *28/950–0100,* FAX *28/950–1950,* WEB *www.luxurycollection.com/algarve. 215 rooms. Restaurant, 3 pools. AE, DC, MC, V.*

$–$$ **Hotel Vila Galé Cerro Alagoa.** Guest rooms here are smartly decorated and have private balconies, some with sea views. It's about a ½-km (¼-mi) walk to the downtown Albufeira, or you can take the courtesy bus service, which also stops at local beaches. The hotel has a health club. ✉ *Rua do Município 26, 8200-916,* ☎ *28/958–8261,* FAX *28/958–3199,* WEB *www.vilagale.pt. 310 rooms. Restaurant, 2 pools. AE, DC, MC, V.*

Armação de Pêra

The straggling resort of Armação de Pêra, 14 km (9 mi) west of Albufeira, has one of the longest beaches in the Algarve, a wide, sandy strand with a pretty promenade. Local boats take sightseers on cruises to the caves and grottoes along the shore.

$ ✕ **The Beach Bar.** A famed lunchtime venue, this beach spot doesn't do dinners, but serves its lunch menu until 9 PM. Fish is the specialty, and it has the best paella for miles around. ✉ *Praia Grande,* ☎ *28/231–6966. No credit cards.*

$$–$$$$ 🏨 **Vila Vita Parc.** The pampering begins as soon as you pass through the wrought-iron gates. Fireplaces, dark woods, and the aura of an exclusive oasis fill this superb cliff-top resort. There is golf and tennis, and landscaped gardens wind down to two sequestered beaches. ✉ *Alporchinhos, Box 196, 8365-911,* ☎ *28/231–5310,* FAX *28/231–5333,* WEB *www.vilavitaparc.com. 172 rooms, 10 suites, 5 villas. 6 restaurants, 3 pools. AE, DC, MC, V.*

$–$$$ 🏨 **Hotel Garbe.** The bar, lounge, and restaurant all have terraces that provide views of the sea at this low-rise, gleaming white hotel. Rooms are modern and smartly furnished. Steps lead from the hotel down to the beach. ✉ *Av. Marginal, 8365-909,* ☎ *28/231–5187,* FAX *28/231–5087,* WEB *www.nexus-pt.com/hotelgarbe. 152 rooms. Restaurant, pool. AE, DC, MC, V.*

Portimão

Portimão, 15 km (9 mi) west of Armação de Pêra, is the most important fishing port in the Algarve; it's cheerful and busy, with shops and open-air cafés. Even before the Romans arrived, there was a settlement here at the mouth of the River Arade. At restaurants along the quay you can sample the local specialty: charcoal-grilled sardines with chewy fresh bread and red wine.

$–$$ ✕ **Safari.** Seafood dishes with a distinct African flavor are served at this lively Portuguese seafront restaurant. ✉ *Rua António Feu,* ☎ *28/242–3540. AE, DC, MC, V.*

$ ✕ **A Lanterna.** Specialties at this pleasant restaurant just over the bridge at Parchal, on the Ferragudo side of town, are duck and fresh asparagus, but the exceptional fish soup and smoked fish are also reason enough for crossing the bridge. ✉ *Largo 1° Dezembro,* ☎ *28/242–3948. AE, DC, MC, V. Closed Sun. No lunch.*

$$–$$$$ ★ 🏨 **Le Meridien Penina.** On 360 manicured, secluded acres off the main road between Portimão and Lagos, this golf hotel with attentive service has an impressive range of activities, a health club, an elegant interior, and a number of rooms with balconies and views of the Serra de Monchique. The beautifully landscaped golf courses were designed by Henry Cotton; greens fees are waived for hotel guests. ✉ *Montes de Alvor, Apartado 146 8501-952,* ☎ *28/242–0200,* FAX *28/241–5000,* WEB *www.lemeridien-hotels.com. 192 rooms. Restaurant, pool. AE, DC, MC, V.*

Praia da Rocha

Now dominated by high-rise apartments and hotels, this was the first spot in the Algarve (3 km/2 mi south of Portimão) to be developed as a resort. On its sheltered beach of fine sand, excellent for swimming and sunbathing, is a wall of huge, colored rocks worn into odd shapes by sea and wind.

$$–$$$ 🏨 **Hotel Algarve-Casino.** A modern hotel, the Algarve-Casino has sizable rooms and an attentive staff. Leisure facilities, including windsurfing, deep-sea fishing, tennis, golf, are within easy reach and there's access to the beach below the hotel's cliff-side perch. The casino has in-

ternational shows and gaming rooms. ✉ *Av. Tomás Cabreira, 8500-802 Portimão Praia da Rocha,* ☎ *28/241–5001,* FAX *28/241–5999,* WEB *www.solverde.pt. 207 rooms. Restaurant, 2 pools. AE, DC, MC, V.*

$$ **Hotel Bela Vista.** Traditional tiles and stained-glass panels infuse this small beachfront hotel with charm. You can relax on the terrace overlooking the beach, and enjoy live music performances in summer. ✉ *Av. Tomás Cabreira, 8500-802,* ☎ *28/245–0480,* FAX *28/241–5369. 13 rooms. AE, DC, MC, V.*

Silves

Once the Moorish capital of the Algarve, Silves, 18 km (11 mi) northeast of Portimão, along the N124-1, ceased to be important after it was almost completely destroyed by the 1755 earthquake.The 12th-century

★ sandstone **Castelo de Silves** (Silves Castle), with its impressive parapets, was restored in 1835 and still dominates the area from its rocky heights above the town. ☎ *28/244–5624.* ⏲ *Daily 9–7.*

The 12th- to 13th-century **Santa Maria da Sé** (Cathedral of St. Mary) was built on the site of a Moorish mosque. ✉ *Rua da Sé.* ⏲ *Mon.–Sat. 8:30–6, Sun. 8:30–1.*

The **Museu Arqueológico** (Archaeological Museum) has a large display of locally excavated artifacts from prehistoric times through the 17th century. ✉ *Rua das Portas de Loulé 14,* ☎ *28/244–2020.* ⏲ *Mon.–Sat. 10–12:30 and 2–6.*

Lagos

The western terminus of the coastal railway that runs from Vila Real de Santo António, Lagos is a bustling holiday resort of pedestrian streets lined with shops, restaurants, and bars. It's still an important fishing port, though it's the nearby cove beaches that attract the crowds. The prettiest, the Praia de Doña Ana, is a 3-km (2-mi) walk from town.Lagos has a venerable history (Henry the Navigator maintained a base here), most evident in its imposing **city walls**, which still survive, and its 17th-century harbor-side **fort** at **Ponta da Bandeira.** ✉ *Av. dos Descobrimentos.* ⏲ *Tues.–Sat. 10–1 and 2–6, Sun. 10–1.*

The 18th-century Baroque **Igreja de Santo António** (Church of St. Anthony) is renowned for its exuberant carved and gilt wood decoration. The **Museu Regional** (Regional Museum) at the church displays mosaics and archaeological and ethnographical items. ✉ *Rua General Alberto Silveira,* ☎ *28/276–2301.* ⏲ *Tues.–Sun. 9:30–12:30 and 2–5.*

$–$$$ ✕ **No Patio.** As its name implies (*no patio* means "on the patio"), this restaurant has a lovely outdoor patio. Run by a Danish couple, Bjarne and Gitte, the restaurant serves international dishes with a Scandinavian flair. Tenderloin of pork with a sherry-mushroom sauce is a house specialty. ✉ *Rua Lançarote de Freitas 46,* ☎ *28/276–3777. AE, MC, V.*

$ ✕ **Dom Sebastião.** Charcoal-grilled fish and shellfish are the star attractions at this cheerful restaurant, and the long wine list has been carefully selected to complement the fare. ✉ *Rua 25 de Abril 20,* ☎ *28/276–2795. AE, DC, MC, V.*

$$ ★ **Hotel de Lagos.** At the eastern edge of the Old Town, this modern hotel is near sights and restaurants. Terraced rooms overlook the pool or across the river to the coast. Traditional tiles are used throughout. A shuttle bus runs to the beach, where the hotel has a private club for guests, with a pool, tennis courts, and a restaurant. ✉ *Rua Nova da Aldeia, 8600-755,* ☎ *28/276–9967,* FAX *28/276–9920. 317 rooms. 3 restaurants, 2 pools. AE, DC, MC, V.*

Sagres

Historians now agree that Prince Henry the Navigator's legendary school of navigation at Sagres is just that: mostly legend. But the 15th-century visionary who opened the era of Portuguese discoveries did have a base in nearby Lagos, and it is not difficult to imagine him standing here, on the windy headland, contemplating uncharted seas. Sagres is 30 km (19 mi) west of Lagos; take the N268 south from the N125 at Vila do Bispo.

★ A small road leads across a promontory above the sea through the tunnel-like entrance to the **Fortaleza de Sagres** (Sagres Fortress). The ruins of this 17th-century fort about 1 km (¾ mi) from the village have been transformed into an ugly modern structure that houses an exhibition center and a cafeteria. Nevertheless, the Sagres site retains a particular magic. A cobblestone wind compass 43 m (141 ft) in diameter is still visible on the flat ground beside the fortress. Archaeologists and historians quibble about its date, but some think the compass was used as a navigational tool by Prince Henry. The crashing of waves and howl of the wind create an apt background for thoughts about Portugal's nautical history. You can also explore the restored 16th-century chapel of Nossa Senhora da Graça or watch fishermen cast their long lines from the surrounding cliffs. ☎ *28/262–0140.* ⏲ *May–Sept., daily 10–8:30; Oct.–Apr., daily 10–6:30.*

$$ ★ ✕🏨 **Pousada do Infante.** Views of the sea and craggy rock cliffs are spectacular at this sprawling pousada. Moderately-sized rooms are well appointed and have small balconies. The restaurant creates tasty regional seafood dishes like *lulinhas fritas* (fried squid) and *almeijoas com carne de porco* (clams with pork). ✉ *8650-385,* ☎ *28/262–4222,* FAX *28/262–4225,* WEB *www.pousadas.pt. 39 rooms. Restaurant, pool. AE, DC, MC, V.*

Cabo de São Vicente

★ Sometimes called *o fim do mundo* (the end of the world), Cabo de São Vicente (Cape St. Vincent), 6 km (4 mi) west of Sagres, is the southwesternmost point in Europe and offers sweeping views. The lighthouse, open to the public, is said to have the strongest reflectors in Europe, casting a beam some 96 km (60 mi) out to sea.

Algarve Essentials

AIR TRAVEL TO AND FROM THE ALGARVE

Portugalia and TAP Air Portugal have daily flights to Faro, the capital of the Algarve, from Lisbon (a 45-minute trip), and flights to Faro from most European capitals are frequent.

➤ AIRLINES AND CONTACTS: **Portugália** (☎ 21/842–5500). **TAP Air Portugal** (☎ 80/820–5700).

BUS TRAVEL TO AND FROM THE ALGARVE

Daily bus and rail service connects Lisbon with the major towns in the Algarve; trips take four to six hours.

CAR TRAVEL

The main east–west highway in the Algarve is the two-lane N125, extending from Vila Real de Santo António, on the Spanish border, to Sagres. It doesn't run right along the coast, but has turnoffs to beachside destinations. A four-lane motorway, the IP1/E1, several miles inland, runs parallel to the coast from the suspension bridge at the Spanish border west to Albufeira, where it joins the main road to Lisbon.

TOURS

Organized guided bus tours of some of the more noteworthy villages and towns depart from Faro, Vilamoura, Albufeira, Portimão, and Lagos.

VISITOR INFORMATION

➤ TOURIST INFORMATION: **Albufeira** (✉ Rua 5 de Outubro, ☎ 28/958–5279). **Armação de Pêrá** (✉ Av. Marginal, ☎ 28/231–2145). **Faro** (✉ Rua da Misericórdia 8/12, ☎ 28/980–3604; ✉ airport, ☎ 28/981–8582). **Lagos** (✉ Largo Marquês de Pombal, ☎ 28/276–3031). **Loulé** (✉ Edifico do Castelo, ☎ 28/946–3900). **Monte Gordo** (✉ Av. Marginal, ☎ 28/154–4495). **Olhão** (✉ Largo da Lagoa, ☎ 28/971–3936). **Portimão** (✉ Largo 1° de Dezembro, ☎ 28/241–9131). **Praia da Rocha** (✉ Av. Tomás Cabreira, ☎ 28/241–9132). **Silves** (✉ Rua 25° de Abril, ☎ 28/244–2255). **Tavira** (✉ Rua da Galeria 9, ☎ 28/132–2511).

25 ROMANIA

BUCHAREST, THE BLACK SEA COAST AND DANUBE DELTA, TRANSYLVANIA

ROMANIA CAN BE A CHALLENGING DESTINATION, but it is among the most beautiful countries in Eastern Europe. Its attractions are varied, from summer play on the Black Sea coast to winter skiing in the rugged Carpathian Mountains. The medieval towns and rural villages of Romania are among the least spoiled in Europe.

Romania, made up of the provinces of Walachia, Moldavia, and Transylvania, borders Ukraine, Moldova, Bulgaria, Serbia, and Hungary. With a population of 23 million, Romania is a Latin island in a sea of Slavs and Magyars—its people are the descendants of the Dacian tribe and of the Roman soldiers who garrisoned this province of the Roman Empire. Barbarian invasions, struggles against the Turks, the Austro-Hungarian domination of Transylvania, and a strong French cultural influence have all shaped Romanian culture.

Romania's largest metropolis, Bucharest, may appear unwelcoming, but its wide, tree-lined avenues and hidden charm can outweigh the effects of rows of drab buildings and depressing neighborhoods. The Romanian Riviera on the Black Sea enjoys unfailing popularity, as do the spectacular wildlife sanctuaries of the nearby Danube Delta. Transylvania is famous for the Dracula legend and its related sights, but the region is also home to Hungarian and German populations with distinctive folk traditions.

The overthrow of the Ceauşescu regime in December 1989 ushered in the country's shift toward Western-style democracy and a market economy. Such adversities as bread lines, food shortages, and empty store shelves have been replaced with rapidly rising prices, which trouble many Romanians and frustrate the current government.

Romania is among the poorest countries in Europe, and petty theft remains a widespread problem; try to conceal jewelry and valuables. Be sure to drink bottled water or mineral water (*apa minerala*), which is readily available. You should bring an emergency supply of toilet paper, a full first-aid kit, a flashlight for poorly lighted streets and corridors, and, in summer, insect repellent. Although many pharmacies carry an assortment of Western medications and vitamins, most hospitals do not meet Western standards.

Romania is likely to remain underexplored until the serious problems caused by the former Ceauşescu regime are resolved. In the meantime, you will see a part of Europe that has not experienced the technological advances and social reforms of the late 20th century.

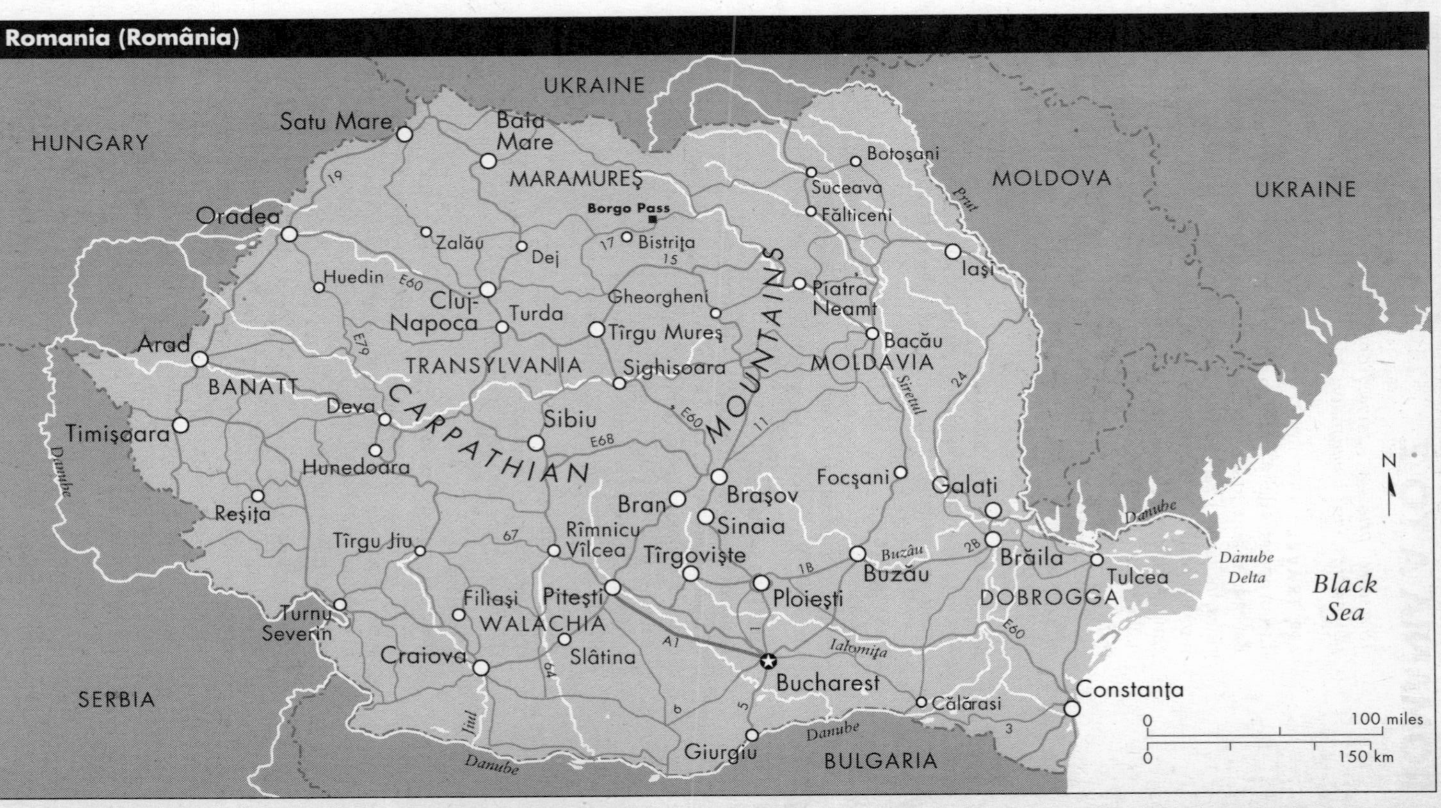
Romania (România)
UKRAINE
HUNGARY
Satu Mare
Baia Mare
MARAMUREŞ
Borgo Pass
Botoşani
Suceava
Fălticeni
MOLDOVA
UKRAINE
Prut
Oradea
Zalău
Dej
Bistriţa
Iaşi
Huedin
Cluj-Napoca
Turda
Gheorgheni
Piatra Neamţ
Tîrgu Mureş
Bacău
Arad
TRANSYLVANIA
Sighisoara
MOLDAVIA
Siretul
BANATT
Deva
CARPATHIAN
MOUNTAINS
Sibiu
Timişoara
Hunedoara
Danube
Focşani
Galaţi
Reşiţa
Bran
Braşov
Sinaia
Rîmnicu Vîlcea
Tîrgu Jiu
Tîrgovişte
Buzău
Brăila
Tulcea
Dănube Delta
Black Sea
Piteşti
Ploieşti
DOBROGGA
Filiaşi
WALACHIA
Turnu Severin
Slâtina
Ialomiţa
Craiova
Bucharest
Constanţa
SERBIA
Jiul
Călărasi
Giurgiu
BULGARIA
N
0
100 miles
150 km

ROMANIA A TO Z

To research prices, get advice from other travelers, and book travel arrangements, visit www.fodors.com.

AIR TRAVEL

Tarom operates daily flights to major Romanian cities from Bucharest's Baneasa Airport. In summer additional flights link Constanţa with major cities, including Cluj and Iaşi. Be prepared for delays and cancellations. International flights can be booked at Tarom Agency's central reservations office, which is open weekdays 8 AM–7:30 PM. You can also make reservation at some major hotels and at travel agencies.

➤ AIRLINES AND CONTACTS: **Domestic flight bookings** (✉ Piaţa Victoriei 1, Bucharest (☎ 01/659–4125). **Tarom Agency central reservations office** (✉ Splaiul Independenţei 17, Bucharest, ☎ 01/337–0208, FAX 01/337–0321).

BOAT AND FERRY TRAVEL

Regular passenger services operate on various sections of the Danube; tickets are available at the ports, including Galaţi and Tulcea.

BUS TRAVEL

Bus stations, or *autogara*, are usually near train stations. Buses are generally crowded and far from luxurious. Tickets go on sale at stations up to two hours before departure.

BUSINESS HOURS

Banks are only open weekdays 9–12:30, but major cities have ATMs. Exchange office hours vary, but most are open weekdays 9–7 and Saturday 9–1; some are open until 7 on Saturday and 1 on Sunday. Museums are usually open Tuesday–Sunday 10–6. Shops are generally open weekdays 10–6. Most state-owned shops close at 2 on Saturday, but private shops stay open until 5 on Saturday and 2 on Sunday.

CAR TRAVEL

An International Driver's Permit is required for all drivers from outside the country for stays of more than 30 days.

GASOLINE

State gas stations are found in towns on main roads. The many new private gas stations charge a bit more than the state stations. Most gas stations sell regular (90-octane), premium (98-octane), *motorina* (diesel), and *fară plumb* (unleaded). Prices remain low compared to those of Western Europe.

ROAD CONDITIONS

A network of main roads covers the country, though the majority allow for only a single lane in each direction. Potholes are common, and a few roads are not paved at all. Farm machinery, slow-moving trucks, horses and carts, and herds of animals often block roads. At night cars without headlights often drive along poorly lit or unlit roads, an enduring legacy of the Ceauşescu regime.

RULES OF THE ROAD

Drive on the right and observe the speed limits: 50 kph (32 mph) in built-up areas and 90 kph–100 kph (56 mph–62 mph) on all other roads. Traffic signs are the same as those used in most of Western Europe. Driving after drinking any alcohol is prohibited. Seat belts are obligatory in the front seat of vehicles, with the exception of taxis. Spot checks are frequent; police can levy on-the-spot fines. Most fines are minimal, but the seat belt fine is approximately $50.

CUSTOMS AND DUTIES

You may bring in a personal computer and printer, 2 cameras, 10 rolls of film, 1 small camcorder/video camera and VCR, 10 video cassettes, a typewriter, binoculars, a radio/tape recorder, a small TV, a bicycle, a stroller, 200 cigarettes, 1 liter of liquor, and 4 liters of wine or beer. You may import or export duty-free gifts up to a value of $1,200. Antiques taken out of Romania must have a receipt and document stating that they are not part of the national treasure. Keep receipts if you want to change money back into your own currency.

DINING

Bucharest is in the throes of a restaurant renaissance. French, German, Italian, Mexican, Middle Eastern, and Asian restaurants are thriving. Traditional Romanian foods are *mamaliga* (corn porridge often smothered with sour cream and cheese), *sarmale* (cabbage rolls filled with meat and rice), *ciorbă* (a slightly spicy and sour soup stock), and sheep's-milk cheeses. Favored meats are usually pork and beef. Outside the capital, options are limited and some restaurants may not even have printed menus. To avoid being overcharged, ask for prices before you eat. Street vendors sell fragrant offerings like *covrigi* (giant pretzels) and roasted chestnuts.

Prices are for one main course at dinner. Because high inflation means local prices frequently change, ratings are given in U.S. dollars, which remain constant. Your bill will be in lei.

CATEGORY	COST
$$$$	over $12
$$$	$8–$12
$$	$4–$8
$	under $4

MEALTIMES

Outside Bucharest and the Black Sea and Carpathian resorts, some restaurants stop serving by 9 PM, although an increasing number have begun staying open until 11 PM or later.

RESERVATIONS AND DRESS

Jacket and tie are advised for the best restaurants and business lunches and dinners. Casual dress is appropriate at other times.

EMBASSIES

All embassies are in Bucharest. Australia maintains a consular office in Bucharest.

➤ CANADA: (✉ Str. N. Iorga 36, Bucharest, ☎ 01/222–9845, FAX 01/312–0366).

➤ UNITED KINGDOM: (✉ Str. J. Michelet 24, Bucharest, ☎ 01/312–0303, FAX 01/312–0229).

➤ UNITED STATES: (✉ Tudor Arghezi, Bucharest, ☎ 01/210–4042).

HOLIDAYS

December 31–January 2; Orthodox Easter; May 1 (Labor Day); December 1 (National Day); December 25–26.

LANGUAGE

If you speak a Romance language, Romanian is likely to sound pleasantly familiar. French and English are widely spoken and understood in Romanian cities, German and Russian less so.

LODGING

The Romanian Tourism License and Control Department oversees hotel ranking and licensing, rating hotels with from one to five stars.

Accommodations have undergone major improvements, but lodging is not Romania's forte. Prices are variable depending on booking arrangements. Prepaid arrangements through Romanian or foreign agencies abroad often entitle you to discounted prices. Some packages, such as fly-drive holidays, come with bed-and-breakfast vouchers. Most state-run facilities accept vouchers; in deluxe hotels you pay a little extra. You can also book accommodations directly with hotels (which may require reservations by fax) or through Romanian travel agencies. The National Association of Rural Ecological and Cultural Tourism (ANTREC) hosts travelers in clean and hospitable homes with meals and tours provided. Rustic cottages may be rented at such ski resorts as Sinaia and Poiana Braşov. Details are available from Romanian tourist offices abroad or the local office in Bucharest. Rooms in private homes, which can be booked through some private agencies, are a good alternative to hotels.

The following hotel price categories are for two people in a double room. Rates usually include breakfast. Because of inflation, ratings are given according to hard-currency equivalents. Some hotels have a dual price system in which foreigners are charged a much higher rate than Romanians; the higher price may not be displayed. The government has discouraged this practice, but many hotels and museums continue to overcharge foreigners. Room rates in Bucharest are much higher than those in the rest of the country.

CATEGORY	BUCHAREST	OUTSIDE BUCHAREST
$$$$	over $200	over $120
$$$	$125–$200	$80–$120
$$	$70–$125	$50–$80
$	under $70	under $50

➤ ORGANIZATIONS: **The National Association of Rural Ecological and Cultural Tourism (ANTREC)** (Str. Maica Alexandra 7, Bucharest, ☎ 01/311–2845; 01/315–3206, WEB www.antrec.i-net.ro).

HOTELS

Standards of facilities, including plumbing and hot water, improve rapidly through the categories but may not be ideal even in expensive lodgings. Ask at the front desk when hot water will be available. Whatever class of property you choose, do not leave valuables in your room and, on departure, check your bill for unnecessary charges.

MAIL AND SHIPPING

Postal codes exist but mail may be delivered without.

POSTAL RATES

Rates increase regularly, so check before you post. A letter to the United States costs 28,900 lei, a postcard 9,300 lei; rates to the United Kingdom are 26,305 lei for a letter and 6,800 lei for a postcard.

MONEY MATTERS

Prices in Western-style establishments can be as high as those in Western Europe, though typical Romanian restaurants and hotels offer reasonable prices. Prices of basic items are often as high as those in the West.

Museum admission usually costs between 15,000 and 75,000 lei; a bottle of imported beer in a restaurant around 30,000 lei; a 2-km (1-mi) taxi ride about 25,000 lei.

CREDIT CARDS

Though major credit cards are now commonly accepted in large hotels, restaurants, and shops, they are not accepted in most independent establishments or in the countryside, nor are traveler's checks. In addition, some restaurants will now refuse credit cards due to recent fraud by unscrupulous employees making duplicate copies of charge forms.

CURRENCY

The unit of currency is the leu (plural lei). There are coins of 500 lei. Banknotes come in denominations of 1,000, 5,000, 10,000, 50,000, 100,000, and 500,000 lei. Do not expect to be given change of less than 500 lei. Inflation and frequent price increases are expected to continue; costs are therefore best calculated in convertible hard currencies such as U.S. dollars, German marks, or Swiss francs. As the U.S. dollar is the most readily negotiated currency, it is a good idea always to keep some with you, especially in smaller denominations. At press time (summer 2001), the official exchange rate was 26,072 lei to the U.S. dollar, 17,439 lei to the Canadian dollar, 38,842 lei to the pound sterling, 24,625 lei to the Euro, 31,268 lei to the Irish punt, 42,345 lei to the Australian dollar, 14,689 lei to the New Zealand dollar, and 3,369 lei the South African rand.

An increasing number of licensed exchange offices compete to offer the best exchange rates. Do not deal with the black market. Retain exchange receipts if you want to exchange lei back into hard currency upon departure from Romania. By law, foreigners must pay for everything except air tickets in lei, though hard currency is widely accepted in hotels and in some restaurants. You may not import or export lei.

PASSPORTS AND VISAS

U.S. citizens need only a valid passport to enter Romania for up to 30 days, but border guards may try to extort money from you anyway; be firm. If you're traveling on a British, Australian, or New Zealand passport, you must pay $33 for a 30-day tourist card when you cross the border. There is no application and you don't need any photos. They prefer U.S. dollars but will accept British pounds or German marks.

SHOPPING

An influx of private shops has introduced additional style and choice to Romania. Bargains can be found on Oriental-style and flat-weave rugs, wool sweaters, crystal, porcelain, and glassware. Traditional folk crafts—painted eggs, handmade lace, and embroidered items—are sold in Artizanat stores, in shopping areas, and in museums. Keep receipts for all antiques purchases, regardless of their legal export status.

TELEPHONES

COUNTRY AND AREA CODES

The country code for Romania is 40. When dialing Romania from outside the country, drop the initial 0 from the regional code.

INTERNATIONAL CALLS

Direct-dial international calls can be made from hotels, the train station, the phone company building on Bucharest's Calea Victoriei, and local post offices. To place long-distance calls out of Romania, dial 00, then the country code and number. Various international operators, the AT&T USADirect international operator, MCI Worldphone, and Sprint can also be reached from Romania.

➤ ACCESS CODES: **AT&T** (☎ 01/800–4288); **MCI** Worldphone (☎ 01/800–1800); **Sprint** (☎ 01/800–0877). **International information** (☎ 971).

LOCAL CALLS

While the Romanian telephone system is old and overextended, it has become much easier to use in the past few years. Most public telephones are orange and require a phone card, which can be purchased at the post office. You can also make local or long-distance calls at the post office. In larger towns, private business offices offer phone, fax, and telex services.

The area code for Bucharest is 1. Long-distance calls within Romania should be prefixed with a 0 followed by the area code for the county or region. For information in Romania, your hotel's front desk or phone book is often your best bet. For local information call ☎ 9311. Most operators speak English.

TIPPING

Most Romanians do not tip, but it is generally expected of foreigners. A 10% tip is appreciated.

TOURS

Guided tours are offered by the major travel agencies and tour operators. A major travel agency and tour operator is Oficiul National de Turism—ONT; office signs in most Romanian towns read AGENŢIA DE TURISM). Also try Albatross Travel.

➤ FEES AND SCHEDULES: **Oficiul National de Turism—ONT** (✉ B-dul Gen. Magheru 7, Bucharest, ☎ 01/314–5160, FAX 01/315–5839; Otopeni Airport, ☎ 01/312–7078; Gara de Nord). **Albatross Travel** (✉ 9 Mai St., Bl. 25, Apt. 3, Sector 6, Bucharest, ☎ 01/221–9556 or 01/221–9557, FAX 01/221–3585, WEB www.albatross-travel.ro).

TRAIN TRAVEL

Romanian Railways (CFR) operates an extensive network of trains. *Rapid* and *accelerat* trains are the fastest, with limited stops; *personal* trains are slow and have many stops. *Expres* designates special international express trains, such as the *Dacia Expres* to Vienna. First class is worth the extra cost. A *vagon de dormit* (sleeper) or cheap *cuşeta,* with bunk beds, is available on longer journeys. It is always advisable to reserve a seat, but you cannot buy the ticket itself at a train station more than one hour before departure. To buy a ticket ahead of time in Bucharest, contact either a travel agency or the CFR Advance Booking Office. You will be charged a small commission, but the process is less time-consuming than buying your ticket at Gara de Nord, which is open weekdays 7:30 AM–7:30 PM, Saturday 8 AM–noon, and closed on Sunday.

➤ FARES AND SCHEDULES: **CFR Advance Booking Office** (✉ Str. Brezoianu 10, ☎ 01/313–2642).

VISITOR INFORMATION

➤ TOURIST INFORMATION: **Oficiul de Promovare a Turismului—OPT** (Romanian Tourism Promotion Office; ✉ Str. Apolodor 17, 5th floor, Bucharest, ☎ 094/410–0991 or 094/410–1262).

WHEN TO GO

Bucharest is at its best during the spring and fall. The Black Sea resorts open in mid- to late May and close at the end of September. Developed ski resorts in the Carpathians, such as Poiana Braşov and Sinaia, are increasingly popular in winter months.

CLIMATE

The Romanian climate is temperate and generally free of extremes, but snow as late as April is not unknown, and the lowlands can be very hot in midsummer. The following are the average daily maximum and minimum temperatures for Bucharest.

Jan.	34F	1C	**May**	74F	23C	**Sept.**	78F	25C
	19	- 7		51	10		52	11
Feb.	38F	4C	**June**	81F	27C	**Oct.**	65F	18C
	23	- 5		57	14		43	6
Mar.	50F	10C	**July**	86F	30C	**Nov.**	49F	10C
	30	- 1		60	16		35	2
Apr.	64F	18C	**Aug.**	85F	30C	**Dec.**	39F	4C
	41	5		59	15		26	- 3

BUCHAREST

According to legend the capital's name comes from one of the first inhabitants of the area, a shepherd named Bucur. The name Bucureşti was first used officially in 1459 by Vlad Ţepeş, the real-life Count Dracula. Two centuries later, this citadel on the Dîmboviţa River became the capital of Walachia, and after another 200 years, it was named the capital of Romania. Bucharest gradually developed into a center of trade and gracious living, with ornate and varied architecture; landscaped parks; busy, winding streets; and wide boulevards. The city was known before World War II as the Paris of the Balkans, but much of its glory now lies buried under decades of neglect and political turmoil.

Nicolae Ceauşescu's megalomaniacal drive to redevelop the capital involved the forced displacement of thousands of people and the demolition of many priceless early houses, churches, synagogues, and other irreplaceable buildings. Piaţa Unirii (Unirii Plaza) was the hub of his enormously expensive and impractical vision. Lined with ornate, gilded fountains, the lengthy Bulevardul Unirii leads west from the plaza to the enormous Palace of Parliament, still flanked by construction cranes. The massive diversion of resources weakened the city's infrastructure, but now efforts are under way to remedy the situation. Bucharest nevertheless contains a good selection of places of historical interest, cafés, cinemas, and performance halls.

Exploring Bucharest

The high-rise Hotel Inter-Continental dominates the main intersection at Piaţa Universităţii; northward, up the main shopping streets, Bulevardul Nicolae Bălcescu and Bulevardul General Magheru, only the occasional older building survives. Along Calea Victoriei, however, you can savor Bucharest's grander past, especially at the former royal palace opposite the Romanian Senate (formerly Communist Party headquarters) in Piaţa Revoluţiei and near the beautifully restored domed National Library. South of Bulevardul Regina Elisabeta along Calea Victoriei is the busy Lipscani trading district, a remnant of the Old City.

Numbers in the margin correspond to points of interest on the Bucharest map.

16 **Arcul de Triumf.** The Arch of Triumph was built in 1922 to commemorate the Allied victory in World War I. Originally constructed of wood and stucco, it was rebuilt during the 1930s and carved by some of Romania's most talented sculptors. ✉ *Head of Şos. Kiseleff.*

11 **Ateneul Român** (Romanian Athenaeum). The restored Ateneul concert hall, with its Baroque dome and Greek columns, has survived much upheaval since 1888; it is still home to the George Enescu Philharmonic Orchestra. ✉ *Str. Franklin 1,* ☎ *01/315–6875.* ⏲ *Tues.–Wed. noon–6, Thurs.–Fri. noon–7, weekends 6 PM–7 PM when there are concerts.*

Bucharest (București)

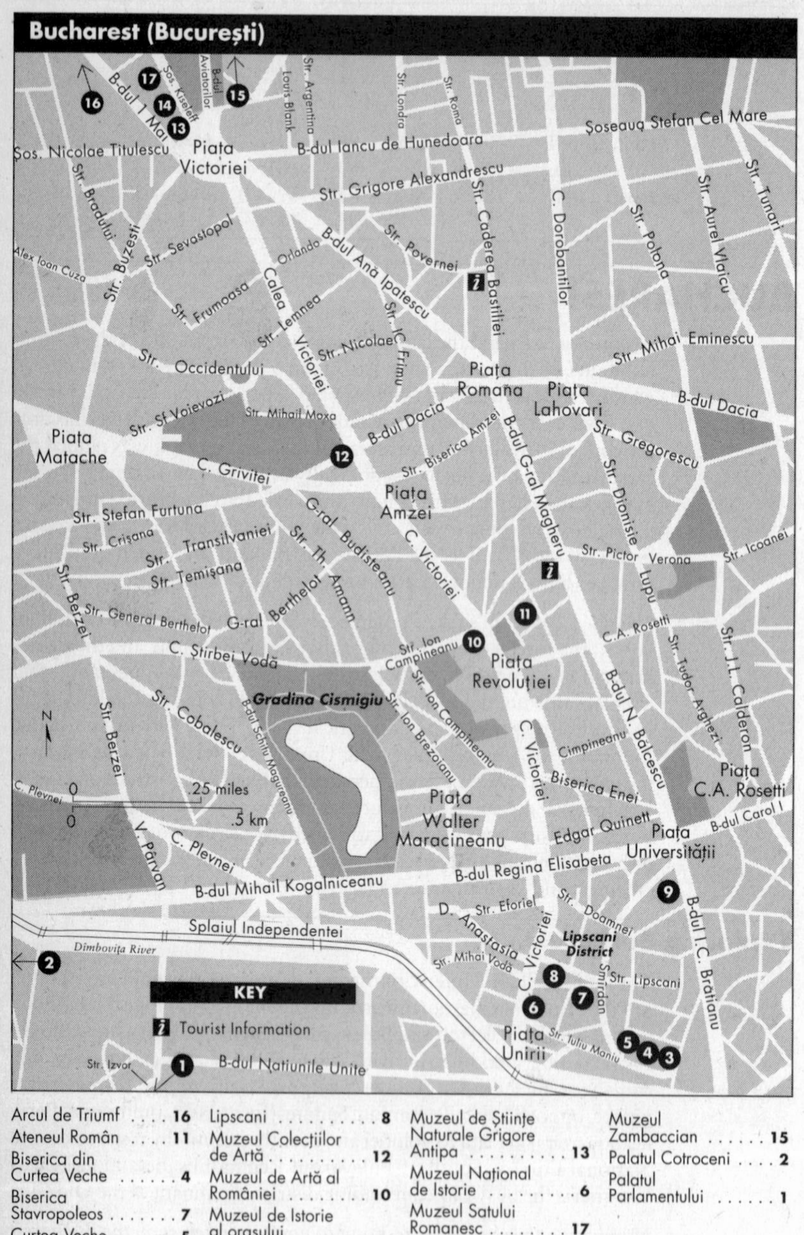

Arcul de Triumf 16
Ateneul Român 11
Biserica din Curtea Veche 4
Biserica Stavropoleos 7
Curtea Veche 5
Hanul lui Manuc 3
Lipscani 8
Muzeul Colecțiilor de Artă 12
Muzeul de Artă al României 10
Muzeul de Istorie al orasului Bucurestului 9
Muzeul de Științe Naturale Grigore Antipa 13
Muzeul Național de Istorie 6
Muzeul Satului Romanesc 17
Muzeul Țăranului Român 14
Muzeul Zambaccian 15
Palatul Cotroceni 2
Palatul Parlamentului 1

4 **Biserica din Curtea Veche** (Church of the Princely Court). The oldest church in Bucharest is ocher with cross-hatched onion domes. This important center of worship was founded in the 16th century beside the Princely Court. ✉ *Str. Selari.*

7 **Biserica Stavropoleos** (Stavropoleos Church). This small, exquisite church combines late-Renaissance and Byzantine styles with elements of Romanian folk art. Inside are superb wood and stone carvings and an ornate iconostasis (the painted screen that partitions off the choir). The inside walls of the church, covered with beautiful frescoes that had turned black from age and pollution, are currently undergoing extensive restoration. Services are held on Sunday at 9:30 AM. ✉ *Str. Stavropoleos.* ⊙ *Sun.–Tues. and Thurs. 6:30–6, Wed. 6:30–4:30, Fri.–Sat. 6:30–5.*

5 **Curtea Veche** (Princely Court). The Princely Court now houses **Muzeul Curtea Veche–Palatul Voievodal** (Old Court Museum–Voivode's Palace), a museum exhibiting the renovated remains of the palace built by Vlad Ţepeş during the 15th century. Tours of the court provide insight into the legend of Dracula. ✉ *Str. Iuliu Maniu 31.* ⊙ *Prearranged visits weekdays 8–5, Sat. 9–2.*

3 **Hanul lui Manuc** (Manuc's Inn). A small hotel and tolerable restaurant operate out of this renovated inn, built in 1808 by a wealthy Armenian merchant named Manuc around a courtyard in traditional Romanian fashion. The 1812 Russian–Turkish Peace Treaty was signed here. ✉ *Str. Iuliu Maniu 62–64,* ☎ *01/613–1415.*

8 **Lipscani.** This charming district is home to a maze of narrow streets, open stalls, and small artisans shops carrying new and used goods. Beware of pickpockets in this area. ✉ *Str. Lipscani.*

12 **Muzeul Colecţiilor de Artă** (Museum of Art Collections). This institution, an affiliate of the National Art Museum, houses an impressive collection of Romanian art from the 19th and 20th centuries as well as carpets, furniture, and icons painted on glass. ✉ *Calea Victoriei 111,* ☎ *01/650–6132.* ⊙ *Wed.–Sun. 10–6 (last admission at 5).*

10 **Muzeul de Artă al României** (National Art Museum). Sculptures by Brancuşi and paintings from the Brueghel school are among the works here. During ongoing restoration, only small exhibits are on display; the major part of the original collection can be viewed at the Muzeul Colecţiilor de Artă. ✉ *Calea Victoriei 53,* ☎ *01/313–3030.* ⊙ *Wed.–Sun. 10–6 (last admission at 5).*

9 **Muzeul de Istorie al Orasului Bucurestului** (Bucharest History Museum). The artifacts, costumes, and pictures in this modern museum capture the rich history of Romania's capital from ancient times to World War I. ✉ *B-dul I. C. Brătianu,* ☎ *01/315–6858.* ⊙ *Tues.–Sun. 10–5.*

13 **Muzeul de Ştiinţe Naturale Grigore Antipa** (Natural History Museum). Natural wildlife exhibits from around Romania and the rest of the world are on display in realistic settings. ✉ *Şos. Kiseleff 1,* ☎ *01/312–8826, 01/312–8863, 01/312–8886.* 🎫 *27,000 lei.* ⊙ *Tues.–Sun. 10–4.*

6 **Muzeul Naţional de Istorie** (National History Museum). This vast, somewhat dreary museum contains an enormous collection dating from the Neolithic period to the 1920s. The Treasury has a stunning trove of gold objects and precious stones—royal crowns, weapons, plates, and jewelry—dating from the 4th millennium BC through the 20th century. ✉ *Calea Victoriei 12,* ☎ *01/315–7054.* ⊙ *Museum Wed.–Sun. 9–4; Treasury Tues.–Sun. 10–6 (last admission at 5).*

★ 17 **Muzeul Satului Romanesc** (Romanian Village Museum). This fabulous open-air museum near Herăstrău Lake is home to more than 300 representations of folk style and architecture taken from peasant villages of different regions and periods. ✉ *Şos. Kiseleff 28,* ☎ *01/224–2759.* ⊙ *Oct.–mid-May, Tues.–Sun. 9–5; mid-May–Sept., Tues.–Sun. 9–8.*

★ 14 **Muzeul Ţăranului Român** (Museum of the Romanian Peasant). Peasant costumes, icons, carpets, and other artifacts from rural life are vividly displayed, along with interiors from two 19th-century wooden churches. ✉ *Şos. Kiseleff 3,* ☎ *01/659–2985 or 01/650–4036.* ⊙ *Tues.–Sun. 10–6.*

15 **Muzeul Zambaccian** (Zambaccian Museum). This unassuming, though lovely, Romanian home contains an astounding collection of art: works by Romanian artists hang alongside paintings by Cézanne, Matisse, Pissarro, and Renoir—all gathered by Armenian-Romanian businessman K. H. Zambaccian. ✉ *Str. Muzeul Zambaccian 21,* ☎ *01/230–1920.* ⊙ *Apr.–Oct., Wed.–Sun. 11–7; Nov.–Mar., Wed.–Sun. 10–6.*

★ 2 **Palatul Cotroceni** (Cotroceni Palace). On the Dîmboviţa River corniche near the Botanical Gardens, this grand building was once the royal residence. Reservations are required for visits. The **Cotroceni National Museum** is in the lower level; ask what's on display here. ✉ *B-dul Geniului 1,* ☎ *01/221–1200.* ⊙ *Tues.–Sun. 9–3:30.*

★ 1 **Palatul Parlamentului** (Parliament Palace). This mammoth structure is among the largest buildings in the world; it is as deep as it is high. Originally meant to house Ceauşescu and his government offices, the unfinished structure is currently the home of the Romanian parliament. The building is closed to visitors during government functions. ✉ *South entrance, Calea 13 Septembrie,* ☎ *01/311–3611.* ⊙ *Daily 10–4.*

Dining

Bucharest's restaurant boom has given rise to a host of delightfully decorated establishments that offer enjoyable, inexpensive fare. You'll find food kiosks, cafés, grills, fast-food chains, and restaurants sprinkled throughout the city. Be sure to check your bill, as it is not uncommon for restaurants to try to overcharge foreigners.

$$–$$$$ ✕ **Byblos Bar and Restaurant.** Step into a modern Mediterranean atmosphere and enjoy seasonal fresh soups and entrées. It's centrally located in the historic district. ✉ *Str. Nicolae Golescu 14–16,* ☎ *01/313–2091. Reservations essential. AE, DC, MC, V.*

$$–$$$ ✕ **La Premiera.** Just behind the National Theater, this restaurant offers a superb mix of international cuisine. The walls are decorated with scenes of Bucharest during the 1920s and '30s. ✉ *Str. Tudor Arghezi 16,* ☎ *01/312–4397. Reservations essential. AE, DC, MC, V.*

$$–$$$ ✕ **Velvet.** Delicately prepared lobster, pheasant, duck, and lamb await you here. This is one of the first restaurants in Bucharest to offer haute cuisine in a formal setting. ✉ *Ştirbei Vodă 2–4,* ☎ *01/311–1736. Reservations essential. AE, MC, V.*

$$ ✕ **Sydney.** This comfortable bar and restaurant offers breakfast all day and Tex-Mex dishes with an Australian twist. There is a wide choice of drinks, including many exotic cocktails and imported beers. ✉ *Calea Victoriei 222,* ☎ *01/312–9670. No credit cards.*

$–$$ ★ ✕ **Bistro Atheneu.** A favorite among both Romanians and expatriates, this Paris-style bistro prepares traditional Romanian dishes such as liver in mushroom sauce, steak, and grilled chicken. ✉ *Str. Episcopiei 3,* ☎ *01/313–4900. Reservations essential. No credit cards.*

$–$$ ✕ **Dragon House.** Sample authentic spicy food in this highly regarded Asian restaurant. The selection of dishes is great, and the "Peking Roast" is particularly recommended. ✉ *Str. Pta. Amzei 1,* ☎ *01/314–7705. MC, V.*

$–$$ ★ ✕ **Il Gattopardo.** Situated in a turn-of-the-20th-century mansion, this stylish restaurant offers a wide selection of elegantly prepared Italian dishes. ✉ *Calea Victorei 115,* ☎ *01/659–7428. Reservations essential. MC, V.*

$–$$ ★ ✕ **Piccolo Mondo.** This haven of Lebanese cuisine serves kebabs, hummus, tabbouleh, *fettouche* (a flavorful Middle Eastern salad), spicy chicken, and a variety of other Middle Eastern dishes. A few Italian and Romanian items are also available. ✉ *Str. Clucerului,* ☎ *01/223–2225. AE, DC, MC, V.*

Lodging

More private hotels are appearing throughout Bucharest. Competition has prompted a boost in service and an improvement in amenities. Hotels fill up quickly during the tourist season and expositions; book early if you can.

$$$$ **Athenée Palace Hilton.** The spacious rooms at this historic hotel are fresh and immaculate; the service is first-rate. ✉ *Str. Episcopiei 1–3,* ☎ *01/303–3777,* FAX *01/315–2121,* WEB *www.hilton.com/hotels/BUHHITW. 257 rooms, 15 suites. 3 restaurants. AE, DC, MC, V.*

$$$$ ★ **Hotel Sofitel.** On the edge of the city en route to the airport, the Sofitel is a Western oasis in Bucharest. ✉ *B-dul Expoziţiei 2,* ☎ *01/224–3000,* FAX *01/211–8688. 91 rooms, 12 suites. 2 restaurants. AE, DC, MC, V.*

$$$ **Continental.** This lovely four-star hotel with turn-of-the-20th-century French decor is convenient to the most historic area of Bucharest. ✉ *Calea Victoriei 56,* ☎ *01/638–5022,* FAX *01/312–0134. MC, V.*

$$$ **Lido.** In the center of the city, this prewar hotel has been privatized and renovated to offer comfortable rooms and good facilities. ✉ *B-dul Gen. Magheru 5,* ☎ *01/314–4939,* FAX *01/312–6544. 107 rooms, 12 suites. Restaurant, pool. AE, DC, MC, V.*

$$ **Capitol.** Well situated near the Continental in one of the busiest sections of Bucharest. What you save in money you lose in ambience: the hotel is built in a 1950's modern style and shows some signs of wear. ✉ *Calea Victoriei 29,* ☎ *01/315–8030,* FAX *01/312–4169. MC, V.*

$ **Triumf.** On a small park near the Arcul de Triumf, this economical, comfortable hotel once served the Communist elite. The more expensive rooms are mini-apartments. ✉ *Şos. Kiseleff 12,* ☎ *01/222–3172,* FAX *01/223–2411. 97 rooms, 3 suites. Restaurant. MC, V.*

Nightlife and the Arts

The Arts

The **Romanian Athenaeum** (✉ Str. Franklin 1, ☎ 01/315–6875) is Bucharest's concert hall, where the George Enescu Philharmonic Orchestra performs regularly. Inside the **Teatrul Naţional** (National Theater; ✉ Piaţa Universitatii, ☎ 01/314–1717), you can see performances by the Ion Dacian Operetta. The **Opera Română** (✉ B-dul Mihail Kogălniceanu 70, ☎ 01/314–6980) stages operas. At the **Radio Hall** (✉ Str. Gen. Berthelot 62–64, ☎ 01/222–4714) you can hear classical music performed by local and visiting musicians.

Nightlife

As Romania's nightlife continues to blossom, new bars and clubs are opening throughout the capital. The **Harp** (✉ Str. Bibescu Vodă 1, ☎ 01/335–6508) Irish pub, a favorite of the Bucharest expatriate community, serves a variety of imported beers. For a lively Romanian bar with good music, try the **Laptaria Enache** (Milk Bar; ✉ Teatrul Naţional,

☎ 01/315–8508) after 11 PM. If dancing is part of your weekend plan, head to **Salsa You and Me** (✉ Str. 11 Iunie 51, ☎ 01/335–5640), where an international crowd moves to a lively Latin beat. For jazz and blues, head to the Lipscani district and **Swing House** (✉ Str. Gabroveni 20, ☎ 01/0922–37093). The new hot spot, **Terminus** (✉ Str. George Enescu 5, ☎ 01/659–7606), attracts an animated group of foreigners and Romanians.

One of the older and better known of Bucharest's 16 casinos is the **Casino Victoria** (✉ Calea Victoriei 174, ☎ 01/659–4913), which also offers a dinner show. Gambling is available in both dollars and lei; admission and drinks are free. The minimum age for admission is 16 years for girls and 18 years for boys.

All foreign films in Bucharest are shown in their original language with Romanian subtitles. One good theater is **Cinema Patria** (✉ B-dul Gen. Magheru 12–14, ☎ 01/211–8625). Just down the street is the clean **Cinema Scala** (✉ B-dul Gen. Magheru 2–3, ☎ 01/211–0372).

If you cannot survive in Romania without e-mail, head to the Internet center in the **Institut Français** (French Institute; ✉ B-dul Dacia 77, ☎ 01/210–0224), which also houses a restaurant, a French film theater, and a space for art exhibits. For Internet access you can also try the British Council (✉ Calea Dorobantilor 14, ☎ 01/211–2346, FAX 01/210–0310).

Shopping

You may legally export art bought at the **Apollo** gallery (☎ 01/313–5010), in the National Theater building. You can also take home art purchased at the galleries of the **Hanul cu Tei** (✉ Off Str. Lipscani, ☎ 01/315–3827).

For local folk arts and crafts, look for Artizanat stores, which specialize in embroidered decorations, dolls, masks, and other crafts made by Romanians. Be sure to consider the carpets, ceramics, and figurines in the **Magazin Amintiri** (✉ Str. Gabroveni 20) in the Lipscani district. For local art try the Artizanat store in the **Muzeul Satului Romanesc** (Romanian Village Museum; ✉ Şos. Kiseleff 28, ☎ 01/224–2759). Arts and crafts are also available in the **Muzeul Ţăranului Român** (Museum of the Romanian Peasant; ✉ Şos. Kiseleff 3, ☎ 01/659–2985 or 01/650–4036).

Romania is well known for its handwoven carpets. For export they must be purchased from an authorized retailer such as **Covoare** (✉ B-dul Unirii 13, ☎ 01/336–2174).

Crystal, porcelain, and china can be great values in Romania. **Sticerom S.A.** (✉ Str. Selari 9–11, ☎ 01/315–7504; ✉ Str. Soarelui 3–5, ☎ 01/314–4066) specializes in magnificent wares at unbelievably low prices.

For a unique shopping experience, explore the department store **Magizinul Unirea** (✉ B-dul Unirii), a Communist-era labyrinth of counters and racks selling everything from CDs to carpets. In contrast, the **World Trade Center** (✉ B-dul Expoziţiei 2) is a small version of a Western shopping mall. The **Bucureşti Mall** (✉ Calea Vitan 55–59, ☎ 01/327–6100) is the first American-style mall in Romania, with more than 80 shops, 20 restaurants, and 8 cinemas.

A central food market is **Piaţa Amzei,** which offers a variety of cheeses, fruits, and flowers and provides a glimpse of animated Romanians bargaining for food.

Bucharest Essentials

AIR TRAVEL TO AND FROM BUCHAREST

Most international flights to Romania land at Bucharest's Otopeni Airport, 16 km (9 mi) north of the city.

AIRPORTS AND TRANSFERS

TRANSFERS

Express Bus 783 leaves the airport for downtown every 30 minutes between 7 AM and 10 PM, stopping in the main squares before terminating in Piaţa Unirii. The journey takes an hour and costs 20,000 lei round-trip. A shuttle service connects the airport to the center of Bucharest: for $10 a person, Sky Services takes passengers to Bucharest's main hotels and the train station. Your hotel can arrange transport by car from the airport. Taxi drivers at the airport seek business aggressively and usually demand payment in dollars; the cost is about $30 with tip.

➤ AIRPORT INFORMATION: **Otopeni Airport** (☎ 01/230–0022). **Sky Services** (☎ 01/204–1002).

BUS, TRAM, AND TROLLEY BUS TRAVEL WITHIN BUCHAREST

Surface transit may sometimes be uncomfortable and crowded, but service is extensive. A one-way ticket can be purchased for 4,000 lei from kiosks near bus stops or from tobacconists; validate your ticket when you board. There are also *abonaments* (day and week passes). You can pay your fare on board the more expensive maxi taxis (minibuses that stop on request) and express buses. The system shuts down at midnight, and buses become scarce around 11 PM.

CAR TRAVEL

Three main routes lead into the city—E70 from the Hungarian border to the west, E60 via Braşov from the north, and E70/E85 from Bulgaria and the south. Streets have few signs and many are one-way.

CONSULATES

➤ AUSTRALIA: (Honorary Consular Section; ✉ 124A Str. Mihai Eminescu, 3rd floor, Apt. 8, Bucharest, ☎ 01/320–9826).

EMERGENCIES

Each sector of Bucharest has a 24-hour pharmacy; ask at your hotel or dial ☎ 961.

➤ EMERGENCY SERVICES: **Police** (☎ 955). **Ambulance** (☎ 961). **Fire** (☎ 981).

SUBWAY TRAVEL

Three subway lines serve the city. Change is available from kiosks inside stations. A two-trip ticket costs 8,000 lei. The system closes at 11 PM on weekdays and midnight on weekends.

TAXIS

You can hail a taxi in the street, but you'll get better taxi rates if you call a dispatcher. Some operators may speak English, but it might be easier to ask the staff at your hotel or a restaurant to call for you. A taxi ride is relatively inexpensive; nevertheless, you should negotiate a price before getting in or ask the driver to turn on the meter.

➤ TAXI COMPANIES: **Taxi dispatch** (☎ 01/9401, 01/9411, 01/9421, 01/9451, 01/9531, or 9851).

TOURS

➤ FEES AND SCHEDULES: **Albatross Travel** (✉ 9 Mai St., Bl. 25, Apt. 3, Sector 6, ☎ 01/221–9556 or 01/221–9557). **Carpatours** (✉ Ion Mihalache 16, ☎ 01/311–0509).

TRAIN TRAVEL

There are five main stations in Bucharest. International lines operate from Gara de Nord. For tickets and information, go to the CFR Advance Booking Office. The authorities may charge people without tickets a 2,000 lei entrance fee to rid stations of vagrants.

➤ TRAIN INFORMATION: **Gara de Nord** (✉ B-dul Gara de Nord, ☎ 01/9521). **CFR Advance Booking Office** (✉ Str. Brezoianu 10, ☎ 01/313–2642).

TRAVEL AGENCIES

➤ LOCAL AGENT REFERRALS: **Albatross Travel** (☞ Tours, *above*). **Magellan Tourism** (✉ B-dul Gen. Magheru 12–14, ☎ 01/211–9650, FAX 01/210–4903). **Medair Travel and Tourism** (✉ Str. N. Bălcescu 16, ☎ 01/312–0699, FAX 01/312–7033). **National Tourism Office—ONT** (☞ Visitor Information, *below*). **Romantic Travel** (✉ Str. Mamulari 4, ☎ 01/310–0401, ☎ FAX 01/312–3056).

TRANSPORTATION AROUND BUCHAREST

Bucharest is spacious and sprawling. The old heart of the city and the two main arteries running the length of it are best explored on foot, but long, wide avenues and vast squares make some form of transportation necessary. It is generally safe on the streets at night, but watch out for potholes and vehicles without headlights.

VISITOR INFORMATION

➤ TOURIST INFORMATION: **National Tourism Office—ONT** (✉ B-dul Gen. Magheru 7, ☎ 01/314–5160, FAX 01/315–5839).

THE BLACK SEA COAST AND DANUBE DELTA

The southeastern Dobrogea region, only 45 minutes by plane from Bucharest (210 km [130 mi] by road), has been important throughout Romania's long history. Within a clearly defined area are the historic port of Constanţa; the Romanian Riviera; the Murfatlar vineyards; Roman, Greek, and earlier ruins; and the Danube Delta, which has become one of Europe's leading wildlife sanctuaries. The rapid development of the resorts and increasing interest in the delta region have led to improvement of tourist facilities and transport.

Eforie Nord, Neptun, Jupiter, Venus, Saturn, and Mangalia

A string of seaside resorts lies just south of Constanţa. Eforie Nord is an up-to-date thermal treatment center; named to evoke the coast's Greco-Roman past, Neptun, Jupiter, Venus, and Saturn were built during the 1960s. The old port of Mangalia is the southernmost resort.

You can take excursions from the seaside resorts to the **Podgorile Murfatlar** (Murfatlar Vineyards) for wine tasting. For tours contact Albatross Travel (☞ Tours in Romania A to Z, *above*). Visits to the ruins of the Roman town at **Trophaeum Trajani** (Trajan's Trophy) can also be arranged.

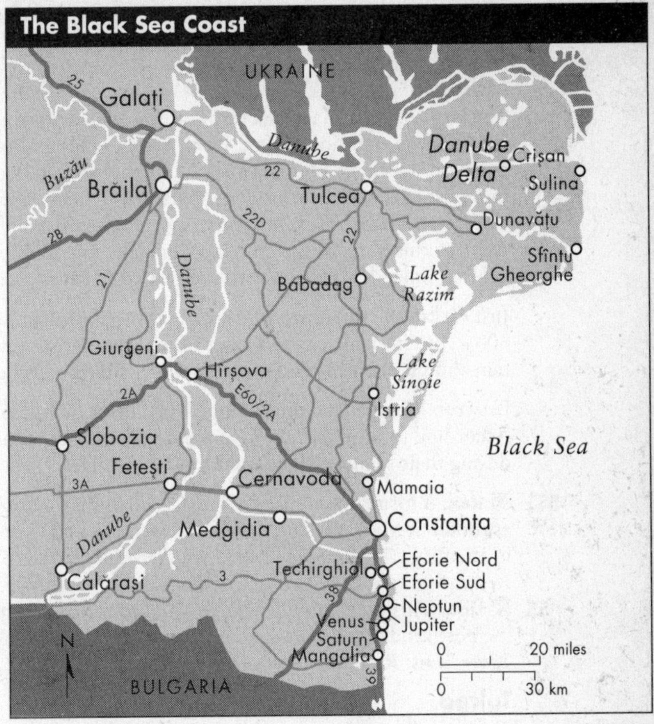

$ ★ ✕🏨 **Panoramic.** Seaside rooms in this beachfront hotel have magnificent views. The restaurant serves good Romanian cuisine. ✉ *Olimp–Neptun,* ☎ *041/731356. 418 rooms. Restaurant, pool. AE, MC, V.*

$ 🏨 **Moldova.** One of many inexpensive hotels near the beach, Moldova has somewhat run-down rooms, but they are clean and the staff is friendly. ✉ *Olimp–Neptun,* ☎ *041/731916. 466 rooms. Restaurant. No credit cards.*

Constanța

Romania's second-largest city has the busy, polyglot flavor characteristic of so many seaports. The poet Ovid was exiled here from Rome in AD 8; a statue of him presides over one of the city's squares.

Famous for its large mosaic floor, the **Edificiu Roman cu Mozaic** (Roman Mosaic Building; ✉ Piaţa Ovidiu 1) is a Roman complex of warehouses and shops from the 4th century. The **Parcul Arheologic** (Archaeology Park; ✉ B-dul Republicii) contains artifacts from the 3rd and 4th centuries, including the remains of Roman baths. Modern attractions in Constanţa include the **Acvariul** (Aquarium; ✉ Str. Februarie 16).The **Muzeul Național de Istorie și Arheologie** (National History and Archaeological Museum) displays statues from the Neolithic Hamangian culture (4000–3000 BC) as well as Greek and Roman artifacts. ✉ *Piaţa Ovidiu 12,* ☎ *041/618763.* ⏲ *Tues.–Sun. 10–6.*

$$ ✕ **Cazinou.** The turn-of-the-20th-century former casino near the aquarium is ornately decorated. You'll find an adjoining bar by the sea. Seafood dishes are the house specialty. ✉ *B-dul. Carpati 2,* ☎ *041/617416. No credit cards.*

$$ 🏨 **Palace.** Near the city's historic center, this gracious renovated hotel has a good restaurant. A terrace overlooks the sea and the tourist port

of Tomis. ✉ *Str. Remus Opreanu 5–8,* ☎ *041/614696,* FAX *041/617532. 102 rooms, 9 suites. Restaurant. No credit cards.*

Mamaia

The largest of the Black Sea resort areas, Mamaia is on a strip of land bordered on one side by fine Black Sea beaches and on the other by the fresh waters of Mamaia Lake. All the resorts along this stretch of the coast have high-rise modern apartments, villas, restaurants, nightclubs, and discos. There are early-morning sea-fishing expeditions as well as cruises down the coast to Mangalia and along the new channel that links the Danube with the Black Sea near Constanţa.

Just 60 km (37 mi) north of Mamaia is **Histria,** which was founded in 600 BC by Greek merchants from Miletus. There are traces of early Christian churches, baths, and even entire neighborhoods here.

Between Mamaia and the Danube Delta town of Tulcea lies **Babadag.** According to local legend, Jason and the Argonauts cast anchor here during their search for the mythical Golden Fleece.

$$$ ★ **Rex.** A former residence of King Carol, this is the largest and grandest hotel in Mamaia. The rooms are spacious and clean, and the staff is attentive. ✉ *Mamaia,* ☎ *041/831595,* FAX *041/831690. 90 rooms. Restaurant, pool. AE, DC, MC, V.*

$$ **Lido.** This hotel stands next to an outdoor pool near the beach at the north end of Mamaia's resort district. ✉ *Mamaia,* ☎ *041/831555. 129 rooms. Restaurant, pool. No credit cards.*

Tulcea

Tulcea is the main town of the Danube Delta and the gateway to the region. Built on seven hills and influenced by Turkish architectural styles, this former market town is now an important sea and river port. It is the center of the Romanian fish industry, famous for processing caviar-bearing sturgeon.

The **Muzeul Deltei Dunării** (Danube Delta Museum) provides a good introduction to the flora, fauna, and way of life of the communities in the region. ✉ *Str. Grigore Antipa 2,* ☎ *040/515866.* ⊙ *Tues.–Sun. 11–4.*

$$ **Delta.** On the bank of the Danube, this spacious, modern hotel has good facilities. ✉ *Str. Isaacei 2,* ☎ *040/514720,* FAX *040/516260. 117 rooms. Restaurant. V.*

The Danube Delta

The **Delta Dunării** (Danube Delta) is Europe's largest wetlands reserve, covering 4,357 square km (1,676 square mi), with a sprawling, watery wilderness that stretches from the Ukrainian border to a series of lakes north of the Black Sea resorts. Romanians have committed themselves to the restoration and preservation of this treasure. While it is home to birds such as the pelican, the Danube Delta is also a refuge for hundreds of species of migratory birds, some from as far away as China and India.

As the Danube approaches the Delta Dunării, it divides into three branches. The northernmost branch forms the border with Ukraine, the middle arm leads to the busy port of Sulina, and the southernmost arm meanders gently toward the little port of Sfintu Gheorghe, a simple holiday spot. From these channels, countless canals widen into tree-fringed lakes and water-lily pools; sand dunes and lush forests are among the region's natural treasures.

$ ☎ **Cormoran.** This unique complex on the St. George branch of the delta, 38 km (24 mi) from Tulcea, includes a floating hotel and special programs for anglers, hunters, and bird-watchers. ✉ *Satuzlina, Comuna Murighiol, Tulcea,* ☎ *094/656372,* FAX *094/736372. 44 rooms. Pool. MC, V.*

Black Sea Coast and Danube Delta Essentials

TOURS

Most hotels in the Black Sea region arrange guided tours throughout the area. Individual and group tours can also be prearranged through travel agencies in Bucharest.

TRANSPORTATION AROUND THE BLACK SEA COAST AND DANUBE DELTA

Travel in this area involves several hours on the road; allow more than one day for a substantive trip. The region is best seen by taking the train to Constanţa, then hiring a taxi or taking a tour.

VISITOR INFORMATION

➤ Tourist Information: **Constanţa** (OPT; ✉ Str. Traian 36, bl. C1, Apt. 31, ☎ 094/655004; Danubius, ✉ B-dul Ferdinand 22/36, ☎ 041/615836). **Mamaia** (ATI—Carpaţi; ✉ B-dul Tomis 46, ☎ 041/614861, FAX 041/611429). **Tulcea** (OPT; ✉ Str. Pacii 20, ☎ 040/510690; Europolis, ✉ Str. Pacii 20, ☎ 040/512443).

TRANSYLVANIA

Transylvania, Romania's western province, contains some of Europe's most beautiful and unspoiled villages and rural landscapes. The Carpathian Mountains, which separate Transylvania from Walachia and Moldavia, shielded the province from the Turks and Mongols during the Middle Ages. Germans and Hungarians settled here during this period, building spectacular castles, towns, and churches. Since the 1980s many ethnic Germans have emigrated, but Transylvania, which was ruled by the Austro-Hungarian Empire until 1920, is still home to a large Hungarian minority and to many of Romania's 2 million ethnic Gypsies. You can best explore the countryside by taking day trips from a major town such as Sibiu, Sinaia, or Braşov.

Sinaia

Prior to World War II and the abdication of Romania's royal family, Sinaia, a tourist attraction on the way to Transylvania, was a summer retreat for the aristocracy. On the mountainside stand many grand summer homes from this period, as well as the **Sinaia Minastire** (Sinaia Monastery), which has operated as a monastery since 1695.

Just up the hill from the monastery is **Castelul Peleş** (Peleş Palace), a 19th-century Bavarian-style palace that served as the summer residence of Romania's first Hohenzollern king, Carol I; inside hang many originals by Gustav Klimt. Tours are available in English. ✉ *Str. Peleşului 2 (take Str. Manastirii uphill and follow signs to castle),* ☎ *044/310918.* ⏲ *Wed.–Sun. 9–3.*

Castelul Pelisor (Pelisor Palace), the summer home of the second Hohenzollern king, Ferdinand, lies just above Peleş Palace. Tours in English are available. ✉ *Str. Peleşului,* ☎ *044/310918.* ⏲ *Wed.–Sun. 9–3.*

$$$$ ★ ☎ **Holiday Inn Resort Sinaia.** One of the grandest provincial hotels in Romania, this resort has a pool and spa, as well as an elegant restaurant serving Romanian fare. ✉ *Str. Toporasilor 1A,* ☎ *044/310440,* FAX *044/310551. 142 rooms, 6 suites. Restaurant. AE, MC, V.*

$ **Economat.** Built in the same Bavarian style as the nearby Peleş Palace, this simple, comfortable hotel is surrounded by mountains. The restaurant serves Romanian and French specialties. ✉ *Str. Peleşului 2,* ☎ *044/311151,* FAX *044/311150. 40 rooms. Restaurant. MC, V.*

Bran

Some locals claim that Vlad Ţepeş once lived in the beautifully preserved **Castelul Bran** (Castle Bran), built in 1377; Vlad's castle actually lies in ruins farther west in Transylvania. The medieval castle has low doorways, tiny winding stairways, wolf skins on the walls, bearskin rugs on the floors, and severe wood and leather furniture. Bran was a trading post during the Middle Ages; nowadays the town's parking lot hosts a lively market Tuesday–Sunday. ✉ *Traiou Moşoiu 498,* ☎ *068/238333,* FAX *068/475607.* ⏲ *Tues.–Sun. 9–4.*

Braşov and Poiana Braşov

To enjoy Braşov, stroll through **Piaţa Sfatului,** the bustling cobblestone square at the heart of the old Germanic city, formerly an important medieval trade center. **Casa Sfatului** (Council's House; ✉ Piaţa Sfatului; ⏲ Tues.–Sun. 8–4) was once the town hall of old Braşov. Built in 1420, it now houses a historical museum. Just off Piaţa Sfatului is the spiraling tower of the newly renovated Gothic **Biserica Neagră** (Black Church). The 15th-century masterwork acquired its name after a fire in 1689 left it black and charred. Opposite the Black Church is **Strada Republicii,** a pedestrian street that provides shopping opportunities.

For a breathtaking view of Braşov, ride the **Telecabina Timpa** (✉ Str. Romer), a cable car that runs to the top of Mount Timpa Tuesday–Sunday 10–6. To find the cable car, leave Piaţa Sfatului on Strada Apollonia Hirscher; take a left onto Strada Castelului; the next right is Strada Romer, which leads to the cable car. Just below the entrance to Telecabina Timpa are some of the remains of the old Braşov city wall. A stroll along the wall will take you to the **Bastionul Ţesătorilor** (Weaver's Bastion), which now holds a museum that is occasionally open to the public.

A 20-minute drive or bus ride (No. 2) from Braşov on St. Stejărişului takes you to **Poiana Braşov,** a mountaintop ski resort that embraces several good restaurants and hotels. In winter Poiana Braşov offers some of the best skiing in Romania, though trails are not groomed and ski lifts are limited. In summer you can follow well-marked hiking trails along the spectacular mountainsides. From the top of the mountain, you'll have a stunning view of the Transylvania Plains. Locals sell handmade wool sweaters in the central parking lot. ✉ *Agenţa Poiana Braşov,* ☎ *068/262389.*

$$–$$$ ★ ✕ **Coliba Haiducilor.** In this classic Romanian lodge whose walls are decorated with hunting trophies, traditional song and dance transport you to an earlier era. Waiters dressed in peasant costume serve boar, bear, venison, and chicken. ✉ *Poiana Braşov,* ☎ *068/262137. Reservations essential. No credit cards.*

$$ ★ ✕ **Sura Dacilor.** Built to look like a traditional Romanian hunting lodge, this restaurant offers garlic chicken, grilled meats, salad, and ciorbă. ✉ *Poiana Braşov,* ☎ *068/262327. No credit cards.*

$$$ **Centrul De Echitatie.** Head for this resort's stable if you'd like to explore the mountainous countryside on horseback or take a sleigh ride. You can rent a clean villa and enjoy barbecues in the woods. It is on the bus line to Braşov and within walking distance of all facilities in

Poiana Braşov. ✉ *Poiana Braşov,* ☎ *068/262161. 10 1- and 2-bedroom villas. No credit cards.*

$$ ★ **Casa Viorel.** Every room in this irreproachable hotel is immaculate, with a balcony and view of the mountains; the service is superb. During ski season, the hotel requires a minimum stay of one week. ✉ *Poiana Braşov,* ☎ *068/262024,* FAX *068/262148. 10 rooms, 2 suites. No credit cards.*

$–$$ **Alpin.** Comfort, cleanliness, and service define this hotel at the top of Poiana Braşov; most rooms have breathtaking views. ✉ *Poiana Braşov,* ☎ *068/262343,* FAX *068/150427. 130 rooms. Restaurant, pool. AE, MC, V.*

Sighişoara

Sighişoara's stone towers and spires can be seen from a great distance. Above the modern town is an exceptionally well preserved medieval **citadel.** Walking up from the city center, you enter the citadel through the 14th-century **Turnul cu Ceas** (clock tower), which is 195 ft tall. The clock still works, complete with rotating painted wooden figures, one for each day of the week. The tower houses the town's **Muzeul de Istorie** (History Museum). From the wooden gallery at the top of the tower you can appreciate a vista of terra-cotta roofs and painted houses. ✉ *Pta. Muzeului.* ⏲ *Tues.–Sun. 9–3:30.*

Along narrow, cobbled streets lined with faded pink, green, and ocher houses, you'll come to a covered staircase that leads to the 14th-century Gothic church and the **Cimitirul German** (German Cemetery), a testament to the town's settlers that extends over the hilltop beyond the city walls. ✉ *Str. Sçolii, Str. Tamplarilor.*

$$–$$$ ✕ **Restaurentul Cetaţe (Casa Vlad Dracul).** Occupying a house where the father of Vlad Ţepeş once lived, this two-story bar and restaurant is the best place in town for a traditional Romanian meal. ✉ *Str. Cositorarilor 5,* ☎ *065/771596. No credit cards.*

$ **Rex.** This clean, modern hotel is the most appealing establishment in town, a few minutes' walk from the center. ✉ *Str. Dumbravei 18,* ☎ FAX *065/777615. 24 rooms. Restaurant. No credit cards.*

Sibiu

Known as Hermannstadt to the Germans, who founded the city in 1143, Sibiu was the Saxon hub in Transylvania. Few ethnic Germans remain, but the city's atmosphere is still distinctly German or Central European. The old part of the town centers on the magnificent **Piaţa Mare** (Great Square), with its painted 17th-century town houses. The **Biserica Romano Catolică** (Roman Catholic Church) on the square is a splendid High Baroque building. Also on the square is the **Brukenthal Museum** (☎ 069/217691), in the palace of its founder, Samuel Brukenthal, Habsburg governor from 1777 to 1787; one of the most extensive collections of silver, paintings, and furniture in Romania is on display.

The second center of the old town is **Piaţa Mica** (Small Square), next to which stands the **Biserica Lutherană**, a massive 14th- to 15th-century Lutheran church with a simple, stark interior.

$$ ★ **Impăratul Romanilor.** In the heart of town, the century-old Romanilor is among Romania's best provincial hotels. Rooms are attractively decorated with paintings and locally made furniture. The restaurant has a lively floor show and discotheque on weekends. ✉ *Str. Nicolae Bălcescu,* ☎ *069/216500,* FAX *069/213278. 182 rooms. Restaurant. MC, V.*

Transylvania Essentials

CAR TRAVEL

Transylvania's rich rural life is best explored by car.

TOURS

Many travel agencies in Bucharest, and those in many hotels throughout Transylvania, lead guided tours of the region. The Transylvanian Society of Dracula arranges unique "Dracula" tours. Albatross Travel will arrange custom tours.

➤ FEES & SCHEDULES: **Transylvanian Society of Dracula** (✉ Str. George Călinescu 20, Apt. 28, Bucharest, ☎ FAX 01/231–4022). **Albatross Travel** (☞ Tours *in* Bucharest Essentials, *above*).

TRAIN TRAVEL

Regular rail travel is available to most Transylvanian towns.

VISITOR INFORMATION

➤ TOURIST INFORMATION: **Braşov** (OPT; ✉ Str. Harmanului 50, Apt. 11, ☎ 094/655007; ✉ Aro-Palace, B-dul Eroilor 9, ☎ 068/142840, FAX 068/150427). **Sibiu** (OPT; ✉ Str. Cetăţii 1, ☎ 069/211788 or 094/655008, FAX 069/217933).

26 SLOVAKIA

BRATISLAVA, THE HIGH TATRAS, AND EASTERN SLOVAKIA

DESPITE MORE THAN 70 YEARS of common statehood with the Czech Republic, not to mention centuries spent under Hungarian and Habsburg rule, Slovakia has shaped a distinct cultural profile. The country's farmlands stretch to an important mountain range. Its culture, steeped in folk tradition, is particularly rich.

Slovaks speak a language closely related to Czech, but they have a strong sense of national identity. United with the Czechs during the 9th century as part of the Great Moravian Empire, the Slovaks were conquered a century later by the Magyars and remained under Hungarian domination until 1918. The Hungarians were not alone in infiltrating the country; after the Tatar invasions of the 13th century, many Saxons were invited to resettle the land and develop the economy. During the 15th and 16th centuries, Romanian shepherds migrated from Walachia into Slovakia. The merging of these varied groups with the resident Slavs further enriched the native folk culture.

Bratislava, the capital of Hungary for nearly 250 years until 1784, and now the capital of the new Slovak republic, was once a city filled with picturesque streets and Gothic churches. A decade after the fall of communism, the streets of the Old Town have undergone rapid revitalization.

The peaks of the High Tatras are a major draw. The smallest alpine range in the world, the Tatras rise magnificently from the foothills of northern Slovakia. Hikers and skiers are the chief visitors here. The area's subtler attractions—the exquisite medieval towns of the Spiš region below the Tatras and the beautiful 18th-century wood churches farther east—are definitely worth the trip.

SLOVAKIA A TO Z

To research prices, get advice from other travelers, and book travel arrangements, visit www.fodors.com.

ADDRESSES

The most common words you'll find on street signs are *ulica* (street, abbreviated *ul.*) and *námestie* (square, abbreviated *nám.*).

AIR TRAVEL

Slovak Airlines has flights from Bratislava to Košice twice daily on weekdays. TLS Air provides charter flights from Poprad to any airport within Slovakia.

➤ AIRLINES AND CONTACTS: **Slovak Airlines** (☎ 02/48575170); **TLS Air** (Poprad airport, ☎ 052/7761626; 0905/342425; 052/7763875).

Slovakia (Slovensko)

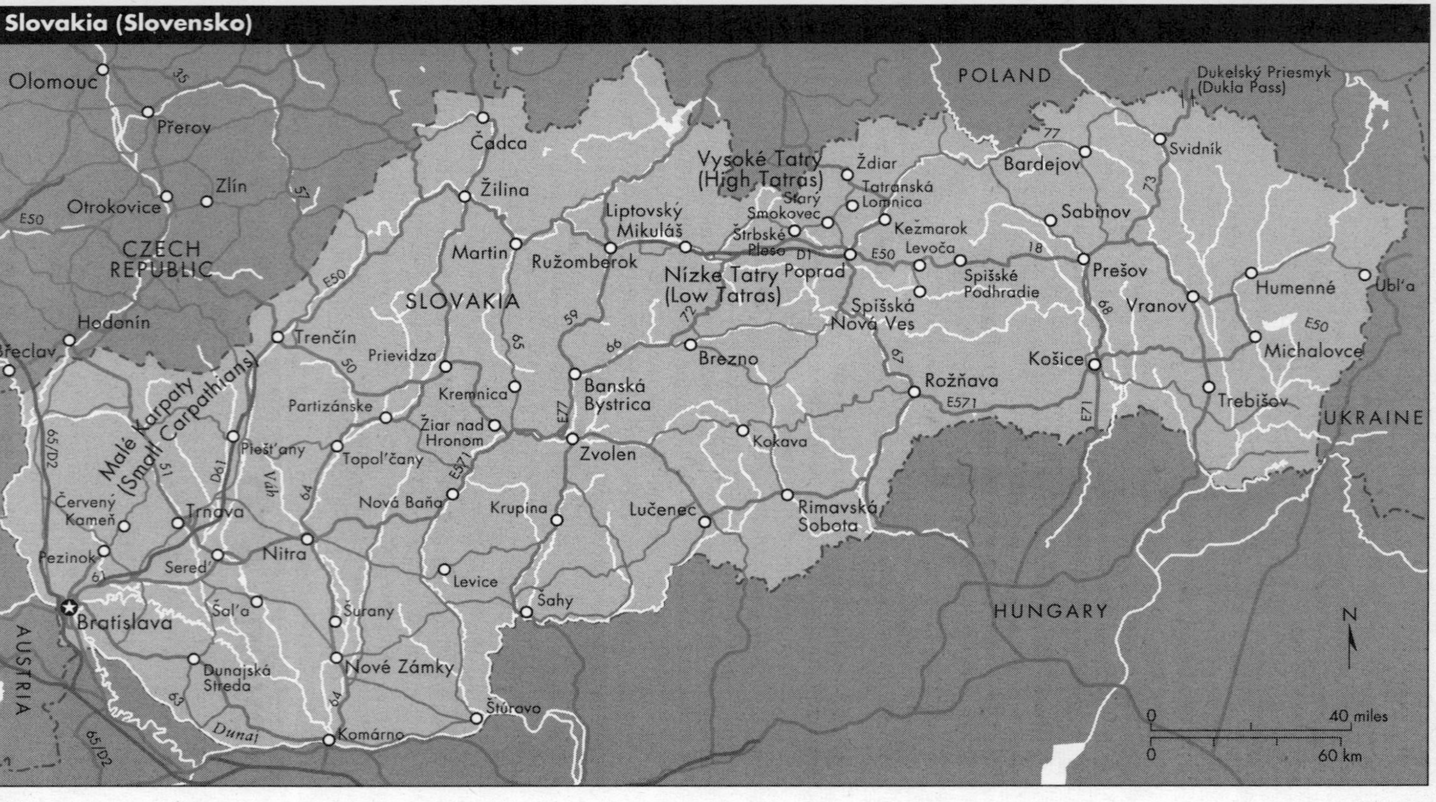

BUS TRAVEL

Bus and tram service in Bratislava is very cheap and reasonably frequent, and you can use it to reach any of the places in the tours below. The timetables can be confusing, so be sure to confirm your itinerary. The bus network in the rest of Slovakia is dense, but service to the smaller towns can be infrequent.

BUSINESS HOURS

Banks are open weekdays 8–4; they remain open through the general lunch hour. Museums are usually open Tuesday–Sunday 10–5. Shops are generally open weekdays 9–6 and stay open slightly later on Thursday; some close between noon and 2. Many are also open Saturday 9–noon (department stores 9–4) and, in big cities, on Sunday.

CAR TRAVEL

EMERGENCIES

In Bratislava or elsewhere, contact the 24-hour repair service. The *Auto Atlas SR* (available at bookstores) has a list of emergency road-repair numbers in various towns. If you have an accident and need an ambulance, call the emergency number.

➤ CONTACTS: **24-hour repair service** ☎ (154; 123). **Emergency** ☎ (155).

GASOLINE

Gasoline is expensive. Service stations are usually along main roads on the outskirts of towns and cities. Finding a station in Bratislava can be difficult, so fill up on the freeway as you approach the city. Lead-free gasoline, known as *natural,* is still available only at select stations.

ROAD CONDITIONS

Main roads are often narrow but adequate. Traffic is light, especially away from main centers. Outside Bratislava, a car is especially useful in central and eastern Slovakia, where many of the sights are difficult to reach by public transportation.

RULES OF THE ROAD

Drive on the right. Speed limits are 60 kph (37 mph) in built-up areas, 90 kph (55 mph) on open roads, 110 kph (68 mph) on expressways, and 130 kph (80 mph) on highways. Seat belts are compulsory; drinking and driving is strictly prohibited.

CUSTOMS AND DUTIES

Enter valuable items such as jewelry or laptops on your customs declaration on arrival so you encounter no problems with customs officials on departure. U.S. or European Union citizens over 18 years old can bring in 250 cigarettes (or their equivalent in tobacco), 2 liters of wine, 1 liter of spirits, and ½ liter of eau de cologne.

There is no limit on the amount of goods purchased for noncommercial use, but to be on the safe side, keep all receipts. You can export antiques (i.e., items more than 50 years old) with a special opinion from a commission at the National Relic and Landscape Center. Commission opinion is based on a court-expert opinion submitted by you; for a list of court experts, call the department of experts and interpreters at the Regional Court in Bratislava.

➤ INFORMATION: **National Relic and Landscape Center** (✉ Bratislava, ☎ 02/54789181). **Regional Court** in Bratislava (✉ Krajský Súd, Záhradnícka 10, 81366, ☎ 02/55424060, 02/55424042, or 02/55571652).

DINING

In Slovakia you can choose between restaurants, *vináreň* (wine cellars), beer taverns, cafeterias, and a growing number of coffee shops and snack bars. Most restaurants are remarkably inexpensive, but the free market is pushing up prices.

Typical main dishes are roast pork, duck, or goose, served with sauerkraut and some type of dumpling or potatoes, generally with a rich gravy. Peppers often spice up bland entrées. Look for *bryndzové halušky*, a tasty Slovak noodle dish with sheep's cheese. Green vegetables and salads come pickled. Be sure to try *palacinky*, delicious crepes stuffed with fruit and cream or jam.

Prices are reasonable by American standards, even in the more expensive restaurants. Prices are for one main course at dinner.

CATEGORY	COST
$$$$	over 400 Sk
$$$	250 Sk–400 Sk
$$	150 Sk–250 Sk
$	under 150 Sk

MEALTIMES

Lunch is usually from 11:30 to 2 or 3, dinner from 6 to 9:30 or 10. Some places are open all day, and in Bratislava it may be easier to find a table during off-hours.

RESERVATIONS AND DRESS

A jacket is suggested for higher-priced restaurants. Otherwise, casual dress is acceptable.

EMBASSIES

➤ CANADA: (✉ Mišíkova 28/d, ☎ 02/52442175 or 02/52442177, FAX 02/52499995).

➤ UNITED KINGDOM: (✉ Panská 16, ☎ 02/54419632 or 02/54419633, FAX 02/54410002, WEB www.britemb.sk).

➤ UNITED STATES: (✉ Hviezdoslavovo nám. 4, ☎ 02/54430861, FAX 02/54418861, WEB www.usis.sk).

HOLIDAYS

January 1 (day of founding of the Slovak Republic); January 6 (12th Night); Good Friday and Easter Monday; May 1 (Labor Day); May 8 (Liberation of the Republic); July 5 (Sts. Cyril and Methodius); August 29 (anniversary of the Slovak National Uprising); September 1 (Constitution Day); September 15 (Our Lady of Sorrows); November 1 (All Saints' Day); December 24–26.

LANGUAGE

Slovak, a western Slavic tongue related to both Czech and Polish, is the official language of Slovakia. English is popular among young people, but German is still the most useful language for visitors.

LODGING

Slovakia has a few new hotels, and many of the older hotels have been privatized by local entrepreneurs. Bratislava and the High Tatras have the highest hotel rates in Slovakia—but prices drop dramatically in the rest of the country. Shortages of hotel rooms are common during the peak season, so make reservations well in advance. Many private room agencies are in operation, and as long as you arrive in a city before 9 PM, you should be able to get a room. Brace yourself for inconveniences from faulty plumbing to indifferent reception clerks.

Prices are for double rooms, generally not including breakfast. Prices apply in peak season. At certain periods, such as Easter or during festivals, rates may increase by 15%–25%.

CATEGORY	COST
$$$$	over 6,000 Sk
$$$	3,000 Sk–6,000 Sk
$$	1,000 Sk–3,000 Sk
$	under 1,000 Sk

CAMPING

In summer, signs that announce *Autokemping* (campsites) crop up along major highways like mushrooms after rain. Year-round campsites are extremely scarce. Plumbing is often primitive, and hot water is a blessing, not a given. The main Satur Tours and Travel office in Bratislava has a rudimentary country-wide directory.

HOTELS

Satur Tours and Travel officially grades hotels from one to four stars in accordance with norms that are not identical with international standards.

PRIVATE ACCOMMODATIONS

Satur Tours and Travel can help you find a private room in Bratislava and other large cities. These accommodations are invariably cheaper (around $20) and often more comfortable than hotels, though you may have to sacrifice some privacy. You can also wander the main roads looking for signs reading ROOM FREE or more frequently, in German, ZIMMER FREI or PRIVATZIMMER.

MAIL AND SHIPPING

POSTAL RATES

First-class (airmail) letters to the United States and Canada cost 16 Sk up to 20 grams, postcards 10 Sk. Airmail (first-class) letters to the United Kingdom cost 12 Sk up to 20 grams, postcards 7 Sk.

RECEIVING MAIL

Mail can be marked "poste restante" and sent to the main post office in Bratislava.

➤ POST OFFICES: **Main Post Office** (✉ Hlavná pošta, Nám. SNP 35, ☎ 02/59393111 or 02/54434055).

MONEY MATTERS

Costs are highest in Bratislava and only slightly lower in the High Tatra resorts and main spas. The least expensive areas are central and eastern Slovakia.

Cup of coffee, 15 Sk–25 Sk; beer (½ liter), 20 Sk; Coca-Cola, 15 Sk–20 Sk; ham sandwich, 30 Sk; 2-km (1-mi) taxi ride, 150 Sk. Admission to museums and castles ranges from 10 Sk to 50 Sk.

CURRENCY

The unit of currency in Slovakia is the crown, or koruna, written as Sk, and divided into 100 halierov. There are bills of 20, 50, 100, 200, 500, 1,000, and 5,000 Sk, and coins of 10, 20, and 50 halierov and 1, 2, 5, and 10 Sk.

At press time (summer 2001), the rate of exchange was 50 Sk to the U.S. dollar, 33 Sk to the Canadian dollar, 71 Sk to the pound sterling, 55 Sk to the Irish punt, 26 Sk to the Australian dollar, 20 Sk to the New Zealand dollar, and 6 Sk to the South African rand.

PASSPORTS AND VISAS

ENTERING SLOVAKIA

Entry without a visa is permitted for citizens of the United States (up to 30 days), United Kingdom (six months), and Canada (90 days). Citizens of Australia and New Zealand need a visa for any visits.

TELEPHONES

If you plan to make several calls, buy a phone card. They can be used for both local and out-of-town calls. You can buy one at most newsstands or at any post office for 100 Sk and 150 Sk.

COUNTRY AND AREA CODES

The country code for Slovakia is 421. When dialing a number from outside the country, drop the initial zero from the regional code.

INTERNATIONAL CALLS

You can dial many countries, including North America and the United Kingdom, from public pay phones. You can also call from Telefón/Telegraf, a public communications office with phone booths inside and out. It's open weekdays 7 AM–9 PM, weekends 8 AM–8 PM. International calls can also be placed via an AT&T USA Direct international operator, or Sprint or MCI operators.

➤ ACCESS CODES: **AT&T** (☎ 00–421–00101). **MCI** (☎ 001–881/422–0042). **Sprint** (☎ 001–881/824–9242). **Telefón/Telegraf** (✉ Kolárska 12, Bratislava); International inquiries: ☎ 0149.

LOCAL CALLS

These cost 2 Sk from a pay phone. Public phones on street corners are often out of order. Try a hotel. For information call ☎ 120 or 121.

TIPPING

Although many Slovaks still tip in restaurants by rounding up the bill to the nearest multiple of 10, higher tipping is beginning to catch on. For good service, 10% is considered an appropriate gratuity on very large tabs. Tip porters and room service 20 Sk. In taxis round up the bill to the nearest multiple of 10. Give tour guides and helpful concierges between 20 Sk and 30 Sk for services rendered.

TRAIN TRAVEL

Train service is erratic to all but the largest cities—Bratislava, Poprad, Prešov, and Košice. Make sure to take the express trains marked "R" or the fast Intercity trains. Reliable, if slow, electric rail service connects Poprad with the resorts of the High Tatras. If you're going just to the Tatras, an electric train will get you there.

VISITOR INFORMATION

➤ TOURIST INFORMATION: **Satur Tours and Travel** (main office, ✉ Jesenského 5, Bratislava, ☎ 02/54410133 or 02/54412904, FAX 02/54410138, WEB www.satur.sk).

WHEN TO GO

Organized sightseeing tours generally run from April or May through October. Some monuments, especially castles, either close entirely or have shorter hours in winter. Hotel rates drop off-season except during festivals. In winter (December–February), skiers from all over Eastern Europe crowd the slopes and resorts of the High Tatra mountains. Visit the mountains in late spring (May or June) or fall and you'll have the hotels and restaurants pretty much to yourself.

CLIMATE

The following are the average daily maximum and minimum temperatures for Bratislava.

Jan.	36F	2C	May	70F	21C	Sept.	72F	22C
	27	-3		52	11		54	12
Feb.	39F	4C	June	75F	24C	Oct.	59F	15C
	28	-2		57	14		45	7
Mar.	48F	9C	July	79F	26C	Nov.	46F	8C
	34	1		61	16		37	3
Apr.	61F	16C	Aug.	79F	26C	Dec.	39F	4C
	43	6		61	16		32	0

BRATISLAVA

In Bratislava you'll find high-rise housing projects, faded supermodern structures, and less-than-inspiring monuments. But everywhere you look new shops are opening and older buildings are under renovation—as if the capital's residents are trying to forget as quickly as possible their past of playing second fiddle to Prague.

Exploring Bratislava

Numbers in the margin correspond to points of interest on the Bratislava map.

Despite its charms, there's no denying that Bratislava is intensely industrial. Avoid the newer, and shabbier, parts of the city and head toward the Danube River to discover the peace and beauty of the Staré Mesto (Old Town) and its Gothic and Renaissance architectural treasures. Walking between the major sites will take just an hour or two.

10 **Dóm svätého Martina** (St. Martin's Cathedral). Construction of this massive Gothic church, with its 280-ft gold-trimmed steeple, began in the 14th century. Between the 16th and 19th centuries, 17 Hungarian monarchs were crowned here. ✉ *Rudnayovo nám.,* ☎ *02/54431359.* ⏲ *Weekdays 10–11:30 and 2–6, Sat. 10–noon, Sun. 2–4:30.*

7 **Hlavné námestie** (Main Square). This enchanting square in the Old Town is lined with old houses and palaces that represent architectural styles from Gothic (No. 2) through Baroque (No. 4) and Rococo (No. 7) to a wonderfully decorative example of Art Nouveau (No. 10). ✉ *Bordered by Radničná ul. and Rybárska brána.*

9 **Hrad** (Castle). Bratislava's castle has been continually rebuilt since its original foundations were laid in the 9th century. The Hungarian kings expanded the castle into a royal residence, and the Habsburgs turned it into a successful defense against the Turks. Its current design, square with four corner towers, dates from the 17th century, although the existing castle was completely rebuilt after a disastrous fire in 1811. In the castle is the **Slovenské národné múzeum** (Slovak National Museum), which displays crafts, furniture and clocks, and silver. ✉ *Zámocká ul.,* ☎ *02/59341626,* WEB *www.hrady.sk/bratislava/.* ⏲ *Castle and museum Tues.–Sun. 9–5.*

2 **Hurbanovo námestie** (Hurban Square). This busy square hides the entrance to the Old Town. A small bridge, decorated with statues of St. John Nepomuk and St. Michael, crosses over the old moat, now blossoming with trees and fountains, into the intricate barbican and past Michalská brána (Michael's Gate). ✉ *Junction of Obchodná, Suché mýto, Michalská, and Námestie SNP.*

4 **Jezuitský kostol** (Jesuit Church). Wild with Baroque detailing on the inside, this church was built by Protestants who, in 1636, received an imperial concession for a place of worship on the condition that it have

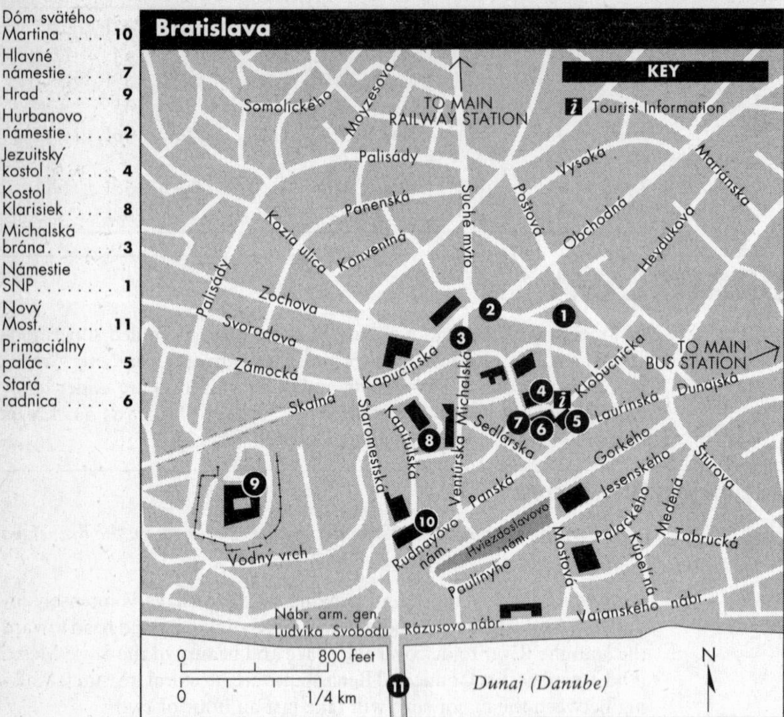

no tower. ✉ *Hlavné nám.,* ☎ *no phone.* ⏲ *Mass weekdays 6:30, 3:15, 4, and 6, Sun. 7, 9, 11, 5, and 6.*

❽ **Kostol Klarisiek** (Church and Monastery of the Poor Clares). Go through the arched passageway at the back of the Baroque **Palác Uhorskej kráľovskej komory** (Hungarian Royal Chamber) on Michalská ulica and you'll come to this church and convent on a tiny square. The one-nave Gothic church is small but still imposing, due to its richly decorated spire. ✉ *Farská ul.,* ☎ *no phone.*

❸ **Michalská brána** (Michael's Gate). Topped with a copper onion dome and a statue of St. Michael, this 500-year-old gate at one entrance to Old Town is the only remainder of Bratislava's three original city gates. ✉ *Hurbanovo nám.*

❶ **Námestie SNP** (SNP Square). An abbreviation for Slovenské Národné Povstanie (Slovak National Uprising), "SNP" appears on streets, squares, bridges, and posters throughout Slovakia. The anti-Nazi resistance movement involved partisan fighting in Slovakia's mountainous areas during the final years of World War II. On the monument that commemorates it in this square, you can often see the Slovak flag (red, blue, and white with a double cross) flying from a partisan's gun. In 1992 the square was the center for demonstrations in support of Slovak independence. ✉ *Bordered by Obchodná ul. and Poštová ul.*

❶❶ **Nový Most** (New Bridge). This futuristic bridge, opened in 1972, was formerly known as Most SNP. The steps under the passageway and up the other side lead in the direction of the historic castle. ✉ *Between Staromestská ul. and Panónska cesta.*

❺ **Primaciálny palác** (Primates' Palace). Go through the back entrance of the Old Town Hall to the **Primaciálne námestie** (Primates' Square), which is dominated by the pale pink, classical elegance of the palace. In the dazzling Hall of Mirrors, Napoléon and Habsburg emperor Francis I signed the Peace of Bratislava of 1805, following Napoléon's victory at the Battle of Austerlitz. ✉ *Primaciálne nám. 1,* ☎ *02/54435151 or 02/59356166.* ⏲ *Tues.–Sun. 10–5.*

❻ **Stará radnica** (Old Town Hall). A colorful jumble of Gothic and Renaissance arcades, archways, and audience halls makes up the Old Town Hall. Walk through the vaulted passageway with early Gothic ribbing into a cheerful Renaissance courtyard. (The hall's interior is not open to the public.) Toward the back of the courtyard, you'll find the entrance to the **Mestské Múzeum** (City Museum), which documents Bratislava's rocky past. ✉ *Primaciálne nám.,* ☎ *02/54435800 museum.* ⏲ *Museum Tues.–Sun. 10–5; wine-growing, pharmacy, and art crafts exhibitions Mon. and Wed.–Sun. 10–5.*

Dining

The long-shared history with Hungary gives Slovak cuisine an extra fire. Bratislava's proximity to Vienna, moreover, has lent a bit of grace and charm to the city's eateries. You'll find a variety of meat dishes, all spiced to enliven the palate and served (if you're lucky) with the special noodles Slovaks call *halušky.* Keep in mind that the city's many street stands offer a price-conscious alternative to restaurant dining. Try some *langoš*—flat, deep-fried, and delicious pieces of dough, which can be seasoned with garlic and other toppings.

$$$$ ✕ **Arkadia.** Arkadia's several dining rooms range from intimate to boisterous and are decorated with period 19th-century furnishings. Come here by taxi and, after fortifying yourself with steak or shish kebab, enjoy the 15-minute and mostly downhill walk back into town. ✉ *Zámocká schody,* ☎ *02/54435650. AE, DC, MC, V.*

$$$$ ★ ✕ **Le Monde.** This Old Town restaurant and cafeteria offers high quality international meals in a large classically minimalistic setting. You can start with sushi, followed by the Russian borscht and tandoori fish. The dinner menu, however, changes every two months to reflect the season and special events. ✉ *Ventúrska ul. 1,* ☎ *02/59227518. AE, DC, MC, V.*

$$$ ✕ **Leberfinger.** Here you'll find a wide choice of genuine Slovak dishes. The traditional furniture evokes the history of the two-story building which served as a road inn at the beginning of the 20th century. Try *kapustné strapačky* (sauerkraut with flour-flakes topped with the Slovak sheep-cheese *bryndza*). This kid-friendly place provides both a kinder-corner inside and teeter-totters at the attached sandy playground. Its location between the Danube River embankment and a major city park makes it a suitable stop of a full-day family trip. ✉ *Viedenská cesta 257,* ☎ *02/62317590. MC, V.*

$$ ✕ **Café Meyer.** Opened in 1997 at the same location downtown as its namesake after more more than a century, this café has brought back with it the Austrian flavor of Pressburg (as Bratislava was known to the Austrians). The great variety of delicious cakes filled with cream and fruit is a reminder of former owner Julius Meyer, a candy supplier to the emperor's court. Its late hours make it an ideal place for a post-theater dinner of such dishes as Wiener schnitzel or hot strudels filled with vegetables, cabbage, spinach, or meat and covered with a vegetable sauce. In July and August, you can sit outside under umbrellas. ✉ *Hlavné nám. 4,* ☎ *02/54411741. No credit cards.*

$$ ✕ **Chez David.** The draw here is kosher food downtown in calm surroundings. Try duck in *sholet* (thick sauce made of potatoes, groats, root crops, and beans) with Austrian wine. David has a great kitchen

and a knowledgeable staff. ✉ *Zámocká 13,* ☎ *02/54413824. AE, DC, MC, V. Closed Sat. No dinner Fri.*

$$ ✕ **Modrá Guľa.** At the top of the Slovenská sporiteľňa bank headquarters building, the rounded restaurant, furnished with metal and blue glass, has a fresh, clean feel. The windows, and in summer, the terrace, afford a good view of downtown. Try a garlic soup served in a *bosniak* (round roll). ✉ *Suché mýto 6,* ☎ *02/58504007. AE, DC, MC, V.*

$$ ✕ **Modrá Hviezda.** A small wine cellar, the "Blue Star" concentrates on regional fare. Try the *bryndzový posúch* (baked sheep's-cheese pie) and *mamičkina špecialita* ("Mother's favorite dish": stewed beef with sour-cream sauce, potato-dough fritters, and cranberries). ✉ *Beblavého 14,* ☎ *02/54432747. No credit cards. Closed Sun.*

$$ ✕ **Prešporská kúria.** The large restaurant, dining hall, and snack bar is housed in three wooden buildings. The cuisine is rich Central European: meats served with potatoes, rice, or dumplings plus vegetable salads. The wooden tables and chairs are simplified Slovak folk art. In summer you can sit outdoors, where wine and beer are served in plastic cups. ✉ *Dunajská 21–23,* ☎ *02/52967981. AE, DC, MC, V.*

$ ✕ **Stará Sladovňa.** This beer hall is known lovingly, and fittingly, as "Mamut" (the word for Mammoth, a huge and ungainly beast) to Bratislavans. Locals come here for the Bohemian beer on tap and for inexpensive, filling meals. The place, which has billiards and slot machines on two floors, seats almost 1,000, so don't worry about reservations. ✉ *Cintorínska ul. 32,* ☎ *02/52921151. No credit cards.*

Lodging

On the whole, Bratislava's hotels are no bargain, and new properties are few and far between. If you're on a budget, investigate the accommodation services at the **Bratislava Tourist Information** branch in the main train station (✉ Hlavná stanica, Predstaničné nám., ☎ 02/52495906)—but stay near the city center, as the fringe areas are a vast sea of block housing.

$$$$ ★ 🏨 **Danube.** Opened in 1992, this French-run hotel on the bank of the Danube has superior facilities and service. The modern rooms are done in tasteful pastels; the public areas gleam. ✉ *Rybné nám. 1, 81338,* ☎ *02/59340000,* FAX *02/54414311,* WEB *www.srs-worldhotels.com. 264 rooms, 16 suites. 2 restaurants, pool. AE, DC, MC, V.*

$$$$ 🏨 **Hotel Forum Bratislava.** The Forum, opened in 1989 in downtown Bratislava, houses three restaurants and several cafés and bars. Rooms are bright and, thanks to twice-daily maid service, very clean. Request a room with a view of the castle or Old Town. ✉ *Hodžovo nám. 2, 81625,* ☎ *02/59348111,* FAX *02/54414645,* WEB *www.forumba.sk. 219 rooms, 14 suites. 3 restaurants, pool. AE, DC, MC, V.*

$$ ★ 🏨 **Grémium.** This small, bright, affordable pension is in the center of Bratislava's Old Town. The friendly staff serves a terminally arty clientele. A Continental breakfast is included in the room rate. Rooms have showers, not tubs. ✉ *Gorkého ul. 11, 81103,* ☎ *02/54131026,* FAX *02/54430653. 5 rooms, 1 suite. Restaurant. AE, MC, V.*

$$ 🏨 **Hotel Turist.** Modern, no-frills, and pleasant, this hotel is a short hop from the city center. A winter stadium and a swimming pool (open in summer) are nearby. Rooms have showers, not tubs. ✉ *Ondavská ul. 5, 82005,* ☎ *02/55572789,* FAX *02/5573180. 95 rooms. No credit cards.*

$$ 🏨 **Penzión SlovAir.** In this apartment building only 1 km (½ mi) from Bratislava airport, the three-room apartments all have kitchens. The clean units have simply upholstered wooden furniture. ✉ *Ivánska cesta 81, 82312,* ☎ *02/43422123,* FAX *02/43423032. 10 apartments. No credit cards.*

Nightlife and the Arts

For listings of events look in Bratislava's English-language newspaper, the *Slovak Spectator,* or ask at **Bratislava Tourist Information** (BIS).

The Arts

The **Slovak Philharmonic Orchestra** stages excellent concerts at the Reduta (✉ Medená 3, ☎ 02/54433351 or 02/54433352). **Slovenské Národné Divadlo** (Slovak National Theater; ✉ Hviezdoslavo nám. 1, ☎ 02/54433890, 02/54433771, or 02/54430402) presents high-quality opera and ballet performances at bargain prices.

Nightlife

Bratislava hosts an annual jazz festival in the fall, but the city lacks a good venue for regular jazz gigs. The **Aligátor** (✉ Laurinská 7, ☎ 02/54418611), downtown, plays rock on Tuesday and Saturday and blues on Thursday. The **Čierny Havran Club** (Black Raven; ✉ Biela ul. 6, ☎ 02/54430717) occasionally has local jazz acts. Good Guinness beer is served at the Irish pub **Dubliner** (✉ Sedlárska ul. 6, ☎ 02/54410706), which has a no-smoking corner. For American-style hard rock try the **Harley-Davidson Club** (✉ Rebarborová ul. 1, ☎ 02/43191095); take Trolleybus 220 from behind the Tesco department store and get off at Ružinovský Cintorín (Ružinov Cemetery).

Shopping

You will find folk-art and souvenir shops along **Obchodná ulica** (Shopping Street) as well as on Námestie SNP. Stores tend to come and go in this fast-changing city.

There are several **Dielo** (✉ Obchodná 27; Obchodná 33; Nám. SNP 12) stores that sell works by Slovak artists and craftspeople at reasonable prices. **Folk, Folk** (✉ Rybárska Brána 2, ☎ 02/54434874) deals in Slovak folk art, including crystal, pottery, handwoven tablecloths, wooden articles, and dolls in folk costumes. **ÚĽUV** (✉ Nám. SNP 12, ☎ 02/52923802) has hand-painted table pottery and vases, wooden figures, and folk costumes.

Bratislava Essentials

AIR TRAVEL TO AND FROM BRATISLAVA

The most convenient international airport for Slovakia is Vienna's Schwechat Airport, approximately 60 km (37 mi) from Bratislava. Nine buses a day run from Schwechat to Bratislava, or you can take a taxi; the journey takes just over an hour, depending on the border crossing. From Prague's Ruzyně Airport you can take a ČSA flight to Bratislava; the flight takes about an hour.

BUS TRAVEL TO AND FROM BRATISLAVA

Buses run frequently between Prague and Bratislava; the trip costs around 300 Sk and takes about five hours. From Vienna there are four buses a day from Autobusbahnhof Wien-Mitte; the trip takes between 1½ and 2 hours. The Autobusová Stanica (Bus Station) in Bratislava is outside the city center; take Trolleybus 217 to Hodžovo námestie in the direction of the Hrad (Castle).

➤ Bus Information: **Autobusová Stanica** (Bus Station; ✉ Mlynské nivy ul., ☎ 0984/222222 or 0984/333333).

BUS TRAVEL WITHIN BRATISLAVA

Bus, trolleybus, and tram service in Bratislava is cheap, fairly frequent, and convenient for getting to the main sights. Buy tickets ahead of time at any newsstand or at automated ticket dispensers for 12 Sk each, or a 24-hour ticket for 70 Sk, or a three-day ticket for 160 Sk, and stamp them when you enter the bus, trolleybus, or tram.

CAR TRAVEL

Good highways link Prague and Bratislava via Brno (D1 and D2); the 315-km (195-mi) journey takes about 3½ hours. The 60-km (37-mi) trip from Vienna (A4 and then Route 8) takes 1½ hours.

Driving can be difficult in Bratislava and parking spaces are at a premium in the city center; foot power is the best way to get around. You can rent a car either at Satur or at the Forum and Danube hotels. Watch out for no-parking zones or your car will be booted and you will have to pay a hefty fine to have the device removed.

EMERGENCIES

Lekárne (pharmacies) take turns staying open late or on Sunday; a list is posted at each pharmacy. For after-hours service, ring the bell; you will be served through a little hatch door.

➤ EMERGENCY SERVICES: **Police** (☎ 158). **Ambulance** (☎ 155).

➤ 24-HOUR PHARMACIES: **Lekáreň pod Manderlom** (✉ Nám. SNP 20, ☎ 02/54432952). **Lekáreň** (✉ Palackého 10, ☎ 02/54419665).

ENGLISH-LANGUAGE MEDIA

➤ BOOKSTORES: **Eurobooks** (✉ Jesenského 5–9, ☎ 02/54417959 WEB www.eurobooks.sk).

TOURS

The best tours of Bratislava are given by Bratislava Tourist Information, which can arrange a tour in a vintage coach or with an individual guide for a very reasonable price. Both BIS and Satur offer one-day tours of castles and the Small Carpathian mountains close to Bratislava.

TRAIN TRAVEL

Bratislava's train station is Hlavná stanica. The tourist information office here provides travel tips and helps find accommodation in the city. Reasonably efficient train service connects Prague and Bratislava (5–6 hours). Unless you crave adventure, take the Intercity trains for their speed and safety. There are several trains a day to and from Vienna (just over 1 hour) and Budapest (3 hours), and one train from Krakow to Bratislava (5½ hours).

➤ TRAIN INFORMATION: **Hlavná stanica** (✉ Predstaničné nám., ☎ 02/50584488 or 02/50584484). **Tourist information office** (☎ 02/52495906).

VISITOR INFORMATION

➤ TOURIST INFORMATION: **Bratislava Tourist Information** (BIS; ✉ Klobučnícka 2, ☎ 02/54434370). **Satur Tours and Travel** (main office, ✉ Jesenského 5, ☎ 02/54410133 or 02/54410129 WEB www.satur.sk).

THE HIGH TATRAS AND EASTERN SLOVAKIA

In the High Tatras region are some of the best hotels in the country (often with saunas to pamper tired skiers), good orientation tours, and stunning mountain scenery laced with well-marked walking trails. Finding a satisfying meal in the Tatras can be difficult, especially in late fall, when some restaurants close. One bright spot is shish kebab made on a *koliba* (open-faced grill). Both an electric train network and

a winding highway (Route 537) link the industrial center of Poprad with the resorts on the lower slopes of the High Tatras.

In the brooding towns of the Spiš region just south and east of the High Tatras (on a map look for the prefix "Spišský" preceding a town name), isolation and economic stagnation have preserved a striking mix of Gothic and Renaissance architecture—Gothic churches with Renaissance bell towers attached are typical of the area. These towns tend to be short on creature comforts.

East of Spiš, the Šariš region is permeated with a unique legacy of 17th- and 18th-century Orthodox and Greek Catholic (Uniate) wooden churches. The splendid walled town of Bardejov makes the best center from which to explore. In contrast, Nazi and Soviet tanks, trenches, and planes, kept as a reminder of the fighting that took place here in 1944, are concentrated near the Slovakia–Poland border at the Dukelský Priesmyk (Dukla Pass).

Spišská Sobota

The beautiful medieval suburb of Spišská Sobota seems light-years away from the Communist apartment blocks of its industrial neighbor Poprad. Once a hub of the historic Spiš empire, the village is filled with steep shingled roofs, high timber-framed gables, and arched brick doorways. The lovely old square—a nearly perfect ensemble of Renaissance houses—has a Romanesque church, **Kostol svätého Juraja** (St. George's Church; ✉ Sobotské Nám., ☎ no phone), rebuilt during the early 16th century. The church's ornate altar is the work of Pavol of Levoča, one of the great wood-carvers of the 16th century. Two doors down from Kostol svätého Jurajá is the **Múzeum** (museum; ✉ Sobotské nám. 33, ☎ 052/7721874), which has a collection that focuses on local history, including the career of Pavol of Levoča. At press time the museum was closed for reconstruction.

Levoča

★ One of the most famous Spiš towns is Levoča, whose layers of Renaissance-on-Gothic architecture are undergoing restoration. The row of facades in Námestie Majstra Pavla, the main square, is particularly striking, especially those of Nos. 43, 45, 47, and 49. **Kostol svätého Jakuba** (St. Jacob's Church) on the main square has an astounding concentration of Gothic religious art, including work by Spiš artist Pavol of Levoča. His carved-wood high altar is monumental in size and exquisite in detail. ✉ *Nám. Majstra Pavla 3,* ☎ *053/4512347.*

Just 16 km (10 mi) east from Levoča along Route 18 is one of the largest castles in Europe: **Spišský hrad** (Spiš Castle). The beautiful views relieve the grim display of torture devices. ✉ *On hill above town of Spišské Podhradie,* ☎ *053/4512786,* WEB *castles.sk.* ⏲ *June–Aug., daily 9–6; May and Sept.–Oct., Tues.–Sun. 9–5.*

$$$ **Hotel Satel.** Inside an 18th-century mansion, the Satel centers on a picturesque courtyard. The guest rooms are bright and modern. ✉ *Nám. Majstra Pavla 55, 05401,* ☎ *053/4512943,* FAX *053/4514486,* WEB *www.pp.internet.sk/satel/Satel_PP_E.htm. 21 rooms, 2 suites. Restaurant. AE, DC, MC, V.*

$$ **Hadušovský Penzión.** Close to the Spiš Castle and 12 km (8 mi) from the ski resort of Plejsy near Krompachy, this pension in a two-story family house offers cozy rooms, horseback riding, and horse-drawn cross-country skiing. ✉ *Hodkovce 14, Spišské Vlachy, 05361,* ☎ *053/4495129,* FAX *053/4495546. 2 suites. No credit cards.*

Smokovec

Smokovec is really three resorts in one: Starý (Old), Nový (New), and Horný (Upper). Starý Smokovec is an excellent place to start exploring the Tatras' hiking trails. Some of the more traveled paths lead to waterfalls, a turn-of-the-20th-century chalet, and alpine lakes. A funicular at Hrebienok can take you back to Starý Smokovec. As soon as there's sufficient snow on the ground, the resort is crammed with skiers (equipment can be rented at **Tatrasport Adam & Andreas:** ✉ Starý Smokovec, Horný Smokovec, ☎ 052/4422110).

$$ ✕ **Restaurant Koliba.** This restaurant's koliba turns out excellent beef, venison steak with cranberry sauce and red wine, and *kapustová polievka* (sauerkraut soup with mushrooms and sausage). A local cimbalom band plays here every night. ✉ *Downhill from train station,* ☎ *052/4422204. No credit cards. Closed Sun.*

$$$ ★ **Grand Hotel.** The town's oldest hotel has an air of faded fin-de-siècle elegance. Large guest rooms have high ceilings, and some have a balcony. A filling buffet breakfast is included in the rate. ✉ *Starý Smokovec, 06201,* ☎ *052/4422154,* FAX *052/4422157. 79 rooms, some with bath; 5 suites. Restaurant, pool. AE, DC, MC, V.*

Tatranská Lomnica

Tiny out-of-the-way Tatranská Lomnica is a peaceful but still convenient spot for hiking and skiing. The **Magistrale** trail (24 km [15 mi]) begins behind the Grandhotel Praha. Along the tree line are dwarf pines and spectacular views, which you can reach with relatively little exertion. At the **Múzeum Tatranského Národného Parku** (Museum of the Tatra National Park), startlingly realistic mounted animals dominate the first floor, while exhibits on local peasant life wait upstairs. ✉ *Štátne lesy TANAP-u, Tatranská Lomnica,* ☎ *052/4467951.* ⏲ *Weekdays 8–noon and 1–4:30, weekends 8–noon.*

$$ ✕ **Zbojnícka Koliba.** This tavern serves a small range of Slovak specialties prepared over an open fire amid rustic decor and accompanied by Gypsy cimbalom music. ✉ *Near Grandhotel Praha,* ☎ *052/4467630. No credit cards. No lunch.*

$$$ ★ 🏨 **Grandhotel Praha.** The multiturreted, turn-of-the-20th-century hotel has spacious, traditionally decorated guest rooms. The restaurant has an unusual air of elegance. ✉ *Tatranská Lomnica, 05960,* ☎ *052/4467941,* FAX *052/4467891,* WEB *www.tatry.sk/grandpraha.html. 83 rooms, 7 suites. Restaurant. AE, DC, MC, V.*

Bardejov

Once astride the trade routes between Poland and Russia, Bardejov (www.bardejov.sk) revolves around its beautiful main square. On the south side of the square is the **Šarišské múzeum** (Šariš Museum), filled with 16th- to 19th-century religious art from local Russian Orthodox churches. ✉ *Radničné nám. 13,* ☎ *054/4746038.* ⏲ *Tues.–Sun. 8–noon and 12:30–4.*

Kostol Svätého Egídia (St. Egidium Church), on the main square, is almost purely Gothic inside and out. Nearly a dozen perfectly preserved Gothic side altars line the nave. ✉ *Radničné nám. 3,* ☎ *054/722595,* WEB *www.unipo.sk/SARIS/BARDEJOV.* ⏲ *Apr.–Sept., Tues.–Sun. 9–5:30; Oct.–Mar., Tues.–Sun. 10–4.*

$ 🏨 **Športhotel.** The rectangular building with a gray facade built in 1989 sits on the Topl'a River bank, among tennis and volleyball playgrounds, just seven minutes from Bardejov's beautiful main square. ✉ *Kutuzovova 34, 08501,* ☎ *054/724949,* FAX *054/728208. 20 rooms. Restaurant. No credit cards.*

The High Tatras and Eastern Slovakia Essentials

AIR TRAVEL

Slovak Airlines has flights from the capital to Košice.

➤ FEES AND SCHEDULES: **Slovak Airlines** (☎ 02/48575170).

CAR TRAVEL

Driving is the quickest and most convenient way to see eastern Slovakia—sometimes it's the only way to reach small villages. Route 537 is the main road between Poprad and the High Tatras resort towns.

TOURS

Satur's seven-day Grand Tour of Slovakia, which leaves from Bratislava every other Saturday from June through September, stops in the High Tatras and a few other towns in eastern Slovakia. The Satur office in Starý Smokovec is also helpful in arranging tours of the Tatras and the surrounding area. TLS Air offers a biplane flight over the Tatras from Poprad airport.

➤ FEES AND SCHEDULES: **Satur** (headquarters, ✉ Miletičova 1, Bratislava 82472, ☎ 02/55422828; Starý Smokovec office ☎ 052/4422710 or 052/4422497). **TLS Air** (☞ Air Travel *in* Slovakia A to Z, *above*).

TRAIN AND BUS TRAVEL

Trains and buses run frequently except on weekends. The electric trains that run between Poprad and the resort towns in the High Tatras leave from the upper platforms of Poprad's main train station, Železničná stanica Poprad-Tatry.

➤ TRAIN INFORMATION: **Železničná stanica Poprad-Tatry** (✉ Wolkerova 496, ☎ 052/7762509).

TRANSPORTATION AROUND THE HIGH TATRAS AND EASTERN SLOVAKIA

Many of the towns in this region have no formal street names; instead, they usually have signs pointing to hotels, restaurants, and museums.

VISITOR INFORMATION

➤ Tourist Information: **Bardejov** (✉ Radničné nám. 21, ☎ 054/4746979). **Poprad** (☎ 052/16186). **Smokovec** (✉ Starý Smokovec, ☎ 052/4423440). **Štrbské Pleso** (✉ Štrbské Pleso, ☎ 052/4492391). **Tatranská Lomnica** (☎ 052/4467951).

27 SLOVENIA

SURGING PEAKS, MYSTERIOUS CAVES, the majestic Old Town of Ljubljana, and a coast dotted with well-preserved Venetian cities of old are the attractions of Slovenia. The combination of Alpine, plain, and coastal geography allows both morning skiing high in the Julian Alps and views of sunset on the Adriatic on the same day. Slovenes' love of their natural surroundings is reflected in the motto they use for their country (fully half of which is covered by forests): "A Green Piece of Europe."

Slovenia's northern border is lined with the jagged peaks of the Karavanke Mountains. The Julian Alps, capped by majestic Mt. Triglav (Three Heads), which rises to 9,393 ft, dominate the northwest. Eastward, the mountains gradually descend to the great Hungarian plain. Lovely lakes nestle in thickly wooded mountain valleys, and vineyards cover low-lying hills farther east.

Slovenia has from earliest times been a frontier region. The Romans came from the coast and marched north; Germanic tribes propelled themselves south. Later Slovenia became a province of Charlemagne's empire; next it served as the Habsburg Empire's bulwark against the Turks. The years during World War II, when Slovenia was annexed by Hitler and Mussolini, were filled with both heroic and unspeakable acts. After World War II, as part of Yugoslavia, Slovenia was at the vanguard of the movement toward democracy and self-determination following Tito's death.

The 2 million Slovenes held a national referendum on December 23, 1990, voting for sovereignty and independence from Yugoslavia, and proclaimed their independence on June 25, 1991. Slovenia gained recognition from other nations and soon set about becoming an active member of the family of European states. Following 500 years as part of the Austro-Hungarian Empire, Slovenes have perfectly combined Austrian efficiency and organization with a genuine and captivating Slavic friendliness. Slovenia's small size (about half the area of Switzerland) can be an advantage: from the centrally located capital, Ljubljana, everything in the country is no more than a three-hour drive away.

SLOVENIA A TO Z

To research prices, get advice from other travelers, and book travel arrangements, visit www.fodors.com.

AIR TRAVEL

There are no direct flights between Slovenia and the United States. Adria Airways, the Slovene national airline, offers regular flights to most major

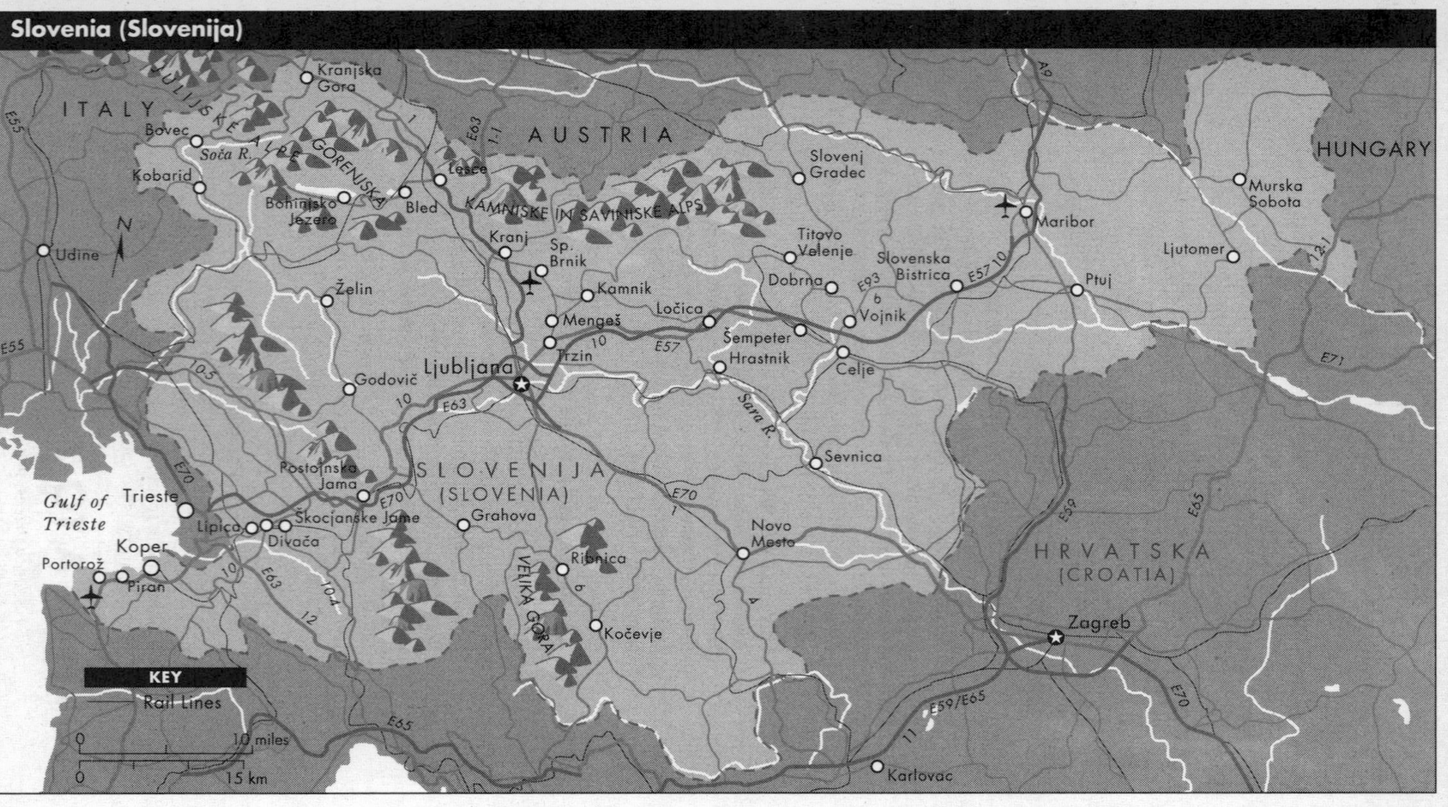
Slovenia (Slovenija)
ITALY
AUSTRIA
HUNGARY
SLOVENIJA (SLOVENIA)
HRVATSKA (CROATIA)
JULIJSKE ALPE
GORENJSKA
KAMNIŠKE IN SAVINJSKE ALPS
VELIKA GORA
Kranjska Gora
Bovec
Soča R.
Kobarid
Bohinjsko Jezero
Bled
Lesce
Kranj
Sp. Brnik
Udine
N
Želin
Kamnik
Mengeš
Trzin
Ločica
Ljubljana
Godovič
Slovenj Gradec
Titovo Velenje
Dobrna
Vojnik
Slovenska Bistrica
Šempeter
Hrastnik
Celje
Sava R.
Sevnica
Maribor
Ptuj
Murska Sobota
Ljutomer
Postojnska Jama
Škocjanske Jame
Grahova
Lipica
Divača
Gulf of Trieste
Trieste
Koper
Portorož
Piran
Ribnica
Kočevje
Novo Mesto
Zagreb
Karlovac
E55
E63
E70
E57
E93
E59
E65
E59/E65
E71
A9
KEY
Rail Lines
0 10 miles
0 15 km

European cities. Austrian Airlines has daily flights from Vienna; Aeroflot and Swissair also have good connections.

➤ AIRLINES AND CONTACTS: **Adria Airways** (✉ Gosposvetska 6, 1000 Ljubljana, ☎ 01/436–2500, WEB www.adria.si).

BOAT AND FERRY TRAVEL

From early March to late October the *Prince of Venice* hydrofoil makes regularly scheduled trips between Venice and Portorož.

From mid-July to mid-September, the Italian firm Adriatica runs a round-trip service from Trieste, calling at Piran and stopping at several towns on the Croatian Adriatic coast.

➤ BOAT AND FERRY INFORMATION: ***Prince of Venice*** (Kompas Turizem; ✉ Obala 41, 6320 Portorož, ☎ 05/617–8000). **Adriatica** (Maona; ✉ Cankarievo nab. 7, 6330 Piran, ☎ 05/673–1290).

BUS TRAVEL

Intercity bus service is regular, cheap, and efficient, reaching even the most outlying mountain villages. For information contact Ljubljana bus station.

➤ BUS INFORMATION: **Ljubljana bus station** (✉ Trg OF 5, ☎ 01/434–3838).

BUSINESS HOURS

Most banks are open weekdays 9–noon and 2–4:30, Saturday 9–11. You can also change money at exchange desks in hotels, gas stations, tourist agencies, supermarkets, and small exchange offices. The main museums are open Tuesday–Sunday 10–6. Larger shops are open Monday–Saturday 10–6, while smaller ones may open mornings only 10–2. Most are closed Sunday.

CAR TRAVEL

An international driver's license is required in Slovenia. Rental for a midsize car costs about US$112 (SIT18,500) for 24 hours, with unlimited mileage.

GASOLINE

Gasoline costs SIT147 per liter and is readily available.

ROAD CONDITIONS

Main roads between large towns are comparable to those in western Europe. Highways charge a toll depending on route and distance traveled. A tunnel speeds traffic through the Karavanke Alps between Slovenia and Austria. From Vienna the passage is by way of Maribor to Ljubljana, with a highway from Graz to Celje. Slovenia's roads also connect with Italy's autostrada highway system.

RULES OF THE ROAD

Slovenes drive on the right. Speed limits are 60 kph (37 mph) in urban areas and 120 kph (74 mph) on motorways. Local drivers are courteous by European standards.

CUSTOMS AND DUTIES

Duty-free allowances are: 1 carton of cigarettes, 1 liter of spirits, 2 liters of wine. The export of historical artifacts is strictly forbidden.

DINING

When you look at a menu remember two key words: regional and seasonal. This is the best way to eat in Slovenia. There are no pretensions at the table, and full respect is paid to traditional peasant dishes. To really get down to basics, eat in a country *gostilna* (inn). Typical dishes are *krvavice* (black pudding) served with *žganci* (polenta) or sausages served with sauerkraut. Another favorite is *bograč,* a peppery stew similar to Hungarian goulash, made from either horse meat or beef. Coffee shops serve the delicious calorie-laden *prekmurska gibanica,* a layered cake combining curd cheese, walnuts, and poppy seeds. Another national favorite is *potica,* a rolled cake filled with either walnuts, chocolate, poppy seeds, or raisins. Slovenes enjoy drinking and produce some excellent wines, notably the red *Teran* and the white *Laški Rizling*.

Prices are for one main course at dinner.

CATEGORY	COST
$$$$	over SIT3,000
$$$	SIT2,000–SIT3,000
$$	SIT1,000–SIT2,000
$	under SIT1,000

RESERVATIONS AND DRESS

Casual dress is acceptable in many restaurants in Slovenia, but Slovenes do tend to dress more formally when going out for the evening.

EMBASSIES

Australia maintains a consulate in Ljubljana.

➤ CANADA: (✉ Miklošičeva 19, ☎ 01/430–3570, FAX 01/430–3575).

➤ UNITED KINGDOM: (✉ Trg Republike 3/IV, ☎ 01/425–7191, FAX 01/425–0174).

➤ UNITED STATES: (✉ Prešernova 31, ☎ 01/200–5500, FAX 01/200–5555).

HOLIDAYS

January 1–2; February 8 (Prešeren Day, Slovene cultural day); Easter; April 27 (National Resistance Day); May 1–2 (Labor Day); June 25 (Slovenia National Day); August 15 (Assumption); October 31 (Reformation Day); November 1 (All Saints' Day); December 25; December 26 (Independence Day).

LANGUAGE

Slovene is the chief language. In the eastern part of the country signs are posted in Slovene and Hungarian; on the Adriatic coast both Slovene and Italian are officially used. English, German, and Italian are spoken in many places.

LODGING

Don't expect Slovenia to be a cheap option: prices are comparable to those in western Europe. During the high season (June–September), many hotels, particularly on the coast, are fully booked.

CATEGORY	COST
$$$$	over SIT30,000
$$$	SIT20,000–SIT30,000
$$	SIT10,000–SIT20,000
$	under SIT10,000

APARTMENT AND VILLA RENTALS

This can be the cheapest option, especially for stays of a week or more. Prices vary depending on region and season. Contact local tourist information centers for details.

HOSTELS

During the summer break, university dorms in Ljubljana and Maribor are open to visitors. There are also a number of youth hostels, generally in country areas, that cater to hikers. For further information, contact the Slovenian Tourist Board.

HOTELS

Many hotels are clean, smartly furnished, and well run. Establishments built under socialism are equipped with extras such as saunas and sports facilities but tend to be gargantuan structures lacking in soul. Hotels dating from the turn of the 20th century are more romantic. Most establishments add a 30% surcharge for stays of fewer than three days.

TOURIST FARMS

Staying on a working farm offers the chance to experience rural life firsthand. "Agritourism" is growing in popularity, especially in Triglav National Park. This is an ideal solution for families with children. Contact the Association of Tourist Farms of Slovenia.

➤ ORGANIZATIONS: **Association of Tourist Farms of Slovenia** (✉ Trnoveljska 1, 3000 Celje, ☎ FAX 03/491–6480).

MAIL AND SHIPPING

Post offices are open weekdays 8–6, Saturday 8–noon. Stamps are also sold at hotels, newsstands, and kiosks.

POSTAL RATES

Airmail postage to the United States is SIT105 for a letter, SIT95 for a postcard. Airmail postage in Europe is SIT80 for a letter, SIT70 for a postcard.

MONEY MATTERS

Costs in general are comparable to those in western Europe. Notable exceptions are public transportation, alcohol, and cigarettes, all of which are cheaper here. Typical prices are as follows: cup of coffee, SIT150; glass of beer, SIT200; slice of cake, SIT200; bottle of house wine, SIT1,500; sandwich, SIT350; admission to museums, SIT200–SIT500.

CURRENCY

The monetary unit in Slovenia is the Slovenian tolar (SIT). One Slovenian tolar is divided into 100 stotin. There are notes of SIT10, SIT20, SIT50, SIT100, SIT200, SIT500, SIT1,000, SIT5,000, and SIT10,000and coins of 1, 2, and 5 Slovenian tolar and 50 stotin.

Exchange rates at press time (summer 2001) were SIT235 to the U.S. dollar, SIT155 to the Canadian dollar, SIT347 to the British pound sterling, SIT268 to the Irish punt, SIT128 to the Australian dollar, SIT99 to the New Zealand dollar, and SIT30 to the South African rand.

PASSPORTS AND VISAS

No visas are necessary for holders of valid passports from the United States, Canada, the United Kingdom, mainland European countries, Australia, New Zealand, or the Republic of Ireland. South African nationals, however, must have a three-month tourist visa.

Telephones

COUNTRY CODE

The country code for Slovenia is 386.

INTERNATIONAL CALLS

To make international calls, dial 00 and then the appropriate country code. International calls can be made from local pay phones or at the post office. To call collect, dial 901. For international directory inquiries, dial 989.

LOCAL CALLS

Pay phones take telephone cards, available at post offices and kiosks. Lower rates apply from 10 PM to 7 AM and all day Sunday. For local directory inquiries dial 988.

TIPPING

Tax is already included in listed prices. Tips are not included in bills, so a 10% tip is customary; if service is especially good, tip 15%.

TRAIN TRAVEL

The internal rail network is limited, but trains are cheap and efficient. Daily trains link Slovenia with Austria, Italy, Hungary, and Croatia. Many are overnight trains with sleeping compartments. For information contact Ljubljana Train Station.

➤ TRAIN INFORMATION: **Ljubljana Train Station** (✉ Trg OF 6, ☎ 01/291–2524).

TRANSPORTATION AROUND SLOVENIA

In Slovenian the words for street (*ulica*) and drive (*cesta*) are abbreviated *ul.* and *c. Nabrežje* (abbreviated *nab.*) means embankment. The word for square is *trg.*

VISITOR INFORMATION

Each region has its own tourist information center (TIC).

➤ TOURIST INFORMATION: **Slovenian Tourist Board** (✉ Dunajska 156, 1000 Ljubljana, ☎ 01/189–1840, FAX 01/189–1841, WEB www.slovenia-tourism.si).

WHEN TO GO

The tourist season runs throughout the year, though prices tend to be lower from November through March. Late spring and fall are best—usually warm enough for swimming but not uncomfortably hot.

CLIMATE

Weather in Slovenia can vary greatly depending upon what part of the country you are in. Temperatures are colder and there is more precipitation in the Alpine regions, while the summers on the coast can be quite hot. Ljubljana and the Pannonian plain have less extreme variations in weather. The following are the average temperatures for Ljubljana.

Jan.	32F	0C	**May**	59F	14.5C	**Sept.**	59F	15C
Feb.	37F	2.5C	**June**	65F	18C	**Oct.**	49F	9C
Mar.	43F	6C	**July**	70F	20C	**Nov.**	40F	4C
Apr.	49F	9C	**Aug.**	68F	19C	**Dec.**	32F	0C

LJUBLJANA

The capital of the republic of Slovenia is on occasion referred to as "Ljubljana the beloved," a play on words: *Ljubljena* means "beloved"; change one letter, and you have the name Ljubljana.

In 34 BC, the Romans founded Emona on this site. Traces of the Roman occupation have been preserved in sections of walls and a complex of foundations complete with mosaics. Slovenes settled here in the 7th century. Later, under the German name Laibach, this became the capital of the Duchy of Carniola, which in 1335 passed into the hands of the House of Habsburg. From then until the end of World War I Ljubljana remained part of the Habsburg Empire. In 1849 the railway linking Vienna and Trieste reached Ljubljana, establishing it as a major center of commerce, industry, and culture.

Influences from the past are apparent in the Ljubljana of today, although you will have to pass through concentric circles like the growth rings of a tree in order to reach the romantic heart of the original Old Town. Vast industrial complexes and high-rise apartments form the outermost

Ljubljana

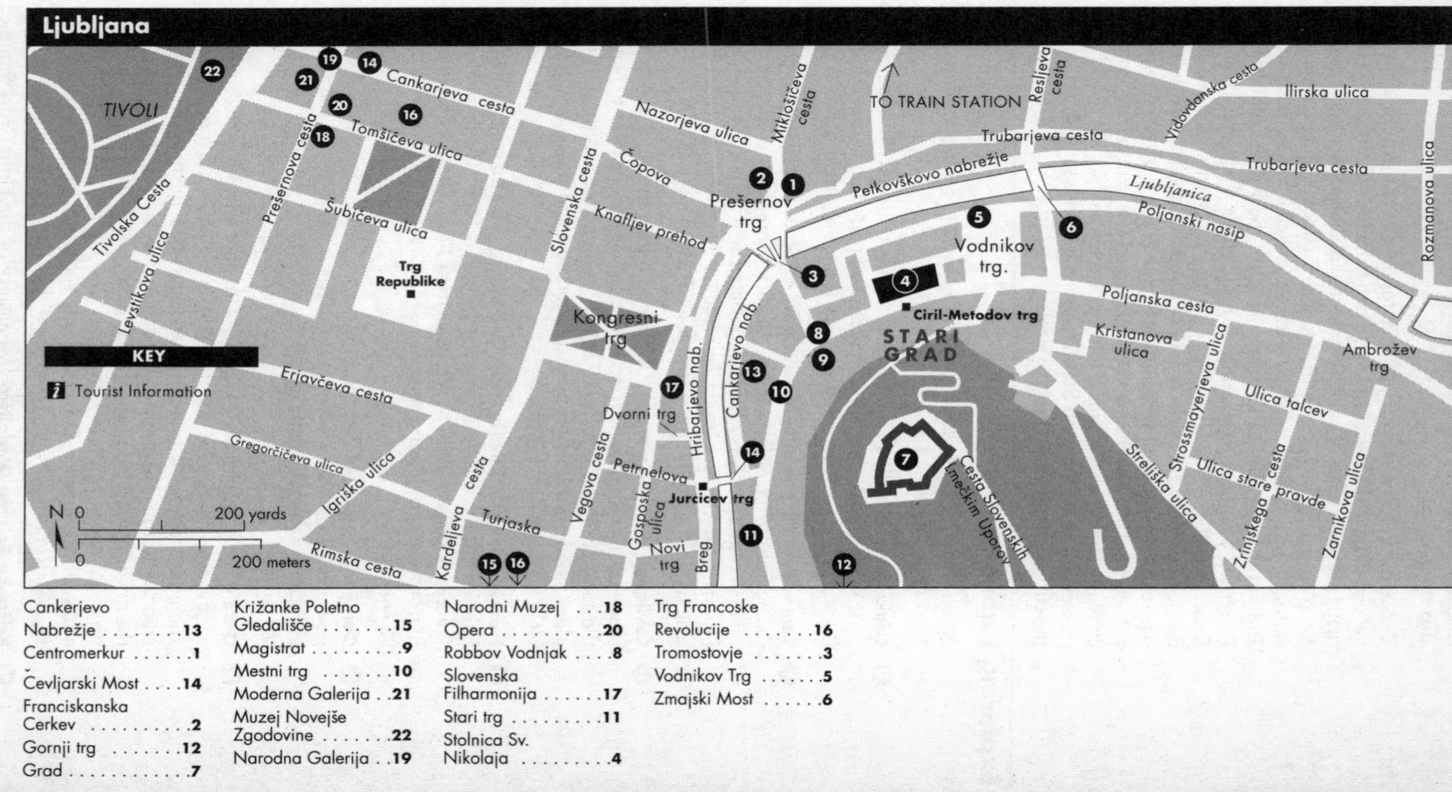

Cankerjevo Nabrežje 13	Križanke Poletno Gledališče 15	Narodni Muzej . . . 18	Trg Francoske Revolucije 16
Centromerkur 1	Magistrat 9	Opera 20	Tromostovje 3
Čevljarski Most 14	Mestni trg 10	Robbov Vodnjak 8	Vodnikov Trg 5
Franciskanska Cerkev 2	Moderna Galerija . . 21	Slovenska Filharmonija 17	Zmajski Most 6
Gornji trg 12	Muzej Novejše Zgodovine 22	Stari trg 11	
Grad 7	Narodna Galerija . . 19	Stolnica Sv. Nikolaja 4	

ring. "Downtown," composed mainly of modern office buildings, is also spread out.

To reach the old, romantic Ljubljana, follow one of the city's main commercial streets, Miklošičeva Cesta, south from the railway station, eventually passing a series of palatial three- and four-story structures in florid Art Nouveau style (Jugendstil), topped by cupolas, spires, and ornate statuary, with facades adorned with extravagant arches, balustrades, and curlicue details. Miklošičeva reaches the River Ljubljanica at Prešernov trg, the square named for Slovenia's greatest poet, France Prešeren (1800–49), whose bronze statue stands here. This expansive, traffic-free square, the banks of the river, and old Ljubljana are the places where this lively city is at its most animated. The narrow cobblestone passageways through the medieval quarter and its 19th-century adjuncts evoke a calmer, quieter time. Here students pedal bicycles to and from classes. Along Mestni and Stari trg green hills rise straight up behind the curve of steeply pitched tile roofs.

Exploring Ljubljana

Numbers in the margin correspond to points of interest on the Ljubljana map.

13 **Cankerjevo Nabrežje.** Numerous cafés line this pretty riverside walkway. When the weather is good, tables are placed outside overlooking the water. *Between Tromostovje and Čevljarski Most.*

1 **Centromerkur.** This magnificent Vienna Secessionist–style building, dating from 1903, is the oldest department store in town. The entrance, off Prešernov Trg, bears a flaring iron butterfly-wing portal and is topped by a statue of Mercury. Inside, extraordinarily graceful curved wrought-iron stairways lead to upper floors. ✉ *Trubarjeva 1,* ☎ *01/426–3170.*

14 **Čevljarski Most** (Shoemaker's Bridge). Linking the old and new sides of town, this romantic pedestrian bridge was built in 1931 to plans by the architect Jože Plečnik (1872–1957). The name is derived from an older wooden structure that once stood here and was lined with cobblers' huts. ✉ *Pod Tranco.*

2 **Franciskanska Cerkev** (Franciscan Church). This massive, pink, High Baroque church was built between 1646 and 1660. The main altar, by Francesco Robba (1698–1757), dates from 1736. The three sets of stairs in front are a popular meeting place for students. ✉ *Prešernov Trg 4.* ⏲ *Daily 8–6.*

12 **Gornji trg.** This cobbled street, now home to some of the capital's finest restaurants, rises up above the Old Town and leads to the wooded parkland surrounding the castle. *End of Stari trg leading up toward the castle.*

7 **Grad** (Castle). Ljubljana's castle sits up on a hill and affords magnificent views over the river and the Old Town's terra-cotta rooftops, spires, and green cupolas. On a clear day the distant Julian Alps are a dramatic backdrop. The castle walls date from the early 16th century, while the tower was added in the mid-19th century. The surrounding park was landscaped by Plečnik in the 1930s. The ramparts shelter a café and summer terrace. ✉ *Uphill from Vodnikov trg via Studentovska Ul.,* ☎ *01/432–7216.* ⏲ *Daily 9 AM–11 PM.*

15 **Križanke Poletno Gledališče** (Monastery of the Holy Cross Summer Theater). The annual International Summer Festival and the Jazz Festival are both held in this unusual open-air theater. Set in the court-

yard of an 18th-century monastery, the space was adapted to plans drawn up by the architect Jože Plečnik and completed in 1976 after his death. There is seating for 1,400 and a movable roof in case it rains. ✉ *Trg Francoske Revolucije.*

9 **Magistrat** (Town Hall). Guarded by an austere facade, this building hides delightful secrets within. The walls of the internal courtyard are animated with murals depicting historic battles for the city, and a statue of Hercules keeps company with a fountain bearing a Narcissus figure. ✉ *Mestni trg 1.*

10 **Mestni trg** (Town Square). This cobbled, traffic-free square extends into the oldest part of the city. Colorful Baroque town houses, now divided into functional apartments, present marvelously ornate facades; carved oak doors with great brass handles are framed within columns, and upper-floor levels are decorated with balustrades, statuary, and intricate ironwork. Narrow passageways connect with inner courtyards in one direction and run to the riverfront in the other. Street-level floors contain boutiques, antiques shops, and art galleries. ✉ *Junction of Ciril-Metodov trg, Stritarjeva ul., and Stari trg.*

21 **Moderna Galerija** (Modern Gallery). The strikingly modern one-story structure contains a selection of paintings, sculpture, and prints by Slovenian 20th-century artists. In odd-numbered years it also hosts the International Biennial of Graphics, an exhibit of artwork by leading artists from as far afield as the United States, South America, and Japan. ✉ *Tomšičeva 14,* ☎ *01/251–4106.* ⏲ *Tues.–Sat. 10–6, Sun. 10–1.*

22 **Muzej Novejše Zgodovine** (Museum of Modern History). The permanent exhibition on Slovenes in the 20th century takes you from the days of Austria-Hungary to World War II, through the victory of the Partisan liberation movement and the ensuing Tito period, and up to the present day. Relics and memorabilia are combined with a dramatic sound and video presentation. You'll find the museum in a pink-and-white Baroque villa in Tivoli Park. ✉ *Celovška 23,* ☎ *01/433–8244.* ⏲ *Tues.–Sun. 10–6.*

19 **Narodna Galerija** (National Gallery). The imposing turn-of-the-20th-century building houses a survey of Slovene art from the 13th through the early 20th century. ✉ *Puharjeva 9,* ☎ *01/426–3109.* ⏲ *Tues.–Sat. 10–6, Sun. 10–1.*

18 **Narodni Muzej** (National Museum). A 5th-century BC bronze urn known as the Vace Situle is the centerpiece here. Discovered in Vace, Slovenia, it is a striking example of Illyrian workmanship. ✉ *Prešernova 20,* ☎ *01/241–4400.* ⏲ *Tues.–Sat. 10–6, Sun. 10–1.*

20 **Opera.** This neo-Renaissance palace with an ornate facade topped by an allegorical sculpture group was erected in 1892. The Opera, home to the Slovene National Opera and Ballet Theater, was originally built for the Theater of the County of Carniola during the time when, as part of the Austro-Hungarian Empire under the Habsburgs, Ljubljana was the county's administrative center. ✉ *Župančičeva 1,* ☎ *01/283–1945.* ⏲ *Weekdays 11–1 and 1 hr before performances.*

8 **Robbov Vodnjak** (Robba's Fountain). When the Slovenian Baroque sculptor Francesco Robba saw Bernini's *Fountain of the Four Rivers* on Piazza Navona during a visit to Rome, he was inspired to create this allegorical representation of the three main Kranjska rivers—the Sava, the Krka, and the Ljubljanica—that flow through Slovenia. ✉ *Mestni trg.*

17 **Slovenska Filharmonija** (Slovenian Philharmonic Hall). The hall was built in 1891 for one of the oldest music societies in the world, estab-

lished in 1701. Associates of the orchestra have included Haydn, Brahms, Beethoven, Mahler, and Paganini. ✉ *Kongresni trg 10,* ☎ *01/251–3554.*

⓫ **Stari trg** (Old Square). More a narrow street than a square, Stari trg is lined with cafés and small restaurants; in good weather tables are set out on the cobblestones. ✉ *Between Mestni trg and Gornji trg.*

❹ **Stolnica Sv. Nikolaja** (Cathedral of St. Nicholas). This proud Baroque cathedral overshadows the daily market on Vodnikov Trg. Building took place between 1701 and 1708, and in 1836 the cupola was erected. In 1996, in honor of the pope's visit, new bronze doors were added: the main door tells the story of Christianity in Slovenia, while the side door portrays the history of the Ljubljana Diocese. ✉ *Dolničarjeva 1.* ⏲ *Daily 7–noon and 3–7.*

⓰ **Trg Francoske Revolucije** (French Revolution Square). When Napoléon took Slovenia he made Ljubljana the capital of his "Illyrian Provinces." This square is dominated by Plečnik's **Ilirski Steber** (Illyrian Column), erected in 1929 to commemorate that time. ✉ *Junction of Rimska c. and Vegova c.*

❸ **Tromostovje** (Triple Bridge). This monumental structure spans the River Ljubljanica from Prešernov trg to the Old Town, taking the fortress on 1,233-ft-high Grajski Hrib (Castle Hill) as its backdrop. The three bridges started as a single span, but in 1931 the two graceful outer arched bridges, designed by Plečnik, were added. ✉ *Prešernov trg at north end; Stritarjeva ul. at Cankarjevo nab. at south end.*

❺ **Vodnikov trg** (Vodnik Square). The big and bustling flower, fruit, and vegetable market is held here Monday–Saturday from 7 to 6. An elegant riverside colonnade designed by Plečnik runs the length of the market, and a bronze statue of the Slovene poet Valentin Vodnik, after whom the square is named, overlooks the scene. ✉ *Resleva c. and Poljanska c.*

❻ **Zmajski Most** (Dragon's Bridge). Four fire-breathing winged dragons crown the corners of this spectacular concrete-and-iron structure. ✉ *Resljeva Ul.*

Dining

You can eat well in Ljubljana, but it won't be cheap. The restaurants listed here serve traditional Slovenian dishes. Foreign restaurants are increasing in number: Italian, Chinese, and Mexican predominate. For a lunchtime snack visit the Vodnikov market. Choose from tasty fried squid and whitebait in the riverside arcade by the fish section or freshly baked pies and cakes at the bakeries on the square.

$$$–$$$$ ✕ **AS.** Now probably the best restaurant in town, AS has a refined menu, impeccable service, and excellent wines. House specialties are seafood and pasta. The ambience is old-fashioned, but the dishes are creative and modern. If you're reluctant to leave, move on to the after-hours bar in the basement. ✉ *Knafljev Prehod,* ☎ *01/425–8822. AE, DC, MC, V.*

$$$–$$$$ ✕ **Spajza.** On Gornji trg, on the way to the castle, you'll find a restaurant with a series of romantic candlelit rooms and bohemian decor. The menu includes venison in cognac sauce with wild asparagus, risotto with porcini mushrooms, and scampi, as well as an inspired selection of salads. They do a great tiramisu. ✉ *Gornji trg 28,* ☎ *01/425–3094. AE, DC, MC, V. Closed Sun.*

$$$ ✕ **Pri sv. Florijanu.** This recently opened restaurant serves up a new generation of Slovenian cuisine. Try the chicken breast with coriander and grilled vegetables, accompanied by an arugula and Parmesan salad. The minimalist interior and background jazz attract a young crowd. ✉ *Gornji trg 20,* ☎ *01/251–2214. AE, DC, MC, V.*

$$–$$$ ✕ **Rotovz.** In the Old Quarter, this restaurant has streetside tables with umbrellas in summer and serves meals in the dark wood interior in colder weather. Order *pastrmka* (trout) with parsley potatoes or a frogs'-leg specialty, along with crisp salad and a bottle of first-rate Slovenian wine. ✉ *Mestni trg 2,* ☎ *01/251–2839. AE, DC, MC, V. Closed Sun.*

$–$$ ✕ **Pivnica Kratchowill.** First and foremost a microbrewery, Kratchowill also serves good food. The interior is modern, but the food is classic: beer sausage and sauerkraut, game dishes, tasty pastas, and a salad bar. The beer is brewed according to old Czech recipes. ✉ *Kolodvorska 14,* ☎ *01/433–3114. AE, DC, MC, V.*

$–$$ ✕ **Zlata Ribica.** This popular bar and bistro is frequented by boisterous stall holders and antiques buffs from the Sunday flea market. The sound menu includes black pudding, squid, and mushroom omelet. In winter, locals enjoy mulled wine here. ✉ *Cankarjevo nab. 5,* ☎ *01/241–0690. AE, DC, MC, V. No dinner weekends.*

Lodging

The hotels listed here are clustered conveniently around Miklošičeva cesta, the main axis running from the train station down to the Triple Bridge. Ljubljana is expensive, but standards are high. In summer you can opt for private accommodation or university dorms for better deals; ask at the **TIC** kiosk (☎ 01/433–9475) in the train station.

$$$–$$$$ **Best Western Slon Hotel.** Close to the river, this hotel on the site of a famous 16th-century inn maintains an atmosphere of traditional hospitality. The breakfast here is among the finest in the city. The rooms are comfortable but not special. ✉ *Slovenska 34, 1000,* ☎ *01/470–1100,* FAX *01/251–7164,* WEB *www.h-slon-bw.si. 185 rooms. 2 restaurants. AE, DC, MC, V.*

$$$–$$$$ **Grand Hotel Union.** This turn-of-the-20th-century hotel occupies a magnificent Jugendstil structure. All facilities have been modernized with great care: decor and furnishings remain typically "Old Vienna." ✉ *Miklošičeva 1, 1000,* ☎ *01/308–1270,* FAX *01/308–1015,* WEB *www.gh-union.si. 233 rooms, 6 suites. 2 restaurants. AE, DC, MC, V.*

$$ **Hotel Turist.** The rooms are basic, but this hotel has the only budget accommodations within the city center and close to the train station. ✉ *Dalmatinova 15, 1000,* ☎ *01/432–2343,* FAX *01/231–9291. 190 rooms. Restaurant. AE, DC, MC, V.*

$$ **Pension Mrak.** Recently reopened after a thorough face-lift, Pension Mrak now offers simple but comfortable rooms and a decent restaurant. It is situated on a quiet side street, close to the Križanke summer theater. ✉ *Rimska 4, 1000,* ☎ *01/421–9600,* FAX *01/421–9655. 30 rooms. Restaurant. AE, DC, MC, V.*

Nightlife and the Arts

The Arts

Ljubljana's **International Summer Festival** (✉ Trg Francoske Revolucije 1–2, ☎ 01/426–4340), running through July and August, is held in Plečnik's open-air Križanke theater. Musical, theatrical, and dance performances attract acclaimed artists from all over the world.

The **Jazz Festival** runs through June. ✉ *Box Office: Cankarjev Dom, Prešernova 10,* ☎ *01/425–8121.*

Nightlife

While Ljubljana University keeps the cultural scene alive, Slovenes old and young alike enjoy music and a few drinks. The nightclubs listed here are all well established and within walking distance of the center. **Club Central** (✉ Dalmatinova 15, ☎ 01/252–1292) stays open until 5 AM, later than any other club in town. The best long-standing nightclub in town is **Eldorado** (✉ Nazorjeva 6, ☎ 01/426–2126). **Jazz Club Gajo** (✉ Beethovnova 8, ☎ 01/425–3206) attracts jazz stars from the United States and Europe: Clark Terry, Sheila Jordan, and Woody Shaw have played here. **K4** (✉ Kersnikova 4, ☎ 01/431–7010), a student-run nightclub attached to the university, is something of an institution, attracting a young and lively crowd.

Shopping

The Sunday-morning flea market is held on Cankarjevo nabrežje, near the Triple Bridge.

Ljubljana Essentials

AIR TRAVEL TO AND FROM LJUBLJANA

Ljubljana's airport is at Brnik, 22 km (14 mi) north of the city. A shuttle bus runs between the airport and Ljubljana and other nearby destinations.

➤ AIRPORTS AND CONTACTS: **Brnik Airport** (☎ 04/206–1981).

BUS TRAVEL WITHIN LJUBLJANA

Tokens are sold at kiosks and post offices. As you board the bus, drop your token into the box by the driver. The cost is a little higher if you pay in change. During the day, buses operate every half hour and cover an extensive network; at night they are less frequent.

CONSULATES

➤ AUSTRALIA: (✉ Trg Republike 3/XII, ☎ 01/425–4252, FAX 01/426–4721).

EMERGENCIES

➤ DOCTORS: **Ljubljana Emergency Medical Services** (☎ 01/232–3060).

➤ EMERGENCY SERVICES: **Ambulance, fire brigade** (☎ 112); **Police** (☎ 113).

➤ 24-HOUR PHARMACIES: **Lekarna Miklošič** (✉ Miklošičeva 24, ☎ 01/231–4558).

ENGLISH-LANGUAGE MEDIA

MK Knjigarna Konzorcij has a good selection of English books and magazines on the upper floor.

➤ BOOKSTORES: **MK Knjigarna Konzorcij** (✉ Slovenska 29, ☎ 01/425–0196).

TAXIS

Private taxis operate 24 hours a day. Telephone from your hotel or hail one in the street. Drivers are bound by law to display and run a meter.

➤ TAXI COMPANIES: **Private taxis** (☎ 01/9700 through 01/9709).

TOURS

Informative and amusing sightseeing walks, organized by Ljubljana Promotion Center, depart from the Magistrat (Town Hall) June–September, daily at 5; October–May, Sunday at 11.

➤ FEES AND SCHEDULES: **Magistrat** (Town Hall; ✉ Mestni trg 1).

TRAIN TRAVEL

The train station, close to the city center, has a tourist office to help travelers find accommodations in hotels, pensions, and apartments.

➤ TRAIN INFORMATION: **Train station** (✉ Trg OF 6, ☎ 01/291–2524).

VISITOR INFORMATION

➤ TOURIST INFORMATION: **Turistično Informacijski Center** (Tourist Information Center [TIC]; ✉ Stritarjeva, ☎ 01/306–1215, WEB www.ljubljana.si).

TRIGLAV NATIONAL PARK AND THE SOČA VALLEY

Northwest of Ljubljana lies a region of mountain and lakeside resorts complete with thermal springs, ski trails, and historic religious shrines. The Julian Alps, lying at the junction of the borders of Italy, Austria, and Slovenia, are contained within Triglav National Park. Lake Bohinj and the small waterside settlement of Ribčev Laz are also within the national park, though Lake Bled and the town of Bled lie just outside the park's boundary. The Alpine village of Kranjska Gora is situated on the rim of the park. The Soča River begins within the park, then flows southwest to form the beautiful Soča Valley. The river passes through Kobarid and snakes south before crossing over into Italy (where it's known as the Isonzo). The region has unspoiled countryside and magnificent mountain walks, many on well-marked trails. Local tourist information centers can supply maps and further details.

Bled

Bled, 50 km (31 mi) northwest of Ljubljana, is among the most magnificently situated mountain resorts in Europe. The healing powers of its thermal springs were known during the 17th century; in the early 19th century the aristocracy arrived to bask in Bled's tranquil Alpine setting. Since the mid-1970s a spate of new hotels and a wide range of recreational facilities have sprung up here; facilities for rowing, hiking, swimming, boating, biking, tennis, and horseback riding are available. In winter there's skiing and ice-skating at the nearby high-altitude resort of Zatrnik.

Blejsko Jezero (Lake Bled), surrounded by forests, is nestled within a circle of mountains, with a castle on one side and a promenade beneath stately chestnut trees on the other. Horse-drawn carriages clip-clop along the promenade while swans glide on the water. On a minuscule island in the lake the lovely **Cerkov Svetega Martina** (St. Martin's Pilgrimage Church) rises from within a circle of red roofs and trees. Graceful, old-fashioned canopied wooden boats called *pletna,* propelled by oarsmen standing aft, carry passengers to the island.

The stately 16th-century **Grad** (Castle) perches above the lake at the summit of a steep cliff, against the backdrop of the Julian Alps and Mt. Triglav. You can climb up to the castle for fine views of the lake, the resort, and the surrounding countryside. Inside is an exhibit tracing the development of the castle through the centuries. Objects on display range from archaeological finds to period furniture. ☎ *04/574–1230.* ⏲ *Mar.–Oct., daily 8–7; Nov.–Feb., daily 9–4.*

The **Vintgar Gorge** was cut between precipitous cliffs by the clear river Radovna, which flows over numerous waterfalls and through pools and rapids. A signed path up the gorge leads over bridges and along wooden walkways and galleries. ✉ *5 km (3 mi) northeast of Bled on road to Pokljuka/Zg. Gorje.*

$$ ✕ **Gostilna Lectar.** At this restaurant with a cozy country-inn atmosphere, you can choose from an impressive array of Slovenian national dishes and wines. Try the pumpkin soup, the "peasant's plate" (buckwheat dumplings, mixed smoked meats, potatoes, and fresh steamed vegetables), and the apple strudel for a cross section of local cuisine. ✉ *Linhartov Trg 2, Radovljica, 9 km (5½ mi) south of Bled on Rte. E61,* ☎ *04/537–4800. AE, DC, MC, V.*

$–$$ ✕ **Gostilna pri Planincu.** This friendly joint is busy year-round. Locals meet here to enjoy morning coffee or a bargain set-menu lunch, or just to drink the cheapest beer in town. While rowdy farmers occupy the front bar, lovers share a candlelit supper in the dining room. Portions are "for people who work all day": roast chicken and chips, steak and mushrooms, black pudding and turnip. Walnut *štrukle* (dumplings) are served with cream. ✉ *Grajska 8,* ☎ *04/574–1613. AE, DC, MC, V.*

$$$$ **Vila Bled.** Yugoslavia's late president Tito used this former royal residence on the lake as a hunting lodge. It was converted into a luxurious small-scale hotel in 1984. Among the elegant touches are hand-embroidered linen sheets, Art Deco furnishings, antique rugs, Oriental vases, and original art. ✉ *C. Svobode 26, 4260,* ☎ *04/579–1500,* FAX *04/574–1320. 10 rooms, 20 suites. Restaurant. AE, DC, MC, V.*

$$–$$$$ **Grand Hotel Toplice.** This elegant, old-fashioned, ivy-covered resort hotel has been favored by British visitors since the 1920s. Directly on the lake, the main building has balconies and big windows that offer dramatic views of the castle and the Julian Alps. The rooms, the lounges, and the bar are all furnished with antiques and heirloom rugs. ✉ *C. Svobode 20, 4260,* ☎ *04/579–1000,* FAX *04/574–1841. 206 rooms. Restaurant, pool. AE, DC, MC, V.*

$ **Bledec Youth Hostel.** Just 5 minutes from the lake and 10 minutes from the castle, Bledec is one of the cleanest and most comfortable youth hostels in Europe. ✉ *Grajska c. 17, 4260,* ☎ *04/574–5250. 13 rooms. Restaurant. MC. Closed Nov.*

Bohinjsko Jezero

A 26-km (16-mi) drive west from Bled will take you to Bohinjsko Jezero (Lake Bohinj) in Triglavski Narodni Park (Triglav National Park). In a valley surrounded by the steep walls of the Julian Alps, at an altitude of 1,715 ft, this deep-blue, 4½-km-long (3-mi-long) lake is even more dramatically situated than Bled and not nearly as developed.

At the lakeside, the small, exquisite 15th-century Gothic church of **Sveti Janez** (St. John), with a fine bell tower, contains a number of notable 15th- and 16th-century frescoes.

At the west end of the lake a cable car leads up **Mt. Vogel** to a height of 5,035 ft. Here you have spectacular views of the Julian Alps massif and the Bohinj Valley and lake. From the cable-car base the road continues 5 km (3 mi) beyond the lake to the point where the waters of the Savica make a tremendous leap over a 195-ft waterfall.

$$ **Hotel Bellevue.** As the name suggests, Bellevue affords wonderful views down over the lake. Agatha Christie fell in love with this old-fashioned hotel and stayed a month here while working on *Murder on the Orient Express.* ✉ *Ribčev Laz 65, 4265,* ☎ *04/572–3331,* FAX *04/572–3684. 76 rooms. AE, DC, MC, V.*

Kranjska Gora

Kranjska Gora, 39 km (24 mi) northwest of Bled, is one of the largest winter tourist centers in Slovenia, in the dramatic setting of some of the country's highest peaks. In summer the resort caters mainly to hiking and mountaineering enthusiasts.

From Kranjska Gora head south over the **Vršič Pass,** 5,252 ft above sea level. You'll then descend into the beautiful Soča Valley, winding through the foothills to the west of Triglav Peak and occasionally plunging through tunnels.

Kobarid

Along the magnificent turquoise-color Soča River, running parallel to the Italian border, is the pretty market town of Kobarid, 41 km (25 mi) from Kranjska Gora.

In the center of town the **Kobariški muzej** (Kobarid Museum) gives a 20-minute presentation of the tragic fighting that took place here during World War I, as recorded in Hemingway's *A Farewell to Arms.* ✉ *Gregorčičeva 10,* ☎ *05/389–0000.* ⏲ *Daily 9–7.*

$$ **Hotel Hvala.** This delightful family-run hotel might be one of the most welcoming places you'll ever stay in. The hotel restaurant, **Restauracija Topli Val**, serves local trout and freshwater crayfish, as well as mushrooms and truffles in season. Italians drive over the border just to eat here. ✉ *Trg Svobode 1, 5222,* ☎ *05/389–9300,* FAX *05/388–5322. 28 rooms, 4 suites. Restaurant. AE, DC, MC, V.*

Triglav National Park and the Soča Valley Essentials

BIKE TRAVEL

You can rent mountain bikes at Bohinjsko Jezero through Alpinum.
➤ Bike Rentals: **Alpinum** (✉ Ribčev Laz 50, ☎ 04/572–3441).

BUS TRAVEL

Hourly buses link Ljubljana to Bled, Bohinjsko Jezero, and Kranjska Gora. There are several buses daily from Ljubljana to Kobarid.

CAR TRAVEL

From Ljubljana a toll road (E63) runs 42 km (26 mi) northwest past Kranj; from there road E651 leads to the resorts of Bled and Kranjska Gora.

TOURS

Alpinum organizes guided mountain-hiking and climbing tours in Triglav National Park, as well as rafting and kayaking trips down the Soča River. Slovenijaturist arranges a trip on a steam locomotive, following the Bohinj line, which runs through the Soča Valley, operating every Thursday mid-June to mid-September.
➤ Fees & Schedules: **Alpinum** (☎ 04/572–3441). **Slovenijaturist** (☎ 01/234–4829).

VISITOR INFORMATION

➤ Tourist Information: **Bled** (✉ C. Svobode 15, 4260 Bled, ☎ 04/574–1122, WEB www.bled.si). **Bohinjsko Jezero** (✉ Ribčev Laz 48, 4265 Bohinjsko Jezero, ☎ 04/572–3370, WEB www.bohinj.si). **Kobarid** (✉ Gregorčičeva 10, 5222 Kobarid, ☎ 05/388–5055). **Kranjska Gora** (✉ Tičarjeva 2, 4280 Kranjska Gora, ☎ 04/588–1768, WEB www.kranjska-gora.si).

ADRIATIC COAST AND KARST HINTERLAND

Adriatic Coast

Backed by hills planted with olive groves and vineyards, this tiny strip of coast, only 42 km (26 mi) long, is dominated by the towns of Koper,

Piran, and Portorož. Following centuries under the Republic of Venice, the region remains culturally and spiritually connected to Italy. The best Venetian architecture of the area can still be seen in the delightful medieval town of Piran. Portorož is a more commercial resort, while Koper is Slovenia's largest port.

Piran

The jewel of the Slovenian coast, the medieval walled Venetian town of Piran stands compact on a small peninsula, capped by a neo-Gothic lighthouse and presided over by a hilltop Romanesque cathedral. Narrow, winding, cobbled streets lead to the main square, Trg Tartini, which in turn opens out onto a charming harbor.

$$ **Hotel Tartini.** The old facade hides a modern interior with a spacious central atrium. The rooms are well furnished and comfortable. The location, overlooking the oval Trg Tartini, is out of this world. ✉ *Trg Tartini 15, 6330,* ☎ *05/671–1000,* FAX *05/671–1665. 43 rooms, 2 suites. Restaurant. AE, DC, MC, V.*

Portorož

Known for its thermal spas, Portorož has a pleasant Mediterranean climate. Its location on a south-facing slope keeps the city warm and blocks cold northern air even in winter. In summer vacationers fill the town in pursuit of the pleasures of the sea and the healing spas.

$$$$ ✕ **Ribič.** Situated 2 km (1 mi) down the coast at Seča, Ribič may just be the best fish restaurant in the area. Specialities include baked sea bass with porcini mushrooms, and risotto Alpe Adria, which combines wild mushrooms from the Alps and fresh scampi from the Adriatic. In summer you can eat in the garden. ✉ *Seča,* ☎ *05/677–0790. AE, DC, MC, V. Closed Tues.*

$$–$$$ **Hotel Palace.** At this modern hotel resort complex the elegant thermal spa center offers massages and medical treatments. Rooms are comfortable and service professional. ✉ *Obala 45, 6320,* ☎ *05/696–9001,* FAX *05/696–9003. 150 rooms. Restaurant, 1 outdoor and 1 indoor pool. AE, DC, MC, V.*

Karst Hinterland

The name of this limestone plateau between Ljubljana and the coast is the source of the word "karst," which describes a geological phenomenon whose typical features include sinkholes, underground caves, and streams.

Postojnska Jama

Postojnska Jama (Postojna Cave) is one of the largest networks of caves in the world, with 23 km (14 mi) of underground passageways. A miniature train takes you through the first 7 km (4½ mi) to reveal a succession of well-lit rock formations. This strange underground world is home of the snakelike "human fish," on view in an aquarium in the Great Hall. Eyeless and colorless because of countless millennia of life in total darkness, these amphibians can live for up to 60 years. Temperatures average 8°C (46°F) year-round, so in summer rent a woolen cloak at the entrance. Tours leave every half hour in summer, hourly the rest of the year. ✉ *Jamska c. 30, Postojna,* ☎ *05/700–0100.* ⏲ *May–Sept., daily 8:30–6; Apr. and Oct., daily 8:30–5; Nov.–Mar., weekdays 9:30–1:30, weekends 9:30–3.*

Škocjanske Jame

The Škocjanske Jame (Škocjan Caves) at Matavun, near Divača, are on UNESCO's list of World Natural and Cultural Heritage sites. These caves require walking, but the beauty of the caverns makes the effort worthwhile. Here, the Reka River thunders along an underground channel, amid a wondrous world of stalactites and stalagmites. One-hour tours leave hourly. ✉ *Matavun 12, 6215 Divača,* ☎ *05/763–0122.* ⏲ *June–Sept., daily 10–6; Apr.–May and Oct., tours daily at 10, 1, and 5; Nov.–Mar., tours weekdays at 10, weekends at 10 and 3.*

Lipica

The **Kobilarna Lipica** (Lipica Stud Farm) in Sežana is the birthplace of the Lipizzaner white horses. Founded in 1580 by the Austrian archduke Karl II, the farm still supplies Lipizzaners to the Spanish Riding School in Vienna. Lipica has developed into a modern sports complex, with two hotels, an indoor riding arena, a swimming pool, and a golf course. The stables are open to the public, and riding classes are available. ✉ *Lipica 5, 6210 Sežana,* ☎ *05/739–1580.* ⏲ *Stables, July–Aug., daily 9–6; Apr.–June and Sept.–Oct., daily 10–5; Nov.–Mar., daily 11–3. Dressage performances Apr.–Oct., Fri. and Sun. at 3.*

Adriatic Coast and Karst Hinterland Essentials

BOAT AND FERRY TRAVEL

See Boat and Ferry Travel *in* Slovenia A to Z, *above.*

BUS TRAVEL

Buses connect the region to Ljubljana and to Trieste in Italy. For information contact Lucija Bus Station, which serves Portorož and the coast.

➤ BUS INFORMATION: **Lucija Bus Station** (☎ 05/677–0468).

CAR TRAVEL

A drive of 52 km (32 mi) west from Ljubljana on the toll road (marked A-10) will bring you to the Karst region; 125 km (78 mi) southwest of Ljubljana (via the A-10) lies the Adriatic Coast.

TRAIN TRAVEL

All trains from Ljubljana to Venice pass through the Karst region, stopping at Postojna, Divača, and Sežana. A train from Ljubljana to Koper serves the coast.

VISITOR INFORMATION

Along the coast, private lodgings provide a cheap alternative to hotels. Owners usually live on the ground floor and let rooms or apartments upstairs. Contact local tourist information centers for details.

➤ TOURIST INFORMATION: **Lipica** (✉ Lipica 5, ☎ 05/739–1580). **Piran** (✉ Trg Tartini 2, ☎ 05/674–8260). **Portorož** (✉ Obala 16, ☎ 05/674–0231). **Postojna** (✉ Jamska c. 30, ☎ 05/728–0788).

MARIBOR AND PTUJ

During the 1st century AD, Poetovio, now known as Ptuj, was the largest Roman settlement in the region. Much later, in the 13th century, Maribor was founded. Originally given the German name Marchburg, the city took its Slavic name in 1836. For centuries the two towns competed for economic and cultural prominence, with Maribor finally gaining the lead in 1846, when a new railway line connected the city to Vienna and Trieste.

Maribor

More geared toward business travelers than tourists, Maribor is Slovenia's second largest city. However, the Old Town has retained a core of ornate 18th- and 19th-century town houses, typical of imperial Austria, and is worth a visit. The heart of the Old Town is **Rotovški**

trg, with the Kužno Znamenje (Plague Memorial) at its center and overlooked by the proud 16th-century Renaissance Rotovž (Town Hall).

From Rotovški trg, a number of traffic-free streets lead down to a riverside promenade, known as **Lent.** It is lined with bars, terrace cafés, restaurants, and boutiques.

A little way upstream from the riverside promenade, an old vine, **Stara Trta,** carefully trained along the facade of a former inn, is believed to date back to the 16th century and thus to be the oldest continuously producing vine in Europe. ✉ *Vojasniska 8.*

The **Vodni Stolp** (Water Tower), a former defense tower, houses the Vinoteka Slovenskih Vin (Slovenian Wine Shop). Here you can sample and purchase more than 500 different Slovenian vintages. ✉ *Usnjarska 10,* ☎ *02/251–7743.*

The **Grad** (castle) has Renaissance and Baroque elements grafted onto its original Gothic core, built in 1478. The castle houses the Pokrajinski Muzej (Regional Museum), with regional costumes and uniforms, Roman relics, an art gallery, and a collection of arms and armor. The main salon, where Franz Liszt (1811–86) gave recitals, is decorated with frescoes and ceiling paintings. ✉ *Grajska ul. 2,* ☎ *02/228–3551.* ⏲ *Mid-Apr.–Nov., Tues.–Sat. 9–5, Sun. 10–2.*

$$ ✕ **Toti Rotovž.** Close to the Town Hall and Plague Memorial, this building has been carefully restored to reveal vaulted brick ceilings and terra-cotta floors. The ground-level restaurant serves typical Slovenian dishes, while the *klet* (wine cellar) in the basement cooks up barbecued steaks. ✉ *Glavni trg 14,* ☎ *02/228–7650. AE, DC, MC, V.*

$$–$$$$ 🏨 **Hotel Orel.** The four-story prewar building on the main square has a pleasant restaurant at street level. The rooms are acceptable, and the service is friendly. ✉ *Grajski trg 3a, 2000,* ☎ *02/250–6700,* FAX *02/251–8497. 146 rooms, 7 suites. Restaurant. AE, DC, MC, V.*

Ptuj

Ptuj, built beside the Drava River and crowned by a hilltop castle, hits the national news each year in February with its extraordinary carnival celebration, known as Kurentovanje. South of Ptuj lie the rolling hills of Haloze, famous for quality white wines.

Ptujski Grad (Ptuj Castle) stands at the top of a steep hill in the center of town. Planned around a Baroque courtyard, the castle houses a museum that exhibits musical instruments, an armory, 15th-century paintings, and period furniture. ✉ *Grajska Raven,* ☎ *02/771–3081.* ⏲ *Summer, daily 9–6; winter, daily 9–4.*

★ **Vinska Klet** (Ptuj Wine Cellars) offers a tasting session with five different wines, bread, and cheese, plus a bottle to take home. You are also given a tour of the underground cellars, and a sound and video presentation takes you through the seasons of wine-making at the vineyards. The wines stocked here come predominantly from the Haloze Hills. ✉ *Trstenjakova 6,* ☎ *02/787–9810.* ⏲ *Daily 8–6; tasting sessions Fri., Sat., and Sun. 11 AM (daily for groups, but call first).*

Maribor and Ptuj Essentials

AIR TRAVEL

➤ AIRLINES AND CONTACTS: **Maribor Airport** (☎ 02/629–1790).

CAR TRAVEL

To reach Maribor from Ljubljana take the E57; to reach Ptuj turn off at Slovenska Bistrica.

TRAIN TRAVEL

Regular service links Ljubljana and Maribor; several international trains continue to Graz and Vienna. Change at Pragersko for Ptuj. For information contact Maribor Train Station.

➤ TRAIN INFORMATION: **Maribor Train Station** (☎ 02/292–2100).

VISITOR INFORMATION

In summer, Maribor university dorms are open to visitors, offering a cheap alternative to hotels. Ask at the tourist information center for details.

➤ TOURIST INFORMATION: **Maribor** (✉ Partizanska 47, ☎ 02/251–1262, WEB www.maribor.si). **Ptuj** (✉ Slovenski trg 14, ☎ 02/787–6230).

28 SPAIN

MADRID, CASTILE, BARCELONA, ANDALUSIA, COSTA DEL SOL AND GIBRALTAR

MUCH MORE THAN flamenco, bullfights, and white hillside villages, modern Spain packs everything from space-age art museums to quaint fishing villages, green highland valleys, soaring cathedrals, medieval towns, designer cuisine, spirited nightlife, and an immense treasury of painting and sculpture.

As most natives are quick to point out, Spain is really several countries in one, each with its own proud character, its own distinctive cuisine, even its own language. Andalusia, in the south, comes closest to postcard images of Spain: rolling hills dotted with whitewashed villages and olive trees. Andalusia's capital, Seville, is known for flamenco music and dance; for the girls dressed in ruffled polka-dot dresses at its April Fair; and for the solemn processions of penitents during Semana Santa (Holy Week). The region is also marked by its Moorish heritage, and remnants of its Islamic past abound, from the red-and-white striped arches of Córdoba's mosque to Spain's most important monument, Granada's Alhambra Palace. Andalusia is known more for tapas than for gourmet cuisine; provincial specialties include mounds of fried fish and shellfish called *frituras,* olives, cured ham, and the sherries of Jerez. On the Andalusian coast, the famed Costa del Sol, you can join the jet set at Marbella.

Spain's vast center is still shaped by its role as a battlefield for centuries of contests between Moorish and Christian armies. Turreted castles overlook the bleak plains of Castile–La Mancha, the land of Don Quixote, and Castile–León, once known as Old Castile. Castile is home to Toledo, where Jews, Moors, and Christians lived and worked together before the Christian Reconquest of the 15th century; and medieval jewels such as Segovia, the university city of Salamanca, and the fortress town of Ávila. The people of Castile are as simple, warm, and hearty as their cuisine—huge portions of roast lamb or suckling pig accompanied by powerful red wines from the Valdepeñas or Ribera del Duero region.

At the hub of it all is Madrid, one of the liveliest capitals in Europe. Madrid is the seat of the Spanish government, a center for the national media, and the home of dozens of embassies, but its sophistication is largely a veneer. Scratch the surface, and beyond Madrid's designer boutiques and chic restaurants you'll find a simple Castilian town. Life here is lived in cafés and rustic taverns; all it takes to become a local is to duck inside.

Madrid is also a magnet for art lovers, with three world-class museums—the Prado, the Reina Sofía, and the Thyssen-Bornemisza—all along a 1-km (½-mi) stretch of leafy promenade. The city's restaurants serve fine cuisine from all of Spain's regions but are probably best known for their seafood, which arrives daily from the coasts and has earned landlocked Madrid an affectionate reputation as Spain's first port.

Catalonia—with a population of 6 million Catalan speakers—is Spain's richest and most industrial region. Its capital, Barcelona, rivals Madrid for power and is generally regarded as the winner in culture and style. Barcelona's tree-lined streets, Art Nouveau architecture, and renovated waterfront still gleam from the scouring they received for the 1992 Summer Olympics—an event that not only focused the world's attention on this Mediterranean port but also provided the city with new museums, sports facilities, and restaurants. The spirit of modernist architect Antoni Gaudí lives on both in his Sagrada Família church, which is still unfinished, and in the Catalan passion for radical, playful design.

Since Franco died in 1975, and since the country joined the European Union (EU) in 1986, Spain has been forced to modernize. The most obvious improvements for the traveler are the fast new nationwide network of superhighways and the high-speed AVE train linking Seville and Córdoba to Madrid (and soon with Barcelona). Happily, though, Spain's uniqueness has not been tossed aside. Real siestas are on the wane these days, but shops still close at midday, and three-hour lunches are commonplace. Young adults still live with their parents until marriage. Bullfights continue despite protests from animal-rights activists. And flamenco is making a comeback.

Most exciting for anyone vacationing in Spain is the nationwide insistence on enjoying life. Whether that means strolling in the park with the family on a Sunday afternoon, lingering over a weekday lunch, or socializing with friends until dawn, a zest for living life to its fullest is Spain's greatest contribution to Europe.

SPAIN A TO Z

ADDRESSES

In addresses, the word *Calle* (street) is abbreviated C.

AIR TRAVEL

Domestic airfares are high by U.S. standards, although deregulation is pushing prices lower. A frequent shuttle service connects Madrid and Barcelona.

CARRIERS

Iberia and its subsidiary Aviaco operate a wide network of domestic flights, linking Spain's major cities and the Balearic Islands. Iberia has its own offices in most major Spanish cities and acts as agent for Aviaco. You can also book flights at most travel agencies. Air Europa offers slightly cheaper service on domestic flights. Spanair is another Spanish domestic airline offering good regional rates. For information on other airlines' flights to and within Spain, call the airline itself, or call the Madrid airport and ask for the airline.

➤ AIRLINES AND CONTACTS: **Air Europa** (☎ 902/401501, WEB www.air-europa.com). **Iberia** (Velázquez 130, Madrid, ☎ 902/400500, WEB www.iberia.com). **Madrid-Barajas Airport** (☎ 91/305–8343 through 91/305–8346). **Spanair** (☎ 902/131415, WEB www.spainair.com).

BUS TRAVEL

Spain has an excellent bus network. There is no national or nationwide bus company, but Enatcar is a consortium of individual, regional bus companies which together cover most of the country. There are

Spain (España)

Bay of Biscay
Ferrol
A Coruña
Vilalba
Ribadeo
Luarca
Gijón
Ribadesella
Santander
Oviedo
Cangas de Onís
Mieres
Santiago de Compostela
Lugo
CANTABRIAN MTS.
PICOS DE EUROPA
Bilbao
Muros
Ponferrada
León
Pontevedra
Vigo
Orense
Astorga
Burgos
Tui
Benavente
Palencia
Valladolid
Duero
Zamora
Tordesillas
Salamanca
Adanero
Segovia
SIERRA DE GUADA
Ávila
Guada
Ciudad Rodrigo
El Escorial
MADRID
PORTUGAL
SIERRA DE GREDOS
Toledo
Plasencia
Talavera de la Reina
Aranjuez
Tajo
Guadalupe
Alcázar San Jua
Cáceres
Trujillo
Guadiana
Mérida
Ciudad Real
Abenójar
Valdepeñas
Badajoz
Almadén
Jerez de los Caballeros
Zafra
Fregenal de la Sierra
SIERRA MORENA
Bailén
Linares
Córdoba
Baeza
Aroche
Jaén
Guadalquivir
Seville
Ecija
Baena
Carmona
Guadix
Huelva
Lucena
Granada
Loja
Sanlúcar de Barrameda
Antequera
COSTA DE LA LUZ
Ronda
Nerja
Torremolinos
Málaga
Motril
Cádiz
Jerez de la Frontera
Estepona
Fuengirola
Marbella
ATLANTIC OCEAN
COSTA DEL SOL
Algeciras
Gibraltar
TO CANARY ISLANDS
Straits of Gibraltar

FRANCE
San Sebastián
Hondarribia
Roncesvalles
Vitoria
Pamplona
ANDORRA
Jaca
PYRENEES
Seu d'Urgell
Figueras
oño
Huesca
Tudela
Barbastro
Gerona
Ebro
Vic
Soria
Manresa
Zaragoza
Lérida
Montserrat
COSTA BRAVA
Calatayud
Barcelona
Medinaceli
Daroca
Alcañiz
Tarragona
Caminreal
COSTA DORADA
Tajo
Monreal del Campo
Tortosa
La Jana
Vinaròs
Balearic Sea
TO MENORCA
Teruel
COSTA DEL AZAHAR
Cuenca
Castellón de la Plana
Palma
Sagunto
Majorca
Requena
Valencia
Jucar
Ibiza
Albacete
BALEARIC ISLANDS
Eivissa
Formentera
Alcaraz
Hellín
COSTA BLANCA
Alicante
Menorca
Segura
Elche
Ciutadella
Mahón
Orihuela
Murcia
Lorca
Manga del Mar Menor
Cartagena
NEVADA
COSTA CALIDA
Mediterranean Sea
Almería
COSTA DE ALMERIA
ALGERIA
N
0
100 miles
0
150 km

also numerous local companies. Buses tend to be more frequent than trains, are sometimes cheaper, and often allow you to see more of the countryside. Some of those on major routes are now quite luxurious; but although they designate no-smoking seats, it's hard to cordon smoke in a bus, so you may be in for a smokier ride than you're used to. On major routes and at holiday times, buy your ticket a day or two in advance. Some cities have central bus stations, but in many of these, including Madrid and Barcelona, buses leave from various boarding points; always check with the local tourist office. Unlike train stations, bus stations usually have facilities for luggage storage.

➤ BUS INFORMATION: **Enatcar** (✉ main office Estación Sur de Autobuses, Calle Méndez Álvaro, Madrid, ☎ 91/754–9950).

BUSINESS HOURS

Banks are open Monday–Saturday 8:30 or 9 to 2 or 2:30 from October through June; in summer they are closed on Saturday. Hours for museums and churches vary; most are open in the morning, but most museums close one day a week, often Monday. Stores are open weekdays from 9 or 10 until 1:30 or 2, then in the afternoon from around 5 to 8. Larger department stores and supermarkets do not close at midday. In some cities, especially in summer, stores close on Saturday afternoon.

CAR TRAVEL

GASOLINE

All rental cars use unleaded gas (*sin plomo*). Gas costs about 150 ptas./€0.90 per liter for super (98 octane) and 135 ptas./€0.81 per liter for regular (95 octane). Many stations are self-service, though prices are the same as those at full-service stations, and there's no need to tip for a simple fill-up. You punch in the amount of gas you want (by price, not in liters), unhook the nozzle, pump the gas, and then pay. At night, however, you must pay before you fill up. Most gas stations accept credit cards.

PARKING

Check locally for parking restrictions. A yellow line along the curb indicates a no-parking zone. Blue markings in the street indicate a metered parking area. Look for the nearest meter, insert coins to cover the time you plan to park, and place the receipt in a visible spot inside the windshield. Beware of parking in no-parking zones or in areas where parking is allowed for residents only; cars are towed promptly. Thefts are common, so it's safer to leave your car in one of the many staffed parking lots; charges are reasonable.

ROAD CONDITIONS

Roads marked *A* are four-lane highways, which can be either toll roads (*autopista*) or freeways (*autovía*). *N* stands for national or main roads and C for country roads. Spain's huge road-improvement scheme has been largely completed, but many N roads are still single-lane, and the going can be slow. Tolls vary but are high.

RULES OF THE ROAD

Spaniards drive on the right. The use of horns and high-beam headlights is forbidden in cities. Front seat belts are compulsory; children under age 10 may not ride in front seats. At traffic circles, cars already in the circle have right of way. Your home driver's license is essential and must be carried with you at all times, along with your insurance card and vehicle registration. If you are bringing your own car into Spain, you will also need an International Driver's License and a proof-of-insurance Green Card. Speed limits are 120 kph (74 mph) on autopistas, 100 kph (62 mph) on N roads, 90 kph (56 mph) on C roads, and 60 kph (37 mph) in cities unless otherwise signposted.

CUSTOMS AND DUTIES

For details on imports and duty-free limits, *see* Customs and Duties *in* Chapter 1.

DINING

Spain offers a choice of restaurants, tapas bars, and cafés. Restaurants are strictly for lunch and dinner; they do not serve breakfast. Tapas bars are ideal for a glass of wine or beer accompanied by an array of appetizers. Cafés, called *cafeterías,* are basically coffee shops that serve snacks, light meals, tapas, and pastries along with coffee, tea, and alcoholic drinks. They also serve breakfast and are perfect for afternoon tea or a cup of thick, creamy hot chocolate.

Spanish restaurants are officially classified from five forks down to one fork, with most places earning two or three forks. In our rating system, prices are for one dinner entrée. Sales tax (IVA) is usually included in the menu price; check the menu for *IVA incluído* or *IVA no incluído.* When it's not included, an additional 7% will be added to your bill. Most restaurants have a prix-fixe menu called a *menú del día*; however, this is often offered only at lunch and at dinner tends to be a reheated version of the same. *Menús* are usually the cheapest way to eat; à la carte dining is more expensive. Service charges are never added to your bill; leave around 10%, less in cheaper (one $) restaurants and bars.

CATEGORY	COST
$$$$	over 3,000 ptas. (€18.03)
$$$	2,400 ptas.–3,000 ptas. (€14.42–€18.03)
$$	1,500 ptas.–2,400 ptas. (€7.51–€14.42)
$	under 1,500 ptas. (€7.51)

MEALTIMES

Mealtimes in Spain are much later than in any other European country. Lunch begins between 1:30 and 2 in the afternoon. Dinner is usually available from 8:30 on, but it's more often taken at 9:30 or 10, especially in larger cities and resorts. Lunch is the main meal. Tapas bars are busiest between noon and 2 and from 8 PM on. Cafés are usually open from around 8 AM to midnight.

RESERVATIONS AND DRESS

In $$$$ restaurants, jacket and tie are appropriate but by no means the norm. Elsewhere, casual dress is fine.

EMBASSIES

The following countries also maintain consular offices in Barcelona.

➤ AUSTRALIA: (✉ Plaza del Descubridor Diego de Ordás 3, Madrid, ☎ 91/441–9300).

➤ CANADA: (✉ Núñez de Balboa 35, Madrid, ☎ 91/431–4300).

➤ NEW ZEALAND: (✉ Plaza de La Lealtad 2, Madrid, ☎ 91/523–0226).

➤ UNITED KINGDOM: (✉ Fernando el Santo 16, Madrid, ☎ 91/700–8200).

➤ UNITED STATES: (✉ Serrano 75, Madrid, ☎ 91/577–4000).

HEALTH

FOOD AND DRINK

Tap water is safe to drink in all but the remotest villages. In Madrid tap water is excellent; in Barcelona it's safe and getting tastier. However, most Spaniards drink bottled mineral water; ask for either *agua sin gas* (without bubbles) or *agua con gas* (with bubbles). A good paella should be served only at lunchtime and should be prepared to order (usually 30 minutes); beware of paella dinners (tourist traps), the frozen offerings of *paelladors,* any restaurant with a pictorial menu out front, or prices that look too good to be true.

HOLIDAYS

New Year's; Epiphany (January 6); Good Friday; Easter; May Day (May 1); St. James's Day (July 25); Assumption (August 15); National Day (October 12); All Saints' Day (November 1); Constitution (December 6); Immaculate Conception (December 8); Christmas.

LANGUAGE

Spanish (called Castellano, or Castilian) is spoken and understood throughout Spain. However, the Basques speak Euskera; in Catalonia, you'll hear Catalan; and in Galicia, Gallego. If you don't speak Spanish, you should have no trouble finding people who speak English in major cities and coastal resorts, but you won't necessarily be able to count on the bus driver or the passerby on the street. Fortunately, Spanish is fairly easy to pick up, and your efforts to speak the local tongue are bound to be graciously received.

LODGING

Spain has a wide range of accommodations, including luxury palaces, medieval monasteries, converted 19th-century houses, modern hotels, coastal high-rises, and inexpensive hostels in family homes. Rates are always quoted per room, not per person. Single occupancy of a double room costs 80% of the usual price. Breakfast is rarely included in the quoted room rate. The quality of rooms, particularly in older properties, can be uneven; always ask to see your room *before* you sign the acceptance slip. If you want a private bathroom in a less expensive hotel, state your preference for shower or bathtub; the latter usually costs more, though many hotels have both. All hotels and hostels are listed with their rates in the annual *Guía de Hoteles,* available from bookstores and kiosks or for perusal in local tourist offices.

Prices are for two people in a double room, not including breakfast.

CATEGORY	MAJOR CITY	OTHER AREAS
$$$$	over 28,000 ptas. (€168.28)	over 23,000 ptas. (€138.23)
$$$	18,000 ptas.–28,000 ptas. (€108.18–€168.28)	15,000 ptas.–23,000 ptas. (€90.15–€138.23)
$$	11,000 ptas.–18,000 ptas. (€66.11–€108.18)	9,000 ptas.–15,000 ptas. (€54.09–€90.15)
$	under 11,000 ptas. (€66.11)	under 9,000 ptas. (€54.09)

**In Gibraltar, $$$$: over £100 (€160.46); $$$: £60–£100 (€96.28–€160.46); not including tax.*

APARTMENT AND VILLA RENTALS

Villas are plentiful all along the Mediterranean coast. A few agencies rent cottages in Cantabria and Asturias, on the north coast; check with the Tourist Office of Spain.

CAMPING

There are about 540 campgrounds in Spain, with the highest concentration along the Mediterranean coast. The season runs from April through October, though some places are open year-round. In summer, especially in August, the best campsites fill with Spanish families who move in with what seems like their entire household. Campgrounds are listed in the annual publication *Guía de Campings,* available from bookstores or tourist offices, and the Tourist Office of Spain has additional information. Reserve the most popular seaside sites with the campground itself or through Federación Española de Campings.

➤ CONTACTS: **Federación Española de Campings** (✉ C. San Bernardo 97–99, Edificio Colominas, Madrid 28015, ☎ 91/448–1234).

HOSTELS

Hostales are rated from three stars to one star; these are not the youth hostels associated with the word in most countries but are usually family homes converted to provide accommodations in one part of the building. A three-star hostel is usually comparable to a two-star hotel; two- and one-star hostels offer basic accommodations.

HOTELS

Hotels are officially classified from five stars (the highest) to one star. Although quality is a factor, the ratings mainly indicate how many facilities the hotel has. A hotel with an *R* on its blue plaque is classified as a *residencia,* and may offer breakfast and cafeteria facilities. The main hotel chains are Barceló, Husa, Iberotel, Meliá Sol, NH, Tryp, and the state-run *paradores* (paradors). Holiday Inn, InterContinental, and Forte also own some of the best hotels in Madrid, Barcelona, and Seville; these, as well as the paradors, and the Estancias de España, a group of lodgings in historic buildings, usually have the most character. The others mostly provide clean, comfortable accommodations in the two- to four-star range.

At many hotels, rates can vary dramatically according to the time of year. The hotel year is divided into *temporada alta, media,* and *baja* (high, mid-, and low season, respectively); high season usually covers summer, Easter, and Christmas plus the major fiestas. IVA is rarely included in the quoted room rates, so expect an additional 7% to be added to your bill. Service charges are not included.

PARADORS

Spain has about 85 state-owned and -run paradors, many of which are in magnificent medieval castles or convents. Most of these are relatively luxurious and are priced accordingly. All have restaurants that specialize in regional delicacies, and you can stop in for a meal or a drink without spending the night. Breakfast, however, is an expensive buffet, and you'll do better to go down the street for a cup of coffee and a roll. Paradors are often booked far in advance. For more information or to make reservations, contact the central reservations office, Paradores, which also has extensive information on—and can reserve—other fine lodgings.

➤ CONTACTS: **Paradores** (✉ Requena 3, Madrid 28013, ☎ 91/516–6666, FAX 91/516–6657, WEB www.parador.es).

MAIL AND SHIPPING

Because mail delivery in Spain can be slow and unreliable, it's best to have your mail sent to American Express. An alternative is to have mail held at a Spanish post office; have it addressed to *lista de correos* (poste restante) in a town you'll be visiting. The address should include the name of the province in parentheses—e.g., Marbella (Málaga). You'll need to show your passport to claim your mail. American Express charges $2 per letter for noncardholders.

POSTAL RATES

To the United States, airmail letters up to 20 grams and postcards each cost 120 ptas./€0.72. To the United Kingdom and other European countries (both EU and non-EU), letters up to 20 grams and postcards each cost 75 ptas./€0.45. Within Spain, letters and postcards each cost 40 ptas./€0.24 ptas. Mailboxes are yellow with red stripes; use the slot marked EXTRANJERO for mail going abroad. Buy your *sellos* (stamps) at a *correos* (post office) or in an *estanco* (tobacco shop).

MONEY MATTERS

The cost of living in Spain is on a par with that of most other European nations. In recent years, however, currency fluctuations have increased the buying power of those visiting from North America and the United Kingdom. A cup of coffee costs between 125 ptas./€0.75 and 166 ptas./€1; a glass of wine in a bar, 100 ptas./€0.60–135 ptas./€0.80; a sandwich 300 ptas./€1.80–416 ptas./€2.50; a local bus or subway ride 125 ptas./€0.75–200 ptas./€1.20; a 2-km (1-mi) taxi ride, about 500 ptas./€3.

CREDIT CARDS

Most hotels, restaurants, and stores accept credit cards. Visa is the most widely accepted card, followed by MasterCard (also called EuroCard in Spain).

CURRENCY

Spain, as one of the euro zone currency countries, will introduce euro (€) notes and coins on January 1, 2002. The euro and the Spanish peseta (ptas.) will circulate simultaneously through March 2002. Banks and ATMs will give all money in euros. Shops and restaurants are encouraged to give change in euros whenever possible. Prices are marked in both euros and Spanish pesetas. Pesetas come in bills of 1,000, 2,000, 5,000, and 10,000, and coins of 1, 5, 10, 25, 50, 100, 200, and 500 pesetas. At press time (summer 2001), the exchange rate was 186.52 ptas. to the U.S. dollar, 119.48 ptas. to the Canadian dollar, 268.29 ptas. to the pound sterling, 211.27 ptas. to the Irish punt, 94.87 ptas. to the Australian dollar, 76.08 ptas. to the New Zealand dollar, 23.27 ptas. to the South African rand, and 166.39 ptas. to the euro.

Visitors may take any amount of foreign currency in bills or traveler's checks into Spain, as well as any amount of euros. When leaving Spain you may take out only €3,000 or the equivalent in foreign currency, unless you can prove you declared the excess at customs on entering the country.

CURRENCY EXCHANGE

The word to look for is CAMBIO (exchange). Most Spanish banks take a 1½% commission, though some less scrupulous places charge more; always check, as rates can vary widely. To change money in a bank, you need your passport and plenty of patience, because filling out the forms takes time. Hotels offer rates lower than banks, but they rarely charge a commission, so you may well break even. Restaurants and stores, with the exception of those catering to the tour-bus trade, generally do not accept payment in dollars or traveler's checks. If you have a credit card with a personal identification number, you'll have no trouble drawing cash from automated teller machines.

TAXES

VALUE-ADDED TAX (VAT)

Value-added tax, called IVA, is levied on most goods and services. It's 7% at hotels and restaurants and 16% on goods and car rentals.

A number of shops, particularly large stores and boutiques in holiday resorts, participate in Global Refund (formerly Europe Tax-Free Shopping), an VAT refund service that makes getting your money back relatively hassle-free. On purchases of more than 14,975 ptas./€90, you're entitled to a refund of the 16% tax (there is no refund for the 7% tax). Ask for the Global Refund form (called a Shopping Cheque) in participating stores. You show your passport and fill out the form; the vendor then mails you the refund, or—often more convenient—you present your original receipt to the VAT office at the airport when you leave Spain. (In both Madrid and Barcelona, the office is near the duty-free shops. Save time for this process, as lines can be long.) Customs signs the original and refunds your money on the spot in cash (pesetas), or sends it to their central office to process a credit-card refund. Credit-card refunds take a few weeks.

TELEPHONES

COUNTRY AND AREA CODES

The country code for Spain is 34.

DIRECTORY AND OPERATOR ASSISTANCE

For the operator and directory information for any part of Spain, dial 1003. The international information and assistance operator is at 025 (some operators speak English). If you're in Madrid, dial 1008 to make collect calls to countries in Europe; 1005 for the rest of the world.

INTERNATIONAL CALLS

You can call abroad from any pay phone marked TELÉFONO INTERNACIONAL. Some are coin-operated, but it is best to purchase a *tarjeta telefónica* (telephone card), available at most newsagents and many shops. A few public phones also accept credit cards. Dial 00, then dial 1 for the United States, 0101 for Canada, or 44 for the United Kingdom, followed by the area code and number. For lengthy calls, go to the *telefónica,* a phone office found in all sizable towns: here an operator assigns you a private booth and collects payment at the end of the call. This is the cheapest and by far the easiest way to call overseas, and you can charge calls costing more than €3 to Visa or MasterCard. Private long-distance companies, such as AT&T, MCI, and Sprint, have special access numbers.

➤ ACCESS CODES: **AT&T** (☎ 900/990011). **MCI** (☎ 900/990014). **Sprint** (☎ 900/990013).

LOCAL CALLS

Note that to call anywhere within Spain—even locally—you need to dial the area code first. All provincial codes begin with a 9.

PUBLIC PHONES

Most pay phones have a digital readout, so you can see your money ticking away. You need at least 25 ptas./€0.15 for a local call, 75 ptas./€0.45 to call another province, and at least 100 pts./€0.60 if you are calling a Spanish cell phone. Some pay phones take only phone cards, which can be purchased at any tobacco shop in various denominations.

TIPPING

Spanish waiters, porters, and taxi drivers appreciate being tipped, but they don't expect American rates. By law, restaurants and hotels are not allowed to add a service charge to your bill, but, confusingly, your bills for both will probably say *servicios e impuestos incluídos* (service and tax included). In restaurants, ignore this unhelpful snippet and leave 10% if you've had a full meal. In humbler eateries, bars, and cafés, leave 5%–10% or round the bill up to the nearest 100 ptas./€1.00. Tip taxi drivers about 5%–10% when they use the meter, otherwise nothing—they'll have seen to it themselves. Train and airport porters usually operate on a posted, fixed rate per bag, around 83 ptas./€0.50. Hotel porters get 83 ptas./€0.50–166 ptas./€1.00 for carrying bags, and waiters get the same for room service. If you stay in a hotel more than two nights, it's customary to tip the maid 100 ptas./€.60 per night.

TRAIN TRAVEL

The Spanish railroad system—usually known by its initials, RENFE—operates several different types of trains: Talgo (ultramodern), electric unit expresses (ELT), diesel rail cars (TER), and ordinary *expresos* and *rápidos.* A few lines, such as the narrow-gauge FEVE routes along the north coast and the Costa Blanca, do not belong to the RENFE network and do not accept international rail passes.

CUTTING COSTS

The RENFE Tourist Card, on sale to anyone who lives outside Spain, buys you unlimited distance over 3, 5, or 10 days' travel. Contact the Tourist Office of Spain for a list of agencies or call RENFE.

FARES AND SCHEDULES

Fares are determined by the kind of train as well as the distance traveled. Of the long-distance trains, Talgos are by far the quickest, most comfortable, and most expensive of the lot; *expresos* and *rápidos* are the slowest and cheapest. The high-speed Alto Velocidad Español (AVE) runs between Madrid and Seville in just 2½ hours, with a stop in Córdoba; fares vary, but the AVE can cost almost as much as flying.

➤ TRAIN INFORMATION: **RENFE** (☎ 34/934–901–122 from outside Spain; 902/240202 from Spain).

VISITOR INFORMATION

For the Tourist Office of Spain in your home country, *see* Visitor Information *in* Chapter 1. For general information on travel within Spain, call Turespaña's information line. For regional and city tourist offices, *see* Visitor Information *in* the Essentials section for the relevant geographic region, *below.*

➤ TOURIST INFORMATION: **Turespaña** (☎ 901/300600).

WHEN TO GO

The tourist season runs from Easter to mid-October. Seasonal events can clog parts of the country, and major fiestas, such as Pamplona's running of the bulls (July 6–15), cause prices to soar. Semana Santa (Holy Week) is the last week in March; this is the time to catch some of Spain's most spectacular fiestas.

CLIMATE

The best months for sightseeing are May, June, September, and early October, when the weather is usually pleasant and sunny without being unbearably hot. In July and August, avoid Madrid and the inland cities of Andalusia, where the heat can be stifling and many places close down at 1 PM. Air-conditioning is not widely used. The one exception to Spain's high summer temperatures is the north coast, where the climate is similar to that of northern Europe. The following are average daily maximum and minimum temperatures for Madrid.

Jan.	47F	9C	**May**	70F	21C	**Sept.**	77F	25C
	35	2		50	10		57	14
Feb.	52F	11C	**June**	80F	27C	**Oct.**	65F	18C
	36	2		58	15		49	10
Mar.	59F	15C	**July**	87F	31C	**Nov.**	55F	13C
	41	5		63	17		42	5
Apr.	65F	18C	**Aug.**	85F	30C	**Dec.**	48F	9C
	45	7		63	17		36	2

MADRID

Dead center in the heart of Spain at 2,120 ft above sea level, Madrid is the highest capital in Europe and one of the continent's most exciting cities. Madrid's famous museum mile boasts more masterpieces per foot than anywhere else in the world. Home of Spain's royal court for the last 500 years, the city's regal palaces and gardens conceal a village-like medieval Madrid with narrow lanes and red-tiled roofs. This is all in contrast to the rowdy Madrid one finds after midnight, when the action really begins; Madrileños are vigorous, joyful people, famous for their defiance of the need for sleep.

Exploring Madrid

Numbers in the margin correspond to points of interest on the Madrid map.

You can see important parts of the city in one day if you stop only to visit the Prado and Royal Palace. Two days should give you time for browsing. You can begin in the Plaza Atocha (Glorieta del Emperador Carlos V), at the bottom of the Paseo del Prado.

★ 1 **Centro de Arte Reina Sofía** (Queen Sofía Arts Center). Spain's Queen Sofía opened this center in 1986, and it quickly became one of Europe's most dynamic venues—a Spanish rival to Paris's Pompidou Center. A converted hospital, the center houses painting and sculpture, including works by Joan Miró and Salvador Dalí as well as Picasso's *Guernica,* the painting depicting the horrific April 1937 carpet bombing of the Basque country's traditional capital by Nazi warplanes aiding Franco in the Spanish Civil War. ✉ *Main entrance, C. de Santa Isabel 52,* ☎ *91/467–5062.* ⏲ *Mon. and Wed.–Sat. 10–9, Sun. 10–2:30.*

10 **Convento de las Descalzas Reales** (Convent of the Royal Barefoot Nuns). This convent, founded by Juana de Austria, daughter of Charles V, is still in use. Over the centuries, the nuns—daughters of royalty and nobility—have endowed it with an enormous wealth of jewels, religious ornaments, superb Flemish tapestries, and the works of such master painters as Titian and Rubens. A bit off the main track, it's one of Madrid's better-kept secrets. Your ticket includes admission to the nearby, but less interesting, **Convento de la Encarnación.** ✉ *Plaza de las Descalzas 3,* ☎ *91/542–0059.* ⏲ *Tues.–Thurs. and Sat. 10:30–12:45 and 4–5:45, Fri. 10:30–12:45, Sun. 11–1:45.*

7 **Fuente de la Cibeles** (Fountain of Cybele). Cybele, the Greek goddess of fertility and unofficial emblem of Madrid, languidly rides her lion-drawn chariot here, watched over by the mighty Palacio de Comunicaciónes, a splendidly pompous, cathedral-like post office. Fans of the home football team, Real Madrid, used to celebrate major victories by splashing in the fountain, but police now blockade it during big games. The fountain stands in the center of **Plaza de la Cibeles,** one of Madrid's great landmarks. ✉ *C. de Alcalá.*

★ 2 **Museo del Prado** (Prado Museum). On the old cobblestone section of the Paseo del Prado you'll find Madrid's number one cultural site, one of the world's most important art museums. Plan to spend at least a day here; it takes at least two days to view the museum's treasures properly. Brace yourself for crowds. The greatest treasures—the Velázquez, Murillo, Zurbarán, El Greco, and Goya galleries—are all on the upper floor. Two of the best works are Velázquez's *La Rendición de Breda* and his most famous work, *Las Meninas,* awarded a room of its own. The Goya galleries contain the artist's none-too-flattering royal portraits, his exquisitely beautiful *Marquesa de Santa Cruz,* and his famous *La Maja Desnuda* and *La Maja Vestida,* for which the 13th duchess of Alba was said to have posed. Goya's most moving works, the *Second of May* and the *Fusillade of Moncloa,* or *Third of May,* vividly depict the sufferings of Madrid patriots at the hands of Napoléon's invading troops in 1808. Before you leave, feast your eyes on Hieronymus Bosch's flights of fancy, *Garden of Earthly Delights,* and the triptych the *Hay Wagon,* both on the ground floor. The museum is adding a new wing, designed by Rafael Moneo, much of which will be occu-

Centro de Arte Reina Sofía 1
Convento de las Descalzas Reales . . . 10
Fuente de la Cibeles 7
Museo del Prado 2
Museo Thyssen-Bornemisza 4
Palacio Real 13
Parque del Retiro 5
Plaza de la Villa 12
Plaza Mayor 11
Puerta de Alcalá 6
Puerta del Sol 9
Real Academia de Bellas Artes de San Fernando 8
Ritz 3
Teatro Real 14

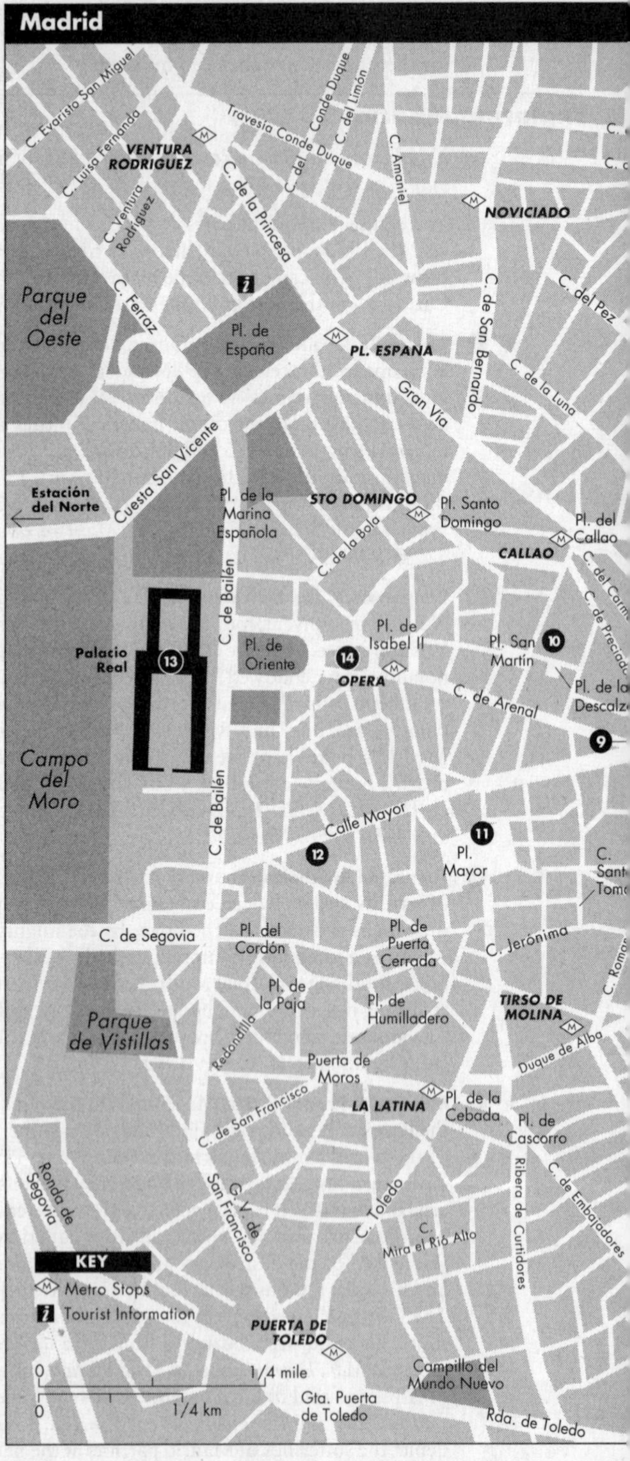

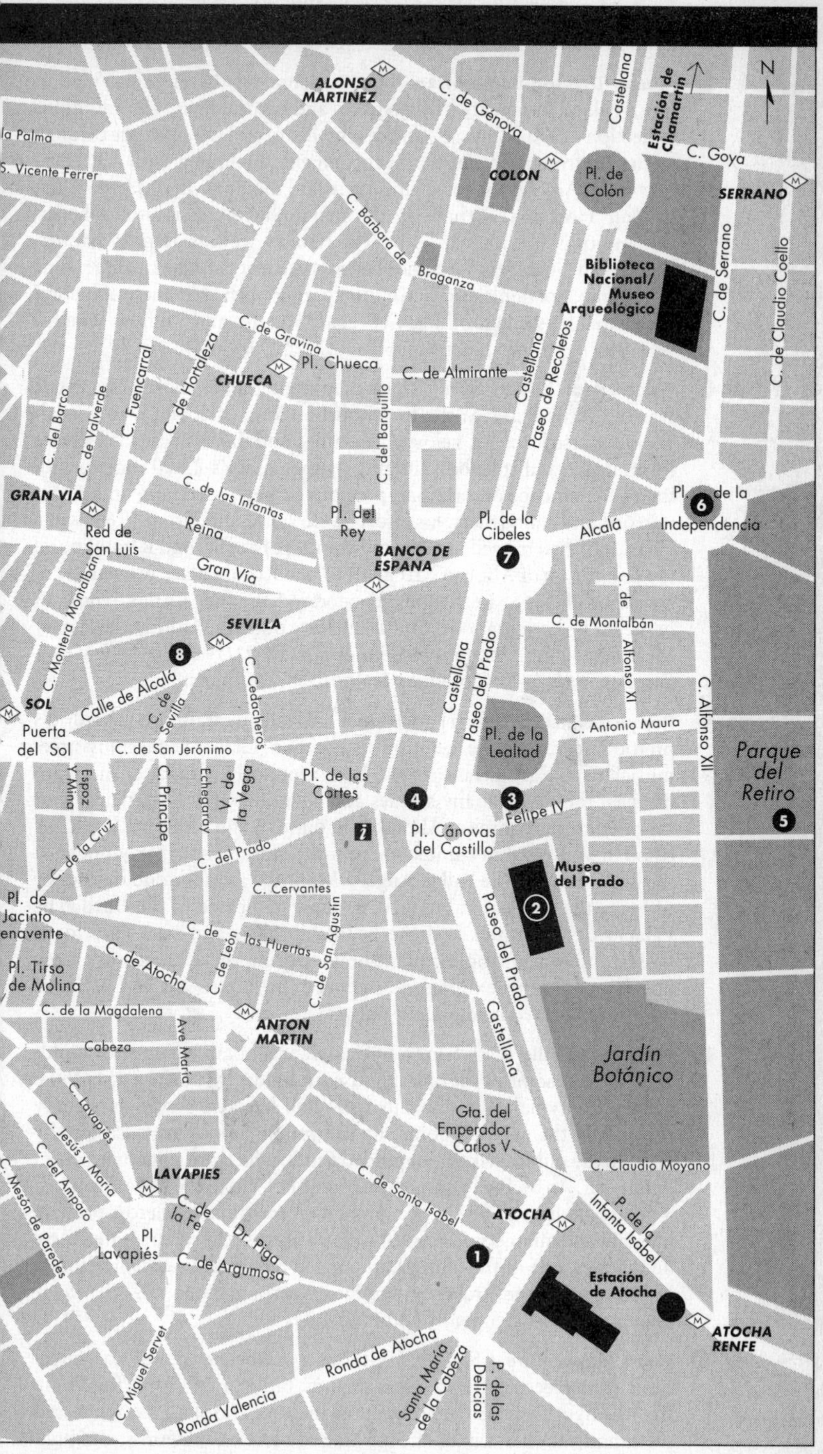
ALONSO MARTINEZ
C. de Génova
Castellana
Estación de Chamartín
N
la Palma
S. Vicente Ferrer
COLON
Pl. de Colón
C. Goya
SERRANO
C. Bárbara de Braganza
Biblioteca Nacional/ Museo Arqueológico
C. de Serrano
C. de Claudio Coello
C. de Gravina
Pl. Chueca
CHUECA
C. de Almirante
Castellana
Paseo de Recoletos
C. Fuencarral
C. de Hortaleza
C. del Barco
C. de Valverde
C. del Barquillo
C. de las Infantas
GRAN VIA
Red de San Luis
Reina
Gran Vía
Pl. del Rey
BANCO DE ESPANA
Pl. de la Cibeles
Alcalá
Pl. de la Independencia
C. Montera
Montalbán
SEVILLA
C. de Montalbán
C. de Alfonso XI
C. Alfonso XII
SOL
Calle de Alcalá
C. de Sevilla
C. Cedacheros
Castellana
Paseo del Prado
Pl. de la Lealtad
C. Antonio Maura
Parque del Retiro
Puerta del Sol
C. de San Jerónimo
Espoz Y Mina
C. Principe
Echegaray
V. de la Vega
Pl. de las Cortes
Pl. Cánovas del Castillo
Felipe IV
C. de la Cruz
C. del Prado
Museo del Prado
C. Cervantes
Pl. de Jacinto enavente
C. de las Huertas
C. de Atocha
C. de León
C. de San Agustín
Paseo del Prado
Castellana
Pl. Tirso de Molina
C. de la Magdalena
ANTON MARTIN
Ave María
Cabeza
Jardín Botánico
C. Lavapiés
C. Jesús y María
C. del Amparo
C. Mesón de Paredes
Gta. del Emperador Carlos V
C. Claudio Moyano
LAVAPIES
C. de Santa Isabel
C. de la Fe
Dr. Piga
ATOCHA
P. de la Infanta Isabel
Pl. Lavapiés
C. de Argumosa
Estación de Atocha
ATOCHA RENFE
C. Miguel Servet
Ronda de Atocha
Santa María de la Cabeza
P. de las Delicias
Ronda Valencia

pied by long-forgotten masterpieces by Zurbarán and Pereda. ✉ *Paseo del Prado s/n,* ☎ *91/420–3768.* ⏲ *Tues.–Sat. 9–7, Sun. 9–2.*

❹ **Museo Thyssen-Bornemisza.** This museum, in the elegant Villahermosa Palace, has plenty of airy spaces and natural light. The ambitious collection—800 paintings—traces the history of Western art through examples from each important movement, beginning with 13th-century Italy. Among the museum's gems are the *Portrait of Henry VIII,* by Hans Holbein. Two halls are devoted to the Impressionists and post-Impressionists, with works by Pissarro as well as Renoir, Monet, Degas, van Gogh, and Cézanne. The more recent paintings include some terror-filled examples of German expressionism, but these are complemented by some soothing Georgia O'Keeffes and Andrew Wyeths. ✉ *Paseo del Prado 8,* ☎ *91/369–0151.* ⏲ *Tues.–Sun. 10–7.*

★ ⓭ **Palacio Real** (Royal Palace). This magnificent granite-and-limestone pile was begun by Philip V, the first Bourbon king of Spain, who was always homesick for his beloved Versailles and did his best to re-create its opulence and splendor. Judging by the palace's 2,800 rooms, with their lavish rococo decorations, precious carpets, porcelain, timepieces, mirrors, and chandeliers, his efforts were successful. From 1764, when Charles III first moved in, until the coming of the Second Republic and the abdication of Alfonso XIII in 1931, the Royal Palace proved a very stylish abode for Spanish monarchs; today, King Juan Carlos, who lives in the far less ostentatious Zarzuela Palace outside Madrid, uses it only for official state functions. ✉ *Bailén s/n,* ☎ *91/542–0059.* ⏲ *Mon.–Sat. 9–6, Sun. 9–3. Closed during official receptions.*

★ ❺ **Parque del Retiro** (Retiro Park). Once a royal retreat, Retiro is Madrid's prettiest park. Visit the beautiful rose garden, **La Rosaleda;** enjoy street musicians and magicians; row a boat around El Estanque; and wander past the park's many statues and fountains. Look particularly at the monumental **statue of Alfonso XII,** one of Spain's least notable kings (though you wouldn't think so from the statue's size), or wonder at the **Monument to the Fallen Angel**—Madrid claims the dubious honor of being the only capital to have a statue dedicated to the Devil. The **Palacio de Velázquez** and the beautiful, glass-and-steel **Palacio de Cristal,** built as a tropical plant house during the 19th century, now host occasional art exhibits. ✉ *Between C. Alfonso XII and Avda. de Menéndez Pelayo below C. de Alcalá.*

⓬ **Plaza de la Villa** (City Square). This plaza's notable cluster of buildings includes some of the oldest houses in Madrid. The **Casa de la Villa,** Madrid's city hall, was built in 1644 and has also served as the city prison and the mayor's home. Its sumptuous salons are occasionally open to the public; ask about guided tours, which are sometimes given in English. An archway joins the Casa de la Villa to the **Casa Cisneros,** a palace built in 1537 for the nephew of Cardinal Cisneros, primate of Spain and infamous inquisitor general. Across the square is the **Torre de Lujanes,** one of the oldest buildings in Madrid; it once imprisoned Francis I of France, archenemy of the emperor Charles V. ✉ *C. Mayor between C. Santiago and C. San Nicholas.*

★ ⓫ **Plaza Mayor** (Great Square). Without a doubt the capital's architectural showpiece, the Plaza Mayor was built in 1617–19 for Philip III—the figure astride the horse in the middle. The plaza has witnessed the canonization of saints, the burning of heretics, fireworks, and bullfights, and is still one of Madrid's great gathering places. ✉ *South of C. Mayor, west of Cava San Miguel.*

❻ **Puerta de Alcalá** (Alcalá Gate). Built in 1779 for Charles III, the grandiose gateway dominates the Plaza de la Independencia. A customs post once stood beside the gate, as did the old bullring until it was moved to its present site, Las Ventas, in the 1920s. At the beginning of the 20th century, the Puerta de Alcalá more or less marked the eastern edge of Madrid. ⊠ *Plaza de la Independencia.*

9 **Puerta del Sol** (Gate of the Sun). The old gate disappeared long ago, but you're still at the very heart of Madrid here, and indeed the very heart of Spain: kilometer distances for the whole nation are measured from the zero marker, a brass plaque on the south sidewalk. The square was expertly revamped in 1986 and now accommodates a copy of **La Mariblanca** (a statue that adorned a fountain here 250 years ago), a statue of Carlos III on horseback and, at the bottom of Calle Carmen, the much-loved statue of the **bear and strawberry tree.** The Puerta del Sol is inextricably linked with the history of Madrid and of Spain; a half century ago, a generation of literati gathered in Sol's long-gone cafés to thrash out the burning issues of the day. Nearly 200 years ago, the square witnessed the patriots' uprising immortalized by Goya in his painting *The Second of May.* ⊠ *Meeting of C. Mayor and C. Alcalá.*

8 **Real Academia de Bellas Artes de San Fernando** (St. Fernando Royal Academy of Fine Arts). Often overlooked in favor of the Prado, the Reina Sofia, and the Thyssen, this surprisingly comprehensive collection covers the masters (Murillo, Zurbarán, Ribera, El Greco, Velázquez, and Goya) with some 19th and 20th-century work (Zuloaga, Sorolla) as well. ⊠ *Alcalá 13,* ☎ *91/522–0046.* ⏲ *Tues.–Fri. 9:30–7, Sat.–Mon. 9:30–2.*

3 **Ritz.** Alfonso II built Madrid's grande dame in 1910, when he realized that his capital had no hotels elegant enough to accommodate his wedding guests. The garden is a wonderfully aristocratic—if wildly overpriced—place to lunch in summer. ⊠ *Plaza de Lealtad 5.*

14 **Teatro Real** (Royal Theater). This neoclassical theater was built in 1850 and has long been a cultural center. Replete with golden balconies, plush seats, and state-of-the-art stage equipment for operas and ballets, the theater is a modern showpiece with its vintage appeal intact. ⊠ *Plaza de Isabel II,* ☎ *91/516–0600.*

Bullfighting

Madrid's bullfighting season runs from March through October. Corridas are held on Sunday and sometimes also on Thursday; starting times vary between 4:30 and 7 PM. The height of the taurine spectacle comes with the San Isidro festival in May, with five weeks of daily bullfights. The bullring is at **Las Ventas,** formally known as the Plaza de Toros Monumental (⊠ Alcalá 237, ☎ 91/356–2200, metro: Ventas). You can buy tickets here before the fight or, for a 20% surcharge, at the agencies that line Calle Victoria, off Carrera de San Jerónimo near Puerta del Sol.

Dining

For details and price-category definitions, *see* Dining *in* Spain A to Z, *above.* Note that some restaurants close for Holy Week.

$$$$ ★ ✕ **La Broche.** Sergi Arola, who trained with celebrity chef Ferran Adriá, has added his own twists and innovations to those of the Catalan master and vaulted directly to the top of Madrid's dining charts. The minimalist dining room clears the decks for maximum taste bud protagonism—a lucky thing as you'll want to concentrate on the hot-cold counterpoints of your codfish soup with bacon ice cream or the marinated sardine with herring roe. The wine list is superb; try a peppery Priorat (Miserere, for example). A full meal with appetizers and wine will run you about 12,000 ptas./€75.12. ✉ *Miguel Angel 29,* ☎ *91/399–3778. Reservations essential. AE, DC, MC, V. Closed Sun. and Easter week. No lunch Sat.*

$$$$ ✕ **Lhardy.** Lhardy looks pretty much the same as it must have on day one (Sept. 16, 1839) with its dark-wood paneling, brass chandeliers, and red-velvet chairs. Most diners come for the traditional *cocido a la madrileña* (garbanzo-bean stew) and *callos a la madrileña* (tripe in spicy sauce). The dining rooms are upstairs; the ground-floor entry doubles as a delicatessen and stand-up coffee bar that fills up on chilly winter mornings with shivering souls sipping steaming-hot *caldo* (chicken broth) from silver urns. ✉ *Carrera de San Jerónimo 8,* ☎ *91/522–2207. AE, DC, MC, V. No dinner Sun.*

$$$$ ✕ **Viridiana.** Viridiana, decorated in black and white, achieves the relaxed atmosphere of a bistro. Iconoclast chef Abraham García creates a new menu every two weeks, dreaming up such varied fare as red onions stuffed with *morcilla* (black pudding), soft flour tortillas wrapped around marinated fresh tuna, and filet mignon in white-truffle sauce. The tangy grapefruit sherbet for dessert is a marvel. ✉ *Juan de Mena 14,* ☎ *91/531–5222. Reservations essential. AE, DC, MC, V. Closed Sun. and Aug.*

$$$$ ✕ **Zalacaín.** A deep-apricot color scheme, set off by dark wood and gleaming silver, makes this restaurant look like an exclusive villa. Zalacaín introduced nouvelle cuisine to Spain and continues to set the pace after 20 years at the top—splurge on such dishes as prawn salad in avocado vinaigrette, scallops and leeks in Albariño wine, and roast pheasant with truffles. A prix-fixe tasting menu allows you to sample the restaurant's best for about 6,500 ptas./€39.07. Service is somewhat stuffy, and jackets are required. ✉ *Alvarez de Baena 4,* ☎ *91/561–5935. Reservations essential. AE, DC, V. Closed Sun. and Aug. No lunch Sat.*

$$$–$$$$ ✕ **Asador Fronton 1.** Long established in Tirso de Molina and now with two branches in northern Madrid, this popular Basque restaurant serves some of the most outstanding meat and fish in the city. Starters include fresh grilled anchovies, *anchos frescas,* and peppers stuffed with cod. The huge chunks of delicious steak, seared on a charcoal grill and then lightly sprinkled with sea salt, are for two or more. Order lettuce hearts or a vegetable to accompany. The *cocochas de merluza,* tender hake morsels in green parsley sauce, are deliciously light. ✉ *Tirso de Molina 7 (rear, upstairs),* ☎ *91/369–1617. Reservations essential. AE, DC, MC, V. Closed Sun.*

$$$–$$$$ ★ ✕ **El Cenador del Prado.** The Cenador's innovative menu has French and Asian touches, as well as exotic Spanish dishes that rarely appear in restaurants. The house specialty is *patatas a la importancia* (sliced potatoes fried in a sauce of garlic, parsley, and clams); other possibilities are shellfish consommé with ginger ravioli, veal and eggplant in béchamel, and venison with prunes. For dessert try the *bartolillos,* custard-filled pastry. Settings are a Baroque salon and a plant-filled conservatory. ✉ *C. del Prado 4,* ☎ *91/429–1561. AE, DC, MC, V. Closed Sun. and Aug. 1–15. No lunch Sat.*

$$$–$$$$ ✕ **Pedro Larumbe.** This excellent restaurant is atop the ABC shopping center between the Castellana and Calle Serrano. It has a lovely summer roof terrace, which is glassed in for the winter, and an Andalusian patio. Owner-chef Pedro Larumbe is famous for the presentation of his modern dishes, such as lobster salad. At lunch there is a salad bar; the dessert buffet is an art show; and the wine list is good. ✉ *Serrano 61/Castellana 34,* ☎ *91/575–1112. AE, DC, MC, V. Closed Sun. and 15 days in Aug. No lunch Sat.*

$$–$$$ ★ ✕ **Casa Botín.** Just off the Plaza Mayor, this is Madrid's oldest (1725) and most famous restaurant. Its decor and food are traditionally Castilian, as are the wood-fire ovens used for cooking. *Cochinillo asado* (roast suckling pig) and *cordero asado* (roast lamb) are the specialties. The restaurant was a favorite of Hemingway's and is somewhat touristy, but it's still fun. Try to get a table in the basement or the upstairs dining room. ✉ *Cuchilleros 17,* ☎ *91/366–4217. Reservations essential. AE, DC, MC, V.*

$$–$$$ ✕ **La Cava Real.** Wine connoisseurs love the intimate atmosphere of this small, elegant restaurant and bar, which was Madrid's first true wine bar when it opened in 1983. There are a staggering 350 wines from which to choose, including 50 by the glass. The charming, experienced maître d', Chema Gómez, can help you select. Chef Javier Collar designs good-value set menus around wines, and the à la carte selection is also plentiful, mainly *nueva cocina* with game in season as well as fancy desserts and cheeses. ✉ *Espronceda 34,* ☎ *91/442–5432. Reservation essential. AE, DC, MC, V. Closed Sun. and Aug.*

$$–$$$ ✕ **La Trainera.** La Trainera is all about fresh seafood. With nautical decor and a maze of little dining rooms, this informal restaurant has reigned as the queen of Madrid's fish houses for decades. Crab, lobster, shrimp, mussels, and a dozen other types of shellfish are served by weight and while Spaniards often share several plates of these delicacies as their entire meal, the grilled hake, sole, or turbot makes an unbeatable second course. Skip the house wine and go for a bottle of Albariño from the cellar. ✉ *Lagasca 60,* ☎ *91/576–8035. AE, MC, V. Closed Sun. and Aug.*

$$ ★ ✕ **La Gamella.** American-born chef Dick Stephens has created a reasonably priced menu at this hugely popular spot. The sophisticated rust-red dining room, batik tablecloths, oversize plates, and attentive service remain the same, but much of the nouvelle cuisine has been replaced by more traditional fare, such as chicken in garlic, beef bourguignonne, and steak tartare à la Jack Daniels. A few signature dishes—such as sausage-and-red-pepper quiche and, for dessert, bittersweet chocolate pâté—remain, and the lunchtime menú del día is a great value. ✉ *Alfonso XII 4,* ☎ *91/532–4509. AE, DC, MC, V. Closed Sun., Mon., and Aug. 15–31. No lunch Sat.*

$–$$ ★ ✕ **Casa Mingo.** This Asturian cider tavern is built into a stone wall beneath the Norte train station. The nearby Ermita de San Antonio de la Florida with its famous Goya frescoes and Casa Mingo are a classic Madrid combination, especially in springtime. Succulent roast chicken, sausages, and salad are the only offerings, along with *sidra* (hard cider). The long plank tables are shared with other diners, while in summer, tables are set out on the sidewalk. ✉ *Paseo de la Florida 2,* ☎ *91/547–7918. No credit cards.*

$–$$ ✕ **La Trucha.** This Andalusian deep-fry specialist is one of the happiest places in Madrid. The staff is perennially jovial and the house specialty, the *trucha a la truchana* (crisped trout stuffed with ample garlic and diced jabugo ham) is a work of art that deserves to be included in one of the nearby national museums. *Chopitos* (baby squid), *pollo al ajillo* (chunks of chicken in crisped garlic), and *espárragos trigueros* (wild asparagus) are among the star entrées here, while the *jarras* (pitchers) of chilled Valdepeñas, a beaujolais-like young claret, seem to act as laughing gas in this magic little bistro. The Nuñez de Arce branch, just down the street from the Hotel Reina Victoria, is usually less crowded, though no less jolly. ✉ *Manuel Fernandez y Gonzalez 3 and Nuñez de Arce 6,* ☎ *91/429–3778. AE, MC, V. Closed Sun. and (at Nunez de Arce only) Aug.*

$–$$ ✕ **Nabucco.** With pastel-washed walls and subtle lighting from gigantic, wrought-iron candelabras, this pizzeria and trattoria is a trendy but elegant haven in gritty Chueca. Fresh bread sticks and garlic olive oil show up within minutes of your arrival. The spinach, ricotta, and walnut ravioli is heavenly, and this may be the only Italian restaurant in

Madrid where you can order barbecued-chicken pizza. Considering the ambience and quality, the bill is a pleasant surprise. ✉ *Hortaleza 108,* ☎ *91/310–0611. AE, MC, V.*

Lodging

For details and price-category definitions, *see* Lodging *in* Spain A to Z, *above.*

$$$$ 🏨 **Ritz.** Once Spain's most exclusive hotel, it is still elegant and aristocratic, with beautiful rooms, spacious suites, and sumptuous public salons furnished with antiques and handwoven carpets. The restaurant is justly famous, and the garden terrace is the perfect setting for summer dining. Weekend brunch is accompanied by harp music, and weekend tea or supper by chamber music from February through May. Near the Parque del Retiro and overlooking the Prado, the Ritz offers unadulterated luxury. ✉ *Plaza Lealtad 5, 28014,* ☎ *91/701–6767,* FAX *91/701–6776,* WEB *www.ritz.es. 158 rooms. Restaurant. AE, DC, MC, V.*

$$$$ ★ 🏨 **Santo Mauro.** Once the Canadian embassy, this turn-of-the-20th-century neoclassical mansion is now an intimate luxury hotel. The architecture is accented by contemporary furniture (such as suede armchairs) in such hues as mustard, teal, and eggplant. The best rooms are in the main building, which also has a popular gourmet restaurant with garden terrace; the others are in a new annex and are split-level, with stereos and VCRs. Request a room with a terrace overlooking the gardens. ✉ *Zurbano 36, 28010,* ☎ *91/319–6900,* FAX *91/308–5477,* WEB *www.ac-hoteles.com. 37 rooms. Restaurant, pool. AE, DC, MC, V.*

$$$$ 🏨 **Villa Magna.** Renowned in the early '90s as the favorite of visiting financiers and reclusive rock stars, the Villa Magna has been humbled by competition. Still, it's one of Madrid's top luxury hotels, its modern facade belying an exquisite interior furnished with 18th-century antiques. With a champagne bar and a top Chinese restaurant, it offers all the amenities you'd expect from an internationally known hotel. All rooms have large desks and VCRs, and all bathrooms have fresh flowers. ✉ *Paseo de la Castellana 22, 28046,* ☎ *91/587–1234,* FAX *91/575–3158,* WEB *www.madrid.hyatt.com. 164 rooms, 18 suites. Restaurant. AE, DC, MC, V.*

$$$$ 🏨 **Villa Real.** English antiques and 19th-century Aubusson tapestries set the tone in the lobby of this very personal hotel. The emphasis is on service and luxurious details. Decor in the rooms is somewhat clubby, with leather sofas and dark-red floral fabrics. The hotel overlooks the Plaza de las Cortes and is convenient to almost all major sights. ✉ *Plaza de las Cortes 10, 28014,* ☎ *91/420–3767,* FAX *91/420–2547,* WEB *www.derbyhotels.es. 94 rooms, 20 suites. Restaurant. AE, DC, MC, V.*

$$$$ ★ 🏨 **Westin Palace.** Built in 1912, Madrid's most famous grand hotel is a Belle Epoque creation of Alfonso XIII. The guest rooms meet today's highest standards; banquet halls and lobbies have been lovingly beautified; and the facade has been finely restored. The Palace is more charming and stylish than ever—and while the glass dome over the lounge remains exquisitely original, the windows in the guest rooms are now double-glazed. ✉ *Plaza de las Cortes 7, 28014,* ☎ *91/360–8000,* FAX *91/360–8100,* WEB *www.westin.com. 465 rooms, 45 suites. Restaurant. AE, DC, MC, V.*

$$$–$$$$ 🏨 **Reina Victoria.** Madrid's longtime favorite among bullfighters, this gleaming white Victorian building across the square from the Teatro Español has been transformed over the last decade into an upscale and modern establishment. The pervasive taurine theme is most concentrated in the bar where stuffed bulls' heads peer curiously over your shoulder. The best rooms are on the top floors, providing the most insulation from noise and great views over the rooftops and the theater.

✉ *Plaza Santa Ana 14, 28012,* ☎ *91/531–4500,* FAX *91/522–0307. 195 rooms. Bar. AE, DC, MC, V.*

$$$ 🏨 **El Prado.** Wedged in among the classic buildings of Old Madrid, this slim hotel is within stumbling distance of Madrid's best bars and nightclubs. Rooms are soundproof, with double-pane glass, and are surprisingly spacious. Appointments include pastel floral prints and gleaming marble baths. ✉ *Prado 11, 28014,* ☎ *91/369–0234,* FAX *91/429–2829,* WEB *www.hotelgreenprado.com. 47 rooms. AE, DC, MC, V.*

$$$ 🏨 **Liabeny.** A large, paneled lobby leads to bars, a restaurant, and a café in this 1960s hotel, centrally located near an airy plaza (and several department stores) between Gran Vía and Puerta del Sol. The large, comfortable rooms have floral fabrics and big windows; interior and top-floor rooms are the quietest. ✉ *Salud 3, 28013,* ☎ *91/531–9000,* FAX *91/532–5306,* WEB *www.liabeny.es. 222 rooms. Restaurant. AE, DC, MC, V.*

$$–$$$ 🏨 **Carlos V.** If you like to be right in the center of things, hang your hat at this classic hotel on a pedestrian street: it's just a few steps away from the Puerta del Sol, Plaza Mayor, and Descalzas Reales convent. A suit of armor guards the tiny lobby, and crystal chandeliers add elegance to the second-floor lounge. All rooms are bright and carpeted, and the doubles with large terraces are a bargain. ✉ *Maestro Victoria 5, 28013,* ☎ *91/531–4100,* FAX *91/531–3761,* WEB *www.carlosv.com. 67 rooms. AE, DC, MC, V.*

$–$$ 🏨 **Inglés.** This hotel was once a favorite with writers and artists, including Virginia Woolf. Though dreary, the rooms are comfortable enough, and the location is key: a short walk from the Puerta del Sol in one direction, the Prado in the other. Inexpensive restaurants and distinctive bars are close at hand. ✉ *Echegaray 8, 28014,* ☎ *91/429–6551,* FAX *91/420–2423. 58 rooms. AE, DC, MC, V.*

$ 🏨 **Mora.** Right across the Paseo del Prado from the Botanical Garden, the Mora rewards your journey with a sparkling, faux-marble lobby and bright, carpeted hallways. Rooms are simple but large and comfortable. Those on the street have great views of the garden and Prado through soundproof, double-pane windows. For breakfast and lunch, the attached café is excellent, affordable, and popular with locals. ✉ *Paseo del Prado 32, 28014,* ☎ *91/420–1569,* FAX *91/420–0564. 61 rooms. AE, DC, MC, V.*

Nightlife and the Arts

Nightlife

BARS AND CAFÉS

Mesónes. The most traditional and colorful taverns are on Cuchilleros and Cava San Miguel, just west of Plaza Mayor, where you'll find a whole array of *mesónes* with such names as Tortilla, Champiñón, and Boqueron. These are the places to start your evening out in Madrid; many serve tapas and raciónes and close around midnight, when crowds move on to bars and nightclubs.

Old Madrid. Wander the narrow streets between Puerta del Sol and Plaza Santa Ana—most are packed with traditional tapas bars. The **Cervecería Alemana** (✉ Plaza Santa Ana 6, ☎ 91/429–7033) is a beer hall founded more than 100 years ago by Germans and patronized, inevitably, by Ernest Hemingway. **El Abuelo** (✉ Victoria 6, ☎ 91/532–1219), or "Grandpa," serves only two tapas but does them better than anyone else: grilled shrimp and shrimp sautéed in garlic. For a more tranquil atmosphere try the lovely, old tiled bar **Viva Madrid** (✉ Fernández y González 7, ☎ 91/429–3640) early in the evening.

Calle Huertas. Once lined with turn-of-the-20th-century bars playing guitar or chamber music, Calle Huertas now has more nightclubs than any other street in Madrid. **Casa Alberto** (✉ C. Huertas 18, ☎ 91/429–9356), a quiet restaurant-tavern with brick walls, has a good selection of draft beers, and tapas. **La Fídula** (✉ C. Huertas 57, ☎ 91/429–2947) often has live classical music. For zest, try the disco **La Fontanería** (✉ Huertas 38, ☎ 91/369–4904), where the action lasts until 4 AM.

Plaza Santa Bárbara. Just off Alonso Martínez, this area is packed with fashionable bars and beer halls. Stroll along Santa Teresa, Orellana, Campoamor, or Fernando VI and take your pick. The **Cervecería Santa Bárbara** (☎ 91/319–0449), in the plaza itself, is one of the most colorful, a popular beer hall with a good range of tapas.

Cafés. Madrid has no lack of old-fashioned cafés, with dark-wood counters, brass pumps, marble-top tables, and plenty of atmosphere. **Café Comercial** (✉ Glorieta de Bilbao 7, ☎ 91/521–5655) is a classic. **Café Gijón** (✉ Paseo de Recoletos 21, ☎ 91/521–5425) is a former literary hangout that offers a cheery set lunch; it's now one of many cafés with summer terraces that dot the Castellana and Paseo de Recoletos. **El Espejo** (✉ Paseo de Recoletos 31, ☎ 91/308–2347) has Art Nouveau decor and an outdoor terrace in summer. For a late-night coffee, or something stronger, stop into the Baroque **Palacio de Gaviria** (✉ Arenal 9, ☎ 91/526–6069), a restored 19th-century palace that often has live jazz. "International" parties are held every Thursday night.

DISCOS AND NIGHTCLUBS

Nightlife—or *la marcha,* as the Spanish fondly call it—reaches legendary heights in Spain's capital. Smart, trendy dance clubs filled with well-heeled Madrileños are everywhere. For adventure, try the scruffy bar district in Malasaña, around the Plaza Dos de Mayo, where smoky hangouts line Calle San Vicente Ferrer. The often seedy haunts of Chueca, a popular gay area, can be exciting (watch your purse), but classy cafés and trendy live music venues occasionally break up the alleys of tattoo parlors, boutiques, techno discos, and after-hours clubs.

Amadis (✉ Covarrubias 42, under Luchana Cinema, ☎ 91/446–0036) has concerts, dancing, and telephones on every table, encouraging people to call each other with invitations to dance. You must be over 25 to enter. Salsa is a fixture in Madrid; check out the most spectacular moves at **Azucar** (✉ Paseo Reina Cristina 7, ☎ 91/501–6107). **El Clandestino** (✉ Barquillo 34, ☎ 91/521–5563) is a low-key bar-café with impromptu jam sessions. Madrid's hippest club for wild, all-night dancing to an international music mix is **El Sol** (✉ C. Jardines 3, ☎ 91/532–6490). **Fortuny** (✉ Fortuny 34, ☎ 91/319–0588) attracts a celebrity crowd, especially in summer, when the lush outdoor patio is open. The door is ultraselective. **Joy Eslava** (✉ Arenal 11, ☎ 91/366–3733), a downtown disco in a converted theater, is an old standby. **Pacha** (✉ Barceló 11, ☎ 91/447–0128), one of Spain's infamous chain discos, is always energetic. **Torero** (✉ Cruz 26, ☎ 91/523–1129) is for the beautiful people—quite literally: a bouncer allows only those judged *gente guapa* (beautiful people) to enter.

FLAMENCO

Madrid has an array of flamenco shows. Some are good, but many are aimed at the tourist trade. Dinner tends to be mediocre and overpriced, though it ensures the best seats; otherwise, opt for the show and a *consumición* (drink) only, usually starting around 11 PM and costing 3,000 ptas./€18.03–3,500 ptas./€21.04. **Arco de Cuchilleros** (✉ Cuchilleros 7, ☎ 91/364–0263) is one of the better and cheaper venues in the city to view flamenco. **Café de Chinitas** (✉ Torija 7, ☎ 91/559–5135) is expensive, but offers the best flamenco dancing in Madrid. **Casa Patas** (✉ Cañizares 10, ☎ 91/369–0496) is a major showplace;

it offers good, if somewhat touristy, flamenco and tapas all at reasonable prices. **Corral de la Morería** (✉ Morería 17, ☎ 91/365–8446) invites well-known flamenco stars to perform with the resident group.

JAZZ CLUBS

The city's best-known jazz venue is **Café Central** (✉ Plaza de Angel 10, ☎ 91/369–4143). **Café del Foro** (✉ San Andrés 38, ☎ 91/445–3752) is a friendly club with live music nightly. **Clamores** (✉ Albuquerque 14, ☎ 91/445–7938) is known for its great champagne list. **Populart** (✉ Huertas 22, ☎ 91/429–8407) features blues, Brazilian music, and salsa. Seasonal citywide festivals also present excellent artists; check the local press for listings and venues.

The Arts

Details of all cultural events are listed in the daily newspaper *El País* and in the weekly *Guía del Ocio*. Two English-language publications, *The Broadsheet* and *In Spain*, are available free in Irish pubs and other ex-pat hangouts and detail mainly ex-pat activities.

CONCERTS AND OPERA

Madrid's main concert hall is the **Auditorio Nacional de Madrid** (✉ Principe de Vergara 146, ☎ 91/337–0100). Beneath the Plaza de Colón, the underground **Centro Cultural de la Villa** (✉ Plaza de Colon s/n, ☎ 91/575–6080 tickets; 91/553–2526 information) hosts an eclectic variety of performances, from gospel, spiritual, and blues festivals to Celtic dance. For ballet or opera, catch a performance at the legendary **Teatro Real** (✉ Plaza de Isabel II, ☎ 91/516–0660), whose splendid facade dominates the Plaza de Oriente.

FILM

Foreign films are mostly dubbed into Spanish, but movies in English are listed in *El País* or *Guía del Ocio* under "VO" (*versión original*). A dozen or so theaters now show films in English. **Alphaville** (✉ Martín de los Héros 14, off Plaza España, ☎ 91/548–4524) shows films in English. **Cines Renoir** (✉ Martín de los Héros 12, off Plaza España, ☎ 91/559–5760) is an old favorite, and shows films in VO. The **Filmoteca Cine Doré** (✉ Santa Isabel 3, ☎ 91/369–1125) is a city-run institution showing different classic English-language films every day. Your best bet for first-run films in the original language is the **Multicines Ideal** (✉ Doctor Cortezo 6, ☎ 91/369–2518).

THEATER

Most theaters have two curtains, at 7 PM and 10:30 PM, and close on Monday. Tickets are inexpensive and often easy to come by on the night of the performance. The **Centro Cultural de la Villa** (☎ 91/575–6080), beneath the Plaza Colón, stages an eclectic range of theater and musical events. In summer, check listings for open-air events in Retiro Park. The **Círculo de Bellas Artes** (✉ Marqués de Casa Riera 2, off Alcalá 42, ☎ 91/360–5400) houses a leading theater. **Sala Triángulo** (✉ Zurita 20, ☎ 91/530–6891) is one of the many fringe theaters in Lavapiés, and is definitely worth a detour if you understand Spanish.The **Teatro Español** (✉ Príncipe 25 on Plaza Santa Ana, ☎ 91/429–6297) stages Spanish classics. The **Teatro María Guerrero** (✉ Tamayo y Baus 4, ☎ 91/319–4769), the home of the Centro Dramático Nacional, stages plays from García Lorca to Els Joglars.

ZARZUELA

Zarzuela, a combination of light opera and dance that's ideal for non-Spanish speakers, is performed at the **Teatro Nacional Lírico de la Zarzuela** (✉ Jovellanos 4, ☎ 902/488–488) October–July.

Shopping

The main shopping area in central Madrid surrounds the pedestrian streets Preciados and Montera, off the Gran Vía between Puerta del Sol and Plaza Callao. The Salamanca district, just off the Plaza de Colón, bordered roughly by Serrano, Goya, and Conde de Peñalver, is more elegant and expensive; just west of Salamanca, the shops on and around Calle Argensola, just south of Calle Génova, are on their way upscale. Calle Mayor and the streets to the east of Plaza Mayor are lined with fascinating old-fashioned stores straight out of the 19th century.

Antiques

The main areas for antiques are the Plaza de las Cortes, Calle Prado, the Carrera San Jerónimo, and the Rastro flea market, along the Ribera de Curtidores and the courtyards just off it.

Boutiques

Calle Serrano has the widest selection of smart boutiques and designer fashions—think Prada, Armani, and DKNY, as well as renowned Spanish designers such as Josep Font-Luz Diaz. **Adolfo Dóminguez** (✉ Serrano 96, ☎ 91/576–7053; ✉ C. Ortega y Gasset 4, ☎ 91/576–0084), one of Spain's top designers, has several boutiques in Madrid. **Jesús del Pozo** (✉ Almirante 9, ☎ 91/531–3646) is one of Spain's premier young fashion designers, a scion of Spanish style for both men and women. **Loewe** (✉ Serrano 26 and 34, ☎ 91/577–6056; ✉ Gran Vía 8, ☎ 91/532–7024) is Spain's most prestigious leather store. **Seseña** (✉ De la Cruz 23, ☎ 91/531–6840) has outfitted Hollywood stars with capes since the turn of the 20th century. **Sybilla** (✉ Jorge Juan 12, ☎ 91/578–1322) is the studio of Spain's best-known woman designer, who designs fluid dresses and hand-knit sweaters in natural colors and fabrics.

Upscale shopping centers group a variety of exclusive shops stocked with unusual clothes and gifts. **Centro Comercial ABC** (✉ Paseo de la Castellana 34) is a four-decker mall with a large café. **Galerías del Prado** (✉ Plaza de las Cortes 7, on the lower level of the Palace Hotel) has fine books, gourmet foods, clothing, leather goods, art, and more. **Los Jardines de Serrano** (✉ C. Goya and Claudio Coello) has smart boutiques. For street-chic fashion closer to medieval Madrid, check out the **Madrid Fusion Centro de Moda** (✉ Plaza Tirso de Molina 15, ☎ 91/369–0018), where up-and-coming Spanish labels like Instinto, Kika, and Extart fill five floors with faux furs, funky jewelry, and the city's most eccentric selection of shoes. **Zara** (✉ ABC, Serrano 61, ☎ 91/575–6334; ✉ Gran Vía 32, ☎ 91/522–9727; ✉ Princesa 63, ☎ 91/543–2415) is for men, women, and children with trendy taste and slim pocketbooks.

Department Stores

El Corte Inglés (✉ Preciados 3, ☎ 91/531–9619; ✉ Goya 76 and 87, ☎ 91/432–9300; ✉ Princesa 56, ☎ 91/454–6000; ✉ Serrano 47, ☎ 91/432–5490; ✉ Raimundo Fernández Villaverde 79, ☎ 91/418–8800; ✉ La Vaguada Mall, ☎ 91/387–4000) is Spain's largest chain department store, with everything from auto parts to groceries to fashions. The British chain **Marks & Spencer** (✉ Serrano 52, ☎ 91/520–0000; ✉ La Vaguarda Mall, ☎ 91/378–2234) is best known for its woolens and underwear, but most shoppers head straight for the gourmet-food shop in the basement. **FNAC** (✉ Preciados 28, ☎ 91/595–6100) is filled with books, music, and magazines from all over the world.

Food and Flea Markets

The **Rastro,** Madrid's most famous flea market, operates on Sunday from 9 to 2 around the Plaza de Cascorro and the Ribera de Curtidores.

A **stamp and coin market** is held on Sunday morning in the Plaza Mayor. Mornings, take a look at the colorful food stalls inside the 19th-century glass-and-steel **San Miguel** market, also near the Plaza Mayor. There's a **secondhand-book market** most days on the Cuesta Claudio Moyano, near Atocha Station.

Gift Ideas

Madrid is famous for handmade leather boots, guitars, fans, and capes. **Seseña** (✉ Calle de la Cruz 23, ☎ 91/531–6840) has outfitted international celebrities in wool and velvet capes. **Tenorio** (✉ Plaza de la Provincia 6, ☎ 91/366–4440) is where you'll find those fine old boots of Spanish leather, made to order with workmanship that should last a lifetime.

Department stores stock good displays of fans, but for superb examples, try the long-established **Casa de Diego** (✉ Puerta del Sol 12, ☎ 91/522–6643), established in 1853, for fans, umbrellas, and classic Spanish walking sticks with ornamented silver handles. The British royal family buys autograph fans here—white kid-skin fans for signing on special occasions. **José Ramirez** (✉ C. La Paz 8, ☎ 91/531–4229) has provided Spain and the rest of the world with guitars since 1882, and his store includes a museum of antique instruments. Two stores opposite the Prado on Plaza Cánovas del Castillo, **Artesanía Toledana** and **El Escudo de Toledo,** have a wide selection of **souvenirs,** especially Toledo swords, marquetry ware, and pottery. Carefully selected handicrafts from all over Spain—ceramics, furniture, glassware, rugs, embroidery, and more—are sold at **Artespaña** (✉ Hermosilla 14, ☎ 91/435–0221). **Casa Julia** (✉ Almirante 1, ☎ 91/522–0270, FAX 91/521–3137) is an artistic showcase, with two floors of tasteful antiques, paintings by up-and-coming artists, and furniture in experimental designs.

Madrid Essentials

AIRPORTS AND TRANSFERS

Barajas Airport, 16 km (10 mi) northeast of town just off the NII Barcelona highway, receives international and domestic flights. Info-Iberia, at the airport, dispenses information on arrivals and departures.
➤ AIRPORT INFORMATION: **Barajas Airport** (☎ 91/305–8343 or 91/393–6000). **Info-Iberia** (☎ 91/329–5767).

TRANSFERS

For a mere 475 ptas./€2.85, there's a convenient bus to the central Plaza Colón, where you can catch a taxi to your hotel. Buses leave every 15 minutes between 5:40 AM and 2 AM (slightly less often very early or late in the day). Watch your belongings, as the underground Plaza Colón bus station is a favorite haunt of purse snatchers and con artists.

The metro is a bargain at 150 ptas./€0.90 per ticket (or 850 ptas./€5.11 for a 10-trip ticket that can also be used on city buses), but you have to change trains twice to get downtown, and the trip takes 45 minutes.

The fastest and most expensive route into town is by taxi (usually about 2,000 ptas./€12.02, but up to 2,500 ptas./€15.02, plus tip in traffic). Pay the metered amount plus the 350-pta./€2.10 surcharge and 150 ptas./€0.90 for each suitcase. By car take the NII (which becomes Avenida de América) into town, head straight into Calle María de Molina, then turn left on either Calle Serrano or the Castellana.

BUS TRAVEL TO AND FROM MADRID

Madrid has no central bus station. Check with the tourist office for departure points for your destination. The Estación del Sur serves

Toledo, La Mancha, Alicante, and Andalucía. Auto-Rés serves Extremadura, Cuenca, Salamanca, Valladolid, Valencia, and Zamora; Auto-Rés has a central ticket and information office, just off Gran Vía, near the Hotel Arosa. The Basque country and most of north-central Spain are served by Continental Auto. For Àvila, Segovia, and La Granja, use Empresa La Sepulvedana. Empresa Herranz serves El Escorial and the Valley of the Fallen. La Veloz serves Chinchón.

➤ Bus Information: **Auto-Rés** (✉ Plaza Conde de Casal 6, ☎ 91/551–7200, metro: Conde de Casal; central ticket office: ✉ Salud 19, ☎ 91/551–7200). **Continental Auto** (✉ Alenza 20, ☎ 91/530–4800, metro: Ríos Rosas). **Empresa Herranz** (✉ 3 Moncloa Bus Terminal, ☎ 91/890–4100, metro: Moncloa). **Empresa La Sepulvedana** (✉ Paseo de la Florida 11, ☎ 91/530–4800, metro: Norte). **Estación del Sur** (✉ Méndez Álvaro s/n, ☎ 91/468–4200, metro: Palos de la Frontera). **La Veloz** (✉ Avda. Mediterraneo 49, ☎ 91/409–7602, metro: Conde de Casal).

BUS TRAVEL WITHIN MADRID

Red city buses run between 6 AM and midnight and cost 150 ptas./€0.90 per ride. After midnight, buses called *buyos* (night owls) run out to the suburbs from Plaza de Cibeles for the same price. Signs at every stop list all other stops by street name, but they're hard to comprehend if you don't know the city well. Pick up a free route map from EMT kiosks on the Plaza de Cibeles or the Puerta del Sol, where you can also buy a 10-ride ticket called a Metrobus (850 ptas./€5.11) that's equally valid for the metro. Drivers will generally make change for anything up to a 2,000-pta./€12.02 note. If you've bought a 10-ride ticket, step just behind the driver and insert it in the ticket-punching machine until the mechanism rings. If you speak Spanish, call the information line listed below.

➤ Bus Information: **General Information** (☎ 91/406–8810).

CAR TRAVEL

The main roads are as follows: north–south, the Paseo de la Castellana and Paseo del Prado; east–west, Calle de Alcalá, Gran Vía, and Calle de la Princesa. The M30 circles Madrid, and the M40 is an outer ring road about 12 km (7 mi) farther out. For Burgos and France, drive north up the Castellana and follow the signs for the NI. For Barcelona and Barajas Airport, head up the Castellana to Plaza Dr. Marañón, then right onto María de Molina and the NII; for Andalusia and Toledo, head south down Paseo del Prado, and then follow the signs to the NIV and N401, respectively. For Segovia, Ávila, and El Escorial, head west along Princesa to Avenida Puerta de Hierro and onto the NVI–La Coruña.

EMERGENCIES

The general emergency number in all EU nations (akin to 911 in the United States) is 112. A list of pharmacies open 24 hours (*farmacias de guardia*) is published daily in *El País*.

➤ Emergency Services: **Ambulance** (☎ 061, 91/522–2222, or 91/588–4400). **Police** (☎ 091 emergencies; 092 Municipal Police [for towed cars and traffic accidents]).

➤ Hospitals: **Hospital 12 de Octubre** (✉ Carretera de Andalucía, Km 5.4, ☎ 91/390–8000). **La Paz Ciudad Sanitaria** (✉ Paseo de la Castellana 261, ☎ 91/358–2600).

ENGLISH-LANGUAGE MEDIA

The International Bookshop carries secondhand books only.

➤ Bookstores: **Booksellers** (✉ José Abascal 48, ☎ 91/442–8104). **Casa del Libro** (✉ Gran Vía 29, ☎ 91/521–2113). **International Bookshop** (✉ Campomanes 13, ☎ 91/541–7291).

SUBWAY TRAVEL

The metro offers the simplest and quickest means of transport and operates from 6 AM to 1:30 AM. Metro maps are available from ticket offices, hotels, and tourist offices. The flat fare is 150 ptas. a ride; a 10-ride ticket, 850 ptas., is also valid for buses. Carry some change (5, 25, 50, and 100 ptas.) for the ticket machines, especially after 10 PM; the machines make change and allow you to skip long ticket lines.

TAXIS

Taxis are one of Madrid's few truly good deals. Meters start at 200 ptas. and add 130 ptas. per km (½ mi) thereafter (150 ptas. per km at night, on weekends and holidays, and beyond city limits). Numerous supplemental charges, however, mean that your total cost often bears little resemblance to what you see on the meter. Supplemental charges—over and above your fare—include 150 ptas. on Sundays and holidays and between 11 PM and 6 AM, 150 ptas. to sports stadiums or the bullring, and 450 ptas. (plus 50 ptas. per suitcase) to or from the airport.

Taxi stands are numerous, and taxis are easily hailed in the street—except when it rains, at which point they're exceedingly hard to come by. Available cabs display a LIBRE sign during the day, a green light at night. No tip is expected, but if you're inspired to give one, 25 ptas. is about right for shorter rides; you may want to go as high as 10% for a trip to the airport. You can call a cab through Tele-Taxi, Radioteléfono Taxi, or Radio Taxi Gremial.

➤ TAXIS & SHUTTLES: **Radio Taxi Gremial** (☏ 91/447–5180). **Radioteléfono Taxi** (☏ 91/547–8200). **Tele-Taxi** (☏ 91/371–2131).

TOURS

Julià Tours, Pullmantur, and Trapsatur all run the same city orientation tours, conducted in Spanish and English. Reserve directly with their offices, through any travel agent, or through your hotel. Departure points are the addresses listed below, though you can often arrange to be picked up at your hotel. Tours leave in morning, afternoon, and evening and cover various selections of sites and activities.

➤ FEES AND SCHEDULES: **Julià Tours** (✉ Gran Vía 68, ☏ 91/559–9605). **Pullmantur** (✉ Plaza de Oriente 8, ☏ 91/541–1807). **Trapsatur** (✉ San Bernardo 23, ☏ 91/302–6039).

BUS TOURS

Trapsatur runs the Madridvision bus, which makes a one-hour tour of the city with recorded commentary in English. No reservation is necessary; catch the bus in front of the Prado every 1½ hours beginning at 10 AM, Tuesday–Sunday. There are no buses on Sunday afternoon. A round-trip ticket costs 1,750 ptas./€10.52, and a two-day pass, 2,500 ptas./€15.03. A similar service with an open-top double decker, is run by Sol Pentours.

➤ FEES AND SCHEDULES: **Sol Pentours** (✉ Gran Vía 26, ☏ 902/303–903).

SINGLE- AND MULTIPLE-DAY TOURS

Julià Tours, Pullmantur, and Trapsatur run full- or half-day trips to El Escorial, Ávila, Segovia, Toledo, and Aranjuez, and in summer to Cuenca and Salamanca. Summer weekends, the popular *Tren de la Fresa* (Strawberry Train) takes passengers from the old Delicias Station to Aranjuez (known for its production of strawberries and asparagus) on a 19th-century train. Tickets can be obtained from RENFE offices, travel agents, and the Delicias Station (✉ Paseo de las Delicias 61). Other one- or two-day excursions by train are available on summer weekends. Contact RENFE for details.

WALKING TOURS

The Municipal Tourist Office leads English-language tours of Madrid's Old Quarter every Saturday morning at 10. The *ayuntamiento* (city hall) has a popular selection of Spanish bus and walking tours under the name Descubre Madrid. Walking tours depart most mornings and visit many hidden corners as well as major sights; options include Madrid's Railroads, Medicine in Madrid, Goya's Madrid, and Commerce and Finance in Madrid. Schedules are listed in the "Descubre Madrid" leaflet available from the municipal tourist office. Tickets can be purchased at the Patronato de Turismo. If you want a personal tour with a local guide, contact the Asociación Profesional de Informadores.

➤ FEES AND SCHEDULES: **Asociación Profesional de Informadores** (✉ Ferraz 82, ☎ 91/542–1214 or 91/541–1221). **Municipal Tourist Office** (✉ Plaza Mayor 3). **Patronato de Turismo** (✉ C. Mayor 69, ☎ 91/588–2900).

TRAIN TRAVEL

Madrid has two railroad stations. Chamartín, in the northern suburbs beyond the Plaza de Castilla, is the main station, with trains to France and the north (including Barcelona, Ávila, Salamanca, Santiago, and La Coruña). Most trains to Valencia, Alicante, and Andalusia leave from Chamartín but stop at the Atocha station as well. Atocha sends trains to Segovia, Toledo, Granada, Extremadura, and Lisbon. A convenient metro stop (Atocha RENFE) connects the Atocha rail station to the city subway system. The old Atocha station, designed by Eiffel, is Madrid's terminal for high-speed AVE service to Córdoba and Seville.

For all train information call or visit the RENFE offices, open weekdays 9:30–8. Ask for an English operator. There's another RENFE office in the international arrivals hall at Barajas Airport, or you can purchase tickets at any of the three main stations or from travel agents displaying the blue and yellow RENFE sign.

➤ TRAIN INFORMATION: **Atocha** (✉ Glorieta del Emperador Carlos V, southern end of Paseo del Prado, ☎ 91/328–9020). **Chamartín** (✉ Avda. Pío XII, ☎ 91/315–9976). **RENFE** (✉ Alcalá 44, ☎ 902/240202, WEB www.renfe.es/ingles).

TRANSPORTATION AROUND MADRID

Madrid is a fairly compact city, and most of the main sights can be visited on foot. If you're staying in one of the modern hotels in northern Madrid, however, off the Castellana, you may need to use the bus or subway.

TRAVEL AGENCIES

➤ LOCAL AGENTS: **American Express** (✉ Plaza de las Cortes 2, ☎ 91/322–5500). **Carlson Wagons-Lits** (✉ Condesa de Venadito 1, ☎ 91/724–9900). **Pullmantur** (✉ Plaza de Oriente 8, ☎ 91/541–1807).

VISITOR INFORMATION

Madrid Provincial Tourist Office is the best place for comprehensive information. The municipal tourist office is centrally located, but hordes of tourists tend to deplete its stock of brochures. Other tourist offices are located at the International Arrivals Hall in Barajas Airport and at Chamartín train station.

➤ TOURIST INFORMATION: **Madrid Provincial Tourist Office** (✉ Duque de Medinaceli 2, ☎ 91/429–4951). **Municipal Tourist Offices** (✉ Plaza Mayor 3, ☎ 91/588–1636; ✉ International Arrivals Hall, Barajas Airport, ☎ 91/305–8656; Chamartín train station; ☎ 91/315–9976; WEB www.munimadrid.es).

CASTILE

The beauty and romantic histories of the towns around Madrid rank them among Spain's greatest sights. Ancient Toledo, Spain's former capital; the great palace-monastery of El Escorial; Segovia's Roman aqueduct and fairy-tale Alcázar; the imposing medieval walls of Ávila; and the magnificent Plaza Mayor of the old university town of Salamanca all lie within an hour or two of the capital.

All of these towns, with the possible exception of Salamanca, are easy day trips from Madrid. But if you've had your fill of Spain's booming capital, you'll find it far more rewarding to leave Madrid altogether and tour from one town to another, spending a night or two in classically Spanish Castile (Castilla). After the day-trippers have gone home, you can enjoy the real charm of these provincial communities and wander at leisure through their medieval streets.

Toledo

If you're driving, head south from Madrid on the N401. About 20 minutes from the capital, look left for a prominent rounded hill topped by a statue of Christ. This is **El Cerro de los Ángeles** (Hill of the Angels), the geographical center of the Iberian Peninsula. After 90 minutes of drab, industrial scenery, the unforgettable silhouette of Toledo suddenly rises before you, with the imposing bulk of the Alcázar and the slender spire of its cathedral dominating the skyline. This former capital, where Moors, Jews, and Christians once lived in harmony, is now a living national monument, holding all the elements of Spanish civilization in hand-carved, sun-mellowed stone. For a stunning view of Toledo as El Greco knew it, begin with a panoramic drive around the Carretera de Circunvalación, crossing over the Alcántara bridge and returning by way of the bridge of San Martín. As you gaze at the city rising like an island in its own bend of the Tagus, you may notice how little its skyline has changed in the four centuries since El Greco painted *Storm over Toledo.*

Toledo is a small city steeped in history and full of magnificent buildings. It was the capital of Spain under both Moors and Christians until Philip II moved the capital to Madrid in 1561. Begin your visit with a drink in one of the many terrace cafés on the central **Plaza Zocódover**; study a map and try to get your bearings, for a veritable labyrinth confronts you as you try to find your way to Toledo's great treasures. While here, search the square's pastry shops for Toledo's typical *mazapanes* (marzipan candies).

Toledo's 13th-century **cathedral** is one of the greatest in Spain, and the seat of the Cardinal Primate. Somber but elaborate, it blazes with jeweled chalices, gorgeous ecclesiastical vestments, historic tapestries, some 750 stained-glass windows, and paintings by Tintoretto, Titian, Murillo, El Greco, Velázquez, and Goya. The cathedral has two surprises: a **Mozarabic chapel,** where mass is still celebrated on Sunday according to an ancient Mozarabic rite from the days of the Visigoths (AD 419–711); and its unique **Transparente,** an ornate Baroque roof that gives a theatrical glimpse of heaven as the sunlight pours down through a hole to a mass of figures and clouds. ✉ *Arco de Palacio 2,* ☎ *925/222241.* ⏲ *Mon.–Sat. 10:30–6:30, Sun. 2–6:30.*

The tiny chapel of **Santo Tomé,** which houses El Greco's (1541–1614) masterpiece the *Burial of the Count of Orgaz,* captures some of the incredible spirit of the Greek painter who adopted Spain, and Toledo in particular, as his home. Do you recognize the sixth man from the left in the painting's earthly contingent? Or the young boy in the left-hand corner? The first is El Greco himself, the second his son Jorge Manuel—

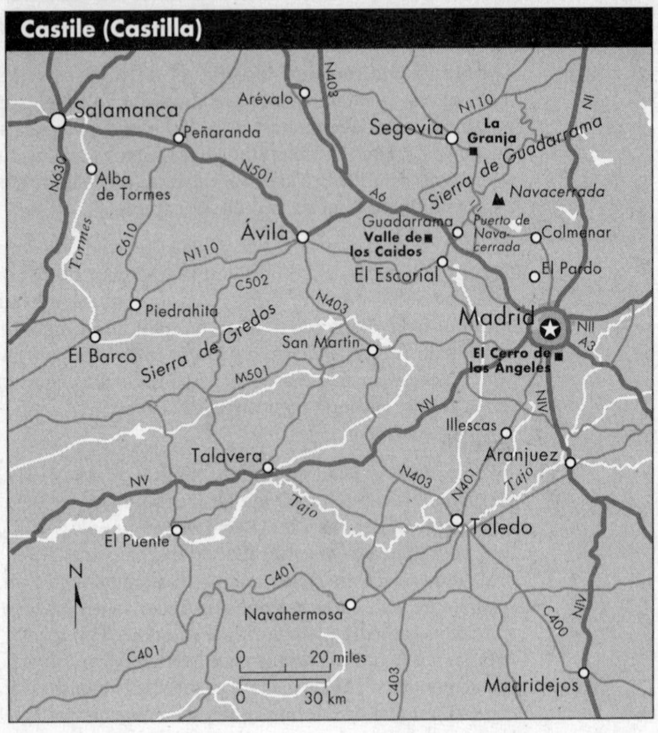

embroidered on the boy's handkerchief you'll see *1578*, the year of his birth. ✉ *Plaza del Conde 4,* ☎ *925/256098,* WEB *www.santotome.org.* ⌚ *May–Oct. 14, daily 10–6:45; Oct. 15–Apr., daily 10–5:45.*

The **Casa de El Greco** (El Greco's House) has copies of the artist's works. The museum next door contains some originals, including a panorama of Toledo with the Hospital of Tavera in the foreground. ✉ *Samuel Levi 3,* ☎ *925/224046.* ⌚ *Tues.–Sat. 10–2 and 4–6, Sun. 10–2.*

The splendid **Sinagoga del Tránsito** (Tránsito Synagogue) was commissioned in 1366 by Samuel Levi, chancellor to Peter the Cruel. The synagogue bears Christian and Moorish as well as Jewish influences in its architecture and decoration; notice the Stars of David interspersed with the arms of Castile and León. The small **Museo Sefardí** (Sephardic Museum) chronicles Toledo's former Jewish community. ✉ *C. Samuel Levi s/n, corner of Reyes Católicos,* ☎ *925/223665.* ⌚ *Tues.–Sat. 10–2 and 4–6, Sun. 10–2.*

Santa María la Blanca (St. Mary the White) was originally a synagogue, founded in 1203. It was consecrated as a church in the early 15th century when it was stormed by a Christian mob led by St. Vincent Ferrer. Except for the 16th-century altarpiece, however, the architecture is neither Jewish nor Christian, but Moorish: the interior has five naves, horseshoe arches, and capitals decorated with texts from the Koran. ✉ *Reyes Católicos 4,* ☎ *925/227257.* ⌚ *Oct.–Mar., daily 10–2 and 3:30–5:45; Apr.–Sept., daily 10–1:45 and 3:30–6:45.*

San Juan de los Reyes, a beautiful Gothic church with fine cloisters, was started by Ferdinand and Isabella in 1476. The iron manacles on the outer walls were placed there for posterity by Christians freed by the Moors. The Catholic Monarchs originally intended to be buried here, but their great triumph at Granada in 1492 changed their plans.

✉ *Reyes Católicos,* ☎ *925/223802.* ⏲ *Oct.–Mar., daily 10–1:45 and 3:30–5:45; Apr.–Sept., daily 10–1:45 and 3:30–6:45.*

The **Museo de la Santa Cruz** (Museum of the Holy Cross) has some splendid El Grecos. ✉ *Cervantes 3, off Plaza de Zocódover,* ☎ *925/221036.* ⏲ *Mon. 10–2 and 4–6:30, Tues.–Sat. 10–6:30, Sun. 10–2.*

The **Hospital de Tavera** (Tavera Hospital), outside the city walls, houses the Duque de Lema museum in its southern wing. The most important works in this miscellaneous collection are El Greco's *Baptism of Christ* and Alonso de Berruguete's exquisitely carved tomb of Cardinal Tavera. ✉ *Cardenal Tavera 2,* ☎ *925/220451.* ⏲ *Daily 10–1:30 and 3:30–6.*

$$$–$$$$ ★ ✕ **Asador Adolfo.** Toledo's most famous restaurant, near the cathedral, is known for its gratifying combination of good food, service, and Old World charm. Parts of the building date from the 14th century; the dining room retains its original wood-beam ceiling and traces of original murals. Try the superb roast meats or the *tempura de flor de calabacín* (zucchini-flower tempura). ✉ *C. de la Granada 6 and Hombre de Palo 7,* ☎ *925/227321. AE, DC, MC, V. No dinner Sun.*

$$$–$$$$ ✕ **Cason López.** No other restaurant in town has such a combination of ambience and cuisine. A vaulted foyer leads to an enclosed patio with marble statues, twittering caged birds, a fountain, and abstract religious paintings. The market-based menu features the finest Castilian and Continental cuisine. Starters such as garlic-ravioli soup are followed by hearty second courses, including braised rabbit with sesame sauce and mashed potatoes. Almond marzipan cake topped with cream cheese is a great way to round out a superb meal. The lunchtime menú del día is 4,500 ptas./€27.05. ✉ *Sillería 3,* ☎ *925/254774. AE, DC, MC, V.*

$$ ✕ **La Abadía.** Perfect for a light lunch, a sandwich, or a round of tapas, this stylish bar-restaurant has vaulted stone ceilings and a huge, old wooden door. The dining room downstairs specializes in shish kebabs, grilled meats, and salads. ✉ *Plaza San Nicolás, Núnez de Arce 3,* ☎ *925/251140. MC, V.*

$$ ✕ **Venta de Aires.** This century-old inn on the edge of town, not far from the Tajo River, is where Toledanos go to eat partridge. Steaks and lamb are also expertly prepared. ✉ *Circo Romano 35,* ☎ *925/220545. AE, DC, MC, V.*

$$$ ★ 🏨 **Parador Nacional de Toledo.** The best and most expensive hotel in Toledo, the Conde de Orgaz is one of Spain's most respected paradors. It's a modern structure built in the traditional Toledan style; perched on a hill across the river (a 15-minute drive from the city center), it commands magnificent views of the city. Book well in advance. ✉ *Cerro del Emperador s/n, 45001,* ☎ *925/221850,* FAX *925/225166,* WEB *www.parador.es. 76 rooms. Pool. AE, DC, MC, V.*

$$ ★ 🏨 **Hostal del Cardenal.** Built in the 18th century as a summer palace for a cardinal, this quiet and beautiful hotel has rooms that overlook a wooded garden and a restaurant that's popular with tourists. It's hard to believe that the highway is so close by. ✉ *Paseo de Recaredo 24, 45004,* ☎ *925/224900,* FAX *925/222991,* WEB *www.cardenal.nacom.es. 27 rooms. Restaurant. AE, DC, MC, V.*

$$ 🏨 **Pintor El Greco.** Next door to the famous painter's house-museum, this friendly hotel fills a building that was a bakery in the 17th century. The interior is warm and modern, with some antique touches such as exposed brick vaulting and terra-cotta tile floors. ✉ *Alamillos del Tránsito 13, 45002,* ☎ *925/214250,* FAX *925/215819. 33 rooms. AE, DC, MC, V.*

El Escorial

In the foothills of the Guadarrama Mountains, 50 km (31 mi) northwest of Madrid and 120 km (74 mi) from Toledo, stands the Monastery of San Lorenzo del Escorial, the burial place of Spanish kings and queens. Built by the religious fanatic Philip II as a memorial to his father, Charles V, El Escorial is a vast, rectangular structure, conceived and executed with a monotonous magnificence worthy of the Spanish royal necropolis. It was designed by Juan de Herrera, Spain's greatest Renaissance architect. The **Pantéon Real** (Royal Pantheon) contains the tombs of all the monarchs since Carlos I save three. Only those queens who bore sons who were later crowned lie in the same crypt; the others, along with royal sons and daughters who never ruled, lie in the nearby **Pantéon de los Infantes** (Princes' Pantheon). The monastery's other highlights are Philip II's magnificent **library,** with 40,000 rare volumes and 2,700 illuminated manuscripts (including the diary of St. Teresa), and the **royal apartments.** Compare the spartan private apartment of Philip II, including the simple bedroom in which he died in 1598, with the beautiful carpets, porcelain, and tapestries with which his less austere successors embellished the rest of his somber commission. ✉ *Junction of Rtes. C600 and M505, northwest of Madrid,* ☎ *91/890–5905.* ⊙ *Tues.–Sun. 10–6 (10–7 in summer), last entry 45 mins before closing.*

$$$–$$$$ ★ ✕ **Charolés.** This elegant restaurant has a terrace above the street for summer dining. Its meat dishes are famous throughout the region; try the *charolés a la pimienta* (peppered steak). Fresh fish is brought in daily from Spain's north coast. ✉ *Floridablanca 24,* ☎ *91/890–5975. Reservations essential. AE, DC, MC, V.*

$$$ ✕ **Parrilla Príncipe.** The scents of roast kid, lamb, chicken, and pork sausage draw crowds with big appetites to this specialist in succulent barbecue. Airier and more modern that most local taverns, the restaurant also has vegetarian paella and pasta on its menu. ✉ *Floridablanca 6,* ☎ *91/890–1611. AE, DC, MC, V. Closed Tues.*

$–$$ ✕ **Mesón de la Cueva.** Founded in 1768, this atmospheric mesón has several small, rustic dining rooms. It's a must for ambience. ✉ *San Antón 4,* ☎ *91/890–1516. MC, V. Closed Mon.*

$$$ 🏨 **Victoria Palace.** The rooms at the back of this grand old hotel near the monastery have balconies and a splendid view toward Madrid. There's also a garden. ✉ *Juan de Toledo 4, 28200,* ☎ *91/890–1511,* FAX *91/896–9896. 88 rooms. Pool. AE, DC, MC, V.*

$$ 🏨 **Miranda Suizo.** With its dark-wood fittings, marble café tables, and main-street location, this charming hotel is straight out of the 19th century. The guest rooms are comfortable. ✉ *Floridablanca 20, 28200,* ☎ *91/890–4711,* FAX *91/890–4358. 52 rooms. AE, DC, MC, V.*

Segovia

★ The golden-stone market town of Segovia has outstanding medieval and Roman monuments, embroideries, and textiles, and excellent cuisine. The majestic **Roman aqueduct,** its huge granite blocks held together without mortar, greets you at the entrance to Segovia. At its foot is a small bronze statue of Romulus and the wolf, presented by Rome in 1974 to commemorate the 2,000-year history of Spain's greatest surviving Roman monument.

The **Ronda de Santa Lucía** leads to the most romantic view of the Alcázar, perched high on its rock like the prow of a mighty ship. Return via the Carretera de los Hoyos for yet another magical view, this time of the venerable cathedral rising from the ramparts.

Calle Real, the main shopping street, passes the Romanesque church of San Martín, with a porticoed outer gallery.

Plaza Mayor, with colorful ceramics shops (good bargains) and pleasant cafés, is set against a backdrop of ancient arcaded houses and one of the loveliest Gothic cathedrals in Spain.

Segovia's **cathedral** was the last Gothic cathedral to be built in Spain (the first was in nearby Ávila). Begun in 1525 by order of Charles V, it has a golden and harmonious interior, illuminated by 16th-century Flemish windows. Its museum, off the cloister, has the first book printed in Spain (1472) and a 17th-century ceiling paneled in white and gold, a splendid example of Mudéjar *artesonado* work. ✉ *Marqués del Arco 1, Plaza Mayor,* ☎ *921/462205.* ⏲ *June–Sept., daily 10–7; Oct.–May, daily 10–6. Closed Wed. afternoon.*

The turreted **Alcázar** is largely a fanciful re-creation from the 1880s; the original 13th-century castle was destroyed by fire in 1862. However, the view from its ramparts—and, even better, from its tower if you can manage the 156 steps—is breathtaking. The Alcázar served as a major residence of the Catholic Monarchs; here Isabella met Ferdinand, and from here she set out to the Plaza Mayor to be crowned Queen of Castile. The interior successfully illustrates the dawn of Spain's golden age. ✉ *Plaza de la Reina Victoria Eugenia s/n,* ☎ *921/460759.* ⏲ *May–Sept., daily 10–7; Oct.–Apr., daily 10–6.*

$$–$$$ ✕ **Casa Duque.** At the end of Segovia's main shopping street, this restaurant has several floors of beautifully decorated traditional dining rooms. There's plenty of local atmosphere, and the food is pure Castilian—roasts are the house specialty. ✉ *Cervantes 12,* ☎ *921/462487. AE, DC, MC, V.*

$$–$$$ ✕ **La Oficina.** Traditional Castilian dishes are served here in two delightful dining rooms that date from 1893. ✉ *Cronista Lecea 10,* ☎ *921/460286. AE, DC, MC, V.*

$–$$ ★ ✕ **Mesón de Cándido.** Tucked cozily under the aqueduct, Segovia's most prestigious restaurant benefits from the ban on traffic by the monument. The dining rooms are full of medieval atmosphere and Castilian memorabilia. Specialties are cochinillo asado and cordero asado, both succulent. Terrace dining is available in summer. ✉ *Plaza Azoguejo 5,* ☎ *921/425911. Reservations essential. AE, DC, MC, V.*

$$$ ★ 🏨 **Parador Nacional de Segovia.** To the north of town, this modern parador offers comfortable, spacious rooms and both indoor and outdoor pools. The views of the city are magnificent, especially at sunset. The rooms are light, with generous amounts of glass. The restaurant serves excellent Castilian food. ✉ *Carretera de Valladolid s/n (off the N601 toward Valladolid), 40003,* ☎ *921/443737,* FAX *921/437362,* WEB *www.parador.es. 113 rooms. Restaurant, pool. AE, DC, MC, V.*

$$ 🏨 **Infanta Isabel.** Right on a corner of the Plaza Mayor, this small, central hotel has a Victorian feel and great views of the cathedral. Guest rooms are light, with painted white furnishings. ✉ *Isabel la Católica, 40001,* ☎ *921/461300,* FAX *921/462217. 37 rooms. AE, DC, MC, V.*

$$ 🏨 **Las Sirenas.** A few steps from the Plaza Mayor, this elegant hotel is in one of Segovia's best locations. The furnishings are slightly faded, but old-fashioned charm and splendid views of the church of Milln make it a hard-to-beat value. ✉ *Juan Bravo 30, 40001,* ☎ *921/462663,* FAX *921/462657. 36 rooms. AE, DC, MC, V.*

Ávila

At nearly 4,100 ft above sea level, Ávila is the highest provincial capital in Spain. Alfonso VI and his son-in-law, Count Raimundo de Borgoña, rebuilt the town and walls in 1090, bringing it permanently under Christian control. It is these walls, the best-preserved military installations of their kind in Spain, that give Ávila its special medieval quality. Thick and solid, with 88 towers tufted with untidy storks' nests, they stretch for 2½ km (1½ mi) around the entire city and make an ideal focus for the start of your visit. For a superb overall view, drive out to the **Cuatro Postes** (Four Posts), ¾ km (½ mi) out on the road to Salamanca. Ávila's other claim to fame is St. Teresa the Mystic, who lived much of her life here in the 16th century.

The **Basílica de San Vicente,** just outside the walls, is one of Ávila's finest Romanesque churches, erected on the spot where St. Vincent and his sisters Sabina and Cristeta were martyred in AD 306. Here, too, St. Teresa is said to have experienced the vision that told her to reform the Carmelite order. ✉ *Plaza de San Vicente,* ☎ *920/255230.* ⏲ *Daily 10–1:30 and 4–6:30.*

Ávila's oldest and most rewarding ecclesiastical monuments predate St. Teresa. The impregnable hulk of the **cathedral** resembles a fortress as much as a house of God. Though of Romanesque origin—the Romanesque sections are recognizable by their red-and-white stonework—it is usually cited as Spain's first Gothic cathedral. Inside is the ornate alabaster tomb of Cardinal Alonso de Madrigal, a 15th-century bishop whose swarthy complexion earned him the nickname of "El Tostado" (the toasted one). ✉ *Plaza de la Catedral,* ☎ *920/211641.* ⏲ *Apr.–Oct. weekdays 10–1:30 and 3:30–7, Sat. 10–5:30, Sun. noon–5:30; Nov.–Mar., weekdays 10–1:30 and 3:30–5:30, Sat. 10–5:30, Sun. noon–5:30.*

The **Convento de Santa Teresa** stands on the site of the saint's birthplace, with an ornate Baroque chapel and a museum with some of Teresa's relics: her rosary, books, walking stick, sandal sole, and preserved ring finger. ✉ *Plaza de la Santa, inside the southern gate,* ☎ *920/211030.* ⏲ *Daily 10–1:30 and 3:30–5:30.*

The **Monasterio de Santo Tomás** was built between 1482 and 1493 by Ferdinand and Isabella, who used it as a summer palace. It houses the tomb of their only son, Prince Juan, who died at the age of 19 while a student at Salamanca, and the tomb of the notorious Inquisitor General Tomás de Torquemada. ✉ *Plaza Granada 1,* ☎ *920/220400.* ⏲ *Cloister daily 10–1 and 4–8. Museum Tues.–Sun. 11–1 and 4–6.*

You can relax in the pleasant **Plaza de Santa Teresa,** with outdoor cafés and a statue of the saint erected for Pope John Paul's visit in 1982.

$$–$$$ ★ ✕ **El Molino de la Losa.** On a quiet spit of land in the Adaja River, this restaurant occupies a restored 15th-century mill and has splendid views of Ávila's walls. In summer you can have a drink and enjoy some tapas outside by the duck pond. Specialties include lamb roasted in a medieval-style wood oven and fresh river trout. ✉ *Bajada de la Losa 12,* ☎ *920/211101. AE, MC, V. Closed Mon.*

$–$$ ★ ✕ **Mesón del Rastro.** This ancient inn tucked into the city walls is Ávila's most atmospheric place to dine. Local specialties include *ternera* (veal) and *yemas de Santa Teresa* (a dessert made from candied egg yolks). ✉ *Plaza del Rastro 4,* ☎ *920/211218. AE, DC, MC, V.*

$$$ ★ 🏨 **Hotel Palacio de los Velada.** A beautifully restored 16th-century palace houses Ávila's top hotel, ideally located in the heart of the city, beside the cathedral. You can relax between sightseeing excursions in the lovely palace courtyard. The attractive rooms are modern and comfortable, and have all the amenities. ✉ *Plaza de la Catedral 10, 05001,* ☎ *920/255100,* FAX *920/254900. 145 rooms. Restaurant. AE, DC, MC, V.*

$$$ 🏨 **Parador Nacional de Ávila.** Superbly set in a 15th-century palace just inside the city's northern walls, this parador has rooms decorated in traditional Castilian style. Some rooms have four-poster beds and views of the city walls. The attractive dining room serves local dishes. ✉ *Marqués Canales de Chozas 2, 05001,* ☎ *920/211340,* FAX *920/226166,* WEB *www.parador.es. 62 rooms. Restaurant. AE, DC, MC, V.*

Salamanca

★ Salamanca is an ancient and gorgeous city, and even your first glimpse of it is bound to be unforgettable. In the foreground as you approach is the sturdy 15-arch Roman bridge, and above this—dominating the view—soar the city's old houses and the golden walls, turrets, and domes of its plateresque cathedrals. The word *plateresque* comes from *plata* (silver), implying that the stone is chiseled and engraved as intricately as that delicate metal. Today, as centuries ago, the University of Salamanca is the dominant influence here, creating an intellectual atmosphere and a stimulating arts scene.

The west facade of the Dominican **Convento de San Estebán** (Monastery of St. Stephen) is superbly plateresque. ✉ *Plaza Concilio de Trento s/n,* ☎ *923/215000.* ⏲ *Daily 9–1 and 4–7.*

Salamanca has two distinct, adjoining **cathedrals,** the **Catedral Vieja** (Old Cathedral) and the grandly carved **Catedral Nueva** (New Cathedral). Inside the sturdy Romanesque walls of the Old Cathedral is a stunning altarpiece with 53 painted panels. Within the splendid **cloister** are a worthy collection of religious art and the **Capilla de Santa Bárbara** (Chapel of St. Barbara, or Degree Chapel), where anxious students sought help the night before their final exams. ✉ *Plá y Deniel s/n,* ☎ *923/217476.* ⏲ *New Cathedral Apr.–Sept., daily 9–2 and 4–8; Oct.–Mar., daily 9–1 and 4–6. Old Cathedral Apr.–Sept., daily 10–1:30 and 4–7:30; Oct.–Mar. 10–12:30 and 4–5:30.*

Founded by Alfonso IX in 1218, Salamanca's **Universidad** (University) is to Spain what Oxford is to England. On the famous facade of the **Escuelas Mayores** (Medieval University), a profusion of plateresque carving surrounds the medallions of Ferdinand and Isabella. See if you can find the famous frog and skull, said to bring good luck to students taking exams. Inside, the **Sala de Fray Luis de León** (Friar Luis's lecture room) has been untouched since the days of that great scholar, and the prestigious **library** holds some 50,000 parchment and leather-bound volumes. ✉ *Patio de Las Escuelas,* ☎ *923/294550, ext. 1150.* ⏲ *Weekdays 9:30–1:30 and 4–7:30, Sat. 9:30–1:30 and 4–7, Sun. 10–1:30.*

The elegant, 18th-century **Plaza Mayor** is Salamanca's crowning glory. Built by Alberto and Nicolás Churriguera, it is widely thought the most beautiful Plaza Mayor in Spain. Here you can browse in stores offering typical *charro* jewelry (silver and black flower beads), head down the adjoining streets in search of colorful tapas bars, or just relax and watch the world go by at an outdoor café.

$$$ ✕ **Chez Victor.** If you're tired of Castilian cuisine, try this chic place, where chef-owner Victoriano Salvador adapts French food to Spanish tastes. Sample the *carrillada de buey braseada con jengibre* (cheek of beef braised in ginger) and outstanding desserts, especially the raspberry-walnut *tarta de chocolate* (chocolate pie) with fresh whipped cream. ✉ *Espoz y Mina 26,* ☎ *923/213123. AE, DC, MC, V. Closed Mon. No dinner Sun. Closed Aug.*

$$–$$$ ★ ✕ **Chapeau.** This chic spot offers both meat and fish carefully roasted in its wood-fire ovens. Try the *pimientos relleños* (stuffed peppers) and, for dessert, the orange mousse. ✉ *Gran Vía 20,* ☎ *923/211–726. AE, DC, MC, V. Closed Sun. Closed Aug.*

$–$$ ✕ **Río de la Plata.** This tiny, long-standing basement restaurant just off Calle de San Pablo retains a warm, old-fashioned character with a fireplace and a local crowd. The food, good-quality fish and meat, is simple but carefully prepared. ✉ *Plaza del Peso 1,* ☎ *923/219005. MC, V. Closed Mon. and July.*

$$$$ **Gran Hotel.** The grande dame of Salamanca's hotels offers stylishly baroque lounges and refurbished, yet old-fashioned, oversize rooms just steps from the Plaza Mayor. ✉ *Poeta Iglesias 5, 37001,* ☎ *923/213500,* FAX *923/213500,* WEB *www.helcom.es/granhotel. 136 rooms. Restaurant. AE, DC, MC, V.*

$$$ **NH Palacio del Castellanos.** Housed in an immaculately restored 15th-century palace, this hotel has an exquisite interior patio and an equally beautiful restaurant. ✉ *San Pablo 58, 37008,* ☎ *923/261818,* FAX *923/261819,* WEB *www.nh-hoteles.com. 62 rooms. Restaurant. AE, DC, MC, V.*

$$ **Hostal Plaza Mayor.** Steps from the Plaza Mayor, this agreeable hostelry has small but modern rooms. The potential drawback is noise on Friday and Saturday nights, when student *tunas* (strolling musicians) sing guitar ballads at nearby cafés until the wee hours. Reserve in advance. ✉ *Plaza del Corrillo 20, 37008,* ☎ *923/262020,* FAX *923/217548. 19 rooms. Restaurant. MC, V.*

Castile Essentials

BUS TRAVEL

All towns are linked by buses; local tourist offices can advise on schedules. Each town has a central bus station.

➤ BUS INFORMATION: **Ávila** (✉ Avda. de Madrid, ☎ 920/220154). **Salamanca** (✉ Filiberto Villalobos 71, ☎ 923/236717). **Segovia** (✉ Paseo Ezequiel González, ☎ 921/427707). **Toledo** (✉ Ronda de Castilla la Mancha, off the road from Madrid, ☎ 925/215850).

CAR TRAVEL

The N403 from Toledo to Ávila passes through spectacular scenery in the Sierra de Gredos, as does the C505 from Ávila to El Escorial. From El Escorial to Segovia, both the Puerto de León and Puerto de Navacerrada mountain passes offer magnificent views. The N501 from Ávila to Salamanca takes you across the tawny plain of Castile.

TRAIN TRAVEL

Trains to Toledo leave from Madrid's Atocha Station; to Salamanca from Chamartín Station; and to Ávila, Segovia, and El Escorial from both stations, although sometimes more frequently from Chamartín. For schedules and reservations call RENFE. Within the region, there's a direct train line between El Escorial, Ávila, and Salamanca; otherwise, train connections are poor, and you'll do better by bus.

➤ TRAIN INFORMATION: **RENFE** (☎ 902/2400202, WEB www.renfe.es).

VISITOR INFORMATION

➤ TOURIST INFORMATION: **Ávila** (✉ Plaza de la Catedral 4, ☎ 920/211387). **El Escorial** (✉ Floridablanca 10, ☎ 91/890–1554). **Salamanca** (✉ Casa de las Conchas, Rúa Mayor s/n, ☎ 923/268571; information booth, ✉ Plaza Mayor). **Segovia** (✉ Plaza Mayor 10, ☎ 921/460334; Plaza del Azoguejo 1, ☎ 921/462–906). **Toledo** (✉ Puerta de Bisagra, ☎ 925/220843).

BARCELONA

As the capital of Catalunya (Catalonia), 2,000-year-old Barcelona commanded a vast Mediterranean empire when Madrid was still a dusty Moorish outpost on the Spanish steppe. Relegated to second-city status only after Madrid was chosen as site of the royal court in 1561, Barcelona more than rivals Madrid for architecture, culture, and nightlife. Industrious, creative and playful in even parts, the citizens of this thriving metropolis are proud to have and use their own language—street names, museum exhibits, newspapers, radio programs, and movies are all in Catalan. An important milestone here was the city's long-awaited opportunity to host the Olympic Games in summer 1992; the Olympics were of singular importance in Barcelona's modernization. Their legacy includes a vastly improved ring road and several other highways; the cleaning-up of four beaches; and the creation of an entire neighborhood in what used to be the run-down industrial district of Poble Nou. In addition, the promontory of Montjuïc gained a sports stadium, several swimming pools, and an adjoining marina. Few cities can rival the medieval atmosphere of the Gothic Quarter's narrow alleys, the elegance and distinction of the Moderniste (Art Nouveau) Eixample, or the many fruits of Gaudí's whimsical imagination. Extraordinarily endowed with two millenniums of art and architecture, Barcelona remains a world center for design.

Exploring Barcelona

Numbers in the margin correspond to points of interest on the Barcelona map.

It should take you two full days of sightseeing to complete the following tour. The first part covers the Gothic Quarter, the Picasso Museum, and Las Ramblas. The second part takes you to Passeig de Gràcia and the church of the Sagrada Família; and the third, to Montjuïc.

The Barri Gòtic (Gothic Quarter) and Las Ramblas

★ 1 **Catedral de la Seu** (Cathedral). Citizens of Barcelona gather on Sunday morning to dance the *sardana,* a symbol of Catalan identity, on Plaça de la Seu, in front of the cathedral. The elaborate Gothic structure was built between 1298 and 1450, though the spire and Gothic facade were not added until 1892. Inside, highlights are the beautifully carved **choir stalls**; Santa Eulàlia's tomb in the crypt; the battle-scarred crucifix from Don Juan's galley in the naval battle of Lepanto, in the **Capella de Lepanto** (Lepanto Chapel); and the cloisters. ⊠ *Plaça de la Seu,* ☎ *93/315–1554.* ⊙ *Daily 7:45–1:30 and 4–7:45.*

12 **Gran Teatre del Liceu.** Barcelona's famous opera house was gutted by fire in 1994 but has reopened, a modern replica of its original self. Built between 1845 and 1847, the old Liceu was one of the world's most beautiful opera houses, with ornamental gilt and plush red-velvet fittings. Anna Pavlova danced here in 1930, and Maria Callas sang here in 1959. ⊠ *La Rambla 51–59,* ☎ *93/485–9900.* ⊙ *Daily 9:45–10:15.*

9 **Monument a Colom** (Columbus Monument). You can ride an elevator to the top for a commanding view of the city and port. Columbus faces out to sea, pointing, ironically, east toward Naples. Nearby you can board the cable car to cross the harbor to Barceloneta or catch it in the other direction up Montjuïc. ⊠ *Portal de la Pau s/n,* ☎ *93/302–5224.* ⊙ *Weekdays 10–1:30 and 3–6:30, weekends 10–6:30.*

15 **Museu d'Art Contemporani de Barcelona** (MACBA; Barcelona Museum of Contemporary Art). Designed by American Richard Meier, the contemporary-art museum is an important addition to Barcelona's treasury of art and architecture. In the once rough-and-tumble Raval district, it and the neighboring **Centre de Cultura Contemporànea** (CCCB; Center for Contemporary Culture) have reclaimed important buildings and spaces as part of the city's renewal of its historic quarters and traditional neighborhoods. ⊠ *Plaça dels Àngels,* ☎ *93/412–0810.* ⊙ *Weekdays 11–7, Sat. 10–8, Sun. 10–3.*

2 **Museu Frederic Marès.** Here you can browse for hours among the miscellany assembled by sculptor-collector Frederic Marès, including

Casa Milà 18
Catedral de la Seu . . . 1
Fundació Miró 22
Gran Teatre del Liceu 12
Mançana de la Discòrdia 17
Mies van der Rohe Pavilion 20
Monument a Colom . . 9
Museu d'Art Contemporani de Barcelona 15
Museu Frederic Marès 2
Museu Marítim 10
Museu Nacional d'Art de Catalunya 21
Museu Picasso 5
Palau de la Música Catalana 4
Palau de la Virreina 14
Palau Güell 11
Plaça de Catalunya . . 16
Plaça del Rei 3
Plaça Reial 8
Plaça Sant Jaume 7
Rambla St. Josep . . . 13
Santa Maria del Mar 6
Temple Expiatori de la Sagrada Família 19

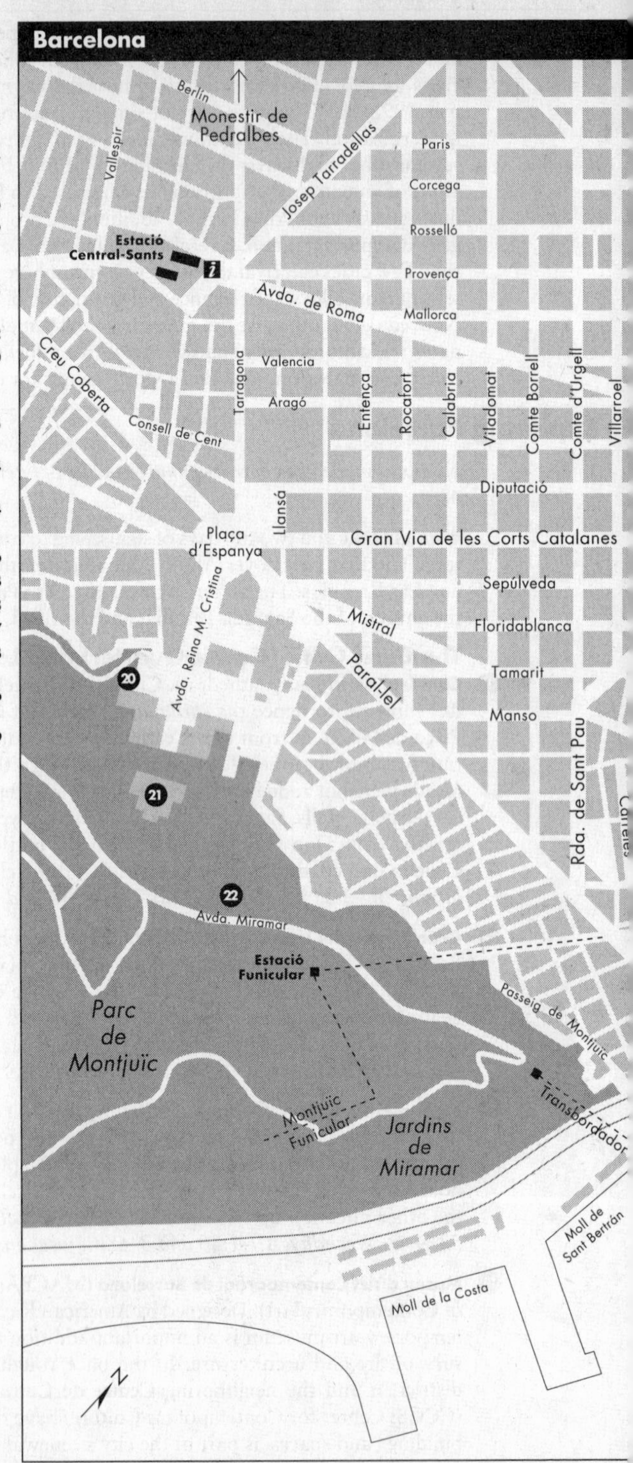

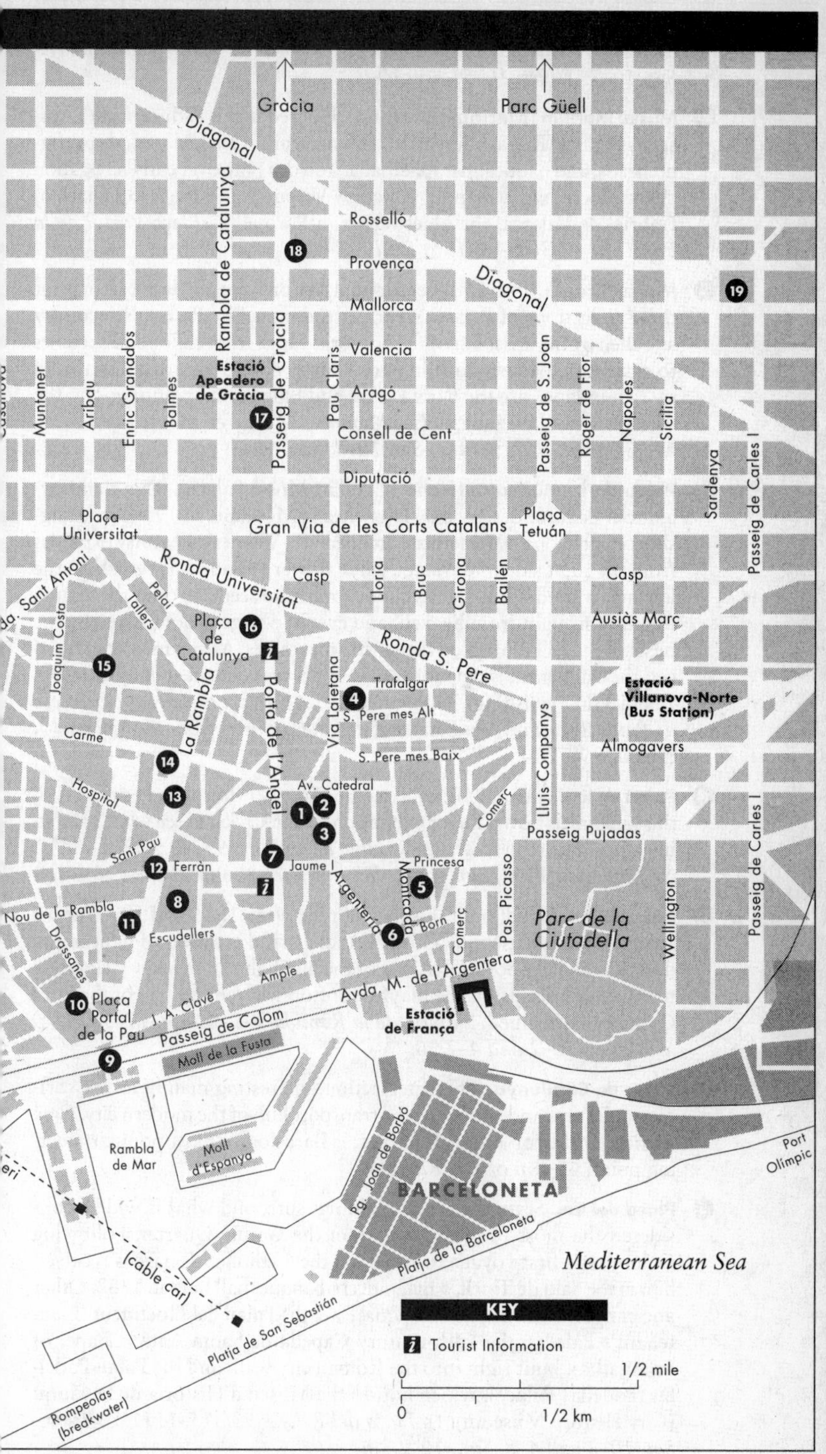
Gràcia
Parc Güell
Diagonal
Rosselló
Provença
Mallorca
Valencia
Aragó
Consell de Cent
Diputació
Gran Via de les Corts Catalans
Casp
Ausiàs Marc
Almogavers
Rambla de Catalunya
Passeig de Gràcia
Estació Apeadero de Gràcia
Muntaner
Aribau
Enric Granados
Balmes
Pau Claris
Passeig de S. Joan
Roger de Flor
Napoles
Sicilia
Sardenya
Passeig de Carles I
Plaça Universitat
Plaça Tetuán
Ronda Universitat
Ronda Sant Antoni
Pelai
Tallers
Joaquim Costa
Plaça de Catalunya
Porta de l'Angel
Via Laietana
Llorìa
Bruc
Girona
Bailén
Ronda S. Pere
Trafalgar
S. Pere mes Alt
S. Pere mes Baix
Estació Villanova-Norte (Bus Station)
Lluis Companys
Carme
La Rambla
Hospital
Av. Catedral
Comerç
Passeig Pujadas
Sant Pau
Ferràn
Jaume I
Princesa
Argentería
Montcada
Born
Pas. Picasso
Parc de la Ciutadella
Wellington
Nou de la Rambla
Escudellers
Drassanes
Ample
Avda. M. de l'Argentera
Estació de França
Plaça Portal de la Pau
J. A. Clavé
Passeig de Colom
Moll de la Fusta
Rambla de Mar
Moll d'Espanya
Pg. Joan de Borbó
BARCELONETA
Port Olímpic
Platja de la Barceloneta
Mediterranean Sea
(cable car)
Platja de San Sebastián
Rompeolas (breakwater)
KEY
Tourist Information
0
1/2 mile
0
1/2 km

everything from polychrome crucifixes to hat pins, pipes, and walking sticks. ✉ *Plaça Sant Iu 5,* ☎ *93/310–5800.* ⊙ *Tues.–Wed. and Fri.–Sat. 10–7, Thurs. 10–5, Sun. 10–3.*

10 **Museu Marítim** (Maritime Museum). Housed in the 13th-century Drassanes Reiales (Royal Shipyards), this museum is packed with ships, figureheads, and nautical paraphernalia. You can pore over early navigation charts, including a map by Amerigo Vespucci and the 1439 chart of Gabriel de Valseca, the oldest chart in Europe. ✉ *Plaça Portal de la Pau 1,* ☎ *93/301–1871.* ⊙ *Daily 10–7.*

★ 5 **Museu Picasso.** Two 15th-century palaces provide a striking setting for these collections of Picasso's early art, donated by Picasso's secretary and then by the artist himself. The works range from childhood sketches to exhibition posters done in Paris shortly before the artist's death. In rare abundance are the Rose Period and Blue Period paintings and the variations on Velázquez's *Las Meninas.* ✉ *Carrer Montcada 15–19,* ☎ *93/319–6310.* ⊙ *Tues.–Sat. 10–8, Sun. 10–3.*

★ 4 **Palau de la Música Catalana** (Catalan Music Palace). This flamboyant tour de force designed by Domènech i Muntaner in 1908 is the flagship of Barcelona's Moderniste architecture. Wagnerian cavalry explodes from the right side of the stage while flowery maidens languish on the left; an inverted stained-glass cupola overhead seems to offer the manna of music straight from heaven, and even the stage is dominated by the busts of muselike Art Nouveau instrumentalists. At any important concert the excitement is palpably thick. Tours are conducted daily at 10:30, 2, and 3 (in English) for 700 ptas./€4.21. ✉ *Ticket office, Sant Francesc de Paula 2 (just off Via Laietana, around a corner from the hall itself),* ☎ *93/295–7200.*

14 **Palau de la Virreina.** Built by a onetime Spanish viceroy to Peru in 1778, this building is now a major exhibition center. Check to see what's showing while you're in town. ✉ *Rambla de les Flors 99,* ☎ *93/301–7775.* ⊙ *Tues.–Sat. 11–8, Sun. 11–2 (last entrance 30 mins before closing).*

★ 11 **Palau Güell.** Gaudí built this mansion between 1886 and 1890 for his patron, Count Eusebi de Güell. Gaudí's artful creation of light in the dark Raval neighborhood is one of the highlights in this key visit along the Ruta Modernista. The playful rooftop will remind you of the later Gaudí of Parc Güell. ✉ *Nou de la Rambla 3–5,* ☎ *93/317–3974.* ⊙ *Weekdays 10–2 and 4–7:30.*

16 **Plaça de Catalunya.** This intersection, interesting mainly for its various sculptures and statues, is the transport hub of the modern city. Café Zurich, at the top of Las Ramblas, is Barcelona's most popular meeting point. ✉ *Top of Las Ramblas.*

3 **Plaça del Rei.** Several historic buildings surround what is widely considered the most beautiful square in the Gothic Quarter. Following Columbus's first voyage to America, the Catholic Monarchs received him in the **Saló de Tinell,** a magnificent banquet hall built in 1362. Other ancient buildings around the square are the **Palau del Lloctinent** (Lieutenant's Palace); the 14th-century **Capella de Santa Àata** (Chapel of St. Agatha), built right into the Roman city wall; and the **Palau Padellàs** (Padellàs Palace), which houses the **Museu d'Història de la Ciutat** (City History Museum). ✉ *Plaça del Rei,* ☎ *93/315–1111.* ⊙ *Tues.–Sat. 10–2 and 4–8, Sun. 10–2:30.*

8 **Plaça Reial.** An elegant and symmetrical 19th-century arcaded square, the Plaça Reial is bordered by elegant ochre facades with balconies overlooking the wrought-iron Fountain of the Three Graces and the lampposts designed by Gaudí in 1879. The place is most colorful on Sunday

morning, when crowds gather to sell and trade stamps and coins; at night it's a center of downtown nightlife. **Bar Glaciar,** on the uphill corner toward Las Ramblas, is a booming beer station for young internationals. The **Taxidermist,** across the way, is a hot new restaurant, while **Tarantos** and **Jamboree** are top venues for jazz, flamenco, and rock. ✉ *C. Colom, off Las Ramblas.*

7 **Plaça Sant Jaume.** This impressive square in the heart of the Gothic Quarter was built in the 1840s, but the two imposing buildings facing each other across it are much older. The 15th-century **ajuntament** (city hall) has an impressive black-and-gold mural (1928) by Josep María Sert (who also painted the murals in New York's Waldorf-Astoria) and the famous **Saló de Cent,** the first European parliament, from which the Council of One Hundred ruled the city from 1372 to 1714. To visit the interior, check with the protocol office. The **Palau de la Generalitat,** seat of the Autonomous Catalonian Government, is a 15th-century palace open to the public on special days or by arrangement. ✉ *Junction of C. de Ferràn and C. Jaume I.*

13 **Rambla St. Josep.** This stretch of the boulevard is one of the most fascinating. The colorful paving stones on the Plaça de la Boquería were designed by Joan Miró. Glance up at the swirling Moderniste dragon on the **Casa Bruno Quadras** and the Art Nouveau street lamps; then take a look inside the bustling **Boquería market** and the **Antiga Casa Figueras,** a vintage pastry shop on the corner of Petxina, with a splendid mosaic facade. ✉ *Between Plaça de la Boquería and Rambla de les Flors.*

★ 6 **Santa Maria del Mar** (St. Mary of the Sea). Simply the best example of Mediterranean Gothic architecture, this church is widely considered Barcelona's loveliest. It was built between 1329 and 1383 in fulfillment of a vow made a century earlier by James I to build a church for the Virgin of the Sailors. The structure's simple beauty is enhanced by a colorful rose window and slender soaring columns. ✉ *Plaça Santa Maria.* ⏲ *Weekdays 9–1:30 and 4:30–8.*

Eixample

Above the Plaça de Catalunya you enter modern (post-1860) Barcelona and an elegant area known as the Eixample (literally, "widening"), built in the late 19th century as part of the city's expansion scheme. Much of the building here was done at the height of the Moderniste movement, a Spanish and mainly Catalan version of Art Nouveau, whose leading exponents were the architects Lluís Domènech i Montaner, Josep Puig i Cadafalch, and Antoni Gaudí. The main thoroughfares are the Rambla de Catalunya and the Passeig de Gràcia, both lined with some of the city's most elegant shops and cafés. Moderniste houses are among Barcelona's drawing cards.

★ 18 **Casa Milà.** This Gaudí house is known as **La Pedrera** (stone quarry). Its remarkable curving stone facade, with ornamental balconies, ripples its way around the corner of the block. In the attic of La Pedrera is the superb **Espai Gaudí,** Barcelona's only museum dedicated exclusively to the architect's work. ✉ *Passeig de Gràcia 92,* ☎ *93/484–5995.* ⏲ *Daily 10–8; guided visits weekdays 6 PM, weekends 11 AM.*

Casa Montaner i Simó–Fundació Tàpies. This former publishing house exhibits the work of preeminent contemporary Catalan painter Antoni Tàpies, as well as temporary exhibits. On top of the building is a tangle of metal entitled *Núvol i Cadira* (*Cloud and Chair*). ✉ *Carrer Aragó 255,* ☎ *93/487–0315.* ⏲ *Tues.–Sun. 10–8.*

17 **Mançana de la Discòrdia** (Block of Discord). The name is a pun on the Spanish word *manzana,* which means both "block" and "apple." The

houses here are quite fantastic: the floral **Casa Lleó Morera** (No. 35) is by Domènech i Montaner, the pseudo-Gothic **Casa Amatller** (No. 41) is by Puig i Cadafalch, and No. 43 is Gaudí's **Casa Batlló.** ✉ *Passeig de Gràcia, between Consell de Cent and Aragó.*

★ 19 **Temple Expiatori de la Sagrada Família** (Expiatory Church of the Holy Family). Barcelona's most eccentric landmark was designed by Gaudí, though only one tower was standing upon his death in 1926. Gaudí's intent was to evangelize with stone, to create an entire history of Christianity on the building's facade. The angular figures on the southwestern Passion Facade by sculptor Joseph Maria Subirach are a stark contrast to Gaudí's Nativity Facade on the opposite lateral facade. With eight towers presently standing, ten more, including the gigantic central tower representing Christ, will complete the project by, according to estimates, the year 2050. Don't miss the museum, with Gaudí's scale models, or the elevator to the top of one of the towers for a magnificent view of the city. Gaudí is buried in the crypt. ✉ *Plaça de la Sagrada Familia,* ☎ *93/207–3031.* ⏲ *Nov.–Mar. and Sept.–Oct., daily 9–6; Apr.–Aug., daily 9–8.*

Montjuïc

The hill of Montjuïc is thought to have been named for the Jewish cemetery once located here. Montjuïc has a fortress, delightful gardens, a model Spanish village, an illuminated fountain, the Mies van der Rohe Pavilion, and a cluster of museums—all of which could keep you busy for several days. The 1992 Olympics were held here.

★ 22 **Fundació Miró** (Miró Foundation). A gift from the artist Joan Miró to his native city, this is one of Barcelona's most exciting galleries, with much of its exhibition space devoted to Miró's droll, colorful works. ✉ *Avda. Miramar 71,* ☎ *93/329–1908.* ⏲ *Tues.–Wed. and Fri.–Sat. 10–7, Thurs. 10–9:30, Sun. 10–2:30.*

20 **Mies van der Rohe Pavilion.** The reconstructed Mies van der Rohe Pavilion—the German contribution to the 1929 Universal Exhibition, reassembled between 1983 and 1986—is a stunning "less is more" study in interlocking planes of white marble, green onyx, and glass: Barcelona's esthetic antonym for the Moderniste Palau de la Música. ✉ *Av. Marquès de Comillas s/n,* ☎ *93/423–4016.* 💳 *450 ptas./€2.70_.* ⏲ *Daily 10–8.*

★ 21 **Museu Nacional d'Art de Catalunya** (National Museum of Catalan Art). In the **Palau Nacional** atop a long flight of steps up from the Plaça Espanya, this collection of Romanesque and Gothic art treasures, medieval frescoes, and altarpieces—most from small churches and chapels in the Pyrenees—is simply staggering. The museum's last renovation was directed by architect Gae Aulenti, who also remodeled the Musée d'Orsay, in Paris. ✉ *Mirador del Palau 6,* ☎ *93/423–7199.* ⏲ *Tues.–Wed. and Fri.–Sat. 10–7, Thurs. 10–9, Sun. 10–2:30.*

Elsewhere in Barcelona

Barceloneta. Take a stroll around what was once the fishermen's quarter, built in 1755. There are no-frills fish restaurants on the Passeig Joan de Borbó. Hike out to the end of the *rompeolas* (breakwater), extending 4 km (2½ mi) southeast into the Mediterranean, for a panoramic view of the city and a few breaths of fresh air. The modernized port is home to the Aquarium, one of Europe's best; the Maremagnum shopping center; the IMAX wide-format cinema; the World Trade Center; and numerous bars and restaurants. The 1992 Olympic Village, now a hot tapas and nightlife spot, is up the beach to the north and is easily identifiable by the enormous, gold, Frank Gehry–designed fish sculpture next to the Hotel Arts. ✉ *East of Estació de França and Ciutadella Park.*

Gràcia. This small, once-independent village within the city is a warren of narrow streets whose names change at every corner. Here you'll find tiny shops that sell everything from old-fashioned tin lanterns to feather dusters. Gaudí's first commission, at Carrer de les Carolines 24–26; Plaça Rius i Taulet, with its clock tower; and the Llibertat and Revolució markets are key sights to seek out. ✉ *Around C. Gran de Gràcia above Diagonal.*

Monestir de Pedralbes. This is one of Barcelona's best visits, a one-time Clarist convent with a triple-tier cloister and now home of the excellent Thyssen-Bornemisza collection of early paintings. ✉ *Baixada Monestir 9,* ☎ *93/203–9282.* ⏲ *Tues.–Sun. 10–2.*

★ **Parc Güell.** This park in the upper part of town above Gràcia is Gaudí's magical attempt at creating a garden city. ✉ *C. D'Olot s/n.* ⏲ *May–Aug., daily 10–9; Sept.–Apr., daily 10–7.*

Port Vell. The Old Port now includes an extension of the Rambla, the **Rambla de Mar,** which crosses the inner harbor from just below the Columbus Monument. This boardwalk connects the Rambla with the **Moll d'Espanya,** which in turn comprises a shopping mall, restaurants, an aquarium, a cinema, and two yacht clubs. A walk around Port Vell leads past the marina to Passeig Joan de Borbó, both lined with restaurants and their outdoor tables. From here you can go south out to sea along the *rompeolas,* a 3-km (2-mi) excursion, or north (left) down the San Sebastián beach to the Passeig Marítim, which leads to the **Port Olímpic.** Except for the colorful inner streets of Barceloneta, the traditional fishermen's quarter, this new construction is largely devoid of character. Take the Golondrinas boat to the end of the breakwater and walk into Barceloneta for some paella.

Sarrià. Originally an outlying village of the Monestir de Pedralbes, Sarrià retains a distinctive local charm. ✉ *North of the western end of the Diagonal (best reached by the Sarrià train from Plaça Catalunya to the Reina Elisenda stop).*

Bullfighting

Bullfights are held on Sunday between March and October at the **Monumental** (✉ Gran Via and Carles I); check the newspaper for details. The **Bullfighting Museum** at the ring is open March–October, daily 10–1 and 5:30–7.

Dining

For details and price-category definitions, *see* Dining *in* Spain A to Z, *above.*

$$$$ ★ ✕ **Botafumeiro.** Barcelona's most exciting seafood restaurant, this Galician spot never fails. Open continuously from 1 PM to 1 AM, Botafumeiro is always filled with ecstatic people in mid-feeding frenzy. The main attraction is the *mariscos Botafumeiro,* a succession of myriad plates of shellfish. Costs can mount quickly. Try the half-rations at the bar, such as *pulpo a feira* (squid on potato) or *jamón bellota de Guijuelo* (acorn-fed ham from a town near Salamanca). ✉ *Gran de Gràcia 81,* ☎ *93/218–4230. AE, DC, MC, V. Closed Aug. 5–25.*

$$$–$$$$ ✕ **Jean Luc Figueras.** Every restaurant that Jean Luc Figueras has touched has shot straight to the top. This one, installed in an elegant Gràcia town house that was once couturier Cristóbal Balenciaga's studio, may be the best of all. For an extra $20 or so, the taster's menu is the best choice. ✉ *C. Santa Teresa 10,* ☎ *93/415–2877. Reservations essential. AE, DC, MC, V. Closed Sun. No lunch Sat.*

$$$–$$$$ ✕ **El Tragaluz.** This is an excellent choice if you've been prowling the Eixample. The roof opens up to the stars in summer, and everything from chairs to utensils has been cleverly invented by some playful designer. There's even good food—modern and light, but hearty. ✉ *Passatge de la Concepció 5,* ☎ *93/487–0196. AE, DC, MC, V. Closed Jan. 5. No lunch Mon.*

$$$–$$$$ ★ ✕ **Tram-Tram.** With chef Isidro Soler at the helm in the kitchen and Reyes Lizán as hostess and pastry chef, Tram-Tram is one of Barcelona's culinary highlights. The excursion northwest to the villagelike suburb of Sarrià is a delight. Order the taster's menu and let Isidro take care of you—you won't regret it. ✉ *Major de Sarrià 121,* ☎ *93/204–8518. AE, MC, V. Closed Sun. and Dec. 24–Jan. 6.*

$$$ ✕ **Can Gaig.** This traditional Barcelona restaurant is well known to Catalonian gastronomes. The market-fresh ingredients combine seafood with upland products in innovative ways. Try the roast partridge with bacon from free-range Iberian pork. ✉ *Passeig Maragall 402,* ☎ *93/429–1017. AE, DC, MC, V. Closed Mon. and Aug. No dinner holidays.*

$$$ ★ ✕ **Can Majó.** On the beach in Barceloneta, Can Majó is one of the premier seafood restaurants in town. The house specialties are *caldera de bogavante* (a cross between lobster bouillabaisse and paella) and *suquet* (fish stewed in its own juices), but whatever you choose will be excellent. In summer, the terrace overlooking the Mediterranean is the closest you can now come to the Barceloneta *chiringuitos* (shanty restaurants) that used to line the beach here. ✉ *Almirall Aixada 23,* ☎ *93/221–5455. AE, DC, MC, V. Closed Sun. night–Mon. except holidays.*

$$$ ✕ **Casa Calvet.** This Art Nouveau space in Antoni Gaudí's 1898–1900 Casa Calvet is Barcelona's only opportunity to break bread in one of the great modernist's creations. The dining room is a graceful and spectacular design display, and the cuisine is light and Mediterranean with more contemporary than traditional fare. ✉ *Casp 48,* ☎ *93/412–4012. AE, DC, MC, V. Closed Sun. and Aug. 15–31.*

$$–$$$ ✕ **El Racó de Can Freixa.** This is one of Barcelona's hottest restaurants, with young chef Ramón Freixa taking the work of his father, José María, in new directions. The cuisine is innovative and yet traditionally Catalan; try one of the game specialties in season. One specialty is *peus de porc en escabetx de guatlle,* pig's feet with quail in a garlic-and-parsley gratin. ✉ *Sant Elíes 22,* ☎ *93/209–7559. Reservations essential. AE, DC, MC, V.*

$$–$$$ ✕ **Los Caracoles.** Just below the Plaça Reial is Barcelona's best-known tourist haunt, crawling with Americans having a terrific time. Its walls are hung thick with photos of bullfighters and visiting celebrities; its specialties are mussels, paella, and of course, *caracoles* (snails). ✉ *Escudellers 14,* ☎ *93/309–3185. AE, DC, MC, V.*

$–$$ ✕ **Agut.** Simple, hearty Catalan fare awaits you in this unpretentious restaurant in the lower reaches of the Gothic Quarter. Founded in 1924, Agut has kept its popularity. There's plenty of wine to go with the traditional home cooking, along with a family warmth that always makes the place exciting. ✉ *Gignàs 16,* ☎ *93/315–1709. AE, MC, V. Closed Mon. and July. No dinner Sun.*

$–$$ ★ ✕ **El Convent.** This small, friendly restaurant hidden behind the Boquería market is a real find, known better to locals than to visitors. Its traditional Catalan home cooking, huge desserts, and swift, personable service all make it a good value. ✉ *Jerusalem 12,* ☎ *93/301–6208. Reservations not accepted. AE, DC, MC, V. Closed Sun.*

Lodging

Hotels around Las Ramblas and in the Gothic Quarter have generous helpings of Old World charm but are weaker on creature comforts; those in the Eixample are mostly '50s or '60s buildings, often more recently renovated; and the newest hotels are out along the Diagonal or beyond, with the exception of the Hotel Arts, in the Olympic Port. The Airport and Sants Station have hotel-reservation desks. For details and price-category definitions, *see* Lodging *in* Spain A to Z, *above.*

$$$$ ★ **Colón.** This cozy, older hotel has a unique charm and intimacy reminiscent of an English country hotel. Rooms are comfortable and tasteful. The location, right in the heart of the Gothic Quarter, is ideal, and front rooms overlook the cathedral and square. ✉ *Avda. Catedral 7, 08002,* ☎ *93/301–1404,* FAX *93/317–2915,* WEB *www.hotelcolon.es. 147 rooms. Restaurant. AE, DC, MC, V.*

$$$$ ★ **Condes de Barcelona.** The Condes is one of Barcelona's most popular hotels, so rooms must be booked well in advance. The decor is stunning, with marble floors and columns, an impressive staircase, and an outstanding bar area. Guest rooms are on the small side. ✉ *Passeig de Gràcia 75, 08008,* ☎ *93/488–1152,* FAX *93/488–0614,* WEB *www.condesdebarcelona.com. 183 rooms. Restaurant. AE, DC, MC, V.*

$$$$ **Hotel Arts.** This luxurious skyscraper, a Ritz-Carlton property, overlooks Barcelona from the Olympic Port, providing unique views of the Mediterranean, the city, and the mountains beyond. A short taxi ride from the city center, it's virtually a world of its own. Rooms are ultramodern, with pale wood, CD players, and Frette linens. Three restaurants serve Mediterranean cuisine, Californian cooking, and tapas, such as *gambas al ajillo* (baby shrimp fried in garlic). Barcelona's casino is now directly under the hotel. ✉ *C. de la Marina 19–21, 08005,* ☎ *93/221–1000,* FAX *93/221–1070,* WEB *www.harts.es. 399 rooms, 56 suites. 3 restaurants, pool. AE, DC, MC, V.*

$$$$ ★ **Hotel Claris.** Widely considered Barcelona's best hotel, the Claris is a fascinating mélange of design and tradition; the rooms come in 60 different layouts. Wood and marble furnishings and decorative details are everywhere, and you can dip into a Japanese water garden, a first-rate restaurant, and a rooftop pool—all near the center of Barcelona. ✉ *Carrer Pau Claris 150, 08009,* ☎ *93/487–6262,* FAX *93/215–7970,* WEB *www.derbyhotels.es. 106 rooms, 18 suites. 2 restaurants, pool. AE, DC, MC, V.*

$$$$ **Majestic.** Right in the thick of the Eixample shopping district, surrounded by high-style boutiques and within sight of two Gaudí creations, the Majestic is a good choice. The rooms are lovely, painted in soothing pastels and decorated very tastefully. ✉ *Passeig de Gráia 70, 08008,* ☎ *93/488–1717,* FAX *93/488–1880,* WEB *www.hotelmajestic.es. 335 rooms. Restaurant, pool. AE, DC, MC, V.*

$$$$ **Princesa Sofía.** The most convenient hotel to the airport, the Sofía is removed from the hue and cry of downtown. For business and convenience, it's one of the city's best options. ✉ *Plaça Pius XII 4, 08028,* ☎ *93/330–7111,* FAX *93/411–2106,* WEB *www.interconti.com/spain/barcelona/hotel_barpri.html. 505 rooms. 3 restaurants, 2 pools. AE, DC, MC, V.*

$$$$ ★ **Rey Juan Carlos I–Conrad International.** Towering over the western end of Avinguda Diagonal, this skyscraper is as much a commercial complex as a luxury hotel: art, jewelry, furs, caviar, flowers, fashions, and even limousines are for sale or hire on site. The garden has a swan-dappled pond and an Olympic-size pool; Barcelona's finest in-town country club, El Polo, spreads luxuriantly out beyond. There are two restaurants: Chez Vous, with French cuisine, and Café Polo, with a sumptuous buffet and an American bar. ✉ *Avda. Diagonal 661671, 08028,* ☎ *93/364–4040,* FAX *93/448–0607,* WEB *www.hrjuancarlos.com. 375 rooms, 40 suites. 2 restaurants, pool. AE, DC, MC, V.*

$$$$ ★ **Ritz.** This classic hotel has maintained or even heightened its splendor over the past few years. The entrance lobby is awe inspiring; the rooms spacious and furnished with Regency furniture; and the service excellent. ✉ *Gran Vía 668, 08010,* ☎ *93/318–5200,* FAX *93/318–0148,* WEB *www.ritzbcn.com. 158 rooms. Restaurant. AE, DC, MC, V.*

$$–$$$ **Gran Vía.** Architectural features are the charm of this 19th-century mansion. The original chapel has been preserved, and you can have breakfast in a hall of mirrors, climb a Moderniste staircase, and make calls from elaborate Belle Epoque phone booths. ✉ *Gran Vía 642, 08007,* ☎ *93/318–1900,* FAX *93/318–9997. 53 rooms. AE, DC, MC, V.*

$$–$$$ ★ **San Agustin.** Just off Las Ramblas in the leafy square of the same name, this inn has long been a favorite for musicians performing at the nearby Liceu opera house. Rooms are modest in size but charmingly decorated. The staff is helpful and polite. ✉ *Plaça de Sant Agustí 3, 08001,* ☎ *93/318–1708,* FAX *93/317–2928. 77 rooms. AE, DC, MC, V.*

$–$$ **Continental.** Something of a legend among cost-conscious travelers, this comfortable hostel with canopied balconies stands at the top of Las Ramblas, just below Plaça Catalunya. The rooms are homey and comfortable, the staff is friendly, and the location is ideal. Buffet breakfasts are a plus. ✉ *Rambla 138, 08002,* ☎ *93/301–2508,* FAX *93/302–7360. 35 rooms. AE, DC, MC, V.*

$–$$ **Jardí.** The rooms at this budget hotel are small but have new bathrooms, powerful showers, and, in most cases, views over the charming, traffic-free Plaça del Pi and Plaça Sant Josep Oriol. Noise can be a problem in summer. The quietest rooms are the highest. ✉ *Plaça Sant Josep Oriol 1, 08002,* ☎ *93/301–5900,* FAX *93/318–3664. 40 rooms. AE, DC, MC, V.*

Nightlife and the Arts

Nightlife

BARS

Champagne Bars. *Xampanyerías,* serving sparkling Catalan *cava,* are a Barcelona specialty. **El Xampanyet** (✉ Montcada 22, ☎ 93/319–7003), near the Picasso Museum, serves cava, cider, and tapas in a lively setting. **La Cava del Palau** (✉ Verdaguer i Callis 10, ☎ 93/310–0938), near the Palau de la Música, has a wide selection of cavas, wines, and cocktails.

Cocktail Bars. The **Passeig del Born,** near the Picasso Museum, is lined with bars. **Dry Martini** (✉ Aribau 162, ☎ 93/217–5072) has more than 80 different gins. **El Copetín** (✉ Passeig del Born 19, ☎ 93/317–7585) has exciting decor and good cocktails. **Miramelindo** (✉ Passeig del Born 15, ☎ 93/319–5376) offers a large selection and often live jazz. **El Paraigua** (✉ Plaça Sant Miquel, behind City Hall, ☎ 93/217–3028) serves cocktails in a stylish setting with classical music.

Tapas Bars. Cal Pep (✉ 8 Plaça de les Olles, ☎ 93/319–6183), near Santa Maria del Mar, is a popular spot, with the best and freshest selection of tapas. **Carrer de la Mercé** is lined with tapas bars, across from the Moll de la Fusta, from Correos (the post office) down to the Iglesia de la Mercé. **Casa Tejada** (✉ Tenor Viñas, near Plaça Francesc Macià, ☎ 93/200–7341) has some of the finest *cazuelitas* (small hot hors d'oeuvres) in town. **Sagardi** (✉ Argenteria 62, ☎ 93/319–9993), near Santa Maria del Mar, is one of many, uniformly good, Basque taverns. **El Irati** (✉ Cardenal Casañas 17, ☎ 93/302–3084), just off Plaća del Pi, is a good, if usually overcrowded, Basque bar. **La Tramoia,** at Rambla de Catalunya and Gran Vía (☎ 93/412–3634), is your best bet on the east side of Passeig de Gràcia, as it is the happy exception to the rest, which generally microwave pre-prepared food. **Ciudad Condal,** across the intersection from La Tramoia (✉ Rambla de Catalunya 24, ☎ 93/412–9414), has a wide variety of appetizing morsels.

CABARET

Barcelona City Hall (✉ Rambla de Catalunya 2–4, access through New Canadian Store, ☎ 93/317–2177) presents sophisticated cabaret in a beautiful music hall.

CAFÉS

The **Café de l'Opera** (✉ Rambla 74, ☎ 93/317–7585), across from the Liceu opera house, is a perennial hangout, open daily until 2 AM. **Café Zurich** (✉ Plaça de Catalunya 1, ☎ 93/302–4140), at the head of Las Ramblas, is Barcelona's number one rendezvous spot. **Carrer Petritxol** (from Portaferrissa to Plaça del Pi) is famous for its *chocolaterías* (serving hot chocolate, tea, coffee, and pastries) and tearooms. Picasso hung out at **Els Quatre Gats** (✉ Montsió 3, ☎ 93/302–4140), which is a great place to people-watch.

DISCOS AND NIGHTCLUBS

Costa Breve (✉ Aribau 230, ☎ 93/414–2778) welcomes all ages, even those over 35. At **Luz de Gas** (✉ Muntaner 246, ☎ 93/209–7711), live guitar and soul shows are followed by dance music and wild abandon. **Oliver y Hardy** (✉ Diagonal 593, next to Barcelona Hilton, ☎ 93/419–3181) is popular with over-35s. **Otto Zutz** (✉ Lincoln 15, below Via Augusta, ☎ 93/238–0722) is a top spot. **Sala Razzmatazze** (✉ Almogavers 122, ☎ 93/320–8200) offers Friday and Saturday disco madness 'til dawn. Weeknight concerts feature international stars such as Ani diFranco and Enya. **Up and Down** (✉ Numancia 179, ☎ 93/280–2922), pronounced "pendow," is a lively classic for elegant carousers.

SALSA

Antilla Barcelona (✉ Aragó, ☎ 93/451–4564) is Cuba-in-Barcelona, with live music, salsa classes and full Caribbean flavor. **Agua de Luna** (✉ Viladomat 211, ☎ 93/410–0440) is a hot Latin American dance spot.

FLAMENCO

El Patio Andaluz (✉ Aribau 242, ☎ 93/209–3378) is a solid option but rather expensive. **Los Tarantos** (✉ Plaça Reial 17, ☎ 93/318–3067) is the most happening flamenco spot. **El Tablao del Carmen** (✉ Arcs 9, Poble Espanyol, ☎ 93/325–6895) hosts touring troupes up on Montjüic.

JAZZ CLUBS

La Cova del Drac (✉ Vallmajor 33, ☎ 93/200–7032) is Barcelona's most traditional jazz venue. The Gothic Quarter's **Harlem Jazz Club** (✉ Comtessa Sobradiel 8, ☎ 93/310–0755) is small but sizzling. **Jamboree** (✉ Plaça Reial 17, ☎ 93/301–7564), downstairs from Los Tarantos, has regular jazz performances featuring top musicians from New York and all over the world.

The Arts

To find out what's on, look in the daily papers or the weekly *Guía del Ocio*. *Actes a la Ciutat* is a weekly list of cultural events published by City Hall and available from its information office on Plaça Sant Jaume, or at the Palau de la Virreina. *El País* lists all events of interest on its *agenda* page.

CONCERTS

The **Auditori de Barcelona** (✉ Carrer Lepant 150, near Plaça de les Glòries) has a full program of classical music, with occasional jazz and pop thrown in. The **Liceu** (✉ Box office: Rambla de Capuchinos 63, ☎ 93/317–4142), Barcelona's opera house, is alive and thriving. The Art Nouveau **Palau de la Música,** whose ticket office is open weekdays 11–1 and 5–8 and Saturday 5–8, is not to be missed. Sunday-morning concerts (11 AM) are a local tradition. Musical events are also occasionally held in some of Barcelona's finest examples of early architecture, such as the medieval shipyards, **Drassanes,** the church of **Santa Maria del Mar,** or the **Monestir de Pedralbes.**

DANCE

El Mercat de les Flors (✉ Lleida 59, ☎ 93/426–1875), not far from Plaça d'Espanya, always has a rich program of modern dance and theater. **L'Espai de Dansa i Mùsica de la Generalitat de Catalunya** (✉ Travessera de Gràcia 63, ☎ 93/414–3133), usually listed simply as "L'Espai" (The Space), is Barcelona's prime venue for ballet and contemporary dance. **Teatre Tivoli** (✉ Casp 8, ☎ 93/412–2063), just above Plaça de Catalunya, hosts major ballet and flamenco troupes.

FILM

Many if not most Barcelona theaters show foreign movies in their original languages—indicated by "VO" (*versión original*). **Casablanca** (✉ Passeig de Gràcia 115), just above Passeig de Gràcia, is a favorite for foreign movies. The Olympic Port's 15-screen **Icaria Yelmo** (✉ Salvador Espriu 61, ☎ 93/221–7585), shows everything in VO **Renoir Les Corts** (✉ Eugeni d'Ors 12), near the Corte Inglés Diagonal, has four VO theaters. The Gràcia neighborhood's **Verdi** (✉ Verdi 32, Gràcia, ☎ 93/237–0516) is a standard VO cinema favorite.

THEATER

Most plays are in Catalan, but top Spanish productions also open in Barcelona. **El Mercat de les Flors** holds theater and dance performances. The **Teatre Lliure** (✉ Montseny 47, Gràcia, ☎ 93/218–9251) has top theater, dance, and musical events. The **Teatre Nacional de Catalunya** (✉ Plaça de les Arts 1, ☎ 93/900–121133) covers everything from Shakespeare to ballet to avant-garde theater. **Teatre Poliorama** (✉ Rambla Estudios 115, ☎ 93/317–7599), on the upper Rambla, holds excellent theater performances. **Teatre Romea** (✉ Hospital 51, ☎ 93/317–7189) is a traditional haven for dramatic events. **Teatre Tívoli** (✉ Casp 10, ☎ 93/412–2063) stages flamenco, ballet, and plays.

Shopping

Elegant shopping districts are the Passeig de Gràcia, Rambla de Catalunya, and the Diagonal. For more affordable, old-fashioned, and typically Spanish-style shops, explore the area between the Rambla and Via Laietana, especially around Carrer de Ferràn. The area around Plaça del Pi from Boquería to Portaferrisa and Canuda is well stocked with youthful fashion stores and imaginative gift shops.

Barcelona has more shopping plazas every year. **El Triangle** mall in Plaça de Catalunya includes FNAC, Habitat, and the Sephora perfume emporium. **Les Glories** (✉ Avda. Diagonal 208, Plaça de les Glories, ☎ 93/486–0639) is near the *encants,* Barcelona's flea market. **L'Illa** (✉ Diagonal 545, between Numancia and Entenza, ☎ 93/444–0000) has everything from FNAC to Decathlon to Marks & Spencer. **Maremagnum** (✉ Moll d'Espanya s/n, Port Vell, ☎ 93/225–8100) is well stocked with shops. **Carrer Tuset,** north of Diagonal between Aribau and Balmes, has many small boutiques.

Antiques

Carrer de la Palla and Banys Nous, in the Gothic Quarter, are lined with antiques shops. An **antiques market** is held every Thursday in front of the cathedral. The **Centre d'Antiquaris** (✉ Passeig de Gràcia 57, ☎ 93/215–4499) has some 75 antiques stores. **Gothsland** (✉ Consell de Cent 331, ☎ 93/488–1922) specializes in Moderniste designs.

Boutiques

Fashionable boutiques line Passeig de Gràcia and Rambla de Catalunya. Others are on Gran Via between Balmes and Pau Claris, and on the Diagonal between Ganduxer and Passeig de Gràcia. **Adolfo Domínguez** (✉ Passeig de Gràcia 89, Valencia 245, ☎ 93/487–3687) is one of Spain's most popular clothing designers. **Joaquín Berao** (✉ Rosselló 277, ☎ 93/218–6187) is a top jewelry designer. **La Manual Alpargartera** (✉ Avinyó 7), just off Carrer Ferran, is a lovely shop specializing in handmade rope-soled sandals and espadrilles.

Loewe (✉ Passeig de Gràcia 35, Diagonal 570, ☎ 93/216–0400) is Spain's top leather store. Lovers of fine stationery will linger in the Gothic Quarter's **Papirum** (✉ Baixada de la Llibreteria 2), a tiny, medieval-toned shop with exquisite hand-printed papers, marbleized blank books, and writing implements. **Zapata** (✉ Buenos Aires 64, at Diagonal, ☎ 93/430–4785) is a major jewelry dealer.

Department Stores

With four locations in Barcelona alone, **El Corte Inglés** (✉ Plaça de Catalunya 14, ☎ 93/302–1212; ✉ Porta de l'Angel 19–21, ☎ 93/306–3800; ✉ Avda. Francesc Macià 58, ☎ 93/419–2020; ✉ Diagonal 617, near María Cristina metro stop, ☎ 93/419–2828) is Spain's great consumer emporium. Both Plaça de Catalunya's Mançana de Oro (a.k.a. El Triangle) and L'Illa include Marks & Spencer and FNAC stores.

Food and Flea Markets

The **Boquería Market** (✉ Las Ramblas between Carme and Hospital) is an exuberant cornucopia, a colorful display of both food and humanity; it's open every day except Sunday. **Els Encants** (✉ end of Dos de Maig, on the Plaça Glòries Catalanes), Barcelona's wild-and-woolly flea market, is held every Monday, Wednesday, Friday, and Saturday, 8–7. **Sant Antoni Market** (✉ end of Ronda Sant Antoni) is an old-fashioned food and clothes market, best on Sunday when there's a secondhand-book market with old postcards, press cuttings, lithographs, and prints. There's a **stamp and coin market** (✉ Plaça Reial) on Sunday morning. An **artists' market** (✉ Placeta del Pi, off Las Ramblas and Boquería) sets up on Saturday morning.

Gift Ideas

No special handicrafts are associated with Barcelona, but you'll have no trouble finding typical Spanish goods anywhere in town. **Xavier Roca i Coll** (✉ Sant Pere mes Baix 24, off Via Laietana, ☎ 93/215–1052) specializes in silver models of Barcelona's buildings.

If your friends back home like fashion and jewelry, you're in the right city—Barcelona makes all the headlines on Spain's booming fashion front. Barcelona and Catalonia passed along a playful sense of design even before Antoni Gaudí began creating shock waves more than a century ago. A number of stores and boutiques specialize in design items (jewelry, furnishings, knickknacks). **Bd** (Barcelona Design; ✉ Mallorca 291293, ☎ 93/458–6909) offers reproduction furniture from many designers. **Dos i Una** (✉ Rosselló 275, ☎ 93/217–7032) is a good source for clever gifts. **Vinçon** (✉ Passeig de Gràcia 96, ☎ 93/215–6050) has a huge selection of stylish housewares.

Barcelona Essentials

AIRPORTS AND TRANSFERS

All international and domestic flights arrive at El Prat de Llobregat airport, 14 km (8½ mi) south of Barcelona just off the main highway to Castelldefels and Sitges. For information on arrival and departure times, call the airport or Info-Iberia.

➤ AIRPORT INFORMATION: **El Prat de Llobregat** (☎ 93/478–5000 or 93/478–5032). **Info-Iberia** (☎ 93/412–5667).

TRANSFERS

The airport-to-city train leaves every 30 minutes between 6:30 AM and 11 PM, costs about 400 ptas./€2.40, and reaches the Barcelona Central (Sants) Station in 15 minutes and Plaça de Catalunya, in the heart of the old city (at the head of Las Ramblas), in 20–25 minutes. From there a short taxi ride of 450 ptas./€2.70–550 ptas./€3.31 will take you to most of central Barcelona's hotels. The Aerobus service connects the airport with Plaça de Catalunya every 15 minutes between 6:25 AM and 11 PM; the fare of 475 ptas./€2.85 can be paid with all international credit cards. RENFE also provides a bus service to the Central Station during the night hours. A taxi from the airport to your hotel, including airport and luggage surcharges, will cost about 3,000 ptas./€18.03.

BOAT AND FERRY TRAVEL

Golondrinas (harbor boats) make short trips from the Portal de la Pau, near the Columbus Monument. The fare is 750 ptas./€4.51 for a 30-minute trip. Departures are Holy Week–September, daily 11–7; October–Holy Week, weekends and holidays only 11–5. It's closed December 16–January 2. A one-way ticket lets you off at the end of the breakwater for a 4-km (2½-mi) stroll, surrounded by the Mediterranean, back into Barceloneta.

➤ BOAT AND FERRY INFORMATION: **Golondrinas** (☎ 93/442–3106).

BUS TRAVEL TO AND FROM BARCELONA

Barcelona has no central bus station, but most buses operate either from the old Estació Vilanova, generally known as Estació del Norte. The Estació Autobuses de Sants also dispatches long distance buses. Julià runs buses to Zaragoza and Montserrat. Alsina Graëlls runs to Lérida and Andorra.

➤ BUS INFORMATION: **Alsina Graëlls** (✉ Ronda Universitat 4, ☎ 93/265–6866). **Estació Autobuses de Sants** (✉ C. Viriato, next to Sants Central train terminal, ☎ 93/490–0202). **Estació del Norte** (✉ end of Avda. Vilanova, ☎ 93/893–5312). **Julià** (✉ Ronda Universitat 5, ☎ 93/317–6454).

BUS TRAVEL WITHIN BARCELONA

City buses run from about 5:30 or 6 AM to 10:30 PM, though some stop earlier. There are also night buses to certain destinations. The flat fare is 155 ptas./€0.93. Route plans are displayed at bus stops. You can purchase a tarjeta multiviatge, good for 10 rides, at the transport kiosk on Plaça de Catalunya (895 ptas./€5.38).

CONSULATES

➤ AUSTRALIA: (✉ Gran Vía Carles III 98, ☎ 93/330–9496).

➤ CANADA: (✉ Elisenda de Pinos, ☎ 93/204–2700).

➤ NEW ZEALAND: (✉ Travessera de Gràcia 64, ☎ 93/209–0399).

➤ UNITED KINGDOM: (✉ Diagonal 477, ☎ 93/419–9044).

➤ UNITED STATES: (✉ Passeig Reina Elisenda 23, ☎ 93/280–2227).

EMERGENCIES

The general emergency number in all EU nations (akin to 911 in the United States) is 112.

➤ DOCTORS AND DENTISTS: **Medical emergencies** (☎ 061).

➤ EMERGENCY SERVICES: **Police** (☎ 091 National Police; 092 Municipal Police). **Tourist Attention** (✉ La Rambla 43, ☎ 93/317–7016 24-hr assistance for crime victims).

➤ 24-HOUR PHARMACIES: **Pharmacies** (☎ 010).

ENGLISH-LANGUAGE MEDIA

BOOKS

BCN Books is one of Barcelona's top spots for books in English. Come In is another good option for English books. El Corte Inglés sells English guidebooks and novels, but the selection is limited. For variety, try English Bookshop. The bookstore at the Palau de la Virreina has good books on art, design, and Barcelona.

➤ BOOKSTORES: **BCN Books** (✉ Aragó 277, ☎ 93/487–3123). **Come In** (✉ Provença 203, ☎ 93/253–1204). **English Bookshop** (✉ Entençan 63, ☎ 93/425–4466).

SUBWAY TRAVEL

The metro is the fastest and easiest way to get around. You can pay a flat fare of 170 ptas./€1.02 or buy a *tarjeta multiviatge,* good for 10 rides (890 ptas./€5.35). Maps of the system are available at main metro stations and branches of the Caixa savings bank.

TAXIS

Taxis are black and yellow. When available for hire, they show a LIBRE sign in the daytime and a green light at night. The meter starts at 410 ptas./€2.64 (which lasts for six minutes), and there are supplements for luggage, night travel, Sundays and holidays, rides from a station or to the airport. There are cab stands all over town, and you can also hail cabs on the street. To call a cab, try one of the numbers listed below, 24 hours a day.

➤ TAXI COMPANIES: **24-hr Service** (☎ 93/387–1000, 93/490–2222, or 93/357–7755).

TOURS

BUS TOURS

City sightseeing tours are run by Julià Tours. Pullmantur also has city sightseeing. Tours leave from the terminals listed below, though you may be able to arrange a pickup at your hotel. Both agencies offer the same tours at the same prices. A morning sightseeing tour visits the Gothic Quarter and Montjuïc; an afternoon tour concentrates on Gaudí and the Picasso Museum. You can visit Barcelona's Olympic sites from May through October.

➤ FEES AND SCHEDULES: **Julià Tours** (✉ Ronda Universitat 5, ☎ 93/317–6454). **Pullmantur** (✉ Gran Viá de les Corts Catalanes 635, ☎ 93/318–5195).

SINGLE-DAY TOURS

Trips out of town are run by Julià Tours and Pullmantur. The principal attractions are a half-day tour to Montserrat to visit the monastery and shrine of the famous Black Virgin; a full-day trip to the Costa Brava resorts, including a boat cruise to the Medes Isles; and, from June through September, a full-day trip to Andorra for tax-free shopping. If you are not an EU citizen, bring your passport with you.

WALKING TOURS

La Ruta del Modernisme (the Modernism Route), created by Barcelona's *ajuntament* (city hall), connects nine key Art Nouveau sites: Palau Güell, the Palau de la Música, the Fundació Tàpies, Casa Milà (La Pedrera), the Museu Gaudí (in the Parc Güell), the Museu d'Art Modern (in Ciutadella), Gaudí's Sagrada Família church, the Museu de la Música, and the Museo de Zoologia (in Doménech i Muntaner's Castell dels Tres Dragins en la Ciutadella). Guided tours, some in English, are included at Palau Güell and the Palau de la Música. At Casa Milá there is one guided tour daily (6 PM weekdays, 11 AM weekends). At the Sagrada Família the guided tour costs extra. Buy your tickets at Casa Amatller, open Monday through Saturday 10–

7, Sunday 10–2. The price, 700 ptas./€4.21, gets you 50% discounts at all nine locations.

The bookstore in the Palau de la Virreina rents cassettes whose walking tours follow footprints painted on sidewalks—different colors for different tours—through Barcelona's most interesting areas. The do-it-yourself method is to pick up the guides produced by the tourist office, *Discovering Romanesque Art* and *Discovering Modernist Art,* which have art itineraries for all of Catalonia. El Consorci Turisme de Barcelona (Barcelona Tourism Cortium) leads walking tours of the Gothic Quarter in English at 10 AM on Saturday. The tour costs 1,000 ptas./€6.01 and includes a visit to the Town Hall.

➤ FEES AND SCHEDULES: **Casa Amatller** (✉ Passeig de Gràcia 41, ☎ 93/488–0139). **El Consorci Turisme de Barcelona** (✉ Plaça de Catalunya 17, lower level, ☎ 906/301282). **Palau de la Virreina** (✉ La Rambla 99).

TRAIN TRAVEL

The Sants Central Station at Plaça Països Catalans is Barcelona's main train station, serving international and national destinations as well as suburban areas. The old and elegant Estació de França (Avda. Marquès de l'Argentera) now serves as the main terminal for certain trains to France and some express trains to points in Spain. Inquire at the tourist office to get current travel information and to find out which station you need. Many trains also stop at the Passeig de Gràcia underground station (at C. Aragó); this station is closer to the Plaça de Catalunya and Rambla area than Sants. Tickets and information are available here, but luggage carts are not. You can also get information on fares and schedules from RENFE with their 24-hour hotline.

➤ TRAIN INFORMATION: **RENFE** (☎ 93/490–0202).

TRAMS AND CABLE CARS

The Montjuïc Funicular is a cog railroad that runs from the junction of Avenida Parallel and Nou de la Rambla to the Miramar Amusement Park on Montjuïc; it's open 10:45 AM–8 PM, except in summer (late June to mid-September), when it runs 11 AM–10 PM. A *teleferico* (cable car) runs from the amusement park up to Montjuïc Castle October–June 21, weekends 11–2:45 and 4–7:30; June 22–September, daily 11:30–9.

The Transbordador Aeri Harbor Cable Car runs from Miramar on Montjuïc to the Torre de Jaume I across the harbor on Barcelona *moll* (quay), and on to the Torre de Sant Sebastià at the end of Passeig Joan de Borbó in Barceloneta. You can board at either stage. Hours are: Oct.–June, weekdays from noon–5:45 and weekends from noon–6:15; and July–Sept., daily from 11–9. A round-trip ticket costs 1,200 ptas./€7.21.

To reach Tibidabo summit, take either Bus 58 or the Ferrocarrils de la Generalitat train from Plaça de Catalunya to Avenida Tibidabo, then the *tramvía blau* (blue tram) to Peu del Funicular, and the *Tibidabo Funicular* from there to the Tibidabo Fairground. The funicular runs every half hour from 7:15 AM to 9:45 PM.

➤ CONTACTS: **El Consorci Turisme de Barcelona** (✉ Plaça de Catalunya 17, lower level, ☎ 906/301282).

TRANSPORTATION AROUND BARCELONA

Modern Barcelona, the Eixample—above the Plaça de Catalunya—is built on a grid system; the Gothic Quarter, from the Plaça de Catalunya to the port, is a warren of narrow streets. Almost all sightseeing can be done on foot, but you may need to use taxis, the metro, or buses to link certain areas, depending on how much time you have. From mid-May to mid-October look for Bus Turistic 100 for low-cost transport between the sights.

El Consorci Turisme de Barcelona (Barcelona Tourism Consortium) sells the very worthwhile Barcelona Card, which costs 2,500 ptas./€15.03 for 24 hours, 3,000 ptas./€18.03 for 48 hours, or 3,500 ptas./€21.04 for 72 hours. Travelers get unlimited travel on all public transport as well as discounts at 27 museums, 10 restaurants, 14 leisure spots, 20 stores, and various other services including walking tours, the airport shuttle, the bus to Tibidabo, and the Tombbus between Barcelona's key shopping areas.

TRAVEL AGENCIES

➤ LOCAL AGENTS: **American Express** (✉ Roselló 257, corner of Passeig de Gràcia, ☎ 93/217–0070). **Bestours** (✉ Diputación 241, ☎ 93/487–8580). **Viajes Iberia** (✉ Rambla 130, ☎ 93/317–9320). **Wagons-Lits Cook** (✉ Passeig de Gràcia 8, ☎ 93/317–5500).

VISITOR INFORMATION

El Prat Airport and Centre d'Informació Turística have general information on Catalonia and Spain. The other offices listed below focus mostly on Barcelona. You can also get general information on the city by dialing 010.

➤ TOURIST INFORMATION: **Ajuntament** (✉ Plaça Sant Jaume, ☎ 93/402–7000 ext. 433). **Centre d'Informació Turistic de Barcelona** (✉ Plaça de Catalunya 17, lower level, ☎ 906/301282, FAX 93/304–3155). **Centre d'Informació Turística** (✉ Palau Robert, Passeig de Gràcia 107, at Diagonal, ☎ 93/238–4000). **El Prat Airport** (☎ 93/478–4704). **França metro station** (☎ 93/319–5758). **Palau de Congressos** (during special events and conferences; ✉ Avda. María Cristina, ☎ 93/423–3101 ext. 8356). **Palau de la Virreina** (✉ Rambla de les Flors 99, ☎ 93/301–7775). **Sants metro station** (☎ 93/491–4431).

ANDALUSIA

Stretching from the dark mountains of the Sierra Morena in the north, west to the plains of the Guadalquivir valley, and south to the mighty, snowcapped Sierra Nevada, Andalusia (Andalucía) rings with echoes of the Moors. Creating a kingdom they called Al-Andalus, these North African Muslims ruled southern Spain for almost 800 years, from their conquest of Gibraltar in 711 to their expulsion from Granada in 1492. To this day the cities and landscapes of Andalusia are rich in their legacy: Córdoba's breathtaking mosque, Granada's magical Alhambra Palace, and Seville's landmark Giralda tower were the inspired creations of Moorish architects and craftsmen working for Al-Andalus's Arab emirs. Outside the cities, brilliant white villages—with narrow streets, heavily grilled windows, and whitewashed facades, all clustered around cool private patios—and the wailing songs of flamenco, vaguely reminiscent of the muezzin's call to prayer, all stem from centuries of Moorish occupation.

The downside to a visit here, especially to Seville, is that petty crime is not uncommon, and thieves often prey on tourists. Purse-snatching and thefts from cars, even when drivers are in them, are depressingly familiar. *Always* keep your car doors *and* trunk locked. *Never* leave valuables in your car. Leave your passport, traveler's checks, and credit cards in your hotel's safe, *never* in your room. Don't carry expensive cameras or wear jewelry. Take only the minimum amount of cash with you.

Seville

Numbers in the margin correspond to points of interest on the Seville map.

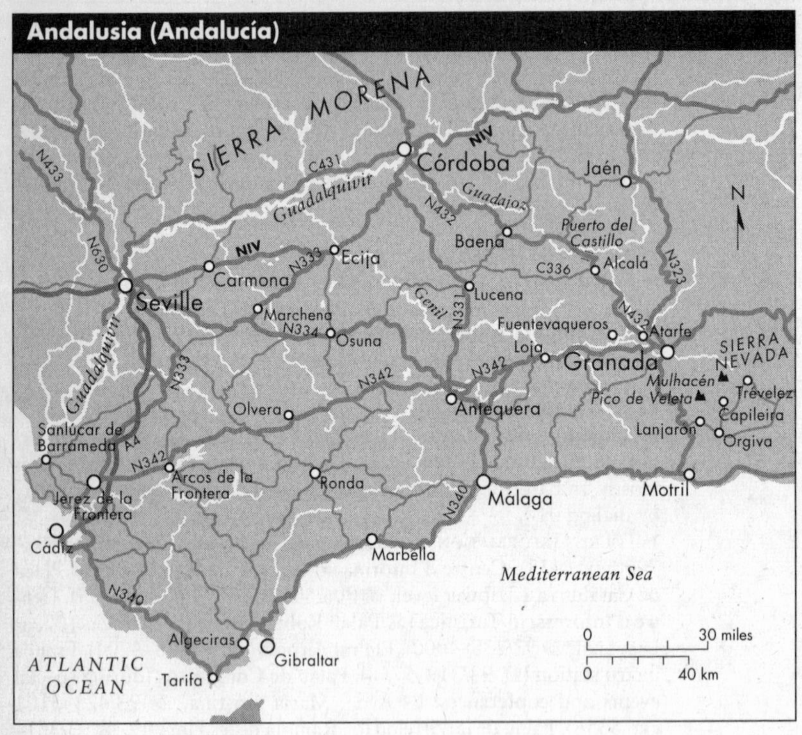

Lying on the banks of the Guadalquivir River, 538 km (334 mi) southwest of Madrid, Seville (Sevilla)—Spain's fourth-largest city and the capital of Andalusia—is one of the most alluring cities in Europe. Famous in the arts as the home of the sensuous Carmen and the amorous Don Juan—and celebrated in real life for its spectacular Semana Santa (Holy Week) processions and April Fair—Seville is the urban embodiment of Moorish Andalusia.

★ ❷ **Alcázar.** The high, fortified walls of this Moorish palace belie the exquisite delicacy of its interior. It was built by Pedro the Cruel—so known because he murdered his stepmother and four of his half brothers—who lived here with his mistress, María de Padilla, from 1350 to 1369. Don't mistake this for a genuine Moorish palace, as it was built more than 100 years after the reconquest of Seville; rather, its style is Mudéjar—built by Moorish craftsmen working under orders of a Christian king. The Catholic Monarchs (Ferdinand and Isabella)—whose only son, Prince Juan, was born in the Alcázar in 1478—added a wing to serve as the administrative center for their New World empire, and Charles V enlarged it further for his marriage celebrations in 1526. Pedro's Mudéjar palace centers on the beautiful **Patio de las Doncellas** (Court of the Damsels), whose name pays tribute to the annual gift of 100 virgins to the Moorish sultans whose palace once stood here. Resplendent with lacelike stucco and gleaming *azulejo* (tile) decorations, the patio is immediately reminiscent of Granada's Alhambra and is in fact the work of Granada artisans. Opening off this patio are the **Salón de Embajadores,** where Charles V married Isabel of Portugal, and the apartments of María de Padilla.

Occupying the upper floors of the Alcázar are the **Estancias Reales** (Royal Chambers), which are the apartments still used by Spain's king Juan Carlos I and his family when they visit Seville. For an additional admission price, you can take the guided tour of the dining room and other protocol rooms and the king's office. Tours, in the morning only, are every half hour in summer and every hour in winter. Next door to Pedro's palace, the Renaissance **Palacio de Carlos V** has a collection of Flemish tapestries.

The fragrant **Alcázar Gardens** are planted with jasmine and myrtle; there's also an orange tree said to have been planted by Pedro the Cruel, and a lily pond well stocked with fat, contented goldfish. The end of your visit brings you to the **Patio de las Banderas** for an unrivaled view of the Giralda. ✉ *Plaza del Triunfo,* ☎ *95/450–2324,* WEB *www.patronato-alcazarsevilla.es.* ⏲ *Oct.–Mar., Tues.–Sat. 9:30–6, Sun. 9:30–2:30; Apr.–Sept., Tues.–Sat. 9:30–8, Sun. 9:30–6.*

★ ❸ **Barrio de Santa Cruz.** With its twisting alleyways, cobbled squares, and whitewashed houses, this intriguing neighborhood is the perfect setting for an operetta. Once the home of Seville's Jewish population, it was much favored by 17th-century nobles and today is home to some of the most expensive properties in Seville. Romantic images of Spain come to life here: every house gleams white or deep ocher, wrought-iron grilles adorn the windows, and balconies and patios are bedecked with flowers. Ancient bars nestle side-by-side with antiques shops. Don't miss the bar **Casa Román,** in Plaza de los Venerables, its ceilings hung thick with some of the best hams in Seville; or the **Hostería del Laurel,** next door, where in summer you can dine in one of the loveliest squares in the city. Souvenir shops and excellent ceramics shops surround the **Plaza Doña Elvira,** where young Sevillanos gather to play guitars around the fountain and azulejo benches. In the **Plaza Alianza,** with its well-stocked antiques shops, a simple crucifix hangs on a wall, framed in a profusion of bougainvillea. ✉ *North of Alcázar Gardens.*

★ ❶ **Cathedral.** Seville's massive cathedral was begun in 1402, a century and a half after Ferdinand III seized Seville from the Moors, and took more than a century to build. It's the largest and highest cathedral in Spain, the largest Gothic building in the world, and the world's third-largest church after St. Peter's in Rome and St. Paul's in London. As if that weren't enough, it has the world's largest carved wooden altarpiece. Despite all this, the inside can be dark and gloomy, with too many overly ornate Baroque trappings. Seek out the beautiful Virgins by Murillo and Zurbarán. In a silver urn before the high altar rest the precious relics of Seville's reconquerer, Ferdinand III. The mortal vestiges of Christopher Columbus are said to be enshrined in the flamboyant mausoleum in the south aisle. Borne aloft by statues representing the four medieval kingdoms of Spain, perhaps the voyager has found peace at last, after the transatlantic quarrels that carried his body from Valladolid to Santo Domingo and from Havana to Seville.

The cathedral's tower, the **Giralda,** is a splendid example of Moorish art and is the symbol of Seville. Originally the minaret of Seville's great mosque, the Giralda was incorporated by the Christians into their new cathedral after the Reconquest and later topped by a bell tower and weather vane. In place of steps, 35 sloping ramps climb the 230 ft to the viewing platform; St. Ferdinand is said to have ridden his horse to the top to admire the view of the city he had just conquered. Seven centuries later, your view of the Golden Tower and shimmering Guadalquivir is just as beautiful. Try to see the Giralda at night, too, when floodlights cast a different magic on this Islamic gem. ✉ *Plaza Virgen de los Reyes,* ☎ *95/4214971.* ⏲ *Cathedral Mon.–Sat. 11–5, Sun. 2–6, and for mass.*

❽ **Museo de Bellas Artes** (Museum of Fine Art). Sevillanos claim that their museum is second only to Madrid's Prado in Spanish art. Opened in 1841,

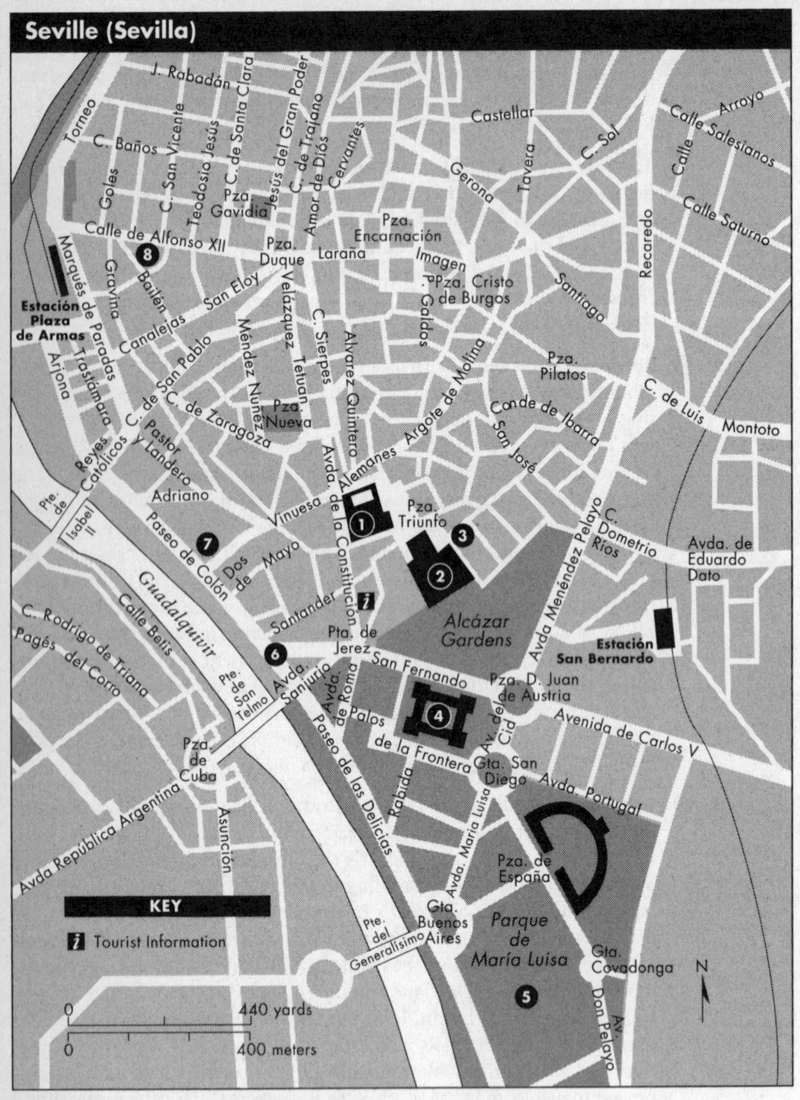

Alcázar 2
Barrio de Santa Cruz 3
Cathedral 1
Museo de Bellas Artes 8
Parque de María Luisa 5
Plaza de Toros Real Maestranza 7
Torre de Oro 6
University of Seville 4

it occupies the former convent of La Merced Calzada. The excellent collection, presented in chronological order on two floors, includes works by Murillo, Zurbarán, Velázquez, Valdés Leal, and El Greco. ✉ *Plaza del Museo,* ☎ *95/422–0790.* ⏲ *Tues. 3–8, Wed.–Sat. 9–8, Sun. 9–3.*

❺ **Parque de María Luisa** (María Luisa Park). The gardens here are a wonderful blend of formal design with wild vegetation, shady walkways, and sequestered nooks. The park was redesigned to house the 1929 Hispanic-American exhibition; the villas you see here today are the fair's remaining pavilions. The centerpiece of the exhibition was the monumental **Plaza de España.** At the opposite end of the park you can feed the hundreds of white doves that gather around the fountains of the lovely **Plaza de América.** Two of the pavilions house the **Museo Arqueológico** (Archaeological Museum; ☎ 95/423–2401), open Tuesday 3–8, Wednesday–Saturday 9–8, and Sunday 9–2; and the **Museo de Artes y Costumbres Populares** (Museum of Folklore; ☎ 95/423–2576), open Wednesday–Saturday 9–8, Sunday 9–2. ✉ *Park entrance, Glorieta San Diego.*

❼ **Plaza de Toros Real Maestranza** (Maestranza Bullring). Sevillanos have spent many a thrilling Sunday afternoon in this bullring, built between 1760 and 1763. *Corridas* (bullfights) are held from Easter through October; the best are during the April Fair. Buy tickets in advance at the ring or from the kiosks on Calle Sierpes (these charge a commission). You can visit the ring and the small **museum** year-round. ✉ *Paseo de Colón 12,* ☎ *95/422–4577.* ⏲ *Daily 9:30–2 and 3–7 (mornings only on bullfight days).*

❻ **Torre de Oro** (Tower of Gold). Built by the Moors in 1220, this 12-sided structure is visible from both sides of the river. During the day you can enjoy a nice view from the tower, which also houses a small naval museum. ✉ *Paseo de Colón, between C. Santander and C. Almirante Lobo,* ☎ *95/422–2419.* ⏲ *Tues.–Fri. 10–2, weekends 11–2.*

❹ **University of Seville.** Between the Alcázar gardens and the Parque María Luisa stands what used to be the Real Fábrica de Tabacos (Royal Tobacco Factory). Built between 1750 and 1766, the factory employed some 3,000 *cigarreras* (female cigar makers) less than a century later, including, of course, the heroine of Bizet's opera *Carmen,* who rolled her cigars on her thigh. The enormous building has been the Seville university's home since the 1950s. ✉ *C. San Fernando,* ☎ *95/455–1000.* ⏲ *Weekdays 9–8:30.*

Seville's regular flamenco clubs cater largely to tourists and cost around 4,000 ptas./€24 per person, but their shows are colorful and serve as a good introduction for the uninitiated. **El Arenal** (✉ Rodo 7, ☎ 95/421–6492) is a flamenco club in the back of the picturesque Mesón Dos de Mayo. You can catch flamenco and other regional dances nightly at **El Patio Sevillano** (✉ Paseo de Colón 11, ☎ 95/421–4120), which mainly serves tour groups. **Los Gallos** (✉ Plaza Santa Cruz 11, ☎ 95/421–6981), an intimate club in the heart of the Barrio Santa Cruz, offers fairly pure flamenco.

$$$–$$$$ ★ ✕ **Egaña-Oriza.** Egaña-Oriza is one of Seville's most fashionable and acclaimed restaurants. The menu changes with the seasons but might include *lomos de lubina con salsa de erizos de mar* (sea bass with sea-urchin sauce) or *solomillo con foie natural y salsa de ciruelas* (fillet steak with foie gras and plum sauce). ✉ *San Fernando 41,* ☎ *95/422–7211. AE, DC, MC, V. Closed Sun. and Aug. No lunch Sat.*

$$$ ★ ✕ **La Albahaca.** In an attractive old house in the heart of the Barrio Santa Cruz, the Albahaca offers plenty of style and atmosphere and original, imaginative cuisine. The menu changes seasonally, but there will always be some variation on *lubina al horno* (baked sea bass) and the restaurant's star dish, *foie de oca salteado* (lightly sautéd goose liver perfumed with honey vinegar). ✉ *Plaza Santa Cruz 12,* ☎ *95/422–0714. AE, DC, MC, V. Closed Sun.*

$$–$$$ ★ ✕ **Casa Robles.** One block north of the cathedral is one of Seville's classic restaurants, established in 1954. The busy bar downstairs does a roaring trade in tapas. The food is classically Andalusian: try the *ensalada de pimientos asados* (roast-pepper salad with tuna) for starters, followed by the herb-flavored *cordero asado* (roast lamb). ✉ *Alvarez Quintero 58,* ☎ *95/456–3272. AE, DC, MC, V.*

$$–$$$ ✕ **El Corral del Agua.** On one of the prettiest streets in the Barrio Santa Cruz, this restaurant is in a restored 18th-century house centered around a delightful patio decorated with a profusion of potted plants and a central fountain. The menu features Andalusian specialities such as *cola de toro al estilo de Sevilla* (Seville-style bull's tail) prepared with modern flair. ✉ *Callejón del Agua 6,* ☎ *95/422–4841 or 95/422–0714. AE, DC, MC, V. Closed Sun. Closed Jan.–Feb.*

$$–$$$ ★ ✕ **Mesón Don Raimundo.** In an old convent close to the cathedral, the Mesón has a deliberately Sevillian atmosphere and decor. Its bar is the perfect place to sample some splendid tapas, and the restaurant, when not catering to tour groups, is one of Seville's most delightful. ✉ *Argote de Molina 26,* ☎ *95/422–3355. AE, DC, MC, V.*

$$ ✕ **El Bacalao.** This popular fish restaurant, opposite the church of Santa Catalina, is in an Andalusian house decorated with ceramic tiles. As the name suggests, the house specialty is bacalao. They once claimed to prepare it 101 different ways, but have since lost count. Try it *con arroz* (with rice) or *al pil-pil* (fried in oil with garlic). Next door is a shop, under the same management, selling Spanish delicacies. ✉ *Plaza Ponce de León 15,* ☎ *95/421–6670. AE, DC, MC, V. Closed Mon., late July, and early Aug.*

$$ ✕ **Enrique Becerra.** This small, cozy restaurant is a short walk from the cathedral. Its lively, crowded bar decorated with Sevillian ceramic tiles is a meeting place for locals, who enjoy its excellent selection of tapas. The menu concentrates on traditional Andalusian home-cooked dishes. ✉ *Gamazo 2,* ☎ *95/421–3049. AE, DC, MC, V. Closed Sun.*

$–$$ ✕ **San Marco.** This restaurant serves Italian-influenced cuisine in an 18th-century mansion with a classic Andalusian patio. Try the *raviolis rellenos de gambas y pesto* (ravioli stuffed with shrimp and pesto), *cordero relleno de espinacas y setas* (lamb with spinach and forest mushrooms), or any of a delectable array of desserts. ✉ *Cuna 6,* ☎ *95/421–2440. AE, DC, MC, V.*

$$$$ ★ ✕🏨 **Los Seises.** This stylish hotel occupies a section of Seville's 16th-century Palacio Episcopal (Bishop's Palace). The combination of modern and Renaissance architecture is striking. Each room is a different shape, and most are split-level. A pit in the center of the subterranean restaurant reveals the building's foundations and some archaeological finds, including a Roman mosaic. The pool and restaurant are in full view of the Giralda. ✉ *Segovias 6, 41004,* ☎ *95/422–9495,* FAX *95/422–4334. 40 rooms, 2 suites. Restaurant, pool. AE, DC, MC, V.*

$$$$ ★ 🏨 **Alfonso XIII.** This ornate Mudéjar-style palace was built for King Alfonso XIII's visit to the 1929 exhibition. It's worth a visit just for its splendid Moorish decor, including beautiful stained glass and the colorful ceramic tiles typical of Seville. ✉ *San Fernando 2, 41004,* ☎ *95/422–2850,* FAX *95/421–6033. 127 rooms, 19 suites. 2 restaurants, bar, pool. AE, DC, MC, V.*

$$$$ 🏨 **Tryp Colón.** The rooms and suites have been very comfortably modernized while retaining much of their old-fashioned style. You're right in the heart of town, near the main shopping area; and on the premises you can dine in the elegant El Burladero restaurant or the more casual

La Tasca. ✉ *Canalejas 1, 41001,* ☎ *95/422–2900,* FAX *95/422–0938. 204 rooms, 14 suites. 2 restaurants. AE, DC, MC, V.*

$$$ **Bécquer.** Conveniently near the main shopping areas, this relatively modern hotel prides itself on attentive service. The guest rooms are traditionally Spanish, with peach-color walls, floral prints, matching woven bedspreads, and carved-wood headboards. There's also a parking garage. ✉ *Reyes Católicos 4, 41001,* ☎ *95/422–8900,* FAX *95/421–4400. 137 rooms, 2 suites. AE, DC, MC, V.*

$$$ **Doña María.** Near the cathedral, the Doña María is one of Seville's most charmingly old-fashioned hotels. Some rooms are small and plain; others are tastefully furnished with antiques. There's no restaurant, but a breakfast buffet is served. The rooftop pool has a good view of the Giralda, just a stone's throw away. ✉ *Don Remondo 19, 41004,* ☎ *95/422–4990,* FAX *95/421–9546. 67 rooms. Pool. AE, DC, MC, V.*

$$$ **Inglaterra.** This classic hotel on the central Plaza Nueva is something of an historic British outpost in Spain, and the room decor might be said to reflect this—furnishings are understated, a bit faded, and sometimes anachronistically floral. The best rooms, on the fifth floor, have spacious balconies. ✉ *Plaza Nueva 7, 41001,* ☎ *95/422–4970,* FAX *95/456–1336,* WEB *www.hotelinglaterra.es. 113 rooms, 1 suite. Restaurant. AE, DC, MC, V.*

$$$ **Las Casas de la Judería.** In the heart of the Barrio de Santa Cruz, this labyrinthine hotel occupies three of the quarter's old palaces, each arranged around inner courtyards. The spacious guest rooms are dressed in tasteful pastels and decorated with prints of Seville. ✉ *Callejón de Dos Hermanas, 41004,* ☎ *95/441–5150,* FAX *95/442–2170. 41 rooms, 16 suites. AE, DC, MC, V.*

$ **Simón.** Housed in a rambling 19th-century town house, the Simón is a good choice for inexpensive, if basic, accommodation, thanks to its location near the cathedral. ✉ *García de Vinuesa 19, 41001,* ☎ *95/422–6660,* FAX *95/456–2241. 29 rooms. AE, DC, MC, V.*

Carmona

Thirty kilometers (19 mi) east of Seville, the NIV brings you to Carmona. This unspoiled Andalusian town of Roman and Moorish origin has a wealth of Mudéjar and Renaissance churches and streets filled with whitewashed houses. At the entrance to the town stands the church of **San Pedro,** begun in 1466, whose extraordinary interior is an unbroken mass of sculptures and gilded surfaces and whose tower, erected in 1704, is an unabashed imitation of Seville's Giralda. Opposite this is the **Alcázar de Abajo** (Lower Fortress), a Moorish fortification built on Roman foundations. In the tower beside the gate is the tourist office. Carmona's most affecting monument is its splendid **Roman necropolis,** where in huge underground chambers some 900 family tombs, dating between the 2nd and 4th centuries AD, were chiseled out of the rock. ✉ *C. Enmedio,* ☎ *95/414–0811.* ⏲ *Mid-June–mid-Sept., Tues.–Sat. 9–2, Sun. 10–2; mid-Sept.–mid-June, Tues.–Fri. 9–5, weekends 10–2.*

$$$$ **Casa de Carmona.** Set in a 16th-century palace, this is one of the most original hotels in Spain, elegantly decorated with fine art, rich fabrics, and antiques. The small pool is in a cool Moorish-style patio. Note, however, that staff can be indifferent and maintenance uneven. ✉ *Plaza de Lasso 1, 41410,* ☎ *95/414–3300,* FAX *95/419–0189,* WEB *www.casadecarmona.com. 30 rooms, 3 suites. Restaurant, pool. AE, DC, MC, V.*

$$$ **Alcázar de la Reina.** This stylishly modern hotel is a welcome addition to the town's hotel scene. The public areas include meeting rooms and a large restaurant and are bright and airy. The rooms are spacious and comfortable. ✉ *Plaza de Lasso 2, 41410,* ☎ *95/419–6200,*

FAX 95/414–0113, WEB www.alcazar-reina.es. 66 rooms, 2 suites. Restaurant, pool. AE, DC, MC, V.

$$$ ★ **Parador Alcázar del Rey Don Pedro.** The beauty of this modern parador is its splendid, peaceful setting, in the ruins of the old Moorish Alcázar on top of the hill above Carmona. The views across the vast fertile plain below are magnificent. ✉ *Alcázar, 41410,* ☎ *95/414–1010, FAX 95/414–1712. 63 rooms. Restaurant, pool. AE, DC, MC, V.*

Jerez de la Frontera

One hundred kilometers (60 mi) south of Seville, Jerez is world headquarters for sherry. The word *sherry,* first heard in Great Britain in 1608, is in fact an English corruption of this town's old Moorish name, Xeres; today, names such as González Byass and Domecq are just as inextricably linked with Jerez. The town's wine-making tradition dates from Roman times and continued under the Moors despite the Koran's condemnation of alcohol.

At any given time more than half a million barrels of sherry are maturing in Jerez's vast, aboveground wine cellars. Most *bodegas* (wineries) welcome visitors, but it's wise to phone ahead for an appointment. If you take a tour, a guide will explain the *solera* method of blending old wine with new, and the importance of the *flor* (a sort of yeast that forms on the surface of the wine as it ages) in determining the kind of sherry. You can finish by sampling and of course you'll be welcome to purchase a few bottles at good prices in the shop.

Domecq (☎ 956/151000) is Jerez's oldest bodega (1730) and makes sherry as well as the world's best-selling brandy, Fundador. You can tour the prestigious **González Byass,** home of Tío Pepe (☎ 956/357000). **John Harvey** (☎ 956/346004) makes the best-selling Harvey's Bristol Cream, a sweet Sherry. **Sandeman** (☎ 956/301100) is a winery famous for its man-in-a-cape logo and Royal Corregidor sherry, their masterpiece.

The **Real Escuela Andaluza del Arte Ecuestre** (Royal Andalusian School of Equestrian Art) stands on the grounds of the Recreo de las Cadenas, a splendid 19th-century palace. Every Thursday (Tuesday and Thursday in summer) the Cartujana horses—a cross between the native Andalusian workhorse and the Arabian—and skilled riders in 18th-century riding costume demonstrate intricate dressage techniques and jumping in the spectacular show "*Como Bailan los Caballos Andaluces.*" On weekdays when there is no show you can visit the stables and tack room, watch the horses being schooled, and witness rehearsals for the show. ✉ *Avda. Duque de Abrantes,* ☎ *956/319635.* ⏲ *Shows Nov.–Feb., Thurs. at noon; Mar.–Oct., Tues. and Thurs. at noon (reservations essential).*

$$–$$$ ✕ **Gaitán.** Within walking distance of the riding school, Gaitán's white walls and brick arches are adorned with colorful ceramic plates and photos of famous diners. The menu is Andalusian, with a few Basque dishes. In season, *setas* (wild mushrooms) make a delicious starter. ✉ *Gaitán 3,* ☎ *956/345859. AE, DC, MC, V. No dinner Sun.*

$$ ★ ✕ **La Mesa Redonda.** Just off Avenida Alvaro Domecq, this small, friendly restaurant serves classic Jerez dishes in what feels like a family dining room. There are only eight tables; the round one at the end of the room gives the restaurant its name. The menu changes constantly; your best bet is to take the advice of the chef's wife, Margarita—who also has an encyclopedic knowledge of Spanish wines. ✉ *Manuel de la Quintana 3,* ☎ *956/340069. AE, DC, MC, V. Closed Sun. and late July–mid-Aug.*

$$$ 🏨 **Royal Sherry Park.** Gleaming, modern, and stylish, the Royal Sherry Park is set back from the road in a large, tree-filled garden. It's designed around several patios filled with exotic foliage, and the light, sunny hallways are decorated with modern paintings. The rooms are bright and airy, and most have balconies overlooking the garden. ✉ *Avda. Alvaro Domecq 11, 11405,* ☎ *956/317614,* FAX *956/311300. 173 rooms. Restaurant, pool. AE, DC, MC, V.*

$ 🏨 **Ávila.** Centrally located but tucked away on a side street, this friendly hotel is a good value. Guest rooms have basic furnishings and tile floors, with beds that are on the small side. The lobby is joined by a TV lounge and bar, providing a convenient break spot. ✉ *Ávila 3, 11401,* ☎ *956/334808,* FAX *956/336807. 32 rooms. AE, DC, MC, V.*

Córdoba

Numbers in the margin correspond to points of interest on the Córdoba map.

Ancient Córdoba (138 km/86 mi northeast of Seville), one of Spain's oldest cities, is the greatest urban embodiment of Andalusia's Moorish heritage. Moorish emirs and caliphs held court here from the 8th to the 11th century, and the city became one of the Western world's greatest centers of art, culture, and learning. Moors, Christians, and Jews lived together in peace here.

5 **Alcázar de los Reyes Cristianos** (Fortress of the Christian Monarchs). Built by Alfonso XI in 1328, the Alcázar is a Mudéjar-style palace with splendid gardens. (The original Moorish Alcázar stood beside the Mezquita, on the site of the present Bishop's Palace.) This is where, in the 15th century, the Catholic Monarchs held court and launched their conquest of Granada. Boabdil was imprisoned here for a time in 1483, and for nearly 300 years the Alcázar served as a base for the Inquisition. ✉ *Plaza Campo Santo de los Mártires,* ☎ *957/421015.* ⏲ *Apr.–Sept., Tues.–Sat. 10–2 and 6–8, Sun. 9:30–3; Oct.–Mar., Tues.–Sat. 10–2 and 4:30–6:30, Sun. 9:30–2:30.*

2 **Judería.** The medieval Jewish quarter is packed with houses, museums, and monuments that best typify Córdoba's storied past. The municipal tourist office is on the **Plaza Judá Leví.** From here, wander along Calle Albucasis and Calle Tomás Conde to the Plaza Maimónides, where you'll find the **Bullfighting Museum** and head up along Calle Judíos. Off here is a statue of the great Jewish philosopher **Maimónides**; farther up is the **Zoco,** a former Arab souk which has pleasant shops and stalls, and a bar that opens in summer. Finally, you reach the **Synagogue.** ✉ *Around C. Judíos.*

★ 1 **Mezquita** (Mosque). Founded by Abd ar-Rahman I (756–788), Córdoba's justly famous mosque was completed by Al Mansur (976–1002) around 987. Inside you'll face a forest of gleaming pillars of precious marble, jasper, and onyx, rising to the red-and-white horseshoe arches characteristic of Moorish architecture. Not even the heavy Baroque cathedral that Charles V built in its midst—and later regretted—can detract from the extraordinary art of the Moorish craftsmen. The mosque once housed the original copy of the Koran and a bone from the arm of the prophet Mohammad, relics that drew thousands of pilgrims before St. Ferdinand reconquered Córdoba for the Christians in 1236. The building opens onto the **Patio de los Naranjos** (Orange Tree Courtyard) and the bell tower, which was the mosque's minaret. ✉ *Torrijos and Cardinal Herrero,* ☎ *957/470512.* ⏲ *Mon.–Sat. 10–7 (5 in winter), Sun. for morning mass and 3:30–7 (5 in winter).*

Córdoba

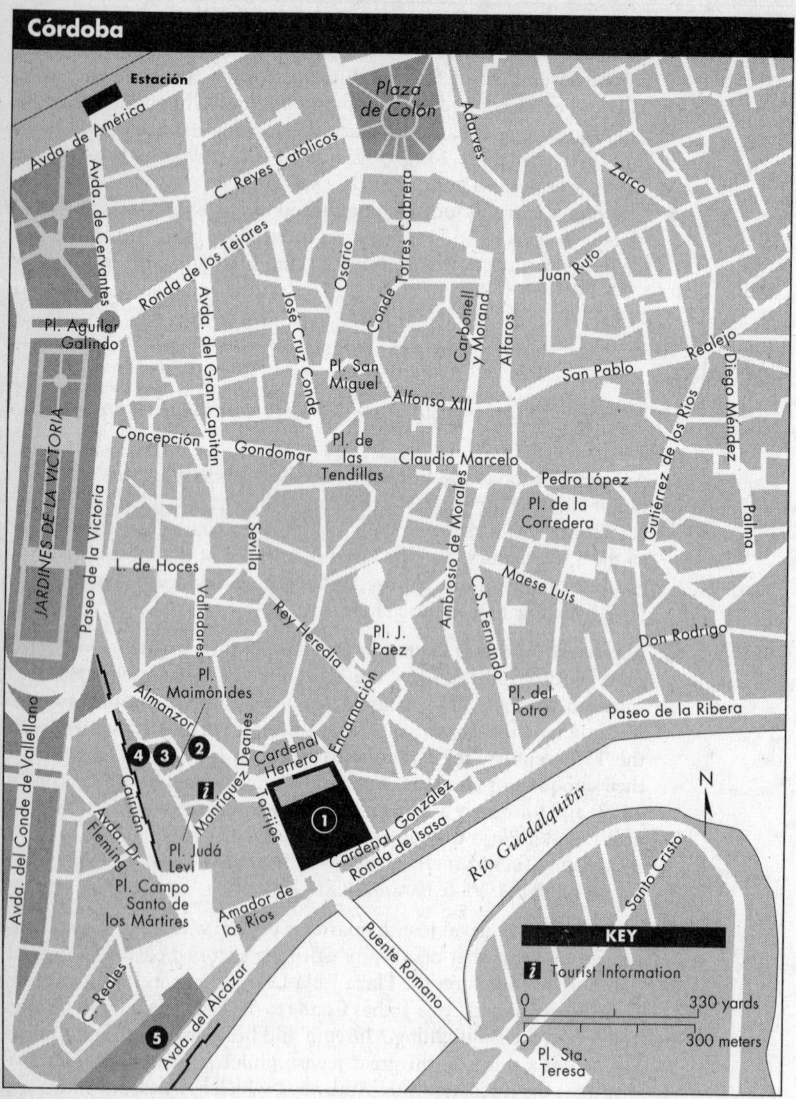
Estación
Avda. de América
Avda. de Cervantes
Plaza de Colón
Adarves
C. Reyes Católicos
Zarco
Ronda de los Tejares
Osario
Conde Torres Cabrera
José Cruz Conde
Avda. del Gran Capitán
Carbonell y Morand
Alfaros
Juan Ruto
Pl. Aguilar Galindo
Pl. San Miguel
Alfonso XIII
San Pablo
Realejo
Diego Méndez
JARDINES DE LA VICTORIA
Concepción
Gondomar
Pl. de las Tendillas
Claudio Marcelo
Pedro López
Gutiérrez de los Ríos
Pl. de la Corredera
Palma
Paseo de la Victoria
Sevilla
Ambrosio de Morales
L. de Hoces
Maese Luis
Valladares
Rey Heredia
C.S. Fernando
Pl. J. Paez
Don Rodrigo
Pl. Maimónides
Almanzor
Encarnación
Pl. del Potro
Paseo de la Ribera
Avda. del Conde de Vallellano
Deanes
Cardenal Herrero
Manriquez
Torrijos
Cairuán
Avda. Dr. Fleming
Pl. Judá Levi
Cardenal González
Ronda de Isasa
Río Guadalquivir
Santo Cristo
N
Pl. Campo Santo de los Mártires
Amador de los Ríos
Puente Romano
KEY
Tourist Information
0
330 yards
0
300 meters
C. Reales
Avda. del Alcázar
Pl. Sta. Teresa

Alcázar de los Reyes Cristianos . . . 5
Judería 2
Mezquita 1
Museo Taurino 3
Synagogue 4

Near the mosque, the streets of Torrijos, Cardenal Herrero, and Deanes are lined with shops specializing in local handicrafts, especially the filigree silver and embossed leather for which Córdoba is known.

❸ **Museo Taurino** (Museum of Bullfighting). Two delightful old mansions house this well-presented collection of memorabilia, paintings, and posters by early 20th-century Córdoban artists. Some rooms are dedicated to great Córdoban *toreros*—one holds the hide of the bull that killed the legendary Manolete in 1947. ✉ *Plaza Maimónides,* ☎ *957/201056.* ⏲ *Tues.–Sat. 10–2 and 4:30–6:30 (6–8 in July and Aug.), Sun. 9:30–2:30.*

❹ **Synagogue.** Córdoba's was the only synagogue in Andalusia to survive the expulsion of the Jews in 1492. One of only three remaining ancient synagogues in Spain—the other two are in Toledo—it has Hebrew and Mudéjar stucco tracery and a women's gallery. ✉ *C. Judíos,* ☎ *957/202928.* ⏲ *Tues.–Sat. 10–2 and 3:30–5:30, Sun. 10–1:30.*

$$–$$$ ✕ **La Almudaina.** This attractive restaurant is in a 15th-century house and former school that overlooks the Alcázar at the entrance to the Judería. It has an Andalusian patio, and the decor and cooking are both typical of Córdoba. ✉ *Campo Santo de los Mártires 1,* ☎ *957/474342. AE, DC, MC, V. Closed Sun. in July and Aug. No dinner Sun.*

$$–$$$ ★ ✕ **Bodegas Campos.** This restaurant in a converted wine cellar offers the complete Andalusian experience in a warren of barrel-heavy dining rooms and leafy courtyards. Regional dishes prepared with flair include *ensalada de bacalao y naranja* (salad of salt cod and orange with olive oil) and *manitas de cerdo relleno com jamón iberico* (pork knuckles with Iberian ham), and the menu also has dishes from elsewhere in Spain. ✉ *Los Lineros 32,* ☎ *957/497643. AE, MC, V. No dinner Sun.*

$$–$$$ ✕ **El Blasón.** This charming restaurant has earned its reputation for fine food and unbeatable ambience. Tucked into an old inn with a pleasant tapas patio and a whole array of restaurants upstairs, it serves specialties such as *salmón con naranjas* (salmon in oranges) and *muslo de oca al vino afrutado* (leg of goose in fruited wine). ✉ *José Zorrilla 11,* ☎ *957/480625. AE, DC, MC, V.*

$$–$$$ ✕ **El Caballo Rojo.** "The Red Horse," near the mosque, is Córdoba's oldest restaurant. The decor resembles a cool Andalusian patio, and the menu features such traditional specialties as *rabo de toro* (bull's tail), *salmorejo* (a thick local version of gazpacho, with chunks of ham and egg), and other exotic creations inspired by Córdoba's Moorish heritage. ✉ *Cardenal Herrero 28,* ☎ *957/478001. AE, DC, MC, V.*

$$–$$$ ★ ✕ **El Churrasco.** In the heart of the Judería, this atmospheric restaurant has a patio and a colorful tapas bar. The steak is the best in town, and the grilled fish is fresh. Specialties are churrasco (a pork dish in pepper sauce) and an excellent *salmorejo.* In a separate house, two doors down the street, is the restaurant's formidable wine cellar, which is also a small museum. Ask your waiter to take you there. ✉ *Romero 16,* ☎ *957/290819. AE, DC, MC, V. Closed Aug.*

$$$$ 🏨 **Conquistador.** This contemporary hotel on the east side of the mosque is built in Andalusian Moorish style, with a charming patio and ceramic decor. Rooms at the front have small balconies overlooking the mosque, which is floodlit at night. ✉ *Magistral González Francés 15, 14003,* ☎ *957/481102,* FAX *957/474677. 99 rooms, 3 suites. AE, DC, MC, V.*

$$$ ★ 🏨 **Amistad Córdoba.** This stylish hotel is built around two former 18th-century mansions that overlook the Plaza de Maimónides. (You can also enter through the old Moorish walls on Calle Cairuan.) It features a Mudéjar courtyard, carved-wood ceilings, and a plush lounge area. The rooms are large and comfortable. The newer wing has a more modern look, with blues and grays and Norwegian wood. ✉ *Plaza de Maimónides 3, 14004,* ☎ *957/420335,* FAX *957/420365. 84 rooms. Restaurant. AE, DC, MC, V.*

$$ **Mezquita.** Located next to the mosque, this hotel occupies a restored 16th-century home. Punctuated with bronze sculptures on Andalusian themes, the public areas reflect the owner's penchant for collecting antiques. The best rooms face the interior patio; their decor is on the plain side. The only real drawback is the lack of parking. ✉ *Plaza Santa Catalina 1, 41003,* ☎ *957/475585.* FAX *957/476219. 21 rooms. Restaurant. MC, V.*

Granada

Numbers in the margin correspond to points of interest on the Granada map.

The graceful city of Granada, 166 km (103 mi) southeast of Córdoba, rises onto three hills dwarfed by the mighty snowcapped peaks of the Sierra Nevada, on which lie the highest roads in Europe. Atop one of these hills, the pink-gold Alhambra Palace, at once terribly imposing yet infinitely delicate, gazes out across the rooftops and gypsy caves of the Sacromonte to the fertile plain, rich in orchards, tobacco fields, and poplar groves. Granada was the Moors' last stronghold, their most cherished city; it fell to the Catholic Monarchs in January 1492.

4 **Albaicín.** Narrow streets wind up steep slopes in the old Moorish quarter, a fascinating mixture of dilapidated white houses and beautiful *cármenes,* luxurious villas with fragrant gardens. Make your way up to the plaza in front of **San Nicolás** church for an unforgettable view of the Alhambra—particularly at night, when the palace is floodlit.

★ 5 **Alhambra.** On a hill overlooking Granada is the grandest and most stunning Moorish monument in Andalusia. Entrance to the interior palace of the Alhambra is restricted to 350 people every half hour, so although you can buy tickets on the same day at the Alhambra ticket office, you may find the tickets for the day have been sold out. The best bet is to reserve them up to a year in advance through any branch of the **Banco Bilbao Vizcaya** (BBV; Plaza Isabel Católica 1, ☎ 34–913/745420 from abroad; 902/224460 within Spain). You can also buy tickets on the same day of your visit during normal banking hours. Pay by Visa or MasterCard, and pick up your tickets at any BBV branch in Spain when you arrive. Your ticket will show the half-hour time slot for your entry; once inside, you can stay as long as you like.

If you're in the mood for a long walk, start from the Plaza Nueva and continue up the steep Cuesta de Gomérez, following the promenade where the duke of Wellington planted shady elms and Washington Irving tarried among the Gypsies, from whom he learned the Moorish legends so evocatively recounted in his *Tales of the Alhambra.* Otherwise, take the minibus from the Plaza Nueva, drive, or take a taxi. Your ticket will show your allotted entry time (if you have a long wait, first visit the **Alcazaba** next to the main palace, and the Generalife gardens). Once you are inside the Alhambra, the legends of the Patio of the Lions, the Hall of the Two Sisters, and the murder of the Abencerrajes spring to life amid a profusion of lacy walls, frothy stucco, gleaming tiles, and ornate domed ceilings. In this realm of myrtles and fountains, festooned arches, and careful inscriptions, every corner holds its secret. Here the emirs installed their harems, awarded their favorites the most lavish of courts, and bathed in marble baths.

In the midst of so much delicacy, the Baroque **Palace of Charles V** would seem an intrusion—heavy and incongruous—were it not for its splen-

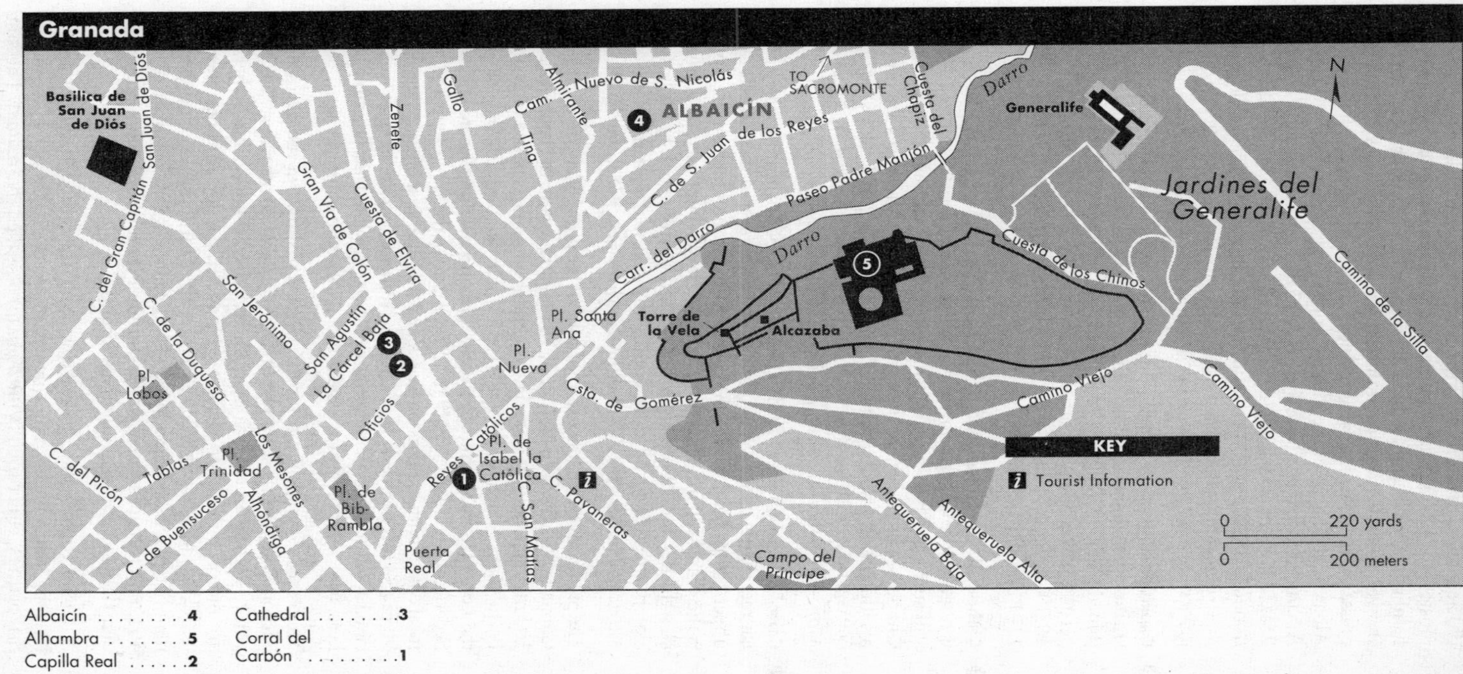
Granada
Basilica de San Juan de Diós
San Juan de Diós
C. del Gran Capitán
Zenete
Gallo
Cam.
Almirante
Nuevo de S. Nicolás
Tina
4 ALBAICÍN
TO SACROMONTE
Cuesta del Chapiz
Darro
Generalife
Jardines del Generalife
C. de S. Juan de los Reyes
Paseo Padre Manjón
Carr. del Darro
Darro
5
Cuesta de los Chinos
Camino de la Silla
Camino Viejo
Camino Viejo
Torre de la Vela
Alcazaba
Pl. Santa Ana
Pl. Nueva
Csta. de Gomérez
Gran Via de Colón
Cuesta de Elvira
San Jerónimo
San Agustín
La Cárcel Baja
3
2
Oficios
C. de la Duquesa
Pl. Lobos
Pl. Trinidad
Tablas
Los Mesones
C. del Picón
C. de Buensuceso
Alhóndiga
Pl. de Bib-Rambla
Reyes Católicos
1
Pl. de Isabel la Católica
C. San Matías
C. Pavaneras
Puerta Real
Campo del Príncipe
Antequeruela Baja
Antequeruela Alta
KEY
Tourist Information
0 220 yards
0 200 meters
N
Albaicín 4
Alhambra 5
Capilla Real 2
Cathedral 3
Corral del Carbón 1

did acoustics, which make it the perfect setting for Granada's summer music festival. Wisteria, jasmine, and roses line your route from the Alhambra to the **Generalife,** the caliphs' summer retreat, where crystal drops shower from slender fountains against a background of stately cypresses. The sweeping view includes the clustered white houses of the Albaicín; the Sacromonte, riddled with gypsy caves; and the bulk of the Alhambra towering above the city. ✉ *Enter on Cuesta de Gomérez,* ☎ *958/220584 or 958/220912.* ⏲ *Mar.–Oct., Mon.–Sat. 9–8, Sun. 9–7; floodlit visits Tues., Thurs., and Sat. 10 PM–midnight. Nov.–Feb., daily 8:30–6; floodlit visits Fri.–Sat. 8–9:30 PM. Ticket office opens 30 mins before opening time and closes 1 hr before closing time.*

★ ❷ **Capilla Real** (Royal Chapel). This ornate Gothic masterpiece is the burial shrine of Ferdinand and Isabella, who have lain here since 1521, later joined by their daughter Juana la Loca, mother of Holy Roman Emperor Charles V. ✉ *C. Oficios,* ☎ *958/229239.* ⏲ *Mar.–Sept., daily 10:30–1 and 4–7; Oct.–Feb., Mon.–Sat. 10:30–1 and 3:30–6:30, Sun. 11–1 and 3:30–6:30.*

❸ **Cathedral.** Commissioned in 1521 by Charles V, Granada's cathedral is a grandiose and gloomy monument, not completed until 1714 but still surpassed in beauty and historic value by the neighboring Royal Chapel—which, despite the emperor's plans, still houses the tombs of his illustrious grandparents. ✉ *Gran Vía de Colón 5,* ☎ *958/222959.* ⏲ *Mar.–Sept., Mon.–Sat. 10:30–1 and 4–7, Sun. 4–7; Oct.–Feb., Mon.–Sat. 10:30–1:30 and 3:30–6:30, Sun. 3:30–6.*

❶ **Corral del Carbón** (Coal Yard). Dating from the 14th century, when Moorish merchants used it as a lodging house and stored their goods on the upper floor, this is one of the oldest Moorish buildings in the city and is the only Arab inn of its kind in Spain. It was later used by Christians as a theater, and at one time it was used to store coal, but it has been expertly restored and now houses the regional tourist office. ✉ *C. Mariana Pineda,* ☎ *958/225990.* ⏲ *Mon.–Sat. 9–8, Sun. 10–2.*

The province of Granada was the home of the poet Federico García Lorca. García Lorca was born on June 5, 1898, in the village of **Fuentevaqueros,** 10 km (6 mi) west of Granada; his childhood home is now a **museum** (✉ Poeta García Lorca 4, ☎ 958/516453). On the outskirts of Granada is the Lorca family's summer residence, **Huerta del San Vicente** (✉ Parque Federico García Lorca, ☎ 958/258466), now also a museum and a cultural center with exhibits on Lorca and his time. Just outside this village, 9 km (5½ mi) northeast of Granada, is **Viznar,** where the poet was executed at the outbreak of the Spanish civil war in 1936. He is probably buried here, in a common grave; a memorial park commemorates him.

There are several "impromptu" flamenco shows in the caves of the Sacromonte, but these can be little more than tourist traps. Go only if you're accompanied by a Spanish friend who knows his or her way around or with a tour organized by a local agency. **Jardines Neptuno** (✉ C. Arabial, ☎ 958/522533) is a colorful flamenco club catering mainly to tourists. **Reina Mora** (✉ Mirador de San Cristóbal, ☎ 958/401265), though somewhat smaller than Jardines Neptuno, offers regular flamenco shows known as *tablaos.*

$–$$ ✕ **Cunini.** Right in the center of town, near the cathedral, this restaurant has long been valued for the quality of its seafood. Try one of the mixed-fish platters, either fried (*fritura mixta*) or grilled (*parrillada*). The long tapas bar up front is popular with locals, the dining room in back small and cozy. ✉ *Pescadería 14,* ☎ *958/250777. AE, DC, MC, V. Closed Mon.*

$–$$ ✕ **Los Manueles.** This old inn is one of Granada's long-standing traditions. The walls have ceramic tiles, and hams hang from the ceiling. There's lots of atmosphere, good old-fashioned service, and plenty of traditional Granadan cooking. ✉ *Zaragoza 2,* ☎ *958/223413. AE, DC, MC, V.*

$-$$ ✕ **Sevilla.** A colorful restaurant in the Alcaicería, beside the cathedral, it has a superb tapas bar at the entrance. The dining room is picturesque, if rather small and crowded. The menu can be somewhat tourist-oriented, but the *sopa sevillana* (fish soup) is excellent. ✉ *Oficios 12,* ☎ *958/221223. AE, DC, MC, V. Closed Mon. No dinner Sun.*

$$$$ ★ **Alhambra Palace.** This flamboyant, ocher-red, Moorish-style palace was built around 1910 and sits halfway up the hill to the Alhambra. The decor offers rich carpets, tapestries, and Moorish tiles. The best rooms overlook the town. ✉ *Peña Partida 2, 18009,* ☎ *958/221468,* FAX *958/226404,* WEB *www.h-alhambrapalace.es. 122 rooms, 13 suites. Restaurant. AE, DC, MC, V.*

$$$$ ★ **Parador de San Francisco.** Magnificently set in an old convent within the Alhambra precincts, San Francisco is the most popular parador in Spain. Queen Isabella was entombed here before the completion of the Royal Chapel. The rooms in the old section are the most elaborate; all need to be reserved four–six months in advance. ✉ *Alhambra, 18008,* ☎ *958/221440,* FAX *958/222264. 36 rooms. Restaurant. AE, DC, MC, V.*

$$$ **Palacio de Santa Inés.** This small hotel is in the heart of the Albaicí, on the two upper floors of a converted 16th-century palace. Each room is uniquely decorated with tasteful antiques and low-key modern art, and some rooms have views of the Alhambra. ✉ *Cuesta de Santa Inés 9, 18010,* ☎ *958/222362,* FAX *958/222465.. 9 rooms, 2 suites. AE, DC, MC, V.*

$$ **América.** A simple but charming hotel within the Alhambra precincts, the América's location is magnificent, and you can linger over breakfast on a delightful patio. It's popular, so reserve months in advance. ✉ *Real de la Alhambra 53, 18009,* ☎ *958/227471,* FAX *958/227470. 13 rooms. Restaurant. MC, V. Closed Nov.–Feb.*

$$ **Reina Cristina.** This hotel occupies an old house near the lively Plaza de la Trinidad. A marble stairway leads to the rooms, which are simply but cheerfully furnished with red curtains and red-and-white-checkered bedspreads. ✉ *Tablas 4, 18002,* ☎ *958/253211,* FAX *958/255728,* WEB *www.hotelreinacristina.com. 43 rooms. Restaurant. AE, DC, MC, V.*

Andalusia Essentials

BUS TRAVEL

Most bus service from Madrid to Andalusia operates out of the Estación del Sur.

Seville has two bus stations. Estación del Prado de San Sebastián has services to Córdoba, Granada, and eastern Andalusia. Estación Plaza de Armas, closer to downtown, has links to western Andalusia and Madrid. In Granada, the main bus station is on Carretera de Jaén. Córdoba's bus station is next to the AVE high-speed train station.

➤ BUS INFORMATION: **Córdoba bus station** (✉ Glorieta de las Tres Culturas, ☎ 957/404040). **Estación del Prado de San Sebastián** (✉ C. Manuel Vázquez Sagastizábal s/n, ☎ 95/441–7111). **Estación Plaza de Armas** (✉ Cristo de la Expiración, by Cachorro Bridge, ☎ 95/490–8040). **Granada main bus station** (☎ 958/185010).

CAR TRAVEL

By car, follow the NIV, which takes you through the scorched orange plains of La Mancha to Córdoba, then along the Guadalquivir River to Seville. The N323 road, which splits from the NIV at Bailén, takes you past lovely olive groves and rolling hills to Granada. Four-lane highways make traveling between the main cities in Andalusia much safer and quicker than relying on secondary roads, and as a result, the scenic routes are less congested. Driving is the best way to enjoy the scenery, although parking is a problem in cities and towns of any size. In cities, seek hotels with parking facilities or use underground parking lots.

TOURS

Guided tours of Seville, Córdoba, and Granada are run by Pullmantur, which has offices in major Spanish cities. Trapsatur has organized tours to southern Spanish destinations, departing from Madrid. In Seville, you may find group excursions to the sherry bodegas and equestrian museum in Jerez.

➤ FEES AND SCHEDULES: **Pullmantur** (☎ 91/541–1807). **Trapsatur** (☎ 91/542–6666).

TRAIN TRAVEL

Seville, Córdoba, and Granada all lie on direct train routes from Madrid. Service is frequent from both Chamartín and Atocha stations in Madrid and includes overnight trains (to Seville and Granada), slower day trains, and express Talgos. In addition, the high-speed AVE train connects Seville, Córdoba, and Atocha station on entirely new track; it's more expensive than any other train, but it's a pleasant whiz of a ride and cuts the inter-province travel time down to 2½ hours.

Seville and Córdoba are linked by direct train service. Buses are a better choice between either of them and Granada, as trains are relatively slow and infrequent and often involve a time-consuming change. Seville's main train station is Santa Justa. Granada's train station is at the end of Avenida Andaluces. Córdoba's train station is on the Glorieta de las Tres Culturas. For general information, call RENFE.

➤ TRAIN INFORMATION: **Córdoba train station** (☎ 957/400202). **Granada train station** (☎ 958/271272). **RENFE** (☎ 902/240202). **Santa Justa** (✉ Avda. Kansas City, ☎ 95/454–0202).

VISITOR INFORMATION

➤ TOURIST INFORMATION: **Córdoba** (✉ Plaza de Judá Leví, ☎ 957/200522). **Granada** (✉ Plaza Mariana Pineda 10, ☎ 958/223528; ✉ Corral del Carbón, C. Mariana Pineda, ☎ 958/225990). **Jerez** (✉ Larga 35, ☎ 956/331150). **Seville** (✉ Avda. Constitución 21, ☎ 95/422–1404; Costurero de la Reina: ✉ Paseo de las Delícias 9, ☎ 95/423–4465).

COSTA DEL SOL AND GIBRALTAR

The Costa del Sol's impoverished fishing villages of the 1950s are now retirement colonies and package-tour havens for northern Europeans and Americans. Fear not; behind the concrete monsters are old cottages, villas, and gardens resplendent with jasmine and bougainvillea. The sun still sets over miles of beaches, and the lights of small fishing craft still twinkle in the distance. The primary diversion here is indolence—swimming and sunning—but when you need something to do, you can head inland to historic Ronda and the white villages of Andalusia or take a day trip to Gibraltar.

Exploring the Costa del Sol

Nerja

Nerja is a small but expanding resort town that so far has escaped the worst excesses of development. Its growth has been largely confined to village-style complexes outside town, such as El Capistrano. There's pleasant bathing here, though the sand is gray and gritty. The **Balcón** ★ **de Europa** is a fantastic lookout, high above the sea. The **Cuevas de Nerja** (a series of stalactite caves) lie off the road to Almuñecar and

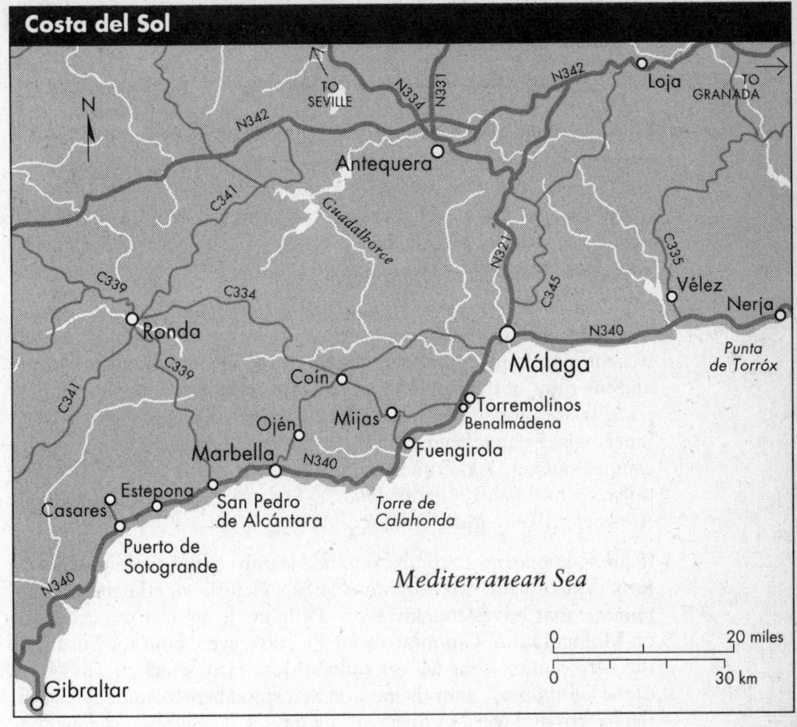

Almería; a kind of vast underground cathedral, they contain the world's largest known stalactite (203 ft long). ☎ *95/252–9520.* ⏲ *Daily 10–2 and 4–6:30 (4–8 in July and Aug.).*

$$–$$$ ✕ **Casa Luque.** One of the most authentically Spanish of Nerja's restaurants occupies a charming old Andalucían house behind the church of Balcón de Europa. Meat and game are featured, but good fresh fish is also served. ✉ *Plaza Cavana 2,* ☎ *95/252–1004. AE, DC, MC, V. Closed Sun.*

$$–$$$ ✕ **Udo Heimer.** A genial German is your host at this art deco villa; his menu is a combination of traditional German dishes and local produce. Try pumpkin stuffed with ham, or prawns wrapped in bacon and served in a curried banana sauce. ✉ *Pueblo Andaluz 27,* ☎ *95/252–0032. AE, DC, MC, V. Closed Wed. No lunch in July and Aug.*

$$$ 🏨 **Parador de Nerja.** A modern structure surrounded by a leafy garden on the cliff's edge, this parador has rooms with balconies overlooking the garden and, obliquely, the sea; those in the newer, single-story wing open onto their own patios. An elevator takes you down to the beach. ✉ *Almuñecar 8, Nerja 29780,* ☎ *95/252–0050,* FAX *95/252–1997. 73 rooms. Restaurant, pool. AE, DC, MC, V.*

$$ 🏨 **Paraiso del Mar.** An erstwhile private villa was expanded to accommodate this 12-room hotel perched on the edge of a cliff overlooking the sea east of the Balcón de Europa. The decor is bright and cheerful. Some rooms have terraces, four have hot tubs, and most have sea views; prices vary accordingly. ✉ *Prolongación del Carabeo 22, 29780,* ☎ *95/2521621,* FAX *95/252–2309. 9 rooms, 3 suites. Pool. AE, DC, MC, V. Closed mid-Nov.–mid-Dec.*

Málaga

Málaga (544 km/337 mi south of Madrid) is a busy port city with ancient streets and lovely villas surrounded by exotic foliage. The central Plaza de la Marina, overlooking the port, is a pleasant place for a drink. The main shops are along the Calle Marqués de Larios.

Málaga's **cathedral,** built between 1528 and 1782 on the site of the former mosque, is unfinished, its construction funds having mysteriously dried up. (One story has it that the money was donated instead to the American Revolution.) Because it's missing one of its twin towers, the cathedral is known as *La Manquita* (the one-armed lady). The lovely, enclosed choir, which somehow survived the burnings of the civil war, is the work of the great 17th-century artist Pedro de Mena. The adjoining **museum** has art and religious artifacts. ✉ *C. de Molina Larios,* ☎ *95/221–5917.* ⏲ *Mon.–Sat. 10–6:45.*

The **Alcazaba** (fortress) was begun in the 8th century, when Málaga was the most important port in the Moorish kingdom. Both the fortress and the ruins of the Roman amphitheater at its entrance were undergoing restoration in 2001; ask which parts are open to the public. The inner palace dates from the 11th century, when the Moorish emirs camped out here for a time after the breakup of the caliphate in Córdoba. ✉ *Entrance on Alcazabilla.* ⏲ *Oct.–Mar., Wed.–Mon. 8:30–7; Apr.–Sept., Wed.–Mon. 9:30–8.*

It takes some energy to climb from the Alcazaba to the summit of **Gibralfaro.** (You can also drive, by way of Calle Victoria, or take the parador minibus that leaves roughly every 1½ hours from near the cathedral on Molina Lario.) Gibralfaro's fortifications were built for Yusuf I in the 14th century—the Moors called it Jebelfaro, which means "rock of the lighthouse," after the beacon that stood here to guide ships into the harbor and warn of invasions by pirates. The beacon is gone, but the parador makes a delightful place for a drink or a meal and has some stunning views. ⏲ *Daily 9–6.*

$$$ ✕ **Café de Paris.** The owner of this stylish restaurant in the Paseo Marítimo area is one of Spain's most awarded chefs. The *menú de degustación* (tasting menu) lets you try a little of everything. Specialties on the ever-changing menu usually include *rodaballo* (turbot) or *lubina* (sea bass) or, in meats, *solomillo de buey* (beef fillet). ✉ *Vélez Málaga 8,* ☎ *95/222–5043. Reservations essential. AE, DC, MC, V. Closed Mon. No dinner Sun.*

$$–$$$ ✕ **Antonio Martín.** This local institution founded in 1886 is right on the beach, one block east of the lighthouse, with a large terrace (glassed in during winter) offering views of the sea. Variations on local dishes mark the culinary theme, with specialities including *zarzuela de pescado y mariscos de la Bahía* (seafood stew) and *solomillo de cerdo estilo Montes de Málaga* (pork fillet Málaga style). ✉ *Plaza la Malagueta,* ☎ *95/222–7382. AE, D, MC, V.*

$–$$ ✕ **El Chinitas.** At one end of Pasaje Chinitas, the most *típico* of Málaga's streets, this dining spot is decorated with colorful Sevillian tiles. The tapas bar is popular, especially for its cured ham. Try the *sopa viña AB* (a fish soup flavored with sherry and thickened with mayonnaise) or *solomillo al vino de Málaga* (fillet steak in Málaga wine sauce). ✉ *Moreno Monroy 4,* ☎ *95/221–0972. AE, MC, V.*

$ ✕ **La Cancela.** At this colorful budget restaurant in the center of town, just off Calle Granada, you can dine indoors or alfresco. The Spanish menu includes *riñones al jerez* (kidneys sautéed with sherry) and *cerdo al vino de Málaga* (pork with Málaga wine sauce). ✉ *Denís Belgrano 5,* ☎ *95/222–3125. AE, DC, MC, V. Closed Wed.*

$$$$ 🏨 **Larios.** This stylish hotel is located in an elegant, restored building on the central Plaza de la Constitución. Rooms have light wood, cream-color fabrics, and black-and-white photographs. ✉ *Marqués de*

Larios 2, 29005, ☎ *95/222–2200,* FAX *95/222–2407,* WEB *www.hotel-larios.com. 34 rooms, 6 suites. Restaurant. AE, DC, MC, V.*

$$$ ★ 🏨 **Parador de Málaga-Gibralfaro.** In a small wood on top of Gibralfaro—3½ km (2 mi) above the city—this cozy parador has spectacular views over the city and bay. Guest rooms have a pleasant mixture of modern comforts and Spanish charm. ✉ *Monte de Gibralfaro, 29016,* ☎ *95/222–1902,* FAX *95/222–1904. 38 rooms. Restaurant, pool. AE, DC, MC, V.*

$$ 🏨 **Don Curro.** Just around the corner from the cathedral, this family classic has an old-fashioned air with its wood-paneled common rooms, fireplace lounge, and the somewhat stodgy, wood-floored guest rooms. The best rooms are in the new wing, at the back of the building. ✉ *Sancha de Lara 7, 29015,* ☎ *95/222–7200,* FAX *95/221–5946. 112 rooms, 6 suites. Restaurant. AE, DC, MC, V.*

$$ 🏨 **Venecia.** This four-story hotel has a central location on the Alameda Principal, next to the Plaza de la Marina. The rooms are simply furnished but spacious. ✉ *Alameda Principal 9, 29001,* ☎ *95/221–3636,* FAX *95/221–3637. 40 rooms. AE, DC, MC, V.*

Torremolinos and Benalmádena

As you approach Torremolinos through an ocean of concrete blocks, it's hard to grasp that it was once an inconsequential fishing village. Today this grossly overdeveloped resort is a prime aesthetic example of 20th-century tourism run amok. The town center, with its brash Nogalera Plaza, is full of overpriced bars and restaurants. Far more attractive is the district of **La Carihuela,** farther west, below the Avenida Carlota Alexandra—here you'll find some old fishermen's cottages, excellent seafood restaurants, and a traffic-free esplanade for an enjoyable stroll on a summer evening. La Carihuela merges with the coastal resort of Benalmádena-Costa, which has a lively yacht harbor and marina; at the western end of the resort is the Torrequebrada casino and golf course, while inland is the surprisingly unspoiled village of Benalmádena itself.

$$–$$$ ✕ **Casa Guaquin.** Casa Guaquin is widely known as the best seafood restaurant in the popular Carihuela district of Torremolinos. Changing daily catches and stalwarts like *coquinas al ajillo* (wedge-shell clams in garlic sauce) are served on a seaside patio. ✉ *Paseo Marítimo 63,* ☎ *95/238–4530. AE, MC, V. Closed Mon. and mid-Dec.–mid-Jan.*

$$–$$$ ✕ **Juan.** Juan is a great place to dine in summer, with a sunny outdoor patio facing the sea. Specialties include the great Costa del Sol standbys: *sopa de mariscos* (shellfish soup), *dorada al horno* (oven-roasted giltheads), and *fritura malagueña* (Málaga's fried fish). ✉ *Paseo Marítimo 29, La Carihuela,* ☎ *95/238–5656. AE, DC, MC, V.*

$$–$$$ ✕ **Mar de Alborán.** This top class restaurant is right next to the Benalmádena yacht harbor. The cheerful dining room is further illuminated by picture windows. Fish dishes such as the Basque-inspired *lomo de merluza con kokotxas y almejas* (hake with cheek morsels and clams) are an imaginative switch from standard Costa fare. Meat and fowl are also also well represented. ✉ *Avda. de Alay 5,* ☎ *95/244–6427. AE, MC, V. Closed Mon. No dinner Sun.*

$$ ✕ **Ventorillo de la Perra.** This old inn (built in 1785) is 3 km (2 mi) from the center of Torremolinos, on the road inland to Arroyo de la Miel. A cozy, rustic atmosphere prevails in both the dining room and the bar. The menu mixes Malagueño specialties and general Spanish fare with international favorites. ✉ *Avda. Constitución, Arroyo de la Miel,* ☎ *95/244–1966. AE, DC, MC, V. Closed Mon.*

$$$ 🏨 **Cervantes.** This busy, cosmopolitan hotel in the heart of Torremolinos has comfortable rooms, good service, and a restaurant on the top floor. Drawbacks: package tours often alight here, rooms on the bottom floors can be noisy, and parking can be a problem. ✉ *Las Mer-*

cedes s/n, 29620, ☎ 95/238–4033, FAX 95/238–4857. 397 rooms. Restaurant, 2 pools. AE, DC, MC, V.

$$$ **Tropicana.** On the beach at the far end of the Carihuela is this comfortable, relaxing resort hotel with several good restaurants nearby. The tropical theme is carried throughout, from the leafy gardens and kidney-shaped pool to the rooms, which have ceiling fans and marble floors. ✉ *Trópico 6, 29620, ☎ 95/238–6600, FAX 95/238–0568. 84 rooms. Pool. AE, DC, MC, V.*

$ **Miami.** Set in an old Andalusian villa in a shady garden west of the Carihuela, Miami is an oasis in the desert of concrete. ✉ *Aladino 14, 29620, ☎ 95/238–5255. 26 rooms. Pool. No credit cards.*

Fuengirola and Mijas

Head west from Torremolinos for the similar but more staid resort of Fuengirola, a retirement haven for Britons and Americans. A short drive from Fuengirola up into the mountains takes you to the picturesque ★ and oft-photographed village of **Mijas.** Though the vast and touristy main square may seem like an extension of the Costa's tawdry bazaar, Mijas does have hillside streets of whitewashed houses whose authentic village atmosphere survived the tourist boom of the '60s largely unscathed. You can visit the bullring, the nearby church, and the chapel of Mijas's patroness, the Virgen de la Peña (to the side of the main square), and shop for quality gifts and souvenirs.

$$$ ✕ **Mirlo Blanco.** Here, in a large Andalusian town-house overlooking the square, you can sample Basque dishes, such as *txangurro* (crab) and *merluza a la vasca* (hake with asparagus, eggs, and clam sauce). The decor and ambience are both pleasantly busy, and in warm weather, you can dine on the terrace overlooking the square in Mijas. ✉ *Plaza Constitución 13, ☎ 95/248–5700. AE, DC, MC, V. Closed Jan.*

$$–$$$ ✕ **Portofino.** This lively restaurant, one of Fuengirola's best, is camouflaged among the brash souvenir shops and fast-food joints on the seafront promenade, just east of the port. The menu is international. ✉ *Paseo Marítimo 29, ☎ 95/247–0643. AE, DC, MC, V. Closed Mon. No lunch July–mid-Sept.*

$$$$ ★ **Byblos Andaluz.** You won't miss any comforts in this luxury spa hotel, set in a huge garden of palms, cypresses, and fountains. The restaurant, Le Nailhac, is known for its French cuisine. ✉ *Mijas-Golf, Fuengirola 29640, ☎ 95/247–3050, FAX 95/247–6783, WEB www.byblos-andaluz.com. 109 rooms, 35 suites. 2 restaurants, 2 pools. AE, DC, MC, V.*

$$$ **Mijas.** This beautifully situated hotel at the entrance to Mijas has views of the hillsides stretching down to Fuengirola and the Mediterranean. ✉ *Urb. Tamisa, 29650, ☎ 95/248–5800, FAX 95/248–5825. 99 rooms, 4 suites. Restaurant, 2 pools. AE, DC, MC, V.*

Marbella and Estepona

Marbella is the most fashionable resort area on the Costa del Sol. It smacks a bit of the Florida land boom, and the town's otherwise charming ancient Moorish quarter is crowded with both upscale boutiques and T-shirt-and-fudge shops; but when people speak of Marbella, they refer both to the town and to the resorts, some more exclusive than others. These stretch some 8 km (5 mi) east of town, between the highway and the beach, and west to San Pedro de Alcántara and Estepona. If you're vacationing in southern Spain, this is the place to stay: in one place you've got championship golf courses and tennis courts, yacht harbors, waterfront cafés, and shopping arcades.

Marbella's Golden Mile (which is, in fact, 5 km/3 mi), with its mosque, Arab banks, and residence of Saudi Arabia's King Fahd, illustrates the ever-growing influence of wealthy Arabs in this playground of the rich. In the plush marina, **Puerto Banús,** flashy yachts, fashionable people, and expensive restaurants form a glittering parade that outshines even St. Tropez.

Estepona is set back from the main highway and lacks the hideous high-rises of Torremolinos and Fuengirola. It's not hard to see the original outlines of this old fishing village. Wander the streets of the Moorish village, around the central food market and the church of **San Francisco,** and you'll find a pleasant contrast to the excesses up the coast.

$$$$ ✕ **La Meridiana.** A favorite with the local jet set, La Meridiana is just west of town and is famous for its original Bauhaus architecture and the superb quality and freshness of its ingredients. ✉ *Camino de la Cruz,* ☎ *95/277–6190. Reservations essential. AE, DC, MC, V. Closed Jan. No lunch June–Aug., or Mon.–Tues. Sept.–May.*

$$$–$$$$ ✕ **El Portalón.** This attractive restaurant combines hearty Castilian roasts and innovative *cocina de mercado,* based on whatever ingredients are freshest at the market. ✉ *Carretera de Cádiz, Km 178,* ☎ *95/286–1075. AE, DC, MC, V.*

$$$–$$$$ ✕ **Santiago.** This busy place on the seafront promenade is known as the best fish restaurant in Marbella. Try the *ensalada de langosta* (lobster salad), followed by *besugo al horno* (baked red bream). ✉ *Paseo Marítimo 5,* ☎ *95/277–0078. AE, DC, MC, V. Closed Nov.*

$$$$ 🏨 **El Fuerte.** The best of the few hotels in the center of Marbella, this one has comfortable rooms with sea views. The 1950s-style building sits in a large garden with an outdoor pool. ✉ *Avda. El Fuerte s/n, 29600,* ☎ *95/286–1500,* FAX *95/282–4411,* WEB *www.hotel-elfuerte.es. 261 rooms, 2 suites. Restaurant, 1 pool. AE, DC, MC, V.*

$$$$ 🏨 **Kempinski.** On the beach just east of Estepona, this luxurious, ocher resort hotel looks like a combination of the Moroccan kasbah and the hanging gardens of Babylon, surrounded by tropical gardens. Rooms are spacious and luxurious, with balconies overlooking the sea. ✉ *Playa El Padrón, Carretera N340, Km 159, 29680,* ☎ *95/280–9500,* FAX *95/280–9550,* WEB *www.kempinski-spain.com. 133 rooms, 16 suites. Restaurant, 1 pool. AE, DC, MC, V.*

$$$$ 🏨 **Las Dunas.** This spectacular hotel rises like a multicolor apparition next to the beach midway between Estepona and Marbella. The setting is palatial, and the large guest rooms are bright and airy, with large easy chairs, hemp carpets, and light-green furniture. ✉ *La Boladilla Baja, Carretera de Cádiz, Km 163, 29689,* ☎ *95/279–4345,* FAX *95/279–4825,* WEB *www.las-dunas.com. 34 rooms, 39 suites, 33 apartments. 2 restaurants, pool. AE, DC, MC, V.*

$$$$ ★ 🏨 **Los Monteros.** This deluxe hotel offers top-notch facilities, including an 18-hole golf course, tennis, horseback riding, and dining in the famous El Corzo Grill. ✉ *Urb. Los Monteros, Carretera N340, Km 187, 29600,* ☎ *95/277–1700,* FAX *95/282–5846,* WEB *www.monteros.com. 159 rooms, 10 suites. 3 restaurants, 3 pools. AE, DC, MC, V.*

$$$$ ★ 🏨 **Marbella Club.** The grande dame of Marbella attracts an older clientele. The bungalow-style rooms run from small to spacious, and the decor varies considerably, from regional to modern, so specify the type you prefer. The grounds are exquisite. Breakfast is served on a patio where songbirds flit through the vegetation. ✉ *Carretera de Cádiz, Km 178, 29600,* ☎ *95/282–2211,* FAX *95/282–9884,* WEB *www.marbellaclub.com. 90 rooms, 36 suites, 10 bungalows. Restaurant, 2 pools. AE, DC, MC, V.*

$$$$ ★ 🏨 **Puente Romano.** A spectacular, modern hotel and apartment complex of low, white stucco buildings 3¼ km (2 mi) west of Marbella (on the road to Puerto Banús), this "village" has a Roman bridge in its beautiful grounds as well as a tennis club, squash courts, and a nightclub. ✉ *Carretera de Cádiz, Km 177, 29600,* ☎ *95/282–0900,* FAX *95/277–*

5766, WEB www.puenteromano.com. 149 rooms, 77 suites. 3 restaurants, 2 pools. AE, DC, V.

Ronda

You arrive in Ronda (61 km/38 mi northwest of Marbella) via a spectacular mountain road from San Pedro de Alcántara, between Marbella and Estepona. Ronda is one of the oldest towns in Spain and the last stronghold of the storied Andalusian bandits. The town's most dramatic feature is its ravine, known as **El Tajo,** which is 915 ft across and divides the old Moorish town from the "new town" of El Mercadillo. Spanning the gorge is the amazing **Puente Nuevo,** built between 1755 and 1793, whose parapet provides dizzying views of the River Guadalevin, far below. Ronda's breathtaking setting and ancient houses are its chief attractions. Stroll the old streets of **La Ciudad**; drop in at the historic **Reina Victoria** hotel, built by the English from Gibraltar as a fashionable resting place on their Algeciras–Bobadilla railroad line. Visit the **bullring,** one of the oldest and most beautiful in Spain; Ronda's most famous native son, Pedro Romero (1754–1839), father of modern bullfighting, is said to have killed 5,600 bulls here during his 30-year career. The **museum** inside has posters dating from the very first fights held in this ring in May 1785. The ring is privately owned now, but three or four fights are still held in the summer; tickets are exceedingly difficult to come by (☎ *95/287–4132*); it's open daily 10–6 and 10–8 in July and August). Above all, don't miss the cliff-top walk and the gardens of the **Alameda del Tajo** (Tajo Park), where you can enjoy one of the most dramatic views in all of Andalusia.

$$$–$$$$ ★ ✕ **Tragabuches.** This restaurant around the corner from Ronda's parador and the tourist office has interesting decor, which, like the food, combines traditional and modern ingredients. Try the *menú de degustación,* a taster's menu of five courses plus two desserts. ✉ *José Aparicio 1,* ☎ *95/219–0291. AE, DC, MC, V. Closed Mon. No dinner Sun.*

$–$$ ✕ **Pedro Romero.** Opposite the bullring, this restaurant is, not surprisingly, packed with colorful taurine decor. The restaurant serves traditional regional recipes; the *tocinillo del cielo al coco* (sweet caramel custard flavored with coconut) is a treat. ✉ *Virgen de la Paz 18,* ☎ *95/287–1110. AE, DC, MC, V.*

$$$ ★ **Parador de Ronda.** One of Spain's newest paradors stands at the very edge of the Tajo gorge, with a modern interior concealed within the shell of the old town hall. The rooms are spacious and comfortable, and the restaurant is justifiably famous. ✉ *Plaza de España, 29400,* ☎ *95/287–7500,* FAX *95/287–8188. 62 rooms, 8 suites. Restaurant, pool. AE, DC, MC, V.*

$$ **Polo.** A cozy, old-fashioned hotel in the center of town, Polo has a reasonably priced restaurant. The staff is friendly, and the rooms are simple but comfortable. ✉ *Mariano Souvirón 8, 29400,* ☎ *95/287–2447,* FAX *95/287–2449. 33 rooms. Restaurant. AE, DC, MC, V.*

Casares

Nineteen kilometers (11¾ mi) northwest of Estepona, the mountain village of Casares lies high in the Sierra Bermeja. Streets lined with ancient white houses perch on the slopes beneath a ruined Moorish castle. Stop for a breather, admire the view of the Mediterranean, and check out the village's thriving ceramics industry.

Between Estepona and Gibraltar, the highway is flanked by new and prosperous vacation developments known as *urbanizaciones.* The architecture here is much more in keeping with traditional Andalusian style than the earlier, concrete stuff. Near Gibraltar, Sotogrande—a millionaire's paradise—is the home of the Puerto de Sotogrande Marina and the Valderrama golf course, which hosted the 1997 Ryder Cup.

Exploring Gibraltar

Numbers in the margin correspond to points of interest on the Gibraltar map.

Gibraltar is the only colony in Europe. It was captured by the British in 1704, and Spain has been claiming it back ever since. Today, it offers a curious mixture of English and Andalusian atmosphere. To enter Gibraltar, simply walk or drive across the border at **La Línea** and show your passport. There may be border delays for cars, and traffic in Gibraltar is congested, so unless you have a good reason for driving it is best to leave your car in a guarded parking lot in La Línea, walk across the border, and take a taxi or bus from there. In theory, drivers need an International Driver's License, insurance certificate, and registration book; play it safe and bring these documents with you to avoid a possible hefty fine. In practice, these requirements are usually waived. Once you reach Gibraltar the official language is English, and the currency is the British pound, but Spanish and pesetas and euros are also widely accepted.

The Rock of Gibraltar acquired its name in AD 711, when it was captured by the Moorish chieftain Tarik at the beginning of the Arab invasion of Spain. It became known as Jebel Tariq (Rock of Tariq), later corrupted to Gibraltar. After successive periods of Moorish and Spanish domination, Gibraltar was captured by an Anglo-Dutch fleet in 1704 and ceded to the British by the Treaty of Utrecht in 1713. This tiny British colony, whose impressive silhouette dominates the strait between Spain and Morocco, is a rock just 5⅘ km (3⅗ mi) long, ¾ km (½ mi) wide, and 1,394 ft high.

Upon entering Gibraltar, you have to cross the airport runway on the narrow strip of land that links the Rock with La Línea, in Spain. A good way to see all the sights is the **"Official Rock Tour,"** available by minibus or taxi.

9 **Apes' Den,** near the Wall of Charles V, can be reached by car or cable car. The famous Barbary apes are a breed of cinnamon-color, tailless monkeys, natives of the Atlas Mountains in Morocco. Legend holds that as long as the apes remain, the British will continue to hold the Rock. Winston Churchill himself ordered the maintenance of the ape colony when its numbers began to dwindle during World War II.

1 **Catalan Bay.** If you turn left (east) at Devil's Tower Road just after you enter Gibraltar, you'll reach a small fishing village founded by Genoese settlers during the 18th century and now one of the Rock's most picturesque resorts.

13 **Gibraltar Museum.** Exhibits recall the history of the Rock throughout the ages. ✉ *Bomb House La.,* ☎ *9567/74289.* ⏲ *Weekdays 10–6, Sat. 10–2.*

10 **Great Siege Tunnel.** These huge galleries at the northern end of the Rock were carved out during the Great Siege of 1779–83, when the French and Spanish attacked. In 1878 the Governor, Lord Napier of Magdala, entertained ex-president Ulysses S. Grant here at a banquet in St. George's Hall. From here the Holyland Tunnel leads out to the east side of the Rock, above Catalan Bay.

7 **Jews' Gate.** Drive down Engineer Road for an unbeatable lookout point over the docks and Bay of Gibraltar to Algeciras. Here you can access the **Upper Nature Preserve,** which includes St. Michael's Cave, the Apes' Den, the Great Siege Tunnel, and the Moorish Castle. The preserve is open daily 9:30–sunset.

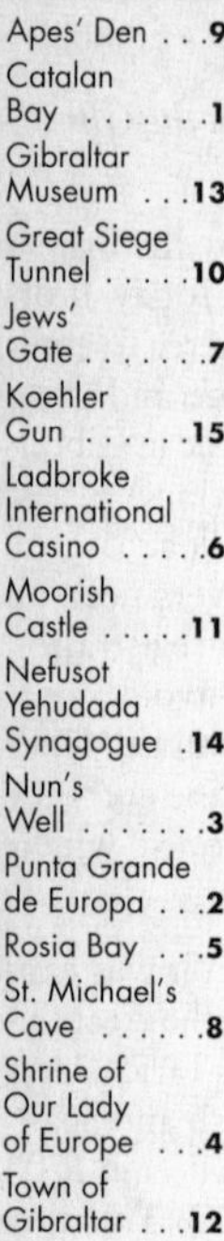

Apes' Den . . . 9
Catalan Bay 1
Gibraltar Museum . . . 13
Great Siege Tunnel 10
Jews' Gate 7
Koehler Gun 15
Ladbroke International Casino 6
Moorish Castle 11
Nefusot Yehudada Synagogue . 14
Nun's Well 3
Punta Grande de Europa . . . 2
Rosia Bay . . . 5
St. Michael's Cave 8
Shrine of Our Lady of Europe . . . 4
Town of Gibraltar . . . 12

15 **Koehler Gun.** Standing in Casemates Square, this is an impressive example of the type of gun developed during the Great Siege. ✉ *Northern end of Main St.*

6 **Ladbroke International Casino.** Perched above the Alameda Gardens, the casino is open for gaming daily until 4 AM. Dress is "smart casual" and children under age 18 are not permitted. ✉ *Europa Rd.*, ☎ *9567/76666.*

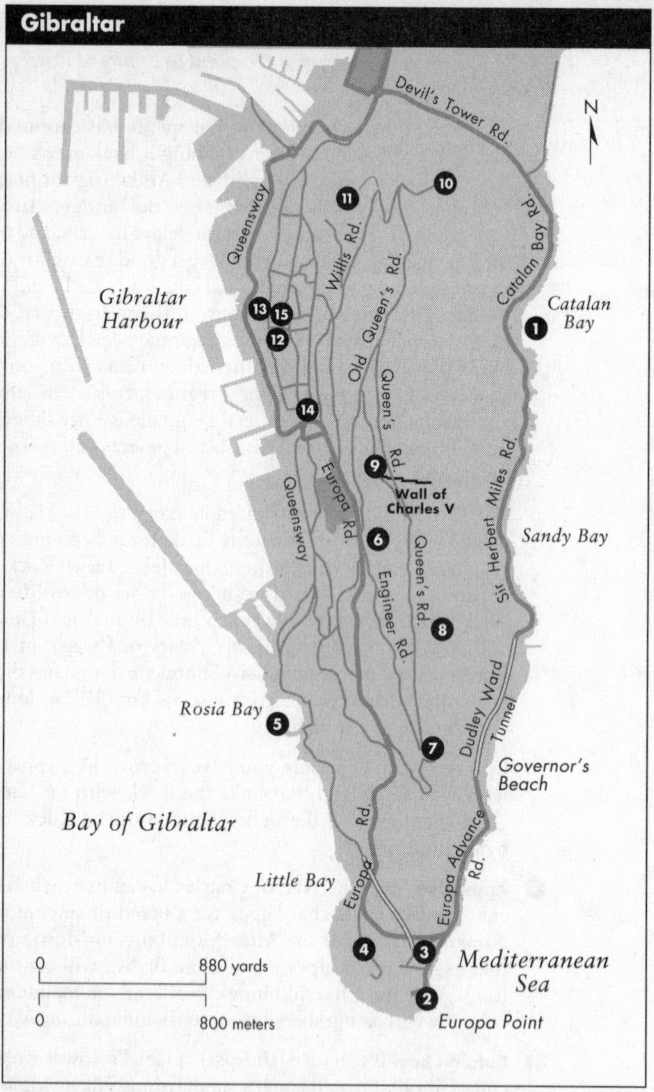

11 **Moorish Castle.** This refuge was built by chieftain Tarik's successors in the 11th century. The **Tower of Homage**, the only bit remaining, was rebuilt by the Moors in 1333. Admiral Rooke hoisted the British flag from its top when he captured the Rock in 1704, and it has flown here ever since. ✉ *Willis Rd.*

14 **Nefusot Yehudada Synagogue.** The synagogue is worth a look for its inspired design. ✉ *Line Wall Rd.*

3 **Nun's Well.** The Nun's Well is an ancient Moorish cistern. ✉ *Europa Flats.*

2 **Punta Grande de Europa** (Europa Point). Stop here at the Rock's southernmost tip to admire the view across the strait to the coast of Morocco, 22½ km (14 mi) away. You are standing on what in ancient times was called one of the two Pillars of Hercules. (The second pillar was just across the water, in Morocco—a mountain between the cities of Ceuta and Tangier.) Plaques explain the history of the gun installations here.

5 **Rosia Bay.** This is where Admiral Nelson's flagship, HMS *Victory,* was towed after the Battle of Trafalgar, in 1805. Aboard were the battle's casualties, now buried in **Trafalgar Cemetery** (✉ southern edge of town), and the body of Nelson himself, preserved in a barrel of rum. Nelson was taken to London for burial in St. Paul's Cathedral.

8 **St. Michael's Cave.** A series of underground chambers adorned with stalactites and stalagmites, the cave makes a wonderful setting for concerts, ballet, and drama. ✉ *Off Queen's Rd.*

4 **Shrine of Our Lady of Europe.** The shrine has been venerated by sailors since 1462. ✉ *Europa Flats.*

12 **Town of Gibraltar.** Britain's dignified Regency architecture blends with the shutters, balconies, and patios of southern Spain in this colorful, congested confluence. Apart from the attraction of shops, restaurants, and pubs on Main Street, yot has not been eradicated from the outer regions, so it's best to take precautions. Inoculations for hepatitis and tetanus should also be up-to-date. If you're a hiker or diver, be aware that these islands are home to a number of dangerous and poisonous creatures—know what to watch out for before you head into the wild.

Owing to the downward spiral of the Indonesian economy and general political dissatisfaction, large public demonstrations and riots have occurred in Jakarta, Bandung, Medan, and Ujung Pueensway Quay, Gibraltar's most fashionable marina. The outdoor terrace is very pleasant. The extensive menu incorporates international dishes, including some Spanish specialties. ✉ *Queensway Quay,* ☎ *9567/40362. MC, V Closed Mon.*

$$–$$$ ✕ **La Bayuca.** One of the Rock's best-established restaurants, La Bayuca is renowned for its onion soup and Mediterranean dishes. ✉ *21 Turnbull's La.,* ☎ *9567/75119. AE, DC, MC, V. Closed Tues. No lunch Sun.*

$$$$ **The Eliott.** The Rock's most modern hotel, the Eliott is right in the center of the town. The rooms are functional and comfortable. ✉ *2 Governor's Parade,* ☎ *9567/70500,* FAX *9567/70243. 114 rooms, 2 suites. Pool. AE, DC, MC, V.*

$$$$ ★ **The Rock.** Overlooking the town and harbor, the refurbished Rock is spiffy enough to qualify as an international hotel while preserving something of its colonial English background. Pink, peach, and a beach theme predominate in the rooms and restaurant, which have ceiling fans. ✉ *3 Europa Rd.,* ☎ *9567/73000,* FAX *9567/73513. 112 rooms, 8 suites. Restaurant, pool. AE, DC, MC, V.*

$$$ **Bristol.** This colonial-style hotel is in the heart of town, just off Gibraltar's main street. Rooms are large and comfortable, and the tropical garden is a haven if you're craving some isolation. ✉ *10 Cathedral Sq.,* ☎ *9567/76800,* FAX *9567/77613. 60 rooms. Pool. AE, DC, MC, V.*

Costa del Sol and Gibraltar Essentials

AIR TRAVEL

Daily flights on Iberia and Aviaco connect Málaga with Madrid and Barcelona. Air Europa and Spanair also schedule wallet-friendly flights.

Iberia, British Airways, and numerous charter airlines offer frequent service from London; most other major European cities also have direct air links. You'll have to connect in Madrid if you're flying from the United States. Flights leave London for Gibraltar daily; as yet there are no flights from Spanish airports.

AIRPORTS AND TRANSFERS

Málaga Airport is 12 km (7 mi) west of the city.

➤ AIRPORT INFORMATION: **Málaga Airport** (☎ 95/204–8804).

TRANSFERS

City buses run from the Málaga Airport to the city every 30 minutes, 6:30 AM–midnight, and cost 150 ptas./€0.90. Portillo bus company has frequent service from the airport to Torremolinos. A suburban train serving Málaga, Torremolinos, and Fuengirola also stops at the airport every half hour, though the station is a long walk from the terminal.

➤ TAXIS AND SHUTTLES: **Portillo** (☎ 95/236–0191).

BUS TRAVEL

Buses are the best means of transportation along the Costa del Sol (as well as from Seville or Granada). Málaga's long-distance station is on the Paseo de los Tilos; nearby, on Muelle de Heredía, a smaller station serves suburban destinations. The main bus company serving the Costa del Sol is Portillo. Alsina-Gräells goes to Granada, Córdoba, Seville, and Nerja.

➤ BUS INFORMATION: **Alsina-Gräells** (☎ 95/231–8295 at the station). **Málaga main bus station** (☎ 95/235–0061). **Portillo** (☎ 95/236–0191).

TOURS

There are plenty of bus tours from Spanish cities. Pullmantur and many smaller agencies run daily tours to Gibraltar (except Sunday) from most Costa del Sol resorts. Portillo runs an inexpensive daily tour to Gibraltar from the Torremolinos bus station, and you can always take the regular Portillo bus to La Línea and walk across the border.

Numerous companies, including Pullmantur, lead one- and two-day excursions from all Costa del Sol resorts to such places as Seville, Granada, Córdoba, Ronda, Gibraltar, and Tangier. Your hotel desk or any travel agent can arrange a reservation.

TRAIN TRAVEL

From Madrid, Málaga is served by half a dozen rapid trains daily. The train station in Málaga is a 15-minute walk from the city center, across the river. Call RENFE for general information.

➤ TRAIN INFORMATION: **Málaga train station** (✉ Explanada de la Estación, ☎ 95/236–0202). **RENFE** (☎ 902/240202).

VISITOR INFORMATION

The most helpful tourist offices (by far) are in Málaga and Marbella. The Málaga office covers the entire province.

➤ TOURIST INFORMATION: **Estepona** (✉ Paseo Marítimo Pedro Manrique, ☎ 95/280–0913). **Fuengirola** (✉ Avda. Jesús Santos Rein 6, ☎ 95/246–7457). **Gibraltar** (✉ Cathedral Sq., ☎ 9567/74950). **Málaga** (✉ Pasaje de Chinitas 4, ☎ 95/221–3445; ✉ Avda. Cervantes 1, Paseo del Parque, ☎ 95/260–4410). **Marbella** (✉ Glorieta de la Fontanilla, ☎ 95/282–2818). **Nerja** (✉ Puerta del Mar 2, ☎ 95/252–1531). **Ronda** (✉ Plaza de España 1, ☎ 95/287–1272). **Torremolinos** (✉ Ayuntamiento, Plaza Blas Infante, ☎ 95/237–9511).

29 SWEDEN

STOCKHOLM, UPPSALA AND THE FOLKLORE DISTRICT, THE WEST COAST, AND THE GLASS COUNTRY

THE NATURAL BEAUTY OF SWEDEN, with its glaciated mountains, vast forest tracts, thousands of lakes and rivers, and unspoiled archipelagoes, stands in stark contrast to the cosmopolitan lifestyle of Swedish towns and cities.

Sweden is Europe's fourth-largest country, encompassing an area of 449,964 square km (173,731 square mi). Watch its environment change dramatically as you travel from the barren Arctic north to the fertile plains of the south, a distance measuring nearly 1,600 km (1,000 mi). Still, Sweden is home to only 8.9 million people. The railway line that runs 2,128 km (1,322 mi) from Trelleborg, in the far south, to Riksgränsen, in the north, is the world's longest stretch of continuously electrified track. Traveling it takes more than 35 hours.

Sweden is a land of contrasts. It has short, warm summers and long, dark, cold winters. Ancient Viking rune stones and 19th-century landmarks coexist with modern skyscrapers. Socialism exists side by side with staunch royalism. Shop windows, full of the latest in consumer goods, attract shoppers who are as at home in the city as they are in the countryside. Swedes seem to like this diversity, big-city living contrasting with the silence of the countryside. Sweden is also a clean country; it is possible to fish for salmon and trout right in the center of Stockholm, just a stone's throw away from the Royal Palace. In downtown Malmö, startlingly large hares hop around in the parks.

Once the dominant power of the Nordic region, Sweden has always been politically independent. During the cold war, it was largely successful in retaining its position as a neutral trading partner of both superpowers. The economic recession of the late 1980s forced Sweden to rethink its comprehensive welfare system, and changes were made down to its very foundations. When the country developed one of Europe's largest budget deficits, the fragile conservative coalition that had defeated the long-incumbent Social Democrats in 1991 attempted further cutbacks. The Social Democrats' power was restored in 1994, but cutbacks have continued at an ever-increasing pace. Sweden joined the European Union (EU) in January 1995, following a closely won referendum preceded by a heated debate. While the domestic benefits of membership have been slow in showing themselves, Sweden has quickly become an influential member of this often divided organization.

Sweden (Sverige)

SWEDEN A TO Z

To research prices, get advice from other travelers, and book travel arrangements, visit www.fodors.com.

AIR TRAVEL

Most major cities are served by SAS and smaller, independent airlines. From Stockholm, there are flights to more than 30 points around the country. SAS offers cut-rate round-trip fares every day on selected flights, including student rebates and discount prices for travelers under 26.

➤ AIRLINES AND CONTACTS: **SAS** (☎ 020/727000).

BIKE TRAVEL

Cycling is popular in Sweden, and the country's uncongested roads and many cycle paths make it ideal for extended bike tours. Bicycles can be rented throughout the country; inquire at tourist information offices. Rental costs average around SKr 80 per day or SKr 400 per week. The Swedish Touring Club can give you information about cycling packages that include bike rental, overnight accommodation, and meals. Cykelfrämjandet (National Cycle Association) has information in English and German about cycling trips around Sweden.

➤ CONTACTS: **Cykelfrämjandet** (✉ Torsg. 31, Box 6027, 102 31 Stockholm, ☎ 08/321680, FAX 08/310503). **Swedish Touring Club** (✉ Kungsg. 2, Box 25, 101 20 Stockholm, ☎ 08/4632200 or 020/292929, FAX 08/6781958).

BOAT AND FERRY TRAVEL

A classic Swedish boat trip is the four-day journey along the Göta Canal between Göteborg and Stockholm, operated by Göta Canal Steamship Company. Children must be at least eight years old to ride aboard the steamship.

➤ BOAT AND FERRY INFORMATION: **Göta Canal Steamship Company** (✉ Box 272, 401 24 Göteborg, ☎ 031/806315, FAX 031/158311).

BUS TRAVEL

Sweden has excellent express bus service that provides inexpensive and relatively speedy transportation around the country. An information and booking office is at Stockholm's station, Cityterminalen. Swebus and Wasatrafik run daily; other private companies operate weekends only. In the far north, postal buses delivering mail to remote areas also carry passengers, providing an offbeat, inexpensive journey.

➤ BUS INFORMATION: **Cityterminalen** (✉ Klarabergsviadukten 72, ☎ 0200/218218; wait on the line for English service).

BUSINESS HOURS

BANKS AND OFFICES

Banks are open weekdays 9:30 to 3; some stay open until 5 in larger cities. Banks at Stockholm's Arlanda Airport and Göteborg's Landvetter Airport are open every day, with extended hours. Forex and Valuta Specialisten currency-exchange offices operate in downtown Stockholm, Göteborg, and Malmö, also with extended hours.

MUSEUMS AND SIGHTS

Museum hours vary widely, but most are open weekdays 10 to 4 or 10 to 5, weekends 11 to 4; they may close on Monday.

SHOPS

Shops are generally open weekdays 9 or 9:30 to 6 and Saturday 9 to 1 or 9 to 4. Some department stores remain open until 8 or 9 on certain evenings, and some are also open Sunday noon to 4 in major cities.

Many supermarkets open on Sunday. Sweden's Systembolaget, the state-run liquor store and only place to buy wine, hard alcohol, or class III beer, is open weekdays 9 to 6. Select stores are open Saturday 10 to 4. Expect a long line on Friday evenings.

CAR TRAVEL

EMERGENCIES

The Larmtjänst organization, run by a confederation of Swedish insurance companies, provides 24-hour breakdown service.

➤ CONTACTS: **Larmtjänst** (✉ Stockholm headquarters, ☎ 08/7837000).

GASOLINE

Sweden has some of the highest gasoline prices in Europe, SKr 9–SKr 10 per liter. Gas stations are self-service: pumps marked SEDEL are automated and accept SKr 20 and SKr 100 bills; pumps marked KASSA are paid for at the cash desk; the KONTO pumps are for customers with Swedish gas credit cards.

PARKING

Park on the right-hand side of the road, but if you want to park overnight, be sure not to do so the night the street is being cleaned; circular signs with a red border indicate when this occurs. Timed ticket machines and, sometimes, meters operate in larger towns, usually between 8 AM and 6 PM. The fee varies from about SKr 5 to SKr 30 per hour; parking is free on weekends. Parking garages in urban areas are mostly automated, often with machines that accept credit cards; LEDIGT on a garage sign means space is available. On the street, a circular sign with a red border and a red diagonal on a blue background means parking is prohibited; a yellow rectangle with a red border means restricted parking. Beware: fines for parking violations are very high in Sweden. City "Trafikkarta" maps, available at many gas stations, include English explanations of parking signs and systems.

ROAD CONDITIONS

Sweden has an excellent network of more than 80,000 km (50,000 mi) of highways. The fastest routes are those with numbers prefixed with an *E* (for "European"). All main and secondary roads are well surfaced, but some minor roads, particularly in the north, are gravel.

RULES OF THE ROAD

Drive on the right, and no matter where you sit in a car, you must wear a seat belt. You must also have at least low-beam headlights on at all times. Signs indicate five basic speed limits, ranging from 30 kph (19 mph) in school or playground areas to 110 kph (68 mph) on long stretches of *E* roads.

CUSTOMS AND DUTIES

For details on imports and duty-free limits, *see* Customs and Duties *in* Chapter 1.

DINING

Traditional Swedish restaurants are giving way to myriad international culinary influences. Fast-food outlets abound, but an impressive range of eateries—from top-class establishments to less expensive places for lunch or a snack—can suit even the most fickle palates and every budget.

Restaurants all over the country specialize in *husmanskost* (home cooking), based on traditional Swedish recipes. Sweden is world famous for its *smörgåsbord,* a word now internationally used as a synonym for diversity. This tempting buffet of hot and cold dishes usually emphasizes seafood, notably herring. You can usually find an authentic smörgåsbord, and eat as much as you wish, for SKr 200–SKr 300. Hotels sometimes serve a smörgåsbord-style breakfast, often included in the room price.

Prices are for a main course at dinner. Service charges and *moms* (value-added tax) are included in the check, but it is common to tip 5%–10%.

CATEGORY	COST
$$$$	over SKr 350
$$$	SKr 250–SKr 350
$$	SKr 120–SKr 250
$	under SKr 120

MEALTIMES

Swedes eat early. Lunch is served from 11 AM, and outside the main cities restaurants often close at 9 PM or don't even open for dinner.

RESERVATIONS AND DRESS

Except for in the most formal restaurants, where a jacket and a tie are preferable, casual—or casual chic—attire is perfectly acceptable.

EMBASSIES

➤ AUSTRALIA: (✉ Sergelstorg 12, Stockholm, ☎ 08/6132900).
➤ CANADA: (✉ Tegelbacken 4, Stockholm, ☎ 08/4533000).
➤ IRELAND: (✉ Östermalmsg. 97, Stockholm, ☎ 08/6618005).
➤ UNITED KINGDOM: (✉ Skarpög. 6–8, Stockholm, ☎ 08/6713000).
➤ UNITED STATES: (✉ Strandv. 101, Stockholm, ☎ 08/7835300).

HOLIDAYS

January 1; January 6 (Epiphany); Good Friday; Easter Monday; May 1 (Labor Day); Ascension (in May); June 21 (Midsummer Evening); June 22 (Midsummer Day); All Saints' Day (first Saturday in November); December 24–26.

LANGUAGE

Swedish is closely related to Danish and Norwegian. After "z," the Swedish alphabet has three extra letters, "å," "ä," and "ö." Note that the letter *w* is pronounced like a *v.* Most Swedes speak English.

LODGING

Sweden offers a variety of accommodations from simple bed-and-breakfasts, campsites, and hostels to hotels of the highest international standard. Major hotels in larger cities cater mainly to business clientele and can be expensive; weekend rates are more reasonable. Prices are usually on a per-room basis and include all taxes, service charges, and breakfast. Apart from the more modest inns and the cheapest budget establishments, private baths and showers are standard. Whatever their size, Swedish hotels provide scrupulously clean accommodation and courteous service. Sweden virtually shuts down during the entire month of July, so make your hotel reservations in advance, especially if you're staying outside the city areas during July and early August.

RATINGS

Prices are for two people in a double room, based on standard rates; tax and breakfast are included.

CATEGORY	COST
$$$$	over SKr 2,700
$$$	SKr 1,800–SKr 2,700
$$	SKr 1,000–SKr 1,800
$	under SKr 1,000

CAMPING

Camping is popular in Sweden. About 750 officially approved sites dot the country, most next to the sea or a lake and offering such activities as windsurfing, horseback riding, and tennis. They are generally open June to September, although some stay open year-round. A free, abbreviated list of sites is published in English by the Sveriges Campingvårdernas Riksförbund (Swedish Campsite Owners' Association).

➤ CONTACTS: **Sveriges Campingvårdernas Riksförbund** (✉ Box 255, 451 17 Uddevalla, ☎ 0522/642440, FAX 0522/642430).

CHALET RENTALS

Accommodations can often be arranged on the spot at tourist offices for 250 chalet villages, all with high standards. Scandinavian Seaways in Göteborg arranges package deals that combine a ferry trip from Britain across the North Sea and a stay in a chalet village.

➤ CONTACTS: **Scandinavian Seaways** (☎ 031/650600).

HOTELS

You can contact major hotel groups through their central reservations services: Best Western hotels can be found throughout the country. Radisson SAS has high-quality hotels often located in city centers. Scandic is one of Sweden's largest hotel chains. Sweden Hotels has about 100 independently owned hotels and its own classification scheme—*A, B,* or *C*—based on facilities.

You'll find comprehensive information about hotel facilities and prices in the official annual guide *Hotels in Sweden,* published by and available free from the Swedish Travel and Tourism Council. Countryside Hotels, 40 select resort hotels, may be restored manor houses or centuries-old inns. Hotellcentralen is an independent agency that makes advance telephone reservations for hotels in Stockholm.

➤ CONTACTS: **Best Western** (☎ 08/56629370 or 020/792752). **Countryside Hotels** (✉ Box 69, 830 13 Åre, ☎ 0647/50680, FAX 0647/51920). **Hotellcentralen** (✉ Central Station, 111 20, ☎ 08/7892456, FAX 08/7918666). **Radisson SAS** (☎ 020/797592). **Scandic** (☎ 08/51751700). **Sweden Hotels** (☎ 08/7017900).

MAIL AND SHIPPING

If you're uncertain where you will be staying, have your mail addressed to "poste restante" and sent to S-101 10 Stockholm. Collection is at Post Office Stockholm 1. American Express offers a poste-restante service free to cardholders and for a small fee to others.

➤ POST OFFICES: **Post Office Stockholm 1** (✉ Drottningg. 53, ☎ 08/7814682).

POSTAL RATES

Airmail letters and postcards to the United States and Canada weighing less than 20 grams cost SKr 8. Postcards and letters within Europe cost SKr 5.

MONEY MATTERS

Sweden is looked upon as an expensive country, although prices are generally in line with the European average. Restaurant prices can be high, but bargains exist: in cities look for the lunch *dagens rätt* (dish of the day) for about SKr 60–SKr 70. Also, check for a recommended two- or three-course menu. Hotels are at their priciest fall through spring; many have special low summer and weekend winter rates. Heavy taxes and excise duties make liquor prices among the highest in Europe.

Some sample prices include: cup of coffee, SKr 15–SKr 25; beer, SKr 30–SKr 49; soda, SKr 15–SKr 25; ham sandwich, SKr 25–SKr 50; 2-

km (1-mi) taxi ride, SKr 60–SKr 80 (depending on the taxi company, day, and time).

CURRENCY

The unit of currency in Sweden is the krona (plural kronor), which is divided into 100 öre and is written as SKr, SEK, or kr. Coins come in values of 50 öre and 1, 5, or 10 kronor; bills come in denominations of 20, 100, 500, and 1,000 kronor. Traveler's checks and foreign currency can be exchanged at banks all over Sweden and at post offices displaying the NB EXCHANGE sign. At press time (summer 2001), the exchange rate was SKr 9.66 to the U.S. dollar, SKr 6.25 to the Canadian dollar, SKr 14.22 to the pound sterling, SKr 11.48 to the Irish punt, SKr 5.13 to the Australian dollar, SKr 4.21 to the New Zealand dollar, and SKr 1.25 to the South African rand.

SHOPPING

Swedish goods are internationally renowned for their style and quality, especially interior design items—such as plastic kitchen tools, glassware, stainless steel, pottery and ceramics—and clothing and furniture. Textiles are also of exceptional quality. You will find a wide selection of top-quality goods, including Swedish-designed clothing, at such major stores as NK, PUB, and Åhléns City in Stockholm. Other clothing stores nationwide are H&M, jc, Vero Moda, and MQ.

For glassware at bargain prices, head for the Glass Country. The major glassworks have large factory outlets where you can pick up seconds at prices well below normal retail. For textiles, the best centers are Borås and Ullered, not far from Göteborg. In rural areas, head to the local Hemslöjd crafts centers for high-quality clothing, woodwork, and needlework.

TAXES

VALUE-ADDED TAX (V.A.T)

Many Swedish shops participate in the tax-free shopping program, enabling visitors to claim a refund of most of the *moms* (value-added tax) paid, a rate of about 25%. Participating shops display a distinctive black, blue, and yellow sticker in the window. (Some stores offer the service only on purchases amounting to more than SKr 200.) The cashier will wrap and seal your purchase and give you a "Tax-Free Shopping Check" equivalent to the tax paid minus a handling charge. This check can be cashed when you leave Sweden and show your unopened packages, either at the airport or aboard ferries. If you're packing your purchases in a suitcase, you can show them at the "Tax-Free" counter at Arlanda airport's check-in lobby and get your refund before you check your luggage. You need your passport when making your purchase and claiming your refund.

TELEPHONES

COUNTRY AND AREA CODES

The country code for Sweden is 46. When dialing Sweden from outside the country, drop the first zero in the regional telephone code.

DIRECTORY AND OPERATOR ASSISTANCE

For international calls, the operator assistance number is ☎ 0018; directory assistance, which costs SKr 16 per minute, is ☎ 118119. Within Sweden, dial ☎ 90200 for operator assistance and ☎ 118118 for directory assistance (this service costs SKr 11 per minute).

INTERNATIONAL CALLS

These can be made from any pay phone. For calls to the United States and Canada, dial 00, then 1 (the country code), then wait for a second dial tone before dialing the area code and number. When dialing the United Kingdom, omit the initial zero on area codes. You can make international calls from Telebutik offices. AT&T, MCI, and Sprint all offer long-distance service from Sweden.

➤ ACCESS CODES: **AT&T** (☎ 020/795611). **MCI** (☎ 020/795922). **Sprint** (☎ 020/799011).

LOCAL CALLS

Telephone numbers beginning with 020 are toll-free within Sweden.

PUBLIC PHONES

Sweden has plenty of pay phones; to use them you'll need SKr 1, SKr 5, or SKr 10 coins, as a local call costs SKr 2. You can also purchase a *telefonkort* (telephone card) from a Telebutik, hospital, or *Pressbyrån* store for SKr 35, SKr 60, or SKr 100. The card can provide a savings if you make numerous domestic calls and is indispensable when you're faced with one of the many public phones that accept only cards.

TIPPING

Tipping in Sweden has become more common in recent years. At hotels it is customary to tip the porter about SKr 5 per item. For taxi rides, SKr 5–SKr 10 is usual. When dining out you must often check your coat or sports jacket, regardless of whether you wish to do so; the tip (or cost) for this is usually SKr 10.

TRAIN TRAVEL

Frequent trains link Stockholm with Göteborg and Malmö. First- and second-class cars are provided on all main routes, and sleeping cars are available in both classes on overnight trains. Most long-distance trains have a buffet car and a playground car for kids. Seat reservations are advisable, and on some trains—indicated with *R*, *IN*, or *IC* on the timetable—mandatory. Reservations can be made right up to departure. Couchette reservations on the regular train cost SKr 95 and beds from SKr 180. The Swedish rail network also operates high-speed X2000 trains from Stockholm to Göteborg, Falun, Malmö, Jönköping, and Sundsvall, and from Göteborg to Malmö.

CUTTING COSTS

There is a 50% discount on *röda platser* ("red," or off-peak, seats) booked at least seven days in advance. ScanRail passes allow unlimited train travel throughout Sweden, as well as to Denmark, Finland, and Norway. Limited ferry passage in and beyond Scandinavia is also included. The pass is available for 21 days, or 5 days of travel within 15 days.

➤ TRAIN INFORMATION: **Reservations** (☎ 020/757575 Swedish recorded message; wait to be served by operator).

TRANSPORTATION AROUND SWEDEN

The basic street-sign terms you'll come across are *gatan* (street, abbreviated to *g.*), *vägen* (road, abbreviated to *v.*), and *gränd* (lane, shortened to *gr.*).

VISITOR INFORMATION

➤ TOURIST INFORMATION: **Swedish Travel and Tourism Council** (✉ Kungsg. 36, Box 3030, 103 61 Stockholm, ☎ 08/7255500, FAX 08/7255531, WEB www.visit-sweden.com/).

WHEN TO GO

The tourist season runs from mid-May through mid-September; many attractions, however, close in late August, when the schools reopen at the end of the Swedish vacation season. The weather can be glorious in the spring and fall, when fewer visitors are around.

CLIMATE

Sweden has typically unpredictable northern European summer weather, but as a general rule it is likely to be warm but not hot from May until September. In Stockholm, the weeks just before and after midsummer have almost 24-hour light, and in the far north, above the Arctic Circle, the sun doesn't set between the end of May and the middle of July.

The following are the average daily maximum and minimum temperatures for Stockholm.

Jan.	30F	– 1C	**May**	58F	14C	**Sept.**	60F	15C
	23	– 5		43	6		49	9
Feb.	30F	– 1C	**June**	67F	19C	**Oct.**	49F	9C
	22	– 5		51	11		41	5
Mar.	37F	3C	**July**	71F	22C	**Nov.**	40F	5C
	26	– 4		57	14		34	1
Apr.	47F	8C	**Aug.**	68F	20C	**Dec.**	35F	3C
	34	1		55	13		28	– 2

STOCKHOLM

Stockholm stands on 14 islands surrounded by water so clean that you can fish and swim in the heart of the city. This cultivated, civilized city has many parks, squares, and wide streets, providing welcome calm in what has become a bustling metropolis. Modern glass-and-steel buildings abound in the city center, but you are seldom more than a five-minute walk from twisting, medieval streets and water views.

The first written mention of Stockholm dates from 1252, when a powerful regent named Birger Jarl built a fortified castle here. The strategic position, where the fresh waters of Lake Mälaren meet the brackish Baltic Sea, prompted King Gustav Vasa to take over the city in 1523, and King Gustavus Adolphus to make it the heart of an empire a century later.

During the Thirty Years' War (1618–48), Sweden became an important Baltic trading state, and the city gained a reputation as a commercial center. By the beginning of the 18th century, however, Swedish influence had begun to wane, and Stockholm's development slowed. It did not pick up again until the Industrial Revolution, when the hub of the city moved north from the Gamla Stan (Old Town) area.

Exploring Stockholm

Numbers in the margin correspond to points of interest on the Stockholm map.

Stockholm's main attractions are concentrated in a relatively small area, and the city itself can be explored in just a few days. If you have only limited time in Stockholm, give priority to a tour of Stockholm's Gamla Stan (Old Town), a labyrinth of narrow medieval streets, alleyways, and quiet squares on the island just south of the city center. Be sure to visit the large island of Djurgården. Although it's only a short walk from the city center, the most pleasant way to approach it is by ferry from Skeppsbron, in Gamla Stan.

13 **Gröna Lund Tivoli.** Stockholm's only amusement park is a family favorite, with traditional rides and new attractions on the waterfront each season. ✉ *Djurgårdsv.,* ☎ *08/58750100,* WEB *www.tivoli.se.* ⌚ *May–Sept., daily. Hrs vary; call ahead.*

9 **Historiska Museet** (Historical Museum). The museum houses some remarkable gold and silver treasures dating from the Swedish Viking era.

Stockholm

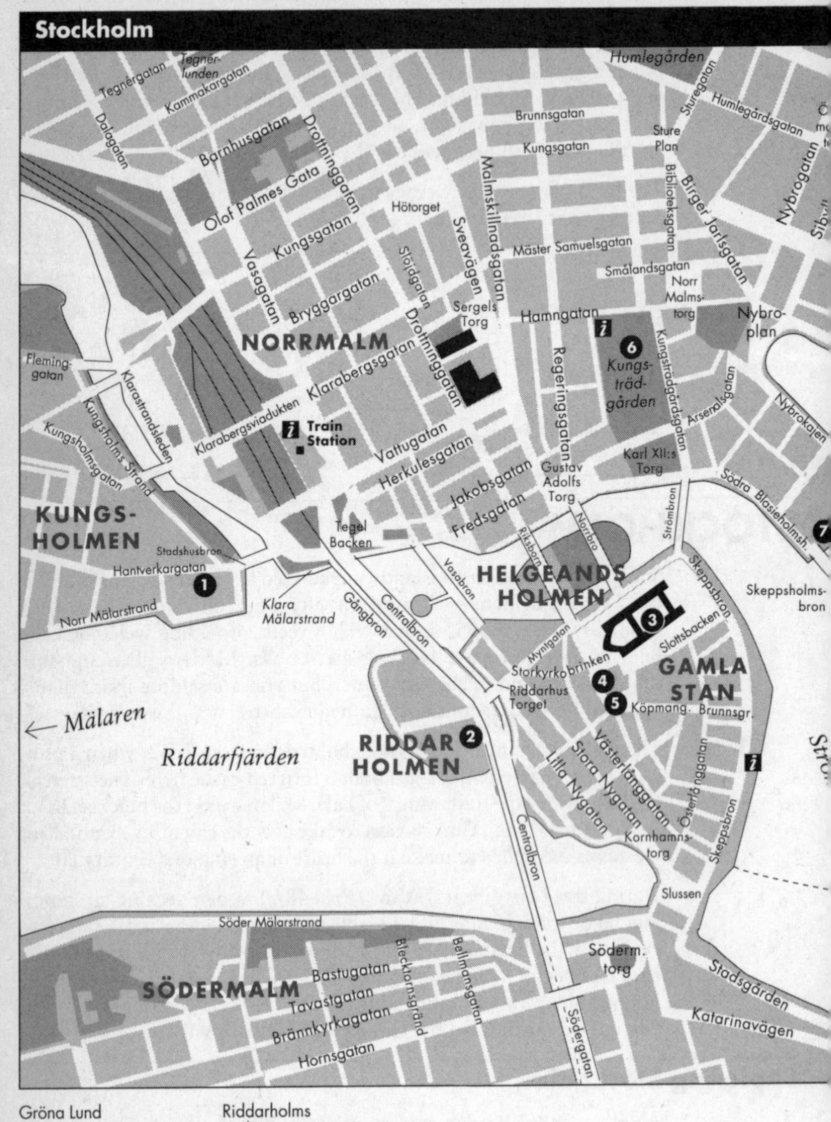

- Gröna Lund Tivoli 13
- Historiska Museet . . . 9
- Junibacken 10
- Kaknästornet 15
- Kungliga Slottet 3
- Kungsträdgården . . . 6
- Moderna Museet . . . 8
- National Museum . . 7
- Nordiska Museet 11
- Riddarholms Kyrkan 2
- Skansen 14
- Stadshuset 1
- Storkyrkan 4
- Stortorget 5
- Vasamuseet 12
- Waldemarsudde . . 16

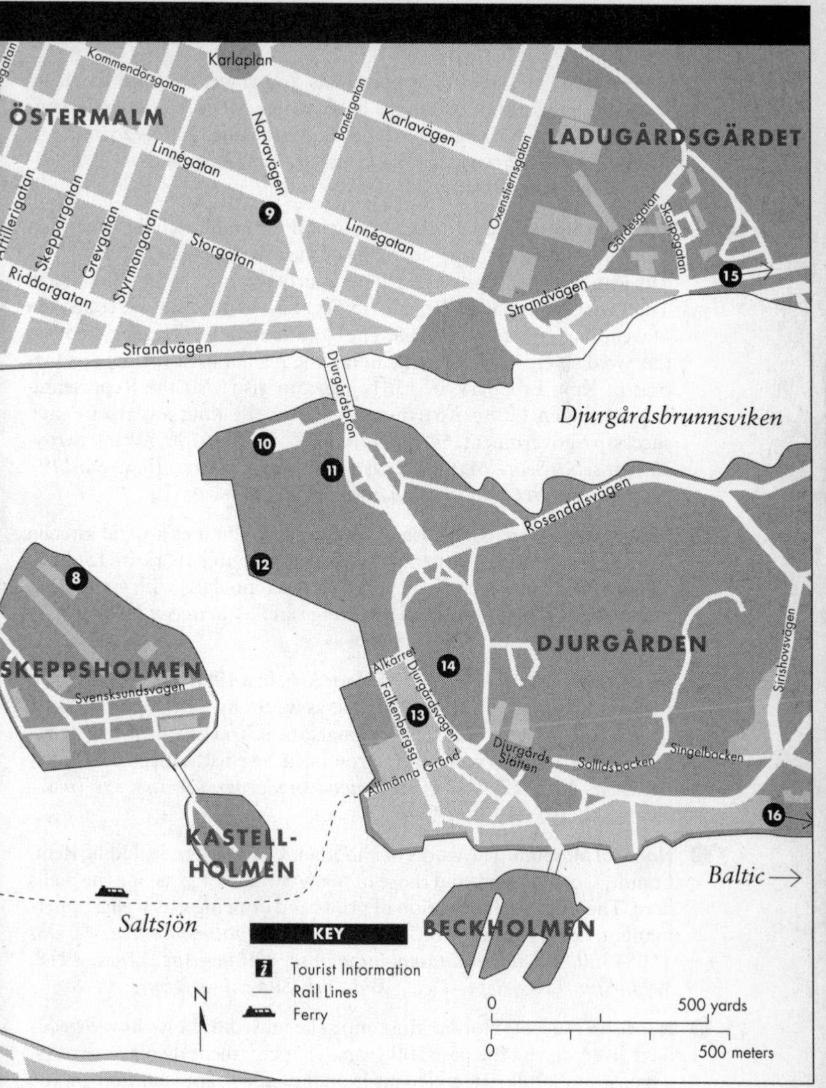
Kommendörsgatan
Karlaplan
ÖSTERMALM
Narvavägen
Banérgatan
Karlavägen
LADUGÅRDSGÄRDET
Linnégatan
Oxenstiernsgatan
Artillerigatan
Skeppargatan
Grevgatan
Styrmangatan
Storgatan
Linnégatan
Gärdesgatan
Skarpögatan
Riddargatan
Strandvägen
Strandvägen
Djurgårdsbron
Djurgårdsbrunnsviken
Rosendalsvägen
DJURGÅRDEN
SKEPPSHOLMEN
Svensksundsvägen
Alkärret
Djurgårdsvägen
Falkenbergsg.
Sirishovsvägen
Djurgårds Slätten
Saltsjöbacken
Singelbacken
Allmänna Gränd
KASTELLHOLMEN
Baltic
Saltsjön
BECKHOLMEN
KEY
Tourist Information
Rail Lines
Ferry
N
0
500 yards
0
500 meters

✉ *Narvav. 13–17,* ☎ *08/51955600,* WEB *www.historiska.se.* ⏲ *Tues.–Wed. and Fri.–Sun. 11–5, Thurs. 11–8.*

★ ⓒ ❿ **Junibacken.** This fairy-tale house lets you travel in small carriages through the world of children's book writer Astrid Lindgren, creator of the irrepressible character Pippi Longstocking. ✉ *Galärvarsv.,* ☎ *08/58723000,* WEB *www.junibacken.se.* ⏲ *June–Aug., daily 9–6; Sept.–May, Wed.–Sun. 10–5.*

★ ❸ **Kungliga Slottet** (Royal Palace). Visit at noon and watch the time-honored yet now superfluous changing of the smartly dressed guards. You can wander at will into the palace courtyard and the building itself. The **Livrustkammaren** (Royal Armory) has an outstanding collection of weaponry and royal regalia. The **Skattkammaren** (Treasury) houses the Swedish crown jewels, including the regalia used for the coronation of King Erik XIV in 1561. You can also visit the **Representationsvåningen** (State Apartments), where the king swears in each successive government. ✉ *Gamla Stan,* ☎ *08/4026130,* WEB *www.royalcourt.se.* ⏲ *Sept.–May 14, daily 10–4; May 15–Aug., Tues.–Sun. 12–3. Prices and hrs subject to change; call ahead.*

❻ **Kungsträdgården** (King's Garden). Originally built as a royal kitchen garden, Kungsträdgården was turned into a public park in 1562. In summer you can watch people playing open-air chess with giant chess pieces. In winter the park has a skating rink. ✉ *Between Hamng. and the Royal Opera in the city center.*

❽ **Moderna Museet** (Museum of Modern Art). In a 1998 building designed by Rafael Moneo, the museum displays works by Picasso, Kandinsky, Dalí, Brancuşi, and other international artists. You can also view paintings and sculptures created by prominent Swedish artists. ✉ *Skeppsholmen,* ☎ *08/51955200,* WEB *www.modernamuseet.se.* ⏲ *Tues.–Thurs. 11–10, Fri.–Sun. 11–6.*

❼ **National Museum.** The works of important Old Masters, including Rembrandt, Goya, Degas, and those of many Swedish artists line the walls here. There is a wide selection of prints and drawings, as well as a permanent design exhibition. ✉ *Södra Blasieholmshamnen,* ☎ *08/51954300,* WEB *www.nationalmuseum.se.* ⏲ *Jan.–Aug., Tues. 11–8, Wed.–Sun. 11–5; Sept.–Dec., Wed., Fri.–Sun. 11–5, Thurs. 11–8.*

ⓒ ⓫ **Nordiska Museet** (Nordic Museum). The museum shows how Swedes have lived during the past 500 years. On permanent display are peasant costumes, folk art, and items from the Sami (Lapp) culture. On the ground floor, there's a delightful "village life" play area. ✉ *Djurgårdsv. 6–16,* ☎ *08/5195600,* WEB *www.nordm.se.* ⏲ *Tues., Thurs. 10–8, Wed., Fri.–Sun. 10–5.*

❷ **Riddarholms Kyrkan** (Riddarholm Church). A legion of Swedish kings is buried in this magnificent sanctuary, a Greyfriars monastery dating from 1270. ✉ *Riddarholmen, Gamla Stan,* ☎ *08/4026130.* ⏲ *May–Aug., daily 10–4; Sept., weekends noon–3.*

★ ⓒ ⓮ **Skansen.** More than 150 reconstructed traditional buildings from all over Sweden and a variety of handicraft displays and demonstrations form this large, open-air folk museum. There is a zoo, with native Scandinavian lynxes, wolves, and elk, as well as an aquarium and an old-style *tivoli* (amusement park). Snack kiosks and a pleasant restaurant make it easy to spend a whole day. ✉ *Djurgårdsslätten 49–51,* ☎ *08/4428000,* WEB *www.skansen.se.* ⏲ *Oct.–Apr., daily 10–4; May, daily 10–8; June–Aug., daily 10–10; Sept., daily 10–5. Prices and hrs subject to change; call ahead.*

★ ❶ **Stadshuset** (City Hall). Architect Ragnar Östberg's ornate 1923 facade is a Stockholm landmark. Lavish mosaics adorn the walls of the **Gyllene Salen** (Golden Hall), and the **Prinsens Galleri** (Prince's Gallery) holds a collection of large murals by Prince Eugen, brother of King Gustav V. Take the elevator halfway up, and then climb the rest of the way to the top of the 348-ft tower for a magnificent view of the city. ✉ *Hantverkarg. 1,* ☎ *08/50829058.* ⏲ *Guided tours only. Tours in English, June–Aug., daily 10, 11, noon, and 2; Sept., daily 10, noon, and 2; Oct.–May, daily 10 and noon.*

❹ **Storkyrkan** (Cathedral). In this 15th-century Gothic cathedral in central Gamla Stan, you will find the *Parhelion,* a painting of Stockholm dating from 1520, the oldest in existence. ✉ *Trångsund 1,* ☎ *08/7233016.* ⏲ *Sept.–Apr., daily 9–4; May–Aug., daily 9–6.*

❺ **Stortorget.** Danish king Christian II ordered a massacre in this square in 1520 that triggered a revolt and the founding of the sovereign state of Sweden. ✉ *Gamla Stan, just southwest of Kungliga Slottet.*

★ ⓬ **Vasamuseet** (Vasa Museum). The 17th-century warship *Vasa* sank ignominiously in Stockholm Harbor on its maiden voyage in 1628 because it was not carrying sufficient ballast. Forgotten for centuries, the largely intact vessel was recovered from the sea in 1961 and now stands sentinel over the harbor in this striking museum; film presentations and exhibits are also on site. ✉ *Galärvarvet,* ☎ *08/51954800,* WEB *www.vasamuseet.se.* ⏲ *Thurs.–Tues. 10–5, Wed. 10–8. English tours available year-round, throughout the day.*

⓰ **Waldemarsudde.** Once the summer residence of Prince Eugen (1865–1947), this museum has a significant collection of Nordic paintings dating from 1880 to 1940, as well as the prince's own works. ✉ *Prins Eugensv. 6,* ☎ *08/54583700,* WEB *www.waldemarsudde.com.* ⏲ *May–Aug., Tues., Wed., and Fri.–Sun. 11–5, Thurs. 11–8; Sept.–Apr., Tues., Wed., and Fri. 11–4, Thurs. 11–8, weekends 11–5.*

Elsewhere in Stockholm

Bergianska Botaniska Trädgården (Bergianska Botanical Garden). North of the city center, this garden and greenhouse has plants from all over the world. The **Victoria House** has the world's largest display of water lilies. ✉ *Frescati,* ☎ *08/162853,* WEB *www.bergianksa.se.* ⏲ *Greenhouse daily 11–5. Herbal Garden May–Sept., daily 8–5; Oct.–Apr., weekends 11–4. Victoria House May–Sept., daily 11–5. Park daily.*

⓯ **Kaknästornet** (Kaknäs TV Tower). Just shy of 511 ft, the tower on Gärdet is the tallest structure in Scandinavia. From its top you have a magnificent view of the city and the surrounding archipelago. Facilities include a cafeteria, restaurant, and gift shop. ✉ *Mörkakroken off Djurgårdsbrunsv. Bus 69 from Sergels Torg,* ☎ *08/7892435.* ⏲ *June–Aug., daily 9 AM–10 PM; Sept.–May, daily 10–9.*

Dining

Stockholm has one of the highest densities of restaurants per capita in Europe. If you're looking for value dining, make lunch your big meal.

$$$$ ★ ✕ **Den Gyldene Freden.** Once a favorite haunt of Stockholm's artists and composers, this restaurant, dating from 1722, has an Old Town ambience. Every Thursday, the Swedish Academy, the group of writers, artists, and scholars that chooses the Nobel Prize winners each year, meets for lunch on the second floor. The menu offers a tasteful combination of French and Swedish cuisines. ✉ *Österlångg. 51,* ☎ *08/109046. AE, DC, MC, V. Closed Sun. and July. No lunch Sun.–Fri.*

$$$–$$$$ ✕ **Edsbacka Krog.** Located 15 km (10 mi) north of Stockholm in a storybook inn that dates from the 1600s, this is the only restaurant in the country with two stars from the Michelin Guide. Expect Swedish cuisine to be taken to new heights. Service is impeccable, and the chef is known to send out small complimentary dishes during a meal. ✉ *Sollentunav. 220,* ☎ *08/963300. Reservations essential. AE, DC, MC, V. Closed lunch Mon. and Sat., closed Sun.*

$$$–$$$$ ✕ **Wedholms Fisk.** You can only get fresh fish and shellfish at this open, high-ceiling restaurant near Berzelli Park, across from the Royal Dramatic Theater. The tartare of salmon and the grilled sole are noteworthy, and portions are generous. The Scandinavian artwork on display is part of the owner's personal collection. ✉ *Nybrokajen 17,* ☎ *08/6117874. AE, DC, MC, V. Closed Sun. and July.*

$$–$$$$ ✕ **Operakällaren.** One of Stockholm's best-known traditional restaurants is found in the elegant Opera House. With both Scandinavian and Continental cuisine on its menu, it is famed for its smörgåsbord, available from June 1, with seasonal variations, through Christmas. In summertime you can dine on the veranda. ✉ *Operahuset, Jakobs Torg 2,* ☎ *08/6765800. AE, DC, MC, V. Main dining room closed July.*

$$–$$$$ ✕ **Ulriksdals Wärdshus.** Top-notch service, a beautiful location—in a castle park on the outskirts of town—and a noteworthy Swedish and international menu highlighting a lunchtime smörgåsbord all make this worth a splurge. Built in 1868, the restaurant was once a country inn, and it hasn't lost a bit of its country hospitality. ✉ *Ulriksdals Slottspark, Solna,* ☎ *08/850815. AE, DC, MC, V. No dinner Sun.*

$$$ ✕ **Bon Lloc.** With a crew of internationally renowned chefs, an elegant and spacious dining area, and a creative Mediterranean-influenced menu, Bon Lloc has established itself as one the hottest restaurants in town. The extensive wine list offers an excellent selection of European wines. ✉ *Regeringsg. 111,* ☎ *08/6606060. Reservations essential. AE, DC, MC, V. Closed Sun.*

$$$ ✕ **Gondolen.** Suspended under the gangway of the Katarina elevator at Slussen square, Gondolen has a magnificent view over the harbor, Mälaren, and the Baltic. The cuisine is international with a range of prix-fixe menus available. ✉ *Stadsgården 6,* ☎ *08/6417090. AE, DC, MC, V. Closed Sun.*

$$–$$$ ★ ✕ **Stallmästaregården.** This historic inn with an attractive courtyard and garden sits in Haga Park, just north of Norrtull, about 15 minutes by car or slightly longer by bus from the city center. In summer fine French and Swedish cuisine is served in the courtyard overlooking Brunnsviken lake. ✉ *Norrtull near Haga, Bus 52 to Stallmästaregården,* ☎ *08/6101300. AE, DC, MC, V. Closed Sun.*

$$ ✕ **Sturehof.** Opened before the turn of the 20th century, Sturehof is one of Sweden's oldest fish restaurants. It has a refurbished (1996) bistro-pub, but the nautically inspired ambience of the main restaurant has been preserved. ✉ *Stureplan 2,* ☎ *08/4405730. AE, DC, MC, V.*

$–$$ ✕ **Il Conte.** A warm, Italian-style restaurant close to Strandvägen, Stockholm's most elegant avenue, Il Conte has delicious Italian dishes and wines served by an attentive staff. The restaurant is tastefully decorated to create an alluring, refined atmosphere. ✉ *Grevg. 9,* ☎ *08/6612628. Reservations essential. AE, DC, MC, V. Call for closing dates.*

$–$$ ✕ **Koh Phangan.** Creative food is served until midnight at this lively Thai restaurant, where you'll be seated in individual "huts," each with a special name and style. Sign up for a table on the chalkboard next to the bar when you arrive. While you can expect a wait on weekends, the food and atmosphere are well worth a visit. ✉ *Skånag. 57,* ☎ *08/6425040,* FAX *08/6426568. AE, DC, MC, V.*

$ ✕ **Örtagården.** One floor up from Östermalms Saluhall market is this attractive, vegetarian all-you-can-eat buffet of soups, salads, hot dishes, and homemade bread plus an inexpensive bottomless cup of coffee—in a turn-of-the-20th-century atmosphere. ✉ *Nybrog. 31,* ☎ *08/6621728. AE, MC, V.*

Lodging

Stockholm has plenty of hotels in higher price brackets, but summer rates—some as much as 50% off—can make even very expensive hotels affordable. The major chains also have bargain plans on weekends throughout the year and weekdays in summer.

More than 50 hotels offer the "Stockholm Package," providing one night's lodging at between SKr 398 and SKr 890 per person, including breakfast and a Stockholmskortet. The package is available June through mid-August, at Christmas and Easter, and Friday through Monday year-round; get details from Hotellcentralen and American Express travel agency. If you arrive in Stockholm without a hotel reservation, Hotellcentralen can arrange accommodation for you.

$$$$ **Berns Hotell.** This cozy yet subtly ultramodern hotel occupies a mid-19th-century building. A new restaurant and bar were installed in a joint venture with well-known restaurant entrepreneur Terence Conran. As a result, the building is regaining the hot-spot status it had at the end of the 19th century. ✉ *Näckströmsg. 8, 111 47,* ☎ *08/56632000,* FAX *08/56632201,* WEB *www.berns.se. 65 rooms. Restaurant. AE, DC, MC, V.*

$$$$ **Grand.** Each year the large, Old World–style Grand accommodates the current Nobel Prize winners. The waterfront hotel dates from 1874 and stands opposite the Royal Palace in the center of town; request a room with a view of the water. The two excellent restaurants—French and Swedish—have harbor views, and the bar serves light snacks. ✉ *Blasieholmshamnen 8, 103 27,* ☎ *08/6793500,* FAX *08/6118686,* WEB *www.grandhotel.se. 307 rooms, 20 suites. 2 restaurants. AE, DC, MC, V.*

$$$$ **Reisen.** This 17th-century building, on the waterfront in Gamla Stan, has been a hotel since 1819; it has a fine restaurant, a grill, tea and coffee service in the library, and a good piano bar. The swimming pool was installed beneath surviving medieval arches in the structure's foundations. ✉ *Skeppsbron 12–14, 111 30,* ☎ *08/223260,* FAX *08/201559. 114 rooms. 3 restaurants, pool. AE, DC, MC, V.*

$$$–$$$$ **Hotel Birger Jarl.** Just outside the city center, this contemporary refuge was recently renovated so that all rooms are decked out entirely in Swedish furniture. Special business rooms make it great for both business travelers and tourists eager to experience modern Swedish design and comfort. ✉ *Tuleg. 8, 104 32,* ☎ *08/6741800,* FAX *08/6737366,* WEB *www.birgerjarl.se. 225 rooms. AE, DC, MC, V.*

$$$–$$$$ **Nordic Hotel.** Opened in early 2001 right next to Central Station, this center for the business traveler is actually two hotels—Nordic Light and Nordic Sea—in one. The first focuses on simplicity. Rooms are a mix of dark wood, gray flannel, and black-and-white tile. Nordic Sea uses lighter wood with lots of blue fabric and mosaic tiles, creating a Mediterranean atmosphere. Both are clean and bright and provide excellent service. ✉ *Vasaplan, 101 37,* ☎ *08/50563000,* FAX *08/50563060,* WEB *www.nordichotels.se. 542 rooms. 2 bars. AE, DC, MC, V.*

$$$–$$$$ **Sergel Plaza.** This basic downtown hotel has a relaxing atmosphere, a piano bar just behind the light, spacious lobby, and an executive floor, a casino, and a body care center. The restaurant offers international haute cuisine. ✉ *Brunkebergstorg 9, 103 27,* ☎ *08/*

226600, FAX 08/215070, WEB www.scandic-hotels.com/. 405 rooms, 11 suites. Restaurant, bar. AE, DC, MC, V.

$$$–$$$$ **Strand (Radisson SAS).** This gracious old-world hotel was built in 1912 and modernized in 1983. No two rooms are alike; all are furnished with antiques. The hotel's Italian restaurant has a superb wine list. ✉ *Nybrokajen 9, 103 27, ☎ 08/50664000, FAX 08/50664002, WEB www.radissonsas.com. 148 rooms. Restaurant. AE, DC, MC, V.*

$$$ **Amaranten.** Not far from the central train station, Amaranten is a large, modern hotel that was renovated in 2000. Rooms with air-conditioning and soundproofing are available at a higher rate. ✉ *Kungsholmsg. 31, 104 20, ☎ 08/6925200, FAX 08/6526248, WEB www.firsthotels.com/go_hotel.asp?hid=21. 410 rooms. Restaurant, pool. AE, DC, MC, V.*

$$$ **Continental.** In the city center across from the train station, the Continental is considered one of the best hotels in town for the business traveler and is especially popular with Americans. ✉ *Klara Vattugr. 4, 101 22, ☎ 08/51734200, FAX 08/51734211, WEB www.scandic-hotels.com. 268 rooms. Restaurant. AE, DC, MC, V.*

$$$ ★ **Diplomat.** This elegant hotel near the city center, Djurgården, and the open-air museum Skansen offers magnificent views over central Stockholm. The turn-of-the-20th-century town house was used by embassies in the 1930s; in 1966 it was converted into a hotel. Be sure to check out the ultra-hip T-Bar downstairs. ✉ *Strandv. 7C, 104 40, ☎ 08/4596800, FAX 08/4596820, WEB www.diplomathotel.com. 133 rooms. Restaurant. AE, DC, MC, V.*

$$$ ★ **Lady Hamilton.** As charming, desirable, and airily elegant as its namesake, the Lady Hamilton opened in 1980 as a modern hotel inside a 15th-century building. Swedish antiques accent the light, natural-tone decor in all the guest rooms and common areas. The subterranean sauna rooms provide a chance to take a dip in the building's original, medieval well. ✉ *Storkyrkobrinken 5, 111 28, ☎ 08/234680, FAX 08/4111148, WEB www.lady-hamilton.se. 34 rooms. AE, DC, MC, V.*

$$$ **Lydmar Hotel.** Just opposite Humlegården in the center of Stockholm lies this modern hotel, a 10-minute walk from the downtown hub of Sergels Torg. The lobby lounge is alive nearly every night with the latest DJs and live musicians. ✉ *Stureg. 10, 114 36, ☎ 08/56611300, FAX 08/56611301, WEB www.lydmar.se. 56 rooms, 5 junior suites. AE, DC, MC, V.*

$$$ **Stockholm Plaza Hotel.** On one of Stockholm's foremost streets for shopping and entertainment, this turn-of-the-20th-century building is furnished in an old-style, elegant manner and has reasonable-sized rooms. ✉ *Birger Jarlsg. 29, 103 95, ☎ 08/56622000, FAX 08/56622020, WEB www.elite.se. 151 rooms. Restaurant, bar. AE, DC, MC, V.*

$$–$$$ **Gamla Stan.** This quiet, cozy hotel is in one of Gamla Stan's 17th-century houses. Each room is uniquely decorated. ✉ *Lilla Nyg. 25, 111 28, ☎ 08/7237250, FAX 08/7237259, WEB www.rica.cityhotels.se. 51 rooms. AE, DC, MC, V.*

$$ **August Strindberg.** A narrow, frescoed corridor leads from the street to the flagstone courtyard, into which the hotel's restaurant expands in summer. Parquet flooring and high ceilings distinguish the rooms, which are otherwise plainly furnished. Kitchenettes are available; some rooms can be combined into family apartments. The four floors have no elevator. ✉ *Tegnérg. 38, 113 59, ☎ 08/325006, FAX 08/209085. 19 rooms. Restaurant. AE, DC, MC, V.*

$$ ★ **Örnsköld.** Just behind the Royal Dramatic Theater in the heart of the city, this gem has the atmosphere of an old private club, with a brass-and-leather lobby and Victorian-style furniture in the moderately spacious, high-ceiling rooms. Rooms over the courtyard are quieter, but those facing the street are sunnier. ✉ *Nybrog. 6, 114 34, ☎ 08/6670285, FAX 08/6676991. 30 rooms. AE, MC, V.*

$–$$ **Långholmen.** This former prison (built in 1724) was converted into a combined hotel and hostel in 1989. The island on which it sits has popular beaches and a prison museum. ✉ *Långholmen, Box 9116, 102 72,* ☎ *08/6680500,* FAX *08/7208575,* WEB *www.langholmen.se. 101 rooms. 3 restaurants. AE, DC, MC, V.*

$ ***Gustav af Klint.*** A "hotel ship" moored at Stadsgården quay, near Slussen subway station, the *Gustav af Klint* is divided into a hotel and a hostel. The rooms are small but clean, with bunk-style beds in both the hotel and hostel rooms; the shared bathrooms are spotless and accessible. You can dine on deck in summer. ✉ *Stadsgårdskajen 153, 116 45,* ☎ *08/6404077,* FAX *08/6406416. 8 hotel cabins, 120 hostel beds. Restaurant. AE, MC, V.*

Nightlife and the Arts

The Arts

Stockholm's theater and concert season runs from September through May, so you won't find many big-name artists in summer. For a list of events, pick up the free magazine *What's On,* available throughout the city and from hotels and tourist information offices. For tickets to theaters and shows try **Biljettdirekt** at Sweden House or any post office.

CONCERTS

The city's main concert hall is **Konserthuset** (✉ Hötorget 8, ☎ 08/102110), home of the Stockholm Philharmonic Orchestra. Also look in the local press for events at **Berwaldhallen** (✉ Strandv. 69, ☎ 08/7845000), a concert hall downtown. In summer many city parks have free concerts; listings appear in the "Events" section of *Stockholm This Week.*

FILM

English and American films predominate, screened with the original soundtrack and Swedish subtitles. Programs are listed in the local evening newspapers, although movie titles are usually given in Swedish. **Filmstaden Sergel** (✉ Hötorget, ☎ 08/56260000) has 18 cinemas under one roof. There are also a number of theaters on Kungsgatan. Most cinemas take reservations over the phone, and the latest releases may well be sold out. The city's annual **Stockholms Filmfestival** is held in early November, screening films from all over the world.

OPERA

Operan (Royal Opera House; ✉ Jakobs Torg 2, ☎ 08/248240) lies just across the water from the Royal Palace. The season runs from mid-August to early June and offers world-class performances. The exquisite **Drottningholms Slottsteater** (Drottningholm Court Theater; ✉ Drottningholm, ☎ 08/6608225) presents opera, ballet, and orchestral music from May to early September; the original 18th-century stage machinery is still used in these productions. Drottningholm, the royal residence, is reached by subway and bus or by special theater-bus (which leaves from the Grand Hotel or opposite the Central Train Station). Boat tours run here in summer.

THEATER

Stockholm has some 20 theaters. **Kungliga Dramatiska Teatern** (Royal Dramatic Theater; ✉ Nybroplan, ☎ 08/6670680), better known as the Dramaten, with great gilded statues at Nybroplan, stages international productions in Swedish. **Vasa Teatern** (✉ Vasag. 19–21, ☎ 08/248240; 08/102363 last-minute bookings) produces whimsical Swedish comedies. Musicals are presented regularly at several city theaters. Productions by the **English Theatre Company** are occasionally staged at various venues in Stockholm; check the local press for details.

Nightlife

BARS AND NIGHTCLUBS

The Red Room, on the second floor of the renovated restaurant-bar **Berns' Salonger** (✉ Berzelli Park 9, ☎ 08/6140550), is where playwright August Strindberg once held court. **Café Opera** (✉ Operahuset, Gustav Adolfs Torg, ☎ 08/6765807) is a favorite meeting place of the suit-and-tie set; at the waterfront end of Kungsträgården, it has the longest bar in town, plus dining, roulette, and dancing after midnight. **Mosebacke Etablissement** (✉ Mosebacke Torg 3, ☎ 08/6419020) is a combined indoor theater and outdoor café with a spectacular view of the city. Royalty and other dignitaries mingle at **Riche** (✉ Birger Jarlsg. 4, ☎ 08/6796840); the grand bar's pedigree stretches back to 1893. **O Bar** (✉ Stureplan 2, ☎ 08/4405730), located inside Restaurant Sturehof, is great for live soul and hip-hop music. **Sture Compagniet** (✉ Stureg. 4, ☎ 08/6117800) is good for drinking and dancing. **Tiger** (✉ Kungsg. 18, ☎ 08/244700) is a club and restaurant with a Latin touch.

Pubs abound in Stockholm. Watch for happy hour, when drinks are cheap. Irish beer enthusiasts rally at **Dubliner** (✉ Smålandsg. 8, ☎ 08/6797707). **Limerick** (✉ Tegnérg. 10, ☎ 08/6731902) is a favorite Hibernian spot. The **Tudor Arms** (✉ Grevg. 31, ☎ 08/6602712) is just as popular as when it opened in the '70s.

CABARET

Stockholm's biggest nightclub, **Börsen** (✉ Jakobsg. 6, ☎ 08/7878500), has high-quality Swedish and international cabaret. **Wallmans Salonger** (✉ Teaterg. 3, ☎ 08/6116622) provides an unforgettable cabaret experience; reservations are essential.

DANCING

Bäckahästen (✉ Kungsg. 56, ☎ 08/4115180) is lively on weekends, catering to a slightly older crowd. **Karlson & Co** (✉ Kungsg. 56, ☎ 08/54512140) is a pub, restaurant, and nightclub for the middle-age set. **Penny Lane** (✉ Birger Jarlsg. 29, ☎ 08/201411) pulls in all ages with music from the '70s.

JAZZ CLUBS

Fasching (✉ Kungsg. 63, ☎ 08/216267) is Stockholm's most popular jazz club, offering both jazz and soul. **Nalens** (✉ Stora Nyg. 5, ☎ 08/4533434) is a mellow jazz and dance club with events four or five nights a week. Tickets for concerts are available through **BiljettDirekt** (☎ 077/1707070); most shows cost SKr 150–SKr 200 or less.

Shopping

Department Stores

NK (✉ Hamng. 18–20, ☎ 08/7628000) is a high-class galleria. **PUB** (✉ Hötorget, ☎ 08/4021611) has 42 boutiques. **Åhléns City** (✉ Klarabergsg. 50, ☎ 08/6766000) is a traditional department store with lots of Swedish and international name brands.

Food and Flea Markets

For a real high-class Swedish food market with such specialties as marinated salmon and reindeer, try **Östermalms Saluhall** (✉ at Östermalmstorg). Another good bet is **Hötorgshallen** (✉ at Hötorget), which is filled with butcher shops, coffee and tea shops, and fresh fish markets. It's located under Filmstaden Sergel.

Glassware

Duka (✉ Sveav. 24/26, ☎ 08/104530) specializes in crystal as well as porcelain. **Gustavsbergs Fabriksbod** (✉ Odelbergs Väg 13, Gustavsberg, ☎ 08/57035655), just outside the city, is a factory shop of quality. For the best buys try **Nordiska Kristall** (✉ Kungsg. 9, ☎ 08/104372).

Handicrafts

For unique Swedish stationery and office supplies in fun colors and styles go to **Ordning & Reda** in NK (✉ Hamng. 18–20, ☎ 08/7628462). Kitchen supplies and interior design items by some of Sweden's best designers are available at **Designtorget** (✉ Kulturuset Sergelstorg 3, ☎ 08/50831520). A good center for all kinds of Swedish wood and metal handicrafts is **Svensk Hemslöjd** (✉ Sveav. 44, ☎ 08/232115). **Svenskt Hantwerk** (✉ Kungsg. 55, ☎ 08/214726) has Swedish folk costumes and handicrafts from different parts of Sweden. For elegant home furnishings and timeless fabrics, try **Svenskt Tenn** (✉ Strandv. 5A, ☎ 08/6701600), best known for its selection of designer Josef Franck's furniture and fabrics.

Shopping Districts

Shop 'til you drop means hitting the stores along **Hamngatan** and **Biblioteksgatan** with a vengeance. The **Gamla Stan** area is best for antiques shops, bookshops, and art galleries. **Sturegallerian** (✉ Stureg.) is an elegant covered shopping gallery on the site of the former public baths at Stureplan.

Side Trips

Skärgården

★ You could sail forever among the 24,000 islands of Stockholm's Skärgården (archipelago). But if you don't have a boat, then purchase the Båtluffarkortet (Inter-Skerries Card, SKr 300) from early June to mid-August, which gives you 16 days' unlimited travel on Waxholmsbolaget (Waxholm Steamship Company) boats. Get the card at the Excursion Shop at the Stockholm Tourist Centre or at the Waxholm Steamship Company terminal.

Fjäderholmarna

The group of four islands known as Fjäderholmarna (the Feather Islets) lies only 20 minutes by boat from the city center. They were formerly a restricted military zone but are now a haven of restaurants, cafés, a museum depicting life in the archipelago, an aquarium with many species of Baltic marine life, handicraft studios, shops, and a pirate-ship playground. Boats leave for the islands from Slussen, Strömkajen, and Nybroplan (April 29–September 17). For boat information and time schedules contact the **Strömma Kanalbolaget** (Strömma Canal Company). Tourism information is available from the islands' info service, **Fjäderholmarna** (☎ 08/7180100).

Mariefred

In Mariefred, on the southern side of Lake Mälaren, about 64 km (40 ★ mi) from Stockholm, **Gripsholm Slott** (Gripsholm Castle), with its drawbridge and four massive round towers, is one of Sweden's most romantic castles. Following the destruction of a castle from the 1380s, King Gustav Vasa built the present structure in 1577. It now houses the state portrait collection. ☎ *0159/10194,* WEB *www.royalcourt.se/gripsholm.* ⊙ *May–Aug., daily 10–4; Sept., Tues.–Sun. 10–4; Oct.–Apr., weekends noon–3.*

An unforgettable boat journey on the recently restored vintage steamer *Mariefred,* the last coal-fired ship on Lake Mälaren, is the best way to get to Gripsholm, but you can also take the train. ✉ *Boat departs quay next to City Hall,* ☎ *08/6698850.* *SKr 170 round-trip.* ⊙ *Mid-May–late Aug., Tues.–Sun. 10 AM (returns 4:30).*

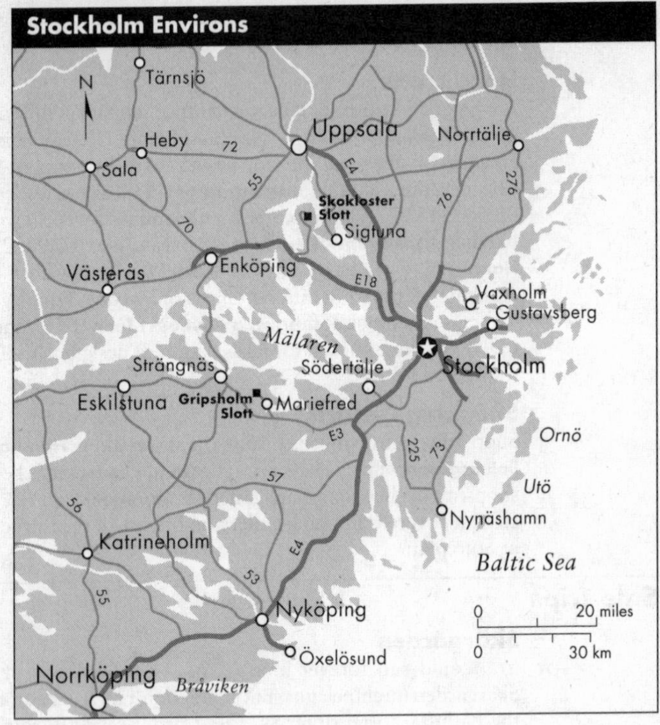

Skokloster

Built by the Swedish field marshal Carl Gustav Wrangel, **Skokloster** (Skokloster Castle) contains many of his trophies from the Thirty Years' War. The palace, about 70 km (44 mi) from Stockholm in Skokloster, also displays one of the largest private collections of arms in the world, as well as some magnificent Gobelin tapestries. Next door to the palace is a **motor museum** housing Sweden's largest collection of vintage cars and motorcycles. ☎ *018/386077.* ⏲ *May–Aug., daily 11–4; Apr., Sept., and Oct., weekdays 1–2, weekends noon–3.*

Skokloster is easily reached by boat. The route follows the narrow inlets of Lake Mälaren along the "Royal Waterway." It stops at **Sigtuna,** an ancient trading center. You can get off the boat here to visit the town, which has medieval ruins and an 18th-century town hall. For boat information contact the **Strömma Kanalbolaget.** ✉ *Boats depart from Stadshusbron (City Hall Bridge),* ☎ *08/58714000.* *SKr 165 round-trip.* ⏲ *Early June–mid-Aug., Tues.–Thurs. and weekends.*

Stockholm Essentials

AIRPORTS AND TRANSFERS

International flights arrive at Arlanda Airport. For information on arrival and departure times, call the individual airlines.

➤ AIRPORT INFORMATION: **Arlanda Airport** (✉ 40 km/25 mi north of city, WEB www.arlanda.com).

TRANSFERS

The airport is linked to Stockholm by a major highway as well as a high-speed train that costs SKr 120 one-way and takes 20 minutes. Families can get a group rate for SKr 240. Trains leave every 15 minutes 6 AM–7 PM and then twice an hour 7–11 PM. Buses, called Flygbusarna, depart for Cityterminalen from the international and domestic terminals every 10–15 minutes between 6:30 AM and 11 PM. The ride costs SKr 60 per person and takes about 40 minutes. A bus-taxi package is available from the bus driver at prices ranging from SKr 150 per person to SKr 220; additional passengers in a group pay only the bus portion of the fare. Ask the bus driver for details. A taxi directly from the airport will cost around SKr 350–SKr 430 (ask the driver if he offers a fixed-price airport-to-city rate before you get into the taxi). Look for Taxi Stockholm, Taxi 020, and Taxi Kurir cabs, and ask the cab line attendant for help. Illegal taxis abound.

BOAT AND FERRY TRAVEL

➤ BOAT AND FERRY INFORMATION: **Waxholmsbolaget** (Waxholm Steamship Company; terminal (✉ Strömkajen, in front of Grand Hotel, ☎ 08/6795830, WEB www.waxholmbolaget.se). **Strömma Kanalbolaget** (Strömma Canal Company; ✉ Boats depart from Stadshusbron [City Hall Bridge], ☎ 08/58714000, WEB www.strommakanalbolaget.com).

BUS TRAVEL TO AND FROM STOCKHOLM

All major bus lines arrive at the Cityterminalen, next to the train station. Bus tickets are also sold at the railroad reservations office.

BUS TRAVEL WITHIN STOCKHOLM

The Stockholm Transit Authority, known as the SL, operates both the bus and subway systems. Tickets for the two networks are interchangeable. The comprehensive bus network serves out-of-town points of interest, such as Waxholm, with its historic fortress, and Gustavsberg, with its porcelain factory. In greater Stockholm there are a number of night-bus services.

EMERGENCIES

➤ DOCTORS AND DENTISTS: **Doctor** (Medical Care Information, ☎ 08/320100). **Dentist** (☎ 08/54551220 8 AM–9 PM). **Private clinic** (✉ City Akuten, ☎ 08/4122960).

➤ EMERGENCY SERVICES: **Ambulance** (☎ 112). **Police** (☎ 08/4010000; 112 emergencies only).

➤ 24-HOUR PHARMACIES: **C. W. Scheele** (☎ 08/4548130).

ENGLISH-LANGUAGE MEDIA

BOOKS

Akademibokhandeln has a wide variety of books in English. If you don't find what you need there, Hedengrens is also well stocked, especially with fiction and poetry.

➤ BOOKSTORES: **Akademibokhandeln** (✉ Mäster Samuelsg. 32, ☎ 08/6136100, WEB www.akademibokhandeln.se). **Hedengrens** (Sturepl. 4/Sturegalerian, ☎ 08/6115132).

SUBWAY TRAVEL

The subway system, known as T-banan (*T* stands for tunnel), is the easiest way to get around. Station entrances are marked with a blue T on a white background. Trains run frequently between 5 AM and 2 AM.

Bus and subway fares are based on zones, starting at SKr 14, good for travel within one zone, such as downtown, for one hour. You pay more if you travel in more than one zone. Single tickets are available at station ticket counters, but it is cheaper to buy the SL Tourist Card, which is valid on buses and the subway and also gives free admission to a number of sights and museums (though not as many as the Stockholmskortet). It can be purchased at Pressbyrån newsstands and SL information desks and costs SKr 70 for 24 hours or SKr 135 for 72 hours.

Also available from the Pressbyrån newsstands are SKr 95 coupons, good for at least 10 bus or subway rides in the central zone.

TAXIS

Typically, a trip of 10 km (6 mi) will cost about SKr 100 between 9 AM and 4 PM on weekdays, SKr 110 on weekday nights, and SKr 120 on weekends. It can be difficult to hail a taxi on the street, so call ahead if possible. Taxi Stockholm is one of the city's biggest taxi companies. Taxikurir also serves the greater Stockholm area, as does Taxi 020.

➤ TAXI COMPANIES: **Taxi Stockholm** (☎ 08/150000). **Taxikurir** (☎ 08/300000). **Taxi 020** (☎ 020/939393).

TOURS

BOAT TOURS

Take a boat trip through the archipelago with the Strömma Kanalbolaget (Strömma Canal Company) or the Waxholm Steamship Company. Trips range from one to three hours each way. One-day excursions include Waxholm, Utö, Sandhamn, and Möja. Conventional sightseeing tours include a one-hour city tour run by Strömma Kanalbolaget and leaving from the Nybroplan quay every hour on the half hour between 10:30 and 5:30 in summer. Don't miss the boat trip to the 17th-century palace of Drottningholm. Trips depart every hour on the hour from 10 to 4 and at 6 PM during the summer from City Hall Bridge (Stadshusbron). Other trips go from Stadshusbron to the ancient towns of Sigtuna and Vaxholm. By changing boats you can continue to Uppsala to catch the train back to Stockholm. Information is available from the boat companies or the Stockholm Tourist Centre at Sweden House.

ORIENTATION TOURS

More than 35 different tours—on foot or by boat, bus, or a combination of these—are available throughout the summer. Some take only 30 minutes, others an entire day. A 90-minute coach tour, costing SKr 130, runs daily. Tickets are available from the Excursion Shop at Stockholm Tourist Centre.

PRIVATE GUIDES

Guide Centralen at the Stockholm Information Service offers individual guides and group bookings.

➤ CONTACTS: **Guide Centralen** (✉ Sweden House, Hamng. 27, Box 7542, 103 93, ☎ 08/7892496).

SPECIAL-INTEREST TOURS

Special-interest tours in the Stockholm area include spending a weekend at a cabin in the archipelago, renting a small fishing or sailing boat, visiting the Gustavsberg porcelain factory, and more. Call the Stockholm Tourist Centre at Sweden House for details.

TRAIN TRAVEL

Both long-distance and commuter trains arrive at Stockholm Central Station on Vasagatan, a main boulevard in the heart of the city. For information and ticket reservations 6 AM–11 PM, call the train information number below. There is a ticket and information office at the station where you can make reservations. Automated ticket-vending machines are also available.

SL runs commuter trains from Stockholm Central Station to a number of nearby locales, including Nynäshamn, a departure point for ferries to the island of Gotland. Trains also run from the Slussen station to the fashionable seaside resort of Saltsjöbaden.

➤ TRAIN INFORMATION: **Train Information** (☎ 020/757575 for recorded message; wait for assistance).

TRANSPORTATION AROUND STOCKHOLM

Maps and timetables for all city transportation are available from the Stockholm Transit Authority (SL) information desks.

Stockholmskortet (Stockholm Card) grants unlimited transportation on city subway, bus, and rail services, and free admission to 70 museums and several sightseeing trips. The card costs SKr 220 for 24 hours, SKr 380 for two days, and SKr 540 for three days. It is available at the tourist information centers at Sweden House, Kaknästornet (TV Tower), and at Hotellcentralen at the central train station.
➤ CONTACTS: **Stockholm Transit Authority** (✉ Sergels Torg; Stockholm Central Station; Slussen in Gamla Stan; ☎ 08/6001000 information, WEB www.sl.se).

TRAVEL AGENCY

➤ LOCAL AGENT: **American Express** (✉ St. Eriksg. 117, ☎ 08/4295600, FAX 08/4294343).

VISITOR INFORMATION

➤ TOURIST INFORMATION: **Stockholm Tourist Centre/Excursion Shop** (✉ Sweden House, Kungsträdgården, Hamng. 27, ☎ 08/7892490). **Stockholm Information Service** (✉ Sweden House, Box 7542, 103 93, ☎ 08/7892400, WEB www.stockholmtown.com). **Stockholm Central Station** (✉ Vasag., ☎ 020757575, WEB www.sj.se). **City Hall** (summer only; ✉ Hantverkarg. 1, ☎ 08/50829000). **Kaknästornet** (TV Tower; ✉ Ladugårdsgärdet, ☎ 08/7892435). **Fjäderholmarna** (☎ 08/7180100).

UPPSALA AND THE FOLKLORE DISTRICT

The "Folklore District" is essentially the provinces of Dalarna and Värmland. With its rural ambience, it's the best place to discover some of the country's most interesting traditions. Dalarna, which has its own special style of handicrafts, can be reached via the ancient city of Uppsala. Return to Stockholm through the Bergslagen region, the heart of the centuries-old Swedish iron industry.

Uppsala

★ Uppsala is well worth exploring. **Gamla Uppsala** (Old Uppsala) is dominated by three huge burial mounds dating from the 5th century. The first Swedish kings, Aun, Egil, and Adils, were all buried here. The church next to the burial mounds was the seat of Sweden's first archbishop and was built on the site of a former pagan temple. At the adjacent Odinsborg restaurant you can sample local mead brewed from a 14th-century recipe.

The impressive **Domkyrka** (cathedral), with its twin towers dominating the skyline, has been the seat of the archbishop of the Swedish church for 700 years. Its present appearance owes much to major restoration work completed during the late 19th century. At the **Cathedral Museum** in the north tower, you can see one of Europe's finest collections of ecclesiastical textiles. ✉ *Domkyrkoplan,* ☎ *018/187201.* ⊙ *Cathedral daily 8–6. Museum May–Aug., daily 9–4:30; Sept.–Apr., Sun. 12:30–5.*

Strategically positioned atop a hill, the august **Uppsala Slott** (Uppsala Castle) was built in the 1540s by King Gustav Vasa. Having broken his ties with the Vatican, the king was eager to show who was actually running the country; he even arranged to have the cannons aimed at the archbishop's palace. ✉ *Borggården,* ☎ *18/274800.* ⊙ *Mid-Apr.–mid-June, daily 11–3; mid-June–mid-Aug., daily 10–5.*

One of the most famous people to emerge from Uppsala was Carl von Linné, known as Linnaeus. A professor of botany during the 1740s,

Uppsala and the Folklore District

he developed the system of plant and animal classification still used today. Visit the **gardens** he designed, as well as his former residence, **Linné Trädgården** (Linné Gardens), now a museum. ✉ *Svartbäcksg. 27,* ☎ *018/109490 garden; 018/136540 museum.* ⏲ *Garden May–Aug., daily 9–9; Sept., daily 9–7. Museum June–Aug., Tues.–Sun. noon–4; May and Sept., weekends noon–4.*

$$ ★ ✕ **Domtrappkällaren.** One of the city's most popular restaurants, Domtrappkällaren is in a 14th-century cellar near the cathedral. The menu includes both French and Swedish fare. ✉ *St. Eriksgr. 15,* ☎ *018/130955,* FAX *018/101740. Reservations essential. AE, DC, MC, V. Closed Sun.*

$$ **Grand Hotel Hörnan.** An old-world hotel opened in 1906, the Grand Hotel Hörnan is in the city center near the train station, with a view of the castle and the cathedral. ✉ *Bangårdsg. 1, 753 20,* ☎ *018/139380,* FAX *018/120311,* WEB *www.eklundshof.se/enghornan.htm. 37 rooms. AE, DC, MC, V. Closed July.*

$$ **Hotel Svava.** In the center of town, just five minutes from the Central Station, this hotel shares the block with a pharmacy, a liquor store and a post office—all a traveler really needs. According to Viking mythology, Svava took care of fallen warriors. Today the hotel simply takes care of fallen travelers. ✉ *Bangårdsg. 24, 751 44,* ☎ *018/130030,* FAX *018/132230,* WEB *www.hotelsvava.com. 120 rooms. AE, DC, MC, V.*

Säter

Säter, one of the best-preserved wooden villages in Sweden, sits northwest of Uppsala on the way to Dalarna in farming country.

Falun

Probably the best place to stay in Dalarna is Falun, the province's capital. Here you can visit the **Falu Koppargruva** (Great Pit), a hole created in 1687 when an abandoned copper mine collapsed. There are working mines in the area and guided tours (requiring good shoes) into some of the old shafts. ✉ *Ask at tourist board on Stora Torget (main square) for directions,* ☎ *023/711475.* ⏲ *May–Aug., daily 10–4:30; Sept.–mid-Nov. and Mar.–Apr., weekends 12:30–4:30.*

The **Stora Kopparberg Museum** tells the story of the local mining industry. ☎ *023/15825 or 023/711475.* ⏲ *May–Aug., daily 10–4:30; Sept.–Apr., daily 12:30–4:30.*

$$ **Hotel Winn.** In the town center, this cozy hotel built in traditional Dalarna style is filled with antiques. ✉ *Bergskolegr. 7, 791 26,* ☎ *023/63600,* FAX *023/22524,* WEB *www.swedenhotels.se. 88 rooms. Restaurant. AE, DC, MC, V.*

$ **Hotel Falun.** This simple, cozy hotel, built in the 1950s in the center of town, offers a clean, less expensive alternative. ✉ *Centrumhuset, Trotzg. 16, 791 71,* ☎ *023/29180,* FAX *023/13006,* WEB *www.hotelfalun.nu. 27 rooms, 15 with shower. AE, DC, MC, V.*

Sundborn

★ Just outside Falun, at Sundborn, is the former home of Swedish artist Carl Larsson, **Carl Larsson Gården.** Here, in an idyllic lakeside setting, you can see a selection of the artist's paintings, which owe much to local folk-art traditions. His great-grandchildren still use the house on occasion. ✉ *Carl Larssonsv. 12,* ☎ *023/60053 summer; 023/60069 winter,* WEB *www.clg.se.* ⏲ *Tours May–Sept., daily 10–5, every 10 min.*

Tällberg

The real center of Dalarna folklore is the area around Lake Siljan, by far the largest of the 6,000 lakes in the province. The attractive lakeside village of Tällberg is a good starting point for a tour.

$$ ★ **Åkerblads.** Near the shores of Lake Siljan, the hotel offers a genuine experience of rural Sweden. In a typical Dalarna farmstead, parts of which date from the 16th century, it is run by the 19th generation of the Åkerblad family and has been a hotel since 1910. ✉ *Sjögatu, 793 70,* ☎ *0247/50800,* FAX *0247/50652,* WEB *www.akerblads-tallberg.se. 58 rooms with bath, 6 rooms with shared WC/shower. Restaurant. AE, DC, MC, V.*

Mora

Mora was the home of the artist Anders Zorn (1860–1920), famous for his distinctive and tasteful paintings of robust, naked women in rural surroundings. His house and **Zorn Museet** (Zorn Museum), exhibiting his paintings, are open to the public. ✉ *Vasag. 36,* ☎ *0250/16560,* WEB *www.zorn.se.* ⏲ *House: guided tours only; call for information and times. Museum: mid-May–mid-Sept., Mon.–Sat. 9–5, Sun. 11–5; mid-Sept.–mid-May, Mon.–Sat. noon–5, Sun. 1–5.*

$$ ★ **Siljan.** Named for the nearby lake, Siljan is a small but up-to-date hotel. Many rooms have a lake view. ✉ *Morag. 6, 792 01,* ☎ *0250/13000,* FAX *0250/13098,* WEB *www.swedenhotels.se. 40 rooms with shower, 2 with WC only. Restaurant. AE, DC, MC, V.*

Rättvik

At midsummer in Rättvik, hundreds of people wearing traditional costumes arrive in longboats to attend midsummer church services—a time-honored tradition. Twelve-man longboat races are held in summer. The *Gustav Vasa* vintage steamboat has trips with nightly dancing and prawn dinners.

Nusnäs

Nusnäs is the home of the brightly colored Dalarna handmade wooden horses, known as *Dalahästar.* Red or blue and painted with traditional floral patterns, the only real Dala horses are made here. One of the biggest workshops is **Nils Olsson** (✉ Edåkersv. 17, ☎ 0250/37200).

Ludvika

This town is an important center of the old Bergslagen mining region, which stretches from the forests of Värmland in the west to the coastal gorges in the east. Ludvika has a notable open-air mining museum, the **Gammelgården.** ✉ *Nilsnilsg. 7,* ☎ *0240/10019.* ⏲ *June–Sept. 3, daily 11–6.*

Music and poetry festivals are held in memory of local poet Dan Andersson in nearby towns. Visit the **Dan Andersson Museum** to learn more about his work. You can also follow signposts to his former home, Luosastugan (Luosa Cottage; ☎ 0240/86050), open mid-May to August, daily 11–5. ✉ *Engelbrektsg. 8,* ☎ *0240/10016.* ⏲ *May–Aug., Tues.–Sat. 10–5; Sept.–Apr., Tues.–Sat. 10–2.*

$$ 🏨 **Grand.** A modern-style hotel, the Grand enjoys a central location. ✉ *Eriksg. 6, 771 31,* ☎ *0240/18220,* FAX *0240/611018,* WEB *www.grand-elektra.se. 102 rooms. Restaurant. AE, DC, MC, V.*

$ 🏨 **Rex.** Built in 1960, the Rex is a basic modern hotel near the city center. ✉ *Engelbrektsg. 9, 771 30,* ☎ *0240/13690. 28 rooms, 15 with shower. AE, DC, MC, V. Closed 1 wk in July.*

Örebro

Örebro nestles on the western edge of Lake Hjälmaren. It received its charter in the 13th century, becoming an important trading center for the farmers and miners of the Bergslagen region. Rising from a small island in the Svartån (Black River), right in the center of town, is the imposing **Örebro Slott** (Örebro Castle), parts of which date from the 13th century. The castle is now the residence of the regional governor and has an excellent restaurant, Slottskrogen. ✉ *Kanslig.,* ☎ *019/212121 (Örebro Tourist Information),* WEB *www.orebro.se/slottet.* ⏲ *Call ahead for hrs.*

$$ ✕ **Drängen.** Decorated in the style of an old Swedish farmhouse, this eccentric restaurant serves a fine mix of international and traditional cuisine. ✉ *Oskarstorget 1,* ☎ *019/323296. AE, DC, MC, V.*

$$ 🏨 **Stora Hotellet.** Across the street from the castle on the Svartån, this Best Western hotel is one of the oldest in Sweden, dating from 1858. It has a cozy cellar restaurant, the Slottskällaren, and an English pub, the Bishop's Arms. ✉ *Drottningg. 1, 701 45,* ☎ *019/156900,* FAX *019/156950. 103 rooms. Restaurant, pub. AE, DC, MC, V.*

Uppsala and the Folklore District Essentials

BUS TRAVEL

For information about bus travel, call Dalatrafik, the region's traffic information center.

➤ BUS INFORMATION: **Dalatrafik** (☎ 020/232425, WEB www.dalatrafik.se).

CAR TRAVEL

A car will give you the flexibility to explore some of the attractions not so easily accessible by public transportation; the drive to Uppsala from Stockholm, via the E4, is about 71 km (44 mi).

TOURS

Uppsala is compact enough to explore on foot, and guided sightseeing tours are available; call the Guide Service at the Uppsala Tourist

Information office. For guided tours of the district, contact the Falun tourist office, which has both package tours and personalized services.

➤ FEES AND SCHEDULES: **Guide Service** (☎ 018/274800).

TRAIN TRAVEL

The train from Stockholm to Uppsala takes only 50 minutes, and service is fairly frequent.

VISITOR INFORMATION

➤ TOURIST INFORMATION: **Falun** (✉ Stora Torget, ☎ 023/83050, WEB www.falun.se). **Ludvika** (✉ Fredsg. 10, ☎ 0240/86050, WEB www.ludvika.se). **Mora** (✉ Ångbåtskajen, ☎ 0250/592020, WEB www.mora.se). **Örebro** (✉ Slottet, ☎ 019/212121, WEB www.orebro.se). **Rättvik** (✉ Torget, ☎ 0248/797210, WEB www.rattvik.se). **Uppsala** (✉ Fyris Torg 8, ☎ 018/274800, WEB www.uppsala.se).

THE WEST COAST AND THE GLASS COUNTRY

Göteborg (Gothenburg) is an important Swedish port on the North Sea. North and south of the city lie scenic stretches of the country's western coast, where you'll find the history-rich town of Helsingborg and the booming city of Malmö. Inland are the lakes and forests of the Glass Country, and beyond stands the medieval fortress town of Kalmar, on the east coast.

Göteborg

This attractive harbor city is Sweden's second largest. Within a 10-minute walk of the industrial waterfront is an elegant modern city of broad avenues, green parks, and gardens. The city was laid out during the 17th century by Dutch architects, who gave it its extensive network of straight streets divided by canals. Only one major canal survives; you can explore it by sightseeing boat. Gothenburgians fondly refer to these short and squat (so they can pass under the city's 20 low bridges) boats as *paddan* (toads).

Passengers embark for the one-hour boat tour at the **Paddan terminal.** ✉ *Kungsportsplatsen.* ⏲ *Departures late Apr.–late June and mid-Aug.–early Sept., daily 10–5; late June–mid-Aug., daily 10–9; early Sept.–Oct. 1, daily noon–3. Closed Oct.–late Apr.*

★ Running through the heart of Göteborg is **Kungsportsavenyn,** commonly called Avenyn (the Avenue). This broad, tree-lined boulevard is lined with many boutiques and eateries. Avenyn ends at **Götaplatsen,** which has a **grand theater,** a **concert hall,** an **art museum,** and a **library** that has a wide selection of English-language newspapers.

Just a stone's throw away from Götaplatsen is the **Liseberg amusement park,** the largest of it's kind in the Nordic region. Liseberg is an excellent place to take kids, and its downtown location makes it convenient for a quick visit. ✉ *Öregrytev. 5,* ☎ *031/400100,* WEB *www.liseberg.se.* ⏲ *Late Apr., weekends 11–8; May–June, Mon.–Thurs. 3–11, Fri.–Sat. 11–11, Sun. 11–8; July–mid-Aug., Sun.–Thurs. 11–11, Fri.–Sat. 11–midnight; mid-Aug.–Sept., Fri. 5–11, Sat. 11–11, Sun. 11–8.*

Trädgårdsföreningen (Garden Association) maintains an attractive park with a magnificent Palm House, built in 1878 and recently restored, and a Butterfly House containing 40 different species. ✉ *Just off Kungsportsavenyn,* ☎ *031/7411111 Butterfly House.* ⏲ *Park daily 9 AM–sundown. Palm House daily 10–4. Butterfly House Oct.–Mar., Tues.–Sun. 10–3; Apr., Tues.–Sun. 10–4; May and Sept., daily 10–4; June–Aug., daily 10–5.*

The West Coast and the Glass Country

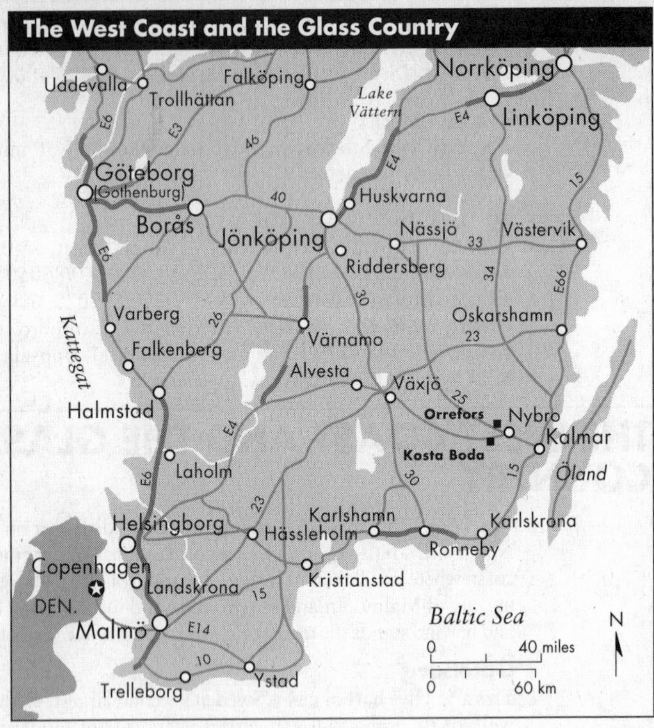

For shopping, try **Nordstan** (✉ entrances on Köpmansg., Nils Ericsonsg., Kanaltorgsg., and Östra Hamng.), a covered complex of shops near the train station.

$$–$$$ ★ ✕ **Westra Piren Restaurant.** Across the river from central Göteborg is this award-winning restaurant, one of the finest in Sweden. Finding it by car can be difficult, so it's best to take a ferry from the city side of the river. ✉ *Dockepiren, Eriksberg,* ☎ *031/519555. Reservations essential. AE, DC, MC, V.*

$–$$ ★ ✕ **Noon.** Combining Swedish and Asian styles in both its menu and atmosphere, Noon has quality seafood and noodle dishes that are served in a simple, modern setting. Try a bunch of their smaller, less expensive appetizers or go all out and have the flounder in lemon ginger sauce with saffron dumplings. ✉ *Viktoriag. 2,* ☎ *031/138800. AE, DC, MC, V. Closed lunch weekdays Sept.–May and lunch weekends.*

$$$ ★ **Radisson SAS Scandinavia Hotel.** Opened in 1986, this is Göteborg's most modern and spectacular international-style hotel. It has an atrium lobby with a central fountain. The international-style restaurant changes its menu each month. ✉ *Södra Hamng. 59–65, 401 24,* ☎ *031/806000,* FAX *031/159888,* WEB *www.radissonsas.com. 344 rooms. Restaurant. AE, DC, MC, V.*

$$ ★ **Eggers.** Dating from 1859, the Best Western Eggers has more old-world character than other hotels in the city. Most rooms are furnished with antiques. ✉ *Drottningtorget, 401 25,* ☎ *031/806070,* FAX *031/154243,* WEB *www.scantours.com/countryside_hotels10sweden.htm. 67 rooms. AE, DC, MC, V.*

$$ **Liseberg Heden.** Not far from the Liseberg amusement park, this is a modern family hotel. ✉ *Sten Stureg., 411 38,* ☎ *031/7506900,* FAX *031/7506930,* WEB *www.liseberg.se/Hotell/ehotell/eindex.htm. 159 rooms. Restaurant. AE, DC, MC, V.*

Helsingborg

Helsingborg, with its twin town, Helsingør (Elsinore in Shakespeare's *Hamlet*), across the Öresund, is a small town with a rich history dating back to the 10th century. Today it comprises a busy industrial waterfront, charming pedestrian streets, and large parks.

All that remains of Helsingborg's castle is **Kärnan** (The Keep). It stands in a park and offers fine views over the Öresund from the top. ✉ *Slottshagen,* ☎ *042/105991.* ⏲ *June–Aug., daily 10–7; Apr.–May and Sept., daily 9–4; Oct.–Mar., Tues.–Sun., 10–3.*

★ **Sofiero Slott** (Sofiero Castle), built in 1864 in the Dutch Renaissance style, is a haven for more than 300 kinds of rhododendron, a large English garden, and art exhibitions. A café (open April through September) and one of southern Sweden's finest restaurants (open March through December) are on the grounds. ✉ *Sofierov. (on the road to Laröd),* ☎ *042/137400.* ⏲ *Apr.–Sept., daily 10–6; guided tours only. Park open year-round.* ☎ *042/140440,* WEB *www.helsingborg.se/sofiero/.*

$$–$$$ ★ ✕ **Gastro.** A long leather booth divides this modern dining room into two halves. The menu, prepared by award-winning chefs, offers Swedish-based international fare. Fish and seafood are the stars. ✉ *Södra Storgatan 11–13,* ☎ *042/243470. AE, DC, MC, V. Closed Sun.*

$$–$$$ ★ **Grand Hotel.** One of Sweden's oldest hotels maintains its longstanding reputation for excellence. Antiques and fresh flowers fill the hotel, which is convenient to the railway station and ferry terminals. ✉ *Stortorget 8–12, 251 11,* ☎ *042/380400,* FAX *042/118833,* WEB *www.radissonsas.com. 117 rooms. Restaurant, bar. AE, DC, MC, V.*

Malmö

Capital of the province of Skåne, Malmö is Sweden's third-largest city. With the completion of the nearly 8-km (5½-mi) bridge from Malmö to Copenhagen in July 2000, the city and much of southern Sweden are experiencing an economic and cultural boom.

The city's castle, **Malmöhus,** completed in 1542, houses the city's major museums. ✉ *Malmöhusv.,* ☎ *040/341000,* WEB *www.museer.malmo.se/.* ⏲ *June–Aug., daily 10–4; Sept.–May, Tues.–Sun. noon–4.*

In Gamla Staden, the Old Town, look for the **St. Petri Church** on Kalendegatan. Dating from the 14th century, it is an impressive example of the Baltic Gothic style, with its distinctive stepped gables.

★ You can learn about Scandinavian art and design at the **Form/Design Centre** just off Lilla Torg, an attractive, small cobblestone square surrounded by restored buildings from the 17th and 18th centuries. ✉ *Lilla Torg,* ☎ *040/6645150,* WEB *www.scandinaviandesign.com/formdesigncenter/.* ⏲ *Aug.–June, Tues., Wed., Fri. 11–5, Thurs. 11–6, Sat. 10–4, Sun. 12–4; July, Tues.–Fri. 11–5, Sat. 10–4.*

★ The **Rooseum,** in a turn-of-the-20th-century brick building that was once a power plant, is one of Sweden's most outstanding contemporary art museums. ✉ *Gasverksg. 22,* ☎ *040/121716,* WEB *www.rooseum.se.* ⏲ *Tues.–Sun. 11–5. Guided tours weekends at 2.*

★ For more (free) modern art go to **Malmö Konsthall.** The gallery is one of the largest in Europe, with about 10 classic and modern exhibitions a year. Other activities at the gallery include theater performances, film presentations, and poetry readings. The café and bookstore are excellent. ✉ *St. Johannesg. 7,* ☎ *040/341286,* WEB *www.konsthallen.com.* ⏲ *Thurs.–Tues. 11–5, Wed. 11–10.*

Rådhuset (Town Hall), dating from 1546, dominates Stortorget, a huge, cobbled market square in Gamla Staden.

$$ ✕ **Johan P.** This popular restaurant specializes in seafood and shellfish prepared in Swedish and Continental styles. White walls and crisp white tablecloths give it an elegant air. ✉ *Saluhallen, Lilla Torg,* ☏ *040/971818. AE, DC, MC, V. Closed Sun.*

$$$ 🏨 **Radisson SAS Hotel.** Only a five-minute walk from the train station, this modern luxury hotel has rooms decorated in several styles: Scandinavian, Asian, and Italian. The restaurant serves Scandinavian and Continental cuisine, and there's a cafeteria for quick meals. ✉ *Österg. 10, 211 25,* ☏ *040/6984000,* FAX *040/6984001,* WEB *www.radissonsas.com. 221 rooms. Restaurant, no-smoking room, sauna, exercise room, meeting room. AE, DC, MC, V.*

Jönköping

Jönköping is an attractive town on the southern shore of Lake Vättern, Sweden's second-largest lake. The town is distinguished not only by its age—it celebrated the 700th anniversary of its founding in 1984—but also as the birthplace of the match-manufacturing industry, established here in the 19th century. **Tändsticksmuseet** (Match Museum), built on the site of the first factory, has exhibits on the development and manufacture of matches. ✉ *Tändsticksgr. 7,* ☏ *036/105543.* ⏲ *June–Aug., weekdays 10–5, weekends 10–3; Sept.–May, Tues.–Thurs. noon–4, weekends 11–3.*

$$ ★ ✕ **Mäster Gudmunds Källare.** This particularly inviting restaurant is cozily nestled beneath the vaults of a 16th-century-style cellar and is only two minutes from the train station. The cuisine is typically Swedish. ✉ *Kapellg. 2,* ☏ *036/100640. AE, DC, MC, V.*

$$ 🏨 **John Bauer Hotel.** This modern Best Western, named for a local artist famous for his fairy-tale depictions of trolls and mystical landscapes, lies close to the center of town and overlooks Munksjön Lake. ✉ *Södra Strandg. 15, 550 02,* ☏ *036/349000,* FAX *036/349050,* WEB *www.johnbauer.se. 100 rooms. Restaurant. AE, DC, MC, V.*

Växjö

The hub of Sweden's Glass Country is Växjö, the main town in Kronoberg County. Some 10,000 Americans visit Växjö each year, drawn here by a desire to see where their ancestors emigrated from in the 19th century. The **Utvandrareshus** (Emigrants' House; ✉ VilhelmMobergsg. 4, ☏ 0470/20120), in the town center, tells the story of the migration period, when close to a million Swedes—a fourth of the entire population—set sail for the promised land across the sea. People of Swedish descent can trace their ancestry in a research center.

Manufacture of Swedish glass dates from the middle of the 16th century, when Venetian glassblowers were first invited to the Swedish court. About 200 years passed before glassmaking became a major Swedish industry. Because the dense forests between Växjö and Kalmar offered an unlimited supply of wood for firing furnaces, the glass industry was centered here. All the major Swedish glass companies still operate in this area, and their plants are open to the public. The factory shops ★ sometimes give huge discounts. Be sure to visit **Orrefors** (✉ follow signposts; ☏ 0481/34195, WEB www.orrefors.se), for quality Swedish crystal. **Kosta Boda** (✉ follow signposts, ☏ 0481/34500 tours, WEB www.kostaboda.se), which has been producing fine glassware for over 200 years, is also worth a visit.

$$ 🏨 **Statt.** A conveniently located traditional hotel, this Best Western attracts tour groups. The building dates from 1853; the rooms themselves are modern but classic. The hotel has a cozy Irish pub and two restaurants. ✉ *Kungsg. 6, 352 33,* ☏ *0470/13400,* FAX *0470/44837,* WEB *www.bestwestern.se. 124 rooms. 2 restaurants. AE, DC, MC, V.*

$ **Esplanad.** This small family hotel in the center of town offers basic amenities. ✉ *Norra Esplanaden 21A, 352 31,* ☎ *0470/22580,* FAX *0470/26226. 27 rooms. MC, V.*

Kalmar

★ In this bustling coastal town the imposing 12th-century **Kalmar Slott** (Kalmar Castle) stands as a reminder of the time when Kalmar was the "lock and key" of Sweden. Situated on the eastern coast, it was often attacked by Baltic raiders. Most of the present-day castle stems from the days of King Gustav Vasa, who rebuilt the fortress in the 16th century. ✉ *Slottsv.,* ☎ *0480/451490,* WEB *www.kalmarslott.kalmar.se.* ⏲ *Apr., May, Sept., daily 10–4; June, Aug., daily 10–5; July, daily 10–6; Oct.–Mar., daily 11–3:30.*

$$ **Scandic Stadshotellet.** Located in the town center, this large hotel is done in traditional English style with smartly decorated rooms. The main building dates from 1907. ✉ *Stortorget 14, 392 32,* ☎ *0480/496900,* FAX *0480/496910,* WEB *www.scandic-hotels.com/. 139 rooms. Restaurant. AE, DC, MC, V.*

$$ **Slottshotellet.** Occupying a gracious old house on a quiet street, Slottshotellet faces a waterfront park and is a few minutes' walk from both the train station and Kalmar Castle. Inside, modern facilities are wrapped in a 19th-century atmosphere. Restaurant service is offered on the terrace in summer. ✉ *Slottsv. 7, 392 33,* ☎ *0480/88260,* FAX *0480/88266,* WEB *www.romantikhotels.com. 36 rooms. Restaurant. AE, DC, MC, V.*

The West Coast and the Glass Country Essentials

AIR TRAVEL

SAS operates hourly flights to Göteborg from Stockholm's Arlanda Airport between 7 AM and 10 PM on weekdays, less frequently on weekends. The flight takes 55 minutes.

BOAT AND FERRY TRAVEL

You can reach Malmö by boat from Copenhagen. The fastest option is one of the hourly hovercraft with Flygbåtarna.

➤ BOAT AND FERRY INFORMATION: **Flygbåtarna** (☎ 040/103930).

CAR TRAVEL

Göteborg is 478 km (297 mi) west of Stockholm along the E20. Malmö is 620 km (386 mi) from Stockholm. Take the E4 to Helsingborg, then the E6/E20 to Malmö and Lund. If you're approaching from Copenhagen take the Öresund Bridge.

TOURS

Summer sightseeing tours around Göteborg usually begin at the city tourist office on Kungsportsplatsen 2 (reserve tickets at the office in advance). Tour boats run frequently in summer; a central reservations service will book you with either Paddans Sightseeing or Börjessons Sightseeing.

➤ FEES AND SCHEDULES: **Central reservations service** (☎ 031/609660).

TRAIN TRAVEL

Regular trains departs from Stockholm's Central Station for Göteborg, Helsingborg, and Malmö. High-speed X2000 trains travel between Stockholm and Göteborg and Stockholm and Malmö. Train service also runs from Copenhagen to Malmö over the Öresund Bridge.

TRANSPORTATION AROUND THE WEST COAST AND THE GLASS COUNTRY

In Göteborg, the best and cheapest way to get around is with the Göteborg Card. It provides free travel on all public transportation, free parking, and free admission to the Liseberg amusement park and all city museums. The card costs SKr 95 for 24 hours.

VISITOR INFORMATION

➤ TOURIST INFORMATION: **Göteborg** (✉ Kungsportsplatsen 2, ☎ 031/612500, WEB www.goteborg.com). **Helsingborg** (Stortorget Södra Storg. 1, ☎ 042/104350, WEB www.visit.helsingborg.se). **Jönköping** (✉ Juneporten, ☎ 036/105050, WEB www.jonkoping.se). **Kalmar** (✉ Larmg. 6, ☎ 0480/15350, WEB www.kalmar.se). **Malmö** (Central Station, ☎ 040/341200, WEB www.malmo.se). **Växjö** (✉ Kungsg. 11, ☎ 0470/41410, WEB www.turism.vaxjo.se).

30 SWITZERLAND

ZÜRICH, GENEVA, LUZERN, LUGANO, BERN, ZERMATT

THE SWISS KEEP COZINESS under strict control: an electric eye beams open a sliding-glass door into a room of carved wood, copper, and old-fashioned rafters. That is the paradox of the Swiss, whose primary impulses pitch high-tech urban efficiency against rustic Alpine comfort.

Alcohol here is measured with scientific precision into glasses marked for 1 or 2 centiliters (⅓ or ⅔ ounces), and the local wines come in graduated carafes reminiscent of laboratory beakers. And as for passion—well, the "double" beds have separate mattresses and sheets tucked firmly down the middle. Politically isolated, culturally self-contained, Switzerland remains economically aloof . . . even Europhobic. As their neighbors pull their wagons in a circle, sweeping away borders to present a unified front to the world, the Swiss continue to choose their apples from bins marked *Inland* (domestic), leaving the *Ausland,* or imported, varieties to humbly rot. Yet Switzerland is many different countries. Not far from the hum of commerce in the streets of Zürich you can listen to the tinkle of cowbells on the slopes of the Klewenalp. While fur-wrapped and bejeweled socialites shop in Geneva, the women of Appenzell, across the country, stand beside their husbands on the Landsgemeinde-Platz, raising their hands to vote in local elections—a right they won only in 1991.

Switzerland combines most of the attractions of its larger European neighbors—Alpine grandeur, urban sophistication, ancient villages, exhilarating ski slopes, and all-around artistic excellence. It's the heartland of the Reformation, the homeland of William Tell; its cities are full of historic landmarks, its countryside strewn with castles. The varied cuisine reflects French, Italian, and German influences.

All these assets have made Switzerland a major tourist destination, and the Swiss are delighted to pave the way. A welcoming if reserved people, many of them are well versed in English. Their hotels and inns are famous for cleanliness and efficiency, and the notoriously high prices do mirror the quality you'll receive in return.

SWITZERLAND A TO Z

To research prices, get advice from other travelers, and book travel arrangements, visit www.fodors.com.

AIR TRAVEL

CARRIERS

Swissair connects airports in Zürich, Basel, and Geneva. The airline's in-house tour operator, Swisspack, arranges flexible packages for the

Switzerland (Suisse, Schweiz, Svizzera)
N
FRANCE
GERMANY
GERMANY
AUSTRIA
LIECHTENSTEIN
ITALY
ITALY
FRANCE
Rhine
Bodensee
Inn
Rhône
Lac de Neuchâtel
Lac Léman
JURA MOUNTAINS
BERNER ALPS
LEPONTINE ALPS
PENNINE ALPS
RHAETIAN ALPS
ENGADINE ALPS
Matterhorn
Grand St. Bernard Pass
Schaffhausen
Kreuzlingen
Basel
Brugg
Baden
Winterthur
Frauenfeld
Arbon
Rorschach
Wil
St. Gallen
Porrentruy
Olten
Aarau
Zürich
Küsnacht
Appenzell
Solothurn
Buchs
Vaduz
La Chaux-de-Fonds
Biel
Zug
Sargans
Neuchâtel
Bern
Langnau
Luzern
Schwyz
Glarus
Murten
Sarnen
Altdorf
Chur
Payerne
Fribourg
Yverdon
Thun
Interlaken
Meiringen
Davos
Scuol
Zernez
Wassen
Grindelwald
Gruyères
Lausanne
Wengen
Andermatt
Gstaad
Vevey
Montreux
Villars
Nyon
St. Moritz
Biasca
Brig
Geneva
Sierre
Visp
Sion
Bellinzona
Locarno
Ascona
Martigny
Verbier
Zermatt
Lugano
0
40 miles
0
60 km

independent traveler who flies at least one way between North America and Europe on Swissair. Crossair is Switzerland's domestic airline, servicing local airports and various Continental cities as well, including Rome, Barcelona, Berlin, Amsterdam, and London.

➤ AIRLINES AND CONTACTS: **Crossair** (☎ 020/7439–4144 in the U.K.; 0848/852000 toll-free within Switzerland). **Swissair** (☎ 800/221–4750 in the U.S.; 020/7434–7300 in the U.K.). **Swisspack** (✉ 106 Calvert St., Harrison, NY 10528, ☎ 800/688–7947).

BIKE TRAVEL

Bikes can be rented at some 200 train stations and returned to most stations. (If you return a bike to a different station from the one where you rented it, there's a service charge of 7 SF per bike if you've notified the station where you've rented in advance and double that if you have not.) Rates for standard or mountain bikes are 27 SF per day, and 130 SF per week. Groups get reductions according to the number of bikes. Individuals must make a reservation by 6 PM the day before they plan to use the bike, groups a week in advance. There is a daily charge of 15 SF (10 SF with Swiss Half-Fare Travel Card) to transport a bicycle on a train.

BOAT AND FERRY TRAVEL

Drifting across a Swiss lake and stopping off here and there at picturesque villages makes for a relaxing day trip, especially if you are lucky enough to catch one of the elegant old paddle steamers (although there is a supplemental charge). Trips are scheduled on most of the lakes year-round, with increased service in summer. Unlimited travel is free to holders of the Swiss Pass. For those not traveling by train, there is also a Swiss Boat Pass (35 SF), which allows half-fare travel on all lake steamers for the entire calendar year. If you don't hold one of the passes, the longest round-trip journey costs 66 SF for first class and 44 SF for second class. For the many short-hop trips also available, prices vary accordingly. For more information, contact the Lake Lucerne Navigation Company.

➤ BOAT AND FERRY INFORMATION: **Lake Lucerne Navigation Company** (✉ Werftestr. 5, Box 4265, CH-6002 Luzern, ☎ 041/3676767, FAX 0413676868).

BUS TRAVEL

Switzerland's famous yellow postal buses (called *postauto* or *postcar*) link main cities with villages off the beaten track. Both postal and city buses follow posted schedules to the minute. Routes and timetables can be found in train timetable books, available in post offices. The Swiss Pass allows you unlimited travel on postal buses, which venture well beyond the rail routes.

BUSINESS HOURS

Banks are open weekdays 8:30–4:30 or 5 but are often closed at lunch. Museum times vary considerably, though many close on Monday—check locally. Shops are generally open 8–noon and 1:30–6:30, though some may have late hours on Thursday or Friday evening. Some close Monday morning and at 4 or 5 on Saturday. In cities, many large stores do not close for lunch. All shops are closed on Sundays except those in resort areas during high season and in the Geneva and Zürich airports and train stations.

CAR TRAVEL

EMERGENCIES

Assistance is available by telephone: dial 140 and ask for *Strassenhilfe/Secours routier.*

GASOLINE

Sans plomb or *bleifrei* (lead-free) gasoline costs 1.34 SF per liter; super costs 1.42 SF per liter. Leaded fuel is no longer available.

PARKING

Areas are clearly marked and parking times are signposted. Blue and red zones, which require a *disque* to be displayed in the windshield, are slowly being replaced by metered white zones. Metered parking is often paid for at communal machines; these vary from city to city. Some machines simply accept coins and dispense tickets. At others, you'll need to punch in your parking space number, then add coins. The parking ticket may or may not have to be placed in your car window; this information is noted on the machine or ticket. The *disques* (provided in rental cars or available from banks, tourist offices or police stations) must be placed clearly in the front window. Make sure that the arrow on the disque is indicating the proper arrival time; the arrow will also indicate the corresponding departure time so you will know how long you may use the space. Parking in public lots normally costs about 2 SF per hour.

ROAD CONDITIONS

Conditions are usually excellent due to well-surfaced roads. Note that roads—especially in the mountains—wind about considerably. Don't plan to achieve high average speeds. When estimating likely travel times, look carefully at the map: there may be only 32 km (20 mi) between one point and another, but there could also be a mountain pass along the way. Switzerland has a well-developed highway network, though some notable gaps still exist in the south along an east–west line, roughly between Lugano and Sion. Under some mountain passes, there are tunnels through which cars are transported by train while passengers remain inside—an experience not unlike riding through the world's longest car wash. A combination of steep or winding routes and hazardous weather conditions may close some roads during the winter, especially over mountain passes. Dial 163 for bulletins and advance information on road conditions.

RULES OF THE ROAD

The Swiss drive on the right. Priority is given to the driver on the right except in roundabouts. In built-up areas, the speed limit is 50 kph (30 mph), and on main highways, it's 120 kph (75 mph). On other roads outside built-up areas, the limit is 80 kph (50 mph). Pass on the left only. Fines for speeding are exorbitant and foreigners are required to pay on the spot—in cash. Children under seven are not permitted to sit in the front seat. The use of seat belts in both the front and rear seats is mandatory. Driving with parking lights is prohibited, and the use of headlights is mandatory during heavy rain and in road tunnels. To use the main highways, you must display a sticker, or *vignette,* which you can buy for 40 SF from Switzerland Tourism before you leave home, at the border stations when you enter the country, or at post offices and most gas stations. Cars rented in Switzerland already have these stickers. Traffic going up a mountain has priority, except when postal buses are coming down (signs showing a yellow post horn against a blue background indicate that postal buses have right-of-way). During the winter, snow chains are advisable—sometimes mandatory. They can be rented in all areas, and snow-chain service stations have signs reading SERVICE DE CHAÎNES À NEIGE or SCHNEEKETTENDIENST.

CUSTOMS AND DUTIES

For details on imports and duty-free limits, *see* Customs and Duties *in* Chapter 1.

DINING

Because the Swiss are so good at preparing everyone else's dishes, it is sometimes said that they have none of their own, but there definitely is a distinct and characteristic Swiss cuisine. Switzerland produces great cheeses—Gruyère, Emmentaler, Appenzeller, and Vacherin—that form the basis of many dishes. Raclette is cheese melted over a fire and served with potatoes and pickles. Fondue is either a bubbling pot of melted cheeses flavored with garlic and kirsch, into which you dip chunks of bread or boiled potatoes, or a pot of boiling broth (*chinois*) or oil (*bourgignon*) into which you dip various meats. *Rösti* is shredded potato sautéed until golden brown. Other Swiss specialties are *geschnetzeltes Kalbfleisch* (veal bits in cream sauce with mushrooms), Italian-style polenta in the Ticino, and fine game in autumn. A wide variety of Swiss sausages or air-dried beef with *pommes frites* (french fries) and salad makes for filling, inexpensive meals, and in every region the breads are varied and superb. Fresh or smoked fish from the many lakes is always a treat.

Dining options range from luxury establishments to modest cafés and *Stübli* (tavern-cafés) specializing in local cuisine. In resorts especially, most restaurants are associated with hotels, and the half-pension plan includes a hot meal in the room rate. Watch for *Tagesteller* or *plats du jour* (prix-fixe lunch platters or menus), enabling you to a taste of the best restaurants without paying high à la carte rates.

Prices are for one main course at dinner.

CATEGORY	ZÜRICH/GENEVA/ RESORT AREAS	OTHER AREAS
$$$$	over 50 SF	over 40 SF
$$$	30 SF–50 SF	30 SF–40 SF
$$	20 SF–30 SF	20 SF–30 SF
$	under 20 SF	under 20 SF

MEALTIMES

At home, the main Swiss meal of the day is lunch, followed by a light snack in the evening. Restaurants are open at midday and at night; often limited menus are offered all day. Dinner hours vary; dinner is served around 6 or 7 PM in the Germanic regions, a bit later in the French- and Italian-speaking areas.

RESERVATIONS AND DRESS

Jacket and tie are suggested for restaurants in the $$$$ and $$$ categories (except in more relaxed ski resorts); casual dress is acceptable elsewhere.

EMBASSIES

For the New Zealand consulate, *see* Geneva, *below.*

➤ AUSTRALIA: (✉ 56 rue de Moillebeau, Geneva, ☎ 022/9182900).
➤ CANADA: (✉ Kirchenfeldstr. 88, Bern, ☎ 031/3573200).
➤ IRELAND: (✉ Kirchenfeldstr. 68, Bern, ☎ 31/3521442).
➤ SOUTH AFRICA: (✉ Alpenstr. 29, Bern, ☎ 031/3501313).
➤ UNITED KINGDOM: (✉ Thunstr. 50, Bern, ☎ 031/3525021).
➤ UNITED STATES: (✉ Jubiläumsstr. 93, Bern, ☎ 031/3577011).

HOLIDAYS

New Year's (January 1–2); Good Friday; Easter Sunday and Monday; Ascension; Whitsunday, Pentecost; National Day (August 1); Christmas (December 25–26). Note that May 1 (Labor Day) is celebrated in most cantons, but not all.

LANGUAGE

French is spoken in the southwest, around Lake Geneva (Lac Léman), and in the cantons of Fribourg, Neuchâtel, Jura, Vaud, and the western portion of Valais; Italian is spoken in the Ticino; and German is spoken everywhere else—in more than 70% of the country, in fact. (Keep in mind that the Swiss versions of these languages can sound very different from those spoken in France, Italy, and Germany.) The Romance language called Romansh has regained a firm foothold throughout the Upper and Lower Engadine regions of the canton Graubünden, where it takes the form of five different dialects. English, however, is spoken widely. Many signs are in English as well as in the regional language, and all hotels, restaurants, tourist offices, train stations, banks, and shops have at least a few English-speaking employees.

LODGING

Switzerland's accommodations range from the most luxurious hotels to more practical rooms in private homes. Pick up the free "Schweizer Hotelführer" ("Swiss Hotel Guide") from Switzerland Tourism. The guide lists all members of the Swiss Hotel Association (SHA).

Most hotel rooms have private bath and shower; those that don't, noted below, are usually considerably cheaper. Remember that the no-nonsense Swiss sleep in separate beds or, at best, a double with separate bedding. For a standard double bed, request a "French bed" or a *lit matrimonial.* Service charges and taxes are included in the price quoted. Continental breakfast is usually included. In resorts especially, half pension (choice of a noon or evening meal) is often encouraged and included in the room price. If you choose to eat à la carte or elsewhere, the management, if notified in advance, will usually reduce your price.

Prices are for two people in a double room with bath or shower, including taxes, service charges, and Continental breakfast.

CATEGORY	ZÜRICH/GENEVA/ RESORT AREAS	OTHER AREAS
$$$$	over 350 SF	over 300 SF
$$$	250 SF–350 SF	200 SF–300 SF
$$	150 SF–250 SF	120 SF–200 SF
$	under 150 SF	under 120 SF

APARTMENT AND VILLA RENTALS

Off-season, per-day prices for a furnished chalet for four are around 50 SF per person; in peak season, prices double. You may save money if you write directly to the village or resort you wish to rent in. You can get a brochure offering apartment rentals with hotel services at Utoring AG. In the United States and Britain, write to Interhome.

➤ RENTAL LISTINGS: **Interhome** (✉ 383 Richmond Rd., Twickenham, Middlesex TW1 2EF, United Kingdom; ✉ 36 Carlos Dr., Fairfield, NJ 07006, United States). **Utoring AG** (✉ Buckhauserstr. 26, CH-8048 Zürich, ☎ 01/4972727, FAX 01/4972760).

HOTELS

The Swiss Hotel Association grades from one to five stars. Always confirm the price before you register, and check the posted price in your room. Often, rates will be quoted on a per-person basis; single rooms are about two-thirds the price of doubles, but this can vary considerably. Romantik Hotels and Restaurants and Relais & Châteaux have premises in either historic houses or houses with some special character. First-class Relais du Silence hotels are usually isolated in a peaceful setting. The E & G (*einfach und gemütlich,* or "Simple and Cozy")

Swiss Budget Hotels are dependable small hotels, boardinghouses, and mountain lodges.

➤ HOTEL INFORMATION: **E & G Swiss Budget Hotels** (☎ 024/4951111, WEB www.rooms.ch). **Relais & Châteaux** (☎ 800/735–2478 in the US; 00800/20000002 in Switzerland, WEB www.relaischateaux.com). **Romantik Hotels and Restaurants** (☎ 049/0696612340 main office, Frankfurt, WEB www.romantikhotels.com).

MAIL AND SHIPPING

If you're uncertain where you'll be staying, you can have your mail, marked "poste restante" or "postlagernd," sent to any post office in Switzerland. The sender's name and address must be on the back, and you'll need identification to collect it. You can also have your mail sent to American Express. This service is free to those holding American Express cards or traveler's checks; others are charged a small fee.

POSTAL RATES

Mail rates are divided into first-class "A" (air mail) and second-class "B" (surface). Letters and postcards to the United States up to 20 grams cost 1.80 SF first-class, 1.40 SF second-class; to the United Kingdom, 1.30 SF first-class, 1.20 SF second-class.

MONEY MATTERS

Switzerland's high standard of living is reflected in its prices. You'll pay more for luxury here than in almost any other European country. Though annual inflation has been less than 2% for years, and the dollar has regained its strength against the Swiss franc, Switzerland's exorbitant cost of living makes travel noticeably expensive. You'll find plenty of reasonably priced digs and eats, however, if you look for them.

Zürich and Geneva are Switzerland's priciest cities, followed by Basel, Bern, and Lugano. Price tags at resorts—especially the better-known Alpine ski centers—rival those in the cities. Off the beaten track and in the northeast prices drop considerably.

Some sample prices (may be more at top resorts) include: cup of coffee, 3 SF; bottle of beer, 3.50 SF; soft drink, 3.50 SF; sausage and Rösti, 16 SF; 2-km (1-mi) taxi ride, 12 SF (more in Geneva, Lugano, Zürich).

CREDIT CARDS

Most major credit cards are generally, though not universally, accepted at hotels, restaurants, and shops. Traveler's checks are almost never accepted outside banks and railroad station change counters.

CURRENCY

The unit of currency is the Swiss franc (SF), divided into 100 centimes (in Suisse Romande) or rappen (in German Switzerland). There are coins of 5, 10, 20, and 50 rappen/centimes and of 1, 2, and 5 francs. Bills come in denominations of 10, 20, 50, 100, 200, and 1,000 francs. At press time (summer 2001), the Swiss franc stood at 1.65 SF to the U.S. dollar, 1.10 SF to the Canadian dollar, 2.40 SF to the pound sterling, 1.95 SF to the Irish punt, 0.89 SF to the Australian dollar, 0.73 SF to the New Zealand dollar, and 0.21 SF to the South African rand.

TAXES

A 7.6% value-added tax (VAT) is included in the price of all goods. Nonresidents spending at least 550 SF at one time at a particular store may get a VAT refund. To obtain a refund, pay by credit card; at the time of purchase, the store clerk should fill out and give you a red form and keep a record of your credit card number. When leaving Switzerland, you must hand deliver the red form to a customs officer—at the customs office at the airport or, if leaving by car or train, at the border. Customs will process the form and return it to the store, which will refund the tax by crediting your card.

TELEPHONES

COUNTRY AND AREA CODES

The country code for Switzerland and Liechtenstein is 41. When dialing Switzerland from outside the country, drop the initial zero from the area code.

INTERNATIONAL CALLS

To dial international numbers directly from Switzerland, dial 00 before the country's code. If a number cannot be reached directly, dial 1141 for a connection. Dial 1159 for international numbers and information. International access codes for the major telephone companies will put you directly in touch with an operator who will place your call. Calls to the United States and Canada cost 0.12 SF per minute; calls to the United Kingdom, Australia, and New Zealand cost 0.25 SF per minute. International telephone rates are lower on weekends.

➤ ACCESS CODES: **AT&T** (☎ 0848/804343). **MCI Worldcom** (☎ 01/5808011). **Sprint** (☎ 155/9777).

PUBLIC PHONES

Calls from booths are far cheaper than those made from hotels. A phone card, available in 5 SF, 10 SF, and 20 SF units at the post office, kiosk, or train station, allows you to call from any adapted public phone. Note that very few public phones accept coins.

TIPPING

Although restaurants include service charges of 15% along with the taxes in bills, a small tip is still expected: a bit of change for a light meal, 1 to 2 SF for a modest meal, 5 to 10 SF for a first-class meal, and at least 10 SF at an exclusive gastronomic mecca in the $$$$ range. When possible, tip in cash. Elsewhere, give bathroom attendants 1 SF and hotel maids 2 SF. Theater and opera-house ushers get 2 SF. Hotel porters and doormen should get about 2 SF per bag in an upscale hotel, 1 SF elsewhere. Airport porters receive 5 SF per bag.

TRAIN TRAVEL

Swiss trains are swift (except through the mountains), immaculate, and punctual. Don't linger between connections: Swiss Federal Railways (CFF/SBB) runs a tight ship. A useful booklet, "Swiss Travel System," available from Switzerland Tourism, describes passes, itineraries, and discounts available to rail travelers. Apply for tickets through your travel agent or Rail Europe.

Inter-City or Express trains are the fastest, stopping only at principal towns. A *Regionalzug/Train Régional* is a local train, often affording the most spectacular views. Meals, snacks, and drinks are provided on most main services. Seat reservations are useful during rush hours and high season, especially on international trains and in second class. Travelers holding tickets or passes on Swiss Federal Railways can forward their luggage to their final destination.

The Swiss Card, which can be purchased in the United States through Rail Europe, is valid for 30 days and grants full round-trip travel from your arrival point to any destination in the country, plus a half-price reduction on any further excursions during your stay (104 SF second-class, 138 SF first-class). For more information, get the free "Swiss Travel System" or "Discover Switzerland" brochure from Switzerland Tourism. You can also get information from Swiss Federal Railways line, which costs 1.19 SF/min.

CUTTING COSTS

The Swiss Pass is the best value, offering unlimited travel on Swiss Federal Railways, postal buses, boats, and the local bus and tram services of 36 cities. It also gives reductions on many privately owned railways, cable cars, and funiculars. Available from Switzerland Tourism and from travel agents outside Switzerland, the card is valid for 4 days (230 SF second-class, 350 SF first-class), 8 days (320 SF second-class, 480 SF first-class), 15 days (380 SF second-class, 580 SF first-class), 21 days (440 SF second-class, 660 SF first-class), or one month (500 SF second-class, 760 SF first-class). There is also a three-day Flexi Pass (220 SF second-class, 330 SF first-class), which offers the same unlimited travel options as a regular Swiss Pass for any three days within a month. A 15% discount is offered for the Swiss Pass and the Flexi Pass for two or more people. The STS Family Card is issued free of charge, upon request; it allows children up to age 16 to travel free with a parent. In some popular tourist areas Regional Holiday Season Tickets are available, providing discounts on fares. Prices vary widely, depending upon the region and period of validity.

FARES AND SCHEDULES

If you plan to use the trains extensively, get a comprehensive timetable (*Offizieles Kursbuch* or *Horaire*), which costs 16 SF, or a portable, pocket version called the *Reka* for 12 SF. Both are available from either Rail Europe or Swiss Federal Railways.

➤ TRAIN INFORMATION: **Rail Europe** (✉ 226–230 Westchester Ave., White Plains, NY 10604, ☏ 800/438–7245). **Swiss Federal Railways** (☏ 0900/300300).

VISITOR INFORMATION

➤ TOURIST INFORMATION: **Switzerland Tourism** (✉ Tödistr. 7, Postfach, CH-8027 Zürich, ☏ 01/2881111, FAX 01/2881205, WEB www.myswitzerland.com).

WHEN TO GO

Switzerland attracts visitors year-round. Winter sports begin around Christmas and usually last until mid-April, depending on snow conditions. The countryside is a delight in spring, when wildflowers are in bloom, and foliage colors (and clear skies) in fall rival those in New England. In the Ticino, or the Italian-speaking region, and around Lake Geneva (Lac Léman), summer lingers late: there is often clear weather in September and October.

CLIMATE

Summer is generally warm and sunny, though the higher you go, the cooler it gets, especially at night. Winter is cold everywhere: in low-lying areas it is frequently damp and foggy or overcast and rainy, while in the Alps above 1,000–1,200 m (3,600–4,200 ft) days are either brilliantly clear and cold, or snowy, although recent winters have seen rain from time to time.

In summer and winter, some areas of Switzerland are subject to an Alpine wind that blows from the south and is known as the *Föhn*. It brings clear but somewhat oppressive weather, which the Swiss claim causes headaches. The wind that blows from the north is called the *Bise* and can create very cool summer days; in winter, it chills to the bone. The only exception to these more general weather patterns is the Ticino; protected by the Alps, it has a positively Mediterranean climate—even in winter.

The following are the average daily maximum and minimum temperatures for Zürich.

Jan.	36F	2C	**May**	67F	19C	**Sept.**	69F	20C
	26	- 3		47	8		51	11
Feb.	41F	5C	**June**	73F	23C	**Oct.**	57F	14C
	28	- 2		53	12		43	6
Mar.	51F	11C	**July**	76F	25C	**Nov.**	45F	7C
	34	1		56	14		35	2
Apr.	59F	15C	**Aug.**	75F	24C	**Dec.**	37F	3C
	40	- 4		56	14		29	-2

ZÜRICH

Stroll around on a fine spring day and you'll ask yourself if this city, with its glistening lake, swans on the river, sidewalk cafés, and hushed old squares of medieval guild houses, can really be one of the great business centers of the world. There's not a gnome—a mocking nickname for a Swiss banker—in sight. For all its economic importance, this is a place where people enjoy life.

Zürich started in 15 BC as a Roman customs post on the Lindenhof overlooking the River Limmat, but its growth really began around the 10th century AD. It became a free imperial city in 1336, a center of the Reformation in 1519, and gradually assumed commercial importance during the 1800s. Today the Zürich stock exchange is fourth in the world, and the city's extraordinary museums and galleries and luxurious shops along the Bahnhofstrasse, Zürich's 5th Avenue, attest to its position as Switzerland's cultural—if not political—capital.

Exploring Zürich

Numbers in the margin correspond to points of interest on the Zürich map.

Although Zürich is Switzerland's largest city, it has a population of only 360,000 and is small enough to be explored comfortably on foot. The Limmat River, crisscrossed with lovely low bridges, bisects the city. On the left bank are the Altstadt (Old Town), the polished section of the old medieval center; the Hauptbahnhof, the main train station; and the Bahnhofplatz, a major urban crossroads and the beginning of the world-famous luxury shopping street, Bahnhofstrasse. The right bank, divided into the Oberdorf (Upper Village), toward Bellevueplatz, and the Niederdorf (Lower Village), around the Central, is young and lively and buzzes on weekends. The latest addition to the city's profile is Zürich West, an industrial neighborhood that's quickly being reinvented. Amid the cluster of cranes, former factories are being turned into spaces for restaurants, bars, art galleries, and dance clubs. Construction and restoration will most likely be ongoing well into 2006.

9 **Altstadt.** Zürich's medieval core is a maze of well-preserved streets and buildings easily explored on foot in a few hours. The area stretches from Bahnhofplatz to Bürkliplatz on the left bank. On the right bank of the city's historic center is a livelier section known as the **Niederdorf,** which reaches from Central to Bellevueplatz.

2 **Bahnhofstrasse.** Zürich's principal boulevard offers concentrated luxury shopping, while much shifting and hoarding of the world's wealth takes place discreetly behind the upstairs windows of the banking institutions. ✉ *Runs north–south, west of Limmat.*

★ 5 **Fraumünster.** Of the church spires that are Zürich's signature, the Fraumünster's is the most delicate, a graceful sweep to a narrow spire. The Romanesque, or pre-Gothic, choir has stained-glass windows by

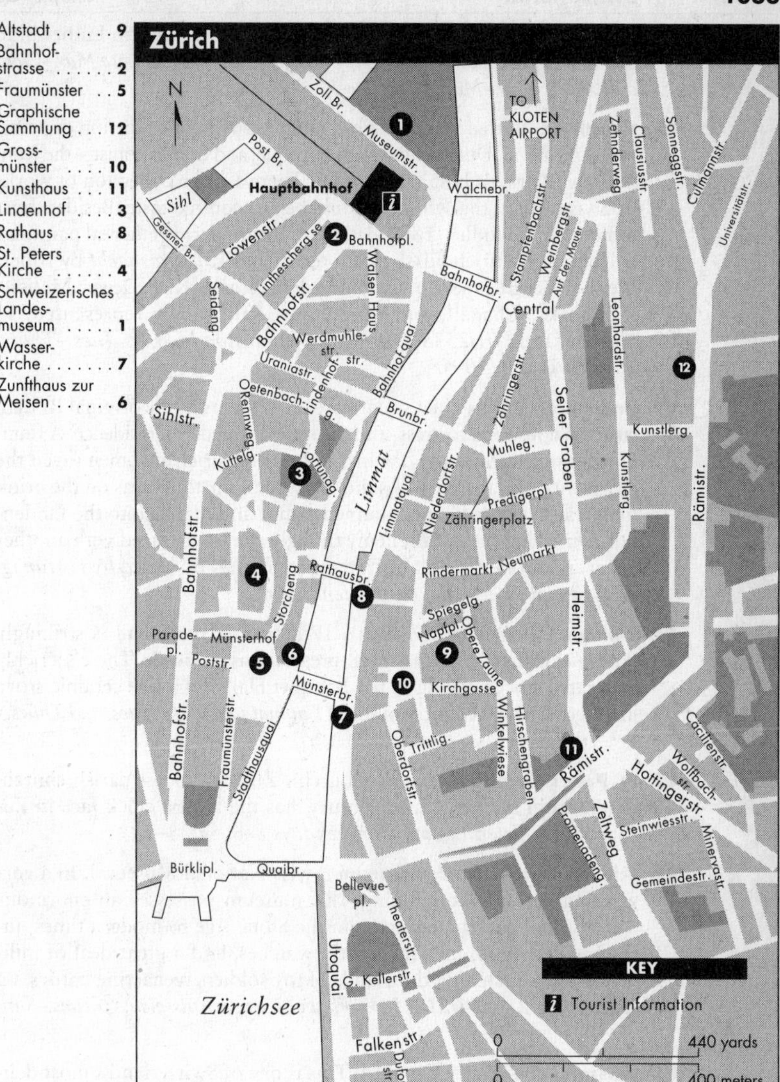

Chagall. ✉ *Stadthausquai.* ⏲ *May–Sept., Mon.–Sat. 9–6; Mar.–Apr. and Oct., Mon.–Sat. 10–5; Nov.–Feb., Mon.–Sat. 10–4.*

⓬ **Graphische Sammlung** (Graphic Collection). This impressive collection of the Federal Institute of Technology displays portions of its vast holdings of woodcuts, etchings, and engravings by European masters such as Dürer, Rembrandt, Goya, and Picasso. ✉ *Rämistr. 101,* ☎ *01/6324046.* ⏲ *Mon.–Tues. and Thurs.–Fri. 10–5, Wed. 10–7.*

★ ❿ **Grossmünster** (Great Church). In the 3rd century AD, St. Felix and his sister Regula were martyred nearby by the Romans. Legend maintains that having been beheaded, they then walked up the hill carrying their heads and collapsed on the spot where the Grossmünster now stands. On the south tower of this 11th-century structure you can see a statue of Charlemagne (768–814), who is said to have founded the church when his horse stumbled on the same site. In the 16th century, the Zürich reformer Huldrych Zwingli preached sermons here that were so threatening in their promise of fire and brimstone that Martin Luther himself was frightened. ✉ *Zwinglipl.,* ☎ *01/2513860.* ⏲ *Late Mar.–Oct., daily 9–6; Nov.–Mar., daily 10–5.*

★ ⓫ **Kunsthaus.** With a varied, high-quality permanent collection of paintings—medieval, Dutch and Italian Baroque, and Impressionist—the Kunsthaus is Zürich's best art museum. There's a rich collection of works by Swiss artists, though some could be an acquired taste. Besides those of Ferdinand Hodler (1853–1918), there are darkly ethereal paintings by Johann Heinrich Füssli and a terrifying *Walpurgisnacht* by Albert Welti. Other European artists, including Picasso, Klee, Degas, Matisse, Kandinsky, Chagall, and Munch, are satisfyingly represented. ✉ *Heimpl. 1,* ☎ *01/2538484,* WEB *www.kunsthaus.ch.* ⏲ *Tues.–Thurs. 10–9, Fri.–Sun. 10–5.*

❸ **Lindenhof.** On this quiet square are the remains of the original Roman customs house and fortress, and the imperial medieval residence. A fountain commemorates the day in 1292 when Zürich's women saved the city from the Habsburgs. As the story goes, the town was on the brink of defeat when its women donned armor and marched to the Lindenhof. On seeing them, the enemy thought they were faced with another army and promptly beat a strategic retreat. ✉ *Bordered by Fortunag. to west and intersected by Lindenhofstr.*

❽ **Rathaus** (Town Hall). Zürich's 17th-century town hall is strikingly Baroque, with its interior as well-preserved as its facade. There's a richly decorated stucco ceiling in the Banquet Hall and a fine ceramic stove in the government council room. ✉ *Limmatquai 55.* ⏲ *Tues. and Thurs.–Fri. 10–11:30 AM.*

❹ **St. Peters Kirche** (St. Peter's Church). Zürich's oldest parish church, dating from the early 13th century, has the largest clock face in Europe. ✉ *St. Peterhofstatt.* ⏲ *Weekdays 8–6, Sat. 8–4.*

★ ❶ **Schweizerisches Landesmuseum** (Swiss National Museum). In a gargantuan neo-Gothic building, this museum possesses an enormous collection of objects dating from the Stone Age to modern times, including costumes, furniture, early watches, and a great deal of military history, including thousands of toy soldiers reenacting battles. ✉ *Museumstr. 2,* ☎ *01/2186511,* WEB *www.musee-suisse.ch.* ⏲ *Tues.–Sun. 10:30–5.*

❼ **Wasserkirche** (Water Church). This is one of Switzerland's most delicate late-Gothic structures; its stained glass is by Augusto Giacometti. ✉ *Limmatquai 31.* ⏲ *Tue.–Wed. 2–5.*

❻ **Zunfthaus zur Meisen.** Erected for the city's wine merchants during the 18th century, this Baroque guildhall today houses the Landesmuseum's exquisite ceramics collection. ✉ *Münsterhof 20,* ☎ *01/2212807,* WEB *www.musee-suisse.ch.* ⏲ *Tues.–Sun. 10:30–5.*

Elsewhere in Zürich

Museum Rietberg. A wonderful representation of art from India, China, Africa, Japan, and Southeast Asia is displayed in the neoclassic Villa Wesendonck (as in *Wesendonck Songs*), where Richard Wagner once lived. ✉ *Gablerstr. 15 (take Tram 7 from city center),* ☎ *01/2024528,* WEB *www.rietberg.ch.* ⏲ *Tues., Thurs.–Sun. 10–5, Wed. 2–5.*

Dining

Over the past few years, new restaurants, both Swiss and international, have been sprouting up all over town. The newcomers tend to eschew the traditional, heavily curtained decor and meat-and-Rösti menus in favor of lighter cuisine and bright rooms, frequently open to the street. Prices are often steep; for savings, watch for posted Tagesteller lunches.

$$$$ ★ ✕ **Petermann's Kunststuben.** This is one of Switzerland's gastronomic meccas, and although it's south of the city center—in Küssnacht on the lake's eastern shore—it's more than worth the 8-km (5-mi) pilgrimage. The ever-evolving menu may include lobster with artichoke and almond oil or Tuscan dove with pine nuts and herbs. Come here for serious, world-class food—and prices to match. ✉ *Seestr. 160, Küssnacht,* ☎ *01/9100715. Reservations essential. AE, DC, MC, V. Closed Sun.–Mon., 2 wks in Feb., and 3 wks in late summer.*

$$$–$$$$ ✕ **La Rotonde.** Even when it's not illuminated by candlelight, the Dolder Grand Hotel's haute-cuisine restaurant is one of the city's most grandiose spots. Housed in a great arc of a room, La Rotonde provides sweeping lake views. The atmosphere is formal, the staff attentive to a fault, the culinary style traditional French with a fashionably light touch—sweetbreads on a bed of gnocchi with asparagus and truffles, for instance. ✉ *Kurhausstr. 65,* ☎ *01/2693000. Reservations essential. Jacket and tie. AE, DC, MC, V.*

$$$–$$$$ ★ ✕ **Kronenhalle.** From Stravinsky, Brecht, and Joyce to Nureyev, Deneuve, and Saint-Laurent, this beloved landmark has always drawn a stellar crowd for its genial, formal but relaxed atmosphere; hearty cooking; and astonishing collection of 20th-century art. Try the herring in double cream, tournedos with truffle sauce, or duck à l'orange with red cabbage and *Spätzli* (tiny dumplings). Have a cocktail in the adjoining bar: anyone who's anyone in Zürich drinks here. ✉ *Rämistr. 4,* ☎ *01/2516669. Reservations essential. AE, DC, MC, V.*

$$$–$$$$ ✕ **Veltliner Keller.** Though its rich, carved-wood decor borrows from Graubündner Alpine culture, this ancient dining spot is no tourist-trap transplant: the house, built in 1325, has functioned as a restaurant since 1551. There is a definite emphasis on the heavy and the meaty, but the kitchen is flexible and reasonably deft with more modern favorites as well: grilled salmon, veal steak with Gorgonzola, and dessert mousses. ✉ *Schlüsselg. 8,* ☎ *01/2254040. AE, DC, MC, V. Closed weekends.*

$$–$$$ ✕ **La Salle.** This is a favorite of theatergoers heading for the new Schiffbauhalle Theater, as it conveniently shares the same building. The glass, steel and concrete interior mixes well with the brick elements left from the original building. Elegantly dressed patrons enjoy delicate dishes such as sole medallions in saffron sauce and rack of lamb with herb fig sauce, beneath an enormous Murano glass chandelier. The hefty wine list can also be enjoyed at the bar, where a smaller version of the menu is available. ✉ *Schiffbaustr. 4,* ☎ *01/2587071. AE, DC, MC, V.*

$$–$$$ ★ ✕ **Oepfelchammer.** This was once the haunt of Zürich's beloved writer Gottfried Keller, and it still draws unpretentious literati. The bar is dark and riddled with graffiti, with sagging timbers and slanting floors; the welcoming little dining rooms have carved oak paneling, coffered ceilings, and damask linens. The traditional meats—calves' liver, veal, tripe in white wine sauce—come in generous portions; salads are fresh and seasonal. It's always packed and service can be slow. ✉ *Rindermarkt 12,* ☎ *01/2512336. MC, V. Closed Sun.–Mon.*

$$–$$$ ★ ✕ **Zunfthaus zur Zimmerleuten/Küferstube.** While the pricier Zunfthaus upstairs is often overwhelmed with conference crowds, at basement level a cozy, candlelit haven dubbed "Coopers' Pub" serves intimate, atmospheric meals in a dark-beamed, Old Zürich setting. Standard dishes have enough novelty to stand apart: braised sole in saffron sauce, roast pork with smoked bacon, and homemade cinnamon ice cream with wine-poached pears. ✉ *Limmatquai 40,* ☎ *01/2520834. AE, DC, MC, V.*

$–$$ ✕ **Adler's Swiss Chuchi.** Right on the Niederdorf's busy main square, Hirschenplatz, this squeaky-clean, Swiss-kitsch restaurant features an airy, modern decor, with carved fir, Alpine-rustic chairs, Big Boy–style plastic menus, and good home-cooked national specialties, particularly fondue. Excellent lunch menus are rock-bottom cheap and served double-quick. ✉ *Roseng. 10,* ☎ *01/2669666. AE, DC, MC, V.*

$–$$ ★ ✕ **Bierhalle Kropf.** Under the mounted boar's head and restored century-old murals, businesspeople, workers, and shoppers share crowded tables to feast on generous hot dishes and a great selection of sausages. The *leberknödli* (liver dumplings) are tasty, *apfelküechli* (fried apple slices) tender and sweet, and the service as wisecracking-cranky as in a New York deli. ✉ *In Gassen 16,* ☎ *01/2211805. AE, DC, MC, V. Closed Sun.*

$–$$ ✕ **Reithalle.** In a downtown theater complex behind the Bahnhofstrasse, this old military horse barn now serves as a noisy and popular restaurant, with candles perched on the mangers and beams and heat ducts exposed. Young locals share long tables arranged mess-hall style to sample French and Italian specialties, many vegetarian, and an excellent, international blackboard list of wines. ✉ *Gessnerallee 8,* ☎ *01/2120766. AE, MC, V.*

$–$$ ★ ✕ **Zeughauskeller.** Built as an arsenal in 1487, this enormous stone-and-beam hall offers hearty meat platters and a variety of beers and wines amid comfortable, friendly chaos. The waitstaff is harried and brisk, especially at lunchtime, when crowds are thick with locals—don't worry, just roll up your sleeves and dig in. ✉ *Bahnhofstr. 28, at Paradepl.,* ☎ *01/2112690. AE, DC, MC, V.*

$ ✕ **Les Halles.** This old warehouse space in Zürich West is less renovated than cleaned and enhanced with an eclectic mix of antiques and '50s collectibles. The fare is health-conscious, made from organic ingredients sold in the attached health food store; try the couscous with vegetables, chicken with peppers, tomatoes, and eggplant. ✉ *Pfingstweidstr. 6,* ☎ *01/2731125. AE, DC, MC, V.*

Lodging

Zürich has an enormous range of hotels, from chic and prestigious to modest. Prices tend to be high, but you will get what you pay for: quality and good service are guaranteed. Deluxe hotels—the five-star landmarks—average between 450 SF and 600 SF per night for a double, and you'll be lucky to get a shower and toilet in your room for less than 140 SF.

$$$$ ★ 🏨 **Baur au Lac.** This is the highbrow patrician of Swiss hotels, with luxurious but low-key facilities—like the Rolls-Royce limousine service. Its broad back is turned to the commercial center, while its front rooms overlook the lake, canal, and manicured lawns of the hotel's private park. The decor is posh, discreet, and firmly fixed in the Age of Reason. ✉ *Talstr. 1, CH-8022,* ☎ *01/2205020,* FAX *01/2205044. 108 rooms, 17 suites. 2 restaurants. AE, DC, MC, V.*

$$$$ ★ 🏨 **Dolder Grand.** A cross between Camp David and Maria Theresa's summer palace, this sprawling Victorian fantasy-palace sits high on a wooded hill over Zürich, quickly reached from Römerhof by funicular railway (free for guests). It's a picturesque hodgepodge of turrets, cupolas, half-timbering, and mansards; the uncompromisingly modern wing was added in 1964. For the authentic grand-hotel experience, a room in the old section is a must. Its restaurant, La Rotonde, excels in traditional French cuisine. ✉ *Kurhausstr. 65, CH-8032,* ☎ *01/2693000,* FAX *01/2693001,* WEB *www.doldergrand.ch. 149 rooms, 34 suites. Restaurant, pool. AE, DC, MC, V.*

$$$$ 🏨 **Splügenschloss.** Befitting its age (built in 1897 in the Art Nouveau style), this Relais & Châteaux property maintains its ornate, antiques-filled decor. One room is completely paneled in Alpine-style pine;

others are decorated in fussy florals. Its location (a 10-minute walk from Paradeplatz) may be a little out of the way for tourists, but atmosphere buffs will find it worth the effort. ✉ *Splügenstr. 2, CH-8002,* ☎ *01/2899999,* FAX *01/2899998,* WEB *www.splugenschloss.ch. 50 rooms, 2 suites. Restaurant. AE, DC, MC, V.*

$$$$ ★ 🏨 **Widder.** One of the city's most captivating hotels, the Widder revels in the present while preserving the past. Ten adjacent medieval houses were gutted and combined to create it. Behind every door is a fascinating mix of old and new—a guest room could pair restored 17th-century frescoes with a leather bedspread and private fax. ✉ *Rennweg. 7, CH-8001,* ☎ *01/2242526,* FAX *01/2242424,* WEB *www.widderhotel.ch. 42 rooms, 7 suites. 2 restaurants. AE, DC, MC, V.*

$$$$ ★ 🏨 **Zum Storchen.** In a stunning central location, tucked between Fraumünster and St. Peters Kirche, this 600-year-old structure has become an impeccable modern hotel. It has warmly appointed rooms, some with French windows opening over the Limmat, and a lovely restaurant with riverfront terrace seating. ✉ *Weinpl. 2, CH-8001,* ☎ *01/2272727,* FAX *01/2272700,* WEB *www.storchen.ch. 73 rooms. Restaurant. AE, DC, MC, V.*

$$$ ★ 🏨 **Florhof.** In a quiet residential area by the Kunstmuseum, this is an anti-urban hotel—a gentle antidote to the bustle of downtown commerce. This Romantik property pampers guests with its polished wood, blue-willow fabrics, and wisteria-sheltered garden. ✉ *Florhofsg. 4, CH-8001,* ☎ *01/2614470,* FAX *01/2614611,* WEB *www.romantikhotels.com/zuerich. 33 rooms, 2 suites. Restaurant. AE, DC, MC, V.*

$$–$$$ 🏨 **Haus zum Kindli.** This charming little bijou hotel could pass for a 3-D Laura Ashley catalog, with every cushion and bibelot as artfully styled as a magazine ad. The result is welcoming, intimate, and a sight less contrived than most cookie-cutter hotels. At the Opus restaurant downstairs, guests get 10% off menu prices, though you may have to vie with crowds of locals for a table. ✉ *Pfalzg. 1, CH-8001,* ☎ *01/2115917,* FAX *01/2116528. 21 rooms. Restaurant. AE, DC, MC, V.*

$$–$$$ 🏨 **Rössli.** This ultrasmall but friendly hotel is set in the heart of Oberdorf. The chic white-on-white decor mixes stone and wood textures with bold textiles and mosaic bathrooms. Extras include safes and bathrobes—unusual in this price range. Some singles are tiny, but all have double beds. ✉ *Rösslig. 7, CH-8001,* ☎ *01/2567050,* FAX *01/2567051,* WEB *www.hotelroessli.ch. 16 rooms, 1 suite. AE, DC, MC, V.*

$–$$ 🏨 **Leoneck.** From the cowhide-covered front desk to the edelweiss-print curtains, this budget hotel wallows in its Swiss roots but balances this with no-nonsense conveniences: tile baths (with cow-print shower curtains) and built-in pine furniture. It's one stop from the Central tram stop, two from the Hauptbahnhof. ✉ *Leonhardst. 1, CH-8001,* ☎ *01/2542222,* FAX *01/2542200,* WEB *www.leoneck.ch. 65 rooms. AE, DC, MC, V.*

$ 🏨 **Limmathof.** This spare but welcoming city hotel inhabits a handsome historic shell and is ideally placed on the Limmatquai, minutes from the Hauptbahnhof. Rooms have tile bathrooms and plump down quilts. There's an old-fashioned *Weinstube* (wine bar), as well as a vegetarian restaurant that doubles as the breakfast room. ✉ *Limmatquai 142, CH-8023,* ☎ *01/2614220,* FAX *01/2620217. 62 rooms. Restaurant. AE, DC, MC, V.*

Nightlife and the Arts

Zürich has a lively nightlife scene, largely centered in the Niederdorf area on the right bank of the Limmat. And despite its small population, Zürich is a big city when it comes to the arts; it supports a top-ranked orchestra, an opera company, and a theater. For information on goings-on, check *Zürich News,* published weekly in English and German. Also check "Züri-tipp," a German-language supplement to the Friday edition of the daily newspaper *Tages Anzeiger.* Tickets to opera, concert, and theater events can also be bought from the tourist office. **Ticketcorner** (☎ 0848/800800) allows you to purchase advance tickets by phone for almost any event. **Musik Hug** (✉ Limmatquai 28–30, ☎ 01/2694100) can make reservations for selected events. **Jecklin** (✉ Rämistr. 30, ☎ 01/2537676) sells tickets for all major concert events, plus it own productions, which showcase small classical concerts and independent artists.

The Arts

During July or August, the **Theaterspektakel** takes place, with circus tents housing avant-garde theater and experimental performances on the lawns by the lake at Mythenquai. The Zürich Tonhalle Orchestra, named for its concert hall **Tonhalle** (✉ Claridenstr. 7, ☎ 01/2063434), was inaugurated by Brahms in 1895 and enjoys international acclaim. Tickets sell out quickly, so book directly through the Tonhalle. The music event of the year is the **Züricher Festspiele** (Zürich International Festival), when, from late June to mid-July, orchestras and soloists from all over the world perform and plays and exhibitions are staged. Book well ahead. Details are available from Info- und Ticketoffice (✉ Postfach 6036, CH-8023, ☎ 01/2154030).

Nightlife

BARS AND LOUNGES

Not just for intellectuals, **I.Q.** has a good selection of whiskies (✉ Hardstr. 316, ☎ no phone). The **Jules Verne Panorama Bar** (✉ Uraniastr. 9, ☎ 01/2111155) shakes up cocktails with a wraparound downtown view. The narrow bar at the **Kronenhalle** (✉ Rämistr. 4, ☎ 01/2511597) draws mobs of well-heeled locals and internationals. Serving a young, arty set until 4 AM, **Odéon** (✉ Am Bellevue, ☎ 01/2511650) is a cultural and historic landmark (Mata Hari danced here and James Joyce scrounged drinks).

DANCING

The medieval-theme **Adagio** (✉ Gotthardstr. 5, ☎ 01/2063666) offers classic rock, jazz, and tango to well-dressed thirtysomethings. **Kaufleuten** (✉ Pelikanstr. 18, ☎ 01/2253300) is a landmark dance club that draws a well-dressed, upwardly mobile crowd. **Paradise** (✉ Theaterstr. 10, ☎ 01/2524481) draws all ages on week nights, and a young crowd on weekends, for funk and soul.

JAZZ CLUBS

Moods (✉ Schiffbaustr. 6, ☎ 01/2768000) hosts international and local acts in the hip new Zürich West district. The **Widder Bar** (✉ Widderg. 6, ☎ 01/2242411), in the Hotel Widder, attracts local celebrities with its 800-count "library of spirits" and international jazz groups.

Shopping

One of the broadest assortments of watches in all price ranges is available at **Bucherer** (✉ Bahnhofstr. 50, ☎ 01/2112635). **Heimatwerk** (✉ Rudolf-Brun Brücke, Rennweg 14 and Bahnhofstr. 2, ☎ 01/2178317) specializes in Swiss handicrafts, all of excellent quality. **Jelmoli** (✉ Seideng. 1, ☎ 01/2204411), Switzerland's largest department store, carries a wide range of tasteful Swiss goods. You can snag some of last season's fashions at deep discounts at **Check Out** (✉ Tödistr. 44, ☎ 01/2027226), which jumbles chichi brands on thrift-shop style racks. If you have a sweet tooth, stock up on truffles at **Sprüngli** (✉ Paradepl., ☎ 01/2244711). The renowned chocolatier **Teuscher** (✉ Storcheng. 9, ☎ 01/2115153) concocts a killer champagne truffle. For the latest couture, go to one of a dozen **Trois Pommes** (✉ Weggengasse 1, ☎ 01/2124710) boutiques featuring top-name designers such as Versace and Armani.

Side Trip from Zürich: Liechtenstein

For an international day trip out of Zürich, dip a toe into tiny Liechtenstein: there isn't room for much more. Just 80 km (50 mi) southeast on the Austrian border, this miniature principality covers a scant 158 square km (61 square mi). An independent nation since 1719, Liechtenstein has a customs union with Switzerland, which means they share trains, currency, and diplomats—but not stamps, which is why collectors prize the local releases. It's easiest to get there by car, since Swiss trains pass through without stopping. If you're using a train pass, ride to Sargans or Buchs. From there, local postal buses deliver mail and passengers across the border to Liechtenstein's capital, Vaduz.

Exploring Liechtenstein

Green and mountainous, with vineyards climbing its slopes, greater Liechtenstein is best seen by car; however, the postal buses are prompt and their routes are extensive.

VADUZ

In fairy-tale Vaduz, Prince Johannes Adam Pius still lives in the castle, a massive 16th-century fortress perched high on the cliff above the city. Only honored guests of the prince tour the interior, but its exterior and the views from the grounds are worth the climb. In the modern town center, head for the tourist information office to have your passport stamped with the Liechtenstein crown.

The black polished-cement block that houses the **Kunstmuseum Liechtenstein** (Liechtenstein Museum of Art), contains paintings, sculpture, and installations, charting the course of modern art from the Barbizon school of 1830 to more recent artists such as Joseph Beuys. It also showcases various segments of Prince Johannes Adam Pius's vast collection, mostly 14th–19th century paintings with a focus on the Flemish school: Rembrandt, Reubens, Van Dyck. ✉ *Städtle 32,* ☎ *2350300.* ⏲ *Tue.–Wed. and Fri.–Sun. 10–5, Thurs. 10–8.*

The **Briefmarkenmuseum** (Stamp Museum) attracts philatelists from all over the world to see the 300 frames of beautifully designed and relatively rare stamps. ✉ *Städtle 37,* ☎ *2366105.* ⏲ *Apr.–Oct., daily 10–noon and 1:30–5:30; Nov.–Mar., daily 10–noon and 1:30–5.*

BEYOND VADUZ

In **Schaan,** just north of Vaduz, visit the Roman excavations and the parish church built on the foundations of a Roman fort. Or drive southeast of the capital to the chalets of picturesque **Triesenberg** for spectacular views of the Rhine Valley. **Malbun** is a sun-drenched ski bowl with comfortable slopes and a low-key ambience.

Dining and Lodging

$–$$ ★ ✕ **Wirthschaft zum Löwen.** It may be tiny, but Liechtenstein has a cuisine of its own, and this is the place to try it. In a farmhouse on the Austrian border, the friendly Biedermann family serves pungent *Sauerkäse* (sour cheese) and *Käseknöpfli* (cheese dumplings), plus lovely meats and the local crusty, chewy bread. ✉ *Schellenberg,* ☎ *3731162. No credit cards.*

$$–$$$ ★ ✕🏨 **Real.** Surrounded by slick modern decor, you'll find rich, old-style Austrian-French cuisine in all its buttery glory. It's prepared these days by Martin Real, son of the unpretentious former chef Felix Real—who, in his retirement, presides over the 20,000-bottle wine cellar. The menu offers game, seafood, soufflés, and an extraordinary wine list. Downstairs is a more casual Stübli for those who don't feel like getting dressed up. Upstairs is a baker's dozen of small, airy rooms. ✉ *Städtle 21, Vaduz FL-9490,* ☎ *2322222,* FAX *2320891,* WEB *www.relaischateaux.ch/real/. 11 rooms, 2 suites. Restaurant. AE, DC, MC, V.*

$$$$ **Park-Hotel Sonnenhof.** A garden oasis commanding a superb view of the valley and mountains beyond, this hillside retreat in a residential district offers discreet luxury minutes from downtown Vaduz. Some rooms open directly onto the lawns; others have balconies. The excellent restaurant is open only to guests. ✉ *Mareestr. 29, Vaduz FL-9490,* ☎ *2321192,* FAX *2320053. 17 rooms, 12 suites. Restaurant, pool. AE, DC, MC, V.*

$$ **Engel.** On the main tourist street, its café bulging with bus-tour crowds, this simple hotel manages to maintain a local, comfortable ambience. ✉ *Städtle 13, Vaduz FL-9490,* ☎ *2361717,* FAX *2331159. 20 rooms. 2 restaurants. AE, DC, MC, V.*

Liechtenstein Essentials

TELEPHONES

Liechtenstein now has its own country code, 423; from Switzerland call 00423 plus the local number.

VISITOR INFORMATION

➤ TOURIST INFORMATION: **Liechtenstein Tourist office** (✉ Städtle 37, Box 139, FL-9490, ☎ 2321443).

Zürich Essentials

AIR TRAVEL TO AND FROM ZÜRICH

Swissair flies nonstop from major international cities. "Fly-Rail Baggage" allows Swissair passengers departing Switzerland to check their bags at any of 120 rail or postal bus stations throughout the country; luggage is automatically transferred to the airplane. At many Swiss railway stations, passengers may complete all check-in procedures for Swissair flights, including picking up their boarding pass and checking their bags.

AIRPORTS AND TRANSFERS

Zürich-Kloten is Switzerland's most important airport. Several airlines fly directly to Zürich from major cities in the United States, Canada, and the United Kingdom.

➤ AIRPORT INFORMATION: **Zürich-Kloten** (☎ 0900/571060).

BUS TRAVEL TO AND FROM ZÜRICH

All bus services to Zürich will drop you at the Hauptbahnhof (main train station), which is between Museumstrasse and Bahnhofplatz. There are also hotel bus services that charge 22 SF per person.

BUS TRAVEL WITHIN ZÜRICH

VBZ Züri-Linie (Zürich Public Transport) buses and trams run daily from 5:30 AM to midnight, every six minutes on all routes at peak hours, and about every 12 minutes at other times. Before you board the bus, you must buy your ticket from one of the automatic vending machines found at every stop. An all-day pass is a good buy at 7.20 SF. Free route plans are available from VBZ offices and larger kiosks.

CAR TRAVEL

Highways link Zürich to France, Germany, and Italy. The quickest approach is from Germany; the A5 autobahn reaches from Germany to Basel, and the A2 expressway leads from Basel to Zürich. The A3 expressway feeds into the city from the southeast.

CONSULATES

➤ United Kingdom: (✉ Minervastr. 117, Zürich, ☎ 01/3836560).

EMERGENCIES

➤ Doctors and Dentists: **Doctor/Dentist Referral** (☎ 01/2616100).
➤ Emergency services: **Ambulance** (☎ 144). **Police** (☎ 117).
➤ 24-hour Pharmacies: **Bellevue** (✉ Theaterstr. 14, ☎ 01/2525600).

ENGLISH-LANGUAGE MEDIA

English-language magazines are available at most large kiosks, especially in the Hauptbahnhof.

➤ Bookstores: The **Bookshop** (✉ Bahnhofstr. 70, ☎ 01/2110444). **Payot** (✉ Bahnhofstr. 9, ☎ 01/2115452).

TAXIS

Taxis are very expensive, with an 8 SF minimum.

TOURS

BUS TOURS

The daily "Trolley Zürich" tour (29 SF) gives a good general tour of the city in two hours. "Zürich's Surroundings" covers more ground and includes an aerial cableway trip to Felsenegg; it takes 3 hours and costs 39 SF for adults. The daily "Cityrama" tour hits the main sights, then visits Rapperswil, a nearby lakeside town; it costs 39 SF. All tours start from the Hauptbahnhof. Contact the tourist office for reservations. This tourist office service also offers day trips by coach to Luzern; up the Rigi, Titlis, or Pilatus mountains; and the Jungfrau.

WALKING TOURS

Two-hour conducted walking tours (18 SF) starting at the train station are given daily from May to October, and Wednesday to Saturday from November to March. You can join a group with English-language commentary, but the times for these tours vary, so call ahead.

TRAIN TRAVEL

Zürich is the northern crossroads of Switzerland, with swift and punctual trains arriving from Basel, Geneva, Bern, and Lugano. All routes lead to the Hauptbahnhof (main train station).

➤ Train Information: **Hauptbahnhof** (✉ between Museumstr. and Bahnhofpl., ☎ 0900/300300).

TRAVEL AGENCIES

➤ Local Agents: **American Express** (✉ Uraniastr. 14, ☎ 01/2287777). **Kuoni Travel** (✉ Bahnhofpl. 7, ☎ 01/2243333).

VISITOR INFORMATION

➤ Tourist Information: **Zürich Tourist Information** (✉ Hauptbahnhof, ☎ 01/2154000). **Hotel reservations** (☎ 01/2154040, FAX 01/2154044).

GENEVA

Geneva shares most of its borders, as well as its language, with France. It also commands postcard-perfect views of the French Alps from its position at the southwestern tip of Lac Léman (Lake Geneva). The combination of Swiss efficiency and French savoir faire gives the city a chic polish; the infusion of international blood from the United Nations adds a cosmopolitan heterogeneity rarely seen in a population of only 180,000.

Geneva was known for enlightened tolerance long before the International Red Cross was founded here (1864) or the League of Nations moved in (1919). The city gave refuge to religious reformers Calvin and Knox and sheltered the writers Voltaire, Hugo, Balzac, and Stendhal. Rousseau was born here; Byron, Shelley, Wagner, and Liszt all fled to Geneva from scandal at home.

The city's history as a crossroads stretches back farther still. Geneva controlled the only bridge over the Rhône north of Lyon when Julius Caesar breezed through in 58 BC; the early Burgundians and bishop-princes who succeeded the Romans were careful to maintain this control. Calvin's rejection of Catholicism in the 16th century transformed Geneva into a stronghold of Protestant reform. The fiercely independent city-state fell to the French in 1798, then made overtures to Bern as Napoléon's star waned. Geneva joined the Swiss Confederation as a canton in 1815.

Exploring Geneva

Numbers in the margin correspond to points of interest on the Geneva map.

Lac Léman bisects Geneva's *centre ville* with graceful precision, then tapers off into the River Rhône. The historic Rive Gauche (Left Bank, on the south shore) mixes museums, shopping streets, and the picturesque Old Town. The International Area, the train station, and sumptuous waterfront hotels dominate the Rive Droite (Right Bank, on the north shore). Most of the main neighborhoods are easily toured on foot. The International Area, on the northern edge of the city, is a short bus or cab ride from downtown.

12 **Auditoire de Calvin** (Protestant Lecture Hall). John Calvin taught missionaries his doctrines of puritanical reform in this sober Gothic chapel in the 16th century; from 1556 to 1559 the Scots reformer John Knox preached here. English, Dutch, and Italian services are held every Sunday. ✉ *1 pl. de la Taconnerie,* ☎ *022/9097000.* ⏲ *Variable.*

★ 10 **Cathédrale Saint-Pierre** (St. Peter's Cathedral). Construction of this cathedral began in 1160 and lasted 150 years, by which time this towering Romanesque structure had acquired Gothic accents. An imposing neoclassical facade was added in 1750. The nave's austerity reflects its 1536 conversion from a Catholic cathedral to a Protestant church; Calvin's followers removed statuary and frescoes like those now restored to the Chapel of the Maccabees. The bird's-eye view from the north tower is worth the climb. ✉ *cour Saint-Pierre,* ☎ *022/3117575.* ⏲ *Oct.–May, Mon.–Sat. 10–noon and 2–5, Sun. 1:30–5; June–Sept., daily 9–7.*

14 **Collections Baur.** Alfred Baur's treasure trove of lovingly preserved Chinese and Japanese ceramics spans more than 10 centuries. Jades from China, lacquerware and sword-fittings from Japan, stoneware tea services, and age-old smoking paraphernalia round out the largest collection of Asian art in Switzerland. ✉ *8 rue Munier-Romilly,* ☎ *022/3461729,* WEB *www.collections-baur.ch.* ⏲ *Tues.–Sun. 2–6.*

7 **Hôtel de Ville** (City Hall). The cantonal government now inhabits this elegant, vaulted compound, Geneva's political seat since 1455. Sixteen countries signed the first Geneva Convention in the ground-floor **Alabama Hall** on August 22, 1864, and the League of Nations convened its first Assembly here in 1920. The tourist office visits the complex on its weekday morning walking tours of the Old Town. ✉ *2 rue de l'Hôtel-de-Ville,* ☎ *022/9097000.*

8 **Maison Tavel** (Tavel House). Geneva's oldest house traces the development of urban life from the 14th to the 19th century. Several rooms have period furnishings; others display artifacts ranging from medieval grafitti to a scale model of the city's elaborate pre-1850 defense walls. Don't

miss the little room full of photographs. ✉ *6 rue du Puits-St-Pierre,* ☎ *022/4183700,* WEB *mah.ville-ge.ch.* ⏲ *Tues.–Sun. 10–5.*

★ ❹ **Monument de la Réformation** (Wall of the Reformers). Conceived on a grand scale and erected between 1909 and 1917, this phalanx of enormous granite statues pays homage to the 16th-century religious movement spearheaded by Guillaume Farel, John Calvin, Théodore de Bèze, and John Knox. It's flanked by memorials to Protestant kingpins Ulrich Zwingli and Martin Luther. ✉ *Parc des Bastions.*

⓭ **Musée d'Art et d'Histoire** (Museum of Art and History). Switzerland's largest collection of Egyptian art, fine 17th-century weapons, and an impressive array of Alpine landscape paintings crown this museum's extensive archaeological, applied arts, and Beaux Arts collections. The enormous building that houses them dates from 1910. ✉ *2 rue Charles-Galland,* ☎ *022/4182600,* WEB *mah.ville-ge.ch.* ⏲ *Tues.–Sun. 10–5.*

❺ **Musée d'Art Moderne et Contemporain** (Museum of Modern and Contemporary Art; MAMCO). Concrete floors and fluorescent lighting set the tone for this gritty collection of stark, mind-stretching, post-1965 art. This museum, housed in a former factory, juxtaposes artists of wildly different cultures and politics. ✉ *10 rue des Vieux-Grenadiers,* ☎ *022/3206122.* ⏲ *Wed.–Sun. noon–6, Tues. noon–9.*

★ ❾ **Musée Barbier-Mueller** (Barbier-Mueller Museum). Josef Mueller began to acquire fine primitive art from Africa, Oceania, Southeast Asia, and the Americas in 1907; today his family's vast, inspired collection of sculpture, masks, shields, textiles, and ornaments spans six continents and seven millennia. A small selection is on view at any given time. ✉ *10 rue Calvin,* ☎ *022/3120270.* ⏲ *Daily 11–5.*

★ ⓯ **Musée International de la Croix-Rouge** (International Red Cross Museum). State-of-the-art media technology illuminates human kindness in the face of disaster in this custom-built bunker. The sometimes grim displays include a reconstruction of a 9- by 6½-ft concrete prison cell that once held 17 political prisoners. The Mur du Temps (Wall of Time), a simple time line punctuated by armed conflicts and natural disasters, puts the overall story into sobering perspective. Commentary is available in English. ✉ *17 av. de la Paix,* ☎ *022/7489525,* WEB *www.micr.org.* *10 SF.* ⏲ *Wed.–Mon. 10–5.*

❷ **Musée Rath** (Rath Museum). Switzerland's original fine-art museum, inaugurated in 1826, hosts up to three major temporary exhibitions each year. Its focus ranges from archaeology to contemporary art. ✉ *1 pl. Neuve,* ☎ *022/4183340,* WEB *mah.ville-ge.ch.* *Up to 10 SF.* ⏲ *Tues. and Thurs.–Sun. 10–5, Wed. noon–9.*

⓰ **Palais des Nations** (Palace of Nations). The core of this monumental compound, the largest center for multilateral diplomacy in the world, was built in the early 1930s to house the League of Nations. Now the European headquarters of the United Nations, it hosts scores of world leaders and hundreds of thousands of delegates each year for conferences on human rights, disarmament, humanitarian aid, development, and environmental protection. ✉ *14 av. de la Paix,* ☎ *022/9074896,* WEB *www.unog.ch.* *8.50 SF.* ⏲ *Apr.–June and Sept.–Oct., daily 10–noon and 2–4; July–Aug., daily 10–5; Nov.–Mar., weekdays 10–noon and 2–4. Closed the last 2 wks of Dec.*

★ ❻ **Place du Bourg-de-Four.** Once a Roman cattle market, later flooded by Protestant refugees, this quintessential Genevois crossroads mixes scruffy bohemia, genteel tradition, and slick gentrification. ✉ *Intersection of rue Verdaine, rue des Chaudronniers, rue Étienne-Dumont, and rue de l'Hôtel-de-Ville.*

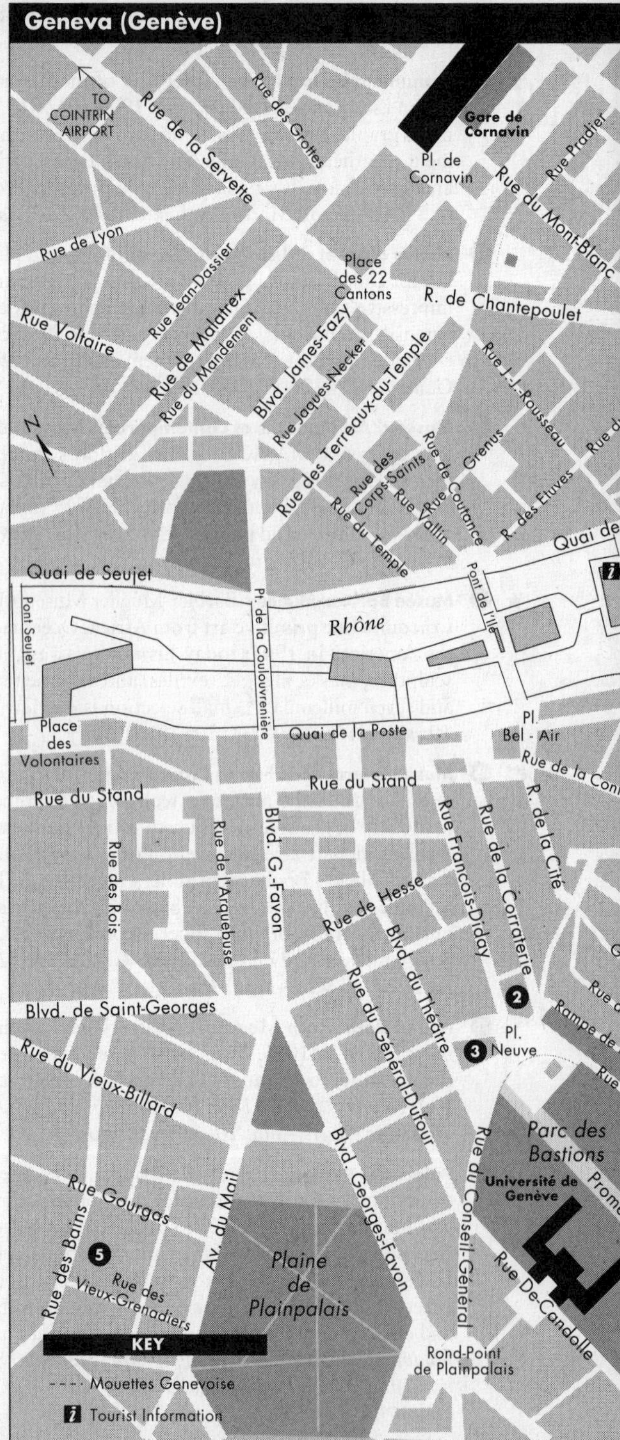

Geneva (Genève)
TO COINTRIN AIRPORT
Rue de la Servette
Rue des Grottes
Gare de Cornavin
Pl. de Cornavin
Rue Pradier
Rue du Mont-Blanc
Rue de Lyon
Rue Jean-Dassier
Place des 22 Cantons
R. de Chantepoulet
Rue Voltaire
Rue de Malatrex
Rue du Mandement
Blvd. James-Fazy
Rue Jaques-Necker
Rue des Terreaux-du-Temple
Rue J.-J.-Rousseau
Rue des Corps-Saints
Rue de Coutance
Rue Grenus
Rue Vallin
Rue du Temple
R. des Etuves
Quai de Seujet
Pont Seujet
Pt. de la Coulouvrenière
Rhône
Pont de l'Ile
Place des Volontaires
Quai de la Poste
Pl. Bel - Air
Rue du Stand
Rue des Rois
Rue de l'Arquebuse
Blvd. G.-Favon
Rue Francois-Diday
Rue de la Corraterie
R. de la Cité
Rue de Hesse
Blvd. du Théâtre
Blvd. de Saint-Georges
Rue du Général-Dufour
Pl. Neuve
Rue du Vieux-Billard
Parc des Bastions
Université de Genève
Rue du Conseil-Général
Blvd. Georges-Favon
Rue Gourgas
Av. du Mail
Rue des Bains
Rue des Vieux-Grenadiers
Plaine de Plainpalais
Rue De-Candolle
Rond-Point de Plainpalais
KEY
Mouettes Genevoise
Tourist Information

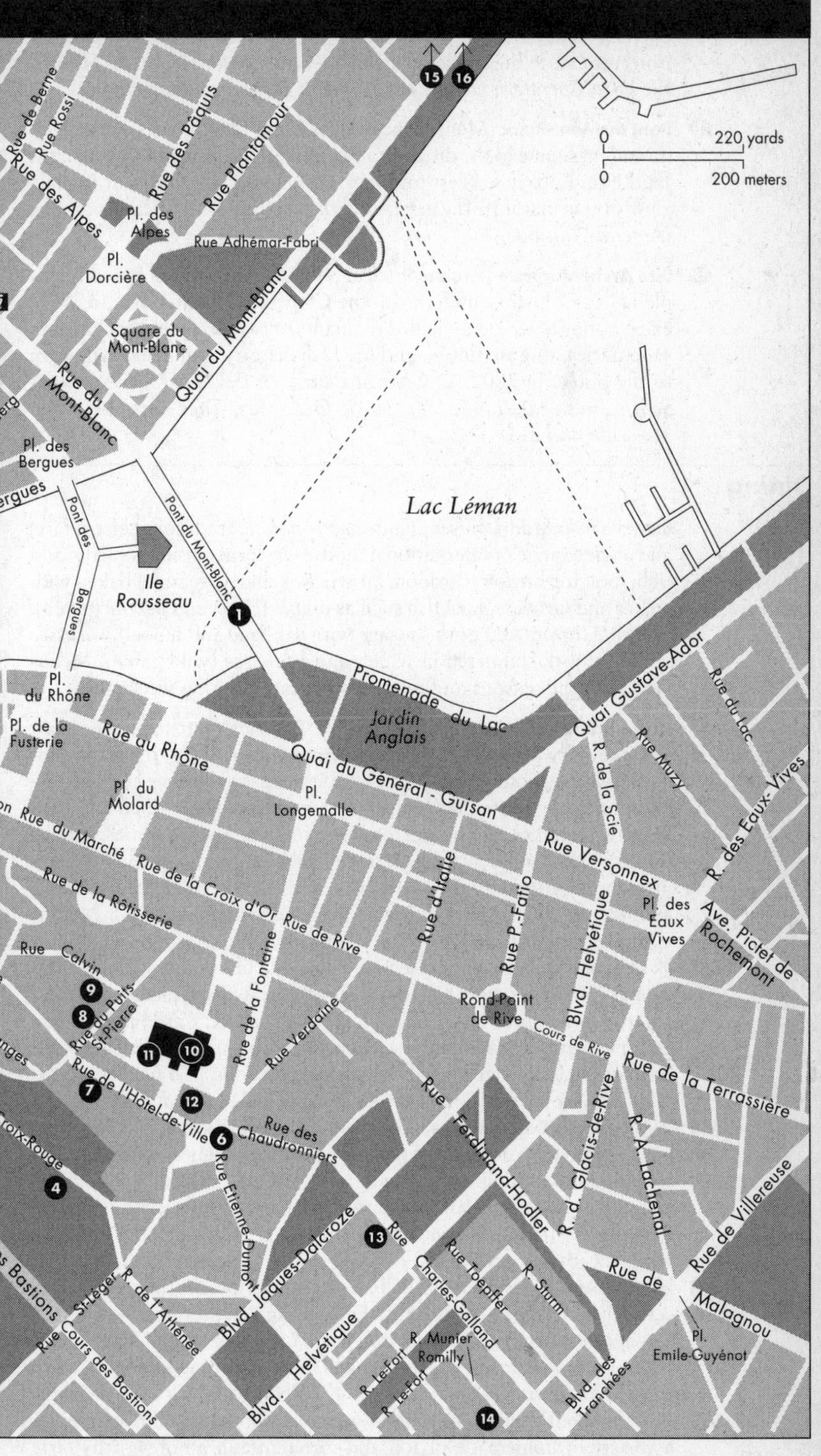

220 yards
200 meters
Rue de Berne
Rue Rossi
Rue des Alpes
Rue des Pâquis
Rue Plantamour
Pl. des Alpes
Rue Adhémar-Fabri
Pl. Dorcière
Square du Mont-Blanc
Quai du Mont-Blanc
Rue du Mont-Blanc
Pl. des Bergues
Pont des Bergues
Pont du Mont-Blanc
Ile Rousseau
Lac Léman
Pl. du Rhône
Pl. de la Fusterie
Rue au Rhône
Promenade du Lac
Jardin Anglais
Quai du Général - Guisan
Quai Gustave-Ador
Rue du Lac
Rue Muzy
R. de la Scie
R. des Eaux-Vives
Pl. du Molard
Pl. Longemalle
Rue du Marché
Rue de la Croix d'Or
Rue de Rive
Rue de la Rôtisserie
Rue d'Italie
Rue P.-Fatio
Rue Versonnex
Blvd. Helvétique
Pl. des Eaux Vives
Ave. Pictet de Rochemont
Rue Calvin
Rue du Puits-St-Pierre
Rue de la Fontaine
Rue Verdaine
Rond-Point de Rive
Cours de Rive
Rue de la Terrassière
Rue de l'Hôtel-de-Ville
Rue des Chaudronniers
Rue Ferdinand-Hodler
R. d. Glacis-de-Rive
R. A. Lachenal
Rue de Villereuse
Croix-Rouge
Rue Etienne-Dumont
Blvd. Jaques-Dalcroze
Rue Charles-Galland
Rue Toepffer
R. Sturm
Rue de Malagnou
Pl. Emile-Guyénot
Bastions
Rue St-Léger
R. de l'Athénée
Rue Cours des Bastions
Blvd. Helvétique
R. Munier Romilly
R. Le-Fort
Blvd. des Tranchées
1
4
6
7
8
9
10
11
12
13
14
15
16

3 **Place Neuve.** Aristocratic town houses overlook the Musée Rath, the operatic Grand Théâtre, the Conservatoire de Musique, and the wrought-iron entrance to the Parc des Bastions. ✉ *Intersection of bd. du Théâtre, rue de la Corraterie, rue de la Croix-Rouge, and rue Bartholoni.*

1 **Pont du Mont-Blanc** (Mont-Blanc Bridge). Mont Blanc hovers like a sugar-dusted meringue in the distance and, between March and October, the **Jet d'Eau,** Europe's tallest fountain, gushes 475 ft into the air in plain view of this major traffic artery. ✉ *Joins rue du Mont-Blanc and quai Général-Guisan.*

★ 11 **Site Archéologique** (Archaeological Site). Archaeologists found multiple layers of history underneath the Cathédrale Saint-Pierre in 1976; excavations have so far yielded remnants of two 4th-century Christian sanctuaries, mosaic floors, and an 11th-century crypt that will open to the public in 2002. ✉ *Cour St-Pierre,* ☎ *022/3117575.* ⏲ *June–Sept., Tues.–Sat. 11–5, Sun. 10–5; Oct.–May, Tues.–Sat. 2–5, Sun. 10–noon and 2–5.*

Dining

Geneva restaurants present *haute gastronomie,* traditional bistro fare, and a wide range of international foods. The local cuisine is earthy and rich; look for *cardon* (cardoon, an artichokelike vegetable) baked with cream and Gruyère, lake fish such as *omble* (char) and *perche* (perch), *longeole* (unsmoked pork sausage with cabbage and fennel), *fricassée de porc* (pork simmered in wine), and *la chasse* (wild game). Menus vary with the seasons and many restaurants close on weekends.

$$$$ ★ ✕ **Domaine de Châteauvieux.** Philippe Chevrier's kitchen, at the heart of Geneva's wine country, has a glowing (and growing) reputation for its simple, elegant, unpretentious quality. Seasonal dishes highlight asparagus in spring, seafood in summer, game come October, and truffles in winter; the cellar houses top local vintages. Ancient beams, antique wine presses, and a summer terrace overlooking the vineyards complete the country setting; a warm welcome is assured. ✉ *Peney-Dessus, Satigny,* ☎ *022/7531511. Reservations essential. AE, DC, MC, V. Closed Sun.–Mon.*

$$$$ ✕ **Le Lion d'Or.** Cologny is Geneva's Beverly Hills with a view, and this culinary landmark takes full advantage of its real estate; picture windows and the summer terrace overlook the city at sunset. Cardons served au gratin with truffles and roasted sea bass are perennial favorites. The dessert cart favors luscious cream and chocolate confections. ✉ *5 pl. Pierre-Gautier, Cologny,* ☎ *022/7364432. AE, DC, MC, V. Closed weekends.*

$$$ ★ ✕ **Bistrot du Boeuf Rouge.** The menu at this brisk bistro offers rich, unadulterated Lyonnaise cuisine. The tender filet mignon barely requires a knife, and andouillettes, *boudin noir* (blood sausage) with apples, and citrus mousse are all superlative. Each dish is presented on a decorated silver tray. ✉ *17 rue Alfred-Vincent,* ☎ *022/7327537. AE, DC, MC, V. Closed weekends.*

$$$ ★ ✕ **Le Vallon.** A rosy facade and hanging grapevines set the scene at this century-old village restaurant. Everything on the menu—whether sausage, terrine, or a succulent tart Tatin (caramelized apple tart) in calvados cream—is made in chef Daniel Huvet's bustling kitchen. ✉ *182 rte. de Florissant,Conches,* ☎ *022/3471104. MC, V. Closed weekends.*

$$–$$$ ✕ **Chez Léo.** Daniel Carugati's tiny, smoky, sunny corner bistro serves a variety of homemade ravioli and tortellini and a noteworthy *tarte au citron* (lemon tart). Intense, trendy locals descend on the old-fashioned bentwood-and-posters setting for lunch, then linger over coffee. ✉ *9 rond-point de Rive,* ☎ *022/3115307. MC, V. Closed Sun. No dinner Sat.*

$$–$$$ ★ ✕ **La Favola.** Run by a Ticinese chef from Locarno, this quirky little restaurant may be the most picturesque in town. The tiny dining room, at the top of a vertiginous spiral staircase, strikes a delicate balance between rustic and fussy. The food mixes country simple and city chic: homemade pastas melt on the tongue, the carpaccio is paper thin, and the tiramisu is divine. ✉ *15 rue Calvin,* ☎ *022/3117437. No credit cards. Closed weekends*

$$–$$$ ✕ **Le Lyrique.** Portraits of Beethoven, Verdi, Strauss, and Liszt watch from under wedding-cake ceilings as pre-theater diners choose homemade pasta with scampi, summer gazpacho, or a nuanced steak tartare. The croissants served from 7 AM are buttery and rich; the Place Neuve setting and the dessert cart make for a terrific afternoon tea. ✉ *12 bd. du Théâtre,* ☎ *022/3280095. AE, DC, MC, V. Closed weekends.*

$$ ✕ **L'Opéra Bouffe.** The mood is casual-chic and friendly. Wine racks stretch floor to ceiling, classical music plays in the background, and opera posters decorate the walls. The Syrian chef rolls out subtle updates of traditional bistro fare.✉ *5 av. de Frontenex,* ☎ *022/7366300. AE, DC, MC, V. Closed Sun.–Mon. No lunch Sat.*

$–$$ ✕ **L'Echalotte.** Artists and journalists jostle for space on the polished wood banquettes, and the seasonal menu stretches from vegetarian options to the namesake *onglet a l'echalotte* (steak in shallot butter). Service is jovial and prompt.✉ *17 rue des Rois,* ☎ *022/3205999. MC, V. Closed weekends.*

Lodging

Hotel prices in Geneva are similar to those in most European capitals, but many hotels offer weekend deals and group rates. Since it's a popular convention center, you'll need to book well in advance; large events can suddenly fill entire hotels.

$$$$ ★ **Des Bergues.** Creamy fabrics, graceful statues, and unpretentious, friendly service give the oldest of Geneva's grand hotels an inner glow. The sumptuous marble bathrooms and Louis-Philippe elegance mesh seamlessly with such modern conveniences as private fax machines and modem connections. ✉ *33 quai des Bergues, CH-1201,* ☎ *022/9087000,* FAX *022/9087090,* WEB *www.hoteldesbergues.com. 107 rooms, 15 suites. 2 restaurants. AE, DC, MC, V.*

$$$$ ★ **President Wilson.** Huge, fragrant flower arrangements punctuate the public areas of this expansive hotel; 17th-century tapestries, colorful paintings, and Greco-Roman stonework complement green marble and sleek wood throughout. Many of the stylish, modern rooms take in sweeping views of the lake, Cologny, or the French Alps. ✉ *47 quai Wilson, CH-1211,* ☎ *022/9066666,* FAX *022/9066667,* WEB *www.hotelp-wilson.com. 203 rooms, 33 suites. 2 restaurants. AE, DC, MC, V.*

$$$ ★ **Cornavin.** The comic book character Tintin made this hotel famous with *L'Affaire Tournesol* (*The Sunflower Affair*). It's now modernized with a spectacular glassed-in breakfast hall, sleek cherry-wood furniture, frosted-glass bathroom walls, and panoramic top-floor views. ✉ *Gare de Cornavin, CH-1201,* ☎ *022/7161212,* FAX *022/7161200,* WEB *www.fassbind-hotels.ch/. 162 rooms, 4 suites. AE, DC, MC, V.*

$$–$$$ ★ **Ambassador.** Don't let the airport-lounge lobby fool you—each room in this central Right Bank hotel is fresh, colorful, and full of natural light. Many of the huge doubles would be called suites elsewhere, and bathrooms gleam with white tile. You'll pay more for a room with a view, but it's worth it to see the sun rise over the Old Town across the river. ✉ *21 quai des Bergues, CH-1211,* ☎ *022/9080530,* FAX *022/7389080,* WEB *www.hotel-ambassador.ch/anglais_situation.htm. 83 rooms. Restaurant. AE, DC, MC, V.*

$$–$$$ **Le Montbrillant.** Front rooms in this family-run hotel behind the train station have a terrific view of trains as they arrive from Paris; double-glazed windows keep it quiet. Nineteenth-century beams and stone walls accent rose fabrics and blue-gray trim throughout. ✉ *2 rue de Montbrillant, CH-1201,* ☎ *022/7337784,* FAX *022/7332511,* WEB *www.montbrillant.ch. 58 rooms, 24 studios. 2 restaurants. AE, DC, MC, V.*

$$ **Suisse.** Colorful trompe l'oeil scenes decorate the elevator doors and a model tall ship or clipper guards the landing on each floor of this stylish corner hotel facing the train station. The lobby is sponge-painted in peach; the sunny, green-accented rooms are soundproof. ✉ *10 pl. Cornavin, CH-1201,* ☎ *022/7326630,* FAX *022/7326239,* WEB *www.hotel-suisse.ch. 57 rooms. AE, DC, MC, V.*

$–$$ ★ **Bel'Espérance.** The Salvation Army owns this former *foyer pour dames* (ladies' boardinghouse) tucked away near place du Bourg-de-Four. Its spectacular terrace, conference facilities, bright yellow and blue rooms, and graceful Louis Philippe–style breakfast salon put it on a par with much pricier hotels. Monthly rates, no-smoking rooms, self-service laundry facilities, and communal kitchen space are available—alcohol is not. ✉ *1 rue de la Vallée, CH-1204,* ☎ *022/8183737,* FAX *022/8183773,* WEB *www.hotel-bel-esperance.ch. 38 rooms, 2 studios. AE, DC, MC, V.*

$ ★ **St-Gervais.** Red tartan carpeting and fresh, creamy linen warm the garretlike rooms in this old Right Bank inn. The tiny, wood-paneled café on the ground floor doubles as a breakfast room. Most major bus lines stop around the corner. ✉ *20 rue des Corps-Saints, CH-1201,* ☎ FAX *022/7324572. 21 rooms, 1 with bath, 1 with shower. AE, DC, MC, V.*

Nightlife and the Arts

Genève Agenda lists concerts, performances, museums, restaurants, and clubs each week in French and English. It is available free from the tourist office. The French and English monthly *Genève Le Guide* profiles current film, theater, music, dance, and museum events and provides a map. Tourist information booths and some hotels offer free copies, or check out their web site at www.le-guide.ch.

The Arts

The **Grand Théâtre** (✉ pl. Neuve, ☎ 022/4183000, WEB www.geneveopera.ch) stages full-scale operas, ballets, and recitals from September to June. **Victoria Hall** (✉ 14 rue du Général-Dufour, ☎ 022/3283573, www.ville-ge.ch) is home to **L'Orchestre de la Suisse Romande** (☎ 022/8070017, WEB www.osr.ch), which plays mostly 20th-century classical compositions along with a couple of older crowd-pleasers; its season runs from September to June.

Nightlife

Arthur's (✉ 20 rte. dePré-Bois, ☎ 022/7917700, WEB www.arthurs.ch) spins house, disco, funk, and salsa and packs 1,500 people onto multilevel dance floors. The **Griffin's Club** (✉ 36 bd. Helvétique, ☎ 022/7351218, WEB www.griffin-span.ch) has a dress code and celebrity clients. **L'Interdit** (✉ 18 quai du Seujet, ☎ 022/7389091) alternates high-voltage techno with flamboyant disco classics. **La Clémence** (✉ 20 pl. du Bourg-de-Four, ☎ 022/3122498) gets packed with university students. Since the bar is only big enough to hold about 25 people, the revelry often spills out into the street. Rarefied opulence lures the jet set to the trendy bar **Le Baroque** (✉ 12 pl. de la Fusterie, ☎ 022/3110515). Luxury hotels such as the **President Wilson** provide piano bars with quiet settings and pricey cocktails. The **Spring Bros. Pub** (✉ 23 Grand-Rue, ☎ 022/3124008) serves Guinness and Strongbow on tap.

Geneva Essentials

AIR TRAVEL TO AND FROM GENEVA

Swissair operates direct service from New York and hourly connector flights to its hub in Zürich. Crossair connects Geneva with Basel, Zürich, Lugano, and most major European cities.

AIRPORTS AND TRANSFERS

Four airlines fly direct from London to Geneva's airport, Cointrin, 5 km (3 mi) northwest of the city center.

➤ AIRPORT INFORMATION: **Cointrin** (☎ 022/7177111, WEB www.gva.ch).

TRANSFERS

Cointrin has a direct rail link with the Gare Cornavin, Geneva's main train station. Trains run about every 15 minutes from 5:30 AM to midnight. The trip takes six minutes; the fare is 5 SF. Regular city bus service between the airport departure level and downtown takes about 20 minutes and costs 2.20 SF. Taxis are plentiful but expensive; you'll pay at least 25 SF to reach the city center, plus 1.50 SF per bag.

➤ TAXIS AND SHUTTLES: **Gare Cornavin** (☎ 0900/300300).

BUS TRAVEL TO AND FROM GENEVA

Long-distance bus lines use the Gare Routière de Genève (bus station).

➤ BUS INFORMATION: **Gare Routière de Genève** (✉ pl. Dorcière, ☎ 022/7320230, WEB www.coach-station.com).

BUS TRAVEL WITHIN GENEVA

Local buses and trams operate every few minutes on all city routes. Buy a ticket from the vending machine at the stop before you board (instructions are in English). The 2.20 SF fare will let you use the system and transfer at will between buses, trams, and the Mouettes Genevoises harbor ferries for one hour. A carte journalière, available for 5 SF from the vending machines and the Transports Publics Genevois booths at the train station and Cours de Rive, buys all-day unlimited city-center travel. Travel with a Swiss Pass is free.

➤ BUS INFORMATION: **Transports Publics Genevois** (✉ ☎ 022/3083434, WEB www.tpg.ch).

CAR TRAVEL

Geneva's long border with France makes for easy access from the south; Chamonix, Annecy, Lyon, and Grenoble are all 1- to 2-hours away on the French A40 (l'Autoroute Blanche). The Swiss A1 expressway is Geneva's northern link to Lausanne and the rest of Switzerland.

CONSULATES

➤ AUSTRALIA: (✉ 2 chemin des Fins, ☎ 022/7999100).

➤ CANADA: (✉ 5 av. de l'Ariana, ☎ 022/9199200).

➤ NEW ZEALAND: (✉ 2 chemin des Fins, ☎ 022/9290350).

➤ UNITED KINGDOM: (✉ 37–39 rue de Vermont, ☎ 022/9182400).

➤ UNITED STATES: (Consular Agent; ✉ 7 rue Versonnex, ☎ 022/8405161).

EMERGENCIES

➤ DOCTORS AND DENTISTS: **Doctor referral** (☎ 022/3222020).

➤ EMERGENCY SERVICES: **Ambulance** (☎ 144). **Police** (☎ 117).

➤ HOSPITALS: **Hôpital Cantonal** (✉ 24 rue Micheli-du-Crest, ☎ 022/3723311, WEB www.hcug.ch).

➤ 24-HOUR PHARMACIES: **Pharmacies *de garde*** (24-hour) (☎ 111).

TAXIS

Taxis are clean and the drivers are polite, but expect a 6.30 SF minimum charge plus 2.90 SF per kilometer (½ mi) traveled. In the evening and on Sundays, the rate climbs to 3.50 SF per kilometer.

➤ TAXI COMPANIES: **Taxi-Phone Centrale** (☎ 022/3314133, WEB www.taxi-phone.ch).

TOURS

BOAT TOURS

Belle Epoque steamers owned by the Compagnie Générale de Navigation ply the lake all year. Swissboat operates guided lake cruises daily from April to October. Les Mouettes Genevoises conduct warm-weather tours of the Rhône and lower lake.

➤ FEES AND SCHEDULES: **Compagnie Générale de Navigation** (☎ 022/3125223, WEB www.cgn.ch). **Les Mouettes Genevoises** (☎ 022/7322944, WEB www.swissboat.com). **Swissboat** (☎ 022/7324747, WEB www.swissboat.com).

BUS-AND-MINITRAIN TOURS

Two-hour bus-and-minitrain tours of Geneva, operated by Key Tours, leave from the place Dorcière bus station daily at 2 PM and also at 10 AM May–October. You may opt to catch the minitrain (independent of the bus tour) at place Neuve for a trip around the Old Town, on the quai du Mont-Blanc for a tour of the Right Bank parks, or in the Jardin Anglais for a ride along the Left Bank quais.

➤ FEES AND SCHEDULES: **Key Tours** (☎ 022/7314140, WEB www.key-tours.ch).

WALKING TOURS

Geneva's Tourist Office organizes a walk through the Old Town every Saturday at 10 AM and, between June 15 and January 1, at 6:30 PM on Tuesdays and Thursdays. Private tours are available upon request from the Service des Guides at the tourist information booth on rue du Mont-Blanc, as are English-language audio tours of the Old Town. Rental of the map, cassette, and player costs 10 SF plus a 50 SF deposit.

➤ FEES AND SCHEDULES: **Service des Guides** (☎ 022/9097030).

TRAIN TRAVEL

Direct express trains from most Swiss cities arrive at the Gare Cornavin every hour. The French TGV provides a fast link to Paris. Thalys leaves for Brussels once a day, and the Cisalpino connects Geneva with Milan and Venice.

➤ TRAIN INFORMATION: **Gare Cornavin** (✉ pl. de Cornavin, ☎ 0900/300300, WEB www.cff.ch).

VISITOR INFORMATION

➤ TOURIST INFORMATION: **Genève Tourisme** (Tourist Office; ✉ 18 rue du Mont-Blanc, ☎ 022/9097000; ✉ Cointrin arrivals terminal, ☎ 022/7178083; Pont de la Machine, ☎ 022/3119827). **Information by mail** (✉ Case Postale 1602, CH-1211, Genève 1,☎ 022/9097000, FAX 022/9097011, WEB www.geneve-tourisme.ch).

LUZERN

As you cruise down the leisurely sprawl of the Vierwaldstättersee (Lake Lucerne), mist rising off the gray waves, mountains—great loaflike masses of forest and stone—looming above the clouds, it's easy to understand how Wagner could have composed his *Siegfried Idyll* while in his lakeside mansion. This is inspiring terrain, romantic and evocative. When the waters roil up you can hear the whistling chromatics and cymbal clashes of Gioacchino Rossini's thunderstorm from his 1829 opera, *Guillaume Tell.* It was on this lake, after all, that William Tell—the beloved, if legendary, Swiss national hero—supposedly leapt from the tyrant Gessler's boat to freedom. And it was in a meadow nearby that three furtive rebels and their cohorts swore an oath by firelight and planted the seed of the Swiss Confederation.

Exploring Luzern

Numbers in the margin correspond to points of interest on the Luzern map.

Luzern's Old Town straddles the waters of the River Reuss where it flows out of the Vierwaldstättersee, its more concentrated section occupying the river's right bank. There are a couple of passes available for discounts for museums and sights in the city. One is a museum pass that costs 25 SF and grants free entry to all museums for one month. If you are staying in a hotel, you may also want to pick up a special visitor's card; once stamped by the hotel, it entitles you to discounts at most museums and other tourist-oriented businesses as well. You can get both passes at the tourist office.

Altes Rathaus (Old Town Hall). This relic overlooking the River Reuss was built between 1599 and 1606 in the late-Renaissance style. ⊠ *Rathausquai, facing north end of bridge, Rathaus-Steg.*

1 **Am Rhyn-Haus** (Am Rhyn House). Also known as the Picasso Museum, the compact Renaissance-style building has an impressive collection of late paintings by Picasso. ⊠ *Furreng. 21,* ☎ *041/4101773.* ⊙ *Apr.–Oct., daily 10–6; Nov.–Mar., daily 11–1 and 2–4.*

9 **Bourbaki-Panorama.** Surrounded by a modern glass cube, this enormous conical wooden structure was created in 1876–78 as a genuine tourist attraction. Its roof covers a sweeping, wraparound epic painting of the French Army of the East retreating into Switzerland at Verrières—a famous episode in the Franco-Prussian War. ⊠ *Löwenpl.,* ☎ *041/4123030,* WEB *www.bourbaki.ch.* 🎫 *6 SF.* ⊙ *Daily 9–6.*

5 **Franziskanerkirche** (Franciscan Church). More than 700 years old, this church retains its 17th-century choir stalls and carved wooden pulpit despite persistent modernization. ⊠ *Franziskanerpl., just off Münzg.*

11 **Gletschergarten** (Glacier Garden). The bedrock of this 19th-century tourist attraction was excavated between 1872 and 1875 and has been dramatically pocked and polished by Ice Age glaciers. A private museum on the site has impressive relief maps of Switzerland. ⊠ *Denkmalstr. 4,* ☎ *041/4104340,* WEB *www.gletschergarten.ch.* 🎫 *9 SF.* ⊙ *Apr.–Oct., daily 9–6; Nov.–Feb., Tues.–Sun. 10–5; March, daily 10–5.*

4 **Historisches Museum** (Historical Museum). Dating from 1567, this building was an armory and today exhibits city sculptures, Swiss arms, and flags; reconstructed rooms depict rural and urban life. ⊠ *Pfisterg. 24,* ☎ *041/2285424,* WEB *www.hmluzern.ch.* ⊙ *Tues.–Fri. 10–noon and 2–5, weekends 10–5.*

12 **Hofkirche** (Collegiate Church). Founded in 750 as a monastery, this Gothic structure was destroyed by fire in 1633 and rebuilt in late-Renaissance style. The 80-rank organ (1650) is one of Switzerland's finest. ⊠ *St. Leodegarstr. 13.*

★ 6 **Jesuitenkirche** (Jesuit Church). Constructed in 1666–77, this Baroque edifice reveals a symmetrical entrance flanked by two onion-dome towers, added in 1893. The vast interior, restored to mint condition, is a rococo explosion of gilt, marble, and epic frescoes. ⊠ *Bahnhofstr., just west of Rathaus-Steg.*

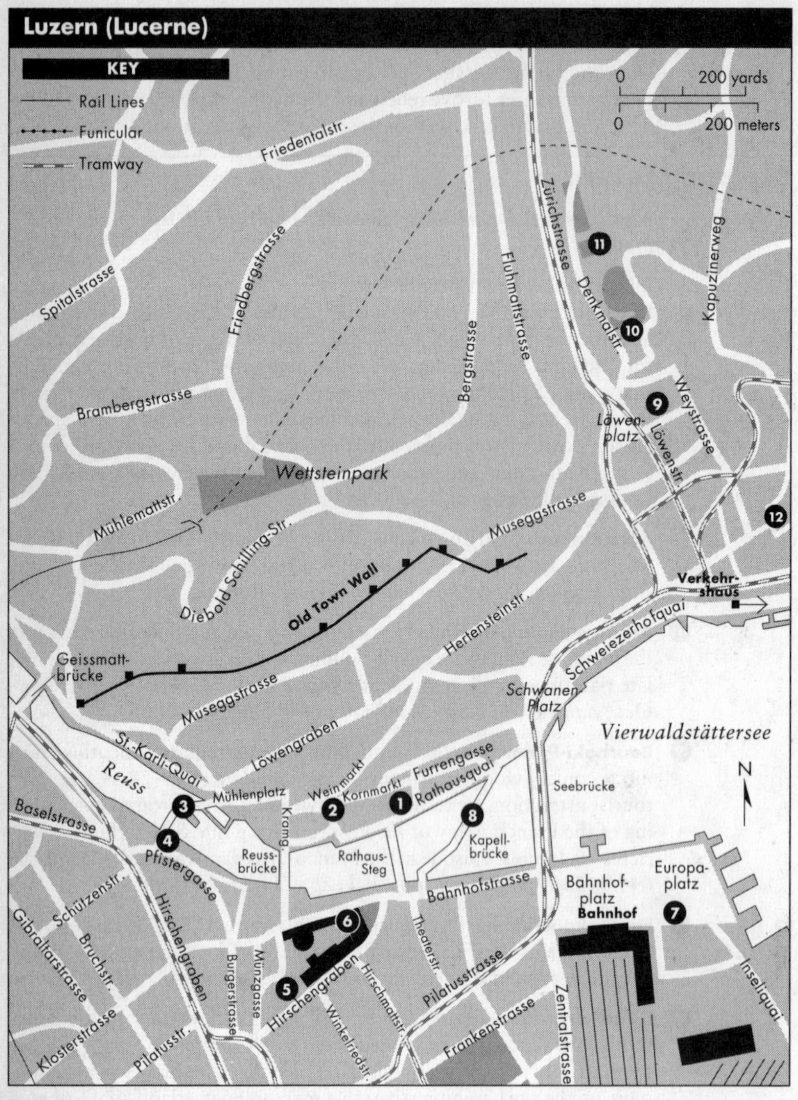

Am Rhyn-Haus 1
Bourbaki-Panorama 9
Franziskanerkirche . . 5
Gletschergarten 11
Historisches Museum 4
Hofkirche 12
Jesuitenkirche 6
Kapellbrücke 8
Kultur- und Kongresszentrum 7
Löwendenkmal 10
Spreuerbrücke 3
Weinmarkt 2

★ 8 **Kapellbrücke** (Chapel Bridge). This bridge snakes diagonally across the water and, when first built in the early 14th century, served as the dividing line between the lake and the river. Its shingled roof and grand stone water tower (now housing a souvenir stand) are to Luzern what the Matterhorn is to Zermatt—but considerably more vulnerable, as was proved by a fire in 1993. Almost 80% of this fragile monument was destroyed, including many of the 17th-century paintings inside; the original 111 gable panels painted by Heinrich Wägmann in the 17th century have been replaced with polychrome copies. The paintings depict scenes from the history of Luzern and Switzerland, legendary exploits of the city's patron saints—St. Leodegar and St. Mauritius—and coats of arms of local patrician families. ✉ *Between Seebrücke and Rathaus-Steg bridges, connecting Rathausquai and Bahnhofstr.*

★ 7 **Kultur- und Kongresszentrum** (Culture and Conference Center). Architect Jean Nouvel's masterful design fits this glass-and-steel building smoothly into its ancient milieu; immense sheets of glass mirror the picture-postcard surroundings. Its concert hall has acoustics so perfect you can hear the proverbial pin drop. ✉ *Europapl.,* ☎ *041/2267070,* WEB *www.kkl-luzern.ch.*

★ 10 **Löwendenkmal** (Lion Monument). The evocative monument commemorates the 760 Swiss guards and their officers who died defending Louis XVI of France at the Tuileries in Paris in 1792. Carved out of a sheer sandstone face by Lucas Ahorn of Konstanz, this 19th-century wonder is a simple image of a dying lion, his chin sagging on his shield, a broken stump of spear in his side. The Latin inscription translates: "To the bravery and fidelity of the Swiss." ✉ *Denkmalstr.*

3 **Spreuerbrücke.** This narrow, weathered, all-wood covered bridge dates from 1408. In its center is a lovely 16th-century chapel looking back on the Old Town. Its interior gables hold a series of eerie, well-preserved paintings by Kaspar Meglinger of the *Dance of Death*; they date from the 17th century, though their style and inspiration—tracing to the plague that devastated Luzern and all of Europe during the 14th century—are medieval. ✉ *Between Geissmattbrücke and Reussbrücke bridges, connecting Zeughaus Reuss-Steg and Mühlenpl.*

2 **Weinmarkt** (Wine Market). One of the loveliest of Luzern's several fountain squares, this former site of the wine market drew visitors from across Europe from the 15th to the 17th century to witness its passion plays. Its Gothic central fountain depicts St. Mauritius, patron saint of warriors, and its surrounding buildings are flamboyantly frescoed in 16th-century style. ✉ *Sq. just west of Kornmarkt, north of Metzgerrainle.*

Elsewhere in Luzern

★ **Verkehrshaus.** The Swiss Transport Museum is one of Luzern's greater attractions. Easily reached by steamer, car, or Bus 2, it's almost a world's fair in itself, with a complex of buildings and exhibitions, including dioramas, live demonstrations, an IMAX theater, and a "Swissorama" (360° screen) film about Switzerland. Every mode of transit is discussed, from stagecoaches and bicycles to jumbo jets and space capsules. If you're driving, turn east at the waterfront and follow the signs. ✉ *Lidostr. 5,* ☎ *041/3704444,* WEB *www.verkehrshaus.org.* 🎫 *21 SF.* ⏲ *Apr.–Nov. 1, daily 9–6; Nov. 2–Mar., daily 10–5.*

Dining and Lodging

Rooted in the German region of Switzerland and surrounded by farmland, Luzern has a native cuisine that's best described as down-home and hearty. The city takes pride in its *Kügelipaschtetli*, puff pastry nests filled with tiny veal meatballs, mushrooms, cream sauce, occasionally raisins, and bits of chicken, pork, or sweetbreads. Watch for lake fish such as *Egli* (perch), *Hecht* (pike), *Forelle* (trout), and *Felchen* (whitefish). A Luzern tradition offers them sautéed and sauced with tomatoes, mushrooms, and capers.

Unlike most other Swiss cities, Luzern has its high and low seasons, and lodgings drop prices considerably in winter.

$$$–$$$$ ★ ✕ **Galliker.** Step past the ancient facade into an all-wood room roaring with local action. Brisk, motherly waitresses serve fresh *Kutteln* (tripe) in rich white wine sauce with cumin seeds; real *Kalbskopf* (chopped fresh veal head) served with heaps of green onions and warm vinaigrette; and the famous simmered-beef pot-au-feu. ✉ *Schützenstr. 1,* ☎ *041/2401002. AE, DC, MC, V. Closed Sun.–Mon. and 3 wks in Aug.*

$$$–$$$$ ★ ✕ **Wilden Mann.** Both dining rooms here—one formal, the other cozily old-fashioned—are excellent, combining old-style local cooking with French cuisine. The Bürgerstube is all dark beams and family crests, while the Liedertafel dining room has soft candlelight and a vaulted ceiling. In both spots the menus and prices are the same; try the whitefish fillets baked in pastry with chive potatoes, or veal tips in green pepper sauce with cheese polenta. ✉ *Bahnhofstr. 30,* ☎ *041/2101666. AE, DC, MC, V.*

$$–$$$ ✕ **Pfistern.** One of the architectural focal points of the Old Town waterfront, this floridly decorated former guildhall offers a good selection of moderately priced meals in addition to higher-priced standards. Lake fish and *Pastetli* (meat pies made with puff pastry) are good local options. ✉ *Kornmarkt 4,* ☎ *041/4103650. AE, DC, MC, V.*

$$–$$$ ✕ **Rebstock/Hofstube.** Across from the Hofkirche, this kitchen offers modern, international fare, including rabbit and ostrich. The lively bentwood brasserie hums with locals lunching by the bar, while the more formal, old-style restaurant glows with wood and brass under a low-beamed herringbone-patterned ceiling. ✉ *St. Leodegarpl. 3,* ☎ *041/4103581. AE, DC, MC, V.*

$$–$$$ ★ ✕ **Rotes Gatter.** This chic restaurant in the Des Balances hotel has a combination as desirable as it is rare: soigné decor, shimmering river views, and a sophisticated menu with fish dishes such as trout with peppers and leeks, or the house specialty, meat and fish fondue. There's a more casual, less-expensive bistro area as well. ✉ *Weinmarkt,* ☎ *041/4182828. AE, DC, MC, V.*

$$$$ ✕🏨 **Palace Hotel.** This waterfront hotel drinks in the broadest possible lake views. Built in 1906, it has been brilliantly refurbished so that its classical look has a touch of postmodernism. Rooms are large enough for a game of badminton and picture windows afford sweeping views of Lake Luzern and Mt. Pilatus. The hotel's elegance infuses its excellent restaurant, Mignon, as well. ✉ *Haldenstr. 10, CH-6002,* ☎ *041/4161616,* FAX *041/4161000,* WEB *www.palace-luzern.com. 178 rooms, 45 suites. Restaurant. AE, DC, MC, V.*

$$$$ 🏨 **Château Gütsch.** Any antiquity in this "castle" (built as a hotel in 1888) is strictly contrived, but honeymooners, groups, and determined romantics in search of a storybook Europe enjoy the Disneyland-like experience. The turrets and towers are worthy of mad Ludwig of Bavaria; a hodgepodge of relics lines the cellars, crypts, and corridors; and beyond the magnificent hilltop site is a private forest. ✉ *Kanonenstr., CH-6002,* ☎ *041/2494100,* FAX *041/2494191,* WEB *www.chateau-guetsch.ch. 28 rooms, 3 suites. 2 restaurants, pool. AE, DC, MC, V.*

$$$$ ★ 🏨 **Des Balances.** This 19th-century riverfront property gleams with style. State-of-the-art tile baths, up-to-date pastel decor, and one of the best sites in Luzern (in the heart of the Old Town) make this the slickest in its price class. The restaurant, Rotes Gatter, is so good, you may want to eat every meal in the hotel. ✉ *Weinmarkt, CH-6000,* ☎ *041/*

4182828, FAX *041/4182838,* WEB *www.balances.ch/index_e.html. 50 rooms, 7 suites. Restaurant. AE, DC, MC, V.*

$$$$ ★ **Wilden Mann.** The city's best-known hotel offers its guests a gracious and authentic experience of Old Luzern, with stone, beams, brass, and burnished wood everywhere. Standard rooms have a prim 19th-century look. The hotel's reputation is matched by its restaurants. ✉ *Bahnhofstr. 30, CH-6003,* ☎ *041/2101666,* FAX *041/2101629,* WEB *www.wilden-mann.ch. 35 rooms, 8 suites. 2 restaurants. AE, DC, MC, V.*

$$$ **Krone.** Spotless and modern, this hotel softens its edges with pastel linens and walls; along the interior walls you may find a stone prayer shrine retained from the original structure. The rooms facing the Weinmarkt have high ceilings and tall windows that let in floods of sunshine. Rooms to the back are less bright but a little larger. The restaurant has a no-alcohol policy. ✉ *Weinmarkt 12, CH-6004,* ☎ *041/4194400,* FAX *041/4194490,* WEB *www.krone-luzern.ch/index_e.html. 25 rooms. Restaurant. AE, DC, MC, V.*

$$–$$$ **Des Alpes.** This historic hotel, with a terrific riverfront location in the bustling heart of the Old Town, has an interior resembling a laminate-and-vinyl chain motel. Rooms are generously proportioned, tidy, and sleek; front doubles, five with balconies, overlook the water and the promenade. ✉ *Rathausquai 5, CH-6003,* ☎ *041/4105825,* FAX *041/4107451,* WEB *www.gersau.ch/hotel-des-alpes. 45 rooms. 2 restaurants. AE, DC, MC, V.*

$$ **Schlüssel.** This spare, no-nonsense little lodging on the Franziskanerplatz attracts young bargain hunters. It's a pleasant combination of tidy new touches (quarry tile, white paint) and antiquity: you can have dinner in a low, cross-vaulted "crypt" and admire the fine old lobby beams. ✉ *Franziskanerpl. 12, CH-6003,* ☎ *041/2101061,* FAX *041/2101021. 11 rooms. Restaurant. AE, DC, MC, V.*

$$ ★ **Tourist.** Despite its friendly, collegiate atmosphere, this cheery dorm-like spot is anything but a backpackers' flophouse. It has a terrific setting around the corner from the Old Town. The coed four-bed, shared-bath dorms (sex-segregated in high season) draw sociable travelers with their rock-bottom prices; there are also seven private-bath doubles. ✉ *St. Karli Quai 12, CH-6003,* ☎ *041/4102474,* FAX *041/4108414,* WEB *www.touristhotel.ch. 35 dormitory rooms, 7 doubles with bath. AE, DC, MC, V.*

Nightlife and the Arts

For information on its concerts and other performances throughout the year, consult the German-English *Luzern City Guide* published by the city seasonally; it's available at the tourist office.

The Arts

The **Luzerner Symphonieorchester** (LSO), the local orchestra in residence, offers a season of concerts from October through June. These are held in the **Kultur- und Kongresszentrum**. Luzern hosts the **International Music Festival** for three weeks in August every year. These performances also take place at the Kultur- und Kongresszentrum. For more information, contact Internationale Musikfestwochen (✉ Hirschmanttstr. 13, CH-6002 Luzern, ☎ 041/2264400).

Nightlife

BARS AND LOUNGES

Château Gütsch (✉ Kanonenstr., ☎ 041/2494141) draws a sedate dinner-and-dancing crowd. The **National Hotel** (✉ Haldenstr. 4, ☎ 041/4190909) serves drinks in both its glossy American-style bar and its imposing lobby lounge. The **Palace Hotel** (✉ Haldenstr. 10, ☎ 041/4161616) has two American-style bars.

CASINO

The most sophisticated nightlife in Luzern is found in the **Casino** (✉ Haldenstr. 6, ☎ 041/4185656), a turn-of-the-20th-century building on the northern shore by the grand hotels. You can visit the Gambling Room (5 SF limit, federally imposed), dance in the **Vegas** club, or have a Swiss meal in **Le Chalet** while watching a folklore display.

FOLKLORE

Nightboat (✉ Landungsbrücke 6, ☎ 041/3194978) sails nightly May through September at 8:45, with drinks, meals, and a folklore show. The **Stadtkeller** (✉ Sternenpl. 3, ☎ 041/4104733) transports you to the Valais Alps for cheese, yodeling, and dirndled dancers.

Shopping

Luzern no longer produces embroidery or lace, but you can find Swiss crafts of the highest quality, and watches in all price categories. **Bucherer** (✉ Schwanenpl., ☎ 041/3697700) represents Piaget and Rolex. **Gübelin** (✉ Schweizerhofquai 1, ☎ 041/4105142) is the exclusive source for Audemars Piguet, Patek Philippe, and its own house brand. **Ordning & Reda** (✉ Hertensteinstr. 3, ☎ 041/4109506) is a Swedish stationer whose store is filled with brightly colored, handmade, recycled paper products. At **Sturzenegger** (✉ Schwanenpl. 7, ☎ 041/4101958), you'll find St.-Gallen-made linens and embroidered niceties.

Luzern Essentials

AIRPORTS AND TRANSFERS

The nearest international airport is Kloten in Zürich, 54 km (33 mi) northeast of Luzern. Swissair flies in most often from the United States and the United Kingdom. Easy rail connections, departing hourly, whisk you on to Luzern within 50 minutes.

➤ AIRPORT INFORMATION: **Kloten** (☎ 0900/571060).

BOAT AND FERRY TRAVEL

It's a crime to see this city and the surrounding mountainous region only from the shore; some of its most impressive landscapes can be seen from the deck of one of the cruise ships that ply the Vierwaldstättersee. The boats of the Schiffahrtsgesellschaft des Vierwaldstättersees operate on a standardized, mass-transit-style schedule, crisscrossing the lake and stopping at scenic resorts and historic sites. The Swiss Pass entitles you to free rides; the Swiss Boat Pass gives you a discount.

➤ BOAT AND FERRY INFORMATION: **Schiffahrtsgesellschaft des Vierwaldstättersees** (☎ 041/3676767).

BUS TRAVEL WITHIN LUZERN

The city bus system offers easy access to sights throughout the urban area. If you're staying in a Luzern hotel, you will be eligible for a special Guest-Ticket, offering unlimited rides for two days for a minimal fee of 8 SF.

CAR TRAVEL

It's easy to reach Luzern from Zürich by road, approaching from the national expressway A3 south, connecting to the A4 via the secondary E41, in the direction of Zug, and continuing on A4 to the city (roads are well marked). Approaching from the southern St. Gotthard Pass route, or after cutting through the Furka Pass by rail ferry, you'll descend below Andermatt to Altdorf, where a view-stifling tunnel sweeps you through to the shores of the lake and on to the city. Arriving from Basel in the northwest, it's a clean sweep on the A2 into Luzern. In case of emergencies or auto breakdowns, contact the Tourist Club of Switzerland or the Swiss Automobile Club.

➤ CONTACTS: **Tourist Club of Switzerland** (☏ 140). **Swiss Automobile Club** (☏ 041/2100155).

EMERGENCIES

➤ DOCTORS AND DENTISTS: **Medical, dental, and pharmacy referral** (☏ 111).
➤ EMERGENCY SERVICES: **Police** (☏ 117).

TAXIS

Given the small scale of the Old Town and the narrowness of most of its streets, taxis can prove a pricey encumbrance.

TOURS

WAKING TOURS

The tourist office provides a two-hour guided walking tour of Luzern with English commentary.

TRAIN TRAVEL

Luzern functions as a rail crossroads, with express trains connecting hourly from Zürich and every two hours from Geneva, the latter with a change at Bern. For rail information, call the Swiss Federal Railways.
➤ TRAIN INFORMATION: **Swiss Federal Railways** (☏ 0900/300300, WEB www.sbb.ch).

TRANSPORTATION AROUND LUZERN

Luzern's modest scale allows you to explore most of the city easily on foot, but you will want to resort to mass transit to visit such noncentral attractions as the Verkehrshaus (Swiss Transport Museum).

VISITOR INFORMATION

➤ TOURIST INFORMATION: **Luzern Tourist Information** (✉ Zentralstr. 5, in the Hauptbahnhof, ☏ 041/2271717). **Tourist information center** (with accommodation service; ✉ Schweizerhofquai 2). **Central Switzerland Tourism Association** (Verkehrsverband Zentralschweiz, ✉ Alpenstr. 1, Luzern, ☏ 041/4184080).

LUGANO

Because of the beautiful, sparkling bay of the Lago di Lugano and dark, conical mountains rising up on either side, Lugano is often referred to as "the Rio of the Old World." The largest city in the Ticino—Switzerland's Italian-speaking region—Lugano has not escaped some of the overdevelopment inevitable in a successful resort town. There's bumper-to-bumper traffic, much of it manic Italian-style; and concrete high-rise hotels crowd the waterfront, with balconies skewed to a view no matter what the aesthetic cost.

Even so, the view from the waterfront is unforgettable, the boulevards are fashionable, and the Old Quarter is still reminiscent of sleepy old towns in Italy. And the sacred *passeggiata*—the early evening stroll to see and be seen—asserts the city's true personality as a graceful, sophisticated Old World resort—not Swiss, not Italian . . . just Lugano.

Exploring Lugano

Numbers in the margin correspond to points of interest on the Lugano map.

8 **Castagnola Parks.** The **Parco degli Ulivi** (Olive Park) spreads over the lower slopes of Monte Brè and offers a romantic landscape of silvery olive trees mixed with cypress, laurel, and wild rosemary; you enter it from the Gandria footpath (Sentiero di Gandria). **Parco San Michele** (St.

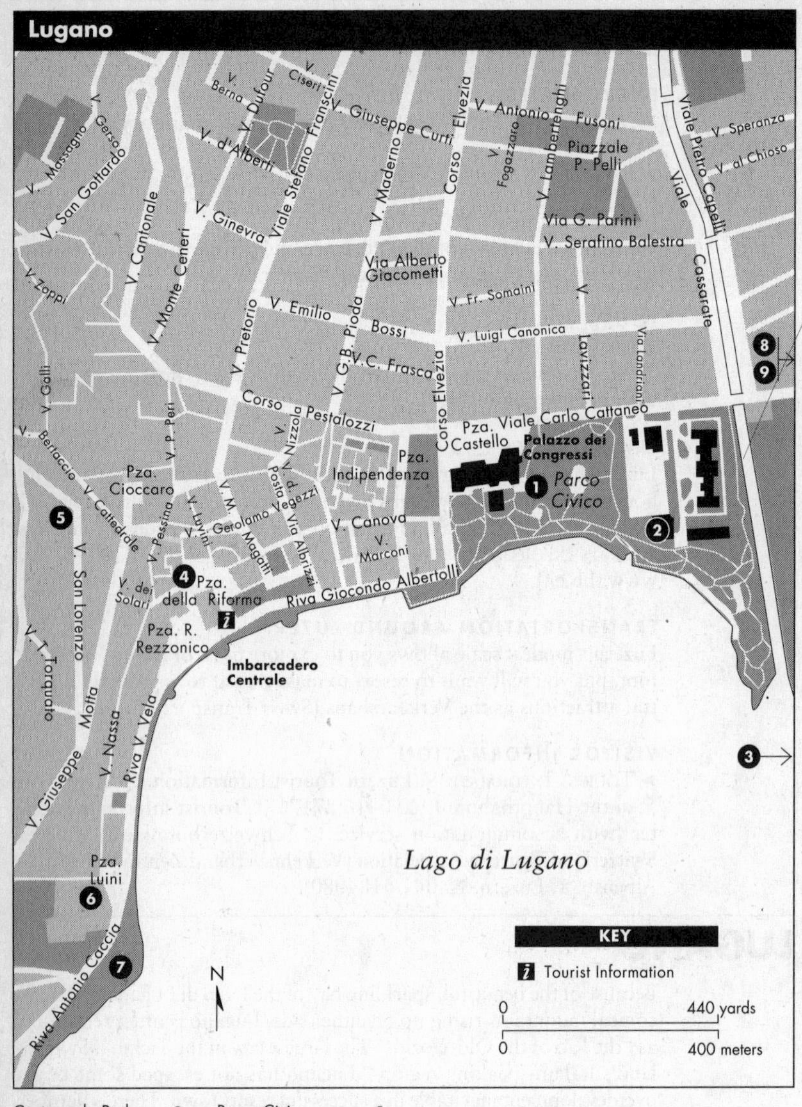

Castagnola Parks . . . 8
Cattedrale di San Lorenzo 5
Chiesa di Santa Maria degli Angioli 6
Giardino Belvedere 7
Lido 3
Museo Cantonale di Storia Naturale 2
Parco Civico 1
Piazza della Riforma 4
Villa Favorita 9

Michael Park), also on Monte Brè, has a public chapel and a broad terrace that overlooks the city; the lake; and, beyond, the Alps. From Cassarate, walk up the steps by the lower terminus of the Monte Brè funicular.

5 **Cattedrale di San Lorenzo** (St. Lawrence Cathedral). With its graceful Renaissance facade, this cathedral contains noteworthy frescoes inside and a lovely view outside. ✉ *Via Cattedrale.*

★ 6 **Chiesa di Santa Maria degli Angioli** (Church of St. Mary of the Angels). Dating from 1455, this church has frescoes of the Passion and Crucifixion by Bernardino Luini (1475–1532). ✉ *Piazza Luini.*

7 **Giardino Belvedere** (Belvedere Gardens). Here you'll see 12 modern sculptures mixed in with palms, camellias, oleanders, and magnolias. At the far west end there's public bathing on the Riva Caccia. ✉ *Quai Riva Antonio Caccia.* ⌚ *Daily.*

8 **Lido.** Along the lake, the municipal stretch of sandy beach includes several swimming pools (heated in spring and autumn) and a restaurant. ✉ *Entrance on right off Viale Castagnola,* ☎ *091/9714041.* 🎟 *7 SF.* ⌚ *May, June, and Sept., daily 9:30–6; July–Aug., daily 9–7:30.*

2 **Museo Cantonale di Storia Naturale** (Cantonal Museum of Natural History). This museum in the Parco Civico has exhibits on the region's fossils, plants, and mushrooms. ✉ *Viale Cattaneo 4 (on the grounds of the Parco Civico),* ☎ *091/9115380.* ⌚ *Tues.–Sat. 9–noon and 2–5.*

1 **Parco Civico** (Town Park). With its cacti, exotic shrubs, and more than 1,000 varieties of roses, this first-rate park also holds fountains, statues, an aviary, a tiny "deer zoo," and a fine view of the bay from its peninsula. Music and events take place here during fair-weather months. **Villa Ciani** has paintings and sculptures from Tintoretto to Giacometti. ✉ *Area south of Viale Carlo Cattaneo, east of Piazza Castello.*

★ 4 **Piazza della Riforma.** Stronghold of Lugano's Italian culture, here you'll encounter modish locals socializing in outdoor cafés. From the piazza one can enter the **Old Town** and follow the steep, narrow streets lined with chic Italian clothing shops and small markets selling pungent local cheeses and porcini mushrooms. Many festivals and concerts take place here. ✉ *Town center.*

★ 9 **Villa Favorita.** This splendid 16th-century mansion in Castagnola houses a portion of the extraordinary private art collection of Baron von Thyssen-Bornemisza. Among the artists represented are Lucian Freud, Edward Hopper, Franz Marc, Jackson Pollock, and Andrew Wyeth. The villa gardens are lush with native and exotic flora. Call ahead; opening hours and entrance fees can change during special exhibitions. ✉ *Strada Castagnola, Via Rivera 14,* ☎ *091/9721741.* 🎟 *10 SF.* ⌚ *Easter–Oct., Fri.–Sun. 10–5.*

Dining and Lodging

The Ticinese were once poor mountain people, so their cuisine shares the earthy delights of the Piemontese: polenta, gnocchi, game, and mushrooms. But as in all prosperous resorts, the mink-and-Vuarnets set draws the best in upscale international cooking. Prix-fixe lunches are almost always cheaper, so dine as the Luganese do—before your siesta. That way you can sleep off the fruity local merlot before the requisite passeggiata through the piazza. For details and price-category definitions, *see* Dining *in* Switzerland A to Z, *above.*

There are few inexpensive hotels in downtown Lugano, but a brief drive into the surrounding countryside increases your options. Since this is a summer resort, many hotels close for the winter, so call ahead. For details and price-category definitions, *see* Lodging *in* Switzerland A to Z, *above.*

$$$–$$$$ ★ ✕ **Al Portone.** Silver and lace dress up the stucco and stone, but the ambience here is strictly easygoing. Chef Roberto Galizzi creates *nuova cucina* (nouvelle cuisine, Italian-style) with ambition and flair, putting local spins on classics such as roast veal kidneys with balsamic vinegar, pasta with white beans and lobster, and seafood carpaccio. ✉ *Viale Cassarate 3, Lugano-Cassarate,* ☎ *091/9235511. Reservations essential. AE, DC, MC, V. Closed Sun.–Mon.*

$$$–$$$$ ★ ✕ **Santabbondio.** Ancient stone and terra-cotta blend with pristine pastels in this upgraded grotto, where superb and imaginative new Franco-Italian dishes are served in intimate, formal little dining rooms and on a flower-filled terrace. Watch for lobster risotto, eggplant ravioli, or scallops in orange-basil sauce. It's a cab ride from town, toward the airport, but worth the trip. ✉ *Via Fomelino 10, Lugano-Sorengo,* ☎ *091/9932388. AE, DC, MC, V. Closed Mon., 1st wk in Jan., and last wk in Feb. No lunch Sat., no dinner Sun.*

$$–$$$ ★ ✕ **Locanda del Boschetto.** The grill is the first thing you see in this no-nonsense restaurant specializing in simple but sensational seafood *alla griglia* (grilled). Crisp linens contrast with rustic wood touches, and the low-key service is helpful and down-to-earth. ✉ *Via Boschetto 8,* ☎ *091/9942493. AE, DC, MC, V. Closed Mon. and first 2 wks of Nov.*

$–$$ ✕ **Da Raffaele.** Having a meal in this family-run Italian restaurant feels like being let in on a neighborhood secret. Start with a pasta, and then try something from the grill, like *gamberoni alla griglia* (grilled shrimp). The restaurant is just outside the city in a residential neighborhood but easily reached by car or by Bus 8 or 9 from the train station to the Viganello stop. ✉ *Contrada dei Patrizi 8/via Pazzalino, Viganello,* ☎ *091/9716614. AE, MC, V. Closed Sun., last wk of July, and 1st 2 wks of Aug. No lunch Sat.*

$–$$ ✕ **Grotto Figini.** This restaurant is in a short stretch of woods on a hill in Gentilino, above Lugano-Paradiso. Locals gather here for a *boccalino* of good merlot and a satisfying, rib-sticking meal of polenta and grilled meats. Don't expect English or other tourists. ✉ *Via ai Grotti,* ☎ *091/9946497. V. Closed Mon. and mid-Dec.–Feb.*

$–$$ ★ ✕ **La Tinera.** This tiny tavern crowds loyal locals, tourists, and families onto wooden benches for authentic regional specialties, hearty meats, and pastas. It's tucked down an alley off Via Pessina in the Old Town. Regional wine is served in traditional ceramic bowls. ✉ *Via dei Gorini 2,* ☎ *091/9235219. AE, DC, MC, V. Closed Sun. and Aug.*

$$$$ ★ 🏨 **Ticino.** This 500-year-old palazzo, protected as a historical monument, is in the heart of the Old Town, just steps away from the funicular to the station. Shuttered windows look out from every room onto a glassed-in garden and courtyard, and vaulted halls are lined with art and antiques. There is a two-night minimum stay. ✉ *Piazza Cioccaro 1, CH-6901,* ☎ *091/9227772,* FAX *091/9236278,* WEB *www.romantikhotels.com/lugano. 18 rooms, 2 suites. Restaurant. AE, DC, MC, V. Closed Jan.*

$$$$ ★ 🏨 **Villa Principe Leopoldo/Hotel Montalbano.** A Relais & Châteaux property, this garden mansion sits on the Collina d'Oro (Golden Hill), offering guests magnificent lake, garden, or pool views. There are scads of facilities, including a fitness room, sauna, and tennis. ✉ *Via Montalbano 5, CH-6900,* ☎ *091/9858855,* FAX *091/9858825,* WEB *www.leopoldo.ch. 70 rooms, 4 suites. 3 restaurants, pool. AE, DC, MC, V.*

$$$–$$$$ 🏨 **Du Lac.** This discreet, simple hotel gives you true lakefront luxury for your money. All rooms face the lake, but the sixth floor is the quietest. The hotel has a private swimming area on the lake, plus a num-

ber of such pampering facilities as a sauna and massage. ✉ *Riva Paradiso 3, CH-6902 Lugano-Paradiso,* ☎ *091/9941921,* FAX *091/9941122,* WEB *www.dulac.ch. 52 rooms, 1 suite. Restaurant, pool. AE, DC, MC, V. Closed Jan.–mid-Mar.*

$$–$$$ **International au Lac.** This big, friendly hotel classic is half a block from the lake, with many lake-view rooms. It's next to Santa Maria degli Angioli, on the edge of the Old Town. ✉ *Via Nassa 68, CH-6901,* ☎ *091/9227541,* FAX *091/9227544,* WEB *www.hotel-international.ch. 80 rooms. Restaurant, pool. AE, DC, MC, V. Closed Nov.–Easter.*

$$ ★ **Park-Hotel Nizza.** This former villa affords panoramic views from its perch on the lower slopes of San Salvatore; it's an uphill hike from town. The mostly small rooms are decorated in styles ranging from repro-antique to modern; there is no extra charge for lake views. A cozy bar overlooks the lake, and the restaurant serves vegetables from its own garden and even wine from its own vineyards—alfresco, when weather permits. There are some no-smoking rooms, and one of the restaurants is no-smoking as well. A shuttle provides service to the nearby town Paradiso. ✉ *Via Guidino 14, CH-6902,* ☎ *091/9941771,* FAX *091/9941773,* WEB *www.castlegate.net/nizza/index.htm. 29 rooms. Restaurant, pool. AE, MC, V. Closed mid-Dec.–mid-Mar.*

$$ **Zurigo.** Handy to parks and shopping, this former bargain-rate hotel has been totally renovated. Rooms are bright and modern with new bathrooms. There's a nice garden in front, too. ✉ *Corso Pestalozzi 13, CH-6900,* ☎ *091/9234343,* FAX *091/9239268. 48 rooms. AE, DC, MC, V. Closed Dec.–Jan.*

$–$$ **San Carlo.** The San Carlo offers one of the better deals in this high-priced town: it's small, clean, quiet, and newly renovated. The location is great, too—right on the main pedestrian shopping street, a block from the waterfront, and just 150 yards from the funicular that takes you to the railway station. ✉ *Via Nassa 28, CH-6901,* ☎ *091/9227107,* FAX *091/9228022. 22 rooms. AE, DC, MC, V.*

$ **Dischma.** The welcoming owners of this hotel make it a bargain worth seeking out. The rooms are clean and bright, with flowers on the balconies; public rooms are a riot of colors, souvenirs, and knickknacks. The restaurant is no-smoking (rare in these parts). ✉ *Vicolo Geretta 6, CH-6902 Lugano-Paradiso,* ☎ *091/9942131,* FAX *091/9941503. 35 rooms. Restaurant. AE, MC, V. Closed Dec.–Feb.*

Lugano Essentials

AIRPORTS AND TRANSFERS

There are short connecting flights by Crossair—the Swiss domestic network—to Aeroporto Lugano-Agno from Zürich, Geneva, Basel, and Bern, as well as from Paris, Nice, Rome, Florence, and Venice. The nearest intercontinental airport is Malpensa, about 50 km (31 mi) northwest of Milan, Italy.

➤ AIRPORT INFORMATION: **Aeroporto Lugano-Agno Airport** (☎ 091/6101212). **Malpensa** (☎ 02/74852200.

TRANSFERS

There is no regular bus service between the local airport and central Lugano, 7 km (4 mi) away, but **Fly Car Lugano** operates a shuttle service. A taxi ride costs about 30 SF to the center.

➤ TRANSFERS: **Fly Car Lugano** (☎ 091/8078520).

BOAT AND FERRY TRAVEL

The Navigation Company of Lake Lugano makes cruise-boat excursions around the bay to the romantic fishing village of Gandria and to the Villa Favorita. You may use these like public transit, following a schedule and paying according to distance, or look into special tickets: seven consecutive days' unlimited travel costs 58 SF, three days' travel within a week costs 48 SF (with half price for the other 4 days), and an all-day pass costs 32 SF.

➤ BOAT AND FERRY INFORMATION: **Navigation Company of Lake Lugano** (☎ 091/9715223).

BUS TRAVEL WITHIN LUGANO

Well-integrated services run regularly on all local routes. Buy your ticket from the machine at the stop before you board.

CAR TRAVEL

There are fast, direct highways from both Milan and Zürich. If you are planning to drive from Geneva, check weather conditions with the automobile associations beforehand.

EMERGENCIES

➤ DENTISTS: **Dental clinic** (☎ 091/9350180).
➤ EMERGENCY SERVICES: **Ambulance** (☎ 144). **Police** (☎ 117).
➤ HOSPITALS: **Civic Hospital** (☎ 091/8056111).

TAXIS

Though less expensive than in Zürich or Geneva, taxis are still not cheap, with a 10 SF minimum.

➤ TAXI COMPANIES: (☎ 091/9712121 or 091/9719191).

TOURS

The tourist office has information about hiking tours into the mountains surrounding Lugano; it provides a wonderful packet of topographical maps and itineraries. Cycling maps are also available. There are bus trips to Locarno, Ascona, Lake Como, Lake Maggiore, Milan, Venice, St. Moritz, Florence, the Alpine passes, and the Italian market in Como.

TRAIN TRAVEL

There's a train from Zürich every hour; the trip takes about three hours. If you're coming from Geneva, you can catch the Milan express at various times, changing at Domodossola and Bellinzona. During the day, there's a train every hour from Milan's Stazione Centrale; the trip takes about 1½ hours. Always keep passports handy and confirm times with the Swiss Federal Railways.

The Holiday Pass gives unlimited free regional travel for three or seven consecutive days on many rail routes and local bus routes and a 30% to 50% discount on PTT buses and other lines. Available at the tourist office or train station, they cost 46 SF for three days, 66 SF for seven days.

➤ TRAIN INFORMATION: **Swiss Federal Railways** (☎ 0900/300300).

VISITOR INFORMATION

➤ TOURIST INFORMATION: **Lugano Tourism** (✉ Palazzo Civico, CH-6901, ☎ 091/9133232, FAX 091/9227653).

BERN

No cosmopolitan nonsense here: the mascot is a common bear, the annual fair celebrates the humble onion, and the president is likely to take the tram to work. Walking down medieval streets past squares teeming with farmers' markets, you might forget the city of Bern is the federal capital—indeed, the geographic and political hub—of a sophisticated nation.

Bern earned its pivotal position with a combination of muscle and influence dating from the 12th century, when the Holy Roman emperor Berchtold V established a fortress on this gooseneck in the River Aare. By the 15th century the Bernese had overcome the Burgundians to expand their territories west to Geneva. Napoléon suppressed them briefly—from 1798 until his defeat in 1815—but by 1848 Bern was back in charge as the capital of the Swiss Confederation.

Today it's not the massive Bundeshaus (Houses of Parliament) that the city is known for, however, but rather its perfectly preserved arcades and fountains—all remnants of its heyday as a medieval power. They're the reason UNESCO granted Bern World Cultural Heritage status.

Exploring Bern

Numbers in the margin correspond to points of interest on the Bern map.

Bern's easily walkable streets run in long parallels east to the Old Town. The original city was founded in a bend of the river and grew westward; those stages of growth are marked by three "towers"—the Zeitglockenturm, the Käfigturm and the Christoffelturm. The city is crisscrossed by *Lauben* (arcades) that shelter stores of every kind and quality.

★ 8 **Bärengraben** (Bear Pits). According to legend, Berchtold V named Bern after the first animal he killed while hunting. It was a bear; in those days the woods were full of them. Live mascots have been on display in the city since the late 1400s. Today they beg for carrots and caper for tourists year-round. ⊠ *East end of Nydeggbrücke.* ⏲ *Summer 9–6, fall and spring 10–4, winter weekends 11–3.*

★ 12 **Bernisches Historisches Museum** (Historical Museum). This castle-like Victorian building houses 15th-century Flemish tapestries and Bernese sculptures as well as 15th- and 16th-century stained-glass windows. Don't miss the novel three-way portrait of Calvin, Zwingli, and Luther. ⊠ *Helvetiapl. 5,* ☎ *031/3507711.* ⏲ *Tues., Thurs.–Sun. 10–5, Wed. 10–8.*

3 **Bundeshaus** (Capitol). This hulking, domed building is the beating heart of the Swiss Confederation and meeting place of the National Council and Council of States. Free guided tours include entry to the parliamentary chambers. ⊠ *Bundespl.,* ☎ *031/3228522.* ⏲ *Tours Mon.–Sat. at 9, 10, 11, 2, 3, and 4; Sun. at 10, 11, 2, and 3. No tours during session or official holidays.*

1 **Christoffelturm** (Christoffel tower). Remains of the city's third gate were uncovered in the train station during construction of a pedestrian passageway. ⊠ *Christoffelunterführung, southernmost entrance to Bahnhofpl.*

5 **Kornhaus** (Granary). At various times a granary, a post office, and a beer hall, this cellar with a magnificent vaulted ceiling now houses a popular restaurant. Upstairs, the Forum for Media and Design hosts exhibitions on architecture, photography, contemporary media, and applied arts. ⊠ *Kornhauspl. 18,* ☎ *031/3129110.* ⏲ *Tues.–Fri. 10–7, weekends 10–5.*

11 **Kunsthalle** (Art Gallery). This groundbreaking contemporary art venue displays the works of living artists, usually before you've heard of them. Built in 1918 in heroic classical style to boost local artists—Kirchner, Klee, Hodler—it grew to attract the young Kandinsky, Miró, Cy Twombly—and a parade of newcomers of strong potential. ⊠ *Helvetiapl. 1,* ☎ *031/3510031,* WEB *www.kunsthallebern.ch.* ⏲ *Tues. 10–9, Wed.–Sun. 10–5.*

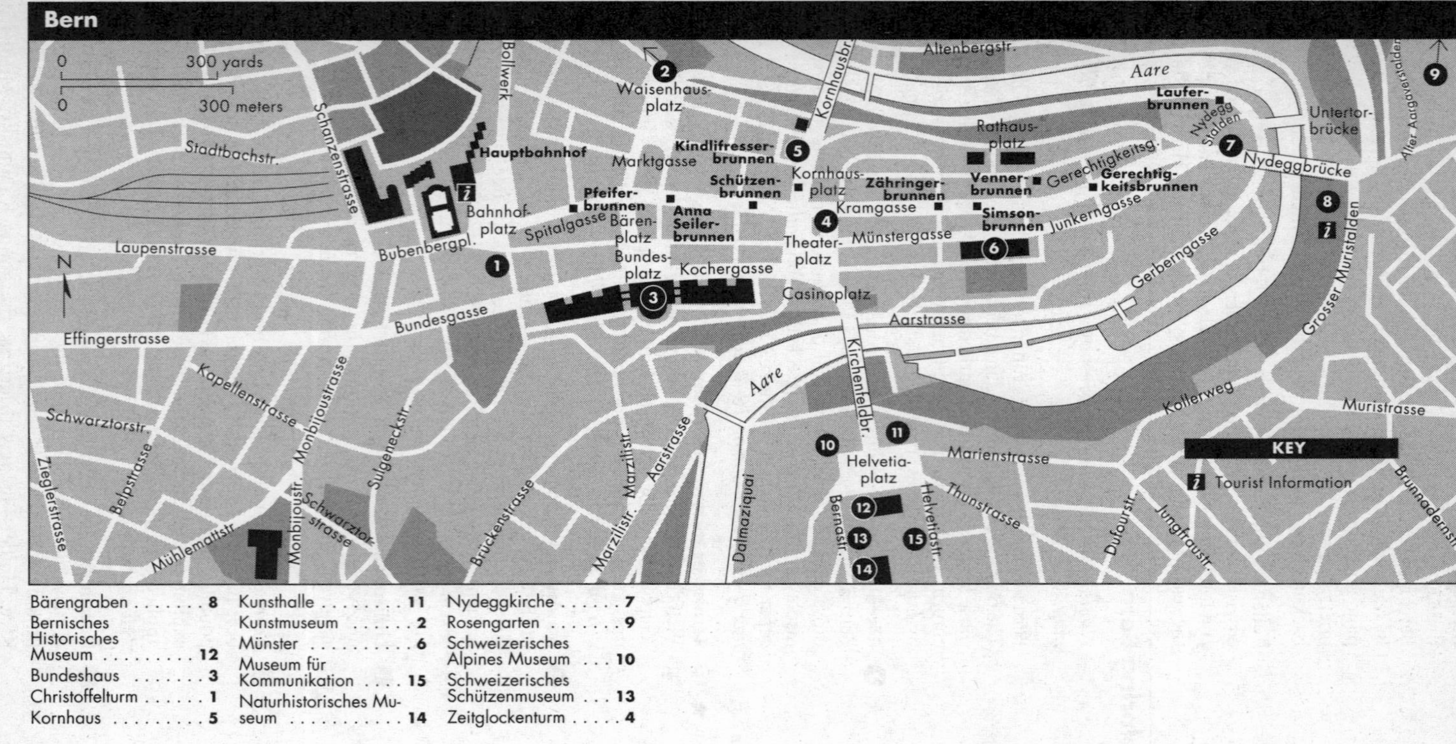

Bärengraben 8
Bernisches Historisches Museum 12
Bundeshaus 3
Christoffelturm 1
Kornhaus 5
Kunsthalle 11
Kunstmuseum 2
Münster 6
Museum für Kommunikation 15
Naturhistorisches Museum 14
Nydeggkirche 7
Rosengarten 9
Schweizerisches Alpines Museum . . . 10
Schweizerisches Schützenmuseum . . . 13
Zeitglockenturm 4

★ ❷ **Kunstmuseum** (Art Museum). Established for the promotion of Swiss artists, this landmark art museum houses an exceptional group of works by Ferdinand Hodler, including some enormous allegories. Fans of Paul Klee have hit the jackpot: the world's largest collection of his work, with more than 2,000 pieces. There is also an impressive collection of Old Masters and Impressionists and a constant turnover of temporary exhibitions. ✉ *Hodlerstr. 8–12,* ☎ *031/3280944,* WEB *www.kunstmuseumbern.ch.* ⏲ *Tues. 10–9, Wed.–Sun. 10–5.*

★ ❻ **Münster** (Cathedral). Begun in 1421, Bern's famous cathedral was planned on lines so spacious that half the population could worship in it at one time; its construction went on for centuries. It has an outstanding painted portal (1490) depicting the Last Judgment, and stunning stained-glass windows, both originals and period reproductions. The steeple, added in 1893, is the tallest in Switzerland. ✉ *Münsterpl. 1,* ☎ *031/3120462.* ⏲ *Easter–Oct., Tues.–Sat. 10–5, Sun. 11:30–5; Nov.–Easter, Tues.–Fri. 10–noon and 2–4, Sat. 10–noon and 2–5, Sun. 11:30–2.*

⓯ **Museum für Kommunikation** (Museum of Communication). This museum dedicated to communication—from signaling by bonfire through the transmission of complex digital information—features interactive exhibits, artifacts related to the history of the post and telecommunications, and the world's largest public display of stamps. ✉ *Helvetiastr. 16,* ☎ *031/3575555,* WEB *www.mfk.ch.* ⏲ *Tues.–Sun. 10–5.*

★ ⓮ **Naturhistorisches Museum** (Museum of Natural History). This slick and spacious natural history museum, considered one of Europe's finest, features enormous wildlife dioramas, exhibits on master builders, and a splendid collection of Alpine minerals. ✉ *Bernastr. 15,* ☎ *031/3507111.* ⏲ *Mon. 2–5, Tues. and Thurs.–Fri. 9–5, Wed. 9–6, weekends 10–5.*

❼ **Nydeggkirche** (Nydegg Church). Built between 1341 and 1571 on the foundations of Berchtold V's ruined fortress, this ancient church marks the founding place of Bern. ✉ *Nydegg.* ⏲ *Mon.–Sat. 10–noon and 2–5:30, Sun. 10–noon.*

❾ **Rosengarten** (Rose Garden). This splendidly maintained garden features a riot of color from April to October, with 27 types of rhododendrons, 200 roses, and 200 irises. There's also a panoramic view of the bridges, roofs, and major buildings of downtown Bern. ✉ *Alter Aargauerstalden/Laubeggstr..* ⏲ *Daily sunrise–sunset.*

❿ **Schweizerisches Alpines Museum** (Swiss Alpine Museum). This museum of the Alps, known for its topographical maps and reliefs, also covers the histories of mountain climbing and life in the mountains. There are fine old photos and a magnificent Hodler mural of the tragic conquest of the Matterhorn. ✉ *Helvetiapl. 4,* ☎ *031/3510434,* WEB *www.alpinesmuseum.ch.* ⏲ *Mon. 2–5, Tues.–Sun. 10–5; closed noon–2 in winter.*

⓭ **Schweizerisches Schützenmuseum** (Swiss Rifle Museum). This unusual (but very Swiss) cultural center traces the development of firearms since 1817 and celebrates Swiss marksmanship beyond the apple-splitting accuracy of William Tell. ✉ *Bernastr. 5,* ☎ *031/3510127,* WEB *www.schuetzenmuseum.ch.* ⏲ *Tues.–Sat. 2–4, Sun. 10–noon and 2–4.*

★ ❹ **Zeitglockenturm** (Clock Tower). This mighty landmark, Bern's oldest building, was built as a city gate in 1191 but transformed by the addition of an astronomical clock on its east side in 1530. At five minutes before the hour, every hour, a delightful group of mechanical figures parades out of the clock. ✉ *Kramg. between Theaterpl. and Kornhauspl.*

Dining and Lodging

Although Bern teeters between two cultures politically, Teutonic conquers Gallic when it comes to cuisine. Dining here is usually a down-to-earth affair, with Italian home cooking a popular alternative to meat and potatoes. Specialties include the famous *Bernerplatte* (sauerkraut with boiled beef, fatty pork, sausages, ham, and tongue), normally served in heaping portions, and the Berner version of *Ratsherrtopf* traditionally enjoyed by the town councillors: veal shank cooked in white wine, butter, and sage.

There's no shortage of hotels in Bern, and those not located in the Old Town are a pleasant walk or a short tram or bus ride away.

$$$$ ★ ✕ **Bellevue-Grill.** When Parliament is in session, this haute-cuisine landmark turns into a political clubhouse. The menu leans to luxury; unusual dishes might include beef fillet with truffle pasta or roast breast of duck with a hint of coffee in the sauce. ✉ *Kocherg. 3–5,* ☎ *031/3204545. Reservations essential. AE, DC, MC, V.*

$$$$ ★ ✕ **Schultheissenstube.** The intimate, rustic dining room of the Schweizerhof hotel may look less like a gastronomic haven than a country pub, but this is formal dining at its best. The cooking is sophisticated, international, and imaginative, such as salmon fillet with a coulis of tomato and black truffles. ✉ *Bahnhofpl. 11,* ☎ *031/3268080. Reservations essential. Jacket and tie. AE, DC, MC, V. Closed Sun..*

$$$–$$$$ ✕ **Eurasia.** More than 300 European and Asian dishes (among them Japanese, Chinese, Thai, and Mongolian specialties) are offered over the course of a year in this intimate restaurant with a panoramic view of Bern and the Alps. ✉ *Hotel Allegro, Kornhausstr. 3,* ☎ *031/3395500. AE, DC, MC, V. Closed Sun.–Mon.*

$$$–$$$$ ★ ✕ **Kornhauskeller.** Entering the Kornhauskeller is like entering a cathedral, except that that spectacular vaulted ceilings and frescoes are all underground. Now a restaurant serving classic Mediterranean cuisine, this historic building was at various times a granary, a post office, and a beer hall. ✉ *Kornhauspl. 18,* ☎ *031/3277272. AE, DC, MC, V.*

$$$–$$$$ ★ ✕ **Zimmermania.** This deceptively simple bistro has been in business for more than 150 years and is a local favorite for authentic French bourgeois cooking. Try the cheese soufflé or veal kidneys in mustard sauce, and be sure to ask for the separate, special French wine list. ✉ *Brunng. 19,* ☎ *031/3111542. AE, MC, V. Closed Sun.–Mon.*

$$–$$$ ★ ✕ **Della Casa.** Affectionately nicknamed "Delli," this unadorned favorite has been serving locals for more than a century in its rowdy, yellowed Stübli and wood-paneled upstairs rooms. It's an unofficial Parliament headquarters, with generous local and Italian specialties—a good place to try the Bernerplatte. ✉ *Schauplatzg. 16,* ☎ *031/3112142. AE, DC, MC, V. Closed Sun. No dinner Sat.*

$$–$$$ ★ ✕ **Gartenrestaurant Marzilibrücke.** Down by the Aare in the quarter known as Marzili you'll find this small, relaxed restaurant where jazz plays in the background and the menu contains something for everyone. Choices range from pumpkin soup to green chicken curry to chestnut mousse with plum compote. In the summer you can eat pizza in the garden behind the house. ✉ *Gasstr. 8,* ☎ *031/3112780. AE, MC, V.*

$$–$$$ ★ ✕ **Lorenzini.** Members of the Swiss parliament meet here monthly for traditional Italian specialties and homemade pastas and desserts. Changing menus represent the specialties of different Italian regions. The café-bar downstairs draws the young and chic. ✉ *Theaterpl. 5/Hotelg. 8,* ☎ *031/3117850. AE, DC, MC, V. Closed Sun.*

$–$$ ✕ **Menuetto.** This refreshing vegetarian oasis serves sophisticated, imaginative cooking. Try *Rouladen* (roulades) of spinach and feta with tamari-sweetened beer sauce. ✉ *Münsterg. 47/Herreng. 22 (2 entrances),* ☎ *031/3111448. AE, DC, MC, V. Closed Sun. and holidays.*

$$$$ ★ 🏨 **Schweizerhof.** Intimate and sophisticated, this landmark steeps in luxury. Lush greens and golds dominate the spacious rooms; original pieces of art add an individual touch. Warm, professional service makes it a pleasure to stay here. ✉ *Bahnhofpl. 11, CH-3001,* ☎ *031/3268080,* FAX *031/3268090,* WEB *www.schweizerhof-bern.ch. 70 rooms, 14 suites. 2 restaurants. AE, DC, MC, V.*

$$$ 🏨 **Allegro.** This cutting-edge hotel offers data ports and a fax in every room. Furnishings range from soothing ("Trend" rooms with original lithographs by local artist Teruko Yokoi) to snappy (red or green "Event" rooms with prints by Warhol and Hopper). "Panorama" rooms have a view of the Alps on clear days. ✉ *Kornhausstr. 3, CH-3000,* ☎ *031/3395500,* FAX *031/3395510,* WEB *www.allegro-hotel.ch. 161 rooms, 2 junior suites. 3 restaurants, 2 bars. AE, DC, MC, V.*

$$$ ★ 🏨 **Belle Epoque.** This novel hotel is more suggestive of fin-de-siècle Paris than you might expect in Germanic Bern: every inch of the arcaded row house is filled with authentic Art Nouveau antiques. Despite the historic look, amenities, including white-tile baths, are up-to-date. ✉ *Gerechtigkeitsg. 18, CH-3011,* ☎ *031/3114336,* FAX *031/3113936,* WEB *www.belle-epoque.ch. 15 rooms, 2 suites. AE, DC, MC, V.*

$$$ 🏨 **Innere Enge.** Eighteenth-century origins and Jugendstil updates are discreetly discernible in this quiet hotel in a pleasant area outside the city center. Guest rooms are spacious, light, and airy thanks to generous windows that face the Bernese Alps. Downstairs, Marian's Jazzroom features top jazz acts. Take Bus 21 (direction Bremgarten) from the train station to the Innere Enge stop. ✉ *Engestr. 54, CH-3012,* ☎ *031/3096111,* FAX *031/3096112,* WEB *www.zghotels.ch. 11 rooms, 15 suites. Restaurant, bar. AE, DC, MC, V.*

$$–$$$ 🏨 **Bern/Continental.** There's a feeling of energy in the lobby of the sleek, modern Hotel Bern. A few doors down is the Bern's less expensive sister lodging, the Continental, which offers quiet cozy rooms. Guests at both hotels receive a discount at the Bern's two restaurants. ✉ *Bern: Zeughausg. 9, CH-3011,* ☎ *031/3292222,* FAX *031/3292299. 97 rooms, 1 suite. 2 restaurants. Continental: Zeughausg. 27, CH-3011,* ☎ *031/3292121,* FAX *031/3292199. 40 rooms. Both hotels: AE, DC, MC, V.* WEB *www.hotelbern.ch*

$$ ★ 🏨 **Zum Goldenen Adler.** From the outside, this 1764 building looks like a patrician town house, but its interior is modern and modest, with linoleum baths and severe Formica furniture. The ambience is comfortable and familial nonetheless; it's been in the same family for 100 years. ✉ *Gerechtigkeitsg. 7, CH-3011,* ☎ *031/3111725,* FAX *031/3113761. 16 rooms. Restaurant. AE, DC, MC, V.*

$–$$ 🏨 **Bern Backpackers Hotel Glocke.** The top two floors of this centrally located hotel contain simple but pleasing single, double, and triple rooms with peach walls, crisp white linens, and a view of the roofs of the Altstadt. On the lower floors are dormitories, a common room, and a shared kitchen. No breakfast. ✉ *Rathausg. 75, CH-3011,* ☎ *031/3113771,* FAX *031/3111008,* WEB *www.chilisbackpackers.com. 24 rooms (2 triples, 4 doubles, 6 singles, 12 dorms), 3 with own bath. MC, V.*

$–$$ ★ 🏨 **Landhaus.** Just across the river from the Old Town, this simple, clean, and bright hotel-hostel offers everything from a dorm-style cubicle to a double room with shower. Cook for yourself in the community kitchen, or dine at the hotel's trendy (and popular) restaurant. ✉ *Altenbergstr. 4/6, CH-3013,* ☎ *031/3314166,* FAX *031/3326904,* WEB *www.landhausbern.ch. 6 double rooms, 2 dormitories. Restaurant, 2 bars. AE, DC, MC, V.*

Nightlife and the Arts

Bern Aktuell, published every two weeks, lists special events, concerts, entertainment, museum exhibits, and a variety of telephone numbers. Portions of the text are in English. The booklet is free from Bern Tourismus and hotels.

Be forewarned: dance clubs often also have a separate "cabaret," but don't expect Liza Minnelli; it's normally a strip joint.

The Arts

The **Bern Symphony Orchestra** (☎ 031/3114242 tickets) is the city's most notable musical institution. Concerts are held at the Casino (✉ Casinopl.) or the Münster. A five-day **International Jazz Festival** takes place in early May, with tickets available through TicketCorner, at the UBS bank (✉ Bärenpl. 8, ☎ 031/3362539).

A variety of theatrical, dance, and opera performances take place at the **Stadttheater** (✉ Kornhauspl. 20, ☎ 031/3295151); tickets are sold next door (✉ Kornhauspl. 18) weekdays 10–6:30, Saturday 10–4.

Nightlife

BARS AND LOUNGES

In the little hotel **Belle Epoque** (✉ Gerechtigkeitsg. 18, ☎ 031/3114336) there's a lovely small bar where you can drink surrounded by Art Nouveau treasures. For history, head for **Klötzlikeller** (✉ Gerechtigkeitsg. 62), said to be the oldest wine bar in Bern. The **Kornhaus Café** (✉ Kornhauspl. 18, ☎ 031/3277270), serving 14 kinds of coffee, pastries, and light meals, is relaxed enough for families during the day and draws a trendy crowd at night.

DANCING

Quality Dance in InSide in the Kursaal (✉ Kornhausstr. 3, ☎ 031/3395148) has dancing on Friday and Saturday nights and on Sunday afternoons. One of the biggest and hottest spots in town is **Toni's the Club** (✉ Aarbergerg. 35, ☎ 031/3115011), with two bars and two dance floors.

Bern Essentials

AIRPORTS AND TRANSFERS

Bern's small airport, 9 km (5½ mi) south of the city in Belp, has flights to and from most European capitals. A convenient shuttle bus running between the airport and the train station costs 14 SF, a taxi about 35 SF.

➤ AIRPORT INFORMATION: **Bern-Belp Airport** (☎ 031/9602111).

BUS TRAVEL WITHIN BERN

The bus and tram service in Bern is excellent; fares range from 1.50 SF to 2.40 SF. Buy individual tickets from the dispenser at the tram or bus stop. Visitor cards for unlimited rides are available for 6 SF a day at the tourist office in the Hauptbahnhof or at the public-transportation ticket office on Bankgässchen (from the train station follow signs for Bus 13). A Swiss Pass allows you to travel free.

CAR TRAVEL

Bern is connected conveniently by expressway to Basel and Zürich via A1, to the Berner Oberland via A6, and to Lac Léman and thus Lausanne, Geneva, and the Valais via A12.

EMERGENCIES

➤ DOCTORS AND DENTISTS: **Emergency medical, dental and pharmacy referrals** (☎ 0900/576747).

➤ EMERGENCY SERVICES: **Ambulance** (☎ 144). **Police** (☎ 117).

TAXIS

This inconvenient alternative to walking or public transportation costs around 18 SF just to travel from the train station to the end of Old Town.

TOURS

BUS TOURS

A two-hour multilingual bus tour covering Bern's principal sights is offered by the tourist office for 24 SF.

WALKING TOURS

From June 1 to September 30 a multilingual 1½-hour tour of the principal sites in the Old Town is offered daily at 11 AM and costs 14 SF. Contact the tourist office.

TRAIN TRAVEL

Bern is a major link between Geneva, Zürich, and Basel, and Intercity trains, which make the fewest stops, leave almost every hour from the Hauptbahnhof. Bern is the only European capital to have three high-speed trains: the ICE from Berlin takes nine hours; the TGV from Paris takes 4½ hours, and the Pendolino from Milan takes 3–4 hours.

➤ TRAIN INFORMATION: **Hauptbahnhof** (☎ 0900/300300, costs 1.19 SF per min.).

VISITOR INFORMATION

The Bern Tourismus location at the Bear Pits offers a multimedia history of Bern.

➤ TOURIST INFORMATION: **Bern Tourismus** (✉ Hauptbahnhof, Bahnhofpl., ☎ 031/3281212, WEB www.bernetourism.ch).

ZERMATT

The ultimate Swiss-Alpine experience is bundled in one tidily wrapped package in Zermatt (5,300 ft): spectacular mountains, a roaring stream, a state-of-the-art transport network, and a broad range of high-quality accommodations—some of them rich in rusticity—plus 230 km (143 mi) of downhill runs and 7 km (4 mi) of cross-country trails. But its ★ greatest claim to fame remains the **Matterhorn** (14,690 ft), which attracts swarms of package-tour sightseers pushing shoulder to shoulder to get yet another shot of this genuine wonder of the Western world.

Exploring Zermatt

Zermatt lies in a hollow of meadows and trees ringed by mountains—among them the broad **Monte Rosa** (14,940 ft), with its tallest peak, the **Dufourspitze** (at 15,200 ft the highest point in Switzerland), of which visitors hear relatively little, so all-consuming is the cult of the Matterhorn. Walking down the main street, Bahnhofstrasse, you'll be deluged by Matterhorn images: on postcards, on beer steins, on candy wrappers. Yet the Matterhorn deserves idolatry: though it has become an almost self-parodying icon, like the Eiffel Tower or the Statue of Liberty, this distinctive, snaggletoothed pyramid thrusting upward in solitary splendor is even more impressive than the photographs suggest.

Despite its celebrity mountain, Zermatt remains a resort with its feet on the ground. It is as protective of its regional quirks as it is of its wildlife and its tumbledown *mazots* (grain-storage sheds raised on stone bases to keep the mice away), which hunker between the glass-and-concrete chalets like old tenements trapped between skyscrapers. Car-free streets twist past weathered wood walls and flower boxes until they break into open country that inevitably slopes uphill.

The cog railway between Visp and Zermatt began disgorging summer tourists in 1891, but it was not until 1927 that it also plowed through in wintertime. What had drawn the first tourists and made Zermatt a household word was Edward Whymper's spectacular—and catastrophic—conquest of the Matterhorn in 1865. Whymper and his band of six managed to reach the summit, but then tragedy struck. On the treacherous descent, four of the men lost their footing and snapped their safety rope, pulling each other 4,000 ft to their death. One of the bodies was never recovered, but the others remain in the grim little cemetery behind the church in the village center.

To experience the exhilaration of standing on top of the world without risking life or limb, you can take the trip up the **Gornergrat** on the *Gornergratbahn,* which does double duty as ski transport and a sightseeing excursion. Completed in 1898 and the highest exposed rail system in Europe, it connects out of the main Zermatt station and climbs slowly up the valley to the **Riffelberg,** which at 8,471 ft offers wide-open views of the Matterhorn. From **Rotenboden,** at 9,248 ft, a short downhill walk leads to the **Riffelsee,** with its pristine reflections of the famous peak. At the end of the 9-km (5½-mi) line, passengers pour onto the observation terraces of the Gornergrat (10,269 ft) to take in majestic views of Gorner glacier, the Matterhorn, Monte Rosa, and scores of other peaks. Be sure to bring warm clothes and sturdy shoes. ✉ *Leaves from Zermatt Station.* 🎫 *63 SF round-trip; 38 SF one-way up and ski or hike down.* ⏲ *Departures every 24 mins 7* AM*–6* PM*.*

Skiing

Zermatt's skiable terrain lives up to its reputation: it is said to guarantee skiers 7,216 ft of vertical drop no matter what the snowfall—an impressive claim. This royal plateau has several less-than-perfect features, however, not least of which is the separation of the skiable territory into three sectors. **Sunegga-Blauherd-Rothorn** culminates at an elevation of 10,170 ft. **Gornergrat-Stockhorn** (11,155 ft) is the second. The third is the region dominated by the **Klein Matterhorn**; to go from this sector to the others you must return to the bottom of the valley and lose considerable time crossing town to reach the lifts to the other elevations. The solution is to ski for a whole day in the same area, especially during high season (mid-December to the end of February, or even until Easter if the snow cover is good). A **ski school** (Skischulbüro; ☎ 027/9662466) runs during the high season. A one-day lift ticket costs 63 SF; a seven-day pass costs 324 SF.

Dining and Lodging

Perched at the German end of the equally French canton of Valais, Zermatt offers a variety of French and German cooking, from veal and Rösti to raclette and fondue. Specialties often feature pungent mountain cheese: *Käseschnitte,* for instance, are substantial little casseroles of bread, cheese, and often ham, baked until the whey saturates the crusty bread and the cheese browns to gold. Air-dried beef is another Valais treat; it's served in thin, translucent slices, with gherkins and crisp pickled onions. Alas, McDonald's has infiltrated this once-isolated retreat, and you now have to climb or ski to find memorable, cut-above dining outside the hotels—which do offer considerable variety.

At high season—Christmas and New Year's, Carnaval to Easter, and late summer—Zermatt's high hotel prices rival those of Zürich and Geneva. But read the fine print carefully when you plan your visit: most hotels include half pension in their price, serving breakfast and your choice of a noon or evening meal. Hotels that call themselves "garni" do not have a full kitchen and serve only breakfast and sometimes light snacks.

Since Zermatt is for the most part a one-street town, street addresses are rarely used. However, hotels are signposted throughout the town.

$$–$$$ ✕ **Grill-Room Stockhorn.** The tantalizing aromas of pungent cheese and roasting meat on the open grill should sharpen your hunger the moment you step inside this low-slung restaurant. This is a great place to fortify yourself with regional dishes; the service and the clientele are equally lively. ☎ *027/9671747. AE, MC, V. Closed mid-May–mid-June and Oct.*

$$–$$$ ★ ✕ **Zum See.** Beyond Findeln, in a tiny village by the same name, Zum See has become something of an institution, serving light meals of a quality and level of inventiveness that would merit acclaim even if the restaurant weren't in the middle of nowhere at 5,794 ft. Regional specialties include wild mushrooms in pastry shells, rabbit, Rösti, and *foie de veau* (calve's liver). ✉ *Zum See,* ☎ *027/9672045. MC, V. Closed Apr.–June and Oct.–mid-Dec.*

$–$$ ★ ✕ **Findlerhof.** This mountain restaurant in tiny Findeln is perched high between the Sunnegga and Blauherd ski areas. The Matterhorn views from the wraparound dining porch are astonishing, the food surprisingly fresh and creative. Franz and Heidi Schwery tend their own Alpine garden to provide spinach for the crisped-bacon salad, and rhubarb and berries for their hot desserts. It's about 30 minutes' walk down from the Sunnegga Express stop, and another 30 minutes back down to Zermatt. ✉ *Findeln,* ☎ *027/9672588. MC. Closed May–mid-June and mid-Oct.–Nov.*

$$$$ ★ ✕🏨 **Monte Rosa.** This was the first inn in Zermatt and the home base of Edward Whymper when he conquered the Matterhorn in 1865. Behind its graceful shuttered facade you will find flagstone floors, brass, stained and beveled glass, honey-gold pine, fireplaces, and an elaborate, fully restored Victorian dining hall. Dinner is a five-course candlelight affair that could have been styled for a Merchant Ivory film. The bar is an après-ski must. Guests have access to the sports facilities at Mont Cervin, and all Seiler restaurants on the members' "Dine-Around" plan. ✉ *CH-3920,* ☎ *027/9663333,* FAX *027/9671160. 44 rooms, 5 suites. Restaurant. AE, DC, MC, V.*

$$$$ ★ ✕🏨 **Zermatterhof.** If you can afford no-limits luxury, then this faultless hotel has a lot to offer. Rooms in multifarious shades and styles of wood have either granite or marble bathrooms where you can lie back and nibble a Matterhorn-shape chocolate while soaking in a whirlpool bath. There's also an indoor pool, health club, and sauna. The formal hotel restaurant serves ambitious French cuisine; in La Broche you can enjoy regional food such as smoked lamb and Walliser cheese. ✉ *CH-3920,* ☎ *027/9666600,* FAX *027/9666699. 60 rooms, 26 suites. 2 restaurants, pool. AE, DC, MC, V.*

$$$–$$$$ ★ ✕🏨 **Julen.** This hotel has shunned the usual regional kitsch in favor of a century-old spruce-wood decor coupled with primary-color carpets and silk curtains. A three-floor sports center includes an elaborate Roman bath room. Besides a restaurant serving international cuisine, there's a welcoming Stübli with unusual lamb dishes (such as lamb's tongue in capers) made from local family-owned flocks. ✉ *CH-3920,* ☎ *027/9667600,* FAX *027/9667676. 27 rooms, 5 suites. 2 restaurants, pool. AE, DC, MC, V.*

$$$$ ★ 🏨 **Mont Cervin Hotel and Residences.** One of the flagships of the Seiler dynasty, this is a sleek, luxurious, and urbane mountain hotel. Built in 1852, it's unusually low slung for a grand hotel, with dark beams and classic decor; a few rooms are full of rustic stucco and carved blond wood. The restaurant is light in decor and tone—a jacket and tie are required only for the Friday gala buffet. Luxurious apartments across the street are accessible through a handy tunnel. ✉ *CH-3920,* ☎ *027/*

9668888, FAX *027/9672878. 100 rooms, 15 suites, 24 apartments. 2 restaurants, pool. AE, DC, MC, V. Closed May–mid-June and mid-Oct.–Nov.*

$$ ☐ **Le Pétit Hôtel.** What this pie-shaped inn lacks in fancy facilities, it makes up in character. Rooms are unfussy and compact. The restaurant is panelled with golden wood and has a stenciled ceiling. It dishes out heart-warming comfort food; your server will likely know you by name after the first order. ✉ *CH-3920,* ☎ *027/9664266,* FAX *027/9664265. 20 rooms. Restaurant, bar. AE, MC, V.*

$$ ☐ **Mischabel.** One of the least, if not *the* least, expensive hotels in this pricey resort town, the Mischabel provides comfort, atmosphere, and a central situation few places can match at twice the price: southern balconies frame a perfect Matterhorn view—the higher the better. Creaky, homey, and covered with *Arvenholz* (Alpen pine) aged to the color of toffee, its rooms have sinks only and share the linoleum-lined showers on every floor. A generous daily menu, for guests only, caters to families and young skiers on the cheap. ✉ *CH-3920,* ☎ *027/9671131,* FAX *027/9676507. 28 rooms. Restaurant. MC, V.*

$$ ☐ **Romantica.** Among the scores of anonymously modern hotels cloned all over the Zermatt plain, this modest structure—unremarkable at first glance—has an exceptional location directly above the town center. Its tidy, bright gardens and flower boxes, its game trophies, and its old-style granite stove give it personality, and the plain rooms benefit from big windows and balconies. You can also stay in one of the two *Walliserstadel,* 200-year-old, tiny (but charming) huts in the hotel's garden. Views take in the mountains, though not the Matterhorn, over a graceful clutter of stone roofs. ✉ *CH-3920,* ☎ *027/9662650,* FAX *027/9662655. 13 rooms. AE, DC, MC, V.*

Nightlife

If you can find a space, squeeze into **Elsie's Place** (☎ 027/9672431), a rustic hut across from the church, for an aged scotch or double martini. **GramPi's Bar** (☎ 027/9677788), on the main drag, is a lively, young bar where you can get into the mood for dancing downstairs with a Lady Matterhorn cocktail. **T-Bar** (☎ 027/9674000), below the Pollux hotel, plays more varied music than the generic disco of most ski resort nightspots.

Zermatt Essentials

AIR TRAVEL

The airports of Zürich and Geneva are roughly equidistant from the nearby town of Brig, which is well-connected by train, but by approaching from Geneva you can avoid crossing mountain passes.

CAR TRAVEL

Zermatt is a car-free resort isolated at the end of the Mattertal, a rugged valley at the eastern end of the Alpine canton of Valais. A good mountain highway cuts south through the Mattertal valley from Visp, the crossroads of the main Valais east–west routes. You can drive up the valley as far as Täsch, but there you must abandon your car in a parking lot and catch the train for the cogwheel climb into Zermatt.

EMERGENCIES

➤ EMERGENCY SERVICES: **Ambulance** (☎ 144). **Police** (☎ 117).

TRAIN TRAVEL

The Brig-Visp-Zermatt Railway, a private narrow-gauge system, runs from Brig to Visp, connecting on to Zermatt. All major rail routes connect through Brig, whether you approach from Geneva or Lausanne in the west, from the Lötschberg line that tunnels through from Kandersteg and the Bernese Oberland, or from the connecting Simplon Pass from Italy.

TRANSPORTATION AROUND ZERMATT

Because Zermatt permits no private cars, electric taxi shuttles operated by hotels are the only means of transportation. The village is relatively small and easily covered on foot. Hiking and skiing are Zermatt's raisons d'être, but you can get a head start into the heights by riding part of the sophisticated network of cable cars, lifts, cog railways, and even an underground metro that carries you above the village center into the wilderness. Excursions to the Klein Matterhorn and Gornergrat are particularly spectacular.

VISITOR INFORMATION

➤ TOURIST INFORMATION: **Verkehrsbüro Zermatt** (✉ Bahnhofpl., CH-3920, ☎ 027/9670181).

31 TURKEY

ISTANBUL, THE AEGEAN COAST, THE MEDITERRANEAN COAST, CENTRAL ANATOLIA, AND CAPPADOCIA

TURKEY IS ONE PLACE to which the phrase "East meets West" really applies. It is in Turkey's largest city, Istanbul, that the continents of Europe and Asia come together, separated only by the Bosporus, which flows 29 km (18 mi) from the Black Sea to the Sea of Marmara. On the vibrant streets of this city of 12 million people, miniskirts and trendy boots mingle with head scarves and prayer beads.

Although 97% of Turkey's landmass is in Asia, Turkey began facing west politically in 1923, when Mustapha Kemal, better known as Atatürk, founded the modern republic. He transformed the remnants of the shattered Ottoman Empire into a secular state with a Western outlook. So thorough was this changeover—culturally, politically, and economically—that in 1987, 49 years after Atatürk's death, Turkey applied to the European Union (EU) for full membership and in December 1999 was finally listed as an official candidate. However, its prospects look dim until Turkey's government implements reforms toward greater democratization as requested by the EU. Full membership is also likely to depend on the resolution of a number of long-standing problems, including 15 years of rampant inflation, social polarization over the role of Islam in public life, and the recognition of minority rights.

For 16 centuries Istanbul, originally known as Byzantium, played a major part in world politics: first as the capital of the Eastern Roman Empire, when it was known as Constantinople, then as capital of the Ottoman Empire, the most powerful Islamic empire in the world, when it was renamed Istanbul. Atatürk moved the capital to Ankara at the inception of the Turkish Republic.

The legacies of the Greeks, Romans, Ottomans, and numerous other civilizations have made the country a vast outdoor museum. The most spectacular of the reconstructed classical sites are along the western Aegean coast and the southwest Mediterranean coast, which are lined with magnificent sandy beaches and sleepy little fishing villages, as well as busy resorts with sophisticated facilities for travelers.

If you have an extra five to seven days, an excursion inland to central Anatolia and the eroded lunar valleys of the Cappadocia area will give you a glimpse at some of the enormous diversity of the landscapes and people of Turkey.

TURKEY A TO Z

To research prices, get advice from other travelers, and book travel arrangements, visit www.fodors.com.

AIR TRAVEL

CARRIERS

Turkish Airlines operates an extensive domestic network. There are at least 14 flights daily on weekdays between Istanbul and Ankara, as well as less-frequent flights to other major cities. In summer additional flights between the cities and coastal resorts are added.

➤ AIRLINES AND CONTACTS: **Turkish Airlines** (THY; ✉ Taksim Sq., Istanbul, ☎ 212/252–1106; 212/663–6363 reservations).

CHECK IN AND BOARDING

Try to arrive at the airport at least 45 minutes before your flight, because security checks, which are rigidly enforced, can be time-consuming. Checked luggage is placed on trolleys on the tarmac and must be identified by boarding passengers before it is put on the plane. Unidentified luggage is left behind and checked for bombs or firearms.

BOAT AND FERRY TRAVEL

A car ferry and cruise service is operated out of Istanbul by Turkish Maritime Lines. Cruises are in great demand, so make your reservations well in advance through the main office in Istanbul. The Black Sea Ferry sails from May through September from Istanbul to Samsun and Trabzon and back, from Karaköy Dock in Istanbul. One-way fares to Trabzon are about $25 for a reclining seat, $50–$80 for cabins, and $85 for cars. The Istanbul-to-İzmir car ferry departs once a week. The price of a one-way ticket with meals included varies between $50 and $80, plus $50 for a car.

➤ BOAT AND FERRY INFORMATION: **Turkish Maritime Lines** (✉ Rıhtım Cad. 1, Karaköy, ☎ 212/249–9222 or 212/293–7454).

BUS TRAVEL

Buses, which are run by private companies, are much faster than trains and provide excellent, inexpensive service. Buses are available, almost around the clock, between all cities and towns. They are fairly comfortable and many are air-conditioned. Companies have their own fixed fares for different routes. Istanbul to Ankara, for instance, varies from $10 to $15; Istanbul to İzmir varies from $12 to $18. *Şişe suyu* (bottled water) is included in the fare. You can purchase tickets at stands in a town's *otogar* (central bus terminal) or at branch offices in city centers. All seats are reserved. There are small variations in fares among the different companies, but it is usually worth paying the 3%–5% extra for companies such as Varan, Ulusoy, and Kamil Koç, which offer no-smoking seating. Many buses between major cities are double-deckers and all of those operated by the larger companies have toilets. For very short trips or getting around within a city, use minibuses or a *dolmuş* (shared taxi). Both are inexpensive and comfortable.

BUSINESS HOURS

BANKS AND OFFICES

Banks are generally open weekdays 8:30 or 9–12:30 and 1:30–5, although increasingly banks are remaining open at lunchtime. Foreign exchange bureaus normally remain open from 9:30 or 10 AM to 6 PM.

MUSEUMS AND SIGHTS

Museums are generally open Tuesday–Sunday 9:30–4:30. Palaces are open Friday–Wednesday 9:30–4:30. Mosques are usually open to the

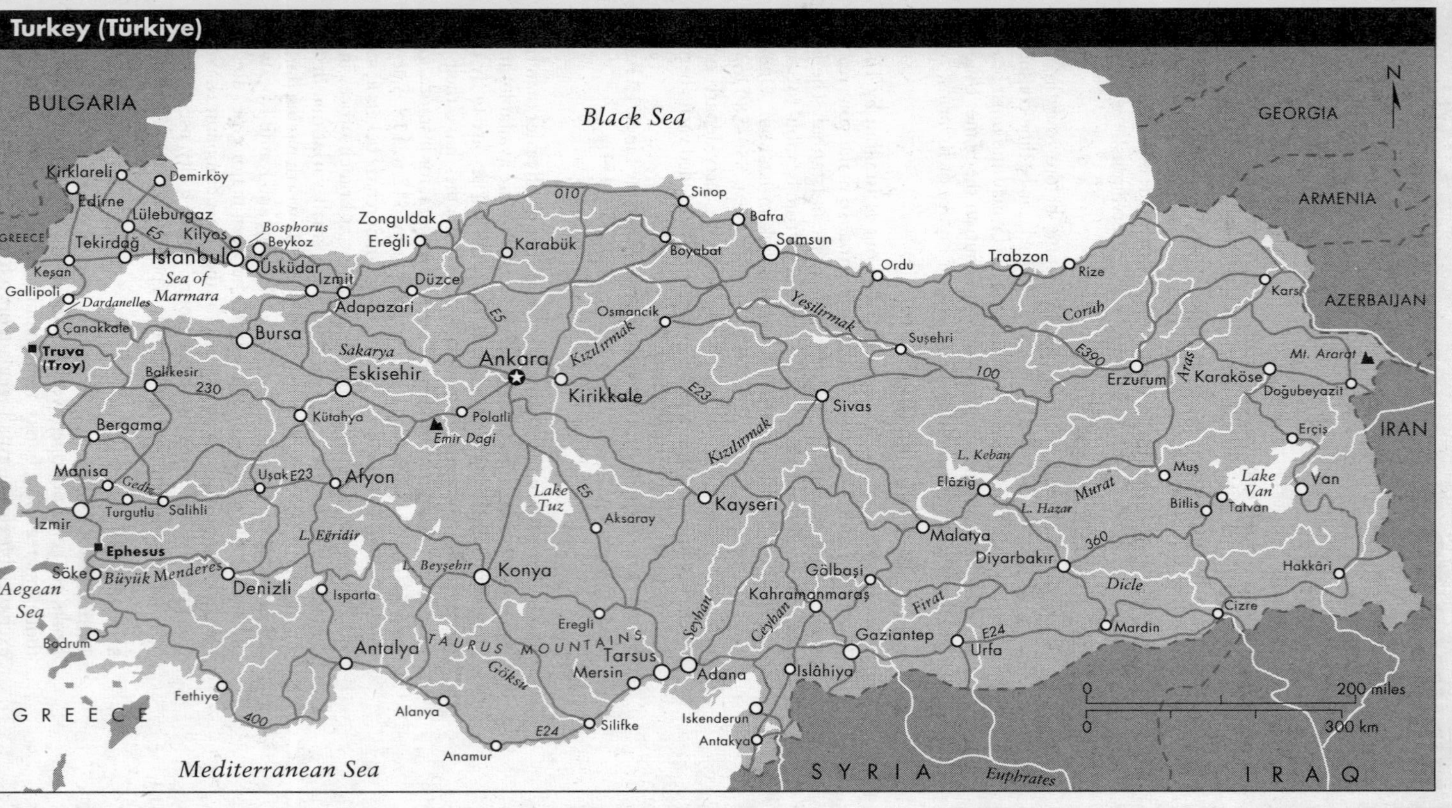
Turkey (Türkiye)
BULGARIA
GEORGIA
ARMENIA
AZERBAIJAN
IRAN
IRAQ
SYRIA
GREECE
Black Sea
Mediterranean Sea
Aegean Sea
Sea of Marmara
Bosphorus
Dardanelles
Lake Van
Lake Tuz
TAURUS MOUNTAINS
Mt. Ararat
Emir Dagi
Istanbul
Ankara
Üsküdar
Kilyos
Beykoz
Izmit
Adapazari
Zonguldak
Eregli
Düzce
Karabük
Bursa
Eskisehir
Kütahya
Afyon
Izmir
Manisa
Bergama
Balikesir
Canakkale
Truva (Troy)
Gallipoli
Kesan
Tekirdag
Edirne
Kirklareli
Lüleburgaz
Demirköy
Ephesus
Söke
Bodrum
Turgutlu
Salihli
Usak
Denizli
Fethiye
Antalya
Isparta
Alanya
Anamur
Konya
Eregli
Aksaray
Mersin
Tarsus
Adana
Silifke
Iskenderun
Antakya
Kayseri
Kirikkale
Polatli
Osmancik
Boyabat
Sinop
Bafra
Samsun
Ordu
Sivas
Susehri
Trabzon
Rize
Erzurum
Karaköse
Kars
Dogubeyazit
Erçis
Van
Tatvan
Bitlis
Mus
Hakkâri
Cizre
Mardin
Diyarbakir
Malatya
Elâzig
Urfa
Gaziantep
Gölbasi
Kahramanmaras
Islâhiye
L. Keban
L. Hazar
L. Egridir
L. Beysehir
Kizilirmak
Yesilirmak
Sakarya
Coruh
Aras
Murat
Dicle
Firat
Euphrates
Seyhan
Ceyhan
Göksu
Gediz
Büyük Menderes
E5
E23
E24
E390
010
100
230
360
400
0
200 miles
300 km
N

public, except during *namaz* (prayer hours), which are observed five times a day. These times are based on the position of the sun, so they vary throughout the seasons between the following hours: sunrise (5–7), lunchtime (noon–1), afternoon (3–4), sunset (5–7), bedtime (9–10). Prayers last 30–40 minutes.

SHOPS

Most shops are open Monday–Saturday 9:30–1 and 2–7. There are some exceptions in the major shopping areas in large cities and resort areas, where shops stay open until 9 PM. Most are closed Sunday, although small grocery stores and a few other stores in the main shopping areas remain open seven days a week.

CAR TRAVEL

EMERGENCIES

If your car breaks down, Turkish mechanics in the villages will usually manage to get you going again, at least until you reach a city for full repairs. In the cities, entire streets are given over to car-repair shops. Prices are not high, but it's good to give a small tip to the person who does the repair work. If you're not in the shop during the repairs, take all car documents with you. The Touring and Automobile Club gives information about driving in Turkey and has a repair service.

➤ CONTACTS: **Touring and Automobile Club** (TTÖK; ☎ 212/282–8140).

GASOLINE

Throughout the country Shell, Total, Elf, and British Petroleum, as well as two Turkish oil companies, have gas stations that are open 24 hours on the main highways. Others are open from 6 AM to 10 PM.

ROAD CONDITIONS

Turkey has 37,500 km (25,000 mi) of well-maintained, paved highways, but signposts are few, lighting is scarce, and city traffic is chaotic. City streets and highways are jammed with vehicles operated by high-speed drivers who constantly blast their horns. In Istanbul avoid the many small one-way streets; you never know when someone is going to barrel down one of them in the wrong direction. Better yet, use public transportation or take taxis. Parking is a big problem in the cities and larger towns.

RULES OF THE ROAD

The best way to see Turkey is by car, but be warned that it has one of the highest accident rates in Europe. In general, Turkish driving conforms to Mediterranean customs, with driving on the right and passing on the left. But watch out for drivers passing on a curve or on the top of a hill. Other hazards are carts and motorcycles weaving in and out of traffic. Archaeological and historical sites are indicated by yellow signposts. Seat belts are required in the front seats.

CUSTOMS AND DUTIES

Turkish customs officials rarely look through tourists' luggage on arrival. You are allowed to bring in 400 cigarettes, 50 cigars, 200 grams of tobacco, 1.5 kilograms of instant coffee, 500 grams of tea, and 2.5 liters of alcohol. An additional 600 cigarettes, 100 cigars, or 500 grams of tobacco may be imported if purchased at the Turkish duty-free shops on arrival. Register all valuable personal items in your passport on entry. Goods at duty-free shops in airports are usually less expensive here than in duty-free shops in other European airports or in-flight offerings. Turkey is extremely tough on anyone attempting to export antiques without authorization or on anyone caught with illegal drugs, regardless of the amount.

DINING

The Turkish people are justly proud of their cuisine. In addition to the blends of spices used, the food is also extremely healthy, full of fresh vegetables, yogurt, legumes, and grains, not to mention fresh seafood, roast lamb, and kebabs made of lamb, beef, or chicken. Because Turkey is predominantly Muslim, pork is not readily available. But there's plenty of alcohol, including local beer and wine, which are excellent and inexpensive. Particularly good wines are Villa Doluca and Kavaklidere, available in *beyaz* (white) and *kırmızı* (red). The most popular beers are Efes Pilsen, Troy, and Tuborg. Miller is also now brewed locally under license and widely available. In major cities and large hotels it is usually possible to find imported beers from Europe and the United States. The national alcoholic drink, *rakı,* is made from grapes and aniseed. Turks mix it with water or ice and sip it throughout their meal or serve it as an aperitif.

Many hotel restaurants have English-language menus and usually serve a bland version of Continental cuisine. Foreign fast-food chains are also becoming increasingly widespread. Far more adventurous and tasty are meals in *restorans* and in *lokantas* (Turkish restaurants). Most lokantas do not have menus because they serve only what's fresh and in season, which varies daily. At lokantas you simply sit back and let the waiter bring food to your table, beginning with a tray of *mezes* (appetizers). You point to the dishes that look inviting and take as many as you want. Then you select your main course from fresh meat or fish—displayed in glass-covered refrigerated units—which is then cooked to order, or from a steam table laden with casseroles and stews. For lighter meals there are *kebabcıs,* tiny restaurants specializing in kebabs served with salad and yogurt, and *pidecis,* selling *pides,* a pizzalike snack of flat bread topped with butter, cheese, egg, or ground lamb and baked in a wood-burning oven.

Prices are for a main course at dinner.

CATEGORY	MAJOR CITIES	OTHER AREAS
$$$$	over $20	over $17
$$$	$12–$20	$10–$17
$$	$6–$12	$5–$10
$	under $6	under $5

MEALTIMES

Lunch is generally served from noon to 3 and dinner from 7 to 10. In cities you can find restaurants or cafés open almost any time of day or night, but in villages, finding a restaurant open at odd hours can be a problem. In more conservative areas restaurants often close during daylight hours in the Islamic holy month of Ramadan (usually falls within November and December), when many Muslims fast.

RESERVATIONS AND DRESS

Except for at the pricier restaurants, where jacket and tie are appropriate, informal dress is acceptable at restaurants in all price categories.

EMBASSIES

Consular offices are in Istanbul. *See* Istanbul Essentials, *below,* for additional information.

HEALTH

Although tap water is heavily chlorinated, it is often not safe to drink. Even when it is, it is often unpalatable. It's best to play it safe and drink *maden suyu* (bottled mineral water) or regular *şişe suyu* (bottled water).

HOLIDAYS

January 1; February 22–25 (Kurban Bayramı, an important sacrificial feast celebrating Abraham's willingness to sacrifice his son to God);

April 23 (National Sovereignty and Children's Day); May 19 (National Youth and Sports Day); August 30 (Victory Day); October 29 (Republic Day); December 5–7 (Şeker Bayramı, "Sugar Feast," a three-day celebration marking the end of Ramadan).

The Islamic religious holidays of Şeker Bayramı and Kurban Bayramı follow the lunar calendar and move forward by approximately 10 days each year. The dates given above are for 2002. Many shops and most companies close at midday on the day before the official beginning of Şeker Bayramı and Kurban Bayramı.

LANGUAGE

Atatürk launched language reforms that replaced Arabic script with the Latin-based alphabet. English and German are widely spoken in cities and resorts. In villages and remote areas you'll have a hard time finding anyone who speaks anything but Turkish. Try learning a few basic Turkish words; your efforts will be appreciated.

LODGING

Accommodations range from international luxury chains in Istanbul, Ankara, and İzmir to comfortable, family-run *pansiyons* (guest houses). Plan ahead for the peak summer season, when resort hotels are often booked solid by tour companies. Turkey does not have central hotel reservations offices.

Hotels are officially classified in Turkey as HL (luxury), H1 to H5 (first- to fifth-class); motels, M1 to M2 (first- to second-class); and P, pansiyons. The classification is misleading because the lack of a restaurant or a lounge automatically relegates the establishment to the bottom of the ratings. A lower-grade hotel may actually be far more charming and comfortable than one with a higher rating. There are also many local establishments that are licensed but not included in the official ratings list. You can obtain their names from local tourist offices.

Rates vary from $10 to more than $200 a night for a double room. In less expensive hotels the plumbing and furnishings will probably leave much to be desired. You can find very acceptable, clean double rooms with bath for between $30 and $70, with breakfast included. Room rates are displayed in the reception area. It is accepted practice in Turkey to ask to see the room in advance.

Prices are for two people in a double room, including 17% VAT and a 10%–15% service charge.

CATEGORY	MAJOR CITIES	OTHER AREAS
$$$$	over $200	over $150
$$$	$100–$200	$100–$150
$$	$60–$100	$50–$100
$	under $60	under $50

MAIL AND SHIPPING

Post offices are painted bright yellow and have PTT (Post, Telegraph, and Telephone or PTT) signs on the front. The major ones are open Monday–Saturday 8 AM–9 PM, Sunday 9–7. Smaller branches are usually open Monday–Friday 8–4:30.

If you're uncertain where you'll be staying, have mail addressed to "poste restante" and sent to Merkez Postanesi (central post office) in the town of your choice.

MONEY MATTERS

Turkey is among the least expensive of the Mediterranean countries. Prices in this chapter are quoted in U.S. dollars, which indicate the real cost to the visitor more accurately than do the constantly increasing lira prices.

Coffee can range from about 50¢ to $2.50 a cup, depending on whether it's the less expensive Turkish coffee or American-style coffee and whether it's served in a luxury hotel or a café; tea, 20¢–$2 a glass; local beer, $1–$5; soft drink, $1–$4; lamb shish kebab, $2–$7; taxi, approximately $1.30 for 2 km (1 mi). Taxi prices are 50% higher between midnight and 6 AM.

CURRENCY

The monetary unit is the Turkish lira (TL), which comes in bank notes of 100,000, 250,000, 500,000, 1,000,000, 5,000,000, and 10,000,000. Coins come in denominations of 25,000, 50,000, and 100,000. At press time (summer 2001), the exchange rate was 672,900 TL to the U.S. dollar, 447,985 TL to the Canadian dollar, 994,081 TL to the pound sterling, 801,093 TL to the Irish punt, 368,896 TL to the Australian dollar, 295,403 TL to the New Zealand dollar, and 84,323 TL to the South African rand. Major credit cards and traveler's checks are widely accepted in hotels, shops, and expensive restaurants in cities and resorts but rarely in villages and small shops and restaurants.

There are no problems changing money back from Turkish lira to other currencies. But because the value of Turkish currency can sometimes fall significantly over a very short period, it is advisable to change enough money for only a few days at a time.

Foreign exchange bureaus are now widespread in Turkey's major cities and resorts (they usually have a sign saying DÖVIZ, Turkish for "Foreign Exchange"). Exchange rates are usually displayed just inside the door. Rates may vary slightly between exchange bureaus but are always better than bank rates and considerably more attractive than rates offered in hotels.

PASSPORTS AND VISAS

U.S. citizens not arriving on a cruise line need visas. These are most easily obtained at the port of entry—just be sure to have cash (U.S. $20). Canadian tourists do not need visas. Visas are required for visitors from the United Kingdom—obtain them at the port of entry for £10 or from any Turkish consulate (the rate will be somewhat higher).

SHOPPING

The best part of shopping in Turkey is visiting the *bedestans* (bazaars), brimming with copper and brass wares, hand-painted ceramics, alabaster and onyx goods, fabrics, richly colored carpets, and relics and icons trickling in from the former Soviet Union. The key word for shopping in the bazaars is "bargain." You must be willing to bargain, and bargain hard. It's great fun once you get the hang of it. As a rule of thumb offer 50% less after you're given the initial price and be prepared to go up by about 25%–30% of the first asking price. It is often advisable to get up to leave, as the best price is invariably the one called after you as you disappear around the corner. You can always think about it for two minutes and, if you are happy about it, return and accept. It's both bad manners and bad business to underbid grossly or to start bargaining if you're not serious about buying. Outside the bazaars prices are usually fixed, although in resort areas some shopkeepers may be willing to bargain if you ask for a "better price." Part of the fun of roaming through the bazaars is having a free glass of *çay* (tea), which vendors will offer you whether you're a serious shopper or just browsing. Beware of antiques: chances are you will end up with an expensive fake, but even if you do find the genuine article, it's illegal to export antiques of any type.

If you decide to buy something that looks antique, ask for documentation from the seller that the item is not an antique.

TAXES

Value-added tax (VAT) is nearly always included in the price. You can claim back the VAT if you buy articles from authorized shops. The net total value of articles subject to VAT on your invoice must be more than a specified amount, depending on the nature of the goods, and these articles must be exported within three months of purchase. The invoice must be stamped by customs. Otherwise, mail the stamped invoice back to the dealer within one month of departure and the dealer should send back a check.

TELEPHONES

All telephone numbers in Turkey have seven local digits plus three-digit city codes. Intercity calls are preceded by 0. The code for the European side of Istanbul is 212; be sure to dial the country code first if you are calling from outside Turkey; otherwise you may reach New York City!

Turkey's two GSM mobile telephone service providers have reciprocal agreements with most of their European counterparts, enabling subscribers to use the Turkish GSM network during their stay in the country. But most subscribers to U.S. and Canadian cellular telephone service providers are currently unable to connect to the Turkish network.

COUNTRY AND AREA CODES

The country code for Turkey is 90. When dialing a number in Turkey from outside the country, drop the initial 0 from the local area code.

INTERNATIONAL CALLS

For all international calls dial 00, then dial the country code, area or city code, and the number. You can use the higher-price cards for this, or reach an international operator by dialing ☎ 132. To reach a long-distance operator call AT&T, MCI, or Sprint.
Access Codes: AT&T (☎ 00800–12277). MCI (☎ 00800–11177). Sprint (☎ 00800–14477).

LOCAL CALLS

Pay phones are blue, push-button models. Most now take phone cards, or occasionally credit cards. However, particularly away from large cities, you can still find the old type phones which take *jetons* (tokens). Multilingual directions are posted in many phone booths.

Telephone cards are available at post offices for around $2 for 30 units, $3.50 for 60 units, and $5 for 100 units. They can also often be purchased for a few cents more from street booths. Tokens are available for 30¢ and $1 for long-distance calls. If you need operator assistance for long-distance calls within Turkey, dial ☎ 131. For intercity calls, dial 0, then dial the city code and the number.

Telephone numbers in European and Asian Istanbul have different codes: the code for European Istanbul (for numbers beginning with 2, 3, 5, 6, or 8) is 0/212; for Asian Istanbul (for numbers that start with 3 or 4), dial 0/216.

TIPPING

Except at the cheapest restaurants, a 10%–15% charge is added to the bill. As the money does not necessarily find its way to the waiter, leave an additional 10% on the table or hand it to the waiter. In top restaurants waiters expect tips of between 10% and 15%. Hotel porters expect between $1 and $4 and the chambermaid about $2. Taxi drivers don't expect tips, although they are becoming accustomed to foreigners' giving them something. Round off the fare to the nearest 100,000 TL. At Turkish baths the staff that attends you expects to share a tip of 30%–35% of the bill. Don't worry about missing them—they'll be lined up expectantly on your departure.

TRAIN TRAVEL

Although there are trains labeled express, the term is usually a misnomer. These trains have several long-distance routes, but they tend to be slow. The best daily trains between Istanbul and Ankara are the *Başkent Expres* and the *Fatih Expres*. The overnight *Yataklı Ankara Expres* has luxurious sleeper cars; the *Anadolu Expres* has cheaper, less comfortable berths. There are overnight trains to Pamukkale as well as daily trains to Edirne from Sirkeci station in Istanbul. Dining cars on some trains have waiter service and serve surprisingly good and inexpensive food.

FARES AND SCHEDULES

Train fares tend to be lower than bus fares. Seats on the best trains, as well as those with sleeping berths, should be reserved in advance. In railroad stations, buy tickets at windows marked ANAHAT GISELERI. Travel agencies carrying the TCDD (State Railways) sign and some post offices sell train tickets, too.

WHEN TO GO

The tourist season runs from April through October. July and August are the busiest and warmest months. April–June and September–October are the best months to visit archaeological sites or Istanbul and the Marmara area because the days are cooler and the crowds are smaller.

CLIMATE

The Mediterranean and Aegean coasts have mild winters and hot summers. You can swim in the sea from late April through October. The Black Sea coast is mild and damp, with a rainfall of 90 inches a year.

The following are the average daily maximum and minimum temperatures for Istanbul.

Jan.	46F	8C	**May**	69F	21C	**Sept.**	76F	24C
	37	3		53	12		61	16
Feb.	47F	9C	**June**	77F	25C	**Oct.**	68F	20C
	36	2		60	16		55	13
Mar.	51F	11C	**July**	82F	28C	**Nov.**	59F	15C
	38	3		65	18		48	9
Apr.	60F	16C	**Aug.**	82F	28C	**Dec.**	51F	11C
	45	7		66	19		41	

ISTANBUL

Istanbul is noisy, chaotic, and exciting. Spires and domes of mosques and medieval palaces dominate the skyline. At dawn, when the muezzin's call to prayer rebounds from ancient minarets, many people are heading home from the nightclubs and bars, while others are kneeling on their prayer rugs, facing Mecca.

Day and night, Istanbul has a schizophrenic air. Women in jeans, business suits, or elegant designer outfits pass women wearing the long skirts and head coverings that villagers have worn for generations. Donkey-drawn carts vie with old Chevrolets and Pontiacs or shiny Mercedes and BMWs for dominance of the loud, narrow streets. The world's most fascinating Asian bazaar competes with Western boutiques for your time and attention.

Exploring Istanbul

Istanbul's Asian side is filled with Western-style sprawling suburbs, while its European side contains Old Istanbul—a wonderland of mosques, opulent palaces, and crowded bazaars. The Golden Horn, an inlet 6½ km (4 mi) long, flows off the Bosporus on the European side, separating Old Istanbul from New Town. The center of New Town is Beyoğlu, a district filled with a combination of modern and turn-of-the-20th-century hotels, banks, and shops grouped around Taksim Square. There are three bridges spanning the Golden Horn: the Atatürk, the Galata, and the Haliç.

The historic Galata Bridge (the original structure has been replaced by a modern drawbridge) is a central landmark and a good place to get your bearings. From here, you can see the city's layout and its seven hills. The bridge will also give you a taste of Istanbul's frenetic street life. It's filled with peddlers selling everything from pistachio nuts and spices to curly-toed slippers fancy enough for a sultan; fishermen grill their catch on coal braziers and sell them to passersby. None of this sits well with motorists, who blast their horns constantly, usually to no avail. If you want to orient yourself in a quieter way, take a boat trip from the docks on the Eminönü side of the Galata Bridge up the Bosporus.

Old Istanbul (Sultanahmet)

Numbers in the margin correspond to points of interest on the Istanbul map.

The triangular peninsula of Old Istanbul is home to most of the oldest sites in Istanbul. Its boundaries of water on two sides and the ancient walls on the other are identical to those of the ancient city first laid out by the Emperor Constantine nearly 1,700 years ago. Although a couple of broad modern highways now cut a swathe through its tumble of stone and concrete buildings, most of Old Istanbul's narrow streets twist and turn over the city's seven hills as they have done for centuries.

★ ❷ **Arkeoloji Müzesi** (Archaeological Museum). This museum houses a fine collection of Greek and Roman antiquities, including finds from Ephesus and Troy. Admission to the Archaeological Museum is also good for entrance to the **Eski Şark Eserleri Müzesi** (Museum of the Ancient Orient), with Sumerian, Babylonian, and Hittite treasures; and the **Çinili Köşkü** (Tiled Pavilion), which houses ceramics from the early Seljuk and Osmanli empires. ✉ *Gülhane Park,* ☎ *212/520–7740.* ⏲ *Tues.–Sun. 9–4:30.*

★ ❸ **Aya Sofya** (Hagia Sophia, Church of the Divine Wisdom). One of the world's greatest examples of Byzantine architecture, it was built in AD 532 under the supervision of Emperor Justinian. The third church on the site, it took 10,000 men five years to complete it. The first was built in 360; both it and its successor were destroyed by fire. The dome of the current church was the world's largest until the dome at St. Peter's Basilica was built in Rome 1,000 years later. Aya Sofya was the cathedral of Constantinople for nearly 1,000 years, surviving earthquakes and looting crusaders until 1453, when it was converted into a mosque by Mehmet the Conqueror. Minarets were added by succeeding sultans. Aya Sofya originally had many mosaics depicting Christian scenes, which were plastered over by Süleyman I, who felt they were inappropriate for a mosque. In 1935 Atatürk converted Aya Sofya into a museum. Shortly after that American archaeologists discovered the mo-

Arkeoloji Müzesi . . . 2
Aya Sofya 3
Çiçek Pasajı 14
Dolmabahçe Cami 15
Dolmabahçe Sarayı 16
Galata Kulesi 12
Hippodrome 5
İstanbul Üniversitesi 9
İstiklâl Caddesi 13
Kapalı Çarşısı 8
Mısır Çarşısı 11
Süleymaniye Cami 10
Sultan Ahmet Cami 4
Topkapı Saray 1
Türk Ve Islâm Eserleri Müzesi 6
Yerebatan Sarnıcı . . . 7

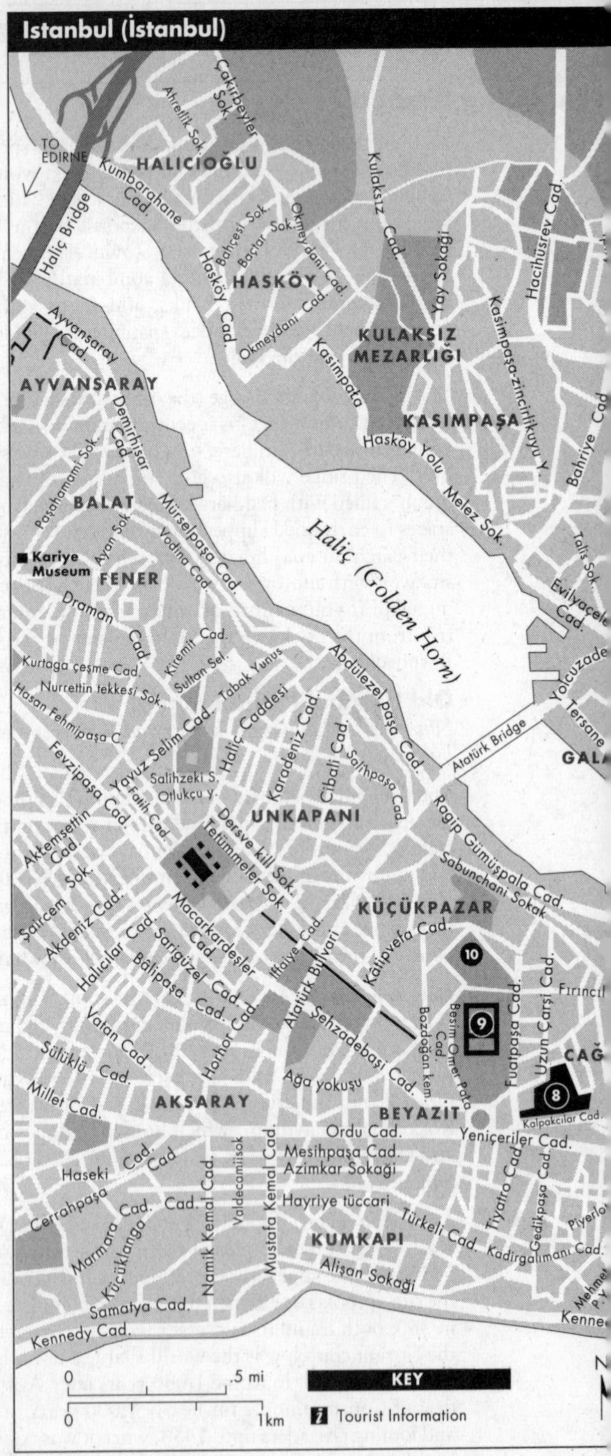

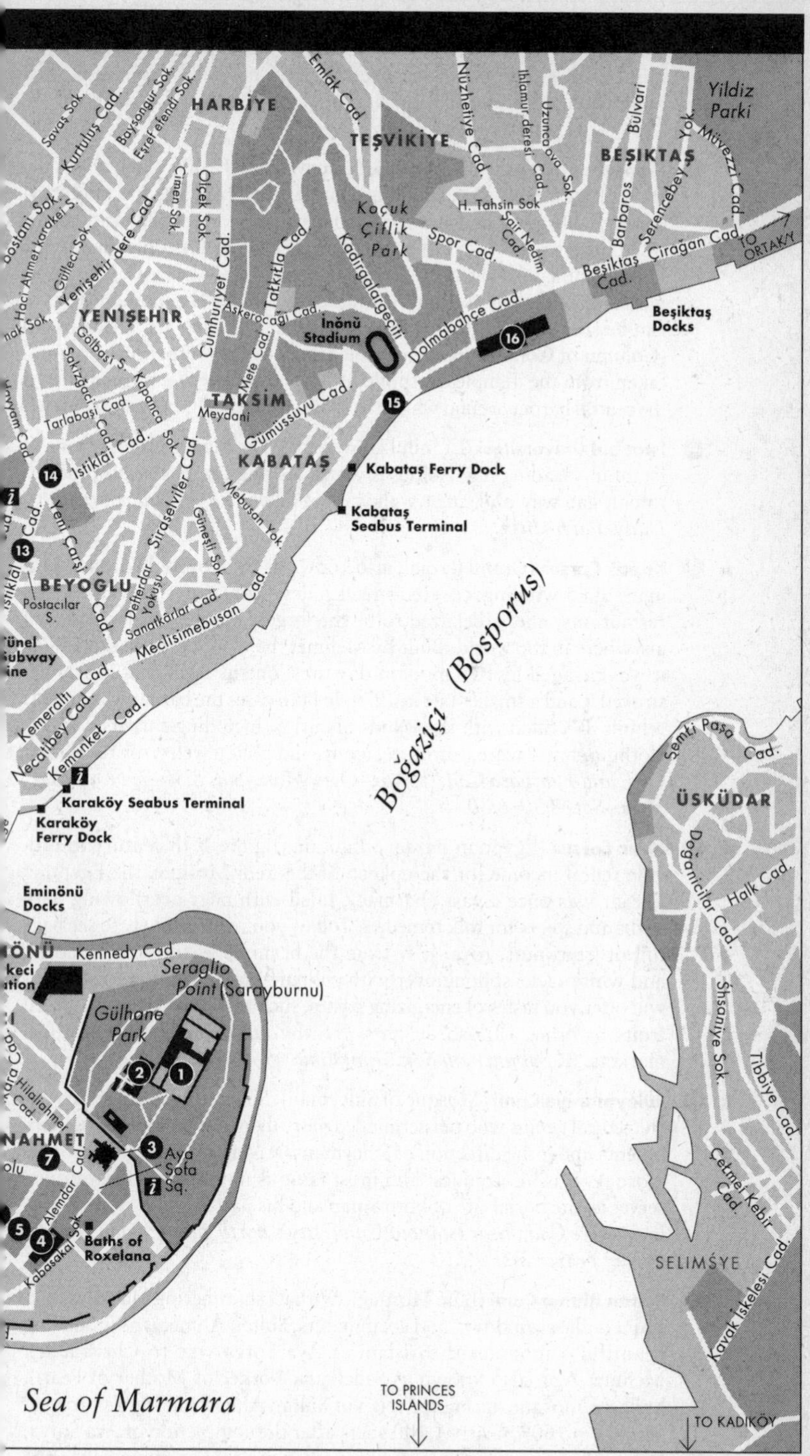
HARBİYE
TEŞVİKİYE
BEŞIKTAŞ
Yildiz Parki
Koçuk Çiftlik Park
YENİŞEHİR
İnönü Stadium
TAKSİM
Meydani
KABATAŞ
Kabataş Ferry Dock
Kabataş Seabus Terminal
BEYOĞLU
Postacılar S.
Beşiktaş Docks
TO ORTAKÖY
Boğaziçi (Bosporus)
ÜSKÜDAR
Karaköy Seabus Terminal
Karaköy Ferry Dock
Eminönü Docks
Kennedy Cad.
Seraglio Point (Sarayburnu)
Gülhane Park
Aya Sofa Sq.
Baths of Roxelana
SELIMŞYE
Sea of Marmara
TO PRINCES ISLANDS
TO KADIKÖY
Emlâk Cad.
Nüzhetiye Cad.
Ihlamur deresi Cad.
Uzuncaova Sok.
Bulvari
Müvezzi Cad.
H. Tahsin Sok
Spor Cad.
Sair Nedim Cad.
Barbaros
Serencebey Yok.
Çırağan Cad.
Beşiktaş Cad.
Dolmabahçe Cad.
Kadirgalargeçiti
Tatkitla Cad.
Askerocaği Cad.
Mete Cad.
Gümüssuyu Cad.
Cumhuriyet Cad.
Olçek Sok.
Cimen Sok.
Savaş Sok.
Kurtuluş Cad.
Baysongur Sok.
Eşref efendi Sok.
Yenişehir dere Cad.
Gülleci Sok.
Haci Ahmet Karakei S.
Gölbasi S.
Sakizğaci S.
Kapanca Sok.
Tarlabaşi Cad.
İstiklâl Cad.
Yeni Çarşı Cad.
Sıraselviler Cad.
Güneşli Sok.
Mebusan Yok.
Defterdar Yokuşu
Sanatkârlar Cad.
Meclisimebusan Cad.
Kemeraltı Cad.
Necatibey Cad.
Kemankeş Cad.
Şemsi Paşa Cad.
Doğanicilar Cad.
Halk Cad.
İhsaniye Sok.
Tibbiye Cad.
Çetmet Kebir Cad.
Kavak İskelesi Cad.
Hilaliahmer Cad.
Alemdar Cad.
Kabasakal Sok
NAHMET
Tünel Subway Line

saics, which were restored and are now on display. According to legend, the Sacred Column in the north aisle "weeps water" that can work miracles. It's so popular that over the centuries believers have worn a hole through the marble and brass column. ✉ *Aya Sofya Meyd.,* ☎ *212/522–1750.* ⏲ *Tues.–Sun. 9–4.*

❺ **Hippodrome.** Once a Byzantine stadium with 100,000 seats, it was the focal point for city life, including chariot races, circuses, and public executions. Disputes between rival groups of supporters of chariot teams often degenerated into violence. In AD 531, 30,000 people died in the Hippodrome in what came to be known as the Nike riots. The original shape of the Hippodrome is still clearly visible. The monuments that can be seen today—the **Dikilitaş** (Egyptian Obelisk), the **Örme Sütun** (Column of Constantinos), and the **Yılanlı Sütun** (Serpentine Column) taken from the Temple of Apollo at Delphi in Greece—formed part of the central barrier around which the chariots raced. ✉ *Sultanahmet Meyd.*

❾ **İstanbul Üniversitesi** (Istanbul University). The main campus of one of Istanbul's leading universities is worth visiting for its magnificent Ottoman gateway and quiet walkways. ✉ *Fuat Paşa Cad., Beyazit.* ⏲ *Daily dawn–dusk.*

★ ❽ **Kapalı Çarşısı** (Grand Bazaar, also known as the Covered Bazaar). This maze of 65 winding, covered streets hides 4,000 shops, tiny cafés, and restaurants, and is believed to be the largest number under one roof anywhere in the world. Built by Mehmet the Conqueror in the 1450s, it was ravaged by two modern-day fires, one in 1954 that nearly destroyed it and a smaller one in 1974. In both cases the bazaar was quickly rebuilt. It's filled with thousands of curios, including carpets, fabrics, clothing, brass ware, furniture, icons, and gold jewelry. ✉ *Yeniçeriler Cad. and Fuatpaşa Cad.* ⏲ *Apr.–Oct., Mon.–Sat. 8:30–7; Nov.–Mar., Mon.–Sat. 8:30–6:30.*

★ ⓫ **Mısır Çarşısı** (Egyptian Bazaar). Built during the 17th century to provide rental income for the upkeep of the Yeni Mosque, the Egyptian Bazaar was once a vast pharmacy, filled with bags overflowing with herbs and spices for folk remedies. Today, you're more likely to see bags full of fruit, nuts, royal jelly from the beehives of the Aegean coast, and white sacks spilling over with culinary spices. Some shopkeepers will offer you tastes of energizing pastes, such as *macun,* as well as dried fruits or other Turkish delights. Nearby are colorful fruit and fish markets. ✉ *Sabunchanı Sok., Eminönü.* ⏲ *Mon.–Sat. 8–7.*

★ ❿ **Süleymaniye Cami** (Mosque of Süleyman). Sinan, the 16th-century architectural genius who masterminded more than 350 buildings and monuments under the direction of Süleyman the Magnificent, designed this mosque. It is his grandest and most famous monument. The mosque serves as the burial site of both Sinan and his patron, Süleyman. ✉ *Süleymaniye Cad., near Istanbul University's north gate.* ⏲ *Daily except during prayer hrs.*

❹ **Sultan Ahmet Cami** (Blue Mosque). With its shimmering blue tiles, 260 stained-glass windows, and six minarets, Sultan Ahmet is as grand and beautiful a monument to Islam as Aya Sofya was to Christianity. Mehmet Ağa, also known as Sedefkar (Worker of Mother of Pearl), built the mosque during the reign of Sultan Ahmet I in eight years, beginning in 1609, nearly 1,100 years after the completion of Aya Sofya. His goal was to surpass Justinian's masterpiece, and some believe he succeeded. Press through the throngs and enter the mosque at the side entrance that faces Aya Sofya. Remove your shoes and leave them at the entrance. Immodest clothing is not allowed, but an attendant will lend you a robe if he feels you are not dressed appropriately. **Hünkar**

Kasrı (Carpet and Kilim Museum; ☎ 212/518–1330) is in the mosque's stone-vaulted cellars and upstairs at the end of a stone ramp, where the sultans rested before and after their prayers; call for hours. ✉ *Sultanahmet Meyd.* ⏲ *Daily 9–5.*

★ ❶ **Topkapı Saray** (Topkapı Palace). The number one attraction in Istanbul stands on Seraglio Point in Old Istanbul, known as Sultanahmet. The palace, which dates from the 15th century, was the residence of a number of sultans and their harems until the mid-19th century. To avoid the crowds try to get here by 9:30 AM, when the gates open. If you're arriving by taxi, tell the driver you want the Topkapı Saray in Sultanahmet, or you could end up at the remains of the former Topkapı bus terminal on the outskirts of town.

Sultan Mehmet II built the first palace during the 1450s, shortly after the Ottoman conquest of Constantinople. Over the centuries, sultan after sultan added ever more elaborate architectural fantasies, until the palace eventually ended up with more than four courtyards and some 5,000 residents, many of them concubines and eunuchs. Topkapı was the residence and center of bloodshed and drama for the Ottoman rulers until the 1850s, when Sultan Abdül Mecit moved with his harem to the European-style Dolmabahçe Palace farther up the Bosporus coast.

In Topkapı's outer courtyard are the **Aya İrini** (Church of St. Irene), open only during festival days for concerts, and the **Merasim Avlusu** (Court of the Janissaries), originally for members of the sultan's guard.

Adjacent to the ticket office is the **Bab-i-Selam** (Gate of Salutation), built in 1524 by Süleyman the Magnificent, who was the only person allowed to pass through it. In the towers on either side, prisoners were kept until they were executed beside the fountain outside the gate in the first courtyard. In the second courtyard, amid the rose gardens, is the **Divan-i-Humayun,** the assembly room of the council of state, once presided over by the grand vizier (prime minister). The sultan would sit behind a latticed window, hidden by a curtain so no one would know when he was listening, although occasionally he would pull the curtain aside to comment.

One of the most popular sections of Topkapı is the **Harem,** a maze of nearly 400 halls, terraces, rooms, wings, and apartments grouped around the sultan's private quarters on the west side of the second courtyard. Forty rooms are restored and open to the public. Next to the entrance are the quarters of the eunuchs and about 200 of the lesser concubines, who were lodged in tiny cubicles, as cramped and uncomfortable as the main rooms of the Harem are large and opulent. Tours begin every half hour. Only a limited number are taken on each tour. During the height of the tourist season it is advisable to try to buy a ticket for the Harem tour soon after you enter the palace.

In the third courtyard is the **Hazine Dairesi** (Treasury), four rooms filled with jewels, including two uncut emeralds, each weighing 3½ kilograms (7.7 pounds), that once hung from the ceiling. Here, too, is the dazzling emerald dagger used in the movie *Topkapı* and the 84-carat "Spoonmaker" diamond that, according to legend, was found by a pauper and traded for three wooden spoons.

In the fourth and last courtyard of the Topkapı Palace are small, elegant summer houses, mosques, fountains, and reflecting pools scattered amid the gardens on different levels. Here you will find the **Rivan Köşk,** built by Murat IV in 1636 to commemorate the successful Rivan campaign. In another kiosk in the gardens, called the **İftariye** (Golden Cage), the closest relatives of the reigning sultan lived in strict confinement under what amounted to house arrest. Such confinement began in the 1800s after the old custom of murdering all possible rivals to the throne had been abandoned. The confinement of the heirs apparently helped keep the peace, but it deprived them of any chance to prepare themselves for the formidable task of ruling a great empire. ✉ *Topkapı Palace,* ☎ *212/ 512–0480.* ⏲ *Wed.–Mon. 9–4:30.*

6 **Türk Ve Islâm Eserleri Müzesi** (Museum of Turkish and Islamic Arts). The museum is housed in Ibrahim Paşa Palace, once the grandiose residence of the son-in-law and grand vizier of Süleyman the Magnificent, Ibrahim Paşa, who was executed when he became too powerful for Süleyman's liking. The collection gives a superb insight into the lifestyles of Turks of every level of society, from the 8th century to the present. ✉ *Atmeydanı 46, Sultanahmet,* ☎ *212/518–1385 or 212/518–1805.* ⏲ *Tues.–Sun. 9–4:30.*

★ 7 **Yerebatan Sarnıcı** (Sunken Palace, also known as the Basilica Cistern). This underground cistern was probably first excavated by Emperor Constantine in the 4th century and then enlarged by Emperor Justinian in the 6th century. It has 336 marble columns rising 26 ft to support Byzantine arches and domes. The cistern was always kept full as a precaution against long sieges. Its echoing vastness and the reflections of the columns in the dark water give it a haunting, cathedral-like beauty, and it is a welcome relief from the heat and noise aboveground. ✉ *Yerebatan Cad.,* ☎ *212/522–1259.* ⏲ *Daily 9–4:30.*

New Town

New Town is the area on the northern shore of the Golden Horn, the waterway that cuts through Istanbul on the European side of the Bosporus. The architecture reflects the city's steady expansion north over the last century. Most of the buildings in Beyoğlu, the neighborhood closest to the Golden Horn, date from the late 19th and early 20th century. The faded grandeur of their ornate stone facades recalls a time when Istanbul was one of the most cosmopolitan cities in the world and over half of its population was non-Turkish. The majority of the buildings to the north in Taksim and Nişantaşı are made from concrete and date from the 1970s and 1980s, while further north are the modern skyscrapers of glass and steel housing the city's current business district.

14 **Çiçek Pasajı** (Flower Arcade). Here is a lively blend of restaurants, bars, and street musicians. ✉ *Çiçek Pasajı, off İstiklâl Cad., Galatasaray.*

★ 15 **Dolmabahçe Cami** (Dolmabahçe Mosque). Founded by Valide Sultan Bezmialem, mother of Abdül Mecit I, it was completed in 1853; the 88-ft-tall clock tower was built a year later. ✉ *Dolmabahçe Cad.* ⏲ *Daily except during prayer hrs.*

16 **Dolmabahçe Sarayi** (Dolmabahçe Palace). Built in 1853, it was, until the declaration of the modern republic in 1923, the residence of the last sultans of the Ottoman Empire. It was also the residence of Atatürk, who died here in 1938. The palace, floodlit at night, is an extraordinary mixture of Hindu, Turkish, and European styles of architecture and interior design. Queen Victoria's contribution to the lavishness was a chandelier weighing 4½ tons. Tours of the palace take about 80 minutes. ✉ *Dolmabahçe Cad.,* ☎ *212/258–5544.* ⏲ *Apr.–Oct., Tues.–Wed. and Fri.–Sun. 9–4; Nov.–Mar., Tues.–Wed. and Fri.–Sun. 9–3.*

12 **Galata Kulesi** (Galata Tower). It was built by the Genoese in 1349 as part of the fortifications for their quarter of the Byzantine city. In this century it served as a fire lookout until 1960. Today it houses a restaurant and nightclub and a viewing tower, offering panoramic scenes stretching across the Golden Horn to Old Istanbul and beyond to the

Sea of Marmara. ✉ *Büyük Hendek Cad., Galata,* ☎ *212/245–1160.* ⏲ *Daily 9–8.*

13 **İstiklâl Caddesi.** Formerly known as La Grande Rue de Pera, İstiklâl Caddesi was the most fashionable street in the city during the 19th and early 20th centuries. Pedestrianized and lined with shops, restaurants, banks, and cafés in turn-of-the-20th-century buildings, the street teems with every human element in Turkey's cultural melting pot, dodging the restored 19th-century tram that runs from Tünel to Taksim Square. In the side streets are Greek and Armenian churches, bars, cafés, and other establishments. ✉ *İstiklâl Cad., Beyoğlu.*

Dining

Most major hotels have dining rooms serving bland international cuisine. It's far more rewarding to eat in Turkish restaurants.

$$$ ✕ **Divan.** Enjoy Turkish and international haute cuisine, elegant surroundings, and excellent service at this restaurant in the Divan hotel. Specialties include *islim kebap* (lamb covered with eggplant and served with Turkish rice). ✉ *Cumhuriyet Cad. 2, Elmadağ,* ☎ *212/231–4100. AE, DC, MC. Closed Sun.*

$$$ ✕ **Körfez.** The specialty here is seafood, with such dishes as bass baked in salt. The garden setting on the waterfront is very romantic, and the restaurant has a boat that ferries you across the Bosporus from Rumeli Hisarı. ✉ *Körfez Cad. 78, Kanlıca,* ☎ *216/413–4314. Reservations essential. AE, DC, MC, V. Closed Mon.*

$$$ ✕ **Le Select.** In an elegant villa in the upmarket Levent neighborhood, Le Select lives up to its name by offering a sumptuous selection of Turkish, French, and Russian cuisine. House specialties include marinated salmon, sea bass with thyme, and steak in wine sauce. ✉ *Manolya Sokak 21, Levent,* ☎ *212/268–2120. Reservations essential. AE, MC, V.*

$$$ ✕ **Tuğra.** This spacious and luxurious restaurant in the historic Çirağan Palace serves the most delectable of long-savored Ottoman recipes, including slices of tender beef cooked in paper, air-dried beef cooked in vine leaves, and desserts such as quince tart in cinnamon syrup. The Bosporus view is framed by the palace's marble columns; the high ceilings support dazzling glass chandeliers. ✉ *Çirağan Cad. 84, Beşiktaş,* ☎ *212/258–3377. Reservations essential. Jacket required. AE, DC, MC, V. No lunch.*

$$ ✕ **Beyti.** This classy, sprawling eatery is famous for inventing the *beyti kebabı* (spicy, skewered meatballs wrapped in pita), but also offers a range of other tasty meat dishes and salads. Over the last 55 years it has grown from a couple of chairs and a table to a dozen ornately decorated rooms and an airy terrace; the photographs of previous diners that line the entrance are like a who's who list of the last half century. ✉ *Orman Caddesi 8, Florya,* ☎ *212/663–2992. MC, V.*

$$ ✕ **Çatı.** On the seventh floor of a building in a Beyoğlu side street, this place serves a range of excellent hot and cold Turkish cuisine and a good open buffet. Its lofty location provides a rare opportunity to appreciate the architectural splendors of İstiklâl Caddesi. Ask the waiter for a list of the day's specialities. ✉ *Orhan Apaydın Sok. 20/7, İstiklâl Cad., Beyoğlu,* ☎ *212/251–0000. AE, MC, V. Closed Sun.*

$$ ✕ **Develi Restaurant.** Established in 1912, the Develi is one of the oldest and best kebab restaurants in Istanbul, with some great views across the Marmara. It specializes in dishes from southeast Anatolia, which are traditionally more spicy than those from the west of the country. Try the *patlıcan kebap* (kebab with eggplants) or the *fıstıklı kebap* (kebab with pistachios). ✉ *Balıkpazarı, Gümüşyüzük Sok. 7, Samatya,* ☎ *212/529–0833. AE, MC, V.*

$$ ✕ **Dört Mevsim.** The "Four Seasons," in a large Victorian building, is noted for its blend of Turkish and French cuisine and for its owners, Gay and Musa, an Anglo-Turkish couple who opened it in 1965. You'll find them in the kitchen overseeing such delights as shrimp in cognac sauce and baked marinated lamb. ✉ *İstiklâl Cad. 509, Beyoğlu,* ☎ *212/293–3941. AE, DC, MC, V. Closed Sun.*

$$ ✕ **Dünya.** The busy traffic of the adjacent Ortaköy Square and waiters balancing appetizer trays is countered by the picturesque Bosporus view, which on summer nights includes passing pleasure boats. The grilled *cupra* (bream) is a must, and the mezes are always fresh and delicious. ✉ *Salhane Sok. 10, Ortaköy,* ☎ *212/258–6385. V.*

$$ ★ ✕ **İmroz.** Tucked away in a side street of similar restaurants behind the Balık Pazarı (Fish Market) in Beyoğlu, this is one of last Greek tavernas in Istanbul. The menu offers high-quality fish and meat dishes. Wooden tables and faded photographs contribute to the cozy, relaxed atmosphere. In summer you can dine at tables set out on the street. ✉ *Nevizade Sokak 24, Beyoğlu,* ☎ *212/249–9073. No credit cards.*

$$ ✕ **Rejans.** Founded by two Russians and a Crimean fleeing the Bolshevik Revolution, and now run by their widows, this restaurant has excellent Russian food and lemon vodka, as well as Turkish dishes. The decor has remained basically unchanged since the 1930s. During World War II, when Turkey remained neutral, diplomats and spies from the Allies and Axis powers used to dine here, glowering at each other from different tables. ✉ *Emir Nevrut Sok. 17, İstiklâl Cad., Beyoğlu,* ☎ *212/244–1610 or 212/243–3882. Reservations essential. V. Closed Sun.*

$–$$ ★ ✕ **Hacıbaba.** This large, cheerful-looking place has a summer terrace overlooking an old Greek church. Fish, meat, and a wide variety of vegetable dishes are on display for your selection. Before you choose your main course, you'll be offered a tray of mezes that can be a meal in themselves. ✉ *İstiklâl Cad. 49, Taksim,* ☎ *212/244–1886 or 212/245–4377. AE, MC, V.*

$ ★ ✕ **Hacı Salih.** This charming, tiny, family-run restaurant has only 10 tables, so you may have to line up and wait—but it's worth it. Traditional Turkish food is the fare, with special emphasis on vegetable and lamb dishes, which change each day. Alcohol is not served. ✉ *Anadolu Pasajı 201, off İstiklâl Cad., Beyoğlu,* ☎ *212/243–4528. MC, V. Closed Sun. No dinner.*

Lodging

The top hotels are mainly around Taksim Square in New Town. Hotels generally include the 15% VAT and a service charge of 10%–15% in the rate. In Old Istanbul, the Aksaray, Laleli, Sultanahmet, and Beyazit areas have many conveniently located, inexpensive small hotels and family-run pansiyons.

$$$$ ★ **Çırağan Palace.** The 19th-century Ottoman palace is the city's most luxurious hotel. The setting is exceptional, right on the Bosporus; the outdoor pool is on the water's edge. Most rooms are in the new wing (ask for one here), though there are 12 suites in the palace. ✉ *Çırağan Cad. 84, Beşiktaş, 80700,* ☎ *212/258–3377,* FAX *212/259–6686,* WEB *www.ciraganpalace.com. 287 rooms, 28 suites. 4 restaurants, pool. AE, DC, MC, V.*

$$$$ **Divan Hotel.** Quiet, but close enough to Taksim Square, this renovated old hotel has some rooms with terraces overlooking the Bosporus. All are clean and functionally furnished and a favorite with visitors on business. The restaurant is renowned for impeccably prepared Turkish and international dishes. ✉ *Cumhuriyet Cad. 2, Elmadağ, 80200,* ☎ *212/231–4100,* FAX *212/248–8527,* WEB *www.divanoteli.com.tr. 180 rooms, 11 suites. 2 restaurants. AE, DC, MC, V.*

$$$$ ★ **Pera Palas.** A grand hotel with a genuinely Turkish feel, the Pera Palas was built in 1892 to accommodate guests arriving on the *Orient Express.* Everyone who was anyone stayed here, from Mata Hari to Agatha Christie to visiting heads of state. Although it has been modernized for comfort, the hotel has retained its original Victorian elegance. Many old features, such as a magnificent antique elevator, are still in working order. ✉ *Meşrutiyet Cad. 98, Tepebaşı, 80050,* ☎ *212/251–4560,* FAX *212/251–4089,* WEB *www.perapalas.com. 145 rooms. Restaurant. AE, DC, MC, V.*

$$$$ ★ **Swissôtel.** Near the city center in a hilltop wood, this hotel has superb views across the Bosporus and beyond to the Sea of Marmara. It also has lavish amenities, including excellent sports facilities and a range of French, Turkish, Japanese, Chinese, and Swiss cuisines at its many restaurants. ✉ *Bayıldım Cad. 2, Maçka, 80680,* ☎ *212/326–1100,* FAX *212/316–1122,* WEB *www.swissotel.com. 600 rooms. 6 restaurants, 2 pools. AE, DC, MC, V.*

$$$ **Hyatt Regency.** This massive but tasteful pink building, reminiscent of Ottoman splendor, houses an upscale hotel. Many rooms have views of the Bosporus. The decor is a combination of earth tones in many textures. The restaurants serve a range of Asian, Turkish, and Italian foods. ✉ *Taşkişla Cad., Taksim, 80090,* ☎ *212/225–7000,* FAX *212/225–7007,* WEB *www.istanbul.hyatt.com. 360 rooms. 3 restaurants, pool. AE, DC, MC, V.*

$$$ **Istanbul Hilton.** One of the best hotels in the chain, it offers a combination of comfort and local color, with reception and public areas decorated with Turkish rugs and large brass urns. Ask for a room overlooking the Bosporus. ✉ *Cumhuriyet Cad., Harbiye, 80200,* ☎ *212/315–6000,* FAX *212/247–0402. 501 rooms. 4 restaurants, 2 pools. AE, DC, MC, V.*

$$$ **Richmond.** A turn-of-the-20th-century building on İstiklâl Caddesi was renovated to create this comfortable hotel. Downstairs is the Lebon patisserie, a remake of the 19th-century pastry shop that once operated here and an excellent place to watch the world pass by. ✉ *İstiklâl Cad. 445, Tepebaşi, 80070,* ☎ *212/252–5460,* FAX *212/252–9707. 109 rooms. 2 restaurants. AE, V.*

$$$ ★ **Yeşil Ev.** Practically next door to the Blue Mosque, the restored 19th-century "Green House" is decorated in old-fashioned Ottoman style with lace curtains and latticed shutters. Its high-walled garden restaurant is a peaceful oasis in the midst of frenetic Istanbul. ✉ *Kabasakal Cad. 5, Sultanahmet, 34400,* ☎ *212/517–6786,* FAX *212/517–6780. 19 rooms with shower. 2 restaurants. AE, MC, V.*

$$ **Ayasofya Pansiyons.** These guest houses are part of an Automobile Club project to restore a little street of historic wooden houses along the outer wall of Topkapı Palace. One of the houses has been converted into a library and the rest into pansiyons, furnished in late Ottoman style. In summer, tea and refreshments are served in the gardens. ✉ *Soğukçeşme Sok., Sultanahmet, 34400,* ☎ *212/513–3660,* FAX *212/513–3669,* WEB *www.ayasofyapansiyonlari.com. 57 rooms. 2 restaurants. AE, MC, V.*

$$ ★ **Hotel Empress Zoe.** Named for an empress who ruled Byzantium during the 11th century, this unusual property is decorated with murals and paintings in that era's style. Rooms, of varying configurations, are brightened with colorful embroidered textiles. The American owner, Ann Nevans, can help you with your itinerary. ✉ *Akbıyık Cad., Adliye Sok. 10, Sultanahmet, 34400,* ☎ *212/518–2504,* FAX *212/518–5699,* WEB *www.emzoe.com. 19 rooms. MC, V.*

$ **Berk Guest House.** Cheerful Güngör and Nevim Evrensel run this clean, comfortable pansiyon in a converted private home. There is a small lounge inside and a terrace offers beautiful views across the Sea of Marmara. Two of the rooms also have balconies overlooking a garden. ✉ *Kutlugün Sok. 27, Sultanahmet, 34400,* ☎ *212/516–9671,* FAX *212/517–7715. 9 rooms with shower. No credit cards.*

$ **Büyük Londra.** This six-story, mid-19th-century hotel has aged gracefully. The rooms are small and comfortably worn, the furnishings heavy and traditional. The dark woods and velvet drapes used in the high-ceiling lobby and dining room evoke an Ottoman Victorian era. ✉ *Meşrutiyet Cad. 117, Tepebaşi, 80050,* ☎ *212/293–1619,* FAX *212/245–0671. 54 rooms. Restaurant. AE, MC, V.*

$ **Hotel Barin.** Modern, clean, and comfortable, the Barin makes up in convenience, functionality, and friendliness what it lacks in atmosphere. The hotel caters to business travelers as well as tourists. ✉ *Fevziye Cad. 7, Şehzadebaşı, 34470,* ☎ *212/513–9100,* FAX *212/526–4440. 65 rooms. AE, MC, V.*

Nightlife and the Arts

The Arts

For tickets to the **Istanbul International Festival**—held late June through mid-July and attracting internationally renowned artists and performers—contact the Istanbul Foundation for Culture and Arts (✉ Kültür ve Sanat Vakfı, İstiklâl Cad., Luvr Apt. 146, Beyoğlu, 80070, ☎ 212/293–3133). Tickets can also be purchased at ticket booths outside some of the venues. Performances, which include modern and classical music, ballet, opera, and theater, are given throughout the city in historic buildings. The season at the city of Istanbul's **Cemal Reşit Rey Concert Hall** (☎ 212/231–5498) runs from September through May and includes classical, jazz, and rock music, as well as ballet performed by visiting and local groups.

CONCERTS

From October through May, the Istanbul State Symphony gives performances at the main concert hall, **Atatürk Kültür Merkezi** (✉ box office, Taksim Sq., ☎ 212/251–5600); tickets are also available here for concerts at Cemal Reşit Rey Concert Hall. Ballet and dance companies perform at this hall, too.

Nightlife

BARS

Bebek Bar (✉ Bebek Ambassadeurs Hotel, Cevdet Paşa Cad. 113, Bebek, ☎ 212/263–3000) has views over the Bosporus and draws locals from the neighborhood and nearby Bosporus University. Sophisticated **Beyoğlu Pub** (✉ İstiklâl Cad. 140/7, Beyoğlu, ☎ 212/252–3842), behind an arcade off İstiklâl Caddesi, has a pleasant garden and a discreet indoor bar. **Hayal Kahvesi** (✉ Büyük Parmakkapı Sok. 19, Beyoğlu, ☎ 212/244–2558) is a bohemian side-street bar with wooden furniture, lace curtains, and live music. The fin-de-siècle decor of the **Orient Express Bar** (✉ Pera Palas Hotel, Meşrutiyet Cad. 98, Tepebaşı, ☎ 212/251–4560) distills the atmosphere of Old Istanbul with the lingering presence of the rich, powerful, and famous who once played here. With its British pub atmosphere and range of imported beers and malt whiskies, the **Sherlock Holmes** (✉ Çalıkuşu Sokak 5, ☎ 212/281–6372) has become a popular haunt for local yuppies and expatriates alike. **Kehri Bar** (✉ Divan Hotel, Cumhuriyet Caddesi 2, Taksim, ☎ 212/231–4100) offers the latest in Turkish music, including live pop and jazz bands.

DANCE CLUBS

Çubuklu 29 (✉ Paşabahçe Yolu, Çubuklu, ☎ 216/322–2829), by the Bosporus on the Asian side, is open mid-June–September. **Havana** (✉ Fargo İş Merkezi, Büyükdere Caddesi, Zincirlikuyu, ☎ 212/213–1036) is the place to be seen for young socialites, although the dancing only really gets going after 10. **Hayal Kahvesi** (✉ Burunbahçe, Çubuklu, ☏ 216/413–6880), a huge, restaurant-bar-disco complex on the Asian shore of the Bosporus, has dancing to live jazz or rock on Friday or Saturday (summer only). The loud and lively three-story **Kemancı Rock-Bar** (✉ Taksim Sitesi, Sıraselviler 69, Taksim, ☏ 212/245–3048 or 212/251–3015) is a favorite with students, who dance to live rock and blues bands. **RA** (✉ Bayıldım Caddesi 2, Maçka, ☏ 212/326–1100) under the Swissôtel plays Turkish pop music and often features live pop stars.

JAZZ CLUBS

Q Jazz Bar (✉ Çırağan Cad. 84, Beşiktaş, ☏ 212/236–2489 or 212/236–2121), the Çırağan Hotel's luxurious jazz bar, has some of the classiest music in town—at equally classy prices. **Harry's Jazz Bar** (✉ Hyatt Regency Hotel, Takışla, Taksim, ☏ 212/225–7000) is popular with both local and expatriate professionals.

NIGHTCLUBS

Galata Tower (✉ Kuledibi, ☏ 212/245–1160) serves dinner followed by a Turkish show and dancing. **Kervansaray** (✉ Cumhuriyet Cad. 30, Elmadağ, ☏ 212/247–1630) has dining, dancing, and belly-dancing shows. The revue at **Orient House** (✉ Tiyatro Cad. 27, Beyazıt, ☏ 212/517–3488) is the spot for some of Istanbul's best-known belly dancers and folk dances from around Turkey.

Shopping

Districts and Malls

In New Town, stores and boutiques line İstiklâl Caddesi, which runs off Taksim Square, and Rumeli, Halaskargazi, and Valikonağı Caddeleri, north of the Istanbul Hilton. Two streets in the Kadiköy area with good shops are Bağdat and Bahariye Caddeleri. **Akmerkez,** the newest of the malls in Etiler, has luxury and designer wear. **Ataköy Shopping and Tourism Center** is a large mall near the airport. In Altunizade on the Asian side, the slick **Capitol** mall has movies and entertainment, too.

Markets

The **Grand Bazaar** is what it sounds like: a treasure trove of all things Turkish—carpets, brass, copper, jewelry, textiles, and leather goods. **Tünel Square,** a quick Metro ride up from Karaköy, is a quaint group of stores with old prints, books, and artifacts. **Çukurcuma,** in the back streets of Beyoğlu, contains several shops specializing in maps and odds and ends from the late 19th and early 20th centuries. **Balıkpazarı** (fish market) is in Beyoğlu Caddesi, off İstiklâl Caddesi. A bustling clutter of narrow covered streets, Balıkpazarı contains stalls and tiny stores, selling everything from spices, vegetables, and fruit to fish, cooked meats, and even pork. Turkish traders are joined by new arrivals from eastern Europe and the former Soviet Union at a flea market held in **Beyazit Square,** near the Grand Bazaar, every Sunday starting at about 10 AM; here you can find everything from cheap electronic goods to Russian boots and hats. A crafts market, with street entertainment, is open on Sunday along the Bosporus at **Ortaköy.** A weekend crafts market takes place on **Bekar Sokak,** off İstiklâl Caddesi.

Istanbul Essentials

AIRPORTS AND TRANSFERS

All international and domestic flights arrive at Istanbul's Atatürk Airport. For arrival and departure information call the individual airline or the airport's information desk listed below.

➤ AIRPORT INFORMATION: **Atatürk Airport** (☏ 212/252–1106).

TRANSFERS

Shuttle buses run from the airport's international and domestic terminals to the Turkish Airlines (THY) terminal in downtown Istanbul, at Cumhuriyet Caddesi, near the THY Taksim office. Buses depart for the airport from the same address. Allow at least 45 minutes for the bus ride. Plan to be at the airport two hours before your international flight because of the lengthy security and check-in procedures. The ride from the airport into town takes from 30 to 40 minutes, depending on traffic. Taxis charge about $15 to Taksim Square and $11 to Sultanahmet.

➤ CONTACTS: **THY Taksim office** (☎ 212/245–2454).

BOAT AND FERRY TRAVEL

Many ferries run between the Asian and European continents. Deniz otobüsü (sea buses) run between the continents and, in summer, to destinations such as the Princes' Islands; they are fast and efficient. For an inexpensive ride take the boat in the direction of Anadolu Kavağı, along the Bosporus to its mouth at the Black Sea. The boat leaves year-round from Dock No. 5 at the Eminönü Docks, next to the Galata Bridge on the Old Istanbul side, at 10:35 AM and 1:35 PM, with two extra trips on weekdays and four extra trips on Sunday from April through September. The fare is $6 (round-trip). The trip takes 1¾ hours one-way. You can disembark at any of the stops and return by land if you wish. Regular ferries depart from Kabataş Dock, near Dolmabahçe Palace on the European side, to Üsküdar on the Asian side; and also from Eminönü Docks 1 and 2, near Sirkeci Station.

➤ BOAT AND FERRY INFORMATION: **Deniz otobüsü** (☎ 216/362–0444). **Sirkeci Station** (☎ 212/244–4233).

BUS TRAVEL TO AND FROM ISTANBUL

Buses arrive in Istanbul at Esenler terminal, northwest of the city center. From the terminal, the major bus companies offer free minibus service to centers such as Sultanahmet, Taksim, and Aksaray. The Hızlı Tren (rapid train) also connects the terminal to Aksaray, though it is often very crowded and can be extremely hot in summer. A few buses from Anatolia arrive at Harem terminal, on the eastern shore of the Bosporus. If you arrive with baggage, it is much easier to take a taxi, which will cost about $10 to Taksim from the Esenler terminal and about $6 to Old Istanbul.

BUS TRAVEL WITHIN ISTANBUL

You need to buy a ticket before boarding a bus. Individual tickets or books of 10 can be purchased at ticket stands around the city. Shoeshine boys or men on the street will also sell them to you for a few cents more. Fares are about 25¢ per ride. On the city's orange privatized buses (Halk Otobüsü), you pay for tickets on the bus. The London-style red double-deckers operate along a scenic route between Sultanahmet and Emigran on the Bosporus and between Europe and Asia and cost about $1 one-way.

CAR TRAVEL

If you drive in from the west, take the busy E5 highway, also called Londra Asfaltı, which leads from Edirne to Atatürk Airport and on through the city walls at Cannon Gate (Topkapı). E5 heading out of Istanbul leads into central Anatolia and on to Syria. You can also take one of the numerous car ferries that ply the Sea of Marmara and the Dardanelles from Kabataş Dock, or try the overnight ferry to İzmir, which leaves from Sarayburnu.

CONSULATES

➤ Australia: (✉ Tepecik Yokuşu 58, Etiler, 80630, ☎ 212/257–7050).
➤ Canada: (✉ Büyükdere Cad. 107/3, Bengün Han, 80300, Gayrettepe, ☎ 212/272–5174).
➤ Ireland: (Honorary; ✉ Cumhuriyet Cad. 26, Harbiye, 80200, ☎ 212/246–6025).
➤ United Kingdom: (✉ Meşrutiyet Cad. 34, Tepebaşı 80050, Beyoğlu, ☎ 212/293–7540).
➤ United States: (✉ Meşrutiyet Cad. 104–108, Tepebaşi 80050, Beyoğlu, ☎ 212/251–3602).

EMERGENCIES

Dial ☎ 118 for information on 24-hour pharmacies in each neighborhood; a notice in the window of every pharmacy lists the name and address of the nearest all-night shop. For a doctor, call one of the hospitals below.
➤ Emergency Services: **Ambulance** (☎ 112). **Tourism Police** (☎ 212/527–4503).
➤ Hospitals: **American Hospital** (✉ Güzelbahçe Sok. 20, Nişantaşı, 80200, ☎ 212/231–4050 through 231–4069). **International Hospital** (Yesilyurt, ☎ 212/663–3000).

ENGLISH-LANGUAGE MEDIA

➤ Bookstores: **D & R** (✉ Nispetiye Cad., Etiler, ☎ 212/263–2914). **Homer** (✉ Yeni Çarşı Cad. 28A, Galatasaray, ☎ 212/249–5902). **Pandora** (✉ Büyükparmakkapı Sok. 3, ☎ 212/243–3503 or 212/243–3504). **Robinson Crusoe** (✉ İstiklâl Cad. 389, Tünel, ☎ 212/293–6968 or 212/293–6977).

TAXIS

Taxis are inexpensive and metered. As most drivers do not speak English and may not know the street names, write down the street you want, the nearby main streets, and the name of the area. Although tipping is not expected, you should round off the fare to the nearest 100,000 TL.

DOLMUŞ

These are shared taxis operating between set destinations throughout the city. Dolmuş stops are indicated by a blue-and-white sign with a large D. The destination is shown on either a roof sign or a card in the front window. Until the mid-1990s all the dolmuş were classic American cars from the 1950s, but they have now been nearly all replaced by modern yellow minibuses.

TOURS

Tours can be arranged through travel agencies. Most companies have a half- or full-day Classical Tour. The half-day tour includes Aya Sofya, the Museum of Turkish and Islamic Arts, the Hippodrome, Yerebatan Saray, and the Blue Mosque; the full-day tour, in addition to the above sights, includes Topkapı Palace, the Süleymaniye Mosque, the Covered or Egyptian Bazaar, and lunch.

TRAIN TRAVEL

Trains from the west arrive at Sirkeci Station in Old Istanbul. Eastbound trains to Anatolia depart from Haydarpaşa Station on the Asian side.
➤ Train Information: **Haydarpaşa Station** (☎ 216/336–0475). **Sirkeci Station** (☎ 212/527–0050 or 212/527–0051).

TRANSPORTATION AROUND ISTANBUL

The best way to get to the various magnificent monuments in Sultanahmet in Old Istanbul is to walk; they're all within easy distance of one another. A tram system runs from Topkapı, via Sultanahmet, to Sirkeci. The Tünel, a tiny underground train, is handy for getting up the steep hill from Karaköy to the bottom of İstiklâl Caddesi. It runs every 10 minutes and costs about 25¢. Trams run the length of İstiklâl Caddesi from Taksim to Tünel and cost about 25¢.

TRAVEL AGENCIES

➤ LOCAL AGENTS: **Fest** (✉ Barbaros Apt. Barbaros Bulvarı 44, Balmumcu, ☎ 212/234–1200). **Intra** (✉ Halaşkargazi Cad. 111/2, Harbiye, ☎ 212/247–8174 or 212/240–3891). **Plan Tours** (✉ Cumhuriyet Cad. 131/1, Elmadağ, ☎ 212/230–2272 or 212/230–8118). **Setur** (✉ Cumhuriyet Cad. 107, Harbiye, ☎ 212/230–0336). **Türk Express** (American Express Travel Service representative; ✉ Istanbul Hilton, Cumhuriyet Cad., Harbiye, ☎ 212/241–0248 or 212/241–0249). **Vip Tourism** (✉ Cumhuriyet Cad. 269/2, Harbiye, ☎ 212/241–6514).

VISITOR INFORMATION

➤ TOURIST INFORMATION: **Atatürk Airport** (☎ 212/663–0793). **Istanbul Hilton** (☎ 212/233–0592). **Karaköy Yolcu Salonu** (International Maritime Passenger Terminal, ☎ 212/249–5776). **Pavilion** (✉ Divan Yolu Cad. 3, Sultanahmet, ☎ 212/518–1802 or 212/518–8754).

THE AEGEAN COAST

Some of the finest ancient Greek and Roman cities, including the fabled Pergamum, Ephesus, Aphrodisias, and Troy, are found in this region of Turkey. Watch for the ubiquitous bright-yellow road signs pointing to historic sites or to those currently undergoing excavation. There are so many Greek and Roman ruins, in fact, that some haven't yet been excavated and others are going to seed. Grand or small, all the sites are best visited early in the morning or late in the afternoon, when crowds are smaller. Escape the heat of the day on one of the sandy beaches along the coast.

It makes sense to begin your exploration of the Aegean Coast in the north at inland Bursa, moving west to Gallipoli and Çanakkale at the Dardanelles. Farther south, past Troy, is the city of İzmir. Follow the southern coast down to Bodrum, with a detour inland to the ruins at Aphrodisias and the natural hot springs of Pamukkale. You'll need 8–10 days to cover the region thoroughly.

Bursa

The first capital of the Ottoman Empire, Bursa is known as Yeşil (Green) Bursa. In recent years rapid growth has meant that Bursa is now surrounded by a sprawl of hastily-built concrete apartment blocks.
★ Its center, however, has retained the many trees and parks and **Yeşil Cami** (Green Mosque) and **Yeşil Türbe** (Green Mausoleum), that gave it its nickname. Both mosque and mausoleum derive their names from the green tiles that line their interiors. ✉ *Yeşil Cad. (Green Ave.).* ⊙ *Daily except during prayer hrs.*

The town square, called Heykel, which means "statue," is named for its statue of Atatürk. Off Heykel is the **Ulu Cami** (Great Mosque) with its distinctive silhouette of 20 domes. ✉ *Atatürk Cad.* ⊙ *Daily except during prayer hrs.*

Bursa is also the site of **Uludağ** (Great Mountain), Turkey's most popular ski resort. To fully appreciate why the town is called Green Bursa, take a ride on the *teleferik* (cable car; ✉ Namazgah Cad.) up the mountain for a panoramic view.

$$ ✕ **Cumurcul.** In a converted old house, this restaurant is a local favorite. Grilled meats and fish are attentively prepared, and there is a good range

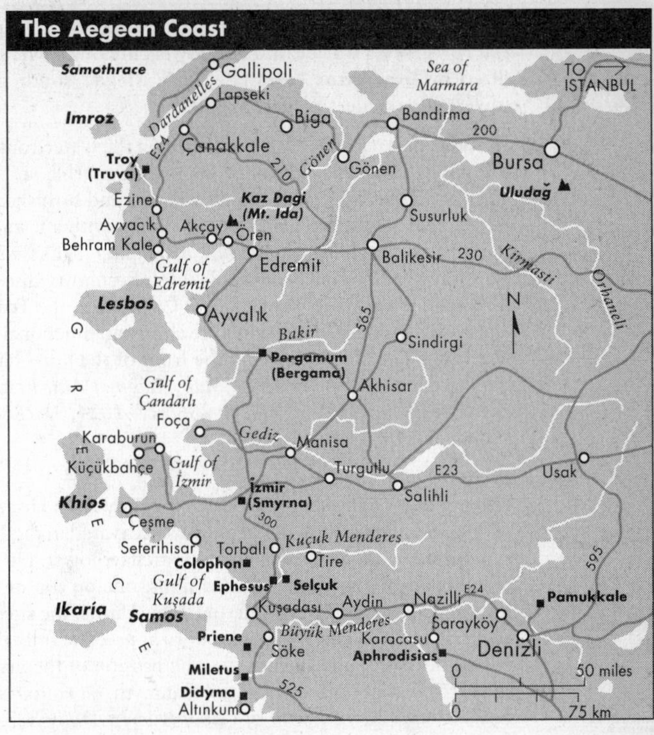

of cold and hot mezes, including *avcı böreği*(hunter's pie), a deep-fried or oven-baked pastry filled with meat or cheese. ✉ *Çekirge Cad.,* ☎ *224/235–3707 or 224/235–3373. AE, MC, V.*

$ ✕ **Kebabcı İskender.** Bursa is famous for the dish served in this 140-year-old restaurant, *İskender kebab* (Alexander's kebab—slivers of skewer-grilled meat and pita bread immersed in a rich tomato sauce and topped with hot butter and yogurt). ✉ *Ünlü Cad. 7, Heykel,* ☎ *224/221–4615. No credit cards.*

$$$$ ★ 🏨 **Çelik Palace.** After you've indulged at this posh hotel's restaurant, casino, and clubs, enjoy a dip in the domed, Roman-style thermal pool fed by local hot springs. The place has a lively 1930s design scheme, and some rooms have balconies. ✉ *Çekirge Meyd. 79, 16000,* ☎ *224/233–3800,* FAX *224/236–1910,* WEB *hotels.wec-net.com.tr/emek. 173 rooms. Restaurant. AE, DC, MC, V.*

$$ 🏨 **Ada Palas.** Thermal baths are on every floor of this Çekirge hotel, and the price is lower than that at the nearby Çelik. Rooms are unexceptional but in good condition. ✉ *Murat Cad. 21, Çekirge 16000,* ☎ *224/233–3990,* FAX *224/236–4656. 36 rooms. Restaurant. V.*

Çanakkale and Gallipoli

Çanakkale is the guardian of the Dardanelles, the narrow straits that separate Europe from Asia and connect the Aegean Sea with the Sea of Marmara. This strategic point has been fought over since the days of the Trojan War. During World War I Britain and France tried to breach Çanakkale's defenses in the unsuccessful Gallipoli campaign. They were defeated by the strategy of Mustafa Kemal—the man who would later be called Atatürk. Thirty-one beautifully tended **military cemeteries** of the Allied dead from World War I line the battlefields.

Nowadays Çanakkale is a drab agricultural center and garrison town, but it serves as the gateway to historic Gallipoli, on the north side of the Dardanelles. At Cape Helles there is a massive, four-pillared memorial to Turkey's war dead. Half-day excursions to Gallipoli are organized by **Troy-Anzac Tours** (✉ İskele Meyd., south side near clock tower, Çanakkale, ☎ 286/217–5849).

$$ **Akol.** This modern hotel is perched on the waterfront in Çanakkale. The lobby is bright and full of cool white marble and brass fixtures. The rooms are fitted with green carpeting and furnished with wooden tables, chairs, and dressers. Ask for a room with a terrace overlooking the Dardanelles. ✉ *Kordonboyu, Çanakkale 17100,* ☎ *286/217–9456,* FAX *286/217–2897. 135 rooms, 2 suites. Restaurant, pool. MC, V.*

$$ **Büyük Truva.** Near the center of Çanakkale, the Truva is an excellent base for sightseeing. Rooms are clean and functional and have large windows. The older section at the front of the hotel has views across the Dardanelles. ✉ *Cevatpaşa Mah. Mehmet Akif Ersoy Cad. 2 Kordonboyu, Çanakkale, 17100,* ☎ *286/217–1024,* FAX *286/217–0903. 66 rooms. Restaurant. AE, MC, V.*

Troy

Long thought to be simply an imaginary city from Homer's *Iliad*, **Troy** (Truva in Turkish, Ilion in Greek) was excavated in the 1870s by Heinrich Schliemann, a German amateur archaeologist. He also found the remains of nine successive civilizations, one on top of the other, dating back 5,000 years. Considering Troy's fame, the site is surprisingly small. It's best to take a guided tour to appreciate fully the significance of this discovery and the unwavering passion of the man who proved that Troy was not just another ancient myth. ✉ *Follow signs from Rte. E87, 32 km (20 mi) south of Çanakkale.* ⌚ *Daily 8–7.*

$$ **Tusan.** Along the beachfront north of Troy at Güzelyalı, and framed by a pine forest, this is one of the most attractive hotels in the area. The two-story stucco and brick structure has nondescript rooms, but the setting is superb. Be certain to reserve well in advance. ✉ *Güzelyalı, 17001,* ☎ *286/232–8210 or 286/232–8746/47,* FAX *286/232–8226,* WEB *www.tusanhotel.com. 64 rooms. Restaurant. MC, V. Closed Nov.–Mar..*

Ayvalık

The charming, sleepy coastal resort just south of the Gulf of Edremit has some of the best examples of 19th-century Greek domestic architecture found anywhere in the Aegean. From Ayvalık you can take boats to **Ali Bey Adası,** a tiny island with pleasant waterfront restaurants, and to the Greek island of Lesbos.

$ **Ankara Oteli.** On Sarımsaklı beach, just a few feet from the surf, this is the cheapest option. Although rooms are nondescript, they do have balconies; book ahead to get one facing the beach. ✉ *Sarımsaklı Plaj, 10425,* ☎ *266/324–1195 or 266/324–1048,* FAX *266/324–0022. 108 rooms. Restaurant. No credit cards. Closed Nov.–Mar.*

$ **Büyük Berk.** Part of a larger complex, this modern hotel sits on Ayvalık's best beach, about 3¼ km (2 mi) from the center of town. Rooms are functional, with low wooden beds and whitewashed walls but all have balconies, most with views across the Aegean. ✉ *Sarımsaklı Plaj, 10425,* ☎ *266/324–1045,* FAX *266/324–1194. 250 rooms. Restaurant, pool. MC, V. Closed Oct.–Mar.*

Pergamum

The windswept ruins of Pergamum (Bergama in Turkish) are among the most spectacular in Turkey. Pergamum's glory peaked during the Greek Attalid dynasty (241 BC–133 BC), when it was one of the world's most magnificent architectural and artistic centers—especially under the rule of Eumenes II, who lavished his great wealth on the city. When the mad Attalus III died, he bequeathed the entire kingdom to Rome.

Because the attractions are spread out over several miles, it's best to take a taxi from one site to the next. The most noteworthy places are the Asklepieion, the Ethnological Museum, the Red Hall, and the Acropolis. The most famous building at the Acropolis is the library, which once contained a collection of 200,000 books, all on papyrus. The library's collection was second only to the one in Alexandria, Egypt. ⏲ *Apr.–Oct., daily 8:30–6:30; Nov.–Mar., daily 8:30–5:30.*

$ ✕ **Bergama Restaurant.** This inexpensive eatery on the main street offers an excellent range of kebabs and starters, including local specialities such as the tasty spicy meatballs *Bergama köftesi,* at tables set amid potted plants around a small indoor pond filled with plump goldfish. ✉ *Bankalar Caddesi 5,* ☎ *232/632–3492. No credit cards.*

$ 🏨 **Asude Hotel.** Some of the rooms at the front of this clean, no-frills hotel on the outskirts of town have distant views of the ancient ruins of Pergamum. The restaurant serves a passable selection of grilled meats. ✉ *İzmir Asfaltı, Fatih Mah., Bergama 35700,* ☎ *232/631–3903,* FAX *232/631–3904. 52 rooms. Restaurant, bar. MC, V.*

$ 🏨 **Hotel İskender.** Although it's plain and modern, this place is right in the center of town and has air-conditioning. The outdoor restaurant serves tasty fresh mezes and grilled foods. ✉ *İzmir Cad. Ilica Önü Mev., Bergama 35700,* ☎ *232/633–2123 or 232/632–9711,* FAX *232/632–9710. 60 rooms. 2 restaurants. MC, V.*

İzmir

Turkey's third-largest city is also its most Mediterranean in feel. Called Smyrna by the Greeks, it was a vital trading port that was often ravaged by wars and earthquakes. The city was almost completely destroyed by a fire in 1922 during the final stages of Turkey's War of Independence against Greece. It was quickly rebuilt and became known by its Turkish name, İzmir. Today it's a lively, modern city filled with wide boulevards, apartment houses, and office buildings. At the center of the city is **Kültürpark,** a large green park that is the site of İzmir's industrial fair from late August to late September (a time when most hotels are full).

Atop İzmir's highest hill is the **Kadifekale** (Velvet Fortress), built in the 3rd century BC by Lysimachos. It is easily reached by dolmuş and is one of the few ancient ruins that was not destroyed in the fire. At the foot of the hill is the restored **Agora,** the market of ancient Smyrna. The modern-day marketplace is in **Konak Square,** a maze of tiny streets filled with shops and covered stalls. ⏲ *Mon.–Sat. 8–8.*

$$$$ 🏨 **İzmir Hilton.** At 34 stories, the Hilton is one of the Aegean coast's tallest buildings. Striking and modern, the structure looms over the city center. From the 10-story atrium to the rooftop restaurant, the public spaces are suitably grand. Guest rooms are plush. ✉ *Gazi Osman Paşa Bul. 7, 35210,* ☎ *232/441–6060,* FAX *232/441–2277. 381 rooms. 4 restaurants, pool. AE, DC, MC, V.*

$$$ 🏨 **Mercure Konak Hotel.** This hotel right on the water has lots of cool marble and greenery. Guest rooms have big windows with views. The city's museums are within easy walking distance. ✉ *Mithatpasa Cad. 128, 35210,* ☎ *232/489–1500,* FAX *232/489–1709. 80 rooms. Restaurant. AE, MC, V.*

Kuşadası

One of the most popular tourist resorts in the Mediterranean, Kuşadası has grown in 30 years from a fishing village into a sprawling town. Although geared to serving thousands of tourists who visit the nearby ruins and beaches, the busy town maintains an easy pace.

$$ ✕ **Ali Baba Restaurant.** The focus is on fish at this simply styled (starched white tablecloths, wooden chairs) waterfront spot with a peaceful view of the bay. Try the marinated octopus salad or the fried calamari, followed by a grilled version of whatever has just been caught. ✉ *Belediye Turistik Çarşısı 5,* ☎ *256/614–1551. Reservations essential. MC, V.*

$$ ★ ✕ **Alize.** A five-minute walk from the waterfront, this excellent bistro more than makes up for its lack of sea view with a superb range of meat, fish, and pasta dishes and live acoustic music in the evenings. It's a favorite hangout for locals, particularly the young trendy set. ✉ *Karagöz Sok. 67, Sağlık Cad.,* ☎ *256/612–0360. MC, V.*

$$$ **Club Kervansaray.** In a refurbished 300-year-old caravansary, this hotel in the center of town is Ottoman in style and loaded with charm and atmosphere. Its restaurant has a floor show and there's dancing after dinner in the palm-fringed courtyard, where the camels were once kept. ✉ *Atatürk Bul. 2, 09400,* ☎ *256/614–4115,* FAX *256/614–2423,* WEB *www.kusadasihotels.com. 26 rooms. Restaurant. AE, DC, MC, V.*

$$$ ★ **Kismet.** Although it's small, this hotel is run on a grand scale. It's surrounded by beautifully maintained gardens on a promontory overlooking the marina on one side and the Aegean on the other. Ask for rooms in the garden annex. Reservations are a must. ✉ *Akyar Mev., Türkmen Mahallesi, 09400,* ☎ *256/618–1290,* FAX *256/618–1295. 107 rooms. Restaurant. MC, V. Closed Nov.–Mar.*

$$ **Efe Otel.** Located on the waterfront a little beyond the path to Pigeon Island, the Efe is small, clean, and comfortable. The rooms are nondescript, with bare walls and low beds with wooden frames, but you can compensate by asking for one with a balcony and a view over Pigeon Island. ✉ *Guvercin Ada Cad. 37, 09400,* ☎ *256/614–3661,* FAX *256/614–3662. 84 rooms. AE, MC, V.*

Ephesus and Selçuk

Ephesus is the showpiece of Aegean archaeology and one of the grandest reconstructed ancient sites in the world. Created by the Ionians in the 11th century BC, Ephesus became a powerful trading port and the sacred center for the cult of Artemis, Greek goddess of chastity, the moon, and hunting. The Ionians built a temple in her honor, one of the Seven Wonders of the Ancient World. Later the city received a visit from St. Paul, who spent two years preaching here and established one of the first Christian communities on the Aegean coast. Over the centuries, heavy silting of the old port finally led to the city's abandonment; the ancient site now lies 3 km (2 mi) inland. Allow yourself one full day for Ephesus. The city is especially appealing out of season, when it can seem like a ghost town with its shimmering, long, white marble road grooved by chariot wheels. Some of the splendors here include the two-story Library of Celsus; houses of nobles, with their terraces and courtyards; a 25,000-seat amphitheater, still used today during the Selçuk Ephesus Festival of Culture and Art; remains of the municipal baths; and a brothel. ✉ *4 km (2½ mi) west of Selçuk on Selçuk–Ephesus Rd.,* ☎ *232/892–6402.* ⊙ *Apr.–Sept., daily 8:30–6; Oct.–Mar., daily 8:30–5.*

In Selçuk, east of Ephesus, on Ayasoluk Hill, stands the restored **Basilica of St. John** (St. Jean Anıtı), containing the tomb of the apostle. Near the entrance to the basilica is the **Ephesus Museum,** with two statues of Artemis and marvelous frescoes and mosaics. ⊙ *Basilica and museum Tues.–Sun. 8:30–6.*

St. Paul and St. John preached in both Ephesus and Selçuk and changed the cult of Artemis into the cult of the Virgin Mary. **Meryemana,** 5 km (3 mi) from Ephesus, has the **House of Mary,** thought by some to have been the place where St. John took the mother of Jesus after the crucifixion and from which some believe she ascended to heaven. ⊙ *Daily 7:30–sunset.*

$$ **Kale Han.** In a refurbished stone building, this is one of the nicest hotels in town, run by a very welcoming family. Rooms are simple, with bare, whitewashed walls and dark timber beams. Ask for one facing the castle behind the hotel. The restaurant is open around the clock. ✉ *Atatürk Cad. 49, Selçuk 35920,* ☎ *232/892–6154,* FAX *232/892–2169,* WEB *www.kalehan.com. 50 rooms with shower, 4 with bath, 1 suite. Restaurant, pool. V.*

$ **Victoria Hotel.** Rooms in this tidy, cheerful hostelry in the center of town have whitewashed walls and honey-color wooden trim. In summer most have delightful views of storks nesting on a nearby aqueduct. The restaurant is a good bet for traditional Turkish fare. ✉ *Cengiz Topel Cad. 4, Selçuk 35920,* ☎ *232/892–3203,* FAX *232/892–3204. 24 rooms. Restaurant. MC, V.*

Priene

Priene, which sits atop a steep hill, was an artistic and cultural center during the Hellenistic period. Its main attraction is the **Temple of Athena,** with five fluted columns and a backdrop of mountains and the fertile plains of the Meander River. The city also has a small amphitheater, gymnasium, council chambers, marketplace, and stadium. ⊙ *Daily 8:30–6.*

Miletus

A thriving port made Miletus one of the greatest commercial centers of the ancient Greek world. It was the first Greek city to use coins for money. It also became an Ionian intellectual center and home to such philosophers as Thales, Anaximander, and Anaximenes, all of whom made contributions to mathematics and the natural sciences. The city's most magnificent building is the **Great Theater,** a remarkably intact amphitheater built by the Ionians and enlarged by the Romans to seat 25,000. Climb to the highest seats in the amphitheater for a view across the city to the bay. ⊙ *Tues.–Sun. 8:30–6.*

Didyma

Once home to one of the most famous oracles in the ancient world, Didyma was a sanctuary dedicated to Apollo. It's still possible to follow the 32-km (20-mi) path of what was known as the Sacred Way, leading from the coast at Miletus to the site of the oracle at Didyma's **Temple of Apollo.** Under the temple courtyard is a network of corridors whose walls would throw the oracle's voice into deep and ghostly echoes. The messages would then be interpreted by the priests. Fragments of bas-relief include a gigantic head of Medusa and a small statue of Poseidon and his wife, Amphitrite. ⊙ *Daily 8:30–6.*

Pamukkale

The place first appears as an enormous chalky-white cliff rising some 330 ft from the plains. Mineral-rich volcanic spring water cascades over basins and natural terraces, crystallizing into white stalactites—curtains of solidified water seemingly suspended in air. The hot springs in the area were popular with the ancient Romans, who believed them to have curative powers. People still believe that the waters cure a variety of ailments, including rheumatism. Accommodations are in the nearby village of Karahayıt, 3 km (2 mi) from the springs, where several hotels have their own thermal pools. You can see the remains of Roman baths among the ruins of nearby **Hierapolis.**

★ It's best to stay in Karahayıt overnight before heading on to the ruins of **Aphrodisias,** a city of 60,000 dedicated to Aphrodite, the Greek goddess of love and fertility. It thrived from 100 BC to AD 500. Aphrodisias is reached via Karacasu, a good place to stop for lunch; fresh trout is the local specialty. Aphrodisias is filled with marble baths, temples, and theaters, all overrun with wild blackberries and pomegranates. Across a field sprinkled with poppies and sunflowers is a well-preserved **stadium**, which was built for 30,000 spectators.

$$$ **Polat Thermal Hotel.** Clean, spacious, and comfortable, with a full range of facilities, the Polat Thermal is almost a thermal resort in itself, consisting of a scattering of one- and two-story buildings around a large outdoor pool. ✉ *Karahay, Denizli 20227,* ☎ *258/271–4111,* FAX *258/271–4092. 296 rooms. 2 restaurants, 2 pools. MC.*

Aegean Coast Essentials

BUS TRAVEL

All the towns are served by direct bus routes, and there are connecting services to the ancient sites.

CAR TRAVEL

The E24 from Çanakkale follows the coast until it turns inland at Kuşadası to meet the Mediterranean again at Antalya.

TOURS

Travel agencies in all the major towns organize tours of the historic sites. Travel agencies along Teyyare Caddesi in Kuşadası arrange escorted tours to Ephesus; Priene, Miletus, and Didyma; and Aphrodisias and Pamukkale.

VISITOR INFORMATION

➤ TOURIST INFORMATION: **Ayvalık** (✉ Yat Limanı Karşısı, 10400, ☎ 266/312–2122). **Bergama** (✉ Hükümet Binası, Zemin Kat, B Blok, 35700, ☎ 232/633–1862). **Bursa** (✉ Ulu Cami Parkı, Orhangazi Alt Geçidi No 1, 16020, ☎ 224/220–1848). **Çanakkale** (✉ İskele Meyd. 67, 17000, ☎ 286/217–1187). **Çeşme** (✉ İskele Meyd. 8, 35948, ☎ 232/712–6653). **İzmir** (✉ Gaziosmanpaşa Bul. 1/C, 35340, ☎ 232/489–9278). **Kuşadası** (✉ İskele Meyd., 09400, ☎ 256/614–1103).

THE MEDITERRANEAN COAST

Until the mid-1970s, Turkey's southwest coast was inaccessible to all but the most determined travelers in four-wheel-drive vehicles or on the backs of donkeys. Today, well-maintained highways wind through the area, and jets full of tourists arrive at the Dalaman Airport.

Thanks to strict developmental control, the area has maintained its Turkish flavor, with low, whitewashed buildings and tile roofs. The beaches are clean, and you can swim and snorkel in turquoise waters so clear that it is possible to see fish 20 ft below. There are excellent outdoor cafés and seafood restaurants, and no shortage of nightlife. But the region isn't just about untainted beaches and charming fishing villages. It also contains ancient cities of Greek, Roman, Arab, Seljuk, Armenian, crusader, and Byzantine vintage.

Seven full days should give you enough time to travel the 560-km (347-mi) route from Bursa to Antalya, stopping at the highlights in between.

Bodrum

Sitting between two crescent-shape bays, Bodrum, known as Halicarnassos in antiquity, was one of the first Greek colonies in Asia, founded around 1000 BC. In modern times it has long been the favorite haunt of the Turkish upper classes. Today the elite are joined by thousands of foreign visitors, and the area is rapidly filling with hotels and guest houses,

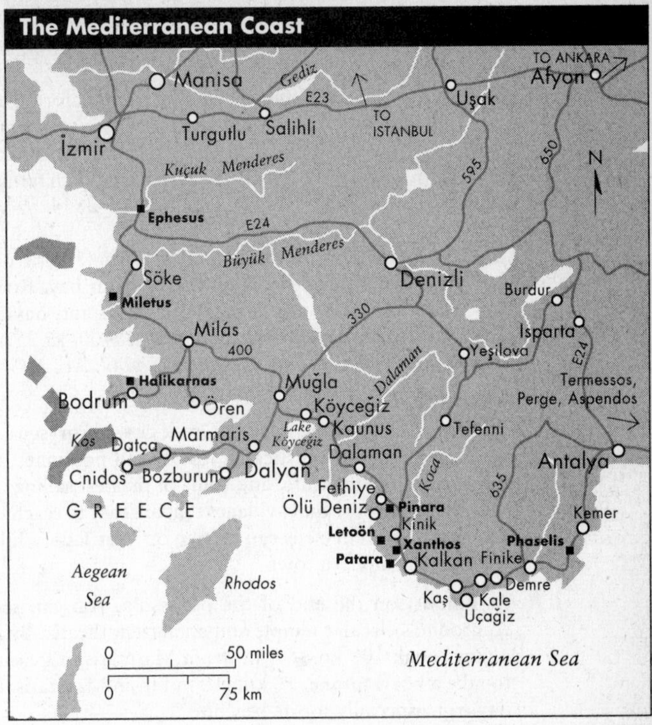

cafés, restaurants, and discos. Many compare it to St. Tropez on the French Riviera. Fortunately, it is still beautiful and unspoiled, with gleaming, whitewashed buildings covered with bougainvillea and magnificent unobstructed vistas of the bays. People flock to Bodrum not for its beach, which is a disappointment, but for its fine dining and nightlife. Beautiful **beaches** can be found in the outlying villages on the peninsula—Torba, Türkbükü, Yalıkavak, Turgutreis, Akyarlar, Ortakent, Bitez, and Gümbet. Easy to reach by minibus or dolmuş, these villages are about an hour's drive away and have clean hotels and plenty of outdoor restaurants.

One of the outstanding sights in Bodrum is **Bodrum Kalesi** (Bodrum Castle), known as the Castle of St. Peter. Standing between the two bays, the castle was built by crusaders during the 15th century. It has beautiful gardens and a **Sualtı Arkeoloji Müzesi** (Museum of Underwater Archaeology). ✉ *Kale Cad.,* ☎ *252/316–2516.* ⏲ *Winter 8–5; summer 8–7.*

$$ ✕ **Amphora.** Beautifully situated in an old stone building decorated with kilims and fishing gear opposite the marina at the edge of town, this eatery offers dazzling options: 20 or so mezes (including eggplant pureed, sautéed with garlic, or in tomato sauce) and two dozen kinds of kebabs. ✉ *Neyzen Tevfik Cad. 172,* ☎ *252/316–2368. Reservations essential in summer. MC, V.*

$–$$ ✕ **Kortan.** This seaside fish restaurant with white tablecloths and candles has outdoor seating with views of Bodrum's castle and the Greek island of Kos off the coast. The better dishes include fish kebabs, calamari, octopus salad, and whatever the catch of the day happens to be, usually grilled. ✉ *Cumhuriyet Cad. 32,* ☎ *252/316–1241. Reservations essential in summer. AE, MC, V.*

$$ 🏨 **Ayaz Hotel.** Less than a five minute drive east of Bodrum harbor, this hotel on a small bay has its own gardens and a beach with a bar where you can listen to the waves. The guest rooms are done in contemporary style and have balconies and sea views. ✉ *On Gümbet Bay 48400,* ☎ *252/316–1174 or 252/316–2956,* FAX *252/316–4751. 96 rooms. Restaurant, bar, pool. V.*

$$ 🏨 **Manastır Hotel Bodrum.** The bar in this comfortable whitewashed-stucco Mediterranean-style hotel was once the site of a monastery. Front rooms have balconies and overlook the Petronion; all are cool and spacious, with whitewashed walls and tasteful, modern furnishings. ✉ *Barış Sitesi Mev., Kumbahçe 48400,* ☎ *252/316–2854,* FAX *252/316–2772. 59 rooms. 2 restaurants, pool. AE, DC, V.*

$ 🏨 **Hotel Anka.** This hilltop hotel, just 2 km (1 mi) from the city center, has commanding views of the Bodrum bay. Rooms, in white-washed bungalows, are simple and clean and have balconies. ✉ *Eskiçeşme Mah. Asarlik Mev., Gümbet 48400,* ☎ *252/316–8217,* FAX *252/316–6194. 85 rooms. Restaurant, pool. AE, MC, V.*

Marmaris

Built on the site of the ancient Greek city of Phryscus, Marmaris has developed into a sophisticated resort with boutiques, elegant restaurants, plenty of nightlife, and some of the best sailing in the Mediterranean. Nearby are quiet villages that are easy to reach by boat or taxi. The remains of Phryscus can be seen on **Asar Tepe,** a hill 1½ km (1 mi) north of the modern town.

★ At **Knidos,** on the end of the peninsula, you can see the ruins of Aphrodite's circular temple and an ancient theater. By road Knidos is a very rough 108 km (67 mi) from Marmaris; it's easier and quicker to take a boat. **Turunç,** 16 km (10 mi) from Marmaris, is also worth a day trip, especially for its beaches.

Dalyan

Tombs from the Carian civilization of the first millennium BC are carved into the cliff that rises behind the Dalyan River in the fishing town of Dalyan, 20 minutes' drive from the airport in Dalaman. The town makes a good base for exploring the 4th-century BC city of **Kaunos,** 10 km (6 mi) to the west. It costs about $20 to rent a boat with a boatman to sail from Dalyan to the ruins and unspoiled **İstuzu beach.** You can also reach freshwater **Lake Köyceğiz** by boat through the reed beds of the Dalyan delta. This entire area is a wildlife preserve, filled with such birds as kingfishers, kestrels, egrets, and cranes.

$$ 🏨 **Dalyan Hotel.** Comfortable and clean, with views across Lake Köyceğiz to the tombs, the Dalyan is surrounded by trees on the shore of the lake. It has an excellent restaurant and a friendly, attentive staff that organizes hiking, bicycling, and motorcycling trips on nearby mountain paths. ✉ *Yalıı Sok., Maras Mahalli, Dalyan 48840,* ☎ *252/284–2239,* FAX *252/284–2240. 20 rooms with shower. 2 restaurants, pool. AE, MC, V.*

$$ 🏨 **Hotel Assyrian.** Beautifully situated at the edge of town with a large pool and views across the delta, the Assyrian has whitewashed single-story units in the style of the local architecture and offers free boat rides to the turtle beaches and medicinal mud baths. ✉ *Maraş Mahallesi, Dalyan 48800,* ☎ *252/284–3232,* FAX *252/284–3244. 34 rooms. Restaurant, pool. MC, V. Closed Nov.–Apr.*

$$ 🏨 **Hotel Özay.** This quiet, modern, efficiently run lakeside hotel is surrounded by lush greenery and palm trees. Its indoor café is in a garden draped with vines, bougainvillea, and jasmine, and its restaurant is above average. Daily boat tours of the lake are available, and Turkish belly-dancing shows take place at night. ✉ *Kordon Boyu 11, Köyceğiz 48800,* ☎ *252/262–4300,* FAX *252/262–2000. 34 rooms. Restaurant, pool. MC, V.*

Ölü Deniz

One of Turkey's greatest natural wonders is Ölü Deniz, an azure lagoon flanked by long, white beaches. There are a few wooden chalets in campgrounds and one beachfront hotel. Opposite the beach are small restaurants with rooftop bars, many with live music all night long.

$$–$$$ ★ ✕ **Ölü Deniz.** Wicker chairs and wooden floors fill this domed restaurant, whose name means "white dolphin." One of the most picturesque restaurants in the area, it commands a promontory overlooking the sea. Continental and Turkish cuisines are imaginatively prepared and presented. ✉ *On bay of Belcekiz, near Padirali,* ☎ *252/617–0068. No credit cards. Closed Nov.–Mar.*

$ ✕ **Asmali Restaurant.** This family-run restaurant serves homemade dishes, which vary from day to day, and cold mezes, grilled meats, and fish. It has a beautiful garden terrace with overhanging vines. ✉ *On road to Meri Oteli,* ☎ *no phone. No credit cards.*

$$ **Meri Oteli.** On a steep incline above the lagoon, this hotel is made up of a series of bungalows with rooms that are a bit down-at-the-heel though clean. But it's the only place to stay at the lagoon. Look for signs for Meri. ✉ *Fethiye, Fethiye 48300,* ☎ *252/617–0001,* FAX *252/617–0010. 84 rooms. Restaurant. MC, V.*

Pinara

In ancient times Pinara was one of the most important cities of the former Roman province of Lycia. Near the ruins of the ancient city, up a steep and strenuous dirt road, are nearly 200 Roman tombs cut honeycomb-fashion into the face of the cliffs. ✉ *Southeast of Fethiye, near Rte. 400.* ⏲ *Daily 8:30 AM–sunset.*

Xanthos

Xanthos was one of the leading cities of the Roman province of Lycia. Its inhabitants developed a fearsome reputation for bravery, twice burning down their own city rather than surrender. The ruins of the city lie down a rough road, but it's still well worth the bumpy ride to see the acropolis, the Tomb of Harpies, some plaster-cast reliefs, and ruins of some Byzantine buildings. ✉ *Off Rte. 400 from Kinik.* ⏲ *Daily 8:30 AM–sunset.*

Patara

Two thousand years ago, Patara, port city of Xanthos, was among the busiest ports in the region. Hannibal and St. Paul both visited, and St. Nicholas, the future Santa Claus, was born here. Today you will find **ruins** scattered around the marshes and sand dunes. The area's long, wide **beaches** remain unspoiled despite the fact that they attract hundreds of Turkish families and tourists.

Kalkan

With its red-tile roofs and waterfront restaurants, Kalkan is a perfect Mediterranean fishing village. Nearby beaches have made it a popular base for exploring the region.

$$ **Hotel Pirat.** This large, modern hotel consisting of a cluster of three-story buildings is beautifully located right on the harbor and a short walk from the swimming platform. Each room has its own private terrace. Ask for one overlooking the water. ✉ *Kalkan Marina, 07960,* ☎ *242/844–3178,* FAX *242/844–3183. 136 rooms. 2 restaurants, 3 pools. AE, MC, V.*

$–$$ **Kalkan Han.** A rambling, clean-lined, restored Ottoman caravanserai in the back part of the village, the Kalkan Han has a special treat: a roof terrace with sweeping views of the bay. It is a splendid place to enjoy breakfast and perfect after dark when it becomes the Star Bar. ✉ *Köyiçi Mev., 07960,* ☎ *242/844–3151,* FAX *242/844–2059. 12 rooms, 2 suites. Restaurant, pool. No credit cards. Closed Nov.–Apr.*

Kaş

Kaş is rapidly developing from a sleepy resort into a major yachting center. Luxury hotels have replaced many of the tiny houses on the hills, though there are still plenty of old-fashioned, budget-priced pansiyons. One of the attractions here is a day trip by boat to the underwater city of **Kekova,** where you can look overboard and see ancient Roman and Greek columns that were once part of a thriving city before the area was flooded. Kekova is especially popular with scuba divers and snorkelers, but to scuba dive or fish in this area, a permit must be obtained from the directorate of the harbor and from the directorate of the ministry of tourism. Boats leave daily at 9:30 and cost about $15.

$$ ✕ **Mercan.** On the eastern side of the harbor, this place serves good, basic Turkish food in an open-air setting. The menu includes whole lamb on a spit, fish, and lobster, as well as vegetarian choices. The water is so close that you can hear fish jumping as you watch the excursion boats heading out to sea. ✉ *Hükümet Cad., Cumhuriyet Meyd.,* ☎ *242/836–1209. MC, V.*

$$ 🏨 **Anı Motel.** From both the rooms and the terrace bar of this hotel in a restored old building you get beautiful views of the sea and the town of Kaş. Traditional furnishings enliven the clean, whitewashed walls. ✉ *Recep Bilgin Cad. 12/B, 07580,* ☎ *242/836–1791,* FAX *242/836–1791. 10 rooms. AE, MC, V.*

Phaselis

Phaselis is the site of some of the most romantic ruins in Turkey, with jumbles of stones dating from the 7th century BC through the Roman period. Overgrown streets descend to the sparkling waters of the Mediterranean, which are ideal for swimming.

Kemer

This town is a center of intensive tourist development, with hotels and restaurants, a well-equipped marina, and club-style holiday villages that may make you forget you're in Turkey.

Antalya

The resort of Antalya is a good base for several worthwhile excursions to major **archaeological sites** at Perge, Aspendos, Side, and Termessos. The city, built around a restored harbor, is filled with narrow streets lined with small houses, restaurants, and pansiyons. On the hilltop are tea gardens where you can enjoy tea made in an old-fashioned samovar and look across the bay to the Taurus Mountains. To the right of the port is the 13th-century **Yivli Minare** (Fluted Minaret).

The first-rate **Antalya Müzesi** (Antalya Museum) displays Turkish crafts, costumes, and artifacts of the classical Greek and Roman eras. ✉ *Konyaaltı Cad., west of town,* ☎ *242/241–4528.* ⏲ *Tues.–Sun. 9–6.*

$$ ✕ **Kırk Merdiven Restaurant.** You can reach this restaurant, which was once the barn of an Ottoman house, from the marina by climbing the 40 stairs from which it takes its name. Choose from the high-quality meats, fish, and large selection of mezes and salads, served either inside or in the garden. ✉ *Musalla Sok. 2Selc*

$$$$ ★ 🏨 **Talya.** At this luxurious resort you reach the private beach by taking an elevator down the side of the cliff. Every angle gives a view of the sea. Rooms are spacious, with big beds and terraces. The hotel is usually full in high season, so plan ahead. ✉ *Fevzi Çakmak Cad. 30, 07100,* ☎ *242/248–6800,* FAX *242/241–5400,* WEB *www.talya.com.tr. 204 rooms. 3 restaurants, pool. AE, DC, MC, V.*

$$ 🏨 **Tütav Türk Evleri.** Part of the old Kaleiçi district, this hotel consists of a row of restored 19th-century Turkish houses joined together. Well-tended gardens surround the inn and its popular restaurant,

which serves French-inspired cuisine and is known for delectable fish stew. ✉ *Mermerli Sok. 2, 07100,* ☎ *242/248–6478,* FAX *242/241–9419. 20 rooms. Restaurant, pool. AE, MC, V.*

Termessos

Writers in antiquity referred to Termessos as the "Eagle's Nest." It's not hard to see why. The only access is a stiff but rewarding climb up a steep, rocky path. Perched atop the mountain, the ruins offer views that are among the most dramatic in Turkey. Difficulty of access means that much of the site is romantically overgrown, and large areas, including virtually the entire Roman city, have never been excavated. You can see an amphitheater built on the mountainside. Organized tours to Termessos leave from Antalya. ✉ *Korkuteli, Rte. 350 off Rte. E87, northwest of Antalya.* ⏲ *Daily 9–5:30.*

Perge

The ruins of the ancient city of Perge, northeast of Antalya, include a superb amphitheater, well-preserved thermal baths, a restored colonnaded street, and a Roman basilica, where St. Paul gave his first sermon, in AD 45. ✉ *North off Rte. 400 at Aksu turnoff.* ⏲ *Daily 9–5:30.*

Aspendos

★ This site contains Turkey's best-preserved Roman amphitheater. The acoustics are so fine that modern-day performers don't need microphones or amplifiers. ✉ *North off Rte. 400 at turnoff past Belkis.* ⏲ *Daily 9–5:30.*

Mediterranean Coast Essentials

BOAT AND FERRY TRAVEL

There are many coves and picnic areas along the coast, accessible only by boat. For a small fee local fishermen will take you to and from the coves; you can also take one of the many water taxis. Or charter a small yacht, with or without skipper, at the marinas in Bodrum and Marmaris. One of the most enjoyable ways to see the coast is to take a one- or two-week cruise on a *gulet,* a wooden craft with a full crew.

CAR TRAVEL

Although the highways between towns are well maintained, the smaller roads are usually unpaved and very rough.

VISITOR INFORMATION

➤ TOURIST INFORMATION: **Antalya** (✉ Cumhuriyet Cad., Özel İdare Altı 2, 07040, ☎ 242/241–1747). **Bodrum** (✉ Barış Meyd. 12, 48400, ☎ 252/316–1091). **Dalaman** (✉ Dalaman Airport, 48770, ☎ 252/792–5291). **Datça** (✉ İskele Mah. Hükümet Binası, 48900, ☎ 252/712–3163 or 252/712–3546). **Kaş** (✉ Cumhuriyet Meyd. 5, 07580, ☎ 242/836–1238). **Marmaris** (✉ İskele Meyd. 2, 48700, ☎ 252/412–1035).

CENTRAL ANATOLIA AND CAPPADOCIA

The archaeological sites of Central Anatolia abound with well-preserved Roman architecture. Cappadocia, an area in the eastern part of Anatolia filled with ruins of ancient civilizations, has changed little over the centuries. People still travel between their farms and villages in horse-drawn carts, women drape their houses with strings of apricots and peppers for drying in the sun, and nomads pitch their black tents beside sunflower fields and cook on tiny fires that send smoke billowing through the tops of the tents.

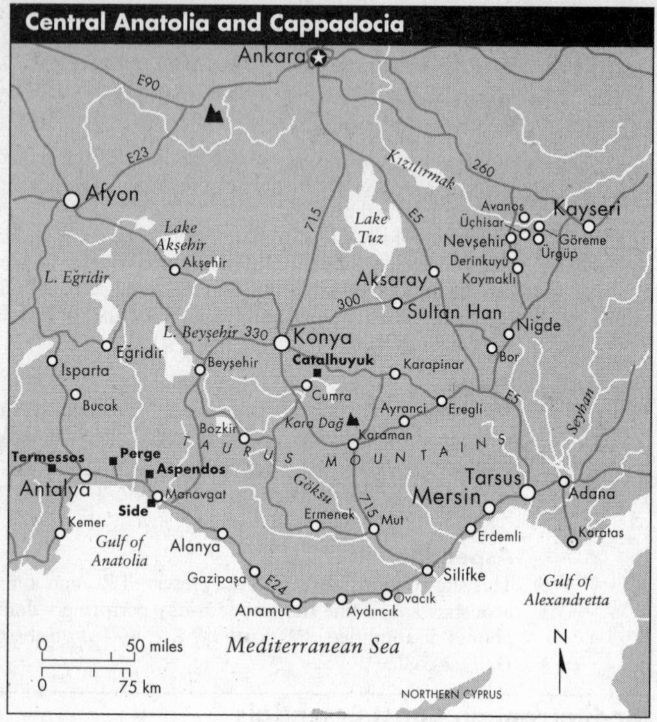

Ankara

From the time it was founded in about 1200 BC through its gradual decline under the Ottomans, Ankara, now Turkey's capital, had an illustrious yet strife-filled existence. By the early 20th century it was little more than a dusty provincial town, the perfect site for Atatürk to build his new capital and establish the new Turkish Republic. Today it is a bureaucrats' city, with functional, uninspired architecture and straight, broad roads. Although it is less frenetic than Istanbul, it is not as orderly as it was a decade ago, and traffic and overcrowding are becoming serious problems.

It was at the **Cumhuriyet Müzesi** (Republic Museum; ✉ Cumhuriyet Bul. off Ulus Meyd., ☎ 312/310–5361) in 1920 that Atatürk was elected chairman of the Grand National Assembly, which would organize the new nation. Housed in a restored 15th-century *bedestan* (covered bazaar and inn) is the superb **Ankara Anadolu Medeniyetleri Müzesi** (Museum of Anatolian Civilizations). The museum is small but packed with masterpieces from the Neolithic and Bronze ages and through the Assyrian, Phrygian, Urartu, Hellenistic, and Roman eras. The heart of the museum is its comprehensive collection of Hatti and Hittite artifacts, dating from the dawn of the second millennium BC. There are also small statues, jewels worked in gold and iron, combs and needles, as well as wonderful bas-relief carvings in stone. The addition in 1998 of several frescoes from the site of Çatal Höyük (first occupied in the 7th millennium BC) offers an opportunity to view art that adorned the walls of homes in the oldest settled community in the world. ✉ Gözcü Sok., ☎ 312/324–3160).

$$$$ ★ 🏨 **Ankara Hilton SA.** The luxurious 16-story Hilton in a quiet, hilly neighborhood on Embassy Row provides many amenities and a view to boot. Expect the standards of comfort and style that you've come to expect from Hiltons the world over, but without many distinguish-

ing characteristics to show that you're in Turkey. ✉ *Tahran Cad. 12, Kavaklıdere, 06700,* ☎ *312/468–2888,* FAX *312/468–0909. 324 rooms. 2 restaurants. AE, DC, MC, V.*

$$ ★ 🏨 **Kent Hotel.** A pleasant, helpful staff distinguishes this hotel in the heart of the city, near the main shopping and business areas. Rooms are pleasant and comfortable, if nondescript. ✉ *Mithatpaşa Cad. 4, Sıhhiye, 06540,* ☎ *312/435–5050,* FAX *312/434–4657. 117 rooms. Restaurant, bar. AE, DC, MC, V.*

$$ ★ 🏨 **King Hotel.** On a quiet street near the Turkish Grand National Assembly, the King Hotel is a favorite with frequent visitors to Ankara. The central location, helpful staff, above-average restaurant, and clean rooms with typical hotel decor all make this hotel a great deal. ✉ *Güvenlik Cad. 13, Aşağıayrancı, 06540,* ☎ *312/418–9099,* FAX *312/417–0382. 36 rooms, 3 suites. Restaurant. AE, DC, MC, V.*

Konya

Konya has always been the religious capital of Turkey. During the Ottoman Empire it was the center of the Islamic mystical order known to the West as the whirling dervishes. The order was founded in the 13th century by Celaleddin Rumi, or Mevlâna, a Muslim mystic, who said, "There are many ways of knowing God. I choose the dance and music." The **Mevlâna Müzesi** (Mevlâna Museum; Mevlâna Meyd., ☎ 332/331–1215) contains the **Mevlâna Türbesi** (Tomb of Mevlâna Celaleddin) as well as displays that illustrate the dervishes' way of life. You can still see the dervishes whirl to the sounds of a flute at the annual commemorative rites held in Konya in early December. Tickets are available from travel agencies or from the Konya tourist information office.

$ ✕ **Hanedan.** Kebabs are the order of the day at Hanedan. Highly recommended are the *tandır* (baked lamb) and the *inegöl köfte* (grilled meatballs). ✉ *Mevlâna Cad.,* ☎ *332/351–4546. No credit cards.*

Cappadocia

Over the centuries the softness of the volcanic rock in the Cappadocia region has been ideal for hollowing out cave dwellings and forming defenses against invading armies. They were begun as early as the 5th century BC. From the 7th through the 10th centuries AD, inhabitants of the Christian kingdom of Cappadocia took refuge from Arab raiders in about 40 underground cities, with some structures as deep as 20 stories underground. The largest of these cities housed 20,000 people. Each had dormitories, dining halls, sewage disposal systems, ventilation chimneys, a cemetery, and a prison. Large millstones sealed off the entrances from enemies.

The magical landscape of Cappadocia consists roughly of the triangular area between Kayseri in the east, Nevşehir in the center, and Niğde in the south. Within that triangle Ürgüp is the center from which to explore the villages on your own or to arrange tours; it is the best place to shop. Because the Cappadocia area is so vast, you'll need at least two days to see the main sights.

In the ruins of the underground city of **Derinkuyu** (✉ Rte. 765, 30 km/19 mi south of Nevşehir, ☎ 384/381–3194) is an unusual Greek church carved out of rock. Equipped with a flashlight, explore the stairways and corridors of the underground city of ★ **Kaymaklı** (✉ Rte. 765, 21 km/13 mi south of Nevşehir, ☎ 384/218–2500). Both cities are open daily 8–5.

Some of the earliest relics of Christianity can be found in the **Göreme Valley,** a couple of miles east of Nevşehir. There are dozens of old churches and monasteries covered with frescoes honeycombed through the soft rock. For a history of the area, visit the ★ **Göreme Açık Hava Müzesi** (Göreme Open-Air Museum). Signs provide information about the site, but bring a flashlight—most churches are illuminated only by the natural light that seeps in. The oldest rock church dates from the 4th century, while frescoes first appeared in the 8th century. ✉ *1 km (½ mi) outside Göreme village on Ürgüp road.* ⏲ *Daily 8:30–5:30.*

$$$$ **Ataman.** Run by a tourist guide and his wife, this hotel is built into the face of a rock. Rooms are connected by maze-like corridors and are individually decorated with kilims and handicrafts. Rates include breakfast and dinner. ✉ *Göreme 50180,* ☎ *384/271–2310,* FAX *384/271–2313,* WEB *www.atamanhotel.com. 38 rooms. Restaurant. MC, V.*

$$ **Alfina.** For the ultimate Cappadocia experience try this hotel, where the rooms are carved out of volcanic rock. Even with a small window in every room it still feels as if you are sleeping in a cave, albeit a fully equipped one with a modern bathroom. ✉ *İstiklal Cad., Ürgüp Girişi 27, Ürgüp 50400,* ☎ *384/341–4822,* FAX *384/341–2424. 26 rooms. MC, V. Closed Nov.–Mar.*

Central Anatolia and Cappadocia Essentials

BUS TRAVEL

A good bus network links most towns and cities; fares are reasonable.

CAR TRAVEL

There are good roads between Istanbul and the main cities of Anatolia—Ankara, Konya, and Kayseri. The highways are generally well maintained and lead to all the major sites. Minor roads are full of potholes and are very rough. On narrow winding roads, look out for oncoming trucks.

TOURS

If you are driving, consider hiring a guide for about $15 to $30 a day. Local tourist offices and hotels can recommend guides and excursions. Taxi drivers are usually willing to take you to historical sites out of town for reasonable fares.

TRAIN TRAVEL

Although there is frequent train service between the main cities, it is almost nonexistent between small towns. It's much quicker to take a bus.

VISITOR INFORMATION

➤ Tourist Information: **Aksaray** (✉ Ankara Cad. Dinçer Apt. 2/2, 68000, ☎ 382/212–5651). **Ankara** (✉ Gazi Mustafa Kemal Bul. 121, Tandoğan, 06050, ☎ 312/229–2631). **Kayseri** (✉ Kağnı Pazari 61, 38000, ☎ 352/222–3903). **Konya** (✉ Mevlâna Cad. 65, Karatay, 42030, ☎ 332/351–1074). **Nevşehir** (✉ Atatürk Bul., 50130, ☎ 384/213–3659). **Ürgüp** (✉ Kayseri Cad. 37, 50200, ☎ 384/341–4059).

WORDS AND PHRASES

DUTCH

English	Dutch	Pronunciation
Basics		
Yes/no	Ja, nee	yah, nay
Please	Alstublieft	**ahls**-too-bleeft
Thank you	Dank u	**dahnk** oo
Excuse me, sorry	Pardon	pahr-**don**
Good morning	Goede morgen	**hoh**-deh **mor**-ghen
Goodbye	Dag	dah
Numbers		
1	Een	ehn
2	Twee	tveh
3	Drie	dree
4	Vier	veer
5	Vijf	vehf
6	Zes	zehss
7	Zeven	**zeh**-vehn
8	Acht	ahkht
9	Negen	**neh**-ghen
10	Tien	teen
Days of the Week		
Sunday	zondag	**zohn**-dagh
Monday	maandag	**mahn**-dagh
Tuesday	dinsdag	**dinns**-dagh
Wednesday	woensdag	**voons**-dagh
Thursday	donderdag	**don**-der-dagh
Friday	vrijdag	**vreh**-dagh
Saturday	zaterdag	**zah**-ter-dagh
Useful Phrases		
Do you speak English?	Spreekt U Engels?	sprehkt oo **ehn**-gls
I don't understand.	Ik begrijp het niet.	ihk be-**ghrehp** het neet
I don't know.	Ik weet niet.	ihk **veht** ut neet
I'm American/ English.	Ik ben Amerikaans/ Engels.	ihk ben am-er-ee-**kahns**/**ehn**-gls
Where is . . .	Waar is . . .	vahr iss

the train station?	het station?	heht stah-**syohn**
the post office?	het postkantoor?	het **pohst**-kahn-tohr
the hospital?	het ziekenhuis?	het **zeek**-uhn-haus
Where are the restrooms?	Waar is de WC?	**vahr** iss de **veh**-seh
Left/right	Links/rechts	leenks/rehts
How much is this?	Hoeveel kost dit?	hoo-**vehl** kohst deet
It's expensive/ cheap	Het is te duur/ goedkoop	het ees teh **dour**/ **hood**-kohp
I am ill/sick.	Ik ben ziek.	ihk behn zeek
Help!	Help!	help
Stop!	Stoppen!	**stop**-pen

Dining Out

Bill/check	De rekening	de **rehk**-en-eeng
Bread	Brood	brohd
I'd like to order	Ik wil graag bestellen	ihk veel khrah behs-**tell**-en
Menu	Menu/kaart	men-**oo**/kahrt
Napkin	En servet	ehn ser-**veht**
Please give me . . .	Mag ik [een] . . .	mahkh ihk [ehn]

FRENCH

English	French	Pronunciation
Basics		
Yes/no	Oui/non	wee/nohn
Please	S'il vous plaît	seel voo **play**
Thank you	Merci	mair-**see**
Excuse me, sorry	Pardon	pahr-**dohn**
Good morning/ afternoon	Bonjour	bohn-**zhoor**
Goodbye	Au revoir	o ruh-**vwahr**
Mr. (Sir)	Monsieur	muh-**syuh**
Mrs. (Ma'am)	Madame	ma-**dam**
Miss	Mademoiselle	mad-mwa-**zel**
Numbers		
1	Un	uhn
2	Deux	deuh
3	Trois	twah
4	Quatre	**kaht**-ruh
5	Cinq	sank
6	Six	seess
7	Sept	set
8	Huit	wheat
9	Neuf	nuf
10	Dix	deess

20	Vingt	vehn
21	Vingt-et-un	vehnt-ay-**uhn**
50	Cinquante	sang-**kahnt**
100	Cent	sahn
1,000	Mille	meel

Days of the Week

Sunday	dimanche	dee-**mahnsh**
Monday	lundi	luhn-**dee**
Tuesday	mardi	mahr-**dee**
Wednesday	mercredi	mair-kruh-**dee**
Thursday	jeudi	zhuh-**dee**
Friday	vendredi	vawn-druh-**dee**
Saturday	samedi	sahm-**dee**

Useful Phrases

Do you speak English?	Parlez-vous anglais?	par-lay **voo** ahn-**glay**
I don't understand.	Je ne comprends pas.	zhuh nuh kohm-**prahn** pah
I don't know.	Je ne sais pas.	zhuh nuh say **pah**
I'm American/ British.	Je suis américain/ anglais.	zhuh sweez a-may-ree-**kehn**/ahn-**glay**
Yesterday	Hier	yair
Today	Aujourd'hui	o-zhoor-**dwee**
Tomorrow	Demain	duh-**mehn**
What is it?	Qu'est-ce que c'est?	kess-kuh-**say**
Where is . . .	Où est . . .	oo ay
the train station?	la gare?	la gar
the subway station?	la station de métro?	la sta-**syon** duh may-**tro**
the post office?	la poste?	la post
the bank?	la banque?	la bahnk
the hospital?	l'hôpital?	lo-pee-**tahl**
Where are the rest rooms?	Où sont les toilettes?	oo sohn lay twah-**let**
Left/right	A gauche/à droite	a goash/a drwaht
I'd like . . .	Je voudrais . . .	zhuh voo-**dray**
a room	une chambre	ewn **shahm**-bruh
I'd like to buy . . .	Je voudrais acheter . . .	zhuh voo-**dray** ahsh-**tay**
How much is it?	C'est combien?	say comb-bee-**ehn**
A little/a lot	Un peu/beaucoup	uhn peuh/bo-**koo**
More/less	Plus/moins	plu/mwehn
I am ill/sick.	Je suis malade.	zhuh swee ma-**lahd**
Help!	Au secours!	o suh-**koor**
Stop!	Arrêtez!	a-reh-**tay**

Dining Out

A bottle of . . .	Une bouteille de . . .	ewn boo-**tay** duh
Bill/check	L'addition	la-dee-see-**ohn**
Bread	Du pain	dew pan
Dish of the day	Le plat du jour	luh plah dew **zhoor**
Fixed-price menu	Le menu	luh muh-**new**
I'd like to order.	Je voudrais commander.	zhuh voo-**dray** ko-mahn-**day**
Is service/the tip included?	Est-ce que le service est compris?	ess kuh luh sair-**veess** eh comb-**pree**
Menu	La carte	la cart
Napkin	Une serviette	ewn sair-vee-**et**
Please give me . . .	Donnez-moi . . .	doe-nay-**mwah**
Waiter!/Waitress!	Monsieur!/ Mademoiselle!	muh-**syuh**/ mad-mwa-**zel**
Wine list	La carte des vins	la cart day **van**

GERMAN

English	German	Pronunciation
Basics		
Yes/no	Ja/nein	yah/nine
Please	Bitte	**bit**-uh
Thank you (very much)	Danke (vielen Dank)	**dahn**-kuh (**fee**-lun dahnk)
Excuse me	Entschuldigen Sie	ent-**shool**-de-gen zee
Good day	Guten Tag	**goo**-ten tahk
Good bye	Auf Wiedersehen	auf **vee**-der-zane
Mr./Mrs.	Herr/Frau	hair/frau
Miss	Fräulein	**froy**-line
Numbers		
1	Ein(s)	eint(s)
2	Zwei	tsvai
3	Drei	dry
4	Vier	fear
5	Fünf	fumph
6	Sechs	zex
7	Sieben	**zee**-ben
8	Acht	ahkt
9	Neun	noyn
10	Zehn	tsane
Days of the Week		
Sunday	Sonntag	**zone**-tahk
Monday	Montag	**moan**-tahk
Tuesday	Dienstag	**deens**-tahk

Wednesday	Mittwoch	**mit**-vokh
Thursday	Donnerstag	**doe**-ners-tahk
Friday	Freitag	**fry**-tahk
Saturday	Samstag/ Sonnabend	**zahm**-stakh/ **zonn**-a-bent

Useful Phrases

Do you speak English?	Sprechen Sie Englisch?	**shprek**-un zee **eng**-glish?
I am American/ British.	Ich bin Amerikaner(in)/ Engländer(in).	ich bin a-mer-i-**kahn**-er(in)/**eng**-glan-der(in)
Where are the rest rooms?	Wo ist die Toilette?	vo ist dee twah-**let**-uh
Left/right	links/rechts	links/rechts
Where is . . .	Wo ist . . .	**vo** ist
the train station?	der Bahnhof?	dare **bahn**-hof
the subway station?	die U-Bahn-Station?	dee oo-bahn-**staht**-sion
the post office?	die Post?	dee **post**
the bank?	die Bank?	dee **banhk**
the hospital?	das Krankenhaus?	dahs **krahnk**-en-house
I'd like to have . . .	Ich hätte gerne . . .	ich **het**-uh **gairn**-uh . . .
a room	ein Zimmer	ine **tsim**-er
a ticket	eine Karte	I-nuh **cart**-uh
How much is it?	Wieviel kostet das?	**vee**-feel **cost**-et dahs?
I am ill/sick.	Ich bin krank.	ich bin krahnk
Help!	Hilfe!	**hilf**-uh
Stop!	Halt!	hahlt

Dining Out

A bottle of . . .	Eine Flasche . . .	I-nuh **flash**-uh
Bill/check	Die Rechnung	dee **rekh**-nung
Do you have . . . ?	Haben Sie . . . ?	**hah**-ben zee
I'd like to order . . .	Ich möchte bestellen . . .	ich **mush**-tuh buh-shtel-en . . .
Menu	Die Speisekarte	dee **shpei**-zeh-car-tuh
Napkin	Die Serviette	dee zair-vee-**eh**-tuh

ITALIAN

English	Italian	Pronunciation

Basics

Yes/no	Sí/No	see/no
Please	Per favore	pear fa-**vo**-ray
Thank you	Grazie	**grah**-tsee-ay
You're welcome	Prego	**pray**-go

Excuse me, sorry	Scusi	**skoo**-zee
Good morning/ afternoon	Buon giorno	bwohn **jor**-no
Good evening	Buona sera	**bwoh**-na **say**-ra
Good bye	Arrivederci	a-ree-vah-**dare**-chee
Mr. (Sir)	Signore	see-**nyo**-ray
Mrs. (Ma'am)	Signora	see-**nyo**-ra
Miss	Signorina	see-nyo-**ree**-na
Hello (over the phone)?	Pronto?	**proan**-to

Numbers

1	Uno	**oo**-no
2	Due	**doo**-ay
3	Tre	tray
4	Quattro	**kwah**-tro
5	Cinque	**cheen**-kway
6	Sei	say
7	Sette	**set**-ay
8	Otto	**oh**-to
9	Nove	**no**-vay
10	Dieci	dee-**eh**-chee
20	Venti	**vain**-tee
50	Cinquanta	cheen-**kwahn**-ta
100	Cento	**chen**-to
10,000	Diecimila	dee-eh-chee-**mee**-la
100,000	Centomila	chen-to-**mee**-la

Days of the Week

Sunday	domenica	doe-**men**-ee-ca
Monday	lunedì	loo-neh-**dee**
Tuesday	martedì	mahr-teh-**dee**
Wednesday	mercoledì	mare-co-leh-**dee**
Thursday	giovedì	jo-veh-**dee**
Friday	venerdì	ven-air-**dee**
Saturday	sabato	**sah**-ba-toe

Useful Phrases

Do you speak English?	Parla inglese?	**par**-la een-**glay**-zay
I don't understand.	Non capisco.	non ka-**peess**-ko
I don't know.	Non lo so.	noan lo **so**
I'm American/ British.	Sono americano/a Sono inglese.	**so**-no a-may-ree-**kah**-no/a **so**-no een-**glay**-zay
What is it?	Che cos'è?	kay ko-**zay**
Where is . . .	Dov'è . . .	doe-**veh**
the train station?	la stazione?	la sta-tsee-**oh**-nay

the subway station?	la metropolitana?	la may-tro-po-lee-**tah**-na
the post office?	l'ufficio postale?	loo-**fee**-cho po-**stah**-lay
the bank?	la banca?	la **bahn**-ka
the hospital?	l'ospedale?	lo-spay-**dah**-lay
Where are the rest rooms?	Dov'è il bagno?	doe-**vay** eel **bahn**-yo
Left/right	A sinistra/a destra	a see-**neess**-tra/ a **des**-tra
I'd like . . .	Vorrei . . .	vo-**ray**
a room	una camera	**oo**-na **kah**-may-ra
How much is it?	Quanto costa?	**kwahn**-toe **coast**-a
A little/a lot	Poco/tanto	**po**-ko/**tahn**-to
More/less	Più/meno	pee-**oo**/**may**-no
I am sick.	Sto male.	sto **mah**-lay
Help!	Aiuto!	a-**yoo**-toe
Stop!	Alt!	ahlt

Dining Out

A bottle of . . .	Una bottiglia di . . .	**oo**-na bo-**tee**-lee-ah dee
Bill/check	Il conto	eel **cone**-toe
Fixed-price menu	Menù a prezzo fisso	may-**noo** a **pret**-so **fee**-so
I'd like . . .	Vorrei . . .	vo-**ray**
Is service included?	Il servizio è incluso?	eel ser-**vee**-tzee-o ay een-**kloo**-zo
Menu	Il menù	eel may-**noo**
Napkin	Il tovagliolo	eel toe-va-lee-**oh**-lo
Waiter/Waitress	Cameriere/ cameriera	ka-mare-**yer**-av/ ka-mare-**yer**-a
Wine list	La lista dei vini	la **lee**-sta **day**-ee **vee**-nee

PORTUGUESE

English	Portuguese	Pronunciation

Basics

Yes/no	Sim/Não	**see**ing/nown
Please	Por favor	pohr fah-**vohr**
Thank you (very much)	(Muito) obrigado	**(moo**yn-too) o-bree **gah**-doh
You're welcome	De nada	day **nah**-dah
Excuse me	Com licença	con lee-**ssehn**-ssah
Good morning!	Bom dia!	bohn **dee**-ah
Good afternoon!	Boa tarde!	**boh**-ah **tahr**-dee
Good evening!	Boa noite!	**boh**-ah **noh**ee-tee

Goodbye!	Adeus!/Até logo!	ah-**deh**oos/ah-**teh loh**-go
Mr./Mrs.	Senhor/Senhora	sen-**yor**/sen-**yohr**-ah
Miss	Senhorita	sen-yo-**ri**-tah
Hello (on the telephone)	Alô	ah-**low**

Numbers

1	Um/uma	oom/**oom**-ah
2	Dois	**doh**ees
3	Três	**treh**ys
4	Quatro	**kwa**-troh
5	Cinco	**seen**-koh
6	Seis	**seh**ys
7	Sete	**seh**-tee
8	Oito	**oh**ee-too
9	Nove	**noh**-vee
10	Dez	**deh**-ees
20	Vinte	**veen**-tee
50	Cinquenta	seen-**kwehn**-tah
100	Cem	**seh**-ing
1,000	Mil	meel
1,000,000	Um milhão	oom mee-lee-**ahon**

Days of the Week

Sunday	Domingo	doh-**meehn**-goh
Monday	Segunda-feira	seh-**goon**-dah **fey**-rah
Tuesday	Terça-feira	**tehr**-sah **fey**-rah
Wednesday	Quarta-feira	**kwahr**-tah **fey**-rah
Thursday	Quinta-feira	**keen**-tah **fey**-rah
Friday	Sexta-feira	**sehss**-tah **fey**-rah
Saturday	Sábado	**sah**-bah-doh

Useful Phrases

Do you speak English?	Fala inglês?	**fah**-lah een-**glehs**?
I don't understand (you).	Não lhe entendo.	nown ly**eh** ehn-**tehn**-doh
I don't know.	Não sei.	nown say
I am American/ British.	Sou americano/ inglês.	sow a-meh-ree-**cah**-noh/een-**glehs**
What is it?	O que é isso?	oh **keh** eh **ee**-soh
Where is . . .	Onde é . . .	**ohn**-deh **eh**
the train station?	a estação de trem?	ah es-tah-**sah**-on deh train
the subway station?	a estação de metrô?	ah es-tah-**sah**-on deh meh-**tro**

the post office?	o correio?	oh coh-**hay**-yoh
the bank?	o banco?	oh **bahn**-koh
the hospital?	o hospital?	oh ohss-pee-**tal**
the bathroom?	o banheiro?	oh bahn-**yey**-roh
Left/right	Esquerda/ direita	ehs-**kehr**-dah/ dee-**ray**-tah
I'd like to buy . . .	Gostaria de comprar . . .	gohs-tah-**ree**-ah deh cohm-**prahr** . . .
How much is it?	Quanto custa?	**kwahn**-too **koos**-tah
A little/a lot	Um pouco/muito	oom **pohw**-koh/ **moo**yn-too
Please call a doctor.	Por favor chame um médico.	pohr fah-**vohr shah**-meh oom **meh**-dee-koh
Help!	Socorro!	soh-**koh**-ho

Dining Out

A bottle of . . .	Uma garrafa de . . .	**oo**mah gah-**hah**-fah deh
Bill/check	A conta	ah **kohn**-tah
Is the tip included?	A gorjeta esta incluída?	ah gohr-**jyeh**-tah ehss-**tah** een-clue-**ee**-dah
Menu	Menu/ cardápio	me-**noo**/ kahr-**dah**-peeoh
Mineral water	Água mineral	**ah**-gooah mee-neh-**rahl**
Napkin	Guardanapo	gooahr-dah-**nah**-poh
Please give me . . .	Por favor me dê . . .	pohr fah-**vohr** mee **deh**
Waiter!	Garçon!	gahr-**sohn**
Wine	Vinho	**vee**-nyoh

SPANISH

English	Spanish	Pronunciation

Basics

Yes/no	Sí/no	see/no
Please	Por favor	pohr fah-**vohr**
Thank you (very much)	(Muchas) gracias	(**moo**-chas) **grah**-see-as
You're welcome	De nada	deh **nah**-dah
Excuse me	Con permiso	con pehr-**mee**-so
Good morning!	¡Buenos días!	**bway**-nohs **dee**-ahs
Goodbye!	¡Adiós!/ ¡Hasta luego!	ah-dee-**ohss**/ **ah**-stah-**lwe**-go
Mr./Mrs.	Señor/Señora	sen-**yor**/sen-**yohr**-ah
Miss	Señorita	sen-yo-**ree**-tah
Hello (on the telephone)	Diga	**dee**-gah

Numbers

1	Un, uno	oon, **oo**-no
2	Dos	dohs
3	Tres	tress
4	Cuatro	**kwah**-tro
5	Cinco	**sink**-oh
6	Seis	saice
7	Siete	see-**et**-eh
8	Ocho	**o**-cho
9	Nueve	new-**eh**-veh
10	Diez	dee-**es**
20	Veinte	**vain**-teh
50	Cincuenta	seen-**kwen**-tah
100	Cien	see-**en**
500	Quinientos	keen-**yen**-tohss
1,000	Mil	meel

Days of the Week

Sunday	Domingo	doh-**meen**-goh
Monday	Lunes	**loo**-ness
Tuesday	Martes	**mahr**-tess
Wednesday	Miércoles	me-**air**-koh-less
Thursday	Jueves	hoo-**ev**-ess
Friday	Viernes	vee-**air**-ness
Saturday	Sábado	**sah**-bah-doh

Useful Phrases

Do you speak English?	¿Habla usted inglés?	**ah**-blah oos-**ted** in-**glehs**
I don't understand (you).	No entiendo.	no en-tee-**en**-doh
I don't know.	No sé.	no seh
I am American/ British.	Soy americano (americana)/ inglés(a).	soy ah-meh-ree-**kah**-no (ah-meh-ree-**kah**-nah)/in-**glehs**(ah)
Yes, please/No, thank you	Sí, por favor/No, gracias	**see** pohr fah-**vor**/ no **grah**-see-ahs
Yesterday/today/ tomorrow	Ayer/hoy/mañana	ah-**yehr**/oy/mahn-**yah**-nah
What is it?	¿Qué es esto?	keh es **es**-toh
Where is . . .	¿Dónde está . . .	**dohn**-deh es-**tah**
the train station?	la estación del tren?	la es-tah-see-**on** del **train**
the subway station?	la estación del metro?	la es-ta-see-**on** del **meh**-tro
the post office?	la oficina de correos?	la oh-fee-**see**-nah deh-koh-**reh**-os
the bank?	el banco?	el **bahn**-koh

the hospital?	el hospital?	el ohss-pee-**tal**
the bathroom?	el baño?	el **bahn**-yoh
Left/right	Izquierda/derecha	iss-key-**er**-dah/ dare-**eh**-chah
I'd like . . .	Quisiera . . .	kee-see-**ehr**-ah
a room.	un cuarto/una habitación.	oon **kwahr**-toh/ **oo**-nah ah-bee-tah-see-**on**
I'd like to buy . . .	Quisiera comprar . . .	kee-see-**ehr**-ah kohm-**prahr**
How much is it?	¿Cuánto cuesta?	**kwahn**-toh **kwes**-tah
A little/a lot	Un poquito/ mucho	oon poh-**kee**-toh/ **moo**-choh
More/less	Más/menos	mahss/**men**-ohss
Please call a doctor.	Por favor llame un medico.	pohr fah-**vor ya**-meh oon **med**-ee-koh
Help!	¡Ayuda!	ah-**yoo**-dah

Dining Out

A bottle of . . .	Una bottella de . . .	**oo**-nah bo-**teh**-yah deh
A glass of . . .	Un vaso de . . .	oon **vah**-so deh
Bill/check	La cuenta	lah **kwen**-tah
Bread	El pan	el pahn
Menu of the day	Menú del día	meh-**noo** del **dee**-ah
Fixed-price menu	Menú fijo o turistico	meh-**noo fee**-hoh oh too-**ree**-stee-coh
Is the tip included?	¿Está incluida la propina?	es-**tah** in-cloo-**ee**-dah lah pro-**pee**-nah
Menu	La carta, el menú	lah **cart**-ah, el meh-**noo**
Napkin	La servilleta	lah sehr-vee-**yet**-ah
Please give me	Por favor déme	pohr fah-**vor deh**-meh
Waiter!/Waitress!	¡Por favor Señor/Señorita!	pohr fah-**vor** sen-**yor**/ sen-yor-**ee**-tah

INDEX

Icons and Symbols

★ Our special recommendations
✕ Restaurant
🏨 Lodging establishment
✕🏨 Lodging establishment whose restaurant warrants a special trip
Good for kids (rubber duck)
☞ Sends you to another section of the guide for more information
✉ Address
☎ Telephone number
⏲ Opening and closing times
Admission prices

Numbers in white and black circles ③ ❸ that appear on the maps, in the margins, and within the tours correspond to one another.

A

C

G

K

L

T